PRAISE FOR THE SCARECRO

"From Fred Astaire to Abbas Kiarostami. From Fritz Lang's *Die Nibelungen* to Todd Browning's *Freaks*. **The Scarecrow Video Movie Guide** contains thousands of different titles, but I feel safe that my own films will not be lost in such a well organized cornucopia."

—Werner Herzog, director of *Nosferatu: The Vampyre, Fitzcarraldo*

✳ "When I walk into Scarecrow Video it's like walking into Treasure Island. Their amazing collection of films is like so many treasured gems. Naturally, their knowledgeable staff are the perfect people to create the essential movie lover's book."

—John Woo, director of *Face/Off, Paycheck, Land of Destiny*

"**The Scarecrow Video Movie Guide** is such good reading, you won't have time to see any of the movies."

—David Zucker, director *Airplane!, Naked Gun 1 and 2½, Ruthless People*

✳ "You must read this book! Scarecrow Video is the tarot of videostores, a labyrinth of mystery and occult knowledge with a great collection of porn."

—Alejandro Jodorowsky, director of *El Topo, The Holy Mountain, Santa Sangre*

"The movie freaks (or movie nuts) at Scarecrow Video know films better than anyone. They played a major role in getting my film *Two-Lane Blacktop* out on video."

—Monte Hellman, director of *Two-Lane Blacktop, Cockfighter, The Shooting,* and producer of *Reservoir Dogs*

THE SCARECROW video MOVIE GUIDE

SASQUATCH BOOKS PRESENTS "THE SCARECROW VIDEO MOVIE GUIDE"
WRITTEN AND COMPILED BY THE STAFF AND FRIENDS OF SCARECROW VIDEO

SASQUATCH BOOKS
SEATTLE

This book is dedicated to George Latsios and Rebecca (Latsios) Soriano, whose vision, eclectic style, and love of movies shaped Scarecrow into what it is today.

Printed in the United States of America
Published by Sasquatch Books
Distributed by Publishers Group West
12 11 10 09 08 07 06 05   6 5 4 3

Book design: Stewart A. Williams
Index: Michael Ferreira
All interior photographs reprinted with permission.

Library of Congress Cataloging-in-Publication Data
The Scarecrow Video movie guide / by the staff and friends of Scarecrow Video.
    p. cm
    ISBN 1-57061-415-6
    1. Motion pictures—Catalogs. 2. Video recordings—Catalogs. I. Scarecrow Video (Firm : Seattle, Wash.)

PN1994.S348 2004
016.79143'75—dc22

2004046734

Sasquatch Books / 119 South Main Street, Suite 400 / Seattle, WA 98104 / (206) 467-4300
www.sasquatchbooks.com / custserv@sasquatchbooks.com

Contents

The Scarecrow Video Movie Guide
A PREFACE

Harry Knowles
head geek, aintitcool.com

On Planet Earth there are very few magical places for film geeks.... Usually these locations are places where movies were shot, perhaps conceived or shown. You know, that theater where you first saw *Star Wars* or *Evil Dead 2*. That sort of thing. Video rental stores, typically, are not magic.

Most people in this world rent at the cold, soulless, tacky corporate video-rental husks called Blockbuster or Hollywood Video. For these sad grubworms of humanity, I mourn. For they have never touched or seen the Monolith of Video Rental Stores. . . . Scarecrow Video!

Being a movie geek means you know of Scarecrow. It's legendary, the Valhalla of Video, the Shangri-La of Cinema. It is the very memory of movies itself. When I first walked in to the store I instantly felt depressed... You see, I'll never live in Seattle, and Scarecrow will never be in Austin.

First off—it is huge. The sections are never-ending, you can twist and turn and never see the same video twice—and you can find titles long-forgotten, never seen... faintly remembered. If you can name it, they have it, and in the age of The Video Store, which all rent pretty much the same 2,000 titles, having a store, one place that has any film "I" can think of, well, it boggles the mind.

After about two hours of wandering the World Cinema areas and realizing that, as a visitor to Seattle, I should be realistic and go look at their For Sale area, instead of the rentals, I began to make a stack. . . . OK,

several stacks—actually, mounds is a better word. DVDs you just can't get anywhere. Like what? Orson Welles's *Don Quixote*. This is one of Welles's lost films. A unicorn of unseen cinema. It was here. Finished in 1992 by cult-schlock wunderchild Jess Franco, the film is unlike anything I've ever seen. It is Welles tearing at the very fabric of narrative film itself. All at once telling the legend of Don Quixote and becoming a new part of that legend. Unfinished dialogue tracks, parts dubbed by Welles himself, some by Franco and some by the actors. Bliss–Heaven–Xanadu. . . Sure the DVD was Region 2, and I wouldn't be able to play it, but Norm—the savant of Scarecrow—he hooked me up with the correct superpowers to break the bonds of arbitrary corporate borders. To be a part of true World Cinema—to see it all, no matter from what continent or corner of this world it is released—now I can and will see it!

Why is this important? Because as a movie lover, do you want any government, any corporation, any limits put on your maddening pursuit of that which you have never seen. To be a film fetishist, it means you never cease searching. The fix is out there, and Scarecrow can help bitchslap the man that is keeping you from treasures unknown.

This brings me to the second title: *La Chute De La Maison Usher* (1928), directed by Jean Epstein; second-unit direction by Luis Buñuel—the year before he helmed *Un Chien Andalou* with Dalí. You cannot see this in America. The DVD comes from far-off lands, never released here. Hell, never mentioned here. A work of Poe touched by the surreal genius of Buñuel and the absinthe fettered visions of late-'20s Spain? My God, man, it is unthinkable that it is not being seen everywhere, but it is here. And now I own it, thanks to Scarecrow.

I also loaded up with Ogami Itto / Baby-cart Samurai films of long ago—but it isn't all vintage. They also have the films being released around the world that you hear rumors about. At the time, *Ichi the Killer* by Takeshi Miike was just hinted at existing with rumors about its audacity and insanity—I got it instantly.

Late that night, Norm took my father and me to dinner with Seattle Cineastes and the conversations that night danced in and out of various genres, 'til finally taking a sustained vacation in the land of Film Noir. Specifically—a subgenre of Film Noir regarding Atomic Energy. Most geeks instantly begin thinking of *Kiss Me Deadly*, which I adore, but my personal favorite is a title that I own a 16mm-film print of, but that nobody anywhere has ever seen. It is called *Split Second* and was directed by that Busby-boy Dick Powell. The title stumped everybody at the table. They'd never heard of it. Never seen it. It was as if I had landed from a far-off planet and began speaking Zweszinese. The next day, when I returned to Scarecrow, Norm set about looking for the title. Sure enough, nestled away in the Noir section was *Split Second*—it had never been rented or seen. That was going to change.

I asked if they had the missing scenes of the spider attack from *King Kong* or Lon Chaney's *London After Midnight*—and for now. . . they don't. However, it might just be mislabeled. Somebody probably put it in the *Milpitas Monster* box—thus it'll go unseen, but safely upon the shelves of Scarecrow. There's magic there—neglected careers, overseen cinema, and titles that boggle the mind.

That's the glory of Scarecrow Video, they are the Ark of Film. There in their halls, side by side go the silents and the sounds of films past, present, and sometimes even future. Filmmakers call, travel, and pay homage there. Want to know everything there is to know about film? I'd recommend going to work there. You wouldn't get rich, but certainly it's one of the best, if not the greatest, trove of titles you could ever work

your way through. It is a sacred place and at least once a week I slip on my ruby slippers and click my heels three times whilst repeating, "There's no place like Scarecrow, There's no place like Scarecrow, There's no place like Scarecrow," but that bitch Dorothy broke these slippers. . . so instead I just end up looking a bit too wong fu.

Scarecrow Video: A History of Sorts
PART ONE

Rebecca (Latsios) Soriano
founding co-owner

> " . . . would you be good enough to
>   explain this outrage? . . .
> " . . . first of all I want to make one
>   thing perfectly clear. . .
>   I never explain anything."

Mary Poppins
Before the Beginning
The founding of Scarecrow Video begins with two people who watched *Mary Poppins* perhaps too many times, spent far too many tuppence on the birds, and believed stepping into chalk paintings was something everyone should do.

Scarecrow was in the mind of George Latsios when I met him in 1983, though I hesitate to use the word brain and scarecrow in the same sentence. He thought video stores were the most fantastic places. I thought he was crazy. He put me under his account at the local video store as soon as he met me, but I was sure I would never use it. I had graduated in fine arts and was a certified arts-snob; and there were no interesting art films on video (yet). Video stores were for people who wanted big, bad, commercially-produced films. George convinced me that maybe I was wrong, and that *Mary Poppins* was really a movie about Zen.

We traveled cross-country in 1983, looking for a place to live and make a video store. Our U-Haul contained a sofa and videos. We liked Seattle, but we didn't know exactly why. Lots of rain, rain and rain, kind of nice on the roof as you watched a video. Just felt like the right place.

Fos

What many people don't know is that the first name George picked for the store was "Fos." In Greek, it means "light," and in 1985 we put together a business proposal for a bank loan to start our video store. We presented it to Rainier Bank, and were promptly laughed out of the bank. Our proposal basically had all of the current Scarecrow ideas, computer kiosks, huge inventory, movie memorabilia, book library, and posters. At that time, there were no video stores like it. What we didn't have was money, equity, or any way to get it. Actually, we presented the idea to three bankers who listened quite politely and then told us no. It did convince George that *Mary Poppins* was right about bankers. One of the three came up to us afterward and told us he personally loved the idea. He later became a customer at our original location.

We ditched the name Fos when we opened Scarecrow Video. It sounded too corporate, and Scarecrow had more of a fun, instantly likeable personality.

In 1986 George put 200 of his own tapes in Backtrack Video in the U District. Mostly horror, sci-fi, cannibal flicks, and a few women-in-prison films. Each and every title at Backtrack was lovingly reviewed on the outside by George. These videos rented really well.

In 1987 we bought a house thinking we could eventually have equity for a loan if we were patient. We were not. Well, George wasn't.

In November 1988 George walked into my office and announced he had quit his job, and had put down a deposit on a storefront in Seattle near Green Lake to open a video store, and too bad, that's just the way it was gonna be. I was speechless. We spent Thanksgiving painting and building shelves, and on December 9 at exactly noon, we opened the doors of Scarecrow Video. We had a huge inventory of 619 films, lots of empty space, and five new customers. We made $36 the first day, it rained (of course) and we took our new-found millions and went next door to the Latona Pub to celebrate.

George set up a desk at the front of the store and became the Green Lake neighborhood's "Doctor of Video Pleasures." He manned the store, and I worked behind the scenes and did other jobs to pay the rent. The store was mostly empty, but people came, and they liked talking to the "Doctor." George genuinely liked talking to the customers, and made them feel their opinions were important. He began to play movies in the store and this was made part of the schedule:

Friday night:*The Good, the Bad and the Ugly* or other Spaghetti Western. (Then later, *Rocky Horror Picture Show*.)

Sat. morning: Japanese animation

Sat. night: *Enter the Dragon* or another kung fu classic, then any Elvis movie. Then, at 9PM or so: *Bladerunner* (original version.)

Sun. at 7PM: *Mary Poppins*

"The Doctor of Video Pleasures"

This is a sign that sat for many years on George's desk in the original location of Scarecrow Video. It sat on the desk where he checked out videos for every customer, and where he recommended movies to most anyone who would listen.

I think it is a title he liked.

The only other term I can use to describe

George is a kind of "Nanny of Video Pleasures." I truly believe he had much in common with Mary Poppins. He was like a video-nanny to adults. It gave him great pleasure to see others get pleasure out of films, and he saw life as a kind of child's game. It was like George was not born, or did not die, but came in on a wind and left when the wind changed. He operated not in the normal person's reality but on his own plane of reality, and what was possible in his world would not necessarily work for anyone else. He didn't abide by the rules most people followed because he didn't feel he had to, and in most cases he didn't. This affected people differently; it did make most people smile, though, because they just wished they could get away with such things. He was like a child in the adult world, and he made the children's rules work in the adult world, and in the process, he created Scarecrow Video.

"That's it. It's like a finger pointing to the moon. Dooooooooon't concentrate on the finger, or you'll miss all that heavenly glory." Bruce Lee—*Enter the Dragon*

Heavenly glory = Widescreen. George discovered it and fell in love. If there was a way to get movie widescreen, he would do it. This led to our addition of laser discs in 1990 as well as other more obscure titles and foreign films, anime, and PAL tapes. We added computer kiosks and more space, and slept on the floor in the horror section at night because it was the only place a person outside wouldn't see you. I liked waking up looking at the Bela Legosi section.

At about this time we began to attract some serious film people, not just locals, or the grunge rockers who kept us in business: Bernardo Bertolucci, Bridget Fonda, Roger Ebert. I still remember the phone call from the customer who couldn't believe that Roger Ebert helped her find a movie.

Over the years at Scarecrow some famous and infamous people visited us. I'm sure there are many more we don't know about.

The beauty of George, though, is that he didn't really care if you were famous or not, he really just wanted you to enjoy the movies.

The Cobains

When we were in the small Latona location, it was a haphazard collection of movies, lots of cult stuff on makeshift shelves. George waited on almost everyone, and signed almost everyone up. One day (very close to the time Nirvana appeared on *Saturday Night Live*) Kurt Cobain and Courtney Love walked in. Courtney spent the next hour on the floor in the documentary section and Kurt explored everything else. When they had decided on their choices they came up to the counter. Everyone behind the counter buzzed (this was *the* Kurt Cobain!) George had no idea who he was and didn't care. George just cared if Kurt picked good movies. George asked him for his credit card, and reviewed the paperwork with him—"So, what do you do?" George asked, as he entered Kurt's gold American Express–card number in the computer. "I'm a musician." Kurt answered. George lifts his gaze to him, goes back to the computer. "Ahhhh, yeah, one of those grunge musicians," George said, very non-excited, not lifting his head.

"Yeah. . . " answers Kurt. And he smiles. He knows George doesn't know who he is and he likes it. He's just a guy renting some movies.

Over the years we used to tease Kurt and Courtney about how much they spent at the store in late fees. We figured they should have a Cobain Wing. It was definitely in the thousands of dollars. One day Courtney came in and she was really pissed off. She immediately went to George and let him have it. She was furious about the amount she had been charged for late fees. (Not that she really cared, but her accountant had given her a lecture about it, and Courtney does not like to be lectured.) She lit into George. None of us could bear to watch. But... the next time we looked, she was giving him a big kiss and leaving with a movie. When we asked him what he said to her, he said he just listened for a while, and then they talked movies. He gave her a copy of *I Claudius*, one of her favorites, and all was forgiven.

The Big Move

In 1993 we ran out of room (again), and went in search of a new space. We found it at the present location of 5030 Roosevelt Way—8,200 beautiful square feet, and a balcony! Felt a bit like being on a big boat. Lots of remodeling later, in November 1994, we moved in our now seemingly enormous 18,000 titles. We added a movie theater, The Sanctuary, in 1995, stressing our commitment to seeing great films in theaters, not just on video. Scarecrow was perhaps the first video store in Seattle to support film festivals and to sponsor film screenings in theaters. This was also about the time we began to bring famous and unknown directors to town, to show their films. Alejandro Jodorowsky was the first, and along the way we saw Nicolas Roeg, John Woo, Wim Wenders, Monte Hellman, Seijun Suzuki, and others. We also put together an incredible animation festival at the Seattle Art Museum. We added DVDs in 1997 and continued adding films at an incredible rate...

...and the wind began to change. That may be when we got into trouble. George was a kid in his own candy store, which was great, but it was just *tooo* much sugar. In 1997 due to too much sugar, Scarecrow needed fillings and a diet overhaul. Enter Sir John and Sir Carl. They did not enter on white horses, but on motorcycles, and they saved Scarecrow from certain doom.

Scarecrow Video is a celebration of people and movies and the connection between the two. The energy of anyone who has ever rented at Scarecrow, or worked there, is in the store and vibrates with imagination. Scarecrow owes its life to the people who rented movies at the beginning and who still do today, and to its truly remarkable employees who share their enthusiasm for connecting people and movies. It could have only happened in Seattle, when the wind changed.

Scarecrow Video: A History of Sorts
PART TWO

Carl Tostevin
co-owner

"Has my DVD arrived yet?"

It was with these words my relationship with Scarecrow started. Oh, we'd seen each other off and on many times over the years, spent hours together reliving memories of the films I'd seen as a kid (I especially like the old Roger Corman/Vincent Price renditions of Poe's stories). But it was when I learned that Scarecrow Video, a legendary Seattle landmark, was in danger of disappearing that I first considered what it might mean to own a video store.

As it turned out, there were really only three things required. First, I needed a like-minded business partner, and I was fortunate to find one in a longtime friend, John Dauphiny. Second, we needed some expertise, and we were pleasantly surprised to find out that everyone associated with Scarecrow wanted to stay with us (and that meant the staff, the previous owners, and most importantly our customers). Third, and finally, we had to buy into the idea that Scarecrow proposes—that even today in the world of vast corporations, seventeen ways to calculate ROI (return on investment), and massive Hollywood studio systems distributing pan-and-scan edited-for-content shadows of filmmakers' children, a business founded on more dream than business plan can survive. That dream is simply this: Scarecrow Video can exist to unite people with film.

What many people don't know is how close to the edge Scarecrow has been in its existence. George and Rebecca Latsios started simply, building from George's personal collection of movies that he lent out to customers who were more like friends. When George was diagnosed with terminal brain cancer, it was an excuse to move up the time line, to accrue as many titles as possible in the time that was left. When the store began bursting at the seams, they found a new building large enough to accommodate ten times the titles (which surprisingly, we have now surpassed—we're again working around space constraints!). When the store managed to make money, it went back to the collection—it also helped to sponsor film festivals, bring filmmakers to the Northwest, and fund trips to foreign countries in quests to find the elusive titles unavailable any other way.

Every year the collection grew, the reputation grew, and the number of customers grew. Unfortunately, stresses also grew. What many people didn't see was bleary-eyed inventory managers desperately entering this week's new titles well past midnight; or the event planners working days on end to make sure a filmmaker showed up on time; or the beleaguered floor staff somehow finding the energy to smile at the line of customers that reached to the door even after working their sixth consecutive 12-hour shift. Scarecrow's existence owes a debt of gratitude to those who worked so hard to keep it alive over the years.

But Scarecrow's dream is contagious that way—people do what must be done to keep it going, often at great personal expense. Between the tireless efforts of our staff and their encyclopedic film knowledge (which borders on the surreal), the pieces to keep Scarecrow alive were all provided to us. We just helped to organize those pieces in a way that has allowed Scarecrow to expand its dream further without losing sight of what's important.

What matters most, ultimately, is our store *and* our customers. The fact that we have been able to expand our dream is something made entirely possible by our customers. We need to keep looking around the world to sustain the dream that Scarecrow is built upon, to bring the rare and unique inventory coming in so that our customers will keep coming back.

But what matters here, in this book, is all those folks you see behind our counters, upstairs in the offices, and walking through the doors every day—you'll hear from them in these pages. And trust me, they're an opinionated bunch. We don't expect you to agree with everything here (half the time they don't agree with each other), nor will we pull our punches (if we hated your favorite film, we'll be happy to tell you why). What we will do is tell you what we think, the same way we would if you dropped by the store. In the end, that's probably the best part of Scarecrow—you can come in and ask, "What did you think of this?" and we'll tell you. It's the common bond between Scarecrow and the customer: shared views of cinematic masterpieces, which makes film special. Hopefully, it's also what will continue to make Scarecrow special for years to come. At the very least, that'll be our goal as long as we hold the reins.

Introduction / User's Guide

Kevin Shannon

"Bringing people and movies together."

So many movies, so little time.

Sure, sometimes you walk into the video store and you know exactly what you want. You hop in the car, head to the video store and go right to where you want to go, "Comedy." You grab *Waiting for Guffman*, you get in line, check out, and you're gone.

But, what happens when *Guffman* is checked out? What now?

Well, you know that you want to see a movie, that's why you're at the video store, for crying out loud, and tonight, well tonight, forget *Guffman*, by God, you're pretty darn sure that you kinda-maybe feel like seeing something comedic but adrenaline-charged: a loaded-gun actioner, you know, not too heavy, and funny too, but not in a Burt Reynolds kind of way, maybe a spy story, or a Western, or maybe something British. Twenty-five minutes go by, yet you are certain it won't be long before you see that one title that'll trigger the usually inaccessible 90 percent of your brain, where you hide that list of movies you've always wanted to see and then finally. . . you're stuck. You actually find yourself starting to think that surfing through 275 channels of cable to end up watching a re-cap of last year's "Winter Beach Volleyball Championships" on ESPN Classics couldn't be so bad. . . right?

You have absolutely no idea what you want.

Well, it is precisely at this moment that you need the help of your trained video-store professional. It is at this moment where anyone worth their salt who works at a video store begins to earn their keep. Go into any video store in the country and more often than not (yes, occasionally even at Blockbuster) you will find someone who wants to help find the right movie for you.

"Bringing people and movies together."

From the day we opened our doors, that's been our motto. That's what we do in Seattle, at Scarecrow Video. And that's what the best videos stores in the country do for you wherever you live. Movie Madness in Portland, Oregon; Video Station in Boulder, Colorado; Vidiots in Santa Monica, California; Le Video in San Francisco; Kim's Video in New York City; and hundreds of other independent video stores across the country are where you will find some of the brightest, cinema crazy people on Earth just waiting to share their favorite films with you.

We aspire to movie nerdom so you don't have to. We watch movies of every ilk, from the thickest and thinnest margins in the realm of cinema, from the tiniest tributaries to the mainstream of film, popular and nearly unknown movies from every nook and cranny of the world. We do this for no other reason than to be able to share these films with our friends and other cinematic adventurers. And, by that, we mean you. (So, *Waiting for Guffman* is checked out? Well, try *Best in Show* or *Living in Oblivion* or, if you're feeling more adventurous, how about *Sharkskin Man and Peach Hip Girl*?)

So, what makes us so special? Why Scarecrow Video?

To answer that, answer this: To what lengths will your local video store go to get you the movie you want to see? You want to see *Henry and June*. Blockbuster won't carry it. (They carry no unrated or NC-17 films, heck Blockbuster even coerced a "Blockbuster-friendly" exclusive-but-edited cut of John Carpenter's *Halloween*.) Hollywood Video sold their VHS copy and had the DVD, but it's missing (and hard to find, it's out of print), and your neighborhood store doesn't have it and the clerk tells you you'll have to talk to the owner if you really want it, which you do and three months pass before they get it on VHS. Well, of course, we have it at Scarecrow, in three formats, in a section for director Philip Kaufman. But wait, that's too easy. Let's try another one.

How about one even we'd never heard of: a customer comes in and asks for *The Legend of Johnny Lingo*. What? We dig around, do a little research, find out it's a short film produced by the Mormon church in the late-60s about a Pacific Island native who trades eight cows, an unheard of high price, for a homely wife whose inner beauty finally shines to the surface when she realizes how prized she is by her new husband. And we buy it, no questions asked, just because one inquiring customer asked us about it. What the heck are we thinking? (It's a pretty good little movie, actually, though it's hardly ever rented.)

So, we'll bring in just about any movie that anyone wants us to, so what? Is this any way to run a business? Well, we think so. And why do we think so? Because founding owner George Latsios told us so, and damned if he wasn't right.

We don't think we're so special. We really don't. We just think we're the way everybody should be. Thank goodness our customers agree with us, otherwise we'd be out of business. Bottom line: movies are special, and our customers are special too. We just love movies, and love bringing movies to people. And that's the all of it, really. It sure doesn't make a business plan, that's for sure, and we have just a whole lot of zero money in our pockets to prove it. But we wouldn't have it any other way.

Another, perhaps crazier, Scarecrow tradition has also remained true from day one: The money we make, we spend on movies. Carpet needs fixing? Yes, but we need to get a Japanese import *Godzilla* DVD box-set that was just made available. Oh, and we just must have the most popular Polish

comedy of the '90s, right? The carpet will wait a bit. So, all right, we are crazy, yes, but just for movies. It is a very pleasant surprise; we are grateful for this each day we open the store, and that our customers think that this is special as well.

Scarecrow began, in 1988, like most any other independent video store, small, very small indeed. In a relatively inexpensive little storefront in a small, out of the way neighborhood in Seattle, with just 619 movies from his personal collection that he just had to share with the world, George and his wife Rebecca started Scarecrow Video with little more than their unbridled enthusiasm. From the very first day of business like has attracted like at Scarecrow.

George's passion for movies was infectious. Everyone he met was exposed to his mania for movies and for people. He would greet customers with "Hello, my friend," and would often refer to movies as the "best film ever made." In spite of the hyperbole, many people would soon find themselves similarly afflicted with George's seemingly insatiable desire for movies. Working each and every day but Christmas, it seemed that the only company George and Rebecca kept were each other and their customers, many of whom became close friends. Finally, after two years without a day off, George and Rebecca allowed themselves to spread their enthusiasm through a few employees as well.

As George and Rebecca gave, they got back in return. Word spread throughout the neighborhood, the city, and beyond, and before long, customers would come from far distances to this little storefront to share their passion for movies. Customer after customer would make movie recommendations to George, and he would bring those titles in, as a matter of policy, no questions asked. Later, as the store expanded into the storefront next-door, Scarecrow hired more employees, each with their own tastes and passions, preaching their own variations of the cinema gospel. And George would take their recommendations as well. This pattern began to reach out very far indeed. Like the old TV commercial said: four friends told more friends who told four friends, and so on and so on and so on. And so, with the support of our customers, the store grew and grew.

It wasn't long before Scarecrow had so many movies they didn't know where to put them. If you were a customer who had to use the bathroom, you needed the leave your bag or purse behind and give a clerk your driver's license as a security deposit. Why? Because they needed to store movies there!

George Latsios's ultimate goal at Scarecrow, his primary promise to his customers, was to make the store better and better day by day striving to become "one of the best video stores in the country, giving 100 percent to film" and hoping one day to offer "the finest selection of films" anywhere in the world. And Scarecrow Video, in our current 8,200-square-foot location since late 1994, amazingly and against steep odds, has come astonishingly close to offering just that.

So why this book?

When George sold his "candy store" to two of the finest film nerds we know, Scarecrow Video continued to grow even more. Under the current ownership of John Dauphiny and Carl Tostevin, with more than 70,000 movies, and over 90,000 customers from Washington State and elsewhere, Scarecrow began to attract even more attention, very often from the most surprising places.

Premiere magazine once wrote of our store dubbing it "the coolest video store in the country." Wow. Who knew? And when the heck were they in the store? Coolest in Seattle, yeah, whatever, okay, but the entire country? In June of 2001, we got a phone call from a customer who told us he was walking to the store from downtown and needed directions. It was an unusually warm spring day, and one of our employees, Bryan W., gave him directions but helpfully included information regarding which were the best bus routes to take to get here. "No that's alright, alright? Best way to see the city is to walk around." Whatever. Well, imagine our surprise when we saw Quentin Tarantino hiking his sweaty butt up the street to our store, sunburned on one side of his face after strolling the 4 miles from downtown! We're not cool, not compared to that, anyway. But Mr. Tarantino walking to our store? That is cool.

We just do what we do. And word gets around. Many of the nice folks at Sasquatch Books are customers at our store, and like many of our customers, they've appreciated the ways in which we've helped them travel, cinematically, to places they'd never dreamed of. Then, enterprising individuals that they are, they started to wonder if it might somehow be possible to take Scarecrow Video and re-create it in book form. A book that will reflect our desire to run to every corner of the globe to amass a video collection that will reflect as many tastes, perspectives, cultures, and behaviors to as many people as we can. Simply put, the publishers wanted to help us to share our take on cinema-by-way-of-video with you. We're happy to oblige. But we've never done anything like this before. We had never even considered it a possibility until the Sasquatch folks came to us.

So, just as Scarecrow Video itself started small, we're starting small here too.

Even so, we know that this book will be like no other video guide yet.

At Scarecrow Video, we've had access to movies that most American moviegoers have never even heard of. But just because *Nang Nak* is completely unfamiliar to you doesn't mean that you should just pass it by. It is a stunningly beautiful film, reviewed in this book, because we think more people need to see it.

It doesn't take much prodding to get us to share what we think about movies. But getting us to write about what we think? That took a little doing. After all, we've all got our day jobs to do (owners included). We've got a store to run. We would have just loved to kick out a book that comes close to offering a full guide to what our store has, to share our relatively extreme scope of cinema. But due to limitations of space, money and time, we can't (at least not yet). But that doesn't mean we think that's a bad thing either. And the why of that, means this:

We offer you the best 4,000 or so reviews that came to our minds. These reviews offer you a guided tour of sorts, through our store and through our minds, of the world of Scarecrow Video.

Compiled by current and former employees, friends, and customers of the store, it's as if we were able to take you by the hand and walk you through the store. So walk through this book with us, these are the films we're most eager to point out to you. We hope these reviews reflect our store, and our tastes and distastes, so that you can browse through this book as you would our store, to whet your appetite for the kind of cinematic experiences that we enjoy, which we want to share with you.

In that vein, this book is a cinema travel-guide that directs you to some of the best of the best and the worst of the worst, and let's you decide where to go from there. Never been to Myanmar? Get a guide. You're only going to be there a few weeks, you won't be able to see everything, so let the guide help you. Want an introduction to explore Korean cinema? We're here to get you started.

We know things have been left out. We know we did not get to reviewing all that we had wanted to. We know that. Our work is not done. But for now, we hope you like what you see.

Using this book: The basics

The best thing to keep in mind about how to approach this guide is this: always keep in mind that you are browsing. Wherever you open this book, there you are. Open the book, you are in the Comedy section. Open the book, you are in the Foreign Films section at Thailand. Open the book again, and you are looking at Documentaries.

Use the table of contents when you know what you're in the mood to see. Looking for a comedy? Check it out. Don't know what you want? Flip through the book, and see what catches your eye.

We have indexed the back of the book by title and director so you can find specific movie reviews more easily, if you are so inclined. There, too, we have provided some odd entertaining lists of movies that over the course of time, from time to time, keep coming to our weird minds. We couldn't resist sharing.

For each individual review, we provide you with the basics: title, year, running time, director and cast, and where the film is located in our store. Occasionally a review has been written by one person that another person thought was bunk. So they added their two-cents worth: dueling reviews. Trust us, sometimes triangulating your position, though it might take just a little longer, is a lot better. Two reviews get you that much closer. The reviewers themselves are listed in each review by their initials; their names can be found in a key at the end of this section.

You can also use this book to prod your local store to purchase films you want. "See what the chuckleheads at Scarecrow said about this Hou Hsiao-Hsien film? You should get it!"

Finding the video store for you

Scarecrow Video is not the only special video store in the world. As stated earlier, in nearly every part of the country, you will find video stores that owe their existence and survival to a willingness to share their zeal for movies with their customers. Go into any major city in the country and ask around: You will find that one or more stores fits the bill. When you can't find that movie you're looking for, where do people tell you to go? Where to go when you're in Tucson? That would be Casa Video.

Every store, no matter what kind, reflects the tastes and aspirations of its owners. In the video business, the cookie-cutter corporate stores like Hollywood or Blockbuster are pretty much about three things: offering convenience, making big money, and driving out the "competition." If you absolutely need to go to one of these stores, well, we understand. You're on vacation someplace, or visiting family in the middle of Iowa, or, it's the only store to be found within miles of your home. Sometimes it's simply the only game in town. But it wasn't always that way.

Back in the day, every video store was independent. Independent beginnings are true of just about any field of business. (When Scarecrow Video first opened its doors, Starbucks only had eight locations. Heck, remember bagel, croissant, or gourmet cookie shops?) Before big corporations are willing to take over any industry, they let the groundwork be done by small businesses, sometimes their own, and sometimes not. Once the small-timers invest their time and passion and sweat equity, and prove their viability through enterprising individuality, the corporations pounce and all too often, and all too soon, substitute unimaginative homogeneity.

These corporations begin to grow (some might say metastasize) and gain huge advantages in the marketplace, buying more "product" with less capital than the independent retailer can ever hope to. They spread out into the world knowing that, on this newly unbalanced playing field, the little guy barely stands a chance. Many of these independent businesses fight to survive, but all

too often, it's not long before they are either taken over wholly by the corporate stores or are wiped out when they open across the street. So, after years of proving themselves and building their businesses, the independent retailers are left to die, either through absorption or by preemptively cutting their losses by closing down.

The only chance the independent video-store owner has ever had to survive corporate invasions takes us back to where we started: the tastes and aspirations of the owners. If you cared first about your customers, giving them the best your business had to offer, if you cared about those things first, and about money later, you had a chance. One of our favorite video stores in Vancouver, B.C., had a Blockbuster open right across the street. In a year and a half, it was Blockbuster that closed its doors. Take that!

The best video stores reflect the tastes and aspirations of its employees and, most importantly, you, its customers. Some smaller stores offer videos for the gourmet. One of the better small stores in Seattle, Maltese Falcon, offers "The 2,000 best movies ever made." Smaller stores that actively focus on the best, as well as the usual New Releases, are great. Other stores that only keep what rents, good or bad, tend to be more generic. (Don't get us wrong, not all corporate chains are evil, but—)

We are pretty certain of this: The best video stores around are your local independent video stores.

The store that speaks its mind, that dares to share that *In the Soup* is a neglected classic, or that *The Cat in the Hat* will do more harm to your children than any porn, that's the store you want. The store that will listen to you, the store that already has or will bring in the movies that you want to see, that is the store you want. Do not accept anything less.

So, grab the phone book, ask around town, and find the store for you. Let them make you better, help you explore the world of the movies. Then share what you find, and then help them get better too.

And please keep in mind. . .

Get thee to a cinema!!! Even in this age of home theaters, the best way to watch any film is in the theater, on the big screen, with other people. The shared experience is so much better than you could ever hope for at home.

Home video is great; you can have access to films you might never otherwise get a chance to see. But if there is a theatrical screening of a film you love, one that you have only seen on video, at all cost you absolutely must go see it! You can spend your time looking at reproductions of paintings in books, but then you have never seen the painting as the painter intended it to be seen. The same applies to movies. See them on the canvases they were meant to be seen on. They don't call it *the big screen* for nothing. (And we don't care how big your TV is, it can't compare.) There is simply no good reason you shouldn't see movies in the theater, to share your experience, in real time, with your peers. To know that there are people who have only watched *The Lord of the Rings* movies, alone, on 15-inch TV screens drives us nuts!

Support your local movie houses, museums, and film festivals!

Thanks for letting us share our thoughts with you,

The staff and friends of Scarecrow Video:

Alex Williams, Andrew Toms, Anissa Bower, Anne Hockens, Anonymous, Anonymous, Brandon Lanich, Brian Blue, Bryan Theiss, Bryan Ward, Carl Tostevin, Chad Day, Chad Perman, Charley Cvercko, Chris Burkhalter, Dagmar Jacobs, David Wingo, Ed Ward, Ellen Osborne, Eric Bauer, Gayle Truax, Greg Olson, Guerren Marter, Ivan Peycheff, J. Brian Pitts, Jae Carlsson, Jaideep Dasgupta, Jane Johnson, Jason Dodson, Jen Koogler, Jenn Schmidt, Jim Chapman, John Dauphiny, John Hicks, Josh Warren, Kevin Clarke, Kevin Shannon, Kin Ferate, Kris Siriwangchai, Kyle Blair, Luke Walker, Marc Burgio, Marc Palm, Mark Steiner, Matt Lynch, Megan McNellis, Mike Harring, Mimi Noyes, Nathan Jensen, Norman Hill, Patrick Mathewes, Rebecca (Latsios) Soriano, Rich Grendzinski, Richard T. Jameson, Robert Graves, Ryan M, Ryan Danner, Ryan Johnson, Sam Franklin, Sean Axmaker, Shade Rupe, Shawn Foster, Spenser Hoyt, Susan Purton, Ted Chen, Tommy Swenson, Trevor Pyle, Tyler Bromley, Wesley Nelson, Zack Carlson.

A KEY TO THE REVIEWERS

AB-Anissa Bower
AH-Anne Hockens
AT-Andrew Toms
AW-Alex Williams
BB-Brian Blue
BL-Brandon Lanich
BT-Bryan Theiss
BW-Bryan Ward
CB-Chris Burkhalter
CBG-Anonymous
CC-Charley Cvercko
CD-Chad Day
CP-Chad Perman
DD-Deep Dasgupta
DJ-Dagmar Jacobs
DW-David Wingo
EB-Eric Bauer
EO-Ellen Osborne
EW-Ed Ward
GM-Guerren Marter
GO-Greg Olson
GT-Gayle Truax
IP-Ivan Peycheff
JBJ-Brian Pitts
JC-Jae Carlsson
JD-Jason Dodson
JH-John Hicks
JJ-Jane Johnson
JK-Jen Koogler
JS-Jenn Schmidt

JW-Josh Warren
KB-Kyle Blair
KC-Kevin Clarke
KF-Kin Ferate
KS-Kevin Shannon
KSI-Kris Siriwangchai
LW-Luke Walker
MB-Marc Burgio
MH-Mike Harring
ML-Matt Lynch
MM-Megan McNellis
MN-Mimi Noyes
MP-Marc Palm
MS-Mark Steiner
NH-Norman Hill
NJ-Nathan Jensen
PM-Patrick Mathewes
RD-Ryan Danner

RG-Rich Grendzinski
RGR-Robert Graves
RJ-Ryan Johnson
RLS-Rebecca (Latios) Soriano
RM-Ryan Miller
RTJ-Richard T. Jameson
SA-Sean Axmaker
SCV-Anonymous
SF-Sam Franklin
SH-Spenser Hoyt
SP-Susan Purton
SR-Shade Rupe
SWF-Shawn Foster
TB-Tyler Bromley
TC-Ted Chen
TP-Trevor Pyle
TS-Tommy Swenson
WN-Wesley Nelson
ZC-Zack Carlson

CHAPTER ONE

Directors

W e begin our book where we begin our store, with the most distinctive filmmakers in the world. People are often perplexed when they're confronted by how we prioritize the arrangement of our store. They want to rent *Being There* but to get it they need to find what? Hal Ashby? Who? A Hal Ashby section? OK, whatever. They also want to rent *High Noon* . . . in the Fred Zinnemann section? Huh?

Why a Directors' section at all?

Well, from A to Z we have nearly 450 directors' sections in six different locations in our store (seven, if you count the filmed operas directed by Peter Sellars). Starting with our feature film directors, we have sections for documentary film directors, experimental directors, animation directors, local directors from the Seattle area, and directors of adult films. Any film that does not fall into one of these directors' sections is distributed to its appropriate section throughout the store.

No other aspect of our store has generated as much controversy as the directors' sections. The first objections tend to regard their very existence. The sections are certain to confuse the uninitiated and confound the experts. Why do we have this director in one of the sections and not that director? There is no doubt that the perception of Scarecrow as an "elitist" video store comes largely from our insistence on *these* section—and we make no claim to being intelligent enough for true elitism.

Yes, the sections are somewhat based on the "auteur" theory of cinema, but we just

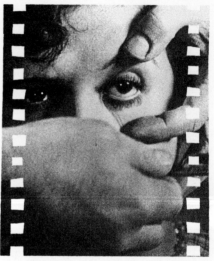

©KINO INTERNATIONAL CORP.

Un Chien Andalou (1929)

like to think it's just our way of celebrating those directors who, for good or ill, have distinguished themselves from the rest of the moviemaking herd. How else would we end up with Ray Dennis Steckler's films next to those of Steven Spielberg? In filmmaking, we believe that the buck stops with the filmmaker. Bookstores arrange books by author and not by publisher, don't they? Of course!

So if you go to the Foreign section called "Japan" looking for *The Seven Samurai,* our apologies. Head to the Akira Kurosawa section, and while you're there why not pick up *Red Beard* as well? That's part of the idea, too: we figure that if you really like the work of a particular director, you should be able to easily find all of his or her films in one place. And that, as they say, is that. Well, not quite.

The directors' sections are organic. Every two years or so, after taking into account the votes of the entire Scarecrow staff (supermajority needed), and sometimes utilizing customer polls, the senior members of our staff meet to decide who should be added to or removed from our esteemed/reviled/populist/elitist sections. These discussions are always impassioned, sometimes volatile. We'll discuss as many as one hundred to two hundred different directors in these marathon sessions and then vote on them. Often, only the thinnest margins decide who's added, who stays, or who goes. And then, just when we think it is over, our inventory manager, bestowed with veto power, will often make judgment calls, adding a director here or there. But hey, we're not perfect—our staff's tastes are as fickle as yours or anyone else's—and it helps keep our store breathing and alive, that's for sure.

Finally, each director we add to our section must have at least four films that are available on video. Over the years, we've found that it's pretty common for a director to have distinguished him- or herself with two or three films. It's only after a fourth film that we begin to see the real makings of a distinguished career in directing. (The rule used to be three films, and those directors who got in with three are still in, but they're on the bubble.) Even so, exceptions have been made to this rule. If we're looking at someone who directed forty films of repute and only two are available on video, they may be given a section. But these cases are rare. We also have a Multi-Directors section, for films that are directed by two or more directors in the section. This section includes films like *Four Rooms*, an anthology with three of its four segments directed by Allison Anders, Robert Rodriguez, and Quentin Tarantino.

And please keep in mind that our store is full of exceptions. For example, Atom Egoyan directed a version of Samuel Beckett's *Krapp's Last Tape* for the BBC, but in our determination Beckett is the dominating factor here, so we've got that film in our Playwrights section under Beckett. But is Roman Polanski's *Macbeth* in the Shakespeare section? No, that's in Polanski's section. Yeah, we know it seems a little goofy but, case by case, whether fair is foul or foul is fair, that's just the way we call it.

Also included in this chapter are reviews from our Experimental and Experimental Directors, Local (Seattle) Films and Local Directors, and Short Film Collections.

BLACK HEAT L: DIRECTORS/ADAMSON, AL (1976) 92M D: Al Adamson. *Geoffrey Land, Russ Tamblyn, Timothy Brown*. Another dubious example of the Adamson/Sam Sherman approach to filmmaking, *Black Heat* played at inner-city theatres as a black action picture. It was retitled *Girl's Hotel* for the drive-ins, and later was renamed *The Murder Gang* when it made yet another round through various lowbrow venues. Though usually labeled blaxploitation, *Black Heat* is more of an urban action flick with an African-American lead, along the lines of *Detroit 9000* or *Across 110th Street* but lacking their dramatic resonance. The narrative is a typical mess and deals with a tough black cop, his TV-journalist girlfriend, a sleazy nightclub, outrageous threads, compulsive gambling, sadistic villains, and exploding toy airplanes. Individual scenes are strewn together without much structure but a lot of gritty stuff happens. As blaxploitation *Black Heat* is pretty weak, but its cast (Tamblyn is especially amusing), scuzzy locations, and that Adamson touch make it an oddly compelling example of full-blown '70s grind house/drive-in exploitation. —*S.H.*

MEAN MOTHER L: DIRECTORS/ADAMSON, AL (1973) 88M D: Al Adamson. *Luciana Paluzzi, Dennis Safren, Al Richardson, Clifton Brown, Marilyn Joi, Lang Jeffries*. The trash-movie tag team of Adamson and Sam Sherman was always on the cusp of pop-culture fads, always ready with a movie to cash in on the current craze. In this case Sherman acquired a boring Spanish/Italian coproduction about jewel thieves, helmed by European journeyman Leon Klimovsky. Adamson shot new footage featuring a badass black dude named Beauregard Jones (Brown, aka soul singer Dobie Gray), drug dealers, wah-wah guitars, lots of muthafuckin' cussing, and more sex. Safren, who starred in the original version, was brought to the United States and parallel plot lines were developed to create the international intrigue.

The movie was then packaged as a blaxploitation action flick to unsuspecting audiences. The film haphazardly trots around the world through various seemingly unrelated incidents. Adamson directed this film under a pseudonym (Albert Victor), and you gotta wonder about a picture that even he didn't want to be associated with! —*S. H.*

SATAN'S SADISTS L: DIRECTORS/ADAMSON, AL (1969)
86M D: Al Adamson. *Robert Dix, Russ Tamblyn, Scott Brady, John "Bud" Cardos, Regina Carrol.* The *Citizen Kane* of biker movies! Adamson's classic story about an evil bike gang and their innocent victims is considered his masterpiece. It features a lot of his recurring actors including the fantastic Tamblyn and Adamson's wife, Carrol. As far as no-budget drive-in flicks go, you'd be hard pressed to do better than the work of Adamson, and this is, indeed, one is his best. —*T. S.*

BAGDAD CAFÉ (AKA OUT OF ROSENHEIM) L:DIRECTORS/ADLON, PERCY (1988) 95M D: Percy Adlon. *Monica Calhoun, Marianne Sagebrecht, CCH Pounder, Christine Kaufmann, Darron Flagg, Jack Palance.* A peculiar and playful film, *Bagdad Café* is about the meeting of minds and different worlds as a German tourist ends up transforming the lives of the people who own a small, run-down café off the highway. A fight with her husband leaves Jasmin (Sagebrecht) alone in the middle of the desert, so she decides to befriend and transform the local motel/diner and its owner, who is at first furious with the interference. Over time, the owner comes to realize the changes in her and her business are in fact needed and welcome. This film is German writer-director Adlon's first American feature, which explains the foreign film quality that imbues the whole production. Quirky, curious, refreshingly light and upbeat, with a subtle touch of magical realism added to the mix, this film is a charmer. —*M. N.*

AKERMANIA, VOL. 1 L: DIRECTORS/AKERMAN, CHANTAL (1992) 89M D: Chantal Akerman. *Chantal Akerman, Maria de Medeiros.* This collection of three short films was to be followed by a second collection that unfortunately never appeared. The first short, *I'm Hungry, I'm Cold* (1984), one of Akerman's more accessible works, deals with two runaways struggling to satisfy such basic needs as food and shelter. In the second, *Saute Ma Ville* (1968), which is Akerman's first film, a young woman cooks, cleans, and then kills herself. Though rough, it firmly establishes a number of interests Akerman would pursue in the following years. *Hotel Monterey* (1972), the third and longest film, is an ambitious piece consisting of largely unpeopled shots of the interior of a New York residence hotel; the footage does not even attempt to satisfy a linear narrative. This excellent short may torment your patience, but it offers a rare look at the type of structuralist

filmmaking practiced by Michael Snow and a number of others whose work you'll have difficulty catching on video. —*C. B.*

CAPTIVE, LA L: DIRECTORS/AKERMAN, CHANTAL (2000) 118M D: Chantal Akerman. *Olivia Bonamy, Sylvie Testud, Stanislas Merhar.* Where many of Akerman's earlier films seemed more conceptual than conventionally cinematic, *La Captive* surprises with masterful acting, stunning visuals, and an all-around elegant film experience. Based on Marcel Proust's *La Prisonniere*, the novelistic plot involves wealthy Simon (Merhar) and his quietly destructive obsession with Ariane (Testud), who as the film's title suggests is his semi-willing captive. Not that he locks her in a dungeon—rather, his jealousy demands constant knowledge of Ariane's every activity and thought. He even arranges for a female friend (Bonamy) for Ariane; she accompanies Ariane on excursions outside the apartment and reports to Simon the details of Ariane's day. This control extends to their sexual relationship as well. Impotent, Simon requires Ariane to feign sleep while he attempts to, well, possess her. Ever pliable, Ariane passively—numbly—bends to his will until the film's tragic, if not unexpected, finale. —*C. B.*

EIGHTIES, THE L: DIRECTORS/AKERMAN, CHANTAL (1983) 86M D: Chantal Akerman. *Françios Beukelaers, Katherine Best, Aurore Clément, Aischa Bentebouche.* Consisting of screen tests culled from the casting of a musical, *The Eighties* has been referred to by Akerman as a kind of "work in progress." Although it's not what one might call entertaining, it's as conceptually serviceable as anything she's done. The auditions start off bland but slowly gain polish. Yet as the acting becomes more dynamic, the material becomes increasingly redundant. Already lacking a solid narrative context for the audience to latch on to, the soap-operatic dialogue is read and reread repeatedly by various auditioning performers until it becomes entirely banal. After about an hour of this, we watch the finished product—a short bubblegum musical set in a shopping mall, which Akerman used as a pilot for her feature-length musical *Window Shopping*. Though challenging to watch, *The Eighties* should be a walk in the park for anyone familiar with Akerman's work. I'd direct the uninitiated to *News from Home*—a film no less demanding, but more rewarding and perhaps more engaging. —*C. B.*

NEWS FROM HOME L: DIRECTORS/AKERMAN, CHANTAL (1976) 85M D: Chantal Akerman. *Chantal Akerman (voice-over).* News from Home collects cinema verité footage of everyday New York settings (the subway, a run-down street corner), over which are read letters from Akerman's mother in Belgium. The letters express loneliness and distress at her daughter's abrupt departure for

New York, and enumerate the routine events of the mother's day-to-day life. Through unbelievably inventive narrative means, the film explores a marginalized experience of home (the public space Akerman resides in and photographs, the domestic space her mother speaks of/from, and the "space" that family constitutes). *News from Home* single-handedly advances the untapped potential of the film medium, and crafts a perplexingly indirect self-portrait (the most impressive example since Roland Barthes wrote *Roland Barthes*). Akerman is one of the most conceptually rich resources in cinema or anywhere, and I couldn't possibly exaggerate the accomplishments of this work. —*C. B.*

RENDEZ-VOUS D'ANNA, LES (AKA **THE MEETINGS OF ANNA**) L: DIRECTORS/AKERMAN, CHANTAL (1978) 127M D: Chantal Akerman. *Helmut Griem, Lea Massari, Jean-Pierre Cassel, Aurore Clément.* Film director Anna (Clément) travels by train from Germany to Belgium to France. Consisting primarily of encounters en route with friends, family, lovers, and strangers, *Les Rendez-Vous D'Anna* is a series not of conversations but bland, flat, unnatural monologues recited at our awkwardly withdrawn protagonist. Serial in structure, the progression of these scenarios defies narrative utility, instead accumulating as an array of stylized contexts for Anna to drift into and out of with little interest or involvement. Holding fixed medium-long perspectives, avoiding point-of-view shots, and favoring stagy blocking, Akerman's hyperrealist mise-en-scene is sanitized of photogenic allure until numb. Add to this an unsettling lack of voice-overs and you've got a systematic denial of character interiority. This rigorous defamiliarization is perhaps the film's key element—it's cinema Akerman describes as "language itself, without parasites, without the possibility of identification." If such cinema is as rich, complex, and effective as this, I'm all for it. —*C. B.*

TOUTE UNE NUIT (ALL NIGHT LONG) L: DIRECTORS/ AKERMAN, CHANTAL (1982) 90M D: Chantal Akerman. *Aurore Clément, François Beukelaers, Natalia Akerman.* Spanning a single night in Brussels, Akerman's deconstructionist romance drastically overclocks its melodrama, literally composing the film entirely of the type of brief crescendos that would normally punctuate a film's climax—for example, a scene in which lovers reunite, dropping luggage and running to one another. A film of quickened paces and spilt drinks, there's much slow-dancing, passionate kissing, even a balcony scene and breakups and betrayals. Frustrating audience expectations, Akerman refuses to anchor the proceedings with consistent characters. We don't follow any of the anonymous people for more than a few minutes, and even when we do return to one, nothing's resolved. A choreography of what Akerman calls "mythological representations of love and desire," these genre clichés become the syntax of a serial romance

film composite wholly disconnected from narrative functionality, identification with characters, progress toward plot resolution, or even a unifying story. Yeah, it's awesome. —*C. B.*

WINDOW SHOPPING L: DIRECTORS/AKERMAN, CHANTAL (1986) 92M D: Chantal Akerman. *Nicholas Tronc, Delphine Seyrig, Myriam Boyer, Fanny Cottençon.* Also released as *Golden Eighties,* this lighter-than-air musical unleashes romance on the witless characters of a shopping mall. Although Robert (Tronc) has captured the hearts of many among the mall's hair-salon staff, he only has eyes for Lili (Cottençon), the salon's glamorous manager. Lili, however, is deeply embroiled in an affair with a wealthy businessman. Robert's mother, Jeanne (Seyrig), has troubles of her own when an old flame happens into her garment store. And, as the mall's finger-snapping Greek chorus will tell you, there's much, much more. Fans of Ackerman's formally challenging early work will be surprised by *Window Shopping*'s conventional plotting, although her handling of generic movie romance is interesting in its emphasis on the purely physical forces driving the heart. Still, this is pretty saccharine stuff, which might have been forgivable had the musical numbers aged a little better. —*C. B.*

FLIGHT OF THE PHOENIX, THE L: DIRECTORS/ALDRICH, ROBERT (1965) 149M D: Robert Aldrich. *Richard Attenborough, James Stewart, Hardy Kruger, Ian Bannen, Ernest Borgnine, Peter Finch.* Stewart is the cranky professional who crashes in the middle of the Sahara with a cargo plane full of men and a radio that refuses to work. It could be your basic survival tale with the usual suspects: the alcoholic navigator (Attenborough), the stiff-upper-lip British martinet (Finch), and a punch-drunk optimist (Borgnine), tossed together in a fight for survival. But with them is a German designer (Kruger), at once dreamer and obsessive visionary. He sets himself to the task of reengineering the spare parts into a workable plane and clashes constantly with the realist captain, while the men do the only thing they can to stay alive: they follow the dream. A tough-minded film directed with a lean, mean style by two-fisted intellectual Aldrich. —*S. A.*

KISS ME DEADLY L: DIRECTORS/ALDRICH, ROBERT (1955) 106M D: Robert Aldrich. *Maxine Cooper, Paul Stewart, Ralph Meeker, Albert Dekker.* One of the most brutal films noir stars Meeker as Mike Hammer, who becomes involved in a violent search for a suitcase filled with radioactive materials. Hammer spends the majority of the film beating people up and getting beat up himself. Most scenes end with him blacking out from drugs or a punch to the head. Meeker is perfect as the tough, sleazy, and unlikable Hammer and the apocalyptic conclusion is a knockout. The DVD restores Aldrich's slightly longer ending that allows Hammer and his secretary/lover,

Velda, to escape, but they've been exposed to excessive radiation so they're doomed anyway. Even if you've never seen *Kiss Me Deadly* you've undoubtedly seen visual references in movies like the glowing trunk in *Repo-Man* and the shiny briefcase in *Pulp Fiction*. —*S. H.*

VERA CRUZ L: DIRECTORS/ALDRICH, ROBERT (1954) 94M D: Robert Aldrich. *Ernest Borgnine, Charles Bronson, Jack Elam, Gary Cooper, Burt Lancaster.* Southern gentleman turned hard-bitten adventurer Cooper and mercenary Lancaster, a perpetually grinning bandit in black, meet in the dust of the southwestern frontier. Conning, robbing, and outwitting one another in games of one-upmanship, they bond in mutual admiration and team up to steal a fortune in gold in the chaos of the Mexican revolution. Then they revert to their old ways, selling out anyone—even each other— to get the treasure for themselves. Played out as a seat-of-the-pants con game of shifting alliances and double crosses, it's a cheerfully ruthless tale that served as a veritable blueprint for the Italian spaghetti Westerns of the '60s. Aldrich is a master at turning cynical opportunists into deviously riveting characters. Only the creeping sentimental attachment to the peasant revolutionaries betrays this otherwise ruthless Western. Borgnine, Bronson, and Elam contribute their share of betrayal as conniving members of the gang. —*S. A.*

ALICE L: DIRECTORS/ALLEN, WOODY (1990) 106M D: Woody Allen. *Kristina Kohoutova, Mia Farrow, Joe Mantegna, William Hurt, Judy Davis.* After remaking *La Dolce Vita* (*Manhattan*), *8½* (*Stardust Memories*), and *Amarcord* (*Radio Days*), Allen decided to put muse/companion Farrow front and center and remake *Juliet of the Spirits*. As Fellini's wife Giulietta Masina did in *Juliet*, Farrow plays Alice, a woman trapped in a suffocating marriage, looking to escape through spiritual means. In Masina's case, she had a séance. Farrow goes to Chinatown on the advice of her trendy upscale friends, and seeks out a Chinese healer who's been known to cure anything. This visit precipitates a wild, liberating, and truly spiritual journey for Alice as she confronts new loves, ghosts of loves past, and ultimately herself. Less fanciful and more down to earth than Fellini's film, *Alice* is a lovely, semi-forgotten Allen/Farrow collaboration that deserves a second look. —*M. S.*

ANNIE HALL L: DIRECTORS/ALLEN, WOODY (1977) 93M D: Woody Allen. *Tony Roberts, Carol Kane, Paul Simon, Woody Allen, Diane Keaton.* *Annie Hall* is Allen's quintessential film. It was such a success (beating out *Star Wars* for Best Picture) that it basically allowed Allen the freedom to do anything he pleased with the rest of his career. Almost single-handedly, Allen made it possible for the romantic lead in a film to be neurotic rather than confident, aloof rather than suave. *Annie Hall* is

an important turning point for the writer/director because it marked not only a new direction for Allen but for the romantic comedy genre itself. —*C. P.*

ANYTHING ELSE L: DIRECTORS/ALLEN, WOODY (2003) 109M D: Woody Allen. *Danny DeVito, Jimmy Fallon, Stockard Channing, Christina Ricci, Jason Biggs, Woody Allen.* *Everything Else* might have been more descriptive as Allen returns to familiar subjects, this time with Biggs playing a junior Woody Allen character. He's a fledgling comedy writer with a passion for the darker side of the human condition (at least philosophically speaking) and the inability to break off unfulfilling relationships (his latest with the flighty, fickle Ricci). Allen himself is the elderly sidekick with a barely sublimated violent streak and life lessons freely illustrated in Borscht Belt jokes. Once upon a time Allen's casts of neurotics were both hilarious and relatable. Now those self-involved figures are just annoying and intermittently funny, but give Allen some credit. He's the funniest of the sad lot. —*S. A.*

BANANAS L: DIRECTORS/ALLEN, WOODY (1971) 82M D: Woody Allen. *Natividad Abascal, Jacobo Morales, Carlos Montalban, Woody Allen, Louise Lasser.* Allen creeps me out these days both due to his lifestyle and yearly production schedule of one lame movie after another, but he used to make some very funny films and *Bananas* is one of his best. Allen plays a nerdy product tester who falls for Nancy (Lasser), a political activist who eventually spurns his advances. Desperately trying to prove his leadership skills, he travels to a Central American country, becomes involved in its revolution, eventually becomes the president, and dresses like Castro. He is reunited with Nancy and Howard Cosell gives a play-by-play of their honeymoon. *Bananas* is more like a Zucker-Abrams-Zucker or Mel Brooks comedy than Woody's later, pretentious films. A lot of the humor is pretty lowbrow, but at least it's funny! —*S. H.*

CRIMES AND MISDEMEANORS L: DIRECTORS/ALLEN, WOODY (1989) 107M D: Woody Allen. *Mia Farrow, Anjelica Huston, Jerry Orbach, Alan Alda, Martin Landau, Woody Allen.* Don't be fooled by the one-liners. Crimes and Misdemeanors, which carries moments of humor familiar to anyone who's a fan of Allen, is actually a serious meditation on morality, punishment, and life. It also happens to be funny. The film follows two stories: a married man (Landau) who considers having his mistress murdered, and a documentary filmmaker (Allen) who falls for a woman (Farrow) with an obnoxious, vain boss (Alda) about whom Allen is making a film. The stories eventually intertwine. Laughs abound—the nebbish in love was virtually invented by Allen—but the story takes some surprising and dark terms, and the accent is more on the bitter than the sweet. A strong cast doing some of its best work doesn't hurt either. —T. P.

EVERYONE SAYS I LOVE YOU L: DIRECTORS/ALLEN, WOODY (1996) 101M D: Woody Allen. *Julia Roberts, Edward Norton, Drew Barrymore, Woody Allen, Goldie Hawn, Tim Roth*. I realized some interesting things while watching this movie. First of all, Allen is a funny guy, if not a little bit off-putting at times. Second, an Allen musical is also funny and a little off-putting at times. The story line is simple, sweet, and ultimately delivers the message that relationships are complicated and kind of stupid, but we're all going to die anyway, so we might as well make the most of it. Thank you for this little pearl of wisdom, Mr. Allen. And thanks for a movie that is just far enough embedded in fantasy that we get a little piece of France, a little convenience-store robbery, and a little Hawn flying through the air, while you manage to get a little piece of both her and Roberts. Fantasy is a beautiful, beautiful thing, and this movie is good-natured fun that reminds us how much of our lives really are ridiculous. —J. S.

HANNAH AND HER SISTERS L: DIRECTORS/ALLEN, WOODY (1986) 103M D: Woody Allen. *Woody Allen, Mia Farrow, Barbara Hershey, Dianne Wiest, Carrie Fisher, Michael Caine*. In 1986, Allen returned, older and perhaps a bit wiser, to territory he had previously mined somewhat in both *Annie Hall* and *Manhattan*. The result was this Oscar-nominated film, a movie inspired by a range of sources, from the plays of Henrik Ibsen to some of the later character studies of Ingmar Bergman (most notably it echoes *Cries and Whispers* with its familial, sisterly themes). The plot of *Hannah and Her Sisters* reads deceptively simple. At its heart is the story of three sisters, their relationships with each other and with the world around them, over the course of a single year. Allen handles these relationships and their complications in a very mature fashion, managing to mix comedy and tragedy in a distinctive synergy that no other director has been able to achieve. This impressive synthesis of style makes *Hannah and Her Sisters* a film that appeals to audiences and remains one of Allen's most popular works. —C. P.

HUSBANDS AND WIVES L: DIRECTORS/ALLEN, WOODY (1992) 107M D: Woody Allen. *Judy Davis, Sydney Pollack, Woody Allen, Mia Farrow*. Let's not kid ourselves here, this is a painful movie to watch. It also happens to be an exceptional one. Farrow and Allen play a married couple that is breaking up (while their real-life relationship was simultaneously falling apart over the Woody/Soon Yi affair). On one level it's fascinating and on another level it's truly awful to watch. Not surprisingly, this was also Farrow's last film with Allen, ending a string of thirteen consecutive films between the two. One of the better films of

the '90s, and Davis is not to be missed (or easily forgotten) in an amazing supporting role. —C. P.

INTERIORS L: DIRECTORS/ALLEN, WOODY (1978) 95M D: Woody Allen. *Geraldine Page, Maureen Stapleton, E. G. Marshall, Mary Beth Hurt, Diane Keaton*. The success of *Annie Hall*—which had garnered Oscars for both Best Picture and Best Director the previous year—allowed Allen the complete artistic freedom he ultimately needed to make a film that was such a bold departure from anything he had ever done. Drawing obvious inspiration from legendary Swedish director Ingmar Bergman, Allen crafted a very slow-paced, quiet, European-style chamber drama focusing on the relationships within a single family. The film somewhat echoed Bergman's *Cries and Whispers* (and to a lesser extent *Through a Glass Darkly*), respecting the dramatic structures of these films and borrowing more than lightly from their stylistic mainstays. While some critics praised Allen (Vincent Camby perhaps most notable among them) and his attempt at pure drama, many more attacked or even completely disregarded the film. They claimed, and somewhat rightfully so, that *Interiors* was precisely the type of intellectually based art film that Allen had poked various fun at earlier in his career. However, bold performances from Keaton, Marshall, Stapleton, and Page make this intriguing character study more than worth your time. —C. P.

MANHATTAN L: DIRECTORS/ALLEN, WOODY (1979) 96M D: Woody Allen. *Diane Keaton, Meryl Streep, Mariel Hemingway, Michael Murphy, Wallace Shawn, Woody Allen*. Allen's love for New York is summed up in his beautiful black-and-white film *Manhattan*. Allen plays Isaac Davis, a neurotic writer who's trying to make it big but can't seem to keep any of his relationships together. Feeding his neuroses is Streep playing his ex-wife who turns out to be lesbian and makes a killing with her own book on her marriage with Isaac. Allen's keen humor is revealed at cocktail parties, in the bedroom, and even in the narrative elucidating his theory that one is most lonely in the biggest city. The music by George Gershwin is also an essential ingredient, making everything about this film perfectly indigenous to Manhattan. —N. J.

RADIO DAYS L: DIRECTORS/ALLEN, WOODY (1987) 89M D: Woody Allen. *Michael Tucker, Mia Farrow, Dianne Wiest, Julie Kavner, Wallace Shawn*. In this nostalgic film Allen does his best through several vignettes to bring to life that innocent time of youth which for him existed before the invention of television. With incredible period detail and typical Allen humor the film depicts the lifestyle of one family, its relationship to society, and its relationship to one of the most important pieces of furniture: the radio. Folks who do remember such days will be taken back by the familiar sounds and culture, and those who don't will get an education on what entertainment was really like in people's living rooms. —*N. J.*

SEPTEMBER L: DIRECTORS/ALLEN, WOODY (1987) 82M D: Woody Allen. *Jack Warden, Elaine Stritch, Dianne Wiest, Denholm Elliot, Mia Farrow, Sam Waterston.* This claustrophobic gloom-fest feels like a play—ceaselessly talky, set almost entirely in a few stagy interiors, with physical action that seems little more than window dressing to the dialogue and a plot that follows something of an act/scene progression. Suicidally mopey Lane (Farrow) tries to hold herself together in a crowded cottage where love is in the air but, typically, not always reciprocated. Looming over the party is a dark secret that some know, some try to learn, and some work to forget. In keeping with Allen's tendency to direct actors to behave like himself, Farrow here does her best anxiety-ridden Woody impression, to uncanny (and, in retrospect, eyebrow-raising) effect. —*C. B.*

SHADOWS AND FOG L: DIRECTORS/ALLEN, WOODY (1992) 85M D: Woody Allen. *Woody Allen, John Cusack, Mia Farrow, John Malkovich.* Allen's bizarre, Kafka-esque tribute to German expressionist thrillers is a visual delight in black and white, and a celebration of the power of fantasy and magic. Though critically dismissed on its release for its awkward transplanting of Allen's world to the murky streets of Fritz Lang's *M,* there are wondrous moments of human comedy (the prostitutes at rest) and classic Allen lines (Cusack's talkative student gets many of them). It's undeniably as weird as Allen's films get, but the handsomely moody sets and shadowy lighting give a unique setting for Allen's brand of comedy. In such a world of doom, sometimes comedy and magic are all we have. —*S. A.*

SLEEPER L: DIRECTORS/ALLEN, WOODY (1973) 88M D: Woody Allen. *Woody Allen, Diane Keaton, John Beck, Mary Gregory, Don Keefer.* Sleeper is Allen's view of the future, a future two hundred years from now. He plays a neurotic patient who survives a bungled surgery only to wake up in another century. There he learns about all sorts of strange things that we in the twentieth century would find surprising, like their gargantuan vegetables, their robotic servants, and the fact that a Volkswagen Bug will start after sitting for two hundred years. There is also the Orgasmatron, which must be seen to be believed. The plot focuses on the protagonist's love interest (Keaton, as the futuristic woman who helps save him) and how he means to improve the world by overthrowing the government ruled by a dictator simply named "The Leader." This is one of Allen's early classics. —*N. J.*

STARDUST MEMORIES L: DIRECTORS/ALLEN, WOODY (1980) 91M D: Woody Allen. *Woody Allen, Charlotte Rampling, Marie-Christine Barrault, Jessica Harper.*

Allen's homage to Fellini's *8½* plays out much in the same way, as Allen creates a skewed version of himself, this time called Sandy Bates. Bates is at a film festival for a retrospective on his career, and throughout the course of the weekend he reflects on his personal life, his past films, and the future of his career, all of which are very similar to Allen's real life. The film itself meanders from reality into the imagination of Bates, though the line is never clearly drawn. *Stardust Memories* can be seen as a chapter break in Allen's career. Throughout the film Bates is plagued by fans saying that they especially like his earlier, funnier movies, as Bates (and thus Allen) attempts to break into more dramatic features. *Stardust Memories* is not given as much praise as many of Allen's other films, but is worth seeing for his critique on cinema in general. —*R. M.*

WHAT'S UP, TIGER LILY? L: DIRECTORS/ALLEN, WOODY (1966) 80M D: Woody Allen. *China Lee, Tatsuya Mihashi, Akiko Wakabayashi, Mie Hama.* Here's a strange kind of movie—or more properly, an un-movie. Allen dispensed with the soundtrack to a Japanese spy film released in 1964 under the title *Kagi No Kag* or *Key of Keys.* What he did was record a different soundtrack in English, thereby changing the original plot concerning espionage to a new one about acquiring a recipe for egg salad. Only Allen's offbeat humor would be capable of sustaining this for an entire film. The music is supplied by Lovin' Spoonful. —*N. J.*

ZELIG L: DIRECTORS/ALLEN, WOODY (1982) 80M D: Woody Allen. *Mia Farrow, Will Holt, G. Mac Brown, Woody Allen, Stephanie Farrow.* One of Allen's most diverse film projects, and coincidentally his shortest film to date, was the pseudo-documentary film released in 1982, *Zelig.* The film, which Allen worked on at the same time as *A Midsummer Night's Sex Comedy,* is a visual marvel and a miniature gem in Allen's filmography. Though he had used a documentary approach somewhat in his first directorial feature, *Take the Money and Run* (1967), it was with *Zelig* that he went "all the way," so to speak. If you were unfamiliar with the faces of Allen and Farrow and stumbled upon this "documentary" on television, it would take quite some time to figure out that it couldn't possibly be true. This is a testament to the rigorous mimicry of the documentary style that Allen creates and employs for the entire eighty minutes of the film. —*C. P.*

ALL ABOUT MY MOTHER L: DIRECTORS/ALMODÓVAR, PEDRO (1999) 101M D: Pedro Almodóvar. *Cecilia Roth, Marisa Paredes, Penelope Cruz, Candela Peña.* The bitter tragedy of a single mother's loss of her child sends her on a journey that will help her come to terms with herself and rejoice in the life of her son. On his seventeenth birthday, Esteban is killed in a car accident trying to get an autograph of his favorite actress. His mother, Manuela (Roth), makes the painful choice to go find his father in Barcelona to tell him what has happened. Along the way, she is reunited with an old friend, who helps her cope with her loss and becomes a shoulder to lean on. Manuela is shocked to discover that Esteban's father is now a woman. And as life is a circle, Manuela comes face-to-face with the actress who was the ultimate cause of Esteban's death, only to befriend her. This is a beautiful story using twists on classic plot devices, weaving a sad tale that will leave its introspective mark on the heart. —R. M.

KIKA L: DIRECTORS/ALMODÓVAR, PEDRO (1993) 115M
D: Pedro Almodóvar. *Erika Remberg, Victoria Abril, Peter Coyote, Veronica Forque.* Another campy Almodóvar sex comedy romp, with a murder mystery wedged in. Kika (Forque), a motor-mouthed makeup artist, is hired to do some pre-funeral touch-up work on the handsome corpse of Ramón (Álex Casanovas). Applying makeup to his face, she revives him and they fall in love. Plausibility cast to the wind, *Kika* tosses out a few convoluted crime subplots and, just for good measure, a comedic rape scene. Generally an Almodóvar fan, I can't stand this obnoxious movie. Perhaps it's that Forque's Kika, whose floating rack the film seems dedicated to, annoys the snot out of me. More likely the problem is that Almodóvar gets bogged down trying to tell a story. Unlike his later efforts, the plot here is nothing special and continually spoils the absurdist fun found in his earlier films. Best avoided unless you've already waded through the bulk of Almodóvar's other work. —C. B.

LABYRINTH OF PASSION L: DIRECTORS/ALMODÓVAR, PEDRO
(1982) 100M D: Pedro Almodóvar. *Cecilia Roth, Antonio Banderas, Imanol Arias, Marta Fernandez-Muro.* Long before winning the Palme d'Or, Almodóvar was dedicated to the frantic exposure of all things suppressed, taboo, and indecent, churning out raucous sex comedies barely held together by ludicrous plots. In *Labyrinth of Passion* Roth plays nymphomaniac punk star Sexilia, daughter of a renowned reproductive specialist. Banderas plays Sadeq, a terrorist in love with Reza—also a punk star and the son of an emperor—whom Sadeq is unfortunately ordered to track and kidnap using his uncanny sense of smell (no, I'm serious). With the help of plastic surgery, Queti trades places with Sexilia, enabling Sexilia to run away with Reza, and Queti to escape her deranged father. It's actually far more confusing than I make it sound, but I doubt you'll mind. *Labyrinth of Passion* finds humor in everything, even and especially the most offensive material. Pure fun you have to see to believe. —C. B.

LIVE FLESH L: DIRECTORS/ALMODÓVAR, PEDRO (1997)
103M D: Pedro Almodóvar. *Javier Bardem, Francesca Neri, Liberto Rabal, Angelo Molina.* Almodóvar matures in a thriller that teeters on the edge of lurid sexploitation but ends up a sensitive essay of jealousy, need, passion, and love. Ex-con Rabal plots his revenge against a crippled cop (Bardem) and his elegant wife (Neri, who transforms from spindly junkie into elegant, confident social worker). The plan is steeped in adolescent sex fantasies, but the convoluted plot (adapted from a Ruth Rendell mystery) takes the vivid gallery of emotionally crippled saints, sinners, and innocents into Almodóvar's favorite territory: grand melodrama. And yes, there's plenty of sex, but not necessarily the lurid, lascivious spectacle we're used to. This is a kinder, gentler Almodóvar. He's transformed the wonderfully garish images and melodramatic excesses of his earlier films into a more controlled style which is just as evocative but more delicate, and it makes for an eye-opening film. —S. A.

TALK TO HER L: DIRECTORS/ALMODÓVAR, PEDRO (2002)
116M D: Pedro Almodóvar. *Rosario Flores, Geraldine Chaplin, Javier Camara, Dario Grandinetti, Leonor Watling.* This is about as good as mainstream art house cinema gets. In a plot too complex to summarize, stoic travel writer Marco (Grandinetti) befriends enigmatic nurse Benigno (Camara) in a hospital where Marco's lover Lydia lies in a coma and where Benigno cares for Alicia, who is also in a coma. Benigno's devotion is abnormally zealous, and he seems incapable of distinguishing his relationship as caretaker to Alicia from what he perceives as something like a marriage. Although never without compassion, Almodóvar pushes his characters into a bottomless moral quagmire that will ultimately alienate some of the audience, while many will find the film profoundly touching. It might just turn out to be the best film you've rented since *All About My Mother.* —C. B.

WHAT HAVE I DONE TO DESERVE THIS? L: DIRECTORS/
ALMODÓVAR, PEDRO (1984) 100M D: Pedro Almodóvar. *Gonzalo Suarez, Chus Lampreave, Carmen Maura, Angel De Andres Lopez, Veronica Forque.* In the center of a wild cast of prostitutes, juvenile drug dealers, kleptomaniacs, pederasts, Hitler biographers, telekinetically powered schoolchildren, and opera enthusiasts is Gloria (Maura), a burned-out housewife who thanklessly cares for a brutish husband, two delinquent children, and a near-senile mother-in-law, as well as handling some outside cleaning work to supplement the dismal household income. In what feels like Almodóvar's *Jeanne Dielman,* the searing indictment of the domestic constraints placed on women makes this the most focused and least delirious of Almodóvar's early work. And yet, characteristic of his early films, a deluge of off-color, near-offensive absurdity bursts forth. Perhaps the biggest problem this movie faces is an inability to reconcile its socially conscious intentions with its ridiculous comedic non sequiturs. There's almost a sense that Almodóvar didn't even attempt a compromise of these distinct trajectories, which in a funny way makes me like this movie that much more. —C. B.

WOMEN ON THE VERGE OF A NERVOUS BREAKDOWN

L: DIRECTORS/ALMODÓVAR, PEDRO (1988) 90M D: Pedro Almodóvar. *Antonio Banderas, Maria Barranco, Kiti Manver, Carmen Maura, Julieta Serrano, Rossy DePalma.* A classic film about love in all of its twisted, peculiar, perverted, and demented beauty. A woman having an affair is dumped over the answering machine, then realizes that she is pregnant. A convoluted tale begins between her, her neurotic friend, the man, his ex-wife, his son, and his girlfriend. Drugged gazpacho, high hysterics, and suicide attempts are only the start of this wild and hilarious roller coaster of a film about women coping the best they can with the pangs and pains of love. My first Almodóvar film and still my favorite. Look out for a very young and nerdy Banderas! —*M. N.*

BREWSTER MCCLOUD

L: DIRECTORS/ALTMAN, ROBERT (1970) 101M D: Robert Altman. *René Auberjonois, Stacy Keach, Michael Murphy, Bud Cort, Sally Kellerman.* Cort plays a boy who wants to fly. He's also a bit of a terrorist. It seems that every person who crosses him winds up getting splattered with bird shit, then killed. Enter high-profile, high-style detective Frank Shaft (a cross between John Shaft and Bullitt), brought in to solve these strange murders, and you've got one wild update of the story of Icarus. A nice, stylish entry from early '70s Altman, mixing slapstick humor with the sad tale of a dreamer. A trippy score by John Phillips and some fine Panavision camera work by Jordan Cronenweth add to the unsettling lunacy, and Keach, Margaret Hamilton, and Auberjonois all turn in memorable supporting roles. —*M. S.*

DR. T & THE WOMEN

L: DIRECTORS/ALTMAN, ROBERT (2000) 121M D: Robert Altman. *Richard Gere, Farrah Fawcett, Helen Hunt, Kate Hudson.* Dr. T (Gere) is the most popular doctor in town; he is also one of the busiest. The film explores the ways in which various women—his wife, his daughters, his patients, his friends—alternately improve and ruin his seemingly charmed life. Fans of Altman will find much to like with this effort, although those who simply never "got" his work won't find anything here to change their minds. For better or for worse, this is most definitely an Altman film—from the roving camera to the overlapping dialogue and everything in between, every scene bears his distinctive stamp. Yet the film itself is fairly trivial. Altman once again demonstrates his dislike for any normal semblance of plot, choosing to subvert his audience's expectations for a cohesive narrative by instead offering a rambling, hectic film that never seems to fully decide where it wants to go. But then again, perhaps that was the point all along. —*C. P.*

GOSFORD PARK

L: DIRECTORS/ALTMAN, ROBERT (2001) 138M D: Robert Altman. *Kelly MacDonald, Emily Watson, Jeremy Northam, Clive Owen, Helen Mirren, Maggie Smith.* Altman's best work in years begins as a sprawling *Upstairs Downstairs* peek into class and transforms into a smartly lampooned Agatha Christie drawing-room mystery. His richest characters since *Nashville* include Oscar-nominated performances by Smith (as a creaky dowager clinging to privilege) and Mirren (the housekeeper who holds court in her little servant fiefdom). Owen provides a piercing turn as a fiercely independent valet, Watson is a tough cookie with a sentimental underbelly as an impulsive but worldly maid, and Northam is effortless as real-life actor and music-hall singer Ivor Novello. Altman's restless camera is sure and more graceful than ever, probing, revealing, catching his characters off guard, and then gliding back into the formal social dance of manners. This portrait of a petrified system crumbling before our eyes offers no real heroes and villains, only people on all levels trapped by their crippling classism. —*S. A.*

JAZZ '34: REMEMBRANCES OF KANSAS

L: DIRECTORS/ALTMAN, ROBERT (1996) 72M D: Robert Altman. *Don Byron, Joshua Redman, David "Fathead" Newman, Craig Handy, Jesse Davis, Ron Carter.* The best part of Altman's narratively challenged *Kansas City* was the free-flowing jam in the Hey Hey Club, a re-creation of the 1934 jazz scene highlighted by the legendary cutting contest between tenor giants Coleman Hawkins and Lester Young. In *Jazz '34* Altman lets go of all narrative pretense and charts the ebb and flow of a night of jazz, capturing the rhythms and cadences of the musicians themselves in a visual texture to match the music. Slow zooms, gentle pans and dollies, and a lazy editing pace ease the piece through some great music and brilliant playing, culminating in the fabulous battle of the tenors (marked by whip pans between the dueling horns) and easing off as the party breaks up and drifts off. Who needs a story? —*S. A.*

KANSAS CITY

L: DIRECTORS/ALTMAN, ROBERT (1996) 115M D: Robert Altman. *Dermot Mulroney, Jennifer Jason Leigh, Miranda Richardson, Harry Belafonte.* It's a wonder it took more than thirty years of filmmaking for Altman to make a movie about jazz. His entire career has basically been one long instrumental riff with the camera, but here he goes back to his hometown to get it right, setting his tale in 1930s Jazz Age KC, where cats like Lester Young, Coleman Hawkins, and Charlie Parker played 'til dawn and rumrunners controlled the city. Altman weaves a tale of kidnapping and corruption around some lovely jazz interludes, with Belafonte, Richardson, and Leigh all providing their own riffs on life back then. Leigh in particular stands out as a trashy flapper doing (in character) a bad Jean Harlow impression. There are so many wonderful moments in this wild, lyrical look at a forgotten era that one wonders why such criticism was heaped on it at the time.

If Leigh gets on your nerves, just sit back and enjoy the music. It's solid. —*M. S.*

I agree with most everything stated above, except that I thought it was a colossally boring failed experiment with great music. I actually fell asleep in the cinema, which I NEVER do. Oh well. *K. S.*

LONG GOODBYE, THE L: DIRECTORS/ALTMAN, ROBERT (1973) 112M D: Robert Altman. *Mark Rydell, Sterling Hayden, Nina Van Pallandt, Henry Gibson, Elliott Gould.* My favorite film, period. This update of Raymond Chandler's (and more cinematically known, Humphrey Bogart's) creation of private dick Phillip Marlowe throws the lead from his swank '40s joint into an unkempt Los Angeles penthouse, circa 1973. Altman delivers Leigh Brackett's screenplay with mood in mind before story. Gould's careless yet moral Marlowe is a hip idealist investigator who talks to and would suffer some for his employer. Unlike Bogart and Lauren Bacall's romance in *The Big Sleep,* Gould has no love interest here. He doesn't care; sex isn't on his mind. His concerns? In the first act he runs a midnight errand to the grocery store to find his cat's favorite brawnd of cat food, then he helps his best friend by giving him a ride to Tijuana at three a.m. A boozed Hayden, druken rants, gambling debts, suicides, double crossings, and the term "albino turd" all ensue. Plotwise, it fits. *The Long Goodbye* plays, on one of its many levels, as homage to classic Hollywood. You'll see. —*Z. L.*

M*A*S*H L: DIRECTORS/ALTMAN, ROBERT (1970) 116M D: Robert Altman. *Elliott Gould, Donald Sutherland.* Irreverence, anarchy, and gushing blood. After more than fifteen years in the business, Altman became an overnight success with a film that broke all of the studio rules. This portrait of war as a madhouse was the first Vietnam satire to come out of Hollywood (it was set in Korea, of course, but that didn't fool anyone) and it was a smash hit, launching not only Altman's career but pretty much every cast member's as well. Sutherland is the closest the film has to a moral center as Hawkeye Pierce and Gould is his slightly more anarchic buddy Trapper John, but unlike their TV counterparts these guys can be downright cruel, which is part of the genius of the film. In war, Altman suggests, you have to be mad to save your sanity. The great ensemble includes Tom Skerritt, Sally Kellerman, Michael Murphy, Gary Burgoff, John Schuck, Rene Auborjonois, and Robert Duvall. —*S. A.*

MCCABE AND MRS. MILLER L: DIRECTORS/ALTMAN, ROBERT (1971) 121M D: Robert Altman. *René Auberjonois, Warren Beatty, Julie Christie, Shelley Duvall, William Devane.* Gambler McCabe (Beatty) is a cocky entrepreneur on a cutthroat business frontier and Christie is the utterly professional bordello madam who manages his unkempt business in Altman's alternately delicate and savage vision

of the old West invaded by modern business. It's only a Western by genre definitions; it's really an Altman film, defined as much by the communal cast that mills through the picture and mutters dialogue as by the story of its charming but over-his-head hero McCabe and the caustic Miller who escapes nightly in a cloud of opium. It has the look and feel of no other Western: time just washes along and people like McCabe and Miller either flow with it or get left behind. One of Altman's masterpieces, and easily one of the finest American films of the '70s. —*S. A.*

NASHVILLE L: DIRECTORS/ALTMAN, ROBERT (1975) 160M D: Robert Altman. *Allen Garfield/Goorwitz, Henry Gibson, Keith Carradine, Ned Beatty, Karen Black, Lily Tomlin.* Altman's satire on country music and, more accurately, a post-Nam/JFK America, *Nashville* features multiple tracks of overlapping dialogue and many chaotic plot threads. A large cast, vaguely connected through politics and the music industry, interacts in the days before a presidential candidate's fund-raising concert. A lot of the characters parody real Nashville singers and situations, and the soundtrack is pretty cool. Gibson plays a Conway Twitty–type singer named Haven Hamilton and Ronee Blakely gives the performance of her career as Barbara Jean, the mentally unstable Queen of Nashville. The ensemble improvised their lines and wrote their own songs, and the semidocumentary style set the groundwork for later films like *Waiting For Guffman.* This was a huge critical success that met mixed reactions from mainstream audiences and is now regarded as one of the seminal films of the mid-'70s. —*S. H.*

POPEYE L: DIRECTORS/ALTMAN, ROBERT (1980) 114M D: Robert Altman. *Shelley Duvall, Robin Williams, Paul Dooley, Geoff Hoyle, Paul L. Smith, Donald Moffat, Bill Irwin, Ray Walston.* Watch this delightful movie! Please! In the wake of images of the hugely popular Williams as Mork from *Mork and Mindy* and exaggerated reports of budget overruns, this movie was so overhyped and over-trashed by critics that it was nearly ignored by audiences in its initial release. It's perfectly cast, smartly written, beautifully designed, and sumptuously shot in super-wide Technovision. And the music ("Everything is Food," "I'm Mean," "He's Large") is delightful. Now, gloriously restored to its original aspect ratio on DVD, this is a must-see movie that the entire family will enjoy. *Popeye* has some of the most vibrant margins in the history of the cinema. Watch every frame: in the background you'll see all manners of monkey business concocted by some of the greatest clowns on the planet. Enjoy this film, hum this music, and spread the gospel! —*K. S.*

Bringing popular cartoons into live action is always a tricky business. It's difficult to say exactly why studios even bother. One thing they all seem to have in common, however, is the portrayal of a familiar cartoon character by a popular and well-known actor. The weak plot of *Popeye* trying to find his father leads the audience through an odyssey of unpleasant-looking characters who, with the help of a costume and makeup department run amok, contort themselves to look as much like cartoons as possible. Far from being a comedy, *Popeye* is more like a train wreck. You can't help staring at it and feeling sorry for the people on board. —*N. J.*

SECRET HONOR L: DIRECTORS/ALTMAN, ROBERT (1985) 90M D: Robert Altman. *Phillip Baker Hall.* A fascinating yet deeply disturbing look at power, insecurity, narcissism, self-destruction, and fame all wrapped up in a misplaced sense of identity using, as its only character, Richard Nixon on the eve of his resignation. Hall gives a veritable tour de force performance as the embattled president at the very end of his term, a man who doesn't know if he should make love to his portrait on the wall or use the loaded gun in his desk drawer. Brilliantly written by Donald Freed and Arnold Stone, this is the kind of performance that sticks with you after you've seen it, for Hall as the president behaves like the kind of mentally unstable guest you can't get rid of. —*N. J.*

SHORT CUTS L: DIRECTORS/ALTMAN, ROBERT (1993) 189M D: Robert Altman. *Bruce Davison, Jack Lemmon, Julianne Moore, Andie MacDowell, Lily Tomlin, Tim Robbins.* Short Cuts is exactly that, short cuts of a variety of people's lives that effectively produce a smorgasbord out of the human condition. This highly serialized film has an exposition that necessarily runs for half the film, intrigue that in numerous ways fuses half the characters, and a very brief conclusion that succeeds in wrapping up only the most annoying of the loose ends. It is probably the only film that daringly attempts to portray the entire cosmos of American society, and within the bearable length of the American attention span manages to get more than halfway there. With *Short Cuts,* Altman proves himself to be one of the greatest modern directors America has produced. The long list of actors eager and willing to work with him is testament to his legacy. —*N. J.*

THIEVES LIKE US L: DIRECTORS/ALTMAN, ROBERT (1973) 122M D: Robert Altman. *Shelley Duvall, Bert Remsen, Louise Fletcher, John Schuck, Keith Carradine.* Altman's take on Edward Anderson's novel (previously filmed by Nicholas Ray as *They Live By Night*) takes the romantic filter off the Depression-era tale of a young criminal (Carradine) who breaks prison with a pair of veteran bank robbers and joins their gang. Where Ray's film, shot in shadowy black and white (usually at night), played the story of doomed love—and lovers—as American tragedy, Altman's is more like a loose folktale populated by characters more oblivious than naive, shot in the daylight where they appear all too human and vulnerable. Yet Altman retains an affection and sympathy for his young lovers (Carradine and Sissy Spacek) and their fumbling, awkward courtship and need for each other's unconditional love. —*S. A.*

THINGS BEHIND THE SUN L: DIRECTORS/ANDERS, ALLISON (2001) 120M D: Allison Anders. *Kim Dickens, Eric Stoltz, Gabriel Mann, Don Cheadle.* This is pretty hardcore for a movie that debuted on television. It's the harrowing story of an adolescent gang rape told through the entanglement of the victim and an accomplice. The spin is that the story's two protagonists are not the average "when bad things happen to good people" types, tortured with grief and insight, waiting for someone to tell them it's OK. They don't seem to understand their experiences and they don't try to set an example, *7th Heaven* style, by talking about how this will all only make them stronger, and how life is so much more beautiful after strife and all that. The movie includes a beautiful performance by Cheadle and a score by Sonic Youth. —*J. J.*

IF. . . L: DIRECTORS/ANDERSON, LINDSAY (1969) 111M D: Lindsay Anderson. *Malcolm McDowell, David Wood, Richard Warwick.* McDowell, in his film debut, plays an older student in a British private school. In the well-established pecking order among the students, he takes pleasure in pestering all the younger children but is the target of stuffy classmates senior to him. Meanwhile, the headmaster is so strict that everyone seems to be living in a form of perpetual captivity. McDowell's cynicism of this tried-and-true social structure becomes tangible and he starts acting out in increasingly violent ways. Anderson uses some interesting techniques from time to time to help explain this rebellious character. The film's soundtrack is also impressive, expressing a cultural explosion that features an African Mass, Buxtehude organ music, and English marches. —*N. J.*

ETERNITY AND A DAY L: DIRECTORS/ANGELOPOULOS, THEO (1998) 132M D: Theo Angelopoulos. *Fabrizio Bentivoglio, Bruno Ganz, Isabelle Renauld.* Is Angelopoulos cheekily throwing down the gauntlet with this title? As his films simultaneously stretch out and compress the passage of time, they can seem like an eternity if you're not keyed into them. But make that connection and they are gorgeous, delicate journeys through time and memory and space. This story takes one day in the life of an aging Greek poet (played by the German Ganz, who is distractingly dubbed into Greek) and his life-changing encounter with a young street kid, a Balkan refugee whose presence sends the poet thinking back on his own Balkan heritage. As the film floats between the cold gray present and sunny blue skies, clear water, and white sands of memory. Angelopoulos's camera glides through the cinematic landscape with almost geometric precision while his characters wander down the same path with very human hesitations and

Michelangelo Antonioni

Born to a bourgeois family in Ferrara, Italy, in 1912, Michelangelo Antonioni was interested in the arts from an early age. At ten his hobby was constructing puppets, and in his teens he took up oil painting. He attended the University of Bologna, where he studied economics and business, but in his off hours he wrote stories and plays and cofounded a student theater group. He also discovered the cinema and wrote reviews for

a local paper. A vocal anti-fascist, he continually ran into censorship problems because of his views and lost many jobs, but despite those problems he began working on films as a writer and an assistant director.

After World War II (during which he was involved with the underground), Antonioni began making his own short films while continuing to write, including co-authoring Fellini's debut *The White Sheik* (1952) (which, it is rumored, he was to have directed himself). His first feature, *Story of a Love Affair* (1950), won several awards at international film festivals and included early signs of Antonioni's mature style: bleak

---

detours. This Cannes-winning film is meditative, introspective, slow, and absolutely beautiful. —*S.A.*

BEAR, THE L: DIRECTORS/ANNAUD, JEAN-JACQUES (1988) 92M D: Jean-Jacques Annaud. *Jack Wallace, Tchecky Karyo.* What a strange film this is. The mesmerizing tale of a bear cub, based on a novel by the great adventure author James Oliver Curwood. The cub, after helplessly witnessing his mother's death in a rock slide, must fend for himself and, just when we're beginning to think that something horrible might happen to him, he comes upon a giant grizzly who, though very reluctant at first, takes him under his care. I won't ruin any story details here, though. This is just a film you'll need to experience for yourself. A veritable textbook in cinematography and editing, this film is so well constructed that you do not mind knowing that the whole of it is so artificial. A final note: my pothead and acid-dropping friends give this film unanimous raves. —*K.S.*

BEYOND THE CLOUDS L: DIRECTORS/ANTONIONI, MICHELANGELO (1995) 112M D: Michaelangelo Antonioni. *Fanny Ardant, Jean Reno, Sophie Marceau, John Malkovich.* Antonioni's 1995 feature turns out to be the best episode of *Red Shoe Diaries* ever put on-screen. Adapted from his story sketchbook "That Bowling Green on the Tiber," the film explores the elusive nature of love, lust, and sex in four brief encounters woven together with the philosophical musings of narrator and Antonioni stand-in Malkovich (the linking scenes are directed by Wim Wenders). Antonioni's camera floats through long, slow takes in the misty chill and we wander, with his characters, through the ethereal beauty of his images. But the vignettes

are unfinished sketches, little more than gorgeous cinematic noodlings, and the film keeps grounding out in portentous declarations, arch theatricality and needless nudity. It all feels very important but winds up lost in the fog. —*S.A.*

BLOW-UP L: DIRECTORS/ANTONIONI, MICHELANGELO (1966) 111M D: Michelangelo Antonioni. *Vanessa Redgrave, David Hemmings, Sarah Miles.* In his first English-language feature, Italian director Antonioni starts with Hitchcock and ends up, brilliantly, nowhere. As the go-to fashion photographer of swinging London, Thomas (Hemmings) has it all—wealth, professional fame, all the "birds" he can bed, a Rolls-Royce convertible—and nothing at all. He moves through this life of riches with an automaton's ennui until, courtesy of Hitchcock, he stumbles upon a mystery. Strolling in a park, he photographs a couple in the distance and is pursued by the woman (Redgrave), who entreats him to give her the film. He refuses, despite her subsequent (and then scandalous) attempt to seduce him. Intrigued by her apparent desperation to destroy whatever it is he's captured on film, he develops it to find what *may* be a murder. Thomas's pursuit of this enigma cuts through his ennui and gives his life, for now, some direction. *Blow-Up* remains a vital meditation on the numbing excesses of modern life. —*C.C.*

L'AVVENTURA L: DIRECTORS/ANTONIONI, MICHELANGELO (1960) 143M D: Michelangelo Antonioni. *Gabriele Ferzetti, Lea Massari, Monica Vitti.* After booing its first screening, the 1960 Cannes Film Festival appropriately gave this landmark film a special award "for its search for a new cinematic language and for the beauty of its images." The plot revolves around the inexplicable disappearance of Anna

exteriors, meticulously composed shots, and long takes with a moving camera. It also signaled Antonioni's interest in the Italian bourgeoisie, which would be his primary focus throughout his Italian features. His subsequent films *The Vanquished* (1953) and *The Girl Friends* (1955) attracted critical attention, but it was *L'Avventura* (1960) that brought him international fame.

In *L'Avventura*, the first in a series of films concerning middle-class alienation and spiritual dislocation, Antonioni created a contemplative, austere film virtually without a story. The focus is on the characters and their emotional lives, explored as much through Antonioni's mise-en-scène as through the dialogue. These themes were continued through *La Notte* (1961)

and *L'Eclisse* (1962), which completed his loose trilogy. He then turned to color in *Red Desert* (1964), where he pushed the themes of isolation and personal dislocation to the breaking point.

Antonioni went to Britain for his next film, *Blow-Up* (released in 1966, and set in swinging London), which became a critical and commercial hit, and then to the United States for two films, *Zabriskie Point* (1970) and *The Passenger* (1975), the latter of which is considered one of his finest achievements. He returned to Italy for the remainder of his career. His productions since have been sporadic and have not found American distributors. In 1985 a heart attack left him partially paralyzed, but he continues to actively seek out projects.   —*Sean Axmaker*

(Massari), friend to Claudia (Vitti) and lover to Sandro (Ferzetti). Wandering through Sicily in search of her, Claudia and Sandro find no clues pointing to Anna's whereabouts, and initiate a relatively dispassionate affair. As Pascal Bonitzer says, "What happens in reality is the disappearance of the disappearance of Anna," an event that frees the film from dramatic conflict and ushers in a new and eye-opening brand of listless realism. The result is a breathtakingly gorgeous, haunting, and exciting masterpiece—absolutely one of the greatest films I know. —*C. B.*

RED DESERT (IL DESERTO ROSSO) L: DIRECTORS/ ANTONIONI, MICHELANGELO (1964) 116M D: Michaelangelo Antonioni. *Richard Harris, Rita Renoir, Xenia Valderi, Carlo Chionetti, Monica Vitti.* The most ambitious project Antonioni had yet undertaken, *Red Desert* is like a *L'Avventura* with the audacious scope of *2001,* set amid the rapid postwar industrialization that alienated the world from itself. Our protagonist Giuliana (Vitti), wife to an engineer and mother to a young boy, is increasingly unable to cope with her environment after a traumatic auto accident. "There's something terrible about reality, and I don't know what," she says at one point, haunted by an uncertain existential displacement throughout the film. Likening alienation with neurosis and even hysteria, as well as cultural and socioeconomic isolation, Antonioni bashes out another masterpiece, each and every aspect of cinema contributing to a tightly focused glacial whole. Perfectly complementing Vitti's screen presence, the camera work amplifies the sense of loneliness and cold inhumanity, while the brilliant sound design underscores Giuliana's confusion and fear. The combined effect is nothing short of chilling. —*C. B.*

JESUS OF MONTREAL L: DIRECTORS/ARCAND, DENYS (1989) 121M D: Denys Arcand. *Lothaire Bluteau, Catherine Wilkening, Johanne-Marie Tremblay.* This is a modernized and extraordinarily metaphorical retelling of the Passion of Christ. To revitalize his parish's annual tradition of a Passion play, the head priest decides to hire a younger troupe of actors. The actors research their subject matter carefully and decide to strive for a different approach using stark realism to bring the story to life—realism that in turn makes the play quite controversial. The role of Daniel, who leads the troupe and plays the role of Jesus, is brilliantly acted by Bluteau. As the controversy of the production generates curiosity among the populace, it likewise generates dissolution among the church. The unchurched members of the play find deeper meaning in what they are enacting, but the priest who hosts them realizes that he has essentially lost his faith and that his occupation is political rather than spiritual. The play is eventually shut down, thus concluding the actual passion this film is about. —*N. J.*

BIRD WITH THE CRYSTAL PLUMAGE, THE L: DIRECTORS/ ARGENTO, DARIO (1970) 98M D: Dario Argento. *Suzy Kendall, Tony Musante.* Argento's first horror film is a *giallo* based on a novel by Edgar Wallace. It's a straightforward mystery as an American writer searches through Rome trying to find a murderer. Argento's beautiful stylistic impulses are more than evident here, even though they are far from refined. The story has plenty of twists and turns and it's a lot of fun to watch, but the best reason to see the movie is to understand Argento's beginnings. To trace his films and watch his skills develop is a singular experience. —*T. S.*

DARIO ARGENTO: AN EYE FOR HORROR L: DIRECTORS/ ARGENTO, DARIO (2000) 60M D: Leon Ferguson. *Asia Argento, Daria Nicolodi.* In the words of this made-for-TV documentary, Italian horror director Dario Argento "changed the face of horror fantasy." Fellow directors John Carpenter and George Romero are among the fans who pay homage to Argento in this well-researched piece that dives into the style and sensibility of his films and tries to dispel his reputation as "the Italian Hitchcock." Though Argento's scenes of terror are painstaking and controlled, Carpenter points out he's more attuned to the surrealists, with plots that don't necessarily make sense and scenes that favor spectacle over narrative logic. Even more disturbing than his penchant for sentencing beautiful actresses to elaborate, sadistic death is his history of ravaging loved ones on the screen. "He's killed my mother a number of times in his films, and my sister once," reflects his daughter and frequent star Asia Argento. Includes plenty of clips of bravura scenes and interviews with Argento and his collaborators. —S.A.

FIVE DAYS OF MILAN L: DIRECTORS/ARGENTO, DARIO (1973) 122M D: Dario Argento. *Adriano Celentano, Enzo Cerusico.* By 1973, Argento felt that the *giallo* film had run its course and decided to make his one deviation from the horror genre. *Five Days of Milan* is an average film that only Argento fans will find intriguing. Its weak story, set during the Italian Revolution of 1848, is reminiscent of some of Sergio Leone's films. This is unsurprising since Argento helped write *Once Upon a Time in the West* and his experiences on that film played a big part in the making of this one. It's nowhere near as engaging as Leone's films, however. The characters are dry, the acting is weak, and there is little to keep you interested in the film. It is fascinating to see Argento's directorial style applied to a non-horror film, but that is pretty much the only appeal. —*T. S.*

FOUR FLIES ON GREY VELVET L: DIRECTORS/ARGENTO, DARIO (1971) 104M D: Dario Argento. *Michael Brandon, Mimsy Farmer.* This is Argento's most bizarre and abstract film, and that's really saying something. Many people are so unsettled by the disjointed story, jarring editing, and bizarre cinematography that they write the film off. But all these aspects are intentional and serve the film well. The film is supposed to be unsettling. The film is supposed to be hard to watch. Everything from the hallucinatory cinematography to the surreal, nonlinear editing gives the film its visual punch. The acting seems uncomfortable and removed. This too works in the film's favor, leaving the viewer with an unstable uneasiness. *Four Flies on Grey Velvet* is one of Argento's less appreciated films and it deserves to be seen and recognized by a much larger audience. —*T. S.*

INFERNO L: DIRECTORS/ARGENTO, DARIO (1980) 107M D: Dario Argento. *Eleonora Giorgi, Irene Miracle, Leigh McCloskey.* The second in a planned trilogy by Argento, *Inferno* is the successor to *Suspiria* only in theme. The film is illogical, but then again that's part of its power. By leaving the viewer without solid intellectual ground to stand on, Argento makes us that much more vulnerable to the horrors he has in store. The dreamlike flow of the film gradually builds until it becomes a feverish nightmare from which there is no escape. The sound and image conspire to keep us riveted in our seats, all lucidity gone, entranced by the eerie madness. Open up to this film and it will slowly devour you, until all that you're aware of is your heart pounding in your chest. —*T. S.*

PHENOMENA (AKA CREEPERS) L: DIRECTORS/ARGENTO, DARIO (1985) 110M D: Dario Argento. *Daria Nicolodi, Dalila di Lazzaro, Patrick Bauchau, Donald Pleasence, Jennifer Connelly.* A girl is lost in the lush meadows and back roads of Switzerland. Argento's camera floats behind like a disembodied observer. It looks like a mysterious romance, directed with the dreamy grace of a fairy tale, until a psychopathic maniac plunges the picture into an exquisite nightmare. Future Oscar winner Connelly is an American teenager who arrives at an exclusive school for girls while a killer stalks the students with a harpoon-like stiletto. The overly dense plot winds her telepathic link with the insect world, her sleepwalking, and the investigative plans of lonely entomologist Pleasence into a rather muddled mystery, but Argento's lyrical cinematography and lovingly choreographed violence give it all a kind of dream logic. —*S. A.*

SUSPIRIA L: DIRECTORS/ARGENTO, DARIO (1977) 98M D: Dario Argento. *Stefania Casini, Udo Kier, Jessica Harper.* Argento's supreme masterpiece, *Suspiria* is one of the finest horror films ever made. Abandoning reason for a quasi-demented dream logic and abandoning sanity for something much more sinister, *Suspiria* assaults viewers' senses with creepy, mind-bendingly beautiful cinematography and a fantastic, ghoulish score by the band Goblin. The intrinsic artistic value of the film is not hard to see but its true genius lies just under surface, an eerie, unnamed lingering that has the power to haunt you long after the final credits roll. —*T. S.*

CREATURE FROM THE BLACK LAGOON, THE L: DIRECTORS/ARNOLD, JACK (1954) 79M D: Jack Arnold. *Julie Adams, Whit Bissell, Richard Denning, Antonio Moreno, Riccou Browning, Richard Carlson.* Arnold hits the right note, taking an essentially throwaway plot (a group of scientists searching for a "missing link" in a hidden lagoon) and creates a tension-filled horror classic, diving into the mythical sexual union between monster and mate. Arguably the last great Universal monster film until Spielberg's similarly themed *Jaws*,

Arnold's Gill Man is akin to King Kong (both the original and remake) or Cocteau's Beast from the 1946 French masterpiece *La Belle et la Bête,* as its existence for thousands of years is tragically brought to an end by his lust, in this case swimming beauty Adams. The underwater scenes (co-directed by TV's *Flipper* creator and Gill Man suit-wearer Browning, who actually held his breath throughout all the underwater scenes, as the costume could not hold an oxygen tank) are the best ever filmed, and the overall production is a marvel of tension and atmosphere, especially when seen in its original 3-D format. —*N. H.*

HIGH SCHOOL CONFIDENTIAL L: DIRECTORS/ARNOLD, JACK (1958) 85M D: Jack Arnold. *Mamie Van Doren, Russ Tamblyn, John Drew Barrymore, Jackie Coogan, Michael Landon.* The funniest juvenile delinquent/beatnik/antidrug movie of all time, *High School Confidential* features lots of choice dialogue, old-looking school kids, weird characters, hipster poetry, and some pretty absurd plot twists. Tamblyn is the tough new kid who maneuvers his way into the "wheelers and dealers" and is soon hooked up with Drew Barrymore's dad and the local drug distributor (Uncle Fester, I mean Coogan). It turns out Tamblyn is working undercover, but for some reason lives with his nymphomaniac "aunt" (Van Doren) who vamps around in a tight sweater. It's a latter-day *Reefer Madness* and, like that film, is preachy yet exploitative and is jam-packed with unintentional humor that is a lot of fun "under the influence." —*S. H.*

IT CAME FROM OUTER SPACE L: DIRECTORS/ARNOLD, JACK (1953) 81M D: Jack Arnold. *Richard Carlson, Barbara Rush, Charles Drake, Russell Johnson.* Often cited as an inspiration for Steven Spielberg's *E.T., It Came From Outer Space* was the first in a series of imaginative, intelligent, science fiction thrillers directed by Arnold and produced by William Alland. In this twist on the alien invasion theme, the visitors are neither marauding killers nor diplomatic emissaries, merely crash-landed space travelers who "recruit" locals to facilitate repairs, temporarily replacing them with zombie-like doubles (shades of *Invasion of the Body Snatchers*!). Only B-movie stalwart Carlson understands that they're just a benign bunch who want to get on their way. The game but flat cast riffles through stiff expressions of fear, wonder, and steely intensity, but that's par for the course. The minimal but striking special effects include an awesome visualization of the alien ship hidden in a mountain cave, and Arnold uses the dark desert setting for all its eerie austerity. It was originally shot in 3-D, but this inventive piece of sci-fi filmmaking needs no such gimmicks to hold your attention. Freely adapted from Ray Bradbury's short story "The Meteor." —*S. A.*

MOUSE THAT ROARED, THE L: DIRECTORS/ARNOLD, JACK (1959) 83M D: Jack Arnold. *Peter Sellers, Jean Seberg.* Arnold will forever be remembered for redefining the science fiction film in the 1950s, but most people forget he made one of the funniest comedies of the era. Reminiscent of the Ealing comedies of the time, Arnold borrows their low-key sense of humor (via a script co-written by *The Man in the White Suit* author Roger MacDougall) and their secret weapon—Sellers, before he became an international star in the *Pink Panther* films—for this clever little political satire. Sellers leads the bow-and-arrow army of the Duchy of Grand Fenwick, the smallest country in the world, in an invasion of the United States. In his frustrated attempts to find someone to surrender to (and thus get American foreign aid) he bumbles into winning the war and finds an unlikely war bride in modern American girl Seberg. Sellers also plays the scheming Prime Minister and the Grand Duchess, a cross between the Queen Mum and a good-natured great aunt. —*S. A.*

THIS ISLAND EARTH L: DIRECTORS/ARNOLD, JACK (1955) 87M D: Jack Arnold, Joseph Newman. *Russell Johnson, Lance Fuller, Rex Reason, Faith Domergue, Jeff Morrow.* Airplanes with no pilots, superscientists with brains so big their heads warp, giant buglike creatures from another planet. This is pulp science fiction at its best, built around an intergalactic conspiracy and the earnest earth scientists (among them Morrow, Domergue, and future *Gilligan's Island* Professor Johnson) innocently working to help one alien race defend itself in a planet-threatening war. The plot is a cut above most '50s science fiction, but it's the eerie images and exotic outer-space delights (in that garish oversaturated color that only Technicolor can provide) that really turn the trick, with solid support from Reason's troubled alien scientist, torn between his desperation to save his people from destruction and his moral qualms about kidnapping Earth's greatest scientists. Real Saturday matinee stuff in all the best ways: imaginative, energetic, inventive, and so much fun to watch. The final scenes were directed (uncredited) by Arnold. —*S. A.*

BEING THERE L: DIRECTORS/ASHBY, HAL (1979) 130M D: Hal Ashby. *Jack Warden, Melvyn Douglas, Shirley MacLaine, Peter Sellers.* Sellers stars as a simpleminded fellow named Chance who has spent his entire life as a gardener and his only knowledge about the outside world is based on television. When his benefactor dies he finds himself let loose on the world and stumbles into the life of an elderly wealthy man (Oscar winner Douglas) and his bubbly wife (MacLaine). His innocence and benevolent nature lead him to unexpected political powers. In many ways Chance is a mirror and the people he encounters see what they want in his blank face. His babbling about gardens and "liking to watch" are interpreted in all

sorts of unexpected ways. This movie works on many levels and can be seen as a political satire, a religious allegory, or a commentary on our media-obsessed society. I see it as another great performance by Sellers and another great film by Ashby. —S. H.

HAROLD AND MAUDE L: DIRECTORS/ASHBY, HAL (1971) 90M D: Hal Ashby. *Vivian Pickles, Bud Cort, Ruth Gordon, Charles Tyner.* Harold (Cort) is an affluent teenager whose mother (Pickles) tries to push him into dating and socializing, but he's not that kind of guy. His main interest is staging gory fake suicides to punish his mother for not understanding him. Things change, though, when he falls in love with seventy-nine-year-old Maude (Gordon), an arty, peace-loving, anti-authoritarian who poses nude, steals trees, and teaches her death-obsessed new friend how to enjoy his life. Many of the themes (and the songs by Cat Stevens) are obviously rooted in the generational clash of the late '60s, but they are still relevant today. I wasn't born until four years after the movie was made, but when I discovered it in high school its dark humor that turns to optimism was a great comfort. —B. T.

LAST DETAIL, THE L: DIRECTORS/ASHBY, HAL (1973) 103M D: Hal Ashby. *Clifton James, Jack Nicholson, Carol Kane, Randy Quaid, Otis Young.* The Last Detail exemplifies Ashby's masterful blend of subtle melancholy and humor. Given the task of taking a young seaman (Quaid) to the brig, navy shore patrolmen "Bad Ass" Buddusky (Nicholson, in his finest performance) and "Mule" Mulhall (Young) decide to show the kid a good time. Half-shot in dreamy overcast grays and snow-bound skies, this kind-of road movie gives way to moody reticence and bleak humor, casting a cold light on what it means to have order and to follow order in one's life. Ashby's use of dissolves is impeccable, and Towne's script is spotless. In the best scene of the movie, Nicholson explodes in a bar when the redneck bartender refuses to serve them. "I am the motherfucking shore patrol, motherfucker! I am the motherfucking shore patrol! Give this man a beer." Amen. —J. D.

SHAMPOO L: DIRECTORS/ASHBY, HAL (1975) 109M D: Hal Ashby. *Jack Warden, Goldie Hawn, Lee Grant, Julie Christie, Carrie Fisher, Warren Beatty.* This brilliant satire of the shallow sexual practices of the '70s actually takes place in late 1968, at the time of Nixon's election. Beatty, lampooning his offscreen persona, stars as a popular hairdresser for the wealthy women of Beverly Hills. Beatty does more than just cut hair, and his complex sexual entanglements and desperate attempts at maintaining his dignity reveal the ugly foundations that lie beneath the "beautiful people" of Southern California. This is one of Beatty's funniest and bravest performances, and the film is much more than a vanity project. Another great

American film directed by Ashby, *Shampoo* led to the bizarre cheapie blaxploitation rip-off *Black Shampoo*, which readily qualifies as a guilty pleasure. —S. H.

BLACK STALLION, THE L: DIRECTORS/BALLARD, CARROLL (1979) 118M D: Carroll Ballard. *Michael Higgins, Kelly Reno, Mickey Rooney, Teri Garr, Clarence Muse, Hoyt Axton.* It's really two films in one. The first film is about a young boy who gets stranded on a deserted island with a wild black stallion. Over time he gains the trust of the horse and they develop a unique and powerful bond. The second story is of Alex and "the Black" after they have been rescued. They fall under the tutelage of an ex-jockey and horse trainer who realizes the amazing strength and speed of the Black, and trains them both, horse and rider. What starts as a curious experiment to tame the Black to the saddle and bridle turns into a plot to try to get this amazing stallion into a race with two of the fastest horses on the racing circuit. The first "film" is definitely the best and most striking. There is no dialogue, just sound and music and unbelievably beautiful visuals of the boy and the horse bonding over sand and sea and water. So different from traditional films and stories, it is both breathtaking and magical. —M. N.

FLY AWAY HOME L: DIRECTORS/BALLARD, CARROLL (1996) 106M D: Carroll Ballard. *Anna Paquin, Jeff Daniels, Dana Delany.* A surprisingly good kids-and-animals movie thanks to director Ballard. After the death of her mother, fourteen-year-old Paquin goes to live with her eccentric father (Daniels). Life is miserable until a nest of orphaned geese becomes imprinted on her. Then father and daughter bond over leading the geese to migrate using ultralight airplanes. The story follows the formula of movies like *The Amazing Panda Adventure* but proves through Ballard's elegant direction that it's all in the execution. —B. T.

DEATH RACE 2000 L: DIRECTORS/BARTEL, PAUL (1975) 78M D: Paul Bartel. *Simone Griffeth, Sylvester Stallone, David Carradine, Mary Woronov.* In the futuristic year of 2000, America is enthralled by the Death Race, a cross-country auto race where the drivers gets extra points for running over pedestrians (a sport later copied in *The Toxic Avenger*). Each of the cars and their drivers and navigators has a comic book-ish motif (Calamity Jane drives a car with bullhorns) and Carradine's heroic Frankenstein wears a leather mask that some believe inspired Darth Vader. It's a lot of fun and full of clever touches, like the rebels who try to dodge the cars. Roger Corman just wanted to cash in on *Rollerball*, but Bartel went and made a smarter (and to this day better regarded) satire of violent sports, leaving the necessary car chases and explosions to the second unit. —B. T.

BLACK SABBATH L: DIRECTORS/BAVA, MARIO (1963) 92M D: Mario Bava. *Boris Karloff, Michele Mercier, Mark Damon, Lydia Alfonsi*. When American International Pictures originally imported Bava's intense horror anthology, they trimmed it, toned it down, rescored it, rearranged the order, and even rewrote one story completely in the dubbing. It's finally been restored to its full glory, and while it's odd to watch host/costar Karloff speak with some else's Italian voice, it's literally a new film. The correctly ordered stories now build from the early, ornate *giallo* thriller *The Telephonet* to the gorgeous and eerie vampire tale *The Wurdulak* (with Karloff as an uncharacteristically demonic patriarch systematically sucking the life from his family, person by person) to the chilling ghost story *The Drop of Water,* a masterpiece of shiver-inducing imagery haunted by the piercing dead eyes of a creepy restless corpse. If it all gets to intense for you, don't worry. Bava reminds us it's only a movie with his playful coda. —*S.A.*

BLACK SUNDAY L: DIRECTORS/BAVA, MARIO (1960) 87M D: Mario Bava. *John Richardson, Ivo Garrani, Andrea Checchi, Barbara Steele*. Steele, her eyes glaring hate even as her face registers terror, spits curses with hellfire as a spiked mask is slowly placed over her face. Suddenly a massive mallet pounds the iron mask and the credits explode in fire. Even in his directorial debut, Bava knew how to grab an audience's attention, and he doesn't let it go. Steele is terrifyingly lovely in a double role as the vengeful witch burned at the stake and her victimized descendant who unwittingly resurrects her with a drop of blood, and she's both innocent and devilishly wicked with equal fervor. The moody, macabre, hauntingly beautiful cult classic of cruelty established the lynchpins of the Italian *giallo*: sex, sadism, and style. —*S.A.*

BLOOD AND BLACK LACE L: DIRECTORS/BAVA, MARIO (1964) 90M D: Mario Bava. *Cameron Mitchell, Thomas Reiner, Eva Bartok*. Bava gave birth to the *giallo*, a distinctly Italian twist on horror, with this elegant slasher picture, combining a poetic, haunting beauty with Grand Guignol gore and a bent of sexual perversity. Forget the plot, which has something to do with a masked stalker hunting the gorgeous models of a Rome fashion house, and just take in the color and style. Bava lovingly delivers every elaborate killing like a dreamy dance of death, choreographed with sadistic precision, delivered in lurid color, spied upon with a restlessly gliding camera. There's an undeniable edge of misogyny to the whole thing, but the psycho-thriller aspects seem beside the point as the narrative melts into abstract moments of dreamy, disconnected beauty. —*S.A.*

5 DOLLS FOR AN AUGUST MOON L: DIRECTORS/BAVA, MARIO (1970) 78M D: Mario Bava. *William Berger, Edwige Fenech, Renato Rossini, Ira VonFurstenberg*. What spices up a swinging weekend on a private island

retreat more than a body count? Bava's mod take on Agatha Christie's *Ten Little Indians* is a silly thriller from a tired script that offers Bava precious few moments of bravura cinematic style. But they are there: a brilliant rack focus from the barrel of a rifle to the eyeball literally floating in close-up in the scope, a cascade of glass bubbles down a flight of stairs and into the bathtub where the next victim lies, and the surreal spectacle of each victim hanging by ropes and wrapped in plastic in a meat locker. Groovy score by Piero Umiliani, great color, and a wry coda that almost makes it all work. —*S.A.*

HERCULES IN THE HAUNTED WORLD L: DIRECTORS/ BAVA, MARIO (1961) 82M D: Mario Bava. *Reg Park, Franco Giacobini, Christopher Lee, Leonora Ruffo*. Bava's surreal muscleman classic was his first color film and it is a beaut, with purple, red, and blue lights on swirls of fog, underworld caves, and moats of glowing lava. The haunted world is, in fact, Hades, where Hercules (Park) and his traveling buddies face witches, hallucinations, and a stone monster on the way to retrieve a magic crystal that will save a princess. Lee is the evil King Lyco, who leads Hercules to the second great set piece of the film, a graveyard chase where the dead rise from the ground and glide through the air with a supernaturally eerie grace in a twilight zone of darkness and mist. For a muscleman film the action scenes are clumsy, but then Bava was always better at wild fantasy. The sets are wonderfully weird and the special effects are gorgeous, the work of a craftsman whose cinematic textures are far more interesting than the "realism" that took over in the '70s. —*S.A.*

KILL, BABY. . . KILL L: DIRECTORS/BAVA, MARIO (1966) 84M D: Mario Bava. *Erika Blanc, Giacomo Rossi-Stuart, Piero Lulli, Fabienne Dali*. The title hardly captures the eerie mood of Bava's stylish ghost story with a homicidal edge. Set in a turn of the century Italian village, Bava floods his handsome sets with red, blue, and green light, a surreal day-for-night look that only increases the otherworldly atmosphere. This fanciful nocturnal world becomes the stage for virtual pageants of death in which the victims become tortured puppets forced to murder themselves by a malevolent spirit. The murders are grotesque and sometimes grueling, but not gory (this is before his shift to more sadistic slasher-style pictures), and he manages to bring a chill to every appearance with the spooky little girl who is death, a creepy vision in white who giggles as she pulls the strings on her victims. The English dubbing deadens the performances and heightens the flat script, but it's a minor flaw in a film that soars on style alone. —*S.A.*

KNIVES OF THE AVENGER L: DIRECTORS/BAVA, MARIO (1965) 85M D: Mario Bava. *Cameron Mitchell, Elissa Pichelli*. Bava, best known, of course, for his mystery-filled hallways drenched in green, red,

Mario Bava

Mario Bava is a horror original. A painter and cinematographer turned director, a craftsman turned celluloid dreamer, an industry veteran who created, almost single-handedly, the uniquely Italian genre of baroque horror known as the giallo, he directed the most graceful and deliriously mad horror films of the 1960s and early 1970s. Always better at imagery than explanation, at set-piece than story, Bava makes films that are both dream worlds and nightmare visions. Check your logic at the door.

Bava was born into the movies in 1914. Italy was at the height of its epic historical spectacles, and Mario's father, Eugenio Bava, was one of Italy's top cameramen (he shot, among others, the blockbuster *Quo Vadis*). Mario trained as a painter but soon followed in his father's footsteps, becoming one of Italy's most in-demand cameramen (Bava disdained the term "cinematographer") and special-effects artist, often working uncredited.

Legend has it that director Riccardo Freda pushed his friend Bava into the director's chair by abandoning not one but two projects for his cinematographer to fin-

---

yellow, and other-colored lights and fog, takes a less-tense turn in this sword-and-sandal actioner. Rurik (Mitchell) is the blade master who rescues a woman and her son from attack with his fast and sharp steel, only to later realize that he had once taken this woman by force and her son may be his own. That story line alone should be causing gasps and oohs and aaahs but instead we're left with mere yawns. Some nice action fights and knife-throwing effects, but an overall tepid job that reaches no new cinematic heights. For the absolute die-hard Bava and sword-and-sandal genre film fans. —*S. R.*

LISA AND THE DEVIL/THE HOUSE OF EXORCISM L: DIRECTORS/BAVA, MARIO (1973) 95M D: Mario Bava. *Alessio Orano, Sylva Koscina, Elke Sommer, Telly Savalas.* On first glance *Lisa and the Devil* is a typically lush Bava shocker: a twisted family haunted by the sins of yesteryear murders the guests of their spooky-of-old manor house. But there's something sinister in Savalas's sardonic, lollipop-sucking butler, manipulating his own behind-the-scenes psychodrama for the benefit of innocent American Sommer. Mixing slasher movie and ghost story conventions with ingeniously playful satanic mind games, Bava drops the bottom out of genre expectations and creates a genuinely surreal nightmare horror film. When the lovely but uncommercial dream shocker proved unreleasable in the United States, new scenes were shot with Robert Alda as a priest exorcising the devil in Sommer and *The House of Exorcism* was clumsily cobbled together—a bizarre mess that nonetheless features a couple of delirious new scenes. —*S. A.*

RABID DOGS L: DIRECTORS/BAVA, MARIO (1974) 96M D: Mario Bava. *Riccardo Cucciolla, Maurice Poli, Lea Lander, Aldo Caponi, George Eastman.* Three ferocious hoodlums hijack a weekly payroll from a man, knifing him dead. Closely followed by police, they grab two women and stab one in front of her horrified friend. They jump into a man's car and squeeze in next to a young, sick boy in the back seat. The sweat runs from brows, heartbeats and breathing quicken, and the desperation and pathos begin for a nonstop thrill ride that never lets up, even after the final frame flickers out. Almost the entire film takes place inside a moving car. We're so close to the action we can damn near smell the killers' sweat. With their vile crotch-grabbing at the woman hostage and ash-tapping in the child's face, the backseat killers create an increasingly hostile environment in the confines of the vehicle. This is Bava's gritty, violent, swan song masterpiece. —*S. R.*

HONOR AMONG THIEVES L: DIRECTORS/BECKER, JACQUES (1954) 94M D: Jacques Becker. *Lino Ventura, Jeanne Moreau, Rene Dary, Jean Gabin.* Smart, tough, poetic gangster flick. After a gold heist, it eventually becomes obvious a suave, aging gangster (Gabin) has the loot. Another gang cleverly but dishonorably plots to take it from him by kidnapping him and his partner and beating the location of the stash out of them. But the wily gangster gets wise, foils the attempt, and tips his soft-in-the-head confederate. Eventually the latter needs to see his girlfriend (Moreau), who is two-timing him with the other gang leader. A straight trade is offered: "your partner's life for gold." But given the evidence so far, is there such a thing as honor among thieves? The stylistic

ish. Based on his uncredited direction on *I Vampiri* (1957) and *Caltiki, the Immortal Monster* (1959), plus his contributions on *Hercules* (1958) and *Hercules Unchained* (1959), Bava was offered a project of his choosing. He decided to adapt Nikolai Gogol's short story "Viy," calling his filmed version *The Mask of Satan*, and thus made his official directorial debut at age forty-six. In the United States, the film was released as *Black Sunday* (1960).

The hauntingly beautiful *Black Sunday* established the linchpins of the *giallo*—sex, sadism, and style. Later films *Blood and Black Lace* (1964) and *The Whip and the Body* (1963) added Grand Guignol gore to the macabre poetic beauty and sexual perversity, and the eerie *Kill, Baby, Kill* and the surreal *Lisa and the Devil* took the *giallo* into new worlds. Murder becomes an elaborate, usually sadistic, tightly choreographed dance of death; plot becomes secondary to spectacle, delivered in lurid color and brought to life with a gliding camera.

Bava directed much more than horror—his filmography includes Westerns, Viking films, spy movies (*Danger: Diabolik* [1968] is a delirious, practically plotless celebration of Bava's visual games), and even his own uniquely fantastical take on the muscleman adventure, *Hercules on the Haunted World* (1961)—but it is the choreography of horror that made his name. Welcome to his dance of death.

—*Sean Axmaker*

---

tone of self-control reigns in the story progression till the very end, which breaks out almost majestically in violence. This film reveals that when it comes to crime only irony rules. —*J. C.*

TROU, LE L: DIRECTORS/BECKER, JACQUES (1960) 131M D: Jacques Becker. *Phillippe Leroy, Raymond Meunier, Marc Michel, Jean Keraudy, Michel Constantin.* Becker's meticulous story of the elaborate escape from a Parisian prison ("the hole") features a cast of nonactors whose etched and sculpted faces tell as much about their characters as their deliberate, restrained performances. The long-simmering escape of four hardened street criminals is interrupted by the arrival of a young neophyte accused of a crime of passion and insisting on his innocence. Becker paces the film deliberately, as attentive to the time it takes to accomplish each task as he is to the minute details and split-second timing of every facet, one of the many things this film shares with another meticulous crime classic, *Rififi*. In a twist on that film's silent robbery sequence, these men spring their plan into action by pounding through the cement floor, risking discovery with every blow that thunders through the cell like a pile driver. The effect is nerve-racking and brilliant. One of the greatest prison films ever made and inspired by a true story, it was the last film by Becker, an unjustly forgotten French master of the 1940s and '50s. —*S. A.*

AUTUMN SONATA L: DIRECTORS/BERGMAN, INGMAR (1978) 97M D: Ingmar Bergman. *Lena Nyman, Ingrid Bergman, Halvar Björk, Liv Ullmann, Gunnar Björnstrand.* Ingrid Bergman's last film features her as a reclusive concert pianist who uneasily reunites with her two daughters. Ullmann plays the daughter who has come to her mother's home to find that her paralyzed sister (Nyman), who is suffering from a congenital nerve disease, has been left to languish in a hospital. So Nyman is brought into the house, where the concert pianist must face up to her maternal responsibilities. The director develops these two main characters much as themes are developed in a sonata, and with his symbolic use of autumn he probes their inner depths as few filmmakers can. The slower pacing of the film may be a little bland for American viewers unaccustomed to Bergman's direction, but the deep impression this film makes is enduring and well worth the viewer's patience. —*N. J.*

FANNY AND ALEXANDER L: DIRECTORS/BERGMAN, INGMAR (1983) 188M D: Ingmar Bergman. *Pernilla Allwin, Bertil Guve, Gunn Walgren, Allan Edwall, Ewa Fröling, Erland Josephson.* Ingmar Bergman's last film is a subtle, mesmerizing story concerning two young children who live in a large upper-class Swedish household at the turn of the century. When their father dies the mother marries a local bishop who proves to be a very strict parent. Over time the children find some escape from their awkward domestic problems through an old family friend and also through some very curious supernatural phenomena. Truly this breathtaking film is a crowning achievement for a long life of filmmaking, and in Bergman's own words it "is the sum total of my life as a filmmaker." And it's not hard to see how true this is considering it won four Academy Awards. Be sure to hunt down the definitive five-hour cut for the fullest effect. —*N. J.*

MONIKA (SOMMAREN MED MONIKA) L: DIRECTORS/ BERGMAN, INGMAR (1953) 96M D: Ingmar Bergman. *Lars Ekborg, Harriet Andersson.* Known for his terse psychological dramas and religious allegories, Bergman was not averse to exercises in sheer eroticism, *Monika* the loveliest and most notorious. A cheeky, adventurous, self-centered girl (Andersson) from a big noisy family uses the pretext of her father's drunken behavior to go live with her boyfriend (Ekborg) on a small boat. Soon bored with their cold and damp life, the boy grabs his vacation pay and the two head to an island of storms, coffee, cigarettes, and cuddles. They swim naked in tide pools, dance on a deserted dock to music from a distant club, and talk of their future life together. But their summer ends and so too their rhapsodic vision of life when reality chills their romantic dreams and the two head down separate roads. The lovely, muted black-and-white photography (Fischer) deftly and ruefully echoes these kids' naive expectations. —*J. C.*

PERSONA L: DIRECTORS/BERGMAN, INGMAR (1966) 100M D: Ingmar Bergman. *Bibi Andersson, Gunnar Björnstrand, Liv Ullmann, Margreta Krook.* *Persona* is one of Bergman's most experimental films. In Ullmann's first film with the great Swedish director, she is cast as an actress who has lost her voice. She goes to a secluded country house where she tries rehabilitating with a nurse (Andersson) who keeps her company with a lot of talking. As the two slowly begin to sour of each other's company, their personalities merge into a single persona. This is accomplished cinematically with shade and lighting and some curious double exposure. The film stops there, not entirely explaining itself but leaving lots of material for film students to muse upon. —*N. J.*

SAWDUST AND TINSEL L: DIRECTORS/BERGMAN, INGMAR (1953) 93M D: Ingmar Bergman. *Åke Grönberg, Hasse Ekman, Harriet Andersson.* Circus folk and sex, clowns and well-endowed women, and a soundtrack of calliopes and carnival melodies—you'd think this was a Fellini film. Then in the opening scene, a rambunctious diva goes to entertain the troops, ends up skinny-dipping with them, and the film takes a turn into the dark night of the soul and we find ourselves in Bergman country. The story of the desperate, doomed yearnings of the tired ringmaster of a failing circus and his disillusioned young lover is considered an early masterpiece. It's a gloomy study in humiliation, filled with portentous performances and symbol-laden imagery under gray skies and rainy days. The overly controlled, overtly world-weary pose is lugubrious despite moments of fine drama, but that shouldn't stop fans and film buffs from seeing this early, self-assured work. Also known as *The Naked Light.* —*S. A.*

SEVENTH SEAL L: DIRECTORS/BERGMAN, INGMAR (1958) 92M D: Ingmar Bergman. *Bengt Ekerot, Max von Sydow.* I've always considered Bergman's masterpiece a horror film of sorts. With its eerie silences and daunting landscapes, not to mention the figure of Death himself, this morality play set during the Crusades is an often chilling look at love, death, God, and the soul of man. Let's just call it a "philosophical horror film." —*C. P.*

VIRGIN SPRING, THE L: DIRECTORS/BERGMAN, INGMAR (1959) 88M D: Ingmar Bergman. *Axel Duborg, Brigitta Pattersson, Gunnel Lindblom, Brigitta Valberg, Max von Sydow.* Bergman takes a very old story and with his use of photography, sound, and storytelling makes it stunningly realistic. Set in the fourteenth century, the film features von Sydow as a mild-mannered father whose daughter is senselessly raped and murdered. Rage overwhelms him and he is possessed with the singular goal of revenge. And the revenge he manages to exact is equally as violent as that perpetrated against his daughter. The violence in this black-and-white film is surprisingly graphic, but what makes it even more shocking is the absence of music. Whereas Hitchcock would be using the visceral compositions of Bernard Herrmann to help deliver his horror, Bergman uses stark silence and lingering camera work to let the tragic reality settle into a deeper part of the viewer's mind. One of Bergman's most striking films, *The Virgin Spring* has influenced countless imitations. —*N. J.*

WILD STRAWBERRIES L: DIRECTORS/BERGMAN, INGMAR (1957) 91M D: Ingmar Bergman. *Victor Sjöström, Gunnar Björnstrand, Bibi Andersson, Ingrid Thulin.* Bergman takes that most venerable of modern genres, the road movie, and transforms it into the contemplative journey of an aging professor (played by legendary Swedish director Sjöström) into his unexamined past. Sjöström gives a vulnerable, moving performance as the crotchety, morally imperious old man who slowly realizes the effect of his inflexibility and hard demands on those around him. Thulin is the professor's daughter-in-law who nudges him along the craggy trail to self-awareness and Andersson is both the love of his early life, revisited in musings and dreams, and the freewheeling modern hitchhiker he meets on the road. The digital master of the Criterion DVD isn't so much a revelation (heck, we all knew it was gorgeous) as a tribute to the imagery of Bergman and cinematographer Gunnar Fischer, from the delicate gray tones of sunlight on leaves to the barely overexposed white-cold intensity of the professor's dreams of death. —*S. A.*

WINTER LIGHT L: DIRECTORS/BERGMAN, INGMAR (1963) 81M D: Ingmar Bergman. *Gunnel Lindblom, Gunnar Björnstrand, Ingrid Thulin, Max von Sydow.* This is Bergman at his best, using minimalist cinema for its most effecting experience. With great performances by Björnstrand and Thulin, Bergman has created a masterpiece about a village priest who finds "God's silence" intolerable. With stark depression the film's slow pace gradually draws the viewer in. Cinematographer Sven Nykvist has captured the coldness of the terrain, small villages shrouded in gray and snow, with beautiful shots of the interiors and emotionally revealing close-ups of silent hells. There are hidden references to the Crucifixion, as the time covered in the movie is the same time Christ spent on the cross. The priest questions his faith, love, death, and God all in a single, bleak afternoon. —B. W.

FOOTLIGHT PARADE L: DIRECTORS/BERKELEY, BUSBY (1933) 104M D: Lloyd Bacon. *Ruby Keeler, Dick Powell, James Cagney.* If you haven't seen a Berkeley musical yet, you have no one to blame but yourself. Though *42nd Street, Dames,* and many others have their merits, this is as good a place to start as any. Cagney can sing and tap-dance with the best of 'em—and here he does just that. Fantastic, surreal scenes and amazing choreography abound. Give it a look. —C. P.

BESIEGED L: DIRECTORS/BERTOLUCCI, BERNARDO (1998) 93M D: Bernardo Bertolucci. *David Thewlis, Thandie Newton, Claudio Santamaria.* An African woman (Newton) flees her country's despotic dictatorship and works for a reclusive British pianist (Thewlis) in his musty Roman villa. The awkwardness of their relationship—his mooning gazes at her, her wary distance while dusting and cleaning—is enhanced by their heavy silences and Bertolucci's use of contrasting music: his European classical piano-playing and her cassette tapes of African pop and traditional songs. Bertolucci turns away from his usually graceful lushness in favor of a stark visual style of intense sunlight and shadowy interiors; a peering, probing handheld camera; and a staccato, abrupt editing pace, all of which create an awkward but intense intimacy. It's a stylistic departure for the aging master, but for all its seeming surface simplicity this is one of the richest films of his late career. —S. A.

CONFORMIST, THE L: DIRECTORS/BERTOLUCCI, BERNARDO (1970) 115M D: Bernardo Bertolucci. *Stefania Sandrelli, Pierre Clémenti, Dominique Sanda, Jean-Louis Trintignant.* This film dazzles you in each and every way a film can. Trintignant's turn as "conformist" Marcello Clerici is haunting as he wanders through life trying to please everyone, especially the Fascists in 1930s Italy as they ask him to kill an old mentor who has been characterized as subversive. Vittorio Storaro's groundbreaking camera work set the bar for nearly everything to follow, as did the tragically unappreciated production design by Ferdinando Scarfiotti. Martin Scorsese has stated that he and his contemporaries in the '70s took the look of this film as a stylistic call to arms. Bertolucci creates magic,

making each jaw-dropping sequence a stylistic comment on the action at hand and creating a psychotically beautiful film for the ages. Restored in 1994, it was rereleased theatrically and even played on cable. Sadly, to date, the only home video release is available in an English-dubbed format. —M. S.

LAST EMPEROR, THE L: DIRECTORS/BERTOLUCCI, BERNARDO (1987) 218M D: Bernardo Bertolucci. *Joan Chen, Victor Wong, Peter O'Toole, Ryuichi Sakamoto, John Lone.* This lavish film is rich with historic detail in its account of the last emperor of China. Emperor Pu Yi assumed the throne at the age of three and grew up knowing only the traditional and highly sheltered life reserved for emperors within the Forbidden City. Communism eventually sweeps the land and the emperor realizes he must relinquish power. And so with the help of a Scottish tutor (O'Toole) the emperor tries to learn about the ways of the Western world. Allowing a learned Western presence inside the Forbidden City gives a very interesting perspective to this slice of history, as does the remarkable location photography, which is in fact the Forbidden City itself deep inside the People's Republic of China. The music by Ryuichi Sakamoto and David Byrne also adds favorably to the sweep of this film. —N. J.

LITTLE BUDDHA L: DIRECTORS/BERTOLUCCI, BERNARDO (1993) 123M D: Bernardo Bertolucci. *Ruocheng Ying, Alex Wiesendanger, Keanu Reeves, Bridget Fonda, Chris Isaak.* This was partially filmed in Seattle, and during production, Fonda and Vittorio Storaro became semi-regular renters at Scarecrow. Towards the end of production, when Tower Records would not rent to Bertolucci because he didn't have proper I.D., he came in as well. I'll never forget the smile on Bridget Fonda's face when she saw us making a slight fuss over him after weeks of enjoying anonymity among the non-instrusive Scarecrow staffers herself. An interesting work for Bertolucci, who, when bringing it back to the Seattle International Film Festival for its world premiere, stated that he wanted to make a film for children through the tale of Siddhartha and his reincarnation. A huge ambition, to be sure, especially when you have Reeves playing Siddhartha. I don't think it's as successful as Bertolucci's greatest work, but it surely is a feast for the eyes and ears, showing Seattle in possibly its best light ever (thanks to Storaro) and stridently telling the tale of Siddhartha for a younger generation. —M. S.

STEALING BEAUTY L: DIRECTORS/BERTOLUCCI, BERNARDO (1996) 118M D: Bernardo Bertolucci. *Jeremy Irons, Donal McCann, Liv Tyler, Sinéad Cusack.* An American teenager (Tyler) comes to an Italian villa to deal with her mother's suicide, lose her virginity, find out who her father is, and hang out with artists. It's an absolutely gorgeous movie, and cinematographer Khondji, best known for dark movies like *Seven* and *The City of Lost Children*, proves that he can also work with the more sunny and traditional beauty inherent in this setting and in this leading lady. The story takes place in a glamorized artist's fantasyland where no one has to work for a living, everyone you meet is working on a sculpture or a poem or something, and every night people stay out late under the stars drinking wine, telling stories, and laughing. —*B. T.*

FEMME NIKITA, LA L: DIRECTORS/BESSON, LUC (1990) 117M D: Luc Besson. *Jean Reno, Jeanne Moreau, Anne Parillaud, Tchéky Karyo, Jean-Hugues Anglade.* Nikita (Parillaud) is a drugged-out teen searching for thrills with her junkie friends. After an armed robbery gone wrong, cop-killer Nikita is condemned to death. But instead of carrying out the sentence, the French government gives her a choice: be an assassin or face execution. She chooses her new life, and after surviving her first assignment—a trap designed to get her killed or prove she's skilled—Nikita decides to fit in until she can escape. Her new life is a paradox as she is forced to work for her agency mentor, Bob (Karyo), whenever he calls, while she enjoys love and true happiness for the first time with her boyfriend, Marco (Anglade). Besson's breakout film, *La Femme Nikita* is an intelligent and creative espionage thriller with a beautiful and strong female lead (Parillaud won the Cesar award for Best Actress). Watch for a brilliant supporting turn by Reno in the role of Victor, the resourceful and vicious "cleaner." —*G. M.*

FIFTH ELEMENT, THE L: DIRECTORS/BESSON, LUC (1997) 127M D: Luc Besson. *Milla Jovovich, Gary Oldman, Bruce Willis, Ian Holm, Chris Tucker.* In the twenty-fifth century, a big ball of evil hurtles toward the earth, occasionally making phone calls to the authorities, introducing itself as "Mr. Shadow." Luckily, various aliens and long-dead archaeologists have already cooked up a battle plan for this particular doomsday scenario. It involves the four elements and a genetically engineered "perfect being" named Leeloo (Jovovich) who literally lands in the flying taxi driven by ex-soldier Willis. From there it's an epic space adventure. At times it's overly silly (Willis's mom keeps calling him on the phone and bothering him), but it's also full of stunning imagery, from the hulking, beetle-like armor of aliens visiting Egypt to the glistening futuristic cities. There's also a great sense of absurdity (Tiny "Zeus" Lister plays the president, Oldman imitates Andy Griffith as a Jean Paul Gaultier–wearing villain named Jean-Baptiste Emmanuel Zorg) and over-the-top performances by Jovovich as the confused superbeing who speaks a language only she knows, and Tucker as a cartoonishly effeminate shock jock. Besson had been dreaming of this story since he was a teenager. The end result is as convoluted as that would imply, but also as rich in detail and imagination. —*B. T.*

LÉON (AKA **THE PROFESSIONAL**) L: DIRECTORS/BESSON, LUC (1994) 136M D: Luc Besson. *Gary Oldman, Natalie Portman, Danny Aiello, Peter Appel, Willie One Blood, Jean Reno.* First off, make sure you get the original version of this, not the watered-down, twenty-six-minutes-short Americanized version called *The Professional*. Trust me, you'll thank me in the end. This stylish thriller showcases a brilliant performance by Portman as a twelve-year-old girl who loses everything and must turn to an assassin for help and protection, all the while wanting much more. Reno is the assassin who reluctantly takes her under his wing. Determined to avenge her beloved brother, she convinces/forces him to teach her the tricks of the trade. What follows is a tale of strangers and strange circumstances, betrayal, infatuation, assassination, murder, revenge, and determination. It's wonderfully morally ambiguous, delightfully twisted, entertainingly brutal, and wickedly intelligent. —*M. N.*

SUBWAY L: DIRECTORS/BESSON, LUC (1985) 98M D: Luc Besson. *Isabelle Adjani, Christopher Lambert, Jean-Pierre Bacri, Jean Reno, Michel Galabru.* Lambert is the spiky-haired, vaguely punk safecracker who takes refuge from the mob in the harshly lit platforms and unending tunnels of the Paris Metro in this stylish and silly lark of a mock-chic romantic crime drama. He flirts with Adjani, the wife of the criminal businessman he's blackmailing, puts together a cheesy rock band while living underground (their debut, performing a mawkishly awful pop tune, is the film's cheesiest moment, unhelped by Besson's utter seriousness), and the film glides from one arbitrary situation to another. This was Besson's second film (after his impressive "silent" sci-fi allegory *Le Dernier Combat*) but was originally meant to be his debut. In his own words, he put the script aside because he "couldn't come up with a story strong enough to counterbalance the decor," a problem even the addition of four extra screenwriters couldn't overcome. —*S. A.*

GET OUT YOUR HANDKERCHIEFS L: DIRECTORS/BLIER, BERTRAND (1977) 109M D: Bertrand Blier. *Patrick Dewaere, Gérard Depardieu, Carole Laure.* Blier has made a career of buddy films in which clueless men haplessly and hopelessly try to understand the women around them, and his social satires have been described as everything from mischievous to misanthropic. In *Get Out Your Handkerchiefs*, Blier's smash hit and Oscar winner for Best Foreign Film, Depardieu is married to the depressed, lethargic Laure, who is so mopey she's virtually inert. Dewaere is the bystander drawn into a stifled romantic triangle by a husband so desperate to make his wife happy he goes looking for a lover for her. What Laure needs is a child, insists Dewaere, and how right he is: she falls in love with a precocious thirteen-year-old genius who seduces her and gives her back her laugh. Blier has a knack for creating deadpan absurdity and he corkscrews the plot twists into a Buñuelian territory by the end, with the now best buddies Depardieu and Dewaere consoling themselves in a friendship more intimate than anything they ever shared with the unresponsive Laure. —S.A.

MY MAN (MON HOMME) L: DIRECTORS/BLIER, BERTRAND (1996) 99M D: Bertrand Blier. *Gerade Lavin, Anouk Grinberg.* Blier loves to hover in the murky area between love and sex, as if trying to trace the connections between the two. His latest foray takes Marie (Grinberg), the proverbial whore with a heart of gold who loves her job so much that she feels compelled to recruit other women, and gives her true love in the form of a homeless man, Jeannot (Lavin), whose sudden sexual dominance turns her rapturously submissive. It looks like another one of Blier's ugly stories of sexual shackles, but he invests this one with some interesting conflicts (which, admittedly, have their own elements of ugliness). Who's really in charge if Jeannot's dominance comes from Marie's bequest? Why does Jeannot spend all his money on another mistress? How does this uneasy relationship balance out? This is one case where Blier makes potentially offensive material work by sheer force of his personality and creative energy. —S.A.

BEHIND LOCKED DOORS L: DIRECTORS/BOETTICHER, BUDD (1948) 62M D: Budd Boetticher. *Thomas Browne Henry, Lucille Bremer, Richard Carlson, Douglas Fowley.* Future cult-Western director Boetticher still used his given name, Oscar Boetticher Jr. when he turned out this low-budget programmer for Monogram studios. Fresh out of the Columbia B-movie grind house, he was already displaying a knack for character and mood, not to mention style, in this mystery about a private detective (Carlson) who goes undercover in a private sanitarium to flush a crook out of hiding. Boetticher creates sparks with his character clashes and drenches the film in menace with swaths of shadow (which also hide his cheap sets), transforming a bargain-basement crime film into a neat little thriller. Look for Ed Wood regular Tor Johnson as the mindless, punch-drunk boxer. —S.A.

RIDE LONESOME L: DIRECTORS/BOETTICHER, BUDD (1959) 73M D: Budd Boetticher. *Randolph Scott, Karen Steele, Pernell Roberts.* From the get-go, this is one of the tightest movies ever made. Scott rides into a tense situation in the opening shot (the memorable rocky location literally starts Scott out between a rock and a hard place) and the tension increases as additional groups of antagonists are added. The interplay between the various antagonists and the determination of Scott propel the picture forward. Scott is the epitome of grace under pressure. The film shows its beautiful precision when he jumps his horse over the low wall where his four companions are sheltering,

collapses his horse onto its side, then turns and begins shooting at the pursuing Mescaleros— gauging each shot purposefully. —P.M.

TALL T, THE L: DIRECTORS/BOETTICHER, BUDD (1957) 78M D: Budd Boetticher. *Skip Homeier, Randolph Scott, Richard Boone, Arthur Hunnicutt, Henry Silva, Maureen O'Sullivan.* Boetticher's best Westerns are models of austerity: tight, tough dramas on an unforgiving frontier. *The Tall T,* adapted by Boetticher's favorite screenwriter from an Elmore Leonard story, is one of his best. The laconic Scott is a struggling rancher who winds up in the hands of stage robbers when a botched heist turns into a kidnapping and they take heiress and aging newlywed O'Sullivan hostage. Boone, the pitiless yet charismatic leader of a small gang of homicidal punks (dim, boyish Homeier and sneering sadist Silva), is the greatest of Boetticher and Kennedy's charming villains: quiet yet commanding, at once alert and relaxed, and almost helplessly drawn to Scott. Scott bluffs and feints to isolate the gang and the screen erupts in shockingly brutal violence. With his vividly realized characters, the rich frontier simplicity of Kennedy's dialogue, and the beautiful yet desolate Lone Pine landscape, Boetticher creates one of the great Westerns of the 1950s. —S.A.

PAPER MOON L: DIRECTORS/BOGDANOVICH, PETER (1973) 102M D: Peter Bogdanovich. *Madeline Kahn, John Hillerman, P. J. Johnson, Ryan O'Neal, Tatum O'Neal.* Director Bogdanovich gives us the story of two Bible hustlers on the run in late 1930s Dust Bowl America, beautifully shot in hard black-and-white by Laszi Kovács. After reluctantly taking orphan Addie (Tatum O'Neal) under his wing, con man Moses Pray (Tatum's real-life dad Ryan) sets off through the Bible Belt in search of hopeless (and often hapless) yokels to sell Bibles to. The two have an almost immediate rapport, which usually consists of Addie outwitting the dim Moses, but all good things end when Moses falls for busty stage performer Trixie Delight (a lascivious Kahn). The story then plays out like a polite Flannery O'Connor story on downers, with a lot of double-crossing and seeming disappointments. But *Paper Moon* is one of the finest films of the 1970s, blending Hollywood sentimentality with a fistful of hard-luck realism. O'Neal won the Best Supporting Actress Oscar for her performance, becoming the youngest-ever Academy Award recipient. —J.D.

TARGETS L: DIRECTORS/BOGDANOVICH, PETER (1968) 89M D: Peter Bogdanovich. *Tim O'Kelly, Boris Karloff.* The genesis of Bogdanovich's debut feature isn't so strange a story, given the road to the director's chair that Roger Corman offered so many of his apprentices. Bogdanovich was given free reign to make whatever he wanted, as long as he used Karloff for a couple of days and incor-

Budd Boetticher

Budd Boetticher stumbled into the movies in the fluky way so many of the two-fisted directors of the silent days landed in the director's chair, but with a high-society twist only Hollywood could have provided. Born Oscar Boetticher Jr., the sports-mad kid from a wealthy family planned a career in athletics until he saw his first bullfight in Mexico City and stayed to learn the sport, under the tutelage of two of the finest and most respected matadors in Mexico. He wound up teaching Tyrone Power how to look good in the ring for Rouben Mamoulian's 1941 remake of *Blood and Sand.*

He worked his way up the ladder, learning his craft on the job—production assistant, second assistant director, first assistant director—and then cutting his teeth on a string of B movies for Columbia until he broke away from the mire of low-budget quickies with his own script.

The Boetticher we know as Budd was born with *The Bullfighter and the Lady* (1951), inspired by his own adventures as a young torero in Mexico (though certainly embellished for the screen) and filled with a reverence for the tradition of torero and a love of the Mexican culture. It earned him a 1951 Academy Award nomination for Best Original Story and catapulted him onto the A list.

The midlist salt mines of his subsequent Universal contract were almost as constraining as his B-movie assignments, but he made some interesting films in his two years there, notably the World War II adventure *Red Ball Express* (1952) and the Westerns *Horizons West* (1952), *Seminole* (1953), and *The Man from the Alamo* (1953). His reputation was made with the terse, austere,

ruthless Western *Seven Men from Now* (1956), written by Burt Kennedy and starring the craggy, lean Randolph Scott. It brought out the best in Boetticher, who pared himself down to the rugged essentials and ratcheted up the tension between the central characters, isolated in the empty desert, with remarkable economy. Boetticher directed Scott in six more films: *Decision at Sundown* (1957); *Buchanan Rides Along* (1958); the otherwise forgettable *Westbound* (1959), a contractual obligation Boetticher directed out of friendship; and, most important, three written by Burt Kennedy: *The Tall T* (1957), *Ride Lonesome* (1959), and *Comanche Station* (1960). Tight, taut, graceful, and visceral, often savage and always rich in character, Boetticher's Kennedy-scripted films, nicknamed the Ranown cycle, are lean stories about men on the dangerous, inhospitable frontier, and they stand next to the greatest works of Anthony Mann and John Ford.

Boetticher made one more film, the offbeat little gangster picture *The Rise and Fall of Legs Diamond* (1960), before he too turned his back on civilization and wandered into his own desert to work on his dream project, a portrait of Mexico's greatest torero, Carlos Arruza, who was working to return to the ring as a *rejoneador,* a bullfighter on horseback. The project took him to Mexico for seven years and almost killed him.

He directed one more feature, the low-budget 1969 Western *A Time for Dying,* and the video documentary *My Kingdom For . . .* (1985), but he never gave up his dream of getting back into Hollywood. He died on November 27, 2001, leaving behind a handful of scripts he had spent decades trying to get produced, and an underrated career of lean, smartly made movies.

—*Sean Axmaker*

porated footage from *The Terror,* a Corman costume thriller starring Karloff. What he came up with was a uniquely American horror inspired by real-life Texas sniper Charles Whitman and wound around the story of an aging scary-movie icon (Karloff, playing "Byron Orlok"). He's determined to retire because his brand of horror is simply no longer relevant in a world where a bland, blank young man could suddenly, numbly, slaughter his family and then take his frozen rage into the streets. It wasn't Karloff's last film, but it's the farewell performance he should be remembered by: he's gentle, funny, sad, and dignified throughout. It's amazing that so serious and powerful a film could arise from such conditions. —*S. A.*

VOYAGE TO THE PLANET OF PREHISTORIC WOMEN
L: DIRECTORS/BOGDANOVICH, PETER (1969) 78M D: Peter Bogdanovich. *Mamie Van Doren, Mary Marr, Paige Lee, Aldo Roman, Margot Hartman.* The 1962 Russian sci-fi film *Planeta Burg* had already been ransacked to make *Planet of Blood* when Roger Corman gave it to his eager assistant Bogdanovich to see what he could make of it. The result is the damnedest example of Corman's cinema recycling. To the original film, about a mission to rescue missing explorers from a storm-ravaged planet, Bogdanovich directs new scenes (under the name Derek Thomas) with Van Doren as the queen of the telepathic Venusian women. These aquatic blond beach-babes dress in hip-hugging bell-bottoms and seashell bikinis, frolic on the sunny beaches of Big Sur, and worship Ptera, the pterodactyl god. A truly strange film, at times campy, at other times simply surreal, as the narrator (Bogdanovich in a weirdly haunting drone) endlessly searches for the woman he hears in his mind but never meets. Bogdanovich plants his signature on the end of the film, a quote from the final shot of *The Lady From Shanghai:* "Maybe I'll forget her. Maybe I'll die trying." —*S. A.*

WHAT'S UP, DOC? L: DIRECTORS/BOGDANOVICH, PETER
(1972) 94M D: Peter Bogdanovich. *Michael Murphy, Austin Pendleton, Kenneth Mars, Madeline Kahn, Ryan O'Neal, Barbra Streisand.* This harkens back to the years of screwball comedies, but manages somehow to avoid a lot of the pitfalls of that genre by moving at a quick and playful pace, rather than hammering in jokes long past the point where they are funny. Streisand is wonderful as a brilliant but crazy-making woman who has fixed her attention upon food and the poor hapless O'Neal. Four plaid bags, one with a diamond collection in it, another with clothes, another with secret government documents, and the last with musical rocks, play the catalyst for chaos as characters beg, borrow, and steal them from each other, bringing an unlikely collection of criminals, miscreants, victims, thieves, and innocent bystanders into a hilarious collision course. —*M. N.*

DELIVERANCE L: DIRECTORS/BOORMAN, JOHN (1972)
109M D: John Boorman. *Ronny Cox, James Dickey, Ned Beatty, Burt Reynolds, Jon Voight.* A group of men decide to go on a rafting trip in a very remote area in the South. Not far from where they intend to set up camp they bump into a few locals, strange hillbillies who act kind of scary. But at least one of them can play a good banjo, and performs "Dueling Banjos" with one of the vacationers. After a rafting accident, one of them is injured and the friends regroup on shore, only to find their horror has just begun. They are kidnapped and tortured by the very hillbillies they just met. Viewers beware: the themes of this movie become disturbing and extremely mature. "Squeal like a pig! Squeal like a pig!" —*N. J.*

EXORCIST II: THE HERETIC L: DIRECTORS/BOORMAN,
JOHN (1977) 118M D: John Boorman. *Max von Sydow, Richard Burton, Linda Blair, Louise Fletcher, Kitty Winn.* This was not the sequel people expected to see after the success of the first film. But in its own inimitable way it is still a very curious, rather campy, yet thoroughly watchable film. Blair, again playing Regan, is hypnotized by her psychologist with a strange pulsating device that is supposed to connect people's minds. Burton plays the priest who happens to connect with her to discover she is still possessed. To save her, von Sydow must be tracked down on the other side of the world where his lifelong struggle with the Demon continues. In the subsequent odyssey that follows, the audience is treated to psychedelic music and effects and very interesting acting through a highly contrived plot. After such a film it's little wonder that by 1990 Blair would team up with Leslie Nielsen for the spoof *Repossessed.* —*N. J.*

HELL IN THE PACIFIC L: DIRECTORS/BOORMAN, JOHN
(1968) 101M D: John Boorman. *Lee Marvin, Toshirô Mifune.* During WWII an American soldier (Marvin) and a Japanese one (Mifune) are stranded on a remote island. At first they fight and try to take each other prisoner, but eventually they realize the futility of their battles and attempt to coexist peacefully. What makes the movie unique (besides having two of the most iconic tough-guy actors as its entire cast) is that each of the characters speaks only his native language, without subtitles; thus it is probably a different movie for Japanese-speaking audiences than it is for English speakers. In one of the most memorable scenes Marvin tries to degrade Mifune by making him fetch a stick like a dog. But when Mifune doesn't seem to understand the concept, Marvin ends up fetching it himself as a demonstration. —*B. T.*

POINT BLANK L: DIRECTORS/BOORMAN, JOHN (1967)
87M D: John Boorman. *Lee Marvin, Angie Dickinson, Keenan Wynn, Carroll O'Connor.* Tough-guy icon Marvin tears apart the screen in this three-fisted art film/action blast hybrid by the venerable

Robert Bresson

Robert Bresson always made a point of calling the performers in his films models—a term specifically culled from painting—rather than actors. The term was fitting, coming from a former painter who envisioned filmmaking as a marriage not of theater and photography, but of painting and music. But it was also descriptive of his method of directing. Bresson drilled his actors to follow his every instruction, to reproduce an action exactly as he created it. There was no room for interpretation in his films, which is likely why he worked only with nonactors or first-time performers since *A Man Escaped* in 1956.

"You can say things mechanically," he explains in the documentary *The Way to Bresson*, "but if you do, soon you will penetrate the character, bringing the mechanics to life." By taking the "noise" of acting from his performers, having them perform in a near monotone with blank faces and conditioned movements, Bresson sought to reveal the soul.

By most accounts, Robert Bresson was born in the Auvergne region of France in 1907 and moved to Paris with his family when he was eight. As a teen he studied philosophy and the classics, and for many years he played the piano and studied to become a painter, a goal he abandoned when he became fascinated by the cinema. After working fitfully on the fringes of the French

---

Boorman. This masterpiece was the inspiration for Soderbergh's *The Limey,* but no revenge epic has neared its barely contained cinematic intensity. Robbed of his cash and fiancée by his so-called best friend, Marvin climbs an endless criminal ladder toward bitter vengeance. Everything in his way is completely demolished: men, cars, lives—even a feather mattress is torn apart in a barrage of gunfire. Mind-numbing colors, daring sound design, and impossibly gripping performances combine to create an amazing example of a film catapulted beyond the limits of its genre. *Point Blank* railroads you like a top-notch Don Siegel script directed by an angrier Jules Dassin. In fact, Marvin's rabid hatred is so palpable you'll swear he's actually killing half the cast! —*Z.C.*

TAILOR OF PANAMA, THE L: DIRECTORS/BOORMAN, JOHN (2001) 109M D: John Boorman. *Pierce Brosnan, Geoffrey Rush, Jamie Lee Curtis.* Set during the trigger-happy days of George Bush Sr.'s reign just after the fall of Noriega, Boorman's adaptation of John Le Carre's novel is a witty, wicked, delightfully cynical bit of global intrigue grounded in vivid characters. Rush is the eponymous tailor whose outrageous tales of revolution and political intrigue spiral into tragedy when a conniving con man of a British agent (Brosnan in an anti-007 turn) passes them on to the conspiracy-hungry western powers. Boorman creates a rich, dense, fresh work, unleashing free and easy flashes of his cinematic youth and spicing the story with sardonic counterpoints, humor-

ous asides, and running conversations with the ghosts of memory. Energetic and inventive, this tricky mix of the sarcastic and the serious is a satirical, smart, grown-up thriller rooted in genuine affection for Rush's weathered sad sack. Curtis, Catherine McCormack, Brendan Gleeson, and Harold Pinter costar. —*S.A.*

ZARDOZ L: DIRECTORS/BOORMAN, JOHN (1974) 106M D: John Boorman. *Niall Buggy, Charlotte Rampling, John Alderton, Sara Kestelman, Sally Anne Newton, Sean Connery.* Connery plays a barbarian human in a highly stylized distant future. He manages to hide within the giant floating head that appears from time to time to instruct his people in the ways of warfare. After flying a long distance he gets out of the head and discovers he is on the other side of the barrier—a large force field that separates the humans from the immortals. The more he investigates the city of the immortals, the more he finds out about them and how the bizarre place came into being. Boorman's visual depiction of this strange future is startling and his use of Beethoven's Seventh Symphony adds even more magic to this curious film. —*N.J.*

SEVENTH HEAVEN L: DIRECTORS/BORZAGE, FRANK (1927) 119M D: Frank Borzage. *Ben Bard, Charles Farrell, Janet Gaynor.* Borzage took home the first Academy Award for direction and leading lady Gaynor copped the Best Actress award for this romantic melodrama, an affirmation of the human spirit and an example of silent cinema at its best. Parisian sewer worker Farrell offers shelter to a

film industry (including a short comedy, in 1934, now lost, called *Les Affaires Publiques*), he completed his first feature in 1943, *Les Anges de Péché*.

Disappointed with the results, he embarked on a campaign to transform his cinema from "filmed theater" to a wholly new kind of experience. With *Diary of a Country Priest* (1951) he created his first masterpiece, mixing documentary-like scrutiny and detail with a harsh spirituality and austere, minimalist performances. In *A Man Escaped* (1956), Bresson's portrayal of a real-life POW prison break, and *Pickpocket* (1959), the Dostoyevsky-inspired story of an arrogant thief, his transformation is complete: performances systematically stripped of affectation and theatrical flourish come alive with a kind of truth very different from the psychologically motivated interpretations of even the greatest actors.

Bresson belonged to no school or movement; he spawned many fans but no disciples. His films range in subject matter from the Arthurian anti-spectacle *Lancelot of the Lake* (1974) to the urban studies of loneliness and alienation in the modern world, *A Gentle Woman* (1969) and *The Devil Probably* (1977). After *L'Argent* (1982), a bitter tale of contemporary crime and punishment loosely based on a story by Tolstoy, Bresson retired to a life of books and concerts.

Bresson died in the closing days of the twentieth century, leaving behind a handful of interviews, a short, staccato book of reflections on his philosophy of cinema titled *Notes on the Cinematographer*, and thirteen films of quiet restraint that explore life, faith, sadness, and transcendence, finding amid the pain of life and the acceptance of death a state of grace.

—*Sean Axmaker*

---

destitute street girl and the two fall in love in their seventh-floor garret, but before they can marry he leaves to fight in WWI. Borzage tells his story as much through visual metaphor as narrative convention, expressing in images what words cannot. Their daily "telepathic" communication across hundreds of miles defies logic, but Borzage makes it believable in the context of his story, which takes place largely in the spiritual realm. A powerful and beautiful film, this is one of Borzage's masterpieces. —*S.A.*

REAL YOUNG GIRL, A L: DIRECTORS/BREILLAT, CATHERINE (1976) 93M D: Catherine Breillat. *Bruno Balp, Rita Meiden, Hiram Keller, Charlotte Alexandra*. This film provides substantial evidence in support of a theory of mine: Girls in France have cooler sexual awakenings than anywhere else in the world. The real young girl is 14-year-old Alice Bonnard (Alexandra), who is home visiting her parents somewhere in the French countryside on her summer holiday. Bored, Alice spends her time shoving random objects in a variety of shapes and sizes "up herself" and stalking Jim, an older local boy who works for her philandering father. With superb direction, Breillat creates a unique sexual landscape of danger and experimentation where the border between fantasy and reality is as fluid as the vomit, urine, and silver jism that free flow over the course of the film. —*D.D.*

DAMES DU BOIS DE BOULOGNE, LES L: DIRECTORS/ BRESSON, ROBERT (1945) 85M D: Robert Bresson. *Maria Casares, Paul Bernard, Elina Labourdette*.

Bresson's second movie stars Casares as a jealous high-society woman who takes revenge on longtime lover Bernard by sacrificing an impoverished young dancer (Labourdette) to a public disgrace. Based on the novel *Jacques le Fataliste et son Maître* by Denis Diderot, with a script polished by Jean Cocteau, this melodrama of love, jealousy, revenge, and redemption is haunted by an uneasy tension between Bresson's ambitions and directorial compromises, notably the stylized dialogue and psychologically shaded performances of classical French cinema that Bresson's later films reject. The director's hand can be seen in the austere sets and compositions, the tempered performances, and the moving, spiritually rich conclusion. —*S.A.*

DIARY OF A COUNTRY PRIEST L: DIRECTORS/BRESSON, ROBERT (1951) 110M D: Robert Bresson. *Jean Danet, Antoine Balpêtré, Léon Arvel, Claude Laydu, Jeanne Étiévant*. Laydu delivers perhaps the finest performance in any Bresson film as the young village vicar who martyrs himself in his desperate, flailing, yet spiritually pure attempts to bring salvation to his self-centered parishioners. In other hands the martyrdom of the dying priest might turn sentimental and superficial, but the restraint and simplicity of Bresson's style and the powerful expressiveness of Laydu's impassive, dour face create a powerful story of spiritual engagement. The world of the French countryside comes alive through the rustling leaves and the blowing wind, which become the soundtrack of the lonely yet alive film. Bresson's first true masterpiece is his calling card to the world of cinema. —*S.A.*

FOUR NIGHTS OF A DREAMER L: DIRECTORS/BRESSON, ROBERT (1971) 87M D: Robert Bresson. *Guillaume des Forets, Isabelle Weingarten.* One of Bresson's last films, this adaptation of Dostoevsky's *White Nights* dabbles a bit too much in contemporary Parisian youth culture, which today renders it painfully dated. That said, we're talking about Bresson here, and no amount of outmoded fashion could diminish the potency of his vision. Jacques (Forets), a romantic young painter, meets Marthe (Weingarten), whom he talks out of suicide. Over four nights, an intensely needy bond forms as Jacques waits with her on the Pont-Neuf bridge for a wayward lover who never arrives. Jacques is trapped between his genuine interest in helping Marthe find happiness and his desire to become her lover. High on mood, low on action, *Four Nights of a Dreamer* is not an easy sell to many viewers. For Bresson fans, however, each of his few films is a work of great importance. —*C.B.*

GENTLE WOMAN, A L: DIRECTORS/BRESSON, ROBERT (1969) 89M D: Robert Bresson. *Jeanne Lobre, Dominique Sanda, Guy Frangin. A Gentle Woman* begins with the suicide of an unnamed girl (Sanda). The rest of the film consists of her husband's account of their miserable marriage as he talks his way toward an understanding of what might have led to her death. Quintessentially Bresson, the film literally begins with its alarming conclusion. From there suspense is further subverted; we see the husband describe an event, and afterwards watch the event unfold in flashback. Although she is the film's focus, by killing herself at the outset the girl cannot narrate her own story. As a result, we know little of her specific motivations for suicide or really of anything going on inside her stoic figure beyond a quiet contempt for her husband. When the film comes full circle and retreads the suicide, nothing about it seems tragic, only practical. Bresson's first color film, this begins the later and less hopeful period of his career. —*C.B.*

MAN ESCAPED, A L: DIRECTORS/BRESSON, ROBERT (1951) 99M D: Robert Bresson. *Charles Le Clainche, Jacques Ertaud, Maurice Beerblock, François Leterrier, Roland Monod.* While it remains a resolutely Bressonian film—"modeled" with impassive restraint accompanied by an uninflected narration and built up with an obsessive attention to minute details—*A Man Escaped* is also a gripping adventure of one man's daring breakout from a war prison. Based on the memoir by André Devigny, the self-possessed loner (renamed Fontaine for the film and played by Leterrier) painstakingly plots his escape with patience and perseverance and is assisted by lucky breaks (divine intervention?), while a pair of fellow prisoners becomes a sort of Greek cho-

rus discussing his chances and progress. Shot on location at the actual prison in Lyon, Bresson's film painstakingly re-creates every detail of Devigny's ordeal while denying us any elements that are extraneous to his purpose. In such austerity the tiniest of details take on a monumental significance —*S.A.*

PICKPOCKET L: DIRECTORS/BRESSON, ROBERT (1959) 75M D: Robert Bresson. *Pierre Leymarie, Marika Green, Dolly Scal, Jean Pélégri, Martin La Salle.* Though the film starts with Bresson's only overt cinematic homage (to Sam Fuller's *Pickup on South Street*), *Pickpocket* owes more to Dostoevsky's *Crime and Punishment* in the story of an isolated loner (the blank-faced La Salle) whose belief in his superiority leads to a criminal existence. More than a job, picking pockets becomes his way of life, thumbing his nose at his victims and the dogged detective who relentlessly pursues him, while grace awaits him in the form of a selfless young woman. Bresson's films aren't for everyone—his austere style, emotionless direction, and minimalist scripts can become frustrating if you don't connect—but there's a purity in his ambition to pare away everything but the essential elements of cinema. A masterpiece from one of the cinema's true originals. —*S.A.*

TRIAL OF JOAN OF ARC L: DIRECTORS/BRESSON, ROBERT (1962) 88M D: Robert Bresson. *Florence Carrez.* This is the most austere and stylistically rarefied film of Bresson's career and, perhaps as a result, isn't one of the best-loved ones. But as the most extreme example of Bresson's aesthetic (and/or ascetic) agenda, it can't be—and shouldn't be—avoided. The film's plot stays stubbornly close to the real facts of St. Joan, to the point that its dialogue is literally quoted from the actual court records of her trial. Any narrative tension must originate in the factual event, whose outcome must already be obvious to any audience. Bresson was fairly outspoken in his distaste for Carl Theodor Dreyer's more melodramatic rendering of the Joan of Arc story. His own version took his trademark distancing effects to new stoic heights and can usefully be taken as the polar opposite of Dreyer's. —*C.B.*

KING OF HEARTS, THE L: DIRECTORS/BROCA, PHILIPPE DE (1966) 101M D: Philippe de Broca. *Pierre Brasseur, Alan Bates, Geneviève Bujold, Jean-Claude Brialy, Micheline Presle.* Bates plays a Scottish soldier in WWI who cautiously enters a small French town occupied by the Germans. To his surprise he discovers the entire city is abandoned save for a handful of very odd people trying to establish their own government. It appears that what they lack is a central, rational leader. A king! As Bates is slowly groomed into that royal position he begins to discover that these aren't regular townsfolk he's liberating, these are all mental patients escaped from the nearby nuthouse! This timeless film is packed with political commen-

tary and a rational perspective on the futility of war. —*N. J.*

MAGNIFIQUE, LE L: DIRECTORS/BROCA, PHILIPPE DE (1973) 90M D: Philippe de Broca. *Jacqueline Bisset, Jean-Paul Belmondo.* Belmondo is a reclusive novelist who imagines he's the dashing spy-hero of his books in this Walter Mitty-meets-James Bond farce by de Broca. While the rumpled slob of a writer clumsily woos his pretty British neighbor (Bissett, a college sociology student fascinated by his sly fantasy novels), his absurdly suave and outrageously manly pulp fiction alter ego Bob St. Clare seduces sexy secret agent Tatania (Bissett again). The fantasy scenes are like a Bond spoof by Tex Avery, full of farcical flourishes and slapstick pratfalls, which only magnify when the writer decides to sabotage his creation in a nutty climactic somersault. The violence plays like a Monty Python take on Sam Peckinpah: henchmen aren't just shot, they're turned into Swiss cheese while Bob's machine gun creates a veritable waterfall of bad-guy blood (in bright, ultra-vivid crimson paint). Even the moments of mean-spirited fantasy revenge are mellowed with de Broca's unfaltering tone of crazy comedy. —*S. A.*

REAL LIFE L: DIRECTORS/BROOKS, ALBERT (1979) 99M D: Albert Brooks. *Charles Grodin, Dick Haynes, Albert Brooks.* Brooks's first film is ostensibly a parody of the British documentary series *American Family,* where a film crew recorded the daily events of an American family, but it's also a proto–*Big Brother.* Grodin is great as the average American pushed to the brink at a slow burn, but Brooks is even more maniacal as the showbiz veteran who can't reconcile the demands of documentary and the desires of entertainment, so he simply creates his own reality. None of the excellent mockumentaries made in the wake of this film have its bite or its cunning take on the intrusive influence of the media. —*S. A.*

BLAZING SADDLES L: DIRECTORS/BROOKS, MEL (1974) 93M D: Mel Brooks. *Gene Wilder, Mel Brooks, Slim Pickens, Cleavon Little, Harvey Korman, Madeline Kahn.* *Blazing Saddles* is a surprisingly raw Western comedy that liberally uses racial epithets in a manner not unlike how they were used in the old West. If you can get past that, you have some classic comedy waiting for you. In order to get a railroad built through the town of Rock Ridge, a railroad baron (Korman) cooks up a scam to scare off the populace by making the governor (Brooks) install a black sheriff (Little). Then he then sends in the worst possible criminals to terrorize people and scare them out of town. All of this makes for some great slapstick done up as only Brooks can conceive. —*N. J.*

LIFE STINKS L: DIRECTORS/BROOKS, MEL (1991) 93M D: Mel Brooks. *Mel Brooks, Jeffrey Tambor, Lesley Ann Warren, Stuart Pankin, Howard Morris.* Brooks plays the richest man on Earth who wants to build his dream project over a downtown Los Angeles slum. To buy out the whole area he makes a bet with its owner to see if the richest man can live as a bum in that district for thirty days. The situation gives rise to broad comedy with an emphasis on the absurdity of class hierarchy. Predictably, Brooks becomes lifelong friends with the truly impoverished, marrying one such lady by the time he is finally able to reclaim his wealth. The film is a bit long for its subject matter, but the final climax featuring two giant bulldozers battling it out just like dinosaurs is worth the wait. —*N. J.*

PRODUCERS, THE L: DIRECTORS/BROOKS, MEL (1968) 85M D: Mel Brooks. *Zero Mostel, Gene Wilder, Kenneth Mars, Dick Shawn.* It's "Springtime for Hitler" in Brooks's debut film, a farce about a threadbare but undeterred veteran Broadway producer (Mostel) and a meek accountant (Wilder) who plot to make money by creating a surefire flop. Loud, brassy, and brimming with bad taste, this burlesque has one of most hilarious moments in the fictional history of showbiz outrageousness: dancing Nazis and showgirl frauleins celebrating Hitler's Third Reich in song, complete with a salute to Busby Berkeley. Jaw-droppingly funny, this paste jewel in the tin crown of Brooks's knockabout comedy sits atop the marvelous camaraderie of Mostel and Wilder. Shawn is wonderfully dippy as the hippie Hitler and Mars is the demented German soldier whose love letter to his Fürher is turned into the craziest musical to ever hit the Great White Way. Brooks won an Oscar for Best Original Screenplay. —*S. A.*

SILENT MOVIE L: DIRECTORS/BROOKS, MEL (1976) 88M D: Mel Brooks. *Dom DeLuise, Marty Feldman, Paul Newman, James Caan, Liza Minnelli, Mel Brooks.* An actual silent movie made in 1976? That's exactly what Brooks's homage to the golden age of slapstick is, a modern silent film about the making of a modern silent film. Brooks plays a former studio executive who, with his associates Feldman and DeLuise, pitches the idea of a silent movie to the current studio executive so as to save the failing studio from being bought out by a company called Engulf and Devour. The current studio executive agrees so long as some major stars sign on to the project, and so begins the list of cameos. All of these stars agree to the project except for the celebrated mime Marcel Marceau, who has the only spoken word in the film: "No!" Hilarious vignettes in the style of old slapstick make this a pleasurable Brooks outing, and like good slapstick it doesn't overstay its welcome. —*N. J.*

SPACEBALLS L: DIRECTORS/BROOKS, MEL (1987) 96M D: Mel Brooks. *Bill Pullman, Mel Brooks, Daphne Zuniga, Rick Moranis, John Candy.* The merchandizing of *Star Wars* and the mania that accompanied that film obviously tempted Brooks, a director famed

Luis Buñuel

Luis Buñuel was born in 1900 in Calanda, Spain, the first of eight children. The son of a wealthy hardware merchant and his aristocratic wife, Buñuel was raised in the town of Saragossa and educated in religious schools until the age of fifteen, when he began to question his faith. To escape his rigid environment, he went to university in Madrid, where he joined a circle of writers and artists (including Federico García Lorca and Salvador Dalí) who influenced him to switch from science to the arts.

A movie fan from an early age, he immersed himself in the cinema after his mother arranged for him to become the secretary to a Spanish diplomat in Paris.

He attended avant-garde filmmaker Jean Epstein's film school and worked on a few films before he made his first production. The surrealist landmark *Un Chien Andalou* (1929) was created in collaboration with Dalí, but they split during their second film, the controversial *L'Age d'Or* (1930). After a brief stint in Hollywood and difficulties with his third film, the documentary *Land Without Bread* (1933), Buñuel spent the next few years dubbing American films and directing (uncredited) for a Spanish company that collapsed after the fascist coup. Moving to America for a brief job in Hollywood, he found work at the Museum of Modern Art dubbing and subtitling films.

Buñuel went to Mexico in 1946 to direct a play (which fell through), but instead found himself actively directing movies again, this

---

for his spoofs. In *Spaceballs* nearly every piece of the film *Star Wars* is deconstructed and scoffed at, from the opening prologue to the characters to most every part of the plotline. Featured is Moranis as Dark Helmet, whose helmet is roughly the size of his body; Candy as a "Mog," a creature that is half man, half dog ("I'm my own best friend."); Zuniga as the princess whose coiled braids are in fact headphones; and a host of others. This slapstick may be too much for fans of Brooks's earlier films, but one could say this film is a bridge to the humor of his later films, which are stylistically much more like this one than *Young Frankenstein*. —*N. J.*

YOUNG FRANKENSTEIN L: DIRECTORS/BROOKS, MEL (1974) 105M D: Mel Brooks. *Marty Feldman, Madeline Kahn, Teri Garr, Peter Boyle, Gene Wilder, Cloris Leachman.* Wilder plays a descendent of Baron Von Frankenstein who hates to acknowledge his familial ties. He insists on being called "FrankenSTEEN." He finds himself inheriting the family castle and all the trappings that come with it, including Igor (a brilliantly cast Feldman). Naturally, young Frankenstein comes to accept his role and becomes something of a chip off the old block. Filmed in black and white so as to better spoof the original Universal horror films, *Young Frankenstein* is lined corner to corner with puns, wit, slapstick, and wordplay. It warrants repeated viewing to uncover all the layers of humor. —*N. J.*

ELMER GANTRY L: DIRECTORS/BROOKS, RICHARD (1960) 146M D: Richard Brooks. *Burt Lancaster, Jean Simmons, Shirley Jones.* Lancaster earned his only Oscar as the wide-smiling, glad-handing, soul-saving charlatan Elmer Gantry, a salesman who turns his gift for preaching into a career on the pulpit. He harnesses all his physical vigor and natural charisma for this role. He even brays like a hound to show the holy spirit within him. With the vigor of an acrobat and the delivery of a gospel singer, he's a showman, pure and simple. While he doesn't fool Sister Sharon (Simmons), a true believer in the Aimee Semple McPherson mold, he does give her a few object lessons in playing the crowd. Jones also earned an Oscar for her supporting role as a blackmailing prostitute, as did Brooks for his screenplay adaptation of the Sinclair Lewis novel. —*S. A.*

DRACULA L: DIRECTORS/BROWNING, TOD (1931) 75M D: Tod Browning. *Edward Van Sloan, Dwight Frye, David Manners, Helen Chandler, Bela Lugosi.* Lugosi's star-making turn as the notorious bloodsucker was the first of the great Universal classic horror films. Preceded only by silent gems such as *Hunchback* and *Phantom,* this early sound picture is an absolute masterpiece of production design, cinematography, and directing. These elements combine to create an atmosphere so distinctly eerie and so madly fun that there are few horror films more enjoyable than this all-time classic. There are so many things about *Dracula* that I

time in the Mexican film industry. Though he made mostly commercial comedies and melodramas, Buñuel brought political overtones and a sense of surrealism to these pictures, and was able to direct more personal productions between his commercial assignments. His most famous picture from this period is the drama *Los Olvidados* (1950), a study of poverty influenced by Italian neorealist films and sprinkled with surrealist moments.

He returned to Spain in 1960 for a Mexican-Spanish coproduction, the controversial *Viridiana*, which was immediately banned in Spain and denounced by the Vatican. Following *The Exterminating Angel* (1962), Buñuel moved to France, where he remained for the rest of his career, collaborating with screenwriter Jean-Claude Carrière. Buñuel was more than sixty years old at this point in his career, and at the height of his critical acclaim.

His last films met with critical success almost without exception, and he attracted the best actors from France. In many ways he returned to the freedom of his first films, except that these surreal pieces are structured around narratives. His thematic preoccupations remained the same: satirizing the church and the bourgeoisie, exploring sexual desire and violent behavior (often together), puncturing social conventions and turning cultural stereotypes on end. His narratives are quirky and unpredictable, but his visual style is surprisingly simple and direct, full of long takes and moving cameras focused on the characters and the action. According to collaborators, Buñuel was an efficient filmmaker, shooting directly from the script with little or no changes, often getting scenes in one take.

After retiring from filmmaking three times, Buñuel died in 1983.

—*Sean Axmaker*

---

could rave about, but what really counts is how it all comes together in the end to create a masterpiece. *Dracula* will never die. —*T. S.*

FREAKS L: DIRECTORS/BROWNING, TOD (1932) 66M D: Tod Browning. *Harry Earles, Wallace Ford, Olga Baclanova, Lelia Hyams, Roscoe Ates.* True to its title, *Freaks* is about a group of freaks in a circus who look after each other yet are ridiculed by the strongman and his trapeze-artist girlfriend. Capitalizing on the success of the horror films of the time, this film uses actual freaks to generate its shock but portrays them as sympathetic characters forced onto the lowest rung of the social ladder. The plot concerns the trapeze artist trying to marry a dwarf solely to steal his money. By the climax of the film, natural human emotion overwhelms these freaks and a suitable revenge is exacted against the strongman and his beautiful girlfriend. Very shocking even by today's standards, this film has repeatedly been banned over the years. —*N. J.*

UNKNOWN, THE L: DIRECTORS/BROWNING, TOD (1927) 61M D: Tod Browning. *Nick De Ruiz, Joan Crawford, John George, Frank Lanning, Lon Chaney, Norman Kerry.* The circus owner's daughter (Crawford) is one sexy wench, pawed all the time by men's hands to the point she's developed a psychological phobia about the arms of men. She hates them all, including the strongman (Kerry). She does not hate the armless man (Chaney), who throws knives with his feet (and lights cigarettes

with his feet and places them in his mouth— amazing!) or the midget who is her confidante. But the armless man has secrets and desires too, and he makes two bad decisions. The plot is a tad contrived and the ironic ending is almost too much, but Browning is expert at building edgy scenes and manufacturing edgy character traits. Given such moments, great silent performers like Chaney and Crawford inevitably shine. Gets way down deep under your skin. —*J. C.*

CHIEN ANDALOU, UN (AN ANDALUSIAN DOG) L: DIRECTORS/BUÑUEL, LUIS (1929) 16M D: Luis Buñuel. *Salvador Dalí, Pierre Batcheff, Luis Buñuel, Simone Mareuil.* The *Evil Dead* of the art world. Watch it so you can tell your colleagues "of course I've seen it." If no one around is familiar, reference it often and poignantly. Make sure to refer to it as Buñuel's film and not Salvidor Dalí's—less people have heard if Buñuel than Dalí and you'll appear smarter than you are, even if you're a huge Dalí fan and think he deserves the credit. Though the film may seem like a hollow series of bizarre sights, there is no denying the strength of the imagery. You won't get bored and you may be inspired. You can see where David Lynch is coming from—would the ear in *Blue Velvet* or the ugly little baby from *Eraserhead* exist without this Buñuel and Dalí collaboration? You'll also finally understand Black Francis's lyrics in the beginning of The Pixies's song "Debaser." —*M. H.*

DIARY OF A CHAMBERMAID L: DIRECTORS/BUÑUEL, LUIS (1964) 97M D: Luis Buñuel. *Georges Géret, Daniel Ivernel, Michel Piccoli, Jean Ozenne, Françoise Lugagne, Jeanne Moreau.* With its stunning use of widescreen, this is the best-looking Buñuel film I've seen (aided enormously by Rialto's restoration efforts), as well as one of my favorites. Celestine (Moreau) takes a servant position at an estate on the French countryside. Her first day on the job is spent dodging sexual advances from the estate's numerous lecherous men, a problem that only gets worse with time. Just as Celestine's had enough, a young girl is discovered murdered. Using her power over male desire, Celestine gathers evidence against the man she suspects is the killer. In part a rich cinematic updating of the Gothic novel, *Diary of a Chambermaid* is additionally a searing (and overt) indictment of French nationalism, further pointing to the moral apathy of the bourgeoisie as making such reactionary movements inevitable. —*C. B.*

DISCREET CHARM OF THE BOURGEOISIE, L: DIRECTORS/ BUÑUEL, LUIS (1972) 100M D: Luis Buñuel. *Stéphane Audran, Fernando Rey, Delphine Seyrig, Jean-Pierre Cassel, Paul Frankeur.* A group of ambassadors and their wives repeatedly schedule dinner parties but are interrupted by increasingly bizarre circumstances before they ever eat. They are so involved in their wine and their social circle that they are not phased by the constant bombings outside their houses. When an anarchist tries to inject her viewpoint it is always drowned out by the sounds of airplanes or typewriters so the upper classes will never have to hear her opinions. Many of the scenes drift off into dreams or dreams within dreams. It's a dead-on class satire but not a particularly angry one. Most of all, it's very funny and plays with cinematic conventions. —*B. T.*

EXTERMINATING ANGEL, THE L: DIRECTORS/BUÑUEL, LUIS (1962) 95M D: Luis Buñuel. *Lucy Gallardo, Silvia Pinal, Cesar del Campo, Claudio Brook, Enrique Rambal.* Social satire is never so harsh and poignant as when it comes from Buñuel. An elaborate formal dinner party is being held at a large estate and not long after all the guests show up, the audience gets the feeling that none of them particularly like each other. They pretend to be friends, but conversation becomes a little nasty, with people subtly ridiculing each other, and the dinner goes quite late because no one is willing to leave the table. Eventually morning dawns and still nobody has left. They ask the butler to bring them breakfast, but he can't seem to leave. As they vainly wait for a rational explanation as to why they are stuck in the room, they begin dropping all social pretenses. A fortnight passes and nobody is able to save them. Eventually the curse lifts. No particular reason is given for their experience, but the social commentary has been

amply made. This is one of Buñuel's finest films. —*N. J.*

NAZARIN L: DIRECTORS/BUÑUEL, LUIS (1958) 92M D: Luis Buñuel. *Rita Macedo, Francisco Rabal, Ignacio Tarso, Marga Lopez, Jesus Fernandez.* Father Nazario (Rabal), an outcast of the Church, goes on a pilgrimage through Mexico with two "apostles" tagging along. Driven purely by Christian faith and an earnest belief in the innate goodness of humanity, Nazario unfortunately brings nothing but trouble to the people he wishes to help. In perhaps the greatest sequence in *Nazarin,* a hungry Nazario stops at a day-labor site to work for a meal, unwittingly enraging the other workers whose already dismal wages are instantly threatened by his humble acceptance of a few tortillas. Effectively a series of parable-form rebukes to the Catholic Church for the impotence of institutionalized spirituality, Buñuel's uncharacteristic civility here makes *Nazarin* a surprisingly sympathetic, not to mention rewardingly rich, meditation on the difficulty of applying ideology to everyday life. —*C. B.*

PHANTOM OF LIBERTY, THE L: DIRECTORS/BUÑUEL, LUIS (1974) 104M D: Luis Buñuel. *Paul Frankeur, Claude Piéplu, Paul Le Person, François Maistre, Jean-Claude Brialy, Monica Vitti.* This truly surreal film actually has no main character. It instead wanders from character to character, scene by scene, showing just how bizarre society is by taking a look at it backwards. One fine example of this is when one character shows up to a formal soiree where a large table holding little more than magazines is surrounded by toilets. All the guests are seated (lifting lids first) and begin socializing while leafing through magazines and relieving themselves. One guest gets hungry and must excuse himself, and in a small locked closet he gorges on a large meaty drumstick. Through a mixture of satire and surrealism this film attempts to unmask the very phantom that our society dubs "liberty." —*N. J.*

THAT OBSCURE OBJECT OF DESIRE L: DIRECTORS/ BUÑUEL, LUIS (1977) 104M D: Luis Buñuel. *Carole Bouquet, Angela Molina, Fernando Rey.* Buñuel was almost eighty when he made this, his final film, the cap on a career that spanned almost fifty years. In this adaptation of Pierre Louys's novel *La Femme et le Pantin,* written in collaboration with his longtime screenwriting partner Jean-Claude Carrière, his shock effects have mellowed but he's as surreal and unpredictable as ever, casting two different actresses (cool French model Bouquet and sensual Spanish actress Molina) to play the part of the ambiguous beauty Conchita. Frequent Buñuel star Rey is the patronizing bourgeois cad who repeatedly tries to buy her favors and justify his actions as he tells his story to a compartment full of train passengers. Josef von Sternberg adapted the same novel for *The Devil Is a Woman* and with all the imaginative transformation the different artists bring to the story, you'd never know. —*S. A.*

VIRIDIANA L: DIRECTORS/BUÑUEL, LUIS (1961) 90M D: Luis Buñuel.
Silvia Pinal, Fernando Rey, Francisco Rabal, Margarita Lozano, Victoria Zinny. Invited back to Spain by no less than Franco, Buñuel made himself unwelcome in a hurry with a film denounced by the Spanish government and the Catholic Church in the same year it won the Palme d'Or at Cannes. A chaste nun, Viridiana (Pinal) is filmdom's Pamela (or Shamela?), her virtue forever in peril. This is easily my favorite of Buñuel's movies, and contains the greatest closing line of any film I can think of. His satirical eye is as busy as ever, but is restrained to a symbolism that is at once heavy-handed and extremely economical. Though interesting as a critique of both Spain and the Church, *Viridiana's* real merit lies in its neoclassical literary style. —*C. B.*

ALADDIN AND HIS WONDERFUL LAMP L: DIRECTORS/ BURTON, TIM (1984) 64M D: Tim Burton.
James Earl Jones, Kristy McNichol, Leonard Nimoy, Robert Carradine. This episode of Shelley Duvall's *Faerie Tale Theater* shows Burton's early experimentation with live action, working with the minimal production values provided by the fledgling Disney Channel. Jones plays a blue-skinned genie years before Robin Williams did, and fans will notice many telltale signs of what would become the Burton style (including some great models by constant Burton collaborator Rick Heinrichs). Unfortunately, the episode is very slow moving—it would work much better if it were trimmed down to half an hour or less. Probably only worthwhile for children and Burton completists. —*B. T.*

BATMAN L: DIRECTORS/BURTON, TIM (1989) 126M D: Tim Burton.
Jack Nicholson, Michael Keaton, Jack Nicholson, Michael Keaton, Kim Basinger, Robert Wuhl, Michael Gough. Although some of it seems dull and stiff today, I believe Burton's take on *Batman* was one of the most influential studio films through the '90s and certainly the template for most comic-book films. The dark shadows, stylized cityscapes, classic Danny Elfman score, and (less successfully) Nicholson's scenery-chewing villainy have all been imitated to the point of becoming their own genre. What works best is the mystery around the Batman showing up in Gotham for the first time and being mistaken for a monster. Frank Miller's *The Dark Knight Returns* and Alan Moore's *The Killing Joke* are always cited as influences on the film, but in many ways it's closest to the earliest Batman stories by Bob Kane. The book *Hit and Run* by Nancy Griffin and Kim Masters tells many interesting stories about notorious producer Jon Peters and the troubled shooting of the film. —*B. T.*

BATMAN RETURNS L: DIRECTORS/BURTON, TIM (1992) 126M D: Tim Burton.
Christopher Walken, Michelle Pfeiffer, Danny DeVito, Michael Keaton. For the first *Batman,* Burton reined in his style and came up with a mainstream hit. For the sequel he insisted on more creative control, which made for one of the weirdest summer event movies ever. Pfeiffer's female avenger Catwoman instantly became the definitive version of the character, but many were disturbed by DeVito's grotesque Penguin, literally a monster from the sewers who through image consulting and a corporate-sponsored recall becomes mayor of Gotham. The script (by *Heathers* scribe Daniel Waters) is piled heavy with genuinely witty lines, political satire, and a mirror motif (Max Shrek lives above the city/Penguin lives below, Bruce Wayne and Selina Kyle wear masks in public/ don't wear masks at a masquerade ball). The movie is weak with some of the elements that make up the best Batman stories—the detective work, especially—but as Burton's expressionistic interpretation of Gotham City, it's brilliant. —*B. T.*

BEETLEJUICE L: DIRECTORS/BURTON, TIM (1988) 92M D: Tim Burton.
Jeffrey Jones, Winona Ryder, Michael Keaton, Alec Baldwin, Geena Davis, Catherine O'Hara. A spooky atmosphere combines with an excellent original soundtrack and fantastic acting to make *Beetlejuice* one of the best films Burton has made. Davis and Baldwin are the Maitlands, a couple that was recently killed and must now spend the next 125 years haunting the house they lived in. When the eccentric Deitz family moves in from New York and rips the place apart, the Maitlands become so desperate to get rid of them they hire Beetlejuice, the self-proclaimed afterlife bio-exorcist. It's at this point that the shit hits the fan and craziness goes down. The dark, Gothic look of the film shows Burton once again for the atmospheric genius that he is, and strong performances by Keaton as Beetlejuice and Ryder as the dark, depressed Lydia Deitz make this movie really fun to watch. More silly than scary, *Beetlejuice* is as good now as it was sixteen years ago. —*J. S.*

ED WOOD L: DIRECTORS/BURTON, TIM (1994) 127M D: Tim Burton.
Johnny Depp, Bill Murray, Patricia Arquette, Sarah Jessica Parker, Martin Landau. Since the 1970s when the notorious Medved brothers declared *Plan 9 from Outer Space* "the worst movie of all time," its director, Ed Wood, has been ridiculed, not only for his bizarrely inept filmmaking style, but for his cross-dressing. Not surprisingly, Burton, whose films are generally about outcasts, paints a more sympathetic portrait of Wood. The film centers on the relationship between Wood (Depp) and the aging Bela Lugosi (Landau, who deservedly won an Oscar for the role), perhaps because it mirrors Burton's own relationship with Vincent Price. Depp portrays Wood as a fast-talking movie lover whose

Tim Burton

A lot of people dislike Tim Burton's films, complaining that they are all style and no substance, that he doesn't know how to tell a story, or that his attachment to outsider-artist characters is juvenile.

I disagree. Burton is my favorite type of Hollywood director: the type who can somehow convince major studios to sink millions of dollars into weird, idiosyncratic art projects packaged as big-budget genre films. How many directors can put as much

of a personal stamp on summer event films as Burton did with *Mars Attacks!* (1996) or *Batman Returns* (1992)? In the latter, he put Catwoman in S&M fetish gear and made the Penguin a deformed pervert with black blood and raw fish guts dripping from his mouth, and McDonald's still made them both into Happy Meal toys.

But Burton is more at home with his own characters, and in those cases it's hard to see where the storytelling criticism comes from. Who else would make a movie about an artificial man with shears for hands coming down from a castle, becoming a subur-

---

passion far exceeds his talent. Burton's best film to date, it shows a deep love for the movies and for people in general. Filmed in black and white with sets that are somehow minimal enough to mimic the look of Wood's film while also being perfect enough to look like a Burton film. First in a trilogy of eccentric biopics written by Alexander and Karaszewski including *The People vs. Larry Flynt* and *Man on the Moon.* —*B.T.*

EDWARD SCISSORHANDS L: DIRECTORS/BURTON, TIM (1990) 105M D: Tim Burton. *Vincent Price, Johnny Depp, Anthony Michael Hall, Dianne Wiest, Winona Ryder.* Depp plays Edward, the pieced-together creation of an inventor who dies before completing him, leaving him with scissors where his hands should be. He is discovered by Peg, an Avon lady who comes to try to sell some cosmetics and instead decides to take Edward home with her. He cuts some shrubs, cuts some hair, wins some hearts, and, of course, deals with some assholes who are reluctant to accept a man who wears all black and has scissors for hands. There are two things that I find really interesting about this movie. The first is Depp, who is, as always, the shit. The second is the use of color. Depp's world at the beginning is dark and muted, and contrasts sharply with the town he is taken to, which is pastel, bland, and uniform. You're left at the end wondering which end of the spectrum is really better. —*J.S.*

FRANKENWEENIE L: DIRECTORS/BURTON, TIM (1984) 29M D: Tim Burton. *Barret Oliver, Paul Bartel, Daniel Stern, Shelley Duvall.* Burton's first foray into live action was another black-and-white short funded by Disney. Oliver plays young Victor Frankenstein, whose dog Sparky is run over by a car. But this isn't *Where the Red Fern Grows* so

he decides to go retrieve Sparky from the pet cemetery and reanimate him. Once the family has accepted the return of Sparky they throw a party to introduce him to the neighbors, who respond with fear and hatred (sort of like *Edward Scissorhands*). Everything takes place in the world of a suburban child but is earnestly filtered through the look and feel of James Whale's Frankenstein films. So the laboratory is partly made out of playground equipment and the climax takes place in a burning windmill at the miniature golf course. The version on the special edition DVD of *The Nightmare Before Christmas* is slightly longer than the separate VHS version. Watch for Sofia Coppola's aerobicizing with her Barbie doll ("Barbie, you're not working hard enough.") —*B.T.*

MARS ATTACKS! L: DIRECTORS/BURTON, TIM (1996) 103M D: Tim Burton. *Pam Grier, Tom Jones, Lukas Haas, Jim Brown, Jack Nicholson.* An Irwin-Allen–style all-star cast inhabits a silly flying-saucer movie as filtered through Burton's peculiar brain (and inspired by the gruesome series of Topps trading cards from the 1950s). There's a lot of good satire (note that the president gets his news from MTV), but the real joy comes from the Martians, depicted through computer animation by Industrial Light and Magic and designed to look like Ray Harryhausen stop-motion. They are ruthless bastards who set cattle on fire, raid nursing homes, and pretend to attempt peace talks with the humans just to fuck with them. It's Burton's first movie where he doesn't seem to have any emotional invest-ment in the characters, but it's hard (and prob-ably morally wrong) not to love a movie where Pierce Brosnan's severed head makes out with

ban haircutting sensation, and then being shunned and going off to invent snow? And what would be a more compelling way to tell the tale of *Edward Scissorhands* than to treat it as a funny, tragic suburban romp turned Gothic fairy tale? Burton invests emotion in the silliest of premises: a cookie machine in love, a man dressed as a bat, a skeleton tired of scaring people.

Indeed, the most recognizably Burtonian of his films, *The Nightmare Before Christmas* (1993), he didn't even direct—Henry Selick did (and brilliantly). No one but Burton could have imagined anything like it, though, or convinced Disney to fund it. The last time I was at Disneyland, I saw more Jack Skellington hats than Mickey ears. It's

because Jack and Sally are, like many Tim Burton creations, those rare fantasy characters we can relate to on a certain level as much as we can to real-world characters on a more literal level.

We love Burton's films not just for their vivid imagery and goofy, cartoonish sense of the macabre, but also for their exaggerated emotions. We can relate to Lydia's drama-queen death obsession in *Beetlejuice* (1988), to Catwoman's violent disgust with the men of Gotham City, to Edward's problem of cutting everyone he tries to embrace. Who cares if the surface is ludicrous, as long as what's underneath is sincere?

—*Bryan Theiss*

Sarah Jessica Parker's head attached to the body of a Chihuahua. —*B. T.*

PEE-WEE'S BIG ADVENTURE L: DIRECTORS/BURTON, TIM (1985) 92M D: Tim Burton. *Pee-wee Herman, Elizabeth Daily, Mark Holton, Diane Salinger.* When Pee-wee's amazing bike is stolen, he makes a cross-country journey to the Alamo to find it. I love the movie-pastiche world of this film where one man (boy?) can harbor a fugitive, befriend a biker gang, get chased through a rodeo, interfere with a Godzilla movie and a Twisted Sister video shoot, save all the animals from a burning pet shop, have a movie based on his life, and much more, all in a couple of days. There really is no way to capture the greatness of this movie in a capsule review; it simply must be seen. If, like me, you always wondered why Pee-wee bought a boomerang bow tie at the magic shop and never used it, be sure to check out the deleted scenes on the DVD. But beware, there is also a scene that explains who Amazing Larry is and why he has a mohawk. —*B. T.*

PLANET OF THE APES (2001) L: DIRECTORS/BURTON, TIM (2001) 120M D: Tim Burton. *Paul Giamatti, Mark Wahlberg, Tim Roth, Helena Bonham Carter, Michael Clarke Duncan, Estella Warren, Kris Kristofferson.* Easily Burton's worst movie, this is a perfect example of his directorial vision being crushed beneath a giant summer-event movie. There are great makeup effects and some funny ideas (I especially enjoy the silly twist ending with Wahlberg being chased down by ape cops) but the smart script of the original is replaced with a mishmash of brainless action scenes that seems like it was made up on the set (which, apparently, much of it was). The original was about the ape society's shock at finding a human

who could talk—in this version all the humans talk, but for no apparent dramatic reason. It does not even live up to Burton's reputation as a visualist. The ape city is particularly disappointing because it is all crammed together on a sound-stage like some cheesy stage show at Universal Studios. Burton directing a remake of *Planet of the Apes* is like Jack Skellington taking over Christmas or Edward Scissorhands living in the suburbs: it seems like a fun idea at first, but it just wasn't meant to be. —*B. T.*

SLEEPY HOLLOW L: DIRECTORS/BURTON, TIM (1999) 105M D: Tim Burton. *Christopher Lee, Christina Ricci, Miranda Richardson, Michael Gambon, Christopher Walken, Johnny Depp.* Team Depp, one of the best character actors currently on the screen, with Burton, the end-all genius of spooky atmosphere, and *The Legend of Sleepy Hollow* takes a swift kick to the teeth. The acting is excellent, with Depp delivering an especially great performance as Ichabod Crane, the goofy constable who is more concerned with scientific gadgetry than solving murders. Even Ricci, who I normally feel like strangling, is great in this film. But more than the acting, the special effects and set design are what make this film fun to watch. This version of *Sleepy Hollow* definitely beats the hell out of the animated one I used to watch on TV as a kid. —*J. S.*

VINCENT L: DIRECTORS/BURTON, TIM (1982) 6M D: Tim Burton. *Vincent Price.* While Burton was a lowly animator at Disney he convinced them to fund his directorial debut, a six-minute, black-and-white stop-motion short. The story involves young Vincent Malloy, a kid obsessed with Vincent Price's Edgar Alan Poe films and who would rather sit in the shadows and brood than play outside. You'll notice that Vincent bears a striking resemblance to Burton. Narrated by Price himself in Seussian rhyme, the macabre humor is reminiscent of Edward Gorey. The look of the film is gorgeous, and it makes a perfect fit on the special edition DVD of *The Nightmare Before Christmas*. Rick Heinrichs (who sculpted the puppets) went on to work on most of Burton's movies, and animator Stephen Chiodo later did the famous Large Marge scene in *Pee-wee's Big Adventure*. —B. T.

ABYSS, THE: SPECIAL EDITION L: DIRECTORS/CAMERON, JAMES (1989) 141M D: James Cameron. *Ed Harris, Mary Elizabeth Mastrantonio, Michael Biehn, Todd Graff. The Abyss* is basically about a deep-sea oil rig coopted by the military to salvage a sunken nuclear submarine during a storm. With the military come some loose-cannon Navy SEALS who take things into their own hands after tragedy befalls the beleaguered rig. Meanwhile, on the surface, WWIII is about to break out and the SEALS think the Russians are after them. All along there are sightings of an unexplained origin, eventually affecting everyone involved. Cameron and crew do an amazing job capturing the darkness and emptiness of a mostly unexplored part of our planet. The special edition DVD includes the longer cut of the film and loads of behind-the-scenes information including storyboards and documentaries on the special effects, cinematography, stunt work, and more. —B. W.

ALIENS L: DIRECTORS/CAMERON, JAMES (1986) 138M D: James Cameron. *Michael Biehn, Carrie Henn, Bill Paxton, Paul Reiser, Lance Henriksen, Sigourney Weaver*. In the first sequel to Ridley Scott's classic *Alien*, Cameron cleverly chose to move beyond the gothic-horror-in-space of the original and into a big, macho, military action movie. Ripley (Weaver) awakens from hypersleep fifty-seven years later only to find that the Weyland-Yutani Corporation has colonized the planet where the alien eggs were found. Nobody believes her story about the alien until communication with the colony is lost and Ripley is sent in as an adviser to a platoon of colonial marines, who end up finding a whole lot more than the one alien that took out Ripley's whole crew in the first film. At times the bravado of the soldiers is hard to take, but there's a brilliant shot of Ripley looking appalled as they discuss "alien poon-tang" in the cafeteria. Ultimately the themes are feminine as Ripley protects her surrogate daughter Newt (Henn) from the alien queen, who in turn is only trying to protect her eggs. Alien designer H. R. Giger did not work on this film, and the new look of the aliens is a little less creepy. However, the creature effects by Stan Winston are very convincing, and the alien queen is among the greatest monsters ever put on film. —B. T.

PIRANHA II: THE SPAWNING L: DIRECTORS/CAMERON, JAMES (1981) 94M D: James Cameron. *Tricia O'Neil, Lance Henriksen, Steve Marachuk*. We all have to start somewhere. This flat-footed sequel, a sloppy horror about flying saltwater piranha with a taste for tourist flesh, is Cameron's directorial debut. Not that you can tell: the script is slapdash and silly, the toothy fish fly with all the realism and grace of a rubber bat from a 1940s Republic horror film, and Cameron's attempts at comedy are embarrassingly amateurish. On the plus side, O'Neil does fine on Adrienne Barbeau duty as the fearless scuba instructor, Henriksen is a welcome sight as the gruff cop taking on corpse duty, and the precredits scuba sex scene is, if nothing else, at least inspired. It's hard to believe his next film was *The Terminator*. —S. A.

TERMINATOR L: DIRECTORS/CAMERON, JAMES (1984) 108M D: James Cameron. *Michael Biehn, Linda Hamilton, Paul Winfield, Lance Henriksen, Arnold Schwarzenegger*. Schwarzenegger is the Terminator, a virtually indestructible robot from the future sent to assassinate Sarah Connor (Hamilton), who is destined to give birth to a child who will become a warrior and topple the future government. This good sci-fi story is not complete without Biehn, who plays a futuristic human trying to alter this alteration of history by following the Terminator back in time and warning and protecting the defenseless woman. The classic horror technique of the killer perpetually coming back to life in the elongated climax works well with this premise. Far from relying on supernatural reasons for a killer's continual resuscitation, this film relies on sophisticated future technologies and the fact that this Terminator is played by Ahnold. —N. J.

TERMINATOR 2: JUDGMENT DAY L: DIRECTORS/CAMERON, JAMES (1991) 139M D: James Cameron. *Edward Furlong, Robert Patrick, Linda Hamilton, Arnold Schwarzenegger*. Cameron is back with this sequel, but this time the studio gave him the entire bank. At $100 million, *Terminator 2* was one of the most expensive films ever made. It also paid off. Schwarzenegger returns as the indestructible robot, but in this story he has traveled to the present day to defend the young future warrior John Connor (Furlong) from being killed by a more advanced Terminator (Patrick) from the future. The sensational computer-graphic effects that Cameron had extensively toyed around with in *The Abyss* are used appropriately and stunningly in this strong story focusing on the destiny of the human race among the rapid sophistication of machinery. The depiction of a nuclear holocaust, for instance, is the best yet seen on screen. —N. H.

TITANIC L: DIRECTORS/CAMERON, JAMES (1997) 195M D: James Cameron. *Leonardo DiCaprio, Kate Winslet, Billy Zane, Kathy Bates, Frances Fisher, Gloria Stuart*. Before *Titanic* came out it was attacked and mocked for its out-of-control budget and delayed release, and most considered it a guaranteed flop. Instead it was an enormous, record-breaking hit and worldwide cultural phenomenon. So then everyone started hating it again. Cameron had been worshiped like a god by young men because of *Aliens* and the *Terminator* films, but as soon as he made a film that was popular with teenage girls he became one of the most hated figures in movie fandom. Like there's something wrong with teenage girls having a movie they like. It's full of corny dialogue, DiCaprio is positively Fievel-esque in the early scenes, Zane is never more than a one-dimensional villain until the very end of the movie, and it would've been wise to cut out all the modern day scientific expedition sequences with Paxton and some Harry Knowles look-alike riding around in submarines showing off their knowledge of scientist jargon. But as an epic disaster melodrama with obsessive-compulsive attention to historical detail, *Titanic* isn't half bad. It's hard not to get wrapped up in the horror of the crumbling ship and the frozen bodies floating in the water. I even found myself getting emotional by the end, asking myself what I would do facing death with a loved one. I don't know what happened to Cameron after *Aliens* either, but *Titanic* doesn't deserve as much hatred as it receives. —*B. T.*

TRUE LIES L: DIRECTORS/CAMERON, JAMES (1994) 141M D: James Cameron. *Jamie Lee Curtis, Arnold Schwarzenegger, Tom Arnold, Bill Paxton.*

Schwarzenegger is an agent so secret that even his wife (Curtis) thinks he's a nerdy computer salesman. Meanwhile Paxton, who actually sells used cars, convinces Curtis that he's a secret agent and can bring her the adventure she's sorely missing. So Schwarzenegger and his buddy (Arnold) kidnap Paxton and force him to wet his pants. Then they all get mixed up in a plot to retrieve nuclear warheads stolen by a group of caricatured Arab terrorists. (Don't worry, there's a token Arab good guy, so it doesn't count as racist. Right?) Cameron had a reputation as the thinking man's action director until he made this big, dumb action comedy. Most of his previous films had an anti-technology theme, this one is like a promo reel for the latest military hardware. He had been known for strong portrayals of action heroines in *Aliens* and *Terminator 2*, but this one is downright misogynistic. One scene has Curtis thinking she has to do a striptease to save her husband's life, when he's actually making her do it for his own amusement. The scene ends with Curtis sobbing and smashing a chair through a mirror, and was widely deemed sexy. There are some amusingly over-the-top action sequences, but the whole thing is too macho and mean-spirited to be any fun. Maybe it wasn't a good idea for Cameron to try a romantic comedy right after a divorce. —*B. T.*

HOLY SMOKE L: DIRECTORS/CAMPION, JANE (1999) 114M D: Jane Campion. *Pam Grier, Tim Robertson, Sophie Lee, Harvey Keitel, Kate Winslet.*

Winslet, a willful but spiritually sincere Aussie teen, and Keitel, a cocky, macho American deprogrammer as urban cowboy, match wits and wills in Campion's libidinous stew of sex, desire, and power in the outback. He's hired by her panicked parents when she falls under the sway of an Indian guru, but far from a routine assignment, their private psychodrama plays out like a warped reflection of *The Piano*. Campion fills the film with delicious images, from garish middle-class cookie-cutter homes to a kitschy heatstroke hallucination of Winslet as a pop Kali, painted in a palette of sun-baked desert colors and hazy imagery punctuated with punches of savage humor. It's a passionate if haphazardly constructed screenplay, but Campion's herky-jerky mix of styles makes this messy, emotionally tumultuous journey beguiling and beautiful, leaving unresolved conflicts still pinging around as the credits roll. —*S. A.*

PIANO, THE L: DIRECTORS/CAMPION, JANE (1993) 121M D: Jane Campion. *Harvey Keitel, Geneviève Lemon, Anna Paquin, Sam Neill, Kerry Walker, Holly Hunter.*

Hunter took the Oscar for her performance as a Scotswoman who moves to the jungles of New Zealand to wed Stewart (Neill) in an arranged marriage. Mute by choice, she communicates primarily through her daughter (Paquin, who also got an Oscar). But her treasured form of communication is music, which is why she's alarmed when her prized piano is left behind on the beach by her husband. Keitel plays the sleazy neighbor who buys the piano and lets her practice on it for what amounts to sexual favors. This film is a cinegraphic delight with all the nineteenth-century detail and formalities one would expect from a period film—that is, except for one. In a movie called *The Piano* we might suppose that a Victorian pianist would be in love with the rich music of Beethoven, Chopin, and Liszt, not the repetitive and two-dimensional music of Michael Nyman exclusively. —*N. J.*

IT HAPPENED ONE NIGHT L: DIRECTORS/CAPRA, FRANK (1934) 105M D: Frank Capra. *Clark Gable, Claudette Colbert, Walter Connolly, Roscoe Karns.*

This was the first picture to win all five major Oscars and became the prototype for every battle-of-the-sexes film that followed. Colbert is an unhappy, runaway heiress who learns how "real" people live during a cross-country trek with boozy, out-of-work reporter Gable. The chemistry between the two leads is electric. This Depression-era screwball classic demonstrates the dignity of the poor and the shallowness of the rich with memorable scenes, such as the "Walls of Jericho" bedroom finale, the donut-eating scene, and Colbert's leggy hitchhiking technique, acted out in the natural and appealing performances by the stars. —*S. H.*

IT'S A WONDERFUL LIFE L: DIRECTORS/CAPRA, FRANK (1946) 130M D: Frank Capra. *James Stewart, Beulah Bondi, Henry Travers, Thomas Mitchell, Lionel Barrymore, Donna Reed*. The main thing is to get past any silliness about *It's a Wonderful Life* being some icky, obligatory yuletide ritual. It's a great—really great—film, so densely well made that to watch any three minutes of it is to realize how paltry the vast majority of movies are by comparison. You know the premise: family and small-business man in an American small town is contemplating suicide on Christmas Eve, so a couple of heavenly presences flash back over his life, then send a somewhat klutzy emissary to give the guy some insight on what that life has meant. Yes, it sounds like something off a Christmas card—a film noir Christmas card before Capra is through with it. The cast is perfection, of course. But look at the intimate map of Old Man Gower's drugstore, what's in focus and what isn't... and on the railroad station platform, the camera movement that gets bumped along with George Bailey when he realizes he isn't going to escape from Bedford Falls after all. . . . We said densely well made and we meant it. See *It's a Wonderful Life* again and get a fresh perspective. —*R. T. J.*

MR. SMITH GOES TO WASHINGTON L: DIRECTORS/CAPRA, FRANK (1939) 130M D: Frank Capra. *James Stewart, Jean Arthur, Claude Rains, Edward Arnold, Guy Kibbee, Thomas Mitchell*. Capra straddles the line between populist idealist and American cynic in this political fable. Stewart is all awed reverence and aw-shucks small-town innocence as the Boy Scout master turned temporary senator who runs afoul of his corrupt party machine and becomes the target of a smear campaign. Arthur is the jaded political aide won over by his pluck and Rains is perfect as the savvy, compromised senator whose tortured soul is exposed by Stewart. The Capra-corn climax gives victory to the American common man, but leaves the corrupt machine quietly whirring in the background. —*S. A.*

PLATINUM BLONDE L: DIRECTORS/CAPRA, FRANK (1931) 89M D: Frank Capra. *Halliwell Hobbes, Loretta Young, Robert Williams, Reginald Owen, Jean Harlow*. Harlow is the titular blonde, a flighty society heiress who falls for a smart-talking newspaper reporter (Williams, in his last role before his untimely death) and tries to make him over into a polished American aristocrat. The gilded cage, however, soon ruffles the feathers of urbane street-bird Williams, and it's not long before his squawking upsets the high-society decorum. This early screwball comedy is Capra's first collaboration with screenwriter Robert Riskin, who is credited with the snappy, wisecracking dialogue and a classic comedy of streetwise pros clashing with upper-class sophisticates. Young plays Williams's tough coworker, a working-class

newswoman who can dish it with the boys: the prototype for the classic Capra heroine. —*S. A.*

STATE OF THE UNION L: DIRECTORS/CAPRA, FRANK (1948) 124M D: Frank Capra. *Van Johnson, Angela Lansbury, Spencer Tracy, Katherine Hepburn*. About twenty minutes into this film, big businessman Grant Matthews (Tracy) stands in front of the White House and launches into his first of several passionate speeches about the power and potential of our great nation. It's then you know the Capra quality has kicked into this charming film. Tracy plays a well-known entrepreneur who gets steered into running for president by newspaper-head Lansbury (playing a villain—creepy!). Hepburn shines as Mary Matthews, Grant's estranged wife who gets caught up in the campaign and ends up in a tug-of-war with Lansbury for his ideals and his heart. Like any great Capra movie, it leaves you with a warm, idealistic feeling about what our nation, and our lives, should be like. If only Capra could have directed real life. —*J. K.*

YOU CAN'T TAKE IT WITH YOU L: DIRECTORS/CAPRA, FRANK (1938) 126M D: Frank Capra. *Edward Arnold, Jean Arthur, Lionel Barrymore, James Stewart*. This film is a Capra/Stewart/Barrymore film without the hearty Christmas overtones. Arthur stars as a young woman from an eccentric family (headed by Barrymore) who falls in love with Stewart, the son of a soulless, greedy banker. When the romance is revealed, the two families' decidedly different lifestyles clash and madcap hilarity ensues. In the end everyone learns a valuable lesson about what is important in our lives and how to live them to the fullest. This film seems especially relevant in today's materialistic atmosphere. —*J. K.*

BOY MEETS GIRL L: DIRECTORS/CARAX, LEOS (1984) 90M D: Leos Carax. *Denis Lavant, Mireille Perrier*. *Boy Meets Girl* shows an unmistakable debt to the French New Wave but, more excitingly, somehow captures the energetic attitude of that movement's first products as well. Wandering through the hollow after-hours of Paris, a rough-edged loner (Lavant) finds companionship with a suicidal woman (Perrier). Both newly single, their repeated encounters seem uncannily willed by fate. Carax was a mere twenty-two years old when he helmed this impressive project. The film's heartbreaking, unpolished, black-and-white photography looks stunning. The dialogue walks a delicate line between serious-as-death melodrama and naive teen angst. Lavant, who seems unbelievably young here, is absolutely fascinating to watch, as always. Carax even throws some Dead Kennedys on the soundtrack. With style to burn, *Boy Meets Girl* is about as hip as movies get. At the same time, its moody expressionism comes off as unerringly sincere. What more could anyone want from a first film? —*C. B.*

CHILDREN OF PARADISE L: DIRECTORS/CARNE, MARCEL (1945) 190M D: Marcel Carne. *Arletty, Jean-Louis Barrault, Louis Salou, Pierre Renoir, Marcel Herrand.* Carne's legendary epic of love, theater, and crime in nineteenth-century Paris is a masterpiece of French cinema and one of the best-loved films of all time. It's been described as the *Gone With the Wind* of France, but that comparison misses the point. This tragic romance is about love of the theater as much as human love. Barrault plays mime Baptiste Debureau, Brasseur is actor Frederick Lemaitre, and Herrand the former criminal turned playwright Lacinaire, all real-life characters thrown together in a fictional love quadrangle with the beautiful actress Garance (Arletty) and her (fictional) patron Count (Salou). Forget that it's three hours long; every moment bursts with love and passion, and the amazing Boulevard du Crime re-creation bustles with the activity of street performers and pickpockets, con men and cops, prostitutes and rubberneckers. An epic in every sense of the word, this soulful tribute to free France and the heart of art was, astoundingly, made in the midst of the German occupation. —*S. A.*

ASSAULT ON PRECINCT 13 L: DIRECTORS/CARPENTER, JOHN (1976) 91M D: John Carpenter. *Austin Stoker, Darwin Joston, Gilbert De la Pena, Al Nakauchi, Laurie Zimmer.* Carpenter's first real movie (*Dark Star* was an expanded student production) combines elements of *Night of the Living Dead* and Howard Hawks Westerns like *Rio Bravo* with an urban gangster spin. After a police ambush, some multiracial gangsters swear an oath of vengeance (or *cholo*) on cops and a police precinct comes under their wrath. Filled with some shocking violence—like a kid getting shot at an ice cream truck—and lots of tense situations, it's a very impressive and carefully constructed film. The heroic characters are interesting, including a black cop (Stoker) and an incarcerated criminal (Joston), and the soundtrack is one of many excellent scores by the director. When director Claire Denis visited Scarecrow, this is the movie she bought! —*S. H.*

BIG TROUBLE IN LITTLE CHINA L: DIRECTORS/CARPENTER, JOHN (1986) 99M D: John Carpenter. *Dennis Dun, Kim Catrall, Kurt Russell.* Big Trouble in Little China is a lot like its hero: loud, fun, and not especially bright. Russell plays the hero, a truck driver who becomes ensnared in a world of magic and evil while trying to rescue a friend's fiancée from thugs. Soon he and his friend encounter martial-arts masters, corpses that haven't aged well, and a villain who can blow up like a balloon animal. It could all be heavy-handed or dull, but Carpenter keeps the film fun, with touches of humor throughout. Especially good is the scene where Russell, pumped up for a climactic battle, fires his gun upward only to have chunks of the ceiling fall on his head and knock him unconscious. —*T. P.*

ESCAPE FROM NEW YORK L: DIRECTORS/CARPENTER, JOHN (1981) 99M D: John Carpenter. *Lee Van Cleef, Ernest Borgnine, Donald Pleasence, Isaac Hayes, Kurt Russell.* Maybe it's not Carpenter's best film, but it's one of his most fun and the premise is irresistible: in the future, Manhattan has been turned into a high-security island prison and Liberty Island is the guard station. Russell hisses out a B-movie–Clint Eastwood impression as he navigates the feral streets to free the American president (Pleasence) from the clutches of cock-of-the-walk Hayes with a motley, not completely trustworthy, crew. Carpenter's dark, garbage-strewn streets lit by bonfires and headlights make for inspired art direction and his synthesizer score is suitably minimalist and moody. Shot for a song with simple but bold model work (some of it created by James Cameron in his Roger Corman days), striking computer graphics, and the rougher parts of St. Louis doubling for Manhattan. It's a hoot. —*S. A.*

ESCAPE FROM LA L: DIRECTORS/CARPENTER, JOHN (1996) 101M D: John Carpenter. *Peter Fonda, Bruce Campbell, Georges Corraface, Steve Buscemi, Kurt Russell, Valeria Golino.* When the president's daughter runs off with her revolutionary boyfriend and her dad's doomsday device, the notorious convict Snake Plissken (Russell) is poisoned and released on the island of LA where he must retrieve the weapon if he wants the antidote. So he must contend with strictly Californian postapocalyptic dangers like a mad plastic surgeon (Campbell) and a glider battle above the ruins of Disneyland. Many fans of *Escape From New York* were profoundly disappointed: this is really more of a remake than a sequel, loosely re-creating the original on a bigger budget and with a Californian theme. But it's still entertaining. Yes, it's ridiculous to see Snake shooting hoops—that's why it's so great that New York's gladiatorial combat is replaced by basketball to the death. And if you really don't think you're supposed to laugh when Fonda suddenly comes surfing into a scene on a big wave then I don't know what to tell you. —*B. T.*

FOG, THE L: DIRECTORS/CARPENTER, JOHN (1979) 90M D: John Carpenter. *Jamie Lee Curtis, John Houseman, Janet Leigh, Hal Holbrook, Adrienne Barbeau.* One night every year a strange, luminescent fog seems to roll ashore and the former colonists of a modern fishing village come to life in order to avenge their wrongful genocide. Or so Houseman tells a group of children over a campfire. Of course, this is a Carpenter film that follows the surprise success of *Halloween,* so the campfire tale would have to come true, and with a decent budget to back it up. Holbrook is well cast as the priest who uncovers the hidden book that accounts for all of this history as well as the gold stolen from the colonists. Somehow the gold must be found and given back before these spirits commit their own

John Cassavetes

For years the raw emotion and explosive spontaneity of John Cassavetes's films have been explained as complex, finely honed improvisations, and Cassavetes has been erroneously burdened with a reputation as a ringmaster of happy accidents and performers' inspirations. Nothing could be further from the truth: Cassavetes directed from carefully prepared scripts and rarely, if ever, deviated from them—at least on the set. (One need only look to *She's So Lovely*, directed by son Nick from his father's script, for evidence of Cassavetes' screenwriting style.) But his reputation is enlightening: no other American director makes films that look so spontaneous, so alive, so immediate, that seem to have been made up in front of the camera, drawn from the depths of his performers' souls.

The Actors Studio–trained Cassavetes was the first modern American independent director, and his debut, *Shadows*, shot on the streets of New York in 1959, inspired young American filmmakers. "It had an emotional truth to it, power. It made me realize I could make a movie," Martin Scorsese confesses to Peter Biskind in his book *Easy Riders, Raging Bulls*. It was the start of a career that could exist only outside of the studios (his brief flirtation with Hollywood resulted in films that chafed against their constraints).

---

genocide. This film has the curious distinction of starring both Curtis and her mother, Leigh. The DVD features two documentaries about the film and commentary by Carpenter. —*N. J.*

GHOSTS OF MARS L: DIRECTORS/CARPENTER, JOHN (2001) 97M D: John Carpenter. *Natasha Henstridge, Ice Cube, Clea DuVall, Jason Statham, Pam Grier.* It was a routine prison transfer, except it was on Mars. The prisoner escaped and the ghosts of dead Martians started possessing people and turning them into self-mutilating Marilyn Manson clones to fight off the Earthling colonists. There's a grain of a great Carpenter movie here, with his trademark driving score, the Western-in-space motifs (there's even a train!), the anticolonialist subtext, and the casting of Ice Cube as ridiculously named antihero Desolation Williams. Unfortunately the villains are silly, the story quickly devolves into dumb, poorly staged fight scenes, and the tension is diffused by a needless wraparound story badly narrated by Henstridge. —*B. T.*

HALLOWEEN L: DIRECTORS/CARPENTER, JOHN (1978) 92M D: John Carpenter. *Donald Pleasence, Jamie Lee Curtis, Nancy Loomis, P. J. Soles, Charles Cyphers.* *Halloween*'s plot is simple: Michael Myers murders his sister. Fifteen years later he escapes from the asylum and returns to his hometown to terrorize a group of teenagers that includes a very young Curtis in her first film role. Veteran horror actor Pleasence pulls off one of the best performances of his career as Michael's doctor who tries to put a stop to the madness. Carpenter's camera and score work together to build a universe of steadily increasing terror and suspense. Rarely has a director made such effective use of every inch of the screen. Carpenter reveals every corner, every shadow where our worst fear may be hiding. The film spawned many sequels and imitations but none have come close to capturing the brilliance of the original film. It is truly one of the most suspenseful movies ever made and is guaranteed to give you the chills. —*S. W. F.*

MEMOIRS OF AN INVISIBLE MAN L: DIRECTORS/ CARPENTER, JOHN (1992) 90M D: John Carpenter. *Chevy Chase, Daryl Hannah, Sam Neill, Michael McKean, Stephen Tobolowsky.* Chase plays a businessman who, walking down the wrong hallway while drunk at an office party, bumbles into a nuclear accident and gets turned invisible. Neill is the CIA agent who knows of his existence and wants to kill him if he won't become a government assassin. So Chase goes into hiding at a friend's vacation home and finds out how hard it is to get by (not to mention fall in love with Hannah) when nobody can see you. The film has some clever pre–*Forrest Gump* computer effects (when he smokes a cigarette, you see the smoke go down his throat and circulate around his lungs before it comes back out). Carpenter didn't really have his heart in the movie, but Chase was taking a big risk by acting in a more serious role. One reason this feels like a studio movie and not a Carpenter movie is that he didn't do his trademark minimalist electronic scoring; instead there's a big orchestral score by Shirley Walker. —*B. T.*

Exploring the frustrations of middle-class adults frustrated by compromised lives and unattained dreams, films such as *Faces* (1968)and *Husbands* (1970) offered up characters who were hard to like but perhaps uncomfortably easy to understand. For his wife, the talented Gena Rowlands, Cassavetes created *A Woman Under the Influence* (1974) and *Opening Night* (1977), powerful studies of emotional dysfunction and alienation. In his (anti-)gangster film *The Killing of a Chinese Bookie* (1976), he dissects the flashy lifestyle and tarnished ethical code of a small-time impresario, guiding Ben Gazzara through one of his finest performances. Cassavetes is an actor's director, and the heart of his films are the rambling scenes of fumbled self-expression in which characters struggle between emotional release and self-restraint—in other words, the scenes cut out of most American films, the scenes about the journey, not the destination.

Like Orson Welles, the true outcast godfather of American independents, Cassavetes acted in almost anything to scrape up the funds to direct his own very personal films. Many of his acting gigs were pure pap, although his electric presence and nervous unpredictability elevated even his worst roles. Given the right character—the wounded victim of *The Killers* (1964), the rebellious punk of *The Dirty Dozen* (1967), the social dropout Prospero of Paul Mazursky's *Tempest* (1982)—he approached genius. In Elaine May's *Mikey and Nicky* (1976), he even re-creates the atmosphere of his own work, playing off Peter Falk as a doomed thug with a sneering bravado that hides a tough guy's embarrassed vulnerability.

—*Sean Axmaker*

THEY LIVE L: DIRECTORS/CARPENTER, JOHN (1988) 93M D: John Carpenter. *Keith David, Roddy Piper*. Underrated Carpenter B movie about the Reagan years. Piper plays the working-class loner who wanders into town and happens to discover a box of special sunglasses belonging to some sort of mysterious underground resistance group. When he puts on the glasses and walks around town he sees the sinister truth beneath the surface: billboards have subliminal slogans like "MATE, SPAWN, AND DIE" or "OBEY"; money says "I AM YOUR GOD"; and all the yuppies, cops, and ladies in fur coats have skeletal alien faces. His response: "It fuckin' figures."It's a great gimmick, and Piper has some classic one-liners (which he claims to have ad-libbed). The film is infamous for Piper's protracted street-wrestling scene with David, which was intended to unseat *The Quiet Man* as the film with the longest uninterrupted fight scene. What most people miss is its spot-on symbolism. All Piper wants David to do is put on the glasses and see what's going on in the world; this is how far we will go to not know the truth. —*B. T.*

THING L: DIRECTORS/CARPENTER, JOHN (1982) 109M D: John Carpenter. *Wilford Brimley, Kurt Russell*. Not to denigrate the talent of the great Howard Hawks or the achievement of the original version of this story, but this is the movie that more faithfully reflects sci-fi author John W. Campbell Jr.'s intent. Where the original was scary and fun, full of typically Hawksian chumminess and tart dialogue as well as his trademark rough-and-tumble action, Carpenter's vision is as bleak, cold, and uncompromising as the Antarctic waste that the story is set in. American films rarely dare to have endings as numbingly ambiguous as this one. —*S. F.*

VAMPIRES L: DIRECTORS/CARPENTER, JOHN (1998) 104M D: John Carpenter. *James Woods, Daniel Baldwin, Sheryl Lee, Thomas Ian Griffith, Tim Guinee*. Woods plays the leader of a squad of professional vampire hunters working for the Vatican. They discover a master vampire (Griffith) who may have found a way to become immune to sunlight. The characters are incredibly macho, spewing misogynistic and homophobic insults and cockily performing their duties like a SWAT team (one technique involves attaching cables to vampires and dragging them out into the sunlight). The attitude is infectious and the movie has a raunchiness rare in '90s horror films, full of graphic violence without aid of CGI (including lots and lots of severed heads). Like most of Carpenter's films it's largely inspired by Westerns, and it's refreshing to see a vampire movie that takes place mostly in a sunny desert. This is also the rare '90s vampire film that does not have Udo Kier in it. —*B. T.*

FACES L: DIRECTORS/CASSAVETES, JOHN (1986) 129M D: John Cassavetes. *John Marley, Seymour Cassel, Gena Rowlands, Lynn Carlin*. An incomparable downer about the ungraceful death of a California marriage, *Faces* is a film composed entirely of tapped nerves. This exhaustingly pessimistic collection of awkward, nervous conversations about nothing involves a cast of characters who, though not particularly bad people, are people we'd rather not be around. Audience discomfort is key to the film's supercharged intensity (kind of a melodramatic road rage), but works only because the tense interactions on-screen seem so exceptionally real. Although improvisation was a large part of the film's development, each scene was meticulously scripted—a notable fact that's at once the film's greatest achievement and most damning liability. Almost convincing in its realism, there's a nagging staginess and theatricality that can't be ignored once the film's exposed as the result of careful planning. But enough nitpicking, this is a hell of a movie. Chances are, you'll be thrilled to have seen it. —*C. B.*

HUSBANDS L: DIRECTORS/CASSAVETES, JOHN (1970) 150M D: John Cassavetes. *John Cassavetes, Peter Falk, Ben Gazzara.* Depending on your perspective, *Husbands* is either a loose, searing critique of masculinity dominated by stellar, frenetic performances by its three leads, or a ridiculous, indulgent mess of mysogynistic machismo and laughably "realistic" dialogue. Probably the truth lies somewhere in between, but certainly *Husbands* is a veritable checklist of blunders for Cassavetes naysayers, and I can't imagine even his most doting fans denying its inferiority to something like *Faces.* Though I tend to side with the "critique of masculinity" camp, I'm inclined to say *Husbands* is a rose-colored celebration of brutish fraternity. If it wasn't, I'm not sure it would be so disarming. *Husbands* is like a rough night spent in a seedy bar—which sounds cool. . . until you actually stop to think about it. Maybe *Husbands* is great, maybe it's atrocious. I'm not sure there's much difference in this case. —*C. B.*

KILLING OF A CHINESE BOOKIE L: DIRECTORS/CASSAVETES, JOHN (1976) 135M D: John Cassavetes. *Seymour Cassel, Timothy Carey, Ben Gazzara.* When Cassavetes released this 1976 venture into the Mafia/crime genre, it was a commercial and critical flop. *Bookie* didn't gorge itself on a procession of tragic death scenes and *Godfather*-esque gangsters. Instead, it used a minimalist story line, devoid of exposition or device. Cosmo Vitelli (Gazzara) is the owner and soul of the Crazy Horse West, a struggling strip joint. He emerges from one debt only to fall into another, this time to some gritty mafiosi who collect in any way they choose. They enlist Cosmo to kill a troublesome bookie in Chinatown, a job he performs with less than professional ability. Cassavetes's pacing is lifelike—sometimes boring, sometimes confused. It is often hard to tell who is talking or shooting, or what will happen next. This chaos solidifies the film's simple evolution—there is no plot agenda, no single image to walk away with. Cosmo Vitelli is a dubious underdog, and the merit of his life is refreshingly negotiable. —*M. M.*

MINNIE AND MOSKOWITZ L: DIRECTORS/CASSAVETES, JOHN (1971) 115M D: John Cassavetes. *Val Avery, Gena Rowlands, Seymour Cassel, John Cassavetes.* Consistently underappreciated among Cassavetes's work, *Minnie and Moskowitz* is an accurately schizophrenic representation of flawed romance between flawed people. The would-be couple is played impeccably by a thundering Cassel and Cassavetes's eternally suffering leading lady (and wife) Rowlands, with the director himself appearing in a supporting role as Minnie's loathsome, jealous beau. This may be the only film that accurately depicts the awkwardness and failings of love, as the characters thrash each others' lives to pieces just trying to keep their emotions above water. Cassel's nagging senile mom is played by Cassavetes's real-life mother, Sheba, and legendary character actor Timothy Carey shows up early in the film as a ranting and heartbroken homeless man. At turns tender, brutal, and hilarious, *Minnie and Moskowitz* is an often-ignored example of a great filmmaker at the height of his abilities. —*Z. C.*

SHADOWS L: DIRECTORS/CASSAVETES, JOHN (1959) 81M D: John Cassavetes. *Lelia Goldoni, Hugh Hurd, Ben Carruthers.* This movie may be a structured improvisation by nonprofessional actors, but it is shrewd storytelling by its director. You follow around a curly-haired kid in a gang of Beat-generation white "jazz musicians" who you never see play instruments but just use that line to pick up girls when not scoring some drugs. You follow a brassy, fair-skinned young "writer" (Goldoni) who blows off her middle-age mentor for a handsome young Italian boy, only for the guy to find out she's a virgin and more. Then you follow a black club singer with his manager, his cool blues vocal style no longer hot enough for contemporary taste. And about the time you begin to wonder how these three stories connect, bang! You realize they are all brothers and sister. The two lighter-skinned ones are passing for white, preferring their crowd to their darkskinned brother's equally hip African-American crowd. The off-balance, seemingly aimless moviemaking style of Cassavetes magically reflects the directionlessness of the three siblings' lives. Wonderful filmmaking. —*J. C.*

HOMICIDAL L: DIRECTORS/CASTLE, WILLIAM (1961) 87M D: William Castle. *Jean Arless, Patricia Breslin, Glenn Corbett, Alan Bunce, Eugenie Leontovich.* If Castle, the carnival showman of horror cinema, imagined himself a B-movie Hitchcock, then *Homicidal* is his *Psycho,* right down to the psychologist's explanation at the end. This devious little gem is an inspired twist on its inspiration, kicking off with a weird little first act that pays off in a shocker of a murder, and then getting stranger, thanks largely to a pair of genuinely unsettling characters: the cooing killer Emily, everyone's worst nightmare of a caregiver, and the awkward Warren, who is tensed and stiff as if coiled and ready to spring. Always armed with a gimmick, Castle created the "Fright Break" for this one, a clock countdown (in Castle's own cheery voice-over) to "allow anyone to leave the theater who is too frightened to see the end of the picture." Or shut off the TV? —S. A.

STRAIT-JACKET L: DIRECTORS/CASTLE, WILLIAM (1963) 93M D: William Castle. *Diane Baker, Leif Erickson, Howard St. John, John Anthony Hayes, Rochelle Hudson, Joan Crawford.* This frightfully good horror film begins with the infamous Crawford scene that nobody could forget once they've seen it. Arriving home earlier than anticipated, Lucy Hurbin peeks into her own bedroom window at night to find her husband sleeping with another woman. Going berserk, she finds an ax in the shed and lops off both their heads! Twenty years later she's released from the mental ward and her daughter takes her in—the same daughter (Baker) who happened to witness the murders as a child. Promising not to pass judgment, the daughter slowly gets reacquainted with her mother. But that's when all the horrible ax murders start happening. This offbeat Castle film will keep you double-guessing all the way to the end. —N. J.

13 GHOSTS (1960) L: DIRECTORS/CASTLE, WILLIAM (1960) 84M D: William Castle. *William Castle, Jo Morrow, Charles Herbert, Margaret Hamilton.* A destitute family inherits a huge old house from an uncle they thought had been dead for years. It turns out the uncle was an eccentric scientist who collected ghosts, and they will be sharing said house with said ghosts. The catch is that the ghosts can only be seen by wearing a special pair of glasses. Appropriately, the movie comes with a special "ghost viewer," which Castle explains is intended to weed out the believers from the nonbelievers. Look through the red if you believe, and through the blue if you don't. What this film lacks in special effects, it makes up for in atmosphere. The cinematography is beautiful, the music is eerie, and even when the acting falls a little bit short, the creativity of watching half the movie on a blue screen full of hologram ghosts makes this a horror classic. —J. S.

TINGLER, THE L: DIRECTORS/CASTLE, WILLIAM (1959) 82M D: William Castle. *Vincent Price, Patricia Cutts, Philip Coolidge, Judith Evelyn, Darryl Hickman.* In the late '50s, film directors tried everything from stereo to 3-D to get people unglued from the novelty of television and come back out to the movie theaters. Castle was shameless in this use of theatrical gimmickry. *The Tingler* was projected in 1959 employing what was called Percepto. Participating theaters would rig some of their seats with electric shocks and deliver a charge to a random group of moviegoers. Meanwhile, on the screen, Price is brilliant playing a doctor who discovers the physical manifestation of fear—a sluglike monster that grows on your spine and constricts you to death unless you scream. Remarkably, as Price tries to self-induce fear, we get to see him dose out on LSD. This is very possibly Castle's finest film and the DVD by Columbia Pictures has plenty of extras and trailers to put it all in the proper perspective. —N. J.

BONNES FEMMES, LES L: DIRECTORS/CHABROL, CLAUDE (1960) 100M D: Claude Chabrol. *Bernadette Lafont, Clotilde Joano, Ave Ninchi, Stéphane Audran, Lucille Saint-Simon.* Hitting the theaters of Paris around the same time as *Breathless* and a number of other Nouvelle Vague splashmakers, *Les Bonnes Femmes*'s slightly moralistic tale delves into the life of the single shopgirl. More precisely, the lives of a whole coterie of shopgirls—good-times girls in search of various romantic ideals of conventional happiness—love, liberty, economic stability, and combinations thereof. Like many of the film's contemporaries, *Les Bonnes Femmes* wears its Hollywood influences on its sleeve (Hawks, Hitchcock). Fellini's *Cabiria* and Cassavetes's *Shadows* seem useful reference points as well. More important is the fact that the movie is excellent in its own right. The characters are maddeningly likable, the dialogue has a great dynamic naturalism, and the photography (shot by Henri Decaë) is gorgeous. If you've already tracked through Godard's and Truffaut's early films, this is a must. —C. B.

BOUCHER, LE L: DIRECTORS/CHABROL, CLAUDE (1970) 87M D: Claude Chabrol. *Stéphane Audran, Pascal Ferone, Jean Yanne, Antonio Passalia.* Audran (Chabrol's wife and longtime collaborator) is a friendly but emotionally distant young schoolmistress who meets a glum butcher (Yanne) at a wedding. Haunted by his years in the army in Vietnam (or Indochina, as he calls it), he rouses to life as he tries to woo her from her shell. Meanwhile a serial killer preys on young women of the area, and the evidence points to the butcher. The crimes are all offscreen and only a single victim is seen; the suspicion and terror are played out entirely on an intimate level between the could-be lovers. Chabrol's delicate restraint warms in his characters and their relationships, the emotional risk that guards their emotions, and the possibilities they offer one another. One of Chabrol's most sublime and austere films. —S. A.

CRY OF THE OWL L: DIRECTORS/CHABROL, CLAUDE (1987) 102M D: Claude Chabrol. *Mathilda May, Jacques Penot, Virginie Thévenet, Jean-Pierre Kalfon, Christophe Malavoy.* Chabrol makes psychological thrillers in the true sense of the term. His characters are psychotic in ways that make them far more disturbing than criminal geniuses, and their psychology is far more enthralling than the twists and turns of his plots. This one is from a novel by Patricia Highsmith (*The Talented Mr. Ripley*), herself a master of psychologically disturbing characters, and the marriage is perfect—a

Claude Chabrol

Considered both "the French Hitchcock" and the progenitor of the Nouvelle Vague, Claude Chabrol has sometimes found his esteemed reputation difficult to live up to, and his career is spotted with as many misses as masterpieces. A filmmaker in the legendary company of Eric Rohmer, Jean-Luc Godard, Jacques Rivette, and François Truffaut, Chabrol began his film career while a critic for *Cahiers du Cinéma* in the 1950s.

He took his lead from Alfred Hitchcock, and his first feature, *Le Beau Serge* (1958)—which he directed, wrote, and produced, and modeled on Hitchcock's *Shadow of a Doubt*—established him as a force to be reckoned with. His follow-up, *Les Cousines* (1959), was another critical success, and the first to employ the character names that Chabrol would return to in many subsequent films—Charles and Paul. His debut in color, *A Double Tour* (also 1959), was the first of many of his films to focus on the convergence of stifling bourgeois values and explosive passion—often leading to violence.

While readily accepted by commercial European markets due to their inherent melodrama, Chabrol's best films—*L'Oeil du Malin* (1962), *Les Biches* (1968), *La Femme Infidèle* (1968—remade in 2002 as *Unfaithful*), *Le Boucher* (1969), *Juste Avant la Nuit* (1971), *La Rupture* (1972), and *Innocents with Dirty Hands* (1974)—are also his most personal, centered on conspiracy and deceit, often in domestic situations. Appropriately,

---

chilly but devastating work about the systematic destruction of one man's life. Malavoy is a depressed but polite and gentlemanly Peeping Tom who introduces himself to the object of his obsession (May) and becomes the target of her pathologically jealous husband, who is egged on by Malavoy's own vindictive former wife. Chabrol's direction is as cool and restrained and preternaturally possessed as Malavoy, which only makes the psychological swamp of mind games, menace, and obsession all the more disturbing, right down to the devastating, unsettling freeze-frame of the final image. —*S. A.*

EYE OF VICHY L: DIRECTORS/CHABROL, CLAUDE (1993) 110M D: Claude Chabrol. *Michel Bouquet (narrator, French version), Brian Cox (narrator, English version)*. In the words of this documentary, directed by Chabrol and constructed almost exclusively from pro-Nazi newsreels created by the puppet government of authoritarian Marshal Pétain, "This film shows France, not as it was between 1940 and 1944, but as Petain and the collaborators wanted it to be seen." The narrative comments by Cox (who fills in for Bouquet in the English-language release) consist mostly of historical background and factual corrections and are largely unnecessary. These clips speak for themselves as they extol the paternal Nazi occupation and the heroic leadership of Marshal Pétain, brand Charles de Gaulle as a traitor and the Allies as enemies to the simple French citi-

zen, and spread the anti-Semitic poison of the Third Reich. Watch for one jaw-dropping piece of Axis propaganda: a cartoon with pirated parodies of Mickey Mouse and Popeye as incompetent bomber pilots dropping their payloads on collaborationist French peasants. —*S. A.*

FEMME INFIDELE, LA (AKA THE UNFAITHFUL WIFE) L: DIRECTORS/CHABROL, CLAUDE (1969) 94M D: Claude Chabrol. *Stéphane Audran, Michel Bouquet, Maurice Ronet, Michel Duchaussoy*. Audran (Chabrol's longtime leading lady and as well as his wife at the time) escapes the tedium of a routine marriage and a dull bourgeois husband (Bouquet) with a lover in the city, until the husband discovers the affair and, in one impulsive movement, kills the lover. Chabrol's coolly observed stories of secrets, guilt, murder, and complacency stripped to primitive impulses may have their roots in the work of Hitchcock, but his films are all his own. This is a psychologically compelling and surprising story where murder and investigation are secondary to the play of secrets and discoveries of husband and wife. Without sharing a word, they become unspoken conspirators, and the excitement of the illicit is the charge that their dead battery of a relationship needs. It was remade in 2002 by Adrian Lyne as *Unfaithful*, which captures the broad story but, in its exploding emotions and melodramatic direction, misses the subtlety and ambiguity that makes Chabrol's crisp production so delicious. —*S. A.*

the love triangles that colored many of Chabrol's films were most often formed by characters named Charles, Paul, and Hélène, with the latter role routinely taken up by Chabrol's muse and longtime wife, Stéphane Audran.

By the early '70s, Chabrol was already showing signs of strain—the obtuse *Ten Days Wonder* (1972), for example, is an adaptation of an Ellery Queen mystery, which despite an excellent cast—Anthony Perkins, Orson Welles, Michel Piccoli, and Marlene Jobert—manages only to be convoluted and stagy. Chabrol's work underwent a significant change in the latter half of the 1970s—he abandoned his insular conceits in favor of television work and international coproductions in which auteur theory had little relevance. He also cleaned house in the cast-and-crew department, replacing stalwarts Michel Bouquet, cinematographer Jean Rabier, composer Pierre Jansen with

new talent, most notably Isabelle Huppert, who first appeared in his acclaimed *Violette Nozière* (1978).

Chabrol continued to be prolific throughout the '80s and '90s, although his films lacked the vitality of his earlier work. *Quiet Days in Clichy* (1990) is a dull and unnecessary remake; *Dr. M* (1990) takes place in a convincing dystopian future but suffers from the weak performances of its lead actors (Jennifer Beals and Jan Niklas). Still, Chabrol has not been without the occasional return to form: *The Story of Women* (1988) is an incredibly complex character-study of a female abortionist (Huppert) who becomes the last woman guillotined in France; *La Cérémonie* (1995) is a nifty domestic thriller that mirrors the sentiment of Joseph Losey's *The Servant*; and his numerous contributions to the *Fantomas mythos* for French TV cannot be overlooked.

—*Kier-La Janisse*

INNOCENTS WITH DIRTY HANDS L: DIRECTORS/CHABROL, CLAUDE (1975) 121M D: Claude Chabrol. *Jean Rochefort, Rod Steiger, Romy Schneider, Paoli Giusti.* A plot by a sexy young wife (Schnieder) and her hunky lover (Giusti) to kill alcoholic husband Steiger turns into a frosty psychological study in Chabrol's hands. He's not so much interested in the plot as in the characters: the camera lingers on the wife's face as she bludgeons her husband, but the rest of the plan is barely glimpsed in brief snippets. As the police start to suspect the lovers, the plot twists with complications reminiscent of *Les Diaboliques,* but in the altogether cooler key of Chabrol's style. Screenplay by Chabrol, from a novel by Richard Neely. —*S. A.*

NADA L: DIRECTORS/CHABROL, CLAUDE (1974) 107M D: Claude Chabrol. *Lou Castel, Fabio Testi, Michel Aumont, Mariangela Melato, Michel Duchaussoy.* Chabrol's scathing indictment of the French government's response to the terrorism of the 1970s begs comparison with Bruno Barretto's idealistic *Four Days in September.* Chabrol's cynical take on a Marxist-driven terrorist cell that kidnaps the American ambassador from a ritzy Paris brothel becomes a grim farce as French police battle competing government agencies for information and try to leverage the standoff into an armed confrontation. With taut direction in the measured style of a policier, Chabrol inflects his usual chilly distance with a jaundiced attitude that becomes downright angry as the film

closes in on its bloody conclusion. While he can't embrace the violent tactics of the terrorists, he finds an honor in their guerrilla campaign that is missing from the expedient duplicity of the so-called law. —*S. A.*

THIS MAN MUST DIE L: DIRECTORS/CHABROL, CLAUDE (1969) 107M D: Claude Chabrol. *Michel Duchaussoy, Caroline Cellier, Jean Yanne, Anouk Ferjac.* Chabrol has been called the Gallic Hitchcock because of his fascination with the Master of Suspense and his career-defining work in the suspense genre. But where Hitchcock is fascinated by doubles and guilty innocents, Chabrol is more interested in the killers and their loved ones, in their inner lives, and in the ambiguous relationships and emotional connections between victims and victimizers. In this revenge drama, a father (Duchaussoy) obsessed with hunting down the hit-and-run driver who killed his young son finally tracks down his suspect (Yanne), a callous, vicious man whose own son wants him dead. No mere revenge drama, this is a modern story of crime and punishment told from the inside out with Chabrol's characteristic elegance, restraint, empathy, and ambiguity. —*S. A.*

ALEXANDRIA TRILOGY, THE L: DIRECTORS/CHAHINE, YOUSEF (1978) 348M D: Youssef Chahine. *Nour El-Cherif, Farid Chawky, Naglaa Fathi, Yehia Chahine.* Chahine, the Egyptian director who first drew international attention to his country's cinema and

Sir Charles Chaplin

Born in 1889 to English music-hall performers, Charles Spencer Chaplin grew up mostly in workhouses after his father died and his mother went insane. He turned to the theater to escape his poverty and at sixteen was starring in a West End production of *Sherlock Holmes*. After landing a spot in a touring revue that took him to the United States, he was spotted by Mack Sennett and signed to the Keystone Company in 1914.

Starting as a member of Sennett's slapstick troupe, Chaplin soon began developing his own unique brand of comedy based on character, emotion, and pathos, and he began directing his own films after less than a year. His character, the Little Tramp, became a sensation with the public and Chaplin was soon offered an enormous salary and freedom to create. In 1916 he signed the first million-dollar contract in Hollywood and began making a series of twelve shorts for Mutual Film Company, a period he once described as "the happiest years of my life." His eighteen-month ten-

---

earned a lifetime achievement award at Cannes 1997, was always a groundbreaker in his domestic cinema. *Alexandria . . . Why?* (1978), Egypt's first autobiographical film, views national history through the eyes of a young man coming of age in a volatile time. It's a fascinating portrait of a country at the crossroads, bustling with color and cultural diversity. *An Egyptian Story* (1982) is Chahine's ruminations on his life in a fantasy mock trial while under the knife during open heart surgery. The premise is a bit absurd but the flashbacks create a complex portrait of the film director taking stock of his successes, failures, and compromises. *Alexandria Again and Forever* (1990), the most elliptical film of the trilogy, stars Chahine himself as his alter ego, winning an award for *Alexandria . . . Why?* while struggling with his balance of art and political action. Chahine (who turns out to be a marvelous actor) performs a marvelous Hollywood song and dance sequence before joining a student strike. The trilogy is rife with film history references, clips from his career, re-creations of film productions, and fantasy sequences of imaginary pictures. They gush with passion and a love of cinema, but also seriously grapple with the compromises made in the name of creating art —*S.A.*

DESTINY L: DIRECTORS/CHAHINE, YOUSSEF (1997) 135M D: Youssef Chahine. *Mahmoud Hemeida, Lalia Eloui, Nour El-Cherif.* A rollicking intellectual adventure with the emotional tenor of a melodrama, Youssef Chahine's passionate tale of real-life twelfth-century philosopher Averroes is ambitiously dense with ideas and rites of passage. In many ways a riposte to the forces that banned his 1994 *L'émigré* in Egypt, Chahine turns his blow against religious extremism and censorship into

a film that is part romance, part political thriller, part musical. "Ideas have wings," predicts Averroes, "No one can stop their flight." Though it sometimes stumbles in its passion and shirks its poorly served women characters, these lapses aren't that apparent in all the swirling action and energy. Each scene flowers with its own passion and every character shines in his or her moment of glory. Chahine carries the electricity of these scenes throughout the picture to create a colorful, dynamic celebration of the joy of knowledge that takes off in it's own cinematic flight. —*S.A.*

CHAPLIN MUTUALS, THE L: DIRECTORS/CHAPLIN, CHARLES (1916) 100M D: Charles Chaplin. *Charlie Chaplin, Eric Campbell, Edna Purviance.* Chaplin called his eighteen months at Mutual "the happiest period of my life," and the twelve two-reel comedies in *The Chaplin Mutuals* remain his finest achievements: slapstick ballets of distilled Chaplin comic genius. Settling the Little Tramp into his final form—equal parts class clown, sneaky bully, downtrodden social outcast, and sentimental softy—Chaplin spins twenty-five-minute works of art from little more than a character, a setting, and a situation: a drunk playboy navigating a hostile home (*One AM*), a scamp in a department store (*The Floorwalker*), a tramp in a high-class spa (*The Cure*). But Chaplin is more than simply a physical clown. Behind the camera Charlie became Charles, a comic poet whose farces began to reflect a social conscience in classics such as *Easy Street* and *The Immigrant*. They remain his purest, funniest films. —*S.A.*

CHAPLIN'S ESSANNAY COMEDIES L: DIRECTORS/CHAPLIN, CHARLES (1915) 136M D: Charles Chaplin. *Charlie Chaplin, Edna Purviance.* The first volume of this collection is a compendium of shapeless Keystone-

ure with Mutual is considered by many to be his single most creative period.

The care with which Chaplin created his shorts set a standard of excellence that was not approached by other filmmakers until the 1920s, but by that time he had moved on to features, beginning with *The Kid* in 1921. As with his shorts, Chaplin lavished time and money on his features, and like his shorts they were smash hits (with the notable exception of his drama *A Woman of Paris* [1923]). Having proved that his Little Tramp could not only carry a feature but also develop as a character, he turned even more toward pathos and sentimentality, and even bucked the changeover to sound with essentially silent films in 1931 and 1936.

His first talking picture, *The Great Dictator* (1940), was his first without the Tramp persona and represented a marked change of genre, a political satire. It was his last popular success, though by no means his last work of art. His films after the silent period were made years apart; meanwhile, he came under increasing scrutiny for his political leanings. He never became a U.S. citizen, and when he left for Europe to promote *Limelight* (1952), during the height of the blacklist, he was denied permission to return to the country. He made two films while in exile from the United States and did not return until 1972, when he was awarded an honorary Oscar. He was knighted in 1975. —*Sean Axmaker*

---

style gags, but with the second volume Chaplin begins working his comedy around a story, injecting pathos into the humor, and turning his often malevolent character into the resourceful, sad Tramp we know and love. In the final shorts, the Tramp is no longer a mischievous aggressor but a hapless whirlwind of disaster and impish impulses, and Chaplin is the director building gags into uproarious cataclysms of comic chaos. Along with his fourteen "official" shorts are two bonus shorts: David Shepard's reconstruction of Chaplin's original two-reel version of *Burlesque on Carmen*, which is returned to the concentrated, cohesive, and very funny comedy Chaplin originally created, and the faux Chaplin short *Triple Trouble*, which was cobbled together by Essanay from an unfinished film and outtakes from other shorts. —*S. A.*

CITY LIGHTS L: DIRECTORS/CHAPLIN, CHARLES (1931) 87M D: Charles Chaplin. *Charlie Chaplin, Virginia Cherrill, Florence Lee, Harry Myers. City Lights* is Chaplin's greatest silent film. Using his familiar character of the Little Tramp, Chaplin spins a convincing romantic comedy. Cherrill plays a blind flower girl who mistakes the Tramp for a wealthy duke. When the Tramp learns that an operation would restore her sight, he does what he can to raise the money. The comedy that ensues manages to land him in jail, but in the process he does get her the money for the operation. Once she can see, she learns about her benefactor, sparking a romance that still brings viewers to tears. Chaplin himself composed the music, and the DVD by Image Entertainment features Carl Davis conducting. —*N. J.*

GOLD RUSH, THE L: DIRECTORS/CHAPLIN, CHARLES (1925) 72M D: Charles Chaplin. *Charlie Chaplin, Mack Swain, Tom Murray, Henry Bergman*. Inspired by the lengths to which gold lust would drive people, Chaplin wrote, directed, and starred in *The Gold Rush*. He plays a fellow whose bad luck follows him at every turn in his quest for gold; he fights a blizzard, other gold diggers, treachery, and most especially hunger. Knowing about the cannibalism that some of these parties of gold diggers resorted to, Chaplin includes a hallucinatory chicken and the famous cooked shoe. This classic comedy shouldn't be missed. —*N. J.*

GREAT DICTATOR, THE L: DIRECTORS/CHAPLIN, CHARLES (1940) 124M D: Charles Chaplin. *Charlie Chaplin, Paulette Goddard, Jack Oakie, Reginald Gardiner.* Like Lubitsch's brilliant *To Be or Not to Be*, Chaplin's classic satirizes fascism and the Third Reich with his own stock-in-trade: vaudeville burlesque. Chaplin leaves the Tramp behind to play (in his first genuine speaking roles) both twentieth-century Napoleon Adenoid Hynkel and a look-alike amnesiac Jewish barber, and Oakie is a dead ringer for a certain Italian dictator as Napaloni of Bacteria. If it soars when Chaplin plays to his strengths (notably a balletic pantomime with Hynkel bouncing a globe like he owns the world), it threatens to sink in his weakness for pathos—his climactic plea for peace, understanding, and tolerance is played so straight-faced you keep waiting for the punch line despite the passion and sincerity of the speech. Chaplin once said that if he'd known the true extent of Hitler's horrors, he would have never made the film, but there's nothing belittling about it. —*S. A.*

LIMELIGHT L: DIRECTORS/CHAPLIN, CHARLES (1952) 141M D: Charles Chaplin. *Buster Keaton, Claire Bloom, Charlie Chaplin, Nigel Bruce.* Casting himself as the aging clown, Chaplin plays Calvero, an entertainer at the very end of his career who meets a young ballerina. This dancer (Bloom) believes she is paralyzed. Calvero's passion for the arts makes him try to inspire the dancer to greater motivation. When the film was first released, Chaplin was already blacklisted and it was banned in some American theaters. It wasn't until 1972, toward the end of the Vietnam War and well after Chaplin moved to Europe, that the film was fully released and won Chaplin an Oscar for Original Dramatic Score. —*N.J.*

MODERN TIMES L: DIRECTORS/CHAPLIN, CHARLES (1936) 87M D: Charles Chaplin. *Charlie Chaplin, Paulette Goddard, Henry Bergman.* Chaplin, the king of silent comedy, aptly dubbed this half silent, half talkie film. It's man against machine as the Little Tramp is employed as a factory worker who must cope with enormous machines, demanding customers, and the unsympathetic taskmaster. This classic film is still predominantly silent and relies on sight gags, yet the synchronization of Chaplin's original score clearly demonstrates his interest to coordinate sound and film for humorous effect. The film also features futuristic technology such as two-way audio/video communication. For the countless fans of Chaplin, seeing him speak at the end of this film must certainly have been proof enough of modern times. It wouldn't be until *The Great Dictator* in 1940, however, that Chaplin would find a character he could play that liked to talk a lot. —*N.J.*

MONSIEUR VERDOUX L: DIRECTORS/CHAPLIN, CHARLES (1947) 124M D: Charles Chaplin. *Martha Raye, Robert Lewis, Allison Roddan, Mady Correll, Charlie Chaplin.* Chaplin playing a serial killer? It would have to be a very dapper and charming serial killer, and popular with the ladies, of course. That is what Chaplin portrays as Monsieur Verdoux, who finds it to be socially and financially expedient to murder wife after wife. The film was certainly ahead of its time (it had to wait for a 1964 rerelease before it was critically acclaimed) yet with this vehicle Chaplin was able to vent his frustrations over his mother-in-law, who performed character assassination on him to legally steal a large portion of his wealth. All considered, this film is a brilliant social satire from a man who knows his subject well. —*N.J.*

RINK, THE L: DIRECTORS/CHAPLIN, CHARLES (1916) 20M D: Charles Chaplin. *Charlie Chaplin, Eric Campbell.* In this silent short the Little Tramp works as a waiter who manages to screw up most everything he does, especially around a certain rotund patron who leaves quite irate. On his lunch hour the waiter goes out roller-skating, thereby making a spectacle of himself and everyone else he rolls into. And of course he rolls into the patron

who hoped to be rid of him. This is one of Chaplin's finest and most famous shorts, which amply demonstrates his unique and humorous agility, even on roller skates. —*N.J.*

YELLOW EARTH L: DIRECTORS/CHEN KAIGE (1984) 89M D: Chen Kaige. *Liu Qiang, Xue Bai, Wang Xueqi, Tan Tuo.* A soldier travels to a rural community in Northern China, literally singing the praises of what Communism will do for the impoverished locals. Interactions with his hosts, a farmer and his two children, make up a sort of dialogue on the limits of Communism (and by extension any nationally embraced ideology) when applied to the day-to-day lives of individuals. Of course "dialogue" really isn't the best word—there's little speaking in this slow-paced, visually dominated film. Cinematographer Zhang Yimou, later a much admired director in his own right, tends to photograph the characters as figures engulfed in the huge expanse of their barren setting, adding to the film an almost purely visual equivalent to literary naturalism. Employing a variety of modest effects, the film has a look like none other, and rewards repeated viewings with a richer appreciation of both the film's photographic achievements and its subtle political critique. —*C.B.*

BELLY OF THE BEAST L: DIRECTORS/CHING SIU-TUNG (2003) 90M D: Ching Siu-Tung. *Byron Mann, Steven Seagal, Russell Wong.* I hate to say it, but the title of this film can only be taken literally: Seagal is starting to look like Sammo Hung these days, but without the agility. After watching Ringo Lam and Tsui Hark suffer with "The Curse of Van Damme" for all these years, Ching decided to break new ground as the first Hong Kong director saddled with task of trying to make Seagal look like an action hero. The result is a bizarre mix of Seagal-style ex-CIA-guy-trying-to-save-kidnapped-daughter movie and Ching-style spiritual kung fu. Seagal teams with a former cop turned Buddhist monk (Mann) to fight terrorists, gangsters, cops, and even a random wire-fu transvestite. Seagal doesn't move around much but his opponents are fairly agile with lots of swords and even a bow and arrow (Seagal shoots one arrow apart in midair and bisects another one with a sword). The climactic battle also involves voodoo dolls and a temple full of praying Buddhist monks, which is unusual for a Seagal film. For Ching completists only. That is, unless you get an ironic kick out of Seagal's films, in which case this is highly recommended. —*B.T.*

CHINESE GHOST STORY, A L: DIRECTORS/CHING SIU-TUNG (1987) 93M D: Ching Siu-Tung. *Leslie Cheung, Joey Wong.* Director Ching, along with producer Tsui Hark, created this fantastic period ghost story that weaves in and out of Chinese legend with ease and jump-started the ghost-romance genre. The bumbling Choi-Sin, endearingly played by

Cheung, is a tax collector who must spend the night at a haunted temple when he is caught in a rainstorm. Wong's performance as trapped ghost Siu-Seen is beautiful as she glides across the screen seducing men for her Tree Demon master to eat. Veteran martial artist Wu Ma takes on the persona of a Taoist priest, and after a rollicking rap song becomes the ally of Choi-Sin as he sets out to save Siu-Seen from her possessor. Tsui's eye for amazing effects takes center stage as the film progresses, with Taoist magic fully showcased. The final scene supposedly gave Sam Raimi part of his inspiration for *Army of Darkness.* —*R. M.*

DRAGON INN L: DIRECTORS/CHING SIU-TUNG (1992) 103M D: Ching Siu-Tung, Raymond Lee. *Tony Leung Ka Fai, Maggie Cheung, Brigitte Lin.* Forget the complicated exposition and political backdrop. This remake of King Hu's classic is all about spies, shifting alliances, greed, power, and romantic fancy. Cheung is the Innkeeper, a flirting thief with a Sweeney Todd sideline of meat buns, who clashes with rebel Lin (in her full androgynous glory) and falls for Lin's lover (Leung Ka Fai) while they battle it out with evil agents and royal troops. Driven with the New Wave playfulness of Tsui Hark's *Peking Opera Blues,* it's full of the madcap energy, furious fight choreography, melodramatic excess, and sheer invention that made Hong Kong cinema the cult choice of adventurous movie buffs in the early '90s. Lee is the credited director, but you can see the fingerprints of action choreographer Ching and producer Tsui Hark (who, uncredited, also shot and shaped much of the film). —*S. A.*

DUEL TO THE DEATH L: DIRECTORS/CHING SIU-TUNG (1982) 86M D: Ching Siu-Tung. *Tsui Siu Keung, Kao Hsiung, Ka Sa Fa.* Oh shee-it, this movie is dope. The top martial artist from Japan does battle with the best from China and the one who lives is the winner. Japan tries to fix the fight, but in the end the best from each nation get to test their skills on each other. Not only does this film have a soundtrack that was probably learnin' the Wu-Tang Clan when they were still in diapers, but it also has some of the sweetest martial arts moves ever. I mean, why didn't anyone tell me that if I wanted to fly all I have to do is jump off my sword? Come to think of it, why didn't anyone ever tell me that in order to defeat a Shaolin monk all I have to do is get a hot chick to prance in front of him naked? —*T. C.*

EAST IS RED, THE L: DIRECTORS/CHING SIU-TUNG (1993) 95M D: Ching Siu-Tung, Raymond Lee. *Brigitte Lin Ching-Hsia, Joey Wong.* Lin plays Asia the Invincible, a badass swordswoman who was once a man. She protects a magic scroll (possibly related to her gender switch?) from various attackers and things get messy when an old girlfriend (Wong) pretends to be her when she was a man. Seeing this without knowing it was the third part in a

trilogy, I really could not follow the characters or story line much at all. And I didn't care one bit. This is an absolutely delirious, flying kung-fu period piece full of fantastic wire fu and surreal imagery like birds flying out of people's mouths and fighters shooting colorful strings and scarves out of their hands. —*B. T.*

EXECUTIONERS L: DIRECTORS/CHING SIU-TUNG (1993) 97M D: Ching Siu-Tung. *Michelle Yeoh, Anita Mui, Maggie Cheung, Damian Lau, Anthony Wong Chau-Sang.* Gloomier, more ambitious sequel to *Heroic Trio,* for which Ching was action choreographer. This time we find Thief Catcher (Cheung), Invisible Woman (Yeoh), and Wonder Woman (Mui) living new lives in a postapocalyptic wasteland. Most of the water has been contaminated by radiation, so the crazed mutant in an iron mask who runs the water company (Wong) raises prices to create chaos and launch a coup. It's up to the trio to come back together to stop Wong and find fresh water for the people. *Executioners* is not quite as fun as the first film, but admirable for its dark themes that reflect the real-life controversy over a nuclear power plant in Hong Kong and widespread fears about the Chinese takeover. *Heroic Trio* director Johnny To codirected this sequel. —*B. T.*

AND THEN THERE WERE NONE L: DIRECTORS/CLAIR, RENÉ (1945) 97M D: René Clair. *Barry Fitzgerald, June Duprez, Roland Young, Walter Huston, Louis Hayward.* Clair takes on Agatha Christie and Hollywood gets one its first slasher films. Ten people are invited to a private party in a large mansion on an island off the stormy English coast by a mysterious host, whose identity remains unknown to everyone attending. One by one the guests die off, each in very gruesome manner. The remaining guests try to figure out who the murderer is before they are next. An often-filmed story of Christie's book *Ten Little Niggers* (remade in 1966, 1975, and 1989 as *Ten Little Indians*), this version sports the best dialogue and acting and is well designed by Clair with the right mix of humor and grisly details. The film is also well edited, building slowly to its climactic ending. —*N. H.*

IT HAPPENED TOMORROW L: DIRECTORS/CLAIR, RENÉ (1946) 100M D: René Clair. *Dick Powell, Linda Darnell, Jack Oakie.* Powell, dapper and cocky in his turn-of-the-century duds and caterpillar mustache, is perhaps too sedate for the more manic moments of this proto–*Twilight Zone* fantasy where the aspiring reporter is shown a succession of early-edition newspapers—tomorrow's in fact. Professional gains turn into personal troubles and a comic insanity that wreaks havoc on his predictable life, but the glories of the picture lie in the quiet scenes, the moments of resignation where Powell sighs and relents in the face of fate. Clair's lolling style works at cross purposes to the manic machinations of the plot, but the characters come alive in wry portrayals and measured performances. —S. A.

NOUS LA LIBERTÉ, A L: DIRECTORS/CLAIR, RENÉ (1931)
87M D: René Clair. *Paul Olivier, Rolla France, Raymond Cordy, Henri Marchand.* Clair was a pioneer of early sound comedy, melding music, sound effects, images, and action into a comic ballet with a spoken libretto. This is a high-spirited farce that satirizes capitalism, Communism, class difference, and the regimentation of modern life. Louis (Cordy) is a natural-born thief who breaks prison and remakes himself into a phonograph tycoon. Former cell-mate Emile (Marchand) unleashes chaos in the regimentation of his prisonlike assembly line (a scene that anticipates Chaplin's *Modern Times,* which the producers sued for plagiarism) but brings his staid old buddy back to hearty life. The film was reportedly directed with only a loose outline and largely improvised by the performers, but it feels completely organic and flows like a dance. It's a delight to see a romantic take on the human spirit that defies conformity yet denies the expected romantic fantasy of a climax. This happy ending has far more spirit and sass. —S. A.

UNDER THE ROOFS OF PARIS L: DIRECTORS/CLAIR, RENÉ
(1930) 92M D: René Clair. *Gaston Modot, Edmond T. Greville, Albert Préjean, Pola Illéry.* Clair's sound-film debut is a sweet lark of a street romance that exudes a sense of community and friendship in the cobblestone neighborhood of a Parisian cul-de-sac. Using silent-film style in long wordless sequences orchestrated to music and setting his camera free to prowl through the streets, up through the windows, and down the halls of the apartment buildings, Clair keeps the grace of silent cinema as he exploits sound with the same expressionist bent he applies to the visuals. The story is completely lightweight and looks forward to more complex and rich films (the delightfully screwball *Le Million* and the glorious social satire *A Nous La Liberté*), but the cinematic flourish, good feeling, and deft sense of character are all here. —S. A.

MADE IN AMERICA: ORNETTE L: DIRECTORS/CLARKE,
SHIRLEY (1985) 80M D: Shirley Clarke. *Ornette Coleman.* Experimental director Clarke was a perfect match for the free-form music of Coleman. As you'd expect, Coleman performs (including with a symphony) and talks about his life and his music. But then the movie suddenly drifts into abstract imagery, reenactments of Coleman's childhood, crude alterations of moon landing footage, or Coleman standing outside playing in front of a bunch of weird mannequins. In many jazz documentaries the musicians talk about the pioneers who influenced them. Coleman apparently is more influenced by architecture than music, so he stands inside a geodesic dome talking about Buckminster Fuller. I hope this impossible-to-find movie will be given a DVD release some day. —B. T.

PORTRAIT OF JASON L: DIRECTORS/CLARKE, SHIRLEY
(1967) 90M D: Shirley Clarke. Jason is an effeminate black gay prostitute who sits down with Clarke, has a few drinks, and tells stories about his life. He's a theatrical guy (in fact much of the conversation is about his cabaret act) so some of the interview may be exaggerated for showmanship. There is a lot to be gleaned about race and sexual preference issues, but Clarke doesn't make it into a message movie. You'll feel less like you're watching a documentary than like you're meeting a stranger who tells you some funny and unusual stories. —B. T.

INNOCENTS, THE L: DIRECTORS/CLAYTON, JACK (1961)
85M D: Jack Clayton. *Deborah Kerr, Michael Redgrave, Martin Stephens, Pamela Franklin.* This is a highly atmospheric version of Henry Miller's *Turn of the Screw.* Ms. Giddens (Kerr) is employed by the owner of an estate (Redgrave) to be the governess for two young children, Flora and Miles. She eventually starts seeing ghosts at odd times and in strange places. At first she's convinced it's all in her head, but soon she thinks that the children see these ghosts as well. However, the children are remarkably unhelpful and insist they cannot see any ghosts. It turns out that these ghosts resemble the former owners of the estate who died horribly and are seemingly possessing the children. Or, Ms. Giddens is going insane! —N. J.

FORBIDDEN GAMES L: DIRECTORS/CLÉMENT, RENÉ (1952)
102M D: René Clément. *Georges Poujouly, Amédée, Lucien Hubert, Suzanne Courtal, Brigitte Fossey.* Often said to be for WWII what Renoir's *Grand Illusion* was for WWI, *Forbidden Games* examines the wreckage of war by focusing on the psychological scarring suffered by children. After adorable five-year-old Paulette (Fossey) is orphaned by an air raid, she's taken in by a family of farmers. Eleven-year-old Michel (Poujouly) develops a childish crush on Paulette, doing everything possible to please her. His first gesture of kindness is to help her bury her dog, also killed in an air raid. Looking for more dead animals to "keep the dog company," Michel turns to killing animals for their budding cemetery, as well as stealing crosses for grave markers. Clever enough to be a serviceable black comedy, but also unsentimental and disarmingly grave. —C. B.

PURPLE NOON (PLEIN SOLEIL) L: DIRECTORS/CLÉMENT,
RENÉ (1962) 118M D: René Clément. *Erno Crisa, Elvire Popesco, Maurice Ronet, Alain Delon, Marie Laforêt.* Based on *The Talented Mr. Ripley* by lesbian writer Patricia Highsmith, *Purple Noon* is homosexual murder-romance thinly veiled as a Hitchcockian thriller. Tom Ripley (Delon) enters the lives of handsome and rich Philippe Greenleaf (Ronet) and his girlfriend, Marge (Laforêt),

Jean Cocteau

Jean Cocteau is a preeminent figure in the history of twentieth-century culture. Well regarded for his work as a novelist, poet, painter, sculptor, and playwright, Cocteau left perhaps his most indelible mark as a filmmaker. He was dedicated to helping define the vocabulary for a poetic cinema.

Cocteau was born Jean Maurice Eugène Clément Cocteau in 1889. From his first film, *Le Sang d'un Poète* (1930), to his last, *Le Testament d'Orphée* (1959), Cocteau was an experimental filmmaker, pushing the boundaries of how film tells a story, all the while acutely aware that "the Muse of Cinema is impatient." Making films, unlike many other forms of art, means being tied to finance: huge sums of money pour into the process, and the people who provide this money expect a swift return on their investment.

Nevertheless, Cocteau found a middle ground, reaching critics and audiences alike with his two greatest and perhaps most enduring films, *La Belle et la Bête* (1946) and *Orphée* (1949). To the end, he believed that cinema would eventually overcome the obstacle of cash, take its rightful place alongside painting, sculpture, poetry, and music, and become a means of expression for all humanity: "Cinematography is an art. It will liberate itself from industrial slavery," he said. This century has seen few artists as pure, true, and visionary, and perhaps revolutionary, as Jean Cocteau.

—*Kevin Shannon*

who are on "permanent" vacation in Italy but are actually hiding from Philippe's aristocratic father. Philippe's father hired Ripley to return his son home to the United States. Ripley gets sidetracked in his mission and quickly becomes blinded by his attraction for both Philippe and his wealthy lifestyle. He squirms his way into the young couple's lives as an uncomfortable third in their relationship. Tensions soar as the three go sailing on the ocean and Ripley murders Philippe, hiding his body and then returning to Italy to masquerade as Philippe. *Purple Noon* is remembered for its beautiful cinematography by legendary cinematographer Henri Decaë and for Delon's strikingly handsome looks. —*N.H.*

MYSTERY OF PICASSO, THE L: DIRECTORS/CLOUZOT, HENRI-GEORGES (1956) 85M D: Henri-Georges Clouzot. *Pablo Picasso.* Clouzot puts the camera on Picasso at work in this utterly unique documentary about the seventy-three-year-old artist. In fact, Picasso is almost entirely offscreen as his sketches appear on the screen (he draws on one side of thin paper suspended in the air as the camera captures the ink bleeding through on the other side) and his paintings build layer upon layer in stop-motion sequences. If the "mystery" of the title is the mystery of creative inspiration, then this one is left unsolved. The work is casual and tossed off, engaged in by Picasso with a playful spirit for the sake of goofing with a gimmick, but how many chances will any of us have to see a master at work or play on the canvas? In 1984 the French government declared this one-of-a-kind film a national treasure. —*S.A.*

QUAI DES ORFEVRES L: DIRECTORS/CLOUZOT, HENRI-GEORGES (1947) 106M D: Henri-Georges Clouzot. *Suzy Delair, Louis Jouvet, Bernard Blier, Simone Renant.* It's easy to forget that Clouzot, who made his name on icy, tense, carefully played out thrillers like *Wages of Fear* and *Diabolique*, was once the director of lively, quirky mysteries. This deftly directed classic stars Delair as an ambitious dance-hall singer and Blier as her jealous piano-player husband. Both believe the other is guilty of murdering the wealthy old lecher who has designs on the singer. Enter Inspector Antoine (Jouvet), a sad little man with a sharp brain and a dogged pursuit of justice. Clouzot's sharp, busy visual design favors the winding streets and cluttered apartments of the tiny neighborhood. He executes the elaborate crime with great precision while unleashing chaos, but it's the ambiguity of trust and the unexpected sacrifices that enliven the mystery and the crazy world around it. Clouzot took the award for Best Director at the 1947 Venice Film Festival. —*S.A.*

BEAUTY AND THE BEAST (1946) L: DIRECTORS/COCTEAU, JEAN (1946) 93M D: Jean Cocteau. *Jean Marais, Josette Day.* Widely regarded as one of the most visually captivating fantasies in the history of film, Cocteau's 1946 masterpiece stands unparalleled in its heartbreakingly lyrical presentation.

The age-old fairytale of love and loss could not have been more perfectly captured. From young Belle's storybook village to the fantastic creatures and catacombs of the Beast's castle, the director creates a delicately somnambulistic wonderland light-years beyond anything in the Disney canon. As the Beast, Marais shines impossibly through his horrific makeup, offering one of the most tragic and sympathetic performances of its era. Conservative cross-dresser Marlene Dietrich was allegedly so repulsed by the openly homosexual actor's human unveiling at the film's end that she stood up at the premiere and shouted, "Bring back my beautiful beast!" —Z. C.

BIG LEBOWSKI, THE L: DIRECTORS/COEN BROTHERS (1998)
127M D: Joel Coen. John Turturro, Steve Buscemi, Philip Seymour Hoffman, Julianne Moore, John Goodman, Jeff Bridges. The Big Lebowski takes two viewings to reveal its humor, and then you can't stop watching it. Bridges gives a too-good-to-be-considered-for-an-Oscar performance as The Dude, a lazy, burned-out ex-hippie who by having the same name as a millionaire finds himself thrust into the role of detective in a Chandler-esque mess involving a kidnapped trophy wife, angry pornographers, and a band of motorcycle-riding nihilists. Try as he may, The Dude can't stay out of it and eventually even starts referring to it as a "case." There is ingenious attention to detail in the language, like the way characters pick up phrases (for example The Dude borrows "in the parlance of our times" from Maude (Moore), and Walter (Goodman) uses George H. W. Bush's "line in the sand" during a bowling dispute). Watch it twice and you'll know why many consider it the funniest movie of all time. —B. T.

BLOOD SIMPLE L: DIRECTORS/COEN BROTHERS (1984) 96M
D: Joel Coen. M. Emmet Walsh, Frances McDormand, Dan Hedaya, John Getz. The Coen brothers' inventive debut film is a sleek, austere neo-noir about an adulterous affair that leads to a complicated web of murder and betrayal in a small Texas town. Their script spins a scrupulously plotted set of misunderstandings into a wicked crossfire, and their inventive style has fun with the material while effectively ratcheting up the tension. It's a smart, stylish, well-turned genre picture. Getz, McDormand, Hedaya, and Walsh (simply oozing perspiration as an oily PI) star and future director Barry Sonnenfeld is the man behind the clever camera work. In 2000 the directors tinkered with the film for rerelease, creating the version they had originally envisioned. The DVD does not have the kooky introduction by the mock historian that preceded the theatrical rerelease, but it does have an absurd and annoying spoof of academic commentary tracks, with a mock intellectual making up ridiculous production "facts" and silly cinematic observations. —S. A.

FARGO L: DIRECTORS/COEN BROTHERS (1996) 98M D:
Joel Coen. Harve Presnell, Peter Stormare, Steve Buscemi, William H. Macy, Frances McDormand. I love every single minute of Fargo, a dark fable for northern America full of barren snowscapes, parkas, family restaurants, frozen windshields, truck stops, icy roads, paintings of ducks, murder, and wood chippers. Opening on a wall of snow, a car slowly emerges to the moody strings of Burwell's score, setting the tone for the rest of the film. With their collaborators, the Coens perfectly re-create a specific time and place (Minnesota, 1987). Cinematographer Roger Deakins captures the bleak beauty of the flat, snow-covered wilderness. The performances are all-around brilliant: Macy as a desperate, scheming car-salesman; Buscemi as a funny-looking guy; and McDormand as kind but strong-willed pregnant police chief Marge Gunderson. She created one of cinema's most interesting characters. The sudden bursts of violence and sardonic humor are what the Coens specialize in, but it's the warm, quiet scenes between Marge and her husband that bring us in from the cold. —K. C.

HUDSUCKER PROXY, THE L: DIRECTORS/COEN BROTHERS
(1994) 111M D: Joel Coen. Tim Robbins, Paul Newman, Jennifer Jason Leigh. The Coens go screwball here, with Joel Silver footing the bill, Newman and Robbins delivering riotous dialogue, and Leigh putting on her most mannered performance ever. So what's not to like?! Actually, this film turned a lot of people off, maybe because they weren't ready for a screwball comedy from the already loony Coen duo. Ultimate stooge and sucker Robbins gets played for a patsy by tycoon Newman when he's promoted from the mail room to run the corporation and take a fall for it as well. Classic rise and fall story, told with the Coen brothers' ripe mixture of charm and lunacy. Homage alert: The fight in the giant clock room was taken directly from John Farrow's lovely film noir The Big Clock. —M. S.

MAN WHO WASN'T THERE, THE L: DIRECTORS/COEN
BROTHERS (2001) 116M D: Joel Coen. Tony Shalhoub, Billy Bob Thornton, James Gandolfini, Michael Badalucco, Frances McDormand. The devious melodrama of adultery, embezzlement, blackmail, and murder is secondary to the crumbled dreams and mechanical lives of its deadened characters in this tale of madness, repression, and soul-suffocating dislocation in 1950s small-town America. It's like a Jim Thompson novel on opium, with Thornton as the cheerlessly amoral so-called hero crawling through a scheme hatched on a whim and watching the lives of those around him get swamped and drowned from the ripples of his crime. Thornton takes the title literally, delivering a character so disconnected and discontented it's as if he'd stepped outside his body and stared it down into numb submission. Perfectly constructed, utterly dispassionate, and directed with uncanny attention

to detail, the Coens do their job too well: for all its brilliance, this dry, deadpan, inhuman comedy is as cold as an ice crystal. Brrrr. —*S. A.*

MILLER'S CROSSING L: DIRECTORS/COEN BROTHERS
(1990) 115M D: Joel Coen. *Gabriel Byrne, Marcia Gay Harden, Albert Finney, Jon Polito, John Turturro, Steve Buscemi.* "What's the rumpus?" 1990 was a big year for gangster movies (Scorses's *Goodfellas* and the disappointing *Godfather III*), but this is probably my favorite of the three. Set during prohibition, the plot is derived from Dashiell Hammett's classic *The Glass Key* but is given an intelligent, fun, and complex spin by the Coens. Tom Reagan (Byrne) is caught in the middle of a complex love triangle with his boss (Finney) and a party girl named Vera (Harden). Vera's brother has been antagonizing a rival gangster and it all leads to lots of violence, bloodshed, and blazing tommy guns. For a guy who doesn't do much, Tom sure manipulates the rest of the characters. You really need to watch *Miller's Crossing* (one of the best movies about hats) more than twice to untangle all the plot intricacies, choice dialogue, and tricky interrelationships. —*S. H.*

O BROTHER, WHERE ART THOU? L: DIRECTORS/COEN
BROTHERS (2000) 106M D: Joel Coen. *Holly Hunter, Tim Blake Nelson, John Turturro, George Clooney, Chris Thomas King, John Goodman.* The Coens take one of the all-time great comedies—Preston Sturges's *Sullivan's Travels*—as a starting point for an exercise in sheer entertainment. In *Sullivan's Travels,* John Sullivan is a rich movie producer who feels guilty that he's not making significant films: films that treat the woes and miseries of real people. His dream is to film the novel *O Brother, Where Art Thou?*, a *Grapes-of-Wrath*–type plunge into the depths of poverty and hopelessness. Accused of ivory-tower hypocrisy, he rubs some dirt on his face and sets out to be an undercover hobo, to learn about the other half from their side of the fence. What he learns, finally, is that the greatest gift he can give to people who live dreary lives is laughter: the laughter he's given them through his "insubstantial" comedies. And now the Coen brothers have made the film of *O Brother, Where Art Thou?* that Sullivan might have made after his epiphany. It has all the surface trappings of a highbrow Depression drama—its heroes are hobos on the run from the law, and it jokes that it's based on Homer's *The Odyssey*—but ultimately it's a fast ride on a wacky horse, with an absolutely fabulous bluegrass soundtrack of wildly entertaining songs. Don't make the mistake Sullivan would have made before his journey of self-discovery and get lost in surface details; take this ride for the sheer fun of it. —*C. C.*

RAISING ARIZONA L: DIRECTORS/COEN BROTHERS (1987)
94M D: Joel Coen. *John Goodman, Nicolas Cage, Holly Hunter, William Forsythe, Trey Wilson.* Cage plays an ex-convict who meets his prison photographer wife (Hunter) over the course of the multiple times he is arrested and thrown in jail. After he turns over a new leaf and leaves his life of crime behind, the two get married and decide they want children, only to find out Hunter's character can't have kids. At first they are devastated, but soon hear about the birth of quintuplets to Nathan Arizona, a rich furniture salesman, and decide to kidnap one to raise as their own. The chemistry between Cage and Hunter in this film is outstanding, and is only topped by a hilarious performance by Goodman as Cage's convict friend. This movie is funny and sweet and manages to be absurd and over the top without resorting to cheap blows and campiness. A big hug to the Coen brothers for a wonderful movie. —*J. S.*

FULL MOON HIGH L: DIRECTORS/COHEN, LARRY (1982)
93M D: Larry Cohen. *Adam Arkin, Roz Kelly, Elizabeth Hartmann, Ed McMahon.* A high-school football player (Adam Arkin) goes with his military father on a short trip to Romania. While dad (McMahon) hogs the hotel room with a prostitute, the young man waits in a restaurant, and after that he waits somewhere outside at night, and ultimately he is bitten by a werewolf. After ten years of lycanthropic travel, he finally returns home to find that all his friends have become adults while he himself is still a teenager with an odd, periodic taste for human flesh! Made three years before Michael J. Fox's *Teen Wolf, Full Moon High* is similar to Mel Brooks's *Young Frankenstein.* It's a veritable sleeper for fans of comic werewolf films! —*N. J.*

BONE (AKA HOUSEWIFE) L: DIRECTORS/COHEN, LARRY
(1972) 95M D: Larry Cohen. *Yaphet Kotto, Andrew Duggan, Joyce Van Patten, Jeannie Berlin.* Cohen became a B-movie maverick of the '70s by sneaking sly political commentary and social satire into exploitation thrillers and drive-in genre pictures. In *Bone,* his little-seen directorial debut, it's more savage and much closer to the surface. Kotto radiates an unspoken, unpredictable threat when he walks into the backyard of an affluent middle-aged white couple in Beverly Hills (Van Patten and Duggan) and demands money, but finds himself a party to the dirty little secrets of their chilly relationship when his threats excite more than frighten them. Van Patten, guzzling umbrella drinks, reveals herself to be more predatory than everyone else, including her scheming husband, and Berlin is great as a shoplifting kook with a harrowing story of childhood trauma. Cohen tweaks stereotypes and twists expectations until the film shifts into

Larry Cohen

arry Cohen is a prolific screenwriter who turned director in 1972 with his first film, *Housewife* (aka *Bone*). A year later he made two blaxploitation films, *Black Caesar* and its sequel, *Hell Up in Harlem*, both filmed in New York. These black mafioso films starring Fred Williamson garnered enough of a cult following over time that many years later Cohen would be recruited to direct an update of the blaxploitation film *Original Gangstas* (1996).

Then, in 1974, came the film that gave Cohen his reputation as the best low-bud-

get horror director since Roger Corman— *It's Alive*. With its unique blend of social satire, cheesy effects, and strong script, *It's Alive* was an immediate B cult classic. Cohen would go on to direct two sequels, *It Lives Again* in 1978 and *Island of the Alive* with Michael Moriarty in 1987.

Directors often develop allegiances with certain actors, and writer/directors are perhaps more inclined to do this, since they often write for the specific talents of certain actors. Andrew Duggan, the husband with decidedly few morals in *Housewife,* was an important character actor for Cohen. He appeared in wonderful supporting roles in many of Cohen's films. But it was Michael

---

an unsettling social satire with caustic humor. —*S. A.*

DEADLY ILLUSION L: DIRECTORS/COHEN, LARRY (1987) 95M D: Larry Cohen. *Billy Dee Williams, Vanity, Morgan Fairchild, John Beck, Joe Cortese.* Williams plays an unlicensed private dick trying to hunt down a murderer while flirting with Vanity. Both of these personalities are wasted (if that's possible) on a script that never quite leaves the starting gate. But then again, what should one expect from a detective film where the private eye is named Hamburger? This joke is not very funny the first time, yet each and every time it's used it falls flatter and flatter, especially as it keeps coming from Williams. —*N. J.*

GOD TOLD ME TO (AKA **DEMON**) L: DIRECTORS/COHEN, LARRY (1976) 92M D: Larry Cohen. *Tony Lo Bianco, Deborah Raffin, Sandy Dennis, Sylvia Sidney.* Cohen's subversive little horror film mixes religion and UFO lore in inventive ways, spinning off von Daniken's *Chariots of the Gods* with a few wild theories of his own for a not-too-radical interpretation of the second coming. Bianco stars as a New York City cop investigating a strange series of murders committed by citizens who have never broken the law before, and who all claim they killed because "God told me to." One of the most interesting science fiction thrillers from the '70s from the always unpredictable and devious low-budget auteur, this is prime pre-*X-Files* alien conspiracy tumbled through with spiritual somersaults, though Cohen's low-budget energy and visceral direction drive the film with an emotional contact unknown to the

cool, self-knowing TV show. Intelligent, creepy, subversive. —*S. A.*

ISLAND OF THE ALIVE L: DIRECTORS/COHEN, LARRY (1987) 91M D: Larry Cohen. *Michael Moriarty, Karen Black, Laurence Landon, Gerrit Graham, James Dixon.* This third installment makes up remarkably for the second in that it develops the original abortion allegory (the first film was released just a year after Roe vs Wade) in a new light. In the projected future of the first two films it is natural to believe that the aging killer infants (now full-blooded monsters, of course) would be extradited to a very remote place—an island that only the military would know about. Enter Moriarty, the daring anthropologist who goes on a risky visit to the island so that some parents can fulfill their dream to check up on their kids. Naturally this in-and-out excursion turns into an all-out survival of the fittest. Perhaps the original allegory has been carried too far . . . or has it? —*N. J.*

IT LIVES AGAIN L: DIRECTORS/COHEN, LARRY (1978) 91M D: Larry Cohen. *Frederic Forrest, Kathleen Lloyd, John P. Ryan, Andrew Duggan, James Dixon.* This sequel adds very little to the first except for the complexity of multiple killer babies. As a result there are multiple parents with multiple perspectives on the issue, including the original parents of the first little monster. It is a well-made variation on a theme, especially when one considers the added killer baby effects and the low-budget killer baby perspective. But overall it is much more of the same save for the showdown ending with the original father trying pathetically to

Moriarty who really made his mark as the lead character in some of the finest Cohen films. This unique combination got its start with Cohen's unparalleled B classic *Q—The Winged Serpent* (1982). As a sorry jazz pianist who does a poor job of scatting, Moriarty goes far by accentuating the underlying comic element of Cohen's script, even as he holds New York hostage over his information about the winged menace. Following this, Moriarty starred in some of Cohen's finest films—*The Stuff* (1985), a film about killer yogurt; *Return to Salem's Lot* (1987); and *Island of the Alive* (1987).

Meanwhile, in the late '80s, Cohen made a valuable team with director William Lustig, penning for him the scripts of *Maniac Cop* (1988) and its two sequels. One of his finest for this director, however, was the bit-ing antiwar satire *Uncle Sam* (1996), which features a right-wing soldier who dies from friendly fire in the Gulf War only to return to his hometown around July 4 as a member of the living dead, dressed as Uncle Sam, to brutally murder anyone with the slightest liberal leanings.

Whereas the heyday of Cohen's directing career may be over, his writing is as prolific and stunning as ever. His script for the film *Phone Booth* was written and filmed before the Washington, D.C., sniper shootings of 2002, but because the script was so similar to the harsh reality of the time, the film's release was delayed by a good six months.

—*Nathan Jensen*

---

save his murderous child from the manhandling of a large SWAT team. —*N. J.*

ORIGINAL GANGSTAS L: DIRECTORS/COHEN, LARRY (1996) 98M D: Larry Cohen. *Fred Williamson, Pam Grier, Jim Brown.* Who said blaxploitation flicks were a thing of the past? Not Cohen. This '90s nostalgia vehicle combines the finest fixtures of the '70s genre into one film: Williamson, Roundtree (*Shaft*), Brown (*Slaughter*), O'Neal (*Superfly*), and of course Grier (*Foxy Brown*). Together they unite to kill the very scum of the earth that passes itself off these days as "gangstas." These black icons *are* the original gangstas! And they're gonna make the streets safe once again for honest ma-and-pa businesses. —*N. J.*

PRIVATE FILES OF J. EDGAR HOOVER L: DIRECTORS/ COHEN, LARRY (1977) 112M D: Larry Cohen. *Broderick Crawford, Dan Dailey, Jose Ferrer, Rip Torn.* This is a different kind of fictionalized biography. But what should you expect from the director who brought you killer yogurt in *The Stuff* and murderous babies in *It's Alive*? Who else is better qualified to direct a biopic on J. Edgar Hoover? The scope of this film is thorough: it begins with Hoover's appointment in the time of Capone and ends with his death in the time of Watergate. Don't expect to see any caches of women's clothing here—this film may be cheap on budget but it's not cheap on subject matter. Instead you will be given a thorough character analysis of a desperately lonely and powerful WASP from the perspective of a Jewish filmmaker who has had friends and mentors stung by the McCarthy hearings. —*N. J.*

Q—THE WINGED SERPENT L: DIRECTORS/COHEN, LARRY (1982) 93M D: Larry Cohen. *Michael Moriarty, Candy Clark, David Carradine, Richard Roundtree, James Dixon.* A two-bit hustler (Moriarty) hatches a get-rich-quick scheme when he stumbles across the nest of a giant winged creature in New York City's Chrysler Building in Cohen's grungy, goofy, tongue-in-cheek horror. The pterodactyl-like, people-snatching menace Q is a throwback to the stop-motion creatures of Saturday matinee movies but the black humor, social satire, and anything goes plot devices are pure contemporary Cohen. Carradine and Roundtree run around the city as New York's finest, trying to solve the rash of mysterious deaths. Only Cohen could make this work because, as apparently only he understands, in his native New York no one looks up! —*S. A.*

RETURN TO SALEM'S LOT L: DIRECTORS/COHEN, LARRY (1987) 96M D: Larry Cohen. *Michael Moriarty, Samuel Fuller, Andrew Duggan, Evelyn Keyes, Jill Gatsby.* This is a perfect gem of a B movie. Casting the great director Fuller as a Nazi hunter turned vampire hunter, Cohen capitalizes on the most salient points of the original plot while getting the most out of a very small budget. The anthropologist (Moriarty) and his son move to Salem in order to make a home. They soon find that the town is completely taken over by vampires and worse, the head vampire (Duggan) insists that the anthropologist document their history or rather, their Bible. Very little is wasted in this film and it smacks of the social commentary Cohen is best at. —*N. J.*

STUFF, THE L: DIRECTORS/COHEN, LARRY (1985) 86M D: Larry Cohen. *Michael Moriarty, Andrea Marcovicci, Garret Morris, Paul Sorvino, Scott Bloom, Danny Aiello.* "Are you eating it, or is it eating you?" This is a tongue-in-cheek horror film about killer yogurt. Cohen has a unique way of presenting a twisted premise while serving up the rest of the film straight. The premise to this film goes something like this: "What's this stuff bubbling up from the ground? Whatever it is it tastes good. Let's sell it!" Of course people find out that it's killing them well after it is monopolized by greedy corporate culture. Is this an allegory for oil? Fast food? Tobacco? Whatever it is it's a good clean parody of American culture. —*N.J.*

WICKED STEPMOTHER L: DIRECTORS/COHEN, LARRY (1989) 90M D: Larry Cohen. *Bette Davis, Tom Bosley, Barbara Carrera, Richard Moll.* This film is the evil stepsister to the film *Trog.* Whereas *Trog* is the embarrassing final contribution to the film world by Joan Crawford, *Wicked Stepmother* is the equally embarrassing final contribution by Davis. Unlike Crawford, she at least had enough self-possession to quit halfway through filming. This left director Cohen in a lurch. He had to rewrite his whole screenplay so that the evil witch stepmother is suddenly turned into a black cat whose intentions are channeled by Carrera. This tragic amalgamation of a film is going to be of interest only to Cohen fans, Davis foes, or film students interested to see how a film can self-destruct yet still be released. —*N.J.*

APOCALYPSE NOW, APOCALYPSE NOW REDUX L: DIRECTORS/COPPOLA, FRANCIS FORD (1979) 153M D: Francis Ford Coppola. *Dennis Hopper, Martin Sheen, Robert Duvall, Lawrence Fishburne, Marlon Brando, Frederic Forrest.* Based on Joseph Conrad's novella *Heart of Darkness,* but the setting changes from darkest Africa to deep in the jungles of Vietnam during the war. Brando plays Kurtz, an officer taken to the razor's edge by the insanity of war. Somehow he convinces local tribesmen that he's some kind of god, becoming their leader and spreading his diseased ideas with vengeful wrath carried out by his faithful servants. Sheen is the "errand boy" sent to terminate his command with extreme prejudice. Truly an amazing piece of cinema, both versions are well worth watching. The original flows better, but *Redux* feels like a more complete story, filling gaps in the plot with added scenes, some which are relevant, some less so. To me this doesn't play as a straight antiwar film; there are other movies out there that do better jobs at that. *Apocalypse Now* is a metaphor for the madness of civilization and how epochs, groups, and nations embrace and justify policies of absolute terror. There are some truly historic moments in this film, like Sheen's mirror-punching scene that triggers a real heart attack, or when the helicopter cavalry attacks the beach with Richard Wagner's "Ride of the Valkyries" playing on loudspeakers. This is a true cinematic experience. —*B.W.*

BRAM STOKER'S DRACULA L: DIRECTORS/COPPOLA, FRANCIS FORD (1992) 128M D: Francis Ford Coppola. *Keanu Reeves, Richard E. Grant, Gary Oldman, Winona Ryder, Anthony Hopkins.* The general feeling toward this version of Dracula seems to be that it is visually impressive and more faithful to the novel, but weakened by the miscasting of Reeves and Ryder. I would go one step further, though, to say that Oldman is miscast as Dracula. The biggest diversion from the novel is a new backstory that gives Dracula a lover. This seems intended to make him a more sympathetic and romantic antihero, and yet he is played by Oldman, whose specialty is over-the-top villains. Still, it's a worthwhile film, with many clever visual tricks and a memorable performance by Hopkins as a slightly insane Van Helsing (which, in my reading, is much closer to the book than the traditional heroic Van Helsing). —*B.T.*

GODFATHER, THE L: DIRECTORS/COPPOLA, FRANCIS FORD (1972) 175M D: Francis Ford Coppola. *Diane Keaton, Marlon Brando, Al Pacino, James Caan, Robert Duvall, John Cazale.* The Godfather has been so highly praised and deeply analyzed since its release that it's easy to forget it's a real movie, not a filmmaking class or a dissertation. But at its heart it's a simple story about the forces that draw families together and splinter them apart. The family in question just happens also be in The Family. Plenty of the film deserves praise, including its lush look, shocking violence, and moving performances from the smallest roles to the largest. *The Godfather* has aged well, and certain scenes, even if viewed over and over again, still have the ability to shock and delight. —*T.P.*

GODFATHER PART II, THE L: DIRECTORS/COPPOLA, FRANCIS FORD (1974) 200M D: Francis Ford Coppola. *Dominic Chianese, Peter Donat, Robert De Niro, Al Pacino, Gianni Russo, Frank Sivero.* Pacino returns as Michael Corleone, now the head of the family, who must grapple with being in control of an enormous crime organization. Interspersed throughout his and the mob's growing pains is the idyllic recounting of how it all began. De Niro plays Vito Corleone, the founder of the family's legacy who made a place for himself in New York's Little Italy after the turn of the century by terminating a loathsome crime lord. In place of this menace, Vito imposes a more benevolent organization, one that enhances the plight of immigrant Italians. Again, the direction of Coppola and the music of Nino Rota add immeasurably to this remarkable expansion of the *Godfather* epic. —*N.J.*

GODFATHER PART III, THE L: DIRECTORS/COPPOLA, FRANCIS FORD (1990) 170M D: Francis Ford Coppola. *Diane Keaton, George Hamilton, Talia Shire, Andy Garcia, Al Pacino, Joe Mantegna.* This third installment of the *Godfather* trilogy was a bit of an afterthought (it was filmed fifteen years after the award-winning *The Godfather Part II.*), yet it is a fitting end to the trilogy. The young Corleone of the first film is now the frail, aging Don Corleone who is riddled with guilt over the life of crime he has ruled over and, more specifically, what may become of his family. Corleone tries setting up a truce with various crime families, but when the attendees are gunned down by helicopter everyone suspects the Corleone family of a setup. One of the most interesting subplots is about the confession of Corleone directly to Pope John Paul I whose truncated papacy is here explained as a hit. Plenty more awaits fans of the first two films, not the least of which is Coppola's daughter Sofia who as an infant was baptized on screen for the first *Godfather* film and who appears here as Corleone's daughter. —*N. J.*

ONE FROM THE HEART L: DIRECTORS/COPPOLA, FRANCIS FORD (1982) 100M D: Francis Ford Coppola. *Raul Julia, Nastassja Kinski, Frederic Forrest, Harry Dean Stanton, Teri Garr.* Toss up the talents of Tom Waits, Coppola, Garr, Stanton, and Kinski, all going for broke in this love story of lost dreams and fantasies never to be, drop it in the middle of Las Vegas, and confine the filming to a soundstage. The rest is pure magic, a bittersweet love ballad of winners and losers. Lots of 'em. —*M. S.*

BUCKET OF BLOOD, A L: DIRECTORS/CORMAN, ROGER (1959) 66M D: Roger Corman. *Antony Carbone, Julian Burton, Barboura Morris, Dick Miller, Ed Nelson.* Reliable Corman regular and future Jonathan Demme good-luck charm, Miller takes his first and only lead as Walter Paisely, a schlemiel bus boy in a beatnik coffeehouse who dreams of artistic greatness. He's all thumbs until he accidentally kills his cat and covers it in clay—a grotesque study in death that becomes the talk of the community. Unfortunately, he has to keep topping himself. Yeah, daddy-o, Corman's madhouse of beatnik poseurs, drug-dealing lowlifes, and poetry-spewing beards is high on the list of B-movie mondo greatness, shot in mere days from a crazy script full of black comedy and hysterical hipness. Makes a great companion with Corman's original *Little Shop of Horrors* (1960), which was tossed together on the sets left over from the shoot. Watch for future game-show host Bert Convy as a narc! —*S. A.*

FRANKENSTEIN UNBOUND L: DIRECTORS/CORMAN, ROGER (1990) 86M D: Roger Corman. *Bridget Fonda, Raul Julia, Jason Patric, Michael Hutchence, Catherine Rabett, John Hurt.* After a lengthy retirement from directing films, Corman decided to make this very curious twist on the old *Frankenstein* story. Hurt plays a nuclear physicist who happens to drive his car back in time, by chance to the time and place of Mary Shelley (Fonda). After making her acquaintance and feebly trying to fit into the past, he makes the startling discovery that Dr. Frankenstein isn't fiction after all. As the two doctors become acquainted with each other they find that the monsters each has created are not so very different. Excellent casting and good direction make this plenty more than just a B movie. —*N. J.*

HOUSE OF USHER L: DIRECTORS/CORMAN, ROGER (1960) 79M D: Roger Corman. *Vincent Price, Mark Damon, Myrna Fahey.* American International's first Poe adaptation was, like many of the others directed by Corman, written by Richard Matheson and magnificently acted by Price. It is the closest in content to Poe's original work, telling the tale of a man who travels to the House of Usher only to discover the horrible curse that has been visited upon the family. Like Poe's work itself, the horror is almost always internal, proving that the greatest of all cosmic terrors comes not from the physical threats, monsters, or madmen, but from within the vast and troubled recesses of the darkest corners of the human mind. Price plays Roderick Usher, a man whose senses have become painfully acute. He epitomizes Poe's traditional protagonist, both a villain and a victim. Credit is owed to Matheson and Corman for making the film so intelligent, subtle, and eerie, but Price is the reason the film remains one of the all-time great pieces of Gothic horror cinema. —*T. S.*

INTRUDER, THE L: DIRECTORS/CORMAN, ROGER (1962) 84M D: Roger Corman. *Beverly Lunsford, Frank Maxwell, William Shatner.* Shatner delivers the most controlled performance of his career as an ambitious white supremacist who heads south to rouse the white rabble of a small town into a mob on the eve of school integration. With a cagey smile and a glad-handing manner, the would-be pedagogue spins a *Music Man*–like sales pitch, only he's hawking hate. In classic Shatner fashion he unravels in spastic histrionics as he loses his grip on the group. Famed as the only Corman film to lose money, this brave (for its time) look at the politics of racism is rife with powerful scenes (many of them including stinging slaps of the "n" word), which makes up for the plastic wrap–thin separation between text and subtext and the overanxious exposition. —*S. A.*

MASQUE OF THE RED DEATH L: DIRECTORS/CORMAN, ROGER (1965) 88M D: Roger Corman. *Vincent Price, Hazel Court, Jane Asher, Patrick Magee, David Weston, Nigel Green.* Price stars as the mad twelfth-century prince in Corman's seventh Poe film. In the midst of the plague, the sadistic Prince Prospero confines himself in his palace along with a masquerade party composed of aristocrats who he detests. In the midst of this stimulating yet stilted party, Death enters unannounced and dressed in red. The prince's interest in this uninvited guest increases, especially as the other guests start dropping like flies. The colors and sets in this film are absolutely spectacular, especially the strange sequential chambers of different colors through which Price chases Asher. Poe films don't get much classier than this. —*N.J.*

RAVEN, THE L: DIRECTORS/CORMAN, ROGER (1963) 86M D: Roger Corman. *Hazel Court, Boris Karloff, Jack Nicholson, Peter Lorre, Vincent Price.* Not so much a horror film as a parody of horror films and characters of such films, *The Raven* is Corman's tongue-in-cheek horror-comedy that utilizes its brilliant cast for its stage presence, characterization, and dazzling elocution. Karloff, Price, and Lorre are all hams by disposition, each of them having played the line between horror and comedy in various ways. Here Corman lets their natural comedy come out in style. The plot is about rival magicians who insist on proving their magical prowess against each other. After endless spoofs and puns a showdown is the inevitable climax. Fifth in Corman's Edgar Allan Poe series. —*N.J.*

TALES OF TERROR L: DIRECTORS/CORMAN, ROGER (1962) 89M D: Roger Corman. *Peter Lorre, Basil Rathbone, Debra Paget, Maggie Pierce, Vincent Price.* This is a great addition to the Corman/Poe film legacy. It is unique in that it is the only film in the series that is an anthology horror piece. The three stories are connected only by the fact that they are based on stories by Poe and star Price. The framework is a simple but fantastic monologue from Price over some creepy images of blood and beating hearts. The best of the three tales is the second, called "The Black Cat" (combining the stories *The Black Cat* and *The Cask of Amontillado*) starring Lorre. *Tales of Terror* is good watching. —*T.S.*

TRIP, THE L: DIRECTORS/CORMAN, ROGER (1967) 85M D: Roger Corman. *Susan Strasberg, Peter Fonda, Dennis Hopper, Bruce Dern.* The quintessential '60s head film presents the acid trip of a burned-out, sold-out TV director (Fonda) as part psychedelic Renaissance fair, part hyperactive city as go-go club (complete with strobe-light editing). Corman (working from a Jack Nicholson screenplay) weaves us in and out of Fonda's fantasies while charting his freaked-out journey through LA to find himself. While much of the imagery is the silliest kind of theatrical surrealism (who really has visions of dwarfs in medieval getups?), its serious subjective exploration is as interesting as the psychedelic freak-out is fun—just ignore the studio-imposed introduction and tampered-with concluding image. To this day Corman decries the studio's interference. —*S.A.*

AMEN L: DIRECTORS/COSTA-GAVRAS (2002) 130M D:Costa-Gavras *Ulrich Tukur, Mathieu Kassovitz, Ulrich Mühe, Michel Duchaussoy, Ian Caramitru.* Tukur is the real-life SS scientist and devout Christian Kurt Gerstein, who tried to tell the world about the Holocaust while he discovered the truth

about the gas chambers (which he, inadvertently, helped develop). Kassovitz plays the (fictional) priest with the Vatican's ear who attempts to bring Gerstein's message to Pope Pius XII. The Vatican turned a deaf ear, as if refusing to hear the words meant that they didn't have to face their moral responsibility. Costa-Gavras is not the subtlest of directors, but he is passionately committed and he pulls no punches in this indictment of the Catholic Church's abdication of moral leadership during WWII. His direction is as blunt as his unholy rage and disgust at this real-life atrocity. —*S.A.*

HIGHWAY PATROLMAN L: DIRECTORS/COX, ALEX (1991) 104M D: Alex Cox. *Bruno Bichir, Pedro Armendáriz Jr., Zaide Silvia Gutiérrez, Roberto Sosa.* Sosa plays an idealistic young Mexican who wants to serve his country and make a difference in the world. He also needs a job, so he enrolls in the National Highway Patrol Academy where he learns many unexpected things. Once he is assigned to patrol the roads of northern Durango with his friend Anibal (Bichir), he finds that corruption is totally pervasive in the police force. The rest of the film is his slow and certain immersion into this culture of back-scratching and profitable bribery. It's a bittersweet ending, for this young man becomes the very image of his ideal for himself and his family, yet what he had to trade for it was likely more valuable. —*N.J.*

REPO MAN L: DIRECTORS/COX, ALEX (1984) 92M D: Alex Cox. *Emilio Estevez, Harry Dean Stanton, Tracey Walter, Fox Harris, Olivia Barash.* *Repo Man* is packed with layers of odd details, strange characters, and enough obscure jokes that it warrants repeat viewings. It's a comic science-fiction film that incorporates punk rock, consumer culture, religious hypocrisy, government conspiracy, and a whole lot more. Estevez (in his best performance) plays Otto, a disenfranchised punk who stumbles into the world of automobile repossession. His Repo Mentor is Bud (Stanton) and all of his fellow Repo Men are named after beer. J. Frank Parnell (Harris) is a crazy scientist driving a '64 Chevy Malibu with space aliens in the trunk that are given the *Kiss Me Deadly* treatment. There are endless quotable lines and a great punk rock soundtrack. —*S.H.*

STRAIGHT TO HELL L: DIRECTORS/COX, ALEX (1987) 86M D: Alex Cox. *Jim Jarmusch, Courtney Love, Zander Schloss, Joe Strummer, Sy Richardson, Grace Jones, Dick Rude.* This film has a terrible reputation among those who take it seriously, and a great reputation among those who join in on the party. Four outlaws (Rude and Richardson of *Repo Man* fame, and Strummer and Love) wander into a south-of-the-border town run by the maniacal coffee-swilling MacMahon clan (aka The Pogues). Hopper, Jones, Jarmusch, Elvis Costello, and most of the cast of *Repo Man* turn up in Cox's valentine to the spaghetti Western.

Invite your friends over, turn down the lights, and make sure you have plenty of tequila and coffee. —*M. S.*

WALKER L: DIRECTORS/COX, ALEX (1987) 95M D: Alex Cox.
Richard Masur, Blanca Guerra, Ed Harris, Keith Szarabajka, Peter Boyle, Marlee Matlin. Harris plays William Walker, an American who declares himself president of Nicaragua in 1855. The intense Harris is perfect in the role because he seems to really believe that his rule is best for the Nicaraguan people, even though all he's doing is oppressing them to make the country safe for big business. It's a graphic and horrifying historical action drama, made more powerful by actually being filmed in Nicaragua. Cox occasionally uses intentional anachronisms to draw parallels between Walker's situation and what went on in Nicaragua the decade the film was made. Unfortunately the political themes are still relevant with today's American foreign policy. —*B. T.*

MAN OF FLOWERS L: DIRECTORS/COX, PAUL (1983) 91M D: Paul Cox.
Sarah Walker, Norman Kaye, Alyson Best, Chris Haywood, Werner Herzog. Kaye stars as a kinky recluse who escapes the ghosts of a troubled childhood through a uniquely individualistic approach to celebrating beauty, which involves (among other things) watching a beautiful artist's model strip naked for his voyeuristic pleasure while playing the church organ in an orgiastic frenzy. Made back in Cox's eccentric early days, this is one of his most offbeat and delicious portraits of the awkward relationships between men and women, this time from the perspective of a man whose appreciation of women has only ever been from a distance. Quirky, clever, and completely unpredictable, the film follows the psychologically troubled man's journey from distanced aesthete to social being as he becomes involved with his model's messy personal life. Herzog can be seen as the father in the foggy home-movie flashbacks. —*S. A.*

HILLS HAVE EYES, THE L: DIRECTORS/CRAVEN, WES (1977) 83M D: Wes Craven.
Robert Houston, Dee Wallace, Susan Lanier, Michael Berryman. If you're ever in a middleclass family driving your Winnebago through a desert that used to be a nuclear testing site, do yourself a favor and don't break down. They got these families of mutant cannibals out there whose values are pretty different from yours. And you won't necessarily get along that well. Craven's harsh cannibal movie is not as perfect as *The Texas Chain Saw Massacre*, but it's a good take on a more tribal version of the deranged-killer family. The huge and weird-looking Berryman (also known for *One Flew Over the Cuckoo's Nest*) is a particularly memorable villain (though my favorite moment is the cameo by producer Peter Locke: "Maybe I'll make a joke like last time and eat the toes."). It's like a way more vicious update of *Hot Rods to*

Hell. There's always something enjoyable about watching bland people get terrorized by weirdo maniacs. —*B. T.*

HILLS HAVE EYES PART 2, THE L: DIRECTORS/CRAVEN, WES (1984) 87M D: Wes Craven.
Michael Berryman, Tamara Stafford, Kevin Spirtas, John Bloom, Janus Blythe. A bunch of motorbike racers run into a group of desert-dwelling cannibals and chase them around. Who knows what shocking secrets will be revealed from their pasts, or whether anybody will get eaten? It's much less raw than the original, with more of a TV-movie feel, and you don't get nearly enough insanity from Pluto and the boys. Only kind of enjoyable as a bad sequel, it is most famous for having the family dog flash back to scenes from the original. —*B. T.*

LAST HOUSE ON THE LEFT L: DIRECTORS/CRAVEN, WES (1972) 83M D: Wes Craven.
Jeramie Rain, Marc Sheffler, Fred Lincoln, Sandra Cassel, David Hess. On the way to a rock concert, two girls get captured, tortured, and killed by a Manson family–inspired gang of escaped convicts. By coincidence, the killers end up staying at the house of one girl's parents and get their just desserts. Craven's debut is a raw and brutal exploitation classic that channels the violence and madness of the Vietnam era. Some scenes are repulsively sadistic while others are unsettlingly goofy. Craven's goal was to create a horror movie where the deaths were long and ugly, like in real life, and he succeeded. The villains are great—note the similarities between Weasel (Lincoln) and Mr. Blonde from *Reservoir Dogs*. —*B. T.*

Craven's first film lives in the sort of notoriety most horror films only dream about. And quite frankly, it doesn't deserve it. The unflinching view of graphic, disturbing events may have been shocking when the film was released but unfortunately, when you get past the imagery, there is little substance to back it up and the film falls flat. In many ways it is a remake of *The Virgin Spring*. But where *Virgin Spring* is a near perfect film, *Last House* is merely exploitation. If that's what you're looking for, great! But there's something about this film that rubs me the wrong way and I find it annoying that it gets so much acclaim. It may have been groundbreaking in its presentation of violence on-screen, but in this desensitized age where horror requires more than simple gore (something even gore-master Lucio Fulci clearly understood) it is pretty clear that this film is completely overrated. —*T. S.*

NIGHTMARE ON ELM STREET, A L: DIRECTORS/CRAVEN, WES (1984) 92M D: Wes Craven.
Robert Englund, Heather Langenkamp, Ronee Blakely, Nick Corri, Johnny Depp, John Saxon. If you can forget about the sequels and Freddy the wisecracking pop icon, the original *Nightmare On Elm Street* stands on its own as a very effective and psychological slasher film. Craven abandoned the

killer-on-the-loose type of horror for a more cerebral approach in which the spirit of a child killer (Englund) haunts the dreams of Nancy (Langenkamp) and friends because their parents burned him alive in an act of vigilante justice. If he hurts them in their dreams he hurts them for real, but he can't come into the waking world. So all they have to do to survive is never, ever sleep. No problem! The dream imagery seems very genuine—odd things like Freddy's arms stretching for no reason, or a goat suddenly walking past Nancy in the hallway at school. Some of the deaths are absolutely brutal, especially the scene where Tina (Amanda Wyss) is stabbed and dragged across the ceiling by an invisible force. This is also notable as Depp's big-screen debut (playing a standard hunky boyfriend). —*B.T.*

PEOPLE UNDER THE STAIRS, THE L: DIRECTORS/CRAVEN, WES (1991) 102M D: Wes Craven. *Brandon Adams, Ving Rhames, Everett McGill, Wendy Robie.* When Fool (Adams, who played the little Michael Jackson in *Moonwalker*) and his mom get evicted from their ghetto home, he decides to break into the cruel white slumlord's house to steal a rumored stash of valuable gold coins. Things get tricky, though, when the landlords (McGill and Robie) turn out to be crazy S-M freaks who cut out people's tongues and wall the folks up under the house. As horror, it's not as effective as Craven's best, but as an allegory it's pretty interesting. The judgmental upper class are more depraved than anyone; they literally live on top of the underclasses and prevent them from speaking out. Craven, a former college professor, often puts a lot of thought into the subtext of his films, but here it comes closer to the surface than usual (scratching on the other side of the wall, I guess). —*B.T.*

SCREAM L: DIRECTORS/CRAVEN, WES (1996) 110M D: Wes Craven. *Matthew Lillard, Jamie Kennedy, Skeet Ulrich, David Arquette, Courteney Cox, Neve Campbell.* Craven continues the postmodernism of *New Nightmare* with this self-referential horror film that revived the slasher subgenre and then, accidentally, sort of ruined it. A group of teens must use their knowledge of horror clichés to match wits with a ghost-masked stalker trying to reenact the themes of "scary movies." If you can separate it from the baggage of its imitators, it's very suspenseful and clever, particularly in the heart-pounding opening sequence that uses Drew Barrymore like *Psycho* used Janet Leigh. Since it has fun with horror formulas, I think many non-horror fans saw it as a parody. But in fact it is downright worshipful of, and works effectively within, the genre. —*B.T.*

SCREAM 2 L: DIRECTORS/CRAVEN, WES (1997) 120M D: Wes Craven. *David Arquette, Courteney Cox Arquette, Sarah Michelle Gellar, Timothy Olyphant, Neve Campbell.* Craven and screenwriter Kevin Williamson go deeper into self-reference in this sequel where a movie based on the events of the first film seems to inspire a copycat killer. There are many allusions to other sequels and, strangely, to the original *Friday the 13th.* They also try to develop the characters a little further, which sometimes works thanks to a strong performance by Campbell. It definitely doesn't match its predecessor but has some clever moments. —*B.T.*

SCREAM 3 L: DIRECTORS/CRAVEN, WES (2000) 116M D: Wes Craven. *David Arquette, Scott Foley, Patrick Dempsey, Neve Campbell, Courteney Cox Arquette.* After the *Scream* movies, *I Know What You Did Last Summer,* and a couple seasons of *Dawson's Creek,* America was sick of Kevin Williamson and never wanted to hear from him again. Then he let Ehren Kruger take over screenwriting duties and end the *Scream* trilogy on an embarrassing note. This time Sidney (the still-quite-good Campbell) moves to California and finds that the actors in a sequel to the movie based on her traumatic past are being killed for real before they film their scenes. There are a few plays on sequel conventions, but too often the characters do the kind of dumb things that previous *Scream* movies made fun of (like using a lighter to see in the dark and causing a gas explosion). The only really memorable scene is when Sidney gets chased through a movie set of her childhood home—a preposterous idea, but one that's pure Craven. —*B.T.*

WES CRAVEN'S NEW NIGHTMARE L: DIRECTORS/CRAVEN, WES (1994) 112M D: Wes Craven. *Robert Englund, Miko Hughes, Tracy Middendorf, Wes Craven, Heather Langenkamp.* After five sequels with little or no involvement, Craven returned to the series that made him famous with an inventive new premise: the Elm Street movies were only movies, but like age-old campfire tales, their telling had weakened some nameless primeval force that had appeared in Craven's subconscious as Freddy. As the sequels got worse, the force regained its strength and now it is up to Craven, Langenkamp, and Englund (all playing themselves) to stop it. It's hard to explain the pre-*Scream* postmodernist plotting without making it sound silly, but it's a smart and serious-minded movie that explores the blurring of fiction and reality while doing some blurring of its own. The plot involves a celebrity stalker (something Langenkamp had dealt with in real life) and earthquakes (which coincidentally happened during filming, allowing Craven the opportunity to get some real shots of LA earthquake debris). Best of all, the more muscular and demonic real-world Freddy is scary again because he abandons the trademark punning of the sequels. —*B.T.*

BROOD, THE L: DIRECTORS/CRONENBERG, DAVID (1979) 90M D: David Cronenberg. *Samantha Eggar, Oliver Reed, Art Hindle.* A psychotic psychotherapist (Reed) shields his prized patient (Eggar) from the rest of the world, presumably for her therapy. Meanwhile her husband isn't permitted to see her even while her parents and others are all murdered by small, munchkinlike terrorists. As it turns out, however, Eggar herself is giving birth to this nasty brood of killer mutants while the psychotherapist goads her to telepathically instruct them to carry out her feelings of rage. Whereas *Rabid* and *They Came from Within* both emphasized the sexual nature of killer parasites, *The Brood* gravitates toward an unsettling maternal aspect of the same, going so far as having Eggar lick the birthing fluids off her newly born parasitic brood! —*N.J.*

CRASH L: DIRECTORS/CRONENBERG, DAVID (1996) 98M D: David Cronenberg. *Holly Hunter, Elias Koteas, James Spader, Deborah Unger, Rosanna Arquette.* Cronenberg directs this adaptation of J. G. Ballard's 1973 novel about a film producer who gets into a car accident. Spader plays the protagonist who meets and falls in love with a very attractive woman, played by Hunter. Over a short period of time, it becomes evident that she has a peculiar kind of fetish—a sexual fetish for car accidents. This strikes Spader as being very odd but he complies, making love to her over the broken frame of his car. Surely enough, she begins to expose him to a whole subculture of people who share the same twisted taste. Among the people they meet are a couple of men who re-create the car accidents of celebrities such as Jimmy Dean and Jayne Mansfield. Needless to say, this peculiar film crashed at the box office. —*N.J.*

DEAD RINGERS L: DIRECTORS/CRONENBERG, DAVID (1988) 115M D: David Cronenberg. *Jeremy Irons, Geneviéve Bujold.* Cronenberg's critically acclaimed film based is on a true story. Beverly and Elliot Mantle (both played by Irons) are twin gynecologists who share everything, even their most intimate sexual experiences. Elliot is the pursuer of women, and when he tires of his current lay he passes her on to his brother without letting her know that they are switching. Eventually they come across a famous actress (Bujold) who captures Beverly's heart, resulting in emotional turmoil and disappointment. The three-way relationship spirals into drug abuse and mental breakdown, causing a split between the seemingly inseparable brothers. The Mantles' practice suffers and their sickness is imposed on their unsuspecting patients with alienlike hand-forged gynecological torture devices. What results is a disturbing loss of touch with reality and a final operation that forever tears the twins apart. This is classic Cronenberg, probably at the height of his film career. His consistent theme of body modification melded with mental breakdown is explored with an eerie mood. The goofy, dated '80s hairstyles and costumes don't detract from the emotional impact of this film. —*B.W.*

DEAD ZONE, THE L: DIRECTORS/CRONENBERG, DAVID (1983) 103M D: David Cronenberg. *Christopher Walken, Brooke Adams, Tom Skerritt, Herbert Lom, Martin Sheen, Colleen Dewhurst.* What better director to bring out all the potential and ambiguities of a Stephen King story than Cronenberg? Here, as in his adaptations of other writers, Cronenberg doesn't change the story to his own liking as much as he influences the mood and story exposition with his own sensibilities in such a way that the final product is something more than either writer would've come up with on his own. Add pre-über-freak Walken in his most subdued and nuanced performance, and what we have is one of the most haunting explorations of loneliness, fate, responsibility, and lost chances you're likely to run across. —*K.F.*

EXISTENZ L: DIRECTORS/CRONENBERG, DAVID (1999) 97M D: David Cronenberg. *Jude Law, Ian Holm, Jennifer Jason Leigh, Don McKellar, Willem Dafoe.* Conceptually, this movie was really cool; it's about a role-playing video game that is so much like reality you're not sure what's real and what isn't. But the pace is tediously slow. There are some strange things that happen and some really good imagery, but not enough. It's a great idea to make things look and feel artificial in this video game caricature of reality, but the flaw here is that you don't know that they're meant to be this way until the end. And by then, you don't give a fuck about them because they're so bland and lifeless. Yeah, the gun that shoots teeth that's made out of mutated amphibians is cool as hell, but I just wished that the characters would use it on themselves. —*M.P.*

FLY, THE L: DIRECTORS/CRONENBERG, DAVID (1986) 96M D: David Cronenberg. *Geena Davis, John Getz, Joy Boushel, Jeff Goldblum, Cosette Lee.* This remake of the 1958 original has exactly the right filmmaker to retell the story: Canadian director Cronenberg, whose cult horror films are all about the corruption of the human body. In this film, a scientist (Goldblum) has perfected his teleportation machine to such a degree that he's willing to try it out on himself. Unfortunately, an ordinary housefly crawls into his pod before he teleports and his DNA merges with the fly's. Slowly he turns into a very unattractive monster. Meanwhile, the poor fly must cope with becoming well mannered. This is a classic that shouldn't be missed. —*N.J.*

NAKED LUNCH L: DIRECTORS/CRONENBERG, DAVID (1992) 115M D: David Cronenberg. *Peter Weller, Roy Scheider, Julian Sands, Ian Holm, Judy Davis.* Using his own script adapted from the novel by William Burroughs, Cronenberg's story is about a bug exterminator (Weller) who becomes addicted to taking his own bug powder and eventually winds up in Interzone. There he types reports with a bizarre roach-typewriter and takes instruction from a large, slimy creature called the

David Cronenberg

David Cronenberg is a Canadian film-maker with a unique style. His films often gravitate toward the unnatural alteration of human flesh, a theme that take many forms, from horror in *Rabid* (1977) to science fiction in *Videodrome* (1983) to drama in *M. Butterfly* (1993).

This theme is already evident in his first feature film *They Came from Within* (1975), in which a nasty parasite invades a hotel resort. Everyone infected becomes a raving sex-maniac and spreads the parasite through direct contact. Cronenberg indulges in gore effects, thereby competing directly with the then-budding American horror industry.

Rabid (1977) and *The Brood* (1979) are horror films in the same vein as *They Came from Within*, although they are quite different in plot. The primary difference is that the two later films feature a single protagonist who faces physical malformation, with accompanying psychological effect.

Scanners (1981) more deliberately shifts Cronenberg's focus toward science fiction. Here a group of telepaths each possess the capability to kill people by making them explode. Virtue over corruption is the ultimate theme, an idea that would be revisited in many of Cronenberg's future films. Yet the director still infuses the film with explicit gore effects, making *Scanners* one of the bloodiest sci-fi films you're likely to see.

Videodrome (1983) finally blends the hor-

Mugwump. By using Weller as a doped-up writer in Interzone, Cronenberg is able to bring out the themes he likes from the book and develop them into a plot. The effects are very shocking and Weller's matter-of-fact reaction to the absolute unreality of the world around him is perfect for the film. Cronenberg goes far with this material to pull viewers out of their perceived reality, and like a landscape by Dalí, it somehow works quite well. —*N. J.*

SCANNERS L: DIRECTORS/CRONENBERG, DAVID (1981) 103M D: David Cronenberg. *Jennifer O'Neill, Michael Ironside, Patrick McGoohan, Stephen Lack.* My childhood was forever scarred by the infamous exploding head that turned this low-budget Canadian sci-fi thriller into Cronenberg's first genuine American hit, the story of a political conspiracy revolving around psychic government agents and a rogue telepathic underground brewing revolution. Cronenberg misses the character dynamics that turn such classics as *The Fly* and *Dead Ringers* into harrowing horrors, and star Lack lives up to his name: he lacks both the charisma and the acting chops to carry the drama. But Cronenberg once again exhibits his excellent use of location and architecture to suggest a claustrophobic otherness. His ideas overcome his cinematic limitations and the supporting cast keeps the film on track between its pyrotechnic highlights. —*S. A.*

SHIVERS (AKA **THEY CAME FROM WITHIN**) L: DIRECTORS/ CRONENBERG, DAVID (1975) 87M D: David Cronenberg. *Barbara Steele, Joe Silver, Paul Hampton, Allan Migicovsky, Lynn Lowry.* Making the limitations of his low budget work for him, Cronenberg turns the bland sets, flat lighting, and colorless performances of his debut feature into a suffocating vision of modern life. With such a vivid presentation of mankind out of touch with its physical and emotional existence, the horror of a designer parasite accidentally let loose on the insular apartment building is almost a release. Part aphrodisiac, part venereal disease, the parasite spreads like the clap (the Typhoid Mary is a philandering teenager screwing her way through the men in the building) and turns the entire population of the self-contained community into a pack of id-driven sex maniacs: night of the living libidos. Like George Romero before him, Cronenberg brought horror into the contemporary world and broke taboos. This was Canada's first domestic horror film. —*S. A.*

SPIDER L: DIRECTORS/CRONENBERG, DAVID (2002) 98M D: David Cronenberg. *Ralph Fiennes, Miranda Richardson, Gabriel Byrne, Lynn Redgrave.* Spider, an adaptation of a novel by Patrick McGrath, was not meant as a case study in schizophrenia, nor is mental illness mentioned specifically. But the film does an interesting job of helping the viewer walk in the shoes of a mentally ill mind. There's brilliant immersion into the main character of Spider (Fiennes), who has been lost in a web of

ror into an articulate psychological construct, from which James Woods must try to escape. It addresses the same theme that makes Cronenberg's later films so interesting: human malformation placed within a complex psychological construct and further complicated by the influence of technology, or at least some very nonhuman antagonism.

Such is the case with Cronenberg's remake of *The Fly* (1986), in which Jeff Goldblum's malformation is due to the blind horror of technology, and his psychological framework is tortured by the DNA of an insect. *Dead Ringers* (1988) concerns twin gynecologists whose minds are joined and who, in a drug-induced state, decide to operate on each other with chillingly archaic operating tools. *Naked Lunch* (1991), a daring realization of the William S. Burroughs novel, features a writer who is physically transformed by ingesting insecticide powder only to be tortured by his own writing.

Crash (1995) is a bit more esoteric in its design. The physical transformation of James Spader is induced by a car crash, the psychological structure is imposed on him by Holly Hunter and her friends, and technology is here represented by automobiles, which experience a variety of accidents.

Lastly, there is *eXistenZ* (1999), which hearkens back to *Videodrome* via *Naked Lunch*. The innocent protagonist's reality is broken down by the grips of an living video-game system. Within the game itself, corruption is uncovered and the virtue of our heroes prevails . . . we think.

Several of these films have been written off as pulp, but a deeper analysis yields a kind of shocking theme and variations. And these variations are by no means run-of-the-mill. —*Nathan Jensen*

---

confusing memories that allow him to believe in illusions of truth that are slowly being cleaned from the attic of his troubled mind. Intentionally, the story is slowly revealed through flashbacks that are both real and fantasy, leaving the viewer as lost and confused as Spider. Richardson takes on three different roles, but the most difficult part is acted by Byrne, who has the daunting task of playing a real character in the film but also playing a fictionalized character based on the fantastic musings of a sick mind. Redgrave rounds out the fine cast as Spider's keeper at a halfway house where he is coming to terms with his past. —*B. W.*

VIDEODROME L: DIRECTORS/CRONENBERG, DAVID (1983) 88M D: David Cronenberg. *Sonja Smits, Deborah Harry, James Woods*. Woods plays the head of a television station that broadcasts both soft and hard pornography. His search for further, more intense viewing material from the underground brings him to a video cabal named Videodrome. On the surface Videodrome seems to be nothing but a small company making very bad snuff films of torture, but upon repeated viewings a strange kind of hallucination starts to take command of the viewer. In an effort to get to the bottom of all of this, Woods finds himself trying to reach Dr. Brian Oblivion, who is apparently the originator of the phenomenon. Soon Woods discovers that he is somehow being controlled through these hallucinations—controlled to allow Videodrome to be broadcast over his own station. Canadian director Cronenberg packs quite the cerebral punch in this cult classic. —*N. J.*

ADAM'S RIB L: DIRECTORS/CUKOR, GEORGE (1949) 101M D: George Cukor. *Spencer Tracy, Katherine Hepburn, Judy Holliday, Tom Ewell*. This sixth pairing of Hepburn and Tracy is generally regarded as the best of their romantic comedies, and there is a lot to recommend. The pair's banter, generously supplied by Ruth Gordon and Garson Kanin, is sophisticated and edgy. Holliday's wild comic turn as a spurned, homicidal wife put her on the map in Hollywood and won her the role that would define her career (as Billie Dawn in *Born Yesterday*). Cukor's simple, unobtrusive direction lets the script and actors shine, using long takes and simple camera setups. Contemporary audiences may gasp at some of the archaic references and humor found in sexism and spousal abuse, but Gordon and Kanin's script assuredly and ultimately indicts sexism, while exploring the nature of feminism at the time through the dissimilar guises of Hepburn and Holliday. —*M. S.*

MARRYING KIND, THE L: DIRECTORS/CUKOR, GEORGE (1952) 92M D: George Cukor. *Aldo Ray, Judy Holliday*. Holliday and Ray are a young married couple in a touching tale that moves from the comic to the tragic and back to the hopeful. The film opens on divorce hearings, but rather than angry or bitter, they just seem exhausted from their travails, which we learn about in flashbacks that take us from deftly funny beginnings to trials that come close to breaking their spirit. Not what you expect from a Holliday film, which may explain its relative obscurity. If you can brace yourself for the pathos, however, it's quite a moving story and Cukor's compassion washes over the performances (including Ray's gruff but boyish leading-man debut). The script is by real-life married Ruth Gordon and Garson Kanin, whose *Adam's Rib* was Holliday's breakthrough Hollywood role. —*S. A.*

MY FAIR LADY L: DIRECTORS/CUKOR, GEORGE (1964) 170M D: George Cukor. *Wilfrid Hyde-White, Audrey Hepburn, Stanley Holloway, Gladys Cooper, Rex Harrison.* Easily one of the best musicals ever to grace the screen, *My Fair Lady* is a Lerner adaptation of George Bernard Shaw's *Pygmalion.* Harrison plays a self-absorbed linguist who develops a theory that high culture has less to do with breeding and more to do with the ability to speak well. His friend wagers a bet with him on this subject and brings in Hepburn, a low-class dame with the worst cockney accent you've ever heard. The rest of the film is the humorous excursion of preparing her for a hoi polloi social engagement and her own personal renewal in the process. This film handily swept the Oscars in 1964, and it's easy to see why. —*N. J.*

PHILADELPHIA STORY, THE L: DIRECTORS/CUKOR, GEORGE (1940) 112M D: George Cukor. *Virginia Weidler, Ruth Hussey, Katherine Hepburn, Cary Grant, James Stewart, Roland Young.* This sophisticated comedy stars Hepburn as an unhappily repressed socialite whose impending marriage is interrupted by her dashing ex-husband (Grant as C. K. Dexter Haven) and a snooping magazine reporter (Stewart, who won an Oscar for the role). Cukor's rhythmic direction of the fiery love triangle and an award-winning screenplay resulted in a box-office smash and restored Hepburn's tarnished career. The three leads are excellent, but I think the outstanding supporting cast is the best part. The scene where Young (star of the *Topper* films) stumbles around with a hangover makes me laugh just thinking about it. *The Philadelphia Story* remains a beloved romantic screwball classic and deservedly so. —*S. H.*

PRISONER OF ZENDA L: DIRECTORS/CUKOR, GEORGE (1937) 101M D: George Cukor. *Madeleine Carroll, Douglas Fairbanks Jr., Mary Astor, David Niven, Raymond Massey, Ronald Colman.* There is a moment in this matchless screen version of Anthony Hope's classic adventure tale when Colman and Carrol join arms and walk down a long, royal staircase to inaugurate a ballroom sequence. The camera is on a crane, tracking back from them as they advance/descend. As the shot and they continue, for what feels like minutes, it seems that they will never run out of stairs, or ballroom, or glorious Hollywood space in which to enact the most splendid of high-toned period fantasies. *The Prisoner of Zenda* is golden-age Hollywood to the max—truly an all-star production on both sides

of the camera. The story is enchantment itself. English gentleman Rudolf Rassendyll (Colman), traveling on the Continent, is enlisted to carry on a short-term impersonation of the rightful ruler of Ruritania, whose spitting image he is. The real monarch has been kidnapped by his archrival, Black Michael (Massey). The people must never know of their nation's peril. And the king must prepare to go on with his marriage to the beauteous Flavia (Madeleine Carrol). And somebody really must knock the stuffing out of that curly-haired Machiavellian, Prince Rupert of Hentzau (Fairbanks in a movie-stealing villain role). Truly, they don't make glossy, swoonworthy movies like this anymore. —*R. T. J.*

ADVENTURES OF ROBIN HOOD, THE L: DIRECTORS/ CURTIZ, MICHAEL (1938) 102M D: Michael Curtiz. *Olivia de Havilland, Errol Flynn, Claude Rains, Basil Rathbone, Eugene Pallette, Alan Hale.* Flynn is the definitive Robin Hood in the most gloriously swashbuckling version of the legendary story. Flynn's confidence and cocky charm make for the perfect Robin Hood and he's paired with his most celebrated leading lady de Havilland, a delight as Maid Marion. On the side of the devils are the regal and haughty Rathbone as the aristocratic Sir Guy of Gisbourne and a smoothly conniving Rains as the decadent Prince John, a pair so oily they inspire Robin to form a medieval guerrilla rebel outfit (he calls them his Merry Men), hide out in Sherwood Forest, and "steal from the rich and give to the poor." Filmed in the rich hues of late 1930s Technicolor, helmed by the quintessential Hollywood artisan Curtiz, and set to the rousing strains of an Oscar-winning Erich Wolfgang Korngold score, this is a celebration of studio filmmaking and old-fashioned craftsmanship at its finest. —*S. A.*

CAPTAIN BLOOD L: DIRECTORS/CURTIZ, MICHAEL (1935) 119M D: Michael Curtiz. *Lionel Atwill, Basil Rathbone, Errol Flynn, Olivia de Havilland.* This was Flynn's first film, and he wasn't even originally slated for the part. Dr. Peter Blood is arrested for offering medical aid to a rebel. Wrongfully convicted of treason and sentenced to death, he is instead sold into slavery. Blood manages to escape with many of his fellow slaves, turning to a life of piracy upon the high seas. Over time he finds that a compatriot pirate captain has captured the woman who purchased Blood in the first place. He is determined to rescue her and win her over to his side. Upon returning her home, he finds the city under siege by the French. When he learns that the rebellion is over and that there is a new king on the throne of England, Blood rescues the city and ironically becomes the new governor. The story is sound, well written, and entertaining, but Flynn brought his good looks and enthusiastic talent to the role, making his mark and starting off his career with a bang. —*M. N.*

CASABLANCA L: DIRECTORS/CURTIZ, MICHAEL (1942) 102M D: Michael Curtiz. *Paul Henreid, Peter Lorre, Humphrey Bogart, Claude Rains, Ingrid Bergman.* *Casablanca* has been quoted, imitated, and parodied so much that it is almost anachronistic unto itself. Each new generation might find this formative film to be absolute kitsch unless they could remove all the copies and parodies from their prejudice. Bogart plays the owner of a gin house in Morocco during World War II. As he is beholden to the Vichy French (who occupy the area) he can't let it be known that he is actually against the Nazi party. It's within this tense environment that Bergman appears, playing his long-lost love. The expressions of tenderness and sacrifice between these two characters were readily understood by most cultures at the time, thereby catapulting this well-made film to the status of cinematic icon. Who could have known, considering that George Raft was preferred over Bogart and that the famous last scene was for all practical purposes improvised? —*N.J.*

EGYPTIAN,THE L: DIRECTORS/CURTIZ, MICHAEL (1954) 139M D: Micheal Curtiz. *Gene Tierney, Michael Wilding, Jean Simmons, Victor Mature.* The ultimate Bible movie isn't a Bible movie at all. When Hollywood moguls ran out of Bible stories, they looked elsewhere for inspiration. So, when Mika Waltari's novel about ancient Egypt's only monotheistic dynasty topped the best-seller charts in the United States for two years running, boy did they get inspired! But was turning Akhenaton into a Christ figure really what they were looking for? Wilding does his beatific best in the title role and a great score and cinematography help, but it's hard to suppress amazed giggles while enjoying this perfectly misguided work. —*K.S.*

KING CREOLE L: DIRECTORS/CURTIZ, MICHAEL (1958) 115M D: Michael Curtiz. *Paul Stewart, Elvis Presley, Carolyn Jones, Vic Morrow, Dolores Hart, Walter Matthau.* When Elvis first started making movies, he usually appeared in fairly serious roles as a tough, misunderstood youth. *King Creole* was a project originally slated for James Dean, and Elvis was a good choice as a replacement. He plays a singing busboy at a cocktail lounge frequented by bad-guy mobster Maxie Fields (Matthau) who wants to use Elvis as the new star at one of his nightclubs. Things get complicated when Maxie's girlfriend (Jones, aka Morticia Addams) takes a shining to the scrappy young singer. Elvis just wants to be happy with cute Nellie (Hart) and use his stardom to help his family. Unfortunately Maxie and his henchmen have other ideas. From the director of *Casablanca*, *King Creole* features plenty of fine acting and a tense plot to go along with the Elvis tunes. Even non–Elvis fans will dig *King Creole*. —*S.H.*

MILDRED PIERCE L: DIRECTORS/CURTIZ, MICHAEL (1945) 111M D: Michael Curtiz. *Joan Crawford, Jack Carson, Zachary Scott, Eve Arden, Ann Blyth.* Crawford won her sole Academy Award and revived her floundering career as the driven single mother who sacrifices everything for her spoiled daughter (already a fatale as a mere child femme, and truly cold-blooded when she grows up) in this James M. Cain adaptation. Mildred falls out of a middle-class marriage and into a demeaning job as a waitress, then climbs up the mountain of success solely to satisfy her daughter's greed and shallow sense of social respectability. Directed in inky shades of night by Curtiz, it's a melodrama seeped in the shadow of noir (or is it a film noir tinged with melodrama?) and a snappy "woman's picture" (thanks largely to the sardonic dialogue tossed off by best friend and gal Friday Arden). Carson and Bennet costar, and Scott plays his trademark gigolo with weasely insincerity. —*S.A.*

WHITE CHRISTMAS L: DIRECTORS/CURTIZ, MICHAEL (1954) 120M D: Michael Curtiz. *Danny Kaye, Bing Crosby, Rosemary Clooney, Vera Ellen.* *White Christmas* mixes the "let's put on a big show to save our beloved but troubled place of business" story with traditional holiday fare. Bob Wallace (Crosby) and Phil Davis (Kaye) are two army buddies who exit the service and enter stardom. They sing, they dance, they write, they produce shows with glitzy, pointless numbers. Enter Betty and Judy Haynes, a "sister act" who want in on a little of the Wallace and Davis action. Davis sees his chance to get a little action of his own, so they follow the girls up to a inn in Vermont for Christmas, where they run into their former general who has fallen on bad times. This movie sometimes feels like a mere showcase for the talents of its stars (how many times do we need to see the impossibly thin Ellen prance around?), but it's not Christmas without it. —*J.K.*

YANKEE DOODLE DANDY L: DIRECTORS/CURTIZ, MICHAEL (1942) 125M D: Michael Curtiz. *James Cagney, Joan Leslie, Walter Huston, Rosemary DeCamp.* Cagney won his only Academy Award playing George M. Cohan in the rousing Curtiz biopic. Cagney was a song-and-dance man before he found fame as a movie tough guy and he returns to his roots with a passion, dancing his way through the role with straight-backed, stiff-legged formality while his body is coiled like a loaded spring about to leap. The story of his spunky rise in the showbiz world is pure Hollywood hogwash, but it's delightful hogwash invigorated by Cagney's cocksure drive. Huston and De Camp play his vaudevillian parents and Leslie is the love of his life (for whom he writes the song "Mary"—"plain as any name can be"). It's a real flag-waver of a showbiz tale, a Fourth of July celebration with Cagney setting off the fireworks. —*S.A.*

BRUTE FORCE L: DIRECTORS/DASSIN, JULES (1947) 102M D: Jules Dassin. *Charles Bickford, Jeff Corey, Hume Cronyn, Sam Levene, Burt Lancaster.* Lancaster's cold, hard career-criminal-behind-bars squares off against the sadistic prison guard Cronyn, whose gentle features hide a menacing, dictatorial monster. Dassin captures the tensions building as the torture (mental and physical), the climate of fear, and the claustrophobia of overcrowded quarters turn the population into a volatile, combustible pressure bomb with a hair trigger. The oppressive atmosphere of the prison—cavernous halls echoing with footsteps and clanking bars, the tiny courtyard overwhelmed by guard towers, the muddy hellhole known as the drainpipe—can be felt in every richly realized frame. An explosive prison drama and one of the most brutal films noir ever made. —S. A.

NAKED CITY L: DIRECTORS/DASSIN, JULES (1948) 96M D: Jules Dassin. *Howard Duff, John Marley, Barry Fitzgerald. Naked City* is arguably the hard-boiled prototype for most of the crime dramas dominating network television today. New York City police investigate the tragic death of a jet-setting young model, with dozens of suspects to sift through. Lt. Dan Muldoon (Fitzgerald), heading the investigation, is as close as we come to a protagonist; *Naked City* is far less interested in following him than it is in the murder investigation. Subsequently, the story trudges through a number of real-life New York locations, moving from one cop to another through various, often mundane, facets of the police proceedings leading to an arrest, as well as through the media's parallel journalistic investigations. Resisting a more human element, *Naked City* never comes close to losing momentum and is more interesting for its lack of personality. —C. B.

RIFIFI L: DIRECTORS/DASSIN, JULES (1955) 118M D: Jules Dassin. *Carl Möhner, Perlo Vita, Robert Manuel, Jean Servais, Magali Noël.* "Rififi means danger," proclaimed the ads for this iconic French gangster film. Close enough. Haggard, worn-jewel-thief Servais is in threadbare suits and down to his last francs but still dapper and elegant when he hatches the perfect plan to rob a jewel shop. The thirty-five-minute heist scene is justly famous, thrillingly executed without a word spoken, and the entire film is meticulously shot with an eye for the dingy beauty of the Paris underworld. American expatriate Dassin's tale of honor among thieves, their patient professionalism, friendship, responsibility, and the romantic code of the "good" crooks and the merciless toll it exacts, established the tone and style of French crime films for years to come. —S. A.

COWBOY L: DIRECTORS/DAVES, DELMER (1958) 92M D: Delmer Daves. *Glenn Ford, Jack Lemmon, Richard Jaeckel.* The title applies: this is the rare Western that really does have some feeling for the working realities and sometimes deep pain of the cowboy's life. Chicago hotel clerk Frank Harris (Lemmon) lets himself in for it when he uses his savings to bail out a Texas cattleman (Ford) who bet on the wrong card. The new partners head south to cattle country, Harris hoping to continue his courtship of a well-born Mexican lady. Happily, *Cowboy* has no time for cutesy-poo romance or any other distraction. The film moves fast and along unexpected vectors, with crisp camera work and crisper editing. This is an original. —R. T. J.

DARK PASSAGE L: DIRECTORS/DAVES, DELMER (1947) 107M D: Delmer Daves. *Agnes Moorehead, Lauren Bacall, Humphrey Bogart, Bruce Bennett, Tom D'Andrea.* An escaped convict (Bogart) gets extensive facial surgery for a new identity and then goes about trying to prove that he was framed for the murder of his wife. For the first half of the film when Bogart is supposed to have a different face, the director chose to use mostly first-person perspective (a technique that was used to its fullest in *Lady in the Lake*). As such, Bogart is really in only half of this film, but the supporting cast is strong throughout. Moorehead plays the bull-headed woman who happens to be his old flame, and Bacall plays the compassionate woman who takes him in. It's a fascinating and rather different sort of film noir. —N. J.

3:10 TO YUMA L: DIRECTORS/DAVES, DELMER (1957) 92M D: Delmer Daves. *Glenn Ford, Van Heflin, Felicia Farr, Leora Dana, Henry Jones, Richard Jaeckel.* A farmer (Heflin), hit hard by a drought, agrees to take in a wanted man (Ford in a wonderfully underplayed performance) for the bounty in this taut Western in the *High Noon* mode. Daves, a former movie all-rounder, found his métier in the Western in the mid-1950s, and this is his best. Set in the barren, parched West, this is a film defined by emptiness and dust, its players alone and vulnerable in the eerie landscape. The story is pure Elmore Leonard, both deflating and celebrating against-all-odds heroism in a well-plotted waiting game as the charming, cunning, and deadly gunman Ford picks at Heflin's confidence while slowly warming to his sense of honor and duty. It's a modest but tense little thriller with excellent turns by Jones (as a town drunk who proves his worth in selfless sacrifice) and Jaeckel (as Ford's smiling second in command). —S. A.

KHARTOUM L: DIRECTORS/DEARDEN, BASIL (1966) 136M D: Basil Dearden. *Richard Johnson, Alexander Knox, Ralph Richardson, Laurence Olivier, Charlton Heston.* Heston is General Charles "Chinese" Gordon in this sweeping story of the 1880 battle between the British and the Madhi (Olivier behind a thick beard and brownface makeup) in the Sudan. Made in the shadow of *Lawrence of Arabia*, it opens with a spectacular desert battle but then depends on the fascinating figure of Gordon to carry it along, and Heston is up to the challenge. He plays the vain Gordon with a cocky flair, as a brilliant maverick with a mystic's passion who routinely disobeys orders at his whim and plays politics with the wiles of a guerrilla statesman. Dearden is no epic director, but he plays the game of wills and wiles with a nice understanding of imperialist realpolitik maneuvering. By the end it's more *55 Days at Peking* than *Lawrence,* less imperialistic than the latter and less subtle than the former, but always compelling. —*S. A.*

BLADE II L: DIRECTORS/DEL TORO, GUILLERMO (2002) 116M D: Guillermo Del Toro. *Ron Perlman, Luke Goss, Kris Kristofferson, Wesley Snipes, Norman Reedus.* The great Mexican director Del Toro (*Cronos, The Devil's Backbone*) managed to perfectly recapture the tone of the first *Blade* and throw in weirder monsters, more sympathetic villains, and a strong cast of new supporting characters. This time Blade (Snipes) must team with a special ops team of vampire badasses to fight a new monster that feeds on both vampires and humans. Del Toro regular Perlman has a great rivalry with Blade, and Hong Kong hero Donnie Yen (who choreographed some of the fights) makes a brief appearance. The fights this time around are more memorable, using innovative computer effects to mimic comic-book-style superhuman combat. One enemy swings Blade around and his head smashes right through a cement pillar! An extremely satisfying sequel. —*B. T.*

CRONOS L: DIRECTORS/DEL TORO, GUILLERMO (1993) 92M D: Guillermo Del Toro. *Ron Perlman, Tamara Shanath, Margarita Isabel, Claudio Brook, Federico Luppi.* Del Toro (*Blade 2*) made his feature debut with this striking twist on the vampire legend. Luppi is a curio shop owner who stumbles upon a clockwork device that looks like some Quay Brothers creation and revives his fading energy while creating a druglike addiction and a craving for blood. As the old man's granddaughter plays angel to the devils of his addiction, a Howard Hughes–like millionaire recluse sends a brutal henchman (Perlman) to retrieve the immortality device. Part melodrama, part morality play, part thriller, it's as much Dorian Gray as Bram Stoker and features a weird, heady alchemic brew of antiquated clockwork mechanism, mutant organisms, demented villains driven by a greed for youth, and one man's struggle for his soul. Cool, creepy, tempered with a clever gallows humor and anchored by a passion for life and love. —*S. A.*

DEVIL'S BACKBONE, THE L: DIRECTORS/DEL TORO, GUILLERMO (2001) 106M D: Guillermo Del Toro. *Fernando Tielve, Eduardo Noriega, Federico Luppi, Marisa Paredes.* Del Toro's eerie, complex ghost story takes place in an orphanage where the kids are stranded between the Spanish Civil War, a stash of gold, an unexploded bomb, and the ghost of a little boy. It's full of people and things trapped in limbo, just like the bomb that is stuck in the ground in the town square but hasn't gone off. It's more along the lines of *Cronos* than Del Toro's other films, but bigger in its cast and scope. Even more so than in *Mimic,* be ready for horrible things to happen to the characters, even if they are kids. There are also some inventive and subtle uses of digital effects. —*B. T.*

MIMIC L: DIRECTORS/DEL TORO, GUILLERMO (1997) 105M D: Guillermo Del Toro. *Mira Sorvino, Jeremy Northam, Josh Brolin, Giancarlo Giannini, Charles S. Dutton.* A New York entomologist (Sorvino) stops an insect-born plague by genetically engineering cockroaches called the Judas Breed. Years later the bugs have adapted so well that they are wandering alleys and sewers mimicking the appearance of humans. Del Toro's first attempt at a studio film is a mixed bag with a script that suffers from some reliance on action clichés, and why do bugs in movies always make loud chirping sounds, anyway? But it has some effective atmosphere and traces of the director's sick imagination. I can forgive any flaws just based on the scene that reveals what the stranger in the subway actually is. —*B. T.*

GREATEST SHOW ON EARTH, THE L: DIRECTORS/DeMILLE, CECIL B. (1952) 152M D: *Gloria Grahame, James Stewart, Dorothy Lamour, Betty Hutton, Cornel Wilde, Charlton Heston.* The next time someone complains how the Oscars have turned commercial, remind them that in 1952 *The Greatest Show on Earth* won for Best Picture. It's not a bad film, but this unwieldy, elephantine mix of melodrama, spectacle, and splashy showmanship is hardly a sterling example of Hollywood classical cinema at its best. So why is it so much fun? Because it's pure C. B. DeMille: sprawling, loud, garish, full of cheeseball melodramatics and big-top thrills, and one of the greatest train wrecks ever. Heston reigns over the chaos as the slow-speaking manager of the Ringling Bros. and Barnum & Bailey Circus, a ringmaster in leather whose terse authority is matched by Grahame's tough but tender girl Friday and part-time elephant girl. Also stars Stewart as a fugitive behind clown white. —*S. A.*

TEN COMMANDMENTS, THE (1956) L: DIRECTORS/ DeMILLE, CECIL B. (1956) 220M D: Cecil B. DeMille. *Anne Baxter, Edward G. Robinson, Charlton Heston, Yul Brynner.* DeMille wanted to shake the world with this live-action version of the life of Moses, which succeeded in becoming a worldwide box-office smash. Remaking his own silent film from 1925, DeMille starts the picture with baby Moses (who grows up to be played by Heston) as a child floating down the Nile in a wicker basket. Saved by members of the Pharaoh's household, Moses grows up a favorite of the Egyptian ruler (Brynner). When Moses learns of his Jewish heritage he must turn against his Egyptian stepfather and lead his people to freedom. The plagues brought down on the Egyptians are filmed like a horror movie, and the parting of the Red Sea is a marvelous effect even today in the era of digital technology. The all-star cast does far better in this than most of the large-screen biblical epics that would follow in the '60s, and the film represents the pinnacle of Heston's career as a leading man. The DVD includes the introduction by Demille and is letterboxed, preserving its Vistavision framing. —*N. H.*

WHY CHANGE YOUR WIFE? L: DIRECTORS/DeMILLE, CECIL B. (1920) 100M D: Cecil B. DeMille. *Bebe Daniels, Thomas Meighan, Gloria Swanson.* A funny, funny social comedy that is smart and revealing about relationships. A proper wife (Swanson) nags at her husband (Meighan), trying to improve him but ending up sending him innocently into arms of another woman, the conniving Daniels. He's tricked and trapped into a painful divorce and grudging second marriage. Now free, his former wife realizes the pettiness of her genteel ways and lets down her hair, lifts up her skirt, and starts to dance with the joy of living. Then, the former couple bumps into each other at a vacation resort. The acting of the three principals is precise and exquisite, and the script is fresh, lively, and deeply intelligent. DeMille is behind it all, winking at you when the moral lesson is expounded. —*J. C.*

CAGED HEAT L: DIRECTORS/DEMME, JONATHAN (1974) 93M D: Jonathan Demme. *Erica Gavin, Juanita Brown, Barbara Steele.* Demme's directorial debut is the greatest women-in-prison movie ever made, a film that both satisfies every requirement of the genre (babes behind bars, gratuitous nudity, showers, and shock treatment) and punctuates it with an underdog burst of grrrl-power rebellion. Demme never tries to pretend it's anything more than what it seems—a trashy, energetic exploitation flick for the drive-in circuit—so there are no "messages" to weigh down the fast and furious action, merely a mean sense of satire and creative flourishes around the edges. Russ Meyer alumnus Gavin and tough-cookie Brown are the brassy babes who make their way out, then plot their break-in to rescue their cell-block sisters from a corrupt prison doctor. The bluesy score is by Velvet Underground veteran John Cale, and cinematographer Tak Fujimoto went on to shoot almost every one of Demme's subsequent films, including *Silence of the Lambs.* —*S. A.*

MELVIN AND HOWARD L: DIRECTORS/DEMME, JONATHAN (1980) 95M D: Jonathan Demme. *Gloria Grahame, Paul LeMat, Jason Robards, Mary Steenburgen, Michael J. Pollard, Joe Spinell.* Based on the true story about a guy named Melvin Dummar (LeMat) who picks up an elderly hitchhiker that turns out to be Howard Hughes (Robards). Howard names Melvin as a beneficiary in his will and a legal battle erupts. Much of the film exists within Melvin's blue-collar world, filled with authentic details like crappy jobs and three-dimensional characters (Steenburgen won the Best Supporting Actress Oscar for her role). The humor is low-key, letting the actors inhabit an

authentic Americana that rings truer than most Hollywood attempts at similar stories. Demme's first mainstream success is one of the best films of the '80s. —*S. H.*

SILENCE OF THE LAMBS, THE L: DIRECTORS/DEMME, JONATHAN (1991) 118M D: Jonathan Demme. *Anthony Hopkins, Scott Glenn, Anthony Heald, Brooke Smith, Jodie Foster.* Based on the novel by Thomas Harris, *Silence of the Lambs* grabbed four Oscars and redefined the genre of the psychological thriller. Foster plays an FBI cadet with a degree in psychology. When a nasty serial killer proves difficult to catch, the GVI asks her to probe the imprisoned psycho-killer Hannibal Lecter (Hopkins). With his disturbed personality, however, it becomes difficult to determine who is analyzing whom. Great direction and stunning acting make this unique story come to life. The sequel *Hannibal* followed ten years later. —*N. J.*

STOP MAKING SENSE L: DIRECTORS/DEMME, JONATHAN (1984) 99M D: Jonathan Demme. *Tina Weymouth, Chris Frantz, Jerry Harrison, David Byrne.* This isn't your average concert video. Demme (*Silence of the Lambs, Philadelphia*) employs a stunning use of camera and editing, such that you'd swear you were in attendance with the best seat in the house. Filmed in December 1983 over three nights at the Pantages Theater in Hollywood, this film features the Talking Heads performing such songs as "Psycho Killer," "Heaven," "Burning Down the House," "Once in a Lifetime," and "Take Me to the River." The sweeping use of the stage, the lighting, and the rear-projected slides give the concert a strong sense of progression. Byrne's costume change near the end into the Big Suit is uproarious. The widescreen DVD has remixed and remastered sound, as well as audio commentary by Demme and the band. —*N. J.*

SWIMMING TO CAMBODIA L: DIRECTORS/DEMME, JONATHAN (1987) 85M D: Jonathan Demme. *Spalding Gray.* *Swimming* is a monologue about Gray's experience as a supporting actor on the film *The Killing Fields.* Clearly, he's more than just an actor; he is a veritable orator and wry comedian who is able to teach us about Cambodia and the U.S. involvement there while making it all quite entertaining and amusing. To this he adds his own personal and uncanny experiences. Demme, who demonstrated his unique eye for the stage with the Talking Heads in *Stop Making Sense,* adds measurably without distracting from Gray's delivery. Two similar Gray vehicles followed the success of this low-budget film, *Monster in a Box* and *Gray's Anatomy.* —*N. J.*

BAY OF ANGELS L: DIRECTORS/DEMY, JACQUES (1963) 85M D: Jacques Demy. *Claude Mann, Jeanne Moreau.* Demy's films never struck me as the most interesting of the early Nouvelle Vague, and certainly this film pales in comparison with such contemporary work as *Breathless* or *The 400 Blows.*

Basically a love story involving two reckless gamblers running wild in Nice, the film draws parallels between their irrational and obsessive desires for love and money, the love affair itself rendered as a game of roulette. A promising premise greatly enhanced by Moreau's typical top-notch performance, it's tragic this film isn't better. Sadly, the film's entirely too topical, with little merit beyond its insights on gambling addiction (which for all I know might be totally off-base) and, again, Moreau's show-stealing. Maybe worth looking into if you've already exhausted the catalog of black-and-white Truffauts and Godards (though I would then steer you toward *Les Bonnes Femmes*). —*C. B.*

DONKEY SKIN L: DIRECTORS/DEMY, JACQUES (1970) 100M D: Jacques Demy. *Catherine Deneuve, Micheline Presle, Jacques Perrin, Jean Marais.* Demy does a wonderful job of faithfully adapting seventeenth-century fairy tale tycoon Charles Perrault's story of the same name, which is pretty impressive considering it features a jewel-shitting donkey, a toad-spitting wench, and other such improbable entities. The story centers around the proverbial beautiful princess (Deneuve) whose mother, the queen (also Deneuve), upon her deathbed asks the king (Marais) to remarry only if he can find a woman more beautiful and talented than her. This proves to be no small task, and the only woman who matches the bill is—*gasp*—his daughter! Much fantastical drama ensues in rainbow-colored glory, including music by the incomparable Michel Legrand. No director captured Deneuve's youthful charm and grace quite like Demy; fans shouldn't miss this one. It's a magical, incest-tinged fairy tale like none other. —*E. O.*

LOLA L: DIRECTORS/DEMY, JACQUES (1961) 90M D: Jacques Demy. *Elina Labourdette, Anouk Aimee, Marc Michel, Alan Scott, Jacques Harden.* Demy's debut feature is a bittersweet musical without the music. It's lyrically shot in his hometown of Nantes in black-and-white CinemaScope by New Wave master Raoul Coutard, and set to a lovely score by Michel Legrand. Aimee, whose appearance in lacy tights, boa, and top hat made her an eternal pin-up dream, is a single mother in Nantes, working her way along the port towns while looking for the father of her child, and only occasionally taking consolation in the arms (and the beds) of the men smitten by her charms. As in so many of his films, Demy reveals himself as both eager romantic and sadder-but-wiser realist, and for all the dashed dreams of the film it still manages to have its swoon-y romantic fantasy come true. The story was practically remade as *The Umbrellas of Cherbourg,* a genuine Technicolor musical, a few years later, but with the emphasis on the bittersweet. —*S. A.*

UMBRELLAS OF CHERBOURG, THE L: DIRECTORS/DEMY, JACQUES (1964) 87M D: Jacques Demy. *Catherine Deneuve, Nino Castelnuovo.* Demy's legendary musical is a film entirely sung (from a libretto by Demy set to Michel Legrand's famed score), a bittersweet story of two young lovers (Deneuve and Castelnuovo) who are separated by the Algerian war, their lives pulled in different directions. The candy-colored sets suggest the great Hollywood musicals: bright, clean, a utopian world, but with a distinctly French flavor. Instead of elaborate numbers, we get intimate staging where every movement becomes like a dance. Instead of a traditional happy ending it's a stoic, moving moment that tempers the romance with the compromises that make real life so unpredictable. —*S. A.*

BEAU TRAVAIL L: DIRECTORS/DENIS, CLAIRE (1999) 90M D: Claire Denis. *Grégoire Colin, Michel Subor, Denis Lavant.* This movie holds top prize for having one of the most mind-fucking endings I have ever seen. It requires some patience (of the three people that watched this film with me, two, my roommates, went to bed). I, however, endured and boy-oh-boy was I ever glad I did. The style and execution of the film is a bit artsy and pretentious, but the last scene nullifies and invalidates any critical quibbles that you might have with its approach. Anyway, I was so flipped out over the ending that I woke my roommates up. —*T. C.*

FRIDAY NIGHT L: DIRECTORS/DENIS, CLAIRE (2002) 90M D: Claire Denis. *Hélène de Saint-Pére, Valérie Lemercier, Vincent Lindon.* American films are self-conscious about physical love and one-night stands, as if embarrassed by the whole idea. Denis feels her way through the fleeting emotions, excited anticipation, and tingling thrill of a one-night stand had by Laure (Lemercier), a nervous single woman apprehensive about a life-changing decision when she meets a handsome stranger (Lindon). We know little of their lives outside of this night. Denis's camera, always in motion, hovers intimately around Lemercier to drink in the symphony of emotions that plays across her anxious, excited face. You can almost feel the textures through the light, shadow, and sounds. *Friday Night* is as sensuous and intimate work of cinema as there is, a film that luxuriates in the immediacy of the moment. There is no guilt to the act, only exhilaration, joy, and freedom. —*S. A.*

NENETTE AND BONI L: DIRECTORS/DENIS, CLAIRE (1996) 103M D: Claire Denis. *Grégoire Colin, Alice Houri, Jacques Nolot, Vincent Gallo.* There's really no question that *Beau Travail* is Denis's most accomplished and perhaps greatest film to date, but *Nenette and Boni* is far more charming, and maybe more exciting. Boni is a hotheaded pizza vendor who fantasizes about the baker's wife, and Nenette is his defiant younger sister who shows up at his place pregnant. We come to know this guarded pair through a series of slight, under-played vignettes captured by Agnès Godard's typically alluring camera work. Although brimming with masterful filmmaking from start to finish, the film's real magic is more difficult to put a finger on. A true work of beauty, the film draws enormously from a contagious fascination with itself. Without question, this is one of the most enchanting films I've ever seen. —C. B.

NO FEAR, NO DIE L: DIRECTORS/DENIS, CLAIRE (1990) 97M D: Claire Denis. *Solveig Dommartin, Jean-Claude Brialy, Isaach de Bankolé, Alex Descas.* Set in France's cockfighting underworld, *No Fear, No Die* follows a pair of West Indies immigrants who train roosters for fights organized by shady entrepreneur Ardennes (Brialy). While Jocelyn (Descas) handles the business end, Dah (de Bankolé) trains the roosters. Dah has a natural talent and a passion for his work, treating the roosters like beloved pets and relating to them better than to people. Attempting to boost excitement at the fights, Ardennes orders lethal razor-blade attachments for the roosters' feet. Normally quiet and introspective, Dah lashes out over this unnecessary cruelty, and the business relationship rapidly erodes. This film could've been an obvious exploration of the connection between masculinity and brutality, but a subdued pace, a distanced tone, and an absorbing sense of the everyday make for something substantial enough to obliterate interest in the social agendas possibly lurking below the surface. —C. B.

CARLITO'S WAY L: DIRECTORS/DePALMA, BRIAN (1993) 141M D: Brian DePalma. *John Leguizamo, Sean Penn, Luis Guzman, Penelope Ann Miller, Al Pacino.* DePalma may have made the loveliest, most dramatic movie of his career back in '93, so understated and off-topic for him that it is still forgotten when people callously refer to him as the "masturbator of suspense." Nothing like that is going on here, as Pacino turns in an achingly restrained, melancholy performance as Carlito, an ex-con trying to go straight. *Mystic River* aside, Penn has never been better than he was here as Pacino's best friend, a scumbag lawyer. Shot on the streets of New York, mostly at night and in the rain, this "little" DePalma film still has some amazing set pieces, but ultimately it is a simple tale of redemption and grace. Guzman and Leguizamo (as well as Viggo Mortenson) add much spice as the various scumbags Carlito has to contend with on his journey to salvation. —M. S.

CARRIE L: DIRECTORS/DePALMA, BRIAN (1976) 98M D: Brian DePalma. *Sissy Spacek, Piper Laurie, Amy Irving, John Travolta.* Carrie is the daughter of a freaky religious zealot, and has tampons thrown at her by scary naked '70s girls when she gets her first period in a high school–locker room shower.

She's sheltered and innocent, and is the object of constant ridicule. What her asshole peers don't realize is that Carrie is also telekinetic, and when they plan a big prank to play on her at the prom involving pigs' blood and public humiliation, we find out exactly what it takes to push an already miserable girl over the edge. Not a traditionally scary movie, *Carrie* packs more of a psychological punch. The characters are strongly stereotyped, but this contributes to the eerie feel of the film. Carrie could very easily be the girl next door, and you could be the guy plastered to a windshield when she finally snaps. —J. S.

DRESSED TO KILL L: DIRECTORS/DePALMA, BRIAN (1980) 105M D: Brian DePalma. *Nancy Allen, Dennis Franz, Keith Gordon, Angie Dickinson, Michael Caine.* Consider this stylistic tour de force DePalma's urban reimagining of Hitchcock's *Psycho* in a world of obsessions and erotic fantasies. Think about it: the reckless heroine murdered in the opening act, the amateur detectives (Gordon and Allen) who team up to find the mysterious killer, the doubles and doppelgangers, even the psychiatrist who explains it all in end. This being DePalma, of course, that's never the end: the nightmare lives on. Dickinson is the sexually frustrated wife whose impulsive midday affair seems to set it all in motion. Caine is the psychiatrist who thinks he knows the killer, a patient of his who torments him with phone calls and taunts him with hints of further murders. DePalma's play with perspective and point of view is stunning and his silky style has a sinister elegance to it. —S. A.

FEMME FATALE L: DIRECTORS/DePALMA, BRIAN (2002) 114M D: Brian DePalma. *Edouard Montoute, Antonio Banderas, Rebecca Romijn-Stamos, Peter Coyote, Eriq Ebouaney.* When we first see Romijn-Stamos, she's disguised as a paparazzo, involved in an elaborate jewel heist/lesbian make-out session in the bathroom at the Cannes Film Festival, and we leave her several years, countries, personas, and out-of-left-field plot twists later with a little bit more understanding of where she's coming from. In other words, this is the ultimate DePalma movie. Rather than trying to reconfigure the studio event movie into his style as he had done with *Mission Impossible* and *Mission to Mars*, DePalma returned to the obsessions of his best thrillers (voyeurism, dualism, mistaken identity, coincidence). This time he puts the audience manipulation into overdrive, forcing you to repeatedly shift your allegiance from character to character, giving you one idea of what they're up to and then showing you that you're completely wrong. At one point there's a plot twist that seems completely absurd, but if you give it a second you'll find that it makes more sense than it appeared to at first glance. It's unusual to see a director this late in his career able to create something like he did when he was young, but better. —B. T.

FURY, THE L: DIRECTORS/DePALMA, BRIAN (1978) 118M
D: Brian DePalma. *Amy Irving, John Cassavetes, Kirk Douglas.* This wonderfully goofy DePalma flick opens with Middle Eastern terrorists kidnapping shirtless Douglas's son on a beach and continues as he (shirtlessly) evades evil government agent Cassavetes. Irving shows up as a psychic teenager and a mystery unfolds involving a school for gifted youngsters, full of trademark DePalma visual flourishes. But the real joy is Douglas's giddy performance as a (mostly) shirtless man searching for his son. He's in full-bore silly mode as he explains how he "killed" Cassavetes's arm with a machine gun, holds a hilarious old woman and her kids hostage, and even feigns mental retardation over the phone to avoid wiretaps. Also, I believe this is the only movie featuring "Exploding Cassavetes." —*K. C.*

HOME MOVIES L: DIRECTORS/DePALMA, BRIAN (1979) 89M
D: Brian DePalma. *Keith Gordon, Nancy Allen, Kirk Douglas.* In this cheesy comedy, Gordon plays a nerd convinced by a famous film professor/cult leader (Douglas) that he is an extra in his own life. He tries to change himself into the star, filming himself as he does it. This is by far DePalma's silliest and most amateurish film, so it's not too surprising that he did it as a project for a filmmaking class at Sarah Lawrence College. His students acted as the crew and got their chance to work with Douglas. It's a throwaway, with none of DePalma's usual cinematic flair, but it still contains many of his primary themes including voyeurism, spy devices, infidelity, and split personalities. —*B. T.*

MISSION: IMPOSSIBLE L: DIRECTORS/DePALMA, BRIAN (1996) 110M D: Brian DePalma. *Ving Rhames, Jon Voight, Tom Cruise, Henry Czerny, Jean Reno, Emmanuelle Béart.* Cruise plays Ethan Hunt, a protégé of the TV series–lead Jim Phelps (Voight), who gets framed as a traitor and has to prove his innocence and catch the real culprit while on the run. He gets what he needs using clever deceits, disguises, and gadgets, and this leads into some breathtakingly tense set pieces like the famous break-in at the CIA headquarters, which leaves Hunt hanging from pulleys in a silent chamber. This is DePalma's most successful foray into mainstream summer-event movies because it works on the level of a normal, crowd-pleasing thriller but contains many distinct DePalma touches and innovations like a scene where Hunt talks about one version of an earlier event while flashing back and realizing what actually happened. Some fans of the TV show were angry about the unexpected turns in the plot, which they felt betrayed the characters and concepts of the show. Imagine—being upset because a *Mission: Impossible* movie was too surprising! —*B. T.*

MISSION TO MARS L: DIRECTORS/DePALMA, BRIAN (2000) 112M D: Brian DePalma. *Connie Nielsen, Tim Robbins, Don Cheadle, Jerry O'Connell, Gary Sinise.* DePalma is a brilliant director of horror and suspense, but evidently not of science fiction. In this film a mission to Mars that includes Robbins, Sinise, and Nielsen accomplishes the goal of locating Cheadle, who had survived an earlier failed mission. They also happen to come across vastly superior intelligent life as well as the very secrets of the cosmos! This epiphany is depicted in the most emotive manner possible, making Spielberg's *E. T.* seem a bit restrained. I left the theater feeling as though I had been slimed. But who knows? Perhaps that's the desired effect. —*N. J.*

PHANTOM OF THE PARADISE, THE L: DIRECTORS/DePALMA, BRIAN (1974) 92M D: Brian DePalma. *Gian Maria Volonte, Paul Williams, William Finley, George Memmoli, Jessica Harper.* This is one of my all-time favorite demented musicals! An up-and-coming composer creates a masterpiece, a musical adaptation of *Faust.* A nefarious producer (with a dark secret) steals the music and claims it as his own for the opening of his new rock-opera club, the Paradise. Desperate to regain what is his, the composer goes through a number of harrowing experiences that leave him crippled, deformed, and determined for revenge. In the end the producer needs the composer and a devilish pact is struck, but neither knows the truth about the other as they pursue their own goals. It's a bizarre, surreal retelling of *The Phantom of the Opera* with wild characters, costumes, music, and madness. —*M. N.*

RAISING CAIN L: DIRECTORS/DePALMA, BRIAN (1992) 95M D: Brian DePalma. *Cindy Girard, Frances Stemhagen, John Lithgow, Lolita Davidovich, Steven Bauer.* A child psychologist (Lithgow) has his own childhood problems. Apparently this fellow's father experimented on him (a plot taken liberally from *Peeping Tom*) and with the help of his evil twin brother, Caine (Lithgow, again), he must use children to continue his father's research. Recycling good plots is common practice in Hollywood; in fact, that alone made DePalma great. But here the plot was clearly overcooked and worse, the main actor who plays multiple roles is encouraged to overact to such a degree that this film cannot even be qualified as a horror film. Or a suspense film. It is at best a comedy, and at that not a very good one. —*N. J.*

Lithgow perhaps never had a greater vehicle than this one, absolutely relishing the chance to play a variation on the Jekyll/Hyde type, chewing on every scene he appears in and doing it at just the right level. Given the script and the ludicrousness of the situations, there's really no way not to overdo things, but if you just sit back and enjoy the ride, you'll have a very wild time. Also worth mentioning is Stephen Burum's majestic cinematography, enhancing the ride even more with gobs of lovely, fluid Steadicam work in and around Northern California. *M. S.*

SCARFACE L: DIRECTORS/DePALMA, BRIAN (1983) 170M D: Brian DePalma. *Al Pacino, Steven Bauer, Michelle Pfeiffer, Mary Elizabeth Mastrantonio, Robert Loggia, F. Murray Abraham.* In updating the 1932 Howard Hawks film DePalma uses as his backdrop the pervasive culture of cocaine in the 1970s. Pacino is cast as a poor Cuban immigrant who can't stand washing dishes for a living. Together with his brother he tries his hand at drug dealing, but his first deal goes very badly as his brother is cut up with a chainsaw right in front of his eyes. Somehow Pacino manages to escape and whack the crooks, suddenly establishing himself in the hierarchy of drug dealing. The rest of the film is about how he rises to the top of the lucrative drug business, cracking heads all the way there. Abraham plays one such obstacle in his path. This film is ridiculously violent, yet Pacino allows you to focus on the twisted character who makes this whole underworld the hell it is. —*N. J.*

SISTERS L: DIRECTORS/DePALMA, BRIAN (1973) 93M D: Brian DePalma. *Charles Durning, William Finley, Margot Kidder, Jennifer Salt, Barnard Hughes.* This is arguably DePalma's finest horror film. Kidder plays a complex character—a Siamese twin whose sister died during separation. Consequently this confused woman is haunted by her sister, who seems to be the motivation for Kidder's violent episodes that culminate in the murder of a visitor to her apartment. She crudely hides this man's body inside the sofa bed and then must play innocent to a reporter who evidently witnessed the murder from outside her window. With Bernard Hermann's music this film quite deliberately has all the wonderful trappings of Hitchcock, a veritable language DePalma would use to great effect in many of his films to follow. —*N. J.*

UNTOUCHABLES, THE L: DIRECTORS/DePALMA, BRIAN (1987) 119M D: Brian DePalma. *Robert De Niro, Andy Garcia, Charles Martin Smith, Sean Connery, Kevin Costner.* Costner plays Eliot Ness, the G-man who brought down Al Capone in 1920s Chicago. De Niro is brilliant as Capone, bringing out all the evil and excess of that personality. The film is suspenseful and stylized, with an unflinching eye toward violence in addition to an incredible view of what the high life must have been like for the inner circle of gangsters during the era of Prohibition. The music by Ennio Moricconne helps make this film rise to nearly epic status. —*N. J.*

BICYCLE THIEF, THE L: DIRECTORS/DE SICA, VITTORIO (1947) 93M D: Vittorio De Sica. *Lianella Carell, Enzo Staiola, Lamberto Maggiorani.* The Italian title actually translates to *Bicycle Thieves,* plural,

which is key to the film. The search for the bicycle stolen from a man on the first day of his first job in two years is largely a symbol-laden vehicle (pun intended) for a portrait of depression-ridden postwar Rome. The etched-by-time face of Maggiorani, a steelworker picked by De Sica to be his everyman protagonist, projects a wounded dignity and desperation that could stand in for the country. In the fifty years since its release the melodrama and sentimentality haven't aged well, but then the strength of the film has never been its plot but the sum of its snapshot-like scenes: the desolate apartments on the outskirts of town, the bustling street markets, and the crowded sidewalks where pedestrians huddle during a flash storm. —*S. A.*

UMBERTO D L: DIRECTORS/DE SICA, VITTORIO (1952) 89M D: Vittorio De Sica. *Lina Gennari, Carlo Battisti, Maria Pia Casilio.* Once held up as an example of a pure everyday cinematic aesthetic, today the film looks like a rather sentimental example of naturalism—which is not to deny that it's excellent. The film opens on a crowd of white-collar pensioners gathered in protest, which gradually thins until Umberto (Battisti) emerges as our singular protagonist, a shorthand representation of an entire social class. Struggling for money, unable to meet his rent or even keep warm at night, Umberto's standard of living erodes until his self-respect and very will to live are in peril. Added to the equation is his controversially adorable dog Flike (who many critics regard as the Jar Jar Binks of neorealism). A quintessential film of Italian neorealism, this disarmingly moving film paved the way for much of the best cinema being made today. —*C. B.*

HOUSE OF WAX L: DIRECTORS/DE TOTH, ANDRÉ (1953) 88M D: André De Toth. *Vincent Price, Frank Lovejoy, Carolyn Jones, Phyllis Kirk.* Price is the co-owner of a wax museum who gets horribly disfigured when his partner burns the place down for the insurance money. But Price manages to get back on his feet a few years later with a new museum that has extremely lifelike dummies who, uh, just happen to look exactly like various missing people connected to his old business partner. Charles Bronson (credited as Charles Buchinsky) plays Price's assistant, Igor. This is one of Price's greatest roles. Unfortunately the great 3-D of the original film cannot be re-created at home (it requires a special projector lens and a silver screen). —*B. T.*

RAMROD L: DIRECTORS/DE TOTH, ANDRÉ (1947) 95M D: André De Toth. *Preston S. Foster, Veronica Lake, Joel McCrea, Donald Crisp, Arleen Whalen.* The Western started going a little nuts after World War II. This one is a full-fledged film noir. However complicated the original Luke Short novel may have been, the movie is a gurgling stew of mixed motives, cross-purposes, deceit, back-shooting, and failures of nerve and/or morality. De Toth builds paranoia and ambiguity right into his mise-en-scène; a favorite tack is to back into a scene ahead of an advancing character and let the sinister possibilities of the unknown terrain disclose themselves one foot at a time. Lake, as a decorous prairie lily turned femme fatale, was married to De Toth at the time. De Toth anticipates his fine late-'50s Western *Day of the Outlaw* with a Western town that really seems like a specific place, in which getting to know the rooms and buildings and how they relate to one another is almost a parallel narrative unto itself. —*R. T. J.*

DEVIL COMMANDS, THE L: DIRECTORS/DMYTRYK, EDWARD (1941) 65M D: Edward Dmytryk. *Amanda Duff, Anne Revere, Richard Fiske, Boris Karloff.* Karloff plays a scientist who makes a machine that can chart brain waves. (Imagine an EKG slowly drawing three-foot zigzags on the wall while electricity arcs in front of the helmeted patient.) After the death of his wife the doctor becomes a veritable mad scientist and attempts to procure help from a spiritualist in order to reach his beloved. While using his machine on her he compels his other assistant to join the electric conduit and accidentally fries him into an Igor-like slave. Karloff moves with his spiritualist and slave to another city where they dig up freshly buried corpses to include in their experiment. The simple townsfolk don't take kindly to their deceased being dug up and so, reminiscent of *Frankenstein*, they charge his laboratory with the usual castle-storming accessories. A hokey film like this can only be pulled off with Karloff in the lead, and he does so brilliantly. —*N. J.*

MIRAGE L: DIRECTORS/DMYTRYK, EDWARD (1965) 109M D: Edward Dmytryk. *Walter Matthau, Diane Baker, George Kennedy, Gregory Peck, Kevin McCarthy.* There should be a moniker for all those post-noir, black-and-white, sun-dappled, shot on location in NYC, usually in winter so it looks even cooler, funkily scored crime/suspense films. Films like *Odds Against Tomorrow, Seconds,* and this one, which seems to get forgotten. Psycho-noir master Dmytryk employs Peck here as an amnesiac in a paranoid nightmare he may be living out for real. A fine score by Quincy Jones; lovely camera work (the blackout's a dazzler) by one of the masters of the lens, Joe McDonald; and a great supporting cast inhabit and elucidate Peck's nightmare. Matthau almost steals the show as the PI and the only person who might believe Peck's loony story, McCarthy is appropriately slimy, and Kennedy's bespectacled thug looks almost too classy, but is a fine sadistic son of a bitch. *Memento* wouldn't have existed without *Mirage*. Check it out. —*M. S.*

MURDER, MY SWEET L: DIRECTORS/DMYTRYK, EDWARD (1944) 95M D: Edward Dmytryk. *Otto Kruger, Claire Trevor, Mike Mazurki, Dick Powell, Anne Shirley.* Dmytryk cast, against type, the oddly perfect Powell as the rumpled, hard-boiled detective

Philip Marlowe, who starts out looking for a dame and uncovers a web of blackmail and murder in this underrated adaptation of Raymond Chandler's *Farewell My Lovely.* Told in flashback, Powell narrates with smart, witty observations and a cynical edge to his voice, and Dmytryk fills the film with expressionist images: tilted angles, sharp contrasts, a world of night illuminated by isolated pools of light. Humphrey Bogart gets all the credit with *The Big Sleep,* but the tone for the next decade of film noir detectives—tough talking, aloof, smarter than your average hood—was set by baby-faced former song-and-dance man Powell in this film, and his vulnerability is closer to the character that Chandler wrote than Bogie's iconic invulnerability. —*S. A.*

YOUNG LIONS, THE L: DIRECTORS/DMYTRYK, EDWARD (1958) 167M D: Edward Dmytryk. *Montgomery Clift, Marlon Brando, Dean Martin, Hope Lange, Barbara Rush.* Clift is a Jewish private fighting racism in the ranks of the U.S. Army and Martin plays a showbiz smoothy pulling strings to avoid front combat in this sprawling WWII drama. Meanwhile, on the other side of the front lines, Brando's idealistic Nazi officer becomes disillusioned with the war and Hitler's megalomania, and shocked by the final solution. Clift's underdog private with a wrought-up, wrapped-up timidity makes him a fidgety pressure cooker, while Martin joked that, "I just played myself. A likeable coward." Clift accused Brando of turning his character into a "fucking Nazi pacifist," and the contrast between the almost saintly officer and his army's "corruption" of his Nazi dream, and Brando's intense, fascinating performance, makes it one of the more curious war films of the '50s. Dmytryk's handsome direction avoids the spectacular war scenes of this era's rousing patriotic pictures to create a much darker drama marked by contradiction and complexity. —*S. A.*

BEDAZZLED L: DIRECTORS/DONEN, STANLEY (1967) 104M D: Stanley Donen. *Dudley Moore, Peter Cook, Raquel Welch, Eleanor Bron.* This is a funny but somewhat dated British variation on *Faust* that was written by the comedic team of Moore and Cook. Moore plays a short-order cook at a greasy spoon called Wimpy Burger who is in love with a waitress (Bron). He makes a pact with the Devil (Cook) to win her heart in exchange for selling his soul, and this leads to several imaginative comedic fantasies in which Moore becomes everything from a housefly to a rock star. Somehow old Scratch always finds a way to screw the mortal over but, over time, the two become friends. Welch plays one of the seven deadly sins, but the movie really belongs to Moore and Cook. My favorite scenes feature the Devil doing his day-to-day activities, like getting birds to poop on people's heads and scratching record albums. Stay away from the pointless remake. —*S. H.*

CHARADE L: DIRECTORS/DONEN, STANLEY (1963) 113M
D: Stanley Donen. *Ned Glass, James Coburn, Walter Matthau, Audrey Hepburn, Cary Grant, George Kennedy.* When Hepburn's estranged husband is murdered, she finds out that he stole $250,000 during the war. She has no idea where it is, but various factions (including her husband's war buddies) think she has it and try to muscle it out of her. She meets Grant, who both flirts with and protects her through the ordeal, but his stories quickly turn out to be lies and she can't be sure he's not after the money too. It's an overseas suspense thriller in the Hitchcock vein with witty dialogue, bouncy music, and an endless amount of twists and turns. Grant and Hepburn are pretty much the most charismatic humans who ever lived and here they are romancing each other at the height of their powers. Donen makes the story dance around as elegantly as the characters in his musicals, and with equally delightful results. Perhaps the most charming movie ever made. —*B.T.*

GRASS IS GREENER, THE L: DIRECTORS/DONEN, STANLEY (1960) 104M D: Stanley Donen. *Jean Simmons, Deborah Kerr, Robert Mitchum, Cary Grant, Moray Watson.* Remember when romantic comedies were about grown-ups? Grant and Kerr are a couple of modest, married British nobles living in his family home, a grand old English estate turned into a tourist attraction to pay the bills, when American millionaire Mitchum crashes into their lives and seduces Kerr. Now the easygoing Grant has to fight for his wife, and he does so with the measured grace that only he could accomplish. Donen directs this very British drawing-room comedy of romantic tempests with a mix of wry, well-mannered wit and American lilt. The slow-paced banter benefits from a crack cast of confident pros who practically dance through the material. It's pure fantasy, of course: adultery and jealousy were never this civilized, but what a portrait of cool, clever, cultured lovers. Simmons is delightful as Kerr's flighty party-girl best friend with an outrageous fashion sense. —*S.A.*

SATURN 3 L: DIRECTORS/DONEN, STANLEY (1980) 88M D: Stanley Donen. *Harvey Keitel, Kirk Douglas, Farrah Fawcett.* Douglas and Fawcett play scientists living on a remote space station. They are unexpectedly visited by another, more sexually aggressive scientist (Keitel) who gets a little grab-assy with Fawcett. Next thing you know Keitel builds a robot that would also do badly in a sensitivity-training workshop. Although *2001* was already two decades old, for some reason the early '80s were rife with cheesy space adventures like this one. It's hard to imagine why Donen chose to direct this film, but even more befuddling was his choice to redub Keitel's voice with that of a different actor. —*B.T.*

SINGIN' IN THE RAIN L: DIRECTORS/DONEN, STANLEY (1952) 103M D: Stanley Donen, Gene Kelly. *Gene Kelly, Donald O'Connor, Jean Hagen, Debbie Reynolds.* Arguably the greatest American musical ever made, and certainly one of the most fun, this is a knockabout look of the transition from silent to sound movies: lousy history but a blast of singing, dancing, romancing energy, and color. Kelly is the vaudeville schlub turned movie stuntman turned matinee idol who falls in love with girl-next-door extra Reynolds, much to the slow-burn anger of leading lady Hagen (in a catty performance done completely with a nasal Brooklyn screech). O'Connor literally climbs the walls in the show-stopping acrobatic dance number "Make 'Em Laugh," and choreographer/codirector/star Kelly goofs on his own character's biography twice—first in a glib radio address with flashback gag punch lines, then again in a glorious set piece dance/ballet—before he stomps, slides, and taps through the water in the title number. —*S.A.*

TWO FOR THE ROAD L: DIRECTORS/DONEN, STANLEY (1967) 111M D: Stanley Donen. *Albert Finney, Claude Dauphin, Gabrielle Middleton, Eleanor Bron, Audrey Hepburn, William Daniels.* It's so refreshing to see a movie that takes a tradition in filmmaking and shakes it up. *Two for the Road* challenges the conventional linear story line, taking the tale of a couple through several years of their lives together, tossing it into a blender, and mixing the whole thing around. We see, in time-travel tidbits, the birth, rise, and fall of a love relationship—from first meeting to attraction to marriage to disillusionment to divorce. The film moves seamlessly through shifts in history and circumstance using landscapes, visuals, sights, and sounds as the catalysts. —*M.N.*

GERTRUD L: DIRECTORS/DREYER, CARL THEODOR (1964) 116M D: Carl Theodor Dreyer. *Ebbe Rode, Bendt Rothe, Baard Owe, Nina Pens Rode.* Beneath the surface of this extremely formal-looking film is some shocking action. Shortly after she announces to her husband that she plans on dumping him, a woman begs her musician boyfriend not to sleep around. She confesses a dream she had where she is running naked through the woods with dogs chasing after her. Later, she sees her dream depicted on the wall behind her as she confides in yet another boyfriend. In the end her desire for autonomy alienates her from everyone. This was Dreyer's last film and was released in the midst of the French New Wave when theatergoers were turning on to fast cuts and flashy colors. This wonderfully visionary film must have seemed quite drab in 1964. —*N.J.*

ORDET L: DIRECTORS/DREYER, CARL THEODOR (1955) 125M D: Carl Theodor Dreyer. *Preben Lerdoff Rye, Henrik Malberg, Emil Hass Christensen.* The tale of young lovers kept apart by the religious differences of their stern, unforgiving fathers smacks of a Scandanavian *Romeo and Juliet,* but the real story lies in the mad son (Rye) who believes he is Christ and preaches the forgiveness of love. Dreyer's exacting style is at its most austere, pruned of stylistic flourish, narrative verbiage, and visual clutter. What's left is sheer perfection, a warm tale of faith, sorrow, and redemption in a chilly world where walled-up feelings are slowly unleashed and a genuine miracle (a moment of true cinematic grace and power) cements the newly formed bonds. One of the most spiritual films ever made. —*S. A.*

PASSION OF JOAN OF ARC, THE L: DIRECTORS/DREYER, CARL THEODOR (1928) 114M D: Carl Theodor Dreyer. *Antonin Artaud, Maurice Schutz, Ravet, Renée Maria Falconetti, Eugène Silvain.* Dreyer's masterpiece is the story of the last days of Joan of Arc's trial. Cinema will never again achieve the expressiveness of Dreyer's stark black-and-white compositions or the wide-eyed pleading looks on Falconetti's face as Joan, realizing she does not stand a chance against the Church. The close-up shots of hands, faces, and body gestures each signify the mood and emotions going through the characters during the trial. Falconetti is well served by the entire cast, especially French author/poet Artaud as the one monk who may be sympathetic to Joan's cause. Dreyer went back to the original trial texts for the dialogue and set the trial to take place on one set and in one room. Despite the simplicity of the setting, it is the combined power of the film's text, Dreyer's editing choices, and Rudolph Mate's magnificent, stark white-and-gray lighting and roaming camera that together create an impassioned spiritual cry. Considered for many years a lost film, a 35mm print was found in the closet of a mental institution in Denmark and is the source for all existing versions of the film. —*N. H.*

BANDERA, LA L: DIRECTORS/DUVIVIER, JULIEN (1935) 96M D: Julien Duvivier. *Pierre Renoir, Jean Gabin, Annabella.* Gabin is both a wanted man and a haunted man who flees Paris for Barcelona and joins the Spanish Foreign Legion, but his past follows him to Africa. Handsomely directed by Duvivier, this is a classic tale of romantic gloom and stoic doom, moved from the shadowy alleys of the urban labyrinth into the bright sun and open landscape of the African desert. There are no surprises in the tough heroism, but Gabin, still at the dawn of his tortured male beauty and intensity, makes every scene worth watching. Renoir is perfect as the Prussian-style captain whose tough-love command earns the respect of all, and Annabella, who has a small but memorable role as Gabin's bedouin gypsy girlfriend, gets top billing. Beware the unusual subtitles in the Vanguard DVD, which contain not a single apostrophe (leaving all those contractions and possessives looking awfully strange). —*S. A.*

PEPE LE MOKO L: DIRECTORS/DUVIVIER, JULIEN (1937) 94M D: Julien Duvivier. *Mireille Balin, Jean Gabin, Gilbert Gil, Gabriel Gabrio, Lucas Gridoux, Marcel Dalio.* Duvivier's pre-noir piece of French poetic realism is a crime thriller steeped in romantic doom and honor among thieves. Gabin is perfect as the gentleman thief at its center. Equal parts elegance and edgy brutality, he's the uncrowned king of the Casbah, a labyrinth of alleys and termite hole dwellings in a bustling, self-contained slum within Algiers that is both his kingdom and his prison. Into this shadowy world, where friendship and trust are everything yet betrayal and duplicity await behind every dark corner, walks a lovely Parisian (the exotic Balin). Pepe steals her jewels and she steals Pepe's heart, a fatal weakness exploited by an undercover inspector determined to bring him in. Just as Pepe exacts a harsh justice on those who defy his code, he pays the price when he breaks his own rules. —*S. A.*

IRON MASK, THE L: DIRECTORS/DWAN, ALLAN (1929) 103M D: Allan Dwan. *Nigel de Brulier, Belle Bennett, Marguerite de la Motte, Douglas Fairbanks.* Fairbanks reprises his role as D'Artagnan, now older and more mature, and reunites his aging Musketeers to avert a plot against young Louis XIV in the lavish sequel to his 1920 hit *The Three Musketeers.* Director Dwan (*Robin Hood*) balances the energy of his breathless chase scenes and jaunty fencing battles with a dimension of melancholy, the slow fade-out on the era of chivalry. The graceful denouement, a scene both ebullient and affecting, becomes not merely D'Artagnan's touching end, but the forty-three-year-old Fairbanks's heartfelt farewell to the silent screen. —*S. A.*

SILVER LODE L: DIRECTORS/DWAN, ALLAN (1954) 81M D: Allan Dwan. *Dolores Moran, Emile G. Meyer, Dan Duryea, John Payne, Lizabeth Scott, Frank Sully.* The usually inexpressive Payne is excellent as the tarnished hero, a small-town rancher loved by all until his reputation is chipped away when scruffy, trail-worn Duryea (in a wonderfully sneering, smarmy performance) rides in with an arrest warrant in his pocket and vengeance in his heart. It may look on the surface to be a routine '50s Western, but this unusual revenge picture turns downright dark and desperate as circumstances and a vicious whispering campaign turn the town into a bloodthirsty mob out to get their adopted favorite son and he scuttles through the shadows seeking evidence to prove his innocence. In hindsight it's one of the more evocative metaphors for the panic of McCarthyism. Scott costars as the loyal good girl and Moran is the no less loyal (and far more fun) "bad girl," whose directness makes for an obvious but undeniably satisfying contrast to the hypocrisy of the town's so-called leading citizens. —*S. A.*

Allan Dwan

Born in 1885 as Joseph Aloysius Dwan, the son of a Toronto clothier, Allan Dwan studied electrical engineering and helped develop the mercury-vapor arc while with the Peter Cooper Hewitt Company. While installing arcs at the Essanay film studio, he became interested in filmmaking and sold a number of stories he wrote in college, which led to a job as a scenario editor with Essanay.

When some Essanay executives broke away to form their own studio, Dwan went with them as a scenarist and production manager. And when a location unit found itself without a director, Dwan took over, turning out more than 250 one- and two-reelers in the next two years. During the teens he worked for Universal, Famous Players, and Triangle as both producer and director, while pioneering such techniques as the dolly shot, the crane shot, and the track shot.

In the 1920s he became one of Hollywood's top directors, with such blockbusters as *Robin Hood* (1922) and *The Iron Mask* (1929, with Douglas Fairbanks), and a series of comedies with Gloria Swanson.

After a short stint directing in Britain at the advent of sound, however, he found himself at the bottom of the Hollywood ladder and relegated to low-budget fare. Though he directed several big productions at the end of the decade, he spent the rest of his career making modestly budgeted comedies, Westerns, and assorted genre films, many of them among his best pictures: *Brewster's Millions* (1945), *The Sands of Iwo Jima* (1945), *Tennessee's Partner* (1955) and *Slightly Scarlet* (1956) among them. His last film, the low-budget science fiction picture *The Most Dangerous Man Alive*, was completed in 1958. Dwan continued to write scripts and develop projects for the next several decades, until his death in 1981 at the age of ninety-six.

Dwan has long been respected as an economical director (both in style and in spending) with a clear narrative sense and a clean, uncluttered visual style, but his career has yet to be explored in depth. Though most consider his silent films to be his best, his unpretentious work of the '40s and '50s includes a number of charming, subtle pictures as well.

—Sean Axmaker

SLIGHTLY SCARLET L: DIRECTORS/DWAN, ALLAN (1956) 99M D: Allan Dwan. *Arlene Dahl, Kent Taylor, Ted de Corsia, Rhonda Fleming, John Payne.* Call it *film rouge,* a shadowy color crime film about an ambitious underworld underling (hunky Payne doing his heavy-lidded, slow-simmer bad-guy number) who turns on his gang leader boss (de Corsia) to worm his way into the graces of a law-and-order gubernatorial candidate (Taylor). As Payne romances the candidate's beautiful secretary (Fleming), whose flaming red hair just about sets fire to the Technicolor, Dahl sasses her way between them as Fleming's shameless klepto sister, sinking her claws into bad-boy Payne. Dwan was an old pro when he made this film and it shows: he slowly turns the day-bright color darker and darker, until night all but swallows corrupt player Payne as his betrayals come back to haunt him. Dwan, helped by legendary noir cinematographer John Alton, makes it look effortless. *—S.A.*

UP IN MABEL'S ROOM/GETTING GERTIE'S GARTER L: DIRECTORS/DWAN, ALLAN (1944/45) 77M/72M D: Allan Dwan. *Mischa Auer, Gail Patrick, Barry Sullivan, Marie McDonald, Dennis O'Keefe.* Practically the same films with a few name changes, Dwan's pleasantly old-fashioned door-slamming, bedroom-hopping farces balance innocence with the suggestion of the illicit. Both films revolve around an intimate memento given years ago to a girlfriend by nervous, tongue-tied professor (B tough-guy O'Keefe channeling Cary Grant's *Bringing Up Baby* performance—in both films!), and the elaborate antics and outrageous explanations involved in hiding the clearly innocent deed from his jealous wife. It's predictable stuff and pretty soon everyone suspects everyone else of infidelities, but Dwan's invisible hand effortlessly gives form to the chaos and keeps the films zipping along smoothly. Don't watch these back to back—you'll think you've seen a rerun. —*S. A.*

BLOOD WORK L: DIRECTORS/EASTWOOD, CLINT (2002) 110M D: Clint Eastwood. *Wanda de Jesus, Anjelica Huston, Jeff Daniels, Clint Eastwood.* Eastwood returns to the gritty police thriller, this time incorporating the age consciousness of his films since *Unforgiven.* He plays a police detective who collapses while chasing a killer and has to get a heart transplant. Later, de Jesus guilts him into working one more case by telling him that his new heart came from her murdered sister. There is some painful wisecracking by asshole cop Paul Rodriguez and one embarrassingly overemphasized clue to the mystery, but other than that it's a classic Eastwood badass crime thriller. —*B. T.*

BRONCO BILLY L: DIRECTORS/EASTWOOD, CLINT (1980) 116M D: Clint Eastwood. *Geoffrey Lewis, Sondra Locke, Bill McKinney, Clint Eastwood, Sam Bottoms, Scatman Crothers.* One of Eastwood's criminally underrated films, this sweet little road movie about a ragged Wild West show in modern Midwest America is like a laconic screwball comedy. Clint is beautiful as a made-up cowboy star, living out his fantasy in a gypsy big top with an inclusive community of dreamers and dropouts. Locke is a spoiled little rich girl who runs away and inadvertently joins his second-rate show. The plot echoes Capra: salt-of-the-earth little guys vs scheming corporate villains, with a runaway heiress between them. Quiet, quirky, and unusually gentle, this delightful little comedy skewers Eastwood's macho image while embracing the power of playacting. —*S. A.*

GAUNTLET, THE L: DIRECTORS/EASTWOOD, CLINT (1977) 109M D: Clint Eastwood. *Sondra Locke, Pat Hingle, William Prince, Clint Eastwood.* Eastwood is a not-so-distinguished cop assigned to escort a hooker (Locke) from Vegas to Phoenix for a Mafia trial. He doesn't know at first that the commissioner (Prince) is corrupt and assigned him only because he's a fuckup who could never succeed with the case. Locke convinces him of what's going on, they fall in love, and together they survive many bombings, chases, and shootouts. A lightweight and somewhat forgettable Eastwood film, it is notable mainly for its exaggerated action scenes. The title refers to the climactic sequence in which the two have to armor a bus and drive it through a mob of heavily armed cops. —*B. T.*

HIGH PLAINS DRIFTER L: DIRECTORS/EASTWOOD, CLINT (1973) 105M D: Clint Eastwood. *Marianna Hill, Mitchell Ryan, Clint Eastwood, Jack Ging, Verna Bloom.* In his first Western as a director, Eastwood once again plays a nameless stranger who wanders into town and ends up getting involved in a dispute with some outlaws. But this is much darker than his Man With No Name films, as you can figure out well before he literally paints the town red and renames it Hell. I wish I didn't have to sit through the rape scene, but this is up there with *Unforgiven* as one of Eastwood's best non-Leone Westerns. —*B. T.*

OUTLAW JOSEY WALES, THE L: DIRECTORS/EASTWOOD, CLINT (1976) 136M D: Clint Eastwood. *Clint Eastwood, Sondra Locke, Chief Dan George, John Vernon.* Eastwood brings warmth and low-key humor to his previously cold-blooded revenge-seeking persona. Josey Wales is a Confederate guerrilla avenging the brutal massacre of his family by Union renegades, hunted after the war for refusing to surrender to the very killer who led the raid. On his trek south he collects more strays than the ASPCA, creating a family-like community that draws his repressed paternal instincts out and pulls him back into life. The explosions of brutal violence and Eastwood's cinematic eye recall Leone, with an image of a changing landscape as dangerous as it is embracing. The hope and loving vision of community are all Eastwood's own. —*S. A.*

PERFECT WORLD, A L: DIRECTORS/EASTWOOD, CLINT (1993) 138M D: Clint Eastwood. *Leo Burmester, Kevin Costner, T. J. Lowther, Clint Eastwood, Laura Dern, Keith Szarabajka.* Costner plays an escaped con on the lam who picks up a fatherless boy as a hostage while he's being pursued by a Texas ranger (Eastwood). This film is a total misfire for Eastwood, who has proven himself to be a brilliant director of psychological suspense—not the reclaiming of childhood innocence. In a perfect world Costner would not be in an Eastwood film. In a perfect Texas an escaped con would spend life behind bars for kidnapping a boy. And in a perfect film the climax wouldn't be so drab and predictable. —*N. J.*

PLAY MISTY FOR ME L: DIRECTORS/EASTWOOD, CLINT (1971) 102M D: Clint Eastwood. *John Larch, Clint Eastwood, Jessica Walter, Donna Mills.* This first film directed by Eastwood clearly shows his knack for psychological suspense along the lines of Don Siegel (who has a cameo). Eastwood plays a radio DJ who starts getting frequent requests from the same odd woman (Walter) to play the song "Misty." Over time it becomes apparent that this woman has some very serious issues since she starts stalking the poor DJ and doing her best to instigate a romance. His lack of feelings for her eventually results in some crazy violence for the climax of the film. Clearly Eastwood knew his trade before directing this debut because it is tightly constructed, highly atmospheric, and downright memorable. —*N. J.*

SPACE COWBOYS L: DIRECTORS/EASTWOOD, CLINT (2000) 130M D: Clint Eastwood. *Clint Eastwood, Donald Sutherland, James Garner, James Cromwell, Marcia*

Gay Harden, Tommy Lee Jones. There's something satisfying in Eastwood's take on the techno-overkill space adventure. The script is pure hokum, of course, as four geriatric retired test pilots (Eastwood is joined here by Jones, Sutherland, and Garner) get their decades-overdue chance at a space shot and save the world in the process. Eastwood wipes it clean of trumped-up patriotism and clears out clumsy subplots and hackneyed conspiracies like the clutter they are (mostly by simply ignoring them). His skills at building tension are slipping and his narrative mechanics could use a little well-placed flash and techno sparkle, but he's still a lean, clean, and sleek storyteller. I guess there's something grizzled old codgers like Eastwood can teach those young hotshots after all. —*S. A.*

SUDDEN IMPACT L: DIRECTORS/EASTWOOD, CLINT (1983) 117M D: Clint Eastwood. *Clint Eastwood, Sondra Locke, Pat Hingle, Bradford Dillman, Paul Drake.* "Go ahead. Make my day." Eastwood directs himself while returning to his familiar role of Dirty Harry for this, the fourth installment of the five-part series. After the opening sequence in which he stops a holdup with the help of his enormous Magnum, he delivers the famous one-liner that helped cement the fame of his character. Eastwood had actually directed several films before he returned to Dirty Harry for the first time since 1976, and here he seems more comfortable with the role than ever. The plot concerns a woman murderer bent on revenge (strains of *Play Misty for Me*). After much psychological analysis he anticipates her last move at a California pier, cruelly exacting her revenge on the psycho who instigated her group rape many years earlier. It is an exhilarating and well-directed contribution to the Dirty Harry series. —*N. J.*

UNFORGIVEN L: DIRECTORS/EASTWOOD, CLINT (1992) 135M D: Clint Eastwood. *Gene Hackman, Jaimz Woolvett, Morgan Freeman, Clint Eastwood, Richard Harris.* When the coldhearted sheriff (Hackman) fails to bring justice to a man who slashes a prostitute's face, her brothel puts together a bounty on the perpetrator's head. A young, aspiring outlaw (Woolvett) thinks he could get the bounty with the help of the legendary outlaw William Munny (Eastwood). It turns out Munny has become a pig farmer and doesn't believe in violence anymore but, needing money for his kids, he reluctantly takes the offer. Justifiably one of Eastwood's most acclaimed films (it won Oscars for Best Picture and Director), *Unforgiven* works on two levels: as a rousing Western, and as a commentary on the violence of Westerns (in particular, those starring Eastwood). Many of Eastwood's later films deal with age and the way it changes one's perspective; this is his most successful examination of that theme. —*B. T.*

CURSE OF THE PINK PANTHER L: DIRECTORS/EDWARDS, BLAKE (1983) 110M D: Blake Edwards. *Harvey Korman, Ed Parker, David Niven, Herbert Lom, Robert Wagner, Ted Wass.* This sequel to the *Pink Panther* films is lamentable as Peter Sellers, the only man who could possibly play Inspector Clouseau, died shortly before production began. Wass fills in as an inspector who, cleverly enough, is *looking for* the Inspector—as if nobody in the audience knew that Sellers had died! To make up for the fact that Wass hasn't half the charisma of Sellers, multiple cameos and flashbacks are utilized, as though everybody watching this sequel could be manipulated by nostalgia alone. It's a pathetic shame that Niven's last film is easily one of the most pointless sequels ever created. Predictably followed by another dud, *Son of the Pink Panther.* —*N. J.*

PARTY, THE L: DIRECTORS/EDWARDS, BLAKE (1968) 99M D: Blake Edwards. *Marge Champion, Claudine Longet, Peter Sellers.* Sellers plays a sweet klutz of an Indian actor who wreaks havoc at a Hollywood party he was never supposed to attend and falls in love with a sweet young thing, starlet Longet. It's like an all-American take on a Jacques Tati comedy, and it was developed almost the same way. Edwards and Sellers walked onto the set with a sketch of a script and proceeded to improvise situations and physical gags that they then honed into an organic symphony of comedy. The opening sequence, a spoof on *Gunga Din* where trumpet blower Sellers simply won't stay dead, is one of Sellers's most hilarious gags. This may be Edwards's most loved film and he manages to keep it grounded in sweetness as the series of minor mishaps tumbles into a freewheeling, fun-loving explosion of chaotic fun. Great score by Henry Mancini. —*S. A.*

PETER GUNN L: DIRECTORS/EDWARDS, BLAKE (1958) 800M D: Blake Edwards. *Hope Emerson, Lola Albright, Herschel Bernardi, Craig Stevens.* Stevens is TV's most debonair private eye, a sardonic small-screen Cary Grant with high-society tastes and underworld connections, in the stylish series created by Edwards. Every episode begins with a concise, cool, often wordless precredits crime, then leaps from the visual punch-line kicker into the now famous brassy theme song. Each thirty-minute show is a veritable digest of B-movie film noir conventions, done up in a strikingly stylized manner on austere, often abstract sets filled with fog and lit in a shadowy twilight haze. Real life and natural locations never intrude upon the self-contained existence of this formalized world. The teasingly elegant Albright is Gunn's classy chanteuse girlfriend, Bernardi is the cynical Lt. Jacobi, and gravel-voiced, hatchet-faced Emerson is the street-smart nightclub owner Mother, whose growling, rubber-mouthed musical performances are series highlights. —*S. A.*

PINK PANTHER, THE L: DIRECTORS/EDWARDS, BLAKE (1964) 113M D: Blake Edwards. *Peter Sellers, David Niven, Robert Wagner, Capucine.* In this classic American comedy a large diamond is held under tight security—a diamond so large it is said that one can actually see the Pink Panther in it. The credit sequence that follows is the now familiar cartoon of the Pink Panther accompanied by the equally familiar theme music by Henry Mancini. A James Bond–style heist takes place and one morning the diamond is missing! Enter Sellers in what is perhaps his most familiar role, the bungling French detective Inspector Clouseau. Sellers brought this detective spoof to life by employing a hilarious language barrier as well as being the endless target of Murphy's Law. However, the viewer will have to wait until the sequel, *A Shot in the Dark,* to see such valuable comic assets as the manservant Kato (played by Burt Kwouk) and the neurotic Chief Detective played by Herbert Lom. —*N. J.*

SHOT IN THE DARK, A L: DIRECTORS/EDWARDS, BLAKE (1964) 102M D: Blake Edwards. *George Sanders, Peter Sellers, Elke Sommer.* Arguably the best film in the Pink Panther series, this follow-up to *The Pink Panther* employed Sellers's comic genius to its fullest extent. Pratfalls aside, the whole secret to Edwards and Sellers's creation and lasting success in this series was Clouseau's utter stubbornness and unwavering commitment to justice, even when he was falling down a flight of stairs or defending someone he believed to be innocent. In this case, the "innocent" was the lovely Sommer, who is by far the most likely murder suspect in the films' cursory whodunit, and who Clouseau seems to take a shine to, letting nothing (including his own ineptitude) stand in his way of finding the real murderer. Sanders and Herbert Lom lend marvelous supporting bits, Henry Mancini contributed a very memorable score (my favorite of the "Pink" films), and William Peter "The Exorcist" Blatty adapted the script from the stage play, which, in fact, had no Clouseau at all. —*M. S.*

10 L: DIRECTORS/EDWARDS, BLAKE (1979) 121M D: Blake Edwards. *Bo Derek, Julie Andrews, Dee Wallace Stone, Brian Dennehy, Dudley Moore.* A year after Moore was made familiar to American filmgoers with *Foul Play* he starred in this Edwards vehicle about a song writer obsessed with finding the perfect woman. Of course, he finds Derek, the very woman he rates ten on his one-to-ten scale. Derek had only recently appeared in *Orca*, where she played human bait, but this film made her a female heartthrob across America. The story's broad sense of humor pokes fun at lust, voyeurism, and the objectification of women, which Edwards pulls off lightheartedly. The film also popularized Ravel's "Bolero," using its growing and incessant theme to parallel and even mock the general premise of the film. —*N. J.*

VICTOR/VICTORIA L: DIRECTORS/EDWARDS, BLAKE (1982) 133M D: Blake Edwards. *Alex Karras, Lesley Ann Warren, Julie Andrews, Robert Preston, James Garner.* Andrews is a woman posing as a man posing as a woman in 1930s gay Paris, "gay" being the operative term in this identity-bending musical comedy. Edwards is in top form as he skewers sexual stereotypes and challenges issues of identity and self-esteem with a deft mix of elegance, dry wit, broad slapstick, and romantic warmth. Garner is the American mobster who questions his own masculinity when he falls for the slim, cross-dressing "boy" (Andrews, with a fog hazing over her crisp voice, really does come off as a smooth-faced youth), and Preston is thoroughly charming as the aging gay entertainer who embraces his sexuality with gusto. In the great tradition of old Hollywood comedies, this is a remake of a 1930s German film. Warren is wonderfully brassy as the American dame on Garner's arm, and Karras is quietly effective as the mob tough inspired to reveal his own secret. —*S. A.*

ARARAT L: DIRECTORS/EGOYAN, ATOM (2002) 115M D: Atom Egoyan. *Marie-Josée Croze, Charles Aznavour, David Alpay, Christopher Plummer, Arsinée Khanjian, Eric Bogosian.* Canadian-Armenian director Egoyan sets the Armenian Genocide of 1915 at the center of his ambitious contemporary drama, which is as much about how we interpret, reconstruct, and struggle with history as it is about history itself. Raffi (Alpay), our ostensible guide, is a confused young Canadian man of Armenian ancestry trying to understand his dead father, an Armenian terrorist, while a well-intentioned director (a paternal Aznavour) turns an epic re-creation of the massacre into hoary and overwrought melodrama. Plummer anchors the film as a customs official whose dedication to "the truth" is complicated by Raffi's story, and Croze and Khanjian costar. A master of intimate miniatures and community portraits, Egoyan is a little overwhelmed by this busy mural, but he explores with seriousness and compassion how history defines individuals and communities, the destructive effect of denial, and the distortions created when history is turned into narrative fiction. —*S. A.*

ALEXANDER NEVSKY L: DIRECTORS/EISENSTEIN, SERGEI (1938) 110M D: Sergei Eisenstein. *Nikolai Cherkasov, Nikolai Okhlopkov, Andrei Abrikosov, Vasili Novikov, Dmitri Orlov.* Unable to find work for years because of his failed attempt to escape the control of Stalin, Eisenstein was tossed *Alexander Nevsky* as a bone to prove his loyalty. Forced to codirect the film with Stalin spy Dmitri Vasilyev, Eisenstein nonetheless achieved a major masterpiece in his first sound film. The Asian Mongols and the German Teutonic Knights invade Russia on both sides. Prince Alexander Nevsky (Cherkasov) is called back into service to raise up the Russian armies and drive out the invaders. Nevsky's armies are successful after a mammoth battle on the fields near Novgorod, where Nevsky wisely drives the Germans onto a frozen lake. Masterfully edited, the film uses carefully drawn compositions and the reversal of black and white to represent good and evil. Composer Sergei Prokofiev, given access to less than perfect equipment, creates a rousing score, mixing battle cries and vocals as if they were instruments. The film was used by Stalin as a propaganda war cry to improve morale in Russia when Germany threatened its borders at the onset of WWII. Eisenstein won the approval of Stalin to move forward directing his final and most epic work, *Ivan the Terrible, Parts 1 and 2. —N. H.*

BATTLESHIP POTEMKIN (AKA POTEMKIN) L: DIRECTORS/ EISENSTEIN, SERGEI (1925) 70M D: Sergei Eisenstein.
Alexander Antonov, Vladimir Barsky, Grigory Alexandrov, Marusov, Mikhail Gomorov. In 1905, sailors on the battleship *Potemkin* revolt against the poor living conditions on their ship. They are fed maggot-filled meat that the ship's doctor declares is fine. The men rise up and take control of the ship after the dissenters who complained about the meat are shot under the direct orders of their admiral. The people of the port town Odessa support the *Potemkin*'s mutiny but are murdered in the film's most famous sequence—the Odessa Steps—when the tsarist Cossack army moves in to stop the revolt. Battleships then appear in Odessa Bay and destroy the *Potemkin*. Eisenstein's montage editing shocked the world with its effective counterpoint use of two images set side by side (a baby, a soldier with a gun) to create a third emotional effect (tension). Considered worldwide to be one of the most significant achievements in the history of filmmaking. —*N. H.*

IVAN THE TERRIBLE, PARTS 1 AND 2 L: DIRECTORS/ EISENSTEIN, SERGEI (1945) 100M D: Sergei Eisenstein.
Vsevolod Pudovkin, Nikolai Cherkasov, Lyudmila Tselikovskaya, Mikhail Nazvanov, Serafima Birman. Ivan the Terrible, Parts 1 and 2 are really one film. Intending to make three films, Eisenstein died having finished only minutes of footage for Part 3. Part 1 starts in 1547, as Ivan IV (Cherkasov) crowns himself Tsar of Russia, marries his wife Anastasia (Tselikovskaya), and begins his campaigns to reclaim Russian territory from the Tartans. Ivan falls sick and is afraid he will die. His Aunt Euphrosyne (Birman) decides that her infantile adult son (Nazvanov) will replace Ivan on the throne. But Ivan recovers, and Euphrosyne attempts to murder him with poison, instead killing his wife. In Part 2, Ivan finds himself alone, remembering his youth. He becomes friends with a priest who attempts to bring Ivan under the control of the Church. However, the priest is also working behind Ivan's back, plotting with the Boyers who are led by Euphrosyne, still attempting to replace Ivan with her son. Unknown to the Boyers, Ivan

secretly plots revenge for his wife's murder. The film's production values are amazing. Stalin gave Eisenstein access to the entire Russian army to create the mammoth battle sequences. Prokofiev creates another masterpiece score. Part 1 was hailed by Stalin as a masterpiece. Part 2 was treated as treason and withheld from distribution for ten years (many people claim Stalin's response drove Eisenstein into his fatal heart attack) because Stalin was furious at Eisenstein for depicting a historic Russian ruler as a plotting murderer. Part 3 was intended to be shot in full color and was going to show Ivan bowing down before God confessing his sins. —*N. H.*

OCTOBER (TEN DAYS THAT SHOOK THE WORLD) L: DIRECTORS/EISENSTEIN, SERGEI (1927) 95M D: Sergei
Eisenstein. *Vladimir Popov, Vasili Nikandrov, Layaschenko.* For all his theorizing about "montage" and use of cinema to reveal social truths, Eisenstein is not beneath melodramatic devices to manipulate viewer response as in his supposed masterwork *Potemkin*. On the surface, *October* is much plainer and more carefully textured intellectually. But deep down it is far more thrilling because the pattern of events builds in the style of contemporary news. Some things are planned and stirring speeches are made, but other events are spontaneous, overwhelming the planning and charging the air with immediacy. The newsreel look of the film puts you in the thick of it and the electric feeling is palpable and genuine. The events push then wane, but the tension subtly builds. When a horse goes off a bridge into the frigid river, the event as both historic fact and visual metaphor earns its role as the epiphany upon which the whole story hinges. This is powerful emotionally honest storytelling. —*J. C.*

QUE VIVA MEXICO/SERGEI EISENSTEIN'S MEXICAN FANTASY L: DIRECTORS/EISENSTEIN, SERGEI (1930) 100M
D: Sergei Eisenstein. *Sergei Bondarchuk, Grigori Aleksandrov. Que Viva Mexico* and *Sergei Eisenstein's Mexican Fantasy* are two separate attempts to reedit the film Eisenstein shot during his stay in Mexico in the 1930s, having been ousted from Hollywood where he was labeled incompatible with the American studio system. The film was produced by writer Upton Sinclair, who took the film away from Eisenstein after a full year of shooting what Sinclair considered to be "unusable footage." Eisenstein was forced to return to Russia, unable to edit the film together. With *Que Viva Mexico,* Eisenstein attempted to capture the beautiful mysticism of the Mexico he had fallen in love with, dividing his film into four pieces: "Sandunga," "Fiesta," "Maguey," and "Soldadera." Each piece was intended to focus on the poverty and religion of the persecuted Mexican workers and the beauty of their simple peasant life. In 1979, Eisenstein's assistant Alexandrov attempted to recut the footage with *Que Viva Mexico,* but his efforts proved very unlike Eisenstein's dynamic editing

style and the results were flat and uninvolving. In 1998, Eisenstein author Oleg Kovalov was more successful in recutting the footage into *Mexican Fantasy,* which proved to be closer to Eisenstein's intentions. Yet neither film is completely successful in attempting to re-create Eisenstein's techniques, leaving only a hint of what could have been the Russian director's greatest achievement. —*N. H.*

ALI: FEAR EATS THE SOUL L: DIRECTORS/FASSBINDER, RAINER (1974) 93M D: Rainer Werner Fassbinder. *Brigitte Mira, El Hedi ben Salem, Barbara Valentin, Irm Hermann, Elma Karlowa.* Fassbinder paid tribute to his mentor Douglas Sirk with this loose adaptation of his *All That Heaven Allows,* replacing society widow Jane Wyman with an aging, lonely charwoman (Mira), and hunky young nature boy Rock Hudson with a silent, stiff Moroccan guest worker (ben Salem). An unlikely romance blooms as they find comfort and happiness in each other's company. Their impulsive marriage outrages her children, upsets his friends, and alienates the entire neighborhood, but when the pressure of community prejudice lifts (for purely mercenary reasons), the strange bedfellows are forced to confront the not-so-pure motivations for their marriage and the cultural and personal gulf between them. Fassbinder's biggest critical hit to that time is also his most stylistically assured, full of gliding camera work and evocative images, and its social commentary and often grotesque caricatures of prejudice in modern Germany are invested with intimacy and tenderness. —*S. A.*

BERLIN ALEXANDERPLATZ L: DIRECTORS/FASSBINDER, RAINER (1980) 930M D: Rainer Werner Fassbinder. *Gunter Lamprecht, Hanna Schygulla, Barbara Sukowa, Gottfried John, Elisabeth Trissenaar.* Fassbinder's epic *Berlin Alexanderplatz* was made for German television and runs more than fifteen hours. Fassbinder's expressionism gives the audience so much of the protagonist's interior monologue that his dreams become ours. The time is late 1920s Berlin. Lamprecht plays Franz Biberkof, a man just released from prison for murdering his wife. The entire series focuses on his attempt to rebuild his life in a society that has completely collapsed. To survive he finds himself working inside some seedy circles, yet most people in Berlin at that time were seedy, which is why the well-dressed Nazis drew such appeal. Seen in full, *Alexanderplatz* is a dream—it's a fantasy, it's a fugue, it's a nightmare—but it's the encyclopedic dream of a simple man in complicated times. If you are able to watch it all, it's unlikely you will be able to forget it. —*N. J.*

BITTER TEARS OF PETRA VON KANT, THE L: DIRECTORS/FASSBINDER, RAINER (1972) 124M D: Rainer Werner Fassbinder. *Margit Carstensen, Irm Hermann, Hanna Schygulla.* Fassbinder adapted his own play for this modern twist on *The Women,* the great all-woman Hollywood classic of sex and social conventions in high society. Carstensen is successful dress designer Petra von Kant; Hermann her silent, obedient secretary/servant/girl Friday Marlene, whom she alternately abuses and ignores. Schygulla is the callow, shallow young Karin, a seemingly naive blond beauty Petra falls in love with and treats as part protégé, part pet. Michael Ballhaus's prowling camera finds Marlene silently hovering on the borders of Petra's dramas, looking in through doors and windows like an adoring lover from afar. Handsome with a touch of aloofness (a pair of bare dress dummies sprawled through each scene adds a note of alienation), it's a quintessentially Fassbinder portrait of doomed love, jealousy, and social taboos, bouncing between catty melodrama and naked emotional need. —*S. A.*

DESPAIR L: DIRECTORS/FASSBINDER, RAINER (1978) 120M D: Rainer Werner Fassbinder. *Klaus Lowitsch, Dirk Bogarde, Andrea Ferreol, Volker Spengler.* Adapted by Tom Stoppard, from the Vladimir Nabokov novel, *Despair* was the first screenplay of a Fassbinder film not written by himself. Fassbinder did not use any members of his stock company for the leads, but instead cast international stars Bogarde and Ferreol, and German leading man Spengler, respectively, as Hermann; his vulgar wife, Lydia; and her penniless cousin, Ardalion, whom she is obsessed with. Hermann, a delusional Russian exile in 1930's Berlin, hatches a plot to murder a man he thinks is his double and collect life insurance, thus escaping his insane life. His increasing madness as the film unfolds reflects the growing insanity of the world as the Nazis came to power. What seemed at first to be an atypical Fassinder project turned out to be a fascinating and extremely autobiographical look into the psyche of a man on the verge of destroying himself and those around him. —*M. S.*

EFFI BRIEST L: DIRECTORS/FASSBINDER, RAINER (1974) 140M D: Rainer Werner Fassbinder. *Hanna Schygulla, Wolfgang Schenck, Ulli Lommel, Lilo Pempeit.* Shot over a two-year period in lush, elegant black and white, *Effi Briest* (adapted from the novel by Theodor Fontane) was Fassbinder's most ambitious film to date and a turning point in his career. Schygulla stars as the naive young Berlin girl who marries a petty government bureaucrat (Schenk) and enters a stifling, lonely existence assuaged only in the attentions of a handsome young count (Lommel), an affair that is doomed to come crashing down upon her. The soft-focus cinematography complements the lovely, purposefully static portrait-style direction that is full of mirrors and frames within frames. Dominated by intrusive narration in place of dialogue, it defines the alienation effects Fassbinder was mastering at the time. Schygulla is lovely and sincere if hollow as Effi, but that

Rainer Werner Fassbinder

In 1982 Rainer Werner Fassbinder, the most famous—some might say notorious—director of Germany's postwar era, died at thirty-seven from a drug overdose. He lived hard, died young, and left behind a pale, bloated corpse that showed the ravages of his excesses: years of overeating, drug and alcohol abuse, and chronic overwork. Yet in a mere thirteen years he directed more than forty films and TV productions (most of which he either wrote or cowrote), wrote eight plays and directed twenty-three, and acted in dozens of films. From his first film, the stark black-and-white gangster riff *Love Is Colder than Death* (1969), to his final film, the outrageously stylized, sunset-colored Jean Genet adaptation *Querelle* (1982), Fassbinder searched for his identity while transforming himself from Germany's young punk of angry, edgy agitprop to the internationally acclaimed auteur of emotionally lush and visually elegant historical melodramas.

Fassbinder was a magnificent contradiction: a charismatic creative artist desperate for love and attention from those around him, and a controlling, abusive dictator who terrorized and manipulated his friends, collaborators, and lovers. Members of his inner circle (which varied depending on his mood and grudge of the moment) have consistently described him as a "monster," an emotional vampire who fed off his friends and enemies alike; yet he created professional collaborations that lasted for years. His emotionally turbulent life was echoed in his films: portraits of desperate, abusive, and unhappy relationships defined by crippling emotional dependency, or of doomed loves destroyed by jealousy and fear.

His early films, such as *The American Soldier* and *Why Does Herr R Run Amok?* (both released in 1970), were raw, acidic satires of a complacent society, directed with an in-your-face style and a confrontational attitude, but he increasingly turned to his personal life for inspiration and characters. His volatile, abusive relationships found reflection in pained dramas of cruel manipulators and needy victims such as *Fox and His Friends* (1975) (starring Fassbinder himself as a gay working-class lottery winner picked clean by predatory upper-class dandies) and *The Bitter Tears of Petra von Kant* (1973).

Around this time he also discovered his mentor, Douglas Sirk, the great Hollywood melodramatist who fled Germany and made his name with a series of baroque, subversive soap operas (*Written on the Wind, Imitation of Life*). Fassbinder embraced both the melodrama and Sirk's stylistic effects for his own explorations of identity in modern Germany, even transforming Sirk's *All That Heaven Allows* into the portrait of racism and ageism in modern Germany *Ali: Fear Eats the Soul* (1974).

With *The Marriage of Maria Braun* (1979) his passions, ambitions, and lush style came together in his first film to connect with both German history and German audiences. Fassbinder was catapulted from cult figure to renowned director, and his succeeding productions reflected his confident new cinematic control: Hollywood gloss married with Fassbinder's passion. That passion was simultaneously creative and self-destructive, but it led the way for the creative rebirth of the German film industry known as the New German Cinema and left a legacy unmatched by any of his contemporaries.   —*Sean Axmaker*

becomes the point: she ultimately allows a critical, shallow society to define her. Though rarely emotionally involving, the tarnished portrait of a society mired in empty convention recalls the work of earlier German melodrama master Max Ophuls. —S.A.

FOX AND HIS FRIENDS L: DIRECTORS/FASSBINDER, RAINER (1975) 123M D: Rainer Werner Fassbinder. *Rainer Werner Fassbinder, Peter Chatel, Kurt Raab, Barbara Valentin, Adrian Hoven, Rudolf Lenz.* While Fassbinder is definitely an acquired taste, *Fox and His Friends,* as pessimistic and downbeat as it is, stands as one of his few films that many audiences can appreciate. It's the story of how Fox (an amazing performance by Fassbinder himself) goes from being a simpleton who wins a lot of money to being a dead body in a subway station. It can be seen as a moral fable on the infallibility of man, an attack on a bourgeoisie culture that lives off the lower classes, or a statement on the greediness of all people. I accept and reject all three views in favor of another one: this is a great film. Even though you know how the whole thing will end, you never once stop watching Fox. You might not root for him but you can understand him, and that's what stings the most. —K.F.

LOVE IS COLDER THAN DEATH L: DIRECTORS/FASSBINDER, RAINER (1969) 85M D: Rainer Werner Fassbinder. *Ulli Lommel, Hanna Schygulla, Katrin Schaake, Ingrid Caven.* Fassbinder's feature debut is a stark black-and-white gangster riff starring Lommel as a handsome small-time gangster who dresses like Alain Delon, Schygulla as a prostitute, and Fassbinder himself as a petty crook and pimp who rejects the syndicate and hooks up with Lommel, much to the frustration of the jealous Schygulla. A simultaneous tribute to and parody of Hollywood gangster movies, directed in the detached, alienating style he had developed in his Anti-Theatre stage company, it coincidentally marks the first appearance of "Franz Walsh," a name Fassbinder reused for characters and pseudonymous credits throughout his career (it's a mesh of Franz Beiberkopf—the hero of the novel *Berlin Alexanderplatz*—and the American director Raoul Walsh). The film was almost universally disliked and only years later, in light of Fassbinder's subsequent acclaim, was it reevaluated as an audacious debut. —S.A.

MARRIAGE OF MARIA BRAUN, THE L: DIRECTORS/FASSBINDER, RAINER (1979) 120M D: Rainer Werner Fassbinder. *Ivan Desny, Hanna Schygulla, Gottfried John, Elisabeth Trissenaar, Gisela Uhlen, Klaus Löwitsch.* Winner of the Silver Bear at the Berlin Film Festival and the closing-night film at the New York Film Festival, the first movie in Fassbinder's BRD (Bundesrepublik Deutschland) trilogy brought his passions, ambitions, and lush style together to become his first commercial hit in Germany. In the months following the end of WWII, Maria Braun (Schygulla) spends her days waiting for her man to return, and her nights doing what it takes to survive in the rubble of her city. Maria's rise to success in postwar Germany parallels the country's own development in the years between 1945 and 1954, but the personal costs to Maria belong to the operatic emotional world of this beloved melodrama, done up with stylistic grace. Fassbinder called it his first "Hollywood film in Germany," and he turned Schygulla into a star—his star. —S.A.

MERCHANT OF FOUR SEASONS, THE L: DIRECTORS/FASSBINDER, RAINER (1972) 88M D: Rainer Werner Fassbinder. *Hanna Schygulla, Kurt Raab, Klaus Lowitsch, Hans Hirschmuller, Irm Hermann, Ingrid Caven.* After years of filmmaking with his stock company, Fassbinder won international acclaim with this bleak working-class melodrama. Jumping back and forth in time, he explores the life of a French Foreign Legionnaire vet turned produce streetpeddler (Hirschmuller) on a downward spiral of depression during the "economic miracle" of the 1950s. Fassbinder invests his chilly but compelling portrait of a mercenary, often unfeeling family desperate to grab a piece of the economic boom with a mix of street realism, melodrama, black comedy, and theatrical flourish, right down to the unforgettable climax: a unique, utterly Fassbinderian escape. —S.A.

MOTHER KUSTERS GOES TO HEAVEN L: DIRECTORS/FASSBINDER, RAINER (1975) 105M D: Rainer Werner Fassbinder. *Peter Kern, Armin Meier, Lilo Pempeit, Brigitte Mira.* A factory worker goes insane and kills the son of his boss and then himself. His widow, Mother Kusters (Mira), refusing to accept what her husband has done, spends the day preparing his homecoming meal with her conniving daughter-in-law, Corinna (Pempeit). The media show up at her door, giving Corinna the opportunity to make herself a star, while a political group of persuasive Communists takes advantage of Mother Kusters's position in the headlines to try and free some of their imprisoned party members. Written by Fassbinder and one of his actors, Kurt Raab, this is a lighter-toned dark comedy that pokes fun at both left- and right-wing politics while maintaining the melodramatic edge of tragedy and suffering abundant in Fassbinder's work. Mira is in top form, giving a performance as sharply tuned as any better-known Hollywood actress. The DVD includes both the "tragic" European ending and the "happy" U.S. ending. —N.H.

QUERELLE L: DIRECTORS/FASSBINDER, RAINER (1982) 109M D: Rainer Werner Fassbinder. *Jeanne Moreau, Laurent Malet, Franco Nero, Brad Davis, Hanno Pöschl.* Fassbinder's badboy final feature is Genet's world stylized by Warhol and channeled through Fassbinder's focus on fucked-up relationships. Querrelle (Davis) wants his brother and can't have him so he disguises a local laborer to resemble his brother and sets him up for murder. The film is filled with giant penis buildings and bright orange backgrounds, which are Fassbinder's tribute to the Vincente Minnelli musical *The Pirate '42.* Hot sweaty men, lustful looks, and soft-focus photography add to the gayest of all films. A must-see. —*N. J.*

VERONIKA VOSS L: DIRECTORS/FASSBINDER, RAINER (1982) 104M D: Rainer Werner Fassbinder. *Annemaire Duringer, Cornelia Froboess, Hilmar Thate, Rosel Zech.* Part of the multi-film swan song of the great Fassbinder, *Veronika Voss* is a lovingly painted ode to the director's obsessions with doomed, tortured relationships and the people who succumb so easily to simple human needs. Opening with the director himself leaning over the shoulders of Ms. Voss (Zech) as she watches one of her own silent films. She then steps out into the rain and meets the kind and simple sportswriter Robert Krohn (Thate), who offers his umbrella. After a bizarre second meeting, Robert finds himself more and more intrigued by this odd, once-famous woman. After learning of her morphine addiction, his inner Prince Charming rises and he decides he must save this poor woman. Bleak and depressing, though treated as the jewel of a film it is by the careful light-and-dark constructions of cinematographer Xaver Schwarzenberger, this is dark melodrama at its finest. —*S. R.*

WHITY L: DIRECTORS/FASSBINDER, RAINER (1970) 95M D: Rainer Werner Fassbinder. *Ron Randell, Katrin Schaake, Ulli Lommel, Hanna Schygulla, Harry Baer, Gunther Kaufmann.* This film is a whacked-out, psycho party "sauerkraut Western" that pokes fun at every standard of the Western genre. Whity is the mulatto servant of Nicholson family in the Wild West. Whity also happens to be the bastard son of the family matriarch, who is dying (but not really. . . he's testing the loyalty of his messed-up sons and wife, each of whom is either seducing Whity or bossing him around). In the end, Whity kills them all, but not before the audience has quite a few dark chuckles over such things as incest, voyeurism, bestiality, machismo, blackface, polyester clothes, and banal pop tunes. *Whity* is one cavalcade of grotesqueries that turns the Western a full 300 degrees farther than Leone ever wanted to. Whether that's a good thing or not is up to you. —*K. F.*

WHY DOES HERR R. RUN AMOK? L: DIRECTORS/ FASSBINDER, RAINER (1969) 88M D: Rainer Werner Fassbinder. *Lilith Ungerer, Kurt Raab.* This is an odious film. It's also a film that, in a deconstructionist vein, challenges the very dramatic structure of what an audience normally expects from film. Herr R. is an ordinary man with an ordinary job. In fact, he is so ordinary that after a brief exposition of him and his family we become rather bored. There is no proper antagonist in this story, and there is no

particular conflict going on. We become bored with Herr R. presumably as much as he becomes bored with himself. And then, for no explainable reason, moments before the film ends, Herr R. guns down his family. Unwittingly the audience is asked to participate to find answers in the unromantic story in order to explain such an overly dramatic conclusion. —*N. H.*

8½ L: DIRECTORS/FELLINI, FEDERICO (1963) 138M D: Federico Fellini. *Marcello Mastroianni, Barbara Steele, Anouk Aimee, Claudia Cardinale, Sandra Milo.* "*8½* is to me the film that captures what it actually is like to be a film director making a movie," says Terry Gilliam in his introduction to the Criterion edition of Fellini's masterpiece. Mastroianni is Fellini's alter ego, a director whose life and art become hopelessly intertwined in his three-ring imagination of sexual fantasies as he ponders his next film. Equal parts self-indulgent quasi-autobiography and cinematic celebration, it's as magical and quintessentially Fellini-esque as ever. In other words, despite—or because of—the worldweary pose, sexist romps, and self-serving portrayal of the artist as a man above the petty concerns of mere mortals, it's a delightful piece of filmmaking full of imaginative flights of creative delirium and accomplished with wit, grace, and a tongue-in-cheek joy. Fellini keeps winking at us, as if not to take it all too seriously. Cardinale, Aimee, Milo, and Steele costar as the women in his life. —*S. A.*

SATYRICON L: DIRECTORS/FELLINI, FEDERICO (1969) 129M D: Federico Fellini. *Capucine, Max Born, Hiram Keller, Salvo Randone, Martin Potter.* Based on the book by the famed Roman writer Petronius, which was deemed the "the most remarkable fiction which has dishonored the literature of any nation," Fellini's film is a remarkable fantasy about two young men in the indulgent time of Nero's Rome. In vivid color and comical accuracy Fellini portrays a sumptuous era marked by rampant sexual deviancy and devotion to classical mythology. From a purely theatrical viewpoint, one of the many things that continues to plague the viewer is the ever-watching ugly eye of bystanders. Off-color bystanders are a certain hallmark of Fellini's films, but in *Satyricon* these strange, half-mad bystanders seem to be on equal footing with the lead characters, neither of whom has much dialogue. The end of the film features one of the young men battling the Minotaur in his labyrinth. It is a suitable climax for what is a hauntingly serpentine film. —*N. J.*

STRADA, LA L: DIRECTORS/FELLINI, FEDERICO (1954) 115M D: Federico Fellini. *Anthony Quinn, Giulietta Masina.* Pitched between the neorealist evocation of everyday life of his earlier work and the carnivalesque fantasies of his later films, Fellini's story of brutish circus strongman Zampano (Quinn) and waiflike simpleton Gelsomina (Masina), whom Zampano literally buys to be his clown, cook, and servant, is enriched with a poetry both magical and tragic. Masina's performance has been compared with Chaplin, but there is an innocence and a spirituality in Gelsomina nowhere to be found in Chaplin's often cruel Tramp. Quinn's gruff physicality perfectly captures the simple, hearty needs of the self-gratifying Zampano: food, drink, sex, sleep (not necessarily in that order). Fellini captures their hard life on the road in all its beauty and pain, and ultimately releases the stony soul of the beastly Zampano in a devastating conclusion. Fellini's first masterpiece remains one of his finest films ever. It won the Silver Lion at the Venice Film Festival and the Oscar for Best Foreign Film. —S. A.

DRILLER KILLER L: DIRECTORS/FERRARA, ABEL (1979) 94M D: Abel Ferrara. *Alan Wynroth, Harry Schultz, Baybi Day, Carolyn Marz, Abel Ferrara.* Ferrara's first feature (discounting the self-starring *Nine Lives of a Wet Pussy*)leads the pack of power-tool killer flicks, and although Jimmy Laine (Ferrara's pseudonym) really drives it home in his murderous rages, the film itself doesn't truly pull it all together. The punk band downstairs that drives Reno (Ferrara) crazy unfortunately makes us a little crazy too, with a way-too-long "let's let the camera roll while we have another joint" scene that could've been better spent with Reno staring and grunting at the painting that he's been promising his agent or pumping his drill in and out. What truly works is Ferrara's outer-orbit commentary session recorded for the DVD. Able is just *not* with us as he giggles to himself every time a character in the film drags on a smoke or puts in their shoes. *Driller Killer* has its flaws, though its true winning grace is getting Ferrara the notice he needed to make the genius *Ms. 45* and his close-to-Hollywood follow-up *King of New York*. —S. R.

KING OF NEW YORK L: DIRECTORS/FERRARA, ABEL (1990) 106M D: Abel Ferrara. *Lawrence Fishburne, Christopher Walken, Wesley Snipes, Janet Julian, Victor Argo, David Caruso.* Walken plays a crime lord just released from a long term in prison. He's anything but reformed—just more careful! He spends his time violently reclaiming his former role as the head of organized crime in New York. Following the bloodbath is Caruso as an NYPD cop. He and his partners know who's committing the sudden rash of murders, but finding evidence proves to be difficult, especially as this crime lord is using all of his money and influence to climb the social and political ladders. This very tense film by Ferrara expertly casts Walken in a perfect role and proves that Caruso is more than a television actor. —N. J.

MS. 45 L: DIRECTORS/FERRARA, ABEL (1981) 81M D: Abel Ferrara. *Steve Singer, Jack Thibeau, Peter Yellen, Zoe Tamerlis.* The jump in aesthetic quality from Ferrara's first horror feature (*Driller Killer*) to the

beauty, grace, and finesse of *Ms. 45* is astounding, from the cinematography to the biting soundtrack to Tamerlis's excellent mute performance as the title character. Tamerlis breathes silent fire into the tragedy of poor Anna, first humiliated by an alleyway rape then by an attempted rape by an intruder in her home. Silent about her problems, Anna slowly succumbs to the weight of these attacks, becoming an avenger against all perpetrators of harm. The only problem is, she doesn't know when to stop. The multiple gang-member killing at Bethesda Fountain in Central Park is a precisely choreographed ballet of feminine violence, but the film never takes a feminist stance. The final, slow-motion dance of death exposes this vigilante as an out-of-control killer, not only debilitated by her muteness, but by her blindness to who the "real" perpetrators are. Ferrara is in fine form. —S. R.

'R XMAS L: DIRECTORS/FERRARA, ABEL (2001) 83M D: Abel Ferrara. *Victor Argo, Ice-T, Drea de Matteo, Lillo Brancato.* Family drama about drug dealers in New York City who live like any other rich family, bringing their daughter to an expensive private school and going to great lengths to buy her the hot toy of the season. When the husband (Brancato) is kidnapped by vigilante cops (including "Cop Killer" Ice-T), the wife (de Matteo) has to come up with ransom money without the help of the other organization members, who are in Puerto Rico for the holidays. It's a refreshingly realistic drug story lacking the usual movie contrivances, and has superb, naturalistic acting by de Matteo and Brancato. Be warned, though, that it ends very abruptly with a title card that manages to be equal parts awkward and pretentious. If you're wondering what the hell the title means, the best theory I've heard is that it's a badly punctuated combination of "Rx" (as in prescription drugs) and "Christmas." —B. T.

ALIEN 3 L: DIRECTORS/FINCHER, DAVID (1992) 114M D: David Fincher. *Sigourney Weaver, Charles S. Dutton, Pete Postlethwaite, Charles Dance, Lance Henriksen.* In his feature debut, Fincher made the brave and foolhardy decision of killing off most of the main characters from *Aliens*—during the opening credits, offscreen, and the one who survived, well, he kills her at the end. This enraged many fans who overlooked the strong atmosphere and originality of the movie for many years, giving it a reputation as a *Highlander II*–style sequel disaster. Then Fincher directed *Seven* and people started to reevaluate. Suddenly *Alien 3* was recognized as a visionary sequel and nobody cared about the muddled chase scenes, the less effective creature effects, the senseless killing of undeveloped characters, and the cast of bald British guys who are hard to tell apart. So *Alien 3* is both underrated and overrated. At least the worst of the series is still well worth watching. —B. T.

FIGHT CLUB L: DIRECTORS/FINCHER, DAVID (1999) 139M D: David Fincher. *Brad Pitt, Helena Bonham Carter, Meat Loaf Aday, Jared Leto, Edward Norton.* Norton plays a nameless insurance company investigator so frustrated with his empty life that he has become addicted to attending support groups for fatal diseases (testicular cancer being a favorite). Then his apartment blows up, he goes to stay with Tyler Durden (Pitt)—the charismatic rogue he just met on a plane—and next thing you know they're starting an underground club where people beat the shit out of each other to find enlightenment. As membership grows, so does Tyler's ambition, and Norton can't stop him from turning Fight Club into a brainwashing cult/playful anarchist terrorist group. Fincher applies the audacity, gallows humor, and stylish execution of his earlier films to more challenging material. The result is an utterly unique, thought-provoking film that both speaks to the angers and disappointments of people in their twenties and questions their methods for dealing with them. It's incredible that a Hollywood studio actually made this primal scream against materialism and corporatism! The special edition DVD has great menus and is loaded with supplemental materials including a commentary track by author Chuck Palahniuk, who almost seems to think the movie is better than his book. —*B. T.*

GAME, THE (1997) L: DIRECTORS/FINCHER, DAVID (1997) 128M D: David Fincher. *Sean Penn, James Rebhorn, Deborah Kara Unger, Michael Douglas.* For his forty-eighth birthday a wealthy investment banker (Douglas) gets an unusual gift from his brother (Penn): the mysterious services of Consumer Recreation Services, an organization that promises to immerse him into some sort of game when he least expects it. He dismisses CRS as "fantasy role-playing nonsense" until their elaborate deceptions and uncanny control of his life cause him to suspect a scam. It's an imaginative and perfectly constructed thriller. Some people hate the emotional ending, but the final twist is what brings all the pieces together and makes the story work both emotionally and as a suspense thriller. —*B. T.*

PANIC ROOM L: DIRECTORS/FINCHER, DAVID (2002) 112M D: David Fincher. *Jodie Foster, Jared Leto, Dwight Yoakam, Kristen Stewart, Forest Whitaker.* When thieves (Whitaker, Yoakam, and Leto) break into their new house, Foster and her daughter (Stewart) lock themselves in the "panic room"—a fortified bunker with security monitors. Unfortunately, what the thieves want is inside the room, and they won't leave without it. This high-concept thriller is a mild disappointment coming from the usually more thoughtful Fincher, but his meticulous execution wrings every possible piece of tension out of the script. With a good performance by Foster; clever, digitally enhanced camera trickery; and tensely staged set pieces, this would be impressive coming from most any other director. —*B. T.*

SEVEN L: DIRECTORS/FINCHER, DAVID (1995) 127M D: David Fincher. *Brad Pitt, Morgan Freeman, Gwyneth Paltrow, R. Lee Ermey. Seven* is a horror movie in the purest sense of the word. It feels no need to create its monster, choosing instead to give the audience a human one. It follows a pair of detectives (Pitt and Freeman) as they hunt a killer who ends his victims in sadistic fashion. Each crime scene reveals that the victim was chosen for his or her violation of one of the seven deadly sins: The first victim, a grossly overweight man, is force-fed for being a glutton, and his stomach explodes. Some of the punishments border on outlandish, but the film's bleak, washed-out look and spirit of crawling, contemplative horror keeps audience members unsettled. And the ending, which offers a dark, meditative take on the notion of punishment itself, will stay coiled beneath your skin. —*T. P.*

CURSE OF FRANKENSTEIN, THE L: DIRECTORS/FISHER, TERENCE (1957) 83M D: Terence Fisher. *Robert Urquhart, Valerie Gaunt, Hazel Court, Christopher Lee, Peter Cushing.* Hammer Studio's first horror hit is a retelling of the Frankenstein story. It's much different than the previous versions as the emphasis is on the obsessed doctor rather than the monster. Cushing stars as Baron von Frankenstein, whose research and lack of morals lead to him make a monster and actually become somewhat of a monster himself. Frankenstein and his associate (Urquhart) discover how to reanimate the dead and they create the ugly stitch-faced fiend (Lee). The doctor relates the story as a flashback to a priest. There were several sequels that allowed Cushing to further develop his unbalanced character. Lee and Cushing teamed up the next year for the even more thrilling *Horror of Dracula.* —*S. H.*

DEVIL RIDES OUT, THE L: DIRECTORS/FISHER, TERENCE (1968) 95M D: Terence Fisher. *Christopher Lee, Charles Gray, Leon Greene, Nike Arrighi.* Lee takes a rare heroic turn as a man of reason. When he discovers that the son of a war buddy has joined a satanic cult lorded over by the quietly malevolent Gray, he risks all to save his young friend. The towering Lee cuts quite a figure, whether leaping through hoards of robed devil worshippers to save a sacrificial victim or holding back the forces of black magic while standing in a giant pentagram. Director Fisher turns Richard Matheson's elegant script into an intellectual swashbuckler, a life-and-death struggle between two masters of the forces of light and darkness. The effects are coarse and dated by today's standards, but the gorgeous period detail, vivid color, and eerie imagery create a sinister ambiance. One of Fisher's—and Hammer's—best films. —*S. A.*

DRACULA: PRINCE OF DARKNESS L: DIRECTORS/FISHER, TERENCE (1966) 90M D: Terence Fisher. *Andrew Keir, Barbara Shelly, Charles Tingwell, Christopher Lee.* The second Dracula film made by Hammer and written by Jimmy Sangster is not as good as the first, but it is in no way overshadowed. The story begins with two traveling British couples who are warned by a cleric (Keir) not to go anywhere near a mysterious castle. But of course they go and spend a night there despite all warnings. Dracula is resurrected and wreaks havoc upon the world once more. Eventually the cleric returns, filling Peter Cushing's shoes as the vampire slayer. The high point is, as always, Lee's Dracula. He goes through the entire film without ever uttering a line yet conveys such a sense of menace that he fills the film with a terrible foreboding and uneasiness. He is able to imbue the character with a tenderness that invokes our sympathy while still making our hair stand on end. An excellent second step in Hammer's Dracula legacy. —*T. S.*

FRANKENSTEIN AND THE MONSTER FROM HELL L: DIRECTORS/FISHER, TERENCE (1974) 93M D: Terence Fisher. *Shane Briant, David Prowse, Bernard Lee, Madeleine Smith, Peter Cushing.* Fisher and Cushing team up for their final Hammer Frankenstein movie. It wasn't the studio's last but it remains the swan song of the series. Fisher's Dr. Frankenstein is less evil and cruel than simply cold and drained of compassion as he blackmails and coerces the corrupt employees of the asylum into complicity with his beastly experiments. Bodybuilder Prowse (who donned the Darth Vader robes in the *Star Wars* trilogy) is once again unrecognizable under the hulking bodysuit of Frankenstein's ape-like creation, and Smith plays angel to his devilish-looking creature. The budgetary constraints show through too often (you can see the seams in the costume) but the claustrophobic set and buzzing, bubbling laboratory make for effective atmosphere, and the stormy graveyard scene, where the misshapen ogre digs up his "other" body, is a highlight of the series. Fisher, Hammer's preeminent director, retired from the movies after this film. —*S.A.*

FRANKENSTEIN CREATED WOMAN L: DIRECTORS/FISHER, TERENCE (1967) 92M D: Terence Fisher. *Robert Morris, Peter Cushing, Susan Denberg.* Hammer Studio's fourth Frankenstein film starring Cushing as the brilliant but crazy scientist provides an emotionally complex monster movie that should appeal to people who normally don't like this kind of stuff. Dr. Frankenstein has settled for his latest round of experiments in a village populated by lots of intolerant jerks. Hans (Morris), the doc's assistant, is in love with a bar wench named Christina (Denberg) who has a burnt face. Hans is unjustly sentenced to death by guillotine and Christina commits suicide. Never missing an undead opportunity, Frankenstein reanimates the dead girl's body and infuses it with the soul of Hans. The Doctor also performs some beauty-enhancing surgery and the sexy blond monster extracts her revenge on the cruel villagers. Former Playboy Playmate Denberg gives a sympathetic performance and Cushing gives another strong turn as the unhinged scientist. My only complaint is the abrupt ending. The title is inspired by Roger Vadim's *And God Created Woman.* —*S. H.*

HORROR OF DRACULA L: DIRECTORS/FISHER, TERENCE (1958) 82M D: Terence Fisher. *Carol Marsh, Christopher Lee, Peter Cushing, Michael Gough.* Hammer's first Dracula production stars the great Lee as the Count and Cushing as Van Helsing. The story more or less follows Bram Stoker's novel, but reaches extraordinary heights due to the two stars' amazing, iconic performances and Fisher's creepy direction in shocking Hammer color. Hammer's trademark Gothic atmosphere merges the visual flair of Universal's most imaginative horror films with an abrasive level of violence and beautiful, bright red blood. Cushing is awesome as always but Lee steals the show, creating the most memorable portrayal of Dracula since Bela Lugosi. It's one of Hammer's greatest pictures, which is great praise, indeed. Gough also lends his excellent acting chops to the picture and Fisher brings it all together with a flair for the macabre. For Gothic chills and thrills, you simply can't do better than classic Hammer horror. —*T. S.*

HOUND OF THE BASKERVILLES, THE L: DIRECTORS/FISHER, TERENCE (1959) 86M D: Terence Fisher. *Peter Cushing, David Oxley, Andre Morell, Marla Landi, Miles Malleson, Christopher Lee.* Hammer's horror franchise swept wide, indeed: even Sherlock Holmes was given the Gothic treatment in this moody adaptation. Cushing is perfectly cast as the great detective, the very embodiment of science and reason (which, incidentally, also made him such a great Van Helsing in the Dracula series). Lee is less at ease as young Lord Baskerville, the last of a cursed family, flitting between fear and apathetic disregard. The film drips with the mood of the moors, mist hanging in the air, the dying vegetation threatening to come to life and trap the next unwary traveler. Another excellent production from Fisher, Britain's master of horror. —*S. A.*

ISLAND OF TERROR L: DIRECTORS/FISHER, TERENCE (1966) 87M D: Terence Fisher. *Sam Kydd, Edward Judd, Carole Gray, Eddie Byrne, Peter Cushing.* Silicates, weird creatures that look like a big turtle-shelled scab with a protruding combination tentacle/trunk, are sucking the bones out of the residents of a remote island off the coast of Ireland. The Silicates reproduce at a frightening rate and when they divide it looks like somebody dumped a can of chicken noodle soup on them. Considering how silly they look, *Island of Terror* is really creepy. The deaths are frequent and gruesome and feature gross, rubbery corpses. You really sense that the island population is doomed because the multiplying creatures are virtually unstoppable. Cushing (who gets his armed chopped off) and Judd play two scientists who must find a way to stop the goddamn monsters before they spread around the world. Similar to executive producer Gordon's equally scary *Fiend Without a Face,* this is Fisher's best non-Hammer horror film. —*S. H.*

MUMMY, THE L: DIRECTORS/FISHER, TERENCE (1959) 88M D: Terence Fisher. *Christopher Lee, Peter Cushing, Yvonne Furneaux.* After successfully remaking *Dracula* and *Frankenstein,* Hammer films applied their lurid Gothic style to *The Mummy.* Cushing stars as an archeologist who desecrates a sacred tomb and is pursued by Lee's mummy, a towering, barrel-chested creature who crashes through the film like a veritable golem. The Egyptian scenes have that cheap, back-lot look to them, but once the film returns to the misty swamps and Victorian mansions of rural England it's back in traditional territory. Lee is the best movie mummy ever: haunted soul, rampaging juggernaut, and hugely powerful monster all in one. Furneaux costars as Cushing's wife who, coincidentally, is a dead ringer for the mummy's ancient love. In the Hammer tradition there's a sadistic twist to the flashback when Lee's transgressive priest has his tongue removed. It's not as gory as it sounds, but there's still a shivering eeriness about it. —*S. A.*

PHANTOM OF THE OPERA (1962) L: DIRECTORS/FISHER, TERENCE (1962) 84M D: Terence Fisher. *Edward de Souza, Michael Gough, Thorley Walters, Heather Sears, Herbert Lom.* This Hammer version of Leroux's classic story is decent, but not great. Fisher, whose films usually benefit because of how sympathetic the monsters are, imbues the Phantom with far too many endearing qualities. As a result the character is overly sympathetic and the movie fails to have the dark and dangerous qualities the story demands. My favorite part of this version is the strange evil dwarf. Despite a few creepy touches, the film fails to come together as it should. —*T. S.*

REVENGE OF FRANKENSTEIN, THE L: DIRECTORS/FISHER, TERENCE (1958) 90M D: Terence Fisher. *Peter Cushing, Francis Matthews, Eunice Gayson, Michael Gwynn.* Fisher's sequel to the successful Hammer resurrection of the Frankenstein franchise is more cold-blooded than *The Curse of Frankenstein.* Cushing escapes the guillotine (sending a priest to donate his head in Frankenstein's place) and sets up shop as a celebrated society physician who runs a charity hospital, which he turns into a parts shop for his latest creation. The centerpiece set is his new laboratory of buzzing devices with a tank for his suspended creature. Fisher makes the most of his limited budget and

even the claustrophobic sets look good in the vivid color of the Hammer style. There are few innocents in the Frankenstein films and this is no different: high-society dandies are hypocrites, poorhouse patients are thieves and opportunists, and of course the driven doctor is willing to sacrifice anything and anyone to achieve his goal. Where the movies once treated him as a well-meaning but misguided scientist, Cushing turns him into a soulless megalomaniac with ice in his veins and a stare that practically dissects, as if he sized up everyone he saw for the potential of their body parts. —*S. A.*

SHERLOCK HOLMES AND THE DEADLY NECKLACE L: DIRECTORS/FISHER, TERENCE (1962) 88M D: Terence Fisher. *Christopher Lee, Thorley Walters.* This German Sherlock Holmes mystery (based on the novel *The Valley of Fear*) imports British Hammer veterans Lee and Walters (as Holmes and Watson) and director Fisher (who directed Lee in the superior Hammer Gothic horror *The Hound of the Baskervilles*). The black-and-white mystery plays more like the Edgar Wallace thrillers that were the rage in Germany; less a brain puzzle than a body-count picture with Holmes battling Moriarty over the cursed necklace of Cleopatra. For all the weird waterfront color, booby traps, and Holmes disguises and undercover identities, this film has little of the mood and tension one would expect from Fisher. A real oddity among Holmes films, this has the added twist of lacking Lee's voice: the English language version was dubbed over by another actor. —*S. A.*

GONE WITH THE WIND L: DIRECTORS/FLEMING, VICTOR (1939) 231M D: Victor Fleming. *Clark Gable, Hattie McDaniel, Vivien Leigh, Olivia de Havilland, Leslie Howard.* This is one of the greatest American films of all time because it employs some of the most timeless actors on a subject extremely time-oriented to the country when it was released. Leigh plays Scarlett, the impressionable belle of the South who naively expects her boyfriend to triumph in the Civil War. Of course, things turn very badly for the South. Her boyfriend becomes cannon fodder, she is burned out of Atlanta, and eventually she must choose between Ashley Wilkes (Howard) and Rhett Butler (Gable)—a choice suggestive of varying allegiances after the war. Historically this movie is doubly important, for countless young men from both North and South had this bigger-than-life film indelibly etched in their minds as they marched off to fight WWII so soon after its release. —*N. J.*

WIZARD OF OZ, THE L: DIRECTORS/FLEMING, VICTOR (1939) 101M D: Victor Fleming. *Jack Haley, Frank Morgan, Judy Garland, Ray Bolger, Bert Lahr.* Garland in her most famous role plays Dorothy, the young woman depicted in the classic Oz novels by L. Frank Baum. The first part of the film is in black and white and portrays Dorothy as a simple farm girl in Kansas. Through the course of a tornado, or perhaps just a dream, she finds herself and her whole house magically transported to Oz, which is in brilliant Technicolor. She's stunned, but is praised by the tyrannized Munchkins for inadvertently killing the Wicked Witch of the East with the drop of her house. She follows the yellow brick road to find the fabled Wizard of Oz, who might transport her back home. On the way she finds a tin man who needs a heart, a scarecrow who needs a brain, and a lion who needs courage. This bizarre entourage, accompanied by her trusty dog Toto, makes its way to the Emerald City despite the obstacles presented by the Wicked Witch of the West, who wishes to avenge her sister. Any enthusiast of this film should be sure to see *Return to Oz*, which continues the original story. —*N. J.*

DONOVAN'S REEF L: DIRECTORS/FORD, JOHN (1963) 109M D: John Ford. *Elizabeth Allen, Jack Warden, Dorothy Lamour, Lee Marvin, John Wayne.* Ford's boisterous comedy, set on a tropical Pacific Island where the free and easy freedoms of old war buddies are threatened by the arrival of a Boston socialite, is yet another of his pictures that explores race and racism. This one is hardly deep, but it is good fun, with Wayne and Marvin as drinking buddies still engaged in adolescent pissing contests and Lamour doing a number on her South Seas Princess stereotype. When it comes to romance Ford is still a chauvinist curmudgeon (Wayne spanking his bride-to-be is embarrassing under any circumstances), but he knows how to throw a tropical party. —*S. A.*

FORT APACHE L: DIRECTORS/FORD, JOHN (1948) 125M D: John Ford. *Henry Fonda, Shirley Temple, Ward Bond, John Agar, John Wayne.* A philosophical Western, but full of exciting sequences and humor and an emotional scope as wide as the Monument Valley landscape where it is filmed. Ford's wraparound story is history as legend, a cavalry unit's valiant stand against overwhelming odds. Then the events are shown as they really happened: a preventable tragedy caused by an arrogant colonel (Fonda) who goes back on his word to a native tribe ready for peace and leads his troops into an ambush. Ford takes a subtle view of history. The realist who saw things straight (Wayne) and protested survives to take over command. But he tells the reporters the legend (not truth) for the sake of service morale as well as to honor the memory of his brave comrades who died. Ford perceives that for history to move forward, legend and truth of necessity must interpenetrate. For this reason and others, *Fort Apache* is by far cinema's greatest cavalry Western. —*J. C.*

GRAPES OF WRATH, THE L: DIRECTORS/FORD, JOHN (1940) 129M D: John Ford. *John Carradine, Russell Simpson, Jane Darwell, Henry Fonda.* Back when the auteur theory first got rolling, the passion for exalting previously undervalued movies, especially genre movies, led Ford partisans to neglect *The Grapes of Wrath,* a prestigious literary adaptation with full Establishment honors. John Steinbeck's left-leaning novel of the Okies who lost their homes to foreclosure and set out on the road to find a new life in California was not what you'd expect a big corporate entity like a major Hollywood studio to bring to the screen, and producer Darryl F. Zanuck deserved every rave review the movie got. For his part, Ford, working with that master of deep-focus composition Gregg Toland, achieved an awe-inspiring fusion of poetry and documentary-style realism in chronicling the Okies' odyssey. Fonda tapped deep into the American soul with his portrayal of Tom Joad, and Darwell—a heretofore-all-but-anonymous small-part player—as Ma Joad created an indelible characterization that brought her an Oscar. Carradine and John Qualen also reached career highs as, respectively, Preacher Casy and Muley Graves. This is one of Ford's great movies, even if the critics, Hollywood, and the Academy knew it from the get-go. —*R. T. J.*

HORSE SOLIDERS, THE L: DIRECTORS/FORD, JOHN (1959) 115M D: John Ford. *Denver Pyle, Strother Martin, John Wayne, William Holden, Constance Towers.* Ford's only Civil War feature is also his most purely enjoyable. The tone is light, the color lush, and the comedy works. Pyle and Martin are the Cheech and Chong of Westerns. Towers holds her own against Wayne (no small feat), and amid all the hoopla, Ford manages to throw in some very strong meditations on the senselessness of war without changing the tone of the film too much. And it's got the great Stan Jones cavalry song, "I Left My Love." —*M. S.*

HOW GREEN WAS MY VALLEY L: DIRECTORS/FORD, JOHN (1941) 118M D: John Ford. *Maureen O'Hara, Anna Lee, Donald Crisp, Roddy McDowall, Walter Pidgeon.* Ford's multiple Oscar–winning classic (including Best Picture and Best Director) is one of his most visually beautiful films, a sentimental but rich tale of a Welsh mining family based on the novel by Richard Llewellyn. McDowall is the young boy who comes of age under the watchful eye of his protective but stern father (Crisp) and the encouragement of the university-educated village preacher (Pidgeon), whose love for the boy's older sister (O'Hara) is forbidden because of a clash with the father's unbending demands. Coming only a year after *The Grapes of Wrath,* Ford skirts the social commentary for a misty-eyed celebration of traditional values in the face of the industrial age. Emotion wells and music swells, but at the core is Ford's fine eye for composition and sure hand with performers. His mix of professionalism and poetry results in the moments of cinema magic that made Ford the dean of American directors. —*S. A.*

MAN WHO SHOT LIBERTY VALANCE, THE L: DIRECTORS/ FORD, JOHN (1962) 123M D: John Ford. *James Stewart, John Wayne, Vera Miles, Lee Marvin.* Stewart

John Ford

John Ford was born Sean Aloysius O'Fearna (the family soon changed its name to O'Feeney) in Cape Elizabeth, Maine, in 1895. In 1914 he joined his brother Francis in Hollywood, where he apprenticed as a production assistant, stuntman, actor, cameraman, and assistant director. Soon after arriving in Hollywood, he changed his name to Jack Ford. He directed his first film in 1917, and with *Cameo Kirby* (1923) his directorial credit read John Ford.

Many critics consider Ford to be America's greatest film director, perhaps even the world's greatest director. In a career spanning more than fifty years, he made over 120 films (sadly, most of his silent films have been lost to time) and a few works for television. During the studio era he was a powerful director who maintained a surprising amount of control over his films. He died at his home in California in 1973.

Most famous for his Westerns and for the landscape of Monument Valley, which he made into his mythic vision of America, Ford has a scope that ranged across dramas, comedies, war films, adventures, and literary adaptations, but his themes and his vision have been consistent across genres. He explored American history and the communities that made up the country with a nostalgia that turned darker in his later films. His images are among the most graceful and beautiful of American cinema. Ford was, as Andrew Sands wrote, "a storyteller and a poet of images. He made his movies both move and be moving."

Ford was nominated for the Academy Award for Best Director for *Stagecoach* (1939), and won it four times, for *The Informer* (1935), *The Grapes of Wrath* (1940), *How Green Was My Valley* (1941), and *The Quiet Man* (1952).

"I never thought about what I was doing in terms of art, or 'this is great' or 'world-shaking' or anything like that," John Ford said in 1969. "To me, it was always a job of work—which I enjoyed immensely—and that's it."

—*Sean Axmaker*

---

is decades too old to play the naive tenderfoot who finds the West a little more wild than he expected, and Ford hardly leaves the confines of the soundstage, giving the film an oddly claustrophobic feeling. Yet this is one of the great Westerns. Ford punctures the heroic myths he helped create in a bitter tale of a freedom-loving gunfighter (Wayne) who dreads the coming of civilization and its structures to the wide-open towns and lawless plains, yet sacrifices himself to make it happen. Ford has never made a darker portrait of the lies and the lives that built the West. —*S.A.*

MY DARLING CLEMENTINE L: DIRECTORS/FORD, JOHN (1946) 97M D: John Ford. *Tim Holt, Walter Brennan, Henry Fonda, Linda Darnell, Cathy Downs, Victor Mature.* Ford's sublime interpretation of the Gunfight at OK Corral rewrites the story as a mythic frontier legend. Fonda is the stiff, moral Wyatt Earp, who accepts the badge to take his vengeance on the barbarous Clanton clan led by a ruthless Brennan ("When you pull a gun, kill a man!" is his motto). Mature is surprisingly effective as the haunted alcoholic Doc Holliday, a tubercular gambler who escapes civilization in the Wild West, only to find that it follows him. Sure, Ford takes great liberties with history, but the result is one of the most classically beautiful Westerns ever made, a lyrical ode to the taming of the West when Manifest Destiny was an unambiguous rallying cry. —*S.A.*

QUIET MAN, THE L: DIRECTORS/FORD, JOHN (1952) 129M D: John Ford. *Barry Fitzgerald, Victor McLaglen, Maureen O'Hara, John Wayne, Arthur Shields.* A retired boxer from America (Wayne) returns to his native Ireland. The culture difference is obvious to all yet he persistently tries to fit in. Some of the largest social clashes are between himself and the equally strong-willed Mary Kate (O'Hara) whom he dates and tries to marry. She has a brother (McLaglen) who attempts to dissuade her from getting married, while friends of the American urge him toward marriage. These two strong personalities, despite their love for each other, eventually come to blows. This spellbinding dramatic comedy is gorgeous to watch and is downright insightful with a colorful understanding of American and Irish cultures. —N.J.

SEARCHERS, THE L: DIRECTORS/FORD, JOHN (1956) 125M D: John Ford. *Natalie Wood, Jeffrey Hunter, Vera Miles, Ward Bond, John Wayne.* Initially received as just another, slightly above average Western, *The Searchers* went on to recognition as one of the Ten Best Films of All Time, the supreme Ford masterwork, the best work ever by Wayne, and a touchstone for the so-called American film renaissance of the '70s. Ford and his cinematographer Winton C. Hoch never framed Monument Valley more dynamically, or had a sharper format than VistaVision to serve the saturated Technicolor or the echoing vastness of the Southwest. Ethan Edwards (Wayne) is authentically a hero, but also some kind of monster, and almost certainly a man with a guilty past. When the woman he has always loved, and the family and home he could never have, are savagely destroyed, Ethan sets out in pursuit of the blue-eyed Comanche chief Scar and the two Edwards nieces he has carried away. His fellow searcher, a part-Cherokee orphan (Hunter) adopted by the family, comes to fear that Ethan's obsessive intention is to kill the girls in the name of racial purity. Long before the "revisionist" Westerns of the '70s, Ford and Wayne wrestled with the demonic side of Western myth and achieved a richer, more deeply disturbing complexity than anyone who came afterward. —R.T.J.

SHE WORE A YELLOW RIBBON L: DIRECTORS/FORD, JOHN (1949) 103M D: John Ford. *Ben Johnson, Harry Carey Jr., Victor McLaglen, Joanne Dru, John Agar, John Wayne.* Capt. Brittles's retirement becomes official after one last patrol to lead women and children to an overland stage station as well as relieve a distant column and connect with his scouts. Indian trouble is brewing. This is fun and games to Miss Dandridge (Drew), the Eastern niece of the post commander, who flirts with Lt. Penell (Carey) to aggravate Lt. Cohill (Agar). She grows up quickly when their destinations yield dead and dying soldiers and the stage station is burned. When the patrol finally finds its way back safely to the fort, Brittles (Wayne) is full of bitter self-reproach regarding his three objectives, "Failure. Failure. Failure." Dandridge has witnessed soldiering at its most honorable. This is one of the most perfectly staged and emotionally powerful moments of cinema. Ford has a handle on failure that few directors do, turning a pretty ordinary story into something profound. —J.C.

STAGECOACH L: DIRECTORS/FORD, JOHN (1939) 100M D: John Ford. *Donald Meek, Berton Churchill, Thomas Mitchell, Claire Trevor, John Wayne, Andy Devine.* If you had to show a Martian—or someone reared on Michael Bay video games—what a real movie looks and feels like, you couldn't top this arguably greatest film of Hollywood's most golden year, 1939. Besides boasting glorious imagery, it *tells a story,* with impeccable craft, of nine travelers thrown together on an overland stage, crossing Apache country with an uprising about to erupt. The script meticulously develops each character and plots their itineraries toward redemption. The casting exemplifies the richness of Hollywood's character-actor corps, especially Trevor as the prostitute Dallas, and Mitchell (Supporting Actor Oscar) as the drunken Doc Boone, the two "dregs of society" who are the best people around; Carradine as a courtly gambler fixated on protecting a Southern lady; and Meek as a timorous whiskey drummer. Wayne steps out of B-movie indentured servitude and into American myth as the Ringo Kid, an escaped convict bent on keeping an appointment in the town of Lordsburg. Conventional wisdom holds that *Stagecoach* peaks with its celebrated chase across the salt flats, and that the final act is anticlimactic. No way: the Lordsburg nighttown sequence is the most brilliantly directed passage Ford had yet achieved. —R.T.J.

THEY WERE EXPENDABLE L: DIRECTORS/FORD, JOHN (1945) 135M D: John Ford. *Robert Montgomery, John Wayne, Donna Reed, Jack Holt, Ward Bond.* Ford was called back from active service in WWII to make this somber classic about the early Pacific campaign in the months after Pearl Harbor. Wayne, not yet the superstar of American cinema, plays Rusty Ryan, second-in-command to the aloof, no-nonsense Lt. John "Brick" Brickley (Montgomery, also a WWII officer). Hotheaded and emotional where Brick is calm and clear-thinking, Ryan is constantly reminded that his duty is to the unit, not his own frustrated sense of helplessness in the face of repeated defeats. Overflowing with Ford's love of military tradition, this is one of his most beautiful films: a rich mix of documentary realism, bold expressionism, and poetic delicacy, all of which add to the poignancy and power of a film that ends not in victory but defeat. It was Ford's reminder to the American public that victory in the Pacific was reached at a tremendous cost in human life. —S.A.

AMADEUS L: DIRECTORS/FORMAN, MILOS (1984) 180M D: Milos Forman. *Elizabeth Berridge, Simon Callow, Christine Ebersole, Tom Hulce, F. Murray Abraham, Roy Dotrice.* Abraham plays the successful Italian court composer Antonio Salieri, who one day meets the ambitious young German composer Wolfgang Amadeus Mozart. After discovering what a womanizer and scoundrel Mozart is, Salieri curses God for choosing such

a gross German as his vehicle of musical expression and goes about destroying the young monster. This film is based on the successful stage play by Peter Shaffer rather than on the actual life of Mozart. Whereas the historic details of music, setting, and costume, as well as several aspects of Mozart's life are accurate to history, the plot of Salieri murdering Mozart is pure fiction. *Amadeus* swept the Oscars in 1984, earning awards for Best Picture, Best Director, and Best Actor for Abraham's unforgettable performance. The longer release in 2002 is an improvement in that a few of the smaller subplots are put back, allowing more sense to be made of character motivations. —*N. J.*

FIREMEN'S BALL, THE L: DIRECTORS/FORMAN, MILOS (1967) 73M D: Milos Forman. *Josef Kolb, Frantisek Debelka, Vaclav Stockel, Josef Svet, Josef Valnoha, Jan Vostrcil.* Forman's follow-up feature to *Loves of a Blonde* is far less gentle in its satire. The aging members of a small-town fire brigade watch their annual fund-raising party unravel in chaos while they ineffectually try to stage-manage everything from an impromptu beauty contest (the girls all flee) to a raffle (all the prizes are nicked by the end of the night). The metaphor wasn't lost on the Czechoslovakian government and its aging politburo, parodied in this film as a bumbling bunch of clowns hopelessly out of touch with the people, and they tried to ban it. It opened two weeks before the Soviet invasion of 1968. —*S. A.*

LOVES OF A BLONDE L: DIRECTORS/FORMAN, MILOS (1965) 85M D: Milos Forman. *Jiri Hruby, Antonin Blazejovsky, Vladimir Mensik, Hana Brejchova, Vladimir Pucholt.* Forman's second feature and first hit (in fact one of the biggest hits in Czech history) is a sweet little story of romantic confusion. A naive factory girl spends the night with a handsome young piano player visiting her provincial little town and decides to follow her new love to the city. . . and is surprised to find her sophisticated big-city swinger living with a protective mother and a numb father in a cramped apartment block. Quiet, nicely observed, and shot in an intimate style in black and white, it's a very funny film with a gentle satire of romantic fancy, idealism, and contemporary Czech Socialism. —*S. A.*

MAN ON THE MOON L: DIRECTORS/FORMAN, MILOS (1999) 118M D: Milos Forman. *Jerry Lawler, Paul Giamatti, Courtney Love, Jim Carrey, Danny DeVito.* Using all his comedic and dramatic chops, Carrey is surprisingly great playing Andy Kaufman. He re-creates Kaufman's most famous characters and, at times, even channels the regular Andy Kaufman voice with uncanny accuracy. The one thing this movie does not entirely capture, however, is the unpredictable, provocative, and sometimes confusing spirit of Kaufman's work. The movie also gives away some of Kaufman's tricks

(like his friendship with supposed enemy Lawler, and having his friend Bob Zmuda [Giamatti] take over his alter ego Tony Clifton). This is a good movie, and it is an interesting notion that Kaufman's tricks caused people to think he was faking it when he actually died of cancer. But coming from Alexander and Karaszewski, who had already made such ingenious biopics of eccentric subjects Ed Wood and Larry Flynt, it is disappointing to see a fairly orthodox biography of a completely unorthodox artist. —*B. T.*

ONE FLEW OVER THE CUCKOO'S NEST L: DIRECTORS/FORMAN, MILOS (1975) 134M D: Milos Forman. *William Redfield, Scatman Crothers, Dean R. Brooks, Danny DeVito, Louise Fletcher, Jack Nicholson.* Before Forman became obsessed with chronicling history's entertainers, he assembled an incredible cast for this adaptation of Ken Kesey's most important novel. *One Flew over the Cuckoo's Nest* is widely considered one of the triumphs of American filmmaking, having won every major Oscar at the time of its release and retaining its impact and relevance throughout the years. Nicholson immortalizes R. P. McMurphy, an arguably unstable roustabout admitted to a mental institution managed by the seemingly soulless Nurse Ratchet (Fletcher). McMurphy's flagrant disregard for authority lands him in ever-increasing disfavor with the hospital staff, especially when his influence over his fellow patients becomes apparent. The supporting cast turn in unbelievable performances, with several familiar faces getting their start here as schizophrenics and sociopaths. Despite taking some liberties with the original work, Forman's first American production is truly deserving of its accolades. —*Z. C.*

PEOPLE VS LARRY FLYNT, THE L: DIRECTORS/FORMAN, MILOS (1996) 129M D: Milos Forman. *Courtney Love, Brett Harrelson, Edward Norton, Donna Hanover, Woody Harrelson, Crispin Glover.* Meet Larry Flynt, publisher of *Hustler* magazine and unlikely champion of the free press in a series of court battles that takes him to the Supreme Court. Harrelson plays the controversial, flamboyant Flint, from his beginnings as a strip-club owner to his success with Larry Flynt Publications. Along the way he is paralyzed by an assassin's bullet (which put him in a wheelchair for the rest of his life) and born again, which apparently didn't end his career as a pornography king. Written by *Ed Wood* screenwriters Scott Alexander and Larry Karaszewski, this is a bawdy burlesque with a crude, smutty, self-promoting clown at the center (at least through most of it), and Harrelson's meat-eating performance is perfect: grotesque, gauche, and hearty. Love won well-deserved raves as his junkie stripper wife, Althea, and Norton plays passion in a much calmer mode as Flynt's lawyer. —*S. A.*

ALL THAT JAZZ L: DIRECTORS/FOSSE, BOB (1979) 123M D: Bob Fosse. *Ben Vereen, Ann Reinking, Roy Scheider.* Fosse's deep self-exploration has never been better. Dark, depressing, and lighthearted in all the right spots, this non-autobiography rarely leaves an unaffected viewer. Scheider's choreographer is working on too many shows, too hard, and with the aid of too many substances, completely damaging every relationship that gets close to his tap-dancing feet. The astonishing Reinking's legs alone require some form of statuette. Erzsebet Foldi as the neglected daughter, Leland Palmer as the pissed-off mom (obviously modeled after Gwen Verdon), the amazing Vereen, and Tony Walton's dazzling fantasy set pieces kick this downbeat flick into high gear. It's wrought with black irony; infused with drug, alcohol, and nicotine abuse; and pierced with scathing song bits and dance numbers that cause goose bumps near your soul, where it counts. From rock numbers to ditties to ultrasexy set pieces to Jessica Lange's coldly beauteous dark-even-in-white angel, *All That Jazz* is an unstoppable, foot-tapping classic. —*S. R.*

LENNY L: DIRECTORS/FOSSE, BOB (1974) 111M D: Bob Fosse. *Stanley Beck, Gary Morton, Jan Miner, Valerie Perrine, Dustin Hoffman.* Hoffman channels the passion of legendary comedian Lenny Bruce, who pushed the envelope of comedy with his excoriating satire and profane language, in Fosse's biographical drama, based on Julian Barry's adaptation of his stage play. Perrine gives the best performance of her career as the sweetly naive street-smart stripper turned spiraling heroine addict Honey Bruce, and earned her only Oscar nomination. It was one of the film's honors, which included nods to Hoffman, Fosse, Barry's script, Bruce Surtees's searing black-and-white photography (his images of Bruce on stage look like a vibrant '50s paparazzi shoot come to life), and the film itself. Moments of glibness stand out in the otherwise intense portrait of the man who used words as weapons, but it's the passion in the face of hypocrisy that drives the film. —*S. A.*

AWFUL DR. ORLOF, THE L: DIRECTORS/FRANCO, JESS (1962) 90M D: Jess Franco. *Howard Vernon, Conrado San Martin.* This is kind of an atypical film for sleaze director Franco because it is fairly well crafted, well made, and well, uh, good. You don't have to rely on camp to enjoy it because it's actually a quality little Gothic thriller. The plot involves a doctor who abducts women and steals their skin to try to fix his deformed daughter's face. It's very atmospheric, well shot, and uses just the right amount of humor to stay creepy. It's a real surprise coming from Franco and any horror fan should enjoy it. —*T. S.*

FEMALE VAMPIRE L: DIRECTORS/FRANCO, JESS (1973) 101M D: Jess Franco. *Lina Romay, Monica Swinn, Jack Taylor.* Franco's nudie-cutie outing with longtime companion Romay has been cut and retitled a few times but Image's domestic release gets the basic point across: Countess Irina needs both blood and sperm to survive. She sports a cape, knee-high leather boots, and a thick leather belt secured above her dark pubic bush, but the costume budget was definitely last on the list in this Franco treat. Romay's Countess is able to seduce anyone who gets anywhere near her. As descriptive rationale for her blood-givers' actions, Franco offers several-minute close-ups of Romay's twitching, undulating, rocking, winking snatch before the blood pounce. One of her victims gets it in the crotch after some outdoor action. Romay also has oral sex with a bedpost, humps a pillow, and shows us everything but her fallopian tubes. —*S. R.*

JACK THE RIPPER L: DIRECTORS/FRANCO, JESS (1976) 92M D: Jess Franco. *Josephine Chaplin, Lina Romay, Klaus Kinski, Andreas Mannkopff, Herbert Fux.* Ripperologists beware: Franco shamelessly rewrites Jack the Ripper history in this '70s Euro-thriller. Sometimes stylish and atmospheric, other times crude and clumsy, and always awash in nudity and gore, its interest lies mainly in the casting of the feral Kinski as the killer. He gets a magnificent entrance, all shadow and mystery until he turns his head in a snap and his unmistakable eyes fill the screen, startled wide with fright and maniacal intensity. The dull Mannkopff is the Scotland Yard detective on the case and Chaplin is his ballerina girlfriend who, for no reason, decides to troll for the Ripper on her own, without even telling her cop boyfriend. It's typical Franco: Scenes of misty beauty are interspersed with blunt gorehound excess and Romay (Franco's muse) gets the film's sadistic spotlight death. Knowing their offscreen relationship only makes the brutal, tortuous assault more perverse. —*S. A.*

JUSTINE L: DIRECTORS/FRANCO, JESS (1968) 124M D: Jess Franco. *Akim Tamiroff, Howard Vernon, Klaus Kinski, Romina Power, Mercedes McCambridge, Maria Rohm.* Franco adapts the Marquis de Sade for this notorious Euro sexploitation classic, one of his first collaborations with Harry Alan Towers, the famous British producer of Euro pulp thrillers with decadent flourishes. The kinky tale of the degradation of a virtuous innocent (Power) is perfect Franco material, though the satire and irony is admittedly buried in sheer excess. She is cruelly treated, robbed, falsely accused, imprisoned, assaulted, beaten, and pursued by all she encounters while her sister (Rohm) indulges in vice, sin, murder, and all sorts of wickedness with such glee that it sends her to the top of society. We periodically cut back to Kinski as the Marquis, madly scribbling in a prison while these visions writhe around him. What surprises isn't the kink and cruelty, it's the handsome style and gorgeous photography, and the unhinged performance of Jack Palance as a malicious monk exploring the carnal limits of pleasure through pain. —S.A.

SUCCUBUS L: DIRECTORS/FRANCO, JESS (1967) 76M D: Jess Franco. *Michel Lemoine, Howard Vernon, Janine Reynaud, Jack Taylor.* One of Franco's early color films is also one of his first to feature extensive nudity. Many of the motifs found in his unique brand of erotic psychedelia are fully realized in *Succubus.* Sexy redheaded Lorna (Reynaud) is a cabaret performer in a Lisbon nightclub called Club Snob. Her stage act incorporates a sensual dance and a tortured mannequin (both familiar Franco devices). She eventually loses touch with reality and may be possessed by a demon. Lorna slides into a trippy world of masks, midgets, Aurora monster models, and murder! There's a typical jazz score and it's very well photographed, though the whole thing is confusing as hell. But nobody in their right mind watches Franco's movies for their plots. —S.H.

VAMPYROS LESBOS L: DIRECTORS/FRANCO, JESS (1971) 89M D: Jess Franco. *Ewa Strömberg, Soledad Miranda.* Filled with all the images that Franco fans have come to expect from this late-'60s period of his filmmaking, *Vampyros Lesbos* succeeds as another high-fetish, sleazy psychedelic groove-fest. Miranda plays the Countess Nadina, a vampiress who lures visitors to her island resort by stripping nightly in a club in Istanbul. The film begins with the sitar/electronic soundtrack blaring while Miranda rolls across a stage with only a mirror, candelabra, and stoic nude blond accomplice as set-dressing. Strömberg is Linda Westinghouse, sent to the Countess's compound to investigate the will of Count Dracula, which leaves everything to the Countess. Linda becomes enraptured by the Countess and quickly falls prey to her. Complete with mad doctors, night-time nightmare visits, screaming blondes, and bloody faces, Franco's twist on the vampire tale, made with low-budget pop art aplomb, would work equally well as background video wallpaper for your own Gothic groove parties. —S.R.

VIRGIN REPORT L: DIRECTORS/FRANCO, JESS (1971) 67M D: Jess Franco. *Hans Hass Jr., Ingrid Steinbach, Diane Winter, Howard Vernon.* You could call this sexploitation "documentary" defloration through the ages. A narrator tells us that "Virginity, purity, innocence" has been replaced by the modern motto "Sex liberates and liberation is good." There's plenty of liberation going here as Franco re-creates scenes of young women "losing it" in seductions, wedding night rituals, sex cult ceremonies, Inquisition tortures (what would a Franco film be without a little sadism and kink?), and other earthy delights. In one anthropological wonder, a jungle boy is hunted down by three naked warrior women decked out in feathers, perfectly coifed hair, and layers of eye shadow. Supposedly an exposé, it's nothing more than titillating exploitation with an edge of satire

and a tongue-in-cheek tone to the direction that clashes with the oh-so-serious narration). Franco regular Vernon makes a couple of appearances, one of them as a lascivious inquisitor. —S.A.

BLOOD OF THE BEASTS L: DIRECTORS/FRANJU, GEORGES (1949) 22M D: Georges Franju. This documentary short is a shocking glimpse into the slaughterhouses of 1940s Paris. It begins with idyllic photography and narration about lovers walking through the city of romance, then dissolves to the inside of the nearby slaughterhouse to show workers joyously singing as they casually hack at the throats of horses. I don't care how much you love to eat hamburgers, it's still unpleasant to see cattle roll their eyes over and drop to the ground. Now it's more than fifty years later and it's still hard to take; even at twenty-two minutes I was surprised I got all the way to the end. If only those French lovers knew what was going on inside! —B.T.

EYES WITHOUT A FACE L: DIRECTORS/FRANJU, GEORGES (1959) 88M D: Georges Franju. *Juliette Mayniel, Pierre Brasseur, Alida Valli, Edith Scob, François Guerin.* Much is made of the surgery sequence in Franju's 1959 classic, but the scene in question, while riveting, is but a small element of the film. The austere Brasseur plays a famed surgeon developing experimental skin graft and transplant techniques in the hopes of being able to give his daughter (Scob), disfigured in a car accident of his doing, a new face. Unfortunately for the lovely ladies of Paris, though, he needs their faces to succeed! Valli costars as Brasseur's victim-hunting assistant. While the whole thing sounds lurid, Franju's masterful direction of Pierre Boileau's script never plays for cheap thrills. While the aforementioned surgery scene is definitely shocking, it serves a purpose in the story, making us question the doctor's motives and the true drive behind this "fatherly devotion." The ethereal scenes of Scob drifting through the house in her expressionless white mask, accompanied beautifully by Maurice Jarre's ominous score, are not soon forgotten. —E.O.

FRENCH CONNECTION II L: DIRECTORS/FRANKENHEIMER, JOHN (1975) 119M D: John Frankenheimer. *Gene Hackman, Fernando Rey.* Better than the original; this time Popeye's in France as a fish out of water and involuntarily addicted to heroin, but that doesn't stop his dogged pursuit of Rey. It just makes him more determined. Hackman's best role ever, and a stunning finale. Wow. —M.S.

GYPSY MOTHS, THE L: DIRECTORS/FRANKENHEIMER, JOHN (1969) 107M D: John Frankenheimer. *William Windom, Deborah Kerr, Burt Lancaster, Gene Hackman.* Frankenheimer's films are filled with characters who face death with stoic professionalism to prove not just their mettle, but that they are alive. This underrated drama about a trio of stunt skydivers who wander the back roads of

America with their death-defying shows has the tone of a William Inge drama (small-town frustrations, regret, and repression) combined with the existential male angst of Frankenheimer. Lancaster is the weary veteran who pushes himself closer to the edge with each jump, Hackman the bottom-line businessman of the group, and Kerr the housewife stifled in a loveless marriage to staid, dull, middle-class Windom. Amid the portrait of showbiz pros weary of the road and dulled by the thrills and the small town there to gawk at their spectacle is Frankenheimer's love of professional detail: the deliberate, exacting way Lancaster packs a parachute, Hackman stage-manages a show, and the team prepares for every jump. —S. A.

HORSEMEN, THE L: DIRECTORS/FRANKENHEIMER, JOHN (1970) 109M D: John Frankenheimer. *Omar Sharif, Leigh Taylor-Young, Jack Palance, Peter Jeffrey.* The setting is Afghanistan—a couple of decades pre-Taliban, though essentially it might be anytime in the past two thousand years. A delegation is being dispatched from a remote mountain village to take part in a contest of all the tribes: thirty, forty, fifty horsemen form about a single headless calf, riding in at a signal to attempt to seize the calf and, further, to retain it while riding across the great arena to drop it in the Circle of Justice. This primitive struggle takes place early in the film. The rest is devoted to the self-punishing return home, through desolate passes and bitter weather, of one crippled rider (Sharif). It had every right to be anticlimactic. That it is not is a tribute to the director's intense fidelity to the code the horsemen live by. This film appeared to be Frankenheimer's conscious attempt at purifying his style of TV-bred mannerisms—no more the cuts back to TV dialogues between characters to nail down the meaning of the exhilarating race driving (*Grand Prix*) or parachuting (*Gypsy Moths*) sequences. There is little to interrupt the sweeping advance of an austere, often beautiful movie. —R. T. J.

ISLAND OF DR. MOREAU, THE (1996) L: DIRECTORS/ FRANKENHEIMER, JOHN (1996) 95M D: John Frankenheimer. *David Thewlis, Val Kilmer, Marlon Brando, Fairuza Balk.* This unfairly maligned adaptation opens with a knife fight on an inflatable raft and gets crazier from there. The highlight is Brando in a brilliant performance as the mad doctor, who he portrays as an eccentric Michael Jackson type. He wears strange makeup and hats to protect himself from the sun, sometimes dons an ice bucket on his head to cool himself off, and is often accompanied by a tiny man dressed like him (the inspiration for Mini-Me in the *Austin Powers* sequels). In the middle of a monologue about his experiments to crossbreed men with animals, he pauses to tell the little guy to get his feet off the table. Later, when the beastmen break into his house at night to kill him, he politely offers them biscuits and plays piano for them.

Some of the insanity may come from a turbulent production; original director Richard Stanley (*Hardware*) wanted to make a film along the lines of *Cannibal Holocaust.* When he was fired and replaced by Frankenheimer, Stanley reportedly camped out in the rain forest and spied on the set disguised as a dog-boy extra. —B. T.

MANCHURIAN CANDIDATE, THE L: DIRECTORS/ FRANKENHEIMER, JOHN (1962) 129M D: John Frankenheimer. *Angela Lansbury, Frank Sinatra, Janet Leigh, James Gregory, Leslie Parrish, Lawrence Harvey.* A group of American POWs from the Korean War have a difficult time acclimating back into their domestic lives. Their nightmares are a little too real and parts of their memories don't seem to fit together properly. Sinatra plays a vet who is bent on solving the mystery, and a large part of which seems to revolve around his unit's leader, whose stepfather is a McCarthy-like politician running for president! The plot gets thicker and extraordinarily suspenseful, and with an all-star cast directed by Frankenheimer you will want to see this classic more than once. —N. J.

99 AND 44/100 DEAD! L: DIRECTORS/FRANKENHEIMER, JOHN (1974) 98M D: John Frankenheimer. *Chuck Connors, Richard Harris.* Note the exclamation mark. It perfectly captures this movie's goofy, misguided comic-book sensibility (the opening credits alone are worth the price of admission). Yeah, I'll admit that I'm a sucker for anything filmed in Seattle in the '70s, but what other film gives you the novelty of Connors with a cat-o'-nine-tails prosthetic? And then there's that great scene where Harris, having rescued the damsel in distress from a hair-trigger booby trap, carries her away from University Heights Elementary and BOOM! Harris just keeps on walking, doesn't even flinch. This was Frankenheimer's favorite moment. —S. F.

PROPHECY (1979) L: DIRECTORS/FRANKENHEIMER, JOHN (1979) 102M D: John Frankenheimer. *Armand Assante, Richard Dysart, Robert Foxworth, Talia Shire, Victoria Racimo.* Assante plays a Native American who is trying to save his people's land from the ecological abuses of modern industry. Shire plays an ecologist who comes to his aid by following up his claims with some research. She finds some strange things going on due to the high level of toxins in the area. Most notably, animal life has been growing to alarming proportions. Naturally it's only a matter of time before they find the really big mutant, or before it finds them! This offbeat, miscast thriller should amply please fans of campy horror. Who would have thought Frankenheimer could have directed something like this? —N. J.

REINDEER GAMES L: DIRECTORS/FRANKENHEIMER, JOHN (2000) 124M D: John Frankenheimer. *Charlize Theron, Donal Logue, James Frain, Dennis Farina, Ben Affleck, Gary Sinise.* Boyish, baby-faced Affleck, an ex-con sprung from the joint in time for Christmas, is the sap who follows his dick into the sack with Theron (all sweetness and sex) and winds up kidnapped by her gangster-wannabe brother (a greasy Sinise) for a casino heist. It's a ridiculous script, engineered with cynical, self-conscious efficiency, but Frankenheimer executes it with the kind of mean, lean mechanics missing from modern action cinema. He turns the silliness of the enterprise to his advantage, playing up the criminal ineptitude of his big-talking, stupid-as-shit cons and the small-time reality of their "big score": a penny ante tribal casino in ski country. From the delicious opening images (five dead red-suited Santas sprawled and bleeding on the snowy ground), Frankenheimer never lets up on the momentum. —S. A.

SECONDS L: DIRECTORS/FRANKENHEIMER, JOHN (1966) 107M D: John Frankenheimer. *Jeff Corey, John Randolph, Salome Jens, Rock Hudson, Will Geer.* When a married, retirement-aged man receives a disturbing phone call late one night, it sets him on a strange and sinister journey from which it is impossible for him to return. *Seconds* explores our cultural obsession with youth and beauty and our fear of growing old. In this age of tucks, peels, lifts, and suctions, the film seems even more relevant today. *Seconds* warns against letting the dreams and ideals of youth dissolve into a life of drudgery and sluggish routine with a message that is neatly tucked into one of the most horrifying and original films ever made. Hudson is excellent here, as is the entire cast. James Wong Howe's cinematography is spectacular and director Frankenheimer (whose audio commentary is featured on the DVD) is working here at the peak of his powers. Don't read the video box before renting this one because it will spoil some of the film's many surprises. —A. W.

SEVEN DAYS IN MAY L: DIRECTORS/FRANKENHEIMER, JOHN (1963) 118M D: John Frankenheimer. *Kirk Douglas, Burt Lancaster, Fredric March, Ava Gardner, Edmond O'Brien.* Frankenheimer's follow-up to *The Manchurian Candidate* takes a less flamboyant approach in its behind-the-scenes battle between militaristic general Lancaster and dove president March. At its best, the offhanded documentary realism of location shooting (the streets of DC, airport terminals, and an underground car park) grounds the drama in a palpable real world, and the effective strategy of having major events happen offscreen creates the feeling of a secret, far-reaching conspiracy. Douglas is at his driven best as Lancaster's protégé, a loyal colonel whose dedication to country forces him to expose his mentor. Rod Serling adapted the novel by Fletcher Knebel and Charles W. Bailey II. —S. A.

DANGEROUS LIAISONS L: DIRECTORS/FREARS, STEPHEN (1988) 120M D: Stephen Frears. *Glenn Close, John Malkovich, Michelle Pfeiffer, Keanu Reeves, Uma*

Thurman. A stunning cast makes this curious story of eighteenth-century aristocratic mind games come to life. Vicomte de Valmont (Malkovich) and the Marquise de Merteuil (Close) decide they need a little excitement in their upper-class love life, so they start instigating extramarital affairs. But what starts as an innocent game eventually turns deadly as this snobbish couple doesn't anticipate the degree to which love and obsession will drive people, even people as morally bankrupt as themselves. Excellent direction and great period detail make this film sumptuous and thoroughly engaging. —N.J.

GRIFTERS, THE L: DIRECTORS/FREARS, STEPHEN (1990) 119M D: Stephen Frears. *Pat Hingle, Angelica Huston, John Cusack, Annette Bening.* Frears brings a creamy daylight palette and an out-of-time warp to Jim Thompson's matter-of-factly ruthless novel of petty con artists and small-time scammers. Huston is the career con whose maternal instincts fight her survival instincts when she's unexpectedly reunited with her estranged son (Cusack), who is happily surviving on his penny ante scams. Bening is the hardened girlfriend who tries to woo Cusack into big-time grifts. Huston and Bening pull their claws out in beautifully played hissing matches as they battle for sway over Cusack, who brings an amiable, modest amorality to his confidence game cub, but no one on screen can match the utter killer instincts of Huston's stone-cold survivor. The superb adaptation by Donald Westlake smoothes over some of the more chaotic weirdness of the written-in-a-fever novel, but perfectly captures the attitude and the tragedy of the characters. —S. A.

HIGH FIDELITY L: DIRECTORS/FREARS, STEPHEN (2000) 113M D: Stephen Frears. *Jack Black, Iben Hjejle, John Cusack, Catherine Zeta-Jones, Joan Cusack, Todd Louiso. High Fidelity* is an oddity within the Hollywood romantic-comedy genre; it says, well, I'm tired of looking for the "right" person, so I'm going to settle for you. Cusack plays Rob Gordon, a pissy record store asshole trying to sort through his relationship failures (think *Say Anything*'s Lloyd Dobler if he'd never gotten back together with Diane Court). Cusack spends most of his time talking to the camera, listening to some really, really good music (Love, The 13th Floor Elevators, Smog, Belle and Sebastian), and figuring out what the fuck he did wrong in his most recent breakup with Laura (*Mifune*'s Hjejle). In the end, Cusack's pasty cynical charm wins over the audience (and the girl). Black gives his best Jack Black impression to date. This film is most appropriate for boys who are obsessed with something (records, movies, comics, ex-girlfriends) and spend most of their time drinking and masturbating. —J. D.

MARY REILLY L: DIRECTORS/FREARS, STEPHEN (1996) 108M D: Stephen Frears. *Glenn Close, John Malkovich, Julia Roberts, Michael Gambon. Dr. Jekyll and Mr. Hyde,* R. L. Stevenson's novella on the duality of human personality, has been retold so often that we watch any new version through layers of memory and expectation. *Mary Reilly* both sidesteps and capitalizes on this by recasting the tale from the point of view of a house servant (Roberts) in Jekyll's employ. Physically and emotionally scarred by an abusive father (Gambon), and gifted with a grave, probing intelligence that sets her apart from her fellow minions, she attracts the master's (Malkovich) attention and gradually becomes a spiritual anchor in his mysterious life. It's assumed we know "the story"— it lurks inside Mary Reilly as Jekyll's secret other self lurks inside him. The production design underscores this interiority: Jekyll's house with its many tiers, an adjoining medical amphitheater that seems to extend deep underground yet also tower higher than the house itself. Made by the gifted team behind *Dangerous Liaisons, Mary Reilly* is too conceptualized for its own good, and it bombed. Such total rejection was ill-deserved. Roberts herself is unexpectedly fine. Pale, fragile, and far from glamorous, her Mary is a portrait of intellectual honesty and moral courage—a hard-won triumph of (no other word will do) self-possession. —*R. T. J.*

PRICK UP YOUR EARS L: DIRECTORS/FREARS, STEPHEN (1987) 110M D: Stephen Frears. *Alfred Molina, Gary Oldman, Julie Walters, Vanessa Redgrave, Wallace Shawn.* This is an honest and brutal look at the life of Joe Orton, a playwright who was murdered at the hands of his jealous boyfriend. Through a series of retellings and flashbacks Oldman brilliantly encapsulates the whole of his life with the performance. Frears also incorporates some of Orton's plays, giving the audience a small taste of the writer's satire. In this film he is largely portrayed as a talented hedonist who accomplishes anything he sets his mind to. By contrast the man he settles with is a bundle of insecurities capable of accomplishing little or nothing. Nothing, that is, except the murder of the protagonist. —*N. J.*

BLUE CHIPS L: DIRECTORS/FRIEDKIN, WILLIAM (1994) 101M D: William Friedkin. *Alfre Woodard, J. T. Walsh, Ed O'Neill, Mary McDonnell, Nick Nolte.* Blue Chips is about four-fifths of a good movie about basketball. The film originally drew attention because it costars NBA superstar Shaquille O'Neal, but it revolves around Nolte's obsessed college basketball coach, a man who ignores his own flaws—as well as rule-breaking by his school—in order to win. Nolte participates in the paying of athletes and their families to snag more glamorous recruits to his school. The team wins, but Nolte's deal with the Devil may be costlier than he originally anticipated. Nolte does good work as a coach wrapped tighter than a

Christmas package, as does the cast around him, but the film's finale, which ends with a long and rambling speech, feels as if it's an act too short. The audience and filmmakers have followed the coach this far—why abandon him to so hasty an ending? —*T. P.*

CRUISING L: DIRECTORS/FRIEDKIN, WILLIAM (1980) 102M D: William Friedkin. *Powers Boothe, Karen Allen, Paul Sorvino, Al Pacino.* Pacino plays a New York policeman who goes undercover as a promiscuous homosexual in order to find who has been cruelly murdering gay men in New York's West Village. This turns into a very different and rather unsettling crime story because to achieve its ends it must employ many of the stereotypes that were used in the time and place of the story, such as Gestapo caps and handlebar mustaches. The true-crime element is effectively directed by Friedkin (known best for his work on *The French Connection*) yet was so true to life that it had many gay groups up in arms, not just because of stereotypes but because of fears of future killer imitators. —*N. J.*

EXORCIST, THE L: DIRECTORS/FRIEDKIN, WILLIAM (1973) 122M D: William Friedkin. *Kitty Winn, Ellen Burstyn, Linda Blair, Max von Sydow, Jason Miller.* Based on the novel by William Peter Blatty and buttressed by the experience of a Catholic priest actually experienced with the phenomenon, *The Exorcist* is a very scary film. Blair is cast as Regan, the young daughter in a wealthy household who somehow gets possessed by an evil spirit. The mother, well played by Burstyn, tries the whole circuit of psychologists but to no avail and eventually agrees to let a priest see her daughter. The priest, played by Miller, soon realizes he's in over his head and manages to get the specialist, von Sydow, to perform the exorcism. Naturally the exorcism takes a great deal of time, especially since this particular demon is one von Sydow has been chasing for some time. The acting and direction are topnotch, but paired with the sound effects and visual effects this film cannot fail to leave the viewer with some strong impressions. —*N. J.*

Although I think *The Exorcist* is a well-made and entertaining horror film, I've always suspected that its reputation as a terrifying, fainting-in-the-theater, shit-your-pants-it's-so-scary nightmare was some sort of a Catholic thing. In other words, all this demon possession business is cool, but if you were raised Catholic then it has the potential to knock you on your ass. That's my theory, anyway, because I wasn't raised Catholic and I wasn't knocked on my ass. It's either that, or the movie is just a little overrated. —*B. T.*

FRENCH CONNECTION, THE L: DIRECTORS/FRIEDKIN, WILLIAM (1971) 102M D: William Friedkin. *Tony LoBianco, Roy Scheider, Eddie Egan, Fernando Rey, Gene Hackman.* Hackman and Scheider play narcotics detectives who happen onto the largest drug ring of all time. As these two slowly put together the pieces of this complicated investigation they finally identify a single Frenchman as the predominant connection to an enormous European drug cartel. Naturally this leads to a lengthy chase scene—one of the greatest ever filmed. The best shots of this sequence were captured simply by the director holding a camera in the back seat of a car driven by a stunt driver who took insanely high speeds through New York traffic. Cut together with the Frenchman trying to elude the detectives in an elevated train, the whole chase scene is the perfect climax to a film that will keep you on the edge of you seat. A sequel, *The French Connection II,* was directed by John Frankenheimer and released in 1975. —*N. J.*

HUNTED, THE L: DIRECTORS/FRIEDKIN, WILLIAM (2003) 94M D: William Friedkin. *Benecio Del Toro, Tommy Lee Jones.* Del Toro goes *Rambo* in the Oregon woods and tracker/father-figure Jones is drafted to hunt him down in Friedkin's lean, mean manhunt thriller. Once Hollywood's golden boy, Friedkin remains a sharp action craftsman with a love of compromised heroes and assignments complicated by ambiguity, though he's been too often saddled with scripts long on high-concept gimmicks and short on dimension. This isn't necessarily better material, but the basic situation gives Friedkin room to do what he does best. Beautifully photographed and tightly engineered, it's all about the action, and Friedkin pares the film to essentials. Explanations are left vague and ambiguous, as if there may be more to the conspiracy theories and covert killing missions than the government claims. *The Hunted* is all about the thrill of the chase, and Friedkin challenges the antiseptic spectacle and fantasy flamboyance of computer-enhanced blockbusters with a gritty, hard-edged style. —*S. A.*

TO LIVE AND DIE IN LA L: DIRECTORS/FRIEDKIN, WILLIAM (1985) 116M D: William Friedkin. *Willem Dafoe, Darlanne Fluegel, John Turturro, Debra Feuer, John Pankow, William L. Petersen.* Friedkin's sleek, bleak thriller about a Secret Service agent (Petersen) who goes rogue to get his revenge on a ruthless counterfeiter (a feral Dafoe in his breakthrough performance) paints a very thin line between the good guys and the bad guys. It makes a perfect bookend to his equally hard-edged early '70s classic *The French Connection.* Stylishly shot in steely blues against hazy red and orange skies by Robby Muller (*Paris, Texas*), it practically defines the era (as does Wang Chung's techno soundtrack) while standing apart from every other crime thriller, and the freeway escape is one of the most ingenious, nerve-racking car chases of all time. Friedkin creates a jittery atmosphere of adrenaline, corruption, and danger and draws savage performances from his entire cast, which includes Pankow as the green partner who hardens under Petersen's tutelage, Feuer as

Dafoe's cool lover, and Fluegel as Petersen's informant and sometime sexual partner. —*S. A.*

BATTLE ROYALE L: DIRECTORS/FUKASAKU, KINJI (2001) 122M D: Kinji Fukasaku *Tatsuya Fujiwara, Aki Maeda, Taro Yamamoto, Masanobu Ando, Kou Shibasaki, Chiaki Kuriyama.* In a near-future Japan, unemployment and civil unrest rage out of control. Fearful of an increasingly disenfranchised populace, the government is forced to take action. And how do they react? With a sweeping domestic policy restructuring plan? Maybe an increase in welfare benefits? No, they sign the Battle Royale Act into law, which allows the government, once a year, to kidnap one random class of kids from a random grade and have them off each other on a remote island until only one person survives. The whole event is broadcast live throughout Japan. How does this help with the country's protesting youth? I don't know either, but it hardly matters. *Battle Royale* is a highly entertaining romp that follows Shuya (Fujiwara) and the rest of his ninth-grade class on one such field trip. Friends quickly become enemies as each is outfitted and the clock starts ticking. . . Oh, did I mention they only have three days to diminish their numbers down to one before all their heads explode courtesy of the tracking collar they wear. Wrongfully billed by some as overly violent, *Battle Royale* is not an exploitation film, but one that challenges our ideas of innocence and friendship. —*R. G.*

BATTLE ROYALE 2: REQUIEM L: DIRECTORS/FUKASAKU, KINJI (2003) 133M D: Kinji Fukasaku, Kenta Fukasaku. *Riki Takeuchi, Tatsuya Fujiwara, Ai Maeda, Shugo Oshinari, Ayana Sakai, Sonny Chiba.* In the first *Battle Royale,* Japanese high school kids were dropped off on an island and forced by the government to fight to the death. Now it's a few years later and the survivors of that game have formed a terrorist group to fight back (taking out many innocent civilians in the process). In a new Battle Royale Act, the government forces another group of schoolkids to hunt down the leader of the terrorists. It's an extremely violent war allegory that is even more outrageous than its predecessor, very clearly taking on governments (especially in the United States) and the so-called war on terror. Director Fukasaku died during filming and was replaced by his son, Kenta, but the film still seems to have a pretty solid vision. It could use some tightening and it's hard to get involved in the characters when they keep getting slaughtered before you even know who's who. But it's about the ballsiest war satire you're likely to see, a blunt attack on our willingness to send our kids to kill each other in our name. —*B. T.*

BLACKMAIL IS MY LIFE L: DIRECTORS/FUKASAKU, KINJI (1968) 89M D: Kinji Fukasaku. *Tomomi Sato, Yoko Mihara, Tetsuro Tamba, Hiroki Matsukata.* Four friends get their piece of the economic miracle in Fukasaku's cynical, spirited satire run through with New Wave style. A cool young swinger (Matsukata) leads the group, which grooves on bad behavior like teenagers in a funhouse and tears through the movie like high-spirited schoolkids on a scavenger hunt. This mercenary society, where blackmail is just another commodity (as are sex and romance) and every one of their targets is up to their eyebrows in illegal activities, makes these amoral but loyal pals the closest the film has to heroes. "It's dangerous. That's why we can't leave it alone," becomes their motto as the punk kids get into the big leagues of corporate and political corruption, ending in a bloody finale that has to be seen to be believed. Satirical to the end, it puts the whole film back into a hollow, chilly society. —*S. A.*

GREEN SLIME, THE L: DIRECTORS/FUKASAKU, KINJI
(1968) 89M D: Kinji Fukasaku. *Robert Horton, Richard Jaeckel, Bud Widom, Ted Gunther, Luciana Paluzzi.* Considering the director, the film's name, and the groovy theme song, *The Green Slime* is a major disappointment. In the near future an asteroid is on a collision course. A nearby space station sends a rocket to the asteroid and the astronauts discover some weird little green blobs. They take a couple of samples (one in a jar and one on a guy's pant leg). The asteroid is destroyed but, back on the space station, the green blobs mutate into stupid-looking, four-foot-tall, energy-sucking monsters that make annoying squeaking sounds. The international team of astronauts must figure out a way to destroy the endlessly reproducing creatures before they spread to Earth. The movie is flatly directed by the usually great Fukasaku, the special effects suck, and the three leads (who are engaged in a trite love triangle) are completely boring. Love that theme song though. —*S. H.*

LEGEND OF THE EIGHT SAMURAI L: DIRECTORS/
FUKASAKU, KINJI (1983) 130M D: Kinji Fukasaku. *Sonny Chiba, Sue Shiomi, Hiroyuki Sanada, Hiroko Yakushimaru, Yuki Meguro.* Another dark Sanada-Chiba adventure movie. Eight fighters need to be located to help save a teenage princess. Each possesses a magic jewel that will collectively aid them in defeating a demon mother and son and their part-human, part-demon army. An effective if rather tedious adventure story with decent and oftentimes quite witty fight sequences, plus gritty effects and a wonderfully lurid evil-castle set. The highlight takes place here where the evil mother, like Countess Bathory, bathes in a large pool of human blood to renew her youth. -*J. C.*

MODERN YAKUZA: THE OUTLAW KILLER L: DIRECTORS/
FUKASAKU, KINJI (1972) 88M D: Kinji Fukasaku. *Bunta Sugawara, Noboru Ando, Mayumi Nagisa, Nobuo Yana.* One who lives by the sword dies by the sword, and one who lives by the gun will die by the gun. Sugawara is Okita, a violent, nearly unsympathetic street gangster who is without

remorse in the way that he lives. After spending five years in prison for killing a member of the Takigawa yakuza family, Okita returns to the streets, reassembles his former gang, and finds a woman he once raped and sold into prostitution to be his own. But the crime world he once knew no longer exists. Okita is still full of rage and begins publicly displaying the violence that was once so pertinent in his life. The city's two yakuza families attempt to control him, but they realize that the only way to keep their new way of life is to kill Okita and his gang. *Outlaw Killer* is at times fairly tough to watch, as it features an unflinching eye toward violence and rape. —*R. M.*

SAMURAI REINCARNATION L: DIRECTORS/FUKASAKU,
KINJI(1981) 122M D: Kinji Fukasaku. *Sonny Chiba, Hiroyuki Sanada, Kenji Sawada.* A sorcerer brings back from hell four evil samurai to carry out a revenge. One samurai is a woman and another still wrestles with his own dark side, which leads to the undoing of the plotted revenge. Morbid film with abundant, often-uncomfortable topless nudity, plus buckets of blood. One of several collaborations between Sanada and Chiba in the early 1980s at Toei, at least three of which Fukasaku directed. All films have sword-and-sorcery and ninja elements, two hot items then in the American market. But this has edgy visuals far more effectively morbid and sleazy than its American and European counterparts, though sometimes (as in this case) with thinner story lines. —*J. C.*

TORA! TORA! TORA! L: DIRECTORS/FUKASAKU, KINJI (1970)
144M D: Richard Fleischer, Kinji Fukasaku *Martin Balsam, So Yamamura, Joseph Cotton, Tatsuya Mihashi, E. G. Marshall.* This ambitious, unprecedented co-production between the United States and Japan details the cascade of events and decisions that resulted in the fateful day that will live in infamy: leadership tugs-of-war, tactical goofs, and the shortsighted planning that gave the Japanese immediate Pacific control but left them vulnerable to a long sea war. Hollywood veteran Fleischer does what all old Hollywood directors do best: wrestles a complicated story with dozens of intertwining plots and a huge cast into a dramatic structure you can follow without resorting to a flow chart. Fleischer sacrifices characters for logistics but that's why you cast stars. This one has plenty (among them Cotten, Marshall, James Whitmore, and Jason Robards) vying for screen time with some of the most spectacular battle footage put to film. —*S. A.*

AENIGMA L: DIRECTORS/FULCI, LUCIO (1987) 85M D: Lucio
Fulci. *Milijana Zirojevic, Lara Naszinsky.* Italian gore-meister Fulci comes up with a psychic shocker about a telekinetic girl (Zirojevic) bullied, humiliated, and ultimately put into a coma by her snobby schoolmates at a ritzy Boston girl's school. She doesn't let that come

between her and her revenge, which includes a girl smothered in a swarm of snails (what, she couldn't outrun these things?), another mugged by a stone statue, and plenty of stabbings and beheadings. It's the Australian *Patrick* (an earlier tale of revenge by a bedridden telekinetic) by way of *Carrie*, except that here our heroine is actually new student Naszinsky, a hot-to-trot blond babe possessed by coma-girl. While sometimes blunt and sloppy it's one of Fulci's better efforts, with some dreamy set pieces and inventive hallucinatory mind-attacks amidst his usual gruesome murder spree. —*S.A.*

BEYOND, THE L: DIRECTORS/FULCI, LUCIO (1981) 87M D: Lucio Fulci. *Catriona MacColl, David Warbeck, Cinzia Monreale, Antoine Saint-John*. Alongside *Zombi 2*, this is Fulci's nightmarish horror masterpiece. In between the opening crucifixion and the heart-stopping final shot is some of the most gruesome gore to be captured on celluloid. The story itself is rather simple, and holds together the killing scenes like glue. A Louisiana hotel is built over a doorway to hell, and the unspeakable abominations behind it want into the land of the living. When the seal cracks, they are given just that opportunity. As the horrific murders escalate, the hotel's new owner Liza (MacColl) tries to figure out what is happening. Fulci's maddening effects are all here and marching in fine fashion, from eye gouging to flesh ripping, acid burning, and human devouring. Be sure to seek out the widely available uncut version, but anyone with a weak stomach should best stick to Hollywood's "safe" horror films. —*R.M.*

VOICES FROM BEYOND L: DIRECTORS/FULCI, LUCIO (1994) 91M D: Lucio Fulci. *Pascal Persiano, Bettina Giovannini, Karina Huff, Duilio del Prete*. Leave it to Italian gore-meister Fulci to spice this Agatha Christie–like murder mystery with bizarre ghost story inflections and moments of grotesque horror. The ghost of a murdered industrialist, a real bastard who gave most of his family plenty of motivation to kill him, exhorts his daughter (through her dreams) to find out who did the deed. As long as his corpse remains intact the spirit can communicate with the daughter, or so the film insists. That gives Fulci license to show the slow decomposition of the body in gooey detail as insects devour the flesh. You also get a dying man coughing up gallons of blood, an autopsy in unnecessary detail, a disturbing nightmare with a child stabbing, and an inspired fantasy flashback involving a restaurant of the dead and eyeball custard. One of Fulci's last productions, this truly weird piece of mystery horror has a compelling ambivalence about justice that pays off in a smartly turned conclusion. It's one of his better directed efforts, but much of the offbeat tone is undercut by indifferent English dubbing. —*S.A.*

ZOMBIE (AKA ZOMBI 2) L: DIRECTORS/FULCI, LUCIO (1979) 91M D: Lucio Fulci. *Richard Johnson, Ian McCulloch, Al Cliver, Auretta Gay, Tisa Farrow*. Fulci's horror masterpiece was marketed in Italy as a sequel to *Dawn of the Dead*. While the only connection between the two is that they both have zombies, the truth is that they are possibly the two greatest zombie films of all time. *Zombie*'s plot is simple yet executed perfectly. The film gained notoriety and popularity among gorehounds due to its excellent use of effects, but what's often overlooked is the sheer perfection of the whole ordeal. The progression and pacing of the story, each sequence perfectly building to the next, makes the film flow with dreamlike ease and fevered intensity. Classic moments such as the eye gouging and the zombie vs shark fight fit in perfectly, and the shocking ending is a final cherry on top of this beautiful sundae. —*T.S.*

ZOMBIE 3 L: DIRECTORS/FULCI, LUCIO (1988) 94M D: Lucio Fulci, Bruno Mattei. *Massimo Vanni, Luciano Piggozi, Ottaviano Dell'Acqua, Beatrice Ring, Deran Sarafian*. This bloated mess was shot in the Philippines to accommodate its meagly budget. Fulci succumbed to an illness soon after finishing his original (and by his standards definitive) forty-five-minute cut of the movie. Unhappy with the length, the producers stepped in and doubled the running time to make the film even more of a tepid wasteland of zombie stupidity. The film begins with unknown (and never elaborated upon later) terrorists, hijacking top-secret zombie-inducing canisters from government officials. An army of Hazmat soldiers, dumber than the zombies themselves, is then sent out to kill everyone. Vacationing kids and young off-duty soldiers also get thrown into the mix to make things more exciting. Supposedly the sequel to Fulci's 1979 masterpiece *Zombie*, which confusingly enough was released in Europe under the title *Zombi 2*, to shamefully mine the success of Romero's *Dawn of the Dead*, which was retitled *Zombi* when distributed throughout Europe. —*A.T.*

BIG RED ONE, THE L: DIRECTORS/FULLER, SAM (1980) 113M D: Samuel Fuller. *Kelly Ward, Lee Marvin, Mark Hamill, Robert Carradine, Bobby Di Cicco, Stephane Audran*. Forget *Saving Private Ryan*. You want a WWII story from a vet's perspective, Fuller is still the man. Spare and suggestive where Spielberg's yarn is packed with gore, Fuller gives us North Africa, Italy, even D-Day on Omaha Beach, mostly in close-ups and deserted locales, charting the fortunes of his own real-life unit through the experiences of four riflemen and a couple hundred replacements whose names they finally give up trying to learn over the four years. Carradine is the director's cigar-chomping, pulp-fiction-writing stand-in who transforms (along with Hamill, Di Cicco, and Ward) from a green volunteer to a hardened survivor. Marvin's tough, taciturn sergeant (we never learn his name) is the character Tom Hanks tried for in Ryan: reserved, gruff, hiding his heart under a helmet and three-day stubble. —*S.A.*

FORTY GUNS L: DIRECTORS/FULLER, SAM (1957) 79M D: Samuel Fuller. *John Ericson, Barbara Stanwyck, Barry Sullivan, Dean Jagger, Gene Barry.* Former journalist, pulp writer, and soldier Fuller made tough-guy films with mad passion and driving energy: he was America's kino-fist with a tabloid sensibility. *Forty Guns* is the purest blast of his cinematic thunder and melodramatic excess. Black-clad rancher baron Stanwyck ("a high-riding woman with a whip," according to her theme song) is challenged by cynical gunfighter turned town marshal Sullivan, but the story is merely a setting for the sexual energy and psychotic violence that explode on-screen in staccato editing, darting camera work, and the maddest expressions of love this side of *Duel in the Sun.* —*S.A.*

STEEL HELMET, THE L: DIRECTORS/FULLER, SAM (1951) 85M D: Samuel Fuller. *Robert Hutton, Richard Loo, James Edwards, William Chun, Gene Evans.* The first of Fuller's many war films found its Korean locations in LA's Griffith Park; the heftiest item in the budget was probably the giant Buddha that watches impassively as a patrol of GIs hold a temple against a company of North Korean soldiers. Dedicated "to the United States Army" and dispensing with the consolation of an end title, *The Steel Helmet* is as raw as any Hollywood movie made to that date. Fuller's battlefield ethos holds that, in the words of Kathleen Murphy, "There are two kinds of people: those who are dead and those who are about to be; men who have ceased to move anywhere and mean anything, and those whose idiosyncratic, even crazy energy keeps them in motion until they too are stopped by an arbitrary bullet or knife. Dead men are just corpses, places you can shop for extra sulfa powder, guns, helmets, and boots—or get blown up by a booby trap." Evans, himself a combat veteran who went on to become a Fuller regular, is excellent—nay, definitive—as the gruff, unkillable Sgt. Zack, who first appears under the bullet-punctured title object. —*R.T.J.*

STREET OF NO RETURN L: DIRECTORS/FULLER, SAM (1989) 92M D: Samuel Fuller. *Marc DeJonge, Andrea Ferreol, Valentina Vargas, Bill Duke, Keith Carradine.* Based on a novel by David Goodis, *Street of No Return* was Fuller's last movie. It's about the rise and fall of a pop singer, played by Carradine. While enjoying wealth and popularity, the singer falls in love with another woman, a woman with an ex-boyfriend who happens to be a gangster. Naturally this creates some problems, and eventually he gets his vocal cords slashed. Years later he finds himself on the street begging winos for alcohol when he finally sees an opportunity for his revenge. The characterizations in this film are done very tongue-in-cheek, apparently to ridi-

cule the status of pop stars and their tired rags-to-riches clichés. —*N.J.*

UNDERWORLD USA L: DIRECTORS/FULLER, SAM (1960) 98M D: Samuel Fuller. *Cliff Robertson, Larry Gates, Dolores Dorn.* Underworld USA is as tabloid in style and tone as its title. Like *Verboten!,* which framed the postwar occupation of Germany in terms of a single sidelined boxcar, the movie begins and ends in the same urban alley where teen punk Tolly Devlin sees his father beaten to death, then proceeds as an adult (a shockingly coarse Robertson) to exact revenge on the small-time criminals responsible. By then they've become executives of a crime syndicate Fuller explicitly likens to a modern corporation, headed by a Jabba the Hutt type played by the swollen Robert C. Emhardt. "CONNORS DEFIES UNCLE SAM," reads a characteristic Fuller newspaper headline (Connors being the Emhardt character), and Fuller justifies the national context by showing how crime—and Tolly's own irredeemable crudeness—blights any hope for carving out a normal family life. The most memorable scene involves a stone killer (Richard Rust) befriending a little girl on a pristine suburban street, then rolling over her shattered body with his big-finned luxury car. —*R.T.J.*

WHITE DOG L: DIRECTORS/FULLER, SAM (1982) 89M D: Samuel Fuller. *Paul Winfield, Jameson Parker, Lynne Moody, Kristy McNichol.* McNichol plays a young model who finds a large stray dog. After trying to find its owner she decides to keep it. The dog is so mild mannered that she decides to bring it to work one day, but suddenly it violently attacks one of her coworkers. This disturbing turn of events prompts her to investigate. She discovers that she owns a "white dog," a dog trained by white supremacists to attack black people. She happens to find a specialized dog trainer who attempts to retrain the animal, and by the end of the film she meets the original owner—Burl Ives! Based on a novel by Romain Gary, this film is truly an eye-opener. —*N.J.*

NAPOLÉON L: DIRECTORS/GANCE, ABEL (1927) 235M D: Abel Gance. *Albert Dieudonné, Edmund van Daele.* One of the greatest, most spectacular silent films ever made, *Napoléon* featured no less than three full screens with three synchronized projectors for its climactic battle. With the help of tinting commonly used at the time, the screens at times were effectively lit as the colors of the French flag. This ambitious four-hour film only covers the life of the young Napoleon, the final battle in fact being his very first military victory at Toulon. Other momentous events depicted in this film happen to the child Napoleon, such as the unforgettable snowball fight where Napoleon is instinctively seized by bold and daring leadership and the strategic genius to win the day. Its monumental restoration and rerelease in 1981

Sam Fuller

Samuel Fuller straddled two generations: he was the last of the old Hollywood tough-guy directors and, along with Orson Welles, one of the first independent mavericks. He spent his formative years in journalism, where he worked his way up from hawking papers on the street to becoming a tabloid crime reporter. During the Depression he churned out pulp novels and slaved over scripts in Hollywood, and he returned from World War II having won the Bronze Star in Italy, the Silver Star in Normandy, and the Purple Heart as member of the First Infantry Division, better known as the Big Red One (immortalized in his autobio-

graphical 1980 film).

Thus Fuller had lived a rough, active life before he directed his first film, *I Shot Jesse James*, in 1949, and he brought that life into his films. Fuller's heroes are everything from social outcasts to psychopaths, but almost all are living lives outside the American dream. Soldiers, cops, pickpockets, prostitutes, two-bit hoods, gunmen and con men, his heroes are more ruthless than his villains because that's what it takes to survive in this violent world.

By his third film, *The Steel Helmet* (1951), Fuller had found his style: jagged cuts, abrupt transitions, and increasingly outrageous cinematic shocks—all the better to shake the audience out of passivity and compel them to engage his films head on.

---

featured a rousing score by Carmine Coppola and Carl Davis. —*N. J.*

LATCHO DROM L: DIRECTORS/GATLIF, TONY (1993) 103M D: Tony Gatlif. A rich, culturally diverse look at the Rom people (gypsies), from all different walks of life and areas of the world. We travel through India, Spain, Egypt, Turkey, Romania, Hungary, Slovakia, and France catching glimpses of these people's lives with little introduction or explanation. There is no narration and no dialogue to speak of, save that of the songs they sing to each other. It's like traveling about the world without a guidebook, simply studying and relishing the music, dance, and age-old traditions of these often misunderstood, criticized, and shunned communities. A wonderful sensory experience that should be seen twice—once to absorb and a second time to watch with an educated eye and ear. —*M. N.*

ADVENTURES OF BARON MUNCHAUSEN, THE L: DIRECTORS/GILLIAM, TERRY (1989) 126M D: Terry Gilliam. *Eric Idle, Sarah Polley, John Neville, Uma Thurman, Oliver Reed, Valentina Cortese.* Four years after the postproduction fiasco of *Brazil,* Gilliam released this ambitious follow-up. Of course he still didn't have final cut, but what is left attests to sheer genius. *Munchausen* is a veritable kaleidoscope of events. The historic and bigger-than-real-life baron this script is based on eventually had a clinical syndrome attached to his name to describe people who travel widely and take on various personas of inflated identity. But,

as Gilliam shows with great casting and outrageous special effects, the original Munchausen did it with style and panache. For instance, to impress the young girl he befriends, he doesn't hesitate to visit the king of the moon. In some ways remade from the 1943 German film of the same name, *Munchausen* is a rampant fugue you simply can't shrug off! —*N. J.*

BRAZIL L: DIRECTORS/GILLIAM, TERRY (1985) 142M D: Terry Gilliam. *Michael Palin, Robert De Niro, Bob Hoskins, Kim Greist, Katherine Helmond, Ian Holm, Jonathan Pryce.* I'm continually baffled by people's perception of this film as science fiction or fantasy. While its perspective is uniquely lyrical and poetic, this movie is entirely about the world we live in right now. At its core its one of the most urgent odes to feelings of betrayal by the world of capitalism and the culture of bureaucracy ever put on film. With its simultaneously nihilistic and optimistic ending, this angry masterpiece ground itself into every level of my consciousness upon first viewing. On days when work and life feel like a prison, the title song begins to cycle in my mind and I know that I am not alone. —*E. W.*

FEAR AND LOATHING IN LAS VEGAS L: DIRECTORS/GILLIAM, TERRY (1998) 119M D: Terry Gilliam. *Christina Ricci, Ellen Barkin, Craig Bierko, Johnny Depp, Benicio del Toro.* It's hard to imagine anyone besides Gilliam pulling off this amazingly faithful adaptation of Hunter S. Thompson's supposedly unfilmable classic. Much of Thompson's

His directing style derived from a combination of his pulp sensibility and his tabloid experiences; he directed from a screenplay you would swear was written in 20-point bold headline type, brimming with passion and anger. He may have been a prime cinematic cold warrior, but he was also one of the rare directors to tackle racism squarely and bluntly in his films.

Fuller moved in and out of the studio system, creating such vivid classics as *Pickup on South Street* (1953) before returning to the indie studios and forged a jagged, ragged Expressionist style that owed more to Godard than Goldwyn for such films as *Verboten* (1959), *The Naked Kiss* (1964), and *Shock Corridor* (1963)—and this before the French New Wave crashed down on American shores. Like Hollywood's most famous iconoclast, Orson Welles, he made independent movies within the Hollywood system when possible, outside when necessary, but his way for better or worse.

In Jean-Luc Godard's *Pierrot le Fou* (1965), Fuller appears in a cameo and answers the question "What is cinema?" with the following line: "Film is like a battleground: love, hate, action, death. . . . In one word, *emotion*." Whether Godard or Fuller wrote the line, Fuller's gruff, cigar-chomping delivery makes it his, and it serves as a fitting epitaph for a career filled with uncompromising films of stylistic audacity, cinematic beauty, and passionate sincerity. Fuller put America under the microscope and found disease eating away at the bone, but he told the story in the most exciting, anarchic visual style to emerge from the American studio system.

—Sean Axmaker

---

writing voice comes through in the often verbatim voice-overs and dialogue, and there are even details like songs on the soundtrack that were mentioned in the book or costumes that are based on specific Ralph Steadman illustrations. But Gilliam lets loose with many outlandish psychedelic flourishes, using CGI in creepy new ways and brilliantly visualizing Thompson's nightmarish portrait of Las Vegas. No one should be surprised by Depp's uncanny embodiment of Raul Duke, but del Toro's maniacal performance as Dr. Gonzo goes beyond mere transformation. I am convinced that the sweaty lunatic pouring beer on his fat belly in the opening shot is the real del Toro. He loses weight for all his other roles. The Criterion DVD has many valuable extras including vintage footage of Thompson and Dr. Gonzo inspiration Oscar Acosta, Depp reading his own correspondence with Thompson, and a hilarious commentary track by Thompson himself in which he occasionally bleats or screams for no reason. *—B.T.*

12 MONKEYS L: DIRECTORS/GILLIAM, TERRY (1995) 129M D: Terry Gilliam. *Bruce Willis, Christopher Plummer, Madeleine Stowe, Brad Pitt.* Though there are actually only eight monkeys, *12 Monkeys* is an interesting film. The basic plot is that a prisoner, James Cole (Willis), is sent back from 2029 to 1996 to stop the spread of a virus that wipes out 99 percent of the population in the year 1997. The numerous plot twists and holes leave the average bloke going, "huh?" Gilliam leaves the viewer guessing instead of handing the story to us on a silver platter with everything spelled out. The concepts aren't exactly original, but it's done with Gilliam's curious retro-futurist look and some believable and entertaining characters. Stowe does a great job as Cole's therapist, Dr. Kathryn Railly, who's trying to come to terms with her feelings and beliefs about the state of reality. Pitt, before his meteoric rise to superstardom, plays a mental case–animal rights terrorist, hell bent on chaos and liberation for the oppressed animals of the world. *—B.W.*

MONTY PYTHON AND THE HOLY GRAIL L: DIRECTORS/GILLIAM, TERRY (1975) 91M D: Terry Gilliam, Terry Jones. *John Cleese, Terry Gilliam, Terry Jones, Michael Palin, Graham Chapman, Eric Idle.* The wacky minds of Monty Python took on the legend of King Arthur for the their first "real" feature film and Camelot has never been the same. Banging coconut shells across the misty English countryside, King Arthur and a band of dotty knights run afoul of abusive Frenchmen, sex-crazed nuns, a killer rabbit, the mysterious Knights Who Say "Nih!," and other typical medieval threats while discussing philosophy, logic, and the average speed velocity of the swallow (African or European?). Probably the cheapest Arthurian adventure ever made (heck, they couldn't even afford horses!), and easily the funniest. The DVD restores an extra twenty-four seconds unseen in the original American release, yet even with the remastering the grimy, drab visuals still look like a big-budget TV show that's been a bit underlit. But these are the Dark Ages, after all, and the models and the English countryside look suitably earthy, muddy, and medieval. —*S. A.*

TIME BANDITS L: DIRECTORS/GILLIAM, TERRY (1981) 110M D: Terry Gilliam. *Ian Holm, Katherine Helmond, Sean Connery, Michael Palin, John Cleese, Shelley Duvall, Craig Warnock.* A young boy (Warnock) confused by the state of his futuristic world and upset by the dysfunction of his family is abducted by a klatch of thieving dwarves who escape supernatural authority by running through doorways in time. With help from members of Monty Python, the scenarios this boy stumbles into are surprising, imaginative, and remarkably funny. Napoleon, Agamemnon, and more are delightfully painted with the brush of British comedy. Excellent special effects are also well used, making this science-fictional comic fantasy satire an excellent film for all ages. —*N. J.*

BAND OF OUTSIDERS L: DIRECTORS/GODARD, JEAN-LUC (1964) 95M D: Jean-Luc Godard. *Sami Frey, Claude Brasseur, Anna Karina.* One of Godard's most cinematically playful films, this is a lark, an anti–*Jules and Jim* crime caper, more in tune with Truffaut's sense of cinematic humor than Godard's later politically bent works. Karina is a veritable innocent sucked into the schemes of two best friends (the confident lothario Brasseur and the shy, subservient pretty boy Frey), bouncing back and forth in her affections until they begin to terrify her, yet she's too smitten to give them up. They, on the other hand, act more interested in each other than in the girl, who is little more than a good time and the key to an impulsive, ill-conceived crime. The chaos of the climax has a fun sense of narrative messiness that Godard never tries to clean up. He merely revels in the complications and leaves them hanging, for they matter not to our live-for-the-moment heroes. —*S. A.*

BREATHLESS (A BOUT DE SOUFFLÉ) L: DIRECTORS/ GODARD, JEAN-LUC (1959) 87M D: Jean-Luc Godard *Jean-Paul Belmondo, Jean Seberg.* Godard's first full-length film heralds the French New Wave in with a bang. Unable to successfully avoid the cops after stealing a car, Michel Poiccard (Belmondo) ends up a cop-killer on the run. All of the traditional genre devices are in place: the femme fatale (played by the hot Seberg), the convoluted narrative, and the hero with the fatal flaw (he trusts the girl). Godard knows and respects these devices, but he won't let them control his film. Instead of being a Bogart character, Poiccard is obsessed with playing Bogart himself, often falling into cheap pantomime and posturing. Seberg is an unwilling femme fatale, ultimately too passive to take any action against Poiccard. It's largely a film about film, often drawing attention to its own technical devices (Godard's disjointed jump cut), setting the precedent for self-aware cinema and a league of imitators to follow. It was remade in 1983 starring Richard Gere. —*J. D.*

CONTEMPT L: DIRECTORS/GODARD, JEAN-LUC (1963) 104M D: Jean-Luc Godard. *Michel Piccoli, Brigitte Bardot, Jack Palance.* Godard's anti-Hollywood sensibility and the showman aesthetic of (uncredited) producer Joseph E. Levine come together in this international coproduction about the clash between art and commerce, the politics of artistic integrity and compromise, and the dissolution of love. To meet his producer's demands, Godard added an opening bedroom scene and inserted pinup-style nude shots of Bardot. He actually makes them work as a comment on the process of filmmaking compromise. Bardot has never been better as a young wife who feels betrayed by her writer husband (Piccoli), who is being courted by the same smug Hollywood producer (a wonderfully crude and arrogant Palance) who seduces his wife. Fritz Lang plays himself, a European legend shooting a version of *The Odyssey* on the Mediterranean. Shot in hard, bright colors on a widescreen canvas, it's stately and controlled where Godard's earlier films immediate and felt off-the-cuff, a gorgeous film in the key of alienation. —*S. A.*

DÉTECTIVE L: DIRECTORS/GODARD, JEAN-LUC (1985) 95M D: Jean-Luc Godard *Laurent Terzieff, Aurelle Doazan, Jean-Pierre Léaud, Nathalie Baye, Johnny Hallyday, Claude Brasseur.* Dedicated to John Cassavetes, Clint Eastwood, and Edgar Ulmer, *Détective* is a B movie done up Godard style. Aging New Wave icon Léaud sneaks around the Hotel Concorde, rifling through the private papers of guests, while debt-ridden boxing manager (former French pop singer Hallyday) tries to extricate himself from the mob. Never leaving the confines of the hotel, Godard toys with genre conventions while indulging in his playful sense of humor: word games, running gags, flippant philosophical pronouncements. The comic mystery is merely a pretense for Godard's convention-busting fun and games—right down to the absurdly pat resolution. —*S. A.*

GERMANY YEAR 90 NINE ZERO L: DIRECTORS/ GODARD, JEAN-LUC (1990) 62M D: Jean-Luc Godard. *Eddie Constantine.* Constantine reprises his *Alphaville* role of Lemmy Caution, now the last Allied spy in Germany. Where most narratives find ways to slip "larger ideas" into focused fictional constructs, Godard's method here is one of extreme diversions away from the story. Voiceovers and printed intertitles take us from caution to an array of shorthand ruminations on Germany, reunification, philosophy, history, cinema, Mozart, Dürer, Brecht, and so on. Godard touches on too much, never devoting sufficient time to any one topic, and barely linking one to another. Although much passes through undigested, some of these seedlike passages inevitably take root and can't be shaken for days. The film's maddeningly dense style, more musical than essayistic, probably demands multiple viewings to properly appreciate it, but is exceptionally rewarding even once. —C. B.

ICI ET AILLEURS (HERE AND ELSEWHERE) L: DIRECTORS/GODARD, JEAN-LUC (1976) 60M D: J. L. Godard, A. M. Miéville, J. P. Gorin.

A collaborative effort of Godard, Miéville, and Gorin, *Ici et Ailleurs* is a heady exploration of the applications of film and video and their usefulness to the politics of war and the ideological battle that is history. In 1970 the group was commissioned to document the living conditions of Palestinian militants. Years later, after many of the Palstinians filmed were killed in the Six-Day War, the filmmakers took the project in an entirely different direction. Juxtaposing a portrait of domestic life in France with that of the Palestinians, the result is an unnervingly dense film essay that's as suspicious of its own means of communication as it is of the institutionalized modes it attacks. If you struggled with *Pierrot le Fou,* this film isn't for you. Even if you didn't, *Ici et ailleurs* may require multiple viewings to properly sort out. —C. B.

MARRIED WOMAN, A (UNE FEMME MARIÉE) L: DIRECTORS/GODARD, JEAN-LUC (1964) 94M D: Jean-Luc Godard

Bernard Noel, Roger Leenhardt, Philippe Leroy, Macha Meril. Charlotte (Meril) juggles a husband (Leroy) and a lover (Noel) without too much trouble, until she unexpectedly finds herself pregnant. Similar in structure to *My Life to Live, Une Femme Mariée* describes itself as "fragments of a film," an elliptical, choppy portrait in broad strokes. Emphasizing the increasing commodification of the female form, extreme close-ups of Charlotte's body are coupled with images of seminude women used for advertising and other commercial purposes. But since this is a Godard project, there are many different philosophical, sociological, and aesthetic currents running through the material. Godard himself describes the film, which he pointedly wanted to call not *Une* but *La Femme Mariée,* as "a film where subjects are seen as objects, where pursuits by taxi alternate with ethnological interviews, where the spectacle of life finally mingles with its analysis: a film, in short, where the cinema plays happily, delighted to be only what it is." —C. B.

MY LIFE TO LIVE L: DIRECTORS/GODARD, JEAN-LUC (1962) 85M D: Jean-Luc Godard

Anna Karina. Karina plays the tellingly named Nana, whose determination to become an actress drives her to prostitution. Godard's film is on the one hand extremely novelistic, and on the other hand more rooted in documentary than any of his previous work. In part a meditation on the notion of identity, the film is by no means a psychologically rich portrait, but rather a series of material documents of Nana's life. The result is one of Godard's most indelible characters. *My Life to Live* finds a very comfortable place between the formal rigor of Bresson (particularly in the film's handling of the relationship of image and text) and the self-aware naturalism of Rossellini (in its insistence on real locations and untreated soundtracks). A true masterpiece. —C. B.

OH WOE IS ME L: DIRECTORS/GODARD, JEAN-LUC (1993) 95M D: Jean-Luc Godard

Gerard Depardieu, Laurence Masliah, Bernard Verley. This film made one critic feel like "the victim of an inebriated channel surfer." I wholeheartedly agree and love it for that. Who would you rather have flipping your channels than the man who introduced channel surfing to cinema, Godard. He would pass a sobriety test even though his control over the images employs a random, fire-at-will style; it's all about the story, nothing is extraneous. Godard knows what he's doing, throwing all this stuff at us. We just need more eyes and ears. —M. S.

PASSION L: DIRECTORS/GODARD, JEAN-LUC (1982) 88M D: Jean-Luc Godard

Jerzy Radziwilowicz, Michel Piccoli, Hanna Schygulla, Isabelle Huppert. "Why must there always be a story?" asks a director (Radziwilowicz) attempting to create a film of beautiful images. Of course he's speaking for the real director, Godard, who returned from his self-imposed video exile with this lush production. Perhaps the most physically beautiful of all of Godard's films, he uses cranes, dollies, an elaborate set, and a vivid palette of rich colors to suggest the styles of the great European directors. But there must be a story, so the fictional director flits between his rich lover and a working-class protester while agonizing over his film. This framework seems like an afterthought, but perhaps that's the point: who needs a story when you have these amazing images? —S. A.

PIERROT LE FOU L: DIRECTORS/GODARD, JEAN-LUC (1965) 110M D: Jean-Luc Godard

Anna Karina, Jean-Paul Belmondo, Graziella Galvani. Sick of suffocated bourgeois life, Ferdinand (Belmondo) and Marianne (Karina) go on a romantic romp through the South of France, leaving a wake of inexplicable carnage as they go. A jarring viewing experience even today, *Pierrot*'s playful transgressions of cinematic propriety make for a film illegible as a realist narrative, careening from one plot trajectory to another, even from one genre to another, spontaneously abandoning each the moment it loses interest. A bombastic "attempt at cinema," the film constitutes a decisive moment not only in Godard's career, but in modern narrative aesthetics, and one senses that the film, and even the characters, know it. Certainly Godard knew it, enigmatically claiming nothing short of "life" and "emotion" as its subjects. This self-conscious swagger helps make *Pierrot* (especially its first and last twenty minutes) not only one of Godard's most entertaining movies, but one of the most inspired and exciting by any director. —C. B.

D.W. Griffith

Born in 1875 in Oldham County, Kentucky, the son of a former Confederate soldier whose death left the family struggling, David Wark Griffith aspired to be a playwright, and took a job as a film actor only as a temporary measure. (His debut, *Rescued from the Eagle's Nest* (1908), was directed by pioneer Edwin S. Porter.)

He soon began writing and directing films for the Biograph Company, averaging two and a half films a week between 1908 and 1913, when he left to make longer films.

His independently produced *Birth of a Nation* (1915) was a huge success. Although controversial for its racist and demeaning portrayals of blacks, it is possibly the single most influential film in cinema for its inventive and sophisticated techniques.

Griffith followed that success with the even more ambitious *Intolerance* (1916), a massive production that was a financial failure. He then turned back to simpler pictures but also continued making grand-scale films throughout the next ten years. Despite a number of successes, of both his epic and intimate pictures, he developed a reputation for extravagance and sentimen-

---

2 OR 3 THINGS I KNOW ABOUT HER L: DIRECTORS/ GODARD, JEAN-LUC (1966) 90M D: Jean-Luc Godard. *Roger Montsoret, Anny Duperey, Raoul J. Lévy, Marina Vlady.* Another masterpiece from that endless resource of cinematic invention, this pivotal entry in Godard's filmography seems nearly as transgressive today as it must have in 1966. Centered on a Parisian housewife (Vlady) who supplements the family income by prostituting herself, a near-plotless tangle of heady digressions and asides is more or less unified by a recurring voice-over that delivers in cautious whispers Godard's more overtly radical agenda. Correlating capitalism with prostitution, and positing consumerism as the single greatest force that structures daily life in Paris, Godard walks a highly verbose line between heavy-handed rhetoric and complex profundity. The finale pairs a haunting diatribe on the numbing effect of advertisements (mentioning Vietnam, Auschwitz, and the rest as realities that commercials allow one to forget) with a shot of neatly arranged commercial cleaning products. Despite the eye-rolling bluntness of the image, it seems an appropriate crescendo to close this expansive and substantial work. —*C. B.*

WEEKEND L: DIRECTORS/GODARD, JEAN-LUC (1967) 105M D: Jean-Luc Godard *Jean Yanne, Jean-Pierre Léaud, Mireille Darc, Juliet Berto, Anne Wiazemsky, Jean Eustache.* From its seven-minute dolly shot of a blood-soaked traffic jam to its cannibal revolutionaries, this episodic road movie is a quasi-lucid collage of absurdist ultraviolence and shouted polemics. Hammering out anti-capitalist social critique in the form of ridiculous spectacle, Godard spares no convention or decency on the highway to the "end of cinema," hailing the death of the "grammatical era" with the advent of "Flamboyance." A self-proclaimed "film found on a dump," *Weekend* has a delicious contempt not only for its despicable characters and its bourgeois audience, but even itself. Continually sabotaging passive viewing, human figures operate alternately as fictional characters and self-aware performers, the score functions as a series of interruptions devoid of narrative purpose, and camera work and editing gleefully disintegrate traditional cinematic propriety. Deeply ambivalent about narrative art and its inevitable reception as consumable product, *Weekend* is ironically some of the best fun the cinema has to offer. —*C. B.*

WOMAN IS A WOMAN, A L: DIRECTORS/GODARD, JEAN-LUC (1961) 90M D: Jean-Luc Godard. *Jean-Claude Brialy, Jean-Paul Belmondo, Anna Karina.* The first time I saw it, I dismissed this slightly silly tribute to Hollywood musicals as a minor and not altogether satisfying work by a great filmmaker. Rialto's lavish theatrical rerelease gave me an excellent opportunity for reconsideration, and this time I was thrilled with it. For the first twenty minutes I found myself in front of the most charming movie I'd seen in months. Though occasionally losing momentum, *A Woman is a Woman* at its worst is still exceedingly fresh entertainment. The plot revolves around Angela (Karina), a young dancer whose desire to have a baby throws her into a love triangle. Light and playful, the film's self-reflexive in-jokes include directly addressing the audience, deliberately misusing film special effects, even name-dropping *Breathless*. Ceaselessly clever, if not especially revolutionary, the film may come

tality, and found work harder to come by. After the financial failure of *Orphans of the Storm* (1921) and *Isn't Life Wonderful* (1924), and problems caused by his own financial mismanagement, he was relegated to turning out "programmers," low-budget, small-scale films over which he was unable to exercise the control he'd become accustomed to. He made only two sound films before he found himself unemployable, and after numerous attempts to engineer a comeback he retired to a gentleman's life in Kentucky. His marriage did not last, however, and he returned to Hollywood, where he died in 1948 in Hollywood's Knickerbocker Hotel.

Most famous for his explorations in editing and crosscutting, Griffith is generally considered to be the father of modern film "language." His refinements include attention to screen composition, the development of a more sophisticated acting style, the use of rhythmic editing to build a scene and create tension, and evocative use of long shots, medium shots, and close-ups. Griffith directed hundreds of films that we know of, and over the course of his career he used many pseudonyms, including Lawrence Griffith, M. Gaston de Trolignac, Granville Warwick, Captain Victor Marier, Marquis de Trolignac, Irene Sinclair, and Roy Sinclair. In 1935 he was awarded an honorary Academy Award for his contributions to the motion picture arts.

—Sean Axmaker

---

off frivolous, but it's certainly good fun—I recommend enjoying it with licorice candy. —*C. B.*

BABY OF MACON, THE L: DIRECTORS/GREENAWAY, PETER (1993) 122M D: Peter Greenaway. *Julia Ormond, Philip Stone.* On a stage in the seventeenth century, the Baby of Macon is about to be born. With fanfare and flourish each and every contraction is announced to the enthusiastic crowd, which cheers for this supposedly virgin birth. Few directors could pull off the shocking pretension built into this film as Greenaway does. He makes it clear that this royal child is not so much human as an object of unending public adoration. As the baby is awarded riches from countries across the world, the stage magnifies with Greenaway's excellent photography and the worthlessness of the masses in the audience becomes increasingly evident. By the end of the film the barrier between the audience in the film and the audience in real life is blurred by an endless camera pullback exposing countless peons perpetually applauding this performance. It would seem one man's hell is another man's pinnacle of art. —*N. J.*

COOK, THE THIEF, HIS WIFE AND HER LOVER, THE L: DIRECTORS/GREENAWAY, PETER (1990) 123M D: Peter Greenaway. *Michael Gambon, Helen Mirren, Tim Roth, Richard Bohringer, Alan Howard.* By far Greenaway's most popular film and arguably his best crafted, *The Cook, The Thief. .* probes the very depths of colorful characters with curious flaws. The thief is an obnoxiously rich man who gorges himself at a marathon banquet while impressing his guests with his wealth and culinary taste. His wife sits next to him, yet she loses interest first. She slips out to meet her lover, who has one thing her husband lacks—a good mind. The cook is about the only rational observer in the drama who is also victim to the whims of the thief. Completing this intricate story of intrigue is unforgettable cinematography and camera work, complete with sets that are as outrageous as the characters. There is also profound music, the best of which is sung by a boy soprano who slaves away in the kitchen. This film resonates on quite a variety of different levels and is a veritable playground for film students. —*N. J.*

DEATH IN THE SEINE L: DIRECTORS/GREENAWAY, PETER (1988) 44M D: Peter Greenaway. *Leonie Beverloo, Lars Crama, Niels Crama, Jean-Michel Dagory, Cor van de Beek.* This short film by Greenaway examines the deaths of those who drowned in the Seine in the years following the French Revolution. Visually re-creating the catalog of two Parisian morticians, Greenaway gives us only the information contained therein. We learn the names of the deceased, how they died, who identified their bodies, and other bits of information. Using multiple frames within frames and a dreamlike color palette, Greenaway draws us into a repetitive hypnotic detailing of corpse after corpse. It is a difficult film to analyze, but even if its purpose is obscure, its bizarre appeal is undeniable. —*T. S.*

PROSPERO'S BOOKS L: DIRECTORS/GREENAWAY, PETER (1991) 129M D: Peter Greenaway. *Erland Josephson, John Gielgud, Michel Blanc, Isabelle Pasco.* Flush from the success of *The Cook, The Thief, His Wife and Her Lover,* Greenaway got to work adapting a film version of Shakespeare's last play, *The Tempest.* Gielgud plays the elderly Prospero who is exiled to an island where he reviews his magical books. Exploiting a range of cinematic techniques, including different film stocks and high-definition video, this film is visually stunning. However, it doesn't stop there. As though the verse of Shakespeare through the baritone of Gielgud needed the further elaboration of mixer-happy sound technicians, monologues are double- or triple-masked. And if that isn't enough, there is the overbearing content of some of these visuals: dancers who appear and disappear for little purpose and the young sprite on a trapeze who continually and monotonously pisses into a pool several feet below. Few films can readily match the pretension of this one, except perhaps Greenaway's following film, *The Baby of Macon*. —N.J.

BATTLE OF THE SEXES, THE L: DIRECTORS/GRIFFITH, D. W.
(1928) 88M D: D. W. Griffith. *Phyllis Haver, Jean Hersholt, Don Alvarado, Sally O'Neil, Belle Bennett*. Griffith somehow earned a reputation in the late 1920s as an old-fashioned holdover of the "primitive" days of Victorian melodrama. This thoroughly modern sex comedy, from a play by Arthur Schnitzer, should dispel that myth. Hersholt is a philandering Wall Street frump lured from the loving arms of his family by a flashy flapper with a taste for the night life (Haver), only to discover his own daughter has fallen for a handsome gigolo who is Haver's partner in gold digging. Deft, witty, and fully engaged with the complexities of his mercurial characters, Griffith's silky visual smoothness and fluid camera work (not to mention his flirtation with jazz-age sex and sin) recall the sophistication of Ernst Lubitsch. The echoes of tragic melodrama, however, are pure Griffith. —S.A.

BIRTH OF A NATION, THE L: DIRECTORS/GRIFFITH, D. W. (1915) 190M D: D. W. Griffith. *Mae Marsh, George Siegmann, Mary Alden, Miriam Cooper, Ralph Lewis, Lillian Gish, Henry Walthall, Miriam Cooper, Mae Marsh, Lillian Gish, Robert Harron*. President Woodrow Wilson supplied the first money quote for a motion picture when he likened D. W. Griffith's *The Birth of a Nation* to "writing history with lightning." The history and politics are largely bogus and wrongheaded; the film's portrayal of the post–Civil War South, the Ku Klux Klan, and the irredeemable naiveté of the black race as potential participants in democracy all conspire to render the film virtually unshowable in a public setting. That's a shame, because it's part of our shared history, sociopolitical and cinematic, and because the "writing with lightning" part of Wilson's accolade still applies. Griffith had a vision of what movies could be, how they could move and mean, how shots and scenes and tones and kinesis and stillness could add up to a persuasive reality in their own right. *The Birth of a Nation* is also the birth of an art form. It should be seen not as a grim obligation, or as an opportunity for politically correct self-congratu-

lation, but for its many moments of still-astonishing beauty and power. —R.T.J.

GRIFFITH, D. W.: YEARS OF DISCOVERY L: DIRECTORS/GRIFFITH, D. W. (1909) 334M D: D. W. Griffith. *Blanche Sweet, Lillian Gish, Mary Pickford, Dorothy Gish, Lionel Barrymore*. Griffith directed more than 450 short films between 1908 and 1913. He literally cranked them out, balancing art with business, but he used this immersion as a laboratory where he experimented with editing ideas, camera technique, composition and performance styles, and basic storytelling grammar, essentially giving birth to the roots of modern cinema. The twenty-two silent shorts in this collection represent the cream of his output and provide a survey of his evolution, from the comic play of the brief three-minute comedy *Those Awful Hats* (1909), a goof set in a movie theater featuring a rare Griffith special-effect matte shot, to the sweeping proto-Western *The Battle of Elderbush Gulch* (1913), a taut half-hour action film that anticipates the climactic rush of *Birth of a Nation* (he considered it his best Biograph production). Landmark productions include *The Girl and Her Trust* (1912), an almost pure "chase" film defined by an amazing sense of momentum, confident and creative crosscutting, and picture-perfect framing, and his protogangtser drama *The Musketeers of Pig Alley* (1912), which features some of Griffith's most dynamic moving images and expands the understanding of screen space that, until then, appeared to end at the edge of the frame. Other highlights include his famous social drama *A Corner in Wheat* (1909), *An Unseen Enemy* (the Biograph debuts of Lillian and Dorothy Gish, 1912), the remarkable *The Painted Lady* (with Sweet going quietly mad, 1912), and *The House of Darkness* (a dark and sensitive drama set in an insane asylum, 1913). —S.A.

WAY DOWN EAST L: DIRECTORS/GRIFFITH, D. W. (1920) 145M D: D. W. Griffith. *Mary Hay, Lowell Sherman, Richard Barthelmess, Lillian Gish*. Country girl Anna (Gish) is romanced by a heartless cad (Sherman) and forgotten. Her baby dies, leaving Anna ostracized and poor. Some kindly farmers take her in, only to have the cad end up hitting on their niece (Hay). Griffith tells a modern story while setting Anna on a mythic odyssey. The dire finale is a brittle metaphor for cold fate that sometimes sweeps poor little things like her away, unless a good man like David (Barthelmess) is there to save her. Emotionally the movie is a mess, except when Griffith focuses on Gish. He frames Anna seated in a lighted alcove sewing as David joins her and attempts to speak his feelings. Griffith then reframes the two from an angle that is only a grade different, turning her sewing into a complex emotion, exposing Anna's fear of being too happy too soon after all she's been through. Such moments are Griffith at his core. —J.C.

FUNNY GAMES L: DIRECTORS/HANEKE, MICHAEL (1997) 108M D: Michael Haneke. *Frank Giering, Ulrich Mühe, Susanne Lothar, Arno Frisch.* This movie is seriously fucked-up. The events in the film are horrific enough on their own: a posh Austrian family takes a trip to their posh lake house, where they'll play tennis with their posh neighbors, and they are subsequently physically and emotionally tortured by two young men, dressed in white tennis shirts and white gloves. It's obvious the men are nihilists and mostly just want to fuck up the status quo, one rich family at a time. But the filmmaker doesn't stop there—he wants us to be in on it as well. At one point, when the mother is looking for their (presumably) dead dog, one of the attackers turns to the camera and winks at us, like some kind of sick Austrian Ferris Bueller. At another point he's disappointed with how the movie has turned out, and quickly rewinds the scene so he can have his way. I can't say I enjoyed *Funny Games,* but it is effective as the most fucked-up movie I've seen. —*K. C.*

FLIRT L: DIRECTORS/HARTLEY, HAL (1995) 85M D: Hal Hartley. *Parker Posey, Miho Nikaido, Harold Perrineau Jr.* *Flirt* is one story played against the backdrops of three different characters in three different parts of the world; three stories of impulsive flirts and the social impressions they leave. The stories become more intriguing as it becomes clear the outcomes may be affected by the characters' sometimes subtle differences. Each character must choose between a fleeing love and a dangerous interest. As the characters wander toward a decision, the inevitable threatens to make both choices impossible. The changes in location and gender give the situation the feeling that it encompasses all hearts and lives; that these three stories represent the unchanging insides of love and pain. —*J. J.*

NO SUCH THING L: DIRECTORS/HARTLEY, HAL (2002) 103M D: Hal Hartley. *Bill Sage, Julie Christie, Helen Mirren, Sarah Polley, Robert John Burke.* American indie hipster Hartley takes on *Beauty and the Beast* in this sardonic fairy tale with metaphysical dimension, set in the modern world of global media and instant celebrity. Polley is the beauty, a young cub reporter who miraculously survives a catastrophic plane crash, tracks the "monster" (Burke in a demonic mask) down in his remote Iceland castle, and takes him back to the Big Apple. With her pigtails and plucky purity, she's an innocent in a thoroughly cynical and corrupt world, just the creature to tame the beast. Hartley's deadpan absurdities and self-aware dialogue don't hide the unusually blunt obviousness of his satire. Mirren's manipulative media baron is such a coldhearted caricature that the viewer loses all interest, and the sadistic actions of the humans make the point of "who's the real monster" so blatant as to be meaningless. —*S. A.*

SIMPLE MEN L: DIRECTORS/HARTLEY, HAL (1992) 105M D: Hal Hartley. *Mark Bailey, Robert John Burke, Bill Sage, Karen Sillas, Elina Lowensohn, Martin Donovan, John A. MacKay.* My favorite film by Hartley, *Simple Men* follows the journey of two brothers. The elder (Burke) is a thief betrayed by his partner and his woman; the younger (Sage), a college student who has decided to drop out of school and find their infamous father (Mackay), an anarchist bomber who recently broke out of jail. The older brother is on the run from the law and determined to seduce and then abandon some arbitrary woman to get revenge for the way he was hurt. So begins a convoluted tale, as each brother seeks to reach his respective goal. They become involved and embroiled in the lives and problems of the people they meet. This quirky film toys with language, imagery, and symbolism. The dialogue is priceless, turning in, around, and back on top of itself in patterns that are more akin to Greek choruses, a poor man's Shakespeare, and theatrical absurdity. —*M. N.*

UNBELIEVABLE TRUTH, THE L: DIRECTORS/HARTLEY, HAL (1989) 90M D: Hal Hartley. *Robert Burke, Chris Cooke, Adrienne Shelly.* Hartley's self-effacingly self-conscious and intellectually playful debut feature passed me by in theaters and I finally caught up to it on video, where its modest charms are right at home. The austerely handsome deadpan farce about rumor, obsession, and truth stars Shelly as a glum high-school neurotic with a doomsday obsession who falls for the tall, dark, and enigmatically terse Burke, a philosophical mechanic who dresses in black and has served time for murder. The ping-pong dialogue has an almost Beckett-like quality by way of a modern beatnik sensibility, but it's Hartley's optimism and his cast's crack performances that make the unbelievable believable. —*S. A.*

TRAIL OF THE LONESOME PINE, THE L: DIRECTORS/HATHAWAY, HENRY (1936) 102M D: Henry Hathaway. *Sylvia Sidney, Henry Fonda, Fred MacMurray.* *The Trail of the Lonesome Pine* is a far-from-great, but oh-so-good, instance of golden-age Hollywood craft. This first feature shot outdoors in three-strip Technicolor somehow retains the special thrill of that breakthrough moment. With his fine pictorial eye (abetted by second-unit director Richard Talmadge) and sturdy storytelling instincts, director Hathaway knew just how to place his casts in dynamic settings without getting fussy about it. The film is an account of a long-running Appalachian feud and its interruption by modernity. Its stars are all so very young and fresh-faced in Technicolor, with solid support from Beulah Bondi, Fred Stone, Robert Barrat, Nigel Bruce—and hillbilly Greek chorus Fuzzy Knight to sing the haunting "Twilight on the Trail." And yes, that eldest Falin boy is none other than Henry Brandon, *The Searchers'* Chief Scar, twenty years younger. —*R. T. J.*

BALL OF FIRE L: DIRECTORS/HAWKS, HOWARD (1941) 111M
D: Howard Hawks. *Henry Travers, Oskar Homolka, Gary Cooper, Barbara Stanwyck.* Stanwyck plays Sugarpuss O'Shea, a sexy, tough, fast-talking, street-smart dame on the lam from gangsters and cops in this funny screwball spin on *Snow White and the Seven Dwarfs.* Cooper leads a group of elderly scholars attempting to write a dictionary. They lack any sense of modern lingo and in comes Sugarpuss to set them straight. The dialogue comes fast and furious and rivals Hawks's *His Girl Friday* for frantic pacing. The topnotch script by Billy Wilder and Charles Brackett features lots of great double entendres and one-liners. There's also some great music courtesy of Gene Krupa. For some reason this movie tends to be overlooked by screwball comedy fans but I think it's one of the best. —*S. H.*

BIG SLEEP, THE L: DIRECTORS/HAWKS, HOWARD (1946) 116M D: Howard Hawks. *Humphrey Bogart, Lauren Bacall, John Ridgely, Martha Vickers, Charles D. Brown.* It's strange to think that Raymond Chandler didn't particularly care for Bogart's interpretation of Phillip Marlowe and that he preferred wimpy Dick Powell because Bogart nails the morally complex character in one of the best adaptations of Chandler's novels. The William Faulkner script probably helps, along with Chandler's choice dialogue, and the perfect cast of leads and supporting roles gives even the smallest characters a life of their own. But it's Hawks's smart direction and attention to detail that bring the dark side of Los Angeles to life in this mesmerizing work. Marlowe is hired by a wealthy man with two daughters, one of whom is being blackmailed. While pursuing the blackmailer Marlowe soon discovers that nothing is ever as simple as it seems and, ultimately, he's been given the runaround from the start. The layers of manipulation and deceit are a delight. Available in its original theatrical version or a slightly longer prerelease cut. —*S. H.*

BRINGING UP BABY L: DIRECTORS/HAWKS, HOWARD (1938) 102M D: Howard Hawks. *Asta, Katharine Hepburn, May Robson, Charlie Ruggles, Cary Grant.* Something has to be the greatest of screwball comedies, and it's hard to see how that could be any movie other than *Bringing Up Baby.* Grant's the paradigmatic ivory-tower academic, a paleontologist waiting to insert the last bone in the massive dinosaur skeleton to which he's devoted his life. Hepburn's a giddy New England princess who long-leggedly crosses his path just at the moment of professional triumph. He gets the missing intercostal clavicle at the same time she gets custody of a South American leopard named Baby. Baby and bone, Kate and Cary, all leave Manhattan and head out into the enchanted Connecticut countryside on a journey assured of disaster several times over. An ivory-tower academic might permissibly point out that this movie's journey follows an itinerary

previously charted in the Forest of Arden school of Shakespearean comedy—the red and green worlds of Hawks, no less. From sublime slapstick to the intricate, deceptively effortless verbal play of one of Hollywood's densest scripts, this is one hilarious *and* profoundly intellectual comedy, in which two of cinema's most enchanting babies court chaos to bring each other up to something touchingly like adulthood. —*R. T. J.*

GENTLEMEN PREFER BLONDES L: DIRECTORS/HAWKS, HOWARD (1953) 91M D: Howard Hawks. *Marilyn Monroe, Charles Coburn, Jane Russell.* Hawks discovers one of the great female screen teams in bubbly gold digger Monroe and wry, man-hungry Russell (what a shame they never reunited) in his flip on buddy-film machismo. It's a delightful, hilarious farce, with great musical numbers (Monroe's iconic "Diamonds are a Girl's Best Friend" and Russell's "Isn't Anyone Here for Love," sung to a bevy of beefy but oblivious bodybuilders) and gorgeously garish color. Hawks photographs them like cover girls and plays the sexual humor for what is surely a male audience, but he never, ever allows them to play second fiddle to the men in the film. These two little girls from Little Rock are thoroughly loyal to each other and always in charge. —*S. A.*

HIS GIRL FRIDAY L: DIRECTORS/HAWKS, HOWARD (1940) 92M D: Howard Hawks. *Ralph Bellamy, Rosalind Russell, Cary Grant.* Hecht and MacArthur's play *The Front Page* has been filmed several times, but this variation is by far the best. Hawks conceived of altering the sex of one of the reporters and created one of the most beloved and successful screwball comedies. A hardworking newspaper editor (Grant) tries to get his retiring ace reporter and ex-wife (Russell) to cover one more important story. Grant's motivation is further complicated by jealousy because Russell plans on marrying an insurance salesman (an absolutely hilarious Bellamy) and settling down. The dialogue comes fast and furious, the plot cooks along at full speed, the humor never lets up, the leads are outstanding, and the cast is filled with the best character actors of the era. Remarkably, Hawks was also able to retain the socially conscious message of the play and its attack on corrupt city officials and an amoral media. —*S. H.*

MONKEY BUSINESS L: DIRECTORS/HAWKS, HOWARD (1952) 97M D: Howard Hawks. *Ginger Rodgers, Cary Grant, Marilyn Monroe.* Hawks's low-key screwball is one of the slyest comedies of classic American cinema. Absent-minded professor Grant and the elegant Rogers are a stable, staid old married couple who get a jolt of youth from Grant's experimental serum. Grant turns collegiate show-off and takes out shapely secretary Monroe, then Rogers dances up a storm as a giggly teen virgin, and finally they both revert back to adolescent hijinks. There may be no funnier moment in American cinema than a playschool-aged Grant

Howard Hawks

Born in 1896 to a wealthy paper manu-facturer, and the grandson of a lumber baron, Howard Winchester Hawks showed an interest in inventions from an early age. This passion led to his two great loves: filmmaking and flying. After graduating from Cornell with a degree in engineering, Hawks began spending his free time in Hollywood at the fledgling film studios, and by 1917 was working as a prop boy on Mary Pickford's films.

After a stint in the Air Corps as a flying instructor, he returned to Hollywood and in 1924 joined producer Adolph Zukor's Famous Players as head of their story department. In 1926 Fox offered him the chance to direct, and he made eight films in three years. In 1929, when his contract came up, Hawks became an independent and never again signed a long-term studio contract.

With the advent of sound, Hawks came into his own. His films exhibited breezy, col-orful dialogue that was far different from the arch, theatrical writing of many early talkies. Hawks rewrote on the set and encouraged improvisation to create a sense of spon-taneity. He also often expressed character through action rather than dialogue; his films are full of moments in which truths are revealed through characters' interaction with objects and people.

He dabbled in many genres but found his calling in male-oriented adventures and dramas, including crime pictures, war films, and Westerns. Censors considered his gang-ster film *Scarface* (1932), made for flying buddy Howard Hughes, so brutal that they refused to release it until changes were made. But while most of his films centered on the relationships between men (often groups of men), there were exceptions. Hawks also found great success with screwball com-edies such as *Bringing Up Baby* (1938) and *Monkey Business* (1952), in which he was able to play with the conventions of mascu-line behavior for comic effect.

Hawks was an active sportsman off the set, and a consummate professional on the set. Both of these qualities showed up in his films. Hawks shows admiration for professionals who do their jobs well, and his protagonists are men of action: flyers, soldiers, race-car drivers, and adventur-ers. His comedies feature role reversals in which the men are often passive characters with quiet careers, while the women are active and exciting. Even in his adventure films, women show a degree of activity and aggressiveness not often displayed in Hol-lywood cinema.

Throughout his career Hawks made films that made money and earned the respect of his Hollywood peers, though it wasn't until the 1960s that critics began to appreciate his films. Ironically it wasn't until after his finest films had been made (*Only Angels Have Wings* [1939], *The Big Sleep* [1946], *Red River* [1948], and finally *Rio Bravo* [1959]) and his career was in decline that suddenly he was the focus of great critical attention. He made films in almost every Hollywood genre, including a notable musical (*Gen-tlemen Prefer Blondes* [1953]) and science fiction film (*The Thing from Another World* [1951]) and he continued making films into his 70s. He was still developing projects almost until his death in 1977 at the age of eighty-one.   —*Sean Axmaker*

torn between tit-for-tat sniping with sweetheart Rogers and playing cowboys and Indians with neighborhood kids, jumping and hooting while he struggles with the primal urges of an adolescent adrenaline bomb. Monroe's part is small but her timing is impeccable and she demands attention. She soon graduated from pneumatic supporting doll to leading lady. —*S. A.*

ONLY ANGELS HAVE WINGS L: DIRECTORS/HAWKS, HOWARD (1939) 121M D: Howard Hawks. *Rita Hayworth, Richard Barthelmess, Thomas Mitchell, Sig Ruman, Cary Grant, Jean Arthur.* American flyboys in the Andes live, love, and risk all to fly the mail over the hazardous mountain pass, come fog, blizzard, or buzzard. Grant is the charismatic, uncompromising leader Papa, who lives out of a bar and never lays in a supply of anything, and Arthur the spunky girl who wins his heart. It's a romantic adventure that could only exist in the movies, pure boys-only pulp complicated by romantic twists out of a soap opera: Papa's ex-wife (Hayworth) flies back into his life on the arm of a rival pilot (Barthelmess). But the rich details of Hawks's cinema, where an action, a gesture, or a even a match is worth a thousand words, bring it to hearty life. The quintessential Hawks movie of male bonding and tough love, where life is lived minute to minute, men are good enough, and the highest compliment one can receive is "professional." —*S. A.*

RED RIVER L: DIRECTORS/HAWKS, HOWARD (1948) 133M D: Howard Hawks. *John Wayne, Montgomery Clift, Joanne Dru, Walter Brennan, Coleen Gray.* Hawks's "Mutiny on the Prairie" is an epic Western, the sweeping tale of a journey that can't be made and the story of a son forced to battle the father he loves and adores. Clift made his film debut opposite grand old icon Wayne, and the opposition of acting styles is electric: laconic elder statesman Wayne wearing his character like a buckskin, dominating the screen as upstart method actor Clift's intensity burns a star right next to him. Hawks's style leans more to Wayne: measured, easygoing, he seems to let the characters take the story along with them, but behind that easy pace is a tale of madness, betrayal, and vengeance that heats to a simmer under the sun of the parched prairie. —*S. A.*

RIO BRAVO L: DIRECTORS/HAWKS, HOWARD (1959) 141M D: Howard Hawks. *Ricky Nelson, Angie Dickinson, John Wayne, Walter Brennan, Dean Martin.* Hawks made this laconic Western drama about a sheriff (stocky Wayne) in response to *High Noon,* to show that a *real* lawman is a professional who would turn down the well-meaning efforts of amateurs. The irony is that he ends up under siege with a drunk (Martin), a green kid who is good with a gun (Nelson), a crippled old man (Brennan), and a showgirl (Dickinson as "Feathers") by his side. With unpretentious ease and a rich sense of camaraderie, Hawks turns out

a classic tale of redemption and creates some of his most memorable scenes (most of them, surprisingly, involving Martin), practically without leaving the soundstage. Realistic it ain't, but it's a beautiful, sublime work of cinema—one of the greatest Westerns ever made and one of my all-time favorite movies. —*S. A.*

SCARFACE L: DIRECTORS/HAWKS, HOWARD (1932) 93M D: Howard Hawks. *Paul Muni, Ann Dvorak, Boris Karloff.* The world of crime is given its full glory in blazing black and white in the gangster film that would be remade more than fifty years later. The underworld mobsters are put in a tough position as the last of the famed gang leaders, Louis Costillo, is killed. The police suspect Costillo's former bodyguard, Tony Camonte (Muni), but since Costillo's body is never found, Tony must be released. Tony quickly fills the void that Costillo has left, and with remorseless violence begins taking over the local rackets and removing the competition, including Gaffney (Karloff) in the beautifully shot bowling-alley execution. Tony's rivals soon decide that he must be killed. With the police and the underworld now after him, Tony is cornered and faces his final curtain call. Hawks breathes life into the mystery gangland and, as a true artist and visionary, stood up against the censor board and released his version without approval. —*R. M.*

THING FROM ANOTHER WORLD, THE L: DIRECTORS/HAWKS, HOWARD (1951) 87M D: Howard Hawks (uncredited). *James Arness, Margaret Sheridan, Kenneth Tobey.* Hawks assigned Christian Nyby, his editor on *To Have and Have Not, The Big Sleep,* and *Red River,* to direct this excursion into sci-fi horror, one of the few genres he hadn't yet worked in. Although the producer gallantly insisted in interviews that Nyby had made a fine job of it, in later years surviving cast members had no hesitation in asserting that Hawks himself did most of the picture. Hawks and Lederer disposed of the Thing's diabolical shape-changing ability that played such a big part in the excellent John W. Campbell Jr. story and would be restored in the 1980 John Carpenter remake. But Arness's incarnation of the towering, literally bloodthirsty "intellectual carrot" is fearsome, and the siege atmosphere of a small band of humans clinging to viability in a distant, frozen ice-world is powerfully realized. A cadre of solid character actors works wonders with the most overlapping dialogue in any Hawks film. The emphasis on the brave resiliency of the human voice in extremis is further underscored by the presence of such familiar voice-over/announcer types as George Feniman and Paul Frees. —*R. T. J.*

TO HAVE AND HAVE NOT L: DIRECTORS/HAWKS, HOWARD (1944) 100M D: Howard Hawks. *Humphrey Bogart, Lauren Bacall, Hoagy Carmichael, Dolores Moran, Walter Brennan.* "You know how to whistle, don't you? You just put your lips together and

... blow." Bogie and Bacall sizzle in their first on-screen pairing. Legend has it that director Hawks boasted to Ernest Hemingway that he could make a good film from the author's worst book, and proceeded to do so with a romantic script that has less to do with Hemingway than *Casablanca*, a film Warner was hoping to replicate. Bogart is a cynical fishing-boat captain in Martinique who reluctantly helps out the French Resistance and falls in love with smoky singer Bacall. It was the nineteen-year-old model's film debut and the beginning of one of Hollywood's greatest love affairs. Brennan is the rummy sidekick ("You ever been bit by a dead bee?") and Carmichael tinkles the ivories in the island bar. William Faulkner cowrote the script. —*S. A.*

TWENTIETH CENTURY L: DIRECTORS/HAWKS, HOWARD

(1934) 91M D: Howard Hawks. *Carole Lombard, John Barrymore, Edgar Kennedy.* Barrymore is a pretentious, egomaniacal theater director who takes a timid unknown (Lombard) and transforms her into a Broadway superstar. Eventually his possessive behavior and constant dramatics drive her away and his career plummets as her stardom rises. As fate would have it, they meet again on a cross-country train filled with crazed passengers and small rooms. The two clash in an eruption of furious verbal squabbles, hurled insults, and slammed doors. *Twentieth Century* was director Hawks's first collaboration with Broadway scribes turned screenwriters MacArthur and Hecht, and is considered by many to be the first screwball comedy as it is one of the first Hollywood films to show the elite as a bunch of ridiculous fools. —*S. H.*

FAR FROM HEAVEN L: DIRECTORS/HAYNES, TODD (2002)

108M D: Todd Haynes. *Patricia Clarkson, Dennis Quaid, Julianne Moore, Dennis Haysbert.* Haynes's deliciously smart tribute to the glossy melodramas of the '50s. Moore plays the ideal homemaker with poise, delicacy, and eager oblivion to her compromises, avoiding any real emotional contact with the outside world. Quaid is the unhappy husband repressing his secrets until they burst the bubble of normalcy both have been trying to nurture. Haynes embraces the exaggerated Douglas Sirk style of magazine-perfect sets and Hollywood-movie costume design (and these are costumes, not clothes) done up with perfect compositions and decorator Technicolors, but empathizes with them in a way satirist Sirk never could. The story is drawn most obviously from *All That Heaven Allows,* but *Written on the Wind* and *Imitation of Life* echo through the characters played by Quaid and Haysbert (the "colored" gardener who befriends Moore, much to the shock of her social circle). To complete the Sirk comparison, Clarkson plays the Agnes Moorehead role to perfection. —*S. A.*

POISON L: DIRECTORS/HAYNES, TODD (1991) 85M D:

Todd Haynes. *Buck Smith, Larry Maxwell, Susan Norman, Millie White, Scott Renderer, Edith Meeks.* Haynes's triumvirate of tales became a cause célèbre when it was attacked by the head of the conservative American Family Association (because it was in part funded by a grant from the NEA), which gave the low-budget 16 mm production a wider audience. It probably needed that kind of publicity because it's an aggressively alienating work that explores taboo subjects in alternately poetic and grotesque imagery in three stylistically distinct sequences. The first is a bizarre, murky black-and-white take on 1950s mad scientist and monster movies with allusions to AIDS; the second a mock news documentary of a seven-year-old boy who shot his abusive father and then flew into the sky; the third the brutal story of a gay prisoner remembering his idyllic past, shot with a lyrical style and inspired by the works of Jean Genet. —*S. A.*

SAFE L: DIRECTORS/HAYNES, TODD (1995) 119M D: Todd

Haynes. *Julianne Moore, James LeGros, Peter Friedman, April Grace.* A great and horrifying film about everywoman Carol White (the riveting Moore) who starts developing physical symptoms of illness, though her doctors can't figure out why. Haynes is smart enough a director to give clues, but he never answers. His cold, static camera work (often likened to Stanley Kubrick) distances the audience, alienating the relationships between on-screen characters and their hypoallergenic environments. At times it isn't clear whether Carol is "allergic" to her social conditions, having bland emotionless sex with her husband, getting her hair done, or hanging out with the other trophy wives and their children. Carol's nose bleeds, she bruises, she can't breathe. But what is the cause? Paranoia prevails in this brilliant and creepy exploration of the modern condition. —*J. D.*

VELVET GOLDMINE L: DIRECTORS/HAYNES, TODD (1998)

124M D: Todd Haynes. *Jonathan Rhys-Meyers, Ewan McGregor, Toni Collette, Eddie Izzard, Emily Woof, Christian Bale.* Welcome to the world of music, filled with sex, nudity, bisexuality, backstabbing, and all the glitter and makeup you could ever hope for! We travel back in time as writer Arthur Stuart (Bale) is assigned a "whatever became of?" piece on glam rock star Brian Slade (Rhys-Meyers), who rose to fame like a rocket and crashed and burned just as hard and fast. The story travels back and forth as our intrepid reporter remembers his youth, interviews those once close to Slade, and learns more and more about this elusive ex-star. At times I felt like I was watching something about David Bowie. The androgynous look and style of Slade and the music! Oh, the music! It's a bit of a mystery, a bit of a love story, and a whole lotta glam and debauchery! Check out the '50s-esque beauty

Two-Lane Blacktop

In 1994, I was invited by Scarecrow Video to come to Seattle to speak at a screening of my film *Two-Lane Blacktop*. In addition to feeding and aggravating my addiction to laser discs, and later DVDs, I made some wonderful new friends, most notably Norm Hill and Rebecca Latsios (manager and former owner of Scarecrow Video). Their falling in love with my movie helped to give it new life and bring it to an even wider audience than the people of Seattle.

They asked me why the movie wasn't available on video. I said that its distributor, Universal Studios, usually gave a number of reasons—the main one being the large number of films in their catalog, and their ability to release only a few of them in any given year. As it turned out, there was an even more powerful reason.

Two-Lane Blacktop was released in 1971. At that time, when music rights were negotiated for films, no one anticipated that films would eventually be released on new media like videotapes or DVDs. So the music rights were obtained just for a theatrical motion picture. If these films were ever to be released on video, the rights to all the popular music on their soundtracks would have to be renegotiated and paid for again. So there was a strong incentive not to bother.

But Rebecca and Norm were not deterred. They wrote up a petition asking Universal Studios to release *Two-Lane Blacktop* on video, then circulated it in the store, collecting several thousand signatures over six months. *People* magazine wrote about the success of the petition, which inspired a couple of other video stores to join the campaign.

The rest is history. Universal eventually gave in to this and other pressure, and allowed Anchor Bay Entertainment to release the movie on video, laser disc, and DVD. Of course, the downside is that so many people have now seen *Two-Lane Blacktop*, it hardly qualifies as a cult movie anymore.   —*Monte Hellman*

---

queen photo behind Izzard and guess who really posed for it! —*M. N.*

COCKFIGHTER L: DIRECTORS/HELLMAN, MONTE (1974) 83M D: Monte Hellman. *Warren Oates, Harry Dean Stanton*. Oates gives an absolute tour de force performance as a man living a thoroughly reckless life as a cockfight trainer. After losing everything he owns gambling on matches, he decides to completely reform his life. He does this, in part, by taking a vow of silence until he can win the championship. With this deliberate change, people in his life start seeing him differently. Oates's ability to shift from a destructive hedonist to a sensitive and resolute man will certainly amuse you. Animal lovers beware: this film has very nasty scenes featuring actual cockfights. —*N. J.*

SHOOTING, THE L: DIRECTORS/HELLMAN, MONTE (1966) 82M D: Monte Hellman. *Millie Perkins, Jack Nicholson, Warren Oates*. Hellman created the first genuinely existential Western in this stylized, abstract little odyssey through a harsh, desolate desert landscape. Oates and Nicholson star as clashing bounty hunters on an obscure, doomed manhunt, the former a thoughtful, time-tested tracker and the latter a sadistic bully hired by the mysterious Perkins. The spare cinematography burns bright and harsh in the sunlight that simmers the already edgy relations, and Hellman directs the ambiguous script with always surprising flourishes. Nicholson is appropriately vicious in a preening sort of way, but Oates is magnetic as a man driven by some fate beyond his comprehension. The film ends with more questions than answers, but it is never less than compelling. —*S. A.*

SILENT NIGHT, DEADLY NIGHT 3: BETTER WATCH OUT! L: DIRECTORS/HELLMAN, MONTE (1989) 90M D: Monte Hellman. *Samantha Scully, Robert Culp, Bill Moseley, Richard Beymer*. A sleazy scientist (Beymer) uses the dreams of a blind psychic (Scully) to communicate with the Santa Claus killer (now played by Moseley), who is in a coma with his brain visible through a glass dome on top of his head. When the psychic goes with her brother and his girlfriend to their grandma's house, the killer wakes up and follows them, leaving a trail of bodies along the way. Unfortunately it's neither a good Hellman movie nor an unintentional laugh fest like the first *Silent Night* sequel. Moseley, so brilliant as Chop Top in *The Texas Chainsaw Massacre Part 2*, doesn't get much to do because he's just an automaton powered by life support built into his head. —*B. T.*

TWO LANE BLACKTOP L: DIRECTORS/HELLMAN, MONTE (1971) 102M D: Monte Hellman. *James Taylor, Harry Dean Stanton, Laurie Bird, Warren Oates, Dennis Wilson.* Imperviously detailed, deceptively simple, and masterfully wrought, American auteur Hellman creates a magnificent portrait of national apathy after the generic turmoil of the 1960s (see *Easy Rider*). Our nameless characters, our undefined "heroes," have one aimless goal: to keep moving forward at the highest speed possible. Brilliant. —*J. D.*

AGUIRRE, THE WRATH OF GOD L: DIRECTORS/HERZOG, WERNER (1972) 94M D: Werner Herzog. *Daniel Ades, Peter Berling, Alejandro Chavez, Klaus Kinski, Daniel Farfán.* Written by a twenty-three-year-old Herzog while traveling home on a bus from a soccer game, this is the film that would put him on the map. It is also responsible for elevating actor Kinski to art-house lead actor and Herzog collaborator. The two would go on to make five more feature films, creating a legendarily difficult relationship on and off the set. As the mad conquistador Aguirre, Kinski appoints himself the leader of a group of Spaniard soldiers searching for the lost treasures of Cortez in the Amazon jungle. Kinski is at his eye-popping maddest, first murdering his own guardsmen, then taking control of the Spaniards only to slowly lose his own control to the wilds of the jungles around him. The final image is an excellent metaphor as the crazed Aguirre pitches wild monkeys off his sinking raft, the jungle having finally beaten him. A classic film, and the head of an unintended trilogy (with *Fitzcarraldo* and *Cobra Verde*) portraying men whose dreams and souls are defeated by the natural world around them. —*N. H.*

COBRA VERDE L: DIRECTORS/HERZOG, WERNER (1987) 110M D: Werner Herzog. *King Ampaw, Salvatore Basile, Klaus Kinski, Jose Lewgoy.* Set in the 1800s, a notorious Brazilian bandit (Kinski) settles as a worker on a large plantation. He gravely upsets the owner of the plantation by sleeping with his daughters, and so he is given the least desirable job in the world—slave trading from the west coast of Africa. The plantation owner figures Kinski will be dead in short order due to a mad, bloodthirsty king who has been ruining the slave-trading business. Yet between playing politics and assembling an army of combat-ready women, Kinski wins over all odds. Too bad for him slave trading becomes illegal just as he establishes his monopoly! —*N. J.*

ENIGMA OF KASPAR HAUSER, THE L: DIRECTORS/ HERZOG, WERNER (1974) 109M D: Werner Herzog. *Bruno S., Walter Ladengast, Brigitte Mira.* In 1828, Kasper Hauser, raised in isolation without any knowledge of language or even other people, wandered into the mountain town of Nuremberg, a quaint nostalgic vision cradled in majestic mountains and misty forests. The inimitable Bruno S., who spent most of his youth growing up in mental institutions and prisons, lends his blank, childlike face and frozen demeanor to Herzog's take on the real-life story of a wild-child savant. He's a blank slate and Bruno S. is poignant in the role. Herzog turns his story into the flip side of Francois Truffaut's *The Wild Child,* the moving tragedy of an innocent adopted, tamed, and, in many ways, destroyed by the "civilizing" influences of language, logic, and social learning. Beautifully photographed with an earthy power, it remains Herzog's sweetest, warmest film. —*S. A.*

EVEN DWARFS STARTED SMALL L: DIRECTORS/ HERZOG, WERNER (1971) 96M D: Werner Herzog. *Erna Gschwendtner, Gerd Gickel, Pepi Hermine, Helmut Döring.* Having been tortured while filming *Fata Morgana* in the African Cameroons, Herzog spent months in agony and torment, suffering from nightmares while he recovered. His most vivid dreams became the source of his most notorious production, the story of mad dwarfs on a volcanic island who wage war over the dwarf-organized authority running the mental institution they all live in. They set fire to flower pots, drive cars in circles, and throw live chickens through windows. The film attacks the subconscious of the viewer at the same level as Salvador Dalí and Luis Buñuel's *Un Chien Andalou* and David Lynch's *Eraserhead.* Not a message film or true exploitation, the film is more of a collaboration between author Herzog and the diminutive actors reaching for something intangible. Reviled during its initial release, the film has built a large cult following worldwide and is truly an experience that must be seen to be believed. —*N. H.*

LESSONS OF DARKNESS L: DIRECTORS/HERZOG, WERNER (1992) 50M D: Werner Herzog. For all appearances a documentary on the burning oil fields left in Kuwait after the Gulf War, *Lessons in Darkness* is an elegiac poem on the human capacity for destruction sculpted in image and sound. With perhaps the most impressive footage of the burning fields ever captured on film, we're shown real-life images of what appears to be hell. There are a few cutaways to pertinent interviews and occasional voice-overs comment on the carnage, but for the most part there's an understanding that what we are seeing is beyond words. What led to this catastrophe is here made secondary to the plain fact that it happened at all. Comprehension is an impossible goal, and rather than try to talk it through, the bulk of the film pairs this nightmarish footage with a haunting score (including some devastating Mahler), and lets us stare in awe. —*C. B.*

MY BEST FIEND L: DIRECTORS/HERZOG, WERNER (1999) 100M D: Werner Herzog. *Werner Herzog, Klaus Kinski.* The deliberate play on words in this title is in direct reference to the intimate yet often tumultuous relationship between Herzog and Kinski. Herzog recalls when they first met in their youth and how crazy Kinski was back then. He then recalls the numerous films they worked on together, such as *Fitzcarraldo,* and how crazy Kinski was then. He then recalls Kinski's later years and how age didn't seem to dampen Kinski's peculiar madness. In Herzog's matchless documentary style we get a rare glimpse at this mad yet talented genius and what his lifelong relationship with director Herzog was able to produce. —*N. J.*

NOSFERATU, THE VAMPYRE L: DIRECTORS/HERZOG, WERNER (1979) 110M D: Werner Herzog. *Klaus Kinski, Isabelle Adjani, Bruno Ganz, Roland Topor, Walter Ladengast.* Herzog's most popular film is a magnificent example of how to remake a classic film without losing the soul of its source material. Herzog literally shoots exact camera angles, dialogue, and facial expressions from F. W. Murnau's silent classic, adding color, music, and dialogue to create a slow-moving but beautifully structured re-creation of the German version of Bram Stroker's *Dracula* story. Kinski is breathtaking in his makeup, each movement and gesture stylized to highlight the alien characteristics of the vampire monster, whom Herzog very wisely portrays as a lost, aging, and lonely creature (rather than a beast). The relationship between Lucy (Adjani) and Dracula is mythic as the doomed lovers bring about their own demise, leaving Jonathan Harker (Ganz) as the "carrier" to continue on the vampire legacy. The final image is magnificent. Unsuccessful in its initial run, it has now developed a large cult following and is finally available in its uncut German language. —*N. H.*

STROSZEK L: DIRECTORS/HERZOG, WERNER (1977) 108M D: Werner Herzog. *Bruno S., Eva Mattes, Clements Scheitz.* A film about outsiders. Three German citizens emigrate to America, full of hopes and dreams. What they find is a rural wasteland, full of culture, with no means to support itself. German director Herzog tapped deep into the roots of American myth to extract a careful meditation on dreams gone awry. A lilting accordion score and the effective use of a Woody Guthrie/Brownie McGhee howl-chat, combined with a romantically photographed record of our heartland, help this film etch itself permanently into your mind as a document of a place you will always be a part of but never embrace. —*M. S.*

HAWAII L: DIRECTORS/HILL, GEORGE ROY (1966) 181M D: George Roy Hill. *Richard Harris, Julie Andrews, Caroll O'Connor, Bette Midler, Max von Sydow.* Based on the novel by James A. Michener, *Hawaii* is about a zealous young Calvinist preacher (von Sydow) who is sent as a missionary in 1820 to be a light to the pagan savages on the Hawaiian Islands. He first marries a young Christian woman (Andrews) and takes her with him. His stiff moral code is not well received by the indigenous people or by the Western sailors who visit from time to time. But his attitudes are somewhat tempered by his wife who also bares him children and together they have their share of successes and failures in trying to convert the people to their faith. It's a wonderful story about faith, cultures, and personal pride with excellent acting and, quite naturally, beautiful locations. —*N. J.*

SLAP SHOT L: DIRECTORS/HILL, GEORGE ROY (1977) 122M D: George Roy Hill. *Paul Newman, Michael Ontkean, Lindsay Crouse, Jennifer Warren, Melinda Dillon.* Newman in *Slap Shot* really could have stepped out of the farthest outpost in minor-league hockey. Foul-mouthed and crazy-eyed, he leads a small-town hockey team to greatness by encouraging violent tactics, most successfully with three goonish, bespectacled brothers. The film has a surprisingly hard edge—its down-on-their-luck inhabitants really are down on their luck—which still gives it bite, and the cast is in fine form, including Ontkean as a star player, Dillon as a lady friend of Newman, and Andrew Duncan, hilarious in every scene he's in as a broadcaster. —*T. P.*

SLAUGHTERHOUSE FIVE L: DIRECTORS/HILL, GEORGE ROY (1972) 103M D: George Roy Hill. *Eugene Roche, Sharon Gans, Ron Leibman, Michael Sacks, Valerie Perrine.* Based on the famous Kurt Vonnegut novel, this film concerns Billy Pilgrim (Sacks) who somehow becomes "unstuck" in time. At one moment he will be back in Nazi Germany in Slaughterhouse Five, the next he'll live parts of his married life, then suddenly he'll jump to the end of his life where he's kept in a large bubble on another planet and watched by an alien. Of course this makes for an interesting exposition and an equally complicated development, which includes his near death from an assassin's bullet. Sacks is excellent playing all the different ages and the music is also quite effective, the only film soundtrack that Glenn Gould ever wrote. —*N. J.*

STING, THE L: DIRECTORS/HILL, GEORGE ROY (1973) 129M D: George Roy Hill. *Paul Newman, Ray Walston, Charles Durning, Robert Redford, Robert Shaw.* In many ways this is simply a clever follow-up to *Butch Cassidy and the Sundance Kid.* Redford and Newman assume roles as con men in 1930s Chicago who practice their trade on many unsuspecting souls and eventually wind up in a complicated plot trying to take a big-time racketeer. Topnotch acting is complemented by an original score of period music—Scott Joplin rags well-arranged for orchestra by Marvin Hamlisch. In fact, after this film was released, Joplin's music and ragtime in general had a surge in popularity they had never enjoyed previously. —*N. J.*

WORLD ACCORDING TO GARP, THE L: DIRECTORS/HILL, GEORGE ROY (1982) 136M D: George Roy Hill. *Jessica Tandy, Glenn Close, John Lithgow, Mary Beth Hurt, Robin Williams.* Based on the novel by John Irving, this is one of the finest dramatic comedies of the '80s. T. S. Garp (Williams) must weather the abrupt changes in his life, his family, and the society around him. This character demonstrates the patience and wherewithal of Job while confronting a variety of problems, not the least of which is his radical-feminist mother (Close) and other relations such as a transsexual friend played by Lithgow. Williams is magnetic as the good-humored optimist, a nice change from playing the dopey Popeye. In fact, this role would be his primary typecast for many films to follow—*Dead Poets Society* and *Patch Adams. —N. J.*

WORLD OF HENRY ORIENT, THE L: DIRECTORS/HILL, GEORGE ROY (1964) 106M D: George Roy Hill. *Merrie Spaeth, Peter Sellers, Tom Bosley, Angela Lansbury, Paula Prentiss, Tippy Walker.* In this delightful comedy Sellers plays a serious and straight-laced concert pianist—a very different role for him. Particularly amusing are two young fans who are madly in love with him and his whole persona. During a concert tour of New York the girls stumble across him, at first while he's making love to a woman in a park and later at other awkward moments. One of the very best scenes in this film is a concert sequence featuring piano and orchestra, which wonderfully parodies "modern" atonal concert music. The story of an adult life vs childhood obsession, this will likely appeal to all ages. —*N. J.*

BIG BIRD CAGE, THE L: DIRECTORS/HILL, JACK (1972) 88M D: Jack Hill. *Candy Roman, Carol Speed, Pam Grier, Sid Haig, Karen McKevic.* Hill's superior semi-sequel to *The Big Doll House* (1972) reunited Grier and Haig and promoted them to starring roles. They play mercenaries with a political bent in an unnamed South American country who engineer a women's prison break from the outside. Why? Because their army is a bunch of lonely guys looking for revolutionary sisters to join their cause. . . and their beds. This is pure B exploitation powered with oddball humor and energetic action—the first heist pulled by Grier and Haig is a corker, and the guards at the women's prison are all gay, which makes Haig's flirty infiltration all the more fun. As a side note: the location for the prison was later used by Francis Ford Coppola for Kurtz's compound in *Apocalypse Now,* where it looked much darker and more menacing. Hill wants you to know: He was there first. —*S. A.*

BIG DOLL HOUSE, THE L: DIRECTORS/HILL, JACK (1971) 93M D: Jack Hill. *Judy Brown, Roberta Collins, Pam Grier, Sid Haig.* Hill went to the Philippines to create a cheap women-in-prison picture for Roger Corman and came back with a film that rewrote the rules of the game: abusive guards, lots of showers, late-night groping, and the pay-back prison break. It's pure exploitation and a bit mean-spirited, but it was a smash hit and practically kicked off the '70s drive-in incarnation of the women-in-prison exploitation genre. It was Grier's first starring role (she also sings the theme song) and her first picture with Hill (who hopped genres with her to make *Coffy* and *Foxy Brown*). Brown and Collins star, with Kathryn Loder as one of the sadistic guards on the all-woman staff, and Haig as a produce vendor with a sideline. —*S. A.*

COFFY L: DIRECTORS/HILL, JACK (1973) 90M D: Jack Hill. *Allan Arbus, Sid Haig, Pam Grier, Booker Bradshaw, Robert Do'Qui, William Elliott.* Grier's third collaboration with director Hill was her breakthrough in a leading role and established her as the baddest, toughest, meanest, sexiest bitch around. She plays a nurse named Coffy whose little sister nearly dies from some bad smack. Coffy is fed up and takes the law into her own hands, and within the first ten minutes exposes her amazing bosom and blows an evil pimp's head off with a shotgun. She kicks ass throughout the movie (and takes her clothes off a lot too!). She shoots people, gets in a cat fight with a blond chick at a buffet, drives a car right into somebody's kitchen, and uncovers a complex drug ring that hits close to home. Vigilante filmmaking at its best! —*S. H.*

PIT STOP L: DIRECTORS/HILL, JACK (1969) 91M D: Jack Hill. *Dick Davalos, Beverly Washburn, Sid Haig, Ellen Burstyn, Brian Donlevy.* This taut, energetic little racing picture is one of Hill's best efforts and a little-seen gem. Davalos is the cool customer lured by promoter Donlevy to try his hand at Figure 8 racing, a deadly mix of stock car and demolition derby. The careening track scenes are so dynamic they overshadow the climactic professional race, but the real story is how Davalos turns from cool competitor to ruthless rival, and his icy stare is perfect. Haig's explosive turn as the preening champ is both wild and wounded, and Burstyn (under the name McRae) delivers a fine early performance. —*S. A.*

SPIDER BABY L: DIRECTORS/HILL, JACK (1964) 81M D: Jack Hill. *Lon Chaney Jr., Sid Haig.* Spider Baby is one of those beautiful flukes of exploitation cinema, an inspired mix of horror and comedy that delivers on both, and more. Think *Lord of the Flies* by way of *Freaks.* Chauffeur Chaney Jr. (in a warm, winning performance) cares for the afflicted children of his old master. They suffer from "Merrye's Syndrome," a disease that causes them to regress mentally and emotionally with the onset of puberty: "The unfortunate result of. . . inbreeding." In Hill's inspired screenplay, the "children" (adult women Jill Banner and

Walter Hill

Walter Hill is a real man's director—not in the epic sense of a John Ford or Sam Peckinpah, but on a street level. His is a milieu colored by bar fights and dime-novel dialogue. Like the works of Sam Fuller and Larry Cohen, his films are always economically scripted and entertaining without sacrificing character development. Indeed, Hill's distinctive action films are chock-full of vibrant characters, from James Coburn's fight pimp in *Hard Times* (1975) to the

much-imitated gangs of *The Warriors* (1979) and the renegade soldiers of *Streets of Fire* (1984). And one "character" who makes an appearance in almost every Hill film is Torchy's Bar, its namesake reputedly being an LA bar that was once the epitome of glamour but soon decayed into a seedy hangout for alcoholics and petty criminals.

Hill's blue-collar ethos stems from his upbringing—he traded his construction hat for a camera, but he would go on to focus on the working class many times in his films. After earning impressive assistant-director credits on *Take the Money and Run* (1969)

Beverly Washburn in schoolgirl frocks and gangly Haig as the bald, infantile Ralph) fall into savagery and explore an innocent but perverse kind of sexual curiosity. Pity their poor relations who come to challenge the inheritance! It's kinky and cruel and oddly sweet all at the same time. Eight minutes of newly discovered footage were added to the film in 2000, mostly unnecessary but harmless exposition. —*S. A.*

SWITCHBLADE SISTERS L: DIRECTORS/HILL, JACK (1975) 90M D: Jack Hill. *Asher Brauner, Robbie Lee, Joanne Nail, Monica Gayle.* Tarantino's Rolling Thunder Pictures rereleased this film in 1999, which is beautiful, although Mr. T's obnoxious ass-kissing whine sadly renders the DVD commentary with Hill unlistenable. The movie follows loner babe Maggie (Nail) as she joins the Dagger Debs, led by Lace (helium-voiced Lee), Patch (Gayle—she lost an eye for the gang!), and other chicks with wacky monikers. The Debs and their male counterparts, the Silver Daggers, have it out for rival gang the Crabs, which culminates in an awesome roller-rink machine-gun showdown. Plenty of classic exploitation clichés are represented here. This is no feminist girl-power fest, as it's sometimes advertised; in fact, it's far from it. This one certainly isn't Hill's best (see *Spider Baby* or anything with Pam Grier), but it's still a lot of fun. —*E. O.*

EXTREME PREJUDICE L: DIRECTORS/HILL, WALTER (1987) 100M D: Walter Hill. *Clancy Brown, Michael Ironside, Powers Boothe, Nick Nolte, Rip Torn, William Forsythe.* So you get the guy who made *Red Dawn*, renowned asshole-maniac John Milius, to write a movie that mixes *The Wild Bunch, Tequila Sunrise,* and *High Noon,* and then you hire Hill, who did *The Warriors,* to direct it with

Nolte in the lead. It sounds absolutely, awesomely nuts, and it is. Nolte, a Texas Ranger, takes on his high-school best friend turned drug kingpin Boothe. Of course, they're both in love with the same girl, and to make matters worse, there's a "Zombie Unit" of black-ops paramilitaries hanging around just waiting to drop the hammer. Several elements set it apart from the average '80s action flick, such as the incredible body count, the dream cast of B-level actors (Brown, Ironside, Forsythe, and Torn), and Powers Fucking Boothe. This man is a god. Not only does he have one of the coolest names on earth, but his face alone is enough to terrify small children for years to come. He's a villain ranked right up there with Hans Gruber and Frank from *Blue Velvet.* This movie is sheer bloody perfection. —*M. L.*

JOHNNY HANDSOME L: DIRECTORS/HILL, WALTER (1989) 96M D: Walter Hill. *Elizabeth McGovern, Forest Whitaker, Lance Henriksen, Ellen Barkin, Mickey Rourke, Morgan Freeman. Johnny Handsome* is true film noir, meaning it features all bad guys plus one good girl. It's the story of a disfigured thief (Rourke) who is shot and left for dead by his compatriots (Barkin, Henriksen). He gets plastic surgery in prison, and returns to the outside world weary and ready for revenge. Soon he finds himself conflicted between seeking his vengeance on those who tried to kill him and remaining true for the girl he falls for (McGovern). It's not the best of the noir revival that seems to take place every decade or so in Hollywood, but *Johnny Handsome* is lively and dark, and features a cast with enough of a nasty bite to hold interest. —*T. P.*

and *The Thomas Crown Affair* (1968), Hill penned the script for Peckinpah's *The Getaway* (1972) before landing his first gig as director with the Charles Bronson boxing vehicle *Hard Times* (1975).

His follow-up was the stylish crime thriller *The Driver* (1978), whose cult following would quickly be supplanted by that of *The Warriors*, which garnered controversy when it was accused of inciting real-life gang activity. But the success of *The Warriors* helped make him his next two films, the period Western *The Long Riders* (1980) and the *Deliverance*-style *Southern Comfort* (1981), in which some Vietnam-era Louisiana soldiers face a war on a different front—the rural American backwoods.

After striking gold with the buddy-cop film *48 HRS.* (1982), Hill found himself moving out of blockbuster territory, but his subsequent films maintained his frequent themes of vigilantism and the ineffectuality of society's valued institutions. *Streets of Fire* was a minor masterpiece that has only recently been reappraised as such. Featuring stunning production design, it also set the standard for modern editing techniques. Highlights of his later career included *Brewster's Millions* (1985), *Extreme Prejudice* (1987), *Johnny Handsome* (1989), and the Kurosawa-inspired *Last Man Standing* (1996), although it was really *Undisputed* (2002) that marked a return to form.

—*Kier-La Janisse*

SOUTHERN COMFORT L: DIRECTORS/HILL, WALTER (1981) 99M D: Walter Hill. *Fred Ward, Keith Carradine, Powers Boothe.* Hill reconfigures *Deliverance* with a weekend-warrior National Guard platoon suddenly under fire from the Cajuns whose swamp they've invaded. Echoes of Vietnam reverberate throughout the ordeal as the soldiers become lost in the foliage and outmaneuvered by a guerrilla army at home in the jungle, but Hill is too smart and too primal a director to overplay his symbolism. He directs with a clean simplicity while examining the dynamics of a platoon of battle virgins about to tear itself apart from fear. Ry Cooder's eerie and haunting score only intensifies the paranoia as the city boys flail around lost in the swamp while gunmen pick them off one by one. Carradine and Boothe are the only soldiers smart enough to understand that they are way out of their depth. —*S. A.*

UNDISPUTED L: DIRECTORS/HILL, WALTER (2002) 94M D: Walter Hill. *Wesley Snipes, Micheal Rooker, Peter Falk, Ving Rhames.* Hill's best film in years is a lean, gritty tale of sin and redemption among the locked-down men of a maximum security prison. Snipes is the undefeated champ of the underground prison circuit with a Zen-like inner calm and stoic acceptance that turns into unshakable focus in the ring. Rhames is the explosive heavyweight champ, a fierce man full of rage, sent to prison for rape (one of Hill's brilliant touches is his ambivalence about the truth of the crime—Rhames is as sincere in his indignation and innocence as the victim is in her fear and anger at the violation). Falk is a fading mafioso legend, the borderline senile lifer who arranges the fight. Hill drives the story with a refreshing cinematic efficiency and a stylistic punch that nonetheless creates a rich backdrop of simmering tensions in the prison population that slowly rallies around its personal champ. Hill shows that every man in this bad-man's world draws his own line. —*S. A.*

WARRIORS, THE L: DIRECTORS/HILL, WALTER (1979) 93M D: Walter Hill. *Tom McKitterick, David Harris, Michael Beck, James Remar, Dorsey Wright, Brian Tyler.* Hill's comic book of an action film plays like a prequel to *Escape from New York*, with the city turned into an after-dark war zone. Good guys and bad guys have no meaning in this urban frontier of warring gangs at a tenuous cease-fire when a spoiler tosses a match into the combustible mix, just to see the fiery fallout. It's a funky, flashy B movie that makes the most of its low-budget graffiti aesthetic, practically abstract in terms of plot and motivation (the Warriors must get through the city after they've been falsely accused of murdering a gangland leader), but executed with the visceral pulp punch Hill mastered in his tough, terse pictures. —*S. A.*

BIRDS, THE L: DIRECTORS/HITCHCOCK, ALFRED (1963) 119M D: Alfred Hitchcock. *Jessica Tandy, Suzanne Pleshette, Rod Taylor, Tippi Hedren.* A lot of movies considered to be horror are notable for those things that are on the edge of reality, so that within a couple days (and in the light), you find yourself laughing at the fact that you were ever scared of them. What makes *The Birds* a truly scary movie is the fact that we're not dealing with the supernatural at all, but nature itself. The birds go crazy, they organize, and they attack. Why couldn't that happen, and if it did, what would we be able to do about it? This movie is characterized by an almost complete lack of soundtrack, a genius move on the part of Hitchcock that makes the noise of the birds that much creepier. For days after watching the movie, I shuddered every

Alfred Hitchcock

Sir Alfred Hitchcock was born in Leystone, England, in 1899, the third son of a modest greengrocer. He left school at fourteen, soon after the death of his father, but continued to study navigation, mechanics, and electricity in London. His interest in drawing and graphics led him to advertising, and then to the film industry as a designer of title cards. He began directing his first film in 1922 for an independent company. It was never completed, but it led to a job as assistant director with a new company, where he also became involved in set design and screenwriting. This led to another shot at directing.

His third film and his first thriller, *The Lodger* (1927), was an enormous popular and critical success, but it would be four years before his second thriller, *Blackmail* (also the first sound film made in England). Hitchcock became England's leading director through the 1930s with such films as

The Man Who Knew Too Much (1934), *The 39 Steps*(1935), and *The Lady Vanishes* (1938). In 1940 he left for Hollywood under contract to David O. Selznick.

He soon earned a reputation as the master of suspense through his popular romantic thrillers and murder mysteries, a reputation he both encouraged and disliked, for it often blinded viewers to the subtleties of his direction. His American output ranged from the romantic *Notorious* (1946) to the dark drama *Vertigo* (1958), with such light fare as *North by Northwest* (1959) to mix it up. In the 1960s he changed his approach with *Psycho* (1960), a gritty black-and-white horror film designed to shock audiences.

Hitchcock's films explore fear and guilt, and he constantly takes complacent characters in comfortable lives and plunges them into the unknown. He deftly mixes humor and terror in many of his films, and even his darkest films often have moments of black or ironic humor. As a technician, his skills are unchallenged.

—Sean Axmaker

---

time I saw a bird, wishing I was inside. As if in the end that really would help. —*J. S.*

FAMILY PLOT L: DIRECTORS/HITCHCOCK, ALFRED (1976) 120M D: Alfred Hitchcock. *Karen Black, Bruce Dern, Ed Lauter, William Devane, Barbara Harris.* I held off on watching this for a long time, not thinking it would be up to snuff, and now can't see how I lived without it. What a lovely way to go out for Hitch. Little bizarre touches that burn themselves into your brain and creep up on you long after seeing any Hitchcock film, great performances by doubly dysfunctional couples Devane/Black and Dern/Harris, and a wealth of colorful side characters make this a very fun ride. Harris steals the show, however, as the bogus psychic who lassos loser boyfriend Dern into a manhunt. Hitchcock always had something else going on besides the plot, and this time he seemed most interested in contrasting a pair of relationships. —*M. S.*

I CONFESS L: DIRECTORS/HITCHCOCK, ALFRED (1953) 95M D: Alfred Hitchcock. *Montgomery Clift, Karl Malden, Brian Aherne, Anne Baxter.* Clift plays a Catholic priest who takes an interesting confession from a guilty man. He confesses having murdered the man who told him about the priest's relationship with a woman before he was ordained. When the police inspector (Malden) comes along, the priest faces two problems: he's not supposed to break the sacred confidence of confession, but if he does he would certainly lose his collar over the ensuing scandal. What follows is all the expected soul-searching, yet the way it's presented by Hitchcock it becomes anything but predictable. —*N. J.*

JAMAICA INN L: DIRECTORS/HITCHCOCK, ALFRED (1939) 108M D: Alfred Hitchcock. *Maureen O'Hara, Charles Laughton.* Hitch's last British film before leaving for Hollywood isn't quite as bad as its reputation suggests—there's mood thick enough to stuff a mattress and a few stunning sequences—but that hardly makes it good. Hackneyed melodrama and a convoluted plot (courtesy Daphne du Maurier's novel) landlocks this strange pirate tale-cum-costume pageant, while Laughton chews the scenery not already hidden by the perpetual nighttime fog. Up against this rogue gallery of caricatures, O'Hara's earnest performance is woefully out of place. Hitch sums it up best in his epitaph for the picture: *"Jamaica Inn was an absurd thing to undertake." —S. A.*

LADY VANISHES, THE L: DIRECTORS/HITCHCOCK, ALFRED (1938) 97M D: Alfred Hitchcock. *Cecil Parker, Margaret Lockwood, Michael Redgrave, Paul Lukas, Dame May Whitty.* Combining a good deal of comedy with suspense, Hitchcock tells the story of a female British spy who is trying to get her message about the Germans back to England. Lockwood plays a woman who meets this undercover spy on a train, but then can't find her moments later. She petitions Redgrave to help her locate this woman, but the two of them can't find anyone who even acknowledges that she ever existed! This all culminates into fantastic action and suspense that only Hitchcock can pull off. —N. J.

MAN WHO KNEW TOO MUCH, THE L: DIRECTORS/ HITCHCOCK, ALFRED (1934) 75M D: Alfred Hitchcock. *Edna Best, Hugh Wakefield, Peter Lorre, Leslie Banks, Frank Vosper.* Lorre is superb as the villain bent on a political assassination ostensibly to start World War II. Lorre's hired gun first eliminates an English spy who had learned of the plot, and this information falls into the hands of an unwitting English couple. Lorre has their daughter kidnapped, so the couple decides to stay quiet, but the father conducts his own investigation. He discovers that the assassination is supposed to happen during a cymbal crash in a performance at Royal Albert Hall. He does all he can to stop the assassination after joining his daughter in confinement. Hitchcock remade this excellent film in 1956 starring James Stewart as the father. It's difficult to say which is better since both are directed by the master, however Lorre's performance as the antagonist seems to edge out Stewart's as the good guy. —N. J.

MARNIE L: DIRECTORS/HITCHCOCK, ALFRED (1964) 130M D: Alfred Hitchcock. *Tippi Hedren, Sean Connery, Diane Baker, Martin Gabel, Louise Latham.* "Doctor, doctor, I am ill," begins the little girl's jump-rope rhyme framing the film, as the little girls innocently play outside Marnie's mom's apartment. What a sorely underrated Hitchcock film. He really turned it up a notch for this one. Bizarre, rococo flourishes abound: giant fake backgrounds, thunderstorms creeping in at the most dramatic moments, obvious rear projection during a horse ride (again, a fake background, no doubt commenting on the "fake backgrounds" our heroine uses to plan her crimes). Nothing was ever a mistake in a Hitchcock film, so when you notice these things, don't laugh at their fakeness. See how they comment on what's going on. Then sit back and enjoy the perversity of Connery trying to "own" Hedren—marrying her, raping her, then attempting to save her from a very troubling psychological trauma. There's a lot to take in in this Hitchcock film, but the rewards are plenty. —M. S.

NORTH BY NORTHWEST L: DIRECTORS/HITCHCOCK, ALFRED (1959) 136M D: Alfred Hitchcock. *James Mason, Leo G. Carroll, Martin Landau, Eva Marie Saint, Cary Grant.* Grant stars as executive Roger Thornhill who is mistaken for someone else by foreign spies. He is curiously framed for murdering a diplomat at the UN building and escapes on a train with sympathetic Saint. To get to the bottom of this confusion he entertains the identity of his look-alike so as to encounter these spies, and this is how he comes to wait for a rendezvous on a farm road in the middle of nowhere, only to be attacked in a famous scene by a crop-dusting plane. In the spirit of the best Hitchcock, plot twists lend a sense of British humor that only helps temper the terror of the situation to provide a dramatic roller-coaster ride. This said, it is clearly the direction which makes the top-notch cast bring this classic to life. —N. J.

NOTORIOUS L: DIRECTORS/HITCHCOCK, ALFRED (1946) 102M D: Alfred Hitchcock. *Ingrid Bergman, Claude Rains, Louis Calhern, Cary Grant.* François Truffaut's late-'60s opinion that *Notorious* is the best of Hitchcock's golden-age films has long since become consensus (though there remain *Shadow of a Doubt* diehards). Without question *Notorious* is the gold standard in the espionage-romance subgenre. Just after World War II, an operative in what we'd now call the CIA (Grant) flies down to Rio with an international party girl (Bergman) whose late father was an unregenerate Nazi. She's supposed to ingratiate herself with an old suitor (Rains) whose mansion is command central for other still-active Hitlerites. The two agents hold each other in contempt, which doesn't stop them from falling in love, which doesn't stop them from sinking ever deeper into mutual contempt. Grant's hero is a very sinister fellow (named Devlin), whereas, up to a point, Rains's diminutive Nazi is the most sympathetic of Hitchcock villains (he has, among other things, a Hitchcock mother to contend with). The emotions and psychology are subtle, tortuous, and sublimely nuanced by the great cast and one of Hecht's most intricately wrought scripts, and Hitchcock's direction exemplifies at every turn how he was the master of much more than suspense. —R. T. J.

PSYCHO (1960) L: DIRECTORS/HITCHCOCK, ALFRED (1960) 109M D: Alfred Hitchcock. *John Gavin, Anthony Perkins, Janet Leigh, Vera Miles.* Film is a voyeuristic art form. Hitchcock plays with this mindset a lot in *Psycho*. The concept of voyeurism is a motif established right from the beginning of the film and is finally given form when we see Norman Bates (Perkins) watching Marion Crane (Leigh) through a little hole in the wall. The camera then takes on the role of voyeur as the audience sneaks a peak at the beautiful Leigh undressing and getting into the shower. The audience relishes this forbidden pleasure, watching from a distance, removed. We see the murderer approaching and the knife being lifted. Suddenly we have a desperate need to intervene. Somebody warn her! But the audience cannot transcend its role as voyeur and is forced to watch in agony. Hitchcock explored the theme of voyeurism even more in *Rear Window*, but not as subtly or as brilliantly as in *Psycho*. His genius shines through in every moment of this classic horror. A true masterpiece. —*T. S.*

REAR WINDOW L: DIRECTORS/HITCHCOCK, ALFRED (1954) 112M D: Alfred Hitchcock. *Raymond Burr, Grace Kelly, James Stewart, Wendell Corey.* Stewart is the wheelchair-bound adventurer who spends his bored hours eavesdropping through his neighbors' windows in Hitchcock's classic tale of voyeurism, suspicion, and sex. There are few true innocents in Hitchcock's thrillers and he perversely chose Stewart—forever remembered as Capra's idealistic everyman despite a rich and varied career—to be his most morally gray figure. Here, he's merely the eternal adult adolescent playing at romance with the elegant Kelly, who Hitch transforms into an earthy angel of sex and glamour. This is a brilliant film about voyeurism, a masterpiece of suspense experienced from the wheelchair of Hitch's most physically helpless hero, shot in a beautifully designed courtyard set through a window the same shape as a movie screen. But it's really—like so many Hitchcock films—about the joy and fear of sex and the perceived emasculating threat of commitment. The story plays out, in so many variations, in every window of the courtyard. —*S. A.*

REBECCA L: DIRECTORS/HITCHCOCK, ALFRED (1940) 130M D: Alfred Hitchcock. *Laurence Olivier, Joan Fontaine, George Sanders, Judith Anderson.* Hitchcock is one of my favorite directors, and *Rebecca* is easily my favorite Hitchcock film. Maxim de Winter (Olivier) is a wealthy gentleman who has recently lost his wife, Rebecca, when he meets a much younger woman (Fontaine) while vacationing. He asks the innocent girl to marry him, and she returns with him to live at Manderley, his huge mansion. The second Lady de Winter does not find a warm welcome awaiting her, and instead soon discovers the degree to which the deceased first Lady de Winters is still controlling the household. Anderson delivers an chilling, absolutely flawless performance as Mrs. Danvers, the maid whose heart belonged to the first lady, and therefore instantly detests the second. The tense, ill-eased feeling of the film mounts slowly to a surprising ending that will immediately make you want to watch the film over again with it in mind. —*J. S.*

ROPE L: DIRECTORS/HITCHCOCK, ALFRED (1948) 81M D: Alfred Hitchcock. *Sir Cedric Hardwicke, James Stewart, John Dall, Joan Chandler, Farley Granger.* Brandon (Dall) and Phillip (Granger) strangle their friend with a rope within the first few moments of the movie, simply out of a desire to commit the perfect murder. They then shove his body into a trunk, just in time for their dinner guests to arrive and be served their meal off that same trunk. The plot is sparse, and most of the action is over with that initial scene. What makes this movie excellent to watch is the way the characters handle the pressure of this secret, and the reactions of the guests as hints are dropped as to why David has not yet arrived for the party. The beauty is completely in the acting, with the cast pulling off excellent, extremely tense performances that leave you wondering not if, but how long until someone will find out what is going on. —*J. S.*

SABATOGE (AKA HIDDEN POWER, THE) L: DIRECTORS/ HITCHCOCK, ALFRED (1936) 76M D: Alfred Hitchcock. *Oskar Homolka, Desmond Tester, Matthew Boulton, Sylvia Sidney, John Loder.* During its initial release, *Sabotage* was not a success, and Hitchcock blamed it on the fact that a child is killed by a bomb. However, it's the viciousness of the boy's death that is most remembered from this lesser Hitchcock film. Theater owner Karl Anton Verloc (Homolka) is an undercover saboteur running his operation through the London movie house with his wife (Sydney) and her young brother, Stevie (Tester). When Scotland Yard sends in a spy named Ted (Boulton), Karl gets nervous. Ted befriends Mrs. Verloc and Stevie, first trying to figure out what they know and then attempting to protect the two from Robert's upcoming arrest. Under orders from the secret organization to make another public "hit," Karl sends Stevie to deliver what looks like a film canister to a local pub across town. The package is really a bomb, Stevie gets delayed along the way, and the bomb goes off. Sydney is excellent as the wife, her beautiful wide eyes openly expressing first her fear and then her hatred as she realizes her husband is responsible for her young brother's death. —*N. H.*

SECRET AGENT L: DIRECTORS/HITCHCOCK, ALFRED (1936) 83M D: Alfred Hitchcock. *John Gielgud, Peter Lorre, Madeleine Carroll, Robert Young, Percy Marmont.* Part of a spy trilogy by Hitchcock (along with *The 39 Steps* and *Sabotage*), this is the slowest and most dialogue-heavy of the three films. A young and handsome Gielgud gives an excellent performance as the well-mannered novelist Edgar Brodie, whose death was faked so he could serve his country tracking down and killing a German agent during WWII. He goes undercover in the Swiss Alps, pretending to be married to fellow spy Elsa Carrington (Carroll) while actually working alongside a hired hit man, the General (Lorre). The two track down and kill the wrong man, leaving Elsa back at the hotel bored. Deciding to return home, she finds herself riding on the train alongside the deadly agent (Young), who previously at the hotel had tricked her into believing he was a friend. The General and Brodie, realizing Elsa has been tricked, board the train in an attempt to warn her, and all three find themselves trapped as the train enters a foreign country. All the while, a German agent is stalking the trio. The four leads are top-notch; Lorre especially stands out as usual as the horny and off-kilter killer for hire. Several elements that would show up later in more well-known Hitchcock films are evident here. —N. H.

SPELLBOUND L: DIRECTORS/HITCHCOCK, ALFRED (1945) 111M D: Alfred Hitchcock. *Ingrid Bergman, Gregory Peck, Rhonda Fleming, Leo G. Carroll, Norman Lloyd.* Directed by Hitch, scripted by Ben Hecht, and inspired by producer David Selznick's adventures in psychoanalysis, this ambitious psychological thriller is as ludicrous as it is intermittently stunning, but in the hands of the master, it's still quite the psychodrama. Peck is the tortured doctor with a repressed secret that psychiatrist Bergman helps him unearth with the help of dream therapy. You can see the push-me, pull-you relationship between producer and director as Hitch attempts to visualize heady concepts in bizarre dream sequences (designed by Salvador Dalí) while the dialogue drags it all back to literalness. —S. A.

STRANGERS ON A TRAIN L: DIRECTORS/HITCHCOCK, ALFRED (1951) 103M D: Alfred Hitchcock. *Ruth Roman, Farley Granger, Robert Walker, Leo G. Carroll.* Strangers is by no means a perfect film but very effective as a noir thriller. Guy Haines (Granger) is a professional tennis player riding alone on a train; Bruno Anthony (Walker) is a seemingly normal passenger who happens to be a tennis fan. Bruno introduces himself to Guy; conversation eventually turns to Bruno's thoughts about the perfect murder. This casts some doubt on his personality, Guy not knowing if he's being facetious or not. Bruno's intentions are gradually revealed as he presses the subject even though Guy doesn't seem interested. Through subtle miscommunication we see the catalyst for murder and blackmail. Hitchcock uses cinematic elements like sound and situational irony to create suspense, giving depth to the film. Manipulating these elements in various ways that directly affect the plot help to carry the meaning and increase the suspense without special effects or useless dialogue. —B. W.

TO CATCH A THIEF L: DIRECTORS/HITCHCOCK, ALFRED (1955) 103M D: Alfred Hitchcock. *Cary Grant, Grace Kelly, Jessie Royce Landis, John Williams.* No one will ever nominate this as Hitchcock at his best, but he knew how to make glamour sparkle and stars smolder with sexual heat, and do they ever in this lighthearted thriller. Grant is a reformed jewel thief on the French Riviera who immediately comes under suspicion when a cat burglar goes to work on the rich and famous staying in the luxury hotels. Heiress Kelly decides to play detective the best way she knows how: by romancing the charming rogue. Hitch applies his touch in a few key scenes (fireworks never felt so erotic) but otherwise favors the lavish sets, classy locations, and unbearably beautiful stars to any pretense of suspense. It's paste jewelry next to Hitchcock's real jewels, but it sparkles nonetheless. Landis (who memorably stubs a ciggie out in a fried egg) costars as the flighty Kelly's down-to-earth mother. —S. A.

VERTIGO L: DIRECTORS/HITCHCOCK, ALFRED (1958) 128M D: Alfred Hitchcock. *James Stewart, Barbara Bel Geddes, Kim Novak.* One of Hitchcock's most vital works, *Vertigo* follows Stewart as retired police detective John "Scottie" Ferguson, an impulsive, obsessive man with poor romantic fortune and a terrible fear of heights. His world spirals from bad to worse when he falls for a woman he's hired to trail, leading to a sequence of plot convulsions and identity flummoxes that possibly display Hitchcock's unique abilities better than any other of his films. Stewart's personage is uncharacteristically curt and unpleasant, and the variation from his standard roles makes the performance all the more engrossing. Especially worthy of note is the partially animated vertigo sequence created by brilliant designer Saul Bass, which momentarily plummets the viewer into a surreal effects-laden world that must have painfully blown the minds of the film's initial viewing audience. —Z. C.

YOUNG AND INNOCENT (AKA THE GIRL WAS YOUNG) L: DIRECTORS/HITCHCOCK, ALFRED (1937) 83M D: Alfred Hitchcock. *Nova Pilbeam, Derrick De Marney, Percy Marmont, Edward Rigby, Mary Clare.* Young and Innocent builds the themes that later made Hitchcock so famous. Wrongly accused of murder, handsome Robert Tisdall (De Marney) hides out in local mill while the chief inspector's daughter Erica Burgoyne (Pilbeam) helps him evade the police, believing Robert to be innocent (as she has fallen for him at first sight in the police station). While the police continue their search, the two hide out by traveling down the English country roads together in Erica's car, seeking out the only clue that can free Robert from his murder charge—his coat, given to a local bum by the real murderer (who used the belt to strangle a woman to death). Filled with a great sense of humor and wonderful interaction between the two young leads, this is Hitchcock at this best, playful and irreverent at one moment, and tense and frightening at the next. An early example of classic Hitchcock. —N. H.

WASHINGTON SQUARE L: DIRECTORS/HOLLAND, AGNIESZKA (1996) 115M D: Agnieszka Holland. *Ben Chaplin, Jennifer Jason Leigh, Albert Finney.* In Holland's adapta-

tion of the Henry James novel, Leigh plays the socially awkward daughter of a wealthy widower (Finney) who is wooed by a poor man (Chaplin) her father suspects to be more interested in her money and position than her own attributes. Leigh's performances are often a dubious triumph of manner over material. Here she makes it work, building her self-consciously clumsy society misfit out of accumulated details, then tearing them down as she exposes the soul of her character. Finney is in fine form as a reserved, disapproving father who has never forgiven his daughter for his wife's death in childbirth, and director Holland creates an uncomfortable tension between the two that informs the entire film. A handsome production and an intelligent film. —*S. A.*

DESTROY ALL MONSTERS L: DIRECTORS/HONDA, INOSHIRO (1968) 90M D: Inoshiro Honda. *Akira Kubo, Yukihiko Kobayashi, Yoshio Tsuchiya, Jun Tazaki.* Sometime in the near future (well, 1999), the UN manages to keep Godzilla, Mothra, Rodan, Minya, Baragon, and several other Toho monsters in captivity, *Jurassic Park* style, on Monster Island. This seems like a great thing but all great things must end, and sure enough some evil aliens unleash the monsters for an all-out attack on the Earth. This is one of the greatest of the classic giant monster films. Most films in this genre get boring at some point, but this one is so loaded with monster action that it always keeps your interest. —*B. T.*

GHIDRAH, THE THREE-HEADED MONSTER L: DIRECTORS/HONDA, INOSHIRO (1964) 81M D: Inoshiro Honda. *Godzilla, Hiroshi Koisumi.* The Godzilla movies really hit their stride with this fun, all-star monster bash. It's pretty much a direct sequel to *Godzilla vs The Thing*, aka *Mothra*, and teams Godzilla, Rodan, and a larval Mothra against a new monster (Ghidrah, the three-headed space dragon). Godzilla and Rodan are hanging out fighting when Mothra shows up and asks them for help. It's pretty funny to think about these monsters talking to each other and even funnier when The Peanuts (Mothra's tiny human friends) scold Godzilla for swearing. The fights are really silly and Godzilla gets zapped in the balls by Ghidrah's lightning ray, but it's this kind of goofy stuff that makes these movies so much fun. This film never takes itself seriously and piles on lots of monster action, secret agents, a sexy chick who thinks she's from outer space and, yeah, a guy who catches a boulder. —*S. H.*

GODZILLA VS MONSTER ZERO L: DIRECTORS/HONDA, INOSHIRO (1965) 93M D: Inoshiro Honda. *Akira Takarada, Yoshio Tsuchiya, Jun Tazaki, Nick Adams, Kumi Mizuno, Akira Kubo.* The follow-up to *Ghidrah, the Three Headed Monster* is the first international coproduction of a Godzilla film. This led to the inclusion of an American actor (Adams) costarring as an astronaut named Glenn who, along with fellow space explorer Fuji (Takarada), travels to the newly discovered Planet X. It seems Planet X is under siege by King Ghidora and they want to borrow Earth monsters Godzilla and Rodan to help defeat the evil space monster. It turns out to be a trick to invade Earth with the monsters. However, Godzilla and Rodan are freed from alien mind-control and the pair team up to fight the three-headed space dragon. *Godzilla vs Monster Zero* is a little plot heavy and light on monster action, though Godzilla does a funny victory dance and pulls some moves that may have been inspired by Mohamed Ali! —*S. H.*

GODZILLA'S REVENGE L: DIRECTORS/HONDA, INOSHIRO (1969) 70M D: Inoshiro Honda. *Machiko Naka, Haruo Nakajima, Tomonori Yazaki.* Toho decided to make a more child-friendly Godzilla film after the big-budget monster blow-out *Destroy All Monsters*. Unfortunately, effects man Tsuburaya being on his deathbed and a shrinking budget forced Honda to use large amounts of stock footage. Most of the monster scenes are culled from *Son of Godzilla* and *Godzilla vs the Sea Monster*, but there is a new fight between Godzilla and a weird-looking blue monster called Gabbara. Coincidently our obnoxious young star, a latch-key child named Ichiro (Yazaki), is tormented by a bully also named Gabbara. Ichiro escapes his depressing world by fantasizing about flying to Monster Island and making friends with Minya, the son of Godzilla. Minya talks to young Ichiro and, in the English version, they both speak in obnoxiously dubbed voices. Eventually both kids (monster and human) learn how to be tough and Ichiro returns to reality where he thwarts some comical gangsters and beats up the human Gabbara. —*S. H.*

KING KONG ESCAPES L: DIRECTORS/HONDA, INOSHIRO (1967) 104M D: Inoshiro Honda. *Rhodes Reason, Eisei Amamoto, Akira Takarada, Mie Hama, Linda Miller.* Cheesy but fun monster action based on an obscure American Rankin-Bass cartoon series. It doesn't really have anything to do with Toho's previous King Kong film (*King Kong vs Godzilla*) though it features many of the same technicians. King Kong is found living on a Pacific Island by the crew of a nuclear submarine. He fights Gorosaurus (a Tyrannosaurus rex–type monster also seen in *Destroy All Monsters*) and falls for a blond chick named Susan (Miller). Meanwhile, at the North Pole a bad guy named Dr. Who (no relation to the British character) has built a robot version of King Kong to dig for a dangerous mineral called Element X. Mecha-Kong soon malfunctions and the real Kong is kidnapped to do his doppelganger's dirty work. It all leads to a typical battle in downtown Tokyo. The Kong costume is pretty stupid-looking but Mecha-Kong was the inspiration for one of Godzilla's most popular adversaries, Mecha-Godzilla. —*S. H.*

KING KONG VS GODZILLA L: DIRECTORS/HONDA, INOSHIRO (1962) 105M D: Inoshiro Honda. *James Yagi, Michael Keith.* In a landmark crossover, Toho Studios pitted the giant lizard Gojira against his similarly large American colleague, King Kong. Japanese executives selling medicinal berries discover the natives from the island where they pick the berries worship the giant gorilla King Kong as a god, so naturally they decide to capture him and bring him back to Japan as a promotional gimmick. Meanwhile, Godzilla gets revived from an iceberg and, you know how it is, no matter how big of an island you're on, if you're a giant lizard you're going to run into the giant gorilla sooner or later. Instead of Willis O'Brien's stop-motion, Kong is a guy in a suit, which looks much better than you'd think it would. There are not really two endings, as many claim; this myth may have been caused by the somewhat ambiguous finale in which one could make an argument for either competitor as the winner. —*B. T.*

MYSTERIANS, THE L: DIRECTORS/HONDA, INOSHIRO (1957) 85M D: Inoshiro Honda. *Kenji Sahara, Yumi Shirakawa, Takashi Shimura.* The Mysterians is sort of the Toho Studios version of *Day the Earth Stood Still*, which means it's not as slow, is more confusing, and there are more lasers and a giant bird-looking robot that sets Japan aflame. The Mysterians of the title are football helmet–wearing dudes who come from the distant planet of Mysteroid 7, which has long since been destroyed. . . 100,000 Earth years ago! So, they've come to our planet with two simple requests, three kilometers of land and five Earth women to mate with, or they'll blow the shit out of us. Sounds like a fair deal, but the Japanese military doesn't agree, attacks the giant bubble the Mysterians live in, and they retaliate in kind with powerful lasers. As the plot unfolds, we find the Mysterians' purpose may be more nefarious than originally thought, and the world unites to combat them. A crazy little slice of old-school Japanese sci-fi. —*K. C.*

WAR OF THE GARGANTUAS L: DIRECTORS/HONDA, INOSHIRO (1966) 92M D: Inoshiro Honda. *Hiroshi Sekita, Haruo Nakajima, Russ Tamblyn.* A King Kong–sized Sasquatch with green fur attacks Tokyo, and everybody seems to think it's the adorable Gargantua that scientist Dr. Paul Stewart (Tamblyn) raised from a pup. But come on, his Gargantua would never horse around in Tokyo like that. He's a peaceful Gargantua. So later, the doctor's Gargantua (the brown Gargantua) actually does show up and tries to chill his brother out. It's Cain and Abel meets Godzilla, and it's one of the all-time great giant monster movies. Although the American version is reedited to be a stand-alone, this was originally a sequel to 1964's *Frankenstein Conquers the World*, in which a giant Frankenstein fights Baragon. At one point in that film the monster

loses an arm, which apparently grows into the other Gargantua. —*B. T.*

FLOWERS OF SHANGHAI L: DIRECTORS/HOU, HSIAO-HSIEN (1998) 120M D: Hou Hsiao-Hsien. *Michelle Reis, Tony Leung Chiu Wai, Carina Lau, Michiko Hada.* Hou's lyrical and beautiful story of the decadent world of late-nineteenth-century Shanghai brothels stars Leung Chiu Wai as an opium-smoking nobleman and Reis and Lau as two of the eponymous "flowers." Directed with a cool delicacy and performed with restrained control, it's an alienated portrait of a life of quiet desperation in an insular world where even daylight is never seen. Shot in rich, vivid color and breathtaking beauty, it's a virtual jewel box of elegant fantasy suffused in sadness and defined by the precise, oh-so-slow camera pans that set the pace and the mood. It's also oblique and measured, the very definition of "art film," and it's harder to follow than Hou's previous (but still demanding) films of urban life in contemporary Taiwan, but you'd be hard pressed to find a lovelier, more visually rich film. —*S. A.*

EASTERN CONDORS L: DIRECTORS/HUNG, SAMMO (1986) 97M D: Sammo Hung. *Sammo Hung, Yuen Biao, Joyce Godenzi, Yuen Wah, Haing S. Ngor.* A secret militia unit formed of military prisoners goes into Vietnam to destroy an abandoned weapons cache in this unabashed reworking of *The Dirty Dozen* by way of Sam Fuller's *China Gate* (with nods to *Apocalypse Now* and *The Deer Hunter,* among others), directed with high-energy Hong Kong style by Hung. In other words, it's nonstop action, elaborate set pieces, and amazing stunt work in an unusually dark tale of jungle fighters and grim heroics. Hung (who also choreographed the action) mixes martial arts with high-powered ballistics for this man-against-military machine adventure, culminating in an impressive free-for-all in a high-tech underground missile silo that could have been left over from a James Bond film. Biao and Ngor are Cambodian refugees who join the motley group and Wah is the hyperactively villainous colonel who giggles maniacally as he tracks the group through the jungle. —*S. A.*

MR. NICE GUY L: DIRECTORS/HUNG, SAMMO (1997) 113M D: Sammo Hung. *Gabrielle Fitzpatrick, Richard Norton, Miki Lee, Jackie Chan.* Chan plays a TV chef who runs into an investigative reporter under attack by gangsters because she possesses an incriminating video. Then the video gets mixed up with one that Chan has, and various fights and shoot-outs ensue. Although directed by Chan's longtime partner Hung (who has a cameo), this is one of Chan's worst efforts ever. All of the weaknesses you overlook in a typical Chan film are more extreme here, with less thrilling action to make up for it. The white thugs in Chan films are always lacking in charisma and presence, but these guys are so unmenacing they seem like they would've been rejected from *El Mariachi*. Most disappointingly, the climax is not a stunt or a fight—Chan just runs over a house with a monster truck. Man, *I* could've done that. —*B.T.*

PRODIGAL SON, THE L: DIRECTORS/HUNG, SAMMO (1981) 104M D: Sammo Hung. *Yuen Biao, Sammo Hung, Lam Ching-Ying.* Yuen is given a chance to prove his worth here in an excellent entry into the then new-wave kung fu genre. He plays a spoiled martial artist wannabe whose wealthy father pays others to lose to him. When a seasoned Wing Chun master reveals his father's scheme to him, Yuen vows to learn kung fu for real. But first he has to persuade the master (Lam) to take him on as a pupil. Rounding out the characters is the master's rival colleague and a mysterious fight-seeking challenger bent on keeping his unbeaten title. This is a solid film in the classic student-teacher training world, and pulls from the Shaw brothers' established plot points while instilling new ideas into the burgeoning new age of Hong Kong action cinema. The fight sequences are most impressive, as are the leads' mastery of their trade. The double flag-jumping sequence alone makes this worth checking out. —*R.M.*

WHEELS ON MEALS L: DIRECTORS/HUNG, SAMMO (1984) 100M D: Sammo Hung. *Jackie Chan, Lola Forner, Biao Yuen, Sammo Hung.* Chan teamed up with Hung (who also directs) and Biao for the second of three action-packed comedies, this time shot on location in Barcelona. Chan and Yuen are a pair of acrobatic street vendors who fall for a kleptomaniac heiress (Forner) that amateur private eye Sammo is tailing. When an evil count kidnaps the beauty, the three join forces to storm the castle and Chan engages in one of his greatest screen battles ever, against the strapping, swift kickboxing champion Benny "The Jet" Urquidez. The camaraderie between the three buddies is evident in the rollicking humor and playful stunt choreography, and the terrific locations—culminating with the castle fortress—create a magnificent, often fantastic backdrop for this lighthearted adventure. Look for American character actor Herb Edelman in a small role as Sammo's boss. —*S.A.*

AFRICAN QUEEN, THE L: DIRECTORS/HUSTON, JOHN (1951) 105M D: John Huston. *Katharine Hepburn, Robert Morley, Humphrey Bogart.* At the beginning of World War II, Charlie (Bogart) is a gin-drinking, scruffy boat captain, who ferries supplies to villages in East Africa. At one of his stops, he learns that the local reverend has died, and that his last request was to get his sister, Rose (Hepburn), out of the jungle and back to civilization. Charlie reluctantly agrees to take this new cargo, but soon realizes that he may have taken on too much, as the prim and proper Rose consistently reprimands him for his lifestyle. As their journey continues, Charlie starts to soften

up to Rose's company and takes on an almost gentlemanly attitude. Rose also lets her hair down as she accepts that there is adventure to be had. The pair's romance, which slowly blossoms as the two take on each other's quirks, is interrupted when they float into Nazi territory. Bogart won his only Academy Award for his role here, in Huston's classic adventure-romance that plays up the melodrama like a finely tuned instrument. —*R.M.*

ASPHALT JUNGLE, THE L: DIRECTORS/HUSTON, JOHN (1950) 112M D: John Huston. *Louis Calhern, Marc Lawrence, Sam Jaffe, Sterling Hayden.* Even people who don't buy into Huston's reputation mostly esteem *The Asphalt Jungle.* The story is a multi-layered account of all the people involved in, and caught up on the periphery of, an ingenious caper to steal a fortune in gems from a big-city jeweler. Andrew Sarris shrewdly observed that the film was a collective triumph for a cast that never achieved the greatness they'd variously aspired to: add Jean Hagen, James Whitmore, and a memorable early supporting role for Marilyn Monroe. The Oscar-nominated Jaffe and Lawrence are especially brilliant as, respectively, the philosopher-king of caper plotters (with a weakness for nubile teens) and the sweaty, small-time hood whose back room becomes a de facto headquarters. The movie remains a classic among crime films. It's also one of Huston's most eloquently composed accounts of how people glance off one another's lives without ever occupying the same plane of existence and awareness. *We Were Strangers* was the title of Huston's previous film, and the effective working title of most of his best pictures. —*R.T.J.*

CASINO ROYALE L: DIRECTORS/HUSTON, JOHN (1967) 137M D: John Huston, Various. *Peter Sellers, David Niven, Woody Allen, Ursula Andress, Deborah Kerr, William Holden, Orson Welles.* James Bond is more than a man—he's a veritable franchise in this comic take on the Ian Fleming novel. Agent 007 Niven winds up recruiting a veritable platoon of Bonds (including Sellers and Allen) to take on the evil SMERSH. Andress, Kerr, Joanna Pettet, and Daliah Lavi number among the femmes fatales and George Raft, Jean-Paul Belmondo, Burt Kwouk, and Peter O'Toole make cameos. Helmed by at least five official directors, it's an inconsistent mishmash, more farce than parody, but there is something irresistible about Allen as a cowardly nebbish of a super-spy with an insidious germ that makes all women beautiful while killing all men over four foot six. —*S.A.*

DEAD, THE L: DIRECTORS/HUSTON, JOHN (1987) 83M D: John Huston. *Helena Carroll, Anjelica Huston, Rachel Dowling, Donal McCann, Cathleen Delaney.* This James Joyce short story from *The Dubliners* was Huston's last film. The story concerns a dead marriage between Huston and McCann. The setting is a Christmas party in 1904 where all the

John Huston

Born in Nevada, Missouri, in 1906 to (then) small-time actor Walter Huston and journalist Rhea Gore, Huston spent much of his childhood on the road with his father (who separated from Gore when the boy was three). He missed much of his early schooling, making up for it in high school, where he threw himself into literature, painting, opera, and boxing (he briefly attended Smith School of Art in Los Angeles).

When his father achieved fame on Broadway, Huston followed and flirted with theater before beginning to write short stories. His first contact with the movies lasted only a few years; he spent many more years wandering about Europe before returning to Warner Bros. in 1937 to begin his career in earnest. After writing the screenplays for such films as *Jezebel, High Sierra, Dr. Ehrlich's Magic Bullet,* and *Sergeant York* (the latter two earning him Oscar nominations), he made his directorial debut in 1941 with *The Maltese Falcon.*

Huston's career spanned decades and most genres (including a series of important war documentaries during World War II), but by and large he chose to adapt works of literature. When his Warner contract expired, Huston chose a more independent route, picking studio projects that appealed to him and even producing his own pictures.

Huston's reputation fell in the 1960s during the rise of auteur criticism, but during the final decade of his life he was reaffirmed as one of America's greatest directors, with a number of masterpieces to his credit, despite a rather uneven, erratic career. One of Hollywood's first writer/directors, Huston often scripted his own films and had a hand in the screenplays of all the others. Though he turned to literature for his stories, his films consistently focused on a hero pursuing a quest against impossible odds, one that often becomes a quest for identity. Huston died in 1987, soon after finishing *The Dead.* —*Sean Axmaker*

---

appropriate formalities of the time are steadily observed by hosts and guests alike. As the evening continues, the conversation around the dinner table begins to indicate that extremely different points of view are being exchanged and if it weren't for social niceties it wouldn't be a party at all but a brawl. The formless train-of-thought writing in the original story is preserved in this adaptation, especially as the married couple leaves and discovers that only these same social niceties keep their marriage together. Extraordinary period detail and visual depth make this one of the finest Joyce adaptations to date. —*N. J.*

FAT CITY L: DIRECTORS/HUSTON, JOHN (1972) 100M D: John Huston. *Nicholas Colasanto, Susan Tyrrell, Stacy Keach, Jeff Bridges, Candy Clark.* Stockton, California's grim world of apartments, hotels, vegetable fields, bars, and, most importantly, boxing rings provides the backdrop for several dead-end lives. Keach plays an over-the-hill boxer who contemplates a comeback after several years of heavy drinking. After helping a promising young boxer (Bridges) get his career started, booze, jealousy, bad luck, and smashed dreams bring their personal and professional lives crashing to the ground. Expertly directed by Huston, *Fat City* features some of ace cinematographer Conrad Hall's best and bleakest photography and a strong supporting cast that includes future *Cheers* Coach Colasanto and Tyrell as one hell of a drunk. This is one of the great "sleepers" of the early '70s. —*S. H.*

MALTESE FALCON, THE L: DIRECTORS/HUSTON, JOHN (1941) 100M D: John Huston. *Humphrey Bogart, Mary Astor, Peter Lorre, Sydney Greenstreet, Ward Bond.* This classic American film noir is the directorial debut of Huston, who would go on to direct some of the very best Bogart films. Here Bogart plays the smooth-talking Sam Spade, a private eye in search of the missing black statue from Malta. Based on the Dashiell Hammett novel, this excellent detective story has all the twists and traps you would expect, and its electric performances (the first time Bogart and Astor appeared together) will keep you riveted to your chair right to the end. As with the best Bogart films, *The Maltese Falcon* begs for repeated viewings. —*N. J.*

MAN WHO WOULD BE KING, THE L: DIRECTORS/HUSTON, JOHN (1975) 129M D: John Huston.
Sean Connery, Shakira Caine, Saeed Jaffrey, Christopher Plummer, Michael Caine. Huston originally wanted to make this film in the late 1950s with Humphrey Bogart and Clark Gable. It would've made a hell of a picture, but I've no complaints. With Connery and Caine as the ambitious soldiers/con-artists/masons turned adventurers, Huston's adaptation of Kipling's story manages to be both intimate and gloriously sweeping, a larger-than-life tale on a magnificent canvas (Morocco's mountains—standing in for Afganistan—create the breathtaking backdrop) grounded in the warmth of friendship and camaraderie. And it's pure Huston: an impossible quest, an out-of-reach grail, and an ironic twist leading to a supremely glorious failure. More than any of his later films, Huston is able to turn their story into a strange sort of triumph by remaining true to his characters, right down to the riveting conclusion and the haunting coda narrated by Caine. One of the most rousing films of the 1970s. —*S. A.*

PRIZZI'S HONOR L: DIRECTORS/HUSTON, JOHN (1985) 130M D: John Huston.
Jack Nicholson, Kathleen Turner, Robert Loggia, William Hickey, Anjelica Huston. Huston's poison valentine mixes black humor with an unexpectedly engaging romance. Nicholson, a thick mob hit man, loses his heart to a mystery woman who turns out to be out-of-town talent, an icy but hearty assassin played with calculating gusto by Turner. Manipulating things behind the scenes is the aging mob princess Huston, whose cagey plotting reveals her as another femme fatale to be reckoned with. Director Huston walks a fine line between satire and spoof, making Nicholson a loyal, lovable lug and Turner his vivacious equal, engaged in a doomed love affair on the battlefield of Mafia politics. Hickey has the role of a lifetime in Papa Prizzi, the family don. "Like a cooo-kie?" —*S. A.*

TREASURE OF THE SIERRA MADRE, THE L: DIRECTORS/HUSTON, JOHN (1948) 126M D: John Huston.
Humphrey Bogart, Walter Huston, Tim Holt, Bruce Bennett, Alfonso Bedoya. Critic James Agee greeted *The Treasure of the Sierra Madre* as "one of the best things Hollywood has done since it learned to talk." After his army experiences as a wartime documentary filmmaker, Huston wasn't disposed to confinement on Burbank soundstages; for this tale of prospectors finding gold and losing something greater in the Mexican backcountry, he went on location well south of the border and stayed there (to studio boss Jack Warner's exasperation) till he got what he was after. As Fred C. Dobbs, Bogart bravely exposed the paranoid flip side of his sardonic hipster persona (and alienated some of his fan base), while Huston pere's

portrait of Old Howard, the veteran prospector who's already "seen what gold does to men's souls," is simply one of the most magically fine performances in the cinema. (Between them, the Hustons earned three 1948 Oscars.) The direction masterfully blends documentary realism, grotesque humor, hallucinatory expressionism, film noir, and a startlingly cheerful absurdism that would remain the keynote of John's career. Specific echoes of this movie inform the work of Robert Altman, Sam Peckinpah, Monte Hellman, and many another latter-day artists. —*R. T. J.*

WISE BLOOD L: DIRECTORS/HUSTON, JOHN (1979) 108M D: John Huston.
Harry Dean Stanton, Brad Dourif. Dourif's preacher, with his own screwy brand of Southern Baptism, believes in his own Church, without Christ. The crazy thing is, while having almost no idea what he is talking about, he has one hundred times more faith than anybody else in the film. Huston goes Southern Gothic—how can you lose? —*M. S.*

DAY OF THE BEAST L: DIRECTORS/IGLESIA, ALEX DE LA (1995) 103M D: Alex de la Iglesia.
Alex Angulo, Terele Pavez, Gianni Ippoliti. The appropriately named Father Angel (Angulo) is in a quandary indeed. The mousy, middle-aged theologian has stumbled across the "true" date of the birth of the antichrist—which is appropriately enough Christmas Eve—but he doesn't know the site. With the earnest determination of a satanic Boy Scout he undertakes bad deeds and destructive acts in hopes of impressing the evil one with his sudden conversion. Accompanied by a grotesque metalhead sidekick and the striking, skeptical host of an occult reality TV show, Angel sets about selling his soul to the Devil, but that's just the beginning of his hilariously nightmarish ordeal. Contemporary Madrid becomes a neon-tinged metropolis on the verge of apocalypse, with a pack of street-thug terrorists as veritable storm troopers from hell clearing the streets of undesirables. Though the film momentarily loses itself in a series of blind alleys and ultimately makes little logical sense, De la Iglesia's sly imagery and devilishly dark humor give this fantasy sharp, feral teeth. —*S. A.*

800 BULLETS L: DIRECTORS/IGLESIA, ALEX DE LA (2002) 124M D: Alex de la Iglesia.
Luis Castro, Sancho Gracia, Carmen Maura. De la Iglesia tones down his style slightly for this heartfelt tribute to spaghetti Westerns and Hollywood productions shot in Spain. When young Carlos (Castro) discovers that his grandfather and deceased father were stunt doubles in spaghetti Westerns, he ditches his ski trip to track down his grandfather, Julian (Gracia), against the wishes of his mother (Maura). Julian lives the life of a drunken cowboy, doing stunts for tourists on an old Western town set and occasionally bragging that he drove the tank in *Patton*. He and his stuntman colleagues live the life 24–7, so at their parties there is a guy

who throws himself through the window, a guy who lights himself on fire, and another guy who hangs from a noose all day and night. Carlos and Julian learn to get along, but this is trouble when mom tracks them down and decides to buy out the land and turn it into an amusement park. Incredibly sweet and imaginative, this is almost like a deranged children's fantasy that ends in a violent standoff. —B.T.

MUERTO DE RISA (DYING OF LAUGHTER) L: DIRECTORS/ IGLESIA, ALEX DE LA (1999) 113M D: Alex de la Iglesia.
Santiago Segura, El Gran Wyoming, Alex Angulo. This giddy black comedy about fame and revenge is so fucking funny. In the '70s, Nino (Segura)and Bruno (Wyoming) have a very simple act: the skinny guy slaps the fat guy in the face. That's it. This simple act skyrockets them to fame and fortune, but seething hatred boils between them over the years. Nino and Bruno have identical houses separated only by a thin wall. They loathe each other through the '80s, yet they are conjoined for life—they cannot survive without each other or their act. De la Iglesia injects sly satire and commentary about comedy into the story. Watching people hurt themselves or others is the purest form of comedy in the world, and the final scene is the epitome of duo comedy, ultimately the only possible end for these two very sad clowns. —K.C.

PERDITA DURANGO L: DIRECTORS/IGLESIA, ALEX DE LA (1997) 121M D: Alex de la Iglesia. *Rosie Perez, Javier Bardem, James Gandolfini.* High-octane madness from cult fave de la Iglesia. Bad girl Perez teams up with black voodoo priest Bardem for some over-the-top mayhem involving transporting human fetuses for use in beauty products. Lawman Gandolfini is hot on their trail. Along the way the outlaw couple grabs a couple young white kids for some emotionally torturing fun. Completely butchered in both the United States and the UK, the two-disc German PAL/DVD set is the only way to see almost the entire film. A hot Simon Boswell score, Screamin' Jay Hawkins as a voodoo show assistant, and lots of screaming, bloody violence and crazy rock music make this Barry Gifford adaptation a reasonable extension to the goings-on in David Lynch's *Wild at Heart,* but in oh so different hands with the maniacally inclined de la Iglesia at the reins. Avoid the butchered U.S. version *Dance with the Devil.* Any version less than 121 minutes does not deserve your time. —S.R.

DR. AKAGI L: DIRECTORS/IMAMURA, SHOHEI (1998) 128M D: Shohei Imamura. *Kumiko Aso, Akira Emoto.* Imamura's delightful comic drama of a family doctor battling a hepatitis epidemic in rural Japan in the waning days of WWII (Germany had already surrendered) is full of quirky detail and delicious characters. The film's defining image is Akagi (Emoto), clad in a white suit and clutching his black bag, dashing from one patient to another across town while a jazzy soundtrack plays. Imamura, over seventy when he made this, allows the story of Akagi and his band of merry misfits to ramble on, but his loving portraits and inventive direction full of surprising and magical imagery create a film that celebrates life in the face of defeat. —S.A.

TAMPOPO L: DIRECTORS/ITAMI, JUZO (1985) 114M D: Juzo Itami. *Mario Abe, Koji Yakusho, Ken Watanabe, Nobuko Miyamoto, Tsutomu Yamazaki, Izumi Hara.* It's about food! It's about sensuality! It's about slurping! But most of all it's about a woman who is determined to learn how to make the best noodles for her restaurant. With the help of a passing truck driver, Tampopo (Miyamoto) is taken to number of different chefs to learn the essentials of each aspect of making noodles: the noodles themselves, the broth, the meat, the vegetables. It is an art form, and she is going to learn how to perfect it. The tale is interspersed with random tales of food, oyster diving, benign torture, sex, table manners, and Japanese life. It's quirky. It's strange. It's bizarre. It's playful. It's ironic. It's fabulous! —M.N.

REMAINS OF THE DAY, THE L: DIRECTORS/IVORY, JAMES (1993) 134M D: James Ivory. *Anthony Hopkins, James Fox, Christopher Reeve, Emma Thompson, Peter Vaughan.* Hopkins strips his actorly, often hammy stock-in-trade to play the purposefully repressed butler who has dedicated his life to capturing the perfect, well-mannered distance of the ultimate gentleman's gentleman. So placid and disconnected is he that he rejects even the intrusion of his own feelings when he becomes attracted to the manor's new housekeeper, the professional yet individual Thompson. Ivory's camera is just as proper as Hopkins's manners, not quite intimate yet fearlessly penetrating; behind the elegant surfaces, under the manners and rituals, and beneath the frozen faces he finds the repression and denials that trap Hopkins's butler and Fox's lord of the manor. Adapted by screenwriter Ruth Prawer Jhabvala from the 1989 Pulitzer Prize–winning novel by Kazuo Ishiguro, this is one of the most powerful and nuanced of the Merchant-Ivory dramas of England's calcified class system. —S.A.

BAD TASTE L: DIRECTORS/JACKSON, PETER (1987) 91M D: Peter Jackson. *Peter Jackson, Mike Minett, Peter O'Herne, Terry Potter, Craig Smith.* A team of elite government agents tries to stop alien invaders from turning the Earth into a fast-food restaurant, and gets horribly mangled in the process. It's an incredibly gory gross-out comedy full of brain eating, vomit drinking, and bad wigs. Jackson's super-low-budget debut was made on the weekends with friends who eventually flaked out enough that he had to make himself into the lead actor. Although not as elaborate or polished as the better known *Dead Alive/Braindead,* it has an impressive array of gore, alien makeup effects

Peter Jackson

For years Peter Jackson was the ideal Scarecrow Video cult director, a sort of Kiwi Sam Raimi who specialized in ridiculously gory comedies full of spectacularly imaginative special effects. My personal favorite of this period is the Monty-Python-with-brain-eating-aliens comedy *Bad Taste* (1987). The obscene puppet musical *Meet the Feebles* (1989) has perhaps a fiercer following, but the one that really brings out the obsessives is *Dead Alive*. Legendary for its impossibly bloody effects and the line "I kick arse for the Lord!," it lured in many a new Scarecrow customer seeking the original, uncut version, *Brain Dead* (1992). And then they'd pick up the faux documentary *Forgotten Silver* (1995), Jackson's tribute to New Zealand's fictional contributions to early cinema, and they were goners.

But now there's that other, less cultish Peter Jackson. The epic Peter Jackson. The one you see on the Oscar broadcasts, who somehow convinced a studio to mount an adaptation of the *Lord of the Rings* trilogy and then pulled it off with awe-inspiring skill.

I would be only half lying to say that we saw it coming. Those of us who have followed Jackson since the vomit-eating and the machine gun–wielding hippos, we knew he had the fortitude to pull *something* off.

(cooked in Jackson's parents' oven), and even miniature models. It's the funniest of Jackson's early period. —*B. T.*

BRAINDEAD (AKA DEAD ALIVE) L: DIRECTORS/JACKSON, PETER (1992) 105M D: Peter Jackson. *Diana Peñalver, Elizabeth Moody, Timothy Balme.* Jackson's gore-comedy splatters across the screen with the glee of a child who's just been given fifty-gallon drums of fake blood. When a bizarre rat-monkey is brought to a New Zealand zoo, it opens the doors to a zombie epidemic of mass proportions! Newly romancing lovebirds Lionel (Balme) and Paquita (Peñalver) are on a date at the zoo to view the new rat-monkey when Lionel's mum gets too close and is bitten. The bite turns her into a decaying zombie who begins to infect the town. As more and more people become infected, Lionel has a harder time concealing the truth. Jackson's no-holds-barred style is a tour de force here, and is simply a must-see. Rev up the lawnmower, prepare to kick ass for the Lord, and stand up to your mum. —*R. M.*

FORGOTTEN SILVER L: DIRECTORS/JACKSON, PETER (1997) 80M D: Peter Jackson, Costa Botes. *Johnny Morris, Sam Neill, Leonard Maltin, Costa Botes, Peter Jackson, Harvey Weinstein.* Who knew that Kiwi film pioneer Colin McKenzie actually beat American inventors to color and sound, and challenged Cecil B. DeMille with his own biblical epic shot on the set he single-handedly built in the middle of the New Zealand jungle? Well he didn't, but Jackson and Botes make a convincing case in their *Zelig*-like documentary spoof, with some of the most beautifully crafted mock vintage footage to see the light of screen. Delivered with wicked deadpan technique, Jackson's "personal journey" is less satire than loving lampoon, a hilarious comedy so low-key that it has rooked more than a few viewers. An absolute delight. —*S. A.*

FRIGHTENERS, THE L: DIRECTORS/JACKSON, PETER (1996) 110M D: Peter Jackson. *R. Lee Ermey, Michael J. Fox, Jeffrey Combs, Jake Busey.* Take Gary Busey, accentuate everything frightening about him, give him blond hair, and you've got Jake Busey—a creepy bastard. *The Frighteners* is a comedy-adventure at heart but it indulges its ghoulish whims. Fox plays Frank Bannister who, with help from some friendly ghosts, makes money by "exorcising" people's houses. His scam is endangered when the evil ghost of Busey starts some trouble and Bannister is blamed. Combs, whose character is frighteningly unbalanced, is sent in by the FBI to investigate. Lots of crazy stuff happens and the plot gets really complicated. But what's great about the film is just how much fun it is. If you like ghosts and antics and such, you will enjoy *The Frighteners*. —*T. S.*

LORD OF THE RINGS, THE: THE FELLOWSHIP OF THE RING L: DIRECTORS/JACKSON, PETER (2002) 208M D: Peter Jackson. *Sean Astin, Viggo Mortensen, Ian McKellen, Elijah Wood, Orlando Bloom, John Rhys-Davies, Liv Tyler, Cate Blanchett.* In his original three-hour theatrical version of *Fellowship*, New Zealand genre-film maverick Jackson accomplished the impossible: he created a faithful, magical, thrill-

Just maybe not something quite as epic as *The Lord of the Rings*.

When we look back on his career, though, the signs are all there. *Bad Taste* showed his enthusiasm for invention and for hands-on filmmaking, for stretching budgets as far as humanly possible. *Meet the Feebles* and *Brain Dead* showed the evolution of his special-effects work, far more ambitious and clever than that of anyone else in his genre. And then *Heavenly Creatures* (1994) revealed his surprising gift for portraying drama and emotion, without turning his back on the fantastic. His first major curveball, it was nominated for a Best Original Screenplay Oscar and introduced the world to Kate Winslet. And yet it was for the fantasy sequences in this film that he founded Weta Digital, whose Oscar-winning effects later made the world of Middle Earth seem so real.

But perhaps it was 1996's intensive special-effects workout *The Frighteners* that gave us the most clues. For the first time, Jackson took money from a Hollywood studio and then filmed far away, in the safety of his native New Zealand. Watch *The Frighteners* and you'll see the ancestors of some of Weta's *Lord of the Rings* effects. The empty-cloak villain the Reaper is not unlike the Nazgûl, and the many cemetery ghosts bear a striking resemblance to the army of the dead in *Return of the King*. This film even shows the origins of Jackson's "extended editions" of the *Rings* films. For the laser disc, he restored deleted scenes to create a longer, alternative version for fans that was not necessarily a director's cut. So he already had all this—just give Jackson a whole bunch of money and time, and Tolkien's story, and you get yourself a classic. —*Bryan Theiss*

---

ing, and compelling film version of J. R. R. Tolkien's great cult fantasy epic. Streamlining the novel's complex story and wealth of detail, Jackson introduced a magical collection of races in a fantasy world with a thousand-year history and dozens of characters, creating a dazzling epic on a mythic scale without losing the soul of the odyssey of the Hobbits and their companions. For the special extended edition, Jackson completely rewove the fabric of the film with even more colors. Here you glimpse the exodus of the elves in a magical scene, witness the Elf Queen Galadriel (Cate Blanchet) bestow gifts upon the Fellowship, and explore the history of Aragorn (Mortensen). The longer version is just as smooth as the original (the film was rescored to match the new shape and pace), and the expanded breadth works perfectly for home video: character, relationships, and story complexity play better than spectacle on the small screen. This is one director's cut that fully earns the title. —*S. A.*

LORD OF THE RINGS, THE: THE TWO TOWERS L: DIRECTORS/JACKSON, PETER (2003) 223M D: Peter Jackson. *Elijah Wood, Orlando Bloom, John Rhys-Davies, Viggo Mortensen, Sean Astin, Ian McKellen, Liv Tyler, Hugo Weaving.* J. R. R. Tolkien's original fantasy trilogy is many things: dense, literate, imaginative, epic, mythic. Jackson's cinematic re-creation of *The Lord of the Rings: The Two Towers* is thrilling, enthralling, and dizzyingly exciting. Jackson finds the soul of the film in Mortenson's wandering warrior-prince Aragorn, reveals the torment in Wood's chosen-one pilgrim Frodo,

and turns the wary relationship between Frodo and the gnarled, psychotically obsessed Gollum (a wonder of computer-generated characterization given soul by Andy Serkis) into the defining drama of Frodo's hopes and fears along the quest. Jackson brings both blood and thunder (notably in the Battle of Helm's Deep, a brief ten-page episode in the novel that he transforms into the turning point of the epic battle) and human scale to a tale so long relegated to the stiff archetypes of myth. His extended version weaves not just deleted scenes back into his vision, but additional background and character insight. It adds the kind of weight that gives the epic even greater heft. —*S. A.*

MEET THE FEEBLES L: DIRECTORS/JACKSON, PETER (1989) 92M D: Peter Jackson. Future *Lord of the Rings* director Jackson tops the bad taste quotient of his debut *Bad Taste* with this notorious sophomore feature, an aggressively, gleefully sick puppet show. Like a *Muppet Show* of junkies, sex addicts, and all breeds of perverted and corrupt creatures, this is a diseased backstage drama twisted into grotesque flourishes, from the porno empire in the basement to the muckraking journalist fly that gets its best scoops while hiding out in the toilet. There's even a Vietnam flashback with a *Deer Hunter* quote. Jackson is audacious, to say the least, and his merciless compendium of squalid and repulsive absurdities makes today's gross-out comedies pale in comparison. But, he's also an unexpectedly deft director: cinematic eye meets demented mind. The result is hilarious, offensive, unclean, and not for the squeamish. —*S.A.*

ELEKTRA, MY LOVE L: DIRECTORS/JANCSÓ, MIKLÓS
(1975) 76M D: Miklós Jancsó. *Mari Töröcsik, György Cserhalmi, Jozsef Madaras.* Transporting the myth of Electra to Hungary, this story picks up from the announcement (met with skepticism) of the death of Orestes. The film is mostly memorable for its intensely choreographed long takes of elaborate rituals rooted equally in religious ceremony and modern theater. Driven by these shots more than a narrative, the film looks like what'd happen if Sergei Paradjanov got into ten-minute tracking shots. Consequently, the reportedly "mind-blowing" finale is hardly jarring after the oddities of the previous hour. All in all, the material ranges from disarmingly eerie to laughable. The latter can mostly be blamed on the throngs of nude, swaying flower children. This, along with the now-dated theatrical modernisms in general, keeps the film from being taken seriously, making it the least satisfying of the Jancsó films I've seen. —*C.B.*

RED AND THE WHITE, THE L: DIRECTORS/JANCSÓ, MIKLÓS
(1967) 92M D: Miklós Jancsó. *Tibor Molnár, András Kozák, Jácint Juhász, József Madaras.* Retreading the style and themes of his previous year's film, *The Round-Up,* Jancsó's meticulously shot Russian Civil War piece dwells on the senseless absurdity of war. The film's full and painterly use of widescreen is breathtaking. Thanks to careful and efficient camera movement and what must have been maddening choreography (often stretching massive swathes of landscape), the film's generally long takes don't bore or even lull. This remarkable visual splendor is put to use pitilessly depicting a hopeless and exhausting string of atrocities. Motivations for the bloodshed are intentionally not indicated, and we're left to see the war simply as an arbitrary excuse for people to exact humiliating death on others. Stark and austere, it should appeal to fans of *The Thin Red Line, Andrei Rublev,* or any of Béla Tarr's '90s work. —*C.B.*

ROUND-UP, THE L: DIRECTORS/JANCSÓ, MIKLÓS (1966) 90M
D: Miklós Jancsó. *András Kozák, János Görbe, Zoltán Latinovits.* In the wake of an 1848 revolt against Austrian rule, suspected Hungarian rebels were collected and detained. *The Round-Up* is set amid the psychological torture that went on as prisoners were openly encouraged to betray one another to their captors simply to prolong their own survival. In a trickle-down economics of cruelty, the victims give up one another all too readily, and we're shown a desperate form of freedom that manifests itself not as a function of living, but as the power to kill. Though not especially graphic, it can be tough to watch (at one point in the film the terror tactics spark an impromptu mass suicide). A clear precedent to the work of fellow Hungarian Béla Tarr, the film's gorgeous black-and-white long takes shouldn't just be admired, they should be studied. —*C.B.*

ANGELIC CONVERSATIONS L: DIRECTORS/JARMAN, DEREK
(1985) 78M D: Derek Jarman. *Robert Sharp, Judi Dench, Christopher Hobbs.* Dench narrates Shakespeare's love sonnets as an expression of Jarman's longings for another man, whom he lays in the background of an experimental feature in his continued crusade to invent a new type of cinema for a gay audience. He cross-utilizes different film formats: 8 mm, 16 mm, 35 mm, and video, a la the experimentalists of the 1960s (like Stan Brakhage or Kenneth Anger) to create a beautiful, optically printed visual "poem," which in sum is the slow-moving filmic equivalent to painting (Jarman's first love, being a painter). He expresses the desire of male love and longing, all saturated with the music of Coil and Dench's melodic readings. This was one of Jarman's personal favorites. —*N.H.*

DEREK JARMAN'S BLUE (AKA BLUE) L: DIRECTORS/
JARMAN, DEREK (1993) 76M D: Derek Jarman. *Tilda Swinton (voice), Derek Jarman (voice), Nigel Terry (voice), John Quentin (voice).* A dying man going blind while attempting to portray the "landscape" around him, Jarman found himself suffering from severe complications due to advanced AIDS infection. His eyesight failed and all he could see were blurring images with a blue color. Instead of giving up his profession as a filmmaker, Jarman relied on his background as a painter and poet and created a film made up of a simple blue screen: a cobalt blue, based on the colors of one of his favorite painters, Yves Klein. *Blue* is just that—seventy-five minutes of blue screen with a narration of multiple voices, all actors and artists directly involved in Jarman's life, including his own narration. Each voice describes a different aspect of the director's physical and emotional deterioration, and lays out a roadway that Jarman follows as he seeks out spiritual understanding of his decaying condition. *Blue* is a poem that attempts to place its audience into the perspective of a gay artist facing his own mortality (Jarman died not long after the film's release). —*N.H.*

EDWARD II (DEREK JARMAN'S EDWARD II) L: DIRECTORS/
JARMAN, DEREK (1991) 91M D: Derek Jarman. *Annie Lennox, Tilda Swinton, Andrew Tiernan, Kevin Collins, Steven Waddington.* Edward II was Jarman's closest attempt at a mainstream feature. Shot almost entirely on 35 mm, the film is an archaized updating of the gay tragedy by Christopher Marlowe. King Edward (Waddington) loves his servant Gaveston (Tiernan). Queen Isabella (Swinton) loves her husband, but bitterness over her husband's "brain sickness" for Gaveston drives her into the arms of Mortimer (Nigel Terry), the head of England's military. Isabella has Gaveston first exiled and then murdered, and the King is imprisoned while Mortimer and

Isabella rule England. Jarman boldly changes the play's tragic ending, giving King Edward a chance to live, thus closing the film with an open plea for gay and lesbian rights. Utilizing several Bretchian theatrical tricks, Jarman mixes modern gay protesting with the fourteenth century and pulls it off successfully. Swinton is magnificent as Isabella, changing in the film from a spurned lover to a literal vampire. Once again, Jarman composer Simon Fisher Turner delivers a fantastic soundtrack, including Lennox who has a cameo in the film singing Cole Porter's "Every Time We Say Goodbye." —N. H.

GARDEN, THE L: DIRECTORS/JARMAN, DEREK (1992) 90M D: Derek Jarman. *Kevin Collins, Roger Cook, Tilda Swinton, Michael Gough.* Two gay men (Mills, Collins) fall in love, are beaten, and then sent to the cross as Christ (Cook) walks the earth, a witness to the tragedy, in this mix of religious symbolism, poetry, and Jarman's own life at Dungeness Spit in England where he has built a magical garden around his cottage with the assistance of his friends and lover (Collins). The film is full of surreal images reflecting the influences of Jarman's favorite directors—Jean Cocteau, Michael Powell, and Pier Pasolini. The beautiful compositions belie Jarman's talents as a painter, and the film above all of his other works achieves the truest expression of his feelings as life is fading away. Its multimedia mix of formats (super 8, 16 mm, 35 mm, and video) will either drive away those viewers unable to handle the narrative disjointedness of experimental form or enrapture those who can appreciate the approach and recognize Jarman's masterful techniques as a filmmaker. —N. H.

JUBILEE L: DIRECTORS/JARMAN, DEREK (1978) 103M D: Derek Jarman. *Jenny Runacre, Jordan, Nell Campbell, Toyah Willcox, Richard O'Brien, Adam Ant.* Queen Elizabeth I (Runacre) asks her court magician to show her England's future and he does so by invoking the angel Ariel, who transports the three to a devastated England overrun by Fascist police and bomb-throwing punks. Buckingham Palace has become a recording studio for punk music, and the world is run by media czar Borgia Ginz (Jack Birkett). The Queen finds surprise in her sympathies for a household of punk-girl rebels, Amyl Nitrate, Mad, and their leader Bod (also played by Runacre), who together steal, commit murder, and teach British history classes. Artist and director Jarman's second feature spits acid at conservative England. While the screenplay is dated, the images are not, remaining strong and unsettling in their voiced hatred of the modern British government. Runacre's rendition of "Rule Britannica" is a classic fuck-you to English aristocracy. A big hit at the time, the film made punk celebrities out of Willcox and Runacre. —N. H.

LAST OF ENGLAND, THE L: DIRECTORS/JARMAN, DEREK (1987) 85M D: Derek Jarman. *Tilda Swinton, Nigel Terry, "Spring" Rupert Audley, Michael Gough, Spencer Leigh,.* Young men stick heroin-filled needles in their arms. Black-hooded terrorists dance in the burning streets, cheek to cheek, having just gunned down innocent victims. A newlywed bride (Swinton) cuts up her dress with a pair of giant scissors as she wails in mourning, the body of her dead husband lying next to her in the gutter. Behind her, all of England burns. Jarman takes his title from the painting by Ford Maddox Brown. Having just found out his HIV-positive status, Jarman attacks the British Empire, mixing super 8, 16 mm, and video to create an angry and frightening apocalyptic vision of an England overrun over by terrorism and anarchy. Terry, Jarman, and Gough narrate over the soundtrack a mix of Jarman's own journals and poetry, spewing acidic anger and hatred over the state of England. —N. H.

WAR REQUIEM L: DIRECTORS/JARMAN, DEREK (1988) 92M D: Derek Jarman. *Nathaniel Parker, Owen Teale, Tilda Swinton, Laurence Olivier.* This remarkable film takes for its soundtrack the entire work of Benjamin Britten's story of a soldier and his lover during WW II, *War Requiem*, as performed by Dietrich Fischer-Dieskau, Peter Pears, Galina Vishnevskaya, The Bach Choir, and Britten himself conducting the London Symphony Orchestra. The music is certainly stunning enough, as all of its poetry is taken from the WWI poet Wilfred Owen, who died in the war. For Jarman to set the entire work with his very unique form of filmmaking brings out another dimension in this music—a visual dimension perfectly congruent with the music. This was Olivier's last film. —N. J.

WITTGENSTEIN L: DIRECTORS/JARMAN, DEREK (1993) 73M D: Derek Jarman. *John Quentin, Karl Johnson, Kevin Collins, Michael Gough, Tilda Swinton.* Jarman tackles the life of Viennese-born, Cambridge-educated philosopher Ludwig Wittgenstein (1889–1951). Instead of giving us a usual blow-by-blow BBC autobiography, Jarman infuses his film with visual anarchism of Wittgenstein's developing understanding of language and its usage, throwing out any concern over period details or narrative structure. The result is a beautiful visual essay on Wittgenstein's philosophy realized in a pictorial series of sketches bouncing around Wittgenstein's life. Far from the boring docudrama approach, the film intellectually challenges the viewer by showing how life challenged Wittgenstein's ideas through his acceptance of his homosexuality and his purpose in life. As in his other films, Jarman imbues the visuals with a painterly sense of bright coloring and mood lighting that raises the film above its limited budget. Screenwriter Terry Eagleton lambasted Jarman's directorial approach to film

Alejandro Jodorowsky

Chilean-born Alejandro Jodorowsky formed a theater troupe, directed a hundred plays, wrote three novels, founded the Panic Movement, and toured the world with Marcel Marceau before directing his first film, *Fando y Lis*, in Mexico at the age of thirty-nine. When it premiered at the 1968 Acapulco Film Festival, the iconoclastic director found himself fleeing the theater, pursued by a rock-throwing mob. An avant-gardist fiercely dedicated to art above all else, Jodorowsky has had a career riddled with clashes (although they have more often been with financiers).

Jodorowsky's second and third films, *El Topo* (1970) and *The Holy Mountain* (1973), became midnight-movie phenomena thanks in part to the drug culture and the admiration of John Lennon, who convinced his manager Allen Klein to buy the former and finance the latter. Jodorowsky and Klein have since had a falling out that prevented the video release of the films and prompted Jodorowsky to give away the negatives to pirates. His later films are *Tusk* (1980) (a French film about an elephant, unreleased in the United States and disowned by Jodor-

---

at its release, infuriated at Jarman's rewriting of the screenplay in a less linear fashion. —*N. H.*

DEAD MAN L: DIRECTORS/JARMUSCH, JIM (1995) 121M D: Jim Jarmusch. *Michael Wincott, Gary Farmer, Johnny Depp, Lance Henriksen, Robert Mitchum, Iggy Pop.* Jarmusch's finest film to date about young accountant Robert Blake (Depp), a man of mistaken identity driven to murder. John Ford's majestic old West has been drained of any color (thanks to masterful cinematographer Robby Muller) and what's left is a muddy shit-hole called Machine, a place where whores give head in the alley, skulls pile in the street, and blood runs thick and black as tar. In a revisionist take on the Western genre (not the historical West), Jarmusch fuses the outlaw with the poetic, allowing Depp's reading of Blake's poetry to resonate through idyllic white cedar groves, through fiery star-filled nights, through the watery passageways of morning. But wait! There are also cannibals, head-squishing, and transsexuals! Perfect! Neil Young's choppy, droning guitar score adds to the mood of this transcendent masterpiece. —*J. D.*

GHOST DOG: THE WAY OF THE SAMURAI L: DIRECTORS/ JARMUSCH, JIM (1996) 116M D: Jim Jarmusch. *John Tormey, Henry Silva, Tricia Vessey, Forest Whitaker.* Completely unique even among Jarmusch's filmography, this is the hypnotically paced tale of a mysterious hit man called Ghost Dog (Whitaker) who lives his life based on the samurai code. When mob bosses decide to take out his master, Ghost Dog has to kill them all first. Although technically a violent crime drama, it's much more about philosophy and multiculturalism. Ghost Dog follows the way of the samurai but is open to all other ways (from European literature to freestyle rappers in the park); his dying tradition is pitted against that of the Mafia, whose biggest scheme these days involves recycling. The elderly mobsters bring a lot of humor to the film, including a recurring joke about one who admires Flavor Flav. This is a movie that offers a variety of interpretations upon multiple viewings. Also notable is the outstanding instrumental hip-hop score by Wu-Tang Clan leader RZA. —*B. T.*

NIGHT ON EARTH L: DIRECTORS/JARMUSCH, JIM (1991) 128M D: Jarmusch, Jim. *Armin Mueller-Stahl, Roberto Benigni, Giancarlo Esposito, Winona Ryder, Rosie Perez. Night on Earth* documents a night of taxi rides in five cities around the world, starting in New York and ending in Helsinki. The stories range from comic to serious, but in the end one thing is abundantly clear—no matter where you are in the world, driving a cab is a crazy job. In New York, cabbie Helmut is a German man who is horrible with directions and driving in general. Halfway through the ride, he switches places with his passenger, Yo-Yo. In Rome, the cabbie picks up a priest and insists on confessing all of his sins, which include some pretty compromising sexual situations. All the while the priest sits nearly unconscious in the backseat. What makes this movie truly enjoyable to watch is that the rides don't feel at all contrived. The acting is so true to life that you could actually picture yourself sitting in the backseat of the cab as the situations take place. —*J. S.*

owsky), the more true-to-form circus tale *Santa Sangre* (1989), and the uncharacteristic work-for-hire *The Rainbow Thief* (1990).

Jodorowsky's films are bizarre, grotesque, theatrical, nonlinear, and highly symbolic. They display an obsession with alchemy, physical deformity, subconscious imagery, the shattering of religious and social taboos, and the concept of the inner journey. They are not for everyone—most would find them overly weird, absurdly pretentious, and even boring—but for those tuned into Jodorowsky's wavelength, they can be everything from filmmaking miracles to religious texts. It's hard to believe they even exist.

Jodorowsky has struggled to produce the sequel *Sons of El Topo* (retitled *Abelcain* due to the ongoing dispute with Klein), which at one point was to be produced by Alfonso Arau and at another was rumored to star Marilyn Manson. The script has El Topo, now a saint, buried on an island paradise in the middle of a postapocalyptic wasteland. Stepping on the island causes volcanic eruptions, unless you have the flesh of a saint with you. So when the mother of El Topo's sons, Abel and Cain, passes away, and they try to transport her to the island, every bandit within miles follows the perfumed scent of her sainted body. Despite repeated attempts, the production has so far failed to get off the ground.

Today Jodorowsky studies and restores tarot cards, writes novels and comics *(Metabarons, The Incal)*, and continues planning new films. Here's hoping he's successful, and that nobody throws rocks at him when he's done.   —*Bryan Theiss*

STRANGER THAN PARADISE L: DIRECTORS/JARMUSCH, JIM (1983) 89M D: Jim Jarmusch. *John Lurie, Eszter Balint, Richard Edson.* This is the film that put minimalist director/writer Jarmusch on the independent movie map. His original style burns across the screen at a snail's pace, in lurid black and white, while the dialogue and lack thereof capture the essence of the characters completely. Willie (Lurie, who also donated the score) is a New York slacker who is visited, much to his dismay, by his Hungarian cousin Eva (Balint) on her way to Cleveland. The first third of the film takes place solely in Willie's apartment, and the cramped yet relaxed feeling gives a taste of what New York living is all about. One year later, Willie and his friend drive out to a snow-buried Cleveland to visit Eva. The trio then makes an impromptu visit to Florida. The completely dreary reality of the film, which is controlled perfectly by Jarmusch, is made all the more entertaining by the bizarre ending the characters wander into. —*R. M.*

FANDO AND LIS L: DIRECTORS/JODOROWSKY, ALEJANDRO (1967) 93M D: Alejandro Jodorowsky. *Diana Mariscal, Sergio Kleiner.* Crowds following individuals, strange rituals, mystic experience, death to rebirth, and more themes of Jodorowsky's work are crowded into this ninety-three-minute film. Reminiscent of *Erendira* at times, David Lynch at others, and the director himself most of all, *Fando and Lis* is one of those rare films you saw at the old repertory theatre before they tore it down for the multiplex. Lis (Mariscal) eats a flower. The story of the city of Tar is read over the illustrated credits. A burning piano is knocked over again and again. Mud bathers gather and rise at the base of a mountain. A little doll's crotch has an opening jabbed in it and a snake is put in the new hole. "Art film" is too loose a term to describe what Jodorowsky is doing here. This is mysticism, alchemy, magic. And the DVD boasts one of the richest commentaries ever. —*S. R.*

HOLY MOUNTAIN, THE L: DIRECTORS/JODOROWSKY, ALEJANDRO (1973) 114M D: Alejandro Jodorowsky. *Richard Rutowski, Horacio Salinas, Alejandro Jodorowsky, Ramona Saunders.* The right words have not been invented to describe this surreal, excessive, bizarre masterpiece. It tells about the inhabitants of various planets and why they are searching for spiritual enlightenment at the holy mountain. Along the way Jodorowsky turns his shit into gold, a busload of tourists laughs at a parade of flayed lambs on crucifixes, and street performers re-enact the conquest of Mexico with frogs in a model city. It is visually overwhelming, with sprawling, artfully designed sets and numerous, epic crowd scenes. There is no plot or logic, just psychedelic imagery and symbolism that will certainly seem like pretentious garbage to the more literal-minded. But when I first saw this all I could think was, *I can't believe this movie actually exists, and that nobody told me about it!* It has never received a legitimate American release and can only be seen in hard to find imports (often edited or optically fogged). —*B. T.*

SANTA SANGRE L: DIRECTORS/JODOROWSKY, ALEJANDRO (1989) 123M D: Alejandro Jodorowsky. *Axel Jodorowsky, Blanca Guerra, Guy Stockwell.* A young man named Fenix is freed from an insane asylum by his mother. Twelve years earlier, she was brutally disfigured by his sadistic circus master father, Orgo, who cut off her arms after he caught her with another woman. Witnessing the horror of the attack is the reason Fenix was committed to the asylum in the first place. The mother/son relationship goes into uncomfortable Freudian territory mixed with fantasies of desire and revenge; he gives her his arms and she takes control of his mind. Jodorowsky seems to transcend genres; sometimes this is a horror film, other times drama and black comedy. We are taken on a tour of the mind and ideas of a master visionary. Immersed in colorful characters, perversion, violence, and lust amidst a Bosch-like circus of the absurd, this is a journey not easily forgotten. —*B. W.*

TOPO, EL L: DIRECTORS/JODOROWSKY, ALEJANDRO (1971) 95M D: Alejandro Jodorowsky. *Paula Romo, Alejandro Jodorowsky, Robert John.* Jodorowsky's most famous film is this bloody, surrealist Western that was adored by potheads (including John Lennon) as a midnight show phenomenon and dismissed by critics for that very reason. At the beginning of the film Jodorowsky is a menacing, black-clad outlaw. It really seems like a Western inspired by Leone and Peckinpah, but with an unusually nightmarish landscape that includes a field of dead rabbits. El Topo starts traveling the desert in a spiral to meet and kill a procession of "masters." Next thing you know he's wearing monk robes and he wakes up underground, where he meets a community of inbred freaks. He leads them on an exodus to the surface, only to see them mercilessly gunned down by the townspeople. The weirdest Western you'll ever see. Unfortunately, you'll have a hard time finding it because disputes between Jodorowsky and producer Allen Klein have prevented it from being released on video or DVD in the United States. —*B. T.*

COMPANY OF WOLVES, THE L: DIRECTORS/JORDAN, NEIL (1984) 92M D: Neil Jordan. *Stephen Rea, David Warner, Angela Lansbury, Sarah Patterson.* Jordan's dreamy rethink of *Little Red Riding Hood,* adapted from Angela Carter's story in collaboration with the author, plunges us into the troubled dreams of an adolescent girl in the hormonal rush of puberty. Patterson is the moody younger daughter who locks herself in her room and loses herself in a fairy tale world of misty tangled woods, thatched cottages with cramped, candlelit interiors, and a bestiary of critters crowding into the frame. Warner is woodcutter dad who has a refreshingly modern outlook on adolescence, while Granny Lansbury spins her cautionary tales of beasts and men and lust unleashed. The mix of fear, fascination, and allure of the wolf is a bittersweet look at the end of innocence, seeing adulthood as a transformation at once scary and satisfying. The dense storybook imagery turns it into one of the most deliciously dark fantasy worlds created for the screen. —*S. A.*

CRYING GAME, THE L: DIRECTORS/JORDAN, NEIL (1992) 112M D: Neil Jordan. *Adrian Dunbar, Stephen Rea, Breffni McKenna, Miranda Richardson, Forest Whitaker, Joe Savino.* What makes this film fabulous is the fact that you probably won't see what is coming unless, of course, someone has spoiled it for you. Which I won't. What is especially great about this movie is that it will surprise you. Fool me once, shame on you, fool me twice, and damn, you're a good movie! At first I thought it was going to be a film about two men, one a prisoner the other his captive, and the relationship that forms between them. I was wrong. And then I thought, OK, it's gonna be about how this guy forms a relationship with the other guy's girlfriend. I was wrong. And then I thought. . . well, never mind what I thought. If you haven't seen this film, see it. 'Cause it's a fun little mind-bender, and we all need to stretch ourselves every so often. —*M. N.*

END OF THE AFFAIR, THE L: DIRECTORS/JORDAN, NEIL (1999) 101M D: Neil Jordan. *Stephen Rea, Ralph Fiennes, Julianne Moore.* This tragic wartime drama about a wife who cheats on her husband with a man whom she falls madly in love with and is doomed to lose is not a movie for those who are prone to waiting patiently for a happy ending. Both beautifully shot and written, this adaptation of Graham Greene's novel left me teary-eyed and with a hollow feeling in my stomach at just how unfair and inescapable destiny can really be. The acting is the driving force, with Moore pulling off an excellent performance as the adulterous wife. Rea plays her husband, a man sad and desperate at losing her, which just further confuses the emotions revolving around the final few scenes. An unusually good tearjerker that proves love doesn't always conquer all. —*J. S.*

GOOD THIEF, THE L: DIRECTORS/JORDAN, NEIL (2002) 108M D: Neil Jordan. *Nutsa Kukhianidze, Nick Nolte, Tchéky Karyo, Marc Lavoine.* An adaptation of the Jean-Pierre Melville classic *Bob Le Flambeur, The Good Thief* stars Nolte as an aging gambler in his attempt for one final perfect heist. Jordan does a good job of pacing the movie, keeping a constantly building momentum throughout. I initially had a very hard time trying to get over the dialogue. Filmed with a largely French-speaking cast, it's one thing trying to fake the funk in your native tongue, but an entirely different bug up your bum when you try to do it in English. As a result, some of the gangsta cop comes off as being a little hokey and it takes some strong wires to suspend this disbelief. Once off the ground however, it's a thoroughly entertaining and engrossing flick with one of the better endings that I have seen in a while. —*T. C.*

INTERVIEW WITH THE VAMPIRE L: DIRECTORS/JORDAN, NEIL (1994) 122M D: Neil Jordan. *Kirsten Dunst, Tom Cruise, Brad Pitt, Antonio Banderas, Stephen Rea, Christian Slater.* Anne Rice's popular novel of brooding vampires in New Orleans was turned into an elegant and atmospheric epic that at its best recalls the tone of classic Universal and Hammer horror. Pitt is the interviewer and Cruise is the interviewee, the vampire Lestat who narrates the story of his life after death. There was great controversy over the casting of Cruise until the movie came out and everyone, including Rice, decided they loved his performance. I'm afraid I have to agree with the initial response by the rabid fans, though, because he's a bit awkward in the role. But the movie around him is good enough to be worth watching. Eleven-year-old Dunst is phenomenally creepy as a vampire bitten when she was a little girl, and there are some beautiful and groundbreaking uses of digital effects (particularly a poetic shot of a vampire dissolving into dust). —*B.T.*

KANSAS CITY CONFIDENTIAL L: DIRECTORS/KARLSON, PHIL (1952) 99M D: Phil Karlson. *Coleen Gray, Preston Foster, Neville Brand, Lee Van Cleef, Jack Elam, John Payne.* Karlson spent his career as a low-budget Raoul Walsh, turning out terse tough-guy heist films and crime melodramas with an edge. This is one of his best, the story of an ex-con (Payne) framed for a bank heist who goes undercover to capture the real criminals. Karlson pulls a snarling performance out of the usually dull Payne, but both he and Foster pale next to the unholy trinity of film noir thugs: Brand, Van Cleef, and Elam. It's a gimmicky but clever heist film with a bang-up opening and a sinister payoff, but it's the scheming rogues gallery and Karlson's steely transformation of thick fall-guy Payne into a ruthless hero that make this so much darkly satisfying fun. —*S.A.*

SILENCERS, THE L: DIRECTORS/KARLSON, PHIL (1966) 102M D: Phil Karlson. *Victor Buono, Daliah Lavi, Stella Stevens, Dean Martin, James Gregory, Arthur O'Connell.* The most shamelessly leering of the swinging secret-agent knock-offs, Martin is the aging spy Matt Helm, who has retired to a life of cheesecake photography for girlie magazines and has a revolving door of scantily clad femmes passing through his high-tech bachelor pad. He's in many ways a prototype for Austin Powers, except he's Rat Pack cool (with a slight layer of sleaze) rather than swinging London as he man-handles a buxom, blundering suspect (Stevens) and romances his partner (Lavi). Buono is the obligatory criminal mastermind out to sabotage the American missile program and Gregory is Helm's humorless boss. This was Martin's first turn as the womanizing agent (he returned in two more films). The tongue-in-cheek tone is furthered by parodies of Martin's signature tunes played over the soundtrack as cheeky commentary. —*S.A.*

INVASION OF THE BODY SNATCHERS (1978) L: DIRECTORS/KAUFMAN, PHILIP (1978) 115M D: Philip Kaufman. *Veronica Cartwright, Jeff Goldblum, Leonard Nimoy, Brooke Adams, Donald Sutherland.* Aliens have invaded Earth and are taking over people's bodies, replacing them with emotionless clones. Through sleep and plant pods the invaders transform humans into drones, working toward a complete takeover of the human race. Elizabeth (Adams) realizes that her husband has changed; she convinces her friend Matthew (Sutherland) that something's very, very wrong. They reveal the encroaching conspiracy to their friends, Jack and Nancy (Goldblum and Cartwright in great supporting roles). Eventually the group is discovered and a deadly cat and mouse chase begins. Great pre-CGI special effects add to the creepy atmosphere of this film, with the dog scene that you won't easily forget. Worth checking out as a triple bill with the original 1956 film by the same name and the more recent remake, 1993's *Body Snatchers*. —*B.W.*.

ARIEL L: DIRECTORS/KAURISMÄKI, AKI (1989) 74M D: Aki Kaurismäki. *Susanna Haavisto, Matti Pellonpää, Eetu Hilkamo, Turo Pajala.* Taisto (Pajala) loses his job, his friend kills himself, he's robbed, and he can't get the top up on his convertible Cadillac. When absurdly bad fortune exhausts the usefulness of mere cynicism, all that's left is a resigned sense of humor, a state that Kaurismäki's films have elevated to an art form. Hope comes in the form of meter maid Irmeli (Haavisto), whom Taisto finds writing him a parking ticket. It's love at first sight. She drops everything, including his ticket, and the two ride off together into the promise of a better tomorrow. Sadly, things don't get any easier for Taisto, who promptly lands himself in jail. There he befriends inmate Mikkonen (Pellonpää) and plots a jailbreak and subsequent heist. With understated wit and boundless compassion that never approaches sentimentality, *Ariel* is an excellent introduction to the world of Kaurismäki, a director you need to know. —*C.B.*

I HIRED A CONTRACT KILLER L: DIRECTORS/KAURISMÄKI, AKI (1990) 79M D: Aki Kaurismäki. *Kenneth Colley, Margi Clarke, Jean-Pierre Léaud.* Jim Jarmusch summed up Kaurismaki perfectly: "Sad enough to make you laugh, and funny enough to make you cry." His assessment fits this suicide comedy like a glove. The loss of employment leaves stuffy office clerk Henri (Léaud of *The 400 Blows*) so profoundly without purpose that he decides to kill himself. A clipped series of attempts at his own life makes for the film's most laugh-out-loud hilarious scene, after which Henri determines that he's unable to complete the job himself and turns to a professional. Soon after, he falls in love and gains a new lease on life. Now he must stop the killer before his frail attempt to escape life's misery turns into a romantic tragedy. This simple story generates an unrelenting succession of blunt but understated punch lines,

Aki Kaurismäki

Aki Kaurismäki, the deadpan farceur from Finland, has been mixing minimalist slapstick, absurdist comedy, and bruised romanticism with rock and roll and road trips for more than twenty years, creating films both ridiculous and sublime. A one-time postman, dishwasher, and film critic, he formed a production company with his older brother Mika (a prolific filmmaker in his own right) called Villealpha (an homage to Jean-Luc Godard's French New Wave classic *Alphaville*). According to one source, the Kaurismäkis are responsible for 20 percent of the film production in Finland. Though Kaurismäki has long been a critics' favorite, it took the delightful, deliciously

stoic romantic farce *The Man Without a Past* (2001)—which won the Jury Prize at the Cannes Film Festival and earned an Oscar nomination for Best Foreign Language Film in 2003—for the rest of the world to take notice of the iconoclastic eccentric.

He made his debut with *Crime and Punishment* (1985), a seriocomic transplant of Dostoyevsky's story to contemporary Helsinki, and found his style early: stories of morose social outcasts and lonely working-class schlubs looking for affection, often set in a cold urban world of unemployment and social indifference and accompanied by a jukebox score of rockabilly, old blues and jazz, and old American rock and roll. That world is Helsinki, a city of bars, cheap rooms, and roving bullies who will beat you up just for existing, where the chain-

---

and accomplishes a modest critique of capitalism in the process. In total, it's an excellent and surprisingly touching film. —*C. B.*

JUHA L: DIRECTORS/KAURISMÄKI, AKI (1999) 77M D: Aki Kaurismäki. *André Wilms, Kati Outinen, Sakari Kuosmanen.* After numerous films where dialogue was scarce and almost incidental to the plot, Kaurismäki finally took the plunge and made a real silent film. Country bumpkin cabbage farmers Juha (Kuosmanen) and Marja (Outinen) meet tragedy when a slick villain (Wilms) seduces Marja with his more urbane and Western qualities, then abandons her to a life of misery in a brothel. One of Kaurismäki's most gorgeously shot films, it's ironically also one of his more dialogue-driven ones. It's not that there's more dialogue (by dialogue I mean intertitles), but that the dialogue carries more narrative weight than it does in most of his other films. Consequently, this film seems further from silent film than, say, his earlier (and technically not silent) *Match Factory Girl*. Best viewed by someone familiar with Kaurismäki already, this exercise is fun for its sly inclusion of American rock-and-roll culture in its faithful homage to silent melodrama. —*C. B.*

LENINGRAD COWBOYS GO AMERICA L: DIRECTORS/KAURISMÄKI, AKI (1989) 78M D: Aki Kaurismäki. *Kari Vaananen, Matti Pellonpää, Nicky Tesco, Jim Jarmusch.* The uproarious follow-up to *Ariel* is

a rollicking road movie that features a grievously untalented and outrageously pompadoured Siberian rock band the Leningrad Cowboys setting out for America where, as their manager puts it, "people will swallow any kind of shit." Endless pitfalls and bad-luck streaks keep the protagonists on the shitty end of the stick throughout the entire film, with some shining moments including the death of their bass player and the Cowboys' purchase of a used car from none other than Jim Jarmusch. This Eastern European *Blues Brothers* homage was marketed to be director Kaurismäki's crossover film for American audiences, and though world renown was not in the cards, the result is a hilarious, light, and engaging entry in the director's filmography. —*Z. C.*

MAN WITHOUT A PAST, THE L: DIRECTORS/KAURISMÄKI, AKI (2002) 97M D: Aki Kaurismäki. *Juhani Niemela, Kati Outinen, Markku Peltola, Sakari Kuosmanen, Annikki Tahti.* With a deeply satisfying blend of blunt humor and underplayed compassion, *The Man Without a Past* tells the story of a welder, traveling on business, who is beaten by thugs and left for dead. Miraculously he survives, but his memory has vanished. He can still speak, cook, drive, and tie his shoes—but he doesn't know his name, where he came from, or what he did for a living. Our resourceful nameless protagonist rents a derelict shipping container to live in, plants some potatoes, and fixes up an abandoned

smoking population drinks to escape their dull, lonely lives and free themselves from social restraints. It's the perfect crucible for Kaurismäki's brand of existential slapstick.

From *Shadows in Paradise* (1986), a story of numb service-industry survivors (played by Kaurismäki favorites Matti Pellonpää and Kati Outinen) who stumble through a relationship without ever losing their hang-dog expression, Kaurismäki proved himself a master of simple, affectionate, minimalist portraits with little dialogue and plenty of wry, dry humor. Along the way he dabbled in road movies (*Leningrad Cowboys Go America* [1989], a back-roads rock-and-roll odyssey through U.S. bars and honkytonks), crime goofs (*Ariel* [1988], about an unemployed Laplander who hits Helsinki with nothing but hope and a Cadillac convertible with a stubborn roof, then falls into petty crime), and even a silent tragedy (*Juha* [1999], a D. W. Griffith–style modern silent melo-

drama shot through with Kaurismäki's off-beat humor). And then there's Kaurismäki's darkest comedy, *The Match Factory Girl* (1990), where a drab, dour Kati Outinen revenges herself on the cruel world in a hilariously bleak plot that holds out no hope for her future.

Kaurismäki's masterpieces remain *The Man Without a Past* and *Drifting Clouds* (1996), his tender tale of middle-class husband-and-wife heroes who struggle to find work during the countrywide unemployment of 1996 but are repeatedly stymied by corruption, opportunism, and exploitation. The blank faces of Kaurismäki's early films were just another comic effect, a deadpan reaction to the absurdities of the universe, but here his actors stiffen with determination, fall with failure, and glow with success, all with just a flicker across their weary, beaten, but unbowed faces.

—*Sean Axmaker*

---

jukebox. Though pleased with this simple life, he must find work—a formidable challenge with no name, much less a résumé. With a deep respect for the human capacity for generosity (as well as a bemusement with the human capacity for greed), this film carves out a unique place for itself in the cinema, yet feels very much like a particularly superb Hollywood classic. —*C. B.*

MATCH FACTORY GIRL L: DIRECTORS/KAURISMÄKI, AKI (1989) 70M D: Aki Kaurismäki. *Kati Outinen.* Iris (Outinen) is the anti-Amélie in this jet-black comedy. As the title suggests, she works a menial job in a factory and lives with conservative and television-numbed parents. Despite painful shyness and a plainness bordering on grotesque, she goes looking for love each weekend at a local dance hall. Sadly, things aren't easy for Iris. Suffering after excessive abuse from a disinterested love interest, a disinterested family, and a disinterested world, she finally turns to rat poison. Kaurismäki's style favors muted acting, minimal dialogue, and a casual pace. This style works all too well alongside the monotony of the film's cruelty, and the audience earns the right to laugh after its capacity for empathy is completely exhausted. Kaurismäki has made better films, but none with such a rarefied worldview. —*C. B.*

TAKE CARE OF YOUR SCARF, TATJANA L: DIRECTORS/ KAURISMÄKI, AKI (1994) 62M D: Aki Kaurismäki. *Kirsi Tykkyläinen, Mato Valtonen, Matti Pellonpää, Kati Outinen.* Two guys in a vintage American car (with a car stereo that only plays 45s!) hit the road, searching for adventure. Valto (Valtonen) drinks coffee nonstop (even installing an instant-coffee maker on his dashboard), while Reino (Pellonpää) guzzles vodka like it's water—details that serve as the source of many recurring jokes. The two would-be badasses pick up a pair of hitchhikers, Claudia (Tykkyläinen) and Tatjana (Outinen), and the foursome quickly sifts into couples. Unfortunately, neither Reino nor Valto have the confidence to properly play their rock-and-roll tough guy roles, and the seemingly inevitable love scenes continually end in awkward silence. With a peculiar nostalgia for outmoded American culture and a warm camaraderie for its socially impotent protagonists, this is one of the best films Kaurismäki made. Often viewed without English subtitles, this is such a visually driven film that dialogue isn't necessary to understand what's going on. —*C. B.*

STREETCAR NAMED DESIRE L: DIRECTORS/KAZAN, ELIA (1951) 122M D: Elia Kazan. *Marlon Brando, Kim Hunter, Vivien Leigh, Karl Malden, Rudy Bond.* In one of his most infamous roles, Brando plays Stanley, the aggressive, bullheaded husband to Stella (Hunter). As if their marriage wasn't already poised to explode, Stella's neurotic sis-

Abbas Kiarostami

The art of Abbas Kiarostami is the art of looking, of seeing. In film after film we watch the landscape change through the window of a moving car, the bustle of life play out on the fringes of action. Most important, we watch the person emerge from underneath the character. Kiarostami's films have only the barest of plots, and the best of his work contains only a sliver of a story, by the standards of Western cinema. That's merely an illusion, though, for his cinema is rich in stories—some only touched upon, others simply hinted at, but all of them vital.

Born in 1940 in Tehran, Kiarostami started making films in 1970, although his career consisted largely of shorts and educational documentaries until *Where Is the Friend's Home* (1987), the story of a schoolboy who discovers that he has accidentally taken home his pal's notebook, then travels to a nearby village (against the express orders of his mother) to return it. A simple story of children, like so many of the Iranian films made in the years after the revolution, the film avoids politics but creates a vivid panorama of life as it is lived in Iran. Like his subsequent films, it is cast with nonprofessionals. The acting is not really realistic; rather, it is akin to

---

ter Blanche du Bois (Leigh) imposes on their hospitality for several nights. Stanley's contempt for his sister-in-law makes for some pretty impressive fireworks. Despite being toned down from the original 1947 Pulitzer Prize–winning Tennessee Williams play, this film earned quite a number of awards including Oscars for Leigh, Hunter, and Malden. —*N. J.*

GENERAL, THE L: DIRECTORS/KEATON, BUSTER (1927) 75M D: Buster Keaton. *Buster Keaton.* Keaton believes in doing the "right thing," by gum. In this case that involves enlisting in an army for which he is ineligible, going behind enemy lines during the Civil War, getting back his stolen train *and* his girl, and completing these tasks with the integrity and precise comic timing that have become his trademarks. —*M. S.*

NAVIGATOR, THE L: DIRECTORS/KEATON, BUSTER (1924) 59M D: Donald Crisp, Buster Keaton. *Buster Keaton, Kathryn McGuire.* Keaton has a knack for turning simple sight gags into a modern form of visual poetry. A rich kid (Keaton) drives his limousine to the house of his gal (McGuire). But the house is across the street, so the car simply turns a U and Keaton gets out. Comment on the rich lifestyle aside, Keaton the director composes the sequence in clean lines, cutting space into flat patterns that rotate at will as if space itself is a machine. It's the same when the rich kid and his gal are on her father's ship adrift at sea, but they can't find each other. She trots along the running board of the upper deck, he the lower, both tracing patterns in space. Keaton is the first filmmaker (followed by Sternberg,

Lang, Lubitsch, and Hawks) to see that empty space has an emotional architecture and lines of "navigation" that clean camera work and moving bodies can sculpt out for you. And humor is an excellent eye through which to see it. —*J. C.*

SHERLOCK JR. L: DIRECTORS/KEATON, BUSTER (1924) 60M D: Buster Keaton, Roscoe Arbuckle *Erwin Connelly, Joe Keaton, Kathryn Maguire, Buster Keaton.* Not to be highfalutin about it, but *Sherlock Jr.* is simply one of those films that defines cinema. Keaton, the projectionist in a small-town movie theater, is falsely convicted of a petty crime and his girlfriend's father forbids him to come around anymore. Reporting for work, the young man falls asleep on his projectionist's stool, whereupon his shade traipses down the aisle of the theater, sits alongside the proscenium watching the movie action, then steps *into* the picture about the time the characters on-screen have changed into the characters in his own personal melodrama. Keaton plays Sherlock Jr. of course, the world's greatest detective and just the man to solve the "case." The lyric possibilities of a dream narrative and the heightened dynamics of a film-within-a-film combine to grant director Keaton full license to push the surrealist envelope—which he does by deconstructing the very logic of editing and mise-en-scène. The visual integrity of the gags is mind-boggling. —*R. T. J.*

STEAMBOAT BILL JR. L: DIRECTORS/KEATON, BUSTER (1928) 71M D: Buster Keaton (uncredited) *Marion Byron, Ernest Torrence, Buster Keaton.* The last film Keaton made before the director-star's personal production company was dissolved and

watching real people "play" themselves in a documentary: so aware of the camera that they perform to it.

Kiarostami's style only became more complex and rich with his following films. In *Close-Up* (1990), the true story of an unemployed, movie-mad printer arrested for impersonating the famous film director Mohsen Makhmalbaf, he re-created the event with the actual participants playing fictionalized re-creations of themselves. The seeming simplicity of technique gives way to a remarkable complexity that he pushes further with *Life and Nothing More . . .* (1992), about a director and his young son who return to Koker (the setting of *Where Is the Friend's Home*) in the wake of the devastating 1990 earthquake, and *Through the Olive Trees* (1995), a fictional drama about

the making of *Life and Nothing More . . . .*

Kiarostami's best-known film is *A Taste of Cherry* (1997), which won the Palme d'Or at Cannes. His meandering drama of a man who drives around the hills outside Tehran looking to hire someone to help him commit suicide evolves from a simplistic tableau into a profound portrait of the human spirit in all its desperation and dignity. The same themes reverberate throughout *The Wind Will Carry Us* (1999), which is similarly sensitive to the rhythms of people, but is also permeated with a dry, deft humor.

"We can never get close to the truth except through lying," maintains Kiarostami, and in his multifaceted layering of reality and fiction, he comes closer than any other director to revealing the truth of the human soul.   —*Sean Axmaker*

---

the star himself indentured to the MGM factory, *Steamboat Bill Jr.* is also arguably the last Keaton masterpiece. Fittingly, the great, you-have-to-believe-your-eyes climax—a cyclone hitting a riverside town—is a throwback to the infant Buster's own legendary encounter with a cyclone that plucked him out of his vaudevillian parents' rented room and plunked him down in the middle of a Midwestern street. The extraordinary comic/spectacular images and events of this sequence—entirely realized in integral camera setups from which Keaton was lucky to escape alive—are still being studied and stolen, but never bettered, by latter-day filmmakers. —*R. T. J.*

CLOSE-UP L: DIRECTORS/KIAROSTAMI, ABBAS (1990) 100M D: Abbas Kiarostami. *Ali Sabzian, Hossein Sabzian, Mohsen Makhmalbaf.* Kiarostami merges fact and fiction into an inquiry of the very nature of cinematic representation. In 1989 in Tehran, a movie-mad young man was arrested for impersonating the famous film director Makhmalbaf after he hooked a family into his fantasy. Kiarostami read about the story in the papers and enlisted Sabzian and the Ahankah family to play themselves in a dramatic re-creation. Strewn through the story are documentary recordings of the actual trial, a series of on-camera interviews, and a meandering survey of life on the fringes of the story (has a director ever recorded a tin can kicked down a street with such fascinated intensity?). All of this blurs the boundaries between documentary and deconstruction, which finally merge into a stunning mix of contrivance, intimacy, distance, and dramatic closure. In the final

scene, questions of performance and spontaneous action are tossed to the wind in a moment of emotional power. What is it about Iranian cinema that inspires such resonant, devastating, and defining final images? —*S. A.*

LIFE AND NOTHING MORE. . . L: DIRECTORS/KIAROSTAMI, ABBAS (1992) 91M D: Abbas Kiarostami. *Farhad Kheradmand, Puya Pievar.* In 1990 a catastrophic earthquake killed more than 50,000 people in northern Iran (20,000 of them children), including the inhabitants of Koker, a rural village where Kiarostami shot an earlier film (*Where Is My Friend's Home?*). Hoping to learn the fates of the young actors of that film, Kiarostami and his son took a life-changing trip to Koker. Five months later Kiarostami returned with a film crew to fictionalize his previous trip, and this film is the result. Interestingly mixing actors (playing himself and his son) with the real-life survivors in Koker, the film allows the personality and narrative structure of fiction, but captures the unsentimental authenticity of documentary. Although *Close-up* was Kiarostami's first "mature" work, *Life and Nothing More. . .* initiates the trademark style Kiarostami is most famous for—a rich, complex, neorealistic aesthetic with tendencies to self-reference, narrative ellipsis, creative juxtaposition of sound and vision, and an unrelenting habit of setting long dialogues inside automobiles. —*C. B.*

TASTE OF CHERRY L: DIRECTORS/KIAROSTAMI, ABBAS (1997) 99M D: Abbas Kiarostami. *Afhshin Khorshid Bakhtari, Homayoun Ershadi, Abdolhossein Bagheri, Mir Hossain Noori, Safir Ali Moradi.* Middle-aged

Mr. Badii searches the outskirts of Tehran to hire someone for a job. After some time it's revealed that Badii plans to commit suicide and needs someone to bury him or, should he fail, help him from the grave he's dug himself. One at a time, he pleads with three men in long conversations inside his ever-moving car. An aesthetic wonder and a rich exploration of the will to live, *Taste of Cherry* tied for top prize at 1997's Cannes Film Festival—a matter of some controversy. Roger Ebert denounced the film as not only boring but "an emperor without any clothes," yet many called it a masterpiece. "We are living in the Age of Kiarostami," proclaimed critic Phillip Lopate, who went on to name Kiarostami "the most important filmmaker working today." Central in this debate is the film's unexpected ending, which I find absolutely exhilarating. —*C. B.*

There's a guy who works here who will never shut the hell up about how wonderful this movie is, proclaiming the brilliance of Kiarostami and the profound allusions to the death of film buried within the picture. What the hell he was talking about I still haven't figured out. I have henceforth become wary of listening to any recommendations from people who collect E.T. stuffed animals. Stay away from these people. —*A. T.*

TEN L: DIRECTORS/KIAROSTAMI, ABBAS (2002) 92M D: Abbas Kiarostami. *Mania Akbari, Amin Maher*. Ten is divided into ten segments, each a conversation between a fashionable Tehran woman (divorced and recently remarried) and others, set entirely inside her moving car. Several of these discussions are with her incensed pre-adolescent son, Amin. Some are with a young girl awaiting a marriage proposal from a long-term boyfriend. Others are with an old woman on her way to a mosque, an obnoxiously giggly prostitute, and the driver's sister. It is a calm slice-of-life portrait of Iranian sexual politics from the cinema's most fascinating humanist. Kiarostami satisfies his desire for "the disappearance of direction" with this film of uncertain (irrelevant?) chronology, in which conflict doesn't generate plot. Using improvised dialogue, and restricting shooting to two dashboard-mounted digital video cameras (additionally, Kiarostami was absent during shoots), *Ten* leaps some formidable formal hurdles on the way to being Kiarostami's most rigorously conceptual project to date. —*C. B.*

THROUGH THE OLIVE TREES L: DIRECTORS/KIAROSTAMI, ABBAS (1994) 99M D: Abbas Kiarostami. *Hossein Rezai, Mohammad-Ali Keshavarz, Zarifeh Shiva, Tahereh Ladanian*. Where *Life and Nothing More* fictionalized Kiarostami's actual search for the stars of *Where Is My Friend's Home?*, this film tells a made-up story about the *Life and Nothing More* shoot. While walking a tightrope stretched between representation and reenactment, the plot centers on Hossein, cast for a part in *Life*, whose unwavering adoration for disinterested costar

Tahereh plagues the production. Working as emissaries between them, Kiarostami (played by Keshavarz) and assistant Mrs. Shiva attempt to negotiate a working relationship for their actors and get on with the filming. Complicated as it sounds, Kiarostami sticks to what he describes as "scenes in which there was 'nothing happening.'" As the movie progresses, Kiarostami critiques his own simplistic coloring of rural populations, pulling off some exquisitely inventive camera work while he's at it. Typically, Kiarostami ends the film unresolved and unclear, inviting us, he says, to "furnish the meaning" with our own imagination. —*C. B.*

WHERE IS MY FRIEND'S HOME? L: DIRECTORS/ KIAROSTAMI, ABBAS (1987) 83M D: Abbas Kiarostami. *Ahmed Ahmed Poor, Babek Ahmed Poor, Kheda Barech Defai, Aruna Irani*. Kiarostami's first and most conventional fictional feature is the tale of a schoolboy (Poor) who discovers he's accidentally taken home his pal's notebook and travels to a nearby village (against the express orders of his mother, Irani) to return it. Impulsive, willful, stubborn, and shy, his face tightens in anxiety as he's confronted, berated, and ignored by adults on his mission of honor. Kiarostami's style is forged with this delicate tale. The performances by his cast of nonprofessionals are akin to watching real people "play" themselves in a documentary, so aware of the camera that they perform to it. As with Kiarostami's best films, it concludes with simple, silent open-ended scene, a sublime moment of human kindness and joy. The first of his Earthquake Trilogy, the characters and village are revisited (in a fashion) in *Life and Nothing More*. —*S. A.*

WIND WILL CARRY US, THE L: DIRECTORS/KIAROSTAMI, ABBAS (1999) 118M D: Abbas Kiarostami. *Behzad Dourani*. An easygoing urban engineer (Dourani, the only professional actor in the cast) comes to a rural village to wait for a funeral ceremony of a dying woman and ends up confronting his own mixed motives and selfish sense of superiority. Kiarostami has become a kind of figurehead in the West for Iranian cinema. His rigorous style has always been sensitive to the rhythms of people and the details of day-to-day existence, and like his best films this unfolds with a remarkable fidelity to (or a convincing facsimile of) real time. What may be surprising to fans of his films is the dry humor that permeates the picture. To Western eyes the pace may seem glacial, yet it allows Kiarostami to explore the spaces between words and the landscape that envelopes his characters' lives. The culmination of such astounding visions is a celebration of the human spirit nothing short of sublime. —*S. A.*

CAMERA BUFF L: DIRECTORS/KIESLOWSKI, KRZYSZTOF (1979) 112M D: Krzysztof Kieslowski. *Jerzy Nowak, Malgorzata Zabkowska, Jerzy Stuhr*. Kieslowski's satirical second feature concerns Filip (Stuhr), who buys an 8 mm camera to capture his new-born daughter on film. As it grows from a hobby to a full-blown preoccupation, Filip's experiments with his new toy produce a prize-winning documentary. Yet his new passion brings him as much trouble as good, highlighted in a sequence in which he films his own hand as his wife, less enthusiastic about the camera's new role in their lives, walks out on him. *Camera Buff* goes beyond the obvious theme of Polish censorship (though it does cover plenty of that), creating a rich portrait of a Stan Brakhage–esque artist whose zealous efforts to satisfy experiential and creative impulses eclipse consideration of the ramifications of his actions on himself and those around him. —*C. B.*

DECALOGUE, THE L: DIRECTORS/KIESLOWSKI, KRZYSZTOF
(1987) 575M D: Krzysztof Kieslowski. *Wojciech Klata, Olgierd Lukaszewicz, Grazyna Szapolowska, Olaf Lubaszenko, Henryk Baranowski, Krystyna Janda.* Kieslowski will remain best known for his lush, plush art-house *Three Colors* trilogy, a celebration of grand emotions from beautiful people, but this ten-part television event is arguably his masterwork: a delicate, intimate epic of tragedy and triumph among the emotionally battered proletariat of a dreary Warsaw apartment complex. The ten stories inspired by the Ten Commandments and loosely connected by place and time are not Sunday-school fables illustrating simplistic moral lessons—the connections to the individual Commandments are not always obvious—but powerful, profound stories of love and loss, faith and fear. Each hour-long drama stands on its own as a fully conceived film. The tales range from the ethereal and elusive to the ambitious and devastating. A web of associations pulls the individual episodes into the fabric of the whole: characters pass through other stories, sometimes only briefly, and themes reverberate through the series. Kieslowski explores ordinary people flailing through inner torments, hard decisions, and shattering revelations, grounding his stories in the faces of his deeply human characters. It's ultimately a personal spiritual investigation into the soul of man and a beautiful, devastating, and profound work of art. —*S. A.*

BARRY LYNDON L: DIRECTORS/KUBRICK, STANLEY (1975)
185M D: Stanley Kubrick. *Ryan O'Neal, Hardy Kruger, Marisa Berenson, Patrick Magee.* Based on the novel by William Makepeace Thackeray, this movie follows the life of Redmond Barry (O'Neal), a gambler in the eighteenth century who moves to England and deftly works his way up the social ladder with his personality, sexuality, and cunning. What really steals this show is the photography. In order to capture the intimacy of candlelit interiors of the time, Kubrick used high-speed Zeiss lenses in such a way that brilliant color images could be filmed in actual candlelight. Sumptuous in every detail, *Barry*

Lyndon is the kind of film you can lose yourself in. —*N. J.*

CLOCKWORK ORANGE, A L: DIRECTORS/KUBRICK, STANLEY
(1971) 137M D: Stanley Kubrick. *Malcolm McDowell, Patrick Magee, Michael Bates, Warren Clarke.* Set in a near-future England, this unsettling film concerns a nasty group of friends whose primary source of amusement is violence. McDowell plays the young leader of this group who one night leads his friends into a rich house and brutally rapes and murders the wife of the owner. He's is caught and put through experimental reprogramming, with very mixed consequences. This strikingly imaginative film is based on the curious novel by Anthony Burgess, and Kubrick's adaptation makes the most of the material with vividly sarcastic narrations by the main character. Music often plays a significant role in Kubrick's films and here he makes use of Wendy Carlos (formerly Walter Carlos), whose electronic emulations of Beethoven tinge the film with a humorous pretext. —*N. J.*

DR. STRANGELOVE OR HOW I LEARNED TO STOP WORRYING AND LOVE THE BOMB L: DIRECTORS/KUBRICK, STANLEY (1964) 93M D: Stanley Kubrick. *Slim Pickens, Peter Sellers, George C. Scott, Keenan Wynn, James Earl Jones, Sterling Hayden.* I don't think it would be possible to make a comedy better than this one—a film that is hilariously-laugh-out-loud funny no matter how many times you watch it, and at the same time makes satirical points that get eerily more relevant as our society "progresses" technologically. We still have General Rippers, General Turgidsons, and Dr. Strangeloves—they are in the news developing smaller nuclear weapons, setting up shadow governments, proposing ideas like Total Information Awareness or the terror futures market. So far they have managed to avoid nuclear holocaust, so they've had time to get pardoned for their war crimes, make millions consulting for corporations, and appear as reliable experts on the news. Even a serious drama that accurately portrays the nightmarish, suicidal lunacy of the people in power would lead to fits of angry, incredulous laughter—that's why *Dr. Strangelove* can make you giggle and give you nightmares at the same time. —*B. T.*

EYES WIDE SHUT L: DIRECTORS/KUBRICK, STANLEY (1999)
159M D: Stanley Kubrick. *Tom Cruise, Nicole Kidman, Todd Field, Leelee Sobieski.* Visually, sonically, and emotionally, *Eyes Wide Shut* seems to exist outside the boundary of time. Neither of the two main characters actually change, but the amorphous drama that ensues brings about deep revelations within each of them. The story (adapted from Authur Schnitzler's novella *Dream Story*) concerns a young well-to-do couple (Cruise and Kidman) who have a typical bedroom spat, sending the husband out to look for a little action. The action he finds is a bizarre psycho-

sexual masquerade cult complete with a sacrificial virgin. Further investigation reveals that several influential men of his social strata are involved, and this confused husband discovers that he is in an intractable position. The simple two-note theme sets the mood of boredom every bit as much as it does the mood of painful inevitability. As Kubrick's last film, *Eyes Wide Shut* is entirely appropriate—a career that blossomed with antiwar themes and blasted off into space ultimately landed in the deepest cellars of the human soul. —*N.J.*

FULL METAL JACKET L: DIRECTORS/KUBRICK, STANLEY (1987) 116M D: Stanley Kubrick. *Matthew Modine, Vincent D'Onofrio, R. Lee Ermey, Adam Baldwin, Arliss Howard.* This is a two-part antiwar epic by the master of antiwar films. The first part concerns boot camp where a group of young men are quite eager to fight the Vietnam war. Ermey is remarkable as the drill sergeant who drives an emotionally imbalanced recruit a little too far. The second part quickly whisks the young men to Vietnam, where their preconceptions of war are further shattered as their friends die in action and their orders don't always make sense. Instead of using film as the pedestal on which to place war heroes or great victories, Kubrick uses film as a magnifying glass on the unsavory complexities of war. —*N.J.*

KILLING, THE L: DIRECTORS/KUBRICK, STANLEY (1956) 83M D: Stanley Kubrick. *Coleen Gray, Elisha Cook Jr., Jay C. Flippen, Timothy Carey, Sterling Hayden, Marie Windsor.* There is much debate over which pictures comprise and define the film noir genre, but it's unlikely that anyone denies *The Killing*'s place at the top of the criminal cinema heap. Directed by twenty-eight-year-old Kubrick in 1956, the film paints a brutal portrait of the "perfect" heist. When coordinating con Hayden's complex plan starts hitting walls, fury and vengeance take the stage. Every ingredient needed for ultimate dark city drama is here in spades, and the movie tears through fisticuffs, infidelity, and blazing bullets with animalistic savagery. Even minor roles are handled with complete mastery by character actor luminaries like Cook Jr. and the immortal Carey. A brilliant plot executed by a true filmmaking legend, *The Killing* cannot be recommended highly enough. If you're still not sold, the tough-as-nails dialogue was provided by legendary hard-boiled novelist Jim Thompson. —*Z.C.*

LOLITA (1962) L: DIRECTORS/KUBRICK, STANLEY (1962) 152M D: Stanley Kubrick. *Sue Lyon, Peter Sellers, Shelley Winters, James Mason.* Still controversial more than forty years after its release, Kubrick's *Lolita* is a definitive example of his early work. Choosing to take a less lurid turn with the material, Kubrick and screenwriter Nabokov created a complex, tortured psychological romance. Humbert Humbert (Mason) rents a room from Charlotte (Winters) and soon encounters her willful young daughter, Lolita. Unable to remove the girl from his mind, Humbert finds himself becoming "closer" to Charlotte, if only to peer that much more clearly into her daughter's world. As expected, things go from bad to worse. Mason's depiction of a rationalizing obsessive pedophile should go down in the history books as one of the all-time classic portrayals of self-destruction. Sellers also turns in two brilliantly performed roles. *Lolita* is a gripping and perfectly realized interpretation of the classic novel. —*Z.C.*

PATHS OF GLORY L: DIRECTORS/KUBRICK, STANLEY (1957) 86M D: Stanley Kubrick. *Kirk Douglas, Timothy Carey, Adolphe Menjou.* Well before the release of *Dr. Strangelove,* Kubrick released this blistering antiwar film, arguably the finest since *All Quiet on the Western Front.* Douglas plays a French officer in WWI who is given a command to charge a cliff heavily fortified with German machine guns. Heavy casualties are inevitable, and scapegoats are chosen to be tried and executed for cowardice—a malevolent strategy that Douglas passionately opposes. Based on the novel by Humphrey Cobb. —*N.J.*

SHINING, THE L: DIRECTORS/KUBRICK, STANLEY (1980) 146M D: Stanley Kubrick. *Jack Nicholson, Scatman Crothers, Danny Lloyd, Shelley Duvall.* To hell with the Stephen King purists (Stephen King included), or the people who say Nicholson is too over-the-top in the beginning to go crazy later on. This is one of the scariest movies ever. Not because of Nicholson's maniacal grin, or the corpse in the bathtub, or the waves of blood lapping out of the elevator, or even those creepy twins in the hallway. It's all about that big empty hotel and the way the all-seeing eye of Kubrick's camera looms slowly through its long, quiet hallways. It doesn't matter what's around the corner or on the other side of the wall, all that matters is you know it's there and you won't see it. And it doesn't hurt that Nicholson has hundreds of pages of the same phrase typed thousands of times, or that Kubrick made some poor schmo type it for real. If I got holed up in that hotel for a while I'd probably get just as unhinged as Nicholson or Kubrick. —*B.T.*

SPARTACUS L: DIRECTORS/KUBRICK, STANLEY (1960) 196M D: Stanley Kubrick. *Lawrence Olivier, Jean Simmons, Peter Ustinov, Charles Laughton, Tony Curtis, Kirk Douglas.* This epic film concerning a renegade gladiator who escapes captivity and builds his own army to fight the Roman Empire is based on a true and very intriguing story. Douglas plays Spartacus, an ordinary slave who is selected to be trained as a gladiator, fighting to the death in the Coliseum as entertainment for Julius Caesar. Through vivid and suspenseful melees, Spartacus rises to the status of celebrity while plotting a means to escape. With a fine cast supported by a classic script and the unforgettable fight sequences (not to mention the phenomenal photography), Kubrick makes this one of the finest of the grand epics. —*N. J.*

2001: A SPACE ODYSSEY L: DIRECTORS/KUBRICK, STANLEY (1968) 139M D: Stanley Kubrick. *Keir Dullea, Gary Lockwood, William Sylvester, Daniel Richter, Douglas Rain.*

Many film nerds consider Kubrick a god, and here he tells the story from the point of view of God looking down on the puny humans doing their silly human business. Early on there is the famous moment when an ape man angrily tosses a bone in the air and it dissolves to a shot of a similarly shaped space station. That may be the greatest edit in the history of cinema, summing up millions of years of human progress in a single cut. This is a monumental cinematic achievement that uses groundbreaking special effects and an unforgettable classical soundtrack to drive home a humbling, detached view of humanity and technology that will haunt you for a long time afterward. Maybe Pauline Kael was wrong when she called *2001* "the biggest amateur movie of them all." —*B. T.*

DERSU UZALA L: DIRECTORS/KUROSAWA, AKIRA (1975) 140M D: Akira Kurosawa. *Maxim Munzuk, Yuri Solomin.*

No other filmmaker translated the physicality of the world into moving images and textures as forcefully as Kurosawa. If light and shadow could be lifted in the hand, we might remove any frame-panel from a Kurosawa movie and expect it to stand with the absoluteness of a wall. When the director took his cameras into the vastness of the great Siberian forest, the Ussuri Taiga, he returned with a unique epic. One cannot speak of the locations where the film drama takes place; the wild mountain country pervades the mood and method of Kurosawa's narrative, and is inextricably bound up with any "meaning" one might posit. The story is simplicity itself, the account of the relationship between an early twentieth-century Russian surveyor (Solomin) and the Mongol hunter (Munzuk) who lends his name to the film. There is no saying whether Kurosawa has taken us to one of the last unknown places on Earth, where the elements take on new forms and obey unfamiliar laws, or whether it is the director's vision that makes us see the world that way. We see men boat among the branches of a tree, snow, and the land itself, and that it is possible to walk on a lake of fire. —*R. T. J.*

DREAMS L: DIRECTORS/KUROSAWA, AKIRA (1990) 119M D: Akira Kurosawa. *Martin Scorsese, Akira Terao, Chosuke Ikariya.*

Based on eight of Kurosawa'a own dreams, this film features beautiful, poignant stories dealing with various human struggles and fears and our relation to nature. Kurosawa had long established himself as a vivid storyteller by the time he released this film, but this is by far the most personal to date: "Sunshine Through the Rain," a small child witnesses the forbidden wedding procession of the fox. "The Peach Orchard," a young boy sees the spirits of a clear-cut peach orchard. "The Blizzard," mountaineers are saved from a blizzard by a strange mountain spirit. "The Tunnel," a man encounters the ghosts of an army platoon. "Crows," an artist enters the world of Vincent van Gogh's paintings (and a great cameo by Martin Scorsese). "Mount Fuji in Red," the great mountain has blown its top, or has it? "The Weeping Demon," a vision of a post-nuclear world populated by radiated deformed humans. "Village of the Watermills," a portrait of a village whose people who live in harmony with nature. Kurosawa really captures the feeling of his dreams with an emotional and unique visual style. Compassion shines through the sometimes nightmarish fantastic visions, revealing the folly of human nature. —*B. W.*

HIDDEN FORTRESS, THE L: DIRECTORS/KUROSAWA, AKIRA (1958) 139M D: Akira Kurosawa. *Misa Uehara, Minoru Chiaki, Toshirô Mifune.*

Flashing swords, thundering horses, giant battles, and intimate duels. Kurosawa melds Western fairy-tale adventure with Japanese history for this pre–Samurai era classic of a young princess and a determined general (the gruff, ruthless, and often comically exasperated Mifune) trying to escape from behind enemy lines with a fortune in royal gold. Long recognized as a primary inspiration for *Star Wars* (among other things, the bickering peasants who wander into the odyssey inspired R2D2 and C-3PO), it's Kurosawa's most purely entertaining film, one of his biggest hits, and his first go at the widescreen format. He proves to be a master at it, dynamically spreading his compositions out to an epic scope and boldly setting his cascade of sharp action scenes against a magnificent landscape. —*S. A.*

IKIRU L: DIRECTORS/KUROSAWA, AKIRA (1952) 141M D: Akira Kurosawa. *Takashi Shimura, Shinichi Himori, Haruo Tanaka, Nobuo Kaneko.*

An executive at a bank gets some bad news from his doctor: he has cancer, and less than a year left to live. He returns to work wondering what he has accomplished with his life and comes up with very little. It's while he is sitting in a park absorbed in this existential dilemma that he meets a young lady who befriends him. Over the course of just a few days she opens his eyes, allowing him to have the one thing he never really had: Ikiru, which means "to live." This is a remarkably deep and touching story that could make a Kurosawa fan of nearly anyone. —*N. J.*

MADADAYO L: DIRECTORS/KUROSAWA, AKIRA (1993) 134M D: Akira Kurosawa. *Tatsuo Matsumura, Hisashi Igawa, Kyôko Kagawa.*

Kurosawa's last film is a gentle, sweet story of a retired professor and his devoted students, who honor him annually in sake-soaked birthday parties. It's a meandering film with a quietly restrained quality, content simply to enjoy the good humor and amiable company as the professor answers their repeated queries if he's ready to retire with a phrase from a child's game: "Madadayo" ("not yet"). Kurosawa captures the reflective spirit one has come to expect in the twilight works of great artists, yet impishly declares that he's not ready to give it up. Sadly, he died two years later. —*S. A.*

RAN L: DIRECTORS/KUROSAWA, AKIRA (1985) 160M D: Akira Kurosawa. *Tatsuya Nakadai, Mieko Harada, Akira Terao, Jinpachi Nezu.* Ran, Kurosawa's final masterpiece, isn't filmed Shakespeare but Shakespearean film. King Lear has been reimagined in film language intrinsic to the director's vision of the world and its ways. "Ran" translates as "chaos," but the aesthetic order that defines that chaos is absolute. For ten years, Kurosawa painted every tower, every gate, every screened chamber and sweep of withered plain; nearly blind by the time he made the movie, he had already imposed his vision on it. Though an exemplary "old man's film," Ran surges and sears with the vitality of a breakthrough work. The very elements seem to become one with the drama of an old king abdicating his throne, then finding himself a homeless ghost in his own land. Even a horrific, spectacular battle scene appears to resolve into an expression of the wind that is such a visible and audible presence throughout the film: a streaming rush of soldiers and arrows and smoke. Nakadai (the strutting young villain of Yojimbo and Sanjuro) makes the film's Lear both hieratic and full-blooded, a soul harrowed by the relentless evidence of his own culpability in the debt his whole bloodline and land must pay. —*R. T. J.*

RASHOMON L: DIRECTORS/KUROSAWA, AKIRA (1950) 88M D: Akira Kurosawa. *Minoru Chiaki, Takashi Shimura, Machiko Kyo, Toshirô Mifune, Masayuki Mori.* Rashomon teaches us that the lie is often in the eye of the beholder. In one of world cinema's most admired and influential films, the camera records exactly what Kurosawa wants it to, and nothing it records is true. The wonder of Rashomon is that nothing it shows us is a lie, either. Three men, sheltering in a temple, discuss a bewildering case: A samurai (Mori) is dead. His wife (Kyo) has been raped. A bandit (Mifune) stands accused. We see scenes from the bandit's trial where each participant testifies. Each believes himself to be responsible for the death of the samurai, and in unreliable flashbacks we learn that each account is true. This means, of course, that each account is also a lie. Kurosawa's genius—helped by the breathtaking black-and-white cinematography of Kazuo Miyagawa—allows us to experience this insoluble mystery without any sense of frustration. Instead we come away with a greater understanding of the fluidity of truth, and thus a greater understanding of ourselves. —*C. C.*

RED BEARD L: DIRECTORS/KUROSAWA, AKIRA (1965) 185M D: Akira Kurosawa. *Tsutomu Yamazaki, Yuzo Kayama, Toshirô Mifune.* The final collaboration between Kurosawa and Japanese icon Mifune is one of the director's most ambitious, personal, and heartfelt films. Gentle under his gruff hide and bearded face but fierce in the face of greed, selfishness, cruelty, and indifference, Dr. Niide, aka Red Beard (Mifune), is the fighting angel of the slums and the moral bedrock of Kurosawa's world. The three-hour film follows the education of a spoiled, insolent young doctor (Kayama) under his patient tutelage. The upstart initially bristles at his unexpected assignment to the impoverished clinic but is startled out of his complacency when brought face-to-face with poverty. He all but takes over the film in the second half as he nurses a skittish, suspicious twelve-year-old girl back to health. While the script at times offers Psych 101 lectures to unnecessarily naive characters, the sincerity of the performances and Kurosawa's compassion grounds the film in a powerful humanity. —*S. A.*

SEVEN SAMURAI L: DIRECTORS/KUROSAWA, AKIRA (1954) 206M D: Akira Kurosawa. *Takashi Shimura, Toshirô Mifune, Seiji Miyaguchi.* Kurosawa's *Seven Samurai,* featuring the magnificent Mifune, is generally agreed to be one of the greatest films ever produced in Japan. In some circles it is considered the greatest film ever made. By its closing shot, it has conveyed these things: Your talents exist to be exploited by lesser men. Your friends will mock you and die. You will not get the girl. Your heroes will fall. Rice is more important than you. It took more than a year to shoot. Its running time is a beefy 206 minutes. Perhaps that seems inefficient. But how long will it take you to learn these things? —*M. L.*

YOJIMBO L: DIRECTORS/KUROSAWA, AKIRA (1961) 110M D: Akira Kurosawa. *Daisuke Katô, Tatsuya Nakadai, Toshirô Mifune.* A masterless samurai (Mifune) wandering through the late nineteenth century meets a dog outside a small town. In the dog's mouth is a severed human hand. The dog looks pleased—and so should you be with this Kurosawa masterpiece, an exhilarating action movie and a brilliant black comedy in which laughs and death-rattles become indistinguishable from one another. The town is the disputed terrain of two criminal gangs, each as reprehensible and irredeemable as the other. Mifune's scruffy *ronin* takes in the situation, mutters "Better if all these men were dead," and sets about arranging that outcome. If the premise sounds familiar, that's because Sergio Leone stole it for *A Fistful of Dollars* and Walter Hill bought it to remake as *Last Man Standing*—though, in fairness, we've always suspected Kurosawa himself might have profited from seeing Budd Boetticher's 1957 *Buchanan Rides Alone,* and reading of Dashiell Hammett's *Red Harvest.* Yojimbo (meaning "bodyguard") towers over all of them with its patient, masterly pacing; its startling, sometimes surreal use of space-collapsing telephoto cinematography; the stubble-textured black-and-white look and asymmetrical widescreen compositions by Miyagawa; and Mifune's splendid, personal-best performance in the title role. He and Kurosawa reprised the same character in the nearly as good *Sanjuro* the following year. —*R.T.J.*

BLACK CAT, WHITE CAT L: DIRECTORS/KUSTURICA, EMIR
(1998) 135M D: Emir Kursturica. *Bajram Severdzan, Zabit Memedov, Sabri Sulejman.* Kusturica came back from his rather brief retirement (partly in response to controversy over his madcap political satire *Underground*) to create the altogether less weighty *Black Cat, White Cat*. Powered by driving wall-to-wall music, this drunken roundhouse of a screwball comedy throws gangsters and con men, double crosses and debts, and star-crossed lovers caught in the conspiracies together in a tale of postwar Yugoslavia. It's a giddy little ditty set at a barreling pace and enlivened by outrageous imagery (an ever-present pig chowing down on a rusting car, a tree stump that gets up and runs away on two legs). It's like a modern fairy tale of gruff but lovable gangsters, Damon Runyon in Eastern Europe, which at times feels a tad misplaced, but it's so infectious it's hard to get too worked up over it. Overlong but great fun. —*S.A.*

UNDERGROUND (1995) L: DIRECTORS/KUSTURICA, EMIR
(1995) 167M D: Emir Kursturica. *Mirjana Jokovic, Lazar Ristovski, Miki Manojlovic.* Imagine there is a conflict going on and people try to avoid it by living underground. When the conflict is over, the "connector" between the outside world and the underground doesn't notify those who live beyond him. They keep producing armament and practicing for emergency evacuations. They grow old, they eat and dance, and it all happens underground. This film has an incredible soundtrack to it. The representation of chaos through loud sounds and the coexistence of humans and animals is great. This is a triumph in working with human senses. It is an incredible experience. —*D.J.*

WHEN FATHER WAS AWAY ON BUSINESS L: DIRECTORS/
KUSTURICA, EMIR (1985) 136M D: Emir Kursturica. *Mirjana Karanovic, Moreno D'Ebartolli, Miki Manojlovic.* When Father (Manojlovic) told his two sons that he went away on business, he was actually sent to do compulsory work in the mines. The story is narrated by his youngest son, Malik (D'Ebartolli). It's dynamic, humorous, and has the bitter taste of the events that took part during the regime in the former Yugoslavia. The ability to show these events through a child's eyes is Kusturica's triumph. —*D.J.*

GABRIEL OVER THE WHITE HOUSE L: DIRECTORS/
LACAVA, GREGORY (1933) 86M D: Gregory LaCava. *Arthur Byron, Walter Huston, Franchot Tone, Karen Morley.* LaCava's New Deal fantasy is one of the strangest political films of Hollywood's golden age. Corrupt President-elect Huston survives a near-death experience through the intervention of an angel and emerges a changed man, a sort of philosopher king whose methods border on dictatorial militarism. I suppose this is the kind of leader Hitler assumed himself to be, but to Depression-era audiences this benevolent dictatorship must have seemed like an answer to their prayers. In retrospect it's a fascinating little film, almost perverse in its vigilante justice, yet oddly engaging with its unusual romantic triangle (Huston, his aide Tone, and mistress Morley) and surprise ending. Believe me, you've seen nothing like this before. —*S.A.*

MY MAN GODFREY L: DIRECTORS/LACAVA, GREGORY
(1936) 94M D: Gregory LaCava. *William Powell, Carole Lombard, Eugene Pallette, Mischa Auer, Alice Brady.* This top-notch screwball comedy stars Powell as Godfrey, a "forgotten man" from Manhattan's hobo jungle who is picked up by a sweet rich girl (Lombard in one of her finest and most charming performances) as part of a scavenger hunt. Immensely charmed by her new discovery, Lombard offers him the job of butler to her incredibly wealthy and somewhat eccentric Park Avenue family. But nothing is really what it seems as we learn about Godfrey's real identity. The rich are very foolish and the poor very noble in this film, which was a welcomed twist for Depression-era audiences. Featuring marvelous comic support from several character actors, including a hilarious ape impersonation by Auer. —*S.H.*

STAGE DOOR L: DIRECTORS/LACAVA, GREGORY (1937)
92M D: Gregory LaCava. *Ginger Rodgers, Lucillie Ball, Katharine Hepburn.* Witty dialogue, snappy comebacks, and nary a false step! This film is a gem with an amazing cast, great acting, and engaging characters that draw you into the world of women trying to make it in the theater. This is one of my childhood favorites that has endured the test of time. —*M.N.*

FULL CONTACT L: DIRECTORS/LAM, RINGO (1992) 98M
D: Ringo Lam. *Chow Yun Fat, Simon Yam, Anthony Wong.* Chow is a steely, smiling bar bouncer who emerges from a double cross like an avenging ghost, *Point Blank*–style, for his cut (and a little payback) in Lam's sleek, stylish, coldly cruel action classic. Wong plays his weak-willed pal and the magnetic Yam is the narcissistic gang leader who plots Chow's demise. Lam makes a great cinematic counterpart to John Woo—pared down and precise, clearing the frame of the extraneous flourishes that enrich Woo's kinetic action paintings to concentrate on violent conflict mano a mano—and he chills Chow's normally warm

Fritz Lang

Friedrich Christian Anton Lang was born in 1890 in Vienna, the only child of middle-class parents, and studied architecture and art before leaving home at nineteen. After traveling the world by sea, he fought in World War I, was wounded (he lost sight in his right eye), and began writing screenplays while recovering in a military hospital. He sold two scripts to producer/director Joe May, and then was hired by Erich Pommer to write for Decla Studios,

where Lang would later direct his first film. Around this time he also met Thea von Harbou, who became his longtime collaborator and, later, his wife.

The success of his scripts and his work as a director made him a famous German talent and gave him the freedom to choose his own projects. *Der Mure Tod* (1921), an allegorical tragedy, brought him international acclaim. His projects became increasingly ambitious and visually complex, and *M* (1931) was his most challenging to date.

His final German film, *Das Testament des Dr. Mabuse* (1933), was a veiled attack

---

presence to an icy intensity. Extremely violent, and one of the most impressive action films to come out of Hong Kong. —*S.A.*

BIG HEAT, THE L: DIRECTORS/LANG, FRITZ (1953) 89M D: Fritz Lang. *Glenn Ford, Jocelyn Brando, Alexander Scourby, Lee Marvin, Gloria Grahame.* Ford is the bland family-man cop driven over the edge when the mob violently kills his wife in a car bomb meant for him. Grahame costars as the willfully blind gangster's moll scarred to the soul in an even more scalding moment of brutality, and Marvin is memorable as a drawling gunman with a nasty vicious streak. Lang, once the master of grand expressionist scenes, directs with a stripped-down style and a lean narrative drive, turning the anonymous apartments and hotel rooms and generic city streets into a shadowy world of corruption, violence, and psychopathic criminals. He builds a real head of steam as Ford's private vendetta turns the usually stiff actor into a real bastard, brought back to earth only by the kindness and courage of others touched by the same evil. A masterpiece of film noir and one of the great American films. —*S.A.*

BLUE GARDENIA, THE L: DIRECTORS/LANG, FRITZ (1953) 88M D: Fritz Lang. *Ann Sothern, Raymond Burr, Richard Conte, Jeff Donnell, Anne Baxter.* Good-girl Baxter (at her virginal blonde best) enters a nightmare of paranoia when her impulsive date with sleazy masher Burr ends in her blackout and his murder. Lang turns a lurid little tale of LA intrigue (the title itself is a play on the notorious Black Dahlia murder) into an innocent's oppressive ordeal of guilt and fear only intensified by our heroine's foggy recollections. Conte's smarmy newsman is an opportunist whose conniving promises boomerang back and knock him

into perhaps his first ethical dilemma. Lang's low budget shows through in cheap sets and limited locations, but he achieves the seediness the tawdry tale deserves. Nat King Cole appears in the night club scene to croon the film's theme song. —*S.A.*

FURY (1936) L: DIRECTORS/LANG, FRITZ (1936) 94M D: Fritz Lang. *Spencer Tracy, Sylvia Sidney.* When celebrated German filmmaker Lang managed to leave the despotism of Hitler for the freedom of prewar America, the first film he made was a thriller about mob psychology! Tracy plays the perfectly innocent man with a beautiful girlfriend (Sidney) and a full life to look forward to when he is suddenly jailed for a kidnapping and murder he did not commit. When the townspeople hear that a child murderer is behind bars, collective rage builds into the fury of a mob, and in the dark of night they storm the jail. Riots like this were not uncommon after World War I, often concerning race or unions. Like a fantasy, however, this film deviates from how American history tends to play out and gives the innocent man an escape so he can come back and seek revenge. This classic will put you on the edge of your seat. —*N.J.*

M L: DIRECTORS/LANG, FRITZ (1931) 111M D: Fritz Lang. *Ellen Widmann, Inge Landgut, Gustav Grundgens, Otto Wernicke, Peter Lorre.* In this film, an early talkie for Lang and based on a true story, Lorre plays a psychopathic child killer who single-handedly turns law enforcement on its ear. As a growing number of children turn up dead, local police crack down on gambling and organized crime such that an honest criminal can hardly make a living. With both police and underground crime eager to have his head, this miserable antagonist

---

on Nazism and was banned by the newly elected Nazi government. Legend has it that Joseph Goebbels then invited Lang to head the Third Reich film industry (both Goebbels and Hitler were big fans of *Metropolis* and *Die Nibelungen*), but Lang promptly caught the first train to Paris, where he arrived broke and alone. (His wife, whom he subsequently divorced, stayed behind to make films for the Nazis.)

He traveled to Hollywood in 1934 and began a successful American career, continuing to explore the themes he had developed in his German films: corruption in society, law, social justice, the struggle of the individual against fate. "Every serious picture that depicts people today should be a kind of documentary of its time," he once said.

Though at the time Lang's American productions were considered of lesser quality than his German films, a critical reassessment that began in the 1960s discovered a consistency through his Hollywood period and a number of masterpieces: *You Only Live Once, Scarlet Street, Rancho Notorious, The Big Heat.* Stylistically, Lang adapted his Expressionist approach to the Hollywood mode without losing the moody, nightmarish quality of his German films. What he lost in the grandeur and epic scope of his German period, he made up for in the intimacy and paranoia of the American films.
—*Sean Axmaker*

---

is finally caught and meagerly defends himself against a makeshift jury. In many ways this film is groundbreaking for its time. Not only does it take on highly sophisticated aspects of horror and criminal psychology, but it is also one of the first films to use sound as an integral aspect of plot. The antagonist is recognized by a blind newspaperman because he incessantly whistles the tune "In the Hall of the Mountain King" by Eduard Grieg. —*N.J.*

METROPOLIS (RESTORED) L: DIRECTORS/LANG, FRITZ (1927) 124M D: Fritz Lang. *Alfred Abel, Fritz Rasp, Rudolf Klein-Rogge, Gustav Fröhlich, Brigitte Helm.* Perhaps the most famous silent film ever made, Lang's visionary sci-fi epic has been, with the help of newfound footage and still photos from missing scenes, reconstructed and restored to its most complete form since its 1927 Berlin debut. Filled out with subplots involving *The Thin Man* (Rasp, whose part is all but absent in previous surviving prints), the decadence and corruption of the topside city Yishiwara (Lang's take on Berlin's cabaret scene?), and the destructive rage of the dictatorial industrialist Joh Fredersen (Abel), it becomes both enriched and thematically confused (no revolutionary film, it's an utterly conservative plea for the paternal responsibilities of the ruling class). It's also magnificent, a visually mesmerizing spectacle on a truly epic scale. Restored by the Murnau Foundation, in collaboration with the Munich Film Museum, it's still missing about 25 percent of its original release footage, but has never felt so rounded and textured. —*S.A.*

NIBELUNGEN, DIE L: DIRECTORS/LANG, FRITZ (1924) 291M D: Fritz Lang. *Paul Richter, Margarete Schoen, Theodor Loos.* Released in two parts as *Kriemheld's Revenge* and *Siegfried, Die Nibelungen* is a four-act visual opera. Siegfried (Richter) defeats a dragon (in an utterly fabulous sequence) to win Kriemhilde (Schoen), then helps his brother (Loos) win as his bride the original ice queen Brunhild (Ralph) using a mask of invisibility. Two acts' worth of (often tedious) intrigue and counter-intrigue follow surrounding Siegried's murder. The powerful and apocalyptic final act of revenge by his widow is mega-nasty! Siegfried's aid to his brother-in-law (moral courage) and Kriemhilde's vengeance (moral terror) reverberate with complicated modern moral contours that make these decisions feel emotionally earned. —*J.C.*

1,000 EYES OF DR. MABUSE, THE L: DIRECTORS/LANG, FRITZ (1960) 99M D: Fritz Lang. *Wolfgang Preiss, Gert Fröbe, Dawn Addams, Peter Van Eyck.* For his final film, Lang returns to the arch criminal he created in the silent era and updates him to the modern era with a nuclear plot and a technological empire. A low-budget throwback to his early thrillers, the fantastic story of a criminal mastermind who spies on the city with a TV surveillance network has the mad invention of a silent-film serial with its crazy cast of characters: a blind psychic, a nosy insurance salesman, an icy silent killer, and an unkillable police inspector (Gert *Goldfinger* Fröbe). The marvelously intricate script is fluffy fun, like a cut-rate Bond thriller where the bad guys have all the gadgets, and Lang leaps from scene to scene with urgency. Though never as visually dense or dramatically potent as his earlier *Mabuse* films, it's a sure, handsome, highly entertaining film with a few grand moments of directorial grace. —*S.A.*

SCARLET STREET L: DIRECTORS/LANG, FRITZ (1945) 104M
D: Fritz Lang. *Joan Bennett, Dan Duryea, Edward G. Robinson.* This innovative, paranoid, and heartbreaking noir thriller is a remake of Jean Renoir's *La Chienne* and reunites the director and stars of *Woman in the Window.* Robinson plays Christopher Cross, a henpecked banker with artistic aspirations and a shrew for a wife. He meets a woman named Kitty (Bennett) on a rainy night and leads her to believe that he's a famous artist. Kitty's heel of a boyfriend (a slimy Duryea), named Johnny Prince, smells money and forces Kitty to lead poor Chris onward into his midlife crisis. Chris steals from his wife, embezzles money from work, and sets Kitty up in a swanky apartment where he paints pictures that Johnny turns around and sells under Kitty's name. The shadow-filled photography emphasizes the murky, manipulative characters and the final scenes of a crazed Robinson are quite memorable. One of Lang's best American films. —*S. H.*

WOMAN IN THE WINDOW L: DIRECTORS/LANG, FRITZ (1944) 99M D: Fritz Lang. *Raymond Massey, Dan Duryea, Edward G. Robinson, Joan Bennett.* Mild-mannered psychology professor Robinson sees off the wife and kids on a summer vacation, then settles in for a spell of bachelorhood in the big city. Caught staring at a woman's portrait in the gallery window next door to his club, he's jokingly advised to behave himself. But when the lady herself (Bennett) mysteriously materializes beside him, he risks having a late-night drink with her. The hours lengthen, a street that had been dry turns moon-silver with rain, and in a startling moment, the professor becomes a killer. Trying to cover up the outcome of his "one false step," the still fundamentally innocent man is drawn deeper into conspiracy and jeopardy. *Woman in the Window* is arguably Lang's finest American film, although his next, *Scarlet Street*—also starring Robinson, Bennett, and knifelike villain Duryea—is his most personal, and some critics complain about *Woman*'s twist ending. The twist is entirely legitimate, and on re-viewing only serves to disclose greater complexities artfully woven into the very fiber of the storytelling. This is the kind of movie you remember all your life, and revisit with increased pleasure. —*R. T. J.*

YOU ONLY LIVE ONCE L: DIRECTORS/LANG, FRITZ (1937) 86M D: Fritz Lang. *Henry Fonda, Sylvia Sidney.* Lang created the outlaw-lovers-on-the-lam genre with this romantic tragedy shot in the shadows of night. Fonda is the ex-con whose efforts to go straight are sunk when he's sentenced for a crime he didn't commit. He kills a man while escaping from prison and hits the road in an endless flight with his pregnant wife (Sidney). One of Lang's films of social protest, it's both strikingly American and quintessentially Lang, with two innocents plunged by fate (and a cor-rupt society steeped in hypocrisy) into a life of poverty and flight, and directed in the same pre-film noir grace as France's 1930s poetic realist crime dramas. —*S. A.*

GREAT EXPECTATIONS L: DIRECTORS/LEAN, DAVID (1946) 118M D: David Lean. *Francis L. Sullivan, Bernard Miles, Anthony Wager, Jean Simmons, Valerie Hobson, John Mills.* Lean's handsome adaptation of Dickens's classic novel of an orphan brought to London society by the secret bequest of a mysterious benefactor captures the warm humor and rich-ness of character that so many filmmakers miss in their reverent re-creations of Victorian England. From the nightmarish opening sequence on the windswept graveyard to the shadowy, musty mansion of the widow Miss Haversham, Lean's elegant expressionism captures a childlike exag-geration of reality as seen by our hero, Pip (Wager as a wide-eyed boy and Mills as a dash-ing young man), and he effectively maintains the heart of Dickens's epic drama while cutting it to its essentials. Studded with a gallery of enchant-ing performances, including Simmons's haughty turn as the teenage beauty who wins young Pip's heart and Alec Guinness's playful film debut as adult Pip's jovial London roommate. The novel's finest cinematic incarnation. —*S. A.*

LAWRENCE OF ARABIA L: DIRECTORS/LEAN, DAVID (1962) 221M D: David Lean. *Jack Hawkins, Peter O'Toole, Alec Guinness, Anthony Quinn, Omar Sharif.* Lean's epic adventure based on the true-life story of T. E. Lawrence (played by O'Toole in a com-pelling, complex performance), the blue-eyed desert warrior dreamer who united the warring Arab factions into a strong guerrilla front in WWI, is one of the most beautiful big-screen films ever made. Lean's use of size and scale and widescreen composition is remarkable, which means that one of its grandest attributes suffers on video no matter how big your home screen is. Other aspects translate better. O'Toole's rise to near messianic proportions and delusions of invulnerability and his fall back into the real world with a fear that over-comes his once resolute moral strength are trag-edy on a scale both human and mythic. The fiercely intelligent drama is brought to life by a stunning cast and a mixture of modern sensi-bility and classical filmmaking. It's one of the most finely crafted and brilliantly directed epics of world cinema. —*S. A.*

GIRL ON THE BRIDGE, THE L: DIRECTORS/LECONTE, PATRICE (1999) 90M D: Patrice Leconte. *Daniel Auteuil, Vanessa Paradis, Demetre Georgalas, Isabelle Petit-Jacques, Frederic Pfluger.* French everyman Auteuil is a world-weary knife-thrower and baby-doll pop star Paradis his waiflike muse in Leconte's rhapsodic fairy tale for bruised romantics. Shot in shimmering black-and-white CinemaScope, it's like 1930s Hollywood glamour by way of a modern fashion shoot: tinsel and spangles come to life in inky midnight blacks and glowing whites. Hardly the stuff of grand romance but it's a gloriously baroque vision. In the film's most wonderfully absurd moment, the telepathically connected would-be lovers sneak off to an abandoned shack and play out their act in private: she purrs and sighs and arches her back in orgasmic gasps with each toss. Knife-throwing is not simply foreplay but a replacement for sex itself. Leconte believes in his sequin-and-sawdust fantasy with such unabashed enthusiasm that he makes it work even through its most absurd moments. —S. A.

MAN ON THE TRAIN, THE L: DIRECTORS/LECONTE, PATRICE (2002) 90M D: Patrice Leconte. *Johnny Hallyday, Jean-François Stévenin, Isabelle Petit-Jacques, Jean Rochefort, Edith Scob.* Leconte's elegiac crime drama is a well-tuned character piece starring Rochefort as a droopy, self-effacing dreamer who would like nothing more than to become a hero of the movies he loves, and French pop icon Hallyday, whose face looks like a couple miles of rough road and whose manner suggests the life that goes with it, as a bank robber in town for a job. Crossing paths, the two become unlikely buddies—the lonely old retiree whose life is a monotony of repetition, and the eternal drifter who has spent a lifetime without setting down roots and has come out the other end just as lonely and lost. Their friendship is touching and genuine—Rochefort gives Hallyday a poem, and Hallyday gives Rochefort shooting lessons. Leconte feeds both the romantic fantasy of the tough-guy genre and the inevitable outcome of lives spent in violent endeavor and quiet desperation. —S. A.

RIDICULE L: DIRECTORS/LECONTE, PATRICE (1996) 102M D: Patrice Leconte. *Fanny Ardant, Charles Berling, Bernard Guirardeau, Jean Rochefort.* Berling plays an honest, earnest young man living on the outskirts of Paris in the seventeenth century. He decides to petition his government for improvements in his district's irrigation, but no matter whom he talks to he is shunned. Eventually losing patience, he deliberately insults the official he's talking with and starts home. He's stopped by a socialite who overheard the interchange and is given a quick lesson of high-class French society: to get anywhere one must ridicule people with humor and wit, and the better one can do so the higher one will rise in the social ranks. With nothing to lose, the young man joins his newfound friend in a variety of upper-class salons, using high-class wit to frame his low-class opinions. He's so successful he eventually gets a visit with the king. This little-known film is well worth seeing as its criticisms of bourgeois aristocracy are as valid today as they were then. —N. J.

CROUCHING TIGER, HIDDEN DRAGON L: DIRECTORS/ LEE, ANG (2000) 120M D: Ang Lee. *Chow Yun Fat, Michelle Yeoh, Zhang Ziyi.* Lee transformed his love of "wuxia pian" (China's epic adventures of martial arts, chivalry, and melodrama of the past age) into a worldwide smash by creating, in his own words, "*Sense and Sensibility* with martial arts." A tragedy of repressed love and the rebellion of a feisty young princess (Zhang) against an arranged marriage, it's also a hot-blooded action film, bubbling with heart, soul, and sheer poetry in motion. Yeoh kicks up a storm while Chow relies on poise, confidence, and minimalist movements to make himself the calm master in the center of frenzied fights. The film soars—literally—with high-flying action scenes that border on magic, but it's the romantic abandon and delirious imagery that give the melodrama its universal appeal. Winner of four Oscars, including Best Foreign Language Film and Best Cinematography. —S. A.

EAT DRINK MAN WOMAN L: DIRECTORS/LEE, ANG (1994) 123M D: Ang Lee. *Kuei-Mei Yang, Sihung Lung, Chien-Lien Wu, Yu-Wen Wang.* This is easily my favorite film by the excellent Lee. The story revolves around a father, his three daughters, and their relationships with each other and food. The father, a famous retired chef who is tragically starting to lose his ability to taste the food that he makes, crafts elaborate and spectacular meals for his unmarried daughters each night. But it is more an exercise in self-indulgence, for there is little closeness or true understanding between them. In turn, looking to break away from home and find fulfillment in their own lives, his daughters pursue the paths before them. The film explores the hurdles and changes of this family along with each member's love life. Overall the film has a positive and hopeful air, which is not always the case with Lee's work. Beautifully filmed, this movie is a charming exploration of family, change, and independence. —

HULK L: DIRECTORS/LEE, ANG (2003) 138M D: Ang Lee. *Nick Nolte, Josh Lucas, Sam Elliott, Jennifer Connelly, Eric Bana.* Lee takes a subversively dramatic approach to adapting the *Incredible Hulk* comics, spending a good half of the movie on characterization and relationships (what the fuck?). Then the movie itself hulks out as Bruce Banner (Bana) turns into the giant green monster of the title and goes on a rampage in the desert, twisting up tanks, spitting missiles out of his mouth, and riding a navy jet into the upper atmosphere. The animated mayhem is joyous and graceful (Lee even wore the motion-control suit to act out many of the Hulk's movements), and just wait until Bruce's father (the brilliantly over-the-top Nolte) turns into a weird energy force and wages an abstract battle in the sky. Like Bruce Banner, the movie has two sides: a *King Kong*–type monster movie with destruction that leaves you giddy and giggly, and a serious story about fathers' relationships with their children. It's amazing (and wonderful) that Lee was able to make this movie. —B.T.

ICE STORM, THE L: DIRECTORS/LEE, ANG (1997) 112M D: Ang Lee. *Sigourney Weaver, Christina Ricci, Katie Holmes, Tobey Maguire, Joan Allen, Kevin Kline, Elijah Wood.* A quiet film that speaks volumes without ever raising its voice, Lee's *The Ice Storm* brilliantly tackles suburban dysfunction in the early 1970s. If there was justice in the world, it would have least been nominated for Best Picture. Still, awards aren't ultimately important—it's touching people's hearts and minds for a couple of hours that is truly important. And that's exactly where this wonderful film succeeds. The cast is to die for, and they all turn in eerily fascinating performances. Though a sad movie for sure, it's also a beautiful one, showing us how complicated life can be and the various ways we devise to get through it. Based on the equally outstanding novel of the same name by Rick Moody. —C.P.

BAMBOOZLED L: DIRECTORS/LEE, SPIKE (2000) 135M D: Spike Lee. *Damon Wayans, Mos Def, Michael Rapaport, Savion Glover, Jada Pinkett Smith.* Wayans plays a TV writer so frustrated with stereotypes in television that he pitches an old-fashioned minstrel show—with black actors in blackface—as a way to get fired. Instead, the show gets picked up, becomes a huge hit, and he even starts to believe in it himself. It's a great satirical premise, but it's wasted in a mostly humorless, wildly unfocused mess. Like all of Lee's movies it has some brilliant touches. Unfortunately those strengths are weighed down by a number of huge misjudgments: Wayans's ridiculous cartoon accent, an overabundance of vintage racial caricature montages, the heavy-handed ending, and the bootleg-quality digital cinematography. Many said that Lee, by using blackface, was making a bold move, but the metaphor only serves to distance him from his real targets. If he's going to call out modern-day entertainers, why not name names instead of digging up archaic stereotypes? —B.T.

Regarding the "number of huge misjudgments": I still think Lee is in control here. The Wayans accent is only as cartoony as Michael Rapaport's white-man blackspeak, and I don't think it loses its focus quite so much as it loses its scope. The "racial caricature" stereotype montages aren't the problem, either; they just aren't complete enough. This film shows you the vintage stuff only; it would have been much more powerful for Lee to bring us all up to the current day (where is J. J. Walker, or Urkel?) and end with the characters in his own film. The problem this film has is much like the problem of Spike Jonze and Charlie Kaufman's *Adaptation*: becoming the very thing you are spoofing or satirizing just doesn't quite pay off the way you'd like it to. Still, this should be required viewing. When I saw this

film in the theater, it provoked a multiracial discussion so engaging we, strangers all, continued the conversation for twenty-five minutes after the last credits rolled by. My favorite film of the year 2000. —K.S.

CROOKLYN L: DIRECTORS/LEE, SPIKE (1994) 112M D: Spike Lee. *Delroy Lindo, Zelda Harris, Alfre Woodard, Carlton Williams.* An obviously autobiographical nostalgia piece about a family of seven in '70s Brooklyn. The father (Lindo) is a jazz pianist who has trouble making ends meet without abandoning his art, and the mother (Woodard) is a teacher who suddenly gets severe health problems. The story is told through the eyes of the one daughter, Troy (Harris), perhaps because the screenplay was co-written by Lee's sister, Joie (along with another sibling, Cinque). More light-hearted than most Lee films, but also very sad, made powerful by a uniformly great cast. The one major misjudgment is the section where Troy goes to stay with her aunt and Lee presents it in eye-straining uncorrected Scope, stretching the whole image out of proportion. —B.T.

DO THE RIGHT THING L: DIRECTORS/LEE, SPIKE (1989) 120M D: Spike Lee. *Giancarlo Esposito, Ossie Davis, Danny Aiello, Spike Lee, John Turturro, Bill Nunn.* It's funny to remember how controversial this movie was in 1989 just for daring to quote Malcolm X at the end. It was definitely topical, being partly inspired by a police beating in Howard Beach, and reflected in racist violence in Bensonhurst shortly after the film's release. Now, many years after Rodney King, the film doesn't seem as explosive, but it still stands as Lee's masterpiece. All the elements of the Lee style are at their most intense here. Full of humor and warmth, anger and passion, it is a very human portrait of escalating racial tensions in the Bed-Stuy neighborhood on the hottest day of the summer. Even as the day starts off laid-back, everything seems amplified: the colors, the camera movements, the costumes, and the Public Enemy anthem "Fight the Power" that plays such an important part. Aiello's unforgettable performance as Sal pokes a huge hole in the oft-repeated claim that Lee is not interested in three-dimensional white characters. For a good laugh, watch the TV version, which replaces the many expletives with gibberish like "mickey fickey" and "mamma jamma"—too bad they didn't include that as an alternative audio track on the Criterion Edition. —B.T.

4 LITTLE GIRLS L: DIRECTORS/LEE, SPIKE (1998) 102M D: Spike Lee. Perhaps Lee's least known film is this powerful documentary about four girls killed in the bombing of a black Birmingham church in 1963. Lee looks at this hate crime, which went officially unsolved for many years despite plenty of evidence as to who was responsible, and puts it in context in the history of the civil rights movement. What makes the film special is that it takes

a very personal look at the girls' lives through the eyes of their friends and relatives, and gives a firsthand account of the movement. I often think of these events in terms of dry history books and old black-and-white news footage. This movie really made me think *wow*, this wasn't that long ago. And these are some of the people who were there. This film should be required viewing in American schools. —*B.T.*

HE GOT GAME L: DIRECTORS/LEE, SPIKE (1998) 136M D: Spike Lee. *Milla Jovovich, Rosario Dawson, Hill Harper, Denzel Washington, Ray Allen.* Spike Lee is an avid basketball fan, and *He Got Game* lingers lovingly on the details of the sport. It praises the good and casts a cold eye on the bad, which makes it an honest movie and a powerful one. The film follows a young high school basketball star, played by real-life NBA star Ray Allen. His father (Washington) is released from prison with a strict edict from the warden: Get your son to sign with the warden's alma mater and you'll get parole. The father-son story is the core of the movie, but the stuff at the margins is equally impressive. In some scenes, Allen revels in the game's joys, both obvious and subtle; in another, a hustler warns Allen of the pitfalls of being a star, a monologue that lays out the tempting and terrifying. Basketball is a hard game to play when you're walking a tightrope. —*T.P.*

JUNGLE FEVER L: DIRECTORS/LEE, SPIKE (1991) 131M D: Spike Lee. *Wesley Snipes, Annabella Sciorra, Spike Lee, Samuel L. Jackson, Ossie Davis, Ruby Dee.* Snipes plays the awkwardly monikered Flipper Purify, an upper-class New York architect who has an office affair with an engaged white temp worker from Bensonhurst (Sciorra). Of course, both of their families have problems with this and judging by the lack of emotional attachment it doesn't seem like Lee is entirely on board with the concept of interracial relationships either. Flipper's parents (Davis and Dee) have enough on their hands dealing with their crack-addicted other son, Gator (Jackson in a breakthrough performance). The relationship story and the addiction story are both powerful on their own, but they don't fit naturally together as one movie, arguably making this Lee's least-focused film (which is saying a lot). —*B.T.*

MO' BETTER BLUES L: DIRECTORS/LEE, SPIKE (1990) 130M D: Spike Lee. *Cynda Williams, Denzel Washington, Spike Lee, Wesley Snipes, Joie Lee.* Lee, whose father is a jazz musician, often complained that jazz movies (like Clint Eastwood's *Bird*) made the musicians look bad because they were always about drug addiction. But then for some reason he made his jazz movie with Washington playing a trumpet player who can't decide between two women (Williams and Joie Lee) and himself playing a gambling addict. It's not one of Lee's best, but the music is great, the atmosphere of the jazz clubs is strong, and Snipes has some good scenes

debating musical issues with Washington. The best Lee moment is the 360-degree rotating sex scene where Washington can't figure out which one of his girlfriends he's in bed with. —*B.T.*

ORIGINAL KINGS OF COMEDY, THE L: DIRECTORS/LEE, SPIKE (2000) 115M D: Spike Lee. *Steve Harvey, D. L. Hughley, Bernie Mac, Cedric the Entertainer.* These four comedians are captured performing onstage in Charlotte, North Carolina, during their hugely successful Original Kings of Comedy tour. Their phenomenal popularity in black communities made this movie possible, but it was the movie itself that launched Mac and Cedric to whiter (er, uh, wider) acceptance, making both into big-time movie and TV stars. Harvey and Hughley already had their own sitcoms, but they proved here they could actually be funny. The stand-up (especially Mac's) is strong, so you get what you came for, but the film itself is pretty weak. Shot on ugly digital video (around the same time as *Bamboozled*) it looks more like a TV special than a concert film. —*B.T.*

RENDEZVOUS L: DIRECTORS/LELOUCHE, CLAUDE (1977) 9M D: Claude Lelouch. Strap yourself onto the hood of a sports car for nine minutes of mother truckin' motor mayhem. Lelouch fulfills every boy-racer's wet dreams as he (or Jacques Lafitte perhaps) careens recklessly through the expansive streets and winding alleyways of early morning Paris. I couldn't help but laugh in bemusement as fellow drivers pull off the road and pedestrians scramble desperately to get out of harm's way. This man is on a mission, as apparently there is no lane too narrow, no light too red. Watch as famous monuments zoom into focus at a tremendous pace, much more convincing than any snap pan could offer (current French directors take note). Who knew the Arc de Triomphe could be so exciting? All you aftermarket speed racer wannabes watch out, this is the real deal. And what's that? It's a Ferrari? Badass. —*T.C.*

ALMOST HUMAN L: DIRECTORS/LENZI, UMBERTO (1974) 90M D: Umberto Lenzi. *Anita Strindberg, Guido Alberti, Gino Santercole, Henry Silva, Laura Belli, Tomas Milian, Ray Lovelock.* Nasty, brilliantly acted ode to a psychopathic killer (Milian). Beaten up by his crew for unnecessarily shooting a traffic cop at a bank robbery, he forms his own crew and devises a plan to kidnap the daughter (Belli) of his girlfriend's boss, keeping the girlfriend (Strindberg) in the dark. His plan works. But one of his confederates shoots their prize's gentleman escort, regrets it, and secretly decides to help the young woman, whom the psycho intends to kill as soon as the ransom is paid. The woman escapes to the house and a nicely choreographed, gut-wrenchingly horrendous scene follows, rightly infamous and bloody unforgettable. The girlfriend has to be dealt with, cops screw up the payoff, and the psycho must bribe and blackmail his old gang into giving him an alibi. The lead cop (Silva) knows better, but how does one do one's job in a system where craziness pays? —*J. C.*

CANNIBAL FEROX (AKA **MAKE THEM DIE SLOWLY**) L: DIRECTORS/LENZI, UMBERTO (1981) 93M D: Umberto Lenzi. *Bryan Redford, John Morghen (Giovanni Lombardo Radice), Lorraine De Selle, Zora Kerowa.* A trio of mindbogglingly idiotic Americans deep in the South American jungle blithely ignore every sign of imminent danger, invite a coked-up, drug-dealing sadist to join them, and face the consequences when a brutalized local tribe hunts them down. One of most notorious examples of the cannibal subspecies of Italian exploitation horror from Lenzi, the film delivers all it promises: Stomachs are gutted, brains eaten, men castrated, and one woman is forced to reenact the initiation scene from *A Man Called Horse.* Though badly acted and bluntly directed, it's neither phony enough to be fun nor smart enough to be interesting. This is a freak show with a better budget than usual. —*S. A.*

EATEN ALIVE! (AKA **EMERALD JUNGLE 2**) L: DIRECTORS/LENZI, UMBERTO (1980) 87M D: Umberto Lenzi. *Janet Algren, Me Me Lai, Robert Kerwin, Ivan Rassimov, Paola Senatore, Meg Fleming.* Amiable Lenzi adventure yarn about a Jim Jones–type religious commune in the jungles of New Guinea with cannibals between commune and civilization. A woman (Algren) hires a guide to find her sister (Fleming) who belongs to this sect, and locates the commune after some close scrapes. But they have to join the commune to stay, and drink mind-control cocktail as part of a ritual. Lenzi borrows spicy footage from other films like Deodato's *Jungle Holocaust* and his own *Man from Deep River* and concocts some delectable sequences of his own (the woman's naked torso painted by topless maidens in preparation for ritual marriage). The sister and a native girl (Lai) escape from the commune only to be captured and disemboweled alive by cannibals. Entertaining if message-less film full of lively, unforgettable imagery. —*J. C.*

IRONMASTER L: DIRECTORS/LENZI, UMBERTO (1982) 98M D: Umberto Lenzi. *Sam Pasco, Elvire Audray.* Boasting one of the best pieces of cover art ever, *Ironmaster* is the epic tale of a prehistoric tribe that develops weapons made of metal. It's a dead-serious story about cavemen. And that's why it's good. Your appreciation of the inherent camp value of this oft-maligned parable and its constant soapbox moralizing will determine whether or not you enjoy the film. But if it's armored cavemen who look like members of a hair-metal band that you want, this film's for you. —*T. S.*

MAN FROM DEEP RIVER, THE (AKA **DEEP RIVER SAVAGES**) L: DIRECTORS/LENZI, UMBERTO (1972) 90M D: Umberto Lenzi. *Ivan Rassimov, Me Me Lai.* First in the cycle of 1970s Italian cannibal movies. A

photographer (Rassimov) wanted for assault and possibly murder escapes upriver in Thailand, only to be captured and enslaved by a primitive tribe with cannibal enemies. As he becomes accustomed to tribal ways and becomes helpful in a crisis he is accepted into the tribe. He tries to escape with his new wife who needs eye surgery, and they are punished. But he redeems himself in the next crisis when cannibals attack and airplanes destroy the village. He helps them to rebuild, finally socializing him to the ways of his chosen people. Superb adventure story with a serious social message and some harsh violence (including real violence toward animals) plus abundant nudity effectively used. —*J. C.*

NIGHTMARE CITY L: DIRECTORS/LENZI, UMBERTO (1980) 92M D: Umberto Lenzi. *Maria Rosaria Omaggio, Mel Ferrer, Laura Trotter, Hugo Stiglitz.* Among the hordes of Italian zombie and cannibal films of the '70s and '80s sits this trashy, bandwagon-hopping thriller that attempts to show the negatives of science through splatter horror. On a reporting assignment at an airport, TV journalist Dean (Stiglitz) witnesses an airplane that lands and spills out its enraged passengers onto the city. These zombie-esque creatures rampage the city with a quickness unseen in most standard zombie films. They are smart, able to plan, and use weapons with ease. Stiglitz tries valiantly to get his wife, Anna (Trotter), out of the city, but soon realizes that they are hopelessly surrounded. Although the acting is wooden, the zombie makeup is horrendous, and the production is cheap, these elements do help give an unintentional style to the film. The gore scenes are still violently shocking, even though they've been done before. —*R. M.*

PARANOIA (AKA **ORGASMO**) L: DIRECTORS/LENZI, UMBERTO (1968) 91M D: Umberto Lenzi. *Lou Castel, Carroll Baker, Colette Descombes, Tino Carraro.* Stand-out erotic thriller with *giallo* elements. A rich recent widow (Baker) is set up in a nice villa by her lawyer (Carraro) who seems a little sweet on her. But she has taken to a brash boy (Castel) whose motorcycle has conveniently broken down at her front gate. Before she knows it she's showering with him and permitting him to move in. Then his "sister" (Descombes) comes to her villa for a visit. Baker portrays the widow as not entirely dense but lusty, enjoying herself for the first time in her life. But it is the raw, sinuous magic between Castel and Descombes that is the naked delight of of this film. And while you see where the film is going, you don't want it to get there too quickly. As compensation the film does leave you with a memorably harsh and cruel concluding image—Lenzi at his best. —*J. C.*

FISTFUL OF DOLLARS, A L: DIRECTORS/LEONE, SERGIO (1964) 99M D: Sergio Leone. *Clint Eastwood, Marianne Koch, Gian Maria Volonte.* In this remake of Akira Kurosawa's *Yojimbo,* Eastwood is the Man With

No Name (he did have a name: Joe), a roaming gunslinger who stumbles into the impoverished town of San Miguel. The town has been torn apart by the war of two rival family gangs, the Baxters and the Rojos, as they smuggle goods and terrorize the citizens. With a quick glare and a quicker pistol, Joe manages to get tangled up in the ever-present fights, and soon realizes how much money there is to be made by playing on both sides of the field. The bullets fly and the coffins mount, all while Joe collects payment after payment, and in the process hopes to destroy both factions of outlaw bandits. *Fistful of Dollars* not only launched both Eastwood and Leone's careers, but has become one of the finest examples of the spaghetti Western ever made. The unconnected sequels, *For a Few Dollars More* and *The Good, the Bad and the Ugly,* are also required viewing. —*R. M.*

FISTFUL OF DYNAMITE, A (AKA DUCK YOU SUCKER)
L: DIRECTORS/LEONE, SERGIO (1971) 162M D: Sergio Leone. *Maria Monti, Rod Steiger, James Coburn.* Leone's most obscure Western, *Fistful of Dynamite* is the story of a bandit who unwittingly becomes involved in the Mexican Revolution after trying to team up with an Irish immigrant to rob a bank. Coburn plays an IRA explosives expert who is on the run and working for the revolution. Steiger plays a Mexican bandit and somehow pulls it off perfectly, balancing the character's greed with an awkward sense of nobility, cowardice, and bravery. Directed to perfection by the great Leone, the film's highest merit is its excellent use of flashbacks to reveal character and underscore dramatic situations. It is not until the very end of the film (or perhaps even later in contemplation) that we truly learn who these characters are and why they do what they do. An excellent story about war and revolution, bravery and heroism, and ultimately friendship. —*T. S.*

FOR A FEW DOLLARS MORE
L: DIRECTORS/LEONE, SERGIO (1965) 130M D: Sergio Leone. *Clint Eastwood, Lee Van Cleef, Gian Maria Volonte, Luigi Pistilli, Klaus Kinski.* The inherent genius of *For a Few Dollars More* is apparent after just one viewing. But the more you watch it, the more you begin to realize you are watching a true masterpiece. The innovative camera work becomes even more astounding. The motifs become clearer and more meaningful. Allegory, metaphor, and irony all rise out of the subtext and add new layers to the film. Whether you approach it from a Freudian angle, examine the religious implications, or just enjoy watching Eastwood blast the life out of some bad motherfuckers, you should definitely watch *For a Few Dollars More* again and again. —*T. S.*

GOOD, THE BAD, AND THE UGLY, THE
L: DIRECTORS/LEONE, SERGIO (1966) 181M D: Sergio Leone. *Eli Wallach, Lee Van Cleef, Clint Eastwood.* Leone perhaps never mixed high comedy and the stench of death

as expertly or as epically as he did in this film, the end to the Dollars Trilogy. Clint is "good," only in that he doesn't randomly kill anyone who doesn't deserve it; Van Cleef is truly bad, looking a bit like the Devil himself; and Wallach is laughably ugly, inhabiting an almost feral quality as the ruthless but clumsy survivalist who alternately runs afoul of Eastwood and Van Cleef as all three men try to find a big pot o' gold left behind by a dead man. All of this occurs during the Civil War, and Leone really exploits that aspect too, almost making our "heroes' " quest insignificant as the soldier's bodies pile up to the point of absurdity. Morricone gave arguably his finest and certainly most memorable score to Leone for this masterpiece, anticipating the next collaboration of director/composer on *Once Upon a Time in the West.* In 2003, MGM restored and released the original three-hour version. —*M. S.*

ONCE UPON A TIME IN AMERICA
L: DIRECTORS/LEONE, SERGIO (1984) 229M D: Sergio Leone. *William Forsythe, Treat Williams, Tuesday Weld, Jennifer Connelly, James Woods, Robert De Niro, Elizabeth McGovern.* Leone's swan song is also his greatest achievement and one of the best films ever made. At four hours plus, this epic story chronicles the life of a gang of Jewish mobsters growing up during the Prohibition era in New York. What makes the film special is the way Leone chooses to tell it, jumping between 1922, 1933, and 1968. As we watch the film we slowly put together the puzzle of the rise and fall of David "Noodles" Aaronson (De Niro), ultimately betrayed by his best friend, Max (Woods). Leone pulls out every filmmaking stop to put us into each time period, utilizing an incredible cast ensemble, amazing set re-creations, realistic makeup, quick cuts, and even time-period music cues in another amazing Morricone soundtrack. This is Leone's *Citizen Kane.* Avoid the butchered shortened version by Warner Bros., who attempted to put the film back into chronological order. —*N. H.*

ONCE UPON A TIME IN THE WEST
L: DIRECTORS/LEONE, SERGIO (1968) 165M D: Sergio Leone. *Henry Fonda, Keenan Wynn, Jason Robards, Claudia Cardinale, Charles Bronson.* After turning the West into the cool, cruel mercenary world of the Clint Eastwood Dollar films and defining the style and attitude of the spaghetti Western, Leone made an honest-to-God American Western epic, still shot largely in Spain but featuring stunning footage of John Ford's mythic wonderland, Monument Valley. Casting Bronson as his slow-talking, harmonica-playing hero, Fonda as a steely, blue-eyed killer, and Cardinale as the fallen woman, Leone transforms Western tropes into a horseback epic of bad guys with hearts of gold and an iron engine that reshapes the landscape as its tracks are laid through the wilderness. Bernardo Bertolucci and Dario Argento co-wrote the screenplay and Ennio Morricone's

operatic score so inspired Leone that he directed and edited to the rhythms of the music. It flopped in release but decades later it stands out as Leone's masterpiece, a sun-baked blast of frontier opera. —*S. A.*

FOUR MUSKETEERS, THE: MILADY'S REVENGE L: DIRECTORS/LESTER, RICHARD (1974) 107M D: Richard Lester. *Frank Finlay, Charlton Heston, Christopher Lee, Faye Dunaway, Richard Chamberlain, Raquel Welch, Michael York, Oliver Reed.* The Three Musketeers was split into two movies, and in many ways this second half is even better than the first. The action is brought more to the foreground in this movie, and the swordfights mean more. The duel between Rochefort (Lee) and D'Artagnan (York) at the climax is one of the most badass duels ever filmed, with two men who want to kill each other using all their strength to accomplish that goal. This half turns darker than the first, as the schemes of Milady De Winter (Dunaway) unfold, but there's comedy too, as in the scene where the Musketeers eat breakfast on a crumbling fort in the middle of a raging battlefield. The Musketeers as portrayed here are cocky, pompous, brilliant antiheroes who cheat, steal, and cause mayhem, but always with a smile and always politely. You'll leave these films with a smile too. —*K. C.*

HARD DAY'S NIGHT, A L: DIRECTORS/LESTER, RICHARD (1964) 87M D: Richard Lester. *Paul McCartney, George Harrison, John Lennon, Wilfrid Brambell, Ringo Starr.* The Beatles and Lester give birth to the modern music video in this timeless classic. Alun Owen's crisp script is punctuated with great one-liners and excellent British terms (like "king mixer," which I'm guessing means a highly mischievous person), and makes the personalities of each Beatle bubble like champagne. It's a clever romp through a typical day on the job for the band, with subtle hints of the more "serious" artists they would soon evolve into. Their jaunt in an empty field (to "Can't Buy Me Love") is one of my favorite scenes in any film. —*J. K.*

HELP! L: DIRECTORS/LESTER, RICHARD (1965) 90M D: Richard Lester. *John Lennon, Paul McCartney, George Harrison, Ringo Starr, Leo McKern, Eleanor Bron.* This is one of the fluffiest of the Beatles' movies, substituting dry wit and style for hijinks and wackiness. Nevertheless, if you like slapstick and screwball comedy sprinkled with what essentially are music videos before there were music videos, you'll have a blast. In this ludicrous film, a fan sends Starr a massive red ring that he cannot for the life of him get off his finger. Unfortunately it is his life that is at risk, as the sacrificial ring belongs to the bloodthirsty cult of Kali and it is decreed that whoever wears the ring must be slaughtered. If that weren't enough, a crazed scientist discovers the ring and is convinced he must have it because with such a ring he could, dare I say, rule the world! This is terribly irreverent and politically incorrect, but I revel in its foolish silliness. —*M. N.*

PETULIA L: DIRECTORS/LESTER, RICHARD (1968) 105M D: Richard Lester. *George C. Scott, Julie Christie.* Petulia (Christie), a hipster who recently married into money, and Archie (Scott), a recently divorced middle-aged doctor, try to initiate an affair and fail miserably. The relationship that forms in its place is the stuff of this movie. Filmed in San Francisco at the tail end of the Summer of Love, *Petulia* is shot through with the letdown of the purported social revolution and the loneliness of consumerism that flower power pledged to overturn. The film's characters are too complicated to fit neatly as characters, much less as narrative devices, and their interactions exude a genuine awkwardness rarely captured in cinema. Gibbs's cubist nonlinear editing complicates things marvelously, elevating *Petulia* to something extraordinary, flashing backward and forward in time in a narrative haunted by the compulsive memory and irrepressible thoughts of regret and failure. —*C. B.*

ROBIN AND MARIAN L: DIRECTORS/LESTER, RICHARD (1976) 107M D: Richard Lester. *Nicol Williamson, Robert Shaw, Sean Connery, Richard Harris, Audrey Hepburn.* Connery's bones creak when he leaps into action as a weathered, over-the-hill Robin Hood returning from the Crusades older, wiser, and far less innocent, to a world that has passed him by—if, in fact, it ever really existed. Just shy of cynical, this wistful epitaph to the age of chivalry and honor is tenderly directed by Lester, who never lets the humor inherent in James Goldman's screenplay overwhelm the autumnal romance between Robin and his old love Maid Marian (played by an aged-to-perfection Hepburn). Even Shaw's rascally Sheriff of Nottingham comes off as a dated romantic in this bittersweet adventure. Williamson is steadfast and wry as the ever loyal Little John and Harris is horrifyingly jaded as the dying King Richard. An elegiac paean to love the second time around and the fading dreams of an idealism that was perhaps only a wish. —*S. A.*

THREE MUSKETEERS, THE: THE QUEEN'S DIAMONDS L: DIRECTORS/LESTER, RICHARD (1973) 107M D: Richard Lester. *Raquel Welch, Richard Chamberlain, Michael York, Christopher Lee, Faye Dunaway, Oliver Reed, Charlton Heston, Frank Finlay.* Lester's *The Three Musketeers* is bawdy, brilliant fun from start to finish, with a great cast and some of the best sword fighting in film history. York is perfectly plucky and insolent as D'Artagnan, who literally runs into the Musketeers on his first day in Paris. Reed is understated as Athos, and Finlay and Chamberlain make a hilarious comic duo. On the villains side, Heston does his thing as Cardinal Richelieu and Lee, as always, is perfect as Rochefort, the Cardinal's cyclopslike right-hand man. Welch and Dunaway bring some much-needed estrogen into the proceedings as the D'Artagnan's bumbling love and the treacherous Milady De Winter, respectively. The production design by Eatwell is truly stunning, even though a majority of the locations were just old Spanish castles. The France of that period was a dirty, weird place, and Lester keeps it authentic. Also rent *The Four Musketeers,* the equally brilliant second half of this movie. —*K. C.*

BROOKLYN BABYLON L: DIRECTORS/LEVIN, MARC (2000) 90M D: Marc Levin. *Bonz Malone, Karen Goberman, Tariq "Black Thought" Trotter.* Trotter is a rapper, Goberman is a Hasidic Jew, and none of their friends or family seem to understand what the hell they are thinking when they fall in love. It's a standard forbidden love story made interesting by the Levin directorial style first seen in *Slam.* Again he bases the movie around a very talented nonactor (Black Thought, lead MC for The Roots), showcasing his lyrical skills but also coaxing a surprisingly good acting performance out of him. Malone, the ex-con journalist who played an inmate in *Slam,* also appears here. Should be of most interest to fans of The Roots: they provide the score, they appear as Black Thought's backing band, and their original beatbox Rahzel acts as the film's narrator. —*B.T.*

SLAM L: DIRECTORS/LEVIN, MARC (1998) 100M D: Marc Levin. *Sonja Sohn, Saul Williams, Bonz Malone.* This utterly unique film stars the brilliant poet Williams, who you may have seen in the documentary *Slam Nation.* Williams plays a young man busted for selling pot who uses his talent for poetry to survive prison, both mentally and physically. Director Levin not only chose to cast nonactors in all the lead roles, but also let them improvise most of the scenes and filmed everything documentary style in real locations. In one scene, Williams makes a beat by hitting a brush against the wall and exchanges freestyle rhymes with the guy in the cell next door—who happened to be a real convict in his real cell, showing off the talents he might have put to better use had he not been convicted of murder. This is an extremely moving film not only in its depiction of lives wasted by violence and unfair drug laws, but also in its illustration of the power of art. Because of the unorthodox method of filmmaking, the director's commentary track is very interesting. There is also a book on the subject. —*B.T.*

BLOOD FEAST L: DIRECTORS/LEWIS, HERSCHELL GORDON (1963) 67M D: Herschell Gordon Lewis. *Connie Mason, Thomas Wood, Mal Arnold, Scott H. Hall, Lyn Bolton, Toni Clavert.* This is a Lewis classic and a must-see for fans of B horror films. A mother wants to host a lavish ethnic dinner for her daughter's birthday party, so she contacts a new Egyptian caterer in town. Little does anyone know, however, that the man enjoys making human sacrifices to the god Ishtar. And so

in his painstaking preparations for the various courses of the meal he requires several different body parts, which he pulls off of random victims in town. With absolutely no budget except for film stock, the gore effects look like they were supplied by a fourth-grader with Heinz ketchup. But of course that's all very intentional, you see, so as to complement the level of acting. —*N.J.*

BLOOD FEAST 2: ALL U CAN EAT L: DIRECTORS/LEWIS, HERSCHELL GORDON (2003) 98M D: Herschell Gordon Lewis. *Mark McLachlan, J. P. Delahoussaye, John McConnell.* For the first time in three decades, godfather of gore Lewis has picked up his camera and brought us a brand-new film, a sequel to his 1963 *Blood Feast* (which is a masterpiece). The story follows Fuad Ramses III (Delahoussaye), who has inherited his grandfather's butcher shop from the first film. Surprisingly, the statue of the Egyptian goddess Ishtar is still there and it quickly usurps his mind and commands him to prepare a blood feast. There is a bumbling detective, his young bride, and a bunch of hot bridesmaids who like to wear lingerie and make lesbian innuendo. Overall, it's pretty crappy. All the humor falls completely flat, the gore is decent but unsatisfying, and the acting from Delahoussaye is really the only plus. It's weird and unnatural, but sometimes funny to watch. Mostly, it just seems like they didn't try. Watching *Blood Feast 2* is almost as painful as being chopped up and eaten. —*T. S.*

JIMMY, THE BOY WONDER L: DIRECTORS/LEWIS, HERSCHELL GORDON (1966) 69M D: Herschell Gordon Lewis. *David Blight Jr., Dennis Jones, Nancy Jo Berg.* Legendary gore genre grandfather Lewis dropped this glorious bomb on America's wee ones in 1966, following a slew of exploitation splatter-thons including *Blood Feast* and *2000 Maniacs.* Jimmy wakes up one morning and wishes time would just stop so he wouldn't have to go to stupid school. The villainous Mr. Fig (played with headache-inducing zeal by a frenzied middle-aged man in a plaid jacket) overhears Jimmy's wish and grants it, causing much discord in a magical land (actually a large brown closet) where apparent Alzheimer's victim The Astronomer watches over The Great Clock. The Astronomer's fairylike daughter Aurora is summoned to aid a seemingly disinterested Jimmy in defeating Mr. Fig's plot to enslave the world. Also thrown in are Native Americans with Bronx accents, a cauldron of jelly beans, slow-motion footage of children playing catch, and an endless cartoon that has nothing to do with anything. This film is useless, wooden and totally unwatchable. I can't recommend it highly enough. —*Z. C.*

JUST FOR THE HELL OF IT L: DIRECTORS/LEWIS, HERSCHELL GORDON (1968) 85M D: Herschell Gordon Lewis. *Agi Gyenes, Nancy Lee Noble, Rodney Bedell.* Directed by my favorite inept director of all time, the genuinely inimitable Lewis (of *Blood Feast* and *2000*

Maniacs fame). The appeal of this film is its purity of spirit. There is practically no pretension whatsoever to plot or characterization and certainly not subtlety. The movie's theme song, "Destruction, Inc." says it all: smash everything. EVERYTHING. Violence, usually directed toward pretty young women in Lewis's other gore films, is here aimed almost at objects. With the exception of the grill-cook's hand. *—S. F.*

PSYCHIC, THE L: DIRECTORS/LEWIS, HERSCHELL GORDON (1968) 90M D: Herschell Gordon Lewis. *Robin Guest, Bobbi Spencer, Dick Genola, Carol Saenz.* This little-known film is a wonderful exercise in cheesy low-budget filmmaking. Genola plays an ordinary fellow who falls off a ladder while doing house repairs and hits himself on the head with his hammer. Soon after this he discovers that he is able to read anything on anyone's mind. At the same time his wife finds him to be suddenly impatient and short on temper. He decides to strike out on his own to see if he can make fame and fortune with his new talent. His exploits bring him wine and women for a song, yet somehow his powers evaporate on national television when he most needs them. Curious narrative voice-over is punctuated with bizarre sex scenes inserted to make the film more saleable. *—N. J.*

SHE-DEVILS ON WHEELS L: DIRECTORS/LEWIS, HERSCHELL GORDON (1968) 82M D: Herschell Gordon Lewis. *Nancy Lee Noble, Ruby Tuesday, Pat Poston.* Lewis's biker pic has quite spirited actors delivering the silliest of lines with as much seriousness as they can muster. Overall, it's one funny movie, and action-packed if you follow the staccato music playing while the women (known as the ManEaters) bike down the road. And bike down the road. And bike down the road. There is a bit of filler in this pic. The twangy '50s/'60s grind beat behind the girls' biking adventures is nice background, especially for the big fight between the ManEaters and a group of male bikers. One scene has the girls picking out their men for the night from a group of eager studs. Is this a feminist film? Hardly. These women are just plain tough and ready to rumble at all times. That's pretty much all they do. Just like real bikers! Except their logo is a big pink kitty. *—S. R.*

2000 MANIACS L: DIRECTORS/LEWIS, HERSCHELL GORDON (1964) 87M D: Herschell Gordon Lewis. *Thomas Wood, Connie Mason.* Historical horror! The residents of a literal ghost town perversely commemorate the Civil War centennial by luring a group of unwitting Yankee tourists to a celebration. A celebration of bloody revenge! Ha! The Northerners learn a new kind of Southern hospitality when they are killed by various inventive and painful means like death by boulder, rolling in a nail-filled barrel, and gleeful dismemberment on a Confederate flag. Yep, this movie has

it all—throw in some hilarious bluegrass music (by the director) and a wooden performance by a Playboy Playmate (Mason) and you have an enjoyably bloody and mean-spirited gore film by the makers of the notorious *Blood Feast.* *—S. H.*

BELLBOY, THE L: DIRECTORS/LEWIS, JERRY (1960) 72M D: Jerry Lewis. *Jerry Lewis, Alex Gerry, Bob Clayton, Sonny Sands, Milton Berle, Walter Winchell.* In Lewis's first film, the opening narration promises something quite new: "A film with no plot and no story." (Of course these days a comedy with a plot would be something new.) Lewis knows that a series of unrelated vignettes shouldn't overstay its welcome, so this film comes in at just seventy-two minutes. Using the brand-new setting of Miami's Hotel Fontainebleau, some of the skits have Lewis playing himself, being perpetually crowded in by an overly enthusiastic group of fans, conducting an imaginary orchestra to a real soundtrack, and so on. There are also a grab bag of offbeat comedians who seem to populate the hotel. As an added effect, the bellboy played by Lewis has no lines. An homage to the silent era of slapstick that he pulls off very well. *—N. J.*

CRACKING UP L: DIRECTORS/LEWIS, JERRY (1983) 83M D: Jerry Lewis. *Dick Butkus, Jerry Lewis, Zane Buzby, Milton Berle, Sammy Davis Jr., Herb Edelman.* This is not the best film Lewis made. Perhaps it was the influence of playing a heartless celebrity in Scorsese's *King of Comedy* a year before, or perhaps he's too old for the bumbling character he had been typecast as when he was a kid—either way the jokes fall flat in this, his last film as a director. Lewis plays a man seeking help from a psychologist (played by Edelman) for his chronic jinxing streak. Certainly Lewis saw a psychologist himself after this film flopped. *—N. J.*

ERRAND BOY, THE L: DIRECTORS/LEWIS, JERRY (1961) 92M D: Jerry Lewis. *Howard McNear, Dick Wesson, Sig Rumann, Brian Donlevy, Jerry Lewis.* Paramutual Motion Pictures is losing money, and it's not at the box office. To investigate this problem the CEO first thinks of using the prestigious law firm of Fumble, Fidget, and Fuss. But in a staff meeting he's convinced a lesser-known figure would work better. Enter the errand boy (Lewis). That's as much plot as you'll get out of this follow-up to *The Bellboy.* The rest is a variety of skits pulled off on a film lot, most of which will be great fun for Lewis fans. *—N. J.*

FAMILY JEWELS, THE L: DIRECTORS/LEWIS, JERRY (1965) 100M D: Jerry Lewis. *Robert Strauss, Milton Frome, Sebastian Cabot, Jerry Lewis, Donna Butterworth.* Two years after the success of *The Nutty Professor,* where Lewis played so many different roles in the same film, it was natural for him to find a vehicle where he could fully play out his chameleon-esque bent. In *The Family Jewels* a young girl inherits a large fortune and must determine which of her six uncles she would like to be legal guardian. Lewis trots out all six personas, making each fantastically different than the last. He also plays the chauffeur who offers a little stability for the girl between each outrageous encounter. —*N. J.*

LADIES' MAN, THE L: DIRECTORS/LEWIS, JERRY (1961) 106M D: Jerry Lewis. *Hope Holiday, Pat Stanley, Kathleen Freeman, Helen Traubel, Jerry Lewis, Jack Kruschen.* Lewis plays Herbert H. Herbert, a young man who is dumped by his girlfriend and develops a sudden phobia of women. Perhaps this has something to do with his parents (both played by Lewis). Down and out, Herbert H. applies for and gets the first job opening he sees only to discover the next day that he's the live-in custodian of. . . a sorority! *The Ladies' Man* is one of Lewis's most polished films. The soundtrack is composed of spectacular big band jazz and the set is a breakaway five-story sorority—a large and breathtaking set to have constructed on a soundstage. Comedy simply isn't filmed like this any more. Excellent cameo by George Raft, who plays himself. —*N. J.*

NUTTY PROFESSOR, THE L: DIRECTORS/LEWIS, JERRY (1963) 107M D: Jerry Lewis. *Stella Stevens, Buddy Lester, Howard Morris, Jerry Lewis, Del Moore, Kathleen Freeman.* Perhaps the best known of Lewis's films after his partnership with Dean Martin, *The Nutty Professor* still manages to employ both personas in a *Jekyll and Hyde* fashion. This story is a nice variation on the R. L. Stevenson plot in that the professor is so pathetic a character that any change in him would be for the better. With a potion of his own concoction the professor becomes Buddy Love, the ego de facto of Martin. In this role Lewis shows he can croon and swoon like the best of them. He's generally witty and charming and even dresses and grooms himself. But then the potion wears off and he slips back into the typecast we're used to. When Lewis directs himself he's able to show that he can play more roles than just the fool. In fact, he shows his versatility by playing several different roles in the same film. —*N. J.*

PATSY, THE L: DIRECTORS/LEWIS, JERRY (1964) 101M D: Jerry Lewis. *Jerry Lewis, Ina Balin, Everett Sloane, Phil Harris, Keenan Wynn.* A year after *The Nutty Professor* and near the height of his popularity, Lewis released *The Patsy*. If nothing else, this film is notable for the fact that it is Lorre's last. In a plot reminiscent of Lewis's *The Errand Boy*, a bunch of producers put their heads together to see whom they can make into the next blockbuster comedian. In an attempt to prove that anybody can fill such shoes, they agree to train the unbelievably inept bellboy. Naturally, this leads to some very rich slapstick that only Lewis could pull off. —*N. J.*

BIG COMBO, THE L: DIRECTORS/LEWIS, JOSEPH H. (1955) 88M D: Joseph H. Lewis. *Richard Conte, Jean Wallace, Lee Van Cleef, Brian Donlevy, Cornel Wilde.* The best films noir aren't simply about greed and violence, but megalomania, sex, and obsession. Lewis tosses in sexual enslavement and sadism in this classic and delivers it with a strikingly claustrophobic style drenched in doom, courtesy of cinematographer extraordinaire John Alton. Stiff, studly Wilde is perfect as an emotionally dead cop who hounds preening mobster Conte for his crimes and tries to free the chilly blond debutante (Wallace) he's made into his emotional slave. Donlevy, the former top gangster turned Conte's hired gun, makes memorable use of his hearing aid. Lewis transforms small-budget sets into an austere, eerily empty world, a deserted city of cops, criminals, and denizens of the night. An underrated noir masterpiece. —*S. A.*

GUN CRAZY L: DIRECTORS/LEWIS, JOSEPH H. (1949) 86M D: Joseph H. Lewis. *Morris Carnovsky, Berry Kroeger, John Dall, Peggy Cummins, Anabel Shaw.* The greatest of the criminal-lovers-on-the-run genre explodes onto the screen in a fury of sex, guns, love, and violence. Nice guy marksman Dall falls hard for sexy sideshow markswoman Cummins. He's a sensitive guy who will do anything to hang on to her; she's a psychotic wildcat whose eyes light up whenever she shoots someone. Lewis's exhilarating B-movie masterpiece burns fast and hot with passion and stylistic ecstasy. Lewis creates one riveting set piece after another on a starvation budget. He photographs one heist—and the subsequent escape—in a single long take without ever leaving the backseat of the car. But what fuels the film is a smoldering passion that burns through the screen as their doomed romance careens out of control down the highway to hell. That's Rusty (Russ) Tamblyn playing the boyhood Dall in the opening scene. —*S. A.*

TERROR IN A TEXAS TOWN L: DIRECTORS/LEWIS, JOSEPH H. (1958) 81M D: Joseph H. Lewis. *Sebastian Cabot, Ned Young, Eugene Martin, Sterling Hayden, Carol Kelly.* How can you go wrong with a Western that opens on a dusty main-street showdown between a gunslinger and a harpoon-brandishing Swede? Hayden delivers an almost comic Scandinavian lilt as the pacifist sailor who leaves the sea to join his father on a Texas farm and finds him murdered for his land by a psychotic young gunman (blacklisted screenwriter Young) hired by evil oilman Cabot. This low-budget Western oddity was the last feature directed by cult auteur Lewis, who brings a noir-ish shadow to the film. Screenwriter Ben L. Perry was actually a front for blacklisted screenwriter Dalton Trumbo. —*S. A.*

BEFORE SUNRISE L: DIRECTORS/LINKLATER, RICHARD (1995) 105M D: Richard Linklater. *Julie Delpy, Ethan Hawke.* While attraction usually starts things off,

I don't think people begin falling in love without good conversation. The greatest feeling in the world is to talk to someone and have everything else be less interesting than that person. Time is meaningless and the world around us exists only as a point of dialogue. This movie is about being in that space with two people as they go though the greatest first date ever. "If there's any kind of magic in this world it must be in the attempt of understanding someone sharing something." —E. W.

DAZED AND CONFUSED L: DIRECTORS/LINKLATER, RICHARD (1993) 103M D: Richard Linklater. *Matthew McConaughey, Parker Posey, Wiley Wiggins, Ben Affleck, Jason London, Joey Lauren Adams, Milla Jovovich.* Dazed and Confused is a less-than-brilliant, ultimately entertaining little piece of retro fun. Spanning a twelve-hour time frame in golden 1976, the film follows a bunch of kids on the last day of school as they fight, drink, smoke, and talk (and a few even get laid) in an attempt to make sense out of their pre-adult lives. Linklater maneuvers through these situations in *Slacker* fashion, moving from one conversation to the next, letting dialogue maintain the force of the action. Boasting a great ensemble cast of then indie unknowns (Posey, Affleck, Adams) and one bona fide movie star (McConaughey), and sporting an even greater rock soundtrack (Alice Cooper, Black Sabbath, Aerosmith, Joan Jett), this film gets to the heart of teenage excitement, fear, and angst. Drunk or sober, in high school or not, *Dazed and Confused* rules. —J. D.

NEWTON BOYS, THE L: DIRECTORS/LINKLATER, RICHARD (1998) 135M D: Richard Linklater. *Matthew McConaughey, Ethan Hawke, Dwight Yoakam, Vincent D'Onofrio, Julianna Margulies, Skeet Ulrich.* Linklater courted the mainstream with this big-budget studio period piece, and nobody (audiences or critics) was interested. I couldn't tell you why, though. It's an unusually amiable true-crime tale about some dimwitted brothers from Texas who, in the '20s, became the most successful bank robbers in American history. The whole cast is good (particularly Hawke and Yoakam), but what really makes this a unique bank robbery story is its lighthearted humor and virtual lack of violence. To the Newton brothers bank robbery isn't serious business—it's just some boys getting into trouble—and their attitude is infectious. Be sure to watch the end credits for an actual talk-show appearance by an elderly Newton brother (which makes you wish there was a documentary about them as well). —B. T.

SCHOOL OF ROCK L: DIRECTORS/LINKLATER, RICHARD (2003) 108M D: Richard Linklater. *Jack Black, Mike White, Sarah Silverman, Joan Cusack.* Kicked out of his band and owing rent money, a lazy slacker (Black) pretends to be his roommate (White) and shows up to substitute teach at a private

school. At first he assigns the kids all-day recess, but when he discovers many of them are musical prodigies he decides to give them instruments and teach them to play Led Zeppelin songs. Although it's basically a formula movie about underdog kids triumphing through determination and innate talent, it's also a vehicle completely crafted around Black's Tenacious D overenthusiastic rocker persona. In other words, it's a whole lot of Black, so those of you who don't find him funny should beware. What really makes the movie special is Linklater's decision to cast real musical prodigies as the kids and to show them playing the music for real. To young kids in band, or just nerdy kids who like to be creative, this is probably the greatest movie ever. —B. T.

TAPE L: DIRECTORS/LINKLATER, RICHARD (2001) 86M D: Richard Linklater. *Robert Sean Leonard, Uma Thurman, Ethan Hawke.* Leonard is a filmmaker returning to his Michigan hometown for a film festival, where he stops by to visit Hawke, an old high school friend who has become a drug dealer. There's an uncomfortable resentment between the two that at first seems to be about their occupations, but gets more complicated when their conversation turns to an old flame (who turns out to be Thurman). This is about as minimalistic as a movie can get, using a three-character play set entirely in a hotel room. I wouldn't want to see too many movies like this, but it's a worthwhile approach to a quickie digital-video side project, and I certainly enjoyed it more than Linklater's *Waking Life*, which he made the same year. —B. T.

WAKING LIFE L: DIRECTORS/LINKLATER, RICHARD (2001) 99M D: Richard Linklater. *Julie Delpy, Wiley Wiggins, Ethan Hawke.* The animation is inventive and at times gorgeous, but I could barely sit through this acclaimed experiment from the usually trustworthy Linklater. It's like being cornered at a party by every obnoxious person you ever knew in college and having to listen to their asinine theories about dreams and reality. Instead of pretending you have to leave, you just turn the thing off. —B. T.

BREAD AND ROSES L: DIRECTORS/LOACH, KEN (2000) 110M D: Ken Loach. *Elpidia Carrillo, Adrien Brody, Pilar Padilla, Jack McGee.* I value the cinema of social justice. The righteous anger of injustice, the thrill of solidarity, and the uplifting message that working-class individuals can and do make a difference is too often missing or candy-coated in American movies. In *Bread and Roses* Loach takes his concerns stateside with a labor drama set among the service workers in the Mexican immigrant community in LA. Padilla stars as a Latina Norma Rae caught up in the struggle that puts her at odds with her sister, and Brody is the passionate but reckless union organizer, a flamboyant personality whose showboating techniques constantly threaten his campaign. Loach is more committed to his message than to his characters, who all too often become mere foils for the social politics of Paul Laverty's simplistic script. Which makes this typical Loach: in some ways quite maddening and simplistic, but politically and socially engaged in a way American films so rarely are. —*S.A.*

LAND AND FREEDOM L: DIRECTORS/LOACH, KEN (1995) 109M D: Ken Loach. *Ian Hart, Rosana Pastor, Icíar Bollaín.* This is a moving film about a British journalist named David Carr (Hart) who goes to Spain to cover their Civil War. After becoming disenchanted with the Communist bureaucracy, he eventually joins an anarchist regiment and fights on the front lines against the Fascists. He is exposed to the "real" revolution through the anarchists' example of personal liberation and collectivist organization. Anarchists in Spain at the time believed that evolution wasn't some utopian dream after the revolution, but a change in consciousness and direct action to take over control of their lives from an imposed power. Seeing and experiencing this conflict firsthand changed Carr's perspective and his life. He also simultaneously falls in love with a fellow revolutionary while becoming embittered by the Communists' betrayal of the revolution. Their fate is intertwined in a bleak look at one of the most fascinating and overlooked situations of the twentieth century. —*B.W.*

SWEET SIXTEEN L: DIRECTORS/LOACH, KEN (2002) 106M D: Ken Loach. *Michelle Abercromby, Annmarie Fulton, William Ruane, Martin Compston.* Loach, who makes films as if he were Britain's social conscience, is back in his element with the devastating *Sweet Sixteen.* Scrappy, gawky Liam (Compston) has grown up in the impoverished, drug-controlled streets of Glasgow, where the accents are so thick they are impenetrable to American ears (you'll want to click on the English subtitles). That's where he intends to make his fortune and put his family back together, away from the reach of his crooked father and his mother's brutal drug-dealing boyfriend. Loach vividly exposes the self-destructive world of crime, broken families, and soured dreams that sucks in the teenage hustler Liam. As Loach shows, the mistakes of the past are not as damaging as the mistakes of the present, especially when you just keep making the same ones over and over again. It won the Best Screenplay award at Cannes. —*S.A.*

DON GIOVANNI L: DIRECTORS/LOSEY, JOSEPH (1979) 176M D: Joseph Losey. *Kiri Te Kanawa, Ruggero Raimondi, Teresa Berganza.* One of the finest operas ever written is adapted for the screen by British director Losey. Far from the staginess one normally associates with the filming of such works, Losey's *Don Giovanni* features the actual locations in Venice as depicted in the opera. Furthermore,

with good subtitling, expert dubbing, and excellent editing and cinematography, the rise and fall of this legendary womanizer is clearly laid out by the magic and dramatic genius of Mozart himself. Certainly, if Mozart could have directed his own movie today it would have been very close to what Losey researched and captured in this version. —*N.J.*

EVA L: DIRECTORS/LOSEY, JOSEPH (1962) 107M D: Joseph Losey. *Stanley Baker, Virna Lisi, Lisa Gastoni, Peggy Guggenheim, Jeanne Moreau.* A Welsh writer (Baker) engaged to a movie producer's assistant (Lisi) in Venice falls hard for a fickle, independent, cruel, indifferent woman (Moreau). Luring him only to spurn him, she later asks him to prove his love by leaving his own engagement party. She then shows up on his honeymoon, forcing the writer into an uncomfortable confession about the novel that made his reputation. Moreau has to be the weirdest woman in cinema on evidence of this film. Putting on a Billie Holliday record in a house she's broken into, she slips off her clothes to its rhythms for her bath. Then, when the house's owner arrives, she icily teases him out of his own bedroom and coldcocks him in the morning when he demands a kiss as payment. *Eva* is a couple films prior to Losey finding his patented visually bleak, psychologically edgy style. This darkly lyrical erotic thriller is Moreau's tetchy showcase through and through. —*J.C.*

MODESTY BLAISE L: DIRECTORS/LOSEY, JOSEPH (1966) 119M D: Joseph Losey. *Terence Stamp, Dirk Bogarde, Monica Vitti, Harry Andrews.* Vitti, the '60s cinema queen of restrained elegance and Italian ennui, puts on the mod and camps it up in this pop-art comic book farce. In fact, apart from the name it has little to do with the newspaper comic-strip spy series. The result is more silly than funny: she changes outfits and hair color with the snap of her fingers while her prissy arch nemesis (Bogarde, having a ball in a platinum coif and dandy-ish suits) plots increasingly more ludicrous schemes. It's impossibly convoluted and deliciously designed, a real visual treat with moments of inspired weirdness, but ultimately it's just empty calories. Think of this lark as a vacation from the usual seriousness of Vitti and Losey films. Stamp is all cockney cheek as the street-smart sidekick and Andrews grins wide as if he's in on the joke. —*S.A.*

MR. KLEIN L: DIRECTORS/LOSEY, JOSEPH (1976) 123M D: Joseph Losey. *Alain Delon, Francine Berge, Juliet Berto, Jeanne Moreau.* Delon balances charm with ruthlessness as an art collector buying the treasures of Jews fleeing France during the German occupation in WWII. It's not that he's vicious, but he has no qualms about taking advantage of people in dire straits. Poetic justice seems at hand when he's mistaken for a Jewish man by the same name who's wanted by the police.

Joseph Losey

Joseph Losey was born in 1909 in La Crosse, Wisconsin. After a brief stint at Harvard, Losey followed his true calling to New York City, where he became involved in theater and independent filmmaking. He was picked by MGM to work on short films but ditched them in 1947 for RKO, who gave him his first feature, *The Boy with Green Hair* (1948). As he slowly established himself in Hollywood, his leftist associations and tendencies caught the attention of the House Un-American Activities Committee, and he soon found himself blacklisted. He relocated to England in 1952 and within a few years was on his way to rebuilding what had begun as a promising career. His first

British feature, *The Sleeping Tiger* (1954), also marked his initial collaboration with actor Dirk Bogarde.

The next year would also feature Losey's first of several collaborations with the Hammer film studio and was, in retrospect, a pivotal point in the development of his interests and aesthetic. *A Man on the Beach* was a twenty-nine-minute casino-heist picture that would soon be followed by *The Intimate Stranger* (1956), the suspense-thriller *Time Without Pity* (1957), and the well-received *Blind Date* (1959). However, it was *The Criminal* (1960) that really opened doors for him. Losey's lurid exposé of the British underworld takes place almost exclusively in a prison and plays out like a chilling '60s complement to HBO's *Oz* series.

Hammer offered Losey the opportunity

As Delon searches for the phantom Mr. Klein, who seems to have led the police to his door, it becomes the opportunity for a spiritual quest, a journey of self discovery, but our poor Mr. Klein seems unable to step outside his bourgeois mindset. Losey creates an uneasy atmosphere in this existential mystery, a would-be thriller that raises more questions than it answers. —*S. A.*

SERVANT, THE L: DIRECTORS/LOSEY, JOSEPH (1963) 112M D: Joseph Losey. *Sarah Miles, Wendy Craig, Dirk Bogarde, James Fox.* Wealthy playboy Tony (Fox) hires Barrett (Bogarde) as his manservant. Barrett wows his employer with his efficiency and attention to detail, but Tony's fiancée (Craig) isn't so sure about him. The plot thickens when Barrett recommends his "sister" Vera (Miles) as a maid, then instigates an affair between Tony and Vera. As an engrossing power struggle develops, one can't deny a vaguely sexual charge driving the master-and-servant relationship between Tony and Barrett. What's truly amazing, however, is the desertion of realism, plausibility, and even the film's own hinted-at psychology by the "third act" as Tony deteriorates into a helpless invalid in Barrett's care. This shift happens quickly but effortlessly, as though the film grabbed the wheel of its own narrative and decided to plow it into the hillside. *The Servant* is like nothing I'd seen before, although the hallucinogenic, macabre scene toward the film's end seems a precursor to some of David Lynch's head trips. —*C. B.*

MERRY WIDOW, THE L: DIRECTORS/LUBITSCH, ERNST (1934) 99M D: Ernst Lubitsch. *Edward Everett Horton, Maurice Chevalier, Jeannette MacDonald.* Lubitsch's best musical, *The Merry Widow* ushered in the era of the sound musical. There have been several filmed versions of this operetta, but Lubitsch's inventive camera work and the great cast make this the superior adaptation. The scholar can study how this film eliminates the staginess characteristic of most musicals through the lush camera movements, becoming the prototype for filmed musicals for decades to come. The musical lover can marvel at the wonderful songs and performances. And the musical hater might just be charmed by the lovely leads and caught off guard by the sophisticated (and sexy) humor. MacDonald is a wealthy widow whose spending keeps a small country afloat. When she goes to Paris to search for a husband, the king sends suave Chevalier to woo her back home. Predictably, controversy and confusion ensue when genuine feelings of love arise. —*S. H.*

NINOTCHKA L: DIRECTORS/LUBITSCH, ERNST (1939) 110M D: Ernest Lubitsch. *Bela Lugosi, Greta Garbo, Melvyn Douglas.* Three ministers of the new Soviet Russia are in Paris to sell state jewels to raise money. When the grand duchess Swana gets an injunction against the sale of her former jewels, the three bumbling Bolsheviks—Ivanoff, Bulyanoff, and Kapowski—settle in Paris, fitting in too well and wasting Moscow's money. So special envoy

to direct the sci-fi thriller *The Damned* (aka *These Are the Damned*) in 1962, but did not give full support to the final product. Losey's downbeat genre effort, with a cast headed by Oliver Reed, was a far cry from the conventional sci-fi picture they wanted, and the film ended up being heavily cut before being released. Losey's greatest disappointment was that his next film, the psychosexual *Eve* (1962) starring Jeanne Moreau, also lost pivotal scenes to the shears of the producers, in addition to shedding its Billie Holiday soundtrack.

Determined to press on, Losey next made the brooding *The Servant* (1963), which was a resounding success. Boasting a screenplay by Harold Pinter (who also made a cameo appearance), *The Servant* stars Dirk Bogarde as a sinister household assistant who drives his master to ruin. Plans are hatched, roles are transgressed and subverted; rarely has the screen been privy to such an exacting

and masterful tale of class revenge. Losey's films benefit greatly from the disconcerting presence of Bogarde, who would also star in Losey's *King and Country* (1964) and the uncharacteristically vivacious pop-art caper *Modesty Blaise* (1966) before headlining Losey's international breakthrough film, *The Accident* (1967), a jazz-fueled meditation on alienation and ivory-tower privilege.

With the exception of *The Go-Between* (1970), which again featured a screenplay by Harold Pinter, as well as assured performances by Julie Christie and Alan Bates, Losey's subsequent films—among them *The Assassination of Trotsky* (1972), *A Doll's House* (1973), *Monsieur Klein* (1976), *Boris Godunov* (1980), and *Steaming* (1985)—fail to impress. Succumbing to the poor health that dogged him for most of his years, Losey died in London in 1984.

—*Kier-La Janisse*

Nina Ivanovna Yakushova, "Ninotchka" (Garbo), is sent to straighten things out. Garbo is perfect in the role of Ninotchka—she is droll, dry and a darling. But Ninotchka finds Paris to her liking as well, and when she falls in love with Leon (a dashing Douglas), she may never go back to her Communist ways. Directed with aplomb by Lubitsch, *Ninotchka* is so well written (in part by Billy Wilder) and executed that it is one of the all-time classic screwball comedies. —*G. M.*

SHOP AROUND THE CORNER, THE L: DIRECTORS/LUBITSCH, ERNST (1940) 99M D: Ernst Lubitsch. *Frank Morgan, James Stewart, Margaret Sullavan.* This enchanting picture was the inspiration for an unpleasant '90s comedy (*You've Got Mail*) but don't let that deter you from watching the original. It's pretty great. Stewart plays a likable but tightly wound clerk at Matuschek's department store in Budapest. When Mr. Matuschek (Morgan) hires a new female clerk (Sullavan), the two instantly start squabbling and competing with each other. Unknowingly, they have been exchanging letters through an anonymous lonely hearts club and, as their annoyance at work grows, they fall in love on paper. Thanks to the fine performances and Lubitsch's ability to bring forth the characters' humanity, this remains one of the best and most beloved romantic comedies ever. —*S. H.*

STUDENT PRINCE IN OLD HEIDELBERG, THE L: DIRECTORS/LUBITSCH, ERNST (1927) 102M D: Ernst Lubitsch. *Ramon Novarro, Philippe DeLacy, Jean Hersholt, Norma Shearer, Gustav von Seyffertitz.* This is a musical without music, a poem without words. The prince (Novarro) leaves his palace cloister behind and goes off to university to debate, drink, laugh, and sing in beer gardens with other students. He falls in love with the innkeeper's daughter (Shearer), but not before the little flirting dance they play with each other. The flowers and the grass on the hillside are sweet, but all things good must pass. The king dies and the prince must return to his palace duties, meaning he must have a proper marriage for his station. Little rhymes and contrasts in Novarro and Shearer's twining performances build the story of their feelings for each other like a Mozart sonata. The humor is subtly layered and totally visual. The pathos of promises made that can never be kept stings deep. Shot for shot, this is as good as cinema ever gets. —*J. C.*

TO BE OR NOT TO BE L: DIRECTORS/LUBITSCH, ERNST (1942) 99M D: Ernst Lubitsch. *Felix Bressart, Jack Benny, Carole Lombard, Robert Stack, Sig Rumann.* It outraged some people that as Hitler stood with his boot on the throat of Europe, Lubitsch chose to make a comedy about the Nazi occupation of Poland, starring Benny yet. The thing is, *To Be or Not to Be* is an unprecedented comedy, a black comedy, a comedy with such an exquisite sense of weight and timing that the viewer is often caught between a laugh and a gasp. Its aim is to demystify Hitler as "just a little man with a mustache"—a process that begins with the mind-boggling double take of an opening sequence. The action centers on a Warsaw theater company whose principal actor is an insufferable ham (Benny). His wife and leading lady (Lombard) is an incurable flirt, and the amatory prize for everyone from an RAF Polish squadron aviator (Stack) to, well, let's just say some top Nazi operatives. The ham is playing Hamlet; it's key to the movie's emotional and political dynamics that the line "to be or not to be" evolves from a cue for adulterous mischief to an index of theatrical illusion-making and ultimately a heartfelt acknowledgment of mortality. Mortality wrapped around the movie meta-cinematically too: Lombard, on a bond-selling tour for the war effort, was killed in a plane crash shortly before the film's premiere. —R.T.J.

TROUBLE IN PARADISE L: DIRECTORS/LUBITSCH, ERNST (1932) 82M D: Ernest Lubitsch. *Herbert Marshall, Miriam Hopkins, Kay Francis, Charlie Ruggles, Edward Everett Horton.* One only need watch this film to see the smooth elegance, continental wit, and winking innuendo that defines the Lubitsch touch. In quite possibly the most sparkling and sexy romantic comedy ever made, Marshall and Hopkins are smooth jewel thieves working the wealthy rubes of Europe's hot spots. Their latest sting hits a snag when suave Marshall falls for flighty heiress Francis, their latest target. Lubitsch creates his films in the fantasy of wealth and splendor, but the desires of his characters—romance, position, money, sex—are utterly earthy. For every minute of this film, he transforms Marshall into the most suave and romantic lover on the planet, a man who could talk a girl out of her heart, her fortune, and her clothes. Lubitsch is never so coarse as to show it, but with a little shadow and wordplay and the most graceful edits of the golden age of Hollywood, he can suggest anyone into bed. —S.A.

MOULIN ROUGE (2001) L: DIRECTORS/LUHRMANN, BAZ (2001) 128M D: Baz Luhrmann. *Jim Broadbent, Richard Roxburgh, John Leguizamo, Nicole Kidman, Ewan McGregor.* An innocuous batch of cotton candy that's crammed so tightly with horrible fads from the past fifty years it's impossible to tell whether Luhrmann's trying to mock or pay homage to them. In the end, he fails to do either. Now, I could go on about aspects of the film (the costumes, the cinematography), but when one's senses have been attacked so relentlessly, it's difficult enough to figure out what the hell the film's about, much less actually care. (For the record, here's the plot, or at least as much as I gathered: young wannabe writer goes to an infamous Parisian brothel and falls in love with their top whore, who's also involved with another guy. Your typical love triangle story,

complete with promiscuousness and ego stroking galore.) Luhrmann beats his audience over the head with all that glitter and gaudiness so furiously and condescendingly to hide the fact that behind the music and the staging is a director trying to figure out what the hell to do with his talent. —K.F.

Oh, give me a break. Luhrmann's style obviously isn't for everyone, but it's refreshing when directors make movies this odd, especially with a big studio budget and stars. It's a huge, gaudy, meticulously designed stage musical, but instead of on a stage it's on the screen, using state-of-the-art digital effects and camera trickery. Sure, the pro-love theme isn't anything new, but then Luhrmann never said it was; in fact, the melding of multiple time periods seems to point to the universality of the message. It could be today or it could be a hundred years ago. I think Luhrmann pulled that off better in *Romeo + Juliet* but I still enjoyed seeing it done up so extravagantly and as a musical. —B.T.

ROMEO + JULIET L: DIRECTORS/LUHRMANN, BAZ (1996) 120M D: Baz Luhrmann. *Leonardo Dicaprio, Claire Danes, Harold Perrineau Jr., John Leguizamo, Pete Postlethwaite, Paul Sorvino.* Filtered through Luhrmann's MTV-style eye for theatricality, the senseless teenage passion at the heart of Shakespeare's play is given new life. Although Dicaprio and Danes at times have to struggle to deliver the dialogue, they are made more convincing by the gaudy world they inhabit, which combines modern iconography, advertising, weaponry, cinematic allusions, and Hawaiian shirts with the societal rules of the original play. Montagues and Capulets bite their thumbs at each other and wave guns engraved with the word "dagger." I was won over by the opening shot: a television floating in a black void, showing a news report. It is delivered in such a standard local news tone that it took me a bit to realize the anchor was speaking in the original language of the play. The subsequent overwhelming display of quick cuts and intertitles is such an absurd juxtaposition with the material that, paradoxically, it seems completely natural. It calms down a bit by the end and loses some of its momentum, but there's no denying the effectiveness of the film's depiction of overwhelming puppy love. I mean, you can say it doesn't work, but I still remember sitting in a theater full of teenage girls with tears streaming down their faces. —B.T.

STRICTLY BALLROOM L: DIRECTORS/LUHRMANN, BAZ (1992) 94M D: Baz Luhrmann. *Pat Thompson, Peter Whitford, Tara Morice, Gia Carides, Bill Hunter, Paul Mercurio.* Ohhhhhh, how I love this film! This is a familiar story about people who dare to be different, who dare to dream, and the obstacles they must face and overcome to be true to themselves. Ballroom dancing is the passion and the vehicle for this film, and it is truly a world unto itself. The dancing, the characters, and the outrageous costumes are by turns ludicrous and exquisite. This is a film not afraid to make fun of itself, or its subject matter and players, but at the same time it is refreshingly honest about dreams, obsessions, obligations, and what is really important—to live life not in fear. Every time I see the final competition and the hero and heroine step onto the dance floor, a smile curls my lips, my feet move to the music, and my heart races with excitement. —*M. N.*

DEATHTRAP L: DIRECTORS/LUMET, SIDNEY (1982) 118M D: Sidney Lumet. *Irene Worth, Michael Caine, Henry Jones, Dyan Cannon, Christopher Reeve.* A writer from New England (Caine) has a murder-mystery stage play flop and soon he comes up with a plan to murder one of his students so as to steal a better play. He ropes his wife into the plot until she dies from a coronary when she finds the student (Reeve) isn't quite dead after all. The two live and write together as a same-sex couple until Caine finds that Reeve is writing a play about the murder exactly as it happened. The plot twists start going a bit crazy from there until the end where it eventually all winds up on stage and is a great success. Ira Levin wrote the actual play, but you must sit through this comic tragedy to see which character survives to write the play within the play! —*N. J.*

DOG DAY AFTERNOON L: DIRECTORS/LUMET, SIDNEY (1975) 124M D: Sidney Lumet. *Penelope Allen, Al Pacino, John Cazale, Charles Durning, Chris Sarandon, Lance Henriksen.* "Attica! Attica!" At one point this phrase referred to the brutal massacre at the famed New York prison; now it is forever engrained in the popular moviegoer's brain as Pacino's war cry in Lumet's lambaste of the media and law enforcement. Based on true events, the film centers on Sonny (a feral Pacino), a somewhat charming barker who botches up a routine bank robbery, taking hostages to manage an escape. A crowd of onlookers and cops amasses, as does the media, who begin to exploit the situation when they find out, among other things, that Sonny is a homosexual. The film never wears its politics on its sleeve; rather Lumet engages in character detail and nuance, allowing the film a methodical pacing and grainy realism, even during its most tense moments. Cazale is great as Sal, Sonny's edgy accomplice. —*J. D.*

EQUUS L: DIRECTORS/LUMET, SIDNEY (1977) 137M D: Sidney Lumet. *Peter Firth, Colin Blakely, Joan Plowright, Eileen Atkins, Harry Andrews, Richard Burton.* Burton was nominated for a Best Actor Oscar for his role as a psychiatrist who becomes obsessed with trying to resolve the inner conflicts of one of his patients. Firth plays the young man whose infatuation with horses has gone a little too far, so much so that he finds it difficult to maintain normal relationships. Peter Shaffer's play is expanded for this film and is perhaps a bit long as it tries to dive into the tragic flaws of both characters. But it is Lumet's direction that unifies everything into a beautiful and strangely compelling film. —*N. J.*

FAIL SAFE L: DIRECTORS/LUMET, SIDNEY (1964) 112M D: Sidney Lumet. *Henry Fonda, Dom DeLuise, Larry Hagman, Walter Matthau, Frank Overton, Fritz Weaver.* Fonda plays the President of the United States in this, the ultimate Cold War film. The United States and the USSR have built up enough nuclear bombs to destroy the world many times over, but by some glitch an American aircraft is sent to drop a bomb on the enemy. Most of the film focuses on the effort to recall the mission, which proves difficult since the pilots are trained to disregard all such calls as Soviet trickery. Released the same year as *Dr. Strangelove,* this film analyzes the chillingly frightful possibilities of what could go wrong with the '60s philosophy of mutually assured destruction. —*N. J.*

GUILTY AS SIN L: DIRECTORS/LUMET, SIDNEY (1993) 120M D: Sidney Lumet. *Rebecca DeMornay, Stephen Lang, Don Johnson, Jack Warden.* This enthralling script by Larry Cohen is perfectly cast. DeMornay plays the beautiful and talented young attorney who decides to take on the case of a very flirtatious widower (Johnson) who is accused of murdering his wife for her lavish fortune. After getting to know her client better the lawyer tries backing out of the case, but the judge reprimands her saying it's too late for such a decision. Meanwhile, her professional relationship with her client devolves into a manipulative quagmire where the two seem to be falling in love with each other while at the same time feeling compelled to stab each other in the back. —*N. J.*

NETWORK L: DIRECTORS/LUMET, SIDNEY (1976) 121M D: Sidney Lumet. *Robert Duvall, Beatrice Straight, Ned Beatty, Peter Finch, William Holden, Faye Dunaway.* This eye-opening dramatic satire concerns the function of news in an era of profit-driven media—a very prophetic film for America in 1976. A large TV news station is sold to a giant network and decisions start being made, not about what news people should know, but rather about what stories will bring the highest ratings. During this corporate birthing process Finch, who plays an anchorman, disappears and shows up days later having seen visions. The station figures out he's gone mad, but the network finds his insane outbursts on TV improve their ratings. The prescience of this film is not only accurate to our times, it underestimates just how far networks will sell out, making this nasty satire seem more like a mild comic matinee for most of today's younger audiences. —*N. J.*

David Lynch

Writer/director/artist David Lynch's Northwest childhood of fear and wonder infuses his adult view of art and life, shaping films of unique visual and emotional power. Born in 1946, Lynch was fascinated as a boy by quirky small-town characters and spooky forests, and perceived "a force of wild pain and decay" hiding behind the everyday world's facade. Though plagued by agoraphobia and sometimes afraid to leave his house, he dedicated himself at a young age to being an painter and to following his muse's call wherever it would take him.

Intrigued by the idea of seeing the figures in his paintings move, Lynch made an animated film (*Six Figures Getting Sick* [1968]) while attending the Pennsylvania Academy of Fine Arts, in which men catch fire, their stomachs bloat, and they vomit blood, thus presaging what would become familiar Lynchian territory: human beings in desperate torment.

As a youth Lynch's obsession with becoming an artist had met with resistance both at home and at high school, fostering a general fear of being kept from thinking, feeling, and doing what he dearly wanted to do. This experience is reflected in his animated short *The Grandmother* (1970), in which a boy who is emotionally and physically abused by his parents grows a kindly grandmother from a seed. The film illustrates both Lynch's extraordinary imagination and his lifelong belief in angelic agents and the transcendent power of love. It also initiates his trademark storytelling style, in which reality, dream, and fantasy seamlessly merge to communicate intense, resonant feelings.

Lynch's first feature, *Eraserhead* (1976), reflects his sense of himself as a confused man overwhelmed by unplanned parenthood. It also exemplifies his characteristic artistic embrace of disturbingly extreme psychological states and behavior. In the 1970s Lynch began to practice transcendental meditation, and *The Elephant Man* (1980), in which a London man's monstrously deformed body contains a sweetly sensitive soul, manifests Lynch's profound interest in spiritual matters and inner consciousness.

Lynch returned to his Northwest lumber-town roots in *Blue Velvet* (1986), in which a young man discovers his dark capacity for sadistic sex and violence, and heroically steers his life in the opposite direction. Another Northwest saga, the groundbreaking TV series *Twin Peaks* (1990–91) and film *Twin Peaks: Fire Walk with Me* (1992), boldly explored the harsh reality of father-daughter incest and murder, and made black coffee and cherry pie, a dancing dwarf in a red-curtained room, and the question "Who killed Laura Palmer?" cultural touchstones. The *Twin Peaks* cycle is also the romantic Lynch's adoring rhapsody to women, be they victims, vixens, sages, or lovers.

Lost Highway (1997) and *Mulholland Drive* (2001) are Los Angeles–resident Lynch's first hometown stories, and both communicate his belief in reincarnation and karmic justice, as killers adopt new identities but cannot escape their dark deeds.

Now fifty-eight, Lynch has retained a young person's wide-eyed vision of the world as a strange and scary, yet beneficent and joyful place. It's a balancing act, and for Lynch, "that's a beautiful thing."

—Greg Olson

SERPICO L: DIRECTORS/LUMET, SIDNEY (1973) 130M D: Sidney Lumet. *Jack Kehoe, Barbara Eda-Young, John Randolph, Al Pacino, F. Murray Abraham.* Pacino plays Frank Serpico, the real-life policeman who single-handedly exposed mass corruption in the New York Police Department. He accomplished this by going undercover and following the drugs and money. His rugged and highly independent approach to detective work made him doggedly pursue criminals and ignore the soft pedaling of his superiors until at last he firmly established a connection between the two. As this movie accurately portrays, Serpico was a pariah within the police force. The top brass, sensing what he was on to, did whatever it took to make him go away. After the whole scandal came out he did go away, to Europe, far away from the corrupt network he broke open. Pacino is perfect in this role, and director Lumet adds his unique touch of suspense and realism. *—N. J.*

12 ANGRY MEN L: DIRECTORS/LUMET, SIDNEY (1957) 96M D: Sidney Lumet. *Henry Fonda, Lee J. Cobb, E. G. Marshall, Jack Warden.* Twelve jurors find themselves with an eleven-to-one guilty verdict in a murder trial as this post-courtroom drama opens up. Fonda is Juror #8, who does an astonishing job as the one who has reasonable doubt, facing the other jurors who would rather get the job done quickly and get on with their lives. As the evidence is inspected once again, doubt begins to creep into some of the jurors' minds, and what was once clearly defining evidence starts to crumble away. Tension mounts as others side with Juror #8, and the clock grows closer to the time the jurors have set to decide if they will have a hung jury or rule in unison on the teenager's fate. *12 Angry Men,* which was originally written as a teleplay in 1954, is brilliantly brought to the silver screen by an amazing ensemble cast, and with the help of a razor-sharp script it was deservedly nominated for four Oscars including Best Picture. *—R. M.*

HITCH-HIKER, THE L: DIRECTORS/LUPINO, IDA (1953) 71M D: Ida Lupino. *Edmond O'Brien, William Talman, Frank Lovejoy.* You can almost feel the grit in Lupino's low-budget thriller; she makes the most of the barren desert setting in this story of a psychotic killer (Talman) who hitches a ride with a pair of vacationing buddies (O'Brien and Lovejoy) on their way to fish the Gulf Coast. In the best film noir tradition, the wide-open plains become a veritable prison to the easygoing everymen as long as their captor has the gun, the car keys, and a spooky deformed eye that never closes. . . even when he sleeps. Their feeling of helplessness gives dimension to the tense tale. Lupino was no stylist, and even her best work suffers from a narrative slackness, but her coarse location shooting and cheap sets create a vivid world, an antidote to the Hollywood gloss. *—S. A.*

BLUE VELVET L: DIRECTORS/LYNCH, DAVID (1986) 120M D: David Lynch. *Jack Nance, Dean Stockwell, Laura Dern, Dennis Hopper, Isabella Rossellini, Kyle MacLachlan.* MacLachlan plays a young man who discovers a severed human ear in a field. He brings the ear to the police and is dismayed to find how unimportant the precinct finds the body part. His earnestness to do good propels him into his own sort of investigation, which soon envelopes him in situations and circumstances well beyond his control. Hopper takes the role of the drug hound who seems to be at the root of the case, but MacLachlan somehow gets deeply involved with a totally imbalanced woman (Rossellini) before finally unlocking the mystery. This is perhaps Lynch's finest film, balancing his taste for mystery and the absurd in some of the most fascinating proportions. *—N.J.*

DUNE L: DIRECTORS/LYNCH, DAVID (1984) 190M D: David Lynch. *Sting, Max von Sydow, Dean Stockwell, Brad Dourif, Kyle McLachlan, Jack Nance.* Even Lynch's worst movie (a label given to *Dune* that is rarely disputed) is still really quite an excellent film. Dismissed by fans of the novel for being a poor adaptation, and dismissed by many Lynch fans for being too influenced by Hollywood (both of which are apt and legitimate complaints), it still has some of the qualities that make Lynch films great. Its bizarre atmosphere and intriguing aesthetics are what really give it spark. *—T. S.*

ELEPHANT MAN, THE L: DIRECTORS/LYNCH, DAVID (1980) 125M D: David Lynch. *John Gielgud, Anthony Hopkins, Michael Elphick, Anne Bancroft, John Hurt.* Hurt is astonishing as John Merrick, the truly hideous man in Victorian England who is removed from a freak show by a philanthropic doctor (Hopkins). The good doctor studies his patient carefully and soon makes a few improvements in the poor man's lifestyle, invariably discovering a gentle human being beneath the coarse shell of a monster. However, the doctor fervently believes that proper education and appropriate dress should be able to acclimate this poor fellow into society as a normal person. This seems to work for a time, but the experiment is not without its pitfalls. Beautifully shot in black and white by a very restrained Lynch, *The Elephant Man* is one of the most sensitive historic dramas you are likely to see. *—N.J.*

ERASERHEAD L: DIRECTORS/LYNCH, DAVID (1978) 85M D: David Lynch. *Jeanne Bates, Laurel Near, Judith Anna Roberts, Jack Nance, Charlotte Stewart, Allen Joseph.* A person could go absolutely crazy trying to analyze this avant-garde film. The narrative structure is intact just enough that most people will walk away knowing the story, but the black-and-white imagery and sound effects clearly point toward something deep and sinister at work. There must be something wrong with the character played by Nance, who seems to be a mentally deficient everyman with big hair.

Or perhaps there is something wrong with his girlfriend (Stewart), who cooks a mean dish of chicken and gives birth to some totally unearthly creature. Or maybe it's the entire society they live in and its perverted filter on reality. Either way this stunning film leaves these interpretations largely up to its audience. Lynch's first feature film will stay in your head for a long time. —*N. J.*

INDUSTRIAL SYMPHONY NO. 1 L: DIRECTORS/LYNCH, DAVID (1990) 50M D: David Lynch. *Michael J. Anderson, Nicholas Cage, Laura Dern, Julee Cruise.* Lynch and Angelo Badalamenti teamed up with their siren Cruise to create this bizarre and beautiful piece of musical theater. It has Michael J. Anderson (the "man from another place"), Cage, and Dern performing. It is everything you want from Lynch: strange, surreal, haunting, moving. It uses pieces of music from *Twin Peaks*, the Cruise/Badalamenti/Lynch collaboration albums *Floating into the Night* and *The Voice of Love*, and some original material as well. This film is a must-see for Lynch fans and a strange and confounding experience for those unfamiliar with his work. —*T. S.*

LOST HIGHWAY L: DIRECTORS/LYNCH, DAVID (1997) 135M D: David Lynch. *Robert Blake, Robert Loggia, Balthazar Getty, Bill Pullman, Patricia Arquette.* Employing a circular logic of symbolism and surrealism, *Lost Highway* tells a story of romantic longing, emotional destruction, and eventual madness. Often considered Lynch's warm-up run for *Mulholland Drive*, *Lost Highway* is actually the superior film. Where *Mulholland Drive* can more or less be figured out, *Lost Highway* remains a mystery. A beautiful, obscure, enchanting, terrifying mystery. Without a definite explanation of the events that unfold, we are invited into the poetic dream-speak of surrealism where every detail has meaning and yet none of it has any meaning at all. Rarely has a film so accurately depicted the unnamable emotions evoked from the deep longing of the soul. The film resides in another world, one where beauty and horror exist simultaneously and love and sadness are entirely inseparable. It is a testament to Lynch's prowess to create art that is at once powerful, challenging, and yet entirely accessible. *Lost Highway* is a landmark achievement that Lynch may never surpass. —*T. S.*

MULHOLLAND DRIVE L: DIRECTORS/LYNCH, DAVID (2001) 147M D: David Lynch. *Ann Miller, Lafayette Montgomery, Justin Theroux, Naomi Watts, Dan Hedaya, Laura Harring.* After the enormous success of the cult series *Twin Peaks*, Lynch set to work on another equally mysterious and bizarre show called *Mulholland Drive*. After the pilot was released to studio officials at ABC they got cold feet and decided that the material was a little too bizarre. *Mulholland Drive* concerns a woman (Harring) who survives a nasty car accident yet suffers from severe amnesia. An aspiring actress (Watts) befriends her and helps her try to piece together her life. Naturally this takes the two of them through many strange scenes. This pilot episode was cut, re-shot, re-edited, and ultimately became a very different vision than the full miniseries as it was originally conceived. This is particularly evident through the second half of the film where loose ends in the story line abruptly pop up in a desperate attempt to conclude the film. —*N. J.*

STRAIGHT STORY, THE L: DIRECTORS/LYNCH, DAVID (1999) 112M D: David Lynch. *Harry Dean Stanton, Sissy Spacek, Richard Farnsworth.* A G-rated, family-friendly tale from America's most subversive filmmaker? Lynch defies expectations once again, putting his measured pacing, out-of-step conversational style, and mesmerizing images to the true story of Alvin Straight, the seventy-three-year-old man who drove for six weeks on a riding mower across two states to patch up a decade-old feud with his estranged brother. Lynch skews this delightful journey with oddball moments of weirdness and wonder, and Farnsworth (as Straight) grounds it with withered wisdom from behind wispy hair and twinkling blue eyes. A luminous Spacek gives a heartbreaking performance as his daughter, turning the lurching rhythm of her speech impediment into something almost musical. It could easily slide into melancholy and sentimentality without Lynch's sensibility, an odd mix of up-by-your-bootstraps American conservatism, on-the-road romanticism, and quiet moments of wonder. Lynch transforms Straight's story into a truly beautiful tale from the American heartland. —*S. A.*

TWIN PEAKS L: DIRECTORS/LYNCH, DAVID (1990) 720M D: David Lynch. *Jack Nance, Peggy Lipton, Richard Beymer, Joan Chen, Michael Ontkean, Kyle McLachlan.* *Twin Peaks* is the miniseries directed by Lynch that became a cult sensation inspiring a feature-length film as a prequel as well as several spin-offs. MacLachlan plays the straight-laced FBI agent who investigates the murder of Laura Palmer in the very quirky Northwest town named Twin Peaks. Over its fifteen episodes a mosaic of interesting characters is introduced, each adding a small piece to the elaborate puzzle. Repeated viewings are almost mandatory for those who want to absorb the full story. And with all the curious subplots and odd characters it's hard not to watch it a second or third time once you have been taken in by its strange magic. —*N. J.*

TWIN PEAKS: FIRE WALK WITH ME L: DIRECTORS/LYNCH, DAVID (1992) 135M D: David Lynch. *Moira Kelly, David Bowie, Harry Dean Stanton, David Lynch, Kyle McLachlan, Sheryl Lee.* As a prequel to the*Twin Peaks* TV series, *Fire Walk With Me* is a curious film that tries at once to be an introduction to those new to the murder mystery as well as a kind of narrative addenda for compulsive fans of the series. However, most everyone watching this film knows Laura Palmer is going to be murdered, so there is more an air of predestination about the film rather than one of suspense. Characters are introduced beyond the familiar ones of the series and there are even more peculiar scenarios that don't explain themselves. By the end one is left with very few answered questions. Once you're done watching, it might be time to watch the show again. —*N. J.*

WILD AT HEART L: DIRECTORS/LYNCH, DAVID (1990) 124M D: David Lynch. *Nicolas Cage, Diane Ladd, Harry Dean Stanton, Crispin Glover, Laura Dern.* Lynch follows the yellow brick road in this bizarre take on the theme of the classic film. Ladd is beyond phenomenal as Marietta Fortune, the crazed mother of Lula (Dern), damning her daughter's boyfriend, Sailor (Cage), who just got out of jail by hiring a hit man (Stanton) to put him out of commission. The pathos Ladd engages on the screen in internal retaliation for her daughter's partner choices is shocking, with makeup smears and bellowing trumpets on the score. The violence is just plain over the top and quite fun, especially when Lula relates a story about her relative Dell (Glover) and his enjoyment of cockroaches in his underwear. This is one kooky couple with great wacky dialogue and a love for thrash-metal music. Hot stuff from a roller coaster of a director, *Wild at Heart* has its own pulse and is "weird on top." —*S. R.*

CAREFUL L: DIRECTORS/MADDIN, GUY (1993) 100M D: Guy Maddin. *Kyle McCulloch, Gosia Dobrowolska, Sarah Neville, Paul Cox.* A slow-developing romance is told in the most unlikely setting: a small village way up in the Alps where everyone is as quiet as they can be lest they start an avalanche. It's the perfect place for a script about repression, and of course there's a whole lot of dirt that nobody wants to talk about. To add to this crazy setting and plot is the highly stylized photography that strangely captures the look of an old silent film complete with printed titles between scenes; and the color of the film appears like some failed color system from an earlier time. This curiously over-the-top independent film is well worth a look. —*N. J.*

DRACULA: PAGES FROM A VIRGIN'S DIARY L: DIRECTORS/MADDIN, GUY (2002) 75M D: Guy Maddin. *Tara Birtwhistle, David Moroni, Cindy Marie Small, Johnny Wright, Zhang Wei-Qiang.* Bram Stoker's *Dracula* was already made into a silent film (the unauthorized *Nosferatu*) and into many ballets, but this is the first time it has been both. Maddin adapts the Royal Winnipeg Ballet's version using almost exclusively the cinematic techniques that were available in the silent era (with occasional flourishes of sound effects, slow motion, colorization, violence, and sexuality).

Maddin's film does not follow the book page by page but features numerous scenes that are left out of most movie versions, such as the blood transfusion scene and the beheading of Lucy. But what really makes this work is the strong presence (and dancing!) of Zhang as Dracula. Obviously this is not for everyone, but then I wouldn't have thought I'd enjoy a silent ballet of Dracula, and here I am. —*B. T.*

TWILIGHT OF THE ICE NYMPHS L: DIRECTORS/MADDIN, GUY (1997) 91M D: Guy Maddin. *Pascale Bussieres, Nigel Whitmey, Shelley Duvall, Frank Gorshin, Alice Krige.* Maddin's color debut is a story of sex and obsession in a hallucinatory forest lit by the golden hues of a perpetual sunset. A mysterious political prisoner returns home to his ostrich farm in the storybook land of Madragora and falls in love with two women—exotic temptress Bussieres and woodland beauty Krige—both under the sway of a sinister hypnotist out of some expressionist German silent. It's an Aubrey Beardsley painting come to life by way of Maddin's unique rhythms, rich textures, and surreal stories, and peopled by his best cast to date: Duvall costars as the hero's sister and Gorshin is her tetchy handyman. Maddin's obsessed hero remains unidentified in the credits, but he's since been identified as the body of Nigel Whitmey and the voice of Ross McMillan. —*S. A.*

BARAN L: DIRECTORS/MAJIDI, MAJID (2001) 96M D: Majid Majidi. *Zahra Bahrami, Hossein Abedini.* The beauty of most Iranian cinema is in its evocative directness and simple poetry. Majidi's story of Latif, a hotheaded young Iranian man working on a construction site teeming with illegal Afghan workers, and the silent, shy Afghan boy who takes his cushy job, has a tendency to veer into obvious, didactic "lessons." The boy, it turns out, is really a girl in disguise, desperately hiding her identity to support her impoverished family, and Latif becomes smitten. Not exactly a convincing turn of events, but it provides the impetus for Latif's growth as he discovers her culture of Afghans without a home caught between the dream of freedom and the pull of homeland, and trapped in a world of poverty either way. Majidi's deft moments of unspoken communication and evocative Spartan imagery give the film a tenderness and a power beyond story. —*S. A.*

CHILDREN OF HEAVEN L: DIRECTORS/MAJIDI, MAJID (1997) 88M D: Majid Majidi. *Mohammad Amir Naji, Mir Farrokh Hashemian, Bahare Seddiqi, Fereshte Sarabandi.* Running errands for the family, Ali loses his sister Zahra's shoes, which he'd taken for restitching. While this sounds like a trivial matter, for this poverty-stricken Iranian family it's a small catastrophe. Knowing his out-of-work father cannot afford to replace the shoes and fearing punishment, resourceful Ali devises a time-sharing plan so that he and Zahra can

both use his shoes, bribing his reluctant sister with a coveted new pencil. Ali and Zahra must sprint to and from school to make each tightly scheduled shoe hand-off. After weeks of this, a school footrace is announced—the third-place prize a new pair of sneakers. Now quite the runner, Ali must be careful not to win the race, but to place third. Sentimental in a good way and similar to *The Bicycle Thief*, this touching human drama may completely alter your vision of the familiar material world around you. —*C. B.*

LOVE AFFAIR, OR THE CASE OF THE MISSING SWITCHBOARD OPERATOR L: DIRECTORS/MAKAVEJEV, DUSAN (1967) 73M D: Dusan Makavejev. *Slobodan Aligrudic, Eva Ras, Zivojin Aleksic.* Switchboard Operator is the most wholly satisfying of Makavejev's films. There are three overlapping narrative layers: the story of a love affair between Isabela the switchboard operator and Ahmed the exterminator, the autopsy of Isabela's drowned body, and a nonspecific discussion of violent sex crime. What's remarkable is how seamlessly *Switchboard Operator* shifts between documentary and narrative modes, allowing the two to affect one another without losing sight of the overriding narrative and without sacrificing stylistic consistency. A cinematic house of mirrors, it seems to use every narrative device within reach for its story of the reconciliation of personal needs with those of the common good. Makavejev's *WR* would take this method further, but *Switchboard Operator*'s gravity (as opposed to *WR*'s delirious camp) and raw black-and-white photography make for a much more appealing movie. —*C. B.*

SWEET MOVIE L: DIRECTORS/MAKAVEJEV, DUSAN (1974) 99M D: Dusan Makavejev. *Pierre Clémente, Anna Prucnal, Carole Laure.* Sweet Movie is the story of two women. One, the winner of the Miss World Virginity contest, escapes from her husband after their honeymoon, during which he urinates on her. She is beaten, shipped to Paris in a suitcase, has a tryst with a rock star, and ends up in a commune, emotionally destroyed. This is intercut with the story of another woman, who captains a ship filled with candy and vats of sugar. While constantly espousing revolutionary ideals she lures boys and men aboard her ship for sex. Then she kills them. Makavejev's satire comments on sexual politics, but its main intrigue is in the images it presents. Surreal and disturbing, *Sweet Movie* is sure to provoke at least some sort of reaction. —*T. S.*

WR: MYSTERIES OF THE ORGANISM L: DIRECTORS/ MAKAVEJEV, DUSAN (1971) 80M D: Dusan Makavejev. *Zoran Radmilovic, Jagoda Kaloper, Milena Dravic.* Unable to satisfactorily complete two very different film projects, Makavejev somehow successfully combined them into a single cohesive film. A campy and sexed-up movie about two idealistic socialist women (which would've been pretty

lame on its own) gains tremendous value from interwoven documentary portions concerning controversial psychologist/sexologist Wilhelm Reich. Disparate threads of fact and fiction combine for an extremely loose piece on revolution, physical needs, socialism, Yugoslavia, sexuality, and seemingly everything in between. Never steering a straight course, *WR* casts unresolved loose ends this way and that, but also maintains an unparalleled freshness. *WR* is guaranteed to be unlike anything you've seen, and though far from a perfect film, it proposes an entirely new model of cinema. Sadly, few made use of Makavejev's trailblazing, and *WR* is ultimately more of a long-forgotten blind alley than a new beginning. —*C. B.*

KANDAHAR L: DIRECTORS/MAKHMALBAF, MOHSEN (2001) 85M D: Mohsen Makhmalbaf. *Hassan Tantai, Nelofer Pazira.* Nafas (Pazira), a Western-living Afghani woman, hides herself under a heavy burka and smuggles herself into her mother country in the days before September 11, when the Taliban's laws still stripped women of civil rights and hope. She witnesses border gangs that rob travelers, crippled victims of land mines awaiting prosthetic limbs in desert hospital tents, and a doctor (Tantai) forbidden to speak with the female patients he can examine only through a hole in a sheet hanging across the room. Clumsy dubbing enhances the awkwardness of the performances, but Makhmalbaf's haunting imagery tells a story of devastation, desperation, and poverty. Men on crutches scuttle across the desert as a helicopter drops prosthetic legs that float through the air under parachutes. Young women play with nail polish and jangly bracelets with the glee of girls playing dress-up for perhaps the last time. An eclipse of the sun sears a stark black-and-white image into the screen. *The Sun Behind the Moon* is the English translation of the original title, and what could better exemplify Nafas's odyssey than hiding the radiant light of the sun behind a veil? —*S. A.*

ONCE UPON A TIME, CINEMA L: DIRECTORS/MAKHMALBAF, MOHSEN (1992) 100M D: Mohsen Makhmalbaf. *Ezzatollah Entezami, Mehdi Hashemi.* Makhmalbaf's valentine to the history of Iranian cinema is a loving celebration of the magic of movies. Loosely organized around the story of a cinematographer (a Chaplin-esque figure in a fez) who introduces cinema to the court of the Sultan around the turn of the century, Makhmalbaf's film is at its best when celebrating the simple pleasures of cinema magic, which he indulges in silent movie techniques (jump cuts, dissolves, mirror trick shots), homages to the silent comics, and his richly textured black-and-white photography. I'm sure there are dozens more references to Iranian cinema lost on Western audiences. The offbeat comedy unravels in the third act but the fantastic imagery never flags

and creative invention results in bold and brilliant moments. —S.A.

BADLANDS L: DIRECTORS/MALICK, TERRENCE (1973) 95M D: Terrence Malick. *Sissy Spacek, Ramon Bieri, Warren Oates, Martin Sheen.* Malick's assured debut draws on the true story of spree killer Charlie Starkweather and his fourteen-year-old girlfriend. Sheen is the unstable twenty-five-year-old who kills the father (Oates) of girlfriend Spacek and hits the road in a doomed attempt to find some romantic idyll in the sunset. Beautifully shot on the American plains, Malick contrasts the matter-of-fact killings by the increasingly unpredictable Sheen with banal, oblivious narration in a hopelessly romantic tenor by Spacek. The utter meaningless of their actions creates the real horror in this anything but romantic take on the criminal-couple-on-the-road genre. —S.A.

THIN RED LINE, THE L: DIRECTORS/MALICK, TERRENCE (1998) 170M D: Terrence Malick. *Nick Nolte, Sean Penn, Adrien Brody, Ben Chaplin, James Caviezel.* This epic three-hour film tries to cash in on the World War II realism inspired by the wake of *Saving Private Ryan.* But instead of focusing on the feelings of a bunch of soldiers around the battle of D-Day, it focuses on the feelings of a bunch of soldiers around the battle of Guadalcanal. It is in effect the remake of a 1964 film based on a James Jones novel. Yet as the soldiers in this film aren't entirely clear why they are there, the audience apparently doesn't need to know either—it seems to be a hallmark of 1990s war films to leave historic detail to documentaries and focus instead on fictitious dramas or the tragedy of the "human condition." —N.J.

ATLANTIC CITY L: DIRECTORS/MALLE, LOUIS (1980) 104M D: Louis Malle. *Kate Reid, Michel Piccoli, Burt Lancaster, Susan Sarandon, Robert Joy.* Faded dreams and frustrated hopes rumble through the lives of a would-be gangster turned threadbare numbers runner (Lancaster) and a spirited waitress (Sarandon) who has pinned her hopes of escape on becoming a croupier. Set in the decay of contemporary Atlantic City, a tarnished old relic being torn down to make way for modern, antiseptic casinos, this is one of the unsung masterpieces of American cinema in the '80s. There's no sentiment or glamour in Malle's assured direction, which brings dignity to the stories of frustrated survivors in the seedy landscape of petty crime and desperate schemes. John Guare's original screenplay earned one of the film's five Oscar nominations (the others going to Lancaster, Sarandon, Malle, and the film itself). This is the kind of project that began to disappear in the increasingly blockbuster-oriented '80s. It stands as an epitaph to the stories of unglamorous souls forgotten by the studios, who themselves tore down old models and remade their industry much in the same way as the real-life Atlantic City. —S.A.

LOVERS, THE (LES AMANTS) L: DIRECTORS/MALLE, LOUIS (1958) 88M D: Louis Malle. *Alain Cuny, Jean-Marc Bory, Jeanne Moreau.* Bored with her husband, Jeanne (Moreau) turns to infidelity for adventure. The plot thickens when she and her increasingly suspicious husband land themselves the awkward social obligation of hosting her lover (among others) at their country villa—a risky scenario Jeanne seems a little excited about. When handsome intellectual Bernard (Bory) turns up, she finds she's not only bored with her husband, but with her entire decadent lifestyle. Despite a straightforward classical style, this was considered a precursor to the French New Wave. What particularly impressed me about the film was the subdued sense of stasis used throughout the love scene between Jeanne and Bernard—at the time quite scandalous, despite the fact that it consisted mainly of a walk in the moonlight. —C.B.

VANYA ON 42ND STREET L: DIRECTORS/MALLE, LOUIS (1994) 119M D: Louis Malle. *Phoebe Brand, Jerry Mayer, Lynn Cohen, Julianne Moore, George Gaynes, Wallace Shawn.* Malle's rather brilliant film starts off as an improvisation of sorts, loosely filming actors and actresses running through various parts of Anton Chekov's famous *Uncle Vanya* in rehearsal for an upcoming performance. We see the actors mess up lines and talk about various things, and then somehow, without us realizing it, they are acting out the play in its entirety. It's amazing to see Chekov's work (adapted here by David Mamet) performed in a dimly lit theatre with no costumes, very few props, and an entirely untheatrical setting. Chekov was a master at capturing real life, as is evident in this compelling nonperformance of one of his greatest works. Moore and Shawn shine especially brightly in the film, but the performances across the board are outstanding. This is definitely one to seek out if you haven't managed to see it yet. —C.P.

APPLAUSE L: DIRECTORS/MAMOULIAN, ROUBEN (1929) 79M D: Rouben Mamoulian. *Helen Morgan, Joan Peers, Henry Wadsworth, Jack Singer.* The film debut of Broadway director Mamoulian was a groundbreaker in the early talkie era. The stylish street musical is set in the tawdry world of burlesque and shot with a fluid camera that prowls through the grimy world where a faded singer (Morgan) sacrifices all for her daughter (Peers). Mamoulian broke away from the static style of stilted talkies by demanding the freedom of the earlier silent years and he got it. He also established an expressive, lyrical style that marked all of his subsequent films, making the most of both New York locations and richly realized studios that re-create the seedy showbiz underworld of tarnished glamour. Morgan is especially moving as a burlesque Stella Dallas, determined that her

daughter won't grow up in the mean streets of her predatory world. —*S. A.*

DR. JEKYLL AND MR. HYDE (1931) L: DIRECTORS/MAMOULIAN, ROUBEN (1931) 97M D: Rouben Mamoulian.

Rose Hobart, Holmes Herbert, Frederic March, Miriam Hopkins. March takes on the double role of the ambitious and arrogant doctor who unleashes the repressed beast within, the beastly id he calls "Mr. Hyde," and won an Oscar for his performance. This version roils in sex and Victorian repression. Jekyll, an engaged society man haunted by the taunting offers of sexy, slutty barmaid Hopkins after a night out slumming with his father-in-law to be, satisfies his pent-up frustration through Hyde's lascivious, sadistic abuse of the girl. Mamoulian's fluid style and hearty direction, and his vivid visualization of the painful transformation, make this far more modern and daring than the glossy Victor Fleming remake with Spencer Tracy in the dual roles. —*S. A.*

MARK OF ZORRO, THE L: DIRECTORS/MAMOULIAN, ROUBEN (1940) 94M D: Rouben Mamoulian.

Eugene Pallette, Gale Sondergaard, Basil Rathbone, Linda Darnell, Tyrone Power. Though neither as dashing as Errol Flynn nor as daring and athletic as Douglas Fairbanks Sr., Power is a natural as the swashbuckling hero in this rousing remake of the Old California adventure. He plays the Spanish swordsman who poses as a foppish aristocrat by day but a nineteenth-century Robin Hood by night: Zorro, the hero of the oppressed. Power pulls it off out of sheer bravado and smoldering determination, and he plays the insufferably indifferent Lord with his trademark self-consciousness, an actor living it up in an absurd role. It fits the character to a Z. Rathbone is perfectly cast as the corrupt ruler who killed Power's father, and Darnell is beautiful and spirited as his lady love. Mamoulian directs with panache. —*S. A.*

ALL ABOUT EVE L: DIRECTORS/MANKIEWICZ, JOSEPH L. (1950) 138M D: Joseph L. Mankiewicz.

Hugh Marlowe, Bette Davis, Gary Merrill, Celeste Holm, George Sanders, Anne Baxter. Mankiewicz's acerbic view askance at the Great White Way is his *Citizen Kane,* a less complex but more cynical portrait of ambition on the boards. The barbed dialogue is witty and wonderful, delivered with tart insolence by Davis as an aging Broadway lioness who watches ruthless cub Baxter pull out her claws to charm, manipulate, and insinuate herself into stardom. Even more seductively sinister is Sanders, who oozes arsenic as a cultured but conniving critic. "Fasten your seat belts, it's going to be a bumpy night." Verbal turbulence was never more fun. Nominated for a record twelve Academy Awards, it went home with six, including Best Picture, Best Director and Best Screenplay (Mankiewicz), and Best Supporting Actor (Sanders). Watch for Marilyn Monroe in a tiny but memorable part as a dim starlet. —*S. A.*

BAREFOOT CONTESSA, THE L: DIRECTORS/MANKIEWICZ, JOSEPH L. (1954) 128M D: Joseph L. Mankiewicz.

Rossano Brazzi, Valentina Cortese, Marius Goring, Humphrey Bogart, Edmond O'Brien, Ava Gardner. Writer-director Mankiewicz populates this Cinderella tragedy with his usual almost-too-sparkling dialogue and stylized performances, but as in his better-known *All About Eve,* these characters breathe real air and cry real tears. That this will not be your everyday rags-to-riches tale is made clear when we first meet Maria Vargas (Gardner): as she's recruited for Hollywood by Harry Dawes (Bogart) and Oscar Muldoon (O'Brien, in an Oscar-winning role), they offer to bring her mother along. "Every girl needs her mother." With her response, "I don't like my mother," Maria gains the upper hand and never loses it. Professionally, that is. In no time flat she's the most beloved movie star in the world. At home, however, she soon learns that fame and fortune are fine, but real love would be better. A decent drama that never quite crosses the line to melodrama (even the colors are richly muted) with excellent performances all around. —*C. C.*

GHOST AND MRS. MUIR, THE L: DIRECTORS/MANKIEWICZ, JOSEPH L. (1947) 104M D: Joseph L. Mankiewicz.

Gene Tierney, George Sanders, Rex Harrison. Tierney is the independent-minded young widow who, desperate to escape her oppressive in-laws, falls in love with a grand seaside house and moves in. Only then does she discover the cantankerous ghost of the hot-tempered Sea Captain (a histrionically flamboyant performance by Harrison) and earn his respect when she stands up to his bellowing attempts to scare her away. Bernard Herrmann's haunting score matches the melancholy black-and-white photography of the picturesque turn-of-the-century New England coast setting. Less ghost story than romantic fantasy of impossible love, Mankiewicz's moody classic is a refreshingly mature and down-to-earth bittersweet romance. —*S. A.*

SLEUTH L: DIRECTORS/MANKIEWICZ, JOSEPH L. (1972) 138M D: Joseph L. Mankiewicz.

Michael Caine, Laurence Olivier. Mystery author Olivier invites hair salon impresario Caine to his palatial home to talk over a little private business, namely Caine's dalliances with Olivier's wife. But of course the master games-player isn't about to let it go that easily, and thus the games begin. Mankiewicz's adaptation of Anthony Schaffer's cat-and-mouse stage play is an actor's paradise: Shakespearean-trained Olivier and cockney working-class Caine play out the eternal class struggle in a battle of wits, harmless fun that turns dark and dangerous. As a mystery it's a little lightweight and I spotted the big twist well in advance (I won't tell), but it's the pairing of Olivier and Caine that really drives the film: not simply two fine actors in a duel of performances, but two completely different styles shaping the characters and essential conflicts. —*S. A.*

BEND OF THE RIVER L: DIRECTORS/MANN, ANTHONY (1952) 91M D: Anthony Mann. *Julie Adams, Rock Hudson, James Stewart.* Mann and Stewart made five Westerns together, and Stewart's resolve dominated each one. This time, he's determined to lead a group of settlers down the Oregon Trail and clear his name too. A fine piece of Northwest history and a great adventure to boot. —*M. S.*

FAR COUNTRY, THE L: DIRECTORS/MANN, ANTHONY (1954) 97M D: Anthony Mann. *Corinne Calvert, James Stewart, Walter Brennan, Ruth Roman, Jay C. Flippen, John McIntire.* The Far Country is Alaska, where a cold-hearted cattleman (Stewart) and a garrulous old codger of a sidekick (Brennan) drive a herd of cattle to cash in on the gold rush. Stewart is the ultimate loner—he watches helpless miners murdered by a gang of thugs without lifting a finger. The film becomes a battle for Stewart's soul, with a fledgling community on one side and a seductive saloon owner (Roman) and her sometime partner, a Roy Bean–like judge and merchant who preys off the miners (McIntire at his most magnetically nasty), on the other. The location shots among the Alaskan peaks are spectacular (the studio sets much less so) and Mann brings an edge to the drama with explosions of cold-blooded violence, capped by a brilliant climactic shoot-out on a split-level plain. —*S. A.*

GLENN MILLER STORY, THE L: DIRECTORS/MANN, ANTHONY (1953) 115M D: Anthony Mann. *George Tobias, Henry Morgan, June Allyson, James Stewart, Charles Drake.* Stewart and Allyson star in Mann's colorful, tuneful portrait of the trombonist and bandleader. Stewart is as lanky and laid-back as the film, a journeyman musician trying to put together his own band while searching for an elusive sound in his head. Morgan helps him find it as his loyal friend and fellow musician, and Louis Armstrong and Gene Krupa make musical appearances. As it turns out, Miller's life isn't all that exciting (though his tragic end makes for good Hollywood melodrama), but his music is rousing and toe-tapping, and it defined an era with classics like "Moonlight Serenade," "A String of Pearls," "Chattanooga Choo-Choo," and of course "In the Mood." —*S. A.*

HE WALKED BY NIGHT L: DIRECTORS/MANN, ANTHONY (1948) 79M D: Anthony Mann. *Whit Bissell, Roy Roberts, Scott Brady, Richard Basehart, Jack Webb, James Cardwell.* Basehart stars as an electronics genius who turns to theft and murder, while a tough guy cop (Brady) tracks him down with the resources of the police department, notably a wisecracking forensics expert (Webb). The stiff, stentorian narration and procedural detail of this film were big influences on Webb when he developed *Dragnet.* Alfred Werker is the credited director, but Mann directed a good portion of the documentary-influenced thriller. Inspired by actual police files and shot largely on location (by the great

poverty-row cinematographer and early Mann collaborator John Alton) with a "you are there" naturalism, it's firmly in the B-movie tradition of stilted, often hackneyed dialogue, abstract sets, and more than a few lesser performances. Yet the spare style and hard edge of the direction combined with Alton's stunning visuals lift the film out of the poverty-row ghetto. —*S. A.*

MAN FROM LARAMIE, THE L: DIRECTORS/MANN, ANTHONY (1955) 104M D: Anthony Mann. *Arthur Kennedy, James Stewart.* Stewart and Mann collaborated in the 1950s to produce some of the most mature, profound, and thoughtful films—not merely Westerns—ever made. These are stories with universal themes, their characterizations and conflicts Shakespearean in their dimensions, their themes biblical. If you think Stewart is such a sweet man, wait till you hear him utter the line, "You scum!" with hatred that burns. —*S. F.*

NAKED SPUR, THE L: DIRECTORS/MANN, ANTHONY (1953) 91M D: Anthony Mann. *James Stewart, Robert Ryan, Ralph Meeker, Janet Leigh, Millard Mitchell.* The Naked Spur is a Western in setting and in context—the verdant, rolling landscape of Colorado gives a performance that almost overshadows the work of the human actors—but not in spirit. It's Greek drama; it's Shakespeare. It's a tale of backstabbing greed, with a MacGuffin that won't shut up. Ryan is Ben Vandergroat, a bad actor worth $5,000 dead or alive. Stewart is Howard Kemp, the tortured man with a past, who needs that money to buy back his old ranch and staunch an old wound. Kemp meets up with a failed prospector (Mitchell) and a shady soldier (Meeker, at his snaky, silky best), who help him capture Vandergroat, along with his hellcat traveling companion and frontier masseuse (Leigh). What follows is a game of manipulation and deceit. The Naked Spur is one of the great anti-Westerns. None of these people are innocent, and the inevitable redemption is hard won and well earned. —*C. C.*

RAILROADED L: DIRECTORS/MANN, ANTHONY (1947) 74M D: Anthony Mann. *Hugh Beaumont, Jane Randolph, Sheila Ryan, John Ireland.* Ireland is a sadistic killer who perfumes his bullets before loading his gun, a man who loves his work. Beaumont, best known as Beaver's father on TV, rides around in his convertible and spits out wisecracks as a tough-guy cop. It's B all the way, with a creaky plot about a framed and burned-out detective who digs around "on a hunch" (and because he's sweet on Ryan, the sister of the accused), but Mann's lean style and hard-edged direction bring a little sensibility and verve to an otherwise standard programmer. —*S. A.*

REIGN OF TERROR (AKA THE BLACK BOOK) L: DIRECTORS/ MANN, ANTHONY (1949) 89M D: Anthony Mann. *Norman Lloyd, Arnold Moss, Arlene Dahl, Richard Hart,*

Anthony Mann

Hollywood's Mann of the West made his name with an edgy, psychologically driven string of 1950s Westerns in which his jutting, jagged landscapes and treacherous trails were more than simply an evocation of a dangerous frontier. They were a reflection of the torment and neurosis and sheer ruthlessness of his characters, heroes and villains both—the land of promise turned film-noir frontier. It should come as no surprise that Mann paid his dues on a handful of B movies and honed his chops—and his eye for sharp composition—on a cycle of hard-edged crime thrillers before springing his dark vision of the American West on Hollywood.

Anthony Mann (born Emil Anton Bundsmann) began his career on the stage, rising from bit-part actor to marginally successful director (his projects included a handful of Federal Theater productions) before David O. Selznick brought him to Hollywood. After an apprenticeship as an assistant director in the Paramount system, he made an inauspicious debut in 1942, cranking out ten films in five years on Hollywood's Poverty Row before he made his first ripple with *Desperate* (1947), followed by a pair of minor noir classics: *Raw Deal* (1948) and *T-Men* (1947).

Working with impoverished budgets but

Richard Basehart, Robert Cummings. The French Revolution as film noir: Basehart's Robespierre is an icy criminal mastermind and Cummings puts on his best sneering tough-guy act as an undercover agent who infiltrates the Committee of Public Safety to break Robespierre's death grip on the revolution. Wouldn't you know that Cummings's Paris contact is his former lover (Dahl)? Moss is Robespierre's mercenary henchman Fouché, an oily, enterprising operative whose allegiance is only to himself. The hard-boiled dialogue and tough-love romantic banter is camp, but the gang war free-for-all seems oddly appropriate to the chaos and cutthroat power struggle of the real-life reign of terror. The delicious mix of cobblestone and carriages with John Alton's urban lighting and extreme angles is irresistible. Director Mann, always one to punctuate his volatile dramas with grotesque blasts of sadistic violence, caps this with one of his most memorable. That it is historically accurate only makes it more delicious. —*S. A.*

T-MEN L: DIRECTORS/MANN, ANTHONY (1947) 92M D: Anthony Mann. *Dennis O'Keefe, Wallace Ford, Charles McGraw.* One of the key partnerships of the American cinema, director Mann and Hungarian-born cinematographer Alton, was formed for this most dynamic entry in the late-'40s cycle of semidocumentary, police-procedural crime-fighting movies. O'Keefe and Alfred Ryder play two Secret Service agents who go undercover to crack a counterfeiting ring. The rhetoric of the voice-over narration is straight-arrow; the visual and psychological

dynamics of the film are anything but. From the moment ace Mann villain McGraw leans forward out of an impenetrably black shadow, then leans back into center screen to become invisible once more, the world of this movie is absolutely *noir.* Mann and Alton employ razor-sharp deep focus, vaulting angularity, brutal close-ups, bold overlays of reflection, and slashing, jagged compositions to create a memorably hostile environment. In an act anticipating the tortured heroes Stewart would play in Mann's great cycle of '50s Westerns, O'Keefe's last act is to commit a revenge murder the movie savors as much as he does. —*R. T. J.*

WINCHESTER '73 L: DIRECTORS/MANN, ANTHONY (1950) 93M D: Anthony Mann. *Millard Mitchell, Dan Duryea, Shelley Winters, James Stewart, Stephen McNally.* The first of seven collaborations between Stewart and director Mann is practically a film noir on the frontier. The plot is really a quite clever gimmick—Stewart's one-of-a-kind rifle is stolen and he tracks it across the West as it changes hands—but the story is a much darker tale of hatred and revenge with a Cain and Abel twist. Fusing the spare style and hard edge of his earlier noir thrillers with the open spaces and frontier violence of the Western, Mann turns the wide-open American frontier into a jagged landscape of danger and death and transforms all-American icon Stewart into a ruthless man of the West. Watch for prefame contract players Rock Hudson and Tony Curtis in supporting roles. —*S. A.*

an extraordinary cinematographer (John Alton), he turned bland sets and anonymous back lots into lonely locations swallowed in fog or lost in the night, lit only by dim pools and slashes of light. And to the scrappy, rough-and-ready stories of sneering, sadistic hoods, hard-boiled cops, and honest working-class mugs whose lives are shanghaied by one false move, Mann brought a mix of grace and grit, punctuated by the most visceral cinematic expression of violence seen on-screen in his day.

The Westerns opened up Mann's claustrophobic style; he showed Hollywood how to shoot the magnificent landscape of a mythic American West, a country where both beauty and danger lay in the jagged mountains, barren deserts, and lush wilderness forests. With *Winchester '73* (1950), his first of seven collaborations with

James Stewart, he fused the spare style and hard edge of his noir thrillers with the open spaces and frontier violence of the Western. Stewart changed the entire arc of his career by playing bitter mercenaries driven by anger, hatred, and revenge in such films as *The Man from Laramie* (1955) and *The Naked Spur* (1953).

Anthony Mann's versatility is often overlooked: he made musicals, biographies, adventures, a war picture, and a pair of handsome costume epics (the superior *El Cid* [1961] and *The Fall of the Roman Empire* [1964]). But to this day he's best remembered for the psychological intensity, psychopathic edge, and violent visions of his edgy films noir and harsh Westerns, in which jagged landscapes and vicious villains explode with startling violence.

—*Sean Axmaker*

ALI L: DIRECTORS/MANN, MICHAEL (2001) 158M D: Michael Mann. *Mario Van Peebles, Ron Silver, Will Smith, Jamie Foxx, Jon Voight.* Muhammad Ali is an icon not so much because of his incredible talent as a boxer, but because of his clever boasts and his knack for living up to those boasts. Ali's ringside rhyming, his conversion to Islam, and his courageous (and costly) refusal to fight in Vietnam were crying out to be made into a biopic. Only one problem though: no actor could ever match the magnetic charisma and presence of the real Ali. Mann finds great drama in Ali's life, and Smith comes incredibly close to capturing the man's voice and personality. The filmmakers have done a great job; the problem comes not in their work but in the impossibility of the task at hand. *Ali* is a nice try, but *When We Were Kings* will remain the great portrait of Muhammad Ali. —*B. T.*

HEAT L: DIRECTORS/MANN, MICHAEL (1995) 171M D: Michael Mann. *Robert De Niro, Val Kilmer, Jon Voight, Tom Sizemore, Al Pacino, Amy Brenneman.* There is a short, quiet scene in *Heat* where De Niro and Pacino talk in a coffee shop. De Niro plays a thief, Pacino the homicide detective trying to catch him. The two men talk about women, the demands of their work, and the possibility they may have to kill each other. The drama is in the silence between the words. For a movie that includes both a terrifyingly immediate gun battle and a brief monologue by Pacino on the appeal of women's buttocks, it's startling to realize that the best scenes have the least noise. But director Mann has crafted an epic crime movie

where showy battle scenes sit side by side with domestic dramas, and where the most climactic moment might be when the sleek, sealed-off De Niro falls quickly and achingly in love. —*T. P.*

INSIDER, THE L: DIRECTORS/MANN, MICHAEL (1999) 157M D: Michael Mann. *Russell Crowe, Christopher Plummer, Rip Torn, Al Pacino.* This film is the cinematic whistleblower on the relationship between big tobacco and the media. Pacino plays the producer of *60 Minutes* and Plummer plays seasoned reporter Mike Wallace. They do phenomenal amount of research about the plight of a former tobacco executive played convincingly by Crowe. With all the information he was privy to, this executive decides to help the prosecution of a class-action lawsuit and turn whistleblower against the tobacco industry. At two hours and forty minutes this film does not exhaust its topic. In fact it merely exposes the tip of an iceberg that the entertainment industry was complicit in trying to hide or ignore. That is the only conclusion one is left with for why actual executives shot down a real episode of *60 Minutes*, which in turn instigated the script for this film. A pertinent story, compelling acting and great direction make this film thoroughly engaging. —*N. J.*

MANHUNTER L: DIRECTORS/MANN, MICHAEL (1986) 120M D: Michael Mann. *William Petersen, Kim Greist, Joan Allen, Brian Cox, Dennis Farina.* Mann's film is doomed to live in the shadow of the Oscar-winning *Silence of the Lambs,* its sequel in essence if not detail. An undeserved fate for such a sharp, coolly attenuated thriller. Petersen gives the performance of his career as the intent, troubled serial killer profiler whose methods literally lead to madness and Cox is, frankly, a more insidiously scary Hannibal Lektor (as his name is spelled in his original cinematic incarnation) than Hopkins's more theatrical take on the character. Mann's direction is a triumph of austerity and cinematic precision, and he shatters the carefully controlled mood in a blistering climax choreographed and cut to Iron Butterfly's "In-A-Gadda-Da-Vida." The director's cut features an additional five minutes of detail. It was remade under the novel's title, *Red Dragon,* with Hopkins as (in that case) Lector. —*S. A.*

CASTLE OF BLOOD L: DIRECTORS/MARGHERITI, ANTONIO (1964) 89M D: Antonio Margheriti. *Georges Rivière, Barbara Steele.* Rivière plays a British journalist who spends a night in the haunted Blackwood castle on a bet with Edgar Allan Poe and the castle's owner. He's a one-man audience to an experimental play written out of order and performed by bloodthirsty ghosts determined to make him a part of the tragic finale. Steele plays a lost soul he finds inside and falls in love with as he becomes witness to the horror that left everyone in the castle dead. Moody and atmospheric, and featuring the searing appearance by Steele, this is one the best films from minor Italian genre auteur Margheriti, who directs from a script cowritten by Sergio Corbucci (*The Great Silence*). The restored international version on the Synapse DVD includes scenes cut from the original U.S. theatrical release (those restored scenes are in French with English subtitles). —*S. A.*

SQUEEZE, THE (AKA **THE RIP-OFF**) L: DIRECTORS/ MARGHERITI, ANTONIO (1978) 99M D: Antonio Margheriti. *Lee Van Cleef, Karen Black, Edward Albert.* Shrewdly plotted, smartly acted caper movie with a lively, upbeat score that is the perfect counterpoint to the film's underlying pessimism. A safecracker (Van Cleef) is brought out of retirement by his former partner's son (Albert), now in financial trouble with German mobsters who want diamonds from a certain safe. The two smell a double cross from the Germans and construct a backup plan. But with the kid in jail and Van Cleef wounded with a noisy neighbor (Black) in his hideout building, things don't look good. Set in New York, this 1970s Italian crime movie by the director of *The Last Hunter* is rollicking good entertainment, better than most of the more highly touted films from the overrated Italian crime genre. There are some startlingly nasty moments to it and it's suffused with an emotional tone that is colored like wet, cold, New York pavements. —*J. C.*

YOR, THE HUNTER FROM THE FUTURE L: DIRECTORS/ MARGHERITI, ANTONIO (1983) 88M D: Antonio Margheriti. *John Steiner, Reb Brown, Corinne Clery.* Deliciously bad performances, laughably epic musical cre-

scendos, and C-grade special effects elevate this ill-conceived science fiction oddity to greatness. By virtue of its unbelievable shoddiness, the film surpasses what I can only assume was an earnest desire on the part of *Yor's* creators to turn celluloid into entertainment gold. Bringing new meaning to the word "episodic," the plot takes Yor (Brown) from battling dinosaurs to battling nomadic ape men to battling androids. It's as though the loincloth-clad, body-waxed Yor were the Candide (or Forrest Gump) of evolution—if not of Earth, than at least of the action genre. But it's pointless to try to piece this story together— every frame is crammed with accidental hilarity, and you'll be too busy blotting tears of laughter from your eyes to understand it as a whole. Your friends will gasp at your brilliance when you bring this to the next movie party. —*C. B.*

AT MIDNIGHT I'LL TAKE YOUR SOUL L: DIRECTORS/ MARINS, JOSÉ MOJICA (1964) 92M D: José Mojica Marins. *José Mojica Marins, Magda Mei.* Mojica Marins's creation Ze do Caixao (Jose of the Grave), known to English speakers as Coffin Joe, has been described as a "national bogeyman" in his native Brazil. That hardly captures this darkly fascinating mix of Dracula, demon, Nietzschean superman, black-hatted bully, misogynist, and gleefully sadistic murderer as folk hero. In Coffin Joe's startling, controversial debut, Marins shocked the Catholic country with a blaspheming antihero. The imagery is bold and genuinely startling: he ties up his wife and watches a tarantula crawl up her wriggling body ("It was a great show" he cackles as she dies), severs the fingers of a poker player with a broken bottle, and clubs then drowns his best friend before the inevitable angry villagers turn on the monstrous hedonist. *At Midnight* has the distinction of being Brazil's first true horror film. —*S. A.*

AWAKENING OF THE BEAST, THE L: DIRECTORS/MARINS, JOSÉ MOJICA (1970) 93M D: José Mojica Marins. *José Mojica Marins.* Mojica Marins's most inspired exploration of his wicked boogeyman is a New Wave/Cinema Novo–influenced mindbender, a banned-in-Brazil look into youth culture, drugs, sex, and the iconographic power of Coffin Joe (who by now was the star of a comic book series and had pop songs written about him; one is in the movie). Marins stars as both himself and his cinematic alter ego, Coffin Joe, now a Freddy Krueger–like dream figure who dominates the acid-laced visions of four subjects in an LSD experiment. Shot on donated film and starring fellow directors and Brazilian stars who donated their time, it's perverse, hilarious, demented, and ingeniously self-aware. The hallucinogenic drug scene is shot in blasting hues of hypercolor that would make Dario Argento jealous. —*S. A.*

AWFUL TRUTH, THE L: DIRECTORS/McCAREY, LEO (1937) 91M D: Leo McCarey. *Joyce Compton, Cary Grant, Irene Dunne, Ralph Bellamy, Asta.* McCarey won a Best Director Oscar for this delightful pairing of Grant and Dunne as a married couple that files for divorce, each assuming that the other has been unfaithful. When they decide on a ninety-day trial separation, each proceeds to meticulously sabotage the other's new relationship and fight for the custody of Mr. Smith, the family dog (Asta, who also appeared in *The Thin Man* and *Bringing Up Baby*). The two stars are hilarious, delivering sophisticated dialogue, improvisation, pratfalls, and physical comedy. A prolonged scene involving a hidden hat, a mirror, and the dog is frigging brilliant and Dunne's dance number is priceless. Once again, Bellamy makes a great thickheaded, unsophisticated counterpart to Grant and steals every scene he's in. One of the best screwball comedies. —*S. H.*

DUCK SOUP L: DIRECTORS/McCAREY, LEO (1933) 70M D: Leo McCarey. *Zeppo Marx, Chico Marx, Harpo Marx, Groucho Marx, Margaret Dumont.* The history books will tell you that WWII was "The Big One," but nothing can measure up to Groucho Marx as Rufus T. Firefly (the newly elected president of Freedonia) waging an all-out war against the people of Sylvania! As you may expect, plot quickly takes a backseat to antics, but the film is held together in an avalanche of belly laughs. The politics-lampooning premises of this film have been borrowed by countless others; possibly inspiring everything from *Dr. Strangelove* to rich fat white man Michael Moore's *Canadian Bacon.* The last film to feature performances by all four Marx Brothers, *Duck Soup* is inarguably one of their funniest, alternating between zany political satire and heart attack–inducing musical numbers. If you can stomach a small dose of passive '30s racism, this is absolutely essential viewing. —*Z. C.*

LOVERS OF THE ARCTIC CIRCLE L: DIRECTORS/MEDEM, JULIO (1998) 112M D: Julio Medem. *Najwa Nimri, Fele Martinez, Nancho Novo, Maru Valdivielso, Peru Medem.* Swooning with romantic abandon, Medem's fateful love story weaves reality, fantasy, and memory into a narrative tapestry of recurring images. Airplanes, cars, gas gauges, and a big red bus forever pulling into the paths of our characters all become motifs enriched with each fresh appearance. Young lovers Otto (Martínez) and Ana (Nimri) narrate their own stories in parallel self-titled chapters, filling in the depth of their own thoughts and feelings only guessed at by the other, and at times offering their own dream variations of events more objectively described by the other. When their destinies appear to scatter and the film momentarily loses itself, the rich cinematic quilt keeps them in the same pattern and pulls all the threads together for an astounding conclusion. Visually mesmerizing and creatively ambitious, the delicacy of Medem's images is sometimes lost on the small screen, but his passion survives. —*S. A.*

SEX AND LUCIA L: DIRECTORS/MEDEM, JULIO (2001) 128M D: Julio Medem. *Daniel Freire, Paz Vega, Najwa Nimri, Tristan Ulloa.* There's good reason sex is in the title of Medem's latest tale of obsessive love, tragic twists, and romantic fate. A waitress (Vega) wins the heart of a blocked novelist (Ulloa), but the joyously earthy couplings of the first act's impulsive young love are followed by self-destructive lust when he discovers happiness is poor inspiration for his art. As the writer turns into an irresponsible, self-pitying artist, the tender and touching healing journeys of the women in his life become the heart of the film. Medem's intricately plotted, time-hopping drama at times feels contrived, but he deftly crisscrosses the characters' destinies and pulls their stories together with lovely visual motifs and the defining sun-bright shores of Spain's Formentera Island. —*S. A.*

TIERRA L: DIRECTORS/MEDEM, JULIO (1995) 122M D: Julio Medem. *Nancho Novo, Carmelo Gómez, Emma Suárez, Karra Elejalde, Silke.* Medem's most vibrant and vivid work opens in the heavens and swoops down to Earth to land in the red dust of a remote wine-growing region, a primal and alien land where an exterminator named Angel (Gómez) has been sent to fumigate the enigmatic wood lice that give the grapes their earthy taste. Angel is watched over by his own personal guardian angel, who tries to council him when he falls in love with both a beautiful, unhappily married young mother (Suárez) and a sexy, aggressive single flirt (Silke). Angel, of course, doesn't listen. Medem doesn't direct so much as weave his films: images, characters, crisscrossing stories, and recurring motifs intertwine, blur, and transform through time and changes of perspective, scale, and even reality. It all coalesces in a lovely and unexpected conclusion where "wrong" choices become an insight into the beautiful contradictions of human nature. —*S. A.*

BOLLYWOOD/HOLLYWOOD L: DIRECTORS/MEHTA, DEEPA (2002) 103M D: Deepa Mehta. *Lisa Ray, Rishma Malik, Jazz Mann, Moushumi Chatterjee, Dina Pathak, Rahul Khanna.* This film was quite a departure from writer/director Mehta's usual work, which tends toward serious dramas with no musical numbers. The story is of a wealthy Canadian Indian family whose eldest son promised on his father's death bed to marry. His mother wants him to marry a traditional Indian girl and holds his sister's impending wedding over his head. If he does not find a suitable girl to marry, then his sister's wedding will be postponed until he does. He meets a forward woman in a bar who confesses that she likes Bollywood films and looks close enough to Indian to be convincing. A plan is hatched that she will play the part of his girlfriend/fiancée, for a price, until his sister is safely married. From there surprises follow, boundaries are blurred, lives are changed, and questions are raised. The film is both an homage to the Bollywood musical and a playful parody of it. —*M.N.*

BOB LE FLAMBEUR L: DIRECTORS/MELVILLE, JEAN-PIERRE (1955) 102M D: Jean-Pierre Melville. *Daniel Cauchy, Howard Vernon, Isabelle Corey, Guy Decomble, Roger Duchesne.* Melville took the romance of the French gangster film into the modern world with this meticulously plotted and smoothly directed crime classic. The wonderfully ironic tale of an aging gambler (gracefully played by Duchenese) who plots an elaborate heist is elegant and elegiac, a winsome wish for the sentimental code of honor among thieves and the friendship and loyalty that are threatened by the mercenary impulses of brazen young punks. Melville has a deft, light touch, a mix of calm confidence and restless ambition mellowed by gentle humor, delightful characters, and a world of trench coats, streetside bars, and gentlemanly manners that exists only in the romance of the movies. Shot in the streets and bars of Montmartre on a low budget, this independently produced tribute to Hollywood film noir with a Gallic flavor has been celebrated as an inspiration to the directors of the French New Wave. —*S.A.*

CERCLE ROUGE, LE L: DIRECTORS/MELVILLE, JEAN-PIERRE (1970) 140M D: Jean-Pierre Melville. *André Bourvil, Alain Delon, Gian Maria Volonte, Yves Montand, Paul Crauchet.* Crime cinema has never been so meticulously and coolly executed as in this heist classic starring Delon and Volonte as professional thieves, Montand as a soused sharpshooter who regains his self-respect when he joins their team, and Bouvril as the unrelenting cop on their trail. This is Melville's world of romantic doom, an irresistible cinema fantasy of loyalty, professionalism, sacrifice, and codes of honor in the lives of classy, uncompromising crooks. Melville's most austere work strips even the characters down to the essence of their professionalism and their integrity. But if the film lacks emotional connection (as in *Bob le Flambeur*) or tantalizing irony (*Le Samourai*), its doomed underworld perfection is, well, perfect. When it was released in the United States more than thirty years ago, its distributor saw fit to hack away forty minutes of its precise structure. This rerelease restores every meticulous second of Melville's cinematic fantasy. —*S.A.*

DOULOS, LE L: DIRECTORS/MELVILLE, JEAN-PIERRE (1963) 108M D: Jean-Pierre Melville. *Jean-Paul Belmondo, Serge Reggiani, Jean Desailly, René Lefevre, Marcel Cuvelier.* Melville's cool, often cruel 1963 classic stars Belmondo as a smiling underworld informer, charming and disarming one minute, cunning and sadistically violent the next, yet unfailingly loyal. The skewed morality tale is a ruthless riff on the criminal code and the chaos that erupts whenever it's betrayed, and there's an exactness to Belmondo's meticulous plotting and

a calm in Melville's style. Not all of the niggling little details add up, but they create a savagely murky moral center in this black-and-white fantasy of cops and crooks and elegant living on the edge of destruction, where male friendship trumps romance and loyalty tops all. —*S.A.*

FLIC, UN (AKA DIRTY MONEY) L: DIRECTORS/MELVILLE, JEAN-PIERRE (1972) 100M D: Jean-Pierre Melville. *Simone Valere, Catherine Deneuve, Richard Crenna, Alain Delon.* Delon serves as Melville's alter ego in an actor/director collaboration that brings out the best of both. Delon plays the Parisian police commissioner Edouard Coleman, who is disillusioned with life. He meets Cathy (Deneuve), a nightclub singer, and falls instantly for her charm and sophisticated manner. Cathy is also seeing Simon (Crenna), the nightclub owner who is the secret head of a gang. The three develop a complicated relationship and gangster and cop end up on opposite sides of each other, forcing Cathy in between. Melville's direction of the gang's bank heists makes this film magic. It opens with a tense bank robbery set during a hurricane and ends with a tautly edited race between a helicopter and a train. Shot with stark blue filters and a deadpan acting style that gives the film a cold, objective tone, *Dirty Money* fits right alongside Melville's other works as another of the master's classic French crime noirs. —*N.H.*

LES ENFANTS TERRIBLES L: DIRECTORS/MELVILLE, JEAN-PIERRE (1950) 105M D: Jean-Pierre Melville. *Renée Cosima, Edouard Dermit, Jacques Bernard, Nicole Stephane.* Melville's film captures the tone and style of Cocteau's excellent novel, seamlessly mixing whimsical naiveté (a "climate of innocence," the novel calls it) with the macabre. Teen siblings Paul (Dermit) and Elisabeth (Stéphane) resist adulthood and isolate themselves in the hermetic universe of their shared bedroom, a world of deliberate childishness intended for their private satisfaction, striving for a fiercely exclusive eternal youth. Locking themselves in this world, the two become inextricably connected, "two sundered portions of a single body." This full-time make-believe turns uncontrollable when they're orphaned by the death of their sick mother and their codependency becomes increasingly obsessive and perverse. A wonderfully singular film experience whose only close comparison is the novel on which it's based, although Wes Anderson has with good reason spoken of the film in relation to *The Royal Tenenbaums.* —*C.B.*

SAMOURAI, LE L: DIRECTORS/MELVILLE, JEAN-PIERRE (1967) 103M D: Jean-Pierre Melville. *François Perier, Nathalie Delon, Alain Delon.* Melville starts his most complicated film with a fake samurai proverb, as if alluding to a higher truth through fiction. Delon is at his iciest as Jef Costello, a French gun-for-hire who expresses his anxiety through acts of violence aimed at those who betray him. Jef's girlfriend, Jane (Delon's wife Nathalie), cares little for him and sleeps around behind his back, leaving a pet canary as his only friend. But Jef doesn't care, because work is his life. When he hits a salon owner and mistakenly leaves behind a live witness, Jef's employer hires out a hit against him and Jef must go on the run. The film builds incredible suspense as Jef is forced to use all his skills just to stay alive, and, like a Japanese samurai warrior, he must fight his battle alone. Melville focuses on the meticulous precision of Jef's work like a painter displaying his brush strokes. We see how Jef picks locks, steals cars, and covers his tracks after a hit. *Le Samourai* is considered the best of the three films Melville and Delon made together. —*N. H.*

AGITATOR, THE L: DIRECTORS/MIIKE, TAKASHI (2001) 150M D: Takashi Miike.
Naoto Takenaka, Mickey Curtis, Masaya Kato, Masatô Ibu. The Agitator is as straightforward a gangster yarn as we've gotten from Miike. What it lacks in over-the-top characterizations, gore, and ludicrous action is made up by a stronger, more coherent story than we usually expect from a Miike crime drama. When Kunihiko Kenzaki (Kato)'s gang (and—let's face it—his livelihood) is threatened with absorption by another, larger yakuza group, our hero won't take it lying down. Instead he goes on a rampage, killing yakuza on both sides of the battle line and refusing to yield to the bosses telling him to fit into the new, downsized organization. Miike's already claustrophobic style comes on super strong in tight, tense situations, pushing into his characters' personal space with an unrelenting camera. *The Agitator* is a thrilling (but overlong) gangster drama, and ultimately more accessible than the more well-known *Audition*. —*G. M.*

AUDITION L: DIRECTORS/MIIKE, TAKASHI (1999) 115M D: Takashi Miike.
Eihi Shiina, Miyuki Matsuda, Ryo Ishibashi, Renji Ishibashi. Audition is Miike's breakthrough film, and the easiest one to find on video. It's the tale of a lonely film producer's search for a new, "perfect" wife to replace his deceased one. A friend arranges for Aoyama (Ishibashi) to "audition" a group of women. After he finds that special someone in Asami Yamazaki (model Shiina) it's time to woo and the film moves into the territory of the getting-to-know-you dating scene. But something is not quite right with Asami and Aoyama begins to get suspicious. At this point the film's languid romance drama begins to unravel with psychotic intent and Asami's inner demons spill out. As the film turns nightmarish we return to the shocking world Miike seems so comfortable with. Thanks to this film's tranquil beginnings, the violent punch of its ending leaves the viewer even more unsettled than your typical Miike gross-out film. —*G. M.*

CITY OF LOST SOULS, THE L: DIRECTORS/MIIKE, TAKASHI (2000) 103M D: Takashi Miike.
Teah, Michelle Reis, Patricia Manterola, Mitsuhiro Oikawa, Koji Kikkawa. City of Lost Souls (aka *Hazard City*) is the most comic book–like of all Miike's movies, though it is actually based on a novel by Seishu Hase. The film is chock-full of hyper action, heroes that apparently can't be hurt, love that can't be stopped, and a multicultural cast of hipsters. The characters in the film speak Portuguese, English, Chinese, and Japanese, sometimes interchangeably. There are a lot of flashy ideas throughout including a CGI cockfight that's not to be missed. Our hero, Mario (Teah), is a Brazilian trying to save his Chinese girlfriend, Kei (Reis), from deportation and his estranged gangster contacts. After breaking her out of detention and surviving a very long fall from a helicopter, they run from the law, estranged lovers, gangsters, and themselves to a future they might not get to enjoy. But, that's OK as long as they are free and in love, right? —*G. M.*

DEAD OR ALIVE L: DIRECTORS/MIIKE, TAKASHI (1999) 105M D: Takashi Miike.
Sho Aikawa, Renji Ishibashi, Hitoshi Ozawa, Shingo Tsurumi, Riki Takeuchi. The first film in Miike's absurd nonconnected trilogy is a ride through a bizarre, blood-soaked yakuza fever dream. Riki leads a small group of thugs hell-bent on taking over the drug trade in the Shinjuku district of Japan by killing the leaders of all the opposing criminal organizations. Sho is the police detective determined to stop them. In true Miike style, *Dead or Alive* is spotted with scenes of sensational violence and complete human degradation. In particular, the film begins and ends with its two best scenes. One, a montage, is poetic in its violence and contains the best use of soup I have ever seen. The other is awe inspiring in its sheer nonsensical brilliance. However, when you take away the flash, you're left with just your usual run-of-the-mill crime drama. Always skirting the edge of greatness, *Dead or Alive* never seems to cross over. But for fans of Miike, it is sure to please. —*R. G.*

DEAD OR ALIVE 2: BIRDS L: DIRECTORS/MIIKE, TAKASHI (2000) 95M D: Takashi Miike.
Sho Aikawa, Riki Takeuchi, Noriko Aota, Edison Chen. It seems the world didn't blow up after all. Sho and Riki reunite with Miike for a very different movie in this name-only sequel. The furious gunplay is put on the back burner until the final act to make room for an offbeat comedy about friends. Otamoko (Aikawa) is a hit man whose latest assignment is interrupted by a mysterious gunman who kills his target. Otamoko takes his payment anyway and flees to his home island, where he discovers the gunman is none other than his childhood friend, Sawada (Takeuchi). The pair reminisces about old times and reverts to childhood ways. But both the yakuza and Chinese Mafia are on their trail, and the duo decides that their skills

would be better used to rid the world of evil. Miike's usual band of misfits rounds out the supporting cast here, with Shinya Tsukamoto performing one of the greatest gunfights in recent memory. —R. M.

DEAD OR ALIVE: FINAL L: DIRECTORS/MIIKE, TAKASHI
(2002) 89M D: Takashi Miike. *Sho Aikawa, Riki Takeuchi.* Known for his superlative outbursts of taboo imagery and violence, Miike has every right to his title as Japan's modern lord of confrontational cinema. Here, he mixes styles and influences with dizzying ability, combining dusty '80s aesthetics with postfuturistic brutality. The eternal grudge match between Takeuchi and Aikawa continues almost as expected, but the surprises make this installment of the conflict well worth watching. Less gritty than the first, less poetic than the second, this film seems to settle into a comfortable niche of its own. *Dead or Alive: Final* picks up the gauntlet thrown down by its predecessors, blasting the viewer into Yokohama circa 2346, where malcontented, pompadoured androids have outlawed human reproduction. Lightning flies from fingertips and heads fly from shoulders as the battle between good and evil rages to encompass the fate of the entire universe. If you're a fan of winged penile bionics, this one's for you! —Z. C.

FUDOH: THE NEW GENERATION L: DIRECTORS/MIIKE,
TAKASHI (1996) 98M D: Takashi Miike. *Tamaki Kenmochi, Shosuke Tanihara, Kenji Takano, Marie Jinno.* *Fudoh: The New Generation* uses a high school and its hip, attractive students as the backdrop and protagonists for the ultraviolent tale of a gangster family and the power struggles within. Riki Fudoh (Tanihara) watches his older brother die at his father's hands to appease fellow yakuza. When it seems that the upstart Riki is to be handed the same fate, he fights back against the yakuza council, his father, and tradition with his own gang of dysfunctional (and sexy) youth. The gallons of blood that flow from this film may or may not be an indelicate satire of difficult high school life (I doubt it), but no matter the message you can't deny the strength of Miike's first major film. —G. M.

FULL METAL YAKUZA L: Directors/Miike, Takashi
(1997) 102M D: Takashi Miike. *Yuichi Minato, Yasushi Kitamura, Takeshi Caesar.* Miike's works can be easily categorized into two sections: his cinematic productions and cheap V-Cinema features. *Full Metal Yakuza* easily belongs in the latter category, and hits all the right notes for those seeking ultraviolence, revenge, cheap effects, and of course, bondage. A low-level yakuza member is seemingly killed by his boss while trying to protect a friend, but is instead resurrected by a mad scientist. As in *Robocop*, to which direct comparisons can easily be made, only the yakuza's head remains (along with some skin from a black tattoo) as he transformed into a cyborg.

After an amusing sequence in which the powers of the full metal body are learned, our hero sets out for his revenge, which is made all the more personal when he realizes his girlfriend has been kidnapped. The carnage in the film is almost nonstop, and multiple sword fights deliver the required arterial sprays for such a production. Fans of Miike will appreciate the style of the film, as many of his trademarks are prototyped here. —R. M.

HAPPINESS OF THE KATAKURIS L: DIRECTORS/MIIKE,
TAKASHI (2001) 104M D: Takashi Miike. *Kiyoshiro Imawano, Shinji Takeda, Keiko Matsuzaka, Kenji Sawada, Naomi Nashida.* Miike has proven himself to be a fan of the extraordinarily violent, and I tend to avoid movies overloaded with gratuitous killing and maiming. However, I had heard this movie was completely different, so I had to see it. This amazing film completely defies genre, falling somewhere into the comedy-horror-musical niche. The Katakuris have just opened up a guesthouse in the mountains and are eager to draw in business. After their first customer commits suicide, they decide the best thing to do is hide the body and not tell anyone. When a second guest also meets his end while staying with them, things become a little problematic. Musical numbers abound, really amazing Claymation/stop-motion sequences come up when you're least expecting it, and by the end of the movie the only thing you'll be thinking is how bizarre the last 104 minutes were. This movie shows Miike for the versatile director he is. —J. S.

ICHI THE KILLER L: DIRECTORS/MIIKE, TAKASHI (2001)
129M D: Takashi Miike. *Nao Omori, Shinya Tsukamoto, Alien Sun, Tadanobu Asano.* *Ichi the Killer* is yet another comic book brought to life by Miike, based on the ultraviolent manga *Koroshiya 1.* This blood-soaked film features the wondrous Asano as Kakihara, a vengeful mob underling who is seeking the brutally murderous Ichi (Nao Omori). Kakihara is a masochist and with his sadistic boss gone and his girlfriend, Karen (Sun), unable to hit him hard enough, he longs to see if Ichi can hurt him the way he likes. The visual prowess and moments of humor (both genuine and bizarre) in this film are eclipsed by the over-the-top killings and horrid mistreatment of women. Ichi is sometimes easy to sympathize with, but overall his brutality toward women makes him a repellant character and it's Kakihara we end up rooting for. *Ichi the Killer's* nonstop violent bent has earned this film some heavy edits, though there is a complete version out there for the hard-core cult fan. —G. M.

VISITOR Q L: DIRECTORS/MIIKE, TAKASHI (2001) 84M D:
Takashi Miike. *Shungiku Uchida, Kazushi Watanabe, Kenichi Endo, Fujiko.* *Visitor Q* is Miike's most disturbing yet ultimately most tender and moving picture. It is the tale of a family that has fallen

apart. Enter Visitor Q, a mysterious stranger who moves in with the family. He proceeds to annihilate what is left of normalcy for this sad bunch and pushes them all completely over the edge. What follows is tragic, disturbing, beautiful, and comedic. Yes, the film is a comedy. In fact, it's downright hilarious. Miike wisely infuses humor into almost every scene. The humor gives the film a much-needed sense of levity, preventing it from turning into a piece of abject horror. Miike's attempts to push the limits of cinema succeed here like nowhere else. He makes absolutely no apologies and, by never flinching once, has crafted a shocking and sensitive film that deserves to be seen by all, even if few can stomach its unbearable madness or understand its bizarre meaning. —*T. S.*

Due to the familial setting in which this twisted little picture takes place, I found *Visitor Q* the most disturbing of Miike's films. When Kiyoshi Yamazaki (Endo), a failing TV reporter, decides to turn his camera on his family for subject matter he uncovers domestic violence, drug use, prostitution, and other tidbits of family fun. As if this were not enough a stranger (Visitor Q, played by Watanabe) moves into the house, sowing chaos and pushing things further. A very strange movie, *Visitor Q* exposes an underbelly of family life that you'd probably like to forget. Oh, and by the way, it's a "comedy." —*G. M.*

ALL QUIET ON THE WESTERN FRONT L: DIRECTORS/ MILESTONE, LEWIS (1930) 103M D: Lewis Milestone. *John Wray, Raymond Griffith, Lew Ayres, Louis Wolheim.* Milestone's 1930 antiwar film has been called didactic, powerful, overlong, gritty, preachy, and more. Director Sergei Eisenstein called it a "good PhD thesis." Whatever you want to say about it, the fact remains that more than seventy years later, this WWI film told from the German point of view still inspires debate about war and the nature of propagandistic filmmaking. The film does seem a little stodgy at times, but this sort of lulls you into a comfort zone before smacking you in the face with the horrors of war. —*M. S.*

GARDEN OF EDEN, THE L: DIRECTORS/MILESTONE, LEWIS (1928) 78M D: Lewis Milestone. *Louise Dresser, Corinne Griffith.* Country-girl Griffith decides "I could never be happy making pretzels all my life" and runs off to join the Paris opera with her diploma in hand (via correspondence school, no doubt), little realizing that the Palais du Paris is a den of sin and showgirls. Providence, in the form of a doting seamstress (Dresser), sweeps her off to Monte Carlo, where she becomes the daughter of the Baroness Rosa de Garcer for two short weeks. A sweet nothing of a romantic bonbon from Milestone, this Cinderella story set in the European aristocracy was scripted by Hans Kraly, the prolific writer of risqué Hollywood comedies and romantic dramas. While it lacks the knowing wit of Kraly's Ernst Lubitsch films,

Milestone strikes the right balance of American innocence and continental sophistication, tossing in sexy flourishes that would disappear in the age of the production code. —*S. A.*

OCEAN'S 11 L: DIRECTORS/MILESTONE, LEWIS (1960) 127M D: Lewis Mileston. *Joey Bishop, Peter Lawford, Sammy Davis Jr., Frank Sinatra, Dean Martin.* The quintessential Rat Pack movie drops Sinatra, Martin, Davis Jr., Lawford, and Bishop in Las Vegas for an epic casino heist. Let's face it, this film just sort of clumps along—veteran director Milestone was more like a baby-sitter than a director, haplessly trying to corral the carousing bunch and left filming their improvised antics when they refused to stick to the script—but you can't deny the zingy moments of Rat Pack zeitgeist; the over-the-top, cigar-chomping fun of Akin Tamiroff; or the terrific cast, including Richard Conte, Cesar Romero, Henry Silva, and a (mostly wasted) Angie Dickinson. Look for cameos by Shirley Maclaine, Red Skelton, and George Raft. —*S. A.*

RAIN L: DIRECTORS/MILESTONE, LEWIS (1932) 92M D: Lewis Mileston. *Joan Crawford, Walter Huston.* Crawford offers a moody, introspective take on party-girl Sadie Thompson in the second film version of W. Somerset Maugham's story. Crawford is sad and wounded where Gloria Swanson was a vivacious, honest free spirit. Huston offers none of the subtle ambiguity that John Barrymore earlier brought to the self-serving, holier-than-thou reformer. Cinematic hotshot Milestone puts a flashy style to the salacious material, which is lovely as the camera glides through sets and distracting when it circles around group shots. Straining under the production code, Milestone is barely able to even suggest the tragic transgression that climaxes the film. There are some gorgeous scenes but it misses the simmering tension Raoul Walsh brought to the material so well in the 1926 silent *Sadie Thompson.* —*S. A.*

STRANGE LOVE OF MARTHA IVERS, THE L: DIRECTORS/ MILESTONE, LEWIS (1946) 116M D: Lewis Milestone. *Lizabeth Scott, Van Heflin, Barbara Stanwyck, Judith Anderson, Kirk Douglas, Ann Doran.* Milestone's sole film noir starts out with a prelude in a *Rebecca*-scaled mansion full of soft shadows and the plotting of unhappy children. It looks like a Gothic melodrama until the film jumps ahead almost twenty years, when the shadows turn hard and the dark, dangerous city takes over. Heflin is at his stocky, stand-up best as the professional gambler who takes an unexpected stopover in this small town and steps right into a viper's nest—his two childhood friends (Stanwyck and Douglas) are now a venomous couple whose distrust of outsiders almost tops their distrust of each other. Milestone's direction is a little too clean and classically handsome for the sleazy subject matter, but his use of actors is superb: Heflin's solid fullback stance and hon-

Kenji Mizoguchi

Regarded, with Yasujiro Ozu and Akira Kurosawa, as one of the three "First Masters" of Japanese cinema, Mizoguchi made more than eighty-five films in a career that spanned more than thirty years. Over fifty of them have been lost, primarily through studio fires, the ravages of war, or poor preservation methods, but those that remain have secured his place as one of the greatest film directors of the century.

Drawn to the cinema through literature and painting (he studied at the Aohashi Western Painting Research Institute), he found employment, through an actor friend, as an assistant director at the Nikkatsu Motion Picture Company. A labor dispute at the studio accelerated the usually long apprenticeship process, and Mizoguchi soon found himself directing films for Nikkatsu. His first films were mostly left-leaning literary adaptations and politi-

---

est mug is quite a contrast to Stanwyck's hard, scheming face and Douglas's cowering carriage. —*S.A.*

ALIAS BETTY L: DIRECTORS/MILLER, CLAUDE (2001) 101M D: Claude Miller. *Sandrine Kiberlane, Nicole Garcia, Mathilde Seigner, Luck Mervil.* Miller's deceptively loose crime thriller, adapted from a novel by Ruth Rendell, stars Kiberlane as Betty, an author and single mother who reunites with her obliviously self-involved mother (Garcia). The tension snaps when Betty's son dies and, in a misguided attempt to make up for her own lifelong maternal lapse, the mother kidnaps a little boy to take the son's place. Seigner's mercenary single mom and working girl acts the bereaved mother while privately treating her son's disappearance as a liberation, and Mervil is the caring father figure for her otherwise neglected son. The crisscrossing trajectories spiral into an utterly satisfying conclusion, a climax that feels less designed than divinely steered, a crime film in a moral universe. There's something beautiful about Miller's simple poetic justice in today's cynical cinematic climate. —*S.A.*

BABE: PIG IN THE CITY L: DIRECTORS/MILLER, GEORGE (1998) 120M D: George Miller. *Mary Stein, Mickey Rooney, James Cromwell, Magda Szubanski.* A much weirder and darker sequel that failed upon its release, despite being a masterpiece of fantasy cinema. When Farmer Hoggett (Cromwell) is injured, the farm is in jeopardy, so his wife, Esme (Szubanski), is forced to take Babe overseas to perform for money. The trip is disastrous and they get stranded in an expressionistic portrait of the big city, where landmarks from all over the world collide and jet planes seem to fly just a few feet above the buildings. They stay in an animal hotel inhabited by clothed circus apes, stray cats, and abandoned dogs, until they are displaced by a devastating animal-con-

trol raid. Miller cowrote and produced the first *Babe,* but this time he directs (the intense chase scenes make more sense once you realize he's the director of the *Mad Max* trilogy). It's not as tightly constructed as the first *Babe,* and gets a little silly in the slapstick finale, but there are only a handful of films in existence that rival its imagination and visual ambition. —*B. T.*

MAD MAX L: DIRECTORS/MILLER, GEORGE (1979) 93M D: George Miller. *Hugh Keays-Byrne, Roger Ward, Steve Bisley, Joanne Samuel, Mel Gibson.* The young, clean shaven Gibson looks a little too innocent for the part of a street-calloused cop driven to bloodthirsty revenge, and the straight line of his vengeance is a kind of postapocalyptic *Death Wish.* Where director Miller scores is in an ambitious direction that aspires to more and an ambience that tells us everything we need to know about a society on the verge of implosion: the streets are empty, the police station sign is falling apart, and the cities are hauntingly sparse. When the film was first released to American theaters in the last days of the drive-in market, distributor AIP decided that Australian accents would be too much for stateside audiences and they dubbed the dialogue with Hollywood talent. The DVD debut features both the American dub track and the original Australian soundtrack: Gibson actually speaks his own lines! —*S. A.*

MAD MAX II: THE ROAD WARRIOR L: DIRECTORS/MILLER, GEORGE (1981) 94M D: George Miller. *Kjell Nilsson, Virginia Hey, Syd Heylen, Michael Preston, Mel Gibson, Vernon Wells.* Miller's follow-up to 1979's fantastic postapocalyptic road-rage drama, *Mad Max II* does something that sequels to great films don't often do: it does better. From the opening sequence, Miller is able to rehash the story of Max (Gibson)—how he lost his family to road thugs and became a rogue vigilante—and balance that backstory with the backstory of the

cally sensitive works that rankled the studio heads and overturned the conventions of Japanese cinema of the time. Although he would not continue his commitment to leftist politics, he would remain a tireless rouser of social and cinematic imaginations.

Mizoguchi's sympathy for and depiction of the exploited and marginalized members of society was profoundly influenced by his family life. Mizoguchi's father horribly mistreated his mother and sister. His mother was beaten and neglected, and his sister was given up for adoption and later sold by her foster parents to a geisha house. Yet although he resented his father's actions, when his sister was fortunate enough to find a wealthy patron who provided her with a house and income, and who later married her when his own wife died, Mizoguchi's conscience was not troubled in the slightest when he became fully dependent upon her.

Some view Mizoguchi as sympathetic to women, others as a conspirator against them. But within the context of his own life and his place in Japanese history, one theme resonates time and again in his work: a man's soul is saved by a woman's love.

—Kevin Shannon

---

world—how violence prevailed over peace, governments crumbled, and fuel became the single commodity worth fighting and dying for. Max is seen as a kind of folk hero, coming to the aid of defenseless gas-worshippers surrounded by gas-hungry road thugs, but what kind of hero is he? His heroic acts are more self-motivated than altruistic; he needs fuel too. With *Mad Max II*, Miller creates the ultimate existential hero of a crisis-bound world in need of a savior. *—J. D.*

WITCHES OF EASTWICK, THE L: DIRECTORS/MILLER, GEORGE (1987) 121M D: George Miller. *Jack Nicholson, Veronica Cartwright, Susan Sarandon, Cher, Richard Jenkins, Michelle Pfeiffer.* If there was ever a man born to play the role of the Devil, Nicholson is it. A trio of lonely friends in a small town, played by Cher, Sarandon, and Pfeiffer, unknowingly summon the Devil while talking about the qualities they all want in a man. There's some sex, followed by a lot of gossip, followed by the ladies deciding that maybe their perfect guy isn't the best thing for them after all. Satan isn't too happy with this, as can be expected, and a bunch of crazy shit ensues. What really makes this movie is the acting. The trio of ladies, as well as Nicholson himself, delivers excellent and wonderfully complementary performances, but they barely hold a candle to Cartwright, a religious zealot who goes crazy when Satan comes to town and ends up vomiting up a ton of cherries because of it. *—J. S.*

BAD AND THE BEAUTIFUL, THE L: DIRECTORS/ MINNELLI, VINCENTE (1952) 119M D: Vincente Minnelli. *Walter Pidgeon, Lana Turner, Kirk Douglas, Barry Sullivan, Dick Powell, Gloria Grahame.* One of the great Hollywood movies about Hollywood movies, this Minnelli melodrama stars Douglas as an ambitious producer who crawls his way up the studio system while betraying his collaborators and friends: movie-star Turner, director Sullivan, writer Powell. His character is an amalgam of some real-life personalities (Val Lewton and David Selznick among them), but the steely eyes and hard, conniving fierceness belong completely to Douglas. Turner gives one of the best performances in her career as the once-naive starlet who toughens under Douglas's tutelage. Grahame won an Oscar for her performance as the Southern flirt married to Powell. *—S. A.*

MEET ME IN ST. LOUIS L: DIRECTORS/MINNELLI, VINCENTE (1944) 113M D: Vincente Minnelli. *Judy Garland, Margaret O'Brien, Mary Astor.* Minnelli was truly an extraordinary filmmaker. Who else could make a movie, more than two hours in length, in which the entire plot hinges on curtains? Superficially, this film seems nearly as insubstantial, with the crux of the plot—what little there is of it—coming nearly an hour into the film. It doesn't matter though; this is a movie about a time and a place long gone. *—S. F.*

ON A CLEAR DAY YOU CAN SEE FOREVER L: DIRECTORS/ MINNELLI, VINCENTE (1970) 129M D: Vincente Minnelli. *Yves Montand, Jack Nicholson, Bob Newhart, Barbra Streisand.* Andrew Sarris gleefully states that this film shows "Vincente Minnelli at his most morbid and Alan Jay Lerner at his most wickedly misogynistic," and that is an endorsement. Well, it got me to see it and wow, was I glad. What a trashy spectacle. Montand's a stiff, Streisand out of place, and Nicholson's a hippie (again), but who cares? With lavish, million-dollar sets that are used for ten seconds and then thrown away, or great lines like, "Do you like painting?" "No, I've gotten used to wallpaper," and Leon Ames's "KEEP THE JUNKIES OFF THE LAWN!" There are many pleasures to be found amidst the wreckage. *—M. S.*

YOLANDA AND THE THIEF L: DIRECTORS/MINNELLI, VINCENTE (1945) 108M D: Vincente Minnelli. *Lucille Bremer, Fred Astaire, Frank Morgan.* From the gloriously insipid opening numbers (crooned by a boy-soprano chorus) to Bremer's near-naked costumes and bubble bath scene, this one flopped with the critics but deserves true cult status as an over-the-top, quirky gem. Astaire and Morgan (*The Wiz*) shine as grifters who aim to take doe-eyed Bremer for everything she's got, but find more than they wanted. —*M. S.*

UGETSU (AKA **UGETSU MONOGATARI**) L: DIRECTORS/ MIZOGUCHI, KENJI (1953) 94M D: Kenji Mizoguchi. *Kinuyo Tanaka, Machiko Kyo, Eitaro Ozawa, Ikio Sawamura, Masayuki Mori.* Ugetsu is the story of two couples in sixteenth-century Japan (a brother and sister and their respective spouses) and the misadventures that befall them when they set out from their village to sell pottery in the city. A hauntingly beautiful meditation on the private but universal struggle between love and greed, *Ugetsu,* which translates as *Tales of a Pale and Mysterious Moon After the Rain,* feels exactly like you'd expect a film with that title to feel: it has the visual texture and depth of Dreyer's greatest films and the comfortable sadness of Ozu's masterpieces. Truly one of the most rewarding moviegoing experiences of my life. —*C. C.*

BEETHOVEN'S NEPHEW L: DIRECTORS/MORRISSEY, PAUL (1988) 103M D: Paul Morrissey. *Wolfgang Reichmann, Ditmar Prinz, Jane Birkin, Nathalie Baye.* Expertly cast as Beethoven, Reichmann depicts the master composer in his later years when it was known that he had become quite paranoid and deaf, as well as hopelessly attracted to his nephew. The historical detail in this little-known film by Morrissey is surprisingly accurate. Even the musicians are actually playing their instruments without having a large union orchestra dubbed over them. With all of these good elements coming into play one cannot help but develop a love/hate feeling toward this complicated character—a feeling very likely shared by his acquaintances in his day. —*N. J.*

BLOOD FOR DRACULA L: DIRECTORS/MORRISSEY, PAUL (1973) 93M D: Paul Morrissey. *Udo Kier, Joe Dallesandro, Roman Polanski, Vittoria De Sica, Arno Juerging.* A remarkably different take on the Bram Stoker story (and also known as *Andy Warhol's Dracula*). Kier plays a Count Dracula who must only drink the blood of virgins (and with Kier's thick accent he enthusiastically pronounces the word "wirgins"). Badly needing fresh blood, Dracula proposes marriage to the oldest of three daughters in a wealthy household. Dallesandro, playing the recently hired groundskeeper of the estate, discovers Dracula's plot and foils him by sleeping with all three daughters before he can get his fangs on them. When Dracula does try to suck their blood he gets very sick and has to vomit

all the blood upon the floor! Filmed alongside its sister film, *Flesh For Frankenstein* (aka *Andy Warhol's Frankenstein*). —*N. J.*

FLESH FOR FRANKENSTEIN L: DIRECTORS/MORRISSEY, PAUL (1973) 95M D: Paul Morrissey. *Monique Van Vooren, Udo Kier, Joe Dallesandro, Vittoria De Sica, Srdjan Zelenovic, Dalila di Lazzaro.* Originally filmed in rather impressive 3-D and also known as *Andy Warhol's Frankenstein,* this is a different take on the Mary Shelley classic. With a very young Kier playing Baron von Frankenstein (despite his thick Romanian accent) and Dallesandro playing the young man who is in search of the missing head of his friend, this film does not disappoint when it comes to overly indulgent gore scenes. In one such scene Frankenstein actually mounts one of his dead victims and makes love to her liver. "One has not lived," he instructs Igor, "until one has fucked a liver!" Of course Frankenstein and his castle are taken down, but not until many more variations of gore and sex are exploited in ways only Andy Warhol would approve of. This was filmed alongside its sister film, *Blood For Dracula* (aka *Andy Warhol's Dracula*). —*N. J.*

HOUND OF THE BASKERVILLES, THE L: DIRECTORS/ MORRISSEY, PAUL (1978) 84M D: Paul Morrissey. *Peter Cook, Dudley Moore, Denholm Elliot, Joan Greenwood, Terry Thomas.* This over-the-top Moore/Cook entry is lined corner to corner with the corniest jokes and puns imaginable! Cook plays Sherlock Holmes, who quickly gives up on the Baskerville case because of better things to do such as visit his mother. Moore, meanwhile, plays Watson, who is more than eager to take on the case even though he can barely put two simple thoughts together. The film lurches hysterically from skit to skit until the end of the film where the original plot is just barely salvaged. After that a nearby volcano explodes. —*N. J.*

SAME TIME, NEXT YEAR L: DIRECTORS/MULLIGAN, ROBERT (1978) 119M D: Robert Mulligan. *Ellen Burstyn, Alan Alda.* The always intelligent direction of Mulligan keeps this film from falling into the sappy melodrama that its musical score seems to hint at. Instead, terrific performances from Burstyn and Alda, as two lovers who take time out from their lives once each year for a weekend affair, provide a strong structure that Slade's script (adapted from his own play) never lets down. A smart and intimate drama. Give it a look. —*C. P.*

SUMMER OF '42, THE L: DIRECTORS/MULLIGAN, ROBERT (1971) 102M D: Robert Mulligan. *Jerry Houser, Oliver Conant, Katherine Allentuck, Jennifer O'Neill, Gary Grimes.* The director of *To Kill a Mockingbird* goes back to themes of youth and memory for a film of great delicacy and cumulative impact. A grown man whom we never see (and whose voice is deliberately un-actorish—Mulligan's own, in fact) recalls the summer of his sixteenth year and the feverish mental and emotional groping of him and two buddies at the threshold of sexual experience. The narrator's teenage self (Grimes) gravitates toward the improbable dream of a young soldier's wife (O'Neill) settling down to sit out the duration on the same Maine island where his family vacations. Mulligan's gift for eliciting warm, spontaneous performances enhances the genuineness of his people. Surtees's Technicolor images have the muted fogginess of nostalgia. There is a careful pan around the young wife's rooms that captures a sense of the boy memorizing the details of the scene forever and the narrator cherishing them from the remove of time and still greater mystery. Otherwise, Mulligan and Surtees consistently use telephoto lenses to do their moving for them: the effect is to suggest moving into past time itself. The only misjudgment is Legrand's music score, superfluously cuing us in on the bittersweetness of it all. —R. T. J.

TO KILL A MOCKINGBIRD L: DIRECTORS/MULLIGAN, ROBERT (1962) 130M D: Robert Mulligan. *Gregory Peck, Mary Badham, Philip Alford, John Megna.* Peck won a Best Actor Oscar for his role in this excellent adaptation of Harper Lee's best-selling novel. Peck plays an Alabama lawyer who takes on the case of a black man accused of raping a white girl. The perspective on this racially charged situation common to the '20s and '30s is provided by the lawyer's two children (Badham and Alford) and their new friend (Megna). They follow Peck around as he collects evidence and they even watch the entire trial from the second-floor gallery along with the allotted blacks. The trial alone is incredible enough, yet with Peck portraying the always patient lawyer battling a flurry of unstoppable emotion and antagonism, this film is apt to stick in your mind's eye for a long time to come. —N. J.

FAUST (1926) L: DIRECTORS/MURNAU, F. W. (1926) 117M D: F. W. Murnau. *Emil Jannings, Camilla Horn, Warner Fuetterer, Gosta Ekman.* Before the introduction of sound in filmmaking, the style of German expressionism in the silent era reached a pinnacle with such films as *Sunrise* and *Faust* by Murnau. The familiar story of a man selling his soul to the devil in exchange for youth is here done up with wonderful sets and remarkable style. The DVD through Kino Video features an excellent original score by Timothy Brock conducting the Olympia Chamber Orchestra. —N. J.

HAUNTED CASTLE, THE L: DIRECTORS/MURNAU, F. W. (1921) 75M D: F. W. Murnau. *Paul Bildt, Lothar Mehnert, Lulu Kyser-Korff, Arnold Korff, Olga Tschechowa.* The Baroness (Tschechowa) arrives at the lodge for a rained-out hunting party. The Count invites himself in; he may have killed her husband and now predicts a shot will be fired. A Holy Father later arrives to mysteriously disappear then later reappear. The Count jokes in bad taste and is ostracized by the other guests at breakfast. More complications occur in and out of the main door and up and down the stairs. Then a shot is fired. As contrived as this seems with at least two mysteries plus secret motives and disguises, Murnau animates the large static set with lyrical but edgy touches that give the shocks some real juice. People are framed in the architecture with touches of backlighting or the momentary contrast of outdoor scenes. The Gothic lodge is modernized, becoming a metaphor for psychological internalization that suffuses the atmosphere. This is Murnau's edgiest film; had he only survived into the days of film noir! —J. C.

NOSFERATU (1922) L: DIRECTORS/MURNAU, F. W. (1922) 84M D: F. W. Murnau. *Alexander Granach, Greta Schröder, Gustav von Wangenheim, Max Schreck.* Considered one of the finest silent films ever made, *Nosferatu* is the very first picture based on the story of Dracula. The title *Nosferatu* was used instead of *Dracula* because Bram Stoker's widow still held the rights. With Schreck playing the vampire and director Murnau's incredible use of photography (including some very effective stop-motion animation), this has got to be the most chilling depiction of the timeless story to date. Hutter (the Jonathan Harker of this film) travels into forbidden territory to sell land to the wealthy count. After this shocking exposition the vampire takes a ship to his new home, killing everyone on board and emptying out his plague-infested rats to lay siege to the whole city. —N. J.

SUNRISE (1927) L: DIRECTORS/MURNAU, F. W. (1927) 95M D: F. W. Murnau. *George O'Brien, Janet Gaynor, Bodil Rosing, Margaret Livingston.* It is this simple: *Sunrise* is one of the greatest films ever made. It should be required viewing for anyone who has ever gone to the cinema. "Sir, is your *Sunrise* card punched yet? No? Sorry, but we can't let you in." Subtitled "A Song of Two Humans," Murnau created a modern mythic love story of timeless, lyrical, heart-rending power. It also astonishes to learn how Murnau and cinematographers Charles Rosher and Karl Struss shot the film. It is an amazing technical and artistic achievement that only gets better when you learn more about it. It should be pointed out that Gaynor was awarded an Oscar for her performances in three films (the only time Oscar did this), the others being *Seventh Heaven* and *Street Angel*; and that the original score by Hugo Reisenfeld is also very powerful, though it did suffer in the postproduction process. Both scores are available on the DVD version. —K. S.

TABU L: DIRECTORS/MURNAU, F. W. (1931) 84M D: F. W. Murnau, Robert Flaherty. *Anne Chevalier, Matahi.* German émigré Murnau, director of the classics *Nosferatu* and *Sunrise,* teamed up with

F. W. Murnau

Perhaps no other director in the history of cinema had a career that shone so brightly yet so briefly as F. W. Murnau. Born Friedrich Wilhelm Plumpe in 1888, Murnau completed twenty-two films between 1919 and 1931—many lost forever, some considered among the greatest ever made.

Though his signature style was to emerge later, Murnau's talents were on display from the beginning. In his earliest films, he seems to be merely learning the craft. But with the Expressionist horror classic *Nosferatu* (1922), Murnau attracted international attention.

Contrary to popular opinion, Murnau was signed by William Fox in Hollywood not after but before the tremendous success of *The Last Laugh* (1924). Having garnered a five-picture deal from Fox only a few weeks after that film's opening in Berlin, Murnau was eager to get to Hollywood, where he would be able to work with all the facilities that a director could dream of. Even so, he stayed in Germany long enough to complete

two more films, *Tartuffe* (1925) and the masterpiece *Faust* (1926).

Murnau's first film in America, *Sunrise* (1927), may have been his greatest. A smashing critical success, *Sunrise* represented the highest aspirations and achievement of the time: a "prestige" film that had universal appeal. As a climax of the silent era, and a shining example of the power of the cinema, this "song of two humans" has withstood the test of time to become one of the most highly regarded films in the history of the art.

Sadly, Murnau never learned how to handle the fiscal and political elements of Hollywood, and his career went into decline. His contract with Fox was broken after only three films. His second, *Four Devils* (1928), has been lost, and his third, *City Girl* (1929), was sabotaged by the advent of sound. Murnau's final film, *Tabu* (1931), used sound effects and music but was otherwise a silent film. Killed in an auto accident a few weeks prior to its opening, Murnau was fated never to explore the cinema of sound, never to demonstrate where he might have taken the medium.   —*Kevin Shannon*

---

documentary legend Flaherty (*Nanook of the North*) to make a portrait of South Seas culture. Sensibilities clashed and Flaherty left the film, leaving Murnau to create his own vision of *Paradise Lost* in the story of young love threatened by tribal law. Murnau uses the clash of cultures to contrast an Eden-like innocence with the corruption of modern society (one seemingly sensitive white soul is more opportunist than romantic). The mythic undertones are more European than Pacific Rim and Murnau's portrayal of the young lovers as Peter Pan–like children of nature is paternalistic at best and downright condescending in parts. But *Tabu* is also astoundingly beautiful, like a black-and-white rendering of Paul Gaugaun's visions of Tahiti through an expressionist sensibility. *Tabu* is classic Murnau, a powerful, poetic story of the doomed struggle against fate. —*S. A.*

HYSTERICAL BLINDNESS L: DIRECTORS/NAIR, MIRA (2002) 96M D: Mira Nair. *Juliette Lewis, Gena Rowlands, Justin Chambers, Ben Gazarra, Uma Thurman. Hysterical Blindness* is brimming with talent. Thurman and Lewis fearlessly tackle two of their most memorable characters as a couple of trashy barflies looking for affection. Thurman takes desperation to a whole new level when she drops all standards to seduce a man who thinks she's garbage. This was an extremely moving piece, emotionally charged with great costumes and gnarly hair. It has an excellent eye for detail, thanks to Nair (*Monsoon Wedding*) and the screenplay by Laura Cahill (from her play). In addition, the costumes, set design, editing, and production design were all done by women. —*R. D.*

MISSISSIPPI MASALA L: DIRECTORS/NAIR, MIRA (1991) 118M D: Mira Nair. *Sarita Choudhury, Denzel Washington.* Much more than just a love story, this film explores prejudice, condemnation, and different generations trying to establish or maintain their places in the world. Beautifully filmed with rich, warm colors, the movie leaves its viewer with hope for the young lovers and possibly the world they live in. —*G. T.*

MONSOON WEDDING L: DIRECTORS/NAIR, MIRA (2002) 115M D: Mira Nair. *Vasundhara Das, Parvin Dabas, Lillete Dubey, Naseeruddin Shah, Shefali Shetty.* Henna and hip-hop: India hits the twenty-first century in Nair's Technicolor culture clash. Imagine *Father of the Bride* by way of Robert Altman's *A Wedding* and transplanted to modern Delhi. This is a world where marriages are arranged by cell phone and young Indian women tenuously strike a balance between cultural expectations and professional careers with the help of advice from *Cosmopolitan.* Nair plays the collision of modern life and tradition for all they're worth, at times losing the skin-deep characters in two hours of bustling stories. For all of its infectious energy and passionate splashes of glowing color, busy spectacle, melodramatic subplots, and driving pace, *Monsoon Wedding* has more in common with Hollywood's Technicolor movie fantasies than the so-square-it's-hip Bollywood musical Nair claims to be taking into the twenty-first century. But perhaps the modern flair of Nair's characters is just their way of preserving their heritage in the bustle of the global economy. —*S. A.*

POSTCARDS FROM THE EDGE L: DIRECTORS/NICHOLS, MIKE (1990) 101M D: Mike Nichols. *Meryl Streep, Shirley MacLaine, Dennis Quaid, Gene Hackman.* Fisher's *Postcards from the Edge* is one of my favorite books, and the film was disappointing. It contains very little of the book's personality, but it would be difficult to translate its wit and truths into film, even if Fisher herself wrote the screenplay. The film centers on Suzanne (Streep), an actress who overdoses, goes through rehab, makes a bad movie, has a fling with a sleazy guy, clashes with her mother, and tries to make sense of her emotions and the absurdities going on around her—just your usual Hollywood problems. Streep does a wonderful job portraying the confusion and craziness of Suzanne's life with defensive humor and sarcasm. MacLaine is also great as Suzanne's also famous, somewhat overbearing mother. My favorite scene (that doesn't appear in the book) involves Hackman as a father-figure director who props up Suzanne's drooping spirits during a looping session. —*J. K.*

WHO'S AFRAID OF VIRGINIA WOOLF? L: DIRECTORS/ NICHOLS, MIKE (1966) 127M D: Mike Nichols. *Sandy Dennis, Elizabeth Taylor, George Segal, Richard Burton.* The script for this film based on Edward Albee's play is an intricate study of psychological mechanisms regarding interpersonal relationships. As a matter of fact, one can simply attain the book *The Games People Play* by Eric Berne, published two years before this film's release, and use it

as a veritable scorecard for what is happening between the nasty husband and wife played by Taylor and Burton. The story is simple enough: a teacher and his wife spend an evening at this couple's house for dinner and conversation. But given the twisted disposition of the hosts and the sadistic pleasure they derive from insulting each other, you'd swear that you have entered a level of Dante's Inferno. The acting is so darned good that one suspects this is how Taylor and Burton normally behaved around each other. Socially it's all one big, long car wreck, yet for these hosts it comes off as just another evening. —*N. J.*

WORKING GIRL L: DIRECTORS/NICHOLS, MIKE (1988) 114M D: Mike Nichols. *Melanie Griffith, Sigourney Weaver, Harrison Ford, Joan Cusack, Alec Baldwin.* At the opening of *Working Girl,* we find birthday-girl Tess McGill (Griffith) poised to take the New York business world by storm, if only someone would give her a chance. Her night-school degree, secretarial work, self-improvement seminars, and perpetual gumption just aren't impressing the snobby higher-ups. Then her boss, Katherine (Weaver), ends up in traction after a ski accident, and it turns out to be a break for both of them. Tess sees her chance and takes on the role of executive, maneuvering an important business acquisition with the help of Jack Trainer (Ford). More than just businesses start to merge, and that's when things get complicated. Your usual movie snafus ensue, but in the end everyone gets what they deserve. A little formulaic and general, but altogether empowering and somewhat inspirational. Cusack certainly deserved the Oscar nomination she received for her role as Cyn, Tess's big-haired, smart-talking best friend. —*J. K.*

ULEE'S GOLD L: DIRECTORS/NUÑEZ, VICTOR (1997) 113M D: Victor Nuñez. *J. Kenneth Campbell, Patricia Richardson, Jessica Biel, Christine Dunford, Peter Fonda, Tom Wood.* Nuñez is an American treasure, a true American independent before the term was hip. For years a chronicler of American life and the seesawing balance between the individual and community, he discovers a universal humanity though his films never leave the confines of Florida. His fourth feature in almost twenty years tackles the story of Ulee (Fonda), a stoic beekeeper raising his granddaughters while his son is in prison. Nuñez turns the crude plot involving the son's former partners coming after some uncovered loot into a catalyst for Ulee's rebirth. Fonda's deceptively minimalist performance focuses our attention on the tiny moments when he lets his emotions through, whether it's a flicker of a smile, a flash of sympathy in his hard eyes, or a quiet explanation to his granddaughter. I swear at times you can see the ghost of his father pass in front of his face. —*S. A.*

LOLA MONTES L: DIRECTORS/OPHULS, MAX (1955) 110M D: Max Ophuls. *Peter Ustinov, Martine Carol.* The tension between genuine emotion and the desire for love that suspends many of Ophuls's films becomes the melancholy center of his final drama, the story of "the world's most scandalous woman" re-created as a veritable three-ring circus. Ophuls's only color film contrasts the outrageous sensationalism of her reputation, garishly performed as a big-top cabaret narrated by ringmaster/emcee Ustinov, with offstage moments of tender candor and poignant, poetic flashbacks of her notorious affairs. Swept along by Ophuls's gliding camera work, her life becomes a cinematic ballet with Ophuls as the choreographer and conductor. Carol's Lola is hardly the most passionate or electrifying of Ophuls's stars—her quiet, private demeanor stands in sharp contrast to her public flamboyance and fits of pique—but it provides a sad core of the woman who loved well, if not too wisely. —*S. A.*

IN THE REALM OF THE SENSES L: DIRECTORS/OSHIMA, NAGISA (1976) 105M D: Nagisa Oshima. *Eiko Matsuda, Tatsuya Fuji.* So, it's like this: you go to the video store and want to rent porn. . . but, you don't "want to rent porn." Because then that sarcastic guy behind the counter will know "This perv watches porn!" The solution: rent *In the Realm of the Senses.* It's like porn, albeit artfully made porn. Since it's actually "about" sexual obsession and not just a string of bland, gratuitous sex scenes, it transcends porn. But, you still have two people fucking on camera. And that geek behind the counter will think you're just renting an art film. —*K. C.*

MAX, MON AMORE L: DIRECTORS/OSHIMA, NAGISA (1986) 94M D: Nagisa Oshima. *Charlotte Rampling, Victoria Abril, Anthony Higgins.* Margaret (Rampling) sleeps with a monkey to get back at her unfaithful husband, British diplomat Peter (Higgins). Peter must accept the situation or face a divorce. He is then forced to adopt the monkey as a part of his family, adding to his shame. Jean-Luc Godard cinematographer Coutard uses slow, static shots to create uncomfortable moments of love between woman and ape. Japanese master director Oshima strikes the perfect absurd balance between fact and fantasy, poking fun at bourgeoisie morality with the same playful tone that screenwriter Carrière brought to the films he wrote for Spanish director Luis Buñuel. A midget in a suit designed by master ape-maker Rick Baker plays the disturbingly realistic monkey. —*N. H.*

MERRY CHRISTMAS, MR. LAWRENCE L: DIRECTORS/OSHIMA, NAGISA (1982) 130M D: Nagisa Oshima. *David Bowie, Tom Contie, Ryuichi Sakamoto, Beat Takeshi Kitano, Jack Thompson.* Oshima teams up with writer Paul Mayersberg (*The Man who Fell to Earth, Eureka*) to bring to the screen Laurens Van der Post's WWII autobiography *The Seed and the Sower,* and the results are spellbinding. Bowie could not be more perfectly cast as the rebellious Major Jack Celliers, who winds up in the Japanese war camp under the watchful eye of Captain Yonnai (Sakamoto). Yonni finds himself first drawn to and then intimidated by Celliers's beautiful blond hair and white skin. Yonni's self-hatred at his own homosexual tendencies is manifest in his sadistically cruel treatment of Celliers and his men. As Oshima's work has done in the past, *Merry Christmas, Mr. Lawrence* brings to the surface hidden feelings of racism and repressed homosexuality, in this case those found in the Japanese war-dominated culture of WWII. A beautifully shot, written, and acted film, even its score by Sakamoto instantly became a classic. —*N. H.*

TOMBS OF THE BLIND DEAD L: DIRECTORS/OSSORIO, ARMANDO DE (1971) 93M D: Armando de Ossorio. *Maria Silva, Veronica Limera, Helen Harp, Jose Telman.* Opening with the Knight Templar ritual of tying a woman down and horse-riding around her while hacking into her flesh, the blood level seems quite high. Many years after the townspeople execute the Knights and leave them for the crows, they are now hungry for revenge. A group of young people wanders into a crumbling monastery and those gray-ragged Templars itch for some sonar action—their eyes long plucked and burned out, they must use sound to locate their victims. Out of all the permutations of the walking dead, the Knights Templar are the slowest of the bunch. Director De Ossario even shoots their night rides in slow motion. And this is what works about these films: the slow rise and fall of the knights' "voices," the beating heart of a victim, the woman screaming while snails beat the Templars to the nubile flesh. Followed by three sequels by the same director. —*S. R.*

8 WOMEN L: DIRECTORS/OZON, FRANÇOIS (2002) 101M D: François Ozon. *Isabelle Huppert, Danielle Darrieux, Catherine Deneuve, Emmanuelle Béart, Ludivine Sagnier, Firmine Richard, Virginie Ledoyen, Fanny Ardant.* Ozon's glamorous diva-fest is a mix of musical, chamber drama, and murder mystery by way of George Cukor's *The Women.* There's a murder at a country estate over the Christmas holidays and no one is above suspicion: the elegant lady of the house and wife of the victim (Deneuve), her dotty mother (Darrieux), two daughters (Ledoyen and the tomboyish Sagnier), and catty old-maid sister (Huppert); the maternal old family cook (Richard); the sexy, defiant parlor maid (Béart); and the victim's bad-girl sister (Ardant). It's choreographed as much as it is directed, staged like a dance on a magnificent central grand room. As the investigation wears on, their secrets come tumbling out, as do songs—a collection of eight French standards that gives each woman her time in spotlight. Ozon's theatrical flourish harkens back to the Technicolor splendor and studio grandeur of '50s Hollywood melodrama, but with a definitively Gallic flavor. It's a lightweight but deft piece of cinematic candy and a rare opportunity to see so many of France's grand actresses wrestle on-screen. —*S. A.*

SEE THE SEA L: DIRECTORS/OZON, FRANÇOIS (1997) 52M D: François Ozon. *Sasha Hails, Marina de Van.* I have never felt so victimized by a film and loved it. Through the vulnerability of a lonely mother in a picturesque house by the sea, *See the Sea* presents a challenging story showcasing both the beauty and twisted horror of women. Director Ozon is able to pull apart everything that I secretly hold sacred and inviolable, then crudely sew it together again to complete a devastating experience. And he does this all with style and humor. I would compare it to a very sad song that you can dance to. —*J. J.*

SITCOM L: DIRECTORS/OZON, FRANÇOIS (1998) 85M D: François Ozon. *Evelyne Dandry, Francois Marthouret, Marina de Van, Adrien de Van, Stephane Rideau.* Imagine *American Beauty* on hallucinogens. Ozon uses the situation comedy as a starting point for social satire, deftly deconstructing convention, conformity, and so-called family values with comic collisions of class, race, gender, and sexual orientation. Ozon nuzzles the borders of bad taste with some seriously deviant episodes as the nuclear family acts out its most extreme, repressed fantasies (bondage, sadomasochism, suicide, incest), but he deftly balances the perversity with a tender sympathy, the wackiness with knowing wit. The result is like a transgressive Luis Buñuel shattering the false fronts of middle-class conventions. Ozon gives their search for identity a touching sincerity. —*S. A.*

UNDER THE SAND L: DIRECTORS/OZON, FRANÇOIS (2000) 95M D: François Ozon. *Charlotte Rampling, Bruno Cremer, Jacques Nolot, Alexandra Stewart, Pierre Vernier.* Rampling stars in Ozon's psychodrama as a middle-class woman whose settled, predictable life is turned inside out when her husband vanishes without a trace. Rampling gives a delicate performance as the elegant but fragile English professor whose denial soon manifests itself in visions of her husband padding through the apartment and smiling bemusedly over breakfast. But don't expect a playful romantic comedy a la *Truly, Madly, Deeply.* Less mystery than metaphysics, this is about loss, desire, and the intricate working of the human psyche in crisis, and Ozon applies a delicate restraint far different from the bright, bold style of his previous features *Water Drops on Burning Rocks* and *Criminal Lovers.* —*S. A.*

AUTUMN AFTERNOON, AN L: DIRECTORS/OZU, YASUJIRO (1962) 112M D: Yasujiro Ozu. *Shin-Ichiro Mikami, Shima Iwashita, Chisu Ryu.* Ozu's final film appropriately places his customary plots and themes in the most industrialized Japan found in his body of work. It's also one of the most extreme examples of Ozu's distinctive style (shunning showy filmmaking and overly dynamic acting), finally eliminating camera motion altogether. Shuhei (Ryu) is an aging widower resistant to marry off his twenty-four-year-old daughter, Michiko (Iwashita), a reluctance he has difficulty justifying as attractive proposals roll in. When an old friend, whose wife also passed away, takes up with a much younger woman, Shehei begins to stew over his own loneliness. Meanwhile Shuhei's son, Kazuo (Mikami), has troubles of his own, infuriating his wife by recklessly splurging on an expensive set of golf clubs. One of Ozu's funniest films, it's also a melancholy reflection on life's disappointments. The poignant combination makes for one of the most satisfying movie experiences I know of. —*C. B.*

EARLY SUMMER (BAKUSHU) L: DIRECTORS/OZU, YASUJIRO (1951) 135M D: Yasujiro Ozu. *Chieko Higashiyama, Chishu Ryu, Sutsuko Hara, Ryudan Nimoto, Ichiro Sugai.* With seasons in the titles of so many Ozu films, it's hard to keep them straight. Worse, this is one of several to involve the marrying off of a reluctant daughter—in this case Noriko (Hara, who maddeningly played another Noriko in 1949's *Late Spring*)—quickly passing marriageable age. And then there's Ozu's uniformity of camera work to contend with. Still, each film is a distinctive pleasure in itself, often remembered more for the plot's minute details than for the story as a whole. Perhaps the most memorable of these in *Early Summer* are Noriko's meetings with friends, which continually end in unserious spats pitting the married girls against the unmarried ones. Delicately weighing tradition against modernity and the needs of the individual against the needs of the family, *Early Summer's* hefty run time allows for nuance and characterization, lending a novelistic richness that's entirely welcome. —*C. B.*

GOOD MORNING (OHAYO) L: DIRECTORS/OZU, YASUJIRO (1959) 93M D: Yasujiro Ozu. *Masahiko Shimazu, Koji Shitara, Yoshiko Kuga, Chishu Ryu.* Ozu's famous film stands as the epitome of Technicolor wholesomeness wrapped in the weight of a bouquet of feathers. Two bratty kids resort to the silent treatment when their parents refuse to buy them a television so they can watch sumo wrestling like the pseudo-American hipster weirdo next-door neighbors. The kids are so damn cute that every time they make a fart joke it's so adorable you can't help laughing, realizing there's no way in hell this would or could have been funny in an American film. The Criterion DVD is vibrant pastel goodness that should not be substituted for VHS, despite the minor scratches from the transfer that pop and crackle every now and then. —*A. T.*

Directors who should have larger followings

WES ANDERSON
(Bottle Rocket, Rushmore,
The Royal Tenenbaums)

KENNETH ANGER
(Fireworks, Scorpio Rising, Lucifer Rising)

MICHAEL BAY
("There, I said it")

KATHRYN BIGELOW
(Near Dark)

FRANK BORZAGE
(China Doll, Till We Meet Again,
A Farewell to Arms)

LARRY COHEN
(It's Alive, The Stuff, Black Caesar, Bone)

SERGIO CORBUCCI
(Django, The Beast, Compañeros)

JOE DANTE
(The Howling, Gremlins, Matinee)

ALEX DE LA IGLESIA
(Day of the Beast, Perdita Durango,
800 Bullets)

GUILLERMO DEL TORO
(Cronos, The Devil's Backbone, Blade II)

KINJI FUKASAKU
(The Green Slime, Battles Without Honor and
Humanity, Message from Space,
Battle Royale)

HRAFN GUNNLAUGSSON
(Revenge of the Barbarians, Witchcraft)

TRENT HARRIS
(Rubin and Ed, The Beaver Trilogy,
The Cement Ball of Heaven and Earth)

TODD HAYNES
(Poison, Safe, Far from Heaven)

WALTER HILL
(Hard Times, The Warriors, The Long Riders)

HOU HSIAO-HSEN
(Summer at Grandpa's, Good Men, Good
Women, Flowers of Shanghai)

DEREK JARMAN
(Sebastiane, The Tempest, Caravaggio, Aria)

SHUSUKE KANEKO
(Gamera 3: Revenge of Iris, Godzilla GMK)

I WAS BORN BUT. . . L: DIRECTORS/OZU, YASUJIRO (1932) 100M D: Yasujiro Ozu. *Seiichi Kato, Tomio Aoki, Tatsuo Saito, Mitsuko Yoshikawa, Takeshi Sakamoto, Hideo Sugawara.* This late silent film is a textbook exercise in perfect filmmaking, generating from one moment to the next a rhythm that gets under your skin, then warping it in a slightly different direction. You follow two grammar school kids walking home from school or running around with the neighborhood gang. The intertitles precisely punctuate the movie's loping pace. There is a paternalistic, such-are-kids humor. The brothers are proud of their dad and say so. But then they witness him kowtowing to his boss and it embarrasses them. They ask their dad why he does it. The question is like a knife in the gut. Dad has no answer. From there the humor darkens and darkens, and you realize Ozu is pointing the same verbal knife back at you. *I Was Born But. . .* is as edgy as they come, the best and blackest comedy ever made. —*J. C.*

LATE SPRING (BANSHUN) L: DIRECTORS/OZU, YASUJIRO (1949) 107M D: Yasujiro Ozu. *Masao Mishima, Hohi Aoki, Kuniko Miyake, Satsuko Hara, Chishu Ryu.* Universally considered one of Ozu's most substantial achievements, *Late Spring* is one of his many stories about a daughter reluctant to marry and a father eager to convince her otherwise before she's too old to attract a suitable husband. In this case the widower father, Shukichi (Ryu), turns to rather extreme tactics, convincing his devoted daughter, Noriko (Hara), that he himself is marrying in order to make her feel unwelcome at home. It works, and Noriko agrees to consider a suitor described emphatically, though not convincingly, as a Gary Cooper look-alike. With a carefully pared-down script and rigorous employment of Ozu's trademark minimal composition (camera movement is shunned, camera positions and framing vary little, and editing is used sparingly), *Late Spring* masterfully renders the melancholy rite of passage that is the parting of parents from their children (and vice versa) with surprising humor and disarming poignancy. —*C. B.*

ALEJANDRO JODOROWSKY
(El Topo, The Holy Mountain, Santa Sangre)

AKI KAURISMÄKI
(Leningrad Cowboys Go America, I Hired a Contract Killer, The Man Without a Past)

ABBAS KIAROSTAMI
(Close-up, And Life Goes On . . . , A Taste of Cherry, The Wind Will Carry Us)

JOSEPH H. LEWIS
(Gun Crazy, Big Combo, Terror in a Texas Town)

NORMAN Z. MCLEOD
(Horse Feathers, It's a Gift, Topper)

JOHN MCTIERNAN
(Predator, Die Hard, The Hunt for Red October)

JIRÍ MENZEL
(Closely Watched Trains, Capricious Summer, My Sweet Little Village)

TSAI MING-LIANG
(The Hole, Rebels of the Neon God, What Time Is It There?)

LUKAS MOODYSSON
(Show Me Love, Together, Lilya 4-Ever)

RAYMOND PETTIBON
(Weatherman '69, Sir Drone, Citizen Tania)

KAREL REISZ
(Isadora, The French Lieutenant's Woman, Sweet Dreams)

TONY SCOTT
(The Hunger, True Romance, Crimson Tide)

DON SIEGEL
(Invasion of the Body Snatchers, Two Mules for Sister Sara, Dirty Harry)

RAY DENNIS STECKLER
(Rat Pfink a Boo Boo, The Incredibly Strange Creatures Who Stopped Living and Became Mixed-Up Zombies, Lemon Grove Kids Meet the Monsters)

JAN SVANKMAJER
(Alice, Faust, Scenes from the Surreal)

LUCHINO VISCONTI
(Rocco and His Brothers, The Witches, Death in Venice, The Innocent)

MICHAEL WINNER
(The Girl-Getters, I'll Never Forget What's 'Isname, Death Wish)

RONNY YU
(The Bride with White Hair, The Phantom Lover, Bride of Chucky)

RECORD OF A TENEMENT GENTLEMAN L: DIRECTORS/ OZU, YASUJIRO (1947) 115M D: Yasujiro Ozu. *Hohi Aoki, Eiko Takamatsu, Chishu Ryu, Shohichi Kawamura, Takeshi Sakamoto.* A young boy (Aoki) is found in a train station, abandoned by his father. Collectively, the middle-class community is all compassion and concern. Individually, no one can be bothered to care for the child. Literally drawing the short straw, Tome (Takamatsu), a childless middle-aged single woman, begrudgingly takes him into her home. Tensions soar as the bizarrely silent boy infuriates Tome by repeatedly wetting the bed. After numerous comical attempts to abandon the boy herself, Tome finally comes to enjoy having him around—at which point his father appears to collect him. Preceding *Tokyo Story* and *Late Spring* (films that would ultimately define the whole of Ozu's not-quite-homogeneous body of work), this film has a pace and a look not seen in his later work. But as always, Ozu's subdued sense of humor thinly conceals a touching social commentary. —*C.B.*

TOKYO STORY (TOKYO MONOGATARI) L: DIRECTORS/ OZU, YASUJIRO (1953) 136M D: Yasujiro Ozu. *Chishu Ryu, Haruko Sugimura, Setsuko Hara, Chieko Higashiyama.* Visiting their children and grandchildren in the suburbs of Tokyo, Mr. and Mrs. Hirayama (Ryu and Higashiyama) find themselves a burden on their busy families. Their children shuffle them from one household to the next, even sending them off for a weekend at a spa to clear them out of the way. Finally they return home, where Mrs. Hirayama soon passes away. A simple plot about life's disappointments that, in Ozu's hands, yields a subtle and poignant masterpiece generally distinguished as the most famous, most beloved, and perhaps greatest of his films. Combining rigorous uniformity of camera work, spare use of editing, and highly stylized performances, *Tokyo Story's* essentialist style squeezes remarkable nuance and more than a little humor from its mundane day-to-day setting, making for a unique film experience that ranks among the best the cinema has to offer. —*C.B.*

DIARY OF A LOST GIRL L: DIRECTORS/PABST, G. W. (1929) 116M D: G. W. Pabst. *Josef Ravensky, Louise Brooks, Andre Roanne, Fritz Rasp, Franziska Kinz.* Brooks, today seen as an icon of the silent era, was merely a bright, vivacious supporting player in Hollywood when German master Pabst brought her to Germany to star in his silent classic, *Pandora's Box*. In *Diary of a Lost Girl*, their second and last collaboration, she plays Thymian, a naive, wide-eyed innocent impregnated by her father's assistant and sent to a repressive reform school by a family that spurns her for her fall from innocence. No better than a prison, it is so spirit-crushing that she escapes and drifts into prostitution. Brooks is an original: her performance is refreshingly free from actorly technique, and her sweetness and sincerity radiate from her very presence. She can even make prostitution seem like a noble profession the way she innocently creates joy with games and good cheer at the high-class bordello. While this lacks the dramatic power of the brilliant *Pandora's Box*, it remains a beautiful and masterfully made social drama. —*S. A.*

JOYLESS STREET L: DIRECTORS/PABST, G. W. (1925) 96M D: G. W. Pabst. *Werner Krauss, Asta Nielsen, Valeska Gert, Greta Garbo.* In post–World War I Vienna, an American soldier and his family are in dire straits, and all their rent money immediately goes to creditors. A nightclub manager (Gert) who rents out private rooms to wealthy men wanting "companions" and women having affairs tells the eldest daughter (Garbo) she can help. It's a tightly wound drama of innocence, decadence, and power, told in bleak but emotionally rich black and white with strange, edgy performances by Gert and Krauss and others (Garbo's restraint is too plain in their company). But the deepest, bleakest moments are Nielsen's; emotion seems to seep from every fold of clothing and hair on her head. She's an uncanny performer in this wickedly cynical essay on the relations between seduction, money, and betrayal. —*J. C.*

PANDORA'S BOX L: DIRECTORS/PABST, G. W. (1929) 110M D: G. W. Pabst. *Louise Brooks, Fritz Kortner, Francis Lederer, Alice Roberts, Gustav Diessl.* Toward the very end of the silent era some of the greatest examples of German expressionism were produced: Murnau's *Sunrise*, Lang's *Metropolis*, von Stroheim's *Queen Kelly*, and Pabst's *Pandora's Box*. Brooks plays Lulu, an attractive woman who happens to destroy every man she meets. Eventually she turns to prostitution, and, as luck would have it, gets a date with Jack the Ripper. Be sure to get Kino Video's DVD, which features the music of Timothy Brock and the Olympia Chamber Orchestra. —*N. J.*

TIME MACHINE, THE L: DIRECTORS/PAL, GEORGE (1960) 103M D: George Pal. *Yvette Mimieux, Alan Young, Rod Taylor, Sebastian Cabot.* In this wonderfully stylized version of the H. G. Wells novel, Taylor plays a scientist who creates a machine capable of going forward and backward in time. After a small dinner party where he unveils his invention, the eminent scientist tries it on for size, taking a little trip to the future. The effects are absolutely stunning as he zips ahead through

the future of world affairs. After WWIII, however, he's completely buried, nuclear war having taken its toll. So the scientist skips ahead to the year 802,701, when the earth has eroded enough around him and he can step out to investigate. He accidentally gets stuck in this strange future where he learns about a whole new society—a society already repeating the mistakes of the distant past. —*N. J.*

COLOR OF POMEGRANATES, THE L: DIRECTORS/ PARADJANOV, SERGEI (1969) 88M D: Segei Paradjanov. *Sofiko Chiaureli, Melkop Alekyan, Vilen Galstyan, Georgiy Gegechkori.* More or less a biography of Armenian poet Sayat Nova, the film appropriately takes a poetic cinematic form. The result is a bold step toward non-narrative cinema, relying wholly on its cryptic and somewhat static images, precisely ordered on the screen like figures painted on a canvas to convey their story. The material is pretty impenetrable, especially so for Western viewers unfamiliar with Armenian folklore or with Nova's work or biography. Quotations from the poet's writings appear throughout the film, but really don't make things any easier to piece together. Still, this is an amazing film experience. Paradjanov's style is utterly groundbreaking, and hasn't seen many followers outside music video. This is absolutely essential viewing for anyone interested in expanding the boundaries of the medium. —*C. B.*

ACCATTONE L: DIRECTORS/PASOLINI, PIER PAOLO (1961) 120M D: Pier Paulo Pasolini. *Adriana Asti, Franco Citti, Franca Pasut, Paola Guidi, Silvana Corsini.* Vitorrio Accattone (Citti) is a homeless pimp who prostitutes his girlfriend for a living and begs for food and money on the streets and alleyways of Italy. Having no moral conscience, he even begs from his local church and from the ex-wife he beats up, who is trying to raise their son away from the influence of his deadbeat father. Accattone meets and falls in love with an innocent peasant worker, Stella (Pasut), hoping she will redeem him. Yet in the end he falls back on his old ways, unable to rise above his subproletarian existence. Pasolini's first film as a director was based on his own novel. The details of Italian street life are so thoroughly depicted that the film was considered shocking when it was released. Its depressing themes and the spiritual struggle of its socially unredeemable protagonist were a major focus in Pasolini's work. —*N. H.*

ARABIAN NIGHTS (AKA **THE FLOWER OF THE ARABIAN NIGHTS**) L: DIRECTORS/PASOLINI, PIER PAOLO (1974) 155M D: Pier Paolo Pasolini. *Franco Citti, Margaret Clementi, Tessa Bouché, Ninetto Davoli, Ines Pellegrini.* Pasolini spent two years freely adapting Sir Richard Burton's translation of the Arabian myths for the last and most rapturous of the three films in the Trilogy of Life series. Aziz (Davoli) has fallen in love with his slave girl, Zumurrud (Pellegrini). But Zumurrud gets stolen away and Aziz must go out into the world to search for her. His travels form the film's many lustful tales as he encounters others who share their stories of lovers lost. The yellow, sand-filled desert locations and bright blue sunny skies of Yemen, Iran, and Eritrea create a sense of period and authenticity rare in cinema. The film was heavily censored during its release and two episodes were cut. The complete version, minus the two missing episodes, runs 155 minutes. The film, as in the case of the other two in the trilogy, received an X rating for its U.S. release. —*N. H.*

CANTERBURY TALES, THE (RACCONTI DI CANTERBURY) L: DIRECTORS/PASOLINI, PIER PAOLO
(1972) 109M D: Pier Paolo Pasolini. *Pier Paolo Pasolini, Tom Baker, Jenny Runacre, Hugh Griffith, Franco Citti.* Pasolini adapted British medieval author Geoffrey Chaucer for the second film in his Trilogy of Life series. Like its predecessor in the trilogy, this is a lustful adaptation taken from six of the twenty-four tales and two prologues, only this time Pasolini's approach and style are much darker then in his previous *Decameron.* Each tale is filled with graphic flatulence, urination, explicit sexuality, and blood. Pasolini starts the film with an ode to Charlie Chaplin's Tramp and ends with a live-action re-creation of Hieronymus Bosch's Hell. Shot on location throughout the lush green hills of England, the film is filled with a British cast, including Pasolini himself in the part of Chaucer, acting out behaviors you would never see in English film. Winner of the Golden Bear award at the Berlin International Film Festival and given an X rating for its U.S. release. Pasolini considered this to be the lesser film of his trilogy. —*N. H.*

DECAMERON, THE L: DIRECTORS/PASOLINI, PIER PAOLO
(1971) 112M D: Pier Paolo Pasolini. *Jovan Jovanovic, Ninetto Davoli, Franco Citti, Pier Paolo Pasolini.* Pasolini begins his Trilogy of Life with this collection of nine stories by medieval author Boccaccio. Pasolini himself plays fresco painter Allievo di Giotto, who realizes his actual work will never equate the vision in his dreams. The painter's tale bridges the other stories selected, including the tale of a Sicilian who ends up rich after being cheated twice, a man who pretends to be deaf and dumb in a convent, and a wife who must hide her lover because her husband has returned home. Each is filled with the lustful imagery of drinking, graphically depicted sexuality, and the muddy, earthly griminess of medieval life. Pasolini also includes several jabs at the Catholic Church. The production is shot around the timeless architecture of Italy. Pasolini once again brings his audience a view of life unshackled by modern taboos. As a result, the film was banned in many countries and received an X rating in the United States. —*N. H.*

GOSPEL ACCORDING TO ST. MATTHEW, THE L: DIRECTORS/PASOLINI, PIER PAOLO (1965) 136M D: Pier Paulo Pasolini. *Enrique Irazoqui, Margherita Caruso, Susanna Pasolini, Marcello Morante, Mario Socrate.* Pasolini's version of the Christ story is an angry film. Taken from the texts of Matthew's Gospels, Pasolini's Christ is a young idealist born into the Italian countryside among prostitutes, pimps, hustlers, and the lower class, many of whom are part of Pasolini's cast. The soundtrack mixes the rhythms of the African Missa Luba with Bach's "St. Matthew Passion" and modern jazz, which, combined with the beautiful black-and-white photography and Italian country landscapes, create a passionate backdrop for this highly personal story of a young Christ who rebels against all social doctrines in Roman society. This film was an inspiration for Martin Scorsese's *Last Temptation of Christ,* and together the two remain the most interesting filmed versions of Christ's life. Pasolini's real-life mother plays the older Mary. —*N. H.*

HAWKS AND SPARROWS L: DIRECTORS/PASOLINI, PIER PAOLO (1964) 88M D: Pier Paolo Pasolini. *Renato Capogna, Ninetto Davoli, Femi Benussi, Totò, Umberto Bevilacqua.* Pasolini wrote this film simply for the opportunity to work with Italian vaudeville comedian Totò before he died. *Hawks and Sparrows* breaks the serious tone of the neo-realist feature films Pasolini had directed thus far and instead develops as a comedic odyssey. Father and son (Totò and Davoli), out walking in the Italian countryside, try to sort out what to do as they are about to be evicted by their landlord. They come across a Marxism-spouting crow who tells them the story of Brother Ciccillo and Brother Ninetto (also Totò and Davoli), who work for St. Francis of Assisi converting the birds of the world over to Christianity. However, each time one of the monks converts a sparrow, a hawk flies down from the sky and eats it. The father and son think the crow's story is full of shit and they kill the bird and eat it, deciding their life will work itself out without the crow's help. An enjoyable romp and an intellectually enlightening experience as well. —*N. H.*

LOVE MEETINGS L: DIRECTORS/PASOLINI, PIER PAOLO (1964) 90M D: Pier Paolo Pasolini. *Alberto Moravia, Pier Paolo Pasolini, Cesare Musatti.* Pasolini hits the streets of Rome with microphone in hand and asks young people to share their feelings on sexuality in this documentary. He confronts both the educated and the working class with questions on where babies come from, their views on homosexuality, acceptance of brothels, and concerns with the Catholic Church over marriage and divorce. Italian intellectuals Moravia and Musatti join in along the way. More of a document of its time, the film still fascinates with its black-and-white shots of a post–WWII Rome and the trendy fashion designs of early '60s Italy, as well as the not-so-definitive and shakily

assured statements by Italy's young people on the film's difficult topics. —*N. H.*

MAMMA ROMA L: DIRECTORS/PASOLINI, PIER PAOLO (1962) 110M D: Pier Paulo Pasolini. *Vittorio La Paglia, Silvana Corsini, Anna Magnani, Franco Citti, Ettore Garofolo.* Mamma Roma attempts to leave her life of prostitution when her abusive pimp runs off to marry a country girl. Momma takes her earnings and becomes a fruit/vegetable vendor, attempting to raise her son Ettore (Garofolo) alone. Mamma dreams only of a better life for Ettore, but sadly he falls in with a group of hoodlums and is lost when he is caught stealing and is shot by the police. Magnani creates in Mamma Roma a fiery, strong woman able to stand up to all life throws at her until her son is killed. Ettore's death is shot like Christ on the cross and the film's black-and-white religious imagery mixes with touches of postwar Hollywood melodrama and Italian neorealism. Declared obscene at its debut at the 1962 Venice Film Festival and edited down for its release in Europe, *Momma Roma* was returned to its original form by director Martin Scorsese for its 1995 U.S. debut. —*N. H.*

MEDEA L: DIRECTORS/PASOLINI, PIER PAOLO (1969) 109M D: Pier Paolo Pasolini. *Margaret Clementi, Massimo Girotti, Giuseppe Gentile, Maria Callas, Laurent Terzieff.* Pasolini uses the landscapes of Africa as the backdrop for this version of the Medea story. It is curious with the casting of Callas that Pasolini did not base his film on the opera by Cherubini, but instead derived his screenplay from the original Greek tragedy by Euripides, mixing in the philosophies of M. Eliade, Frazer, Levy-Bruhl, and the modern works on ethnology and anthropology. Medea, tricked by Jason into helping him win the golden fleece, returns to her homeland in Greece to become his partner and mother to his sons. She finds herself abandoned when Jason decides to marry a younger, more wealthy princess. Medea reveals her powers as a sorceress, poisoning Jason's wife-to-be and murdering her children by him, leaving Jason forever cursed. Callas is top-notch in her solo acting debut. The film is filled with Third World imagery and music that brings a primal energy to the Greek tragedy. —*N. H.*

OEDIPUS REX L: DIRECTORS/PASOLINI, PIER PAOLO (1967) 119M D: Pier Paolo Pasolini. *Carmelo Bene, Alida Valli, Julian Beck, Silvana Mangano, Franco Citti.* Pasolini modernizes his autobiographical version of the Sophocles play, opening in prewar Italy as a young couple has a baby boy. The father quickly grows jealous of his young son and has the baby taken to the desert to die. The boy is rescued and brought up as a prince by the King and Queen of Corinth. The Oracle of the land warns Oedipus that he will sleep with his mother and kill his father. Oedipus goes blindly forward and does just that. The film takes on a deeply

mystical and spiritual feeling with African landscapes as its background. When Oedipus realizes what he has done and pokes his eyes out, he then wanders into contemporary Italy. Pasolini destroys all concepts of the story's time, showing that Sophocles' essay on incest and self-guided destiny is as contemporary now as when it was first written. —*N. H.*

PORCILE (PIGSTY) L: DIRECTORS/PASOLINI, PIER PAOLO (1969) 99M D: Pier Paulo Pasolini. *Jean-Pierre Léaud, Marco Ferreri, Pierre Clémenti, Franco Citti, Ugo Tognazzi.* A young man (Clementi) wanders away from society after murdering his father. He stumbles into the remains of a battlefield and comes across a wandering soldier whom he attacks and kills, eating his body. A second story intertwines with the first as another young man, Julian (Léaud, from Truffaut's films), leaves his fiancée because he can only achieve an orgasm if he is fucking pigs. Living in modern Italy and the son of a German industrialist, Julian is bitter over his father's bourgeois ideals and decides to work for a former Nazi scientist who collects skulls from the war in order to study brain matter. At a party, Julian slips out to get off in the pigsty and is eaten by the pigs. Both stories are combined in an uncomfortable commentary on the corruption of upper-class society. —*N. H.*

SALO, OR THE 120 DAYS OF SODOM L: DIRECTORS/PASOLINI, PIER PAOLO (1975) 117M D: Pier Paulo Pasolini. *Caterina Boratto, Marco Bellocchio, Umberto P. Quinavalle, Paolo Bonacelli, Laura Betti.* Salo was a brave attempt by Italian director Pasolini to put the corruption and collapse of society on display through the overpowering and perverting of innocent youth by a Fascist government. The audience itself is degraded as we watch armed guards kidnap a group of innocent youth and bring them to a hidden mansion, where they are forced to endure the Four Circles of Hell. Each Circle inflicts a more severe form of debauchery, attacking all levels of the youths' humanity: sexual, emotional, spiritual, and physical. A film that may even today shock and horrify, others will find it boring and be disappointed that it is not as sick and disgusting as its reputation. Pasolini's final film, *Salo* is a testament to the genius and prophetic nature of his work, proving that society has indeed reached a level of desensitization where graphic images of torture and rape no longer affect us as they should. —*N. H.*

TEOREMA (THEOREM) L: DIRECTORS/PASOLINI, PIER PAOLO (1968) 98M D: Pier Paolo Pasolini. *Terence Stamp, Silvana Mangano, Massimo Girotti, Anne Wiazemsky, Laura Betti.* An unknown handsome young man (Stamp) suddenly arrives at the home of a bourgeois upper-class family in Milan and proceeds to sleep with all of them (the father, mother, son, daughter, and the maid). He then wanders into town and performs miracles while the family falls apart without him, their structure destroyed.

The maid becomes a saint, the son an artist, and the father races through the town ripping off his clothes and running naked into the countryside. Was the visitor Christ or Satan? Was his purpose to free the family or destroy it? Pasolini wisely dodges such questions and creates a morally ambiguous essay on the repressed desires of a modern upper-class society. A seminal role for Stamp, whose handsome face and deep blue eyes add to the mysterious spirituality the film evokes. Pasolini adapted the screenplay from his own novel. —*N. H.*

BALLAD OF CABLE HOGUE, THE L: DIRECTORS/PECKINPAH, SAM (1970) 122M D: Sam Peckinpah. *Jason Robards Jr., Stella Stevens, David Warner.* A desert rat whose name most emphatically is Cable Hogue (a sublime Robards) gets abandoned in the desert by his partners, left to die. A contrary cuss, he walks, stumbles, and scrabbles his way into a waterhole that wasn't supposed to exist halfway between Deaddog and Gila. Noting wagon tracks nearby, Cable realizes that the waterhole could be a gold mine. Goin' in among 'em (i.e., to town), he files a claim, secures a loan from a shrewd banker, and promptly invests five dollars of it in a visit to a golden-haired whore named Hildy (Stevens). Yes, it *is* a Peckinpah movie, after all—his personal favorite among his films, and one of his best. Although a satisfactory number of killings ensues, and Cable's major preoccupation is waiting for his old partners Taggart (L. Q. Jones) and Bowen (Strother Martin) to come by on that road so he can settle his old score, this is a joyous, bounteous, life-affirming movie, and an exultant celebration of filmmaking as lyric play. If you think you know what "Bloody Sam" Peckinpah was all about, you have some happy surprises coming. —*R. T. J.*

BRING ME THE HEAD OF ALFREDO GARCIA L: DIRECTORS/PECKINPAH, SAM (1974) 112M D: Sam Peckinpah. *Isela Vega, Kris Kristofferson, Robert Webber, Warren Oates, Gig Young.* Peckinpah abuses veteran character actor Oates in this violent melodrama about a guy (Oates) who is hired by a Mexican crime lord to bring him the head of Alfredo Garcia, some local punk who impregnated his daughter. Along the way Oates gets the chance to drink a lot of tequila, beat up on his girlfriend, drive around the Mexican countryside, and talk smack to a severed head covered in flies. *Bring Me the Head of Alfredo Garcia* never gets bogged down in plot, the Achilles' heel of most Peckinpah films, but instead chooses to show you the action all the way down to its blood-soaked, riddled-with-bullets climax. Look for country superstar Kristofferson as a would-be rapist. —*J. D.*

GETAWAY, THE L: DIRECTORS/PECKINPAH, SAM (1972) 122M D: Sam Peckinpah. *Al Lettieri, Steve McQueen, Bo Hopkins, Sally Struthers, Ben Johnson, Ali MacGraw.* Doc McCoy (McQueen) gets paroled by a corrupt politician (Johnson) in exchange for

doing one last robbery. But when he finds out his partners (Lettieri and Hopkins) are going to betray him, Doc and his wife (MacGraw) head for Mexico with the money. In typical Peckinpah fashion, women and weak men are treated horribly, violence is filmed beautifully, and children are left staring at the aftermath. But all this only adds to the gritty atmosphere of one of McQueen's greatest badass films. In one classic scene, Doc goes to buy a radio to keep up with the news. The clerk recognizes him from a mug shot, so Doc walks out to the car to warn MacGraw that there's trouble, then strolls into a gun shop to buy a shotgun. The excellent script is by Walter Hill, based on the novel by Jim Thompson. —*B. T.*

JUNIOR BONNER L: DIRECTORS/PECKINPAH, SAM (1972) 103M D: Sam Peckinpah. *Joe Don Baker, Steve McQueen, Ben Johnson, Ida Lupino, Robert Preston.* McQueen plays Junior Bonner, a former rodeo star who left his family and the whole town behind to pursue a different life. After several years he decides he made the wrong decision and opts to return to his family and try to reclaim his former life. His old friends welcome him immediately and press him to ride in the upcoming rodeo. His children are slower to accept him, and after dogged perseverance by Bonner, his wife comes around. But the hardest to win over is his hard-drinking father, played brilliantly by Preston. Throughout the tense drama we get Peckinpah's action-packed scenes of the rodeo, which serve as a metaphor for this protagonist wrestling with his own demons. —*N. J.*

PAT GARRETT & BILLY THE KID L: DIRECTORS/PECKINPAH, SAM (1973) 122M D: Sam Peckinpah. *James Coburn, Katy Jurado, Bob Dylan, Kris Kristofferson, Slim Pickens.* My favorite Peckinpah, period. I know he might have made "better" films, but this one just feels so right. Coburn and Kristofferson are Pat and Billy, longtime friends who find themselves on opposite sides of the law as big business begins to move West and flush out outlaws like Billy. The film seems to focus on this change in power through its characters, and in doing so becomes a sort of elegy to the old West. The film has so many pleasures—a lovely, jangly Bob Dylan score; Dylan himself as a trickster; and a supporting cast featuring Jurado, Pickens, R. G. Armstrong, Chill Wills, L. Q. Jones, and Dub Taylor—that it's hard to take how truly sad the entire weight of the film really is. In my mind, this is Peckinpah's most lyrical vision: a melancholy, achingly beautiful masterpiece. —*M. S.*

RIDE THE HIGH COUNTRY L: DIRECTORS/PECKINPAH, SAM (1962) 94M D: Sam Peckinpah. *Joel McCrea, Randolph Scott, Mariette Hartley, Ron Starr, James Drury.* Peckinpah's first great Western stands as one of the high-water marks of the genre. *Ride the High Country* incorporates many of the themes that would permeate the best Peckinpah films

Sam Peckinpah

Sam Peckinpah was born in 1925 in Fresno, California, the son of a lawyer (later a Superior Court judge) and grandson of a pioneer rancher. After a stint in the Marines, he attended Fresno State College, then earned a master's degree in theater from USC. He directed live theater and worked at a TV station before landing a job in the movie industry, working as an assistant to Don Siegel on three films and as a dialogue director at Allied Artists. It was during this period that he began writing television Westerns (he created two series, *The Rifleman* and *The Westerner*), which led to opportunities to direct for television. He made his first film, *The Deadly Companions*, in 1961. His second film, *Ride the High Country* (1962), survived studio interference to open to enthusiastic reviews and good business.

Peckinpah developed a reputation for being difficult after troubles on *Major Dundee* (1965), but salvaged his career and cemented his reputation with the controversial *The Wild Bunch* (1969). He became famous for his "poetry of violence," but attention to this often overshadowed other notable aspects of his films, such as his nostalgia for the mythic Old West and his gentler, more intimate side, evidenced in a number of films and dominant in *The Ballad of Cable Hogue* (1970) and *Junior Bonner* (1972).

An alcoholic for years and prone to fighting with producers and studio executives, Peckinpah found it harder to get assignments later in his career. Many of the films he did make suffered from studio tampering, most notably *Pat Garrett and Billy the Kid* (which was finally restored to his original cut years after his death) and *Cross of Iron*. He died in 1984 of a heart attack at the age of fifty-nine. —*Sean Axmaker*

and marks the end of the "old-school" Western as it presents two of its most beloved stars (McCrae and Scott) symbolically riding off into the sunset and making way for the many revisionist Westerns to follow. At the beginning of the twentieth century we find two old-timers refusing to let go of their ways and trying to find a place in this new society. The pair is hired to transfer a load of gold across the Sierras. Things get complicated with the inclusion of a spunky young woman (Hartley), her involvement with the scummy Hammond brothers, and some unexpected greed. The scenery is beautiful, the performances are consistently top-notch, there are countless memorable scenes, the script provides many plot twists, and the film remains consistently entertaining up until the atypical final shootout. —*S. H.*

STRAW DOGS L: DIRECTORS/PECKINPAH, SAM (1971) 118M D: Sam Peckinpah. *Dustin Hoffman, Susan George, Peter Vaughan, T. P. McKenna, David Warner.* Even more controversial upon release than Peckinpah's earlier *The Wild Bunch*, *Straw Dogs* displays the troubling ambivalence toward violence that makes Peckinpah so truly fascinating. Hoffman is a meek American mathematician in rural England with his wife (George), a former local girl who falls back in with the rough boys of her youth. Suffering under their bullying, Hoffman finally explodes in a mixture of territorialism, principle, and pent-up rage when a drunken gang storms his house as he shelters a retarded man wanted for a crime. Hardly a simple hero defending his home from invaders, his perverse, bloodthirsty glee as he racks up a body count verges on savagery and Peckinpah's double-edged attitude manages to find the hero and horror tied up in one troubling package. Be forewarned: this movie contains one of the most brutal portrayals of rape on screen. —*S. A.*

WILD BUNCH, THE L: DIRECTORS/PECKINPAH, SAM (1969) 145M D: Sam Peckinpah. *Ernest Borgnine, Robert Ryan, William Holden, Edmond O'Brien, Warren Oates, Ben Johnson.* In many ways *The Wild Bunch* is the last great Western. It stars some of the best aging actors of the time and features a complex moral palate sprinkled with heroics, loyalty, and bloodshed. Unfortunately, the imitative and less skilled later-day filmmakers who only latched on to the violence of Peckinpah's controversial film essentially undid the beloved genre. An aging gang of outlaws fumbles a bank robbery and is pursued by some scuzzy bounty hunters led by an ex-partner. They end up affiliated with a shifty Mexican general and it all culminates in a bloody gunfight. While the violence is plentiful, at the soul of this film is the failed friendship between Holden and Ryan. This is Peckinpah's best-known Western. —*S. H.*

ALICE'S RESTAURANT L: DIRECTORS/PENN, ARTHUR (1969) 111M D: Arthur Penn. *James Broderick, Pat Quinn, Arlo Guthrie, Pete Seeger.* Penn turns Arlo Guthrie's folk-epic song "The Alice's Restaurant Massacre" into a loose, loving, bittersweet portrait of the unraveling of the 1960s. Guthrie's awkward sweetness and on-camera modesty are hardly electric—the sharp, bubbling performances by professionals Quinn and Broderick as hippie communal leaders Alice and Ray serve that function—but his presence in the film is nonetheless essential. His commentary track on the DVD is disarmingly acute, the recollections of a first-time actor watching his life turned into a fiction and revisiting it thirty years later: "You gotta understand that this is old peoples' version of what we were doing." He has nothing but praise for Penn and his vision, but Guthrie makes the case that while Penn's film is about fracture and failure, their real lives are a success story. —*S. A.*

BONNIE AND CLYDE L: DIRECTORS/PENN, ARTHUR (1967) 111M D: Arthur Penn. *Warren Beatty, Faye Dunaway, Gene Hackman.* In reality, Bonnie and Clyde were a ruthless pair of bank robbers whose string of crimes turned the Southwest sky blood-red. But thirty years later, with the help of a little cinema magic and the '60s revolution, they have become heroes of the independent spirit and the forerunners of anti-establishment. Clyde (Beatty) has just been released from prison and decides that bank robbery is his newest career. He quickly seduces and sweeps up a young country girl, Bonnie (Dunaway), and together they begin their spree of crime. As their robberies become bolder, so do the cops' attempts to capture them. Bonnie and Clyde's romanticized exploits helped capture the spirit of antigovernment, though in the end their punishment must come. And what a punishment it is. At the time of the film's release, the hail of gunfire was possibly the most violent sequence ever filmed, and still holds that same raw power today. —*R. M.*

LITTLE BIG MAN L: DIRECTORS/PENN, ARTHUR (1970) 139M D: Arthur Penn. *Martin Balsam, Dustin Hoffman, Chief Dan George, Richard Mulligan, Jeff Corey, Faye Dunaway.* Hoffman is Jack Crabbe, a 121-year-old survivor who narrates his adventures of the old West and surviving Little Big Horn, in Penn's modern classic, a revisionist Western adapted from Thomas Berger's novel. Adventure, comedy, social satire, and tragedy are rolled together in this unforgettable, often rollicking tour of the old West through the eyes of a man who lived among both the settlers and Indians (as the adopted son of a Cheyenne chief, played with easy charm by George). Penn deftly balances the shifts in tone and creates a film that manages to be warm, winning, and unendingly entertaining while still delivering a painful lesson in America's genocide of the Native American population. Dunaway costars as his adopted white "mother" (whose interest in the young man rescued from the redskins is more than maternal) and Mulligan almost steals the film as the flamboyant and borderline insane General George Custer. —*S. A.*

PENN & TELLER GET KILLED L: DIRECTORS/PENN, ARTHUR (1989) 89M D: Arthur Penn. *Penn Jillette, Teller.* Jillette (the loud, tall one), while performing on television with his silent partner, Teller, invokes a stalker simply by stating that he wished someone was trying to kill him so he really had something to worry about. After several prank murders played on each other, Penn and Teller stop for a bit of psychic surgery debunking, until real bullets chip the concrete around them. Hiding out in a converted black-and-white, noir-driven reality, mostly of Penn's verbal conjuring, the duo lose themselves in slipped-up ninja fantasies and semi-Beat fever dreams. A unique denouement finds our heroes living out an odd working of the title of the film. *Penn & Teller Get Killed* cracks a window in the viewer's head, shakes a few things around, fires a synapse or twelve, and dances off with a gleeful smirk. —*S. R.*

LOULOU L: DIRECTORS/PIALAT, MAURICE (1980) 110M D: Maurice Pialat. *Isabelle Huppert, Gérard Depardieu, Guy Marchand, Humbert Balsan, Bernard Tronczyk.* Pialat offers a portrait of middle-class dissatisfaction in Paris in the affair between cultured Huppert and urban drifter and small-time thug Depardieu. She leaves her explosively jealous husband and high-class social circle for a life of cheap apartments, easy living, and great sex. Depardieu is effortlessly charming and defiantly unconcerned with social obligations, while Huppert is at once freed and frustrated by her new existence. It's a narratively uneventful film directed with an easy, lolling intimacy and driven by emotional turbulence, full of tender detail and often painful observations, and of course a bohemian attitude toward sex and propriety. The final sequence is both heartbreaking and uncomfortably dead-on. —*S. A.*

BITTER MOON L: DIRECTORS/POLANSKI, ROMAN (1992) 139M D: Roman Polanski. *Kristin Scott Thomas, Peter Coyote, Emmanuelle Seigner, Hugh Grant.* A half-mad writer (Coyote) reflects on his relationship with his wife (Seigner) during conversations with a newly married and naive young man (Grant) on a cruise ship. Over lengthy chats in which the wheelchair-bound writer is thoroughly self-absorbed, flashbacks detail his account about how he met his wife, fell in love with her, became overly obsessed with her, and finally how the obsession imploded to physical and psychological torture resulting in his crippling among several other things. With each chapter in this man's story things become more and more horrifying. By the end of the film the young man and his new bride can't help but be sucked into this veritable black hole of obsession. A chilling psychological shocker from Polanski, the master of paranoia. —*N.J.*

CHINATOWN L: DIRECTORS/POLANSKI, ROMAN (1974) 131M D: Roman Polanski. *Jack Nicholson, Faye Dunaway, John Huston.* Polanski and writer Robert Towne weave a detective story that drips with the cold sweat of 1930s hard-boiled pulp thrillers, from the perfect style to the light filtering through the venetian blinds and rolling cigarette smoke. The production is top-notch as it puts the viewer in a perfect period setting, and Polanski's direction is at its best in his last film made in the United States. Nicholson embodies private eye J. J. Gittes with a flawless performance, while Dunaway makes a stunning moll as Evelyn. The plot twists and turns with the flip of every rough page, as Gittes finds himself investigating a routine adultery case that avalanches into an insidious realty plot that involves murder, betrayal, and deceit in the deserts of Los Angeles. To give away any more would ruin this grizzled mystery. *Chinatown* was most deservedly nominated across the board at the 1975 Oscars, and won for Best Screenplay. —*R.M.*

FEARLESS VAMPIRE KILLERS, THE (OR PARDON ME, BUT YOUR TEETH ARE IN MY NECK) L: DIRECTORS/POLANSKI, ROMAN (1967) 98M D: Roman Polanski. *Roman Polanski, Alfie Bass, Jessie Robbins, Sharon Tate, Jack MacGowran.* The alternate and lengthier title of this comedy better conveys its general tone: *Pardon Me, But Your Teeth Are in My Neck.* In this burlesque, Tate is kidnapped by vampires and taken to a large castle. Trying to rescue her is Professor Abronsius (MacGowran) and his assistant Alfred (Polanski), the bungling vampire killers. As it turns out, some of their superstitions are proven to be inadequate, such as when they find a Jewish vampire who won't react to a crucifix! That's the sort of broad comedy that consumes this film where laughs can be found around every corner. —*N.J.*

KNIFE IN THE WATER L: DIRECTORS/POLANSKI, ROMAN (1962) 94M D: Roman Polanski. *Jolanta Umecka, Zygmunt Malandowicz, Leon Niemczyk.* Polanski's first film is a daring psychological suspense story relayed with impressive black-and-white photography. A writer and his wife take a hitchhiker with them on an outing in a sailboat. Of course, it turns out that this hitchhiker is pathologically dangerous. Similar to Hitchcock's *Lifeboat*, nearly all the action of this film takes place on the boat itself, which is very demanding on the filmmaker. Yet Polanski pulls it off brilliantly,

reflecting the astounding artistry that would follow him in his long career. —*N.J.*

NINTH GATE, THE L: DIRECTORS/POLANSKI, ROMAN (1999) 127M D: Roman Polanski. *Johnny Depp, Frank Langella, Lena Olin, Emmanuelle Seigner.* A rare book dealer (Depp) is asked to hunt down three originals of a seventeeth-century book that, as he slowly discovers, supposedly contains the means of conjuring the Devil. Conspiracy and paranoia brew together as layer after layer of this strange plot is exposed. The fiery and outrageously paranormal ending is an apt conclusion to the cryptic story. Good casting, spectacular sets, and dead-on performances enhance what seems to be a rather offbeat film for Polanski. —*N.J.*

PIANIST, THE L: DIRECTORS/POLANSKI, ROMAN (2002) 150M D: Roman Polanski. *Adrien Brody, Thomas Kretschmann.* Nary a page of Wladyslaw Szpilman's story of the bombing and takeover of Warsaw is lost in this transition to the screen. Polanski had a strong vision of what life was like in Warsaw in the early '40s, and he creates a vista of despair and hope. Eschewing ideas of autobiography, Polanski nevertheless holds memories of ghetto life as he escaped an incarcerated childhood by running from the Krakow ghetto. Brody is the proud then destitute final survivor of his family, his only skill being his fingers conjuring beautiful sound on the piano. Foregoing the obvious and expected clichés of Nazi=Demon and Jew=God, Polanski instead invokes a reality of lone survival from the Poles coping with their destroyed city, to Jews alone against the world, to Germans fighting for reasons they're not so sure of. Truly breathtaking actions during the ghetto fighters' revolts and classic Polanski scenes make for a gripping film. —*S.R.*

REPULSION L: DIRECTORS/POLANSKI, ROMAN (1965) 105M D: Roman Polanski. *Catherine Deneuve, Ian Hendry, John Fraser, Patrick Wymark, Yvonne Furneaux.* Deneuve plays a beautiful yet somewhat disturbed beautician's assistant. She lives with her sister, who is well aware of her emotional instability and visceral repulsion toward sex. When her sister leaves for a vacation with another man this poor woman is left alone with her terrible train of thought. Soon the beauty parlor has to let her go because of her horrible mistakes, and with nothing else to do she sits at home and becomes a victim of her own insane repression. To this end the camera is more than willing to oblige. The already tenuous distinction between reality and chaos begins to dissolve, and the audience is allowed to see the deep insecurities that consume this seemingly innocent woman alive. —*N.J.*

ROSEMARY'S BABY L: DIRECTORS/POLANSKI, ROMAN (1968) 136M D: Roman Polanski. *Ruth Gordon, John Cassavetes, Mia Farrow.* This is a masterpiece of drama, suspense, and horror all mixed into one

Roman Polanski

Roman Polanski displays a seemingly innate understanding of film language and its ability to express his characters' deepest fears and uncertainties. Despite the paranoia of his films and the numerous tragedies that marked his personal life, he contends that both he and his films are ultimately optimistic.

Polanski's tumultuous life behind the camera is a drama as compelling as any he has put on screen. Born in 1933, he spent his youth in Nazi-occupied Poland, where he saw his Jewish parents taken away to concentration camps. Left alone, he would often hide out in the darkness of the cinema. This inspired him to both act and direct, and in 1954 he was accepted into a prestigious five-year program at the Lodz Film School. The short work he produced there was award-winning and allowed him to make his first feature, *Knife in the Water*, in 1962. *Knife* established many of Polanski's obsessions: tension between the sexes, claustrophobic settings, and pointed use of music. Though acclaimed overseas, the film was panned in Poland, and Polanski retreated to England for his next three films. The last of these, *Fearless Vampire Killers*, starred his wife-to-be, Sharon Tate. They wed in 1968, the year Polanski's first U.S. production, *Rosemary's Baby*, hit theaters, but the following year Tate was murdered by the Charles Manson cult. She was eight months pregnant at the time.

Polanski then filmed *Macbeth* (1971), a gory adaptation of Shakespeare's play that most critics read as a reaction to the murder. His next film, *Chinatown*, was an homage to film noir and is generally considered to be his best work. After directing and starring in *The Tenant*, he again got himself into trouble: in 1977 he was arrested in California for having had sexual relations with a minor. He subsequently fled the United States illegally and has not returned since.

After adapting the Thomas Hardy novel *Tess of the d'Urbervilles* in 1979, he took a five-year break from film to direct and star in the acclaimed stage production of *Amadeus*; in recent years his on-screen performances have been as frequent and notable as his work behind the camera.

—*Sean Axmaker*

film. Starring Farrow and Cassavetes, it's about the birth of the Antichrist to an unsuspecting mother. Maybe it's the gritty '70s look or the blunt style of Polanski's direction, but this was a damn scary movie for its time (pre-*Exorcist*), and somewhat controversial as well. With scenes supervised by Anton LaVey (The Satanic High Priest himself), there is nothing "holy" or "virtuous" about this film. —*E. B.*

TENANT, THE L: DIRECTORS/POLANSKI, ROMAN (1976) 126M D: Roman Polanski. *Isabelle Adjani, Claude Dauphin, Shelley Winters, Lila Kedrova, Roman Polanski, Michel Blanc.* Polanski stars in this offbeat film about a new tenant in an apartment building. The tenant learns that the woman who used to live in his flat jumped out the window to her death. This concerns him, but not as much as the increasingly odd behavior of his neighbors. He slowly becomes convinced that there is some sort of conspiracy going on, especially as he starts finding strange things in his flat cryptically left by the former tenant. His friends assure him that it's all in his head, but by this point he's having a difficult time distinguishing fact from hallucination. This quirky film has all the hallmarks of Polanski and seeing him act out the title role makes it all the more effective. —*N. J.*

WIDE BLUE ROAD, THE L: DIRECTORS/PONTECORVO, GILLO (1957) 99M D: Gillo Pontecorvo. *Alida Valli, Francisco Rabal, Yves Montand.* Pontecorvo's directorial debut, set and shot in the island fishing communities off Italy, plays like the evolutionary second step for Italian neorealism. To save his family from poverty, a renegade fisherman (Montand) breaks the law and the code of the fishing community to go dynamite fishing, splitting his family as the town turns against him. Beautifully shot in deep blues and sunny yellows, the film swims in the local color of location shooting (the marble quarry is astounding) but its drama arises from the tension of desperate men in dire poverty driven to conflict when the lone wolf threatens the livelihood of the village. Montand practically radiates passion and heat as he struggles with his decision and tries to hold his family together. —*S. A.*

CONTRABAND L: DIRECTORS/POWELL, MICHAEL (1940) 88M D: Michael Powell. *Conrad Veidt, Valerie Hobson, Joss Ambler, Raymond Lovell, Hay Petrie.* Veidt, whose glaring eyes and severe, hawklike features made him an eternal screen villain, portrays a striking hero in this inventive wartime espionage thriller. Set during the London blackouts of 1939 (thus the American title *Blackout*), Powell uses the inky darkness to great effect. Veidt romances his lovely "prisoner" Hobson with a charming, nightclub-hopping tour of the bustling, big city nightlife and they stumble into a Nazi spy ring. Stylish, witty (the resourceful captain navigates his way through London by the stars), and fast paced, Powell's film transforms the usual clichés (ordinary citizens and proud immigrants band together for king and country against the Nazi menace) into a delightful romantic adventure. —*S. A.*

EDGE OF THE WORLD, THE L: DIRECTORS/POWELL, MICHAEL (1938) 75M D: Michael Powell. *Belle Chrystall, Eric Berry, Niall MacGinis, Finlay Currie, Kitty Kirwan, John Laurie.* After a decade of B-movie programmers, Powell made his name with this independently produced dream project, a magnificently photographed drama set against the primal landscape of the windswept island of Foula (renamed Hirta in the film) in the Outer Hebrides in the North Sea. Laurie and Curry play two family patriarchs who struggle over the future of the isolated island community and its hard, traditional way of life as the modern cities of the mainland draw the young men away. While the elders debate, the younger generation decides to settle the question in a breathtaking race up the sheer cliffs, with tragic results. It's more stately and still than the cinematically playful and stylistically vibrant films Powell became famous for in later years. Yet there's a poetry to his images, and Powell directs with a coiled energy that suggests the urgency, desperation, and danger of life on the island. —*S. A.*

GONE TO EARTH (AKA **THE WILD HEART**) L: DIRECTORS/ POWELL, MICHAEL (1950) 90M D: Michael Powell. *Sybil Thorndike, David Farrar, Jennifer Jones, Cyril Cusack.* Based on the novel by Mary Webb, the film portrays beautiful Hazel Woodus (Jones), who lives in a dirty cabin with her toothless, drunken Pa (Knight) and her wild pet fox, Foxy. Life is relatively quiet for Hazel until she meets lecherous town squire Jack Reddin (Farrar). She's superstitious and promises the mountains to marry the first man who asks her. Fate decides that the man is not Reddin, but instead the local town parson, Edward Marston (Cusack). Hazel marries "Edrd" but soon runs off to have an affair with Reddin. Marston, who is as obsessively in love with Hazel as Reddin is, soon comes after her and the two men have a confrontation that sends poor Hazel off again, hiding away in the hills confused by her love for them both. The dark nature of the story, heavy cockney accents, and period setting did not bode well at the British box office and Selznick decided to have the film completely re-edited under the title *The Wild Heart.* —*N. H.*

I KNOW WHERE I'M GOING! L: DIRECTORS/POWELL, MICHAEL (1945) 92M D: Michael Powell. *Roger Livesey, Wendy Hiller, Pamela Brown.* Modern material-girl Hiller plots her social-climbing marriage with mercenary efficiency until a storm, a raging whirlpool, and the gentle charm of penniless Scottish laird Livesay upset her carefully arranged plans with messy emotions. Set in a rough, windswept Scottish village, this lively, earthy romantic drama brims with vivid, offbeat characters (notably the scrappy, lovelorn Brown and her pack of bloodhounds) in a world that's part tradition and part myth. Powell brings his lively manner and bold visual invention to the creation of his beautiful but harsh primal paradise, culminating in the awesome spectacle of a massive whirlpool that could be the work of the "legend of Corryvreckan," or the stormy embodiment of Hiller's hysterical heart. Awash in the mystic power of ancient castles and chanted legends, it's one of the most deliriously romantic films of Powell's magical career. —*S. A.*

LIFE AND DEATH OF COLONEL BLIMP, THE L: DIRECTORS/POWELL, MICHAEL (1943) 163M D: Michael Powell. *Roger Livesey, Anton Walbrook, Deborah Kerr.* This dashing, deft epic is one of the masterpieces of The Archers: Powell and Emeric Pressburger. Major General Clive Wynne-Candy (a curmudgeonly Livesay in a bald cap and walrus mustache) is an old soldier ambushed by the new young army in an attempt to jolt him out of his outdated notions of a "gentleman's war" against the Nazis. In flashbacks that show us how Candy got there, Livesay is warm and witty as an ambitious young officer who becomes devoted to his German rival (Walbrook) and falls in love with a series of beautiful women (all of them played by Kerr) as the world changes around him. Winston Churchill tried to stop the film from being made but made it was, in beautiful Technicolor and sweeping, grand style that defied the budget. Though cut in subsequent years, the British Film Institute restored the film to its complete 163-minute running time and correct flashback structure. That's the beautiful specimen on the Criterion DVD. —*S. A.*

Michael Powell

François Truffaut once remarked that "the terms 'British' and 'cinema' are mutually exclusive." But, flying in the face of the stodgy, stage-bound tradition of British filmmaking, director Michael Powell crafted films that expanded the expressive boundaries of the cinematic art.

In 1938, after Powell had directed almost two dozen British "quota-quickie" thrillers, he met Imre (Emeric) Pressburger, a Hungarian émigré who had fled Germany as Hitler rose to power. Powell was set to direct *The Spy in Black* for mogul Alexander Korda when he encountered Pressburger at a script conference. Powell was thrilled when the Hungarian "stood the story on its head," switching the genders of characters, boosting the suspense, and twisting

the ending. Powell loved to tell stories with images, and was glad that Pressburger "only used dialogue to advance the plot." Powell made a vow to himself: "I'm not going to let him get away."

The Spy in Black began the pair's seventeen-year partnership, in which Pressburger wrote the screenplays that Powell fine-tuned and directed, though in 1942 when they formed their own company, the Archers (with its famous arrow logo thudding into the target), they uniquely shared credit for writing, directing, and producing. *The Spy in Black*, set in the wilds of Scotland, also initiated the partners' love of filming in far-flung locations, as well as their daring fascination for the heroic and willful Teutonic personality at a time when Germans were the bullyboys of the world.

With a bigger budget, and actors Lau-

continued on page 202

MATTER OF LIFE AND DEATH, A (AKA STAIRWAY TO HEAVEN) L: DIRECTORS/POWELL, MICHAEL (1946) 100M D: Michael Powell. *David Niven, Kim Hunter, Richard Attenborough.* Filled to the brim with clever lines, brilliant ideas, and true romance, *A Matter of Life and Death* is one of the greatest films released during the 1940s. English WWII-pilot Peter Carter (Niven) is about to die. He is stuck alone, in the cockpit, plane on fire, without a parachute. He puts in a final call to the flight headquarters. On the other end is June (a luminescent Hunter), a Boston born and bred girl working at the army base. Carter is facing certain death, and a heartbroken June falls in love with him as he speaks his final words over a radio from his plane. Then, sans parachute, Carter jumps. But wait! He is alive, floating in the water where he landed. Someone upstairs has messed up big time. Originally commissioned as a kind of propaganda film to ease American/English tensions after WWII, *A Matter of Life and Death* is one of the more surreal, affecting, beautiful, and graceful films ever made. —*C. P.*

PEEPING TOM L: DIRECTORS/POWELL, MICHAEL (1960) 101M D: Michael Powell. *Karl Heinz Böhm, Moira Shearer, Maxine Audley, Anna Massey.* Released the same year as *Psycho*, this film received much more negative criticism and is admittedly creepier. It's so twisted, in fact, that it effectively

ended Powell's career in Hollywood. The ultimate voyeuristic film in the most voyeuristic of mediums, *Peeping Tom* tells the story of a man obsessed with capturing death on film by whatever means necessary. Creepy and awkward in every way. The main character, polite and crazy, will scare you. —*C. P.*

PURSUIT OF THE GRAF SPEE L: DIRECTORS/POWELL, MICHAEL (1957) 106M D: Michael Powell. *Patrick Macnee, Ian Hunter, Bernard Lee, Peter Finch, Anthony Quayle, John Gregson.* This is an intense look at battleship warfare early in World War II. In the late 1930s, British supply ships in the Atlantic were routinely sunk by U-boats and fast Nazi battleships. The fastest of the Nazi battleships was the Graf Spee, which was caught by a flotilla of English battleships just outside the River Plate in South America. The battle scenes are shocking: enormous cannons blast shells from miles away, then the audience must wait a good ten seconds to see if they hit their mark. Historically accurate, this Powell/Pressburger film is a must-see for any WWII enthusiast. —*N. J.*

RED SHOES, THE L: DIRECTORS/POWELL, MICHAEL (1948) 136M D: Michael Powell. *Anton Walbrook, Moira Shearer, Marius Goring, Leonide Massine, Robert Helpmann.* Victoria Page (Shearer) is a young and talented ballet dancer who is in love with Julian Craster

rence Olivier, Leslie Howard, and Eric Portman in tow, Powell and Pressburger crafted the ambitious *49th Parallel* (1941), in which a German submarine is sunk and its crew is chased across Canada, from Hudson Bay through the Rockies to British Columbia. Powell and Pressburger appreciated fine food, clothes, and cars, but they also harbored anti-materialistic sentiments, which were first expressed in this film, as one of the fleeing Germans is charmed by an Alberta Hutterite community that lives simply, close to the land, and bakes its own bread.

The Archers' first masterpiece, 1943's *The Life and Death of Colonel Blimp*, is a satirical yet warmly affectionate portrait of British military life that centers on a certain soldier (played by husky-voiced Roger Livesey, Powell's frequent cinematic alter ego). With great generosity of spirit, the film follows Livesey's journey from young Boer War firebrand to mellow World War II Home

Guard commander. Over the years he learns his gentlemanly code of honor and chivalry.

Powell believed in "beauty, truth, and the heart of England," and for him that heart was located in the woods and fields of Kent, where Chaucer's fourteenth-century *Canterbury Tales* pilgrims walked. Designed to show Britain and America the "spiritual values and traditions we were fighting for" in World War II, *A Canterbury Tale* (1944) is a typically quirky Powell and Pressburger story in which a man who pours glue on women's hair in the dark, and some young English folk and an American on their way to Canterbury Cathedral communicate the mysteries of faith, love, and landscape, and the reveries of Powell's boyhood.

Powell loved Americans and their Constitution and culture, and *A Matter of Life and Death* (1946), also called *Stairway to Heaven*, centers on the love between English fighter-pilot David Niven and American-WAC Kim Hunter. The Archers make

---

(Goring), a young and talented composer. Both of them are hired by the same ballet company. Things look particularly good when the ballet they do together is a success. However, Victoria is eventually forced to choose between love and success. Consequently her own ballet shoes drive her mad! With the twenty-minute ballet piece that shows off great dancing, imaginative cinematography, and stunning use of color, this film has been an inspiration for countless young women to enroll in ballet classes. —*N.J.*

TALES OF HOFFMANN, THE L: DIRECTORS/POWELL, MICHAEL (1951) 125M D: Michael Powell, Emeric Pressburger. *Pamela Brown, Robert Helpmann, Anne Ayars, Frederick Ashton, Robert Rounseville, Moira Shearer.* A favorite of filmmakers such as Martin Scorsese, Brian DePalma, and George Romero, this beautifully filmed version of Offenbaeh's opera tells the story of Hoffmann (Rounseville), a university student who always fails at love. He falls for Parisian mechanical doll Olympia (Shearer), then Venetian courtesan Giulietta (Ludmilla Tchérina), and finally Greek singer Antonia (Ayars), and loses them all. In real life, he also loses actress Stella (Shearer), which serves as the link that brings the stories together. Filmed in gorgeous Technicolor and featuring the dancing choreography of Sir Frederick Ashton, *Tales of Hoffmann* is a magical, mystical celebration of filmmaking surpassing even the

Powell/Pressburger achievements in *The Red Shoes* and never again equaled in cinema. The Criterion laser disc and Homevision VHS are the most complete versions, though they are still missing footage from this memorable classic. —*N.H.*

THIEF OF BAGDAD, THE L: DIRECTORS/POWELL, MICHAEL (1940) 106M D: Michael Powell. *June Duprez, Sabu, John Justin, Rex Ingram, Conrad Veidt.* At least four directors helmed pieces of this lavish *Arabian Nights* fantasy produced by British mogul Alexander Korda, including Powell in his color-film debut. Sabu stars as the vagabond street kid who fights the evil Grand Vizier (Veidt in high-villain mode) with the help of his giant genie in the bottle (Ingram, joyfully hamming it up). Romantic leads Justin and Duprez feel like dull afterthoughts next to the flamboyant fun had by these three. The glorious art direction by William Cameron Menzies creates an amazing world for the fantastical wonders of flying carpets, mechanical horses, and a fifty-foot genie with a bellowing laugh. It won Oscars for its vivid, fairy-tale color cinematography (by George Perinal), art decoration, and special effects. For the record, Ludwig Berger and Tim Whelan were the other credited directors, Zoltan Korda has recently been "officially" acknowledged as an uncredited director, and Alexander

this simple equation gloriously complex, as Niven jumps from his plane without a parachute but doesn't die, due to a logistical mistake in the Other World. Niven's friend (Roger Livesey) argues before a celestial tribunal that "the rights of the uncommon man" must be respected, and that Niven and Hunter should be allowed to enjoy many years together. Powell brilliantly visualizes the earthly scenes in color and the heavenly ones in a pearlescent monochrome. This was Powell's favorite film, and it's bursting with a springtime, post–World War II feeling of renewed life.

Black Narcissus (1947), the Archers' delirious meditation on the primacy of both spirit and flesh, joins a group of Anglican nuns led by Deborah Kerr as they attempt to run a school in the high Himalayas. Their pious Christian faith collides with indecently exotic foliage, an ancient yogi silently meditating day after day, and the erotic urges of the locals and of their own bod-

ies. Aside from being another Technicolor milestone, *Black Narcissus* was Powell's first "composed film," in which he choreographed the action and emotion of scenes to match music, rather than composing a soundtrack inspired by filmed images.

The Archers' most famous film, *The Red Shoes* (1948), blends the nightmarish Hans Christian Andersen fairy tale (about a woman swept away by bewitched dancing shoes) with a love triangle and the backstage world of ballet. Powell the puckish pagan believed that dance was the oldest art, older than religion, and his film captures the primal awe that attends this ritual of inspired movement. The film's twenty-minute *Red Shoes Ballet*, one of the director's greatest stylistic achievements, seamlessly combines dance, narrative drama, surrealistic design, and painterly color in a vision that flows like music. It's easy to see why this film moved countless young people to take up ballet. —*Greg Olson*

Korda and Menzies are also said to have contributed scenes. —*S. A.*

ADVISE AND CONSENT L: DIRECTORS/PREMINGER, OTTO (1962) 142M D: Otto Preminger. *Henry Fonda, Walter Pidgeon, Don Murray, Franchot Tone, Lew Ayres, Charles Laughton.* Preminger's sprawling document of old-fashioned politics in contemporary Washington has it all: backroom deals, politico parties, factional squabbles, and even a scandal or two as the pressure from an ailing president to push through an unpopular cabinet candidate (Fonda) creates a series of crises in the hallowed halls of the Senate. Preminger's cool distance and dispassionate dramatics can't make the homophobia palatable and George Grizzard's strange left-wing Fascist is a plastic Cold War stereotype, but the rest of the film is fabulous. Laughton's scheming, scrappy conservative and Pidgeon's party-quarterback anchor a rich set of characters and a marvelous cast. "Son, this is a Washington, D.C., kind of lie. It's when the other person knows you're lying and also knows you know he knows." —*S.A.*

BONJOUR TRISTESSE L: DIRECTORS/PREMINGER, OTTO (1958) 94M D: Otto Preminger. *Geoffrey Horne, Mylene Demongeot, Deborah Kerr, David Niven, Juliette Greco, Jean Seberg.* In the late '50s and early '60s, no American director melded classic Hollywood style and modern European elegance better

than producer/director Preminger. His handsome films are celebrations of introspection and stylistic remove, and his best work is defined not by heroes and villains, but by complex, flawed, achingly sympathetic characters. This is one of his chilliest masterpieces. Adapted from the novel by Françoise Sagan by playwright Arthur Laurents, the film explores the repercussions of a rift between a gadabout bachelor playboy (Niven) and his partner-in-partygoing daughter (Seberg) when a smart, sensible, and mature lady (Kerr) enters their lives. Told in flashback from a sleek but shadowy black-and-white Paris, the film erupts in vivid Technicolor to explore the gorgeous French Riviera, though the story is anything but sunny. Seberg flatly drones her narration but her impish, often petulant performance is perfect for the spoiled teenager. Kerr's middle-aged working woman seems puritanical compared to the irrepressible jet-setters but is never less than honest, true, and forthright. —*S. A.*

CARDINAL, THE L: DIRECTORS/PREMINGER, OTTO (1963) 175M D: Otto Preminger. *John Saxon, Carol Lynley, Ossie Davis, John Huston, Romy Schneider, Tom Tryon.* The education of a Catholic cardinal (the stolid and stiff Tryon) takes the viewer through twentieth-century social history on his journey from Rome to Boston and back in the years between the World Wars. The story is episodic and

Tryon's moral posture is forever overshadowed by the passion of his colorful supporting cast (including Huston as an irascible Boston archbishop who teaches him humility, Schneider as his would-be love interest, and Davis as a priest from Georgia fighting segregation and racial terrorism in the '30s). Preminger's subdued, coolly observed religious epic is intelligent, intimate, stately, graceful, and magnificently composed. It's an extraordinarily handsome CinemaScope production defined not by spectacle, but isolation: one man walking a moral and spiritual path through defining moments in history. For a film suspicious of Catholic dogma, Vatican politics, and church timidity, it becomes an even more remarkable story of faith and duty. —S. A.

IN HARM'S WAY L: DIRECTORS/PREMINGER, OTTO (1965) 165M D: Otto Preminger. *John Wayne, Kirk Douglas, Patricia Neal.* Opening with the attack on Pearl Harbor (re-created in amazing detail) and ending a couple of years later with America's return to the South Pacific in force, Preminger packs a lot into the 165 minutes of this sprawling WWII drama. He's a master at organizing huge casts and busy scripts, sacrificing the expected rousing battle thrills for a detailed but removed look at the complexities (physical, emotional, and political) involved in launching a battle campaign. The script veers to melodrama a few times, but Preminger's cool restraint, helped by Loyal Griggs's handsome black-and-white photography, keeps the film in check. Wayne and Douglas star as a career naval captain and his self-pitying second officer, and Saul Bass provides the impressive closing credits sequence, a veritable short film in its own right that creates drama from the power unleashed in the stormy sea. —S. A.

LAURA L: DIRECTORS/PREMINGER, OTTO (1944) 88M D: Otto Preminger. *Clifton Webb, Vincent Price, Gene Tierney, Dana Andrews.* Detective Mark McPherson (Andrews) is too cool for school, but when he immerses himself in a murder investigation, he finds himself falling in love with the victim, Laura Hunt (Tierney), without ever having met her. As his obsession deepens, *Laura* takes on *Vertigo*-like proportions, and the film really takes off when the "murdered" Laura shows up, alive and well. One of film noir's genuine gems, with some of the genre's most memorable dialogue, a gripping plot, and great performances all around. —C. B.

BELL, BOOK AND CANDLE L: DIRECTORS/QUINE, RICHARD (1958) 103M D: Richard Quine. *Kim Novak, Jack Lemmon, Ernie Kovacs, James Stewart.* This light dramatic comedy focuses on Novak, who plays a witch trying her best to wean herself from her coven and live a normal human life. Stewart plays a man who moves into her building, and she casts a spell on him to make him fall in love with her. Despite the mounting evidence, he has

a difficult time accepting the fact that he has been enchanted. She eventually agrees to quit casting spells and together the two face witchcraft like any other addiction until the climactic ending. The title is a reference to the old rite of excommunication in the Catholic Church, yet was also used in the '50s for casting a ne'er-do-well out of one's life. —N. J.

PUSHOVER, THE L: DIRECTORS/QUINE, RICHARD (1954) 88M D: Richard Quine. *Dorothy Malone, Philip Carey, Kim Novak, Fred MacMurray.* The Pushover is noir by the numbers, and I mean that in the best sense. Detective Paul Sheridan (MacMurray) is assigned to keep an eye on gangster girlfriend Lona McLane (Novak). He quickly falls for her, but it remains to be seen whether she loves him back or is just using him to get at her boyfriend's stolen cash. A favorite of Godard's, it is also Novak's first major film. Interestingly, the film's stars give a pretty fair impression of what to expect. The plot is undeniably close to *Double Indemnity*'s, and a number of scenes seem ripped right out of *Vertigo*, although it should be noted that *The Pushover* preceded the latter film by four years. —C. B.

HEAD L: DIRECTORS/RAFELSON, BOB (1968) 86M D: Bob Rafelson. *Victor Mature, Teri Garr, Michael Nesmith, David Jones, Micky Dolenz, Peter Tork.* The Monkees took the money they made from their TV show and did *Head* as a big "FUCK YOU" to their critics and the general public. I was never much of a fan of the band until I saw this wild, psychedelic, and goddamn funny movie. In an unstructured, surreal plot the band attacks conformity, the Vietnam War, commercialism (a Coke machine is blown up), apathy, the Man, and many other targets. Many of the film's wild cast of guest stars put in brief cameos and tell the band how much they suck. The songs are pretty good and the movie takes a very counter-culture approach to its story (co-written by Jack Nicholson, who makes a brief appearance complaining about how his script is being mangled). With a title like *Head*, an anti-establishment message, and some shocking war footage, it's hard to believe this movie was rated G, but it's not surprising it bombed during its initial theatrical release. —S. H.

ARMY OF DARKNESS L: DIRECTORS/RAIMI, SAM (1992) 77M D: Sam Raimi. *Richard Grove, Bruce Campbell, Embeth Davidtz, Ian Abercrombie, Marcus Gilbert.* The third in the *Evil Dead* series is enough of a stand-alone that it has become popular even with people who don't know it's a sequel. The film picks up more or less from the classic left-field ending of *Evil Dead 2*, in which Ash was sucked through a portal into the fourteenth century. Because he seems to fulfill a prophecy, he becomes a Chosen One and leads his followers into battle against an army of demonic skeletons called Deadites. Since Ash is a self-centered asshole, he takes advantage of his followers, who he calls "primitive screwheads," and most of the humor comes from his cocky one-liners. The movie is more openly comic than its predecessors and loses a little bit of focus as it becomes more about the skeleton battles than the character of Ash. But it's still a whole lot of fun, and deserving of its worshipful following. —*B. T.*

CRIMEWAVE L: DIRECTORS/RAIMI, SAM (1985) 83M D: Sam Raimi. *Paul L. Smith, Sheree J. Wilson, Brion James, Bruce Campbell, Reed Birney.* Raimi and writers Joel and Ethan Coen disown this comedy because of studio interference. Raimi was left out of the editing and his chosen composer was rejected in favor of a forced "funny" score. The studio also wouldn't let him cast Campbell in the lead because he wasn't established enough, so instead they went for uncharismatic Birney. I'm sure they could have made a better movie if they were left alone, but the result is still a unique and very funny retro comedy with all kinds of classic Coen brothers dialogue. The story involves two sleazy exterminators (Smith and James) hired as hit men. Birney is the hapless nerd framed for their crimes. Smith and James are great, getting involved in all kinds of cartoonish mayhem; my favorite is a little boy trying to impress the police by saying that his "pop" is responsible for the dead body they just found. This was also released as *The XYZ Murders* and—my favorite—*Broken Hearts and Noses. —B. T.*

DARKMAN L: DIRECTORS/RAIMI, SAM (1990) 96M D: Sam Raimi. *Liam Neeson, Frances McDormand, Larry Drake.* Long before *Spider-Man*, Raimi did this darker and lower-budget comic book–inspired revenge thriller. Neeson plays a scientist working to perfect a liquid skin formula for burn victims. When gangsters attack, he is burnt beyond recognition, washes away in a river, and ends up as a John Doe in a hospital, where surgeons sever his nerve endings to prevent him from feeling pain. Naturally, he escapes and sets up a makeshift laboratory where he uses the imperfect liquid skin (which melts away after 99 minutes in sunlight) to disguise himself as his enemies to play them against each other. Meanwhile he tries to return to his fiancée (McDormand) without revealing his condition or his new, more psychotic attitude. It's a little bit *Batman*, a little bit *Phantom of the Opera*, with lots of clever *Mission: Impossible*-style trickery. Most memorable scene: Neeson mangles a carnival worker's hand in a dispute over a stuffed elephant. —*B. T.*

EVIL DEAD, THE L: DIRECTORS/RAIMI, SAM (1981) 85M D: Sam Raimi. *Sarah York, Ellen Sandweiss, Hal Delrich, Bruce Campbell, Betsy Baker.* Raimi labeled his lively debut feature "The Ultimate Experience in Grueling Terror" in mock-pretension, but he wasn't too far off. The bravura cinematic inventiveness of *The Evil Dead* is too much fun to be genuinely grueling, but this unrelenting parade of funhouse terrors and creative, low-budget effects is one of the most entertaining American horror films of the past two decades. Raimi rummages through decades of haunted-house and demon-possession movies for inspiration, playing with a virtual catalog of clichés (creaky doors, banging shutters, fog-drenched forests, unexplained lights) before twisting them into his own stylish roller coaster of a horror movie, and unleashing it full-on like an assault on his bloody, battered lantern-jawed hero Bruce Campbell. Much of the energy is supplied by the "shaky-cam," a gliding, swooping, rushing camera that suggests a dislocated, otherworldly point of view while injecting a lively if spooky fleetness to the pace. Though it's no comedy, Raimi's dry wit and cinematic cleverness pervades the entire film. —*S. A.*

EVIL DEAD 2: DEAD BY DAWN L: DIRECTORS/RAIMI, SAM (1987) 84M D: Sam Raimi. *Theodore Raimi, Kassie Wesley, Dan Hicks, Sarah Berry, Bruce Campbell.* "Hyper-surreal" might be a good adjective for this over-the-top remake of Raimi's *Evil Dead*. Campbell returns in his familiar role of the vacationer who retires to a cabin with his girlfriend only to have his relaxation wrecked by an evil book of magic lying about the cabin. This book of the dead, "The Necronomicron," springs to life in the most unpredictable ways. After his girlfriend is possessed, Campbell finally murders her, but then his own hand is possessed. He lops that off with the help of a chainsaw only to have the dismembered hand chase after him like a demented spider. With effects far superior to the first film and keen editing which amplifies the humor of this horror-comedy, *Evil Dead 2* is one of those crazy films you'll never forget. —*N. J.*

QUICK AND THE DEAD, THE L: DIRECTORS/RAIMI, SAM (1995) 105M D: Sam Raimi. *Leonardo DiCaprio, Sharon Stone, Gene Hackman, Russell Crowe.* This underrated (though inconsequential) Western was Raimi's first film with major Hollywood stars. Stone (in a role inspired by Charles Bronson's in *Once Upon a Time in the West*) enters a gunfight tournament ostensibly to prove her skills, but in fact to get revenge on a tyrannical mayor (Hackman) who always wins the tournament. Most impressive is the way Raimi's visually playful montages and camera angles manage to keep the numerous gun duels from seeming repetitive. I also enjoy Raimi's willingness to push the violence to cartoonish extremes, especially in the scene where Keith David gets a grapefruit-sized hole blasted all the way through his head. The one thing in the movie I cannot understand is how Stone gets a perm before the finale. —*B. T.*

SPIDER-MAN L: DIRECTORS/RAIMI, SAM (2002) 121M D: Sam Raimi. *Willem Dafoe, James Franco, Kirsten Dunst, Tobey Maguire, Cliff Robertson.* High-flying whoosh, gymnastic spectacle, and graphic comic book punch: What more could you want in a *Spider-Man* movie? Maguire, buffed up from everyman to superman, is transformed from shy science geek Peter Parker into a mutant, wall-crawling muscleman from the bite of a radioactive spider. He finds his nemesis in the cackling, rocket-powered gremlin, The Green Goblin (Dafoe). While the costumed incarnation battles muggers, thieves, and the megalomaniac Goblin, the former high-school nerd struggles with his unrequited love of girl-next-door Mary Jane (Dunst, under flaming red tresses). Raimi delivers the goods in film that faithfully translates the teenage melodrama of alienation and tortured secrets that redefined comic book heroes in the 1960s with the zip and zoom of modern movie-making magic. There have been slicker superhero films, but none with as much heart, unabashed charm, and kinetic joy of speed. —*S. A.*

IN A LONELY PLACE L: DIRECTORS/RAY, NICHOLAS (1950) 93M D: Nicholas Ray. *Frank Lovejoy, Humphrey Bogart, Gloria Grahame, Carl Benton Reid, Martha Stewart.* One of the best uses of Bogart I've seen, this bleak love/murder story casts him as cocky, disillusioned screenwriter Dix Steele, busy with a commissioned adaptation of an overwrought popular novel. A combination of coincidence, circumstances, and fate lead the police to suspect Dix of a heinous murder. As it happens, the homicide investigation romantically unites Dix to his beautiful neighbor, Laurel Gray (Grahame). Seemingly a match made in heaven, there is no happiness available to this pair, as haunting suspicions of Dix's involvement in the crime and allegations of past violence slowly crush any and all trust that once existed between the two. A thoroughly perfect motion picture, this crushing tale of alienation folds epic melodrama and a profoundly frustrated hopelessness into what might've otherwise been a forgettable movie matinee. In other words, another fine Ray picture. —*C. B.*

REBEL WITHOUT A CAUSE L: DIRECTORS/RAY, NICHOLAS (1955) 111M D: Nicholas Ray. *Jim Backus, Sal Mineo, James Dean, Natalie Wood.* It's hard to keep James Dean separated from the role he played in *Rebel Without A Cause.* He plays Jim, a lonely high school kid from a dysfunctional family who has just moved to yet another new town. After a game of "chicken" results in the death of a kid named Buzz, Jim finds himself even more alienated from his parents and hides out with his new friends Judy and Plato (Wood and Mineo). The trio hangs out in a deserted mansion and Judy and Jim pretend to be Plato's parents, but this family is just as messed up as every other one in the movie and Plato ends up going crazy. It's kind of a hopeless film that reflects the disenfranchised feelings that many young people of the era (like my dad, who loves this movie) shared. —*S. H.*

THEY LIVE BY NIGHT L: DIRECTORS/RAY, NICHOLAS (1949) 92M D: Nicholas Ray. *Cathy O'Donnell, Farley Granger.* Before Clarence & Alabama, Bonnie & Clyde, or Thelma & Louise, there was Bowie & Keechie, two star-crossed lovers on the run whose stars weren't lined up exactly right. Ray's dazzling debut feature about two loners who find each other for a short, happy while, is as dark as it is romantic, but hey, they live by night. It's a Depression-era, lovers-on-the-run crime drama, and also an intensely personal and very unique tale of outsiders fighting to stay on the fringe of their world—an issue that Ray would deal with for the rest of his life. —*M. S.*

THIRD MAN, THE L: DIRECTORS/REED, CAROL (1949) 104M D: Carol Reed. *Joseph Cotten, Alida Valli, Orson Welles, Trevor Howard.* There have been few better movies in the history of the planet than *The Third Man,* and fewer still as brilliantly directed from second to second. Welles played the title role, and his omnivorous legend has tended to engulf the film. But it was directed by Reed and written (except for a Wellesian riff on the Borgias) by Grahame Greene, and the credit for this half-century-old masterpiece is properly theirs. Theirs and Cotton's; for cheekily awesome as Welles is, his *Citizen Kane* second banana is onscreen here about six times as much, and he uses every minute to create one of the most distinctive (if also forlorn) of modern heroes. At this cinematic moment Reed was the hottest director going, and you can still see why in every frame, feel it in your nerve endings. In its on-location filming, *The Third Man* is so vivid in its canny mix of gray semidocumentary and insanely angular, Expressionist/Surrealist chiaroscuro that it seems to have imagined not only the postwar thriller but also postwar Europe itself singlehandedly. —*R. T. J.*

CRIME OF MONSIEUR LANGE, THE L: DIRECTORS/ RENOIR, JEAN (1935) 90M D: Jean Renoir. *Jules Berry, Florelle, René Lefèvre, Sylvia Bataille.* The Crime of Monsieur Lange has long been a touchstone film in Europe, but American viewers remain mostly unaware of it. It's a rather scruffy thing compared with the majestic *Grand Illusion* and *Rules of the Game,* and it seems to straddle genres and tones—sometimes wackily funny, sometimes starkly tragic. So underrating it is understandable. But not, finally, forgivable: this is one of Renoir's very greatest films. Lefèvre plays a shmoe with a secret night life: he writes penny-dreadful Western stories. When his publisher boss, an equal-opportunity exploiter named Batala (Berry), finds out, he starts exploiting Lange too. But Batala has to take it on the lam when the law gets on to him, and in his absence Lange and his fictional creation "Arizona Jim" ride to the rescue of Batala's publishing house and its much-abused employees. The screenplay by Jacques Prévert anticipates his later *Children of Paradise* with poetic/pixilated crossovers between life and fiction, and the ending has haunted—and inspired—later generations of French filmmakers. —*R. T. J.*

GRAND ILLUSION L: DIRECTORS/RENOIR, JEAN (1937) 114M
D: Jean Renoir. *Marcel Dalio, Pierre Fresnay, Erich von Stroheim, Jean Gabin, Charles Spaak.* Made on the eve of WWII but set during WWI, Renoir's tale of French POWs in Germany is ostensibly a prison camp escape adventure but is really about class, race, and cultural identity among a quartet of officers: working-class Gabin (whose early career was built on such proletariat heroes), cultured aristocrat Fresnay, Jewish nouveau-riche Dalio, and Prussian blueblood von Stroheim, their German jailer. Renoir and co-scenarist Spaak aren't particularly subtle, the script far too often voices the obvious, but Renoir brings his points home in moving moments woven through the film. (The final scene between von Stroheim and his prisoner Fresnay, with whom he feels more at ease than his own men, is one of the most poignant in his career). It's an elegant, lovingly detailed, but ultimately safe, drama brought to life through the richness of Renoir's humanity. With a long overdue restoration from Criterion, the DVD looks amazing and supplements include commentary by film historian Peter Cowie, rare film and radio clips (including a late-1950s introduction by Renoir), and essays. —*S. A.*

RULES OF THE GAME, THE L: DIRECTORS/RENOIR, JEAN (1939) 110M D: Jean Renoir.
Nora Gregor, Paulette Dubost, Marcel Dalio, Roland Toutain, Julien Carette, Jean Renoir. Reviled and condemned upon its release and declared a rediscovered masterpiece when the butchered film was restored in 1959, Renoir's bittersweet classic is at once savage social satire and a compassionate comedy of manners with a fatal, feral undercurrent. Set in the dying days of the 1930s, as the Third Reich cast a long shadow over a seemingly impotent France, the ironic drama of life, love, class, and the social code of manners and behavior—"the rules of the game" of the title—finds its microcosm of French society in farcical romantic triangles that play out during a weekend in the country hosted by a bloodless, bored, philandering aristocrat (Dalio). While a sophisticated bedroom comedy plays out upstairs with his wife (Gregor) and a lovesick aviator (Toutain), another plays out in the servants' quarters as a garrulous rabbit poacher (Carette, playing his part like an impulsive imp) proceeds to seduce the flirtatious young wife of a humorless Teutonic gamekeeper. The famous catch-phrase "everyone has their reasons" transforms from a statement of tolerance to an apologist's impotent excuse for the tragic conclusion. There is not a more perfect, more profound, or more inexhaustible film in Renoir's amazing career. —*S. A.*

SOUTHERNER, THE L: DIRECTORS/RENOIR, JEAN (1945) 91M D: Jean Renoir.
Beulah Bondi, Betty Field, Zachary Scott, J. Carrol Naish. Sam (Scott) and Nona (Field) try to make a home for themselves, their two children, and Sam's cranky grandmother (Bondi) out of a derelict shack on a neglected piece of Texas property. Through hard labor they strive to cultivate a healthy cotton crop. Trouble is, regardless of their diligent efforts, their success is always at the mercy of the elements. An unabashed celebration of American values (hard work, determination, and the rest), *The Southerner* somehow never takes a false step. Certainly this can be attributed to director Renoir's unwavering respect and sympathy for the family's struggle for independent financial means (Sam repeatedly turns down opportunities to work in a nearby factory). The film isn't without corny moments, but it never stoops to sentimentality, and never comes off as insincere. —*C. B.*

HIROSHIMA, MON AMOUR L: DIRECTORS/RESNAIS, ALAIN (1959) 90M D: Alain Resnais.
Emmanuelle Riva, Eiji Okada. *Hiroshima, Mon Amour* starts out with flashes of the destruction from Hiroshima, which mixes actual footage of the blast zone with the dead and dying, along with staged scenes of victims in shock from their wounds. This sets the stage for an intense but brief love affair between a Japanese man and a French woman filming a movie in Hiroshima ten years after the bomb was dropped. The love affair becomes a vehicle for the woman to reveal the emotional devastation of a past relationship between her and an occupying German soldier killed in an attack back in her hometown, and the abuse and alienation to which she was subjected by the local townspeople and her family. As with most love affairs, the characters are drawn into more emotional turmoil than was intended. All the suffering is justified. The French woman connects with the trauma experienced by her Japanese lover, which draws out the poisonous trauma eating away at her psyche. —*B. W.*

LAST YEAR AT MARIENBAD L: DIRECTORS/RESNAIS, ALAIN (1961) 94M D: Alain Resnais.
Delphine Seyrig, Giorgio Albertazzi, Sacha Pitoeff. In a monstrous old luxury hotel where the rich idle away their time, a married woman becomes wrapped up with a mysterious stranger whom she may or may not have had an affair with the previous year. The film is a beautiful treatise on loneliness, love, memory, and time itself. Its haunting, lyrical beauty seduces the audience, thanks in large part to master Sacha Vierny's amazing cinematography. A hypnotic study of subjective memory, *Marienbad*'s success depends on how much you are willing to give over to the film. Like all great art, it improves upon each viewing as more nuances are noticed and its beauty becomes more solidified. Or perhaps more transient and unnamable. Either way, it is an amazing film. —*T. S.*

NIGHT AND FOG (NUIT ET BROUILLARD) L: DIRECTORS/
RESNAIS, ALAIN (1955) 32M D: Alain Resnais. Resnais
agreed to direct this documentary about the concentration camps in Auschwitz and Majdanek
only under the condition that poet/novelist Jean
Cayrol (himself a concentration camp survivor)
write the narration. The result is less an exorcism of traumatic memories than a frustrated
meditation on the impossibility, and perhaps
uselessness, of representing the catastrophes
of the Holocaust. Grasping at the unthinkable,
Cayrol's oppressively numbed commentary
bares an anxiety precisely matched by Resnais's
formal perfectionism and intensified by the nau-
sea summoned by horrific archival footage. I
consider it one of the twentieth century's most
substantial aesthetic accomplishments, but I'll
leave the experts to convert the unconvinced.
Phillip Lopate: "Aesthetically sophisticated
and ethically irreproachable." Serge Daney:
"Unimpeachable witnesses of our modernity."
Jonathan Rosenbaum: "*Schindler's List* is a cartoon alongside it." Youssef Ishaghpour: "*Night
and Fog* and the accumulated horror of history
reduce to a lie any work that does not speak of
them." François Truffaut: "The greatest film ever
made." —*C. B.*

STAVISKY L: DIRECTORS/RESNAIS, ALAIN (1974) 112M D:
Alain Resnais. *Charles Boyer, Jean-Paul Belmondo.*
Belmondo, in high-charm mode, is Serge
Alexander, aka Stavisky, the small-time con man
turned high-rolling businessman whose ambitious sting weakened the French government
before WWII: Horatio Alger gone corrupt.
Could it be more timely? Director Resnais, with
Jean-Luc Godard, is the most formally adventurous of the New Wave directors, but where
Godard is impulsive, energetic, and emotional
amid his political inquiries, Resnais is studied,
elegant, and intellectually cold. Stavisky's story
is viewed through a kaleidoscope of flashbacks
and woven through the tapestry of 1933 Europe
and the world: Trotsky exiled in France, the
Fascists rising to power in Germany, Italy, and
Spain, the depression in America. Yet *Stavisky*
is one of Resnais' warmer works, largely due to
Belmondo's seductive performance and a beautiful turn by Boyer as his loyal friend, the Baron,
played with quiet dignity and tired irresponsibility. Watch for Gérard Depardieu in his single
scene as an inventor. Features a lovely (if at times
too insistent) score by Broadway legend Stephen
Sondheim. —*S. A.*

LOOK BACK IN ANGER L: DIRECTORS/RICHARDSON, TONY
(1958) 115M D: Tony Richardson. *Richard Burton, Claire
Bloom, Mary Ure.* Burton was a bit old to play
the quintessential angry young British intellectual in Richardson's adaptation of the acclaimed
John Osborne play (which Richardson originally
directed on stage), but his searing performance of
self-loathing turned outward is powerful enough
to make you forget. Ure is his long-suffering

wife whose youthful glow has been deadened
by his contempt, and Bloom is her best friend,
who turns from Burton's antagonist to his lover.
Burton never tries to be likeable but he is compelling, burning with frustration and indirection
and self-loathing, making a show of middle-class
derision with his working-class affectation, but
unable to really embrace or understand his so-
called comrades. —*S. A.*

MADEMOISELLE L: DIRECTORS/RICHARDSON, TONY (1966)
100M D: Tony Richardson. *Jeanne Moreau, Umberto
Orsini, Ettore Manni, Keith Skinner. Mademoiselle,*
directed by Tony "Natasha's Dad" Richardson,
is based on a Jean Genet story adapted for the
screen by Marguerite Duras and stars the young
Moreau in a kind of proto-Verhoeven film about
the dangers of sexual repression. At least at first.
The quiet madness of the demure schoolmistress, a passionless sadism that brought to mind
Mark Twain's darkest work, "The Mysterious
Stranger," is ultimately unleashed by the fulfillment of her desires. A powerful melodrama about
the power of female sexuality—Mademoiselle
is explicitly labeled a goddess at one point—
Mademoiselle wears its Freud on its sleeve: when
Mademoiselle's passions burst, they burst the
dam. And the snake means exactly what you
think it means. —*C. C.*

HUD L: DIRECTORS/RITT, MARTIN (1963) 111M D: Martin Ritt.
*Patricia Neal, Paul Newman, Brandon De Wilde,
Melvyn Douglas, White Bissell.* Newman plays
the cynical, hard-drinking, good-time son of
an aging rancher (Douglas), a callous rebel on
a windswept plain. Beautifully photographed
by James Wong Howe in black and white, and
etched into a widescreen frame dominated by
a lonely plain and empty skies (Howe won an
Oscar for his work), this excellent adaptation of
Larry McMurtry's modern Western about the
collapse of the frontier also earned Oscars for
Douglas and Neal as the ranch housekeeper who
escapes her lonely life in Hud's bed. De Wilde
is Hud's wide-eyed cousin, who worships Hud
and his free-wheeling ways but is also devoted to
his stern, old-world uncle. But the film is owned
completely by Newman and his lazy, insolent
performance. —*S. A.*

LONG, HOT SUMMER, THE L: DIRECTORS/RITT, MARTIN
(1958) 115M D: Martin Ritt. *Lee Remick, Paul Newman,
Angela Lansbury, Orson Welles, Anthony Franciosa,
Joanne Woodward.* Newman brings his piercing
blue eyes to the role of Ben Quick, suspected
barnburner and notorious charmer, who wafts
into a small Southern town controlled by Will
Varner (Welles) and begins wooing the old man's
spinster schoolteacher daughter (Woodward)
in this sweltering adaptation of three William
Faulkner stories. Ritt gets the hothouse atmosphere right and directs Newman to a blue-eyed
devil of a performance as the latter throws sparks
in his first on-screen pairing with Woodward.

Directors we truly hate

An unscientific poll of the Scarecrow staff predictably finds JOEL SCHUMACHER our most hated director. He is responsible for *Batman and Robin, 8MM, Phone Booth*, and *Falling Down*.

OTHER HATED DIRECTORS:
WOODY ALLEN
ROBERT ALTMAN
GREGG ARAKI
DARREN ARANOFSKY
DARIO ARGENTO
MICHAEL BAY
JANE CAMPION
SACHA GUITRY
HAL HARTLEY
RON HOWARD
JOHN MCTIERNAN
MICHAEL MOORE
GASPAR NOÉ
ALAN PARKER
GUY RITCHIE
LARS VON TRIER

Franciosa is the Varner heir who becomes deathly jealous as Quick chips his way into the family, and Remick is all sexy sass as Franciosa's flirtatious wife. —*S. A.*

CELINE AND JULIE GO BOATING L: DIRECTORS/RIVETTE, JACQUES (1974) 193M D: Jacques Rivette. *Marie-France Pisier, Barbet Schroeder, Dominique Labourier, Juliet Berto, Bulle Ogier*. *Alice in Wonderland* meets Henry James meets *Fantomas* in Rivette's playful postmodern fantasy (he draws from Alfred Hitchcock, haunted-house thrillers, and slapstick comedy as well). The story involves two strangers who meet by chance, become fast friends, and find that after visiting a mysterious mansion they have no memory of their past hours, their only clue a piece of hard candy in their mouths. A tale of mystery, magic, and adventure ensues as they unravel the story of the haunted mansion (a veritable film within a film) while swapping roles in their real lives. Rivette developed this complex, multilayered story of mystery, magic, and adventure with his two stars (Berto and Labourier) and screenwriter Eduardo de Gregorio, creating a script as dense as it is playful and entertaining. Enchanting and inventive, Rivette's lengthy, intimate epic is a one-of-a-kind film and a masterpiece of the 1970s. —*S.A.*

GANG OF FOUR, THE L: DIRECTORS/RIVETTE, JACQUES (1988) 160M D: Jacques Rivette. *Fejria Deliba, Bulle Ogier, Laurence Côte, Benoit Regent, Inês de Medeiros, Bernadette Giraud*. A group of acting students (Côte, Deliba, Giraud, de Medeiros) become involved with a mysterious stranger who may be a cop and a dark secret inside the small house outside of Paris where they all live. "I can't find the secret for you," comments their teacher (the marvelous Ogier), who could be describing their lives as much as their roles. This is classic Rivette, a weave of mysteries and flirtations in a world where theater and role-playing merges with life. The overarching mystery that envelopes them becomes all the more vague and unknowable as they dig deeper into the details. —*S.A.*

PARIS BELONGS TO US L: DIRECTORS/RIVETTE, JACQUES (1960) 120M D: Jacques Rivette. *François Maistre, Françoise Prévost, Gianni Esposito, Betty Schneider*. Though a favorite of some of the best film critics I've ever read, I find Rivette impenetrable and generally not especially interesting. *Paris Belongs to Us*, his first film and one of the earlier films of the Nouvelle Vague, strikes me as possibly the least satisfying of the Rivette films I've seen (which is hardly all of them, I should point out). Mixing formal experimentation, philosophy, and espionage, the film has an incredibly rough look edging on amateur. Lacking both the complexity of his later work and the enthusiastic charm of the early films of some of his cohorts, this is only worth a look if you're interested in the first films of the Cahiers du Cinema set, otherwise I can't really recommend it. —*C. B.*

SECRET DEFENSE L: DIRECTORS/RIVETTE, JACQUES (1998) 170M D: Jacques Rivette. *Sandrine Bonnaire, Grégoire Colin*. Rivette likes to take his time when he tells his odd littlwwwwe stories, so for an hour he spins the Elektra myth into a contemporary revenge drama. Research scientist Sandrine Bonnaire discovers her father's accidental death may have been murder and races to beat her hot-headed brother (Colin) to the suspected killer. The story doesn't twist and turn as much as drift through odd little eddies, and you can gauge your interest in the film with a long love-it-or-hate-it sequence where Bonnaire steels herself for the job as she ponders, fidgets, and knocks back vodkas on the long series of train rides to the country. Despite its structure, this is no murder mystery. Rivette is less interested in the obscure clues and conspiratorial edges than the smallest details of human behavior and the physical manifestations of ambivalence and unease. But then Rivette's stories have always been about metaphysical mysteries and unfathomable conspiracies. This is one of his most unfathomable, a compelling emotional journey through suspicion, guilt, family secrets, and moral duty that turns into a devastating cycle of vengeance. —*S. A.*

VA SAVOIR L: DIRECTORS/RIVETTE, JACQUES (2001) 154M D: Jacques Rivette. *Jeanne Balibar, Hélène de Fougerolles, Marianne Basler, Jacques Bonnaffé, Sergio Castellitto.* All the world's a stage in the films of Rivette, and his players are forever slipping in and out of character. Like a musical comedy without the music, Rivette's delightful story of lovers who change partners and dance has the crazy intertwining threads of performance and real life, romance and fancy, and wacky farce, played with easy, real-time pace and loving warmth. The magical Balibar, with her gawky beauty and comedienne's grace, is the leading lady of an Italian troupe run by her boyfriend (Castellitto), and their love is on the rocks as they return to her Paris home—a perfect place for the lover to stray and experiment. This is prime Rivette: vaguely dissatisfied characters in petrified relationships who flirt with romantic thrills of old loves, new enchantments, and seductive rakes before finding true love with. . . well, that would be telling. But then the surprises aren't in the plotting (which Rivette fudges at times) but in his choreography of the lovers and the deft, playful zigzags of their journey. This is subdued and mellow Rivette serenity. —*S. A.*

DESPERADO L: DIRECTORS/RODRIGUEZ, ROBERT (1995) 103M D: Robert Rodriguez. *Steve Buscemi, Salma Hayek, Joaquim de Almeida, Cheech Marin, Antonio Banderas.* In this bigger budget (about $7 million) studio sequel to *El Mariachi,* the character (now played by Banderas) has transformed into a legendary outlaw who wanders the Mexican border towns with a guitar case full of guns killing off drug dealers. Filling his first real movie with stylistic homages to Woo, Leone, Peckinpah, and even Tarantino (who gets his head blown off in a cameo), Rodriguez nevertheless establishes his own recognizable style and themes. The mariachi is a wronged-artist character who because of his mistreatment has become destructive instead of creative. But he shows artistry in his violence, and the movie is particularly great when he calls upon two other mariachis (including *El Mariachi* star Carlos Gallardo) to help him out using guitar-case-shaped rocket launchers and machine guns. These sorts of exaggerated scenes are treated completely deadpan (part of what makes them more effective than Rodriguez's later, more comedic films). Underrated, and easily one of the best American action films of the '90s. —*B. T.*

FROM DUSK TILL DAWN L: DIRECTORS/RODRIGUEZ, ROBERT (1996) 107M D: Robert Rodriguez. *Quentin Tarantino, Harvey Keitel, Ernest Liu, Juliette Lewis, George Clooney.* Clooney and Tarantino play the notorious Gecko brothers, bank robbers who take Keitel's family and RV hostage on their run for the Mexican border. At first it's a tense crime movie, but then the characters arrive at a Mexican bar called The Titty Twister, where, completely out of the blue, everybody turns into vampires. It's a fun experiment by Rodriguez and Tarantino, but the two-movies-in-one concept makes for poor pacing; it feels more like two halves of separate movies, with the serious themes of the first half left unfinished and the exhaustion you should feel at the end of the second half nonexistent. Despite this, it's a fun movie that improves with repeat viewings. It was the role that turned Clooney into a movie star, the only good acting performance by Tarantino, and an enjoyably excessive display of special effects makeup. Thanks to Tarantino's participation it has lots of funny hard-boiled dialogue, a morbid sense of humor, and appearances by genre icons like Fred Williamson, Tom Savini, Michael Parks and John Saxon. —*B. T.*

MARIACHI, EL L: DIRECTORS/RODRIGUEZ, ROBERT (1992) 81M D: Robert Rodriguez. *Carlos Gallardo, Consuelo Gomez, Peter Marquardt.* A young mariachi (Gallardo) looking for work in a Mexican border town is confused with a similarly dressed gunman and ends up in a one-man war against a drug gang led by Marquardt. Rodriguez's energetic and charmingly handmade debut is known more for the story of its production than for the actual movie. Delivered to the studio for $7,000, it was intended for the Mexican straight-to-video market and funded partly by Rodriguez subjecting himself to medical experiments (which is where he met Marquardt). Nevertheless it stands up as an entertaining movie, and the low production values and nonactor cast are a refreshing change for action fans raised on nearly two decades of *Die Hard* rip-offs. It has an endearingly goofy sense of humor and a constant drive to achieve exciting action without the aid of money, special effects, or stuntmen. Best of all, Gallardo really is a regular guy thrust into extraordinary circumstances, not an actor playing one. —*B. T.*

ONCE UPON A TIME IN MEXICO L: DIRECTORS/RODRIGUEZ, ROBERT (2003) 101M D: Robert Rodriguez. *Antonio Banderas, Salma Hayek, Mickey Rourke, Ruben Blades, Willem Dafoe, Johnny Depp.* Rodriguez turns his *El Mariachi* trilogy in a more epic direction with this story of a deranged CIA operative (Depp) who hires the mariachi (Banderas) to kill a corrupt military general immediately after a coup de tat. It's a convoluted story but any lack of narrative clarity is made up for with the Leone-esque atmosphere and strong use of music (this time composed by Rodriguez himself). The mariachi's hand has healed, so he now hides out in a town of guitar makers and walks around playing beautifully even while people are trying to kill him. As a fan of the series, my one complaint is that the mariachi is overshadowed by Depp's hilarious character who wears tacky thrift-store t-shirts, delivers bribe money in a *Clash of the Titans* lunchbox, and assumes ridiculous disguises for no reason. This is one of the best uses of high-definition digital video to date, and the DVD is full of great featurettes on the process (I was amazed to learn how many digital effects were used in this seemingly organic movie). —*B. T.*

ROADRACERS L: DIRECTORS/RODRIGUEZ, ROBERT (1994) 95M D: Robert Rodriguez. *William Sadler, David Arquette, Jason Wiles, John Hawkes, Salma Hayek.* Rodriguez's second feature (made for cable) shares that same spark of ingenuity and off-beat humor that made *El Mariachi* so much fun. Slowing down his usual breakneck pace to a gentle stroll, this tale of a leather-clad small-town rebel with a rockabilly heart is all broad strokes and bright colors, a '50s exploitation knock-off with a '90s sensibility. Casting sleepy-eyed Arquette as the rebellious loner hero, thumbing his nose at authority in public, and thoughtfully plucking his electric guitar in private, Rodriguez proceeds to re-create the juvenile delinquent melodrama in equal parts reverence and playful irony. It's *Rebel Without a Cause* by way of *Invasion of the Body Snatchers,* a tale of nonconformity and rock and roll versus the homogenization of American society. OK, so that's a little profound for a film where the hero paints a roller rink floor with a head full of pomade (you gotta see it to believe it), but the elements are all therein this never-never land of fast cars, twangy guitars, and malt-shop philosophy. —*S. A.*

SPY KIDS L: DIRECTORS/RODRIGUEZ, ROBERT (2001) 88M D: Robert Rodriguez. *Alan Cumming, Daryl Sabara, Alexa Vega, Antonio Banderas, Carla Gugino.* One-man filmmaking whirlwind Rodriguez brings a sense of whimsy to his hit family adventure of a battling brother/sister team (Vega and Sabara) who discover their parents (Banderas and Gugino) are really international spies. They join the family business when mom and dad are kidnapped by an evil mastermind (a nefarious children's TV show host played by Cumming) with a machine that turns people into wild mutant creatures. Rodriguez has a real affinity with kids and fills their odyssey with such real-world hurdles as sibling rivalry and lack of self-confidence in addition to the wicked supervillains, enemy spies, and double agents. Imaginative, energetic, and rich with adolescent fantasy life, it's a junior James Bond goof with spy gadgets more like toys than weapons and lots of slapstick humor. The ambitious digital effects that looked a little ragged on the big screen are not as much a problem on DVD. —*S. A.*

SPY KIDS 2: THE ISLAND OF LOST DREAMS L: DIRECTORS/RODRIGUEZ, ROBERT (2002) 100M D: Robert Rodriguez. *Antonio Banderas, Carla Gugino, Ricardo Montalban, Steve Buscemi, Daryl Sabara, Alexa Vega.* The *Spy Kids* have grown up, if just a little, in Rodriguez's inevitable sequel to his junior James Bond adventure. Spunky schoolkid siblings Vega and Sabara are now veteran agents whose new assignment takes them to the realm of pure fantasy: a genetic mix-and-match *Jurassic Park* and misfit *Island of Dr. Moreau* (this one run

by one Dr. Romero, played by Buscemi in high nebbish mode) hidden in the Bermuda Triangle. The preposterous dream-creatures are hatched with a childlike love of puns (spider-monkey, bull-frog, and could that flying sow be one of Pink Floyd's pigs on the wing?) and raised with digital technology. This delightful tribute to the fantastic creations of Ray Harryhausen even borrows the famous fighting skeletons for a swash-buckling bit of action, done up with Rodriguez's goofy sense of humor. The adult world subplots are flat under the frenzied direction, but the whimsy and imagination of this high-energy, high-tech wish-fulfillment adventure empowers its young audience while delighting them with an amusement park ride of an adventure. —*S. A.*

I wish Rodriguez was a better artist. So much of the world of the *Spy Kids* movies, from the logos of corporations to the CGI creatures, is based on his crude cartoon sketches. In stylized live action like the *Mariachi* films he has a great eye for visuals, but when he gets into outlandish special effects he starts drifting toward The Island of Bad Drawings You Made in High School Art Class. It's impressive how hands-on he is with every aspect of the series (both sequels were mostly shot digitally on his ranch!) but I think in this case his ambitions are a little higher than his skills. Still, the goofy spirit of the films is hard not to enjoy. —*B. T.*

BAD TIMING: A SENSUAL OBSESSION L: DIRECTORS/ROEG, NICHOLAS (1980) 117M D: Nicholas Roeg. *Denholm Elliot, Harvey Keitel, Theresa Russell, Art Garfunkel.* Roeg is known for directing some very controversial films, and *Bad Timing* is no exception. Rank, the distributor of the film, branded it "a sick film made by sick people for sick people." Consequently it is very hard to find. The story is largely told in non-chronological flashbacks which the audience must necessarily assimilate. Garfunkel plays a kind of spy assisting NATO intelligence. Russell plays the woman he falls in lust with, but beyond the physical she has very little in common with him. The infamous climax features an outrageous rape scene where Garfunkel takes advantage of Russell when she is unconscious. Explaining his film, Roeg has said, "You cannot intellectualize yourself out of obsessions." More disjointed than most Roeg films, *Bad Timing* is a kaleidoscope waiting to spring upon a patient and thinking audience. —*N. J.*

DON'T LOOK NOW L: DIRECTORS/ROEG, NICHOLAS (1973) 110M D: Nicholas Roeg. *Donald Sutherland, Julie Christie.* *Don't Look Now* is perhaps the most underrated horror film of the '70s. It's in the same miraculous league as Peter Weir's *The Last Wave.* An eerie, mysterious film, it plays on human instincts to read the workings of super-natural forces into events and also to deny their presence. It is slow-paced and takes its time to develop the characters, their relationship and their fears, so when the action plays out in the film's final act we see it through the characters' eyes. Roeg subtly creates a subjective reality where we feel fear but cannot name its source. —*T. S.*

EUREKA L: DIRECTORS/ROEG, NICHOLAS (1984) 130M D: NICOLAS ROEG. *Rutger Hauer, Theresa Russell, Gene Hackman, Mickey Rourke, Joe Pesci. Eureka* is a movie of extremes. It is the crazy story of Jack McCann (Hackman), whose rise to extreme wealth is followed by his extremely violent demise. The movie begins in the sub-zero climate of the Arctic and ends on a tropical island paradise. There are moments of gruesome action as well as tender silences. Given this pattern of extremes set by the movie, it only makes sense that audience response is just as polarized. You either hate it or love it. I love it. —*D. D.*

INSIGNIFICANCE L: DIRECTORS/ROEG, NICHOLAS (1985) 110M D: Nicholas Roeg. *Tony Curtis, Gary Busey, Michael Emil, Theresa Russell.* The characters in this interesting Roeg film are not named. However it is perfectly obvious that as American archetypes they stand for Albert Einstein, Marilyn Monroe, Joe DiMaggio, and Senator Joe McCarthy. The film asks: What if these people all happened to stay in the same hotel on the same night? This deliberate fantasy probes the nature of fame and politics in 1950s America. As such, the film has the fun of balancing bigger-than-life personalities against each other, such as when Einstein explains to Monroe his theory of relativity and she tries explaining it back to him with a curious demonstration, much to his surprise. Only Roeg's direction could keep this oddity alive and breathing. —*N. J.*

MAN WHO FELL TO EARTH, THE L: DIRECTORS/ROEG, NICHOLAS (1976) 140M D: Nicholas Roeg. *Candy Clark, Rip Torn, Buck Henry, David Bowie.* David Bowie plays Thomas Jerome Newton, a peaceful alien who comes to Earth seeking help for his dying planet and family by exchanging technology for water, only to lose everything when he falls in love with a woman, Mary Lou (Clark), who distracts him from his work. Meanwhile meddling professor and NASA employee Nathan Bryce (Torn) figures out who Newton really is. Newton ends up losing his planet, being tricked by his own investors, and captured by the U.S. government, which experiments on and tortures him until he becomes trapped in the form of a reclusive rock star. Roeg has fashioned a complicated, multileveled approach to Walter Tevis's cult science-fiction novel, utilizing quick cutting and cross-narrative structure that jumps back and forth in time and between our world and the alien world. Bowie is excellent in his first movie role, as are the rest of the actors. The film's explicit sex scenes and its structure, considered indecipherable at the time, resulted

in up to twenty minutes of forced cuts. Shot in Cinemascope, this modern masterpiece should only be viewed in the uncut widescreen version on DVD. —*N. H.*

PERFORMANCE L: DIRECTORS/ROEG, NICHOLAS (1970) 105M D: Nicholas Roeg, Donald Cammell. *Mick Jagger, Anita Pallenberg, James Fox.* Chas (Fox) is a performer, a real act, and he has his own personal spotlight, which doesn't rub his homosexual gangster buddies in the way they prefer. After taking one too many jobs in his own hands, specifically the murder of a former pal, Chas takes refuge in the flat of Turner (Jagger), a man who has "lost his demon," and Chas may be just the man to help him find it. Anita Pallenberg is a true sunshine joy as a flower child, and Michele Breton is pepper to Anita's salt throughout. Fox and Jagger are reported to have tripped on the short-term LSD-like DMT during the shooting of the film, and the whole experience was just too much for Mr. Fox, who went into a hermetic retirement soon after. —*S. R.*

TRACK 29 L: DIRECTORS/ROEG, NICHOLAS (1988) 90M D: Nicholas Roeg. *Theresa Russell, Sandra Bernhard, Colleen Camp, Christopher Lloyd, Gary Oldman.* Russell plays a very confused and lonely woman whose husband works long hours and who has an overactive imagination. Oldman appears out of nowhere playing her long-lost son whom she doesn't entirely remember having, and he plays up the role in the most peculiar way while regressing into infantile instincts with the mother he never knew. Other people evidently cannot see her demanding and clutching son. Lloyd plays her husband, a doctor by day and a man who totally ignores her by night due to his passion for toy trains, which he has erected throughout the house. Bernhard plays this man's favorite nurse and mistress who will indulge his strangest fantasies in the middle of the day and in any empty hospital room. Roeg is the director of this outrageous classic, and his unique filming and editing only amplifies the strangest elements of these characters, painting a story as surreal as it is heartfelt. —*N. J.*

TWO DEATHS L: DIRECTORS/ROEG, NICHOLAS (1996) 102M D: Nicholas Roeg. *Sonia Braga, Michael Gambon.* A return to form for Roeg, this film, like many of his other works, is constructed on a James Joyce-like narrative structure of past and present colliding together in the story of physician Daniel Pavenic (Gambon), who attempts to hold his annual dinner for twelve of his closest friends while war explodes around his home in a fictional country somewhere in Eastern Europe. Only three of his friends are brave enough to show up. During dinner they find themselves caught in the sado-masochistic relationship between Pavenic and his once-beautiful house servant (Braga), which they find out has been going on for years. The more stories they hear

Eric Rohmer

After more than forty years of feature film-making, Eric Rohmer, the old man of the French New Wave, is still one of the greatest practitioners of the fine art of conversation on film. A former teacher and film critic, he contributed to *Cahiers du Cinéma* with younger writers François Truffaut, Jean-Luc Godard, Claude Chabrol (with whom he wrote his classic study of the films of Alfred Hitchcock), and others. Like his fellow critics, he made short films and even a feature (*The Sign of Leo*, 1959), but his recognition came with a cycle of films he called his "Moral Tales," which Rohmer described as dealing "less with what people do than with what is going on in their minds while they are doing it."

His earlier films were variations on this theme, examining the interior life of the protagonist, beginning with a pair of short films (*The Girl at the Monceau Bakery* [1963] and *Suzanne's Career* [1963]). He hit his stride—and found his audience—with the delightful *My Night at Maude's* (1969), in which Jean-Louis Trintignant portrays a smug intellectual torn between his idealized image of blond beauty Marie-Christine Barrault and the earthy, intelligent, sexually aggressive Maude (Antoine Vitez), who challenges Trintignant in a long evening of philosophical debate and flirting. The same mix of sexual attraction, romantic triangles, and endless intellectualizing, Rohmer-style, continues through *Claire's Knee* (1970) and *Chloe in the Afternoon* (1972)

Comedies and Proverbs, Rohmer's second series, trades the first cycle's troika-based plots and male-centered narratives for largely female-driven ensemble work, creating romantic comedies with headstrong characters, mismatched couples, and the crisscrossing plots of a Shakespearean farce. Featuring delicately delivered ruminations on modern love, his films mellow in tone over the course of the decade, from the bittersweet irony of *The Aviator's Wife* (1980) and *Full Moon in Paris* (1984) to the giddy happy endings of *Boyfriends and Girlfriends* (1987) and the magical *Summer* (1984), a largely improvisational film marked by easy rhythms, a gentle naturalism, and an effervescent, romantically sublime climax.

Between the two cycles, he created two of his most unusual and unique feature films: *The Marquise of O* (1976), an eighteenth-century costume drama that is stately where his other films are relaxed and easy, and directed in painterly compositions from a removed distance, and *Perceval* (1979), a strange, sophisticated blend of theater, the storytelling traditions of the Middle Ages, story-song, and cinema. Greeted with derision upon release, it remains one of the most unique expressions in modern cinema, bound to frustrate as many viewers as it delights.

Rohmer concluded his third cycle, a quartet of lovely romantic films called "The Four Seasons," at the age of seventy, before embarking on another adventurous experiment: *The Lady and the Duke* (2001), the true story of a defiant Englishwoman in the French Revolution. The film eschews all pretense of realism: the actors play against oil paintings created in period style, lending a startling and beautiful texture, as if the figures of a painting had come to life to tell their stories. The effervescent sparkle and naturalistic lilt of Rohmer's dialogue has, like fine wine, aged to perfection.

—*Sean Axmaker*

about the cruelty and love between the master and his servant, the more the three look back on their own dark secrets. Based on the book *The Two Deaths of Senora Puccini* by Stephen Dobyns. Beautifully shot and acted, the film was co-produced for the BBC by Luc Roeg, the director's son. —*N. H.*

WALKABOUT L: DIRECTORS/ROEG, NICHOLAS (1971) 100M D: Nicholas Roeg. *David Gulpilil, Lucien John, Jenny Agutter.* For years unavailable on video, *Walkabout*, like most of Roeg's work, is a mix of visual mysticism and spiritual journey played out by its characters, in this case, a beautiful young teenage British girl (Agutter) and her brother (John) who are abandoned in the Australian outback after their father takes them on a picnic with plans to murder them, but ultimately kills himself, leaving the two children alone in the middle of nowhere. As they venture into the sandy dunes, they come across an aboriginal teenage boy (Gulpilil) on a Walkabout, learning to survive away from his people alone in the desert. Unable to communicate, the boy figures out the two need to be brought back to civilization and helps them return. Magnificently shot, the film focuses on social taboos that disappear in the wilds as children become adults and learn to survive the outback's hellish conditions. *Walkabout* drips with budding sexuality as the girl finds herself drawn to the aboriginal boy, and he to her. Heavily censored when first released, the Criterion DVD restores *Walkabout* to its original cut, the only way to see this truly landmark film. —*N. H.*

WITCHES, THE L: DIRECTORS/ROEG, NICHOLAS (1990) 92M D: Nicholas Roeg. *Jasen Fisher, Mai Zetterling, Anjelica Huston, Rowan Atkison.* A boy (Fisher) staying in a hotel with his grandma (Zetterling) discovers that the Royal Society For the Prevention of Cruelty to Children meeting going on in the convention room is actually a front for witches planning to turn all the children of the world into mice. He gets found out and turned into a mouse, but still manages to foil their plot. Huston is memorably sinister as the Grand High Witch, who removes her mask to reveal a hideous face with a nose so long it had to be folded up to fit inside the mask. The imaginative mythology (witches all wear wigs and hate the smell of children) and nasty humor come from the great book by Roald Dahl, while the animatronic mouse effects are supplied by Jim Henson (for his last film). The only significant flaw is a happier ending than the one in the book, added as a favor to the knuckleheads who attended the test screenings. —*B. T.*

LADY AND THE DUKE, THE L: DIRECTORS/ROHMER, ERIC (2001) 129M D: Eric Rohmer. *Leonard Cobiant, François Marthouret, Jean-Claude Dreyfus, Lucy Russell.* Where so many sumptuous historical dramas appear to have leapt out of a painting, Rohmer

has his actors step into one, literally, in this fresh take on the French Revolution costume drama. Russell is Englishwoman abroad Lady Grace Georgina Elliot, the real-life royalist who refused to keep her views private during the French Revolution's reign of terror and lived to tell. Dreyfus is Prince Philippe, the Duke of Orleans, her former lover and an outspoken revolutionary leader. Lady Grace is a maddening yet fascinating figure, with her defiant, unapologetic embrace of aristocratic privilege and affectionate but antagonistic relationship with Prince Philippe. Eschewing all pretense of realism, Rohmer places his characters against—in fact, inside—period-style oil paintings, creating a startling and beautiful texture with a mix of old-fashioned technical trickery and state-of-the-art digital magic, as if the very figures of a painting came to life to tell their stories. —*S. A.*

MARQUISE OF O, THE L: DIRECTORS/ROHMER, ERIC (1976) 100M D: Eric Rohmer. *Bruno Ganz, Edda Seippel, Edith Clever, Peter Lühr, Otto Sander.* A handsome and dashing Count (Ganz in a quietly intense performance) rescues a beautiful young Marquise (Clever) from certain assault during the Russian invasion of Italy in the Napoleonic wars. The chivalrous savior guards her over the long night and returns to court her. Only when he leaves does she discover that she is, unaccountably, pregnant. Adapted from a story by Heinrich von Kleist, this eighteenth-century costume drama is an anomaly in Rohmer's career, stately where his other films are relaxed and easy and directed in painterly compositions from a removed distance. It's an assured, gorgeous piece of cinema and, as with *Perceval*, Rohmer breaks with his usual style to play with period and language (it's in German), resulting in one of his "orphans," a film his fans don't quite know what to do with. Yet its story of innocence, honor, corruption, and the shades between that lay within even the best of men, is thoroughly Rohmer, shaped by carefully sculpted dialogue, informed by a sense of irony, and directed with forgiveness and understanding. —*S. A.*

MY NIGHT AT MAUD'S L: DIRECTORS/ROHMER, ERIC (1969) 110M D: Eric Rohmer. *Françoise Fabian, Jean-Louis Trintignant, Marie-Christine Barrault, Antoine Vitez.* Rohmer elevated smart talk to an artform with his "Six Moral Tales" cycle, loose little stories of the decisions made (or not) in brief moments of time. *My Night at Maud's*, his third feature and his breakthrough film, is the best of the series. Trintignant stars as a rigorous Catholic and a studious intellectual who falls in love with a "pure" young blonde (Barrault) he has only fleetingly seen. The night of the title, however, is spent with the seductive and fascinating Maud (Fabian), a recently divorced woman who proves to be not merely his philosophical equal but more frank and honest in a night that turns out to be mostly talk: small talk, serious talk, introspection, and finally rationalization when surfaces prove to be deceiving. Which only proves that the well educated and erudite aren't so different from us, they just manage to make it sound better. A sly, smart little film, shot in wintry black and white, that captures the choices, regrets, and moments leading up to them that most movies pass right over. —*S. A.*

PAULINE AT THE BEACH L: DIRECTORS/ROHMER, ERIC (1983) 95M D: Eric Rohmer. *Féodor Atkine, Rosette, Simon de La Brosse, Pascal Greggory, Amanda Langlet, Arielle Dombasle.* The third film in Rohmer's "Comedies and Proverbs" cycle delights in the folly of love and impulsive, illogical instincts of human nature, all seen through the eyes of teenage Pauline (Langlet). Her gorgeous cousin (Dombasle) is a vivacious, flirtatious blond goddess looking for fun now that her divorce is almost final, and two men—her decent but jealous former boyfriend (Greggory) and a charming but shallow intellectual (Atkine) who treats love as a game and Dombasle as a delightful fling—vie for her affections. True to form, Rohmer doesn't judge, and his generosity of character rounds out everyone caught up in the tangled affairs and mistaken identities. A delightfully light-fingered look at the games people play with love and sex. —*S. A.*

PERCEVAL L: DIRECTORS/ROHMER, ERIC (1978) 140M D: Eric Rohmer. *Fabrice Luchini, André Dussollier, Marie-Christine Barrault, Marie Rivière, Arielle Dombasle.* Rohmer's most unique feature is a strange, sophisticated mix of theater, storytelling traditions of the Middle Ages, story-song, and cinema. Luchini is all naive innocence and wide-eyed wonder as the child-man Perceval. The ignorant but well-meaning young lord vows to become a knight after catching his first sight of what he believes to be godly beings but he knows nothing of the world he now faces, which leads to awkward, humorous, and sometimes tragic consequences on the road to King Arthur's court. Adapted from the twelfth-century book by Chrétien de Troyes and played out completely on a circular stage ringed with flat sets and a neutral background, the film looks like a medieval painting come to life, but plays like theater, coming alive in excellent performances and enchanting stories, all performed in rhyming couplets. It was greeted with derision upon release but looks better and more revolutionary with each passing year. Rohmer's odyssey into the very nature of stories and storytelling remains one of the most singular expressions in modern cinema and a fascinating, delightful experience. —*S. A.*

SUMMER L: DIRECTORS/ROHMER, ERIC (1986) 98M D: Eric Rohmer. *Lisa Heredia, Vincent Gauthier, Marie Rivière, Beatrice Romand.* The willowy Rivière is Delphine, a gloomy, insecure Parisian who faces her summer vacation alone and miserable. A combination of romantic idealism, headstrong determination and uncompromising demands, she sabotages one getaway after another with her impossible standards, moping lonely and wanting until she meets a handsome young man. Rohmer changed his shooting style for this largely improvisational film, which he constructed and created in collaboration with his actors. But the easy rhythms, gentle naturalism, and genuine affection for the characters, foibles and all, is vintage Rohmer. The original French title of the film is *Le Rayon Vert*, a reference to the legendary green ray that can sometimes be seen in the dying light of the setting sun. The ephemeral phenomenon informs the delicate conclusion, an almost mystical experience that is at once magical, tender, and sublime. It may be his finest film ever, and it is certainly his most romantically hopeful and emotionally effervescent. —*S. A.*

FASCINATION L: DIRECTORS/ROLLIN, JEAN (1979) 83M D: Jean Rollin. *Brigitte Lahaie, Franca Mai.* Rollin's masterwork, *Fascination*, is beautiful. There are many frameable images in just the first few minutes at the abbatoir, where all classes of people are consuming cow blood to stave off anemia. A bandit makes off with shared booty and holes up in a castle with two strange young women, one a beautiful sex kitten (Lahaie). After much teasing and game-playing, the robber must succumb to the mad desires of the women in the castle, culminating in a lesbian orgy of diaphanous-nightie-wearing vampires crawling over each other for a taste of blood. Magnificent images abound in this Rollin masterpiece, including Lahaie wielding a large scythe, slashing her way towards the castle. The doomed romanticism is heightened by the film's low budget, relying on strong imagery of near-naked, bloodthirsty young women against the solemn locale of the castle. Philippe D'Aram's amazing score, classic in its force and power, opens the film, quickly setting the tone for this lovefeast of horror cinema. —*S. R.*

GRAPES OF DEATH, THE L: DIRECTORS/ROLLIN, JEAN (1978) 90M D: Jean Rollin. *Felix Marten, Serge Marquand, Marie-Georges Pascal.* French horror fantasist Rollin puts an environmental twist to Romero's *Night of the Living Dead* in this oddball little zombie movie. As surreal as the rest of his films, this one is set in the vineyard region of southern France, where the eerily empty countryside explodes with bloodthirsty villagers covered in oozing sores. Only these zombies are haunted by the human damage of their destructive sprees and uncontrollable drive to kill the ones they love. Considered the first French gore film, Rollin brings a graceful dreaminess to his violence (at least compared to the blunt bludgeoning of Italian goremeisters Lucio Fulci and Umberto Lenzi), and a purely emotional illogic to the impulsive actions of prey and predator alike. Pascal stars as the terrified out-of-towner driven off the train and into the infestation, and Rollin regular Brigitte Lahie costars as an unbalanced human who wanders among the staggering monsters in a white nightdress, accompanied by two noble hounds, like a queen in the land of the dead. —*S. A.*

LIVING DEAD GIRL, THE L: DIRECTORS/ROLLIN, JEAN (1982) 86M D: Jean Rollin. *Mariana Pierro, Françoise Blanchard.* This Rollin film is a moving, bloody story about friendship, reluctant monsters, and naked chicks. Throughout his career, Rollin has been obsessed with sexuality and lesbian vampires. His films are a unique combination of poetic visuals, campy gore, and unrestrained passions. *The Living Dead Girl* is the story of two childhood friends, Helene (Pierro) and Catherine (Blanchard), whose longtime love for each other is almost ended by Catherine's surprising death. Even more surprising is Helene's discovery that Catherine is still alive and has become some sort of bloodthirsty vampire that's been getting naked, seducing, and killing local men. The relationship between the two women is quite touching and Catherine makes an unusually sympathetic creature of the night. Nobody makes movies like Rollin and this is a good starting point for those uninitiated with his sensual European horror films. —*S. H.*

NIGHT OF THE HUNTED L: DIRECTORS/ROLLIN, JEAN (1980) 93M D: Jean Rollin. *Vincent Garder, Brigitte Lahaie, Dominique Journe.* A fairy-tale figure (Lahaie) clad in a flimsy white nightgown flees through a misty forest in the dead of night, running from a horror that she can't remember. The imagery echoes with the gothic elements of classic horror fantasy until Rollin takes a hairpin turn into a paranoid tale of insanity, collective amnesia, and haunted souls grasping at stories to replace their dissipated memories. Imagine Sam Fuller's *Shock Corridor* by way of David Cronenberg. Blank-eyed inmates shuffle through the impersonal white hallways and empty rooms of an antiseptic skyscraper asylum known as "Black Tower," living zombies somewhere between shock and stupor slowly losing their minds. Being a Rollin film, science fiction merges with sexploitation for gratuitous nude scenes, and a disconnected series of gory murders punctuate a story that never really makes sense in the first place. But then Rollin has always been more attuned to mood and texture than narrative, and this bubbles with atmosphere. His ethereal, poetic imagery and stark landscapes create an unsettling, alienated world out of time and place, a perfect setting for his ambiguous conspiracies and enigmatic psychodramas. —*S. A.*

RAPE OF THE VAMPIRE L: DIRECTORS/ROLLIN, JEAN (1976) 91M D: Jean Rollin. *Solange Pradel, Ursula Pauly.* French erotic horrormaster Rollin's debut feature may just be the lost New Wave horror film,

a simultaneous rebellion against the old-horror guard and narrative coherence. Often cited as the first French vampire film, it was originally conceived and executed as a surreal short about madness and manipulation, a modernist twist on classic conventions: crumbling estates and secret passages, angry villagers roused to mob action, haunted girls wandering through delirious rituals in white nightgowns, and their obligatory disrobing. Narrative is of secondary concern to images and Rollin hops from one gorgeously composed shot to another. Given the funds to expand it into a feature, Rollin added an entirely new story involving a cackling vampire queen with a convertible and an antiseptic laboratory where scientists toil to find a cure for vampirism. If the first half is surreal, this is simply senseless. Rollin seems to be making it up as he goes along, bringing back dead characters and killing them off yet again, but he also sends the film spinning in mind-bending directions and climaxes with a revolutionary act that channels Jean Vigo by way of Jean-Luc Godard. —*S. A.*

REQUIEM FOR A VAMPIRE L: DIRECTORS/ROLLIN, JEAN (1971) 88M D: Jean Rollin. *Mireille Dargent, Louise Dhour, Philippe Gasté, Dominique Toussaint.* Two nymphets in clown garb blast handguns from the back of a getaway car careening down a country road. This opening recalls Godard at his most playfully bizarre, but the meandering, abstract narrative is pure Rollin. The adolescent heroines wander dreamily through a graveyard (where one falls into a freshly dug grave and is almost buried alive!) and into the castle of a tired, sorry-looking vampire desperately attempting to perpetuate his race with fresh blood. As they awaken to their sexuality, the nightmarish threat of the sexually depraved vampires looms. The lyrical first half, with its fairy-tale imagery, surreal poetry, and eerie beauty, gives way to astonishingly brutal scenes of kinky decadence and brutal nastiness (the vampire's ogre-ish henchmen molest women chained up in their dungeon), but Rollin's ethereal mood gives the largely wordless film a delicacy and a surprisingly melancholy conclusion. It's a gorgeous picture that follows the loony logic of a waking dream. —*S. A.*

SHIVER OF THE VAMPIRES L: DIRECTORS/ROLLIN, JEAN (1970) 96M D: Jean Rollin. *Michel Delahaye, Sandra Julien, Jacques Robiolles, Dominique.* One of Rollin's most deliriously dense and full films, *Shiver of the Vampires* is a showcase of Euro-horror energy and images. Opening with a strange burial ceremony rendered in black and white, the film then moves into lurid, bright color. In his closest moment to Welles, Rollin's camera moves through an open castle doorway and shows the vampire's two assistants in ready for their master. Encountering him in deathly repose at the top of a staircase, he admits that his race must be destroyed, and only the two girls can save him from the menace of his disease. The haunting Dominique is an ultracreepy and sexy vampiress, appearing from within a grandfather clock's bowels, loosing herself into the castle via levitation and magically appearing behind bedroom curtains, brazing them open as if on a Broadway stage. A thick script for Rollin, rife with notations on the vampire's lifestyle of the dead, is churned into a chunky brew with the visuals and tweaked-out groovy psychedelic rock score provided by Acanthus. —*S. R.*

ZOMBIE LAKE L: DIRECTORS/ROLLIN, JEAN (1981) 90M D: Jean Rollin. *Howard Vernon.* Rollin worked on this French horror film (originally slated for Jess Franco) about Nazi zombies in a haunted lake preying upon skinny-dipping girls. You can see his hand in the underwater scenes, which are oddly lovely. The weird reunion between a sentimental zombie soldier and his living French daughter is as tweaky as it gets: the green-faced corpse strolls down a country lane hand-in-hand with the cloying moppet to maudlin music. But Rollin's dreamy, surreal touch is nowhere else to be seen throughout the rest of this clumsy, blunt production. The makeup wouldn't pass muster at a pre-school Halloween party, the performances are embarrassingly amateur, and the dubbing is so bad it's painful. —*S. A.*

CRAZIES, THE L: DIRECTORS/ROMERO, GEORGE (1973) 103M D: George A. Romero. *Will MacMillan, Lane Carroll, Lynn Lowry, Lloyd Hollar, Harold Wayne Jones.* Romero's fourth film is a paranoid reworking of themes explored in his legendary debut *Night of the Living Dead.* Another community suddenly turns mad and violent, but here the trigger is a military virus accidentally unleashed on the local water supply. Of course the military isn't about to let this secret out, so in addition to fighting infection and infected neighbors, the survivors have the military to worry about. They're an army of faceless, radiation-suited killers more terrifying than the rampaging citizens. The theme of normalcy suddenly turned into a nightmare isn't new, but Romero communicates the terrifying alienation in addition to delivering visceral horror. The independent production was shot in Romero's home state of Pennsylvania with a cast of unknowns and costarring minor cult actress Lowry. —*S. A.*

CREEPSHOW L: DIRECTORS/ROMERO, GEORGE (1982) 120M D: George A. Romero. *Adrienne Barbeau, Leslie Nielsen, Stephen King, Robert Harper, Tom Atkins.* The most high profile of all horror anthology films, this King/Romero creation is a lot of fun. Taking its inspiration from classic E.C. Comics, the suburban framework is what really makes *Creepshow* great. When a kid's dad throws out the trashy comics that the kid loves so dearly, he cooks up some wicked revenge. There are many good stories here, but the one about cockroaches gave me nightmares when I was little and still creeps me

out. This also has King's largest acting role ever as the hick who becomes a plant. Good stuff. —*T. S.*

DAWN OF THE DEAD L: DIRECTORS/ROMERO, GEORGE (1978) 126M D: George A. Romero. *Ken Foree, Gaylen Ross, David Emge, Scott Reiniger.* The first sequel to 1968's *Night of The Living Dead* takes place a few weeks after the zombie apocalypse began, yet it also takes place in the world of 1978. Rather than following the same characters or time line, each *Dead* film is an allegory about the time in which it was made. A group of survivors holes up in an abandoned shopping mall, where they can take advantage of leftover consumer goods. But they also have to blow away hundreds of zombies who keep returning to the mall because "it was a place that was important to them." It's a funny movie but by no means tongue-in-cheek; the humor comes from the recognition that in the same situation you might also find yourself running around a mall stealing luxury items and getting a little too much joy out of killing zombies. It takes every kid's fantasy of staying the night in a mall and combines it with an extremely well-thought-out disaster movie. It's hard to say if it's better than *Night of The Living Dead* or not. So instead let's just say it's one of the best movies ever made. —*B. T.*

DAY OF THE DEAD L: DIRECTORS/ROMERO, GEORGE (1985) 91M D: George A. Romero. *Lori Cardille, Terry Alexander, Joseph Pilato, Antone DiLeo Jr., Richard Liberty, Howard Sherman.* The third in Romero's *Dead* trilogy is the weakest, but it's still great. This time, a larger group holes up in a military base where soldiers corral zombies into underground tunnels and a doctor conducts experiments to find a solution to the zombie problem. The most memorable character is Bub (Sherman), a chained-up zombie that has been trained to mimic some elements of human behavior. It's almost as violent as *Dawn of The Dead* but with less colorful, more gruesome effects. The only thing holding it back is embarrassing overacting by some of the military characters, especially Pilato, who comes off as one of the most unlikable actors of all time. —*B. T.*

KNIGHTRIDERS L: DIRECTORS/ROMERO, GEORGE (1981) 145M D: George Romero. *Tom Savini, Gary Lahti, Amy Ingersoll, Patricia Tallman, Christine Forrest, Ed Harris.* With *Knightriders*, Romero brings his social and artistic commentary to the forefront and builds a film around his feelings on corporate sponsorship. The plot deals with a group of showmen who put on medieval jousting matches, except they ride motorcycles. And yes, that is as cool as it sounds (if that's what you were thinking). As their show becomes popular they are approached and offered big money by a sponsor. Savini (in one of his biggest acting roles) wants to make the show bigger and better but the noble king Harris vows never to sell out. A struggle for artistic integrity ensues and Romero shows why the independent must stay independent. An excellent film. An excellent message. And, knights on bikes. —*T. S.*

MARTIN L: DIRECTORS/ROMERO, GEORGE (1978) 94M D: George Romero. *John Amplas, Lincoln Maazel, Christine Forrest, Tom Savini.* Not to be confused with that horrible sitcom starring Martin Lawrence, this Martin is a gawky Pittsburgh teenager (Amplas) who stalks women, drugs them, then cuts them with razor blades and sucks their blood. Dracula's exploits were chronicled in Mina Harker's diaries, but Martin's become fodder for a talk radio-show he calls regularly. He believes he is the victim of a family vampire curse, as does his uncle Cuda (Maazel) who wants to stake him. The movie leaves it ambiguous, but you get the feeling that really there are no vampires and both of them are crazy. It's a very unique approach to vampire films, with the usual gothic flourishes replaced by working-class realism and vulnerable, emotionally scarred humanity. The opening sequence on a train is particularly disturbing. Generally considered Romero's best non-*Living Dead* film. —*B. T.*

MONKEY SHINES L: DIRECTORS/ROMERO, GEORGE (1988) 108M D: George Romero. *Stephen Root, John Pankow, Kate McNeil, Christine Forrest, Jason Beghe.* A quadriplegic is given a trained monkey to be his hands and legs. However, the psychological rage of the wheelchair-bound protagonist is readily absorbed by the remarkably perceptive monkey. As such, the helping hands of the helpless man turn murderous, very much like the infamous hands of Dr. Orlac. Only here, in this fascinating plot, the helping hands also turn shockingly on their master, such as in the memorable scene when the enraged monkey urinates on its helpless master's lap. Clearly not for the faint of heart, this horror film surely packs a wallop! —*N. J.*

NIGHT OF THE LIVING DEAD, 30TH ANNIVERSARY SPECIAL EDITION L: DIRECTORS/ROMERO, GEORGE (1998) 96M D: George Romero, John Russo. *Judith O'Dea, Duane Jones.* For this special DVD release of the classic film, world-class idiot Russo went back and shot some scenes that were originally going to be in the film but were scrapped because of budget restraints. They also added a bunch of new stuff never intended to be in the first film but they thought would be good. This includes a raving minister who appears in a scene after the original ending, totally changing the effect of the movie. In fact, all these scenes totally change the effect of the movie. They change it to CRAP. With the possible exception of the first scene where we see the origins of the first creepy zombie, everything they add is worthless and only detracts from the merit of the original. On top of ruining the film with a bunch of superfluous, poorly shot, poorly acted, poorly integrated foolishness, they also added a new score. Luckily, they included

the original version of the film in this release as well. Otherwise it would be a complete and utter waste. Then again, you can get the original version with a much nicer transfer and a bunch of extras in the millennium edition. —*T. S.*

EUROPA 51 L: DIRECTORS/ROSSELLINI, ROBERTO (1952) 110M D: Roberto Rossellini. *Giulietta Masina, Alexander Know, Ingrid Bergman.* One of Rossellini's notorious Bergman vehicles, this film is in many ways a modern update of his previous film, *The Flowers of St. Francis.* After her son's abrupt death, Irene (Bergman) obsessively dedicates herself to helping the sick and the poor. Her zealous devotion and fierce independence ultimately cause her family to declare her insane. Featuring what Eric Rohmer named "the most beautiful tears ever shed on a screen," *Europa 51* is often compared to Carl Dreyer's *Passion of Joan of Arc*, in part for obvious thematic similarities, but also for its tormented "documentary of the face" close-ups. As the title indicates, Irene represents the European bourgeoisie at large in the years when the damage of WWII was less physical than moral, psychological, and spiritual. *Europa 51* is largely neglected probably because its style, straddling realism and expressionism, fails to match the *Open City* aesthetic generally associated with Rossellini. —*C. B.*

GERMANY YEAR ZERO L: DIRECTORS/ROSSELLINI, ROBERTO (1947) 71M D: Roberto Rossellini. *Edmund Moeschke, Ingetraud Hinze, Franz-Otto Krüger.* A high point of neorealism, Rossellini's film about the decay of Germany in the years following WWII examines the rift between the fascist exaltation of strength and the weakened state of Germany and its desperate people. With no script (but with some specific images in mind) and using German non-actors, Rossellini shot this loose film amid the rubble of the truly decimated Berlin. The camera's almost indifferent gaze is substituted for a psychologically rich script, and we are left with a naturalist composition that follows a young boy through the remains of the Nazi capital, not as a character in a landscape but a character of a landscape. —*C. B.*

MESSIAH, THE L: DIRECTORS/ROSSELLINI, ROBERTO (1978) 145M D: Roberto Rossellini. *Toni Ucci, Flora Carabella, Carlos de Carvalho.* The last film directed by Rossellini makes the unending speculation about his relationship with Catholicism unavoidably pertinent. Not interested in setting the issue to rest, Rossellini applies his neorealist aesthetic to a film with an unassuming matter-of-factness far removed from the celebration of miracles. Though I'd never think of using the word "secular," there's no denying that Rossellini presents the life of Christ as a historical event rather than a mythic one, offering Jesus's teachings as practical wisdom rather than stacking the deck with the Word-of-God card. It's Rossellini's decision to end the movie abruptly at the opening of Jesus' post-Crucifixion tomb that throws the film back into the arena of faith. Cutting the story short before the Resurrection, Rossellini removes his film from denominational debate and wisely leaves the viewer to his or her own faith, in the process capping an unparalleled career. —C. B.

STROMBOLI L: DIRECTORS/ROSSELLINI, ROBERTO (1950)
117M D: Roberto Rossellini. *Mario Sponza, Mario Vitale, Ingrid Bergman.* Initiating one of film's most notorious scandals, Bergman traveled to Italy to work with Rossellini and became pregnant with his child. *Stromboli* itself is the story of an urbane, Lithuanian woman living on a rural Italian island, whose conservative inhabitants scorn her modern sensibilities. A remarkable drama about the needs of the individual versus those of the community, *Stromboli*'s behind-the-scenes story is even juicier. With the shoot over-budget and long over-schedule, producer Howard Hughes literally kidnapped an incomplete print, drastically editing it, and released it in the United States. Ridiculous advertising posters (promptly banned) capitalized on the scandal, depicting Bergman writhing beside an absurdly phallic volcano. Meanwhile, "the first lady of the screen" pressed on with Rossellini's staunch aesthetic, working without a written script, enduring appalling heat, and managing her own hair and makeup—even badly scalded herself while shooting on an active volcano. —C. B.

VOYAGE TO ITALY L: DIRECTORS/ROSSELLINI, ROBERTO
(1953) 83M D: Roberto Rossellini. *George Sanders, Ingrid Bergman.* Bergman and Sanders play a married couple taking a tour of Italy. Much of their time is spent in and around Pompeii, taking advantage of all the archaeological discoveries in the area. Over time it becomes increasingly obvious that their marriage is falling apart, and that their attempts to resuscitate the relationship are as difficult as the work to restore Pompeii. After discovering a couple holding hands in the ruins, they subsequently lose themselves in an avalanche of people celebrating a religious occasion, a beautifully harmonized analogy to end the film. —N. J.

ALL THE KING'S MEN L: DIRECTORS/ROSSEN, ROBERT
(1949) 109M D: Robert Rossen. *Mercedes McCambridge, John Ireland, Broderick Crawford.* Based on Robert Penn Warren's Pulitzer Prize-winning novel and inspired by real life Louisiana Governor Huey Long, Rossen's Oscar-winning drama is a dark, cynical look at political demagoguery and corruption. Crawford (who also won an Oscar for his portrayal) brings blustery charm and oversized performance to charismatic populist politician Willie Stark, who turns his back on ideals when he discovers the real currency of political power. Rossen's savage screenplay, with its folksy rhetoric, and documentary-like direction gives an immediacy to the drama. Excellent performance by McCambridge (who took home an Oscar for her film debut) as the cool mistress-turned-calculating assistant, and Ireland as the newsman-turned-political flack, help make this film an American classic. —S. A.

HUSTLER, THE L: DIRECTORS/ROSSEN, ROBERT (1961)
135M D: Robert Rossen. *Murray Hamilton, Piper Laurie, Paul Newman, Myron McCormick, George C. Scott, Jackie Gleason.* Newman plays Eddie Felson, a hotshot pool shark tired of all the pool players he has taken. More than money, he wants a better game of pool. Quite simply, he wants to be known as the best. To do this he needs to challenge Minnesota Fats, brilliantly played by Gleason. The challenge goes on all through the night and into the wee hours of the morning—thousands of dollars trade hands back and forth. In the end it seems Eddie has bitten off more than he can chew. Newman played Felson again in the sequel, *The Color of Money.* —N. J.

LILITH L: DIRECTORS/ROSSEN, ROBERT (1964) 114M D:
Robert Rossen. *Peter Fonda, Warren Beatty, Jean Seberg, Kim Hunter.* Beatty plays Korean War-veteran Vincent, who takes a position at a mental hospital and immediately becomes captivated by Lilith (Seberg), a long-term hospital resident whose shaky grasp of reality hasn't impeded her from calculatingly manipulating numerous other patients. Though sincere in his efforts to help her, ulterior motives lurk below the surface, and he slowly falls madly and deeply in love with the seemingly helpless black widow. The precarious distinction between sanity and insanity is the crux of this dismally undervalued suspense classic. A true master of his craft, Rossen flawlessly directs what would be his final film with streamlined efficiency, allowing us to forget we're watching a film and thoroughly immerse ourselves in the story. Absolutely superb performances are delivered by the whole cast—watch for a cameo by a very young Gene Hackman. —C. B.

AFTERGLOW L: DIRECTORS/RUDOLPH, ALAN (1997) 119M D:
Alan Rudolph. *Julie Christie, Nick Nolte, Lara Flynn Boyle, Jonny Lee Miller.* Two alienated couples (Christie and Nolte, Boyle and Miller) secretly change partners and dance in awkward affairs in a postmodern sex farce so low-key it's positively chilly. Nolte is all gruff charm as a burly teddy bear of a handyman and Christie is a fragile ice queen as a retired B-movie starlet living in blissed-out denial. But otherwise Rudolph's wispy drama is as sterile as the glass and steel surfaces in Boyle and Miller's alienating apartment. Rudolph knows what he's doing, he's just not letting any of us in on it. Christie earned a Best Actress Oscar nomination for her performance. —S. A.

BREAKFAST OF CHAMPIONS L: DIRECTORS/RUDOLPH, ALAN (1999) 110M D: Alan Rudolph. *Albert Finney, Bruce Willis, Nick Nolte, Barbara Hershey, Glenne Headly.* Breakfast of Champions is definitely an experience. It is chaotic and messy in much the same way that *Fear and Loathing in Las Vegas* is. Basically, if you're not familiar with Kurt Vonnegut's work at all, or if you're currently taking a whole bunch of drugs, you won't like this film much. If you like the book, you'll probably make it through. It's a sometimes entertaining, sometimes unsettling film, often too surreal for its own good. But when it works, it really works, and the audience I saw it with gave it many laughs and much applause. Director Rudolph and Willis have created something here, but I'm still not sure whether it's intelligent or idiotic. —*C. P.*

CHOOSE ME L: DIRECTORS/RUDOLPH, ALAN (1984) 114M D: Alan Rudolph. *Rae Dawn Chong, Geneviève Bujold, Keith Carradine, Patrick Bauchau, John Larroquette, Lesley Ann Warren.* Robert Altman protégé Rudolph had found his voice in such smooth ensemble pieces as *Welcome to LA*, but he perfected his pitch and delivery with the elegant *Choose Me*. Rudolph is a pure romantic in a beautifully fabricated, studio-built modern world of neon and night. Warren's emotionally bruised bar owner is the closest the film has to a lead character, a sadder-but-wiser working girl with the bright, inviting personality of a hostess offset by a certain defensiveness. Bujold almost steals the film from her as a romantically frustrated sex therapist whose intellectual approach to relationships takes a sudden turn after a passionate affair lights her fire. Carradine is a smooth-talking stranger ready to commit to the first woman who wins his heart. And then the second. And then the third. Directed with the lazy ease of a jazz piece (the score is by jazz saxophonist Phil Woods), the film recalls the multifaceted works of Altman but has a romantic sweetness all its own. Teddy Pendergrass provides the soulful original songs. —*S. A.*

NIGHTMARE CIRCUS (AKA BARN OF THE NAKED DEAD) L: DIRECTORS/RUDOLPH, ALAN (1973) 86M D: Alan Rudolph. *Gil Lamb, Manuela Thiess, Andrew Prine.* Say, isn't that a hairy nuclear mutated retiree in that there shed? Prine positively shines as Andre, a rural maniac with a showgirl fixation and a chained, fuzzy, flesh-eating daddy. When three young ladies get trapped out on Andre's circus property/nuclear-test site, Pop gets hungry, Andre gets angry, and everyone else gets naked and dead! Well, actually, there's no nudity at all in the film, but there are plenty of other ways to offend Grandma: severed heads, chained ladies, lewd acts on the part of a snake... yeesh! In addition to this, expect liberal doses of tight pants, bullwhips, inept police work, cougars, and a mind-chewing-noise rock score that will transport you to a dimension that you will not want to escape.

Could a movie get any more exciting? Yes! But *Nightmare Circus* does a fine job of entertaining any fan of mid-impact '70s, drive-in sleaze. Partially directed by the otherwise fairly respectable Rudolph. —*Z. C.*

COMEDY OF INNOCENCE L: DIRECTORS/RUIZ, RAÚL (2000) 98M D: Raúl Ruiz. *Edith Scob, Charles Berling, Jeanne Balibar, Isabelle Huppert, Nils Hugon.* On his ninth birthday, precocious, only-child Camille becomes Paul and insists that his mother (Huppert) take him to his "real" home and his "real" mother: Isabella (Balibar), who lost her son two years ago. Is it a ghost story or a psychological thriller? Director Ruiz isn't telling, at least not until he reveals his hand in the last act. Until then this is a low-key example of Ruiz's stock in trade: stories where identity is up for question and narratives swirl around in their own cinematic worlds of logic. The mood and mystery are more intriguing than the story itself, but the emotional dynamic of the two mothers sharing the boy creates as fascinating an askew family portrait as you're likely to see. Huppert is lovely in her repressed panic of loss and the gawky/graceful Balibar glows both angelic protectivenes and desperate loneliness under her childlike smiles. —*S. A.*

GENEALOGIES OF A CRIME L: DIRECTORS/RUIZ, RAÚL (1997) 114M D: Raúl Ruiz. *Catherine Deneuve, Andrzej Seweryn, Melvil Poupaud, Michel Piccoli, Bernadette Lafont.* At once playful and poised, Ruiz's study of psychotherapy and gamesmanship is like a surreal tennis match between fate and free will, the ball lobbed back and forth in the most imaginative ways. Poupaud, a human guinea pig for theories of genetic predestination, makes good on his psychotherapist aunt's prediction that he'll become a killer. Deneuve is both commanding and unusually understated in twin roles, as both the boy's aunt and the boy's attorney. The two merge through Ruiz's bizarre mix of slapstick and therapeutic recreation. Though somewhat overlong, the film makes for an always inventive mind game. —*S. A.*

HYPOTHESIS OF THE STOLEN PAINTING, THE L: DIRECTORS/RUIZ, RAÚL (1978) 66M D: Raúl Ruiz. *Jean Rougeul.* Under the guise of a documentary, *Hypothesis* investigates the purely fictional mystery of a series of seven canvases painted in the nineteenth century by fictional artist Tonnerre. The seventh of these paintings no longer exists, if in fact it ever did, and there are no concrete records of what it depicted. An avid collector provides an exhaustive analysis of the six extant works, focusing on aesthetic peculiarities that, he maintains, connect the paintings in a delicately unified set with implications reaching well beyond art history. However, this theory only holds up if the existence of the seventh canvas can be assumed. The scenario's fascinating Borgesian puzzle is something of a cinematic anomaly, but the film's greatest accomplishment is its plunge into the melancholy of uncertainty that constantly looms over the study of aesthetics. —*C. B.*

THREE LIVES AND ONLY ONE DEATH L: DIRECTORS/RUIZ, RAÚL (1996) 123M D: Raúl Ruiz. *Marcello Mastroianni, Melvil Poupaud, Anna Galiena, Marisa Paredes.* If movies are dreaming with your eyes open, then the imaginative Ruiz is a dream weaver, telling fantastic tales with stunning and unexpected imagery and a surprise at every turn of the plot. Ruiz presents four separate stories (bridged by the narration of a radio storyteller) featuring Mastroianni in different roles, a loose anthology that tightens with the telling. At first it's just a couple of references that jump from story to story, then characters blow back and forth, and before it's over the film intertwines each tale like lace. Beguiling and hilarious, and Marcello is magnificent in one of his final screen appearances: dignified, charming, funny, and utterly convincing in a series of roles he pulls together in a delicious conclusion. —*S. A.*

TIME REGAINED L: DIRECTORS/RUIZ, RAÚL (1999) 169M D: Raúl Ruiz. *Catherine Deneuve, Emmanuelle Béart, Vincent Perez, Pascal Greggory, John Malkovich, Marie-France Pisier.* "Then one day, everything changes." No phrase better captures the sense of flux and fluidity of experience and memory in the swirl of subjective remembrance, at least as expressed by Ruiz in his adaptation of the final volume of Marcel Proust's epic *Remembrances of Things Past.* Book-ended by two high-society salons, where a small circle of acquaintances meet (Greggory's gentleman gadabout and his neglected wife Béart, her luxury-loving mother Deneuve, an insolent Malkovich [who beautifully captures the bored decadence of an arrogant aristocrat], the pianist Perez, and the eternal social busybody Pisier), the film ricochets through the remembrances of "the narrator" (a not-so-thinly veiled Marcel Proust, played by lookalike actor Marcello Mazzarella but voiced by Patrice Chereau). Past and present swirl together with dazzling bravura as sights, sounds, and thoughts trigger flashbacks that Ruiz gracefully weaves into a gorgeous evocation of early-twentieth-century Paris salon society. It's a brilliant match of sensibilities and a sublime masterpiece: wry, sad, thoughtful, beautifully shot, densely layered, and cinematically breathtaking. —*S. A.*

FLIRTING WITH DISASTER L: DIRECTORS/RUSSELL, DAVID O. (1996) 92M D: David O. Russell. *Patricia Arquette, Mary Tyler Moore, George Segal, Alan Alda, Téa Leoni, Ben Stiller.* Stiller is happily married to Arquette, but the fact that he's adopted (by Segal and Moore) has been nagging at him, so he decides to seek out his birth parents. He brings along Leoni, who's videotaping the journey for her research, and to whom he is clearly attracted. Meeting his family for the first time,

Stiller accidentally knocks over a shelf of priceless heirlooms, then figures out that there was a mistake, and he's not related to them at all. The movie is full of absurd and humiliating scenarios like this, which are Stiller's forte. This is an extremely funny movie with uncanny insights into human nature, difficult relationships, family squabbles, and cultural tensions. —*B. T.*

THREE KINGS L: DIRECTORS/RUSSELL, DAVID O. (1999) 115M D: David O. Russell. *Spike Jonze, Nora Dunn, Ice Cube, Mark Wahlberg, George Clooney.* Stuck in the desert at the end of the first Gulf War, a group of American soldiers finds a map to a stash of Saddam's gold. They're just waiting around anyway, so why not look? But in their search for the loot they discover the plight of the Iraqi opposition groups abandoned by George Bush and have to decide between their conscience, their greed, or the rules of their military. *Three Kings* was one of the first movies about the Gulf War and made some important points about the conflict that were not yet acknowledged by the American mainstream. But its greatest success is in capturing the dark absurdities and dreamlike images of modern warfare: massive hording and looting, a cow exploded by a landmine, a crashed tanker that causes a flood of milk. It's also notable for a very funny acting performance by Jonze (in the same year he directed *Being John Malkovich*). —*B. T.*

ALTERED STATES L: DIRECTORS/RUSSELL, KEN (1980) 103M D: Ken Russell. *Dori Brenner, Charles Haid, Bob Balaban, William Hurt, Drew Barrymore, Blair Brown.* This film's title is not remotely deceiving. The credits are shown over the experiment of a sensory deprivation tank in which Hurt hopes to achieve some kind of breakthrough. Analyzing his experience, he foreshadows deeply religious and highly personal encounters with evolutionary memory, heightened by his use of highly potent, mind-altering drugs. Such a story is perfect material for director Russell, whose style of filmmaking is highly visual and extremely over-the-top, not to mention laced with mythic and sexual imagery. Much disagreement accompanied the shooting of this film, including the abandonment of novelist Paddy Chayefsky, but nobody would be the wiser given Hurt's impeccable performance. —*N. J.*

CRIMES OF PASSION L: DIRECTORS/RUSSELL, KEN (1984) 101M D: Ken Russell. *Anthony Perkins, Bruce Davison, Annie Potts, Kathleen Turner, John Laughlin.* Over the top, even by the standards of Russell, *Crimes of Passion* dives into the underworld of sexual deviancy and religious hypocrisy. Turner plays a fashion designer who, by day, moonlights as a prostitute willing to act out the most bizarre fantasies of her clientele. Perkins, meanwhile, plays a completely whacked itinerant preacher who somehow develops a fixation with Turner's character. The twisted electronic music by Rick

Wakeman (from the group Yes) adds just one more layer of craziness. Be sure to watch the uncut version since much of the nasty bits of this film are thematic and not merely for shock. —N.J.

DEVILS, THE L: DIRECTORS/RUSSELL, KEN (1971) 111M D: Ken Russell. *Gemma Jones, Murray Melvin, Oliver Reed, Max Adrian, Dudley Sutton, Vanessa Redgrave.* Reed is at his sexiest as a priest accused of congress with the Devil and subjected to various tortures to pull out a confession among a bevy of repressed nuns. While he may not be sharing brews with Satan, Reed's Father Grandier is somewhat of a louse, impregnating a teen and leaving her to her own devices. Sadly for Grandier, Redgrave's Sister Jeanne is a bit hot under the habit and it's easy to blame Grandier for those late-night itches in public. Derek Jarman's sets are an incredible hearth for Russell's demonic fire, and frame after frame oozes with sumptuous unease. Grandier walking on the water for prostrated Redgrave is salivation central, and Peter Maxwell Davies's wild raucous score furthers the flames. Sister Jeanne's cleansing with a very large bellows and wonder elixir, the frenzied naked nuns screaming in the chambers, and Grandier's melting flesh are just a few of Russell's retina-burning mindscapes. —S.R.

GOTHIC L: DIRECTORS/RUSSELL, KEN (1987) 87M D: Ken Russell. *Julian Sands, Gabriel Byrne, Timothy Spall, Natasha Richardson, Myriam Cyr.* One legendary night in 1816, a curious sort of party was held with five famous guests: Lord Byron (Byrne), Percy Shelley (Sands), Shelley's fiancée Mary (Richardson), her stepsister Claire Clairemont (Cyr), and Byron's friend Dr. John Polidori (Spall). They exchange stories, the relating of which is enhanced by the mind-altering drug laudanum, and with Russell's uncanny knack for filming altered states, the visions of these guests spring to life in colorful detail. Shelley's fiancée, who would later be inspired to write *Frankenstein*, expresses her fear of being buried alive and Lord Byron his fear of leeches. Polidori would also be inspired to write *The Vampyre* which would in turn be an influence on Bram Stoker's *Dracula*. For fans of gothic horror this inventive film is a must. —N.J.

LAIR OF THE WHITE WORM L: DIRECTORS/RUSSELL, KEN (1988) 93M D: Ken Russell. *Sammi Davis, Catherine Oxenberg, Peter Capaldi, Amanda Donohoe, Hugh Grant.* James D'Ampton (Grant) takes up lodging as lord in his family's castle in England. The legend concerning the estate is that one of his ancestors slayed a dragon with a taste for virgins. He has no interest in such folklore, yet an archaeological dig on the estate seems to support much of the story. When his girlfriend disappears he decides to investigate by visiting the cavern believed to be the lair of the worm. Mixing both

humor and horror with typical Russell verve, this colorful adaptation of a Bram Stoker story also dabbles in paganism and Christianity. —N.J.

LISZTOMANIA L: DIRECTORS/RUSSELL, KEN (1975) 106M D: Ken Russell. *Sara Kestelman, Ringo Starr, Paul Nicholas, Roger Daltrey, Fiona Lewis.* This film on the life and enormous popularity of Franz Liszt is likely to be one of the most outrageous film bios you're likely to see. Russell also parodies quite a number of other famous composers while he's at it, saving most of his punch for Richard Wagner, whom he depicts as a vampire. Casting Daltrey as Franz Liszt would normally be an enormous error, but because of the way Russell chose to depict the famous pianist, as a bit of a rock star in his own time, Daltrey becomes the ideal choice. It would help the viewer, however, to know something about the actual life of Liszt to better interpret these surreal scenes. —N.J.

MAHLER L: DIRECTORS/RUSSELL, KEN (1974) 111M D: Ken Russell. *Robert Powell, Richard Morant, Rosalie Crutchley, Georgina Hale, Lee Montague.* With his wife Alma, an elderly Gustav Mahler reminisces upon his productive and turbulent life while on a train to his native Austria. The flashbacks are treated in the unique style Russell is known for, brilliantly combining sumptuous music of the composer with beautiful photography and poignant symbolism. Among the many topics of Mahler's life touched upon are his marriage, his affairs, and his rejection of Judaism. Powell is well cast as Mahler and pulls off both the drama and crazy, dreamlike musical scenes quite well. It helps, however, for the viewer to know about Mahler's life before seeing this film as it is not by any means a proper documentary, but rather a tribute. —N.J.

MUSIC LOVERS, THE L: DIRECTORS/RUSSELL, KEN (1971) 122M D: Ken Russell. *Glenda Jackson, Cynthia Albritton, Richard Chamberlain, Izabella Telezynska, Kenneth Colley, Max Adrian, Christopher Gable.* The Music Lovers is Russell's film about the life of Peter Ilyich Tchaikovsky. Chamberlain plays the celebrated Russian composer, going so far as to actually learn how to play Tchaikovsky's First Piano Concerto for the film. That scene is one of the most memorable because of its use of flashbacks, but also because of its remarkable use of camera and editing. The film goes on to show Tchaikovsky's struggle to become accepted as a composer, only to have the discovery of his homosexuality interfere with his social aspirations. Russell directs this classic with dazzle but also a certain restraint, at least when compared to *Lisztomania*. —N.J.

PRISONER OF HONOR L: DIRECTORS/RUSSELL, KEN (1991) 90M D: Ken Russell. *Richard Dreyfuss, Oliver Reed, Jeremy Kemp, Brian Blessed, Peter Vaughn, Peter Firth.* Dreyfuss produced and starred in this interesting historic account of the Dreyfus

Affair, the scandal that seized France in the 1890's when French general Alfred Dreyfus, who was Jewish, was found guilty of treason despite little evidence. Dreyfuss does not play the general, but rather the head of counterintelligence who, despite his own anti-Semitism, must conclude that the Jewish general is in fact innocent. He discovers the actual traitorous general, but the army doesn't pursue the matter; they are more interested in putting the whole thing behind them. More and more trials and appeals ensue as the government tries to cover its ass. Dreyfuss sticks out at first since his American accent doesn't blend in with the smooth English accents around him, but as it continues he seems proficient as the besieged director who spends his life working for justice. —*N. J.*

SALOME'S LAST DANCE L: DIRECTORS/RUSSELL, KEN (1987) 89M D: Ken Russell. *Glenda Jackson, Stratford Johns, Nickolas Grace, Douglas Hodge.* Russell tackles Oscar Wilde with imagination and suitable flair. Grace plays Wilde whose play *Salome* was banned from the London stage. He gives a private performance at a brothel where he can enjoy his own work and provide his own commentary throughout the play. The cast, including Johns as Herod and Jackson as Herodias, stunningly pulls of this play within the movie. Herod, during an evening of debauchery, grants his daughter Salome anything she would like for a most seductive dance. By the prompting of her conniving mother she asks for the head of the insurgent John the Baptist. This play is rich with social satire and Russell goes all out to accentuate it through the surreal setting, the outrageous acting, and a dance you'll never forget. —*N. J.*

TOMMY L: DIRECTORS/RUSSELL, KEN (1975) 111M D: Ken Russell. *Oliver Reed, Eric Clapton, Roger Daltrey, Ann-Margret, Elton John.* Tommy is the famed rock-opera by The Who. This film version is brought to life with full participation of the rock group, including Daltrey as Tommy, and with all the flare you might expect from director Russell. The story, related entirely through music, details how young Tommy learns about the death of his father, a fighter pilot in WWII, and soon catches his mother sleeping with Reed. Tommy clams up, becoming blind, deaf, and mute. As he grows up, his stepfather does all he can to break this spell, which leads to some very interesting scenes. Eventually it is discovered that Tommy is a pinball wizard, and that playing pinball not only delivers him out of psychological bondage but builds him into a Christ-like figure for the masses. This film used all the right combinations of talent in the production of something truly unique and unforgettable. —*N. J.*

VALENTINO L: DIRECTORS/RUSSELL, KEN (1977) 127M D: Ken Russell. *Rudolph Nureyev, Leslie Caron, Michelle Phillips, Carole Kane.* The famous dancer Rudolf Nureyev plays the role of silent-film-star Rudolph Valentino. Beginning with the shocking announcement of his death at age thirty-one and the tumultuous outpouring of public grief, a reporter at Valentino's wake bumps into a bevy of young ladies who knew him well. In this manner flashbacks of various parts of his life are created, chronologically describing his rise to stardom. Included is the pink-powder-puff scandal and Valentino's boxing match with a newspaper reporter. With characteristic flare befitting the subject, Ken Russell pulls out the stops making this bigger-than-life celebrity bigger than life. —*N. J.*

MATEWAN L: DIRECTORS/SAYLES, JOHN (1987) 132M D: John Sayles. *Kevin Tighe, Will Oldham, Mary McDonnell, James Earl Jones, Chris Cooper, David Strathairn.* This story deals with class and race issues surrounding the operation of coal miners struggling to form a union in the early 1920s in Mingo County, West Virginia. The miners are up against company operators and gun thugs, while African and Italian miners brought in by the company to break the strike get caught between the two forces. A Wobbly union organizer confronts locals and outsiders working in the mines, convincing them their only chance at dignity is to work together to fight for their way of living. Eventually, they take up self-defense against the company operators and hired gunmen, which climaxes with violence. Great performances by the whole cast rounds out a very believable period piece. Sayles does an amazing job with the story based on actual events and people. Haskell Wexler's cinematography is breathtaking, and captures the time and feel of the situation with stunning grace. —*B. W.*

MEN WITH GUNS L: DIRECTORS/SAYLES, JOHN (1997) 128M D: John Sayles. *Damián Alcázar, Dan Rivera González, Damián Delgado, Federico Luppi, Tania Cruz.* I don't know how John Sayles does it, but every time this film seems to be heading off into "well-intentioned liberal tract" territory he turns back on his characters and anchors his political voyage of discovery in the human experience. Set in an unnamed Latin American country (though shot entirely within Mexico), distinguished Argentine star Luppi plays a liberal city doctor blind to the repression and atrocities committed in his country until he travels into the jungle to find his old students and finds most of them dead, along with many of the natives they have vowed to help. Populated with characters more iconic than individual, Sayles creates an almost existential archetype for the terrors of living in a South American dictatorship. Think of a magical realist rendition of "Heart of Darkness," told with the passion of a man who believes in the power of the human spirit. Sayles wears his heart on his sleeve, and it beats powerfully and passionately. —*S. A.*

SUNSHINE STATE L: DIRECTORS/SAYLES, JOHN (2002) 141M D: John Sayles. *Tom Wright, Angela Bassett, Edie Falco, Timothy Hutton, Mary Steenburgen, James McDaniel.* Using a large (and excellent) ensemble cast, Sayles loosely connects an armload of disparate stories, in the process staging a snapshot portrait of the tangled social reality that is Plantation Island, Florida. Though a bit contrived, it goes down well, thanks in part to Sayles's skill for writing doubly-functional dialogue (working in service of the plot while brazenly voicing the film's political agendas). *Sunshine State* is one of the best showcases of Sayles's talent for charging seemingly banal settings with dramatic politics and long-forgotten history. The problems Sayles faces are that making a movie "about Florida" is an almost insurmountable task, and the fact that his movies, formally speaking, are fairly wooden. Still, Sayles seems most effective when he casts aside the art of fiction and gets downright didactic—something you'll certainly see here. Perhaps a weaker film than *Lone Star, Limbo,* or *Matewan,* but not to be overlooked. —*C. B.*

COLD COMFORT FARM L: DIRECTORS/SCHLESINGER, JOHN (1995) 95M D: John Schlesinger. *Sheila Burrell, Rufus Sewell, Joanna Lumley, Ian McKellen, Kate Beckinsale, Eileen Atkins.* The heroine, Flora (Beckinsale), having lost her parents, looks for the most interesting set of relations with whom she can move in. She finds a most unique and bizarre collection at Cold Comfort Farm, where there have always been Starkadders and where the matriarchal grandmother once saw "something nasty in the woodshed," which has forever colored the lives of the inhabitants there. Flora comes in like a breath of fresh air and, through clever manipulations, subtle suggestions, high-society connections, and brilliant intuition, micromanages everyone's life for the betterment of all. The humor is quirky, the acting top-notch, and the film is overall a foolish and playful romp through the bizarre world of human nature. —*M. N.*

DARLING L: DIRECTORS/SCHLESINGER, JOHN (1965) 124M D: John Schlesinger. *Laurence Harvey, Dirk Bogarde, Julie Christie.* This is one of several Christie vehicles to focus on the 1960s and the much-advertised sexual revolution. Christie won an Oscar for her portrayal of Diana, a driven model/actress in London who lives her life moment-to-moment for herself and no one else. As Diana moves from one suitor to another (and back again), guided by her needs more than her emotions, the contemporary mania for liberation is seen as a newly evolved form of materialism. Though Diana is the epicenter of the film's satire of Swinging Sixties England, she's such a vivid and three-dimensional figure we never lose sight of her as a person, even as we accept her as narrative shorthand for an entire cultural phenomenon. —*C. B.*

ENGLISHMAN ABROAD, AN L: DIRECTORS/SCHLESINGER, JOHN (1983) 63M D: John Schlesinger. *Coral Browne, Alan Bates.* This is a true hidden gem of a film that will stay with you for quite a while. The film depicts a real-life, 1958 meeting between exiled British spy Guy Burgess and famous British actress Coral Browne. The two met by chance when Browne was performing in Russia, where Burgess was exiled, and ended up spending the day together. As the two get to know each other, Burgess (played here by Bates) reveals a true and deep sadness for things lost through his exile, and Browne (playing herself) reaches out to him as best she can. Filmed on the wintry streets of Moscow, clocking in at a trim 63 minutes, and featuring more hidden emotion on Bates's face than you can imagine, this chamber piece is surely Schlesinger's, *and* Bates's, great forgotten film. —*M. S.*

MIDNIGHT COWBOY L: DIRECTORS/SCHLESINGER, JOHN (1969) 113M D: John Schlesinger. *Dustin Hoffman, Jon Voight.* The late Schlesinger provided this ode to male prostitution way back in 1969, where the film received Oscars for Best Picture, Director and Adapted Screenplay. A young and handsome Voight stars as the young and handsome Joe Buck, a Texas-to-NY transplant intent on raking in some perfumed cash with his good looks (as well as some nonexistent charm and sharp thinking). It's not long before reality catches up and Joe finds himself living in sexless squalor with his newfound partner-in-misery, "Ratso" Rizzo, played to the tuberculonic hilt by Hoffman. The film moves forward relentlessly, with its characters being driven ever downward by everything from impotence to drugged-out love-ins to fanatically religious homosexual schizophrenics. In fact, so many unsavory topics are addressed in this modern MGM masterpiece that it was originally released with an X rating, which was dropped two years later for a more marketable R. Depressed balladeer Harry Nilsson provides the film's recurring theme song, "Everybody's Talkin'." —*Z. C.*

LEGEND OF RITA, THE L: DIRECTORS/SCHLÖNDORFF, VOLKER (2000) 103M D: Volker Schlöndorff. *Bibiana Beglau, Mario Irrek, Martin Wuttke, Harald Schrott, Nadja Uhl.* Schlöndorff returns to his roots in this drama inspired by the Baader-Meinhof gang, the notorious revolutionaries of Germany's volatile 1970s. Beglau plays Rita, the young German anti-capitalist terrorist who escapes to East Germany after a youth spent robbing banks in the name of *la revolucion.* Beglau is marvelous as the idealist who champions the working class and embraces the dream of East German communism that her repressed coworkers despise, yet is willing to resort to killing when her own freedom is on the line. The East German Stasi support of these middle-class leftists-turned-guerrilla rebels is a marvelous, real-life twist, and the tarnished idealism of the Stasi agent enamored of their convictions, and willing to repress his own people to protect their identities, is a haunting mirror of the terrorist's own campaign. From the vantage point of the year 2000, after the fall of the Berlin Wall, Schlöndorff beautifully confronts the contradictions of political ideals and the realities of the Cold War from both sides of the iron curtain. —S. A.

OGRE, THE L: DIRECTORS/SCHLÖNDORFF, VOLKER (1996) 117M D: Volker Schlöndorff. *Volker Spengler, John Malkovich, Gottfried John, Marianne Sägebrecht, Heino Ferch.* Schlöndorff (adapting the novel *The Erl King* by Michael Tournier) rethinks the Third Reich as a feast of glorious storybook paintings: misty plains and swamps with castles in the horizon, verdant forests out of Die Niebelungen, a Teutonic fantasy come to life. It's the brilliant key to understanding the draw of Hitler and the Nazi party, a fantasy of perfection that transforms Malkovich's misfit childman into a loving but terrifying demon childsnatcher, plucking future Hitler youth from the bosoms of their mothers. It's a seductive, stylized portrait, perhaps too much so, but in that beauty lies the film's power: evil has never looked so inviting. —S. A.

TIN DRUM, THE L: DIRECTORS/SCHLÖNDORFF, VOLKER (1979) 141M D: Volker Schlöndorff. *Daniel Olbrychski, Mario Adorf, David Bennent, Angela Winkler.* Young Oskar is a peculiar child. He is given a tin drum for his birthday but then, almost like magic, the boy stops growing. Over time his parents explain to people that he simply fell down the stairs. The real reason, however, is the stifling atmosphere of prewar Nazi Germany. The boy's primary form of expression is his drum, which he uses to express his resentment, and he beats it loudly for the marching Nazis who in turn see him as a patriotic youth. Based on the novel by Gunther Grass, this story paints a human perspective for the trapped citizens of Nazi Germany, citizens whose silence was ominously interpreted as enthusiastic support for the cause. This film won the Oscar for Best Foreign Film in 1979. —N. J.

CHANG L: DIRECTORS/SCHOEDSACK, ERNEST (1927) 69M D: Merian C. Cooper, Ernest B. Schoedsack. *Ladah, Nah, Chantui, Bimbo, Kru.* Part adventure and part documentary, Cooper and Schoedsack's *Chang* was a smash hit upon its release and is considered a classic of the genre. It's not hard to see why: the directors took their cameras to the wilds of Thailand and captured sights that still have the power to awe. Of course the usual condescending attitude toward tribal peoples runs rampant through the film ("We be mighty hunters, Kru," comments one warrior in an intertitle, as if their own language is but some pidgin dialect), and the filmmakers fill the loose story with goofy comic relief and a veritable petting zoo of furry little pups and cubs. So forget the story

and enjoy the sights: hunters building deadfalls and spring traps, a leopard charging through the woods, a tremendous herd of elephants ford a river like a rampaging army. —S. A.

KING KONG L: DIRECTORS/SCHOEDSACK, ERNEST (1933) 102M D: Ernest B. Schoedsack, Merian C. Cooper. *Sam Hardy, Bruce Cabot, Fay Wray, Robert Armstrong, Frank Reicher.* The granddaddy of the giant monster films. Willis O'Brien had already stunned the world with his stop-motion animation for the silent classic *The Lost World*, but no one was prepared for his follow-up work with *Kong*. Silent jungle documentarians Schoedsack and Cooper joined forces with O'Brien to create "the Eighth Wonder of the World," mixing their own sense of adventure (having shot several wild-animal documentaries in Africa) with O'Brien's stop-motion techniques so that together they could bring to life the story of a group of moviemakers searching the lost Skull Island in the Pacific, in hopes of finding the "big one" to capture on film. Hollywood producer Robert Armstrong (Denham), actress wannabe Anne Darrow (Wray), and first mate "Jack" Driscoll (Cabot) have no idea what they are getting into, but begin to figure it out when they come across local natives and the gigantic wall they built to keep "something really big" out of their village. The film crew captures the Mighty Kong and bring him back to New York City, where he escapes, kidnaps Ann, and finally meets his doom atop the Empire State Building. The metaphors are rich, the film incredibly well designed, and the stop-motion work has never been topped (though O'Brien's protégé Ray Harryhausen has come very close. —N. H.

AFFLICTION L: DIRECTORS/SCHRADER, PAUL (1997) 114M D: Paul Schrader. *Willem Dafoe, Nick Nolte, Mary Beth Hurt, Sissy Spacek, James Coburn.* The best adaptation to date of a Russell Banks novel, Schrader's powerfully depressing film features career-defining performances from both Nolte and Coburn (who won an Oscar for his work here). The film takes an unflinching look at the life of Wade Whitehouse (Nolte), a small-town cop investigating a local hunting death while his own world begins to unravel around him. Depression, alcoholism, domestic violence, and the sins of the father being passed down to the son are all touched upon; the result is at once completely real and completely horrifying. You want painful, powerful, alcoholic-fueled family dysfunction, you got it. Easily one of the best films of 1997. —C. P.

BLUE COLLAR L: DIRECTORS/SCHRADER, PAUL (1978) 114M D: Paul Schrader. *Cliff DeYoung, Harvey Keitel, Lane Smith, Ed Begley Jr., Richard Pryor, Yaphet Kotto.* Three frustrated autoworkers rob their union's safe and end up with some incriminating information. Their blackmail scheme destroys their friendship and their lives. Schrader's directorial debut (after writing *Taxi Driver* and others), about powerless blue-collar workers is an engrossing condemnation of corrupt unions. The three leads (Pryor, Keitel, and Kotto) are excellent. They seem to share a genuine friendship that makes the film's final betrayals even more devastating. Schrader spends a lot of time developing the characters, their relationships, and the factory life atmosphere. Watch this in a double feature with *Roger and Me* and prepare to be pissed at the auto industry. —*S. H.*

Much of the response to this film centers on Pryor's dramatic turn as Zeke Brown, a jive-talkin' would-be radical who ends up ratting out his buddies to save his own butt. Compelling as Pryor's performance may be, Schrader's overwrought script often mocks our blue-collar heroes by injecting superfluous religious metaphor (yes, one of the three main characters gets "crucified"). Schrader's best work as a screenwriter (*Taxi Driver, Raging Bull*) has always tried to incorporate a Calvinist upbringing with a street-smart sensibility, but with *Blue Collar*, his intuition as director often leads this film to loaded speeches and abysmal cliché. —*J. D.*

CAT PEOPLE L: DIRECTORS/SCHRADER, PAUL (1982) 119M D: Paul Schrader. *Ruby Dee, Ed Begley Jr., Annette O'Toole, Malcolm McDowell, Nastassja Kinski, John Heard.* Schrader's kinky feline horror is less a remake than a new take on the ideas of Jacques Tourneur's moody horror classic. This one has its own perverse psycho-sexual horror and unique sense of mood suggested in dreamy visuals designed by Bernardo Bertolucci's former art director, Ferdinando Scarfiotti. ("The most important man in the credits" says Schrader in his DVD commentary track.) Kinski is the nervous virgin who comes "home" to the brother she's never met (McDowell, who appropriately swaggers like a cat even in human form) in New Orleans and discovers the legacy of their bloodline. The whole "cat people" mythology doesn't make any logical sense, but it sure looks good in surreal flashbacks seeped in dream colors. Schrader, working from a script by Alan Ormsby, forgoes all the ambiguity of the original for an orgy of style and blasts of sex and death wrapped up in one another. Giorgio Moroder's score is as elegant and sexy as the visuals. —*S. A.*

FOREVER MINE L: DIRECTORS/SCHRADER, PAUL (1999) 115M D: Paul Schrader. *Ray Liotta, Vincent Laresca, Gretchen Mol, Joesph Fiennes.* Schrader's tribute to classic Hollywood melodrama and romantic film noir proved just too emotionally lush for modern Hollywood to gamble on a theatrical release. Too bad. While it's hardly as tight or as psychologically rich as his best work, there's an emotional intensity and purity to the film that recalls the romance of nineteenth-century epics. Fiennes is a marvelously haunted hero and Mol could have stepped out of a WWII pinup, but

Liotta feels underbaked as the workaholic councilman turned corrupt politico with a vicious streak. Shot in glowing colors and scored by Angelo Badalamenti in a darkly romantic key that recalls the classic age, it really captures the romantic abandon and intensity of the great Universal soaps of the fifties. —*S. A.*

HARDCORE L: DIRECTORS/SCHRADER, PAUL (1979) 109M D: Paul Schrader. *Leonard Gaines, George C. Scott, Dick Sargent, Season Hubley, Peter Boyle.* Taxi Driver, schmaxi driver! Scott is a bitter rectangle of blazing righteous fury in Schrader's true masterpiece of moral vengeance. Scott brilliantly portrays a Calvinist widower whose only child disappears on a church road trip. Several weeks later, smirking hired detective Boyle screens the grieving father a reel of a new porn film starring his adolescent daughter. Denouncing God and sanity, Scott tears off to Los Angeles to retrieve his sullied offspring at any cost, eventually recruiting a prostitute sidekick to aid him in his search. Scenes of Scott infiltrating the skin trade in a polyester shirt and fake mustache are genuinely surreal, but the real star here is the unapologetically graphic brutality and filth pervading nearly every scene. Rarely has a man of such advanced years inflicted so much violence on-screen, and Scott's overall performance absolutely ranks among the finest I've ever seen. —*Z. C.*

MISHIMA: A LIFE IN FOUR CHAPTERS L: DIRECTORS/SCHRADER, PAUL (1985) 121M D: Paul Schrader. *Ken Ogata, Kenji Sawada, Yasosuke Bando.* Mishima: A Life in Four Chapters attempts to paint a portrait of the celebrated and controversial Japanese writer by juxtaposing stylized interpretations of his works against realistic dramatizations of his life. This film interprets Mishima as an artist struggling with his identity in dramatically changing times. He was not only a fanatical supporter of the traditional Japanese Empire but also a renaissance man of art, film, and literature. On top of all this he was also homosexual. The music by Glass assists in expressing the timelessness of this dramatic enigma. —*N. J.*

PATTY HEARST L: DIRECTORS/SCHRADER, PAUL (1988) 108M D: Paul Schrader. *Frances Fisher, Ving Rhames, William Forsythe, Natasha Richardson, Jodi Long.* Schrader's *Patty Hearst* is a riveting account of the abduction and brainwashing of the granddaughter of famed newspaper mogul William Randolph Hearst. Based on Hearst's book *Every Secret Thing*, this film tries to focus on what most papers of the '70s omitted—the precise reasons for why the Symbionese Liberation Army would execute such a daring scheme. But the SLA essentially was just a handful of people run by feuding henchmen. And even though they pulled off the kidnapping and brainwashing, this so-called army began to self-destruct when it came to forcing their hand. Patty Hearst eventually was seen as a wild card, and ever since her guilt and innocence have been hotly debated. —*N.J.*

GENERAL IDI AMIN DADA L: DIRECTORS/SCHROEDER, BARBET (1974) 90M D: Barbet Schroeder.

This is a very curious documentary about Uganda's infamous dictator Idi Amin. The documentary was filmed in 1974 by Schroeder with Amin's full cooperation. The camera follows a friendly Amin to his conferences, speeches, and public apperances. Along the way he espouses his bizarre political beliefs. Amin is primarily known for killing an estimated 300,000 people in Uganda between 1971 and 1979, but here we see him playing accordion and having swim races. —*D.J.*

MORE L: DIRECTORS/SCHROEDER, BARBET (1969) 116M D: Barbet Schroeder.

Mimsy Farmer, Michel Chanderli, Heinz Engelmann, Klaus Grunberg. Schroeder's directorial debut is an odd mix of counterculture holiday and anti-drug drama. Grunberg is a German drifter who begins a life of crime, falls for cool American blond Farmer, and discovers drugs all in the same week. They drift to the Mediterranean where the days of sun and dope lead to a crippling heroine addiction and a twisted reliance on a former Nazi turned drug dealer. Schroeder isn't sure who's at fault, amoral hedonist Farmer or naive obsessive Grunberg, but beneath the naked romps, druggy Pink Floyd score, and deadpan bursts of languid narration is a startlingly conservative view of the European counterculture. —*S.A.*

OUR LADY OF THE ASSASSINS L: DIRECTORS/SCHROEDER, BARBET (2000) 98M D: Barbet Schroeder.

Manuel Busquets, German Jaramillo, Anderson Ballesteros, Juan David Restrepo. Schroeder's grim look at life on the streets in Medellín, Colombia, offers a portrait of violence and poverty so rampant it makes gang-banger films from New York slums look positively utopian. This story of a jaded gay writer who ends a thirty-year exile and returns home to Colombia ("To die," he tells his friends) and his troubling but often tender relationship with a violent street kid is intense and unsettling. Jaramillo's hypocritical writer is hardly a hero; his lip service about nonviolence is undercut by his verbal abuse and his world-weary cynicism borders on misanthropic intolerance. Ballesteros (as his young lover) is not so much a rebel without a cause as a gun-toting hustler without a future, part naive teenager, part hardened veteran of drug-cartel-dominated war-zone streets of Medellín. Shot on DV (Digital Video), it has the look of an especially handsome TV movie: carefully lit, artfully composed, vivid and sharp, giving a heightened realism to the chaotic mix of crowded, clogged streets, quiet churches, and violence that explodes with as little as an insult. Adapted from the novel by Fernando Vallejo. —*S.A.*

AFTER HOURS L: DIRECTORS/SCORSESE, MARTIN (1985) 97M D: Martin Scorsese.

Linda Fiorentino, Tommy Chong, Griffin Dunne, Rosanna Arquette, Verna Bloom. This is a strangely surreal film depicting one night in the life of a young man who, in search of diversion, finds himself in a loopy maze of Escher-like proportions. It all starts when Paul Hackett (Dunne) bumps into a beautiful young lady (Arquette) at a café very late one night in New York. He takes her up on an invitation to her apartment but winds up learning some uncomfortable things about her and her strange roommate. He decides to pick up and leave, but every time he tries to do so, a strange Murphy's Law takes hold and he is unable to escape. Consequently he finds himself continually meeting the same strange people and a growing number of even stranger acquaintances. His empathy for the characters in this mad menagerie wears thin, especially by the time he is fingered by an irate ice-cream truck driver and chased by a vigilante mob. Brilliant casting and tight direction make this curiosity worth watching several times. —*N.J.*

AGE OF INNOCENCE, THE L: DIRECTORS/SCORSESE, MARTIN (1993) 138M D: Martin Scorsese.

Daniel Day-Lewis, Michelle Pfeiffer, Winona Ryder, Richard E. Grant, Joanne Woodward, Geraldine Chaplin. No director making films today finds as much excitement in sheer cinema as Scorsese, and this foray into Merchant-Ivory territory is no exception. From the opening sequence, a social tour of nineteenth-century New York society and manners that recalls both Orson Welles's *The Magnificent Ambersons* and his own *GoodFellas*, through the sheer restrained beauty of Scorsese's portrait of repressed desires under elegant fronts and the possibility of freedom fleetingly glimpsed in the cracks of individual masks, this is an exhilaratingly cinematic work. Day-Lewis is impeccable as the social, straight-arrow lawyer whose carefully plotted career and marriage are suddenly thrown into doubt by an affair of the heart—something for which this rigid, intellectual man is unprepared. Pfeiffer is both fragile and hardened as the "compromised" woman who dares upset convention in the name of personal freedom. Scorsese defied expectations with his mixture of restraint and bravura, always reaching for the cinematic expression of the internal conflicts that plague his characters, and if he stumbles in places he soars in others and makes this his most poignant film ever. —*S.A.*

ALICE DOESN'T LIVE HERE ANYMORE L: DIRECTORS/SCORSESE, MARTIN (1974) 113M D: Martin Scorsese.

Ellen Burstyn, Harvey Keitel, Alfred Lutter, Kris Kristofferson, Diane Ladd. Always riffing on something, Scorsese here decided to take on the classic Hollywood "woman's picture," casting Burstyn as newly widowed Alice Hyatt, forced by circumstance and gusto to seek a new life for herself and her son Tommy. Closer to his previous effort (*Mean Streets*) than one might think, this film is really all about making choices and taking responsibility; all things we watch Alice do with varying degrees of success. Kristofferson and Keitel play the men who tenuously enter in and out of Alice's life, and Ladd earned an Oscar playing Alice's coworker, Flo. Still a vital, charming effort from Scorsese and company thirty years later. —*M. S.*

BOXCAR BERTHA L: DIRECTORS/SCORSESE, MARTIN (1972) 88M D: Martin Scorsese. *Barry Primus, Victor Argo, John Carradine, Bernie Casey, David Carradine, Barbara Hershey.* Hershey is the title character in this Depression-era drama about a young woman who becomes a fugitive along with a union leader (David Carradine) on the run from railroad magnates. This mix of true story and exploitation drama was Scorsese's second feature (after his student indie, *Who's That Knocking at My Door*), a straight work-for-hire job for AIP's Roger Corman. It will never be mistaken for a forgotten Scorsese masterpiece (the rebellious spirit and social message behind the sex and violence is more Corman than Scorsese), but it's a key film in his oeuvre nonetheless: his audition for Hollywood, and he passes with high marks. *Boxcar Bertha* is a successful exercise in storytelling, an energetic, fast-paced exploitation picture with evocative music, scruffy, stylish photography, and solid performances. His follow-up picture was the jittery, passionate streetwise study *Mean Streets.* —*S. A*

BRINGING OUT THE DEAD L: DIRECTORS/SCORSESE, MARTIN (1999) 121M D: Martin Scorsese. *Ving Rhames, Tom Sizemore, John Abrahams, John Goodman, Nicolas Cage, Patricia Arquette.* Bringing Out the Dead is a beautiful, if ultimately unfulfilling, ode to suffering and redemption in New York City. Collaborating with screenwriter Paul Schrader for the first time since 1988's *The Last Temptation of Christ*, Scorsese's adaptation of Joe Connelly's semi-autobiographical novel promised to be a sort of *Taxi Driver* set in an ambulance. Of course, any film would be hard pressed to match the sheer visceral force and raw brilliance of *Taxi Driver*, and Scorsese wisely steers clear of potential parallels between the two. *Bringing Out the Dead* has a look all its own, and a main character, Frank Pierce (Cage), who deals with the the NYC nightlife in a vastly different manner than *Taxi's* Travis Bickle. The film, though, ultimately just is not at the same level. A victim of high expectations and an overreaching grasp, it is not a bad film, but neither is it a great one. —*C. P*

CAPE FEAR L: DIRECTORS/SCORSESE, MARTIN (1991) 128M D: Martin Scorsese. *Joe Don Baker, Juliette Lewis, Jessica Lange, Nick Nolte, Robert De Niro.* Scorsese did something new in remaking the 1961 film *Cape Fear*. He had Elmer Bernstein restore Bernard Herrmann's score for the original movie and recorded it with modern sound equipment, thus capturing much of the unrelenting spirit of the original film. Add to that the acting of De Niro, who plays a psychopathic ex-con who stalks his former defense attorney (Nolte), and a great supporting cast (complete with cameos by Robert Mitchum and Gregory Peck, who played the leads in the original film), and you end up with a very powerful and unique remake. Scorsese reaches for deeper and more mature themes in this version, making De Niro's character even more despicable than the ex-con of the first film. —*N. J.*

CASINO L: DIRECTORS/SCORSESE, MARTIN (1995) 179M D: Martin Scorsese. *Sharon Stone, Robert De Niro, Don Rickles, James Woods, Joe Pesci.* Accounting for how the mob lost its stranglehold on Las Vegas, Scorsese's *Casino* is an eye-opening portrayal of casino manager Sam "Ace" Rothstein (De Niro). Rothstein has an out-of-control wife (Stone) and an old friend, Nicky (Pesci), who is new to town and impatient for his slice of the money pie, often stepping on toes. While casino patrons are winning and losing large sums, casino owners gamble loosely with such stakes as limitless wealth or a small hole in the desert. Rothstein excels within this tense environment, until local politics catch up with him and his wife and his friends pull him down, spelling the beginning of the end of the mob in Las Vegas. As the final part of Scorsese's underworld crime trilogy (preceded by *Mean Streets* and *GoodFellas*), *Casino* is just as nasty as its predecessors. —*N. J.*

COLOR OF MONEY, THE L: DIRECTORS/SCORSESE, MARTIN (1986) 118M D: Martin Scorsese. *Forest Whitaker, Tom Cruise, Mary Elizabeth Mastrantonio, Helen Shaver, John Turturro, Paul Newman.* In this sequel to the 1961 film *The Hustler*, Newman returns as a much older Eddie Felson. Having retired from shooting pool, he happens across a young, headstrong pool shark named Vincent (Cruise). Eddie sees a little bit of himself in this misdirected fellow and over time decides to take it upon himself to show him all the tricks of the trade. Their partnership eventually brings them to the much celebrated 9-ball competition. Great acting highlights the personalities behind the game, and great direction makes the game itself bigger than life. —*N. J.*

GANGS OF NEW YORK L: DIRECTORS/SCORSESE, MARTIN (2002) 166M D: Martin Scorsese. *Leonardo Dicaprio, Daniel Day-Lewis, Cameron Diaz, John C. Reilly, Jim Broadbent.* Gangs of New York supposedly stars DiCaprio, but the real star is Day-Lewis, whom Scorsese courted for the role of Bill the Butcher. The plot finds DiCaprio seeking revenge on Day-Lewis, who killed his father (Liam Neeson) years before. The reason to watch is the rollicking, enthusiastic, and epic portrayal of New York and the people who populated it during the Civil War. Outfitted in a top hat and glass eye and boasting an accent culled from a rare wax recording of Walt Whitman, Day-Lewis rules the film as effectively as his character rules the Five Points section of New York. His performance is so magnetic it virtually drowns out fine work by the supporting cast (including Diaz as a pickpocket who falls for DiCaprio) and almost dwarfs the extensive, expensive sets. —*T. P.*

GOODFELLAS L: DIRECTORS/SCORSESE, MARTIN (1990) 146M D: Martin Scorsese. *Robert De Niro, Joe Pesci, Ray Liotta, Lorraine Bracco, Paul Sorvino.* Based on the life story of mobster Henry Hill, *GoodFellas* accounts for the rise and fall of a young man (Liotta) within the society of organized crime. Scorsese's photography and unique sense of storytelling goes far in depicting the nature of such a tight-knit society, where gangster hierarchy and the code of ethics are clearly defined. Nasty violence punctuates this film at almost random intervals as the gangster world keeps itself in check. The introduction of drugs as a viable source of profit for organized crime shifts this film dramatically toward the end. As the protagonist starts selling and using drugs against the wishes of the mob he finds himself frantically avoiding cops and criminals at the same time. In the end he fizzles out, joining the Witness Protection Program as the criminal society crumbles beneath him. —*N. J.*

KING OF COMEDY, THE L: DIRECTORS/SCORSESE, MARTIN (1983) 101M D: Martin Scorsese. *Robert De Niro, Sandra Bernhard, Jerry Lewis.* Following the massive critical success of *Raging Bull*, Scorsese and De Niro teamed up yet again for this bizarre, disturbing black comedy. *The King of Comedy* is a difficult film to watch (think *Taxi Driver* played like a comedy). De Niro plays awkward, aspiring comedian and would-be, talk-show host Rupert Pupkin, a sad little man with dreams that exceed his talent. Unable to break into showbiz in any conventional manner, he takes matters into his own hands—by kidnapping a popular late-night talk-show host (Lewis) and holding him hostage. A horrible failure upon its original release, it has managed to grow in stature—and deservedly so—in the two decades since it first reared its rather strange head. —*C. P.*

KUNDUN L: DIRECTORS/SCORSESE, MARTIN (1997) 134M D: Martin Scorsese. *Gyurme Tethong, Robert Lin, Tencho Gyalpo, Tsewang Migyur Khangsar, Tanzin Thuthob Tsarong.* This true-life story about the Dalai Lama has an excellent cast of Tibetan actors. The film begins with a search for the newborn Dalai Lama. (Tibetan Buddhists believe in reincarnation and that their spiritual and political leader returns to them as a child after he dies.) Once he is found, the fourteenth Dalai Lama is brought up in the monastery through deeply troubled times, as Red China sets out to invade Tibet. The nation's very young leader tries negotiating with Chairman Mao Tse-tung, but to no avail. Prior to China's occupation, the Dalai Lama flees to

India, where he remains beyond China's control while hoping to return to his homeland. This film is both stunningly beautiful and thoroughly educational, and the music by Glass fits the subject and mood extremely well. —*N. J.*

LAST TEMPTATION OF CHRIST, THE L: DIRECTORS/ SCORSESE, MARTIN (1988) 163M D: Martin Scorsese. *Harry Dean Stanton, David Bowie, Verna Bloom, Willem Dafoe, Harvey Keitel, Barbara Hershey, Andre Gregory.* Scorsese's most personal (and controversial) film examines the power of faith. Scorsese and screenwriter Paul Schrader bring Nikos Kazantzaki's novel to life to examine the conflicts between Jesus the man and Christ the God and the idea that the Christ was both God and man. In many ways it is also Scorsese's own spiritual journey; he works out his own spiritual conflicts through this very human Christ (Dafoe) and passionate, sympathetic Judas (Keitel). The film brings the Christian myth to earth with full-blooded characters (who speak in American street vernacular in an attempt to give the ancient story a connection to contemporary audiences) and gives Christ's ultimate sacrifice a mortal, primal dimension. Shot in the empty, open Moroccan desert, Scorsese's visuals are at their most subdued, given a simple beauty by Michael Ballhaus's cinematography, while Peter Gabriel's percussive score drives the drama with an insistent beat. Hershey costars as Mary Magdalene. —*S. A.*

MEAN STREETS L: DIRECTORS/SCORSESE, MARTIN (1973) 110M D: Martin Scorsese. *Harvey Keitel, Robert De Niro.* Never again did Scorsese, De Niro, or Keitel pack this much vitality into such a tight little film as *Mean Streets.* It all started here, and they went for broke. The tracking shots, De Niro's powder-keg personality, Keitel's intense yet compromised moral quest; all these little things were born in a movie camera in Little Italy in 1973, and still resonate today throughout American cinema. —*M. S.*

NEW YORK, NEW YORK L: DIRECTORS/SCORSESE, MARTIN (1977) 163M D: Martin Scorsese. *Mary Kay Place, Liza Minnelli, Barry Primus, Robert De Niro, Lionel Stander.* In this grand scale, big-band musical, De Niro plays a saxophonist and Minnelli a singer who fall in love despite their different backgrounds. Their tenuous relationship doesn't last, however, as they become rivals, artistically and professionally. Consequently the music they perform together has a distinctly different meaning for these two characters, including "You Brought a New Kind of Love to Me," "I'm Getting Sentimental Over You," "But the World Goes 'Round," and "Avalon." Impeccable musical performances, fine acting, and keen direction put this on par with some of the great musicals of the cinema. —*N. J.*

Martin Scorsese

Martin Scorsese is a brilliant yet unassuming director who proves that in America today, a filmmaker can be successful through perseverance, enthusiasm, and lots of friends—and an endless knowledge of film and film history doesn't hurt either.

Scorsese essentially began as a student of cinema. His first film was *Who's That Knocking at My Door?* (1968), which was actor Harvey Keitel's first film as well. This somewhat autobiographical story of Italian American life foreshadows many of the concepts and perspectives Scorsese would develop throughout his career. Scorsese

was also hired as an editor for the musical documentary *Woodstock* in 1969–70. This experience helped him develop not only a greater knack for editing but also a perspective and sensitivity for music that many young film directors lack.

Mean Streets (1973) was the first of his many films on Italian American crime. In fact, with the films *GoodFellas* (1990) and *Casino* (1995), he established a remarkable trilogy of films about organized crime across America.

In *Taxi Driver* (1976), Scorsese created a vivid cinematic portrait of a perfectly lonely yet highly imperfect hero. (Unfortunately, this particular portrait was so successful that it inspired a mentally unbalanced man

PERSONAL JOURNEY WITH MARTIN SCORSESE THROUGH AMERICAN MOVIES, A L: DIRECTORS/ SCORSESE, MARTIN (1998) 226M D: Martin Scorsese. This British-produced documentary is as idiosyncratic a text on American cinema as there is, but therein lies its strength and charm. Scorsese, cowriter and codirector as well as host and narrator, uses his own love of American cinema to guide his journey, featuring his favorite directors to illustrate his own unique groupings of film artists: Storytellers (John Ford, Raoul Walsh), Illusionists (F. W. Murnau, Frank Borzage), Smugglers (Douglas Sirk, Sam Fuller), and Iconoclasts (Orson Welles, Stanley Kubrick). Full of film clips (with Scorsese's commentary) and interviews with major directors (many of them archival), this is a genuinely personal journey, a stroll with Scorsese through classical Hollywood and wonderful films and filmmakers through the years. His personal remembrances and excitement bring an immediacy to the films and provide a window on history. Made as part of the BFI's "A Century of Cinema" celebration, Scorsese overshot his assigned target length of 52 minutes by quite a distance: the three-part production runs just under four hours (and what a way to spend an evening!). —S.A.

RAGING BULL L: DIRECTORS/SCORSESE, MARTIN (1980) 128M D: Martin Scorsese. *Joe Pesci, Cathy Moriarty, Frank Vincent, Nicholas Colasanto, Theresa Saldana, Robert De Niro.* In one of the greatest performances of his career, De Niro plays boxer Jake LaMotta in a story of the latter's rise and fall, both in the ring as well as in his per-

sonal life. Moriarty plays his beautiful wife who endures his physical and emotional abuse. Pesci plays LaMotta's always supportive brother who picks up the broken pieces of Jake's life. This delicate balance lasts just long enough for Jake to win the championship. After that, everything begins to unravel. The boxing scenes are shockingly intense, and the brilliant black and white photography heighten the effect. De Niro actually packed on an unhealthy amount of weight in order to played the aged boxer. The actual Jake LaMotta served as consultant for the making of this gruelingly insightful film. —N.J.

TAXI DRIVER L: DIRECTORS/SCORSESE, MARTIN (1976) 112M D: Martin Scorsese. *Harvey Keitel, Cybill Shepherd, Robert De Niro, Jodie Foster.* De Niro plays Travis Bickle, a half-mad taxi driver in New York who provides a rolling narrative on his existential view of life and the city, all to a haunting Bernard Herrmann score. Travis's attention becomes riveted to a beautiful woman (Shepherd) who happens to work for the election campaign of a prominent politician. A few awkward dates between them show how incompatible they are, but the creepy antihero simply doesn't get it. Meanwhile, he becomes obsessed with trying to save a child prostitute (Foster) from her pimp (Keitel). Once Travis is rudely dumped by Shepherd, his need to accomplish some kind of good in this world leads him to violence. This atmospheric film allegedly inspired John Hinkley Jr. to stalk Foster, leading to his assassination attempt on President Ronald Reagan. —N.J.

to try to assassinate President Reagan in an effort to "impress" actress Jodie Foster, who plays a prostitute in the film.) Scorsese's lonely and imperfect protagonist seems to resurface in such films as *Raging Bull* (1980), *King of Comedy* (1982), and Scorsese's highly criticized, Catholic-leaning film *The Last Temptation of Christ* (1988).

Yet another aspect of Scorsese's dramatic sense can be seen in *Alice Doesn't Live Here Anymore* (1974). This film is all about displacement, as even its title suggests. The story of the physical and often permanent alienation of a protagonist from her place in the world was actually begun in Scorsese's lesser-known *Boxcar Bertha* (1972) and continues in *Alice*, which concerns the displacement of a widow with a child who starts a diner in Phoenix. Later Scorsese films sharing this theme include *After Hours* (1985);

The Color of Money (1986), his sequel to *The Hustler*; *The Age of Innocence* (1993), which transports the theme of *Alice Doesn't Live Here Anymore* to the nineteenth century; and *Kundun* (1997), which portrays the displacement of the Dalai Lama.

An important element in Scorsese's filmmaking is his love of music, which is conveyed not least through *Woodstock* but also in *New York, New York* (1977) and *The Last Waltz* (1978), a documentary about the rock group The Band.

It's impossible to predict what Scorsese may do next—perhaps return to a largely musical form, since he has done relatively few such films. Whatever he chooses, it is sure to merit, like most of his other work, repeated viewings in order to fully appreciate this accomplished director's vision.

—*Nathan Jensen*

ALIEN L: DIRECTORS/SCOTT, RIDLEY (1979) 117M D: Ridley Scott. *Yaphet Kotto, Veronica Cartwright, Ian Holm, Tom Skerritt, Sigourney Weaver, Harry Dean Stanton.* This is where it all began....*Alien* didn't come out of a vacuum though. Some of the ideas had been used before in a few early sci-fi films; some were successful, some less so. What makes this film work is the combination of the feeling of a haunted house in deep space and the terror of being stalked by an unknown enemy. This psychological thriller created a tension rarely seen in horror films. The cast was extremely believable, too; instead of an orderly clean ship and crew, one sees a disheveled, class-conscience group of people just trying to do their jobs, get paid, and get home in one piece. Add Scott's brilliant pick of Swiss Surrealist painter H. R. Giger as the creature's designer, and you have a match made in the depths of a pure archetypal hell. This film launched a franchise that has had its ups and downs, but to experience the essence of pure alien terror, I suggest going with the genesis. —*B. W.*

BLADE RUNNER (DIRECTORS CUT) L: DIRECTORS/SCOTT, RIDLEY (1982) 117M D: Ridley Scott. *Daryl Hannah, Harrison Ford, M. Emmet Walsh, Rutger Hauer, Sean Young, Edward James Olmos.* The world Scott has created here is haunting and bleak. The plot revolves around a group of androidlike replicants who rebel against their human creators, looking for extended life after becoming conscious of their own pre-programmed mortality. What is memory, what is truth, whose truth is your truth? Do machines, androids, robots of the

future deserve the same rights as humans? In general, we already treat animals as objects to be exploited, consumed, and discarded; will we do the same to the A.I. we construct in the future? Scott does an amazing job adapting Philip K. Dick's original story, albeit with major changes. Ford plays Deckard, a classic noir detective assigned to terminate the rogue replicants. Scott's director's cut omits the obvious narrative voice-over from the Hollywoodized version, adds slightly greater detail to the romance between Rachel (Young) and Deckard, and includes the unicorn dream-scene suggesting that Deckard may be more human than human. Hauer's quote at the end of the film sums up the hopelessness of the replicants plight, "All these moments will be lost in time, like tears in rain. . . time to die." —*B. W.*

GLADIATOR L: DIRECTORS/SCOTT, RIDLEY (2000) 154M D: Ridley Scott. *Richard Harris, Derek Jacobi, Oliver Reed, Connie Nielsen, Russell Crowe, Joaquin Phoenix.* I cannot argue with anyone's emotional response to this movie about a would-be emperor turned slave who kills a bunch of people in gladiatorial combat until he can start a revolution and then die tragically and make everyone sad because he's played by ruggedly handsome Crowe. But I really can't understand all the hoopla, let alone the Best Picture Oscar. Sure it's a decent enough mythic story arc, it brings back a genre we haven't seen for a while, and some of the digital recreations of historical detail are impressive. But then you could say all those things about *The Mummy* and nobody tried to claim that was a classic for the ages. Where this film suffers most is in the place it could most reasonably be expected to excel: the gladiator battles. They are shot with shaky cameras and lots of close-ups, leaving the viewer confused and uninvolved. —B. T.

LEGEND L: DIRECTORS/SCOTT, RIDLEY (1986) 89M D: Ridley Scott. *Mia Sara, Tim Curry, David Bennent, Billy Barty, Tom Cruise.* This is one of those films that exists only as a shadow of what was intended. It's difficult to say what the film's planned running time was supposed to be (the recent director's cut runs nearly two hours), yet for a variety of reasons the film was cut down to a mere 89 minutes (other versions are also floating around). Jerry Goldsmith's score was largely replaced with the music of Tomita. What remains is a visually stunning film with a simple story of good and evil—evil being the Prince of Darkness (Curry) who tries nabbing an innocent girl (Sara) over the intervention of a boy who loves her (Cruise). Try to find the director's cut, or at least the longest cut available. The images of this incredible fantasy will be sure to stay with you. —N. J.

BEGUILED, THE L: DIRECTORS/SIEGEL, DON (1971) 109M D: Don Siegel. *Geraldine Page, Jo Ann Harris, Clint Eastwood, Elizabeth Hartman.* Eastwood plays a badly wounded Union soldier in the Civil War taken in and cared for by a small Southern school for girls. The head of this school, played by Geraldine Page, hides him from Confederate soldiers and the Yankee quickly discovers the reason: she has a crush on him. Then again, so do all the women old enough to entertain such feelings. As the wounded soldier recuperates, he begins getting up at night and sleeping around in different rooms. But this only stirs up all sorts of jealousies, and eventually the jilted headmistress decides she needs to perform a hasty operation on him. And it all gets worse from there! Stunningly directed and excellently performed, this film amply shows that a very young Eastwood doesn't always have to be typecast as a vigilante gunslinger. —N. J.

CHARLEY VARRICK L: DIRECTORS/SIEGEL, DON (1973) 111M D: Don Siegel. *Joe Don Baker, Sheree North, John Vernon, Andy Robinson, Walter Matthau, Jacqueline Scott.* Siegel's best movie was underrated when it came out and is now vaguely written off as simply a Matthau vehicle. Wrong, wrong, wrong. Clean, fascinatingly and unfussily detailed, beautifully paced, *Charley Varrick* is a model of movie craftsmanship—the culmination of a filmmaking career that began thirty years earlier in the montage department at Warners (*Casablanca, The Roaring Twenties, Gentleman Jim,* et al.). The first quarter-hour, the buildup to and grenade-like misfire of a bank holdup in a sleepy Southwest town, never misses a beat, and the fallout from the crime affords ample room for great character work by an exceptional cast.

It may or may not be significant that Matthau's "last of the independents" resembles Siegel in appearance: rumpled, crumpled, consummately sly. Certainly Matthau turns in an exemplary Siegel performance, harkening back to the dour sheriff of *Lonely Are the Brave* and similar inspired supporting roles that endeared him to moviegoers in the early '60s. Among the sharp cast are North (gorgeously past her starlet prime and even more watchable as a character actress), Scott (wonderfully subtle as Varrick's wife), and especially Baker as a Stetsoned, suit-wearing, pipe-smoking gunman whose most lethal gesture is to smile. —R. T. J.

DIRTY HARRY L: DIRECTORS/SIEGEL, DON (1971) 103M D: Don Siegel. *Clint Eastwood, Harry Guardino, Reni Santoni, John Vernon, Andrew Robinson, John Larch.* The collaboration of Siegel and Eastwood (including *Coogan's Bluff, Two Mules for Sister Sarah,* and *The Beguiled*) eventually yielded an enduring character worthy of many sequels. In this, the first *Dirty Harry* film, hard-nosed San Francisco cop Harry Callahan is given a new partner, a subplot most of the sequels have in common. This new partner learns the hard way how this cop got his nickname. Together they investigate a serial killer who sends cryptic letters to the precinct. Harry eventually gets his man, but not without stepping on a lot of toes and resorting to tactics more befitting a vigilante than a police officer. —N. J.

INVASION OF THE BODY SNATCHERS (1956) L: DIRECTORS/SIEGEL, DON (1956) 80M D: Don Siegel. *Dana Wynter, Carolyn Jones, Jean Willes, Kevin McCarthy, Larry Gates, King Donovan.* It's not at all surprising that after the McCarthy era, Hollywood would echo themes of conformity and paranoia. Hence, *The Red Planet, I Married a Monster from Outer Space,* and *The Blob* were all produced in this era. *Invasion of the Body Snatchers* was in many ways just one of many, yet the way it dealt with issues of allegiances and insurgency was as shocking as it was familiar. In this film, alien beings secretly descend to Earth and assume the form of the humans they destroy. In this way a whole society can be conquered by stealth and a new intelligence put in its place. Similar themes were taken on in the '70s, most notably the 1978 remake of this film and *The Stepford Wives.* —N. J.

KILLERS, THE (1964) L: DIRECTORS/SIEGEL, DON (1964) 95M D: Don Siegel. *John Cassavetes, Ronald Reagan, Clu Gulager, Lee Marvin, Angie Dickinson, Norman Fell.* Reagan as the bad guy? In 1962 Reagan had changed his political party from Democrat to Republican. Before he became popular with Republicans for his involvement in the California Goldwater committee, he took the advice of his agent and appeared as the antagonist in this suspenseful Siegel film. Marvin plays a hired gun who assassinates Cassavetes at the beginning of the film. But the hit didn't seem quite right to him—the marked man was expecting it and didn't even try to run. Suspecting he was set up to kill an innocent man, Marvin figures he'll get to the bottom of it all by following the money. Based on a Hemingway story, this film is fantastically violent and suspenseful. —*N.J.*

CRIMSON PIRATE, THE L: DIRECTORS/SIODMAK, ROBERT (1952) 105M D: Robert Siodmak. *Burt Lancaster, Eva Bartok, Nick Cravat, Leslie Bradley.* Lancaster puts tongue in cheek and grins his way through the greatest comic swashbuckler ever made. He puts his acrobatic talents to use in a flamboyant performance and his diminutive circus buddy Cravat makes his second appearance as a mute sidekick, miming conversations like a clown. The tale involves a beautiful woman (Bartok), a corrupt royal governor (Bradley), and kooky scientist whose inventions give the peasants a modern armory for their revolution. But really, this about Lancaster in action. Swinging from mast to mast, leaping and somersaulting through one scrap after another, and playing the high-seas con man with glee, Lancaster is bigger than life and loving it, a Caribbean pirate king as colorful as the title suggests. —*S.A.*

KILLERS, THE L: DIRECTORS/SIODMAK, ROBERT (1946) 103M D: Robert Siodmak. *Burt Lancaster, Sam Levene, Albert Dekker, Edmond O'Brien, Ava Gardner.* Lancaster smolders his way onto the screen in his film debut as the brooding, vulnerable Swede, awaiting his execution with doomed resignation. Gardner shed her ingénue image to play a slinky sexpot with a heart of ice. Neither of them are actually very good—Lancaster is rather callow and Gardner is a viper without venom—but they don't need to be. The camera loves them, every curve on their bodies, every shadow on their faces. It turns their images into icons: the wounded romantic with a beefcake build and the temptress pulling the heartstrings of innocents merely by staring up from under those long lashes in a calculated nonchalance. The first fifteen minutes may be the most faithful Hemingway adaptation ever put on screen, but after that it's pure Hollywood invention at its best, a web of deceit and double crosses in the shadow world of noir. It's Siodmak's finest film and a model film noir. —*S.A.*

SPIRAL STAIRCASE, THE L: DIRECTORS/SIODMAK, ROBERT (1946) 83M D: Robert Siodmak. *Elsa Lanchester, Sara Allgood, Kent Smith, Ethel Barrymore, Dorothy McGuire, George Brent.* This film starts out with a rather harrowing murder in a small town, stirring up some fright in a large house where Helen Capel (McGuire) is a servant. Helen is mute, a condition she developed after seeing her parents burn in a fire. Barrymore plays Mrs. Warren, the ailing matriarch who takes a liking to her and tells her to leave the house (despite a wicked thunderstorm) because she knows the mur-

derer must be somebody under her own roof. But Helen has fallen in love with a young doctor who promised to take her away for tests. Will he return in time to save her from this worsening situation? Based on the novel *Someone Must Watch* by Ethel Lina White, this film will likely keep you on the edge of your seat. —*N.J.*

ALL I DESIRE L: DIRECTORS/SIRK, DOUGLAS (1953) 79M D: Douglas Sirk. *Maureen O'Sullivan, Barbara Stanwick, Richard Carlson.* Naomi Murdoch (Stanwyck) abandoned her husband and children to make it big as an actress. Returning home years later for her daughter's performance in a school play, she has much to own up to. Despite what she's let her small-town family believe, her fame as an actress was slight and brief. She's surprised to find that she rather likes being back home, but her past choices continually haunt the possibility of a present happiness with her family. *All I Desire* covers familiar Sirk terrain as Naomi faces the loneliness of liberty and ambition. —*C.B.*

ALL THAT HEAVEN ALLOWS L: DIRECTORS/SIRK, DOUGLAS (1955) 89M D: Douglas Sirk. *Rock Hudson, Jane Wyman.* Widow Cary Scott (Wyman) wants to date the gardener. Only trouble is, the gardener is none other than semi-bohemian, Thoreau-follower Ron Kirby (Hudson), and the ladies at the country club don't quite approve. Deer, television, and, of course, Hudson all help Wyman decide. But is she too late? Watch and find out. This is a quirky one, best seen in the winter. —*M.S.*

IMITATION OF LIFE L: DIRECTORS/SIRK, DOUGLAS (1959) 125M D: Douglas Sirk. *Robert Alda, Susan Kohner, Sandra Dee, John Gavin, Lana Turner, Juanita Moore, Ned Sparks, Rochelle Hudson, Claudette Colbert, Louise Beavers, Warren William.* The most successful film in the career of Hollywood legend Sirk ostensibly concerns the rise of an ambitious actress on the New York stage (Turner, in a career-reviving role). But it's the story in the shadows, so to speak, that makes this glossy melodrama so memorable and resonant. Kohner plays a light-skinned African-American girl who turns her back on her mother (Moore), who is Turner's loyal, maternal maid, and denies her race to pass for white. Sirk's films are all about surfaces and social masks, and his style—impeccable compositions, portentous angles, gaudy color, and performances that ping-pong between simmering repression and overwrought emotional turbulence—tells the real story. This film plays its themes closer to the surface than his early work, but if it's a weepie you want, this delivers the waterworks. Gavin is Turner's handsome, stolid, and bland cardboard leading man, the equivalent of the Bond girl: an object of desire of the dynamic female hero. Perhaps that, too, explains the tremendous commercial success of Sirk's unique Hollywood soap opera. —*S.A.*

LURED L: DIRECTORS/SIRK, DOUGLAS (1947) 103M D: Douglas Sirk. *Joseph Calleia, George Sanders, Lucille Ball, Charles Coburn, Sir Cedric Hardwicke, Alan Mowbray.* Ball is an American showgirl in London persuaded by Scotland Yard to act as bait to catch a killer. Sirk makes the most of his limited budgets with elegantly drawn set pieces and moody fog-drenched night scenes (this is London after all) in this stylish Victorian melodrama/murder mystery. In his grace he's left out the tension and the terror, replaced with a refreshingly sophisticated mind game. The film clues us in to the real killer and then plays a cat-and-mouse game with both the audience and the target. Sanders is at the top of his form—when the cultured ladies' man finds a worthy romantic adversary in Ball, who simultaneously abandons and encourages him, his smiles register appreciation, sheepish embarrassment, and respect. —*S. A.*

MAGNIFICENT OBSESSION L: DIRECTORS/SIRK, DOUGLAS (1954) 89M D: Douglas Sirk. *Barbara Rush, Agnes Moorehead, Rock Hudson, Jane Wyman, Otto Kruger.* The story concerns a careless auto accident caused by Hudson's character. He inadvertently kills a man and blinds the man's wife (Wyman). Suddenly this unabashed hedonist develops a change in character and goes so far as to become a doctor with the hope of one day being able to restore the woman's sight. One might conclude that this medical pursuit is the "magnificent obsession." But according to Kruger, playing a friend to the protagonist, most of this newfound inspiration is actually generated from a man two thousand years ago who died on a tree. —*N. J.*

SCANDAL IN PARIS, A (AKA **THIEVES' HOLIDAY**) L: DIRECTORS/SIRK, DOUGLAS (1946) 100M D: Douglas Sirk. *George Sanders, Signe Hasso, Carole Landis.* "Only the heartless succeed in crime, as in love," muses suave con man and criminal mastermind Vidocq (Sanders) with mix of bemusement, blasé, and aristocratic poise. Based on the (highly dubious) memoirs of the real-life rascal turned lawman in nineteenth-century Paris (the debonair master criminal works his way up to chief of police of Paris while continuing his life of crime), this immensely entertaining romantic comedy is an early American production for Sirk. His continental wit and playfulness and Sanders' droll delivery and impeccable manners add a knowing wink to the production. The sumptuous sets are cramped but richly dressed with the merest suggestion of a world outside the frame, giving it the feeling of a miniature. The great Eugen Shuftan gave uncredited assistance to the lovely cinematography. —*S. A.*

WRITTEN ON THE WIND L: DIRECTORS/SIRK, DOUGLAS (1956) 99M D: Douglas Sirk., *Rock Hudson, Lauren Bacall, Robert Stack, Dorothy Malone.* Sirk was paradoxically one of the most revered and mis-understood directors from the silver age of the American studio system. A stubbornly caustic artist, Sirk produced and directed films in several genres, all linked by vibrant colors and an almost abrasive flair for melodramatic social criticism. He pulls out all the cinematic stops in this wrenching story of the very, very rich whose lack of morality lead to ruin and death. Stack portrays a tornado of a man, Kyle Hadley, a well-to-do ne'er-do-well bringing about the wreckage of his family's empire through endless carousing and violent fits of brutal jealousy and self-loathing. Joining Stack on his downward spiral is an amazing cast that includes Bacall as his long-suffering wife, the sinful Malone, and Sirk's favorite virtuous everyman, Hudson. The tension between characters becomes so strong that the dialogue is often nearly obscured by gritting teeth and furrowed brows. Lust, hatred, and envy whiz through this film like white-hot bullets. Often considered his masterpiece, Sirk's *Written on the Wind* must be seen to be believed. —*Z. C.*

HE WHO GETS SLAPPED L: DIRECTORS/SJÖSTRÖM, VICTOR (1924) 95M D: Victor Sjöström. *Norma Shearer, John Gilbert, Lon Chaney.* In the silent era, Europe was the home of expressionist adventurism and Hollywood the hallmark of professional gloss. Swedish master Seastrom (nee Sjöström) married the two wonderfully in *He Who Gets Slapped*, an at-times histrionic melodrama inflected by a performance from Chaney that borders on madness. As a scientist betrayed by his benefactor and his wife and ridiculed by the Academy of Science, he sinks into a life of self-abasement as a renowned clown named simply He, whose entire grotesque act is based on humiliation—slapstick boiled down to pure, malevolent abuse—much to the delight of roaring crowds. The film gets sidetracked by an uninspired romance between Shearer and Gilbert (both rather pale next to Chaney's energetic performance) but comes to life in Chaney's scenes, where Sjöström's inventive direction turns the film into a gloriously overblown masterpiece. —*S. A.*

OUTLAW AND HIS WIFE, THE L: DIRECTORS/SJÖSTRÖM, VICTOR (1918) 102M D: Victor Sjöström. *John Ekman, Edith Erastof, Victor Sjöström.* This tragic tale from eighteenth-century Iceland builds in a contrived stage-by-stage fashion like the play it is based on. A runaway convict (Sjöström) finds work with a widowed woman (Erastoff), and when he's exposed the two flee into a life of deprivations in the mountains to be hunted and die. What makes *The Outlaw and His Wife* a supremely powerful early silent film is the key characters' naturalistic acting styles richly performed and shot entirely on location, mostly outdoors. The landscape magnifies their emotions to near cosmic dimensions. —*J. C.*

WIND, THE L: DIRECTORS/SJÖSTRÖM, VICTOR (1928) 74M D: Victor Sjöström. *Lillian Gish, Montague Love, Edward Earle.* Letty (Gish) travels from Virginia to Texas to stay with her cousin Beverly (Earle—despite the name, he's a he). Beverly's jealous wife Cora treats Letty brutally, finally forcing her to marry one of Beverly's hired hands. All the while, an unceasing and fierce wind rages outside. Letty is told that this wind has driven many to madness, and by the film's violent climax the wind (or maybe just the Texas hospitality) has exactly that effect on her. A happy ending was unfortunately tacked on, but it in no way ruins this glorious picture, which some consider Hollywood's greatest silent drama. The video includes a short, informative intro by Gish describing her large role in the movie's conception and the extreme conditions of its production, shot in the scorching Mojave Desert using stationary single-engine airplanes as wind-machines. —*C. B.*

SHOUT, THE L: DIRECTORS/SKOLIMOWSKI, JERRY (1978) 87M D: Jerzy Skolimowski. *Tim Curry, Robert Stephens, Susannah York, John Hurt, Alan Bates.* Hurt plays an organist at a local church who spends plenty of time at home recording a variety of sounds and noises and amplifying them for experimental recordings. One day after church he runs into Bates, who plays a very mysterious man returned from fifteen years in aboriginal Australia. This man proceeds to shock Hurt and York (as Hurt's wife) by telling them about his odd beliefs and experiences. The acoustician would like to hear the aboriginal shout that Bates has learned to perform—the legendary shout that can kill. So the two go to a very distant location and, armed with a pair of earplugs, Hurt listens to Bates. With a curious script and excellent acting, this strange film is oddly compelling and memorable. —*N. J.*

DELLAMORTE DELLAMORE (AKA **CEMETERY MAN**) L: DIRECTORS/SOAVI, MICHELE (1994) 105M D: Michele Soavi. *Rupert Everett, Anna Falchi, François Hadji-Lazaro.* Weaving its haunting spell of dark beauty, this film pulls you into a dreamworld where the differences between the dead and living get less distinguishable by the minute. The film is a dark comedy infused with love, longing, existentialism, and loneliness. Oh yeah, and zombies. It's gorgeous, surreal, unnerving, and ultimately very powerful. Everett is perfect as the undertaker lost in a world where nothing seems to matter, but forced to keep plowing through life anyhow. When the dead begin to return to life, he must send them back to their graves, but he really could care less. The only thing able to stir his meaningless existence is the presence of the beautiful Falchi, whom he begins to obsess over. Imagine a Beckett play rewritten by George Romero with production design from Tim Burton and you'll start to get the picture. This is a film about zombies and killing them

that somehow manages to be poetic. A rare and admirable achievement indeed. —*T. S.*

ERIN BROCKOVICH L: DIRECTORS/SODERBERGH, STEVEN (2000) 131M D: Steven Soderbergh. *Aaron Eckhart, Cherry Jones, Marg Helgenberger, Albert Finney, Julia Roberts.* Based on a true story, Roberts plays the title character, a working-class single mother of three who, despite her lack of a legal education, helped a community win a landmark water-pollution settlement from a gas company. Especially compared to other Soderbergh films, this is a fairly routine, stick-it-to-the-man crowd-pleaser, but the director's camera work and his knack for bringing out the best in Roberts somehow elevate the material. Maybe he should've gotten the best director Oscar for this instead of *Traffic*, because in anyone else's hands it wouldn't have been anything special. —*B. T.*

FULL FRONTAL L: DIRECTORS/SODERBERGH, STEVEN (2002) 101M D: Steven Soderbergh. *Nicky Katt, Mary McCormack, Julia Roberts, David Hyde Pierce, Catherine Keener, Blair Underwood. Full Frontal* is a series of partially improvised vignettes about a group of tangentially connected people in Hollywood. The story involves extramarital affairs, a midlife crisis, an unexpected death, and a really bad one-man show about Hitler. There are lots of amusing celebrity cameos and in-jokes and a thematic interest in the differences between movie reality and real-life reality (including some swipes at the portrayal of black heroes in films, a few costarring Roberts). Soderbergh made this quickie experiment between *Ocean's 11* and *Solaris* using a set of Dogme 95-inspired rules. The actors had to do their own makeup and hair, drive themselves to the set and arrive without entourages, and they did not have trailers or catering. Except for the movie-within-the-movie, the film was shot on handheld digital video with natural lighting, giving it a so-ugly-it's-kind-of-interesting muddiness. It's certainly self-indulgent (how many experimental movies can Hollywood people make about Hollywood people, anyway?), but since it's Soderbergh it's clever and funny enough to make up for that. Definitely not for everyone (or even very many people at all), but worthwhile for Soderbergh fans. —*B. T.*

KAFKA L: DIRECTORS/SODERBERGH, STEVEN (1991) 98M D: Steven Soderbergh. *Jeremy Irons, Theresa Russell, Ian Holm, Alec Guinness, Joel Grey.* This film delves into the fear induced by living in the shadow of a totalitarian system, symbolized by a castle brooding over a claustrophobic city. When one of Kafka's coworkers is murdered he becomes drawn into an underground group of stereotypical anarchists who are responsible for numerous bombings around the city. The group wakes Kafka from his tedious day-to-day routine as an insurance worker subtly dehumanized by his looming bureaucratic boss (Guinness). Most of

Josef von Sternberg

Born Jonas Sternberg in 1894, the eldest child in a poor Orthodox Jewish family in Vienna, Sternberg spent his first seven years in Vienna. He and his family then moved to New York but returned to Vienna after three years. Finally, in 1908, the family moved back to New York for good. After leaving home at seventeen (at which time he adopted the name Josef), he took odd jobs and studied art until he landed a job projecting and repairing film. After a stint editing films in New York and making training films for the Signal Corps in World War I, he apprenticed as an assistant director on a number of productions in the United States and Europe, and added the "von" to his name.

Sternberg made his directorial bow with a low-budget production, *The Salvation Hunters* (1925). The film was not well received by the public, but his attention to mise-en-scène and pictorial beauty brought him to the attention of Charlie Chaplin and MGM. After two troubled MGM productions, he made *A Woman of the Sea* (1926) for Chaplin, who showed it only privately and ultimately destroyed it to claim a tax loss. Sternberg resorted to working as an assistant at Paramount, where he was entrusted to a small gangster picture written by reporter Ben Hecht, *Underworld* (1927). The film's huge

---

the film is shot in black and white, with scenes in the breached castle shot in color. (The contrast works as a metaphor for illuminating the experiments, control, and conspiracies perpetrated against the people of the city.) While not for everyone, I think this is one of Soderbergh's more interesting and overlooked films. —*B. W.*

LIMEY, THE L: DIRECTORS/SODERBERGH, STEVEN (1999) 89M D: Steven Soderbergh. *Peter Fonda, Leslie Ann Warren, Luis Guzmán, Terence Stamp.* Stamp is a cool, cruel cockney thug on the sun-bright streets of LA, one minute disarmingly charming, the next a bulldog with his teeth locked on his latest quarry. Soderbergh weaves the past into the present with flashbacks and voice-overs as if it all exists at once. Perhaps it does in the haunted mind of Stamp's single-minded ex-con as he hunts his daughter's killer. He sets his task to divining the secret that terrifies ex-hippie record executive Fonda, picking up allies like a lost puppy attracts lonely kids. It's an austere, elegant picture, at times so precise and removed it cools Stamp's driving passion, but it's always engaging and at times astounding. The flashbacks are from Ken Loach's 1967 directorial debut *Poor Cow.* —*S. A.*

OCEAN'S ELEVEN L: DIRECTORS/SODERBERGH, STEVEN (2001) 116M D: Steven Soderbergh. *George Clooney, Brad Pitt, Julia Roberts, Andy Garcia, Don Cheadle, Matt Damon.* Soderbergh and his cool cast accomplish what Lewis Milestone couldn't with the Vegas playboy Rat Pack: they swing to the beat of the heist. Clooney is all easy charm as the adorable bad boy who masterminds the impossible ultimate score and Pitt has a smart-alecky rapport with Clooney as his dutiful lieutenant. Their jokey by-play greases the gears of the group's smooth interaction. Soderbergh, handling his own camera, gives the film crisp compositions and keeps it moving with gliding camera work and a wandering eye that easily and elegantly hones in on the essential details of the scene. Yet he somehow fails Julia Roberts: Hollywood's most photogenic star loses her glamour in his lens. Just for the record, the gang is rounded out by Garcia, Gould, Damon, Cheadle (uncredited but unmistakable as a cockney dynamite man), Casey Affleck, Scott Caan, Bernie Mac, Carl Reiner, Eddie Jemison, and Shaobo Qin. —*S. A.*

OUT OF SIGHT L: DIRECTORS/SODERBERGH, STEVEN (1998) 122M D: Steven Soderbergh. *Luis Guzmán, Don Cheadle, Ving Rhames, Jennifer Lopez, George Clooney, Steve Zahn.* Clooney and Lopez give some of their best performances as a fugitive bank robber and a federal marshall who fall in love. Based on the book by Elmore Leonard, this is a funny and upbeat crime story despite the inevitable doom of their relationship. There are many great performances and memorable characters (especially Zahn and Guzmán) but the success of the movie really stands on the great chemistry of the two leads and the Cary Grant-like charm of Clooney. With a great director, script (by Scott Frank), and a funky score (by David Holmes),

success launched Sternberg's long career at Paramount, where he also developed a reputation as a perfectionist and a tyrant on the set.

German star Emil Jannings brought Sternberg to Universum Film A.G. to direct him in that studio's first sound film, *The Blue Angel* (1930). It was a worldwide smash, making a star of Marlene Dietrich, who accompanied Sternberg back to Hollywood. They worked together on six more films through the early 1930s, considered by many critics to be Sternberg's richest period. These lavish, lush films combine ornate set design, delicate lighting, and a battery of scrimlike devices (such as hanging nets, smoke, and cross-hatched bamboo and wooden slats) to create a dense visual style. Critics have charged that Sternberg creates his "visual poetry" at the expense of narrative, and certainly he shows more

concern than do most directors with mood and character, but it is also true that his films consistently explore issues of sexuality and power. In addition, Sternberg creates a unique kind of glamour in his films with Dietrich that has never been replicated by any other director.

Though critically acclaimed today, Sternberg's last three Dietrich films were critical and financial disappointments, and his career never recovered from the disastrous experience of the unfinished *I, Claudius* (described in the documentary *The Epic That Never Was*). Though his films thereafter were few and far between, two independent productions, *The Shanghai Gesture* (1941) and *Anatahan* (1954), are considered among his best. His final years before his death in 1969 were devoted to leisure, teaching (at UCLA), and writing his autobiography.

—Sean Axmaker

---

this is easily one of the best crime movies of the '90s. It's also Soderbergh's most crowd-pleasing movie, more fun than *The Limey* and smarter than *Ocean's Eleven.* —*B. T.*

SCHIZOPOLIS L: DIRECTORS/SODERBERGH, STEVEN (1996) 99M D: Steven Soderbergh. *Mike Malone, Betsy Brantley, Dave Jensen, Steven Soderbergh.* Although Soderbergh had already received an absurd amount of media attention for *Sex, Lies, and Videotape* and more subdued acclaim for films like *King of the Hill, Schizopolis* was the first real sign of his mad brilliance. Soderbergh himself stars in the nonglamourous role of a speech writer for an L. Ron Hubbard-like cult leader. But there isn't really a plot here—it's more a series of strange vignettes and skits loosely applying the theme of communication. A favorite episode involves Soderbergh seeing his doppelganger and following him home. ("I'm having an affair with my own wife!") In some scenes the characters talk complete gibberish, or are dubbed into other languages, or describe their sentences instead of actually speaking them ("bland greeting" instead of "Hello," for example). Then, suddenly, some guy will be running around with no pants on. It took a lot of balls for the designated Future of Independent Cinema to follow up a series of gloomy dramas with this highly intelligent, completely silly, no-budget movie starring himself and his friends. Perhaps what's most surprising about *Schizopolis* is what a great comic actor Soderbergh is. In 2003 he showed off those skills again on the Criterion Edition

director's commentary in which he, completely deadpan, interviews himself and claims that this movie reinvented the language of cinema. —*B. T.*

SOLARIS (2002) L: DIRECTORS/SODERBERGH, STEVEN (2002) 99M D: Steven Soderbergh. *George Clooney, Natascha McElhone, Jeremy Davies.* Perhaps since Tarkovsky's masterpiece *Solaris* is not an original work but is based on Stanislaw Lem's magnificent novel of the same name, the idea of basing another film on it is not such a terrible idea. Tarkovsky certainly left out many elements but added many more, and all was for the better, since his film is one of the greatest science-fiction pictures of all time. Soderbergh's uninspired remake seemed like a bad idea, though, and indeed it was a terrible mistake. Here witness the complete Hollywoodization of a profound story. By leaving out all elements of yearning, spirituality, expanded consciousness, and basically everything that made the original film so inspiring, Soderbergh has stripped it of its soul, if not of its heart. Because indeed it has heart by the bucketload. This *Solaris* has become an unabashed love story revolving around Chris Kelvin (Clooney) and the apparition of his dead wife (McElhone). By absurdly playing up the melodramatic element and leaving out the transcendent qualities, the film is left a limp mess of nothing that has no real purpose, no real aim, no real reason to exist. —*T. S.*

TRAFFIC L: DIRECTORS/SODERBERGH, STEVEN (2000) 147M D: Steven Soderbergh. *Don Cheadle, Catherine Zeta-Jones, Erika Christensen, Benicio del Toro, Topher Grace, Michael Douglas, Luis Guzmán.* Soderbergh tackles the drug trade with startling clarity, turning a complex checkerboard screenplay into a unified piece with color-coded environments to match dramatic temperatures. Taking the viewer from Tijuana to Washington, with side trips to Middle America and border crossings, Soderbergh explores the instability and corruption that make the drug war so futile. Douglas stars as the well-meaning but impotent drug czar, and Zeta-Jones is a pregnant socialite turned lioness, but the heart belongs to Del Toro, a Tijuana cop ambiguous to the final scene, playing the opportunist while hiding his passion and disgust under a mask of indifference. Soderbergh, too, never lets his anger overflow into the film, but his emotional restraint makes this critical portrait of a doomed struggle even more cutting. It's been awhile since such a smart, demanding film has come out of Hollywood. —*S. A.*

HAPPINESS L: DIRECTORS/SOLONDZ, TODD (1998) 139M D: Todd Solondz. *Ben Gazzara, Dylan Baker, Jane Adams, Jared Harris, Philip Seymour Hoffman, Lara Flynn Boyle. Happiness* is brilliantly written and acted but extremely difficult to watch. Joy (Adams) is a thirty-year-old unmarried woman whose relationships are dysfunctional and pathetic at best, which her two sisters and mother are more than happy to tell her. The irony becomes clear as the movie progresses, and we learn that the husband (Baker) of one of the sisters is a pedophile who fantasizes about mass killings, the mother (Louise Lasser) is on the verge of divorce because her husband is just tired of being married, and the other sister (Boyle) is obsessively lusted after by her neighbour (Hoffman). Ultimately, it is anything but happiness lurking below the surface, and every character is so uncomfortably awkward and sad that the film becomes a car wreck from which you want to turn away but somehow cannot. —*J. S.*

STORYTELLING L: DIRECTORS/SOLONDZ, TODD (2001) 88M D: Todd Solondz. *Selma Blair, Leo Fitzpatrick, Robert Wisdom, Paul Giamatti, Mark Webber, John Goodman.* Solondz seems to both defend and question himself in this two-part study divided into "Fiction" (about a writing student's affair with her professor) and "Non-Fiction" (about a documentary filmmaker following a teenage stoner and his family). Filled with the type of cruel characters and uncomfortable situations that are Solondz's trademark, it also brings up a number of questions about this type of work. Is it better to lie and pretend something is OK, or be honest and be a total asshole? How do you discern whether a movie is being sympathetic toward its characters or exploitative of them? Solondz makes this second question more dif-

ficult by including Mike Schank of *American Movie* in a cameo. It doesn't feel as complete as *Happiness* (perhaps because a third story starring James Van der Beek was removed from the film), but it has the same uniquely creepy vision of the world and uses its shock value to provoke thought about questions with no easy answers. —*B. T.*

I'm afraid to tell people I don't like this movie. There are people who love Solondz so aggressively that I usually try anything to avoid the fifteen minutes of "Well, his characters really remind me of myself," or "You really have to be marginalized by society to understand." I didn't think the two stories were tight or complementary enough to be presented within the frame of "Fiction" and "Nonfiction." The first, shorter story, "Fiction," tries to convey the irony of a somewhat unbelievable situation when the non-fiction narrative is presented to an audience that finds it. . . well, unbelievable. The second story explores the exploitation of a confused teenager by an aging filmmaker. Many of the characters were potentially real and endearing, but they were disposed of before they had a chance to become intriguing. There was one highlight— Mike Schank's cameo—and that came at the very beginning of "Nonfiction," so if you make it that far, you've reached the peak. And Lupe Ontiveros, the maid in *Goonies* and in countless other, plays a maid, again. —*J. J.*

WELCOME TO THE DOLLHOUSE L: DIRECTORS/SOLONDZ, TODD (1995) 87M D: Todd Solondz. *Brendan Sexton Jr., Eric Mabius, Heather Matarazzo.* As the working title *Faggots and Retards* suggests, *Welcome to the Dollhouse* is a dark comedy/drama that does an excellent job of showcasing Solondz's characteristic cruel, sarcastic wit. Dawn is an unattractive, nerdy seventh grader teased by kids at school (a situation not helped by the fact that her last name is Wiener) and ignored by her parents in favor of her cute younger sister and supersmart older brother. She can't seem to do anything right. The acting is good, and Dawn is portrayed as a character of whom you would probably make fun yourself. After the first hundred times that Dawn gets shit on, however, the movie starts to become painful to watch, and you find yourself wishing Solondz would cut the girl at least one break. As a man who prefers brutal reality to escapism, however, he draws the movie to an uneventful close. Dawn's life still sucks, and you leave feeling disconcerted. —*J. S.*

A.I.: ARTIFICIAL INTELLIGENCE L: DIRECTORS/SPIELBERG, STEVEN (2001) 145M D: Steven Spielberg. *William Hurt, Frances O'Connor, Jude Law, Haley Joel Osment, .* For years we read about this movie *A.I.* that Kubrick was planning to do now that he felt CGI made it possible, and we tried to imagine what that meant. While everyone else was trying to make dinosaurs and dragons, Kubrick must've been cooking up a way to do something much more interesting. We'll never get to see what Kubrick would've done, because Spielberg ended up writing and directing based on Kubrick's outline, using a real kid (Osment) to play the robot boy David. This strange frankenkubrick film is highly underrated. The first stretch, where a family buys a robot son, then discards it like an old toy when their real son comes home from the hospital, is especially creepy. But my favorite part (and the most Kubrick-esque) is the last act, which skips forward thousands of years to a post-human age where walking liquefied television screens rule the world and poor David still wants his mommy. It's a unique and sometimes awe-inspiring film, and I almost buy the line that it will be better understood and appreciated years from now. —B. T.

CLOSE ENCOUNTERS OF THE THIRD KIND L: DIRECTORS/SPIELBERG, STEVEN (1977) 152M D: Steven Spielberg. *Richard Dreyfus, François Truffaut, Teri Garr, Melinda Dillon.* A very well-crafted science-fiction film from Spielberg which combines his talent for suspense with his yearning for drama. Strange, unexplained phenomena happen to a variety of people in this film, causing select characters to become obsessed with a particular mountain, ultimately resulting in a pilgrimage of these characters to Devil's Tower, Wyoming, where an encounter with benevolent aliens occurs. A very well-chosen cast brings this interesting script to life. Where the suspense is topnotch, the drama at times becomes a bit syrupy, especially by the end. Spielberg expands much more upon such drama in his film *E.T.* five years later. —N. J.

DUEL L: DIRECTORS/SPIELBERG, STEVEN (1971) 90M D: Steven Spielberg. *Dennis Weaver, Lucille Benson, Cary Loftin, Eddie Firestone, Jacqueline Scott.* Even the worst critics of Spielberg would have to admit that this is one of his best films. It is also his first. With very little budget, Spielberg amply proves he is able to manipulate audience fear quite well. Weaver plays a man on a long road trip who is hunted down by a belligerent truck driver—or is it a truck come to life, a la Stephen King? Either way the suspense becomes perfectly palpable as this thriller shifts forward. Spielberg's masterful use of sound and music only heightens the tension and foreshadows his future use of sound to evoke audience emotion. Beyond introducing a celebrated directorial career, this film stands perfectly on its own merits as a spine-tingler. —N. J.

EMPIRE OF THE SUN L: DIRECTORS/SPIELBERG, STEVEN (1987) 153M D: Steven Spielberg. *Christian Bale, John Malkovich.* This beautifully shot, sensitive film concerns the plight of a British boy (Bale), the son of a diplomat in China, who is taken prisoner by the Japanese at the outset of World War II and must live apart from his parents in a prison camp. This adaptation of J. G. Ballard's novel marks Spielberg's return to serious drama.

The acting and script are perfectly captivating, and the photography is spellbinding. However, the pacing and music lack subtlety, and on some occasions ruin the potential effect of the film. Example: When the young protagonist befriends a Japanese boy on the other side of the perimeter fence, they communicate through their own sign language, with the dramatic effect over-exaggerated by John Williams's music. The effect would be much more genuine and intimate if either background noise or simple silence were employed instead. As a master of suspense, though, Spielberg is more comfortable manipulating emotions rather than telling the story in a straightforward manner. All the same, it is a brilliant, if slightly flawed, picture. —N. J.

E.T. THE EXTRA-TERRESTRIAL L: DIRECTORS/SPIELBERG, STEVEN (1982) 115M D: Steven Spielberg. *Robert MacNaughton, Peter Coyote, Dee Wallace Stone, Henry Thomas.* One of the all-time great family films, *E.T.*'s portrait of a broken yet functional family has none of the contrivances of similar films. This family must cope and grow and move on. Spielberg manages warmth and wonder without painting too brightly. He allows rough edges and a real threat and fear without demonizing the scientists seeking E.T.—few family films suggest opposition is anything short of evil. When E.T. must leave, the emotions you feel are earned, not manufactured. Most spectacularly, nothing about the film seems childish or pandering. This is a director in top form. From an FX standpoint, Carlo Rambaldi's creature is one of the most original created for the screen. Although E.T. has been assimilated as another adorable pop-culture icon, the creature is notably homely, perhaps appealing in its resemblance to a grandparent yet far from a soft cuddly. —M. H.

Avoid the touched-up, 121-minute twentieth-anniversary version, though. The digitally altered effects aren't necessarily bad, but you have to draw the line at removing guns from policemen's hands. There are scenes where officers run around with their hands in a rifle position but they're only holding walkie-talkies or flashlights. How stupid does Spielberg think his kids are? —B. T.

INDIANA JONES AND THE LAST CRUSADE L: DIRECTORS/SPIELBERG, STEVEN (1989) 127M D: Steven Spielberg. *River Phoenix, Alison Doody, Sean Connery, Denholm Elliot, John Rhys-Davies, Harrison Ford.* This third entry of the Indiana Jones trilogy is a modest improvement over the second in that it costars Connery as the archaeologist father of Ford's hero. Still, the writing is not much better than for the second film, and the story is absurd and laughable at best. After Indiana Jones and his father reunite, they combine their investigations and soon get captured by Nazis who tie them back-to-back in chairs just like Batman and Robin in old TV shows. After the predictable

escape, more and more adventures occur until a "surprise" arrives at the end. —*N. J.*

INDIANA JONES AND THE TEMPLE OF DOOM L: DIRECTORS/SPIELBERG, STEVEN (1984) 118M D: Steven Spielberg. *Harrison Ford, Kate Capshaw, Ke Huy Quan, Amrish Puri.* Here's a film that seems to prove the rule of thumb that the sequel to a good film is never so good as the first. The Oscar-winning special effects in this movie hold very little value when the dialogue and acting are so painfully bad. The story has Indy drop (literally) into India and onto an evil Kali cult, and wanders with an irritating Capshaw following Ford around, who must maintain a straight face through the awful script. But there's always the special effects that indulge in shock value with no bearing on the story; monkey brains, for instance, eaten from open skulls at a formal Third World dinner party. —*N. J.*

It's true that this film overuses the creepiness and gore *Raiders* employed sparingly and to good effect, and downplays the human qualities that gave the first film its appeal. It's like Lucas and Spielberg decided everyone's favorite part of *Raiders* was the snakes and face-melting scenes, so they quadrupled the gross elements for the sequel. But it isn't as bad as my colleague makes it sound. The script isn't great and Capshaw's character is grating right from the start, but Ford proves he can carry himself with dignity through anything, and the movie delivers just the right amount of adventure and heart-pounding scenes. —*J. K.*

JAWS L: DIRECTORS/SPIELBERG, STEVEN (1975) 120M D: Steven Spielberg. *Roy Scheider, Lorraine Gary, Robert Shaw, Richard Dreyfuss.* The film is about a Giant Shark that eats people. The shark facts are mostly bullshit (creating a worldwide hatred of sharks). The shark looks like shit. Is it still fun to watch? Yup. Was it the successful movie of its day? Yup. Did the book by Peter Benchley suck? Yup. Did it launch the career of Hollywood's most manipulative filmmaker? Yup. Should it have gotten a PG rating? NFW! Is it, along with *Raiders of the Lost Ark* and *Duel,* one of the few good films by Hollywood mogul/director Steven Spielberg? Yup! —*N. H.*

1941 L: DIRECTORS/SPIELBERG, STEVEN (1979) 142M D: Steven Spielberg. *Lorraine Gary, Ned Beatty, Christopher Lee, Toshirô Mifune, John Belushi, Murray Hamilton.* Jaw-droppingly bad. This glorious train wreck of a movie is almost entirely devoid of humor, with some of the gags so unsuccessful they are literally painful to watch. Everybody on this project seems to be laboring under the misconception that smashing things and shouting are inherently funny. There are some scenes, though—particularly the dance competition—that are really, really alive. And Williams's score is one of his best. —*E. W.*

SCHINDLER'S LIST L: DIRECTORS/SPIELBERG, STEVEN (1993) 197M D: Steven Spielberg. *Liam Neeson, Ralph Fiennes, Ben Kingsley.* Perhaps I went in a little guarded to this film, having grown up with my older relatives showing me pictures of large, smiling groups of ancestors in prewar Europe, then telling me that they were all wiped out in the Holocaust. I had heard how emotionally powerful this film was, and as I sat there in the darkness, watching the titular German industrialist risk life and limb to save hundreds of Jews from being shipped off to concentration camps, the strangest thing happened. I felt so distanced from the story of my ancestors and that particular time in history. Instead, I just felt very aware that I was watching a well-made movie, replete with dazzling camera work, lovely nuanced performances, skilled direction, and a resoundingly emotional score. It bothered me, this numbness. Then, after the story concluded, something very strange happened. Spielberg chose to show us the real people that Schindler saved, standing around his grave. The reality set in, as did the emotions I'd perhaps been suppressing for 197 minutes, and I sat there in the darkness blubbering like a baby, those last three "real" minutes drawing out the entire emotional weight of the film. I've never had an experience quite like that in cinema. —*M. S.*

LEMON GROVE KIDS MEET THE MONSTERS L: DIRECTORS/ STECKLER, RAY DENNIS (1965) 78M D: Ray Dennis Steckler. *Cash Flagg, Carol Brandt.* Ray Dennis Steckler (acting under his on-screen pseudonym of Cash Flagg) is the Huntz Hall to Mike Kannon's Leo Gorcey in this goony, loving tribute to the Bowery Boys movies (with a little Beach Movie nuttiness a la Baron von Zipper tossed in). It's not actually a feature but a collection of three utterly innocent, engagingly silly comedy shorts, the most unabashedly joyous films in Steckler's career. In the first, a cross-country race with a rival gang transforms without explanation into a monster mash farce, complete with gorilla suit (courtesy of Bob Burns) and unbilled appearance by long-underwear-superhero Rat Pfink. Brandt costars as a vampire who teams up with green-skinned aliens in the second, and in the third plays a starlet on the decline kidnapped by gangsters straight out of 1940s B-movies. But she's upstaged by the cute-as-the-dickens Little Lemon Grove Kids, wee ones who waddle through the episodes without a trace of self-conciousness. And, yes, they are shot in lifelike "laugh-o-color." —*S. A.*

RAT PFINK A BOO BOO L: DIRECTORS/STECKLER, RAY DENNIS (1965) 72M D: Ray Dennis Steckler. *Ron Haydock, Titus Moede, Bob Burns, Carolyn Brandt.* Yeah, it's spelled right. *Rat Pfink a Boo Boo!* Harnessing a schizophrenic mania unmatched before or since, B-movie godfather Steckler (*The Thrill Killers*) shocked and befuddled audiences with this drive-in—era classic. What do a pockmarked middle-

aged rock star and his gardener do when pushed to the emotional brink by kidnappers? Become costumed crime-fighters Rat Pfink & Boo Boo, of course! The outfits alone would send any producer to the exit door, but somehow Steckler succeeded in bringing this aimless wonder to the silver screen. Half goofy and half immersed in an unidentifiably sleazy glaze, there is absolutely no other film to compare this to. "Remember Boo-Boo. We have just one weakness." "What's that Rat Pfink?" "... mmm ... Bullets!" Wild guitars, fistfights, sidecars, and ape suits abound in this inconceivably zany movie experience—filmed in REGULARSCOPE! —*Z. C.*

BLUE ANGEL, THE L: DIRECTORS/STERNBERG, JOSEF VON
(1930) 106M D: Josef von Sternberg. *Marlene Dietrich, Emil Jannings.* Von Sternberg went to Germany to guide Jannings through his nervous transition from silent to sound cinema and returned to Hollywood emboldened with an international hit and a new star: Marlene Dietrich. Not exactly what Jannings had in mind, but then how could he know that the theatrical thickness of his gesture-laden silent film–style would come across as simply old-fashioned next to the brash, lazy, sensual quality of Dietrich's easy screen presence and modern performance. It's of course a perfect pairing: the repressed petty provincial schoolteacher Rath, so obsessed by appearance and authority, and the happy-go-lucky showgirl Lola. With such a strong tale behind von Sternberg's layered visual style, it becomes his most dramatically driven and intense sound film, and his most tragic. The luscious spray of nets and scrims and artful clutter is on gorgeous display in the nightclub scenes, which are simultaneously cheap and exotic, tawdry, and enticing: a marvelous, messy contrast to the neat regimentation of Rath's everyday life. —*S. A.*

DEVIL IS A WOMAN, THE L: DIRECTORS/STERNBERG,
JOSEF VON (1935) 79M D: Josef von Sternberg. *Alison Skipworth, Marlene Dietrich, Lionel Atwill, Cesar Romero, Edward Everett Horton.* Von Sternberg's final collaboration with muse Dietrich is at once his most visually splendid and narratively austere. A dense web of veils, nets, shutters, and screens, von Sternberg's dreamiest film suffers from the blank performances of leads Atwill and Romero, the rivals in pursuit of Dietrich's calculatingly disdainful lady of Spain. Von Sternberg appears to have ignored the men completely in his total fixation on Ms. Dietrich. The director's Hollywood swan song pushes the limits of style as substance. It's maddeningly uninvolving on a narrative level, yet composed of images so ethereal you can float away on them. —*S. A.*

DOCKS OF NEW YORK, THE L: DIRECTORS/STERNBERG,
JOSEF VON (1928) 76M D: Josef von Sternberg. *Mitchell Lewis, George Bancroft, Betty Compson, Olga Baclanova, Clyde Cook.* On a pier at night, the camera looks at the rolling water below. A reflec-

tion of a figure standing above wavers in the water, then disappears. The water ripples. It cuts to ship's stoker (Bancroft) on shore leave. He takes a final puff on his cigarette, then jumps into the bay to rescue the destitute girl (Compson) from the water. So begins visually the most redolent movie of the silent era. Von Sternberg's smoggy, atmospheric lighting finesses an emotional linkage between the harbor environment and the characters inhabiting taverns and flophouses there. The stoker provides the girl a room and steals clothes for her, later mock-marrying her in a big party before shipping out. Von Sternberg places architectural objects between his camera and its target creating a tension between audience detachment and involvement. Which is also how he has Bancroft, Compson, and Baclanova (so magnificently) play their scenes, painting very modern, morally conflicted psyches in a story that takes no easy ways out. Emotionally as rich as they come. —*J. C.*

SCARLETT EMPRESS, THE (AKA CATHERINE THE
GREAT) L: DIRECTORS/STERNBERG, JOSEF VON (1934) 104M D: Josef von Sternberg. *Sam Jaffe, Marlene Dietrich, Louise Dresser, C. Aubrey Smith, John Lodge.* This is a semi-fictionalized life of Catherine the Great (Dietrich), who was forced into a marriage with the mad Grand Duke Peter of Russia (Jaffe). She runs away from her crazy husband and straight into the arms of the handsome captain of the guard (Lodge), while also climbing and clawing her way up the Russian hierarchy to become Empress of Russia. As is the case of most of von Sternberg's works, the story is not important to the overall film. What is best remembered from *The Scarlet Empress* is the lavish costume design, soft focus, pre-noir lighting design reminiscent of the era of silent German cinema (where von Sternberg springs from), and the highly stylized sets with gothic gargoyle statues and white silk curtains. They propel *The Scarlet Empress* out of the standard Hollywood biopic and into a more Neogothic art film, anchored by the central performance of Dietrich in her greatest role. —*N. H.*

ALICE ADAMS L: DIRECTORS/STEVENS, GEORGE (1935)
99M D: George Stevens. *Fred MacMurray, Katharine Hepburn, Fred Stone, Evelyn Venable.* Hepburn is lovely and delicate as the social-climbing Alice, ashamed of her family's white-collar shabbiness as she elbows her way into high society. The first two-thirds of this drama is deftly accomplished by Stevens, who broke out of his B-movie prison and rose to the challenge of the material. Hepburn's Alice is brazen and status-obsessed, yet still vulnerable and sympathetic, as are her callow, good-time brother and nagging mother. The film sets the family on a collision course with disaster, and then pulls back for an utterly unconvincing and emasculated conclusion. Until then, however, it's a fine, knowing portrait of a past age. —*S. A.*

GIANT L: DIRECTORS/STEVENS, GEORGE (1956) 201M D: George Stevens. *Rock Hudson, Carroll Baker, Dennis Hopper, Elizabeth Taylor, James Dean.* When Bick (Hudson) returns to Texas after buying a horse from a wealthy family in Maryland, he returns not only with the family's horse, but also their beautiful, bright, and outspoken daughter, Leslie (Taylor). The flat, barren Texas landscape is a shocking contrast to the rolling green hills of Leslie's Maryland home, but she settles in and the couple begins to face the changes that the next thirty years will bring to their family, friends, land, and each other. Majestic, captivating, and ahead of its time, *Giant* is one of the best American films of the '50s. It's a genuine pleasure to watch a film that holds its characters' integrity in such high regard while giving great actors roles in which they can really shine. —*A. W.*

GREATEST STORY EVER TOLD, THE L: DIRECTORS/STEVENS, GEORGE (1965) 196M D: George Stevens. *Shelley Winters, Charlton Heston, José Ferrer, Robert Loggia, Max von Sydow, Dorothy McGuire.* What went wrong with Stevens's Christ epic is hard to say: perhaps too many expensive, large Hollywood Bible stories tested audience patience to the point that anything short of perfection could not be tolerated. *The Greatest Story* is anything but perfect, but it is not awful. Shot for the then-enormous budget of $20 million, the film follows all the basic points of Christ's life, from an opening shot of von Sydow painted as Christ on the Sistine Chapel, to his birth, death, and resurrection. Along the way almost every major star from that time has a part or cameo, and this is where the film really falls: von Sydow as Christ with a Swedish accent, Ferrar as Herod, Winters as the Woman with no Name, Sidney Poitier as Simon of Cyrene, Telly Savalas as Pontius Pilate, and (most infamously) John Wayne as a Roman Centurion. The mix of accents and acting styles certainly had audiences laughing. The magnificent widescreen cinematography and beautiful filmmaking techniques harken back to the great films of the silent era, but were lost on the television generation and the film died a painful death at the box office. Recently restored to DVD, the film is an interesting oddity; it's more fascinating to watch the making (and unmaking) of Stevens's greatest passion than to watch the film itself. —*N. H.*

PLACE IN THE SUN, A L: DIRECTORS/STEVENS, GEORGE (1951) 121M D: George Stevens. *Montgomery Clift, Raymond Burr, Shelley Winters, Elizabeth Taylor.* Stevens won an Oscar directing this elegant American classic, a handsome adaptation of Theodore Dreiser's *An American Tragedy*. Clift is at his most wounded and sensitive as an ambitious poor boy who falls for elegant society woman Taylor (who has never been more heavenly), but gets his factory girlfriend Winters pregnant. Marry her, kill her, what's an honest kid to do to clear his way for social advancement and take his shot at the American Dream? Stevens's stately direction is heavy-handed at times and the gloomy doom turns downright gothic, but he achieves the kind of exaggerated, baroque magic that could have only come from the film noir influence of classical Hollywood filmmaking. Burr does a pre-*Perry Mason* turn as the D. A. The picture won six Oscars, including well-earned statues for Michael Wilson and Harry Brown's screenplay, William C. Mellor's cool, handsome cinematography, and Franz Waxman's moody score. —*S. A.*

TALK OF THE TOWN, THE L: DIRECTORS/STEVENS, GEORGE (1942) 118M D: George Stevens. *Edgar Buchanan, Ronald Colman, Cary Grant, Jean Arthur.* There's a real populist bent to this comedy about a stuffy legal scholar (Colman) dragged out of his ivory tower of abstract philosophy and into the real world of human justice by a bubbly landlady (Arthur) and a social activist on the run from a phony murder charge (Grant). But this film is from Stevens, not Frank Capra, and his heavier hand drowns the screwball comedy in social debate. Not a problem for this magnificent cast, who makes the dialogue dance and the contrived script feel more deft than it really is. Grant is oddly miscast as a working-class agitator, but Colman is perfect as the erudite intellectual and has a twinkling playfulness as he debates law and justice with Grant. Arthur, torn between the two unexpected comrades, is her usual befuddled, adorable self. Buchanan is marvelous as Grant's gravel-voiced attorney. —*S. A.*

ANY GIVEN SUNDAY L: DIRECTORS/STONE, OLIVER (1999) 156M D: Oliver Stone. *Cameron Diaz, Al Pacino, Dennis Quaid, Jamie Foxx, James Woods.* Sometimes Stone crafts movies, and sometimes he bludgeons them into bloody, dazed submission. *Any Given Sunday* falls into the second category, and that's probably just as well. Stone has selected a subject, professional football, that is deserving of his technique. The plot follows an old-school coach (Pacino), a veteran quarterback (Quaid) and a brash newcomer (Foxx). Characters, plot lines, and themes crash into each other like loosened railroad cars, allowing Stone to turn his gaze on arrogance, pride, leadership, race, and money. It's pro football as ancient Rome. While Stone turns the volume up too loud on some of his themes—if I'm not mistaken, Pacino gives three inspirational speeches in the final hour—the pageantry of football, which hypes itself outlandishly, meshes nicely with the director's own love of the big stage. —*T. P.*

DOORS, THE L: DIRECTORS/STONE, OLIVER (1991) 138M D: Oliver Stone. *Val Kilmer, Meg Ryan, Kyle MacLachlan, Kathleen Quinlan, Frank Whaley.* You can't go wrong with a fictionalized biography of a dead rock star as long as you have the rights to use that star's music. The only other obstacle is casting someone who can pass as that dead rock star, something Kilmer does fairly well. Of course, the supporting cast isn't nearly as important in this respect, which is why MacLachlan is able to be passed off as keyboardist Ray Manzarek. Once all of this is set up, there's that pesky thing known as a story. Leave it to Stone (famed for his controversial *JFK*) to tell it like it was: drugs, sex, and maybe even some rock and roll! Throw in some supernatural visions of American Indians and you've got yourself a major motion picture. —*N.J.*

JFK L: DIRECTORS/STONE, OLIVER (1991) 189M D: Oliver Stone. *Kevin Bacon, Kevin Costner, Tommy Lee Jones, Sissy Spacek, Donald Sutherland, Jack Lemmon.* Stone damns the findings of the Warren Commission and makes up a few "facts" of his own in order to do so. Characters and situations have been invented to strengthen his position, and others are underdeveloped to simplify things. Anyway, the point is, it worked. The film reopened examination of the incident by the public and the government. Art or propaganda? You make the call. —*S.C.V.*

NATURAL BORN KILLERS L: DIRECTORS/STONE, OLIVER (1994) 119M D: Oliver Stone. *Woody Harrelson, Juliette Lewis, Tommy Lee Jones, Tom Sizemore, Robert Downey Jr.* Mickey and Mallory (Harrelson and Lewis) are lovers on a serial killing spree who become celebrities on Downey's tabloid TV show. Switching manically from super-8 to video to black and white to animation, and assaulting viewers with moral ambiguity, overacting (Tommy Lee Jones in a test run for his awful performance in *Batman Forever*), and *Evil Dead*-like camera trickery, Stone attempts to create some sort of an impressionistic portrait of modern television. Working loosely from an early Quentin Tarantino script, there are some clever moments (Lewis's horrible childhood is depicted as a sitcom starring Rodney Dangerfield), and Harrelson gives another great performance that makes you wonder why he's not more respected as an actor. Still, as well-intentioned as it may be, it's a heavy-handed, stylistically obnoxious stab at an obvious point: the media exploits violence. This same material was already covered more effectively in *Man Bites Dog* and *Serial Mom*. Hell, maybe even *Death Race 200* and *The Running Man*. —*B.T.*

NIXON L: DIRECTORS/STONE, OLIVER (1995) 191M D: Oliver Stone. *Anthony Hopkins, Joan Allen, Powers Boothe, Ed Harris.* Casting Hopkins as Nixon, Stone portrays the scandal-ridden U.S. president as misunderstood, lonely, embattled. In a scene based on an actual event, Nixon shows his deep and generous heart one night to a bunch of Vietnam protestors at the Lincoln monument. Yet by the time he holes himself up in the White House feeling sorry for himself for having to resign, most of the audience not obsessed with the

'60s will be glancing at their watches wondering if the film will ever be over. There are more interesting and even more truthful versions of the later years of Nixon, such as *Secret Honor* by Robert Altman. —*N.J.*

GREED L: DIRECTORS/STROHEIM, ERIC VON (1925) 140M D: Erich von Stroheim. *Gibson Gowland, Zasu Pitts.* Greed is one of the most harrowing and intense silent films ever. It's the story of how winning the lottery unravels the lives of two lovers. Sadly enough, von Stroheim had his masterpiece taken away and butchered by studio heads. Now, Rich Schmidlen, after his success with saving *Touch of Evil*, works his magic once again. Yes, a lot of original shots are gone forever, but the still photos are a haunting reminder of what might have been. —*K.*

QUEEN KELLY L: DIRECTORS/STROHEIM, ERIC VON (1929) 101M D: Erich von Stroheim. *Seena Owen, Tully Marshall, Walter Byron, Gloria Swanson.* The lavish, kinky silent epic that destroyed the Hollywood directing career of famed monomaniacal auteur von Stroheim (or so his legend had become) was for years a Hollywood ghost. It remained unfinished (he was kicked off the film by Swanson and her lover/producer Joseph Kennedy when he had a costar drool tobacco juice on Swanson) and unsalvageable (Swanson released a cobbled-together version in Europe briefly), and was briefly glimpsed in teasing clips in Billy Wilder's *Sunset Boulevard*. The story of a convent girl's corruption at the hands of a lascivious prince, a jealous queen, a mercenary aunt, and a syphilitic brothel owner was finally reconstructed in 1985 with stills and descriptions filling out the unfilmed sequences. It's still essentially incomplete, yet remains von Stroheim's most perversely dazzling film. —*S.A.*

WEDDING MARCH, THE L: DIRECTORS/STROHEIM, ERIC VON (1928) 113M D: Erich von Stroheim. *Erich von Stroheim, Fay Wray, Zazu Pitts.* Excellent romantic tragedy where nobody dies except in the soul. Rakish aristocrat (von Stroheim) loves his expensive pleasures: "marry for money" his parents cynically but realistically insist. Then he becomes infatuated with an innkeeper's daughter (Fay Wray) and imprisons her testy boyfriend, the guy her mother thinks is suitable for her to marry. In a lovely, atmospheric evening scene, the girl takes the jaunty aristocrat's words of love with a grain of salt, making him fall deeper than his initial glib infatuation. But pressed into an arranged marriage with a wealthy but unattractive cripple, he succumbs to practicality. Once out of jail, the boyfriend plans a bullet for the aristocrat as a wedding gift, and the only way the girl can stop it is to marry this brute she hates. This is von Stroheim's ode to love. —*J.C.*

BAD DAY AT BLACK ROCK L: DIRECTORS/STURGES, JOHN (1955) 84M D: John Sturges. *Anne Francis, Ernest Borgnine, Dean Jagger, Robert Ryan, Spencer Tracy, Lee Marvin.* Tracy stars as a one-armed stranger who uncovers a small desert town's dark racist secrets. Using new Cinemascope techniques and a fantastic cast (with Ryan portraying the main, manipulative heavy), director Sturges creates a tense thriller that imbues a modern Western with themes of racial hatred, group conformity, and individual responsibility. Produced in the midst of the McCarthy era, *Bad Day at Black Rock* can be seen as an allegorical attack on the Hollywood blacklist. No matter what the subtext may be, this is a tightly constructed, suspenseful motion picture with vivid characters, incredible photography, and a thought-provoking script. —*S. H.*

SATAN BUG, THE L: DIRECTORS/STURGES, JOHN (1965) 114M D: John Sturges. *Frank Sutton, George Maharis, Richard Basehart, Anne Francis, Dana Andrews, Edward Asner.* Anti-war activists go just a little too far in this unusual suspense film. Using the government's own top-secret intelligence, a group of men infiltrate a secret government base and steal the Satan Bug, a dormant virus that if let loose, could literally kill everyone on the planet. They intend to use it unless the secret military base is closed down. The plot culminates in a lengthy and suspenseful chase to Los Angeles to stop the spread of the virus in time. Good casting and strong direction make this film every bit as tense as *The Andromeda Strain.* —*N. J.*

CHRISTMAS IN JULY L: DIRECTORS/STURGES, PRESTON (1940) 67M D: Preston Sturges. *Ellen Drew, Dick Powell.* Though short and simple, this film is a rollercoaster ride of emotional highs and lows. Head-in-the-clouds office clerk Jimmy (Powell) lays all his hopes on a major coffee company's contest for a new advertising slogan. Two coworkers fake a telegram for laughs, notifying Jimmy that his slogan submission is the winner! Based solely on this forgery, Jimmy is given a major promotion, receives a sizable prize check, and launches a spending spree buying gifts for all his family and friends. When the ruse is discovered, Jimmy finds himself humiliated and in debt. His promotion is yanked from him and his very sense of self-worth is lost. A genuine heart-warmer that's pure Sturges, it's hard to imagine anyone not liking this film, and when the inevitable happy ending (complete with moral) finally comes, it absolutely feels earned. —*C. B.*

LADY EVE, THE L: DIRECTORS/STURGES, PRESTON (1941) 97M D: Preston Sturges. *Henry Fonda, Barbara Stanwyck, Eugene Pallette, William Demarest, Charles Coburn.* A sheer screwball delight. Tough, confident, bold Stanwyck has always been underrated as a comediane, but she's never been better than as the smooth, sexy con-woman who falls in love with her socially awkward stiff-of-a-mark Fonda (perfectly cast as a millionaire scion with a love of snakes). She commands every scene, no matter what her persona, as she first melts in the innocent presence of the sincerely naive buffoon, and then runs him through the ringer in a delicious revenge after he dumps her. Only Sturges could make such a situation work: with nothing but a British accent and a change of mannerisms, she convinces the dope she's someone else. That he transforms it into a hilarious and unexpected lesson in love is proof of his genius. One of the funniest mixes of slapstick and sophistication in classic Hollywood—with a little sex in it (to borrow a phrase from another Sturges classic). —*S. A.*

MIRACLE OF MORGAN'S CREEK, THE L: DIRECTORS/STURGES, PRESTON (1944) 99M D: Preston Sturges. *Eddie Bracken, Betty Hutton, Brian Donlevy, Porter Hall, Akim Tamiroff, William Demarest.* A small-town floozy, wonderfully played by wholesome Hutton, does her patriotic duty by partying with a bunch of soldiers preparing to go to war. During the wild, drunken night, she gets married to and knocked up by a soldier. Unfortunately, she was so loaded she can't remember his name and it's up to a local schnook (Bracken) to save her honor. An onslaught against American morals, small-town life, and WWII-era patriotism, *Miracle of Morgan's Creek* was shot back to back with the equally amusing *Hail the Conquering Hero* and features a hilarious cameo by Adolph Hitler. Considering the lead character is a slut named Kockenlocker, it's truly amazing that this film made it past the censors of the day. —*S. H.*

SULLIVAN'S TRAVELS L: DIRECTORS/STURGES, PRESTON (1941) 90M D: Preston Sturges. *Robert Warwick, Joel McCrea, Veronica Lake, William Demarest.* Sturges simultaneously lampoons and embraces Hollywood in this comic masterpiece about a popular Hollywood director (a low-key McCrea) of lowbrow hits like *Ants in Your Pants of 1939*, who decides to make a serious film about social strife and human suffering called *O Brother, Where Art Thou* and hits the road as a hobo to research the film. Nobody marries crackling wit and spirited slapstick like Sturges, who brings a sassy edge to this satirical road movie through Depression-era America and the out-of-touch plenty of La-La-land, yet imbues his heroes with a loving dignity. The celebration of simple joys of Hollywood comedies may seem like a self-serving defense of Sturges's art, but it's so magical and genuine and full of hilarious ego-puncturing moments that it overcomes the overly sentimental finale. Lake gives a career-best performance as the sadder-but-wiser starlet wannabe who joins his odyssey, and the whole darn Sturges stock company checks in with marvelous jewels of character bits. A masterpiece from Hollywood's master of the satiric, and the most personal film of his career. —*S. A.*

BRANDED TO KILL (KOROSHI NO RAKUIN) L: DIRECTORS/
SUZUKI, SEIJUN (1968) 91M D: Seijun Suzuki. *Jo Shishido,
Koji Nanbara, Isao Tamagawa, Anne Mari.* Even
by 1960s standards, this clean-lined, fashion-
conscious film about competing contract killers
is one of the most bizarre movies ever made.
A hit man muffs his new assignment from the
Deathwish Lady and now there is a contract
on his life. The triggerman turns out to be his
always-naked wife, but she only gets him in the
belt-buckle. He tracks her to his boss' place and
shoots her a tad lower, finishing her between her
eyes and then leaves her hair swirling in the toilet bowl. Five killers are set to finish him but he
is tipped off by another hit man, and so begins
the moves and countermoves that leads to a bout
between these two. The compositions, camera
angles, editing, and performances are so stylishly
right-on that the experience is one dumbfounding, long, nihilistic, savory treat. *—J. C.*

FIGHTING ELEGY L: DIRECTORS/SUZUKI, SEIJUN (1966) 86M
D: Seijun Suzuki. *Isao Tamagawa, Hideki Takahashi,
Yusuke Kawazu, Takeshi Kato.* When repressed
school-boy Takahashi channels his adolescent
lust for the Catholic girl in his boarding house
into street-brawling, he finds an affinity for
fighting that soon takes over his life. The meek,
lovesick kid transforms into a tough rebel who
flirts with Japan's 1935 Fascist movement. The
historical background and period specifics may
be lost to American viewers (as they were on
me), but the insistent corollary between sexual
energy and violence works in every culture. Less
stylistically outrageous than most of Suzuki's
work, it still packs a wallop with startling attacks,
outrageous sexual metaphors, and moments of
serene beauty amid the explosions of pent-up
energy. *—S. A.*

GATE OF FLESH L: DIRECTORS/SUZUKI, SEIJUN (1964) 90M
D: Seijun Suzuki. *Satoko Kasai, Yumiko Nogawa, Kayo
Matsuo, Tamiko Ishii, Misako Tominaga, Jo Shishido.*
A luscious color sexploitation film from Japan,
edgy and cruel but never quite sordid. Five
tough whores in postwar Japan live together by
a strict code in a bombed-out castle: no free sex.
Offenders are trussed up naked and thrashed
bloody (front and back) with bamboo sticks.
Thieving to stay alive, an ex-soldier (Shishido)
tangles with an American. He kills the G.I., and
the whores hide him and care for his wounds
while the occupying force offers a reward for his
capture. When one of the whores starts falling
for him, the table is set for tragedy. The camera
angles, flow of action, colors, and close-up of
faces (foul-mouthed, noisy, confident, truculent,
vengeful), as well as the startlingly naked flesh,
make *Gate of Flesh* an astonishingly original film
for 1965. One of the first pink films made, and
perhaps the very best. *—J. C.*

PISTOL OPERA L: DIRECTORS/SUZUKI, SEIJUN (2002) 112M
D: Seijun Suzuki. *Makiko Esumi, Sayoko Yamaguchi,
Kan Hanae, Masatoshi Nagase, Mikijiro Hira.*
Stray Cat (Mekiko) is the #3 killer in her organization, but she wants to become #1. This whole
movie is one big tournament where assassins
with colorful gimmicks try to off each other to
improve their ranking. There's an especially good
chase scene with a wheelchair-bound badass,
and as the story goes on it becomes stranger and
more theatrical. Stray Cat is mentored by the
protagonist of *Branded to Kill* (now known as #0
and played by Mikijiro), making this a sort of
sequel. Suzuki's first film in eight years, it takes
his style to its logical conclusion with absolutely
gorgeous colors and designs. Although I found it
difficult to follow at times, and ultimately rather
exhausting, I didn't really care because it's one
of the best-looking films I've ever seen. If you
really like *Kill Bill* and you want something in a
similar spirit, this might come close. *—B. T.*

TOKYO DRIFTER L: DIRECTORS/SUZUKI, SEIJUN (1966) 83M
D: Seijun Suzuki. *Tetsuya Watari, Chieko Matsubara,
Hideaki Nitani, Ryuji Kita.* High-contrast black-
and-white photography explodes into candy-
colored comic book images in Suzuki's almost
incomprehensible tale of a hit man named
Phoenix Tetsu (Watari). The last honorable man
in a corrupt world where the criminal code has
no meaning, he leaves the mob and goes his own
way, whistling his own theme song as he dodges
assassins sent by his old gang and former rivals.
His odyssey takes him from impossibly stylized nightclubs drenched in delirious color to
the serene snowy plains of Northern Japan and
he leaves a trail of corpses in his wake. It's like
the insane collision of a Technicolor Hollywood
musical and a self-destructing Jean-Pierre
Melville gangster film. The extreme stylization,
jarring narrative leaps, insane plot devices, and
wild parodies of gangster clichés combine to
create a pulp fiction on acid, at once alienating,
abstract, engrossing, and utterly whacked out.
—S. A.

YOUTH OF THE BEAST L: DIRECTORS/SUZUKI, SEIJUN
(1963) 92M D: Seijun Suzuki. *Jo Shishido, Misako
Watanabe, Ikuko Kimuro.* Suzuki's delirious
pulp gangster film leaps from quiet black and
white to loud color and even louder jazz music
in a cityscape of random violence and bustling
citizenry in the first few minutes, then makes a
style of that driving pace and jagged narrative
leaps. In yet another twist on *Yojimbo* (itself
rooted in Dashiell Hammet's *Red Harvest*), a
brutally effective hoodlum (Shishido) becomes
the number one henchman for an ambitious
mobster, then joins up with his rival and feeds
them both information. The ridiculously twisted
plot is only enhanced by astounding colorscapes,
surreal images (the boss's back yard is a howling
desert), and cinematic excess. Yowza! *—S. A.*

Takeshi Kitano

The multitalented "Beat" Takeshi Kitano is best known throughout the world as one of Japan's greatest modern directors. His nickname comes from his years as a comedian in the early 1970s, when he performed as part of a duo called the Two Beats. He still uses the nickname as an actor today, although he uses his formal name as a director.

Takeshi Kitano got his first chance to direct in the late 1980s, when Kinji Fukasaku had to drop out of a cop thriller Kitano was to star in. He tweaked the script, and the result was his incredible debut, *Violent Cop* (1989). From the beginning, Kitano's directing had an identifiable style that was immediately linked to his name. He offers well-crafted long takes and minimal dialogue along with bursts of raw violence and subtle humor to make each movie uniquely his.

Following directly on the heels of *Violent Cop* came the revenge piece *Boiling Point* (1990), in which a loser encounters the fury of the yakuza (Japanese mafia) and must stand up for himself. Here Kitano put most of his energy into directing, keeping only a minor character for himself, and showed that his directorial skill was a force to be contended with. He followed that up the next year with *A Scene by the Sea* (1991), about a deaf-mute garbageman who learns to surf and finds love on the shores of Japan.

It was the internationally recognized *Sonatine* (1993) that put Takeshi Kitano's name on the lips of critics around the world. He received his first award, the Critics Award of the Cognac Festival du Film Policier, for this tale of yakuza revenge in which he also played the lead character. Kitano's ability to blend humor and violence is at its early best here, as most of the film features ousted gangsters goofing off.

In 1994 Kitano suffered a near-fatal motorcycle accident that left half of his face paralyzed, the reason for his subtle facial expressions in his later films. After his recovery, he reached back into his comedic years to create *Getting Any?* (1995), an absurdly raunchy comedy about a loser who

---

BOILING POINT L: DIRECTORS/TAKESHI KITANO (BEAT) (1990) 98M D: Takeshi Kitano. *Masahiko Ono, "Beat" Takeshi, Yuriko Ishida, Takahito Iguchi.* Kitano's second directorial effort, and first original screenplay, is the meandering tale of a passive gas-station attendant and baseball team benchwarmer (Ono) who rebels from a life of submissive deference by striking a rude customer who just happens to be yakuza. When the gangsters start taking it out on both his coworkers and his teammates, Masaki sets out to buy a gun and take care of the problem. Takeshi appears as a disgraced gangster and fun-loving brute in a rambling subplot that delivers the film's most electric and eclectic scenes. The narrative almost dissolves in abstractions and digressions before the startling conclusion, but it remains a fascinatingly warped look at the uniquely Japanese culture of violence. —*S.A.*

BROTHER L: DIRECTORS/TAKESHI KITANO (BEAT) (2000) 112M D: Takeshi Kitano. *Takeshi Kitano, Ren Ohsugi, Masaya Kato, Claude Maki, Omar Epps.* Taking place mostly in Los Angeles, spoken mostly in English, and costarring Epps, you'd think this would be Kitano's big try at American crossover success. His sellout movie. Quite to the contrary, *Brother* completely retains Kitano's deadpan black humor, his artfully static camera-work, his themes of honor and brotherhood, and his playful use of games, and it has more graphic and brutal violence than most of his Japanese films (maybe that's what he thinks Americans want). Kitano plays another yakuza character, this time one who flees to the U.S. after his gang gets wiped out. Staying with his low-level street thug half-brother, he decides to use his yakuza knowledge to turn his new American friends into a powerful crime syndicate. It seems like a pretty good idea until they come head to head with the Mafia and, due to their Japanese sense

just wants to have sex and tries any means to get it. It is to this day Kitano's most laugh-out-loud comedy, and again shows his limitless potential. The following year, he became solely a director for the dramatic *Kids Return* (1996), about two high school dropouts who reminisce about their younger days while waiting for their past to catch up with them.

With *Fireworks* (aka *Hana-Bi*) in 1997, Kitano once again tasted international acclaim. Possibly his finest work, this tragic tale of an ex-cop haunted by his partner's death and his wife's leukemia drew tears from audiences and praise from critics, and won a host of awards around the world. After a year's break from directing, Kitano stepped behind the camera once more for the beautiful cross-country drama *Kikujiro* (1999), in which a young boy desperately searches for his mother.

Kitano took a huge chance to make his next film, *Brother* (2000): he went off to Los Angeles to not only make but star in the movie, even though he hardly spoke any English. The multiracial cast, which included Omar Epps, helped create a believable portayal of the thriving gangster rivalry in LA and made the movie accessible to an English-speaking market, thus finally bringing Kitano's brilliance to U.S. shores. Unfortunately, it was edited for domestic release; this is a film that needs to be seen in the original version to deliver its full impact.

In 2002, Kitano stepped behind the camera as director only for *Dolls*, a film he has said he wasn't sure if he could pull off but had to challenge himself to make. The film entwines three separate stories, all connected by a theme of lost love, into a moving piece of art that flows slowly across the screen. It is certainly a new direction for Kitano and has received mixed reviews from fans, but has garnered appreciation from critics and several award nominations. More recently, Kitano is working on a new film starring Zatoichi, a blind swordsman who becomes caught up in a town's diabolical rule by gangsters.

Takeshi Kitano remains a name that can be trusted to expand the world of cinema with each release, whether it is a yakuza film (arguably what he is best known for), a comedy, or a dramatic tragedy. His sense of style, again arguably unique in a world of ever more fast and furious editing, remains constant and pure. He shows no sign of slowing down and is always looking for his next challenge. —*Ryan Miller*

---

of honor, walk straight into a suicidal gang war. (Kitano has claimed the movie is about World War II.) —*B. T.*

DOLLS L: DIRECTORS/TAKESHI KITANO (BEAT) (2002) 114M D: Takeshi Kitano. *Carrie Lorraine, Guy Rolfe, Hilary Mason, Bunty Bailey, Stephen Lee, Ian Patrick Williams, Miho Kanno, Hidetoshi Nishijima, Tatsuya Mihashi, Chieko Matsubara, Kyoko Fukada*. Kitano gives us three stories of unresolved love. A man takes his former lover through the countryside in a half-conscious, dreamlike state in an attempt to rekindle their love. Another returns to his lover to continue their relationship that has been on hold for several decades but does not let her know that it is him. The last goes to extremes of physical deformity in order to get close to the pop star he loves. The opening sequence begins in a Japanese puppet theater. The movie immediately takes a surreal tone as the verisimilitude of the puppets is simultaneously astonishing and just a little bit creepy. This is a very patient movie, but besides that, I didn't really care for some of the character dynamics, especially the one between the pop star and her fan. The camera also seems too self-aware, but this is a gorgeously shot film and still worth a look. —*T. C.*

FIREWORKS (HANA-BI) L: DIRECTORS/TAKESHI KITANO (BEAT) (1997) 103M D: Takeshi Kitano. *Ren Osugi, Kayoko Kishimoto, Susumu Terajima, Beat Takeshi*. Known as *Hana-Bi* to many, *Fireworks* represents the culmination of auteur Kitano's cinematic styles and story motifs into a sweeping work of art. Takeshi takes on the role of Nishi, a cop who is haunted by the memories of an arrest gone horribly wrong. His waking hours are far worse as he must watch his wife slowly succumb to leukemia. With a mounting debt to a vicious loan shark, Nishi devises a broad-daylight bank robbery to pay off the loans, and uses the remaining money to take his wife on a final vacation across Japan that shows the diverse landscape of the island nation.

Takeshi's subtle offbeat humor and stoic acting is at its apex here, and proves that by saying nothing one is able to say everything. Takeshi's body of artwork, which he created for the movie, also appears throughout the film, as the projects of Nishi's ex-partner. —R. M.

GETTING ANY? L: DIRECTORS/TAKESHI KITANO (BEAT) (1994) 105M D: Takeshi Kitano. *Dannkann, Shouji Kobayashi, Tetsuya Yuuki, Yuuji Minakata, Ren Osugi.* Those who know Beat Takeshi as only a self-destructive gangster or policeman should definitely see this film and get to know his lowbrow, comedic roots. Although he only makes a brief appearance, Takeshi's role as a mad scientist is the high point of the film. The rest of the movie centers around Asao, who spends the entire film trying to figure out a way to get laid, and deals with his out-of-touch thoughts on what women want in a man. This is the main theme that connects the short skitlike feel of the film, as Asao goes through various desperate attempts to get women. He robs a bank, steals an armored car, joins the yakuza, hunts for buried treasure, becomes a *Zatoichi* extra, and eventually becomes a human guinea pig for science experiments. My only gripe with the film, which comes with many subtitled comedies, is that some of the wordplay is probably lost in translation. Aside from that, this is a milk-out-of-the-nose laugh riot. Don't expect any thought-provoking long takes, melodic scoring by Jan Hisaishi, or suicidal endings, and you'll do just fine. —R. M.

KIDS RETURN L: DIRECTORS/TAKESHI KITANO (BEAT) (1996) 107M D: Takeshi Kitano. *Ken Kaneko, Hatsuo Yamaya, Masanobu Ando, Leo Morimoto.* Kitano's first film since his motorcycle accident is a quieter, more introspective drama than his previous gangster films, but it's also typical Kitano in many ways. Two troublemaking dropouts (Ando and Kaneko) grow apart when their paths take them into separate dead-ends. One turns to boxing, ignoring his coach for the misguided advice of a loser on the way down, while the other becomes a fumbling, low-level yakuza. As they reunite, fellow failures killing time on their old stomping grounds, the next generation of restless students watch them out the school window with misplaced envy. With deadpan humor and understated drama, this is a portrait of characters doomed to their fates by their very personalities, but in this world such doom leaves them drifting through life untethered rather than dead. —S. A.

KIKUJIRO L: DIRECTORS/TAKESHI KITANO (BEAT) (1999) 122M D: Takeshi Kitano. *Beat Takeshi, Yusuke Sekiguchi, Kayoko Kishimoto.* Kikujiro (Takeshi) is a loutish criminal whose wife volunteers him to take a lonely nine-year-old boy (Sekiguchi) on a trip to find his mother. Wackiness ensues. Somehow filtering it through his style of static camerawork and deadpan black comedy, Kitano elevates what could be a formulaic comedy to the level of

poetry. It almost works as a kid's movie, but then there is the occasional brutal beating or run-in with a child molester. Kikujiro is more like a troublemaking kid than a responsible adult. In one hilarious scene he sets up a booby trap to pop the tire of a passing vehicle, planning to help the driver change his tire and then get a ride from him. The car crashes, so he panics and runs off. This is an underrated film and a refreshing attempt by Kitano to get away from the yakuza genre. —B. T.

SCENE AT THE SEA, A L: DIRECTORS/TAKESHI KITANO (BEAT) (1991) 101M D: Takeshi Kitano. *Nenzo Fujiwara, Sabu Kawahara, Hiroko Oshima, Kuroudo Maki.* An altogether different kind of film for Kitano, the stand-up comic, talk-show host, movie star, and director best known for his offbeat gangster films of explosive violence and quirky, quiet interludes, this is a film composed almost completely in the sublime quiet of the deaf-mute hero's singular focus to become a surfer. The camera takes a contemplative distance and we spend more time watching the surfer and his deaf-mute girlfriend sitting on the beach and staring into the sea than seeing actual surfing. And that's just fine; more is communicated in those silent moments through glances, smiles, relaxed body language, and Maki's serene face than all the action, dialogue, and sly comic relief of the rest of the picture. —S. A.

SONATINE L: DIRECTORS/TAKESHI KITANO (BEAT) (1993) 94M D: Takeshi Kitano. *Tetsu Watanabe, Aya Kokumai, Beat Takeshi.* This would be a fairly typical story about a violent yakuza war, except for what happens when Kitano and his men show up in a beach town to wait for the men who are coming to try to kill them. There is a long section of the movie where these hard-boiled gangsters have nothing to do but run around and play games on the beach. There is an unrestrained joy in these scenes; it's like winning a contest to go on a beach vacation with Beat Takeshi. It seems as though the actors really just played around in the sand—joking, inventing strange new competitions, shooting Roman candles at each other—and just filmed their fun. The themes of romanticism, sudden bursts of violence, long takes, and deadpan humor are trademark Kitano, but it's this silly tangent in the plot that most reflects what he's all about. —B. T.

VIOLENT COP L: DIRECTORS/TAKESHI KITANO (BEAT) (1989) 103M D: Takeshi Kitano. *Beat Takeshi, Maiko Kawakami, Makoto Ashikawa, Shirô Sano.* Kitano exploded onto movie screens with this visceral, violent directorial debut. As director he sets a tone of stillness and calm that the serene, wryly smiling actor shatters with brutal attacks. Playing police detective Azuma, a vigilante force of pure reflex hiding behind teddy-bear eyes, he earns the film its title many times over while hardly cracking his calm, bemused deadpan mask. Even when the battle becomes personal and the hair-trigger cop goes on his rogue rampage, he maintains that serenity, hardening just a bit, his crook of smile straightening out to a taut determination suggesting just a touch of bitterness and sadness. Kitano stepped in as director at the last minute and leapt out of the gate with a powerful, fully developed style. He completely transformed the genre screenplay, a cops-and-gangsters tale of corruption and revenge, into a jaundiced, cynical vision. —S. A.

JACKIE BROWN L: DIRECTORS/TARANTINO, QUENTIN (1997) 155M D: Quentin Tarantino. *Pam Grier, Robert Forster, Samuel L. Jackson, Robert De Niro, Bridget Fonda.* Tarantino's thoughtful adaptation of Elmore Leonard's *Rum Punch* stars Grier as an aging flight attendant caught smuggling drugs for the small-time but dangerous Ordell Robie (Jackson). Forster is the straight-laced bail bondsman who falls for her and helps her maneuver Ordell against law enforcement. Brimming with Tarantino's usual wit and bottomless bag of cinematic tricks, it also boasts an uncharacteristic emotional maturity. Although it certainly works as a crime story and a blaxploitation homage, it's really about loneliness, longing, and fear of growing old. Grier and Forster received much-deserved acclaim for their performances, but you also have to hand it to De Niro's ticking-time-bomb character, who steals scenes even when he's sitting stoned on a couch. —B. T.

KILL BILL VOL. 1 L: DIRECTORS/TARANTINO, QUENTIN (2003) 111M D: Quentin Tarantino. *Daryl Hannah, Sonny Chiba, Vivica A. Fox, Lucy Liu, David Carradine, Uma Thurman, Michael Madsen.* The Bride (Thurman) is left for dead (along with the rest of her wedding party and her unborn child) on her wedding day by Bill (Carradine) and the Deadly Viper Assassination Squad, of which the Bride was once a member. After a four-year coma, she awakens and makes a death list; and much like Santa, goes down the list seeking revenge. Pretty simple plot, but it invites some of the most audacious action scenes ever. It doesn't pussyfoot around the gore either; these fights are brutal and chock full of geysers of gorgeous, crimson blood. The action in here is not *Crouching Tiger* poetry-of-motion-martial-arts; it's two people who are out for blood just fucking each other up with katanas. A whole half-hour is dedicated to "Chapter 5: Showdown at the House of the Blue Leaves," which features the Bride versus GoGo Yubari, killer O-Ren Ishii's personal bodyguard army, no less than fifty Japanese swordsmen fighting the Bride in an orgy of severed limbs, all followed by a badass duel between the heroine and O-Ren (Liu). All the actors are great, but the standout in Vol. 1 (besides Thurman, who carries the film with her sad, steely gaze) is Chiba as Hattori Hanzo, the master swordmaker, who gets the best lines: "I can tell you without ego that this is my best sword. If on your journey you were to meet God, God would be cut." —K. C.

PULP FICTION L: DIRECTORS/TARANTINO, QUENTIN (1994) 154M D: Quentin Tarantino. *Bruce Willis, Uma Thurman, Samuel L. Jackson, John Travolta, Ving Rhames.* So, there I was, opening night of *Pulp Fiction*. And somewhere between the bombastic opening surf-rock and the mellow closing surf-rock, my brain had been switched. I didn't sleep that night. At school the next week, I wouldn't shut the fuck up about the movie, and I only wanted to listen to surf rock. I went again the next weekend, and again, until it left town. I don't care who Tarantino was ripping off, all I know is *Pulp Fiction* got me excited about movies in a way I didn't know was possible, and I haven't looked back since. It was the catalyst that sent me scouring my small town for whatever was weird and great—any cool cinema I could find from John Woo (not too weird now, I know) to *Dead Alive* (somehow our Blockbuster had the unrated edition). Maybe he was just channeling Godard, and Woo, and Melville, and Sam Fuller ... but Tarantino and *Pulp Fiction* are the reasons I watched any of their movies in the first place. I owe my love of movies to that first time I saw *Pulp Fiction*. —K. C.

RESERVOIR DOGS L: DIRECTORS/TARANTINO, QUENTIN (1992) 100M D: Quentin Tarantino. *Tim Roth, Lawrence Tierney, Chris Penn, Steve Buscemi, Harvey Keitel, Michael Madsen.* Tarantino's quotable blast of postmodern crime-movie cool is one of the most attention-grabbing directorial debuts in history. Keitel, Roth, Madsen, and Buscemi regroup in an empty warehouse in the aftermath of a jewel heist gone bad that left two dead and another bleeding his life away. This is very much a first film: exceedingly violent, virulently macho, and bubbling with sexist, racist, unapologetically amoral criminal characters. Tarantino has too much fun in the pulp world of tough guys to scratch beneath the surface of romantic gangster tropes. The key word, however, is fun. Tarantino lifts ideas from dozens of movies (the plot itself is an ingenious rethinking of the Hong Kong crime classic *City on Fire*), then makes it his own with narrative surprises, striking characters, and some of the most enjoyable movie dialogue and pop culture patter to show up in the movies in ages. Precisely plotted and engagingly juggled into a rich swirl of flashbacks, this is the work of a director who loves movies and a storyteller engaged with the art of telling stories. —S. A.

WHO DO YOU THINK YOU'RE FOOLING? L: DIRECTORS/TARANTINO, QUENTIN (1994) 11M D: Mike White. This crappy home-made short is just a series of clips from *Reservoir Dogs* and Ringo Lam's *City on Fire* edited together to show that the basic plot and many of the details of Tarantino's film were lifted from portions of Lam's. The short played many underground film festivals and gained a

Andrei Tarkovsky

Haunting, stark, beautiful, eerie—all these words describe Andrei Tarkovsky's films, but none quite capture the essence of his work. Tarkovsky is an extremely intense and personal filmmaker. His films, be they war movie, science fiction, or historical biography, are explorations into what it means to be living in this world. He gives us no answers. What we see instead is his struggle to answer, his attempt to place himself in relation to what is around him.

Tarkovsky was born in Zaurazhie, Russia. His father, Arseniy Alexandrovich Tar-

kovsky, a well-regarded poet and translator, left for the Front in 1941 and subsequently abandoned his children and wife. Andrei and his sister left Moscow, where they had been attending school, and moved back to the country for the duration of the war. Tarkovsky's stunning and most challenging film, *Mirror*, is made up of images, dreams, and memories of his childhood and his mother, actress Maria Ivanova Vishnyakova. Back in Moscow, Tarkovsky rather unceremoniously finished school and began work as a surveyor, traveling through less developed areas of the Soviet Union. It was during a year of traveling that Tarkovsky decided to pursue film directing. He was

---

certain amount of notoriety as a backlash grew against Tarantino's status as "rock star director" and media icon. It makes a convincing case, but it's not clear what the point is: Even if *Reservoir Dogs* was an outright remake, it would clearly be a very good one. What pushes director White over the line from overzealous film geek to obsessed nutcase is his follow-up, *You're Still Not Fooling Anybody*, also included on this tape. White split-screens little lines and shots from *Pulp Fiction* with the films they reference—or plagiarize, according to him: the glowing briefcase is shown beside the one from *Kiss Me Deadly*, for example. By the way, this is not the same Mike White who wrote *Chuck and Buck* and *School of Rock*, but it is the one who did a film zine called *Cashiers Du Cinemart*. —B.T.

ANDREI RUBLEV L: DIRECTORS/TARKOVSKY, ANDREI (1966) 205M D: Andrei Tarkovsky. *Anatoli Solonitsin, Ivan Lapikov.* When people talk about encounters with this austere epic, it often sounds like they're describing a religious experience. Regularly met with awe for its stark photography, poetic imagery, dreamlike narrative, and mythic status, this is a massive masterpiece of virtuoso filmmaking. An impressionistic swath of scenes details medieval icon-painter Rublev's journey to a commissioned job, on his way becoming Tarkovsky's witness to the violent transition of fifteenth-century Russia. As he questions the purpose of art in the face of such brutality, Rublev's spiritual restlessness becomes the unifying theme, matched flawlessly by the cinematography. The camera wanders through scenes as a withdrawn but profoundly affected presence (and make no

mistake, it's most certainly a *presence*). For many this is the film's most engaging element, and certainly it's a crucial part of the unshakably haunting force that is *Andrei Rublev*. —C.B.

SOLARIS L: DIRECTORS/TARKOVSKY, ANDREI (1972) 169M D: Andrei Tarkovsky. *Natalya Bondarchuk, Donatas Banionis, Juri Jarvet.* Famously promoted as the anti-*2001*, Tarkovsky's meditative adaptation of Stanislaw Lem's novel is less science fiction than metaphysical trance. A psychologist (Banionis) travels to a deep-space station to discover why the crew has broken contact and discovers a skeletal crew (the others have killed themselves or fled) teetering on the edge of sanity. Curiously, it shares a relentlessly tracking camera and a fascinatingly sterile technological environment (though this space station is trashed and thrashed and virtually abandoned) with Kubrick's masterpiece, but Tarkovsky invests his work with emotion that overwhelms its characters. This is a study in grief and guilt and second chances, set aboard a space station haunted from the past, orbiting an enigmatic planet that may be alive. —S.A.

STALKER L: DIRECTORS/TARKOVSKY, ANDREI (1979) 163M D: Andrei Tarkovsky. *Nikolai Grinko, Anatoli Solonitsin, Aleksandr Kajdanovsky.* Stalker is the story of three men traveling through the mysterious "Zone" toward a room where, if they enter, their deepest wish will be granted. There is a writer, a science professor, and their leader, the Stalker, one who knows how to travel safely in the Zone. The great Tarkovsky leads us through a world of poetic symbolism where exploring the nature of

accepted into the All Russian State Institute for Cinematography (VGIK), where he met Andrey Konchalovsky, with whom he would later collaborate on a number of films. Their first coscripted work was Tarkovsky's award-winning student (diploma) film *The Steamroller and the Violin* (1960).

Tarkovsky made five more films in the Soviet Union. All of them met with resistance in distribution and delays in final release. Almost every one of these films went on to receive international awards. His films revolve mostly around the artist's duty to his world and to his gift of vision, and how these two duties clash. *Andrei Rublev* (1971), considered by many to be his most important film, is the most obvious in presentation and treatment of this theme. It presents the story of a sixteenth-century icon painter and his struggle with the world around him. The struggle is both internal and external, and reflects the struggles that Tarkovsky himself would face.

Due to mounting pressures and roadblocks from Gosinko, Tarkovsky went to Italy to film *Nostalghia* (1983). There he was free to oversee all aspects of the film without having to fight censors to maintain the integrity of his vision. From Italy, Tarkovsky went to London, where he officially defected. His last film, *Sacrifice* (1986), was filmed in Sweden, a tribute to Ingmar Bergman who, along with Luis Buñuel and Robert Bresson, was a major influence on Tarkovsky.

Andrei Tarkovsky died in Paris in 1984 of cancer. He was fifty-four years old.

—*Breta Yvars*

---

human existence, our suffering and our yearning, takes precedent over linear storytelling. As the characters make the dangerous journey through the Zone, they are forced to make an even more dangerous spiritual journey. Tarkovsky lets the drama naturally unfold as the characters carry on their metaphysical debates, focusing his camera on the floor of a flooded room. Beneath the water are hypodermic needles, religious icons, and other representations of how humanity seeks to escape from itself. The dialogue fades away and we are left watching insects skirt aimlessly along the surface of the pool, the Stalker at one with its earthy flow. It becomes clear that we are these insects, the problems and conflicts debated are ours, and the water is the evidence and physical apprehension of the ultimate mystery. All filmmakers deal with these insects. Tarkovsky alone films the water. —*T. S.*

STEAMROLLER AND THE VIOLIN, THE L: DIRECTORS/ TARKOVSKY, ANDREI (1960) 45M D: Andrei Tarkovsky. *Marina Adzhubei, Vladimir Zamansky, Igor Fomchenko.* This delicate little forty-five-minute debut film by Tarkovsky (made as his diploma film) has more in common with the visual poetry of Soviet classics like *The Cranes Are Flying* than the complexity and density of his later works. You can take the title as a handshake between the worker and the artist, which the film presents in a brotherly friendship between a lonely seven-year-old violin student and a young road worker who stops bullies from taunting the boy and takes him along on his steamroller. The boy's awe of the young man's brawny job is returned in the latter's delight in his companion's ability to cre-

ate music. The mutual admiration is sweet and understated, the images are lovely (the demolition of buildings becomes a symphony of promise as the last bricks fall away to reveal the grandeur of a stately structure in the background), and the pastel colors have a quiet subtlety rarely seen on the screen. —*S. A.*

DISORDERLY ORDERLY, THE L: DIRECTORS/TASHLIN, FRANK (1964) 90M D: Frank Tashlin. *Alice Pearce, Glenda Ferrell, Susan Oliver, Everett Sloane, Jack E. Leonard, Jerry Lewis.* Lewis plays an orderly who empathizes so strongly with the patients that he physically begins to feel their pain. This concept makes for a perfect Lewis vehicle, especially as he plays off the head nurse who badly wants to fire him. But she is stopped by the administrator who remembers the orderly's father as an eminent doctor. The slapstick in this film is vintage Lewis: the hospital's silent ward has subtitles, and the TVs have snow—real snow! —*N. J.*

HOLLYWOOD OR BUST L: DIRECTORS/TASHLIN, FRANK (1956) 95M D: Frank Tashlin. *Pat Crowley, Anita Ekberg, Dean Martin, Jerry Lewis.* How is it possible that Steve (Lewis) and Malcolm (Martin) have the exact same winning raffle ticket for a new car? Whatever the reason, management decides they will have to share the car. It turns out both want to go to Hollywood, so they pack up and take Dino's dog along with them. This was Martin and Lewis's last film together and it's fitting they did a road film to Hollywood. They were probably driving each other crazy the whole time. —*N. J.*

Jacques Tati

If Frenchman Jacques Tati (born Jacques Tatischeff in 1908) had been better at math, the world would have been deprived of a master cinematic comedian. For generations Tati's family had crafted frames for painters like van Gogh and Toulouse-Lautrec, but Jacques dropped out of trade school. A tall youth with large hands, he pursued his interest in sports and entertaining instead, performing pantomimes that portrayed athletics as a theater of the absurd. Watching him work, literary lioness Colette was moved to declare, "He plays on your imagination with the skill of a great artist."

After a compulsory stint in the army, Tati acted in a few films and made a comedy short about a school for postmen, which he expanded into his first feature, *Jour de Fête* (1948). Tati plays the mailman in a sleepy rural village who, after watching a documentary about American workers' speed and efficiency, decides to streamline his methods—with hilarious results. In this film Tati set aesthetic and thematic stan-

dards that he would maintain throughout his career.

Tati the actor contorts his long, gangly body with the precise control of a ballet dancer, and as a director he steps back, avoiding close-ups and creating distanced perspectives so that viewers can discover their own points of interest within the frame. For Tati, sound "is of capital importance," and the sequence in which the postman dodges the angry attacks of a buzzing hornet is a classic.

Jour de Fête aroused laughter wherever it was shown and brought Tati international fame. In addition to showcasing Tati's genius for silent-film–level visual humor, the film reveals his predilection for melancholy poetry, a wistful affection for an old-fashioned, agrarian France assailed by modernity. The director had a gift for creating and playing iconic characters, and his frantically bicycling postman is lovingly referenced in Sylvain Chomet's *The Triplets of Belleville* (2003).

Tati's most famous character is Monsieur Hulot, who appeared in four films over a span of eighteen years. The director's penchant for meticulous preplanning explains

---

MON ONCLE L: DIRECTORS/TATI, JACQUES (1958) 110M D: Jacques Tati. *Jacques Tati*. The second appearance of Tati's loping, pipe-smoking M. Hulot drops the distracted gentleman (and Hulot is always a gentleman) into the modern world of empty consumerism, social status, and gadgets that take on a life of their own. Tati's films have been long compared to the work of Charlie Chaplin and Buster Keaton, and Hulot does indeed share both Keaton's gangly physicality and polite, gentlemanly dissonance with the world and Chaplin's man-out-of-time war with modern mechanics. But Tati also creates a unique little world around his awkward beanpole of a bachelor, a pocket of silent film comedy and pantomime set-pieces where the entire cast become vivid characters with their own quirks and personalities. Tati's style is effortless as he conducts his comic symphonies of sight gags, and the color photography by Jean Bourgoin is lovely. —*S. A.*

MR. HULOT'S HOLIDAY L: DIRECTORS/TATI, JACQUES (1953) 85M D: Jacque Tati. *Lucien Fregis, Rene Lacourt, Jacques Tati, Nathalie Pascaud.* This first appearance of Tati's alter-ego, Hulot, is perfect. Episodic in style, the movie comes to you like comedic visual postcards that allow you to share, delightfully, a vacation at the beach. Classic bits of near-silent comedy (what sound there is, though, is perfectly tuned to vibrate the funny bone) make train-catching, card-playing, boating, dancing, dining, or even tennis more hilarious than you could ever have thought possible. While this film's carefully composed comedy might suffer a bit on the small screen (those with huge TVs shouldn't have a problem) the comedy in this film is pure gold: what might be mere amusement on TV, well, in the theater, it nearly caused my girlfriend's dad to throw up, he was laughing so hard. Plain and simple: one of the greatest comedies ever made from one of the greatest of

the long gaps between pictures, but Hulot's character remains constant: a pipe-smoking, middle-aged man bending forward at the waist, investigating the world with a courteous, well-meaning, eager-to-help attitude—yet causing chaos wherever he goes. In *Monsieur Hulot's Holiday* (1953), his wet spare tire with leaves stuck to it is assumed to be a wreath, and he's pulled into a funeral procession; then, hiding from some dogs in a hut, he accidentally sets off a fireworks display before it's due.

Tati's subtle comedy is born of believable, realistic situations: eschewing exaggerations, grotesquerie, and sentimentality makes his observations of people's recognizable foibles and errors of perception all the more potent. Using the language of images, Tati shows us vivid portraits of a workaholic businessman, a besieged waiter, a henpecked husband. Hulot often irritates people his own age, but children and an old man appreciate his innocent nature.

Tati has said that his films "express what is leading to the suppression of personality in an increasingly mechanized world." In *Mon Oncle* (1958), Hulot champions the organic French life of fermented wine and cheese, the patina of venerable street corners, and the "accidental architecture" of old-quarter apartments, while his sister and her family live a regimented, fast-paced life of sterile patterns dictated by the geometric lines of their modern metal house. Even devout worshipers of high technology soon feel the profound impact of Hulot's gentle subversiveness.

The director's warm-hearted yet critical look at modern life continued with *Playtime* (1967), in which Paris has been engulfed by steel-and-glass structures, though spontaneous human error and high spirits can still erupt at a fancy restaurant opening. *Traffic* (1971), Tati's last widely released film, finds his absurdist wit and sharp perceptions gamboling on the "efficient" new freeways and meandering byways of his beloved France.

Crisp, dry, and precise, the impeccably designed scenes in Tati's films are created by a man full of affection for the messy muddle of life. He doesn't worry about what it all means because he's too busy enjoying the show. Tati found his vision most clearly by paying attention to what everyone else was doing. Hulot never really has a job: he spends his time being idle, an occupation that generates and nurtures culture, and that's an activity at least as important as making widgets and money.

—*Greg Olson*

---

all film comedians. One way or another, on your shelf or just in your heart, or both, this is a film everyone should own. —*K. S.*

PLAYTIME L: DIRECTORS/TATI, JACQUES (1967) 120M D: Jacques Tati. *Jacques Tati.* Tati's masterpiece places his ever-popular, gangly, pipe-smoking bachelor M. Hulot in the big city, just one of many in a huge group of French sightseers, American tourists, and urban businesspeople whose paths crisscross through a largely plotless film. Tati's humor graduates from the inspired to the sublime, his gags layered through every wide, deep-focus shot as the characters confront the world on their own terms and unite in a brilliant, inclusive third act that moves like a comic ballet. It's sheer grace, and it was Tati's most beautiful film (thematically as well as visually) and the most expensive film made in France up to that time. *Playtime* was a financial disaster upon release but has since been recognized as one of the most unique and loving human comedies put to film. —*S. A.*

CAPITAINE CONAN L: DIRECTORS/TAVERNIER, BERTRAND (1996) 130M D: Bertrand Tavernier. *Samuel Le Bihan, Bernard Le Coq, Catherine Rich, François Berleand, Philippe Torreton.* Tavernier powerfully captures the contradictions of war in this WWI drama about an unconventional officer whose misfit soldiers become the army's most successful tactical unit under fire, but degenerate into gangsters and hooligans off the field of battle. Working-class Conan (a scrappy Torreton) is disliked by the career officers for his disdain of protocol and affinities with his soldiers, which comes close to destroying him when he defends men from his unit tried for robbery and murder in a garrison town. Rich in bitter irony, Tavernier's bleak view of war and its warriors echoes themes from the late films of John Ford (Conan is Tavernier's version of Tom Doniphon from *The Man Who Shot Liberty Valance*, necessary in battle but discarded in peacetime), recast in the historical events of France. —*S. A.*

CLOCKMAKER, THE L: DIRECTORS/TAVERNIER, BERTRAND (1973) 105M D: Bertrand Tavernier. *Philippe Noiret, Jean Rochefort, Jacques Denis, Julien Bertheau.* Tavernier's low-key debut is ostensibly a murder mystery (he adapted it from a Georges Simenon novel), but it focuses on the internal drama of single father (Noiret) when he discovers his teenage son is wanted for murder. We don't even see the boy until the end; the central relationship is between Noiret and investigating cop Rochefort, a sympathetic and even likable guy who obviously feels for the distraught father but has a job to do. Noiret's performance is a masterpiece of understatement: he suggests devastation and desperation by stripping away all expression of emotion. When father and son finally meet, the whole of their life together is beautifully captured in glances and body language. —*S. A.*

COUP DE TORCHON L: DIRECTORS/TAVERNIER, BERTRAND (1981) 128M D: Bertrand Tavernier. *Stéphane Audran, Eddy Mitchell, Philippe Noiret, Isabelle Huppert, Jean-Pierre Marielle.* In adapting Jim Thompson's grim yet funny novel, *Pop. 1280*, director/screenwriter Tavernier transfers the action from the rural southern United States to a French colony in Africa in the late 1930s and manages to capture the essence of Thompson's dark prose in an apt new setting. Noiret plays an apparently simple-minded white cop in a small town. Virtually everyone underestimates his intelligence and vindictiveness, but it is soon evident that he has been playing dumb in order to distract his cheating wife and the general populace from his true nature. His facade of stupidity allows him the space to trick everyone into believing his innocence while he murders and manipulates to get what he wants. The truly scary part is that he believes he is doing the right thing and never really feels any guilt or regret. Noiret, with his hound-dog face and sad eyes, makes a great antihero and the colonial setting mirrors his treatment of his fellow humans. Also known as *Clean Slate*, *Coup De Torchon* is one of the more unique examples of modern film noir. —*S. H.*

D'ARTAGNAN'S DAUGHTER (AKA **REVENGE OF THE MUSKETEERS**) L: DIRECTORS/TAVERNIER, BERTRAND (1994) 125M D: Bertrand Tavernier. *Claude Rich, Sami Frey, Philippe Noiret, Sophie Marceau.* Tavernier took over the directing reins on this film from buddy Riccardo Freda after Marceau demanded Freda be taken off the project. The result is certainly Tavernier's most straightforward, entertaining, and commercial film. Funny then, that, upon picking it up for U.S. distribution, Miramax demanded Tavernier shorten it. He refused and Miramax promptly buried the film, releasing it only on home video, absurdly retitling it *Revenge of the Musketeers*, and giving Marceau breast-implant surgery for the eventual U.S. pan-and-scan video release cover art. The DVD was finally released in 2004 in proper letterboxed format. Far from being a hired gun on this one, Tavernier still interweaves his perennial themes of contempt for greed and class separation, parent-child relations, and a beautiful pantheism seemingly inherited from fellow countryman Renoir. —*M. S.*

'ROUND MIDNIGHT L: DIRECTORS/TAVERNIER, BERTRAND (1986) 133M D: Bertrand Tavernier. *Lonette McKee, Dexter Gordon, François Cluzet, Gabrielle Haker, Sandra Reaves-Phillips, Christine Pascal.* More of a slowly unfolding blues than a frantic bebop, *Round Midnight* is the story of an aging saxophone player who develops a friendship with a young, avid French fan. The musician is played elegantly by Gordon, the real-life saxophone player who spent years abroad before making a triumphant return to the U.S, and other jazz figures, including Herbie Hancock, Bobby Hutcherson, and Wayne Shorter, round out the cast and play moving, original music in the movie itself. (In another bit of inspired casting, Martin Scorsese has a supporting role.) The plot meanders, starting in Europe and making a side trip to New York, but it's to be watched more for the sense of nostalgia, the feel of the city streets, and most of all the music. —*T. P.*

ST. MICHAEL HAD A ROOSTER L: DIRECTORS/TAVIANI BROTHERS (1972) 90M D: Paolo Taviani, Vittorio Taviani. *Renato Scarpa, Giulio Brogi, Daniele Dublino.* The Taviani Brothers are Italy's neorealist hipsters, presenting simple, direct images and earthy stories with a decidedly offbeat spin. With this story by Tolstoy, the Tavianis give us practically a one-man show. Intellectual humanist/anarchist Giulio Manieri (Brogi) is a revolutionary preaching to his followers, and when stuck in solitary confinement for ten years, he is his own audience as he recreates a semblance of his former life. His unflagging energy and almost religious devotion to his cause is contagious, and the inventive cinema and unexpected humor round out a loving, passionate portrait, all the more powerful when, after a decade in solitary, he finds his cause a vestigial historical curiosity outmoded in the industrial revolution and the fledgling labor movement. Like the best works of the Tavianis, you never know what's coming next, but when it happens it seems just perfect. —*S. A.*

MY FAVORITE SEASON L: DIRECTORS/TÉCHINÉ, ANDRÉ (1993) 125M D: André Téchiné. *Daniel Auteuil, Marthe Villalonga, Catherine Deneuve.* Téchiné's novelistic picture tells the story of two siblings (Deneuve and Auteuil), now adults, who shared an intensely deep bond as children. Both were very bright and full of potential. Living up to that potential, they naturally drifted apart and settled into their respective professional/adult roles, but neither have found much happiness. When their aged mother's health turns for the worse, the siblings' reunion unearths reminders of the happiness they enjoyed together as children—reminders weighted with the sad recognition of a vanished past. *My Favorite Season* is classically refined cinema, a character drama constructed with the precision and delicacy of an exceptional novel, and fueled by absorbing, complex performances and masterfully understated direction. —C. B.

ANTONIO GAUDI L: DIRECTORS/TESHIGAHARA, HIROSHI (1984) 72M D: Hiroshi Teshigahara.

With no narration and minimal titles, Teshigahara creates a flowing cinematic study that complements the rippling organic style of Spanish architect Antonio Gaudi. His camera caresses the statues and spirals that festoon the facades and snake around the honeycombed designs, then pulls back to show the intricate detail blur into the flowing lines of the overarching construction. While short on history and background information, this loving tribute to Gaudi's work is astoundingly tactile and immediate and the careful inclusion of people working, playing, and living within his structures is an excellent reminder that, for all their astounding beauty, Gaudi designed dwellings and public spaces for the people. —S. A.

BLUE KITE, THE L: DIRECTORS/TIAN, ZHUANGZHUANG (1993) 138M D: Tian Zhuangzhuang. Wenyao Zhang, Xiaoman Chen, Tian Yi.

A lacerating portrait of China under Mao's unforgiving rule in the '50s and '60s, Tian's drama of the lives destroyed by brutal and seemingly arbitrary political policies was banned in China and resulted in the effective blacklisting of the director. It was almost ten years before he was permitted to make his next film. In the meantime this beautiful, subtle film has been overlooked in the wake of more visually arresting and dramatically gripping productions, and undeservedly so. As seen through the eyes of a boy who grows up in the troubled times and watches three fathers disappear from his life, this is more potent for what remains unsaid, from the quiet sacrifices of loved ones to the unspecified charges that condemn the victims. —S. A.

FULLTIME KILLER L: DIRECTORS/TO, JOHNNY (2003) 101M D: Johnny To. Andy Lau, Takashi Sorimachi, Kelly Lin, Simon Yam.

Lau is a flamboyant, reckless young hit man in the Hong Kong underworld who decides to take out his cool, careful rival (Sorimachi), the old pro at the top of the killing game, and become the number one assassin in Asia. Lin is the woman caught between the dueling killers and Yam is the Interpol cop on the veteran killer's trail whose obsession finally cracks him up. Underworld opera of the bravura kind, this is driven (like most Hong Kong action) more by emotion than logic. The dreamy

flow through time and memory and the shifting point of view across four narrators cast the sleek stylistics of twenty-first-century Hong Kong cinema between tortured existential heroics, tall tale, and post-modern gangster fantasy. The melodramatic excess is all there, as are the shootouts and the daring escapes, but there's also a ruthlessness to the romantic conventions of hit men and hired killers. The outlaw melodrama snakes along so seductively that it's easy to lose yourself in the cinematic textures and the crime movie fantasy. —S. A.

HEROIC TRIO, THE L: DIRECTORS/TO, JOHNNY (1993) 82M D: Johnny To. Michelle Yeoh, Anita Mui, Maggie Cheung, Damian Lau, Yee Kwan Yan.

All that needs to be said about this movie is that Cheung is Thief-Catcher, Yeoh is Invisible Woman, and Mui is Wonder Woman, and they are superheroes trying to stop an evil master's plot to kidnap babies and turn them into an army of super-cannibals. The whole movie is completely berserk, combining crazy, cartoonish wire-assisted action with occasional bits of gruesome horror (bad things can and do happen to babies in this film). Laws of gravity do not apply, so the trio and their foes are able to fly around on motorcycles, on flaming barrels, or just on their own. This is one of my favorites. Followed by the darker but also great sequel *Executioners* directed by Ching Siu-Tung (who choreographed the action for this one). —B. T.

LIFELINE L: DIRECTORS/TO, JOHNNY (1997) 110M D: Johnny To. Lau Ching-Wan, Alex Fong, Carman Lee, Ruby Wong.

This Hong Kong[-]styled *Backdraft* is a dramatic exploration in the lives of firemen and -women, who must make decisions everyday that will not only affect their own safety, but the lives of their company and those they must protect. Lau proves his might once again as the boss of a firefighting unit that is considered jinxed. An incredible firefighting sequence in a burning building is an exhilarating and nail-biting emotional ride, as the company must decide to press on to save the trapped people or save their own lives. The most impressive thing about *Lifeline* is that all the actors do their own stunt work, and the fire was filmed on location. To takes another unique direction here, as there are no true antagonists save for the characters' uncertainty that they can do their jobs. This is an easy pick as one of the highlights for 1997. —R. M.

MISSION L: DIRECTORS/TO, JOHNNY (1999) 81M D: Johnny To. Anthony Wong Chau-Sang, Francis Ng.

To delivers the most handsome Hong Kong action film since John Woo left for Hollywood. The story is generic gangster stuff—five disparate professionals are hired to protect a mob boss targeted by assassins and they bond under fire —but the execution is topnotch. To's lean, precise style is the opposite of Woo's explosive action frenzies. He has an unerring eye for composition and creates tension from stillness as his badass bodyguards patiently wait for their opponents to make the first move, then strike swiftly with surgical precision. The gangster code of loyalty is tested when one of them commits a grievous sin against the honor of the boss and duty is put up against friendship. The story is slim but the film is rich with character (especially Wong's retired pro and Ng's hotheaded up-and-comer) and directed with a steely edge. —*S. A.*

PTU L: DIRECTORS/TO, JOHNNY (2003) 88M D: Johnny To *Simon Yam, Lam Suet, Ruby Wong, Maggie Siu.* After a slew of romantic comedies, To returns to what his fans love best and weaves a dramatic and suspenseful thriller that takes place over the course of a night for the Police Tactical Unit (PTU), led by Yam. The evening's events are set off when a law-bending detective named Lo (Lam) discovers his gun is missing after a tumble with a local triad gang. This is a serious offense and could cost him his job. His only hope is the PTU, which takes pity on Lo and decides to help him recover his gun. As their search continues, they are hounded by the Anti-Vice Squad and a Homicide Unit, who are competing for recognition, and become caught up in a gang turf struggle that is about to explode. To masterfully weaves his characters in a beautiful ballet, and brings them all together in the end for one climatic standoff that will have his followers rejoicing. —*R. M.*

RUNNING OUT OF TIME L: DIRECTORS/TO, JOHNNY (1999) 93M D: Johnny To. *Andy Lau, Lau Ching-Wan.* A box office smash in Hong Kong, this cat-and-mouse thriller is at times absurdly plotted and the twists are engineered without much thought to logic, but then that's hardly the point. To directs with steely seriousness and a sleek style, but like the best Hong Kong pictures it's driven by pure character. A mysterious, brooding criminal genius strings a brilliant supercop along in a battle of wits and a crazy series of crimes. Forget the elaborate if unlikely heist and just enjoy the melodrama of John Woo[-]style male bonding and a debt of honor paid in full. —*S. A.*

RUNNING OUT OF TIME 2 L: DIRECTORS/TO, JOHNNY (2001) 91M D: Johnny To, Law Wing-Cheung. *Lau Ching-Wan, Ekin Cheng, Kelly Lin, Lam Suet.* To (joined by co-director Law) takes a jaunty approach to this sequel as he pits impulsive genius police inspector Lau in a battle of wits against Cheng, a benevolent magician with a Robin Hood complex and a showman's love of performance. Both more lightweight and more fun than the first *Running Out of Time,* the absurd twists put strains on suspension of disbelief, but the playful direction, creative asides (the smiling magician's coin-tossing response to gambling cop Suet's crippling addiction is a lunatic bit of mad mental medicine), and complete lack of seriousness

give it a gentleness and a coolly comic dimension. —*S. A.*

WHERE A GOOD MAN GOES L: DIRECTORS/TO, JOHNNY (1999) 90M D: Johnny To. *Lau Ching-Wan, Lai Yiu-hung, Ruby Wong.* Lau is the former crime boss just released from prison who wants to rebuild his crime base but winds up falling for the widowed landlady (Wong) who runs the dive of a hotel he lives in. Less an action film than a melodrama of a man torn between his old life of hot-tempered violence and criminal scams and a possible new beginning promised by romance and fatherhood (he practically adopts the woman's young boy), it's pretty hammy and often overwrought as young punks and egotistical cops get in his face and torment his woman, but Lau gives a simmering performance. —*S. A.*

CAT PEOPLE L: DIRECTORS/TOURNEUR, JACQUES (1942) 71M D: Jacques Tourneur. *Simone Simon, Tom Conway, Jane Randolph, Elizabeth Russell.* Tourneur and producer Val Lewton were a classic thrill-making team, with unstoppable combined talents that most fortunately gave us three films. Irena (Simon) is the softly felined femme-fatale fashion designer who marries Oliver (Smith) but fears consummation of the marriage due to what may be a neurotic conjuring of strange memories of ancestral ties with a Balkan sect, where the women become fanged panthers when sexually excited. Oliver offers her a meeting with his friend Dr. Louis Judd (Conway) who works on Irena's problems quite closely, so closely that he attempts to cuckold his friend with the strange cat lady, of course ending in his doom. Randolph, as Oliver's office friend Alice, carries quite a few scenes, notably the scariest late-night solo pool dip ever, with cat growlings rumbling out of the shadowed darkness, solely illuminated by shimmering circles of light from the water's surface. Although forced by the studio to include actual shots of a panther, Tourneur and Lewton are able to prove that great fear need not be seen to be felt. —*S. R.*

CURSE OF THE DEMON, OR NIGHT OF THE DEMON L: DIRECTORS/TOURNEUR, JACQUES (1957) 95M D: Jacques Tourneur. *Peggy Cummins, Niall Mac Ginnis, Dana Andrews, Athene Seyler.* In a sleepy English town, a satanic cult appears to have been calling on demons to dispose of its various enemies. Skeptical psychologist John Holden (Andrews) works to debunk the theory that supernatural forces are behind the murders. Unfortunately, his investigations could make him the next victim. What's cool about this movie is that it maintains its suspense despite a dearth of action. The conflict between Holden and ominous cult leader Julian Karswell (Mac Ginnis) plays out predominately in calm conversations debating the contradictions of clinical science and superstitious mysticism. Good performances, a creepy musical score, and a fantastic screenplay make this is a pretty impressive little thriller, although it never approaches the sheer brilliance Tourneur brought to *Cat People* or *Out of the Past.* —*C. B.*

WAR GODS OF THE DEEP L: DIRECTORS/TOURNEUR, JACQUES (1965) 85M D: Jacques Tourneur. *David Tomlinson, Vincent Price. War Gods of the Deep* is an unmitigated failure that is perhaps the worst film of both director Tourneur and star Price's careers. But it's still fun. The plot centers on an underwater civilization of smugglers who never age and have gill-men for slaves. It's absolutely ridiculous. Poorly written, poorly acted, and with uninspired direction, *War Gods* is B-Movie through and through; it just has a big-name star and a reputable director. Price's uninspired performance is paired with too many underwater scenes and too many special effects. It's all a mess and everyone involved fully understood that. American International forced the production through too quickly and cheaply, refusing to let the script be improved. The result is a cinematic oddity, an absurd footnote to the careers of two great men. —*T. S.*

BLUE BIRD, THE L: DIRECTORS/TOURNEUR, MAURICE (1918) D: Maurice Tourneur. *Tula Belle, Robin Macdougall, Lillian Cook.* The richly tinted, blue night-tones set the mood for this allegory for children. A fairy in the shape of a crone (Cook) provides two kids (Belle and Macdougall) with magic clothing so they can see into the soul of fire and water and milk and sugar. With a dog and cat as companions, they search for the "blue bird of happiness" that will make the crone's sick daughter happy. After many adventures visiting dead relatives and a "house of luxury" with little happiness in it, they return home to find the Blue Bird. The film leaves you with a good, serious message and contains wonderful *Wizard of Oz*-like encounters, shot with sparkling photography. —*J. C.*

LAST OF THE MOHICANS L: DIRECTORS/TOURNEUR, MAURICE (1920) 73M D: Maurice Tourneur, Clarence Brown. *Wallace Beery, Barbara Bedford, Lillian Hall, Alan Roscoe, Theodore Lorch, Harry Lorraine.* Great, deep emotions are conveyed through astonishing visuals in this rich, powerful telling of the James Fenimore Cooper classic. A scout (Lorraine) during the French and Indian War leads a British officer (Woodward) and two women (Bedford and Hall) through the wilds to their father's fort, aided by the last two living members of the Mohican tribe (Roscoe and Lorch). Along the way, a native guide (Beery) who knows the terrain but is of questionable loyalty is foisted upon them. Adventures and betrayals ensue, and affection between the Mohican youth and one of the girls slowly and credibly blossoms. There's great deep-focus photography and lighting, particularly in a march out of the fort and during a grueling, ten-minute massacre sequence. Perhaps no film ever has etched such profoundly

moving scenes as this masterpiece of the silent cinema. —*J. C.*

BREAKING THE WAVES L: DIRECTORS/TRIER, LARS VON (1996) 159M D: Lars von Trier. *Stellan Skarsgård, Emily Watson.* I pop this into my player and about a half hour later pause to make myself some lunch. I watch about another half hour and I decide to start some laundry, another thirty minutes, I stop to call a friend, another thirty minutes, I decide to clean my room, thirty minutes, I wash the dishes, then I finally sit down and finish the damn thing. When the last credits roll off the screen, I lay down on my couch, pause for several seconds, and suddenly burst into uncontrollable tears for the next twenty minutes. This film is one of the hardest things I have ever had to sit through and I will never watch it again. —*T. C.*

DOGVILLE L: DIRECTORS/TRIER, LARS VON (2003) 177M D: Lars von Trier. *Philip Baker Hall, John Hurt, Paul Bettany, Stellan Skarsgård, Nicole Kidman, James Caan.* What's truly remarkable about this film is its set. Though the action is supposed to take place in the '30s in Dogville, a fictional town in the American Rockies, the set is simply one large empty soundstage with lines and names in the floor to indicate where buildings are supposed to be. Within this curious setting a plot unfolds. A young woman flees from some gangsters who are after her by hiding in an abandoned mineshaft in town. Once the gangsters leave, the protagonist convinces her and the whole town that staying in Dogville would benefit everyone. Slowly she wins the acceptance of the town and the town shifts from ignoring her to using her to abusing her. Von Trier has found a very good story to probe one of his favorite themes: the corruption of the individual as perceived by group psychology. —*N. J.*

IDIOTS, THE L: DIRECTORS/TRIER, LARS VON (1998) 117M D: Lars von Trier. *Bodil Jorgensen, Anne Louise Hassing, Troels Lyby, Jens Albinus.* It's hard for many folks to watch Dogme films, with handheld cameras and natural lighting. But it's strange that it's easier for many people to watch a movie with awful acting than a movie that doesn't have the obvious marks of high-budget filmmaking. Therein lies the importance of *The Idiots.* It's at least partially adherent to Dogme rules, allowing for the film's focus to be the acting, which *The Idiots* does better than any other film I've seen. Von Trier is able to get the type of acting on screen that allows you to feel who the characters are without a lot of story development. You can sense what his characters want and what they've experienced through a mere glimpse into their eyes. I'd sit through eight hundred shaky films for that. —*J. J.*

KINGDOM, THE L: DIRECTORS/TRIER, LARS VON (1995) 279M D: Lars von Trier. *Ernst Hugo Jarogard, Soren Pilmark, Ghita Norby, Kristen Rolffes, Udo Kier,*

Holger Juul Hansen. This is a fascinating serial about a haunted hospital in Denmark. The characters are well balanced and expertly cast. They include an elderly woman who checks herself into the hospital and finds she is able to communicate with the murdered child who haunts the facility, a Swedish doctor who despises Denmark and longs for his own country, the morgue attendant who hordes mood-altering medicines and experiences the chronic disruptions caused by the ghost, and a variety of strange patients and personnel who make this lengthy film anything but tiresome. It was made for Danish TV but also released theatrically. *—N. J.*

KINGDOM 2, THE L: DIRECTORS/TRIER, LARS VON (1997) 286M D: Lars von Trier. *Holger Juul Hansen, Kristen Rolffes, Ghita Norby, Udo Kier, Ernst Hugo Jarogard, Soren Pilmark.* Kier steals the show in this hospital soap-turned-carnival. Within an intricate circle of strange characters, Kier plays a newborn baby who immediately develops the power of speech (albeit strained and annoying) and grows at such an accelerated rate that his ten-foot limbs must be supported by makeshift scaffolds. He whines and pleads for assistance, but most of the staff are caught in awkward problems of their own, such as the neurosurgeon experimenting with a voodoo potion from Haiti, and the head of the hospital who has some sort of erectile fetish. This film is by far more bizarre than its predecessor, yet for fans of von Trier it is all the more exhilarating. *—N. J.*

ZENTROPA L: DIRECTORS/TRIER, LARS VON (1992) 112M D: Lars von Trier. *Max von Sydow, Jean-Marc Barr, Barbara Sukowa, Udo Kier, Eddie Constantine.* A conductor on a train in 1945 post-WWII Germany falls in love with one of the passengers. As the young lady begins to win the confidence of this conductor, she begins to trust him with a plot of which she is a part—a group of Nazi sympathizers intend to destroy a bridge while the train passes over it. Knowledge of this plotted sabotage causes great turbulence for the conductor's sense of morality and allegiance. All of this is stylistically conveyed through dynamic black-and-white photography while the hypnotic voice of von Sydow narrates both internal and external aspects of this unique story. Originally titled *Europa,* it was changed in the U.S. to avoid confusion with *Europa, Europa. —N. J.*

MARIANNE AND JULIANE L: DIRECTORS/TROTTA, MARGARETHE VON (1981) 106M D: Margarethe von Trotta. *Barbara Sukowa, Jutta Lampe, Doris Schade, Rudiger Vogler.* This is a look at two German sisters working and fighting for social change during the late '60s, and how the different tactics used divides the community. The close relationship between the two sisters is affected by one of the sisters going underground, causing alienation and frustration in the family. One of them, Marianne (Sukowa), is a journalist writ-

ing about ideas and theories for change, while Juliane (Lampe) goes underground and becomes a member of the feared and legendary Baader Meinhof group. Fans of New German Cinema will love this film; the tone is bleak and it does a great job of setting up scenes. It focuses a little much on the emotional tests of Marianne, when the more interesting story is with Juliane and the exploits of the Baader Meinhof group. Any good film that deals with a historical narrative will ultimately drive the viewer to find out more about a situation in history, and this is one of those films *—B. W.*

ROSA LUXEMBURG L: DIRECTORS/TROTTA, MARGARETHE VON (1986) 122M D: Margarethe von Trotta. *Barbara Sukowa, Daniel Olbrychski, Otto Sander, Adelheid Arndt.* "All history is based on people deciding the fate of others, and that is deeply rooted in the conditions of our material existence. The only way to change this is by painful upheaval." *Rosa Luxemburg* is an inspiring and powerful portrait of a Polish-German, Socialist/Communist activist who lived from 1872–1919. Using flashbacks, we follow her work and arrest in Warsaw, her move to Berlin, her friendships, and two love affairs. Sukowa plays Rosa with fire and grace, embodying her drive, her speeches, the articulation of her ideas, her empathy, and her purpose with inspiration. When the war ends she seems vindicated and is released from prison, but fate has other things in store. She was eventually murdered for her beliefs during the unsuccessful Spartacus rebellion in Germany, right after its defeat in World War I. If we could only have more Rosas amongst us now perhaps the state of the world would not be so grim. We could use some painful upheaval. *—B. W.*

SECOND AWAKENING OF CHRISTA KLAGES, THE L: DIRECTORS/TROTTA, MARGARETHE VON (1978) 92M D: Margarethe von Trotta. *Marius Müller-Westernhagen, Sylvia Reize, Tina Engel.* Von Trotta didn't so much burst onto the German filmmaking scene as work her way up from actress to scenarist to codirector (with husband Volker Schlöndorff on *The Lost Honor of Katrina Blum*). Her first solo effort grapples with elusive political and social issues in an intelligent and thoughtful manner, and her direction of performances is excellent. Based on a true story, the film chronicles the journey of a dedicated social worker and young mother (Engel) who turns to bank robbery to save her child's day-care center when it runs out of money. Becoming a fugitive, her escape takes her full circle to a surprising conclusion. This is an excellent debut, but the power is in the words and performances, and von Trotta's points are made bluntly yet eloquently. *—S. A.*

SHEER MADNESS L: DIRECTORS/TROTTA, MARGARETHE VON (1983) 100M D: Margarethe von Trotta. *Hanna Schygulla, Peter Striebeck, Angela Winkler.* Von Trotta is the most aggressively political director of the New

German Cinema to emerge onto the international scene, but it's her vital characters and their rich relationships to one another—and to themselves—that make her films such exciting celebrations of women empowering themselves. In *Sheer Madness* (beautifully shot by Fassbinder's cinematographer, Michael Balhaus) she again examines the relationship between two women, a confident college professor (Schygulla in one of her best performances) and a withdrawn, suicidal artist (von Trotta regular Winkler), and charts the complexity of relations between and within the sexes.But this one is more troubling, more elusive. Where von Trotta's previous films have rewarded their protagonists with the clarity of insight and revelation at their conclusions, this takes a surprising turn that suddenly redefines the entire film. Her brilliant signature of cutting back to the film's title after the final shot only reinforces that thinking. —*S. A.*

ANTOINE AND COLETTE L: DIRECTORS/TRUFFAUT, FRANÇOIS
(1962) 30M D: François Truffaut. *Rosy Varte, François Darbon, Jean-Pierre Léaud, Marie-France Pisier.* Truffaut's classic is about a boy (Léaud) in love with a girl (Pisier). The center of Antoine's infatuation, Colette, just wants a friend, and Antoine is left to pace at home with his parents as she dates other young beaus. The optical effects, which Truffaut used on occasion but never so often or as concentrated as here, makes clear his joy of the filmmaking process. —*M. H.*

BED AND BOARD L: DIRECTORS/TRUFFAUT, FRANÇOIS
(1970) 95M D: François Truffaut., *Jean-Pierre Léaud, Claude Jade, Jacques Cottin, Hiroko Berfhauer.* Just as *Stolen Kisses* is no *400 Blows*, *Bed and Board* is no *Stolen Kisses*. But let's face it, *Stolen Kisses* was pretty great. *Bed and Board* may not be one of Truffaut's essential moments, but it is surely one of the more inventive, entertaining, and interesting French relationship comedies around. Antoine (Léaud) is updated into married life with Christine (Jade), yet seems not much different than the kid from *The 400 Blows*. Christine becomes pregnant, but Antoine turns his attention to writing a novel and having an affair. The characters are as likable as in *Stolen Kisses,* and the film is awash in small, near-perfect moments. While watching the film you might be disappointed that it doesn't hold up to the previous Antoine Doinel episodes, but afterward its likely to be a film you'll look back on fondly. —*C. B.*

DAY FOR NIGHT L: DIRECTORS/TRUFFAUT, FRANÇOIS
(1973) 116M D: François Truffaut. *Jean-Pierre Léaud, Nathalie Baye, Jean-Pierre Aumont, Jacqueline Bisset, Valentina Cortese, Dani, François Truffaut.* Truffaut's Oscar-winning love letter to cinema celebrates the glorious chaos and creative heartache of making movies. Truffaut himself reigns over the on-screen cinema circus as a director named Ferrand, an aloof figure juggling produc-

tions delays, budget cuts, and the personal crises of his cast and crew as he tries to get his film made.But he's more ringmaster than featured player: In the center ring are an impulsive young actor (Léaud, evoking a decade of roles in the films of the French New Wave), plus a famous French lover (Aumont), an Italian diva who can hardly remember her lines (Cortese), and a fragile American actress (Bisset). Holding it all together is production assistant Joelle (Baye in her screen debut), playing everything from cast nursemaid to crew foreman to Ferrand's girl Friday. Truffaut revels in the parade of minor disasters that often as not provide a spark that will later enrich the film—a line, a script change, a different way of attacking a scene—and in the friendships, quick affairs, and camaraderie turn them all, for a brief moment, into a festive filmmaking family. —*S. A.*

JULES AND JIM L: DIRECTORS/TRUFFAUT, FRANÇOIS
(1962) 105M D: François Truffaut. *Henri Serre, Vanna Urbino, Jeanne Moreau, Oskar Werner.* Werner is the Austrian Jules, a vibrant young biologist whose slow, melancholy slide to emotional compromise is charted in his increasingly sad eyes and resigned face. Serre plays his best friend, the Parisian writer Jim, as more of an enigma, guarded and introspective. Both are eclipsed in the glare of Moreau's radiant performance as the impulsive and reckless Catherine, the sensual and destructive woman steeped in mystery who turns their duo into a trio. A scandal upon its release for its unapologetic treatment of a ménage-à-trois, Truffaut's creative adaptation of Henri-Pierre Roche's novel uses the stylistic freedom of New Wave techniques (zooms, flash-cuts, handheld shots taken literally on the run by Raoul Cotard) to contrast the scenes of carefree youth with the somber, subdued "adult" years of impermanence. The handsome period-piece jackrabbits through the story with concentrated scenes interspersed with newsreel footage and montages, pulled together by an interpretive "literary" narrator who layers the film with an added richness. A confident, compelling work. —*S. A.*

MISTONS, LES L: DIRECTORS/TRUFFAUT, FRANÇOIS (1957)
22M D: François Truffaut. *Michel François (narrator), Gerard Blain, Bernadette Lafont.* Truffaut's 1957 short (roughly translated to "The Brats") is early testament to his affinity with kids. Five boys palling around one summer fall for a teen beauty, but as the narrator (one of the five remembering back) describes, "Too young to love Bernadette, we decided to hate her—and torment her." Which they do, between their worshipful watches. These adolescent boys are neither cute nor innocent, but Truffaut sympathizes with their frustration, born of budding hormones and sexual mystery. With the limitations imposed by the project (a running time of twenty-two minutes, a voice-over in place of dialogue) he never

Movies we like from directors we usually hate

ANNIE HALL	JAWS
(Woody Allen)	*(Steven Spielberg)*
BAMBOOZLED	THE KEEP
(Spike Lee)	*(Michael Mann)*
BLADE RUNNER	MCCABE AND MRS. MILLER
(Ridley Scott)	*(Robert Altman)*
BUGSY MALONE	PHENOMENA
(Alan Parker)	*(Dario Argento)*
CHINATOWN	THE PILLOW BOOK
(Roman Polanski)	*(Peter Greenaway)*
DC CAB	PREDATOR
(Joel Schumacher)	*(John McTiernan)*
THE DOORS	REPULSION
(Oliver Stone)	*(Roman Polanski)*
DUEL	SPLASH
(Steven Spielberg)	*(Ron Howard)*
FAT GIRL	SPLENDOR
(Catherine Breillat)	*(Gregg Araki)*
FEMME FATALE	THE STRAIGHT STORY
(Brian DePalma)	*(David Lynch)*
THE HILLS HAVE EYES	THE 25TH HOUR
(Wes Craven)	*(Spike Lee)*
THE INCREDIBLE SHRINKING WOMAN	TIGERLAND
(Joel Schumacher)	*(Joel Schumacher)*

creates individual personalities—the boys exist only as a pack—and Bernadette and her boyfriend (future New Wave performers LaFont and Blain) are more icons than characters.But that works just fine in the context of this haunting yet tender remembrance. —*S.A.*

SHOOT THE PIANO PLAYER L: DIRECTORS/TRUFFAUT, FRANÇOIS (1960) 85M D: François Truffaut. *Nicole Berger, Marie Dubois, Michèle Mercier, Charles Aznavour.* Truffaut's second film is a constantly surprising combination of film noir fatalism and comic absurdism that pinballs all around before settling into a mood of soul-shattering doom. Aznavour is a seedy bar pianist with a shadowy past that hangs over him like a perpetual night and a waitress lover (Dubois) who needs his help. The source is David Goodis's pulp crime novel *Down There*, but the film is all Truffaut's. Shot on the streets of Paris and in the snowy wilderness of Southern France, the film is alternately seedy, elegant, and picturesque, interspersed with slapstick silliness sprung from Truffaut's imagina-

tion. But it's Aznavour's dour face, a cigarette dangling from his listless lips as he hunches in a resigned slump over his piano, that ultimately defines the film's tone. —*S.A.*

SOFT SKIN, THE L: DIRECTORS/TRUFFAUT, FRANÇOIS (1964) 118M D: François Truffaut. *Jean Desailly, Françoise Dorléac, Nelly Benedetti.* Literary critic Desailly doesn't have adultery on his mind when he becomes entranced with a lithe, lovely young stewardess (Dorléac) who keeps crossing his path on a speaking engagement. He's happily married with a wife and daughter, but he plunges ahead with an affair that, despite his best efforts, begins to unravel all of their lives. It's not a thriller in any generic sense of the term; Truffaut invests this bitter tale of an affair and its repercussions with curious elements of Hitchcock, some very effective (a meticulously plotted sequence of just-missed connections) and others merely offbeat (a drive to the airport backed by a *Psycho*-like violin theme). Shooting in creamy black and white with a smooth, chic elegance, Truffaut surrounds the film with the trappings of lush romanticism before stripping away the idealized elements. Desailly's middle-aged adulterer emerges not so much sordid as vain and pathetic, but the change in tone hardly prepares the viewer for the furiously calamitous conclusion. Watch for the scene with the kitten who licks off a plate set out for room service—Truffaut recreated it for his film-within-a-film in *Day For Night*. —*S.A.*

STOLEN KISSES L: DIRECTORS/TRUFFAUT, FRANÇOIS (1969) 90M D: François Truffaut. *Jean-Pierre Léaud, Claude Jade, Delphine Seyrig, Michael Lonsdale.* The third and definitely most well-rounded of Truffaut's five-part introspective series. The film begins with a slightly less naive Antoine Doinel (Léaud) waiting to be released from a military prison, only to make a beeline to the nearest brothel. Unable to find another job, Doinel becomes a private investigator who must pose as a shoe clerk to uncover the reason why all the employees talk so much shit about their boss. Every movie in this group of Truffaut's is without a doubt worth seeing, yet this one sticks out the most as we finally see Doinel as a carefree, barely mature, grown man who still hasn't really jumped into any commitments or engagements—something that Truffaut seemed constantly stuck on and attempted to shake throughout his career. If he had his choice, I'm thinking he would be perpetually stuck in this film, surrounded by hookers, alluring discontent housewives, and pretty, young French girls with rosy cheeks. —*A.T.*

HOLE, THE (1998) L: DIRECTORS/TSAI MING-LIANG (1998) 95M D: Tsai Ming-Liang. *Lin Kun-huei, Kang-sheng Lee, Tien Miao, Kuei-Mei Yang, Hui-Chin Lin.* At the brink of the millennium, the city must deal with a plague that is said to turn people into cockroaches. It doesn't physically cause the victim to grow antennae or suffer some grotesque metamorphosis, but the disease actually infects the behavior or spirit of the vermin into the person, causing him or her to avoid social contact and seek refuge in dark places. If it weren't for the stark pacing and slow delivery, these scenes of middle-aged men and women scurrying around floors could otherwise seem quite ridiculous. These moments are enhanced by the intermittent musical scenes, which explode out of nowhere and return back into the somber continuity as quickly as they came. —*A.T.*

WHAT TIME IS IT THERE? L: DIRECTORS/TSAI MING-LIANG (2002) 116M D: Tsai Ming-Liang. *Lee Kang-Sheng, Cecilia Yip, Chen Shiang-Chyi, Miao Tien.* Lee is a street-side watch vendor in Tapei who reluctantly sells his own dual-time watch to Paris-bound Chen. This portrait of delicate connections and disconnections has all the charms of Tsing's earlier films—a story of loneliness and social isolation, unrequited longing, obsession, and family splintering, caught with an unmoving camera that

reveals the most telling details in its long hard looks—with a sense of dry whimsy and absurdity. Lee's mother awaits her deceased husband's reincarnation with such single-minded focus that she loses touch with life around her and Lee resets every clock he comes across to Paris time after watching *The 400 Blows* on video. (To complete the roundelay, Chen wanders about Paris and meets *The 400 Blows* star Jean-Pierre Léaud in a delicious cameo.) This film is as much about time passing while characters stand still as about any explainable story. If you can settle into the decidedly unique rhythm and quiet detail, it rewards with amazing textures of time and emotion. —*S.A.*

BLADE, THE L: DIRECTORS/TSUI HARK (1995) 104M D: Tsui Hark. *Moses Chan, Zhao Wen-Zhuo, Xiong Xin-Xin.* Tsui's hyperactive remake of the Shaw brothers' *One-Armed Swordsman* stays true to the original source, while effortlessly making a unique film with his stamp all over it. On (Zhao) is a master swordmaker who works for the Sharp Manufacturer sword factory, which pays tribute to a broken blade every year. On, who is the least popular worker, has been appointed the new master of the factory, but instead of taking the position, he sets out to find his father's killer. His first encounter with the tattooed madman leaves him without an arm. His quest for vengeance leads him to steal the broken blade and learn sword technique from a half-destroyed ancient book, before setting out again for the final duel. Zhao is quite believable as a one-armed man, and Tsui's kinetic and frantic editing goes against the grain of swordplay filming, which is a dizzying treat to take in. Sadly, this is one of Tsui's last movies worth watching. —*R.M.*

CHINESE FEAST, THE L: DIRECTORS/TSUI HARK (1995) 106M D: Tsui Hark. *Anita Yuen, Leslie Cheung, Kenny Bee.* Hark's culinary comedy combines martial-arts movie tropes with *Iron Chef*-style duels. Cheung is the former gangster turned cooking-school drop-out (actually he was kicked out for incompetence) who turns to a retired master chef (Bee) to take on an evil restaurateur in a grand contest. Yuen goes new wave as the chef's rebellious daughter with an old-fashioned heart (could true love be brewing?). Hark directs it like an action movie, with furious pacing, wicked editing, and wacky twists, but his pacing is pure comedy. The humor is often broad and slapstick, but Hark always remembers to keep it grounded in gags, and his timing is dead-on. —*S.A.*

DOUBLE TEAM L: DIRECTORS/TSUI HARK (1997) 91M D: Tsui Hark. *Dennis Rodman, Natacha Lindinger, Mickey Rourke, Paul Freeman, Jean-Claude Van Damme.* The great Hong Kong director/producer Tsui came to Hollywood and, like John Woo and Ringo Lam before him, got saddled with Van Damme. But instead of toning down his style for the United States, he turned the dial up until it broke, creating perhaps the most insane vehicle ever for an American action star. The first half of the movie has Van Damme captive on a *Prisoner*-like island for super spies. Then he escapes and finds himself in a buddy movie with Rodman as an arms dealer who inexplicably uses a parachute shaped like a basketball. It's hard to explain but suffice it to say that the climactic battle involves Rourke, a baby, a motorcycle, a Roman coliseum, a Coke machine, landmines, a tiger, and a monastery of subterranean computer experts called "cybermonks." Tsui and Van Damme later reteamed for the arguably even weirder *Knock Off*. —*B. T.*

GREEN SNAKE L: DIRECTORS/TSUI HARK (1993) 98M D: Tsui Hark. *Maggie Cheung, Joey Wong, Man Cheuk Chiu, Wu Hsing-Kuo.* Sexy snake-sisters Wong (the philosophical one) and Cheung (the impulsive one) shed their skins for a little fun in human bodies while a humorless monk (a holier-than-thou Chiu) finds their exploration of, um, the fleshy pleasures a decidedly sinful pursuit and vows to kill them. Directed with grandiose flash and high-energy drive by Hong Kong New Wave godfather Hark, this umpteenth remake of the classic Chinese myth is a sexy hoot. The ambitious special effects are a bit ragged but the spirited performances, bright visual palette, and a flamboyant sense of fantasy turn this myth into a new portrait of Eden. Innocence experiments with sex: What a discovery! —*S. A.*

KNOCK OFF L: DIRECTORS/TSUI HARK (1998) 91M D: Tsui Hark. *Paul Sorvino, Lela Rochon, Jean-Claude Van Damme, Rob Schneider.* Hong Kong director Tsui re-*Double Team*-ed with Van Damme for this fever dream of an action movie before returning to the motherland for the more respectable *Time and Tide*. Van Damme plays a fashion designer (!) who, along with undercover CIA agent Schneider (!!), tries to stop a convoluted terrorist plot involving exploding jeans (!!!). Writer Steven E. de Souza intended this as an obliteration of the *Die Hard*-on-a-blank genre, but it seems like it's supposed to be serious, even when Van Damme pulls a rickshaw and Schneider whips him with an eel, yelling "Move that beautiful ass!" Like many Hong Kong films it was shot non-synch, so you get to see Hollywood actors like Schneider and Sorvino with all of their dialogue looped. There is also a POV shot from inside a shoe. —*B. T.*

LEGEND OF ZU, THE L: DIRECTORS/TSUI HARK (2001) 104M D: Tsui Hark. *Sammo Hung Kam-Bo, Cecilia Cheung, Louis Koo, Kelly Lin, Ekin Cheng.* This movie is like a video game accompaniment to the original film, *Zu: Warriors of the Magic Mountain*. Loosely connected to the original, *Legend* doesn't really hold its own in terms of storytelling and construction, if one were to compare the two, but that's not really the point. The story line has been inflated to operatic proportions, and the

special effects will have any CG buff creaming silicon out their pants as the movie stacks one big climactic moment on top of another. Alas, one can only endure so much eye candy, and after awhile the overwhelming pace gets to be, well, overwhelming. Nonetheless, this is what *Final Fantasy*, the movie, should have/could have been. —*T. C.*

ONCE UPON A TIME IN CHINA L: DIRECTORS/TSUI HARK (1991) 134M D: Tsui Hark. *Jet Li, Rosamund Kwan, Yuen Biao, Jacky Cheung.* Tsui's sweeping martial-arts epic is a historical action-picture presented as new wave pulp. Li rose to stardom as Chinese folk hero Wong Fei-hung: healer, teacher, and—when his mild mannered ways are pushed to the limit—wicked scrapper. That's easily done when the British, the Americans, and the French bring gunboat diplomacy to 1875 China. The history is pure, flag-waving heroics, but the set pieces are masterful and the color and choreography are magnificent. Watch Li get almost airborne while fighting on ladders swooshing back and forth in a grain elevator and then chopped down to kindling while the foes fight it out on splinters. Biao and Cheung costar, and Kwan is his Westernized Auntie Yee, who stirs feelings in the boyish hero that go far beyond family devotion. —*S. A.*

ONCE UPON A TIME IN CHINA 2 L: DIRECTORS/TSUI HARK (1992) 112M D: Tsui Hark. *David Chiang, Rosamund Kwan, Jet Li.* After the rousing anti-imperialist adventure showcased in the first film, Tsui makes the villains of this first sequel a pious band of isolationist zealots, sort of a radical fringe of the Boxers led by a self-proclaimed messiah. That gives healer/martial artist/folk hero Wong Fei-hung (the calm, graceful action whirlwind Li) a chance to play multicultural ambassador, and the film a chance to introduce another real-life hero: Sun Yat-sen. The slam-bang climax, directed with Tsui's trendsetting flash and flair, features Li leaping about a church and fighting atop a rickety tower of tables, then engaging in a breathtaking pole fight that almost tops the airborne bravura of the first film. Kwan returns as the Westernized Auntie Yee to continue their shy courtship. —*S. A.*

PEKING OPERA BLUES L: DIRECTORS/TSUI HARK (1986) 104M D: Tsui Hark. *Sally Yeh, Paul Chu, Kenneth Tsang, Cherie Chung, Brigitte Lin, Ma Wu.* Tsui's stylish, high-energy genre cocktail mixes slapstick, romance, espionage, politics, history, and Chinese Opera into a frenzied screwball adventure. Young turn-of-the-century revolutionary Lin (the boyish daughter of a military warlord) teams up with a scheming courtesan (Cherie Chung) and an aspiring actress (Yeh) in a traveling theatrical troupe as the opposition to the invading dictator gathers and chaos erupts around the city. Hark's tone runs the gamut from lighthearted mistaken identity mix-ups to gallows humor to out-and-out sadism (a grim, prolonged torture scene), all of it driven by an acrobatic style and a rollicking pace. He never lets the pace lag while juggling the crisscrossing story-lines, and the sumptuous visuals are never less than gorgeous. A landmark film in the Hong Kong New Wave, and a delirious delight. —S. A.

TIME AND TIDE L: DIRECTORS/TSUI HARK (2000) 113M D: Tsui Hark. *Wu Bai, Candy Lo, Cathy Tsui, Couto Remotigue, Nicholas Tse, Anthony Wong Chau-Sang*. Clever, witty, stylish, and action packed; this offering is a feast for the eyes and the mind. The convoluted tale traces the path of two men; one is determined to support the woman he accidentally impregnated whether she wants him to or not. Desperate to make some quick cash, he joins a bodyguard service only to find himself embroiled in something much more dangerous. The other man is a disillusioned mercenary determined to start a new life with his new wife. The two men collide, and fate twists their lives together as they work to thwart an assassination attempt. From there, the strands divide to wild and chaotic results. This film is a frenzy of explosions, gunfire, and top-notch martial-arts action with a final scene that has to be seen to believed. I for one will never look at my refrigerator the same way again. The tag line says it all: "No tigers, no dragons—just a hell of a lot of bullets." —M. N.

ZU: WARRIORS OF THE MAGIC MOUNTAIN L: DIRECTORS/TSUI HARK (1983) 95M D: Tsui Hark. *Hoi Mang, Adam Cheng, Moon Lee, Brigitte Lin, Biao Yuen*. This is how it should be done! Continuity takes a back seat as action sequences frenetically jump from cut to cut in mid-movement. The visual language is initially jarring and confusing, but once you let go of trying to make sense of everything, it turns into this unsettlingly gorgeous hyper-ballet. I have never seen such a sublime use of color and cloth in a kung fu flick. —T. C.

HEAVEN L: DIRECTORS/TYKWER, TOM (2002) 96M D: Tom Tykwer. *Cate Blanchett, Giovanni Ribisi*. German director Tykwer takes on a screenplay by the late, great Kieslowski and his writing partner, Piesiewicz. Designed as the first film in a trilogy (*Purgatory* and *Hell* being the later entries), *Heaven* is similar to Kieslowski's Three Colors trilogy in that it takes a major theme (redemption) and turns it inwards, making it personal and humanizing it. Blanchettt plays a British teacher living in Italy who accidentally kills four innocent people while attempting revenge on a local drug lord. Ribisi is the translator for her interrogation by the corrupt police department. He helps her to escape and the rest of the film chronicles their run from the law and Blanchett's struggle to come to terms with her crime. After a tense opening scene, the action plays out with a languid pace but there is beauty in its meditative forward momentum. Heightened with beautiful photography and excellent multilin-

gual acting from the stars, *Heaven* never seems quite as important or transcendent as any of the scripts Kieslowski directed himself, despite its lofty intentions. But overall, *Heaven* is a very rewarding effort, the closest to a posthumous Kieslowski film that we can get. —T. S.

PRINCESS AND THE WARRIOR, THE L: DIRECTORS/TYKWER, TOM (2001) 135M D: Tom Tykwer. *Benno Fürmann, Franka Potente*. Tykwer sets the cinematic bravura of *Run, Lola, Run* at the dreamy pace of his earlier *Winter Sleepers* for this gorgeous but sedate tale that reunites him with *Lola* star Potente. She's an emotionally inert nurse whose careful life is uprooted by a near-fatal traffic accident and the haunted thief (Fürmann) who saves her life. I'm at a loss to explain why it takes the thrill of crime to break through lives of quiet desperation and find love on the run, but such clichés of outlaw romantic aside it's a lush, rich film. Full of sleek and often stunning images and thrilling effects set to the constant throbbing of an electronic score, it's downright hypnotic at its best and sedate and slow at its worst. Tykwer oversells his simple and familiar story of forgiveness, sacrifice, and emotional healing, but when he connects it's exhilarating. —S. A.

RUN, LOLA, RUN L: DIRECTORS/TYKWER, TOM (1998) 81M D: Tom Tykwer. *Franka Potente, Mortiz Bleibtreu, Herbert Knaup*. In a world just outside of reality, Lola (Potente) is given three chances to save the life of her boyfriend, Manni (Bleibtreu), when she receives a frantic call from him. Manni, who has lost a huge sum of money due to a mob boss, must make his payment in twenty minutes or he will die. Lola is given the responsibility of replacing the funds, but where does one find $50,000 in such a short amount of time? Fate sets her out on her exploration, and only a chance in hell will get her out alive. When one attempt fails, Lola is thrown back in time to try again, and it is debatable whether she "realizes" this or not. Watching the film is a surreal experience that is a lesson in how to keep a heartbeat going at breakneck speed for eighty-one minutes. The story unfolds almost in real time, and the techno beat makes every step in Lola's race all the more emphasized. —R. M.

WINTER SLEEPERS L: DIRECTORS/TYKWER, TOM (1997) 122M D: Tom Tykwer. *Josef Bierbichler, Marie-Lou Sellem, Ulrich Matthes*. Wandering home drunk from Sleepers' Bar on the day after Christmas, Rene (Matthes) steals an unlocked car and drives out onto the icy highway. To avoid an oncoming truck, Rene slams on the brakes and skids over the embankment into a snowdrift. Theo (Bierbichler) discovers that his daughter has stowed away in the truck when he sees her body lying in the snow. Tykwer focuses on the coincidences that often link the most unsuspecting strangers. Laura (Sellem), Theo's nurse at the hospital, meets Rene at Sleepers'. Theo, just a step behind, plasters the streets with flyers describing and blaming Rene for his daughter's death. Each character suffers an affliction that adds to *Sleepers'* drowsy mood. Laura drops into a dead faint without warning. Rene's reality is blurred by chronic memory loss. Only Theo, enlivened by his quest, breaks out of this sleepy haze and instead wrestles with insomnia. *Winter Sleepers* uses an expectant score and atmospheric set to invite us completely into its dream world. —*M. M.*

CARNEGIE HALL L: DIRECTORS/ULMER, EDGAR (1947) 136M D: Edgar Ulmer. *Frank McHugh, Martha O'Driscoll, Marsha Hunt, William Prince.* How do you get to Carnegie Hall? Practice! Or watch Ulmer's tribute to the famed New York concert hall, the story of an immigrant mother (Hunt) who pushes her son (Prince) to become a classical musician, only to turn her back on him when he turns to popular music. The director's dream project is overlong but not as ponderous as you might expect. A few sequences are delicate and lovely (the little immigrant girl who sneaks out on stage during a Carnegie Hall performance is magical), but the story is pure hokum. Its claim to history is the roll call of '40s music-greats performing on the hallowed stage. Ulmer manages musical appearances by Artur Rubenstein, Leopold Stokowski, Jascha Heifetz, Harry James, Vaughn Monroe, Rise Stevens, Lily Pons, Ezio Pinza, Jan Peerce, Gregor Piatigorsky, Bruno Walter, and the New York Philharmonic. —*S. A.*

DAUGHTER OF DR. JEKYLL, THE L: DIRECTORS/ULMER, EDGAR (1957) 70M D: Edgar Ulmer. *Gloria Talbott, Arthur Shields, John Agar.* Another of Ulmer's six-day wonders, this is less Robert Louis Stevenson than Universal gothic horror, complete with angry villagers and an ever-present mist licking an ancient English manor. Think of it as a werewolf film by way of *Gaslight*, with the Jekyll name merely an ingenious Macguffin. Talbott is the titular offspring of the infamous mad scientist who is terrified that she's inherited her father's curse. Ulmer brilliantly stage-manages his budget with lavish art direction in a few key scenes while obscuring the rest of his sets (yes, that eternal fog). It's at times silly and the low-rent monster makeup is rather shaggy, but Ulmer is a master of mood and mise-en-scène, teasing beautiful imagery from his ramshackle sets and the beautiful face of tortured heroine Talbott. —*S. A.*

DETOUR (1945) L: DIRECTORS/ULMER, EDGAR (1946) 67M D: Edgar Ulmer. *Ann Savage, Claudia Drake, Edmund MacDonald, Tom Neal.* Handsome, down-on-his-luck Al (Neal) hitches his away across America to meet up with his sweetie Sue (Drake) in LA, hoping to marry her. Along the way he catches a ride with Charles Haskell Jr. (Macdonald), whom Al notices sports a nasty set of scratches along his cheek. Haskell dies from a heart condition along the way, and so Al takes Haskell's clothes and car onward. But Al makes a fatal mistake: he picks up the lovely Vera (Savage) along the way, and finds out the beauty is a beast. Vera rode with Haskell the day before and was the one who scratched his face off. She suspects Al murdered Haskell, and without proof to the contrary, Al allows Vera to blackmail and boss him around until he finally can't take it anymore. All the classic noir elements are here: the innocent man, a poor shmuck only guilty in his mind and a victim of circumstances beyond his control; the femme fatale who drives him to commit crime; and, of course, murder. Told completely in flashback, *Detour* is even more amazing to watch when you realize Ulmer was forced to shoot the entire film in three days for twenty thousand dollars. Neal and Savage are topnotch, as is the direction in this little film that is perhaps more famous than any other noir. —*N. H.*

MAN FROM PLANET X, THE L: DIRECTORS/ULMER, EDGAR (1951) 70M D: Edgar Ulmer. *Robert Clarke, William Schallert, Margaret Field.* Ulmer's moody, poverty-row sci-fi thriller put a twist in the usual B-movie fluff. A lone alien lands in the fog-bound Scottish Highlands to seek human help in saving his doomed planet, but his peaceful quest is corrupted by an evil scientist (B-movie stalwart Schallert). It's an unusually beautiful film, full of Ulmer's odd camera angles and impeccably lit scenes, and the ever-present fog creates a nervous suspense while obscuring his spare sets (actually leftovers from the 1948 *Joan of Arc*). Most affecting, however, is his sensitive direction of the unnerving and silent alien and the miscommunication that leads to an unexpectedly bitter conclusion. —*S. A.*

MONSOON (AKA **ISLE OF FORGOTTEN SINS**) L: DIRECTORS/ULMER, EDGAR (1943) 83M D: Edgar Ulmer. *John Carradine, Gale Sondergaard, Sidney Toler.* Ulmer was the only director besides John Ford to make the most of lanky, laconic Carradine. Here he's a South Seas con man with a partner he can't trust and a plot to steal $3 million from someone even more corrupt than he. It's a sea adventure done on the cheap—cheesy models stand in for diving boats, tropical lagoons, and the obligatory hurricane in a goldfish bowl—but the double-crossing, conniving characters would make *The Usual Suspects* check their wallets. B-movie auteur Ulmer makes it all enormously entertaining and makes Carradine a most magnetic, good bad guy. —*S. A.*

STRANGE ILLUSION L: DIRECTORS/ULMER, EDGAR (1945) 87M D: Edgar Ulmer. *Regis Toomey, Jimmy Lydon, Sally Eilers, Warren William.* A B-movie update of *Hamlet* in suburbia with a psychiatric bent. Lydon is a gee-whiz kid plagued with nightmares of a mysterious man who comes into the life of his widowed mother (Eilers) and brings death along with him. They all come true in the form of a thoroughly wolfish William (in the Claudius role), a smooth operator with a disturbing taste for teenage girls. When the ghost of his father tells Lydon to protect her, he even pretends to be crazy to get dirt on this guy! It's one of the best from the true King of the Bs: Ulmer does wonders with mood on the low budget, and even the dialogue is better than most of his PRC productions. Toomey costars as a family friend and trusted doctor. —S.A.

SWEET SWEETBACK'S BAADASSSSS SONG L: DIRECTORS/VAN PEEBLES, MELVIN (1971) 97M D: Melvin Van Peebles.
Melvin Van Peebles, West Gale, John Dullaghan, Hubert Scales, Simon Chuckster. Sweetback (Van Peebles) becomes a fugitive after attacking some abusive white cops. Though the title might imply a silly action movie, it's actually a serious and quite gloomy primal scream against racism and despair. Angry, intense, and completely hallucinogenic in its editing and scoring, *Sweetback* feels like nothing else in the blaxploitation genre it spawned. The story and characters are uninvolving, but if you're in the right mood it's an interesting spectacle. Whatever its worth as a film, its cultural significance is undeniable; it was the film that inspired a generation of black independent filmmakers. —B.T.

DRUGSTORE COWBOY L: DIRECTORS/VAN SANT, GUS (1989) 104M D: Gus Van Sant. *Matt Dillon, James Remar, James LeGros, Kelly Lynch, Heather Graham.* Van Sant's downbeat tale of gypsy drug addicts, shot on the streets of Portland, Oregon, and surrounding areas, mixes low-key style and hallucinatory imagery with the grungy details of the sleepy day-to-day life of dead-end druggies in the early 1970s. Dillon turns around his teen-rebel image as the heist mastermind and group leader, and Lynch, as Dillon's lover, partner-in-crime, and frustrated co-pilot (and might I add quite striking in knee boots and mini-skirts) was never better. LeGros and Graham are the flighty kids who become his crew, and the quartet drifts from highs to heists and back again. William S. Burroughs makes a memorable appearance as the aging junkie Tom the Priest. An electric drama of a placid existence, and to my mind still Van Sant's best movie. —S.A.

GERRY L: DIRECTORS/VAN SANT, GUS (2002) 103M D: Gus Van Sant. *Casey Affleck, Matt Damon.* Damon and Affleck get lost in a Van Sant film. As abstract an American film as you'll ever see starring a Hollywood golden boy, this is less a story than a striking and compelling experiment in filmmaking. There is neither a sense of fear or danger as their day hike takes a wrong turn and they plunge deeper and deeper into the beautiful desolation of Death Valley without food or water, only a rumbling frustration, as if they've just gotten lost in one of their epic video games. Death has all the drama of a reboot, but as the days roll by their mortality weighs heavier and

heavier as they hike on, parched, exhausted, hallucinating. The purposefully pointless dialogue signifies little (besides the private language that gives the title its real meaning) but the formal beauty of Van Sant's photography, composed in long unbroken shots, isolates his Gerries with a terrifying sense of helplessness and aloneness in the universe. The cracking, creaking, hauntingly lonely soundscape only intensifies the feeling. —S.A.

GOOD WILL HUNTING L: DIRECTORS/VAN SANT, GUS (1997) 126M D: Gus Van Sant. *Stellan Skarsgård, Minnie Driver, Robin Williams, Matt Damon, Ben Affleck.* Will Hunting is the name of a custodian at MIT (played by Damon) who sees a complicated yet incomplete math problem on a chalkboard. Being an unsung genius, he finishes the problem and goes on with his chores. The rest of the film concerns how a professor (Skarsgard) and a psychologist (Williams) try tempering the built-in rage of this young genius with the goal of prying him away from his blue-collar roots for greater use elsewhere. In the end it's just a feel-good, teen-angst film, the content of which is several notches lower than *Dead Poet's Society*. The script is the first by Damon and Affleck. —N.J.

MALA NOCHE L: DIRECTORS/VAN SANT, GUS (1985) 75M D: Gus Van Sant. *Robert Lee Pitchlynn, Tim Streeter, Doug Cooeyate, Nyla McCarthy, Ray Monge.* Van Sant's first "real" film, the rarely screened *Mala Noche*, is a unique experience. Based on the novel by Walt Curtis, the film tells the tale of a Portland liquor-store clerk who develops a crush on a young, poor Mexican street kid who speaks very little English. Though its story is at times muddled and somewhat sluggish, the way in which Van Sant presents the tale allows it to often rise above its own low-budget standards. *Mala Noche* also marks a turning point in the director's career, as it was the first film of his that was recognized and praised on a semi-national level. His success with this low-budget film allowed him to make *Drugstore Cowboy* a few years later, a film which would win him nearly universal praise and launch his career in Hollywood (for better or for worse). A true diamond in the rough, *Mala Noche* is one to seek out, especially if you liked *Drugstore Cowboy* or *My Own Private Idaho*. —C.P.

MY OWN PRIVATE IDAHO L: DIRECTORS/VAN SANT, GUS (1991) 102M D: Gus Van Sant. *William Richert, Keanu Reeves, Udo Kier, James Russo, River Phoenix, Flea.* *My Own Private Idaho* is an experience as much as it is a film. It draws you into a world you most likely know little about, then humanizes it in every way and finds the moments of beauty—as well as pain— inherent in such a lifestyle choice. Phoenix is beyond phenomenal here, and every time I watch this film (which is often), I mourn, selfishly, all the things he could have given us had he not died so young. As narcoleptic street pros-

Worst movies by favorite directors

BAMBOOZLED	**ICHI THE KILLER**
(Spike Lee)	*(Takashi Miike)*
CECIL B. DEMENTED	**KING IN NEW YORK**
(John Waters)	*(Charles Chaplin)*
CHRISTINE	**LAND OF THE PHARAOHS**
(John Carpenter)	*(Howard Hawks)*
GHOSTS OF MARS	**MILLION DOLLAR HOTEL**
(John Carpenter)	*(Wim Wenders)*
G.I. JANE	**MISSION: IMPOSSIBLE 2**
(Ridley Scott)	*(John Woo)*
HARD TARGET	**MONKEY BONE**
(John Woo)	*(Henry Selick)*
HOLLOW MAN	**NEW YORK, NEW YORK**
(Paul Verhoeven)	*(Martin Scorsese)*

titute Mike Walters, wandering his way around the world in search of his mother and home, Phoenix finds the truth of his character in a way few can. Ending as powerfully as it began—say what you might about its random diversion into Henry IV for the film's middle act—*My Own Private Idaho* is a deeply personal film by a director at the top of his powers and an actor at the peak of his short-lived career. "I'm a connoisseur of roads. I've been tasting roads my whole life. This road will never end. It probably goes all around the world. . ." —*C.P.*

PSYCHO (1998) L: DIRECTORS/VAN SANT, GUS (1998) 120M D: Gus Van Sant. *William H. Macy, Julianne Moore, Viggo Mortensen, Vince Vaughn, Anne Heche.* I don't care what anyone says, I admire Van Sant for this failed experiment. It takes a courageous director to follow up a mainstream hit like *Good Will Hunting* with a stunt as audacious as a shot-for-shot remake of a universally loved masterpiece. Obviously it's not as effective as the original, but it's an unusual experience of déjà vu watching such familiar scenes exactly re-created with different actors. Actually, it's not exactly shot-for-shot; there is the occasional added flourish like flashes of stock footage during the shower scene or a shot of Norman masturbating while he spies on Marion. Vaughn is good as Norman, but not good enough to withstand comparisons to Anthony Perkins. Mortensen actually improves on the original in the supporting role of Sam Loomis. —*B.T.*

BONHEUR, LE L: DIRECTORS/VARDA, AGNÈS (1965) 77M D: Agnès Varda. *Marie-France Boyer, Olivier Drouot, Jean-Claude Drouot, Sandrine Drouot, Claire Drouot.* The lone woman of the French New

Wave boy's club, Varda came from a very different tradition from her *Cahier*-spawned brethren, a world of art and photography. Those inspirations come to the fore in the lush, impossibly idyllic world of her controversial *Le Bonheur*, a lovely tale of a tragic love triangle. The matter-of-fact double life of a young carpenter (Jean-Claude Drouot) with a wife and family who takes a mistress on the side is told with a cool distance, quite a change from the warm immediacy of *Cleo from 5 to 7*. Filled with flashcuts, out-of-focus portraits, and visual wordplays, it's like an impressionist painting come to life with playful New Wave style, a sun-drenched Eden where even tragedy is transformed into a happy ending. —*S.A.*

CLEO FROM 5 TO 7 L: DIRECTORS/VARDA, AGNÈS (1962) 90M D: Agnès Varda. *Michel Legrand, Corinne Marchand, Antoine Bourseiller, Dominique Davray, Dorothée Blank.* Varda, a key director of the French New Wave, never belonged to the group proper—by her own admission she had seen less than two dozen films before she embarked on her own first feature. Her second feature made her reputation. Shot on the streets of Paris, it charts ninety minutes in the life of a flighty pop singer (Marchand) as she awaits the results of a cancer test. Restless and nervous, she leaves the lonely protection of her almost antiseptic apartment and joins the flow of the Parisian streets. As she weaves through the crowds, Varda leads us beyond Cleo's callow surface to explore the fears and vulnerability she masks from the world while simultaneously treating us to the rhythm of life in Paris with a delicate naturalism. The city has never looked more lovely, and Cleo sees it with different eyes as she firmly embraces

OSTERMAN WEEKEND
(Sam Peckinpah)

THE PARADINE CASE
(Alfred Hitchcock)

PLANET OF THE APES
(Tim Burton)

QUERELLE
(Rainer Werner Fassbinder)

REINDEER GAMES
(John Frankenheimer)

ROSEBUD
(Otto Preminger)

THE SERPENT'S EGG
(Ingmar Bergman)

STARMAN
(John Carpenter)

STARSHIP TROOPERS
(Paul Verhoeven)

TITANIC
(James Cameron)

TRAFFIC
(Steven Soderbergh)

VANILLA SKY
(Cameron Crowe)

WEATHERMAN '69
(Raymond Pettibon)

WINDTALKERS
(John Woo)

WITCH HUNT
(Paul Schrader)

---

life in the face of possible death. Watch for an uncredited Jean-Luc Godard in the silent film-within-the-film. —*S.A.*

GLEANERS AND I, THE L: DIRECTORS/VARDA, AGNÈS (2001) 82M D: Agnès Varda. Varda takes her lightweight digital video camera on the road for this first-person documentary that examines the evolution of gleaning (traditionally, the act of gathering grain left behind the reapers) in modern life. From urban scavengers and dumpster divers to junk sculptors and multimedia artists of found objects to the still active gleaners who pick the leaving of mechanical harvesters, Varda explores these all-but-ignored cultures of recycling with an appreciative, fascinated curiosity. She captures both a culture gripped in unnecessary waste and the wanton dumping of "imperfect" products and a portrait of hardy people living off the land and sometimes returning a little something in the bargain. Between subjects she turns the camera inward, photographing one wizened hand with another, studying her face in a mirror, musing over her own aging (she was 72 when she made this film). Whether Varda is truly a "gleaner" herself is open to question, but the spirit is there and her cinematic gleanings are dead on. She captures the overlooked, the discarded, and the ignored and illuminates them for us. The DVD features the exclusive sixty-minute long follow-up, *The Gleaners and I: Two Years Later.* —*S.A.*

ONE HUNDRED AND ONE NIGHTS L: DIRECTORS/VARDA, AGNES (1994) 101M D: Agnès Varda. *Michel Piccoli, Emmanuel Salinger, Mathieu Demy, Julie Gayet, Marcello Mastroianni, Henri Garcin.* Varda's tribute to cinema's centennial is a love letter to the movies. Piccoli plays 100-year-old director Simon Cinema, who hires a young film buff (Gayet) to indulge in his passion for discussing movies and jog his failing memory, whereupon he becomes each remembered legend: Luis Buñuel, Orson Welles, Gene Kelly, even. . . Michel Piccoli! The dense patchwork of remembered scenes, film quotes, in jokes, film clips, and cameos galore (from Alain Delon to Hannah Schygulla to Robert De Niro) is framed by Godard-like introductions but moves with the magic of a musical. Those not in on the joke will be scratching their heads, but anyone who lives for the movies will laugh in delight at this film-lover's fantasy. Other cameos include Anouk Aimée, Jane Birkin, Catherine Deneuve, Gérard Depardieu, Leonardo DiCaprio, Harrison Ford, Jean-Pierre Léaud, Gina Lollabrigida, Jeanne Moreau, Assumpta Serna, Martin Sheen, and Harry Dean Stanton. —*S.A.*

VAGABOND L: DIRECTORS/VARDA, AGNES (1985) 105M D: Agnès Varda. *Sandrine Bonnaire.* A young homeless woman is found frozen to death in a small French town. In a style similar to *Citizen Kane,* *Vagabond* pieces together the story of the drifter (played phenomenally by Bonnaire) through the marks she left on those who met her. The writer/director of the first film of the Nouvelle Vague maintains a carefully distant but curious position from her subject, continuing an ongoing interest in the relationship between fiction and documentary. Grappling with such complicated issues as homelessness, liberty, and femininity, as well as cinematic representation, Varda offers no explanations or solutions. In the end, what we know of Mona is restricted to material facts and second-hand impressions. —*C.B.*

FOURTH MAN, THE L: DIRECTORS/VERHOEVEN, PAUL (1983) 105M D: Paul Verhoeven. *Dolf de Vries, Thom Hoffman, Renée Soutendijk, Jeroen Krabbé.* Verhoeven's ultrasexy, early, trippy thriller is just perfect. Krabbé plays the author, Gerard Reve, who has a bit more interest in men than women. He becomes interested in a widow (Soutendijk), though only to gain access to her dreamboat boyfriend Herman (Hoffman). Amusing himself with Soutendijk's body by concealing her breasts and imagining her as a man, Krabbé makes do with fevered lusty images of Herman on the cross. After a night of drunkenness, Gerard finds a movie projector and a bit of history that sets his already blistering mind in motion. Gerard is a lovely sleazebag, as enjoyable as a couple of slabs of bloody, dripping meat laid against a reddest-rose-strewn, grayed graveyard. His descent into madness is one we take with him. *The Fourth Man* was shot by Jan de Bont before his breakthrough direction on *Speed.* —*S. R.*

HOLLOW MAN L: DIRECTORS/VERHOEVEN, PAUL (2000) 113M D: Paul Verhoeven. *Kevin Bacon, Elisabeth Shue. Hollow Man* makes the fatal mistake of being serious when it has no right to be. Unlike director Verhoeven's previous film, *Starship Troopers*—an obvious and intelligent satire that allows us to be in on the joke—this offering seems to think it is much more important than it is. The astonishing special effects are matched only by the astonishing gaps in plot and character motivation. Taking the lowbrow approach to a truly interesting question—what would you do if no one could see what you did?—*Hollow Man* lets us down time and again. Apparently, Sebastian Crane (Bacon) spent all of these years working to devise a way to make himself invisible, just so he might be able to engage in sexual activities with his ex-girlfriend (Shue). Perhaps on some level this is an interesting study of base male desire, but it can hardly be the intent of the filmmaker; as soon as a theme starts to emerge, he moves away from it, as if afraid to make a point. However, little else in this film suggests a fear of being over-the-top. —*C. P.*

I enjoyed this widely hated take on the invisible man story because it's Verhoeven's perverted version of the dumb-scientist-action-movie genre that includes *Jurassic Park* and *Deep Blue Sea.* Bacon turns invisible and quickly becomes depraved because, as he says, he doesn't have to look in the mirror anymore. Verhoeven is nothing if not audacious, so he throws in a scene of a breast being fondled by invisible hands, finds a way to show "Kevin's bacon" a couple times even though his character is invisible, and has Shue lean over too far in the obligatory falling-elevator scene and take off a chunk of meat. You can have your "guilty pleasure" dumb-cop movies; I'll have my insane Verhoeven invisible-man thriller. —*B. T.*

ROBOCOP L: DIRECTORS/VERHOEVEN, PAUL (1987) 103M D: Paul Verhoeven. *Miguel Ferrer, Dan O'Herlihy, Nancy Allen, Peter Weller, Ronny Cox, Kurtwood Smith.* Verhoeven's corporate *Frankenstein* hasn't lost its edge over the years, though for my money it wimps out at the end for a nasty (though very funny) little gag. The satirical sci-fi story of the near future posits big business running city services like a factory, complete with downsizing and cost cutting. When an effective alternative to human crime fighting is created (the reanimated corpse of mutilated cop Weller, revived with computer circuitry and robotic limbs), it's up to the head honchos to stop it before it threatens real profits in cost overruns, spare parts, and a cut on the drug and prostitution money around new construction sites. Mean-spirited and very violent, Verhoeven's stylish satire manages to be funny and intelligent amid the carnage. —*S. A.*

SHOWGIRLS L: DIRECTORS/VERHOEVEN, PAUL (1995) 131M D: Paul Verhoeven. *Gina Gershon, Elizabeth Berkeley, Kyle MacLachlan. Showgirls* is a wicked piece of satire that went over everyone's head on its first release in 1995. French director Jacques Rivette defends *Showgirls* as the best and most personal of Verhoeven's American films. Yes, Elizabeth Berkeley, as the small-town girl who vies for stage dominance as a stripper-dancer, is awful. But we don't object when John Waters uses bad actors intentionally. Perhaps that's because Waters is ultimately very affectionate toward his characters, while Verhoeven clearly hates just about everyone. It's crucial to Verhoeven's vision that Berkeley's character, Nomi, be unable to convince us of her character's humanity, because Nomi (no me?) is inhuman. In a deeply subversive twist on the Hollywood cliché of the stage-struck ingénue's rise to stardom, Nomi finally achieves her full potential when she stops pretending to be human and embraces her inner monster. Please, don't wait for the French to point out our myopia once again: see and reevaluate *Showgirls* as a film that perfectly fulfills its every intention, unpalatable as those intentions may ultimately be. —*C. C.*

I'm not sure about that, but *Showgirls* does not deserve the reputation it has as an *unwatchably* bad movie. It's not as if Verhoeven was unaware of the absurdity of loosely remaking *All About Eve* as the first big-studio NC-17 sex romp, but you still have to wonder what he was thinking in over-the-top moments like the sex scene with MacLachlan and Berkley violently flopping around in a swimming pool. But it really doesn't matter what he was thinking—it's that relentless excessiveness that makes the movie so much fun. I think the most audacious touch is the hunky lounge-singer character who is obviously based on Michael Bolton, but who turns out in the end to be a rapist. Michael Bolton is a real guy! I wonder if he ever saw *Showgirls.* . . —*B. T.*

SPETTERS L: DIRECTORS/VERHOEVEN, PAUL (1980) 123M D: Paul Verhoeven. *Han van Tongeren, Renée Soutendijk, Toon Agterberg, Maarten Spanjer.* "My dad always said life is like a croquette: you wouldn't like it if you knew what was in it." Verhoeven's story of three young dirt-bike dreamers in a small Dutch town is anything but nostalgic. This story of working-class ambition is crammed with sex, rejection, humiliation, a crippling accident, suicide, and a very persuasive sexpot (Soutendijk) who tries to hitch her fortunes to the three boys. You can see her internal calculator adding up a potential scheme behind her sly fox of a smile. This is prime Verhoeven territory: we get gay bashing, brutal, invasive revenge, humiliation, and suicide before it pulls out for, of all things, a happy ending (of sorts) in the face of the failure and tragedy. Rutger Hauer and Jeroen Krabbé costar as the national dirt-bike champ and the glib TV sportscaster, respectively. *—S. A.*

STARSHIP TROOPERS L: DIRECTORS/VERHOEVEN, PAUL (1997) 129M D: Paul Verhoeven. *Casper Van Dien, Dina Meyer, Denise Richards, Jake Busey, Neil Patrick Harris.* A group of bland Aryan 90210-like teens from futuristic Buenos Aries join the military, fly into space, and slaughter (or get slaughtered by) giant insects. In a style reminiscent of his own *Robocop*, Verhoeven uses envelope-pushing violence, groundbreaking special effects and deadpan satire (especially in the propagandistic media segments) to depict a bloodthirsty future society that is depressingly similar to our own. If Verhoeven had waited four more years, there's no way he could have gotten $100 million from a studio to make a sarcastic war film, and it's surprising he was even able to do it in 1997. Many critics profoundly misunderstood the movie at the time, even claiming that it was pro-fascist. Adapted loosely from a book by Robert A. Heinlein, Verhoeven's film inspired violent hatred in fans who missed the robotic power-suits of the book and/or were offended by what they saw as a perversion of its politics. *—B. T.*

TOTAL RECALL L: DIRECTORS/VERHOEVEN, PAUL (1990) 109M D: Paul Verhoeven. *Arnold Schwarzenegger, Sharon Stone, Ronny Cox, Michael Ironside, Rachel Ticotin.* Loosely based on a Philip K. Dick short story, *Total Recall* concerns a secret agent (Schwarzenegger) who has been severely brainwashed. False memories have somehow been implanted over real ones, leading him to believe he has a happy wife in a happy home far away from his actual duties on Mars. Beginning with a subconscious yearning to return to the Red Planet, the film slowly develops as he learns bit by bit who he actually is and what his objectives are as a secret agent. Scripted by the creators of *Alien*, this film packs quite the punch. *—N. J.*

DUEL IN THE SUN L: DIRECTORS/VIDOR, KING (1946) 144M D: King Vidor. *Jennifer Jones, Joseph Cotton, Gregory Peck, Lionel Barrymore, Herbert Marshall, Lillian Gish.* Condemned by every church group in America, this steamy Western is really a sultry, overheated melodrama in chaps. Jones, who won an Oscar just a few years before as a saintly virgin with religious visions in *The Song of Bernadette*, becomes the hot-blooded, half-Mexican orphan torn between Cain-and-Abel brothers: bad-boy Peck and cultured gentleman Cotten. It would be silly if it wasn't so maniacally over-the-top. Peck has never been so animated, relishing every villainous deed with a smirk and a wink, and Barrymore creates a power-mad ancestor for his *It's a Wonderful Life* villain, Mr. Potter, as the cattle-baron father willing to go to war over barb wire. Vidor is the credited director and Josef von Sternberg was one of many uncredited participants, but this is really producer David O. Selznick's baby. *—S. A.*

ATALANTE, L' L: DIRECTORS/VIGO, JEAN (1934) 89M D: Jean Vigo. *Louis Lefebvre, Dita Parlo, Jean Dasté, Michel Simon.* Recently restored and available in its original form, Vigo's masterwork (he died at 29 during postproduction) beautifully renders the story of young newlyweds trying to maintain their marriage while living on a barge. The main focus of the film is Juliette (Parlo) and her latent desire to see the city of Paris and, even more so, gain her own individuality and freedom. This isn't to say that she wants to leave her husband, Jean (Dasté); she wants to gain some ambiguous freedom, a freedom stifled by Jean's jealousy and ritual control. Juliette, however, finds her way to Paris, leaving a tearful Jean on the brink of suicide. Often mixed between the surreal and the real, the dreamlike and the waking, Vigo expresses the power of a love between two people and their ability to forgive one another. Supporting character Pere Jules (brilliantly played by Simon) provides tender comic relief (especially in a scene where he shows Juliette all the items he has gathered from his travels), balancing out the oft-heavy dramatic tension between the couple. *—J. D.*

ZERO FOR CONDUCT L: DIRECTORS/VIGO, JEAN (1933) 44M D: Jean Vigo. *Jean Dasté, Delphin, Robert Le Flon, Louis Lefebvre.* Vigo caught the rebellious spirit of adolescent boys captivated by magic tricks and word games in this anarchic little gem, the first masterpiece of prepubescent self-actualization. Set in a strict boy's school run by creaky, cranky petty tyrants, it's a strange and wonderful film full of unbridled imagination, flights of fantasy, and lovely images, such as a pillow fight that turns into a kind of snow-globe scene. The final rebellion is completely surreal and utterly fascinating, as the boys pelt stiff authority figures (some of them literally mannequins) with schoolbooks and shoes before taking over the school like adolescent pirates. *—S. A.*

BELLISSIMA L: DIRECTORS/VISCONTI, LUCHINO (1951) 110M
D: Luchino Visconti. *Anna Magnani, Arturo Bragaglia, Gastone Renzelli, Walter Chiari, Tina Apicella.* Italian great Magnani plays Maddalena, a zealously driven woman convinced that her young daughter Maria (Apicella) has all the makings of a star. When a famous director holds an audition for a part in his next movie, Maddalena is disappointed to learn that few share her enthusiasm. Still, it's clear she will stop at nothing until seeing her daughter become a Shirley Temple-caliber celebrity. The bulk of the film is driven by fairly effective comedy, but there's a sincerely touching story of human struggle running through it all that simply refuses to stay below the surface. Very nearly a masterpiece, *Bellissima* is graced with the grandeur and artistry that would blossom into something truly special in later Visconti films like *Rocco and His Brothers*. Highly recommended to fans of *Nights of Cabiria.* —C. B.

DEATH IN VENICE L: DIRECTORS/VISCONTI, LUCHINO (1971) 130M D: Luchino Visconti. *Marisa Berenson, Dirk Bogard, Sylvana Mangano, Mark Burns.* Based on the Thomas Mann novel, Visconti's *Death in Venice* is a fascinating character study about an artist in search of the perfection of beauty. Bogard plays Gustav Aschenbach, the aging composer who moves to Venice for solitude hoping that some time alone on the beach will improve his health and state of mind. Instead, he finds that Venice is trying to recover from an outbreak of cholera, and even as he walks the city, lye is being thrown about the streets to help kill the disease. Suddenly, his eye catches that of a boy, and his mind wanders. . . could this be the absolute personification of pure beauty that he has been seeking? Most of this story is told quite visually with its emphasis on nonverbal acting. The music of Gustav Mahler adds to the incredible use of atmosphere as only Visconti could conjure. This film won a special 25th Anniversary prize at the 1971 Cannes Film Festival. —N. J.

OSSESSIONE L: DIRECTORS/VISCONTI, LUCHINO (1942) 135M D: Luchino Visconti. *Dhia Cristani, Juan de Landa, Clara Calamai, Massimo Girotti.* Handsome grifter Gino (Girotti) stops for a meal at a roadside restaurant and meets hot-to-trot Giovanna (Calamai), quickly resulting in a passionate, lusty, and obsessive affair. Giovanna convinces Gino that their love can flourish only after the murder of Bragana (de Landa), Giovanna's older, unattractive, oafish, but relatively wealthy husband. This top-notch adaptation of *The Postman Always Rings Twice* is considered by many to be the first great work of Italian neorealism, though its epic scope and tendency for melodramatic crescendo set it apart. —C. B.

ROCCO AND HIS BROTHERS L: DIRECTORS/VISCONTI, LUCHINO (1960) 168M D: Luchino Visconti. *Annie Giradot, Renato Salvatori, Alain Delon, Katina Paxinou.* An epic masterpiece of "operatic realism," this gritty melodrama chronicles the migration of the Parondi family (widow Rosaria and her five sons) from Italy's rural south to its industrialized north (a move 9 million made between 1955 and 1971). Two of the older sons, Rocco (Delon) and Simone (Salvatori), achieve minor fame in boxing. The movie becomes their story, including their parallel careers in the ring and their tormented rivalry over the love of prostitute Nadia (Giradot). Balancing monumental theatrical crescendos with biting social commentary, Visconti's novelistic ode to bygone values is an awesome and elating cinematic experience. We laugh with the hopeful and hard-working Parondis at the beginning, the middle hits like a fist to the gut, and the near-biblical finale aches with tragic anguish straight out of Shakespeare. —C. B.

SIBERIAN LADY MACBETH L: DIRECTORS/WAJDA, ANDRZEJ (1962) 93M D: Andrzej Wajda. *Kapitalina Eric, Ljuba Tadic, Olivera Markovic.* Wajda directs this harsh tragedy about a ruthless woman having an affair with a drifter who then poisons her father-in-law to keep her secret, and then has to face down the rest of her family as suspicions rise. This is unusual territory for Wajda, an emotional melodrama against a severe, almost primitive landscape. It makes for some stunning images: the wind-whipped snowflakes that swirl around the mill ground, a dust storm seemingly driven by one man's overwhelming guilt, the fog that swallows a boatload of prisoners at the conclusion. The drama is less sure; this Lady Macbeth is not so much ambitious or calculating as she is lonely, but her passions create a woman equally as ruthless. Effective if not quite affecting, with a haunting conclusion. —S. A.

BIG TRAIL, THE L: DIRECTORS/WALSH, RAOUL (1930) 108M D: Raoul Walsh. *Ian Keith, Tully Marshall, Tyrone Power Jr., John Wayne, Marguerite Churchill.* Shrugged off upon original release, this widescreen experiment from the dawn of the sound era was effectively "lost" for more than half a century. Considering its historical interest as a forerunner of the CinemaScope era, a superproduction directed by Walsh in his lusty prime, and the first starring vehicle for Wayne, there was a lot to lose. Happily, when the movie was restored in the late 1980s, film festival audiences loved it, and it's gone on to win more friends on video and through showings (letterboxed and not) on cable TV. Wayne —Duke Morrison rechristened for the occasion—is an especially pleasant surprise, giving a charming performance and looking drop-dead gorgeous at age twenty-two. It really is a Big Trail, wending from the Mississippi to the Grand Canyon to the snowy Northwest. And knowing you're seeing the first-ever widescreen movie remains a genuine thrill. —R. T. J.

HIGH SIERRA L: DIRECTORS/WALSH, RAOUL (1941) 101M D: Raoul Walsh. *Alan Curtis, Humphrey Bogart, Henry Hull, Ida Lupino, Joan Leslie, Arthur Kennedy.* Bogart stepped up to his first starring role in Walsh's grim and gritty gangster classic. Bogie plays leathery prohibition-era gangster Roy "Mad Dog" Earle, who steps out of prison and into another job with a pair of short-fuse punks and finds that the times have passed him by. Lupino is a hardened survivor who warms to the gravelly professional, but his heart goes out to a young crippled woman (Leslie). There's a sense of romance in the idea of the criminal code of years past now swept away by the punks who infest the landscape, but ultimately the film owes more to the weary resignation and doom of film noir than the rat-a-tat energy of the early Warner gangster thrillers from which it sprouts. John Huston cowrote the script with author W. R. Burnett and apparently liked what he saw in Bogie; he cast Bogart in his directorial debut *The Maltese Falcon.* —*S. A.*

OBJECTIVE, BURMA! L: DIRECTORS/WALSH, RAOUL (1945) 142M D: Raoul Walsh. *George Tobias, Henry Hull, William Prince, James Brown, Errol Flynn.* Walsh's taut thriller of American paratroopers stranded behind enemy lines in Burma is one of the darker adventures to come out of WWII. Flynn gives a superior performance as the platoon captain whose successful mission turns sour when their escape route is cut off and their position discovered. It's a tough, grim, war-is-hell take on the classic platoon drama, peopled with familiar faces (including Tobias as the typical urban grunt and Hull as the aging war correspondent itching to get into action, until he does). Walsh drives it with a relentless momentum that makes it feel far shorter than its 142-minute running time. —*S. A.*

PURSUED L: DIRECTORS/WALSH, RAOUL (1947) 105M D: Raoul Walsh. *Dean Jagger, Alan Hale, Judith Anderson, Teresa Wright, Robert Mitchum.* The laconic Mitchum is at his best as an orphan haunted by half-remembered images from a traumatic childhood event and hunted by a hateful one-armed man (Jagger) who has dedicated his life to murdering him. Part Western noir, part frontier Freud, this revenge thriller is one of the most unusual and evocative Westerns ever made, thanks to the shadowy cinematography by James Wong Howe, understated direction by Walsh, and an increasingly tormented performance by Mitchum. His sleepy eyes communicate a tortured helplessness as everyone around him, including his adoptive family—protective Ma (Anderson), jealous "brother" (Rodney), and loving "sister" (Wright, who loves him as more than a brother)—all turn against him for reasons he can't comprehend until he revisits his past and puts a story to those foggy images. —*S. A.*

SADIE THOMPSON L: DIRECTORS/WALSH, RAOUL (1928) 96M D: Raoul Walsh. *Gloria Swanson, Raoul Walsh, Charles Lane, Lionel Barrymore, Blanche Friderici.* Swanson does her best jazz-baby vamp as a San Francisco hooker stuck in Pago Pago in Walsh's adaptation of W. Somerset Maugham's story. Barrymore is lean and weather-beaten as the "professional reformer" who clashes with the willful party girl and Walsh steps in front of the camera to play the two-fisted marine who woos the worldly woman. Walsh creates a world filled with innuendo and sultry atmosphere and is refreshingly ambiguous with his heroes and villains, suspicious of the reformers who take a churlish delight in smiting their sinful opponents yet are open to the possibility of salvation. There is significant damage to isolated stretches of the film, and the Kino disc reconstructs the lost final reel from stills, film clips, and excerpts from the 1932 remake *Rain.* —*S. A.*

CENTER OF THE WORLD, THE L: DIRECTORS/WANG, WAYNE (2001) 88M D: Wayne Wang. *Molly Parker, Carla Gugino, Balthazar Getty, Peter Sarsgaard.* Wang collaborated with experimental video artist Miranda July, novelists Paul Auster and Siri Hustevedt to write this tale of a disconnected computer geek (Sarsgaard) who falls for a young stripper (Parker) and tries to buy her love on a weekend trip to Vegas. For all the explicit content (which would have earned the film an NC-17 had the distributors not chosen to go unrated), this shot-on-video tale of alienation in the modern, hard-wired world is sober and serious and downright glum. Wang has tossed a little technology and a lot of sex into an otherwise familiar portrait of lonely souls unable to break through their own isolation, but he hasn't anything new to bring to the conversation. —*S. A.*

CECIL B. DEMENTED L: DIRECTORS/WATERS, JOHN (2000) 90M D: John Waters. *Maggie Gyllenhaal, Lawrence Gilliard Jr., Melanie Griffith, Stephen Dorff, Alicia Witt.* Dorff leads a Manson-family-style sect of "Cinema Terrorists" who kidnap a movie star (Griffith) and force her at gunpoint to star in their independent film. Like Patty Hearst (who has a part in the movie) Griffith gets into the spirit of things as they commit extreme acts like assaulting an audience watching the director's cut of *Patch Adams.* In an era where mainstream movies are more about the bottom line than ever, it's a lot of fun to watch people who remain abstinent in the name of filmmaking and tattoo the names of their favorite directors on their arms. They are so passionate about film that they are willing to light themselves on fire for it. —*B. T.*

DESPERATE LIVING L: DIRECTORS/WATERS, JOHN (1977) 90M D: John Waters. *Edith Massey, Susan Lowe, Liz Renay, Mink Stole.* This is the first Waters film without Divine, and while his/her presence is missed, Waters still delivers a thoroughly filthy, sick, hilariously perverted comedy. Stole stars

John Waters

John Waters has seemingly enjoyed the kind of rags-to-riches Hollywood career that people dream about. But his path to fame deviated a bit from the fable: he first won fame as a filmmaker in Baltimore, Maryland, and rather than rise to prominence with the help of a dramatically photogenic cast, he became famous by working with a 300-pound transvestite named Divine who, in one of Waters's first films, laid claim to being the most disgusting person on Earth.

Welcome to the concept of cinematic shock-value, a provocative style of filmmaking first practiced by the likes of the godfather of gore Herschell Gordon Lewis (*Two Thousand Maniacs, Taste of Blood*). In his own unique manner, and with the help of a singular group of individuals, Waters greatly expanded this territory. As he began working more and more with the film industry, the shock value of his oeuvre gradually lessened.

Waters's first two films, *Mondo Trasho* (1969) and *Multiple Maniacs* (1970), are extremely experimental and lack some of the most basic elements of sound and editing, probably because they were essentially made at the director's parents' house, with funding from his father. What little money he made from those went into *Pink Flamingos* (1972), which on a more technical level is Waters's first film. It also happens to be his most shocking, featuring people from Baltimore vying for the aforementioned title of the most disgusting person on Earth.

In Waters's autobiography, *Shock Value*, he admits to being an avid spectator of the criminal court—the more sensational the trial, the better. (He particularly enjoyed the Patty Hearst trial, which may explain

as a mad middle-class housewife who runs off with her sassy black maid after killing her husband (the four-hundred-pound maid smothers him with her buttocks) and enters the twisted kingdom of Queen Carlotta (Massey), the criminal shantytown of Mortville (which looks like a ramshackle Pee-wee's Playhouse from the wrong side of the tracks). This is just as clumsy as Waters's previous films, but has great trash art direction and pushes the envelope with oodles of nudity and extreme perversions: a baby in the refrigerator, an eye gouged out with a spike heel, necrophilia, cannibalism, and an on-camera castration. Waters earns his self-imposed X rating. —*S. A.*

DIVINE TRASH L: DIRECTORS/WATERS, JOHN (1998) 97M D: Steve Yeager. *John Waters, Jeanine Basinger, Steve Buscemi, Ken Jacobs.* Village Voice critic J. Hoberman calls *Pink Flamingos* "the most important underground film made since *Chelsea Girls*." Director Yeager, a John Waters intimate, gives us an in-depth look at the film's evolution, the man who made it, and the bizarre filmmaking family he nurtured. Dedicated to Waters' early career, *Divine Trash* features a wealth of behind-the-scenes footage and interviews, a loving portrait of Divine ("the Godzilla of drag queens"), and a

priceless interview with "the last film censor in America," Mary Avara, who hasn't the words to describe her complete disgust with Waters, but gamely tries. There hasn't been a more loving or hilarious portrait of trash filmmaking since *Ed Wood*. —*S. A.*

FEMALE TROUBLE L: DIRECTORS/WATERS, JOHN (1974) 97M D: John Waters. *Mink Stole, Divine.* "Crime is beauty." Divine is a high school girl who runs away from home when she doesn't get her Cha Cha heels for Christmas, gets raped on the road (by a motorist played by. . . Divine!), gives birth to a child who grows up to become Mink Stole, and re-creates bloody car wrecks for fun. Directed with the same ramshackle spirit of *Pink Flamingos*, this film once again lets Divine loose in a wild, eye-rolling performance as a demented diva who locks her mother-in-law in a giant birdcage and then massacres the opening night audience of her nightclub act. There's no polish to this production, which is part of its charm, but there is passion and sheer creative energy. If the celebrity fates had a sense of humor, then middle-class rebel John Waters would be the Andy Warhol of our generation, and the anything-for-a-shock casts of his outrageous midnight movies

why he enjoyed casting Hearst in many of his later films.) And so the topic of his follow-up to *Flamingos* should not be at all surprising: *Female Trouble* casts Divine as a woman who kills for the sake of fashion. When she is sent to the chair, she is most concerned about how she looks.

Polyester (1981) was Waters's first real foray into the more industrial side of film-making. Casting Tab Hunter along with Divine, Waters manufactured a surreal story about a woman's survival against all domestic odds. The film was released in Odorama, and moviegoers were issued scratch-and-sniff cards to be used at key moments in the film.

It took some time, but Waters finally worked his way into the mainstream with his script and concept for *Hairspray* (1988), which downplays the vulgar aspects of his characters and plays up the youthful nostalgia for bandstand music of the '50s. Divine died the year the film was released and thus never got to witness its popularity (it even inspired a successful Broadway musical in 2002). *Cry-Baby* (1990), with Johnny Depp, has a similar style and themes, especially the strong focus on '50s musical nostalgia.

Just when Waters's fans were convinced he had sold out to the blandness of the film industry, he released *Serial Mom* (1994), whose very title suggests a twisted kind of humor. This film, with Kathleen Turner as a serial killer and Patty Hearst as her sympathetic juror, blends the most shocking black humor with the social gloss of *Leave It to Beaver*. *Pecker* (1998) is essentially Waters's *Radio Days* in that he autobiographically waxes nostalgic on the time, place, and manner of his own evolution, with odd characters (including Patty Hearst) lurking around almost every corner.

The more recent films by Waters seems to indicate that strangely familiar films may well be waiting for his fans in the future. *Cecil B. Demented* (2000) tells the story of a group of cinema terrorists who kidnap a top actress to advance their utopian ideals of art in film.

—*Nathan Jensen*

---

would be the hipster celebrities of a gross-out art scene. —*S. A.*

HAIRSPRAY L: DIRECTORS/WATERS, JOHN (1988) 92M D: John Waters. *Deborah Harry, Colleen Fitzpatrick, Ricki Lake, Divine, Ruth Brown, Sonny Bono.* Before Ricki Lake was chastising twelve-year-old mothers and incestuous rednecks on her now-defunct, television talk show, she was Tracy Turnblad, a 1960s hairhopper who danced her way into the heart of millions on *The Corny Collins Show*. When the show refuses to integrate, however, Tracy takes a stand against segregation. Although this movie does present a bit of a social commentary about a time when America was even more stupid than we are now, the general tone is overall light and fun. Segregation, interracial dating, dancing rivalry, overweight drag-queen mothers, and psychotic carnival-owning fathers are all delivered with humor and good grace. The cast includes both Sonny Bono and Divine, contributing to the absurdity that characterizes Waters films and makes them so much fun to watch. This is why we love John Waters, and this is why I love this film. —*J. S.*

MONDO TRASHO L: DIRECTORS/WATERS, JOHN (1969) 95M D: John Waters. *Divine, Mary Vivian Pearce, David Lochary, Mink Stole.* Waters' first film is quite raw and experimental. It stars the all-new sex symbol Divine—a three-hundred-pound transvestite who drives a 1959 Cadillac convertible while seductively chewing gum. This fragmented film charts a day in the life of this strange fashion fanatic through gutters and Laundromats of Baltimore. On her way she meets a number of very strange people, such as a foot fetishist who sucks on her toes, a nude hitchhiker, and the crazed Dr. Coat Hanger. The film is virtually silent with lots of '50s rock music in the soundtrack. It will appeal primarily to fans of Waters who like to indulge in shock value. —*N. J.*

MULTIPLE MANIACS L: DIRECTORS/WATERS, JOHN (1971) 70M D: John Waters. *David Lochary, Mink Stole, Susan Lowe, Divine, Mary Vivian Pearce, Edith Massey.* One of Waters's greatest influences was Herschell Gordon Lewis, and this film is an homage to the Lewis classic *2000 Maniacs*. Here Waters's uses the unique latitude produced from a crazy cast, a disturbed imagination, and no budget to relate the story of a traveling freak show that enjoys murdering its audience. The narrative becomes segmented into large vignettes, such as the nightmarish scene when Divine is led into a Catholic sanctuary to have lesbian sex with a parishioner implementing a rosary, while the Passion of Christ is related in an equally outrageous fashion. And of course, who could forget the attack of the monstrous killer lobster at the end of the film? If you find you really enjoy all this, then you are unquestionably a John Waters fan. —N. J.

PECKER L: DIRECTORS/WATERS, JOHN (1998) 86M D: John Waters. *Edward Furlong, Christina Ricci, Lili Taylor, Martha Plimpton, Mary Kay Place.* Pecker (Furlong) takes pictures with an old camera he got from his mom's store. A hungry-for-love art-gallery director from New York sees his pictures and decides to sponsor a show for him. Pecker decides he can do without the "perks" of instant fame that seem to be alienating him from all of the people he cares about, and goodness prevails. Waters creates really vibrant, dynamic characters, and this movie is full of them. Pecker's girlfriend, Shelley (Ricci), is a feisty, Laundromat workaholic, his grandma has a puppet Virgin Mary that speaks to her, his little sister eats bags of sugar at a time, and his best friend Matt aspires to be a professional thief. Plot highlights include lots of balls on foreheads, the pubic hair of a stripper, and sex in a voting booth. Ask yourself, is there *really* anything else you want in a movie? —J. S.

PINK FLAMINGOS L: DIRECTORS/WATERS, JOHN (1972) 95M D: John Waters. *Edith Massey, Danny Mills, Mink Stole, David Lochary, Divine, Mary Vivian Pearce.* In many ways this is the quintessential cult film. Though it is nearly impossible to please absolutely every audience, it is also just as difficult to offend absolutely every audience—and that's exactly what this film does. What makes this possible is the bizarre cast and the plot, which focuses on a family advertising itself to be the most offensive people on the planet. —N. J.

POLYESTER L: DIRECTORS/WATERS, JOHN (1980) 86M D: John Waters. *David Samson, Divine, Tab Hunter, Edith Massey, Mink Stole, Stiv Bators.* Divine wants little more than to be an ordinary housewife with an ordinary family in Baltimore. Of course, it doesn't help that her husband owns the X-rated theater in town, that her daughter is trying to induce an abortion, or that her son is the notorious Baltimore Foot Stomper! But every family has their share of problems and Divine seems to keep it together rather well—that is until she suddenly falls in love with Tab Hunter. This film is Waters's first entry into mainstream moviemaking, yet it retains enough of his peculiar shock value to keep the average viewer totally slack-jawed throughout. Originally presented in "Odorama," where moviegoers were given a scratch-and-sniff card. —N. J.

SERIAL MOM L: DIRECTORS/WATERS, JOHN (1994) 93M D: John Waters. *Matthew Lillard, Kathleen Turner, Sam Waterston, Mink Stole, Ricki Lake.* Turner plays Beverly Sutphin, the picture-perfect middle-class housewife who loves to take care of her perfect middle-class family. There doesn't seem to be anything particularly extraordinary about her at first, until she shows herself for the crazy bitch she really is, ready to attack anyone who fucks with her or her family. She makes obscene phone calls to a neighbor who cut her off in a parking lot, runs over a math teacher, and gouges out the liver of a guy who cheated on her daughter. The body count keeps rising higher and higher as Beverly finds new reasons why some people just deserve to die. A little campy, and a little over the top, this is a must-see for Waters's fans as well as those who don't know they are yet. —J. S.

LAST WAVE, THE L: DIRECTORS/WEIR, PETER (1977) 106M D: Peter Weir. *Richard Chamberlain, David Gulpilil.* Australian director Weir first came to international attention with this heady tale of Aboriginal tribal religion, prophecy, and visions, and the skeptical outsider who is drawn into "the dreamtime" and begins having visions of apocalyptic events. Chamberlain stars as the Australian lawyer who takes on the defense of a group of Aborigines accused of killing one of their own. He's convinced it was in retribution for violating a tribal taboo, but slowly begins to see outside his reductive view of their culture and religion as his visions intensify. The rational, "civilized" man gets in touch with the primal roots and it scares the bejesus out of him. The spookiness of Weir's film comes from the slightly out-of-kilter imagery and the way it slowly and subtly reveals a world horribly out of balance, beginning with a freak hailstorm in Sydney and climaxing with—well, that's best left experienced. —S. A.

MASTER AND COMMANDER: THE FAR SIDE OF THE WORLD L: DIRECTORS/WEIR, PETER (2003) 138M D: Peter Weir. *Russell Crowe, Paul Bettany, James D'Arcy, Billy Boyd.* This film rocked and rolled, swayed from side to side, and up and down. You could almost feel the ocean spray, smell the salt air, and hear the boards creaking under foot. *Master and Commander* is based on Patrick O'Brian's novels about a fictional British Frigate, in this case engaging and chasing a much larger French warship off the coast of South America during the Napoleonic wars. This is a huge production, with tons of money and a major star, but it does not go into the realm of cheesy, tongue-in-cheek humor or blatant emotional manipulation, as so many big films do. The CGI effects are seamless and Crowe, who plays Captain Jack Aubrey, does not detract from this great seafaring action film. While still a Hollywood film full of pomp and bigger-than-life scenes, much attention is also paid to characters and the relationships between

men living in close quarters on the high seas for months at a time. —*B. W.*

CITIZEN KANE L: DIRECTORS/WELLES, ORSON (1941) 119M D: Orson Welles. *Joseph Cotton, Agnes Moorehead, Orson Welles, Everett Sloane, Ruth Warrick. Citizen Kane* has been so longed hailed as "the greatest film ever made" that it has become a dry truism. With the American Film Institute imprimatur stamped on it like some official seal, it's in serious danger of becoming the least seen masterpiece around, and with its creator (and let's face it, Pauline Kael has simply wrong: this is Welles's creation) the legends surrounding the film have long overshadowed the actual production. Above all, Welles was a showman. *Citizen Kane* is a three-ring circus of cinematic ingenuity, a startlingly entertaining blend of dimestore melodrama, historical biography, detective story, political drama, storytelling confabulation, and plain old theatrical flourish. Years ahead of its time in its layered use of sound and score, stunningly designed and brilliantly conceived, *Citizen Kane* is a vital, moving, exciting moment of American cinema brought back to life with every screening. —*S. A.*

F FOR FAKE L: DIRECTORS/WELLES, ORSON (1974) 85M D: Orson Welles. *Oja Kodar, Laurence Harvey, Joseph Cotton, Orson Welles.* It's hard to tell if this is a spoof in the form of a documentary or a documentary about spoofs. Either way, Welles's prosaic narration, as profound as it may seem, is of no help whatsoever and he knows it. Describing the mysterious life of an art forger whose identity is entirely uncertain, who may or may not have had a daughter, who may or may not have been involved in further unexplained conspiracies, the audience is encouraged to entertain thoughts about the veracity of the interviewer and the whole concept of documentaries in the first place. Whereas most documentaries construct a subject for the consumption of the audience, this is a documentary which deconstructs its audience for lack of a subject! At the end of this film the audience walks away empty-handed and perfectly robbed. —*N. J.*

LADY FROM SHANGHAI THE L: DIRECTORS/WELLES, ORSON (1946) 86M D: Orson Welles. *Everett Sloane, Rita Hayworth, Orson Welles.* Welles is Michael O'Hara, a misguided vagabond and would-be writer who unwittingly, but not entirely unwillingly, becomes involved in a complex murder plot full of back-stabbing and dirty deals. The streetsmart, working-class innocent is at the mercy of the lies, false faces, and scheming plots of Elsa (a bleached-blond Hayworth, Hollywood's girl-next-door auburn beauty turned cold-killer bitch) and her Iago-like grotesque-of-a-husband, Arthur Bannister (Sloane, rocking along with his canes and leg braces). It's a strange portrait in a career of corrupt figures, shady charlatans, and tragic fools, yet this unlikely Welles project is a wonderfully Wellesian film, a nightmare world of labyrinthine danger culminating in the dazzling, justly celebrated hall of mirrors. He shatters and distorts the world with the bravura of a visual artist at the height of his craft, and in the process essentially ended his directing career in the United States: the film lost money and "tarnished" Columbia-star Hayworth, who divorced Welles during the shoot. —*S. A.*

MAGNIFICENT AMBERSONS, THE L: DIRECTORS/WELLES, ORSON (1942) 88M D: Orson Welles. *Agnes Moorehead, Ray Collins, Tim Holt, Joseph Cotton, Anne Baxter.* For all its reputation as one of the great "lost films" of American cinema, *The Magnificent Ambersons* is a masterpiece—possibly Welles's greatest film—and one of the greatest evocations of turn-of-the-century America. Where *Kane* was fast and frenetic, the clipped pace of a city-based newspaper drama, *Ambersons* revels in sweeping long takes and Griffith-like compositions, the evocation of the gentle pace of small-town life, an idyll shattered by the coming of the automobile and a melancholy remembrance of a simpler past that may only have existed in memory. There's also a personal connection: author Booth Tarkington, a friend of the family, reportedly based the character of inventor Eugene Morgan on Welles's father. As would be the case with several of Welles's features to follow, *Ambersons* was heavily re-edited by the studio (RKO) after a disastrous audience preview. Alternative scenes were shot, a happy ending tacked on, and the negative and film from the deleted scenes was destroyed, preventing Welles from ever being able to reassemble the original cut. Yet even in its truncated form, *The Magnificent Ambersons* remains one of his greatest achievements. —*S. A.*

OTHELLO (1952) L: DIRECTORS/WELLES, ORSON (1952) 90M D: Orson Welles. *Orson Welles, Michael MacLiammoir, Robert Coote, Suzanne Cloutier.* Welles plays the passionate yet confused Moor in this remarkable black-and-white Shakespearean classic. The story concerns how Othello's most trusted friend, Iago (MacLiammoir), plots to turn him against his own wife (Cloutier) by spreading lies and distortion. The film features some of the most stunning photography imaginable. Each and every shot is composed as a veritable work of art, from suffocating close-ups of Iago to the shadows of iron bars cutting across Othello's wife in anticipation of the inevitable. This film had an extraordinarily difficult production with many scenes, even separate shots of single scenes, being filmed in a variety of countries over a period of several years. —*N. J.*

TOUCH OF EVIL L: DIRECTORS/WELLES, ORSON (1958) 105M D: Orson Welles. *Charlton Heston, Janet Leigh, Orson Welles.* It was the picture that would be remembered as the last page in Hollywood's true film-noir book, as Welles directs and costars

Orson Welles

George Orson Welles was born in 1915 in Kenosha, Wisconsin, the son of an inventor, engineer, and itinerant gambler father and a concert pianist mother. His mother died when he was six, and he traveled around the world with his father until 1925, until his father killed himself. Welles then entered the progressive Todd School, where he began his lifelong association with theater. Upon graduating, he traveled around Europe and joined the Gate Theater in Dublin before returning to the United States and joining the touring company of Broadway star Katherine Cornell. He also directed his first film at this time, a short spoof of surrealist and avant-garde films.

Welles began his New York stage career in the mid-'30s with the Federal Theater Project, staging his famous *Voodoo Macbeth, Horse Eats Hat,* and *Doctor Faustus* before forming the Mercury Theater, one of the most influential and controversial companies in the history of Broadway, with John Houseman. Welles also began lending his voice for radio productions, first to raise funds for his theatrical productions, and later for his own radio shows. The Mercury Theater of the Air became the most prestigious radio company in the country, and their production of *The War of the Worlds* made his name legend.

Welles had been turning down offers from Hollywood for many years, but when his theater company ran short of funds he accepted a generous offer from RKO, which gave him an unprecedented amount of control for a first-time director. His first film, which he produced, directed, co-wrote, and starred in, was *Citizen Kane* (1941), perhaps the most written-about film in the history of Hollywood. Despite critical success and multiple Oscar nominations, it lost money on its initial release. Though *Kane* didn't introduce any technical innovations, Welles's inventive use of sound, deep-focus photography, Expressionist lighting, and set design—along with his approach to editing and story structure—influenced the look of countless Hollywood productions. His follow-up picture, *The Magnificent Ambersons* (1942), was taken from his hands and radically recut (more than forty minutes were removed), but it is still considered a masterpiece. It was a huge financial failure, however, and Welles and his troupe were kicked off the RKO lot.

Welles's career as a director continued intermittently for a few years, but his services as an actor were much in demand. For the rest of his life he used money from his performances in other people's films to fund his own productions, many of which remained unfinished at the time of his death. Among these personal projects are *Othello* (1952), *Chimes at Midnight* (1965), and the unfinished *Don Quixote.*

He returned to Hollywood in 1958 to direct the film noir thriller *Touch of Evil,* but most of his later productions were European projects, for which he sacrificed budgets and technical support for creative freedom. Even his most impoverished films are notable for their inventiveness and complexity, their lighting and photography, their dense soundtracks and fragmented editing. His best films use these elements to explore characters in positions of power or authority marked by contradiction and caught up in a changing world.   *—Sean Axmaker*

in a grueling story of murder and revenge on the U.S./Mexico border. Heston plays Ramon Vargas, a Mexican narcotics officer on a honeymoon in a U.S. town with Susan (Leigh). The trip is cut short when the notorious, drug-dealing Grande family harasses Vargas and a car bomb sends him into a deep investigation back in his Mexican town. When he discovers U.S.-cop Quinlan (Welles) planting evidence against a Mexican national, a bitter rivalry between the two ensues, and leads to the thrilling climax. Welles's mastery of film is on perfect display here as he takes the elements of noir, which had almost become farcical, and makes them completely new and fresh again. The film was originally cut against Welles's approval upon initial release, but was reedited in 1998 using a letter he had written describing how he envisioned the film. —R. M.

TRIAL, THE L: DIRECTORS/WELLES, ORSON (1963) 118M D: Orson Welles. *Anthony Perkins, Jeanne Moreau.* Based on the story by Franz Kafka, a story which all too clearly mocks the justice system of over-bureaucratization, a simple and ordinary man (Perkins) is imprisoned without charge. He is brought to trial and still no particular crime is established and yet the defendant is still found guilty. With the help of dark and ominous photography, claustrophobic interiors and a remarkable use of the protagonist's narrative over nerve-wracking periods of solitude, Welles is able to express some of the deepest aspects of this poignant story. —N. J.

HIGH AND THE MIGHTY, THE L: DIRECTORS/WELLMAN, WILLIAM (1954) 147M D: William Wellman. *Claire Trevor, Robert Stack, Jan Sterling, Laraine Day, John Wayne.* Hugely popular with '50s audiences, this "*Grand Hotel* on an airliner" dropped off the radar after John Wayne's death in 1979; the film was among the star's personal productions and so sat in the vaults for decades, along with many another Batjac property. The movie loomed large in the Duke's legend (they played its theme for his final public appearance at the 1979 Oscars), so it's a little disappointing to discover that, apart from the growing possibility of crashing in the mid-Atlantic, it's a rather formulaic talk-fest of a movie. Although bewilderingly Oscar-nominated, director Wellman hasn't a clue how to fill the new CinemaScope screen with tourist-class spectacle. Wayne, as a pilot who survived the plane crash that killed his family, mostly stays in the cockpit with Stack. The well-cast ensemble back in the cabin includes Oscar nominees Claire Trevor and Jan Sterling, Laraine Day, Robert Newton, Paul Kelly, and John Qualen. —R. T. J.

LADY OF BURLESQUE L: DIRECTORS/WELLMAN, WILLIAM (1943) 91M D: William Wellman. *Michael O'Shea, Gloria Dickson, Marion Martin, J. Edward Bromberg, Barbara Stanwyck, Iris Adrian.* Brassy Barbara Stanwyck drives this energetic murder mystery with cocky confidence as the headlining stripper who becomes a suspect when her costar is found strangled with her own G-string. She's a saucy little firecracker as the slumming vaudeville queen in a second-rate theater, clashing with the has-beens and would-be stars who think they own this venue. Stanwyck plays second bill to nobody, on or off stage. Wellman struggles against code censorship and mostly wins, dropping saucy suggestions throughout the backstage drama. The film never quite catches fire but it smolders well enough to entertain and the excellent backstage/onstage play is worthy of a film in itself. Based on a novel by legendary, real-life stripper Gypsy Rose Lee. —S A.

STORY OF G.I. JOE, THE L: DIRECTORS/WELLMAN, WILLIAM (1945) 108M D: William Wellman. *Robert Mitchum, Wally Cassell, Freddie Steele, Burgess Meredith.* The quintessential platoon film is less a story than a string of anecdotal incidents and character moments in an American infantry unit, strung together by the travails of real-life war correspondent Ernie Pyle (Meredith), whose dispatches inspired the film. This is a glamourless and harsh portrait of war, an unending march through mud and blood and the everyday reality of death. Wellman's blunt, documentary-like photography gives it the immediacy of a newsreel. Though out of step with 1945 audiences caught up in the tide of victory, it was then, and is still, considered one of the most important and accurate depictions of the soldier's experience. —S. A.

AMERICAN FRIEND, THE L: DIRECTORS/WENDERS, WIM (1977) 125M D: Wim Wenders. *Bruno Ganz, Sam Fuller, Nicholas Ray, Lisa Kreuzer, Dennis Hopper, Gerard Blain.* Hopper is a very different kind of Tom Ripley in Wenders's adaptation of Patricia Highsmith's novel *Ripley's Game* (the sequel to *The Talented Mr. Ripley*). Yet just as in the novel, Ripley is spurred to take revenge on art-restorer Jonathan Zimmerman (Ganz) after nothing more than being slighted at their first meeting, but then comes to his rescue as the revenge mires him in a series of murders. Their ensuing relationship is genuine and fraternal even as it arises from deceit, but Ripley's victims are not merely criminals. This is as introspective and psychologically tangled as thrillers come, and no less riveting for it. Wenders regular Kreuzer is excellent as Zimmerman's wife, whose suspicions of Ripley prove completely founded. Ray is haunting as the aging New York art forger, and Fuller barks orders as an American gangster. *The American Friend* became Wenders's first truly international film (the first of many) and a critical and commercial success. —S. A.

END OF VIOLENCE, THE L: DIRECTORS/WENDERS, WIM (1996) 122M D: Wim Wenders. *Gabriel Byrne, Pruitt Taylor-Vince, Traci Lind, Loren Dean, Bill Pullman,*

Wim Wenders

Born in Düsseldorf in 1945, just months after Germany's surrender to the Allies in World War II, Wim Wenders grew up in a society gripped by historical and cultural amnesia. Living in a succession of small towns, he found that his entertainment outlets consisted of listening to rock-and-roll music on American Forces Radio and playing pinball at the local ice cafés (ice cream shops).

Wenders discovered the cinema while attending art school in Paris, where he watched as many as five features a day at the Cinémathèque Française. As with rock and roll (which to this day plays an integral role in his films), foreign cinema captured Wenders's interest and prompted his desire to make films, with influences from directors John Ford, Nicholas Ray, Anthony Mann, Sam Fuller, and Howard Hawks guiding his first films, and later Fritz Lang and most significantly Yasujiro Ozu becoming important influences.

Wenders's films during his first decade of directing deal primarily with Germany and German identity in a culture where American influences have filled in the gaps left by the country's historical denial. Like most of his contemporaries, Wenders has avoided dealing directly with Germany's fascist past, instead making tentative references in such films as *Wrong Move* (1975), *Kings of the Road* (1976), and *Faraway, So Close!* (1993), to name but a few. But the specter of Germany's past, and the culture's denial of that painful history, hangs over many of his films in the form of the rootless, dislocated individuals that populate them. The drifter, the wanderer, the searcher is at the heart of Wenders's films.

Wenders makes films about travelers,

Andie MacDowell. The overreaching story tries to take in too many characters and the well-meaning screenplay borders on trite in moments, but like so many Wenders films the accumulation of moments, images, and ideas becomes something more than the sum of its parts. Byrne is a computer/audio/video genius secretly wiring Los Angeles up for Big Brother-style surveillance while wrestling with his conscience, especially after catching glimpses of a possible murder. Pullman is an action-film producer who disappears into the LA underclass and Dean is the cop whose search for the man leads him to a romance with stuntwoman Lind. A complex web of relationships and personalities transforms the film into an internalized thriller, trading physical violence for moral conflict. Wenders twists what little on-screen violence there is into either coldly distanced observations or abrupt but anonymous killings, creating an odd but often touching and unnerving ethereal thriller. —*S.A.*

KINGS OF THE ROAD L: DIRECTORS/WENDERS, WIM (1976) 176M D: Wim Wenders. *Rüdiger Vogler, Hanns Zischler.* If it's true that all Wenders films are road movies, then this is the greatest of them all. A traveling repairman (Wenders's alter-ego, Volger) literally pulls a loner out of the lake and together they hit the road. A search for personal and national identity through the backroads and small towns of West Germany, repairing film projectors and confronting injured relationships. A truly redemptive work of cinema, with beautiful cinematography by Robby Müller. —*S.A.*

LISBON STORY L: DIRECTORS/WENDERS, WIM (1994) 100M D: Wim Wenders. *Teresa Salgueiro, Patrick Bauchau, Rüdiger Vogler.* Wenders's love letter to Lisbon is one of his lesser efforts, but the charming humor, gorgeous location shooting, and wonderful music (by Madredeus, who play themselves) keeps the film fun and engaging. Longtime Wenders regular Vogler plays a movie soundman called to help a director shooting a film in Lisbon, but after driving across Europe (in a terrific credits sequence that takes us through practically every border between Germany and Portugal) he finds only pieces of the unfinished film in an empty apartment. Wenders quotes his earlier film *The State of Things* and gives homage to Portuguese director Manuel de Oliveira, Charlie Chaplin, and the hundredth anniversary of cinema, but the film is at its best when succumbing to the simple pleasures of making cinema as Vogler

people on the move, and he continually returns to the road film: *Alice in the Cities* (1975); *Wrong Move*; *Kings of the Road*; *Paris, Texas* (1984); and *Until the End of the World* (1991). In other films, travel becomes a central element of the narrative: *The Goalie's Anxiety at the Penalty Kick* (1972), *The American Friend* (1977), *The State of Things* (1982), *Lisbon Story* (1994), and, of course, the journeys from heaven to earth in *Wings of Desire* (1988) and *Faraway, So Close!* (1993). His world is a landscape of winding country roads through fields and forests, urban cityscapes, railroad tracks and speeding trains, coffee shops, hotels, jukeboxes, and photo booths and other roadside attractions. The road serves as both an escape and a way back: the route for escape from responsibility, and the winding path back to self. From the self-exiled wanderer to the determined traveler, Wenders's characters find that the road ultimately becomes a pathway to (or the possibility of) grace.

Wenders's films are generally stylistically austere by American standards, but they are always concerned with the visual and the concept of "seeing." A number of his films refer to cinematic devices, characters are always taking photographs, and the camera is continually looking at the world through the windows of a moving car. An artist concerned with "the disease of images," Wenders continually reconnects himself with cinema through simple, direct images.

Wenders is an international filmmaker in the greatest sense of the term: he makes his films all over the world, and he uses his camera to blur the artificial constraints of national borders to focus on the global community. Part of his success in this endeavor must be attributed to his fierce independence, which has allowed him to make his films with a minimum of compromises. Another important element is his loyal group of collaborators, some who have worked with him for more than twenty years. Perhaps most importantly, Wenders finds his own identity on the road, a traveler on a quest: the external journey to discover the world, and an inward journey to the soul. —*Sean Axmaker*

leads us on a journey through the sights and sounds of Lisbon, tracking the missing director via the pieces of film he has left behind. —*S. A.*

PARIS, TEXAS L: DIRECTORS/WENDERS, WIM (1984) 147M D: Wim Wenders. *Harry Dean Stanton, Nastassja Kinski, Dean Stockwell, Hunter Carson, Aurore Clement.* Film is, indeed, a collaborative medium and rarely is that more beautifully illustrated than with a film like *Paris, Texas*. Shepard's deceptively simple script is brought heart-breakingly to life with a magnificent cast, including two absolutely amazing performances from Stanton and Kinski. Frequent Wenders collaborator Robby Müller captures sublimely beautiful images of everything from landscapes of the Mojave Desert to the interiors of a sex club with the deft skill of a true master. Ry Cooder's slide-guitar score is nostalgic and tender and aptly captures the emotion of the film. Wenders's direction just slides quietly into the background. He hangs on to his shots, not wanting to cut away, giving full life to the characters and his scenes. The end result of all this is that the pieces fall perfectly into place and create a real masterpiece. *Paris, Texas* is a gentle film of enormous power. —*T. S.*

TOKYO-GA L: DIRECTORS/WENDERS, WIM (1985) 88M D: Wim Wenders. *Chris Marker, Werner Herzog, Chishu Ryu, Yuuharu Atsuta.* Wenders's passion for the films of director Yasujiro Ozu takes him to Japan, a country he knows little of outside what he's seen in movies. *Tokyo-Ga* should appeal to Ozu fanatics, particularly the interview with Ozu regular Ryu. The film tries to stay loose enough to be affected by the material, but often loses sight of its Ozu preoccupation completely, for better or worse. A rather aimless documentary, it does include conversations with Herzog and Marker—fairly incidental to the material, but a bonus for film aficionados. Marker's interview is notable, conducted as he completed his masterpiece, *Sans Soleil* (Wenders is shown a rough cut). Unfortunately, mere mention of *Sans Soleil* decimates Wenders's own already weak film. Given their striking similarities, it seems unavoidable to point out that *Tokyo-Ga*'s ambling, pedestrian observations simply can't keep up with *Sans Soleil*'s rich cerebral workout. —*C. B.*

UNTIL THE END OF THE WORLD L: DIRECTORS/WENDERS, WIM (1991) 158M D: Wim Wenders. *Solveig Dommartin, William Hurt, Sam Neill.* Until the End of the World is a sprawling road movie shot on location in four different continents and eight countries. It is a science-fiction film set in 1999, when a nuclear satellite comes crashing to earth, supposedly destroying civilization. Also, a doctor has developed an apparatus that can project people's dreams. But at its heart, it is a story about humans and how they relate to each other. Its epic scale lends it a great feeling of adventure. The soundtrack is perfect, filled with original songs by U2, Peter Gabriel, Nick Cave, and others. The film's lengthy running time hides the fact that the available version is actually a drastically cut film. Almost two hours of film have not been included. I've never seen this uncut version and I imagine it fills out the story immensely, creating an entirely different film. As it is, *Until the End of the World* is fascinating but has many flaws and does not really come together in the end. Still, it's leagues above most science-fiction stories. —*T. S.*

WINGS OF DESIRE L: DIRECTORS/WENDERS, WIM (1988) 130M D: Wim Wenders. *Solveig Dommartin, Otto Sander, Peter Falk, Bruno Ganz, Curt Bois.* Wenders's surreal masterpiece details the plight of a working angel over modern-day Berlin. Ganz plays angel Damiel who, with another angel, keeps watch over an aging poet (Bois), a trapeze artist (Dommartin), and an American actor (Falk). As witness to their deepest thoughts, this angel develops thoughts of his own—thoughts that maybe the people in his charge are simply writing off the very miracle of life, thoughts that he himself could appreciate the work of God better on his own if only he were human. This remarkable film features brilliant black-and-white as well as color photography, and incredible asides to the audience including excerpts of such great poets as Rilke. *Wings of Desire* is an absolute classic of modern German expressionism that nobody should miss. —*N. J.*

BRIDE OF FRANKENSTEIN, THE L: DIRECTORS/WHALE, JAMES (1935) 75M D: James Whale. *Boris Karloff, Ernst Thesiger, Valerie Hobson, Colin Clive, O. P. Heggie, Elsa Lanchester.* This is a sequel that somehow, amazingly, finds a way to surpass the original in every respect, certainly no small task. Its opening with Lord Byron and the Shelleys is a perfect segue back into the story of the first film. The Monster's experience with the blind old man is touching and profound, his persecution is sad, his rage is horrifying, and his ultimate fate is deeply tragic. Everything about this film comes together to make something so much more than its parts. The writing, the directing, and cinematography, the acting, the effects, the art design—everything is perfect. This is truly one of the great horror films of all time and possibly one of the best films ever made. —*T. S.*

FRANKENSTEIN (1931) L: DIRECTORS/WHALE, JAMES (1931) 71M D: James Whale. *Mae Clarke, Colin Clive, John Boles, Edward Van Sloan, Boris Karloff,*

Dwight Frye. The original movie is often considered one of the greatest horror films of all time. I'm certainly not going to challenge that; I wholeheartedly agree, but it's wise to remember the importance of the sequels, especially *Bride of Frankenstein* and *Son of Frankenstein.* It's not just this original film but all the films that comprise the greatest horror series of all time. This first work doesn't quite pack the emotional punch of some of its successors, but thematically and atmospherically it is genius. Everything, from the creepy studio graveyards to the cutting down of the corpse to the awakening of the monster to the windmill finale, is perfectly imagined and executed. Karloff creates the ultimate archetype of the tortured, misunderstood monster. Here's to the house of Frankenstein! —*T. S.*

INVISIBLE MAN, THE L: DIRECTORS/WHALE, JAMES (1933) 71M D: James Whale. *Henry Travers, William Harrigan, Gloria Stuart, Claude Rains.* Although perhaps the least popular of the Universal monsters, I think the Invisible Man is right up there with Dracula and Frankenstein's monster. Rains plays the scientist whose invisibility formula drives him to madness. It's not as memorable a performance as Lugosi or Karloff, because for almost all of the film he's either not on screen at all or wrapped completely in bandages (and that cool bathrobe). But this is the edgiest of these films because the guy is so devious. He has a far higher body count than the other Universal monsters, and he takes obvious pleasure in it. It's hard to feel sorry for him. While certainly less atmospheric than Whale's Frankenstein films, it moves at a fast pace that makes it feel much more modern and energetic. —*B. T.*

OLD DARK HOUSE, THE L: DIRECTORS/WHALE, JAMES (1932) 70M D: James Whale. *Melvyn Douglas, Gloria Stuart, Charles Laughton, Boris Karloff, Lillian Bond.* Universal's foray into the old-dark-house genre is a runaway success. This is clichéd gothic fun on par or surpassing other films such as *The Bat* or *Bat Whispers.* Based on a novel by J. B. Priestly (rather than one by Mary Roberts Rinehart), we are hardly offered a unique twist on the traditional premise, although this one is masterfully crafted and excellently acted with a mad butler played by Karloff. It also includes the beautiful actresses Stuart and Moore. A great Universal horror treat. —*T. S.*

ACE IN THE HOLE L: DIRECTORS/WILDER, BILLY (1954) 111M D: Billy Wilder. *Kirk Douglas, Jan Sterling, Porter Hall, Frank Cady, Robert Arthur.* In Wilder's darkest film, Douglas gives one of his best performances as cynical newspaperman Chuck Tatum. In one of the best entrances since Rita Hayworth's in *Gilda*, Chuck arrives in a small Arizona town riding in his towed, broke-down convertible. He fast-talks his way into a temporary job on the local paper. . . just until a story comes along that's big enough to carry him back to the big time. Cut to a year later, and Chuck's still stuck in Podunk. Then, out to cover a trivial local story, he stumbles upon a gold mine (almost literally: the title is a cynical reference to a man trapped underground by a mine collapse). The film darkens as Tatum's desperation—he's tied his entire future to this story—leads him to manipulate events and, ultimately, endanger the other participants. Sterling plays Lorraine Minosa, a local married woman who hitches her fortunes to Tatum's. *Ace in the Hole* was such a box office bomb (Wilder's first) that the studio almost immediately retitled it *The Big Carnival*, a reference to the media circus that swirls up under Tatum's orchestration. It's never been available on video. —*C. C.*

APARTMENT, THE L: DIRECTORS/WILDER, BILLY (1960) 125M D: Billy Wilder. *Jack Lemmon, Shirley MacLaine, Fred MacMurray, Ray Walston, Jack Kruschen.* Wilder is at the helm of this romantic masterpiece about young insurance worker C. C. Baxter (Lemmon), who industriously attempts to climb the corporate ladder by lending out his apartment key to adulterous bosses. Baxter's plans go awry when he discovers the girl he is in love with (the sprightly MacLaine) is having an affair with the big boss man (the awesome MacMurray). At once clever romantic comedy and biting social critique, the film never lets go of its warmth, humor, and pathos for characters injured or ennobled by their ideals of love. Wilder won Oscars for both directing and writing this film. —*J. D.*

DOUBLE INDEMNITY L: DIRECTORS/WILDER, BILLY (1944) 107M D: Billy Wilder. *Fred MacMurray, Barbara Stanwyck, Edward G. Robinson.* For anyone looking to dive into the gritty world of film noir, start here. All the plot twists, hidden innuendoes, film devices, and cinematography are as fresh as ever in this biting thriller. The blacks are as pitch as night, while the whites eerily hide the truth. The story quickly gets up to speed as Walter Neff (MacMurray) lies dying on his office floor. With a dictaphone, he records his story of deception, murder, and betrayal, and the movie unfolds as a continuous flashback. Phyllis (Stanwyck) is the married woman Walter falls for when he goes to have her husband sign some insurance contracts. From there, a plot to murder her husband unfolds, as the pair's affair heats up. When greed gets the best of them they decide to enact the double-indemnity clause to double the insurance payment. But Walter's best friend and coworker, Barton, can tell that something doesn't add up, and begins to do some investigating on his own. From the beginning shot to the closing fade-out, every frame oozes with what would become standard crime pulp. —*R. M.*

FEDORA L: DIRECTORS/WILDER, BILLY (1978) 114M D: Billy Wilder. *Frances Sternhagen, José Ferrer, Hildegarde Neff, Marthe Keller, William Holden.* This is basically a sequel to *Sunset Boulevard*, which in its own way is as shocking as the original. The manic-depressive actress Norma Desmond has died and an American reporter flies out to Italy where her family has an open-casket funeral for the celebrity so her fans can pay their last respects. The reporter (Holden, who played the screenwriter in *Sunset Boulevard*) goes undercover as a friend of the deceased and soon discovers so much dirt that even he is uncomfortable with the story. Great acting abounds in this off-beat gem, and lots of odd cameos in the endless queue of mourners. —*N. J.*

FIVE GRAVES TO CAIRO L: DIRECTORS/WILDER, BILLY (1949) 96M D: Billy Wilder. *Franchot Tone, Anne Baxter, Erich von Stroheim.* Oh. . . Anne Baxter, you eternal cutie, how you make me go. . . BOING! If you think all Wilder ever did was comedy, think again. This is an intelligent, involving WWII espionage–suspense film with deftly drawn characters and a seemingly endless supply of snappy dialogue. And don't forget von Stroheim as Field Marshall Rommel. —*S. F.*

FOREIGN AFFAIR, A L: DIRECTORS/WILDER, BILLY (1948) 116M D: Billy Wilder. *Millard Mitchell, John Lund, Marlene Dietrich, Jean Arthur.* Wilder, with his caustic wit, looks into the American occupational forces in post-WWII Germany for this toast to corrupted innocence. The innocence this time is naive Iowa Congresswoman Phoebe Frost (Arthur), a prim idealist who storms into Berlin for a good housecleaning and comes out a little less prim and a lot more fun. Dietrich, belting out cabaret tunes for food and favors, vamps it up as a poverty-stricken survivor getting by any way she knows how. Forget colorless Lund, who plays the opportunistic American officer who hides his black-market sideline from the investigating committee, and join corn-fed Arthur in singing the Iowa fight song! —*S. A.*

IRMA LA DOUCE L: DIRECTORS/WILDER, BILLY (1963) 143M D: Billy Wilder. *Jack Lemmon, Bruce Yarnell, Lou Jacobi, Shirley MacLaine.* Only Wilder could have gotten away with it: Lemmon is the rookie gendarme who loses his job, wins the heart of streetwalker MacLaine, and becomes the most successful pimp in Paris, all in the same day. Wilder adapted the Broadway musical with his regular collaborator I. A. L. Diamond, removing the songs to replace them with Wilder slyness, and spoofing sweetness bubbling under all the corruption and hypocrisy of this turn-of-the-century Gay Paree. It's like a farcical remake of his earlier *The Apartment*, with Lemmon pushed to even more extremes as a straight-laced naif so jealous of his lover's clients that he poses as one himself, and then becomes jealous of his own creation! MacLaine is delightful and Jacobi is earthy yet somehow above it all as the philosophical barman and commentator. Wilder pushes the boundaries of bourgeois morality with a mix of ribald suggestion and fairy-tale innocence, all in a gaudy re-creation of a fantasy Paris underworld. —S. A.

KISS ME, STUPID L: DIRECTORS/WILDER, BILLY (1964) 126M D: Billy Wilder. *Dean Martin, Felicia Farr, Kim Novak, Ray Walston.* Wilder began the 1960s winning three Oscars and became a near-pariah with *Kiss Me Stupid* four years later. The plot is a farcical concoction about a would-be song-writer (Walston) in the pit-stop town of Climax, Nevada, who passes off local prostitute Polly the Pistol (Novak) as his wife so that he can detain a lecherous Las Vegas star (Martin) long enough to audition his creations. Often praised for his envelope-pushing daring, Wilder was univer-sally deemed on this occasion to have gone way beyond the pale comedy-wise, morality-wise, and bad-taste-wise. The movie was released without a Code Seal of Approval and bombed with press and public alike. Within a few years, community standards had changed enough that *Kiss Me Stupid* could be shown on network TV in prime time without cuts or apology, and what had once seemed crude and scandalous now seemed almost... sweet? *Kiss Me Stupid* still isn't one of Wilder's best films, but it's not the out-rage it was taken for. In its tortuous fashion, and its instinct for the need for fantasy, it's as star-tlingly beautiful as it is caustic. With Farr (Mrs. Jack Lemmon) as the real wife. —R. T. J.

LOST WEEKEND L: DIRECTORS/WILDER, BILLY (1945) 101M D: Billy Wilder. *Jane Wyman, Ray Milland.* Wilder's classic drama is notable in more ways than one. Released in 1945, audiences at the time weren't sure how to react to this searing, brutal, honest portrait of an alcoholic. Wilder, known much more for his comedies (*The Apartment, Some Like it Hot*) pulls no punches whatsoever in depict-ing the life of a drunkard who has managed to be "left alone" for one horrendous weekend. Don Birnam (Milland), a writer waiting for the inspiration to write, attempts to make alcohol his muse. However, over the course of many years, he's never managed to write a book and has instead become a hopeless addict. Admirably portrayed by Milland (in an Oscar-winning per-formance), Birnam is able to come across as both repulsive and sympathetic, a deft juggling act of viewer emotions handled professionally and assuredly by Wilder. The supporting roles are also handled well, though they come across as slightly dated in a twenty-first-century context. —C. P.

ONE, TWO, THREE L: DIRECTORS/WILDER, BILLY (1961) 109M D: Billy Wilder. *Pamela Tiffin, Liselotte Pulver, Arlene Francis, James Cagney, Horst Buchholz.* Loud and relentless, this movie employs a much more assaultive style of comedy than Wilder is usually known for. The characters are more archetypes than actual people but the ways they

collide with each others' lives are always funny. —E. W.

SABRINA (1954) L: DIRECTORS/WILDER, BILLY (1954) 113M D: Billy Wilder. *Humphrey Bogart, William Holden, Audrey Hepburn.* Sabrina isn't the strongest of Wilder's films, but that's more of a testament to him than a dig at this charming Hepburn vehicle. She plays a chauffeur's daughter in love with the rake (Holden) her father drives around. When she returns from cooking school in Paris, she's blossomed, and draws the attention of both Holden and his serious, business-minded brother (Bogart). While it doesn't have the ten-sion or cutting wisecracks of *Some Like It Hot* or *The Apartment*, the film features lively dialogue and a cast in top form: Holden is charming as the playboy, Bogart is surprisingly effective as the stone-faced mogul, and Hepburn is ach-ingly beautiful, never more so than when she spies on an elegant party from the branches of a tree. —T. P.

SOME LIKE IT HOT L: DIRECTORS/WILDER, BILLY (1959) 120M D: Billy Wilder. *Tony Curtis, Marilyn Monroe, Joe E. Brown, Jack Lemmon.* Over forty years since its production, Billy Wilder's *Some Like it Hot* still stands as one of the greatest screen com-edies of all time. Hilarious performances from Lemmon, Curtis, and Monroe, among others, highlight Wilder's superb script and razor-sharp wit. When Lemmon and Curtis accidentally wit-ness a mob killing, they find themselves the next target. In order to hide out, they join and all-female jazz band, dressing in drag to fit in. A joy to watch from start to finish; this film has lost none of its magical touch. —C. P.

SUNSET BOULEVARD L: DIRECTORS/WILDER, BILLY (1950) 110M D: Billy Wilder. *Nancy Olson, Erich von Stroheim, William Holden, Gloria Swanson.* The blackest of Hollywood's self-portraits is an old dark house of a ghost story inhabited by the living shadows of its discarded stars. Swanson is magnificent as Norma Desmond, the former silent-movie queen living in her memories while plotting a fantasy of a comeback, and she understands both the mon-strous and pathetic dimensions of her demented diva. Holden is equally good as the failed screen-writer with a mercenary streak who plays the gigolo to hide from creditors. Director/cowriter Wilder makes his scabrous and acidic exposé of Hollywood's living graveyards both ghoulish and tragic, thanks largely to the quiet devotion of von Stroheim's performance as her butler and, once upon a time, her director. It was a biting in-joke for Tinseltown historians at the time—von Stroheim's directorial career was destroyed by Swanson's lover, who fired him from *Queen Kelly*, and Wilder even fit some of that footage into the "home movie" scene. —S. A.

WITNESS FOR THE PROSECUTION L: DIRECTORS/WILDER, BILLY (1957) 116M D: Billy Wilder. *Charles Laughton, Tyrone Power, Marlene Dietrich.* Wilder adapts and directs one of the best and most entertaining Agatha Christie films. A twisting little courtroom drama, it stars Laughton as a barrister who only takes cases that intrigue him, and defending shady Power against a charge of murder intrigues him because the prosecution's chief witness is the defendant's wife (Dietrich). Laughton revels in the part with his usual mix of sardonic humor and unforced authority and Dietrich puts on a great act as Dietrich, but Power is the unheralded key to the film as the charming rogue with a callous soul. The Old Bailey centerpiece set is a marvel. —S. A.

ANDROMEDA STRAIN, THE L: DIRECTORS/WISE, ROBERT (1971) 131M D: Robert Wise. *David Wayne, James Olson, Paula Kelly, Kate Reid, Arthur Hill.* The Andromeda Strain is an extraterrestrial virus which has been quarantined to a certain desert area of the southwestern United States. The viewer is given a tour of a small town killed off by this particular virus—people's blood actually turns to powder in their own veins. In a secret, underground government facility nearby, a team of experts is assembled to find a vaccine. But can it be done before the virus exponentially multiplies? This is a tremendous suspense film within a very convincing science-fiction plot. —N. J..

BODY SNATCHER, THE L: DIRECTORS/WISE, ROBERT (1945) 77M D: Robert Wise. *Boris Karloff, Bela Lugosi, Henry Daniell, Edith Atwater.* In the late nineteenth century, medical science was developing at a very rapid pace, so rapid that neither religion nor politics could keep up with it. So it was no surprise that in real-life Scotland, a nasty murder case transpired involving two men who normally robbed graves for their medical clientele, but for improved business turned to murdering old people. A writer contemporary to this intriguing murder case, R. L. Stevenson, penned a story which painted the horrors of the scenario. This film is based largely on that story, with Karloff well cast as the creepy body snatcher. Handsomely filmed, this story probes that moral gray area where one man's death can profitably be used for the life of another. It is also the last film with both Karloff and Lugosi. —N. J.

DAY THE EARTH STOOD STILL, THE L: DIRECTORS/WISE, ROBERT (1951) 92M D: Robert Wise. *Michael Rennie, Sam Jaffe, Hugh Marlowe, Patricia Neal.* Wise's Christ parable is the perfect Easter film, the story of a messenger from the heavens with a mission of peace, his message from a powerful force in the Universe. Killed by the people of Earth, he rises from the dead for a last sermon and returns to the heavens. As science fiction it ain't too bad either, with a great space ship and the best movie robot ever: the unstoppable Gort. Rennie makes a striking American film debut as Klaatu, the

well-spoken stranger from outer space, and Jaffe goes Einstein as the peace-loving scientist to whom Klaatu reaches out. Wise, ever the professional, places the fantastic elements in a scrupulously realistic Washington, D. C., setting, and gives the film the dramatic weight and narrative elegance it deserves. —S. A.

HAUNTING, THE L: DIRECTORS/WISE, ROBERT (1963) 112M D: Robert Wise. *Julie Harris, Claire Bloom, Richard Johnson, Russ Tamblyn.* Wise has dabbled consistently in the cinema of the fantastic but isn't really a master of the genre. He's a craftsman, and this is finely crafted film: beautifully designed and handsomely shot in black-and-white widescreen, with the eeriness of the ghost house suggested in the simplest of effects, from bumps (or rather pounding thumps) in the night to doors that close when the head is turned to cold spots visible only in the fog of breath. In fact, the house becomes a central character, the primary antagonist in the story of a determined supernatural researcher (Johnson in college-professor mode), two women with paranormal gifts (Harris and Bloom), and the glib young heir-to-be (Tamblyn) of the haunted mansion who come together to explore the creepy qualities of the manor, which picks the already unstable and emotionally fragile Harris for its attention. The theatrical drama looks at times overwrought, but as Wise underplays the horror it all balances out in a strange way. —S. A.

HINDENBURG, THE L: DIRECTORS/WISE, ROBERT (1975) 126M D: Robert Wise. *George C. Scott, Anne Bancroft, William Atherton, Roy Thinnes, Gig Young, Burgess Meredith.* The fiery explosion of the German air ship Hindenburg over American soil in 1937 is perfectly rife material for a Nazi-conspiracy story. Extensive footage of the remarkable tragedy already exists with an impressive audio track of an announcer detailing the event. The only thing missing is the intricate story of sabotage. To this end a great cast arouses the kind of suspense and intrigue which was expected of disaster films of the mid-'70s. Cutting in the familiar footage at the climax was simply a must, as clearly the decision to use black-and-white film was based around the very concept. —N. J.

SOUND OF MUSIC, THE L: DIRECTORS/WISE, ROBERT (1965) 174M D: Robert Wise. *Julie Andrews, Christopher Plummer.* How do you solve a problem like Maria? She's bursting with naiveté, so much so she's outside running around on Austrian mountaintops singing when she should be inside praying and studying to be a good nun. She's got to settle down a little before she can marry God, so the head nun sends her off to watch seven kids, children of navy captain von Trapp (Plummer), who is Maria's complete opposite, very stern and stiff. But Maria's innocent charm melts his tough exterior, and after some misunderstandings with a pinecone, they make out in a gazebo,

John Woo

John Woo began his moviemaking career in Hong Kong, where he started as a film critic, then began making short experimental films while attempting to crack the studios. His breakthrough came after an apprenticeship with the noted Hong Kong martial arts director Zhang Che at Shaw brothers. His debut film, the independently produced *The Young Dragons* (1973), was initially banned in Hong Kong for its extreme violence, but it impressed enough people to land him a contract at Golden Harvest film studio. His early career was a succession of period adventures, martial arts films, and goofy comedies.

He moved to Cinema City Studios in the early 1980s, but the creative freedom he had hoped for never materialized. Friend and fellow director Tsui Hark agreed to produce Woo's dream project through Tsui's fledgling production company, Film Workshop. *A Better Tomorrow* became Hong Kong's biggest moneymaker up to that time, and John Woo's career exploded.

Three years later, *The Killer* introduced American audiences to Woo's gangster melodramas, and Woo left Tsui to form his own production company with partner Terence Chang. Their first film together

get married, and flee the Nazis. And let's not forget the kids. Liesl is sixteen and she's just fallen in love with a boy. He kisses her and immediately after she yells "Whee!" Then she finds out a few weeks later that he's dumped her for Hitler. What a jerk! All the kids are forced to wear uniforms, and when they are told they don't have to anymore, they end up in clothes made out of some tatty old curtains. No wonder they need constant reminding of their favorite things. This timeless film, full of catchy tunes, scenic vistas, and genuine pluck, has earned its reputation as a classic. —*J. K.*

STAR TREK: THE MOTION PICTURE L: DIRECTORS/WISE, ROBERT (1979) 143M D: Robert Wise. *George Takei, James Doohan, Stephen Collins, DeForest Kelley, Leonard Nimoy, William Shatner.* Not long after the impossible success of *Star Wars*, it was natural for space operas to suddenly flood the market. And so it made perfect sense to trot out Gene Roddenberry's *Star Trek*. The full cast of the long-running television series was reunited, and given better uniforms, a better ship, and state-of-the-art special effects to boot. This film starts with a very long exposition explaining what has happened to these aged characters and their ship over the last many years. But eventually the Earth is threatened by a strange phenomenon in space, and Admiral Kirk takes over the Enterprise to save the day. —*N. J.*

ASHES OF TIME L: DIRECTORS/WONG KAR-WAI (1994) 99M D: Wong Kar-Wai. *Tony Leung Ka Fai, Tony Leung Chiu Wai, Maggie Cheung, Brigitte Lin, Leslie*

Cheung, Charlie Yeung, Jackie Cheung. Wong Kar-Wai, arguably Hong Kong's most exciting and complex director working today, turns a period adventure-epic centered around old friends and rival swordsmen into an introspective existential essay in a melancholy key. Malicious West (Leslie Cheung) and Evil East (Tony Leung Ka Fai) meet once a year to examine their lost opportunities and drink to forget their losses. Brigitte Lin costars as the enigmatic pair Yin and Yang, who morph back and forth across identity and gender. Full of flash-forwards and flashbacks, enigmatic characters, and stunning visuals (courtesy of cinematographer Christopher Doyle), the story circles back to the beginning, the rivals trapped by their fates into repeating their mistakes. Or are they second chances? The film is so rich and dense, with narrating chores split between its central protagonists, that it may take repeated viewings to unpack it all. —*S. A.*

CHUNGKING EXPRESS L: DIRECTORS/WONG KAR-WAI (1994) 102M D: Wong Kar-Wai. *Takeshi Kaneshiro, Brigitte Lin Ching-Hsia, Tony Leung Chiu Wai, Faye Wong.* Wong first burst onto the international scene with this jazzy little cinematic improvisation with themes of love, loss, connection, and the craziness of emotion. The two stories revolve around cops, but any resemblance to the usual Hong Kong action fare ends there. In the first story, rookie Kaneshiro falls for a femme fatale in a blond wig (Lin). In the second, ladies' man Leung Chiu Wai finds himself the object of the affections of big-eyed pixie Wong (a popular Cantopop chanteuse who makes her film

was Woo's very personal Vietnam film (and Tiananmen Square allegory) *Bullet in the Head.* After the release of their biggest, most action-packed film to date, *Hard Boiled,* Woo and Chang relocated to the United States, where Woo made his American directing debut with *Hard Target* at the request of star Jean-Claude Van Damme.

What defines a Woo film is style: an exhilarating display of visual aesthetics, a dance of color and movement, a celebration of kinetic energy. Thematically, he explores values such as honor, duty, family, and friendship, which are central to the traditional historic epics and period adventures of Hong Kong cinema. His films have attitude and passion, gliding cameras and lightning-fast edits, gunshots and explosions, cool heroes and hotheaded villains, honor, trust, respect, and betrayal. This marriage of surface aesthetics and an articulated vision has made Woo a cult director the world over.

As of this writing, Woo's American productions have lacked the passion and power of his great Hong Kong gangster epics. The differences between those self-scripted productions and the assembly-line genre screenplays handed to him in America are evident and immense: Woo cares for his characters. He develops intense emotional bonds between his heroes, and he makes his audience care about them. For this reason, the best of his films border on tragedy. Life has value when put on the line for a higher ideal: love, integrity, respect. However, Woo's recent successes in Hollywood, along with the formation of his own stateside production company, may allow him the freedom to make his own films in an American context. —*Sean Axmaker*

---

debut here and sings a Cantonese version of The Cranberries' song "Dreams"). A unique peek into the urban flavor of one working-class suburb in the crowded island nation of Hong Kong, this film sways to its own beat with unusual, infectious rhythms and the smeary/stuttered visuals of cinematographer Christopher Doyle. —*S. A.*

FALLEN ANGELS L: DIRECTORS/WONG KAR-WAI (1995) 96M D: Wong Kar-Wai. *Leon Lai, Michelle Reis, Takeshi Kaneshiro, Charlie Yeung, Karen Mok*. Wong carves a splinter originally written for *Chungking Express* into a crime film viewed through a kaleidoscope. Two stories of disconnected individuals cross paths. In one, a hit man (Lai) falls in love with the woman (Reis) who arranges his contracts, though they've never met (she does clean his apartment while he's on assignment). In the other, a mute, unemployed ex-con (Kaneshiro) breaks into businesses after hours so he can "practice" running them, and meets a volatile girl (Yeung) during his adventures. Wong punctuates the melancholy narrative with odd humor and unexpected explosions of shocking violence, all shot in those wonderfully saturated colors captured by cinematographer Christopher Doyle. —*S. A.*

HAPPY TOGETHER L: DIRECTORS/WONG KAR-WAI (1997) 96M D: Wong Kar-Wai. *Tony Leung, Leslie Cheung, Chen Chang*. This collaboration of Wong and cinematographer Christopher Doyle is one of the most aesthetically rich and visually stunning films of the decade. This story of two capricious lovers begins with their vacation to Buenos Aires and the perpetual fallouts and make-ups they go through as they decide whether or not cut their losses and return to Hong Kong. Like most of Wong's films, *Happy Together* rarely seems to follow any direction, instead relying on Doyle's cinematography. Doyle's trademark style creates an atmosphere of murkiness matched with excessive whiteouts and layers of highly saturated hues that, along with the erratic and often impatient movement of camera work, mirrors the indecisive and rash behavior of the two characters. *Happy Together* is much more visually diverse and sporadic than any of the director's other films, and a strikingly gorgeous work. —*A. T.*

IN THE MOOD FOR LOVE L: DIRECTORS/WONG KAR-WAI (2001) 96M D: Wong Kar-Wai. *Maggie Cheung, Tony Leung Chiu Wai*. There may be no more sensual director in the world today than Hong Kong's Wong Kar-Wai and this is his richest work yet, a shadow dance of would-be lovers sketched in suggestions and intimations. Cheung and Leung Chiu-Wai star as next-door neighbors in a crowded apartment building, a tiny community bustling with chit-chat, potluck dinners, and all-night mah-jongg games. When they suspect that their spouses are having an affair, they meet to compare notes, but even in friendship and growing affection they keep their social faces in place. Wong shoots the film from around corners, under tables, through doorways and windows, eavesdropping on a life. Slivers of scenes dissolve into one another as time is lost to mood and emotion; the film doesn't progress as much as spiral lazily around the characters. Wong remains on the outside looking in, but his gliding camera finds a grace in their sadness and his simmering colors allow their repressed emotions to burn their way into the screen. —*S. A.*

BETTER TOMORROW, A L: DIRECTORS/WOO, JOHN (1986) 95M D: John Woo. *Waise Lee, Chow Yun-Fat, Leslie Cheung, Lung Ti.* Woo came to world attention for this film's jaw-dropping action sequences, as did Chow for his performance as the once-cocky, now crippled Mark, who refuses to quit. But at its core this is a brilliant and heart-rending crime film. Ho (Ti) and Mark operate a lucrative counterfeiting operation for their bosses, with Ho showing clumsy Shing (Lee) the ropes. Trouble is, Ho has a brother Kit (Cheung) who is a cop trying to make his mark. He becomes fierce in his dedication and bitterly angry when his brother is arrested in Taiwan. Kit's girl Jackie (Chu) tries to patch things up as Ho tries to go straight. But Kit is targeting Shing, now a smooth operator in charge of counterfeiting. And word gets out that Shing is now targeting back. The emotions are crisp and hard with a very sweet center. There is suspense but the violence cuts loose like a string of firecrackers going off. And you become overwhelmed with a sense of lost innocence that can never be redeemed. An action crime-flick that reaches every sinew of your being. Unsurpassed. —*J. C.*

BULLET IN THE HEAD L: DIRECTORS/WOO, JOHN (1990) 136M D: John Woo. *Simon Yam, Tony Leung Chiu Wai, Jacky Cheung, Waise Lee.* Woo's hard-hitting tale of friendship, betrayal, and tragedy blends his trademark action and heroic bloodshed to a perfect concoction, and the performances he evokes from his leads are almost heartbreaking to watch. A trio of childhood friends, who realize they have no future in Hong Kong after they kill a gangster, sneak into Vietnam to find their fortune in black-market smuggling, and become embroiled in the Vietnam War. When the Viet Cong trap them, they are imprisoned, endure torture beyond imagination, and face the horrific game of Russian Roulette previously made famous in *The Deer Hunter.* During their escape, the titular bullet in the head is received. Though Frank (played perfectly by Cheung) survives, the lodged bullet causes him to slowly go mad, and though he cannot bring himself to do it, Frank knows that he must be killed before he goes into complete psychosis. His quest leads to an ending that could only be made in Hong Kong, and only brought to life by Woo. —*R. M.*

FACE/OFF L: DIRECTORS/WOO, JOHN (1997) 138M D: John Woo. *Nicolas Cage, Joan Allen, Alessandro Nivola, Dominique Swain, John Travolta.* It's too complicated to explain how a cop (Travolta) and a psychotic criminal mastermind (Cage) get their faces surgically switched. So you'll just have to take my word for it that Woo has taken this preposterous premise and turned it into by far his best American film. So Cage plays Travolta undercover trying to get the location of a bomb out of Cage's accomplice brother (Nivola), while Travolta plays Cage pretending to be Travolta and taking better care of his wife (Allen) and daughter (Swain) than the real guy did. Like the best Woo films, it shows how the cop and the criminal have more in common than they think; it also has the most emotion and over-the-top action of any of Woo's post–Hong Kong films. Cage is spectacular as the hammy, maniacal villain and as the nice guy disguised as the villain. The best scene has him revealing to his wife who he really is while looking like the man who killed their son. —*B. T.*

HARD-BOILED L: DIRECTORS/WOO, JOHN (1992) 128M D: John Woo. *Bowie Lam, Chow Yun-Fat, Tony Leung Chiu Wai, Kwan Hoi-Shan.* Tequila (Chow) is a cop who breaks too many rules, and Tony (Leung) is a deadly assassin who also happens to be an undercover cop. They form a reluctant partnership to stop a crime syndicate, which culminates in an incredible shootout in a hospital where Chow must run around with a newborn baby in one hand and a gun in the other. To those not initiated into Woo's Hong Kong films, this is an absolute mindblower. There are endless gun battles, each of which probably has more bullets fired than in the entire *Die Hard* and *Lethal Weapon* franchises combined. But somehow, between the outrageous scenes of operatic mayhem there is also an emotional center. Tequila's bond with Tony and Tony's bond with the boss he has to betray are much more affecting than you would get in an American action movie, including those by Woo. —*B. T.*

KILLER, THE L: DIRECTORS/WOO, JOHN (1989) 110M D: John Woo. *Kenneth Tsang, Chu Kong, Sally Yeh, Chow Yun-Fat, Danny Lee.* Chow is a hit man who accidentally blinds a night-club singer (Yeh) and decides it's his duty to get the money to pay for her eye surgery. Lee is the cop trying to catch him but ends up sort of becoming his buddy. While obviously paying tribute to Jean-Pierre Melville and Sam Peckinpah, *The Killer* itself became extremely influential with its poetic slow-motion, show-off shooting styles, tremendous body count, and male bonding melodrama that blurs the line between heroes and villains. It was and still is great to see such a potent combination of thrilling action and sincere emotion. This was the movie that made many American filmgoers fall in love with John Woo, with Chow Yun-Fat, and with Hong Kong film in general. An essential classic of the action genre, it somehow spends most of its running time being artful and sentimental and still packs in three times as much violence as most of its American counterparts. —*B. T.*

MISSION: IMPOSSIBLE 2 L: DIRECTORS/WOO, JOHN (2000) 123M D: John Woo. *Tom Cruise, Thandie Newton, Dougray Scott, Richard Roxburgh, Ving Rhames.* Brian DePalma's take on *Mission: Impossible* involved only a few gunshots, so the choice of Woo to direct the sequel caused a lot of curiosity. Would he defy his fans, who would expect a violent shoot-'em up, or would he take the series in an entirely new direction? Well, it's closer to the second one, I guess. The first was a smart thriller based around clever ruses—this one is just dumb, over-the-top action with an occasional digitally enhanced latex disguise. Although it is a disappointment coming from Woo, it can be enjoyed as campy, brainless action. That said, there are a few trademark Woo touches that make it seem slightly more elegant. There is a car chase with Newton that comes across more like a tango, and a scene where the disguised Scott discovers his lover has betrayed him and removes his mask to reveal a tear dripping down his face. I can't imagine any other director including something like that. *—B.T.*

ONCE A THIEF L: DIRECTORS/WOO, JOHN (1990) 104M D: John Woo. *Cherie Chung, Leslie Cheung, Chow Yun-Fat.* Woo does Hitchcock in this romantic caper film, his homage to Truffaut's *Jules and Jim* by way of *To Catch a Thief*, with references to *North by Northwest* and *The Godfather*. Chow (oozing Cary Grant–like charisma) is the charming "big brother" to Cheung and Chung. They're a trio of street-smart orphans turned international art thieves who undertake heists the world over and play practical jokes between jobs. Woo's cool elegance goes hot when the film climaxes in an action-packed gunfight (there is a body count, but no exit wounds). Charming, funny, and very suave between bouts of slapstick goofiness, it's Woo at his most lighthearted. *—S.A.*

WINDTALKERS L: DIRECTORS/WOO, JOHN (2002) 134M D: John Woo. *Christian Slater, Nicolas Cage, Adam Beach, Frances O'Connor, Noah Emmerich, Mark Ruffalo.* Cage plays an injured WWII marine who manages to get back into the war by agreeing to an unusual assignment: protecting a Navajo soldier (Beach) who is valuable because his native language is being used as a code to keep communications hidden from the Japanese. The catch is that if Beach is captured, Cage is instructed to kill him to protect the code. Naturally there is a bond built between the two and Cage must decide whether to honor his duties as a soldier or as a friend. It's the perfect premise for a great American John Woo movie, but sadly this is not that. The predictable plot hits every possible WWII or Native American cliché, any potential tension in the battle scenes is destroyed by James Horner's overwrought score, and Cage's performance is at times unbearably over-the-top. It's probably not the worst of Woo's American films, but it's the most frustrating because it

seems like one he should be able to hit out of the park. *—B.T.*

GLEN OR GLENDA? L: DIRECTORS/WOOD, ED (1953) 65M D: Ed Wood Jr. *Delores Fuller, Lyle Talbot, Bela Lugosi, Daniel Davis, Ed Wood Jr.* Wood's debut is the one that best sums up what is so fascinating about his films. You could argue that *Plan 9 from Outer Space* is funnier, but it's hard to top this film's stale educational film story line randomly sliding into Lugosi's inexplicable scenes as a demonic puppet master who yells the infamous line, "Pull de stling! Pull de stling!" Of course there's the non-sequitur stock footage. (Why would you superimpose a buffalo herd over that?) But what makes this one my favorite is that, beneath the deranged tastelessness and unimaginable ineptitude, there is a courageous autobiographical element. It's hard to believe that a director in 1953 would be brave enough to star in a straight-up defense of cross-dressing. Even today you don't see a whole lot of movies about regular old female impersonation, as opposed to campy drag queens. This film has more artistic merit than most films by first-time directors. *—B.T.*

PLAN 9 FROM OUTER SPACE L: DIRECTORS/WOOD, ED (1953) 67M D: Ed Wood Jr. *Duke Moore, Tom Keene, Bela Lugosi, Vampira, Gregory Walcott.* It's difficult to say that this is the worst movie ever made for the reason that it is the best film Ed Wood Jr. ever directed! It's a compelling story about how badly dressed aliens plan to take over the Earth by raising the dead to do all their dirty work for them. In a very real way, Wood did just that! Lugosi had died before the film started shooting, but by the use of old footage and a much-too-tall stunt double, Wood indeed brings back the dead in an attempt to conquer Hollywood. Of course, it's possible that he succeeded. What else could begin to explain the cost, size, and breadth of bombs coming out of Hollywood since that time except for an alien Ed Wood Jr. hovering in his flying saucer calling all the shots? *—N.J.*

BEN-HUR L: DIRECTORS/WYLER, WILLIAM (1959) 212M D: William Wyler. *Charlton Heston, Jack Hawkins, Haya Harareet, Martha Scott, Sam Jaffe.* Throughout the fifties the threat of Communism prompted McCarthy and Hoover to start blacklisting prominent people in Hollywood. Since church attendance was also at an all-time high, some of the safest films for the industry to produce were religious epics. *The Robe* ('53), *The Ten Commandments* ('56), and this film set the tone for more to follow, including *King of Kings* and *El Cid* (both '61). Heston stars as Ben-Hur, a Palestinian Jew and miserable slave to the Roman occupation whose life story occurs at the same time as Christ's and in some ways even parallels it. The famous chariot race is a truly remarkable and absolutely classic climax. (And there's nothing to the rumor that a Volkswagen Bug can be seen in the distance of this scene!) *—N.J.*

Ed Wood

Is Ed Wood the worst director who ever lived? Harry and Michael Medved gave the cross-dressing auteur that dubious honor in their backhanded tribute to trash cinema *The Golden Turkey Awards*, and his reputation has since grown to mythic proportions. No director has become more famous, even beloved, for bargain-basement sets, laughable special effects, surreal dialogue, and an angora fetish.

A World War II hero, transvestite, and one-time carny, Ed Wood Jr. kicked around Hollywood as an actor and writer—picking up bit parts, staging theatricals, and directing several short films—before he landed his first feature: the jaw-dropping "documentary" *Glen or Glenda* (1953), a bizarre confessional starring Wood himself as a misunderstood transvestite.

Initially intended to cash in on the famous sex-change operation of Christine Jorgensen, Wood's film brought in horror icon Bela Lugosi (whose career was at rock bottom) as a smirking godlike narrator to watch over this mix of mock documentary and hoary melodrama, with a mad bondage-and-babes-filled dream sequence tossed in for good measure. "Pull ze strings!" shouts Lugosi, and Wood (under the pseudonym Daniel Davis) exposes his angora fetish and passion for women's underwear to the world. *Bride of the Monster* (1955), a howler of a horror picture, reunited Wood with

---

BEST YEARS OF OUR LIVES, THE L: DIRECTORS/WYLER, **WILLIAM (1946) 172M D: William Wyler.** *Dana Andrews, Harold Russell, Virginia Mayo, Myrna Loy, Fredric March, Cathy O'Donnell.* Three veterans fresh from victory in World War II get acquainted in a cab that drops them off in their hometown. Andrews plays a captain who lives in dire poverty compared to the two men ranked below him. His financial woes and his broken relationships are complicated by his difficulty coping with war experiences on a bomber. The banking executive (March) also has a difficult time adjusting to post-war life even though he is quite wealthy. But worse still is the young man (Russell) who lost his hands and must live with prosthetic hooks. He tries desperately to live a normal life with a normal girlfriend (O'Donnell). Not surprisingly, this sensitive and beautifully shot film won seven Oscars, including best film. *The Best Years of Our Lives* simply must be considered one of the finest pictures ever made. —*N.J.*

BIG COUNTRY, THE L: DIRECTORS/WYLER, WILLIAM (1958) **165M D: William Wyler.** *Charlton Heston, Burl Ives, Jean Simmons, Charles Bickford, Gregory Peck.* I've always preferred the edgy to the epic, especially when it comes to Westerns, but Wyler makes poise and polish work in *The Big Country*. Peck is a sea captain who comes west, smack in the middle of a range war: cattle baron Bickford and trusted foreman Heston versus a scruffy family of desert rats led by Ives. Peck shows stiff sincerity as the noble hero, but the supporting cast steals the show, especially Ives as the crusty white-trash patriarch with a sense of honor even stronger than his sense of family. The grand sweep and a primal sense of landscape matches the jagged explosions of hate and passion, and Jerome Moross's rousing score is one of the best of the '50s. —*S.A.*

COLLECTOR, THE L: DIRECTORS/WYLER, WILLIAM (1965) **119M D: William Wyler.** *Samantha Eggar, Mona Washbourne, Terence Stamp.* Here's a curious kidnapping story. Stamp plays an avid collector of butterflies. He knows everything about them and has many framed and hanging on his walls. It becomes readily apparent, however, that he is also a lonely and insecure man. But he has a plan to fix all that. He's had his eye on a certain woman for quite a while, and he's made all the necessary preparations in his cellar: furniture, carpet, all the amenities, including a cast-iron cage. If he can just keep a woman for a certain period of time, she will simply fall in love with him. Right? —*N.J.*

FUNNY GIRL L: DIRECTORS/WYLER, WILLIAM (1968) 151M **D: William Wyler.** *Barbara Streisand, Omar Sharif.* *Funny Girl* is Streisand's first film, but you can't tell by the way she charmingly and effortlessly maneuvers through Fanny Brice's rise to stardom as a Ziegfeld Girl. Sharif plays Nicky Arnstein, Fanny's love interest. The two share a

Lugosi. Hulking Swedish wrestler turned B-movie icon Tor Johnson made his first Wood appearance as the lumbering beast Lobo (he almost knocks over the set in one scene!) tamed by the touch of angora.

But the clumsy, nearly incoherent, and ridiculously cheap *Plan 9 from Outer Space* (1959) remains Wood's cult masterpiece. Bela Lugosi died after a few days of shooting and was replaced with his wife's tall, skinny, blond chiropractor, who looks *nothing* like Lugosi ("he had the same skull structure as Lugosi," Wood offered in an interview). Cardboard gravestones wobble as the actors walk by, and the flying saucer is a Cadillac hubcap doused with lighter fluid.

Tim Burton's affectionate film biography *Ed Wood*, a celebration of Wood's unflagging spirit and the group of eccentrics and outsiders who formed his misfit filmmaking family, ends on a note of triumph—the release of *Plan 9 from Outer Space*, his most enduring and endearing work—but the real story wasn't so pretty. An alcoholic whose drinking simply got worse, Wood and his wife, Kathy, were evicted from one apartment after another. After his 1960 Hollywood melodrama *The Sinister Urge*, he was reduced to cranking out cheap-sex paperbacks and exploitation scripts with only the occasional industrial short or pornographic feature. His 1978 death didn't even merit an obituary in the trade magazines.

But Wood achieved his immortality, albeit belatedly. Midnight revivals and video releases of his pictures introduced a whole new generation to his campy classics. The Medveds were wrong. Wood's films are campy, clumsy, often incoherent, and hysterically inept, but no picture made with so much love and brimming with so many laughs—earned or not—can be all that bad.

—*Sean Axmaker*

Scarlett and Rhett-like romance full of passion and emotional turmoil. Some of the songs make me snicker, like Sharif's stumbling through "You are Woman, I am Man," but most fill me with the glee only a great musical can muster. —*J. K.*

LITTLE FOXES, THE L: DIRECTORS/WYLER, WILLIAM (1941) **116M D:** William Wyler. *Richard Carlson, Patricia Collinge, Dan Duryea, Teresa Wright, Herbert Marshall, Bette Davis.* Davis could freeze almost anyone with her icy stare, the practiced look of a woman who has learned how to operate in the man's world of business at the turn of the twentieth century. Lillian Hellman's chilly play of greed and power in a Southern clan on the edge of financial ruin is perfect material for the classical precision and dramatic control of Hollywood master Wyler (at the top of his craft in 1941). The part of the ruthless Regina, who battles her brothers (Charles Dingle and Carl Benton Reid) and her sickly, estranged husband (Marshall) for control of a dwindling family business, seems written with Davis in mind—hard, conniving, cunning. The dialogue glints like the edge of a knife and the razor-sharp images of Gregg Toland's deep-focus photography turns the old-world splendor of the family mansion into a cold, lonely world ruled by an utterly pitiless matriarch, a woman ready to sacrifice her daughter (Wright) to the family fortune. —*S. A.*

ROMAN HOLIDAY L: DIRECTORS/WYLER, WILLIAM (1953) **118M D:** William Wyler. *Audrey Hepburn, Gregory Peck, Eddie Albert.* In her first starring role, Hepburn is absolutely stunning as a fair young princess who, on a visit to Rome, tires of her royal obligations. She finds a way to escape the palace she's staying at and while feebly trying to hide her identity shares a full day on the town with a reporter (Peck) who, with his cameraman (Albert), also tries hiding his identity from her. Incredible location photography abounds in this film, one of the first major studio features to be shot in full in a foreign city. By the end, a deep romance completes the film. Hepburn was awarded the best-actress Oscar for her performance. The story was by Dalton Trumbo, blacklisted at the time, and he was posthumously awarded his well-deserved Oscar in 1993. —*N. J.*

YI YI (AKA A ONE AND A TWO) L: DIRECTORS/YANG, EDWARD (2000) **173M D:** Edward Yang. *Wu Nien-Jen, Kelly Lee, Elaine Jin, Chen Xisheng, Jonathan Chang.* It can't be coincidence that Yang's sublime, serene, deeply personal drama of one family frustrated by the alienating effects of modern Taiwan society struck a chord throughout the world. Leisurely paced at three hours, it winds us through the complications of family relations, the stresses of Taiwan's rickety economy, and the larger mysteries of life—love, death, faith, knowledge—in a way that is unique to contemporary Taiwan and universal to the human condition.

This is not a drama of Big Events, but of small details and delicate emotions, and Yang lets them seep through the fabric of the film with such sincerity and feeling that I couldn't help but feel, in my own small way, redeemed by this vision. Winner of the Best Director prize at the 2000 Cannes Film Festival —*S. A.*

BRIDE OF CHUCKY L: DIRECTORS/YU, RONNY (1998) 89M D: Ronny Yu. *Brad Dourif, Jennifer Tilly, Katherine Heigl, John Ritter.* In this fourth *Child's Play* movie we learn that serial-killer-stuck-in-the-body-of-a-doll Chucky left behind an also-murderous girlfriend named Tiffany (Tilly). Now he goes back for her and connives to get her into the body of a doll to force her to go on a cross-country murder spree with him and help him do a voodoo spell. Whoever thought up the idea of recruiting Hong Kong émigré Yu (best known for *Bride With White Hair*) to direct a *Child's Play* sequel should get some kind of medal. He was probably hired because of his experience with state-of-the-art animatronic puppetry in *Warriors of Virtue,* but he also brought along a completely fresh approach to the slasher movie. Some scenes are almost John Waters[-]like camp while others take a more operatic approach with stylized visuals and high emotion portrayed by puppets. The first *Child's Play* is a legitimately good horror film—this one is more of a ridiculous comedy. —*B. T.*

BRIDE WITH WHITE HAIR, THE L: DIRECTORS/YU, RONNY (1993) 92M D: Ronny Yu, Philip Kwok. *Nam Kit-Ying, Leslie Cheung, Brigitte Lin.* Yu, before making a name for himself stateside, brought to Hong Kong this violent fantasy drama about sword-wielding star-crossed lovers using a variant on the Romeo and Juliet story line. Cheung plays Zhuo, a member of the Wu Dong clan, who tells the story of the movie as a flashback. The usually androgynous Lin is the feminine yet powerful Lian, who is an assassin and follower of Mo Curt. When Zhuo and Lian meet, it is love at first sword clash, yet tragedy is inevitable. Lian warns Zhuo that if he ever stops trusting her she will be cursed with white hair and her heart will become dead. This setup pays off in spades when Zhuo discovers his entire clan has been slaughtered and the few survivors claim it was Lian. Lian holds to her innocence, but when Zhuo doesn't believe her, her hair indeed turns white. The brutal bloodbath that ensues still keeps the film's artful eye, even as limbs are severed and soldiers are impaled on flying hair. *Bride* is considered a staple of modern Hong Kong cinema, and is definitely a must-see for the dynamic themes it portrays. —*R. M.*

FREDDY VS JASON L: DIRECTORS/YU, RONNY (2003) 97M D: Ronny Yu. *Jason Ritter, Robert Englund, Ken Kirzinger, Monica Keena, Kelly Rowland, Katharine Isabelle.* When I was in middle school I remember my friend Robby saying, "You know what would be awesome? If they made Freddy versus Jason!" And I said, "They would never do that, because it would be stupid." Well, I was sort of right on the second count, but adult-me still loved this entertainingly ridiculous crossover between the Elm Street and Crystal Lake mythos. Freddy (Englund, as always) is stuck in hell, powerless because the modern Springwood teens don't know about him and thus don't fear him. So he connives to resurrect Jason (newcomer Kirzinger, one of the best Jasons) and send him to Nancy's old house on Elm Street to kill some teens, causing the authorities to fear the return of Freddy. Their fear gives him the power he needs to start haunting dreams again—the only trouble is that Jason is on the loose and keeps killing the kids before Freddy gets the chance. Although a little more straight-faced than *Bride of Chucky* or *Jason X,* it's in a similar vein of slasher absurdism, with plenty of unique Yu visuals and even a beautiful slow-motion wire shot of Freddy leaping out of Crystal Lake. I believe this is also the first film where Freddy kicks or elbow drops anyone. —*B. T.*

PHANTOM LOVER L: DIRECTORS/YU, RONNY (1995) 100M D: Ronny Yu. *Jacqueline Wu Chien-Lien, Leslie Cheung.* Yu's last Hong Kong film before leaving for Hollywood is a lush and lovely rethinking of *Phantom of the Opera,* but it's only partly successful. Those parts feature Cheung as the impresario/architect/1920s stage idol who becomes the mysterious, scarred phantom haunting his burned-out theater. Less successful is the pallid story of the young heartthrob he grooms as his successor—and his stand-in to woo a now-mad lover (Wu Chien-Lien). The flashbacks are vivid and vibrant, directed by a flamboyance and an unhinged melodramatic sweep that once defined Hong Kong cinema, but the contemporary story only comes alive in the moments Cheung and Wu show the kids just how real movie stars command the screen. —*S. A.*

WARRIORS OF VIRTUE L: DIRECTORS/YU, RONNY (1997) 101M D: Ronny Yu. *Chao-Li Chi, Dennis Dun, Angus MacFadyen, Marley Shelton, Mario Yedidia.* Yu (*The Bride with White Hair*) made a bizarre American debut with this children's fantasy about, believe it or not, kung fu kangaroos. Despite a muddled story about a bullied kid stumbling into a fantasy world, it occasionally impresses with a combination of stunning cinematography (by Peter Pau, who later did *Crouching Tiger, Hidden Dragon*) and elaborate wire fu. This was before *The Matrix,* and performed by fighters wearing animatronic animal masks! The groundbreaking lip synch technology used in the film helped land Yu his next gig, directing *Bride of Chucky.* —*B. T.*

So your kids desperately want to see *Kill Bill,* but you're terrified about the whole dismemberment of limbs thing. With live-action kangaroos as heroes, *Warriors of Virtue* is about as "family" as kung fu gets. An evildoer is even taken out by a flower. The sadistic but still PG-rated villain is trapped in the hell of his own heart and, like so many punk-asses before him, is doomed to a luxurious life as lord of an evil kingdom. With special effects that rectify the horror of *Kangaroo Jack,* it's one of the only recent family releases that doesn't make me pity the youth of the new millennium. And it has a great moral: It's OK to be crippled. We all have something that doesn't work. If you're lucky, it's not your heart. —*J.J.*

DRUNKEN MASTER L: DIRECTORS/YUEN WOO PING (1978) 111M D: Yuen Woo Ping. *Simon Yuen Jr., Hwang Jang Lee, Jackie Chan, Dean Shek.* The film that made Chan the undisputed king of comic kung fu, this comic take on folk hero Wong Fei Hung (whose adventures had previously been chronicled in over a hundred films), is a semi-sequel to *Snake in the Eagle's Shadow.* This time, Chan and director refine the mix of comedy and kung fu and push the stunts to crowd-wowing levels. The plot is an eminently familiar martial-arts formula: a wild youth enters a grueling training regime under a master teacher (a red-nosed Yuen, the director's father) and ultimately defends the honor and lives of his loved ones in a deadly battle to the finish, but not before generous amounts of brawling, practical joking, and of course epic drinking. The infectious mix of slapstick sequences and amazing martial-arts moves breathes new life into the old school of Hong Kong action. —*S.A.*

IRON MONKEY L: DIRECTORS/YUEN WOO PING (1993) 85M D: Yuen Woo Ping. *Yu Rong Guang, Donnie Yen.* The *Matrix* choreographer Yuen directs this colorful, high-flying Hong Kong *Zorro.* Yu Rong (in a rare turn as a hero) is the meek town doctor who dons a black mask at night. Yen, a wandering healer (and father to future folk-hero Wong Fei-Hung), befriends the doctor but is blackmailed by the corrupt governor to tackle the outlaw. This splashy, colorful martial-arts extravaganza has some of the best choreography this side of Jet Li, plenty of over-the-top aerial wire work, and a suitably spectacular finale in a fiery inferno. Yuen is a better choreographer than director, at least in terms of narrative logic, but that amazing work is the reason to see this fun, action-filled film. —*S.A.*

SNAKE IN THE EAGLE'S SHADOW L: DIRECTORS/YUEN WOO PING (1978) 98M D: Yuen Woo Ping. *Simon Yuen Siu-tien, Jackie Chan.* This is the film that made Chan a star. He plays a menial servant in a school for martial arts who saves the life of an aged vagrant, Yuen Siu-tin (the director's father), who just happens to be a martial-arts master on the run. Cut to training sequence, toss in the sight gags, and unleash Chan's Chinese Opera style. Up to this film, he'd been unsuccessfully promoted as "the next Bruce Lee" in a series of stiff, serious revenge adventures. Here Chan gets to display

the gymnastic martial-arts style that made his name, in addition to exhibiting his facility for physical humor. It created (along with his follow-up *Drunken Master,* also directed by Yuen) a whole new approach to martial-arts movies: the comic kung fu adventure. Chan himself became the clown prince of kung fu. —*S.A.*

CATAMOUNT KILLING, THE L: DIRECTORS/ZANUSSI, KRZYSZTOF (1974) 93M D: Krzysztof Zanussi. *Patricia Joyce, Chip Taylor, Louise Caire Clark, Ann Wedgeworth, Horst Buchholz, Polly Holliday.* "What kind of life? To be killed slowly. Viciously. Day by day." A new bank manager, angered at his assignment to a small Vermont town, plots to rob his own bank on its big payroll day. When things don't go as planned, the unthinkable happens, the most grueling and horrendous murder ever put on film. The scheme eventually works, but unravels anyway. Zanussi's palate is dour. The colors are heavy, not luminous like in his pre-Solidarity films that followed. —*J.C.*

HERO L: DIRECTORS/ZHANG YIMOU (2002) 96M D: Zhang Yimou. *Donnie Yen, Daoming Chen, Ziyi Zhang, Maggie Cheung, Tony Leung Chiu Wai, Jet Li.* This movie makes *Crouching Tiger, Hidden Dragon* look like an OK flick. Don't be deceived by the seemingly simplistic beginning. The film is far more complex and layered than it first appears to be, telling and retelling a story of how one man managed to defeat three of the greatest assassins in all of China. The choreography and martial arts are fantastic, the characters are fascinating and compelling, and the cinematography is breathtaking. The story is told with a high sense of myth, with a grandeur befitting the epic tale being spun. But most striking and delightful is the use of color as a metaphor for the emotions, situations, and characters, with red for passion, light blue for reason, green for youth, and white for the truth. An amazing cast. An amazing film. It stole my breath away. —*M.N.*

DAY OF THE JACKAL L: DIRECTORS/ZINNEMANN, FRED (1973) 142M D: Fred Zinnemann. *Alan Badel, Terence Alexander, Michel Auclair, Edward Fox.* Based on the Frederick Forsyth best-seller, *Day of the Jackal* is a fantastic suspense film, directed by Zinnemann (*High Noon*), one of the masters of the form. An assassin is hired to kill Charles de Gaulle and in the clever process of avoiding the detectives the hit man demonstrates nearly all the tricks of the trade. His disguise as a one-legged veteran is truly stunning, and so is the process through which the French detectives eventually solve the case. This one has to be seen to be believed. The 1997 film *The Jackal* is supposedly some kind of remake, but nothing could top this original. —*N.J.*

FROM HERE TO ETERNITY L: DIRECTORS/ZINNEMANN, FRED (1953) 118M D: Fred Zinnemann. *Burt Lancaster, Deborah Kerr, Donna Reed, Frank Sinatra, Ernest*

Borgnine, Montgomery Clift. You know the scene: Lancaster and Kerr rolling around the beach as the surf crashes around them and the foamy tide washes around their clenched bodies. It's a cliché now, but it's as primal as erotic scenes got in the production-code days, and it helped transform Zinnemann's classy adaptation of Jones's novel of soldiers in Hawaii in the days before the bombing of Pearl Harbor into an American screen classic. Clift made his own splash as the troubled, sensitive bugler terrorized by his commanding officer, earning his third Oscar nomination. Acting awards went to supporting performers Reed (as his "dance hall" girlfriend) and Sinatra (as the lanky Brooklyn soldier bullied by Borgnine). It won eight Academy Awards in all, including Best Picture and Best Director. —*S. A.*

HIGH NOON L: DIRECTORS/ZINNEMANN, FRED (1952) 89M D: Fred Zinnemann. *Katy Jurado, Gary Cooper, Grace Kelly, Thomas Mitchell.* Cooper is the long, lanky sheriff who stands tall to face a killer while the town he once defended scatters to the shadows. One of the best-loved westerns of all time, it's been called an old-fashioned celebration of courage and responsibility in the face of impossible odds, an ironic dissection of the Western myth, and a blast of moral outrage at the silence and passivity of American citizens. Howard Hawks claimed this film inspired him to make *Rio Bravo*, because he couldn't fathom a sheriff who went around begging for help. There's so much loaded weight attached to the film (from famously right-wing lead Cooper to famously liberal screenwriter Carl Foreman, who was blacklisted by Hollywood) that it can overwhelm what is essentially a lean, dusty Western classic set to the real time of a ticking clock, counting down the minutes until a gang of killers pulls up on the noon train, looking for revenge on Sheriff Cooper. Kelly costars as Cooper's violence-abhorring Quaker bride. —*S. A.*

ARIA L: DIRECTORS/MULTI-DIRECTORS (1988) 90M D: Various. The directors involved in this incredible pastiche are as brilliant as they are diverse: Ken Russell (*Altered States*), Jean-Luc Godard (*Breathless*), Robert Altman (*Short Cuts*), Derek Jarman (*Last of England*), Nicholas Roeg (*Don't Look Now*), and more. Each director takes as inspiration an aria of some famed opera and incorporates it into their episode in the style that most befits them. Godard chops up an aria from *Armide* by Lully while two tormented women witness men pumping iron at a gym. Julien Temple pushes Buck Henry through a bizarre rendition of Verdi's *Rigoletto,* complete with a glimpse of an Elvis impersonator lip-synching. And Jarman lovingly photographs Swinton with his distinctive filmmaking to music of Charpentier's *Depuis le Jour.* There is something here for every fan of cinema, and there is most everything here for any fan of opera! —*N. J.*

BOCCACCIO '70 L: DIRECTORS/MULTI-DIRECTORS (1962) 145M D: Various. *Sophia Loren, Luigi Giuliani, Anita Ekberg, Romy Schneider, Peppino De Filippo, Tomas Milian.* A collection of three medium-length films inspired by and relating to the stories of Italian writer Giovanni Boccaccio (*The Decameron*). De Sica's story is about the much-ogled Zoe (Loren), who offers herself as the prize in a shooting game to help her impoverished family. Visconti directs a comic chamber drama about a wealthy playboy (Milian) who faces the biting scorn of his wife (Schneider) when his reckless dalliances become public scandal. Fellini's contribution, the only film he made in the defining period between *La Dolce Vita* and *8½*, is a fantastic satire involving a puritanical professor (Filippo) who zealously fights the installment of a mildly lurid billboard advertisement outside his apartment window. Though all three are worth your time, I highly recommend the Visconti segment in particular. —*C. B.*

EARLY AUTEUR FILMS L: DIRECTORS/MULTI-DIRECTORS (1961) 98M D: Various. This collection of early films by some of the greats of cinema—Jean-Luc Godard, Roman Polanski, François Truffaut, Orson Welles, Alberto Cavalcanti, and Michelangelo Antonioni—offers a glimpse at the genesis of brilliance. Some of these works that preceded the directors' full-length features are quite excellent, while some struck me as boring. I imagine reactions will vary depending on the viewer's interest in each director's later work. Probably none of them hold up as substantial examples of their creator's best work, but this is essential viewing for fans of the included directors. I enjoyed the Antonioni short "Nettezza Urbana" for its hints of preoccupations that would appear more boldly in something like *L'avventura*. Godard's contribution, the twenty-one-minute "All the Boys Are Called Patrick," is my pick for the most entertaining on the video. A comedy set amid Parisian café culture, it introduces the brand of Coca-Cola-swilling matinee dwellers that would people his early-1960s work. —*C. B.*

FOUR ROOMS L: DIRECTORS/MULTI-DIRECTORS (1995) 102M D: Various. *Bruce Willis, Quentin Tarantino, Tim Roth, Ione Skye, Antonio Banderas.* This anthology was meant to showcase a "new wave" of independent filmmakers who first hit it big and became friends at film festivals in the early '90s. Each of the four directors does one segment set inside a hotel, tied together by Roth's character, Ted the bellhop. While the sequences by Allison Anders and Alexandre Rockwell are amusing at best, Robert Rodriguez's "The Misbehavers" is excellent: a morbid, live-action cartoon in which the children of a suave gangster (Banderas), left alone for an evening, manage to light the room on fire and discover a decomposing corpse. Quentin Tarantino's segment about a self-absorbed movie-star character is more

The Scarecrow Video Movie Guide

controversial. Some claim it is a rip-off of the *Alfred Hitchcock Presents* episode "Man from the South." This is a silly notion since the episode is explicitly discussed throughout the segment, and the segment itself was taken from the short story by Roald Dahl. —*B.T.*

NEW YORK STORIES L: DIRECTORS/MULTI-DIRECTORS (1989) 124M D: Various. *Talia Shire, Mae Questel, Mia Farrow, Woody Allen, Nick Nolte, Rosanna Arquette.* The directorial anthology is a rare thing, and this particular one may indicate why. The three directors here are some of the finest the film industry could offer: Woody Allen, Martin Scorsese, and Francis Ford Coppola, all New Yorkers. And yet these three films couldn't be more different. In "Life Lessons," Scorsese details the angst of a painter (Nolte) who tries to contain his girlfriend (Arquette); in "Oedipus Wrecks," Allen endlessly dogs his own mother; and in "Life Without Zoe" you will simply be bored stiff. It's hard to say this is a bad anthology, but it's certainly not all that it's cracked up to be. —*N.J.*

1:99 L: DIRECTORS/MULTI-DIRECTORS (2003) 70M D: Various. *Tony Leung, Daniel Wu.* Having dealt with the SARS epidemic that nearly quarantined and ostracized the country from the rest of the world, Hong Kong filmmakers were asked to make short films that acted as public service announcements in an attempt to restore morale and general happiness to a place that had lived in constant fear. Most of these shorts are around two minutes long, featuring well-known directors like Chow and Lau along with mainstay actors Leung and Wu. While some of these are pretty damn goofy, the DVD as a whole remains very interesting, allowing us to see how a country overcame a modern-day plague. The documentary that precedes the short films and examines SARS from the standpoint of the filmmakers and crew has a running time that is twice as long as the combined shorts, yet it bears almost more importance, giving an honest depiction of how severely the Hong Kong film industry was affected by the epidemic. —*A.T.*

SEVEN DEADLY SINS, THE L: DIRECTORS/MULTI-DIRECTORS (1962) 113M D: Various. *Dany Saval, Marina Vlady, Eddie Constantine, Marie-José Nat, Nicole Mirel, Claude Brasseur.* A who's who of French directors created this anthology with segments representing each of the seven deadly sins. It's much more humorous than the better-known anthology *Spirits of the Dead* (which also had a Vadim contribution), particularly in the case of Jean-Luc Godard's "Sloth," about a movie producer so lazy he tries to pay a guy to tie his shoe. The opening "Anger," directed by Sylvain Dhomme and written by Ionesco, is also very funny, showing how flies in everyone's soup lead to the destruction of the world. Out of print on

VHS and not yet on DVD, but well worth tracking down. —*B.T.*

SIX IN PARIS (PARIS VU PAR) L: DIRECTORS/MULTI-DIRECTORS (1965) 95M D: Various. *Jean-Pierre Andréani, Gilles Chusseau, Stéphane Audran, Jean-François Chappey, Nadine Ballot, Claude Chabrol.* In 1965 six young French directors contributed short sketches of Parisian neighborhoods for a compilation film. The resulting collection remains one of the best anthology films made. The strongest short comes from Claude Chabrol, whose "La Muette," a shiver-inducing slice of urban life in a splintered upper-class family, only briefly ventures out of the oppressive hallways and too-small rooms and into the streets. Chabrol concludes the otherwise lighthearted collection on a devastating, dark note. Eric Rohmer's goofy contribution is endearingly slight and silly, and Jean-Luc Godard's lolling romantic sketch is all unexpected lightness and sweet irony. The revelation comes from Jean-Daniel Pollet's "Rue Saint-Denis," a hilariously understated comedy of a mousy man who brings a brassy streetwalker to his dumpy apartment. A delight. —*S.A.*

SPIRITS OF THE DEAD L: DIRECTORS/MULTI-DIRECTORS (1968) 117M D: Various. *Marina Yaru, Alain Delon, Jane Fonda, Terence Stamp, Brigitte Bardo.* Originally released as *Histoires Extraordinaires* in France, this is a trio of short films based on Edgar Alan Poe stories, one each directed by Roger Vadim, Louis Malle, and Frederico Fellini. Vadim kicks things off with *Metzengerstein,* the least effective of the three. Fonda stars, wearing various trashy outfits, providing a good example of Vadim's weird obsession with casting his wives/lovers as bitchy, half-naked harlots. Malle's *William Wilson* fares far better. Delon is great as the icy Wilson; Bardot also makes an appearance. Fellini truly takes the cake here, though, with *Toby Dammit,* starring Stamp as a drug-addled star traveling to Italy to claim a souped-up Ferrari (who knew they had Ferraris back in Poe's day?). The bad dubbing into French even works well with the weird tone of this eerie, dreamlike short. Yaru is especially creepy as the recurring girl/devil character. *Spirits* is definitely worth a look, even if you can only appreciate it as eye candy. —*E.O.*

TWILIGHT ZONE: THE MOVIE L: DIRECTORS/MULTI-DIRECTORS (1983) 120M D: Various. *Larry Cedar, Scatman Crothers, Jeremy Licht, Dan Aykroyd.* Get some big-name directors to remake four episodes from Rod Serling's original TV show from the '60s, and you get this movie: a film with entertainment value, but one that doesn't feel entirely right to the *Twilight Zone* aficionado. The first sequence, which shows a racist guy getting tossed back in time to experience what racism is truly like, comes across as less than memorable. The next has a bunch of elderly people playing kick-the-can-back-to-their-youth; it loses all of its original eeriness in the hands of Steven

Spielberg. The third is the one with the creepy kid who takes a teacher back to the house that he controls and creates entirely with his mind. And finally, there's the good old "creature on the wing" episode. There's something about the television medium that is really conducive to eerie, twisting sci-fi, and that something gets lost in this movie. —*J. S.*

TWO EVIL EYES L: DIRECTORS/MULTI-DIRECTORS (1990) 120M D: Various. *Adrienne Barbeau, E. G. Marshall, John Amos, Harvey Keitel.* Loosely based on a couple of Edgar Allen Poe stories, *Two Evil Eyes* is directed by two of the most celebrated horror directors of all time. George Romero's selection, "The Facts in the Case of Mr. Valdemar," details how the daughter of a rich old man and her fiancé murder her father and hide the corpse. But of course, Romero loves the living dead too much to let it all stop there. Dario Argento directs "The Black Cat," where a crime-scene photographer is driven mad by the black cat his girlfriend has taken in. He decides to murder her but the black cat has its own design. The two short stories are adapted with surprisingly different perspectives. Where Argento takes the traditional stance of weaving a scary horror yarn, Romero stabs at more humorous and schlock-filled comic horror. After all, a frozen, bullet-riddled corpse walking around yelling, "They're coming for you, Jessica!" is certainly more spectacular than a cat supernaturally besting a photographer! —*N. J.*

EXPERIMENTAL DIRECTORS/FILMS, SHORTS, AND LOCAL FILMS

EAUX D'ARTIFICE (WATERWORKS) L: EXPERIMENTAL DIRECTORS/ANGER, KENNETH (1953) 12M D: Kenneth Anger. *Carmila Salvatorelli.* A drag-queen dwarf (Salvatorelli) plays the Water Witch in eighteenth-century dress and face mask, running throughout the Gardens of the Villa d'Este in Tivoli, Italy, at night while water cascades around her from waterfalls, sprinklers, and out of the faces of statues of water gods. Vivaldi's "Waterworks" plays over the soundtrack of this silent filmic poem shot with a green gel, and the watery imagery is edited to the beat of Vivaldi's music. In 1993, the Library of Congress selected it to be part of the National Film Registry. —*N. H.*

FIREWORKS (1947) L: EXPERIMENTAL DIRECTORS/ANGER, KENNETH (1947) 20M D: Kenneth Anger. *Kenneth Anger, Bill Seltzer, Gordon Gray. Fireworks* is pure homoeroticism, stylistically reminiscent of the work of great French authors Jean Genet and Jean Cocteau. A young and very handsome Anger (who was only seventeen when he made the film) awakens from a bad dream with a hard-on (a statue under his sheets) and goes out for a walk on the town to try and cool down, only to be accosted by a group of sailors who beat him up and rape him. Shot in a blue-filtered haze, *Fireworks* is ripe with dreamlike imagery, scattered snapshots of a young sailor carrying the beaten-up Anger, and a Roman candle exploding from a sailor's zipper. These Dionysian images of lustful young sailor men, death, and rape fill the screen and transform Anger's character into a homoerotic icon. —*N. H.*

INAUGURATION OF THE PLEASURE DOME L: EXPERIMENTAL DIRECTORS/ANGER, KENNETH (1954) 40M D: Kenneth Anger. *Sampson De Brier, Curtis Harrington, Anaïs Nin, Marjorie Cameron.* Dedicated to occult author Aleister Crowley, of whose work Anger is a devote follower, this phantasmagorical visual essay of psychedelic colors, black backgrounds, costuming dance, and performance visually invokes the gods Shiva, Pan, Hecate, Kali, and the sleepwalker from *The Cabinet of Dr. Caligari* in a orgiastic ritual masquerade at which Pan is the prize. A big influence on filmmakers from Roger Corman to Martin Scorsese at the time of its release, it is still the best visual representation of magic and ritual ever captured on film. It stars filmmaker Harrington (*Games, What's the Matter with Helen*) as the sleepwalker and author Nin, the former lover of writer Henry Miller (*Tropic of Capricorn*). —*N. H.*

INVOCATION OF MY DEMON BROTHER L: EXPERIMENTAL DIRECTORS/ANGER, KENNETH (1969) 12M D: Kenneth Anger. *Bobby Beausoleil, Mick Jagger, Brian Jones, Kenneth Anger.* A close-up shot of a towheaded white boy waking up to find he has a tattoo intercuts with a scene of a group of hippies smoking grass and is followed by a barrage of images of Anger conducting a midnight Mass as the red-robed Magus invoking Lucifer. As Anger says, the film is a "conjuration of pagan forces coming off the screen in a surge of spiritual and mystical power." Anger mixes in shots of the Rolling Stones in concert, the burning of a cat, and scenes of Hell's Angels. Anger had Jagger compose the pulsating, throbbing soundtrack on a Moog synthesizer, creating a meditative trance feeling to go with Anger's jarring and startling imagery. —*N. H.*

LUCIFER RISING L: EXPERIMENTAL DIRECTORS/ANGER, KENNETH (1973) 40M D: Kenneth Anger. *Marianne Faithful, Miriam Girbil, Donald Cammell, Kenneth Anger. Lucifer Rising*'s hypnotic soundtrack (by Manson family–murderer Bobby Beausoleil) pulsates throughout the mystical imagery of moons, sun, pyramids, erupting volcanoes, Stonehenge, and rock stars as the Egyptian gods Isis and Osiris summon forth Lucifer, "the Angel of Light." They partake in ritual magic, calling forth not only Lucifer but also, at the film's climax, a sky full of pink spaceships passing over the pyramids as the gods of past and future come together in the "dawning of the Aquarian Age, the Aeon of

Horus." Shot at famous "magical" locations in Egypt, England, and Germany. —*N. H.*

RABBIT'S MOON L: EXPERIMENTAL DIRECTORS/ANGER, KENNETH (1950) 7M D: Kenneth Anger. *Claude Revenant, Nadine Valance, André Soubeyran.* Anger's poem to the silent fantasy films of Georges Méliès and turn-of-the-century cinema, *Rabbit's Moon* is about a moon-driven Pierrot (Soubeyran) lover out in the forest, whose affections for a beautiful ballerina Columbine (Valance) are thwarted by the evil Harlequin (Revenant). Pierrot turns his love instead to a magic lantern he finds that projects images out in the forest. Never finished, the film is very theatrical in its sets, face makeup, and acting, and is dialogue free. Anger recut the film in the '70s to a pounding rock soundtrack that leaves the resulting imagery closer to a beautiful music video than silent film. —*N. H.*

SCORPIO RISING L: EXPERIMENTAL DIRECTORS/ANGER, KENNETH (1964) 38M D: Kenneth Anger. *Johnny Sapienza, Bruce Byron.* Meth-popping biker boy Scorpio (Byron) defaces a church and attends an all-guy biker party, where the leather-clad riders torture and rape one of their own. Scorpio then leaves the party and dies wrecking his bike. Images of swastikas, comic books, Christ figures and the Cross, Hitler, Satan, a leather-clad Marlon Brando, death, and motorcycles crosscut in a montage that pulsates to the soundtrack of '50s pop tunes and motorcycle-engine vrooming. Anger's postmodern essay of male '50s biker culture giving rise to homosexual fascism worshiping death and depravity is a reflection of Hollywood icons James Dean and a young Marlon Brando as the biker in *The Wild One,* whose legendary homoerotic iconography creates the flavor to Anger's most famous work. *Scorpio Rising* has been out of distribution for several years due to music rights claims by the record mogul bastard Allen Klein, owner of ABKCO Entertainment, who has also held back Jodorowsky's films *El Topo* and *Holy Mountain* from being distributed on video in the United States. —*N. H.*

TRIBULATION 99 L: EXPERIMENTAL/BALDWIN, CRAIG (1991) 48M D: Craig Baldwin. About as credible as a Mexican wrestling picture (mentioned because they're frequently mined for images here), *Tribulation 99* is like a lecture from a caffeine-mad *X-Files* zealot blessed with the ability to distinguish verified facts from irrational hallucinations. Beginning immediately with less-than-plausible conspiracy theories, the film quickly advances to rabid paranoia (largely involving extraterrestrial government intervention, but not failing to include killer bees). Although delivered deadpan, none of this is meant to be taken literally—the inclusion of B-grade science fiction and, again, Mexican wrestling film clips make this clear. Effectively *Tribulation 99* is a film generated entirely from stock footage, with a raving voice-over to further dizzy the already perplexing proceedings.

Admittedly the joke runs on a little long, but don't let that dissuade you from checking out this genuine oddity. —*C. B.*

BRAKHAGE, STAN: HAND PAINTED FILMS L: EXPERIMENTAL /BRAKHAGE, STAN (1993) 44M D: Stan Brakhage. The title is quite precise—Brakhage actually painted on film, and the flickering results of its projection are like nothing the cinema has seen before or since. Referred to by Brakhage as "an adventure in perception," the closest approximation I can offer is that it's like a cross between a kaleidoscope and an abstract-expressionist painting that moves—with all the emotional amplitude of that school of painting complemented by the sheer exhilaration of motion. Certainly among the finest non-representational works of the man who turned the notion of filmmaking on its head. A few but not all of these short films can be found on the monumental *By Brakhage* DVD set, but I find this tape particularly effective for its clustering of films that share a similarity of appearance, method, and chronology. —*C. B.*

BY BRAKHAGE: AN ANTHOLOGY L: EXPERIMENTAL/ BRAKHAGE, STAN (2003) 243M D: Stan Brakhage. Over half a century, Brakhage made literally hundreds of films, expanding our understanding of not only the potential of the film medium, but visual perception itself. Some consider him the greatest poet the cinema has seen. Others classify him as "merely" a brilliant innovator. To create his absorbing rhythmic abstractions, Brakhage often painted, etched into, oven-baked, and even attached moth wings to film strips, working refreshingly free of the constraints of traditional realism. Most of these films were scarcely available on VHS or DVD until the good folks at Criterion compiled this brilliantly transferred, four-hour collection of Brakhage' greatest hits, including *Cat's Cradle, The Dante Quartet Mothlight,* even the monumental *Dog Star Man.* Although certainly much is missing, this collection should be more than sufficient to satisfy any viewer's appetite for what Brakhage suitably defines as "a world alive with incomprehensible objects and shimmering with an endless variety of movement and innumerable gradations of color." —*C. B.*

DOG STAR MAN L: EXPERIMENTAL/BRAKHAGE, STAN (1964) 78M D: Stan Brakhage. *Stan Brakhage, Jane Brakhage.* This wildly ambitious avant-garde film attempts to construct an epic creation myth out of images unfixed from conventional representational value. Overlapping, marring, and transforming footage as well as employing numerous convulsive framing and editing practices, *Dog Star Man's* manic poetics aren't what you'd call conventionally lucid. The film seems to reinvent, if not scramble, even its own intuitive methods several times before abruptly reaching an end. More remarkable is the film's sheer forward thrust. Frequently rushing past flashes of breathtaking beauty, the film eventually slows things down, sorts them out, makes sense of them. Better to let waves of light and color wash over you, and to become somewhat acclimated to the film's rhythm. Like a roller coaster ride, watching this film is a willful demand for exceptional experience, hopefully all the more exhilarating for defying expectations and disrupting passive comfort. —*C. B.*

JETEE, LA L: EXPERIMENTAL/MARKER, CHRIS (1962) 28M D: Chris Marker. *Davis Hanich, Jean Negroni, Étienne Becker, Jacques Ledoux, Hélène Chatelain.* Underground survivors of a future nuclear holocaust subject prisoners to time-travel experiments. One prisoner clings to a memory of a boyhood visit to the Orly airport, where he witnessed an unknown man's murder. Unusually vivid, this memory is especially valuable for projection through time. Things come full circle when a visit to the past returns the prisoner to the Orly airport, allowing him to retread his mysterious childhood memory. The most striking aspect of this exceptional, politically charged science fiction is its unique "photo-roman" composition—the film is made up of a series of still photos shown in succession, like a slide show. We quickly become accustomed to this unusual narrative style, and in so doing prove that cinematic language is merely a form of audience conditioning. *La Jetee* is guilty of totally and irrevocably changing my relationship with film. —*C. B.*

JOLI MAI, LE L: EXPERIMENTAL/MARKER, CHRIS (1963) 124M D: Chris Marker. In the early 1960s it was impossible to show a film in France that was critical of the government or military, particularly if Algeria was mentioned. As a result, Marker's documentary on France's Algerian military campaigns makes almost no direct reference to Algeria, instead capturing the general denial on the part of the French people. In a series of interviews we watch French citizens continually not talking about Algeria. Along the way, Marker characteristically sabotages any claim to objective authority, quite deliberately. Late in the film we see early seeds of what we now know as the trademark Marker style—a series of essaylike musings, observations, and questions rambling over various images, all of it fascinating. —*C. B.*

LAST BOLSHEVIK, THE L: EXPERIMENTAL/MARKER, CHRIS (1992) 120M D: Chris Marker. Named by critic Howard Hampton as the best film of the 1990s, *The Last Bolshevik* is ostensibly a movie-letter from Marker to a friend, early Russian filmmaker Alexander Medvedkin. Typically, the end result is a boundlessly complex essay-film, weaving a mythology of Medvedkin's life from an array of film clips and interviews. Submitting Medvedkin as a man inseparable from his setting, a man "notched by history," Marker uses Medvedkin's story as both a parable of the history of Soviet Union and a much more general portrait of the struggles of reconciling art and politics. From this emerges a thoughtful retrospection on the role of the Left in the twentieth century, and an elegy for the idealism (not only collective, but intensely personal) that suffered in the process. Fascinating from start to finish, this is arguably the most accomplished work of Marker's unparalleled career. —*C. B.*

SANS SOLEIL L: EXPERIMENTAL/MARKER, CHRIS (1982) 100M D: Chris Marker. A personal meditation on time, memory, travel, thinking, and feeling; this film is a beautiful work of art. As images collected from around the world (with a heavy focus on Japan) are paraded before us, we witness these captive pieces of time with only a rare moment of complete lucidity. For most of the film we fall subject to the dreamlike movement of unstructured memory. The visual cues that trigger emotional responses are juxtaposed with the reading of a traveler's letters by the woman to whom they were written. In many ways inspired by Hitchcock's *Vertigo*, the film echoes *Vertigo*'s concern with time, history, and memory, and even includes clips from Hitchcock's film. But where *Vertigo* is a modernist masterpiece, *Sans Soleil* is a postmodern treatise on all that has come before and all that will follow. In essence, all that is within the realm of experience. —*T. S.*

KOYAANISQATSI L: EXPERIMENTAL/REGGIO, GODFREY (1983) 87M D: Godfrey Reggio. Combining the unique talents of music composer Philip Glass and photographer Ron Fricke, this film tries to express the Hopi concept of Koyaanisqatsi or "Life Out of Balance." Glass's minimalist style by itself has a hypnotic quality, yet when viewed with Fricke's incredible photographic techniques, which include time-lapse and slow motion, the effect is quite stunning. For a non-narrative film of this nature there is still a general structure: nature followed by people followed by society and finally, Koyaanisqatsi. This truly incredible film was followed five years later with *Powaqqatsi*. —*N. J.*

POWAQQATSI L: EXPERIMENTAL/REGGIO, GODFREY (1988) 97M D: Godfrey Reggio. Once again combining the talents of Philip Glass and Ron Fricke, *Powaqqatsi* is an excellent sequel to *Koyaanisqatsi*. The theme to this non-narrative venture is "Life in Transformation," expressed by juxtaposing views of third-world life against views of "civilized" life. Once again the combined effect of music and photography is quite stunning, and just as the subject of the photography has changed in this film so has the pulse and character of the music. *Naqoyqatsi*, or "Life as War," completes the trilogy. —*N. J.*

BEGOTTEN L: EXPERIMENTAL/EXPERIMENTAL CINEMA (1991) 78M D: E. Elias Merhige. *Donna Dempsey, Stephen Charles Barry, Brian Salzberg.* This dark and foreboding experimental film captures the essence of human suffering through director

Merhige's visionary creation myth. The mood and atmosphere it creates is bleak and beautiful. "God Killing Himself" is a scene of pure imagination, while the journey in "Son of Earth" is one of isolation and pain. Some knock this film as pretentious art; it is definitely art, but I would rather sit through a thousand years of this than to be subjected to another second of the commercially excessive waste of resources, time, and energy that is constantly shat out of Hollywood. Merhige created his own filters to convey its unusual grainy black-and-white visual look, and the sound is a subtle texture of noise that creates a spacious ambience. It's an amazing example of the possibilities of film as true artistic expression, like looking at an evolving canvas with sound. This was a labor of love and pure visionary expression from a brilliant mind. —*B.W.*

I'm pretty sure this movie is the sole reason why many people tend to not take experimental film seriously, ignoring the section altogether. Many people (myself included) have issues with the severely graphic violence and squirm-inducing gore this film is drenched in; the gruesomeness would be perfectly fine if it seemed to carry any relevance beyond being a glorified Marilyn Manson video. This is a movie that Hot Topic Goth kids would secretly pass along to each other during high school, hiding it under their beds from their parents. *Shadow of the Vampire* also seemed a lot more interesting and engaging before I actually spent the hour and a half dredging through hopes of seeing any resolution or ending. Led by characters with names such as "God Killing Himself" and "Son of Earth-Flesh On Bone," *Begotten* is a hundred times more painful an experience. —*A.T*

BILL AND COO L: EXPERIMENTAL/EXPERIMENTAL CINEMA (1948) 61M D: Dean Rieser. *Ken Murray, Elizabeth Walters, George Burton.* Bill lives on the wrong side of the tracks, working as a cabbie to earn enough to marry his beloved—and well off—Coo. Their story collides with the evil Black Menace, a social deviant bent on the destruction of the entire town. The entire cast is made up of TRAINED BIRDS. Brilliant. Just when you thought all was wrong with the world, a movie like this comes along and makes everything right. —*M.H.*

CHANT D'AMOUR, UN L: EXPERIMENTAL/EXPERIMENTAL CINEMA (1950) 25M D: Jean Genet. Rarely seen until recently, this silent short is Genet's lone foray into cinema (though much of his written work has been adapted to film). Influenced by Jean Cocteau and Kenneth Anger, *Un Chant D'Amour* is heavily steeped in the poetically charged imagery familiar to his readers. Set inside a prison, isolated inmates sweat over their respective sexual fantasies. A guard watches it all, and adds his own fantasy of domination. Though not especially experimental, it's not without disarming

moments. Twice a prisoner plucks a straw from under his bedroll and pierces the concrete wall with it, blowing cigarette smoke through it to the prisoner in the neighboring cell. Perhaps more disarming to some will be the frequent and frank images of the prisoners' masturbation rituals (trust me, the film pulls no punches there), something that made trouble for Jonas Mekas when he championed the film. —*C.B.*

CHRISTMAS YULE LOG FIREPLACE L: CINEMA/HOME CINEMA (2000) 180M There is a whole genre of fireplace movies, perhaps the best known being *Fireplace: Visions of Tranquility*. The plots of these films usually involve a match being struck, some wood being lit, and then the wood slowly burning to embers. One might be tempted to trace the genre's roots back to Andy Warhol's experimental films like *Empire* and *Sleep*. However, the true ancestor is *The Yule Log*, a three-and-a-half-hour feature from 1966, originally aired on New York TV station WPIX. First filmed at the Gracie Mansion, it was remade at a Californian fireplace in 1970 and for this video release in 2000. Although the 2000 version is a faithful and well-constructed update, it would be great to see a remastered version of the 1966 original, preferably in a deluxe Criterion Edition with director's commentary. That would be really cool, at least for people who like watching a log burn on TV. —*B.T.*

REMINISCENCES OF A JOURNEY TO LITHUANIA L: EXPERIMENTAL/EXPERIMENTAL CINEMA (1972) 82M D: Jonas Mekas. Best known as a critic and champion of underground cinema, Mekas also made a number of films. In this particular one, he returns to his homeland after a twenty-seven-year absence. Combining footage shot over two decades, this autobiographical work shows Mekas at home in New York, visiting family in Lithuania, and returning to the site of a forced-labor camp in Austria where Mekas was held before he emigrated to the U.S. Dealing in the highly personal territory of his own memory, Mekas more or less shrugs off the formal obligations of classical cinema, and hardly seems concerned with flexing his avant-garde cred. A truly independent production and a very basic film, *Reminiscences* looks more like a home movie than the product of a man well-acquainted with the work of Kenneth Anger, Maya Deren, and Andy Warhol. —*C.B.*

MONEY BUYS HAPPINESS L: LOCAL/LOCAL FILMMAKERS (1999) 109M D: Gregg Lachow. *Jeff Weatherford, Cynthia Whalen, John Holyoke, Megan Murphy.* Three days in the breakup of a ten-year marriage through the offbeat, independent eye of Seattle filmmaker Lachow. Weatherford searches for meaning in the modern world by embracing spirituality in small steps (starting with the observance of the Sabbath, his first), while his wife (Murphy) tracks down a former secret admirer to hopefully find true, pure love. On the verge of breakup, they reconnect on an unlikely weekend that involves a ten-year-old love letter, a friend's sudden suicide, and a seventy-block journey pushing an upright piano—an interesting metaphor for a relationship if I ever saw one. Weatherford is easy and charming but Murphy is stiff and posed, and Lachow has a tendency to belabor a scene. Yet there's more honesty in the film's final image than many movies manage in ninety minutes. —*S. A.*

DEFINITELY NOT HOLLYWOOD: EXTREME L: SHORT FILMS/SHORT FILM COLLECTIONS (1999) 57M D: Various. *Tom Fahn.* This is a decent collection of short films. Don't miss the gripping, dramatic, and over-the-top tear-jerking tale of *Saving Ryan's Privates,* where an entire platoon goes on a mission to retrieve private James Ryan's manhood from the battlefield. There are many laughs as well in a funny Martin Scorsese–style spoof called *Fast Food,* starring a not-too-shabby De Niro look-alike played by Fahn. The short *Boy Next Door* is a great little story about a brother and a sister who fall in love with their new sexpot neighbor. When they both start pining over him, they turn against each other, only to find out he really didn't care for either of them. —*R. D.*

JONZE, SPIKE: THE WORKS OF L: SHORT FILMS/SHORT FILM COLLECTIONS (2003) M D: Spike Jonze. Jonze himself (along with fellow visionaries Michel Gondry and Chris Cunningham) have formed a partnership to release collections of their music-video work. This DVD includes legendary classics like the Beastie Boys' "Sabotage" (in the style of a '70s cop-show intro), Fatboy Slim's "Praise You" (Jonze and "The Torrance Community Dance Group" dancing in front of a crowded movie theater) and "Weapon of Choice" (Christopher Walken tapdancing and flying). And then there are lesser knowns like the Pharcyde's "Drop" (filmed backward) and Notorious B.I.G.'s "Sky's the Limit" (Hype Williams–style rap-video clichés acted out by a cast of children). Each video includes a commentary by the musicians, some have additional info and the B-side of the disc has rarities and documentaries. The best of those is the poignant thirty-minute "What's Up Fat Lip?" taped during the making of the video of the same name by the MC kicked out of the Pharcyde. —*B. T.*

CHAPTER TWO

Foreign Films

The Foreign Films section is one of the most frustrating sections in our store. Not just for our customers, but also for us. There are 8,000 films in the section and that just isn't enough. We want more and more and more! But not enough is available! Has Jerzy Skolimowski's *Barrier* ever been released? Or what about Ariane Mnouchkine's *Molière*? What about films from directors out of Brazil or Mexico or the entire continent of Africa, for crying out loud. Come on! Open it up! We want to watch your movies! Whether you've got the rights to films from Norway, the Czech Republic, Indonesia, or Mali, there is an international audience for your films! (Hey, and since we're not all Charles Berlitz, don't forget those subtitle tracks on the DVDs, OK?) Now hop to it! Thanks!

A Better Tomorrow (1986)

ARGENTINA

FUNNY DIRTY LITTLE WAR L: FOREIGN/ARGENTINA (1983) 80M D: Hector Olivera. *Federico Luppi, Hector Bidonde, Victor Laplacep.* The title gets it right on both counts: Olivera's scathing satire of rightist Peronists plotting to oust the leftist Peronist mayor in a fictional Argentine town, set during the vicious internal struggle in the wake of President Juan Peron's death in 1974, blossoms into a small, farcical revolution complete with death squads, hostages, and torture. Luppi (*The Devil's Backbone*) stars as the righteous mayor who fights back like he's in a Western, holing up in the city hall and taking shots at the cops surrounding the building. The political dirty tricks and Keystone Kop street battles soon erupt into a battle between a government goon squad practicing its own brand of door-to-door Fascist justice and a leftist guerrilla brigade unleashing a reign of terror. Simultaneously horrifying and hilarious, Olivera deftly twists the satirical knife (both sides chant "Viva Peron" while killing their former friends and neighbors) without losing the black humor, the gut-wrenching irony, or the humanity of the victims. —*S.A.*

NINE QUEENS L: FOREIGN/ARGENTINA (2002) 115M D: Fabian Bielinsky. *Gaston Pauls, Leticia Bredice, Ricardo Darín.* There is no honor among thieves in the code of Marcos (Darín). The world is a mercenary place, he instructs his new acolyte (Pauls). To illustrate, the camera turns to the Argentine urban jungle around them and reveals a feeding frenzy of thievery played out by the human vultures and hyenas preying on the weaker members of the pack. Whether it's justification or explanation we don't know, but Marcos, a con man with a history of turning on his partners, is out for every penny he can bilk out of the world and he's just stumbled onto the sting of a lifetime. If Bielinsky's entry into the cinema of scam doesn't bring anything new to the table, he has a smartly engineered scheme and a good poker face, and he has mastered the essential art of misdirection. There are enough surprises and wry revelations, right down to the last play, to make this a most satisfying cinematic confidence game. —S. A.

AUSTRALIA

ADVENTURES OF PRISCILLA, QUEEN OF THE DESERT, THE L: FOREIGN/AUSTRALIA (1994) 103M D: Stephan Elliot. *Guy Pearce, Bill Hunter, Terence Stamp, Hugo Weaving.* After aging transsexual Bernadette Bassenger (Stamp) finds herself a widow when her young husband asphyxiates while dying his hair, she opts for a change of scenery and a return to her glory days as a stage performer when she agrees to accompany two drag queens, Mitzi Del Bra (Weaving) and Felicia Jollygoodfellow (Pearce), as they travel by bus across the outback to Alice Springs for a drag show. A lot of movies that focus on drag queens tend to show fairly shallow characters that are only depicted from the angle of glamorous stage performances and elaborate costumes. While this movie definitely has its fair share of those, it also offers insight as to who the three main characters are offstage through their personal tribulations and eventual reconciliation of them. The dialogue is full of one-liners and witty attacks, the costumes are fabulous (this may be your only chance to see Weaving wearing a dress made entirely of flip-flops), and the soundtrack features a ton of good songs, particularly from the genius of ABBA. This is a really fun, great movie that will leave you humming for days. —J. S.

BABE L: FOREIGN/AUSTRALIA (1995) 94M D: Chris Noonan. *James Cromwell, Magda Szubanski, Miriam Margolyes, Christine Cavanaugh.* In this beautifully realized fantasy where animals can talk to each other (a la *Charlotte's Web*), a little pig named Babe (voice of Cavanaugh) goes to live with a stoic sheep farmer (Cromwell). When a cruel cat tells Babe he has no purpose on the farm other than to become meat, he decides to learn how to herd sheep. Unfortunately that confuses the sheep, angers one of the dogs, and humiliates the farmer's wife when he decides to enter the pig in a televised sheep dog competition. *Babe* is a perfect movie. It takes a genre you couldn't possibly have high expectations for (the talking-animal movie) and executes it so deftly and with such conviction from the first frame to the last that you never even question it. Its sweet morals (don't let anyone stop you from doing what you want to with your life; being nice helps you get what you want) seem completely sincere. The storytelling is flawlessly constructed to climax and then immediately cut to the credits—no lingering around. I can't watch it without getting at least a little teary-eyed when Farmer Hoggett comes out of his shell to dance for the pig, or when he says, "That'll do, pig" triumphantly at the end. —B. T.

BAD BOY BUBBY L: FOREIGN/AUSTRALIA (1993) 112M D: Rolf De Heer. *Nicholas Hope, Claire Benito, Ralph Cotterill, Syd Brisbane, Carmel Johnson.* This movie sincerely blew my mind. I like to describe it as watching *Dancer in the Dark* backwards because it starts out overwhelmingly grim but lightens up as it goes along. Poor Bubby; his mom has imprisoned him with her in a window-less room for about thirty years, conned into believing the outside air is poisonous gas. When his real father comes to town for the first time and sees Bubby and his mother's incestuous relationship, Bubby is forced to hit the road and discover the world. This is an awesome character-awakening movie. Bubby comes a long way from accidentally murdering his own cat, to finally finding some friends and eventually becoming a very popular singer for a local rock band. It doesn't get cooler than that. —R. D.

CHOPPER L: FOREIGN/AUSTRALIA (2000) 94M D: Andrew Dominik. *Eric Bana, David Field, Simon Lyndon, Vince Colosimo.* Bana plays Mark "Chopper" Read, an infamous Australian criminal who murdered other thieves in acts of quasi-vigilantism and later became a best-selling author. The early prison scenes where he shanks a man, then apologizes, can best sum up Chopper's personality. Don't think he's soft, though; to escape retribution, he has a friend cut off his ears, an injury that will earn him a transfer to a different prison. Later he gets out and terrorizes those who betrayed him by going to them and acting friendly. It's a small story that seems to be over before it really begins, but what makes this movie unforgettable is a brilliant performance by former stand-up comedian Bana (who you will not recognize if you only know him as the Hulk). Even during acts of brutal violence he never stops being funny and charismatic, which makes him all the more terrifying. —B. T.

DEAD END DRIVE-IN L: FOREIGN/AUSTRALIA (1986) 92M D: Brian Trenchard-Smith. *Ned Manning, Natalie McCurry, Peter Whitford, Dave Gibson, Wilbur Wilde, Sandie Lillingston.* In the chaos of the economically devastated future in Australia, the authorities hit upon a brilliant solution to contain the frustrations of the young and the unemployed: turn the local drive-in into a concentration camp and ply the inmates with a diet of snack-bar meals and evening movies. Except one of the prisoners (Manning) decides he wants out and plots his escape. Like an Australian variant on a Roger Corman sci-fi drive-in adventure with *Mad Max* art direction, some sharp political and social observations (when the authorities get worried that the restless youth may soon tire of incarceration, they distract them by creating and encouraging racial division) are woven through the action and color of the low-budget action satire. —S. A.

DISH, THE L: FOREIGN/AUSTRALIA (2000) 101M D: Rob Sitch. *Sam Neill, Kevin Harrington, Patrick Warburton, Tom Long.* This quiet and unassuming little film is a total charmer. Based on the true story behind the second satellite used as the Southern hemisphere contact with the first Apollo moon landing, it is an exploration of the differences between Australian and American cultures. The satellite was given the honor mainly because it was the only one large enough and in the right location, but NASA was concerned about the rural sheep-farming area that it was built in and worried that something might go wrong out there in the outback. And they were right. The characters blessedly don't feel like caricatures, but like quirky and honest representations of the Australian culture. Playful, entertaining, witty and even at times gripping, this film is worth watching because it actually bothers to have a story and characters over action and sex. What a concept! —*M. N.*

GHOSTS OF THE CIVIL DEAD L: FOREIGN/AUSTRALIA (1998) 93M D: John Hillcoat. *Mike Bishop, Chris DeRose, David Field, Nick Cave.* I waited for a long time to see this film, not because of lack of interest but lack of access to it. When I finally did see it, I was a bit let down. It was built up too much over a long period of time, and the type of cinematic violence portrayed in this film has become more commonplace over the years. Presumably based on actual events, this is a harsh dramatization of life in certain maximum-security prisons throughout the world. It shows in a sped-up fashion how a prison with perhaps too many freedoms loses control of its inmate population. Then it turns around and clamps down to the point of driving the inmates mad like feral animals in cages. When you take away dignity and respect you get bitter hatred that will find a release in one form or another. The form in this case is violence against themselves, other inmates, and ultimately the corrections officers. In a series of flashbacks, narration, and interviews we see how the twenty-four-hour-a-day lockdown came to pass and what instigations provoked the hostilities between inmates and guards; we find that the omnipotent unseen administration is behind the manipulation of the system of control. If you can get your hands on this film, it's well worth the watch, if for no other reason than to see it for what it was in the context of the time and place it was made, and to perhaps see this as a metaphor for greater systems of control and manipulation throughout society. —*B. W.*

LOVE SERENADE L: FOREIGN/AUSTRALIA (1996) 101M D: Shirley Barrett. *George Shevtsov, Miranda Otto, Rebecca Frith.* Barrett's writing-directing debut makes a hypnotically daft addition to the offbeat Aussie dossier. In the remote burg of Sunray, surrounded by empty flatlands and situated on a river in which a dead forest unaccountably

stands, two sisters named Dimity and Vicki Ann lead what passes for a life. Anywhere else, they'd probably be institutionalized. Dimity (Otto) claims to be twenty but comes across as a hopelessly backward teen. Vicki Ann (Frith) is a few years older, wears grown-up clothes, and puts on a credible-enough adult face to hold down a job at the beauty parlor. Into the life of Sunray rolls Ken Sherry (Shevtsov), who used to be a media superstar but, after some unspoken difficulty (possibly involving one of his ex-wives) has signed on as the new local deejay. Naturally, both Dimity and Vicki Ann fall for him. Barrett deploys an imperturbably deadpan widescreen style, whether appreciating the spatial peculiarities and architectural banality of her frontier town, or savoring the endlessly renewable varieties of perversity and self-delusion our species is heir to. —*R. J.*

METAL SKIN L: FOREIGN/AUSTRALIA (1994) 115M D: Geoffery Wright, Chris Odgers. *Nadine Garner, Petru Gheorghiu, Chantal Contouri, Tara Morice, Aden Young, Ben Mendelsohn.* Metal Skin, by the Australian director of *Romper Stomper,* is a cool, gritty movie about young, drag-racing kids who can barely afford to keep their cars running. It's all about atmosphere; Wright sets the tone with quirky camera shots, off coloring, and a driving score. I found it similar to *Crash* in that with creative filming techniques, you can have lots of cool stuff going on without much plot and still come out with an enjoyable movie. Too bad that never works for director Gregg Araki. —*R. D.*

QUIET ROOM, THE L: FOREIGN/AUSTRALIA (1996) 92M D: Rolf De Heer. *Chloe Ferguson, Paul Blackwell, Celine O'Leary, Phoebe Ferguson.* This is a sweet, thought-provoking story of a young girl who has stopped talking after a traumatic experience. Her silence goes on for years, with only a few moments of uncontrolled giggling. Her caring parents are having problems, and though she doesn't say much, she is constantly thinking about everything. This is a good family study told though a child's point of view. —*R. D.*

SHINE L: FOREIGN/AUSTRALIA (1995) 105M D: Scott Hicks. *Geoffrey Rush, Lynn Redgrave, Armin Mueller-Stahl, Noah Taylor, John Gielgud.* Based on the life of concert pianist David Helfgott, *Shine* is the story of the rise and fall and rise of a fine musician. Rush plays the role of Helfgott, who escapes his tyrannical father in Australia to attend a music conservatory in London and study with Cecil Parkes (Gielgud). Yet as he achieves success, his demand for perfection causes him to have a nervous breakdown. He is summarily confined to a mental ward. Redgrave plays the outside character who develops an interest in him and releases him from the institution with hopes that he can resume his career. The film ends on an open, positive note about his future potential, yet this same brilliant pianist who performed his own soundtrack in the film and stirred quite the flurry of interest was a one-season wonder with actual concertgoers. As inspirational as this film is, perhaps it could use a bit less "spit with its shine." —N. J.

BALKAN STATES

CABARET BALKAN L: FOREIGN/BALKAN STATES (1999) 102M D: Goran Pasakaljevic. *Ana Sofrenovic, Nebojsa Glogovac, Miki Manojlovic.* Pasakaljevic's *Cabaret Balkan* (released in the rest of the world as *The Powder Keg*, a title that Kevin Costner registered in the U.S., then didn't use) is as black a portrait of Belgrade as ever was seen on the screen. The trajectories of a dozen or so characters, mostly men, intertwine over the course of one night as they accost, beat, rape, kidnap, hijack and murder citizens (often women) for fun and profit. It's an assured, passionate film, laced with black humor and cutting satire, but it's not pretty. In fact it's unrelentingly grueling and features not a single sympathetic character. Pasakaljevic makes a case for a culture of misogyny and machismo gone mad, and unwittingly implicates himself by making the handful of women that are victimized by the brutality almost all passive, flat figures. Only a few receive even a token personality, while the men are energetic, volatile, active. It's a man's world indeed. —S. A.

BELGUIM

MAN BITES DOG L: FOREIGN/BELGIUM (1992) 95M D: Remy Belvaux, Andre Bonzel. *Benoit Poelvoorde, Remy Belvaux, Andre Bonzel, Jean-Marc Chenut.* First and foremost, be sure to watch the uncut version of this pitch-black comedy masterpiece for the purest enjoyment of the film. This pseudo-documentary can in retrospect be seen as a harbinger for the clout of reality-based TV shows that started plaguing the airwaves only a few years after the film's release. The story picks up as a trio of filmmakers document the life of a serial killer in a small Belgium town. The killer, Ben, is an extremely thoughtful (if at times misled) man, who in between his brutal killings shares his ideas on the world around him. The crew crosses paths with an identical crew following another criminal, showcasing the copycat simplicity of entertainment. As Ben's ambitious slayings, which have no boundary or reason, begin to pile up, the crew realizes that they have become part of a horrible experiment of their own creation, and only their footage may survive to tell the tale. —R. M.

MA VIE EN ROSE (MY LIFE IN PINK) L: FOREIGN/BELGIUM (1997) 88M D: Alain Berliner. *Jean Philippe Ecoffey, Michele Laroque, Helen Vincent, George Du Fresne.* Seven-year-old Ludovic is not your ordinary boy. He constantly dresses like a girl, acts like a girl, thinks like a girl, and knows in his heart that some day he will be miraculously changed into a girl. It's a very unusual phase for a boy to go through, but after much probing, questioning, and anxiety, his parents slowly begin to think that these feelings are actually all quite genuine. Acceptance proves to be a difficult thing for the parents, even more so for the neighbors, yet it seems quite easy for the grandmother, who is often available to listen to her grandson/daughter's viewpoints. In his film debut, Berliner does very well in expressing a child's perspective on such a divisive topic. This film won the Golden Globe for Best Foreign Language Film. —N. J.

ROSETTA L: FOREIGN/BELGIUM (1999) 95M D: Jean-Pierre Dardenne, Luc Dardenne. *Emilie Dequenne, Fabrizio Rongione, Olivier Gourmet.* The film that beat *All About My Mother* at Cannes, *Rosetta* is easily one of the finest films of the 1990s. The movie begins as the intense eighteen-year-old Rosetta (Dequenne) loses her job. The remainder of this whirlwind of a film is spent literally following Rosetta in a desperate search for employment. Determined to be a useful member of Belgian society, the need to work is for Rosetta nothing less than a struggle for survival. Pursuing their subject with shaky handheld cameras, the Dardennes reveal their character solely through up-close observation of her daily struggles for work. The Dardennes are narrative essentialists, and know precisely where to begin and end a scene (or for that matter a whole movie). When *Rosetta* halts in conclusion, the viewer is almost out of breath, immersed for ninety-five minutes in a frantic chase of a character whom we never fully know yet come to love very much. —C. B.

SON, THE (LE FILS) L: FOREIGN/BELGIUM (2002) 103M D: Jean-Pierre Dardenne, Luc Dardenne. *Morgan Marinne, Olivier Gourmet, Isabella Soupart.* *The Son* begins with the enrollment of a new student, fresh from juvenile prison, at the trade school where our protagonist Olivier teaches carpentry. As the parable-like story slowly reveals the horrific history behind their difficult relationship, the film takes on a massive, near-biblical moral gravity. With the Dardennes' most rigorous and evolved style to date, *The Son* progresses through deep immersion in Olivier's world. The camera literally pursues him, generally shooting from behind and at extremely close range. Strictly maintaining this singular perspective, we're denied access to Olivier's inner workings—we seldom even see his face. We understand him through his work, watching him toil through mundane daily tasks, performed not merely as vocation or even fondness for his students, but as self-preservation. Far and away the single greatest film experience I had in 2003, this unequivocal masterpiece has the capacity to leave its audience emotionally devastated yet exhilarated by the human capacity for compassion. —C. B.

BHUTAN

CUP, THE L: FOREIGN/BHUTAN (1999) 93M D: Khyentse Norbu. *Neten Chokling, Orgyen Tobgyal, Jamyang Lodro, Lama Chonjor, Godu Lama.* Lodo (Chokling) and Orgyen (Lodro) are two small boys studying at a Tibetan Buddhist monastery in northern India. They and their fellow exiled monks pray, study, and go about their monasterial duties all the while longing to watch the 1998 World Cup. They follow the games as best they can, but when the final game approaches the boys risk their future as monks in an effort to bring a TV into the monastery so everyone can watch the match. When the senior abbot gives the nod they race about the countryside trying to find a satellite dish they can rent for the night of the match. Locally cast with nonactors and real monks, *The Cup* features honest characters portrayed without pretense. The scenery is beautiful and well captured by first-time director Norbu (also the writer and a monk himself!). *The Cup* is a genuine treat. An unexpectedly good film from tiny Bhutan with a universal story everyone especially soccer fans will enjoy. —*G. M.*

BOSNIA-HERZEGOVINA

NO MAN'S LAND L: FOREIGN/BOSNIA-HERZEGOVINA (2001) 97M D: Danis Tanovic. *Branko Djuric, Rene Bitorajac, Filip Sovagovic, Katrin Cartlidge, Simon Callow.* Former documentarian Tanovic takes an unexpected tack in his first fiction film. He turns the racial hatred and the international mess of the Balkans in 1993, at the height of the bloodshed, into an acidic black comedy grounded in the brutality and horror of war. Set largely in an abandoned trench between enemy lines, where a Serb and a Bosnian play the blame game in a comic tit-for-tat struggle while pinned by enemy fire, Tanovic takes a big bloody bite out of the insanity that erupts. A wounded soldier lays on a bouncing betty land mine that will blow them all if he moves, the UN forces play politics in a situation they want nothing to do with, and a British news crew turns the squabble into a media event. Tanovic's bold metaphors and wild chaotic complications may not be subtle, but there's no need for them to be. He paints the war in vivid terms that are alternately wickedly funny and horrifying without sacrificing the power of either pole. It deservedly took home the Oscar for Best Foreign Language Film. Callow is perfect as the bombastically ineffectual UN commander. —*S. A.*

BRAZIL

ANTONIO DAS MORTES L: FOREIGN/BRAZIL (1969) 100M D: Glauber Rocha. *Odette Lara, Mauricio de Valle, Othon Bastos.* Hired to kill leaders of a plantation labor uprising, assassin-for-hire Antonio das Mortes slowly comes to sympathize with the idealistic peasants he's pitted against, eventually joining them in the fight against their feudal landowners. A landmark of Brazil's Cinema Novo movement, the film's combination of ritualistic violence and radical politics is a daunting package. Director Rocha defends violence as "normal behavior for the starving," and describes its power in the film as "the moment when the colonizer becomes aware of the existence of the colonized." A bizarrely stylized mutation of the Western, *Antonio das Mortes* mixes deliberately theatrical acting, implausibly staged bloodbaths (Brechtian violence anyone?), and an exhausting use of long takes as tension builders-the results being more expressionistically affecting than coherent. Although this was a deliberate choice on Rocha's part, it's sort of baffling to watch. —*C. B.*

BEHIND THE SUN L: FOREIGN/BRAZIL (2001) 92M D: Walter Salles. *Rita Assemany, Rodrigo Santoro, Ravi Ramos Lacerda, Luis Carlos Vasconcelos, José Dumont.* Salles, the acclaimed Brazilian director of the Oscar-nominated *Central Station*, has best intentions but the worst instincts in this Tragedy (with a capital T) of two once mighty clans gripped in a hate-fueled cycle of murder and retribution in 1902 rural Brazil. Rugged, soulful Santoro is ordered to avenge the death of his elder brother by his father (Dumont), a man battered into a hard knot of blind hate. Not only is Dad ready to sacrifice what's left of his family for some meaningless precept of honor, he becomes his son's jailer while they await their nemesis clan to execute his death sentence. The grim absurdity is almost suffocating. Salles's visceral, vivid imagery burns through the screen like the sun that bakes the parched desert of the setting, but it overwhelms the near-abstract story and smothers what passes for characters. —*S. A.*

PIXOTE L: FOREIGN/BRAZIL (1981) 122M D: Hector Babenco. *Fernando Ramos Da Silva, Edilson Lino, Jorge Juliano, Gilberto Moura.* Equal parts exposé and social drama, Babenco's gritty portrait of juvenile poverty dramatizes the plight of millions of homeless children on the streets of Brazil, ground up and spit out of a system that breeds hardened criminals from juvenile delinquents, but its power comes equally from a stunning performance by da Silva. A real-life slum kid cast from the streets, he's a natural, creating a childlike and vulnerable character left emotionally hardened and morally adrift by his brutal experiences. The at-times melodramatic portrait is shocking and affecting, but no more so than da Silva's real-life story: after completing the film he sank back into poverty and crime and died on the streets. Despite the outcry this film inspired, things haven't changed, and that only makes the film more powerful. —*S. A.*

BRITISH COMEDY

BEND IT LIKE BECKHAM L: FOREIGN/BRITISH COMEDY (2002) 112M D: Gurinder Chadha. *Anupam Kher, Keira Knightley, Jonathan Rhys-Meyers, Juliet Stevenson, Shaheen Khan, Parminder K. Nagra.* This is one of those movies where afterward a small voice in my mind whispers, "There is no WAY things would ever work out that smoothly," but this time around I just told that voice to shut the fuck up and enjoyed the warm fuzzy feeling surrounding my heart. Jess Bharma (Nagra) is an Indian teenager who wants nothing more than to play professional soccer. Her traditional parents don't think it's appropriate for an Indian girl to play soccer; they want her to marry and learn to be a good bride. Jess meets Juliette (Knightley) and secretly joins her soccer team. Both girls have a little bit of a thing for the coach, Joe. There's a bunch of drama about people thinking the girls are lesbians. An American soccer scout is expected to be at a game, but Jess isn't sure she can find a good enough lie to able to go. Drama, drama, drama. In the end, everything works out, of course. Little voice be damned, because it made me feel really good. —*J. S.*

BRASSED OFF L: FOREIGN/BRITISH COMEDY (1996) 109M D: Mark Herman. *Philip Jackson, Pete Postlethwaite, Tara Fitzgerald, Ewan McGregor, Stephen Tompkinson, Jim Carter.* This British film got swamped by the wave caused by *The Full Monty* and as such never got the attention or exposure that it so justly deserved. The story is of a small town in northern England fighting the government for the right to dig coal. If the coal mine is closed, it means the people of the town will have to find other forms of work and will likely be forced to move, thus endangering the Grimley Colliery brass band, which has been in existence for one hundred years, nearly as long as the town and coal mine have been. The bandmaster struggles to keep the group together despite the financial troubles they are all in, dreaming of competing with the other local brass bands and winning for a change. While at times dramatic and tragic, the film also has a bright and stubborn sense of humor as these people refuse to be put down or in their place. Definitely worth watching! —*M. N.*

BRIDGET JONES'S DIARY L: FOREIGN/BRITISH COMEDY (2001) 116M D: Sharon Maguire. *Colin Firth, Hugh Grant, Renée Zellweger, James Faulkner, Gemma Jones, Jim Broadbent.* Bridget Jones's Diary is definitely a chick flick because Bridget Jones is a woman's woman, the kind that nearly everyone can relate to on some level. She's awkward, rambles painfully, speaks her mind all the time (even when it's not appropriate), she smokes and drinks constantly, and is (unbelievably) a little on the chubby side. And, of course, she's looking for love in all the wrong places. She starts a tumultuous relationship with her shithead boss,

played by Grant, but keeps running into quiet, sullen, and sexy Firth, a friend of her family whom she secretly wants a piece of. This is just a lighthearted, feel-good movie, and Zellweger is absolutely charming. That's good enough for me. —*J. S.*

EXPRESSO BONGO L: FOREIGN/BRITISH COMEDY (1959) 111M D: Val Guest. *Yolande Donlan, Cliff Richard, Laurence Harvey, Sylvia Syms.* A drummer turned self-styled promoter (Harvey) has his feet in two worlds: He talks like a cross between a beat poet and a huckster, but he knows how to hustle. . . or so he thinks. When he spots a bongo-playing crooner (Richard) in a local juke joint, he thinks he's got his meal ticket: "Bongo" Herbert, teen sensation. Unfortunately for our naive would-be manager, he's swimming with the sharks and doesn't have the teeth. Ultimately neither does the film, which for all its sardonic humor and irony misses the tremendous opportunities of the conclusion. But the ride is terrific: Harvey is all slippery charm and Donlan is terrific as a sincere but savvy aging American sexpot attempting a comeback in the face of younger rivals. —*S. A.*

I'LL NEVER FORGET WHAT'S 'IS NAME L: FOREIGN/BRITISH COMEDY (1967) 99M D: Michael Winner. *Oliver Reed, Orson Welles, Michael Hordern, Harry Andrews, Carol White.* Reed strolls through London in a designer suit with an ax slung over his shoulder and a devious smile on his lips. He chops his desk into kindling as a groovy guitar score rocks across the soundtrack, quits his wildly successful career as an advertising executive, and goes off to "find himself." Winner's "angry young man" social satire is set firmly in London's swinging '60s, but for all his grand gestures and ambitious talk, Reed's character is neither angry, young, nor particularly sincere. He's just empty and desperate, trying to chuck his empty life of money and mistresses for a more meaningful existence but failing miserably. Winner doesn't quite pull it all together, but his sharp images and shrewd direction kindle a passion matched by Reed's brooding charm. —*S. A.*

IMPROMPTU L: FOREIGN/BRITISH COMEDY (1991) 107M D: James Lapine. *Julian Sands, Judy Davis, Hugh Grant, Mandy Patinkin, Bernadette Peters, Ralph Brown.* A most entertaining flick with a fantastic cast examines the foibles, quirks, and social interactions of a group of artists, writers, and musicians. Central to the story is the infamous George Sands, a racy author who is in fact an authoress. Upon hearing him play the piano, she becomes enamored of the delicate and ethereal Frederic Chopin and decides to woo and win him. But she is not the only one interested in winning him over. Struggling to balance her independent nature and her wish to attract Chopin, we are led through a dizzying chase of lovers, fools, and friends. An early role for Grant and one that suits him well. Davis is fabulous as the feisty and determined George Sands. —*M. N.*

MAGIC CHRISTIAN, THE L: FOREIGN/BRITISH COMEDY
(1969) 101M D: Joseph McGrath. *Peter Sellers, Ringo Starr, Caroline Blakiston, Christopher Lee, Raquel Welch.* Sellers is Guy Grand, a wealthy eccentric who uses his money and power to set up elaborate pranks that expose the depth of human greed and depravity. For example he builds a giant vat, fills it with feces, urine, and hundred dollar bills, then posts a sign that says "Free money" (sadly, Grand's point is made every day now on reality television). It's based on the satirical novel by Terry Southern, which Sellers was so enamored with that he gave it to everyone he knew. The movie's not nearly as sharp as the book, and more dated (Starr's adopted son character was invented for youth appeal), but Sellers makes it a lot of fun. The title refers to the name of a rigged cruise ship that plays a more important role in the movie than in the book. —*B. T.*

MAYBE BABY L: FOREIGN/BRITISH COMEDY (2000) 93M D:
Ben Elton. *Joely Richardson, Joanne Lumley, Rowan Atkinson, Hugh Laurie, Dawn French.* The directorial debut of Britain's embarrassingly prolific comic scribe Elton (cocreator of *Blackadder*) is an entertaining baby-blues comedy. He adapted his own novel, milking laughs from fertility tests and the discomfort of invasive medical examinations (made easier when you cast Atkinson as a gynecologist). His hero, a sardonic TV producer (Laurie) also milks their pain when he starts writing a satirical script based on their experiences, against the expressed wishes of his sunny, sexy wife (Richardson). Low-key and lots of fun, this comedy of infertility, frustration, and the loss of romance caused by the regimentation of a sex life around charts and rituals is hardly as insightful as it could and should be, but Elton doesn't cop out on how Laurie's emotionally invasive games tear the trust of his marriage. Emma Thompson has a bit as a dippy hippy singing the praises of fertility rites. —*S. A.*

NUNS ON THE RUN L: FOREIGN/BRITISH COMEDY (1990)
95M D: Jonathan Lynn. *Lila Kaye, Eric Idle, Robbie Coltrane, Camille Coduri, Janet Suzman, Doris Hare.* A fun, slapstick-styled comedy that avoids taking jokes too far and getting annoying, which is truly an art unto itself. The story revolves around two thieves who find they've been set up by their gangster boss to be taken out after they help out with robbing a Triad group, taking their ill-gotten drug-dealing profits. Taking their lives into their own hands, Brian (Idle) and Charlie (Coltrane) decide to literally take the money and run, but with gangsters to the left of them and cops to the right, there is nowhere else to go. . . except to a nunnery! Disguising themselves as visiting nuns, they manage to hide from both the law and the lawless, and naturally wacky hijinks ensue. It's silly and foolish and delightfully

funny. If you want something light and fluffy and British comedy is your thing, then this is a definite must-see. —*M. N.*

RULING CLASS, THE L: FOREIGN/BRITISH COMEDY (1972)
154M D: Peter Medak. *Peter O'Toole, Arthur Lowe, Alastair Sim, Harry Andrews, Coral Browne.* O'Toole gives an eye-opening performance as Jack, a man recently released from the nuthouse to claim a giant inheritance and massive estate. Clearly not entirely rehabilitated, Jack has some very abrupt relapses where he believes he is Jesus Christ. This is done up complete with a large wooden cross he has installed in his living room and climbs onto whenever he feels persecuted. And of course relatives who think the inheritance was not willed appropriately persecute him. After much satire on the class system in England punctuated with mad rants and musical numbers, Jack eventually comes to believe that he is actually Jack the Ripper, finally turning his persecution complex into something a bit more violent. The DVD by Criterion features plenty of extras including commentaries by O'Toole, director Medak, and the writer Peter Barnes. —*N. J.*

TRULY, MADLY, DEEPLY L: FOREIGN/BRITISH COMEDY
(1991) 106M D: Anthony Minghella. *Alan Rickman, Juliet Stevenson, Christopher Rozycki, Jenny Howe, Michael Maloney, Bill Paterson.* "I can't believe I have a bunch of dead people watching videos in my living room!" Grieving widow Stevenson spends her hours talking to dead husband Rickman, and suddenly he's back. . . sort of. Called "the thinking man's *Ghost*" by many critics, this delightful and often painful romantic comedy finds a beautiful metaphor for mourning and denial in a love affair that only seems to continue after death but in reality mires the living in the frozen-in-time nothingness of the spirits that congregate in his place. Until she meets Maloney, a part-time magician who brings her heart back into the world of the living. Minghella (*The English Patient*) made his directorial debut from his original screenplay with this warm and very down-to-earth romantic comedy about life, death, and carrying on in the face of both. —*S. A.*

24 HOUR PARTY PEOPLE L: FOREIGN/BRITISH COMEDY
(2002) 117M D: Michael Winterbottom. *Steve Coogan, Lennie James, Shirley Henderson, Paddy Considine, Andy Serkis.* The rise and fall of Factory Records and the Manchester music scene is presented as a decade-long party hosted by journalist-turned-entrepreneur, record producer, and bon vivant Tony Wilson (British comedian Coogan). Winterbottom's sprawling, jagged film is happily, even willfully unreliable as history and a bracing portrait of a time, a place, and a social phenomenon. Coogan's Wilson weaves in and out of the story as main character, master of ceremonies, and commentator (at one point even stepping

out of character to point out the cameos made by the real-life figures in the story) while cinematographer Robby Müller brings a little focus to the clichéd use of frantically wandering handheld camera, jump cuts, and mixing textures of film and video. Winterbottom, a chameleon with the uncanny ability to reinvent his style with almost every film, mixes it into his most entertaining and invigorating film to date. —*S.A.*

YOUNG POISONER'S HANDBOOK L: FOREIGN/BRITISH COMEDY (1995) 106M D: Benjamin Ross (I). *Hugh O'Conor, Ruth Sheen.* A highly dramatized account of a true story, this movie definitely falls into the category of dark comedy. O'Conor plays Graham Young, a teenage boy whose first love is his chemistry set. He becomes fascinated with the subject and decides to take his experiments to a new level, testing them out on the people in his life he dislikes, starting with his mother. He is sent to a rehabilitation center, where he convinces the doctor that he is, in fact, already cured and ready to be released. You can take the poison away from the crazy guy, but can you really take the crazy away from the poisoner? O'Conor really makes this movie, pulling off the role beautifully. You are so sucked in by his calm demeanor and delusions of sanity that you often find yourself sympathizing with him over his victims. Although most of the darker scenes are pulled off with a humorous twist, you'll still find yourself a little disturbed by their cruelty and apathetic deliverance. —*J.S.*

BRITISH DRAMA

BILLY ELLIOT L: FOREIGN/BRITISH DRAMA (2000) 111M D: Stephen Daldry. *Gary Lewis, Jamie Bell, Jean Heywood, Jamie Driven, Julie Walters.* Billy Elliot (Bell) is a boy with dancing on his mind. Living in working-class Manchester, England, he is allowed to take boxing as a sport but his eyes are on the dance class next door. The dance instructor soon notices his interest and, eager to have a boy in her class, she invites him to dance. He does—quite badly—but over time he improves, especially since the teacher gives him private lessons for free. He doesn't tell his father for fear that this education would come to an end. Finally, just before his big recital, his father finds out, leading to the inevitable climax. This film has some great dances but more importantly, it does well in showing a young man's enthusiasm for dance and how he's able to win acceptance through perseverance. —*N.J.*

BIRTHDAY GIRL L: FOREIGN/BRITISH DRAMA (2001) 90M D: Jez Butterworth. *Nicole Kidman, Matthieu Kassovitz, Ben Chaplin, Vincent Cassel.* From Russia with love: a seductive mail-order bride (Kidman) doesn't speak English, but she manages to light the fire of her dull British suitor (Chaplin) with the international language of sex and bondage. Kidman is almost incandescent as the emotionally bruised dolly who shows that she's much more than meets the eye as the film morphs from awkward romance to noir-ish crime film to oil-and-water road movie. Butterworth's across the pond *Something Wild* costars Cassel as an explosive, scary con man and Kassovitz as his happy-to-follow-along partner, but the film never quite recovers from Chaplin, who plays dour hangdog mopeyness so well his wet blanket smothers the sparks around him. Utterly inconsequential but fun in a weird way, and Kidman manages to make some unusually unromantic come-ons sexy and sweet. —*S.A.*

BORSTAL BOY L: FOREIGN/BRITISH DRAMA (2000) 93M D: Peter Sheridan. *Shawn Hatosy, Michael York.* This adaptation of Brendan Behan's autobiographical novel is sweet but heavy-handed. Brendan, a teenager in a veteran IRA family, gets arrested for smuggling a bomb across England's border. After a brief, brutal stint in prison, he's sent to Borstal reformatory. Under the watchful but kindly headmaster, Brendan fulfills his "duty as a POW" and plans escape. He learns to trust his new friends despite their unfamiliar backgrounds and taboo sexual preferences. But the film undermines his accomplishments with glorified "coming-of-age" stereotypes-swelling music and lengthy shots of boys learning teamwork through sports. —*M.M.*

CHRISTIE MALRY'S OWN DOUBLE ENTRY L: FOREIGN/ BRITISH DRAMA (2000) 89M D: Paul Tickell. *Nick Moran, Neil Stuke, Kate Ashfield, Mattia Sbragia.* I enjoyed this film quite a bit. It revolves around the main character, Christie (Moran), who has nothing really exceptional going on in his life . . . except that his mom is dying. He decides to take a course on bookkeeping. The course changes his life when he decides to use the credit-debit system for more karmic purposes. Instead of keeping records of money spent versus acquisitions, he starts keeping track of being mistreated, either personally or by the government. At first he starts out getting even in small ways, like keying the car of his boss who was rude to him. Soon he realizes he can get ahead of the game by inflicting destructive chaos on a massive scale. Very interesting indeed. —*R.D.*

ELIZABETH R L: FOREIGN/BRITISH DRAMA (1972) 540M D: Claude Whatham. *Glenda Jackson, Robert Hardy, Ronald Hines.* Jackson is absolutely stunning in the role of Queen Elizabeth I. The miniseries begins at the deathbed of her younger brother, Edward VI, and then accounts for her difficult subsistence under her older sister, Mary I. At length Mary dies leaving Elizabeth to become the "Virgin Queen." In her forty-year reign miniseries, we get to see her secret relationship to Lord Essex; her decision to behead her cousin Mary, Queen of Scots; her trust in Sir Francis Drake to fight the Spanish Armada; and lots and lots of other details. Jackson does a remarkable job showing the progression of age and makeup on the much-loved queen. Leave it to the BBC to get their English history right! —*N. J.*

ENIGMA L: FOREIGN/BRITISH DRAMA (2002) 117M D: Michael Apted. *Dougray Scott, Kate Winslet, Saffron Burrows, Jeremy Northam.* A mix of conspiracy thriller and real-life code-breaking puzzle, Michael Apted's WWII drama is a smartly directed picture that demands a little more of the viewer than most. Dougray Scott is a math genius and code-breaking legend recovering from a nervous breakdown and returning to work at Bletchley Park, code-breaking central for Britain's war effort. When the willowy blonde who threw him over (Burrows) disappears, he uncovers a conspiracy with the help of her dowdy roommate (Winslet) while sinister agent Jeremy Northam (who puts real menace in his scheming smile) is hot on his trail. Scripted by Tom Stoppard from the novel by Robert Harris, it's a slow-moving but intriguing premise and the conspiracy actually gets in the way of the real history: cracking the Enigma code. Now that's a story worth making a film about. John Barry provides a lovely score with an ominous undercurrent. —*S. A.*

FAIRYTALE: A TRUE STORY L: FOREIGN/BRITISH DRAMA (1997) 99M D: Charles Sturridge. *Paul McGann, Peter O'Toole, Harvey Keitel, Phoebe Nicholls, Bill Nighy, Elizabeth Earl, Florence Hoath, Bob Peck.* Treated with a light enough hand that it doesn't become maudlin, sappy, or annoyingly cute, FairyTale is a charming film based on a true story of two girls in 1917 who manage to capture pictures of fairies with a camera. The film proceeds to follow the story of their lives, their families, and the controversy that follows the discovery of their photographs, as some believe them to be scientific proof of the existence of fairies while others maintain that somehow they are fakes. I did have a hard time buying Harvey Keitel as Harry Houdini, but the rest of the film is told with a bright and vivacious air and manages to be satisfying even without taking a firm stand on whether the photos are indeed real or fake, though they are pretty clear about the existence of fairies. —*M. N.*

FINAL CUT, THE L: FOREIGN/BRITISH DRAMA (1995) 200M D: Mike Vardy. *Ian Richardson, Isla Blair, Paul Freeman, Brian Baines, Diane Fletcher, Nick Brimble.* This is the final film in the trilogy that documents the life of fictitious Prime Minister Francis Urquhart (Richardson), his rise to power, and his tyrannical abuses of that power. Having previously murdered a young reporter and politically forced the abdication of a king, Urquhart and his wife try planning for their comfortable retirement. For the kind of money they want to retire with, they fix the decision of a peace settlement in Cyprus such that they are able to profit from offshore oil reserves. But of course, oil and politics always make a rather messy mix.

For best effect this film should be seen together with the other parts of the trilogy, *House of Cards* and *To Play the King.* —*N. J.*

FIRELIGHT L: FOREIGN/BRITISH DRAMA (1997) 103M D: William Nicholson. *Stephen Dillane, Sophie Marceau, Joss Ackland, Kevin Anderson, Dominique Belcourt, Lisa Williams.* An elegant, stylish, and charming period romance that begins from the most unlikely of places. A woman, desperate to pay off her beloved father's debts, agrees to act as a surrogate mother, sleeping with a man she does not know and giving birth to a child she will never see again. While the affair is loveless and an act of convenience for both, a bond is forged between the pair. Unable to forget her daughter she manages to track the mysterious man down and applies for the position of governess, swearing that she will not reveal her true identity to her daughter. But circumstances change, forged bonds remain compellingly strong, and by firelight all secrets and dreams can be revealed safely. I find myself drawn to this movie and its simple honesty and pursuit of love. A little reminiscent of *Jane Eyre* at times. —*M. N.*

GIRL GETTERS (AKA **THE SYSTEM**) L: FOREIGN/BRITISH DRAMA (1966) 93M D: Michael Winner. *Oliver Reed, Jane Merrow, Barbara Ferris, David Hemmings.* Boys on the make, flirty girls in bikinis, sandy seashores, the summer sun, and the Searchers thrashing out '60s guitar rock: the makings of a frothy beach movie. Enter brooding Reed as the twenty-something Tinker, a fliptalking bohemian pickup artist with an identity crisis. Tinker is out to (in the parlance of the film) pluck the birds that fly through his resort town, until he meets a worldly model whose sophistication blows his hip facade away. As he wakes up one morning next to a clueless sweet young thing (his latest conquest) chirping about true love it finally sinks in: he's simply another self-centered cad with a smooth line. Shot by later director Nicolas Roeg in handsome black-and-white and sporting a few splashy tricks from *A Hard Day's Night, The Girl Getters* turns the fun-and-frolic youth film on its ass with frank discussions of sex and a mood that turns from sunny irresponsibility to moody melancholy in the dying days of summer. —*S. A.*

HOUSE OF CARDS L: FOREIGN/BRITISH DRAMA (1990) 225M D: Paul Seed. *Ian Richardson, Miles Anderson, Susannah Harker.* Based on the novel by Michael Dobbs, this is a fascinating story of the abuses and excesses of power. At the beginning of this three-part British drama, Francis Urquhart (Richards) is a Tory whip in Parliament who befriends a young female reporter and leaks inside information to her that helps to ruin the new prime minister. And so, who should take the reins of government except Urquhart (who is also known as FU)? This seasoned politician gleefully tells you what's on his cruel, conniving mind through intermittent voice-over monologues. Followed by *To Play The King*(1993) and *The Final Cut*(1995). —*N. J.*

I, CLAUDIUS L: FOREIGN/BRITISH DRAMA (1976) 650M D: Herbert Wise. *Derek Jacobi, John Hurt, George Baker, Brian Blessed, Sian Phillips.* One of the great TV events and a landmark drama, this grandly written, finely performed thirteen-part adaptation of Robert Graves's historical portrait of the Roman Caesars has more backstabbing intrigue than a dozen soap operas. Jacobi stutters and slinks his through the background of epic treachery and unthinking decadence, a noble historian hidden in a crippled body, keeping stock of the secret alliances and stashes of poison as his "loving" family members murder one another in their grab for power. Phillips is ruthless as matriarch Livia and Hurt almost hijacks the series as the mad, depraved Caligula, licking his chops and laughing like a madman through the most outrageous humiliations and displays of power he could muster. Like most British TV productions of the time, it was shot on video, but once you get caught up in the drama you barely even notice. —*S. A.*

LAST MINUTE, THE L: FOREIGN/BRITISH DRAMA (2002) 104M D: Stephen Norrington. *Max Beesley, Emily Corrie, Tom Bell, Jason Isaacs.* An artist of some kind (it's left up to the imagination) becomes an overnight star, hobnobbing with high-powered agents and appearing on Japanese talk shows. But the next day the public turns on him, his girlfriend kicks him out of their apartment, he projectile vomits on a cab driver, and before he knows it he's living underground with a gang of tough-talking pickpocket children. This surreal tale of an artist's woe is director Norrington's low-budget, semi-autobiographical follow-up to *Blade*. At times it's pretentious and the storytelling gets murky, but it's worthwhile for the vivid cinematography and the occasional great idea. I especially love the elite nightclub where VIPs sit in illuminated inflatable chairs surrounded by masochists having surgery. —*B. T.*

MRS. BROWN L: FOREIGN/BRITISH DRAMA (1997) 105M D: John Madden. *Judi Dench, Billy Connolly, Geoffrey Palmer, Antony Sher.* Dench is astounding in the role of Queen Victoria. When her husband, Prince Albert, dies in 1861, Victoria was thrust into a perpetual state of mourning. She would continue visiting her large Scottish estate at Balmoral, but without her husband nothing seemed quite the same. As she began to rely more heavily on her servants for company she soon discovered that she most preferred the company of a certain Scotsman she simply called Mr. Brown. He was a humble servant at Balmoral who had the charge of taking the Queen out for horse rides in the countryside. Her interest and trust in him began to run so deep that she soon brought him to London. He

became so much a part of her immediate company that the merciless newspapers eventually began referring to her as "Mrs. Brown." Largely based on her extensive writings, historical fact, and newspaper stories, this film is a remarkably well-balanced story reflecting the more private side of an older Queen Victoria. —*N. J.*

NEIL GAIMAN'S NEVERWHERE L: FOREIGN/BRITISH DRAMA (1996) 180M D: Dewi Humphreys. *Paterson Joseph, Laura Fraser, Hywel Bennett, Clive Russell, Tanya Moodie, Gary Bakewell.* This TV series by writer and comic-book author Neil Gaiman unfortunately did not get the quality treatment it deserved. While Gaiman wanted it to be shot on film, the limited budget forced him to contend with shooting on video and cutting some of his original concepts. Still, despite this and other cheap decisions made by the production company (like the Beast of London being. . . a bull), the series is still striking and compelling because of Gaiman's extraordinary writing. With a blend of modernism, magic, and mythology, Gaiman brings to life the world of NeverWhere, the place where those who have slipped between the cracks of this world find themselves. Average everyday working joe Richard (Bakewell) finds himself dragged into this world when he chooses to help a young girl named Door (Fraser) who is running for her life. Suddenly unseen by the rest of the world, Richard must find Door and help her in order to regain his life. It's a twisted, dark fairy tale of a series, with a complicated world all its own where there are rules to be followed, others to be broken, and dangerous adversaries at every turn. The show is especially a delight for anyone familiar with London, for Gaiman utilizes actual places, such as abandoned subway stations, giving their strange names new (and also old) meanings. —*M. N.*

PHOTOGRAPHING FAIRIES L: FOREIGN/BRITISH DRAMA (1997) 106M D: Nick Willing. *Toby Stephens, Emily Woof, Ben Kingsley, Frances Barber.* In Charles Sturridge's *FairyTale: A True Story*, the real-life tale of two little girls and a photograph that fired up a nation, the factual existence of fairies is secondary to the discovery of the fairies within us. Willing's *Photographing Fairies* (from the novel by Steve Szilagyi and inspired by the same true story) takes the same essential point in a completely different direction. Where *Fairy Tale* blossoms into a warmhearted family film about the power of imagination, faith, and innocence, *Photographing Fairies* burrows into the mourning soul of a British photographer (Stephens), numb from the death of his newlywed wife and hardened by the horror of WWI, who finds a startlingly different kind of salvation. A hallucinogenic flower unlocks the ability to see the fairies, contact with them unleashes pent-up sexuality in erotic and vivid dreams, and belief seems to draw one toward death. Willing's sophisticated mix of memory, dream, fantasy, and hallucinogenic imagery is a decidedly adult fairy-tale, an elegantly told excursion into the dark reaches of one man's haunted soul. —S. A.

RATCATCHER L: FOREIGN/BRITISH DRAMA (1998) 93M D: Lynne Ramsay. *Willam Eadie, Tommy Flanagan, Mandy Matthews.* Ramsay's unhurried debut is set in Glasgow's housing projects during the 1973 sanitation strikes. The film's most jarring drama is dispensed with minutes into the film, and from then on *Ratcatcher* maintains a comfortable stasis. Through the eyes of preteen protagonist James, *Ratcatcher's* portrait of childhood takes the form of a collection of scenes of family life. Out of what seems like a genuine fascination with her characters (perhaps more precisely with her cast and script), Ramsay shows a palpable affection for all her characters, while at the same time exposing their imperfect human nature. *Ratcatcher's* unsentimental beauty relies on atmosphere (largely through Alwin Kuchler's excellent cinematography) over melodrama, with a tone reminiscent of Terrence Malick or Terence Davies. The extras-packed DVD includes Ramsay's excellent early shorts. —C. B.

SINGING DETECTIVE, THE L: FOREIGN/BRITISH DRAMA (1986) 415M D: Jon Amiel. *Michael Gambon, Patrick Malahide, Joanne Whalley, Lyndon Davies.* Pulp author Philip Marlow (Gambon) is an angry, sharp-tongued misanthrope hospitalized for a debilitating skin rash that has turned his entire body into a lobster-red mass of scabbed and peeling skin, as if all his guilt and self-loathing have bubbled to the surface. Battling pain and boredom, Marlowe retreats from his gloomy hospital ward by imagining himself into the cold-blooded hide of a suave private-eye hero of a hard-boiled detective fantasy, but it's no safe haven from himself. Hallucinations break into his reality, repressed memories interrupt his mystery, and soon his subconscious seems to take over the story. Dennis Potter's multiple narratives start to blur at the edges as names and faces reappear and resonate across stories, and events are reimagined and replayed from one narrative to another. Gone are all pretenses of a traditional mystery (or a linear narrative for that matter) as a far more complex story is created out of the latticework, connections strung out across the stories like a cobweb. Director Amiel (*Queen of Hearts*) blends it all with simple but striking images and a dream logic: the world through Marlow's guilt-colored glasses. —S. A.

THEY MADE ME A FUGITIVE L: FOREIGN/BRITISH DRAMA (1947) 103M D: Alberto Cavalcanti *Sally Gray, Trevor Howard, Renee Ray, Mary Merrall.* Probably the closest the British cinema ever came to creating a true film noir, Cavalcanti's grimy crime thriller stars Howard in a superb performance as a reckless ex-serviceman who turns to crime for a lark. Double-crossed and framed for murder by a narcissistic mob boss (Jones), he escapes a hard,

bitter, ruthless figure, his cheery old self buried under scar tissue of hate, vowing vengeance as the cops close in. Cavalcanti's British underworld is a claustrophobic and shadowy, with rain-slicked streets and dark alleys, and his edgy direction has never been more taut and violent. Underneath this stark style bubbles the true psychosis of noir characters driven by anger, fear, and just plain sadism. —S. A.

TO PLAY THE KING L: FOREIGN/BRITISH DRAMA (1993) 212M D: Paul Seed. *Ian Richardson, Bernice Stegers, Kitty Aldridge, Diane Fletcher, Michael Kitchen.* In this, the sequel to *House of Cards*, Prime Minister Urquhart (Richards) uses all of his political influence to rid himself of a liberally minded king. In this futuristic fiction, the queen has died and the new king (it's not said to be Charles) has serious marital problems (with a woman who looks like Diana) and tries asserting his authority over the conservative prime minister. Through Machiavellian tactics and a forced election, Urquhart comes out on top and embarrasses the king to force an abdication. The young prince (it's not said to be William) takes the throne. Followed by *The Final Cut.* —N. J.

TRAFFIK L: FOREIGN/BRITISH DRAMA (1990) 360M D: Alastair Reid. *Lindsay Duncan, Bill Paterson, Julia Ormond, Linda Bassett.* The popularity of the film *Traffic* in 2000 is owed to this six-part English TV miniseries. A Tory antidrug minister (the equivalent in America to a Republican drug czar) cracks down as hard as he can on drug trafficking from the Middle East and eventually discovers that his own daughter is hooked on the very drug he is trying to curb. Faced with members of his party insisting that he legislate stiff prosecution for users, this minister broadens his education into the larger picture of the drug world in order to save his daughter. This excellent series has plenty of time to develop subplots, especially those plots concerning a grower of poppies in Pakistan and his German dealer. —N. J.

TWICE UPON A YESTERDAY (AKA **THE MAN WITH RAIN IN HIS SHOES**) L: FOREIGN/BRITISH DRAMA (1998) 96M D: Maria Ripoll. *Douglas Henshall, Lena Headey, Penelope Cruz.* In the magic land of the United Kingdom, if one is confronted with hopelessness, happens to be at the dump, dons a blindfold, and spins about in a circle, amazing and mysterious things can happen, like time travel. Sounds like *Dr. Who*, but it's a romantic comedy about an out-of-work actor and his philandering. Generally, I think blending time travel, or a whole lot of fate crap, or angels, with romance can only end in disaster, but somehow this movie seems to rise above its own shaky plot, and you have a really cute guy with a Scottish accent just trying to protect his guitar. —J. J.

VERY BRITISH COUP, A L: FOREIGN/BRITISH DRAMA (1989) 153M D: Mick Jackson. *Ray McAnally, Alan MacNaughtan, Keith Allen, Geoffrey Beevers.* Mr. Smith goes to 10 Downing Street in this delicious British miniseries. McAnally's Harry Perkins is a working-class miner turned politician and Labor Party leader, swept into office by a landslide as Britain's first Socialist Prime Minister. Smart, savvy, and witty, he's no one's patsy, which is good because the establishment (from career government leaders to conservative industrialists and monopolists) has declared a covert war on his party. Cynical and devious and clear-eyed about the reality of politics, it's not really a comedy because all the dark, satirical humor underlies the devious games and dirty tricks. It's a fantasy grounded in ideals and idealism: a portrait of a government of the people, by the people, and for the people. —S.A.

WICKER MAN, THE L: FOREIGN/BRITISH DRAMA (1973) 117M D: Robin Hardy. *Christopher Lee, Britt Ekland, Edward Woodward, Ingrid Pitt.* This cult classic is a fun jab at conservative ideology and religious morality. The film takes place on the island of Sommersisle off of Scotland in the early '70s when an anonymous letter to a policeman on the mainland (Woodward) brings his attention to a missing twelve-year-old girl. A thorough policeman, he gets on his plane to go investigate the missing child. He receives a less than enthusiastic welcoming party and what proceeds is a series of misleading conversations, misinformation, and lies. The officer smells a cover-up, and he's going to get to the bottom of things. Meanwhile, his WASP ethics are challenged by the pagan whores that romp around naked and free, testing his virgin will and tormenting his thoughts. Although a dated film with its cheesy summer-of-love tone and equally hard to listen to music, it still manages to capture an element of the eerie and strange and has a rather unexpected shock ending. If you have the opportunity make sure to watch the 2001 director's cut-it's well worth the extra scenes. —B.W.

WONDERLAND L: FOREIGN/BRITISH DRAMA (1999) 108M D: Michael Winterbottom. *Gina McKee, Shirley Henderson, Molly Parker.* McKee is heartbreaking as the desperately seeking single Nadia, the closest to a center Winterbottom has in his delicate portrait of family, friends, and lovers in South London. Along with her sisters (single mom Henderson, a mix of adolescent passion and emotional scar tissue, and the married, pregnant, and on the edge of hysterics Parker) she careens through the streets of London over a long weekend. Winterbottom draws sensitive, intense performances and captures a nervous spontaneity with his shot-on-the-street immediacy. While there's little new or surprising in the intertwining stories, Winterbottom's intimacy makes their ache and sadness all the more palpable and invests the script's lucky coincidences with a dramatic

power that overcomes the clichés. It transforms the fog of melancholy into a celebration of hope, of chance, and the promise of possibility in a new day. —S.A.

BRITISH TELEVISION

BLACK ADDER: THE COMPLETE COLLECTOR'S SET L: FOREIGN/BRITISH TV (1989) 860M D: Mandie Fletcher. *Tony Robinson, Rowan Atkinson.* Spanning four distinct periods of English history, *Black Adder* is about as British as British humor can get. The first period concerns the would-be Richard IV, the Black Prince who was defeated in the battle of Bosworth Field in 1485. In these episodes the prince survives and becomes king because of the ineptitude of Edmund, Duke of Edinburgh (Atkinson). The second period, naturally, is the time of Queen Elizabeth circa 1570s. Atkinson plays Lord Edmund who tries to curry favor from the crazy queen. The third period concerns the Prince of Wales, son of King George III, whose manservant is Edmund Blackadder Esq. Curiously, as Prince George was supposed to be extremely rotund, the very skinny Robinson playing him didn't dress big but simply delivered his lines as though everyone would simply know he was fat, presuming most English would understand the stretch. The fourth period concerns World War I, where Captain Blackadder wants to escape the throes of war without seeming to betray the cause. His other men, played by all the familiar actors, are none the wary. The BBC Complete Collector's Set on DVD includes the feature-length film set in the twenty-first century where Lord Blackadder is able to time-warp to all the places of English history he would have loved to have parodied but didn't get a chance to. For instance, Atkinson gets to curse Shakespeare for writing all that stuff he was forced to study. This DVD set also includes lots of extras the die-hard fan will not want to miss. —N.J.

CHOCKY L: FOREIGN/BRITISH TV (1984) 30M D: Victor Hughes, Christopher Hodson. *Zoe Hart, James Hazeldine, Prentis Hancock, Glynis Brooks, Annabel Lorrell.* Chocky is an alien who has traveled far from home to teach the world about cosmic energy. He is only able to communicate with certain children. These children then become best friends with Chocky, and with his help they are able to see the world in a different way. They start baffling scientists with their unorthodox, groundbreaking discoveries. Its like *Escape from Witch Mountain* meets *Little Man Tate*. Genius kid stories rule. Make sure to also look for the second and third series called *Chocky's Children* and *Chocky's Challenge*. —R.D.

COUPLING: SEASON 1 L: FOREIGN/BRITISH TV (2000) 175M D: Martin Dennis. *Ben Miles, Jack Davenport, Gina Bellman, Sarah Alexander, Kate Isitt, Richard*

Coyle. Hitting the magical mixture of sex, smarts, satire, and smutty humor that every American sex farce aspires to, this hilarious British sitcom is less about the war between the sexes than the ongoing negotiations. Davenport and Alexander lead the sextet of thirtysomething singles as a brave couple who try to maintain a stable relationship while temptation looms and their friends continue their randy ways. Coyle stands out as the man-child with a theory for every occasion. The damnably clever scripts by Steven Moffat are grounded in the clash between the head, the heart, and regions south, and he suggests all those words you can't utter on TV so deviously that you practically hear them in your mind's ear. But behind the laughs and cockeyed comedy are inspired observations of women and men and the difficult compromises a single person makes to couple. Being a British production, this "complete season" runs all of six episodes on a single disc, but it packs more laughs in those half-dozen episodes than most American sitcoms get in their twenty-plus episode season. —*S. A.*

FAWLTY TOWERS L: FOREIGN/BRITISH TV (1975) 500M D: Howard Davies, Douglas Argent, others. *John Cleese, Prunella Scales, Andrew Sachs, Connie Booth.*
This classic British comedy series features a bed and breakfast run by Basil Fawlty (Cleese) and his wife, Sybil (Scales). Among their hired hands is a young maid (Booth) and a Spanish bellhop (Sachs) whose English is never quite up to snuff. Even though it only ran for twelve episodes, the situation comedy that results is one of the finest ever crafted for broadcast. Some of the highlights include "The Germans," where German guests are accidentally yet constantly reminded of the war by a confused Basil; "The Anniversary," where Basil plans a surprise for his wife's anniversary and everything backfires; and "The Kipper and the Corpse," where Basil and Manuel try to hide a deceased guest. If you speak the English language and are capable of laughing, this series will not disappoint. —*N. J.*

HITCHHIKER'S GUIDE TO THE GALAXY TV L: FOREIGN/BRITISH TV (1981) 190M D: Alan J. W. Bell. *Mark Wing Davey, Sandra Dickinson, David Dixon, Simon Jones, Peter Jones.*
This adaptation of Douglas Adams's humorous interstellar comedy was made for the BBC with a rather slim budget. The computer cutaways and graphic demonstrations accompanied by Jones's wonderful narration are right on target, but the mechanical papier-mâché head of Bieblebrox is about as embarrassing as special effects can get. But all the original humor of the novel and the remarkable radio series is here intact, so fans of the book would do well to put up with some desperation of production in order to see these great actors realize this hilarious sci-fi story. —*N. J.*

I'M ALAN PARTRIDGE L: FOREIGN/BRITISH TV (1997) 180M D: Dominic Brigstocke. *Steve Coogan, Felicity Montagu, Barbara Durkin, Simon Greenall, Sally Phillips.*
"A-ha!" Alan Partridge: motivational speaker, TV talk-show host, and now early morning radio-show host in Norwich, residing in a roadside motel. Coogan has created a brilliant character: egotistical, narcissistic, hurtful, pigheaded, stupid, yet retaining just enough humanity that we still like him. . . a little. The joy of the show is watching Alan make an ass out of himself. Whether offending Irish television execs ("Sunday, bloody Sunday!") or interrupting a funeral to talk on his cell phone, Alan's always victorious, at least in his mind. This is the funniest show to come out of England in a long time. —*K. C.*

LOUIS THEROUX'S WEIRD WEEKENDS L: FOREIGN/BRITISH TV (1997) 114M D: Geoffrey O'Connor. *Louis Theroux.*
When he was on *TV Nation*, Louis Theroux was funny because he could get people to trust him and then say horrible things. For example, there was one where a white supremacist showed him a racist birthday card. He pretended to not understand the joke and got the guy to go through point by point and explain why he thought it was funny. What makes Theroux's BBC series *Weird Weekends* even better is that he is much more sympathetic toward his subjects, no matter how strange their lifestyles are. Each week he explores an American subculture (gay porn stars, UFO watchers, demolition-derby drivers, gangsta rappers) and then tries to involve himself in its activities. When he gets a shot at selling a paper shredder live on QVC he doesn't condescend at all—instead he tries his best and seems devastated when his pitch is not very successful. It's a very funny, very human, and occasionally very sad portrait of the people around you who you may not have known you'd want to meet. Unfortunately it has not been released on an American format (just two "best of" volumes on PAL code 2 DVD). —*B. T.*

MONTY PYTHON'S THE MEANING OF LIFE L: FOREIGN/MONTY PYTHON (1983) 107M D: Terry Gilliam, Terry Jones. *Graham Chapman, John Cleese, Terry Gilliam, Eric Idle, Terry Jones, Michael Palin.*
The final creative reunion of the five overeducated British comics (and one American illustrator and humorist turned animator and director) better known collectively as Monty Python's Flying Circus is a return to the sketch format of their television days, but with no holds barred: sex education with practical illustrations, bloody organ transplants from reluctant live donors, death by topless nubile young joggers, and a tribute to the sacredness of sperm. The latter, a high-energy, brightly colored song-and-dance production number that could have come from a kinky remake of *Oliver!,* is one of the highlights of a film that is admittedly inconsistent but often inspired and hilarious. The infamous "Mr. Creosote" sketch

mixes gag and gag reflex equally ("Just a way-fur theen meent!") and Terry Gilliam's contribution "The Crimson Permanent Assurance," a swashbuckling pirate parody with white-haired accountants mutinying against their uptight bosses and sailing their skyscraper into high seas of high finance, is a short film in itself, played as a short subject before the film proper. According to Terry Jones, that is what landed them their Jury Prize at Cannes. —*S. A.*

MONTY PYTHON: THE LIFE OF BRIAN L: FOREIGN/MONTY PYTHON (1979) 94M D: Terry Gilliam. *Eric Idle, Graham Chapman, Terry Gilliam, Terry Jones, Michael Palin, John Cleese.* Here's a peculiar comedy concerning misidentification. In this irreverent film, a baby is born just down the road from the infant Jesus and a group of admirers drop into the wrong place. For the rest of his life, Brian tries fending off fanatic believers who insist he is the Christ and believe everything he says except when he says he's not their savior. To rigid Christian fundamentalists, there is nothing in this film to enjoy. For the rest of the world this is an excellent and memorable parody about exactly those kind of people. —*N. J.*

MR. BEAN L: FOREIGN/BRITISH TV (1989) 30M D: John Birkin, Paul Weiland. *Rowan Atkinson.* Evidently, good slapstick is not quite dead. Mr. Bean (brilliantly played by Atkinson) is the absurdly simpleminded fellow who always seems to turn everyday activities into impossibly labyrinthine chores. Something as simple as building a sandwich or doing his laundry or going out for a swim is somehow twisted into an epic struggle of man vs nature. And then, just in case you may have missed his sensitive human side, Mr. Bean will pull out his trusted teddy bear, which easily demands our empathy for simply being in the care of such a clod. This series inspired a feature film as well as a bizarre cartoon series. —*N. J.*

OFFICE, THE L: FOREIGN/BRITISH TV (2001) 180M D: Ricky Gervais, Stephen Merchant *Ricky Gervais, Lucy Davis, Martin Freeman, Mackenzie Crook.* Creator/co-writer/codirector Gervais is David Brent, the insufferably self-satisfied office manager of a paper company branch who fancies himself a born comedian and a natural leader. He's wrong about both, naturally, but his yes-man team-leader Gareth (Crook), a brownnoser with delusions of competency, hasn't noticed, and white-collar joker Tim (Freeman) is too worried about his job to say anything to his boss. Apart from the interviews interspersed through the shows, Gervais and his cocreator Stephen Merchant underplay the mockumentary affectation as they eavesdrop casually on the workplace. Everyone forgets about the camera but Brent, who can't help but bray and play to his audience, mouthing off inanities while he pontificates as the voice of wisdom. This wicked look at workplace politics and oblivious middle management dares to make you wince and squirm with every laugh. In other words, it's a comedy that only British TV could get away with. All six half-hour first-season episodes of pure genius are included on the two-disc DVD set. —*S. A.*

RED DWARF L: FOREIGN/BRITISH TV (1988) 30M D: Various. *Danny John-Jules, Craig Charles, Robert Llewellyn, Chris Barrie.* A mesh of comedy and science fiction, *Red Dwarf* is raunchy, corny, cheesy, and full of bad jokes in the best tradition off British comedy. The music is annoying, the laugh track is turned all the way up, and I love every cotton-picking minute. A radiation leak kills everyone on board the space ship Red Dwarf. Three million years later, Dave Lister (Charles), the chicken soup–machine repairman, emerges from suspended animation. The only other occupants of the ship are a hologram representation of Lister's archenemy Arnold Rimmer (Barrie), a swanky dude who evolved from a cat (John-Jules), and Kryten (Llewellyn), a mechanoid guy. The fact that this series has a fucking *mechanoid* should sort of give you an idea of the geek factor. Not that that is a bad thing. In fact, I recommend renting several episodes and wallowing in the fact that yes, you are a huge fucking nerd. —*J. S.*

RIPPING YARNS L: FOREIGN/BRITISH TV (1995) 90M D: Various. *Michael Palin, Terry Jones.* By far the most difficult way to put together a television series is to dispense with a regular cast of characters and create each episode from scratch (*Twilight Zone* and *Outer Limits* are examples). But in comedy it's a harder sell since an audience prefers the return of funny characters. The short-lived British series is unique in that way. Palin and Jones (from Monty Python) create some of the most peculiar comic situations ever seen on television. "Escape from Stalag Luft 112B" accounts for the unlikely escape of a British prisoner in WWII with the help of hundreds of toilet paper cores; "The Curse of the Claw" parodies most every aspect of British gothic horror; and "Tomkinson's Schooldays" features an old-style English boarding school with a perfectly masochistic headmaster and ridiculously sadistic upperclassmen. If you're in any way a fan of Monty Python then *Ripping Yarns* is a must-see. —*N. J.*

YEAR IN PROVENCE, A: WINTER/SPRING L: FOREIGN/BRITISH TV (1993) 180M D: David Tucker. *Gabrielle Anwar, Lindsay Duncan, John Thaw, Jean-Pierre Delage.* I was beginning my freshman year in high school when I saw this with my best friend at the request of his mom. I actually remember it being very interesting; I hadn't really been exposed to anything French at the time so I was eager to sponge the cultural fodder it was providing: "Oh how interesting, they're using pigs to find truffles." I saw that we had a copy in the store the other day and decided to pick it up. Never had I seen such mass bourgeois indulgence so shamelessly on display, this side of Merchant and Ivory at least. The overgeneralizations made on the culture and people of Southern France in this miniseries are too many and too laughable to repeat. After seeing this again, I can't even begin to imagine what a dickhead I must have been in high school. —*T. C.*

YOUNG ONES, THE: EVERY STOOPID L: FOREIGN/BRITISH TV (1982) 400M D: Paul Jackson, Geoff Posner. *Christopher Ryan, Rik Mayall, Adrian Edmondson, Nigel Planer, Alexei Sayle.* The Young Ones was a wild twelve-episode BBC comedy series that celebrated (and spoofed) anarchistic punk rock attitude, slapstick violence, and the slacker college lifestyle. Four students (a hippy, a punk, a pseudo-socialist poet, and a slick ladies man) share a flat in England. Each episode features a ridiculous plot (like a nuclear bomb landing in the kitchen) and a guest band (some are great, like Motorhead, and some are pretty bad, like the "body popping" guy). Some of the jokes don't make much sense (being either dated or too British-specific) but the humor comes so fast and furious that it doesn't matter. Every episode is packed with strange asides and other odd touches that make the stories unpredictable and dense with funny details. My favorite is probably "Bambi," where the boys are on a college quiz show, but hell, they're all pretty damn great! As a bonus the DVD comes with an extra disc with documentaries and a couple other related TV shows. —*S. H.*

BURKINA FASO

YAABA L: FOREIGN/BURKINA FASO (1989) 90M D: Idrissa Ouedraogo. *Fatimata Sanga, Noufou Ouedraogo, Adama Ouedraogo, Roukietou Barry.* A slight film shot in a tiny village on a barren-looking West African landscape, Yaaba is a fable-like movie about the relationship between Bila, a young boy generally dismissed as a troublemaker, and Sana, a withered old woman rumored to be a witch. Its folklore preoccupation isn't always especially engaging, and it is at its best when focused on the tendency of petty personal dramas to escalate into turmoil affecting the whole community. Western audiences will probably recognize these people's day-to-day problems as not much different from their own-which brings up an interesting issue. Watching Yaaba, one wonders to what degree West African director Ouedraogo is addressing the West African people the film depicts, and to what degree he's specifically addressing a Western audience. In my opinion, it is chiefly this question, concerning nothing less than the limitations of the film medium, that makes Yaaba an intriguing film. —*C. B.*

CANADA

BETWEEN STRANGERS L: FOREIGN/CANADA (2002) 98M D: Edoardo Ponti. *Sophia Loren, Mira Sorvino, Deborah Kara Unger, Pete Postlethwaite, Klaus Maria Brandauer, Malcolm McDowell.* Ponti, the son of Italian producing legend Carlo Ponti and cinema icon Sophia Loren, makes his feature debut with this intimate but unreal portrait of three women. Sorvino is an award-winning war photographer whose missing memory of a battlefield photo holds the key to her unhappiness. Unger (her face hard and tortured) is a cellist who has abandoned her family to stalk a lonely, empty old man (McDowell) just released from prison, and Loren is deeply affecting as an aging woman numb from the years of dismissive treatment from a bitter wheelchair-bound husband (Postlethwaite). Haggard and worn, her eyes sunken into resignation, the tired lines of her face etching a lifetime of disappointment, Loren brings depth to a woman looking to connect with her past through her drawings, and delicacy to a very careful film that tries so hard yet rarely gets past the textured surface. —*S. A.*

BIG CRIMEWAVE, THE L: FOREIGN/CANADA (1986) 80M D: John Paizs. *Eva Kovacs, John Paizs.* From the north comes this tragically obscure movie with a great vintage look, about Steven Penny (played by the director), a screenwriter with a severe case of writer's block. He wants to make the "best color crime-movie ever" but can only think of the beginnings and endings of a story. Kim (Kovacs), his young neighbor and the film's narrator, helps Steven find his perfect "middle." Inspired by '50s educational films, crime movies, pulp fiction, and Fellini's 8½, it features an unpredictable plot in which Steven is threatened by a weird serial killer and visited by many of his fictional characters, including an Elvis impersonator. Originally titled *Crime Wave*, the *Big* was added later to ease confusion with the Coen brothers/Sam Raimi film of the same title. —*S. H.*

CLEARCUT L: FOREIGN/CANADA (1992) 100M D: Ryszard Bugajski. *Ron Lea, Graham Greene, Michael Hogan, Rebecca Jenkins.* Greene plays Arthur, a pissed-off North American Indian man who wants revenge for the clear-cutting of an old-growth forest on a reservation. The object of his anger is the corporate executive who's responsible. In the middle is a leftist lawyer whose idiotic liberal guilt guides his feeble attempts at mediation. Although Arthur seems to be ruled by his anger, his revenge and desire for redemption are justified by the actions of corporate terrorists. The story takes place in the beautiful Canadian wilderness and the viewer sees some heart-wrenching shots of old-growth forests, before and after. Pay attention to the opening and closing water scenes, as well as the sweat lodge. Is Arthur just

a man or the manifestation of something deeper and more spiritual? —*B. W.*

FAST RUNNER, THE L: FOREIGN/CANADA (2001) 172M D: Zacharias Kunuk. *Natar Ungalaaq, Sylvia Ivalu, Peter-Henry Arnatsiaq.* Winner of the 2001 Caméra d'Or at Cannes and the first feature to be made in the Inuktitut language, this mythic struggle of good and evil on the endless horizon of a beautiful and unforgiving frozen desert is more than just a primal adventure. Inspired by an ancient Inuit myth of evil spirits and human greed, the evocative but simple story revolves around young hunter Atanarjuat (the jovial, personable Ungalaaq) who is sent running for his life, barefoot and naked, across the barren plain, when a pathologically jealous rival turns malevolent and murderous. Director/cowriter Kunuk immerses the viewer in the very texture of the land, the rituals, and the pace of the Inuktitut culture. Like the best of foreign cinema, this is as much about the way a culture tells and understands its stories as it is about the story itself. For almost three hours, *The Fast Runner* invites the viewer to experience a timeless culture on the edge of an unforgiving earth, and a world that moves at its own measured pace. The result is epic, entrancing, and utterly spellbinding. —*S. A.*

MAZES AND MONSTERS L: FOREIGN/CANADA (1982) 100M D: Steven Stern. *Tom Hanks, Wendy Crewson, Chris Makepeace, David Wallace, Lloyd Bochner.* This paranoid TV movie is a time capsule of the days when parents were afraid Dungeons & Dragons would drive their children to murder. (I wonder what would have happened if those parents could've peeked into the future to see *Grand Theft Auto*?) The plot involves a group of clean-cut college students who play the fictional fantasy role-playing game of the title. They become increasingly more addicted until one of the group is driven insane and wanders New York thinking he's on a magical quest. What makes this amusing to modern-day audiences is that he's played by two-time Academy Award winner for Best Actor Hanks. —*B. T.*

MEN WITH BROOMS L: FOREIGN/CANADA (2002) 102M D: Paul Gross. *Leslie Nielsen, Peter Outerbridge, Paul Gross, Molly Parker.* Think *The Full Monty* on ice. Canada's most famous TV Mountie, Gross (*Due South*) puts tongue firmly in cheek as he applies the old underdog sports-team formula to that great Northern obsession: curling. (You thought hockey was the national obsession? So did Canada). Gross directs, cowrites, produces, and stars as the amiable team skip (that's curling talk for captain) who reunites his estranged teammates to fulfill a dead man's last request, win glory for their fictional hometown, and earn back their hibernating self-respect. Parker is his old drinking buddy with an unresolved crush and Nielsen (playing a real character for a change) is his estranged father turned crotch-

ety coach. Don't expect any surprises along the way, just settle back for the deadpan delivery of a modest and, yes, entertaining little film with big stones and the biggest herd of beavers you've ever seen. —*S. A.*

PROJECT GRIZZLY L: FOREIGN/CANADA (1996) 72M D: Peter Lynch. *Troy Hurtubise.* Naturalist by education, macho mountain man by temperament, obsessive by nature, Hurtubise is driven to recapture the rush of his first against-all-odds survival of a face-to-face with a wild grizzly. So he builds himself a robo-suit and field tests the Buzz Lightyear–looking contraption by pummeling it with logs, speeding trucks, and drunks with baseball bats. Hurtubise is completely serious, staggering about like Robbie the Robot in the deep woods, and while director Lynch's deadpan delivery paints the entire enterprise as somewhat off-balance (and often quite hilarious), Hurtubise retains a queer Quixotic dignity that the constant setbacks and failures can't deny. —*S. A.*

WRONG GUY, THE L: FOREIGN/CANADA (1997) 94M D: David Steinberg. *Colm Feore, David Higgins, Dave Foley, Jennifer Tilly, Dan Redican, Kevin McDonald.* This is one of the funniest movies I have ever seen, and maybe the only movie I've ever actually laughed so hard at that I cried. If you are a fan of *Kids in the Hall* and Dave Foley, you will love this film. He stars as Nelson Hibbert, the oblivious dorky guy who is engaged to his boss's second favorite daughter, which he believes should entitle him to a promotion to company president. When Ken Daley (Redican), the fiancé of the boss's first favorite daughter, is given the promotion instead, Nelson becomes enraged and threatens to kill him. When the boss turns up dead at the hands of someone else and Nelson is the one to discover the body, he instantly assumes everyone will think he is the murderer and flees from the law, certain they are after him. The rest of the movie shows Nelson "on the run" from the police who aren't after him as he accidentally keeps ending up in situations with the real killer. Throw in a narcoleptic Jennifer Tilly, and you've got a total masterpiece. —*J. S.*

CHINA

GREAT WALL, A (AKA **THE GREAT WALL IS A GREAT WALL**) L: FOREIGN/CHINA (1986) 102M D: Peter Wang. *Peter Wang, Sharon Iwai, Kelvin Han Yee, Qinqin Li.* Taiwanese-born Wang directs and stars in this gentle culture clash comedy of a thoroughly Americanized Chinese-American family gone to China to meet the relatives. The "first American comedy shot in China," as it was promoted in 1986, takes an innocent peek behind the wall, possible only before the Tiananmen Square massacre; the cultural revolution and social repression are but fleeting shadows in the background. The lessons of the film are nothing revolutionary—teenagers are the same the world over, communication is not simply a matter of language, and a healthy cultural cross-fertilization can only make us richer—but Wang comes to them with a warmth. —*S. A.*

QUITTING L: FOREIGN/CHINA (2001) 112M D: Zhang Yang. *Chai Xiuling, Jia Fengsen, Jia Hongsheng.* "This is a true story," proclaims the film as the last image fades out. The actual participants in this story of Chinese film idol turned heroine-addicted dropout Jia—his parents (veteran stage actors themselves), sister, and even director Zhang—re-create their real-life roles in interviews and dramatic re-creations. This act of exploration and dramatic reinterpretation adds an evocative level to an already compelling portrait of paranoia, alienation, and mental breakdown. Zhang's modernist mosaic jumps through time and through perspectives, yet hews to a surprisingly conservative message: the self-destructive rebellion of a youth culture transformed by Western influence is healed by the devotion of family. The complexity sometimes becomes confusing and clues that might seem obvious to a Chinese audience can be vague to us, but the total effect is mesmerizing, an eye-opening tour of modern Beijing culture in a journey of rebellion, retreat into oblivion, and return. —*S. A.*

SHOWER L: FOREIGN/CHINA (1999) 92M D: Yang Zhang. *Xu Zhu, He Zeng, Wu Jiang, Quanxin Pu.* Old and new China collide in the award-winning drama of a family-run bathhouse in a crumbling Beijing neighborhood marked for demolition. The proprietor's estranged eldest son, now part of China's modern business culture, returns home for what begins as a wary reunion but ultimately turns into a warm reconciliation. The title of the film nicely captures the central struggle between the traditional and the modern: the long, soothing baths in a communal setting are supplanted by the energy- and time-efficient shower. Zhang populates his film with neighborhood characters and creates a lovely sense of community moving at the speed of lazy conversation. It's more of a sentimental swan song for a dying way of life than a portrait of a culture in transition, but it's a real heart-warmer and a favorite at festivals around the world. —*S. A.*

SO CLOSE TO PARADISE L: FOREIGN/CHINA (1998) 90M D: Wang Xiaoshuai. *Guo Tao, Tong Wang, Yu Shi.* Wang Xiaoshuai (*Frozen*), a member of the "Sixth Generation" of Chinese filmmakers, directs this modern Chinese take on a classic American film noir, a story of small-time criminals on the outskirts of the bustling port city of Wuhan (in Central China) that reverberates with a sense of doom. Narrated by naive country boy Dong Zi (Shi), in the city to make money as a manual laborer (a "shoulder pole" who hauls things to the river and back), he reports on the ambitions of his more urbane pal, Gao Ping (Tao),

who loses a small fortune in a failed scheme and spends the film trying to recover the loot. In the process he kidnaps, rapes, and seduces would-be nightclub singer Ruan Hong (Wang), a karaoke romantic who loses her dashed dreams in a few moments caught in the spotlight. This has a shaggy slickness in comparison to Wang's earlier underground films, but his restless handheld camerawork and grimy locations have a tawdry glamour, from the neon colors cutting through the night to the sunlight flooding daytime rooms with a dusty haze. —*S. A.*

SUZHOU RIVER L: FOREIGN/CHINA (2000) 83M D: Ye Lou. *Hongshen Jia, Xhou Xun, Zhongkai Hua.* The polluted, garbage-strewn river that snakes through Shanghai makes for an inspired metaphor in Lou's melancholy meditation on love, memory, and obsession. At once romantic and repulsive, the Suzhou River is described by the narrator as "the lifeblood of Shanghai," which explains the diseased, crime-ridden world of this mysterious drama and the sense of dislocation and betrayal established by Lou. Moto-delivery boy Mardar (Jia) falls in love with the schoolgirl daughter (Xun) of a smuggler and betrays her trust when he kidnaps her. Meanwhile, the unnamed, unseen narrator, whose world is defined solely by the images he records on his video camera, romances model turned performing mermaid Meimei (also Xun), but it's closer to voyeurism than passion: he likes to watch. Somewhere along the line the stories become impossibly tangled: The two women are played by the same actress and Mardar is either too confused, too obsessed, or too guilt-ridden to tell the difference. With its bobbing camera, lunging jump cuts, interweaving story lines, slipping back and forth in time, and lonely voice-over, it recalls the early work of the Hong Kong master of doomed love and disconnected lovers, Wong Kar Wai. —*S. A.*

CUBA

BITTER SUGAR L: FOREIGN/CUBA (1996) 102M D: Leon Ichaso. *René Lavan, Mayte Vilán, Miguel Gutiérrez.* Ichaso paints an unrelentingly grim portrait of modern Cuba: poverty stricken, repressive, corrupt. Our hero, an idealistic young Marxist somehow blind to the injustice around him, tries to defend his principles in the face of brutal police reprisals against his rebellious rocker brother and the contradictions he finally confronts during a passionate affair with an earthy young dancer. Ichaso's simplistic structure makes his attack at least a little suspect, and his protagonist is practically a straw figure set up for a hard fall. Yet he invests his characters with passion and his images with rich detail (though part of the film was somehow shot in Cuba, Santo Domingo doubled for Havana through the bulk of the feature). If this film were made in America I'd call it didactic and heavy-handed, but Ichaso brings his experience and anger to the film with such force that I can't help but feel his rage. —*S.A.*

LIFE IS TO WHISTLE L: FOREIGN/CUBA (1998) 106M D: Fernando Perez. *Isabel Santos, Coralia Veloz, Claudia Rojas, Bebe Perez, Luis Alberto Garcia.* Every Cuban film that comes to the United States-and there are precious few-arrives loaded with the social and political baggage that we wouldn't dream of heaping on a film from any other country. Any portrait of the tiny island country that has become America's poster child for religious intolerance, political repression, and social despair seems fodder for propaganda. Perez's colorful tapestry of mother Cuba confronts its own identity crisis from within. It's a love letter to Cuba, an earthy and erotic mix of fantasy and street realism full of magic and color and music, by an abandoned child searching for his real mother country, and finding-I'm not exactly sure what. The stories of three orphans searching for happiness become metaphors for Cuba herself, a gorgeous (but overlong at times), abstract journey through one man's ambivalent feelings toward a mother country in an identity crisis. —*S.A.*

CZECH REPUBLIC

DIVIDED WE FALL L: FOREIGN/CZECH REPUBLIC (2001) 122M D: Jan Hrebejk. *Jiri Pecha, Jaroslav Dusek, Boleslav Polivka.* Hrebejk brings a richly humanist vision to the nightmare of the Nazi occupation of Czechoslovakia. A childless Christian couple hides a Jewish concentration camp escapee in an alcove of their apartment while a petty Nazi bureaucrat who counts the couple as his only friends (and pines for his friend's wife) constantly visits and snoops. The fate that ties them all together is full of delightful surprises. Wry humor and moments of slapstick are used to marvelous effect, but it's the fear, weakness, and moments of terror that tear at the resolve of these heroes that makes their drama compelling and their sacrifices all the more affecting. The oddly lurching quality of the image in moments of high tension gets distracting, but the tender core of this lovely portrait of loyalty, forgiveness, and love overcomes such weaknesses. It won every major Czech film award and was nominated for Best Foreign Language film at the 2001 Oscars. —*S.A.*

KOLYA L: FOREIGN/CZECH REPUBLIC (1996) 105M D: Jan Sverak. *Irena Livanova, Ondrej Vetchy, Andrei Khalimon, Zdenek Sverak.* This Oscar-winner for Best Foreign Language Film is one of those fuzzy, warmhearted productions where the cute little kid melts the heart of a crusty old codger and makes everyone feel good. Along the way, though, director Sverak and writer/star Sverak (the director's father) explore some interesting territory, namely the tensions between the Czech citizens and the Russian army that seems to be everywhere. The character of Czechoslovakia in the years leading up to perestroika comes through nicely and there's some good music to boot. There's nothing here you haven't seen before, but the Sveraks do it well. —*S.A.*

DENMARK

ITALIAN FOR BEGINNERS (DOGME #12) L: FOREIGN/DENMARK (2000) 97M D: Lone Scherfig. *Ann Eleonora Jorgensen, Sarah Indrio Jensen, Peter Gantzler, Anette Stovelbaek, Anders W. Berthelsen, Lars Kaalund.* Sherfig, the first woman to make a Dogme-certified film, warms the normally chilly world of prickly characters and damaged souls these films usually encourage with a romantic comedy about the power of love to heal emotional wounds. The six lonely thirtysomethings of a small Denmark town who meet for an Italian-language evening course have survived abusive parents, tragic love lives, and suffocating lives of quiet misery (except for hot-tempered Kaalund, whose misery is anything but hushed), and Sherfig rewards them with bonds of friendship, discovery of lost family, and touching moments of connection. What could be more appropriate than the language of love to thaw these frozen hearts? Sherfig has a fine feel for character and social dynamics, and she takes the onus off the Dogme label by celebrating the triumph of survivors who overcome the gloom, nastiness, and depression around them, and find happiness. —*S.A.*

KING IS ALIVE, THE (DOGME #4) L: FOREIGN/DENMARK (2000) 106M D: Kristian Levring. *Janet McTeer, Bruce Davison, Romaine Bohringer, Jennifer Jason Leigh, David Bradley.* The fourth official film to carry the Dogme 95 seal returns to the favorite theme of the collective: troubled groups put under glass and examined as emotions under pressure are pushed to feral extremes. In this case a disparate group of travelers in the North African desert are stranded in an abandoned village without food, radio contact, or hope, so they stage a production of King Lear to keep up their spirits. Behind-the-scenes tensions, jealousies, and power games mirror the drama with monstrous results. What is starvation next to the destructive potential of the human animal? The desert setting, with its blank canvas surrounding the players like an empty stage, is a natural for the digital video production, which tends to abstract backgrounds as it favors the human face. The unrelenting portrait of human cruelty and pettiness can be overwhelming and alienating at times, but the performances are mesmerizing and Leigh brings a heart to it as the guileless, impulsive Gina (the Cordelia of the group). —*S. A.*

ECUADOR

RATAS RATONES RATEROS L: FOREIGN/ECUADOR (1999) 107M D: Sebastian Cordero. *Irina Lopez, Carlos Valencia, Fabricio Lalama, Marco Bustos.* Naive street punk Salvador (Bustos) finally gets his fatally reckless cousin Angel's number in this down and dirty social drama (you can almost feel the grunge on the film). It tells a familiar story of wrecked lives and doomed spirals of self-destruction, but director Cordero gives his raw tale a real sense of panic as his petty crooks run from one disaster to another, too caught up in the momentum (and in Angel's case the sheer rush of playing the bad boy) to get a fix on their lives. What makes this one different is the sense of hope when Salvador wises up, even as Angel's poisonous influence continues to destroy every life he touches. And it's set to a great soundtrack of Latin punk. —*S. A.*

FRANCE

ADVENTURES OF FELIX, THE L: FOREIGN/FRANCE (2000) 95M D: Olivier Ducastel, Jacques Martineau. *Pierre-Loup Rajot, Ariane Ascaride, Patachou, Sami Bouajila.* The jazzy Blossom Dearie tune that plays as we first see Felix gliding along the seaside on his bicycle perfectly sets the tone for this wonderfully clever and creative gay-themed film from France. When Felix unexpectedly loses his job, he decides to set off on foot across the French countryside in order to visit his estranged father. Along the way, he encounters various people who form a sort of surrogate family for him and provide the adventures referred to in the film's title. Subjects such as race, age, monogamy, homosexuality, HIV, and the dynamics of relationships are handled here in such a natural way that they don't become "issues" as in so many other films, but only various aspects of a full and interesting life. The people Felix encounters on his journey are refreshingly realistic; they have mood swings and don't always say or do just the right thing. *The Adventures of Felix* is a beautiful, breezy film that is free from the constraining influences of genre conventions-a film that seems to understand life is full of endless possibilities. —*A. W.*

AFFAIR OF LOVE, AN L: FOREIGN/FRANCE (1999) 80M D: Frederic Fonteyne. *Jacques Viala, Sergi López, Nathalie Baye.* The original French title is *A Pornographic Affair* but there's nothing pornographic here, only a melancholy memory of love in a physical no-strings-attached relationship that becomes briefly and beautifully intimate. Baye and Lopez recall their affair for an unseen interviewer as Fonteyne jumps between their recollections and flashbacks. Baye is stunning, confident, and vulnerable as her shy smiles soon radiate sheer joy, and Lopez nicely straddles the line between nonchalant openness and emotional defensiveness. Fonteyne captures a sense of discomfort

and anticipation that turns relaxed and passionate as their relationship deepens, then discards his naturalism for an almost surreal vision of the hotel: they pass through a hellish crimson red hall before entering their room, a cool blue sanctuary. It sounds obvious but the imagery is gorgeous and he manages to make it work. —*S. A.*

AMÉLIE (AKA LE FABULEUX DESTIN D'AMÉLIE POULAIN) L: FOREIGN/FRANCE (2001) 122M D: Jean-Pierre Jeunet. *Rufus, Dominique Pinon, Audrey Tautou, Mathieu Kassovitz, Artus de Penguern, Yolande Moreau.* Many, many people loved this heartwarming tale of a sexually dissatisfied French idiot savant named Amélie (lovingly played by cow-eyed beauty Tautou). Director Jeunet manipulates his cast through an idyllic, racially purified Paris: marvel as Amélie helps out a retarded grocery clerk, squeal as Amélie comes to the aid of a sad, lonely artist (oh, he also has brittle-bone disease), gawk as nymphette Amélie stalks a geeky porn-store employee in search of "true love." This is a heartwarming tale of the purest male fantasy, filled with spoons, raspberries, yard gnomes, and a woman-child who can't wait to find a Mr. Right that will debunk her other two pump chumps. The best part is she rarely talks, so she might not ever tell you if you've been mistreating her. —*J. D.*

There are a few movies in this world that you would have to be kind of an asshole to hate. *Amélie* is the standard romantic comedy formula elevated to far greater heights than you'd ever think it could go. You wouldn't have to have read it somewhere to know that Jeunet went through years of journals full of little anecdotes and details to create this screenplay brimming with coincidences, pranks, and rich fantasies. You could watch some slapdash piece of shit with Sandra Bullock or Julia Roberts misleading some guy or getting misled but managing to fall in love and overcome her troubles. Or, you could watch a timeless classic so full of imagination and beauty that you walk out feeling intoxicated. It's your pick. —*B. T.*

AND GOD CREATED WOMAN L: FOREIGN/FRANCE (1956) 92M D: Roger Vadim. *Jean-Louis Trintignant, Jeanne Marken, Christian Marquand, Curt Jurgens, Brigitte Bardot.* Vadim's directorial debut is more titillation than continental cool, but it broke box office records and censorship taboos and gave the world the original sex kitten Brigitte Bardot: earthy, innocent, and all fleshy curves. The story of a precocious girl pursued by rich widower Jurgens and torn between the earnest, innocent young man she married (Trintignant) and his brawny older brother (Marquand) is pure paperback melodrama. The teasing display of sex and eroticism in the sunny vacation playground of the St. Tropez seashore and Bardot's pouty child-woman frolicking through the film with nary a self-conscious moment are the real show. It's worth it just for the climactic mambo, where Bardot's pent-up frustration and sexual confusion explodes in a mad dance as bongos pound away on the soundtrack. Vadim remade the film in 1988 with Rebeca DeMornay, but lightning did not strike twice. —*S. A.*

ANY NUMBER CAN WIN L: FOREIGN/FRANCE (1963) 118M D: Henri Verneuil. *Maurice Biraud, Jean Gabin, Viviane Romance, Carla Marlier, Alain Delon.* Gabin, thick and doughy but still elegant as a working-class master criminal, plots the heist of a lifetime with his former cellmate, a leather-jacketed Delon, in Verneuil's cool widescreen caper. Playing high-rollers at a Cannes casino, Delon woos the ladies (after a well-tipped bartender gives him the lay of the land in a hilariously frank overview) while Gabin scopes out the club's vault. Verneuil made this in the heart of the French New Wave, but behind the swinging score and modern flourishes is a classic, tightly scripted, cleanly directed crime picture, and behind the continental cool is a genuine respect of craft that shows in every handsome frame. —*S. A.*

AUBERGE ESPAGNOLE, L' (THE SPANISH APARTMENT) L: FOREIGN/FRANCE (2002) 122M D: Cedric Klapisch. *Romain Duris, Audrey Tautou.* Xavier (Duris) is a young French man who goes off to live in Barcelona for a year to hang out and study finance. He ends up in a flat with other students like himself from all over the European Union (Italy, Denmark, the UK, and Germany to name a few). They argue the finer points of language (using English as their lingua franca), relationships, cleanliness, and beer. Many critics see this film as a microcosm of EU politics, but the story is more personal than that. Xavier grows up a lot over his short time in Barcelona, realizing his true ambitions through many nights of drinking and hijinks with his roommates, learning things about himself one can only really know by venturing outside one's usual way of life. By the end of his course, he is rich with memories that will shape his future. Tautou plays his girlfriend who stays in Paris and watches him slowly drift away. —*J. K.*

BAISE MOI L: FOREIGN/FRANCE (2000) 76M D: Virginie Despentes, Coralie Trinh Thi. *Raffaela Anderson, Karen Bach.* This is an ultraviolent, nihilistic revenge movie only well known because it's a "legitimate" movie containing actual hardcore porn scenes. You always have to wonder how things will turn out when a guy rents this with a porn movie-you hope he's not planning to, uh, enjoy it. The movie starts with a brutal rape scene made much more disturbing because it's acted out by porn stars who are really having sex. When the victim (Anderson) tells a friend what happened he gets macho and wants to know who did it so he can beat them up. She says, "Bastard! You didn't even ask me if I was OK!" and shoots him dead. Later she makes a new friend (Bach) and the two go on a crime spree, along the way picking up men, having sex with them, and then

killing them. Although it's shot on crappy digital video it's well acted and edited to a driving rock score. Still, I wouldn't recommend it as anything other than an artistic warning shot from angry French porn stars. —*B. T.*

BEAST, THE (LA BÊTE) L: FOREIGN/FRANCE (1975) 94M D: Walerian Borowczyk. *Lizbeth Hummel, Sirpa Lane, Guy Trejan, Elizaba Kaza, Pierre Benedetti.* Written, edited, and directed by Polish filmmaker Borowczyk, *The Beast* is a shocking film concerning an American woman who inherits an estate with a strange past. Through a variety of disparate clues and increasingly vivid dreams, the heiress learns about the woman who lived there two hundred years ago. She also finds out about the strange beast who lived in the nearby woods and possessed a giant phallus and an insatiable lust. She discovers the beast is still among the living, and is quite fertile. This outrageously disturbing film was banned for many years, but is now available on DVD from Cult Epics. The harpsichord music by eighteenth-century composer Domenico Scarlatti contributes not only to the strange tension in the film, but also to its absurdity. —*N. J.*

BROTHERHOOD OF THE WOLF L: FOREIGN/FRANCE (2002) 144M D: Christophe Gans, Pascal Laugier. *Emilie Dequenne, Vincent Cassel, Monica Bellucci, Samuel Le Bihan, Mark Dacascos.* This undeniably entertaining mix of eighteenth-century costume epic, action thriller, and arcane conspiracy movie was a box-office sensation in France. Le Bihan is a butt-kicking naturalist back from the New World with his Iroquois blood-brother (played by Japanese-American martial-arts star Dacascos). He issent by Louis XV to Southern France to stop the "Beast of Gevaudan," a real-life creature that killed more than one hundred people in eighteenth-century France and disappeared, becoming a resonant national legend. The movie is less horror than stylistically flamboyant adventure, spun around an absurd plot and punctuated with the ancient Iroquois art of kickboxing. Gans directs like a junior Ridley Scott with a pulp fiction soul, but the mix of atmospheric imagery, over-the-top action, and hyperkinetic editing is less a Gallic *Gladiator* than an outrageous collision between a weighty, overlong continental epic and an ambitious monster movie. Dequenne is the baby-faced love interest and Bellucci steals her scenes as a Mata Hari–like courtesan. —*S. A.*

CITY OF LOST CHILDREN, THE L: FOREIGN/FRANCE (1995) 112M D: Jean-Pierre Jeunet, Marc Caro. *Ron Perlman, Judith Vittet, Daniel Emilfork, Dominique Pinon, Claude Dreyfus.* In a dark fantasy world somewhere between Jules Verne and the Brothers Grimm, a withered old scientist kidnaps children and steals their dreams to make himself younger. One of the missing children is the brother of One (Perlman), a dim-witted but kindhearted circus strongman who teams up with Miette (Vittet), an orphan pickpocket, to save the kids. It's a movie inhabited by clones, cyborgs, Siamese twins, and a talking brain in a jar. Rarely has an artificial world been so perfectly imagined on film. It's full of pioneering special effects and elaborate chain reactions, but it also has more beneath the surface than most people give it credit for. "Adults" in this movie are cruel people who can't even remember how to dream. Those who would penalize *The City of Lost Children* for being so imaginative and visually arresting might as well be stealing dreams from children. —*B. T.*

CRIMSON RIVERS L: FOREIGN/FRANCE (2000) 106M D: Mathieu Kassovitz. *Vincent Cassel, Nadia Fares, Jean Reno.* Reno is the maverick cop from Paris sent to investigate an elaborate torture/murder in the insular college town in the French Alps in this stylish, slick, eerily gruesome pulp mystery. Director Kassovitz creates an unsettling mood amid the icy blue glaciers and blinding snow and keeps the film on track with solid pacing and just enough action, even as the story strains credibility. Cassel costars as a leather-jacketed, dopesmoking junior detective; Fares is the mountain-climbing babe who helps the investigation; and Dominique Sanda makes a memorable cameo as a mad nun with milky-blind eyes. —*S. A.*

DANGEROUS LIAISONS (1960) L: FOREIGN/FRANCE (1960) 106M D: Roger Vadim. *Jeanne Moreau, Annette Vadim, Jean Valerie, Gérard Philipe, Simone Renant.* Vadim is a master of showcasing glamorous beauties, especially cruel ones, so what better idea than for him to adapt this novel and put Moreau in the lead? It's a stylish but fairly straightforward adaptation with Philipe playing Valmont and Vadim (one of the director's many leading-lady wives) as the naive girl the two manipulate. What really makes this movie memorable is the superb jazz score by Art Blakey and the Jazz Messengers featuring Thelonious Monk. Blakey and his band also appear in the movie performing at a party. —*B. T.*

DELICATESSEN L: FOREIGN/FRANCE (1991) 95M D: Marc Caro, Jean-Pierre Jeunet. *Ticky Holgado, Karin Viard, Jean-Claude Dreyfus, Marie-Laure Dougnac, Dominique Pinon.* Surreal and brilliantly executed, *Delicatessen* is the story of Louison (Pinon), a young ex-clown who comes to an apartment building looking for work in a postapocalyptic city where food is very short in supply. The landlord, a butcher, takes in young Louison and offers him work as a handyman. What Louison doesn't know is that the butcher is in the business of fattening up passing handymen in order to kill and sell them as meat to the bizarre, famished tenants of his building. When Louison falls in love with the butcher's daughter, things become complicated, and the battle between love and hunger begins. Visually, this movie is stunning, with every shot carefully planned. The zany, over-the-top acting is effective in producing an otherworldly, sci-fi-type feel, and as the plot escalates further and further into craziness, you find yourself hoping that our young hero will keep both love and his life. —*J. S.*

DEMONLOVER L: FOREIGN/FRANCE (2002) 130M D: Olivier Assayas. *Charles Berling, Connie Nielsen, Chloë Sevigny, Dominique Reymond, Gina Gershon.* The exotic spy thriller is injected into the modern corporate world, then veers off into an expressionistic portrait of high-tech porn and exploitation. Nielsen plays a double agent manipulating two entertainment conglomerates that are fighting over a 3-D CGI anime porn that they expect to be all the rage. When Reymond gets kidnapped, Sevigny aids Nielsen-or maybe not, since she's obviously suspicious of her. No one knows whom they can trust until all of the cards have been laid out on the table, and even then it's a bit sticky. Slickly shot (sometimes with intentionally disorienting digital video), most of the film is very gripping and tense, especially when it erupts into some pretty brutal violence. But right when it seems to have reached a fairly satisfying conclusion, Assayas launches into a half hour of *Lost Highway*–style incomprehensible gloominess and sadism. —*B. T.*

DESTINÉES, LES L: FOREIGN/FRANCE (2000) 180M D: Olivier Assayas. *Charles Berling, Isabelle Huppert, Emmanuelle Béart.* After a short career of lilting contemporary dramas directed with a generous understanding of the chaos, confusion, and second-guessing missteps of modern life and modern love, Assayas steps out of his métier for this intimate costume epic. Yet it's the same Assayas behind the camera of this sprawling three-decade-long story of a venerable family whose porcelain legacy circles around the dedicated son (Berling), who rejects the business for the church and then returns to guide it through depression and WWI. It has an understated grace, the sun-dappled beauty of Southern France and Switzerland in the springtime, and a camera that dances with its characters. You feel the three hours, but as with the best of Assayas, the film lives in its moments of grace. The glorious ballroom scene features Assayas's camera floating through the throng to pick out the characters as they turn their emotions into a slow dance. —*S. A.*

FARINELLI: IL CASTRATO L: FOREIGN/FRANCE (1994) 110M D: Gérard Corbiau. *Elsa Zylberstein, Enrico Lo Verso, Caroline Cellier, Marianne Basler, Stefano Dionisi.* Visually stunning with a rich soundtrack, this dramatic interpretation of the life of the renowned eighteenth-century castrato Carlo Broschi, more commonly known as Farinelli, is well worth watching. Castrated as a young boy in order to preserve his beautiful singing voice, Farinelli grows to be a famous opera singer. His brother, Riccardo, also shares a love for music and works as a composer, writing pieces for Farinelli to perform. But as time goes on, it becomes evident that Carlo is by far the more talented of the brothers. The portrayal of the tension this rift brings to the brothers' relationship is tender, candid, and ultimately tragic. This in combination with a illustrious, if not slightly dramatized, musical history makes *Farinelli* a great film, as long as you can get past the gratuitously large amount of sex scenes. —*J. S.*

HATE (AKA LA HAINE) L: FOREIGN/FRANCE (1995) 96M D: Mathieu Kassovitz. *Hubert Koundé, Saïd Taghmaoui, Vincent Cassel.* This movie deals with three friends from different cultural backgrounds living in the projects outside of Paris during a period of street revolts, the choices they make after one of their comrades is hospitalized by the police, and what they do when one of them finds a gun. I love this film; it captures the rawness of the streets with a modern French hip-hop soundtrack, and plays with the harsh realities of class and race in a contemporary urban setting. I can't say I really liked the machismo of any of the characters, but I related to the anger and frustration of their poverty and oppression. The daily cat-and-mouse intrusions into "the hood" are being played out in inner cities throughout the world, so the conclusion is one that many people can relate to. It could also be seen as a metaphor for state terrorism and unilateral pre-emptive wars waged on the planet. Sometimes, the pigs paralyze people with fear and at times the people react with anger, but other times they respond with well-deserved hate. —*B. W.*

HE LOVES ME, HE LOVES ME NOT L: FOREIGN/FRANCE (2002) 92M D: Laetitia Colombani. *Isabelle Carré, Eric Savin, Clément Sibony, Sophie Guillemin, Audrey Tautou, Samuel Le Bihan.* If you think of Tautou as the sweet, innocent, earnest Amélie, you're in for a real shock with this movie. Tautou is Angelique, a young French student who is in love with a married doctor. For the first half of the movie we watch as Angelique's heart is repeatedly broken by the aloof Loic (Le Bihan), as he refuses to leave his pregnant wife and strands Angelique at an airport before a romantic getaway. What an asshole, right? Then the movie heads back to the beginning, and we see things from Loic's perspective. A creepy, thought-provoking drama that shows everything is in how you perceive it. This movie will leave you with the uncomfortable feeling of having been duped. Tautou shows herself to be a dynamic and versatile actress as well. —*J. S.*

HORSEMAN ON THE ROOF L: FOREIGN/FRANCE (1995) 135M D: Jean-Paul Rappeneau. *Olivier Martinez, Juliette Binoche, François Cluzet, Pierre Arditi, Claudio Amendola, Jean Yanne.* This is an extremely beautiful movie about a very ugly time, when cholera was ravaging the south of France in 1832.

An Italian soldier running from the Austrian secret police comes upon an exquisite young woman who is determined to find her husband, even though it means she must delve deeper and deeper into quarantine and disease-infested areas of the country. As determined as she is to reach her husband, so is the soldier to go with her and protect her as best he can. While watching this film I kept shaking my head at this woman's persistence, which to be honest is more often foolhardy insanity. I had the urge to smack her upside the head to bring her to her senses, and could not for the life of me understand why this handsome dashing soldier would find her quest, or her for that matter, so irresistible that he could not abandon her. Over and over again I whispered inside my head, "She's crazy! She's married! You can do better! Dump the crazy bitch and get on with your life!" Probably just as well—would have made for a pretty dull movie otherwise. And it is, without a doubt, an exceedingly well-made and gorgeous film, with amazing landscapes, architecture, costumes, and people. —*M. N.*

HUMANITÉ, L' L: FOREIGN/FRANCE (1999) 148M D: Bruno Dumont. *Séverine Caneele, Emmanuel Schotté, Philippe Tullier.* The controversial Cannes award-winning film by Dumont is a stark, sedate portrait of an empathic cop investigating the brutal murder of an eleven-year-old girl. With his unnervingly wide eyes and slow, careful speech of a child, Schotté behaves more like a mentally challenged village idiot than a detective. Dumont makes the film purposefully obscure; it unnecessarily defies logic and affronts the audience with startling violence and explicit carnality. The mystery is but an excuse to set the emotionally devastated Schotte on an odyssey that the camera unblinkingly records. Yet it's a beautiful and compassionate work-at once stark, sensory, and spiritually grasping-that challenges us to forgive even the most monstrous sins. —*S. A.*

Ostensibly a police drama, *L'Humanité* contains maybe three scenes remotely essential to the plot. Instead a loftier meditation on human-nature-at-large unravels. The quiet pace and austere cinematography seem well suited to the task, and the word "transcendental" seems poised to lend its generous services. What's unfortunate is that over the 148 minutes, so little of interest actually happens on either level. I have no idea why anyone wanted to make this film.—*C. B.*

I STAND ALONE (AKA SEUL CONTRE TOUS) L: FOREIGN/ FRANCE (1998) 81M D: Gaspar Noé. *Frankye Pain, Martine Audrain, Blandine Lenoir, Philippe Nahon.* Hatred. Unfettered, pure, and raw. Watch as anti-hero "The Butcher" goes from bad to worse to so far gone it's sickening. *The Sound and The Fury* meets *Taxi Driver* in what is essentially a ninety-minute internal monologue about the agony, rage, and ferocity of this misogynistic, racist, and incestuous pedophile. Then, after experiencing ugly atrocities in the form of a blizzard of scurrilous language and imagined violence that results in complete emotional implosion, we find a great chasm of nothingness gaping at us on the other side. Here is the darkness of the human spirit. This is daring and important filmmaking marred only slightly by Noe's extreme pretension and self-awareness. —*T. S.*

This film is such a cop-out. Despite all the venom coming from the Butcher, he is unable to carry off any of the world-ending plots he conceives. The shocking "end" is preceded by a countdown, giving the weak time to leave the theater. It's either the most pretentious device or the lamest, and probably both. But it's not the end, only another of the Butcher's impotent fantasies. In the real finish, he decides a life of illegitimate sex with his half-retarded daughter is his happy ending. Give me a break! A French guy decides to fuck his daughter and we are supposed to be shocked? *I Stand Alone* totally betrayed me. I LOVED this film for eighty minutes. It is amazing, heated, and strangely beautiful, only to turn into clichéd claptrap. It was like getting punched in the stomach when you least expect it. Ugh.—*G. M.*

IN THE LAND OF THE DEAF L: FOREIGN/FRANCE (1993) 99M D: Nicolas Philibert. The lingering pace of this engrossing documentary on France's insular deaf communities allows scenes to open up and exist as something more substantial than mere illustrative cogs, lending the film an exciting sense of lived experience that's carefully preserved by the total lack of narration. Not much interested in depicting the struggles of the disability, a focus on the day-to-day shows how deafness is simply a way of life for some, even in a world designed for the hearing. Perhaps most fascinating is the film's assertion of sign language as not merely a compromise of spoken language, but a distinct and parallel form of communication. This is best represented by the unbelievably expressive deaf teacher Jean-Claude Poulain, who has enormously enriched his signing with something close to pantomime. An affecting and beautiful film, this is easily one of the finest documentaries I've seen in recent years. —*C. B.*

IRMA VEP L: FOREIGN/FRANCE (1996) 97M D: Olivier Assayas. *Maggie Cheung, Jean-Pierre Léaud, Nathalie Richard.* While it always seems just a hair away from delving headfirst into its own complete pretension, *Irma Vep* manages to hold strong and stay focused throughout as a light, mindless, and completely fluffy depiction of the goings-on behind and during a horribly organized remake of the classic silent film *Les Vampire.* Cheung (playing herself) arrives in Paris to shoot the film after being pursued by a hilariously tragic Léaud, serving as the decaying and delusional visionary director of the doomed remake. As the filming spirals out of control, Cheung is forced to deal with the meltdown of Léaud and the crew in between wandering through Paris and creeping around hotel rooms in her skintight latex costume during the night. Listening to Cheung speak English in a British accent makes it even the more wonderful. —*A. T.*

IRREVERSIBLE L: FOREIGN/FRANCE (2002) 97M D: Gaspar Noé. *Monica Bellucci, Phillipe Nahon, Albert Dupontel, Vincent Cassel.* Cinema provocateur Noé (*I Stand Alone*) uses the cinema as an assault weapon to tell the story-in reverse-of a loving couple (Bellucci and Cassel) destroyed by a random rape and the boyfriend's rage-fueled revenge, like a fever-induced nightmare reimagining of *Memento.* The soundtrack throbs and pounds, the camera jerks and tilts and swings so violently it may cause motion sickness, and the screen burns furnace red as Noe unleashes one of the most sadistically brutal scenes of human violence ever executed on screen. It's a brutal, harrowing ordeal (he records the prolonged graphic-though not explicit-rape of Bellucci with an unflinching eye), but the film stair-steps back, the jittery camera-work calms down, the soundtrack eases up, and a delicate tenderness glows from Cassel and Bellucci at play, a loving couple full of hope and happiness. The grace of the final images is made all the more poignant by the violence we know awaits them. It's not a film that can be dismissed or easily put out of mind. The question is, do you want to put yourself through such an ordeal? —*S. A.*

LATE AUGUST, EARLY SEPTEMBER L: FOREIGN/FRANCE (1998) 112M D: Olivier Assayas. *Mathieu Amalric, Virginie Ledoyen, François Cluzet, Jeanne Balibar, Alex Descas, Arsinée Khanjian.* Self-conscious, stumbling intellectual Amalric is on the verge of thirty desperately looking for a way out of whatever drain he's spiraling down. He's ended one affair (with the delightfully gawky yet graceful Balibar) and started another (with sweet and sour Ledoyen, a restless wild-child with the temper of a diva). Cluzet plays his reluctant mentor, the insular "old timer" of the bunch. Assayas directs his sublime story of Parisian adults grappling with commitment, indecision, and crises of confidence as if he's constantly searching for a better, more revealing look. His camera never settles down, quietly gliding through scenes as if to catch his characters off guard or break through their defenses, and he sneaks in and out of his dramas like an eavesdropper. The title doesn't refer to a time of year but a feeling, a tone, and a sense of passage which Assayas deftly and delicately captures with his intimate glimpses and quirky sensibility. —*S. A.*

MATTER OF TASTE, A L: FOREIGN/FRANCE (2000) 90M D: Bernard Rapp. *Florence Thomassin, Bernard Giraudeau, Jean-Pierre Léaud, Jean-Pierre Lorit.* The temptations of gourmet food, fine wines, and a luxurious lifestyle are secondary to the more powerful seduction that awaits working-

French Crime Films: Gallic Gangsters

Leave it to the French to bring dignity and delicacy to a genre of blood and bullets. When the gangster movie exploded onto American screens with *Little Caesar* (1931), the country found a new kind of antihero: gutsy, energetic, a powder keg of ambition and violence charging to success with a hail of gunfire. The French gangster film couldn't be more different. Where American criminals scuttled out of the gutter and into the nightclubs at the rat-a-tat-tat pace of a tommy gun, the French antiheroes blew in from the fog and forged friendships and alliances in an underworld founded on respect and respectability.

Jean Gabin, the angry young working-class man of 1930s French cinema, embodied the original Gallic gangster in his role as the AWOL soldier seeking escape from a harsh world in *Le Quai des Brumes*, and as the aristocratic crime boss *Pépé le Moko* trapped in the catacombs of the Casbah. He's a combination of cool confidence and emotional volatility wrapped up in a handsome, haunted package, a proto–film noir protagonist whose desperation and doom were reborn behind the eyes of Robert Mitchum and Burt Lancaster.

The French gangster all but disappeared

---

class Lorit. An industrialist aesthete (the sinisterly seductive Giraudeau) hires him as his taster, and then transforms him into a kind of double at his beck and call, and at his mercy. Director Rapp elegantly melds Rainer Werner Fassbinder and Alfred Hitchcock for this sadomasochistic relationship, told in flashback as a judge (Léaud) reconstructs "the scene of the crime." Exactly what crime is kept hidden until the climax, but this is less a thriller than a study of intimacy (they share food, secrets, and even women) more powerful than sex, somewhere between friendship, mentorship, and willing, even invited, emotional possession. —*S. A.*

MOTHER AND THE WHORE, THE L: FOREIGN/FRANCE (1973) 210M D: Jean Eustache. *Jean-Pierre Léaud, Françoise Lebrun, Bernadette Lafont, Isabelle Weingarten.* Possibly *the* film on the sexual revolution, *The Mother and the Whore* uses Léaud brilliantly as Alexandre, for all practical purposes Antoine Doinel, who divides his time between two girlfriends. Alexandre is very frank with both women, even occasionally sleeping with both at once. Despite his best efforts to ride the wave of the sexual revolution, Alexandre is unshakably conservative and judgmental, and only ends up tormented by his own actions. Both the liberation and obligation of the post-1968 political, social, and sexual milieu are discussed at length in this almost nauseatingly personal autobiographical film. But before you write this off as another agonizing three-and-a-half hour French café talk-fest about a ménage à trois, let me point out that it is in fact an exceptional three-and-a-

half hour French café talk-fest about a ménage à trois. —*C. B.*

MY LIFE AND TIMES WITH ANTONIN ARTAUD L: FOREIGN/ FRANCE (1993) 90M D: Gerard Mordillat. *Valerie Jeannet, Marc Barbé, Sami Frey, Julie Jezequel.* This film is a fictional account of the relationship between "theater of cruelty" founder/surrealist champion Antonin Artaud and fellow surrealist follower Jacques Prevel. It takes place in postwar Paris, but for some reason this film always feels like an early '80s New York punk film. There is the same "suffering for art" mentality, plus plenty of drugs, sycophantic behavior, and melancholy to go around (and a mistress with bleached hair and bad roots to boot). —*J. K.*

PEUT-ÊTRE L: FOREIGN/FRANCE (1999) 109M D: Cédric Klapisch. *Jean-Paul Belmondo, Julie Depardieu, Romain Duris, Riton Liebman, Geraldine Pailhas, Vincent Elbaz. Peut-Être* is a really neat movie. The film takes place at a house party where a young man finds a hole in the ceiling of the bathroom that leads him into the future. In this future, he meets his own seventy-year-old son and his family. The son begs him to go back to the party, because that's the night he is supposed to be conceived. The confused man knows his girlfriend wants to get pregnant but he doesn't feel ready. Can he be convinced, or will his future family keep disappearing? I especially like the fact that the time portal stays open throughout the film, so other people from the future come to hang out at the party. I thought this movie was fun and original. —*R. D.*

with World War II and the German occupation, but the genre was reborn in the mid-1950s with a pair of classics: *Touchez pas au Grisbi*, starring an older, wiser, oh-so-dapper Jean Gabin, and Jules Dassin's magnificent caper classic *Rififi*. Measured and moody, these are films about aging professionals whose codes and friendships are threatened in a world of brazen young punks. Jean-Pierre Melville took the gangster film into the modern world with his meticulously plotted and smoothly directed crime classics, beginning with the elegant, elegiac *Bob le Flambeur*, the wonderfully ironic tale of an aging gambler (gracefully played by Roger Duchesne) who plots an elaborate heist; reaching its apex in the austere, existential *Le Samourai*, starring Gabin's heir apparent Alain Delon as the ultimate professional loner; and coming back with the most Mel-villian of Melville's crime films, *Le Cercle Rouge*.

Melville continued to make his increasingly handsome crime classics right up to his death in 1973, but his passing marked the end of a tradition. Jean-Luc Godard's 1959 debut *Breathless* (which paid tribute to Melville with a generous cameo) turned the genre on its head with stylistic experimentation and a rough, jazzy quality, and François Truffaut's *Shoot the Piano Player* reworked the fatalism of American film noir with invigorating bursts of humor and creative invention. Today the genre is the home of the self-aware stylistics and cinematic energy of Jean-Jacques Beineix's candy-colored *Diva* and Luc Besson's slick, stylish *La Femme Nikita*: French crime cinema redefined for a new generation.

—*Sean Axmaker*

PLACE VENDOME L: FOREIGN/FRANCE (1998) 117M D: **Nicole Garcia**. *Emmanuelle Seigner, Catherine Deneuve, Jean-Pierre Bacri, Jacques Dutronc.* Deneuve is a tired alcoholic who rouses back to life in Garcia's thriller about stolen diamonds and the conspiratorial web that spins around them, but the twisting plot and clash of criss-crossing interests are underplayed in favor of the story of three middle-aged characters (Deneuve, Bacri, and Dutronc) whose lives have brought them to strangling dead ends, and for a young woman (Seigner) at a turning point on the same road. Deneuve has aged into one of France's great actresses, her once flawless face now a beautiful mystery: still, serene, masking a turbulent and unhappy life with clenched resolve. As a thriller it's rather modest and slight and the emotional stories of the characters don't always come mesh with the complicated plot, but Garcia's redemptive vision is explored with passionate but understated grace. Her dialogue is wonderfully crafted, short, sharp, and resonant, and her elegant direction is delicate and handsome. —*S. A.*

SET ME FREE (EMPORTE-MOI) L: FOREIGN/FRANCE (1999) 95M D: **Lea Pool**. *Alexandre Mérineau, Karine Vanasse, Miki Manojlovic, Charlotte Christeler, Pascale Bussières, Nancy Huston.* *Set Me Free* was the sixth feature film of Québecois writer-director Pool's twenty-year career, and the first to win a U.S. release. Although often breathtaking to look at, and focused on the delicate theme of a young girl taking hesitant steps toward womanhood, Pool's film is blessedly free of candy-box prettiness, cloying gentility, and anything else that would dishonor its deeply felt, sensitively observed memoir. Hanna (Vanasse) is the thirteen-year-old daughter of an expatriate Polish Jew (Manojlovic) and the Québecois Catholic (Bussières) he has never got round to marrying. Hanna's brother Paul (Mérineau) is that rare sibling, a soul mate rather than a rival. But Hanna finds herself looking to other females for reinforcement: a beautiful teacher (Huston, who cowrote the film), a classmate (Cadieux) who can't decide whether she's more attracted to Hanna or to Paul. The inference that Hanna may ultimately gravitate to a lover of the same sex is invited without coyness, tendentiousness, or special pleading. What matters is that it's her life to live. It's a life you'll be glad you looked in on. —*R. T. J.*

SHORT FILMS OF PASCAL AUBIER L: FOREIGN/FRANCE (1986) 40M D: **Pascal Aubier**. French filmmaker Aubier is the master of the short film and has been called "the great hope of French cinema" by the one and only Andrei Tarkovsky. This videotape collects six of Aubier's best and reflects the director's humor and humanity. Frequently set in blue-collar working environments, Aubier shows quite a bit of sympathy for his downtrodden protagonists clinging to their humanity in a modern world. The films make their points simply and humorously with minimal dialogue and silent comedy techniques. For example, in *Les Petits Coins* a factory worker escapes the tedium of an automobile assembly line by entering into a fantasy accessible through a bathroom window.

A typical film for Aubier, it features a grim view of cold modern technology that is counterbalanced with a beautiful world filled with genuine human connections. —*S. H.*

TASTE OF OTHERS, THE L: FOREIGN/FRANCE (2000) 112M D: Agnes Jaoui. *Anne Alvaro, Jean-Pierre Bacri, Agnes Jaoui, Gérard Lanvin.* Jaoui, writing with her husband and longtime writing/performing partner Bacri, makes a deft directorial debut in this lovely romantic drama about adults caught in the midst of their own personal evolutions years after they thought they'd stopped changing. Bacri becomes the heart of the film as a gauche petit-bourgeois businessman whose confined, shallow world explodes after a theater performance moves him to tears, while Jaoui is a worldly waitress in a dead-end affair with Bacri's cynical bodyguard. They're just two of a small group of Parisians caught in the painful joy of reassessment and rediscovery. Jaoui and Bacri have a knack for exploiting the annoying edges of characters for comic exaggeration while simultaneously exposing their vulnerabilities, and Jaoui's lightness helps spin the familiar situations into a new look at age-old frustrations and the clumsy but sincere search for meaning and intimacy in the modern world. —*S. A.*

TIME OUT L: FOREIGN/FRANCE (2001) 132M D: Laurent Cantet. *Aurélien Recoing, Karin Viard, Serge Livozet, Monique Mangeot, Jean-Pierre Mangeot.* *L'Emploi du Temps (Time Out)* is the story of Vincent (Recoing), who hides the fact that he has been fired from his wife and family. With no job to go to, Vincent idles his time driving from one random location to another, pausing to call his wife on his cell phone and fill her in on fabricated details about his busy work schedule and pseudo–company meetings. Without the means to financially support his family, Vincent devises a scam involving third world investments to swindle money from those closest to him. Vincent's lies become more and more intricate as his victims begin to question him about the investment returns. The tension mounts as Vincent's lies spiral out of control and the truth threatens to expose itself. A quiet and terrifying film, perfect for what it is. —*J. D.*

TO BE AND TO HAVE (ETRE ET AVOIR) L: FOREIGN/FRANCE (2002) 105M D: Nicolas Philibert.. A documentary with universal appeal, this film centers on Georges Lopez, a calm teacher in a single-room rural schoolhouse who teaches children of a variety of ages and grade levels as a single class. The filmmakers spent about six months with Lopez and his pupils, catching numerous exceptional (dare I say "heartwarming") moments unraveling with surprisingly little awareness of the camera. Repeatedly stealing the show is Jojo, an easily distracted little boy with a hyper-expressive face and an innocent nose for mischief-the sort of dynamic indelible character most fiction films

would kill for. Hardly an exposé-style investigation, the film wisely stays on the surface of things (there's only one interview in the entire film, and no narration) and, in so doing, succeeds at being not only a superb documentary but really an exceptionally beautiful film. —*C. B.*

TOM AND LOLA L: FOREIGN/FRANCE (1990) 97M D: Bertrand Arthuys. *Catherine Frot, Cecile Magnet, Mélodie Collin, Marc Berman.* With the beauty of a Bjork video, Arthuys tells a fantastic tale of two bubble children. This film is underrated and rarely seen, but it's really beautiful. Tom and Lola are science experiments/subjects. They've lived their whole ten years hairless and naked in bubbles, next to each other in a huge lab surrounded by voiceless, faceless doctors. They've learned how to communicate with the doctors but also have developed their own language. They get to watch some TV but it's only a rerun of an Alaskan documentary. They pick up ideas and words from the video much like we use quotes from *The Simpsons*. With that, they have their own inside jokes. They observe a way to escape their bubbles and do so night after night. The imagery may have been ahead of its time for 1990,and the lighting and compositions are great, creating a necessary bleakness and cold feeling. Tom and Lola are pale, shorn of all hair, and innocently beautiful. Their playfulness keeps the movie warm. —*M. P.*

TOWN IS QUIET, THE L: FOREIGN/FRANCE (2000) 132M D: Robert Guédiguian. *Jean-Pierre Darroussin, Gérard Meylan, Ariane Ascaride.* In Guédiguian's vivid but somber portrait of Marseilles, the town may be quiet, but the once prosperous port city, now deep in rampant unemployment, poverty, and crime, is far from peaceful. The spirited neighborhood eccentrics (among them Ascaride, Meylan, and Darroussin, all from Guédiguian's earlier *Marius and Jeannette*) who once pulled together to survive have hardened into mercenary individualists born of desperation, frustration, and simmering resentment. This sprawling slice of life resembles one of John Sayles's ambitious social portraits with big, interlocking casts, quilted together with more passion than grace, and rumbling with lost idealism, the collapse of working class solidarity, and the rise of reactionary xenophobic politics. Shot in the unflinching, hard-edged style of a documentary, it makes for a film that is far more than simply its message. His fumbling characters find that survival is not a matter of economics alone, it's also a matter of hope. —*S. A.*

VENUS BEAUTY INSTITUTE L: FOREIGN/FRANCE (1999) 105M D: Tonie Marshall. *Nathalie Baye, Samuel Le Bihan, Bulle Ogier, Audrey Tautou.* Baye stars as a jaded beautician who has given up on love and settles for anonymous sex and the workaday autopilot of her job until a hunky bohemian (Le Bihan) falls madly in love with her. Most of the drama takes place in the salon of the film's title,

a storybook shop in baby blue and neon pink that could have been dropped in from a Jacques Demy musical, and writer/director Marshall has a marvelous feeling for the women who work and visit the place. Ogier is excellent as the shop's chirpy but bottom-line owner and the adorable Tautou's role as a naive shopgirl cutie was a star-making turn, but Baye is the bittersweet soul of the film as the haunted and lonely middle-aged "girl" who holds on to those emotions rather that risk intimacy. —*S. A.*

VIDOCQ L: FOREIGN/FRANCE (2001) 98M D: Pitof. *André Dussollier, Gérard Depardieu, Ines Sastre, Edith Scob, Guillaume Canet.* Depardieu plays Vidocq, the pioneering French detective turned pulp hero. In this version Vidocq is killed in a duel with the Alchemist, a man in a mirrored mask who has also caused a series of deaths by lightning. A journalist (Canet) tries to write a book about the detective, but each of the people he interviews ends up dead shortly afterward. Is the Alchemist trying to stop him from getting to the truth? First-time director Pitof was the genius behind the special effects in *City of Lost Children*, so it's not surprising that this is a fun, visually impressive comic book of a movie. It was shot on high-def digital video and the images are heavily manipulated-even the clouds in the sky are given an exaggerated, stylized look. The story is pretty lightweight so I guess it must be the French equivalent of a big Hollywood summer movie. But if so it's a particularly clever and cool-looking one. —*B. T.*

If A&E filed for bankruptcy and merged with the SciFi channel, this would be the first mess of a movie that would come out of their union. The effects look like they were stolen from the cutting-room floor of the Dungeons and Dragon movie (which are far superior). And Gérard Depardieu? C'mon. —*A. T.*

WASABI L: FOREIGN/FRANCE (2001) 94M D: Gerard Krawczyk. *Jean Reno, Ryoko Hirosue, Michel Muller, Carole Bouquet.* A playful, entertaining film about an ex-special forces operative who now makes his living as a cop whose measures lean more toward the extreme. Still pining for the love he lost nineteen years ago, he is shocked to learn that she has died and he is the sole legate of her will. He flies to Japan, where he learns that she was keeping a great deal more secret from him than just her whereabouts. It's no Oscar winner and the storyline is for the most part very predictable, but it is FUN! Reno is wonderful as always, with tough and yet retiring characters as his strong suit. Hirosue is utterly adorable, VERY *kawaii*, and an excellent foil to Reno's austere characterization. Your reaction to this film will likely be akin to Reno's to wasabi: there's not very much kick and it won't leave you gasping, but it's very tasty. —*M. N.*

WITH A FRIEND LIKE HARRY. . . L: FOREIGN/FRANCE (2000) 117M D: Dominik Moll. *Sophie Guillemin, Laurent Lucas, Sergi López, Mathilde Seigner.* One can't help but call on the ghost of Hitchcock to describe Moll's black comedy thriller. The ominously overfriendly Lopez stars as a hero-worshiping nerd and nouveau-riche bumpkin who ingratiates himself with the family of old school-chum Lucas and starts bumping off the "distractions" in his pal's life. The title recalls *The Trouble with Harry*, a black comedy of a corpse that won't go away, and the story of a vague acquaintance turned into a twisted fairy godfather echoes with suggestions of *Strangers on a Train*. But Moll doesn't quote Hitchcock as much as explore the same thematic territory of fantasy, obsession, and the terrifying realization that one's most repressed, guilty wishes are coming true. He creates a satirical look at middle-class frustrations grounded in the intimate chemistry of family reunions and marital relations. —*S. A.*

YAMAKASI L: FOREIGN/FRANCE (2001) 90M D: Ariel Zeitoun, Julien Seri. *Charles Perrière, Guylain N'Guba-Boyeke, Yann Hnautra, Malik Diouf, Williams Belle, Châu Belle Dinh.* The Yamakasi are a real-life troupe of urban acrobats and free climbers (featured in some Nike ads). This film fictionalizes their exploits, turning them into modern-day Robin Hoods out to save a young boy's life. It's a creative, fun film with a multicultural cast of urban youth and without overt violence, guns, or other things that make American family films so anti-family. —*G. M.*

ZOU ZOU L: FOREIGN/FRANCE (1934) 92M D: Marc Allegret. *Pierre Larquey, Josephine Baker, Jean Gabin.* Baker never made an American film, but as the highest paid entertainer in France during the '30s she made a handful of French musicals, silly little confections that blossomed through her infectious enthusiasm. In the 1934 *Zou Zou*, she stars as a former circus performer who becomes a laundress, falls in love with her adopted brother (Gabin, the epitome of working-class cool), and becomes an overnight success on the stage. Toss in a love triangle, a death in the family, and a murder, and there's enough plot for a handful of movies. Allegret can't quite find the narrative center of this busy screenplay, but if the movie wanders around the edges at least it has Baker to pull it back together, if only when she's on-screen. She may speak French like an American (fluent but flat), but her incandescent glow nearly eclipses Gabin (no mean feat) and her energy drives the fitful narrative even at its most tangled. —*S. A.*

GERMANY

ANATOMY L: FOREIGN/GERMANY (2001) 100M D: Stefan Ruzowitzky. *Franka Potente, Sebastian Blomberg,*

Holger Speckhahn, Anna Loos, Benno Fürmann, Traugott Buhre. A medical school is the perfect setting for a horror movie, because after all, the misuse of science is pretty fucking creepy, right? Potente is Paula Henning, a smarty-pants who just got admitted to a prestigious medical school in Heidelberg. At first, all is well and things are cool. When the body of a guy she knows turns up dissected, however, Paula is suspicious and decides to find out what happened. Things get crazy. She finds out the school has a secret society that likes to dissect people while they are still alive for better body-part preservation, and as she comes closer and closer to finding out who is responsible for the freaky shit happening on campus, the closer she comes to being the target of freaky shit herself. Although the story idea isn't really that original, this movie is good fun, suspenseful, and creepy, and what's worse is that it could really happen. Stay away from medical schools and medical school students. —*J. S.*

CHRISTIANE F. L: FOREIGN/GERMANY (1982) 120M D: Uli Edel. *Thomas Haustein, David Bowie, Natja Brunkhorst.* Ah, the magic of dubbing. Bad English voice-overs manage to turn this deadly serious German drama about teen drug use into a comedic tour de force! Brunckhorst stars in the title role as a fourteen-year-old girl in 1970s Berlin who, after being drawn into the evil world of disco, descends into a life of drugs and prostitution. After seeing the horrible and hilarious dubbed version on video (you'd swear the voice-over actors were on drugs themselves), I mentioned it to a couple of German acquaintances, who were less than amused when I started mercilessly mocking the picture. It seems that Germany is still very taken by this film, based on a true story originally told in a book of the same title. Fortunately, it was recently released on DVD featuring the original German audio so that you can appreciate it in all its true, gritty glory. A Bowie soundtrack (in his post–Ziggy Stardust prime) is beautifully exploited. Bowie (or "Bahwee," as they call him in the dubbed track) himself appears in a concert scene. —*E. O.*

DAS BOOT L: FOREIGN/GERMANY (1981) 216M D: Wolfgang Petersen. *Jurgen Prochnow, Martin Semmelrogge, Hubertus Bengsch, Klaus Wennemann, Herbert Gronemeyer.* Petersen's WWII epic, originally a six-hour miniseries on German TV, was edited by more than half for theatrical release. In 1997, Petersen prepared a director's cut for a theatrical rerelease that brought the film to more than three and a half hours. The story remains the same-the ordeal of a German submarine crew in 1942, when the American battleships started turning the tide of the "Battle of the Atlantic." The biggest change is in the detail of life on a sub: the waiting, the stress, the boredom of endless hours on the sea, and ultimately the numb-ing tour of duty in a claustrophobic metal coffin. In the theatrical version, the scene of the damaged sub plummeting to the bottom of the sea as the men race the clock to repair it is a suspenseful highlight, a gritty countdown that tests frayed nerves and the crew's ingenuity. In the director's cut it becomes an intense ordeal where the protracted wait, silent but for the sounds of the bending metal, is enriched with this new luxury of time. —*S. A.*

EAST SIDE STORY L: FOREIGN/GERMANY (1997) 78M D: Dana Ranga. *Margarita Andrushkovich, Chris Doerk.* More than simply kitsch, this celebration of that rare artifact-the Socialist musical-turns up everything from *Twilight Zone*–like takes on the Hollywood production number (with synchronized tractors no less) to the 1960s rock musical, *East German* style. Director Ranga celebrates their energy and joy while charting the Soviet bloc's uneasy truce with this most decadent Western art form. Packed with effervescent clips ranging from early Socialist attempts to celebrate the five-year plan to glitzy backstage musicals to an Eastern bloc beach movie (*Hot Summer*, with the East German equivalents of Frankie and Annette giving a musical lesson in collective responsibility), it actually creates a nostalgia for a genre that this country never even knew existed-until now. —*S. A.*

EXPERIMENT, THE L: FOREIGN/GERMANY (2002) 120M D: Oliver Hirschbiebel. *Oliver Stokowski, Christian Berkel, Moritz Bleibtreu, Wotan Wilke Mohring.* What is "The Experiment"? A group of men answer an ad for a government experiment without really knowing the details. They end up in a prison where they are split into two groups, the guards and the inmates. Then they are all locked up together for a week, under surveillance to see how they cope with the challenges. Each man has his own breaking point and eventually, the experiment backfires beyond anyone's predictions. Superbly acted, fast-paced, shocking, and inventive. I can't believe this was based on an actual event. —*R. D.*

HARMONISTS, THE L: FOREIGN/GERMANY (1997) 115M D: Joseph Vilsmaier. *Ulrich Noethen, Meret Becker, Ben Becker, Kai Wiesinger, Max Tidof.* Vilsmaier dramatizes the true story of the Comedian Harmonists, a fabulously popular multiethnic, multinational vocal group during the flowering of freedom and tolerance in Germany before Hitler's racial purges. It's enormously entertaining, if at times hackneyed, like an old Hollywood biography: lush, grand, spread to very edges of its CinemaScope dimensions, and reverberating with the plots of dozens of Hollywood showbiz movies. The legacy of the Harmonists, popular to this day in Europe, is lost on American audiences, but Vilsmaier displays their impact and their music (the film features their actual his-

torical recordings) effectively in this cheerfully old-fashioned melodrama. —*S. A.*

HITLER: A FILM FROM GERMANY L: FOREIGN/GERMANY
(1977) 450M D: Hans-Jürgen Syberberg. *Peter Luehr, Helmut Lange, Peter Moland.* Attempting to confront "the oppressive curse of guilt" that Hitler's legacy constitutes for Germany, *Our Hitler* is both an in-depth exploration of the very idea of German identity and a self-aware struggle to create a monumental work of art. Rather than fictionalize Hitler's biography or document his atrocities, Syberberg audaciously employs "all the possibilities that cinema offers" over its seven hours, combining archival material, poetic musing, and academic inquiry in a bizarre series of Brechtian sound-studio stagings involving elaborate costumes, puppets, projected images, overlapping photography-anything within reach. The antithesis of *Night and Fog, Our Hitler* tries to say EVERYTHING in a deluge of discourse not meant to leave you convinced of something, but dizzy with it. Picked up in the middle, left unfinished, watched piecemeal or as a whole, the force of its style and gravity of its topic is felt even in small doses and gets no easier with prolonged exposure, only less alarming. —*C. B.*

HOT SUMMER L: FOREIGN/GERMANY (1967) 91M D: Joachim
Hasler. *Chris Doerk, Hans-Michael Schmidt, Frank Schoebel, Regine Albrecht.* Communist East Germany pop stars Doerk and Schoebel sing, dance, flirt, and romance on the sands of the Baltic coast in the first (and only) rock-and-roll beach movie from behind the iron curtain. The silly, spirited teen musical starts with boys-versus-girls shenanigans, half flirting and half competing on the road to the beach and gripped in a war of practical jokes until they all decide to make puppy love, not war. That's where it transforms into a love triangle pushed to soap opera extremes. When their romantic escapades land them in trouble with those hard-line adults, it takes this rousing line to pull together the fractured group: "Are we a collective or just an ordinary gang?" There's a bouncy song every few minutes (some better than others) and a few guitar rock tunes that are actually quite catchy, and even when the music takes a break the group dynamics are choreographed into an elaborate mating dance. —*S. A.*

HOW TO LIVE IN THE GERMAN FEDERAL REPUBLIC L:
FOREIGN/GERMANY (1980) 83M D: Harun Farocki. As evidence that an increasingly modern workplace demands an impersonal and effectively mechanized human work force, we're shown footage of instructional classes-role-playing exercises readying future bank tellers for various customer service scenarios, mock raids preparing police officers for real raids, an exotic dancer practicing a new striptease routine. Not limiting labor to employment, we're also shown Lamaze classes, CPR training, even children meeting with devel-

opmental specialists. There's no narration and no interviews, and though the footage is scrupulously neutral (distanced, indifferent to ideology or argument-to all appearances, stock footage found in the back of a TV studio), it's given deliberate, ham-fisted significance by its juxtaposition beside images of automated product-testing (crash-test dummies of course, as well as durability testing of recliner chairs). Though a bit monotonous, the result is highly persuasive social critique, and a cautionary examination of the divisive nature of documentary (or really any nonfiction medium). —*C. B.*

JACOB THE LIAR L: FOREIGN/GERMANY (1975) 100M D:
Frank Beyer. *Vlastimil Brodský, Armin Mueller-Stahl, Henry Huebchen, Erwin Geschonneck.* Brodský is Jakob, a Jewish prisoner of the Warsaw ghetto who overhears a radio broadcast of a Russian victory while he's detained by gestapo. Soon the ghetto buzzes with stories of a hidden radio and he's forced to make up more "news" stories. Not a comedy in any accurate sense of the word, but a wistful drama of prisoners of the Warsaw ghetto escaping the daily nightmare through memories, fantasies, and the desire to believe. The bitter irony of the film is that no one will believe Jakob heard the news from the police-station radio-you simply don't return alive from such a visit-but they are more than willing to embrace the heroic risk of a forbidden hidden radio set. Jakob's lies give these sad, shuffling humans reason to continue in the face of certain doom, and that's what gives the picture its haunting power. A 1976 Oscar nominee for Best Foreign Film. —*S. A.*

KILLER CONDOM L: FOREIGN/GERMANY (1997) 107M
D: Martin Walz. *Leonard Lansink, Udo Samel, Peter Lohmeyer, Marc Richter.* Shot in bleeding color on the streets of New York, where everyone suddenly speaks German, this aggressively trashy spoof is not really a Troma picture but fits right into the family, cultural whiplash and gay pride aside. A race of snaggletoothed rubbers take a painful bite out of the Big Apple and it's up to slovenly detective Luigi Mackaroni (Samel), hard-boiled and hung like the Empire State Building, to stop them. Martin Walz's comic horror picture is short on gore and the monster resembles a sock puppet with teeth (amazing, as H. R. Giger is listed as a "creative consultant" and corpse-obsessed goremeister Jörg Buttgereit executed the special effects), but castration anxiety has never been more humorously palpable. —*S. A.*

MOSTLY MARTHA L: FOREIGN/GERMANY (2001) 106M D:
Sandra Nettelbeck. *Martina Gedeck, Ulrich Thomsen, August Zirner, Sergio Castellitto, Maxime Foerste.* Martha is an exact woman, and she needs to be in order to cook for one of the finest restaurants in town. Martha's sister dies in a car wreck and leaves behind a daughter for Martha to fend for

while they search for her long-departed Italian father. During this time, Martha is forced to endure the hijinks of a new Italian chef in her restaurant. But none of this really matters too much because this movie sucks. It's like one of those movies that you rent because you heard something about it and at the end of it you're like, "Well, that blew." The story is formulaic and predictable, yet the magnitude of its crapiness is still surprising. This type of moviemaking should have died with the nouvelle cuisine craze of the '80s. Food: 2 stars; ambience: 2 stars; service: 3 stars; disappointment: 5 stars. —T. C.

MUNCHAUSEN L: FOREIGN/GERMANY (1943) 110M D: Josef von Baky. *Kaethe Kaack, Hermann Speelmanns, Hans Albers, Leo Slezak.* This curious German film produced in the midst of World War II was certainly ambitious. Celebrating its twenty-fifth anniversary, the film studio UFA assembled its best actors and some huge production expenses for this stunning fantasy about the legendary Baron Munchausen who was famed for traveling everywhere with the help of his hot-air balloon-even to the moon! The sets in this film are dazzling and the peculiar early color system (Agfacolor) gives the film an extra aura of surrealism. Unfortunately for the film studio, Germany needed something more than a fantasy to get out of the enormous war that engulfed every aspect of its society. —N. J.

STALINGRAD L: FOREIGN/GERMANY (1992) 134M D: Joseph Vilsmaier. *Jochen Nickel, Dominique Horwitz, Thomas Kretschmann.* Stalingrad depicts one of the bloodiest battles in world history, in which Soviet forces successfully held back the German army for several months during a brutal Russian winter. Conversely objective and sympathetic, the film follows a group of freshly recruited young Nazis on a downward spiral from induction to, ultimately, destruction. Sadistic superiors, terrified opposition, and brutal climates rally against the protagonists as their dedication to their cause is replaced by the will to merely survive. Vilsmaier's crushing film goes as far as cinema can in showcasing the carnage and stupidity of modern warfare, while still conveying the hopes, dreams, and stories of terrified young men. —Z. C.

TENDERNESS OF THE WOLVES L: FOREIGN/GERMANY (1973) 87M D: Ulli Lommel. *Kurt Raab, Rainer Werner Fassbinder, Jürgen Prochnow.* The first feature film from German child-star and Fassbinder actor Lommel, who teamed up with co-Fassbinder–actor Raab to re-create a more accurate portrayal of the WWII child-murderer Fritz Haarman, (aka The Vampyre of Hanover) than what Fritz Lang had used for the basis of his film *M* (and the Joseph Losey remake of *M*). Lang had changed the victims to little girls; Lommel and Raab change it back to wayward street boys. The story becomes a fascinating study of a gay

serial killer, similar to Jeffrey Dahmer. Haarman worked for the German police force in postwar Germany as an informant. Roaming the train stations at night, Haarman would pick up homeless young teenage boys and take them home with promises of a good meal and money. Instead, he murdered them, had sex with their bodies, and chopped them up for meat which he then sold to local street vendors. Lommel and Jürges wisely choose the tone of a macabre fairy tale, portraying Haarman as a grisly, bald-headed troll praying on innocent youth. Filmed with leftover money from other Fassbinder productions and shot on weekends while the actors were working on more well-known Fassbinder film productions and stage plays, *Tenderness* is a lost horror gem with moments of sheer terror. —N. H.

TUVALU L: FOREIGN/GERMANY (1999) 101M D: Veit Helmer. *Denis Lavant, Chulpan Khamatova, Philippe Clay, Terrence Gillespie.* Helmer's imaginative, unusual, and stylistic charmer features lovely tinted black-and-white photography, minimal dialogue, and enchanting silent comedy technique. The film is set in a rundown public bath where a young man (Leos Carax-regular Lavant) tries to keep the decaying building intact and convince his blind father that the baths are as popular as ever. When a beautiful young woman (the incredibly cute Khamatova who likes to swim naked with her pet goldfish) and her sea captain father arrive, tension builds between Lavant, his greedy brother, and the woman (who wants to steal the pool's water pump). Clearly patterned in the silent-film tradition, *Tuvalu* is a technically stunning treat reminiscent of "dream" films like *Eraserhead* and *Delicatessen* with a dash of Eastern European surrealism a la Jan Svankmajer. —S. H.

VIDEOGRAMS OF A REVOLUTION L: FOREIGN/GERMANY (1992) 107M D: Harun Farocki, Andrei Ujica. *Nicholae Ceaucescu.* When Romania's Ceaucescu regime fell in 1989, armed revolutionary forces headed straight to the nearest TV station. Consisting solely of Romanian television broadcasts aired during these turbulent days of transition (both before and after the station was seized), *Videograms* explores the boundless effects of the media on daily life. Here the control of information played a far more important role in social change than the actual overthrow of the regime. Farocki shows how mass communications work not merely as a transmission of facts, but in this case as a lethal political weapon. —C. B.

WHAT TO DO IN CASE OF FIRE L: FOREIGN/GERMANY (2002) 101M D: Gregor Schnitzler. *Til Schweiger, Martin Feifel, Sebastian Blomberg, Nadia Uhl.* The energetic opening, set in 1987, is all defiance and rebellion, shot to look like a guerrilla documentary by way of MTV and German punk music: Berlin Calling, and these shaggy revolutionaries answer the call. Fast-forward fifteen years when one of their dud bombs suddenly ignites. The angry not-so-young leader (Schweiger, in a close-cropped bleach job) contacts the old comrades, now all sold out to the system, and offers them a choice: clear out of the country before the cops link them to the bomb, or gear up for one last action. Schnitzler directs this *Big Chill* reunion of a would-be Baader-Meinhof Gang, except that these guys are more harmless pranksters than political activists. There's no teeth to the satire, and no ideology to the good fight, but there is style, fun-loving attitude, and lots of bonding after all those years of brooding. —*S. A.*

HONG KONG

AND I HATE YOU SO L: FOREIGN/HONG KONG (2000) 96M D: Yee Cheung-Man. *Kelly Chen, Aaron Kwok.* Remember back in grade school, where if a kid liked someone, he would usually tease and torment her to get her attention? Well, two adults use that same technique in this romantic melodrama, when a used record brings together radio DJ Kwok and newspaper columnist Chen. Kwok, who hosts a romance talk-show, uses Chen's sentimental attachment to the record to his advantage, and uses it on the air. Chen, in response, writes a column to counterattack. The pair go back and forth attacking each other until they realize that they could be in love. The plot is fairly predictable and includes the often-used Hong Kong plot device of the woman deciding to move to Canada, but it is the charm that both Kwok and Chen carry that makes this film very enjoyable. Interspersed between the main couples bantering is a cute subplot between the unattractive Eric Tsang and Teresa Mo, who decide to start dating each other because they can't find anyone else. This is a great watch for anyone who needs to have their faith in romance jump-started. —*R. M.*

ANOTHER MELTDOWN (AKA **BI XIE LAN TIAN**) L: FOREIGN/ HONG KONG (1998) 92M D: Allun Lam. *Chiu Man-Cheuk, Ken Wong, Qi Shu.* There's plenty of action, if not much old Hong Kong–style heart, in the story of a dedicated Chinese cop who winds up in the (fictional) independent Soviet state of Lavernia. As he fights a deadly Japanese cult leader who is waging a private war against the sins of humanity, he finds he's being made a pawn in a political power play. Made right after the 1997 Hong Kong handover to China (and the film industry exodus that accompanied it), it stars soft-spoken, soft-featured Chiu, who was being groomed to replace Jet Li. His moves are good but he lacks any real screen definition either as an actor or an action dynamo, which makes him a bland figure to pin a film on. Qi has almost nothing to do as his girlfriend, who fled China in fear after Tiananmen Square and wants to reconnect. Ching Siu Tung provides the largely unmemorable fight choreography. —*S. A.*

AVENGING FIST, THE L: FOREIGN/HONG KONG (2001) 105M D: Andrew Lau. *Sammo Hung, Yuen Biao, Kristy Yang, Lee-Hom Wang.* In the bleak, black-sky future universe of an Asian *Blade Runner–The Fifth Element*, a brother and sister superhero team (Wang and Yang) discover that their special gifts come from the genetic legacy of a government "Power Glove" experiment that ultimately claimed their father (Biao). When dad reemerges after twenty years as a mindless, silver-masked supersoldier and fellow test subject turned supercop, Hung (who has to endure an unending parade of fat jokes) combats his bid for world domination, and a complicated family melodrama ensues. Frankenstein morality and superpower doom (the Power Glove sucks the user's life force every time it's used) is churned into a flashy, high-tech action thriller with terrific cement-and-neon warehouse sets and a cathode-ray neon blue color scheme. Lau directs this live action adaptation of the *Tekken* video game and subsequent anime series, and Corey Yuen Kwai choreographs the action. —*S. A.*

BIO ZOMBIE L: FOREIGN/HONG KONG (1998) 94M D: Wilson Yip. *Angela Tong Ying-Ying, Jordan Chan, Sam Lee.* Like a comic Asian mix of *Dawn of the Dead* and *Return of the Living Dead*, this is a gooey black comedy about a motley bunch stuck in a chintzy mall when a zombie (who was infected by a bio-weapon stored in a soda can) starts biting everyone (cops, security guards, soccer players) and infecting the population. Stars Chan and Lee are the loudmouth hooligans who turn heroic just about the time their bickering and whining starts to get annoying, and Ying-Ying plays the flirty beautician whose love/hate clash with Chan takes a turn under threat of flesh-eating ghouls-especially the lovesick Sushi Boy whose moony-eyed silence doesn't prevent him from proposing to the sexy Ying-Ying. The film spins its wheels in a slow-to-start first half, but director Yip picks things up once limbs start flying and the blood starts flowing, keeping the tone with some clever video game references. Great ending, too. —*S. A.*

BLACK CAT L: FOREIGN/HONG KONG (1991) 91M D: Stephen Shin. *Simon Yam, Jade Leung, Thomas Lam.* This shamelessly unabashed *La Femme Nikita* rip-off takes the Gallic girl-with-guns classic practically scene for scene, then warps it into an action-movie *Twilight Zone*. Surly Leung pouts and poses in place of a performance as she's beaten, shot, thoroughly abused, and dumped into a top-secret government training facility-and that's before she emerges as a super-assassin. Her graduation exercise is a hit at a Jewish wedding where all the guests are sporting private arsenals, and her specialty becomes killing VIPs with shards of ice. The always reliable yet curiously ambiguous Yam is her smitten handler. Powered by over-the-top action excess and absurd levels of melodrama (and accompanied by cheesy electronica with a sentimental pop bent), this is hard to beat for sheer outrageous Hong Kong fun. —*S. A.*

BLACK MASK L: FOREIGN/HONG KONG (1997) 96M D: Daniel Lee. *Jet Li, Anthony Wong, Patrick Lung Kang, Jet Li, Karen Mok, Lau Ching-Wan, Françoise Yip.* Li plays a librarian who was genetically modified to be a super-soldier in a failed military experiment (that's why he can fight like Jet Li as choreographed by Yuen Woo Ping). When he finds out that some of the other test subjects are now using their powers for crime, he puts on a Kato mask and tries to stop them. It would be nice to have a few more fights in this film, but the ones that are there are great and the dark comic book tone is a lot of fun. While Miramax usually shortens Hong Kong imports before releasing them in the United States, Artisan actually made *Black Mask* a few minutes longer for its American theatrical release, restoring some gore that had been cut from the original. On the other hand, they dubbed it into English and completely rescored it with a hip-hop soundtrack. I happen to think the new score works great as a weird crosscultural hybrid-they even got Roc Raida of the X-ecutioners to scratch on it-but most fans tend to view it as a horrible bastardization. —*B. T.*

BRASSIERE, LA L: FOREIGN/HONG KONG (2001) 111M D: Patrick Leung, Chan Hing-kai. *Gigi Leung, Louis Koo, Lau Ching-Wan, Carina Lau.* This delightful romantic comedy that puts men at odds with women has a heartwarming effect, even as the male species is put in its place. A bulk of the lighthearted comedy comes from the screenplay, which pokes at man's inability to understand women, but that should not deter men from seeing the movie. In fact, the film could help men understand women better. Johnny (Lau) and Wayne (Koo) are hired by Sis, a lingerie design company, and are given the task to design the world's best bra. They quickly set out to their task, while also trying to date all of the women in the office. As romance begins to bloom, they soon find themselves wearing their own product in order to test it. As they continue, both Johnny and Wayne learn what it is really like to have breasts, as well as the different perceptions both men and women have of them. —*R. M.*

CHAMPIONS, THE (1983) L: FOREIGN/HONG KONG (1983) 100M D: Brandy Yuen. *Yuen Biao, Kwok Keung Cheung, Moon Lee, Dick Wei, Eddy Ko.* This Yuen Biao film is a great comedy for any age and was my all-time favorite Chinese soccer movie (OK, it's a small category), until it was eclipsed by *Shaolin Soccer*. In fact there are many ideas that Stephen Chow borrowed from *The Champions.* Biao plays Lee Tong, a young man from a rural town who runs barefoot in the river, scaring the fish into the shallows to catch them. His footwork lends itself naturally to the game of soccer and his talents are noticed by a club team when he moves

to the "big city." Tong and his team eventually face off with the evil King (Wei) and his team of ruffians for the championship. A driving rainstorm ensues and the players are unable to use their skills effectively, except for Tong who sheds his shoes and guides the soccer ball gracefully through the rain with his bare feet. Thanks fish! A highly adept martial arts–based cast makes for some of the most acrobatic, thrilling, yet naturalistic soccer sequences ever filmed. Underrated and overlooked, *The Champions* is a great little film to seek out and love. —*G. M.*

CHINESE ODYSSEY 2002 L: FOREIGN/HONG KONG (2002) 97M D: Jeff Lau. *Vicki Zhao, Chang Chen, Tony Leung Chiu Wai, Faye Wong.* Historical romance and Ming-era action meet goofball farce in Lau's comedy of rascally royal siblings who dress up and sneak out of the palace for innocent shenanigans. Princess Wong dresses as a man and falls for the failed outlaw Bully the Kid (Leung), who of course wants to set "him" up with his scrappy sister (Zhao), while the Prince (Chen) becomes a fashion guru who anticipates platform shoes and afros by a couple of centuries and moonwalks through one of the handful of musical numbers. Sweet, silly, and often unexpectedly funny, it's like a Bugs Bunny cartoon of a martial-chivalry epic, complete with energetically animated performances, inspired anachronisms, and gender confusion that could happen only in the movies. —*S. A.*

CITY HUNTER L: FOREIGN/HONG KONG (1992) 105M D: Jing Wong. *Jackie Chan, Joey Wang, Gary Daniels, Kumiko Goto, Chingmy Yau, Leon Lai.* This is definitely one of Chan's more goofy flicks, and considering his work, that's really saying something. Based on the Japanese manga of the same name, *City Hunter* is about a self-indulgent private investigator who is hired to keep an eye on a powerful businessman's wild teenager. Her hijinks lead him onto a cruise ship, where hijackers take the ship and its passengers hostage, wreaking havoc and chaos. With the assistance of his lovely young ward (the now grown-up daughter of his ex-partner), his client's daughter, two undercover female cops, and a devilishly good gambler who has more up his sleeves than just cards, Chan fights to save the crew and passengers from the deadly terrorists. There are even parodies of fighting video games and martial arts movies in this often hilarious and ludicrous comedy. —*M. N.*

COME DRINK WITH ME L: FOREIGN/HONG KONG (1966) 95M D: King Hu. *Pei-pei Cheng, Chen Hung Lieh, Biao Yuen, Hua Yueh.* I was both surprised and pleased with the quality of the story, dialogue, martial arts, and most of all the humor of this 1966 Hong Kong movie. The story revolves around a young woman who is an almost legendary law enforcer known as the Golden Swallow. She is on a mission to rescue her brother and the son of the governor from a group of villains who are holding them as ransom, demanding the release of their leader. Along the way she meets a seemingly useless bum known as Drunken Cat, who is more than he appears, giving her crucial hints in drunken ditties and becoming her ally on more than one occasion. Eventually she meets Jade Tiger, the first in command, and finds that perhaps this time she has met her match. Some of the martial arts are a bit cheesy (she swings her sword and everyone explodes away from her!), but it is a wonderful flick, with delightfully playful characters. Everyone really lives up to their name too: Smiling Tiger almost always has this shit-eating grin on his face, Drunken Cat is usually, well, drunk, and Jade Tiger is terribly femme in appearance, unusually pale and ever-so-slightly green in complexion. —*M. N.*

CONTRACT KILLER L: FOREIGN/HONG KONG (1997) 98M D: Stephen Tung Wai. *Eric Tsang, Jet Li.* Li is a country boy who comes to Hong Kong to become an assassin and Tsang is the failed pro who bluffs his way into becoming his agent. Li carries this often-forced action comedy by sheer good-natured charm (he finds that his only problem is that he's just too darn nice for the job), but the best moments belong to a collection of absurd parodies introduced in the opening scenes: hilarious versions of *La Femme Nikita* and *Léon* (from *The Professional,* complete with potted plant) show their stuff as they compete with assassins from all over Asia for a big money hit. Director Tung Wai can't sustain that tone, which collapses in a city mouse/country mouse tale that straddles comedy and tragedy with mixed success. But Li is a marvel in action. —*S. A.*

COP ON A MISSION L: FOREIGN/HONG KONG (2001) 89M D: Marco Mak. *Suki Kwan, Daniel Wu, Eric Tsang.* Wu (also known as Daniel Ng) is an ambitious cop who goes undercover in the Triads and discovers he's got a real talent for crime. Wu is excellent as this corrupted *Donnie Brasco* with a ruthless streak, a young actor with matinee idol looks that harden into fierceness as he embraces the violence of his new life. Popular comic star Tsang gives crime boss Tin a marvelous mix of personable charm, cool-headed smarts, and an unexpected capacity for payback. We know where the tale is headed from the film's brilliant opening image of a bound figure in an open grave awaiting his burial, but the pitiless narration that accompanies his journey to hell rings with a hollow doom. It's one of the better gangster dramas to emerge from Hong Kong since John Woo checked his guns at the door and left for Hollywood. —*S. A.*

CRAZY SAFARI (AKA **THE GODS MUST BE CRAZY III**) L: FOREIGN/HONG KONG (1991) 96M D: Billy Chan. *Lung Chan, Stephen Chow, N!xau.* It stars the African tribesman Xixo (N!xau) and it's like *The Gods Must Be Crazy* but instead of a Coke bottle falling out of

an airplane, there is a vampire. Naturally, hijinks ensue. Kung fu action, magicians, blood-sucking conundrums, and powerful spirits all await. The highlight is when Xixo becomes possessed by the ghost of Bruce Lee and takes care of some shit. Also, it is narrated by Stephen Chow. In light of Xixo's recent death, I feel it is important to look at his entire canon of work and ponder why he chose to stay a San bushman rather than continue in the filmmaking business. This film, I think, provides some insight. —*Tommy*

DOUBLE VISION L: FOREIGN/HONG KONG (2002) 110M D: Chen Kuo-fu. *David Morse, Tony Leung Kar-Fai, Rene Liu, Leon Dai.* Morose Hong Kong cop Leung, shunned by his fellow officers and alienated from his wife (Liu), and American FBI profiler Morse team up to stop a spooky serial killer in Taiwan. Three seemingly unrelated deaths straddle the supernatural, the spiritual, and the scientific: a businessman freezes to death in a sweltering office, a woman is burned to a crisp in an otherwise scorch-free apartment, and a Catholic priest has his intestines removed, washed, and replaced while he is alive, without a sign of struggle or spilled blood. Connecting the deaths are a mysterious fungus with psychotropic properties, an ancient Taoist prophecy of immortality, and a cult constructed around a girl with double pupils. As strange a thriller as you'll ever see, Kuo-fu's moody little piece unfolds with leisurely style and takes such surreal turns that it defies all conventional logic while constructing its own alternate world. In the past few years Asain cinema has plunged head-first into the *Seven*-inspired thriller, right down to the unnerving stylistic jitters and CGI-enhanced visions. This strange entry doesn't always make sense, but it does offer tantalizing intrigue. —*S. A.*

DRAGON LIVES, THE (AKA **BRUCE LEE: THE MAN, THE MYTH**) L: FOREIGN/HONG KONG (1976) 88M D: Ng See Yuen. *Bruce Li, Caryn White.* Li (one of the better Bruce Lee imitators) stars in a humorously shoddy telling of Lee's life story. In this version, Lee's primary concern is proving that his Chinese kung fu is superior to other nationalities and fighting styles, whether that be Japanese karate, Thai kickboxing, or just some fat Italian-American guys harassing him. There is even a scene where he attaches electrodes to himself and keeps turning the voltage up higher to prove he can take it. His marriage and fatherhood are completely skipped except for one scene where his wife and a blonde Brandon walk in and say hello. At the end, a narrator explains, "Many believe Bruce Lee is still alive, a recluse, preparing to return in 1983, ten years from the day of his disappearance." —*B. T.*

DRUNKEN MASTER II (AKA **THE LEGEND OF THE DRUNKEN MASTER**) L: FOREIGN/HONG KONG (1994) 102M D: Chia-Liang Liu. *Jackie Chan, Chia-Liang Liu, Lung*

Ti, Ken Lo, Felix Wong, Anita Mui. This is the best film Chan ever made. It truly is the pinnacle of his talent, having some of the most brilliant and innovative martial arts choreography, an interesting and entertaining storyline, and all the angst, fighting, humor, and excitement you could possibly ask for. Returning with his father from a shopping expedition for medicines, Feihung (Chan) finds himself embroiled in a complicated struggle between foreigners who wish to illegally export ancient Chinese artifacts and the Chinese loyalists who want to protect their country's heritage. He is urged to use his fighting abilities to aid his countrymen, but his true strength comes out when he practices "drunken boxing." His father, however, is ashamed of his son for this drunken display of talent and bans him from ever practicing it again. And so Fei-hung is torn between his loyalty toward his father and his need to help in this struggle against these cultural thieves. Go watch the original-*Drunken Master 2*, not the U.S. release *Legend of the Drunken Master.* You'll be glad that you did. —*M. N.*

EBOLA SYNDROME L: FOREIGN/HONG KONG (1996) 90M D: Herman Yau. *Shing Fui-On, Anthony Wong, Vincent Wan.* Wong does what he does best, playing a psychotic anti-hero, in this grisly, ruthlessly exploitive feature. Ah Kai (Wong) is a short-tempered man who flees to Africa after he kills his wife and her lover in Hong Kong. He makes a quiet living for himself at a restaurant, and after an unconsenting encounter with a young woman, he becomes infected with the Ebola virus and soon finds that he is immune to its effects. When his temper gets the best of him, his employer is quickly dispatched. Ah Kai returns to Hong Kong to start eliminating those he felt had done him wrong, and in the process possibly infects the whole city. Yau and Wong, who previously worked on *The Untold Story*, bring their Category III expertise to the table to push Ebola to the limits of acceptability. Unfortunately, and tragically, those extremes have been expunged from the film by Hong Kong's censors, and may have been lost to the ages. —*R. M.*

ENTER THE DRAGON L: FOREIGN/HONG KONG (1973) 99M D: Robert Clouse. *Bruce Lee, John Saxon, Kien Shih, Angela Mao.* This international coproduction was released just after Lee's untimely death. It established him as the first martial arts superstar and kicked off a worldwide kung-fu craze that resulted in countless rip-offs and was eventually parodied in *Kentucky Fried Movie.* Already an established movie star in Hong Kong, Lee was known to American audiences for his portrayal of Kato in *The Green Hornet* TV series. After starring in a series of great martial arts films back in Asia he returned to the States to star in this outstanding action film. He plays a special agent who infiltrates a martial arts tournament at an island fortress run by a claw-handed

master criminal named Han who is secretly manufacturing heroin. A wide variety of martial arts styles are demonstrated in the tournament while Lee investigates Han's illegal activities. It all ends with a thrilling battle between Lee and Han in a roomful of mirrors. Lee is a magnetic screen presence and the cast is nicely filled out by American actors like Kelly and Saxon as well as many of the top stars of Hong Kong action cinema. —*S. H.*

FEARLESS HYENA L: FOREIGN/CHAN, JACKIE (1979) 94M D: Jackie Chan. *Yam Sai-Kun, Jackie Chan.* Chan makes his directorial debut with this comic kung fu adventure, which is virtually a copy of his breakthrough hit *Drunken Master.* Jackie ("Jacky" on the credits) is a rascally kung fu student who gambles, street fights, and opens his own kung fu school. When an evil warlord murders his grandfather, he gets serious and gets revenge. Jackie also choreographs the film, which is full of complicated fights with slapstick undertones and the now traditional, elaborate training sequences. He mugs his way through a series of comic contests in costumes (once even in drag as a geisha). In the pirate tradition of Hong Kong knockoffs, the score is cribbed from a variety of Hollywood films, including *The Pink Panther* and *Superman.* —*S. A.*

FLASH FUTURE KUNG FU L: FOREIGN/HONG KONG (1980) 82M D: Kirk Wong. *Johnny Wang, Eddy Ko Hung, Ray Lui Leung-Wai.* The students of a poor but honorable martial arts master battle the bullying soldiers of a neo-Nazi-styled organization bent on city domination through surgically implanted computer chips that turn its victims into zombie soldiers. Or something like that. Shot in dark, smoky rooms lit by the pale blue reflection of video monitors, this odd, early Wong action thriller drops gang fights and grudge matches into the artful techno-poverty of a *Blade Runner*-esque future. Made on the cusp of the Hong Kong new wave, this bizarre mix of old-school martial arts melodrama ("You beat the master of my school and now you must pay!") and grunge-noir cyberpunk stylings doesn't make much sense, but why let that get in the way of the fun? —*S. A.*

FULL THROTTLE L: FOREIGN/HONG KONG (1996) 108M D: Derek Yee. *Andy Lau, Chin Ka-lok, David Wu, Gigi Leung.* As with many motorcycle films, this one gives the viewer an exhilarating and breathtaking ride during the racing scenes and drags when the lead characters are not speeding down the streets. Lau is a motorcycle junkie who becomes first friends, then rivals with hotshot biker Wu, who is looking to make a name for himself among the professional racers who hang out at a local bar. To complicate matters worse, not only does Wu join Lau's estranged father's racing team (the father refuses to let his own son race), but Lau's longtime girlfriend (Leung) gives him an ulti-

The Real and Reel Wong Fei-Hung

Over the course of the twentieth century, martial artist Wong Fei-Hung was revered and turned into a patriotic folk hero who some now say is only a legend and never truly existed. But Wong Fei-Hung was very much a real person. He was born in 1847 into the Wong lineage. His father, Wong Kay-Ying, was a member of the Ten Tigers of Canton, and practiced medicine in the small village of Xiqiao near Canton. Fei-Hung was taught in both external and internal medicinal practices in his father's famous clinic, Po Chi Lam, and given a strong sense of self-worth. At an early age, Fei-Hung became interested in kung fu and was determined to learn martial arts.

Fei-Hung's true master has become lost to time. While some say that his father passed on his martial skills, which were rooted in the practices of Shaolin monks, others claim that Fei-Hung's father refused to teach him in order to keep him safe from harm, and that it was in fact Wong Kay-Ying's master who became Fei-Hung's teacher. As Fei-Hung's skills improved, he started performing in the street for money. By his early twenties, he had mastered the Hung Gar form and also created a new form combining tiger and crane studies. Fei-Hung eventually came into the service of the local army, where his extraordinary mastery of martial arts led him to become the instructor of thousands of soldiers as well as generals. He eventually rose to be assistant to the governor of the Fujian province.

As the assistant to Governor Tang, he

continued on page 334

matum: he must stop racing, or she'll leave him. When a drag race goes wrong, Lau is severely hurt, and it seems like Leung's wish has come true. But a tragic accident forces him to face his fears, and Lau must once again stare down the broken yellow line of fate. The race scenes are the primary reason to seek out this film; they were choreographed by master stuntman Bruce Law and feature cameras mounted on helmets and the actual motorcycles to give an extra rush of speed. —R. M.

GEN-X COPS L: FOREIGN/HONG KONG (1999) 113M D: Benny Chan. *Daniel Wu, Eric Tsang, Toru Nakamura.* After a shipment of explosives is stolen, the Hong Kong police are at ends attempting to discover what has happened. A veteran policeman (Tsang), who is the laughingstock of his squad, is given permission to try to send undercover cops into the triad to get information. His choices are three police academy cadets who are about to be expelled. They are given a trendy Gen-X outfit and equally Gen-X nicknames, and sent into to fray to learn the location of the explosives. They are soon caught up in a power struggle between two equally hip criminals, which sets the stage for the final climactic conclusion. Although the action does tend to meander into U.S. straight-to-video country, it remains fresh and well laid out for most of the film. Fans of any of the leads

will have a blast following the trio's exploits, and the final multilevel fight sequence is worth the wait. Jackie Chan, who produced the film, also gives a cameo performance. —R. M.

GOD OF COOKERY L: FOREIGN/HONG KONG (1997) 95M D: Stephen Chow, Li-Lik-Chu. *Karen Mok, Stephen Chow, Ng Man Tat.* Chow gives a frantically paced, laugh-till-it-hurts performance as the head of a Hong Kong restaurant chain who has lost the spirit of cooking in the search of a higher profit margin. When he is suddenly usurped and outcast by his assistant, Chow finds himself alone in the streets. A chance encounter with a disfigured noodle-stall owner (Mok) leads him to create a new chain of restaurants and a fantastic new dish, Pissing Beef Balls. As the annual God of Cookery championship comes, Chow heads into China to find a secluded cooking school, but disappears when his rival attempts to have him assassinated. This is one of Chow's best comedies and shows off his unique humor. It pays homage to *Iron Chef* while farcing it completely, and throws in parodies of *The God of Gamblers* and *The Chinese Feast*, which can not fail to entertain those familiar with the films. —R. M.

GOD OF GAMBLERS L: FOREIGN/HONG KONG (1989) 126M D: Wong Jing. *Chow Yun-Fat, Shing Fui-On, Joey Wong, Andy Lau.* A seminal classic in all

became quite popular among the people, and a champion for the weak. He became so popular that the people rallied around both him and the governor to become the next leaders of Canton. Unfortunately, the revolution was squashed and Fei-Hung fled back to his hometown, where he became the proprietor of the Po Chi Lam clinic, and secretly aided Ching revolutionaries.

The specific details of Fei-Hung's later life are few, but one fact that is certain is that one of his sons died during a raid by the drug gang Dai Fin Yee. Hawn-Sun had been taught by his father the same principles and martial arts that had been passed down to Fei-Hung, but while standing up for the weak and protecting the innocent, Hawn-Sun was gunned down. It is said that after that, Fei-Hung refused to teach his remaining nine children martial arts in order to protect them. He had finally learned the lesson that his father had attempted to teach him so many years before.

Fei-Hung lived his remaining years in his hometown, where he died of natural causes in 1924. Though he was revered as a patriot and helped to usher in the modern style of martial arts, it is the fictitious stories written and legends spread about him, after his death, that catapulted him into folklore forever. The first of these stories began running in a local paper, which printed both fictional and embellished chronicles of Wong Fei-Hung's life. The stories became so popular that they were adapted into plays and screenplays.

Between one hundred and two hundred films have now been made featuring Wong Fei-Hung as the central character. Films have dramatized every phase of his life, from young boy to old man, and have portrayed him as everything from a patriotic savior to a drunken idiot. The first man to portray Fei-Hung was a former Peking Opera performer named Kwan Tak-Hing. Tak-Hing would return to the screen for the next two decades in nearly a hundred films, portraying what was becoming the

---

categories, this is indeed the god of gambling movies, as Yun-Fat brings to life Ko Chun, a master gambler with an almost supernatural ability to win. When Ko Chun is involved in an accident, he becomes a semi-amnesiac with the mental state of a child, and can only remember how to gamble. Knife (Lau) takes Ko Chun in, and although he helps take care of him, he also abuses Ko Chun's power for profit. After Ko Chun's enemies finally discover what has happened to him, they plan to beat him at the tables, and a final duel is set up to see who indeed is the God of Gamblers. The gaming action in the film is a sight to be seen, and the comedic aspects of Ko Chun's condition are not forced. Jing's cinematic direction is also at its best here. The film was so popular, it spawned not one, but two different sets of sequels, with Yun-Fat reprising his role in *God Of Gambler's Return*. —R. M.

GORGEOUS (BOR LEI JUN) L: FOREIGN/HONG KONG (1999) 121M D: Vincent Kok. *Jackie Chan, Shu Qi, Ken Lo, Richie Ren, Tony Leung Chiu Wai*. Is it possible to have a Jackie Chan film that a) doesn't really have any villains in it; b) does have good fight scenes in it; c) is a romantic comedy with Jackie as the romantic lead; and d) is still good? Why yes! Bu is a young woman from Taiwan who finds a bottle with a message in it saying "I love you" from a man in Hong Kong. But when

she gets there the fantasy quickly ends, leaving her uncertain as to what to do. She meets Chan, a single businessman who spends more time working than living, and becomes quickly fond of him. Young, impetuous, silly, and full of life, she injects a breath of fresh air into his stale existence and reminds him the worth of a smile, play, and simple pleasures. It's light, fluffy, and charming for the most part. Nothing to get super excited about, but the fight scenes, which are more a question of comparing skill than expressing any malice or urge to maim, are still great even if Jackie has lost some of his speed with age. Low on angst, high on perky. Take a break from the usual fare. —M. N.

HIGH RISK L: FOREIGN/HONG KONG (1995) 100M D: Corey Yuen, Wong Jing. *Jet Li, Chingmy Yau, Jacky Cheung, Charlie Yeung*. Jacky Cheung is an almost libelous satire of Jackie Chan in this Jet Li *Die Hard* takeoff. Li plays a former demolition expert who retires from the social world (see brief flashback for details) and becomes the bodyguard (and secret stunt-double) of womanizing movie superstar Frankie (Cheung), but his secret-and his emotional distance-are forced into the open when high-tech jewel thieves invade a society party and take both Li and Cheung hostage. Wong Jing (one of Hong Kong's most prolific directors) is a shamelessly slapstick-oriented

commonly accepted version of Wong Fei-Hung's persona.

In the last quarter of the twentieth century, Wong Fei-Hung achieved legendary status on the silver screen. In *Drunken Master* and its sequels, two of Hong Kong's most beloved martial artists, Jackie Chan and Jet Li, would take the character in different directions, while at the same time remaining true to the central ideals so vital to the real Wong Fei-Hung.

The *Drunken Master* phenomenon began in 1978, when director Yuen Woo-Ping took a martial artist who was rising in popularity, Jackie Chan, and teamed him with the director's father, Yuen Siu-Tien, to add a new twist to the legend of Wong Fei-Hung. Chan, whose mixture of comedy and kung fu had garnered him early attention, portrayed Wong as an undisciplined, out-of-control young man who is sent by his father to learn drunken boxing from Sam Seed. The film was so successful that it catapulted Jackie Chan to stardom and solidified Yuen

Woo-Ping's action direction as some of the best in Hong Kong cinema.

Jackie Chan would return to the screen sixteen years later, in 1994, to reprise his role as a goofy Wong Fei-Hung in the semi-sequel *Drunken Master 2*. The film set a high bar in terms of pure kung fu action and is to this day a standard against which all other films in the genre are measured. Fei-Hung, who has been taught drunken boxing by his father, is a shiftless layabout who has no ambitions. But when he is caught up in a battle against foreigners stealing treasures from his town, he finds his true calling as a champion for the people. The climatic battle, in which Fei-Hung must drink industrial alcohol to gain the strength to fight, could be considered one of the top fight scenes in modern Hong Kong cinema. The film was so successful that part 3 was quickly filmed and released later that year, but without Jackie Chan, and with a much more serious attitude.

continued on page 336

director, but he knows how to stage an action scene-gunplay, explosions, terrific martial arts battles, and a spectacular helicopter stunt highlight this comic action picture. —*S.A.*

INFERNAL AFFAIRS L: FOREIGN/HONG KONG (2002) 97M D: Andrew Lau, Alan Mak. *Tony Leung Chiu Wai, Sammi Cheng, Kelly Chen, Anthony Wong Chau-Sang, Andy Lau, Eric Tsang.* This dark and intelligent crime thriller traces the path of two men, each living a lie. In their youth, they were deliberately placed undercover. One man secretly works for a crime boss while entering the police academy and advancing himself up to detective. The other, apparently having been kicked out of the academy, enters into a life of crime and begins to move up along the thug ladder, secretly still working for the police. Ten years later, their paths finally cross in a case where the undercover cop is working for the same crime lord the fake officer is trying to protect. A twisted film about each man working at cross-purposes trying to determine the identity of the other, their lives intersect with dramatic and unexpected results. —*M.N.*

INFRA-MAN (AKA SUPER INFRA-MAN) L: FOREIGN/HONG KONG (1976) 92M D: Hua-Shan. *Terry Liu, Wang Hsieh, Lin Wen-wei, Li Hsiu-hsien.* Primarily known for their period martial arts films, here the Shaw

brothers try out the Japanese-style giant monster genre a la *Ultraman*. Infra-Man is a man in a robot suit who can enlarge himself to battle giant bugs and plants controlled by the wicked Princess Dragon Mom. The movie is crammed full of enough monsters and fights to fill several movies, making it perhaps the most berserk movie of its type outside of *Space Monster Gamera*. This goofy, colorful, and sometimes surprisingly violent film is endlessly fun no matter how many times you watch it. One video release tacks on a cheesy opening credits montage that retitles the movie *Infra-Man* vs. *The Sci-Fi Monsters*. If you can play region 2 DVDs, look for it as *Super Infra-Man* from the Shaw Brothers Collection. Although it is lacking the hilarious English-dubbed version, it is a revelation to see this film widescreen, subtitled and gorgeously remastered. —*B.T.*

INTIMATE CONFESSION OF A CHINESE COURTESAN L: FOREIGN/HONG KONG (1972) 86M D: Chu Yuan. *Lily Ho, Fan Mei Sheng, Betty Ting Pei.* Ho is the feisty, proud young woman kidnapped and sold to a brothel run by a ruthless lesbian madam, where she is tortured, sold to the highest bidder, and deflowered. This is no Mizoguchi melodrama of a fallen woman, but a kinky revenge tale of an innocent turned seductive assassin: pure exploitation with a tasteful canvas. The elegantly

Although Chan's embodiment of the legend is highly regarded, it is Tsui Hark's fictional accounts of Wong Fei-Hung that are truly the finest interpretation. In 1991, Tsui Hark tapped Jet Li to portray Fei-Hung in *Once Upon a Time in China*. The straightfaced Li's performance as a much more serious and patriotic Fei-Hung is perhaps one of his finest on-screen roles, both as actor and as martial artist. In *China*, Li's Fei-Hung takes a steady stance against Western influence, and as riots escalate between the local militia and foreign soldiers, he joins in to protect the ideals and ways of his homeland. Jet Li returned to the role in *Once Upon a Time in China 2* (1992), *Once Upon a Time in China 3* (1993), and *Once Upon a Time in China and America* (1997) to further the visions of director and producer Tsui Hark. Li also created his own interpretation in *Last Hero in China* (1993), which he both directed and starred in. After Li left the *China* series, Zhao Wen-Zhou took up the helm for part 4 and part 5, but failed to equal Li's intensity.

Wong Fei-Hung's childhood also got some screen time in the early 1990s. The aforementioned *Drunken Master 3* features a younger, and historically inaccurate, Fei-Hung helping to save a princess in the early years of the Chinese revolution, which in reality would have been toward the end of Fei-Hung's life. A more accurate portrayal of young Wong Fei-Hung and his mastery of martial arts comes in Yuen Woo-Ping's *Iron Monkey* (1993). Although in this film Fei-Hung's saga takes a backseat to his father's story, the powerful relationship between the two is shown as they become entangled with local corruption and the title hero.

During his life Wong Fei-Hung became a symbol of patriotism, a champion for those who could not defend themselves, and a philosopher of modern ideals. The Wong Fei-Hung of Chinese entertainment has helped to keep alive those ideals, as the footsteps of one of the greatest martial arts stars continue to echo in the halls of legend and imagination. —*Ryan Miller*

---

composed widescreen shots have the quality of a screen painting that suddenly explodes into martial arts frenzies. The weird mix of sensibilities bleeds into the soundtrack, where traditional instruments are joined by '60s fuzz-guitar stings and sassy strip-club saxophones. It's not exactly good, but it's gorgeous and mad and more fun that it should be. —*S. A.*

KIDNAP L: FOREIGN/HONG KONG (1974) 122M D: Ching Gong. *Fan Mei Sheng, Lin Wei-Tu, Lo Lieh*. Lo takes a break from his period films to star in the Shaw brothers's ultragritty modern tale of greed and brutal justice. As a gas-station attendant, Lo conceives what he believes to be a quick way to get some money out of his stingy boss. With the help of his friends, he plots to kidnap the boss's son, demand the ransom money, and make a quick exchange. But the plan is spoiled from the beginning, and when blood is spilled, the quartet of kidnappers becomes wanted by the police for murder. Lo's girlfriend is also pulled into the web and is forced to become an accomplice to get Lo out of Hong Kong along with his friends. Many standard '70s crime thrillers are spiced up here, with car chases, police escapes, and detective-work cutaways. In the end, as is clear from the beginning, Lo must face up to his responsibilities and make amends with the swift and pitiless justice system as he counts down his final hours. —*R. M.*

LADY PROFESSIONAL, THE L: FOREIGN/HONG KONG (1971) 80M D: Matsuo Akinori. *Lily Ho, Shen Chan*. The always desirable Ho plays the title character in this gritty revenge-thriller. When a gangster is released from jail to testify against his former mob boss, a hit is put out on the gangster's life to keep him from telling his tale and exposing the textile company owner's true identity. The gangsters blackmail café owner/hit woman Tian-Li, whom they have incriminating evidence on, to kill the stool pigeon. But when the hit is complete, an accident is set up for Tian-Li to die in a car wreck. She is able to survive, and plots her revenge against the men who would not only kill her but, she discovers, had previously killed her father as well. The Shaw brothers are certainly known for their martial arts films, but their crime pictures deserve equal accolades, and this is no exception. The opening car chase would make even Steve McQueen envious, the double-crossings are well thought out, and the revenge is oh-so-sweet. —*R. M.*

MAN CALLED HERO, A L: FOREIGN/HONG KONG (1999) 105M D: Andrew Lau. *Yuen Biao, Shu Qi, Nicholas Tse, Ekin Cheng, Kristy Yang*. Following on the heels of *Stormriders*, Lau reunites many of the film's cast and crew here. When Hero (Cheng) returns from an initiation ceremony, he finds that his family has been slain by foreigners searching for the legendary Red Sword, his family's heirloom treasure. Hero's vengeance is swift and complete, but in the process he becomes wanted by the police and flees to America. Years later, Hero's son makes the same journey to America, to look for a father he does not know. He quickly learns that America is not the land of opportunity, and that many of those who followed before him are now slave to a coal mining company that keeps them under an iron thumb. Though Hero is nowhere to be found, a mysterious man of the people knows where he might be. The effects here one-up their predecessor, and emotions run high throughout the film as it questions the treatment of immigrants. The final fight, which takes place on the Statue of Liberty, is well worth the wait. —*R. M.*

MAN CALLED TIGER, A L: FOREIGN/HONG KONG (1973) 70M D: Lo Wei. *Maria Yi, Jimmy Wang Yu, Kawai Okada, Tien Chun.* Two years after Wei directed Bruce Lee to stardom in *The Big Boss* he directed this well-known but overrated yawner. In Japan trying to discover who killed his father and why, Chinese tough-guy Wang Yu feigns beating up a friend as a ticket into the gang world. Two women are also looking for their fathers, one a dice cheat and other a knife assassin. Everyone watches the dice game between two gang-bosses except two different women more interested Tiger. In the end the answer lies at the dice table but in between the pace is awkward. The wooden, dubbed dialogue is just time filler. And the sexiness of Wang Yu and the four women actresses is neither played up nor drawn out sufficiently to stir much inside you. Wang Yu's fight scenes make for good watching as you would expect, but every twist and turn of the big kick-fight finale is 100 percent predictable. —*J. C.*

MASTER OF THE FLYING GUILLOTINE L: FOREIGN/HONG KONG (1975) 93M D: Jimmy Wang Yu. *Jimmy Wang Yu, Kam Kang, Chia Yung Liu.* Seeking revenge, the blind, bushy-eyebrowed Master of the Flying Guillotine (a slick weapon which is basically a spinning, bladed hat that chops people's heads off) vows to kill every one-armed boxer in China. After several heads fly, he finally tracks down *the* One-Armed Boxer (played by the director and '70s martial arts superstar), leading to an incredible showdown in a booby-trapped coffin factory. Featuring one of the greatest kung fu movie soundtracks (a combination of pirated Kraut rock and original electronic music), *Master of the Flying Guillotine* piles one exciting fight after another. The film's centerpiece is a lengthy martial arts tournament featuring lots of bizarre characters and unusual fighting techniques. Immensely fun and action packed, *Master* supplies plenty of thrills, kicks, punches, and chops for all you kung fu theater fans. —*S. H.*

MIRACLES (aka BLACK DRAGON) L: FOREIGN/CHAN, JACKIE (1989) 127M D: Jackie Chan, Benny Chan. *Jackie Chan, Anita Mui, Yah-Leh Gui.* Chan's uncredited remake of Frank Capra's *Lady for a Day* is slapstick comedy in costume, punctuated by his unique brand of acrobatic action. He's a country boy in 1930s Shanghai who rescues a mob boss and is given a nightclub and his own gang as a reward. Mui plays the hot-headed singer he alternately romances and rebuffs, until the two band together to make an aging flower-seller (whom Chan believes is the source of his good luck) into a society woman for a day. Being a Chan film, the usual disasters are punctuated by a gang war, which leads to the usual gymnastic battles and rubber-faced mugging for the camera. The warfare in this film is definitely in a comic vein. Chan has cited this as his personal favorite among the films he directed. —*S. A.*

MOMENT OF ROMANCE, A L: FOREIGN/HONG KONG (1990) 88M D: Benny Chan. *Andy Lau, Wu Chien-Lien.* From start to finish, this film has all the makings of a great Hong Kong film, including production by Johnnie To. Lau plays Wah-Dee, an orphan who has grown up on the mean streets of Hong Kong and has become a triad member specializing in vehicles, zipping around on a motorcycle or in a car with ease. He is hired to be the getaway driver for a robbery that goes horribly wrong, and must take Jo Jo (Chien-Lien) hostage in order to escape. An instant connection is made between the two, and Wah-Dee saves her from certain death at the hands of his gang. Although Wah-Dee is reluctant to accept the affection that Jo Jo is so willing to give, he eventually gives in to what will indeed become a moment of romance. When the police identify Jo Jo as being the former hostage, they bring her in for questioning, and the triad decides that she must die. Wah-Dee forsakes his triad to protect her, and single-handedly stands against them in the name of love. Although the film at first seems like a slice-of-life triad drama, the romantic aspects pull it into another direction, and conclude as a tragedy that is sure to make the heart weep. —*R. M.*

MR. VAMPIRE L: FOREIGN/HONG KONG (1985) 96M D: Ricky Lau. *Moon Lee, Ricky Hui, Chin Siu-Hou, Lam Ching-Ying.* This is the film solely responsible for igniting the hopping vampire craze that swept across Hong Kong cinema in the late '80s and early '90s. It also created the typecast role for Ching-Ying, who would go on to forever be remembered as the One Eye-Browed Priest. This is a Hong Kong horror in the purest sense, and successfully pulls off the blend of scares and laughs required. As the movie starts, a Taoist priest has been called upon to inspect the reburial of a businessman's grandfather. The priest realizes that the corpse has become a vampire, and begins his preparations to put the soul to rest. But the body awakens before he can finish his magic spells, and escapes to spread ter-

ror in the town. Meanwhile, one of the priest's assistants has fallen under the spell of a ghost and must be saved before he forever becomes her slave, while the other has become infected by a vampire bite. The film goes into incredible detail portraying the rites of a Taoist priest, and fight scenes are incredibly fun as the hopping vampires get out of control. Many sequels and rip-offs followed, but few came close to capturing the initial impact of their originator. —R. M.

MY FATHER IS A HERO L: FOREIGN/HONG KONG (1995) 100M D: Corey Yuen. *Jet Li, Tsue Miu, Anita Mui.* A boy (Miu) who is a martial arts champion always has faith in his deadbeat father (Li) even though he's always late to his tournaments, and even though he gets busted, goes to prison, and breaks out. Although the kid doesn't know it, he is actually right: his dad is a cop who has gone deep undercover in a gang of arms dealers. When his mom dies, the boy goes to Hong Kong to find his dad and gets mixed up in the investigation. In a great scene that acts as both the action climax and the emotional climax, father and son fight side by side. Li even gets to tie Miu to a rope and spin him around like a weapon. This is a sentimental, somewhat downbeat martial arts drama. —B. T.

MY SCHOOLMATE, THE BARBARIAN L: FOREIGN/HONG KONG (2001) 90M D: Wong Jing, Billy Chung. *Stephen Fung, Nicholas Tse.* This action goof featuring award-winning stunt choreography by Ching Siu-Tung starts off with echoes of *Volcano High* and *Battle Royale,* but soon turned into Hong Kong's answer to *My Bodyguard.* Fung is the straight-A rich kid who, through the kind of screwy mix-up rife in Hong Kong movies, lands in a violent school overrun with delinquents who solve every conflict with private battles on a "mat" of school desks. Tse is the brooding Rock, the former fight king who has vowed never to fight again but teaches the young genius how to defend himself. Wong's penchant of cartoon-y comedy, often sped up to silly extremes, is all over the film, and the story is nonsense, but the fights are very stylishly done. —S. A.

NAKED KILLER L: FOREIGN/HONG KONG (1993) 93M D: Clarence Fok. *Simon Yam, Yiu Wai, Carrie Ng, Yau Chingmy.* Is it pure exploitive trash, or one of the finest examples of Hong Kong's Category III films, and more importantly, does it really matter? Yau takes on the title role as Kitty, a woman whose bursts of violent crimes against men gains the eye of Sister Cindy (Yiu), who brings Kitty under her wing to be taught the arts of sex and murder. Kitty is given a new identity and starts her career as a professional hit woman. But she keeps a part of her past as she continues flirting with Tian (Yam), a cop on the trail of her brutal killings. Things heat up when one of Cindy's ex-students, Princess (Ng), along with her lesbian lover, Baby, are assigned to kill her

and Kitty, and the deadly duo make their mark on Cindy's mansion. Fok titillates his audience exactly as needed here and lays on the explosive gunplay, steamy lesbianism, and gutter humor to exponential proportion. Be sure to seek out the director's cut of this classic film from Hong Kong's modern heyday. —R. M.

ONE ARMED SWORDSMAN L: FOREIGN/HONG KONG (1967) 109M D: Chang Cheh. *Jimmy Wang Yu.* The title pretty much says it all: a gifted but proud martial arts student (Yu, previously known as Wang Yu) overcomes the loss of a limb (sliced off by a confused young woman) and defends his teacher from a ruthless rival bent on revenge. Cheh's martial arts drama favors clashing swords and brutalized bodies over the beauty of the bodies in motion and the romance and grace of King Hu's *Come Drink with Me.* With its petty jealousies, rival martial arts schools, and gimmicky weapons, it launched the harder-edged style of '70s martial arts movies, but this film has a touch of Zen missing from those leaner, meaner films. —S. A.

PEACE HOTEL L: FOREIGN/HONG KONG (1995) 98M D: Wai Ka-Fai. *Chin Ho, Cecilia Yip, Chow Yun-Fat.* This would be Chow's last Hong Kong film before relocating to the United States, and with Johnnie To's frequent collaboration behind the camera, it makes for a fine departing swan song. Set during the 1920s in a cobbled-together hotel, the King of Killers (Chow) has set up a sanctuary where anyone can stay protected from harm. His patience, and only rule of not kicking anyone out, is put to the test with the arrival of a lying, conniving, penniless swindler (Yip) who is wanted by a vicious gang for their boss's murder. Now he must decide whether to keep his promise to protect anyone who stays at the hotel and risk an all-out war with the gang, or ask her to leave and fend for herself. Chow gives a solid performance as the hotel's proprietor. The intricate set piece makes for an excellent stage for the final showdown as the patrons valiantly fight for their lives. —R. M.

POM POM AND HOT HOT L: FOREIGN/HONG KONG (1992) 90M D: Joe Cheung. *Lam Ching-Ying, Jacky Cheung, Stephen Tung, Loletta Lee.* Using a dangerous technique of taking what would be the first half of one film and splicing it with the second half of another film, *Pom Pom and Hot Hot* starts out as a bumbling-cop comedy of errors, only to switch gears halfway through into a balls-to-the-wall bullet ballet action movie. Two unorthodox cops who share an apartment are visited by their cousins from the mainland, which starts the grueling comedy ball rolling. The two repeatedly wreak havoc on their cases, and end up having to be bailed out of hot water by their stoic commanding officer and mentor (Lam). The comedy is then picked up and thrown in the trash as the pair are given a drug-related murder case and

Things That Go Hop in the Night

The hopping vampire is a relative new-comer to the Hong Kong screen, though its origin is buried deep within Chinese belief and spiritualism. This vampire is very different from the Western character of the same name: it is a corpse that has undergone rigor mortis and must hop around. A hopping vampire can result either from a Taoist priest's magic as he prepares to transport the body to its final resting place, or from a buried body that has become cursed due to an improper burial. As with the Western vampire, a bite from a hopping vampire will slowly kill the victim and turn him or her into a vampire as well.

The hopping vampire, like its Western counterpart, can be warded off, controlled, or destroyed by a long list of items. First, and most necessary, is yellow parchment paper with spells written on it. When such a paper is attached to a hopping vampire's forehead, the creature becomes subdued and under control. Other spells can be used to control the movement of hopping vampires. Sticky rice can be spilled on the floor to block their movement, as they cannot step on it. Sticky rice can also be used to slow humans' transformation into vampires, if the humans hop on it. When combating a hopping vampire, martial arts are essential, as the vampire has its own form of kung

continued on page 340

get down to crime-stopping business. As they close in on their target in a claustrophobic warehouse, two-gun-fisted, bullet-spitting mayhem rips across the screen. Don't forget to pick up your jaw when the movie is done. —*R. M.*

PROJECT A 2 L: FOREIGN/CHAN, JACKIE (1987) 102M D: Jackie Chan, Benny Chan. *Rosamund Kwan, Maggie Cheung, Jackie Chan.* Chan directs and stars in this turn-of-the-century adventure. Gangsters, revolutionaries, corrupt cops, and ax-wielding pirates all want a piece of royal policeman Dragon Mao (Chan), who takes on all comers with acrobatic energy and gymnastic grace. The slapstick highlights include a bedroom farce hideaway with a dozen characters scurrying for cover and a *Defiant Ones*-style chase where Jackie dodges knives while handcuffed to his nemesis. The messy plot is not as elegant as his best adventures, but it has good-natured humor and cockeyed optimism to spare. It's Chan's own swashbuckling *Peking Opera Blues*, a nostalgic lark without the absurdist irony. —*S. A.*

QUEEN BOXER L: FOREIGN/HONG KONG (1974) 92M D: Yu Fung Chi. *Pai Lai Lee, Peter Yang Kwan, Ling Chia.* Man (Kwan) beats up protection goons who lean on his and his brother's food stand while a young lady customer (Chia) looks on. The man later removes these same middlemen from the dockyards, pleasing both owner and workers. But when he threatens the gang's big income from the gambling dens he goes too far. His brother and a large innocent family are massacred, and the gang-boss (Lee) and his two associates are too good at fighting for him to handle alone. The lady also has a grudge with the boss and also fails taking him on alone. But she now must to rescue the man who has impatiently fallen into their trap. The fight choreography is first rate particularly at the end, bringing on the nastiest deaths imaginable. —*J. C.*

RETURN OF THE DRAGON L: FOREIGN/HONG KONG (1973) 91M D: Bruce Lee. *Bruce Lee, Chuck Norris. Return of the Dragon* was actually filmed before Lee's international breakout hit, *Enter the Dragon*, but wasn't released until after his untimely demise. The title would lead you to think it's a sequel, but the film isn't related to any of Lee's other movies. In this film (which he also wrote and directed) Lee plays a likable, naive guy from Hong Kong who travels to Rome to help a friend run a Chinese restaurant. He encounters racism, violent gangsters, and Japanese kung fu masters. . . and beats the shit out of all of them! It all culminates in the famed fight between Lee and a very hairy Norris with the Roman Coliseum ruins in the background. —*S. H.*

ROBOTRIX L: FOREIGN/HONG KONG (1991) 94M D: Jamie Luk. *David Wu, Chikako Aoyama, Billy Chow, Amy Yip.* The old saying "they don't make 'em like they used to" certainly holds its weight in gold in this

fu that it uses. Octagonal mirrors, swords made of Chinese coins, and bells are also used to subdue a vampire. If the vampire is still in its coffin, a special ink can be placed on the coffin, which will create a cage that keeps the vampire in.

The legend of the hopping vampire first appears on screen in the Shaw Brothers's 1979 film *The Spiritual Boxer 2* (aka *The Shadow Boxing*). Although the Western vampire first appeared in Hong Kong in 1973's *Legend of the Seven Golden Vampires, Spiritual Boxer 2* offered the viewer a whole new mythology. In the film, a Taoist priest, who is referred to as a corpse herder, is preparing to take his clients to their hometown for burial. The opening sequence goes into incredible detail about Taoist magic as the corpses are prepared for their travels. After the bodies are washed, they are dressed in what would become the classic garb, the Mandarin robe, and controlled by the spell-inscribed yellow

paper. In the movie, Gordon Liu fakes being a hopping corpse to avoid capture, and high jinks ensue as he attempts to impersonate his hopping companions.

While *The Spiritual Boxer 2* does incorporate kung fu, it is not the actual vampires that perform it, but the limber corpse herders and finally the amazing Gordon Liu. However, in the action-horror hybrid *Encounters of the Spooky Kind* (1981), Sammo Hung goes one-on-many as he battles some lively hopping vampires who remember their martial arts moves. These vampires would make another cameo appearance in *Spooky Encounters 2* (1990), then take a well-needed rest and resurface in the career-making *Mr. Vampire.*

In 1986 Hong Kong opened the floodgates for the hopping vampire, as *Mr. Vampire* hit the screen. It not only contained the horror-oriented element of uncontrollable corpses, but also included a side plot about

---

gleeful Hong Kong exploitation masterpiece that easily spans the width of all genres. Lifting from the underlying basis of *Robocop*, a female officer is who is gunned down in secretly given a second chance when her mind is transplanted into a robotic clone of her body by an experimental scientist and her assistant. She resumes her work as a police officer and attempts to keep her relationship going with her boyfriend while hunting down the sadistic madman who took her life. This is one of most well-made trash films out there and offers a bit of something for everyone. Yip delivers in fine form as usual, displaying her ample talents while keeping a bit for the imagination. Aoyama is the star of this show, however, easily outdoing Yip's teasing ways and locking in the Category III rating. —*R. M.*

ROYAL WARRIORS L: FOREIGN/HONG KONG (1986) 93M D: David Chung. *Michelle Yeoh, Michael Wong, Hiroyuki (Henry) Sanada.* This second *In the Line of Duty* flick is by far the hardest and nastiest. A prisoner is being transported by passenger airliner; his buddy frees him and the two take over the plane. But not for long as a Japanese cop (Sanada), a security officer (Wong), and a HK female detective (Yeoh) also happen to be aboard, making for a great, tense fight sequence. There are three more members of the gang with top military training and a blood bond that is so compelling you almost want to root for them. Willing to die to avenge their two comrades, they become

powerful adversaries. Complicating matters, the Japanese cop has his own agenda and the security cop has the unreciprocated hots for the detective. Heart-pounding suspense alongside edgy guns-and-kicks fight scenes and an interesting tangle of relationships drives the plot along like a loudly banging hammer. The plexus of emotion tightens into a visceral knot as you hope against hope that somehow things will end better than you expect them to. —*J. C.*

RUMBLE IN THE BRONX L: FOREIGN/HONG KONG (1995) 105M D: Stanley Tong. *Jackie Chan, Anita Mui, Bill Tung, Françoise Yip.* If he didn't have extraordinary fighting skills and Batman-like leaping and climbing abilities, Chan would be just a regular Hong Kong cop who comes to a suspiciously Vancouver-looking New York for a wedding. He just wants to hang out and help Mui with her newly purchased grocery store, but when some cartoonish street thugs come in and cause trouble, he gets mixed up with them and a hunt for stolen diamonds. Next thing you know he's getting involved in elaborately choreographed fights and stunts where he jumps through shopping carts and pinball machines or leaps off of a parking garage onto a balcony across the street. Dubbed into English, this was the movie that finally made Chan into a superstar in the United States (dropping him into a downward spiral that would lead to crappy buddy movies with less fighting and more CGI than actual

ghostly love, offered comedic reflections on human love, and sprinkled strange British customs throughout to lighten the mood. In the film, Lam Ching-Ying plays a no-nonsense Taoist priest who not only herds corpses but offers insights on Taoist rites as well. Lam, who got his start as a martial artist in Bruce Lee's movies, played the part so successfully that he was typecast (willingly) as the One-Eyebrowed Priest for the rest of his career, until his untimely death in 1997 from cancer.

The "Mr. Vampire" in the movie is the grandfather of a local businessman who is reburying his ancestor, as he has been instructed to do by a previous priest. In doing so, Kou (Lam Ching-Ying) realizes that the body was buried improperly and is about to turn into a vampire. Kou and his assistants must use all of their skills to stop it, including using hopping vampires they have under their control. *Mr. Vampire*

goes into detail about Taoist magic and lore, much as *Spiritual Boxer 2* did, from the yellow parchment with inscribed spells, to the specially mixed ink, and of course the power of sticky rice.

With the success of *Mr. Vampire*, a wave of sequels, spoofs, and rip-offs would come to the screen into the early '90s, when the craze began to wear off. A sequel was quickly drafted and filmed to keep the series going, and *Mr. Vampire 2* made its mark in 1986. Lam Ching-Ying reprises his role as the Taoist priest attempting to guide a family of hopping vampires to their grave, with Yuen Biao costarring. Not only does this film move the setting to modern-day Hong Kong, but it also introduces the "cute kid" vampire as a comedic element, making it perhaps the bane of the hopping vampire subgenre.

The following year, *Mr. Vampire 3*

continued on page 342

---

stunts). Outside of his classier period pieces (like *Drunken Master 2*) this is one of his more entertaining movies, with all kinds of jaw-dropping stunts, physical comedy, and enjoyably goofy portrayals of American criminals. —*B. T.*

SAMURAI FICTION L: FOREIGN/HONG KONG (1998) 111M D: Hiroyuki Nakano. *Morio Kazama, Mitsuro Fukikoshi, Tomoyasu Hotei, Tamaki Ogawa.* On the surface, *Fiction* makes for an excellent entry into in the samurai genre. Anyone who has knowledge of samurai films, though, will find this straight-faced parody/homage a delectable treat that tweaks the cinema world of feudal Japan just enough to succeed in its quest. First off, as with any great samurai movie, it is filmed in black and white. The costume and set designs are dead-on, and the instrumental heavy metal soundtrack offers a unique adrenaline to the sword fights. The plot could have easily been lifted from Japan's golden age of samurai films, and involves rogue samurai Kazamatsuri (Hotei), who steals a sword from a lord he has been charged to protect. The lord's young son, Heishiro (Fukikoshi), quests to return the sword but finds his heart bent on revenge when Kazamatsuri murders one of his friends. Subtle subplots involving peace, forgiveness, and love are also torn from the pages of samurai cliché to round out this fantastic story. —*R. M.*

SAVIOUR OF THE SOUL L: FOREIGN/HONG KONG (1992) 98M D: Corey Yuen. *Anita Mui, Andy Lau, Carina Lau, Gloria Yip, Aaron Kwok, Kenny Bee.* There are comic book films-those movies that leap off the edge of narrative credibility and into the abyss of exaggeration and dreams-and then there is *Saviour of the Soul.* Myth and melodrama and superheroes and spies wrapped in a psychedelic quest of revenge and redemption, this is pulp adventure on acid. Masked villain Kwok plots his revenge on Mui and her lover Lau crawls through broken glass to win her back (and somehow winds up with Pet Lady Lau instead). Does it make sense? Only in a purely emotional and visceral way: the plot is a madhouse of sacrificing lovers and mistaken identities in "spy vs spy" world. But love conquers all and then some-in the most surreal burst of Hong Kong viscera, it even conquers narrative. —*S. A.*

SEX AND ZEN 2 L: FOREIGN/HONG KONG (1996) 90M D: Chin Man-Kei. *Ben Ng, Loletta Lee, Shu Qi, Elvis Tsui.* The master of farce and exploitation, Wong Jing takes Tsui Hark's *The Lovers*, and makes it all his own. An overprotective father (Tsui) forces his daughter, Lee, to wear a custom chastity belt and dress as a man before she is allowed to go to school. But her charms cut through the disguise and capture the heart of a young scholar who introduces her to the world of sex. Meanwhile, her father has taken on yet another wife (Shu), and her unending appetite for sex quickly makes

returned the Taoist priest to his period setting and attempted to put a little scare back into the film. Richard Ng plays a Taoist priest imposter who uses two ghosts to con unknowing villagers, thus setting off the film's events. *Mr. Vampire 3*, along with 1989's *Vampire vs. Vampire*, which features the inevitable pairing of a Taoist priest fighting a Western vampire, are some of the best post–*Mr. Vampire* films to hunt down.

In the early '90s, the movies began to mix up vampire lore to keep things fresh. The parody *Dr. Vampire* (1990) incorporates both the Western and hopping variety into its story, spoofing other horror films and styles as well. *Vampire Kids* (1991) brings in five cute child vampires to hunt down the voluptuous Amy Yip for their master. The *Mr.* series gets one more sequel before calling it quits: *Mr. Vampire 1992*, in which a band of explorers seek out a curative powder made from vampires' teeth. N!xau, the lead actor of *The Gods Must Be Crazy*, even came to Hong Kong in 1991 to star in the hopping vampire comedy *Crazy Safari* (aka *Vampires Must Be Crazy*), in which a plane transporting a corpse crashes near his village.

The hopping vampire films took a backseat to other movies in the later '90s, as the *Troublesome Night* series began its run and countless ghost-seeing films made their way to the screen. A few vampire films surfaced in the early 2000s, as *Vampire Controller* (2000) and *The Vampire Combat* (2001) attempted to revive the subgenre. Unfortunately, neither film succeeded in stirring up any emotions or chemistry among fans of hopping vampires, so it is uncertain whether the corpses will hop again in the future. It is entirely up to how properly the subgenre was buried, and whether it plans to rise for revenge.

—*Ryan Miller*

---

her his favorite. But this woman has a ulterior motive, and his daughter and new lover decide to learn the truth about the mysterious sex fiend. They discover that she is actually a sex demon who sucks the life out her lover. Lee takes on the sex demon in a lesbian duel that must be seen to be believed. —*R. M.*

SHAOLIN SOCCER L: FOREIGN/HONG KONG (2001) 112M D: Stephen Chow. *Man Tat, Vicki Zhao, Stephen Chow.* When down-on-his-luck Shaolin master Steel Leg (Chow) meets a crippled and disgraced soccer coach Golden Leg (Tat), they decide to round up all the old Shaolin masters and turn them into a soccer team. Like the Mighty Ducks or somebody, they start out as wacky losers, but then they learn how to use each of their kung fu specialties as soccer superpowers. The movie takes place in an exaggerated comic book world (the rival team is so evil they're just called Team Evil) so the games are full of over-the-top computer effects. Players flip and fly through the air and the ball spins so fast it tears the grass out of the ground or burns off all of the goalie's clothes. One of the most imaginative and crowd-pleasing comedies to come along in years. —*B. T.*

STORM RIDERS, THE L: FOREIGN/HONG KONG (1998) 128M D: Andrew Lau. *Aaron Kwok, Ekin Cheng, Shu Qi, Sonny Chiba.* With its incredible special effects, stunning cinematography, and star-studded cast, this comic book adaptation easily became Hong Kong's movie of the year in 1998. The story pulls highlights from its comic roots, and Lau's groundbreaking digital work makes it a highly enjoyable ride. At the beginning of the movie, the Conqueror (Chiba) is told that "Wind and Cloud will make and break you." The Conqueror sets out to find two young boys named Wind (Cheng) and Cloud (Kwok) and molds them into his perfect soldiers. At first the pair work in harmony, doing the Conqueror's bidding, but after his ten-year reign of terror, he is told that these two will ultimately betray him. The Conqueror hopes to alter destiny and sets out to destroy the master swordsmen before fate plays its final hand. *Storm Riders* became a film phenomenon and proved to the world that Hong Kong could compete against Hollywood's dazzle, and launched Lau into a series of films that would continue to top one after the other in the realm of special effects. —*R. M.*

SUPER CAR CRIMINALS L: FOREIGN/HONG KONG (1999) 84M D: Lau Koon Wai. *Louis Koo, Michael Wong, Roy Cheung, Simon Lui.* A crew of former race-car drivers have turned into a brazen gang of daylight car thieves: even the police inspector gets his sports car nicked, and by his own undercover operative (Koo) at that. Koo has finally landed a spot in heist mastermind Wong's gang, but too late he realizes he likes and respects the guy, and even falls madly in bed with the man's giggly sister. This tepid mix of *City on Fire* and *Gone* in *Sixty Seconds* (the remake, not the original) is flashy but too noble for its own good (Wong's ethics may land him in trouble, but they make for little dramatic tension) and lacks the edge and hard-hitting action that someone like Ringo Lam would bring to the tale. There's not even a passable car chase. —*S. A.*

36TH CHAMBER OF SHAOLIN L: FOREIGN/HONG KONG
(1978) 111M D: Liu Chi-Liang. *Lung Chan, John Cheung, Norman Chu, Hou Hsiao, Billy Chan.* Idealistic student revolutionary Gordon Liu flees the Manchu militia occupying Canton when his group is betrayed, and seeks refuge in a Buddhist monastery to learn the secret martial arts. Chi-Liang's trendsetting classic mythologizes the true story of a monk who took his martial teaching out of the temple and into the secular world as it boils the revenge drama down to almost abstract levels. Gone are fiery drive and emotional fury, replaced by the dispassionate focus of our wide-eyed young scholar as he gains wisdom, confidence, maturity, and kick-ass moves on his journey through the chambers, each one dedicated to a single skill. This pure physical triumph becomes the real drama of the film, and the inevitable showdown becomes mere exhibition. —*S. A.*

TWENTY SOMETHING TAIPEI L: FOREIGN/HONG KONG
(2002) 97M D: Leon Dai. *Stanley Huang, George Chang, Jill Yu, Yu Jung Huang, Chin Hua Yang, Vivi Wang.* When people talk shit about Asian films, this is probably what they are referring to. This melodrama follows the story of several twenty-something Taipeiers in their personal journey for success (the mighty dollar), love (a piece of sweet ass), and fulfilled dreams (a mighty piece of sweet-ass money). It seems like this movie was executed with serious intent, which makes it all the funnier or sadder depending on how you want to take it. Basically it's about a bunch of Taiwanese socialites getting wasted, getting naked, and trying their damnedest to M. N.c Hong Kong, but why would anyone want to do that anyway? —*T. C.*

UNKNOWN PLEASURES L: FOREIGN/HONG KONG (2002)
113M D: Jia Zhangke. *Zhao Tao, Zhao Wei Wei, Wu Qiong, Zhou Qing Feng, Wang Hong Wei.* With a casual naturalistic style, *Unknown Pleasures* follows four bored teens preoccupied with American popular culture, who spend large portions of the film imitating characters from *Pulp Fiction.* Time and place play huge roles here. Set in the small city of Datong in early 2001, it was a defining year for China when, among other events, a downed American plane sparked the Bush administration's first substantial diplomatic standoff. Cleverly self-reflexive, the film heavily employs humor only accessible to Westernized audiences. Indeed, the *Pulp Fiction* homages are enacted by characters who didn't actually catch the name of the film. In one sequence, a found American

dollar is mistakenly thought to be worth a fortune. In another, an explosion is assumed to be an American attack. Excluding the protagonists, these in-jokes between film and audience mire the film in satire, which works against the film's sincere portrait of a China in transition. —*C. B.*

WESLEY'S MYSTERIOUS FILE, THE L: FOREIGN/HONG KONG (2001) 87M D: Andrew Lau. *Beverly Hotsprings, Roy Cheung, Andy Lau, Shu Qi, Rosamund Kwan.* A bizarre mix of *The X-Files, Men in Black,* and *E.T.* (among many other influences), Lau's techno-babble sci-fi thriller pits UN alien specialist Lau against the FBI's own alien unit, where there's a conspiracy brewing, while they all chase the mysterious blue-blooded Kwan. As if she doesn't have enough problems, the Warlock Toxin Gang is after her and her long lost brother to recover the long lost Blue Blood Bible. For those who miss the good old days of crazy action, arbitrary plot twists, and shameless Hollywood rip-offs in colorful Hong Kong cinema, this one is for you. It's absurd, inane, totally ridiculous, and has some translation gaff doozies in the subtitles (and, for that matter, the title). It was shot largely in San Francisco, where the *real* Area 51 is located at the top of a city skyscraper (and all this time we've been fooled into thinking it was in New Mexico!). —*S. A.*

WHO AM I? L: FOREIGN/CHAN, JACKIE (1998) 108M D: Jackie Chan, Benny Chan. *Michelle Ferre, Mirai Yamamoto, Jackie Chan.* You can basically ignore the first thirty minutes of this Chan vehicle. It's the typical "secret-agent who-can't-remember-who-he-is" story. Once the film gets past the meandering setup, there are a number of outstanding moments that make it worth watching. Chan plays "Whoami" (We never learn his real name), on the run to Amsterdam with operatives hot on his trail. (And he's wearing leather pants with suede ass-pockets.) A fight featuring a barefoot Chan stepping into wooden clogs to take on some thugs is a great one, especially with it's near-miss, pedestrian-vs-truck moment that I had to watch over and over. There is also a great rooftop fight scene between Jackie and two well-dressed thugs whose wardrobe gets turned against them. And "the why is he wearing those pants?" question finally gets answered when our hero slides a long way down the angled side of a glass building, a feat that would have been impossible without sexy suede pockets. Not quite the '80s Chan, but still a fun ride and one of his last good Golden Harvest productions. —*G. M.*

YES, MADAM! L: FOREIGN/HONG KONG (1985) 93M D: Corey Yuen. *Tsui Hark, Michelle Yeoh, Cynthia Rothrock, John Sham, Hoi Mang.* This is truly a mishmash of a movie that surprisingly comes off very well. An accountant of a crime boss is killed and his microfilm is on the loose, in the hands of small-time thieves. The lady inspector (Yeoh) is on its trail. Then a Scotland Yard detective (Rothrock)

comes along with a different agenda on the plate, pushing people around. The two gals don't see eye to eye until push comes to shove as their cases converge. Some clumsy attempts at humor in Rothrock's first film fall flat. But her fighting style more than makes up for it-so muscular and quick compared to Yeoh's fluidity and finesse in a role (as actress and as martial artist) that rightly made Yeoh a star. The real comedy relief comes from Tsui as a passport forger, imaginatively hiding from killers within the clutter of his tiny room. *Yes, Madam!* started a Hong Kong cycle of female cops out-kicking their male counterparts, this one with double barrels. Good stuff. —*J. C.*

ICELAND

COLD FEVER L: FOREIGN/ICELAND (1995) 83M D: Fridrik Thor Fridriksson. *Lili Taylor, Fisher Stevens, Masatoshi Nagase, Gisli Halldorsson, Laura Leigh Hughes, Seijun Suzuki.* "Sometimes there's a man-I won't say a hee-ro because what's a hee-ro . . . sometimes there's a man who, well, he's the man for his time 'n' place, he fits right in there" (*The Big Lebowski*). And sometimes there's Atsushi Hirata, a young, successful (and beautiful) Japanese businessman forced to abandon a golfing trip to drive across Iceland to honor the spirits of his parents. I've never seen two cultures treated more respectfully by a director. The balance between allowing the cultural conflicts to unfold naturally, without exploiting one world or the other, and showing the painstaking similarities between Hirata's personal spirituality and his mystical surroundings creates a rare glimpse of how strange our world is. —*J.J.*

SEA, THE L: FOREIGN/ICELAND (2002) 109M D: Baltasar Kormakur. *Hélène de Fougerolles, Hilmir Snær Guðnason, Gunnar Eyjolfsson, Kristbjörg Kjeld.* From Kormakur, director of *101 Reykjavik*, comes a film about damaged family worthy of a Dogme 95 project. Eyjolfsson is the iceberg-hard father who calls his grown children together for an announcement about the family business, a failing fish plant propped up by government subsidies. Gudnason is the favored son who reluctantly returns to the poisonous atmosphere he fled long ago. *King Lear* this ain't-his three children won't even feign affection for the old hypocrite and he's hardly the generous type, despite his self-image as benevolent monarch of a feudal village. The anger of abandonment, neglect, and betrayal soon erupts like lava through the frozen town. Not a pretty film, but uncompromising in its portrait of facing up and moving on. —*S. A.*

INDIA

ASOKA L: FOREIGN/INDIA (2001) 150M D: Santosh Sivan. *Shah Rukh Khan, Rahul Dev, Ajit, Kareena Kapoor, Danny Denzongpa.* Sivan, most famous in America for his powerful political drama *The*

Terrorist, is no stranger to the Bollywood formula of romance, melodrama, and energetic musical numbers and he brings old-fashioned spectacle and modern flair together for this sweeping historical epic. Khan and Kapoor, two of India's biggest stars, topline this epic adventure inspired by a true story of the third-century warrior prince exiled from his kingdom by his half brother. The real life King Asoka is a legendary figure with almost mythic status, and this sweeping spectacle feeds the myth over the history. At a mere 165 minutes, this lush production is short by India's Bollywood standards, yet packed with more action and spectacle than most and shot with a stunning eye for images. —*S. A.*

BANDIT QUEEN L: FOREIGN/INDIA (1994) 119M D: Shekhar Kapur. *Seema Biswas, Agesh Markam, Ajai Rohilla, Aditya Srivastava.* An amazing film based on the life of India's most notorious bandit turned politician, Phoolan Devi. Her story is the perfect example of a life from degradation to liberation, and with a story like that, plus acting that is superb all around and a setting that seems impeccable, you can't go wrong. Phoolan grows up in the lowest caste in India, is sold into marriage at age eleven, is forced to suffer the indignities of her husband, and after this is gang raped by upper-caste men in her village. Bandits eventually take in Phoolan and she rises to be the leader of the group, which goes on to exact revenge upon the upper-caste men in retribution for what they did to her. The revenge aspect of this film is a very cathartic act, and probably one of the only ways to regain some sort of dignity against such an oppressive situation. Phoolan was touted as a modern-day Robin Hood in the local press before she was captured, and ended up spending more than ten years in prison. After this film was released Phoolan went on to be elected into the Indian Parliament and became a successful advocate of human rights. In 2001 unknown assailants assassinated her, a heart-breaking ending to an inspiring life. —*B. W.*

COMPANY L: FOREIGN/INDIA (2002) 145M D: Ram Gopal Varma. *Ajay Devgan, Antara Mali, Mohanlal, Vivek Oberoi, Manisha Koirala.* Varma knows just how to create a great, swelling crime-action-romance picture, and this tale from the heart of Bollywood is perhaps his magnum opus. Oberoi makes his film debut here as Chandu, a rising gangster who becomes part of a lethal organization of crime and assassinations, and is pushed up the ranks by the watchful Mallick, deviously portrayed by Devgan. Their "company" becomes so successful in its business practices that it becomes an international conglomerate, with branches spreading out across southern Asia. Chandu becomes the head of the Hong Kong branch, but after a misunderstanding between him and Mallick, a bitter and nihilistic rivalry sparks between them, and as their friendship crumbles, so does the strength of their empire.

From start to finish, *Company* has a hard-hitting sense of doom to it, so much so that Varma cut out the prerequisite breaks to musical numbers found in most Indian films, to keep a steady dark mood. There are a few songs spread throughout, but instead of just being randomly inserted they are built into the story's reality. The film has a great appeal, not only for fans of Bollywood, but for anyone starving for an intense and brutal drama. —*R. M.*

DEVDAS L: FOREIGN/INDIA (2002) 181M D: Sanjay Leela Bhansali. *Madhuri Dixit, Smita Jaykar, Kiron Kher, Shah Rukh Khan, Aishwarya Rai, Jackie Shroff.* Called the most expensive Bollywood musical ever made, *Devdas* has all the elements of the genre: star-crossed lovers, lavish costumes, grand sets, sweeping music, dramatic dance scenes, tortured souls, betrayal, salvation, loss, all done in a tearfully melodramatic style of operatic proportions. It's difficult to get too emotionally attached to the characters or their woes due to the high drama and the fact that some of them, well, kinda got what they deserved. I felt the most drawn to and compassionate toward the lovely courtesan played with great playfulness, charm, and sincere emotion by Dixit. She also dominated the arena of resplendent costumes and breathtaking dance scenes. *Devdas* definitely should be seen on as large a screen as possible in order to enjoy the fantastic visual splendor this film provides. —*M. N.*

KHUDAH GAWAH (GOD IS MY WITNESS) L: FOREIGN/INDIA (1992) 193M D: Mukul Anand. *Amitabh Bachchan, Sridevi.* I love this movie. It is a "Scarecrow Classic." This is the only film Scarecrow Video ever put out on video itself, and it sent two of its staff to India to get it. We eluded Indian mafia, hotel pet rats, and bad water to bring this movie back to Seattle. This film is pure, beautiful Bollywood at its best! Everything happens to fabulous Indian music and everybody dances. Two of India's biggest stars, Amitabh Bachchan and Sridevi, play lovers doomed to spend years apart in different lands for the sake of honor. It is their story and their journey to return to each other's arms. On this journey there are weddings, evil Indian mafia, a game of Bakshi, lots of action, and even more dancing. The music is one of the best things about the film; I have watched it hundreds of times, sometimes just to listen the music. —*R. L. S.*

LAGAAN: ONCE UPON A TIME IN INDIA L: FOREIGN/INDIA (2001) 224M D: Ashotosh Gowariker. *Aamir Khan, Kulbhushan Kharbanda, Suhasini Mulay, Paul Blackthorne, Rachel Shelley, Gracy Singh.* Nominated for an Oscar for Best Foreign Film in 2001, this movie is a lavish production recalling the wonders of India's history, beauty, culture, and rich tradition of spectacular cinema. It's brimming with expressive music, choreography, and dance. The story revolves around a challenge between an Indian farming community and an English cantonment. The village must play a game of cricket to determine its survival during a season of drought and poverty. Should the farmers win, they are free from paying the tax (the *lagaan*) for three years, but if the English win then the farmers must pay triple the tax. Despite this rather peculiar premise, or perhaps because of it, I spent the entire 224 minutes (almost four hours long!) watching with pleasure, delight, and unbelievable anticipation and have watched it several times over since. Quite easily one of my favorite films of all time! —*M. N.*

VAASTAV L: FOREIGN/INDIA (1999) 145M D: Mahesh Manjrekar. *Sanjay Dutt, Mohnish Bahl, Mohan Joshi, Reema Lagoo.* Dutt gives a powerhouse performance here as Raghu, a fun-loving slacker who finds himself the leader of an underground mob. Raghu, who has forever lived in his brother's shadow, is finally given a chance when he opens a food stall. Business is good, until one day a misunderstanding with a local mobster's brother leads to a shooting. Raghu becomes a wanted man by Bandya, but Bandya's rival Vitthal takes Raghu under his wing, and brings him into dark side of the city. Raghu's transformation is swift and complete into a force to be reckoned with, and soon Bandya's men fall before his might. However, Raghu is not invulnerable, and when a minister's illegal activities are brought into the spotlight, he plans on using Raghu as his fall guy to make his getaway. Bollywood's ability to mix gritty violence, romance, and comedy is shown in top form here. Fans of modern mobster films will feel quite at home with the tragic epic. —*R. M.*

IRAN

CIRCLE, THE L: FOREIGN/IRAN (2000) 90M D: Jafar Panahi. *Nargess Mamizadeh, Elham Saboktakin, Fereshteh Sadr Orafai, Maryiam Parvin Almani, Monir Arab.* Banned in Iran, Panahi's drama of women's lives under the strictures of Islamic law in Iranian society is a harrowing portrait that resembles a police state. Women scramble through streets, dodging cops like fugitives and searching for a land where they too have rights. Even a quiet moment with a cigarette is denied. A mix of the poetic and the polemic, the film is oddly abstract and untethered, with men little more than anonymous authority figures and women rarely more than roughly sketched martyrs. It's Panahi's passion, his anger, and most importantly his sensitivity to moment-by-moment sensations and the more subtle realities of these women's status that bring the film alive as it returns, full circle, to where it began, ready to start the cycle over again. —*S. A.*

LAST ACT, THE L: FOREIGN/IRAN (1991) 105M D: Varuzh Karim-Masihi. *Niku Kheradmand, Farimah Farjami.* Echoing elements of *Hamlet* and *Les Diaboliques*, this ostensible thriller of a brother and sister who plan an elaborate living-theater pageant to drive their sister-in-law mad turns into a jubilant tribute to the glory of theater and storytelling. Directed as a play within a play, with a troupe of actors playing the servants, this is calculated and carefully observed where most Iranian films are loose and seemingly improvisational. The mind-game mystery intertwines with a police investigation that seems headed into *Columbo* territory, but the thriller aspects, which are clever if drawn out, give way to the communal magic of theater. Varuzh Karim-Masihi's directorial debut is ultimately about, if you'll pardon the cliché, the theater of life and the healing powers of art. —*S. A.*

LEILA L: FOREIGN/IRAN (1996) 129M D: Dariush Mehrjui. *Turan Mehrzad, Mahnaz Ansarian, Mohammad Reza Sharifinia, Jamileh Sheikhi, Ali Mosaffa, Leila Hatami.* Mehrjui, considered the Godfather of Iranian cinema, continually pushes taboo subjects in his portraits of modern life. In this discreet melodrama he explores the pressures of tradition on modern life when a happily married but childless couple is destroyed by the interference of the man's mother, who demands the family name continue. Mehrjui's understated direction beautifully captures the quiet desperation and the sense of helplessness they feel as the husband (Mosaffa) buckles under pressure to choose a second spouse and his wife, Leila (Ansarian), quietly retreats into herself. Amid the feelings of abandonment, betrayal, and manipulation is a devastating, delicately realized, all-too-human tragedy. —*S. A.*

MIRROR, THE L: FOREIGN/IRAN (1997) 93M D: Jafar Panahi. *Mina Mohammad Khani, Kazem Mojdehi.* School lets out and little Mina's mother isn't there to pick her up. Mina is confident she can make her way home on Tehran's public transportation system but takes a bus in the wrong direction. Turning to strangers for help, she ends up more confused. Kiarostami collaborator Panahi takes Iranian neorealism to its naturalist limit when, at the forty-minute mark, his young star turns to the camera and screams that she's had enough. Abandoning the shoot, "real-life" Mina tries to walk back to her real-life home, but encounters more or less the same problems her fictional character did. The opportunistic-even antagonistic-camera follows her home as the film turns self-reflexively on itself. By turns hilarious and cruel, *The Mirror* is a consistently fascinating treatise on the moral problems of fashioning cinema out of reality. —*C. B.*

NARGESS L: FOREIGN/IRAN (1992) 100M D: Rakhshan Bani-Etemad. *Atefeh Razavi, Farimah Farjami.* A petty thief (Farjami) falls in love with and marries a social naif (Razavi) in the slums of Tehran, but his efforts to go straight are thwarted by his record, his life on the streets, and a former lover who leverages his desperation and pulls him into

one last job. Bani-Etemad turns what appears to be a typical social-realist melodrama into a generous story of three complex individuals caught in a complicated web of love, anger, and desperation, a product of pasts that seem to determine their future. This is an Iran rarely seen on the screen, a city of filthy alleys cluttered in junk, crowded tenements, and rundown hovels. Amid the poverty and unemployment Bani-Etemad examines the struggle between dreams and reality, dignity and desperation, through the choices of characters she both loves and understands. —*S. A.*

SECRET BALLOT L: FOREIGN/IRAN (2001) 105M D: Babak Payami. *Cyrus Abidi, Nassim Abdi.* The lyrical grace of Iran's serene cinema gets a shot of offbeat comedy in Babak Payami's look at the rocky road to the election process. Steered by a bickering odd couple-a naive young female election agent (Abdi) driven to take the ballot box to every last resident by idealistic passion, and a provincial, literal-minded soldier (Abidi) more concerned with smugglers than the secret ballot-this mosaic adds a shot of offbeat comedy to the lyrical grace of Iran's serene cinema. The couple confronts indifference, suspicion, and women whose religious fundamentalism forbid them to vote without the permission and guidance of their men. Enlivened with an absurdist bent, rich characters, and human comedy, and seeped in evocative images and the unmistakable texture of time passing before our eyes in the changing light from dawn to dusk, this is an education hiding in a comedy. But what could easily turn into a polemic becomes a sharply observant and gently satirical study of a culture caught in transition. —*S. A.*

IRELAND

FUNNY BONES L: FOREIGN/IRELAND (1995) 128M D: Peter Chelsom. *Lee Evans, Leslie Caron, Jerry Lewis, Oliver Platt, Richard Griffiths.* This is a brilliant drama that uses the very sources of comedy as its internal structure. *Funny Bones* is ultimately about the hopes and aspirations of two sons of different comedic families who, finding each other, are able to find themselves and their rightful places in their respective families. The film begins in Las Vegas where Tommy Fawkes (Platt) fails miserably in trying to follow in his father's (Lewis) comedy footsteps and, even more embarrassingly, is bailed out onstage by his father. He flees to his hometown in Blackpool, England, to sort out his career and his comic roots. Once there, he learns much, much more about himself and his father than he could have ever imagined. He discovers family ties to another performing family, the Parkers, who are experiencing pains of their own. The collision of these two families results in deeply moving comedic drama. This is a film that splits, and sticks to, your ribs. Chelsom has been a little snakebit with his career choices after this so don't judge him by his filmography: This movie is fabulous. With great performances by Platt, Lewis, and the (why isn't this guy more famous?) wonderfully strange and whimsically talented Evans. —K. S.

MAGDALENE SISTERS, THE L: FOREIGN/IRELAND (2002) 114M D: Peter Mullan. *Dorothy Duffy, Nora-Jane Noone, Anne-Marie Duff, Geraldine McEwan, Eileen Walsh.* Mullan's portrait of the now defunct Magdalene Asylums of Ireland is a work of outrage. Run by the Sisters of Mercy for decades, they were homes for wayward girls that were run as holier-than-thou prisons, and Mullan's film follows the ordeal of three young women. Their "crimes": pride, unwed motherhood, and the "sin" of being raped. Their sentence: a regime of dreary laundry work, obedient silence, and ritual humiliation and punishment. It's hardly subtle (the self-righteous Sister Bridget hardly looks up from counting her money when the girls are brought in) but the stories are drawn from real experiences and told with a furious sense of holy betrayal. It won the Golden Lion at Venice and roused protests from the Vatican. That's two more reasons to see it. —S. A.

MAN OF NO IMPORTANCE L: FOREIGN/IRELAND (1994) 99M D: Suri Krishnamma. *Rufus Sewell, David Kelly, Michael Gambon, Tara Fitzgerald, Albert Finney, Brenda Fricker.* What should by all rights be nothing more than a wry, twee little BBC-style production becomes a charming, heartfelt story that makes you laugh and sigh. It isn't the direction, the editing, or anything else (which is all fairly plodding and by-the-book, to be honest). It's the acting. The actors all breathe life into characters that feel like they were written paper-thin. Sewell and Fitzgerald both make you wish that they'd get better roles than the ones they've had since this film, and Fricker is dead-on as the spinster sister. But this movie really belongs to Finney. From the get-go, he holds on to your attention without your even noticing it. Alfred Byrne, instead of being a cardboard pastiche of wronged homosexuals that we've been inundated with by horrible made-for-TV films, becomes, in Finney's hands, a sad and wonderful human being who we grow to know and love. —K. F.

ISRAEL

KIPPUR L: FOREIGN/ISRAEL (2000) 123M D: Amos Gitai. *Yoram Hattab, Uri Ran Klauzner, Juliano Merr.* Gitai's defiantly subjective account of the 1973 Yom Kippur War follows the experience of two young soldiers lost in the chaos of the invasion and overwhelmed by the noise and panic of the battlefield. Simultaneously immediate and alienated, the film captures a chaotic portrait of the war with no glory, only the confusion, fear, and fatigue of a tour under fire. Its effectiveness is undercut only by the pretentious framing device and the meandering discussions of soldiers in downtime-stilted scenes of graceless chatter that come off as phony and forced next to the numbing scenes of soldiers slogging through the war zone. Gitai must have felt compelled to give the viewer a reprieve from the monotony of war, and no wonder: at over two hours *Kippur* is something of an ordeal. As it should be. —S. A.

TIME OF FAVOR L: FOREIGN/ISRAEL (2000) 101M D: Joseph Cedar. *Tinkerbell, Idan Alterman, Assi Dayan, Aki Avni.* "The land of Israel is bought with pain." Michal (Tinkerbell), the fiercely independent daughter of West Bank rabbi Meltzer (Dayan), is quoting her ultranationalistic father, whose teachings are sprinkled with an almost militaristic zeal. To him, it's a prayer; to her the curse that has defined her life. Cedar's drama of politics, religion, and militarism in the Israeli West Bank settlements is an unusual thriller shot through with a romantic triangle that, far from distracting, actually helps define the issues of personal desire subsumed under religious direction and nationalistic fervor. Avni stars as the yeshiva-student-turned-soldier drafted by the rabbi to lead a settlement unit (under the rabbi's tacit direction?). He struggles with his attraction to Michal, whom the rabbi has promised to his gifted student-scholar Alterman. There is not a Palestinian face to be seen, which has the effect of focusing the film wholly on the struggle within the Israeli community, as well as lending a powerful punch to the film's final shot. Though a bit narratively muddled, it is clear-eyed in its message. Winner of six Israeli Academy Awards, including Best Picture. —S. A.

YANA'S FRIENDS L: FOREIGN/ISRAEL (1999) 90M D: Arik Kaplun. *Evelyn Kaplun, Nir Levy, Shmil Ben Ari, Mosko Alkalai.* Sweet, sexy, and unexpectedly enchanting, this little feel-good comedy from Israel set in the largely Russian immigrant community of Tel Aviv during the 1991 Gulf War, won ten Israeli Academy Awards. First-time feature director Kaplun modestly stirs the story of Russian émigré Yana (a fragile, frail-looking Kaplun, his real-life wife) who has been abandoned by a scheming husband who fled back home to Russia, leaving her three months pregnant and holding the bag for a large loan. The bustling neighborhood quiets only when air-raid sirens whine and the populace dives inside and dons gas masks for the scud attacks from Iraq. It feels right that love would bloom huddled in the safe room, faces hidden in the masks while fingers tear off clothes and caress skin for comfort as much as for intimacy. Kaplun doesn't offer any surprises in his slice-of-life ensemble piece, but it's a charming, modest delight full of heart and humanity. —S. A.

BEST MAN, THE L: FOREIGN/ITALY (1998) 101M D: Pupi Avati. *Inés Sastre, Dario Cantarelli, Cinzia Mascoli, Diego Abatantuono.* The millennium is just around the corner for the golden-hued, candlelit world of 1899 rural Italy. It's New Year's Eve day and the occasion is marked with an arranged wedding between the dreamy young daughter of a financially strapped family and a boorish entrepreneur. As the bride's family fulfills centuries-old Catholic customs, the bride is ready to call it off—headstrong and independent, she wants to marry for love. When the groom's handsome best man arrives, she's convinced she's found it. Avati sets Old World customs and new ideas on a collision course, creating a world of modest contradictions and conflicts, but such issues give way to the real focus of the film: a lush, old-fashioned romance. Avati hangs too much on the slim story, but in a film crammed with loving details perhaps these ideas are simply part of the rich atmosphere, easily the strongest element of the film. —S. A.

L'AMERICA L: FOREIGN/ITALY (1994) 116M D: Gianna Amelio. *Michele Placido, Piro Milkani, Carmelo Di Mazzarelli, Enrico Lo Verso.* Amelio, director of the fine drama *Stolen Children*, follows up with another journey rich in culture and character. Italian hustlers Gino (Verso) and Fiore (Placido) hit the economically destitute Albania to cash in on government incentives with a phony business scheme and a puppet chairman. The plan collapses when their pawn, a former political prisoner, rejects their manipulations and disappears. Gino finds himself adrift, an alien trapped in a violent world, just another refugee on the road. Amelio directs with low-key sincerity, observing Gino's transforming journey with humble deference to the desperation around him. Like the Italian neorealist directors before him, Amelio creates a vivid world around his hero with an almost documentary-like offhandedness, given shape by his hero's experience. —S. A.

NIGHT PORTER, THE L: FOREIGN/ITALY (1974) 122M D: Liliana Cavani. *Philippe Leroy, Dirk Bogarde, Charlotte Rampling.* The sexiest self-destructive relationship ever. Often lumped in with *Love Camp 7* and *Women's Camp 119*, Cavani's intent is of an entirely different sort. Exploitation? Not quite. Perverse? Sure. Bogarde's Max is a former Nazi hiding out as a porter in a fancy hotel when his eye catches a guest entering, his former lover at a concentration camp. Rampling cinches her dominance of the screen with her broken-down, corrupted Jewish "little girl" who seeps deep into a re-creation of the original tortuous relationship of victim/tormentor, and becomes the dominator of Max's heart and soul. Locking themselves in a room together, terrified to leave and get food, the two are as doomed as they were during the War years. Deep, spiraling love eats away at the couple until their final, definite end. Mesmerizing and intricate, *The Night Porter* crosses many boundaries and cements itself as an eternal classic meditation on the power of love, and its eventual destruction of the practitioners. Rampling's sexy, topless Nazi cabaret scene outdoes any other in Nazi-flick history. —S. R.

SACCO AND VANZETTI L: FOREIGN/ITALY (1971) 120M D: Giuliano Montaldo. *Gian Maria Volonté, Riccardo Cucciolla, Cyril Cusack, Rosanna Fratello.* Based on actual events in the early '20s in Boston when two Italian anarchist immigrants were framed for a robbery and murder they didn't commit. This story is about the international outcry against this injustice and the revealing of the conspiracy and policies behind their eventual murder by the state. It is a timely film to be watching at the beginning of the twenty-first century, for these times are starting to look again like the hysteria of the '20s, '50s, and the '60s in the United States. The didacticism of the film can inspire individuals to keep vigilant of government oppression under the guise of national security. This film handles the subject with great humanism and empathy, without feeling like it's trying to shove a particular political agenda down the viewers' throats. Ennio Morricone does a superb job with a musical score that contributes to the emotional power of the story and is easily one of his best. It's interesting to watch a film that is actually sympathetic to anarchist ideas and gives a rare glimpse into a seldom referred to time in U.S. history. —B. W.

SCARLET DIVA L: FOREIGN/ITALY (2001) 91M D: Asia Argento. *Herbert Fritsch, Gianluca Arcopinto, Jean Shepard, Asia Argento.* Actress and Italian sex symbol Asia Argento (daughter of Dario) makes her directorial debut with this story she penned about an actress and sex symbol who has written an autobiographical script she aspires to direct. It only appears self-reflexive. Self-indulgent is more like it. In this screechy diva piece, Asia gets naked (frequently), sleeps around, looks for affection in casual sex, has flashbacks of her life before fame, and suffers alienating nightmares after she becomes pregnant by a rock star even more self-involved than she is. "I'm the loneliest girl in the world," the unbearably self-pitying superstar whines while she inhales drugs to calm her fears about impending motherhood. Yeah, she's gonna be a great mom. —S. A.

SCENT OF A WOMAN L: FOREIGN/ITALY (1974) 103M D: Dino Risi. *Vittorio Gassman, Moira Orfei, Agostina Belli, Alessandro Momo.* Neither kinder nor gentler than the American remake, nor as meaty—and that's ultimately a plus. The original, which received Oscar nominations for Best Foreign Film and Best Adapted Screenplay, is a miniature centered on the blind Captain (played with hearty machismo by Gassman, who won an award at Cannes for his performance). The embittered officer tours Italy guided by his young aide and his nose, sniffing out beauties and sating his libidinous appetites as he brings his life to a kind of closure. He's a crass old man, hiding his loneliness behind bravado and sex. There's no sentimentality and rousing speeches here, but a drama that ends with the harsh, introspective whimper of reality, not the bang of Hollywood cliché. —S. A.

JAMAICA

HARDER THEY COME, THE L: FOREIGN/JAMAICA (1973) 103M D: Perry Henzell. *Jimmy Cliff, Ras Daniel Hartman, Carl Bradshaw, Janet Barkley.* Cliff plays Ivan, a spaghetti Western–loving musician trying to break into a corrupt business who, after finding he can't make it by talent alone, resorts to crime and finds fame as a "rude boy" outlaw. In many ways *The Harder They Come* parallels the blaxploitation genre that was exploding about the same time in the States but features a gritty authenticity not found in similar American movies. The plot wanders a bit as Ivan tries to seduce a preacher's daughter, deals with his newfound fame, rides a motorcycle around the beautiful Jamaican countryside, and shoots some cops. The soundtrack is fantastic and I love the ending that inverts the viewing experience and shows an audience reaction to the on-screen thrills. The Jamaican accents are pretty thick, so it's best viewed with subtitles. A must-see for fans of reggae, ska, and rock steady as well as people who dig black action films. —S. H.

JAPAN

ASSASSIN, THE L: FOREIGN/JAPAN (1977) 87M D: Yukio Noda. *Sonny Chiba, Callan Leung.* If you dig Chiba like I do, then pretty much anything he appears in is worth watching. Unfortunately he starred in lots of stinkers but you gotta watch them anyway. *The Assassin* would almost fall into this category but, then again, it's pretty weird and is never boring so you could do a lot worse. Not only is the video badly dubbed, several scenes aren't even dubbed at all! So unless you understand Japanese the nonsensical plot makes even less sense. It's a comical, action-packed buddy film about pot smugglers in Japan. Chiba and some other guy wear big ugly hats, shoot lots of people, and get their pants burnt off. He's a tough guy, but Chiba isn't his usual badass self, and he looks pretty silly wearing some outrageously dated '70s threads. It's goofy stuff but *The Assassin* is a must-see for Chiba maniacs. —S. H.

BAYSIDE SHAKEDOWN L: FOREIGN/JAPAN (1999) 119M D: Katsuyuki Motohiro. *Chosuke Ikariya, Soichiro Kitamura, Miki Mizuno, Eri Fukatsu, Toshirô Yanagiba, Yuji Oda.* Detective Aoshima (pop star Oda) seems bored by his job as a police-man. It's the bureaucracy that's got him down, the hierarchy of the job, keeping track of his receipts week after week. The routine at Bayside Precinct is broken when a body is found in the river (with a teddy bear in its stomach), the chief gets kidnapped, and Aoshima's receipts are stolen right off his desk. As he tries to keep track of each investigation he gets wrapped up in all three. This police procedural drama (a spin-off of a popular Japanese TV show) is original and witty fare and there are some nice twists to the cops-at-work motif. But in the long run, *Bayside* is just not very thrilling; the "virtual killer" murder mystery falls flat. The kidnapping of the Commissioner takes center stage and it doesn't make our hearts race either. The film is pretty good but it is too scattered, with too many plot strings to tie up. When *Bayside* was released in Japan, moviegoers couldn't get enough, making it the top-grossing domestic film of 1998. The actual title translates as "Dancing the Major Investigation Line." —G. M.

BEAUTIFUL BEAST L: FOREIGN/JAPAN (1995) 86M D: Toshiharu Ikeda. *Kaori Shimamura, Takeshi Yamato.* Ikeda directs this Japanese *La Femme Nikita* knockoff about a savage and sexy assassin (Shimamura) from China who comes to Japan to hunt down the yakuza mobster responsible for her sister's death. Of course she takes time off to have sex with a bartender and former yakuza soldier (Yamato), who hides her from his former boss, and she briefly becomes the plaything for the sadistic crime boss in an unnecessary torture scene. Shimamura delivers the necessary hard-edged sexiness and single-minded drive, letting her emotional walls down ever so briefly for the necessary exposition. Another in the parade of straight-to-video boobs-and-bullets thrillers in the Japanese market, it doesn't bring anything new to the genre, but it adds to the strange mystique of moral ambiguity and doomed retribution-with a little sex thrown in. —S. A.

BEAUTIFUL MYSTERY L: FOREIGN/JAPAN (1983) 60M D: Genji Nakamura. *Tatuya Nagatomo, Kei Shuto, Akira Yamashina.* An idealistic young man joins a small, closely knit militia for the love of country. However, as he slowly becomes indoctrinated, he soon finds that the life of a militiaman is much different than he expected. The intense physical training and the long hours of study were no surprise, but the nocturnal activities of these men require a little getting used to. The young man's assigned mentor initiates him one night by drinking down a lot of sake, tying him up, taking down his pants, and applying a liberal amount of lubricant. And over a short period of time nearly everyone wants a piece of the new recruit. Once the young man has been around and once he finally settles with his preferred militiaman, the two stay up all night admiring each other and each other's uniforms until they sleep past the alarm and miss the entire operation scheduled the next day. This film is strange, funny, and perverted all wrapped up in one. —*N. J.*

BLACK ANGEL (1997) L: FOREIGN/JAPAN (1997) 107M D: Takashi Ishii. *Riona Hazuki, Jinpachi Nezu, Reiko Takashima.* Asian cinema is drowning in *La Femme Nikita* knockoffs, but this revenge thriller by Ishii (*Gonin*) takes the bullets-and-babes genre into new territory. Hazuki is Ikko, a twenty-year-old orphan who returns from the United States with a sidekick and a mission to avenge the death of her yakuza boss father. She's part giddy schoolgirl (the groovy dance number in the hotel room is pure youthful passion) and part apprentice hit woman, with dead-shot skills and gymnastic fighting abilities apparently learned in her American private school. It gets more interesting in the complicated web of sisterhood bonding and maternal impulses between Ikko, the real Black Angel (now a pathetic drug addict under the control of the man who killed Ikko's father), and Ikko's conniving half sister, who now runs the family business. Ishii's style is sleek and dark, taking the aesthetics developed in the low-budget V-cinema training ground to a higher level. While this has none of the madness and desperation that drove his two *Gonin* films, it still manages to pull out a few surprises and end with a tragic emotional twist. —*S. A.*

BLACK TIGHT KILLERS L: FOREIGN/JAPAN (1966) 84M D: Yasuharu Hasebe. *Chieko Matsubara, Akima Kita, Yuriko Sawanouchi, Akira Kobayashi.* Anyone who enjoys bubble-gum pop culture, skintight bodysuits, and '60s spy/gangster films is sure to eat this film right up. A Japanese photographer (Kobayashi) is out to save his girlfriend, Yoriko (Sawanouchi), when aligned Japanese and American gangsters kidnap her. Right behind him is a quintet of female assassins who masquerade as go-go dancers (or is it the other way around?), and are seeking out the gangsters for their own purposes. They wind up helping and hindering the photographer as the film progresses. The sexy assassins have records and chewing gum among their arsenal of weapons, and are not afraid of looking good while killing those who get in their way. Tension builds when it is discovered that Yoriko's grandfather hid a stash of gold before World War II, and the gangsters are now determined to get it. The film culminates in an island mansion, complete with an electrified pool of water keeping the half-naked Yoriko captive, and the expected explain-it-all speech by the main boss. Hasebe takes many film pointers from pop-art master Seijun Suzuki here, using lighting and camera-angle techniques, and throws in enough straight-faced gangster film spoofing to keep you smiling, even as the body count rises. —*R. M.*

BLIND BEAST L: FOREIGN/JAPAN (1969) 86M D: Yasuzo Masumura. *Noriko Sengoku, Eiji Funakoshi, Mako Midori.* Art house eroticism meets exploitation kink in this pop-art remake of *The Collector* by way of *In The Realm of the Senses.* A blind sculptor (Funakoshi as a grown mama's boy, sort of like a sightless Norman Bates under the sway of a still-living mother) kidnaps artists' model Midori and imprisons her in his warehouse studio, a wild set where sculpted body parts reach out of the walls to the two giant female torsos that lounge in the center of his cavernous tactile playground. Apart from peeks at black-and-white nude studies and sculptures, there's actually no real explicit nudity in new-wave director Masumura's adaptation of Edogawa Rampo's notorious tale, but there is plenty of consensual sadomasochistic experimentation in this twisted tale. Great color, wild art direction, and a gorgeous transfer. —*S. A.*

BRIGHT FUTURE L: FOREIGN/JAPAN (2003) 128M D: Kiyoshi Kurosawa. *Tadanobu Asano, Jo Odagiri, Tatsuya Fuji.* Supposedly a departure from the smartness of Kiyoshi Kurosawa's patent Japanese post-horror films that keep kicking everybody's ass. Starring Asano as an apathetic kid who along with his best friend doesn't really give a shit about anything except their pet jellyfish. Somewhere along the line, a brutal murder occurs and hordes of CGI-mutated glowing jellyfish begin to overrun and attack people throughout Tokyo. Teenage "gang members" wearing matching white dress-shirts also make their way into the film to reinforce the cultural issues of youth gone wild in modern Japan, a topic that has reared its head quite often, evident in recent Japanese films such as Shinji Iwai's *All About Lily Chou Chou* and Shinji Aoyama's *Eureeka.* —*A. T.*

CHAOS L: FOREIGN/JAPAN (1999) 104M D: Hideo Nakata. *Ken Mitsuishi, Masato Hagiwara, Miki Nakatani, Miki Nakatani, Ken Mitsuishi, Masato Hagiwara.* Nakata is best known for his über-creepy horror films *Ringu* and *Dark Water.* This twisty little crime thriller couldn't be more different. The coolly observed story of a kidnapping gone bad keeps jumping back in time to complicate the seemingly straightforward story with new perspectives. Victims and villains flip-flop with each new revelation of mercenary motives and cold-blooded manipulation. A calm, controlled kidnapper with an eye for the angles (Hagiwara), an all-business executive (Mitsuishi), and a gorgeous young trophy wife who vanishes from plain sight (Nakatani): no one is what they seem. Cleanly and crisply directed, this *Chaos* is anything but chaotic: every step of the film has a lean precision and an austere architecture. Though it lacks the resonance of Nakata's horror films, which are seeped in guilt and ghosts and shadowy menace, this ingeniously engineered sun-bright thriller is damnably clever. —*S. A.*

FEMALE CONVICT SCORPION: JAILHOUSE L: FOREIGN/JAPAN (1972) 89M D: Shunya Ito. *Meiko Kaji, Fumio Watanabe, Kayoko Shiraishi.* The women-in-prison genre has never been so much fun. Gonzo doesn't begin to describe this mad mix of outrageous exploitation, flamboyant art movie, and energetic comic-book craziness. Kaji gives a near silent performance as the smoldering heroine who defies the sadistic warden and brutal guards with burning stares and sudden strikes. An innocent systematically abused, tortured, and humiliated by the vengeful warden, she escapes with a chain gang and watches her comrades get cut down by the trigger-happy posse, but not before they take a few with them. Striking and at times breathtakingly beautiful, exploitation has never looked so carefully painted or sensitively composed. But as artful as it is, this is still prime exploitation, full of sadistic mayhem and bloody death. —*S. A.*

GIANTS AND TOYS L: FOREIGN/JAPAN (1958) 95M D: Yasuzo Masumura. *Hitomi Nozoe, Hiroshi Kawaguchi.* Masumura's satire of Japanese corporate culture and media manipulation was made in 1958, in the adolescence of the Japanese economic miracle. It couldn't be more timely in the wake of its collapse. The battleground of this sprightly, brightly colored blast is the Japanese caramel candy market, which three rival companies try to dominate with prizes, promotions, and old-fashioned barnstorming stunts. Fresh-faced Nishi (Kawaguchi), the college grad gofer to the ruthless publicity chief Goda (a go-go-go young executive who pushes himself so hard he's coughing up blood in the final reels), enters the fray with all the naive energy of a true believer, and watches the opportunistic antics with growing revulsion as friends and rivals alike double-cross one another with a shrug. Nozoe is the giggly working-class girl with bad teeth and a girlish spirit turned into an overnight pop sensation by Goda. It doesn't take long for her to develop the mercenary instincts of the callow operators around her. Behind Masumura's buoyant direction and the hilarious pop-culture wars lays a cutting portrait of greed, opportunism, and the sheer weirdness of Japanese TV and media culture. —*S. A.*

GONIN L: FOREIGN/JAPAN (1995) 122M D: Takashi Ishii. *Koichi Sato, Jinpachi Nezu, Naoto Takenaka, Beat Takeshi.* Ishii twists the familiar heist-gone-bad picture into a mind-bendingly weird and nightmarishly violent piece of yakuza madness. The title translates to "five," the number of nothing-to-lose amateurs who team up to heist the mob and face the vengeance of the steely, unflappable enforcer "Beat" Takeshi. Ishii directs with an edge of desperation;, visceral action; bright, searing colors; and a dark cloud of doom hanging over the picture. He spares nothing in the gruesome display of beatings, interrogations, and bloody murder, but he really goes round the

bend in a demented homecoming scene with a delirious daddy sweet-talking his family of crimson corpses. Truly demented. The DVD features good, punchy Dolby Digital sound and a decent picture that emphasizes the grain of Ishii's photography to surprisingly good effect. —*S. A.*

IREZUMI L: FOREIGN/JAPAN (1989) 102M D: Yoichi Takabayashi. *Yusuke Takita, Tomisaburo Wakayama.* *Irezumi* is an interesting and fascinating tale of sexual obsession and fetishism. A beautiful young woman tries to satisfy her lover's fetish for tattooed women. She agrees to have her back covered in an elaborate tattoo by an old retired tattoo artist, but he will only do it if she lets him use a special technique, by which his assistant keeps her mind off the pain while the old man does his work. She must be made love to while being tattooed! She agrees to go through with the process for the sake of her lover and the pain. The intensity increases as she becomes emotionally attached to her new lover while still not abandoning the old. After the tattoo is completed, a shocking discovery of how the old man mastered his technique shatters the emotions of all involved. This erotic flick is a good choice for a date movie if your date is open to a little sexual pain and moral deviance. It's not your average love story; leave it to the Japanese culture to push boundaries within the context of what is acceptable in relationships and how women should or shouldn't behave in a society. *Irezumi* moves a little slow but is worth a watch if you're in the mood. —*B. W.*

LONE WOLF AND CUB: SWORD OF VENGEANCE L: FOREIGN/JAPAN (1972) 83M D: Kenji Misumi. *Tomisaburo Wakayama, Akhiro Tomikawa.* Ogami Itto is a stoic with a sword and a baby to take care of. After he is forced from his post as shogun's head executioner by political intrigue of the Yagyu clan and his wife is murdered by its shadow-clan ninjas, Ogami (Wakayama) hits the road as a sword for hire. While pushing his child, Daigoro (Tomikawa), along in a bamboo baby cart full of secreted weapons, he is always wary of passersby who may be shadow-clan assassins. Based on the manga by Kazuo Koike and Goseki Kojima, so begins by far the finest series of B movies produced anywhere. Beautifully paced, the action scenes are as casual and matter-of-fact as the rolling baby cart. The violence is bloody, with flying hands, spraying blood, and severed limbs. The suspense is in the waiting and the clarity of sword work. —*J. C.*

MABOROSI L: FOREIGN/JAPAN (1995) 110M D: Hirokazu Kore-eda. *Makiko Esumi, Takashi Naitô, Gohki Kashiyama, Tadanobu Asano.* If still waters run deep, then this film is an ocean: a glassy, gorgeous surface concealing an unfathomable depth. With quiet grace, director Kore-eda explores the feelings of loss that young mother and widow Yumiko (Esumi) endures after the sudden death

(a possible suicide) of her husband, and the melancholy that envelopes her years later. Delicate images and an easy naturalism create a serene world of understated beauty in long, placid takes while silhouette, darkness, and scenes caressed with natural light give a painterly quality to the images. Kore-eda achieves a delicate intimacy with his privileged moments of everyday sorrows and joys. A sublime masterpiece of profound emotional power. —*S. A.*

NINJA WARS (IGA NINPOUCHO) L: FOREIGN/JAPAN (1982) 100M D: Mitsumasa Saito. *Hiroyuki Sanada, Noriko Watanabe.* This is a lurid fairy tale with stunning fight sequences and two scenes that knock your socks off. Twin girls (Watanabi) are separated at birth; one became a princess and the other a ninja. The ninja is kidnapped by five devil-monks, one of whom can bring the others back to life when killed. Together they do the bidding of a sorcerer who serves an ambitious lord in need of the girl's tears as an ingredient of love potion to make the princess fall in love with him. The girl's ninja boyfriend (Sanada) follows only to find her dying body, which contains her soul but has a different head on it—a scene you must see to believe! The boy promises to keep her dying wish to warn and protect her twin sister. Complicating matters, the body-soul of a crafty concubine is running around with the twin girls' face atop it with a nasty seduction ambush in store for the boy—among other twists on road toward keeping his promise. A dazzling B movie. —*J. C.*

NOBODY L: FOREIGN/JAPAN (1999) 100M D: Shundo Ohkawa, Toshimichi Ohkawa. *Masaya Katoh, Jimpachi Nezu, Hideo Nakano, Riki Takeuchi.* Three smug businessmen are caught mocking a trio of tough-looking young suits, and the homicidal game of cat and mouse begins. Shundo Ohkawa's bizarre nightmare thriller is almost abstract: austere, empty Tokyo locations, mysterious assailants who may be cops or criminals or ruthless corporate young turks, and a methodical campaign of terror that is never explained. His approach is cool and deliberate, sleek and slick and very slow until it's startled by shrieking bursts of violence. There isn't a likable character in the bunch and Ohkawa's chilly detachment makes this the most alienating of Japan's new wave of violent thrillers. In a perverse way, that makes it all the more fascinating. —*S. A.*

NON-STOP L: FOREIGN/JAPAN (1996) 82M D: Sabu. *Shinichi Tsutsumi, Tomorowo Taguchi, Diamond Yukai.* Yasuda (Taguchi) is a loser, but he's got a gun and a plan. Cowardly as he is he's going to rob a bank, and he's been practicing. However, on the night of the holdup he accidentally robs the corner convenience store instead. The clerk, Aikawa (Yukai), gets shot in the arm and the terrified Yasuda drops his gun and runs. Aikawa grabs the piece and gives chase. The sprinting

pair run smack dab into small-time gangster Takeda (Tsutsumi), and he's got a knife. Now the three of them are on the run across Tokyo for no good reason. Aikawa chases Tatsumi, Tatsumi chases Yasuda, and I don't think any of them have any idea what they'll do if they stop. Sabu's slick direction makes a simple premise a lot of fun. Nothing happens in this film except that three sweaty lads won't stop running, but in the minds of the characters Sabu shows us a lot more. At one point as the men run by a pretty lady adjusting a high-heel strap, they look down her bosom and with their leering glances we are transported to a fantasy world where each man in turn has his way with her, each in a different fashion. A snappily paced film, you won't regret the time you spend with it. —*G. M.*

ONIBABA L: FOREIGN/JAPAN (1964) 103M D: Kaneto Shindô. *Taiji Tonoyama, Jukichi Uno, Kei Sato, Nobuko Otowa, Jitsuko Yoshimura.* One of the two or three best horror movies ever made. Not only does it have a shrewd and ultimately very nasty little story, but the visuals are stunning. The reeds grow ten feet tall, diminishing humans. People seem like mice in grass. An old woman (Otowa) and her (probably widowed) daughter-in-law (Yoshimura) eek out a living harvesting the weapons and battle armor from dead and dying soldiers and selling them to a merchant. Not above finishing the weary soldiers off, the elder woman is worried when the younger woman (her meal ticket and her soldier son's wife) nurses one soldier back to health. She rises nightly and runs naked through the wildly blowing reeds to a tryst with the man, the image of uncontrollable young lust. But now a demon from an ancient well arises to stop her from these nightly trysts. Her husband? Her guilt? Or what? The eroticized visuals suck you in so powerfully and the story ends so perfectly that *Onibaba* will buzz inside you for days and weeks after. There's nothing quite like it. —*J. C.*

PARTY 7 L: FOREIGN/JAPAN (2000) 104M D: Katsuhito Ishii. *Masatoshi Nagase, Keisuke Horibe, Tadanobu Asano.* Ishii's follow up to 1998's fantastic *Shark Skin Man and Peach Hip Girl* wants so badly to be just as good, but unfortunately misses the bar. The "seven" are introduced at the start of the film in a hyperkinetic anime sequence that pumps up the pace, which quickly drops when the film switches to the real world, only to build back up later. The characters congregate toward a reclusive hotel and set the stage for a wild ending as they all come together in the same room. While the yellow-clad, masked Mr. Banana teaches his new assistant Mr. Yellow (an innocent-looking Asano) the arts of peeping, a thief who has stolen from the mob meets with his ex-girlfriend at the hotel. Behind them is her obsessive boyfriend, a gangster sent to retrieve the money, and another mob hit man sent to kill everyone. This is a solid second film from Ishii,

The Scarecrow Video Movie Guide

who uses his genre actors to the best of their ability, and closes them in a claustrophobic setting to wait for the pressure to burst. —R. M.

PING PONG L: FOREIGN/JAPAN (2002) 114M D: Fumihiko Sori. *Shido Nakamura, Yosuke Kubozuka, Koji Ogura, Arata, Sam Lee*. I never thought I would find the game of ping-pong interesting, let alone a whole movie about it, but I am totally sold on *Ping Pong*! Funny, bizarre, entertaining, philosophical, and playful, this flick charmed the paddles right out of my hands. A story of two teenagers, one who loves ping-pong more than anything and the other who does it solely to kill time and plays too nice for his own good. Each meets his match and is challenged both at the table and in his life to make decisions about what he wants, who he is, and what is worth going for. Ultimately it's a tale of heroes, what the true heart of sports is, and how the game really can and should be more important than winning or losing. —M. N.

SCORPION: DOUBLE VENOM L: FOREIGN/JAPAN (1998) 180M D: Riyoji Nimura. *Chiharu Komatsu*. Nimura directs this pair of direct-to-video exploitation thrillers loosely inspired by the *Female Convict Scorpion* series of the 1970s, with a twist of *The Fugitive*. Komatsu is the Scorpion, a female doctor who finds the man who murdered her little sister and kills him, but not before learning he had a one-armed partner still at large. Sent to one of those horrid prisons the cinema saves for the degradation of comely, naked actresses, she deals with a sadistic lesbian warden, a butch cellblock queen, and plenty of pent-up babes looking for love while she plots her escape. The convoluted plot is executed with a grim bluntness and little style, but it does deliver the goods and a wacko ending involving a hanging, CPR, and live electrical wires. The sequel, *Scorpion 2*, picks right up where the first leaves off, with our hero now a fugitive hiding under a dirty blond wig in a strip club while searching for the one-armed man. The sequel contains more action and curious twists, including a hit man in a police uniform and a secret drug-testing program behind bars (which prompts her to break back in to jail), and is dutifully entertaining if impersonal and undistinguished. —S. A.

SHARK SKIN MAN AND PEACH HIP GIRL L: FOREIGN/JAPAN (1998) 108M D: Katsuhiro Ishi *Tadanobu Asano, Sie Kohinata*. American audiences might call it "Tarantino-esque," but Ishii's wild-card crime blast, with its deadpan black humor and runaway plot is pure Japanese manga-inspired madness. The hurtling pace and surf-punk score of the opening scenes level off as we spend time with yakuza defector Asano, who grabbed 100 million yen of mob money on his way out, and meek hotel-clerk runaway Kohinata, fleeing from a pathologically possessive manager who thinks he's going to marry her. A cute couple indeed:

Asano's grinning glee is surprisingly charming and Kohinata's shows the only joy in her life when she impulsively throws in her lot with him. Add a hit man with knife holsters strapped to his chest, the yakuza chief's punk son with the nose of a bloodhound, a gang of underlings distracted in meaningless conversations that circle endlessly, blood spatter, and banged-up cars, and you've got an instant cult movie. It's not nearly as wild or wicked as Miike Takashi's genre explosions, but it's a good time set to a great beat and flashy style. —S. A.

SHOGUN'S NINJA L: FOREIGN/JAPAN (1982) 115M D: Noribumi Suzuki. *Hiroyuki Sanada, Sue Shiomi*. After the very bloody, beautifully rendered suicide of the mother, the father and virtually the whole clan are massacred. The child prince is tossed in the sea, presumably lost only to return as an adult (Sanada) from China. He is followed by his stepfather and stepsister (Shiomi), with a mere half minute of flashbacks on the movie's dubbed cut to explain those years. Remnants of the clan that have gone underground now rise up to follow the prince like Robin Hood, only to all die again at the end. The story hinges on two swords that together hold the map of the clan's secret gold mine that could finance its return-or their final destruction if their enemies get it first. Wistfully apocalyptic film with dazzlingly choreographed martial arts battles. —J. C.

SLEEPY EYES OF DEATH 4: SWORD OF SEDUCTION L: FOREIGN/JAPAN (1964) 87M D: Kazuo Ikehiro. *Shiho Fujimura, Raizô Ichikawa*. The first three in this series are nicely photographed and lyrically told stories of a bitter Christian half-breed who tries to mind his own business but has no compunction whatsoever about killing for pay or sometimes just because he dislikes someone. He has a sword trick where he moves the blade in an arcing circle and the opponent will always die before the arc is complete. That builds suspense, but the fight choreography is smart and watchable at all times. This fourth episode takes an unbelievably dark turn. Nemuri (Ichikawa) learns about his dark birth, which is the source of his bad dreams (priests and rape and crucifixion) matched by contemporary events that are equally as bloody and dark: a court official's drug-crazed daughter murders her handmaidens and tosses their naked corpses into the river. But this amoral man never acts out of righteous indignation unless something befalls him. And the ending threatens sentimentality as he finds a long-lost sister. Guess again! Wild, wicked but ultimately very compelling fare. —J. C.

STREET FIGHTER, THE L: FOREIGN/JAPAN (1974) 92M D: Shigehiro Ozawa. *Sonny Chiba, Waichi Yamada, Masashi Ishibashi*. Chiba's *Street Fighter* is an amoral Japanese karate mercenary, and not only is he a motherfucker martial arts master, he'll sell your sister into prostitution if you can't pay the bill. No shit. And if he wants, for shits and giggles, he'll come to your dojo, fuck up all the students, attack your niece, and fuck you up, just so you'll hire him to protect her ass. And you will, too! Because, if the gangsters are trying to rape her... HE'LL RIP THEIR FUCKING BALLS OFF! No shit. The yakuza doesn't scare him. He doesn't play by the fucking rules; if he needs to, he'll pop your eyeballs or tear your fucking throat out. He can do it. There's not much else to say; he's not a good guy, not a bad guy, just a badass who wants to get paid, and kill every fucker that gets in his way. —*K. C.*

STREET FIGHTER'S LAST REVENGE, THE L: FOREIGN/JAPAN (1979) 80M D: Shigehiro Ozawa. *Gerald Yamada, Sonny Chiba, Sue Shiomi, Bruce Li, Etsuko Shihomi.* Fast-paced fun in a story that (true to form in this series) makes little sense. Terry (Chiba) is hired to steal two tapes that alone are meaningless but together contain a formula for the cheap manufacture of heroin. He is double-crossed so he steals one back. Somebody else wants in and there is a crooked cop who wants everything and a straight cop (Shihomi) who falls in love with him. And then, Wow! There is the boss's daughter (Ike) who tries to seduce him at the same time she sends a Mexican strongman to kill him with magic tricks. Twice! Those are great scenes. Ike starred in a string of "girl-boss" movies in the early '70s (unavailable on video) and it is easy to see why she was popular: she's glib, sensual, and confident. Chiba and Shihomi each have edgy, nicely choreographed, nasty fight sequences. All in all a smart, rich movie nearly the equal of the legendary *Street Fighter*. —*J. C.*

SUICIDE CLUB (AKA JISATSU CIRCLE) L: FOREIGN/JAPAN (2002) 94M D: Shion Sono. *Ryo Ishibashi, Rolly, Akaji Maro, Masatoshi Nagase, Takashi Nomuri.* Fifty-odd schoolgirls hold hands, chant, and leap in front of an oncoming subway train, and that's just the beginning of the wave of youth suicide that grips Tokyo. "Suicide Club. We're charter members," explains one girl who, as part of another group, is determined to top the mass suicide record. This mad Japanese horror of alienation and mass insanity is messier than most of this unique genre (count *Pulse, Uzumaki,* and *Kikashi* among its numbers) and is rather unfocused, but it has some great elements: the utter adolescent glee of these kids as they plan and execute their suicides, the insidious conspiratorial undertones of the preteen girl pop band that inspires listeners to kill themselves through their cheery bubble-gum music, a death-rock band whose lyrics compare life to a Bresson film. And yes, the gore and grotesque methods of suicide increase with the body count. What it lacks is a haunting story behind the bloody spectacle. —*S. A.*

SWALLOWTAIL (AKA SWALLOWTAIL BUTTERFLY) L: FOREIGN/JAPAN (1996) 148M D: Shunji Iwai. *Hiroshi Mikami, Chara, Ayumi Ito, Yosuke Eguchi, Andy Chi-On Hui, Atsuro Watabe.* In a bleak, industrial, and vaguely familiar dreamland lies Yentown, the setting for this genre-consuming film by Japanese director Iwai. Unfortunately, his work mysteriously remains elusive to most American audiences. Much more diverse and attentive to aesthetic than most of his other films, *Swallowtail* involves a group of lower-class misfits weaving through the slums and shanties of Yentown, until they stumble across a super-secret machine inside a corpse's body, which allows them to steal money from vending machines. Amid this amazing discovery, members of the group deal with aspirations of being famous, like Gilco (played by real-life yesteryear Japanese pop star Chara), who longs to one day become a rock star. Mobsters and a host of other shady people attempt to steal back the device, forcing the group to decide how valuable it really is to them. In doing so they help the film retain its oddly sincere and dreamy quality. —*A. T.*

TOKYO FIST L: FOREIGN/JAPAN (1996) 87M D: Shinya Tsukamoto. *Kahori Fujii, Koji Tsukamoto, Shinya Tsukamoto.* Shinya Tsukamoto's full-on, bloody bout with flesh, muscle, and self-mutilation is like a boxing picture as reconceived by Clive Barker as a schizophrenic melodrama. Insurance salesman Tsuda (played by Tsukamoto himself), an empty automaton going through the motions of his job and his relationship with a live-in fiancée, is jerked out of his stupor when a former schoolmate turned pro-boxer blows into his life. Kojima (the director's real-life brother Koji Tsukamoto) bullies Tsuda and puts the moves on his girl, like a repetition of a decades-old cycle of aggression, but this time Tsuda turns to the boxing club to beat his body into a match for his once and future rival. And beat is right: faces are pummeled into bloody pulp, boxers beaten and broken in the ring, bodies ritually pierced and tattooed. Tsukamoto's vision of modern Tokyo is an alienated world of disconnected zombie-citizens repressing raw emotion under a social veneer of manners and passivity. Pull back that cover and WHAM! *Raging Bull* meets *Eraserhead* in an all-out sensual assault. The film runs down before the conclusion, but until then it's an unbelievably visceral ride. —*S. A.*

TOKYO MAFIA: YAKUZA WARS L: FOREIGN/JAPAN (1995) 90M D: Seiichi Shirai. *Riki Takeuchi.* Japanese action heartthrob Takeuchi is the renegade yakuza who starts his own criminal collective that thrives on the fringes of the underworld while trying to keep a restless peace. But he's no Gandhi: finally he's forced to fight back. Rather a slack and generic gangster drama under Shirai's slick and impersonal direction, this abstract thriller is highlighted only by Takeuchi's swaggering confidence and smoldering star power. With his slicked-back pompadour and curled sneer, he looks like a cross between a snazzy-dressing punk thug and a 1950s juvenile delinquent, but

he's got the charisma and control to pull it off.
—*S. A.*

TURN L: FOREIGN/JAPAN (2001) 112M D: Hirayama Hideyuki. *Riho Makise, Mistuko Baisho, Kitamura Kazuki. Turn* is based on a novel by Kitamura Kaoru, and features a story reminiscent of *Groundhog Day*, though it is much more drama-oriented than its comedic American counterpart. Maki (Riho) is an artist who one day is in a severe accident. Instead of dying, however, she is transported back exactly one day and must repeat the twenty-four-hour cycle again and again. But in this world, she is the sole inhabitant. One day, she receives a mysterious phone call from someone who has tapped into her bizarre new world. Now this daily call is her one connection to the outside world, and may be the only way out of the revolving cycle. The bulk of the story takes place in Maki's lonely city and attempts to show the extent one would go to in order to make one's life as normal as possible. The use of sound and static shots helps bring the viewer into Maki's world, and as the film progresses, so does the heightened sense of her solitary existence. —*R. M.*

UNDO L: FOREIGN/JAPAN (1994) 47M D: Shinji Iwai. *Tomorowo Taguchi, Etsushi Toyokawa, Tomoko Yamaguchi.* Iwai's first film about a woman's spiraling obsession that involves wrapping things up and tying them together with string. Fruit, pet turtles, people, whatever. She starts small before eventually working her way up, just like those nerdy girls in elementary school who used to entwine each other's hands while I was running around the playground pretending I was a Transformer. In its short running time, Iwai's film manages to beautifully depict a detailed implosion of a young Japanese couple's relationship as they increasingly become unfamiliar with each other. As characteristic of many early works by directors, *Undo* is at times disjointed-the lighting fluctuates nonsensically from whiteout bright to radiant deep red hues while the camera work stilts and stutters from impatience. Yet the awkwardness of the film also seems to wonderfully parallel the weirdness experienced between the young couple as they attempt to make sense of the newfound void developed between them. —*A. T.*

VERSUS L: FOREIGN/JAPAN (2001) 119M D: Ryuhei Kitamura. *Hideo Sakaki, Tak Sakaguchi, Kenji Matsuda.* The plot is promising: two reincarnated samurai brothers fulfill their destiny by reuniting for a battle they began five hundred years ago. Their duel takes place in the Forest of Resurrection, where one brother hopes to open the 444th portal and bridge another dimension. His sibling, known only as Prisoner KSC2-303, escapes from jail with the help of yakuza crime lords. The yakuza rendezvous with the prisoner in the forest, but an argument leads to an ultra-stylized shoot-out. When they realize that the forest is bringing their casualties back to life, the gang nevertheless follows the prisoner into the wilderness-where they have been dumping bodies for years. Kitamura understands the need for balance between horror and comedy in a good zombie flick. Zombies don't really scare audiences anymore, so they have become a platform for anything from gratuitous gore to satire. Kitamura's fight scenes mime Hong Kong action films with a ballet of slow motion and sideways gunfire-but the action is repetitive. If there's anything classic zombie-film heroes rely on, it's ingenuity and originality. *Versus*'s hero may look cool, but he can't come up with anything new. The plot becomes formulaic, too, following uninteresting characters whose allegiances switch from good to evil for no better reason than needing another body to throw on the pile. —*M. M.*

WIFE TO BE SACRIFICED L: FOREIGN/JAPAN (1975) 80M D: Masaru Konuma. *Terumi Azuma, Naomi Tani, Nagatoshi Sakamoto.* The most famous example of Japanese S&M, this is the story of a violent, abusive fugitive who kidnaps his ex-wife and tortures her in a series of elaborate scenes. She comes to like it so he kidnaps a young couple to join in their games. The so-called hero is also a pedophile and the conclusion leaves him free to continue his violent ways. Full of bondage, nudity, and transgressive sexual torment, this is a shockingly graceful film, beautifully shot and lovingly realized by Konuma, lending a dreamlike quality to the whole thing. You ain't never seen nothing like this, and you may not want to, but it's a film that Scarecrow founder George Latsios would have loved. —*S. A.*

WILD ZERO L: FOREIGN/JAPAN (2000) 98M D: Tetsuro Takeuchi. *Guitar Wolf, Drum Wolf, Bass Wolf, Masashi Endo, Makoto Inamiya.* This is my all-time favorite Asian zombie movie. It's more ridiculous than even *Kung-Fu Zombie*, and a hell of a lot funnier than the very funny *Biozombie*. *Wild Zero* is a complete mess of styles and genres all thrown into the notoriously rickety framework of the rock musical. Real Japanese punk band Guitar Wolf play themselves (yes, their names really are Guitar Wolf, Drum Wolf, and Bass Wolf) as they help a young would-be rock star named Ace battle alien zombies attempting to take over Earth. Along the way they have to avoid a crazy crime boss named The Captain (Inamiya), in the best sex-fiend villain performance since Simon Yam in *Full Contact*. This film is full of cool music, excellent low-budget gore and makeup, and reaches a level of absurdity that constantly ups itself. It stumbles from scene to scene with only the flimsiest of connective tissue for a plot, and punctuates every other character beat with the heroic Guitar Wolf extolling the virtues of ROCK. It's obnoxious, violent, stupid, and more fun than just about any American film I've seen in ages. —*M. L.*

ZATOICHI: THE TALE OF ZATOICHI L: FOREIGN/JAPAN
(1962) 96M D: Kenji Misumi. *Shintarô Katsu, Shigeru Amachi.* Katsu stars as the legendary blind swordsman in his first appearance. Ichi wanders into a gangster-run town like a wry con man, fleecing the dim-bulb thugs and sponging off a local mob boss preparing for a gang war with a rival town syndicate. He may be a scoundrel, but Ichi is modest about his abilities (he won't fight for show). As he befriends the samurai warrior hired by a rival town, he reveals a code of honor missing in the lackeys surrounding him. Director Misumi has a steady hand that keeps Ichi from showing his talents until the very end, where his spare, sudden style makes a startling contrast to the flashing swords and furious movements of the fighters we've seen up till then. You can't avoid comparisons to Akira Kurosawa's *Yojimbo* (released in the same year); *Zatoichi* shows a certain coincidental similarity in parts (even down to the lone gun pulled out among the battery of swords), even if Kurosawa's film is easily the more cynical and sharp. —*S. A.*

ZATOICHI: THE TALE OF ZATOICHI CONTINUES L:
FOREIGN/JAPAN (1962) 72M D: Kazuo Mori. *Shintarô Katsu, Yoshie Mizutani, Masayo Mari.* Mori creates a tighter and more action-packed picture in the direct sequel, which takes place on a return trip to the corrupt town one year later and takes the character and the series in another direction. Ichi is hunted by both a government goon squad and the gang they hire to finish the job, but more deadly (and more personal) is the mysterious one-armed swordsman whose fate is twined with the blind swordsman. The sequel deepens the character of Ichi, hinting at his troubled past in a tender yet sad interlude with a kindly geisha, and gives his antics a more melancholy twist. Katsu returned as Ichi in twenty-five sequels and a long-running TV series. —*S. A.*

ZATOICHI 3: NEW TALE OF ZATOICHI L: FOREIGN/JAPAN
(1963) 91M D: Tokuzo Tanaka. *Shintarô Katsu, Mikiko Tsubouchi.* The first color film in the series finds the wandering blind masseur and master swordsman (Katsu, in the role that made him a legend) returning to his home village. Redemption waits just out of reach in the form of his former master's sister, who offers herself to the humble hero. But his corrupt master will have none of it, and a showdown between master and pupil is inevitable. Ichi's transformation from womanizer, gambler, and all-around rascal continues. He tries to put his past behind him, but the past of a yakuza is not so easily escaped: he enters every battle, whether fighting vicious bandits or avenging warriors, with a reluctance that turns to sadness on his inevitable victory. Director Tanaka brings a visual beauty to the series, especially in the many forest scenes, and remains true to Ichi's unique lightning-strike style: a fight with Ichi rarely lasts more than a single stroke. —*S. A.*

ZERO WOMAN (AKA ZERO WOMAN 2) L: FOREIGN/JAPAN
(1995) 90M D: Daisuke Gotoh. *Saori Iwama, Kane Kosugi, Natsuki Ozawa.* I'm hooked by this Japanese series, a *La Femme Nikita* knockoff with a strange mix of slick violence, softcore exploitation, and empty style. Ozawa plays the hard-bitten nymph of an assassin in *Zero Woman*, which is actually the second film in the series. She slinks around in a little black dress (which impossibly hides an arsenal) while stalking a trio of dim street punks and the mob boss whose secrets-laden briefcase they heisted. Better looking than most video productions, with a sharp, sleek design, it's often maddeningly clichéd and indifferently acted, with a nihilistic edge that is more fashionable than heartfelt, but it builds to a bitter bleakness that most American films wouldn't dare touch. It's hardly great, but it makes for a funky series that (perhaps accidentally) tightens around its mythology with each succeeding chapter. Watched as pieces of a whole it becomes unaccountably compelling. —*S. A.*

KOREA

ATTACK THE GAS STATION! L: FOREIGN/KOREA (1999)
109M D: Sang-Jin Kim. *Sung-jae Lee, Oh-seong Yu, Seong-jin Kang, Ji-tae Yu.* This curse-riddled slacker comedy is a truly funny and original movie. *Attack* is centered around four bored tough-guys, each with a checkered past-which we get to see as vignettes that show them failing and floundering through life-who decide to rob and ultimately take over a filling station, tormenting employees, customers, and passersby alike. They take hostages, make customers buy a full tank of gas no matter what they've come asking for, and have a running battle with a Chinese food delivery guy whom they refuse to pay, but keep ordering food from. With moments of ingenious camera work and an original story, *Attack* is a delightful surprise and not to be missed, if only for its Mexican (Korean?) standoff ending that pits our four heroes against a hundred cops and bikers. *Attack* was voted best comedy at Fantasia Film Festival the year it debuted. —*G. M.*

BAD GUY L: FOREIGN/KOREA (2001) 100M D: Ki-duk Kim.
Won Seo, Duek-mun Choi, Yun-tae Kim, Jae-hyeon Jo. Damn freakin' weirdest love story. Tough guy (Jo) forcibly kisses a college girl (Seo) he is attracted to on a college park bench. Uniformed soldiers peel him off her and attempt to force him to apologize. He won't. She spits on him. He secretly follows her into a bookstore and plants a thick wallet in plain sight. She looks around and grabs it, taking the money. A man chases and traps her; she returns the several hundred dollars to him. "There was $10,000. Where's the rest?" She is forced to go to a loan shark, then into prostitution till the loan is paid back. Guess who's the leader of the gang that controls the house of prostitution? That's right. He watches her through a one-way mirror a former gang

used in a blackmail racket. One of his buddies falls for her, leading to trouble. Angry love. Violent loyalty. Weirdest affection. Twisted sentimentality. And a happy ending, of sorts. —*J. C.*

BEAT L: FOREIGN/KOREA (1997) 114M D: Sung-su Kim. *Woo-sung Jung, So-young Ko, Oh-seong Yu.* The opening shot of this film lasts two minutes. It's a gloriously long tracking shot of an incredibly chaotic gang fight that introduces us to our hero Min (Jung) and his best friend Taesoo (Yu). This film has more edits than most Korean films and it lends a frenetic pace to its story of friendship and obligation. *Beat* is a tale of a couple of friends in Korea who have dropped out of school. The story follows Min trying to cope with his ever-changing life as he moves from high school dropout to gang initiate. His mother is a drunk and he desperately seeks escape. Caught between the love of an upper-class college-bound girl, Romi (Ko), and his loyalty to his gangster friend, Taesoo, Min becomes trapped by a life he can't control. *Beat* delivers a pretty typical story of a young man caught between a life of crime and the love (and lifestyle) of girl who is out of his league, but it does it with such flash and energy that you forget its "been done before" plot and settle back to watch the fast cuts of fights, love, and slick kids riding motorcycles through tunnels. —*G. M.*

BICHUNMOO L: FOREIGN/KOREA (2000) 118M D: Sung-su Kim. *Shin Hyun-Joon, Kim Hee-Seon.* Prepare a box of tissues before sitting down to watch this violent love tragedy. In the mid-1300s, as the Huns, Mongolians, and Korya migrants begin to stake their claim for land, a brief romance is held between Jinha and Soli after he saves her from an attack. When Soli is taken away, Jinha vows to wait for her, and to reclaim their love. Fifteen years later the now-adult Jinha (Shin) learns that Soli (Kim) has been married to a wealthy family. He braves his life to return to her arms, and as swords are drawn, the power of his love shines stronger than ever. The film is beautiful to look at, and no detail has been spared for the scenery, lighting, cinematography, and score, while action scenes and swordplay choreography are gorgeous to watch. The only drawback to the film is the story itself, which becomes incoherent at times, as cuts were forced in order to get a running time suitable for the cinema. A second viewing of the film may be needed to take it all in. —*R. M.*

CHUNHYANG L: FOREIGN/KOREA (2000) 120M D: Im Kwon-Taek. *Seung-woo Cho, Hyo-jeong Lee.* Im turns an epic Korean folktale into a mix of story-song performance and sweeping cinema in this gorgeous, thoroughly old-fashioned love story. Though it was saddled with the misleading tag "A South Korean *Gone With the Wind*," it's really more of a Victorian melodrama a la D. W. Griffith: a pure-hearted woman (Lee) tormented by a corrupt blackheart, a spoiled lover (Cho) who abandons her yet rides to the rescue as a paragon of virtue, and a thoroughly unironic reverence for a story steeped in chauvinism and tradition. In this world, a woman's lot is to wait and suffer in dignity, and her reward is at the hands of benevolent patriarchy. Im takes a cue from the New Chinese Cinema and creates a lush, lavish melodrama, but lacks the irony and introspection of those works. —*S. A.*

CONDUCT ZERO L: FOREIGN/KOREA (2002) 100M D: Geun-shik Jo. *Seung-beom Ryu, Hyo-jin Kong, Eun-kyeong Lim.* Joong Pil (Ryu) is the king of Moonduk High. Sang Mahn, the badass newcomer to the school, is itching to take his place at the top. Who's gonna win? But wait! First there's the problem of whether Joong Pil will ever get his first kiss! This movie satirizes the power of gossip, especially through the mouths of adolescent teens. The reputations of both fighters progressively get bigger as they move from the lips of one student to the next. We are treated to *Shaolin Soccer*–level battles to accompany all this hype. The last fight scene between the two is expectedly underwhelming and hilarious-except for the part where one of them gets knifed in the back. What is it with Korean films that they think they can pull this shit outta nowhere without fucking changing the whole mood of the movie? Kids these days... —*T. C.*

GINGKO BED L: FOREIGN/KOREA (1996) 88M D: Je-gyu Kang (aka Jacky Kang). *Hye-jin Shim, Hee-kyung Jin, Suk-kyu Han, Hyeon-jun Shin.* Popular but overrated middlebrow horror/romance that spans a thousand years. Needing a bed for his studio, a dream leads an artist (Han) to a bed frame carved of gingko wood with a headboard in the shape of two lovers. Ancient story has it that a musician won the heart of a lady only to lose his head to the sword of his romantic rival, but the lovers were reincarnated in the gnarly windings of the gingko tree. Suddenly the artist's doctor-lover starts having problems; turns out the rival from the deep past travels across time to win the lady again and she appears to the artist in dreams. Nicely told Hollywood-style sentimental folktale with wrathful but understandable villain and saccharin-sweet love object too pure for this world. Edgeless melodrama. —*J. C.*

GREEN FISH L: FOREIGN/KOREA (1997) 111M D: Chang-dong Lee. *Sung-keun Moon, Suk-kyu Han, Hye-jin Shim.* Harsh, bitter, sad film. Young returnee from military duty (Han) wants to bring his fragmenting family back together in some small business. He retrieves the scarf of a girl on a train (Shim). A gang beats him up when he tries to return it. But the boss (Moon) is impressed and hires him. Breaking his hand, he stages a fight with a politician realistic enough that the boss can squeeze the guy for concessions. The returnee becomes boss's confidant, the boss being a man who had

DVD region codes and video standards

The invention of DVD technology has opened up the pleasures of cinema to people all over the world. Now, with a little effort or searching, you can find a copy of some lost classic in Russia or the newest Thai epic with subtitles.

Unfortunately, getting these DVDs to work in your player might be somewhat of a problem. Media companies have invented region codes as a way to control the sales and marketing of their releases in different parts of the world. Most DVDs are hard-coded with information about the region they were manufactured in:

Region 1: Canada and the United States

Region 2: Europe, Japan, the Middle East, and South Africa

Region 3: Southeast Asia

Region 4: Australia and South America

Region 5: Africa, Russia, and the rest of Asia

Region 6: China

This coding can stop a disc made in one area of the world from playing in a DVD player made in another part of the world. Region coding is not mandatory, however, and many companies do not encode a region into their DVD releases.

Many countries also have a different video standard (the way the actual video signal gets to a TV). The two main power frequencies widely used around the world, 50Hz and 60Hz, divide the world's TV systems into two distinct systems: the twenty-five-frames-per-second system (50Hz) and the thirty-frames-per-second system (60Hz). PAL will not play in an NTSC VCR/DVD player (or vice versa) without a video signal converter or internal converting hardware inside the player (which most players do not have).

—*Joshua Warren*

---

dreams too and had made sacrifices to work his way up. "We are not gangsters," the boss tells his crew, allowing himself to be humiliated in front of them by a local crime boss fresh out of prison. But the pressure builds and so too the almost-relationship with the boss's girl. The boss and the returnee strike a devil's bargain...Even with a strong undercurrent of sentimentality there is an incredible bitterness underlying Green Fish, and a remarkable sweetness too. —*J. C.*

HI, DHARMA!! L: FOREIGN/KOREA (2001) 95M D: Park Cheol-Kwan. *Park Shin-Yang, Jeong Jin-Yeong.* There are no surprises in this South Korean comedy of urban gangsters on the lam who hide out in a rural Buddhist monastery and clash with the young monks, but this feel-good fantasy of chaos and order colliding like rival school gangs on the playground is lightweight fun. There are lessons to be learned by all—about respect, about patience, about loyalty, and most of all about the choices one makes in life—but not before the urban gangsters try to muscle into the monastery like it was a rival's turf. The not-quite-so-peaceful monks show their competitive streak in a series of sporting contests. The wager: whether the gangsters are allowed to stay or not. Good-natured, amiable, and utterly forgettable, this knockabout goof was a smash hit in Asia. —*S. A.*

ISLE, THE (SEOM) L: FOREIGN/KOREA (2000) 89M D: Ki-duk Kim. *Yoosuk Kim, Jung Suh, Sung-hee Park.* This was another one of those semi-overhyped, domestic-adapted foreign thrillers. Unlike its other "new Korean cinema" counterparts, however, *The Isle* remains consistent in both style and substance all the way until the end. In a semi-isolated fishing resort, a mute woman manages tiny floating houseboat rentals that double as brothels for local hookers who the drunken vacationing fishermen import nightly. The mute woman also deals with the rowdy fishers, lurking under the water and creeping through creeky outhouse hatches of the boats, before eventually being smitten by one of the mysterious visitors. The desolate setting of the backwoods lake and lopsided characters creates an uneasy atmosphere the film relies on as it walks the border between suspense and full-blown horror. Like *Sympathy for Mr. Vengeance, The Isle* is brutal at times, but in all fairness, it avoids any misogynistic themes director Ki-Duk Kim has been accused of conveying. Fishhooks for everyone! —*A. T.*

JOINT SECURITY AREA L: FOREIGN/KOREA (2000) 110M D: Chan-wook Park. *Song Kang-Ho, Lee Byeong-Heon, Lee Young-Ae.* JSA, as it is also known, is as much a political allegory for the current state of Korea as the action-romance film *Shiri*, and was Korea's number one film in 2000. On the border between North and South Korea in the demilitarized zone are guardhouses for both sides. After a firefight breaks out, it leaves two North Korean soldiers dead and one South Korean soldier in custody. A neutral Swiss team is brought in to investigate, and as they begin compiling the evidence an elaborate idea is created to describe what purportedly happened. The truth, which is never fully given as the *Rashomon*-esque denouement unravels, is much more simple, and infinitely more tragic. Director Park asks his fellow Koreans some hard questions for which they don't have easy answers. The notion of one people and two countries, and the limitless compassion that brotherhood evokes, are at the heart of the film, and it is clear that Park wonders if his people's soul will ever heal and become whole again. —R. M.

KICK THE MOON L: FOREIGN/KOREA (2001) 118M D: Sang-Jin Kim. *Hye-su Kim, Seung-won Cha, Seong-jae Lee.* In their youth, Park was a school intellect, who was constantly bombarded by the thuggish Choi, who enjoyed nothing more than a good brawl in the streets. As adults, Park (Lee) has become a leader in an organized crime syndicate, while Choi (Cha) has become a teacher who still employs violence to keep kids straight. When Park returns to their town for some business, a chance meeting between the two begins a rivalry for the heart of a local noodle stall owner. Park has a suave demure to him, which overcomes Choi's outbursts and antics, and it seems that Park has finally gotten his childhood revenge. But when he starts to hire Choi's students as incoming criminals, Choi decides to take on Park with his best weapon, his fists. This is Kim Sang-Jin's follow-up to *Attack The Gas Station*, which proves to be just as enjoyable, as he freely uses the bigger budget to over-stylize his film. —R. M.

LIES L: FOREIGN/KOREA (1999) 112M D: Jang Sun-Woo. *Lee Sang Hyun, Kim Tae Yeon, Jeon Hye Jin.* There's something fitting about Jang's notorious South Korean erotic drama winding up in Paris for a last tango, so to speak. Based on the novel *Tell Me a Lie*, which was immediately banned in South Korea and its author Jang Jung Il jailed for obscenity, the film flies in the face of national censorship. It's the story of a purely physical affair between an eighteen-year-old high school girl and a forty-year-old artist that escalates from awkward sex to an addictive sadomasochistic relationship. Jang directs with a purposeful banality, with prosaic first-person narration and an almost clinical approach to the taboo material, making even two hours of kinky and violent sex repetitive and numbing. Their home lives are almost unknown. The only emotion they seem to feel is the visceral thrill of breaking cultural taboos. The film seems designed solely to affront sensibilities; less a dramatic exploration than a political statement. It makes for quite a con-

versation piece (you'll be talking about the "ho stick" for days) but an uninvolving film. —S. A.

MEMENTO MORI (AKA WHISPERING) L: FOREIGN/KOREA (1999) 98M D: Kim Tae-Yong, Min Kyu-Dong. *Park Yeh-jin, Kim Min-sun.* Think *Carrie* as a Korean ghost story with a lesbian subtext. Schoolgirl Min-sun discovers an abandoned diary and reads about the delicate relationship between two of her classmates, one of whom leapt off the roof of the school to her death. The bitchy portrait of high-school-girl social cliques is dead-on (and far more convincing than the oddly similar Canadian film *Lost and Delirious*) and a perfect crucible for ghostly revenge. The flashback structure is admittedly hard to follow, but it's worth the effort. The imagery is gorgeous, the narrative weave is rich, and the ghost story has a wonderfully earthy grounding. —S. A.

MUSA (AKA MUSA, THE WARRIOR) L: FOREIGN/KOREA (2001) 158M D: Sung-su Kim. *Sung-kee Ahn, Ziyi Zhang, Woo-sung Jung, Jeong-hak Park, Yong-woo Park, Ji-mo Ju.* This is one seriously intense flick! *Gladiator* looks like a bunch of guys in skirts having a tea party in comparison. A group of Korean diplomats, hoping to offer good will and establish diplomatic relations in China, are met with suspicion and hostility and branded as spies. Arrested and banished, they are unexpectedly freed by a group of roving Mongols. The group becomes divided. Some wish only to return home to Korea, but the general in command wants to rescue a Chinese princess in the hope it will gain them the trust of the Chinese emperor and restore their honor. This film is ferociously tragic, drenchingly bloody, piercingly poignant, fiercely violent, blindingly honorable, and viciously action packed. —M. N.

MY SASSY GIRL L: FOREIGN/KOREA (2001) 137M D: Jae-young Kwak. *Ji-hyun Jun, Tae-hyun Cha.* The first three-quarters of this movie are hilarious. The main actress throws up on a guy with a toupee. She also punches people and it's really funny. The main actor has the best "sour face" I have ever seen since the animated version of *GTO*. Anyway, the first three-quarters of the movie will have you crapping your pants. The last quarter, however, feels twice as long as the first three-quarters and it's shit-achingly melodramatic. It made me long to be in relationship even though I already had a girlfriend. —T. C.

NOWHERE TO HIDE L: FOREIGN/KOREA (1999) 112M D: Lee Myung-Sae. *Choe Ji-woo, Jang Dong-Kun, Ahn Song-Gi, Park Joong-Hoon.* Myung-sae put South Korean action cinema on the map and leapt to the top of the glitz-noir heap with his always-in-motion, jittery-with-nervous-energy police manhunt thriller. It's ostensibly a mystery, the search for a deadly Mafia assassin, but maverick cops Joong-Hoon and Dong-Kun do little actual investigating as the film leaps from one flashy, high-energy set piece to another. They do, however, pick a fight with every thug on the street and spend hours chain smoking and trading tough-guy aphorisms and dime-store philosophical insights in dramatic backlit poses. The grainy high-contrast black-and-white inserts, skip-frame–action cutting, obligatory slow-mo, and pounding rock score create the slickest-looking action since John Woo and the glitziest use of gimmicks outside of Hollywood. —*S.A.*

This movie was a drag, typifying the burgeoning Korea film industry and proving how fricking boring a movie can be regardless of flashy, contrived effects. Convoluted Hong Kong action + wannabe glossy Japanese production = a complete mess of tedious shite.—*A.T.*

PEPPERMINT CANDY L: FOREIGN/KOREA (2000) 130M D: Lee Chang-dong. *Kim Yeo-Jin, Mun So-ri, Sul Kyoung-Ku.* At a railroad bridge over a stream, a man (Sul) stumbles onto a reunion picnic. Limping and half out of his mind, he joins them. Then the story goes backward three days to how he got to this spot, and backward three more years to a failing job and a failing marriage. The story goes backward again and again, delving further into his past. By twenty years back, the seeds of not just his personal discontent but the anguished recent history of his country become clear, showing South Korea as a nation undergoing the brutal growth pangs of rapid industrialization. It's an incisive, deeply affecting film, stylistically clear-eyed, sharply acted, harshly ironic, and unsentimental. One of the finest films made anywhere in the last few years. —*J.C.*

PULGASARI L: FOREIGN/KOREA (1958) 106M D: Sang-ok Shin, Chong Gon Jo *Chang Son Hui, Ham Gi Sop, Jong-uk Ri, Kenpachiro Satsuma.* Communist North Korea's answer to Godzilla isn't much different from his capitalist cousin. Metal-eating lizard god Pulgasari grows from cute little doll to towering freedom fighter, leading the peasant rebellion and stomping the armies of the evil emperor. Satsuma, the man in the Godzilla suit from 1984 on, looks more awkward than awesome as he waddles around in this tubby creation. The dramatics are strictly juvenile melodrama, overwrought and campy, but the epic amounts of property damage are dutifully delivered. Just like the video box proclaims, this film was banned for a decade, but don't expect a hidden subversive political message. President Kim Jong II put the epic on ice out of sheer pique when its director defected. —*S.A.*

QUIET FAMILY, THE L: FOREIGN/KOREA (2000) 105M D: Kim Ji-un. *Song Kang-ho, Park In-hwan, Na Mun-heui.* Kim's morbidly dark comedy about a dysfunctional family that finds its latent talents after taking over a mountain lodge. As innkeepers they are fitfully successful-there are simply no customers this far from civilization-but when the rare guests all wind up dead they become

pros at hiding the bodies (death is bad for business). As the parents become increasingly complicit in the cascade of death, the family starts to splinter and the mayhem grows more frequent, often accompanied by an inspired selection of American rock-and-roll tunes, from the Stray Cats to Love and Rockets to the Partridge Family's "I Think I Love You." Kim keeps the tone deadpan, which Takashi Miike turned on its head in his 2002 remake *The Happiness of the Katikuris*, a madcap musical with outrageous set pieces and a strangely innocent quality. Don't expect innocence here, but you might find an unspoken forgiveness. —*S.A.*

RING VIRUS, THE L: FOREIGN/KOREA (1999) 108M D: Dong-bin Kim, Mauricio Dortona. *Eun-Kyung Shin, Seung-hyeon Lee, Jin-young Jeong, Du-na Bae, Chang-wan Kim.* People who watch an odd videotape get a telephone call then inexplicably die horribly exactly one week later unless they pass it on to someone else who also sees it, like a virus. This remake of the Japanese cult-horror classic *Ringu* is better than the American version and every bit as good as the Japanese original. It's not as eerie and uncanny but visually and emotionally cleaner and more scientific in its storytelling, which gives the telekinetic angle and the art gallery connection more prominence and the characters and backstory more edge. Also the Korean version's moral harshness makes it perhaps even scarier deep down at an existential level. —*J.C.*

SEX IS ZERO L: FOREIGN/KOREA (2002) 96M D: Je-gyun Yun. *Chang Jung Lim, Ji-won Ha.* So there's this Korean miniseries about two families who get their kids mixed up in a hospital, and the boy falls in love with his sister who really isn't his sister, but he already has a girlfriend who tries to kill herself. Anyway, his sister who isn't his sister dies of cancer in the end. It sucks and makes you cry. This movie is not like that at all, but its level of fucked-itude reminds me of the other one. How do they come up with these combinations? It seems to adhere to the dartboard philosophy of plot construction, e.g., throw in some bawdy sex humor and pepper it with some abortion melodrama. In any case, you'll laugh your ass off and then feel guilty about it. Shit. —*T.C.*

SHIRI L: FOREIGN/KOREA (1999) 125M D: Jacky Kang. *Han Suk-Kyu, Choe Min-Sik, Song Kang-Ho, Kim Yeo-Jin.* Call it *Die Hard* on the DMZ, a high-tech action thriller built on the same cheesy conventions and impossible twists as most American blast-happy movie roller coasters, yet rooted in a very real and resonant political powder keg. The secret agent cat-and-mouse game between earnest South Korean investigators Ryu (Han), a handsome young veteran with a dreamy optimism, and his impulsive younger partner Lee (Song). A feral female North Korean assassin named Hee leads them to a plot to heat the Korean cold war up to boil. Kang directs with a funereal seriousness (which underscores the high stakes while inadvertently highlighting the silly action-movie clichés) and a breathless sense of velocity. This is an unmistakable Asian variant on the action movie, a sleek, slick espionage thriller in the John Woo mold, with high melodrama and emotional hysteria between the bloody urban assaults and really big explosions. —*S. A.*

SORUM (AKA GOOSEBUMPS) L: FOREIGN/KOREA (2001) 100M D: Jong Chan-Yun. *Jin-Young Jang, Myeong-Min Kim.*

I rented this movie thinking it was some sort of haunted-house story, but what I got was a vague and utterly boring stab at the sort of socially conscious thriller that Japan has been turning out for a while. A South Korean taxi driver moves into a new apartment, whereupon he becomes slowly entwined in the lives of the building's tenants, a motley bunch of morbidly depressed wackos, each suffering from some hidden past trauma. He gets involved with a neighbor girl after helping her bury the corpse of her abusive boyfriend. Blah, blah, blah. You've all seen this crap before. *Sorum* badly wants to be suspenseful and careful, but its "deliberate" pace just ends up leading to repetitive scenes of people spouting expository dialogue, followed by a twist ending that, robbed of any context by the meandering plot, is totally meaningless. It's *Sympathy for Mr. Vengeance* or *Audition* without the meticulous attention to detail, the shocking brutality, or the social relevance. —*M. L.*

SYMPATHY FOR MR. VENGEANCE L: FOREIGN/KOREA (2002) 129M D: Chan-wook Park. *Du-na Bae, Ha-kyun Shin, Kang-ho Song, Ji-Eun Lim.*

This movie is brutal. I can probably count on one hand the number of scenes that weren't completely psychologically debasing, and still have enough fingers left over to poke out my own eyeballs. Ryu (Shin) is a deaf-mute whose sister is slowly dying from kidney failure. He can't pay for his sister's transplant operation, though, because he's been recently laid off. So he and his revolutionary-wannabe girlfriend concoct a scheme to kidnap the daughter of a wealthy factory owner (yes, the same factory from which Ryu was let go). And of course it wouldn't be much of a movie if things went smoothly. When the little girl is accidentally killed, her father can think of nothing but revenge. But any of these characters could be "Mr. Vengeance." The film is full of people you know to be generally decent human beings who have been so utterly emotionally mangled by suffering and loss that they're prepared to do absolutely repugnant things to each other. In the end, though, the "sympathy" part is just irony ... even these well-intentioned people are capable of the worst kind of evil. The gorgeous cinematography, deliberately glacial pace, and numbing brutality are more than enough to turn most folks off. Stick with it and you'll get one of the best films ever about why bad things happen to good people. —*M. L.*

TELL ME SOMETHING L: FOREIGN/KOREA (1999) 118M D: Yoon-Hyun Chang. *Eun-ha Shim, Suk-kyu Han.*

My favorite scene in this movie is when a playful boy breaks open a trash bag and *lots* of blood and body parts come washing out. Don't worry, I haven't given away the goriest bits-there are plenty of them to go around in this film. *Tell Me Something* is the dark, creepy, and definitely not for the weak-stomached tale of a jaded cop, Detective Cho (Suk-kyu Han), who is investigating a string of grisly murders. When he begins protecting Chae (Eun-ha Shim), a female witness in the case, he puts his heart and his life at risk. No one is sure if the woman he's begun to love is the killer or just a hapless victim. It's a pretty standard plot turn, but *Tell Me Something* escapes from mediocrity, succeeding as a highly stylized, moody thriller. Beautiful cinematography adds a lot to this film and helps it transcend the simplistic murder-mystery genre it is a part of. —*G. M.*

VIRGIN STRIPPED BARE BY HER BACHELORS L: FOREIGN/KOREA (2000) 126M D: Sang-soo Hong. *Sun-keun Moon, Myeong-gu Han, Eun-Joo Lee, Bo-suk Jung.*

Arty black-and-white film detailing a developing relationship between a young insecure gallery owner (Jung) getting close to a screenwriter (Lee) and to a film director, complicated by the screenwriter's virginity and distrust of the commitment of the wealthy young man. The movie breaks down into segments. Scenes perceived from the man's perspective are repeated, this time seen through the woman's eyes. Different details come to light with a differing emphasis on what is important: a dropped fork is remembered by the other as a spoon. Places and even different dating partners get transposed, providing the film and the pair's wobbly but developing relationship a rich contour. The discomfort feels right; their mutual trust develops then falters then awkwardly reestablishes itself. Smart, wistful, forgiving movie. —*J. C.*

VOLCANO HIGH L: FOREIGN/KOREA (2001) 120M D: Kim Tae-gyun. *Kim Su-ro, Shin Min-a, Jang Hyeok.*

In the wake of deadly Teacher Wars, a hero arises from the halls of high school to defend the students against the dark forces of oppression, authoritarianism, and detention. Set in a postapocalyptic high school where homework has been displaced by conspiracies and extracurricular clubs vie for ultimate power against a cabal of teachers and a scheming vice principal, this high-flying, tongue-in-cheek collision of historical martial arts epics, *Rebel Without a Cause* and *The Matrix*, is an audacious, genre-bending action spectacle. Director Kim balances his hilarious, mock-epic tone perfectly with the melodramatic machinations of the plot, the tortured moral struggle of its juvenile delinquent hero (a reluctant superhero-think Luke Skywalker by way of Spider-Man-who gets a mini-movie of a flashback dedicated to his origins), and the eye-popping action.

No wonder South Korea has become the action-movie giant of Asia. —S.A.

YONGARY, MONSTER FROM THE DEEP L: FOREIGN/KOREA (1967) 79M D: Ki-duk Kim. *Kwang Ho Lee, Soonjai Lee, Yungil Oh, Moon Kang, Chungim Nam.* If you're like me, the prospect of a Korean *kaiju* (giant monster) movie is pretty exciting, but you are likely to be disappointed and bored by *Yongary, Monster from the Deep.* Mysterious earthquakes are caused by Yongary, a legendary monster that pops out of the ground and starts destroying Seoul. He's a Godzilla-type lizard that drinks gasoline, shoots lasers out of a horn on his nose, and breathes fire from a clearly visible nozzle in his mouth. An annoying kid in short-shorts discovers that Yongary digs rock and roll, and the shots of Yong getting down are the most amusing in the movie. Eventually the monster dies a slow, agonizing death after being doused with some scientifically designed powder. The end! This was remade in the late '90s as an all-digital monster movie (retitled *Reptilian* in the States) to cash in on the sucky American Godzilla film. —S.H.

MACEDONIA

BEFORE THE RAIN L: FOREIGN/MACEDONIA (1994) 113M D: Milcho Manchevski. *Silvija Stojanovska, Labina Mitevska, Grégoire Colin, Katrin Cartlidge, Rade Serbedzija.* Malchievski presents a conflict between two Macedonian families that is based on religious grounds as a puzzle. His fascination with photography is represented through the main character, a Macedonian photographer living in London who decides to move back to his home country. The plot of this film is circular. Its connection between time, events, and places is clever and open-minded. The concern with violence, the repetition of mistakes humans make, their hate, and the timelessness of these qualities is powerful. A great film with beautiful music and landscapes. —D.J.

GOODBYE, 20TH CENTURY L: FOREIGN/MACEDONIA (1999) 89M D: Darko Mitrevski, Aleksandar Popovski. *Lazar Ristovski, Vlado Jovanovski, Sofija Kunovska, Dejan Acimovic, Nikola Ristanovski.* Stylish, pessimistic Macedonian film about the brutality of man. Starts out in a postapocalyptic wasteland with Jodorowsky-esque violence and depravity (the protagonist survives an execution, then has sex with the portrait of a saint). Suddenly it jumps back to a party on New Year's Eve of 1999 and a story about a depressed man in a Santa costume. Very much captures the turmoil and millennial fears of the time. —B.T.

MEXICO

ALL OF THEM WITCHES L: FOREIGN/MEXICO (1995) 100M D: Daniel Gruener. *Susana Zabaleta, Ricardo Blume,* *Alejandro Tommasi, Delia Casanova.* Daniel Gruener's creepy supernatural thriller takes its title from *Rosemary's Baby* (the movie plays in the background on TV at one point) and pings with reverberations from Polanski's classic: an apartment building with strange doings, a mysterious husband, bizarre hints of black magic all around. But this moody piece goes its own way as scared mouse Zabaleta turns to witchcraft for empowerment, transforming herself into a confident woman who confronts her demons. Gruener has a great eye for images: expressive sets and striking scenes are masterfully mixed together for a potent witch's brew of moody horror. Winner of three Mexican Academy Awards. —S.A.

AMORES PERROS L: FOREIGN/MEXICO (2000) 153M D: Alejandro González Iñárritu. *Emilio Echevarría, Gael Garcia Bernal, Goya Toledo, Álvaro Guerrero, Jorge Salinas.* This trilogy of stories connected by a crippling car wreck is quite literally a portrait of the violent dog-eat-dog world of Mexico City. The jittery, jagged style of the opening scene aside, Iñárritu directs with a slow, methodical pace and a sureness of tone, the better to get under the skin of his unsettled characters. And unsettled they are: an aimless but gentle boy in love with the schoolgirl bride of his angry, abusive street-criminal brother; a glamorous model crippled and scarred in a car wreck; a street person with a violent past and a murderous sideline who prowls garbage dumps with a pack of stray dogs. At times Iñárritu allows his pretensions to overtake the raw power of the passionate characters, and at 153 minutes focus tends to dissipate, especially in the final story, but it's an invigorating film filled with vivid performances, haunting scenes, and messy, intense emotions. The volatile portrait in frustration and helplessness is also quite violent and the many scenes of animal cruelty may upset some viewers, despite the repeated insistence that no animals were harmed during the making of the film. —S. A.

BETWEEN PANCHO VILLA AND A NAKED WOMAN L: FOREIGN/MEXICO (1995) 87M D: Sabina Berman, Isabelle Tardan. *Arturo Ríos, Jesús Ochoa, Diana Bracho.* Pancho Villa becomes a loaded symbol in this witty look at sex, love, and identity in modern Mexico. To successful businesswoman Bracho, he's a fiery romantic figure of manly power. To intellectual writer and revolutionary Ríos, he's the embodiment of Mexican machismo. When he appears as an apparition (Ochoa) to help Ríos woo back girlfriend Bracho, who has left him for a younger, more sensitive lover, he becomes a clownish symbol of chauvinism and outdated clichés of nineteenth-century masculinity. Its views on modern relationships are universal and not new, but its inventive channeling of Mexican culture gives it a distinctive slant and a specific twist, and hearty performances and deft direction give it gusto. —S. A.

CHAC: THE RAIN GOD L: FOREIGN/MEXICO (1975) 95M D: Rolando Klein.

Pable Canche Balam, Alonzo Mendez Ton. Chilean director Klein learned filmmaking at UCLA, then went on a pilgrimage to the Tzeltal villages in Chiapas, Mexico, where he lived for two years and put together this film, his only feature to date. Though it takes place in contemporary times, the traditional culture and ancient beliefs of the Tzeltal villagers could be a flashback to thousands of years ago. . . until one dubious villager pulls out a flashlight in the midst of a meeting. Thus faith and fact, tradition and technology battle in the soul of the town leader unable to embrace the magic of ceremony and the wisdom of the spiritual elder they turn to for help in bringing back the rains. Primal, unadorned, yet striking and beautiful, this mystical odyssey through the primal landscape of the Chiapas region is a sumptuously photographed film that moves at its own pace. This cult film still holds a primal power. —S. A.

CRIME OF PADRE AMARO, THE L: FOREIGN/MEXICO (2002) 119M D: Carlos Carrera.

Gael García Bernal, Ana Claudia Talancón. Bernal (*Y Tu Mamá También*) is Amaro, the liberal, idealistic, and well-meaning young priest whose ambition and hubris make him easy prey to the corruption of internal politics in the Catholic Church of Mexico. The passionate, earthy rush of his secret affair with a good Catholic girl and virginal catechism teacher (Talancón) is troubling enough. As he learns from his elders to compromise in the name of the "greater good" and measure sin (especially his own) on a sliding scale, his moral compass is sent spinning. Carrera's direct, unadorned style bristles with passion, anger, and a palpable sense of betrayal. Though condemned by the Catholic Church, this scathing indictment of power, politics, and organized religion became the most successful domestic production in Mexican film history. —S. A.

DOÑA HERLINDA AND HER SON L: FOREIGN/MEXICO (1985) 90M D: Jaime Humberto Hermosillo.

Marco Antonio Trevino, Guadalupe Del Toro, Leticia Lupersio. Hermosillo's subversive little comic drama of tolerance and acceptance, while still keeping up appearances, is so sly and subtle it's beguiling. "As a child Ramon was left-handed, but I taught him to use his right. I made him perfectly ambidextrous," boasts Doña Herlinda (Del Toro). That's the closest she comes to admitting his homosexuality, but in her mission to have it all she moves her son's gay lover into their home for his happiness ("Rodolfo's bedroom is big," she smiles with convincing innocence), just as she marries him off to an eligible and smart woman. Herlinda projects naive innocence while determinedly stage-managing her unconventional family unit. It's a truly astounding portrait of

acceptance and determination, all engineered by a mother who wanted it all and got it: an absolutely loving utopian family. —S. A.

SINGLE ACTION L: FOREIGN/MEXICO (1997) 79M D: Carlos Gallardo.

Óscar Castañeda, Carlos Gallardo, Alejandra Prado, Miguel Gurza, Manuel Vela. Fans of *El Mariachi* probably noticed the original Mariachi Gallardo's bit part in the 1995 sequel *Desperado.* But did they know he also wrote, directed, produced, and starred in this modern-day Western made on a budget only a few thousand dollars more than that of *El Mariachi*? Gallardo plays a man-with-no-name-type stoic drifter (also revealed to be some sort of government agent) who wanders into a small town and (with the occasional help of two old men) takes on a cartel that is apparently involved in some political assassinations. It feels very much like a slightly more serious *El Mariachi*, taking obvious influence from it and its sequel. I love the scene where Gallardo slides across a cable shooting at two gunwomen in a car, who in turn call him a bitch. A major drawback though is that Gallardo, who was so great as an ordinary guy mixed up in violence, this time pretty much just casts himself as Clint Eastwood. Sure, he's a little more grizzled than he was in *El Mariachi* (and so are the bad guys) but he's so self-conscious about chewing on that cigar that it becomes distracting. In the final scene his new love takes the cigar out of his mouth and throws it away, which is kind of a relief. —B. T.

WHO THE HELL IS JULIETTE? L: FOREIGN/MEXICO (1997) 91M D: Carlos Marcovich.

Yuliet Ortega, Fabiola Quiroz, Jorge Quiroz, Victor Ortega, Salma Hayek. The real-life stories of rebellious Cuban schoolgirl Yuliet and Mexican model Fabiola, two women with nothing in common but a shared music video and an absent father, are rewritten as staged documentary: *This Is Your Life* as Godardian comic meditation. Less subjects than performers interpreting their lives on film, they increasingly interact with the filmmaker as in a Bugs Bunny cartoon, calling into question director Marcovich's assertions, correcting subtitles, and revealing the artifice behind the verisimilitude. Through the revelations of rehearsals and retakes, director Marcovich lays bare the manipulations and challenges the representation to find the person between fact, fiction, fantasy, and the tough pose Yuliet offers the camera. —S. A.

Y TU MAMÁ TAMBIÉN L: FOREIGN/MEXICO (2001) 105M D: Alfonso Cuarón.

Diego Luna, Maribel Verdu, Gael García Bernal. The Mexican story of two sex-obsessed, dope-smoking teenage boys (Bernal and Luna) on a raunchy road trip with a sexy, worldly young Spanish woman (Verdu) reads like a transplanted American teen-sex comedy on the surface, but it's far more than that. Working-class Bernal and rich-kid Luna are utterly unselfconscious in their portrayal of boys on their last blast of irresponsible fun, bringing just a touch of tension to their screen friendship, while Verdu emerges as the heart and soul of the picture. Under her smiling front of confidence and fun-loving impulsiveness, Luisa is sad and lost, and she thrives on the unbridled energy and naive innocence of the immature, cocky, sex-mad boys. Framing the giddy teenage explosion of energy are the comments of an omniscient narrator, whose ironic insights offer background color and flash-forward reality checks, and the political and social tensions of modern-day Mexico in the periphery of their road trip. Like all road movies, this is a journey to self, and Cuarón both celebrates and mourns the passing of their youth deftly, thoughtfully, and with sharp, aggressive style. It feels honest. —*S. A.*

NETHERLANDS

EVERYBODY'S FAMOUS L: FOREIGN/NETHERLANDS (2001) 92M D: Dominique Deruddere. *Eva Van der Gucht, Werner De Smedt, Thekla Reuten, Victor Low, Josse De Pauw.* In yet another take on the lunge for Andy Warhol's promised "fifteen minutes," Deruddere takes a satirical setup and turns it into harmless, toothless fun, sweet where it calls for sour. Imagine a working-class version of *Gypsy* with a modern-media twist. Blue-collar stage dad De Pauw kidnaps a famous pop star and ransoms her, not for money but for an audition for his daughter Van der Gucht (sort of a Belgian Ricki Lake) with the pop star's manager. The sleazy showbiz pirate stage-manages De Pauw's naive plot into a live melodrama of hysterical tabloid TV. Deruddere shamelessly sugarcoats his cynicism, turning the kidnapping into a kind of liberation, and the out-of-control plan into a venue for emotional healing. Forget the potential in the story of a dad who pushes his alienated daughter to fulfill his own dreams; Deruddere transforms it into a feel-good working-class fairy tale. —*S. A.*

VANISHING, THE L: FOREIGN/NETHERLANDS (1988) 107M D: George Sluizer. *Johanna ter Steege, Benard-Pierre Donnadieu, Gene Bervoets.* This is the scariest movie I have ever seen, and it is truly one of the best love stories I have ever seen. Sluizer minimizes blood and gore and opts for a more subtle form of horror. This movie is about obsessive love and the random terror (human terror) that ultimately threatens to destroy that love. It is at once irrational and deeply searching, reminding us of the consuming beauty and morbid danger of life. —*J. D.*

NEW ZEALAND

ONCE WERE WARRIORS L: FOREIGN/NEW ZEALAND (1994) 99M D: Lee Tamahori. *Taungaroa Emile, Rena Owen, Temuera Morrison, Mamaengaroa Kerr-Bell.* When I first heard about this film, I was living in Berlin. My friends saw it and said it was one of the most powerful dramas they had ever seen, and that some people got up and walked out of the screening. Its reputation preceded itself and I wasn't let down when I finally saw it. The film deals with a Maori family's domestic violence and abuse. Fueled by racism, poverty, and alcohol, we experience a descent into the maelstrom of a destroyed people and a family in decay. Jake (Morrison) is a raging alcoholic with frequent outbursts of violence, one son is in trouble with the law, another is on the verge of joining a gang, and a daughter has a secret she can no longer keep inside. The only saving grace is the strength of a mother's love. Watching *Once Were Warriors* is an emotional roller coaster, and it's meant to be. If you value cinema's power to communicate and transfer an experience to those who never have been exposed to a situation different than their own, then this film is well worth your time. —*B. W.*

QUIET EARTH, THE L: FOREIGN/NEW ZEALAND (1985) 91M D: Geoff Murphy. *Bruno Lawrence, Alison Routledge, Pete Smith.* One day Lawrence wakes up and gets ready for work, but when he leaves his house, nobody is around. Once he figures out that most of the human race has disappeared, he moves into a better house. As he gets more lonely he starts to do odd things like setting up an audience of cardboard standees and making a speech to them. But then he finds a woman (Routledge). They immediately fall in love and have all the world as their playground. Stories about people finding themselves alone on Earth are always fun, and this is one of the better ones. —*B. T.*

UTU L: FOREIGN/NEW ZEALAND (1983) 120M D: Geoff Murphy. *Tim Elliot, Kelly Johnson, Bruno Lawrence, Anzac Wallace.* A Maori man who works as a guide for the occupying British army of his native New Zealand finally snaps at the sight of the ongoing atrocities against his people. The film opens with a horrific massacre of a Maori village. The guide, Te Wheke (Wallace) swears a blood vendetta ("utu") against the white man. What results is a purifying orgy of violence against a deserving victim. Although the film lacks some historical narrative as to why the massacre takes place or how Te Wheke came to his conclusion, this doesn't take away from the old Western feel, or the justification for revenge. Lt. Scott (Johnson) is charged with introducing new commando tactics from the Boer War, and Williamson (Lawrence) is a gun-obsessed homesteader who swears his own oath of vengeance against Te Wheke after he kills his wife. All in all this is worth seeing if for nothing else than to witness the beautiful cinematography shot in the dynamic rugged landscapes of New Zealand. —*B. W.*

WHALE RIDER L: FOREIGN/NEW ZEALAND (2002) 101M D: Niki Caro. *Mana Taumaunu, Keisha Castle-Hughes, Rawiri Paratene, Vicky Haughton, Cliff Curtis, Grant Roa.* This is a wonderful and powerful film about a Maori tribe whose leading elder is desperate for a successor. His family is descended from a long line of chiefs reaching back through time to their ancestor, who swam over the oceans to New Zealand. He grew tired and weary and was rescued by a whale, which he rode the rest of the way to shore. With neither of his sons to succeed him, and no male heir to come, he turns to the young boys in the village to train and determine which of them will become the leader. All the while his granddaughter dares to ask why she cannot be the next leader and chooses to defy tradition to prove her worth and rightful place. The only thing that bothered me is that the girl has to prove herself through divine means. I would have been happier if she could have proven herself through pure determination and skill. It is a remarkable film about a culture that is desperately trying to survive a modern world, a man who must see past tradition to truth, and a girl who believes in the power within herself and the power of change —*M. N.*

WHAT BECOMES OF THE BROKEN HEARTED? L: FOREIGN/NEW ZEALAND (1999) 108M D: Ian Mune. *Temuera Morrison, Nancy Brunning, Clint Eruera, Pete Smith, Rena Owen.* This follow-up to *Once Were Warriors* is not as intense or dramatic as the first, but it's engaging nonetheless. When I first heard there was going to be a sequel I assumed that the story would follow the mother (Owen) from the first film, as her character was the most redeeming, but surprisingly the story decided to follow the character you loved to hate, Jake (Morrison). Jake is the epitome of a male patriarchal violent bastard, and after many tragedies in his life he is finally trying to come to terms with his uncontrollable violent nature. His oldest son falls victim to a gangland murder, while the younger brother, Sonny (Eruera), seeks vengeance by infiltrating the gang his brother was in, taking on his older brother's girlfriend (Brunning) in the process. Meanwhile Jake confronts himself by coming to terms with his Maori background and finding friendship in his search for answers. Jake finally wakes up to what matters to him most: redemption to his family. But can he help himself and thus his son in time? —*B. W.*

NORWAY

ELLING L: FOREIGN/NORWAY (2002) 90M D: Peter Naess. *Marit Pia Jacobsen, Sven Nordin, Per Christian Ellefsen.* Paranoid, socially challenged Elling (Ellefsen) is a self-described forty-year-old "mommy's boy" sent to a psychiatric hospital after his mother's death. The articulate, educated obsessive finds an unlikely best friend in his simple orangutan of a roommate (Nordin) and they hit the big city of Oslo together as a some-times contentious but always supportive odd couple. Naess's quirky little comedy about oddballs navigating such real-world crises as crossing the street and using public toilets hits every cliché we've come to expect in comedies about childlike and innocent "crazy people." It's also cute and sweet and often very funny. Ellefsen's prissy Elling and Nordin's beefy sex-obsessed virgin are endearing characters who build their own communal family of equally neurotic characters. A 2002 Oscar nominee for Best Foreign Language Film. —*S. A.*

PATHFINDER L: FOREIGN/NORWAY (1987) 88M D: Nils Gaup. *Mikal Gaup, Svein Scharffenberg.* This ancient tale from northern Scandinavia is made into a beautiful and spellbinding film of adventure and growing up. Aigin, a teenage boy who has been out hunting, returns to his family's remote home to find that they have been slaughtered by bandits. He makes a narrow escape and finds a small camp to take refuge in. He tells this group of people of the bandits and they reluctantly let him stay with them. Meanwhile the men from the camp are desperately hunting for meat of any kind to feed their people and are coming up with bones. Soon the boy's tracks are found by the murderers and they will stop at nothing to kill him and pillage the people he has hidden with. The people decide to flee and this is when Aigin decides he must stay and take his revenge on his family's killers. —*A. B.*

ZERO KELVIN L: FOREIGN/NORWAY (1995) 118M D: Hans Petter Moland. *Bjørn Sundquist, Gard B. Eidsvold, Stellan Skarsgård.* Moland's story of an idealistic young writer (Eidsvold) looking for adventure and story ideas as a fur trapper in remote Norway is no *Never Cry Wolf.* Facing a year in a one-room cabin with two antisocial hunters, cut off from all civilization, this learned young lad has a whole new education in front of him. Almost immediately he crosses Randbek (a marvelously tempestuous Skarsgård), an experienced hunter with a mean streak and violent temper. As the year drags on, brief moments of merriment and spontaneous joy are invariably turned into new confrontations when the writer's moral dander meets Randbek's barely controlled hate-as if the misanthropic Randbek has taken refuge from the social world only to have it follow him here in the form of a know-it-all kid. The rage that he radiates practically melts the frozen frontier. —*S. A.*

POLAND

SARAGOSSA MANUSCRIPT, THE L: FOREIGN/POLAND (1965) 182M D: Wojciech Has. *Jonanna Jedryka, Iga Cembrzynska, Zbigniew Cybulski, Franciszek Pieczka, Leon Niemczyk.* Six degrees of separation? Go one better in this deliriously labyrinthine cult tale within a tale within a tale, a multilayered story that becomes a dazzling commentary on storytelling itself. Adapted from Count Jan Potocki's nineteenth-century novel with ornate flourishes and droll humor by Has. It's ostensibly the story of a Belgian captain (Cybulski) who gets lost in the landscape of seventeenth-century Spain and winds up lost in stories, dreams, adventures, riddles, and a mysterious book he stumbles across. This mad mix of ghost story, love story, allegorical adventure, myth, and conspiracy is wrapped in a dream play and layered in reality and storytelling that become impossibly and hilariously complicated even before the stories begin to blur and crisscross. Has creates a visually dense and deliriously ornate world and directs with a lilting grace: his camera is always gliding, tracking, tilting, keeping the film flowing through its next narrative maze with forward momentum (even if the story is moving back). It's all damnably clever and very wry, a tongue-in-cheek trip through the metaphysics of storytelling. —S. A.

PORTUGAL

PARTY L: FOREIGN/PORTUGAL (1996) 95M D: Manoel de Oliveira. *Rogerio Samora, Leonor Silveira, Michel Piccoli, Irene Papas.* Piccoli is both sad and endearing as the aging lothario whose poetic flirtations find their match in Silveira's verbal volleys, and Papas is regal as the impresario who longingly watches Piccoli's games with young women. They aspire to an imagined world of Noel Coward wit and verbal deftness, forever circling one another while using words to fend off real communication. De Oliveira directs this portrait with an arch, awkward, stagy stiltedness, as if it's all a phony pose. He never quite overcomes the hollow center for all the grace of his cast, but he directs like a master choreographer whose design becomes clear in the final movement. —S. A.

VOYAGE TO THE BEGINNING OF THE WORLD L: FOREIGN/PORTUGAL (1997) 91M D: Manoel de Oliveira. *Marcelo Mastroianni, Jean-Yves Gautier, Leonor Silveira.* Restrained, wistful, and confidently generous, Mastroianni performs in *Voyage to the Beginning of the World* as if he knew it would be his last film. Playing a famous Portuguese filmmaker (an alter-ego for Oliveira, who was eighty-eight when he made this film) shooting a picture in land of his youth, he turns raconteur, hosting a pair of his actors on a journey through his past. This inspires his leading man (Gautier), a French actor with Portuguese ancestors, to seek out his father's sister and discover his own roots. Olivera directs this tale of memory, family, and connecting the past and the present with the patience of someone who has lived a long life: savoring every moment, he pauses to watch the waves break on shore and turns to share it with his friends. As Mastroianni steps to the background to allow his costar his moment, his smiling eyes still steal every scene with the sparkle of warm understanding. —S. A.

RUSSIA

BALLAD OF A SOLDIER L: FOREIGN/RUSSIA (1959) 88M D: Grigori Chukhrai. *Vladimir Ivashov, Zhanna Prokhorenko, Antonina Maksimova, Nikolai Kryuchkov, Yevgeny Urbansky.* Chukhrai's WWII tale, a deliriously romantic story of a six-day pass, is from the early days of the Russian thaw, a brief period during the Cold War when censorial standards were eased, creating the first flowering of Soviet cinematic freedom between WWII and perestroika. Ivashov is the radio operator turned hero by happenstance who journeys home to fix his mother's roof, and becomes continually waylaid as he helps out loyal comrades, fellow soldiers, and salt-of-the-earth civilians along the way to his village and his hardworking mother. Think of it as the poetic odyssey of an accidental hero through the ideals of the Soviet state pulling together in times of hardship, with (again) a few raised eyebrows at the shirkers and unfaithful spouses on the home front. Delicately photographed (life during wartime has rarely looked so beautiful), deftly paced, and populated with delightful characters, this road trip is good company. —S. A.

BROTHER L: FOREIGN/RUSSIA (1997) 96M D: Alexei Balabanov. *Sergei Bodrov Jr., Viktor Sukhorukov, Svetlana Pismichenko.* Bodrov Jr. is an appealing baby-faced soldier who makes the transition to civilian life by putting his skills to use as a hit man in consumer-crazy St. Petersburg. He's the lone man with a code in a cutthroat world of fast-buck street sellers, extortionists, and businessmen-mobsters, but the irony of this loyal kid turned efficient killer twists like a knife by the conclusion of this amazing drama. The unusual mix of lanky neorealist drama and harsh gangster violence has striking parallels to the Oscar nominated *A Friend of the Deceased*, but goes its own way with a story of cynicism, satire, and innocence lost in opportunism. —S. A.

CRANES ARE FLYING, THE L: FOREIGN/RUSSIA (1957) 95M D: Mikhail Kalatozov. *Svetlana Kharitonova, Tatiana Samoilova, Alexei Batalov, Alexander Shvorin, Vasily Merkuryev.* Kalatozov, most famous for his daring cinematic essay *I Am Cuba*, was something of a throwback to the silent Soviet masters when he created *The Cranes Are Flying.* A romantic tale of Russian heroism during hardship, a tribute to fallen heroes, and a celebration of hope for the future (along with a more ambivalent condemnation of the "traitors" who shirk their responsibility for fleeting comfort), it's the story of almond-eyed brunette beauty Veronica (Samoilova), whose storybook courtship is shattered by war when her lover, an idealistic architecture student, enlists. Her journey takes her from the sunny Baltic shore to snowy Siberian hospitals and back again, and she seems to wilt as she awaits some word from her MIA lover. It was the first Russian film in years to break past the borders and capture the international community, as well as the Palm D'Or at the 1958 Cannes Film Festival, and it proclaimed the end of Russia's cinematic dry spell under Stalin's reign with a return to the poetry and humanism practically unseen since the heady days of experimentation and optimism in the silent and early sound years. —S. A.

MOTHER AND SON L: FOREIGN/RUSSIA (1997) 75M D: Aleksandr Sokurov. *Gudrun Geyer, Aleksei Ananishnov.* Nick Cave boasts of having cried through the whole film. *Mother and Son* consists entirely of the intimate last moments between a dying mother and her adult son, who continually cradles her in a remarkable reverse pietà. With little dialogue, no flashbacks, no voice-over narration, and no plot twists, the film's emotional and dramatic weight demands from the audience only the most basic recognition of the relationship-a mother and her son. Rather like the pair in the film, the audience inhabits a finite pocket of time as something like a reverie, until it ends. A composition less of narrative than of a tangible sense of time, *Mother and Son* could only exist in the film medium, which is to say that it is brilliant cinema. —C. B.

RUSSIAN ARK L: FOREIGN/RUSSIA (2002) 96M D: Aleksandr Sokurov. *Maria Kuznetsova, Sergei Dreiden, Leonid Mozgovoy, David Giorgobiani, Alexandr Chaban.* Aleksandr Sokurov's tribute to the Hermitage Museum through time and space, created in a single unbroken shot, is far more than an astounding technical achievement-though that achievement is nothing less than sublime. Our guide is a spindly time traveler who flits through history as if at home in each era, and the camera is the kino-eye of our narrator. A delirious piece of cinema, it glides back and forth in time as we cross the thresholds from one room to another, moving from contemporary patrons appreciating the masterworks on the walls to a carpenter constructing coffins for the dead of WWI, from visits with Catherine the Great to eavesdropping on Cold War–era curators discussing to the difficulties in preserving the heritage in the face of a Soviet government intent on rewriting history, and finally dancing through a nineteenth-century ballroom. The breathtaking finale is as graceful as ballet and suffused with a luxurious nostalgia that is as poignant as it is ambiguous. A staggering work of cinematic art. —S. A.

VIY, OR SPIRIT OF EVIL L: FOREIGN/RUSSIA (1967) 105M D: Konstantin Yershov. *Vadim Zakharchenko, Leonid Kuravlev, Natalya Varley, Alexei Glazyrin.* A rascally drunkard of a theology student escapes the clutches of a cackling crone of a witch and beats her near to death, but she concocts her revenge by transforming herself into the young daughter

of a noble lord and demanding the callow student come to perform her death rites. It's based on the short story by Nikolai Gogol, which earlier inspired Mario Bava's *Black Sunday,* but the real creative delight comes from the contributions of its cowriter, artistic director, and special effects designer: fantasy legend Aleksandr Ptushko (*The Day the Earth Froze*). The opening scenes with the student transformed into a flying beast of burden are hardly realistic but they are lovely and lyrical, and the magical assault she unleashes as he reads over the restless corpse for three consecutive nights climaxes with a parade of hellish ash-gray minions crawling over every surface. The lumbering Viy himself looks like a Golem from a Maurice Sendak nightmare. The moments between aren't nearly as compelling, but the pastoral countryside and its rustic peasants give it a simple serenity that the students shatter in their reverie. —S. A.

SCOTLAND

ABERDEEN L: FOREIGN/SCOTLAND (2000) 103M D: Hans Petter Moland. *Lena Headey, Ian Hart, Charlotte Rampling, Stellan Skarsgård.* Skarsgård is an alcoholic retired oil-rigger and Headey his hostile, tightly wound coke-addict daughter in this road-trip drama that takes them from Norway to Scotland to mother (a serene and sublime Rampling), who is dying of cancer. You wonder if darling mother has a little of the trickster in her as she reunites her frayed family through guilt, manipulation, and subversion. This road trip takes some familiar turns and sentimental stops, but director Moland avoids the usual movie clichés of addiction and abuse to create a searing and scary look at dysfunction and moving story of reunion. Hart, one of Britain's most underrated and surprising character actors, is marvelous as a truck driver who helps the dysfunctional couple get to their destination. —S. A.

SPAIN

BETWEEN YOUR LEGS L: FOREIGN/SPAIN (1999) 120M D: Manuel Gómez Pereira. *Sergi López, Victoria Abril, Javier Bardem, Carmelo Gómez, Juan Diego.* Another gloriously overheated Spanish melodrama of sex, jealousy, lust, passion, and murder. Abril plays a radio talk-show screener with a penchant for picking up men for quickies and Bardem is a screenwriter hooked on phone sex. Their eyes meet at a group for sex addicts. It isn't long before they're tearing off their clothes in a passionate affair that becomes entwined with a murder investigation headed by Abril's husband (Gómez). Then it gets complicated with almost absurd subplots involving a plane crash, a cop suicide/murder, blackmail, revenge, and black-market sex tapes. What saves it is the atmosphere of musk and pheromones (so thick you could swim through it) created by director Pereira. —*S.A.*

CANNIBAL MAN L: FOREIGN/SPAIN (1971) 98M D: Eloy De La Eglesia. *Eusebio Poncela, Emma Cohen, Vicente Parra.* De La Eglesia's perversely entertaining thriller is an absurdist portrait of homicidal madness. Hot-tempered butcher Parra accidentally kills a man in a drunken brawl and keeps on killing to keep his crime a secret. The working-class grunt, living in a stark, sun-baked desert town, starts off angry and aggressive, but as the momentum of his murders spins out of control, his soul crumbles under the strain. Structured like a farce but heavy with despair, it's an unusually melancholy thriller of a man who ends up killing everyone he cares about until he turns numb and hollow. Not your usual horror fare. —*S.A.*

DREAM OF LIGHT, THE L: FOREIGN/SPAIN (1992) 138M D: Víctor Erice. *Antonio López García.* Not quite a documentary but certainly no work of fiction, this staged cinematic essay obsessively details Spanish artist García as he struggles to paint a young quince tree in the dying days of autumn. Directed by Erice (*Spirit of the Beehive*), this Cannes Jury Prize winner is about the art of creation in the face of aging and the cycle of life. It's a rich work, lush and lovely and bustling with activity but paced at a contemplative stroll, like a time-lapse recording in first gear. The slow seasonal shedding of the quince tree marks is more than a metaphor, it's life captured and shaped into a work of art. —*S.A.*

IN A GLASS CAGE L: FOREIGN/SPAIN (1985) 110M D: Agustín Villaronga. *Günter Meisner, David Sust.* If you can stomach most horror films, perhaps enjoy them, and think you have seen it all, then try this Spanish thriller on for size. Most rational people will not be able to sit through it. It begins with a Nazi child-torturer beating his last victim before throwing himself off a cliff. Little does he know, however, that he is being followed by a former victim! Of course, the fall doesn't quite kill him and he's forced to live in an iron lung to stay alive. The family puts out an ad for a nurse, and guess who applies? This new presence in the house starts taking more and more control of things, and at night he forces the former Nazi to reexperience his experiments with the detailed help of his own handwritten diary. And I can only say things get much worse from there. —*N.J.*

INTACTO L: FOREIGN/SPAIN (2001) 109M D: Juan Carlos Fresnadillo. *Mónica López, Eusebio Poncela, Leonardo Sbaraglia, Max von Sydow.* Luck is both a blessing and a curse in a world where the lucky are often haunted and lonely survivors. Such is the unusual horror of Fresnadillo's tale of corruption and power, where luck is a charge that can be stolen and staked in games of chance. von Sydow is "God of Chance," a fierce but weary demon-king who reigns over a karmic casino like an old West gunfighter, forever defending the title of the luckiest man alive from all comers. A bank robber (Sbaraglia) is plucked from oblivion by von Sydow's former protégé (Poncela), who has been doomed to an eternity of bad luck and wants his revenge. Fresnadillo's morality tale is played out in secular terms, but the metaphysical implications are downright demonic: these karmic vampires steal the souls of luckless victims and pitch them like chips in unholy wagers. Clever dramatic design and broad but intense emotional strokes make Fresnadillo's odysseys of temptation, revenge, and redemption more affecting than you might expect. —*S.A.*

LOVE CAN SERIOUSLY DAMAGE YOUR HEALTH L: FOREIGN/SPAIN (1997) 117M D: Manuel Gomez Pereira. *Penelope Cruz, Gabino Diego, Ana Belén, Juanjo Puigcorbé.* Former lovers Belén and Puigcorbé clash thirty years after their first madcap meeting and sparks fly, sending them back into memories of years earlier, when she (played by a perky, delightfully flighty Cruz) sneaks into John Lennon's hotel room and he (a flustered, boyish Diego) is the bellboy who grapples with her—under Lennon's bed! From that point in it's a screwball series of extramarital trysts with a melancholy undercurrent: in this case, love can't overcome character. Belén brings a mercenary quality to her social-climbing socialite, whose ambition constantly trumps her passion, while Puigcorbé brings an exasperation to his lovesick working-class slob who decides he can't keep making all of the sacrifices to spend a few passionate hours with his mercurial lover. —*S.A.*

MAD LOVE L: FOREIGN/SPAIN (2002) 118M D: Vincente Aranda. *Pilar López de Ayala, Daniele Liotti, Rosana Pastor.* Spain's answer to *Elizabeth* is a sixteenth-century political-conspiracy drama turned hot-blooded bodice ripper, inspired by the true story of the passionate Queen Joan "the Mad." Brown-eyed Spanish beauty Ayala looks every inch the innocent sacrificed on the altar of political marriage as the virginal naif transformed into the sexually insatiable lover and tempestuously jealous wife of Normandy's swarthy Prince Philip (Liotti-think Fabio as a royal womanizer). Ayala brings a fiery, full-blooded passion to her transformation from demure porcelain beauty to insatiable lover to tempestuously jealous wife and fulfills the "Mad"-ness of the title with impulsive, obsessive spectacle. This volatile package of emotional nitroglycerin gives birth in a royal commode (chewing through the umbilical cord like a feral she-wolf) and crawls over her husband's bedsheets like a bloodhound to sniff out his lover. Aranda gives Pedro Almodóvar a run for his money in the arena of self-destructive love, obsessive passion, sweaty cinematic sex, and deliriously melodramatic spectacle. It makes for lustiest costume drama in years. —*S.A.*

MOON CHILD L: FOREIGN/SPAIN (1989) 120M D: Agustín Villaronga. *Maribel Martin, Lisa Gerrard, Enrique Saldana.* Twelve-year-old David (Saldana) is a psychically gifted child who attends a special school run by occultists in Europe. He learns of a prophecy about a new Messiah child to be born in Africa under a full moon. David believes he is this child and feels he must escape from his school, as the occultists believe the Moon Child must be kept under their control so they themselves can harness the power of the moon. An employee of the school helps David escape, and soon he joins up with Georgina (Gerrard from the group Dead Can Dance), the supposed mother of the Moon Child. Together they travel to Africa where David tries to survive and fulfill his destiny as the Moon Child. A mystical movie, similar in tone to the alchemical films of Dario Argento (*Suspiria, Inferno*) though not nearly as violent, Villaronga takes a different turn with this film from his other works (*In a Glass Cage, El Mar*). Here, the Spanish director/screenwriter focuses more on the theme of mystical experience as ancient prophecies unfold before the reality of the world around us. As with Villaronga's other work, the film is beautifully shot and contains a rare soundtrack by the alternative group Dead Can Dance. Given its unusual subject matter, *Moon Child* was rarely screened anywhere worldwide and is very difficult to find on video. —*N. H.*

NICO AND DANI (AKA **KRÁMPACK**) L: FOREIGN/SPAIN (2000) 91M D: Cesc Gay. *Fernando Ramallo, Chisco Amado, Esther Nubiola, Marieta Orozco, Jordi Vilches.* Seventeen-year-old best friends (Ramallo and Vilches) plot to lose their virginity one unsupervised summer at the seaside in this Spanish coming-of-age drama. In the United States, this kind of film usually takes the form of either heavy melodramatic romances or leering, wacky sex comedies, but this is in the more earthy, naturalistic European mode. Gay, adapting Jordi Sanchez's play *Krámpack*, shows a sensitivity to the hormonally driven boys and their awkward attempts at seduction in his presentation of playful energy, romantic confusion, and blossoming sexual identities. It's a modest but frank look at adolescent lust, both heterosexual and homosexual, but the refreshingly matter-of-fact presentation is also bluntly macho and almost exclusively from a male perspective. —*S. A.*

OTHER SIDE OF THE BED, THE (AKA **EL OTRO LADO DE LA CAMA**) L: FOREIGN/SPAIN (2002) 114M D: Emilio Martinez Lazaro. *Ernesto Alterio, Paz Vega, Guillermo Toledo, Natalia Verbeke, Alberto San Juan, Maria Esteve.* This is cute, but nothing to write home about. First thing I'll say is this: musicals from Spain are . . . different. Be aware of that going into the flick. The music was, for the most part, not catchy or interesting and, in general, just didn't seem to fit the rest of the film. The choreography was also

fairly pedantic. Some of the lyrics were funny and entertaining, and there is a clever bit where a song moves from person to person to person in totally different situations and settings. It's basically one of those bed-swapping stories where everyone is fooling around with everyone else. There were some very funny moments though and I definitely laughed often. —*M. N.*

RUNNING OUT OF TIME (DIAS CONTADOS) L: FOREIGN/ SPAIN (1994) 93M D: Imanol Uribe. *Javier Bardem, Karra Elejalde, Ruth Gabriel, Carmelo Gómez, Candela Peña.* Gómez (Julio Medem's favorite leading man) is an insolent Basque terrorist who comes to Madrid for his latest assignment and falls in lust with his next-door neighbor, an exhibitionist junkie hooker (Gabriel) who spends much of the movie buck naked. Bardem costars as a cocky pimp with greasy hair and a moral backbone even more rotten than his teeth. Set in the sleazy Madrid underworld, it is loosely inspired by *Carmen,* but goes its own way with a (surprisingly) more romantic twist to the inevitable tragedy. The thriller takes a backseat to the hothouse passions and erotic displays that post–Franco Spanish cinema has become famous for. —*S. A.*

SEA, THE (EL MAR) L: FOREIGN/SPAIN (2000) 107M D: Agustín Villaronga. *Angela Molina, Simon Andreu, Roger Casamajor, Antonia Torrens, Bruno Bergonzini.* From the Spanish cult director of *In A Glass Cage* comes this dark and frightening morality tale set in a tuberculoses hospital on the island of Mallorca during the Spanish Civil War. Handsome and violent Andreu (Molina) arrives at the hospital in the beginning stages of TB. There he meets his childhood friend Manuel, who is suffering from advanced stages of TB and has turned to Christianity in a desperate attempt to find meaning to his illness (and avoid a growing lustful attraction to Andreu). Andreu is also reunited with Francisca, his boyhood sweetheart who lost her virginity to him years before and now resides as nun working with the sick and dying youth. His past slowly pervades into his life in the hospital, and soon Andreu is caught up in both acts of theft and murder. As in the case of *In a Glass Cage,* director Villaronga films with terrifying images of innocent youth being victimized (in this case by disease) and striking out in desperation. The film is both beautifully shot and acted, and drips with undertones of unexpressed sexuality and despair. —*N. H.*

SPIRIT OF THE BEEHIVE, THE L: FOREIGN/SPAIN (1973) 95M D: Víctor Erice. *Isabel Telleria, Ana Torrent, Teresa Gimpera, Fernando Fernán Gómez.* Set in an isolated village in the wake of the Spanish Civil War, the film opens with a screening of James Whale's *Frankenstein.* Hardly able to distinguish the movie from reality, little Ana (Torrent) is utterly captivated, but also profoundly upset over the angry mob's brutal attack of the misunderstood monster. Ana's older sister improvises

Victor Erice's *The Spirit of the Beehive*

I've just finished a semester teaching directing at the University of Southern California's Graduate School of Film. I used scenes from a number of movies to illustrate points I was trying to make. One of those movies was Victor Erice's *The Spirit of the Beehive* (1973).

I discovered *Beehive* through Nestor Almendros, who recommended its cinematographer, Luis Cuadrado, to me when I was about to make a film in Spain. I later learned that Cuadrado had since died of a brain tumor, and that he had lit *Beehive* when he was nearly blind. He had had his assistant describe the sets to him, and then told him where to put the lights and how intense each should be.

I have now seen the film over twenty times—more than any other of my favorite films. I never tire of it. I discover something new each time I see it. It reveals its secrets slowly.

It is a secret and mysterious work, concerned with the biggest mysteries of all: creation and death. It is also concerned with family relationships—husband and wife, father and daughters, sister and sister—and with each character's attempts to communicate, as well as with their ultimate isolation and loneliness. Finally, it is about cinema itself, and the power of cinema to invade our dreams and awaken our knowledge and fears.

There are no accidental images or extraneous scenes. The opening shot of the father, his face distorted by the screen of the beekeeper's hood, foreshadows the scene near the end where he becomes the Frankenstein monster in his daughter's fantasy. In other scenes the children create their own monster in the classroom by adding heart, lungs, and eyes to a chart of the human body, having seen the film in which Dr. Frankenstein does the same. Even the image of the hex-

---

an explanation to calm her, claiming that the monster lives on as a spirit in a nearby derelict barn. Ana makes daily pilgrimages to the barn until, by chance, she encounters a war deserter hiding there, and believes she's finally found the gentle monster. Unsettling and fascinating, Ana's thoughts and motivations are appropriately withheld, unknowable as they are, until she becomes as mysterious to us as the Frankenstein monster is to Ana. Considered by some critics the single greatest achievement of Spanish cinema, haunting cinematography, flawless performances, and a foreboding pace make this a truly special film. —*C. B.*

THESIS L: FOREIGN/SPAIN (1996) 121M D: Alejandro Amenabar. *Fele Martinez, Eduardo Noriega, Ana Torrent, Xavier Elorriaga, Migel Picazo.* Winner of numerous Goya Awards (the Spanish Oscar equivalent), including Best Picture and Best Director, Amenabar's (*The Others*) debut feature is an unsettling mystery that delves into the social fascination with sensational violence.

University student Torrent discovers a snuff film in the school archives, and a conspiracy of murder and sadism for sale that may include her grungy pirate-video partner, a handsome but sinister beau, and her thesis advisor. Amenabar's points about the draw of the dark side of human evil fall to the wayside as the spiraling mystery draws us into a first-person nightmare, but even if it's thematically murky, the edgy direction creates a riveting psychological thriller. —*S. A.*

VIVA LA MUERTE L: FOREIGN/SPAIN (1970) 87M D: Fernando Arrabal. *Nuria Espert, Mahdi Chaouch.* Set in the carnage and violence of the aftermath of the Spanish Civil War, playwright Arrabal's directorial debut is a surreal portrait of a child, Fando (the boy shares the same name as the protagonist of his play *Fando and Lis*, which Alejandro Jodorowsky adapted into a film in 1967), trying to come to grips with his Republican father's arrest at the hands of his mother, who betrayed him to the authorities. His lessons emerge in violent games and obscure fantasy sequences

agonal cells of the honeycombs is repeated in the small hexagonal windowpanes and the hexagonal screening of the apiary.

The central character of the film is a five-year-old girl, Ana, who along with her slightly older sister, Isabel, sees the movie *Frankenstein* and is profoundly affected by it. Ana is disturbed by the killing of the little girl in the film and doesn't understand why the monster is also killed. Isabel pretends to have the answers to Ana's questions, but when pressed later, she can say only this: They're not really dead. It's only a movie, and nothing is real. Besides, she's seen the monster. He's a spirit, and she can make him appear whenever she calls him.

In subsequent scenes, the children play with and at death. Isabel experimentally attempts to strangle her cat, stopping when the cat scratches her. She applies the blood on her finger to her lips, as if it were lipstick. Later she pretends to be dead to frighten Ana. Finally, Ana experiences the death of a real person, a deserter from the army whom she befriended. We feel Ana's crisis as our own, for we have all passed from innocence to knowledge of mortality at some time in our own childhood.

The adults remain more enigmatic.

The wife, Teresa, writes letters to a soldier, perhaps a former lover. The husband, Fernando, listens to a crystal radio before writing in his journal late at night, eventually falling asleep in his chair. Teresa goes to the train station to mail her letter and sees another soldier sitting in the train as it slowly pulls away. They are separated by the glass window of the railway car as they watch each other, each in their own soundproof universe, isolated.

It was exciting for me to see the movie again, freshly, through the eyes of my students. One of them asked a question I had never thought about before: was the letter Teresa burns at the end *to* or *from* her lover? I looked at the scene again, and it's clear it's *to*, not *from*. My student also raised the question of whether the deserter was Teresa's lover, which I couldn't answer. One of the greatnesses of *Beehive* is that it's completely without exposition, other than what would be revealed to an observer in life. Nothing is added purely for the benefit of the audience. Consequently, it fulfills Jean Cocteau's definition of a work of art: it must hide its riches, to reveal them little by little over a long period of time.

—*Monte Hellman*

(shot in blurry videotape and transferred to film through color filters), but the adults are just as tormented (his aunt has the boy flagellate her naked back). The portrait of madness and hysteria is rather bluntly directed-Arrabal has little subtlety but lots of twisted images (see a man sewn into a cow's carcass!). He gets his point across. —*S. A.*

SWEDEN

FAITHLESS L: FOREIGN/SWEDEN (2000) 142M D: Liv Ullmann. *Lena Endre, Erland Josephson, Krister Henriksson.* Ingmar Bergman wrote this painful autobiographical drama about a writer (named Bergman and played by Josephson) trying to come to grips with a tragedy caused by his own monstrous and unforgivable actions decades before. He tells the story to a woman (Endre) who may be a ghost, a memory, or an actress playing the part in a theater exercise. Perhaps too personal for Bergman to direct himself, he allowed Ullmann to helm this script and she does so beautifully.

Henriksson plays the director in the past, a cocky young man in the midst of a relationship with a married woman who is assaulted by her separated husband and abandons her in her time of need. The haunting story is even more devastating when set against Bergman's own history. But this is no mere act of atonement. Bergman's script is powerful and uncompromising, and Ullmann's direction is sensitive and responsive to the hard emotions at work. —*S. A.*

LILYA 4-EVER L: FOREIGN/SWEDEN (2002) 109M D: Lukas Moodysson. *Artyom Bogucharsky, Oksana Akinshina.* Director Moodysson continues to improve, perhaps establishing himself as an heir to Ingmar Bergman, as some critics suggest. If he is of that cloth, here he is a Bergman of the streets. Capturing perfectly the tale of two abandoned souls, Lilya (Akinshina), left behind in the Soviet Union by her America-bound mother, and Volodya (Bogucharsky), a twelve-year-old dreamer cast out of his violent home as a nuisance, this story follows each of their downward spirals as they struggle to escape their desperate predicaments. With no one else to lean on, they adopt each other, comforting, consoling, and keeping alive their thin attachments to dreams of a better life. Akinshina and Bogucharsky give documentary-like performances that stun, numb, exalt, and deny us. Moodysson's sure-handed writing and direction allow us to experience it all as truly great art. The only thing that bothered me about this film is how little attention it received here in the United States, where Sundance festival darling, the artificial and forced *Thirteen*, grabbed most of the ink. If you watch this after having seen *Thirteen*, you will recognize the difference between good cinema and great cinema. —*K. S.*

MAN ON THE ROOF, THE L: FOREIGN/SWEDEN (1976) 110M D: Bo Widerberg *Carl-Gustaf Lindstedt, Sven Wollter, Thomas Hellberg.* Widerberg's policier is a refreshingly modest tale rooted in character rather than glitz and gore. Lindstedt plays the rumpled police detective Martin Beck, an aging homicide investigator whose meticulous plodding reveals more than the legwork by the department's younger men. A gruesome murder at a hospital turns into something much more when the chief suspect suddenly takes to a rooftop with a high-powered rifle and starts picking off cops and only cops. Widerberg's easy pace and loose direction lend a sense of familiarity to the film (not unlike American TV shows *NYPD Blue* and *Homicide*, except no handheld camera), and he eschews the sensational for genuine drama and character conflict. A meaty, methodical cop thriller with a real feel for character. —*S. A.*

THEY CALL HER ONE EYE (AKA THRILLER: A CRUEL PICTURE) L: FOREIGN/SWEDEN (1974) 104M D: Alex Fridolinski. *Christina Lindberg, Heinz Hopf.* A young girl is raped (off -camera, I guess) by someone who I thought was her grandpa at first, until the police dragged him away for raping her. This trauma causes her to be mute for the rest of her life. Flash forward several years to the girl, now a beautiful teenager, working on a farm with her dad, I think. She's misses her bus and is promptly picked up by a sleazebag who hooks her on heroin, and pimps her out to other Swedish slime. At one point she retaliates against a "client," and her pimp cuts out one of her eyes, which leads to her stylish color-coded eye patches. That'll teach her! Or will it? No. As a show of good faith, the pimp lets her have two days a week for herself, to do with what she will. What she does is learn how to kill, and seeks revenge on her pimp and his clients in several slow-motion shoot-outs. Like most Swedish cinema, *They Call Her One Eye* is slow and depressing; unlike most Swedish cinema, this movie has XXX porno and shotguns. —*K. C.*

BETTER THAN SEX L: FOREIGN/TAIWAN (2002) 92M D: Chao Pin Su, Lee Feng-bor. *Leon Dai, Bobby Chen, Ginny Liu, Michael Wong, .* While I was in Taiwan, there was this pop singer named Michael who was ruling the pop charts. He had all the Taiwanese teenyboppers wrapped around every sugary sweet lyric that oozed out of his emasculated mouth. I thought to myself, "How can such shitty music be so universally popular?" This movie is about a porn-obsessive, donkey-dicked genius and his wacky search for true love, and it stars none other than Michael. Now, after seeing this movie, I think to myself, "How can such a fruity man be so fuckin' rad?" —*T. C.*

PERSONALS, THE L: FOREIGN/TAIWAN (1999) 104M D: Chen Kuo-fu. *Ku Paoming, Chin Shi-chieh, Wu Pai, Chen Chao-Jung, Rene Liu.* Chen Kuo-fu's modern romantic comedy stars Liu as a strong-willed but lonely-eyed doctor who takes out a personal ad to find Mr. Right and winds up in a series of blind dates with many Mr. Wrongs, among them a foot fetishist, a pimp, and a movie actor in disguise "doing research." It sounds like a lighthearted comedy, but Kuo-fu underlines the film with a sense of pathos and loneliness, much of it due to Liu's melancholy phone calls to a lost lover, which become monologues to his answering machine. It's often very funny, but as the film develops an affecting sadness takes over. Liu is an amazing actress with an expressive face that anchors the film in her experience as she sits through an increasingly pathetic and lonely stream of men with increasing awkwardness and discomfort. —*S. A.*

TOUCH OF ZEN, A L: FOREIGN/TAIWAN (1969) 180M D: King Hu. *Shih Chun, Feng Hsu.* Hu's romantic chivalry adventure is a masterpiece of Hong Kong cinema, a magnificent epic with grand battles and one of the films that inspired *Crouching Tiger, Hidden Dragon*. The story of modest but honorable scholar Ku (Chun) who helps a princess in exile (Hsu) against the forces of a corrupt Eunuch is a three-hour experience that flows like a lazy river with a swirling undertow just beneath the placid surface. The Zen comes in with a brotherhood of monks dedicated to defending the innocent with nothing but bare hands against swords. The acrobatics are more graceful than athletic; our heroes somersault through the air, leap up trees and over walls, and float like feathers to the ground. Hu accomplishes it through editing and camera work, without resorting to elaborate wirework or other special effects. The colors are delicate, like they've been painted, and the atmosphere is painstakingly created with mist and falling leaves, sunlight that floods the lens, and darkness that shrouds the visual world in shadow. One of the most beautiful martial arts movies you've ever seen, every frame of the film is worth hanging on a wall. —*S. A.*

THAILAND

BANGKOK DANGEROUS L: FOREIGN/THAILAND (1999) 105M D: Oxide Pang Chun, Danny Pang. *Premsinee Ratanasopha, Pawalit Mongkolpisit.* The Pang Brothers take Hong Kong flash to Thailand for this flashy, splashy piece of action melodrama. The story of a deaf-mute master assassin (Mongkolpisit) with an innocent heart and a puppy-love attachment to a sweet young pharmacist is little more than a structure to hang a series of snazzy set pieces on. The characters are simply sketched but acted with conviction, and the romantic nihilism and blood-spattered chivalry is delivered with more energy and invention than conviction. They're John Woo and Wong Kar-wai fans emulating their cinematic mentors, and they have the stylistic chops if not the soul. In this case that's enough, because they manage to pull almost every technique in the book together into a coherent, energetic, flamboyantly show-offy crime thriller. —*S. A.*

EYE, THE L: FOREIGN/THAILAND (2002) 98M D: Oxide Pang Chun, Danny Pang. *Angelica Lee, Lawrence Chou, Chutcha Rujinanon, Yut Lai So.* A blind girl undergoes an eye transplant to be able to see again. She enters the world of sight, but with one little stipulation. The eyes have a history of their own, and she starts seeing the things that they have seen. . . as well as dead people. Understandably frightened, she teams up with the sexy young doctor who wants to jump her bones, to find out who the young woman was whose eyes were able to see the aforementioned dead people. Eerie and suspenseful, this film proves once again that Asia does atmospheric horror in a way that America repeatedly fails to. You're lulled into a false sense of security with a pseudo-happy ending right before the actual super-creepy ending comes along and punches you in the face. A film to watch with the lights off. —*J. S.*

Having received full-bore acclaim from almost every major critic who saw it, *The Eye* should have been a million times better than anyone ever promised it to be. Moody? Not really. Haunting? Hmm. Nope. Better than most Hollywood horror movies? Probably. But damn, what a letdown anyway.—*A. T.*

IRON LADIES, THE L: FOREIGN/THAILAND (2000) 104M D: Youngyooth Thongkonthun. *Jesdaporn Pholdee, Sahaphap Tor, Ekachai Buranapanit.* Inspired by a true story, this Thailand tale of a volleyball team of transvestites, cross-dressers, and a pre-op transsexual who spike and screech their way through the national championships and became folk heroes along the way is pure, energetic movie hokum, and became the all-time second-highest grossing film in Thailand history. Director Thongkonthun tangles even the simplest exercises in narrative coherence but drives through his sloppy direction with sheer energy and flamboyance. Too shrill and silly to take seriously, its high spirits and naive message of tolerance make for an odd, innocently winning comedy. Not bad for a scrappy, sloppy little film running on mincing, wince-inducing performances and tired sports-movie clichés. —*S. A.*

KILLER TATTOO L: FOREIGN/THAILAND (2001) 111M D: Yuthlert Sippapak. *Suthep Pongam, Somchai Kemglad, Sornsutha Klunmalee.* In the near future (though aside from a few throwaway shots you'd never know it), assassin Buffalo Gun has just been released from prison and is immediately hired to kill the chief of police in Bangkok. He rounds up three other assassins (a sniper, an explosives madman, and an M16-toting Elvis fanatic) to assist him, unaware that the hit has been double booked with another assassin, Kit Silencer. The two assassins choose the same venue for their hit, and in the confusion cause a near riot with the police. They continue to harass each other until a common enemy unites them, but Kit's quest for the identity of his parents' killer may have them once again turning their guns on each other. At first, this violent and over-the-top crime comedy seems like a hodgepodge of excellent Hong Kong action scenes that have been seen before. However, it quickly and seamlessly changes gears into a much more tragic tone, as each of the characters' pasts are revealed, and a search for redemption and love ends in a bloody, tear-jerking finale. —*R. M.*

LEGEND OF SURIYOTHAI L: FOREIGN/THAILAND (2001) 185M D: Chatrichalerm Yukol. *Marisa Anita, Mai Charoenpura, Sarunyu Wongkrachang, Johnny Anfone, M. L. Piyapas Bhirombhakdi, Sorapong Chatree.* This is a huge epic film out of Thailand that traces its history and struggle, focusing on the life and true story of the legendary Princess Suriyothai. She is beloved by her people for sacrificing herself in order to save her husband's life and, thus, all of Thailand. Watch the full-length version if you can though (185 minutes versus 142), because the Coppola release is cut (for shame, Mr. Coppola!) and feels truncated, especially early on as they go through her youth, marriage, and so forth with increasingly short and pointless scenes. The rest of the film is rather reminiscent of watching a Thai version of *I, Claudius: Murder. Betrayal*, with an ever-shifting seat of power revolving from one member of the royal family to the next, and various battles with their bordering enemy, Burma. The costumes, sets, and landscapes are breathtakingly beautiful and the story is enjoyable and entertaining, although Suriyothai feels more like an observer through most of it, rather than an active player. —*M. N.*

NANG NAK (AKA **GHOST WIFE**) L: FOREIGN/THAILAND (1999) 100M D: Nonzee Nimibutr. *Intira Jaroenpura, Winai Kraibutr.* This is as much a love story as it is a ghost story. Mak leaves his newly pregnant wife and goes off to fulfill his duty as a soldier to fight in the Chiang Toong War. A serious wound leaves Mak recovering in Bangkok for many months until he is strong enough to return home. There he reunites with his devoted wife, Nak, and finally sees their infant son. However, it soon becomes evident that Nak's labor pains caused a transformation in her. The other villagers have come to fear Nak, for good reason. For some viewers of recent ghost films from Hollywood such as *The Sixth Sense* and *The Others*, the transformation we witness might not be wholly unexpected. Shot in the beautiful Thai jungle and countryside with some interesting horror special effects, this is an all-around enjoyable movie. With the one exception of Nak and Mak crying each other's names one too many times. —*B. W.*

PHRA APAI MANI L: FOREIGN/THAILAND (2002) 91M D: Chalart Sriwanda. *Ying Juraluk.* This fantasy-enhanced Thai adventure is a good starting place for those curious about Thailand's rich folktale culture. After two princes are exiled from their kingdom they become caught up in a fantastic voyage across the kingdoms. When a shape-shifting sea-witch kidnaps one brother, the other brother and a trio of swamis follow in pursuit. Along the way, they get tangled up in a war between two rival kingdoms and must fight to save a princess. Meanwhile, the captured prince encounters a family of mermaids who decide to help him escape from his island prison. When the two brothers finally reconvene, they must stand against the sea-witch's true, gigantic form that is able to deflect any physical assault. The effects-laden fight sequences, of which there are plenty, only add to the martial arts powers that the leads have mastered. Almost all of the action and effects are physically based, with computer effects added on top and well-crafted green-screen shots to create the magical world. The final product feels like an almost perfect blend of Ray Harryhausen's classic effects and Andrew Lau's CGI-heavy works. —*R. M.*

TEARS OF THE BLACK TIGER L: FOREIGN/THAILAND (2000) 110M D: Wisit Sasanatieng. *Sombat Metanee, Arawat Ruangvuth, Supakorn Kitsuwon, Chartchai Ngamsan, Stella Malucchi.* This movie is nuts. It takes place in Thailand and the old West (which is apparently in Thailand), and some kind of revolution is going on, and there's a love story and lots of bloody squibs. So, it's like a Thai spaghetti Western. . . a Thaighetti Western. I'm sorry, that was lame. But, this movie isn't. The director makes great use of color, and the set designs are very stagey but perfect for this film. At one point a soldier is shot with a rocket, flies backward, hits a wall, and explodes. And for some reason, the bandits have a midget in their gang. The plot revolves around Dum (aka Black Tiger, the bandit) and his longtime love,

Rumpoey (who is about to marry a police captain), and other betrayals in the bandit gang, all of which are taken very seriously by the actors, which makes the whole production that much cooler. Watch it! NOW! —*K. C.*

TIBET

HIMALAYA L: FOREIGN/TIBET (1999) 108M D: Eric Valli. *Gurgon Kyap, Lhakpa Tsamchoe, Karma Wangiel, Karma Tensing Nyama Lama, Thilen Lhondup.* Director Valli, a former *National Geographic* documentarian, hauled his crew up to the high passes and mountain lakes of the Himalayas to shoot this simple, almost mythic survival adventure, but this is no documentary. It could be two or two hundred years ago that this tribe makes its trade pilgrimage through the mountains to the lowland. At stake is the stubborn pride of the old former chief who reclaims his position when his son is killed, and the sense of responsibility of the rebellious young leader when he sees blind emotion leading the old man's determination to make the journey without him. There's a certain hint of a European creator turning the adventure of an almost primitive culture into a pseudo-mythic journey, and the simplicity of this tale threatens to collapse into cliché at times, but the iconic power and directness of the nonactors and the sheer magnificence of the imagery pulls this caravan over the trickiest terrain. —*S. A.*

VIETNAM

CYCLO L: FOREIGN/VIETNAM (1995) 120M D: Tran Anh Hung. *Tony Leung Chiu-Wai, Tran Nu Yên-Khê, Le Van Loc.* Tran Anh Hung followed the lyrical *The Scent of Green Papayas* with a vision as violent and dark as *Scent* was delicate and hopeful. His gliding camera effortlessly takes us through the claustrophobic streets and grimy slums of Ho Chi Minh City, following the desperate lives of a teenage boy (Van Loc) sold into a life of crime and his older sister (Yên-Khê) whored out by her gangster boyfriend, Poet (the smoldering Leung). Under the sad eyes and thoughtful silences of Poet rages a tempest that explodes in the film's most startlingly violent scene, just as Tran exposes a thoroughly degraded world that threatens to close in and destroy all who enter with grace and tenderness. An amazing film. —*S. A.*

VERTICAL RAY OF THE SUN, THE L: FOREIGN/VIETNAM (2000) 112M D: Tran Anh Hung. *Le Tuan Anh, Chu Hung, Tran Manh Cuong, Tran Nu Yên-Khê.* Tran Anh Hung brings his poetic elegance and lush, delicate imagery to a domestic melodrama of four siblings in modern-day Hanoi. The two eldest sisters are married, though their apparent happiness is possibly not as perfect as it seems, while the younger brother and sister share an apartment and a sometimes eerily intimate relationship (which Tran never quite explains). "It's tranquility I look for in a photograph," explains one of the husbands, a nature photographer, and he could be speaking to Tran's graceful, nonjudgmental direction. There's an almost stoic attitude toward the frustrations, discontent, wandering hearts, and unhappy lives that rumble under his exquisite surfaces while he revels in the momentary joys of their lives. His elegantly gliding camera eases past each conflict and lulls the film into a lovely, lyrical state of inertia. —*S. A.*

CHAPTER THREE

Action, Adventure, War & Westerns

f it moves fast or shoots fast, or if it runs away fast—whether on foot, horseback, automobile, boat, or any other odd type of vehicle—it ends up here.

Adventures in all manner of exotic places; action dramas of cop and/or criminal ilk; tales of the American West; and wars, real or imagined make up the reviews in this chapter. We hope that most of the section-name meanings are self-evident, but here's a brief explanation of a few:

Peplum refers to the skirts that those saucy Greeks and Romans wore.

Bang! was the best fit for our old computer system's small location field, way back when, for our tribute to legendary film critic Pauline Kael's book *Kiss Kiss Bang Bang.*

Chopsockie is a section of American-made martial arts pictures. If you don't know about Cynthia Rothrock, one of the best-paid actresses of any genre in the '80s, you owe it to yourself to check out her films, and you'll find more than a few of them here.

Populated with characters like Dolemite and John Shaft, actors like Ron O'Neal, Raymond St. Jacques, Pam Grier, and Fred Williamson, all the Afros, Macs, and Zodiacs in late-twentieth-century Black American Cinema make badass appearances in our Blaxploitation section.

The Rednecks section refers nonpejoratively to a particular brand of Southern cinema where moonshiners, whiskey-runners, gator-baiters, hillbillies, kissin' cousins, and others rule their cinematic days.

A spaghetti Western is that marvelous

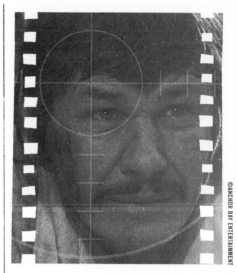

Violent City (1970)

breed of Italian-made films from the '60s and '70s set in the American West of the late 1800s. Think Leone and Eastwood, then imagine Sergio Corbucci and Klaus Kinski instead, and you begin to get the idea.

The Westerns section also contains one of only two "star" sections in the store, where you'll find some of the biggest stars of Western films and serials. In Adventure you'll find certain authors' works collected. Great writers whose works tended toward adventure: H. Rider Haggard, Edgar Rice Burroughs, and Jack London.

ADVENTURES OF BRISCO COUNTY, JR. (PILOT) L: WESTERN TV/WESTERN TV (1993) 95M D: Bryan Spicer. *Bruce Campbell, Julius Harris, Kelly Rutherford, R. Lee Ermey, Billy Drago.* The same year and night of the week that they introduced *The X-Files,* Fox spent one measly season on this lighthearted Western with sci-fi undertones. The pilot introduces Campbell (still a cult figure at the time and not recognizable to the mainstream) as a bounty hunter hired to capture those who killed his legendary father (Ermey). Along the way he gets in some shoot-outs, jumps out windows, meets those who would become the supporting cast of the series, and encounters a mystical object called "The Orb." A good showcase for Campbell's cocky one-liners and a precursor to other period shows with modern humor such as *Hercules* and *Xena* (both of which featured Campbell as a recurring guest star). Unfortunately, the rest of the series has not been released on video (let alone DVD). —*B.T.*

ALWAYS OUTNUMBERED, ALWAYS L: BANG! (ACTION)/ BANG! (ACTION) (1998) 120M D: Michael Apted. *Laurie Metcalf, Bill Cobbs, Bill Duke, Laurence Fishburne, Natalie Cole.* Fishburne brings an edgy intensity to ex-con Socrates Fortlow, an angry, intimidating figure with his bald pate and trim goatee, his haunted memories keeping his violent streak in check—just barely. Author Walter Mosely, who adapted his own novel, is best known for his period detective novels, and this modest but rich character study turns a slice-of-life drama into a compelling tale of redemption. Soc slowly integrates himself into his community, allowing himself to love again, making a difference for the first time. When it's over you'll agree with his best friend: "You're the closest thing to a hero I ever met." In the violent world of South Central LA, that's quite an accomplishment. —*S.A.*

ANY GUN CAN PLAY L: WESTERNS/SPAGHETTI WESTERNS (1967) 105M D: Enzo G. Castellari. *George Hilton, Edd Byrnes, Gilbert Roland, Stefania Careddu.* The legacy of *The Good, the Bad, and the Ugly* is all over Castellari's spaghetti Western about three scoundrels (folk-hero outlaw Roland, bank officer Byrnes, and bounty hunter Hilton) chasing a fortune in stolen gold hidden somewhere in the countryside. Castellari has neither the style nor sweep of Sergio Leone, nor the cold-blooded edge or cynicism of Sergio Corbucci, but his twisty little story of suspicions and betrayals and shifting alliances has a pleasantly lighthearted tone, helped immensely by Roland's easy performance. Byrnes cuts a surprisingly effective figure as the stuffy Eastern bank officer turned scheming crook, and he looks plenty hard and ruthless with a gun in his hand. In the overstuffed buffet of spaghetti Westerns, this is one of the few worth dishing up. —*S.A.*

ART OF ACTION: MARTIAL ARTS IN THE MOVIES L: BANG! (ACTION)/CHOPSOCKIE DOCS (2002) 96M D: Keith Clarke. *Samuel L. Jackson (narrator), Bruce Lee, Jackie Chan.* Jackson narrates this unusually rich made-for-cable documentary about the history of martial arts action in the movies. Where most such productions skim over the greatest bits of Bruce Lee and Jackie Chan, this one begins from the roots of the philosophy, the art of martial combat, and the gymnastic spectacle of Peking Opera and follows the development of screen action. Beautiful, rare silent-film clips, scenes from the 1950s Wong Fei Hong films, and some gorgeous clips from King Hu's landmark *Come Drink with Me* give an amazing (if brief) history lesson, and the work of Chang Cheh (*One Armed Swordsman*) and Lau Kar Leung (*36 Chambers of Shaolin*) is spotlighted along with more familiar contemporary directors (Tsui Hark, John Woo, Ang Lee) and martial artists (Sammo Hung, Jet Li, Donnie Yen). A crash course in Hong Kong action cinema that spotlights some of the greatest and grandest films and will leave audiences wanting more. There are a few Hollywood clips sprinkled in as well, to show how the action has made its way across the Pacific. —*S.A.*

ART OF WAR, THE L: BANG! (ACTION)/BANG! (ACTION) (2001) 116M D: Christian Duguay. *Cary-Hiroyuki Tagawa, Wesley Snipes, Marie Matiko, Anne Archer, Maury Chaykin, Michael Riehn.* The premise is absurd (the UN has a covert "dirty tricks" force that blackmails world leaders into playing nicely) and the story utter nonsense (top agent Snipes is framed for murder and must uncover a conspiracy to clear his name and save his life). Yet director Duguay and producer/star Snipes mold the espionage action thriller into a sleek, sly, and at times smartly made little picture. Snipes doesn't showboat the role, dispatching bad guys with smooth efficiency, and Duguay applies a sharp eye and kinetic editing skills to modest yet impressive action scenes. By the time it winds up to reveal the ludicrous conspiracy, it's created a movie logic so marvelously gonzo that it works. —*S.A.*

BAADASSSSS CINEMA L: BANG! (ACTION)/BLAXPLOITATION (2002) 56M D: Issac Julien. *Melvin Van Peebles, Pam Grier.* Subtitled *A Bold Look at '70s Blaxpoitation Films,* Julien's made-for-cable documentary puts the short-lived burst of exploitation cinema with African-American stars into focus with a rich array of interviews from the founding fathers and muthas (among them directors Van Peebles and Cohen, and stars Fred Williamson, Richard Roundtree, Grier, and Gloria Hendry), commentary from contemporary critics and fans (Elvis Mitchell, Armond White, Samuel L. Jackson, and of course Quentin Tarantino), and a wealth of film clips. It's fascinating to watch how the edgy (and at times revolutionary) stand of the first films (notably *Sweet Sweetback's Baadasssss Song*) was tamed when Hollywood took the reins. Role models, fashions, and urban stereotypes are dissected and dissed, but all agree: for a few years, it was the only game in town where black characters could stand up to white power and win. —*S.A.*

BALLISTIC: ECKS VS SEVER L: BANG! (ACTION)/BANG! (ACTION) (2002) 91M D: Kaos. *Lucy Liu, Gregg Henry, Antonio Banderas, Ray Park.* Banderas is Ecks, a retired souse of an FBI man roused from retirement to take on a rogue operative from a covert CIA division (Liu) and turn the city of Vancouver, Canada (which somehow becomes the Mecca for outcast American agents), into rubble. Thailand helmer Kaos directs his video game of a movie with a certain technical facility and it all looks very cool, especially the twenty-first-century bat-cave-gone-tech-noir mad scientist laboratory, with its erector set–like constructs of catwalks and cages and steaming vats of fog—for mood, I'm sure. The story of lost loves, staged murders, stolen children, and righteous revenge would qualify as spy opera if there was any feeling to it, but for all the epic property damage and fallen soldiers, this is simply bloodless and utterly humorless. It makes you wonder if all the human moments were trimmed away to get to this abstract, frantic exercise in empty flourish. —*S. A.*

BAND OF BROTHERS L: WAR/WWII (2001) 705M D: Tom Hanks, David Frankel. *Donnie Wahlberg, Ron Livingston, Damian Lewis, Matthew Settle, Neal McDonough.* After *Saving Private Ryan* in a single mission, Steven Spielberg and Hanks teamed up to produce a chronicle of the European theater of WWII from a soldier's-eye view on a vast canvas. The resulting made-for-HBO, ten-hour miniseries is one of the most powerful and entrancing portraits of men at war put on screen. Shot in the same khaki and gray tones and combat staccato flicker of *Ryan,* as if viewed through the adrenaline-enhanced fear and you-are-there hyperalert eyes of a soldier under fire, it plays down the melodrama to focus on the texture of battle, the dynamics of platoon life, the wear of fatigue and experience, and the sudden bursts that break a lull. This is not a pretty WWII film: violence and blood are both more and less than you might expect, and the finality of death is disturbing whether it's enemy or fellow soldier. Lewis is the beating heart of the film, a drawling professional who slowly rises in rank due to his calm sense of the big picture, and Livingston is his best friend, fellow officer, and closet alcoholic who hides his liquor in Lewis's footlocker. But it's the sprawling cast and the interplay that builds through the course of the war that give meaning to the title. Bonding under fire is no cliché here. It's a simple matter of survival. —*S. A.*

BEVERLY HILLS COP L: BANG! (ACTION)/BANG! (ACTION) (1984) 105M D: Martin Brest. *Eddie Murphy, Judge Reinhold, John Ashton, Lisa Eilbacher, Ronny Cox, Bronson Pinchot.* There was a time when Brest (*Gigli*) made good movies. After debuting with the charming, melancholy *Going in Style* in 1979, Brest teamed with "blast-boy" producers Don Simpson and Jerry Bruckheimer to develop this fish-out-of-water story originally slated for Clint Eastwood. Squint said no, as did a few other action stars, and, adding a whole new element to the "fish out of water," along came Murphy, fresh off the big hits *Trading Places* and *48 Hours.* What's so refreshing about this film is that it's really not a dumb excuse for an action comedy. There's actually some edgy moments of action here, and Murphy, out to get his partner's killer, brings a pathos to the character most others might eschew in favor of machismo. —*M. S.*

BIG BAD MAMA L: BANG! (ACTION)/VROOM (CHASES & RACES!) (1974) 83M D: Steve Carver. *Angie Dickinson, William Shatner, Tom Skerritt, Susan Sennett, Robbie Lee.* A Depression-era mama (Dickinson) with her two teenage girls in tow (Sennett and Lee) hits the road and finds it only leads to crime. Mama hooks up with a bank robber (Skerritt) and pulls a kidnapping. On the run with the law close behind, she holes up in a farm and fucks a con man (Shatner). The film can't end well. But this comedy-action flick nonetheless bounces along on amiable good spirits down the bumpy back roads of hard-luck America like a hopped-up jalopy, taking its edge from the tough, focused driver at the wheel. This film is something of a classic in its own right. But what is compelling about *Big Bad Mama* are the little details that build eventually into a portrait of the new woman of the feminist 1970s. Aging but sinewy and sexual and persevering, staring down the dusty road while boring full-throttle into the future. It's a period (not the '30s but the '70s) worth remembering, with Dickinson's image here as good as any to remember it by. —*J. C.*

BIG HIT, THE L: BANG! (ACTION)/BANG! (ACTION) (1998) 91M D: Kirk Wong. *Lou Diamond Phillips, Bokeem Woodbine, China Chow, Mark Wahlberg.* Wahlberg plays a sensitive hit man who falls for the girl he kidnaps and has to fight off his colleagues, who have names like Crunch, Cisco, and Gump. It's an awkward combination of clever action sequences and embarrassingly bad comedy, with lots of self-conscious post–*Pulp Fiction* "we're criminals but it's just a regular job to us" dialogue and an uncomfortably over-the-top performance by Phillips. But Wahlberg proves his appeal as a comedic action hero. In my favorite action scene he bungee jumps out of a window just before an explosion, but times it wrong so that he bounces back up into the fireball. Screenwriter Ben Ramsey explored similar territory in 2002's straight-to-video hit man comedy *Love and a Bullet.* —*B. T.*

BILLY JACK L: BANG! (ACTION)/BANG! (ACTION) (1971) 120M D: Tom Laughlin. *Tom Laughlin, Delores Taylor, Clark Howat, Bert Freed.* Director/star Laughlin took his Billy Jack character from the biker film *Born Losers* and gave him his own action series that is still unique for its badass hippie vibe. Half Native-American Vietnam vet Billy Jack and his wife (Laughlin's real-life wife, Taylor) run an alternative "Freedom School" and their students often get into trouble with the racist ranchers in the area. Luckily, they have Billy Jack to walk in, say something real quietly, and slowly take off his cowboy boots to indicate that a righteous karate ass-kicking is about to occur. The film-making is endearingly crude and there are many noisy documentary-like crowd scenes, including a town meeting and various performances of emotional hippie folk music. You can't deny that it's silly and pretentious, but it's great to see a dumb action movie that stands for left-wing values instead of the usual all-this-bureaucracy-is-preventing-me-from-killing-the-scum themes of the genre (Steven Seagal later tried to do this with less success in the obviously Billy Jack–influenced On Deadly Ground). Warning: Don't expect to enjoy the movie for camp value—there is a brutal rape scene. —B.T.

BILLY JACK GOES TO WASHINGTON L: BANG! (ACTION)/ BANG! (ACTION) (1977) 155M D: Tom Laughlin. *Tom Laughlin, Delores Taylor, E.G. Marshall, Sam Wanamaker, Terasa Laughlin.* Laughlin brought his hippie action movie series to its zenith with this straight-faced remake of *Mr. Smith Goes to Washington.* Billy Jack becomes Senator Billy Jack, and although there is one karate scene, the biggest set piece is the filibuster. With Congress depicted as whores to the core, and the primary villains being energy companies, the themes are as relevant now as they were then. This movie is usually a source of ridicule, but the oddity of a liberally slanted action movie coupled with the obvious sincerity of the filmmakers makes it charming. —B.T.

BLACK DOG L: BANG! (ACTION)/BANG! (ACTION) (1998) 89M D: Kevin Hooks. *Randy Travis, Meat Loaf, Patrick Swayze, Brian Vincent, Gabriel Casseus.* Black Dog is a very funny movie, which in a way is unfortunate because it's not a comedy. But it's hard not to chuckle when a few of the characters, who are truckers, discover the federal law enforcement tracking device that has been planted in their truck. The device is a good-sized box that help-fully has a blinking red light on it. Apparently federal law enforcement agents aren't big on subtlety. In *Black Dog,* Swayze plays a trucker who gets involved with some very bad people and has to go on a dangerous, illegal trucking run. Country singer Travis does a decent job playing his sidekick, but the film's acting award goes to villain Meat Loaf, who has a trucking duel with Swayze at the climax that is almost worth seeing the movie for. —T.P.

BLACK GESTAPO L: BANG! (ACTION)/BLAXPLOITATION (1975) 88M D: Lee Frost. *Rod Perry, Charles P. Robinson, Phil Hoover.* A superbly nasty exploitation film, casu-ally toned, crudely brutal, and deeply harsh. The benevolent "Peoples Army" provides medicine to the black community and feeds the poor in the ghetto. The General (Perry) would like to curb drug use, gambling, and prostitution. The Colonel (Robinson) strikes at the Mafia with his shock troops with ambitions to take over their illegal businesses. A battle with the Mafia ensues and the clueless General finally figures out the gambit. When the Colonel fails to assassinate him, there is all hell to pay, which in the end puts the Mafia right back in charge of the ghetto. Plenty of edgy action, exactingly choreographed, makes *Black Gestapo* a minor masterpiece of blood, bullets, pointy tits, and shitty attitude. Unbelievably funky fun. —J.C.

BLACULA L: BANG! (ACTION)/BLAXPLOITATION (1972) 92M D: William Crain. *Gordon Pinsent, William Marshall, Vonetta McGee, Thalmus Rasulala, Denise Nicholas.* It's understandable that *Blacula* has a reputation as a silly blaxploitation movie, but it's actually a successful crossbreeding of the genre with serious, classic horror. The title refers to Manuwalde, an African prince bitten by a white supremacist Dracula while on a diplomatic mission to end slavery. Cursed with the racist "Blacula" designation, he is resurrected from his coffin in 1970s Los Angeles and courts a woman he thinks is the reincarnation of his wife. Shakespearean actor Marshall brings consider-able class to the production, making it feel like an Afrocentric Hammer film. (You may recog-nize Marshall as the original King of Cartoons on *Pee-wee's Playhouse.*) Followed by the sequel *Scream Blacula Scream,* which is also good and has the added bonus of Pam Grier. —B.T.

BLIND RAGE L: BANG! (ACTION)/CHOPSOCKIE (1978) 81M D: Efren C. Pinon. *D'Urville Martin, Leo Fong, Fred Williamson.* A transpacific oddity that features a blind pimp, a blind magician, a blind kung fu master, and a blind Mexican rancher hired by yachting enthusiasts to commit a $15 million bank heist. Scenes of the sightless criminals in training, firing guns at mannequins, are truly amazing. Braille Seikos, sound-triggered karate chops, and ocular acid baths are among the rancid treats found here. The actor who funds the rob-bery speaks more haltingly than ten Christopher Walkens, and the police chief may have the most perfectly round head ever captured on film. Williamson, the 1970s drive-in icon, shows up in the last eight minutes to chew on his skinny cigar in a half-assed supporting role that snags him top billing in the closing credits. Half the production crew has the last name "Uy." From Pinon, director of the far superior epic *Killing of Satan.* —Z.C.

BLOOD, GUTS, BULLETS, AND OCTANE L: BANG! (ACTION)/ VROOM (CHASES & RACES!) (1988) 87M D: Joe Carnahan. *Ken Rudulph, Dan Leis, Joe Carnahan.* Sure, it's more of a promo reel for aspiring director Carnahan than a real movie, but you have to hand it to him for making a hip thriller that looks fine, maintains its momentum, and manages to entertain, all for a mere $8,000 (or so). It's no worse than films

Movies that didn't seem that great until we saw them more than once

AKIRA

THE BIG LEBOWSKI

(and pretty much every Coen brothers movie)

CABIN BOY

CASINO

CHATTERBOX

THE DEVIL *(1981)*

THE EXORCIST

FACES

FEAR AND LOATHING IN LAS VEGAS

FOR A FEW DOLLARS MORE

FRIDAY

THE INNOCENTS

LOST HIGHWAY

MINNIE AND MOSKOVITZ

NASHVILLE

NEW YORK, NEW YORK

SCHIZOPOLIS

THE STONE KILLER

STRANGE DAYS

TO LIVE AND DIE IN LA

VERTIGO

WAITING FOR GUFFMAN

WINGS OF DESIRE

that cost hundreds of times more. Unfortunately it's often no better either. The overstretched story concerns partners in a failing used-car lot who are offered $250,000 for merely parking a convertible on their lot, no questions asked and no touching—the car is wired to explode. The snaky conspiracy loses its way more than once and clumsy writing damages the overreliance on complicated exposition. It's not bad, at times it's quite inventive, and I wouldn't have seen that climax coming in a million years, but how long do you want to watch two white, high-pressure used-car salesman unreel their spiel on clients and yell at each other in sub–David Mamet rants? Carnahan has gone on to better work—check out *Narc.* —S.A.

BULLET FOR SANDOVAL, A L: WESTERNS/SPAGHETTI WESTERNS (1970) 96M D: Julio Buchs. *George Hilton, Ernest Borgnine.* Hilton is the Confederate officer who deserts to marry his Mexican girlfriend (and thus save her name) before she gives birth, and slowly degenerates into a vengeful killer when his girl dies, her father (Borgnine, teeth clenched and eyes mad with hate) abandons the infant, and a heartless world refuses to feed his dying baby boy. A typically violent spaghetti Western, it's an anti–Robin Hood, complete with a loyal Little John sidekick and a Friar Tuck. His mission has little to do with stealing from the rich and everything to do with wiping out all he blames for the infant's death, while his band of followers are vicious cutthroats in it for the loot and the notoriety. Director Buchs (who is, according to many sources, assisted by uncredited codirector Lucio Fulci) is no stylist and has no sense of irony or tragedy, but he embraces the nihilism inherent in more extreme versions of the genre, right down to an epic massacre that climaxes the film. —S.A.

BULLETPROOF L: BANG! (ACTION)/BANG! (ACTION) (1996) 84M D: Ernest Dickerson. *Damon Wayans, Adam Sandler, Kristen Wilson, James Caan.* Wayans and Sandler are the best of friends. Or that's what Sandler thinks, until he finds out Wayans is an undercover cop trying to get to his boss (Caan). So Sandler shoots Wayans in the head, and now they both have a reason to hate each other. Later, Wayans (now with a plate in his head) has to bring Sandler in, but both are on the cartel's hit list, so they squabble until they begin to bond and do action scenes together and all the usual crap. Although Sandler works bits of his comedy into the role, he is utterly unconvincing as a high-ranking criminal, and Wayans is even worse as a tough-talking cop. Sandler and Wayans haven't even mastered their comedies yet, and here they are trying to transcend the cliché-ridden script of a serious action movie. It's sad to see Dickerson, once a great cinematographer for Spike Lee, wasting his time doing throwaway crap like this. —B.T.

BULLITT L: BANG! (ACTION)/VROOM (CHASES & RACES!) (1968) 113M D: Peter Yates. *Steve McQueen, Don Gordon, Jacqueline Bisset, Robert Vaughn.* McQueen is at his steely-eyed best as Detective Lieutenant Frank Bullitt. Set in late-1960s San Francisco, we follow Bullitt as he attempts to protect a gangland witness/rat from a bunch of thugs who don't want him to confess. Something happens, though, and the rat is killed. And then we find out the rat isn't who we thought he was. The plot really doesn't make that much sense, and it doesn't matter. What matters here is (a) McQueen and (b) McQueen's souped-up 390 Mustang. McQueen did most of his own stunt driving (as did famed Hollywood stunt driver Bill Hickman) and that gritty realism pays off in the end. McQueen's performance is never tender; he is just as hollow and void of emotion as we expect a cold-blooded action hero to be. —J.D.

CAT BALLOU L: WESTERNS/WESTERNS (1965) 96M D: Elliott Silverstein. *Jane Fonda, Lee Marvin, Michael Callan, Dwayne Hickman, Nat "King" Cole, Stubby Kaye.* When Catherine Ballou (Fonda) comes home from college, her father is struggling to keep the family farm under threats from the railroad company. He's killed by a gunman (Marvin) who wears a prosthetic nose to replace the one that was bitten off. So Cat gets some guns and forms a posse, including a pathetic, alcoholic ex-gunman (also Marvin), to get her revenge. Despite the typical Western plot, it's a light-hearted comedy framed by scenes of Cole and Kaye telling the story and singing "The Ballad of Cat Ballou." Fonda's comic timing is excellent (this is her best comedy) and Marvin's dual role is irresistible (he even won the Best Actor Oscar for it). —B.T.

CAVALRY CHARGE (AKA THE LAST OUTPOST) L: WESTERNS/ WESTERNS (1951) 88M D: Lewis R. Foster. *Ronald Reagan, Hugh Beaumont, Noah Beery Jr., Rhonda Fleming, Bruce Bennett.* Cheer on Reagan, the smiling Confederate guerrilla ambushing Union patrols and supply trains along the Santa Fe Trail in this low-budget programmer Western. Bennett, the biggest cinematic stiff in the history of the movies, plays his Union officer brother and Fleming is his old flame, and guess what? They all show up in the same outpost town! The plot stretches credulity with absurd twists and a kid-gloves approach to war, but the politics between settlers and Indians are more complwicated than most and the climactic battle carries it with ironies that appear to be lost on director Foster. Chalk that up to screenwriters Winston Miller (*My Darling Clementine*) and Daniel Mainwaring (*Out of the Past*). Beery Jr. and Beaumont costar as Reagan's loyal men. —S.A.

CHARLIE'S ANGELS L: BANG! (ACTION)/BANG/TV (2000) 98M D: McG. *Drew Barrymore, Cameron Diaz, Lucy Liu, Bill Murray, Sam Rockwell, Crispin Glover.* Faced with the task of adapting an outdated TV show, the oddly named music video director McG and producer/star Barrymore came up with a unique tone that is definitely not a straight adaptation, but also not exactly a parody. Instead it is an absurdly over-the-top action comedy that makes no bones about its utter silliness. Barrymore, Diaz, and Liu are the multitalented agents working for a mysterious voice on a speaker box to solve mysteries and kick ass. They do lots of wire fu (choreographed by Yuen Cheung-Yan), dress up in all kinds of disguises, make lots of sexual innuendos, and spontaneously burst into dance (in one case wearing Spider-Man Underoos). Murray is funny (if somewhat constricted) as their associate Bosley, but Glover steals the show as the mute villain The Thin Man, whose theme

song, appropriately, is Prodigy's "Smack My Bitch Up." —B.T.

CHARLIE'S ANGELS: FULL THROTTLE L: BANG! (ACTION)/ BANG/TV (2003) 111M D: McG. *Demi Moore, Crispin Glover, Lucy Liu, Bernie Mac, Drew Barrymore, Cameron Diaz.* McG takes the same formula (and some of the same jokes) from his original pop confection and tries to push it to the next level. This is like Cool Ranch *Charlie's Angels* or *Charlie's Angels* Extreme. It has the same outlandish tone, but with far more ridiculous action (which is a good thing). At one point they crash a stolen truck off of a bridge but, while plummeting to the earth, discover that there is a helicopter in the back of the truck, which they use to escape. There is also a midair shoot-out during a motocross race, and a scene where they crash through a roof and use debris from said roof like skateboards to slide down a handrail and land safely. The people who loathed this movie (and there were many of them) may not be in possession of human hearts. How can you hate something so utterly joyful? It's like telling your grandpa to shut up because one of his puns was bad. He knows they're bad, that's why he says them. —B.T.

CLEOPATRA JONES L: BANG! (ACTION)/BLAXPLOITATION (1973) 89M D: Jack Starrett. *Shelley Winters, Antonio Fargas, Brenda Sykes, Bernie Casey, Tamara Dobson.* Cleopatra Jones (Dobson) isn't your usual blaxploitation heroine—she's a glamorous, globe-traveling secret agent who in the opening scenes burns down poppy fields in Turkey to stop the flow of heroin into the neighborhood. Those poppies belonged to Mommy (Winters) though, and she takes her revenge by sending the police to shut down the rehab center run by an old flame of Cleopatra's (Casey). So Cleopatra comes back to the neighborhood to take on Mommy and her thugs. Dobson is great, Winters is wonderfully over the top, and the whole proceedings are much more colorful and exaggerated than you normally expect from this genre. The script, by The Mack himself, Max Julien, is full of clever jokes and social satire. One of the funniest blaxploitation films there is. —B.T.

COMPAÑEROS L: WESTERNS/SPAGHETTI WESTERNS (1970) 118M D: Sergio Corbucci. *Tomas Milian, Fernando Rey, Jack Palance, Iris Berben, Franco Nero.* The new government in Mexico and various factions want the Professor (Rey) liberated from an American jail either to kill him because he's a dangerous man or to get the combination to an impenetrable safe full of riches. A Swedish businessman (Nero), a bandit (Milian), and girl-revolutionary (Berben) each want the treasure for their own reasons and are willing to fight off half the Mexican army plus one nasty, black-clad bounty killer with a hawk on his shoulder and a score to settle (Palance). An excellent follow-up to Corbucci's *The Professional Gun* with a deeply

political plot underlying the adventure yarn. *Compañeros* is slow but compelling and strangely humorous, evincing strong emotions by the end as both the Swede and bandit undergo serious life changes despite the ironies that underlie their dreams. All haunted by Ennio Morricone's score and infested with wildly cathartic action sequences. —*J. C.*

CON AIR L: BANG! (ACTION)/BANG! (ACTION) (1997) 115M D: Simon West. *John Malkovich, John Cusack, Ving Rhames, Steve Buscemi, Danny Trejo, Nicolas Cage.* Dangerous prisoners take over a plane, and even more dangerous filmmakers brutally beat the audience over the head with one of the most grating action movies of the '90s. In what became known as the "Bruckheimer style," an all-star cast struts around in slow motion and spits out wads of dialogue so unnatural the screenwriter must be dictating it phonetically to the actors through an earpiece. I mean, just look at that cast! How could you possibly have that many great actors and still make a movie this awful? I don't know, but it helps to edit the shots quickly and at random so that it is virtually impossible for anyone not raised with a Gameboy attached to his or her face to comprehend where the characters are standing or what exactly they are doing. —*B. T.*

COOL AS ICE L: BANG! (ACTION)/BANG! (ACTION) (1991) 92M D: David Kellogg. *Vanilla Ice, Kristen Minter, Michael Gross, Sidney Lassick, Dody Goodman.* Asinine movie vehicle for the notorious white rapper Vanilla Ice. Vanilla and his all-black posse get stranded in a small town when one of their motorcycles breaks down. The posse hangs out at the repair shop dancing and playing cards while Vanilla goes out to fall in love and save a child from kidnappers. The condescending racial themes and awkward slang provide big laughs from beginning to end. Director Kellogg would disavow the film eight years later when he directed his first "real" movie, *Inspector Gadget.* —*B. T.*

CORRUPTOR, THE L: BANG! (ACTION)/BANG! (ACTION) (1999) 110M D: James Foley. *Ric Young, Chow Yun Fat, Mark Wahlberg, Paul Ben-Victor, Jon Kit Lee.* A white rookie cop (Wahlberg) teams with a cynical Chinese-American cop (Chow) to stop a gang war in New York's Chinatown. When the Triads try to buy out Wahlberg, he begins to realize that Chow is not exactly a clean cop. Although not nearly on the level of, say, his work with John Woo, *The Corruptor* deserves credit as the one American Chow vehicle that showcases his depth as an actor. His character is not just the cocky badass, he's also the jokester, the brooder, the guy who's been betrayed, the guy who cooks. In the end he's a bad guy, but you like him anyway, and you understand why Wahlberg does too. —*B. T.*

DAY OF ANGER (AKA **DAYS OF WRATH**) L: WESTERNS/ SPAGHETTI WESTERNS (1967) 109M D: Tonino Valerii. *Giuliano Gemma, Lee Van Cleef.* There is no movie genre I love more than the spaghetti Western, and it's been my long-held opinion that Van Cleef is without question better than Clint Eastwood. Nobody did bad as good as Lee. *Day of Anger* features his absolute best performance. Gemma plays the local bastard, Scott. He literally cleans horseshit from the streets and gets nothing but beatings and cursing from the "good people" of Clifton. All that changes when Frank Talby (Van Cleef) shows up and takes a shine to Scott. Together the two of them basically take over the town, killing anyone who gets in the way. It's almost a variation on the old "new kid teaches the school nerd how to stand up for himself" formula, except the nerd has a violent streak and an unlimited supply of hot lead. Van Cleef is a GOD in this film. He's the spaghetti Western version of Darth Vader: ruthless, calculating, and most assuredly evil, but with an obvious humanity that makes his hold on Gemma all the more convincing, while ratcheting up the tension as the film builds toward their inevitable showdown. *Day of Anger* was directed by Sergio Leone protégé Valerii, and it displays all of Leone's signature elements, but without his leanings toward social relevance or his tendency to belabor his points. —*M. L.*

DEAD POOL L: BANG! (ACTION)/BANG! (ACTION) (1988) 92M D: Buddy Van Horn. *Clint Eastwood, Liam Neeson, David Hunt, Patricia Clarkson, Evan Kim.* The last of the Dirty Harry films has Eastwood playing an older Inspector Callahan investigating a celebrity "dead pool." Beyond the questionable morality of gambling on the odds of when people die, two other problems surface. The first is that some murderer is up to making a killing off the list, and the second is that Dirty Harry's name is on it! The borderline humor of previous films goes well over the line here. One of the primary mechanisms used to kill people is a tiny remote-controlled sports car that stops under a targeted vehicle and explodes like a ton of dynamite. The climax of this film, it follows, includes a high-speed chase between Dirty Harry and this deadly remote-controlled toy on the streets of San Francisco. What better way to end a five-part series about a near-vigilante cop? —*N. J.*

DEATH WISH L: BANG! (ACTION)/BANG! (ACTION) (1974) 93M D: Michael Winner. *Charles Bronson, Hope Lange, Jeff Goldblum, Vincent Gardenia.* After his wife is murdered and his daughter raped, liberal architect Paul Kersey (Bronson) has a change of his bleeding heart and decides to dish out some vigilante justice and make the punks on the street bleed for a change. Bronson means business and when you rent a Bronson picture you know you're not going to get any lame subplots or superfluous love stories—just Bronson, his moustache, and a pistol in your face. Playing his archetypal avenger role with brutal success, Bronson owns the picture. Night after night he takes to the streets and busts some heads, leaving a wake of terror behind him. A vehemently pro-gun, balls-to-the-wall revenge movie, Bronson's charisma is enough to convince you that *he* is the true hand of justice. This tough as nails, mean-spirited, good old-fashioned action movie will kick your ass and leave you out of breath, down on the floor, covered in blood, and begging for more. —*T. S.*

DEER HUNTER, THE L: WAR/VIETNAM WAR (1978) 183M D: Michael Cimino. *Robert De Niro, Christopher Walken, Meryl Streep, John Savage, John Cazale.* The Deer Hunter swept the Oscars in 1978, and deservedly so. It's a brilliant film that cemented the repu-tation of all of its main actors and catapulted rookie director Cimino to the top of his field. De Niro, Walken, and Savage play Northeastern steel workers who are shipped off to the Vietnam War and whose lives are changed forever. Savage is a soldier whose legs are blown off and can't adjust to life back home. Walken stays behind and is brainwashed by the Vietcong. De Niro returns to a party, takes Walken's girlfriend (played by Streep), and returns to Vietnam in search of his friend. But it is Cimino's relentless use of real-time action that brings a curious sense of realism and, with the help of the cast, expression to this American classic. —*N. J.*

DESTRY RIDES AGAIN L: WESTERNS/WESTERNS (1939) 95M D: George Marshall. *James Stewart, Brian Donlevy, Irene Hervey, Marlene Dietrich, Mischa Auer, Charles Winneger.* The story of Destry, the peace-loving deputy sheriff created by Max Brand, has been made many times, but Stewart created the definitive portrayal of the lawman who liked to keep his gun holstered. Easygoing, charming, drawling jokes while disarming violent situa-tions, he's the nice guy with nerves of steel and a promise to keep, and the rough-and-tumble town of Bottleneck isn't going to make it easy on him. Dietrich (who copped top billing) proved that she, too, was a natural comic, spoofing her exotic image as a spirited saloon singer (she belts out "The Boys in the Back Room" in one high-light). Marshall takes a gentle hand to the whole thing, making a comedy that spoofs clichés without becoming a parody. Donlevy is the town heavy and Auer is unforgettable as the wannabe gunfighter whose dreams of shoot-out glory are momentarily put on hold when his wife hides his pants! One of the best loved comic Westerns. —*S. A.*

DETROIT 9000 (DETROIT HEAT) L: BANG! (ACTION)/ BLAXPLOITATION (1973) 106M D: Arthur Marks. *Harry Rhodes, Robert Phillips, John Nichols, Alex Rocco.* Damn, what a movie! Black politician carefully amplifies charity ball into fund-raiser for his race for governor. Black ladies freely donate their jewels and men their cash, all going into a basket.

But the basket is then ripped off by a well-orga-nized gang, masked and gloved to hide their race. An experienced white cop (Rocco) with a sick wife to worry over lands this thankless case, with a black cop (Rhodes) foisted on him as partner. With plenty of credible thrills along the way, they crack the case together. Their linchpin: the call girl Ruby. In two powerhouse scenes Vonetta McGee gives this character such an eerie, cheeky, world-weary pathos that it is somehow not sur-prising that all the pieces drop cleanly into place, save one unresolved question at the end still lin-gering in the black cop's mind. This audacious mystery thriller is easily the smartest blaxploita-tion film of the '70s and one of the best B mov-ies ever. —*J. C.*

DIE HARD L: BANG! (ACTION)/BANG! (ACTION) (1988) 114M D: John McTiernan. *Alan Rickman, Bonnie Bedelia, Bruce Willis.* Willis is an action hero with jet lag on Christmas Eve, caught in an office building taken over by terrorists, wearing no shoes. He sneaks around, walks over broken glass, and picks off bad guys one by one, like *Alien* in reverse. But he's also a cynical smart-ass as he talks to himself, to the terrorists over their walkie-talk-ies, or to the one cop (Vel Johnson) who knows what's going on in the building. The humor goes over well because it is the type that people use to get through stressful ordeals more than it is formulaic punning and one-liners. Watching it now there are certainly dated elements (you have to enjoy the limo driver blasting Run DMC's "Christmas in Hollis") but it holds up surpris-ingly well for a movie so imitated that it has become a genre of its own (in fact some of Van Damme and Seagal's *Die-Hard*-in-a-blank mov-ies were rejected scripts for *Die Hard* sequels). —*B. T.*

DIE HARD 2 L: BANG! (ACTION)/BANG! (ACTION) (1990) 124M D: Renny Harlin. *Franco Nero, Bruce Willis, William Atherton, Bonnie Bedelia, Bill Sadler.* After *Die Hard* I knew they were making a sequel, and I wondered how they would explain John McClane getting involved with another terrorist attack. I thought he'd probably become a terror-ism expert and get sent in to help instead of hav-ing it just come to him. Nope—the filmmakers made it a coincidence, just to get it over with. "How can the same shit happen to the same guy twice?" McClane asks rhetorically. This time McClane is having a bad day as he goes to the airport to meet his wife and sees some suspicious packages. A group of American mer-cenaries have taken over the airport, forcing planes to circle endlessly, using up all their fuel. McClane runs around in a borrowed snow jacket with a torch and still manages to fight them all off himself. Obviously this type of movie has been done to death, but *Die Hard 2* is one of the better examples of the genre. —*B. T.*

DIE HARD WITH A VENGEANCE L: BANG! (ACTION)/BANG! (ACTION) (1995) 128M D: John McTiernan. *Jeremy Irons, Bruce Willis, Samuel L. Jackson.* After bombing New York City, terrorists request the attention of McClane, who, despite his heroic past, happens to be suspended and drunk at the time. McClane is forced (with the aid of Jackson, a shopkeeper he meets during a particularly arduous task) to run around the city following clues and solving puzzles to prevent more bombs from going off. It works on the strength of the character and the villain's devious games, but it starts to stretch credibility a little too much in the last act. In the other two films McClane is an everyman who gets involved because he happens to be trapped inside and he has to save his wife. But here he has a perfect chance to let the authorities take over and instead he hops in a helicopter and keeps chasing the bad guy. Worse, they dubbed his "yippee kai yay" catchphrase over the climactic explosion, as if he would really think to reference back to his previous encounters with terrorists. Still, it's an above-average action movie, more so considering it's a sequel, and it's good to see this character outside of the terrorism-in-confined-space formula that started the series. —*B.T.*

DIVINE ENFORCER L: BANG! (ACTION)/BANG! (ACTION) (1991) 90M D: Robert Rundle. *Erik Estrada, Jan-Michael Vincent, Jim Brown, Don Stroud, Michael M. Foley, Judy Landers.* This is a really bad, low-budget horror/action/comedy about an ass-kicking vigilante priest. The cast and synopsis were all I needed to know and, depending on your tastes, *Divine Enforcer* is a must-see even though it's pretty lousy. The mysterious Father Daniel (Foley) shares a house with fellow priests Vincent and Estrada and housekeeper Landers. Father Daniel is secretly a nocturnal crime fighter, exterminating wrongdoers with his martial art skills and crucifix daggers. He wastes some gangsters and drug dealers but almost meets his match with a serial killer. Stroud plays the "vampire" who kills women so he can drink their blood and eat cereal out of their skulls. He looks horrible, really overacts, and the movie spends too much time with this ranting maniac. Still, the kung fu priest is awesome, the action scenes are ludicrous, and Vincent and Estrada are absolutely stupefying. I nearly blew beer out my nose when Father Daniel said, "God forgives. . . I don't!" before killing a guy. —*S.H.*

DJANGO L: WESTERNS/SPAGHETTI WESTERNS (1966) 90M D: Sergio Corbucci. *Loredana Nusciak, Franco Nero, Eduardo Fajardo, Jose Bodalo.* Nero plays Django, a quiet visitor to an old Western town who stands out because he drags a coffin with him everywhere he goes. When asked about his coffin, he explains it's simply a reminder of his own inevitable demise. At the local saloon he discovers that an outlaw cruelly controls the city with help from a handpicked militia of fifty men. Django promises to remedy this situation, which

he promptly does by whipping out a brand-new Gattling gun from his coffin and mowing down the entire group. Of course the leader escapes with his life to seek revenge, but not until Django has unearthed the gold he's come for. This is an excellent spaghetti Western by Corbucci, one of the masters of the genre. —*N.J.*

DJANGO KILL. . . IF YOU LIVE, SHOOT! L: WESTERNS/SPAGHETTI WESTERNS (1967) 100M D: Giulio Questi. *Ray Lovelock, Piero Lulli, Tomas Millan.* Django Kill doesn't have anything to do with the original *Django*, nor does it feature a character named Django. Despite these minor title problems, *Django Kill* is as good if not better than the original. A great opening shows our hero (who I'll refer to as Headband due to his choice of stylish forehead fashion) digging himself out of a shallow grave in the desert. Some Indians stumble across him while looting the stuff left behind by the bandits who double-crossed Headband, the story of which is quickly covered in a flashback involving stealing gold from the Union Army. Anyway, the Indians nurse him back to health and make solid gold bullets from Headband's gold. What follows is a tale of revenge in a creepy town, full of self-righteous pricks who want the gold from the bandits, suicidal teenagers, and a land baron who makes his men all dress the same. . . like gay cowboys. If violent, nihilistic spaghetti Westerns are your thing, you could do worse than *Django Kill: The Adventures of Headband and His Indian Friends.* —*K.C.*

DOLL SQUAD, THE L: BANG! (ACTION)/BANG! (ACTION) (1973) 101M D: Ted V. Mikels. *Tura Satana, Michael Ansara, Sherri Vernon, Francine York.* Female assassins have a timeless quality as seen in the '70s-flick-revisioned *Kill Bill.* Mikels took a different curve with his band of bold babes by having them assigned by computer, and with variant professions from librarian, scientist, karate instructor, and (gosh!) erotic dancer. York, Vernon, and Satana (Varla from *Faster Pussycat, Kill! Kill!*) are three kick-ass babes and while they're a bit lost in the no-budget convolutions of the pencil-thin story line, they know how to pull a flick like this off, deftly employing flame-throwing cigarette lighters and long legs to stomp on the bad guys. For those looking for a hot spy-action thriller, I don't want to steer you wrong—this writer adored *The Almighty Isis* and Linda Carter as Wonder Woman as a wee one. Chicks with attitude have me by the balls, and *The Doll Squad* has declared snooker on my privates. —*S.R.*

DRIVE L: BANG! (ACTION)/CHOPSOCKIE (1996) 110M D: Steve Wang. *Kadeem Hardison, Tracey Walter, John Pyper-Ferguson, Mark Dacascos, Brittany Murphy.* Dacascos proves once again here that not only is he a martial arts master and action-film star waiting to happen, but his comedic timing pretty dead on. Dacascos stars as Toby Wong, an

Blaxploitation

Blaxploitation. The term, coined during the 1970s boom in low-budget action and genre films with African-American stars, was never meant to be flattering or sensitive. But despite its dubious origins, the word still conjures up visions of Shaft, Superfly, Black Caesar, Foxy Brown, and Dolemite, jive-talking heroes who take no shit. It stands for a priceless 1970s time capsule of soul cinema, as campy and contrived as it was raw and funky.

Hollywood historically ignored black audiences. Apart from the "race" cinema that flourished in urban centers from the 1920s to the 1940s, African-American audiences had no celluloid heroes of their own, and precious few films that addressed their communities.

Then came *Sweet Sweetback's Baadas-* *ssss Song.* Writer/director/star Melvin Van Peebles had made films in France (*The Story of a Three Day Pass*) and Hollywood (*The Watermelon Man*), but he went guerrilla in 1971 to make this angry, passionate picture so inflammatory by industry standards that it was "Rated X by an All White Jury," which the ads proudly touted. The searing political content married with raw violence and steamy sexuality excited black audiences and made white audiences uneasy, and it broke box-office records.

Hollywood took notice and a genre exploded overnight. African-Americans became action film heroes, horror film heavies, and even cowboys for the first time since the 1940s. Within a year, *Shaft* and *Superfly* made stars of Richard Roundtree and Ron O'Neal. Both films were helmed by African-American directors (Gordon Parks Sr. and Jr., respectively), but Hollywood soon put its stable of industry vets behind the camera.

---

enhanced human being who is trying to reach his wife while the company that created him attempts at first to get him back at any cost, and then to destroy him at any cost. Along Wong's journey, he picks up a less than willing, "stereotypical" black sidekick, Malik (Hardison). Malik becomes Wong's driver as they make their way along the California coast. Behind them are bounty hunters and corrupt cops who have been ordered to bring Wong in. The Hong Kong–styled action sequences are flat-out incredible, and Dacascos easily performs with and without wires with total fun and understanding of the over-the-top choreography. Hunt down the full cut of the film to see the directors' original vision, and not what the producers thought the public wanted to see. —*R. M.*

FACE TO FACE L: WESTERNS/SPAGHETTI WESTERNS (1967) 110M D: Sergio Sollima. *William Berger, Carole Andre, Tomas Milian, Gian Maria Volonté.* Hard, intelligent story of an eastern professor (Volonté) with bad lungs going West to die or regain his health. Giving water to a notorious bandit (Milian), he inadvertently helps him to escape. Nursing the bandit back to health, the professor regains his own in the process and builds a bond between them. The bandit puts together the old gang with one new inclusion, Siringo (Berger), who may or may not be a Pinkerton man. Their safe haven in the hills is a kind of natural anarchist enclave of outsider types until the professor starts organizing it like a socialist dictator, knowing that the law will eventually bring the battle to them. It's a compelling and involving story, thoughtfully dealing with big issues and swaggering action sequences, which are poignantly punctuated by Ennio Morricone's score. One of top five spaghetti Westerns to come out of Europe. —*J. C.*

FAST AND THE FURIOUS, THE L: BANG! (ACTION)/VROOM (CHASES & RACES!) (2001) 107M D: Rob Cohen. *Vin Diesel, Michelle Rodriguez, Jordana Brewster, Rick Yune, Paul Walker.* Director Cohen thought he was really capturing the zeitgeist with this slick B movie about the secretive subculture of rich kids who street race their souped-up, neon-colored Toyotas. Instead he happened to cast Diesel at just the right time in a role that took full advantage of his macho charisma. The star, though, is Walker, a cop going undercover as a racer to investigate Diesel and his friends, and who may be involved in a series of robberies. No wonder he didn't get upset when he lost his car in a bet! He didn't have to pay for it, our tax dollars did.

The results were often ludicrous: flamboyant fashion statements, outrageous mock-jive dialogue, and films populated by pimps, hookers, pushers, and gangsters, a white industry's stereotype of the ghetto. Drop "Black" in front of the title and you had yourself a blaxploitation movie: *Black Samson, Black Samurai, Black Shampoo, Black Mama White Mama*, and, of course, *Blacula*.

The best of these films rumbled with a gritty edge and pulsing energy. Larry Cohen's explosive gangster films *Black Caesar* and *Hell Up in Harlem* made Fred "The Hammer" Williamson a star. Jack Hill launched Pam Grier's career with *Big Doll House* and made her a kick-ass action icon with *Coffy* and *Foxy Brown*. Arthur Marks had a hit with *Detroit 9000*, an edgy cop drama about black and white cop partners on a volatile case, and continued making offbeat black cast pictures like *Bucktown, Friday Foster*, and *J. D.'s Revenge*.

The Mack puts a human twist on the cliché of the mack-daddy pimp: behind the

gold chains and platform shoes and surreal street slang is a surprising thoughtfulness. But of all the macho hustlers and two-fisted heroes, the baddest and maddest of them all is Rudy Ray Moore's rapping martial artist/pimp *Dolemite*, a jaw-droppingly insane and profane comic with his own private all-girl army of kung fu killers.

Blaxploitation lived and died within a few years. African-American stars soon crossed over into mainstream cinema, and the low-budget action pictures were ultimately reborn as direct-to-video "urban action" gangsta films. But the old school is not forgotten: Keenan Ivory Wayans's 1988 spoof *I'm Gonna Git You Sucka* lovingly pokes fun at the fashions and the tough-guy clichés, and Larry Cohen's 1996 *Original Gangstas* reunites Fred Williamson, Pam Grier, Jim Brown, Richard Roundtree, and Ron O'Neal to take on modern gangbangers. They aren't as young or outrageous as they once were, but they've got attitude, charisma, and soul.

—*Sean Axmaker*

It's a dumb movie, but some of it is fun thanks to Diesel's conviction. When he makes asinine boasts like "We live life a quarter-mile at a time," he seems completely serious. —*B. T.*

FIRST BLOOD L: BANG! (ACTION)/BANG! (ACTION) (1982) 94M D: Ted Kotcheff. *Sylvester Stallone, Richard Crenna, Brian Dennehy*. Stallone plays John Rambo, a drifter who walks into a small town to visit one of his Vietnam buddies (it turns out his friend has died of cancer caused by Agent Orange). On his way out of town he runs into the sheriff (Dennehy), who treats him condescendingly. The two stubborn personalities butt heads, one thing leads to another, and the next thing you know Rambo is on the run and using his expert combat training to slaughter all the police that are after him. The movie has an engaging sense of escalating mayhem as things lead logically from a run-in with the cops to a one-man war. After the colonel who trained Rambo (Crenna) is called in, Rambo breaks down for a cathartic, somewhat incomprehensible monologue about the horrors of war. With the popular sequels, Rambo became a symbol of macho American military aggression, so it's easy to forget that he started out as a critique of the Vietnam War and the toll it took on soldiers. The DVD includes

an interesting commentary by David Morrell, author of the book. He says that he wanted to "bring the Vietnam War home" and discusses the ironic way that pop culture twisted the meaning of the Rambo character. —*B. T.*

FORCE 10 FROM NAVARONE L: WAR/WWII (1978) 118M D: Guy Hamilton. *Robert Shaw, Carl Weathers, Harrison Ford, Edward Fox, Barbara Bach, Franco Nero*. This tight, bouncy B-action sequel is actually better than the watchable but pretentious big movie *The Guns of Navarone*. During WWII an American officer (Ford) and British bomb specialist (Fox) are parachuted into Yugoslavia to help outnumbered partisans blow up a strategic bridge. With them is a British intelligence officer (Shaw) with a different mission: assassinate a heroic partisan (Nero) believed to be a German spy. Also with them is a black GI (Weathers) who chose the wrong airplane to go AWOL on. Being captured by German allies posing as partisans is just the first of many obstacles to overcome. What should register as ridiculous is actually an exercise in smooth storytelling. The wildly differing character types help make the solution to one problem just believable enough to carry you on to the next. Bach's low-burn sexiness as a resourceful but gullible partisan adds spice to the pot. A fun ride. —*J. C.*

FOUR FEATHERS, THE (2002) L: ADVENTURE/ADVENTURE
(2002) 130M D: Shekhar Kapur. *Wes Bentley, Djimon Hounsou, Kate Hudson, Heath Ledger.* Ledger is the "coward" soldier who questions the imperialist charge of Britain and is spurned by his friends and his fiancée (Hudson) when he resigns his commission rather than go to war against the desert "savages" of the Sudan. Kapur's rousing, handsome, and seriously confused adaptation of A. E. W. Mason's adventure classic at once embraces the British tradition of honor and duty while puncturing the soldiers' blind patriotism and the colonialist precepts of the British Empire. It's Britain's own Vietnam film: the so-called civilized army trapped in an alien landscape, outfought by an enemy they continually underestimate, and constrained by their own superiority complex. You can feel the director fight his material, and the result is a film that tries to have it both ways and fails both, falling back on pure sentiment and simplistic portraits of their Sudanese enemies. Finally, what they are fighting for is embodied in Hudson's innocent, feather-brained smile. —*S. A.*

FREEWAY II: CONFESSIONS OF A TRICK BABY. L:
BANG! (ACTION)/BANG! (ACTION) (1999) 97M D: Matthew Bright. *Maria Celedonio, Vincent Gallo, David Alan Grier, Michael T. Weiss, John Landis, Max Perlich, Natasha Lyonne.* Lyonne plays White Girl, an inmate at a youth correctional facility who is headed for the big house. This film follows the tradition of the first *Freeway* when White Girl hooks up with Cyclona, a lifer with an escape plan. Together they go searching for Cyclona's safe place, a church in Mexico where she spent a lot of her childhood. Cyclona turns the psycho knob up to eleven when she stops taking her meds and has to murder a few people along the way while prancing around in their bloody carcasses. When they finally reach their destination, it's not quite how she remembered. This film is much more of a horror film than the first *Freeway*, but fans of the sick and bizarre will dig it. This is also Gallo's most unusual character; his part is short but probably weirder than the entire movie. —*R. D.*

FRIDAY FOSTER L: BANG! (ACTION)/BLAXPLOITATION (1975)
90M D: Arthur Marks. *Pam Grier, Yaphet Kotto.* Friday (Grier) prepares for her bath, and a killer pulls his knife. Friday runs for it, scared and dripping. A freelance photographer shooting a black fashion show, she is too close to a conspiracy she doesn't see the contours of. She saves a black millionaire's life and buddies up with a private dick (Kotto), and together the three of them will get to the bottom of it. But not before more majestically lush brown skin is seen draping across Friday's bed. Based on the Jim Lawrence/Jorge Longaron comic strip, *Friday Foster* is another smart and raucous Marks and Orville Hampton blaxploiter. Ambitious like *Detroit 9000* but with the storyline wandering all over before slamming home at the end. The gaudy clothes, the bitchy banter, the bare flesh are all about attitude, dude! A three-ring circus of the cool-black mind. —*J. C.*

GATOR BAIT L: BANG! (ACTION)/REDNECKS (1976) 88M D:
Beverly Sebastian, Ferd Sebastian. *Claudia Jennings, Sam Gilman, Douglas Dirkson.* Deep in the bayou lives a girl named Desiree. She spends her days poaching to feed her family. When the son of the local sheriff tries to rape her and accidentally dies, she is blamed for murder. Now the law is after her and her family, but she won't take it lying down. Imagine if the Dukes of Hazzard all got combined into one hot girl who likes to take off her shirt and isn't afraid to kill some motherfuckers and you start to get the picture. —*T. S.*

GONE IN 60 SECONDS L: BANG! (ACTION)/VROOM (CHASES
& RACES!) (1974) 98M D: H.B. Halicki. *Marion Busia, Jerry Daugirda, H. B. Halicki.* This is the ultimate drive-in car-chase movie. If that sounds like a backhanded compliment, then you don't know the sheer, pure visceral thrill of a great car-crunching, tire-squealing, speed-demon piece of auto outlaw cinema. Writer/producer/director/star/stunt driver Halicki is all thumbs when it comes to directing his nonprofessional cast, but he's a natural performer and has a confident efficiency in showing the mechanics of the car theft biz. All that, of course, is mere framework for the film's famous forty-minute car chase finale as his vehicle—a souped-up yellow 1973 Ford Mustang Mach 1 named Eleanor—gets banged, bashed, and smashed into a crinkled wreck. It's a masterpiece of stunt driving, driver's seat photography, and sharp, spirited editing, and more fun that it has any right to be. —*S. A.*

GREAT SILENCE, THE L: WESTERNS/SPAGHETTI WESTERNS
(1968) 105M D: Sergio Corbucci. *Vonetta McGee, Jean-Louis Trintignant, Klaus Kinski, Frank Wolff, Luigi Pistilli.* Trintignant stars as a mute gunslinger in this spaghetti Western in the snow-covered high plains set to the haunting sounds of an Ennio Morricone score. Beautiful and bleak, the trademark cynicism of director Corbucci (*Django*) is complicated by the nature of its ruthless nemeses: the vengeance-hungry mercenary Trintignant (whose silence is the result of a bounty hunter's knife) and bounty killer leader Kinski, who plays everything by the letter of the unforgiving frontier law. Kinski gives one of his most engaging performances and Trintignant brings a real enigma to his role, with tender blue eyes that grow hard and cold on the job. Wolff is affable and interesting as a sheriff with no love of bounty killers and McGee makes her film debut as a widow out for revenge. One of the best and most unusual examples of the genre. —*S. A.*

HACKERS L: BANG! (ACTION)/BANG! (ACTION) (1995) 104M
D: Iain Softley. *Jonny Lee Miller, Angelina Jolie, Jesse Bradford, Matthew Lillard, Lawrence Mason, Fisher Stevens.* Laughable teen rebellion movie (I'm sure the filmmakers called it a "cyber thriller," though) about teen supergenius computer hackers with names like "Acid Burn" (Jolie) and "Cereal Killer" (Lillard) being framed by a diabolical computer security expert supervillain called "The Plague" (Stevens). This is the kind of movie where outsiders wear asinine clothes and hairdos meant to represent futuristic punk fashion, and where accessing computer files involves flying through fanciful computer-animated cityscapes. It's a depiction of teen life and modern technology so ludicrous it makes *Pump Up the Volume* look like a BBC documentary. —*B. T.*

HALF PAST DEAD L: BANG! (ACTION)/BANG! (ACTION) (2002) 98M D: Don Michael Paul. *Steven Seagal, Ja Rule, Morris Chestnut, Nia Peeples.* Seagal, who resembles the Pillsbury Doughboy more than the action star he once was, is the undercover agent in New Alcatraz who takes on a mercenary squad that breaks into prison. The details are largely unimportant, at least as far as the script is concerned. It's all an excuse for a gun-toting, bomb-bursting, helicopter-crashing, cell-block rumble, and a sorry, silly, singularly banal one at that. The talent and charisma of Chestnut is wasted as a second-rate sociopath mastermind and the dialogue is the literary equivalent of gristle, which the cast doesn't deliver so much as chew up and spit out. Just to clear up any possible confusion, the title *Half Past Dead* doesn't actually refer to Seagal's gasping-for-air film career, it's merely a lucky coincidence. —*S. A.*

HEAVEN'S GATE L: WESTERNS/WESTERNS (1981) 220M D: Michael Cimino. *Christopher Walken, Kris Kristofferson, Isabelle Huppert, Brad Dourif, Mickey Rourke, John Hurt.* *Heaven's Gate*'s script is loosely based on the famous Western battle known as the Johnson County War. United Artists went so far as to give Cimino their entire bank expecting huge results. What they got was a production rife with problems and a film that bombed so badly on opening night in New York that they pulled it before it could screen hours later in Los Angeles. The biggest flaw is the miscasting—De Niro was busy doing *Raging Bull*, Pacino was busy doing *Godfather*, so Kristofferson was apparently third on Cimino's list. The rest of the cast works quite well—Walken, Hurt, and Sam Waterston are all perfect. But perhaps outshining the cast is the cinematography by Vilmos Zsigmond that captures the incredible surroundings of Montana (cleverly pretending to be Wyoming). The action scenes are at once stunning and enthralling, using Cimino's sense of realism. Any fan of *The Deer Hunter* should watch this film, especially the director's cut on DVD. For a fantastic education of studio filmmaking and the demise of United Artists as a result of this production, read the book *Final Cut* by Steven Bach. —*N. J.*

HELLBENDERS L: WESTERNS/SPAGHETTI WESTERNS (1967) 92M D: Sergio Corbucci. *Julián Mateos, Gino Pernice, Norma Bengell, Joesph Cotton, Angel Aranda.* This film has one of the most shocking introductions you're likely to see in any spaghetti Western. Cotten plays a die-hard Confederate interested in reigniting the Civil War who leads an ambush against a federal gold transport. After gunning down every single man in the convoy, this Confederate veteran and his sons gun down their own hired hands to keep all the gold for the cause. They spend the rest of the film smuggling the gold to the South in a coffin, pretending to be returning a Confederate soldier to Tennessee for burial. They go through a variety of fake widows who help along the way as they all narrowly avoid Yankee detection. Eventually they bump into a priest who knew this Tennessee soldier and wants to bury him himself. Gripping action by one of the masters of spaghetti Westerns. —*N. J.*

HELL'S ANGELS ON WHEELS L: BANG! (ACTION)/BIKERS (1967) 95M D: Richard Rush. *Adam Roarke, Jack Nicholson, Sabrina Scharf, Jana Taylor.* Poet (Nicholson) is a restless gas station attendant who takes his job and shoves it to join biker king Roarke in this Joe Soloman–produced knockoff of *The Wild Angels.* Directed by Rush (*The Stunt Man*), the episodic, somewhat rambling tale of cheap thrills, easy sex, bar fights, and gang wars becomes a buddy film of rootless rebels without a life. Nicholson's scrappy energy impresses Roarke, but it's also what leads these newfound friends into an inevitable showdown. That, and Roarke's despotic leadership of the gang. The climax is more dramatically potent than cinematically convincing, but Rush neatly carves a portrait of hollow activity passing for freedom. Scharf costars as the girl in the middle and Laszlo Kovacs, who went on to shoot *Easy Rider*, is the cinematographer. —*S. A.*

HIRED HAND, THE L: WESTERNS/WESTERNS (1971) 90M D: Peter Fonda. *Warren Oates, Peter Fonda, Verna Bloom, Robert Pratt, Severn Darden.* Returning to the wife (Bloom) he abandoned seven years earlier, Harry Collings (Fonda) finds that he isn't welcomed with open arms, and that things aren't exactly as he'd left them. Advancing its elliptical narrative at a languid pace, this minimal and highly atmospheric "revisionist Western" has much to recommend itself. The film looks fantastic thanks to legendary cinematographer Vilmos Zsigmond's contributions, as well as to its notable borrowings from the American avant-garde (reportedly the result of Fonda's friendship with artist/filmmaker Bruce Conner). The latter thankfully smoothes over the hippie-dippie mysticism that could easily have spoiled everything. Despite occasional rickety dialogue,

Alan Sharp's screenplay greatly enriches its stock stoic frontier characters with a palatable sense of world-weary regret, and even takes a well-intentioned, if simplistic, stab at progressive sexual politics. Finally, incomparable actor Oates lends his services as Collings's riding companion Arch, and very nearly steals the show. —*C. B.*

HOOPER L: BANG! (ACTION)/BANG! (ACTION) (1978) 99M D: Hal Needham. *Burt Reynolds, Sally Field, Jan-Michael Vincent.* There was one movie theater within biking distance from where I grew up and no matter what was playing there, I'd go see it every weekend. I must have seen *Hooper* at least ten times. Burt was the king of cool and no matter how many times I saw it, I always got chills up my spine when Reynolds, the aging stuntman with a back injury, makes his one final stunt, a do-or-die car jump. Did he make it. . . or did he die? If you don't know, good luck. If you do, you're a genius and you've earned the right to guiltlessly watch this inane piece of trash. —*M. S.*

IF I WERE KING L: ADVENTURE/SWASHBUCKLERS (1938) 101M D: Frank Lloyd. *Ronald Colman, Henry Wilcoxon, C. V. France, Ellen Drew, Frances Dee, Basil Rathbone.* Colman's lilting voice speaks Preston Sturges's mellifluous dialogue like a slumming Don Juan. As vagabond poet François Villon he's almost that: a rascal, a rogue, and an underworld wit whose barbed tongue reaches all the way to Rathbone's beleaguered but streetwise Louis XI. Rathbone is no slouch with a speech himself, and the film's highlights are the verbal sparring matches between king Rathbone and knave Colman. It's a winning mix of swashbuckling adventure and courtly romance with finely penned dialogue and two marvelous voices that give it life. —*S. A.*

IRON EAGLE L: BANG! (ACTION)/BANG! (ACTION) (1985) 117M D: Sidney J. Furie. *Tim Thomerson, Louis Gossett Jr., David Suchet, Caroline Lagerfelt, Jason Gedrick, Larry B. Scott.* An aimless local boy makes good by joining the Air Force. This movie is especially noteworthy for getting me into some serious trouble by introducing me to two foul terms that would later become indispensable members of my vocabulary: "bastard" and "son of a bitch." I guess my teacher didn't appreciate it when I exercised these useful phrases on the playground because it wound me up on the sidelines considering what I had done wrong. She wouldn't even explain what was wrong with calling classmates "little bastard" or screaming "I'll get you, you son of a bitch" on the playground at the top of my lungs. The experience taught me the power of these words, though they haven't carried the same awesome weight since. —*M. H.*

J. D.'S REVENGE L: BANG! (ACTION)/BLAXPLOITATION (1976) 95M D: Arthur Marks. *Louis Gossett Jr., Glynn Turman.* Marks (*Detroit 9000*) directs this well-done mix

of supernatural possession and gangster revenge thriller. Turman (*Cooley High*) stars as an easygoing law student possessed by the vengeful spirit of a flashy 1940s gangster, turning the gentle kid into a ruthless killer, a regular Jekyll and Hyde who wakes up with a hole in his memory. Sharp writing and nicely turned characters make it work: when Turman awakens after one of his alter ego's rampages, he makes you feel the terror of his realization that he may harbor a killer in his soul. Gossett Jr. costars as a fire-and-brimstone preacher whose dark past is intricately tied up with J. D.'s murder. —*S. A.*

JUNKMAN, THE L: BANG! (ACTION)/VROOM (CHASES & RACES!) (1982) 98M D: H. B. Halicki. *H. B. Halicki, Christopher Stone, Hoyt Axton.* Director/writer/producer/stunt man Halicki stars as a fantasy version of himself, a stunt-driving movie mogul chased through the back roads of Southern California by assassins. Less a sequel than an ambitious follow-up to his lean, mean speed machine of outlaw cinema *Gone in 60 Seconds*, Halicki expands his tire-squealing repertoire with a complicated plot that juggles multiple stories and a murder mystery, which is the film's biggest weakness. Halicki is better at directing cars than actors, and he's best when executing the elaborate chases and jaw-dropping stunts that range from the farcical to the spectacular. The film never recovers from the adrenaline rush of the first act, but Stone (as Halicki's easygoing publicist) and Axton (as his easygoing self) help keep the sliver of a story rolling. For all the spectacular wrecks and twisted metal (the 150 cars destroyed put him in the *Guinness Book of World Records*), Halicki is the rare action director who takes pains to show his bystanders emerging unscathed as the film roars on. The sound remix is terrific and the new score unmemorable but energetic and appropriate to the material. —*S. A.*

KENTUCKIAN, THE L: WESTERNS/WESTERNS (1955) 104M D: Burt Lancaster. *Burt Lancaster, Dianne Foster, Diana Lynn, John McIntire, Una Merkel, Walter Matthau.* Lancaster was a prolific producer, but this story of a single frontiersman dad who takes his son to a small town for schooling and civilizing was his only go at directing. Lancaster, the most physically expressive of the Hollywood greats, anchors the picture with his grinning confidence more than with his often airy direction. The film's best scenes feature him in action, and Lancaster the director makes the most of Lancaster the actor: leaping from a riverboat after outsmarting a slick gambler with a hick act, taking on the bullwhip-toting villain (Matthau) with his bare hands, and a brilliant long take of Lancaster racing around the lake to take a would-be ambusher before he reloads his single-shot rifle. —*S. A.*

KISS OF THE DRAGON L: BANG! (ACTION)/BANG! (ACTION) (2001) 98M D: Chris Nahon. *Bridget Fonda, Tchéky Karyo, Jet Li.* Li is the humorless Chinese cop

Our favorite war movies

ASCENT

BAND OF BROTHERS

THE BATTLE OF ALGIERS

CASUALTIES OF WAR

THE DEER HUNTER

DEVILS ON THE DOORSTEP

THE DIRTY DOZEN

FULL METAL JACKET

THE GENERAL

HELL IS FOR HEROES

HELL IN THE PACIFIC

HOPE AND GLORY

PATHS OF GLORY

PLATOON

RED DAWN

who tracks a drug ring to its Paris source and winds up framed for murder by corrupt French detective Karyo (in full-on, wild-eyed supervillain mania). Cue epic amounts of property damage in five-star hotels, hundreds of bystanders mowed down by seething crooked cops, and Li's almost-romance with wounded, makeup smeared Fonda, the Midwest American farm girl coerced into prostitution by the ever more blackhearted Karyo. (Hissssss!) Luc Besson cowrote and produced this absurd but undeniably entertaining, French-inflected martial arts romp. Unpretentious and sleek, the plot is nonsensical, but who cares? Director Nahon knows how to stage an action scene for full visceral punch, and that's the only reason I can fathom for watching a Jet Li movie. Watch for Burt Kwouk (the mock martial arts maniac Cato from the *Pink Panther* movies) as Li's homesick contact in the Paris underground. —*S. A.*

LADY COCOA L: BANG! (ACTION)/BLAXPLOITATION (1975) 93M D: Matt Cimber. *Millie Perkins, Gene Washington, James A. Watson Jr.* First-rate B movie with young black cop (Washington) and old white lieutenant (Alex Dreier) escorting reluctant convict-witness (Lola Falana) to testify against her hoodlum boyfriend. But for her it is just a vacation from prison, a chance to dress up and eat nice food. She plays head games with the black cop, sees her jail-shy boyfriend, and flips off the judge. But two hit men are already stalking her and her boyfriend gives her the kiss of death. She doesn't realize it until a hotel maid steps in front of a bullet meant for her. A mere tinkle of

glass, then the shock of mortality on the white maid's face as she slips bleeding to the floor. All this adds up to one of the gnarliest B-movie scenes ever! From here the movie turns exciting then sensual then clever, making for a very solid production that should have made Falana a genuine star. Still one dandy of a movie. —*J. C.*

LAND THAT TIME FORGOT, THE L: ADVENTURE/BURROUGHS, EDGAR RICE (1975) 90M D: Kevin Connor. *Anthony Ainley, Keith Barren, Godfrey James, Doug McClure, John McEnery, Susan Penhaligon.* Don't expect the best dinosaur effects in this science fiction film. Instead look for a wonderfully crafted story by Edgar Rice Burroughs. A German U-boat in the '30s sinks an English passenger ship, only to become pirated by a handful of the ship's survivors. After days grappling over control of the submarine, the two parties are helplessly lost somewhere deep in the south of the Atlantic. By chance they stumble upon the fabled land of Caprona. In the time it takes them to cooperate, find oil, and refine it for their voyage back, they have also discovered the strange evolutionary patterns of life on this forgotten land. Altogether this turns out to be a wonderful character analysis on the psychology and anthropology of war. —*N. J.*

LAST BOY SCOUT, THE L: BANG! (ACTION)/BANG! (ACTION) (1991) 105M D: Tony Scott. *Bruce Willis, Noble Willingham, Taylor Negron, Damon Wayans, Chelsea Field.* The Last Boy Scout may be the most macho movie ever. You want a violent, wisecrack-studded flick that features a down-on-his-luck private detective? Why don't you pull up a seat at the tea party, Mavis? Try this—it's a violent, wisecrack-studded flick that features a down-on-his-luck private detective AND a down-on-his-luck former pro quarterback. Willis plays the detective, and Wayans the quarterback. Both were bounced from their respective jobs for various reasons and now spout laconic one-liners as if they were raised on James Cain novels. They have to team up to solve a murder, and from there things get hyped up on testosterone. There are car chases, explosions, high-powered rifles, and one of the most hilariously contrived finales ever. Here's a hint: To save the day, Wayans must throw a football. —*T. P.*

LAWMAN L: WESTERNS/WESTERNS (1971) 99M D: Michael Winner. *Sheree North, Robert Duvall, Lee J. Cobb, Robert Ryan, Burt Lancaster.* Director Winner left the world of British social satires and quirky psychological dramas for Hollywood and a career of hard-edged Westerns and ruthless crime films, most famously the *Death Wish* films. This is one of his first American productions, an old-fashioned Western in the age of *The Wild Bunch* (he even resorts to Peckinpah zooms). Lancaster (in a hard, driven performance) is a morally inflexible sheriff who battles an entire town to bring in a group of otherwise respectable citizens wanted for murder in another county. It's the end of frontier justice, the age when the legendary gunslingers are getting old and the firebrands of the past are mellowing. Winner's style is lean and tough, with a streak of "passing of an era" melancholia. Ryan plays the local sheriff torn between duty and obligation, and Cobb is the local cattle baron. —S. A.

LEATHER BOYS, THE L: BANG! (ACTION)/BIKERS (1964) 108M D: Sidney J. Furie. *Colin Campbell, Dudley Sutton, Rita Tushingham, Gladys Henson.* Tushingham and Campbell are a pair of fun-loving teen-age biker rebels who cut loose from home and marry, but find their newfound freedom devolve to irresponsible freewheeling—without each other. Furie's supposedly frank exploration of an ill-conceived marriage by two immature youths became sensation in its day for its oblique look at leather-clad culture and the homosexual underground, but the mix of "kitchen sink" drama and rebel exploitation movie is at its best capturing the details of working-class life in claustrophobic apartments, pubs and cafés, and the uniquely British holiday camps. Today neither aspect is developed enough to carry its drama forward. Tushingham, the diva of Britain's social realist films, delivers a marvelously giggly performance, and Campbell is appropriately soft-spoken and lost throughout. Their performances far outstrip the story and the subtext. Today it's largely a curious time capsule. —S. A.

LONESOME DOVE L: WESTERNS/WESTERNS (1989) 384M D: Simon Wincer. *Tommy Lee Jones, Anjelica Huston, Danny Glover, Robert Duvall, Rick Schroeder, Robert Urich, Diane Lane.* Duvall is the man in *Lonesome Dove*; he is at once rugged, funny, tough, lazy, charming, and good-natured. *Lonesome Dove* is a fine Western, a simple tale of retired U.S. marshals McCrae (Duvall) and Woodrow Call (Jones, as an old dude), who decide to drive a herd of cattle from their one-horse Texas town to Montana. McCrae goes along with this fool idea, out of pure boredom it seems. Old friend Jake Spoon (Urich) tags along to avoid gambling-debt collectors and in the saddest scene is on the receiving end of some old West justice, dispensed by his friends McCrae and Call, who ethically can't let him get away with something just out of friendship. The girl is Lorena (Lane), who works as a whore in the saloon and is deeply in love with McCrae, even though he's about a hundred years older. Schroeder, Huston, and some others are along for the ride, but at the heart of the story is McCrae, and Duvall chews the scenery every chance he gets. This miniseries would only be OK if not for his performance; no other actor could truly embody this man. —K. C.

LOVE AND A BULLET L: BANG! (ACTION)/BANG! (ACTION) (2002) 100M D: Ben Ramsey. *Treach, Walter Jones, Sam Scarber, Charles Guardino.* Treach (of the once-popular rap group Naughty By Nature) plays a professional hit man who made his reputation by gunning down some dangerous gangsters because they showed up late for a meeting. Now he's in an apartment watching his boss's girlfriend through a scope, waiting to shoot her as soon as he gets the word, and he narrates the story of how he got there with many tangents along the way. It's in the style of that sort of self-conscious, post-Tarantino world of bickering hit men who treat murder as an occupation, but for that sort of thing it's actually pretty funny. The best scene involves having to assassinate someone while preparing a Thanksgiving dinner. Ramsey also wrote the similar hit-man comedy *The Big Hit*, which had better action scenes, but this one is funnier. Treach's character was also spun off into a flash animation series that was released on DVD as *The Contract.* —B. T.

MACK, THE L: BANG! (ACTION)/BLAXPLOITATION (1973) 110M D: Michael Campus. *Max Julien, Carol Speed, Richard Pryor, Roger E. Mosley.* It's no wonder that *The Mack* is a favorite of gentlemen of leisure, rap stars, and black action fans everywhere. It presents a fairly serious approach to the art of pimping and, while it features plenty of outrageous threads and funky bitches, avoids some of the sillier elements of the blaxploitation genre. Julien gives a great performance as Goldie, a charismatic pimp just out of the joint and looking to get some action going in Oakland. He partners up with his old buddy (Pryor in a fairly serious role) and his militant brother (Mosley—later on *Magnum P.I.*) and hits the motherfuckin' jackpot of hos and benjamins. Unfortunately there are a couple of asshole honky cops and some jealous pimps to incite a spate of nasty violence, and ultimately Goldie learns the lesson that pimpin' ain't easy. —S. H.

MACKENNA'S GOLD L: WESTERNS/WESTERNS (1969) 128M D: J. Lee Thompson. *Eli Wallach, Edward G. Robinson, Burgess Meredith, Telly Savalas, Julie Newmar, Gregory Peck, Omar Sharif.* Like other "super-movies" of the '70s (*Airport, Earthquake*), this one featured a virtual panoply of veteran character actors whose parts, in many cases, add up to little more than cannon fodder. It's fun and a little sad too, kind of like blowing up your Micronauts with firecrackers. For those of you interested in seeing "Catwoman" Newmar naked, this is as close as you'll ever get (though it's a little hard to really see much in that murky water). Also, you see Sharif's butt (but no, no Gregory Peck-ary). I guess part of this film's appeal for me is just the sight of all that extravagance (cast, explosions, 70 mm film stock) on a film almost universally reviled. —S. F.

MADE IN USA L: BANG! (ACTION)/BANG! (ACTION) (1988) 82M D: Ken Friedman. *Jacqueline Murphy, Christopher Penn, Adrian Pasdar, Lori Singer.* Penn and Pasdar play leather jacket–wearing, working-class punks who leave their rundown mining town in Pennsylvania for a stolen-car road trip. There are themes about unemployment and industrial pollution–poisoning towns, but they don't amount to much. Most notable for the excellent location scouting of poverty-stricken towns and burned-down houses. The score is by Sonic Youth. —*B. T.*

MAGNUM FORCE L: BANG! (ACTION)/BANG! (ACTION) (1973) 122M D: Ted Post. *Clint Eastwood, Hal Holbrook, Mitch Ryan, David Soul, Tim Matheson.* What's interesting about this first Dirty Harry sequel is how it openly questions the values of its predecessor. In fact it challenges the audience by opening with a reprise of the famous "Do you feel lucky?" speech but instead of pointing the Magnum .45 at the head of a "punk," Harry points it directly at us. The first film institutionalized the cliché of the cop-who-plays-by-his-own-rules, but this one shows the danger of said cops when Harry has to stop a circle of his colleagues who have been executing criminals (a mere three decades before the LAPD Rampart Division scandal). This storyline is especially surprising coming from talented but notoriously right-wing writer John Milius (who later directed *Red Dawn* and inspired the character of Walter Sobchak in *The Big Lebowski*). —*B. T.*

MARK OF ZORRO, THE L: ADVENTURE/ZORRO (1920) 96M D: Fred Niblo. *Robert McKim, Noah Beery Sr., Marguerite de la Motte, Douglas Fairbanks, Eugene Pallette, Gale Sondergaard, Basil Rathbone, Linda Darnell, Tyrone Power.* Fairbanks turned himself into the first action hero playing Old California's Robin Hood in this dashing silent swashbuckler. In his secret identity as the foppish Don Diego, Fairbanks slouches, shuffles, and gives the dim, dull air of a bored dilettante who can hardly be bothered to wake up, while clueing us in to the charade with smiling asides and playful parlor tricks and games. Behind the mask of Zorro, however, he comes alive with a zesty smile and an acrobatic performance, vaulting through windows and over walls and declaiming his pantomime speeches with every muscle in his body. You can almost hear him through the silence (or is that silents?). —*S. A.*

MASK OF ZORRO, THE L: ADVENTURE/ZORRO (1998) 136M D: Martin Campbell. *Antonio Banderas, Catherine Zeta-Jones, Anthony Hopkins, Stuart Wilson.* Hopkins plays Don Diego de la Vega, who secretly dons the mask of the anonymous revolutionary known as Zorro. The film opens with his thrilling final ride before his rival Don Raphael Montero (Wilson) kills his wife, steals his daughter, and imprisons him. Years later, the broken hero escapes and meets a young bandit (Banderas) whom he trains to become the new Zorro and exact his revenge. A humorous and well-staged action adventure in an old-fashioned vein. The

stunts are great and it's certainly the best sword fighting put on screen during the '90s. —*B. T.*

MASTER GUNFIGHTER L: WESTERNS/WESTERNS (1975) 110M D: Tom Laughlin. *Barbara Carrera, Tom Laughlin, Ron O'Neal.* Laughlin plays the master gunfighter of the title, but that's misleading because he's trained in martial arts and is more fond of using swords. At any rate, he continued the themes of his *Billy Jack* series in this more elegantly shot period piece that takes place along the Western coastline, a uniquely wet setting for a Western. Laughlin's character is basically a conscientious objector who abandons his home after he fails to prevent a massacre of Native Americans, but comes back to fight when he finds out it's happening again. O'Neal (best known as the lead in *Superfly*) makes a great villain because he's so charismatic, and his character has a believable motivation; he really believes what he's doing is right. —*B. T.*

MECHANIC, THE L: BANG! (ACTION)/BANG! (ACTION) (1972) 100M D: Michael Winner. *Charles Bronson, Keenan Wynn, Jan-Michael Vincent.* The late, great Bronson and *Death Wish* director Winner provide the ultimate thinking man's tough guy movie. Bronson plays Arthur Bishop, a veteran hit man whose intricate methods of assassination have earned him the position of top "cleaner." Hounded by the overzealous son of a recent victim and anxious to retire, Bishop eventually takes the young man under his wing to teach him the profession. Naturally, explosive complications ensue. Sure, this sounds like typical '70s action fare, but the understated likeability of Bronson's character and deliberately mounting tension between leads make *The Mechanic* more of a character study than a macho crime drama. For instance, Bronson visits a prostitute (played by his wife Jill Ireland) and pays her to pretend she's in love with him. Later, he gives a suicidal teenager tips on how to slit her wrists most effectively and watches sympathetically as she slips away. Wooden acting by Vincent and Wynn doesn't hurt here, but rather showcases the restrained talents of the film's star. Overall, *The Mechanic* is an impossibly human film about professional killers and is, in my opinion, Bronson's greatest work. —*Z. C.*

MIAMI BLUES L: BANG! (ACTION)/BANG! (ACTION) (1990) 97M D: George Armitage. *Alec Baldwin, Fred Ward, Jennifer Jason Leigh.* Baldwin is such a bizarre character in *Miami Blues* that it's hard to take him seriously in any other role. It's also strange that he seems to suck, except for in this movie. But, it's not everyday he gets to be in such a strange movie, a sort of Elmore Leonard slapstick farce. Baldwin is Fredrick Frenger (although he has several fake names during the movie), a freshly released sociopath convict who lands in Miami and promptly kills a Hare Krishna by breaking his finger. This draws the attention of the Miami

PD, specifically Sgt. Hoke Moseley (Ward), who has fake teeth. Stuff happens and Baldwin ends up with the sergeant's gun and badge, then runs rampant around Miami arresting people and robbing people and causing general mayhem. Leigh is in here too, playing a white-trash Florida hooker. But the movie belongs to Baldwin. He chews the scenery and spits it at us. I wish he'd be this funny and good again. Maybe he just needs another weird script like this. —*K. C.*

MIDWAY L: **WAR/WWII** (1976) 132M D: Jack Smight. *Hal Holbrook, Henry Fonda, Charlton Heston, Robert Mitchum, James Coburn, Toshiro Mifune.* Midway was the strategic turning point in World War II for the battle of the Pacific, and this film has all the historical details of strategy and tactics as its central plotline. As a result, the tension and suspense that build in this film are over enormous stakes in the Pacific theater. Four U.S. aircraft carriers that happened to survive Pearl Harbor confront a fleet of four Japanese aircraft carriers in 1942 near Midway—an atoll west of Hawaii. The United States gains the upper hand in a game of cat and mouse and then manages to deliver a fatal blow to the Japanese Navy in a very shocking battle sequence. Some of the effects are actual color stock footage from this battle. With good editing and direction and a remarkable cast this film comes together as a brilliant action film as well as a veritable history lesson. —*N. J.*

MR. MAJESTYK L: **BANG! (ACTION)/BANG! (ACTION)** (1974) 104M D: Richard Fleischer. *Charles Bronson, Paul Koslo, Lee Purcell, Al Lettieri, Linda Cristal.* All Bronson wants to do is get back to his farm and pick the watermelons before the whole crop goes bad. So why do people always have to fuck with him? If it takes escaping from jail, turning the tables on the police, and outfoxing the mafia, so be it. He needs to pick those watermelons. Based on a book by Elmore Leonard. This is an entertaining and dryly humorous spin on macho '70s action pictures. —*B. T.*

NINJA III: THE DOMINATION L: **BANG! (ACTION)/CHOPSOCKIE** (1984) 92M D: Sam Firstenberg. *Shô Kosugi, James Hong, Dale Ishimoto, David Chung, Jordan Bennett, Lucinda Dickey.* A hilarious time capsule of the early '80s that combines ninjas, aerobics, video games, earthquakes, leg warmers, and *Exorcist* rip-offs to create a memorable entry in a forgettable series of martial arts films from Cannon Studios. An evil black ninja kills some guys on a golf course then gets shot by a bunch of cops. His spirit enters the body of an athletic aerobics instructor (played by Dickey, star of *Breakin'* and *Breakin' 2: Electric Boogaloo!*) who proceeds to enact his revenge. Things get complicated when our heroine falls for a cop with a hairy back (Bennett) and a mysterious ninja with an eye patch (played by Kosugi, "one of the world's most popular action adventure stars")

begins to uncover Dickey's weird possession. After she kills a lot of cops, the spirit is exorcised and returned to his evil body just in time for the two ninjas to have a big showdown. —*S. H.*

NO RETREAT, NO SURRENDER L: **BANG! (ACTION)/CHOPSOCKIE** (1986) 85M D: Corey Yuen. *Kurt McKinney, Jean-Claude Van Damme.* A dumb white kid in Seattle (McKinney) gets picked on by bullies who make fun of his karate club. So he does what any kid would do: he visits Bruce Lee's grave until Lee's ghost begins to train him in kung fu. Later, he proves his mettle by entering a tournament and facing Ivan the Russian (Van Damme), a silly rip-off of *Rocky IV*'s Ivan Drago who, because he's played by Van Damme, does the splits across the ropes. This movie is obviously trying to be *The Karate Kid*, even though Lee does Jeet Kune Do. It's a fun, bad '80s movie—there's even a breakdancer and a mean fat kid. —*B. T.*

ON DEADLY GROUND L: **BANG! (ACTION)/BANG! (ACTION)** (1994) 101M D: Steven Seagal. *Joan Chen, Steven Seagal, John C. Mcginley, Michael Caine, R. Lee Ermey.* Seagal's directorial debut is a well-meaning but unintentionally hilarious attempt at a pro-environment dumb action movie. Seagal plays an ex-CIA oil-fire-putter-outer who is down with the Eskimos. Oscar-winner Caine, who enjoys money, plays the evil oil company CEO villain. If you've ever gotten a laugh from a bad action movie, then this is a must-see, full of preposterous dialogue ("I want you to guard this entrance like it was your sister's cherry"), asinine action (Seagal is the expert they call in an emergency to go in and push a button that puts out the fire), and laughable pretension (it ends with Seagal giving a speech about American dependency on oil and possibilities for alternative energy). Keep an eye out for Oscar-winner Billy Bob Thornton, who adds a little personality to the handful of lines he has as a mercenary who is hunting Seagal. —*B. T.*

OUT FOR A KILL L: **BANG! (ACTION)/BANG! (ACTION)** (2003) 88M D: Michael Oblowitz. *Steven Seagal, Michelle Goh, Corey Johnson.* Here's how you know this is one of Seagal's funniest: he plays a professor of Chinese archaeology at Yale. In fact, he's introduced as "our most distinguished academician." And later he turns out to also have a past as an international art thief known as "The Ghost." Framed as a drug smuggler by Chinese gangs, he gets to fly around in planes and drive jeeps and then punch some guys. It's great to see Seagal's response to the popularity of wirework in modern action movies, which is to stand on the ground and punch his acrobatic foes when they happen to flip near him. —*B. T.*

PAID IN FULL L: **BANG! (ACTION)/BANG! (ACTION)** (2002) 97M D: Charles Stone III. *Cam'ron, Mekhi Phifer, Esai Morales, Kevin Carroll, Wood Harris, Chi McBride.*

ALIEN QUADRILOGY. This incredible nine-disc set has two versions, commentary tracks, and in-depth "making of" featurettes for each film in the series. Of course, the first two films are the best, but some of the disc's most fascinating features are those associated with the much-maligned Alien 3, including a newly created longer cut based on David Fincher's workprint.

BEASTIE BOYS VIDEO ANTHOLOGY (CRITERION COLLECTION). Eighteen videos with alternative audio tracks, including forty new remixes, band commentary, and director commentary. Many have alternative angles with raw footage from the video shoots. Other extras include the fake interview show Ciao L.A.!, in which Sofia Coppola interviews the stars of the Sabotage video.

BLACK NARCISSUS. Michael Powell and Emeric Pressburger discuss one of their most acclaimed films.

BLADE II. The menu for deleted scenes is hosted by director Guillermo del Toro, who calls the section "mostly crap." His and Wesley Snipes's commentaries are entertaining, there are all kinds of behind-the-scenes featurettes, and one deleted scene features a vampire interrupted while fondling a bag of intestines—a part originally intended for Michael Jackson.

BLOOD SIMPLE. The head of the fictional Forever Young Films tells ludicrous stories about how the film was supposedly made.

continued on page 396

Gritty crime drama inspired by three real-life drug dealers in 1986 Harlem. Harris is excellent as a dry cleaner who gets swept up in the early crack industry, then has to maneuver his way out *Superfly* style. Rapper Cam'ron also has a Tupac-in-*Juice*–style turn as the psychotic Rico. The screenplay was rewritten from one by the real guy Harris is playing, so it comes from his perspective of the events. Director Stone did the more widely seen *Drumline* in the same year, but this film is more impressive. —*B.T.*

PATTON L: WAR/WWII (1970) 171M D: Franklin J. Schaffner. *George C. Scott, Tim Considine, Michael Strong, Karl Malden, Stephen Young.* This movie swept the Academy Awards in 1970 and it's easy to see why. Scott plays the role of the four-star general George Patton in the European theater of World War II. Patton is a man obsessed who pushes his army deep into German territory trying to get to Berlin in order to claim victory before the Russians do so from the east. With battle scenes that are riveting and stunningly realistic, the real battles in this plot are between Patton and Montgomery, Patton and Eisenhower, and Patton and anyone who doesn't see the path to victory the same way he does. Malden is well cast as General Omar Bradley, who is perhaps the only person Patton feels he can confide in. Given its success there's little doubt that *Patton* defined the genre of war films for years to come, and it also was a much-needed patriotic shot in the arm for a country sunk in Vietnam, where

the war was getting much more complicated and confused from day to day. —*N.J.*

PAYBACK L: BANG! (ACTION)/BANG! (ACTION) (1999) 101M D: Brian Helgeland. *Gregg Henry, Maria Bello, Mel Gibson.* Underrated adaptation of Richard Stark's *The Hunter*, which was also the basis for *Point Blank*. Gibson is at his most cold-hearted and likeably unlikable since the Mad Max days as a single-minded thief attempting to recover his take from a robbery (no more, no less). His one-man badass quest brings him up the bureaucratic ladder of an organized crime outfit run like a corporation. Helgeland (who previously won an Oscar for writing *L.A. Confidential*) creates a timeless but '70s-inspired world where rotary car phones and nose rings can coexist awash in a strange blue tinge. Gibson got cold feet before the release of the movie, took over from Helgeland, and rejiggered the entire last act. The director's cut has not been released officially, but both versions have their pluses and minuses. —*B.T.*

PEARL HARBOR L: WAR/WWII (2001) 183M D: Michael Bay. *Ben Affleck, Josh Hartnett, Kate Beckinsale, Cuba Gooding Jr., Jon Voight, Alec Baldwin.* Compare this film to *Tora Tora Tora* or *Midway* and you will see just how far war movies have retreated into the safety of special effects, TV drama, and lack of historical perspective. Clearly this "epic" was trying to ride the coattails of the historic disaster film *Titanic*, with the drama of a love triangle to carry the plot. It's a bizarre kind of

CANNIBAL: THE MUSICAL. Trey Parker and Matt Stone entertainingly reminisce about their Troma musical.

CHOPPER. The real Mark "Chopper" Read gives advice on shanking and speaks about the characters in the movie as if he thinks they're the actual people.

EVEN DWARVES STARTED SMALL. Werner Herzog explains his fear of chickens. "Have you ever looked a chicken in the eye, Norm?"

EVIL DEAD 2. Bruce Campbell's humorous track provides great insight into the making of the film while also taking preemptive swipes at things he assumes Sam Raimi will say on his track.

FANTASIA. The restored cut of the Disney masterpiece includes a "commentary track" constructed largely from interviews with Walt Disney. There is also an extensive "making of" documentary. The three-disc Fantasia Anthology set also includes Fantasia 2000 and the Fantasia Legacy disc, which includes more in-depth and scene-specific background information as well as artwork, test footage, and rejected sequences.

FEAR AND LOATHING IN LAS VEGAS (CRITERION COLLECTION). Highlights include vintage documentaries on Hunter S. Thompson, a book reading by Oscar Acosta, Johnny Depp reading his correspondence with Thompson, and a crazed commentary track by Thompson.

FIGHT CLUB. The best of the four commentary tracks is the one with the book's author, Chuck Palahniuk. Also enlightening are

---

historical rewrite that leaves out all the cigarette smoking of World War II. Furthermore, while the effects of the bombing of Pearl Harbor are quite brilliant, no particular reason is given for the Japanese to attack. This film will awaken very little in the audience; there is absolutely nothing to be learned about the history of this battle. The drama is as deep as a pie pan and about as interesting. —*N.J.*

PETEY WHEATSTRAW (AKA THE DEVIL'S SON-IN-LAW) L: BANG! (ACTION)/BLAXPLOITATION (1978) 95M D: Cliff Roquemore. *Rudy Ray Moore, Jimmy Lynch, Wildman Steve.* Petey Wheatstraw (Moore) is a famous comedian who gets gunned down at a funeral by his rivals, Leroy and Skillet. The Devil offers to let him live again, he just has to marry the Devil's daughter. So he comes back with magic powers, gets revenge on Leroy and Skillet, and tricks the Devil so he won't have to marry his "ugly bitch" daughter. This is my favorite Moore film because it combines his usual ridiculous blaxploitation tall tales with magical elements and a larger portion of rhyming dialogue. The DVD includes what might be the funniest commentary track ever if it didn't have twenty-minute gaps between comments. —*B.T.*

POINT BREAK L: BANG! (ACTION)/BANG! (ACTION) (1991) 122M D: Kathryn Bigelow. *Keanu Reeves, Patrick Swayze, Lori Petty, Gary Busey.* On the one hand it's one of the most ridiculous action films of the '90s. On the other, it's male bonding overdrive and pure action ecstasy from the underrated director Bigelow. Leave it to a woman to get under the skin of male bonding, even through the metaphysical rap of Zen-surfer and danger junkie Swayze and the breathy California-dude speak of Reeves, the eager young agent who goes undercover to bag a band of bank robbers. Busey at least gives it some grounding as Reeves's FBI mentor. At times, the sheer exhilaration and adrenaline make you forget just how silly it is. —*S.A.*

POINT OF NO RETURN L: BANG! (ACTION)/BANG! (ACTION) (1993) 108M D: John Badham. *Bridget Fonda, Harvey Keitel, Anne Bancroft, Miguel Ferrer, Gabriel Byrne, Dermot Mulroney.* An utterly empty and unneeded remake of Luc Besson's now classic *La Femme Nikita, Point of No Return* fails even on the most basic action movie levels. A clearly miscast Fonda stars clumsily as Maggie, a young punk turned government assassin. Byrne does passable work as her mentor in the agency, Bob. The real crime here is not the talented cast members who should have known better, but the thin, slapdash direction by Badham. Scenes that are lifted wholly from the original film seem either pale rip-offs or overblown, cheesy spectacle. Where is the muted coolness of *Nikita*? Even Keitel's turn as Victor the Cleaner is shallow, wasted. Of course the plot gets changed as well, including a less than subtle tweak to the ending. The heart of Besson's film—the contrast of a young woman skillfully learning how to live in a society while ignoring its rules and coldly killing whomever she's told—is mostly ignored.

the detailed "making of" featurettes, which make use of alternative angles and optional commentary tracks. The menus are well designed, and there's even a hidden catalog of Fight Club merchandise (what the hell is that—a subversion of a subversion?).

HEART OF GLASS. More weird Herzog commentary: "No, Norman, that is bullshit."

IN THE MOOD FOR LOVE (CRITERION COLLECTION).

THE KILLERS (CRITERION COLLECTION).

THE LIMEY. Director Steven Soderbergh and writer Lem Dobbs squabble hilariously about the finished film, with Soderbergh continually trying to egg Dobbs on.

THE LORD OF THE RINGS (EXTENDED VERSIONS). In addition to boasting the more fleshed-out versions of the films, these ultra-deluxe versions include, hands down, the most extensive "making of" documentaries ever on DVD.

OUT OF SIGHT. With a cast this great, it's exciting to see cast interviews. With a movie this perfect, it's exciting to see deleted scenes. And Steven Soderbergh's commentaries are always entertaining.

PETEY WHEATSTRAW. Although Rudy Ray Moore is silent for most of the film, the twenty or so minutes of commentary he does provide is priceless.

POWERPUFF GIRLS: THE MANE EVENT. Evil monkey supergenius Mojo Jojo complains about the girls foiling his plot but also demon-

continued on page 398

Instead things blow up and Bridget gets sweaty. Jeesh. —*G. M.*

PRIME CUT L: BANG! (ACTION)/BANG! (ACTION) (1972) 86M D: Michael Ritchie. *Lee Marvin, Sissy Spacek, Gene Hackman.* Legendary badass Marvin plays collections agent Nick Devlin, hired to squeeze money from a Kansas cattle rancher enigmatically named Mary Ann (Hackman). Arriving in Kansas, Devlin learns that Mary Ann's involved in various sordid illegalities, up to and including grinding foes into sausage (and I mean that literally) and auctioning nude teenage girls, drugged and sold out of livestock pens. Devlin hardly cares what Mary Ann does, so long as he gets the money. So when Devlin seizes prize stock Poppy (a very young Spacek), it's unclear whether it's a rescue or a repo. Although the performances are riveting, if not Oscar caliber, the plot is far from lucid, which actually makes it all the more entertaining. An excellent movie night selection, *Prime Cut* is sure to elicit a long string of "What the hell?"s. —*C. B.*

PRISONER OF ZENDA, THE L: ADVENTURE/SWASHBUCKLERS (1952) 101M D: Richard Thorpe. *James Mason, Jane Greer, Louis Calhern, Robert Douglas, Deborah Kerr, Stewart Granger.* This is my favorite version of this classic film, probably due to the swoonable performance of Granger and the wonderfully wicked and dastardly performance of Mason. An Englishman has the good, or rather bad, luck of being nearly identical to the soon-to-be-crowned King Rudolf. Alas, the heir apparent has a bit of a drinking problem, a problem with responsibility, and a younger brother who is eager to sit on the throne in his stead. So when said brother takes advantage of the heir's drinking problem, hoping to have him miss his coronation and be disgraced in front of his subjects, naturally the double is requested to save the day. Though shot with a light hand and simple acting, the beautiful settings and costumes help make it an entertaining and fun swashbuckling romp. —*M. N.*

PSYCHOMANIA (AKA THE DEATH WHEELERS) L: BANG! (ACTION)/BIKERS (1971) 95M D: Don Sharp. *George Sanders, Beryl Reid, Nicky Henson, Mary Larkin, Roy Holder, Robert Hardy.* This British prepunk horror film concerns "The Living Dead," a gang of bikers whose leader Tom (Henson) decides to boldly pursue a life after death. With help from his occult-driven mother (Reid) and the frogs she worships, Tom commits suicide by riding his bike off a bridge, fully anticipating to rise from the dead. His biker friends bury him themselves, situating him upright on his bike in a very shallow grave. Later on, Tom pops a wheelie out of his grave and compels his biker friends to commit suicide and join him. This brings out quite a few suicides, each one more absurd than the last. Once all the bikers are reunited, Tom's mother decides that she doesn't like her son's designs, so with the help of her butler (Sanders) she finally puts a stop to them. This is truly a classic cult film of low-budget horror, not to be missed if playing somewhere at midnight. —*N. J.*

strates his film literacy. "This reminds me of a shot in High Noon."

THE ROYAL TENENBAUMS (CRITERION COLLECTION).
This disc includes all kinds of great interviews and galleries, but the two highlights are The Peter Bradley Show, in which the movie's Charlie Rose–like interviewer talks to some of the bit players in the cast, and With the Filmmaker, an enlightening Albert Maysles documentary following Wes Anderson for a day on the set.

SCHIZOPOLIS (CRITERION COLLECTION).
It may be a stretch to call this one "extras-packed," but among the three or so extra features is an absolutely priceless commentary track in which director/star Steven Soderbergh interviews himself and makes himself out to be a complete jackass.

SNOW WHITE AND THE SEVEN DWARFS.
Lots of artwork, animation tests, and behind-the-scenes featurettes make this disc worth sifting through the needless crap (Barbra Streisand singing "Someday My Prince Will Come"?). The best part is the elaborate magic mirror–themed menus.

STYLE WARS.
Many of the young graffiti artists from this classic 1982 documentary returned twenty years later to do interviews and provide impressive galleries of their work. These features give the disc a fascinating 7 Up angle.

TITUS.
The forty-nine-minute "making of" documentary is one of the best ever, created from footage shot during the production rather than interviews after the fact. You will be amazed by director Julie Taymor's passion, especially during the rehearsals.

QUICK AND THE DEAD, THE L: WESTERNS/WESTERNS (1987) 91M D: Robert Day. *Sam Elliott, Tom Conti, Kate Capshaw, Kenny Morrison.* When the sun set on the big-screen Western and closed down the theatrical frontier, the genre found a new home on the small screen. Originally made for HBO, this Louis L'Amour adaptation stars Elliott as a grizzled trail veteran who becomes the gruff guardian angel with a gun to a family of good-hearted pioneers. Scottish storekeeper Conti is the pacifist father leading his family from Pennsylvania to a homestead in Wyoming while a scraggly bunch of bushwhackers and barfly criminals (led by Matt Clark) dog their trail. Whether he's initially driven by an innate sense of responsibility to protect this naive woman or simply in love with Conti's wife, Capshaw ("a handsome woman," he repeatedly remarks), Elliott becomes entwined with the trio as pride, jealousy, and rivalry give way to respect. The musical lilt of Conti's Scottish burr makes a marvelous contrast to Elliott's gravely drawl, just as the stunning meadow where the family makes its home and its last stand is a beautiful contrast to the savage violence that descends upon them. —S.A.

RAGE L: BANG! (ACTION)/BANG! (ACTION) (1972) 100M D: George C. Scott. *George C. Scott, Richard Basehart, Martin Sheen, Barnard Hughes, Nicolas Beauvy.* Scott directs and stars in this clumsy and slow-moving rural revenge "thriller" about a man getting even for the government's unintentional murder of his son. What was marketed as a brutal epic of parental retribution crawls along for an hour before a hint of the much-ballyhooed rage is seen on-screen. Sheen walks through his role as a corrupt doctor. Eventually, after trudging through endless dialogue and some mildly amusing incontinence, *Rage* lets loose with a little violence—but by that point it really isn't enough to keep the viewer awake. The most effective moment in the film takes place when Scott shoots a cat off a chair. A disappointment after his epochal vengeance-fueled performance in the far superior *Hardcore* from Paul Schrader. —Z. C.

RAISE THE TITANIC L: ADVENTURE/ADVENTURE (1980) 112M D: Jerry Jameson. *Anne Archer, Richard Jordan, Jason Robards Jr., Alec Guinness, David Selby.* The plot of this film has very little to do with the Titanic. The U.S. military decides it can use the little-known mineral byzanium for missile defense and it so happens to be found only on a small Arctic island. Upon exploration it is discovered that back in 1912 the mineral had been totally mined and shipped from Europe to the United States on the Titanic. The rest of the film focuses on finding the Titanic and then raising it with airbags and explosives while the Soviets do their best to interfere. With all that's been learned about the Titanic since this film was released, the suppositions made stretch far beyond absurdity. However, if you can buy the premise you might also buy the physics concerning its special effects. —N.J.

RAW FORCE (AKA **SHOGUN ISLAND**) L: BANG! (ACTION)/ CHOPSOCKIE (1982) 86M D: Edward D. Murphy. *Cameron Mitchell, Vic Diaz, Jewel Shepard, Hope Holiday, Jillian Kesner, Carl Anthony.* A swinging singles/ martial artist cruise ship captained by Mitchell accidentally sails to a mysterious island inhabited by virgin-eating monks who are creating an army of kung fu zombies. Sound preposterous? Hell, that stuff is just for starters—throw in a Hitler look-alike, piranhas, a gratuitous trip to a Philippine whorehouse, plenty of cornball humor, white slavery, lots of dumbfounding kung fu (with an emphasis on the "dumb"), exploding toy boats, slapstick gore, and great mounds of boobies, and you are barely scratching the surface of what makes *Raw Force* such an incredibly shitty but irresistible action comedy. I wish they spent more time with the preposterous zombie/ monk plot instead of the goofball heroes, but it ends promising a sequel (!) so there's always hope. —*S. H.*

REPLACEMENT KILLERS, THE L: BANG! (ACTION)/BANG! (ACTION) (1998) 86M D: Antoine Fuqua. *Chow Yun Fat, Kenneth Tsang, Danny Trejo, Mira Sorvino, Jürgen Prochnow, Michael Rooker.* An accomplished assassin (Chow) backs down from killing the seven-year-old son of a cop (Rooker), thus bringing the wrath of his boss upon him. He teams with a document forger (Sorvino) and fires many guns. Chow's first American film is also the directorial debut of Fuqua, whose roots in music videos are evident. Perhaps due to his limited English skills, Chow's character has much less depth than those he is known for playing in Hong Kong. This film is watchable for one reason alone: the magnetic, badass charisma of Chow as he struts through the movie with a gun in each hand and a grim look on his face. Too bad there's nothing beneath the surface. Strangely, Fuqua went on to acclaim directing Denzel Washington and Ethan Hawke in *Training Day*, which has a plot very similar to Chow's second (and better) American vehicle, *The Corruptor.* —*B. T.*

REVOLVER (AKA **BLOOD IN THE STREETS**) L: BANG! (ACTION)/BANG! (ACTION) (1973) 110M D: Sergio Sollima. *Oliver Reed, Fabio Testi, Agostina Belli.* Reed is a violent prison warden whose beautiful young wife (Belli) is kidnapped by a gang that demands the release of notorious criminal Testi, but that's just the beginning of their ordeal. The two become unlikely partners when they get caught in the midst of a vast conspiracy that spans from the underworld to the government. Reed's voice is unfortunately dubbed by some American voice actor, an all-too-common frustration with Italian productions, but his bearish body language communicates his rage, his inner struggle, and the entire murky morality of this lean Sollima (*Violent City*) production. A smartly done Italian thriller. —*S. A.*

ROAD HOUSE L: BANG! (ACTION)/BANG! (ACTION) (1989) 114M D: Rowdy Herrington. *Sam Elliott, Patrick Swayze, Kelly Lynch, Ben Gazzara.* There aren't many action movies as cheerfully divorced from reality as *Road House*, which is the story of a thoughtful bouncer taking on a small-town crime boss. The bouncer (Swayze) boasts a philosophy degree and an uncanny ability to break the limbs of opponents. If that combination of character traits seems incongruous, the movie happily whisks over it like a water bug over a pond. Despite the fact that the film hails from the sluggish '80s, there's a lack of weight to it, a sly sense of fun that trumps the ponderous, sloth-slow films that rose and died in that decade. There are fistfights, trashy women, and horrible but entertaining dialogue; there's bar house music, big hair, and a scene featuring a monster truck. This is a movie to enjoy while drinking beer out of cans. —*T. P.*

ROLLING THUNDER L: BANG! (ACTION)/BANG/TV (1977) 99M D: John Flynn. *William Devane, Linda Haynes, Tommy Lee Jones, Lisa Richards, Dabney Coleman.* Paul Schrader was undeniably responsible for scripting the toughest, bleakest films of the '70s, and *Rolling Thunder* is thankfully no exception. Devane plays Charles Rane, an army major recently released from a Vietnam POW death camp along with his friend Johnny Vohden (played by a young and impossibly handsome Jones). Upon returning home to San Antonio, Rane's life is shattered in a series of events that leave him without his family and right hand. Fitted with a sharpened hook, he draws on the resolve gained from years of torture while planning revenge. What sounds like the plot for countless lousy action films is elevated to masterpiece status by Schrader's dialogue and Devane's seething, bitter performance. Once the major unleashes his vengeance, the film moves relentlessly forward toward a vicious conclusion that eclipses even the finales of Schrader's other violent epics of the time. Fans of savage cinema take note: This one is *crucial.* —*Z. C.*

ROMULUS AND REMUS (AKA **DUEL OF THE TITANS**) L: ADVENTURE/PEPLUM (1961) 89M D: Sergio Corbucci. *Virna Lisi, Steve Reeves, Gordon Scott.* Though it conflates some events (the Rape of the Sabine Women) and borrows from other cultures' national epics (*Exodus*), this film is a reasonably accurate and highly entertaining representation of the humble beginnings of the Eternal City. Not to mention that it features what is probably "Hercules" Reeves's best performance (with able script assistance from none other than Sergio Leone). —*S. F.*

ROUGH RIDERS L: WAR/OTHER CONFLICTS (1997) 240M D: John Milius. *Tom Berenger, Sam Elliott, Gary Busey, Brad Johnson, Illeana Douglas.* This made-for-TNT miniseries is quintessential Milius, the story of heroism under fire and the honor of battle during the Spanish-American War. The cavalry units sent to Cuba at the turn of the century (one of them commanded by future President Teddy Roosevelt, played by Berenger) become a microcosm for an idealized American melting pot: East and West, North and South, rich and poor, white, black, red, and brown form the new brotherhood of America. For Milius this is a defining moment for the country, America's first battle since the Civil War, and he's probably the only domestic director who can put on such a straight-faced display of patriotic passion with such energy and heart. I could have used a little more of his brief ironic asides—even yellow journalist William Randolph Hearst (who does indeed utter the line "You provide the stories, I'll provide the war") escapes this one with dignity—but the final image doesn't pull any punches in its understanding of the real reason America went to war. —*S. A.*

RUDE L: BANG! (ACTION)/BLAXPLOITATION (1980) 80M D: Cliff Roquemore. *Rudy Ray Moore.* Before he started making his weird blaxploitation classics, Moore was a comedian. He was known for his cockily delivered, obscene, and sexist jokes as well as clever rhyming toasts about folk heroes like Shine, Dolemite, and Petey Wheastraw (the latter two, of course, he turned into movie characters). This attempt at a concert film showcases a lot of his best material, but awkward editing, some fake audience reaction shots, redubbed routines, and obvious audience plants make the film seem very unprofessional. For some that might make it more amusing. —*B. T.*

RUSH HOUR L: BANG! (ACTION)/BANG! (ACTION) (1998) 98M D: Brett Ratner. *Chris Tucker, Jackie Chan, Philip Baker Hall, Elizabeth Peña, Tom Wilkinson, Chris Penn.* Following up their collaboration on *Money Talks*, director Ratner and star Tucker went for another retro-'80s multiracial buddy movie, but with the inspired twist of replacing the white buddy (Charlie Sheen in the case of *Money Talks*) with Jackie Chan. Chan plays a Hong Kong detective trying to save his friend's kidnapped daughter; Tucker plays the fuckup LAPD detective sent to keep Chan out of the way. And of course these two get past their cultural differences, learn to work together, and save the day. But the movie does subtly subvert the *Lethal Weapon*/*Beverly Hills Cop* formula in a couple of ways. Usually in a buddy movie there is a black buddy, but there is a white buddy who the white audience is supposed to relate to more. Here there is a black buddy, an Asian buddy, and a Latina who helps them. No white buddy at all. Also, when Tucker tries to play by his own rules, as cops in these movies always do, it's not portrayed as cool—the other cops even make fun of him for it. This is a fun movie, but Chan's stunts are pretty slight compared to his Hong Kong movies, and Tucker is funnier in rated-R movies. —*B. T.*

RUSH HOUR 2 L: BANG! (ACTION)/BANG! (ACTION) (2001) 91M D: Brett Ratner. *Jackie Chan, Chris Tucker, Ziyi Zhang.* Chan and Tucker (the moves and the mouth) collide once again in a globe-trotting action adventure, this time set in Hong Kong, and the sequel lives or dies on Chan's martial arts prowess and physical magic (especially his great use of props in fight scenes) and Tucker's motormouth. Both are in fine form, even if the script is a bit shaggy. Director Ratner appears to have let them work over the screenplay on the fly, which energizes the film and sparks their scenes together. Otherwise it's a generic adventure thriller where the casting props up the narrative weaknesses. Guest villain Ziyi (*Crouching Tiger, Hidden Dragon*), who speaks not a line in English, burns with both a mysteriousness and a ruthlessness. —*S. A.*

SAVAGE ABDUCTION L: BANG! (ACTION)/BIKERS (1972) 83M D: John Lawrence. *Tom Drake, Amy Thomson, Kitty Vallacher, Bill Barney, Tanis Gallik, Stephen Oliver, Joe Turkel, Sean Kenney.* A fairly tame scuzzball kidnapping film from the early '70s that, despite having all the ingredients, fails to deliver the grim sadism, perverse thrills, extreme violence, brutal humiliation, tortured teenagers, vengeful castrations, and gratuitous nudity usually found in movies like this. Turkel (*The Shining* and *Blade Runner*) plays Harvey, a goofy psycho necrophiliac in ugly-ass clothes who blackmails an amoral lawyer into providing women for his sick needs. The lawyer employs the lamest biker gang ever, the Savages (a three-man gang with only two motorcycles), who kidnap a couple of innocent youngsters. The bikers and the girls go to the gang's hangout and "party." Tension builds between the gang members and, eventually, Harvey shows up and is such a pervy weirdo that he even freaks out the Savages. It all seems to be building to a grim nihilistic finale where everyone (even the innocent) dies, but no, the movie cops out and discards a pessimistic ending that would put *Savage Abduction* in the category of other disturbing abduction films. There are lots of seedy elements present but *Savage Abduction* only manages to generate laughs instead of cheap thrills. —*S. H.*

SCARAMOUCHE L: ADVENTURE/SWASHBUCKLERS (1952) 111M D: George Sidney. *Stewart Granger, Eleanor Parker, Janet Leigh, Mel Ferrer.* The second big-screen adaptation of Rafael Sabatini's swashbuckling adventure stars Granger as a leader of the French Revolution who vows revenge on the cruel aristocrat (Ferrer) who murdered his best friend in a duel. While Granger hones his skills with a blade, he takes on the identity of a legendary stage clown to get into the halls of power. There he falls in love with an aristocratic cutie (Leigh, who just may be his sister) and flirts with all-woman temptress Parker. Director Sidney was an MGM musical specialist and his gifts for choreography and color serve him well in this spirited adventure, which boasts one of the greatest swordfights ever put on screen. —*S. A.*

SCORPION KING, THE L: ADVENTURE/ADVENTURE (2002)
92M D: Chuck Russell. *The Rock, Steven Brand, Michael Clarke Duncan, Kelly Hu.* WWE veteran The Rock is dropped into the sands of ancient Egypt with a wicked cutlass and a quip-heavy arsenal of blunt pronouncements and flip wisecracks in this barbarian film spin-off from *The Mummy Returns.* He looks like he was poured from a life-size action figure mold and acts as if born to the part. He throws his entire body into every lunge and leap, brawls and brandishes a broadsword with the brute power of an ogre, and speaks in the granite voice of a brawny Batman who doesn't take any of this tough guy stuff seriously. No reason he should; the story, a series of set pieces and stock situations cribbed from decades of pulp adventures, is pure pulp junk, but so what? The Rock is surprisingly charismatic and Russell directs with breathless action, borderline camp comedy, and high-tech flair. If it's not exactly exciting, it's at least fast, furious, slick fun. Hu is a visionary sorceress whose wardrobe is so strategically revealing it must have been glued on. —*S. A.*

SCREAM IN THE STREETS, A L: BANG! (ACTION)/BANG!
(ACTION) (1972) 96M D: Carl Monson. *John Kirkpatrick, Linda York, Con Covert, Frank Bannon.* You gotta love the grind house recipe of this bizarre exploitation cocktail: part gritty, in-your-face, mean streets police story and part skin flick, it's a mix of *Dirty Harry* and *Adam 12* as a kinky softcore sickie. Bannon and Kirkpatrick are plainclothes cops after the "freaks" and scum of the city: a neighborhood voyeur who peeps on lesbian housewives, a slimy sadist who goes berserk at a massage parlor, and a cheerful cross-dressing serial killer whose hobby is hacking up ladies in a local park. This drive-in thriller is pure sexploitation with plenty of nudity, groping, and body-on-body contact just short of X, and a little hotheaded police brutality and suspect beatings tossed in for variety. —*S. A.*

SHAFT L: BANG! (ACTION)/BANG! (ACTION) (2000) 99M D:
John Singleton. *Samuel L. Jackson, Jeffrey Wright, Christian Bale, Vanessa L. Williams, Richard Roundtree.* In this update, Jackson takes on the role of John Shaft (although Roundtree has a supporting role as his uncle, also named John Shaft—you can interpret that how you will). Beginning as an NYPD detective, the new Shaft dramatically quits in disgust, throwing his badge into the wall of a courtroom like it was a throwing star, then becomes the private dick we remember. With a screenplay by Richard Price, it manages to be both gritty '90s police drama and faithful wah-wah-infused '70s homage. Wright chews and spits out every piece of scenery that comes between him and his Dominican drug lord character Peoples, and Busta Rhymes is annoying as

Shaft's sidekick. But really, the movie is one long showcase for the ineffable coolness of Jackson. One glimpse of him with his bald head and leather outfit is enough to prove that a remake of Shaft was a worthwhile endeavor. —*B. T.*

SHAOLIN DOLEMITE L: BANG! (ACTION)/BLAXPLOITATION
(1999) 104M D: Robert Tai. *Rudy Ray Moore, Jimmy Lynch, Alice Tseng, Robert Tai, Eugene Thomas.* In one of his most ridiculous projects ever, Moore takes what appears to be an old-school Shaolin kung fu flick and dubs it Dolemite style. The black villain (Thomas) becomes "Two-Pack of the Dolemite Clan" and the woman becomes "Ninja Ho." Best of all, Moore added a few scenes of himself as "Monk Ru Dee" interfering with the story, or sometimes just reacting to the fight scenes ("That mothafucka is outta sight!"). The kung fu footage appears to be of '70s vintage, but maybe they just faked it—the credited director's debut was 1984's *Mafia vs Ninja.* There are a couple of very over-the-top fights, most notably the topless battle where Ninja Ho uses her breasts as weapons. —*B. T.*

SHIELD, THE: SEASON ONE L: BANG! (ACTION)/BANG!/TV
(2002) 614M D: Brad Anderson, Paris Barclay, John Badham, others. *Catherine Dent, Benito Martinez, Walton Goggins, Michael Chiklis, Michael Jace, Jay Karnes.* The Shield debuted on the FX cable channel early in 2002 and shook up television as it blurred the line between good cop and bad cop. Chiklis took home a well-deserved Emmy Award for his fearless performance as a maverick officer at once corrupt and dedicated, violent and protective, and utterly passionate in his job even while he's skimming the evidence. Captain Aceveda (Martinez) is the driven leader with naked ambition who pulls out a glib face for the press, Dutch (Karnes) is an intellectual social geek in a blue-collar station whose abilities are ridiculed until a painful interrogation reveals more than anyone ever expected, and Officer Lowe (Jace) is a churchgoing cop tortured by denial and self-repression. The explosive first episode (directed by former *Homicide* detective Clark Johnson) sets the volatile chemistry, but the fine writing and jagged, jumpy direction of the next twelve episodes builds on the edgy characters by sketching out fascinating relationships and shifting levels of loyalty among the squad. —*S. A.*

SIMON SEZ L: BANG! (ACTION)/BANG! (ACTION) (1999) 85M
D: Kevin Elders. *Dennis Rodman, Dane Cook, Natalia Cigliuti, Filip Nicolic, John Pinette.* If you enjoy bad action movies, obviously it is very exciting to learn that Rodman, after teaming with Jean-Claude Van Damme in Tsui Hark's bizarre *Double Team*, was able to star in his own movie. Here he plays an Interpol agent trying to save a kidnapped girl. Xin Xiong is the action director (he choreographed the fights for *Double Team*) but it just doesn't have the same berserk quality or nonstop, laugh-out-loud ridiculousness.

Worse, Rodman's line delivery has gotten a little less awkward, so you don't get to laugh at him as much. That said, there are a couple of humorously over-the-top fight scenes and a gratuitous motorcycle flip to keep you occupied. Director Elders was the writer of the *Iron Eagle* trilogy. But you probably already knew that. —*B. T.*

SINBAD OF THE SEVEN SEAS L: ADVENTURE/PEPLUM (1989) 90M D: Enzo G. Castellari. *Lou Ferrigno, John Steiner, Leo Gullotta, Teagan Clive.* The prologue to this film set to a corny synthesizer score tells you everything you need to know. Summoning the visage of Edgar Allen Poe, the story *The Thousand and Second Tale of Scherherezad* is cited to cast the film in an authentic light. And then to open the film a mother is reading the story to her sleepless daughter. No doubt you will be sleepless too after seeing this sleeper of überschlock! The mother becomes the narrator of this tale while the rest of us are subjected to the casting of Ferrigno as Sinbad and Steiner as Jaffar. Dialogue and action alike are tortured with bad acting and a fantastically low budget. The final conflict is carried out on the moon! Either you'll laugh or cry, but you will do one of the two thoroughly. —*N. J.*

SLAYGROUND L: BANG! (ACTION)/BANG! (ACTION) (1983) 89M D: Terry Bedford, Dennis Bosher. *Peter Coyote, Mel Smith, Billie Whitelaw, Philip Sayer.* Based on one of Richard Stark's Parker novels, this one finds Parker (here called Stone, played by Coyote) on the run from a hit man hired by the father of a girl accidentally killed during an armored car robbery. Unlike the Parker of the novels, Stone shows emotions and remorse for his deeds, which makes him a more ordinary protagonist. Not nearly on the level of *Point Blank* or even *Payback*, but still fun to watch, especially during the climactic chase through an abandoned amusement park. —*B. T.*

SPEED L: BANG! (ACTION)/BANG! (ACTION) (1994) 115M D: Jan de Bont. *Sandra Bullock, Keanu Reeves, Joe Morton, Jeff Daniels, Dennis Hopper.* *Speed* was made in an era of *Die-Hard*-in-a-blank movies (often starring Steven Seagal or Jean-Claude Van Damme), but it was more successful than the others for a number of reasons. For one thing, there's the audacity of the premise. *Die Hard* on a bus? How do you even pull that off? Bullock has to drive a bus full of people no slower than 50 mph, or Hopper's bomb will blow them all up. Poor bastard cop Reeves is on the bus, so he figures maybe he should do something about it. Although the capabilities of the bus get ridiculous at times (could that thing really jump a bridge?), screenwriter Graham Yost does a fine job of building tension through escalating action set pieces, which are well staged and timed by first-time director de Bont (who at the time seemed like he showed promise). This is also an influential movie in that it established Reeves

Our favorite antiwar movies

APOCALYPSE NOW

ASCENT

ASHES AND DIAMONDS

BATTLE ROYALE 2

BLACK RAIN

COMBAT SHOCK

COME AND SEE

COMING HOME

DEATHDREAM

THE DEER HUNTER

DR. STRANGELOVE

DUCK SOUP

FIRES ON THE PLAIN

FIRST BLOOD

FULL METAL JACKET

THE GRAND ILLUSION

GRAVE OF THE FIREFLIES

JOE

KING OF HEARTS

THE OUTLAW JOSEY WALES

STARSHIP TROOPERS

THE TIN DRUM

TO BE OR NOT TO BE

as an action star, paving the way for *The Matrix* (or maybe it was *Johnny Mnemonic* that did the trick?). —*B. T.*

STINGRAY L: BANG! (ACTION)/VROOM (CHASES & RACES!) (1978) 100M D: Richard Taylor. *Chris Mitchum, Sherry Jackson.* You know, Mitchum is as big a star in Europe as his dad is. Yeah, of course he's nowhere near as cool, but then, who the hell is? This is one of those films that I came across on cable late one night while babysitting for some neighbor kids (I'd put them to bed after letting them stay up and watch *First Blood*). In it I discovered the magnificent Jackson, who plays an absolutely ruthless hit woman (witness how she deals with a jerky guy in a bar, using only his drink and a lighter—ouch!) who'll stop at nothing to retrieve the missing dope and money. —*S. F.*

STRANGE DAYS L: BANG! (ACTION)/BANG! (ACTION) (1995) 145M D: Kathryn Bigelow. *Ralph Fiennes, Juliette Lewis, Angela Bassett, Tom Sizemore, Michael Wincott, Vincent D'Onofrio.* It's 1999, but in this case a little more violent and with some higher-tech gadgets than we actually had in 1999. An ex-cop turned hustler has a product for sale that is usually only meant for the police force: a new technology that allows one to record the brain activities of an individual such that it can be played back to anyone and he can feel the experience as if it were actually happening to him. Mix that up with a kick-ass bodyguard chauffer, some determined cops, a crazy music mogul, a bad-news ex-girlfriend, the murder of a prostitute, and a gang killing of an infamous rap star, and you have the makings of a gritty, intense, and stylish movie. It's a movie of lost love, lost dreams, lost hope, all mixed up in a world gone a little wild and a lot dangerous. —*M. N.*

SUBSTITUTE, THE L: BANG! (ACTION)/BANG! (ACTION) (1996) 114M D: Robert Mandel. *Tom Berenger, Ernie Hudson, Diane Venora.* In a fit of deranged brilliance, somebody decided to combine the white-teacher-makes-a-difference-in-inner-city-school genre with cheeseball action, and I'm so glad they did. When ex-mercenary Berenger's teacher girlfriend (Venora) gets attacked by a gang leader at school, he decides to create a new identity as a teacher and go in to substitute for her. At first he tries to work with the troubled students, and he does find some common ground with them when comparing his Vietnam scars to their drive-by-inflicted bullet wounds. But when push comes to shove, and especially when the suck-up principal (Hudson) tries to sell a suitcase full of cocaine in the gym during parent-teacher night, the substitute has no choice but to bring in a platoon of heavily armed buddies (including the great Luis Guzmán) for a pre–Columbine high school bloodbath. —*B. T.*

SUDDEN DEATH L: BANG! (ACTION)/BANG! (ACTION) (1995) 111M D: Peter Hyams. *Jean-Claude Van Damme, Powers Boothe, Raymond J. Barry.* One of the more entertaining *Die Hard* rip-offs, *Sudden Death* is *Die Hard* in a hockey arena. Van Damme plays John McCla. . . er, I mean, Darren McCord, an ass-kicking fire inspector who happens to bring his kids to the Stanley Cup game where terrorists kidnap the vice president and plan to blow up the arena if they don't get their ransom by the end of the game. Made at a time when Van Damme could still get decent production values, it's actually pretty fun, throwing its hero into absurd situations like fighting a terrorist in a mascot costume or hiding out on the ice disguised as one of the team's goalies. —*B. T.*

SUPERCHICK L: BANG! (ACTION)/BANG! (ACTION) (1973) 95M D: Edward J. Forsyth. *John Carradine, Candy Samples, Joyce Jillson, Tony Young, Uschi Digard, Louis Quinn.* Before Jillson became Nancy Reagan's trusted astrologer (!) she had a brief career in sleazy sex movies like this. She stars (and narrates) as Tara B. True, a horny jet-set chick with a man in every port. As a stewardess (yep, this was made back in the swinging stewardess years) she disguises herself in a brunette wig and travels between lovers. Once on land she lets her blonde hair down and has various "sexy" adventures. Along the way she introduces a soldier to the mile-high club, kicks ass in her karate class, gets hassled by an S&M–crazed old pervert played by Carradine ("Somebody must have slipped some acid in your Geritol," Superchick quips), goes disco dancing, beats up some bikers, screws a bunch of guys, and, eventually, thwarts a terrorist attack on her airplane. It's all pretty lightweight and inept. There's lots of nudity (a disclaimer: you're not always seeing Jillson's boobs!) and some sorry attempts at humor. *Superchick* is worth a few laughs but isn't nearly as amusing as it should be. —*S. H.*

THOU SHALT NOT KILL. . . EXCEPT L: BANG! (ACTION)/BANG! (ACTION) (1987) 84M D: Josh Becker. *Sam Raimi, Tim Quill, Brian Schulz, John Manfredini, Robert Rickman.* The surviving members of a Vietnam War platoon get together for beers. One of them has a dog named Whiskey who wanders off into the woods. When they go looking for Whiskey, they happen to run across a Manson-style cult of murderous hippies, led by Raimi. Then it's an all-out bloodbath. There's a raw tone and an impressive period feel considering how low the budget is, but the bad acting and dialogue prevent it from reaching its potential as an entertaining exploitation picture. Still, it's recommended for Raimi completists. Becker is one of the group of old friends who made *The Evil Dead* and many lesser films (this being one of those). Bruce Campbell, Scott Spiegel, Ted Raimi, and Joseph Lo Duca were also involved. —*B. T.*

TOMBSTONE L: WESTERNS/WESTERNS (1993) 135M D: George Pan Cosmatos. *Kurt Russell, Val Kilmer, Michael Biehn, Powers Boothe, Robert John Burke.* It may not be the best film made about the real-life Gunfight at the OK Corral, but it's likely the most historically accurate, and the cast makes it one of the most entertaining. Russell doesn't try to make Wyatt Earp into an American hero, merely a legendary lawman whose reputation and family loyalty draw him into a feud that should never have started. Kilmer smirks and sneers as the impudent, Southern-educated rogue Doc Holliday, a consumptive gambler who takes to the square-shouldered Earp. In the process Kilmer steals the film from under Russell. Cosmatos is a blundering director, but the sets, the costumes, and the players are so good that they overcome the shapelessness of the film with sheer bravado. Bill Paxton and Sam Elliot play the Earp brothers and Boothe, Biehn, and Stephen Lang stand together on the other side of the lines drawn in the dirt streets. —*S. A.*

TRAINING DAY L: **BANG! (ACTION)/BANG! (ACTION)** (2001) 120M D: Antoine Fuqua. *Ethan Hawke, Denzel Washington, Tom Berenger, Harris Yulin, Snoop Dogg.* In order to join an elite narcotics squad, Hawke's LA cop must go on a ride-along with veteran cop Washington, a character modeled at least partially on the corrupt antigang unit involved in the LA Rampart Division scandal. The relationship between the two characters is interesting at first, with Washington pushing Hawke's buttons by doing things like smoking a joint while on duty, ridiculing him for being upset about it, then turning sweet and apologizing. Unfortunately, the plot veers into ridiculous racial fantasy when Hawke gets stuck in black and Hispanic neighborhoods, an experience presented as roughly equivalent to a big, juicy fish flopping around in a bear's den. Then he provides evidence that he's a cool white guy and suddenly everyone in the neighborhood becomes his guardian angel. Both Hawke and Washington are good until Washington turns into the villain and goes so over the top he spits. It's too bad Washington had to finally get his best actor Oscar from this and not *Malcolm X*, or even *He Got Game.* —*B.T.*

TRANSPORTER, THE L: **BANG! (ACTION)/BANG! (ACTION)** (2002) 92M D: Louis Leterrier, Corey Yuen. *Ric Young, Doug Rand, Jason Statham, Qi Shu, Matt Schulze, François Berléand.* There is nothing I hate more than a film that starts off cool, stylish, and swank and then pisses it all away. And that, alas, is exactly what *The Transporter* is. His job description is simple—transport anything, anywhere, for a price. He has three rules. Rule #1, once a deal is made, it cannot be altered or renegotiated. Rule #2, no names. Rule #3, never look in the package. But of course through a number of circumstances and curiosity, he breaks his own rule and looks in the package. This leads to a number of complications and disasters, events colliding one into another like dominoes tumbling down in a row. And it's great! He's a little amoral, a man who just wants to do his job and live his life peacefully and alone. Too bad the bad guys are dull and uninteresting villains with stupid evil plans, henchmen too numerous, incompetent, and without an ounce of interesting characterization in them. So here's my advice. Watch the movie for the first forty-eight minutes and then turn it off before it devolves into a mindless action film filled with clichés, overhyped fight scenes, and a pathetically redundant storyline that you've seen fifty times by now. —*M.N.*

I feel the reverse: I think it starts out terrible but somewhat makes up for it with some amusing fight scenes later on. It's more like *The Big Hit* than *To Catch a Thief*—how many times can filmmakers expect to impress us by having hit men or thieves who think of themselves as professionals and talk about their rules and codes all the time? It's not a novelty anymore, guys.

But at least there's a fight scene where he dumps a bunch of grease on the ground and uses it to slide around on the floor, and that means my ninety-two minutes weren't entirely wasted. *B.T.*

TRUCK TURNER L: **BANG! (ACTION)/BLAXPLOITATION** (1974) 91M D: Jonathan Kaplan. *Isaac Hayes, Yaphet Kotto.* Awkwardly directed, and Hayes as Truck is a little slower than all the other players, but this piece of blaxploitation zings nonetheless! Skip-tracer Hayes and his buddy track a wanted pimp they have to kill. This causes a tall blond with bouncing breasts to run out and stab the buddy. The madam who runs the pimp's stable of girls wants Truck dead and she offers the whole stable to the pimp, who brings Truck down. Ambushes and quite bloody shoot-outs follow and leave Truck still standing, so a wily SOB (Kotto) brings in pros. When they fail in a hospital shoot-out that is good and mean, Truck nails the escaping SOB in the back, giving Kotto a wonderfully long death scene. With friends hurt and some killed in place of him, the only thing left for Truck is to shoot the bitch-whore boss through the heart. The violence throughout is good and mean: bad and bloody as violence should be. One hard-ass good ride. —*J.C.*

TRUE ROMANCE L: **BANG! (ACTION)/BANG! (ACTION)** (1993) 120M D: Tony Scott. *Brad Pitt, Dennis Hopper, James Gandolfini, Christian Slater, Patricia Arquette, Christopher Walken.* Drawing not so subtly from all the great couple-on-the-run road movies (from *Bonnie and Clyde* to *Badlands*), Quentin Tarantino's raw, hip, and overly energetic script turns a good film into a great film. Slater and Arquette get mixed up with the wrong guys and things just keep getting worse as Tarantino's screenplay hints at the "genre cut and paste" that made *Pulp Fiction* the classic it is. Scott has never directed a finer film (*Top Gun* included!). —*C.P.*

VIGILANTE L: **BANG! (ACTION)/BANG! (ACTION)** (1983) 90M D: William Lustig. *Robert Forster, Don Blakely, Richard Bright, Fred Williamson, Rutanya Alda.* Forster is excellent in this B-movie spin on *Death Wish* about a blue-collar guy who turns reluctant rebel when the killer who murdered his child and assaulted his wife is set free by a corrupt judge. Forster, the almost-star of the late '60s turned exploitation film stalwart, has an everyman face and an easy assuredness on-screen; he comes off as just another working-class guy whose life is turned upside down and whose soul is put through the ringer after an unjust prison term (where guest star Woody Strode gives him the lessons of survival inside). Williamson costars as Forster's buddy who forms his own little vigilante unit that faces its own problems, such as targeting the wrong man. Director Lustig brings a little style to the rough, disturbing violence of the tough-minded, hard-edge, low-budget film, and a lot more ambivalence and complexity than any of the *Death Wish* films. —*S.A.*

VIKINGS, THE L: ADVENTURE/VIKINGS & MONGOLS (1958) 116M D: Richard Fleischer. *James Donald, Kirk Douglas, Alexander Knox, Tony Curtis, Janet Leigh, Ernest Borgnine.* Would you believe Curtis as Eric the Viking? The slave of King Ragnar (a lusty Borgnine having the time of his life) is not only the illegitimate heir to the British throne, he's the bastard son of Ragnar, and thus half brother to Viking Prince Douglas (Ragnar's only son in wedlock), his hated rival in the fight over princess Leigh. Silly? You bet: an absurd amount of bearskin melodrama and medieval conspiracy is packed into this gorgeously filmed blood and thunder adventure, but it is grand, goofy fun. Douglas grins a ferocious smile as he works his caveman seduction technique on Leigh, and snarls his threats to pretty boy Curtis after losing an eye to the scrappy little slave. Director Fleischer manages to keep a straight face through it all. The other star of the picture is cinematographer Jack Cardiff, who fills the screen with Technicolor splendor, from the lush blue waters and thick green forests of Norway to the homely castle to Britain's craggy windswept coast to the obligatory Viking funeral. —*S. A.*

WHERE EAGLES DARE L: WAR/WWII (1968) 155M D: Brian G. Hutton. *Clint Eastwood, Richard Burton, Michael Hordern, Mary Ure, Patrick Wymark.* Eastwood plays straight man and action sidekick to Burton in the WWII military caper concocted by Alistair MacLean, who made it his goal to make the most exciting, action-packed cliffhanger thriller to date. The story, about a seven-man team that parachutes into a castle deep in the Bavarian Alps to rescue an Allied officer, is less gritty and more swift than *The Dirty Dozen* and more coolly serious than *Kelly's Heroes*, with head games galore in the opening half and a nonstop escape in the second as they overcome one impossible situation after another while the Nazis give ferocious chase. Hutton directs with effective anonymity, providing breathless momentum in place of actual excitement but never letting up the pace. —*S. A.*

WISEGUY: SONNY STEELGRAVE AND THE MOB ARC L: BANG! (ACTION)/BANG/TV (1987) 11 Hours D: Various. *Ray Sharkey, Ken Wahl, Jonathan Banks, Robert Miranda, Jim Byrnes, Gianni Russo.* This late-'80s series revolved around the life of undercover cop Vinnie Terranova (Wahl), his cases, his family,

and his friends. But it was really all about the villains. *Wiseguy* had some of the most interesting and entertaining villains to be found on television, each with their own strengths and foibles, and played by some major names in Hollywood (Kevin Spacey and Tim Curry, to name a few). Made up primarily of story arcs with a few interspersed stand-alones, the series had an entertaining blend of characters, corruption, and the fine line between the criminal world and the legal one, where loyalties and boundaries are not always clear. This DVD set contains the first story arc and Vinnie's first case, where he goes undercover for the mob and against all odds (and the orders of his superiors) manages to insert himself as the right-hand man for Sonny Steelgrave, one of the leaders of the East Coast Mafia. Determined to do his job, Vinnie finds that getting that close to Steelgrave is more dangerous than he expected, and it's not only his life on the line. —*M. N.*

ZULU L: ADVENTURE/ADVENTURE (1964) 138M D: Cy Raker Endfield. *Michael Caine, Stanley Baker, Jack Hawkins, James Booth. Zulu* is an epic masterwork from director Endfield and unfortunately one of his last films. It tells the true tale of the Battle of Rorke's Drift, where a garrison of fewer than 150 British soldiers withstood a prolonged attack from well over 4,000 Zulu warriors. Lieutenants John Chard (Baker) and Gonville Bromhead (Caine) are faced with the impossible task of coordinating the defense of their lonely outpost from the encroaching Zulu horde. Chard is the experienced soldier, Bromhead new to his assignment, but they combine their wits and rally their disparate men to turn the Zulus back. This is one of the first roles for Caine, who was reportedly almost dismissed by Endfield for being too stiff. Yet Caine's acting wins through and his Lt. Bromhead is the perfectly reserved British soldier even when surrounded by the horror and confusion of the unending clash. Endfield makes the expansive South African veldt a grand backdrop for the well-coordinated battle scenes. The Zulus are not a faceless mob either. Endfield imparts a dignity and nobility to the warriors who fight with honor and skill as well as ferocity. *Zulu* is a stirring, sweeping tale and the direction and acting carry the story perfectly. —*G. M.*

CHAPTER FOUR

Comedy & Television Comedy

"D ying is easy. Comedy is difficult."

"Tragedy is when something horrible happens to you. Comedy is when it happens to someone else."

"Comedy is an escape, not from truth but from despair."

"The world is a comedy to those that think, a tragedy to those that feel."

Yeah yeah whatever... comedy makes you laugh. Some comedy comes cheap. (Soupy Sales takes a cream pie in the face.) Some comedy comes for a price. (You dress up in your best clothes for a glorious night at the snootiest nightclub in town, and you're there for tewnty-five minutes before someone points out that your fly is open and there's toilet paper stuck to your shoe.)

Ever since the first time ink hit paper, philosophers have written stacks and stacks of books pounding their minds to discover the roots and define the branches of what we all call "comedy." This is a very noble pursuit. But had these philosophers only pounded each other over the heads with their books....You get the idea.

Comedy peels back our illusions. Comedy bares truth. Whenever we get a little full of ourselves, whenever we get caught not looking at what's coming, whenever we start to get feelings of superiority, pride, desire, or whenever we get more than a little lazy about ourselves, comedy will be there to help right the ship.

Even so, it's all a matter of degree. Some comedy is high (*The Importance of Being Earnest*), some comedy is low (*Snow White and the Three Stooges*), and some low comedy

©ANCHOR BAY ENTERTAINMENT

Heathers (1989)

is high (*Dude, Where's My Car?*).

Whether Satire, Farce, Slapstick, Romantic Comedy, Comedy of Manners, Tragicomedy, Comedy of the Absurd, Parody, or Spoof, it all boils down to this: How much does it make you laugh, and how much does it reveal about our character? Comedy is humankind's safety valve: we should never get too serious about ourselves because comedy is lurking around the next corner, pie in hand.

So, fundamentally, this chapter is full of what came to our minds when we thought about what made us laugh, whichever and however it made us do it. We hope you enjoy these films as much as we did.

Note: The Comedy section is a catch-all

section by default. They are the "best (and worst) of the rest," you might say, as many of the best comedies are to be found in the Directors section. So, as is true anywhere, here there is a huge variance of quality in this section. Some of the films here are painfully bad and some are truly great, which basically means the section is great for browsing. How else would you find out that Harry Shearer's directorial debut was *The History of White People in America*?

Also, Comedy TV shows end up in our Television section; Stand-Up, Sketch Comedy, and Comedy Teams have their own sections; plus we distinguish Classic Comedy as those films made before the Motion Picture Arts and Sciences instituted its rating system (G, PG, R, NC17) in the late 1960s. Films produced by major studios are classified in Comedy; independently produced films are placed in our Independent Comedy section.

ABBOTT AND COSTELLO MEET FRANKENSTEIN L: COMEDY TEAMS/ABBOTT & COSTELLO (1948) 83M D: Charles Barton. *Bud Abbott, Lou Costello, Lon Chaney Jr., Bela Lugosi, Glenn Strange.* Abbott and Costello meet Frankenstein, Dracula, the Wolfman, and even the Invisible Man! Ooh, scary. Or just plain hilarious, and mighty convenient for the team that they happened to work at the same studio where all these monsters resided, providing themselves with some of the best comic inspiration of their long careers. The monsters (Dracula in particular) pursue a brain donor for Frankenstein's monster. Naturally, the target is the feeble-minded Costello. Lugosi and Chaney Jr. reprise their roles as Dracula and the Wolfman, respectively, though Boris Karloff's monster is here portrayed by Strange. Ironically, this is the only other film besides the original *Dracula* in which Lugosi actually played the big bad Count. —*M. S.*

ABOUT SCHMIDT L: COMEDY/COMEDY (2002) 124M D: Alexander Payne. *Jack Nicholson, Kathy Bates, Dermot Mulroney, Connie Ray, June Squib, Hope Davis.* Shortly after Warren Schmidt (Nicholson) retires from his nine-to-five job at an insurance company for which he's worked all his life, his wife Helen (Squib) very suddenly passes away, and Warren sinks into depression. Feeling like he has little to show for his life, he decides the best thing he can do is to keep his daughter Genie (Davis) from making the mistake of marrying a mulleted dysfunctional mattress salesman

(Mulroney). Throughout the movie, Warren's feelings are narrated through his correspondence with a child he is sponsoring in Tanzania, a relationship that ultimately defines Warren's happiness. Nicholson delivers an excellent performance as gloomy, tender Warren. The cinematography is great, the plot is slow and methodical, and the story is sentimental and sweet. This is one of my favorite films of 2002. —*J. S.*

ADAPTATION L: COMEDY/COMEDY (2002) 114M D: Spike Jonze. *Nicolas Cage, Chris Cooper, Meryl Streep, Brian Cox, Tilda Swinton.* When Charlie Kaufman was hired to adapt Susan Orlean's *The Orchid Thief*, he quickly realized he was not up to the task, and instead flipped out and submitted a script about trying to write the script with his fictional twin brother. That script was great, and Jonze turned it into a movie. Kaufman (Cage) is sweaty and neurotic, dedicated to making a smart, noncommercial movie, but not knowing how the hell to do that with a book about flowers. His twin brother Donald (also Cage) is more confident and better with women, but is a hack writer with horrible taste in movies based on bad Hollywood formulas. When Charlie lets Donald help him with his screenplay, the realistic world of *Adaptation* itself begins to turn into a Hollywood movie complete with drugs, sordid love affairs, and alligator attacks. Even with the bizarre meta-premise and so much cleverness on display, Kaufman has created a deeply personal story about relationships, self-image, and writer's block. Cooper won a well-deserved Supporting Actor Oscar for his role as John Laroche, the orchid thief of the book. —*B. T.*

AIRPLANE! L: COMEDY/COMEDY (1980) 88M D: Jerry Zucker, David Zucker, Jim Abrahams. *Leslie Nielsen, Robert Hayes, Julie Hagerty, Lloyd Bridges, Peter Graves.* The Zucker brothers's first big film spoofed the extremely tired '70s disaster film genre while propelling Nielsen's career as a remarkable comedian. The story, such as it is, concerns a former pilot (Hays) who must take the controls of an airplane after the cockpit crew is struck with food poisoning. Hays is instructed on how to land the plane by the most bizarre and inept air controllers imaginable. There is about one joke every ten seconds and dozens of surreal one-liners fans will chant for days after seeing this comedy classic. —*N. J.*

AIRPLANE 2: THE SEQUEL L: COMEDY/COMEDY (1982) 84M D: Ken Finkleman. *Robert Hayes, Julie Hagerty, Lloyd Bridges, William Shatner, Peter Graves.* This sequel is not by the Zucker brothers, nor does it feature Leslie Nielsen, but it is every bit as wall-to-wall funny as *Airplane*. Instead of a proper airplane, passengers board a space shuttle this time and head to the moon. Hays returns as the hero, this time to save the shuttle from a mad bomber (Sonny Bono). He is assisted by a starship commander (Shatner, of course), and a couple of crew members from TV's *Love Boat* provide on-board courtesy despite the tragedy. Great fun for all fans of disaster spoofs. —*N.J.*

ALL OF ME L: COMEDY/COMEDY (1984) 93M D: Carl Reiner. *Steve Martin, Lily Tomlin, Victoria Tennant.* Martin is one of the greatest physical comedians of all time and Tomlin is one of the most uniquely funny women in Hollywood. Together they starred in one of the biggest hits of 1984. The ultra-wealthy Mrs. Cutwater is a recluse who has found a way to transmit her soul into a younger body with the help of a spiritual dude and his magic bucket. Along the way her soul enters Mr. Cobb, and all hell breaks loose. Few actors have the physical ability of Martin—he belongs to a tradition that includes Don Knotts, Jerry Lewis, Michael Richards, and the guy who has done more to mainstream this brand of humor than anyone else, Jim Carrey. —*R.D.*

AMAZON WOMEN ON THE MOON L: COMEDY/COMEDY (1987) 85M D: John Landis, Joe Dante, Carl Gottlieb, Robert K. Weiss, Peter Horton. *Arsenio Hall, Michelle Pfeiffer, B. B. King, Steve Allen, Rosanna Arquette, Steve Guttenberg.* In the spirit of *The Kentucky Fried Movie, Amazon Women on the Moon* capitalizes on a variety of unrelated, utterly hysterical vignettes. For much of the film we are teased with glimpses of "regular programming" (the B-movie parody *Amazon Women on the Moon*), which is repeatedly interrupted by channel surfing. Ed Begley Jr. does well in an alleged bit from *Son of the Invisible Man*, giving more than a glimpse of the title character. Likewise, a stripper who considers herself an artist thinks she blends in splendidly at church wearing nothing but a purse and a string of pearls. The film is a delicious plate of appetizers rather than an entrée. —*N.J.*

AMERICAN GRAFFITI L: COMEDY/COMEDY (1973) 109M D: George Lucas. *Ron Howard, Candy Clark, Cindy Williams, Richard Dreyfuss, Harrison Ford, Wolfman Jack, Paul Le Mat.* Before catapulting into the stratosphere and beyond with all things *Star Wars*, Lucas cut his Hollywood teeth on this sweet, unassuming coming-of-age film set in 1962 centering on a bunch of California teens cavorting through pre-Vietnam America. There are more than a few similarities between *Graffiti* and *Star Wars*: both concern a bunch of drifting youths racing around in the dark and looking to escape the lame future ahead of them. Curt (Dreyfuss) chases a mystery girl with whom he's fallen in love after just one glimpse, much like Luke Skywalker chases after his fair princess. Both he and Steve (Howard) yearn, like Luke, to leave home for institutions of higher learning and adventure, and both sets of characters are watched over by an incredibly hirsute, hip daddy-o: Wolfman Jack (*American Graffiti*) and Chewbacca (*Star Wars*). The resemblance is striking. Lastly, both films earn their charm by innocently clunking along with these spunky

characters, having a boat-load of fun along the way. —*M.S.*

AMERICAN JOB L: COMEDY/INDEPENDENT COMEDY (1996) 90M D: Chris Smith. *Charlie Smith, Randy Russell, Tom Wheeler, Matt Collier.* This deadpan comedy from the director of *American Movie* follows an aimless worker on a self-defeating, self-perpetuating downward spiral from one atrocious minimum-wage job to another. Our poor hero works on an assembly line, suffers at a fast food restaurant, engages in phone soliciting, and cleans hotel rooms. Smith perfectly captures the tedium and awkwardness of dead-end jobs as well as strange co-workers and idiotic middle managers. Shot in the Midwest and using nonprofessional actors (Randy, the lead character, is especially spot-on), *American Job* moves along at a deliberate pace and is simultaneously stark, weird, realistic, provocative, and funny as hell. —*S.H.*

AMERICAN PRESIDENT, THE L: COMEDY/COMEDY (1995) 113M D: Rob Reiner. *Michael Douglas, Annette Bening, Martin Sheen, Richard Dreyfuss, Michael J. Fox, Samantha Mathis.* Everyone loves a good fantasy movie, but everyone has a different definition of fantasy. I like to fantasize about a world in which the government doesn't make me cringe. So when I need to escape frustrations with politics, I often watch *The American President*. Douglas plays Andrew Shepard, a widowed president smitten with environmental lobbyist Sydney Ellen Wade (Bening). As Shepard woos her, his approval rating plummets, his policies fall apart, and his staff turns against him. Everyone tries to talk him out of falling in love because it isn't politically savvy. Shepard's character gets picked apart, especially by Republican challenger Bob Rumson, played with subtle wickedness by Dreyfuss. When it appears the two lovers are doomed to succumb to political pressures, Shepard strikes with a classic Sorkin speech telling everyone to get off his back. I still smile and get a little teary every time I watch it. That's the kind of president I dream about. —*J.K.*

ANDY KAUFMAN: I'M FROM HOLLYWOOD L: COMEDY/STAND-UP COMEDY (1992) 60M D: Lynn Margulies, Joe Orr. *Jerry Lawler, Andy Kaufman.* Archival footage and latter-day interviews chronicle Kaufman's legendary stint as a professional wrestler. Known to most at the time as a star of *Taxi*, Kaufman began wrestling women and making outrageously sexist comments in his post-match interviews. This led to a feud with an actual pro-wrestler, Jerry "The King" Lawler, with Kaufman playing the spoiled Hollywood villain who, instead of threatening bodily harm, threatens to sue. The clips of Kaufman's interviews are classic; he put such a good spin on the villain-you-love-to-hate that most people thought he was for real, even when he was kicking an unconscious woman, yelling, "It doesn't matter, she's poor, she doesn't have money, she can't sue me! I can do anything

Screwball Comedy

In the grim, dark times following the Great Depression of 1929, when poverty, hunger, rootlessness, suicide, and fear gripped America, the country needed a good laugh, and the movies provided it. Some of Hollywood's best writers, directors, and performers responded to America's sad and sour mood with films that were like effervescent champagne cocktails. Movies about brides and heiresses who run away from responsibility, everyday guys and gals who strike it rich through no effort of their own, and wealthy folks who lose fortunes and find that there are plenty of compensations in just being alive.

In days of desperate scarcity, money was a key theme, and screwball comedies had a field day portraying wealthy families as motley conglomerations of spoiled, irresponsible, foolishly eccentric people with superficial values who could scarcely tie their own shoelaces. The simple conclusion: money is wasted on the rich, as the classic *My Man Godfrey* (1936) plainly

shows. But if you're a wholesome working girl with a good head on your shoulders, like Jean Arthur in *Easy Living* (1937), then somehow it seems only right that, while riding in an open-topped bus, a fur coat should fall from the sky and land on your head. And that every merchant in New York should mistake you for a tycoon's mistress and ensconce you in a penthouse with all the trimmings.

Even when the rich were shown to be fools and rogues, viewers got vicarious comfort from visiting all their glittering townhouses, ocean liner staterooms, upstate ski lodges, opulent ballrooms, and private train dining cars for a few hours. Screwball comedy was born in the high-art era of black-and-white cinematography, when cameramen were capable of rendering flashy cars, fizzing cocktails, and Jean Harlow's slinky gowns in dazzling silver light. And screwball comedies overflow with the luscious curves and elegant geometries of art moderne and art deco interiors and objects.

The allure of money and the tension between the haves and have-nots were important to screwball comedy, but the

---

I want!" The documentary itself is intentionally deceptive. It later became common knowledge that Lawler and Kaufman were friends and coconspirators. In *I'm from Hollywood*, however, Lawler plays along as if he really hated Kaufman and wanted to punish him for degrading professional wrestling. I think Robin Williams is playing along in his interviews too, but Tony Danza seems to genuinely not get it. —*B. T.*

ANIMAL, THE L: COMEDY/COMEDY (2001) 84M D: Luke Greenfield. *Rob Schneider, Norm Macdonald, Adam Sandler, Colleen Haskell, John C. Mcginley, Ed Asner.* If you watch this particular Schneider movie first, you might be disappointed. He's an easy target for critics and even *South Park*. The only drawback to Schneiders's films are the plots are almost too ridiculous to sink your teeth into. If he could put together a comedy with a little more substance, I think it would really take off. Watch *Deuce Bigelow* or *The Hot Chick* first; if those make you laugh, you probably will find

The Animal good enough to howl over. My favorite part comes at the end, when Macdonald plays a disgruntled, angry-mob enthusiast who travels around looking for new mobs to join—regardless of what they're after. —*R. D.*

ARTHUR L: COMEDY/COMEDY (1981) 117M D: Steve Gordon. *Liza Minnelli, Dudley Moore, Geraldine Fitzgerald, John Gielgud, Jill Eikenberry.* Arthur Bach (Moore) is a millionaire who has nothing to do with his life but drive around town creating chaos and drinking everything in sight. His faithful butler Hobson (Gielgud) tidies up after him with witty remarks and a caring heart. Arthur is destined to marry Susan (Eikenberry), from another wealthy family, but that plan is derailed when he meets Linda (Minnelli), a "nobody-from-Queens" waitress. Then tragedy strikes and Arthur is forced to sober (and grow) up. Moore makes a loveable sot, Minnelli is true to her character, and, with his Oscar-winning performance, the amazing Gielgud proves he can play comedy

films' primal driving force was the battle of the sexes. And we do mean battle, for in these pictures men and women most often express their strong feelings for each other through active hostility. A contrary attitude escalates to traded wisecracks, hurled insults, and thrown objects aimed at heads: surely it must be love.

Emotions that we all can empathize with are expressed with an outrageous intensity and in an almost surrealistically different-from-normal form. How many of us, as in *Bringing Up Baby* (1938), are a stuffy paleontologist who've had our prize dinosaur bone stolen by a wire-haired terrier and spend our days and nights with a daffy heiress chasing a runaway leopard that likes to have "I Can't Give You Anything But Love" sung to it? We feel Cary Grant's frustration, anger, and utter exasperation as Katharine Hepburn puts him through endless trials that only increase in absurdity. In the end he realizes that he can't escape this female force of nature, so he gives up. And, almost like magic, he realizes that Hepburn has liberated him from his ossified, overly controlled existence and awakened him to the spontaneous thrill of unexpected love and sheer fun.

Screwball comedy poses an existential question. If normal, logical, sane life gives us ulcers, wars, economic catastrophes, and emotional and sexual repression—why be rational and sensible? These films show us that a devil-may-care outlook, witty repartee, moonstruck romance, and loony behavior are vibrant, spirit-freeing expressions of the life force, and that a happy dose of craziness keeps us truly sane.

Times changed, though. With World War II came the Holocaust and the horrifying first use of nuclear weapons, obliterating the late-1930s sense that the world could be fixed and stay fixed. Funny films became more sober and earthbound, less insouciant, sophisticated, and deliriously wacky. But mix a martini anyway, because the golden legacy of the screwball comedy era lives on.

Fifteen more beauties: *It Happened One Night* (1934), *The Thin Man* (1934), *Twentieth Century* (1934), *Mr. Deeds Goes to Town* (1936), *Theodora Goes Wild* (1936), *The Awful Truth* (1937), *Nothing Sacred* (1937), *Holiday* (1938), *You Can't Take It with You* (1938), *His Girl Friday* (1940), *The Philadelphia Story* (1940), *The Lady Eve* (1941), *The Major and the Minor* (1942), *The Palm Beach Story* (1942), and *The More the Merrier* (1943).

—*Greg Olson*

---

every bit as well as he can classical drama. The script is full of classic scenes, such as Arthur's drunken conversation with a mounted moose head. —*J.K.*

AT WAR WITH THE ARMY L: COMEDY TEAMS/MARTIN & LEWIS (1950) 93M D: Hal Walker. *Dean Martin, Polly Bergen, Jerry Lewis, Mike Kellin, Jimmie Dundee.* In this early film from the famous comedy team, Martin plays a sergeant and Lewis plays a dim-witted, lowly private. As the two get to know each other, they decide to put together a comedy act. Everything this private does goes wrong somehow. The funniest moment finds Lewis in drag, wearing a low-cut dress with lots of chest hair exposed. Complete with a horrible wig, he does a very convincing Marlene Dietrich. The comedy routine by Martin and Lewis at the end is also quite good, likely taken from material they'd already performed for live audiences. —*N.J.*

AUSTIN POWERS: INTERNATIONAL MAN OF MYSTERY L: COMEDY/COMEDY (1997) 89M D: Jay Roach. *Mike Myers, Elizabeth Hurley, Ron Kuby, Michael York, Robert Wagner, Seth Green, Mimi Rogers.* It's hard to think of this movie apart from its catch phrases, but the truth is it was a nice surprise from Myers, who hadn't done much of interest since his *Saturday Night Live* days. The fish-out-of-water premise ('60s-swinger secret agent gets revived in the '90s and tries to continue his free-loving, sexual-harassing ways) is a good vehicle for his style of humor and for Roach's throwback to colorful spy films such as the Flint series. But the real kicker is Myers's other character, the supervillain Dr. Evil. His confusion over inflation and his idea for sharks with lasers on their heads are priceless. —*B.T.*

AUSTIN POWERS: THE SPY WHO SHAGGED ME L: COMEDY/COMEDY (1999) 95M D: Jay Roach. *Mike Myers, Seth Green, Heather Graham, Rob Lowe, Verne*

Troyer. The first *Austin Powers* film did not do particularly well in theaters, but became a cult hit on video. New Line decided to make a sequel with a bigger budget. It follows some of the ideas from the Bond series like having a different love interest (Graham), and a colorful new villain (Myers, wearing a fat suit, as Fat Bastard). The film does not have a strong comedic premise, reprising some of the same innuendos and catch phrases from the first film, relying too much on fat jokes, farting, and shit-eating. However, there is one very inspired bit of insanity that makes it all worthwhile: the introduction of Troyer as Dr. Evil's Oompa Loompa–like undersized clone Mini Me (a riff on Nelson de la Rosa's character Magi in the 1997 version of *Island of Dr. Moreau*). —B. T.

AUSTIN POWERS IN GOLDMEMBER L: COMEDY/COMEDY
(2002) 94M D: Jay Roach. *Mike Myers, Verne Troyer, Seth Green, Beyoncé Knowles.* Myers was funny on *Saturday Night Live*, but he got stuck in a pattern of repeating himself, every character built on an accent and an often nonsensical catch phrase. By the time he was playing Linda Richman, a not even remotely funny character based on his mother-in-law, and even talking about turning her into a movie, it seemed clear that he had gone insane and could never be trusted to make us laugh again. The first *Austin Powers* was a much needed revival, but the sequels (while certainly amusing at times) show he's up to his old tricks again. Each time he follows the same formula, repeating the same jokes and lines and adding a new villain with heavy makeup and a European accent. This time it's Goldmember, a flaky-skinned, Dutch roller-disco freak with the self-conscious catch phrase, "I'm Dutch. Isn't that veird?" Though a weak installment, it is nice to see Green taking his Scott Evil character to its logical conclusion, and Knowles does a great young Pam Grier imitation as Foxxy Cleopatra ("You're under arrest, sugah!") —B. T.

BABY BOOM L: COMEDY/COMEDY (1987) 103M D: Charles
Shyer. *Diane Keaton, Harold Ramis, Sam Shepard, Sam Wanamaker, James Spader.* I'm confused. The film begins with narration telling women they have the power to succeed in the working world without worrying about the pressures of being "incomplete" because they don't have children. J. C. Wyatt (Keaton, always wonderful no matter how mediocre the movie is, and I sat through *The Other Sister* so I should know) is a New York corporate "tiger lady" who works eighty hours a week and shares a stark apartment with her equally frigid boyfriend. She inherits a baby and immediately loses her footing on the corporate ladder. Wyatt struggles to raise her new daughter among yuppie snobs who look upon children as either the enemy or a clone of their evil ideals. She eventually chucks it all and moves out to the country, meets a hot veterinarian, and succeeds in her own right. The movie implies that it's OK

to have a career, but wouldn't you be much better off having a kid and a man, too? You can do it, and your life will be enriched. Oh, OK. —J. K.

BAD NEWS BEARS L: COMEDY/COMEDY (1976) 102M D:
Michael Ritchie. *Ben Piazza, Erin Blunt, Chris Barnes II, Tatum O'Neal, Walter Matthau, Vic Morrow.* They just don't make kids' movies like this anymore. The Bad News Bears are a misfit bunch of Little Leaguers who can barely catch a ball. Matthau is an alcoholic, ex-minor league pitcher who gets a whole lot more than he bargained for when he decides to coach the team. In one scene Matthau gets so wasted during practice he actually passes out on the mound, leaving the kids to their own mischief. The Bears appear to have no hope of winning the pennant, let alone making it through one inning, until Matthau recruits a couple of ringers, an eleven-year-old girl with a killer screwball and the rebel kid she helps convince to join the team. I loved this movie as a kid, but parents should be warned that Matthau's alcoholism, a major part of his character, never gets addressed. There are also many racist comments by the tough little character, Tanner, who will fight anything, including the entire seventh grade. —R. D.

BAD NEWS BEARS IN BREAKING TRAINING L: COMEDY/
COMEDY (1977) 99M D: Michael Pressman. *William Devane, Jackie Earle Haley, Jimmy Baio, Chris Barnes II, Clifton James.* In the first *Bad News Bears* sequel, the Little League team continues its underdog-to-champion tradition. With the help of Haley's character Kelly Leak (and his motorcycle), the Bears run off their new drill sergeant coach after he writes "ASSUME" on the chalkboard and says, "Never assume anything or you might make an 'ass' out of 'u' and 'me.'" With the help of a groundskeeper posing as coach, the kids con their parents into letting them take an unchaperoned road trip to the Houston Astrodome to play the undefeated Toros. While in Houston, Kelly recruits his father, who left him when he was five, to coach the Bears, all the while trying to reconcile their relationship. The cast of the Bears changed a little and I was sad to see the tomboy pitcher not return. She was replaced by Jimmy Baio, who looks and sounds a lot like Paris Themmen (*Wonka*'s Mike Teevee.) —R. D.

BAD NEWS BEARS GO TO JAPAN L: COMEDY/COMEDY
(1978) 102M D: John Berry. *Tony Curtis, Tomisaburo Wakayama, Jackie Earle Haley, Antonio Inoki.* I was really disappointed with the third installment of the *Bad News Bears* trilogy. My main gripe is with Curtis. He plays a money hungry, swindling coach who continually lies and disappoints the Bears. The underdog-to-champion formula gets sorely diluted with way too many political tangents and not enough charm. In 1979 Bill Murray was making *Meatballs*; why the hell wasn't he in this movie? —R. D.

BEING JOHN MALKOVICH L: COMEDY/INDEPENDENT COMEDY (1999) 112M D: Spike Jonze. *John Malkovich, Catherine Keener, Cameron Diaz, John Cusack.* Too weird to win any Oscars, this triumph of mad hatter creativity is a devastatingly funny portrait of human sadness and desperation. Cusack's puppet master finds the ultimate marionette when he enters the cranium of John Malkovich through a mysterious portal (kudos to Malkovich for being such a good sport) and finds himself battling a veritable army of souls seeking eternal life and true love, willing to sacrifice anything or anyone to get it. What better way to explore the vicious things we do for love than through laughter? Jonze and screenwriter Charlie Kaufman so richly visualize this world that the fantastic (and happily unexplained) details take on a wild life of their own. —*S. A.*

BELA LUGOSI MEETS A BROOKLYN GORILLA L: CLASSIC COMEDY/CLASSIC COMEDY (1952) 74M D: William Beaudine. *Bela Lugosi, Sammy Petrillo, Duke Mitchell.* When two jackasses (who are really bad clones of Martin and Lewis) land on the mysterious tropical island of Cola-Cola, they become subjects of the mad Dr. Zabor's terrible experiments in evolution. Jealous of Mitchell for hooking up with the chief's beautiful daughter, Lugosi turns him into an ape. This brings up many questions worth probing, but the biggest and most pertinent is "What ever happened to the ape-on-the-loose movies?" I'm not talking about cute and funny monkeys like *Monkeys Go Home* or *Dunston Checks In.* I mean big, scary, hairy fucking apes! Everything from *Murders in the Rue Morgue* to *King Kong* to *Planet of the Apes* to *The Beast That Killed Women* fully exploited the storytelling potential of apes. After all, as this film shows us, the line between beast and man is woefully thin. Bring back the ape movie! And not that Disney *Mighty Joe Young* crap either. —*T. S.*

BEST IN SHOW L: COMEDY/COMEDY (2000) 90M D: Christopher Guest. *Christopher Guest, Jay Brazeau, Eugene Levy, Catherine O'Hara, Parker Posey, Fred Willard, Michael Hitchcock.* It's time again for the Philadelphia Mayflower Kennel Club Dog Show, and there is no shortage of colorful, crazy characters to compete for the coveted title of Best in Show. The action covers everything from the competitors' preparations for the trip to Philadelphia through the final moment when one lucky dog gets the giant trophy and blue ribbon. Throughout, we follow the trials, tribulations, and over-the-top zaniness of owners and their champions-in-waiting dogs. Among the human hopefuls are the trophy wife of an ancient invalid, an uptight couple straight out of L. L. Bean, a flamboyant gay pair who pack eight kimonos for the trip, and a suburban couple whose female half finds old boyfriends everywhere they stop. Guest is the master of the mockumentary, and this one is not to be missed. —*J. S.*

BETTER OFF DEAD L: COMEDY/COMEDY (1985) 97M D: Savage Steve Holland. *John Cusack, David Ogden Stiers, Kim Darby, Demian Slade, Scooter Stevens, Diane Franklin, Curtis Armstrong.* This well-received 1980s Cusack film transcends teen genre boundaries and is equally enjoyed by adults. Full of charm and inventiveness, *Better Off Dead* offers accessible themes of popularity, dating, parenting, social structures, and rejection. Lane (Cusack) loses his girlfriend and with her his reason for living, until a beautiful French foreign exchange student persuades him to get off his ass and win her back. Lane must challenge the local skiing legend (who stole his girl) to a difficult, near-suicidal downhill race. In the process, Lane slowly discovers how great this new girl is and falls head over heels for her. If you like to own movies, your '80s collection would be severely lacking without this treasure. —*R. D.*

BIG L: COMEDY/COMEDY (1988) 98M D: Penny Marshall. *Tom Hanks, John Heard, Robert Loggia, Elizabeth Perkins.* I do not like Marshall much as a director, but it's hard not to like this film, largely because of Hanks, who lives and breathes the thirteen-year-old boy into whom he evolves. Marshall, at this time in her career, was still capable of understatement and does a fine job bringing sweetness and sadness to the story of a boy who wants to grow up fast, and does physically, if not mentally. *Big* also benefits from the lovely camerawork of Barry Sonnenfeld who, like Marshall, once used his talents well but then grew up to be a ham-handed director of crap. Come to think of it, wouldn't it be swell if those two just kinda jumped into the film and stayed young, just like Hanks's character? The world would be spared the viewings of *Wild Wild West* and *Renaissance Man*! —*M. S.*

BIG TROUBLE L: COMEDY/COMEDY (2002) 85M D: Barry Sonnenfeld. *Tim Allen, Stanley Tucci, Johnny Knoxville, Jason Lee, Dennis Farina, Rene Russo, Tom Sizemore.* Director Sonnenfeld returns to *Get Shorty* territory with this smart-alecky, rat-a-tat crime comedy based on the debut novel by humorist Dave Barry. Allen and Russo headline a sprawling cast of cartoonish characters tangled in a story of a corporate sleaze (Tucci) who embezzles from the mob, a hit man (Farina) hired to knock him off, idiot street thugs (Sizemore and Knoxville), a ticking atomic bomb, and an airport security staff manned by rejects from the Keystone Kops. This film has nothing to do with terrorism, but jokes about a bomb smuggled through airport security got *Big Trouble* delayed from its original post-9/11 release date. The inventive farce plays like a tongue-in-cheek Elmore Leonard caper without the edge or danger. Funny and harmless, this brisk screwball thriller is as substantial as a tub of popcorn with extra butter. Lee is our dippy conarrator, a corn-chip-munching hippie who lives in a tree and compares the story to the tale of Noah. —S. A.

BILL AND TED'S BOGUS JOURNEY L: COMEDY/COMEDY
(1991) 98M D: Peter Hewitt. *Keanu Reeves, William Sadler, Pam Grier, George Carlin, Joss Ackland, Alex Winter.* Far superior to the original, *Bill and Ted's Bogus Journey* is an endlessly inventive film. Don't believe me? Our wannabe rockstars, saviors of the future, and borderline-retarded heroes, Bill S. Preston Esq. and Ted Theodore Logan, are murdered by evil robot doubles from the future. They "melvin" Death (a most excellent performance by Sadler), end up in hell, defeat Death at Battleship, Clue, Electronic Football, and Twister, swing up to heaven, meet a brilliant Martian scientist, and pop back to Earth and build good robots to kill the evil ones, just in time for the Battle of the Bands and to save all mankind. Still not convinced? Well, you're no fun anyway. I don't know why I'm even talking to you. —K. C.

BLAST FROM THE PAST L: COMEDY/COMEDY (1999) 111M
D: Hugh Wilson. *Brendan Fraser, Alicia Silverstone, Christopher Walken, Sissy Spacek, Dave Foley.* This very silly movie is a surprisingly witty, charming, and entertaining little flick. Walken is an engineering genius with great paranoia. One day while in his massive fallout shelter (an exact replica of his home), an airplane crashes into his house. Fearing that war has broken out, Walken seals himself and his pregnant wife (Spacek) inside to protect them from nuclear fallout. Thirty-five years later the parents send their son (Fraser) out to collect enough provisions to keep them going. Naturally, wacky hijinks ensue. Fraser is great as a sweet, innocent young man who knows nothing of the real world and was raised with all sorts of good old-fashioned manners. This sweet romantic comedy really holds its own, though it gets a little tiresome toward the end, with a predictable freakout when Fraser tells the truth about himself. Still, it's fun, playful, and a lot better written than I would normally give something like this credit for. —M. N.

An overqualified cast is wasted on a brainless, unbelievable love story between one-dimensional characters. Walken portrays a commie-fearing nutcase who has driven his wife to alcoholism. The '50s sitcom values with which he's brainwashed his poor son are supposed to be a shining beacon of light in the ill-mannered '90s, causing women to fall to his feet giggling and Foley to stare at him in awe as he explains the importance of etiquette. The one actor not above the material is Silverstone, who was so great in *Clueless* but is completely unconvincing here as a bitchy LA fashion maven who—for no other reason than to accidentally meet Fraser's character—works in a baseball card shop! From the director of *Police Academy*, by the way.—B. T.

BOB ROBERTS L: COMEDY/INDEPENDENT COMEDY (1992)
105M D: Tim Robbins. *Tim Robbins, Alan Rickman, Gore Vidal, Jack Black, Giancarlo Esposito, Ray Wise.* Bob Roberts (Robbins) is a folk singer who rebelled against his hippie parents by becoming an extreme right-wing nut. The movie takes the form of a campaign documentary/concert film as Roberts runs for the Senate. Many observant points are made about politics as show business, dirty campaigning, and the co-option of the counterculture. Esposito (as an underground journalist) and Vidal (as the Democratic incumbent) occasionally verge on tipping Robbins's political cards, but otherwise this is a very effective satire. Roberts's creepy right-wing folk songs are dead on, right down to the smarmy smile he gives as he sings the jokey lines. Black is hilarious in his first screen role (playing one of three young Republicans obsessed with Roberts). The movie is also eerily similar to the later, actual documentary *A Perfect Candidate*. In order to live up to his liberal reputation, Robbins included on the DVD an audio track with Alexander Cockburn and Jeffrey St. Clair of CounterPunch discussing not the movie, but the history of Iran/Contra and CIA drug smuggling. —B. T.

BOEING BOEING L: CLASSIC COMEDY/CLASSIC COMEDY
(1965) 102M D: John Rich. *Jerry Lewis, Tony Curtis, Thelma Ritter, Christiane Schmidtmer, Dany Saval, Suzanna Leigh.* Rapid improvements in jet travel are cramping the style of an American reporter (Curtis) in Paris. The three stewardesses with whom he's involved are getting more and more difficult to keep apart. With the newer, faster Boeing planes, they are showing up at his apartment more quickly and more often. Even his maid (Ritter) is losing patience with covering up for him. Eventually, while meeting one fiancée and avoiding another, he bumps into a fellow reporter (Lewis), who would like a place to stay in Paris. Naturally this brings out some very broad humor from the excellent combination of Lewis and Curtis. —N. J.

BOWFINGER L: COMEDY/COMEDY (1999) 97M D: Frank Oz.
Steve Martin, Eddie Murphy, Heather Graham, Christine Baranski. Martin has come a long way since *The Jerk*, but his best work in the past ten years has been his screenplays. *Bowfinger* is a loving lampoon in the vein of *Ed Wood*, the story of a ridiculous ploy by a wannabe filmmaker (a calmly cartoonish Martin) to put Hollywood's biggest action star in his movie without him ever knowing. Murphy is all bravado, masking raging paranoia as superstar Kit Ramsey, but his heart is in the geeky Jif, a fast food fry cook and Ramsey look-alike who just wants to be one of the gang. Oz mixes the insider gags with absurd visual jokes and outrageous show-biz clichés and comes up with a Mickey and Judy film for the cinema-savvy '90s, cynical and romantic all at once. "Hey kids, let's put on a show. I know

TV series we wish were on DVD

THE ADVENTURES OF PETE AND PETE

ALFRED HITCHCOCK PRESENTS

BATMAN *(1960s)*

CHIC-A-GO-GO

LOUIS THEROUX'S WEIRD WEEKENDS
(region 1 version)

MAX HEADROOM

MISFITS OF SCIENCE

THE MUNSTERS

NIGHT GALLERY

POLICE SQUAD!

SQUARE PEGS

SUPERMAN: THE ANIMATED SERIES

WILD, WILD WEST

where Kit Ramsey is having lunch and I can borrow a camera!" —*S. A.*

Yeah, but it's the poor man's *Ed Wood.* The only thing sadder than *this* being one of Martin's best movies in years is watching a satire based more on leftover clichés from other comedies than on the reality it is supposedly skewering. The kung fu movie parody at the end, for example, suggests that Martin and friends have lost track of the past twenty years of filmmaking. It's nice to see Murphy playing a role without heavy makeup or fart jokes, but nothing in *Bowfinger* ever rises above mediocrity.—*B. T.*

BOX OF MOONLIGHT L: COMEDY/INDEPENDENT COMEDY (1996) 111M D: Tom DiCillo. *John Turturro, Sam Rockwell, Catherine Keener, Lisa Blount, Dermot Mulroney.* This is a real funny and uplifting movie about a stuffy guy from the city who learns how to let loose when he meets a carefree soul from the forest. Turturro plays Al, the anal-retentive electrical engineer who gets sidetracked by the crazy Kid (Rockwell). It turns out the Kid is lonely and does anything to get Al to stay with him for a couple more days, including sabotaging his rental car. Al is always in a hurry and wants to get back to his normal life, but the Kid finally starts chipping away Al's prudish layers and helps him really start living. Very sweet and positive. —*R. D.*

BREAKFAST CLUB, THE L: COMEDY/COMEDY (1985) 97M D: John Hughes. *Judd Nelson, Ally Sheedy, Molly Ringwald, Anthony Michael Hall, Paul Gleason, Emilio Estevez.* This entire movie takes place in a high school library where five students are spending their day in Saturday detention. The spectrum of the high school class system is represented by the group: Claire (Ringwald) is a popular prom queen-type, Allison (Sheedy) is an odd outcast, Brian (Hall) is a nerd, Andrew (Estevez) is a jock, and John (Nelson) is a bad-boy rebel. At first glance it appears they have nothing in common. As the day progresses, however, their differences melt away to show they are more similar than they first believed. One of John Hughes's more serious films, *The Breakfast Club* is extremely well-acted, especially by Estevez and Hall. While it is far from action-packed, the dialogue is excellent and interactions are tender and realistic. The exploration of social structure is as relevant now as it was when this film was first released. —*J. S.*

BRING IT ON! L: COMEDY/COMEDY (2000) 99M D: Peyton Reed. *Kirsten Dunst, Jesse Bradford, Eliza Dushku, Clare Kramer.* Dunst is captain of her cheerleading squad, national champions for several years running. She is shocked to learn, from a new girl on the squad, that all their award-winning cheers have been stolen from the Clovers, a squad from a high school in Compton. What follows is ninety-nine minutes of crap in which Dunst and her fellow cheerleaders bust their asses to prove that they can come up with original material and still be the best. The characters are clichéd and flat, the dialogue contrived and trite. However, portions of the movie showing the cheerleading competitions are pretty impressive, and there are a few moments that caused me to laugh in spite of myself. The short skirts and shiny hair will have young boys drooling all over themselves, while the rest of us wonder why it is we're watching this movie in the first place. —*J. S.*

BRINGING DOWN THE HOUSE L: COMEDY/COMEDY (2002) 105M D: Adam Shankman. *Steve Martin, Queen Latifah, Eugene Levy, Joan Plowright, Jean Smart.* Martin plays Peter, a lonely upper-class schmo who meets Charlene (Latifah) on the Internet. Peter thinks she is the woman of his dreams. When he meets her in person, however, Charlene turns out to be an escaped convict who wants to use him to get her record cleaned of a crime she didn't commit. The rest of the movie is basically your typical fluffy comedy with crazy anecdotes and a happy ending. I really didn't like this movie. Much of the "humor" is built entirely around negative racial stereotypes. It's offensive, and parts of the film that could have been endearing, such as the interaction between Latifah and Levy, are completely negated by the messages this film sends about African-Americans. I wasn't expecting much from this movie, but I got even less. —*J. S.*

BUBBLE BOY L: COMEDY/COMEDY (2001) 84M D: Blair Hayes. *Jake Gyllenhaal, Swoozie Kurtz, Marley Shelton, Danny Trejo, John Carroll Lynch.* Gyllenhaal has done a lot of cool movies lately, like the awesome *Donnie Darko*. *Bubble Boy*, made the same year, is severely underrated. Anyone, I believe, would enjoy its charm. The plot concerns Jimmy (Gyllenhaal), who falls in love for the first time and runs away from home across country to be with his new love. After being trapped in a germ-controlled bubble environment his whole life, he has a lot to learn about the real world. Luckily Jimmy is so likeable he gets help along the way from some odd allies, including carnival freaks. I love the part when he gets all excited just to step in dog crap. This was as funny as *Dumb and Dumber* and as charming as *Election*. Two cheers for fun, lighthearted comedies. —*R. D.*

BUFFY THE VAMPIRE SLAYER L: COMEDY/COMEDY (1992) 98M D: Fran Rubel Kuzui. *Kristy Swanson, Luke Perry, Paul Reubens, Donald Sutherland, Rutger Hauer.* An airhead cheerleader (Swanson)—the type that often was the victim in bad '80s horror films—finds out she's the chosen one and must fulfill her destiny to fight off vampires. There was a time when it seemed weird that they were making a TV series of this movie, but after seven years of the TV series it seems weird that it all started with *this*. Apparently the script was written as a serious horror movie with comic undertones, but was directed by Kuzui as a comedy not meant to be taken seriously on any level. Ironically, while screenwriter Joss Whedon instilled a more dramatic horror tone in the series, he also had a much funnier cast and better sense of comic timing. If you've seen the TV show, the movie only really works as an oddity, a rough draft where vampires fly like *Lost Boys* and the heroine isn't very smart. Still, there are some good moments, such as a famously long death scene for Reubens's character, and when Buffy dares him to clap even though he only has one arm. —*B. T.*

BULL DURHAM L: COMEDY/COMEDY (1988) 108M D: Ron Shelton. *Kevin Costner, Susan Sarandon, Tim Robbins, Robert Wuhl, Trey Wilson.* Baseball and lust mix amiably in this comedy about a fireballing minor-league pitcher (Robbins), a seasoned catcher (Costner) brought in to tutor him, and a baseball groupie (Sarandon) who has her eye on both of them. Director Shelton, typically a sure hand at sports comedies, does some of his best work here, adding layers of baseball texture on top of deft performances by his cast. Robbins is satisfyingly goofy, but it's Costner's wise catcher and Sarandon's cagey fan who create the film's sparks. The baseball bits are perfect, including an obligatory grizzled manager and a mound conference that veers hilariously off topic. You don't have to love baseball to like *Bull Durham*, but it probably will help. —*T. P.*

BULWORTH L: COMEDY/COMEDY (1998) 107M D: Warren Beatty. *Warren Beatty, Halle Berry, Don Cheadle, Oliver Platt, Paul Sorvino.* This political satire is almost admirable. Beatty plays a senator who, after days without sleep, snaps and starts telling the truth. The trouble comes when he decides to start rapping. The only thing more excruciating than his microphone skills is the condescending treatment of the black supporting characters. Two interns follow him around worshipfully, waving their arms in the air and playing beats on handheld tape decks. At the end Berry actually tells him, "You my nigga." Guaranteed to induce squirms. Somehow Beatty got poet Amiri Baraka to play a supporting role, and the movie cleverly combines an Ennio Morricone score with classic angry hip hop songs. —*B. T.*

CABIN BOY L: COMEDY/COMEDY (1994) 81M D: Adam Resnick. *Chris Elliot, Andy Richter, Ritch Brinkley, Brian Doyle-Murray.* Elliot plays Nathaniel Mayweather, a prissy, wig-wearing "fancy lad" asshole who, fresh out of finishing school, mistakenly boards a fishing boat called "The Filthy Whore" thinking it's a novelty cruise ship. He's lived a ridiculously pampered life (he's never broken a sweat before and screams at the sight of a bunny), so the fishermen throw cans at him and make him wash the boat with his tongue ("It tastes oddly like marzipan!") before the film drifts into a surreal riff on Sinbad movies. In the dangerous Hell's Bucket region the crew encounter a half man/half shark named Chocki (Russ Tamblyn), a tobacco-spitting cupcake, and a working-class giant (Mike Starr) who complains, "All I sold today was an electric toothbrush to a flyin' leprechaun." Widely hated at the time, even by people who liked Elliot's show, *Get A Life*, perhaps because the protagonist is such a complete jackass. But let's be honest, this is one of the funniest and most visually interesting comedies of its decade. —*B. T.*

CABLE GUY, THE L: COMEDY/COMEDY (1996) 95M D: Ben Stiller. *Jim Carrey, Matthew Broderick, Leslie Mann, Jack Black.* I never really thought Carrey was cool until he made this movie. He plays Chip Douglas, a lonely cable guy obsessed with two things: television and his new buddy Steven (Broderick), whom he meets on the job. At first Steven tries to be nice, even though it's weird when the guy who installed his cable starts showing up to play basketball with him and inviting him to hang out. But slowly he realizes that Chip is a dangerous stalker and that his attachment to television is not so much nerdiness as dementia. Carrey's performance is humorously over the top (you don't take this as seriously as, say, *The King of Comedy*) but Broderick plays it straight and holds the movie together by being completely uncomfortable. Stiller provides strong direction of this somewhat dark comedy with light satirical undertones that scared away mainstream audiences who just wanted to see Carrey stick things in his nose and talk out of his ass. —*B. T.*

CADDY, THE L: COMEDY TEAMS/MARTIN & LEWIS (1953) 95M
D: Norman Taurog. *Dean Martin, Jerry Lewis, Donna Reed, Barbara Bates, Joseph Calleia.* The Caddy is one of the best-known Martin-Lewis films and in some ways is a classic example of '50s light humor. Mixing together the right balance of situation comedy, romance, slapstick, and music, Martin and Lewis are perfect in this story about a golfer being coached by his idiot-savant caddy. Of course the two of them make it all the way to the finals. There are plenty of cameos by famous golfers. But the film's true claim to fame is Dino's wonderful crooning on "That's Amore." —*N. J.*

CAMP L: COMEDY/INDEPENDENT COMEDY (2003) 115M D: Todd Graff. *Daniel Letterle, Joanna Chilcoat, Robin De Jesus, Tiffany Taylor, Sasha Allen.* Run, don't walk, to see this movie! This is possibly one of the funniest, most charming, and entertaining coming-of-age/reveling-in-one's-weirdness/musical/going-to-camp movies ever made! It's based on real-life experiences of director/writer/actor Graff and his years at an acting camp, where most of the attendees were kids in the "misfit category." If you were one of those kids, and especially if you were into singing, theater, and all that creative stuff, this film is a nostalgic blast. I laughed my ass off, clapped repeatedly at brilliant, often brutally Machiavellian acts and moments of pure inspiration and striking realism. However, if you hate musicals and never did the theater thing, this whole movie will likely be an inside joke that you'll just never get. You have to be willing to forgive the predictable and cheesy parts. None of the kids in the cast ever acted in film or television prior to *Camp*, and they were all amazing. The film is not flawless, and I'm probably hyping it, but I just had such a good time. —*M. N.*

As for me, though I never went to camp, I was part of the theater crowd and I thought this movie was clichéd garbage. Many of the cast members are exceptionally talented, but let's face it: this is a film from the "genius" who brought us *The Beautician and Beast*. It is a film of little imagination and less ingenuity, crippled by cliché after cliché stacked upon each other like pieces of rancid meat. As I was watching this film, I believe I could feel cancer cells growing around my heart. How they ever got Stephen Sondheim to do a cameo I'll never know. (My evil mind reels—Stephen? Theater camp? Young Men?) Execrable. —*K. S.*

CAN'T HARDLY WAIT L: COMEDY/COMEDY (1998) 98M D: Deborah Kaplan, Harry Elfont. *Ethan Embry, Jennifer Love Hewitt, Charlie Korsmo, Seth Green.* Can't Hardly Wait is obvious, unoriginal, formulaic tripe. And that's why it works far better than any spoof or parody ever could. Relying on every cliché in the teen-movie book, *Can't Hardly Wait* unabashedly relishes in its simplicity. We watch as the shy boy wins the popular girl, the geek becomes popular,

the jock is humbled and a bunch of other stupid crap happens. But its über-obviousness is overcome by honesty. The film takes itself seriously and that's what makes it work. Where *American Pie* is gross, aggressive, and mean-spirited, and *Not Another Teen Movie* is redundant, stupid, and insulting, *Can't Hardly Wait* is warm, humorous, and fun. It's poor cinema to be sure, but it's the sort of poor cinema that a bunch of kids can get together and watch without feeling like the filmmakers have raped them in the ass. —*T. S.*

CAVE GIRL L: COMEDY/COMEDY (1985) 84M D: David Oliver. *Daniel Roebuck, Larry Gabriel, Cindy Ann Thompson, Bill Adams, Jeff Chayette.* Imagine a collision of *Land of the Lost* and *Caveman*, but as a teen sex comedy. *Cave Girl* isn't really as good as all that—the dull farce isn't so much sloppy as inert and it mostly sits there while things just sort of happen on the screen—but there are some minor pleasures to be had, not the least of which is the delightful Thompson as the titular prehistoric honey. Bad jokes aside, she's a sunny, sweet presence whose innocent smiles and cooing voice spark the film to life. Roebuck is fine as the nerdy science student who wanders back in time and falls for this cave cutie in an animal-skin bikini, but Oliver's bland direction leaves him (along with the rest of the cast) to fend for himself, and the script offers very little comic ammunition. —*S. A.*

CHAMPAGNE FOR CAESAR L: CLASSIC COMEDY/CLASSIC COMEDY (1950) 99M D: Richard Whorf. *Ronald Colman, Barbara Britton, Celeste Holm, Vincent Price, Art Linkletter.* Colman is an unemployed genius who takes his revenge on an eccentric corporate visionary (Price, fading in and out of trances in a hilarious performance) by winning his empire from under him through a TV quiz show. Colman's dry geniality and prickly doggedness makes for a fine comic performance (a rarity in his career), while Holm makes a sunny femme fatale sent by Price to distract the hero. Linkletter is perfectly cast as a glib host who gets in on the conspiracy but then falls for Colman's sister. A modest but merry forgotten comedy, this wry little low-budget piece is clever and just a touch kooky, and well worth reviving. —*S. A.*

CHASING AMY L: COMEDY/COMEDY (1997) 111M D: Kevin Smith. *Ben Affleck, Joey Lauren Adams, Jason Lee, Kevin Smith, Jason Mewes.* A lot of people love this semi-autobiographical relationship drama about a comic book artist (Affleck) who falls for a lesbian (Adams), but this is the one that permanently turned me against Smith. It has to be Smith's dialogue that built him his cult following (it sure as hell isn't the visuals), but I having a hard time with all those long speeches, as all of his characters seem to have the same voice. I find myself imagining him sitting there typing all the dialogue as the characters say it, sometimes with his pants around his ankles. Worse, it seems like Affleck's character is supposed to be a reasonable, sympathetic person who makes the kind of mistakes we all do. He's not; he's a complete jackass, and he still achieves every macho asshole's goal of bringing a lesbian over to the dark side, at least temporarily. —*B.T.*

CHATEAU, THE L: COMEDY/INDEPENDENT COMEDY (2001) 91M D: Jesse Peretz. *Paul Rudd, Sylvie Testud, Didier Flamand, Maria Verdi, Donal Logue, Romany Malco.* Rudd and Malco are mismatched American brothers who inherit a French chateau and a kooky staff that could have stepped out of a thirties French farce in this fluffy, flaky croissant of a culture clash comedy. Of course they both fall in love with the doe-eyed, delicate young maid (Testud). Director Peretz shoots on lightweight digital video that's all the indie filmmaking rage, and in some respects this is exactly the kind of project suited to the medium. The ensemble cast has an improvisational spontaneity, creating a genial atmosphere for this modest story. But the DV downside—the murky colors and soft images—fights the character of the chateau and the beauty of the countryside. Given all that, this is a pleasant shaggy dog tale that promises little and delivers just a little more. —*S.A.*

CHUCK & BUCK L: COMEDY/COMEDY (2000) 99M D: Miguel Arteta. *Mike White, Paul Weitz, Chris Weitz, Maya Rudolph, Beth Colt, Lupe Ontiveros.* Screenwriter White plays Buck, a young man obsessed with reuniting with his childhood best friend. Once he finds Chuck (Weitz), it becomes quite clear that the feelings are not exactly mutual. Chuck is engaged to be married and Buck interrupts at the most awkward moments and in the most awkward ways. He wants to talk about some of the most awkward events in Chuck's life, such as a time when Chuck and Buck were just a little bit more than best friends. Meanwhile, Buck manages to occupy himself with staging a play he wrote about his childhood love for Chuck! This story is told empathetically from Buck's perspective and as such it will make your skin crawl. Shot entirely on digital video, *Chuck & Buck* was the first teaming of White and director Arteta, who went on to do *The Good Girl.* —*N.J.*

CITIZEN RUTH L: COMEDY/COMEDY (1996) 102M D: Alexander Payne. *Laura Dern, Kelly Preston, Mary Kay Place, Kurtwood Smith, Swoosie Kurtz.* Director Payne (later known for *Election* and *About Schmidt*) debuted with this funny, button-pushing comedy about abortion. You may wonder how exactly one could make a funny movie about abortion, and the answer is by portraying both "pro-life" and "pro-choice" activists as boobs and crackpots. Ruth Stoops (Dern) is a pregnant glue-sniffer in trouble with the law and offered a lighter sentence by a judge if she will abort her baby. The decision begins a media controversy, so activists on both sides of the abortion debate pretend to be her friend and use her for their causes, going to such ridiculous lengths as wearing disguises and going undercover as their opponents. No one seems to care at all about the well-being of Ruth herself, or her baby for that matter. This very funny and brave satire gives a good indication of where newcomer Payne was headed. —*B.T.*

CLERKS L: COMEDY/COMEDY (1994) 92M D: Kevin Smith. *Brian O'Halloran, Kevin Smith, Jeff Anderson, Marilyn Ghigliotti, Jason Mewes.* Budget is all in what you do with it. This film isn't bad because of the fact that it was made with, like, $14, it's bad because it's poorly written, poorly acted, and completely overrated. It also shows us that a filmmaker really can make a career of using the same jokes over and over again, and the novelty never dies. OK, I'm lying. The novelty has died, been buried, and rotted back into the foul earth from whence it came. A day in the life of a couple disgruntled retail clerks? Hmm, I have no idea what that would be like. At least the people I work with are funny. —*J.S.*

CLOCKWATCHERS L: COMEDY/INDEPENDENT COMEDY (1997) 100M D: Jill Sprecher. *Parker Posey, Toni Collette, Alanna Ubach, Lisa Kudrow, Josh Malina.* What starts out as a conventional, albeit cynical, indie comedy slowly gives way to a massive downer on the dehumanizing effects of modern corporate employment. When Iris (Collette) takes a temp job in the numb offices of Global Credit, she is immediately taken in by a band of female temps sharing a mutual hatred of their jobs. A likable and seemingly indivisible clique forms, but as work conditions become increasingly oppressive, the friendships suffer. Despite Posey's familiar manic cynicism, this film is unusually subdued, from the dialogue and performances right down to the lighting and camerawork. *Clockwatchers* is tough to shake and a film I keep coming back to. —*C.B.*

COMEDIAN L: COMEDY/STAND-UP COMEDY (2002) 100M D: Christian Charles. *Jerry Seinfeld, Greg Geraldo, Sherrod Small, Jim Norton, Geoffrey Danchimah.* Enter the world of Seinfeld as he retires his tried-and-true stand-up comedy act and builds a new one from the ground up. Charles followed Seinfeld (who also produced the film) for over a year as he honed his act at comedy clubs, and picked a glib, grating, hungry young comic named Orny Adams for contrast, letting him spout off about his dues while he tried to make his mark. This is not a comedy concert film, it's about the hard work of creating comedy, the glare of the spotlight, the rush of a good performance, and the heartsink of comic meltdown on stage. Watching Seinfeld lose his place and fall silent in the middle of an act is almost unbearable, yet like a car wreck you can't help but watch with perverse fascination. Fellow comics Colin Quinn, Chris Rock, Ray Romano, Kevin Nealon, Jay Leno, Robert Klein, Garry Shandling, and Seinfeld's hero Bill Cosby all add their insights to the philosophy of stand-up. —S. A.

COMIC BOOK VILLAINS L: COMEDY/INDEPENDENT COMEDY (2002) 92M D: James Dale Robinson. *Natasha Lyonne, D. J. Qualls, Donal Logue, Michael Rapaport, Eileen Brennan, Cary Elwes.* The owners of rival comic book stores—one a comic-obsessed hardcore nerd (Logue), the other an entrepreneur (Rapaport) who's more into selling baseball cards—both find out about a shut-in who died and left behind a treasure trove of mint condition, golden-age comics. Separately, they visit the mother and try to get her to sell the comics, but she turns them down, and things eventually get nasty. So it's sort of a take on *Treasure of the Sierra Madre,* set in the world of comic book collectors. Screenwriter/director Robinson is a well-known comic book writer and knows this world. I especially like the detail within the two comic book shops: Rappaport's is small and neat, Logue's is messy with boxes stacked to the ceiling. *Villains* may strive too hard to be a serious crime film, but it's still a surprisingly good direct-to-DVD feature. —B. T.

COMPANY MAN L: COMEDY/COMEDY (2000) 81M D: Douglas McGrath, Peter Askin. *Alan Cumming, Woody Allen, John Turturro, Sigourney Weaver, Anthony LaPaglia, Douglas McGrath.* McGrath (who cowrote *Bullets Over Broadway* with Allen) lured the Woodman to costar as a neurotic American agent in this screwball satire of the CIA, the Cold War, and Cuba. McGrath gives a cheerfully gee-whiz performance as a high school teacher who inadvertently causes the Bay of Pigs fiasco in this cheeky collision of fifties sitcom Americana with sixties Cold War farce. The comic timing, witty wordplay, and rat-a-tat pacing of the first half ultimately devolves into a series of disconnected skits and one-note characters but the film never stalls, thanks to the lunatic energy of the cast: Turturro (as a bellowing, adrenaline-pumped guerrilla), Weaver (as McGrath's social-climbing wife), and Cumming (an effeminate, interior-design-obsessed General Batista). —S. A.

CONFESSIONS OF A DANGEROUS MIND L: COMEDY/COMEDY (2002) 113M D: George Clooney. *Sam Rockwell, Drew Barrymore, Julia Roberts, George Clooney, Rutger Hauer.* Rockwell is superb as game show pioneer Chuck Barris in this straight adaptation of his "unauthorized autobiography" in which he claims to have moonlighted as a CIA assassin between creating *The Dating Game* and *The Gong Show.* The movie is entertaining in its depiction of the game show world, playing things completely straight, as if the filmmakers really believe it's a true story. Like all of Charlie Kaufman's scripts, it's full of depression and self-loathing, and the secret agent business is an interesting way to show Barris's shame for his actual occupation. The script sat in development purgatory for years, reputed to be brilliant but unfilmable,

until Clooney finally took the plunge and signed on as director just to get it made. His style borrows liberally from some of the directors he's worked with (Soderbergh, Coen, Russell) but he also contributes some cleverly designed transitions, such as dividing one set between two locations to achieve a mock split-screen phone conversation. —B. T.

CORKY ROMANO L: COMEDY/COMEDY (2001) 85M D: Rob Pritts. *Chris Kattan, Peter Falk, Richard Roundtree, Fred Ward, Peter Berg, Vinessa Shaw, Chris Penn.* "Better than I thought it would be" is the average comment about this decent comedy starring *Saturday Night Live* favorite Kattan. The film runs smoothly and has a lot of funny situations that make it worth a second look. Kattan plays Corky, the discarded, embarrassingly bizarre relative of a major crime family. When the family gets into deep trouble with the law and they have nowhere to turn, they recruit the naive Corky to find out secret information by infiltrating the FBI. Through some accidental successes with solving crime, Corky convinces the FBI that he's legit and sets the tone for some totally silly stuff. There are a lot of laughs, but they are overshadowed by the film's ace-in-the-hole scene where Corky has to give a speech to a bunch of kids after snorting up a bag of "evidence." Wacky, wacky fun and shallow enough to stay in the kiddie pool the whole time. —R. D.

CRAZY PEOPLE L: COMEDY/COMEDY (1990) 90M D: Tony Bill. *Dudley Moore, Daryl Hannah, J. T. Walsh, Paul Reiser, David Paymer.* I'm not particularly attracted to the talents of Moore or Hannah, but they are decent in this film. The real stars are the crazy people and the unconventional ads they devise. Moore plays Emory, who is committed following a breakdown from his tedious advertising job. Emory stirs things up at the mental ward when he gives everybody a morale-boosting opportunity to help him come up with new, more realistic ads, such as "Volvo: They're Boxy, But Good." This is an uplifting movie that focuses on patients' feelings when the profiting corporations dismiss their efforts. —R. D.

CRAZYSITTER, THE L: COMEDY/COMEDY (1995) 91M D: Michael J. McDonald. *Lisa Kudrow, Carol Kane, Ed Begley Jr., Beverly D'Angelo, Steve Landesberg, Phil Hartman.* By no means is this a good movie, but it definitely has a few moments. Edie (D'Angelo) doesn't want to leave the comfortable surroundings of the jail cell in which she's spent most of her life, but she's forced out due to budget cuts. She winds up taking a nanny position supervising some horribly undisciplined children. While watching television, she sees a way of making a fortune by selling the children on the black market. This movie aims for charm with a side order of lewdness, but falls short on both. I like the crude attempts the best: the salesman's (Hartman) infatuation with chunky women, the

clueless parenting of Paul (Begley Jr.) and Treva (Kane) Van Arsdale, Kudrow as the snappy talk show host, and (most of all) the all-too-sterile White Family who had their genitals removed and sealed up because it's just too meesy down there. Yuck. —R. D.

CROSS, DAVID: LET AMERICA LAUGH L: COMEDY/STAND-UP COMEDY (2003) 93M D: Lance Bangs. *David Cross.*
Rather than make a traditional concert film, Cross had director Bangs follow his tour and document the downtime between shows. There are bits of stand-up, but most of the movie focuses on the weird people Cross ran into while on the road: idiotic fans, drunks on the street, walkouts, irate club owners, even a farting hippie. The highlight is a spat with a stubborn Nashville club owner whom Cross mentions in his act and then has to face afterward. In another scene, Cross gets invited to a stoner party at a video store, and decides to go just to see what will happen (the answer: a bunch of people sit around smoking pot and spout bullshit philosophy to the camera). Most of all you see Cross going from city to city encountering people who really don't understand why a celebrity might not want to hang out with them at the drop of a hat. *Let America Laugh* is a potent combination of funny and depressing. It serves as a powerful reminder that you are not necessarily that one person who is cool enough to be instant buddies with your favorite entertainer. Next time I meet a celebrity I'm not going to say a word. —B. T.

DARK BACKWARD, THE L: COMEDY/INDEPENDENT COMEDY (1991) 97M D: Adam Rifkin. *Bill Paxton, Judd Nelson, Lara Flynn Boyle, Rob Lowe, Wayne Newton.*
Nelson plays a talentless, completely uncharismatic comedian who suddenly becomes famous when, for no apparent reason, a third arm grows out of his back. He does the same lame jokes but periodically turns around to show the extra arm and everyone claps. Paxton has his funniest role ever as Nelson's abusive accordion player and sidekick who enjoys eating rotten food and in one scene licks a corpse he finds in the garbage dump. Part of the film's appeal (or nonappeal) comes from exaggerated, ugly settings where every character is heartless and sweaty, every window is cracked and splattered, and every street is strewn with garbage. —B. T.

DAYTRIPPERS, THE L: COMEDY/COMEDY (1996) 87M D: Greg Mottola. *Liev Schreiber, Stanley Tucci, Hope Davis, Parker Posey, Anne Meara, Pat McNamara.*
Mottola's loose, character-driven piece begs comparison to *Big Night*. Both films feature marvelous casts, excellent understated performances, strands of personal stories brought together in a simple plot, low-key humor, and the participation of Tucci and the vastly underutilized Campbell Scott. The whole thing is set in motion when worried young wife Davis discovers a love note in the pocket of husband Tucci's pants and her

nosy mom insists on driving into New York to confront him—with the entire family in tow. With a parade of strangers met along the scavenger hunt–like search for hubby, there's plenty of opportunity for sweet little scenes, off-beat moments, and unexpected confrontations. This little gem got lost in the box office shuffle on its release, but its modest charms translate nicely to the small screen. —S. A.

DEATH TO SMOOCHY L: COMEDY/COMEDY (2002) 109M D: Danny DeVito. *Catherine Keener, Robin Williams, Edward Norton.*
Children's show host Rainbow Randolph (Williams) is fired after being caught taking a briefcase partly filled with wadded up ten-dollar bills from parents who want their "little booger eaters" in his studio audience. Post-scandal Randolph becomes increasingly unhinged and begins stalking his idealistic replacement, Smoochy (Norton, in a rhinoceros costume). Writer Resnick (*Cabin Boy, Get a Life*) likened his story to *Serpico*, with Smoochy being the idealistic newcomer who gets swallowed up by the corruption of his industry. It's not a bad concept, and there are a few funny lines, but most of the humor is as obvious as the lame Barney parody at the center of the plot. On the positive side, Williams is less obnoxious than usual as the deranged former host, and he has a couple of nice scenes where he dances and ice skates. —B. T.

DELICATE DELINQUENT, THE L: CLASSIC COMEDY/CLASSIC COMEDY (1957) 100M D: Don Mcguire. *Jerry Lewis, Darren McGavin, Robert Ivers, Martha Hyer, Horace McMahon.*
After breaking off a ten-year partnership with Dean Martin, Lewis was cast in this film about a jinxed young man caught up with juvenile offenders. McGavin plays the good-hearted policeman set on proving that he can reform juveniles through mentoring. Of course he chooses Lewis's character, the hardest nut to crack. This film is certainly not as good as Lewis/Martin vehicles, but it has many things to recommend it: a smashing big-band jazz score, excellent photography, dancing a la *West Side Story*, and an infamous skit with Lewis discovering, and accidentally playing, a theremin. —N. J.

DEUCE BIGALOW: MALE GIGOLO L: COMEDY/COMEDY (1999) 88M D: Mike Mitchell. *Rob Schneider, William Forsythe, Eddie Griffin, Arija Bareikis, Oded Fehr.*
Don't knock it until you've watched it. Schneider is my guilty pleasure; his movies are the perfect example of being so stupid that they're funny. Deuce is a guy who cleans fish tanks, left to watch over the apartment of Antoine (Griffin), a famous man-whore who has gone to Europe. When Deuce breaks Antoine's expensive fish tank and floods his apartment, he freaks out and resorts to becoming a man-whore himself to make the money he needs to fix the tank. This movie is totally absurd, but really funny. By the time the credits roll, you may just find yourself

reconsidering all those horrible things you've thought about Schneider. Or maybe not. But at least you'll laugh. —J. S.

DINNER AT FRED'S L: COMEDY/INDEPENDENT COMEDY

(1999) 93M D: Shawn Thompson. *Gil Bellows, Parker Posey, Kevin McDonald, John Neville.* Bellows (*Ally McBeal*) plays a normal guy heading for a weekend in the country with his fiancé. He winds up instead trapped as the forced guest of a crazy family that looks like every member stopped taking their medications at once. With funny performances by *Kids in the Hall's* McDonald, indie favorite Posey, and Christopher "Flux Capacitor" Lloyd. This would be a good holiday movie to watch with relatives. —R. D.

DIRTY ROTTEN SCOUNDRELS L: COMEDY/COMEDY

(1988) 110M D: Frank Oz. *Michael Caine, Steve Martin, Barbara Harris, Glenne Headly.* Martin is a sloppy, brash American con man who tramples on Caine's territory on the French Riviera, where the latter elegantly separates rich single women from their jewelry. Oz directed this remake of the 1963 comedy *Bedtime Story* and improved upon it, making a hilarious comedy that looks both marvelously refined and brightly exaggerated (thanks to the great photography of Michael Ballhaus). Oz really makes the clash between Martin's bumptious American cockiness and Caine's quiet, refined understatement into an inspired battle of wits and wiles, letting Martin do his wild and crazy exaggerations while Caine makes his comedy out of glances, grace notes, and underplayed line deliveries. Headly is wonderfully simple and naive as the American abroad who becomes their target in a winner-take-all con-test, and Harris is great in a small role as an heiress who is an early mark of Caine's. Oz hasn't made a film this funny since. —S. A.

DOOM GENERATION L: COMEDY/INDEPENDENT COMEDY

(1995) 84M D: Gregg Araki. *Rose McGowan, James Duval, Johnathon Schaech, Margaret Cho, Lauren Tewes.* McGowan, Duval, and Schaech play a twisted threesome who knock over a convenience store, murder its clerk, and flee from the law to a destination that is really no more specific than Hell. Through all the misplaced sex, homoerotic allusions, and totally overstylized violence, evil omens seem to follow them—most especially the peculiar number 666, which mockingly appears at random moments. The audience is treated to a very bumpy roller coaster ride as the three protagonists abandon their conscience in an attempt to widen the hellbound path carved by the likes of Bonnie and Clyde. This is the second film in a trilogy by director Araki, preceded by *Totally F***ed Up* and followed by *Nowhere.* —N. J.

The Doom Generation is absolutely, without hyperbole, one of the worst films ever shat into this world, and its director, the unfathomably talentless Araki, should be labeled a criminal against humanity for inflicting this pretentious

crap upon us all. You've got three main characters named, I shit you not, Red, White, and Blue, who rob convenience stores, have a lot of sex, and irritate Neo-Nazis. That is the whole film. Eighty-five minutes of stultifying "shock" moments and sub-Troma gore effects mixed in with a lot of topless shots of McGowan. It's not funny, it's not shocking, it's not insightful, and it's not cool. It's just pathetic and boring. This film should be wiped from existence—the negative burned, all tapes and DVDs destroyed, and any memory, good or ill, of this piece of shit exiled into the void for all eternity. —M. L.

DOWN WITH LOVE L: COMEDY/COMEDY (2003) 94M D:

Peyton Reed. *Ewan McGregor, Renée Zellweger, David Hyde Pierce, Sarah Paulson, Jeri Ryan.* I absolutely adore movies that seem to get high off the sheer exuberance of movies themselves, movies that wrap you up, plunk you down somewhere new (or in this case, somewhere old and already explored but not quite in the same way), and keep you swept up in the little world they have created. *Down with Love* is exactly that kind of film. And, while its story may be silly or slight or implausible, that's not the point. The point is the film itself, the images and the colors, the innuendo and the re-creation of movies past, the fine line between homage and satire. Throw in a McGregor here and a Zellweger there and you've got yourself quite a wonderful way to spend a couple of hours. A recommended treat for fans of '60s sex comedies, the rather obvious template for this slight but ultimately winning film. —C. P.

DREAM A LITTLE DREAM L: COMEDY/COMEDY (1989) 114M

D: Marc Rocco. *Corey Feldman, Corey Haim, Harry Dean Stanton, William McNamara, Meredith Salenger, Piper Laurie, Jason Robards.* This marks the last good "Corey" movie. *Dream a Little Dream* is a cool '80s film that was really popular with both guys and girls. Girls had the Coreys and guys were mesmerized by the full figured Salenger, who tantalized us with her gymnasium leotard number. Back in 1989, it was a profitable venture to recruit the Feldman/Haim duo after monopolizing the teen market with hits like *The Lost Boys*, but sadly all good things must come to an end. This film does have some quality acting by Robards and Stanton, but my favorite line is by McNamara, who plays the school's hottest guy. When Feldman tells him the girl he is after is not his type, he replies, "I'm every girls' type." —R. D.

DREAM FOR AN INSOMNIAC L: COMEDY/INDEPENDENT

COMEDY (1996) 108M D: Tiffani DeBartolo. *Michael Landes, Seymour Cassel, Ione Skye, Leslie Stevens, Jennifer Aniston, Sean Blackman.* This blandly conventional and pathetically implausible romantic comedy concerns Skye's overly selective taste in men, and the emotional challenge she faces upon meeting the man of her dreams. So much of the talky film is set inside a cafe that it seems this might've been planned as a play—or, more likely, a sitcom. It comes across as an elitist feature-length retread of *Friends*—complete with Aniston, here playing a fingernails-on-chalkboard aspiring actress who affects a different foreign accent each day to keep in practice. Ugh. The acting's so overdone and the dialogue so groan-worthy that it hardly matters that this movie isn't even funny. —*C. B.*

DREAM TEAM, THE L: COMEDY/COMEDY (1989) 120M D: Howard Zieff. *Michael Keaton, Christopher Lloyd, Peter Boyle, Stephen Furst, Dennis Boutsikaris.* This comedy delivers lots of chuckles and boasts some great character actors. You take a couple of guys who should never have left the hospital, add hotheaded Keaton as their chaperone, and I'm interested. There aren't any weak links in this film, but I like Jack (Boyle), who takes Christianity to another level when he believes he is doing God's work, and Henry (Lloyd), who believes he is a doctor. Made just after *Beetlejuice* and released the same year as *Batman*, this is another opportunity to see Keaton in top form during his most successful years. —*R. D.*

DROP DEAD GORGEOUS L: COMEDY/COMEDY (1999) 97M D: Michael Patrick Jann. *Kirsten Dunst, Denise Richards, Ellen Barkin, Kirstie Alley, Allison Janney.* Drop Dead Gorgeous is the kind of movie that can't help poking fun at all its characters, whether the audience is rooting for them or not. It's a mockumentary that follows several small-town beauty pageant contestants, including a sweet girl from the wrong side of the tracks (Dunst) and a stunning vamp from the town's wealthiest family (Richards). As the pageant approaches, the pressure rises—one contestant is dispatched in a mysterious tractor accident—and the true colors of the girls and their families become clear. *Drop Dead Gorgeous* is no classic, but it has enough wit and slickness to rise above other films of its type. It's worth seeing for the pageant, especially the scene in which Richards (who proves to be a spry comic actress) debuts a musical number with a startling choice for a dance partner. —*T. P.*

DUETS L: COMEDY/COMEDY (2000) 112M D: Bruce Paltrow. *Gwyneth Paltrow, Andre Braugher, Scott Speedman, Maria Bello, Paul Giamatti, Huey Lewis.* One can't help but wonder what the people behind this film were thinking. Surely, no matter what marketing tests they're running these days in Hollywood, there seems no possible way that their findings revealed that moviegoers were looking for a film having anything to do with karaoke or starring the indomitable Lewis. It sounds bad on paper and it plays even worse on screen. The only way to pull off a story this horrible is to have it revel in its own badness, and to go for the cheesy, schmaltzy fun that can be had with such unflinchingly stereotypical characters and plot lines. But *Duets* decides to go the

other way. As a result, the audience still ends up laughing—it's just that the film itself isn't in on the joke. With all the depth of a wading pool, the film unfortunately imagines itself to be a sort of *Nashville* for the karaoke crowd, a story packed with interweaving characters, full of life in all its strange manifestations. Thus, in its own sincerity it becomes a truly awful film and one that you should do your very best to avoid. —*C. P.*

DUMB AND DUMBERER: WHEN HARRY MET LLOYD L: COMEDY/COMEDY (2003) 85M D: Troy Miller. *Cheri Oteri, Eugene Levy, Eric Christian Olsen, Derek Richardson, Luis Guzman.* This painful sequel is actually a complex commentary on itself. It's supposed to be about two dumb kids, high school versions of Harry and Lloyd from the first film. At first it seems strange that every single character is just as idiotic as they are, but only at first. As you watch, it becomes clear what the filmmakers are trying to say: if you are exposed to absolute stupidity on a regular basis, you no doubt will become stupid yourself. So we can see that *Dumb and Dumberer* is actually a cautionary picture, a warning against the adverse effect of constantly exposing an entire generation to absolutely worthless, insulting tripe. *Dumb and Dumberer* shows what being inundated with crap will do to someone. Crap like *Dumb and Dumberer.* —*T. S.*

EARTH GIRLS ARE EASY L: COMEDY/COMEDY (1988) 100M D: Julien Temple. *Geena Davis, Jeff Goldblum, Michael McKean, Julie Brown, Jim Carrey, Damon Wayans.* Wow, they really scored with this one. It's hard to mix sci-fi with comedy; it rarely works. Even the great film *The Adventures of Buckaroo Bonzai* isn't as popular as I would expect it to be, but *Earth Girls* transcends these genres to explode with brilliance. The cast kicks ass; this marks the first film where Carrey starts exploring the extremes of physical comedy on camera before *In Living Color* made him a household name the following year. Goldblum gets a chance to explore his lighter side. This was cowritten by the team of Julie Brown and Charlie Coffrey, who wrote the amazing spoofs *Attack of the 5'2" Woman* and *Medusa: Dare to Be Truthful.* —*R. D.*

EASY LIVING L: CLASSIC COMEDY/CLASSIC COMEDY (1937) 88M D: Mitchell Leisen. *Jean Arthur, Ray Milland, Edward Arnold, Mary Nash, Luis Alberni, Franklin Pangborn.* Preston Sturges's sly screenplay is a screwball Cinderella story for the modern world. Mary (Arthur), a clerk-typist, becomes a social princess when a mink coat falls into her lap—literally—and her attempt to return the fur to banking tycoon Edward Arnold backfires. New York high society pegs her as the banker's mistress ("Where there's smoke, there's someone smoking"), and soon the jobless girl is living—penniless—in the lap of luxury for reasons she can't fathom. That's the key to Sturges's comedy: a mix of sophisticated sexual innuendo

and simple innocence. Director Leisen's smooth direction emphasizes people over pratfalls, but the picture has both in plenitude, anchored in Arthur's girl-next-door charm. —*S. A.*

ELECTION L: COMEDY/COMEDY (1999) 103M D: Alexander Payne. *Matthew Broderick, Reese Witherspoon, Emily Martin, Phil Reeves, Chris Klein, Loren Nelson.* *Election* is a great comedy and was one of the best movies of 1999. Broderick plays a teacher who supervises a student election that includes some troublesome candidates. The worst is Tracy Flick, played to a T by Witherspoon, so obnoxiously determined to win the election that she almost drives Broderick to the loony bin. Tracy is so spunky and infectious that she even starts invading Broderick's personal life and his dreams. This film is honest, outrageous, and beautifully crafted, worth seeing again and again. —*R. D.*

EMPIRE RECORDS L: COMEDY/COMEDY (1995) 100M D: Allan Moyle. *Maxwell Caufield, Liv Tyler, Anthony LaPaglia, Renée Zellweger, Rory Cochrane, Johnny Whitworth.* This is just like an old Mickey Rooney/Judy Garland "let's put on a show in my uncle's barn to save (insert financially troubled institution here)" only it's EXTREME! Wait, this came out before extreme was in. . . OK, it's INDIE! No, it's completely homogenized and devoid of anything unpredictable. Hell, it's silly fun! That's the ticket! —*J. B. P.*

FISHING WITH JOHN L: COMEDY/INDEPENDENT COMEDY (1991) 147M D: John Lurie. *John Lurie, Dennis Hopper, Jim Jarmusch, Willem Dafoe, Matt Dillon, Tom Waits.* Actor/musician Lurie (*Stranger than Paradise, Down by Law*) had the brilliant idea to take some of his really cool friends fishing, thereby creating one of the most paradoxically intoxicating and funny television shows ever to hit the air waves. By gathering the likes of Waits, Jarmusch, Dafoe, Dillon, and Hopper, Lurie blurs the line between celebrity roasting and reality TV, showing his guests sticking fish down their pants, wondering why they are there, and even . . . dying. Not much makes sense here, but anything goes. Robb Webb is great as the obtuse, dead-pan narrator with lines like, "Both fishermen are covered with sores and boners." —*J. D.*

FREAKED L: COMEDY/COMEDY (1993) 79M D: Tom Stern, Alex Winter. *Megan Ward, Alex Winter, Randy Quaid, Michael Stoyanov.* Everyone's favorite movie superstar, Ricky Coogan (Winter), has just signed a lucrative promotional deal for the new fertilizer Zygrot-24. Ricky travels to South America with his pal Ernie (Soyanov) to visit the man responsible for its creation, Elijah C Skuggs (Quaid). Along the way they pick up plucky environmental protestor Julie (Ward) who, as it happens, was on her way to sling cow shit at Ricky for promoting the environmentally unfriendly Zygrot-24. Together they discover Mr. Skuggs's true purpose, to create the ultimate freak for the ultimate freak show. Stern and Winter, fresh off their minor television victory *The Idiot Box,* team up again to write and direct one of the best forgotten comedies of the '90s. Full of incredible make-up effects and a great soundtrack (original music by Henry Rollins, George Clinton, and others), *Freaked* deserves a second look, or at least, a first. —*R. G.*

FREDDY GOT FINGERED L: COMEDY/COMEDY (2001) 87M D: Tom Green. *Tom Green, Rip Torn, Marisa Coughlan, Eddie Kaye Thomas, Harland Williams.* Almost unanimously panned as worthless shock-value garbage—but what the hell does everyone in the whole world know, anyway? Green plays a twenty-eight-year-old skateboarder living in his parents' basement and following his dream of creating an animated TV series. His hothead father (Torn) wants him to move out and get a respectable job like his younger brother, Freddy (Thomas). Father and son battle it out, and as the conflict heats up Green does everything from making false allegations of child molestation to uprooting the entire house and moving it to Pakistan while his dad is asleep inside. The humor comes from taking the standard look and formula of modern lowbrow comedy and infusing it with surreal non sequiturs (a fancy musical contraption made of string and sausages), envelope-pushing tastelessness (a gory baby-delivery scene, after which Green tapes the umlilical cord to his own belly for sexual kicks), and John Waters–style shock humor (jerking off a horse). There's also a surprisingly emotional side. For all its silliness, the film clearly says a lot about Green's relationship with his father. Funnier than the movie itself is Green's commentary, in which he argues—not entirely unreasonably—that the masochistic nymphomaniac girlfriend character is a breakthrough portrayal of the disabled. —*B. T.*

FREE ENTERPRISE L: COMEDY/INDEPENDENT COMEDY (1998) 108M D: Robert Meyer Burnett. *William Shatner, Rafer Weigel, Eric McCormack, Audie England.* First off, any movie starring William Shatner playing William Shatner is a must-see. Second, if you are into science fiction films, action figures, *Star Trek,* TV shows, and/or comic books, this film is not only about people like you, it's about people you probably know. It's about two men trying to make a movie (*Bradykillers,* a film about a serial killer going after Marcia, Jan, and Cindy), and about dealing with turning thirty, struggling with relationships, trying to make ends meet, meeting a screen idol for the first time, and realizing that longtime fantasies are not necessarily reality. If you're the right age or belong to this particular subculture, this movie is hilarious and filled with in-jokes that only you and your friends will likely get. If you're not part of this subculture. . . well, watch it anyway! —*M. N.*

FRIDAY L: COMEDY/COMEDY (1995) 89M D: F. Gary Gray. *Ice Cube, Tom "Tiny" Lister Jr., Chris Tucker, John Witherspoon.* A day in the life of Craig (Cube) and his weed-dealing friend Smokey (Tucker) as they struggle to get the $200 the latter owes to Big Per... I mean Big Worm (Faizon Love). You have to forgive some dumb bathroom humor, and while you're busy with that the low-key charm sneaks up on you, making this an addictive cult classic. These were breakthrough roles for Cube and Tucker (who steals the movie), and there are very funny appearances by Witherspoon as Craig's ranting, dogcatcher father, and Lister as the bicycle-riding behemoth who terrorizes the neighborhood. Although the "'hood comedy" has since become a genre unto itself, it was refreshing in 1995 to see a movie about black people in LA that had no gangs or deaths and wasn't heavy-handed in its moralizing. None of the sequels or imitations have managed to successfully capture the atmosphere of the neighborhood or the slice-of-life feel. —*B.T.*

NEXT FRIDAY L: COMEDY/COMEDY (2000) 98M D: Steve Carr. *Ice Cube, Mike Epps, Don "DC" Curry, Tom "Tiny" Lister Jr., John Witherspoon, Justin Pierce.* After *Rush Hour*, Chris Tucker was declared a $20 million leading man. So it's no surprise that he didn't appear in this sequel to the cult classic *Friday* (his character Smokey is in rehab). Debo (Lister) just got out of prison, so Craig (Cube) goes off to the suburbs to hide out with his cousin Day-Day (Epps) and Uncle Elroy (Curry), who recently won the lottery. Epps is funny, and he and Cube have a good chemistry, but they just can't match the laughs that Tucker was able to generate. Nor is music video director Carr up to the task of filling F. Gary Gray's shoes. Worst of all, poor Witherspoon (as Craig's dad) is treated utterly without dignity, spending the entire film with dog shit on his back and at one point stuck in traffic with diarrhea. Still, Cube has an easy-going charm, and this is an amusing enough film if you don't have high expectations. —*B.T.*

FRIDAY AFTER NEXT L: COMEDY/COMEDY (2002) 82M D: Marcus Raboy. *Ice Cube, Rickey Smiley, John Witherspoon, Clifton Powell, Don "DC" Curry, Mike Epps.* This second sequel to *Friday* proves that there is not a lot of potential in making sequels to *Friday*. Craig (Cube) and Day-Day (Epps) have finally moved out of their parents' houses and gotten an apartment together, but when their rent money is stolen by a thief dressed as Santa Claus (Smiley), they resort to getting jobs as security guards to earn the money back. Meanwhile, Craig's dad (Witherspoon) and uncle (Curry) open up a barbecue restaurant. The film is mildly admirable for adding a few new elements to the mix: a Christmas setting, animated opening credits, and an orchestral-sounding score. But it's not quite as funny as

Next Friday, which itself was not nearly as funny as *Friday*. —*B.T.*

GET OVER IT! L: COMEDY/COMEDY (2001) 86M D: Tommy O'Haver. *Kirsten Dunst, Ben Foster, Ed Begley Jr., Sisqo, Melissa Sagemiller, Colin Hanks, Martin Short.* Riding the wave of the *Bring It On!* fame, Dunst stars in another decent comedy. The film is very formulaic but moves along quickly and has a lot of charm. Dunst is hot and Foster successfully plays the cute but shy kid who discovers hidden courage and self-confidence when love inspires him. Martin Short nails another funny supporting role as a flamboyant and eccentric theater instructor. If you liked *Bring It On!*, you should not be disappointed with *Get Over It*. It's just entertaining enough, and equally forgettable, that it's fun to watch a second time. —*R.D.*

GHOST AND MR. CHICKEN, THE L: CLASSIC COMEDY/ CLASSIC COMEDY (1966) 90M D: Alan Rankin. *Don Knotts, Dick Sargent, Liam Redmond, Joan Staley.* "Attaboy, Luther!" Knotts is Luther Heggs, a weak-kneed typesetter at the local paper with big dreams of becoming the hottest reporter in Laurel, Kansas. But to prove his mettle (and win the heart of the beautiful Alma Parker), Luther must spend an entire night in the most haunted house in town! YIKES!!! Countless supernatural sight gags meet ol' bug-eyes head-on in Knotts's uproarious first feature following his stint as Barney Fife on *The Andy Griffith Show*. Surprisingly, the plot of this warm-hearted vehicle revolves around a bloody murder, but that doesn't keep Don from hammin' and googlin' up a storm. Yeah, there's one movie funnier than this one, and that's *The Love God?*, starring (you guessed it) Mr. Don Knotts. —*Z.C.*

GIGLI L: COMEDY/COMEDY (2003) 121M D: Martin Brest. *Ben Affleck, Jennifer Lopez, Lenny Venito, Justin Bartha, Christopher Walken, Al Pacino.* Affleck swaggers under a crooked, cocky grin as a thick-headed underworld contractor who thinks he's the Springsteen of Italian-American street thugs. He winds up more of a Sonny Bono when his loan shark boss foists upon him a sassy Cher—actually a yoga-practicing lesbian named Ricki (Lopez)—with whom he kidnaps a retarded kid to extort his powerful brother. Then real-life sweethearts Affleck and Lopez generate all the heat of a snowball. Walken momentarily steps in from Walkenland for a single scene, and Pacino (apparently paying back director Brest for his *Scent of a Woman* Oscar) tosses his past performances into a blender and pours out a growling Pacino gangster smoothie for one scene. It's not the worst film of 2003, but it's close. There is no histrionic excess or crackpot camp, only painfully hoary sentiment, the puppy-dog cuteness of the mentally handicapped, and the proposition that the "cure" for lesbianism is one good man brave enough to get in touch with his inner cow. —*S.A.*

GIRLS JUST WANT TO HAVE FUN L: COMEDY/COMEDY (1985) 90M D: Alan Metter. *Sarah Jessica Parker, Helen Hunt, Lee Montgomery, Jonathan Silverman, Morgan Woodward, Shannen Doherty. Girls Just Want To Have Fun* is one of my wife's '80s favorites. Parker delivers truckloads of energy as Janey, a dance-obsessed teenager stuck in a Catholic school. Janey and her best friend Lynne (Hunt) spend every day after school watching their favorite show, *Dance TV*. When they announce a dance contest in which the winner will become a regular on the show, Janey knows she is good enough to win but her father forbids her to try out. Lynne urges her to break the rules for once and go for it. *Girls* is one the most uplifting, musically driven, and fast-paced comedies that is, for sure, like, totally '80s. —*R. D.*

GOOD GIRL, THE L: COMEDY/COMEDY (2002) 93M D: Miguel Arteta. *Jennifer Aniston, Jake Gyllenhaal, John C. Reilly. The Good Girl* is both humorous and depressing, though the latter sums up the overall feeling one gets from viewing the film. The humor, while frequent, is at times uncomfortable and other times just plain mean to the characters. There is an overreliance on Southern clichés, but it should be noted there are plenty of instances when laughs are earned in more honest ways. The film is unexpectedly moving at times, especially in quiet moments where Aniston is allowed to express her character through small actions or gestures. She truly does give her best film performance to date, and she more than matches the cast around her, all of whom turn in excellent performances. Mostly well-written—if a bit unsatisfying at the end—*The Good Girl* is a film that deserves to be seen, though it will surely be met with mixed reactions. —*C. P.*

GREASER'S PALACE L: COMEDY/INDEPENDENT COMEDY (1972) 91M D: Robert Downey. *Allan Arbus, Elsie Downey, Larry Moyer, John Paul Hudson, Alex Hitchcock, Jackson Haynes, Don Smolen.* Rife with anachronisms (they're kind of a leitmotif), this film could only be from the end of the '60s. *Greaser's Palace* stars Arbus (of TV's *M*A*S*H*) as the zoot-suited Jessy, who drops out of the sky—with a modern parachute—into the Old West. A series of perplexing but hilarious non sequiturs reveals he is trying to find his way to Jerusalem to be a "singer/actor"; that he (rather perfunctorily) heals the sick and raises the dead; that he dances better on the surface of a lake than on a stage; and that bleeding from the palms of his hands is his likeliest ticket to fame. The dusty little town is run by the inexplicably named Seaweedhead Greaser, who keeps his loving mother in a cage, kills his son Lamy Homo every time Jessy resurrects him, and is inordinately proud of his daughter Cholera, who really packs 'em in at the Palace. Confusion reigns, but it's a hoot nonetheless. Oh, plus there's Toni Basil riding a horse topless. —*C. C.*

GRIFFIN, EDDIE: DYSFUNKTIONAL FAMILY L: COMEDY/STAND-UP COMEDY (2003) 83M D: George Gallo. *Eddie Griffin.* After *Undercover Brother*, Griffin was able to theatrically release this concert film. The concert scenes are shot on real film, not the crappy video they usually use for concert films now, and he comes out all cocky in leather like old Richard Pryor and Eddie Murphy movies. It's not for the sensitive—Griffin makes ignorant comments about Arabs, gays, and retarded people, and uses the n-word probably hundreds of times—but the more he gets into it, the more likely he is to win you over. One thing that makes this movie a little different from other concert films is that it is interspersed with interviews with the family members who inspire Griffin's jokes (his mother, a porn-obsessed uncle, etc.). You see one of his uncles going to rehab, then sitting in the audience watching as Griffin jokes about him shooting up. Some of the deleted footage on the DVD really fleshes things out, with Griffin spending more time talking with his relatives, kids, and strangers on the street. —*B. T.*

GROSSE POINTE BLANK L: COMEDY/COMEDY (1997) 107M D: George Armitage. *John Cusack, Joan Cusack, Minnie Driver, Hank Azaria, Dan Aykroyd, Alan Arkin.* Cusack plays a former military assassin gone independent, now experiencing an early midlife crisis, so he hits his high school reunion and confronts the sweetheart (the delightful Driver) he abandoned for a life of human target shooting. Director Armitage (who was last heard from helming the underrated *Miami Blues*) gets the mix of wry humor and edgy violence dead on, and cowriter/coproducer Cusack's cocked-grin charm and earnest determination tells us not to take it too seriously. Cusack's sister Joan almost steals the film in a few brief scenes as his deliriously sunny but ruthlessly efficient secretary, and Arkin is at his understated best as a reluctant shrink offering such sage advice as "Don't kill anybody for a while." A darkly humorous examination of '80s values refracted through '90s ironic humor. —*S. A.*

GROUNDHOG DAY L: COMEDY/COMEDY (1993) 103M D: Harold Ramis. *Bill Murray, Andie MacDowell, Stephen Tobolowsky, Chris Elliot.* Imagine having to live the lamest day of your life over and over and over again for all eternity, waking up to the same lame song every day and running into the same lame people in the same lame scenarios. Murray plays Phil, a weatherman who has been sent for about the billionth year in a row to report on whether or not the groundhog will see his shadow. The day keeps replaying on a loop, and no one seems to notice except Phil. At first this seems like a cool trick, and he exploits it to his advantage, but when Phil realizes he very well might be living this day for all eternity, he runs the gamut from depressed and suicidal to resigned. If you enjoy the sarcastic wit of Murray, this movie will give you plenty of opportunity to see it happen. Maybe you won't laugh at his first reaction to the situation, and maybe not even to his twenty-third, but the twenty-seventh time will get you for sure. —*J. S.*

HAPPY ACCIDENTS L: COMEDY/INDEPENDENT COMEDY (2000) 110M D: Brad Anderson. *Marisa Tomei, Vincent D'Onofrio, Nadia Dajani, Tovah Feldshuh, Holland Taylor.* "You're so old-fashioned. He's from the future. What do you see in each other?" Tomei is an unlucky-at-love New Yorker who finds true love with sensitive, sweet D'Onofrio, who is either a time traveler from the future or simply another kook in her life. Writer/director Anderson (*Next Stop, Wonderland*) rethinks the cult time-travel film *La Jette* as a delirious traditional romance. D'Onofrio's accumulation of faded photos, scribbled pictures, and unassailable (and unprovable) logic make him seem credible in one scene and bonkers in the next, and puts some real, troubling questions on the line: When does humoring end and enabling begin? Where do we draw the line, and why, and is it all worth it? Not to worry: Anderson is a hopeless romantic in a cynical world. He embraces romantic abandon and the craziness of life and, for a brief moment, makes the case that true love is the only power that can crack time and space. —*S. A.*

HAPPY CAMPERS L: COMEDY/COMEDY (2002) 94M D: Daniel Waters. *Brad Renfro, James King, Peter Stormare, Dominique Swain, Emily Bergl, Jordan Bridges.* Renfro and Swain are just two of the opposites who attract in this summer camp comedy written and directed by *Heathers* screenwriter Waters. While hardly as subversive as that cult classic, this farce of raging hormones and clashing personalities takes some surprising turns on familiar roads. Left to their own devices when the camp's sole adult supervisor (Stormare) goes catatonic after lightning zaps him, the two sexy leads go at it like rabbits and the young campers get a sex education they will never forget. The camp becomes powered by the sparks they give off, and sputters into chaos when their physical thrill is complicated by emotional baggage. *Happy Campers* is really about the hurt we can do from indifference and fear of intimacy. Not bad for a film that otherwise delivers the requisite camp clichés: the picked-on nerds, the kid-hating counselor who bonds, and of course the camp babe who likes to skinny dip. —*S. A.*

After his classic debut with *Heathers*, Waters had a stint as the Hollywood go-to writer to give your big studio movie clever quips and subversive or satirical undertones. *Batman Returns* has a chaotic storyline but it's crammed full of funny lines and unexpected weirdness, and I've always suspected Waters was responsible for the occasional laughs in multiple-screenwriter messes like *Demolition Man* and *Hudson Hawk*. Unfortunately, Waters's directorial debut doesn't

deliver on the promise of his earlier work. There are one or two laughs and a somewhat admirable attempt to mess with the formula of the summer camp genre, but the end result is completely forgettable. —*B. T.*

HAPPY GILMORE L: COMEDY/COMEDY (1996) 92M D: Dennis Dugan. *Adam Sandler, Carl Weathers, Frances Bay, Christopher McDonald, Julie Bowen.* Every time I mention I hate *Happy Gilmore*, I get ten people defending this piece of shit. "Oh, it's not great, but what about the Bob Barker scene... that's funny!" Yeah, Uncle Gary murdered five people, but remember when he told that joke and then punched Bob Barker in the face... Ha! And then I'm the bad guy, as if I'm the one who made the movie shitty. All I did was not laugh. If I want a good golf comedy, I'll watch *Caddyshack*. If I want a hilarious, gross-out, pseudo-sports movie, I'll watch *Kingpin*. Those movies are actually funny. You don't have to like *Happy Gilmore* just because "they" say it's funny; sometimes it's OK not to laugh. Sometimes everyone else is wrong. Leave me alone. —*K. C.*

HAPPY TEXAS L: COMEDY/COMEDY (1999) 104M D: Mark Illsley. *Steve Zahn, Jeremy Northam, William H. Macy, Ally Walker, Ron Perlman, Illeana Douglas.* *Happy, Texas* is a great uplifting comedy, sorely underrated. In recent years, Zahn has edged his way onto the A-list with his great comic timing and honestly funny characters. The film includes memorable supporting roles by Douglas, Macy, and Perlman. The plot is funny as well: two small-time crooks escape from jail and land in a small town, where they masquerade as beauty pageant coordinators. At first their only concern is staying out of sight, but as the children start to pull on their heartstrings, they begin embracing their new jobs. While pretending to be a gay couple, they start learning a few things about themselves, and with a little success build their self-esteem and make some new friends to boot. —*R. D.*

HEATHERS L: COMEDY/COMEDY (1989) 102M D: Michael Lehmann. *Winona Ryder, Christian Slater, Kim Walker, Lisanne Falk, Shannon Doherty.* *Heathers* was one of the biggest teen favorites of the early '90s. Almost everyone I knew was doing their best Slater or Ryder impressions and quoting lines from the film long after its theatrical release, and for good reason. Teens didn't really have a lot to call their own after John Hughes finished his teen run with *Ferris Bueller's Day Off*. *Heathers* had a darker, more biting style. It spoke our language and accurately mirrored high school social pressures. Underneath all its morally incorrect behavior, crass language, and homicidal tendencies, this film has one great underlying message: Be yourself. —*R. D.*

HICKS, BILL: SANE MAN L: COMEDY/STAND-UP COMEDY
(1989) 80M D: Kevin Booth. *Bill Hicks.* Crass, crude, incendiary, offensive. These epitaphs have been used to describe the late Hicks. There's another that leans closer to the truth: genius. Hicks was, quite simply, one of the greatest stand-up comedians ever. With an acidic wit and an acerbic attitude, Hicks waged an unrelenting attack on all that was illogical in modern existence. He not only paved the way for such comedians as Eddie Izzard, Joe Rogan, and Denis Leary, he also showed that stand-up (if done right) is not only an art form, but a weapon to be reckoned with (bringng up constant comparisons to Lenny Bruce, George Carlin, and Richard Pryor). *Sane Man* is the perfect primer for noninitiates. While not as poignant as *Revelations* or as sharp as *Relentless, Sane Man* is Hicks at his best: edgy, observant, and caustic as all fuck. Not only will you understand why he was the only person to have his appearance on the David Letterman show excised after taping, but why his legions of fans keep growing exponentially. —*K. S.*

HICKS, BILL: UNITED STATES OF ADVERTISING (AKA BILL HICKS: CAPZEYEZ INTERVIEW) L: COMEDY/STAND-UP COMEDY (1993) 80M D: Not credited. *Bill Hicks.*
In October 1993, while in Austin for a show, Hicks appeared on a public access show called *CapZeyeZ.* Just him and some rocker dude named Dave Prewitt and some goofy phonecallers who ask about everything from that one joke he told that one time to the situation in Israel and Palestine. Hicks gives the scoop on the time his entire routine was censored from David Letterman (repeatedly, since callers keep saying they missed the beginning of his explanation) and talks very candidly about the state of his career afterward. He says people like Letterman tell him they like him because he's edgy, then ask him to come on their show and tone it down. He didn't want to do that, so he ended up doing a show at a place called The Laugh Stop and talking on public access between crappy local videos. This was his last taped interview before he died of cancer. (Available from the website for his production company, Sacred Cow.) —*B. T.*

HIGH SCHOOL HIGH L: COMEDY/COMEDY (1996) 86M D: Hart Bochner. *Jon Lovitz, Tia Carrere, Mekhi Phifer, Louise Fletcher.* High School High is full of enjoyable parodies and sight gags. Lovitz plays a new teacher who really cares for his kids and his responsibilities. He gets a job at a problematic school where the students have control and the cowardly teachers pass the time making little educational effort. Lovitz gracefully takes a few punches and eventually earns the student's respect, as well as the admiration of his sexy coworker Carrere. —*R. D.*

HIGH STRUNG L: COMEDY/COMEDY (1994) 93M D: Roger Nygard. *Steve Oedekerk, Kirsten Dunst, Jani Lane, Denise Crosby, Fred Willard, Thomas F. Wilson, Jim Carrey.* High Strung is a little too obnoxious for most people, but I love it. It stars writer and comic actor Oedekerk. Throughout the film, his easily irritated character, Thane Furrors, barrages the audience with complaints and insights. Oedekerk has a unique, extremely sarcastic comic style. *High Strung* has a few notable cameo roles by Wilson (*Back to the Future*'s Biff), Crosby (*Star Trek: TNG*'s Lieutenant Natasha Yar), and Lane (lead singer of Warrant, in his only film appearance). You can also get a glimpse of a twelve-year-old Dunst, a rubberfaced Carrey, and my favorite cameo by Willard (*Best in Show, Waiting for Guffman*) as a naive insurance salesman. This is not an easy movie to find, unfortunately, because it was out of print for a long time. But if you get a chance, check it out—it's really funny. —*R. D.*

HISTORY OF WHITE PEOPLE IN AMERICA, THE L: COMEDY/COMEDY (1986) 100M D: Harry Shearer. *Martin Mull, Mary Kay Place, Steve Martin, Fred Willard.* Much has been said about the history of minorities in America. Asian, African-American, Pacific Islander, Latino—these people have roots and histories that are worth documenting. But what is to be said about white people? What roots and history do they have in America worth mentioning? This mockumentary seeks to answer the real question: what does it mean to be white? The result is hilarious interviews and staged conversation about the most important aspects of being white, featuring a thorough analysis of the white man's love of mayonnaise and BBQ. Oh, and don't forget—they really, really love dairy, so bring that sweet cow juice *on.* A documentary about white people is the silliest concept in the world, which is what makes this film totally fucking hilarious. In case you don't get enough of making fun of white people the first time around, you can always watch the sequel. —*J. S.*

HORSE FEATHERS L: COMEDY TEAMS/MARX BROTHERS (1932) 67M D: Norman Z. McLeod. *Groucho Marx, Chico Marx, Harpo Marx, Zeppo Marx, Thelma Todd, David Landau.* This Marx Brothers's film features Groucho as the new president of Huxley College. Through confusion and delusion he helps gangsters rig an all-important football game, but not in the way they expected. Instead of using the two players they chose, Groucho uses Chico and Harpo. You can imagine the problems. Zeppo plays a student who tries adding rationality and romance. Chico and Harpo show off their musical prowess on the piano and harp. Altogether this is classic Marx Brothers and fun for all ages. —*N. J.*

HOT CHICK, THE L: COMEDY/COMEDY (2002) 102M D: Tom Brady. *Rob Schneider, Anna Faris, Mathew Lawrence, Robert Davi.* Schneider is right up there with Tom Green and Adam Sandler in stupid humor, so when you're in the mood for a stupid movie

that will appeal to your crude, silly side, this one will hit the spot. A bitchy, beautiful cheerleader steals some magical earrings and sets off a spell that causes her to switch bodies with a dirty criminal loser. The rest of the movie finds the beautiful, bitchy cheerleader trying to figure out where her body is and who is in it before she is forced to remain a burly, unattractive man forever. *The Hot Chick* has no intellectual merit whatsoever, but when you want to put your brain on the shelf for the evening, Schneider is your woman. —*J. S.*

HOT DOG...THE MOVIE! L: COMEDY/COMEDY (1984) 92M
D: Peter Markle. *David Naughton, Frank Koppala, Shannon Tweed, John Patrick Reger, Tracy Smith, Patrick Houser.* There is no question that *Hot Dog . . . The Movie* warped my fragile little thirteen-year-old mind. This movie has way too much nudity for a child, and only recently when I watched it on DVD did I realize how horrible it really is. The skiing footage is decent, but overall the film has about as much depth as a porno, but without all the good stuff. I had always remembered the classic lines, "Hey Rudy, you can kiss my ass, not on this side, not on that side, but right in the middle" and "Whatas is the fukas is a Chinese downhill?" My coworker Rich accurately described this movie as being like *Porky's* on skis. —*R. D.*

HUMAN NATURE L: COMEDY/COMEDY (2001) 96M D: Michel
Gondry. *Tim Robbins, Rhys Ifans, Patricia Arquette, Miranda Otto, Robert Forster.* Written by Charlie Kaufman, this film wasn't as well received as his *Being John Malkovich* or *Adaptation.* Nevertheless it is a very funny yet depressing satire about an uptight scientist (Robbins), a nature writer with a rare hair disease (Arquette), and a man raised by apes (Ifans). Notions of civilization clash between two extremes: the characters see life as a choice between fanatical adherence to table etiquette or running around naked sniffing women's butts and masturbating compulsively. There are also some absurd narrative tricks: one of the movie's three narrators speaks from beyond the grave, but offers virtually no insight into the events. —*B. T.*

HYSTERICAL L: COMEDY/COMEDY (1983) 87M D: Chris
Bearde. *Bill Hudson, Mark Hudson, Brett Hudson, Cindy Pickett, Richard Kiel, Bud Cort.* This is one of those really cheesy, really funny, and outrageously creative slapstick cult favorites. It features the Hudson Brothers, who shared moderate fame in music and television (*The Hudson Brothers Show*). After honing their talents on the tube, the team brought comic genius to this film. *Hysterical* offers a lot of great parodies of hit films like *Indiana Jones, The Exorcist, The Shining, Friday the 13th*, and at least a dozen more. The writing is so ridiculous. When people start turning into zombies, for instance, they immediately put on turtlenecks and repeatedly say, "What difference

does it make?" This movie is weird enough, bad enough, and constantly funny enough to earn a truly cult classic reputation. —*R. D.*

I LOVE YOU TO DEATH L: COMEDY/COMEDY (1990) 110M
D: Lawrence Kasdan. *Tracey Ullman, Joan Plowright, River Phoenix, William Hurt, Keanu Reeves, Kevin Kline.* This is a keeper, one of those hilarious films to watch every year. The cast is amazing, starting with Kline, who plays Joey, a man with more than eyes for the many women frequenting his pizza joint. Joey's sexual excursions are finally discovered by his loving wife (Ullman), who first contemplates suicide, then decides to murder her husband instead. With the aid of her "I can fix anything" mother (Plowright), she devises various plans to do the deed, the funniest involving the hiring of two stoned discount hit men (Hurt and Reeves). Truly a role made for Reeves! But Joey is not a normal man and just won't die. To top it all off, the film is based on a true story! —*R. D.*

IGBY GOES DOWN L: COMEDY/COMEDY (2002) 104M D: Burr
Steers. *Amanda Peet, Kieran Culkin, Claire Danes, Jeff Goldblum, Susan Sarandon, Bill Pullman.* Culkin is Igby, the almost-eighteen-year-old son of a institutionalized schizophrenic father (Pullman) and a self-absorbed, cold mother (Sarandon). Igby is kicked out of every school he attends. Frustrated with his life and harboring a lot of ill feelings toward his mother, Igby moves to New York and hides out with the strung-out mistress of his rich godfather, D. H. (Goldblum). For the rest of the movie, we watch as this child of fucked-up parents goes further down the path to being fucked up himself, until the movie climaxes with no real resolution. *Igby* is extremely overindulgent, but it doesn't particularly move me. Every character is so overwhelmingly tragic that tragedy starts to negate itself, and the interactions feel quirky and contrived. On a side note, I'm sure I'm not the only one who feels the Culkin kids should be locked in a hole somewhere and never allowed to act again. —*J. S.*

I'M GONNA GIT YOU SUCKA L: COMEDY/INDEPENDENT
COMEDY (1988) 90M D: Keenen Ivory Wayans. *Keenen Ivory Wayans, Bernie Casey, Antonio Fargas, Steve James, Isaac Hayes.* This good-natured *Airplane*-style blaxploitation parody stars the director (Wayans) as a goody-two-shoes war hero named Jack Spade who returns home and is soon out for revenge against Mr. Big (John Vernon), whose illegal dealings caused Spade's brother to O.G. (over gold). Casey plays Jack's mentor, and the latter also gets some help from Hammer and Slammer (Hayes and Jim Brown). There's so many jokes you won't care that some of them aren't very funny. My favorite scene finds Fargas at a pimp convention reading his poem, "Bitch Better Have My Money." There are lots of great bits by then-upcoming actors like Chris Rock (in a funny scene at a rib joint), Kadeem Hardison,

and Damon Wayans. There was a short-lived TV series spin-off called *Hammer, Slammer, and Slade* before Wayans went on to produce the *In Living Color* TV show and the pretty lame *Scary Movie* films. —*S. H.*

IMPOSTORS L: COMEDY/COMEDY (1998) 101M D: Stanley Tucci. *Lili Taylor, Steve Buscemi, Teagle F. Bougere, Stanley Tucci, Oliver Platt, Elizabeth Bracco, Campbell Scott, Tony Shalhoub, Allison Janney.* This is a movie to watch with friends because you are going to quote it for days afterward. Each member of the large cast is given their own moment to shine, and the actors run with them as far as they can. Scott is hilarious, Platt is brilliant as always, and Taylor is more beautiful than I have ever seen her. The final shot of the movie—which runs over the closing credits—is the perfect ending, leaving me feeling happy, sparkly, satisfied, and eager for more. —*E. W.*

IT'S A GIFT L: CLASSIC COMEDY/CLASSIC COMEDY (1934) 71M D: Norman Z. McLeod. *W. C. Fields, Jean Rouverol, Baby Le Roy, Tammany Young, Kathleen Howard, Julian Madison.* For W. C. Fields fans there's only one real argument: is the Great Man's most sublime movie *The Bank Dick* or *It's a Gift*? The latter, a chronicle of the trials of Harold Bissonette of Wappinger's Falls, is little more than an hour in length, but every minute is golden. Walking through life, you find yourself ambushed at odd intervals by memories of. . . Harold losing possession of his own bathroom in mid-shave. . . la famille Bissonette at table. . . the patient exasperation of Mrs. B lying abed reciting a litany of life's disappointments while Harold tries to fall asleep. . . the blind man and his cane in the general store. . . the road trip to California. . . the early-morning quest of a stentorian gentleman seeking one Carl LaFong. . . . It doesn't get any better than this. —*R. T. J.*

JAWBREAKER L: COMEDY/COMEDY (1999) 90M D: Darren Stein. *Rebecca Gayheart, Chad Christ, Julie Benz, Rose McGowan, Judy Greer.* This hateful homage to *Heathers* and *Carrie* was made by filmmakers who clearly don't understand what made those movies powerful. The dialogue is painfully self-conscious, the shock humor embarrassingly forced, and the one character who's supposed to be sympathetic agrees to cover up a murder in exchange for a makeover. You get the feeling this director watched every movie ever made about high school but never actually attended one. I hate this fucking movie. —*B. T.*

JAY AND SILENT BOB STRIKE BACK L: COMEDY/COMEDY (2001) 104M D: Kevin Smith. *Kevin Smith, Jason Mewes, Ben Affleck, Shannon Elizabeth, Shannon Doherty.* Jay and Silent Bob, the peripheral stoner duo from Smith's other movies, take center stage in this embarrassingly unfunny vehicle for amateurish film nerd self-indulgence. In *Chasing Amy* the two became the basis for a cult comic book. Here they find out that comic is being turned into a movie, so they head to Hollywood to interfere. Along the way, they find all kinds of wacky movie in-jokes and excuses to call people "pole smoker." Ha ha, Ben Affleck plays a character who insults Ben Affleck! Get it? Because he *is* Ben Affleck! That's why it's funny! To be fair, this might be a fun time for hardcore Smith fans after a couple of tokes, several beers, and twelve hard punches to the head. It's basically a nonstop parade of cameos and references to Smith's other films, sandwiched between obvious parodies of *Star Wars, Planet of the Apes, Charlie's Angels,* and *Scooby Doo.* Leslie Nielsen was unavailable for comment. —*B. T.*

JERK, THE L: COMEDY/COMEDY (1979) 94M D: Carl Reiner. *Steve Martin, Bernadette Peters, Jackie Mason, M. Emmet Walsh.* Martin's movie debut combines lots of his stand-up comedy routines and puts them into the framework of a Jerry Lewis comedy. It's pretty dumb, but *The Jerk* is funny as hell and I refer to it in my day-to-day life with alarming regularity. When someone gets excited about a phone book, it's hard not to think of *The Jerk.* Navin Johnson (Martin), a dimwitted, misfit white guy who lives with a family of black sharecroppers, hears some easy-listening music on the radio and embarks on a quest to find his way in the world. Along the way he works at a gas station, a carnival, falls in love with Bernadette Peters, makes millions of dollars with a stupid invention and, in my favorite scenes, gets chased around by Walsh. —*S. H.*

JERRY AND TOM L: COMEDY/INDEPENDENT COMEDY (1998) 106M D: Saul Rubinek. *Joe Mantegna, Sam Rockwell, Maury Chaykin, Ted Danson, Charles Durning, William H. Macy, Sarah Polley. Jerry and Tom* has a cool script (adapted from a play), great actors, and creative editing. Mantegna plays a seasoned hit man who reluctantly takes on a prodigy (Rockwell). These hit men are far from professional and share many hilarious scenes, including an argument over how to work a chainsaw on one of the bodies. Their victims are played by the likes of Danson and Macy, among other great supporting actors. Fans of *Fargo* will definitely enjoy this black comedy. Movie joke: "A grasshopper walks into a bar and the bartender says 'Hey, we have a drink named after you'—and the grasshopper says 'What, you have a drink named Kevin?'" —*R. D.*

J-MEN FOREVER L: COMEDY TEAMS/FIRESIGN THEATRE (1979) 73M D: Peter Bergman, Philip Proctor, Richard Patterson. *Philip Proctor, Peter Bergman, M. G. Kelly.* If you were born after 1970, you may not have heard of Firesign Theatre, but if your parents were hip they probably have an old Firesign Theatre record stuck in the basement. Similar to Cheech and Chong, Monty Python, and the later MST3K posse, these guys made up crazy characters for radio, records, and short films. They had been polishing their act for about ten years before *J-Men Forever* came out. The film consists of old black and white, sci-fi action serials spliced together and dubbed to create a different plot in which rock and roll threatens to take over the world. There's a plethora of funny one-liners and enough cool footage to help brighten up any Sunday afternoon. Favorite song lyric: "Off I go wearing my tight pajamas, flying high, this is the life." —*R. D.*

JOE DIRT L: COMEDY/COMEDY (2001) 91M D: Dennie Gordon. *David Spade, Christopher Walken, Kid Rock, Adam Beach, Brittany Daniel, Dennis Miller.* I like Spade. He's a funny guy, and because he is a funny guy, he makes *Joe Dirt*—a silly, kind of stupid movie—actually pretty fucking funny. Joe, a big-hearted redneck with a mullet wig fused to his skull, is working as a janitor in a radio station when an asshole DJ decides to have him tell his story on the air simply to make fun of him. As Joe tells his story, however, from when he was "accidentally" left at the Grand Canyon by his parents, all the way to his budding romance with backwoods hottie Brandy and the discovery that his deadbeat parents are wanks, Joe goes from being the butt of a joke to a source of inspiration, retaining his optimism and good nature through all of the shit. Yeah, it's corny, but it feels good, and has a lot of giggles along the way. *Joe Dirt* is my guilty pleasure. —*J. S.*

JOE VERSUS THE VOLCANO L: COMEDY/COMEDY (1990) 106M D: John Patrick Shanley. *Tom Hanks, Meg Ryan, Lloyd Bridges, Robert Stack, Abe Vigoda.* Unfairly slighted and maligned upon its initial release, this film is actually well worth a viewing (or a second viewing, if need be). Much more than the bizarre comedy it would seem to suggest, it reveals itself to be a moving story of one man's quest for meaning (and love) in an increasingly isolated and oversaturated consumer society.... Plus it's funny and romantic. —*C. P.*

JUMP TOMORROW L: COMEDY/INDEPENDENT COMEDY (2001) 95M D: Joel Hopkins. *Hippolyte Girardot, James Wilby, Patricia Mauceri, Natalia Verbeke.* Gentle, shy, buttoned-down Tunde Adebimpe is a Nigerian born but thoroughly American, white-collar wage slave who seems uncomfortable with his own body, which tends to collide with anything in his orbit. Already engaged, he falls for an impulsive, sunny young Spanish woman (Verbeke) and takes a detour on the way to his own wedding to follow his heart. The feature debut of NYU graduate Hopkins is an old-fashioned screwball road-trip romance with a modern flair and a funky lounge score. Imagine a Hal Hartley film with a rich, multicultural canvas in place of the self-conscious irony. The film's a bit stiff and stilted at times, a common quality of first-time directors who try too hard to sculpt every scene, but it's refreshingly bereft of slick cynicism and smart-ass snideness. Hopkins has

a passion that's hard to resist and his romantic abandon smoothes over the bumps and familiar twists on this road to love. —*S. A.*

Much less overtly stylized than the trailers lead one to believe. Not horrible, but just another semi-generic indie comedy that tries to throw a half-assed high five in the direction of Wes Anderson, who just looks the other way and leaves the room without saying anything. —*A. T.*

JUST MARRIED L: COMEDY/COMEDY (2003) 94M D: Shawn Levy. *Ashton Kutcher, Brittany Murphy, Christian Kane.* Girl meets Guy. Girl and Guy date for a very short time, and then decide to get married. Rich family of Girl objects, but they marry anyway. Guy and Girl go on honeymoon. Lots of shit goes wrong. Guy and Girl return from honeymoon wishing they had never met. Guy and Girl realize that, oh yeah, marriage is hard sometimes, and they really do love each other, even though he's a dirt poor lame ass and she's a snotty rich princess. Sound good? It's not. Not at all. The story has been done before, and much better. Funny moments are few and far between, and the acting leaves much to be desired. So what good can I possibly say about it? Kutcher is HOT, and he takes his pants off. Owwwww! —*J. S.*

JUST ONE OF THE GIRLS (AKA **ANYTHING FOR LOVE**) L: COMEDY/COMEDY (1993) 94M D: Michael Keusch. *Corey Haim, Sheelah Megill, Alanis Morissette, Johannah Newmarch, Cameron Bancroft, Nicole Eggert.* This marks the last enjoyable Corey Haim movie. He stars as Chris (turned "Chrissy") who runs around dressed up as a girl to avoid fighting the school bully (Bancroft, *Beverly Hills, 90210*). This film takes a lot of dorky, obvious jabs at gender swapping from a guy's point of view (such as how he can get away with being in the girl's locker room). But sometimes I just want to let my mind wander, and there's a lot of room for that here. There's also a noteworthy cameo by Alanis Morisette, sporting mammoth hair. The film's biggest downfall is that even though Haim sure looks girly, he doesn't make a very believable female. Oh well, you can't win them all. —*R. D.*

JUST ONE OF THE GUYS L: COMEDY/COMEDY (1985) 100M D: Lisa Gottlieb. *Joyce Hyser, Clayton Rohner, Sherilyn Fenn, Billy Jacoby.* Just One of the Guys is an endearing high school comedy about Terry (Hyser), who thinks by masquerading as a man she will be taken seriously as a writer. This movie doesn't rely too heavily on obvious gender-swapping gags and has more heart than laughs. My favorite character is Buddy (Jacoby), Terry's brother, who teaches Terry some of the finer things about being a guy. The most memorable scene is where he shows her how to shift her package. This film was directed by a woman and the result is a more emotional story featuring characters to whom you can relate. This also has an early performance by a twenty-year-old

Fenn, one year before she was in *The Wraith* and *Thrashin'*. —*R. D.*

KEEPING THE FAITH L: COMEDY/COMEDY (2000) 128M D: Edward Norton. *Edward Norton, Jenna Elfman, Ben Stiller, Anne Bancroft, Milos Forman.* Not your usual love triangle, this romantic comedy has both heart and wit in abundance. Norton (in his directorial debut) and Stiller play best friends Brian and Jake, who happen to be a priest and a rabbi. Their interfaith congeniality is shaken by a visit from their childhood friend Anna (Elfman), for whom they both end up falling. The film follows their mutual growing infatuation with Anna and the restrictions their religions place on their feelings. Brian is a Catholic priest, so obviously he can't even think about being with her. But while Jake's Judaism allows him to hook up, dating outside the faith is highly frowned upon by his congregation. While feelings intensify and love blooms, Brian and Jake's relationship strains under the pressure. Bancroft is wonderful as Jake's mother, and Forman shines briefly as Brian's priest-mentor. *Keeping the Faith* kept me drunk off its charms for days after viewing it. —*J. K.*

KENTUCKY FRIED MOVIE, THE L: COMEDY/SKETCH COMEDY (1977) 90M D: John Landis. *Donald Sutherland, George Lazenby, Henry Gibson, Bill Bixby, Tony Dow, David Zucker.* There is a whole week's worth of laughs contained here in one of the greatest sketch comedy films of all time (though you might have to lower your taste level a bit). The gratuitous nudity tends to be a deterrent for some folks, but it's tasteful and obviously just for laughs. Amid the boob jokes and potty humor there is a shimmering gem. The *Enter the Dragon* parody, *A Fistful of Yen*, makes up most of the movie. It's an intelligent, ridiculous, and important piece that was an inspiration to many future parody filmmakers. I'm sure they upset a few people when they made the Bruce Lee character sound like Elmer Fudd. Cowritten by Jim Abrahams and David Zucker (the team who three years later changed the world with *Airplane!*), it's also the second film directed by Landis, who would go on to direct *Animal House* the following year and the wonder hit of 1980, *The Blues Brothers.* —*R. D.*

KINGPIN L: COMEDY/COMEDY (1996) 113M D: Bobby Farrelly, Peter Farrelly. *Woody Harrelson, Vanessa Angel, Randy Quaid, Bill Murray.* There is no film that epitomizes America better than the Farrelly brothers's *Kingpin.* We get everything here: bowling, severed hands, rubber hands, road trips, the Amish, bull-masturbation, cool '70s hairdos, cool '90s comb-overs, sluts, dudes getting it in the scrotum, women getting punched in the boobs, *The Jeffersons on Ice*, anal-rape fantasies, Chris Elliot, Jack Daniels, Murray, and especially bowling, the most American of "sports." Everything that makes America great. —*K. C.*

LAST AMERICAN VIRGIN, THE L: COMEDY/COMEDY (1982) 90M D: Boaz Davidson. *Lawrence Monoson, Diane Franklin, Steve Antin, Joe Rubbo.* This 1982 teen sex comedy is one of the best of the era, up there with *Fast Times at Ridgemont High* in terms of its humor, honesty, and poignant coming-of-age story. It also has comic antics of a teens-chasing-tail movie. But it is emotionally true, confronting the fact that being a teenager is not always fun and full of hilarious romps, but often shitty and depressing. A great, unparalleled ending makes the characters seem all the more real, and that's what sets this film apart. *The Last American Virgin* is a silly romantic comedy, but because we're dealing with real life, everything gets fucked up and it all falls apart. It's funny because it's true. —*T. S.*

LAST DAYS OF DISCO, THE L: COMEDY/INDEPENDENT COMEDY (1998) 120M D: Whit Stillman. *Chloë Sevigny, Kate Beckinsale, Christopher Eigeman, Matt Keeslar, MacKenzie Astin, Robert Sean Leonard.* *The Last Days of Disco* takes place later in the post–*Saturday Night Fever* portion of the disco era, when the phenomenon was devoured by cultural changes of the early '80s. The protagonists are pretentious yuppies who spend the movie talking and worrying about their clothes, their apartments, the mistakes of their college years, and the right cocktail for their image. Sevigny gives the most sympathetic performance as a young woman struggling in the publishing world. The least sympathetic character is debatable; it's probably the full-of-shit womanizer Eigeman, but there's also Astin (*The Garbage Pail Kids Movie*), who works in advertising and brings his clients to the disco to seem cool. These characters are like old friends you now realize are assholes, but you still find yourself hanging out with them. On paper it sounds like a movie I'd hate, but it's an oddly captivating look into a world I'm glad I missed. —*B. T.*

LAST SUPPER, THE L: COMEDY/INDEPENDENT COMEDY (1995) 94M D: Stacy Title. *Cameron Diaz, Ron Eldard, Annabeth Gish, Jonathan Penner, Courtney Vance.* Essentially, this is a modern-day retelling of *Crime and Punishment*, but instead of a Russian intellectual, the protagonists are a bunch of American college roommates. Instead of feeling guilt over their murders, they rationalize the extinction of right-wing conservatives as a boost to society. The bodies of their dinner guests are buried in their garden, but with each killing, the inevitable question arises: when exactly does a stated opinion become a crime punishable by death? Early in the film the answer is a slam dunk, but the further along these characters go, the less certain they are about their reasoning. This is a rather daring first film for Title, but in retrospect it is really just a political reaction to some of the themes of the Clinton administration. To really do the theme justice, there ought to be a sequel at John Brown University where

those opposed to the Bush administration are invited for quail hunting. —*N.J.*

LITTLE NICKY L: COMEDY/COMEDY (2000) 90M D: Steven Brill. *Adam Sandler, Patricia Arquette, Harvey Keitel, Rhys Ifans, Tom "Tiny" Lister Jr.* Sandler plays Satan's devoted, doofus son, a socially retarded headbanger who leaves Hell for New York City to save his dad (Keitel, more amiable trickster than evil incarnate) from a coup staged by his demon brothers (Ifans and Lister). For all the high-concept gags and elaborate digital magic, there are no fall-down-funny laughs, but there's a steady stream of amusing asides, nutty gags, crude humor, and lewd references, all tempered by Sandler's gawky goofball innocence. The film is also full of fun character bits, and Keitel brings both a noblesse oblige and a sly sense of humor to the Prince of Darkness. Stupid? Well, yeah. Clumsy? Brill is no Scorsese. Funny? Sure. No one does doofus humor like Sandler. —*S.A.*

It's nice to see Sandler step away from the assembly line and try something a little more ambitious with his comedies (a supernatural storyline with numerous special effects), but in doing so he seemed to lose the low-key charm of his smaller films like *Billy Madison* and *Happy Gilmore*. Despite the extra effort and the good cast, this movie just isn't very funny. —*B.T.*

LIVING IN OBLIVION L: COMEDY/INDEPENDENT COMEDY (1995) 91M D: Tom DiCillo. *Steve Buscemi, Catherine Keener, Dermot Mulroney, Danielle von Zerneck, James LeGros, Peter Dinklage.* Being my favorite modern comedy, this is sort of a calibrating movie for me. I use it to measure other films—"Would this character be funnier with an eye patch?" or "Could James LeGros do that better?" It's funny that casting for the movie was based in part on who could put up money for its production. Broken into three sections, the film concerns three dreams of characters interwoven by their work, i.e., they're making a movie together. The story flows well as each dream brings us to a more intimate view of the characters' romances and oddities. Dinklage is the sassiest and sexiest midget I've ever seen. —*J.J.*

LIVING ON TOKYO TIME L: COMEDY/INDEPENDENT COMEDY (1987) 83M D: Steven Okazaki. *Minako Ohashi, Ken Nakagawa, Mitzie Abe, Bill Bonham, Brenda Aoki.* Green card marriages were a pretty popular movie theme in the '80s. *Living* breaks from the rest by glimpsing a culture with honesty and fairness, a culture that was exploited (e.g., *Gung-Ho*) before anime became the commercial force that it is. Kyoto, a Japanese immigrant fleeing from conflicted ideas about love and marriage, agrees to marry Ken, a really cute Japanese American who knows nothing of his "roots," but all about how to rock. OK, so he doesn't really rock that hard, but he has a lot of cool, punk rock shirts. Kyoto needs a green card and Ken needs some

action. Reality engulfs the two characters as they fumble through living together with nothing in common and little communication. —*J.J.*

LIVING OUT LOUD L: COMEDY/COMEDY (1998) 93M D: Richard LaGravenese. *Danny DeVito, Holly Hunter, Martin Donovan, Queen Latifah.* LaGravenese, the screenwriter best known for *The Fisher King*, made a strong directorial debut with this quiet, understated look into the fantasies and lives of two lonely people residing in a New York apartment building. Hunter lives mostly in her head after leaving her cheating husband, but she is able to have conversations with a sympathetic night club singer (Latifah) and an elevator operator (DeVito) who is even more troubled than she is. The richness of Hunter's character and her alternately uncomfortable and sweet relationship with DeVito's are rarities in studio films of this era. This one deserves more recognition than it has received. —*B.T.*

LONGEST YARD, THE L: COMEDY/COMEDY (1974) 121M D: Robert Aldrich. *Burt Reynolds, Eddie Albert, Michael Conrad, Ed Lauter, Richard Kiel.* A former football star (Reynolds) disgraced in a point-shaving scandal lands in prison after a drunken scuffle with police. He is forced to coach a team of prisoners against the semi-pro prison guard team. If Reynolds throws the game he gets a pardon, but he decides instead to earn back the dignity he lost during his career and help his prison buddies humiliate their oppressors. It's very contrived and full of broad character types, but it's still a fun version of the underdog sports movie formula. Reynolds is charismatic in his cockiness, reminding you why he was once such a popular sex symbol. —*B.T.*

LOVE GOD?, THE L: CLASSIC COMEDY/CLASSIC COMEDY (1969) 101M D: Nat Hiken. *Don Knotts, Anne Francis, Edmond O'Brien, James Gregory, Maureen Arthur.* Upped to PG-13 by the American ratings board twenty-five years after its release, this one is sure to redefine your entire goddamn life. Knotts shocked and alienated his fans with this film, which, by his own admission, had "a tinge of the naughty in it." No kiddin', Don, this is hot stuff! In fact, in his autobiography, Knotts blames the public's disinterest in this surprisingly steamy film for his faltering career *and* the sudden fatal heart attack of writer/director Hiken! Knotts plays Abner Peacock IV, a virginal small-town publisher who is unwittingly vaulted overnight to the Hefner-esque role of millionaire skin-mag magnate, irresistible to every woman on Earth. See Abner dance, romance, and punch people out *three* separate times! Wha?!!! The performance by semi-illiterate mob boss B. S. Pulley is without a doubt the most hilarious acting ever caught on film. I swear to god, this is the funniest movie you will ever see. —*Z.C.*

LOVELY AND AMAZING L: COMEDY/COMEDY (2001) 91M D: Nicole Holofcener. *Catherine Keener, Emily Mortimer, Brenda Blethyn, Jake Gyllenhaal, Raven Goodwin.* The title of this story of mothers and daughters is also an accurate description: a lovely and amazing portrait of self-image, insecurity, emotional need, and unquestioned devotion to family ties in a community of women. Holofcener has a startling honesty and her performers respond with fearless portrayals: Keener as the abrasive older sister, a self-obsessed would-be artist so full of hostility she drives everyone from her orbit; Mortimer as the self-doubting actress and younger sister, obsessed with the "imperfections" of her petite body; Blethyn as the mothering matriarch who goes in for liposuction to feel better about her own plus-size; and Goodwin as Blethyn's adopted youngest daughter, a chubby African American acutely aware of her difference from her sisters and her devoted mother. Characters so rarely live with such a vivid glow, and their clashing, colliding relationships zing with the chaotic off-handedness of lived-in history and the forgiving acceptance of family. —*S. A.*

LUNATICS: A LOVE STORY L: COMEDY/INDEPENDENT COMEDY (1992) 87M D: Josh Becker. *Deborah Foreman, Theodore Raimi, Bruce Campbell, George Aguilar, Brian McCree.* This is a fun and totally quirky indie comedy staring cult film legend Sam Raimi's brother, Ted. He plays Hank Stone, a delusional and paranoid guy who starts to come out of his protective tinfoil shell when he accidentally befriends a girl on the run with nowhere to go (played by *Valley Girl*'s Foreman). Together they help each other overcome some issues, all the while battling Hank's uncontrollable hallucinations. —*R. D.*

MAKING MR. RIGHT L: COMEDY/COMEDY (1987) 95M D: Susan Seidelman. *John Malkovich, Ann Magnuson, Laurie Metcalf, Ben Masters, Glenne Headly.* *Making Mr. Right* is a charming love story about Jeff Peters (Malkovich), a reclusive scientist who doesn't have a clue about women. He also plays Ulysses, an android Jeff created in his own likeness, a virtual information sponge with a lot to learn. Magnuson plays the lonely woman who teaches Ulysses a few things that weren't originally in his curriculum. Along the way she falls in love with the android and eventually teaches Mr. Peters a few things about relationships. There's a lot of female insight presented here by director Seidelman, who previously directed the smash hit *Desperately Seeking Susan*. More recently, she's directed the *Sex and the City* pilot and *Gaudi Afternoon*. —*R. D.*

MALLRATS L: COMEDY/COMEDY (1995) 96M D: Kevin Smith. *Jeremy London, Kevin Smith, Jason Mewes, Shannon Doherty, Jason Lee, Claire Forlani.* I have mixed feelings about *Mallrats*. T. S. (London) and Brodie (Lee) are best friends who have recently been dumped by their girlfriends. Brodie because he's a video-game-obsessed, immature slacker, and T. S. because his girlfriend's dad doesn't think very much of him. To soothe their broken hearts, the boys go to the mall, their favorite hangout, and spend the day trying in various ways to get their girlfriends back. I don't know; the acting is fine, the story is fine, the cinematography is fine. The humor though is the kind of stuff my little brother finds funny, and as the plot gets more and more zany, I just start to feel more and more tired. —*J. S.*

I disagree. The story and cinematography are not fine. The reason for this film's infamy is that Smith had the resources of a real movie studio behind him and still made a shitty amateur movie. Many may believe that it's OK for a movie to look like crap as long as it's a comedy, but I think that's just pure laziness. The contrivances of this plot are cringe inducing, and the physical comedy (swinging on a rope like Batman) is the type of humor that only passes on videos you made with your buddies. Even Smith admits *Mallrats* is bad, and he won't say that about most of the other garbage he is responsible for. There is one significant thing that this film can be credited for, though: it was the first significant acting role for the former pro-skateboarder Jason Lee. He may forever be doomed to play the wacky best friend of the leading man, but he's very good at playing charismatic assholes, even in this embarrassing mess. Perhaps he is one of the reasons for this film's otherwise inexplicable cult following, and perhaps they in turn are responsible for his continued career in films like *Almost Famous*. —*B. T.*

MAN OF THE CENTURY L: COMEDY/COMEDY (1999) 80M D: Adam Abraham. *Brian Davies, Gibson Frazier, Susan Egan, Cara Buono.* Frazier is Johnny Twennies, a fast-talking, hard-boiled reporter who's part con man, part big city softy, all 1930s urban smoothy. Problem is, he's living in 1999 and doesn't realize he's behind the times, much to the frustration of his swept-off-her-feet girlfriend (Egan), who still can't get him to kiss her, let alone, well. . . . Looking like David Arquette by way of Harold Lloyd, Frazier is all zippy energy, but director Abraham can't seem to set the film to his wavelength. Frazier kicks up his heels and soars on snappy patter that could have come from a Ben Hecht script, circa 1930s, while he dodges deadly mobsters, avoids his editor, and woos his sweetheart. The film just clumps trying to catch up with him. —*S. A.*

MATINEE L: COMEDY/COMEDY (1992) 98M D: Joe Dante. *John Goodman, Cathy Moriarty, Kellie Martin, Omri Katz, Lisa Jakub, Simon Fenton.* Director Dante is known for his movie in-jokes and B-movie roots (he got his start cutting trailers for Roger Corman) but this film is explicitly about movies themselves. Set during the Cuban missile crisis, *Matinee* tells the story of a kid (Fenton) who escapes the boredom and depression of his life on a military base by going to every horror and sci-fi movie he can. He befriends Lawrence Woolsey (Goodman), a filmmaker obviously based on William Castle, who has brought his new film *Mant* to town and is promoting it with a variety of gimmicks and deceptions. Woolsey even has an actor (Dick Miller, who appears in all of Dante's movies) playing a protester to drum up fake controversy around the film. Contrasting the manufactured fear of spook show theatrics with the real fear of potential nuclear war, this is Dante's most thoughtful film and easily one of his best. —*B.T.*

ME, MYSELF & IRENE L: COMEDY/COMEDY (2000) 117M D: Bobby Farrelly, Peter Farrelly. *Jim Carrey, Renée Zellweger, Robert Forster, Chris Cooper, Michael Bowman, Anthony Anderson.* Don't think too hard about this comedy. It's one of the many films that pays a comic injustice to the mentally ill and it gets away with it, this time because of the brilliance of Jim Carrey. Carrey plays a nice police officer who develops a very bad side in order to cope with his job. To get him out of the office, he's given the assignment of driving Irene from his precinct in Rhode Island to upstate New York. On the way Irene falls for Clark, the mild-mannered policeman, yet finds herself sleeping with Hank, Clark's alter ego with a fetish for dildos. Irene and Clark/Hank are accused of a Bonnie and Clyde–like crime, becoming outlaws. Beyond all the bathroom humor, schizophrenia jokes, and, of course, dildos, this comedy basically relies on a few good skits and some Jim Carrey caricatures. If that's all it takes to make you happy, knock yourself out. —*N.J.*

MEET THE HOLLOWHEADS L: COMEDY/INDEPENDENT COMEDY (1989) 89M D: Thomas R Burman. *John Glover, Nancy Mette, Richard Portnow, Matt Shakman, Juliette Lewis.* Unique black comedy about a Cleaver-esque family in a post-apocalyptic wasteland, or another planet, or another dimension…it's not really clear. Outside it's always dark and wanderers run the risk of falling off "the edge," so everything a family needs is shipped into their house through pneumatic tubes. Since director Burman and his family are veteran FX artists, there's a mutant dog and tentacles that come through the tubes for medical purposes. Unfortunately the story and characters aren't as clever as the world they live in. —*B.T.*

MEET THE PARENTS L: COMEDY/COMEDY (2000) 108M D: Jay Roach. *Ben Stiller, Robert De Niro, Blythe Danner, Teri Polo, James Rebhorn, Owen Wilson.* Greg (Stiller) is a male nurse going with his girlfriend Pam (Polo) to stay with her parents, Jack and Dina Byrnes (De Niro and Danner), for Pam's sister's wedding. Greg's nervous because he's meeting the Byrneses for the first time, and because he plans to propose to Pam during the weekend. Of course, things go badly, and there is an escalating series of physical and mental humiliations, from having to explain why it's OK for a man to be a nurse, to breaking a bridesmaid's nose during a water volleyball game, to accidentally destroying most of the parents' house. Most of this isn't his fault, but that doesn't matter to De Niro, an overprotective ex-CIA agent who decides to give Greg a lie detector test and ask him about drugs and pornography. Stiller is made for this type of role. He is a human degradation machine who can shoulder gargantuan humiliations while remaining sympathetic, even as he explodes in anger and makes matters worse. —*BT.*

MIDNIGHT L: CLASSIC COMEDY/CLASSIC COMEDY (1939) 94M D: Mitchell Leisen. *John Barrymore, Don Ameche, Mary Astor, Claudette Colbert.* Soon after hiring on at Paramount Pictures as a screenwriter, erstwhile New Yorker theater critic Charles Brackett found himself teamed with a newly emigrated Polish-Austrian-German Jew named Billy Wilder. An urbane gentleman of the old school (Brackett) and an irreverent wisecracker (Wilder) who'd learned English from jazz and pop lyrics, movies, and other unabashedly vernacular sources made for an unlikely (and often fractious) pairing, yet within very few years Brackett-Wilder would be a trademark for smart, sophisticated, impeccably constructed screenplays. *Midnight* is one of their best, and certainly most enchanting, scripts, elegantly brought to the screen by Paramount's glossiest director. Colbert is literally radiant as an American showgirl who, stranded penniless in Paree, is taken up by an outrageous "fairy godmother" (a baron played by Barrymore) and brought to the ball as a means of winning back his errant wife (Astor). Romanian cabdriver Ameche also becomes embroiled in the masquerade, one of the crowning achievements of '30s screen comedy, and a precursor of the classics Brackett-Wilder would soon be creating as producer and director, respectively. —*R.T.J.*

MONEY TALKS L: COMEDY/COMEDY (1997) 95M D: Brett Ratner. *Chris Tucker, Paul Sorvino, Charlie Sheen, Heather Locklear.* Before *Rush Hour,* Tucker and Ratner collaborated on this similar, but funnier, '80s-style buddy movie. Tucker plays a ticket scalper unfairly blamed for the murder of a cop. He escapes and teams with an obnoxious TV reporter (Sheen) to prove his innocence. The plot doesn't really matter, though. What makes this work is Tucker's hilarious (and probably improvised) dialogue. The film is full of throwaway jokes and asides, such as when Tucker walks past an armed prison guard and says, "Hey man, loan me your gun." He's such a good actor that when he says something ridiculous, he makes you believe that he really believes it, or that he really expects you to believe it. The R-rating allows him to be much funnier than in the *Rush Hour* films. You may be thinking, yeah, but why would I trade Jackie Chan for fucking Charlie

Sheen? Luckily, with the exception of the very last scene, the movie never pretends that you should like Sheen's character. —*B. T.*

One of those all-too-common atrocious urban comedies whose infrequent highlights are exhausted by an inescapable garrison of television advertisements weeks before the movie actually opened. The ludicrous (and relatively racist) plot will doubtless insult the intelligence of even the most adolescent audience (reaching its pinnacle with bazooka-wielding street gangs). Additionally, the film relies both too much and not enough on the comedic stylings of Tucker. Too much because he isn't up to the task of carrying a ninety-five-minute film. Not enough because there's no reason to let the groan-inducing plot run off with the movie—the audience came to see Tucker act a fool, and all this business about jewel thieves only distracts. —*C. B.*

MONKEYBONE L: COMEDY/COMEDY (2001) 92M D: Henry Selick. *Brendan Fraser, Bridget Fonda, Whoopi Goldberg, Dave Foley, Chris Kattan.* Only the director's commentary on the DVD can explain how animator genius Selick wound up directing this ineptly assembled pile of garbage about a dying cartoonist befriending an obnoxious farting monkey. Apparently the original story was about a puppeteer who goes into a coma and finds himself turned into a puppet, living in a world of puppets, all depicted in stop-motion animation. But executive producer Chris Columbus said audiences couldn't relate to an animated character, so the puppeteer would have to be in live-action, and the animated world of puppets would have to be a live-action world with some animated characters and some people in giant masks. So suddenly they had no premise, but they made the movie anyway. There are some great makeup effects and some small bits of animation, but the plot jumps all over, the fantasy elements are barely explained, and most of the characters don't seem to have any purpose. It makes Ralph Bakshi's *Cool World* seem coherent. —*B. T.*

MOONSTRUCK L: COMEDY/COMEDY (1987) 102M D: Norman Jewison. *Cher, Nicolas Cage, Vincent Gardenia, Olympia Dukakis, Danny Aiello, John Mahoney.* Hands down, this is one of the best romantic comedies ever. It eschews annoying and predictable story lines, it follows the love lives of both the beautiful and the not-so-beautiful, and it is brimming over with sardonic, witty, and oh-so-New York characters and humor. Loretta's (Cher) first marriage ended in tragedy. Determined to change her luck, she agrees to marry a man she likes OK, so long as they wed properly. He asks only one favor of her—invite his brother (Cage) to the wedding and end the siblings' bad blood. But Cage is not what she expects, and she finds herself falling for his determined passion for her. If that weren't enough, her fiancée is in Italy to see his dying mother, there's something fishy

going on with her father, and her mother has been seen with a younger man. Love abounds, as do wisecracks, in this wonderfully written, acted, and executed film. If you don't think this film is for you, then all I have to say is, "Snap out of it!" —*M. N.*

MORON MOVIES L: COMEDY/SKETCH COMEDY (1985) 60M D: Len Cella. *Len Cella.* This is one hour of uncontrolled brain leakage from Bramhall, Pennsylvania's camcorder-bearing, middle-aged idiot savant, Cella. In each short film, the frowning, gray-haired Cella plays all roles, often shirtless for no reason, and narrating in a nasal voice-over. Each film is about eight seconds long, with titles like "How to Kick Yourself" and "Jello Makes a Lousy Doorstop." Nine out of ten are agonizingly unfunny, but the winners are among the most brilliant works in the history of the film medium (i.e., "Shark Complaint"). Cella was "discovered" by the entertainment reporter at the Bramhall newspaper, which somehow led to a few of his shorts being screened on *The Tonight Show with Johnny Carson* in 1985. In 1987, after the release of *More Moron Movies* and a handful of additional television appearances, he faded back into obscurity. —*Z. C.*

MOTHER, JUGS & SPEED L: COMEDY/COMEDY (1976) 95M D: Peter Yates *Bill Cosby, Raquel Welch, Larry Hagman, Allen Garfield, Harvey Keitel.* For some reason, very few people are aware that this little guilty pleasure even exists. But tell me your curiosity isn't more than a little piqued when I mention that the three leads are Cosby (Mother), Welch (Jugs), and Keitel (Speed). And that all three work at a private ambulance dispatch company. When *Mother, Jugs & Speed* was released, it was described by some as "*M*A*S*H* in an ambulance"—and director Yates does try to do what Altman did so wonderfully in *M*A*S*H*: the deft blending of tonalities, fluctuating from bizarre comedy to dead serious drama and back again. But Yates isn't quite the director Altman is. So, while it's admirable that he assembled this cast to make this film, he would have been better off sticking with straight-ahead broad comedy or with greater drama, perhaps focusing on the lifestyle of an ambulance driver. Instead, Yates jams the two styles together, and it winds up more like a train wreck. —*C. P.*

MOTORAMA L: COMEDY/INDEPENDENT COMEDY (1991) 120M D: Barry Shils. *Jordan Christopher Michael, John Diehl, Mary Woronov, Garrett Morris, Drew Barrymore.* I liked this road movie about Gus, a ten-year-old boy who drives himself around the country using homemade stilts and visiting sponsoring gas stations to collect all the pieces to a game called "Motorama." Along the way he meets a whole bunch of weird people who try to help him out. It's fun to see Gus try to beat the odds and actually get all the pieces he needs (like when Charlie finds the Golden Ticket in *Willy Wonka*), even if the game he is trying to win expired a long time ago. I just wish they didn't put Barrymore on the box cover because she barely makes an appearance. —R. D.

MOVING VIOLATIONS L: COMEDY/COMEDY (1985) 90M D: Neal Israel. *John Murray, Fred Willard, Jennifer Tilly, James Keach, Brian Backer, Ned Eisenberg. Moving Violations* does for driver's education what *Police Academy* did for law enforcement. You take a mixed bunch of bad drivers who can't get their licenses for all kinds of reasons, give them a couple of masochistic instructors with an agenda to fail the entire class, and, voilà, you've got comedy. Murray leads the ensemble cast, playing the sarcastic underdog who really knows how to annoy his uptight instructors. Also starring are Tilly as the Rocket Scientist and Willard as Doc Williams, who accidentally convinces one of the students to drink a whole bottle of cooking oil and go running out onto the freeway. There's also a supporting role by Clara Peller of "Where's the Beef?" fame, but my favorite character is the horror film fanatic who gets a little too excited by the scare videos for class, like *Blood Runs Red on the Highway*. —R. D.

MR. BLANDINGS BUILDS HIS DREAM HOUSE L: CLASSIC COMEDY/CLASSIC COMEDY (1948) 94M D: H. C. Potter. *Melvyn Douglas, Cary Grant, Myrna Loy.* Grant's filmography is so rich, there's plenty of room to admit that *Mr. Blandings* isn't among his very best work and still insist that it's well worth seeing. The droll account of a successful Madison Avenue adman aspiring to move his family from Manhattan to bucolic New England is American Dream stuff for the privileged classes, but there's also a universal core of aspiring to a cozy home of one's own. Besides, comedic playing doesn't come any more relaxed and elegant than that of Grant, Loy as the patient, musical-voiced wife, and Douglas as the lifelong suitor who still loves her without ceasing to be Grant's best friend. In its way, this movie is a loving time capsule of a world we know only by rumor. As such, it has a certain enchantment. —R. T. J.

MRS. 'ARRIS GOES TO PARIS L: COMEDY/COMEDY (1992) 97M D: Anthony Shaw. *Diana Rigg, Omar Sharif, Lothaire Bluteau, John Savident, Angela Lansbury.* A paragon of guilty pleasure, this overwhelmingly feel-good, made-for-TV Lansbury vehicle (directed by her son, no less) won the surly teenage hearts of both my brother and myself when it first aired. Lansbury plays Londoner Mrs. 'arris (that's "Harris" with some overdone cockney flair), who has saved for years to buy what she considers the ultimate in luxury: a Dior gown. She travels to Paris to make her dream come true, and touches more than a few Parisian hearts along the way. Laughable English and French stereotypes abound, but try to hold a frown on your face through this irresistibly wholesome, Cinderella-esque ham-fest. —C. B.

MRS. DOUBTFIRE L: COMEDY/COMEDY (1993) 125M D: Chris Columbus. *Robin Williams, Pierce Brosnan, Sally Field, Harvey Fierstein.* Daniel (Williams) is a struggling actor who has just gone through a less-than-amicable divorce. His ex-wife (Field) painted him as a no-good slacker, so he can't spend the quality time he longs for with his three children. So what does he do? Get a job? Appeal to the courts? No, apparently the only solution is to dress up as an elderly woman to be his kids' nanny! Daniel becomes Mrs. Doubtfire, and uses his disguise to dote on his children. Since this is a cross-dressing comedy, the usual gags appear: trying to be in two places at once, having to hear digs about himself, parts of his man-ness accidently showing through the costume, and the stock "I feel like I've known you for years" lines his family utter. Since it's a Columbus film, there is a beautifully lazy montage of Mrs. Doubtfire playing soccer with the son and vacuuming to the music of Aerosmith's "Dude Looks like a Lady." The whole thing is pretty predictable, but the film does save a bit of face by not having the parents get back together in the end. Sure it has its moments, but how this formulaic film made it to number 67 on the American Film Institute's "100 Years. . . 100 Laughs" list (above such classics as *Caddyshack* and *Auntie Mame*) is beyond me. —J. K.

MY BREAKFAST WITH BLASSIE L: COMEDY/STAND-UP COMEDY (1983) 60M D: Linda Lautrec, Johnny Legend. *Andy Kaufman, Fred Blassie, Lynn Elaine.* Kaufman's stints in Hollywood were all disastrous, but luckily this no-budget independent film still exists as a testament to his genius. Made as a response to *My Dinner with Andre* and not long after Kaufman was body slammed on *The Late Show with David Letterman*, the movie is just Kaufman meeting the legendary wrestler "Classy" Freddie Blassie for breakfast at a Sambo's restaurant. Blassie is a hilarious character, from his condescending banter with the waitress to his obsessive-compulsive rants about the hygiene of handshaking. He might be playing up his personality, but it sure seems real. The young woman Kaufman hits on is director Legend's sister Lynn Margulies, who he really was meeting for the first time, and who would eventually be played by Courtney Love in *Man on the Moon*. —B. T.

MY FAVORITE YEAR L: COMEDY/COMEDY (1982) 92M D: Richard Benjamin. *Peter O'Toole, Mark Linn-Baker, Jessica Harper, Joseph Bologna, Lainie Kazan, Bill Macy.* "I'm not an actor, I'm a movie star!" Set in the vital days of live TV in the bustling center of American civilization (New York City, of course), and inspired by the creative excitement generated by the landmark sketch comedy series *Your Show of Shows*, this delightful comedy melds nostalgia, rich period detail (the NYC exteriors are exceptional), and an infectious joie de vivre, set to bouncy Les Paul and Mary Ford tunes. O'Toole is hilarious as the aging Errol Flynn-ish

actor whose failing career gets a boost when he's cast as the guest star on a live TV comedy show. All he has to do is stay sober and out of trouble, and even with junior writer Linn-Baker babysitting him there is little hope that this defiantly alcoholic womanizer will manage either. Bologna costars as the Sid Caesar–like host, Harper is the darling apple of Linn-Baker's eye, Kazan is great as his Jewish mother, and Macy is perfectly weasely as the ass-kissing head writer. —*S. A.*

NEW GUY, THE L: COMEDY/COMEDY (2002) 89M D: Ed Decter.
DJ Qualls, Zooey Deschanel, Lyle Lovett, Eliza Dushku, Eddie Griffin. Gawky, gangly Qualls (the eager-to-please nerd with a wild streak in *Road Trip*) is the über-dork high school underdog who makes himself over into the most unlikely campus bad boy. Qualls is called upon to make a fool of himself, and he does so with such uncontained glee he almost makes this movie fun to watch. But the film just seems to happen around him with no discernible direction, despite the best efforts of some good actors, especially Dushku as the sassy cheerleader with a sincere streak struggling to get out. The slapdash comic flailing of TV scribe-turned-director Decter is only compounded by a script so disconnected you have to wonder if pages were lost on the way to the set. —*S. A.*

NOT ANOTHER TEEN MOVIE L: COMEDY/COMEDY (2001) 88M D: Joel Gallen.
Chyler Leigh, Eric Christian Olsen, Mia Kirshner, Chris Evans, Jaime Pressly. This spoof needed to be made for a long time. Teen movies exaggerate characters and stories superbly. Teen movies in themselves follow so many clichés they are almost parodies to begin with, so when the ruse of being a good film is shamelessly stripped away, my normal critiques turn into appreciation. I know most people would not agree, but there's definitely no lack of cheesy material to make fun of. It's too bad they didn't use the working title *Ten Things I Hate About Clueless Road Trips When I Can't Hardly Wait to Be Kissed.* —*R. D.*

"Teen movies in themselves follow so many clichés that they are almost parodies to begin with." Exactly! Which is why this terrible, unfunny movie has no reason to exist. —*T. S.*

NOTHING BUT TROUBLE L: COMEDY/COMEDY (1991) 93M D: Dan Aykroyd.
Chevy Chase, Dan Aykroyd, Taylor Negron, John Candy, Demi Moore, Valeria Bromfield. Chase and friends get pulled over in the bizarre, apparently inbred, backwoods town of Valkenvania, where they face an insane, decrepit judge (Aykroyd) whose verdict is that Chase must marry his daughter (Candy). Aykroyd's first and almost certainly last work as a director has an underground maze, obese mutant twins, wacky dual roles, and a well-deserved reputation as an obnoxious, unfunny mess. However I must admit that I enjoyed Digital Underground (the entire group, including Tupac) getting pulled

over in their limo and forced to perform at the wedding. —*B. T.*

OFFICE SPACE L: COMEDY/COMEDY (1999) 90M D: Mike Judge.
Jennifer Aniston, Ron Livingston, Ajay Naidu, David Herman, Gary Cole. Anyone who has spent more than two days working a cubicle job knows what it's like to feel your brain slowly leak out of your ear and to watch your dignity walking out the door. This movie does such a great job portraying the tedium of white-collar work that in the end you want to take that pencil you're pushing and poke yourself in the eye with it. Don't despair though, because at least one geek gets ahead in the end. Kind of. One of my favorite scenes involves the movie's main cubicle-occupying character (Livingston) who has a nightmare about his slimy, condescending boss having sex with his girlfriend. He's got a leg in one hand, a coffee cup in the other, and the same smug expression on his face as when he's dictating orders in the office. The movie is funny, so you'll laugh, but more important you'll relate. —*J. S.*

OH, GOD! L: COMEDY/COMEDY (1977) 98M D: Carl Reiner.
George Burns, John Denver, Paul Sorvino. Burns plays an absolutely wonderful God in this slightly corny, feel-good movie in which Denver, a supermarket employee, is chosen to help God spread his message that the world can work with what it has been given. Of course nobody believes him, and he is forced to decide whether to stay true to God and his faith or put his trust in the superficialities and nonbelievers around him. This film delivers a sugarcoated dose of morality in a good-natured and refreshing way. The plot lacks any real twists and turns, and is almost completely dialogue driven. The long conversations between God and Jerry (Denver) keep viewers interested, and the final scenes, in which good conquers evil, will have viewers cheering in their seats. —*J. S.*

ONE FINE DAY L: COMEDY/COMEDY (1996) 108M D: Michael Hoffman.
George Clooney, Michelle Pfeiffer, Charles Durning, Robert Klein. This is the perfect Hollywood romantic comedy if Meg Ryan and Tom Hanks are too cute for you. Melanie (Pfeiffer) is an architect and single mother of Sammy. Jack (Clooney) is a newspaper columnist and single father of Maggie. Both have residual reservations about the opposite sex due to their failed marriages. Due to a misunderstanding, they meet when both their kids miss a school field trip. Stranded with their children on a work day, they must compromise and take turns looking after the kids while coping with chaotic work schedules. Tension builds as Melanie and Jack's personalities clash under pressure. Pfeiffer and Clooney are an edgier version of the adorable Meg and Tom and, as a result, easier to relate to. —*J. D.*

100 GIRLS L: COMEDY/INDEPENDENT COMEDY (2000) 95M
D: Michael Davis. *Jonathan Tucker, Larisa Oleynik, Emmanuelle Chriqui, Jaime Pressly, Marissa Ribisi, Katherine Heigl.* Tucker is a college freshman who finds true love in a girl's dorm during a blackout—but forgets to get the girl's name! Oleynik, Chriqui, Pressly, and Heigl are just a few of the one hundred girls in the dorm he has to work through to find her again. While it reads like a typical male-centered teen sex comedy, there's something refreshingly frank and funny in the way director/writer Davis explores the dynamics of young men and women, first impressions, expectations, and sex, all from the perspective of an inexperienced, "tragically glib" freshman boy. And yes, it is male-centered, but in a curious, open, eager-to-learn way. —*S. A.*

ONE NIGHT AT MCCOOL'S L: COMEDY/COMEDY (2001) 93M D: Harold Zwart. *Matt Dillon, Liv Tyler, Paul Reiser, John Goodman, Michael Douglas.* Tyler is a mix of leggy femme fatale, innocent urchin, and buxom sex fantasy as a conniving con woman, and Dillon, Reiser, and Goodman are the men under her sway in this screwball crime thriller. No one is exactly innocent, but Stan Seidel's script reserves judgment. You might say he has it both ways—Tyler holds onto a simplicity and purity of purpose that imbues her clichéd character with a soul, however misguided and impulsive. But Seidel makes it work, helped immensely by the screwball spirit of director Zwart's comic warmth and crack timing. While it doesn't add anything new to the genre, *McCool's* toys with expectations and captures a tough-to-master balance of film noir and black comedy, the latter with a knowing wink and playful sympathy. —*S. A.*

OPPOSITE OF SEX, THE L: COMEDY/INDEPENDENT COMEDY (1998) 120M D: Don Roos. *Christina Ricci, Martin Donovan, Lisa Kudrow, Lyle Lovett, Johnny Galecki.* Ricci's smart-mouthed misanthrope, a conniving little vamp who moves in with her gay half-brother (Donovan) and seduces his boyfriend, drives this film with her manipulations and moxie. When she's offscreen the film tends to drag, even with Kudrow's hilarious turn as a mocking cynic whose sardonic punctuations are scattered through the picture. Lovett is unexpectedly tender and lovely as the straight man to the bent bunch, a sheriff hopelessly in love with the emotionally blind Kudrow (she, of course, is smitten with her gay colleague). Director Roos kicks the film off with a knowing wink of self-aware narration, satirical asides, and a promise of a little playful skewering of cinematic protocol. He doesn't completely deliver on the last, but his smart writing and sassy characters are so inviting that you won't really care. —*S. A.*

ORGAZMO L: COMEDY/COMEDY (1997) 94M D: Trey Parker, Matt Stone. *Trey Parker, Dian Bachar, Robyn Lynne, Matt Stone, Ron Jeremy.* You don't have to love porn to love *Orgazmo*. The hilarious script and prop gags are only matched by its no-budget feel. Parker plays the lead role of Orgazmo, the Mormon-turned-porn-star and superhero kid from Salt Lake City trying to make some money to please his ultra-straight wife back home. There are some familiar faces from *Cannibal the Musical,* such as Bachar as Choda Boy and Masoa Maki as G-Fresh. There is a fun soundtrack, too, with Wu-Tang Clan, Ween, Primus, and DVDA (Parker and Stone's band), who wrote the title song, "Now You're a Man." This film celebrates the directing duo of Parker and Stone. Much of the same creativity that makes *South Park* so enjoyable comes through in this live-action favorite. —*R. D.*

PAPER, THE (1994) L: COMEDY/COMEDY (1994) 112M D: Ron Howard. *Michael Keaton, Glenn Close, Robert Duvall, Marisa Tomei, Jason Robards. The Paper* may have a moviemaker's heart, but its saving grace is its journalist's brain. The story follows a New York tabloid editor (Keaton) and a cast of eccentric newspaper people through a single day as some try to prove a pair of murder suspects are innocent and others get in the way. The cause is noble enough for a movie, but it's the stuff on the margins (the bickering, the pettiness, the street patter) that adds texture. Characters argue about headlines, money, and sentence structure; they swill coffee, mainline Coca-Cola, and have drinks at the end of the day. When a reporter buys a therapeutic chair, his co-workers replace it with a wooden stool; when a character gets to yell, "Stop the presses!" and mean it, both he and the audience thrill. —*T. P.*

PARENTS L: COMEDY/INDEPENDENT COMEDY (1989) 81M D: Bob Balaban. *Randy Quaid, Mary Beth Hurt, Sandy Dennis, Bryan Madorsky. Parents* is truly a cult classic. This lightweight horror-comedy set in the '50s revolves around a young boy and his curiosity about the strange meat his dad brings home from his job at the hospital. He asks the question, "Dad, what were the leftovers before they were leftovers?" His dad replies, "Leftovers-to-be, son." What will happen when he finds out what he's been eating? Find out in this creative feast for the senses as well as the dinner table. —*R. D.*

PEE-WEE HERMAN SHOW, THE L: COMEDY/STAND-UP COMEDY (1982) 60M D: Marty Callner. *Paul Reubens, John Paragon, Phil Hartman.* Reubens originated his Pee-wee Herman character with the sketch comedy group the Groundlings, creating a buzzed-about live show that was turned into this HBO special. Fans of *Pee-wee's Playhouse* will recognize the sets by cartoonist Gary Panter, the puppets Pterry and Globey, and characters such as Miss Yvonne and Captain Karl. This version is more adult-oriented (Pee-wee looks up girls' skirts with mirror shoes), but Pee-wee is a little more childlike and ends the show flying and singing,

"I am the luckiest boy in the world, the birds envy me, because I'm Pee-wee." —*B.T.*

PLEASANTVILLE L: COMEDY/COMEDY (1998) 124M D: Gary Ross.
Reese Witherspoon, Joan Allen, Jeff Daniels, Tobey Maguire, William H. Macy, Don Knotts. Jennifer (Witherspoon) and her brother David (Maguire) are as different as day and night. Jennifer, a typical teenage clique-chick, likes things the way they are, while David would rather the world be like his favorite TV show, *Pleasantville*, where everyone is nice and things are simpler. Their lives are drastically changed when they are given a special TV remote control that puts them in the places of Bud and Mary Sue Parker, lead characters on *Pleasantville*. At first David is in heaven and Jen is in hell, but they soon learn that what they do and say can change this naive little town in ways they never could imagine. The mixed use of black and white and color footage is brilliant, the color playing as much a role in the film as the actors do. This is a great story about influence and responsibility, exploring the power of knowledge and the risks and rewards of change. A clever, humorous, and compelling film that examines the path of personal growth and the mixed blessing that is freedom of choice. —*M.N.*

POLICE ACADEMY L: COMEDY/COMEDY (1984) 96M D: Hugh Wilson.
Steve Guttenberg, G. W. Bailey, George Gaynes, Michael Winslow, David Graf, Bubba Smith, Kim Cattrall. In 1984, who knew there was such a thing as a Police Academy, except cops? Probably nobody. But after this daring expose, we all knew just what went on there. . . hilarious pranks mostly. Guttenberg brilliantly portrays Mahoney, a petty crook whose punishment is to attend the Police Academy. Well, he won't take this sitting down, no matter who he pisses off. Whether spying on girls showering, stealing cars, or hiding a hooker in the podium to give the Commandant a blowjob during his speech, Mahoney is the heart and soul of *Police Academy*, an impish rogue akin to Shakespeare's Puck or Bugs Bunny. All he wants is to get kicked out of the Academy for some reason and get it on with Cattrall. Is that so wrong? —*K.C.*

POLICE ACADEMY 2: THEIR FIRST ASSIGNMENT L: COMEDY/COMEDY (1985) 97M D: Jerry Paris.
Steve Guttenberg, David Graf, George Gaynes, Michael Winslow, Bob Goldthwait, Bubba Smith. The unnecessary, continuing adventures of Mahoney and the gang heat up in this second installment as they leave the comforts of the Academy for the mean streets of downtown. There, they face off with a gay-punk-junkyard-biker gang led by Goldthwait, and Mahoney continues his crusade against authority. This sequel truly "builds" on the first: Tackleberry falls in love with a fellow psychopathic gun nut, we learn that Jones is a master of sound and karate, and there are some other exciting subplots. This one is also notable

as the last *Police Academy* film to feature gratuitous nudity, so look carefully. —*K. C.*

POLICE ACADEMY 3: BACK IN TRAINING L: COMEDY/COMEDY (1986) 83M D: Jerry Paris.
Steve Guttenberg, Michael Winslow, Tim Kazurinsky, Bob Goldthwait, George Gaynes, David Graf, Bubba Smith. No gratuitous nudity in this one. But, there is a jet ski chase. I can't think of another movie with a jet ski chase. Nothing much happens in this installment with the exception of Zed (Goldthwait), the leader of the gang from Part 2, joining the *Police Academy* gang as they go back in training. . . as the title says. Plus, there's a jet ski chase. —*K.C.*

POOTIE TANG L: COMEDY/COMEDY (2001) 81M D: Louis C. K.
Lance Crouther, Chris Rock, Robert Vaughn, Wanda Sykes, J. B. Smoove, Jennifer Coolidge. Everybody, and I mean, EVERYBODY, loves Pootie Tang (Crouther). He is the king of cool, a singing sensation so great he doesn't even need to make a sound to produce a hit record. The quintessential ladies man, he's a bad-ass crime fighter trying to teach the world right from wrong by using nothing but his magical belt. Pootie, along with his sidekick Trucky (Smoove) and his lady-in-waiting Biggie Shorty (Sykes), take on corporate America in this silly and endearing film. The results are nothing short of what you would expect from a guy of Pootie Tang's caliber. Watch this movie with a group of friends, and be prepared to quote Pootie's nonsense phrases for the next few weeks. Movies this fun are rare. —*J. S.*

PORKY'S L: COMEDY/COMEDY (1981) 94M D: Bob Clark.
Dan Monahan, Cyril O'Reilly, Kaki Hunter, Mark Herrier, Tony Ganios, Wyatt Knight. Porky's became a very popular drive-in film due to its sheer irreverence for its subject. Beginning with a teenage boy measuring his elongated member and affixing this data to a nearby chart, this film does not for a moment deflect from the issue of sex. At the Florida high school he and his sex-obsessed friends attend in the '50s, girls are simply objects and adults are cold-hearted barriers to them. Creativity must therefore be applied, such as peepholes to the women's shower. Shocking by most standards, this film spawned two inferior sequels but is surprisingly original and genuinely funny. —*N. J.*

PRYOR, RICHARD: LIVE AND SMOKIN' L: COMEDY/STAND-UP COMEDY (1971) 47M D: Michael Blum.
Richard Pryor. Originally just called *Smokin'*, this was Pryor's first concert film, and it shows. It captures him at a time when he was really starting to come into his own, using material from his own life instead of imitating the type of jokes other comedians were making. For that reason it's very interesting for Pryor fans, but it's still a poor example of his skills. He seems nervous in front of the camera and his timing is not as natural as in later years. If you're looking for an

introduction to Pryor's brilliant stand-up, watch *Richard Pryor Live in Concert* instead. —*B.T.*

PRYOR, RICHARD: LIVE IN CONCERT L: COMEDY/STAND-UP COMEDY (1979) 78M D: Jeff Margolis. *Richard Pryor.*
If you don't understand the point of a stand-up comedy concert film, give this one a shot. Pryor is at his most brilliant, giving voice and physical presence to every character, including his own, once-unhealthy heart. Some of the black-people-are-like-this, white-people-are-like-this jokes seem trite after years of Def Comedy Jams, but most of the humor is timeless. There is a story about his pet monkeys and a neighbor's dog that I wish I could do justice to. The first Pryor concert film released, and also the best. —*B.T.*

PRYOR, RICHARD: LIVE ON THE SUNSET STRIP L: COMEDY/STAND-UP COMEDY (1982) 82M D: Joe Layton. *Richard Pryor.*
Pryor returns to the stage after his freebasing accident wearing a bright-red suit and treated as a rock star (as Eddie Murphy would be in his concert films soon after). There are some great routines about run-ins with the mafia as a teenager, his trip to Africa, his experiences in prisons filming *Stir Crazy*, and most of all his addiction. He's a master at performing any character (even inanimate objects); here he portrays himself while high, his friend Jim Brown trying to help him get off drugs, and a sinister pipe trying to convince him otherwise—all in one story. —*B.T.*

PUMPKIN L: COMEDY/COMEDY (2002) 121M D: Adam Larson Broder, Tony R. Abrams. *Christina Ricci, Dominique Swain, Brenda Blethyn, Hank Harris.*
Crap crap crap. I *hated* this movie. Ricci plays Carolyn McDuffy, a bitchy sorority princess who, along with her sorority sisters, is forced to "endure" working with a team of mentally challenged athletes in order to win Sorority of the Year. When she meets her particular mentally challenged athlete, Pumpkin, she is at first repulsed, but gradually finds herself falling in love with him, much to the chagrin of her sisters and Pumpkin's mother. Did I mention *crap*? Ricci's evolution from hatred to a love that causes her to be shunned by everyone she cares about is choppy and unconvincing, and the film is 100 percent lacking in emotional resonance. Shallow, poorly written, and dripping with stereotypes, I spent more of the film cringing than laughing. CRAP. —*J.S.*

REAL GENIUS L: COMEDY/COMEDY (1985) 108M D: Martha Coolidge. *Val Kilmer, Patti D'Arbanville, Jon Gries, William Atherton, Michelle Meyrink, Gabriel Jarret.*
One of the few films that truly examines what it means to be a geek, a nerd, and a freak. Based in part on some honest-to-goodness geeks, *Real Genius* shows the full range of the culture. Forget *Revenge of the Nerds*! Here the geeks are brilliant, obsessive, compulsive, charismatic, shy, neurotic, outrageous, playful, and out there. Sure, it's a goofy '80s movie with a silly plot, stylin' period music, and stereotypes of villains and morons and geniuses, but it's got a surprising amount of honesty to it. While in a study group, one member loses it and starts screaming. Everyone looks at him, watches him run out of the room, and then goes back to studying like nothing happened. Besides, having Kilmer in a movie only means one thing: fun, fun, fun. —*M.N.*

REAL JOB, A L: COMEDY/INDEPENDENT COMEDY (2001) 94M D: Ana Barredo. *Alan Natale, Heather Hiltermann, Pramod Mishrekar, Sharon Repass, Paul Kolsby.*
Kolsby is a thirty-eight-year-old video store clerk who quits his fun-loving position to get a real job and impress the girl of his dreams (Repass), only to find his new job is not only taking over his life, it's threatening to swallow his old video store. This indie romantic comedy with a movie geek foundation was written and directed by Barredo, herself a professional in the video industry. Working from a starvation budget, this shot-on-video production shows its limitations with indistinct sets and under-populated settings, but finds its strengths in two charismatic and likable leads and a script that, for all its *Clerks*-like asides, is closer to old-fashioned romantic comedy. In the interests of full disclosure, I confess that Ms. Barredo is a friend of mine. I'm happy to say that for all the technical limitations and first-feature stylistic hiccups, it's an enjoyable film that favors story and character over the flash and contrivances of so many "calling card" productions. —*S.A.*

RELUCTANT ASTRONAUT, THE L: CLASSIC COMEDY/CLASSIC COMEDY (1967) 101M D: Edward J. Montagne Jr. *Don Knotts, Arthur O'Connell, Jesse White, Joan Freeman, Leslie Nielsen.*
Roy Fleming (Knotts) operates a space-themed carnival ride for kids, but is so deathly afraid of heights he can barely climb the ladder to his "space capsule." When his boastful "war-hero" father (O'Connell) gets him accepted to the astronaut program, no one realizes that it's as a janitor, not a space pilot. While Roy is thrilled with not having to go into orbit, he lets his small town—and small-town love, Ellie (Freeman)—believe he's an astronaut-in-training and hero-to-be. Roy is eventually chosen as the first "layman" to go into space and we are treated to some pioneering wire-work as he fights weightlessness, squeezable peanut butter, and a malfunctioning computer on the way to a successful mission and triumph. This is pretty typical fish-out-of-water Knotts fare and Don plays his usual good-natured schnook. Not as funny as his later films, but still worthwhile, especially for fans. —*G.M.*

REVENGE OF THE NERDS L: COMEDY/COMEDY (1984) 90M D: Jeff Kanew. *Anthony Edwards, Robert Carradine, Timothy Busfield, Curtis Armstrong, John Goodman, Andrew Cassese.*
Revenge of the Nerds is a great comedy. Yeah, it's really stupid, but it has a lot of

funny performances and monologues. I can think of no other movie that better glorifies the typical "if we all work together, we can beat anything" speech from '80s cinema. This film makes it easy to like the nerds and dislike the jocks; when the nerds finally show everyone they can totally rock, you feel like cheering. *Nerds* was so well received, it started a sequel avalanche, but sadly, none of the sequels ever matched the potency of the original. *Nerds* is one of Goodman's earliest films, made the same year as *C.H.U.D.* The film gets a little sappy only when the nerds finally come out and say, "Look, I'm a nerd and I'm proud of it." —*R.D.*

ROAD TO MOROCCO, THE L: CLASSIC COMEDY/CLASSIC COMEDY (1942) 83M D: David Butler. *Bing Crosby, Bob Hope, Dorothy Lamour, Anthony Quinn.* The *Road to Morocco*, third in the series of Hope-Crosby "Road pictures" that kept Paramount in the black through the '40s, was made at that sublime moment when the elements, shtick, and cast rapport of the franchise had thoroughly shaken down, but before the formula could turn mechanical and complacent. This is an endearingly silly, engagingly relaxed, and very funny comedy that was one of the biggest hits of its year and is still abundantly entertaining. No matter how many bad-dad stories one has heard about Der Bingle, no matter how thankless the memories of Hope's behavior during the Vietnam War, there's just no resisting the camel-back duet of "We're off on the Road to Morocco," both the straight and the warped deliveries of "Moonlight Becomes You," or Ski-Nose's realization that he's become a sex object in an Arabian slave market. —*R.T.J.*

ROGER DODGER L: COMEDY/COMEDY (2002) 104M D: Dylan Kidd. *Campbell Scott, Jesse Eisenberg, Elizabeth Berkeley, Isabella Rossellini, Jennifer Beals.* Take an uneasy lesson from Scott's charismatic cad in this sharply written character study. Roger is a combination con man, life of the party, and compulsive pick-up artist with a gift for dead-accurate psychological profiles, a line for every occasion, and a darkness that pushes seduction into misanthropic rants. Eisenberg is his young nephew who lands in the big city for a lesson in womanizing from his notorious Uncle Roger. Under the clipped delivery, confident air, and mask of impenetrability of this glib charmer is a sour, self-loathing pessimist who projects his own misery and unhappiness on the world, and then passes judgment on it, one person at a time. Sharply written and confidently directed, Kidd's debut feature is the kind of character study in romantic cynicism that actors live for, and Scott owns the film from scene one. He savors every word and allows us to see the calculating mind behind every sharp glance as he sizes up his next conquest, and the miserable soul scratching to get out from behind his self-created caricature. —*S.A.*

ROMY AND MICHELE'S HIGH SCHOOL REUNION L: COMEDY/COMEDY (1997) 92M D: David Mirkin. *Mira Sorvino, Lisa Kudrow, Julia Campbell, Alan Cumming, Janeane Garofalo.* This is a great ditzy comedy, the kind of movie that rewards you for not taking yourself too seriously. Romy and Michele are best friends who, like pretty much everyone else in the world, were shunned by the popular kids in high school. When they hear their high school reunion is coming up, they decide they need to come up with a story to impress their classmates. So they pretend they invented Post-its and built their own successful business. The acting is fantastic, the soundtrack contains what seems like every good song from the '80s, and the high school flashbacks will make you glad that graduation is far behind you. Laughing is guaranteed, and, like me, you may just want to watch it six or seven times in a row, too. —*J.S.*

ROYAL TENENBAUMS, THE L: COMEDY/COMEDY (2001) 109M D: Wes Anderson. *Gene Hackman, Luke Wilson, Owen Wilson, Angelica Huston, Gwyneth Paltrow, Bill Murray.* Anderson proves once again that he's the modern American master of happy-melancholy with his third film, *The Royal Tenenbaums*, a dramatic comedy about the dysfunctional Tenenbaum family of geniuses. The cast is perfect, ranging from veteran Hackman, as titular patriarch Royal Tenenbaum, to the reluctant GQ-cover boy Owen Wilson (who also cowrote the film), as the childhood neighbor and famous Custer-revisionist-author Eli Cash. Anderson fills the frame with an absurd amount of familial detail, with each character clothed to fit their personality, each room designed to denote some kind of personal history. The soundtrack is breathless, featuring Nico, the Velvet Underground, the Ramones, the Clash, Elliott Smith, and Nick Drake; the score is by ex-Devo Mark Mothersbaugh. Anderson's obsessive attention to nuance and mood adds to the emotional poignancy of the film, and is a rare trait in today's bland and emotionally vacant cinema. —*J.D.*

RUBIN AND ED L: COMEDY/INDEPENDENT COMEDY (1992) 82M D: Trent Harris. *Crispin Glover, Howard Hesseman, Karen Black.* This is one of my all-time top-ten movies. Hilarious, absurd, sarcastic, and psychedelic. Watch as Rubin (Glover) kidnaps Ed (Hesseman) to help him bury his dead frozen cat in the desert. Watch as Ed tries to recruit Rubin in his "Power Through Positive Real Estate" seminars. Quite possibly, you'll find out who really spray painted "Andy Warhol Sucks The Big One" on Ed's car. —*R.D.*

RUN RONNIE RUN! L: COMEDY/COMEDY (2002) 86M D: Troy Miller. *David Cross, David Koechner, Nikki Cox, Bob Odenkirk.* Ronnie Dobbs (Cross) is a wife-beating drunk who gets arrested on a *COPS*-like TV show so many times that faux-British-accented Hollywood producer Terry Twillstein

Funniest movies ever

AIRPLANE!

AN AMERICAN WEREWOLF IN LONDON

ANIMAL CRACKERS

ARTHUR

THE AWFUL TRUTH

BALL OF FIRE

THE BANK DICK

THE BIG LEBOWSKI

THE BLUES BROTHERS

BRINGING UP BABY

DR. STRANGELOVE

DUCK SOUP

FERRIS BUELLER'S DAY OFF

FLIRTING WITH DISASTER

FORBIDDEN ZONE

FUBAR

HALF BAKED

HELLZAPOPPIN

JERRY AND TOM

THE LOVE GOD

MONTY PYTHON AND THE HOLY GRAIL

MONTY PYTHON'S LIFE OF BRIAN

MR. HULOT'S HOLIDAY

MY MAN GODFREY

OFFICE SPACE

ONE, TWO, THREE

ORGAZMO

PEE-WEE'S BIG ADVENTURE

RUBIN AND ED

SHAOLIN SOCCER

SOME LIKE IT HOT

SURF 2

THIS IS SPINAL TAP

VALLEY GIRL

VERNON, FLORIDA

WAY OUT WEST

WRONG GUY

YOUNG FRANKENSTEIN

(Odenkirk) takes him under his wing, gives him his own show, and turns him into a superstar. But fame goes to Ronnie's head and he loses his touch, stops drinking, gets a pony tail, and lives in a frou-frou mansion. Expanding from a great sketch on their sketch comedy show *Mr. Show*, Cross and Odenkirk fought to get the movie released, then fell out with the director over editing disagreements and gave up long before it was unceremoniously dumped on video. Many *Mr. Show* fans hate the movie because it doesn't seem to live up to the promise of Cross and Odenkirk's comedic minds, and perhaps also because it recycles some jokes from their old sketches. But the truth is that it's still a funnier-than-average movie with plenty of inspired moments, such as Mandy Patinkin performing in *Ronnie Dobbs: The Musical*, a goat-wielding Ronnie nonsensically telling a cop, "*You* put the goat down," and a nostalgic montage that includes a dog eating vomit. Also pay attention to the song on the end credits in which Jack Black sings about the end credits. —*B. T.*

RUSHMORE L: COMEDY/COMEDY (1998) 93M D: Wes Anderson. *Bill Murray, Jason Schwartzman, Olivia Williams, Brian Cox, Mason Gamble, Seymour Cassel. Rushmore* excites me and moves me in a way that almost no other film can. The character of Max Fischer, brought heart-breakingly to life by Schwartzman, is the most accurate cinematic portrayal of adolescent confusion and ambition I have ever seen. Murray delivers a most understated, hilarious, and tragic performance. The script, by Anderson and Owen Wilson, is nothing short of brilliant. Anderson's fluid direction is clearly feeding off a strong sense of cinema history, especially the French New Wave. But what's really special about *Rushmore* is the way it fills you with such joy and yet a great underlying sadness. Few films have moments that are convincingly awkward, funny, or sad. Even fewer have moments that are awkward, funny, and sad all at once. The emotional honesty is awe inspiring. It finds my heart and speaks to my sadness, but ultimately leaves me joyful and punch-drunk. —*T. S.*

RUSSIANS ARE COMING, THE RUSSIANS ARE COMING, THE L: CLASSIC COMEDY/CLASSIC COMEDY (1966) 126M D: Norman Jewison. *Brian Keith, Alan Arkin, Eva Marie Saint, Carl Reiner, Jonathan Winters.* Jewison directed this Cold War comedy about the chaos and paranoia unleashed in a small New England town when a Russian submarine accidentally runs aground on the coast. Hapless marrieds

(Reiner and Saint) and a town sheriff (Keith) try to keep the Americans calm while Arkin (who earned an Oscar nomination in his film debut) is the voice of reason on the Russian side. Less a satire than an amiable comedy about escalating paranoia fed by miscommunication and mutual mistrust, it costars Winters as a hysterical deputy, Theodore Bikel as the Russian captain, and John Phillip Law as the blue-eyed Soviet crewman who falls in love with the American girl next door. —S.A.

SAY ANYTHING L: COMEDY/COMEDY (1989) 100M D: Cameron
Crowe. *John Cusack, Ione Skye, John Mahoney, Lili Taylor, Amy Brooks.* I love this movie, and even though it may be a little contrived and formulaic, I'm willing to forgive it because it is one of the best, most genuine romantic comedies ever made. Cusack is wonderful as Lloyd Dobbler, an underachieving high school student whose ambition is to date brainy bombshell Diane Court (Skye). The two go out and begin to fall in love (because after all, how could you *not* fall in love with Cusack) and then have to deal with the trials and tribulations that come when their worlds collide. A classic premise for '80s movies, yeah, but what makes this movie exceptional is the amazing chemistry between Cusack and Skye. Their performances are so tender and realistic that even the most jaded viewer will be drawn in spite of themselves, and the timing of their interactions is flawless. —J.S.

SCENIC ROUTE L: COMEDY/INDEPENDENT COMEDY (1978)
76M D: Mark Rappaport. *Randy Danson, Marilyn Jones, Kevin Wade.* Rappaport's loose modernization of the Orpheus and Eurydice myth was appropriately named by the British Film Institute as the Most Original and Innovative Film of 1978. It tells the story of Estelle (Danson), who finds herself in a cruel love triangle when her sister Lena (Jones) unwittingly takes up with Estelle's former lover (Wade). *Scenic Route*'s would-be melodrama becomes something more intimate through the continuous use of voice-over monologues (by and large Estelle's, but frequently allowing Lena's voice to complicate the narration). Something of an American aesthetic milestone, this sorely overlooked masterwork all but disregards realism, relying instead on a psychologically rich narrative that seems at once exceedingly literary, theatrical, cinematic, even painterly—but always intensely modern. With a metropolitan sensibility and a defensive ironic wit, it almost fits in Woody Allen's niche, but is far too complex and formally courageous for the comparison to stick for long. —C.B.

SECOND CIVIL WAR, THE L: COMEDY/COMEDY (1997)
97M D: Joe Dante. *James Coburn, Phil Hartman, Beau Bridges, Elizabeth Peña, Joanna Cassidy, James Earl Jones.* Set in the dangerously near future, Dante's daring satire puts the melting pot of America into a pressure cooker, cranks it up to full boil, and steps back to watch it blow. Anchored in the nerve center of twenty-four-hour channel NewsNet, the world watches a renegade governor (Bridges) close his state borders to a planeload of orphaned refugee children while the decision-impaired president (Hartman) reaches to his media handler for guidance. Before you can say "Remember the Alamo," the microscopic lens of NewsNet sets off a wave of ethnic uprisings across the country as the lines are drawn. In the best tradition of satire, Martyn Burke's screenplay is pointedly scathing and devastatingly funny, finding an edgy humor in the most unlikely issues. Dante balances the fine line between comedy and tragedy with his sympathetic handling of vivid characters, foolish and foibled but lovingly realized. As *The Second Civil War* carries the tragi-comedy of errors to the bitter end, it's this investment in characters that gives the gutsy conclusion its punch. —S.A.

S.F.W. L: COMEDY/INDEPENDENT COMEDY (1994) 92M D:
Jefery Levy. *Stephen Dorff, Reese Witherspoon, Jake Busey, Joey Lauren Adams, Pam Gidley.* Dorff plays a Gen-X slacker who becomes a media celebrity during a televised robbery. After the ordeal is over, his favorite foul-mouthed phrase (abbrivated as "S.F.W.") becomes a popular catch phrase and he becomes a media darling. *S.F.W* is so bad that it will make you detest not only Stephen Dorff, but people who look like Stephen Dorff. —T.P.

SHAFTED! L: COMEDY/INDEPENDENT COMEDY (1999) 90M D:
Tom Putnam. *Morgan Rusler, Angelle Brooks, Hayley Man, David James Alexander.* Jive-talkin', would-be love machine Steven Byzinsky (Rusler), aka John Shat, is definitely *not* the man in this high-spirited parody of blaxploitation and kung-fu movies, with a little *Taxi Driver, Apocalypse Now,* and *Night of the Living Dead* tossed in for good measure. Rusler hits just the right balance of bad attitude and bad hair as the deluded white boy living out a '70s fantasy of swaggering black urban hero, with a cross-dressing client (Man) and a frumpy social worker (Brooks) making her own transformation into Dr. Foxy Brown. Swimming in '70s references and packed with inventive absurdities, Putnam's shot-on-the-cheap spoof (watch for the crayon artwork intro) is one funny, bad mother-shut-yo-mouth! —S.A.

SHAKES THE CLOWN L: COMEDY/INDEPENDENT COMEDY
(1992) 83M D: Bob Goldthwait. *Bob Goldthwait, Julie Brown, Adam Sandler, Robin Williams.* Shakes the Clown is the king of alcoholic clown movies. Shakes is a pretty decent clown, as long as he's got some booze and friends to help him through it. There's plenty of sick humor and a few moments of sincerity from Goldthwait. This film has a cult following and helped create an audience for later works by such tasteless humor teams as the Farrelly brothers. Most people who watched this when it first came out have for-

gotten that Sandler plays one of Shakes's best friends. Brown is terrific as Shakes's ditsy girlfriend who works at a diner and thinks she is on her way to becoming a professional bowler. I like how this film takes a break from slapstick to give the audience a glimpse of the ugly underbelly of alcoholism. —R. D.

SHALLOW HAL L: COMEDY/COMEDY (2001) 114M D: Bobby Farrelly, Peter Farrelly. *Gwyneth Paltrow, Jack Black, Jason Alexander.* A teaming of Black and the Farrelly brothers seemed like a dream come true. . . until it turned out to be a lame fat-suit movie. Black is a sexist jerk who, during an elevator encounter with Anthony Robbins, (long story) gets hypnotized to see only a person's inner beauty. Soon after, he falls in love with the charming Rosemary, who is skinny little Paltrow to him and is three-hundred-pound Paltrow-in-a-fat-suit to everyone else. I think this was genuinely intended as a counter to fat-joke movies like the Eddie Murphy version of *The Nutty Professor.* It's all about not judging people by their looks, and the usual fat movie scenes like chairs breaking are treated as tragic humiliations, not jokes. Most of the humor comes from Black's misunderstanding (during a love scene he watches skinny little Paltrow pull off a giant pair of panties and says, "Get over here, Houdini!"). But if fat women are OK, then why does the fat woman protagonist have to be a special effect? More important, shouldn't a comedy have more jokes in it? —B. T.

SHORT CIRCUIT L: COMEDY/COMEDY (1986) 98M D: John Badham. *Steve Guttenberg, Ally Sheedy, Tim Blaney, Fisher Stevens.* I can't do the Robot, and I've never been able to do the Robot. When I was ten, a traveling band of hippies came to my school to teach us about recycling. They completely won me over by doing the Robot, and dressing and talking like robots. They brought with them a real robot named R3U2, which was a complete rip-off of Number 5, the character from *Short Circuit* (although I did not know this at the time). R3U2 had the same voice as Number 5 and he repeated "recycle-ycle-ycle-ycle" with the same urgency as "Number 5, still alive!" When I finally saw *Short Circuit,* I really wanted to be a robot, so I could do the Robot. I also wanted to recycle, although I didn't know why at the time. —J. J.

SIMONE L: COMEDY/COMEDY (2002) 117M D: Andrew Niccol. *Al Pacino, Winona Ryder, Jay Mohr, Catherine Keener, Rachel Roberts, Pruitt Taylor Vince. Simone* is a good idea for a film, in theory. On paper it probably even read quite well, save for the final twenty minutes or so, which any beginning screenwriter could have made better. One would be inclined to let writer/director Niccol off the hook if he hadn't previously written one of the better scripts in the past ten years (*The Truman Show*) as well as a decent sci-fi film (*Gattaca*).

Struggling director Viktor Taransky (Pacino) is having a helluva time getting his latest film made. Once a big shot in Hollywood, he finds himself at the mercy of actors more worried about the size of their trailer than the artistic merit of a filmmaker's vision. Under pressure from the studio and his producer (who happens to be his ex-wife), Taransky turns to a virtual actress (Roberts) who could fool any audience. Many problems (of the moral and ethical variety) arise. It's just too bad that we stop caring less than halfway through. —C. P.

SINGLES L: COMEDY/COMEDY (1992) 100M D: Cameron Crowe. *Campbell Scott, Kyra Sedgwick, Bridget Fonda, Matt Dillon, Sheila Kelley. Singles* is always hailed as the classic "grunge" movie, but aside from a few brief glimpses of Soundgarden and Alice in Chains (and Dillon's flannel), there isn't a whole lot of grunge in this film. Instead, Crowe gives us a sweet tale of hip urban relationships against the backdrop of Seattle. His script perfectly captures the frustration and elation of attraction. He also gets little details of normal interaction and conversation just right, and the actors play these out with ease. This movie came out when I was sixteen and provided me with a blueprint for my twenties, everything from the boyfriend-induced traumas and drunken evenings, right down to their apartments. *Singles* made me fall in love with my city and made me want to find someone to fall in love with. —J. K.

SLEEP WITH ME L: COMEDY/INDEPENDENT COMEDY (1994) 86M D: Rory Kelly. *Craig Sheffer, Meg Tilly, Parker Posey, Eric Stoltz, Quentin Tarantino.* Yeah, there's a lot of talking and not much sex, which pisses people off, but the dialogue is actually funny. I appreciate romantic comedies with the guts to explore relationships at any stage other than the beginning, without mucking it up with a ridiculous amount of philandering. Six or more characters sleeping together without any realization that something is afoot until the end is just absurd. *Sleep with Me* concerns that part of a relationship where lovers tend to forget what they really need or want from each other: marriage, with just the right amount of infidelity. Tarantino gives a talk on *Top Gun* and the subversive battle between Kelly McGillis and "the gay way." He sounds a lot like a video store employee. —J. J.

SLUMS OF BEVERLY HILLS L: COMEDY/COMEDY (1998) 90M D: Tamera Jenkins. *Natasha Lyonne, Alan Arkin, Marisa Tomei, Charlotte Stewart, Eli Marienthal, David Krumholtz. Slums* is a movie about a family just weird enough to be interesting and normal enough to believe in. Women who direct comedies have a great sense of finding the humor in real situations rather than exaggerating them. Lyonne plays a very believable teen; her embarrassment about her parents is just one of the elements that connects the viewer to her character. I really like the cringingly awkward scene where she lets a boy from the apartment touch her breast in the laundromat. This is the way first experiences usually are, way too nervous to be sexy. —*R. D.*

SO I MARRIED AN AXE MURDERER L: COMEDY/COMEDY
(1993) 93M D: Thomas Schlamme. *Mike Myers, Amanda Plummer, Nancy Travis, Anthony LaPaglia.* Charlie is a guy who has some relationship problems. He meets Harriet, they cut meat together, it seems like love. They decide to get married. Charlie starts to think that maybe Harriet is psycho. Like an axe murderer psycho, who marries a bunch of dudes just so she can axe them to death, as axe murderers are prone to do. Is he just being paranoid, or will he really lose his head over this girl? The plot is ridiculous, and I love it. Myers, as usual, is extremely funny. Maybe even funnier than normal. Travis does a great job of making it next to impossible to tell whether or not she's a nut job, all the way until the very end. —*J. S.*

SPECIALS, THE L: COMEDY/COMEDY (2000) 82M D: Craig
Mazin. *Rob Lowe, Jamie Kennedy, Paget Brewster, Thomas Haden Church.* What a concept: a superhero movie with no fighting, little melodrama, and nary a super power on display until literally the final shot. The "sixth or seventh greatest superhero team in the world" doesn't get much action, which leads to plenty of downtime and clubhouse bickering and backbiting as strutting team leader Church tries to keep up morale ("Remember when we caught and drained The Blister?"). The flat TV direction of Mazin is dull and draggy but it's unwittingly part of the charm: it's such a low-key parody that the undercurrent of deadpan nuttiness and sheer invention just sneaks up on you. *Mystery Men* has the budget, but this is armed with a real appreciation for the absurdity of superhero melodrama in the suburban world. —*S. A.*

SPLASH L: COMEDY/COMEDY (1984) 111M D: Ron Howard.
Tom Hanks, Daryl Hannah, John Candy, Eugene Levy. Howard is the king of totally predictably movies and epitomizes everything I usually loathe about American films. But somehow *Splash* made a "splash" with me. It probably wasn't the acting prowess of *Bosom Buddies* star Hanks or the sexy Replicant from *Blade Runner*, Hannah. It probably wasn't Howard, who previously directed *Night Shift* starring Henry Winkler and Michael Keaton, either. So that leaves the story, even though you can pretty much tell what is going to happen from the get-go. There is enough action, special effects, and hope for nudity for the guys. There is enough romance and chivalry for the girls, topped off by enough silliness from Levy and Candy to complement the seriousness of loving and losing those pesky but perky mermaids. —*R. D.*

STRANGE BREW L: COMEDY/COMEDY (1983) 91M D: Dave
Thomas, Rick Moranis. *Dave Thomas, Rick Moranis, Max von Sydow, Paul Dooley, Mel Blanc, Lynne Griffin.* After the flop premiere of their movie *The Mutants of 2051 A.D.*, Bob and Doug McKenzie, two beer-loving hosers, attempt to blackmail free beer from Ellsinore Brewery. Soon the donut-fueled Canadians are involved in a *Hamlet* variation involving a beer heiress battling an egomaniacal brewmeister (von Sydow). Some highlights: Bob, trapped in a vat of beer, drinks his way to freedom; Doug gets a bloody nose from laughing too hard in the court room; and Hosehead the flying dog saves the world from poisoned beer by scaring partygoers at Oktoberfest. As the McKenzie brothers admit, *Strange Brew* is shot in 3-B—three beers—and it looks pretty good, eh? So pop a cold one and prepare to enjoy one of Canada's greatest cinematic achievements. —*S. H.*

STRIPES L: COMEDY/COMEDY (1981) 101M D: Ivan Reitman.
Bill Murray, Warren Oates, Harold Ramis, P. J. Soles, Sean Young, John Candy. Stripes is a comedy about a bunch of likeable losers who discover self-respect through teamwork and eventually get revenge on The Man. Sound familiar? Yes, this is a tried-and-true theme (*Police Academy*, *Revenge of the Nerds*, etc.) but no one does it better that Murray. *Stripes* has great one-liners, spies, sex, mud wrestling, and mischief. My favorite character is nicknamed Psycho, who insists on putting everyone on his death list and threatens to kill anybody who touches him, touches his stuff, or calls him Francis. —*R. D.*

STUART SAVES HIS FAMILY L: COMEDY/COMEDY (1995)
95M D: Harold Ramis. *Al Franken, Vincent D'Onofrio, Laura San Giacomo, Harris Yulin, Shirley Knight.* For some reason, Franken took his cartoonish *Saturday Night Live* self-help guru Stuart Smalley and put him in the middle of a fairly serious family drama. Surprisingly, it works. Stuart's tensions with his family (particularly D'Onofrio as his tough guy brother) are uncomfortably true to life. The ridiculous public access show from the *SNL* skits ("I'm good enough, I'm smart enough, and doggone it, people like me") is put into a context so you understand where it's coming from and don't really want to laugh at it anymore. Of course it's no *Blues Brothers*, but it's definitely one of the better movies based on *Saturday Night Live* skits. —*B. T.*

STUDENT BODIES L: COMEDY/COMEDY (1981) 86M
D: Mickey Rose. *Richard Brando, Joe Talarowski, Matthew Goldsby, Kristen Ritter.* Before *Scary Movie*, before *Repossessed*, about the same time as *Wacko* and just after *Airplane!*, a little horror parody film came and went. I don't even know if it ever played in theaters. I saw it on television when I was about fourteen. The minimal plot is the standard teenagers + sex = murder, but the movie has much more to offer. It is stu-

pid, it is crude, it is damn funny: the principal is addressing the high school over the PA system, discussing a recent string of murders. "And now a special appeal to the killer. Let's stop all this senseless killing; can't we have a murder that makes sense?" He continues, saying all scheduled events will go on normally because, "even the dead love a parade." The ending may suck, but its a fun ride until then. . . and you'll never think about sex or horse head bookends in quite the same way. —R. G.

STUPIDS, THE L: COMEDY/COMEDY (1996) 93M D: John Landis. *Tom Arnold, Jessica Lundy, Christopher Lee, Mark Metcalf, Alex McKenna, Bug Hall.* Landis may have lost the manic brilliance of his youth, but a laugh-a-minute script by *Simpsons* vet Brent Forrester makes this one worthwhile. Sprung from the pages of a children's book series, the Stupids are a family of nice people without so much as a drop of common sense between them. They go through life mistaking every day events for surreal adventures. At one point they mistake a museum elevator for a time machine, and the janitor for God. In the opening scene, Stanley Stupid (Arnold) notices that, just like every week, his garbage has disappeared, so he sets out to discover who stole it. At first it seems like a throwaway joke, but then you realize it's the plot of the movie. As Stanley follows the garbage men he thinks he's uncovered a conspiracy involving the military, the postal service, and a bee. If you don't hate this movie, you will laugh until you cry. —B. T.

SUDDEN MANHATTAN L: COMEDY/INDEPENDENT COMEDY (1996) 89M D: Adrienne Shelly. *Adrienne Shelley, Tim Guinee, Roger Rees, Louise Lasser.* It should come as no surprise that Shelly's directorial debut reverberates with Hal Hartley's offbeat American indie explorations of urban angst, fear of commitment, and trust in the modern world. After all, Ms. Shelly was the red-headed pixie star of his first two features. This little romantic goof is a hip NY indie comedy full of surreal moments, bizarre coincidences, and offbeat humor. Shelly stars as a mopey, neurotic goofball who falls in love with an impotent guy (Guinee) who reads Russian authors to her in bed. When she witnesses a series of murders in the streets of her Greenwich Village neighborhood that no one else sees, she turns to morbid gypsy fortune teller Lasser (who is no help, but is undeniably funny). Shelly proves quite deft with her ensemble cast while appearing in every scene. Her script is less sure, whimsical but rather scattered, and plays more like a dry run for her superior follow-up *I'll Take You There*. It lacks the focus and direction of Hartley, but bounces quite nicely on its own. —S. A.

SUPER TROOPERS L: COMEDY/COMEDY (2001) 103M D: Jay Chandrasekhar. *Kevin Heffernan, Steve Lemme, Erik Stolhanske, Jay Chandrasekhar, Brian Cox.*

"Desperation is a stinky cologne." It's not smart, it's not serious, and it has all the dignity of a fat naked man covered in powdered sugar, but *Super Troopers* is funny. At least most of the time. Written and performed by the comedy group Broken Lizard, the skit-like piece behaves like smart-alecky, anything-goes comedies of the '70s, but instead of rebels defying authority, these are authority figures as pranksters. It's like the *Animal House* boys joined the State Troopers, and found a new rivalry with local small-town cops. The plot has something to do with an impending shut down of a trooper station and a marijuana smuggling ring. But the fun is in the stunts and inspired mind games pulled on unsuspecting motorists, such as a car full of stoned college boys worked into paranoid hysteria. The direction is slapdash but the attitude is consistent. —S. A.

SUPERSTAR L: COMEDY/COMEDY (1999) 82M D: Bruce McCulloch. *Molly Shannon, Will Ferrell, Glynis Johns, Mark McKinney, Harland Williams, Elaine Hendrix.* Add this one to the ranks of *Saturday Night Live* skit-turned-movie. If you like *SNL*, and you like Molly Shannon, you will like this. It's not a masterpiece, but it has the absurd, over-the-top thing down to an art. Sometimes cheap humor is what you want, and *Superstar* delivers in spades. Shannon plays Mary Katherine Gallagher, a frumpy high school student who wants nothing more in life than to be kissed. The lucky guy she has her eye on is Sky Corrigan (Ferrell), and she figures the only way they will ever suck face is for her to become a superstar. Mary Katherine enters a talent show and hilarity ensues. The best part is that you never feel like Gallagher is misunderstood; she's a huge dork who gives everyone reason to laugh at her, which is all part of her charm. —J. S.

SWEETEST THING, THE L: COMEDY/COMEDY (2002) 84M D: Roger Kumble. *Christina Applegate, Cameron Diaz, Selma Blair, Parker Posey, Thomas Jane.* Watching *The Sweetest Thing* is similar to watching a horse dive off a platform at the circus: you know what you're watching is supposed to be entertaining, but instead it leaves you feeling uncomfortable. The film is a gross-out comedy seemingly inspired by *There's Something About Mary*. It has all the requisite jokes about sex, bodily functions, and characters who can't find love, and it even has Diaz. But while *There's Something About Mary* was content to let characters embarrass themselves, *The Sweetest Thing* pours humiliation on its characters like torments on Job. (One character is publicly humiliated so often you will be convinced the filmmakers were having a feud with the actress.) Cruel comedies can work, but only if paired with depth or style or wit. *The Sweetest Thing* has none of that. It doesn't have much of anything. —T. P.

SYKES, WANDA: TONGUE UNTIED L: COMEDY/STAND-UP COMEDY (2003) 60M D: Paul Miller. *Wanda Sykes.* I didn't really catch on to Sykes until I saw *Pootie Tang.* She is hilarious as Biggie Shorty, Pootie's dancing sidekick. She's more impressive as a stand-up, though—insightful and cutting, but with the kind of charisma that makes it impossible to take offense. This program from Comedy Central is extremely funny. Sykes is especially great when she tackles post-9/11 topics: terror alerts, incriminating FBI memos, airport security, the perception that Bush somehow turned smart the moment tragedy struck. She can almost make you laugh your anger away. The DVD extras include an older special (*Comedy Central Presents Wanda Sykes-Hall*) and a February 2001 appearance on *The Daily Show* so you can see her prophetically make fun of Bush's lack of foreign policy skills. —*B. T.*

TADPOLE L: COMEDY/COMEDY (2002) 78M D: Gary Winick. *John Ritter, Sigourney Weaver, Bebe Neuwirth, Aaron Stanford.* High school philosopher Tadpole (Stanford) is a brooding intellectual with a passion for literature and a pining for his wistful stepmother (Weaver). Twenty years ago this tale of a kid who loses his virginity to mom's sexy best friend (Neuwirth) and spends the long Thanksgiving weekend sorting out messy emotions and complicated relationships would have been an R-rated farce for the drive-in date crowd. In the age of the Dutch Dogme 95 Manifesto and digital video production, it's an ensemble piece with delicious performances (Neuwirth almost steals the film with her wry smiles and teasing glances), unexpected intimacy, and a sneaky sense of humor. Director Winick may sidestep the knotty issues of bedding an underage boy, but he doesn't shirk the emotional fallout from the romantic follies. It's an appealing mix of an old Hollywood movie world of Upper East Side sophisticates with the character-driven spontaneity of a modern American indie, all very slight and light but deftly done. —*S. A.*

TEACHING MRS. TINGLE L: COMEDY/COMEDY (1999) 96M D: Kevin Williamson. *Katie Holmes, Helen Mirren, Jeffrey Tambor, Barry Watson, Marisa Coughlan.* Holmes plays a perfect honor student trying to escape her small town through good grades, and Mirren plays her monstrous, impossibly evil history teacher who seems to want nothing more than to ruin the girl's life. Naturally, Holmes and friends set off a wacky series of events that leaves them with no choice but to kidnap the teacher and keep her tied to a bed for two days. Williamson's directorial debut (his prize for the success of *Scream* and *Dawson's Creek*) is a squirm-inducing, juvenile affair that can only lead you to believe he has never gotten over some grudge he had against one of his own teachers. The saddest part is that if you judged him based on this movie, you'd have to assume his teacher was right about him. —*B. T.*

TEEN WITCH L: COMEDY/COMEDY (1989) 94M D: Dorian Walker. *Robin Elaine Lively, Dan Gauthier, Joshua Miller, Caren Kaye, Dick Sargent.* Louise is your typical brainy high school student who spends much of her time daydreaming about the captain of the football team. The twist here is that Louise is descended from witches and will come into her powers on her sixteenth birthday. Upon gaining those powers, she chooses to use them to get all the kids, including the captain of the football team, to like her. You can already see where this is going. This fairly generic teen flick has heart but is poorly executed. —*S. W. F.*

TEEN WOLF L: COMEDY/COMEDY (1985) 92M D: Rod Daniel. *Michael J. Fox, James Hampton, Jerry Levine, Scott Paulin, Susan Ursitti.* Fox is a nerd who's not very good at basketball, but suddenly he finds out that his whole family (including him) are werewolves. Turning hairy brings out his natural manliness and suddenly he knows how to dunk. Everyone thinks he's really cool because he's a werewolf with a basketball jersey. (I think someone once told me this was an allegory about puberty.) Fox also has a "cool" friend named "Stiles" who likes to "surf" on top of a van and tells a wacky story about a guy getting his dick stuck in a shop vac. This horrible movie was apparently shelved and released to brutally negative reviews only after the success of *Back to the Future.* —*B. T.*

THREE SMART GIRLS L: CLASSIC COMEDY/CLASSIC COMEDY (1937) 84M D: Henry Koster. *Deanna Durbin, Ray Milland, Binnie Barnes, Alice Brady.* Time seems to have passed Durbin's films by, and that is just plain terrible. There has rarely been a more radiant child star in all of American cinema (and that includes Shirley Temple, Judy Garland, and Elizabeth Taylor!). It is all pretty much standard Hollywood clichés and pleasantries, but somehow Miss Durbin brings a purity of emotion and heart to fore that is undeniable. If you have a preteen daughter, or if you're just a sentimental old hanky-wringer, this film is for you. —*K. S.*

THREE STOOGES: CURLY CLASSICS L: COMEDY TEAMS/THREE STOOGES (1945) 108M D: Various. *Joe DeRita, Larry Fine, Moe Howard.* This collection of six Stooges shorts from their prime years all feature Curly (everyone's favorite Stooge) in a prominent role. *Woman Haters* is the gang's first film on their own and the dialogue is entirely in rhyme. The plot deals with one of those "he-man woman-haters clubs." The other five films find the Stooges posing as doctors, plumbers, boxers, and football players. The disc's highlight is *Micro-Phonies* in which Curly gets mistaken for a female opera singer named Señorita Cucaracha. The disc features several different language audio tracks, and it's really weird to watch the Three Stooges in Portuguese. —*S. H.*

THREE STOOGES: MERRY MAVERICKS L: COMEDY TEAMS/THREE STOOGES (1951) 99M D: Edward Bernds. *Shemp Howard, Moe Howard, Larry Fine.* This Shemp-heavy Three Stooges collection features four Western comedy shorts and a couple of the best Shemp outings. Most people regard Curly as the superior third stooge and brother Shemp is frequently dismissed as a greasy-haired goon with a weird "meep-meep-meep" vocal tick. But detractors should check out this DVD. Shemp is vastly superior to both Joe Besser and Curly-Joe, and his career is filled with interesting non-Stooge appearances (like *Hellzapoppin*). Curly stars in only one of the six films, *Cactus Makes Perfect*, in which he invents a gold detector and the Stooges head west to make their fortune. The remaining shorts star the disparaged Shemp and other Stooges as clumsy cowboys, bad plumbers, and private detective impersonators. For a strange and surreal time I recommend watching these films dubbed in Portuguese with English subtitles. —*S. H.*

THROW MOMMA FROM THE TRAIN L: COMEDY/COMEDY (1987) 88M D: Danny DeVito. *Danny DeVito, Billy Crystal, Kim Greist, Kate Mulgrew, Anne Ramsey.* Owen (DeVito) has a mom who is an overbearing bitch. Larry (Crystal) has an ex-wife who is an overbearing bitch. Larry teaches a writing class. Owen is his student who can't write. Larry recommends Owen watch a Hitchcock film to help him understand plot and motive. After watching *Strangers on a Train*, Owen thinks he knows what Larry is trying to tell him: They should each kill each other's overbearing bitch, thus obscuring individual motive and assuring that both of them get away with it. This movie is just good-natured fun, and though the plot is a little shallow and predictable, the really funny moments are enough to make one overlook the rest. The scenes from Larry's writing class are what really make the film, and Owen is such a sweet, childish character you just want to give him a big hug, even after he's just shoved a woman off a boat. —*J. S.*

TOP SECRET! L: COMEDY/COMEDY (1984) 90M D: Jim Abrahams, David Zucker, Jerry Zucker. *Val Kilmer, Lucy Gutteridge, Peter Cushing, Omar Sharif, Jeremy Kemp.* This was the Zucker brothers' mother's favorite out of all of their films! Honest! Though *Top Secret!* did not receive the same acclaim that *Airplane!* or *Airplane 2* did, this rough little gem is still worthy. Kilmer plays rock-and-roll star Nick Rivers, who is touring East Germany during WWII. While there he finds himself embroiled in kidnapping, politics, espionage, and the French Resistance as he tries to aid a beautiful young woman. Poking fun at various rock styles and idols along with WWII war and spy films, *Top Secret!* takes you on a ridiculous roller coaster ride with all sorts of twists and bends. Nothing is sacred. There is a brilliant song, "Skeet Shooting" done a la The Beach Boys, with Rivers gyrating his hips and pelvis in homage to the King. There are parodies and rip-offs of a number of famous and infamous films, including *The Great Escape* and *The Blue Lagoon*. Cheesy good fun to be had by all! —*M. N.*

TOPPER L: CLASSIC COMEDY/CLASSIC COMEDY (1937) 97M D: Norman Z. McLeod. *Cary Grant, Constance Bennett, Roland Young, Alan Mowbray, Eugene Pallette, Billie Burke.* Topper sees dead people and they're out for a good time in this screwball ghostly encounter of the comic kind. Grant and Bennett get top billing as the irresponsibly impulsive high society swells who live only for fun and the high life, even after they die. And fun they are as responsible banker Cosmo Topper (Young), a man just waiting to tear out of his safe, predictable routine, discovers when they adopt him as their project. Young is perfect as the old-before-his-time fuddy-duddy flirting with reckless abandon; and Grant is in his element as the devil-may-care eccentric, but Bennett is the retro-find. Like Carole Lombard by way of Myrna Loy, she is one of the most delightful and enchanting women to tease her way through a romantic comedy. —*S. A.*

TOYS L: COMEDY/COMEDY (1992) 121M D: Barry Levinson. *Robin Williams, Joan Cusack, Donald O'Connor, Robin Wright Penn, Michael Gambon, LL Cool J.* This is the quirky and surreal little story of a great toy company that gets split between two men with very different ideals. The son (Williams) believes in his father's dream, wanting only to make great toys and make children happy. The General (and Williams's uncle, played by Gambon), however, sees an opportunity for the government to use children as soldiers through battle games that in fact control remote tanks and weapons. This is one of those films you either love or hate. I think it's fantastic, with whimsical creations and sets, crazy characters, and a bizarre story. With music by Tori Amos and Thomas Dolby, the whole atmosphere is peculiar and perverse. This is a weird, with a capitol W, and wild, crazy ride of a flick. —*M. N.*

28 DAYS L: COMEDY/COMEDY (2000) 103M D: Betty Thomas. *Sandra Bullock, Viggo Mortensen, Steve Buscemi, Elizabeth Perkins, Dominic West.* Alcoholism, and all its inherent tragedy and romanticism, is a potentially dangerous subject for a star-centered Hollywood vehicle. Successful, even great films focusing on alcoholics have been made (*The Lost Weekend, Days of Wine and Roses*), but these films have often worked because of their honesty, showing the destruction such a disease can cause. But of course, this is Hollywood in the twenty-first century, and this is also a Bullock vehicle. The chances of truth surviving this combination are small. Which is not to say that *28 Days* does not have its share of painful moments; it just rarely earns them. Bullock plays an alcoholic woman who causes trouble wherever she shows up. She wakes up in a rehab center after a particularly wild night. As Hollywood would have it though, this is no ordinary rehab center, it's packed with eccentrics and other hackneyed stereotypes: the grouchy older man, the serious, tortured young drug addict, the crazy foreign guy (with a decidedly strange accent that seems to come from no country in particular), the tough but sweet nurse, and, somehow, Buscemi as the head counselor. —*C. P.*

UNCORKED (AKA AT SACHEM FARM) L: COMEDY/INDEPENDENT COMEDY (1998) 110M D: John Huddles.
Rufus Sewell, Nigel Hawthorne, Minnie Driver. Sewell is a well meaning but utterly incompetent businessman who may well lose his family's fortune. ("We'll double our money in a week. I speak metaphorically, of course.") An eccentric uncle (Hawthorne) steps off his pedestal (literally—he lives on top of a giant stone column in the middle of the yard like a geriatric *Simon of the Desert*) to bring his nephew back to reality, with the help of Sewell's girlfriend (Driver). Director Huddles goes overboard with distracting stylistic flourishes (skip frames, slo-mo, sped-up scenes, and too many dissolves) in this sweet, kooky, and thoroughly unconvincing little offbeat indie comedy of British family on a California estate. At least it distracts from a "follow your heart" story that gets lost in its own eccentric asides. —*S. A.*

UNDERCOVER BROTHER L: COMEDY/COMEDY (2002) 87M D: Malcolm D. Lee.
Eddie Griffin, Dave Chappelle, Denise Richards, Chris Kattan, Aujanue Ellis. Griffin plays a stuck-in-the-'70s, Afro-sporting subversive who goes to work for the secret organization The B.R.O.T.H.E.R.H.O.O.D. to fight The Man and his master plan to demean people of color. When a respected general, obviously modeled after Colin Powell (Billy Dee Williams), announces that he is opening a new chain of fried chicken restaurants, Griffin must go undercover to find out what the scheme is. Although the film sometimes seems overly inspired by the *Austin Powers* franchise and plays like a mainstream version of *Pootie Tang*, it is also an endearingly silly satire about racial politics. The supporting cast includes Neil Patrick Harris as a white intern (due to affirmative action) at the B.R.O.T.H.E.R.H.O.O.D. and Richards plays a character called "White She-Devil." —*B. T.*

UNHOOK THE STARS L: COMEDY/COMEDY (1996) 103M D: Nick Cassavetes.
Gena Rowlands, Marisa Tomei, Jake Lloyd, Gérard Depardieu, Moira Kelley. Cassavetes (son of John) makes his directorial debut with this showcase for his mother, Rowlands. She's a widowed mom suffering empty nest syndrome who practically adopts the darling son of feisty working-class party-girl Tomei. Cassavetes doesn't direct like his dad, but he does have a nice feel for personalities that should clash and instead make a strange kind of music together,

and he helps his cast feel their way through their parts. Tomei is excellent as the emotionally frayed crisis junkie, and Depardieu is sweet as a bearish French-Canadian trucker who woos Rowlands (a hearty August-November antidote to the forced May-December pairings of young sexy actresses and middle-aged icons). But the film belongs to Rowlands as a woman learning how to stop wrapping her life around others and live for herself. —*S. A.*

USED CARS L: COMEDY/COMEDY (1980) 113M D: Robert Zemeckis.
Jack Warden, Kurt Russell, Deborah Harmon, Frank McRae, Gerrit Graham. Zemeckis went on to make some of the most famous blasts of American pop culture cinema—*Back to the Future* and *Forrest Gump* among them—but none portray the cynical underside of the American dream with the gleeful anarchic pleasure of this hilariously nasty satire. Russell is the epitome of the smiling mercenary selling lemons to suckers with dirty tricks and phony promises, aided ably by his superstitious buddy (Graham). The outrageous stunts (illegally jamming the Super Bowl with a guerrilla commercial and hiring strippers to bump and grind on the cars like a Vegas sideshow) are more than simply high concept gags: Zemeckis and writer Bob Gale squeeze the limits of bad taste out of these lemons for a deliciously tart cinematic lemonade. Warden has a field day playing twin brothers and McRae is hilarious as the giant adrenaline-pumped mechanic. The crotch-grabbing Mexican junk car wholesaler is none other than Alfonso Arau, the ubiquitous character actor and director of *Like Water for Chocolate*. —*S. A.*

VALLEY GIRL L: COMEDY/COMEDY (1983) 95M D: Martha Coolidge.
Nicolas Cage, Deborah Foreman, Elizabeth Daily, Michelle Meyrink, Michael Bowen, Cameron Dye, Heidi Holicker. *Valley Girl* is many things. It's both an electrifying love story and one of the best '80s time capsules. Cage and Foreman have so much hot chemistry, I think it blew up my Beta player. Coolidge brilliantly explores social pressure and how all-consuming first loves can be. *Valley Girl* has one of the greatest soundtracks of all time and helps to define the decade. Whether you watch it for the music, the great performances, or for the "that's exactly how I felt when I first fell in love" feeling, you will for sure have a, like, totally tubular time every time you pop in your copy of this treasure. It is amazing from start to finish. —*R. D.*

VAMPIRE'S KISS L: COMEDY/COMEDY (1989) 103M D: Robert Bierman.
Nicolas Cage, Jennifer Beals, Bob Lujan, Kasi Lemmons, Maria Conchita Alonso, Elizabeth Ashley. Cage is absolutely over the top in this peculiar film about a literary agent convinced he is becoming a vampire. He admits to his therapist that he has strange dreams and the rest of the people at his office can see he's beginning to act odd. But once he gets it in his mind

that he's been bitten, he begins to change his flat into a dark tomb, he fears garlic, avoids mirrors, and, not satisfied with the size of his own bicuspids, buys himself a set of fangs he eventually uses on an unsuspecting female. Alonso is perfect as his secretary, Alva, who must deal with the worst of his personality disorder. Cage actually ate a cockroach while immersed in this role. —*N. J.*

VERMONT IS FOR LOVERS L: COMEDY/INDEPENDENT COMEDY (1992) 86M D: John O'Brien. *Marya Cohn, Euclid Farnham.* This is one of those movies that feels like a cross between documentary and fiction. Sometimes these movies are really boring. It's a good thing this one has yuppies, marriage, and old people. *Vermont* is armed with enough strong conflict and interesting actors that it never lulls into feeling like a movie about some people who like making movies about themselves. The East Coast couple who are about to wed in the country are a wonderful match and makes for an interesting story as he blunders and stresses, and she bickers and looks warily upon their future. And they both get some excellent advice from very old farmers. —*J. J.*

WAITING FOR GUFFMAN L: COMEDY/COMEDY (1997) 84M D: Christopher Guest. *Christopher Guest, Eugene Levy, Catherine O'Hara, Parker Posey.* From the man who helped bring you the mockumentary *This Is Spinal Tap*, Guest writes, directs, and stars in this spoof about small-town musicals. Playing an effeminate musical theater director from New York named Corky, Guest descends on the fictitious town of Blaine, Missouri, which is preparing for its 150th anniversary celebration. Corky writes a musical for the event, holds auditions, assembles a cast, and begins rehearsals. All this is done in the documentary style of *Spinal Tap*, but the humor is a bit more subtle, heavy on stereotypes of small-town musical theater. Corky gets word from the Oppenheimer Foundation that famous theater critic Guffman will come out to see their performance. Will this mean Broadway for the no-budget production? You'll have to suffer through the show to find out. —*N. J.*

WAY OUT WEST L: COMEDY TEAMS/LAUREL & HARDY (1937) 86M D: James W. Horne. *Stan Laurel, Oliver Hardy, Sharon Lynne, James Finlayson.* This has to be my favorite Laurel and Hardy film. A lot of fans single out *Sons of the Desert* but, while I love that film, it is *Way out West* that makes me laugh the hardest. Stan and Ollie travel way out west to deliver the deed to a gold mine but end up giving it to an imposter. They have to get it back from a saloon singer and her shifty accomplice (Finlayson, master of the double take and speaker of the first "D'Oh!"). There are lots of funny scenes, including a frantic, tickle-filled battle for the will, and another when Ollie gets his head stuck in a trap door. The boys also offer up a cute little shuffle and song in front of some

obvious rear projection. Out of all their features, *Way out West* comes closest to capturing the free-wheeling slapstick of the duo's shorts. —*S. H.*

WEEKEND AT BERNIE'S L: COMEDY/COMEDY (1989) 101M D: Terry Kotcheff. *Jonathan Silverman, Andrew McCarthy, Terry Kiser, Catherine Mary Stewart, Don Calfa.* From the director of *Rambo: First Blood* and the writer of *National Lampoon's European Vacation* comes this super-powered comic hybrid, *Weekend at Bernie's.* Two guys, Larry (McCarthy) and Richard (Silverman), work for this jerk named Bernie (Kiser). Bernie gets taken out (i.e., iced) by Paulie, a stereotypical Italian-American mobster, played by the amazing Calfa. Larry and Richard find Bernie dead and then exploit his beach place, but they have to maintain the illusion that he's alive. But what to do with a corpse? Well, you'll find out. But it's funny, man, I mean really funny. —*T. B.*

WEEKEND AT BERNIE'S 2 L: COMEDY/COMEDY (1993) 97M D: Robert Klane. *Andrew McCarthy, Terry Kiser, Jonathan Silverman, Troy Beyer.* This is the greatest film of all time! The dynamite duo of Silverman and McCarthy are back playing Richard and Larry, those well-intentioned, bumbling, fun-loving guys. And guess who else is back to make your sides split and your heart warm? That's right, it's Bernie Lomax (Kiser)! Yep, he's still dead but now he's out and about and dancing like a fool! Oh, and there's a plot in there somewhere. Some moronic petty criminals are hired to do something bad, but Bernie inadvertently and hilariously foils their fiendish plan (with a little help from Richard and Larry). Directed by screenwriter and *Bernie's* creator Klane. If you're looking for funny, this is funny, really funny. Also, for those of you who just watch movies for scantily clad ladies, there's plenty here for you, too. —*T. B.*

WEIRD SCIENCE L: COMEDY/COMEDY (1985) 94M D: John Hughes. *Anthony Michael Hall, Robert Downey Jr., Ilan Mitchell-Smith, Kelly LeBrock, Bill Paxton.* Hughes's nerd fantasy banner waved its highest with this ultimate pubescent digital daydream. Teen virgin outcasts Hall and Mitchell-Smith harness the awesome power of their Commodore 64 to create the ultimate woman in a dazzling bastardization of the Frankenstein legend. Never before has such a spandex-laden, blast-packed, calculator-age geekstorm been unleashed upon the PG-13 screen. This '80s cultural implosion features early performances by Paxton and Downey Jr., as well as hairless mutant Michael (*The Hills Have Eyes*) Berryman and most of the villainous bikers from *The Road Warrior.* And, if that's not enough, the soundtrack twitches and squirms with endless new wave hits, including the title track from Danny Elfman's seminal, pogo-inducing outfit Oingo Boingo. "You're stewed, buttwad!!" —*Z. C.*

WET HOT AMERICAN SUMMER L: COMEDY/COMEDY
(2001) 97M D: David Wain. *Janeane Garofalo, David Hyde Pierce, Michael Showalter, Paul Rudd.* This tongue-in-cheek tribute to the silly summer camp movies of the '70s and '80s is harmless, amiably entertaining, and completely pointless. The film is at its best with deadpan readings and long stares by Garofalo, and the klutzy shyness of Hyde Pierce (not to mention the sheer weirdness of camp cook Christopher Meloni, a Vietnam vet with a thing for kitchen appliances). But even when the ideas are inspired, the execution resembles an off episode of *Saturday Night Live*. Director Wain and cowriter/costar Michael Showalter obviously love the innocent summer camp comedies they riff on in this goofy feel-good spoof. The coliseum rock soundtrack, passionate French kissing around every corner, girls in bikinis and tight T-shirts, and fashion statements right out of *Dazed and Confused* capture the look and feel of a 1981 drive-in feature, right down to the lazy, laid-back pace and amusing sense of comic absurdity that doesn't quite take off. —*S. A.*

WHATEVER IT TAKES L: COMEDY/COMEDY (2000) 94M
D: David Raynr. *James Edward Franco, Colin Hanks, Marla Sokoloff, Jodi Lyn O'Keefe, Julia Sweeney, Shane West.* This is your usual, run-of-the-mill teen romance comedy. It tries to evoke Cyrano de Bergerac but falls very short of the target. Ryan (West) desires his next-door neighbor Ashley (O'Keefe), whose bedroom balcony is conveniently arms-length from his own bedroom balcony. While trying to win her over, Ryan doctors his voice over the phone to sound like the school jock (Franco). The romantic scenes are flat and the comedy stoops to repeated blows to the groin. If ever a romantic comedy were intended for a grade-school mentality, this is it. —*N. J.*

WHITE MEN CAN'T JUMP L: COMEDY/COMEDY (1992)
115M D: Ron Shelton. *Woody Harrelson, Wesley Snipes, Rosie Perez, Cylk Cozart, Tyra Ferrell.* White Men Can't Jump was billed as a rollicking, trash-talking comedy, and it has several moments that back it up. What's surprising about it is that the comedy is fueled by actual characters, with real wants and quirks and personalities. A pair of basketball hustlers (Snipes and Harrelson) prey on unsuspecting hoopsters in California; the gag is that Harrelson pretends to be the goofy, wide-eyed hick until after the bets are made. Along the way, Snipes and Harrelson bicker, talk, and try to understand their mates. While the film has its share of Hollywood moments, including a rousing showdown Snipes and Harrelson have with a pair of legendary basketball players, director Shelton allows the personalities to dictate the story, infusing even small characters with depth and allowing drama to take over. Notice how Harrelson's relationship with his girlfriend (Perez) has a startling resolution. —*T. P.*

WHO IS CLETIS TOUT? L: COMEDY/INDEPENDENT COMEDY
(2002) 92M D: Chris Ver Weil. *Christian Slater, Tim Allen, Portia de Rossi, Richard Dreyfuss, Billy Connolly.* "I have a story. A good story. It's got it all: a jewel heist, a prison break, a girl." Director/writer Ver Wiel tries to do a Tarantino number on this mix of heist movie, romance, and black comedy starring Slater as a small-time forger mistaken for the titular wanted man, and Allen as the movie-mad hit man on his trail. He ends up with a crisscrossing plot, an awkward mix of sentimental romance and brutal murders played for laughs, and a surface cleverness that loses itself in a fudged plotline and Ver Wiel's utter lack of imagination. The barrage of film references simply reminds us of better films. Dreyfuss is more charming and quietly sweet than he's been in over a decade in his supporting role. —*S. A.*

WIFE, THE (1995) L: COMEDY/INDEPENDENT COMEDY (1995)
103M D: Tom Noonan, Fletcher Christian. *Julie Hagerty, Tom Noonan, Wallace Shawn, Karen Young.* Noonan wrote, directed, edited, starred in, and composed original music for this psychological comedy. Jack (Noonan) and Rita (Hagerty) are a married couple who run a psychotherapy clinic. Without warning, one of Jack's patients, Cosmo (Shawn), pays them an uninvited visit when he decides on his own that he needs more counseling. At the point when the patient starts to drive the psychologists crazy, the film is reminiscent of *What About Bob?*. This movie is written well enough that it doesn't need to have a lot of settings, characters, flashy camerawork, or a driving soundtrack. —*R. D.*

WITH FRIENDS LIKE THESE . . . L: COMEDY/INDEPENDENT
COMEDY (1998) 105M D: Philip Frank Messina. *Adam Arkin, Robert Costanzo, Beverly D'Angelo, Elle MacPherson, Amy Madigan, Laura San Giacomo, David Strathairn, Jon Tenney.* This amiable comedy about second-tier working actors in Hollywood did well on the festival circuit but never broke out. It's a shame: despite its jabs of cynicism and wealth of Hollywood in-jokes (some of them very funny), it's really a sweet film about friendship, ambition, and the schism that occurs when they collide. In this case, it's when an ambitious but underemployed character actor (Costanzo) lands a secret audition for a Martin Scorsese film and winds up competing with his best friends (Arkin, Strathairn, Tenney) for the role. The great cast of character actors knows their milieu of struggling middle-aged guys stuck in a career of goombahs, goons, and victims, but despite their constant state of insecurity and jealousy, they're at heart husbands, fathers, and friends. You won't be wowed, but you will be entertained. Scorsese plays himself with wry unease. —*S. A.*

WIZARD OF SPEED AND TIME, THE L: COMEDY/
INDEPENDENT COMEDY (1988) 95M D: Mike Jittlov. *Mike Jittlov, Richard Kaye, Philip Michael Thomas, Paige*

Moore. This strange little independent film became a cult classic over the years, the tale of a man who wants nothing more than to create films with delightful special effects and the battles he fights to do so. Ironically the movie is not far from the truth, with the rat-bastard producer in the film being played by the actual producer of this film, who allegedly stole the rights right out from under director Jittlov's artistic nose. This is a movie best seen once just for the fun of it, and then again if you have a laserdisc copy or a good VCR. Why? Because most of the special effects are stop-motion animation and there are secret messages and things to see if you shift through them slowly. Be sure to check out the bicycle security scenes. If you ever wanted to make a movie, watch this one. Many of the scenes and descriptions of the rules of business are tragically true, not made up! —*M. N.*

WOO L: COMEDY/COMEDY (1998) 84M D: Daisy von Scherler Mayer. *Tom Davidson, Dave Chappelle, Jada Pinkett Smith, Paula Jai Parker.* One of the least funny films I've seen in my adult life, *Woo* walks the delicate line between cheery racism and pure inanity. Claudette (Parker) and Lenny (Chapelle) find a romantic evening ruined when Claudette's loud, demanding, and street-smart cousin Woo (Pinkett) shows up. Lenny persuades uptight friend Tim (Davidson) to take Woo out, a proposition Tim soon realizes he may not be up to. The worst—and therefore best—of *Woo* is a bizarre peripheral plot involving Lenny's noble but ill-fated attempts to unite his greatest passions: fried chicken and booty. Some versions of the video include a bonus Nate Dogg & Warren G music video, which features perhaps (make that hopefully) West Coast rap's lone foray into synchronized swimming. —*C. B.*

WORLD'S GREATEST SINNER L: COMEDY/INDEPENDENT COMEDY (1962) 82M D: Timothy Carey. *Timothy Carey, Gil Barreto, Betty Rowland, James Farley.* You don't have to be a Carey fan to enjoy the bizarre, one-of-a kind *World's Greatest Sinner,* but it sure helps. This dream project for the unusual actor (who's worked with everybody from John Cassavetes to William Asher) is a wild social satire made on a shoestring budget. Most scenes are poorly lit and the sound quality varies wildly, but if you can get over these technical shortcomings you'll be treated to the crazy story of a man who changes his name to God (but keeps his last name so his new moniker is God Hilliard), then becomes a rock star/public speaker, makes a deal with the devil, and runs for political office. Carey spends much of the movie making out with women of various ages (fourteen to sixty-something). The best parts are his musical performances where he strums one guitar string, shakes his body and says, "Please! Please! Please! Take My Heart!" and then surfs the crowd. —*S. H.*

ZAPPED! L: COMEDY/COMEDY (1982) 96M D: Robert J. Rosenthal. *Scott Baio, Willie Aames, Scatman Crothers, Felice Schachter.* This teen rampage makes *Teen Wolf* look like *Turner & Hooch.* Baio and Aames (both from *Charles in Charge*) star in this '80s sci-fi comedy that put the "t" and "a" in "telepath." Baio is granted superhuman mental abilities after a bizarre science class mishap. Where most red-blooded Americans would use these powers for the advancement of mankind, our hero bursts blouses and levitates bullies. Baio's parents assume he's possessed and spend half the movie trying to exorcise Satan from their household. Meanwhile, high school janitor Crothers (*The Shining*) accidentally inhales an iron stove full of marijuana and hallucinates that he and Albert Einstein are being chased on bicycles by Crothers's obese wife, who is firing enormous sausages out of a bazooka from her horse-drawn chariot. If this doesn't sound entertaining, get the hell out of my house. —*Z. C.*

ZOOLANDER L: COMEDY/COMEDY (2001) 89M D: Ben Stiller. *Ben Stiller, Owen Wilson, Andy Dick, Christine Taylor, Milla Jovovich, Will Ferrell.* "I'm sure there's more to life than just being really, really, really good looking," proclaims Derek Zoolander with spacey, breathless affectation, "and I plan on finding out what that is." Stiller purses his lips, contorts his face, and spikes his hair into the blow-dried coif of an '80s pop band refugee to play Zoolander: a male model, fashion icon, and intellectual pygmy. Stiller spins gags around his harmless idiot and enlists friends and acquaintances to join in on the fun, including Wilson as fast-rising flower child model and mystic goober Hansel, Ferrell as bitchy fashionista Mugatu, dad Jerry Stiller as Zoolander's manager (who yammers on like a Catskills comedian), and Dick, under pounds of latex, playing a flabby German hausfrau-masseuse. That doesn't even touch the film's parade of celebrities, from Winona Ryder to David Bowie to male model incarnate Fabio. Christine Taylor (Stiller's real wife) plays straight man to this catwalk circus. —*S. A.*

A kid told me a story about when he was young, his family was running away from the erupting plumes of Mount Saint Helens when he accidentally fell face first into a pile of volcanic ash. The entire week after, he would wake up crying every night, his eyes crusted over by his irritated tear ducts trying to remove all the ash. Watching this movie may induce similar sensations. But watching a volcano explode would be way cooler. —*A. T.*

TELEVISION COMEDY

BRADY BUNCH MOVIE, THE L: TELEVISION SHOWS/COMEDY TELEVISION (1995) 88M D: Betty Thomas. *Henriette Mantel, Michael McKean, Jennifer Elise Cox, Shelley Long, Gary Cole, Christine Taylor.* Throughout the '90s grunge movement, Gen-Xers raised on endless reruns of *The Brady Bunch* reflected on how such archetypes might fit into their modern world. Thanks to the genius of director Betty Thomas, we all now have a pretty good idea about this: they would stand out like the sore thumbs they are! With a select and clever cast looking enough like the original actors yet taking their performances a little over the top, *The Brady Bunch Movie* has an outrageous script robbing liberally from the TV series. The central plot concerns the children trying to raise $20,000 to save their beloved house from a corporate buy-out. All the subplots are lined with continuous jokes that will make you want to check this film out two or three times. Just imagine the family catching the butcher staying over with Alice (Mantel) for the night and asking him why he's there. He proudly replies, "Just delivering the meat!" —*N. J.*

EERIE, INDIANA L: TELEVISION SHOWS/COMEDY TELEVISION (1991) 75M D: Joe Dante, Sam Pillsbury. *Mary-Margaret Humes, Justin Shenkarow, Omri Katz.* This is the first collection of a short-lived, little-known kids show with imagination and quirky humor on par with the more popular *The Adventures of Pete and Pete.* Marshall Teller (Katz) moves from New Jersey to a seemingly normal Indiana suburb that only he and his new friend Simon (Shenkarow) realize is actually "the center of weirdness for the entire planet." In each episode they encounter a different "weird" phenomenon and save some sort of memento for their evidence locker. On these first three episodes they discover people who live forever by sleeping in giant Tupperware, find a retainer that allows its wearer to read the minds of dogs, and discover an artificially intelligent ATM machine that gives Simon all the money he wants. —*B. T.*

KIDS IN THE HALL: BRAIN CANDY L: TELEVISION SHOWS/ COMEDY TELEVISION (1996) 88M D: Kelly Makin. *Dave Foley, Bruce McCulloch, Kevin McDonald, Mark McKinney, Scott Thompson.* Can you buy happiness in the form of a pill? The Kids in the Hall ask exactly this question in *Brain Candy*, a comic, sarcastic look at how a quick fix to problems can deliver happiness, but at a very high cost. Dr. Chris Cooper (McDonald), a scientist at a prestigious pharmaceutical company, has invented a cure for depression. Before he can properly test this drug, it is pushed into production by the company's money-grubbing president and forced out as an over-the-counter drug. At first everything seems like it's working out, but soon the shit hits the fan, and Dr. Cooper is forced to decide whether to work for or against the evil, money-grubbing corporation. The Kids in the Hall are as funny as ever in a movie that essentially comes across as a longer version of one of their skits. If you think this is just fluff, look again. It's witty, intelligent fluff. —*J. S.*

KIDS IN THE HALL: SAME GUYS, NEW DRESSES L: TELEVISION SHOWS/COMEDY TELEVISION (2000) 86M D: David Foley. *Dave Foley, Scott Thompson, Kevin McDonald, Bruce McCulloch, Mark McKinney.* Foley directed this documentary on the Kids's 2000 North American tour, giving fans a glimpse of their stage show and the background dramas that unfold. While I'd like to believe Kids all get along, that misguided notion vanishes quickly but quietly as group members passive-aggressively crawl through their tour. From Dave's "controversial" laser eye surgery to Scott's preempted Conan O'Brien show appearance, it was evident these folks really do care about one another, but sometimes would like to give each other a good slap across the face. Dave says it best during one of the film's more uncomfortable scenes, a shared dinner where the Kids talk about their future projects. He says when they are writing, the Kids compete against each other, but when they are onstage, they try to do what's best for one another. I guess that's why we all thought they were such good friends. —*J. K.*

KOVACS, ERNIE: BEST OF L: TELEVISION SHOWS/COMEDY TELEVISION (1952) 360M D: Ernie Kovacs. *Edie Adams, Ernie Kovacs.* Kovacs was a true original who never really achieved the fame he deserved. In the midst of a mediocre Hollywood career that consisted of small supporting roles in movies like *Bell Book and Candle* and *North to Alaska*, Kovacs died in a car carsh on the way home from a party. Still, it's his work on TV that really shines. Whether through a surreal visit with The Nairobi Trio or his hilarious, dialogue-free half-hour short *Eugene*, I can't think of anybody as wild, imaginative, ingenious, and just plain flat-out funny as Kovacs. His groundbreaking show consists of sketches that include short, otherworldly gags and longer parodies. He also liked to set odd visual interludes (such as an office coming to life) to unique music by Esquivel and others. Kovacs paved the way for *Monty Python's Flying Circus* and *Saturday Night Live*, and this multi-disc collection features some of his greatest bits. —*S. H.*

LARRY SANDERS SHOW, THE—THE ENTIRE FIRST SEASON L: TELEVISION SHOWS/COMEDY TELEVISION (1992) 332M D: Various. *Garry Shandling, Jeffrey Tambor, Rip Torn.* Insecurities, egos, vanity, and other show-biz ailments abound in this scathingly funny portrait of a TV talk show. Created for HBO by star/writer Shandling, this acidic, sneaky satire quickly became Hollywood's favorite cult show, attracting an astounding array of guest stars all happy to send up themselves and their images in increasingly clever appearances. The guest list (including Carol Burnett, Dana Carvey, Robin Williams, and Billy Crystal) plays it more subdued in the thirteen episodes of the first season, but the regular cast goes for the jugular in biting comments, venal pranks, and a torrent of sadistically funny backbiting. The show is made by Tambor's sharp-as-a-wet-sponge sidekick Hank (perfectly played with blowhard vanity and oblivious babbling) and Torn's smiling wolf of a producer Artie: loyal, fiercely protective, a veteran schmoozer quick to smile and quicker to toss off an epithet-laden insult. Smart, sharp, cutting, cynical, and buoyed by just enough sensitivity, sincerity, and genuine kindness to keep you with the characters, it's the best comedy ever made about the business we call show. —*S. A.*

MIKE DOUGLAS SHOW, THE: VOLUME 2 L: TELEVISION SHOWS/COMEDY TELEVISION (1974) 70M D: Arthur Forrest. *Sly Stone, Muhammad Ali, Mike Douglas.* This July 17, 1974, episode of the legendary daytime talk show is great for two reasons: the guest cohost is Sly Stone (of Sly and the Family Stone) and one of the guests is his friend Muhammad Ali. Sly is all fun and flower power, but Ali (who is preparing for the Rumble in the Jungle) comes out unamused and unwilling to participate in the usual talk show phoniness. He talks bluntly about white people wanting him to smile and tell jokes and calls Sly a clown. Performing his duties as cohost, Sly tries to keep things light, especially after Congressman Wayne Hays comes out and Ali starts grilling him about race. It's a fascinating time capsule where a great musician and an American hero pit their differing philosophies against each other right there on your TV. And if that's not enough, the Family Stone come out and perform at the end. —*B. T.*

NORTHERN EXPOSURE: "CICELY" L: TELEVISION SHOWS/ COMEDY TELEVISION (1990) 46M D: Rob Thompson. *Rob Morrow, Janine Turner, Barry Corbin, John Corbett, John Cullum, Yvonne Suhor, Cynthia Geary.* My obsession with *Northern Exposure* evolves from those novels for young readers about surviving in the wild with wolves and hatchets. Although there are no hatchets in *Northern Exposure*, there is a sense that in Cicely, Alaska, the natural world affects the daily routine. This episode explains the significance of the town's name and includes references to Roslyn, Washington, the town where the show was filmed. The story of how Cicely came to be reveals the strange link the town has to artists and rejected minds from around the world. The episode also tackles girl-on-girl love, long before *Xena*, with two really hot chicks. —*J. J.*

THE ORIGINAL GHOSTBUSTERS VOL. 1 L: TELEVISION SHOWS/COMEDY TELEVISION (1975) 72M D: Norman Abbott, Larry Peerce. *Forrest Tucker, Larry Storch.* Nine years before Bill Murray and Dan Aykroyd busted out their proton packs to snare specters, ex-Hollywood leading man Tucker and goof-ass Storch (*F-Troop*) pioneered the art. Joining them on their Krofft-esque haunt hunts was Tracy the Gorilla, an enormous hairy suit occupied by horror über-nerd Bob Burns, who years earlier had designed and filled the bulb-headed *Invasion of the Saucer Men* costumes. Each of the sixteen

shot-on-video episodes consisted of bad vaudeville routines alternating with worse slapstick as the three 'busters chased down everything from werewolves to a dead Mafioso. Guest stars were apparently easy to come by back in '75, and some of the featured spooks included world-famous little person Billy Barty, *Car 54*'s Joe E. ("Oo! Oo!") Ross, and *Caddyshack*'s Ted Knight. Three episodes were collected on video and released by anything-for-a-buck exploitationeers Continental Video following the success of the Ivan Reitman blockbuster in 1984. —*Z. C.*

SMOTHERED: THE GREAT SMOTHERS BROTHERS CENSORSHIP WARS L: TELEVISION SHOWS/COMEDY TELEVISION (2002) 92M D: Maureen Muldaur. *Tom Smothers, Dick Smothers, Joan Baez, Pete Seegar.* The Smothers Brothers Comedy Hour butted heads with network censors for three years, not for pushing the boundaries of sex or violence or language, but for daring to tackle political satire and social commentary in their comedy. With Tommy Smothers leading the rallying cry of free expression, the fight leapt out of CBS's backrooms and into the popular press, embarrassing the network with every sketch and song they censored. This slice of cultural history offers the anatomy of a controversy, drawing upon contemporary interviews with many of those involved on both sides of the fight. The film also uses a wealth of clips as evidence, from sleepy-eyed Pat Paulsen's deadpan editorials and presidential campaign to performances of folk songs deemed too rebellious by conservative network executives. —*S. A.*

SON OF THE BEACH L: TELEVISION SHOWS/COMEDY TELEVISION (2000) 588M D: Various. *Timothy Stack, Jaime Bergman, Leila Arcieri, Roland Kickinger, Kim Oja.* If you think *Baywatch* is already such a self-parody that spoofing is redundant, you haven't seen *Son of the Beach*, an uproarious farce that revels in juvenile idiocy, bawdy puns, and the skimpiest wardrobe on prime time. Stack is "the world's greatest lifeguard" Notch Johnson, a paunchy, pasty, middle-aged boy scout who proudly claims that while he may not have the biggest unit on the beach, he has the best. He's talking about his bikini-clad lifeguard team, of course. These fearless lifeguards risk life, limb, and overexposure to battle the everyday dangers of beach life—toxic waste, insidious cult leaders, mobsters, and randy sea monsters—and shamelessly exploit every social and ethnic stereotype with a barrage of gleefully tasteless jokes. The first twenty-one episodes feature guest spots by Mark Hamill, Corbin Bernsen, Erik Estrada, and, in the unforgettable episode *Queefer Madness*, David Arquette, Lucas Haas, and Neil Patrick Harris as a biker gang of BMX beatniks. —*S. A.*

SPORTS NIGHT—THE COMPLETE SERIES BOXED SET L: TELEVISION SHOWS/COMEDY TELEVISION (1998) 17 Hours D: Robert Berlinger, Thomas Schlamme, others. *Robert*

Guillaume, Peter Krause, Josh Charles, Felicity Huffman, Sabrina Lloyd, Joshua Malina. This semi-sitcom was underappreciated by audiences and its network, but has since found a following on DVD, helped by the popularity of Aaron Sorkin's well-received *The West Wing*. Casey McCall (Krause), alongside Dan Rydell (Charles), hosts *Sports Night*, a nightly cable sports highlight show. The series follows the group of dedicated, talented, and often downright crazy people who make the show happen, capturing their camaraderie and conflicts, office romances, battles with the network, and power struggles aplenty. Sorkin's trademark writing style, fast paced and peppered with quick, witty banter, more than keeps up with the hustle of producing the fictional live television show. Through his words and the great ensemble cast's performances, you get a real sense of the bond created by their trials. If you can get past the laugh track in the first set of episodes, you're in for a treat. —*J. K.*

STRANGERS WITH CANDY: SEASON 1 L: TELEVISION SHOWS/COMEDY TELEVISION (1999) 246M D: Various. *Stephen Colbert, Amy Sedaris.* Originally broadcast on Comedy Central, this show is extremely funny. Sure, the humor can be a little raunchy at times, and political correctness is a concept the writers threw out the window. But these are the things that make *Strangers with Candy* beautiful. Sedaris is Jerri Blank, a forty-six-year-old high school freshman who spent thirty-two years of her life as a drug-addicted prostitute loser, but has finally decided to pick her life up exactly where she left off. The dialogue is sarcastic and witty, and all the characters are extremely colorful and flamboyant. Jerri deals with everything from peer pressure and sex to racism and motherhood, all with the same trashy resilience and rude charm that won our hearts during the three very short seasons that *Strangers with Candy* stayed on the air. —*J. S.*

SURVIVING GILLIGAN'S ISLAND L: TELEVISION SHOWS/COMEDY TELEVISION (2001) 85M D: Paul A. Kaufman. *Russell Johnson, Sherwood Schwartz, Bob Denver, Dawn Wells.* Wells—*Gilligan's Island*'s Mary Anne—produces and hosts this combination TV-movie and series remembrance with her former costars Denver (Gilligan) and Johnson (The Professor). The program is actually quite entertaining and frothy as it bounces between the real stars dishing stories and trivia and the docu-humor recreations of behind-the-scenes events. But there's something truly odd about celebrating the long, hard road producer Schwartz took to sell one of the most absurdly mindless shows in TV history to the network. Don't expect tell-all melodrama or back-stabbing gossip. Even glamour queen Tina Louise's star fits are less a matter of cast friction and more a quirky personality trait straight out of a TV sitcom. —*S. A.*

TENACIOUS D: THE COMPLETE MASTERWORKS L: TELEVISION SHOWS/COMEDY TELEVISION (2003) 140M D: Spike Jonze, Liam Lynch, others. *Jack Black, Kyle Gass, Dave Grohl.* This collection contains just about anything you could want on the first DVD release by the hilarious folk/metal act who sing intense ditties about themselves and, occasionally, Ronnie James Dio. The "For Fans" disc has a full-length, professionally shot concert at the Brixton Academy and all six episodes of their HBO series. Each episode begins with the D at an open mic night, then follows the duo's unpredictable adventures from stalking a fan to jamming in a cave with Bigfoot (Oscar nominee John C. Reilly). *Mr. Show*'s Bob Odenkirk and David Cross were producers on the show, which is similar to their style of humor and storytelling. The "For Psycho Fans" disc includes three shorts made for HBO, three TV appearances (including their anatomically correct puppet counterparts on *Crank Yankers*), three videos, and humorous documentaries about recording the album with Dave Grohl and the Dust Brothers, and going on tour. Has anyone else noticed that Black played a kid obsessed with a right-wing folk singer in *Bob Roberts*, and then built his career on his own parody folk music? I wonder if that's where it all began. At any rate, he's taken it far, as this DVD proves. —*B. T.*

TICK, THE: THE ENTIRE SERIES L: TELEVISION SHOWS/COMEDY TELEVISION (2001) 201M D: Hank Tucker, Art Vitello, others. *Nestor Carbonell, Patrick Warburton, David Burke, Liz Vassey.* Warburton is the big blue bug of justice in a molded body suit and fidgety antenna feelers in Barry Sonnenfeld's inspired adaptation of Ben Edlund's cult comic book (which previously spawned a hilarious animated series). Perfectly cast as the muscle-bound moron whose aphorisms and gnarled metaphors push the English language into the Twilight Zone, the blankly innocent Warburton might as well be animated himself. His cohorts are much more down to Earth. . . albeit an Earth where superheroes are so commonplace they need a license to operate. Burke is the white-suited, rabbit-eared Arthur (Tick's only real anchor to reality), Vassey the well-endowed and romantically reckless Captain Liberty, and Carbonell is inspired as the self-promoting Batmanuel, a hero who apparently has never actually done anything heroic but doesn't let that get in the way of his ongoing PR campaign. The superhero sitcom was canceled after a mere nine episodes. All of them are collected on this two-disc DVD set. —*S. A.*

WONDER YEARS, THE: BEST OF L: TELEVISION SHOWS/COMEDY TELEVISION (1988-1993) 71M D: Michael Dinner. *Fred Savage, Danica McKellar, Josh Saviano, Daniel Stern, Dan Lauria.* For a show that aired for what felt like 470 years, I find it tragic that this "best of" DVD only contains THREE episodes. The first is a collage of highlights, and after seeing all of the corny-yet-touching scenes in which Kevin Arnold (Savage) blossoms from a young boy into an upstanding boy-man, I was all geared up for hours and hours of watching old episodes. Disappointment followed. Instead of providing years of the programs that followed, we jump right to the final two-part episode in which Winnie (McKellar) and Kevin realize that maybe they aren't meant to be together forever. I cried as they sat together in the barn making out, both because I was watching young love die and because the people who released the DVD denied me all the episodes where young love lived. —*J. S.*

CHAPTER FIVE

Drama, Television Drama & Gay Cinema

I f a film moves you to varying degrees of emotional highs, as long as it is not too suspenseful, or overly focused on murder or mystery (see Murder/Mystery/Suspense), one way or another Drama will cover it.

I don't know. I've always felt that Drama was a category to be filled with all those stories that just couldn't quite qualify for pure tragedy.

But that's fine. Not everybody can be or wants to be the next Arthur Miller. And not every audience member wants to be mainlining tragedy full-time. So, sometimes you take your drama lite: *Once Around* or *Big Wednesday* might suffice. And sometimes you are in the mood for something heavy: *Monster's Ball* or *River's Edge*. But either way, drama stirs your emotions, riles you up, makes you cheer or makes you mad, it educates you or makes you sad. Simply: drama is dramatic. It is born of conflict or injustice, stories of life out of order and needing to be made right.

Like comedy, the Drama section is comprised of the best films not found in other sections of the book: the Foreign Film and Directors sections. The regular Drama section contains films made after the institution of the ratings system, and were produced by major studios, while Independent Drama films were, and weren't. Classic Drama contains those films produced prior to the institution of the Academy of the Motion Picture Arts and Sciences ratings system in the late 1960s. Precode

The Stunt Man (1980)

©ANCHOR BAY ENTERTAINMENT

Dramas were made before the infamous Hays code (look it up online for its details of self-regulating Fascist fun!), which put married people into separate beds and unmarried people seemingly nowhere near one another, and pretty much banned drug use, unpunished crime, and swearing. Yiddish cinema was just that; and the Harlem Renaissance section is full of films made by black producers with all-black casts for all-black audiences to be shown in black-owned cinemas.

This chapter also includes reviews of comedies, dramas, and documentaries that are gay-themed and intended for gay, lesbian, and transgender audiences.

DRAMA

ALL THE PRESIDENT'S MEN L: DRAMA/DRAMA (1976) 139M D: Alan J. Pakula. *Robert Redford, Dustin Hoffman, Jack Warden, Martin Balsam, Hal Holbrook, Jason Robards.* A compelling drama, with excellent performances and script. Rightly regarded as a classic, this is the best of director Pakula's collaborations with cinematographer Gordon Willis. From the gorgeous, brightly lit offices of the *Washington Post* to the bold nighttime exteriors, Willis's photography pushes the limits of filmstock and viewer expectations. Where most movies are afraid of letting actors fall too deeply in shadow, Willis provides contrarian relief. Francis Ford Coppola once called Willis a "conservative" photographer, but Willis's distinctive style is about taking risks with the medium. Of course, the strength of the photography is that it is just one part of the film and so organic you probably won't notice it without a conscious effort. Enjoy the film and take the extra effort to consider the image, you'll get that much more out of it. —*M.H.*

ALL THE REAL GIRLS L: DRAMA/INDEPENDENT DRAMA (2003) 105M D: David Gordon Green. *Paul Schneider, Zooey Deschanel, Patricia Clarkson, Shea Whigham, Benjamin Mouton, Maurice Compte, Danny McBride.* Playing out like the hiss-static love song in one's mind, indie auteur Green's sophomore effort is a sojourn to young love, and even more, the autumnal fall from it. Schneider is good as Paul, the local ladies' man with a heart of gold, but the real props go to Deschanel, whose blue eyes dart, linger, and sparkle, managing a kind of dreamy rapture that only a star could muster. Tim Orr's camerawork is spotless, seeped in honey yellows and golds; never has a North Carolina morning looked better. Though the script sometimes feels trying, Green allows his secondary characters to pull and hold their own weight (particularly McBride as the hilarious Bust-Ass, and the ever-awesome Clarkson as Paul's strong and weary mom). David Wingo and Michael Linnen's score pulls this piece together, finding a fine balance between sentimentality and down-to-earth naturalism. —*J.D.*

ALMOST FAMOUS: THE BOOTLEG CUT L: DRAMA/DRAMA (2000) 162M D: Cameron Crowe. *Patrick Fugit, Kate Hudson, Philip Seymour Hoffman, Jason Lee, Frances McDormand, Billy Crudup.* Crowe's thinly fictionalized autobiography is deftly poised between rosy affection, thoughtful remembrance, and giddy adolescent awe, as perhaps it should be. Revisiting the midseventies rock scene, the story of fifteen-year-old William (Crowe's alter ego, played by Fugit), sent by *Rolling Stone* to tour with an up-and-coming band called Stillwater, has the sensory immediacy of a treasured memory, from the crackle of vinyl on a bedroom turntable to the view of an arena concert from the stage. Crowe exposes the sex, drugs, infighting,

and indiscretions of the music scene (perhaps with more discretion than necessary) without ever losing faith in the power of music. Hudson glows as the giving, impulsive, always surprising Penny Lane, the young groupie (or, as she would say, "Band-Aid") in love with Stillwater guitarist Crudup. Hoffman is marvelous as William's (and Crowe's real-life) mentor, Lester Bangs. None of the extra thirty minutes in the "bootleg cut" are essential. They "thicken" the experience with often lovely and poignant detail, but in filling out the stories around William, they distract from William himself. —*S.A.*

AMERICAN BEAUTY L: DRAMA/DRAMA (1999) 122M D: Sam Mendes. *Kevin Spacey, Chris Cooper, Annette Bening, Thora Birch, Wes Bentley, Mena Suvari.* Bathetic American tragedy about disgruntled family man Lester Burnham (Spacey), who decides one day to quit his job in favor of smoking pot in his garage, driving a muscle car, pumping iron, working at a fast food joint, and lusting after a teenage girl (Suvari). The gimmick (as in *Sunset Boulevard*) is that Burnham is already dead when narrating. The movie plays out as a desperate apology for all the things Burnham has taken for granted: his cheating wife (Bening), his voluptuous beatnik daughter (*Ghost World*'s Birch), his cookie-cutter suburban home, and his sad-sack job. This film has complete disrespect for humanity of any kind, assaulting homosexuals, reducing women to mongrel clothes-whores, and making teenage angst look like a drug-addled boobfest. Clichéd, static, and loaded with self-satisfied bullshit, this is the worst film ever to almost sweep top honors at the Academy Awards. —*J.D.*

ANGELS OVER BROADWAY L: CLASSIC DRAMA/CLASSIC DRAMA (1940) 78M D: Lee Grames, Ben Hecht. *Douglas Fairbanks Jr., Rita Hayworth, John Qualen, Thomas Mitchell.* Fairbanks Jr. produced and starred as a street hustling "Broadway scavenger" in Hecht's tale of tarnished angels on the streets of NYC. Hayworth (not yet the inimitable mix of sex goddess and all-American girl she would become) is a breathy ingénue trying to play it like a streetwise dame, and Mitchell is a silver-tongued playwright turned drunken flop artist. The three are linked in an unlikely scheme to rob a gambling hoodlum and save a suicidal stranger, just the kind of doomed gesture a soused romantic might hatch on a long night of bingeing. Hecht wrote plenty of films that were wittier, more clever, and more hardboiled, often all at once. He's gone a little soft for this tale, but it's the story's littleness that makes this film so winning when characters pick themselves up and greet the new day with a little less cynicism and a little more hope. —*S.A.*

ANNIVERSARY PARTY, THE L: DRAMA/INDEPENDENT DRAMA (2001) 115M D: Alan Cumming, Jennifer Jason Leigh. *Alan Cumming, Jennifer Jason Leigh, Jane Adams, Mina Badie, Jennifer Beals.* Writers/directors/

stars Leigh and Cumming play a married show-biz couple with a rocky history celebrating their sixth anniversary in ensemble drama. A year's worth of dramatic conflicts are condensed into a single night, capped by a drug-fueled journey into emotional abandon. Kevin Kline, Phoebe Cates, John C. Reilly, Parker Posey, and Gwyneth Paltrow costar, but Adams upstages them all as Reilly's neurotic, self-medicating wife, whose distracted comments and nervous energy invigorate the film with a constant stream of unexpected invention. Shot on digital video by Hollywood pro John Bailey (*Mishima*), this may be the best looking DV production ever made. He works the washed-out color of video-to-film transfer into the look of the film and brings a grace to handheld wanderings through groups of partygoers. Though overlong and overly familiar, Leigh and Cumming ultimately bring a sincere sensitivity and understanding to the material, as it they've been through these crises before and understand that you survive these things, forgive, and embrace. —*S. A.*

ANOTHER DAY IN PARADISE L: DRAMA/INDEPENDENT DRAMA (1998) 120M D: Larry Clark. *Melanie Griffith, James Woods, Vincent Kartheiser, Natasha Gregson Wagner, James Oris.* Clark's most mainstream film to date is this *Drugstore Cowboy*–like crime-on-the-road picture. Woods and Griffith are drug dealers and thieves who act as parental figures and mentors to a young junkie couple (Kartheiser and Gregson Wagner). The film is beautifully shot, full of lurid, real-life details (taken from an ex-con's unpublished manuscript and Clark's own junkie past), and Clark's trademark perversity (at one point Kartheiser wears his pants so low his pubes stick out). More surprising is that Griffith works great as the bubbly shopaholic auntie who occasionally needs to wield a shotgun. —*B. T.*

APOLLO 13 L: DRAMA/DRAMA (1995) 140M D: Ron Howard. *Tom Hanks, Kevin Bacon, Bill Paxton, Gary Sinise, Ed Harris, Kathleen Quinlan.* Based on actual events, this film by Howard makes the greatest use of 20-20 hindsight in effects, script, and casting. The real Apollo 13 was the lunar mission that went awry in 1970. Between an air leak, power loss, and who-knows-what else, the crew seemed doomed, never to return to Earth. Yet with round-the-clock work at NASA, the crew managed to survive against all odds. The film captures the drama that transpired on Earth, as well as the one in space. The astronauts's harrowing journey is the sort of thing only movies can re-create. —*N. J.*

AROUND THE FIRE L: DRAMA/INDEPENDENT DRAMA (1998) 96M D: John Jacobsen. *Devon Sawa, Eric Mabius, Tara Reid, Bill Smitrovich, Charlayne Woodard.* Simon (Sawa) is a high school kid with a troubled home life. He falls into a crowd of recreational drug users during his first year at a boarding school and lets the new experiences overwhelm his judgment and his life. This portrait of drug addiction makes a holistic observation about "harmless" recreational drugs: "My friends drop acid and don't have a problem with it," complains over-the-edge Simon while in rehab. "I don't care about your friends," his counselor responds. "I need to find what works for you." The script paints the Deadhead community as a warm, affirming, alternate lifestyle without poking fun. The family melodrama is forced in places, but this is ultimately an understanding and accepting film, and a thoughtful response to the politics of "Just say no." —*S. A.*

AWAKENINGS L: DRAMA/DRAMA (1990) 120M D: Penny Marshall. *Robin Williams, Robert De Niro, Max von Sydow, John Heard, Julie Kavner.* Williams plays a kind-hearted doctor (based on Oliver Sacks) at a mental asylum who uses an experimental drug on De Niro, a catatonic patient. The drug rouses De Niro and is passed out to everyone else in the ward. For one summer, the patients enjoy clarity of mind and reengagement with the world. They go on various outings together and learn about their lost pasts. The drug eventually loses its effectiveness, however, and things end very similar to how they began. De Niro steals the show with a sterling performance of a man who slowly comes to his senses and wins control of his body, only to lose it all again. —*N. J.*

BABY BOY L: DRAMA/DRAMA (2001) 129M D: John Singleton. *Tyrese Gibson, Taraji P. Henson, Omar Gooding, Snoop Dogg, Adrienne-Joi Johnson, Ving Rhames.* Tyrese plays Jody, a grown man who lives with his mom even though he has two kids with different mothers. He's a flawed protagonist, but you root for him as he tries to get a job and straighten out his relationships with his mother and girlfriends. Singleton's return to the "hood movie" is most interesting in comparison to his debut, *Boyz 'N the Hood*. In those days he saw his gangster villains as scary and somewhat glamourous. Now that he's older, he portrays them as immature losers; the main villain (Snoop Dogg) leeches off his girlfriend and spends most of his time playing video games. Model-turned-singer-turned-actor Tyrese is surprisingly good in his acting debut, and Rhames has one of his best and most multilayered performances as Jody's mom's scary new boyfriend. —*B. T.*

BASKET, THE L: DRAMA/INDEPENDENT DRAMA (1999) 101M D: Rich Cowan. *Peter Coyote, Karen Allen, Robert Karl Burke, Amber Willenborg.* Writer/director Cowan effortlessly evokes the rural simplicity of WWI in this story of two German orphans taken in by a local pastor in rural Eastern Washington. But the pastor's kindness comes at the worst time; the first casualties of the war are returning, and anti-German sentiment has turned to racism. Cowan captures the look and feel of simple agricultural land, with windblown fields of golden hues under rich blue skies. But he also fills this basket so full of stories and details (including a fictional German opera that grips the town and a re-creation of basketball, circa 1915) that the film slips from homespun drama to mock-*Rocky* with a sentimental twist. Which is too bad: the family-friendly, beautifully shot *The Basket* is woven from such promising threads that you wish it were better. —*S. A.*

BASQUIAT L: DRAMA/DRAMA (1996) 108M D: Julian Schnabel. *Gary Oldman, Michael Wincott, Jeffrey Wright, Benicio del Toro, David Bowie, Claire Forlani. Basquiat* resembles a book of short stories more than a movie, and that's probably for the better. It's the story of Jean-Michel Basquiat, the artist who rocketed to fame in the 1980s before his untimely death at twenty-eight following a heroin addiction. The film is filled with episodes and amazing scenes; if the movie seems studded with cameos, it's because Basquiat's life was that way, too. If there is a thread through the movie, it is the powerful, mesmerizing performance by Wright, who plays Basquiat. He is well-supported by the cast, including Oldman as Julian Schnabel (a contemporary of Basquiat who also directed the film) and Bowie (who gives a vivid, funny performance as Andy Warhol). —*T. P.*

BEDFORD INCIDENT, THE L: CLASSIC DRAMA/CLASSIC DRAMA (1965) 102M D: James B. Harris. *Richard Widmark, Sidney Poitier, James MacArthur, Martin Balsam, Wally Cox.* Suspenseful, tense, and directed with a hard intelligence by Harris (fresh from producing three of Stanley Kubrick's early acclaimed features), this is one of the best Cold War thrillers of its era, and one of the most overlooked. Widmark (who coproduces the project) delivers one of his best performances as the fierce warrior captain of an atomic submarine whose tactical skills are matched only by his daring and dedication to his loyal crew. Poitier is the civilian reporter who doesn't hide his concerns when his assignment puts him in the midst of a cat-and-mouse game between American and Soviet submarines loaded with nuclear arms. The film never lets you forget what is at stake in this "personal" meeting of minds, whose real-life chess game heats up the Cold War. —*S. A.*

BETTER LUCK TOMORROW L: DRAMA/INDEPENDENT DRAMA (2002) 101M D: Justin Lin. *Parry Shen, John Cho, Roger Fan, Karin Anna Cheung, Jason J. Tobin.* I don't know why I sat through this damn movie. The Ivy League Asian teens in this movie are negative and undeveloped. The narration from the main protagonist serves no function except to annoy the viewer, as nothing interesting or insightful manages to escape his mouth. This long, long movie suffocates the viewer like the fog of exhaust doom that clogs rush hour traffic until one is too lost in its sloppy cinematography to pay attention to the insipid, flat plot. There is violence, and it might shock some that the vio-

Most depressing movies

ALL THAT HEAVEN ALLOWS

AMORES PERROS

BERLIN ALEXANDERPLATZ

BOWLING FOR COLUMBINE

BREAKING THE WAVES

BULLET IN THE HEAD

THE CONFORMIST

THE CONVERSATION

CRUMB

DANCER IN THE DARK

DEAD RINGERS

THE ELEPHANT MAN

THE END OF THE AFFAIR *(1999)*

FULL METAL JACKET

THE GREAT SILENCE

HAPPINESS

JUDE

LAST TANGO IN PARIS

THE MATCH FACTORY GIRL

NAKED

PERDITA DURANGO

RETURN TO OZ

ROCCO AND HIS BROTHERS

SOLARIS *(2002)*

VIOLENT COP

lators are Asian. But this film's most shocking effect is its uncanny ability to put you to sleep. —*T. C.*

BICENTENNIAL MAN L: DRAMA/DRAMA (1999) 132M D: Chris Columbus. *Robin Williams, Sam Neill, Embeth Davidtz, Oliver Platt.* It's really too bad we can't just forget 1998 and 1999, for Williams's sake. After all, this is the man who charmed us on *Mork and Mindy*, made us laugh as *Popeye* (admittedly not for all tastes), showed us his serious side in *The World According to Garp*, received an Oscar nomination for *Dead Poet's Society*, and won an Oscar for *Good Will Hunting*. How then could an actor with such tremendous gifts turn out *What Dreams May Come, Patch Adams, Jakob the Liar*, and *Bicentennial Man* in quick succession? At what point did he stop reading scripts before agreeing to make a film? To be fair, *Bicentennial Man* isn't entirely Williams's fault. In fact, a great deal of the blame belongs to director Columbus, who took a thoughtful, curious piece of fiction by Isaac Asimov and turned it into dull, uninspiring, sentimental garbage. Columbus seems content to let Williams spout immature one-liners and ludicrous speeches that try to pass themselves off as deep and important (or so the background music would have us believe), while never attempting to delve into the potentially interesting questions that Asimov's story raises. —*C. P.*

BIG WEDNESDAY L: DRAMA/DRAMA (1978) 126M D: John Milius. *Gary Busey, Barbara Hale, Sam Melville, William Katt, Jan-Michael Vincent.* Three teenage surf bums (hot-dogging Vincent, serious and stable Katt, and mad misfit Busey) live at the beach in the summer of 1963, under the sway of a surfboard maker (Melville) who is equal parts guru, mentor, and keeper of the lore. But the times they are a changin'. The shadow of Vietnam and the responsibilities of adulthood threaten to pull these friends apart while they face hard decisions. Milius mixes the innocent nostalgia (well, as innocent as Milius will ever get) of his own personal *American Graffiti* with the macho reverence of a John Ford cavalry drama. Surfing becomes a kind of spiritual quest, spoken of in awed, mythic tones and photographed with the epic grandeur of a rite of passage. The film might come off a little too reverent for some tastes, but Milius is true to his macho stylings and philosophical musings, capping it all with spectacular surfing footage. —*S. A.*

BILL L: DRAMA/DRAMA (1981) 97M D: Anthony Page. *Mickey Rooney, Dennis Quaid, Harriet Rogers, Largo Woodruff.* What happens when funding is cut from the mental health industry? An aged, mentally retarded man named Bill (Rooney) is booted out of an institution and Quaid is there to film his own reality show about it. What starts as a worthwhile film project with award potential slowly turns into a deep friendship. In fact, the filmmaker becomes so preoccupied with his new friend that it puts a crimp in his relationship with his girlfriend. Rooney won an Emmy, and deservedly so. His performance single-handedly rescues the challenging script from dreadful camp. He makes this little film worth watching. —*N. J.*

BLUE CAR L: DRAMA/INDEPENDENT DRAMA (2003) 96M D: Karen Moncrieff. *Margaret Colin, Agnes Bruckner, David Strathairn, A. J. Buckley, Frances Fisher.* Bruckner is a high school senior with a crippling lack of self-esteem who falls for her sad-eyed poetry teacher (Straithairn) in Moncrieff's coming-of-age film. You can see the fantasy behind her adoring eyes, turning the paternal teacher into something more. As her home life melts

down (she rebels against her mother and worries over her self-lacerating, troubled little sister) and she pours out her heart to her teacher, you can see the fantasy in his eyes, too. Moncrieff's portrayal of awkward, clashing relationships between daughter and mother, and sister and sister, and her clear-eyed look at the idealization of an inspirational teacher by a student in need of a daddy, have an unsettlingly honest feel. The dreary, half-lit photography reveals the film's low-budget indie origins, but the dusky, anonymous apartment evocatively captures the emotional murkiness of two girls who feel abandoned by their parents. —*S. A.*

BLUE CRUSH L: DRAMA/DRAMA (2002) 105M D: John Stockwell. *Kate Bosworth, Michelle Rodriguez, Sanoe Lake, Matthew Davis.* Stockwell's grrrl power surf melodrama is a summer movie that knows it's a summer movie. The *Rocky*-in-paradise story of a surfer girl confronting her fears to conquer the waves delivers bikini-clad babes, sun, sand, surf photography as beautiful as it is breathtaking, and a little PG-13 romance. Stockwell, however, is a smart director with a good head for character and a wonderful feel for the vivid milieu of minimum-wage, tourist-industry workers as well as the makeshift family of beach buddies. Bosworth and Rodriguez (full of sass and loyalty) even look and ride like athletes, and real-life surfing champ Lake holds her own as an actress. The story is pure pulp, but the film has more life than you'd expect from a bikinis, babes, and surfboards lark. —*S. A.*

BOY IN THE PLASTIC BUBBLE, THE L: DRAMA/DRAMA (1976) 100M D: Randal Kleiser. *John Travolta, Glynnis O'Connor, Diana Hyland, Robert Reed, Ralph Bellamy.* Before *Saturday Night Fever*, Travolta starred in this made-for-TV film about a teenager with a disease of the immune system that prohibits his character from breathing regular air. Confined to his own little environment, a plastic bubble, he attends school by way of a television monitor and becomes popular enough that he gets a girlfriend. Of course, they can only touch each other with plastic gloves fitted to his wall. There's an excellent cameo by Buzz Aldrin, who explains to the boy that being stuck in a plastic bubble isn't as bad as being stuck on the moon. —*N. J.*

BOYS DON'T CRY L: DRAMA/INDEPENDENT DRAMA (1999) 116M D: Kimberly Peirce. *Hilary Swank, Peter Sarsgaard, Chloë Sevigny, Alison Folland, Brendan Sexton Jr.* Based on a true story, Swank (who won an Oscar for her performance) plays Brandon Teena, who was born a woman, passed for a man, and was raped and murdered when found out by her deceived friends. Obviously this makes for unpleasant viewing, but the film also has a Romeo-and-Juliet forbidden romance angle that's ultimately very moving. Sevigny (who was nominated for a Supporting Actress Oscar) plays

Brandon's girlfriend who may or may not know the latter's gender but is far more interested in who he/she is inside. If you watch the documentary *The Brandon Teena Story*, it's easy to see that this cast accurately captured the personalities of their characters. —*B. T.*

BRAVE, THE L: DRAMA/INDEPENDENT DRAMA (1997) 123M D: Johnny Depp. *Johnny Depp, Nicole Mancera, Cody Lightning, Marlon Brando, Luis Guzman, Clarence Williams III.* Depp plays Raphael, a Native American ex-con living in extreme poverty in a trailer near a junkyard. He would literally die for his wife and two children—we know this because when Brando offers to give him $50,000 to be tortured and killed in a snuff film, he accepts. The movie chronicles the last week of his life as he tries to earn back the respect of his family before making the ultimate sacrifice for them. There are a lot of long scenes with little dialogue, but also surprising, magical moments such as the night he spends building an electric junk carnival for his kids. It's actually kind of sweet and light-hearted for a movie with such a grim topic, which I guess reflects Depp's personality. The movie was so hated at Cannes that it was never released in theaters or on video in the United States. Too bad, because it's a good debut and it would be interesting to see if Depp could evolve as a director. —*B. T.*

BREAKING AWAY L: DRAMA/DRAMA (1979) 100M D: Peter Yates. *Dennis Quaid, Dennis Christopher, Paul Dooley, Daniel Stern, Jackie Earle Haley, Barbara Barrie.* This little gem of an independent film from 1979 has not lost any of its charm or style. Christopher plays Dave, a young man in love with bicycling, and especially the Italian Cinzano racing team. Dave rides and tends to his own bike religiously, studies Italian, and listens to opera. He and his friends, all recent high school graduates, are struggling to decide what to do with their lives. They live in a college town, but regard college as a lofty dream or a waste of money. Looked down upon by the college students, Dave and his pals are determined to make something of themselves and prove their worth. In the end they place all their hopes on competing against a fraternity in an annual bike race, where winning it is the only option. With excellent performances and an entertaining, believable story, this film about the pursuit of dreams, acceptance, and a place of one's own is something to which everyone can relate. —*M. N.*

BUFFALO '66 L: DRAMA/INDEPENDENT DRAMA (1998) 120M D: Vincent Gallo. *Vincent Gallo, Christina Ricci, Ben Gazzara, Anjelica Huston, Kevin Corrigan, Jan-Michael Vincent.* Gallo stars (and writes and directs and scores) as Billy, a homophobic greaseball fresh out of jail with the single-minded intention of killing some dumb football player who caused him to lose a $10,000 bet on the Buffalo Bills. The story is completely and

totally absurd, including the anti-hero's kidnapping of, and eventual bonding with, Ricci. The entire film is too underlit, too overwrought, and too über-indie. —*J. D.*

I disagree. By most reports Gallo is a genuine asshole, and I bet that's why he's so effective in this role. It's a '70s-style film in its dirtiness and willingness to linger. But it also experiments with new, show-off techniques, including bullet time (before *The Matrix*) and a few less successful tricks. It is undeniably pretentious, and Huston's performance is so weird that the first time I saw it I honestly thought she was Gallo's real mother who had never acted before. But it's a well-made look into a depressing world, no matter how big an ego created it. —*B. T.*

BUSINESS OF FANCYDANCING, THE L: DRAMA/INDEPENDENT DRAMA (2002) 103M D: Sherman Alexie. *Swil Kanim, Michelle St. John, Evan Adams.* Northwest American Indian writer Alexie takes on both writing and directing this adaptation of his own poetry. Seymour (Adams) is a successful, gay Indian poet from Spokane who must confront his past when he returns to his childhood home on the reservation to attend the funeral of an old friend. He's faced with resentment from those who never left the rez and jealousy because of his success. Seymour is haunted by memories of his lost friend Mouse (Kanim), an amazing violin player slowly suffocated by substance abuse. St. John does an amazing job as Agnes, Seymour's former lover and old friend. *The Business of Fancydancing* uses flashbacks in an interesting way and never really loses pace. There are some very tender scenes between Seymour and his partner, and great moments revealing how pathetic and simpleminded white liberals can be. While there are holes in the screenplay and the acting isn't always believable, this wonderful indie flick captures the essence of DIY filmmaking at its best, taking risks with stereotypes of both race and sexuality that a mainstream film wouldn't have the guts to approach. —*B. W.*

BUSINESS OF STRANGERS, THE L: DRAMA/INDEPENDENT DRAMA (2002) 84M D: Patrick Stettner. *Stockard Channing, Julia Stiles, Frederick Weller.* Channing is a harried, high-powered corporate executive who spends an evening of games and dares with insolent, angry young Stiles. Writer/director Stettner's theatrical drama plays out in artificial environments of glass and steel and plastic, giving it the hemmed-in feeling of a play, with the actors improvising around each other in a show of intimacy. The film plays largely like a performer's showpiece, with showboating and not-so-surprising character twists, but Stettner comes out the other end with a pleasantly modest and satisfying revelation. Behind the accusations and psychodramas and revenge fantasies that play out through the night is a sense that the two women got each other's number, but no understanding of one other. We never know these women and nothing really changes, but we can appreciate the way they come to grips with the featureless, smothering world they live in; they play the game and get on with their lives. —*S.A.*

CHEATERS L: DRAMA/INDEPENDENT DRAMA (2000) 108M D: John Stockwell. *Paul Sorvino, Jeff Daniels, Luke Edwards, Blake Heron, Jena Malone.* Who would have thought such an incisive dissection of the American dream gone sour could have been waiting in the 1995 Steinmetz scandal, where an Academic Decathlon team from a crumbling Chicago school was caught cheating? This clear-eyed portrait doesn't just cut through the hysterical media sensationalism, it turns it back onto the entire drama. Writer/director Stockwell never justifies their action but he takes to task the hypocrisy and double standards that our culture has embraced as "real life." These kids just learned their lessons early: it's not the cheating that's so bad, it's the getting caught. Daniels gives his best performance in a decade as their morally torn teacher. —*S.A.*

CITY OF GHOSTS L: DRAMA/DRAMA (2002) 117M D: Matt Dillon. *Stellan Skarsgard, Gérard Depardieu, James Caan, Matt Dillon, Natascha McElhone.* Dillon is a tortured con man tired of the con. His plans to get out of the game are delayed when he finds his mentor and spiritual father (Caan) deep in the shark-infested waters of international crime and political graft in Cambodia. First-time director Dillon directs at a lazy lope, but what he lacks in narrative expediency, he makes up for in the atmosphere of exotic squalor. The bobbing camerawork is constantly wandering off into the faces of dusty Cambodia mean streets: impoverished locals hustling up business and desperate foreigners hustling everybody else. It's pure pulp fantasy, a story of honor, betrayal, and sacrifice according to some imagined underworld code, and Dillon falls prey to the irresistible clichés of the gutter tragedy. His saintly but not-too-wise guy Jimmy is played like a fiddle, yet redeemed by his sincerity. —*S.A.*

CLAIRE DOLAN L: DRAMA/INDEPENDENT DRAMA (1998) 95M D: Lodge Kerrigan. *Katrin Cartlidge, Vincent D'Onofrio, Colm Meaney, John Doman.* Kerrigan's second film (his first was the astounding, haunting *Clean, Shaven*) is almost too austere and chilly—a world of anonymous, chalky white rooms seen reflected in mirrors and spied upon through windows—but his dedication to leaving things unsaid and unexplained is compelling. Cartlidge's still, careful performance as a New York call girl is a revelation, and D'Onofrio takes another daring role as an earthy but ultimately impotent cab driver whose love for her is crippled by doubt and distrust. Meaney is the pimp who keeps her under his thumb with a debt she'll never repay. Cartlidge doesn't expose the

emotion hidden under her social armor, but she communicates it beautifully nonetheless. —*S.A.*

CLEAN, SHAVEN L: DRAMA/INDEPENDENT DRAMA (1994) 79M D: Lodge Kerrigan. *Peter Greene, Megan Owen, Jennifer MacDonald.* Peter (Greene) is a schizophrenic trying to get his daughter back from her adoptive mother. He is a man lost in his own mind, barely coping with daily routine, tormented by voices and his own image, and struggling to hold onto his one clear goal of finding his daughter. Enter a detective on the trail of a suspected child murderer and you have an interesting tale of criminal investigation, one that only lets you think you know what's going on. Almost everything about this film is disturbing, not in the shocking syle of Japanese cinema, but in an emotionally meditative way. The sounds and abrasive noisescapes throughout the film add to the tension and mental texture of an unsound mind. *Clean, Shaven* is a well-written, thoughtful independent film that shows what kind of movie can be made with a good script and a clear idea. —*B.W.*

COMING APART L: DRAMA/INDEPENDENT DRAMA (1969) 110M D: Milton Moses Ginsberg. *Rip Torn, Lois Markle, Viveca Lindfors, Darlene Cotton, Sally Kirkland.* Torn stars as Joe, a displaced psychiatrist and womanizer who gets his kicks from secretly filming himself and his sexual exploits. Every night there is a different woman: some ask him to burn cigarettes on their breasts, some he asks to dance naked in front of a crying baby, some just come for the old in-and-out. Joann (Kirkland), however, a hopped-up piece of hippie trash who starts to invest a bit of heart into Joe, becomes a heavy load for him to handle. Joann becomes annoying as the film progresses, forcing Joe to "turn the camera" on himself. *Coming Apart* is shot entirely through Joe's secret camera, with Joe turning the camera off between affairs. This film may be a bit too arty for some but the violent climax, and the funny and tragic episodes in between, are well worth the static. —*J.D.*

CQ L: DRAMA/DRAMA (2002) 98M D: Roman Coppola. *Giancarlo Giannini, Gérard Depardieu, Angela Lindvall, Élodie Bouchez, Jeremy Davies.* There's a real love of 1960s movie lore in Coppola's feature film debut, a sort of *81/2* with echoes of *Day for Night* and stirred through with French New Wave, Italian cool, and British mod. Davies is the American-in-Paris hero, an aspiring director in the funky days of 1969. By day he edits a pop-art, sci-fi spy adventure while at home he obsessively films his own life in cinematic journal entries, using the camera to avoid intimacy with his stewardess girlfriend (Bouchez) while his fantasies wander to the spy movie's luscious leading lady (Lindvall). Giannini plays the Italian producer as a high-living Dino De Laurentis, and Depardieu is his mentor, the obsessive director whose increasingly erratic behavior gets him fired and promotes Davies to the director's chair. If the film is slight, the details are right, from the opulent, outrageous sets to the meticulously retro special effects (reminiscent of the beauty and grace of his effects for his father's *Dracula*) to the groovy music by Mellow. —*S.A.*

CRIMSON TIDE L: DRAMA/DRAMA (1995) 115M D: Tony Scott. *Gene Hackman, Denzel Washington, James Gandolfini, George Dzundza, Viggo Mortensen.* Hackman is first in command and Washington second on a nuclear submarine. They have opposing backgrounds and philosophies. After an incident involving Russians and missile silos, the crew receives both an order to fire and a message that cannot be deciphered. Hackman wants to fire, Washington doesn't. Lots of dramatic yelling ensues, and the crew of the submarine must decide whether to follow orders and start a nuclear war or mutiny with Washington. This is an intense and unusually smart thriller from director Scott and producer Jerry Bruckheimer. Quentin Tarantino did an uncredited rewrite on the script, which explains why there are conversations about *Star Trek* and Jean "Moebius" Giraud's stint on *The Silver Surfer*. —*B.T.*

CRUEL INTENTIONS 2 L: DRAMA/DRAMA (2000) 87M D: Roger Kumble. *Amy Adams, Mimi Rogers, Robin Dunne, Keri Lynn Pratt.* This film began life as the first two episodes of *Manchester Prep*, a Fox TV series based on *Cruel Intentions*. But a network executive was so bothered by a scene where a girl has an orgasm while riding a horse that the show was pulled before it aired. Add one nude scene and a couple swear words and, voilà, you've got a straight-to-video sequel. Kumble made some changes that may have been smart for an ongoing series but don't work in movie form. He tried to make Sebastian (the Valmont character) likable, even gave him a working-class background. This may shock you, but *Cruel Intentions 2* is not really worth your time. —*B.T.*

DEBUT, THE L: DRAMA/INDEPENDENT DRAMA (2000) 88M D: Gene Cajayon. *Dante Basco, Eddie Garcia, Tirso Cruz III, Gina Alajar.* Familiar yet heartfelt, Cajayon's Filipino-American take on the immigrant American story has the old-fashioned feel of a 1950s melodrama dropped into contemporary LA society. Rebellious son (Basco) clashes with immigrant father (Cruz) and distances himself from his provincial family before learning to appreciate his legacy and culture one busy night. Cajayon invests his drama with such earnestness he often trips over his intentions. But he pulls the bright, broad performances together into a loose, often fractious, extended family and jump-starts the film with a lively look at a youth culture straddling traditional Filipino culture and the usual concerns of American teenagers. —*S.A.*

DIAMOND MEN L: DRAMA/INDEPENDENT DRAMA (2000) 100M D: Dan Cohen. *Robert Forster, Donnie Wahlberg, Bess Armstrong, Jasmine Guy.* Forster is a veteran diamond salesman who has a heart attack on the job. No longer trusted to carry around a million dollars' worth of diamonds in his trunk, he convinces his boss to let him have one last job training his young replacement (Wahlberg) on the road. Don't be fooled by the guns on the cover—the crime aspect is a small part of the film. Mostly this is a character-driven comedy about the relationship between the older man and his idiot protégé. Forster's performance is arguably even better than in *Jackie Brown*. Watching his face every time Wahlberg inadvertently makes him feel old is priceless. The movie itself is only slightly above average, but Forster really excels. —*B.T.*

DONNIE DARKO L: DRAMA/DRAMA (2001) 122M D: Richard Kelly. *Jake Gyllenhaal, Maggie Gyllenhaal, Mary McDonnell, Patrick Swayze, James Duval, Holmes Osborne, Jena Malone.* Sleepwalking out of his house one night, Donnie Darko (Jake Gyllenhaal) meets Frank (Duval), a giant bunny who tells him that the world will end in 28 days, 6 hours, 42 minutes, and 12 seconds. When he returns to his house the next morning, a jet engine from a plane that no one can seem to locate has crashed into the room where he would have been sleeping. After his narrow escape from death, Donnie slips deeper and deeper into mental illness, with frequent visits from Frank, who leads Donnie on destructive rampages he barely remembers. Over time, the contrast between Donnie's ever-growing detachment from reality and the superficial activities of the people around him grows stronger and stronger, ultimately leading to a frantic, dreamlike feel that weaves through the storyline. The time travel elements of the story lead to an amazing climax that will leave you thinking long after the credits roll. Excellent cinematography, and a great soundtrack. —*J.S.*

EASY RIDER L: DRAMA/INDEPENDENT DRAMA (1969) 94M D: Dennis Hopper. *Peter Fonda, Dennis Hopper, Jack Nicholson, Karen Black, Phil Spector.* The amazing thing about this film is how coherent and entertaining it really is, considering that it was largely made on the road, improvised, with the entire cast and crew stoned out of their gourd during much of the shooting. Hopper and Fonda make a big drug deal with Spector and, with their newfound cash, set out to find "America" and the proverbial dream that goes with such a goal. There are many things to have fun with here: Nicholson's turn as a middle-class drop-out turned stoner overnight, Hopper's whacked-out antics, or the bitchin' score that features Hendrix, Steppenwolf, and The Byrds in all the right places. Yet, the filmmakers' ultimate goal is to make a slightly sobering point about the freedom our two heroes think they have found, but will ultimately lose. —*M.S.*

EVE'S BAYOU L: DRAMA/INDEPENDENT DRAMA (1998) 119M
D: Kasi Lemmons. *Samuel L. Jackson, Meagan Good, Jurnee Smollett, Diahann Carroll, Debbi Morgan, Lynn Whitfield.* Lemmons's directorial debut is a moody tale of love, betrayal, and adolescent anxiety one summer on the Louisiana Bayou. Jackson (who also produced this low-budget, independent production) stars as a successful small-town doctor carrying on an affair with a married woman under the nose of his long-suffering wife (Whitfield). As seen through the eyes of nine-year-old Eve (Smollett), this adult world is portrayed in a series of emotional colors, often changing abruptly from scene to scene or turning radically on a word. The film's intense mood and conflicting emotions give *Eve's Bayou* a special immediacy, childlike wonder, and larger-than-life gravity. Lushly shot and directed with great sensitivity for all the characters and their private sufferings, large and small. —*S. A.*

FALLING DOWN L: DRAMA/DRAMA (1993) 112M D: Joel Schumacher. *Michael Douglas, Robert Duvall, Barbara Hershey, Rachel Ticotin, Tuesday Weld.* Douglas plays a desk-job Rambo who flips out after being laid off from his job at the Defense Department. He abandons his car in the gridlock and wanders Los Angeles with automatic weapons, exacting revenge on racial minorities, minimum-wage workers, and (just to balance it out) some rich guys on a golf course. The movie is designed to exploit the audience's deepest prejudices and frustrations, so it depicts a nightmare world where a guy can't walk down the street without being harassed by gangstas and oppressed by fast-food employees and Korean store owners. Upon its release, *Falling Down* was hailed by some as an important, zeitgeist-riding cultural event that finally set things straight for the poor, victimized white men of America. Some claimed that Douglas's character was not meant to be glamourized, but I wonder why Schumacher (who is gay) would have the protagonist stand up for a gay man and then turn around and brutalize every other minority he encounters. This is obviously a movie designed to push buttons, but for me it pressed the wrong ones. —*B. T.*

FIVE EASY PIECES L: DRAMA/DRAMA (1970) 96M D: Bob Rafelson. *Jack Nicholson, Susan Anspach, Karen Black, Sally Struthers.* Nicholson stars in this superb and complex character study of an alienated cultural misfit. Though a gifted pianist, Nicholson's character prefers slumming in a California oil field and shacking up with his dizzy sexpot waitress girlfriend (Black). Family troubles bring him back home and force him to confront his true background as well as his own temper and instincts. Though filled with funny moments and characters, most people remember the "chicken salad" scene where Jack berates a bitchy waitress. But there are plenty of other amusing scenes, and there's a pervasive sadness that marks this key American film, much of which was shot in the Pacific Northwest. As far as the five easy pieces of the title go, are they the songs played or the women charmed? —*S. H.*

FOLLOWING L: DRAMA/INDEPENDENT DRAMA (1998) 71M
D: Christopher Nolan. *Jeremy Theobald, Lucy Russell, Alex Haw.* This first feature by Nolan (*Memento*) is a black-and-white mind game about Bill (Theobald), a young man obsessed with following people who is drawn into the world of Cobb (Haw), a break-in artist who likes to peek into the personal lives of his victims. Bill becomes a strange companion to Cobb: part student, part confessor, and part evil twin. Russell costars as a victim who becomes an intimate, and sends the junior second-story man on his first big job. Nolan (who also wrote and photographed the film) draws inspiration from *Body Heat* and *The Usual Suspects* for his debut, creating a quirky little film noir with a too-clever twist at the end. But you can also see the seeds of *Memento* in his fascination with alienation, urban loneliness, and the shuffled story structure. It's as if the troubled hero is still working everything out as he tells all in a kind of confession. —*S. A.*

FORREST GUMP L: DRAMA/DRAMA (1994) 142M D: Robert Zemeckis. *Tom Hanks, Sally Field, Gary Sinise, Robin Wright.* Forrest Gump (Hanks), whose lack of intelligence is more than compensated for by his enthusiasm and pure dumb luck, tells the story of his life. Forrest, with his box of chocolates and ceaseless patter, was a war hero, a world-class Ping Pong player, and a millionaire. Milking nostalgia for all it's worth, Zemeckis shows us the greatest hits of American history (Kennedy, Vietnam, the '70s) through Gump's innocent eyes, and explores his longtime love for the elusive Jenny (Wright) and her own struggles with the darker side of our times. Zemeckis knows all the right heart strings to tug, and Forrest's unaffected, cheerful recollection of pivotal events and important figures in the life of America makes this film all the more poignant. It may all boil down to cheesy, sentimental goo, but I understand why it won Best Picture. Audiences love flashbacks and montages set to period music. —*J. K.*

FREEWAY L: DRAMA/DRAMA (1996) 102M D: Matthew Bright. *Reese Witherspoon, Kiefer Sutherland, Wolfgang Bodison, Amanda Plumer, Brittany Murphy, Brooke Shields, Bookeem Woodbine, Dan Hedaya.* Before Witherspoon was ruling the school in *Election* or infecting us with fashion in *Legally Blond,* she was kickin' some serial killer butt in *Freeway.* Our story begins when her character's mom (Plummer) gets arrested for propositioning a cop. Then the cops haul her child-molesting, crack-smoking stepfather away too, leaving her with nothing to do but run from the Child Protection lady. She meets a ton of disturbing characters, like a school counselor (Sutherland) who offers her a ride, intending to add her to his list of freeway victims. Everybody who messes with Witherspoon in this movie gets more than they can handle. This movie represents true girl power without the pumps or matching handbag. —*R. D.*

FRESH L: DRAMA/INDEPENDENT DRAMA (1994) 115M D: Boaz Yakin. *Samuel L. Jackson, Sean Nelson, Giancarlo Esposito, Ron Brice, N'Bushe Wright.* A unique take on the '90s urban crime film, *Fresh* is the story of a young kid (Nelson) who survives life in a New York ghetto by delivering drugs. When his bosses turn on him, he uses his knowledge of chess strategy to play them against each other and save himself. It's a subtle film with strong (and disturbing) performances by its young actors. First-time director Yakin went on to direct more commercial films such as *Remember the Titans* and *Uptown Girls. —B. T.*

FUN L: DRAMA/INDEPENDENT DRAMA (1994) 105M D: Rafael Zielinski. *William R. Moses, Alicia Witt, Renee Humphrey, Leslie Hope.* As in "girls just wanna have," though in this case "fun" is a little unsettling. Director Zielinsky takes familiar elements and themes (two kids incarcerated for murder, a psychologist digging for the "truth," a headline-hunting reporter mining a story) and brings a seriousness and sensitivity to the material, playing down sensationalistic elements and concentrating on the characters. Witt and Humphrey deliver deceivingly layered performances as vulnerable adolescents masking their fears with bravado and attitude. The flashback structure saves the murder for the end, but far from a lurid payoff, it serves as a painful reminder of what these girls have turned into. A Sundance Festival Jury prize winner. —*S. A.*

GEORGE WASHINGTON L: DRAMA/INDEPENDENT DRAMA (2000) 90M D: David Gordon Green. *Donald Holden, Candace Evanofski, Paul Schneider, Eddie Rouse.* In one of the most haunting and rich film debuts in recent history, director Green turns his camera on the (mostly black) children and (mostly white) adults who hang around the rusted ruins of an old train yard in a simultaneously lush and dilapidated Deep South community one summer. It's a strange film with an insular and unreal quality to it, yet Green brings passion and integrity to his story. The largely unprofessional cast is simultaneously awkward and honest. Especially good are Evanofski as Nasia, the philosophical young girl in love with the quiet George (Holden), and Rouse as the angry, aggressive, animal-hating Damascus, who lives his life at a slow simmer, always threatening to boil over. Shot in sharp, almost overly bright color and gorgeous widescreen compositions, the film is both clumsy and compelling, a unique vision of surreal beauty and a kind of naive, naked, and open American film no longer made. —*S. A.*

GIRL, INTERRUPTED L: DRAMA/DRAMA (1999) 127M D: James Mangold. *Winona Ryder, Angelina Jolie, Clea Duvall, Brittany Murphy, Jared Leto, Vanessa Redgrave, Whoopi Goldberg.* Ryder is Susanna, a recent high school graduate with no plans for the future. After an attempted suicide, she's sent for a rest at Claymore, a local mental institution. Here Susanna befriends her fellow patients, including Georgina (Duvall), her pathological roommate, and Lisa (Jolie), a self-proclaimed "lifer." As Susanna's relationships begin to build, particularly with Lisa, she is left to decide whether she is going to allow herself to slip into insanity or try to make something of her life. This dark, emotional film does an excellent job of exploring the path to repairing a broken human spirit. *Girl, Interrupted* ends on a hopeful, positive note that allows this film to cover the entire emotional spectrum. Ryder, Jolie, and Murphy all shine. —*J. S.*

GO ASK ALICE L: DRAMA/DRAMA (1973) 74M D: John Korty. *Ruth Roman, Mackenzie Phillips, Andy Griffith, Charles Martin Smith, Julie Adams, William Shatner, Jamie Smith-Jackson.* Based on an allegedly real diary of a fifteen-year-old girl, this TV production paved the way for countless after-school specials and movies about teens on drugs or in peril. In many ways, *Go Ask Alice* is a throwback to delirious antidrug classics such as *Reefer Madness* and deserves a cult following. Alice, a naive and self-conscious girl, moves to a new town with her peppy but clueless family. She makes one nerdy friend at school, but during the summer goes to a party and drinks a spiked bottle of soda pop. Immediately she's popping pills, smoking weed, having promiscuous sex, selling drugs to junior high schoolers, running away from home and getting ripped off by creeps. After bottoming out, she meets a sympathetic priest (Griffith) and tries to straighten out her life. It leads to a somewhat duller second half, but still features plenty of juicy melodrama and a psychotic babysitter. Shatner is relatively restrained as Alice's dad—they should have had him freak out on drugs too! —*S. H.*

GRIDLOCK'D L: DRAMA/DRAMA (1997) 91M D: Vondie Curtis-Hall. *Tupac Shakur, Thandie Newton, Charles Fleischer, Howard Hesseman, Tim Roth.* Stretch (Roth), Spoon (Shakur) and Cookie (Newton) are a jazz trio who shoot up together after a New Year's Eve show. After Cookie overdoses and lands in a hospital, Stretch and Spoon decide it's time to kick the habit. But while wandering from treatment center to hospital to detox, they find that getting help is more complicated than just asking for it. "I'm sorry, you can't come here if you're not on welfare." "This facility is only for alcoholics." "What kind of insurance do you have?" *Gridlock'd* is not entirely successful as a drama, but it makes a powerful satiric point about our society's poor approach to drug reha-

Movies we wish were on DVD

Anything by Kenneth Anger	GAMERA SUPER MONSTER
BAD BOY BUBBY	THE GIRL CAN'T HELP IT
BERLIN ALEXANDERPLATZ	INFRA-MAN
(THE BIG) CRIMEWAVE	*(region 1 version, with English audio track)*
BLADE RUNNER *(theatrical cut)*	THE KILLING OF SATAN
BODY SNATCHERS FROM HELL	LONDON AFTER MIDNIGHT
BONJOUR TRISTESSE	MALPERTUIS
BRING ME THE HEAD OF ALFREDO GARCIA	A MAN ESCAPED
BRUCE CONNER'S FILMS	PICKPOCKET
BUNNY LAKE IS MISSING	POINT BLANK
THE CONFORMIST	RITUALS
DARK OF THE SUN	ROLLING THUNDER
DEATH RIDES A HORSE *(decent transfer)*	RUBIN AND ED
DEVIL FETUS	SALO *(uncut)*
EL TOPO AND THE HOLY MOUNTAIN	SKIDOO
(remastered and in an American format)	THE THRILL-KILLERS
EXTERMINATING ANGEL	TRISTANA

bilitation. Also, it's weird to see Shakur playing bass. —*B. T.*

GUMMO L: DRAMA/INDEPENDENT DRAMA (1997) 89M D: Harmony Korine. *Chloë Sevigny, Max Perlich, Harmony Korine, Jacob Reynolds, Nick Sutton, Jacob Sewell.* New York–based wunderkind Korine directs this haphazard film about the carny citizens of Xenia, Ohio, left to their own wits after a devastating tornado. Borderline exploitation (a retarded prostitute, an albino fan of muscle cars, a couple of cat-killings, a muscle-bound black Jewish midget) muddies the often beautiful camerawork (by Leos Carax's cinematographer, Jean-Yves Escoffier). The film's disjointed narrative plays out less like a movie and more like an installation piece, making *Gummo* more of a guest book for Korine's art-school buds (sloe-eyed Sevigny, skater and artist Mark Gonzales) than any kind of documentation of subculture reality. Granted, the film does have its moments: nowhere else in cinema history can you see two six-year-old hicks shooting cap guns at a waifish boy in pink bunny ears. —*J. D.*

GUYANA TRAGEDY: THE STORY OF JIM JONES L: DRAMA/ DRAMA (1980) 192M D: William A. Graham. *Powers Boothe, Rosalind Cash, Brad Dourif, Ned Beatty, Randy Quaid, Veronica Cartwright, James Earl Jones.* This is a poignant depiction of Pastor Jim Jones (Boothe) and the rise and fall of his People's Church, which collapsed in a spectacular mass suicide in South America. This film is essentially a character study of a mad and complicated man. At the beginning, he works squarely against pervasive racism, helping minorities and inviting them to his church. After moving his organization to San Francisco, Jones develops a national following. As his power grows, so grows his talent for manipulating individuals and groups. Totally convinced that a nuclear Armageddon is around the corner, he moves his church and hundreds of followers to Guyana. When word leaks out to Congressman Leo J. Ryan (Beatty) that some people are being held against their will, he goes to investigate. Tragedy erupts shortly thereafter. Boothe won an Emmy for his stunning performance in this TV film. —*N. J.*

HIDDEN IN AMERICA L: DRAMA/DRAMA (1996) 93M D: Martin Bell. *Shelton Dane, Beau Bridges, Bruce Davison, Frances McDormand, Jena Malone.* Bell, the director of *Streetwise* and *American Heart*, continues his exploration of citizens falling through society's cracks with this story of a widower (played by the underrated Bridges) with two kids, no savings, and a minimum-wage job, leaving him a paycheck away from hunger. Bell's drama manages to make all its points without losing sight of the characters, and the film is at its best exploring the emotional toll on the kids and their father, whose self-respect becomes the biggest barrier to seeking help. Produced in association with the End Hunger Network, the film is a fine educational tool, but it's also good drama made with love and conviction. —*S.A.*

HIGHER LEARNING L: DRAMA/DRAMA (1995) 127M D: John Singleton. *Omar Epps, Tyra Banks, Laurence Fishburne, Kristy Swanson, Ice Cube, Michael Rapaport.* After *Boyz 'N the Hood* and the less successful *Poetic Justice*, Singleton turned his eye toward the college campus. The story follows a multiracial ensemble cast and rather heavy-handedly attempts to tackle white supremacy, date rape, feminism, and lesbianism all during the beginning of a school year. Rapaport is surprisingly good as a confused skinhead, Fishburne is in his element as a righteous professor, and Cube plays the opposite of his *Boyz* character, a preachy, Afro'd campus activist named Fudge. Singleton sets the story at Columbus University and includes shots of a Christopher Columbus statue looking down on the students, as if to imply that all this turmoil dates back to the colonialist roots of our country. —*B.T.*

HIGHWAY L: DRAMA/INDEPENDENT DRAMA (2001) 97M D: James Cox. *Jake Gyllenhaal, Jared Leto, Selma Blair, Jeremy Piven, John C. McGinley.* Silly attempt at an "edgy" teen road picture about brain-dead stoners (Gyllenhaal and Leto) on the run from a group of mobsters called "Miranda's Pandas." They pick up a hooker-with-a-you-know-the-rest (Blair), see McGinley running around naked with cornrows, and visit a sideshow attraction in rural Oregon. Ultimately they end up at the Seattle Center during the Kurt Cobain memorial. I suppose as far as crappy straight-to-video movies go, this could've been worse—especially considering some of the painful dialogue writer Scott Rosenberg has penned for other movies (*Disturbing Behavior, Con-Air*). The cinematography is somewhat stylish (in a derivative, MTV sort of way), and Gyllenhaal is always likable in these type of dumb-guy roles. —*B.T.*

HOUSE OF CARDS L: DRAMA/DRAMA (1992) 109M D: Michael Lessac. *Kathleen Turner, Tommy Lee Jones, Shiloh Strong, Esther Rolle, Asha Menina.* This beautiful, rare example of American magic realism actually works, but slipped by the public. After losing her archeologist husband in a freak accident, Ruth Matthews (Turner) and her family return home to the United States. Suddenly her daughter, an unusually intelligent and articulate child capable of speaking several languages, lapses into silence and autistic behavior. Jones plays a doctor determined to treat the girl with conventional methods. Ruth, however, is determined to figure out what her daughter is trying to communicate. It's a graceful waltz through spiritual and creative expression, touching upon mythology and magic and bringing into play the world of science and logic. —*M.N.*

HUMORESQUE L: CLASSIC DRAMA/CLASSIC DRAMA (1946) 123M D: Jean Negulesco. *Joan Crawford, John Garfield, Oscar Levant, John Abbott, J. Carrol Naish, Joan Chandler.* Garfield plays a brilliant young violinist who has a difficult time finding work. But with the help of an interested benefactor, he is able to get a leg up in the music world and soon becomes a success. Crawford, in a brilliant performance, plays his patron, manipulating the violinist into more of a relationship than he bargained for. The excellent soundtrack for these performances is provided by the phenomenal Isaac Stern. —*N.J.*

I'LL TAKE YOU THERE L: DRAMA/INDEPENDENT DRAMA (1999) 93M D: Adrienne Shelly. *Ally Sheedy, Alice Drummond, Alan North, Reg Rogers.* The sophomore feature by Shelly, Hal Hartley's pixie diva turned director, is a kind of *Something Wild* for the New York indie set. Sheedy hijacks a callous blind date (Rogers) at gun point, and his desperate road trip to win back his flighty wife turns into a strange courtship between two wounded souls. Shelly loses the mannered cleverness of her first feature *Sudden Manhattan* for this sweet meditation on love and accountability: "We're all responsible for each other." Drummond and North costar as Sheedy's sassy, vivacious grandmother and her devoted, adoring companion in the film's best scenes. There's a certain staginess to the script but the dialogue is unforced and easy and the direction relaxed. Shelly seems to be losing her Hartley influence and finding her own voice, and it's worth hearing. —*S.A.*

IMITATION OF LIFE L: CLASSIC DRAMA/CLASSIC DRAMA (1934) 111M D: John M. Stahl. *Claudette Colbert, Robert Alda, Susan Kohner, Sandra Dee, John Gavin, Lana Turner, Juanita Moore, Ned Sparks, Rochelle Hudson, Louise Beavers, Warren William.* This early '30s tearjerker (based on a novel by Fannie Hurst) is ostensibly about the rise of a single mom turned successful businesswoman (Colbert) and her soapy romance with a tuxedoed ichthyologist (William). Yet the most compelling story belongs to Colbert's loyal black maid (Beavers) and her light-skinned daughter (Fredi Washington), who attempts to pass for white. The latter actresses' billing comes fifth and sixth, respectively, which hints at the contradictions this film both addresses and to which it falls victim. Washington's attempts to pass for white, and the effects it has on her self-image and on her mother, was a bold issue to address in 1934; the mere suggestion of its implications overpowers the rest of the film. It is a frustrating but forgivable weakness that director Stahl never really plumbed the depth of the issue. Douglas Sirk remade the film in 1959 with Lana Turner. —*S.A.*

JO JO DANCER, YOUR LIFE IS CALLING L: DRAMA/DRAMA (1986) 97M D: Richard Pryor. *Richard Pryor, Debbie Allen, Art Evans, Fay Hauser, Carmen McRae.*

Part of what made Pryor's stand-up so great was how personal it was; how he was able to tell long stories about his freebasing accident, or his addiction, or his heart attack. He was actually able to personify his deepest personal problems, literally give them a voice, and make them into funny characters. *Jo Jo Dancer* is his attempt to do that in a narrative film. The story is a barely veiled autobiography about a famous comedian named Jo Jo Dancer, who sets himself on fire in a freebasing accident and subsequently reflects on his life. The story is pretty familiar if you've read Pryor's autobiography: growing up in a brothel, fighting his way up the comedy ladder, then throwing away his success on troubled relationships and drug abuse. At its best, the film is simultaneously funny and tragic, such as an early scene in which Jo Jo phones a friend in a desperate attempt to score drugs but tries to play it like a casual social call. Some of the filmmaking is awkward, but you could say the same thing about a lot of Pryor's commercial movies of the '80s. This one is a must-see for anyone interested in Pryor (although not as important as *Richard Pryor: Live in Concert*). —*B.T.*

JUICE L: DRAMA/DRAMA (1992) 95M D: Ernest Dickerson. *Cindy Herron, Omar Epps, Tupac Shakur, Jermaine Hopkins, Khalil Kain.* A group of teens, including an aspiring DJ named Q (Epps), decide to buy a gun and rob a store, with predictable results. Other than the great photography (first-time director Dickerson had been Spike Lee's longtime cinematographer), this is a fairly routine urban drama. One unique touch is the score by the Bomb Squad, the legendary production team behind most of Public Enemy's albums and Ice Cube's classic solo debut *Amerikka's Most Wanted*. But *Juice* will always be remembered for the debut performance of Shakur as the psychotic Bishop, who pushes the group into violence. His fascination with James Cagney in *White Heat* is an observant touch, as the Hollywood glamour of white gangsters would be a theme in rap videos for years to come. —*B.T.*

JULIEN DONKEY-BOY L: DRAMA/INDEPENDENT DRAMA (1999) 94M D: Harmony Korine. *Chloë Sevigny, Werner Herzog, Ewen Bremner.* Korine continues somewhat in the vein of *Gummo*, but this time with professional actors. The story (and there sort of is one) centers around the schizophrenic Julien (Bremner) and his dysfunctional family. If I didn't know Bremner from *Trainspotting*, I'd probably think he wasn't acting. But Herzog manages to steal the show in a rare acting performance as the bizarre, abusive father who humiliates his kids by spraying them with a hose and also delights in reciting dialogue from *Dirty Harry. Julien Donkey-Boy)* is not nearly as fun (if that's the word) as *Gummo*, and it is most notable for its innovative cinematography. Being a Dogme film, it's shot on low-resolution digital video, but the image is abused and

degraded, exaggerating the inherent ugliness of the medium until it takes on an eerie, impressionistic beauty. —*B.T.*

KEN PARK L: DRAMA/INDEPENDENT DRAMA (2002) 96M D: Larry Clark, Edward Lachman. *James Ransone, Tiffany Limos, Stephen Jasso, James Bullard, Mike Apaletegui, Harrison Young.* Ken Park blows his brains out at a skate park in the first five minutes of the movie. What's left is the story of his friends and their terminally fucked-up lives. Written by Harmony Korine before he wrote *Kids, Ken Park* is similar but with more sex, drugs, violence, and a bit more narrative. Korine's antistory is about the implosion of these kids' lives and the nothingness at their center. Crossing the line from provocative to exploitative without looking back, the film contains such scenes as a father performing oral sex on his son, a kid murdering his sleeping grandparents, and a boy masturbating while strangling himself. The entire film lies somewhere between child pornography and important art dealing with the struggles of contemporary youth. It constantly asks whether any of this misery is necessary. It doesn't provide any insight and is not really a cautionary tale. It just presents the facts, lets us know the characters, and leaves it at that. —*T. S.*

KIDS L: DRAMA/INDEPENDENT DRAMA (1995) 91M D: Larry Clark. *Leo Fitzpatrick, Chloë Sevigny, Justin Pierce, Rosario Dawson.* "Virgins! I love 'em! No skank, no disease, just pure pussy!" This is the motto of *Kids'* young teenage lead, Telly (Fitzpatrick), and there is nothing more important to him than trying to deflower as many virgins as possible, the younger the better. When one of these young girls, Jenny (Sevigny), who has only had sex with Telly, finds out that she is HIV positive, she sets out to find Telly and let him know before he finds another virgin. More than just a glimpse into the world of unprotected sex among the young, *Kids* presents a startling look into juvenile delinquency, and it is so well-acted and realistic that it feels more like a documentary than a fiction drama. Young kids getting trashed, fucking, getting high, puking, passing out, and spreading diseases? You'll find yourself wondering where all the parents are, but don't bother. Just sit back and enjoy a movie that is well made, realistic, and offers no chance of escapism whatsoever. —*J. S.*

LEGEND OF BILLIE JEAN, THE L: DRAMA/DRAMA (1985) 92M D: Matthew Robbins. *Helen Slater, Keith Gordon, Dean Stockwell, Peter Coyote, Christian Slater.* After her brother has trouble with the law, teenager Billie Jean is forced to go on the run, becoming a local legend and hero to all the kids. Sporting a rad theme song by Pat Benatar, the film is ridiculous but lots of fun, too. Billie Jean's rise to fame and the gathering of support around her is inspiring to watch. The way the film plays out is so absurdly fun it will have you cheering and laughing. Billie Jean is a rebel of the MTV age, and the basic message of this film is that it's all about the attitude. Her crusade for justice isn't half as important as how cool she is. And you gotta give her credit, man. —*T. S.*

L.I.E. L: DRAMA/INDEPENDENT DRAMA (2001) 97M D:Michael Cuesta. *Bruce Altman, Paul Franklin Dano, James Costa, Brian Cox.* L.I.E. stands for the Long Island Expressway, the place where Howie's mother died in a car accident. Sans direction, Howie (Dano) returns there several times since his father seems too busy with work and a new woman. Howie's primary mentor becomes Gary (Billy Kay), a young man with questionable associations. They decide to rob the house of an ex-marine (Cox) who turns out to be Gary's pedophile pimp. They don't find any cash in his basement, but they do find his gun. *L.I.E.* is unsettling because the characters, despite taking action to liberate themselves, remain directionless and chained to their original, hopeless situation. All the same, this is a well-made film that casts light on a new generation neglected by society. —*N. J.*

LONELY WIVES L: CLASSIC DRAMA/PRE-CODE DRAMA (1931) 85M D: Russell Mack. *Laura La Plante, Patsy Ruth Miller, Edward Everett Horton.* Everett Horton plays two roles with astonishingly effective split-screen effects in this pre-Code bedroom farce about a philandering lawyer and the show biz impersonator who covers for him. He's hilarious as both the temperamental would-be Romeo and the befuddled play-actor, but the door-slamming comedy becomes a bit forced. It's more sizzle than sex, with most of the innuendo turning out far too innocent, but jazz baby Miller is all wiggles and winks and a sashay full of promise. Platinum blonde La Plante's social-naïf-turned-giggly-flirt is Marilyn Monroe twenty years before Norma Jean invented her. —*S. A.*

LOVE & BASKETBALL L: DRAMA/DRAMA (2000) 124M D: Gina Prince-Bythewood. *Omar Epps, Alfre Woodard, Sanaa Lathan, Dennis Haysbert, Debbi Morgan.* Using sports as a metaphor for life and love is nothing new, but director Prince-Bythewood, a former college athlete, puts a different spin on the story of b-ball lovers. Lathan plays a fierce, hot-tempered competitor playing her soul out to tiny audiences in small gyms and second-rate auditoriums, while cocky Epps plays in huge courts to cheering, sold-out crowds. Lathan is great, taking us through moments of elation and disappointment with convincing pride and vulnerability. This is the rare sports film that favors the woman's struggle over the man's in a male-dominated sport; and an even rarer one to reveal such a sharp, savvy contrast. Spike Lee produces. —*S. A.*

LOVE LIZA L: DRAMA/DRAMA (2002) 93M D: Todd Louiso. *Philip Seymour Hoffman, Jack Kehler, Sarah Koskoff, Kathy Bates.* Hoffman plays Wilson, a young web designer trying to cope with the recent suicide of his wife Liza. As his grief intensifies, Wilson turns to huffing gas and building model airplanes to keep himself from opening the suicide letter that Liza left. Wilson becomes increasingly detached from reality as well as from the people trying to offer him comfort. An honest, painful depiction of loss and tragedy, this film owes all of its emotional resonance to Hoffman. His character is so horribly dejected at times that it almost aches to watch him, and his bizarre, quirky behavior is seamless. Bates is also excellent as Wilson's mother-in-law, Mary Ann, and the dynamic between the two actors makes *Love Liza* one of the most tragic, emotional movies in a long time. —*J. S.*

MEDIUM COOL L: DRAMA/INDEPENDENT DRAMA (1969) 110M D: Haskell Wexler. *Robert Forster, Peter Boyle, Verna Bloom, Peter Bonerz.* Late 1960s Chicago must have been a tough place to live, especially for women, children, and playboy cameramen. Famed cinematographer Wexler writes/directs/shoots this middling metaphoric piece of self-indulgent metacinema about a cameraman (a strapping Forster) torn between his somewhat high-profile career (insert: "womanizer") and an earthbound relationship with a poor woman (the lovely Bloom) and her skinny kid. Wexler is smart enough to steer clear of the film's simplistic narrative, and lets his camera flit about, capturing random scenes of political demonstrations, hippie campaign debates and the childlike wonder of riding the L train. The movie's intentions are always mixed, but it is so well shot and crafted, that you forget all that, and just marvel at what beauty a camera can make. —*J. D.*

MILLIE L: CLASSIC DRAMA/PRE-CODE DRAMA (1931) 85M D: John Francis Dillon. *Joan Blondell, James Hall, Helen Twelvetrees, Lilyan Tashman, Robert Ames.* "I pay my own way," insists thoroughly modern Millie, a single mother and sexually liberated dame in the not-so-modern 1930s. Twelvetrees, a real firecracker of an actress, takes Millie from small-town idealist to disillusioned big-city flirt to cynical boozy floozy, without ever sacrificing her independence or dousing her sexy spark. When a former beau plots to seduce her sixteen-year-old daughter, the worn, sad woman becomes an avenging angel. Full of sex, adultery, free-flowing Prohibition liquor and a nonjudgmental attitude toward it all, this has everything that makes pre-Code movies great, including a dynamic, tough leading lady. —*S. A.*

MONSTER'S BALL L: DRAMA/INDEPENDENT DRAMA (2001) 112M D: Marc Forster. *Billy Bob Thornton, Halle Berry, Peter Boyle, Heath Ledger, Coronji Calhoun, Sean Combs.* Berry's Oscar-winning performance is the soul of Forster's drama about two souls who break the cycle of hate and grief in a small, Southern prison town. Letitia (Berry) is a worn and frustrated single mom, numb from overwork and drained by her visits to her husband (Calhoun) on death row. Hank (Thornton) is the corrections officer who's had the life whipped out of him by racist father (Boyle) and who has, in turn, been feeding the poison to his own son (Ledger). Raw moments of naked emotion rip through the contrived tragedies and Forster's careful control and choreography. The director is so determined to expose the evils of racism and hate passed from father to son like a virus that he smothers the spontaneity out of the picture. Yet this is an often affecting film with a powerful message. In the tender quiet of the final act, two scarred souls step up to take control of a life they've let someone else drive into a dead end. It's a lovely moment of hope, well deserved after all the hate we've slogged through, but it's all a little too contrived to fully embrace. —S. A.

NARC L: DRAMA/DRAMA (2002)105M D: Joe Carnahan. *Jason Patric, Ray Liotta, Chi McBride, Busta Rhymes.* Narc is a movie full of big themes, big violence, and big acting. It's on full volume right from the beginning, and doesn't ever let up. Within the first few minutes, Patric guns down a drug-dealer and, inadvertently, a pregnant bystander. The plot involves a slain narcotics officer and the truth behind his death, and the way Patric tries to balance family life with his nasty job, justice, and dirty cops. The real reason to watch Narc is Liotta. He put on forty pounds and a wolf-like goatee for this role, and his piercing stare suggests menace just waiting to explode. His performance raises this sometimes melodramatic film above the bar, and gives him his best role ever. —K. C.

NIGHT AT THE GOLDEN EAGLE L: DRAMA/INDEPENDENT DRAMA (2002) 87M D: Adam Rifkin. *Vinny Argiro, Natasha Lyonne, Donnie Montemarano, Ann Magnuson, Vinnie Jones.* Rifkin, known (in some circles) for dark comedies like *The Dark Backwards* and *Mousehunt*, tries his hand at a '70s-style gritty character piece, with mixed results. The story involves two friends, one just out of jail, staying in a hotel the night before they plan to leave for legitimate jobs in Vegas. The exaggerated awfulness of life is funny in Rifkin's comedies, but in a drama it tends to feel pretentious and overblown. Take for example the scene where a fourteen-year-old hooker with braces comes on to an old man even though her face is completely smeared with makeup and tears. Still, Montemarano and Argiro, apparently real-life best friends (and one a nonprofessional ex-con), add an authenticity to the movie that almost makes it work. —B. T.

NORTH DALLAS FORTY L: DRAMA/DRAMA (1979) 119M D: Ted Kotcheff. *Mac Davis, Nick Nolte, Charles Durning, Dabney Coleman, Dayle Haddon.* This scathing look at the meat grinder of professional football is adapted from the novel by former Dallas Cowboy Peter Gent, and may be the most cynical take ever on the sport. The film feels, at least in parts, genuine: Nolte plays an aging, bench-warming wide receiver who prays for his own team to drop the ball so he can get into the game. Nolte is thoroughly convincing as the smart-mouthed veteran staving off the ravages of time with pills, shots, sex, and the occasional joint, but with no ready defense against the manipulations of management. The bigger surprise is Davis, whose easy-going facade hides a cagey, opportunistic game player both on and off the field. —S. A.

ONCE AROUND L: DRAMA/DRAMA (1991) 115M D: Lasse Hallström. *Holly Hunter, Richard Dreyfuss, Gena Rowlands, Laura San Giacomo, Danny Aiello.* An early gem from Hallström (*My Life as a Dog, Chocolat*), this film surprises viewers with a kind of emotional misdirection that in the end becomes very affecting. Great performances all around, but Dreyfuss is perfectly cast as Hunter's annoying, hard-to-like suitor. Be patient with this one, and don't be too quick to judge it or its characters, and you'll be gently and touchingly rewarded. —K. S.

OUR SONG L: DRAMA/INDEPENDENT DRAMA (2002) 97M D: Jim McKay. *Anna Simpson, Kerry Washington, Melissa Martinez.* More than simply a title, *Our Song* is a statement of purpose. Like writer/director McKay's previous film *Girls Town*, this is a look into the private worlds of girls, this time concerning three high school kids in Crown Heights, Brooklyn. Washington, Martinez, and Simpson are best friends with plenty in common: single parent households, mixed-race parents, and membership in the Jackie Robinson Steppers, the real-life marching band whose rehearsals run through the film. McKay isn't as interested in a definitive portrait as a quick, sketchy snapshot of a time in life when the girls are on the verge of growing up, growing self-aware, and growing away from one another. He beautifully shapes the stories around the rhythms of their performances and the texture of life in Crown Heights. As the final credits roll, you realize that McKay didn't share the "a film by" credit out of magnanimity but acknowledgment of a true creative collaboration. It's not clear who is telling whose story, but this song belongs to them all. —S. A.

PARTY MONSTER L: DRAMA/INDEPENDENT DRAMA (2003) 98M D: Fenton Bailey, Randy Barbato. *Macaulay Culkin, Seth Green, Wilmer Valderrama, Chloë Sevigny, Natasha Lyonne.* I read a lot of magazines and the only thing that seems to be consistent between them is that most of the people who write for these mags don't know what the fuck they are talking about. Take *Party Monster* for example. *The Rules of Attraction* got a ton of buzz and we can comfortably agree that it was grand crock of poo. When the focus shifted to Culkin's new vehicle, I still hadn't learned my lesson. Why do I listen to these people? Over and over again I get suckered into the possibility that maybe this time they know what they are talking about, but I guess that I just don't know no better. Maybe it's the types of magazines that I read. Am I a shallow fuck? The only thing that I will say for this movie is that I hate myself for watching it. —*T. C.*

PERMANENT MIDNIGHT L: DRAMA/INDEPENDENT DRAMA (1998) 90M D: David Veloz. *Ben Stiller, Elizabeth Hurley, Maria Bello, Owen Wilson, Lourdes Benedicto. Permanent Midnight* is a mixed bag of an addiction drama based on the memoir of Jerry Stahl, the acclaimed writer whose severe drug habit made him stoop to bringing his baby along while scoring heroin, and, worse, writing for sitcoms. Stiller is quite good as Stahl. He usually channels his anger and self-doubt into comedy, but here he brings it right to the surface. There are also some great scenes of drug-induced awfulness. Stahl was a writer for *ALF*, so we see him high out of his mind doing an insane pitch for a fictionalized version called *Mr. Chompers*. Later the Chompers puppet haunts him in his hallucinations (if only they could've gotten the rights to use the real ALF puppet!). Despite those scenes, this just isn't a particularly compelling story and doesn't have much new to say about addiction. —*B. T.*

PEYTON PLACE L: CLASSIC DRAMA/CLASSIC DRAMA (1957) 157M D: Mark Robson. *Lana Turner, Hope Lange, Arthur Kennedy, Terry Moore, Lee Philips, Russ Tamblyn, Lloyd Nolan, Diane Varsi. Peyton Place* in essence is the very first soap opera. With an enormous cast, this serialized film focuses on a number of relationships in a quiet, small town. Turner plays Constance MacKenzie, an unwed mother who does everything she can to keep the truth of her daughter's origin unknown. Her daughter Alison (Varsi) does everything she can to figure out this mystery, only to have the shocking truth come out in a court case. A perfectly timeless movie. Turner was nominated for a Best Actress Oscar. —*N. J.*

PLACE CALLED TODAY, A L: DRAMA/DRAMA (1972) 105M D: Don Schain, Bruno Barreto. *Janet Leigh, Herbert Kerr, Lana Wood, Richard Smedley, Tim Brown.* A smart, socially committed black lawyer (Kerr) is running for mayor on a platform of equality in a small city that is 40 percent black. He needs an edge in order to win against the current administration and their rich backers who have promised "progress," building urban towers and creating jobs. Kerr's character makes a devil's bargain with revolutionaries to step up their bombing, publicly pledging to stop their violence while expressing sympathy for "the poverty and frustration where violence comes from." The dialogue and political attitudes are a time capsule from another era, and while the melodramatic ending presumes high tragedy, the issues are intelligently and seriously laid out. The candidate and others go through credible shifts in their worldview. Verbal obscenities and one unbelievably nasty murder make it all street real. This is harsh, near-profound cinema. —*J. C.*

POETIC JUSTICE L: DRAMA/DRAMA (1993) 110M D: John Singleton. *Janet Jackson, Tyra Ferrell, Joe Torry, Tupac Shakur, Regina King.* Having successfully cast Ice Cube in *Boyz 'N the Hood*, it's not too surprising that Singleton offered Jackson and Shakur starring roles in his second film. Jackson plays Justice, a young poet grieving over her recently murdered boyfriend. She goes on a road trip to Oakland with a group that includes Shakur, a guy who often hits on her at her job. Jackson (whose poems, by the way, are written by Maya Angelou) is surprisingly strong, but the standout performer is Shakur. Although the film itself is forgettable, it is often cited as evidence of the late Shakur's potential as an actor. It is a good example of the alternately tough and sensitive qualities of his persona that made him into such an icon. —*B. T.*

PRETTY IN PINK L: DRAMA/DRAMA (1986) 96M D: Howard Deutch. *Molly Ringwald, Jon Cryer, Andrew McCarthy, James Spader, Annie Potts, Harry Dean Stanton.* Ringwald plays Andie, a high school student whose family isn't particularly loaded, but who falls in love with Blane (McCarthy), a classmate whose family is especially loaded. Blane falls in love with Andie, and when his friends start to question his judgment, things get ugly. We are left to wonder if love will be able to bridge the gap between poor kids and rich kids. What really makes this movie shine, and what makes the ending suck, is Duckie (Cryer), Andie's best friend. He's a huge goofball and totally in love with Andie. Where is the love for Duckie? This is what I want to know. Why doesn't Andie realize that Duckie is the guy every girl secretly wants? I guess she's too busy kissing her rich boyfriend's ass. —*J. S.*

PUMP UP THE VOLUME L: DRAMA/DRAMA (1990) 105M D: Allan Moyle. *Christian Slater, Samantha Mathis, Ellen Greene.* Slater stars as a shy-by-day, loud-by-night high school student who has a pirate radio show starring himself as DJ Happy Harry Hard On. Harry takes on everything with his antiestablishment message: parents, suburbs, society, and the evil high school he attends. Mathis plays Nora, a doting fan of Harry's show who becomes his partner in crime. The film doesn't necessarily hold up years after its release. These days, it's all I can do not to roll my eyes at Slater's simplistic, preachy speeches. "All the good themes have been used up, turned into theme parks." Oh, please. —*J. K.*

REAL WOMEN HAVE CURVES L: DRAMA/INDEPENDENT DRAMA (2002) 93M D: Patricia Cardoso. *America Ferrera, Lupe Ontiveros, Brian Sites, George Lopez, Ingrid Oliu.* Ana is a Mexican-American teenager trying to overcome her overbearing mother, her negative body image (derived from repeatedly being told she is fat), and her almost comically traditional family to become her own woman. Blah blah blah. I have nothing against a good overcoming-the-odds, coming-of-age story, but this movie was painful to watch. Ana really doesn't give us a reason to sympathize with her. She's got a chip on her shoulder that makes her constantly behave like a bratty asshole, and she never misses an opportunity to preach a flat and unconvincing message about body image. Everyone's acting feels forced, and the plot is so contrived as to make one wonder what reality these people are living in. —*J. S.*

REDS L: DRAMA/DRAMA (1981) 200M D: Warren Beatty. *Warren Beatty, Diane Keaton, Jack Nicholson, Edward Herrmann, Maureen Stapleton.* The romance between famed leftist journalists John Reed (Beatty) and Louise Bryant (Keaton), *Reds* expands into an epic history of a tight group of American radicals, including Eugene O'Neill (Nicholson), Emma Goldman (Stapleton), Max Eastman (Herrmann), and numerous others. Though not always faithful to the actual events, there is much to recommend about *Reds*, most notably interviews interspersed through the film with real-life friends and acquaintances of John Reed. The interviewees' various (and often contradicting) anecdotes become, in the words of critic Jonathan Rosenbaum, "the conscience" of *Reds. Reds* drummed up twelve Oscar nominations, winning in several categories. —*C. B.*

RIVER'S EDGE L: DRAMA/INDEPENDENT DRAMA (1987) 99M D: Tim Hunter. *Crispin Glover, Keanu Reeves, Dennis Hopper, Ione Skye, Daniel Roebuck.* A group of teenagers discovers one of their friends has murdered his girlfriend. What follows is how they deal with the situation and how it affects their lives. Most of these kids are so disillusioned and nihilistic that they aren't even moved by repeated viewings of the corpse. I love the feel of this film; it was shot in a small town somewhere in the Northwest during the rainy season. Everything seems shrouded in a dank mist and the river that flows outside town is high, kind of like the kids in the movie. The cast is great, especially Glover as Layne, the hyper metal dude trying to save his friend from the cops, and Hopper as Feck, an ex-biker and drug dealer on the lam. Reeves plays Matt, who juggles a fucked-up home life, a delinquent little brother, and his conscience. The killer, Samson, is played straight and cold by Roebuck. Slayer was used for most of the soundtrack! —*B. W.*

ROCKY L: DRAMA/DRAMA (1979) 119M D: John G. Avildsen. *Sylvester Stallone, Carl Weathers, Burgess Meredith, Burt Young, Talia Shire.* Stallone wrote and stars in this story of a humble, half-punchy prizefighter who gets a shot at greatness. This movie is so inspirational, so simply told, and in its time as much an underdog as Stallone's character. Never mind the sequels, this one is the keeper. In addition to Stallone's charming lead, Shire is lovely as his dowdy, lovable girlfriend, and Meredith won over a whole new generation of fans with his portrayal of Rocky's wide-eyed, fiery trainer, Mickey. Forget everything Stallone's been involved in since (except maybe *Demolition Man*), and watch this one-time-sleeper-turned-'70s-classic. —*M. S.*

ROUNDERS L: DRAMA/DRAMA (1998) 125M D: John Dahl. *Matt Damon, Edward Norton, John Malkovich, Famke Janssen, Gretchen Mol, John Turturro.* Although not as well-known as Dahl's *Red Rock West* or *The Last Seduction*, this thriller about high-stakes poker stars Damon as Mike, who lost all his money gambling with the Russian mafia. He kicked the habit, straightened up his life, and went to law school. But the second his buddy Worm (Norton) is out of prison and they start hanging out, Mike's whole life goes down the toilet again. Damon's performance is solid, but Norton steals the movie as the devil that he knows he ought to swat off of his shoulder, but can't. Excellent noir atmosphere, thanks in part to cinematographer Jean-Yves Escoffier (who also did *Gummo*) and a jazz score by Christopher Young. —*B. T.*

RUSH L: DRAMA/DRAMA (1991) 120M D: Lili Fini Zanuck. *Jennifer Jason Leigh, Jason Patric, Sam Elliott, Gregg Allman.* First-time director Zanuck brings an accomplished style (her opening scene recalls Scorsese's *GoodFellas*, then takes its own unpredictable course) to this tough adaptation of Kim Wozencraft's autobiographical story about working as an undercover narcotics officer in a rural Texas town. Patric is excellent as the brooding realist who likes the thrill too much, and Leigh takes a gripping journey from naive idealist to scarred survivor. Allman is memorable in an almost wordless performance as a shady bar owner. The setting is perfectly captured in unglamourous locations, a well-chosen soundtrack of roadhouse rock, and a bluesy score by Eric Clapton. Zanuck slowly builds tension until the threat of sudden death hangs over every drug deal, and the self-destructive spiral of addiction threatens to suck the characters into the black hole of their assignment. One of the grittiest and grimmest portraits of undercover work made for the big screen. —*S. A.*

SEARCHING FOR BOBBY FISCHER L: DRAMA/DRAMA (1993) 111M D: Steven Zaillian. *Joan Allen, Joe Mantegna, Max Pomeranc, Ben Kingsley, Laurence Fishburne.* Josh (Pomeranc) is really good at chess. Bobby

Fischer was also really good at chess. While the story of Josh's entrance into the chess world is told, parallels between Fischer and Josh are constantly drawn, bringing an ominous feel to this film, because, after all, Bobby Fischer just disappeared one day. Josh's coach (Kingsley) pushes him, his father (Mantegna) pushes him, and while the chess part of the movie is interesting, it is these interactions that really make the film dynamic. —*J. S.*

SIROCCO L: CLASSIC DRAMA/CLASSIC DRAMA (1951) 98M D: Curtis Bernhardt. *Humphrey Bogart, Märta Torén, Lee J. Cobb, Everett Sloane, Zero Mostel, Nick Dennis.* Bogie returns to the desert for a more mercenary and less romantic pseudo-prequel to *Casablanca,* set in the midst of the French/Syrian war in Damascus, 1925. Harry Smith is a merchant, black marketeer, and gun-runner for the Syrian rebellion. Cast in the cold pessimism of America's postwar malaise, this film puts the "anti" in antihero. The romance between Bogart and exotic European beauty Torén ("You're so ugly. How can a man so ugly be so handsome?") is far from convincing, but he creates a ruthless desperation when Smith flees the underground as his shady business collapses. The film lacks the conviction of its own cynicism, but Bogie never betrays his calculating character. Mostel and Dennis stand out as a toadying merchant and Smith's boisterous sidekick, respectively. —*S. A.*

SKINS L: DRAMA/INDEPENDENT DRAMA (2002) 87M D: Chris Eyre. *Eric Schweig, Gary Farmer, Graham Greene.* *Smoke Signals* director Eyre pulls no punches in his angry portrait of life on the impoverished Pine Ridge Reservation, a community awash in poverty, drugs, and alcoholism. Schweig is excellent as the frustrated Reservation cop whose bottled-up rage explodes in missions of midnight vigilante justice, with catastrophic consequences. Anchoring this knotty drama (based on the novel by Adrian C. Louis) is a contentious relationship between the zealous cop and his drop-out older brother (Greene), a Vietnam vet turned bitter drunk, and the legacy of their pasts. Sixty miles from Mount Rushmore, Pine Ridge encompasses the notorious site of the Wounded Knee massacre, and its legacy (which Eyre movingly parallels with My Lai) seems to permeate the land. Eyre confronts his issues bluntly and boldly (if not always deftly), and his fury and fiery passion make this portrait burn with indignation. This is a film about anger, shame, and helplessness. It offers no answers, merely hard questions and angry challenges. —*S. A.*

SLAUGHTER RULE, THE L: DRAMA/INDEPENDENT DRAMA (2002) 112M D: Alex Smith, Andrew J. Smith. *Ryan Gosling, Clea Duvall, David Morse.* "My father told me if I was hard enough I wouldn't break. He was wrong. Everything breaks." Gosling is a passive, careful, second-string high school quarterback who keeps life at arm's length after the death

of his father. Morse is the coach who scouts the boy to lead his dream of a six-man squad in a small rural league. Set in the high desert, the writer/director team captures the crisp air and the lonely Montana plain with a widescreen frame that drinks in open sky while bringing discomforting ambiguity to relationships on the ground. As Morse ignites the alpha-wolf behind Gosling's protective sheep's clothing, their roughhouse relationship takes on intimate shades. While the title reads like some brutal, warrior-sport metaphor for life, the film is simply about staying the course, surviving to the end of the game. —*S. A.*

SLC PUNK L: DRAMA/INDEPENDENT DRAMA (1999) 97M D: James Merendino. *Matthew Lillard, Annabeth Gish, Christopher McDonald, Devon Sawa, Til Schweiger, Jennifer Lien, Michael A. Goorjian.* Lillard talks to the camera in this movie, a lot. Almost constantly. This is OK, though, because the basic premise of this movie is a guy's struggle with the meaning of a punk-rock lifestyle and its conflicts with changes in his own life. Lillard is Stevo, and Stevo believes in anarchy and chaos. Stevo also just graduated from college and has been accepted into Harvard law school (even though it was his Dad who applied for him). How will Stevo reconcile these things? *SLC Punk* will make you think, and it will also make you laugh hysterically. The soundtrack is awesome, Stevo's friends are colorful and energetic, and there are plenty of punks and Mormons to satisfy everyone. —*J. S.*

SPRING FORWARD L: DRAMA/INDEPENDENT DRAMA (2000) 110M D: Tom Gilroy. *Ned Beatty, Liev Schreiber, Campbell Scott, Ian Hart, Peri Gilpin.* Beatty and Schreiber are both perfect in this beautifully restrained and understated film about two city employees who form an unlikely friendship. The script hits all the right notes and, more impressively, avoids all the wrong ones in allowing the duo to carry this profoundly simply film. Amazingly perceptive and easily one of the best indies of the past several years. —*D. W.*

STUNT MAN, THE L: DRAMA/DRAMA (1980) 131M D: Richard Rush. *Steve Railsback, Peter O'Toole, Alex Rocco, Adam Rourke, Allen Garfield, Barbara Hershey.* "If God could do the tricks that we can do, he'd be a happy man!" Rush's brilliant little backstage drama of illusion and reality leapt from legendary unreleased masterpiece to classic cult film. Railsback is intense and haunted as Cameron, the Vietnam vet on the run both from his ghosts and some mysterious crime. He winds up sheltered by a megalomaniac movie director (O'Toole), who hires Cameron as his film's new stunt man. When Cameron falls in love with the leading lady (Hershey) and tries to understand the alternately charismatic, sincere, manipulative, monstrous, and mysterious movie director, he loses the ability to tell what's really happen-

Our favorite remakes

A LITTLE PRINCESS *(1995)*

ALI—FEAR EATS THE SOUL
(remake of All That Heaven Allows*)*

THE BLOB *(1986)*

CAPE FEAR (1991)

A FISTFUL OF DOLLARS
(remake of Yojimbo*)*

THE FLY *(1986)*

GOOD MORNING
(remake of I Was Born But . . .*)*

INVASION OF THE BODY SNATCHERS *(1978)*

LATHE OF HEAVEN *(2002)*

MAGNIFICENT 7
(remake of Seven Samurai*)*

NIGHT OF THE LIVING DEAD *(1990)*

OMEGA MAN
(remake of Last Man on Earth*)*

PAYBACK
(remake of Point Blank*)*

PSYCHO *(1998)*

THE RING
(remake of Ringu*)*

THE TEN COMMANDMENTS *(1956)*

THE THING *(1982)*

12 MONKEYS
(inspired by La Jetée*)*

ing and becomes convinced the filmmakers are out to kill him. The film twists and turns, carrying the audience on the same whirlwind mind game as Cameron. A devious exploration of the line between art and life, *The Stunt Man* is one of the great movies about the movies. —*S. A.*

SURRENDER DOROTHY L: DRAMA/INDEPENDENT DRAMA (1998) 90M D: Kevin DiNovis. *Peter Pryor, Jason Centeno, Kevin DiNovis.* Trevor (Pryor), a frustrated dishwasher with a crippling fear of women, takes in a friend, a homeless junkie named Lanh (DiNovis), and then takes out his frustrations on the listless addict. Trevor's cruel but relatively harmless humiliation of Lanh (dressing the latter in a waitress smock with the name "Dorothy" stitched on the front) escalates into a nasty bit of gender-bending role playing: Trevor blackmails Lanh into becoming Dorothy at all times, com-

plete with a new wardrobe, make-up, and shaved legs. For all its humor, this isn't a comedy but an effectively unsettling drama that takes on gender issues, reinforced behavior, and power relations, especially domestic violence as a form of mind game and control. The twist is that it's about a pair of heterosexual men. This down and dirty, shot-on-grainy-16mm psychodrama is the kind of edgy, adventurous film that independent cinema used to be. —*S. A.*

TEVYE L: CLASSIC DRAMA/YIDDISH (1939) 93M D: Maurice Schwartz. *Miriam Riselle, Maurice Schwartz, Rebecca Weintraub.* The original *Fiddler on the Roof*—a great Yiddish film and love story of universal profundity; truer to Sholom Aleichen's story, better than any "fiddling." —*K. S.*

THREE SEASONS L: DRAMA/INDEPENDENT DRAMA (1999) 110M D: Tony Bui. *Harvey Keitel, Don Duong, Nguyen Ngoc Hiep.* Modern-day Saigon is the setting for a collection of marginally related stories involving characters of different economic and social spheres. Each story is corny as hell and the camerawork, dialogue, and music continually rub the overstated "tragic beauty of it all" in your face. Worse, the film's social and international politics are about as thoughtful and complex as a tubesock, its sexual politics range from laughable to offensive, and its liberal breast-striking is far too self-congratulatory. The first U.S. film shot in Vietnam in decades, *Three Seasons* is nevertheles a regrettable movie experience. —*C. B.*

TIME CODE L: DRAMA/INDEPENDENT DRAMA (2000) 97M D: Mike Figgis. *Xander R. Berkeley, Saffron Burrows, Richard Edson, Salma Hayek.* Figgis tried an interesting experiment—shooting four continuous improvised takes on digital video, then dividing the screen into four sections and running them all simultaneously. For some reason, these kind of experiments are always about self-absorbed Hollywood types betraying each other and having affairs. The characters are loosely connected, so their stories occasionally overlap, and there is a good old California earthquake so all the characters can experience the same thing at the same time while in different places. It seems like a good gimmick but it doesn't really work, and Hayek (usually so charming) turns out to be horrible at improv. —*B. T.*

TIME TO KILL, A L: DRAMA/DRAMA (1996) 150M D: Joel Schumacher. *Matthew McConaughey, Sandra Bullock, Kevin Spacey, Brenda Fricker, Oliver Platt, Samuel L. Jackson.* McConaughey (in his first lead role) plays a newjack lawyer in the South defending a father (Jackson) who killed the white supremacists who raped his daughter. Based on a novel by John Grisham, this sensational courtroom drama seems unusually proud of its racial themes. (Hey Schumacher, dude, we're *all* against the KKK.) It's ironic that Grisham, who later tried to sue Oliver Stone because he thought *Natural Born*

Killers had inspired a murder, would write a story that straight-up justifies vigilantism. But the most offensive thing about this movie is an apparent change from the novel. In his tearful summation speech, McConaughey describes what happened to the little girl in graphic detail. Then he says, "Now imagine that that little girl... was white," and this wins over the jury. (Like they were thinking it wasn't all that bad until they imagined the girl white.) In discussions of his Batman films, people often point to *A Time to Kill* as evidence that Schumacher is a good director. I respectfully disagree. —*B. T.*

TOMORROW'S CHILDREN **L: CLASSIC DRAMA/PRE-CODE DRAMA (1934) 70M D: Crane Wilbur.** *Diane Sinclair, Donald Douglas, Sterling Holloway, Sarah Padden.* An exploitation thriller about forced sterilization! Seriously! Wilbur directed this seventy-minute shocker starring Sinclair as the girl whose reproductive future is in the hands of a judge who thinks her genetic pool is a danger to society because her family is full of "idiots and cripples." Blandly directed and flatly acted, the bluntness and clumsiness of this film only enhances the nightmarish horror of her predicament, condemned to sterilization without a chance to defend herself. The climactic race to the rescue is a perverse twist on D. W. Griffith's cross-cutting cliché, topped only by the perverse morality of the moral. —*S. A.*

TONIGHT OR NEVER **L: CLASSIC DRAMA/PRE-CODE DRAMA (1931) 80M D: Mervyn LeRoy.** *Gloria Swanson, Melvyn Douglas, Ferdinand Gottschalk.* Reliable craftsman LeRoy summons up all his drawing room sangfroid for this pre-Code celebration of sex, all suggested via witty innuendo. The camera fades out on opera-singing virgin Swanson, a diva who has no passion and goes looking for some in suave Douglas (making his film debut), as he woos her in his locked apartment. She returns home the next day, bouncy, ecstatic, and singing her best ever. Has sex ever seemed so innocent? With a script by Ernst Lubitsch–regular Ernest Vajda, a debonair and silkily suggestive performance by Douglas, and Swanson at her best, LeRoy pulls it together with a grace rarely seen in his work. It's a sly, double entendre–laced romantic confection. —*S. A.*

TRAGEDY (AKA SURVIVING) **L: DRAMA/DRAMA (1985) 120M D: Waris Hussein.** *Paul Sorvino, River Phoenix, Molly Ringwald, Zack Galligan, Ellen Burstyn, Heather O'Rourke.* This TV movie stars Ringwald as a depressed suburban teen who teams up with her neighbor (Galligan) for some unhealthy wallowing in their adolescent pressures and disillusionment over their parents' dysfunction. This film is just another TV portrait of crumbling families and personalities. But the melodrama and the not-so-subtle portrayal of the warning signs of suicide are laughable. What? Lonnie wants to paint her bedroom walls *black*!?! —*J. K.*

TRAVELLER **L: DRAMA/INDEPENDENT DRAMA (1996) 101M D: Jack N. Green.** *James Gammon, Bill Paxton, Julianna Margulies, Mark Wahlberg.* Paxton's labor of love is a funky little tale of gypsy con artists in the rural South preying on farmers, homeowners, and other unsuspecting victims. Paxton stars as a charismatic loner who takes on a young novice from the outside (Wahlberg). The latter is claiming his birthright; although his father left the group, he's still got traveller blood in his veins. Oscar-winning cinematographer Green makes a fine directing debut, setting a meandering pace and keeping everything low key as Wahlberg learns the tricks of the trade: small cons and simple stings, until an outlaw gypsy with an elaborate ruse lures Paxton on board. For a while this turns into a low-rent variant of *The Sting*, but it never loses its earthy charm or modest focus. —*S. A.*

TREASURE ISLAND **L: DRAMA/INDEPENDENT DRAMA (1999) 86M D: Scott King.** *Lance Baker, Nick Offerman, Jonah Blechman.* Two British cryptographers on San Francisco's Treasure Island naval base concoct an elaborate plot to drop a dead body, stuffed with phony information, off the coast of Japan just before an American invasion at the close of WWII. Despite that intriguing idea, this 1999 Sundance Film Festival Freedom of Expression Award winner soon turns its focus on the sexual fears and fantasies of its two code-cracking leads. Writer/director King doesn't just set the film in 1945, he gives it a whole framing sequence styled in the old Hollywood mode (complete with fake newsreel and shadowy titles sequence). Yet the film is anything but classical. The style is a mix of period perfection and low-budget austerity, while the direction favors a mix of mundane realities and frustrated fantasies. Though it's not exactly haunting, the way the blank corpse comes to life, filled with our heroes' own hidden desires and fears, it is unsettling and genuinely offbeat. —*S. A.*

TULLY **L: DRAMA/INDEPENDENT DRAMA (2000) 102M D: Hilary Birmingham.** *Anson Mount, Glenn Fitzgerald, Julianne Nicholson.* Birmingham earned Best Director and Best Screenplay nominations at the Independent Spirit awards for this low-key story of a Midwest Romeo (Mounts) dealing with his first serious romance while facing the secrets of his family's past. Romeo's a bit like the eponymous *Hud* in a minor key, light on smug cynicism and heavy on recreational romance. Eventually he sparks to his brother's gal pal Ella (red-headed Nicholson), whose sureness, unlike Tully's, comes from a strong an idea of where she's going and what she wants. The revelations of *Tully* (adapted from the short story by Tom McNeal) are not in the plot but in the rhythm of life and the pace of days (brought to life perfectly in the crisp, bright, sunlit photography). Understated performances bring out the quiet dignity of the characters. —*S. A.*

TWIN FALLS IDAHO L: DRAMA/INDEPENDENT DRAMA (1999) 111M D: Michael Polish.

Mark Polish, Michael Polish, Michele Hicks, Jon Gries. A strong directorial debut by Michael Polish (who cowrote and costars with his twin brother Mark), *Twin Falls Idaho* is unlike other films. Its most distinguishing feature is its main characters: Siamese twins (the Polish brothers) in their late twenties. Odd as that might sound, there is a distinct beauty to this film, an almost David Lynch–like revelry beneath the eccentric plot. In lesser hands, *Twin Falls Idaho* could have become a freak show, shocking us just to get a reaction, forsaking character development and plot along the way. Yet it rarely makes a false step, establishing an eerie, intriguing tone early and allowing it to continue through the story's duration. If you let yourself become enchanted and drawn in, it will stay with you long after the final credits. —*C. P.*

UNBREAKABLE L: DRAMA/DRAMA (2000) 107M D: M. Night Shyamalan.

Bruce Willis, Samuel L. Jackson, Robin Wright Penn, Spencer Treat Clark. When Willis survives a spectacular train wreck completely unscathed, he realizes he is one of a rare breed of humans who are nearly indestructible. He meets his opposite in Jackson, a comic book collector so fragile that if he falls his bones shatter. The story and some of its details deliberately mimic comic book superhero formulas. But Shyamalan treats it with a dead seriousness, deliberate pacing, and relative realism that in no way resembles what you would think of as a "comic book movie." *Unbreakable* is an ambitious concept that really pays off, largely due to Shyamalan's almost Kubrickian cleverness in communicating mood through the movements of his camera. One of my favorite touches is a long take of Willis answering questions in a hospital room after the train wreck. In the foreground, out of focus, is the breathing chest of the only other survivor. As the conversation continues, the chest begins to gradually grow red with blood, but it never comes into focus. —*B. T.*

VALLEY OF THE DOLLS L: CLASSIC DRAMA/CLASSIC DRAMA (1967) 123M D: Mark Robson.

Barbara Parkins, Sharon Tate, Patty Duke, Lee Grant, Susan Hayward. A deliriously tacky, endlessly entertaining adaptation of Jacqueline Susann's novel about three beautiful women who dream of stardom but fall victim to Hollywood excesses. Drugs, pornography, unhappy love affairs, egomania, big hair, incurable diseases, wimpy men, suicide, booze, and hysterics of all kinds bring down an all-star cast. Duke is particularly hilarious as a wholesome tomboy who becomes a pill-popping megabitch, and I love her drunken "boobies, boobies, boobies" monologue. Tate is pretty spooky as a vacant, curvaceous blonde who also talks about her "boobies" and ends up starring in soft-core French sex movies. There are two *Valley of the Dolls* TV movies as well as Russ Meyer's parody/nonsequel *Beyond the Valley of the Dolls.* —*S. H.*

WORLD TRAVELER L: DRAMA/INDEPENDENT DRAMA (2002) 103M D: Bart Freundlich.

Billy Crudup, Julianne Moore, Cleavant Derricks, David Keith, James LeGros, Mary McCormack. Cal (Crudup) is an amiable but skin-deep fellow who has surfed through his social life on good looks and charm without ever tossing out the anchor of meaningful engagement. He abandons his wife and child as he tries to outrun his own conscience and self-loathing. It inevitably catches up with him in time to betray, seduce, and abandon everyone he meets along the way, until he finds an even more troubled soul (Moore) living in a fantasy created by unendurable guilt. Freundlich is yet another thirtysomething male director indulging himself in the overworked genre of adult men who flee responsibility, playing the over-age Peter Pan as a tortured romantic rebel. Though well acted and full of nicely crafted moments, this film fails to shed any new light on the subject and neglects the damage left in the wake of Cal's tear. Keith is nicely cast as Crudup's absent father. —*S. A.*

A basic requirement for any story is a character to identify with and/or root for. Even with antiheroes there must be something to like, something that makes you hope they find what they are looking for. The overwhelming problem with *World Traveler* is that it focuses on a character who doesn't deserve our sympathy to begin with, and never earns it along the way. The eventual explanation for his lousy behavior feels a bit tacked on. Thus, aspiring screenwriters would be one of the few groups to whom I'd recommend this film, so they could see how badly a movie will fail if there's nothing to like about the main character. Crudup, a respectable, good-looking actor, couldn't overcome his character's basic narcissistic and unlikable nature purely on his own power, without a good script. And that is why the film, despite a few moments of beauty, a decent soundtrack, and a great performance by Moore, ultimately fails. —*C. P*

XX/XY L: DRAMA/INDEPENDENT DRAMA (2003) 91M D: Austin Chick.

Mark Ruffalo, Kathleen Robertson, Maya Stange, Petra Wright, Kel O'Neill. Coles (Ruffalo) is a commitment-shy animator who, ten years after snapping a college affair off in a cold display of sexual independence, runs into his old flame, Sam (Stange), and finds the embers stirred back to life. Never mind that he's already in a long-term relationship with a devoted, hopeful girlfriend of five years (Wright), Coles likes to keep his options open. It's choosing that's the trouble. Coming off his breakthrough performance in *You Can Count on Me,* Ruffalo brings to Coles his trademark fidgeting discomfort and look of gnawing disappointment. Ruffalo's free-and-easy man-child floats on the surface of relationships with easygoing charm and shrugging resignation. Writer/director Chick, observant and unusually sensitive to the textures of experience, is refreshingly adamant in his refusal to let Coles off the hook with an easy epiphany and painless happily-ever-after. —S.A.

YIDDLE WITH HIS FIDDLE (AKA YIDL MITN FIDL) L: CLASSIC DRAMA/YIDDISH (1936) 92M D: Joseph Green. *Leon Liebgold, Molly Picon, Max Bozyk.* Yiddle with His Fiddle is the first klezmer film ever made (a "klezmer" is a Jewish band paid to play at weddings, etc.). This unique view of Jewish musicians inside Warsaw, Poland, has a plot that evokes not just the music of the time, but also the culture. Yidl is a young woman who plays quite the mean fiddle. She plays in the streets to try to raise money for her poor father. But when the two of them are evicted she devises another plan. Women cannot join klezmer bands, so Yidl dresses as a man with her father's tacit approval. He plays bass, she plays violin, and they pick up a clarinetist on their journeys with whom she slowly falls in love. Wait a minute—doesn't this sound just like *Yentl?* Anyone interested in genuine klezmer music and its prewar culture absolutely must see this film! —N.J.

YOUR FRIENDS & NEIGHBORS L: DRAMA/INDEPENDENT DRAMA (1998) 100M D: Neil LaBute. *Catherine Keener, Ben Stiller, Nastassja Kinski, Aaron Eckhart, Amy Brenneman, Jason Patric.* Following the success of *In the Company of Men,* LaBute continues his ravaging of humanity with this awful, derisive piece. Typical of LaBute, morality and decency have been obliterated in this film, and the rich scum of the earth have taken over with a single-minded mission: to fuck everyone. The bulk of this film centers on Cary (Patric), a cocksure young professional who works out, sweats, and hunts women (beware his monologue where he describes the best sex in the world). LaBute's crummy dialogue and unmotivated camera bring little value here, neither in content or presentation. If this is a directorial comment on the present human condition, or lack thereof, I'd rather go howl at the moon. —J.D.

ZIGZAG L: DRAMA/INDEPENDENT DRAMA (2002) 101M D: David S. Goyer. *Wesley Snipes, Natasha Lyonne, Sam Jones III, Oliver Platt, John Leguizamo.* An autistic kid nicknamed ZigZag (Jones) steals money from the diner where he works, and his abusive, crack-addict dad (Snipes) steals the money from him. Not wanting the kid to get in trouble, his Big Brother (Leguizamo) tries to steal the money back from Snipes and return it to the diner. The directorial debut of *Blade* writer Goyer is refreshingly subtle in some aspects. Jones is great; his ZigZag is neither tragic underdog nor savant. He's just a disabled kid people treat like shit. In his small but crucial role, Snipes reminds you of the dramatic acting chops that established him before he started concentrating on action movies. —B.T.

ALL OVER ME L: GAY/GAY (1997) 90M D: Alex Sichel. *Alison Folland, Wilson Cruz, Cole Hauser, Tara Subkoff.* Director Alex Sichel and screenwriter Sylvia Sichel have crafted a rare gem: an introspective coming-of-age tale that treats its characters with respect, understanding, and sensitivity. Two fifteen-year-old girls, best friends from troubled homes, seek comfort and love from one another until they face a crisis of conscience that causes a rift in their relationship. Claude (Folland) is the quiet, introspective one, afraid of her own feelings and suddenly left out when Ellen (Subkoff) starts dating a drug-dealing thug who murders a friend of Claude's. Avoiding the usual dramatic clichés of tense confrontations and explosive shouting matches, the Sichels give their performers room to express themselves quietly, more through actions than words, and more through their faces than their actions. The desperation of adolescence has rarely been presented with so much understated insight. —S.A.

BIG EDEN L: GAY/GAY (2000) 117M D: Thomas Bezucha. *Louise Fletcher, Arye Gross, Eric Schweig, George Coe.* A big film festival award winner, *Big Eden* is a sweet, romantic drama set in a fictional Montana town where the rugged individualists and plain-spoken folk not only accept prodigal gay son Henry (Gross) when he returns home from New York, they play matchmaker as well. While Henry acts on a fumbling attraction to his straight best friend from high school, the shy Native American proprietor (Schweig) of the general store secretly woos Henry through lovingly prepared gourmet meals. The town helps out: they don't care about this closeted gay man's orientation, only his happiness. As a portrait of a homophobia-free heartland the title is right on—this is an Eden, all right. The film may not win points for realism, but it isn't about how things really are, it's a fantasy of a world we'd like to see. —S.A.

BUT I'M A CHEERLEADER L: GAY/GAY (1999) 81M D: Jamie Babbit. *Natasha Lyonne, Eddie Cibrian, Douglas Spain, RuPaul, Cathy Moriarty, Clea DuVall.* Lyonne is Megan Bloomfield, a high school cheerleader who has a few too many pictures of girls laying around, listens to a lot of Melissa Ethridge, and doesn't really enjoy kissing her boyfriend. Before it even occurs to her that she might be a lesbian, her friends and family intervene and send her to True Directions, a camp that will "cure" her and make her straight again. This movie relies solely on stereotypes for its humor, and no one is exempt. Homosexuals, heterosexuals, women, and men, everyone is squeezed into a mold, and in the end, no one really fits. The film definitely has an underlying social commentary, but it is delivered with witty, biting humor that you'll either love or hate. Lyonne ultimately falls in love with DuVall's character, another camper

who needs a little straightening out, and the romantic subplot adds another layer to a movie already trying to say a lot. —*J. S.*

QUEER AS FOLK—THE COMPLETE FIRST SEASON (US VERSION) L: GAY/GAY (2000) 825M D: Alex Chapple.
Randy Harrison, Scott Lowell, Peter Paige, Hal Sparks, Thea Gill, Gale Harold, Sharon Gless. Based on the UK show of the same name, *Queer as Folk* is a funny, endearing, and at times shocking look at the lives of five gay friends living it up in Pittsburgh. The characters are: Brian (Harold), the hunky asshole sexpot we see fuck about fourteen times an episode; Ted (Lowell), an inoffensive, sensitive, aging guy constantly rejected at the clubs but keeps coming back for more; Michael (Sparks), the sweet narrator who is not-so-secretly enamored with Brian; Emmett (Paige), the flamboyant gay stereotype of the group; and Justin (Harrison), the young high school student who become Brian's boy toy. The women of the bunch include Michael's mom, Debbie (Gless), and a couple of lesbians who are raising a baby (fathered by Brian) together. Love, lust, drugs, friendship, a healthy dose of gay issues and politics, with huge amounts of sex make it exciting to watch. —*J. S.*

STICKY FINGERS OF TIME, THE L: GAY/GAY (1997) 82M D: Hilary Brougher *Nicole Zaray, Terumi Matthews, Belinda Becker.* "Where are all the good time-traveling lesbian films nowadays?" the world lamented. And hearing her cries, Brougher delivered. After receiving an envelope containing two severed fingers, Tucker (Matthews), a pulp crime novelist, decides she needs some coffee. But before she can make it to the store, she gets transported forty-five years into the future, to the year 1997. There she meets her doppelganger, Drew (Zaray), and learns she is/was murdered on her way for coffee forty-five years ago, the very same trip that landed her in the future. Could all this have something to do with the atomic bomb test Tucker recently covered, back in 1952? Although this story involves time travel, it contains no elaborate special effects. In fact, the entire film was made on a very small budget. But Brougher uses what she has to great effect without resorting to B-movie cheese. Different eras are easily distinguished by color and black and white film, which may seem hokey, but it leaves you able to concentrate on the characters rather than nuances of time travel. The excellent screenplay combined with an able cast of relative unknowns are the best reasons to see this great, underrated sci-fi noir. —*R. G.*

SWOON L: GAY/GAY (1991) 95M D: Tom Kalin. *Daniel Schlachet, Michael Stumm, Michael Kirby, Ron Vawter, Craig Chester.* This is a stylish, black and white retelling of the notorious Leopold and Loeb's 1924 murder of the young boy Bobby Franks. In many ways the story plays out much like *Crime and Punishment* with two gay men

(Chester and Schlachet as Leopold and Loeb, respectively). The killers' trial reveals very little motive behind the kidnap and murder. By all accounts it would seem the two young men committed the act just to prove to each other it could be done, perhaps as a reprieve from their mundane, upper-class existence. However, homosexuality is clearly seen at the time as being one of the leading factors, and this film attempts to tackle that social prejudice. Kalin's well-made directorial debut is hard to forget. —*N. J.*

TIMES OF HARVEY MILK, THE L: GAY/GAY (1983) 90M D: Robert Epstein. *Harvey Milk.* Winner of the Oscar for Best Feature Documentary in 1983, this film presents the story of Harvey Milk, the first openly gay supervisor for the city of San Francisco. Starting with Milk's humble beginnings at his camera store in the Castro district, the film focuses on his developing taste for politics and race for the supervisor's seat for his district. While Milk's homosexuality is not a problem for Mayor Moscone, it is a major concern to another supervisor, Dan White, a former police officer and born-again Christian. White assassinated both Milk and Muscone, claiming at his trial that he was not responsible for his acitons, having endured a sugar high from eating too many Twinkies. (The veteran cop was given a lenient sentence.) Director Epstein shows the ensuing protests and updates us to the year of filming, 1983) on the status of everyone involved. This film is sensitive yet shocking, a story about the ultimate value of the human spirit and the blatant evil of misplaced morality. —*N. J.*

TWILIGHT GIRLS, THE L: GAY/GAY (1957) 90M D: Radley Metzger. *Agnes Laurent, Christine Carere, Estella Blain.* This saucy French import from the days of early Eurotica, originally imported and dubbed by Radley Metzger for his distribution company, Audubon Films, is one of the French all-girl private school dramas of the 1960s that birthed the notorious American "student nurse" films of the 1970s. It's all there: the hothouse of budding sexuality, crushes on hunky young teachers, and of course the endlessly titillating experiments in lesbian petting. This early entry, about a young woman (Laurent) tempted by the love of a classmate, doesn't have much substance to offer, but it captures a uniquely Gallic mix of teenage girl innocence and eroticism and was initially banned in New York for it's lesbian scenes. Ooh la la! Also notable for the film debut of Catherine Deneuve; at the ripe age of thirteen. —*S. A.*

TELEVISION DRAMA

CORNER, THE L: TELEVISION SHOWS/DRAMA TV (2000) 360M D: Charles Dutton. *T. K. Carter, Khandi Alexander, Sean Nelson, Antonio D. Charity.* Dutton directs this lucid and painfully human portrait of a year set on a drug-dominated corner in the

Baltimore slums. Based on the non-fiction book by former *Homicide* scriptwriter David Simon and Edward Burns, it focuses on the struggles of three members of a family so fractured by life in the slums that hope is replaced by the drive to simply survive. Fran (Alexander) is a functioning addict and single mom, whose desire for a fix gets the best of her need to set an example. Husband Gary (Carter) has left home to live in the streets with a mercenary addict girlfriend, stealing scrap metal to scrape together enough scratch for his next fix. Their hustling teenage son DeAndre (Nelson) is on the verge of following in their footsteps as he slings drugs from the corner. This provocative portrait of the world of poverty and predators and their cycle of self-destruction is told from the inside out. Dutton directs with an empathy that never justifies but lets the viewer understand, and he brings out a raw texture to life on the corner. —*S. A.*

FELICITY—FRESHMAN YEAR COLLECTION L: TELEVISION SHOWS/DRAMA TV (1998) 990M D: Jeffrey Abrams, others.

Keri Russell, Scott Speedman, Scott Foley, Amy Jo Johnson, Tangi Miller, Amanda Foreman. On the day of her high school graduation, Felicity Porter (Russell) makes a rash decision to follow a cute boy (Speedman) she doesn't even know to college in New York. Dumb idea, but exactly the dumb idea she needed at that age. Although *Felicity* aired on the WB, it was sort of an anti–*Dawson's Creek*, with realistic behavior and characters who stammer and mutter instead of deliver fanciful monologues. Felicity is a sympathetic heroine, even when she makes bad decisions, and there is a good cast of believable but colorful supporting characters. Especially likable is her crazy goth roommate Megan (Foreman), who is always afraid Felicity opened her mysterious box while she was gone. A favorite episode is the two-parter "Todd Mulcahy," about a goofy kid from Felicity's childhood who tracks her down, showers her with nostalgia-inducing gifts, and asks her to kiss him to see if they have chemistry. She turns him down harshly, and as he explains that he has not given up yet, he backs into the street and gets nailed by a bus. —*B. T.*

FELICITY—SOPHOMORE YEAR COLLECTION L: TELEVISION SHOWS/DRAMA TV (1999) 990M D: Mark Buckland, others.

Keri Russell, Tangi Miller, Amy Jo Johnson, Scott Foley, Scott Speedman. In the middle of the second season of *Felicity,* star Russell cut her trademark long curly hair short. WB executives publicly blamed dropping ratings on the haircut, despite the fact that they had repeatedly changed the timeslot and even put it up against *The Simpsons*. Despite all this, the show became more confident in its second season, feeling freer to experiment with its format and expand on the weird humor it developed in the first season. (It also delves into some *90210*-style subject matter like Ben's gambling addiction, but oh well.) —*B. T.*

MY SO-CALLED LIFE L: TELEVISION SHOWS/DRAMA TV (1994) 1140M D: Various.

Claire Danes, Jared Leto, Bess Armstrong, Wilson Cruz. Danes is Angela, a fifteen-year-old dealing with parents, slutty addict friends, closeted homosexuals with shitty parents and emotional baggage, prissy perfect princesses with '80s bangs and stupid boyfriends, and nerdy, nosy neighbors who just happen to be in love with her. An average day in the life of a teenage girl, right? Or better said, an average day in the so-called life of a teenage girl. This show was great because every single character was fucked up, Angela's problems were all realistic, and conflicts and tension never just suddenly fixed themselves and disappeared. Danes is excellent as the angst-ridden, bratty, emotional Angela, and the supporting cast is great as well. Too bad there are only nineteen episodes. —*J. S.*

SIX FEET UNDER—THE COMPLETE FIRST SEASON L: TELEVISION SHOWS/DRAMA TV (2001) 780M D: Various.

Peter Krause, Michael C. Hall, Frances Conroy, Lauren Ambrose, Rachel Griffiths, Freddy Rodriguez. HBO's hit series is based on the trials and tribulations of a family who operates a funeral home following the accidental death of their husband and father. The writing and acting are excellent: between the psycho girlfriend character; the closeted gay, religious brother; the tragic, misunderstood daughter; the frigid, sexually repressed mother; and the brother who has begrudgingly inherited part of the business, the plot leaves nothing to be desired. —*J. S.*

24—SEASON ONE L: TELEVISION SHOWS/DRAMA TV (2001) 24 hours D: Jon Cassar, others.

Kiefer Sutherland, Dennis Haysbert, Leslie Hope, Elisha Cuthbert. 24 is a great action movie that just happens to be twenty-four hours long (in real time) and a TV show. This will not stop you from watching it as if it were one movie, though. Sutherland gives his best performance as Jack Bauer, who works for a fictional government agency, CTU (Counter Terrorist Unit). His daughter is kidnapped and the whirlwind plot about presidential assassination, betrayal, and personal vendettas begins and doesn't let up for the next twenty-three hours or so. The story is full of twists and surprises, and each episode ends with a brilliant cliffhanger, which means you "have to" see the next episode. You'll save yourself much lost sleep if you take it all at once, trust me. —*K. C.*

WEST WING, THE—THE COMPLETE FIRST SEASON L: TELEVISION SHOWS/DRAMA TV (2000) 16 hours D: Various.

Rob Lowe, Moria Kelly, Dule Hill, Richard Schiff, Allison Janney, John Spencer, Martin Sheen, Bradley Whitford. *The West Wing* follows the trials and numerous tribulations of the White House senior staff under the so-liberal-he-must-be-fictional President Josiah Bartlett (Sheen). This first season introduces the ensemble and throws them hard into the political arena. Sheen and the rest of the cast hit the ground running; they work out the usual first season awkwardness quickly, so by the fifth or sixth episode the dynamics are set and the actors seem comfortable with their characters. The highlight of this show is creator Aaron Sorkin's writing. His scripts paint a broad picture of partisan politics, government issues, and citizenship, then fill in the details with well-drawn characters and agile dialogue. Sorkin's attention to detail, along with strong and enthusiastic performances, make *The West Wing* a powerful program. Two standout episodes are "Take This Sabbath Day," where the president struggles to decide whether he should grant a stay to a prisoner due to be executed, and "In Excelsis Deo," a poignant Christmas episode about a funeral for a homeless veteran. —*J.K.*

CHAPTER SIX

Documentaries

Filmmakers want to tell stories. Some do it with fiction, and some fictions are based on actual events. But documentary filmmakers tell their tales using the real stories of real people or real events, filmed in real time. These filmmakers then do what any other filmmaker does: they edit together all the collected pieces of their stories and then weave them into a whole. Are documentaries objective? No, not entirely. But the best documentarians tend to allow the stories they focus upon to tell themselves, to reveal their own truths. Presenting truth, by presenting answers or by framing questions, is the goal. Revealing truth to the viewers, or clarifying these questions, is the method.

Some directors are better than others. Some subjects are better than others. Some films are surprising, others are disappointing. In short, you can expect just about anything when it comes to documentaries. From collectors of 8-track tapes to teenage Texans struggling to make a drill team; from deep-sea life in the trenches of the Pacific Ocean to the different monkey cultures of the world's jungles, you will never walk away from a selection of documentaries empty-handed.

Can't find a fiction film to watch? Trust us, in the documentary section, you will always find something you'll want to see. This chapter also includes a few fictionalized portrayals of nonfiction subjects, such as the civil rights movement.

Hell House (2001)

AMERICAN PIMP L: DOCUMENTARIES/AMERICAN CULTURE (1999) 87M D: Albert Hughes, Allen Hughes. While researching an adaptation of Iceberg Slim's autobiography *Pimp: The Story of My Life*, it occurred to the Hughes Brothers that the conversations they were having with real pimps were more interesting than any dramatization could be. So they decided to instead make this documentary where pimps and prostitutes (only some of them reformed) explain "The Game" to the outside world. Some have criticized the directors for not providing a counterargument to the pimps, but the interviews are so extreme that trying to point that out to the audience would insult its intelligence. Most of the pimps are very charismatic—still, part of what makes them appealing is their complete cluelessness. With their outlandish clothes, their awards banquets, and their sentences that both begin and end with "bitch," they show that their world is as insular and silly as those of *Trekkies* or *Beyond the Mat*. HBO's documentary *Pimp's Up, Ho's Down* is also interesting, but *American Pimp* has more cinematic photography and a great '70s funk and soul soundtrack. —*B. T.*

ATOMIC CAFE, THE L: DOCUMENTARIES/ATOMIC DOCS (1982) 88M D: Kevin Rafferty, Jayne Loader, Pierce Rafferty.

The Atomic Cafe is little more than a compilation of U.S. government propaganda during the Cold War in the '50s, with pointers on how to protect yourself in the event of a nuclear bomb exploding nearby. Today, post-Chernobyl, all of this information and advice is clearly useless and potentially dangerous, but you still have to love the animated turtle who tells you what to do when you see the bright flash in the sky (duck and cover). And, of course, with a little song we get to see the turtle demonstrate while children follow his example. Feel safer yet? Neither do I. But this film goes far to explain the whole American culture of the time we thought we could simply live with the bomb. —*N. J.*

AWFUL TRUTH, THE: THE FIRST SEASON VOL. 1 L: DOC. DIRECTORS/MOORE, MICHAEL (1999) 100M D: Michael Moore.

Made for the Bravo network, this is sort of an extension of what Moore was trying on network TV with *TV Nation,* with the only major format change being the addition of a live audience there with Moore between the taped segments. Many people who hate Moore say that he is just taking cheap shots, surprise-attacking receptionists instead of tackling the real villains. I would point them to "HMO Funeral," about a man suffering from cancer of the pancreas whose HMO uses a loophole in their policy to avoid giving him the transplant he needs to live. With Moore's help, the man goes to the HMO's corporate headquarters to mock-happily invite everyone to his funeral. You do feel sorry for the receptionists, who obviously aren't responsible for the decision, but then you wonder what the company would have to do before they would feel guilty working for them. And at the end of the segment it is revealed that the stunt caused the company to relent, so the man is alive and well in the studio audience. How can you dismiss a show that is extremely entertaining, asks profound questions, and even *saves a man's life*? I think at the point where it saves a man's life it is safe to say this is a great TV series. —*B. T.*

BEHIND THE VEIL: NUNS L: DOCUMENTARIES/WOMEN'S DOCS (1984) 131M D: Margaret Wescott. *Gloria Demers (narrator).*

Nuns are so far removed from popular culture today that they seem almost on the same level as fairy tale characters. On a logical level, we know they do exist, but it's a lifestyle that most of us can't relate to at all. What do they *do* in those cloisters? And how could *anyone* take a vow to go the rest of her life without having sex? The rest of your life is a really, really long time. This documentary takes a candid, interesting look at what exactly it means to be a nun, and what life in the cloister is like. As opposed to simply looking at the religious, devotional side of being a nun, *Behind the Veil* looks at nuns as individual people, as women with passions, desires, and full, fruitful lives. And yes, there is even some discussion of that whole sex thing. —*J. S.*

BEYOND THE MAT L: SPORTS/WRESTLING (1999) 144M D: Barry Blaustein.

Blaustein, writer of *Police Academy 2* and the Eddie Murphy *Nutty Professor* movies, somehow also directed this fascinating documentary about the business of professional wrestling. Best-selling author/Leatherface-themed-wrestler Mick Foley steals the show, contrasting his seemingly normal family life with his insane wrestling antics. You learn that although it's all acting, it's also very dangerous; in perhaps the most memorable scene, Foley's wife and children cry in horror as they watch him get hit over the head with a chair. There is also a tragic look at the life of Jake "The Snake" Roberts, who was once a superstar but now wrestles in high school gyms and is addicted to crack and sex. Blaustein's quasi–Michael Moore narration gets grating, but it's all so interesting you're left wishing there were whole movies about each of the characters. —*B. T.*

BIGGIE AND TUPAC L: DOC. DIRECTORS/BROOMFIELD, NICK (2002) 107M D: Nick Broomfield.

Beginning with a rare photo showing the two murdered rappers together, Broomfield attempts to trace how Tupac Shakur and the Notorious B.I.G. went from being friends to enemies who were separately shot to death. He interviews many of their friends and relatives (including Biggie's outspoken mother, Voletta Wallace), their former security guards, and most interestingly former LAPD detective Russell Poole, head investigator of the Biggie case. Poole becomes the center of the story because he uncovered evidence that both murders were arranged by Death Row Records CEO Suge Knight and carried out by corrupt LA cops who were also mixed up in the notorious Rampart scandals. His theories are laid out in more detail in the book *Labyrinth.* There are some great characters and some surprising moments, particularly the jaw-dropping climax where Broomfield shows up uninvited at the penitentiary and proceeds to interview Knight (who we've been hearing horror stories about for the entire movie). For the most part this is a crime story, but it's also a human story about the tragically short lives of two talented and charismatic people. —*B. T.*

BLIND SPOT: HITLER'S SECRETARY L: DOCUMENTARIES/NAZIS (2002) 87M D: André Heller, Othmar Schmiderer.

In 1942, Traudl Junge was an apolitical twenty-two-year-old German woman chosen from a clerical pool to work as one of Adolf Hitler's private secretaries. For three years she handled his personal correspondence and followed him to the bunker, shielded from the reality of the outside world (in the center of the hurricane of the Third Reich, she was actually in a "blind spot"). In 2001 she broke her fifty-plus-year silence with an interview stripped bare of excuses and justification, and directors Heller and Schmiderer match her naked honesty by stripping away every barrier between subject and audience. The distance between the discomforting nostalgia for Hitler's paternal warmth and the acknowledgment of her personal responsibility is collapsed into the bracing portrait of a woman taking responsibility for her inaction and still trying to forgive herself for being charmed into passive complicity. In light of Leni Reifenstahl's death in 2003, denying her complicity to her grave, Frau Junge's stand feels all the more courageous, honest, and astounding. —*S. A.*

BLOOD IN THE FACE L: DOCUMENTARIES/NAZIS (1991) 78M D: Anne Bohlen, Kevin Rafferty, James Ridgeway. *Blood in the Face* is a rather straightforward documentary about white supremacists in Idaho. A variety of them are interviewed at length and some even allow the filmmakers into their meeting halls, where there's a bust of Hitler and other Nazi memorabilia adorning the walls. A "well-organized militia" is also interviewed, which is just a few guys who are anything but organized. At one point an older man, sensing that the filmmakers were not completely in sympathy with his racial views, explains one important thing that distinguishes blacks from whites: he says that with black skin a person cannot blush, therefore he can lie and it wouldn't register in his face. For anyone new to the world of white supremacists, this documentary will be sure to give you a shock. —*N. J.*

BOWLING FOR COLUMBINE L: DOC. DIRECTORS/MOORE, MICHAEL (2002) 119M D: Michael Moore. It's a constitutionally protected freedom that all of us as Americans are entitled to: the right to bear arms. This documentary takes a candid, critical look at what this freedom really means, and how warped the American conception of protection has become. Filmed in the aftermath of the Columbine shootings, Moore interviews NRA officials, average citizens, and the people connected to some of the Columbine victims to substantiate his overall point—guns fucking suck. Although I agree with this fact, the main problem I had was that rather than fighting for the people most adversely affected by current gun laws, namely the children who are injured and killed by gun shots each year, it seems like Moore exploits them for the sake of making a point. This aside, however, I think *Bowling for Columbine* effectively illustrates that guns are tragic, and it's not really Charlton Heston who has to feel the impact of this. —*J. S.*

BOYCOTT L: DOCUMENTARIES/CIVIL RIGHTS (2001) 118M D: Clark Johnson. *Carmen Ejogo, Jeffrey Wright, Terrence DaShon Howard, CCH Pounder. Basquiat's* Wright stars as Rev. Martin Luther King in this powerful made-for-cable historical drama about the Montgomery Bus Boycott, the first volley in the modern civil rights struggle. He plays King as a modest young minister thrust into the leadership of what was expected to be a short citywide protest. Wright is rousing on the pulpit, capturing King's charisma and fiery oratory skills. He draws his resolve from the thousands of heroes who hold the boycott fast, the strength of the people "doing the walking," and the network of ministers, activists, and political leaders who overcome dissension and differences. That's the strength of this astounding film portrait as well. As rousing as King's speeches are, the film isn't about words but action: the courage and commitment of ordinary people moved to extraordinary action and resolve in the face of intimidation, harassment, and violence. Director Johnson fills the film with experience, as if trying to bring a legendary event down to earth, to ground history in the experience of the people involved in it at all levels. —*S. A.*

BRANDON TEENA STORY, THE L: DOCUMENTARIES/ AMERICAN CULTURE (1998) 88M D: Susan Muska, Gréta Olafsdottir. The real-life story on which the dramatic film interpretation *Boys Don't Cry* was based, this documentary packs a serious emotional punch and is extremely difficult to watch more than once. Teena Brandon was brutally raped and murdered by a couple of young men who were a part of the circle of friends that she had convinced she was a young man named Brandon Teena. Much more matter-of-fact than the movie interpretation, the sensitive nature of the documentary leaves the viewer feeling a little uncomfortable and extremely shocked at the intensity of this hate crime. Told predominantly through interviews with the people who knew her (including her female lover) and trial footage, this documentary simply gives you the facts and allows you to sit back and feel their emotional impact. —*J. S.*

BRIEF HISTORY OF TIME, A L: DOC. DIRECTORS/MORRIS, ERROL (1992) 85M D: Errol Morris. I first watched this film in my high school physics class. It starts out with a star field, then Stephan Hawking's computer-generated voice comes in, asking, "Which came first, the chicken or the egg?" Then, a chicken pops up from the bottom of the screen. Everyone laughed and I was hooked. Morris balances the story of Stephen Hawking's life and work with explorations of questions usually reserved for drug-induced ramblings at parties. When did the universe start? When will it end? What would happen if you jumped into a black hole? For the answer to that question, Hawking quotes Dante, saying, "Abandon all hope, ye who enter here." The one that gets to me the most is, "When the universe starts to contract, will we remember tomorrow?" Morris presents Hawking's story with interviews from his family (including his mother, Isobel), colleagues,

Les Blank

Les Blank is an anthropological documentarian whose camera eye frequently rests on peripheral pockets of rich ethnic culture. Born in Tampa, Florida, Blank set off on his road to independent filmmaking by earning degrees in theater and English literature from Tulane University in New Orleans, followed by a PhD in film from USC. To finance his first films—*Dizzy Gillespie* (1964), *God Respects Us When We Work But Loves Us When We Dance* (1968), and *The Blues According to Lightnin' Hopkins* and *The Sun's Gonna Shine* (both 1969)—Blank hired out his skills, making promotional documentaries for companies and organizations such as Holly Farms Poultry, Archway Cookies, and the National Wildlife Federation.

Early in his career, Blank set the tone for the intimate portraits he was to become known for—whimsical, anthropological studies of people who derive pleasure from their traditions of music, food, and various modes of creativity. He has taken as his subjects rural Louisiana French musicians and cooks (*Yum Yum Yum!* [1990], *J'ai Été Au Bal Went to the Dance* [1989], *Always for Pleasure* [1978], *Dry Wood* [1973], *Hot Pepper* [1973], *Spend It All* [1972], and *Marc and Ann* [1991]), San Francisco garlic fiends (*Garlic Is As Good As Ten Mothers* [1980]), and every type of ethnic music that has settled in North America, from Serbian to Polish, Hawaiian to Cuban (*Ziveli: Medicine for the Heart* [1987], *Puamana* [1991], *Sworn to the Drum* [1995], *In Heaven There Is No Beer?* [1984]), as well as more traditional Americana such as Appalachian fiddlers (*Sprout Wings and Fly* [1983]) and Texas bluesmen (*A Well Spent Life* [1971], *Cigarette Blues* [1984]).

The poetic lamentations and unique Southwestern streetscapes, with their contrasts of breezy pastel colors and peeling paint, form the heart of *Del Mero Corazón* (1979) and *Chulas Fronteras* (1976), Blank's observations of Mexican American life. *Gap-Toothed Women* (1987) examines the mythology and mystique surrounding women with diastemas. A colorful cast of characters (including actress/cover-girl Lauren Hutton and the late comic artist Dori Seda) discuss/dismiss notions that gap-toothed women are more artistic or more sexually proficient, and probe misguided standards of beauty.

Werner Herzog Eats His Shoe (1980) documents Herzog's fulfillment of a strange promise to budding director Errol Morris: upon completion of Morris's film *Gates of Heaven*, Herzog would voluntarily eat his own shoe.

Blank's seminal work is *Burden of Dreams* (1982), which details the myriad difficulties that plagued Herzog's production of *Fitzcarraldo*—from on-set casualties and tribal wars to Klaus Kinski's threat to murder the director. *Burden of Dreams* may be the greatest movie about the making of a movie—most others of its ilk pale drastically in comparison. The real curiosity in Blank's catalog, however, may be his surreal documentation of a *Huey Lewis and the News* video shoot in Hawaii (*Be-FORE*, 1986).

Blank has also been a creative force, either as cameraman or editor, on many films by other well-known visionaries, including *Easy Rider* and Dusan Makavejev's *Hole in the Soul* (1995). In 1990, Les Blank received the American Film Institute's Maya Deren Award for outstanding lifetime achievement as an independent filmmaker.　　　　　*—Kier-La Janisse*

and Hawking himself. From his childhood to his marriage to his deteriorating health and ever-inquisitive research projects, we learn about the universe both around us and inside Hawking's mind. —*J. K.*

BURDEN OF DREAMS L: DOC. DIRECTORS/BLANK, LES (1982) 94M D: Les Blank. The making of *Fitzcaraldo* is documented in this fascinating film. Director Blank followed this very unique production deep into the Amazon and caught director Werner Herzog's and actor Klaus Kinski's reactions to many of the problems that plagued the shooting of the film. The main difficulty of the production was the attempt to haul a steamship over a mountain, a feat accomplished largely with the assistance of the native people. But of primary interest is the tumultuous relationship between Herzog and Kinski and what they say about each other in the heat of the jungle, giving rise to a variety of curious anecdotes. To properly balance this film with the benefit of hindsight, one should listen to the audio commentary with Werner Herzog and Norman Hill on the DVD of *Fitzcaraldo* by Anchor Bay Video. Of further interest is the documentary *My Best Fiend,* which presents Herzog's postmortem on the life of Kinski. —*N. J.*

CANADIAN BACON L: DOC. DIRECTORS/MOORE, MICHAEL (1994) 95M D: Michael Moore. *Alan Alda, John Candy, Rhea Perlman, Kevin Pollack, Rip Torn, Kevin O'Connor.* Whenever a president seems to be invading a country to get people to forget about a scandal or a poor economy, people tend to refer to it as a "wag the dog" situation, after the movie of the same title. But I think of it more in terms of this broad comedy about suicidal laid-off factory workers set off by a new Cold War against Canada. As absurd and exaggerated as the premise is, the pro-war propaganda depicted in the movie is not all that far from what we saw on TV leading up to the invasions of Iraq both before and after this film was made. There are too many cheap jokes about Canadian stereotypes and the whole feel is pretty cheesy, despite the best efforts of cinematographer Haskell Wexler and composer Elmer Bernstein. But Moore says he was going for something in between *Dr. Strangelove* and *Animal House,* and I think he landed somewhere in that general vicinity for this, his only attempt at a fiction film so far. —*B. T.*

CANE TOADS L: DOC. DIRECTORS/LEWIS, MARK (1988) 65M D: Mark Lewis. When Australian scientists decided to introduce the cane toad into their environment as a way to get rid of the cane beetles that were destroying their crops, they had no idea what they were getting into. The toads not only didn't get rid of the cane beetles, but someone forgot to tell those crazy Australians that cane toads like nothing more than to make baby cane toads. So the toads get their groove on, and now you've got lots and lots of cane toads. They spend all of their time fucking and eating everything but the cane beetles, and the poison in their skin keeps anything except cars from preying on them. This comical documentary explores how Australians dealt with the aftermath of purposely introducing a worthless creature into their environment, and by the end you'll have to decide for yourself whether you feel more like running one over or dressing it like a doll and keeping it as a pet. —*J. S.*

CAPTURING THE FRIEDMANS L: DOCUMENTARIES/ AMERICAN CULTURE (2002) 107M D: Andrew Jarecki. Child pornography found in the home of schoolteacher Arnold Friedman leads to the arrests of Arnold and his son Jesse on dozens of counts of child molestation. This documentary exposé covers the story through a tapestry of testimonies and evidence. Given the passionate reactions these accusations provoke, objectivity is scarce, and the film never allows us to know—even intuitively—what did or did not happen. What makes this documentary notable is the bizarre fact that Arnold's family compulsively filmed its intense "family meetings" throughout the ordeal. Although unquestionably compelling, there's an inescapable feeling that this footage really isn't something we should be seeing—that there is something skewed in our desire to watch it, in the Friedmans' willingness to expose it, and its packaging as entertainment. And yet this is what makes for a great film that the audience can't shake for weeks. —*C. B.*

CHRISTO'S VALLEY CURTAIN L: DOC. DIRECTORS/MAYSLES BROTHERS (1973) 28M D: Albert Maysles, David Maysles, Ellen Giffard. If you don't know who Christo is, you've probably heard jokes about him. He's the Bulgarian-born, New York–based artist known for wrapping, surrounding, or draping things in fabric—not just small objects, but whole buildings and landmasses. First he makes a series of drawings, paintings, photo collages, and models of what the piece will look like, then he sells those pieces to fund construction of the temporary installation. In this first in a series of Maysles films about Christo and his wife/partner, Jeanne-Claude, the project is 142,000 square feet of orange nylon, peaking at 365 feet tall, stretched across a valley in Rifle, Colorado. It requires a crew of thirty-five construction workers and sixty-four other helpers. The Maysles intercut quiet scenes of Christo alone in his studio with dramatic scenes of him pacing around angrily yelling, "PULL!" as workers risk their lives suspended hundreds of feet in the air to put up the curtain. Most of the entertainment in this film comes from the culture clash between the heavily accented artist following a vision and the working-class Coloradans just doing a job. Some of the workers sit around talking shit about Christo and about how drunk they're going to get afterward, but when it's done they say it's beautiful and give him hugs. (Followed by *Running Fence*.) —*B.T.*

CHRISTO'S RUNNING FENCE L: DOC. DIRECTORS/MAYSLES BROTHERS (1978) 58M D: Albert Maysles, David Maysles, Charlotte Mitchell Zwerin. This second Maysles film about the installation artist Christo (after *Christo's Valley Curtain*) follows his quest to build a temporary 24-mile-long, 18-foot-tall white nylon fence in rural California. This time the drama is centered around obtaining the legal right to do the project. He's going to put $2 million of his own money into the county but he has to first convince them to give him the permits. For some reason, people find the project threatening, so at the public hearings the locals angrily declare that the fence is not art and that Christo is an idiot. It's very moving when more sympathetic ranchers (encouraged, I'm sure, by the money they will get for letting him use their property) defend him at a later hearing. Environmental concerns threaten to shut down the project even after it has begun, making for a tense construction. In the end, all the fighting seems to dissolve when you see and hear the fence fluttering and pinging in the wind, following the natural contour of the land. Note that the opening uses a version of the Rolling Stones song "Wild Horses," a reference to one of the most famous Maysles films, *Gimme Shelter*. (Followed by *Christo's Islands*.) —*B.T.*

CHRISTO'S ISLANDS L: DOC. DIRECTORS/MAYSLES BROTHERS (1983) 57M D: Albert Maysles, David Maysles, Charlotte Mitchell Zwerin. In the third Maysles film about Christo (after *Christo's Valley Curtain* and *Running Fence*) the ambitious installation artist attempts three projects: wrapping the Pont Neuf, wrapping the Reichstag, and surrounding a series of islands outside of Miami with floating fabric in shapes reminiscent of lily pads. Like *Running Fence*, most of the film documents the bureaucratic process of getting permission, this time facing a passionately divided Miami City Council and politicians including then-mayor of Paris Jacques Chirac. After much negotiation and debate about "the legitimacy of the art form itself," as one city council member puts it, the Paris and Berlin projects have to wait, but Christo and his collaborators do succeed in placing 6.5 million square feet of pink woven polypropylene fabric around eleven islands. Christo compares his work to a rainbow—if you're lucky, you get to see it before it's gone. The end result is beautiful, but the film is not so much about capturing that image as it is about forcing people to reexamine their definition of art. (Followed by *Christo in Paris*.) —*B.T.*

CHRISTO IN PARIS L: DOC. DIRECTORS/MAYSLES BROTHERS (1990) 58M D: Albert Maysles, Deborah Dickson, Susan Fromke, David Maysles. The fourth Maysles film about Christo begins near the Pont Neuf in Paris, where lovers admire the bridge and artists

paint it. The opening perfectly encapsulates this most intimate entry in the series, which documents the wrapping of the Pont Neuf (a project begun in the previous film, *Islands*), but also tells us more than before about Christo as he and his wife/partner, Jeanne-Claude, reminisce about their lives together. We even get to see Jeanne-Claude's mother, a duchess, tell the story of how she hired Christo to paint her portrait, at which point Jeanne-Claude called him "another one of mother's stray dogs." Like the other films in the series, this is also a thought-provoking essay about the meaning of art, and in the most impressive scenes we see crowds standing on the wrapped Pont Neuf, passionately debating its merits with strangers. (Followed by *Christo's Umbrellas*.) —*B.T.*

CHRISTO'S UMBRELLAS L: DOC. DIRECTORS/MAYSLES BROTHERS (1994) 90M D: Henry Corra, Grahame Weinbren, Albert Maysles. In the last and longest Maysles film about Christo, the artist and his wife/partner, Jeanne-Claude, try their most expensive and ambitious project to date: placing hundreds of giant blue umbrellas in Japan, then flying to California to set up yellow ones. This time there's no trouble getting permission, and no debate about whether or not what they're doing is art. Christo is treated with complete reverence; many of the locals are either afraid to talk to him or amazed at how approachable he is, and once the umbrellas are opened the people start to cry. The central question is whether Christo's work is selfish, or if perhaps he's even defying nature by decorating the environment with his artificial creations. While he's in the serene California desert enjoying the sun shining on the umbrellas, poor Jeanne-Claude is left in Japan with a small crew trying to save the umbrellas from a typhoon. Incredibly, a freak windstorm later hits the California section as well. It's a depressing and tragic end to the series, but as always, the gorgeous images of the final work seem to brush away the rest of the world and leave you in Christo's place of irrationality, enjoying the unusual sight of hundreds of enormous umbrellas. —*B.T.*

COVERUP—BEHIND THE IRAN-CONTRA AFFAIR L: DOCUMENTARIES/POLITICS (1988) 76M D: Barbara Trent, David Kasper. This film mainly covers the many atrocities the United States orchestrated during the Reagan-Bush years. We learn about the CIA's involvement in cocaine trafficking, how Reagan deliberately delayed the release of hostages in Iran to coincide with his inauguration, and that the CIA once had plans to round up and detain political dissidents in the U.S. Such extreme allegations could be dismissed as leftist propaganda/paranoia. *Coverup*, however, nicely retains integrity by avoiding narration and relying almost entirely on interviews with such impressive inside sources as U.S. Congressmen (both Dem. and Rep.), Reagan-Bush campaign managers, formerly high-ranking CIA operatives, and *New York Times* editors. Archived press conference footage also shows the likes of Reagan and North idiotically incriminating themselves. An easy way to bone up on some of the horrors of recent American history. —*C. B.*

CROCODILE HUNTER: COLLISION COURSE L: DOCUMENTARIES/NATURE DOCS (2002) 89M D: John Stainton.
Steve Irwin, the excitable Aussie who throws himself into his hit TV nature programs with the physical abandon of a schoolboy rugby star, leaps, dives, and wrestles his way onto the big screen without ever noticing his change of venue or the spy movie that has invaded his nature show. Director Stainton ping-pongs between the two like he's channel surfing between the Discovery Channel and a late-night made-for-cable action movie. If the conceit is clever—the competing movies don't mesh so much as collide, refusing even to acknowledge the other when they inevitably overlap—the execution is flatfooted and painfully amateur. If you like Irwin's acrobatic brand of stand-up naturalism, then this is your film. Otherwise it's dumb, mate. Real dumb. —*S. A.*

CRUISE, THE L: DOCUMENTARIES/AMERICAN CULTURE (1981) 76M D: Bennett Miller.
Timothy "Speed" Levitch whines through a Gershwin tune to kick off his bus tour of New York City, then proceeds to spin a spiel of historical oddities and offbeat observations. His nasal voice cuts through the traffic din, and the rim-shot click of his microphone punctuates his punch lines. I have no idea how many of his foreign tourists follow even half of what he's saying, but Levitch raises the level of tour guide commentary to performance art in what are easily the most entertaining moments of the film. Get him off the bus, though, and he becomes another New York character. Do we really want to know this much about a bohemian street poet who has orgasms at the sight of terra-cotta brocades on Big Apple architecture? Levitch is never less than entertaining and for such a modest documentary portrait, perhaps that's enough. —*S. A.*

DARK DAYS L: DOCUMENTARIES/AMERICAN CULTURE (2000) 81M D: Marc Singer.
Amazingly intimate documentary about the "mole people" living in a shantytown beneath the New York subways. They take great pride in their tiny cardboard houses, most of which are actually hooked up to electricity. Director Singer was already accepted into the community when it occurred to him he could learn how to use cameras and make a movie about his friends. As a result the subjects seem incredibly candid and open. They discuss their drug addictions, family troubles, even their methods of cooking rats. It's an upclose look at human despair, but never fear—the ending is surprisingly upbeat. —*B. T.*

DERBY L: SPORTS/ROLLER DERBY (1971) 91M D: Robert Kaylor.
Little-known documentary ostensibly about the world of roller derby but more about American culture in the early '70s. It starts out following a factory worker who decides to quit his job and pursue professional roller derby with the blessings of his supportive wife. Later, he casually reveals on-camera that he cheats on his wife, and it gets weirder from there. Reminiscent of everything from the Maysles Brothers to *Gummo*, it only stumbles in a few awkward scenes that appear to be staged. —*B. T.*

DEVIL'S PLAYGROUND L: DOCUMENTARIES/AMERICAN CULTURE (2002) 77M D: Lucy Walker.
At the age of sixteen, Amish children are let out of the confines of their world and begin "rumspringe," the time in which they must choose whether they want to remain within the Amish community and join the church, or leave and become part of the world at large. This documentary follows several different Amish kids as they drink, smoke, party, and sleep around, all in an effort to decide whether these things will be a part of their future. The hands-off and strictly observational approach used in filming makes for a candid, unbiased look at what this type of experience might be like, and at no point does it seem obvious what choice the kids are going to make. What choice is really for the best? At the end, you find out that an extremely large percentage of Amish children decide to join the church after their rumspringe, and it really doesn't come as much of a surprise. —*J. S.*

DOGTOWN AND Z-BOYS L: SPORTS/SKATEBOARDS & SKATING (2001) 91M D: Stacy Peralta.
Sean Penn (narrator). More than simply a portrait of early extreme sports, this hotdogging, high-flying, and at times airborne peek into the '70s skateboard revolution is as much social anthropology as skateboard documentary. The Z-Boys are the Zephyr Skate Team, a misfit family of aggressive surf rats in Dogtown, the crumbling barrio of south Santa Monica and Venice Beach. Turning to sidewalk surfing on homemade boards, they re-created a practically dead sport with their own style and attitude, incubated it in the isolation of their insular "dirty, filthy paradise," and unleashed it on the youth culture of America like a virus. Director Peralta was also one of the most influential Z-Boys and a pioneer of the wild-style skate video. He's hardly an objective observer and he tends to inflate the cultural impact these rough and ready barrio kids had on the world at large, but his personal connection makes for a passionate and often playful piece of nonfiction cinema. Set to a bracing soundtrack of '70s rock and roll and driven with an amped-up, jittery cinema graffiti style, this collision of skate punk and pop culture archeology is riveting slice of cultural history. —*S. A.*

EYES OF TAMMY FAYE, THE L: DOCUMENTARIES/AMERICAN CULTURE (2000) 80M D: Randy Barbato, Fenton Bailey. Truly, this is a remarkable documentary. Tammy Faye was the eccentric wife to the high-profile TV evangelist Jim Bakker, and through extensive interviews with her and lots of footage from their popular *PTL* (or *Praise the Lord*) show, many of the sordid events of the Christian TV industry are exposed. Things are explained chronologically with a young Bakker getting his own show on Pat Robertson's Christian TV channel while Tammy Faye was still doing puppetry. Jim, however, was a visionary and wanted to expand the function of Christian TV. He created the *700 Club*, a Christian news source that Robertson soon stole from Bakker. Undaunted, the Bakkers got their own channel and even raised enough money to launch a satellite. Soon their *PTL* show became extremely popular. Jerry Falwell steps in, sets up Bakker with a hooker, then accuses him of being homosexual. Bakker goes to prison, Falwell gets the satellite. Sounds like nice God-fearing men? Behind all that makeup, Tammy Faye can fill you in with painful accuracy. —*N. J.*

FALLEN CHAMP: THE UNTOLD STORY OF MIKE TYSON L: DOC. DIRECTORS/KOPPLE, BARBARA (1993) 93M D: Barbara Kopple. I keep thinking of George Carlin's line regarding the U.S. government's position on Muhammad Ali's imprisonment for resistance to the Vietnam War ("Well, if you won't kill people, we won't let you beat them up."), and I wonder if we should be letting people beat each other up at all. Academy Award–winning documentarian Kopple dares you to look at the strange engines that drove boxing, Tyson, and our culture down a very unpretty road. —*K. S.*

FAST, CHEAP, AND OUT OF CONTROL L: DOC. DIRECTORS/ MORRIS, ERROL (1997) 82M D: Errol Morris. Morris's passionate celebration of four modern-day iconoclasts-two keeping alive eccentrically antiquated art forms (lion tamer Dave Hoover and topiary gardener George Mendonca), two engrossed in admittedly arcane scientific exploration (insect-influenced robot designer Rodney Brooks and the world's foremost expert on the blind, bald mole rat, Ray Mendez)—is perhaps his most unusual documentary to date. That's saying a lot for the nonfiction rebel. Cutting between his devoted dreamers and their work, interspersed with offbeat imagery set to a calliope-gone-mad score (Caleb Sampson doing his best Philip Glass impression), it's less essay than elusive exploration of the creative drive. Perhaps Morris sees something of himself in these four. Label him the fifth dreamer. —*S. A.*

FEED L: DOCUMENTARIES/MEDIA (1992) 80M D: Kevin Rafferty, James Ridgeway. This unique, somewhat hypnotic documentary tells the story of the 1992 New Hampshire presidential primary through found footage from live feeds of the candidates before they went on the air for speeches and press conferences. Using the tools of the media itself, the documentary breaks down the illusion of media and shows the candidates in more candid and vulnerable states, like when they rehearse the same line over and over again because they can't get it right. —*B. T.*

FILMS OF JEFF KRULIK AND FRIENDS, THE L: DOC. DIRECTORS/KRULIK, JEFF (2000) 88M D: Jeff Krulik. Krulik is best known for his hilarious, arguably exploitative short "Heavy Metal Parking Lot" (included here), which is sort of an anthropological document of the people hanging out in the parking lot before a big Judas Priest concert in 1986. Most of his work is along similar lines—interviews and home videos of odd people he meets, often through working at a public access studio. Other highlights on this collection include "King of Porn" (about a man who wants to donate his enormous porn collection to the Library of Congress—The Daily Show did a segment on him years later) and a short version of "Mr. Blassie Goes to Washington" in which Krulik takes a hint from My Breakfast With Blassie and brings the loudmouthed wrestler on a trip to our nation's capital. There's also a twenty-five-minute version of "Ernest Borgnine on the Bus" (a forty-five-minute version was released separately by Good Times Home Video). —*B. T.*

42 UP L: DOCUMENTARIES/BRITISH DOCS (1998) 134M D: Michael Apted. "Give me the child until he is seven, and I will give you the man." This acclaimed sociodocumentary began as a portrait of fourteen seven-year-old British children from diverse backgrounds that Apted continued to revisit every seven years. The seventh installment is the most fascinating and compelling yet. On the surface it's a study of an inflexible class system and the compromises ("I think the English classes police themselves in subtle ways," comments one subject), shifting values, and changing priorities of the people who grow up in it. Apted has generations of footage for contrast and comparison, but where he once used such opportunities for ironic comment, he now mines the material for insight on the strength and character of the human spirit. —*S. A.*

FRONTLINE: MERCHANTS OF COOL L: DOCUMENTARIES/ MEDIA (2001) 55M D: Barak Goodman. This is one of the most important documentaries available about media and how it influences youth. It explains how major companies and cable networks like MTV hunt down the next big thing by interviewing trendsetters to find out what's hot. Then, these once somewhat original ideas are polished up and fed back to the public on a massive scale, making it not cool anymore, just standard. I moved to Washington state from Alaska when I was in high school in 1990. Before I met anybody, I went to the mall and bought a trendy $40 stupid trench coat because I thought I would stand out too much in my dirty flannels, holey jeans, and hiking boots. Then Grunge broke and everybody from Washington state to Washington, D.C., went running out to buy really expensive flannel shirts and jeans with holes in them already. Now when I think back, I bet 90 percent of all high school kids felt as unwanted as I did. This documentary might help kids realize that only you can make you cool, not your clothes, friends, or bank account. —R. D.

GAP-TOOTHED WOMEN L: DOC. DIRECTORS/BLANK, LES (1987) 30M D: Les Blank, Maureen Gosling, Susan Kell, Chris Simon. From its title you might expect this to be one of the strangest documentaries ever made. And it is. This film actually chronicles women with a noticeable gap between their front two teeth. Famous as well as not famous, and living as well as historical women with such a gap are documented. Included are those who opt for orthodontic work and those who are perfectly comfortable with their smile. Ultimately, by selecting as its subject something so ridiculously mundane, this documentary seems to poke fun at the whole concept of documentaries, or at least the excesses of the documentary style. At any rate, it's the perfect quirky home video to throw on to amuse or bewilder a party. —N. J.

GATES OF HEAVEN L: DOC. DIRECTORS/MORRIS, ERROL (1978) 85M D: Errol Morris. Why bother trying to make a bizarre mockumentary about strange people when you can just go to Southern California and make an actual documentary with strange people in their natural habitat? Morris, who would later make *The Thin Blue Line* and *A Brief History of Time*, polished some of his documenting techniques with this film about an actual pet cemetery. Morris interviews the founder, who fully explains why he started it. He gives you a glimpse of several headstones, interviews many of the people who paid for those headstones, and talks to the current caretaker, who occupies his dead time by recording and playing his own rock tunes. If this isn't just about the strangest documentary you've ever seen, I'll mail you a bridge. —N. J.

GAY AGENDA, THE L: DOCUMENTARIES/CONSPIRACY (1992) 20M D: Ty Besson, Jeannette Beeson. Boy, am I glad I watched this little baby. It really opened my eyes to what's going on right under my nose. It clued me in to horrifying facts such as that gay people have gay SEX! I couldn't believe it! And if my kid's school counselor is gay and my son comes to him and tells him he has homosexual impulses he will actually ENCOURAGE him to ACCEPT them rather then suppress them like I do! There is a conspiracy afoot. But thanks to counselors like the ones showcased in this informative video, even people lost in sin can get help and change their ways. Gee, thanks guys, for telling me all this stuff. In fact, this video was so good I think I'm going to make all the little kids

at Sunday school watch it. Even though they are five years old, they need to know that licking another man's asshole and then having that man defecate on your face is wrong. And, according to this video, apparently all homosexuals really enjoy being shat on. I think I'm going to send whoever made this video $50 so they can continue to distribute it all over America and spread God's good word. Stupid assholes. This is no *Reefer Madness*–style fun. It's just disturbing. —T. S.

An "honest and informative documentary" that purports to tell the truth about what those pesky homos are REALLY up to. I haven't had as many belly laughs since watching snake handlers live in action. If any of the gay people I knew had sex lives that were even half as interesting as the lives all gay people are supposed to have according to this documentary, I'd hate them too, but it'd be out of jealousy more than anything else. —K. F.

GIMME SHELTER L: DOC. DIRECTORS/MAYSLES BROTHERS (1970) 95M D: Albert Maysles, David Maysles. The magical, musical 1960s come to a surefire end in this documentary by the Maysles Brothers (and Charlotte Mitchell Zwerin) capturing the tragic final moments of the Rolling Stones 1969 tour at Altamont. Just four months after Woodstock, concert promoters and organizers thought it would be a good idea to have another hippie/love/music fest on the West Coast. What they got, however, was a Northern California drug-addled blood bath. Hiring the Hell's Angels as festival security, the Stones thought their bad boy image could live up to the real thing. This visage quickly folds as we see a somber Jagger watching the Maysles's dailies of one of the concertgoers getting stabbed. Despite a whoo-hoo soundtrack featuring the likes of Jefferson Airplane, The Grateful Dead, and The Flying Burrito Brothers, this film is all doom from the get-go, painting a portrait of excess and a culture latent with violence. —J. D.

GRASS L: DOC. DIRECTORS/MANN, RON (2000) 80M D: Ron Mann. Mann's documentary is less a social history of marijuana than a portrait of the American government's campaign to demonize the devil's weed via newsreels, hysterical educational scare films, and campy overheated features like *High on the Range*. Contrasting this campaign of disinformation are two official (and subsequently ignored) government studies which find the drug relatively harmless. ("We've found that they experience mild euphoria, disorientation, and they get sleepy. Pretty much what the pot smokers have been telling us all along.") Mann's low-key matter-of-factness is helped greatly by pot poster boy Woody Harrelson's conversation narration, but he edits in punch lines, and the official record gives him plenty of material. Charged with raucous energy and a satirical slant, this witty history lesson is preaching to the converted, sharing a knowing wink with everyone who's ever inhaled. For all its smartly catalogued history, it ultimately aspires to be the thinking man's *Reefer Madness* for the pro-pot movement. —*S. A.*

GREETINGS FROM DOWN SOUTH L: DOCUMENTARIES/ AMERICAN CULTURE (1972) 25M D: Elliot Erwitt.

Greetings From Down South is a compilation of three short films, all of which are entertaining and informative, but one that is essential. *Kudzu* and *Grits* each engagingly document ubiquitous parts of Southern culture, but *Beauty Knows No Pain* is the ripping tale of the Killgore College Rangerettes. Famous for setting the standards for Texas female poise and beauty, the Rangerettes possess a tryout boot camp that I'm sure would put the Radio City Musical Hall Rockettes to shame. In twenty-five amazing minutes, director Erwitt (barely heard from since) captures scene after scene of the competitive cat-fighting drive of girls striving with all their might to make the squad. But there are only so many squad positions, and the scenes as the final lists are posted are perfect: simultaneously showing joyous victory and agonizing rejection in one heart-stirring shot. Is your kid thinking of trying out for something? Show him or her this! —*K. S.*

GREY GARDENS L: DOC. DIRECTORS/MAYSLES BROTHERS (1975) 94M D: Ellen Hovde, Albert Maysles, David Maysles, Muffie Meyer.

Feeling antisocial with nothing better to do on a Thursday night, my roomie and I put this into our player. This film documents the lives of Edith Bouvier Beale (a cousin to the Kennedys) and her daughter, Edith Jr. (Little Edie). The two inhabit a mansion leaning on its last post situated somewhere in the East Hamptons. An exercise on what can happen when one hermetically seals oneself off from the world, this film displays the Beales in all of their filthy glory. The disjunction between their self-image and how we see them elicits simultaneous feelings of shock, shame, and empathy. When you listen to Edie's erudite New England accent as she sifts through the garbage in her room for a can of potted meat, you can't help but think of your own misgivings. Anyway, after watching this, my roomie and I immediately went to the closest bar we could find and got tanked. —*T. C.*

HANDS ON A HARD BODY L: DOCUMENTARIES/AMERICAN CULTURE (1997) 94M D: S. R. Bindler.

For three days or so the entire world revolves around a brand new, fully loaded Nissan pickup for twenty-four contestants in an unusual annual event in Longview, Texas. All they have do is stand around that car with at least one hand firmly planted on it at all times—no sitting, no leaning, and if you remove your hand for any reason during the contest, you're disqualified. "They say it's a contest of stamina," shares former winner Benny Perkins, who's back for a second vehicle, "but it's who can maintain their sanity the longest." Bindler

constructs a surprisingly involving documentary around the 1995 contest, turning a potential freak show into a character drama. As the contestants move from tired to sore to numb, and from boredom to hallucinations, you'll find yourself feeling sympathy pains. When the half dozen contestants winnow out to a hard-core handful by the third day, you may even start to care who wins. —*S. A.*

HARD ROAD, THE L: SPORTS/CYCLING (2003) 120M D: Jamie Paolinetti.

A rather tepid documentary on the life of a professional cycling team on the U.S. circuit. Team Net Zero is a brand-new team joining the U.S. calendar event schedule, which runs from early March through the fall. March alone features fifteen races in twenty-nine days. We get to see some of the struggles of the riders and how the life affects them and their families. What we don't get to see is a lot of great racing, riding, or even crashing. Writer, director, and cameraman Paolinetti is also a rider on the team, and it's a good thing he's a professional cyclist 'cause his career as a director or documentarian isn't going anywhere. The glimpse he gives us into the life of cycling is surprisingly shallow. We learn a lot about the racing schedule and the travel involved, but not much else. Advertised on the cover as "A Feature-Length Documentary," *The Hard Road* might have been better if it were half as long and twice as deep. Even the curiosity of narration by Keith David doesn't save it. —*G. M.*

HARLAN COUNTY, USA L: DOC. DIRECTORS/KOPPLE, BARBARA (1976) 104M D: Barbara Kopple.

In 1973, workers of the Brookside mine in Harlan, Kentucky, signed with the United Mine Workers of America. Their employers, Duke Power Co. and its subsidiary, Eastover Mining Co., refused to recognize the contract, resulting in a worker strike. In addition to union recognition and wage increases, workers sought updated mine safety (far below global standards), improved housing (many company-provided units were without indoor plumbing), and medical care (particularly addressing prevalent lung problems). The strike wouldn't end until an Eastover employee murdered a striker, the company suddenly eager to discreetly end the standoff. Unbelievably dynamic journalism, this Oscar-winning documentary details the conviction of UMW president Tony Boyle (generally suspected of unethical collaboration with the coal companies) for the murder of an opposing union presidential candidate and his family, and even catches on film Eastover foreman Basil Collins firing his pistol at Harlan strikers. —*C. B.*

HEAVEN L: DOCUMENTARIES/AMERICAN CULTURE (1987) 80M D: Diane Keaton.

Here's a very different approach to a documentary: assemble a bunch of strange and ordinary people from all walks of Southern Californian life and ask them some very general

Different ways to watch

An aspect ratio is the ratio of width to height of a film image. It's part of the answer to those questions you're always asking: "Why are there black bars surrounding my movie? Why should I watch widescreen movies?" Most of the aspect ratios discussed below aren't used by filmmakers anymore but are useful to know about because the films are still shown on TV or have been released on DVD.

ACADEMY RATIO—1.33:1 OR 4:3

The Academy ratio was the original aspect ratio. Most movies were shown in this ratio until the early '50s. When you watch a film such as *Citizen Kane* on a television, you are actually seeing the film as it appeared in the theater. Example: *The Bat Whispers* (1930)—it was shot in 4:3 and Cinemascope simultaneously. The DVD contains both versions.

CINEMASCOPE—2.35:1

Invented by Twentieth Century Fox, Cinemascope used to be one of the most commonly used methods of filming movies. Now Fox is the only studio that still uses Cinemascope. Example: the Star Wars trilogy.

PANAVISION—2.40:1 OR 1.85:1

Panavision is one of the most common widescreen formats. Ninety-five percent of widescreen films are shot with Panavision lenses. Example: *Three Days of the Condor*.

SUPER 35

This process does not involve special lenses; rather, it involves framing the picture to fit the ratio of the screen. The top and bottom of the frame are "matted" out in postpro-

continued on page 494

---

questions about heaven! Get them to answer separately on a variety of strangely lit sets and then edit it all together with a bunch of old movie footage depicting heaven as former generations have envisioned it. Extras include some 1950s religious TV shows, one of which features a dwarf in her wheelchair singing, "One of these days I'll be caught up and saved!" By the time the film is over you will have heard so many fervently believed opinions about heaven that you'll start doubting any opinion you yourself may have entertained about the place. Keaton even allows herself to be interviewed among the throng of zanies. —*N. J.*

HELL HOUSE L: DOCUMENTARIES/AMERICAN CULTURE (2001) 85M D: George Whittenburg Ratliff. Enter the evangelical "House of Horrors" and know the hell of a godless life. Ratliff profiles the controversial Halloween sideshow created by the Trinity Assembly of God Church in Texas, and the earnest, fun-loving, church-going folk who have become the performance artist rabble-rousers of the Christian Fundamentalism moralists. Ratliff plays it straight with his subjects, who believe in their moral lessons—that the Devil-inspired dangers of everything from drugs and drink to homosexuality and abortion will send your soul on a one-way dive to hell—and deliver them with gusto and passion. But by the end of the tour you still get the queasy feeling that the moral of their story (accept Jesus Christ as your

savior and you go to heaven, despite your sins) makes this more of a cult than a spiritual philosophy. Fascinating. —*S. A.*

HESTON, CHARLTON: CELEBRITY SHOOT L: DOCUMENTARIES/AMERICAN CULTURE (1992) 60M D: David McKenzie. In this cheesy promotional video, stars ranging from Paul Sorvino to Chuck Norris to Erik Estrada get together to shoot at clay targets and talk to the cameras about shooting being a legitimate sport. It's a competition for charity (the cause being the Olympic shooting team) but the celebrities keep saying it's for things like safety awareness or "the good of America." There are also many gun fans (including a subculture of referees who "like to dress cowboy") who talk about how important it is for celebrities to promote guns. This is the only place you will see Jason Priestley and Richard Crenna lead a team together. Also keep an eye out for veteran character actor M. Emmet Walsh. Too bad this isn't a direct cinema–style documentary, but it's still pretty fascinating as it is: a lame entertainment magazine format with two smiling hosts who pretend to be overly competitive about shooting. —*B. T.*

HIDDEN WARS OF DESERT STORM L: DOCUMENTARIES/ WAR DOCS (2000) 60M D: Audrey Brohy, Gerard Ungerman. This documentary challenges the official account of the motives behind the 1991 Gulf War. It also explores the negative consequences of sanctions

duction or a theater, resulting in a wide-screen picture. When released on home video or shown on television, many of these films are presented in their unmatted format. Unfortunately, some of these releases tend to be versions that the director did not intend to be seen by the public. Example: *The Age of Innocence*—the VHS and television versions of this film are not matted.

VISTAVISION—1.70:1 (APPROXIMATELY)

This aspect ratio was invented by Paramount Studios. Films shot in VistaVision were photographed on a double-width frame of 35mm film running right to left horizontally. The uncropped aspect ratio was 1.5:1. The films were generally reduction-printed to 35mm, four-perforated (four sprocket holes per frame) in dye-transfer Technicolor and projected with a 1.85:1 ratio—the image area extracted optically from the full frame. For some theaters, the double-frame 35mm film was cropped to 1.85:1 during projection. Example: Alfred Hitchcock's *Vertigo*.

CINERAMA—2.77:1 TO 3.00:1

This format was shot with three cameras and projected with three projectors. The most popular film shot in this format was *How the West Was Won*. Seattle is home to the Cinerama, one of the only Cinemascope theaters in the world.

OTHER FORMATS

There are many, many other formats: Superscope, Technoscope, Shawscope, Todd A-O, Technorama, and more. Some of these "formats" have been used only once; watch a bunch of old films, and you will often see a bunch of formats no one ever used again.

Most movies are shown in ratios between 1.66:1 and 3:1, but a television screen is a

---

on Iraqi civilians and the theory that depleted uranium weapons used by the U.S. military were the cause of Gulf War Syndrome. It's basically an instructional video with no artistic or cinematic aspirations, but it is full of invaluable information you'll have a hard time finding in the mainstream press. —*B. T.*

HITMAN HART: WRESTLING WITH SHADOWS L: SPORTS/ WRESTLING (1998) 95M D: Paul Jay. This Canadian TV documentary is an even more fascinating look into professional wrestling than the better-known *Beyond the Mat*. Hart is a popular WWF champion who looks up to his boss, Vince McMahon, as a father figure. But he is ultimately betrayed and his career sabotaged. The story is so moving and archetypal that you could probably hate wrestling and still enjoy it. In one of many interesting developments, Hart's wrestling character bad-mouths American culture, making him a villain in the United States and a bigger hero than ever in Canada. You find that these ringside rants communicate Hart's actual opinions—in other words, that wrestling is more real than you might think. —*B. T.*

HOME PAGE L: DOCUMENTARIES/AMERICAN CULTURE (1999) 99M D: Doug Block. This documentary follows a number of people involved in writing diaries on the Internet at a time in the mid-'90s when mainstream America was just signing onto the Internet revolution. At the center is Justin Hall, a college kid who writes openly about his sexual encounters, including one with himself, for all on campus to read. More interesting than the issues that sites like his raise (how can people give away their intimate secrets to strangers on the Internet but not to their own friends and family?) is the fascination that people had with those issues at the time. With his crude website Hall garners international media attention, goes on a speaking tour, and gets paid by author Howard Rheingold to... sleep on his couch and, uh. . . it's not clear what else. When pressed, Rheingold calls Hall his "guru." *Home Page* is an interesting (if sometimes cringe-inducing) time capsule because it was made at a time when people still had a naive enthusiasm for the seemingly limitless possibilities of the Internet. It was a time when corporations thought every other computer nerd was a pioneer or a visionary, and should be paid to develop some, you know, online kind of. . . interactive, uh, something. —*B. T.*

HOOLIGANS & THUGS: SOCCER'S MOST VIOLENT FAN FIGHTS L: SPORTS/SOCCER (2003) 60M D: Steve Jones. This video highlights nearly forty years of soccer hooliganism: stadium riots, bloody brawls, and alcoholism—all the things a true "fitba" fan loves. The DVD's host, Steve Jones (of The Sex Pistols), blithely introduces each segment wearing a funny costume and a wry smile. He dresses up as a Mexican bandito to introduce the segment on South America's fans—you get the pic-

ratio of 4:3 or 1.33:1. When films are transferred to video, they have to fit inside this television ratio. Below are three examples of what can happen when theatrical film prints are transferred to video.

TELEVISION: LETTERBOXED

All films shot in the Academy ratio—primarily pre-1960 films—look the same on a television as they did in the movie theater. Most modern films, however, are shot in a ratio different to a television. When these are transferred to video, the original rectangular print is cropped to fit on a television screen. When such a film is not cropped when viewed on a television, it is typically called letterboxed. You'll notice letterboxed films have black bars on the top and bottom of the film's image.

TELEVISION: PAN-AND-SCAN

This is a television-only format. The original, widescreen version of the film is reshot or reedited so that it can fit on a standard television screen. Most viewers are missing between a third and half of a film when watching a pan-and-scan version of it on a TV. Luc Besson's *The Professional* is a good example of a pan-and-scan film. The camera makes unnatural movements across wide shots, indicating that it was created by a computer.

TELEVISION: ANAMORPHIC / 16X9 / 1.78:1

Have you seen the term "anamorphically enhanced" on some of your DVDs? This means that the video has a higher resolution. That way, when it is played on a widescreen television, the image will fill the television screen without losing its quality. When a 16 x 9 enhanced DVD is viewed this way, you will see little or no letterboxing.

—*Joshua Warren*

---

ture. This video is actually funnier and a lot less exploitative than I had predicted. It's fun to watch '70s-era footage of Björn Bjorg–looking motherfuckers kicking each other about the pitch. That jaunty mood is only marred by the Leeds United v. Galatasaray violence that sparked up at their UEFA Champions League matches. Two Leeds fans died in Turkey after being stabbed by unknown Galatasaray supporters and that violence boiled over to the match in England as well. This video (decidedly English as it is) is quick to condemn the Turkish fans, while giving a friendly wink to England's own as merely rowdy boys. The overall message of this "documentary" is confused but one thing is clear: alcohol and football do not mix well. —*G. M.*

HOT PEPPER L: DOC. DOCUMENTARIES/BLANK, LES (1973) 54M D: Les Blank. Filmed in and around Lafayette, Louisiana, the home of zydeco music and its crowned king Clifton Chenier, *Hot Pepper* shows plenty of footage of Clifton and his band (which includes his brother on rub board) performing their fun Creole dance music at various clubs and bars. Clifton hangs out and talks with friends and neighbors in homes, businesses, on his tour bus, and out in the country. The residents of Lafayette are in the movie almost as much as Clifton. There's lots of talk about integration and individuality interspersed with all the great music. Blank also includes his beautiful footage of scenic southern Louisiana, which meshes perfectly with Clifton's songs. —*S. H.*

HOW CAN I TELL IF I'M REALLY IN LOVE? L: DOCUMENTARIES/HUMAN SEXUALITY (1986) 51M D: Rick Hauser. *Justine Bateman, Jason Bateman, Ted Danson.* Of all the "so bad, they're good" health films teens are forced to watch in school, this has got to be one of the best. Based on a book by Dr. Sol Gordon, the video says it delivers "straight talk" about sex, dating, and the confusing emotions that go along with being an adolescent, but delivers nothing but a mishmash of catch phrases and clichés. The Bateman siblings, Dr. Gordon, and a group of students from University High School tell viewers what love is (the popular answer is "Happiness!"), lines boys say to get you to do it, things girls can say to get boys to stop wanting to do it, and how to tell if you have a "mature" or "immature" relationship. Danson is featured as the "cool" older guy with experience who warns girls about the myth of "pulling out in time." And if all that wasn't enough to make you giggle and squirm, there's some bad clip art and neon figures floating around the screen at inopportune moments, awkward editing that repeats the same peoples' comments over and over again, and some truly ridiculous original songs. —*J. K.*

HUNTERS AND GATHERERS L: DOCUMENTARIES/AMERICAN CULTURE (1994) 52M D: Darrell Varga. The stories of compulsive collectors—people who horde everything from Betty Boop knickknacks to pieces of dead people's hair. The movie is made up almost entirely of talking head interviews (interspersed with shots of the collections being discussed) and doesn't go deep enough to really feel like a feature documentary, but there are some interesting people on display. The two most memorable are a pretentious artist who collects junk and says (somewhat convincingly) that he works "in the medium of American culture," and another who has spent most of his life collecting Titanic memorabilia. The latter is the oddest character in the movie; he admits that his obsession ruined his marriage and in the end reveals that he doesn't like water and has turned down several opportunities to see the real Titanic. —B.T.

IRON CHEF USA L: DOCUMENTARIES/FOOD & SPIRITS (2001) 92M D: Bud Schaetzle, James Yukich. Americans are fat. They eat partially hydrogenated everything all day every day, and most of it comes out of boxes and cans. They spread this fast-food mentality across the globe and as a result, the world is getting fatter. That sucks. They also created peanut glue and evil. Japanese people are skinny. They stress out way too much but at least it makes them do things faster—have you ever seen them go at it in the work place? *Damn!* They also invented the throwing star and tuna. This is why the Japanese version kicks the shit out of the American version. —T. C.

KESTREL'S EYE L: DOCUMENTARIES/NATURE DOCS (1998) 89M D: Mikael Kristersson. Nature documentaries are forever peering into secret lives—humans looking at the world from the outside. Kristersson's film doesn't merely throw out the expectations of nature documentaries (voice-overs, interviews, reaction shots of humans looking up at the birds). It begins at a bird's-eye view, on high in a church tower looking down at the humans. Forget the dry descriptions of life cycles and mating habits and just look and listen. Kristersson's astoundingly intimate portrait presents a systematic life of survival with a soundtrack of communicating chirps and clicks and a kestrel's-eye view of the world. It's a completely different experience: rich, rewarding, and enthralling. —S.A.

LAND OF LOOK BEHIND L: DOCUMENTARIES/WORLD CULTURE (1982) 88M D: Alan Greenberg. Greenberg provides a very intimate look at the lives of the indigenous people of Jamaica. Originally intended to be a documentary on the funeral of Bob Marley, this film ultimately became an anthropological and ethnomusicological glimpse into Rastafarian life. The spotlight in this film is on villagers living outside the busy city. These are deeply spiritual Christians with a special connection to the earth and the supernatural, which in some ways is augmented with copious amounts of ganja. The

documentary does come around to the bustling city as well as the Marley funeral, but not before this society is put into proper perspective. This is one of those unique documentaries that begs for repeated viewing. —N.J.

LIFE + DEBT L: DOCUMENTARIES/BUSINESS & MONEY (2001) 86M D: Stephanie Black. *Belinda Becker (narrator), Jamaica Kincaid (narrator).* "If you come to Jamaica, this is what you'll see," promises the narrator: verdant green jungles, deep blue seas, and white sandy beaches that sparkle in the golden sun. The ironic narration and the startling contrasts between this tourist's playground and the poverty in the cities and countryside verge on the didactic, but it's merely prelude to Black's sharp and insightful study of the floundering island economy of Jamaica in the wake globalization and the policies of the IMF and the World Bank. Adapted from Kincaid's nonfiction book *A Small Place, Life and Debt,* Black makes her study both instructive and impassioned by taking her camera to the people, who describe in practical terms the effects of the stringent conditions demanded by the IMF in return for a loan. This is a smart, instructive work of political cinema that tackles complex issues of globalization with practical examples and vivid images, and presents its effects in immediate human terms. It makes its pleas without recourse to emotion, but its effect is rousing nonetheless. —S.A.

LIFESTYLE, THE L: DOCUMENTARIES/AMERICAN CULTURE (1999) 78M D: David Schisgall. *Wild Bill Goodwin, Nina Hartley.* Swingers. You would think this would be an interesting topic. Lots of people get together, have parties, fuck each others' wives, and then talk about "the lifestyle" on video. Sexual liberation! Ugh. If this documentary was your only basis for formulating an opinion on swingers, you would think that they are all old, gross, and BORING. We hear a few interviews with people who enjoy "sport fucking," and they don't really have anything interesting or informative to say. We see some sex parties where a bunch of old people have sex with a bunch of other old people, which appears to be completely gratuitous. And then they fast-forward to a year later where we listen to a couple tell us how having group sex has been kind of bad for their marriage. Well, no shit. *Lifestyle* takes a potentially interesting subject and turns it into something boring and a little nauseating. Maybe monogamy isn't natural, but neither is a woman my grandma's age in a thong and high heels strapped in a harness suspended from the ceiling. —J. S.

MANUFACTURING CONSENT: NOAM CHOMSKY AND THE MEDIA L: DOCUMENTARIES/MINDS (1993) 168M D: Peter Wintonick, Mark Achbar. This documentary is not a biography of the famed linguist turned political dissident, but a primer on his theories about the way media works as a form of brainwashing in the United States. If you're one of those people who believes Chomsky is a nutcase because he holds the American government to the same standards he holds others to, then you owe it to yourself to at least watch this movie and consider its arguments. It's a well-made documentary and the filmmakers come up with some interesting ways to depict the information visually. For example, when Chomsky mentions how many more inches of *New York Times* column space were spent on genocide in Cambodia than in East Timor, they literally unroll the columns side by side on a large floor. It's a fascinating movie and a perennial renter here at Scarecrow, especially whenever a new war starts up. —*B. T.*

MARJOE L: DOCUMENTARIES/AMERICAN CULTURE (1972) 92M D: Sarah Kernochan, Howard Smith. Oh my. If you only know Marjoe Gortner from his appearances in such classics as *Earthquake, Food of the Gods,* or *Starcrash,* you will delight in his life story as an enigmatic child-evangelist. Hugely popular in the South, he performed/appeared in tent shows and revival houses, reaping huge financial rewards from deeply faithful religious folk. Like its fictional counterpart *Elmer Gantry,* this is a classic document of hucksterism. Taking money from the blind faithful to fill the pockets of financial prophets is practically an American tradition and, as depressing as this film can be, it is always fascinating. Oscar winner for Best Documentary. —*K. S.*

ME & ISAAC NEWTON L: DOCUMENTARIES/MINDS (1999) 110M D: Michael Apted. "Uncharted territory is the only one worth going into," proclaims Maja Materic, an artificial intelligence researcher in the field of robotics. She's one of the seven renowned scientists whose inspirations, philosophies, and dreams are celebrated in Apted's documentary. Also featured are theoretical physicist Michio Kaku, a superthinker working on string theory who seeks nothing less than "a unified theory of all creation that would allow us to read the mind of God"; environmental physicist Ashok Gadgil, whose "hunger for learning how the world is put together" has led him to hatch practical solutions to the problems that plague poverty-stricken India; cancer researcher Karol Sikura (who lost his father to the disease); cognitive scientist Steven Pinker ("Language's Bad Boy" proclaims one headline in his scrapbook); primatologist and conservationist Patricia C. Wright (inspired by the child-rearing observations of her pet owl monkeys); and the Nobel Prize–winning pharmaceutical chemist Gertrud Elion, whose research has saved the lives of countless leukemia victims. Apted's interest is less in the specific details of their achievements than in their passion for exploring the unknown. He's clearly in awe of these people but his hero worship is tempered with a concerted effort to humanize them. If ever there was a film made to inspire school kids to the sciences, it's this fascinating, loving, and genuinely inspirational portrait. —*S. A.*

MICHAEL BOLTON'S WINNING SOFTBALL L: SPORTS/SOFTBALL (1993) 55M D: Michael Bolton. You thought Bolton was just some long-haired meathead who sings horrible quasi-soul shit they play in the dentist's office. But you were wrong! Right there under your nose he was touring the nation, making women faint, but after the shows he was going out and playing charity softball with his equally coifed team the Bolton Bombers, who "take softball very seriously." On this video he talks passionately about how he loves softball almost as much as music and why slowpitch is more manly than real baseball (the ball doesn't have much momentum so you have to hit it harder). Over Ken Burns–style photograph montages he introduces his instructor, Carroll, who he proudly says played for Skoal as well as the apparently historic 1974 Howard's Furniture team. There is actual instructional material but don't worry, most of it is him talking about himself, so it's very funny. And if you actually like Bolton you'll have a good time too because he acts like he's your buddy and includes a clip of himself singing the national anthem at the World Series in 1993. —*B. T.*

MISSISSIPPI BURNING L: DOCUMENTARIES/CIVIL RIGHTS (1988) 127M D: Alan Parker. *Gene Hackman, William Dafoe, Frances McDormand, Brad Dourif, R. Lee Ermey.* Based on the true story from 1964, this film details the demise of three antisegregation activists and the resulting investigation by two FBI agents (Hackman and Dafoe). The real focus of the film, however, is the social fabric that makes possible the deaths of these activists as well as the perpetual derailment of the investigation. The earnestness of the investigators is countered at every turn by the passionate black-and-white thinking of the local whites, while the local blacks can only leave or live in fear. Heavyhanded at times, Parker's direction does a brilliant job imparting all points of view in a visually sumptuous film. —*N. J.*

MONKEY PEOPLE L: DOCUMENTARIES/NATURE DOCS (1989) 85M D: Gérard Vienne. *Susan Sarandon (narrator).* This is as much footage of monkeys and cute little monkey babies as I have ever seen in one sitting. With light narration, the monkey madness is unbroken by things like structure and thesis. It's just monkeys eating and playing. And yes, there are some animal mating scenes, but nothing romanticized with silly music, and no uncomfortably long close-ups. —*J. J.*

MOVING THE MOUNTAIN L: DOCUMENTARIES/WORLD HISTORY (1994) 83M D: Michael Apted. One of the most compelling documentary films I've seen, *Moving the Mountain* is a look at the Chinese Democracy movement and Tiananmen Square riots. With interviews from many of the student-led movements' leaders and participants, the film really pleads a strong case for freedom. —*L. W.*

MR. DEATH: THE RISE AND FALL OF FRED A. LEUCHTER, JR. L: DOC. DIRECTORS/MORRIS, ERROL (1999) 96M D: Errol Morris.

Mr. Death starts out as a morbidly funny look at Fred A. Leuchter Jr., an expert on execution devices. He first got involved in the capital punishment business because he wanted to make it more humane, but now here he is in the unpleasant position of getting excited about his work, talking passionately about which methods of execution are best. But then see Leuchter getting involved in an even more grotesque hobby: Holocaust denial. Called in to defend a Nazi sympathizer, Leuchter goes to the death chambers at Dachau and takes samples, which he thinks prove there was no gas chamber because he can't find any traces of cyanide in them. It's interesting to see the human face behind this kind of madness. This movie will make you rethink whether to trust the "experts" that get trotted on TV and quoted in articles every day. —*B. T.*

NAKED STATES L: DOCUMENTARIES/AMERICAN CULTURE (2000) 80M D: Arlene Donnelly.

America is probably the most prude country in the world, and people turn red in the face at even the mere mention of public nudity. This is what makes a documentary about an artist whose passion and vision are tied up in taking photos of people nude in public places so interesting. *Naked States* documents photographer Tunick as he travels across the country in an attempt to get people to take their clothes off on camera in every state. From a hundred people laying naked in the middle of the streets of New York at sunrise to a pair of women embracing while standing on top of an American flag, Tunick's photographs are tasteful and incredibly poignant. More than the photos themselves, however, is the message behind the endeavor. Tunick tackles nudity head-on, exposes it in the public eye, and shows it to be something beautiful and artistic as opposed to something to be ashamed of. —*J. S.*

NATURAL HISTORY OF THE CHICKEN L: DOC. DIRECTORS/ LEWIS, MARK (2001) 60M D: Mark Lewis.

Before watching this documentary, most of my thoughts on chickens had to do with what type of sauce to dip them in. I suspect Lewis was thinking of people just like me when he decided to take this interesting and innovative look at chicken life, exposing the bird as more than just appetizer, but also as pet and friend, victim and nuisance. The story is told through a series of narrations by a group of people so interesting and colorful that you find yourself at times wondering if the whole thing is a spoof. There's the lady who takes her pet chicken (in a diaper) to the grocery store, and another woman uses mouth-to-beak resuscitation to bring a frozen chicken back from the dead. Not all of the tales are heart-warming,

however, and the more gruesome side of chicken life is depicted as well. Never preachy and always informative, this is a great look at one of nature's most underappreciated animals. —*J. S.*

NIGELLA BITES L: DOCUMENTARIES/FOOD & SPIRITS (1999) 158M D: Dominic Cyriax, Ben Warwick.

Welcome to the new wave in British cooking, inspiring housewives everywhere to dust the webs out of their KitchenAids and awaken new flavors from their fridges and spice racks. Nigella Lawson demonstrates just how effortlessly you can concoct bold new creations out of simple ingredients and easy preparations. Once you get over the frenetic jump-cutting and slick production, the recipes are pretty straightforward. It is refreshing and disarming to see someone on TV with no formal technique—notice how the knife seems to hack rather than cut—but the food ends up looking great. Timid folks beware, she makes no bones about using fat in her recipes. To say that Lawson is curvy is an understatement; however, she is not large in the American fast-food syndrome sense, but rather in a high-baroque, dewy-goddess painting kind of way. This is one supersexy woman and it definitely comes out in her cooking. —*T. C.*

NIGHT MAIL L: DOCUMENTARIES/BRITISH DOCS (1936) 24M D: Harry Watt, Basil Wright.

This fascinating documentary describes the complex inner workings of the UK's train-powered postal system (which I imagine has since changed tremendously). Mailbags are hung from racks along the railways and captured by nets attached to passing trains, where they're opened and sorted en route. The sorted mail is then bagged and hung outside the still moving train, where rail-side nets nearer the mail's final destination grab it. Ostensibly a documentary, *Night Mail* is composed much like a fictional feature, the most noticeable difference being the official-sounding narrator's voice-over. Largely due to the limits of available film technology, a number of scenes seem extremely contrived—indeed some seem altogether staged. This fact alone makes it an interesting piece of film history, but there's no shortage of reasons to check out this fantastic little film. Featuring notable contributions from Benjamin Britten and W. H. Auden. —*C. B.*

OLIVER, JAMIE: HAPPY DAYS TOUR LIVE! L: DOCUMENTARIES/FOOD & SPIRITS (2001) 108M D: Brian Klein.

Someone told me that, even though he comes from an upper-middle-class background, Jamie Oliver fakes a working-class accent when he does his shows. Frankly, who gives a shit because the motherfucker can cook. And to prove it, he's gonna go on stage live for a few hours to show you how to do it. Watch as he whips up fresh homemade pizza in a matter of minutes, witness as envelopes of seafood pasta seemingly fall from the sky straight onto your dinner plate, and be astonished as he concocts a killer curry and accompanies it with a ditty on the drums. The dishes he makes are undoubtedly "pukka," as he puts it, but after watching him for an extended period of time, I can't help but notice that his food always seems inextricably linked with sex. Cheeky bugger. —*T. C.*

OUR FRIEND MARTIN L: DOCUMENTARIES/CIVIL RIGHTS
(1999) 60M D: Rob Smiley, Vincenzo Trippetti. Two boys travel back in time and meet Dr. Martin Luther King Jr. in this well-meaning but misguided animated tribute. The *Back to the Future* gimmick works to a point as two modern kids face a G-rated version of racism in yesteryear's Deep South, but the "what if King had never lived" alternate future is insulting, hackneyed, and frankly denies the achievements of thousands of activists and millions of citizens. Give the filmmakers credit for attempting to contemporize King's achievements and show a slice of history—the thoughtful use of photographs and newsreel footage helps ground the animated re-creations in recognizable reality—but they should give kids more credit. —*S. A.*

PANAMA DECEPTION, THE L: DOCUMENTARIES/POLITICS
(1992) 90M D: Barbara Trent. I was a teenager when the United States invaded Panama, and I didn't like the idea of invading another country. But I remember watching the news reports and thinking, well, it was very clean, hardly anyone died—it's probably for the better. So it was enlightening to watch this documentary which explores, through eyewitness accounts, a much messier picture: 4,000 killed, U.S. soldiers burning down homes street by street, the execution of journalists, Noriega's past with the CIA, the increased drug traffic under the U.S.-installed puppet regime. Most enraging are the media reports (which mourn the U.S. casualties and don't even mention the rest) and the clips of blatant lies in Bush's speeches. I think this should be required viewing in American classrooms. Of course, it includes extremely graphic footage of dead civilians, but if Americans had learned their lesson from the Panama invasion maybe we could've avoided the first Gulf War, the second Gulf War, and. . . —*B. T.*

PARIS WAS A WOMAN L: DOCUMENTARIES/WOMEN'S DOCS
(1995) 75M D: Greta Schiller. What starts out as a short series of thumbnail sketches weaves into the story of a unique society of women who helped shape the literary world of the 1910s and 1920s from the Paris Left Bank. Beginning with brief portraits of Gertrude Stein and Alice B. Toklas (complete with addresses), director Schiller builds a cast of artists and impresarios (mostly American women, but also some French) and follows their relationships, both personal and professional, through the next couple of decades. Both succinct and rich, Schiller's documentary captures, through historical recordings and interviews with participants, the excitement and energy of a time and place defined by women who defied convention to create their own world. —*S. A.*

PERFECT CANDIDATE, A L: DOCUMENTARIES/POLITICS
(1996) 105M D: R. J. Cutler, David Van Taylor. Hilarious horror show documentary about Oliver North's unsuccessful run for the Senate in 1994. North—whose name we only know because he lied to Congress, traded arms, trained an army of terrorists, and trafficked drugs into the country—runs on a platform of "giving the government back to the people." What's worse, he has hundreds of dedicated followers who buy it. North let the filmmakers follow him along the campaign trail, and interviews with his obnoxious campaign manager reveal a sort of democracy-as-football mind-set. There's even a scene where North deflects a question about his defense of the Confederate flag by saying that he saw his Democratic opponent wearing a Confederate flag tie—a charge that seems to be completely made up! The opponent isn't a notorious war criminal, but he's not exactly a leader who inspires confidence either, so the story of this race makes for a depressingly potent symbol of the current crisis in American politics. —*B. T.*

PIMPS UP, HO'S DOWN L: DOCUMENTARIES/AMERICAN
CULTURE (1999) 94M D: Brent Owens. This lesser "pimpumentary," released the same year as *American Pimp*, is really just a series of interviews cobbled together without much direction. The music, cinematography, and editing are much cheesier than the Hughes Brothers's more carefully crafted film. Still, some people prefer this one because the subjects (a white pimp, a lady pimp, a "Player's Cruise") are so much more ridiculous. These people are completely deluded freaks, and you don't even have to feel guilty for laughing at them because, after all, they pimp hos. That's what they do. Director Owens has done a series of documentaries about prostitution, beginning with *Hookers at the Point*. —*B. T.*

POINT OF ORDER! L: DOC. DIRECTORS/DE ANTONIO, EMILE
(1964) 93M D: Emile de Antonio. Wisconsin Senator Joseph McCarthy's witch hunt for Commies had a rough backlash when the U.S. Army, under fire for its alleged Communist infestation, countered that McCarthy's Committee on Investigations abused its authority by seeking special treatment from the Army for David Schine, a committee investigator. The resulting 1954 Senate hearings became television's first blockbuster trial, a prototype for the sort of media circus we now expect of our political scandals. *Point of Order* condenses dozens of hours of television broadcasts into a narrator-free highlights reel (certainly with a liberal slant—but anything else would seem comical under the circumstances). Not merely a useful document on McCarthyism, the film captures the death rattle of the simpler days of information transmission, and is a sur-

prisingly entertaining lesson in the relationship between politics and media (which is to say, politics and entertainment). —C. B.

POST NO BILLS L: DOCUMENTARIES/POLITICS (1992) 57M D: Clay Walker. Competent documentary about the San Francisco poster artist known for his grotesque portraits of hated political figures like Ronald Reagan, Daryl Gates, and Oliver North. Although Robbie Conal is a good artist, the documentary (and the interest in his work) is more about his guerrilla techniques: he prints up hundreds of the posters and puts together teams who paste them around cities late at night. There is a funny scene where police try to stop him from putting up his posters and he pretends to have no idea what the law is concerning the matter, as if he hasn't done this hundreds of times. —B. T.

PUMPING IRON L: DOC. DIRECTORS/BUTLER, GEORGE (1977) 85M D: George Butler. Fascinating documentary about the world of competitive bodybuilding. Young Lou Ferrigno is the sympathetic underdog who challenges the reigning champion, Arnold Schwarzenegger. The champ offers Ferrigno mentorly tips, then confesses to the camera that he is purposely giving bad advice. Perhaps the most telling image is when the Aryan Adonis Schwarzenegger is waited on by several black waiters in apartheid-era South Africa without any apparent moral discomfort. Ferrigno's dad, Matty, is also an interesting character as he transparently tries to live through his more successful son. Warning: there's an extremely bad song in the opening credits. —B. T.

QUAYLE SEASON L: DOCUMENTARIES/POLITICS (1992) 27M Fans of Lewis Black's acerbic commentaries on *The Daily Show* and his Comedy Central stand-up specials might be interested to know that earlier in his career he wrote and narrated this short attack on then–vice president Dan Quayle. Quayle, of course, had a reputation as a shockingly ignorant moron and self-proclaimed C-average student who had somehow become vice president—a chilling foreshadowing of future presidencies, it turns out. Despite the corny painted cover that gives the appearance of a blooper tape, this is actually a cleverly constructed montage of hilarious/horrifying Quayle moments strung together by sarcastically triumphant music and biographical narration by Black. You can imagine the disgusted look on Black's face as he introduces the clip where Quayle discusses the Holocaust, which he appears to believe happened in the United States during the 1800s. There is also a brief song about the Gulf War by Harry Shearer. —B. T.

ROGER & ME L: DOC. DIRECTORS/MOORE, MICHAEL (1989) 91M D: Michael Moore. Whenever I start to feel numb to the fact that the world is a shitty place where the exploitation of people, usually the very poor,

happens every day in the name of profit, I watch one of Moore's documentaries and I feel the anger and frustration creep back in. *Roger and Me* takes a look at the effect Roger Smith and the General Motors corporation had on Flint, Michigan, when they decided to close their plant there and lay off workers in favor of cheaper labor south of the border. We watch as families with children are thrown out on the streets because they can't pay their rent, and a woman tells how she used to keep rabbits for pets, but now sells them for meat to make enough money to buy groceries for herself. In the background, CEOs tell us how they hold no responsibility, and that corporations do what they have to for profit. The way Moore approaches a topic is humorous, but the information he exposes is far from funny. —J. S.

RUSH II '90 TOUR L: DOCUMENTARIES/POLITICS (1990) 90M D: John Reither. I wondered what exactly Rush Limbaugh would do in front of a stadium of fans, so I took this video home. Turns out he basically does stand-up. He struts the stage in a tuxedo, making zany jokes about the people he hates most: environmentalists, feminists, homeless people, and gays (whom he says stick gerbils in their rectums). He keeps laughing about some activist he says died recently—I guess you had to be there. In the most condescending segment, Limbaugh welcomes Clarence "Frogman" Henry and his band to perform their homeless blues anthem "Ain't Got No Home," with Limbaugh on sarcastic lead vocals. There are also a few in-the-studio clips, with his producers smirking and rubbing their hands together as they listen. I wish there were interviews with the members of the audience, many of whom are shown sitting stone-faced as Limbaugh tells his jokes. It would be interesting to hear why they were there and whether they got what they wanted. —B. T.

SALESMAN L: DOC. DIRECTORS/MAYSLES BROTHERS (1969) 85M D: Albert Maysles, David Maysles, Charlotte Mitchell Zwerin. The Maysles Brothers and Zwerin followed door-to-door bible salesman Paul "The Badger" Brennan and his colleagues for six weeks to create this landmark cinema verité documentary. Don't expect a how-to manual or a feel-good portrait: Brennan is the real-world equivalent of *Death of a Salesman*'s Willy Loman, a veteran salesman losing his passion, his faith, and his self-confidence as younger men rise up through the ranks. We see him making his hard-sell pitches to true believers, swapping stories with his fellow salesmen, and getting through sales conferences and motivational meetings, but the film's most poignant moment is quiet and intimate: he prays in a small diner, gathering strength and steeling his soul for the coming day. —S. A.

SHOAH L: DOCUMENTARIES/JEWISH INTEREST (1985) 570M
D: Claude Lanzmann. A grand achievement in the
advance of documentary filmmaking, *Shoah*
remodeled the way the Holocaust is remembered. Eschewing the usual grainy black-and-
white footage of striped uniforms, Lanzmann
goes for present-day folks who remember the
times of deportation. Often clucked down by
long-documentary-wary filmies as nine and a
half hours of talking heads, Lanzmann enrap-
tures the viewer with his fine cutting and amazing pronouncements of the public's incredible blindness to the annihilation of the Jewish.
Questions to modern Poles who inhabit now-
empty, once-Jewish homes illuminate how banal
the experience was for those not living in the
ghettos or the camps; how watching neighbors
dragged from their homes and shot in the street
could become something perfectly common.
Highlights include Abraham Bomba's recounting of cutting women's hair at the entrance to
the gas chambers at Treblinka, and SS man
Franz Suchomel debating Lanzmann's figure of
18,000 murdered each day, with his more conservative figure of 15,000 lives taken daily at the
death camp. An astonishing, powerful motion
picture experience. —*S. R.*

SOCIAL LIFE OF SMALL URBAN SPACES L: DOCUMENTA-
RIES/AMERICAN CULTURE (1979) 60M D: William H. Whyte.
William H. Whyte (narrator). This wonderful
documentary done by the Municipal Art Society
of New York in the late '70s explores how our
citizens use parks, plazas, and other common
areas of cities. Whyte and his crew use time-
lapse photography and meticulous charting
methods to show how people cluster together,
where they tend to gather, and what they do
while there. Using excellent pre–Power Point
graphs, the team shows us what makes an area
successful and what makes an area inhospitable.
This film is charming because of the little details
it includes, like showing how some people stand
alone in the middle of an open space for no
apparent reason ("life swirls about and they just
let it all pass by") and because it reveals a larger
portrait of our human "choreography." The '70s
fashion alone is worth a look. —*J. K.*

SOLDIERS IN HIDING L: DOCUMENTARIES/WAR DOCS
(1984) 60M D: Malcolm Clarke. A moving and harrowing portrait of the scars war leaves on young
men, *Soldiers in Hiding* is a must-see. Clarke's
1984 documentary tells the stories of men, now
in their thirties, who as teenagers went to war
and returned feeling lost, more connected to
Vietnam than to the United States. These men
live alone for the most part—in the woods, on
boats, on buses. A man named Scott grows marijuana in the wilds of Hawaii; he and his wife stay
one step ahead of the law. She says he would have
been an artist if he hadn't gone to Nam. One of
Scott's drawings found its way into the hands of
another vet; the simple line drawing hangs on a

tree in the wooded acreage the vet bought with
his pension; now it is where he hides. These men
hide more from themselves and the fear of what
they could inflict upon society than from society
itself. Some contemplate suicide, still obsessed
with the cult of death that surrounded them in
their formative years. All are outspoken about
their love for their fellow soldiers and their
hatred for the senseless war they were sent to
fight. If you don't shed a tear along with these
men you have no tears to shed. —*G. M.*

SOUND AND FURY L: DOCUMENTARIES/HEALTH (2000) 80M
D: Josh Aronson. Aronson's fearless and often devastating documentary begins as an exploration
of a revolutionary new technology—the cochlear
implant—and ends with a philosophical quandary as two sets of parents (one pair deaf, the
other hearing) in an extended family grapple
with the options for their deaf children. The deaf
parents fear that such a device would destroy
their child's sense of identity, in effect losing her
to the hearing world, while the hearing parents
see the deafness in their son as a disability keeping him from entering their world and limiting
his options. Aronson shows how fear, ideology,
and the parents' need to have a child in their
own cultural circle have a strong impact on the
decisions. The decision tears apart brothers and
alienates siblings from parents. There may be no
more revealing look into the proud and insular
culture of the deaf community as they protect a
unique culture that technology may sweep away,
and Aronson doesn't take sides, allowing the
arguments and emotions to illustrate the conflicts. —*S. A.*

**SOUTH: ERNEST SHACKLETON AND THE ENDURANCE
EXPOSITION** L: DOCUMENTARIES/ADVENTURE DOCS (1919)
81M D: Frank Hurley. Short on narrative drive and dramatic structure but filled with striking images,
this record of the ill-fated 1915 Shackleton
Expedition to the Antarctic is all the more powerful for its tragic authenticity. The images of the
icebreaker *Endurance* frozen in place and slowly
crushed by piling ice floes were captured by a
cameraman watching his lifeline to home splinter and sink before his eyes. The ensuing survivalist drama of men making a grueling hike over
an expanse of unstable ice and a desperate 800-
mile voyage to civilization in a lifeboat is marred
only by overwrought intertitles and a pointless
(but cute) interlude celebrating the family life of
a penguin. —*S. A.*

SPECIALIST: PORTRAIT OF A MODERN CRIMINAL L:
DOCUMENTARIES/NAZIS (1999) 128M D: Eyal Sivan. Director
Sivan was inspired by Hannah Arendt's book
*Eichmann in Jerusalem: A Report on the Banality
of Evil,* and that guides his portrait of the ruthlessly efficient bureaucrat, culled from five hundred hours of video footage from his 1961 trial
shot by Leo Hurwitz. The balding, middle-aged
Adolf Eichmann looks as scary as an accoun-

Leni Riefenstahl

Leni Riefenstahl's more than 100 years of living were filled with tremendous success, critical acclaim, and, for most of that time, public castigation. Had she not documented and propagandized Hitler's 1936 Nuremberg rally in the film *Triumph of the Will*, Riefenstahl might have escaped the taint of her relationship with the Nazi party, although she would have also missed out on the worldwide notoriety accorded her because of that work.

Born as Helene Bertha Amalie Riefenstahl on August 22, 1902, in Berlin, Riefenstahl began in the creative arts as a dancer.

Her performances were so notable that theater director and producer Max Reinhardt hired her for his Deutsches Theater in Berlin. A knee injury halted Riefenstahl's dance career, though she was able to move into screen acting; her first role in a feature was in Alexander Korda's *Tragedy in the House of Hapsburg* (1924).

But it was the mountain films of Arnold Fanck, notably *The Holy Mountain* (1926), that paved the way for her film career. After acting in several mountain films with Fanck, Riefenstahl starred as Junta in the self-directed *The Blue Light* (1932), a film that caught the attention of Adolf Hitler. His offer to have her direct a filmed record of his Nuremberg rally would cinch

---

tant as he snaps to attention for every question, reading from records or repeating his mantra: "I had to obey, I was a soldier." Eichmann claims to have abhorred his duty, but the only emotion he shows is a creepy pride in his meticulous attention. If that's the real Eichmann, then he's genuinely monstrous in a way no horror film will ever manage to capture. —*S. A.*

STORYVILLE! THE NAKED DANCE L: DOCUMENTARIES/ AMERICAN CULTURE (1997) 60M D: Maia Harris. A fascinating documentary about the famous Red Light district in New Orleans, which ended in the early part of the twentieth century. It is also about the birth of jazz and how the two are connected. I didn't know King Oliver was a pimp! Includes wonderful pictures and music. —*A. B.*

STREETWISE L: DOCUMENTARIES/SEATTLE INTEREST (1985) 92M D: Martin Bell. Mary Ellen Mark chose Seattle for the location of a *Life* magazine photo essay on homeless teens because, at the time, it was rated one of America's most livable cities. Later she returned with her husband, director Bell, to produce this amazing cinema verité documentary about the troubled kids she met. We see them together where they hang out in front of a graffiti wall (a spot now in a tourist area of Seattle) but then they wander off to panhandle, dumpster dive, fight, sneak into abandoned buildings, jump off bridges, or visit their parents in prison. Most of them are prostitutes or addicts, victims of child molesters and alcoholic parents. Their troubled lives seem predestined, but you root for them to find a way out. *Streetwise* will haunt you

long after you see it; walking on the blocks where this movie takes place, I often wonder if maybe those kids are still around somewhere. —*B. T.*

SURPLUS: TERRORIZED INTO BEING CONSUMERS L: DOCUMENTARIES/POLITICS (2003) 52M D: Erik Gandini. John Zerzan's name was tagged to this documentary, so I assumed that with him and the title of the film it would be anticapitalist and have a primitive slant to it, which it does. As a whole it felt kind of like an MTV film done by Situationists, which isn't all bad. Some of the speeches with the head of Adbusters speaking, and the visuals of various heads of state and corporate CEOs that are synched to his words, work brilliantly. Also, a standout line delivered by the bastard Bush himself, "We must not let the terrorists scare people. . . to the extent where they don't shop." Steve Ballmer (of Microsoft fame) has some of the most chilling footage; he appears to be a man truly possessed by business. The repeated words got to be a bit much, kind of like beating a dead horse. In general the focus of the film is worthy: capitalism consumes until there is nothing left but miles and miles of garbage heaps and a permanent underclass that slaves in poverty and pollution for nothing. We get that point driven into us, but it never really has a dialogue about how or why. This is really a noninformative documentary that is a kind of a sound bite video for those who already "get it." —*B. W.*

TEXAS CHAINSAW MASSACRE 20TH ANNIVERSARY CAST REUNION L: DOC. DIRECTORS/KRULIK, JEFF (1994) 100M D: Jeff Krulik. Unlike the more standalone

Riefenstahl's career.

Hitler gave Riefenstahl carte blanche in shooting the rally. Special camera mounts were created under her direction, and with Third Reich–architect Albert Speer's participation, Riefenstahl obtained coverage from three huge pillars, their ascending shots disclosing a mammoth silence as Hitler, Himmler, and Goering marched down an aisle forged between the 800,000-strong membership of the Nazi party. Riefenstahl's direction created an image for Hitler that a desperately empty German populace craved: a sight of fearsome power, yet also a calm in the storm.

Riefenstahl's initial shot, taken from Hitler's plane as it enters the skies of Nuremberg from the clouds on high, forces a perspective of Hitler, and of Germany, that continues in the film's structure of wide, to less wide, to an eventual pinpoint, to the final bellowing incantation, "Hitler is Germany! Germany is Hitler!," the camera rising and filling the screen with the fierce eagle of the Nazi party.

Until her death, Riefenstahl maintained that she herself had no allegiance or interest in the Nazi party. She also stated that had she been aware of how the film and its Nazi connections would haunt her throughout her life, she would never have taken the project. Even her magnificent ode to the human form, the documentary of the 1936 Berlin Olympics known as *Olympia*, could not redeem her. What we are left with is an amazing film that altered the way documentaries are made, and alerted us to how easily the media can be used to manipulate public opinion.

—Shade Rupe

Family Portrait, this home video (not even really a documentary) is for those who are completely obsessed with the original *The Texas Chainsaw Massacre* (as most reasonable people are). Krulik (known for his humorous documentary shorts like "Heavy Metal Parking Lot") apparently shares our obsession with the movie. That's why he went to a small movie-poster convention where the cast was signing autographs, kept his camcorder on for pretty much the whole thing, and then released his raw footage to the public. The attendance is small and it's sad to see old Siedow (the cook) and his wife in a nearly empty room screening his classic film. Neal (the hitchhiker) turns out to be a movie poster dealer and, somewhat disappointingly, seems more sane than he did in *Family Portrait* (the director of which is also interviewed here). It's too bad Krulik didn't bring a real film crew because there are a couple of classic, couldn't-have-planned-it-better scenes. Just waiting around, Krulik happens to ask another fan about his "Ed Gein Fan Club" button and ends up with a deranged interview worthy of its own movie. —*B. T.*

THIN BLUE LINE, THE L: DOC. DIRECTORS/MORRIS, ERROL (1988) 101M D: Errol Morris. This documentary saved an innocent man's life. *The Thin Blue Line* begins with the shooting of a Texas police officer. The details are given as the police themselves interpret the incident. Also giving his story is a man behind bars, the suspect who insists he wasn't at the scene of the crime. He eloquently tells his tale, finishing up with the nightmare he went through while the police nearly tortured him for a confession. Further information is offered, and everything points directly to another man serving time in prison for another charge. That felon is also interviewed and basically confesses to said crime right there. So why is this other man in prison? That's what everyone wanted to know after the film was screened. The music of Philip Glass proves to be ideal as the audience tries to suspend belief and make sense of all the information. —*N. J.*

TRIALS OF HENRY KISSINGER, THE L: DOCUMENTARIES/ POLITICS (2002) 80M D: Alex Gibney, Eugene Jarecki. Examining Henry Kissinger's role in numerous atrocities abroad, this interview-driven documentary is based largely on a book of the same name by journalist Christopher Hitchens. Structured as a biography, the film casts Kissinger sympathetically as a hyperintelligent loner, if only to counter its more resonant portrayal of him as a morally indifferent sociopath with an insatiable mania for power. The viewer will doubtless struggle to comprehend the motivations for some of Kissinger's more destructive—and often inexplicable—diplomatic decisions. Naturally Kissinger had no part in this documentary, which really only adds strength to the claims. What's unfortunate is that it relies so heavily on interviews with Hitchens. Certainly he's an expert on the subject, but he's also wholly dismissed by conservatives (though ironically he was one of George W. Bush's biggest supporters during the Desert Storm sequel), which relegates this credible and informative piece to the Siberian wasteland of "liberal paranoia." —*C. B.*

TRIUMPH OF THE WILL L: DOC. DIRECTORS/RIEFENSTAHL, LENI (1935) 110M D: Leni Riefenstahl. Perhaps you've heard about this Nazi propaganda film but haven't had the interest, time, or nerve to watch it. Whatever the reason, maybe this review can elucidate a few important details. First of all, there are plenty of sound effects and rousing German music, but there is absolutely no dialogue in it. Second, Hitler doesn't appear immediately in this film as the savior of the German race. Instead, the film starts from the view of a plane above the clouds, and then within the clouds (clearly this passenger must be descending from heaven) followed by beautiful views of the German countryside. Third, once the Führer finally touches down and walks amongs his people, he doesn't yell and gesticulate. Rather, he smiles at everyone, pets German shepherds, coos at Aryan infants; in other words he wins the hearts of his people in much the same way as our democratically elected politicians do today. To be honest, I did not make it much past the first sixty minutes or so. With no script fuelling the propaganda and no verbal logic for me to dissect, I began longing for something a bit more familiar. Like maybe the five o'clock news. —*N. J.*

TV NATION: VOLUMES ONE AND TWO L: DOC. DIRECTORS/ MOORE, MICHAEL (1994) 120M D: Michael Moore. Long before *Bowling For Columbine* or the best-selling book *Stupid White Men,* Moore expanded on his *Roger & Me* techniques with this short-lived, extremely entertaining political TV series. Moore would introduce segments by correspondents like Karen Duffy and Louis Theroux, which were generally either friendly interviews with extremists or humorous satirical stunts. One memorable example of the latter is when Yaphet Kotto (distinguished, award-winning actor) tries to hail a cab in NYC but is repeatedly passed by in favor of a white man (who happens to be a convicted felon). The show also introduces Crackers the Corporate Crime Fighting Chicken (a costumed mascot who goes to corporate offices to confront them about corrupt policies) and Theroux (who went on to create the superb *Weird Weekends* for the BBC). —*B. T.*

UNDERGROUND L: DOC. DIRECTORS/DE ANTONIO, EMILE (1976) 88M D: Emile de Antonio, Mary Lampson, Haskell Wexler. The slogan "the future will be what we the people struggle to make it" appropriately appears throughout this documentary. During the '60s and '70s, the left-wing Weather Underground's "by any means necessary" model of reform included detonating bombs in banks, government offices, and prison administration buildings. Consisting largely of a discussion with five Weathermen, *Underground*'s social critique is a give and take of impassioned eloquence and adolescent bullshitting. Extremely polarizing material, the five Weathermen are idealistic enough (and charismatic enough) to strike a chord with more than a few viewers. Unfortunately, none of

it is tempered by a voice of opposition (though certainly such a voice was so dominant at the time as to be implicit). Probably a vital document at one time, *Underground* survives strictly as a supplement to more balanced material benefited by hindsight, such as 2003's excellent *Weather Underground.* —*C. B.*

VERNON, FLORIDA L: DOC. DIRECTORS/MORRIS, ERROL (1981) 55M D: Errol Morris. Morris's second film is a frequently hilarious visit with the (mostly elderly male) residents of a small town in the Florida panhandle. It's fairly low-key as most of the people discuss their lives, religion, and local history. Probably the funniest guy is the obsessive turkey hunter who relates several anecdotes, but the preacher's sermon on the word "therefore" and the old guy who explains about having a "four-track mind" are some of my all-time favorite scenes in a nonfiction film. Morris has taken some heat for a condescending approach but only some oversensitive, bleeding-hearted PC nut would make that sort of claim. A must-see for fans of Jesco White and Les Blank, *Vernon, Florida* makes a great double-bill with the *Cane Toads* documentary. —*S. H.*

WALKING WITH DINOSAURS L: DOCUMENTARIES/SCIENCE (1992) 230M D: Jasper James. *Kenneth Branagh (narrator).* This is a typical, well-made BBC nature documentary, with camera crews following animals in their daily lives as narrator Branagh explains what's going on. The weird thing, though, is that the animals they're following are dinosaurs, which (if I'm not mistaken) were already extinct kind of a while before film was invented. Could be wrong on that one. Actually, not-quite-*Jurassic Park*-level-but-still-quite-good computer animation and puppetry is used to depict the various species of dinosaurs in their travels, battles, feeding, mating, etc. I don't understand how scientists could possibly know this much detail about the way dinosaurs lived, but the stories are fascinating and the documentary conceit is endlessly entertaining. I brought this home planning to just watch one or two episodes and see what it was like, but I couldn't stop myself from watching the whole thing. —*B. T.*

WEST MAUI SURFING ACADEMY: L: SPORTS/SURFING (1994) 30M D: Not credited. It was suggested to me by a coworker that I watch this video before I attempted surfing for the first time. This has got to be one of the most uncomfortable things I have ever had to sit through. It's basically two instructors giving tips on how not to fall off a surfboard. As I watched them stumble through their lines, I was amazed at how such a rad sport can induce such narcolepsy. Despite it being only thirty minutes long, I passed out about five times during the video. Anyway, I went surfing the next day and actually managed to stand on the board for a good bit of the time. Maybe it's true that you retain information better in your sleep. —*T. C.*

WHEN WE WERE KINGS L: SPORTS/BOXING (1996) 94M D: Leon Gast. Filmed in 1974 but finished twenty-two years later, this is the incredible story of Muhammad Ali vs. George Foreman in the Rumble in the Jungle. The fight is legendary for Ali's upset over Foreman, but the film also shows the lead-up in which Ali paints Foreman as an Uncle Tom and arrives in Zaire to crowds chanting what they say translates to "Ali, kill him!" When the fight was delayed, the filmmakers were stuck in Africa and were able to record the concurrent music festival featuring James Brown, B. B. King, and the Pointer Sisters. The interviews and press conference footage (full of Ali's charisma and rhyming boasts) surrounding this great underdog story and all its cultural and political context paint an unforgettable portrait of a great icon and American hero. —*B. T.*

WILD RIDES L: DOCUMENTARIES/AMERICAN CULTURE (1982) 27M D: Robert C. Hughes. *Matt Dillon (narrator)*. A young, *Over the Edge*–era Dillon goes to different amusement parks and, in the worst cue-card reading performance ever put to film, tells you what's so awesome about the various roller coasters. Then you are treated to various skits that involve young people riding the roller coasters in question, all put to '80s pop songs. This is, in my opinion, Dillon's most entertaining performance. —*D. W.*

WINGED MIGRATION L: DOCUMENTARIES/NATURE DOCS (2001) 98M D: Jacques Cluzaud, Jacques Perrin, Michel Debats. This film is very pretty. This film is produced very badly. Shot by the same crew who did *Microcosmos*, *Winged Migration* tracks the flight of several species of birds. Besides its unbelievably gorgeous shots, one has to sit through an hour and a half of annoying new age music, accompanied by a foppishly French narrator who says nothing important. Also mixing things up in this crusty concerto are computer-generated interludes that I guess provide narrative linkage but instead end up looking like dingleberries in an otherwise beautiful movie. I wish they would have turned the "fruity and patronizing" knob a little lower for this one. For your micro/macro animal kicks, watch *Blue Planet* instead. —*T. C.*

WOMAN'S WARRIOR WORKOUT, THE L: DOCUMENTARIES/ SHAPE UP! (WORKOUT VIDS) (1998) 38M D: Melanie Murphy. So, you hate the gym. You want to exercise, but

you hate classes. You tried running, but it kind of made you feel like someone punched you in the chest after you'd gone about three blocks. This video is the solution to your workout problems, and I'll tell you why. First of all, you can do it in your living room, where no one can see you except your cats and maybe a neighbor or two. Second, because it's intended to make you strong like a bull so that you can defend yourself, it is fucking HARD, and you will be sore for three days afterward, just in time to do it again. Third, it's supposed to help you be mentally and spiritually strong as well, although honestly you probably won't care too much about that when you're lying in a pile panting on the floor. —*J. S.*

AILEEN WUORNOS: THE SELLING OF A SERIAL KILLER L: DOC. DIRECTORS/BROOMFIELD, NICK (1992) 87M D: Nick Broomfield. Wuornos was a prostitute convicted of a grisly series of murders in Texas. Some held her as a sort of militant feminist icon because she claimed to only murder men who had raped her. Broomfield was able to interview her in prison before her execution, but as the title implies, the story becomes less about her and more about the way the people in her life take advantage of her infamy. There's an amazing cast of characters including a born-again Christian woman who adopts her and a pothead lawyer who calls himself her "agent" and makes self-conscious jokes to relieve the discomfort of accepting money on camera for her interviews. As her "friends" make money off of her and politicians grandstand on the issue of her execution, Wuornos begins to seem like the most honorable person in the movie when she asks them just to execute her and get it over with. —*B. T.*

YEAH RIGHT! L: SPORTS/SKATEBOARDS & SKATING (2003) 40M D: Ty Evans, Spike Jonze. Holy shit! Once more we are reminded that brains are better than brawn, or in this case, a little ingenuity kicks the ass of a big budget. Just look at that opening sequence. DAMN! Who knew that some close-ups of a skater's feet in slow motion could produce such an awe-inspiring effect? The damn Wachowski brothers couldn't have done it better. Bullet time? Yeah right! There are a few other notable sequences in this video. One riffs off a Nike ad where one skater tosses the deck out of one frame to another skater in the next frame. The other features skaters on boards that have been digitally removed from the shot so it looks like they are wearing hover shoes. Sweet shit. —*T. C.*

CHAPTER SEVEN

Movies for Kids

Why is it so easily forgotten that kids are just little people? Just inexperienced adults, in a way? And why do we need reminding that a kid's taste in movies is in many ways no less refined than our own? That is who the films in this chapter are generally made for. The themes are more broadly stated sometimes, but at their best these films are as intellectually and emotionally complex as many films intended for older audiences.

And do we need to mention that the world's greatest animators have always tested the mettle against younger audiences? Think about it, until the age of music video, can you recall many major developments in animation that were not put before audiences of young people? From *Gertie the Dinosaur* to *Finding Nemo*, animators have continually pushed themselves to the limits while creating entertainment with the broadest popular appeal.

But kids' films are made for adults, too. After all, how can we keep our eyes on our kids at the cinema if we've fallen asleep from boredom? We adults are all like those Russian nesting dolls; deep inside we are all of our previous incarnations. We wear our life experiences like layer over layer over layer on top of that little kid we are too easily lulled into believing we used to be. Well, we are all still that little kid, and nothing proves it more than a great kids' movie. So watch by yourself, or with older or younger friends, and enjoy an entertaining reminder that all you could ever hope to be is young at heart.

Mad Monster Party? (1967)

ADVENTURES OF ICHABOD AND MR. TOAD, THE L: CHILDREN'S/DISNEY ANIMATION (1949) 68M D: James Algar, Clyde Geronimi. *Basil Rathbone, Bing Crosby, Eric Blore, Pat O'Malley.* After WWII and a troublesome animator strike, Disney created a series of forgettable, lower-budget anthology films as a quick way to make more money for the studio. This is the last of those films, a two-parter that adapts scenes from *The Wind and the Willows* and *The Legend of Sleepy Hollow*. The latter makes great Halloween viewing just for the scene where Ichabod Crane walks through the woods seeing phantoms in the trees and hearing the frogs and crickets call his name. The former is also fun but is most significant for introducing the villainous gangster weasels used in *Who Framed Roger Rabbit* and for inspiring a classic dark ride at Disneyland. —B.T.

ADVENTURES OF PETE & PETE, THE L: CHILDREN'S LIVE/CHILDREN'S LIVE ACTION (1993) 30M D: Nicholas Jacobs, Damon Santostefano. *Michael C. Maronna, Danny*

Tamberelli. This is my all-time favorite children's show. I loved it when I was a kid and I love it now. Two brothers, both named Pete, live in the small town of Wellsville. Filled with bizarre and memorable characters, the show chronicles the adventures of the young boys as they suffer through growing up. It is frequently quite touching in the most honest and commendable way, treating its audience (kids) with respect rather than pandering to them. It's a show from a child's perspective, yet intelligent, perceptive, and brimming with imagination. It blends the commonplace with the fantastic and in so doing creates a poetic and comical dreamspace. One that resembles my fondest childhood memories. *Pete & Pete* is the sort of show that is at once funny and tragic, expressing the full range of human emotion with the smallest of gestures. Watch it and return to a magical world where summer seems to last forever and dodgeball is the sport of gods. —*T. S.*

ADVENTURES OF PINOCCHIO, THE L: CHILDREN'S/ CHILDREN'S ANIMATION (1984) 90M D: Ippei Kuri, Jim Terry. *Danielle Romeo, Cindy Kozacik, Pearl Terry, Lacoya Newsome.* In this retelling of Carlo Collodi's tale (apparently cobbled together from episodes of an anime series called *Mock*), we see many adventures that weren't in the Disney version: cruel rodents steal Pinocchio's gold coin; he becomes the spoiled son of a governor; he turns into a tree and sings a whiney song called "Why Me?" The film also has the addition of a cheesy '80s synth and guitar rock score, typical English-dubbed anime voices, and the subtraction of beautiful animation and characterization. Oh, who are we fooling? Unless your kid is a huge Pinocchio completist, you don't want to rent this disposable crap. —*B. T.*

ALICE IN WONDERLAND L: CHILDREN'S/DISNEY ANIMATION (1951) 75M D: Clyde Geronimi, Hamilton Luske, Wilfred Jackson. *Kathryn Beaumont, Felix Aylmer, Pamela Brown, Ernest Milton, Carol Marsh, Stephen Murray, Jerry Colonna, Sterling Holloway, Ed Wynn.* This famed children's story by Lewis Carroll has been filmed over the years with a variety of approaches and styles. But Disney's feature film of 1951 stands out for a variety of reasons. Taking the woodcuts of the novel as templates, the film animates the characters in the shapes and proportions originally conceived. By adding excellent voices to such odd characters as the Caterpillar and the Cheshire Cat (and who can forget the Queen of Hearts?), this remarkable animation is greatly enhanced. What is more, this children's film, as in the novel, does not shy away from veiled references to hallucinogenic drugs, such as the two sides of the mushroom. At any rate, if films indeed comprise a collective memory, Walt Disney's *Alice in Wonderland* surely deserves a place deep in the subconscious. —*N. J.*

ALL I WANT FOR CHRISTMAS L: KIDS HOLIDAY/KIDS XMAS (1991) 92M D: Robert Lieberman. *Harley Jane Kozak, Jamey Sheridan, Ethan Randall, Thora Birch, Lauren Bacall.* Nothing guilty about this holiday pleasure! All precocious little Hallie (Birch) wants for Christmas is for her divorced parents to get back together. Concerned older brother Ethan (Randall) fails to convince her that romance is out of Santa's range. Scrambling to save his sister's faith in Christmas, he takes matters into his own hands (and naturally, his plan involves mice and ice-cream trucks). *All I Want for Christmas* makes New York City at Christmas seem like a genuinely magical place, a metropolitan wonderland so bountiful that it just might have what's needed to make Hallie's Christmas wish come true. Bacall very nearly steals the show as the children's movie star grandmother, but the show's just too darned good to be stolen. —*C. B.*

ANASTASIA L: CHILDREN'S/BLUTH, DON (1997) 94M D: Don Bluth, Gary Goldman. *Christopher Lloyd, Meg Ryan, Hank Azaria, John Cusack, Kelsey Grammer.* What the hell happened to Don Bluth? Is this really the same rogue Disney animator who tried to change the course of American feature animation with *The Secret of NIMH*? Audiences and critics gave him a condescending pat on the head for taking the story of the woman who's forgotten she's the czar's daughter and turning it into a reasonable facsimile of a bad Disney musical. On the very surface it may pass muster, but Bluth's character animation is obnoxious—the humans look semi-realistic, but constantly flail their arms cartoonishly and spin in circles to emphasize every word that comes out of their mouths. And what kind of a nutcase thinks it's a good idea to turn Rasputin—an actual historical figure—into a wacky, supernatural villain with removable eyes? One of the most tellingly misjudged scenes has Rasputin making a dramatic entrance in a shadowy room. . . with a cute, white cartoon bat (Azaria) on his shoulder. —*B. T.*

ATLANTIS: THE LOST EMPIRE L: CHILDREN'S/DISNEY ANIMATION (2001) 95M D: Gary Trousdale, Kirk Wise. *Michael J. Fox, Leonard Nimoy, James Garner, Cree Summer.* It seems promising on paper: a nonmusical, Jules Verne–like adventure designed by the great comics artist Mignola (creator of *Hellboy*), about a museum worker in the early 1900s discovering the lost continent of Atlantis. It could have been a breath of fresh air from Disney, but the story is completely muddled, most of the characters range from annoying to embarrassing, and very little of Mignola's distinct drawings were able to make it past the Disney house style. Completely lacking the focus or drive of the better Disney films, it makes you yearn for the old musical formula. Even *The Emperor's New Groove* is better. —*B. T.*

BAMBI L: CHILDREN'S/DISNEY ANIMATION (1942) 69M D: David Hand, James Algar, Samuel Armstrong, others. *Bobby Stewart, Cammi King, Sterling Holloway, Stan Alexander, Peter Behn.* This is the quintessential children's film, the one most movies and TV programs aspire to when personifying animals. What makes *Bambi* timeless is its highly realistic story combined with remarkable hand-crafted animation—two very rare commodities in most animation today. Bambi is the newborn deer who becomes acquainted with a circle of friendly creatures in the forest. Each creature mimics the attributes of its respective animal personality, most notably Thumper the rabbit. Classic Disney musical numbers punctuate this innocent melodrama, including "Little April Shower," "Love Is a Song," and "Let Us Sing a Gay Little Spring Song." The forest-fire ending, sure to horrify the youngest audience members, leaves poor Bambi an orphan. (Many of Walt Disney's protagonists were orphans, with whom he apparently identified since he believed for most of his life that he was one, too.) —*N.J.*

BAREFOOT EXECUTIVE, THE L: CHILDREN'S LIVE/DISNEY LIVE ACTION (1971) 96M D: Robert Butler. *Kurt Russell, Joe Flynn, Harry Morgan, Heather North, Wally Cox.* Ah, poor Steven Post (Russell). He dreams of being a success but is stuck in a bit of a rut, working a fairly menial job in the mailroom at a television network. If anyone ever needed a chimp who could pick hit television shows, it is Steven. And wouldn't you know it! He babysits his girlfriend's neighbor's pet chimp—don't ask me to explain this—and in the course of events, he notices the little guy goes a bit crazy when all the top performing shows are on. Steven quickly decides how to best use him to his own advantage. Keep in mind, this is a Disney film, so you basically know once he starts passing off the chimp's brilliant television prognosticating as his own, something will certainly happen to teach him (and viewers) a lesson. That message seems to be: don't use your girlfriend's monkey to do your job for you. It's a lesson I keep in mind to this day. And it has saved me plenty of headaches, you can be sure. —*C.P.*

BEDKNOBS AND BROOMSTICKS L: CHILDREN'S LIVE ACTION/DISNEY LIVE ACTION (1971) 117M D: Robert Stevenson. *Angela Lansbury, David Tomlinson, Roddy McDowall, Sam Jaffe.* Lansbury is exceptional as the governess of two young children in World War II England who learn she is also an amateur witch. Fortunately, she is a benevolent witch; unfortunately, she cannot keep her magical incantations straight, and a lot of strangely comic scenarios result. The one thing Lansbury's character can do with some consistency is escape a situation, as long as everybody is on a certain bed while someone turns the bedknob! The only thing is that she has no idea where they will wind up; among other adventures, these travelers happen to stop a Nazi plot to invade England.

Excellent children's story, with fantastic, psychedelic animation when the bed travels. —*N.J.*

BEST OF DR. SEUSS, THE L: KIDS' LITERATURE/DR. SEUSS (2003) 56M D: Robert Clampett, Ralph Bakshi. *Charles Durning, Tim Curry.* If this really were the best of Dr. Seuss, it would just have *How the Grinch Stole Christmas* and *The Lorax* on it. Instead, it has Bakshi's only-pretty-good 1989 adaptation of *The Butter Battle Book* and the not-really-even-worth-watching 1994 Hanna Barbera production *Daisy-Head Mayzie* (a story adapted from discarded, unfinished notes found after Theodor Geisel's death). Despite that, I highly recommend this DVD to Seuss fans because of the inclusion of one of the earliest and least known adaptations, Bob Clampett's 1942 Merry Melodies short *Horton Hatches the Egg!* It's odd to see Looney Tunes humor in a Seuss cartoon, an elephant sitting on a nest on the back of a boat, a fish announcing "Now I've seen it all!" and committing suicide. Now if they'd only release George Pal's stop-motion version of *The 5,000 Hats of Bartholomew Cubbins* we'd all be happy. —*B.T.*

BEST OF ROGER RABBIT, THE L: CHILDREN'S/DISNEY ANIMATION (1996) 25M D: Rob Minkoff. *Charles Fleischer.* After *Who Framed Roger Rabbit*, Disney attempted to revive the tradition of theatrical animated shorts with a series of Roger Rabbit cartoons bearing the logo of the fictional Maroon Cartoons studio. Much like the "Somethin's Cookin'" short that opens the original film, these are retro-styled slapstick in which Roger tries to look after Baby Herman and winds up repeatedly mauled by elaborate physical gags, reacting to the mayhem by contorting his body into weird Tex Avery–inspired shapes. They also repeat some popular elements from the movie—ending each short in live action on a studio soundstage and inserting cameos for both Jessica Rabbit and Droopy. Included are "Tummy Trouble," "Rollercoaster Rabbit," and "Trail Mix Up" (also included as extras on the special edition DVD of *Who Framed Roger Rabbit*). The latter is mediocre but the other two are well-executed tributes to the physical comedy of classic animated shorts. It's too bad theatrical cartoons didn't catch on again after these. —*B.T.*

BIG TOP PEE-WEE L: CHILDREN'S LIVE/PEEWEE HERMAN (1988) 86M D: Randal Kleiser. *Paul Reubens, Kris Kristofferson, Penelope Ann Miller, Valeria Golino.* Like the Three Stooges or Mickey Mouse, Pee-wee Herman lives a life with no continuity. He's an iconic character who can be at home in any world or time period. Instead of the '80s pastiche of *Pee-wee's Big Adventure* or the surreal Puppetland of *Pee-wee's Playhouse*, here he's a small-town farmer who finds a circus has blown into his backyard. Underrated due to comparisons to the unmatchable *Big Adventure*, and an unwillingness to accept Pee-wee as an old-fashioned leading man (with two love interests). My favorite touch is the way Pee-wee's pig Vance starts talking about ten minutes into the movie, and it's treated as if this shouldn't be a surprise. Look for Benicio Del Toro in his screen debut as Duke the Dog-Faced Boy. —*B. T.*

BINGO L: CHILDREN'S LIVE/CHILDREN'S LIVE ACTION (1991) 90M D: Matthew Robbins. *Cindy Williams, Glenn Shadix, David Rasche, David French, Robert J. Steinmiller Jr.* Although marketed (and apparently taken) as a genuine *Benji/Lassie/Air Bud*–type movie, this is actually a lowbrow and quite funny parody of the heroic dog genre. Bingo is an escaped circus dog left behind by his owners when they move across the country. Not wanting to lose his best friend, the boy (Steinmiller) leaves a trail of urine so that Bingo can track them and have many adventures along the way. Bingo is such a talented dog that he is able to perform CPR, use Morse code, testify in court, drive a car, visit his parents' grave, and even survive in a human prison. Pretty dumb, but I must admit that I laugh just thinking about it. From the director of *Corvette Summer.* —*B. T.*

BLACK CAULDRON, THE L: CHILDREN'S/DISNEY ANIMATION (1985) 82M D: Ted Berman, Richard Rich. *Grant Bardsley, Nigel Hawthorne, Freddie Jones, John Hurt, Susan Sheridan.* Young, awkward Taran (Bardsley) is an assistant pig keeper who discovers his pig Hen Wen is an "oracular pig"—she can sense things and create psychic images when she touches water. That would be pretty cool except that the nefarious Horned King (Hurt) plans to steal Hen Wen, track down the Black Cauldron, and raise an army of "cauldron born" (resurrected corpses), which one suspects he would not use purely for matters of national defense. The first Disney animated film rated higher than G, it is notable for its gruesome images of the horned king and his skeletal army. Unfortunately, there are some overly cartoony sequences and the overall story and characters are on the bland side. It's tempting to say the film failed because the world wasn't ready for a darker Disney, but more likely it's just because the movie isn't that great. Based on the first two installments in Lloyd Alexander's series of "Prydain" fantasy novels. —*B. T.*

BLACK HOLE, THE L: CHILDREN'S LIVE ACTION/DISNEY LIVE ACTION (1979) 97M D: Gary Nelson. *Robert Forster, Roddy McDowall, Ernest Borgnine, Joseph Bottoms, Anthony Perkins, Yvette Mimieux, Maximillian Schell.* After the unprecedented success of *Star Wars*, everyone had to jump on the gravy train, including Disney. *The Black Hole* was a very bold movie, not only because of its enormous budget but because this giant movie studio that had always been geared toward all ages released its very first PG film. The risk was worth taking and the money well spent, if for no other reason than the effects are spellbinding for any film released

at the time. That said, this is still a Disney film. A mad scientist in charge of a massive spaceship and a legion of menacing androids takes in an errant crew of astronauts. After impressing them with his brilliance, he shocks them with his insanity, charting a course directly into a black hole. The rest of the film is filled with astronauts escaping imminent danger, zapping androids as they go. Whether you love it, hate it, or both, this likely will be the most interesting Disney live-action film you'll see. —*N. J.*

BRAVE LITTLE TOASTER, THE L: CHILDREN'S/DISNEY ANIMATION (1987) 90M D: Jerry Rees. *Timothy E. Day, Jon Lovitz, Phil Hartman, Deanna Oliver.* I think everyone experienced the Raggedy Ann–induced fear that toys and inanimate objects sense rejection as we carbon-based life forms do, and feel isolation in obsolescence. *The Brave Little Toaster* preys upon this, as a sparky little toaster embarks upon a search for his master. With celebrity voices and writers from *Who Framed Roger Rabbit* and *Miami Vice, The Brave Little Toaster* presents a sorrowful story that made me cry, even though my five-year-old sister didn't quite understand the implications of being left behind to watch life through a tear-stained window, while the years pass and youth withers like shrink wrap, waiting for that one special someone to return and toast something. —*J. J.*

BUDDY L: CHILDREN'S LIVE ACTION/CHILDREN'S LIVE ACTION (1997) 84M D: Caroline Thompson. *Robbie Coltrane, Renee Russo, Alan Cumming.* Gertrude Lintz (Russo), a wealthy eccentric in 1920s New York, raises animals as if they are her children. The plot, based on a true story, centers around the adoption of Buddy, a baby gorilla, who Lintz dresses in human clothes and teaches etiquette. Inevitably, Buddy grows larger and starts to act like a wild gorilla, becoming ever more dangerous until she can no longer control him. Thompson is the author of *Edward Scissorhands*, and the parallels are numerous, but here the story doesn't quite work—it seems to be missing an act. There are some nice emotional moments, and the effects by the Jim Henson Creature Workshop are great, so it's not entirely a waste of time. —*B. T.*

CARE BEARS MOVIE II: A NEW GENERATION L: CHILDREN'S/CHILDREN'S ANIMATION (1986) 77M D: Dale Schott. *Maxine Miller, Pam Hyatt, Hadley Kay, Cree Summer.* There's some plot about saving the world from badness, but who really cares? The real problem with this film is that it's built on the shaky assumption that its audience is incapable of recalling the first *Care Bears Movie*, where the full-grown Care Bears traveled to a faraway land and met the Care Bear Cousins (who looked like Care Bears, except they weren't bears, but rather a menagerie of inappropriately hued animals), who helped save the world from badness. Yet this sequel begins with a montage showing the Care Bears and their Cousins growing up together from infancy to full Care Bear maturation—nullifying everything that happened in the first movie. Plus, there's an excruciating scene where the Care Bears turn to the audience and plead for help in the form of excessive and focused caring. Protect your children. This movie ruined me when I was eight, and clearly I never fully recovered. —*C. B.*

CHARLIE BROWN CHRISTMAS, A L: CHILDREN'S/PEANUTS (1965) 25M D: Bill Melendez. *Bill Melendez, Christopher Shea, Kathy Steinberg, Tracy Stratford, Peter Robbins.* When I think of Christmas, I think of this short little cartoon. *A Charlie Brown Christmas* is a part of my family's Christmas festivities every year, and even after nearly forty years, it continues to deliver a heartfelt message on the true meaning of Christmas for the individual and the whole family. Charlie Brown is fed up with the commercialization of Christmas and sets out to discover what it really means. He becomes involved with the Christmas pageant and has to find a good tree to make the show perfect. The little tree he brings home is more like a single branch that can't take the weight of a single ornament, but it is this sad little tree, and a little biblical insight from Linus, that show everyone what Christmas is really all about. A sweet cartoon that has been warming hearts for years, *A Charlie Brown Christmas* is great for young and old alike. —*J. S.*

CHARLOTTE'S WEB L: CHILDREN'S/CHILDREN'S ANIMATION (1973) 94M D: Charles A. Nichols, Iwao Takamoto. *Pamelyn Ferdin, Henry Gibson, Debbie Reynolds, Paul Lynde.* Wilbur is born the runt of a litter of pigs, but Fern saves him from the axe. She raises him until he is large enough to be sold to a neighboring farm. Fern comes to see him every day, and although it's difficult for him to relate to the other animals after spending his life living with a person, he gets used to things and makes some friends. He even meets a talking spider, Charlotte. It isn't long before Wilbur finds out he will one day be slaughtered, and he becomes really depressed. Charlotte comes up with a plan to save him, however. A tender, touching story about life and death, this film will sit best with younger children. —*J. S.*

CHIPMUNK ADVENTURE, THE L: CHILDREN'S/CHILDREN'S ANIMATION (1987) 76M D: Janice Karman. *Susan Tyrrell, Dody Goodman, Janice Karman, Ross Bagdasarian Jr., Anthony de Longis.* Away from Dave's supervision, the Chipmunks are tricked into a shady jewel-smuggling plot deftly disguised as an around-the-world hot-air balloon race. This quickly degenerates into a gender battle against the Chipettes, with musical interludes. Bizarrely, the numbers "one million" and "one hundred thousand" are used interchangeably throughout the movie in reference to the race's coveted cash prize. There is no plausible explanation for this, and doubtless millions of children suffered for it.

If you want to see just how much the entertainment industry thinks of your kids, check out this winner. I hasten to add that as a child I watched it something like a hundred times. —*C. B.*

CHITTY CHITTY BANG BANG L: CHILDREN'S LIVE ACTION/CHILDREN'S LIVE ACTION (1968) 142M D: Ken Hughes. *Dick Van Dyke, Sally Ann Howes, Lionel Jeffries, Gret Forbe, Anna Quayle.* This children's musical fantasy is in the spirit of *Mary Poppins* and *Bedknobs and Broomsticks*, and features an old car that Van Dyke makes airborne with the help of little wings jutting out below the running boards. The title refers to the choking, wheezing sound the car makes, which serves as rhythm to the theme song, "Chitty Chitty Bang Bang." (Van Dyke and his two children sing this whenever they fly the car.) Van Dyke takes his kids to a land where children are not permitted and where they find an evil Benny Hill and a cache of unmemorable Sherman and Sherman tunes. Good photography and great effects still make this worth a small person's afternoon. Based on an Ian Fleming story and written by Roald Dahl, this musical was dusted off for the stage in 2003. —*N. J.*

CINDERELLA L: CHILDREN'S/DISNEY ANIMATION (1950) 76M D: Wifred Jackson, Clyde Geronimi, Hamilton Luske. *Ilene Woods, William Phipps, Eleanor Audley, Verna Felton, Claire Du Brey, James MacDonald.* Walt Disney found fertile ground for storytelling in a variety of places: children's novels, original stories, popular themes, experimental media. But the fairy tale was the basis for his most interesting films. In *Cinderella,* the story he tells is not simply about the stepsister enslaved to domestic chores while others go off to the ball. It is also about the poor, friendly mice enslaved with her who try to help her out of her grim predicament. With guardian angels from the lowest point of the animal kingdom, this timeless story is retold with a youthful enthusiasm for that knowledge of destiny that belongs to youth and innocence. —*N. J.*

CONDORMAN L: CHILDREN'S LIVE ACTION/DISNEY LIVE ACTION (1981) 90M D: Charles Jarrott. *Oliver Reed, James Hampton, Barbara Carrera, Michael Crawford.* Comic book writer Woody (Crawford) is so devoted to delivering authentic superhero stories that he won't let his characters do anything he hasn't actually done himself. When a buddy in the CIA (Hampton) asks for a little help smuggling a glamorous Russian spy (Carrera) through Europe, Woody submits a detailed list of Bondish gadgets he'll need to complete the mission. As the adventure unfolds, Woody's comics finally achieve the epic grandeur for which he's strived. Unfortunately, they also enable his foes to predict his every move. Yeah, the plot's ludicrous, but evidently the CIA's pretty hard-up for good help. In the end, *Condorman* is a D-grade film that's loads of fun—a cornball comedy almost as clever as it is inane, with ridiculously silly action sequences that are actually pretty cool. —C. B.

DAISY-HEAD MAYZIE L: KIDS' LITERATURE/DR. SEUSS (1995) 30M D: Tony Collingwood. *Fran Smith, Tim Curry, Henry Gibson.* Young Daisy McGrew sprouts a flower from her head, becoming the ridicule of the school. But then a sleazy agent-type named Finagle (Curry) signs her up and makes her famous. Of course show business life doesn't turn out to be all that great. If you're wondering why you've never heard of this story, it's because it was the first posthumous Dr. Seuss book, put together from old notes and sketches. The book is obviously unfinished, with some awkward rhymes and a story that plays like a retread of *Gerald McBoing-Boing*. It's not completely unwatchable, but it's obviously just an exploitation of Seuss's old scraps, not a genuine Seuss story. —B. T.

DINOSAUR L: CHILDREN'S/DISNEY ANIMATION (2000) 82M D: Eric Leighton. *Ossie Davis, D.B. Sweeney, Alfre Woodard.* An allosaur raised by lemurs leads the evacuation as extinction-causing meteors approach the Earth. Although the dinosaurs talk, they don't sing like in *The Land Before Time* and they are created in quasi-photorealistic computer animation, sometimes with live-action backgrounds. This is a prime example of studio cluelessness about the use of computers. Disney spent more than $200 million to create a technically impressive but completely empty film. Who cares how realistic the dinosaurs look if the movie doesn't even have a fraction of the character, emotion, humor, or style of a Pixar film? It's hard to imagine who Disney thought their audience for this film was anyway, with dinosaur fights too scary for younger kids and a story too juvenile for anyone else. —B. T.

DR. SEUSS ON THE LOOSE L: KIDS' LITERATURE/DR. SEUSS (1973) 25M D: Hawley Pratt. *Allan Sherman, Hans Conried, Paul Winchell.* Directed by Looney Tunes veteran Pratt, this great TV special is a Cat in the Hat–hosted anthology that tells three Seuss stories: "The Sneetches," "The Zax," and "Green Eggs and Ham." The highlight is "The Sneetches," a racism allegory about a con man who tricks the self-conscious, bird-like Sneetches into paying to go through a machine that adds or removes the stars from their bellies, whichever is considered genetically superior at the time. It's great to see Seuss's strange contraptions animated—unfolding, chugging, steaming. Watching this as a teenager made me realize there was more to Dr. Seuss than simple nonsense rhymes, and I've been somewhat obsessed ever since. —B. T.

DUMBO L: CHILDREN'S/DISNEY ANIMATION (1941) 63M D: Ben Sharpsteen, Samuel Armstrong, Wilfred Jackson, others. *Berna Felton, Herman Bing, Edward Brophy, Sterling Holloway.* In the days of the mass popularity of P. T. Barnum's Circus, absolutely everyone knew about Jumbo, the enormous elephant who was billed as the largest breathing and walking thing in the whole world. And so, it's only a small play on words for circus animals in this Disney film to deride the baby elephant with big ears as Dumbo. But once it turns out that these ears that look so funny are the same ears enabling the ridiculed elephant to fly, Dumbo becomes the new celebrity of the circus. This classic Disney feature includes such songs as "Pink Elephants on Parade," "Baby Mine," and "I See an Elephant Fly." —N. J.

EMMET OTTER'S JUG BAND CHRISTMAS L: CHILDREN'S LIVE/MUPPETS (1977) 48M D: Jim Henson. *Eren Ozker, Jim Henson, Richard Hunt, Dave Goelz, Marilyn Sokol, Frank Oz, Jerry Nelson.* Emmet Otter is one sweet movie. It's a classic tale of an otter mom and son who have nothing but give everything. Emmet and his mother are gifted singers, and when the opportunity arises for them to earn some much-needed money at a talent show, they decide to part with their few possessions to get materials for their act. This movie has a wonderful message for kids about how truly unimportant possessions are when compared to love and giving. The movie has killer songs as well, performed by the group competing in the talent show, The Riverbottom Nightmare Band. This was probably the first time I really heard heavy rock with growly, evil singing and bad attitudes. I bet those heavy riffs unknowingly influenced a lot of people. I have always secretly wanted to be in The Riverbottom Nightmare Band. —R. D.

EMPEROR'S NEW GROOVE, THE L: CHILDREN'S/DISNEY ANIMATION (2000) 78M D: Mark Dindal. *David Spade, Eartha Kitt, John Goodman, Patrick Warburton, Wendie Malick, Kellyann Kelso.* This was going to be a serious Disney musical—with dramatic plot and random spontaneous bursts into songs by Sting. Thank God the whole thing went to pot and they had to look at the animation and say to themselves, "This will never work. . . what do we do now?" What they did was create a comic delight that feels, looks, and sounds more like a classic Warner Brothers cartoon than anything even vaguely Disney-esque. So don't be fooled! I remember when it came out in theaters I thought to myself, "Oh. . . that can't be good." But it is! It is gut-bursting-with-laughter good! If you miss the tongue-and-cheek wit of the classic Bugs Bunny cartoons, check out this flick and get yourself a fresh new fix. —M. S.

FAMILY DOG (THREE VOLUMES) L: CHILDREN'S/CHILDREN'S ANIMATION (1993) 45M D: Chris Buck. *Cassie Cole, Martin Mull, Molly Cheek, Zak Huxtable Epstein.* This short-lived prime-time animated series began as a stand-alone 1987 episode of Steven Spielberg's anthology series *Amazing Stories* and was later expanded into the series by Spielberg and Tim Burton. A commercial played

during the Super Bowl described it as "from the creators of *Batman* and *Jurassic Park*," but before its premiere the two decided they had failed and went back to rework all the episodes before they finally aired with little fanfare in 1993. These three tapes each contain two episodes about the Binford family and their "small, rat-like dog," who live in an *Edward Scissorhands*-like suburb. The big-adventure episodes don't work as well as the simpler stories—the uniqueness of the series comes from the more down-to-earth themes, like the episode entirely about the dog trying to get a drink of water. Most of the humor is in the way the family and dog always misunderstand each other: one great scene has the whole family yelling at the dog while he smiles and pants because he's happy to see them. It also gets a lot of mileage out of the realistic obnoxiousness of the two young kids who have none of the precociousness of the Simpsons. I love Billy's delighted laugh when he thinks a neighbor's dog has eaten his dog. "The Doggone Girl Is Mine/Family Dog Goes Homeless" contains the two weakest episodes, so start with one of the other volumes. —*B. T.*

FANTASIA L: CHILDREN'S/DISNEY ANIMATION (1940) 120M D: James Algar, Samuel Armstrong, Ford I. Beebe, others. *Leopold Stokowski, Deems Taylor, Walt Disney (voice)*. Walt Disney was ahead of his time marrying animation with classical music in this unique experimental feature. Disney animators took famous classical pieces and created animation to the music—sometimes telling stories, other times building mood and atmosphere. Most people remember "The Sorcerer's Apprentice" (with Mickey Mouse and an army of living brooms) and perhaps "Night on Bald Mountain" (with a mountain turning into the demon Chernabog—a classic image of cinematic horror). My other favorite is the eerie candlelight vigil of "Ave Maria." *Fantasia* has a well-deserved reputation as a misunderstood masterpiece. It was poorly received upon its initial release, said to be heartbreaking for Disney (although he was able to do more music-oriented shorts in anthology films like *Melody Time* and *Make Mine Music*). Even recent re-releases have caused problems with clueless parents seeing Mickey on the poster and expecting a traditional narrative with dialogue. Disney's only mistake was assuming that mainstream audiences respected animation as a medium and not just as a formula for children's entertainment. *Fantasia* is a masterpiece, but it's not for everyone, and it's not for all moods. —*B. T.*

FANTASIA 2000 L: CHILDREN'S/DISNEY ANIMATION (1999) 90M D: James Algar, Gaetan Brizzi, Paul Brizzi, others. *Steve Martin, Bette Midler, Quincy Jones, James Earl Jones*. If the 1940 Disney experiment *Fantasia* had been better received, he might have gone forward with his plan of updating it periodically, removing episodes and replacing them with new

ones. Sixty years later, the company cashed in on Uncle Walt's dream, with mostly good results. "The Sorcerer's Apprentice" (with those famous marching brooms) is the only short left from the original, now joined by seven new pieces. The animation styles vary widely, ranging from abstract geometric (Beethoven's "Symphony No. 5") to detailed 3-D computer animation (*The Steadfast Tin Soldier*, to Shostakovich's "Piano Concert No. 2") to the traditional Disney style (*Noah's Ark* starring Donald and Daisy Duck, to "Pomp and Circumstance"). My favorite is the elemental, almost *Mononoke*-esque life cycle of "The Firebird Suite." Also memorable is Gershwin's "Rhapsody in Blue," which is animated in the style of Al Hirschfeld's iconic characters. The only truly bad parts are the live-action celebrity intros with Bette Midler, Steve Martin, and the like. Originally released in Imax format, the film is not quite as impressive on video. —*B. T.*

FERNGULLY: THE LAST RAINFOREST L: CHILDREN'S/ CHILDREN'S ANIMATION (1992) 72M D: Bill Kroyer. *Samantha Mathis, Christian Slater, Tim Curry, Robin Williams*. Pop environmentalism runs amok in this animated kid flick, where money-hungry loggers threaten to destroy Ferngully, which as the title indicates, is the Last Rain Forest and the only refuge for countless fairy folk. Upping the dramatic ante substantially, the loggers endanger the rainforest, not so much by cutting down all the trees, as by unwittingly releasing the demonic Hexxus (Curry), the cartoon embodiment of destructive corporate greed. Williams nearly bests his *Aladdin* performance as Batty Koda, a zany fruit bat liberated from an animal testing facility. If you haven't caught on yet, this movie lays it on pretty thick, but I guarantee kids go nuts for this movie, thanks in large part to Williams's contributions (though it would be foolish not to give some credit to Tone Loc's reptilian musical cameo). —*C. B.*

FINDING NEMO L: CHILDREN'S/DISNEY ANIMATION (2003) 100M D: Andrew Stanton, Lee Unkrich. *Albert Brooks, Willem Dafoe, Ellen DeGeneres, Alexander Gould*. I love Pixar movies, but I had low expectations for *Finding Nemo*— how exciting can a story about fish be? But the Pixar geniuses had so much fun working in encounters with divers, pelicans, turtles, sharks, and, best of all, a dentist's aquarium where the little lost clownfish Nemo finds himself face to face with a brace-faced little brat just as terrifying as *Toy Story*'s Sid. The story is full of the gentle humanity and humor in which Pixar excels, and is endlessly inventive all the way through the hypnotic end credits, which are sort of like a funny version of those aquarium screensavers that used to be popular. The animation is stunning. Most of the film is seen through murky water, so it's a shock when the fish come up to the surface—their colors are bright and their scales are wet, just like real fish. This sort of attention to detail wouldn't matter if the story and characters weren't so great, but since they are, the film rises to the level of an animated classic. —B.T.

5,000 FINGERS OF DR. T. L: KIDS' LITERATURE/DR. SEUSS
(1953) 89M D: Roy Rowland. *Hans Conried, Peter Lind Hayes, Tommy Rettig, Mary Healy.* The only true live-action Dr. Seuss movie (because he wrote and designed it), this film is second only to *Willy Wonka* as a creepy cult classic kids' movie. It's a paranoid nightmare where Bart's mom is brainwashed by his evil piano teacher Dr. Terwilliker, who has locked up five hundred kids to make them perform his masterpiece on a giant round piano. The dialogue and acting are of the corny variety you'd expect from a movie starring the kid from Lassie, but you'll love it anyway for the surreal sets and Seussian touches like the evil roller-skating Siamese twins connected at the beard. Dr. Seuss hated the movie and never wanted to return to Hollywood. Upon his death he was cremated so that his body would not spin when Ron Howard made a movie about the Grinch. —B.T.

FROSTY THE SNOWMAN L: CHILDREN'S/RANKIN & BASS
(1969) 30M D: Jules Bass, Arthur Rankin Jr. *Jimmy Durante, Jackie Vernon, Billy De Wolfe, Paul Frees.* I'm like anybody else. I watch this special most years and I get nostalgic. But it still must be said that this is the worst of the Christmas specials that have caught on as yearly traditions. *How the Grinch Stole Christmas* is a legitimate masterpiece of animated storytelling, and *A Charlie Brown Christmas* is full of insights into human nature and satirical points about modern attitudes toward the holiday. *Frosty* is more contrived kiddy animation, especially in the case of the obnoxious sound-effect-producing bunny. That sort of lame humor is less forgivable without the novelty of the usual Rankin-Bass stop-motion animation. Oh well, it's still sad when Frosty melts. This DVD also includes 1992's *Frosty Returns*, directed by Bill Melendez, the genius behind the Charlie Brown specials, but it's about as bad as you'd expect from a twenty-years-later sequel to *Frosty.* —B.T.

GARBAGE PAIL KIDS MOVIE, THE L: CHILDREN'S LIVE/
CHILDREN'S LIVE ACTION (1987) 100M D: Rodney Amateau. *Anthony Newley, Mackenzie Astin, Kate Barberi, Ron MacLachlan.* Astin plays a (homeless?) kid who accidentally opens "Pandora's Pail" in an antique shop, unleashing a group of magical peeing and farting midgets who become his friends. He makes them sew clothes for him in a sweat shop to impress a much older girl. Meanwhile, he has to hide them from drug dealers who steal his lunch money and save the other Garbage Pail Kids before they are executed in the State Home For the Ugly (a mission at which he fails, but just shrugs off). The filmmakers seemed to be going for a genuine kids' movie in the produced-but-not-directed-by-Spielberg vein. And it's a

musical! The first movie based on trading cards and, perhaps not coincidentally, one of the worst movies you will ever see in your life. Highly recommended. —B.T.

GERALD MCBOING-BOING L: KIDS' LITERATURE/DR. SEUSS
(1950) 29M D: Robert Cannon. *Marvin Miller.* Gerald McBoing-Boing is a little boy who speaks only in sound effects. At first his parents consider it a sort of speech impediment, but then he turns out to be a godsend to the world of radio drama. Seuss, in collaboration with Bill Scott and Phil Eastman, wrote the charming rhyming story, but it's animated in UPA's trademark stylized, limited animation. It's a great Seuss story that could only be told in animation because actually hearing the sounds is crucial to the humor. This tape includes the original Oscar-winning short plus three others starring the character, all of which are amusing. —B.T.

GOBOTS: BATTLE OF THE ROCK LORDS L: CHILDREN'S/
CHILDREN'S ANIMATION (1985) 75M D: Ray Patterson. *Margot Kidder, Roddy McDowall, Telly Savalas, Frank Welker.* GoBots were the greatest toy ever. They were like little Matchbox cars, but you would pull this part here and that one there and then flip this over and pull these two little things out—suddenly, voilà! It's a robot! Every kid loved them, until we saw an animated commercial for the Marvel comic book, *The Transformers,* showing much more impressive vehicles-that-change-into-robots, and the next thing we knew there was a toy line and they were bigger and more elaborate than those stupid baby toy GoBots. After that, nobody liked the GoBots except my babysitter's youngest son. This star-studded theatrical GoBots movie might have impressed him, but for adults, it is virtually impossible to sit through. It has the obnoxious rhythm and sound of a Saturday morning in the '80s. The story has something to do with a planet of rocks that transform into robots. Fortunately, there are some funny Tolkein parallels, including a villain trying to steal the magic rocks from each tribe so he can rule them all. The one thing that is great about this movie is the dramatic opening credits sequence, which names the celebrity voices next to animation of their characters transforming into robots. There's something precious about hearing a bombastic symphonic score as the screen says, "Clubhouse Pictures presents. . . a Hanna-Barbera Production. . . in association with Tonka." —B.T.

GOOD BURGER L: CHILDREN'S LIVE/CHILDREN'S LIVE ACTION
(1997) 95M D: Brian Robbins. *Kenan Thompson, Abe Vigoda, Linda Cardellini, Kel Mitchell, Sinbad, Shar Jackson.* It is always a challenge to find quality movies for kids that are relatively intelligent and don't pander to lower forms of humor. *Good Burger* manages to entertain without causing adults to roll their eyes. Kenan and Kel work at your friendly neighborhood Good Burger stand;

Song of the South

Song of the South is Disney's most contro-versial film. This live-action/animation combo would be quite good if you could get past the condescending racial attitudes (and a lot of white people are happy to do that). Johnny (Bobby Driscoll) is a white kid whose father abandons him on a plantation with his mother and grandmother. Johnny decides to run away, but a kindly black man named Uncle Remus (James Baskett) tells him a story about "Br'er Rabbit" that con-vinces him otherwise. As the film continues, Bobby has various problems that are solved by Uncle Remus's fables. As Uncle Remus begins each story, we see him wandering into animated backgrounds, interacting with butterflies, letting the bees buzz along with him as he sings "Zip-a-dee-doo-dah." He encounters Br'er Rabbit, Br'er Fox, and Br'er Bear, and their stories continue with the beautiful artistry you would expect from vintage Disney animation.

Last rereleased theatrically in 1986, Dis-ney has never made *Song of the South* avail-able on video in the United States. You might consider this a sign of genuine com-mitment to racial sensitivity, except that they've put it out on laser disc in Japan and PAL-VHS in Europe as recently as 2001. Because Scarecrow specializes in rare videos, people regularly call us just looking for *Song of the South*. They often say that the film is misunderstood or "from a more polite time" and profess to not understand why anyone would be offended by it.

The problem is that the film creates a Disneyland version of the Reconstruction era. Its harshest critics say it paints slavery as fun and romantic, but the story is actually set after slavery was abolished. The reason for the confusion is that there is no men-tion of slavery or any hint of racial tension. The white characters (except for Ginnie's poor family) live in a mansion and wear froofy get-ups (Johnny is quite comical going frog hunting in his lace collar) while the black characters live in shacks, if they have homes at all, and wear fetishistically tattered clothes. Yet all of them get along perfectly and the whites love to watch the blacks sit around the campfire and sing white-as-hell Disney choruses that sit in for Negro spirituals.

It's nice to see Johnny's color blindness, but this is a world where no whites seem to have a problem with black people at all. They think they're just adorable as long as they wear those patched-up clothes. They just stay out there and mind their own busi-ness, most of them seeming to not have families or jobs, except for Hattie McDan-iel, who is the family's servant. It's unclear, but it seems to me like all the black charac-ters may be former plantation slaves who get along so well with their former masters that they still like to hang around now that they don't have to.

The NAACP put it best upon the film's release, when they criticized "the impression it gives of an idyllic master-slave relation-ship" while also recognizing its "remarkable artistic merit." Perhaps some day Disney will release it in one of their collectable tins with documentaries that explain the controversy and put it in historical context. Until then you can enjoy Uncle Remus's songs and characters at Splash Mountain in Disneyland, where the weird racial baggage is removed and replaced by a thrilling five-story waterfall drop.

—*Bryan Theiss*

Kenan does so to pay for hilarious damages to his teacher's car (Sinbad plays the teacher, but don't let that stop you from watching the movie). Good Burger's future is threatened by the opening of a corporate burger chain across the street, so the kids get up the gumption to fight to save their store. An important lesson about supporting independent business is crucial for any child to learn (especially if there's a Wal-Mart opening anywhere near you). —J. K.

GOONIES, THE L: CHILDREN'S LIVE/CHILDREN'S LIVE ACTION

(1985) 114M D: Richard Donner. *Corey Feldman, Sean Astin, Martha Plimpton, John Matuszak, Josh Brolin, Jeff Cohen.* A group of kids are facing permanent separation as a housing development is set to be built where they live, and they don't have the money to keep it from happening. While messing around in the attic of one of their houses one day, they come across an old map for the hidden treasure of One-Eyed Willy! They set out to find the treasure in an attempt to save their homes, but what they don't know is a bunch of criminals are after the treasure, too, and they just might be in for the adventure of their lives. *The Goonies* was one of my favorite movies when I was a kid, and still is. Everybody loves *The Goonies*. It's a fun, exciting adventure for the young'ns and otherwise. Plus, there is a great Cyndi Lauper soundtrack! —J. S.

Actually, I hate the fucking *Goonies*. I loved it as a kid, too, and I'm sure its blend of smartass kids, bumbling criminals, and subterranean pirate adventure still works for kids today. But as an adult, it bugs the shit out of me. I think Donner was going for the approach to child actors that Spielberg perfected in *E. T.*, in which the kids interact in real kid language and overlap each other. Unfortunately these kids are all obnoxious, whiney little brats and the hero, Mikey (Astin, whom I forgive due to his role in the *Lord of the Rings* trilogy), never stops complaining. I just don't want to be around these kids for two hours. —B. T.

GREAT MOUSE DETECTIVE, THE (AKA THE ADVENTURES OF THE GREAT MOUSE DETECTIVE) L: CHILDREN'S/ DISNEY ANIMATION (1986) 74M D: Ron Clements, Burny Mattinson, Dave Michener, John Musker. *Vincent Price, Barrie Ingham, Val Bettin, Susanne Pollatschek, Candy Candido.* Olivia Faversham (Pollatschek) is left alone when her toymaker father is kidnapped by a one-legged bat (Candido). She finds her way to the famous rodent detective, Basil of Baker Street (Ingham), who traces the crime to his arch-nemesis Professor Ratigan (Price). The mystery is played fairly straight with plenty of shadowy, atmospheric background paintings and a dramatic score by Henry Mancini. What makes it so great is the egotistical characterizations of the hero and villain. Price has a ball playing an insecure sewer rat who tries to pass for a distinguished mouse. As in *Theater of Blood*, he

menaces his prey with a deadly Rube Goldberg contraption, but this time he also gets to do a musical number. This forgotten Disney gem was the first to combine computer animation with traditional hand-drawn animation; animators traced over computer-generated footage to create an amazing chase through the gears of Big Ben. —B. T.

GREAT MUPPET CAPER L: CHILDREN'S LIVE/MUPPETS

(1981) 95M D: Jim Henson. *John Clesse, Peter Falk, Peter Ustinov, the Muppets, Charles Grodin, Diana Rigg.* Watch *The Muppet Movie* as a warm-up, then dive into this masterpiece, and forget their following efforts (although *Muppets Take Manhattan* has a little charm). After Henson and his imagination checked out early, Oz's imagination should have taken over. Kermit should have departed on a vision quest or sabbatical, freeing the rest of the crew. There could have been a spin-off of Dr. Teeth's band struggling along the Chitlin' circuit, or the story of Statler's & Waldorf's desperate lives at home in Manhattan. After Henson departed, the rest of the Muppet creators continued with the same basic cast and formula, but forgetting they were truly gifted at filtering human experiences through puppets. This film has great moments, from Miss Piggy upstaging Diana Rigg to Kermie trying to zip up his fly. —B. L.

GRINCH GRINCHES THE CAT IN THE HAT, THE L: KIDS' LITERATURE/DR. SEUSS (1982) 25M D: Bill Perez. *Mason Adams, Bob Holt, Frank Welker.* Although Seuss did write this obvious crossover special, it was weak programs such as this that disillusioned him about working in television and movies. Instead of being the anarchic trickster who wreaks havoc in a home, the Cat becomes a bland good guy out for a picnic. It's also very difficult to accept the Grinch when he's not animated by Chuck Jones or narrated by Boris Karloff. And Seuss must've known it was a bad idea to take him out of his timeless Christmas tale and turn him into a generic villain (he builds a machine that pollutes the world with noise). Would anybody want to know what Ebenezer Scrooge does during the summer? Would they want to see him face off with Oliver Twist? Probably not, because it would be as gloomy and forgettable as this. —B. T.

GUS L: CHILDREN'S LIVE/DISNEY LIVE ACTION (1976) 96M

D: Vincent McEveety. *Ed Asner, Liberty Williams, Tim Conway, Gary Grimes, Don Knotts.* It's difficult to say which aspect of this Disney film is more absurd, a mule kicking field goals for a losing football team or Bob Crane desperately taking a bit part beneath Don Knotts and Dick Van Patten. Of course the successful mule gets kidnapped by the opposing team. But this is a Disney film, so everything must be resolved in the end. The mule is retrieved by its team, the team wins the climactic game, and Crane pretends to be very excited about all of this as he announces it all next to Tom Bosley. —*N. J.*

HALLOWEEN IS GRINCH NIGHT L: KIDS' LITERATURE/DR. SEUSS (1977) 25M D: Gerard Baldwin. *Hans Conried, Henry Gibson, Hal Smith, Gary Shapiro.* Think of it this way: *How the Grinch Stole Christmas* was from the director of the classic Wile E. Coyote cartoons, but this director was a producer on *The Smurfs.* If you go in with that in mind, this special is not all that bad. It's about a young boy from Whoville who has to face his fears and go outside during the sour-sweet winds of Grinch Night. It's got a certain spooky quality and the story is less forced than *The Grinch Grinches the Cat in the Hat,* but it's still disappointing to see the Grinch with lesser animation and the voice of Conried instead of Boris Karloff. —*B. T.*

HAPPIEST MILLIONAIRE, THE L: CHILDREN'S LIVE/ DISNEY LIVE ACTION (1967) 164M D: Norman Tokar. *Fred MacMurray, Geraldine Page, Tommy Steele, John Davidson, Lesley Ann Warren.* This was the last production Walt Disney personally oversaw before his death. Though the current video version runs 164 minutes, it was originally an 172 minutes long! This is a movie that is so utterly wholesome, it begins to approach the outer reaches of perversity. Just look at Steele's teeth (no, he doesn't look like any Irishman I've ever seen either). Now look at MacMurray's gray cable-knit turtleneck sweater. Davidson's immaculate pompadour. Warren's breasts. Now look again. OK, maybe this movie isn't so wholesome after all. Well, anyway, it'll have you humming inane tunes until you want to take a salad fork and put your own eyes out. Fun for the whole family! —*S. F.*

HAROLD AND THE PURPLE CRAYON L: KIDS' LITERATURE/ CHILDREN'S CIRCLE (1969) 30M D: Weston Woods. Based on the Crockett Johnson book, *Harold and the Purple Crayon* is the charming story of Harold, a little boy who has the entire world at his fingertips through the use of his purple crayon. With the moon as his guide and friend, and a really big imagination, Harold draws his way into different worlds and adventures. The story line is simple and easy enough to follow for even the youngest viewers, and in fact, the youngest audience is the one who will enjoy Harold's adventures the most. The animation and dialogue are sweet and simple, providing no flashy distractions for the viewer, making it easy for them to think along and feel like they are a part of Harold's adventures. —*J. S.*

HARRIET THE SPY L: CHILDREN'S LIVE/CHILDREN'S LIVE ACTION (1996) 101M D: Bronwen Hughes. *Michelle Trachtenberg, Gregory Smith, Vanessa Lee Chester, Rosie O'Donnell, Eartha Kitt.* In this update of the Louise Fitzhugh novel, future *Buffy the Vampire Slayer*–kid sister Trachtenberg plays the young, aspiring writer who spies on her friends

and neighbors. She keeps detailed journals about what she observes, but gets in trouble when her subjects read what she wrote. The look is very stylized, with lots of kinetic camera work and a funky soundtrack, but it's also very smartly written and delves into dark emotions you might not expect to find in the first Nickelodeon feature film. Harriet is a multilayered character; a wise-beyond-her-years kid who realizes that honesty is important to her writing even if it angers her friends, but she's also a brat who can be cruel when she gets upset. During the sad section of the film, there's a scene where she stares out the classroom window while everyone else watches a clunky old health film; a classic moment that makes you feel you're sitting in a school desk again, and simultaneously reminiscent of a scene an adult character might have in an old melodrama. This is a very unique and smart children's film that has not been given nearly the recognition it deserves. —*B. T.*

HOLES L: CHILDREN'S LIVE/DISNEY LIVE ACTION (2003) 117M D: Andrew Davis. *Shia Labeouf, Patricia Arquette, Jon Voight, Tim Blake Nelson, Sigourney Weaver, Henry Winkler.* Holes is a totally fun, surprisingly dark, expertly written Disney live-action movie that "rocks" from start to finish. A boy is sent to a youth correctional facility, where every day he and the rest of the inmates are required to dig one huge hole in the sweltering sun and survive on only slave rations. The kids are bossed around by a cranky old sourpuss played to a T by Voight. The warden (Weaver) was traumatized as a child, forced to dig relentlessly for the family treasure, and is still determined to find it no matter the cost. The child actors are awesome. LaBeouf plays Stanley Yelnats, the smartest of the kids, who teaches his friend Zero how to read against the warden's wishes and leads the kids in figuring out just what they're digging for. *Holes* is a great family adventure film in the *Goonies* tradition, with lots of heart, action, courage, suspense, and buried treasure. —*R. D.*

HORTON HEARS A WHO! L: CHILDREN'S/JONES, CHUCK (1970) 26M D: Chuck Jones. *Hans Conried, June Foray.* It turns out that Whoville (which Jones already brought to life in *How the Grinch Stole Christmas*) is so tiny that it's contained on a speck of dust, but only Horton the elephant is sensitive enough to hear their cries. He carries the speck on a tiny flower, but everybody else thinks Horton is a nutcase hearing voices, and they do everything to ridicule him for it short of burning him at the stake. The story may not be as simple and mythic as *The Grinch,* but it's another great Seuss allegory brought to life in collaboration with Jones. Both of Jones's collaborations with Seuss stand light years ahead of the other Seuss adaptations. —*B. T.*

HOW THE GRINCH STOLE CHRISTMAS! L: KIDS' LITERATURE/DR. SEUSS (1966) 26M D: Chuck Jones, Ben Washam. *June Foray, Boris Karloff.* Jim Carrey has nothing on Boris Karloff when it comes to the Grinch, and live action just couldn't do justice to this animated classic. Living in a cave on a mountain above the Who village is the Grinch, a grumpy guy with an itty-bitty heart who hates Christmas more than anything else in the world. This year, instead of bitterly sitting by as everyone below enjoys themselves, the Grinch has come up with a plan: dress up as Santa and steal every trace of Christmas from the little Whos! When Christmas morning rolls around, however, and the Whos wake up to celebrate without a single present, Christmas ball, or Christmas ham, the Grinch finds himself contracting a little bit of the Christmas spirit himself. A truly classic cartoon, whether at Christmas or in June, this cartoon makes my heart all warm, fuzzy, and just a little bit larger. —*J. S.*

HUNCHBACK OF NOTRE DAME, THE L: CHILDREN'S/ DISNEY ANIMATION (1996) 86M D: Gary Trousdale, Kirk Wise. *Kevin Kline, Tom Hulce, Demi Moore.* This loose adaptation of the Victor Hugo novel is the ultimate example of the confusion within the Disney corporation. While talented animators pour their hearts into a project they hope they can be proud of, sinister figures in board rooms insist on sticking their fingers in the pie. The result is an attempt at a serious Quasimodo opera for adults combined with a toy commercial for young children. One moment a menacing priest is standing in front of a fire singing about his lust, the next minute wisecracking gargoyles are making fart jokes with the hunchback they have nicknamed "Quasi." It's well animated, of course, and didn't quite mark the decline of Disney animation (that would come a few years later). But it's frustrating to watch the studio flirt with adult drama and then turn around and run like cowards in the other direction. —*B. T.*

ICE AGE L: CHILDREN'S/CHILDREN'S ANIMATION (2002) 81M D: Chris Wedge, Carlos Saldanha. *John Leguizamo, Ray Romano, Denis Leary.* An unlikely trio of prehistoric beasts—growling but good-hearted Manfred the mastodon (Romano with a gruff and grumpy foghorn voice), motormouth rascal Sid the sloth (Leguizamo as a twittering chatterbox on caffeine), and scheming spy Diego the sabertoothed tiger (a slow and smoky Leary)—interrupt their migration to deliver a foundling man cub back to his "herd." Think *The Jungle Book* with a case of frostbite. This entertaining if derivative computer-animated comic adventure is visually on the bland side. The personality emerges from the voice cast, while the slapstick asides of a jittery, bug-eyed prehistoric squirrel enliven the journey. —*S. A.*

IN SEARCH OF DR. SEUSS L: KIDS' LITERATURE/DR. SEUSS (1994) 90M D: Vincent Paterson. *Patrick Stewart, Billy Crystal, David Paymer, Matt Frewer, Kathy Najimy, Robin Williams.* When Seuss died, there was no one to protect his work from embarrassing commercial exploitation, and one of the first danger signs was this cheesy TV biography. Najimy is a reporter trying to uncover the details of Seuss's life, which she ends up narrating in a condescending tone to which Seuss's children's books never stooped. Then a bunch of celebrities in half-assed costumes pretend to be The Cat in the Hat, the Onceler, etc. I'm sure a lot of hard work went into the props but Seuss deserves much better than this. The director is a choreographer who worked on *Moonwalker, Evita,* and *Dancer in the Dark.* His other work includes *Suzi Lonergan's Power Pilates!* —*B. T.*

INCREDIBLE MR. LIMPET, THE L: CHILDREN'S LIVE/ CHILDREN'S LIVE ACTION (1964) 102M D: Arthur Lubin. *Don Knotts, Carole Cook, Andrew Duggan.* The flawless Knotts strikes gold again in this musical, half-animated aquatic epic. This time out, he's henpecked Henry Limpet, a mild-mannered loser with an unhealthy fixation on oceanic life. For absolutely no reason, Henry is transformed into a fish and uses his newfound form to fall in love with scaly females, as well as lead the Navy into battle against opposing forces! This may all sound like a mess, but Knotts and director Lubin (*Francis the Talking Mule*) pull it off without a hitch. So rarely is a "magical film for the whole family" even worth watching that I think *Mr. Limpet* deserves a little more recognition than it's received. To hell with Disney. This movie makes me want to have kids just so I can watch it with them every day of the week. —*Z. C.*

IRON GIANT, THE L: CHILDREN'S/CHILDREN'S ANIMATION (1999) 86M D: Brad Bird. *Eli Marienthal, Jennifer Aniston, Harry Connick Jr., Vin Diesel, Christopher McDonald.* The best American animated film in the past ten years, *The Iron Giant* is a sweet fantasy about a mysterious, gentle robot-man (who may or may not be a devastating war-machine) and his friendship with young Hogarth Hughes in 1957 Maine. Paranoia sets in as Sputnik is launched. Special Agent Kent Mansley, a man obsessed with finding the truth in the name of "national security," arrives to investigate the strange reports of a "giant metal man," and even though Mansley is the antagonist in the story, it's made abundantly clear the real enemy is blind fear and not the government. Nuclear paranoia is heavy stuff for a kids' movie, but Bird keeps things lively through period references and atmosphere, rather than cheap sight gags, dumb-ass sidekick characters a la Disney movies, or Top 40 songs. This film has it all: horror movies, "duck and cover" films, Superman, the Army, nuclear war, beatniks, rock and roll, true friendship, self-sacrifice, and arguably the coolest robot ever. Certainly the nicest. —*K. C.*

IT'S THE GREAT PUMPKIN, CHARLIE BROWN L: CHILDREN'S/PEANUTS (1966) 25M D: Bill Melendez. *Peter Robbins, Christopher Shea, Sally Dryer, Kathy Steinberg, Bill Melendez.* Go Linus! Way to believe in something, and way to stand up to all those prematurely mature, cynical Peanuts characters, who are always trying to do what society tells them instead of exploring the true meaning of holidays. Linus rules! —*M. S.*

JACK FROST L: CHILDREN'S LIVE/CHILDREN'S LIVE ACTION (1998) 102M D: Troy Miller. *Christopher Allport, Shannon Elizabeth, Joseph Cross, Henry Rollins, Mark Addy.* Not to be confused with the serial killer snowman in the stalkers section, this Jack Frost is the ghost of a kid's dad come back to spend more time with him in the body of a snowman. Unfortunately, this can only turn ugly since, if I'm not mistaken, snow melts pretty easily. Anyway, Jack spent too much time jamming with his band of middle-aged white blues musicians when he was alive, so it's only through this delicate winter-time surrogate that he can teach his son to be better at hockey. The snowman puppet by Jim Henson's Creature Workshop is quite good, but otherwise this is a painful and forced piece of juvenile melodrama. Strangely, it evolved out of Sam Raimi's planned live-action *Frosty the Snowman*, which would've starred George Clooney. Director Miller went on to direct segments of *Mr. Show* as well as their movie *Run Ronnie Run!* —*B. T.*

JAMES AND THE GIANT PEACH L: KIDS' LITERATURE/DAHL, ROALD (1996) 79M D: Henry Selick. *Susan Sarandon, Paul Terry, Simon Callow, Richard Dreyfuss, Jane Leeves.* Visually stunning adaptation of Roald Dahl's classic children's novel about an orphan and some oversized bugs flying around the world on a giant peach tied to some birds. The film starts out in highly stylized live action, switches to stop-motion animation, and ends with a combo when the animated characters make it to New York. The story deviates quite a bit from the book, and the bugs are made much more lovable. But the adaptation has a lot of clever touches, even turning the book's throwaway line about James's parents being killed by a rhinoceros into a very effective recurring scare. It's the best visual depiction of Dahl's world in a movie yet, thanks partly to the character designs by the great children's book illustrator Lane Smith. Some people complain about the preponderance of Randy Newman's songs, but they forget that the book itself was a musical, the lyrics for one song coming straight from those pages. Watch for Jack Skellington's cameo in the underwater sequence. —*B. T.*

JIMMY NEUTRON: BOY GENIUS L: CHILDREN'S/CHILDREN'S ANIMATION (2001) 82M D: John A Davis. *Debi Berryberry, Martin Short, Patrick Stewart.* Little Jimmy Neutron is an Einstein in short pants with the vision of a junior Jules Verne in this animated adventure full of fantastical imagery and gee-whiz fantasy. Think *Mars Attacks* for the adolescent set, with Jimmy leading his schoolmates into battle against a demented race of goopy green aliens. In most childhood sci-fantasies, the kid wakes from such Tom Swift dreams a la Walter Mitty and trudges into the real world of normalcy, but the charge of *Jimmy Neutron: Boy Genius* is that it's all true, at least for the candy-colored eighty-two minutes. There's a real kick to the fantasy of being the brainiest kid on the planet, a down-to-earth quality to Jimmy and his not-so-bright but ever-so-stalwart best buddies, and an innocent joy to their rambunctious energy and rebellion. —*S. A.*

JUNGLE BOOK, THE L: CHILDREN'S/DISNEY ANIMATION (1967) 78M D: Wolfgang Reitherman. *Bruce Rethermann, Phil Harris, Sebastion Cabot, Louis Prima, George Sanders.* This film marks the end of an era, as it was the last animated Disney feature supervised by Walt Disney himself. The story, based on Rudyard Kipling's classic novel, measures up squarely to the general theme with which Disney was obsessed his whole life: an orphan trying to find its place in the world. Here a young boy is raised by wolves and has to decide if he wants to live in the jungle with all his friends or in civilization with human beings. The animal caricatures are some of the best Disney has to offer. The songs include "I Wanna Be Like You," "Trust in Me," and, of course, the song that became the favorite, "Bare Necessities." —*N. J.*

KIM POSSIBLE: THE SECRET FILES L: CHILDREN'S/CHILDREN'S ANIMATION (2002) 71M D: Various. *Will Friedle, Christy Carlson Romano, Jean Smart, Gary Cole, Nancy Cartwright, Tahj Mowry.* So many cartoons these days are made primarily for kids, the humor lacking the wit and intelligence of the golden years when cartoons were written with adults in mind, too. So imagine my shock and surprise when the Disney Channel put out *Kim Possible*, the adventures of a high school cheerleader who does it all. She fights villains bent on taking over the world! She defeats killer robots! She puts to shame false "real life extreme action" shows! But she's also still a high school girl, struggling to ask a boy to the dance and unable to tame the blender in her home ec class. Along with her best friend Ron and his pet naked mole rat Rufus, Kim fights evildoers and foolish villains, saving the day with a little help from her friends. The dialogue is hilarious, the characters witty and entertaining, and there is even *gasp!* continuity! I agree with Ron, who once told Kim, "Without the Ron Factor, you're just another teenage superhero with a website!" —*M. N.*

KIRIKOU AND THE SORCERESS L: CHILDREN'S/CHILDREN'S ANIMATION (1998) 74M D: Michel Ocelot. *Theo Sebeko, Kombisile Sangweni, Antoinette Kellermann.* This charming and unique French animation based on a West African folk tale tells the story of Kirikou (Sebeko), a baby so plucky he climbs out of his mother's womb, announces his own name, saves the village from a wicked sorceress (Kellermann), and gets married. I guess you would have to call him some sort of a prodigy. Since it takes place in Africa, most of the characters are nude or partially nude, and this is probably the sole reason that the film isn't as well known in the prudish United States as other imports, like *Wallace and Gromit* or *My Neighbor Totoro*. But it's one of those rare children's movies that will captivate kids, their parents, and even adults who don't have any kids. Director Ocelot also did the silhouette animation feature *Princes and Princesses*. —*B.T.*

LADY AND THE TRAMP L: CHILDREN'S/DISNEY ANIMATION (1955) 75M D: Hamilton Luske, Wilfred Jackson, Clyde Geronimi. *Bill Thompson, Barbara Luddy, Peggy Lee, Larry Roberts.* The romantic love story between Lady, a female cocker spaniel, and Tramp, a "wrong side of the tracks" mongrel, is another magical feature from Walt Disney. The film rivals any live-action studio flick from the '50s for high romance, as best seen in the famous alley dinner scene behind an Italian restaurant. Two evil Siamese cats, Si and Am, and the dogcatcher are the main villains, but Walt keeps the film centered on the love, as Tramp tries to free Lady from the bondage of her wealthy household and show her how to live life as a free dog. Much like *Beauty and the Beast* forty years later, the romantic plot of *Lady* appealed to both kids and adults, and its many memorable songs are still as lush and lovely half a century later. Avoid the 2001 straight-to-video sequel, *Lady and the Tramp II*. —*N.H.*

LAST UNICORN, THE L: CHILDREN'S/RANKIN & BASS (1982) 92M D: Jules Bass, Arthur Rankin Jr. *Alan Arkin, Mia Farrow, Jeff Bridges, Tammy Grimes, Christopher Lee, Angela Lansbury.* Based on a book by Peter S. Beagle, this animated film is little known but remarkably good. The animation and story are enchanting and delightful, and the voices are perfect for each of the main characters. A unicorn notices one day she hasn't seen any of her kind in a long time, tending to her small forest as she does. She asks a passing butterfly if he has seen any unicorns in his travels, and between foolish rhymes and playful nonsense he offers oblique hints that her kind have met a terrible fate. Unwilling to accept she is the last, she goes in search of other unicorns and meets friends and foes along the way. The magician Schmendrick turns her into a woman to save her, and suddenly the last unicorn must save not only her own kind, but herself before she forgets who she really is and becomes mortal forever. The few terrible musical moments are worth enduring for this excellent film. —*M.N.*

Best movies starring animals

ALLIGATOR

ANY WHICH WAY YOU CAN

AU HASARD BALTHAZAR

BABE

BABE: PIG IN THE CITY

THE BEAR

BENJI

BENJI THE HUNTED

BILL AND COO

THE BLACK STALLION

A BOY AND HIS DOG

BRINGING UP BABY

THE CAT FROM OUTER SPACE

DAY OF THE ANIMALS

EVERY WHICH WAY BUT LOOSE

FLY AWAY HOME

GOING APE

GRIZZLY

THE INCREDIBLE JOURNEY *(1963)*

JAWS

LANCELOT LINK

WILLARD *(1971)*

LIFE & ADVENTURES OF SANTA CLAUS, THE L: CHILDREN'S/RANKIN & BASS (1985) 50M D: Jules Bass, Arthur Rankin Jr. *Earl Hammond, Bob McFadden, Lynne Lipton, Earle Hyman, Larry Kenney.* A council of immortals meets to discuss whether or not to grant immortality to Santa Claus. Making his case, the Great Ak tells us the history of Santa Claus, including his tough childhood and why he started making toys for orphans. Based on a book by L. Frank Baum, this clever story puts the Santa Claus myth into a fantasy context. Made much later than the more famous Rankin-Bass Christmas specials, it has some great character designs and animation, but also some of the leaden pace that weakens most of the studio's work. Children of the '80s will be amused to realize it stars pretty much the entire voice cast of *Thundercats*, including Mumm-Ra as Santa, Lion-O as Commander of the Wind Demons, and Snarf as Tingler. —*B.T.*

LIKE MIKE L: CHILDREN'S LIVE/CHILDREN'S LIVE ACTION (2002) 100M D: John Schultz. *Morris Chestnut, Johnathan Lipnicki, L'il Bow Wow, Robert Forster.* Adolescent hip-hop star L'il Bow Wow is an orphan who puts on magic sneakers and becomes a Tasmanian devil on the basketball court, turning from an attendance gimmick for the local team to the youngest and shortest player in the league. The plot follows a predictable connect-the-dots course, but director Schultz adds some evocative coloring and draws surprisingly shaded performances, creating a picture as much about emotional abandonment as adolescent fantasy. Chestnut is the hard-shelled hero who becomes the kid's reluctant roommate, Forster is the fatherly coach, and Lipnicki the mop top best friend. —*S.A.*

LILO & STITCH L: CHILDREN'S/DISNEY ANIMATION (2002) 85M D: Chris Sanders, Dean DeBlois. *Kevin McDonald, David Ogden Stiers, Tia Carrere, Chris Sanders, Daveigh Chase, Ving Rhames.* Lilo is a troubled Hawaiian girl being raised by her sister, and Stitch is the weird koala-like alien weapon of mass destruction she keeps as a pet. Many of the supporting characters are badly designed and animated, but the two title characters are instant Disney icons. Far from the usual statuesque princesses, Lilo is a short, stalky troublemaker who gets in a fist fight right in the beginning and is well voiced by Chase (who later played the scary girl in the remake of *The Ring*). *Lilo & Stitch* is not a classic like *The Iron Giant* (which seems to be a primary influence), but it has a low-key charm missing from many of the Disney films of the late '90s and early 2000s. —*B.T.*

LION KING, THE L: CHILDREN'S/DISNEY ANIMATION (1994) 87M D: Roger Allers, Robert Minkoff. *Matthew Broderick, Ernie Sabella, James Earl Jones, Jeremy Irons, Rowan Atkinson, Nathan Lane.* Often considered the high watermark for Disney's modern era, I would argue it's actually their most overrated film. Yes, there are some majestic uses of animation, and some great dramatic moments—in particular, the wildebeest stampede and the death of Mufasa. And yet you can't help wonder how much better this movie would be if they followed that story instead of going off on a tangent about a smart-ass meerkat and his friend the farting warthog. You are begging for relief from the schmaltzy Elton John ballads, but all you get is "Hakuna Matata," which is largely about farting. This is a triumph of catchy tunes that sell soundtracks over actual musical numbers that tell the story or add depth to the characters. It's not a terrible movie, and Disney has certainly made worse since, but it doesn't deserve its reputation as one of the all-time-great animated films. In fact, *Tarzan* is a more successful drama about a father-son relationship in the hierarchy of animals, with more impressive animation and less intrusive comic relief (although you just

exchange the Elton John songs for Phil Collins). —*B.T.*

LION, THE WITCH AND THE WARDROBE, THE L: CHILDREN'S/CHILDREN'S ANIMATION (1979) 95M D: Bill Melendez. *Beth Porter, Stephen Thorne, Rachel Warren, Susan Sokol.* I watched this movie not as a fan of the C. S. Lewis book, but as someone who figured director Melendez must've had something to do with the greatness of all those wonderful classic *Peanuts* specials. Sure, Charles Schultz is behind the great personalities and the way they look, but what about Charlie Brown's little dance, or the gibberish the adults speak? No doubt Melendez's TV adaptation of *The Chronicles of Narnia* must be worth watching. Unfortunately, it is not. This story of children who find a portal to a magic land inside their mother's closet is rather dull and ugly. The first hour or so takes place mostly inside bland living rooms and empty snowscapes. The human characters (and some of the monsters) are so crudely drawn (lumpy blobs with only a vague resemblance to actual anatomy) that their sword fights are downright laughable. I do kind of like the way they draw the lion, though, and most of the children's voices sound refreshingly like real kids. —*B.T.*

LITTLE MONSTERS L: CHILDREN'S LIVE/CHILDREN'S LIVE ACTION (1989) 100M D: Richard Greenberg. *Fred Savage, Howie Mandel, Rick Duccommun, Daniel Stern.* This film is a glorious ode to devilish little kids. Actually, maybe not glorious. But I thought so when I was little. Savage is always getting in trouble with his dad (Stern) for things he hasn't done. Well, guess what? It's the monsters who live under the bed who make all the messes, break all the rules, and get you in trouble. When Savage captures one the monsters (Mandel), he is invited to join their world of excess and goes on a marvelous spree of pranks and antics. But soon, young Savage begins to become a monster himself and has to fight for his life. Watching it now, the film is pretty bad (especially Mandel), but it's also a fun bit of '80s nostalgia for the juvenile delinquent in all of us. —*N.J.*

LITTLE PRINCESS, A L: CHILDREN'S LIVE/CHILDREN'S LIVE ACTION (1995) 97M D: Alfonso Cuarón. *Liesel Matthews, Eleanor Bron, Liam Cunningham, Rusty Schwimmer.* In this reworking of the Frances Hodgson Burnett story, a rich girl gets into trouble at a strict boarding school by riling up the children with fantastic stories about Indian mythology. When word comes back that her father has been killed in the war and there are no funds for her tuition, she is forced to become a servant at the school and is treated cruelly, even by those who were once her friends. The young actors are great, the script is very intelligent, and the photography is absolutely gorgeous, particularly during the colorful fantasy sequences. When you consider the boarding school setting, the impressive performances by young actors, and the imaginative special effects (there's even a CGI ten-headed monster), it seems very fitting that Cuarón was later hired to direct *Harry Potter and the Prisoner of Azkaban*. —B.T.

LONELIEST RUNNER, THE L: CHILDREN'S LIVE/CHILDREN'S LIVE ACTION (1976) 75M D: Michael Landon. *Brian Keith, Michael Landon, Lance Kerwin, Melissa Sue Anderson, DeAnn Mears.* This made-for-TV movie, directed by Landon, is a *very* serious treatise on bed-wetting and the trauma it can cause a young man. . . especially if said young man's mother is the most ridiculously evil, castrating woman on Earth. The subject of the film is a fourteen-year-old boy who still has a problem with urinating in his slumber. He tries to hide this from his parents because his mother is not very understanding and hangs his sheets out the windows so the whole damn block knows he wets his bed, and screams, "HE DOES IT BECAUSE HE'S TOO LAZY TO GO TO THE BATHROOM!!" So he runs home from school every day so he can take down the sheets before anyone sees, and this leads him to eventually become a gold-medal-winning marathon runner (after he firsts learns to control his bladder). If this sounds slightly familiar, there's a *Mr. Show* skit I'm betting was inspired by this movie. This was a rather personal statement from Landon; on the back of the box it goes so far as to divulge that he himself was a bed wetter. Yikes. —D.W.

LORAX, THE L: KIDS' LITERATURE/DR. SEUSS (1972) 30M D: Hawley Pratt. *Athena Lorde, Bob Holt, Harlan Carraher.* Perhaps Seuss's sharpest and most relevant allegory, this is the story of big industry destroying the environment in the name of mindless consumerism. The Lorax is the one voice standing up for the trees and the animals, but nobody listens to him. The forests are all cut down in the production of a literally useless product called a Thneed. "You need a Thneed!" the advertisements declare. I always think about Thneeds when I see commercials trying to convince me there is a reason for ridiculous products like drinkable yogurt, cell phone walkie talkies, premade peanut butter sandwiches, or Cinnapie. This is not at all upbeat like *The Cat in the Hat*, but it's the best special made from his darker, more political stories. —B.T.

MAC AND ME L: CHILDREN'S LIVE/CHILDREN'S LIVE ACTION (1988) 95M D: Stewart Raffill. *Jade Calegory, Christine Ebersole, Tina Caspary, Jonathan Ward, Lauren Stanley.* Criticism of this late-'80s family film is not possible; instead I offer a partial synopsis. (1) A naked, whistling alien baby is sucked into a NASA landing module and accidentally brought to Earth. (2) A chubby kid in a wheelchair falls off a cliff. (3) The naked whistling alien parents stand in the desert and whistle, naked. (4) The divorced mother of the handicapped adolescent complains about her car. (5) The whistling alien

baby, hiding inside an enormous unstuffed teddy bear, goes to McDonald's and performs a dance number with all the employees and patrons. Ronald McDonald himself is on hand, and points at the alien baby/plush toy while shaking his own hideous clown ass. (6)The FBI storms the McDonald's and kidnaps the move-busting teddy bear, thinking it a threat to national security. OK, I don't want to ruin the end for you, and by now I'm sure it's clear that *Mac and Me* created a new high mark for fast food–sponsored kids' sci-fi epics. See it with your own fat nerdy child. —Z.C.

MAD MONSTER PARTY? L: CHILDREN'S/RANKIN & BASS (1967) 95M D: Jules Bass. *Allen Swift, Phyllis Diller, Boris Karloff, Gale Garnett.* What do you get when you combine Boris Karloff, *Mad Magazine*, and *Rudolph the Red-Nosed Reindeer*? The most insanely wonderful "children's" film ever made, of course! *Mad Monster Party?* features all the classic Universal Monsters and then some (stylized by *Mad* alum Jack Davis), getting together for a far-out shindig at Karloff's castle. See Frankenstein get drunk and punch out Dracula! See the monsters go bowling with Peter Lorre's head! Rankin and Bass, known mostly for their Christmas classics *Rudolph* and *Frosty the Snowman*, use their "animagic" to create a psychedelic monster-puppet show. With a stripper-jazz score by Maury Laws (who did the music for most of the Rankin and Bass specials), an all-corpse air force, and a catfight between buxom, panty-clad puppets, you'd think *Mad Monster Party?* was aimed at the Mario Bava crowd, but this was actually made for kids! —P.M.

On the plus side are the Rankin and Bass–animated Mad Scientist, Dracula, Frankenstein, the Mummy, the Wolf Man, and the Creature. But on the down side is this whole plot about some pharmacist who goes to Monster Island, the evil Francesca, and crappy '60s lounge music. All I want is the monsters! Jeez, come on! —T.S.

MADELINE L: CHILDREN'S LIVE/CHILDREN'S LIVE ACTION (1998) 88M D: Daisy von Scherler Mayer. *Ben Daniels, Frances McDormand, Nigel Hawthorne, Hatty Jones.* Loving adaptation of Ludwig Bemelmans's picture books about a rebellious little girl in a Paris boarding school. It's amazing how many details from the books (Pepito, the bad hat, Genevieve the dog, the painter, the Eiffel Tower's proximity to the school, etc.) they manage to use while still maintaining some semblance of a real-world plot. The charm of the movie (and maybe what has kept it from being very popular) is its old-fashioned storybook feel. The events are not epic (despite an abduction by clowns), the setting is timeless, and the music is by Michel Legrand. I never would have pictured McDormand playing the nun Miss Clavel, but she certainly works. —B.T.

MAKE MINE MUSIC L: CHILDREN'S/DISNEY ANIMATION (1946) 75M D: Clyde Geronimi, Joe Grant, Hamiton Luke, others. *Sterling Holloway, Benny Goodman, Nelson Eddy, David Lichine, Dinah Shore.* This was the first of the anthology films to which Disney resorted to save money after WWII and the animator's strike. It's in the tradition of *Fantasia*, but instead of classical music, it used popular music from the era. You probably remember "Peter and the Wolf" and maybe "Willy, the Whale Who Wanted to Sing at the Met" (all the segments were released separately as shorts), but others are good, too; especially the two Benny Goodman jazz tunes, "All the Cats Join In" and "After You've Gone." It's definitely worthwhile for animation buffs and hardcore Disney fans, but probably not for occupying the kids. The DVD includes three earlier music-related shorts as extras, including the excellent first Mickey Mouse cartoon made in color, "The Band Concert." Unfortunately, *Make Mine Music* was "edited for content"—the opening seven-minute segment, "A Rustic Ballad," was cut because it showed guns. —*B. T.*

MARY POPPINS L: CHILDREN'S LIVE/DISNEY LIVE ACTION (1964) 140M D: Robert Stevenson. *Julie Andrews, Dick Van Dyke, Karen Dotrice, Mathew Garber, Glynis Johns, David Tomlinson, Ed Wynn.* In this classic Disney musical, Julie Andrews makes her film debut as the new nanny who is "practically perfect in every way." The story is set in early 1890s London, where Mrs. Banks (Johns), mother of two, has occupied herself with the women's suffrage movement while Mr. Banks (Tomlinson) toils at the bank. Mary Poppins is hired as nanny, and from there the magic begins. For every little problem there is an answer, often with a song (e.g. "A Spoonful of Sugar"). She takes the children on a fantastical outing, meeting up with a chimney sweep (Van Dyke), and together they spend an afternoon within chalk drawings outside Hyde Park. Great fun for all ages. —*N. J.*

MATILDA L: KIDS' LITERATURE/DAHL, ROALD (1996) 93M D: Danny DeVito. *Pam Ferris, Embeth Davidtz, Rhea Perlman, Danny DeVito, Mara Wilson.* Matilda (Wilson) is a gifted young girl who enrages her cruel, uncultured parents (DeVito and Perlman) just by reading lots of books. Even worse than her parents is Miss Trunchbull (Ferris), the manly, drill-sergeant-like headmistress who terrorizes and abuses her at school. But Matilda's Dickensian life is improved by two factors: the kindly intervention of her teacher Miss Honey (Davidtz) and a sudden discovery of telekinetic powers (which she uses a little more responsibly than Carrie White did). This movie offended some parents with its faithful rendition of Dahl's theme that most adults are cruel, ugly, horrible monsters lacking in taste or imagination—which is of course the movie's greatest strength. DeVito's dark sense of humor works great for the movie, though he taints what could

be a timeless world with unneccessary product placements and dated references. —*B. T.*

MELODY TIME L: CHILDREN'S/DISNEY ANIMATION (1948) 75M D: Clyde Geronimi, Hamilton Luske, Wilfred Jackson, Jack Kinney. *Roy Rogers, Trigger, Dennis Day, Buddy Clark.* Another anthology of Disney shorts, similar to *Make Mine Music.* One advantage with the format is that Disney was able to experiment with different animation styles, like the simple, abstracted style of "Bumble Boogie" (a jazzy version of "Flight of the Bumble Bee"), or the gorgeous, painterly ode to nature, "Trees." The most memorable segments are the more traditional ones, "Johnny Appleseed" and "Pecos Bill." These are well-told tales, and the latter is introduced by Roy Rogers and the Sons of the Pioneers, who appear as their live-action selves in front of painted backgrounds. Donald Duck also gets to jam with the live-action Ethel Smith in "Blame It on the Samba." If you love Disney animation, you'll find these well-crafted, lesser-known films an interesting chapter in the studio's evolution. A warning for purists: for the DVD release, Disney digitally removed a cigarette from Pecos Bill's mouth. —*B. T.*

MIGHTY MORPHIN POWER RANGERS: THE MOVIE L: CHILDREN'S LIVE/CHILDREN'S LIVE ACTION (1995) 95M D: Bryan Spicer. *Paul Freeman, Karen Ashley, Steve Cardenas, Amy Jo Johnson, Johnny Yong Bosch, Jason David Frank.* Mighty Morphin Power Rangers was an absurdly amateurish TV series made by awkwardly combining stock footage from Japanese giant robot shows with *Saved by the Bell*esque scenes of actors playing American teens. When this cheap-ass show somehow became a phenomenal hit, someone thought it was possible to transfer it to the big screen with Hollywood production values. The spandex costumes became elaborate plastic armor, the people in robot suits became crude, shiny computer animation, the wailing guitar soundtrack became a collection of songs by the likes of Devo and The Red Hot Chili Peppers. They even got a director who had done *X-Files* episodes and veteran character actor Freeman to play the hammy villain Ivan Ooze. The one thing they didn't get was a reason why the asinine mythology of the Power Rangers should be taken seriously. But it's even funnier to see this material trying so hard to be mistaken for a real movie. It's just too bad the computer effects are so bad—it will be nice some day to see some really good CGI robot fights. —*B. T.*

MONSTERS, INC. L: CHILDREN'S/DISNEY ANIMATION (2001) 92M D: Peter Docter, Lee Unkrich, David Silverman. *Billy Crystal, Jennifer Tilly, John Goodman, Steve Buscemi, James Coburn.* An extremely creative story line comes together with excellent computer-generated animation to make one of the cutest movies of all time. The monster world relies on the screams of children as its main source of power, and master scarer Sully is great at scream-collecting. When he catches coworker Randall trying to collect a few extra screams to boost his numbers and take Sully's record, chaos is unleashed. Sully ends up accidentally allowing a little girl into the monster world, and everyone knows that children are extremely dangerous—one touch can kill you! As Sully and his buddy Mike try to hide the little girl, affectionately nicknamed Boo, until they can decide what to do with her, they learn that maybe scaring children isn't so important after all. Well-written and featuring an all-star vocal cast, *Monsters, Inc.* is a movie everyone can enjoy. —*J. S.*

MOUSEHUNT L: CHILDREN'S LIVE/CHILDREN'S LIVE ACTION (1997) 97M D: Gore Verbinski. *Lee Evans, Vicki Lewis, Christopher Walken, Nathan Lane.* Verbinski (who directed the American version of *The Ring* and *Pirates of the Caribbean*) debuted with this stylish dark comedy about heirs to a string factory who have their lives ruined by a mouse. It's marketed for kids, but the story (by *Dark Backward* director Adam Rifkin) is all about people trying to kill animals. Walken plays an exterminator so obsessed he tastes mouse shit to see how fresh it is. —*B. T.*

MUPPET CHRISTMAS CAROL, THE L: CHILDREN'S LIVE/ MUPPETS (1992) 120M D: Brian Henson. *Michael Caine, the Muppets, Steven Mackintosh, Meredith Braun.* After being bought out by Disney for the first time, the Muppets went through a short phase of adapting classic stories instead of playing themselves in movies. This first attempt is a surprisingly straightforward take on the Dickens story, with Caine as Ebenezer Scrooge and Kermit as Bob Cratchit. Miss Piggy plays Mrs. Cratchit, but fortunately Tiny Tim is just a little frog and not some hideous frog-pig hybrid. There is a bit of comic relief provided by the Great Gonzo, who plays Charles Dickens and narrates the story while Rizzo the Rat follows him around and bothers him. But for the most part, it's treated seriously, and this works well, thanks to the timelessness of the story and the great oversized puppets portraying the ghosts. The songs by Paul Williams are all right, but the movie stumbles when two nonpuppet characters sing to each other. Who wants to see that crap in a Muppet movie? —*B. T.*

MUPPET MOVIE, THE L: CHILDREN'S LIVE/MUPPETS (1979) 98M D: James Frawley. *The Muppets, Charles Durning, Edgar Bergen.* In this big-screen debut of the Muppets, we see Kermit leave his home in the swamp to chase his dream of sharing music with the world. On his path he meets Fozzy, Gonzo, and Rowlf, falls in love with Miss Piggy, hooks up with Dr. Teeth and the Electric Mayhem, encounters many celebrity cameos, and has to outrun Doc Hopper (Durning), a restaurant bigwig trying to force him to endorse frog legs. It's full of inventive puppet gimmicks, parodies of cinematic clichés, and deliberately bad puns. But

what really makes it work is that it's so obviously close to the hearts of Henson and Company, who also followed their dream to put on a show and avoid commercialism and other money-oriented industry bullshit. So in the big finale, when the Muppets sing, "Life's like a movie, write your own ending, keeping believing, keep pretending, we've done just what we've set out to do," it's so sincere that it makes me tear up every time. The purity of this Muppet movie makes it impossible to top. —*B. T.*

MUPPET TREASURE ISLAND L: CHILDREN'S LIVE/ MUPPETS (1996) 99M D: Brian Henson. *The Muppets, Billy Connolly, Kevin Bishop, Tim Curry.* Another Muppet adaptation of classic literature, this time bringing along Curry as Long John Silver, Connolly as Billy Bones, and some pretty choir boy (Bishop) as Jim Hawkins. And I mean choir boy literally because the kid sings some syrupy falsetto songs that seem to be designed to test the patience of the audience. There are too many humans and not enough Muppet humor, but it's perhaps the most stylish Muppet movie, with many beautiful sets and clever digital effects for full-body Muppet shots. The most brilliant joke may or may not be intentional. Kermit and Miss Piggy sing the ballad "Love Led Us Here" while hanging upside down over a cliff. In that context, the song is clearly intended as a joke, but on the end credits it's reprised as an adult contemporary duet by John Berry and Helen Darling. I'm not sure whether that's a parody of Disney's unique brand of crass commercialism or a prime example of it, but either way it makes me laugh. —*B. T.*

MUPPETS FROM SPACE L: CHILDREN'S LIVE/MUPPETS (1999) 88M D: Tim Hill. *The Muppets, F. Murray Abraham, Jeffrey Tambor.* You:18–34-year-old in search of things you loved in your youth, but disappointed with recent versions of childhood favorites. Me: 88 minutes long, full of zany, subversive humor, and featuring a talking prawn. Check me out and see if you fall in love with puppets again. —*J. B. P.*

MUPPETS MAGIC FROM THE ED SULLIVAN SHOW L: CHILDREN'S LIVE/MUPPETS (1966) 68M D: Various. Before they became the stars of *Sesame Street*, the Muppets debuted on the Ed Sullivan Show on September 18, 1966, with "Instant Rock and Roll Band" and became frequent guests, performing surreal skits (who can forget the indescribable "Ma-Na-Ma-Na"?) with a bizarre company of malleable, amorphous, shape-changing characters. Among the highlights of this collection, which features over a dozen appearances of the Muppets (and fleeting glimpses of Henson), are a proto-Cookie Monster eating a computer, a "Wow man" hippie Kermit teaching a square how to visualize abstract thought, a reindeer snow dance that merely brings rain ("We are rain-deer after all"), and of course "Ma-Na-Ma-Na." —S. A.

MY LITTLE PONY: THE MOVIE L: CHILDREN'S/CHILDREN'S ANIMATION (1986) 100M D: Michael Joens. *Sheryl Bernstein, Susan Blu, Danny DeVito, Tammy Amerson, Charles Adler, Michael Bell.* It's spring in Ponyland, and the annual pony Spring Festival is about to begin, but little does anyone know that this year things won't run as smoothly as normal. The evil witch Hydia, up in the Volcano of Doom, has set out to destroy the ponies' happiness, releasing a gloom-inducing purple substance called Smooze over Ponyland, infecting everyone with a serious case of the blues. The ponies have to combat their gloom, find their runaway friends, and team up together to get rid of the Smooze, or Ponyland will never be happy and carefree again. A cutesy, fluffy story that will cause adults to roll their eyes but lift the hearts and imaginations of kids, this movie is silly fun. Admittedly, the animation isn't that great, and the dialogue isn't very thought-provoking, but that is adult criticism. I loved this as a little girl in the '80s, and it still has a special place in my heart. —J. S.

OLIVE, THE OTHER REINDEER L: CHILDREN'S/CHILDREN'S ANIMATION (1999) 69M D: Steve Moore. *Ed Asner, Dan Castellaneta, Tim Meadows, Michael Stipe, Joe Pantoliano, Drew Barrymore, Jay Mohr.* Olive (Barrymore) is a little dog who misunderstands the lyric "all of the other reindeer" on the radio and thinks she has to go to the North Pole to help Santa (Asner). That may seem like a dumb mistake, but it turns out it happens to a lot of people, including a bus driver (Meadows) who says, "I used to think the pledge of allegiance was about me, Richard Stands." This contemporary equivalent of the classic Rankin-Bass holiday specials is a very funny expansion of the charming picture book by Vivian Walsh and J. Otto Siebold. It uses a unique 2-D approach to computer animation to faithfully render Siebold's Adobe Illustrator-based art style. —B. T.

101 DALMATIANS L: CHILDREN'S/DISNEY ANIMATION (1961) 79M D: Clyde Geronimi, Wolfgang Reithermann, Hamilton Luske. *Rod Taylor, Pat O'Malley, Betty Lou Gerson, Martha Wentworth.* One of the highest grossing animated films of all time, Disney's *101 Dalmations* concerns a certain Cruella de Vil, who kidnaps Dalmatian puppies in order to make herself a spotted coat. A variety of animals come together to help save the day, and they find this evil woman has collected no less than 101 of these adorable puppies. The songs include "Dalmatian Plantation," "Remember When," and a very jazzy "Cruella de Vil." —N. J.

OSMOSIS JONES L: CHILDREN'S LIVE/CHILDREN'S LIVE ACTION (2001) 98M D: Bobby Farrelly, Peter Farrelly. *Chris Rock, David Hyde Pierce, Bill Murray, Molly Shannon, Chris Elliot, Lawrence Fishburne.* In one of the least compelling high concepts of the modern animation era, Rock voices a wisecracking white bloodcell who is a cop inside Murray's body. He teams up with a pill (Pierce, basically playing Buzz Lightyear) to stop a sinister virus (Fishburne). There are good gross-out laughs in the live-action segments (you can't really go completely wrong with the Farrelly brothers directing Murray and Elliot) but not enough to make it worth sitting through an endless series of lame bodily function puns. —B. T.

PARENT TRAP, THE L: CHILDREN'S LIVE/DISNEY LIVE ACTION (1961) 127M D: David Swift. *Maureen O'Hara, Brian Keith, Hayley Mills.* "Let's get together, yeah, yeah, yeah!" Mills and Mills star (via the magic of split screen) as twin sisters separated in infancy by divorced parents (O'Hara and Keith). The girls meet up at summer camp and hatch a plan to get mom and dad back together. This Disney favorite was remade in 1998 but the new version can't touch the original classic, with its East-meets-West/rock-and-roll-meets-classical-culture sensibility, and the summer camp shenanigans and romantic manipulations of impish girls at play. Spirited and sassy, Mills (both of them) is a real scene stealer, even up against pros like Keith and O'Hara, and her energy has a lot to do with this comedy's success. —S. A.

PEE-WEE'S PLAYHOUSE CHRISTMAS L: CHILDREN'S LIVE/PEEWEE HERMAN (1988) 49M D: Wayne Orr, Paul Reubens. *Paul Reubens, Little Richard, k. d. lang, Grace Jones, The Del Rubio Triplets, Frankie Avalon.* Knowing his kitsch better than anyone, Pee-wee Herman made a Christmas special in the classic variety show sense, cramming the format of his show with absurd celebrity cameos and musical numbers by everyone from Charo to Oprah Winfrey. The production values seem even higher than on an ordinary episode—there is a soundstage ice-skating scene—and at the end he opens up a whole new wing of the Playhouse made out of fruit cake (OK so that last part is just a matte painting). If you enjoy Pee-wee, this is a must-see. —B. T.

PETER PAN L: CHILDREN'S/DISNEY ANIMATION (1953) 76M D: Hamilton Luske, Clyde Geronimi, Wilfred Jackson. *Bobby Driscoll, Heather Angel, Kathryn Beaumont, Hans Conried.* Peter Pan was the perfect animated Disney vehicle. Based on the J. M. Barrie story about a child who never grows up, Disney animated this story far more spectacularly than any stage adaptation could. Furthermore, animation accentuated the bizarre fugue the author most certainly had in mind for the children who escape their upper-class home in favor of the fantastic Neverland. However, in this far off place of fantasy, evil does exist—in the form of Captain Hook. Although the children could seemingly rescue themselves out of this strange land, Peter Pan is ultimately beholden to it. —N. J.

PINOCCHIO L: CHILDREN'S/DISNEY ANIMATION (1940) 87M D: Hamilton Luske, Walt Disney, Ben Sharpsteen, others. *Cliff Edwards, Christian Rub, Dick Jones, Evelyn Venable.* Disney's second feature is my very favorite. The superb craftsmanship of that era's Disney animators was put to great use animating puppet shows, cuckoo clocks, boys transforming into mules, the glimmering Blue Fairy, the gargantuan whale Monstro, and numerous lushly painted multiplane backgrounds. The story of Pinocchio learning to be a real boy by obeying his conscience is still relevant; the scenes where J. Worthington Foulfellow tempts him with fame and fortune might as well have been made today. I never did understand why Jiminy Cricket looks more like a man than a cricket, but oh well. They don't make 'em much better than this. —*B. T.*

PINOCCHIO IN OUTER SPACE L: CHILDREN'S/CHILDREN'S ANIMATION (1964) 71M D: Ray Goossens. *Peter Lazer, Arnold Stang, Conrad Jameson.* At the end of Carlo Collodi's story, Pinocchio (voiced here by Lazer) earned the right to be a real boy. But in this somewhat entertaining sequel, we find he turned out to be a real asshole, picking on his dog and banging other kids' heads together until the karmic nature of Blue Fairy magic reverted him to puppet form. To become a real boy again, he teams up with a turtle-like alien named Nerdle (Stang) and takes on a giant mutant "rogue whale in space" called Astro. The drawing style and references to space are very '60s, and there's even a beatnik cat named Groovy. It's nowhere near the quality of the Disney classic, but it's surprisingly good for some guys from New York you've never heard of who made a bunch of drawings and shipped them off to Belgian animators. Unlike the Disney film, this DVD has some extra features (an overly serious deleted prologue and even a commentary track). —*B. T.*

PIRATES OF DARK WATER: THE SAGA BEGINS L: CHILDREN'S/HANNA-BARBERA (1991) 90M D: Don Lusk. *George Newborn, Tim Curry, Jodi Benson.* This surprisingly good fantasy series by Hanna-Barbera centers on Ren (Newborn), a young Luke Skywalker–type on the aquatic planet Mer who discovers he is the son of King Primus of Octopon. His father failed his quest to collect the Thirteen Treasures of Rule, which magically control a deadly plague of "dark water" that devours anything in its path. So Ren puts together a crew and sets sail to gather the treasures. His chief obstacles include the grotesque pirate Bloth and the dark water itself. Unlike other action cartoons of the era, *Dark Water* was serious, well written, and had a certain amount of craft in its character animation and watercolor backgrounds. It seemed genuinely concerned with characters and stories, not with selling toys—there's even an episode about slavery. This video collects the five-episode mini-series originally called *Dark Water* (the *Pirates of* was added when it became a short-lived series). When the

series originally aired, the monkeybird Niddler was voiced by Roddy McDowall. Unfortunately, when the series started, Frank Welker took over with a squeaky, Snarf-like voice, so they redubbed the original episodes for continuity's sake. —*B. T.*

PIRATES OF THE CARIBBEAN: THE CURSE OF THE BLACK PEARL L: CHILDREN'S LIVE/DISNEY LIVE ACTION (2003) 143M D: Gore Verbinski. *Johnny Depp, Geoffrey Rush, Orlando Bloom, Keira Knightley.* When the crew of the Black Pearl stole Aztec gold, they were cursed to turn into skeletons in the moonlight and, worse, to never enjoy their plundering and pillaging. Now they're trying to retrieve all the gold and a certain type of blood to end the curse, which necessitates the kidnapping of a governor's daughter (Knightley). Trying to stop them is the drunken former captain of the Black Pearl, Captain Jack Sparrow (Depp). It's a rousing old-fashioned adventure spruced up by great ILM skeleton effects and an instantly classic comic performance by Depp, who says he based his character on Keith Richards and Pepe Lepew. It's a fun story (pirates trying to *give back* treasure instead of steal it) and the villains are great, but Depp's performance is so weird and brilliant that it's hard to come out talking about anything else. Only loosely inspired by the Disneyland ride (one of the great works of art of the twentieth century). —*B. T.*

POCAHONTAS L: CHILDREN'S/DISNEY ANIMATION (1995) 90M D: Mike Gabriel, Eric Goldberg. *David Ogden Stiers, Mel Gibson, Linda Hunt, Russell Means, Irene Bedard.* Few things outrage some people as much as Disney-fying historical events. But this fairy tale version of how Pocahontas nonviolently saved the life of John Smith is much better than anyone acknowledges. The animators sat the epic, digitally enhanced theatrics of movies like *The Lion King* on the shelf next to historical accuracy, and instead concentrated on the less showy aspects of animation. Backgrounds are simple and subdued, and the characters are stylized in the vein of *Sleeping Beauty*. The great Glen Keane acted as lead animator for the character of Pocahontas, and he seemed to pay extra attention to the way Pocahontas's hair blows spectacularly in the wind; he's also responsible for the first encounter of Pocahontas and Smith, when the two stare at each other in awe. The songs are good, going for emotion and plot advancement over catchy singalongs. Sure, there's something tasteless about Disney prettying up John Smith, but give them credit for making a cartoon about colonialism and genocide—it's certainly an improvement over the Indians in *Peter Pan!* —*B. T.*

POGO SPECIAL BIRTHDAY SPECIAL, THE L: CHILDREN'S/ JONES, CHUCK (1969) 26M D: Chuck Jones. *June Foray, Les Tremayne, Chuck Jones, Walt Kelly.* It's the month of Octember, so all the animals in the swamp are busy celebrating their favorite holidays. But for Porky Pine, a "natural born norphan," it's a sad time because he has no family to celebrate with. Pogo (Foray) feels bad so he decides to assign Porky a birthday and throw him a surprise party. "Written by Mister Walt Kelly," according to the credits, it's full of the elaborate nonsense and wordplay for which Kelly's comic strip was known. The animation is very faithful to his precise linework—there are very few Chuck Jones–ified characters. At the same time, there is a lot of classic Jones physical humor, such as Porky's sweaty presentation of a Valentine's Day cactus to Ms. Hepzibah. A nice, all-purpose holiday special. —*B.T.*

POWERPUFF GIRLS MOVIE, THE L: CHILDREN'S/CHILDREN'S ANIMATION (2002) 74M D: Craig McCracken.

E. G. Daily, Roger L. Jackson, Tom Kane, Cathy Cavadini, Tara Strong. In this theatrically released spinoff of the *Powerpuff Girls* TV series we see the creation of the superhuman preschoolers and how they learned to use their powers. We also see the beginnings of the evil, big-brained monkey Mojo Jojo, who initially wore a paper bag on his head instead of a turban and tricked the girls into helping him build his volcano lair. Director and series creator McCracken stays true to the simple, thick-lined 2-D animation style of the show, but also created elaborate action scenes with intricate, computer-enhanced camera moves, crowd scenes, etc. The best set piece is when the girls play a super-powered game of tag and level all of Townsville in the process. This is a funny movie for fans, but probably obnoxious to the uninitiated and too violent for very young kids (there are literally hundreds of monkeys beaten unconscious). Keep an eye out for obscure *Big Lebowski* references. —*B.T.*

POWERPUFF GIRLS: THE MANE EVENT L: CHILDREN'S/CHILDREN'S ANIMATION (2001) 133M D: Craig McCracken.

Tara Strong, E. G. Daily, Cathy Cavadini, Roger L. Jackson, Tom Kane. There are several episode collections of the adorably designed preschoolers who fly around Townsville mangling evil. This is my favorite because it was the first to include lots of special features. The highlight is "Slumbering with the Enemy" because it includes a commentary track by the evil monkey Mojo Jojo. He mostly complains about the Powerpuff Girls' behavior, but also makes comparisons to *High Noon, Gone with the Wind,* and the films of Frank Capra, and compliments the use of tertiary colors. "Muhahaha! Very expressionistic-looking use of shadows!" This DVD also include McCracken's original student film in which they were called the Whoopass Girls. —*B.T.*

POWERPUFF GIRLS—MONKEY SEE, DOGGIE DO L: CHILDREN'S/CHILDREN'S ANIMATION (1998) 60M D: Robert Alvarez, others. *Cathy Cavadini, Elizabeth Daily, Tara Strong, Tom Kane, Tom Kenny, Roger L. Jackson.* This VHS offering has a mix of episodes, some of which are so-so ("Telephonies," "Mime for a Change") and others that are excellent. Anything with Mojo Jojo is an instant win, so "Monkey See, Doggie Do" is, of course, brilliant, as the marvelously mad monkey decides to control the world by turning everyone into dogs and making them obey his commands. "Mommy Fearest" features the debut of the wicked Sedusa, but best of all is "Bare Facts," which was nominated for an Emmy (Outstanding Animated Program). In this episode, the girls tell the tale of how they saved the mayor. Each girls' version of the story is animated in a unique artistic style. My favorite is Bubbles's story, told through childish crayon drawings, colorful commentary, and cheerful delight. —*M.N.*

PRINCE AND THE PAUPER, THE L: CHILDREN'S/DISNEY ANIMATION (1990) 24M D: George Scribner. *Wayne Allwine, Bill Farmer, Arthur Burghardt, Tony Anselmo.* A straight adaptation of the Mark Twain story, but starring Mickey Mouse (as both title characters) and friends (in the supporting roles). It's too bad Donald and Goofy don't bring more humor to the mix, but this is pretty good for today's bland Mickey. Excellent background paintings and moody effects help give *The Prince and the Pauper* a somewhat epic feel. Originally released to theaters with *The Rescuers Down Under.* —*B.T.*

RACE FOR YOUR LIFE, CHARLIE BROWN! L: CHILDREN'S/PEANUTS (1977) 75M D: Bill Melendez, Phil Roman. *Greg Felton, Duncan Watson, Bill Melendez, Liam Martin, Gail Davis, Stuart Brotman.* When I was little, we lived on the other side of the country from my grandparents. My Grandma used to make me tapes of the best cartoons. I'd watch them over and over again until the tapes refused to work anymore. *Race for Your Life, Charlie Brown!* was one of those shows, and to this day it holds a special place in my heart as one of the best cartoon movies I can think of. A sweet, simple storyline, not quite as somber as some of the shorter Peanuts sketches, this movie is well animated, fun, and will prompt people of any age to cheer along and see if Charlie Brown and his rafting team survive the trials and tribulations of the river and make it to the finish line first. —*J.S.*

RAGGEDY ANN & ANDY: A MUSICAL ADVENTURE L: CHILDREN'S/CHILDREN'S ANIMATION (1977) 84M D: Richard Williams. *Didi Conn, Arnold Stang, Mark Baker, Fred Stuthman.* One of the many jobs director Williams took to fund his life's work, *The Thief and the Cobbler,* this bizarre animated musical shows his love for animation technique but little else. Many legendary animators took part, including Grim Natwick and Art Babbitt; the lead animators are listed in the opening credits along with the characters they play. For animation buffs, it's fun to stare at the detail of the drawings, but the

story is unabashedly juvenile and the saccharine songs by *Sesame Street*'s Joe Raposo are almost nonstop. I'm not sure if the creepy singing dolls and the disgusting villain made of melted candy make it better or worse. It's probably great for very young kids, but could give adults horrible nightmares. —*B. T.*

RESCUERS DOWN UNDER, THE L: CHILDREN'S/DISNEY ANIMATION (1990) 77M D: Hendel Butoy, Mike Gabriel. *Bob Newhart, George C. Scott, Adam Ryen, John Candy, Eva Gabor.* One of the best of the post–*Little Mermaid* era, this underrated sequel takes heroic mice Bernard (Newhart) and Bianca (Gabor) to Australia to save a lost child (Ryen), himself trying to save a giant eagle from the poacher McLeach (Scott). The Rescuers Society now has UN–like headquarters, a restaurant inside a chandelier staffed by insects, and a worldwide telecommunications system. The character animation is superb, especially the eagle Marahute (animated by the great Glen Keane), and there are thrilling, groundbreaking camera movements for the flight scenes. CGI and rotoscoping are used wisely to depict the nightmarish machinery of McLeach's off-road vehicle. This was the first film to use Disney's CAPS system, meaning it was colored on a computer (making the colors look more vivid than anything before it). Unfortunately, this nonmusical action-adventure tale was not a huge success, so Disney reverted to the musical fairy tale formula of *Little Mermaid* for years after. —*B. T.*

RUDOLPH, THE RED-NOSED REINDEER L: CHILDREN'S/ RANKIN & BASS (1964) 47M D: Kizo Nagashima, Larry Roemer *Stan Francis, Paul Soles, Billie Mae Richards, Larry D. Mann, Burl Ives.* Rudolph is an outsider, rejected by the other reindeer and even Santa because of his shiny, squeaky, red nose. Rudolph leaves the other reindeer and their reindeer games in shame, and runs into another outcast, Hermey, a little elf who wants to be a dentist. On their adventure, they run into a scary abominable snowman (who may be the cutest thing ever given stop-motion life), and end up on the Island of Misfit Toys, a place where they belong, full of outcasts like themselves. But Christmas is in jeopardy because Santa's sleigh has been fogged in; he may need help from a reindeer with a shiny, glowing nose after all. A cute story that shows being different is sometimes the best of all. The jerky stop-motion characters, the excellent set design, and a great soundtrack make this movie a Christmas classic. —*J. S.*

SCOOBY DOO'S ORIGINAL MYSTERIES L: CHILDREN'S/ HANNA-BARBERA (1969) 110M D: Joseph Barbera, William Hanna, others. *Frank Welker, Casey Kasem, Don Messick, Nicole Jaffe.* The Mystery Machine packs up its Scooby Snacks and travels back for the first five shows of the teen sleuths' Saturday morning cartoon. Not so much good as nostalgic, the episodes still have a certain charm as Shaggy

(the "like, wow man" beatnik voiced by Kasem) and talking (sort of) Great Dane Scooby Doo shiver in comic terror with knees knocking and teeth chattering as they confront phony ghosts and manufactured ghouls. Anyone who grew up on the show should get a jolt out it, and they sure beat the grating Scrappy Doo era. "I would have gotten away with it, too, if it weren't for you meddling kids!" —*S. A.*

SCOOBY-DOO MEETS BATMAN L: CHILDREN'S/HANNA-BARBERA (1972) 82M D: William Hannah, Joseph Barbera *Casy Kasem, Don Messick.* These two episodes of *The New Scooby-Doo Movies* are "funny" in that trademark clumsy Hanna-Barbera style. The villains are obvious, in the classic Scooby way. The addition of the Joker and the Penguin just makes lame jokes out of two of Batman's most tenacious foes. Batman and Robin themselves are totally ineffective as crime fighters, either getting rescued or outsleuthed by Fred and the gang. There is "good" comedy, though. Classic. Batman assuages Robin's fears in a haunted house, assuring his young ward the sounds they hear are "merely sound effects, Robin, recorded on tape by talented professional thespians." Batman also apparently has a "boy and his dog" fetish. He lauds the useless Shaggy and Scooby for their bravery, treats them to the previously unheard of "Bat Snacks," and searches for them instead of the victim of a kidnap plot. Batman fans stay away, Scooby fans pass that bong! —*G. M.*

SCOOBY-DOO L: CHILDREN'S/HANNA-BARBERA (2002) 86M D: Raja Gosnell. *Linda Cardellini, Matthew Lillard, Sarah Michelle Gellar, Rowan Atkinson, Freddie Prinze Jr.* Equal parts remake and spoof, this tongue-in-cheek live-action resurrection finds the old cartoon gang split over personality clashes and reunited years later to investigate the zombie teens of Spooky Island amusement park. It's really little more than an excuse to pile on big-screen special effects and poke fun at the stiff personas of the ageless animated characters, especially Fred (Prinze under a blond job and an ascot), now a preening pretty boy with a rock star ego, and Daphne (*Buffy*'s Gellar), the eternal damsel in distress in a magenta mini-dress and matching maxi-boots. In contrast to these flamboyant spoofs are Cardinelli, who is startlingly true to Velma while giving the sexless brain some real sex appeal, and Lillard, who *is* the adenoidal beatnik Shaggy. Give Lillard credit for more than just gangly slapstick; he makes his loyal-to-the-end friendship with talking dog Scooby Doo (an impressive computer animated figure) the most convincing relationship in the whole two-dimensional goof. Zoinks! —*S. A.*

SEALAB 2020 L: CHILDREN'S/HANNA-BARBERA (1972) 50M D: Various. *Ross Martin, Josh Albee, John Stephenson, Ann Jillian, Pamelyn Ferdin.* A bland, environmental adventure story about scientists (and

Movies you'd have to be kind of an asshole to hate

AMÉLIE

BABE

CHARADE

THE MUPPET MOVIE

MY NEIGHBOR TOTORO
(or any Miyazaki film)

TOY STORY

their kids) studying sealife in an underwater laboratory. The only reason it's notable today is that Cartoon Network has reworked it into the hilarious Adult Swim series, *Sealab 2021*, recycling character designs and pieces of animation from the original series and putting them into more absurd situations. All of *2021*'s main characters, and some guest stars, can be seen on this tape, although in very different form. The story involves a disabled kid who comes to the lab, learns how to dive, and interferes with shark hunters. Unfortunately, the shot on the back cover showing people riding on the backs of sea turtles does not actually occur in the episode. —*B. T.*

SECRET OF NIMH, THE L: CHILDREN'S/BLUTH, DON (1982) 82M D: Don Bluth. *Dom DeLuise, Elizabeth Hartman, John Carradine, Hermione Baddeley, Derek Jacobi.* A widowed mouse needs to move her family before a farmer's tractor destroys their home, but her son is too sick to travel. She has no choice but to ask for help from the feared Rats of NIMH (escaped lab rats with humanlike intelligence building a society inside a large rose bush). The book (*Mrs. Frisby and the Rats of NIMH* by Robert C. O'Brien) worked a little better without the inclusion of magic powers, but this is a very effective animated film with a somber tone, similar to *Watership Down*. At the time, Bluth was a rebel who had abandoned Disney to chart his own path. (Maybe we should pretend he retired after this one and never made *Rock-a-Doodle, A Troll in Central Park, Anastasia, Titan A.E.*, etc.) Avoid at all costs the wretched, cute-ified direct-to-video sequel. —*B. T.*

SINBAD: LEGEND OF THE SEVEN SEAS L: CHILDREN'S/ CHILDREN'S ANIMATION (2003) 86M D: Patrick Gilmore, Tim Johnson. *Michelle Pfeiffer, Joseph Fiennes, Catherine Zeta-Jones, Brad Pitt, Dennis Haysbert.* The plundering pirate of myth and legend returns in the DreamWorks animated adventure with the voice of Pitt and the cocky charm of an aquatic delinquent. His odyssey involves the stolen "The Book of Peace" (apparently some sort of supernatural home defense system against the capri-

cious gods and goddesses of the ancient world), a journey to the edge of the earth, and a battle of wits with the Goddess of Chaos (Pfeiffer in a purring, playful performance). And of course flirtatious sparring with a lovely diplomat who has the untapped heart of a tomboy adventuress (Zeta-Jones). Even with the limitless possibilities of modern animation techniques at their disposal, directors Johnson and Gilmore fail to deliver anything close to the awe and wonder of Ray Harryhausen's old stop-motion fantasies, and the ploddingly literal screenplay doesn't help matters. —*S. A.*

SLEEPING BEAUTY L: CHILDREN'S/DISNEY ANIMATION (1959) 75M D: Clyde Geronimi, Eric Larson, Les Clark, others. *Barbara Luddy, Mary Costa, Eleanor Audley, Taylor Holmes, Verna Felton, Bill Shirley.* *Sleeping Beauty* is one of the darkest Disney films ever produced. With barely enough comic relief to keep the story buoyant, Disney plays up the character of the evil witch, who is equal to the devil in *Fantasia*'s "Night on Bald Mountain" segment. As in the fairy tale, Sleeping Beauty is not the main character—it is the witch, who casts a spell on the fair princess as a grudge against the king. Imagine the shock of this horrible antagonist when a prince comes along and kisses the sleeping beauty, dispelling the curse. This feature is more epic than most Disney films, a fact underscored by the Super Technorama 70 mm process. Yet it is the film's dark elements that perhaps explain why it is a bit of a black sheep among classic Disney works. —*N. J.*

SNOW WHITE AND THE SEVEN DWARFS L: CHILDREN'S/ DISNEY ANIMATION (1937) 83M D: Walt Disney, Willian Cottrell, David Hand, others. *Moroni Olsen, Lucille La Verne, Adriana Caselotti, Roy Atwell.* Disney's first feature (and by some accounts the first animated feature ever), *Snow White* is a towering achievement. The lush, atmospheric background paintings, iconic characterizations, and mythic moments of fairy tale terror will probably never be forgotten. It is truly a great movie, but sadly that doesn't change the fact that Snow White herself just plain bugs the shit out of me. I don't want all Disney heroines to be the book-loving, daddy-defying princesses of the post–*Little Mermaid* era, but that would be better than this passive, squeaky-voiced girl who sings and does laundry for dwarves while she waits for some bland royal oaf to come sweep her off her feet. I wonder what the hell the those two even do together while they live happily ever after. I guess he just stands there and looks handsome while she feeds the birds all day. Sadly, I'd rather hang out with the wicked stepmother. She may enjoy cutting out little girl's hearts, but at least she has a personality. —*B. T.*

SPACE JAM L: CHILDREN'S/WARNER BROTHERS (1996) 87M D: Joe Pytka. *Michael Jordan, Bill Murray, Wayne Knight.* When animated aliens attempt to abduct Bugs Bunny and his associates and force them to work at their theme park, Bugs challenges them to a basketball game to decide their fate. The Looney Tunes load their team with NBA ringers, but the aliens transform into giants who call themselves the Mon-Stars. I think we can all agree it's not a good idea to take the classic Looney Tunes characters, redo them in a live-action world with computer-generated three-dimensional shading, and make them play basketball and exchange modern references with Michael Jordan. Who wants to see Yosemite Sam in a *Pulp Fiction* parody? But *Space Jam* is not without its charms, most notably Murray, who, as Jordan's golf buddy, pushes himself into the role of coach. At one point he refers to Bugs and his new love interest as "the gray bunny" and "the girl bunny." —*B. T.*

STUART LITTLE L: CHILDREN'S LIVE/CHILDREN'S LIVE ACTION (1999) 92M D: Rob Minkoff. *Hugh Laurie, Geena Davis, Michael J. Fox (voice), Jonathan Lipnicki, Nathan Lane (voice).* This live-action debut by the director of *The Lion King* was a big hit and is considered to be a better family movie that won't bug the shit out of the parents. I'm merely an uncle, but it did bug the shit out of me. Stuart (voiced by Fox) is a perky little mouse adopted by human parents (in the classic book by E. B. White they actually gave birth to him, but we can't have that in the movie I guess). He is treated just like another kid, but with smaller clothes and furniture. The smarmy cat, Snowbell (Lane, reprising his *Lion King* role of providing annoying comic relief) wants to eat him. The computer effects are undeniably great and the design of Stuart is downright adorable. But in case that doesn't get you, the overbearing score by Alan Silvestri tries to remind you, "Look at this! This is whimsical! This part is fun!" Instead of going for the timeless feel of the book, it is full of modern references and poo-humor. From what I remember of the book, which I loved as a child, I don't think White would approve of this one. Hopefully he's too busy rolling in his grave over grammar-related issues to notice this outrage. (At least it's not *Charlotte's Web 2.*) —*B. T.*

SWALLOWS AND AMAZONS L: CHILDREN'S LIVE/CHILDREN'S LIVE ACTION (1974) 92M D: Claude Watham. *Virginia McKenna, Ronald Fraser, Brenda Bruce, Suzanna Hamilton.* In this fantastic Disney Channel staple from the days before that tramp Hilary Duff came along, four resourceful siblings vacation in Britain's Lake District. Their parents are so cool they let the kids take a four-day unsupervised trip in a small sailboat named The Swallow. The kids sail to a nearby island and set up camp, naming their discovery "Wildcat Island" and pretending it's an uncharted wilderness, even referring to the English locals as "natives." Soon they run into spunky preteen pirates calling themselves the Amazons (lead by Ruth, who tries to pass herself off as "Nancy," having been

told that real amazons were "ruthless"), and a good-natured naval war is declared between the two crews. —*C. B.*

SWAN PRINCESS, THE L: CHILDREN'S/CHILDREN'S ANIMATION (1994) 90M D: Richard Rich. *Howard McGillin, Michelle Nicastro, John Cleese, Steven Wright, Steve Vinovich, Jack Palance.* Prince Derek and Princess Odette knew from the time they were children that one day they were to be married. At first, they detest each other, but as time goes on, they eventually fall in love. Before their wedding, however, Prince Derek makes an offensive remark to the princess, and she leaves. She's kidnapped by an evil enchanter who wants her kingdom and condemns her to spend her days on a lake as a swan, only turning human again when she's exposed to the moonlight. The prince, realizing his mistake, vows to rescue Odette and win her hand in marriage, but will he be able to avoid the wrath of the enchanter? A sweet, simple story based on *Swan Lake*, the music is endearing and the characters entertaining. This is a great movie for kiddies, and for the parents of said kiddies who want a little break from Disney. —*J. S.*

SWISS FAMILY ROBINSON L: CHILDREN'S LIVE/DISNEY LIVE ACTION (1960) 126M D: Ken Annakin. *Dorthoy McGuire, John Mills, James MacArthur, Janet Munro, Sessue Hayakawa, Tommy Kirk.* Things have changed since those wholesome, live-action Disney films from the late '50s and '60s. For example, it wouldn't be considered politically correct these days to have a big group of Asian pirates communicate by making squawking noises similar to the aliens in *Mars Attacks!* Despite these uncomfortable moments, this film is excellent for families looking to take a break from animation and movies with hip tween soundtracks. Mills and the lovely McGuire (who call each other "Mother" and "Father") and their three boys are shipwrecked on their way from Europe to New Guinea. They raid the wreckage of their ship for everything from two huge dogs to a pipe organ, build a tree house, ride around on the backs of elephants, catch tigers, and tussle with pirates. There's plenty of adventure without getting too scary, and there's even some kissing so the little kids can cry, "Eww!" —*J. K.*

TARZAN (1999) L: CHILDREN'S/DISNEY ANIMATION (1999) 88M D: Chris Buck, Kevin Lima. *Tony Goldwyn, Minnie Driver, Glen Close, Brian Blessed, Lance Henriksen.* Tarzan of the Apes gets the Disney treatment with surprisingly good results. The story is treated dramatically, with emphasis on the father-son relationship with the gorilla Kerchak, played by Henriksen. The filmmakers also take full advantage of their medium: for the first time, Tarzan can really move like an animal, walking on his knuckles and using his feet like hands while swinging spectacularly through the jungle. Comic relief by Rosie O'Donnell and Wayne Knight is unnecessary (Driver is already very funny as Jane), and I could do without the Phil Collins soundtrack. Still, *Tarzan* is easily one of the best of the modern Disney era, and perhaps technically among the best animation ever created. Disney debuted a new computer technology to create three dimensional backgrounds that still look like paintings, an ideal use of digital technology combined with traditional cel animation. —*B. T.*

THUNDERCATS: EXODUS L: CHILDREN'S/RANKIN & BASS (1985) 75M D: Katsuhito Akiyama. *Larry Kenney, Earl Hammond, Earle Hyman, Lynne Lipton, Bob McFadden, Peter Newman.* In this pilot for a crappy action cartoon I loved in fifth grade, a race of cat people called the Thundercats escape their exploding home world of Thundera and crash down on a scorched planet called Third Earth. Unfortunately, there's an evil mummy named Mumm-Ra already living there in a big pyramid so he gets pissed and sends his idiotic mutant-animal henchmen to fight these newcomers. At the beginning, the Thundercats are all naked kids. They enter cryo-sleep chambers for their space travel and inexplicably emerge all grown up, except Wily Kit and Wily Kat, who stay the same age they were at the beginning. Panthro (the badass with the nunchakas) is voiced by Earle Hyman, aka Grandpa Huxtable on *The Cosby Show.* —*B. T.*

TITAN A.E. L: CHILDREN'S/BLUTH, DON (2000) 95M D: Don Bluth, Gary L. Goldman. *Drew Barrymore, Matt Damon, Bill Pullman.* As a boy, Damon survives the destruction of Earth, not realizing that he carries the map to a space station called Titan, which could some day replace his home planet. Then there are aliens, spaceships, adventures, etc. The story (written in part by *The Tick* creator Ben Edlund and *Buffy* creator Joss Whedon) has its moments, but as usual Bluth screws everything up with characters who spasm and jerk to overemphasize every other word. His lame alien designs are mostly just talking cartoon turtles or bugs. It wouldn't even need the awkwardly combined computer and cel animation to be an affront to the art form. Bluth's misguided attempt at serious animated sci-fi just gave clueless studio executives another excuse to stick to the kiddie-musical formula. —*B. T.*

TOY STORY L: CHILDREN'S/DISNEY ANIMATION (1995) 80M D: John Lasseter. *Tim Allen, Tom Hanks, Jim Varney, John Ratzenberger, Don Rickles, Wallace Shawn.* Pixar's computer animation debut is a masterpiece. Some day the computer rendering will look crude, and it will be even more obvious the movie's popularity comes less from the new style of animation than from flawless storytelling and character chemistry. My favorite scene is the one built around Randy Newman's song, "I Will Go Sailing No More," where Buzz Lightyear sees a TV ad for himself and realizes he is not a real spaceman, merely a toy one. He tears off what

he'd thought was a wrist communicator, now understanding it's a cheap decal. But when he sees a bird outside, he leaps off the banister, spreading his spring-loaded wings triumphantly. His face saddens as he realizes he is not flying, but plummetting to the floor. These are characters made of rubber and plastic who have more emotional resonance than many movie characters of genuine flesh and blood. —*B. T.*

TOY STORY 2 L: CHILDREN'S/DISNEY ANIMATION (1999) 92M D: John Lasseter. *Tim Allen, Tom Hanks, Joan Cusack, Kelsey Grammer, Don Rickles.* A sequel to a near-perfect movie like *Toy Story* seems like a bad idea. Disney pressured Pixar into making a direct-to-video sequel, but during the production the filmmakers were so happy with the story that they turned it into a theatrical feature. Their instincts were right. With the same loving care invested in the characters and storytelling, they somehow came up with one of the most satisfying sequels ever. While worrying about the inevitability of Andy outgrowing his toys, Woody is stolen by a doll collector—it turns out Woody's a valuable antique. While Buzz Lightyear leads Andy's other toys to save their friend, Woody is tempted to join the rest of his Woody's Roundup doll line in a museum display (the doll equivalent of eternal life). The story is loaded with clever ideas complemented by genuinely emotional scenes. I particularly like the montage in which Jessie's owner grows up, starts wearing nail polish, and eventually donates her to Goodwill. —*B. T.*

TRON L: CHILDREN'S LIVE/DISNEY LIVE ACTION (1982) 96M D: Steven Lisberger. *Jeff Bridges, David Warner, Bruce Boxleitner, Barnard Hughes, Cindy Morgan.* Bridges plays a renegade computer programmer whose programs for video games have been stolen by a computer CEO (Warner). When Bridges breaks into headquarters to get control of one of their high-level computers, he is sucked through the circuits and winds up in ENCOM. In this artificial world, he is just one of many digital gladiators who play lifelike videogames to the death at the whim of Master Control. Ultimately, this character proves to be like Spartacus, leading a small rebellion out of ENCOM. Excellent music and graphics help make this film a tremendous digital fantasy. —*N. J.*

TURBO: A POWER RANGERS MOVIE L: CHILDREN'S LIVE/CHILDREN'S LIVE ACTION (1997) 99M D: Shuki Levy, David Winning. *Jason David Frank, Steve Cardenas, Johnny Yong Bosch, Catherine Sutherland, Nakia Burrise.* *Mighty Morphin Power Rangers* was a hit American show that cheesily combined new footage with fight scenes and special effects from Japanese giant robot shows. At the height of the show's popularity, they made *Mighty Morphin Power Rangers: The Movie* with a real soundtrack album, big soundstage sets, and almost-state-of-the-art special effects, like the computer-animated robots that replaced the clunky costumes

from the show. It didn't work, so for the second movie they went back to stock footage and TV production values and came up with a silly, amateurish mess of a type not seen in about twenty years. But it actually was a hoot to see this on the big screen. —B. T.

20,000 LEAGUES UNDER THE SEA L: CHILDREN'S LIVE/ DISNEY LIVE ACTION (1954) 127M D: Richard Fleischer. *Kirk Douglas, Paul Lukas, James Mason, Peter Lorre.* The grandest, most glorious of Disney's live-action adventures. Two stars compete for attention in this rousing adaptation of the Jules Verne classic: Mason's anguished Captain Nemo, an uncharacteristically sympathetic madman out to save the human race by destroying its warmongers, and his Victorian-era submarine, the *Nautilus,* a warship with the ferocious look of a sea demon on the prowl. Douglas is the brawny, brawling seaman Nemo picks up at sea along with a kindly professor (Lukas) and his Man Friday (Lorre). Douglas's knockabout sense of fun provides the comic relief and the human heroics. Time hasn't dulled the thrill of the set pieces (the giant squid wrestling the *Nautilus* in a storm-ravaged sea as Douglas attacks with a harpoon and a holler is still a classic piece of adventure fantastique) or the scale of the magnificent special effects. —S. A.

WHERE THE TOYS COME FROM L: CHILDREN'S LIVE/ DISNEY LIVE ACTION (1984) 58M D: Theodore Thomas. *Sab Shimono, Erin Young, Jon Harvey.* Peepers and Zoom (both wind-up toys) begin to suffer from the age-old existential anxiety of where-did-I-come-from. Somehow they learn how to travel back in time, and return to the toy factory in Japan where they were originally created. Reminiscent of something out of *Mr. Rogers' Neighborhood, Where the Toys Come From* uses this fictional premise to illustrate the process of mass-producing wind-up toys (beginning with the design of prototypes and going on to assembly and shipping). Along the way, there are musical numbers and a suspense scene involving ZOIDs. For more discerning audiences, it's still pretty interesting to see the wind-up toy designers at work. Made in 1984, this film features an eBay-treasure-chest load of long-forgotten '80s wind-ups. —C. B.

WILLY WONKA & THE CHOCOLATE FACTORY L: KIDS' LITERATURE/DAHL, ROALD (1971) 100M D: Mel Stuart. *Gene Wilder, Peter Ostrum, Jack Albertson.* Wilder is a dark and disturbed man. Hidden behind his façade of humor there seems to linger a great sadness, and when it is allowed to surface, it becomes horrifying. Take the scene in which Wonka's boat begins to speed through a tunnel and Wilder's monologue gets madder, and madder, and madder until it borders on the absolutely insane. It's an unforgettable moment. Just one of many in this fantastic bit of whimsy. —T. S.

WORST WITCH L: CHILDREN'S LIVE/CHILDREN'S LIVE ACTION (1986) 70M D: Robert M. Young. *Fairuza Balk, Diana Rigg, Tim Curry, Charlotte Rae.* HBO used to show this movie twice a day in the week leading up to Halloween when I was young, so watching it has become a bit of a tradition. At a school for young witches, Mildred Hubble (Balk) has trouble with her studies and is teased by her snobby classmates. She stumbles upon a group of bad witches hatching a plan to take over the school, rallies to stop them, and becomes a hero. Wait a minute. That sounds familiar. If anything, you should watch this film for the cast. In addition to Balk, there's Rae (Mrs. Garret from *Facts of Life* in a dual role!), Rigg as a stern professor of potions (wait, that sounds familiar, too), and Curry as the Grand Wizard, who comes in at the end to sing a truly awful song about Halloween and make the ladies swoon. —J. K.

ZEUS AND ROXANNE L: CHILDREN'S LIVE/CHILDREN'S LIVE ACTION (1997) 98M D: George Miller. *Steve Guttenberg, Kathleen Quinlan, Arnold Vosloo, Miko Hughes, Dawn McMillan.* Don't let your children watch this film. It stars a dog and a dolphin but also features Guttenberg (*Police Academy*) and Quinlan. Guttenberg plays a widower with a son and a dog. Quinlan plays a single mom with two girls and a dolphin. It's like the Brady Bunch happens upon Lassie and Flipper in one episode! But if that's not enough, there is an extra-heavy dose of syrupy sweetness in the mix as the children entice their single parents to date each other. And then there's that special interspecies romance between the dog and the dolphin, and. . . Oh, just never mind. —N. J.

CHAPTER EIGHT

Anime, Nonchildren's Animation & Comics

So where were you during the renaissance? The global animation renaissance, so woefully represented in too many North American minds as a by-product of Pokemon, has actually been thirty years in the making. Japanese culture has so fully embraced animation that there is virtually nothing in their collective psyche, real or imagined, sane or insane, that has not been represented by animators. The rest of the planet is only now beginning to catch up.

Often based on popular manga comic books, Japanese anime can astonish with its breadth of scope, genre, and style. It can be made, like Pokemon, for very young people, or it can venture past the borders of pornography. It is rich with series after series of high-quality storylines, made as TV shows (some short, some long, some very long) and as many feature films of distinction. But it's not all good, and it's certainly not all meant for your particular tastes. So tread carefully, but not shyly, and trust this: there are great treasures to be found here.

Most of this chapter is comprised of animation not intended for children. Yet many of the films in this chapter are among the best films ever made for kids. That is because this is also the place where we collect another director's section: Animation Directors. Here are some of the giants of world cinema: Miyazaki, Iwerks, Fleischer, Park, and Williams have all created works of genius for kids of all ages. Bakshi, the Quay Brothers, Svankmajer, Plympton, and McLaren have reached out to a more

Fantastic Planet (1973)

seasoned crowd. But all the animators here have distinguished themselves with great, pioneering, original, and influential films, and you would be remiss not to take time to explore their work.

If all you think about when you hear the word "animation" is "Disney," then prepare yourself for a brave new world. Once you learn that Ub Iwerks created Mickey Mouse, and see that the heralded Disney imagination pales in comparison to the great Miyazaki.... Need I say more? Your world will be expanded. The works of these animators place them among the greatest artists ever to have used the big screen as their palette. This chapter also includes live-action movies based on comic books.

ADVENTURES OF PRINCE ACHMED, THE L: N/C/A DIRECTORS/REINIGER, LOTTE (1928) 67M D: Lotte Reiniger. Disney's *Snow White and the Seven Dwarfs* is often credited as being the first full-length animated feature film, but it came out nine years after Reiniger's animation fantasy, *The Adventures of Prince Achmed*. Based loosely on *The Arabian Nights*, Prince Achmed flies a magical horse, falls in love with a princess, and battles with an evil sorcerer. The film is animated entirely with stop-motion cut-outs, with each piece moved infinitesimally for each frame, resulting in a film that took years to complete. The animation is fluid and smooth, and the painstaking care taken to make this film is evident in every scene. An original soundtrack accompanies the film, resulting in a sweet, entertaining story that will appeal to a wide audience. Animation buffs must watch this film. —*J. S.*

AKIRA L: MANGA/MANGA (1988) 124M D: Katsuhiro Otomo. *Mitsuo Iwara, Nozomu Sasaki, Taro Ishida, Mami Koyama.* Director Otomo adapts his own manga epic to create a neo-Tokyo as vivid and bleak as *Blade Runner*'s Los Angeles, a dystopia where biker gangs ravage the city and government experiments produce a race of psychically superpowered humans who threaten the existence of civilization. Groundbreaking in its time, this mix of science fiction and apocalyptic fantasy is given an explosive treatment with some of the most exciting animation ever to hit the screen: the camera dives, swoops, and swirls through the dense, decaying urban landscape with dizzying swiftness. The plot, condensed from the sprawling manga epic into a single feature-length film, is a bit murky and mystical, but the experience is never less than enthralling. It remains a cyberpunk landmark and the first introduction for many American viewers to contemporary Japanese anime for grown-up audiences. —*S. A.*

ALICE L: N/C/A DIRECTORS/SVANKMAJER, JAN (1988) 86M D: Jan Svankmajer. *Kristina Kohoutova, Mia Farrow, Joe Mantegna, William Hurt, Judy Davis.* Svankmajer's dark and creepy take on Alice in Wonderland surrounds a live-action Alice (Kohoutova) with stop-motion puppets, inanimate objects, and living meat—all of which come off like resurrected corpses. The white rabbit, in fact, is a stuffed rabbit with sawdust spilling from his seams. Svankmajer attempts a more straightforward literary adaptation than his *Faust*, but the story allows him to stay true to his trademark nightmare style of animation. It's not necessarily appropriate for most young kids, but if you show it to them they'll probably remember it forever. —*B. T.*

ALICE IN WONDERLAND L: NONCHILDREN'S/PUPPET ANIMATION (1950) 83M D: Dallas Bower, Lou Bunin. *Felix Aylmer, Pamela Brown, Ernest Milton, Carol Marsh, Stephen Murray, Jerry Colonna, Sterling Holloway, Kathryn Beaumont, Ed Wynn.* This live-action

stop-motion adaptation of the Lewis Carroll classic isn't very well-known because it was overshadowed by the Disney film that came out a year later. This version includes a live-action wraparound story involving Carroll (Murray), who likes to take photos of his students, including Alice (played by twenty-one-year-old Marsh, so there are no creepy pedophilic vibes). Once Alice falls into the hole, she is surrounded by stop-motion characters who are fairly faithful to their literary counterparts. Unfortunately, the songs and performances aren't very appealing, and some crude visual effects can take you out of the fantasy world in a way that doesn't happen with hand-drawn animation. But it's definitely worth watching for fans of stop-motion animation. The cards and the marching fish are especially cool. —*B. T.*

ALLEGRO NON TROPPO L: N/C/A DIRECTORS/BOZZETTO, BRUNO (1976) 85M D: Bruno Bozzetto. *Maurizio Nichetti, Néstor Garay, Maria Luisa Giovanni.* Allegro non *Troppo* begins as a parody of Disney's *Fantasia*, but ends up just as sincere as its inspiration. The Disney movie is technically superior—the animation in *Allegro* is not as fluid or crisp, but the film seems to have something more than just a stylish show on its mind. Bozzetto uses his film to comment on everything from our need to conform, to homelessness, unrequited love, greed, and, materialism. In a direct play on *Fantasia*, one segment shows human evolution (sort of) from the "primordial muck" (a discarded soda bottle). . . but in a much different light than the Disney version. *Allegro* also contains one of the saddest cartoons I've ever seen, about a lost, homeless kitten imagining (or remembering) living in an old, condemned house. Both films contain unnecessary live action; those in *Fantasia* are boring and stiff, the ones in *Allegro* are irritating. Nonetheless, both are worthwhile for anyone who loves pure visual filmmaking at its best, and strangest. —*K. C.*

AMERICAN POP L: N/C/A DIRECTORS/BAKSHI, RALPH (1981) 96M D: Ralph Bakshi. *Lisa Persky, Marya Small, Ron Thompson, Jerry Holland.* American Pop is in many ways Bashki's masterwork. Zalmie is the first of a family of Russian Jews to emigrate to the United States. He attempts to get into Vaudeville during WWI, but was injured during the war and can no longer sing. His son, Benny, joins a jazz ensemble, but dies fighting in WWII. Benny's son, Tony, falls into the beatnik scene and hippie rock in San Francisco and fathers an illegitimate son, Pete. When Tony dies, Pete becomes a rock star, the first in his family to find real success. Bakshi pulls out all the stops in his *Citizen Kane*, melding time and reality together to force out a structure of the emergence of the twentieth-century music through the lives of his characters. Utilizing his controversial rotoscoping techniques of animating over live movement, *American Pop* is a purely adult look at the world of music told in animated form at a level that will likely not be seen again in American animation. —*N.H.*

The rotoscoping technique is controversial because it seems so pointless—if you're going to trace over live-action footage why not just use the live-action footage, especially in a real-world story like this one? We know Bakshi knows how to animate, as shown in superior works like *Heavy Traffic, Fritz the Cat,* and *Street Fight.* Rotoscoping is distractingly realistic while still lacking the humanity of a well-animated character. You have to admire what Bakshi is trying to achieve with this multi-generation epic (it's certainly unlike anything else I've seen in animation), but ultimately I think it is a failure, especially in the ludicrous finale where a mowhawked punk rocker plays cheeseball rock to a stadium full of fans. —*B.T.*

AMERICAN SPLENDOR L: COMIX/COMIX (2003) 100M D: Shari Springer Berman. *Paul Giamatti, Hope Davis, Judah Friedlander, Cameron Carter, James Urbaniak, Daniel Tay, Mary Faktor.* This quirky, fascinating film is part documentary, part traditional movie, and part biographical exploration of comic book writer Harvey Pekar. Pekar wrote the comic series "American Splendor," which was illustrated by R. Crumb, among others. There is a charming mix of animated comic book characters (usually his internal dialogue) mixed with regular footage, some interview-esque interwoven cuts of Pekar himself (and his friends), bits of actual footage from him on the David Letterman show, and voice-overs. While I admired the way the film was made and found it very funny and very interesting at times, in the end it left me feeling cold and a little depressed. I think this is because of who Pekar is: when he and his wife are being interviewed, they're talking about his outlook on life, what he writes about, and the fact that misery loves company. She says, "And here I just thought he had this really great sense of humor." To which Harvey replies, after a pause, "Boy. . . I sure had you fooled." —*M.N.*

ANGEL'S EGG L: N/C/A DIRECTORS/OSHII, MAMORU (1985) 71M D: Mamoru Oshii. *Rainbow Dolan, Keiichi Noda.* A little girl wanders a dark, empty, Gothic city, carrying an ostrich-sized egg under her shirt. Perhaps she believes that its hatching will bring light to her barren world. There is very little dialogue, though a mysterious nomad accompanies her and at one point delivers a monologue about Noah's Ark. The only other living things are the masked warriors who chase after shadows of fish that float down the streets. This enigmatic anime art film uses the elegant designs of Yoshitaka Amano and an incredible soundtrack of eerie choral music and atmospheric sounds. Oshii's direction is so masterful he gets away with long, nearly static shots—like a motionless drawing of the two asleep while a fire burns out in front of them. For many, including anime fans, it is probably a colossal bore. But for those tuned into Oshii's frequency, it is a haunting masterpiece of environment, sound, subtle animation, and delicate linework. —*B.T.*

ANIMATRIX, THE L: MANGA/MANGA (2003) 102M D: Peter Chung, Andy Jones, others. *Clayton Watson, Hedy Burress, Olivia D'Abo.* An anthology of short films by top animation directors, each tied to the world of *The Matrix.* Some are scripted or plotted by the Wachowski brothers, others only take inspiration from the concepts in their films. There is a wide variety of tones and animation styles, but all look superb. "The Second Renaissance" (directed by Mahiro Maeda) is a detailed history lesson about the Machine War that preceded the *Matrix* films, full of disturbing imagery and historical allusion, yet adding enough gray area to the storyline to make even a dyed-in-the-wool human like myself sympathize with the machines. My favorite is "Matriculated," directed by Chung, the creator of *Aeon Flux.* His distinct animation style is updated with digital enhancements and a CGI robot character who, in a reversal of the matrix concept, is plugged into a human dream. It turns into a psychedelic freakout while making a statement about the possible difference between humanity and machinery. Like all of Chung's work, it makes more sense the more times you watch it—an ideal use of the DVD format. —*B.T.*

AVALON L: N/C/A DIRECTORS/OSHII, MAMORU (2001) 107M D: Mamoru Oshii. *Malgorzata Foremniak, Wladyslaw Kowalski, Jerzy Gudejko.* Oshii took nearly two years to complete this dazzling CGI/live-action hybrid that takes place in Poland, and is filmed in Polish, although it is a Japanese production. It is set in a rundown future, where virtual-reality game players vie for fame and fortune in a complex, all-encompassing world called Avalon. Ash (Foremniak) is one of the system's stars and considered a loner among the team-oriented players. Her constant quest for higher levels leads her to the discovery of a hidden door to a level unknown to most players. But in order to get there, she'll have to return to the comrades she left behind and a meeting with one she thought she'd never see again. The use of color and effects to push the limits of the game's world is a perfect example of anime in reality, and a career accomplishment for Oshii, who has made his name in animation. —*R.M.*

BAMBI MEETS GODZILLA L: NONCHILDREN'S/ANIMATION FESTIVALS (1969) 3M D: Marv Newland. This socio-political commentary is as pertinent today as when it was made. After the opening credits, the small figure of Bambi appears on the screen accompanied by the bucolic music of Mendelssohn. After a moment, it is ruthlessly stomped on by the giant reptilian foot of Godzilla. The music descends to chaos, the toenails of said antagonist clench, and all that is left for us is the closing credits. "But what does it mean?" artisans ask each other in coffee-houses after the screening. Power over innocence? Perhaps. This classic animated short packs quite the punch, for it still has us guessing. You'll find it on *Rocketship Reel*, a collection of Canadian animation. —*N. J.*

BATMAN (1966) L: COMIX/COMIX (1966) 105M D: Leslie Martinson. *Adam West, Burt Ward, Burgess Meredith, Lee Meriwether, Cesar Romero, Frank Gorshin.* If you prefer the humorous, tongue-in-cheek Batman and Boy Wonder over the brooding Dark Knight, this film is very much for you. In this feature-length film inspired by the TV series, the Penguin, the Riddler, the Joker, and Catwoman combine forces to get rid of Batman and Robin so they can accomplish their real goal: the molecular dehydration of all the members of the United World Security Council. A lot of action and a lot of corny jokes ensue. Who can forget Batman and Robin being saved at the last moment from a torpedo by a wayward porpoise? Or the disabled Batcopter dropping miraculously into a Foam Rubber Wholesalers Convention? Meanwhile, Bruce Wayne falls in love with Catwoman, who poses as a Russian journalist. Well worth repeated viewings for all ages. —*N. J.*

BATMAN & ROBIN L: COMIX/COMIX (1997) 125M D: Joel Schumacher. *Uma Thurman, Alicia Silverstone, George Clooney, Chris O'Donnell, Arnold Schwarzenegger.* Possibly the worst big-budget event movie ever, which is saying a lot. After the financial (if not artistic) success of *Batman Forever*, Schumacher went all out in making Batman campier and gayer than anyone thought possible. He put nipples on the batsuit, spectacularly miscast Schwarzenegger as heartbroken scientist Mr. Freeze, and cajoled Thurman into a home-video-style performance that must have seemed funny at the time. There are batroller-skates, bat-credit cards, even a muscleman in a pink angora gorilla suit. Despite the title, the story is about Batman and Robin and Batgirl, and Silverstone does nothing to suggest that her performance in *Clueless* was anything other than a fluke. Schwarzenegger delivers a dramatic monologue so similar to Bela Lugosi's in *Bride of the Monster* that the movie might be intended as an Ed Wood tribute. The aftermath: Schumacher became the Internet's most hated director, then started making smaller movies (*Tigerland* and *Phone Booth*). Clooney was so humiliated he vowed to do only movies he believed in (*Out of Sight* and *O Brother Where Art Thou*). The series was derailed, and it took Warner Brothers seven years to make another DC Comics movie. But Akiva Goldsman won an Oscar for Best Adapted Screenplay (for *A Beautiful Mind*), making him to the Academy Award what Henry Kissinger is to the Nobel Peace Prize. —*B. T.*

BATMAN BEYOND: RETURN OF THE JOKER L: COMIX/COMIX (2000) 74M D: Curt Geda. *Will Friedle, Kevin Conroy, Mark Hamill, Angie Harmon, Dean Stockwell.* A fine direct-to-video feature based on the animated series where an elderly Bruce Wayne mentors a young new Batman in a *Blade Runner*–like future Gotham. The Joker, whom Wayne killed years ago, is somehow alive again, and the new Batman has to find out how. Flashbacks bridge *Batman Beyond* with the earlier, present-day Batman series. The animation is better than on the TV show, and there are some great action sequences and dramatic revelations about some of the iconic Batman characters. Beware of the original release, which manages to completely muddle the story by censoring an act of violence crucial to the plot. —*B. T.*

BATMAN-SUPERMAN MOVIE, THE L: COMIX/COMIX (1998) 64M D: Toshihiko Masuda. *Clancy Brown, Arleen Sorkin, Mark Hamill, Kevin Conroy, Timothy Daly.* Originally titled "World's Finest" when it aired as a three-part episode of the *Superman* animated series, this is a more satisfying, better scripted story than either superhero has ever found in live action. The writers go all out finding dramatic ways to bring together the characters of Gotham and Metropolis; debonair Bruce Wayne even dates Lois Lane, apparently just to piss off Clark Kent. A lot of the fun comes from the rivalry between the two superheroes. Batman pulls Kryponite on Superman when they first meet and uncovers his secret identity in a matter of minutes. —*B. T.*

BEAVIS AND BUTT-HEAD DO AMERICA L: NONCHILDREN'S/MTV ANIMATION (1996) 80M D: Mike Judge, Yvette Kaplan, others. *Mike Judge, Robert Stack, Demi Moore, Bruce Willis.* Beavis and Butt-head's world is turned upside down when the unthinkable happens: their TV is stolen. Through a series of moronic misunderstandings, they end up delivering a portable doomsday weapon cross-country, thinking they are going to "score" with a trailer park femme fatale played by Moore. The crude animation and suburban-character-based humor of the show is expanded onto the canvas of a road picture/terrorist thriller. There are still plenty of laughs with their hippie teacher and retired neighbor (who now sounds distractingly like Hank Hill) but the boys leave the living room to experience car chases, strip searches, an encounter with Chelsea Clinton, a psychedelic trip-out animated by Rob Zombie, and even David Letterman as Beavis and Butt-head's long lost fathers (former Motley Crue roadies). This is a funny movie. Whatever happened to the sequel? —*B. T.*

BIG O, THE L: MANGA/MANGA (1999) 30M D: Kazuyoshi Katayama. *Sherry Lynn, Mitsuru Miyamoto, Akiko Yajima.* Mix two parts *Cowboy Bebop* and one part *Evangelion* and what do you get? Nothing too special, apparently. This series straight robs the plot and thematic construction of those two titles and several others, but it fails to elicit even a lingering residual interest. The story arcs are predictable and uncompelling. The robots are moderately large and that's fairly cool, but nothing cool really happens to them. The most interesting part of this series is its hokey title sequence. Big O? O No. —*T. C.*

BLADE L: COMIX/COMIX (1998) 121M D: Steve Norrington. *Kris Kristofferson, Stephen Dorff, N'Bushe Wright, Wesley Snipes, Donal Logue.* At the time, the combination of Snipes, Marvel Comics, vampires, martial arts, and electronica seemed deadly. But somehow, this Shaft-meets-Van Helsing tale is a slick, clever crowd-pleaser. Snipes is the stoic, trench-coated "Daywalker," a half-man/half-vampire dedicated to killing off the vampires who live secretly among us. Despite his hatred for the vampire half, he doesn't really fit in with humans either, and does things like walk around town with a sword on his back or shoot a cop in broad daylight in front of a crowd of witnesses. He is more comfortable kicking ass, like slaughtering dozens of vampires covered from head to toe in blood without getting a single drop on himself. As the movie unfolds, all goes so well you're afraid it's leading to some *Mortal Kombat*-style CG monster, but thankfully, it doesn't. Along the way, Snipes shows himself to be a surprisingly decent martial artist, and spouts some classic one-liners (as does Kristofferson as his vulgar mentor). *Blade* also has imaginative, though low-budget, CGI fighting effects that may have been an influence on *The Matrix*. —*B. T.*

BLOOD: THE LAST VAMPIRE L: MANGA/MANGA (2000) 48M D: Hiroyuki Kitakubo. *Joe Romersa, Rebecca Forstadt, Saemi Nakamura, Youki Kudoh.* It's a good thing this movie is so short, since there's not much to it, really, except that the animation is fucking dope. One of the better attempts at fusing a hand-drawn style with computer-generated movements, the animation is convincingly fluid and surprisingly lush. Check out the imposed depth of field when the helicopter is hovering over the burning warehouse—*damn.* There is little character or plot development, but rather vignettes or moments, so suppress any attempts to puzzle anything deeper out of the story, unless you're a wanker. There's also tons of blood, which makes sense, given the title. —*T. C.*

BUTTER BATTLE BOOK, THE L: N/C/A DIRECTORS/BAKSHI, RALPH (1989) 30M D: Ralph Bakshi. *Charles Durning.* It might seem odd that Bakshi would direct a Dr. Seuss adaptation, but this is the one about the Cold War and the arms race. The Yooks and the Zooks share a walled-up border and hate each other due to a disagreement over whether the butter should go on the top or the bottom of toast. They continually develop more powerful weapons (increasingly elaborate Seussian devices) as a deterrent, but all that does is make

the other side invent something more powerful. The book was controversial for its grim subtext and unresolved ending, so naturally Bakshi turned it into a musical TV special, having fun filling it with ridiculous jingoistic anthems. The animation has a sketchy, Xeroxed look that makes it stand out a little from the other Seuss adaptations. It worked better as a scary children's book than as animation, but it's such a great story that it's worth seeing anyway. —*B. T.*

CAMERAMAN'S REVENGE, THE L: N/C/A DIRECTORS/ STAREWICZ, WLADYSLAW (1912) 12M D: Wladyslaw Starewicz. Animation fans will find this short film to be absolutely extraordinary. Starewicz, a Russian animator who began working long before Walt Disney (but did not receive nearly the same level of recognition), presents a simple tale of an adulterous married beetle couple and the vengeful cameraman whose interference helps to expose them both. The characters are all insects animated through an incredibly realistic and virtually flawless stop-motion technique, and the story is complimented by an instrumental soundtrack that makes it very reminiscent of live-action silent films of the same era. Starewicz was an animation genius, and after over ninety years, this film still stands up as an important staple of early animation. —*J. S.*

CAPTAIN AMERICA II: DEATH TOO SOON L: COMIX/COMIX (1979) 98M D: Ivan Nagy. *Connie Sellecca, Reb Brown, Christopher Lee.* Apparently the second live-action TV movie about Captain America, this is the only one with a video release (and a fancy painted cover, it should be noted). Brown plays a hunky blond painter who occasionally puts on a red, white, and blue costume (with a motorcycle helmet instead of a mask) and drives around on a motorcycle holding (and sometimes throwing) a huge round shield. He happens to be staying in a small town helping small children and animals near diabolical terrorist Miguel (Lee), who has hatched a plot to poison the water supply with an age-acceleration formula if the government doesn't give him a bunch of money. Then there are motorcycle stunts. Good for some laughs if you're in the right mood. —*B. T.*

CAPTAIN SCARLET L: N/C/A DIRECTORS/ANDERSON, GERRY (1967) 880M D: Gerry Anderson. *Francis Matthews.* After the worldwide success of *Thunderbirds*, Anderson turned his gadgets, fantasy vehicles, and "SuperMarionation" puppets to the first (and still the greatest) paranoid conspiracy adventure series for kids. The "shoot first and ask questions later" panic of the first humans to explore Mars turns curious aliens into ferocious enemies bent on the destruction of Earth, and they choose a most insidious method: possessing the agents of Spectrum (all names after colors, of course) and turning them into (dare I say it?) puppets controlled by the strings of the Mysterons. The blandly good-looking Captain Scarlet (the Cary

Grant of the marionettes) is Spectrum's secret weapon, an indestructible fellow who literally dies and comes back to life in practically every episode, and the straight-faced presentation only makes it all the weirder. Anderson and company take all the action and spectacle of the hour-long *Thunderbirds* and compact it into tight half-hour episodes with more impressive effects and better looking and articulated marionettes. —*S. A.*

CARDCAPTOR SAKURA L: MANGA/MANGA (1998) 30M D: Morio Asaka. *Aya Hisakawa, Kikuko Inoue, Sakura Tange, Megumi Hayashibara.* This anime title was released in the States as *Cardcaptors*, but this is the real thing and much more worthwhile than the severely edited domestic release. Young Sakura accidentally releases a deck of magical cards she must find, defeat, and reclaim before they do any damage or mischief. This lengthy, charming series was made for children, but is rather uplifting for adults, too. After all, the best thing Sakura has going for her is her cheerful nature. Even once Sakura has captured all the cards, the creators of the series managed to continue logically in a new direction, without resorting to some foolish plot device such as having her accidentally lose them again. It's sweet, it's perky, it's insanely kawai, and it's very, very Japanese anime. But it has a way of sneaking under your skin and warming your heart. —*M. N.*

CARTOONS THAT TIME FORGOT: THE UB IWERKS COLLECTION L: N/C/A DIRECTORS/IWERKS, UB (1933) 236M D: Ub Iwerks. Iwerks is a hidden animation genius. He's the other genius behind Mickey Mouse. . . the real genius, in my opinion. He left Disney early on to make his own mark. Unfortunately, he's long been forgotten by Hollywood, Disney, and everyone. These two wonderful DVDs feature some of the most inventive, off-the-wall, free-association cartoon craziness ever. His down-and-out Flip the Frog is a kind of amoral Mickey Mouse, always looking out for number one. Iwerks was a pioneer who brought a level of surrealism to cartoons, an influence that is visible in the Warner Brothers cartoons all the way to *Ren & Stimpy*. Watch these discs and be amazed. —*K. C.*

CASTLE OF CAGLIOSTRO L: N/C/A DIRECTORS/MIYAZAKI, HAYAO (1980) 109M D: Hayao Miyazaki. *Bob Bergen, Yasuo Yamada.* A series of chance encounters land Lupin III, a notorious thief generally known as The Wolf, and Jigen, a sharpshooter formerly tied to the Yakuza, in a mysterious town where they hope to rescue a damsel in distress, crush a corrupt counterfeiting operation, and make off with some long lost treasure. A deliriously entertaining mix of every action genre within reach, *Cagliostro* realizes early on that plausibility isn't in the cards, and opts instead for (appropriately) cartoonish flamboyance. Along with *Porco Rosso*, this gets my vote for the most fun to be had in Miyazaki's catalog, with a cast of characters too

brilliant to describe and an endless arsenal of unlikely gadgets that gives new meaning to the word "rad." —*C. B.*

CAT RETURNS, THE (NEKO NO ONGAESHI) L:MANGA/ MANGA (2002) 86M D: Hiroyuki Morita. *Chizuru Ikewaki, Yoshihiko Hakamada, Tetsu Watanabe, Takayuki Yamada, Tetsuro Tamba, Aki Maeda.* While it is a Studio Ghibli film produced by the amazing Miyazaki, he clearly did not direct this one. It begins with the potential to be as cool and delightful as *Spirited Away*, but doesn't take the catnip ball and run with it. A young girl rescues a cat from traffic and discovers he is the Prince of Cats. His father, the King of Cats, lavishes her with gifts of catnip, cattails, and gift-wrapped mice. When she discovers he plans for her to marry his son, she realizes she needs help. It's as if it started off as a Miyazaki film, but then got confused with the anime film *Catnapped*, a very odd and funny movie, but not in the same class as most of Studio Ghibli's work. Worth seeing, for sure, but just don't watch this one with your usual Miyazaki viewing standards. —*M. N.*

CHICKEN RUN L: N/C/A DIRECTORS/PARK, NICK (2000) 84M D: Nick Park, Peter Lord. *Lynn Ferguson, Julia Sawalha, Mel Gibson, Jane Horrocks, Tony Haygarth, Miranda Richardson.* The world of animation, particularly claymation, is one that requires a large amount of skill, attention to detail, and, above all, patience. It is these things that make *Chicken Run* the amazing film it is. Created by the same guys responsible for *Wallace & Gromit*, this movie tells the story of a group of chickens trying to escape a farm before they end up as part of a chicken pie. The only problem is that they can't fly, and they spend most of the movie trying to get around this little technicality. The animation is excellent, especially when you take into account the amazing feat of producing a feature-length claymation film, and the characters are incredibly endearing. This is a really fun, really entertaining movie that's good for kids and those who wish they still were. —*J. S.*

CHRISTMAS CAROL, A L: N/C/A DIRECTORS/WILLIAMS, RICHARD. (1971) 30M D: Richard Williams. *Melvyn Hayes, Alastair Sim, Michael Redgrave.* This incredible Oscar-winning short has a very original animation style with unusually realistic figures and settings. Oftentimes they are shaded with intricate crosshatches, making them look like appropriate illustrations for the Dickens book. Williams is known for animating painstakingly detailed drawings, and there are plenty of knockout sequences in this one, including a meticulously hand-drawn opening that soars over the village. Most impressive, though, are the spooky depictions of the three spirits. Even the Ghost of Christmas Past is scary, her face a three-eyed blur of two faces, like she's stuck in two different time periods simultaneously. And wait until you see the two shriveled-up kids hiding beneath

Best comic-book movies

THE ADDAMS FAMILY

AMERICAN SPLENDOR

BABA YAGA

BARBARELLA

BATMAN *(1966)*

BATMAN *(1988)*

BATMAN: MASK OF THE PHANTASM

BATMAN RETURNS

BLADE

BLADE 2

FRITZ THE CAT

GHOST WORLD

HELLBOY

HULK

LI'L ABNER

LONE WOLF AND CUB

MEN IN BLACK

THE ROCKETEER

SPIDER-MAN

SUPERMAN II

SUPERMAN III

TANK GIRL

UZUMAKI

X2: X-MEN 2

Christmas Present's robe! This was released on video by Anchor Bay, but with a cover that doesn't really give an idea of how great it is. Trust me—seek this one out next Christmas. —*B. T.*

COCKPIT, THE: KAMIKAZE STORIES L: MANGA/MANGA (1994) 60M D: Yoshiaki Kawajiri, Takashi Imanishi. *Kenyû Horiuchi, Hikaru Midorikawa.* A mediocre anime anthology featuring three stories about Japanese soldiers during WWII. The first story has the most traditional anime look and is a tale of a "cowardly" pilot escorting an atomic bomber and his hard decision of honor versus morality. The second drops us into the cockpit of a kamikaze. The pilot wants nothing more than to die for his country, yet, as he's bulleting toward his target, realizes too late the emptiness of war. The third is the most "cartoony" and takes us out of the air and onto a small island near the end of the war. A young soldier wants to get back to his airbase, even though he knows it's been overrun with Allied troops and his motorcycle is broken. An older, funnier, more world-weary soldier fixes his motorcycle and joins him for the ride, which turns out to be kind of predictable and sentimental. A mixed bag, but worth checking out. —*K. C.*

COLORFUL L: MANGA/PORNIME (2002) 110M D: Shun Nakahara. *Koki Tanaka, Sawako Agawa.* This show is about panties!!! Or, is it actually a satire about the odd male obsession with panties? It's hard to tell. But, it doesn't matter since the end product is so much fun no matter how you view it. It has you hooked right from the hyper-obnoxious opening credit music. What the show lacks in character development, story, or social relevance, it more than makes up with sheer energy and insanely hilarious panty peeping. The animation is very free and vibrant, some of the best I've seen. Watch for Steve, the American tourist (in case you thought Japanese men were the only perverts), as he butchers the hell out of the Japanese language. —*K. C.*

COWBOY BEBOP COMPLETE SERIES COLLECTION L: MANGA/MANGA (1998) 650M D: Shinichiro Watanabe. *Ai Kobayashi, Tsutomu Isobe, Aoi Tada, Unsho Ishizuka, Megumi Hayashibara, Koichi Yamadera.* While *Cowboy Bebop* sports many elements found throughout other anime series—high-speed chases, savage gunfights, futuristic settings, striking antiheroes, and martial arts action—it has something most series cannot quite achieve: style with a capital S. Crafted with such care and details, it is unique, simply because no one has pulled this kind of series off with such excellence. The music is the first remarkable aspect, used as punctuation, rich seasoning, and nostalgic romance throughout. The cinematic styles of camera angles, flashbacks, and dramatic poise lend maturity. Add wicked humor, rich and layered characters, a well-developed world with intelligent scientific applications, and a perfect balance between the serious and the playful, and you have one of the best written, animated, and conceived anime ever made. —*M. N.*

COWBOY BEBOP: THE MOVIE—(AKA COWBOY BEPOP: KNOCKIN' ON HEAVEN'S DOOR) L: MANGA/MANGA (2001) 114M D: Shinichiro Watanabe. *Ai Kobayashi, Koichi Yamadera, Unsho Ishizuka, Megumi Hayashibara, Tsutomu Isobe, Aoi Tada.* A stylish piece of anime cinema, based on the popular Japanese *Cowboy Bebop* series. The story takes place at some indeterminate point in time (a few episodes before the end of the series). Once again, while in search of a bounty, the crew of the Bebop becomes embroiled in something much bigger than they suspected. All the signature elements of the series are here: gunfights, martial arts, fantastic chases, a killer soundtrack, and (of course) a dark, brooding overtone mixed with humor and keen perception of human nature. A mysterious individual commits random attacks of biological terrorism, causing Spike to pursue the truth. He seeks to determine just who this person is, how his agent of destruction works, and why he is planning to kill everyone on the planet. While familiarity with the series and its characters enhances viewing, the movie holds its own as a stand-alone piece. —*M. N.*

CRITIC, THE L: Nonchildren'S ANIMATION/Nonchildren'S ANIMATION (1994) 30M D: Various. *Jon Lovitz, Nancy Cartwright, Christine Cavanaugh, Charles Napier.* The first somewhat successful knock-off of the *Simpsons*'s style of humor, this short-lived animated series revolved around Jay Sherman (Lovitz), an egotistical New York City movie critic. While most series of this type are about families, Jay is a divorcé always looking for love and raising his son Marty (Cavanaugh) alone. The show has too many fat jokes (Jay is overweight and bald as an homage to both Siskel and Ebert), and some of the movie parodies are too obvious or arbitrary. But many supporting characters (such as Jay's insane Ted Turner—like boss Duke [Napier]) are funny; and for film buffs especially, it's fun to see a show with jokes about directors, classic films, and ridiculous movie trends. My favorite episode is "Siskel & Ebert & Jay & Alice," guest starring Siskel and Ebert as themselves in a story about a rift in their friendship. This surprisingly touching episode was a weird treat—as if Gene and Roger decided to make an animated Valentine's Day special. —*B. T.*

CROW, THE L: COMIX/COMIX (1994) 102M D: Alex Proyas. *Brandon Lee, Ernie Hudson, Michael Wincott, Rochelle Davis.* The debut film from director Proyas is a visceral look into one man's fight for love and revenge, made all the more bittersweet by the fact that Lee gave his life for the movie. Based on a graphic novel by James O'Barr, and fantastically adapted, it is one of the greatest examples of a comic successfully transformed into film. The supernatural plot is universal and follows the path of Eric (Lee), who has returned from the dead one year after being murdered along with his girlfriend. He seeks revenge, targeting a band of remorseless hoods. In his quest, Eric also returns to the lives of those he once knew to bring them peace. Lee's performance is right on the mark, and one can tell he truly cared for the character. Proyas, who has a natural ability to play with light and dark, sets the uneasy Gothic mood. —*R. M.*

CRYING FREEMAN L: COMIX/COMIX (1995) 102M D: Christophe Gans. *Mark Dacascos, Julie Condra, Tchéky Karyo, Masaya Kato.* In a live-action adaptation of the popular manga, Dacascos plays an innocent potter abducted, tattooed, and brainwashed by a cult to become a badass assassin. When he kills people it's against his will, so tears stream down his face. A painter witnesses one of his hits, so he goes after her next, even though both are clearly attracted to each other. This nicely shot film was made as an homage to the John Woo style before he came to the United States. Unfortunately, it was shelved until long after slow-motion shoot-outs and conflicted hitmen became old hat in the United States, and even now you have to import it from Canada if you want to see it. Gans received a lot of buzz in horror magazines at the time, but never made good on it until 2001's *Brotherhood of the Wolf*, which featured Dacascos in a supporting role. —*B. T.*

DAREDEVIL L: COMIX/COMIX (2003) 104M D: Mark Steven Johnson. *Colin Farrell, Michael Clarke Duncan, Jennifer Garner, Ben Affleck.* Blinded by toxic waste, Affleck's other senses become so hyper-attuned that he decides to dress up in an asinine red S&M motorcycle outfit and fly around the city fighting crime. Then one day he has an adorably flirtatious kung fu battle with the deadly assassin Elektra (Garner), but sadly her father is killed by Bullseye (Farrell), whose superpower is flicking paper clips and peanuts to kill people (seriously). Director Johnson (whose previous garbage includes the *Grumpy Old Men* movies and the nonslasher snowman movie *Jack Frost*) tries to play off the shadows and seediness of Frank Miller's famous Daredevil stories, but it comes across more like a lame imitation of *The Crow*. Farrell makes the proceedings even more embarrassing by channeling the Joel Schumacher school of villainy for his ludicrous character. Your reaction may vary—some comic book fans have been uncharacteristically forgiving of this film despite its casting of girl-next-door Garner as the cold-hearted Greek über-badass. —*B. T.*

DARIA: IS IT FALL YET? L: NONCHILDREN'S/MTV ANIMATION (2001) 75M D: Karen Disher, Guy Moore. *Tracy Grandstaff, Wendy Hoopes.* Daria was a character on *Beavis and Butthead* ("Diarrhea, cha-cha-cha!"), so I was skeptical when this show debuted on MTV in 1997. Wouldn't a spin-off be just as ridiculous? It proved to be the opposite of its origins, pitting the intellectual, antisocial Daria against her bubbly, popular sister Quinn and the trials of surviving high school when you aren't part of the in crowd. *Is It Fall Yet?* takes place over the summer as Daria deals with more than just grating classmates. She's estranged from her best friend and cohort in misery, Jane Lane, for stealing her boyfriend Tom; and her parents force her to get a job at the "It's OK to Cry" camp. Jane goes to an artist's colony and is sickened by the pretension, while Quinn gets a tutor to prove to herself she's more than just the Fashion Club Vice-President. I wish *Daria* had been on when I was in high school; I can only hope it helped a few teens before MTV cancelled it in favor of more hip programming. And I must admit, I had a little crush on Jane's slacker-musician brother Trent. —*J. K.*

EIGHT CRAZY NIGHTS L: NONCHILDREN'S ANIMATION/ NONCHILDREN'S ANIMATION (2002) 76M D: Seth Kearsley. *Adam Sandler, Jackie Titone, Austin Stout, Kevin Nealon, Rob Schneider.* Unlikely to ever wind up on a network Christmas line-up, *Eight Crazy Nights* (named after a line in Sandler's "Hanukah Song") is a steady stream of fart gags and foul language, belches and butt-cracks, animal droppings and urine stains, penned and produced by the man-boy of adolescent toilet humor and juvenile sex jokes. He voices a drunken thirty-three-year-old misanthrope who makes the Grinch look like George Bailey, as well as Whitey, his oblivious dwarf of a guardian and Whitey's kvetching fraternal twin sister Eleanore. Some of the comedy is inspired, but Sandler fills the film with a barrage of product placements and ultimately wallows in the soppy sentiment he sends up. Take note of the rating before picking this up for the kids: the PG-13 is for frequent crude and sexual humor, drinking and brief drug references. —*S. A.*

EL HAZARD: THE MAGNIFICENT WORLD L: MANGA/ MANGA (1995) 235M D: Hiroki Hayashi. *Ryôtarô Okiayu, Tetsuya Iwanaga, Kôji Ishî, Rio Natsuki, Tomo Sakurai, Yuri Amano.* This is the first, and by far the best, OAV of this anime story that tells the tale of Makoto, a high school student who is transported to the world of El Hazard by a strange woman who begs him to save her world. A teacher, a friend, and a boy who considers Makoto his archrival are transported with him. The first two join Makoto to help the people of El Hazard try to defeat the invading Bugrom race. Makoto's rival has given his support to the Bugrom. They race to reach the ultimate weapon—Ifurita, the woman who sent Makoto there in the first place. But what's this? Ifurita does not recognize Makoto now and has become his enemy! Looks like someone other than the Bugrom are creating havoc! The animation is beautiful, the story complex and entertaining, the characters thoroughly enjoyable and often quite wacky, creating an excellent piece of anime storytelling. Highly recommended! —*M. N.*

FAMILY GUY, THE L: NONCHILDREN'S ANIMATION/ NONCHILDREN'S ANIMATION (1999) 30M D: Various. *Seth McFarlane, Alex Borstein, Mila Kunis, Seth Green.* This oft-cancelled prime-time cartoon series has built up quite a following on video. I couldn't tell you why. Creator MacFarlane worked at Hanna-Barbera during its groundbreaking modern era that birthed the influential Tartakovsky-McCracken style seen in *Dexter's Laboratory* and *The Powerpuff Girls*, and yet the guy draws like a kid copying Garfield comics onto his Pee-Chee. The main character (a fatter, less funny, asshole-y version of Homer Simpson) has repulsive bulbous feet and either an ass or a pair of testicles on his chin. There is the occasional clever joke, but it always follows the template of *The Simpsons*, except when it involves baby Stewie, and then it's just *Pinky and the Brain*. After the success of *The Simpsons* and *King of the Hill*, there is no excuse for an animated family show with so little imagination. And there has never been an excuse for character designs this ugly. For crying out loud this was on television! People had to look at it. —*B. T.*

FANTASTIC PLANET L: N/C/A DIRECTORS/LALOUX, RENE (1973) 72M D: Rene Laloux. *Cynthia Adler, Barry Botswick.* This beautifully animated film became a huge hit in the '80s on the late-night cable show *Nightflight*. French painter Laloux and a group of animators created this amazing film from cut-out figures that were stop-motion animated, creating a strange, silent film effect. Written by surrealist author Roland Topor (*The Tenant*), this David and Goliath story is about the Oms, miniature humanoids ruled over by the giant blue-skinned Traggs, who keep the Oms as domesticated pets. When the Oms revolt, they travel to the Fantastic Planet, where the Traggs secretly go to procreate. The Oms threaten to destroy the Traggs unless they are freed from their slavery and given equality. Filled with beautiful imagery and an amazing soundtrack, *Fantastic Planet* is an excellent exercise in surrealist imagery that remains timeless in its design and structure. Winner of the 1973 Grand Prix award at Cannes, Roger Corman distributed it in U.S. theaters in an English-language dubbed version. The DVD restores the French track and includes several short films by Laloux and Topor. —*N. H.*

FINAL FANTASY: THE SPIRITS WITHIN L: NONCHILDREN'S /COMPUTER ANIMATION (2000) 106M D: Hironobu Sakaguchi. *Ming-Na Wen, Alec Baldwin, Ving Rhames, Steve Buscemi, Donald Sutherland.* In this strangely misguided video game adaptation, groundbreaking photo-realistic computer animation is used to tell a story that easily could have been done in live action. A group of scientists and soldiers try to save the Earth from beings they have nicknamed "phantoms," and which they are later shocked to realize actually are phantoms, like the audience assumed. The characters are eerily lifeless, like mannequins or Thunderbirds, making for an uncomfortable moment when two of these soulless automatons clumsily kiss. At the same time, they look enough like real people that it is distracting to hear their dialogue dubbed by recognizable voices like Buscemi or Baldwin. Even if you could set aside the creepy animation, you would be left with an incredibly dull story with little in the way of humor or emotion. —*B. T.*

FIRE AND ICE L: N/C/A DIRECTORS/BAKSHI, RALPH (1983) 81M D: Ralph Bakshi. *Stephen Mendel, Susan Tyrrell, William Ostrander, Maggie Roswell.* Fire and Ice is a basic good-versus-evil story as the world enters a second ice age and all that survives of humankind are barbarian races. Half of the world is covered in ice, and evil Ice Lord Nekron begins destroying villages in the warmer North, attempting to take over with his armies of ape men. Larn, a young warrior orphaned by Nekron's armies, seeks out Nekron to avenge the destruction of his people. Graphic artist Frank Frazetta, known for his covers for *Heavy Metal* magazine and science fiction and fantasy novels, designed the film and his style of large-breasted women and barrel-chested barbarian men, very popular in the '80s, fits the plot like a glove, while also stylistically separating the film from other Bakshi works. The film does, however, include Bakshi's controversial use of rotoscoping (tracing over live action). A cult film, it is refreshing to see a fully animated feature work geared to adults. —*N. H.*

FIVE STAR STORIES L: MANGA/MANGA (1989) 125M D: Kazuo
Yamazaki. *Ryo Horikawa, Kazuhiko Inoue.* When I was about thirteen, I came across this model builders magazine that had these crazy models of psychotic-looking robots with wings and jets and cannons attached to them. I thought to myself, "Holy shit, this is intense!" Of the droves of robotic machinations, one series stood out from the rest of the mecha herd like a gleaming rail-gun pointing the way to sweet, savage salvation. The *Five Star Stories* robots permanently imbedded a sense of awe upon my eager developing brain. Several years later, with my admiration for these machines still firmly cemented, I came across a *Five Star Stories* anime at a rental store. I was so psyched, but after watching it, I wondered, "Can anyone tell me what the fuck this is about?" I still don't know. —*T. C.*

FLASH GORDON L: COMIX/COMIX (1980) 111M D: Mike
Hodges. *Sam Jones, Max Von Sydow, Brian Blessed, Ornella Muti, Melody Anderson, Topol.* Starring former porn actor Jones as Flash Gordon and Von Sydow as Ming the Merciless, this film could hardly miss becoming the camp sci-fi classic it is today. Add the remarkably corny dialogue and special effects, plus the rock group Queen performing the original soundtrack, and it's easy to see how this film made its own following in the midst of so many other *Star Wars* imitators! The moon is being pulled out of its orbit by strange energy waves emanating from the planet Mongo. Dr. Hans Zarkow flies his rocket to the planet, accidentally bringing along Flash Gordon, quarterback for the New York Jets, and Dale Arden (Anderson). On Mongo they find Ming the Merciless, who must be destroyed to save the Earth. Overacting, zany effects, and post-disco music save the day! —*N. J.*

FLCL (AKA FURI KURI) (AKA FOOLY COOLY) L: MANGA/
MANGA (2000) 180M D: Kazuya Tsurumaki. *Izumi Kasagi, Mayumi Shintani, Jun Mizuki.* I've watched the brilliant anime series *FLCL* several times now,

and I'm still not sure what the title means. But I have unconditional love for the crazy world of *Fooly Cooly*, six episodes of pure exuberance, creativity, and sheer insanity. It's a fairly simple coming-of-age story about a teenage boy, his involvement with his brother's girlfriend, Mamimi (while his brother is in America playing baseball), Haruko, a beautiful Vespa-riding alien, the TV-headed robot that sprung from his head when Haruko hit him with her gas-powered Rickenbacker 4001 bass guitar, and a bizarre government (?) man after Haruko for intergalactic crimes. . . I guess. The genius animators at Gainax and Production I.G. have concocted a Japanese pop-art explosion, and it's the most fun you'll have watching anything. . . ever. FLCL!! New Style-Crazy! Are You Ready?! Are You Waiting!? Time For Rock And Roll!! —*K. C.*

FRITZ THE CAT L: N/C/A DIRECTORS/BAKSHI, RALPH (1972)
77M D: Ralph Bakshi. *Skip Hinnant, John McCurry.* Bakshi's interpretation of R. Crumb's underground comic is famous as the first X-rated cartoon. Although it has a big orgy scene near the beginning, it is mostly a high-minded satire about racial politics, brutish cops, and pretentious white college students who only talk revolution to get in somebody's pants. In one of the best scenes, Fritz starts a riot in the ghetto and then hides, popping his head out occasionally to yell catch phrases about "the bosses" and "the iron thumb on the head of the proletariat." It's great to see a cartoon deal with this subject matter, even if it had to throw in lots of tits and marijuana for anyone to pay attention. When I recommend this film, some say, "R. Crumb hated it so much he killed off the character." I say, "Yeah, but did you see *Crumb*? Do you really think you have the same tastes in movies as that guy?" —*B. T.*

GHOST WORLD L: COMIX/COMIX (2001) 111M D: Terry
Zwigoff. *Steve Buscemi, Bob Balaban, Illeana Douglas, Brad Renfro, Scarlett Johansson, Thora Birch.* Based on the Dan Clowes graphic novel, *Ghost World* is the story of two cynical, trendy teenagers who recently graduated from high school and are getting an apartment together instead of going off to college—the thing that everyone else is doing. When the two play a mean prank on Buscemi, a lonely older man, their lives are changed forever. Enid finds a kindred spirit in the dorky old guy, and Rebecca has to face the fact that things with Enid might not work out exactly as she planned. A dark, humorous coming-of-age story with a little twist, *Ghost World* excels at showing how bumpy the transition to adulthood can be. The dialogue is excellent, and Clowes and *Crumb* director Zwigoff are gifted screenwriters. Birch is excellent as Enid, but Buscemi steals the show as Seymour, the painfully shy, awkward record collector whose life is turned upside down by his relationship with Enid. —*J. S.*

Anime 101

Animation from Japan used to be referred to as Japanimation, but "anime" is the current and more popular term, derived from the French word for animation. When it comes to anime, either you're in the know or you're not. So readers well acquainted with anime, feel free to move on, but newbies, stick around! The U.S. releases of *Princess Mononoke* and the Academy Award winner *Spirited Away* expanded awareness of anime in this country, but the genre is still a mystery to most Americans. Because it is animation, anime has often been relegated to the status of "cartoons"; but it actually constitutes a separate genre, far more interesting and complicated than you might think.

One of the first things to remember is that anime is not just for kids. In the United States, animation is considered a lower form of film and television art—a medium primarily for children, with only a few exceptions. In Japan, however, anime is made for all ages, genders, and preferences, from eight-year-old girls to thirty-five-year-old housewives. Anime is born out of the visual art of *manga*, a sort of "comic book" that is as prevalent, varied, and accepted in Japan as books and magazines are in the United States. In Japan there is no stigma attached to a story that is drawn and accompanied by dialogue, as there is in the United States.

Anime in Japan is made in a variety of different media. The highest form is film,

continued on page 544

GRAVE OF THE FIREFLIES L: N/C/A DIRECTORS/TAKAHATA, ISAO (1988) 93M D: Isao Takahata. *Tsutomu Tatsumi, Ayano Shiraishi.* This is the heartbreaking story of a boy and his little sister trying to survive the bombing in Japan during WWII. Although their father is in the navy, it seems for a while like the war only really affects what they eat. Then their mother is killed and they end up trying to live on their own. One of the few war movies that takes the point of view of the civilians caught in the middle, it's a precise depiction both of the innocent people who become "collateral damage" in war and of people's tendency to ignore and fear those worse off than they are. Studio Ghibli made this and *My Neighbor Totoro* at the same time, and both are masterpieces. —B.T.

GREEN GOBLIN'S LAST STAND, THE L: COMIX/COMIX (1992) 114M D: Dan Poole. *Dan Poole, Jimi Kinstle, Bob Tull.* A home-made video by a Spider-Man fan who wanted to star in the Hollywood *Spider-Man* movie then being developed by James Cameron. Poole and his friends pulled out all the stops to depict Spider-Man and Green Goblin jumping, web-slinging, and sky-sledding without a budget. It doesn't look like a real movie, of course, but what they were able to pull off is incredible. Poole recklessly endangered himself for many stunts, including a swing around the corner of a seven-story building with no harness or safety net. He clearly has studied the Spider-Man comics in detail—every move he makes seems pre-cisely modeled on a pose from the comics. More interesting than the movie itself is the making-of documentary where Poole's obsession really comes across. Also you learn that when police see a guy swinging off a building in a Spider-Man costume they assume he's supposed to be doing that. Available only from the filmmaker's website. —B.T.

GTO—GREAT TEACHER ONIZUKA (VOL. 1) L: MANGA/ MANGA (1998) 650M D: Various. *Aimi Nakamura, Hiroyuki Ikeuchi, Yosuke Kubozuka, Takashi Sorimachi, Miki Kuroda, Nanako Matsushima.* Twenty-two-year-old Onizuka has been many things. A rebel. A motorcycle gang leader. A troublemaker. Now he wants to be a teacher. Though he's not terribly bright and never took the educator's exam, Onizuka believes in his students, no matter how troublesome they might be. This faith gets him a position at a private school, in charge of a class that has driven other teachers to quit. But Onizuka is no ordinary teacher! He manages, through personality, actions, determination, and often sheer dumb luck, to jump the hurdles thrown in his path, slowly winning over the class. It's a slightly different slant from the usual "high school drama" animes out there, since the focus is upon Onizuka as much as his students. The animation style is annoying at times, but the stories are entertaining, the character charming, and

with Studio Ghibli reigning supreme among the fine-art animation studios in Japan, making full-length feature films almost exclusively. A great deal of anime is made for television, and it is considered just as worthy as other television programs. Finally, some anime is made for direct sale to the public, showing on neither the big screen nor television but available for purchase only on DVD and VHS.

When choosing and watching anime, one should keep a few important things in mind.

Anime is not simply a cartoon or an animated movie or TV show; it is a foreign film. As such, it will contain aspects of culture, humor, and language that are uniquely Japanese. Ideally, you will find these elements interesting, entertaining, and enjoyable.

Because of cultural differences, anime may contain ideas that Americans would consider inappropriate or unmarketable for a certain age group. The series *Cardcaptor Sakura*, for example, was heavily edited for its American release as *Cardcaptors*. The U.S. version of this youth-oriented anime begins with the introduction of the major male character, Li, under the assumption that boys would not watch the show if it began with a cast primarily made up of girls. The editors also variously altered and deleted episodes that displayed Li's crush on a high school boy, Yuki.

Your reaction to one anime film or series will not guarantee that you will have the same reaction to others. There are many kinds of anime, and it's just like any other kind of show or film; some stories will appeal to you, and some won't. In addition, because anime is often made for a specific age group, there are subgenres within the genre. To find the right kind of anime for you, you may want to get some recommen-

---

the situations often hilarious. Definitely a must-see for anime fans! —*M. N.*

GUMBY: THE MOVIE L: NONCHILDREN'S/CLAYMATION (1995) 90M D: Art Clokey. *Alice Young, Bonnie Rudolph, Janet McDuff, Manny la Carruba.* When Gumby's dog Lowbelly (who rides around on a skateboard, probably so his feet don't have to be animated) hears music, he cries and his tears turn to pearls. So the Blockheads steal the dog and replace him with a robot double. But it turns out that not just any music makes Lowbelly cry, only the music of Gumby's band, The Gumbys. The Blockheads replace The Gumbys with robots one by one until things come to a head and Gumby has a *Star Wars*–style showdown with his evil robot twin. You have to admire Gumby creator Clokey for maintaining ownership of the character and producing and directing this film independently. It's defiantly slow-paced and charmingly anachronistic, so it's not for everybody. But it's refreshing to see a G-rated film that's not trying to be for everybody, and if you're like me, you might get a kick out of the casual surrealism. —*B. T.*

HEAVY METAL 2000 L: NONCHILDREN'S ANIMATION/ NONCHILDREN'S ANIMATION (2000) 88M D: Michael Coldewey. *Julie Strain, Michael Ironside, Billy Idol.* If the term "adult animation" means something only a thirteen-year-old boy of below-average intelligence could like (and even then only in passing), then *Heavy Metal 2000* is adult animation. Telling a single story (unlike its anthology predecessor) about a half-naked female warrior (Strain) fighting a psychotic muscleman (Ironside) in space, this is one of the crappiest and most brain-dead animated films. If you expect to find one clever scene or moment, one character who is not obnoxious, or even one well-drawn action scene, you're looking in the wrong place. However, if a bunch of crudely drawn tits and blood backed by shitty '90s metal bands like Insane Clown Posse give you a boner, maybe this one is worth your while. It's basically a vanity project for Strain's producer/husband Kevin Eastman, who thinks showing off his Playboy model wife will make everybody forget he created the fucking Ninja Turtles. —*B. T.*

HEAVY TRAFFIC L: N/C/A DIRECTORS/BAKSHI, RALPH (1973) 76M D: Ralph Bakshi. *Joseph Kaufmann, Beverly Hope.* Bakshi's second feature is the semiautobiographical story of a cartoonist who takes inspiration from the turmoil that surrounds his life in New York City. He hangs out on the rooftops with delinquents and homeless people, or at a bar inhabited by thugs, a drag queen, and an overpossessive double-amputee. Anything to avoid going home to his nagging mother and his abusive Mafioso father. Finally he takes his bartender girlfriend and tries to escape the city. Some will find the story plodding and pretentious, but I think this is Bakshi at his best. He really was doing something different with the

dations based on themes and stories you enjoy.

Dubbed or subtitled? It's a personal choice. I personally prefer subtitled, just as I would with a foreign film. Anime dialogue can sometimes sound silly in an American voice because the conversation and phrasing is often uniquely Japanese. In addition, the actors who dub anime are often not very skilled. On the other hand, many people prefer dubbed translations because they make it easier to watch the animation and thus keep up with the story. Give each a try, and see which you prefer.

FREQUENTLY ASKED QUESTIONS:

What the heck does OAV stand for, and what does it mean?

OAV stands for original animated video. OAVs are made for direct sale to the public and, as such, are not shown on television or in theaters. OAVs are also made with higher-quality animation than is seen in shows made for television.

When you look through a series you like, some of the videos may be marked "OAV" while others are not. What does this mean? Which came first? That, alas, depends a great deal on the show in question. Sometimes the OAV is made first, as in the case of *El Hazard: The Magnificent World* or *Tenchi Muyo*. If an OAV is successful, the story is often remade for television. But beware! Just because the title is the same or similar does not mean that the story is the same. The television series *Tenchi Muyo* featured the same characters that were first released in an OAV series but changed many of their roles and completely changed the history and the story, much to the annoyance and disappointment of fans of the OAV. *El Hazard* likewise inspired *El Hazard: The Wanderers*, which featured the same char-

continued on page 546

---

medium. He was experimenting with different animation and live-action techniques, and also creating the type of deeply personal portraits of urban despair that Scorsese and friends were doing in live action. *Heavy Traffic* is completely unique among animated films. —*B. T.*

HIS AND HER CIRCUMSTANCES L: MANGA/MANGA (1998) 30M D: Hideaki Anno. *Yuki Watanabe, Maria Yamamoto, Chihiro Suzuki, Atsuko Enomoto.* This high school anime series in no way, shape, or form resembles my own experience, but I find watching it a bizarrely nostalgic experience. It traces the lives of two students driven to success due to different circumstances. Rivals at first, their relationship changes as they get to know one another. Their affection allows them to be themselves rather than the facades they were maintaining. Based on a Japanese manga, the style is referential to its roots, using lovely stills and illustrations along with animation. There is a surprising amount of text to be read on screen, in deference to its literary roots. It definitely enhances the storyline, but it's not essential, so don't fret if you can't keep up. Playful, quirky, and vastly entertaining, the stories touch upon painful truths, tender emotions, and ludicrous scenarios, but rarely delve too far into the foolish, maudlin, or melodramatic. A sheer delight! —*M. N.*

HOWARD THE DUCK L: COMIX/COMIX (1986) 110M D: Willard Huyck. *Lea Thompson, Jeffrey Jones, Tim Robbins.* When I was a kid, George Lucas, Steven Spielberg, and Jim Henson were my Holy Trinity. Anything they touched was golden to my seven-year-old eyes. . . even *Howard the Duck*, probably my favorite movie that year, and, at the time, possibly ever. Even though this movie is pretty abysmal to watch now, it still has the only anthropomorphic duck nudity on film. I still think it's the best "foul-mouthed duck-guy from an egg-shaped planet, who knows 'quack-fu' teamed up with Marty McFly's mom and Robbins vs. evil slime creatures and Jeffrey Jones" movie ever made. Plus, if IMDB (Internet Movie Database) is to be trusted, it took eight people to bring Howard to glorious life. —*K. C.*

HUBLEY COLLECTION, THE—VOL. 1 L: N/C/A DIRECTORS/ HUBLEY, FAITH & JOHN (1991) 118M D: Faith Hubley. *Emily Hubley, Georgia Hubley.* Very fresh, different, and thought provoking. This DVD showcases the work of Faith Hubley, her husband John, and their children Emily, Georgia, Ray, and Mark. Some of it is just plain strange, some is remarkable, some is magical. The animation is often simplistic and childlike, with strong stylistic imagery that reminds me of the works of Klee, Chagall, Picasso, and a lot of Miró. Much is also reminiscent of the more psychedelic moments in *The Yellow Submarine*. Faith is influenced greatly by poetry, with spoken words and music accom-

acters and some of the same basic ideas and storylines, but was in fact a brand-new story that did not follow the original.

Some series, however, treat OAVs as stand-alone movies. They take place at some undefined time during the series and remain true to the characters, the history, and the plotlines. There are several *Ranma* OAVs that exemplify this cooperative relationship. Often when a television series finally ends, a number of OAVs will be released to bring closure, tell a new story that picks up where the television story left off, or tells some of the backstory (events that occurred before the series began). These generally remain true to the original characters, stories, and plotlines.

What's with those big eyes? And that hair?

Many attribute the large eyes to the early influence of Betty Boop on Japanimation filmmakers. Often the size of the eyes is used to indicate the innocence and "goodness" of the character. Those with large, expressive eyes are generally sweet and innocent, and characters with narrow eyes are often villainous and evil—although, as with any generalization, there are exceptions to this rule. Characters often have brightly colored hair with wild and extreme hairdos, mostly to help define the characters and clearly distinguish them from one another, so you can tell at a glance whom you are looking at. Fancy ribbons and bows are yet another defining "look" for a character, and are commonly worn by Japanese girls as well.

Why are all the girls' voices so high-pitched?

This is a cultural phenomenon. In Japan, high voices are considered cute, sexy, and desirable in women—so much so that many companies specifically instruct their receptionists to answer the phone with a

---

panying the animation. John's work is more linear with an illustrative quality in telling a story. Some of her stuff I loved, and some didn't reach me. But it almost always inspired a strong reaction, provoked questions and curiosities, and often sparked a sense of sheer delight. —*M. N.*

I MARRIED A STRANGE PERSON L: N/C/A DIRECTORS/ PLYMPTON, BILL (1997) 74M D: Bill Plympton. *Tom Larson, Charis Michaelson.* Plympton is one of the wilder animators out there and it's amazing to think he drew each and every cell of this crazy movie. A recently married guy develops a bump on his neck that gives him telekinetic power over other people and also allows his imagination to become reality. This leads to lots of wild sex with his new bride, plus lots of other surprises. Sinister government agents and military men try to intrude on the newlywed's bliss, which results in plenty of comical gore and more twisted sexual humor. *I Married a Strange Person* works both as a highly imaginative slapstick comedy and as an artistically unique, nonchildren's animated film. I like everything Plympton does, but this is my favorite. Funny stuff! —*S. H.*

IRRESPONSIBLE CAPTAIN TYLOR, THE L: MANGA/MANGA (1993) 30M D: Koichi Mashimo. *Koji Tsujitani, Yuri Amano, Sho Hayami, Hiroko Kasahana, Maya Okamoto, Toshihiko Seki.* This uproarious anime series tells the tale of a young man looking for a life of ease and fun, so he joins the Space Navy.

Through bizarre circumstances, insanely impossible luck, and wily good charm, Tylor gets promoted to captain aboard one of the navy's worst and most problematic ships. Better yet, they are on the precipice of war with another space-faring nation. The irresponsible captain flies in the face of proper decorum and military regulations on a regular basis, with apparently no tactical knowledge or skills. His crew believes he is clearly a fool and an idiot, but is he? Is it genius or sheer dumb luck that makes Tylor so uncannily successful against his enemies, both on and off his own ship? Judge for yourself. You'll be hard-pressed at times to figure out just how Tylor is going to get out of the next scrape. —*M. N.*

JIN-ROH (AKA JIN-ROH: THE WOLF BRIGADE) L: MANGA/ MANGA (1998) 102M D: Hiroyuki Okiura. This grim, alternate-reality thriller set in a quasi-fascist Japan may startle stateside viewers used to the exquisitely detailed machinery of massive proportions clashing and exploding in elaborate science fiction and fantasy epics. All the vivid imagery and detailed design is shrouded in a murky atmosphere and put in the service of a socio-political suspense tale, a deadly game of political sabotage where rival government factions sacrifice their own in a savage grasp for power. Directed with a stunning seriousness by Okiura (the character designer on *Ghost in the Shell* and *Akira*), this is more like a John Le Carré conspiracy novel than metaphysical sci-fi, with dense layers of subter-

high-pitched, girlish voice. Naturally, this is a generalization, and many females have perfectly "normal" voices. But in cases where cuteness is called for, female voices will be squeaky and high.

What is *pornime*, and what's up with all those tentacles?

Pornime is a term created by Scarecrow Video to denote anime that features graphic sexual situations and would require an R or NC-17 rating in the United States. It is referred to in Japan as *hentai*, which means "pervert." Some of it is silly; some is graphic or violent. It is definitely not for children, and some adults as well may find it upsetting or offensive.

Those who boldly venture into the world of *pornime* may notice a recurring theme of tentacles doing, uh, naughty things. Anime has a variety of rules and taboos about what can and cannot be shown, depending on the year the anime was made and the studio that made it. Sometimes sex organs cannot be displayed, so they are whited out, merely symbolized, or simplified. In the case of tentacles, it's a simple case of substitution, likely inspired by the fact that Japan is an island with a strong reliance upon the sea and its bounties. Tentacles have a long history in Japanese culture and art, so it's a strangely logical result.

Exploring anime is quite an adventure, and there is much to choose from. So choose wisely, and remember that just as with any other type of movie or TV show, your mileage may vary. Try not to judge all anime by any one experience, whether it is good, bad, or indifferent. Anime is a vast world of entertainment that is only now, finally, receiving greater representation and distribution in the United States.

—*Mimi Noyes*

---

fuge and a sometimes bewilderingly complex set of shifting alliances and betrayals. It can be hard to follow at times, but the script by Mamoru Oshii is searing and smart, folding in references to *Little Red Riding Hood* (the undiluted, borderline grotesque version) as a haunting symbol of innocence sacrificed. You can feel the soul of its hero crack and wither in the final haunting moments. —*S. A.*

JOE 90 (4 VOLUMES) L: N/C/A DIRECTORS/ANDERSON, GERRY (1969) 720M D: Peter Anderson, Leo Eaton. *Keith Alexander, Sylvia Anderson, Rupert Davies.* Gerry and Sylvia Anderson's follow-up to the paranoid conspiracy adventure *Captain Scarlet vs. The Mysterons* is a truly mind-bending Cold War series. Joe, a nine-year-old guinea pig in his father's intelligence transference experiments, turns into a secret agent when he dons a pair of glasses that plug him into the super computer (named BIG RAT) that feeds him the brain waves of the world's greatest geniuses. With the blessing of his father, he leaps into deadly situations under the direction of World Intelligence Network officer Uncle Sam. The puppetry and gadgetry are Anderson's most sophisticated yet, and the adventures are pure schoolboy fantasy: who wouldn't want to become a super spy, brain surgeon, military pilot, and rocket scientist (to name just a few of his brief professions)? The foundation of the show isn't merely absurd, it's criminal. Or it would be, if it weren't all in the name of protecting our freedoms from the dreaded, devious Commie menace. —*S. A.*

JUNKERS COME HERE L: MANGA/MANGA (1995) 105M D: Junichi Sato. *Brittney Wilson, Lisa Ann Beley, Sean Campbell.* Sato's delightful animated feature, adapted from the novel by Naoto Kine (who also composed the music for the film), is the story of a sixth-grade girl with a crush on her handsome tutor, her mostly absent parents on the cusp of divorce, and a talking dog. The deft balance of fantasy and drama sacrifices neither the magic of the premise nor the seriousness of the emotional stress on the schoolgirl, helpless as she watches her parents' marriage unravel in front of her eyes. Like so many of the best fantasies, the line between imagination and magic, between what is dreamed and what is real, is left to the viewer to decide. It will remind many viewers of Hayao Miyazaki's work, no doubt in part because of the delicate and expressive work of animator-director Kazuo Komatsubara (who previously served the same capacity on Miyazaki's *Nausicaa: The Valley of the Wind*). A lovely and tender film. —*S. A.*

KIKI'S DELIVERY SERVICE L: N/C/A DIRECTORS/MIYAZAKI, HAYAO (1989) 102M D: Hayao Miyazaki. *Minami Takayama, Rei Sakuma.* Kiki is a young witch who, following a tradional witch rite of passage, goes to live on her own in the city for a year. At first she is lonely but she befriends the proprietors of a bakery and uses her flying broom to deliver their pastries. It's a slight premise that doesn't sound like much, but Miyazaki's sensitive and observant characterization makes it something extraordinary. He has a knack for little visual touches, like the way Kiki drops onto her bed when she's sad—true-to-life touches that make the drawings come to life. The flying scenes are among Miyazaki's most exhilarating. It's fruitless to try to choose a favorite Miyazaki film, but for me, when it's not *Porco Rosso* it's this sweet, moving fable. The English-dubbed version is very good—Kirsten Dunst is so perfect for Kiki it's hard to believe she's not the original voice. But many fans are hostile toward Phil Hartman's portrayal of Kiki's cat, Jiji. —*B.T.*

KING OF THE HILL: SEASON ONE L: NONCHILDREN'S ANIMATION/NONCHILDREN'S ANIMATION (1997) 30M D: Various. *Mike Judge, Kathy Najimy, Pamela Segall, Brittany Murphy, Johnny Hardwick, Stephen Root.* This show is funny. Really, really funny, because Judge, its creator, is a funny guy. The show takes place in Arlen, Texas, a town inhabited by many, many rednecks. Hank Hill is your average lawn-loving, beer-drinking, propane and propane accessory salesman, with sassy line-dancing wife Peg and twelve-year-old goofball son Bobby. His niece Luanne is a ditzy blond airhead barely making it through beauty school, and his best friends are a divorcé who secretly cries himself to sleep at night, a paranoid convinced the world is out to get him, and a guy who speaks mostly gibberish. Crazy shenanigans in a redneck town and funny redneck characters result in a show that is just really fucking funny. Like this one time, where Bobby makes out with a plastic head, and this other time where Peggy is Texas state Boggle champion, and so on. —*J.S.*

I disagree with the description of these characters as "rednecks." One of the many things that makes this show so refreshing is its positive (but not at all preachy) depiction of regular working-class Texans. Hank has many silly characteristics—his obsession with lawnmowers and propane, his fear of talking about sex or bodily functions—but these are part of a sympathetic, three-dimensional character. It makes you care about people that you might never think about getting to know. Despite being so uptight, Hank is an inherently decent person who usually acts as the voice of reason in his neighborhood (especially in later seasons as Peggy turns increasingly insane). Judge takes the type of insightful, observational satire that peppered *Beavis and Butthead* and gives it more humanity. —*B.T.*

LEAGUE OF EXTRAORDINARY GENTLEMEN, THE L: COMIX/COMIX (2003) 110M D: Steve Norrington. *Sean Connery, Shane West, Richard Roxburgh, Stuart Townsend, Peta Wilson, Jason Flemyng.* What if the great adventurers and monsters of English literature (Alan Quatermain, Mina Harker from *Dracula*, Captain Nemo, Dr. Jekkyl, the Invisible Man, etc.) were teamed up by a secret British agency to stop threats from the likes of Fu Manchu or the Martian invaders from *War of the Worlds*? That was the premise of two comics mini-series by Alan Moore and Kevin O'Neil—a sort of highbrow Justice League with Mr. Hyde as the Incredible Hulk and an unpredictable psychopathic Invisible Man. The movie is much less literary and British. They dumped the heavily researched feel of the comics for audience-insulting one-liners like Connery saying, "How operatic!" when a villain is introduced as "The Phantom," and added an American (West as Agent Tom Sawyer) who hops into the first-ever car and already knows how to "go for a spin." This is one of those big, expensive, incredibly dumb messes that feels as if it were written during filming to incorporate the conflicting ideas of fifteen different studio executives. With *Blade*, Norrington took a nothing comic and turned it into a classic movie—here he goes the opposite direction, turning a great comic into crap. —*B.T.*

LITTLE NEMO: ADVENTURES IN SLUMBERLAND L: COMIX/COMIX (1992) 85M D: Masanori Hata, William T. Hurtz. *Gabriel Damon, René Auberjonois, Mickey Rooney.* Winsor McCay was an animation pioneer who made films like *Gertie the Dinosaur*, drawing each frame himself by hand, background and all. He was also a renowned cartoonist, his most treasured creation the surreal *Little Nemo in Slumberland*, in which a boy in his pajamas travels through a bizarre fantasy world of dreams. Other than some shorts by McCay himself, this Japanese children's feature is the only attempt to adapt *Little Nemo* to the big screen. It's a decent film with imaginative ideas taken from the comic strips, but McCay's drawings are adapted into traditional Japanese cartooning style and the story fits the usual children's film template, working against the unpredictable, dreamy feel you want from Slumberland. I hope some day some more ambitious animators will see the potential of a *Little Nemo* feature, but until then check this one out and dream about what a great movie it could have been. —*B.T.*

LITTLE OTIK L: N/C/A DIRECTORS/SVANKMAJER, JAN (2000) 126M D: Jan Svankmajer. *Pavel Nov, Jaroslava Kretschmerova, Jan Hartl, Veronika Zilkova.* Based on a Czech fairy tale, *Little Otik* is the story of a young couple who can't have children. When the husband decides to cheer the wife up one day by carving her a "baby" out of a log, the wife goes totally crazy, convinced the baby is real and alive. She showers the log with affection until it really does come to life and starts eating everything in sight, getting larger and larger and demanding more and more food all the time. The log-baby Otik is animated through stop-motion, and as usual, Svankmajer is brilliant here. However, the movie runs for over two hours, and, animation aside, has a plot that gets a little tiresome after the first ninety minutes or so. —*J.S.*

LORD OF THE RINGS, THE L: N/C/A DIRECTORS/BAKSHI, RALPH (1978) 130M D: Ralph Bakshi. *William Squire, Christopher Guard, John Hurt, Michael Sholes.*

This film is not the entire *The Lord of the Rings* story, just *The Fellowship of the Ring* and half of *The Two Towers.* Having lost funding to finish the film, the producers unwisely left off at the battle of Helm's Deep, with a great deal of storyline still to go, and leaving several characters (such as Treebeard) to be only cameos. Yet Bakshi should be given major credit for being the first to attempt a mostly successful adaptation, written by *Last Unicorn* author Peter Siegel, of the mammoth works of Tolkien and for following many of Tolkien's own illustrations and remaining true to the characters. The film is well animated and edited, following the plot carefully. In fact, some of Peter Jackson's scenes even seem cribbed from Bakshi's. He has achieved a high level of craftsmanship that succeeds beyond all his previous work, and belongs alongside Jackson as the first major attempt by an artist to adapt the most famous fantasy trilogy in the twentieth century. And once again, Bakshi supplies an animated film for an adult audience seeking something more than cartoons for children. —*N. H.*

LUPIN III: THE FUMA CONSPIRACY L: MANGA/MANGA (1987) 73M D: Masayuki Ozeki. *Mami Koyama, Shigeru Chiba, Seizo Kato, Kaneto Shiozawa, Banjo Ginga, Toshio Furukawa.* One of the best of the *Lupin III* films (not to be mistaken with the series, which has much lower-quality animation). Lupin must aid his samurai friend Goemon in recovering his fiancée, who was kidnapped during their wedding ceremony by a rival family bent on stealing the ancestral treasure of her family. An ancient vase holds the secret to a vast wealth—a hidden castle made of gold—which her family has sworn to protect with their lives. With some of the best Lupin car chases ever and an almost *Indiana Jones*-esque journey through the booby-trapped caves and castle, this film is sure to please any Lupin fan, and even likely to seduce the unsuspecting into the stylish, humorous, and sly world of Lupin III, one of the most entertaining anime thieves ever. —*M. N.*

MACROSS PLUS L: MANGA/MANGA (1995) 160M D: Shôji Kawamor, Shinichiro Watanabei. *Megumi Hayashibara, Banjô Ginga, Rica Fukami.* Macross Plus is like animated *Top Gun*, but it's good. Really good, full of all the staples of transforming-robot action anime, with a great, simple story of the battle for manly supremacy. In the air, they are test pilots for experimental jets, one controlled by artificial intelligence, the other by a regular dude, both vying for a space on the manufacturer's table. Their rivalry continues on the ground as they fight over a woman they've both loved since childhood. Yes, it's all very soapy, but it works. The woman is the manager for an A.I. Singing Superstar, which weaves into the plot and becomes a dark part of the narrative up until the

climax. Make sure to watch the entire series and not the shortened movie version. —*K. C.*

MASK, THE L: COMIX/COMIX (1994) 97M D: Chuck Russell. *Jim Carrey, Peter Greene, Richard Jeni, Cameron Diaz.* Aside from turning the title character from a homicidal, bloodthirsty maniac into a lovable and likable goof, this is one of the better comic book translations in the world of cinema. Carrey pulls off the role extremely well, as he overplays his energetic Mask alter-ego with a great lust, while downplaying the hapless Stanley to keep the roller-coaster feel of the film going at a manic pace. Stanley is a banker whose dumb luck (or perhaps fate) lands him in the possession of a mask that pulls his id to the surface. At first he uses his powers for fun, but finds a higher purpose when gangster Tyrell (Greene) wants to get his hands on the mask as well. The special effects presented here pushed the boundaries of what CGI could do in the early '90s, and helped make the subtly dark humor all the more visceral. —*R. M.*

MAXX, THE L: COMIX/COMIX (1995) 120M D: Yeol Jung Chang, Gregg Vanzo. *Glynnis Talken, Michael Haley.* Amazingly faithful (but still somehow superior) MTV adaptation of the Sam Keith comics series about a huge purple guy, his relationship with a social worker, and their fantasy (?) about an alternate world called the Outback. The animation is very limited, but so detailed you are happy to admire the drawings while they are static. Like many comics of the time, it needlessly has a tenuous connection to the superhero genre (like it's supposed to be some sort of revisionism or postmodernism) but it's imaginative and strange enough to stand out from the pack. Definitely one of the best of the failed MTV animated series. —*B. T.*

MEMORIES L: MANGA/MANGA (1996) 110M D: Kouji Morimoto, others. A three-part animated anthology written by *Akira* director Katsuhiro Otomo. The first (and best) story, "Magnetic Rose," involves a derelict space station haunted by the ghost of an opera singer. The second, "Stink Bomb," is more of an epic slapstick comedy about a guy who swallows a biological weapon that gives him a deadly stench, causing mayhem wherever he goes. The third is "Cannon Fodder," about a family in a militaristic society built around a gigantic cannon. For those who can appreciate a loosely connected trilogy of shorts, this is very high-quality anime. The animation and direction is top-notch, especially in the case of the haunting first story. —*B. T.*

METROPOLIS L: MANGA/MANGA (2001) 109M D: Rintaro. *Yuka Imoto, Kei Kobayashi.* This deliriously dense animated thriller is not a remake of Fritz Lang's futuristic silent classic, but like Lang's film this retro-futurist visual feast transforms the New York skyline into a visionary labyrin-

thine cityscape and turns on a robot girl created by an outlaw scientist for an ambitious industrial megalomaniac. The dizzying plot of political conspiracies and betrayals, adapted by Katsuhiro Otomo (*Akira*) from Ozama Tezuka's 1949 graphic novel, can be confusing, but it's smarter and more resonant than you might expect in the way it mingles the fears and horrors of post-WWII Japan with the tensions of contemporary society. The imagery is astounding, a mix of space-age technology and 1930s devices set to a swinging jazz score and explored with swooping camerawork. The echoes of countless films, from *Sunrise* to *Dr. Strangelove* to *Blade Runner* to *Ghost in the Shell*, reverberate throughout. Science fiction fans and adventurous filmgoers will find this ingenious explosion of retro-cyberpunk a compelling dystopian vision with a gleam of hope. —*S. A.*

MILLENNIUM ACTRESS L: MANGA/MANGA (2001) 87M D: Satoshi Kon. *Hirotaka Suzuoki, Miyoko Shoji*. Here's something we don't expect from animated cinema, though perhaps we should. Satoshi Kon's animated drama, a fictional biography of a reclusive actress whose recollections of her life and career quite literally sweep her interviewer into her story, is as loving and perceptive a tribute to the power and legacy of movies as I've ever seen. Kon deftly weaves history, film, and memory into an imaginative meditation on how the movies become a part of our lives, and he does it with a rich style and spellbinding shifts in texture and design that wind us in and out of the different period styles of the great Japanese genres. His cunning understanding of how animation can straddle the literal and the metaphorical without forcing the audience to choose one over the other marries the fantasy of the movies and the dreams that make us a part of them with intelligence, understanding, and empathy. —*S. A.*

MY NEIGHBOR TOTORO L: N/C/A DIRECTORS/MIYAZAKI, HAYAO (1988) 86M D: Hayao Miyazaki. *Shigesato Itoi, Chika Sakamoto, Noriko Hidaka*. Few would disagree that Miyazaki is the finest living animator, and to anyone that does I would show them *My Neighbor Totoro*. The story is simple. Mai, her older sister Satsuki, and their father move to the country to be closer to their sick mother. During their stay, the girls have several adventures with the benevolent forest spirits known as Totoros. For me, it is not the story that captivates, but the way Miyazaki brings it to life. His animation is superb and never ceases to astonish. You can almost feel the wind as it rips the fire wood from Satsuki's hands. You can sense the smugness of the blue Totoro as he saunters through the forest, thinking he has outsmarted Mai. You can see the wonder in Mai's eyes as she stares, bewildered, at the empty bottle in the stream. Add to this the playful song of the soot sprites, the Catbus, and all the other wonderous imagery, and what you are left with is, in my opinion, the

finest animation ever made. Although available from Twentieth Century Fox, I recommend the Japanese import DVD. Not only is it in widescreen and the original language, but there are several small edits made on the Fox release that do make a difference. —*R. G.*

MY NEIGHBORS, THE YAMADAS L: N/C/A DIRECTORS/ TAKAHATA, ISAO (1999) 104M D: Isao Takahata. *Toru Masuoka, Yukiji Asaoka, Masako Araki, Naomi Uno*. There has never been a more charming, understated piece of animation than Studio Ghibli's *My Neighbors, the Yamadas*. Based on a daily comic strip about a Japanese family that seems to exist somewhere between reality and *The Simpsons*, this film is economically animated with simple, stylized characters and minimal background detail. Told with a focus on character in quick, hilarious, sometimes poignant episodes with no plot, it feels as if we're watching a comic strip. Occasionally, the film segues into vivid fantasies involving bobsledding, undersea adventures, hot-air balloons, and giant snails as metaphors for life's journey. One standout sequence, involving the father's impotence to confront a gang of young thugs, followed by a fantasy about being the motorcycle hero Masked Rider, is particularly touching and highlights the film's depth of emotion. —*K. C.*

NAUSICAÄ OF THE VALLEY OF WIND L: N/C/A DIRECTORS/ MIYAZAKI, HAYAO (1984) 116M D: Hayao Miyazaki. *Gorô Naya, Sumi Shimamoto, Hisako Kyôda*. Nausicaä is the prototypical Miyazaki heroine: a brave young princess tough enough to hold her own in a battle and wise enough to lead her people to peace. And of course, like most Miyazaki protagonists, she loves to soar through the skies (in her case on a glider). The story takes place in a polluted, postapocalyptic wasteland gradually being overrun by forests full of toxic spores and giant insects. Nausicaä is one of the few brave enough to explore the forests, and when she returns home to the Valley of Wind, she must protect it not only from pollution, but from various attackers. The animation is not as smooth as in later Ghibli films (this was their first) but the drawings are exquisite. As with *Star Wars* or *Lord of the Rings*, this is a fantasy world filled with so much detail, texture, and history you feel it could have really existed. Miyazaki adapted from his own manga serial, which he continued long after the film, so if you want to see it get even more epic you should pick up the paperbacks. Unfortunately, the only American release so far is a notorious, twenty-one-minutes-shorter version called *Warriors of the Wind*. —*B. T.*

NEON GENESIS EVANGELION (26 EPISODES) L: MANGA/MANGA (1995) 30M D: Hideaki Anno. *Megumi Ogata, Megumi Hayashibara*. *Evangelion* is the best anime series of the '90s, possibly one of the best TV series, period. The creators use, abuse, subvert, and transcend every anime cliché in this

Best animated movies for adults

AKIRA	THE IRON GIANT
ALICE	THE LORD OF THE RINGS
ALLEGRO NON TROPPO	MONSTERS INC.
AMERICAN POP	MUTANT ALIENS
ANGEL'S EGG	THE NIGHTMARE BEFORE CHRISTMAS
THE CASTLE OF CAGLIOSTRO	PERFECT BLUE
CAT SOUP	PORCO ROSSO
COWBOY BEBOP: THE MOVIE	REJECTED
FANTASTIC PLANET	THE SECRET ADVENTURES OF TOM THUMB
FINDING NEMO	SPIRITED AWAY
GHOST IN THE SHELL	THE TIME MASTERS
GRAVE OF THE FIREFLIES	WIZARDS
HEY GOOD LOOKIN'	YELLOW SUBMARINE
I MARRIED A STRANGE PERSON	

apocalyptic tale of insecure Shinji, introverted Rei, overconfident Asuka, and the Evangelion Project, Earth's last line of defense against the attacking "Angels." What begins as a standard giant-robot-versus-giant-alien-invaders plot eventually weaves itself into a story about teen angst, government conspiracies, faith, death, rebirth, loss, betrayal, pop-psycho-babble, and the fate of the world resting on the shoulders of unstable fourteen-year-old kids piloting unstable monsters. The most harrowing, tragic anime series ever created, it'll rip your heart out, and may not give it back. —K.C.

NIGHT ON THE GALACTIC RAILROAD L: N/C/A/JAPANESE LITERATURE (1985) 113M D: Gisaburo Sugii. *Mayumi Tanaka, Chika Sakamoto.* An unusually somber fantasy, director Sugii's adaptation of Miyazawa Kenji's children's fantasy is suffused in imagination and sadness. Giovanni (Tanaka) is a dreamer who looks after his ailing mother while father is away and escapes the loneliness of his life looking up into the stars. One day a mysterious galactic train picks him up for a ride across the galaxy with his equally somber school chum Campanella (Sakamoto) and a series of unusual characters who live, work, and play among the stars. Far more melancholy and introspective than you'd expect from a family film, it tackles poverty, loss, and death sensitively and finds hope in imagination and intellectual exploration, and it never becomes trite or preachy. The animation lacks the rich detail of Miyazaki's fantasies, but it has a quiet grace all its own and the ambient echoes of a heavenly railroad reverberates through the film like a distant storm. —S.A.

NIGHTMARE BEFORE CHRISTMAS, THE L: N/C/A/PUPPET ANIMATION (1993) 76M D: Henry Selick. *Danny Elfman, Chris Sarandon.* Tim Burton usually gets credit for this film, because the story idea is his and he produced it, but he did not direct it. In any case, the film drips with Burton's influence, in everything from the setting to the characters themselves. The film has a dark, macabre feel, fitting for a plot that features Halloween Town and its master of terror, Jack Skellington, the Pumpkin King. Sick of the same routine year after year, Jack stumbles upon Christmas Town and, completely fascinated, decides to kidnap Santa Claus and try to do Christmas the Halloween way. The plot is told largely through musical numbers that you'll either love or hate, but the animation is fantastic, leaving no room for complaint. This film is a great accomplishment for Burton, and for director Selick. —J.S.

NINJA SCROLL L: MANGA/MANGA (1995) 94M D: Yoshiaki Kawajiri. *Kôichi Yamadera, Toshihiko Seki.* When I was a kid, my friends and I liked Japanimation, or "anime." Yes, that means we were nerds, but it also means we were stupid, since you can't find anime in Montana. So we were stuck with *Akira* or whatever else Blockbuster had lying around, one episode of shitty anime after another. But then *Ninja Scroll* came and kicked our ass. It was the greatest anime we'd seen—violent, sexual, weird, full of ninjas with superpowers, and a dude with bees in his back! It's been a while, but I think the story is just Jubei running around, getting into violent ninja swordfights and balls-to-the-wall anime style. Since then I've discovered more anime, stuff that's not ninja pulp fiction, but *Ninja Scroll* was the catalyst; *Ninja Scroll* didn't give a shit. It was awesome, plain and simple. —*K. C.*

NOW AND THEN, HERE AND THERE L: MANGA/MANGA (1999) 300M D: Akitarô Daîchi. *Akemi Okamura, Kaori Nazuka.* This one sort of baffles me. It takes young, headstrong Shuzo from his normal world, to a world where boys are trained as soldiers (or much worse, if you're unlucky enough to be a girl). A megalomaniac rules a giant city/weapon called Hellywood in a desolate, war-torn country. He wants nothing more than to get his hands on a charm worn by LaLa Ru, a mostly speechless girl. Shuzo is enlisted in the ranks of the little soldiers who go off to war and die, and a little girl is raped (off camera) by soldiers and escapes to the desert. The show makes you truly contemplate war, hatred, and the exploitation of children, but the "anime fantasy" elements keep popping up. Our hero being from "our" world is unnecessary; why can't he just be from the horrible "alternate" universe? In the end he doesn't learn anything from his brief trip to hell. And what of Lala Ru's "magic" jewel? Are anime fans so lame that they need some fantasy in their story to not make them just break down and sob into their cheez-puffs? A sort of brilliance is here, if the creators had allowed themselves out of the anime pigeonhole, this film could have been as powerful as *Grave of the Fireflies*, but it just ends up being a mixed blessing. —*K. C.*

NUTCRACKER FANTASY L: NONCHILDREN'S/PUPPET ANIMATION (1979) 82M D: Takeo Nakamura. *Melissa Gilbert, Michelle Lee, Dick Van Patten, Roddy McDowall, Christopher Lee.* This extrapolation of E. T. A. Hoffmann's *Nutcracker* story would be fairly standard children's fantasy material, except it is elevated by superb animation. Director Nakamura was an animator on the 1970 Rankin-Bass special *Santa Claus Is Comin' to Town.* The puppets here aren't radically different than those in the Rankin-Bass films, but the lighting and photography are significantly more cinematic. *Nutcracker* is full of smooth camera movements, stylish rack focus, and varied angles, more like a live-action film. There are many night scenes lit as if by moonlight, including a very effective hiding-under-the-covers sequence that could have come from a horror film. The score gets cheesy at times, though, especially when it disco-fies Tchaikovsky's compositions. The film was produced by the Sanrio company, so watch for a weird cameo by Hello Kitty. —*B. T.*

PERFECT BLUE L: MANGA/MANGA (1999) 80M D: Satoshi Kon. *Junko Iwao, Masaaki Ôkura, Rica Matsumoto, Shinpachi Tsuji.* This ambitious animated psycho-thriller plunges us into the schizophrenic perspective of a former pop idol in an identity crisis gone berserk. As the squeaky clean bubble-gum singer turns serious actress and nude

pinup, and her fans start to turn on her, a psychotic alter-ego appears, skipping through her consciousness like a conscience turned moral hitman. It's an intelligent and compelling use of animation—we watch her days blur together and dreams meld with reality from her own muddled, nightmarish perspective. If the psychosis and anxiety is swept away in a pat, too-cute ending, it's still more imaginative than most American thrillers. —*S. A.*

PHANTOM, THE (1996) L: COMIX/COMIX (1996) 100M D: Simon Wincer. *Billy Zane, Treat Williams, Kristy Swanson, James Remar, Cary-Hiroyuki Tagawa, Catherine Zeta-Jones.* Zane is perfect in this defiantly old-fashioned superhero story. Sort of an anti–Indiana Jones, The Phantom fights off archaeologists in Africa, then goes to museums and steals back ancient relics. Zeta-Jones plays an evil air-pirate who joins the good guys after being asked why she can't just be nice. It's probably too much for many viewers, but some will love the movie's sincere cornball spirit. —*B. T.*

PHANTOM 2040: THE GHOST WHO WALKS L: COMIX/COMIX (1994) 137M D: Vincent Bassul, Bertrand Tager Kagan, others. *Jeff Bennett, Mark Hamill, Margot Kidder, Scott Valentine.* The Phantom, Lee Falk's classic comic strip character, was a purple-clad jungle superhero who passed down his mantle from generation to generation, creating the illusion of an eternal "ghost who walks." In this futuristic animated series, he is young Kit Walker (Valentine), who has trouble defending nature because he lives in the city of Metropia and only knows of trees and animals from virtual reality museums. This first collection of episodes introduces some clever characters and concepts; my favorite is Maxwell Madison Jr., effeminate son of the corporate villain, who attributes all his comments to his cat, Baudelaire. You may recognize the style of the weirdly elongated characters because they were designed by *Aeon Flux* creator Peter Chung. —*B. T.*

PINCHCLIFFE GRAND PRIX, THE L: NONCHILDREN'S/PUPPET ANIMATION (1975) 88M D: Ivo Caprino. *Wenche Foss, Per Theodor Haugen.* This film is a completely original, well-made animated puppet film. I was thrilled right from the start of this innovative Norwegian picture. Inventor and bicycle repairman Theodore Rimspoke lives on top a lonely hill with his bird friend Sonny Duckworth and hedgehog buddy Lambert. Everything is super until they hear news of the world's newest, most fantastic race driver, Rudolph Gore-Slimey. Gore-Slimey is a former apprentice of Rimspoke and is obviously using stolen ideas and inventions for his 12-cylinder super car. Rimspoke reluctantly decides to build his own car and challenge Gore-Slimey in a race to prove who's faster, smarter, and a nicer guy. With the help of the enigmatic and out-of-place merchant Sheik Abdul Ben Bonanza who finances the project, this team of misfits builds a top-secret rocket-engined racing machine. But the reason to watch this movie is the race itself. The speed and realism of driving is captured amazingly well by stop-motion filming. Point-of-view shots are handled with ease by the technically imaginative filmmakers, adding an "in-car camera" feel to the racing. This film is an absolute surprise and delight. My only wish is that I could see the film in its original language rather than in this English-dubbed version. —G. M.

PLAGUE DOGS L: NONCHILDREN'S ANIMATION/NONCHILDREN'S ANIMATION (1982) 103M D: Martin Rosen. *John Hurt, Nigel Hawthorne.* I dare anyone to remain unmoved or unprovoked by this beautifully conceived and realized animated feature. From the same team that produced the more palatable *Watership Down,* this film was sparsely released in 1982 and went virtually unnoticed. But ever since I saw it then at the Seattle International Film Festival, its place in my heart has grown with each passing year. I dare you to see if it will find such a place in yours. —K. S.

POM POKO L: N/C/A DIRECTORS/TAKAHATA, ISAO (1994) 119M D: Isao Takahata. *Yuriko Ishida, Makoto Nonomura, Shincho Kokontei.* This wonderful release from Studio Ghibli, Japan's premier animation studio, tells the tale of two raccoon clans who stop fighting each other and start working together when they realize the real threats to their lives are the encroaching humans who are starting to build on their lands. Seeking out ancient and wise raccoons to help them in their struggles against the humans, they learn the art of shapeshifting and use this skill to try to scare and fool the humans into stopping construction. Alas, there are always more workers to replace the ones they have scared off, or unscrupulous promoters to take credit for the racoons' amazing displays of shapeshifting. A tale that is simultaneously funny, tragic, and thought-provoking as it shows how the human need to develop impacts cruelly upon nature, as well as how nature can sometimes adapt in order to survive. One of Ghibli's best films! —M. N.

PORCO ROSSO L: N/C/A DIRECTORS/MIYAZAKI, HAYAO (1992) 93M D: Hayao Miyazaki. *Shuichiro Moriyama, Tokiko Kato.* Dashing Italian war hero Porco Rosso, who enigmatically has the head of a pig, keeps busy thwarting vicious air pirates with his Red Baron–esque twin-engine airplane. When his plane is damaged in the line of duty, our hero must employ the help of master mechanic Piccolo and his handy apprentice/granddaughter Fio. Time is of the essence, as the plane must be repaired in time for a high-octane dogfight against a smarmy rival. To get the job done in time, Porco Rosso puts his faith in the fiery Fio, who has taken quite a shine to him but will tolerate none of his sexist condescension. Absolutely hilarious, genuinely exciting, and not even slightly dumbed-down for younger audiences, *Porco Rosso* is entertainment at its best. I can't imagine this film disappointing even the most discerning viewer, and kids go freaking nuts for it. —C. B.

PRINCE OF THE SUN: HORUS' GREAT ADVENTURE L: N/C/A DIRECTORS/TAKAHATA, ISAO (1968) 82M D: Isao Takahata. *Eijirô Tono.* A wonderful early Japanese animated film by Takahata, the other half of Studio Ghibli. The animation is great, on par with anything being produced in America at the time. It has a European storybook feel to it, somewhat simlar to early Disney, but more Japanese and with cooler action sequences (and more of them). Unfortunately, there are no subtitles, so the story is confusing at times. It opens with our hero, Horus, fighting a pack of wolves using his trusty hatchet, but he's interrupted by a giant rock monster with a sword in his shoulder. Horus removes the sword and heads home, just as his sick father is dying. Horus and a cute talking bear cub are then taken on an adventure north, where he faces off with a nasty ice-wizard and more wolves. With or without subtitles, this is a must-see for fans of Takahata and Miyazaki, or just fans of great animation —K. C.

PRINCES ET PRINCESSES L: NONCHILDREN'S ANIMATION/ NONCHILDREN'S ANIMATION (2000) 70M D: Michel Ocleot. *Adam Sandler, Jackie Titone, Austin Stout, Kevin Nealon, Rob Schneider.* Through clever futuristic technology and devices, three people tell six tales of princes and princesses, both fantasy and fact, from the past and from the future. The animation is all silhouette, like shadow puppets, which is both striking and unusual, giving it a very theatrical quality. Some of the stories are laugh-out-loud hilarious. My favorites include the Prince and Princess who find that kissing leads to all SORTS of trouble, and the Medieval tale of a young villager who decides he will win the hand of the Princess by meeting the challenge of breaking into a dangerous sorceress' castle. It's an unexpected treasure and delight. —M. N.

PRINCESS MONONOKE L: N/C/A DIRECTORS/MIYAZAKI, HAYAO (1997) 133M D: Hayao Miyazaki. *Yuko Tanaka, Tsunehiko Kamijo, Kaoru Kobayashi, Yuriko Ishida, Yoji Matsuda, Masahiko Nishimura.* One of Miyazaki's finest works, this film addresses the issue of war, examining the motivations of each side and revealing the complexity and tragedy that results. It is an epic story, looking back to a time when gods still walked the earth, when animals talked, and when magic was alive and vibrant. Man is just beginning to alter the balance of nature, using technology to turn the tide to his favor. We see this conflict through the eyes of an innocent man whose life has been destroyed by the ripples of this war, who comes to see the truth of the situation with "eyes unclouded by hate." It is a moving, intense, and passionate film about life, the will to survive, honor, and man versus nature. It is as gripping and powerful as any movie made and stands as a testament to the fact that animation is not just a medium for children. —*M. N.*

RAHXEPHON L: MANGA/MANGA (2002) 30M D: Yutaka Izubuchi. *Maaya Sakamoto, Ayako Kawasumi, Houko Kuwashima, Aya Hisakawa.* I'm watching this and I think, "OK, what the heck is going on? Who's that chick? Oh, I got it. No wait, how did they get there?" The beginning of the third episode finally explains how aliens called the Mu surrounded Tokyo with a strange force field that looks like Jupiter. There is a battle against the Mu and the Mulians, who apparently can look human, or they take over human bodies, or something, and they have blue blood so that's how you tell them apart, or maybe not. It didn't take long before I was completely lost again. To me, this is a good thing. It is clear there is an underlying plot, structure, and background, but not all the pieces of the picture have been revealed. It's anime crack—very addictive. I could have stayed up all night watching this show, determined to unravel the mystery. Beautiful animation, haunting music —*M. N.*

REX THE RUNT L: NONCHILDREN'S/CLAYMATION (1999) 260M D: Richard Goleszowski. *Andrew Jeffers, Steve Box, Andrew Franks, Elisabeth Hadley.* Consider the twenty-six episodes of the adventures of four plasticine dogs as a bowl of cinematic candy: the episodes are under ten minutes a piece and it's easy to scarf up the entire collection in a single sitting. Rex is, in the words of the theme, a robbly, bobbly, iggly, squiggly dog who lives with mates Wendy (the unappreciated brains of the outfit), Bad Bob (a gun-toting slob whose eye patch roves from eye to eye), and the unhinged Vince (who suffers from Random Pavarotti disease and, in one episode, marries a vacuum cleaner and raises a little dust buster). It has the same off-kilter, anything-goes sense of humor we've come to expect from the producer, Aardman Animations, only a little more so ("This delusion isn't too bad." "It's not a delusion, we really are being chased by groceries."), and it even verges on rude and randy at times. Mostly, however, it's just plain absurd, inventive, and hilarious. —*S. A.*

ROUJIN Z L: MANGA/MANGA (1991) 87M D: Hiroyuki Kitakubo. *Nicolette McKenzie, Ian Thompson.* The spirit of an invalid man's dead wife takes over an experimental machine designed to care for the elderly in this anime mix of social satire and huge spectacle of destruction. Witty and slightly off-center, director Kitakubo and writer/designer Katsuhiro Otomo (screenwriter of *Metropolis* and director of *Akira*) make this coldly methodical machine the conscience of the film. When a lonely, alienated old man cries out for his wife, the atomic powered learning machine hacks into a computer and pulls out a ghost, turning

itself into a gargantuan robot to fulfill his wish to see the sea again, but destroying the city in its march to the shore. The reflection of real social problems—caring for an aging population and the impersonal solution of machines to replace human attention—is no less an issue here in the good old USA than it is in Japan. —*S. A.*

RUROUNI KENSHIN L: MANGA/MANGA (1996) 25M D: Kazuhiro Furuhashi. *Mayo Suzukaze, Yuji Ueda, Mina Tominaga, Mika Doi, Yoku Shioya, Miki Fujitani.* Set around 1870, this is the story of a samurai who fought during the revolution as Himura Battosai, The Manslayer. Now Japan is at peace and carrying a sword is forbidden. The time of the samurai is past. To atone for his bloodlust and slaughter during the revolution, the infamous Battosai has become Rurouni Kenshin—a wanderer who helps those in need. He still wears a sword, but has sworn to use it only for the protection of others, never to kill again. The first season introduces the characters as Kenshin stops wandering and settles down in Tokyo. After a while the stories feel like poor copies of one another—a tough bad guy shows up, or someone from Kenshin's past, there's a fight, Kenshin wins, yada yada yada. But the second season sees the beginning of a major story arc and some serious character development that is vastly rewarding and wonderful to watch. —*M. N.*

SAMURAI JACK: THE PREMIERE EPISODE L: NONCHILDREN'S ANIMATION/NONCHILDREN'S ANIMATION (2002) 90M D: Genndy Tartakovsky. *Phil Lamar, Mako.* Although drawn in a cartoony style, with few outlines, almost like paper cutouts, *Samurai Jack* is a serious, dramatic action show about a samurai who travels to the future to slay the all-powerful demon Aku. The juxtaposition of a samurai epic with the Tartakovsky style (especially when you get to the race of talking dogs) takes some getting used to, but soon you'll be drawn into its mythic story of a stoic, honor-bound warrior struggling in a world he does not comprehend. It is one of the most strikingly designed cartoons of recent years, and the most cinematic. Clearly influenced by Sergio Leone and Akira Kurosawa, it's packed with extreme close-ups of eyes, wide shots of landscapes, split screens, dramatic letterboxing, and long scenes with little or no dialogue. The highlight of this pilot movie is a ten-minute, dialogue-free, uninterrupted fight between Jack and an army of robotic bugs. Jack starts out in a full suit of armor and ends wearing only a loincloth and a coating of robot blood. —*B. T.*

SCENES FROM THE SURREAL L: N/C/A DIRECTORS/ SVANKMAJER, JAN (1989) 58M D: Jan Svankmajer. Svankmajer is an amazing animator, his work characterized by a dark, surrealistic mix of claymation, stop-motion, and live-action animation that is both beautiful and slightly disturbing at times. *Scenes from the Surreal* showcases three of his shorts, and is a must-see for any fan of his longer works. In "Darkness/Light/Darkness," a man pieces himself together slowly as one clay body part enters the room at a time. "Male Games" begins with a man watching a soccer game from his home, as one of the soccer teams literally destroys members of the other team. The third, "Death of Stalinism," is a clever look at Czech history and the fall of communism, and shows a bust of Stalin being cut open to reveal all of his insides. A short documentary on Svankmajer himself is included. For any serious animation fan, this is a rental well worth the time. —*J. S.*

SERIAL EXPERIMENT: LAIN L: MANGA/MANGA (1998) 24M D: Ryutaro Nakamura. *Ayako Kawasumi, Rei Igarashi, Chiharu Tezuka, Yoko Asada, Kaori Shimizu, Ryunosuke Obayashi.* This anime series is a surreal trip through the mind and experiences of a young girl who slowly begins to question the world around her and her own true nature. There is an eerie quality about the whole show—part horror, part science fiction, and part coming-of-age. It easily could take several viewings to catch all the details and imagery of this complex puzzle being assembled one piece at a time. By the end, I was in a complete fugue state trying to understand what had happened, what I had just seen, my reason for being, my place in this world, and the importance of my actions upon both myself and those around me. *Lain* definitely proves once again that anime is not the same as children's animation and what Americans generally define animation to be. —*M. N.*

SIMPSONS, THE: COMPLETE FIRST SEASON L: NONCHILDREN'S ANIMATION/NONCHILDREN'S ANIMATION (1989) 300M D: Various. *Dan Castellaneta, Julie Kavner, Nancy Cartwright, Yeardley Smith, Hank Azaria, Harry Shearer.* Remember when Homer Simpson was a man of average intelligence who sounded kind of like Walter Matthau and who made a genuine attempt to be a good father? It's hard to believe how normal he really was in the early episodes, before "D'oh!" was in the dictionary and before the voice inside his head could be heard walking out and shutting the door behind it. A lot of people can't watch the first season episodes anymore because the humor is lighter and the stories are something closer to being serious, but I still enjoy them. It's also nice that they thought enough of the fans to include commentary tracks on every single episode. —*B. T.*

SIMPSONS, THE: COMPLETE SECOND SEASON L: NONCHILDREN'S ANIMATION/NONCHILDREN'S ANIMATION (1990) 300M D: Various. *Dan Castellaneta, Julie Kavner, Nancy Cartwright, Yeardley Smith, Hank Azaria, Harry Shearer.* The second season of *The Simpsons* has a number of landmarks: the first "Treehouse of Horror" Halloween special, the unforgettable Homer-falling-into-the-ravine scene in "Bart the Daredevil," and the introduc-

tion of Comic Book Guy in "Three Men and a Comic Book." This DVD set is also a great document of Simpsons-mania at its height. Remember "Do the Bartman?" "Never lay a finger on my Butterfinger?" How about the Simpsons presenting at the Emmys? The most bizarre extra is a pregnant Nancy Cartwright wearing a mask to appear as Bart on the American Music Awards. The optional commentary track with the producers is mostly embarrassed laughter. —*B. T.*

SOUTH PARK: BIGGER, LONGER AND UNCUT L: NONCHILDREN'S ANIMATION/NONCHILDREN'S ANIMATION (1999) 81M D: Trey Parker. *Trey Parker, Matt Stone, Issac Hayes, George Clooney, Minnie Driver, Mike Judge.* Right from the beginning this film pokes fun at the whole animated-musical genre that Disney dominates. But you don't have to watch much to discover that despite the grand music and orchestrations, the children's world of South Park is quite lurid. For instance, its second catchy show tune comes from a movie the children sneak in to see. The song is "Uncle Fucker," and they sing it all the way home. Their alarmed parents picket the theaters. Since the film was supposedly a Canadian production, they sing another catchy musical number, "Blame Canada," in protest. Things devolve from there. One of the children dies on the operating table and descends to hell, where he learns about Saadam Hussein's intention to take over the world. This uproarious film is for big children with a slender view of the world who no longer have to worry over what their mothers may think. —*N. J.*

SPAWN L: COMIX/COMIX (1997) 97M D: Mark A. Z. Dippé. *Michael Jai White, John Leguizamo, Martin Sheen, Theresa Randle.* A murdered man goes to hell and makes a deal with the devil: he can return to Earth as a demon to get revenge. To make up for his misdeeds, he uses his limited demonic powers to fight evil, including a three-foot, obese, demonic clown (Leguizamo). In contention with *Batman & Robin* for worst comic book movie of all time, this is a moronic mess of video-game-level CGI, bad acting, and asinine dialogue. The comic book is a dumb musclefest that gained some credibility when a few issues were farmed out to acclaimed writers like Neil Gaiman and Alan Moore. For the movie, they decided to go with a script dumber than even your average issue of the comic. At one point Spawn has the line, "I'm gonna nail that asshole." OK, fair enough. But shortly thereafter he also has the line, "I'm gonna nail that dirtbag." You have to sort of admire Leguizamo for being game enough to walk around on his knees wearing hundreds of pounds of makeup (probably how he got the role of Toulouse-Lautrec in *Moulin Rouge*), but that's the best the movie has to offer. —*B. T.*

SPEED RACER: FIRST ELEVEN EPISODES L: MANGA/ MANGA (1966) 120M D: Hiroshi Sasagawa, others. *Katsuji Mori, Jack Curtis.* Go, Speed Racer, go! The popular animated action series about a teenage race car driver and his death-defying race adventures also features the mysterious Racer X (secretly Speed's older brother Rex, who ran away from home years ago). Four two-part stories tell the origins of Speed's career, and the mad three-parter, *The Most Dangerous Race,* claims almost all the competitors (they crash and burn on the alpine mountain roads) while Speed finishes the race driving blind—literally! Dubbed with a rapid fire delivery (to fit all that exposition in mouths that race like the cars on the track) and animated in a limited style that favors speed and violent motion, it's a bizarre mix of gee-whiz teenage melodrama and fatal crashes—probably the only animated kids TV hit with a body count. —*S. A.*

SPIRITED AWAY L: N/C/A DIRECTORS/MIYAZAKI, HAYAO (2001) 125M D: Hayao Miyazaki. *Rumi Hîragi, Miyu Irino, Mari Natsuki, Yasuko Sawaguchi.* A scene near the beginning of *Spirited Away* provides a perfect example of why Miyazaki is the greatest living animation director. Our young heroine, Chihiro, is walking beside her mother through a strange, deserted town. Chihiro's mom gets a little farther ahead of her daughter with each step. Chihiro notices and picks up the pace a bit, only to fall behind again. It's a small thing; obviously a child is slower than her mother. But this is animation. These people don't exist in a physical world. Someone "made" Chihiro slower than her mother. *Spirited Away* is full of some of the most beautiful and fanciful imagery I've seen—dragons, giant babies, ghost trains, talking frogs. But it's the attention to real-life detail that separates Miyazaki's films from other cartoons. It isn't enough that we're taken on a wild ride, they took the time to draw reality into the fantastic images. —*K. C.*

STINGRAY: THE COMPLETE SERIES L: N/C/A DIRECTORS/ANDERSON, GERRY (1963) 975M D: David Elliot, John Kelley, others. *Don Mason, David Graham.* "Stand by for action!" After two successful sci-fi Supermarionation productions, Anderson turned to undersea action with this series about the World Aquanaut Security Patrol (WASP), aquanaut agents fighting the menace of the Aquaphibians from the underwater city of Titanica in souped-up submersibles. *Thunderbirds* it ain't—Anderson hadn't yet mastered the fine art of magnificent miniature spectacle and the kooky subterrestrial conspiracies are awkward to say the least—but it does have a deep sea tyrant who seeks guidance from a bug-eyed fish, a silent slave princess saved from peril by stalwart hero Troy Tempest, and the blue-skinned progeny of Peter Lorre sniveling plans into a radio set. —*S. A.*

STREET FIGHT (AKA **COONSKIN**) L: N/C/A DIRECTORS/ BAKSHI, RALPH (1975) 82M D: Ralph Bakshi. *Philip Michael Thomas, Barry White, Charles Gordone, Scatman Crothers.* Song of the South remade as blaxploitation, and as a sometimes shocking deconstruction of racial stereotypes. Instead of Br'er Rabbit, Thomas plays Brother Rabbit, a pitch-black humanoid rabbit in a slick white suit, sort of like Superfly reborn as a bunny. He and his anthropomorphic cohorts leave the South for Harlem and take over the crime world. The movie was the source of fierce controversy—not surprising considering the original title and the ugly portrayals of blacks, gays, women, Italians, cops, you name it. It's more of an interesting oddity than a good movie, but I think Bakshi was sincere about the movie being an attack on the stereotypes it's steeped in. (In fact, he hired many young, unproven black animators, which could not be said about other animation studios). —*B. T.*

SUPER DIMENSIONAL FORTRESS MACROSS L: MANGA/MANGA (1982) 100M D: Noboru Ishiguro. *Mika Doi, Arihiro Hase, Mari Îjima.* An epic space/ soap opera revolving around the people of the Macross, a giant spacecraft caught in a battle with the giant, humanoid Zentradi, a race bred for war. Despite ongoing skirmishes in space, we are shown the only way to actually win this war is through an understanding and acceptance of other cultures. There is a great moment in the middle of this cheaply animated spectacle when three of the warmongering Zentradi are speechless after hearing some pop music. It's a shitty, annoying song, but it's something they've never heard before, and it changes their perspective on the war. It's a small, important moment in the best series (animated or live action) to address war, hatred, love, and the duality of a strong military force all at once. —*K. C.*

SUPERMAN L: N/C/A DIRECTORS/FLEISCHER, MAX (1941) 100M D: Dave Fleischer. *Joan Alexander, Bud Collyer.* Grace incarnate. Superman never looked more beautiful in flight or heroic in action than in the seventeen animated shorts produced by the Fleischer brothers (producer Max and director Dave) in the early days of WWII. Painted in rich, deep colors, these superhero noir pieces suggest more the dark mood of Batman than the squeaky clean Man of Steel image we've come to expect. Heavy shadows, night crimes, dead bodies... these are comic books for big kids, combining giddy stunts and last-minute rescues with creepy horrors and deadly killers (along with the odd giant rampaging robot). With a real live villain bent on world domination at the time, these fantasies might have hit closer to home than we presently realize. —*S. A.*

SUPERMAN—THE MOVIE L: COMIX/COMIX (1978) 152M D: Richard Donner. *Christopher Reeve, Margot Kidder, Marlon Brando, Gene Hackman Ned Beatty.* This

The Thief and the Cobbler: The Animated Epic That Got Away

Richard Williams is one of animation's most talented and visionary directors. But what does he have to show for it? Almost his entire career was spent doing work-for-hire gigs (such as the animated titles for *What's New Pussycat?* and *Casino Royale*) to fund just one ongoing project: the Arabian Nights–inspired fantasy *The*

Thief and the Cobbler.

Begun in 1968 but not released until 1995, *Thief* is a visual marvel, with influences from Persian art, M. C. Escher, '60s psychedelia, and Op Art, but its most striking feature is its meticulous attention to detail. It was made before the days of digitally enhanced animation, so every little thing had to be drawn in by hand, and yet the thief of the title has a cloud of flies buzzing around his head for the entire movie, the villainous Grand Vizier Zig Zag has a pair of curled shoes that unfurl and then roll back up each time he takes a step, and the camera often soars through the sky, around buildings and characters. There is a ten-minute sequence, involving the piece-by-piece destruction of a giant war machine,

continued on page 558

---

was an extraordinarily expensive film, and on the whole the money was well spent. Perfect casting and stunning special effects combine to relate the origins of the famous DC Comics hero. Superman's father (Brando) jettisons his child into space to save him from the death of planet Krypton. Reeve plays the adult Superman, who, as Clark Kent, gets a job at the *Daily Planet,* where he meets Lois Lane (Kidder). Lex Luthor (Hackman) tries to take advantage of the weaknesses he learns about Superman. This two-and-a-half-hour film is well paced and spawned three sequels. With dazzling effects and spectacular music by John Williams, *Superman* was able to boast the longest credits sequence of the time. It was also the measuring stick to which most films about comic book heroes were calibrated. —*N. J.*

SUPERMAN: LAST SON OF KRYPTON L: COMIX/COMIX (1996) 75M D: Bruce Timm, Curt Geda, Dan Riba. *Tim Daley, Dana Delany, Clancy Brown.* After the success of the Batman animated series, the same team turned their attention to the Superman legend, starting with this origin-story pilot. It opens with the politics of Krypton, continues with Kal El's evacuation to Earth, and ends with a young Superman getting used to his powers and his role as a hero. Batman, with his deranged foes and atmospheric turf, offered a lot more for these talented storytellers to work with, but their serious treatment of Superman is very appealing. The story stays faithful to the traditional comics ori-

gin, but Clark Kent is less of a nerd, Lois Lane is a lot feistier, and Superman's powers are less godlike. In my favorite scene, Superman chases a team of jetpacked terrorists. He dodges one of their missiles, but then realizes it's headed for a passenger jet. When he grabs the damaged jet to bring it to safety, he accidentally tears off the tail. Finally he must abandon the terrorists all together in order to save the passengers. So it's Superman who actually has to put some effort into saving the day. —*B. T.*

TALES FROM THE FAR SIDE L: COMIX/COMIX (1994) 23M D: Marv Newland. *Doug Parker, Kathleen Barr, Lee Tokar, Dale Wilson.* The seeming impossibility of translating Gary Larson's one-panel syndicated comic strip into twenty-three minutes of animation makes this creepy short all the more impressive. Originally aired (only once) as a Halloween special, it took years to find its way to video on Larson's own website. Like the strip, there is no plot, just a series of vignettes. The camera drifts around through numerous visual gags and scenes about people, farm animals, insects, and even eggs. There is no dialogue, only a little narration and a lot of groans, buzzes, and snorts. Director Newland is best known for *Bambi Meets Godzilla,* but this shows he's grown into a real director who can create a spooky atmosphere despite completely silly subject matter. Followed by an equally great sequel, which only played at a few film festivals. —*B. T.*

that alone took a year to produce.

In short, it's the kind of amazing spectacle you'd expect from a team of legendary animators (including Art Babbitt, Ken Harris, Emery Hawkins, and Grim Natwick) who worked on a movie for twenty-six years. It proves that anything is possible in animation, provided that you have a group of geniuses who are willing to work on it for years.

It may very well be the best animation you'll ever see, but you still might have a hard time watching it. Because it's full of lame wisecracks, insidious musical numbers, and slapdash storytelling, many critics who saw it during its 1995 theatrical run as *Arabian Knight* thought it was just a quickie rip-off of Disney's *Aladdin*. And, in a sense, they were right.

Thief was at first funded by Sufi mystic Idries Shah and Saudi prince Mohammed Faisil, and it was Williams's impressive work as animation director for *Who Framed Roger Rabbit?* that convinced Warner Bros. Animation to fund its completion. But despite the long history of the project, they were surprised when Williams continued to lag behind schedule, and when they saw his workprint, they fired him and his staff and handed the movie over to Fred Calvert, an animation producer whose company had created such 1970s specials and series as *The Mini-Munsters* and *I Am the Greatest: The Adventures of Muhammad Ali*. Calvert reordered the footage, cut twenty minutes, and added the poorly animated musical sequences that undeniably ape the themes of *Aladdin*. His version was released in Australia and South Africa to dismal returns.

To make matters much worse, Miramax bought the film, cut out more of the original footage, and hired celebrities to redub some of the characters—even though the

---

TANK GIRL L: COMIX/COMIX (1995) 104M D: Rachel Talalay. *Lori Petty, Don Harvey, Naomi Watts, Jeff Kober, Malcolm McDowell, Ice-T.* This movie is all about the cheese. And I'm not talking Gouda or Cheddar.... I'm talking the kind that comes in a can. Just because it's incredibly bad doesn't mean it can't be good, too. Based on a comic book by the same title, this flick is irreverent, bizarre, silly, and full of babes kicking ass. Best of all are the soundtrack and the interspersed bits of imagery from the comic, which looks way cooler than the live-action stuff. Heck, they should have made an animated film from the comic. But you'll just have to settle for this I guess. —*M. N.*

TEENAGE MUTANT NINJA TURTLES II: THE SECRET OF THE OOZE L: COMIX/COMIX (1991) 88M D: Michael Pressman. *Paige Turco, David Warner, Francois Chau, Ernie Reyes Jr.* After success with one other live-action movie about martial artists in rubber costumes eating pizzas, New Line Cinema brought us this even more crassly commercial quickie sequel. The "ooze" is what mutated ordinary pet turtles into the humanoid Ninja Turtles, and now the evil Shredder uses it to make his own mutant henchmen and to enlarge himself into "Super Shredder." I asked my seven-year-old nephew why, when the ooze turned Shredder giant, it also turned his suit of armor giant. He was stumped. I didn't ask him about the scene where Vanilla Ice "invents ninja rap" with the Turtles, because it's best that the

youth don't learn about these things. Think about this: New Line Cinema built up its coffers on the Ninja Turtles and the *Nightmare on Elm Street* franchise. Miramax almost financed the *Lord of the Rings* series (as two movies) for Peter Jackson, but backed out, and it was New Line who eventually took the risk of financing the entire trilogy. That means had there been no Freddy or Ninja Turtles, there would be no *Lord of the Rings* on film. So on behalf of all filmgoers, I would like to thank Freddy and the Ninja Turtles for their great financial contribution to the artform. —*B. T.*

THIEF AND THE COBBLER, THE L: N/C/A DIRECTORS/ WILLIAMS, RICHARD (1995) 72M D: Richard Williams. *Matthew Broderick, Vincent Price, Jonathan Winters, Donald Pleasence, Jennifer Beals.* Made over thirty years by some of the best animators who ever lived, this incredible hand-animated spectacle is unfortunately only available in an incomplete, heavily bastardized form. It takes place in a fairy tale Baghdad (called the Golden City in this version), where the magic orbs protecting the city have been stolen, leaving it vulnerable to the scheming grand vizier Zig-Zag (Price) and the barbarian hordes of King One-Eye. Our heroes are a humble cobbler named Tack (Broderick) and a nameless kleptomaniac (dubbed over by Winters, but clearly intended to be silent). Because of the intrusive dubbing, watch the film on mute—just turn up the vol-

original characters didn't talk! The most painful example is Jonathan Winters, who provides wall-to-wall wisecracks as the thief. Picture Wile E. Coyote, in a classic Roadrunner cartoon, constantly making modern references and jokes that attempt to explain what he has already explained in pantomime. And without his lips moving. At the end, after the thief inadvertently saves the day by stealing the magical golden orbs, an awkward insert explains that he went to jail anyway, because he was a thief.

But maybe he wasn't the only one who should have gone to jail. Clearly, the celebrity wisecracks and dumbing-down of the plot were added to make the movie more commercial, right? Good job guys—it made $300,000 in its six-week run. Miramax bastardized a movie that was twenty-seven years in the making, crushing a man and his lifelong ambition, all in the name of *$300,000*. They failed even as heartless businessmen.

The gutting of *The Thief and the Cobbler* is one of the greatest artistic injustices in the history of cinema, and the damage is most likely irreparable. Bootlegs of Williams's workprint apparently do exist, but that may be the closest we ever get to a director's cut. During the editing process, whole sections of the film were simply discarded. Roy O. Disney was once rumored to be planning a reconstruction of the film, but his resignation from Disney in 2004 makes such a project highly unlikely.

After the release of the film, Williams went into seclusion, refusing to do interviews or to take on new assignments. He is said to be working on a new animated feature, but this time he's playing it safe—he's animating it entirely by himself.

—*Bryan Theiss*

---

ume when you see Zig-Zag, who speaks entirely in rhyme. It's worth watching for the unique stylization and mind-boggling meticulousness of the animation, which achieves brilliant, computerlike feats entirely by hand. Filmed in Cinemascope, it looks best on the Code 2 DVD or the laser disc; otherwise it's full-frame VHS. Storywise, the best version is the Australian (PAL/Code 4) *The Princess and the Cobbler*, still bastardized but without the Winters/Broderick dub job added by Miramax. —*B. T.*

THUNDERBIRDS MEGASET (COMPLETE 12-VOLUME SET) L: N/C/A DIRECTORS/ANDERSON, GERRY (1964) 156M D: Brian Burgess, David Elliott, others. *Sylvia Anderson, Ray Barrett.* Thunderbirds go in Gerry Anderson's Supermarionation action series of a private rescue organization with really cool vehicles. You could see the strings of the puppet stars, but their jet planes, space shuttles, high-tech monster trucks, and other mechanical marvels were the greatest fleet of fantasy vehicles a kid ever saw. At its best an inspired mix of Japanese monster movie mayhem and British stiff-upper-lip attitude, this series brings a new meaning to the term "wooden" (the marionette stars are a rather bland and interchangeable family of clean-living Hardy Boys). The high-tech toys are big-kid fantasies come alive and the awestruck seriousness of the direction is quaint and cool in these days of hyperactive cartoons. All thirty-two episodes are available on twelve discs. F.A.B.! —*S. A.*

For those of us who didn't grow up on Gerry Anderson's shows, this is a surreal headscratcher, something you only watch because you can't believe it really exists. How did kids ever put up with these slow-moving, expressionless puppets? My favorite part is the dream sequence with the flying car and the puppet band playing in a diner.—*B. T.*

TICK, THE: THE ENTIRE SERIES L: COMIX/COMIX (2001) 250M D: Boris Damast, Mel Damski, others. *Nestor Carbonell, Patrick Warburton, David Burke, Liz Vassey.* This live-action version of the comic book and animated cartoon did not survive prime-time television. A pity—the writing was witty, the characters were true to their origins, the costumes were silly, and the stories were wacky and ridiculous. Fortunately, all nine episodes are available on DVD. *The Tick* is similar in some ways to *Mystery Men*, where bumbling and randomly skilled superheroes try to make the world safe from evil. The cartoon's American Maid morphed into Captain Justice and Die Fledermaus became Batmanuel. While the former is, alas, not as cool, the latter was a brilliant change. Full of macho sexism and Latino hormones, Batmanuel often stole whole scenes throughout the series. And Warburton IS the Tick! He has the build, he has the voice, and he has the ability to utter completely ludicrous lines with a straight face and booming voice. "Sticky pink devil! You are now my bitch!" —*M. N.*

TIME MASTERS, THE L: N/C/A DIRECTORS/LALOUX, RENE (1982) 78M D: Rene Laloux. *Jean Valmont, Michael Elias.* Director Laloux and artist Jean Moebius Giraud (known mostly in the United States for his work on *Alien* and *Heavy Metal* magazine) joined forces to direct this unfinished feature film about Jaffar, a mercenary space traveler who travels across the galaxy to help Piel, the only survivor of an attack by giant hornet creatures, who is alone on the desert planet Perdide. Jaffar finds himself drawn into trying to stop the Masters of Time from turning back the clock and stealing his home planet. Mobius and Laloux did not finish the film as funding ran out (though it was finally released to French television). Even though the film feels unfinished, many of the character drawings and some of the sequences are beautifully recreated from the Moebius drawings and are simply gorgeous. The story is based on the novel *The Orphan of Perdide* by Stephan Wul (*Light Years*). —*N. H.*

TWICE UPON A TIME L: NONCHILDREN'S ANIMATION/ NONCHILDREN'S ANIMATION (1997) 75M D: John Korty. *Lorenzo Music, Marshall Efon, James Cranna, Julie Payne, Hamilton Camp.* Done in a unique animation style called Lumage, this flick is a witty, charming, entertaining adventure of two unlikely, desperately determined heroes who struggle to defeat—but accidentally aid—the villain in his plot to take over the world using endless nightmares. With characters such as Ralph, the all-purpose animal; Synonymous Botch, the arch-nemesis; Flora Fauna, the aspiring actress; and Rod Rescueman, the perspiring superhero, how can you go wrong? —*M. N.*

USHIO & TORA: COMPLETE COLLECTION L: MANGA/ MANGA (1992) 300M D: Kunihiko Yuyama. *Jessica Boone, Jessica Calvello, Mandy Clark.* Ushio and his grandfather live by a temple that they tend. He often hears he is descended from a great samurai warrior who once trapped Tora, the most evil and dangerous of all demons, with the Beast Spear. But Ushio has never believed this, not until he goes into the temple basement and finds Tora pinned to the wall by said spear! When even more demons appear, Ushio must take the risk and free Tora to battle them. But once Ushio holds the Beast Spear, he transmutes into the Samurai Warrior. He cannot let Tora disappear and has threatened to kill him if he does anything evil. Tora stays by Ushio's side, lying in wait for the day the boy lets down his guard and can be slain. This anime series is clever, entertaining, playful, and by turns surprisingly gory and violent, but in that happy, fun, excellent kind of way. —*M. N.*

VAMPIRE HUNTER D: BLOODLUST L: MANGA/MANGA (2000) 103M D: Yoshiaki Kawajiri, Tai Kit Mak. *Andrew Philpot, Dwight Schultz, John Rafter Lee, Wendee Lee, Pamela Segall.* A sequel to the popular 1985 anime, but you needn't have seen the original for this to make sense. D is a super badass half-vampire with a face on his hand that talks to him. He wanders the Leone-meets-Goth wastelands as a vampire hunter for hire. This time he's trying to save a girl supposedly kidnapped by a vampire. Things get more complicated when he learns the girl is actually in love and went willingly; in fact her vampire boyfriend is so dedicated to her that he walks through the sun, skin bubbling like an egg on a frying pan, just to embrace her. But D continues on his quest, making *him* the kidnapper. Full of ambiguous morality and exquisitely detailed animation, this is one of those rare anime films that transcends the genre and will appeal to many of us who are not generally interested in anime. —*B. T.*

WALLACE & GROMIT: A CLOSE SHAVE L: N/C/A DIRECTORS/PARK, NICK (1995) 30M D: Nick Park. *Anne Reid, Peter Sallis.* For the first time, Wallace has a love interest: Wendolene, the owner of a wool shop whose windows he and Gromit wash as part of their new high-tech business. So it's a tad uncomfortable when the two discover a cruel sheep rustling racket being run by Wendolene's pet bulldog. As in *The Wrong Trousers*, Park does an incredible job of creating live-action-style camerawork in stop-motion animation. With plenty of gadgets and set pieces, this is the most action packed of the series. —*B. T.*

WALLACE & GROMIT: A GRAND DAY OUT L: N/C/A DIRECTORS/PARK, NICK (1991) 23M D: Nick Park. *Peter Sallis.* If you're not familiar with the Wallace & Gromit films, just trust me. Go watch them. They are among those timeless, ageless classics (think *Babe, Toy Story,* or Miyazaki) so smartly made and universally appealing that it's difficult to find someone who has seen them and doesn't love them. Although a little more crude and homemade than the later shorts (you can even see fingerprints in the clay), *A Grand Day Out* is the charming introduction of the cheese-obsessed inventor Wallace and his long-suffering dog sidekick, Gromit. In this story, Wallace runs out of cheese so he decides to build a rocket ship and have a picnic on the moon. The real story begins, though, when they run into a sentient refrigerator. As brilliantly conceived as the relationship is between Wallace and Gromit, Park is even better at portraying the thoughts of creatures like the refrigerator without the aid of dialogue or facial expressions. —*B. T.*

WALLACE & GROMIT: THE WRONG TROUSERS L: N/C/A DIRECTORS/PARK, NICK (1993) 30M D: Nick Park. *Peter Sallis.* Wallace and Gromit sublet their house to a penguin, unaware that (when wearing a rubber glove on his head to look like a rooster) he is the notorious criminal Feathers McGraw. Worse, McGraw uses a pair of remote-controlled mechanical pants Wallace invented to steal a precious diamond. Arguably the best of the Wallace and Gromit films, *The Wrong*

Trousers is a perfectly crafted cartoon thriller. There's something hilarious about seeing classic Hitchcock-style filmmaking techniques lovingly recreated on miniature models. Gromit's annoyance at Wallace and Wallace's obliviousness of said annoyance are very funny; Wallace doesn't understand that giving a robotic walker to his dog as a birthday present is an insult. What, you don't want to walk it yourself? But the show is stolen by a supporting character—you know there's scheming going on behind the deadpan expression on that tiny penguin face. It's actually kind of creepy. —*B. T.*

WATERSHIP DOWN L: NONCHILDREN'S ANIMATION/ NONCHILDREN'S ANIMATION (1978) 78M D: Martin Rosen. *Richard Briers, Ralph Richardson, Zero Mostel, John Hurt, Denholm Elliott.* Based on the novel by Richard Adams, *Watership Down* concerns the displacement of rabbits whose home is devastated by human modernization. Their exodus produces a political division among them regarding where they should resettle. In their travels, they encounter predatory larger animals, which demands some quick solutions. This animated feature would seem to be for children, but the themes are clearly allegorical, making the film somewhat like *Animal Farm*. The distinctly non-Disney animation is quite good and the voices of these rabbits include a host of top-notch actors. —*N. J.*

WHISPER OF THE HEART L: MANGA/MANGA (1995) 111M D: Yoshifumi Kondo. *Youko Honna, Kazuo Takahashi, Takashi Tachibana, Shigeru Muroi, Shigeru Tsuyuguchi.* This is one of the sweeter, quieter films to come out of Studio Ghibli. A young girl notices that one person has checked out all the books she has borrowed from the library and attempts to figure out who. Impulsively following an unusual cat she meets on the subway, she comes to an intriguing store filled with strange and beautiful objects. She becomes enchanted by a statue of a cat wearing a suit with tails and a top hat called The Baron. A boy from her school lives there and he is the one she seeks. Their mutual love of music draws them together. Learning he plans to study violin-making in Italy, she questions what she has done, and not done, with her life, leading her to tackle the difficult task of writing a book about The Baron. The story is about being young, finding your path in life, making connections, and falling in love. As such, it is often rather rambling and disjointed, as life itself is. Charming and gentle, this film is probably too thoughtful for children, but a worthwhile journey for teenagers or older viewers. —*M. N.*

WHO FRAMED ROGER RABBIT? L: N/C/A DIRECTORS/ WILLIAMS, RICHARD (1988) 104M D: Robert Zemeckis/Richard Williams. *Bob Hoskins, Charles Fleischer, Christopher Lloyd, Joanna Cassidy, Kathleen Turner.* This fantasy detective story is set in the American animation industry of the 1940s, using cartoon characters (or "toons") as real beings who perform for human camera crews and live in a physics-defying ghetto called Toontown. Human detective Eddie Valiant (Hoskins) is harassed into helping famed Maroon Cartoons star Roger Rabbit, accused of killing novelty toy salesman Marvin Acme. This groundbreaking combination of live action and animation was a rare case where the filmmakers showed respect for iconic characters of the past, not modernizing them or treating them as corporate mascots. They even wrangled the legal rights to use Looney Tunes characters alongside Disney characters (allowing for once-in-a-lifetime meetings of Bugs Bunny with Mickey Mouse, and Donald Duck with Daffy Duck). Based loosely on a book by Gary K. Wolf, the writers devised clever uses of cartoon logic (including an anthropomorphic car riding inside another car) and crowd-pleasing toon cameos. Genius animation director Williams, with the help of shading effects created by Industrial Light and Magic, created a three-dimensional look to the animation that new technology has not been able to match. *Roger Rabbit* was the beginning of the modern era of American animation, and it holds up pretty well today. —*B. T.*

WIND IN THE WILLOWS, THE L: N/C/A DIRECTORS/HALL, MARK (1983) 74M D: Mark Hall, Chris Taylor. *Richard Pearson, Ian Carmichael, David Jason.* Kenneth Grahame's book is beautifully brought to life with stop-motion animation. Mole and Ratty become good friends over tea and decide to trundle down the river to meet Toad at Toad Hall. Toad has quite the penchant for race cars, and as he is fabulously wealthy, he buys such a car only to wreck it immediately. Once he has done this several more times, he is institutionalized and that is when Toad's estate is abandoned and eventually taken over by the Hyenas. The goal of Ratty and Mole, who have come to know Toad, is for Toad to escape and win back his estate. The animation in this film is top-notch and the humor distinctly English. The magical character of Toad was designed by Barry Purvis, the stop-motion animator who brought you the designs of the Martians in *Mars Attacks! —N. J.*

WONDERFUL DAYS L: MANGA/MANGA (2003) 87M D: Moon Saeng Kim. *Ji-Tae Yu, Hee-Jin Wu, Joon-Ho Chung.* Set in the clouded industrialized future of an Earth recovering from ecological disasters, *Wonderful Days* tells the simple, contemplative, and well-paced story of two people whose contrasting worlds collide. Jay and Shua were childhood sweethearts who grew up in very different ways. Jay is a security officer on the ecologically sound cloud city Ecoban. Shua and his little brother are denizens of Marr, the overpolluted, overpopulated city built by the people who were turned away from Ecoban. Jay's search for a would-be terrorist leads her to, and reunites her with, Shua, who pulls her into a rebellion against the forces that oppress humanity. Made with a budget of 13 billion won (approx. $11 million), *Wonderful Days* is the most stunning and ambitious anime to come from Korea, a country quickly showing its prowess for the animated art form. Traditional flat and CGI-aided 3-D animation are blended with miniatures and actual film footage of weather phenomena to truly stunning effect. This grand, groundbreaking work is my favorite animated film of 2003 and not to be missed. —*G. M.*

WORLD'S GREATEST ANIMATION L: NONCHILDREN'S/ ANIMATION FESTIVALS (1994) 105M D: Nick Park, Bill Plympton, others. *Maureen McElheron, Julie Sedgewick.* There are some extremely good shorts on this compilation. All sixteen either won or were nominated for an Academy Award, and they represent a wide variety of animation forms that result in something enjoyable for nearly everyone. One of my favorites is "Balance," a slightly dark, thought-provoking short depicting six men who live their lives carefully balanced on a floating platform. When the balance is thrown off by a large musical trunk, the men must figure out how to regain it so they don't plunge to their deaths. "Creature Comforts," about animals in a zoo sharing their thoughts on being in captivity, once again shows Park for the claymation genius he is. Most of the shorts are not intended for children, particularly "Tango," which has several minutes of nonanimated nudity, but for the adult with a soft spot in his or her heart for good animation, this compilation definitely delivers. —*J. S.*

X L: MANGA/MANGA (1996) 98M D: Rintaro. *Ken Narita, Junko Iwao, Tomokazu Seki.* There's a gang war between Heaven and Hell being played out in Tokyo like a comic book superhero turf war, but the "final battle for the future of Earth" boils down to a Cain and Abel grudge match. Why? This film never answers that question, or dozens of others for that matter. The first half of this splashy animated fantasy bops between symbolically loaded visions (a boy dreams his naked mother pulls a sword out of her womb and charges him with a quest before she explodes in a torrent of blood—talk about childhood trauma!) and breakneck exposition spewed out in staccato bursts. There's a novel's worth of backstory crammed into a few loaded minutes, but not to worry. It's so flashy that story, character, and other nonessential matters are pushed aside in a celebration of kinetic fury and visual flash. —*S. A.*

X-MEN L: COMIX/COMIX (2000) 104M D: Bryan Singer. *Anna Paquin, Hugh Jackman, Famke Janssen, Ian McKellen, Patrick Stewart, Halle Berry.* Director Singer was apparently never a fan of the X-Men comics before he started developing this movie. I'm not sure whether that makes it more impressive or understandable that he could create a movie satisfying to both X-Men fans and normal people at the same time. The number of genetic mutants with strange abilities is on the rise. Humans fear and oppress them, and they fight back in different ways. Dr. Xavier (Stewart) and his X-Men run a private school for mutants, training them to use their powers to help people (mutant or otherwise). His former colleague, Magneto (McKellen), is much more militant, and leads a band of mutant terrorists (who, if you pay attention, make more progress for the cause than the X-Men). The heart of the movie would be the philosophical rivalry between Xavier and Magneto, but the movie is completely stolen by then-unknown Clint Eastwood–look-alike Jackman as Wolverine. Never has an actor been a more perfect fit for a comic book role. Growing up, I could never relate to my friends who obsessed over X-Men and drew macho pictures of Wolverine and his claws. Jackman made me understand completely. —*B. T.*

X2: X-MEN UNITED L: COMIX/COMIX (2003) 133M D: Bryan Singer. *Hugh Jackman, Ian McKellen, Famke Janssen, Alan Cumming, Patrick Stewart, Anna Paquin.* This is the best possible sequel to the original movie. The story still revolves around mutant oppression and the evil of ignorance, but armed with a bigger budget and better script, it is a more thoughtful action movie. The opening sequence, where Nightcrawler invades the White House, is one of the most poetic action scenes I've seen. What really makes *X2* rock for me is that Wolverine kills the shit out of a lot of people. I could go on and on about how the depth of character relationships and the politics of the story are better than the first one, but it's really about Wolverine killing people, which he didn't do in the original. Ever since I first read *X-Men*, I've wanted to see Wolverine kick ass in a movie theater, and now I have. —*K. C.*

ZIGGY'S GIFT L: N/C/A DIRECTORS/WILLIAMS, RICHARD (1983) 30M D: Richard Williams. *John Gibbons, Tony Giorgio.* I cannot explain the popularity of Tom Wilson's comic strip *Ziggy*, about a short bald guy and his pets who observe cute things about life. But Williams is such a talented director that he can make lush, three-dimensional animation out of Wilson's crudely drawn strip. For this Emmy-winning Christmas special he draws Ziggy and his dog the same as in the strip, but gives them very realistic movements and surrounds them with more detailed characters and settings. Ziggy (who does not talk in this incarnation) gets involved in a Christmas charity scam, but manages to make things better. That's about as much plot as you get in an episode of *Teletubbies*, and since the script is by Wilson there aren't a whole lot of laughs either. But it's definitely worth seeking out if you admire good animation, and Williams fans will especially get a kick out of it since there is a silent thief character who moves exactly like the one in *The Thief and the Cobbler*. —*B. T.*

Murder, Mystery & Suspense

A constant in the human con-dition is crime. Murder, robbery, espionage, embezzlement, rape, drug dealing, poisoning, assault, blackmail, and adultery have been part of the human experience ever since someone got to feeling like a third wheel. And if you believe your Bible, violent crime only had to wait one generation in the human family before it reared its ugly head. So what does it all mean? Well, we're not going to get into that here. The most we'll say is that ever since the first human crime was committed, people have been trying to solve crimes as well.

Everyone loves a mystery is how the saying goes. It may well be true. Sometimes, though, we just want to get wound up so tightly in a story that the only release is justice. We want to be brought to the brink of death, literally or figuratively but always vicariously, so that we might quicken our hearts, sharpen our minds, or steel our souls, and come to be relieved that, by hook or by crook, even we are capable of raw survival. That is what these films should do for you.

But, first and best, they should entertain. Great mysteries allow you to play along, to solve the case or think you've solved it, and to be the hero, the savior, or the survivor. The best spy stories take you to places you will never go, expose you to secrets or technologies you were not meant to know, to fight enemies as heartless, faceless, and soulless as have ever existed. The Caper film puts you in the antihero's seat: here you want the crime to be committed, and the more complicated that crime is to pull

Sudden Fear (1952)

off the better, as long as you are somehow allowed to stick it to the man. The Noir film puts you in the place of the innocent, who somehow gets blood on his hands, gets in over her head, or is cornered inextricably by fate and must fight his way out, or die trying.

When asked to describe one of his works, Russian author Nikolai Gogol said that he wanted to "force you into the sewer to take a bath." This sums up our Crime sections. It's a prison cell of a genre, designed to put you, rather uncomfortably, up to your neck in the criminal element. You are initiated into gangs, shot, stabbed, raped, beaten, and mentally, physically, and spiritually dragged deeper and deeper into the most demeaning, dehumanized, and demented worlds of human creation so that by film's end you might appreciate your freedom. There are times when a customer walks out of the store with a movie about which you can't really say "Enjoy!" though you believe nonetheless they will. Well, these films are those. "Enjoy!" (I guess.)

AMBUSHERS, THE L: SPY/SPY (1967) 102M D: Henry Levin. *Dean Martin, Senta Berger, Janice Rule, Albert Salmi, James Gregory.* The third Matt Helm film is just as mediocre as the others. Martin plays the swinging secret agent called back into action by series regular Gregory. It seems a U.S. government flying saucer (that rides on train tracks) has been hijacked by sinister beer-brewers. There are lots of gadgets, booze, dumb jokes, and a fight at a brewery. *The Ambushers* would make a good double bill with *Strange Brew.* Berger plays a curvaceous double agent and Rule plays the wholesome but sexy pilot of the flying saucer. I like the Flint series better, but I'm a Dino fan and get a kick out of his drunken superagent. In a post–Austin Powers world, Helm gets very little respect. —*S. H.*

ANIMAL FACTORY L: CRIME/MEN IN PRISON (2000) 90M D: Steve Buscemi. *Seymour Cassel, Edward Furlong, Mickey Rourke, Steve Buscemi, Willem Dafoe.* Buscemi's second film as a director is this gritty prison story about a young pretty boy (Furlong) locked up for a minor drug offense who convinces a feared old-timer (Dafoe) to protect him from rapists and teach him the ropes. It's a fairly standard prison movie but feels very authentic and includes some colorful performances, most memorably Rourke as a cross-dresser. The DVD has a pretty interesting commentary by executive producers/real-life ex-cons Eddie Bunker and Danny Trejo (Bunker also wrote the movie and both appear in the cast). —*B. T.*

AVENGERS '65 AND '66, THE L: SPY/SPY TELEVISION (1965) 104M D: Various. *Patrick Macnee, Diana Rigg.* Dapper and oh-so impeccably mannered John Steed (Macnee with a twinkle in his eye) met his match in svelte, sassy partner Mrs. Emma Peel (Rigg), the "talented amateur" to his "top professional" (though what profession we're never quite sure) in the fourth and finest season of the show. The low budgets and cheap sets turn into coolly elegant examples of restrained decor, abstract design, and studies in contrast. James Bond conspiracies, science fiction plots, austere imagery, and surreal moments of parody gone to absurd extremes mix it up in the tongue-in-chic height of 1960s TV culture. The Oscar Wilde–ish drawing room wit, flirty repartee, and subtle physicality are all here, but the real draw is Rigg dudded out in Carnaby street fashion, black leather gear, and, in "A Touch of Brimstone," an episode determined too racy for American TV, dressed down as a dominatrix in a black lace corset and fishnet stockings. It's all about attitude with style, and Steed and Peel have it to spare. —*S. A.*

BABY, THE L: MURDER/MYSTERY/SUSPENSE (1972) 85M D: Ted Post. *David Manzy, Ruth Roman, Anjanette Comer.* There has never been a more disconcerting PG film. Long before adult baby-ism became a socially acceptable fetish, director Post's story of a full-grown man in diapers made impressive use of its limited budget and premise. A social worker (Comer) is shocked to learn that a client's so-called baby is actually older than her, kept in a crib for decades, and deprived of any kind of education. Baby is loved by his overprotective mother and two shut-in sisters, but doomed to a life of warm milk and baby talk until do-gooder Comer decides to liberate him from his cheerfully decorated prison. This is, of course, when the poopy hits the fan, and the film suddenly shifts into bitter horror vengeance mode without losing any momentum. Manzy's infant-aping performance should have been recognized by the Motion Picture Academy; one scene of Baby suckling his hesitant teenage babysitter is almost enough to make you crawl under your blanky. —*Z. C.*

BELLY L: CRIME/GANGS & GANGSTAS (1998) 120M D: Hype Williams. *Nas, Tionne "T-Boz" Watkins, DMX, Taral Hicks, Method Man.* Hip-hop video director Williams makes a cumbersome but gorgeous feature film debut. Later teaming with Jet Li and Steven Seagal, DMX first showed a strong screen presence alongside fellow rapper Nas as the protagonists of this urban crime saga. The line delivery is often awkward and so is some of the storytelling, but the cinematography (which takes advantage of the high-contrast silver-retention film also used in *Seven*) is absolutely stunning. It doesn't feel like anything else from this genre and has many great touches. Highlights include an indecipherable Jamaican drug lord and an all black-and-white living room where DMX brings his friends after a shoot-out and tries to get them to watch *Gummo.* —*B. T.*

BEST SELLER L: MURDER/MYSTERY/SUSPENSE (1987) 95M D: John Flynn. *James Woods, Brian Dennehy, Victoria Tennant, Allison Balson.* Woods once again brings charm to the role of a pathologically vindictive hit man who goes to a Joseph Wambaugh–like cop/author (Dennehy) to expose his former employer. This narcissist wants to be the hero of Dennehy's next book. Exploitation movie king Larry Cohen cannily mixes social satire and genre twists in his clever screenplay of an unlikely friendship between two men with more history than they realize; his dialogue has a bite and an unforced wit that hovers somewhere between B-movie gangster dramas and buddy pictures. It was not a success upon release but this smart, lean thriller found an audience on home video and remains a minor gem of the modern crime genre. —S. A.

BLACK ANGEL L: NOIR/FILM NOIR (1946) 80M D: Roy William Neill. *Broderick Crawford, Peter Lorre, June Vincent, Dan Duryea, Constance Dowling, Wallace Ford.* B-movie veteran and Sherlock Holmes series director Neill brings his clean efficiency to Cornell Woolrich's dark world of innocence ensnared. Duryea, traditionally a smarmy noir villain, brings his sass and smart talk to this rare protagonist role, a self-pitying songwriter and pianist who falls for the pretty young wife (Vincent) of the man convicted of the crime and joins her search for his wife's real killer. Sleek set design, modestly effective writing, and an achingly vulnerable performance from Duryea pull this neglected noir gem from the B-movie origins. Neill creates a tight, stylish mystery that's more uneasy mood than literal menace. Not to give anything away, but this is one mystery where the answer can be found in the bottom of a bottle. —S. A.

BODY OF EVIDENCE L: MURDER/MYSTERY//MURDER/ MYSTERY/SUSPENSE (1993) 99M D: Uli Edel. *Madonna, Willem Dafoe, Joe Mantegna, Anne Archer, Julianne Moore.* "She is not only the defendant, she is the murder weapon itself!" Falling somewhere between a *Basic Instinct* knockoff and a preview of Madonna's book *Sex,* this kinky erotic thriller is more concerned with sweaty sex, hot wax, and broken glass than any actual murder mystery. Madonna is the sexy, icy-blond murder suspect with a voracious sexual appetite and a thing for dominance, and Dafoe is the straight-arrow lawyer she seduces (along with about half of the cast). Edel directs this handsome production, but can't get any heat out of the erotic spectacle. Madonna hasn't the burning intensity necessary to become anything more than a cinematic exhibitionist. —S. A.

BORDERLINE L: NOIR/FILM NOIR (1950) 88M D: William A. Seiter. *Fred MacMurray, Claire Trevor, Raymond Burr.* MacMurray was well into his smart-talking tough guy phase when he made this south-of-the-border thriller about drug smugglers and undercover cops. Trevor is the overeager agent who goes to Mexico to get next to American drug lord (Burr) and winds up MacMurray's moll while Burr relentlessly chases them back to the border. Imagine *It Happened One Night* as a dusty, sun-baked crime picture with a little grit and a lot of hard-boiled attitude. It never quite achieves the film noir edge but is plenty fun anyway. —S. A.

BOTTLE ROCKET L: CRIME/CAPERS (HEISTS) (1996) 92M D: Wes Anderson. *Owen Wilson, James Caan, Lumi Cavazos, Luke Wilson, Robert Musgrave.* Dignan. That's his name. It's a strange name for a strange man (Owen Wilson), a lovable loser who has a fifty-year plan to become a thief, something he knows next to nothing about. But he knows Mr. Henry (Caan), a notorious burglar (apparently) who runs a landscaping "front" called the Lawn Wranglers. When they rob a bookstore, it comes off more like a self-actualization exercise than a robbery. Dignan may not be brilliant, but he means well. He's not a liar and he cares about his friends—the type of guy you just want to hug. Anderson's *Bottle Rocket* is a tribute to true friendship, oddballs, yellow jumpsuits, and language barriers, and it's the most winning, good-natured crime movie you'll ever see. —K. C.

BOUND L: CRIME/CAPERS (HEISTS) (1996) 107M D: Andy Wachowski, Larry Wachowski. *Christopher Meloni, Gina Gershon, Jennifer Tilly, Joe Pantoliano, Barry Kivel.* Like the Coen brothers before them, the Wachowski brothers made their debut with a stylish and darkly humorous low-budget neo-noir. An ex-con repairing an apartment building hooks up with a mobster's girlfriend. They come up with a scheme to steal $2 million of Mafia loot, and mayhem ensues. The twist is that both lovers are women (Gershon and Tilly), which makes for some humorous situations like when Pantoliano shakes Gershon's hand right after it has been. . . uh. . . you-know-where. It takes a bit to get used to Gershon as the male-fantasy version of a butch lesbian, but the clever camerawork and skillfully constructed suspense will win you over. My favorite moment is when a mess has to be cleaned up in the apartment before another character shows up. The camera floats down the hallway to the elevator, you hear the "ding" of the elevator arriving, and before the doors even open the camera heads back for the apartment. —B. T.

BREAKDOWN L: MURDER/MYSTERY/SUSPENSE (1997) 95M D: Jonathan Mostow. *Kurt Russell, J. T. Walsh, M. C. Gainey, Kathleen Quinlan, Jack Noseworthy.* Walsh was a talented character actor with one of those faces that was always recognized and delighted in when it appeared on the screen. As the villain in *Breakdown,* he gets to inch closer to the center stage he probably deserved. The film stars Russell as a man whose wife hitches a ride with a trucker (Walsh) after their car breaks down. She doesn't return, and soon Russell is roped into a plot involving kidnapping, extortion, and—maybe—the local police. The twists and turns aren't likely to surprise anyone who has watched movies, but they are expertly maneuvered by the director, crew, and cast. And Walsh, who played sinister about as well as anyone, looks terrifying behind a pair of huge sunglasses. —T. P.

BUGSY L: CRIME/GANGS & GANGSTAS (1991) 134M D: Barry Levinson. *Warren Beatty, Annette Bening, Ben Kingsley, Elliott Gould, Harvey Keitel.* There is a scene in *Bugsy* where Benny "Bugsy" Siegel (Beatty) is standing in front of a sunset. The sunset is fake—a backdrop on a Hollywood set—and Bugsy has just been rejected by a beautiful woman. As if on cue, the sunset dims. It's a neat visual moment, and *Bugsy* is full of them. It's less of a thick Russian novel than *The Godfather* and more of a gorgeous valentine. It's not a story about a thug as much as an ode to Hollywood glamour and mobster movies. It's also beautiful to look at. Whether it's Bening stalking down a hallway, attended by curls of cigarette smoke, or Beatty slipping behind a screen, his silhouette caught in bold black and white, you won't find many gangster movies that look as good as this one. —*T. P.*

BULLY L: CRIME/TRUE CRIME (2001) 111M D: Larry Clark. *Brad Renfro, Rachel Miner, Nick Stahl, Bijou Phillips, Michael Pitt, Leo Fitzpatrick.* Although it is based on a true story, Clark's hilariously over-the-top teenage murder conspiracy tale plays like a parody of his sensationalistic earlier film *Kids.* The bully of the title (Stahl) is a psychotic rapist whose friends and acquaintances get fed up and plot to kill him. What's unusual is that there's no moral character to serve as the audience's entry into the story. Just empty-headed morons who indulge in hard drugs, S-M, orgies, phone sex, and gay strip-club dancing right beneath the noses of their oblivious parents, then rationalize up a storm when they stab and beat their friend to death and feed him to the alligators. You might have to take a shower afterward, or you might disagree with me that the humor is intentional. But you will probably find its trashy excess alluring. It's the foul-smelling, X-rated peep show that all true-crime TV movies wish they could be. —*B. T.*

CAMBRIDGE SPIES L: SPY/SPY (2002) 240M D: Tim Fywell *Toby Stephens, Tom Hollander, Samuel West, Rupert Penry-Jones.* The true story of Anthony Blunt, Kim Philby, Guy Burgess, and Donald Maclean—British upper-class activists recruited out of Cambridge to be Soviet spies in the dark days of the mid-1930s—is given an unusually sympathetic treatment in this four-hour British miniseries. "Fascism or Communism, these are the choices," proclaims college golden boy Burgess as he watches the conservative ruling class embrace Hitler. Thus they begin twenty years of shipping British secrets off to Mother Russia. The ordeal of their treason takes its toll in different ways. Burgess (Hollander), the flamboyantly gay and emotionally volatile early leader, falls into the bottle and becomes reckless while the cool, in-control Blunt (West) distances himself from the group, leaving Philby (Stephens) to babysit Burgess and Maclean (Penry-Jones) as they crack under the pressure. Their stories have been told again and again in British films and television plays; it's as if the country can hardly believe that these privileged men would betray their country, or worse yet, their class. This ambitious retelling, which follows their course

from college to the collapse of their covers, is a fine addition to the collection. —*S. A.*

CAPE FEAR (1962) L: NOIR/FILM NOIR (1962) 106M D: J. Lee Thompson. *Gregory Peck, Robert Mitchum, Polly Bergen, Lori Martin, Telly Savalas, Martin Balsam.* Scorsese remade it in 1991, but the original thriller is still the best. Ex-con Mitchum hunts down the lawyer (Peck) whose testimony sent him to jail and exacts his revenge on Peck's innocent family. Though not really a film noir, it's a dark, edgy thriller that still causes chills today, due in large part to a script ripe with suggestion and an eerily charismatic performance by Mitchum that brings those suggestions to life with a smirking sneer and a nasty stare. Martin acquits herself well in a role director Thompson wanted Hayley Mills for. It was Peck's first film as a producer and he chose top-notch material (the novel *The Executioners* by John D. MacDonald) and a good journeyman director who did the best work of his career. —*S. A.*

CELL, THE L: CRIME/SERIAL KILLERS (2000) 107M D: Tarsem Singh. *Jennifer Lopez, Vince Vaughn, Vincent D'Onofrio, Jake Weber, Dylan Baker.* D'Onofrio is a whacked-out serial killer who kidnaps women and tortures them with elaborate Rube Goldberg devices. After hiding away his latest victim he falls into a coma, so child psychologist Lopez enters his dream world through virtual reality and tries to find out the girl's location. Thanks to music-video director Tarsem Singh (who often just uses his first name), the killer turns out to have some incredible surrealist imagery floating around in his head, even if a lot of it is ripped off from modern artists. The movie is very impressive on a visual level but that doesn't stop it from being just another brainless take on the *Seven*-style serial killer thriller. Even after proving herself in *Out of Sight*, Lopez comes across more like a cosmetics model than an actress. At least Vaughn tries something semi-interesting as an FBI agent who always looks like he just got out of bed and still has a fierce hangover. —*B. T.*

COMPULSION L: CRIME/SERIAL KILLERS (1959) 77M D: Richard Fleischer. *Bradford Dillman, Orson Welles, Dean Stockwell, Diane Varsi, E. G. Marshall.* Stockwell and Dillman play two arrogant college students who commit murder to prove to themselves that they are above morality, then pretend to help the police with the investigation. Of course they get caught, so the second half of the movie is a rousing courtroom drama in which Welles (as the defense attorney) delivers a powerful monologue against capital punishment. Like Hitchcock's *Rope, Compulsion* is inspired by the real-life case of Leopold and Loeb, so it's interesting to see how similar the characters are in both fictionalized accounts. It's also easy for modern audiences to see a little bit of Columbine in the superior attitudes of the killers. —*B. T.*

CONFIDENCE L: CRIME/CAPERS (HEISTS) (2003) 98M
D: James Foley. *Rachel Weisz, Andy Garcia, Paul Giamatti, Morris Chestnut, Edward Burns, Dustin Hoffman.* The usually glib Burns makes a convincing con man in this devious Foley-directed shell game. He's a would-be smoothy who opens the film confessing his sins with a gun to his head while flashbacks take us to an update of *The Sting* with a fashionably cynical sheen. "You can't tell when you're lying," admires sleazy, rodent-like wannabe kingpin Hoffman (in a performance that out-hams Al Pacino), which is what makes Burns so well cast as a shyster but underwhelming as a criminal hero. The plot swims in entertaining distractions—jinxes, double crosses, betrayals—and turns on the almost precognitive ability of Burns to predict the minutiae of human behavior, while Foley's momentum and misdirection enable the disbelief. If you don't look too closely, the film delivers a clever confidence game, if not much else. Weisz costars as a fellow grifter with a taste for unlucky red and Garcia plays it loose and borderline insane as an obsessive federal agent. —S. A.

COOL HAND LUKE L: CRIME/MEN IN PRISON (1967) 126M
D: Stuart Rosenberg. *Paul Newman, George Kennedy, J. D. Cannon, Clifton James, Strother Martin, Jo Van Fleet.* One of my all-time favorite movies is part of our collective subconscious. Whether you've seen the movie or not, you've undoubtedly encountered the "What we've got here is a failure to communicate" line (spoken by Martin) that is one of many memorable quotable moments in *Cool Hand Luke*. Luke (Newman in one of his best roles) becomes a sort of messiah among prisoners on a chain gang. His sacrifices, leadership, and stubborn rebellion inspire his fellow inmates (including Kennedy in an Oscar-winning role). Sit in awe when Luke eats fifty eggs, sing along to "Plastic Jesus," cry when the poor old guard dog dies, and kick yourself squarely in the ass if you've never watched this film. Filled with religious symbolism and outstanding cinematography, *Cool Hand Luke* makes an excellent double bill with *One Flew Over the Cuckoo's Nest.* —S. H.

COTTON COMES TO HARLEM L: DETECTIVES/JOHNSON/GRAVEDIGGER (1970) 97M D: Ossie Davis. *Godfrey Cambridge, Redd Foxx, Raymond St. Jacques, Calvin Lockhart, Judy Pace.* This enjoyable adaptation of the Chester Himes novel was made a couple of years before the blaxploitation craze and has a much different and restrained approach to black action cinema. "Coffin Ed" and "Gravedigger" Jones were two tough Harlem cops that appeared in several Chester Himes novels. They are somewhat softened in this film but are well played by St. Jacques and Cambridge, respectively, and the two repeat the roles in the worthy sequel *Come Back Charleston Blue.* Lockhart is a charismatic but crooked preacher who is scamming the public with a "Back to Africa" campaign. He loses

a bunch of money hidden in a bale of cotton, and Coffin and Grave pursue the bale around Harlem. They encounter various eccentrics (including Foxx, a garbage-collecting homeless man) and troublemakers (pimps, gangsters, crooked cops), and engage in the occasional gunfight and car chase. Coffin Ed and Gravedigger also appear, in greatly reduced roles, in 1991's *A Rage in Harlem.* —S. H.

CRIMINAL, THE L: WHODUNITS/WHODUNITS (1999) 96M
D: Julian Simpson. *Eddie Izzard, Steven Mackintosh, Natasha Little, Bernard Hill.* Simpson's contemporary Brit-noir drops the viewer into the shadowy underworld of blighty thugs, damp alleys, and dark London nights, then pulls the rug out from under the audience. Mackintosh is the innocent on the run, accused of a murder he didn't commit. He's chased by a relentless dinosaur of a detective (Hill) and shadowed by a shady gang whose promises of help ring false as the corpses pile up around him. One of the more ingenious films to sprout from the recent crop of British gangster movies, this is a kind of *North by Northwest* set in the realpolitik world of free-market espionage. Cynical, sleek, and styled in gray, steel blue, and all the colors of the night, this devious thriller is somewhat contrived but terrifically paranoid with a claustrophobic atmosphere that practically swallows the patsy of a hero. —S. A.

DAUGHTER OF HORROR L: NOIR/FILM NOIR (1955) 56M D: John Parker. *Ed McMahon, Adrienne Barrett, Bruno Ve Sota, Richard Barron.* This is an incredible low-budget gem. Mostly silent, but for occasional narration by McMahon (?!) and a groovy, sleazy soundtrack by Shorty Rogers (and his Giants), it plays out like an hour-long nightmare, a never-ending loop of sweating, twitching dementia (the film's alternative title). If you've ever stayed up all night on Benzedrine and Stolli's, this film will bring back some sour memories. —S. F.

DEAD MAN WALKING L: CRIME/MEN IN PRISON (1995) 120M D: Tim Robbins. *Sean Penn, Susan Sarandon, Robert Prosky, Raymond J. Barry, R. Lee Ermey.* Sarandon plays real-life nun/activist Sister Helen Prejean, who visits and counsels a murderer (Penn) before his execution. This painful, superbly acted drama makes an extremely powerful humanist statement because it so steadfastly refuses to stack the deck. Penn's Matthew Poncelot is a racist, and he's apparently guilty of the rape/murder he's accused of, though he claims innocence. But Prejean sees him as a person and therefore worthy of mercy. Director Robbins probably agrees, but he still doesn't make it easy; there are some very emotional, confrontational scenes with the families of the victims. Some people in the media have cast Robbins as an ignorant Hollywood boob to downplay the validity of his occasional antiwar statements, but they'd have a harder time saying that with a straight face if they'd seen this intelligent, incredibly moving film. Same goes for Penn who, with this performance, solidified his reputation as one of the best actors of his generation. —*B. T.*

DEAD PRESIDENTS L: CRIME/CAPERS (HEISTS) (1995) 119M D: Albert Hughes, Allen Hughes. *Chris Tucker, Larenz Tate, Keith David, N'Bushe Wright, Freddy Rodriguez.* The Hughes Brothers's underrated second film begins with a heist, then flashes back to tell the story of how a group of black Vietnam veterans turned to crime. The directors themselves have criticized the movie, saying they were too young to tell that particular story. Still, most of it works and it's worth watching just for the performances. *Menace II Society's* Tate plays another sympathetic outlaw, and David is particularly great as a one-legged crime lord who at one point beats an attacker with his artificial leg. Perhaps most notable is the pre–*Rush Hour* Tucker in a great dramatic performance as a doomed heroin addict. —*B. T.*

DEAD RECKONING L: NOIR/FILM NOIR (1947) 105M D: John Cromwell. *Humphrey Bogart, Lizabeth Scott, William Prince, Morris Carnovsky, Charles Cane, Wallace Ford.* Any resemblance to Bogart classics *The Maltese Falcon* and *The Big Sleep* is anything but coincidental ("A guy's buddy gets killed, he oughta do something about it," Bogie explains in a line that echoes of Sam Spade) in this murder mystery of deception and double crosses. Narrating in his distinctive, gravely lisp, Bogie plays a war hero who collides with femme fatale Scott while investigating the death of his all-American, Medal of Honor buddy. For all her ambivalence and smoky-voiced delivery, Scott is soggy next to Bogie's tight-lipped, war-hardened intensity, and the B roster of supporting actors keeps this from A-movie territory. Cromwell is too polite a director to sleaze this up as it should be, yet the generic everytown setting and undernourished sets lend an appropriate tawdriness to the tarnished portrait of small-time hoodlums with big dreams. A minor but satisfying example of American film noir. —*S. A.*

DEADLIER THAN THE MALE L: DETECTIVES/BULLDOG DRUMMOND (1967) 98M D: Ralph Thomas. *Elke Sommer, Richard Johnson, Sylva Koscina, Steve Carlsen, Nigel Green, Suzanna Leigh.* Suave insurance investigator Hugh "Bulldog" Drummond (Johnson) chases a trail of dead executives from foggy London to the sunny Mediterranean and finds a pair of sexy assassins (cold professional Sommer and flirty klepto Koscina). They are part of a dastardly business that removes "obstacles" to corporate plans. One of the most inspired James Bond spoofs, this film has a light touch with the comedy and a perfectly cool, quipping gentleman in Johnson. The concept and execution are only slightly undercut by a budget that can't support its ambitious effects

ideas, and fight scenes that too often have the look of a high school wrestling match. The fun is all in the performances, the high-concept goofiness of the inspired murders, and, of course, in the revealing wardrobe of the curvaceous killers. Thomas directs from a script cowritten by Hammer stalwart Jimmy Sangster. —*S. A.*

DEEP END, THE L: MURDER/MYSTERY/SUSPENSE (2001) 101M D: David Siegel, Scott McGehee. *Josh Lucas, Raymond Barry, Jonathan Tucker, Tilda Swinton, Goran Visnjic.* Swinton is brilliant as the mother whose protected middle-class world is shattered by a handsome blackmailer (Visnjic) who targets her teenage son while her Navy officer husband is away at sea. This remake of Max Ophuls's film noir classic *The Reckless Moment* (sadly still unavailable on home video in any format as of this writing) is transplanted from '50s LA to modern-day Nevada and is smartly directed by McGehee and Siegel (*Suture*), from their screenplay. Swinton's closed-in performance lacks the necessary emotional connection with Visnjic to make the melodrama's romantic twists believable, but she beautifully creates a shell of toughness that cracks under the pressure of the crisis and her family's emotional needs, tearing at her heart while she's most vulnerable. —*S. A.*

DERANGED L: CRIME/SERIAL KILLERS (1974) 82M D: Jeff Gillen, Alan Ormsby. *Cosette Lee, Pat Orr, Roberts Blossom, Robert Warner.* I don't know why some sick fuck would turn the life of cannibal serial killer Ed Gein into a black comedy, but it sure works. Blossom is perfect as the dimwitted, socially awkward Gein (here called Ezra Cobb), who doesn't completely understand the problems with digging up graves or killing women and wearing their skin. As happened in real life, he tells everybody what he's been up to, but they assume he's joking. Tom Savini provides the very graphic makeup effects but, being based on real murders, these have a hard time being as fun as his work on *Dawn of the Dead.* But they try. This is about as close as you'll get to the true story that inspired *Psycho, The Texas Chain Saw Massacre,* and Buffalo Bill from *Silence of the Lambs,* although the later *Ed Gein* is also pretty good. —*B. T.*

DETOUR L: NOIR/FILM NOIR (1992) 89M D: Wade Williams. *Lea Lavish, Tom Neal Jr., Susanna Foster.* Against all rational thought, somebody remade Edgar Ulmer's grimy little poverty masterpiece. With the blessing of the original story author Martin Goldsmith and the participation of original star Tom Neal's even less talented son, B-movie veteran Williams set about his remake, expanding the story but otherwise slavishly aping Ulmer's existential film noir thriller of a second-rate piano man who hitchhikes to his doom. It's a misguided but loving effort, smartly designed and shot in gorgeous faux period color, but where Neal delivers the blank doom of a corpse waiting to expire, all bland Junior can muster is dull mopeyness. The new scenes chart the corruption of Neal's girlfriend in Hollywood, an interesting but distracting subplot that adds a level of irony at the cost of the original story's sucker punch ending. —S. A.

DIAMONDS ARE FOREVER L: SPY/007 (JAMES BOND) (1971) 120M D: Guy Hamilton. *Sean Connery, Lana Wood, Jill St. John, Charles Gray, Jimmy Dean.* After the release of *On Her Majesty's Secret Service,* producers Albert Broccoli and Harry Saltzman realized they needed a better Bond or they needed Connery back. And so with a million-dollar offer plus extras, by far the largest price tag for an actor at the time, Connery came back as the ideal 007. In *Diamonds Are Forever,* Bond confronts his nemesis Blofeld (Gray) in Las Vegas, where he is hoarding precious stones so as to build a satellite laser. Bond's female interest is Tiffany (St. John), a particularly ditsy Vegas girl. Among the highlights is the Mustang Mach 1 car chase that culminates in Bond eluding police with a two-wheel stunt down a narrow alley. *Diamonds Are Forever* would be Connery's last Bond film until he was talked into a revival twelve years later for *Never Say Never Again,* after which he said "Never again." —N. J.

DOA L: NOIR/FILM NOIR (1949) 83M D: Rudolph Mate. *Edmond O'Brien, Luther Adler, Lynne Baggett, Pamela Britton, Beverly Campbell.* In this film noir classic, O'Brien plays a man who is given a slow-acting poison. The whole of the film concerns his frantic quest to find who poisoned him and what motive such a person could have for doing so. The more time he loses the more intense and suspenseful this film gets. Excellent photography and great performances help make this a brilliant white-knuckle ride. It was remade as *Color Me Dead* in 1969 and again as *D. O. A.* in 1988 with Dennis Quaid and Meg Ryan. —N. J.

DR. NO L: SPY/007 (JAMES BOND) (1962) 111M D: Terence Young. *Sean Connery, Ursula Andress, Joseph Wiseman, Jack Lord, Bernard Lee.* The very first James Bond film captured the formula for success right from the start. With the plot of a mad doctor sabotaging the U.S. space program (taken from Ian Fleming's popular novel), it was important for producers Albert Broccoli and Harry Saltzman to give it proper cinematic shape. Connery was cast as the suave British detective agent 007, the remote locale of Jamaica was the mad doctor's hideout, and the stunningly beautiful Andress played the female interest, Honey Ryder. After the release of the film it became very clear that the love interest was every bit as important as the charisma of agent 007, and both were dead-on with this Bond premiere. *Dr. No* is rare because very few films that could trigger a lengthy series have nearly all the recognizable elements intact so that a Pierce Brosnan Bond

fan today would resonate with a Bond entry made more than forty years ago. —N. J.

ED GEIN L: CRIME/SERIAL KILLERS (2001) 90M D: Chuck Parello. *Carrie Snodgrass, Steve Railsback, Sally Champlin, Carol Mansell.* The most accurate movie about real-life cannibal/necrophiliac Ed Gein, the Wisconsin serial killer whose horrific behavior inspired *Psycho, The Texas Chain Saw Massacre,* and *Deranged.* It's hard to do a classy telling of a story about a guy who dug up his mother's grave, ate human hearts, and wore human skin that belonged to somebody else, but these filmmakers come surprisingly close. Without using a huge amount of gore (if you want that, watch *Deranged*) they delve into the psyche of this dim-witted farm boy who tells his neighbors about his crimes many times before they realize he's not joking. Railsback (who also portrayed Charles Manson) is great. He seems completely oblivious to the social rules he is violating by making furniture out of people he found in the graveyard. —B. T.

EIGHT-TRAY GANGSTER: THE MAKING OF A CRIP L: CRIME/TRUE CRIME (1993) 70M D: Thomas Lee Wright. This raw, 16 mm documentary is a shockingly intimate portrait of two brothers who are members of the LA Crips. They explain what the gang meant to them growing up and why they see it as a radical political group like the Black Panthers. They're even shown practicing shooting in a field somewhere. It's a rare and nonjudgmental look into the mentality of a gangster. One of the two brothers, "Monster Kody" Scott, went on to write his autobiography and appear in a much more amateurish gang documentary called *War Stories.* Cinematographer Jean de Segonzac also did great work on the similarly gritty but fictional TV series *Homicide: Life on the Street.* —B. T.

EXECUTIONER, THE (AKA MASSACRE MAFIA) L: CRIME/GANGS & GANGSTAS (1978) 84M D: Duke Mitchell. *Dominic Micelli, Duke Mitchell, Vic Caesar, John Strong, Jim Williams, Lorenzo Dodo, Sonny Chiba.* Based on a true story, this low-budget *Godfather* is big on violent shock value and rather short on drama. The film relates the story of Mimi (Mitchell) who goes to America to take revenge on the mob for exiling his father to Sicily. Perhaps the best part of the film is the beginning, which is a ridiculously violent opening credits sequence. After that it begins to drag slowly until its even more violent and hysterical conclusion. This is a film clearly designed for fans of schlocky gore who have the patience to weather some very bad pacing. —N. J.

EYE SEE YOU (AKA D-TOX) L: MURDER/MYSTERY/SUSPENSE (2002) 92M D: Jim Gillespie. *Sylvester Stallone, Tom Berenger, Sean Patrick Flanery, Charles S. Dutton, Polly Walker, Kris Kristofferson.* Stallone's career has fallen so far he's now reduced to playing the grunting, tortured hero in an adult version of a teenage stalk-and-slash movie (directed, appropriately enough, by *I Know What You Did Last Summer*'s Gillespie). He's an FBI profiler who hits the bottle after a cop-killing serial killer murders his wife, and he ends up in the most depressing rehab facility in the history of mankind: an ex-military compound run by tough-love counselor Kristofferson. Coincidentally it gets snowed in just as the supposedly dead killer revs up a new campaign. A good cast (Berenger, Jeffrey Wright, Robert Patrick, Courtney B. Vance, Stephen Lang) is staked out as potential victims without the benefit of character development behind their twitches and affectations. Delayed for years and only released theatrically in Europe, it stabbed its way into a DVD debut. —*S. A.*

FAREWELL MY LOVELY L: DETECTIVES/PHILIP MARLOWE (1975) 97M D: Dick Richards. *Robert Mitchum, Harry Dean Stanton, Charlotte Rampling, John Ireland, Anthony Zerbe, Sylvia Miles.* Mitchum's aging Philip Marlowe is neither pastiche nor homage, but a kind of wistful remembrance of an imagined past created in the midst of the '70s revisionism craze. Once again Marlowe heads out into the mean streets of LA yesteryear, searching for a lost dame and landing in a tangled web of politics, murder, and the usual vices of the urban underworld. While Richards is oddly more faithful to the original novel than the 1944 adaptation *Murder My Sweet*, what he creates isn't Raymond Chandler's Marlowe but a version unique to the movies, at once a part of the '50s milieu and on the outside looking in, old enough to know better and honest enough to hope for something better. Ultimately it's more romantic than the noir classics Mitchum starred in early in his career, a rough valentine to a time gone by. —*S. A.*

FEVER L: MURDER/MYSTERY/SUSPENSE (1999) 95M D: Alex Winter. *Bill Duke, David O'Hara, Teri Hatcher, Henry Thomas.* Thomas (still a good actor now that's he's grown up) plays an art teacher living in a squalid apartment complex whose landlord is murdered. Under suspicion by a detective (Duke, of course) he grows increasingly sick and delusional. Director Winter (yes, the same guy from *Bill and Ted's Excellent Adventure*) creates a great atmosphere for this grim neo-noir—you can almost feel how hot it is to live in that building. The sound design is especially effective because you can always hear the machinery of the building as if it's a beating heart or a growling stomach. You really can say that the building is a character in the movie without sounding pretentious. —*B. T.*

FLETCH LIVES L: DETECTIVES/FLETCH (1989) 95M D: Michael Ritchie. *Chevy Chase, Hal Holbrook, Julianne Phillips, Cleavon Little, R. Lee Ermey.* Fletch Lives, obviously a sequel to the funnier and more inspired *Fletch* (1985), provides Chase with an opportunity to do what he does best: play the bumbling fool. Not that Irwin Fletcher is a dumb man; he manages to solve a remarkable amount of crimes. But Chase, as Fletch, found a role that seemed tailor-made for him. So here's how it breaks down: Fletch finds out that his aunt has died and left him her Bel Air estate. Of course, once he arrives it is hardly what he had expected. The "estate" is a run-down, poorly tended dump of a mansion, guarded by a local servant. Fletch inhabits a multitude of characters in his attempt to peel away the layers of mystery ultimately surrounding his estate. It seems quite a few people—including the KKK and the local TV reverend—are looking to get their hands on this hot property. As Fletch digs and digs, in his wonderfully bumbling way, he is finally able to see what's going on all around him. But not before a brief stay in prison, of course. —*C. P.*

FOR YOUR EYES ONLY L: SPY/007 (JAMES BOND) (1981) 127M D: John Glen. *Roger Moore, Carole Bouquet, Julian Glover, Lynn-Holly Johnson, Topol.* Apparently producer Alfred Broccoli felt that maybe he went a bit too far with the previous Bond entry, *Moonraker,* and so by adapting a couple of Ian Fleming stories into the film, the emphasis was intended to be more realistic and a return to the "classic" James Bond. Bond is sent to retrieve a nuclear submarine control system that sunk with a British ship. There are fewer gadgets and more emphasis on stunt work, such as Bond being tied to his love interest, Melina (Bouquet), and dragged by motorboat over a coral reef. So much for realism. All the same, this film is far superior to its predecessor and stands out as one of Moore's best Bond films. —*N. J.*

FORCE OF EVIL L: NOIR/FILM NOIR (1948) 80M D: Abraham Polonsky. *John Garfield, Roy Roberts, Thomas Gomez, Marie Windsor, Beatrice Pearson.* Corrupt lawyer Joe Morse (Garfield) becomes the middleman between his mob boss and his estranged brother, Leo (Gomez), a petty numbers banker too virtuous to survive in the depraved underworld he's found himself in. A profoundly cynical film, the unscrupulous brother feeds his greed but keeps everything technically legal, while the ethical brother must work as a criminal to support his family and provide jobs for his friends. Dismissing the gritty realistic chatter attempted by most of its contemporaries, *Force of Evil* endlessly dispenses dialogue that, though perfectly functional to the narrative, seems not merely melodramatic but downright poetic. At an early screening one critic reportedly cried out, "My God, it's written in blank verse." Through the dialogue and some top-notch performances, this gangster film swells to a masterpiece that's as much Shakespearean tragedy as it is film noir. —*C. B.*

FRAILTY L: CRIME/SERIAL KILLERS (2002) 99M D: Bill Paxton. *Bill Paxton, Matthew O'Leary, Matthew McConaughey, Powers Boothe, Jeremy Sumpter.* Marvelously off-balance and under-the-skin creepy from the first few minutes, this twist on the serial killer Gothic puts us in the position of the emotionally tortured son (O'Leary) of a blue-collar joe (Paxton) turned fanatical executioner following the instructions of God through divine whispers and holy visions. It's all told in flashback on a particularly gloomy night by grown son McConaughey to FBI agent Boothe. Paxton, who directs (it's his debut feature) as well as stars, paints it in dungeon gray and all the colors of the night, and keeps the film rooted in a madness that he refuses to reveal as either divine or demonic. But it's his performance that seals the deal: his intent, straight-ahead, blue-collar delivery makes him utterly sincere, and thus terrifying. —*S.A.*

FROM HELL L: CRIME/SERIAL KILLERS (2001) 137M D: Albert Hughes, Allen Hughes. *Johnny Depp, Robbie Coltrane, Ian Holm, Heather Graham, Ian Richardson, Jason Flemyng.* I never would've imagined that the Hughes Brothers would decide to do a period thriller about Jack the Ripper, but I would've figured it would be better than this. Based very loosely on the graphic novel by Alan Moore and Eddie Campbell, this adaptation drops the deranged historical, anatomical, and architectural detail of the book and adds a trite psychic-detective plotline. Depp is good, as always, and at times it's visually gorgeous, but nothing keeps it from being just another goddamn Jack the Ripper movie. The only little touch that makes it stand out is that the hookers are cartoonishly haggish instead of glamorized (well, all except for romantic lead Graham). —*B.T.*

FROM RUSSIA WITH LOVE L: SPY/007 (JAMES BOND) (1963) 115M D: Terence Young. *Sean Connery, Robert Shaw, Pedro Armendáriz, Lotte Lenya, Daniela Bianchi.* The success of *Dr. No* gave producers Albert Broccoli and Harry Saltzman carte blanche to film any of the numerous Fleming novels for their sequel. They quickly struck while the iron was hot, using *From Russia with Love,* a novel known to be one of President Kennedy's favorites and a story that would have been politically poignant considering the state of the Cold War. Connery returns as the unstoppable 007. As it turns out he isn't really up against Russian spies, but rather spies from Fleming's fictitious evil organization, S.P.E.C.T.R.E. The plot to seize a decoding machine takes 007 through a boat chase, a helicopter attack, and a deadly trip on the Orient Express. Yet it is the beautiful Russian spy (Bianchi) that makes this film so intriguing. If *Dr. No* was the film that established the form of 007 movies, *From Russia with Love* most certainly cemented it, creating certain expectations that would have to be met with future films. —*N.J.*

FUN WITH DICK AND JANE L: CRIME/CAPERS (HEISTS) (1977) 100M D: Ted Kotcheff. *Ed McMahon, George Segal, Dick Gautier, Jane Fonda, Alan Miller.* Likable comedy about a bourgeois suburban couple (Segal and Fonda) who resort to armed robbery to maintain their lifestyle after the husband loses his job. It could probably work as a satire with despicable protagonists, but somehow the charisma of Fonda and Segal helps you to forgive the characters' shallowness and root for them to get away with it. McMahon is also very entertaining as Segal's sleazy boss. Director Kotcheff went on to direct *First Blood,* but also *Weekend at Bernie's.* I guess this one is somewhere in between. —*B.T.*

GILDA L: NOIR/FILM NOIR (1946) 110M D: Charles Vidor. *Glenn Ford, Rita Hayworth, Joseph Calleia, George Macready.* The premise should sound familiar to Tarantino fans: cocksure Johnny Farrell (Ford) is assigned the task of keeping an eye on his boss's new wife. In this case, the boss is Ballin Mundson (Macready), a casino owner with fingers in a number of sublegal pies, and the wife is a sultry redhead by the name of Gilda (Hayworth), who just happens to be Johnny's former lover. Naturally Mr. Mundson has not been informed of this past relationship, which makes things a bit tricky for Johnny. Gilda, the dictionary definition of "femme fatale," does her level best to make things even worse, igniting Johnny's jealousy in the process. The genius of the film is its rapid-fire spew of film noir dialogue so slick I couldn't keep a smile off my face for even a minute, a condition last experienced during my first viewing of *Double Indemnity.* —*C.B.*

GIRL HUNTERS, THE L: DETECTIVES/MIKE HAMMER (1963) 97M D: Roy Rowland. *Mickey Spillane, Shirley Eaton, Lloyd Nolan, Hy Gardner, Scott Peters.* Spillane plays his own pulp fiction creation Mike Hammer in this low-budget, black-and-white CinemaScope production, where the soused, self-pitying Hammer pulls himself out of a seven-year alcoholic binge to track down his former secretary, Velda. Spillane has the grace of a trained monkey and the sex appeal of a Bronx cheer. He interacts with smooth, charismatic actors as if he was a street bum at a cocktail party, and in a strange sort of way, it works. Studio veteran Rowland never had much style and his messy little production works best when on location in city streets and dark alleys, the true home of the thuggish PI. The rest is entertaining if lax, written with a prosaic flatness that begs for more pulp passion. —*S.A.*

GOLDFINGER L: SPY/007 (JAMES BOND) (1964) 110M D: Guy Hamilton. *Sean Connery, Gert Fröbe, Honor Blackman, Harold Sakata, Shirley Eaton, Bernard Lee.* The third James Bond film was viewed as the release of a third novel with the same primary characters, a radically different plot, and newer and deadlier antagonists. A gold-obsessed criminal named Goldfinger (Fröbe) gets very tired of humdrum robbery and with his own militia creatively sets his sights on the gold mine of all gold mines, Fort Knox. Bond is equipped by Q (Desmond Llewelyn) with every specialized weapon he needs. As it turns out, he is also equipped with Pussy Galore, a voluptuous female played by Blackman. Most of the hallmarks of what makes a good Bond movie were well established by this film, making the popularity of its sequels almost certain. —N. J.

GRAND SLAM L: CRIME/CAPERS (HEISTS) (1968) 121M D: Giuliano Montaldo. *Edward G. Robinson, Klaus Kinski, Janet Leigh, Robert Hoffmann, Riccardo Cucciolla, Adolfo Celi.* Acclaimed as one of the great heist movies, this rather overlong but meticulously engineered production hits all the right notes. Robinson opens the picture as a gentle schoolteacher who follows his teary retirement ceremony by pitching a daring Rio de Janeiro diamond robbery to a New York mobster, and then drops after putting together his crack team. Kinski snarls through the rest of film as the authoritarian military and nominal leader, and they must have worked hours to make Leigh, a bank secretary with a crucial key, look so severe and plain. The heist itself is launched in the color and chaos of Carnivale, which makes for a lively set piece and a nicely handled contrast to the quiet patience and split-second timing of the robbery. Montaldo (*Sacco and Vanzetti*) directs and Ennio Morricone provides a swinging score. —S. A.

GUNMAN IN THE STREETS L: NOIR/FILM NOIR (1950) 88M D: Frank Tuttle. *Dane Clark, Simone Signoret, Robert Duke.* This gritty little shot-in-Paris film noir, about an American gangster (Clark) on the run from the French cops, is practically a genuine lost-and-found film. Clark is a different kind of American in Paris, a U.S. Army deserter turned black market thug and gang leader who escapes from police custody on the way to court. Signoret is great as the loyal moll who shakes off the police to help her old lover as the cops cut off his escape routes. Tuttle (*This Gun for Hire*) and cinematographer Eugen Schufftan fill this modest production with atmosphere (the scenes shot on the streets of Paris have a real immediacy to them) and rifle it with moments of startling brutality (watch Clark kick a cop on the ground as he escapes in the chaos). This American/French coproduction never received a theatrical release in the United States, but it did play Britain, Canada, and France in a cut edition. The DVD restores all of those cuts. —S. A.

HENRY: PORTRAIT OF A SERIAL KILLER L: CRIME/ SERIAL KILLERS (1990) 86M D: John McNaughton. *Michael Rooker, Tracy Arnold, Tom Towles.* Rooker is very calm and subdued as he puts on the character of Henry Lee Lucas, an intense ex-con who brings his dim-witted roommate Otis on a killing spree.

Arnold plays Otis's sister who is creeped out by his new roommate. The killings start when Henry and Otis pick up a couple of prostitutes. Henry casually kills his and the other prostitute flees. Naturally they have to hunt her down. Like some alluring drug, the killing continues and Otis gets into it so much he starts recording the crimes with a video camera scored from a family they killed off. What this film tries to do is put a human face on the reality of serial killers. As gruesome as it is, it succeeds by interjecting the innocent and honest character played by Arnold who, like the rest of society, doesn't believe it until it's simply too late. —N. J.

HOPSCOTCH L: SPY/SPY (1980) 105M D: Ronald Neame. *Walter Matthau, Glenda Jackson, Ned Beatty, Sam Waterston, Herbert Lom.* Smart, spry, and executed with a deft touch, this lighthearted yet thoroughly grown-up satire of the intelligence community is one of the most underrated films of its era. Had it been made twenty years earlier, Cary Grant would have turned worldly CIA rebel Miles Kendig into a suave jokester with a twinkle in his eye. Matthau, with his hangdog face and prankster's glee, twists the film into a different sort of cynical playfulness that winks at the Cold War shenanigans and corruption of power. This frustrated field man doesn't just threaten to embarrass the agency with a tell-all memoir, he teases them with every chapter and dares them to stop him—it's his last globe-hopping assignment and he loves every second of it. Beatty is perfect as the red-faced, bureaucratic blowhard with less sense than self-preservation, Waterston is Matthau's clearheaded former apprentice whose own sense of humor is tickled by his mentor's chutzpah, and Lom underplays Matthau's Soviet opposite agent. Jackson's snappy, crisp performance as Matthau's lover and coconspirator is unfortunately wasted in an underdeveloped role, but still a treat. —S. A.

IMPACT L: NOIR/FILM NOIR (1949) 111M D: Arthur Lubin. *Brian Donlevy, Ella Raines, Charles Coburn, Helen Walker, Anna May Wong.* Lubin's murder mystery falls in the fringes of film noir—it lacks the shadowy visual world of urban menace and the psychotic edge of desperation—but it's an entertaining picture for all that. Donlevy lacks both charisma and charge as the industrialist whose philandering wife (Walker) plots to kill him, but his thick gruffness plays well off the perky tomboy brightness of small-town widow Raines, the woman who takes in the ragged stranger. Donlevy survives the murder with lingering amnesia, only slowly waking to a shattered life he would rather forget. Lubin's direction is leaden but the film perks up with a boomerang third act. Coburn is sly as a sharp police detective, but he's reined in to an amble when he should be trotting ahead. —S. A.

Film Noir

Film noir is low-down, sexed-up, over the speed limit. It's the juvenile delinquent child of German Expressionist–cinema aesthetics and American pulp fiction, godfathered by post–World War II malaise, timeless moral corruption, and the workings of a capricious fate. It's a night wind blowing down a dark alley, whistling a blues tune that goes like this:

With their five-o'-clock-shadow faces, you can't see them when they stand in the shade, hiding their whiskey-bruised eyes from the sun. But after midnight, when big black sedans float past on rain-silvered streets, you can't miss the night crawlers. Guys who've seen it all and done most of it. Men with pasty faces and lost eyes who made a wrong turn back there somewhere. They've got nowhere to go, but they tremble when one of the black cars slows to a stop, afraid that some voice will offer them a ride.

You don't have time to worry about these men. They're victims of the night, and you're a winner. You've got plans and dreams and your step quickens as you see the neon wink of the bar up ahead. At the threshold you step into a dusky smudge of cigarette smoke and humid, cool jazz. It's dark in here, but you smell her perfume—

continued on page 574

INSOMNIA L: MURDER/MYSTERY/SUSPENSE (2002) 118M D: Christopher Nolan. *Al Pacino, Robin Williams, Hilary Swank, Maura Tierney, Martin Donovan.* Pacino's LA cop Will Dormer arrives gaunt, tired, and sleepy-eyed in a quiet Alaskan village to investigate a murder, and his eyes just get blearier and more hollowed-out as the sleepless nights go by. Nolan's (*Memento*) remake of the icy, sunbright 1997 Norwegian noir of the same name is built on an evocative motif: the twenty-four-hour daylight of an Alaskan summer as the unblinking light of truth, a visual scream that blasts through Dormer's hotel room every sleepless night. Nolan shifts the moral ground from the snowballing moral corruption of the original to shades of guilt and accountability, filtered through the increasingly blurred and hallucinatory perspective of Dormer. Williams is unsettling as the killer who blackmails Dormer with damning evidence and Swank is the hero-worshipping rookie investigator who plays angel to Williams's devil. Don't expect a nail-biter; the moody style creates action scenes more evocative and entrancing than adrenaline pumping, but it features dreamy imagery, a compelling story, and Pacino's best performance in years. —*S.A.*

INTO THE NIGHT L: MURDER/MYSTERY/SUSPENSE (1985) 115M D: John Landis. *Jeff Goldblum, Michelle Pfeiffer, Richard Farnsworth, Irene Papas, Kathryn Harrold.* Goldblum comes home early from work to find his wife knocking boots with someone else. This incident starts a chain of events that spill Goldblum into a world of terrorists, intrigue, and Pfieffer. At times it drags, but it's got some great moments, including when Goldblum, face to face with a terrorist about to do some damage, relates all the mishaps and disasters that have torn apart his life during a single day, culminating with the terrorist turning the gun on himself. While not leaving the cultural impact of *Animal House, Into the Night* (along with *An American Werewolf in London*) shows the potential Landis had as a filmmaker. If he had continued on this path and avoided the particularly nasty incident from *Twilight Zone: The Movie,* Landis might have been a great American director. —*M.H.*

JACOB'S LADDER L: MURDER/MYSTERY/SUSPENSE (1990) 116M D: Adrian Lyne. *Tim Robbins, Pruitt Taylor Vince, Matt Craven, Elizabeth Peña, Danny Aiello, Ving Rhames, Jason Alexander.* Inspired by *Occurrence at Owl Creek Bridge* and rumors of government experimentation with LSD on soldiers during the Vietnam War, this film succeeds where most modern suspense/horror fails, in that it takes itself seriously from start to finish with disturbing flashes of demonlike visions coupled with *X-Files*–esque conspiracy. Jacob (Robbins) is just your ordinary postal worker, who happens to be a Vietnam vet. All is fine until he starts having flashbacks of what really happened in Nam mixed with hallucinations of strange demonic beings. He contacts fellow vets and finds they are having similar experiences; they decide to bring a class action suit against the government to get to the bottom of what happened. After an "accidental" death and other strange events everyone drops out of the suit, leaving Jacob frustrated but still driven to get to the bottom of what's gong

her body's tawny musk and that faraway tropical scent that makes you think of the palm trees and white beaches she's always talking about. And the way her words stroke your imagination and make you smell her sea scent and the surging warm saltwater as you and she stand naked, pressed together in the surf, kissing forever.

You're in the city, where it's cold and winter clouds people's faces, but as you slide into the back booth next to her warm body, that beach doesn't seem so far away.

She loves you, of course. Or you know she will when she gets what she needs. Maybe there's a dull or cruel husband standing between you and her and the tropics. Or some way you can help her work the angles to get a big pile of money. Greenbacks held by a bank or gamblers or fat-cat businessmen: chumps with no flair or heart's desire,

no fire like your love for the woman, no gnawing dream of escape to freedom and renewal.

Of course you'll help her, it'll be easy, just take a few minutes. Just fix it so hubby sleeps forever at the bottom of his swimming pool, or the jewelry store courier never makes it to work, or the insurance company never misses that half a million smackers.

You do it. For her and you, you splash someone's life on the concrete or snatch goods that aren't yours, and it goes down bad, eating at your gut and stealing your sleep. But you've got the woman, and she's worth all the pain and guilt in the world.

She doesn't return your calls, but surely she's just being careful, laying low so you and she can soon lie on those beaches of eternal summer. You figure it's safe to visit her at night and can't understand why

---

on. He gets lost between the past and present, nightmares and reality. The only saving grace is Jacob's friend/chiropractor (Aiello), who is both his psychologist and guardian angel, grounding him in his search for truth. Jacob's journey leads him to a person with a key to his past and ultimately the key to his future. *Jacob's Ladder* keeps you engaged on a journey into a confused and troubled mind seeking redemption. —*B. W.*

KLUTE L: WHODUNITS/WHODUNITS (1971) 114M D: Alan J. Pakula. *Donald Sutherland, Jane Fonda, Charles Cioffi.* Pakula's stark, alienated neo-noir is best remembered for Fonda's Oscar-winning performance as the would-be actress turned high-class call girl stalked by a killer, but the film is actually named for the repressed private detective John Klute (Sutherland). In classic film-noir fashion, Klute is a small-town outsider who delves into the streets and slums of the city looking for a missing person. The trail leads to Bree and her mysterious stalker (Cioffi). The tough-talking, streetwise swinger is a front, a pose to protect the vulnerable woman underneath, and Fonda runs with it, while Sutherland contrasts her with a quiet, thoughtful, restrained performance. The chilly, aloof cinematography by Gordon Willis, shot on location in New York, beautifully enhances the morbid voyeurism and paranoia while brilliantly building the tension. It's a cliché, but they simply don't make thrillers like this anymore. —*S. A.*

LADY IN WHITE, THE L: MURDER/MYSTERY/SUSPENSE (1988) 92M D: Frank LaLoggia. *Len Cariou, Lukas Haas, Katherine Helmond, Alex Rocco.* A charming, creepy little film about a young boy in 1962 who gets locked in the supposedly haunted school cloakroom on Halloween. The victim of a schoolyard prank, Frankie Scarlatti (Haas) meets the ghost of a young girl and witnesses the ghostly reenactment of the day she was strangled in that very closet ten years earlier. If that were not frightening enough, suddenly someone starts stalking and trying to kill Frankie himself. With the little girl's ghost begging for his help, Frankie finds himself compelled to unravel the mystery of her murder, leading him to an old house where the mysterious Lady in White lives. As he slowly begins to learn the truth, he becomes aware that the murderer might in fact be someone very close to him. With a stylized visual look and a delightfully sinister air, this film is not too frightening, which is good for us scaredy-cats. —*M. N.*

LEAVE HER TO HEAVEN L: NOIR/FILM NOIR (1946) 110M D: John M. Stahl. *Gene Tierney, Mary Philips, Cornel Wilde, Jeanne Crain, Vincent Price.* This splashy, Technicolor film noir melodrama features Tierney at her nastiest as she lays waste to everything in her path, taking no prisoners. Wilde is perfect as the poor schmuck who falls for her, and Price is dead-on as her ex who knows better. —*M. S.*

there's some mousy girl living in her apartment. Your mind races—there's got to be a reason. She must've gotten scared and is hiding just around the corner. She'll come to you, she will. She'll bring the money and you'll fly and fly into the West.

But she's gone. And now you're the sorriest fool who ever staggered down these shadowed streets, whiskey stains on your shirt, searching women's faces for a glimmer of tropical light.

Or maybe she comes to your shabby room and you two count the money and stand and kiss like you will in paradise, but a glint of something catches your eye and you look down to see the little nickel-plated pistol in her hand pump fire into your belly. Or her husband is tougher than he looks and when you try to force him into the pool and hold him under, he wrestles you

off-balance and you fall sideways, smashing your skull on the pool's edge and slipping under water that's warm as the tropics, beginning your big, big sleep in a spreading circle of red.

And you dream you're watching one of those old movies about night and the city, where men with desolation-row faces walk rainy streets and dream of a lone woman waiting by a palm tree.

Fifteen big ones: *The Maltese Falcon* (1941), *This Gun for Hire* (1942), *Double Indemnity* (1944), *Murder, My Sweet* (1944), *Detour* (1946), *The Woman in the Window* (1944), *The Big Sleep* (1946), *The Killers* (1946), *Kiss of Death* (1947), *Out of the Past* (1947), *DOA* (1949), *Gun Crazy* (1949), *On Dangerous Ground* (1951), *The Big Heat* (1953), and *Kiss Me Deadly* (1955).

—*Greg Olson*

LIVE AND LET DIE L: SPY/007 (JAMES BOND) (1973) 121M D: Guy Hamilton. *Roger Moore, Jane Seymour, Yaphet Kotto, Geoffrey Holder, Clifton James.* Once Sean Connery stepped aside, the producers needed a veritable saint to fill his shoes. Moore was their best bet, since he starred in the British series *The Saint.* In case Moore's charisma wasn't enough, the producers went out of their way to get Paul McCartney to sing the title song. In this film, James Bond goes down to Louisiana to take on the crazed Dr. Kanaga (Kotto), who wants to take over the world with voodoo and a particular drug that turns people into addicts. The love interest is the antagonist's underling, Solitaire (Seymour). Over time Bond is able to seduce her, thereby allowing him to work his way into the criminal circuit. A lot has been made over the differences between Moore and Connery, but considering that each made seven films in the series, most of which were blockbusters, the two should really be viewed for their own merits. —*N. J.*

LIVING DAYLIGHTS, THE L: SPY/007 (JAMES BOND) (1987) 130M D: John Glen. *Timothy Dalton, Maryam d'Abo Jeroen Krabbé, Art Malik, John Rhys-Davies, Joe Don Baker.* I don't know if I honestly think that Dalton was the best Bond, but I do know that when I saw this film I was both impressed and delighted. Perhaps it was because after the travesty that was Roger Moore, Dalton was a breath of fresh air. Perhaps, having read the books voraciously, I recognized the edgy and human performance of Dalton, which was more true to Ian Fleming's Bond than Connery's cold and

sardonic portrayal. In the end, I will say this for *The Living Daylights*: the plot is surprisingly interesting, layered, and complex, and there is a good balance between intelligence, abilities, and gadgets. I can't say it's the best Bond film, but it is definitely one of the good ones and worth seeing if you haven't already. —*M. N.*

LOCK, STOCK AND TWO SMOKING BARRELS L: CRIME/CAPERS (HEISTS) (1998) 105M D: Guy Ritchie. *Jason Flemyng, Dexter Fletcher, Nick Moran, Jason Statham, Steven Mackintosh, Vinnie Jones.* Four young British guys lose £500,000 in a card game to a guy called Harry the Hatchet, and they have a week to pay it off. Their attempts to get the money in time do not go particularly well, and they end up in a complex war between two gangs, some pot dealers, and the Hatchet's henchmen. This is a kinetic, stylized crime movie full of crazy coincidences, misunderstandings, and colorful characters like Big Chris (former soccer star Jones), a brutal enforcer who brings his young son Little Chris with him on the job. It's so beautifully shot and cartoonishly plotted that it almost feels like what would happen if Jean-Pierre Jeunet tried to make a pulpy crime movie. In the tradition of *Pulp Fiction,* it inspired a slew of painfully bad imitators. —*B. T.*

LOOKING GLASS WAR, THE L: SPY/SPY (1969) 107M D: Frank Pierson. *Christopher Jones, Susan George, Anthony Hopkins, Paul Rogers, Ralph Richardson, Pia Degermark.* In this adaptation of John le Carré's Cold War thriller, a Polish defector (Jones) is promised political asylum in

England, but first he has to go back behind the Iron Curtain to confirm the existence of a suspected missile. Or so he's told, as they fashion him into a brutal agent able to kill his way to his target. Typical of le Carré's jaundiced view of international espionage and political gamesmanship, surfaces aren't merely deceiving, they are utterly false fronts for devious endgames where the human factor is the most expendable one. Richardson is the chess master moving the pieces around with cold calculation, Degermark the German contact with whom he falls in love, and Hopkins (in one of his earliest film roles) is a dedicated agent who still clings to the belief that he's doing some good. It's not a belief that lasts long in this game. —*S. A.*

MAN WITH THE GOLDEN GUN L: SPY/007 (JAMES BOND) (1974) 123M D: Guy Hamilton. *Roger Moore, Christopher Lee, Britt Ekland, Maud Adams, Herve Villechaize, Lois Maxwell.* Moore's second James Bond film features Lee as the antagonist Francisco Scaramanga, an assassin who prefers to murder people with his precious gold gun. This fantastically rich villain steals the Solex Agitator, an apparatus capable of harnessing the power of the sun. His assistant is Nick Nack, played by Villechaize, famous for his role as Tattoo on *Fantasy Island.* There are also fantastic stunts, including a unique 360-degree spiral jump off an AMC Hornet X. This was the last Bond film Harry Saltzman produced with Albert Broccoli, ending a truly legendary thirteen-year collaboration. —*N. J.*

MEMENTO L: MURDER/MYSTERY/SUSPENSE (2000) 113M D: Christopher Nolan. *Guy Pearce, Carrie-Anne Moss, Joe Pantoliano.* "You see, I have this condition...." *LA Confidential*'s Pearce is Leonard, a detective who has no short-term memory and relies on notes he tattoos on his body to find his wife's killer. In this method, of course, lies madness, but it's a mind-bending ride to the end, or rather, to the beginning. Nolan's ingenious thriller is wonderfully dark and wickedly clever: the film starts at the end of the story and works back in stair-step fashion, throwing us into every scene blind and trying to figure where we are, just like Leonard. We, however, can see the brewing tragedy as we fit the pieces together. The ground shifts beneath this postmodern film noir in every jump, but more affecting is the sense of loss, loneliness, and disconnection behind Leonard's makeshift realities. —*S. A.*

MISTER SCARFACE L: CRIME/GANGS & GANGSTAS (1976) 86M D: Fernando Di Leo. *Jack Palance, Harry Baer, Al Cliver, Enzo Pulcrano, Edmund Purdom, Gisella Hahn.* An Italian Mafia flick inspired by *The Godfather* but with more violence, a dune buggy, and badly dubbed voices. A kid sees his old man get shot by a mean gangster (Palance). He grows up to be a low-level hood in the protection business. He hooks up with a South American

guy with a red dune buggy, and a sort of funny retired Mafioso (Vittorio Caprioli). They decide to rip off their boss and flee the country, but then revenge becomes even more of a motivation when Palance becomes involved. There's lots of action (including some half-assed martial arts and a showdown in a meatpacking factory) and laughable dialogue. *Mr. Scarface* is not bad-good like the jaw-dropping *The Executioner* and it's far from Coppola's classy gangster epic, but it does feature plenty of cheap laughs, some interesting Italian locations, and lots of crazy '70s threads. —*S. H.*

MONEY KINGS L: CRIME/GANGS & GANGSTAS (1999) 96M D: Graham Theakston. *Colm Meaney, Lauren Holly, Freddie Prinze Jr., Peter Falk, Timothy Hutton.* Yeah, I know it looks like just another straight-to-video action flick, but it's not. Really. This is a gritty story of life on the streets in Boston, oozing with authentic atmosphere. Italian mobsters (Prinze) clash with Irish gangsters (Falk) and the lives of the "little" people (Holly and Hutton) are crushed in between with the inheritability of a Greek tragedy. Serious without being bleak, this one's definitely worth a look. —*S. F.*

MOONRAKER L: SPY/007 (JAMES BOND) (1979) 136M D: Lewis Gilbert. *Roger Moore, Bernard Lee, Micheal Lonsdale, Lois Chiles.* Influenced by the success of *Star Wars,* producer Albert Broccoli backtracked on his promise to make *For Your Eyes Only* after *The Spy Who Loved Me,* and instead got to work on this film. The result is what many consider to be the end of the age of great James Bond films and the beginning of insanely improbable stories done thoroughly tongue in cheek in order to have some reason to show off stunts and special effects. Case in point: Lonsdale plays Drax, a man bent on destroying the world. With Chiles as a CIA agent providing the necessary love interest, Bond is propelled across the world trying to save humankind and at one point even gets kidnapped by Amazon women. It's no wonder why Mike Myers (or anyone else for that matter) would spoof such a series once it had devolved to this. —*N. J.*

MURDER BY DECREE L: DETECTIVES/SHERLOCK HOLMES (1979) 120M D: Bob Clark. *Donald Sutherland, Genevieve Bujold, James Mason, Christopher Plummer, David Hemmings.* Played with good humor and warmth by Plummer and ably abetted by Mason as his loyal Watson, Holmes is drafted by a citizen's committee to stop the Ripper, clashing with Scotland Yard as he uncovers a conspiracy that leads to the top levels of Britain's government. This fiction borrows only the characters from Doyle, yet Plummer's Holmes and Mason's Watson are truer to the author's original characterizations than previous cinematic incarnations. Intelligently written, modestly directed by Clark (his best work in a maddeningly inconsistent career that spans from *A Christmas*

Story to *Porkys, Rhinestone,* and *Baby Geniuses*), and crisply performed by a marvelous cast that includes an intense, tortured turn by Sutherland as a psychic and Bujold as a hysterical inmate driven mad in an asylum. This is one of the best Holmes movies ever. —*S. A.*

NEW BEST FRIEND L: MURDER/MYSTERY/SUSPENSE (1999) 90M D: Zoe Clarke-Williams. *Mia Kirshner, Meredith Monroe, Dominique Swain, Rachel True, Taye Diggs.* Dumped into theaters after years on the shelf and buried in an avalanche of damning reviews, this slick, sometimes self-consciously arch college-clique thriller was never given a chance, which is a shame. This story of class envy, social acceptance, and the seduction of privilege in the young adult world is both stylish and smart. The familiar elements are all there: haughty, hedonistic rich kids (led by ice-princess ringleader Monroe), the local working-class girl (doe-eyed innocent Kirshner) pulled into their fold, booze-fueled parties rippling with sex and drugs, and the tensions created when the outsider distills the rich-bitch rules so well she becomes the new party-girl diva. Less familiar is the sensitivity of director Clarke-Williams, who digs beyond the usual portrayals of good kids and bad seeds to reveal a more ambivalent set of characters and motivations. It opens with Kirshner in a drug-induced coma and works back as earnest young sheriff (Diggs) pieces her story together in puzzle-piece flashbacks, shaking up a complacent Ivy League school with his discoveries. Refreshingly free of glib moralizing, this is a breath of fresh air in a stale genre. —*S. A.*

NEW KIDS, THE L: CRIME/JUVENILE DELINQUENTS (1985) 90M D: Sean S. Cunningham. *Lori Loughlin, James Spader, Shannon Presby, John Philbin.* Two citified youths relocate to a Florida suburb where they are immediately targeted by a swampland delinquent gang led by Dutra (played by an inexplicably albino-esque Spader). The relentless harassment from the wayward teens grows increasingly ugly as the blood starts spilling. Drugs, assault, foaming attack dogs, and arson are just tools of the trade for Dutra and his criminal cronies. See a young Eric Stoltz get brutalized by the venomous horde! Spader's sneering, screaming performance is so villainously over the top that he should have won some kind of major award, but the real star here is the bespectacled young hood who looks like a giant ten-year-old and gets chewed to death in his briefs. Plus, this may be the best portrayal you'll ever see of people being murdered with carnival rides. Totally insignificant and unoriginal, *The New Kids* is also persistently entertaining and comes highly recommended. Also marketed as *Striking Back.* —*Z. C.*

NIGHT OF THE HUNTER, THE L: NOIR/FILM NOIR (1955) 93M D: Charles Laughton. *Robert Mitchum, Shelley Winters, Lillian Gish, Peter Graves, Billy Chapin, Evelyn Varden.* A brilliant mix of German expressionism, American film noir, Grimm fairy tale, and Southern Gothic sensibilities, *Night of the Hunter* is the story of two young children relentlessly pursued by the diabolical Rev. Harry Powell, played brilliantly by the always magnificent Mitchum. With the words LOVE and HATE tattooed across his fists, he roams across the South bringing God's word wherever he goes and also bringing evil and cunning. After learning of a buried treasure from the children's imprisoned and dying father, the Reverend tries to get the money for himself, but only the children know where it is. With jaw-droppingly astounding cinematography and a haunting, beautiful score, one of *Night's* most unique aspects is the highly stylized performances which lend it an air of imagination, as if everything is being viewed from the eyes of the children. As they are forced to run and make their way across the country, the film excellently communicates the overwhelming fear only children can experience. *Night of the Hunter* is a simple children's tale but also a fantastically creepy, beautiful, magical tale about good and evil and how the two can be deceiving. —*T. S.*

NINTH CONFIGURATION, THE L: MURDER/MYSTERY/SUSPENSE (1979) 115M D: William Peter Blatty. *Stacy Keach, Ed Flanders, Neville Brand, Scott Wilson, Moses Gunn, Jason Miller, Robert Loggia.* Blatty (who wrote *The Exorcist*) wrote and directed this film about a psychiatrist who goes to work at a mental asylum for veterans. Most of the patients suffer psychological effects from the Vietnam War. Keach plays the psychiatrist who deals with each of them on a one-on-one basis, proving himself to be kind, patient, and deep as the topics discussed get rather existential. But he himself suffers from some pretty serious nightmares that are complicated and existential. He thinks about the ninth configuration of the protein molecule necessary to begin life on the planet and the astronomical odds that it could form from any random process. He concludes that this nearly impossible happenstance is far more impressive than simply believing in God. The curious plot twists wildly and by the end you wonder who is really the psychiatrist and who is really the patient. —*N. J.*

NORMAL LIFE L: MURDER/MYSTERY/SUSPENSE (1996) 101M D: John McNaughton. *Luke Perry, Ashley Judd, Bruce Young, Jim True.* McNaughton has never really lived up to the potential shown by his debut, *Henry: Portrait of a Serial Killer,* but his feel for true crime grit is put to good use in this above-average made-for-cable thriller. Perry is a cop who decides to rob banks with the help of his deeply troubled girlfriend, Judd. The depressing tone of the movie is best summed up by the scene in which Judd humiliates Perry by showing up to a funeral late, obviously high and wearing roller blades. —*B. T.*

OCTOPUSSY L: SPY/007 (JAMES BOND) (1983) 141M D: John Glen. *Roger Moore, Maud Adams, Desmond Llewelyn, Louis Jourdan, Kabir Bedi. Octopussy* is in many ways the final result of 007's growing pains. The producers ran out of Ian Fleming books, titles, and anything else that could be attributed to Fleming, thus *Octopussy* was a market-driven product with very little story. Yet by this time the British agent had grown out of story and was kept alive solely by gadgets, stunts, female interests, and something pronounced in this film—stunning locations. Bond is dispatched to stop a mad Soviet general from starting nuclear war. The plot stops there. Enter resplendent scenery in the form of Udaipur, India. Enter also a bevy of female interests, most notably Octopussy (clearly an inside reference to *Goldfinger*'s Pussy Galore). —*N. J.*

ON HER MAJESTY'S SECRET SERVICE L: SPY/007 (JAMES BOND) (1969) 144M D: Peter R. Hunt. *George Lazenby, Diana Rigg, Telly Savalas, Gabriele Ferzetti, Ilse Steppat, Lois Maxwell.* This was the most belittled of the Bond films, yet it is one of my favorites. It had three strikes against it: a new actor playing the part of Bond, a true love story, and a tragically sad ending. No one wanted a new Bond after Connery and poor Lazenby just didn't have a chance. What was worse, no one wanted a Bond that was going to break the rules of Bond-dom by falling in love, losing, showing emotion, and crying. Bond? Lose? Never!! But he does, and perhaps that is what endears the film to me—it makes Bond more human and tangible. There are other flaws—Savalas as Blofeld for one. Lazenby acting like a foppish genealogist and wearing a goofy-looking kilt is another. But the music is fantastic, the chase scene skiing down the mountain at night is thrilling, and overall the film does hold together. Alas, the combination of so many changes in the genre and a new actor killed the film before anyone got the chance to see it. —*M. N.*

OUR MAN FLINT L: SPY/SPY (1965) 108M D: Daniel Mann. *James Coburn, Lee J. Cobb, Gila Golan, Edward Muhare.* Coburn is Derek Flint—Renaissance man, sensitive new age playboy, and freelance secret agent—in this most famous of James Bond parodies. Called upon by ZOWIE (a sort of covert UN) to save the world, the notorious maverick and nonchalant genius, armed with only a gadget-filled cigarette lighter with eighty-two functions ("Eighty-three if you want to light a cigarette"), tracks down the secret organization that holds the world hostage with its weather-control device. Of course there are stunning women, a curmudgeon of a boss (Cobb), international locations, and a spectacular finale. Though hampered by an obviously restricted budget and helmed by the game but decidedly unhip Mann, it's a swinging spy spoof with great decor, an incoherent plot full of crazy twists, and a meaty performance by Coburn, whose blinding grin and matter-of-fact authority give the spoof a strong, manly center. These groovy details are the primary inspiration for *Austin Powers*. —*S. A.*

PARADISE LOST: THE CHILD MURDERS AT ROBIN HOOD HILLS L: CRIME/TRUE CRIME (1996) 150M D: Bruce Sinofsky, Joe Berlinger. *Damien Wayne Echols, Jessie Miskelly, Jason Baldwin.* This HBO documentary chronicling the trial of three teenagers arrested for the murder of three young children is a terrifying piece of cinema. The teens were arrested on suspicion and prosecuted with circumstantial evidence, and the film illustrates the frightening ignorance and injustice of the American legal system. The key piece of evidence is a confession, later rescinded, obtained from a retarded teenager after he spent a prolonged period of time in questioning with police where no recording equipment was allowed. Commendably, the documentary maintains an absolutely neutral stance in what is clearly a witch hunt. This film and its sequel have made the West Memphis Three into a national cause for concern, drawing support from numerous celebrities and charity funds. However, what's more terrifying than the documented plight of these teens and their damaged community is the ever present possibility of other cases, equally outrageous, that have quietly slipped through the cracks. —*T. S.*

PARADISE LOST 2: REVELATIONS L: CRIME/TRUE CRIME (2000) 130M D: Bruce Sinofsky, Joe Berlinger. *Jason Baldwin, John Mark Byers, Damien Wayne Echols, Jessie Miskelly.* The sequel to the 1996 documentary about child murders in West Memphis, Arkansas, *Revelations* follows the aftermath of the trial, the convicted teenagers' attempts to get a retrial, and, most eerily, the life of John Mark Byers, the father of one of the murdered boys. Less objective than the first film, the sequel is equally as shocking in its portrayal of the miasmic situation in which no one can remain neutral, and anger and pain run rampant on all sides. The future of the accused teenagers, one currently on death row, is constantly in the balance as lawyers, investigators, and the filmmakers uncover shocking evidence that points to their innocence. Juxtaposed with the frightening and suspicious behavior of Byers, whom many suspect is guilty of the crime, the documentary becomes an alarming look at the continuing horrors of one of the most infamous contemporary murder trials. Infamous not because of tabloid-selling superficialities but because of how it underscores the injustices of the American system and the fear and biases of those involved. —*T. S.*

PHONE BOOTH L: MURDER/MYSTERY/SUSPENSE (2002) 81M D: Joel Schumacher. *Kiefer Sutherland, Colin Farrell, Forest Whitaker, Radha Mitchell, Katie Holmes.* Farrell reaches deep within to find his inner sleazebag to play a slimy publicist whose cell phone is his office. He lies, connives, and wheedles his days away until he steps into the last old-fashioned standing phone booth in New York City and ends up on the line with a sniper. Schumacher jazzes up and dumbs down Larry Cohen's high-concept script, which really should have been a jagged low-budget piece rather than a slick big-budget movie. It's weirdly effective nonetheless as it keeps the audience trapped on the same cordoned-off street scene as Farrell begs for his life with the caller, the cops, and loved ones who have gathered with the crowd, but it takes an incomprehensible turn when his "crime" is revealed. You realize that this rifle-toting avenging angel in New York City is setting his sights awfully low on the scale of sinners, and wonder why Schumacher plays it so deadly seriously. —*S. A.*

POSTMAN ALWAYS RINGS TWICE, THE L: NOIR/FILM NOIR (1946) 103M D: Tay Garnett. *John Garfield, Lana Turner, Leon Ames, Cecil Kellaway, Hume Cronyn.* Turner is a vision in white in her most famous role as the femme fatale in the original film version of James M. Cain's sultry crime classic. The restless platinum blonde is luminous as she insolently steps into the film and raises the temperature of the room when she meets the scrappy, swaggering Garfield. It's glossier looking than most films noir of the period and, as it's 1946, Garnett can do little more than suggest the adulterous shenanigans these two are up to behind her cuckolded husband's back, but their libidinous desires burn up the screen nonetheless and their wicked plot to do the lug in is charged with excitement and guilt. Garfield is great as the smart-talking but sincere loner whose lust turns to love, and Turner radiates repressed sexuality and uncontrollable passion that finds salvation in Garfield. A chilly, conniving Cronyn is their heartless, calculating lawyer, who only increases our sympathy for the murderous couple. —*S. A.*

PRIME SUSPECT 1 L: WHODUNITS/WHODUNITS (1991) 207M D: Christopher Menaul. *Helen Mirren, Tom Bell, John Benfield, John Bowe, Zoë Wanamaker.* Mirren is DCI Jane Tennyson, a tough, capable investigator battling the sexist old boys' network of the London police department who is finally handed her first case and finds her fellow officers (notably a sneering, sleazy Bell, the original investigator) working against her. As they obscure evidence and manipulate the investigation, the murders continue and Tennyson finds she's pursuing a serial killer. The vivid four-hour mystery scripted by Lynda La Plante roils with dark mystery, sharp character study, gritty street drama, and smart insights to sexual and racial relations in the workplace, and launched

a long-running series of sequels that reinvigorated Mirren's career. Tom Wilkinson and Ralph Fiennes appear in small roles. —*S. A.*

RED ROCK WEST L: MURDER/MYSTERY/SUSPENSE (1992) 98M D: John Dahl. *Nicolas Cage, Lara Flynn Boyle, J. T. Walsh, Dennis Hopper, Dwight Yoakam.* Cage plays a drifter living out of his car who comes into the town of Red Rock looking for work. Asking bar-owner Walsh about a job, he is mistaken for "Lyle from Dallas" and plays along out of desperation. The job, of course, turns out to be killing Walsh's wife (Boyle). What ensues is a masterfully escalating series of mistakes and coincidences that cause Cage to sink deeper and deeper with every move he makes. The "Welcome to Red Rock" sign is a recurring image reminding us that Cage's luck is so bad he keeps almost but not quite leaving town. It's hard to decide which villain is more menacing between Walsh, Hopper, and Yoakam. Possibly the best neo-noir not directed by the Coen brothers. Director Dahl got even more acclaim for *The Last Seduction,* but has failed to capture this level of quality since. —*B. T.*

REMO WILLIAMS: THE ADVENTURE BEGINS L: SPY/ SPY (1985) 121M D: Guy Hamilton. *Fred Ward, Kate Mulgrew, Wilford Brimley, Joel Grey, J. A. Preston.* The adventure begins, and ends, with this movie. James Bond veteran Hamilton was drafted to launch this screen debut of the character created by Richard Sapir and Warren Murphy in the modern paperback adventure series *The Destroyer,* but he had lost his knack for big set pieces and slick action by this point in his career. Ward is fine as the tough New York cop pronounced dead and "resurrected" to serve as the muscle in a covert government organization, but he's a bulky, clumsy boy in a part that calls for a convincing kung fu fighter, and Grey's professionalism never overcomes his Charlie Chan smart-ass fortune cookie lines (or his Asian makeup) as the Korean martial arts master. Awkward and silly, it's the last gasp of B-movie action before *Lethal Weapon* slickness put low-budget action cinema out of business. Yet it still has its own small following. —*S. A.*

The most treasured of the action movies that I used to see with my dad in the military base theater as a kid. Ward is Remo Williams, the ultimate schmo turned hero. Made apprentice to Chiun (Grey), Remo becomes the ultimate unarmed fighting machine as he learns to dodge bullets and run over liquid cement. A totally catchy orchestral theme only adds to the excitement. Go ahead, I dare you not to have fun with this one. However, on one down note, MGM, which has been pretty good in the past, made the knuckleheaded choice to release this DVD full-frame instead of widescreen. —*M. H.*

ROAD HOUSE L: NOIR/FILM NOIR (1948) 95M D: Jean Negulesco. *Ida Lupino, Cornell Wilde, Celeste Holm, Richard Widmark*. Although it usually slips through the cracks when it comes to film noir recommendations, this is an excellent example of the style and genre before it became a cliché. All the usual ingredients are here, including the fatal love triangle and the dark/light imagery-as-character that is so well associated with the true film noir genre. At a road house that has both a lounge and a bowling alley, the owner, Jefty (Widmark), hires a tough-as-nails singer, Lily (Lupino), for the bar against the advice of his manager, Pete (Wilde). Jefty soon falls for this newest dame, though Lily finds herself falling for Pete, who uneasily avoids her advances. When Pete finally succumbs to her moves, Jefty becomes enraged with jealousy and plans his revenge against the lovebirds. Unknown to most is that this is perhaps the perfect representation of the subgenre "bowling noir," and is a testament to the mystical power the lanes hold. —*R. M.*

ROMEO IS BLEEDING L: MURDER/MYSTERY/SUSPENSE (1993) 108M D: Peter Medak. *Gary Oldman, Lena Olin, Roy Scheider, Annabella Sciorra, Juliette Lewis*. Violent and flamboyant, *Romeo Is Bleeding* manages to inject the sometimes moribund film noir genre with some liveliness. A corrupt cop (Oldman) narrates his tragic tale, which also includes a mob boss (Scheider) and a sinister female killer (Olin). The film doesn't shoot for the moon, but instead is satisfied to be fast moving, slickly made, and well acted. The cast is filled with actors and actresses happy to chew the scenery, but none is as hungry as Olin. Her character, who attempts to choke one victim between her thighs (!), is as vibrant as any villain in recent years; listen for her creepy, echoing laugh in her final scene. —*T. P.*

Although Olin has a few memorably over-the-top scenes, I think this film falls victim to that old Hollywood myth that it is OK to cast Oldman in a role that is supposed to be sympathetic. His macho asshole character isn't even good at being a corrupt cop—he thinks with his dick too much to get away with anything—so we need an actor of extraordinary charisma to make us care what happens to him. Instead we have Oldman, the brilliant portrayer of villains and slimeballs. I would've liked to see this asshole get his comeuppance in the opening scene. —*B. T.*

RUNNING TIME L: CRIME/CAPERS (HEISTS) (1997) 69M D: Josh Becker. *Gordon Jennison, Jeremy Roberts, Anita Barone, Stan Davis, Bruce Campbell*. Campbell, fresh out of prison, gets picked up by his old high school friend (Roberts) and they head straight for their next bank robbery. Shot with handheld cameras and carefully planned to look like one continuous shot, it has a raw, immediate feel that makes it much better than most of Campbell's

non–*Evil Dead* projects. It does suffer from an unconvincing love story and preoccupation with what happened to the characters in high school, and Becker is an ass for claiming that it's better than *Rope*, but you can't go too wrong with the combination of Campbell, armed robbery, and the real-time gimmick. —*B. T.*

SADIST, THE L: CRIME/JUVENILE DELINQUENTS (1963) 95M D: James Landis. *Marilyn Manning, Helen Hovey, Richard Alden, Arch Hall Jr*. Hall was one of the most ridiculous prefabricated teen idols and the majority of his movies are terrible, but not *The Sadist*. It's a tight, tense, and uncompromising thriller about three schoolteachers on the way to a Dodgers game who are terrorized by Hall and his mute girlfriend (Manning, who starred with Hall in the god awful *Eegah!*). The sniveling Hall is effectively threatening and scary and the script is consistently edgy and brutal, providing plenty of plot twists and unexpected events. The real star of this film is Vilmos Zsigmond's incredible photography. Nearly every beautiful black-and-white image is impeccably composed and shot and it's no wonder he moved on to bigger things. *The Sadist* is one of many films based on the Starkweather-Fugate murder spree (also the basis for Terrence Malick's *Badlands*). —*S. H.*

SECRET AGENT (AKA DANGER MAN) L: SPY/SPY TELEVISION (1964) 2820M D: Various. *Patrick McGoohan, Peter Madden*. Before McGoohan was *The Prisoner*, he was John Drake, the maverick agent of Britain's top-secret M9 security force. Much like the U.S. series *The Man from U.N.C.L.E.*, this cool, clever black-and-white show is a Cold War spy series built of elaborate espionage shell games and diplomatic chicanery, and McGoohan is the ingenious con man behind the bluffs and feints. The DVDs feature the original British version of the series, with its harpsicord theme and *Danger Man* title, but organizes them according to the order of the American broadcasts. All forty-seven episodes of the hour-long format (superior to the first season of less skeptical thirty-minute shows) are available on thirteen DVD volumes, including the only two episodes made in color ("Koroshi" and "Shinda Shima," which were combined and turned into the TV movie *Koroshi*). —*S. A.*

SEXY BEAST L: CRIME/CAPERS (HEISTS) (2000) 88M D: Jonathan Glazer. *Cavan Kendall, Amanda Redman, Ian McShane, Ray Winstone, Ben Kingsley*. Kingsley, the man who was Gandhi, Simon Wiesenthal, and Moses, is almost unrecognizable as the bald, wiry London gangster in this fierce yet refreshingly understated entry to the recent spate of British gangster films. He's a tensed-up ball of anger with a 100-yard stare and an ego ready to blow at any moment, and he's come to the Spanish desert to find fleshy British gangster Winstone and take him back to London for one last job. Glazer directs his first film with confidence and leanness. He delivers the edgy explosions of cold-blooded violence and the obligatory yet ingeniously inventive high-concept heist without the self-satisfied showboating that pervades too many crime capers, and turns the tension of social gatherings invaded by Kingsley into the real drama of the film. Winstone is genuinely moving as the devoted husband willing to sacrifice his soul to save his wife and Kingsley is amazing as the blunt, crude thug unleashed. —S. A.

SHACK OUT ON 101 L: NOIR/FILM NOIR (1955) 80M D: Edward Dein.
Frank Lovejoy, Terry Moore, Whit Bissell, Keenan Wynn, Lee Marvin. A Cold War, Red Scare noir about spies, double agents, sexy waitresses, and greasy spoons. Down the road from a government lab is a seaside diner that is a hotbed of activity for Commies and secret agents. Wynn is good as the tough-talking boss, Moore (Mighty Joe Young and also known for dating Howard Hughes) is the sexy waitress everyone wants to shag, and Lovejoy is a mysterious restaurant patron. Marvin steals the show as "Slob," the restaurant's short-order cook. He's got the best lines and is alternately scary and funny. A reasonably tense little thriller, Shack Out on 101 takes place almost entirely on one small set and features lots of "patriotic" pro-American rhetoric. —S. H.

SNATCH L: CRIME/CAPERS (HEISTS) (2000) 102M D: Guy Ritchie.
Benicio del Toro, Brad Pitt, Jason Statham, Dennis Farina, Vinnie Jones. Director Ritchie continues in the vein of Lock, Stock and Two Smoking Barrels with a story about three groups of lowlifes all searching for the same stolen diamond. There's a lot of great imagery, and some amusing characters (especially Pitt as an incomprehensible boxer), but the story and characters are completely muddled. With all kinds of camera trickery but little in the way of narrative drive, it feels more like a collection of music videos than a movie. Lock, Stock was a good example of style successfully trumping substance, but Snatch is like the empty remake of that already hollow movie. —B. T.

SNEAKERS L: CRIME/CAPERS (HEISTS) (1992) 125M D: Phil Alden Robinson.
Sidney Poitier, Ben Kingsley, Dan Aykroyd, Robert Redford, Mary McDonnell, David Strathairn, River Phoenix. Keeping the technology down to earth makes this "hackers" film all the more great, as anyone with a bit of tech knowledge will realize that the characters could actually do what they do in the film. A small organization that is hired to break into supposedly unbreakable security systems is blackmailed into retrieving the ultimate code breaker by the U.S. government. But soon the band of rogues, led by Bishop (Redford), realizes that they could be in the middle of an international controversy. This is pure intrigue excitement at its best, which uses the then post–Cold War political strain to help fuel the unease of the situation. Each character is well-thought-out and has a place, skill, and quirk that help solidify the unification of the team. The acting is top-notch, with a host of actors that are a treat to watch in every scene. —R. M.

SOMEONE BEHIND THE DOOR L: MURDER/MYSTERY/SUSPENSE (1971) 92M D: Nicolas Gessner.
Charles Bronson, Jill Ireland, Anthony Perkins, Henri Garcin. If you are masochistic enough to be excited about a movie starring Bronson and Perkins then you are probably too stubborn to heed my warnings of impending boredom. Perkins is a brilliant neurosurgeon with a cheating wife (Ireland) and Bronson is a mysterious amnesiac who may be the solution to the doctor's marital problems. Perkins manipulates Bronson's fractured mental state hoping to get Ireland's lover killed. Like other memory thrillers (Memento, Spellbound) most of the suspense derives from what we know and what our forgetful protagonist doesn't know. Unfortunately most of this sleep-inducing film consists of tedious conversations between our turtleneck-wearing leads. Made before Bronson's Death Wish breakthrough, Someone is light on asskicking and tough talk as Chuck spends most of the film stumbling around with a confused look on his face. —S. H.

SORRY, WRONG NUMBER L: NOIR/FILM NOIR (1948) 88M D: Anatole Litvak.
Barbara Stanwyck, Burt Lancaster, Wendell Corey, Harold Vermilyea, William Conrad, Ed Begley Sr. Bedridden heiress Stanwyck overhears what she believes are two men plotting murder and spends the night trying to track down the source, only to discover that she is the target. Stanwyck won an Oscar for her performance as the terrified woman who becomes more and more hysterical as she tries to reach help with her only connection to the outside world: the telephone. Litvak opens up this adaptation of Lucille Fletcher's hugely successful radio thriller with flashbacks and location changes (cutting to the other side of the conversation), but can't quite overcome the static nature. The result is still compelling, an interesting marriage of melodrama and film noir with a terrific cast that seems somewhat constrained by the film's gimmick. A still very young Lancaster is Stanwyck's henpecked trophy husband, and the Hollywood diva all but blows him off the screen in their scenes together. —S. A.

SPY WHO LOVED ME, THE L: SPY/007 (JAMES BOND) (1977) 125M D: Lewis Gilbert.
Roger Moore, Richard Kiel, Barbara Bach, Curd Jurgens. This is the first James Bond film not based on an Ian Fleming story. Instead, producer Albert Broccoli chose the title of a Fleming spy novel and created a Bond story using all the hallmarks everyone had come to expect from these films. And to that end The Spy Who Loved Me does not let down. Even

before the opening credits there is a spectacular stunt where Bond skis off a cliff and deploys his Union Jack parachute. He teams up with Russian spy and love interest Anya Amasova (Bach). Together they try to get to the bottom of the mystery of disappearing submarines, leading them to the underwater lair of billionaire Karl Stromberg (Jurgens). The greatest gadget in this feature is an amphibious Lotus Esprit that is armed to the teeth. There is also the billionaire's dreaded bouncer, Jaws (Kiel), with teeth so scary that he returns for the next Bond film, *Moonraker. —N. J.*

SUBURBIA L: CRIME/JUVENILE DELINQUENTS (1983) 99M D: Penelope Spheeris. *Timothy Eric O'Brien, Bill Coyne, Chris Pederson, Wade Walston, Jennifer Clay.* Undeniably the greatest achievement in the history of punk film, *Suburbia* burst out of nowhere at the height of punk's downhill slide, chronicling the doomed lives of America's then truly ostracized Mohawked set. Directed by Spheeris (*Decline of Western Civilization*), *Suburbia* tells the not-too-fictional story of a handful of bitter, disenfranchised, and socially disowned street kids who band together under their own rules, only to be torn apart from all sides. The film contains shockingly convincing performances from actual hard-luck LA punk teens selected by Spheeris herself from suburban malls, shows, and record stores. There are also performances from arguably important LA punk bands TSOL, D.I., and the original Vandals. Sincere, tragic, violent, and hilarious, *Suburbia* is the ultimate '80s teen movie. —Z. C.

SUDDEN FEAR L: NOIR/FILM NOIR (1952) 110M D: David Miller. *Joan Crawford, Jack Palance, Bruce Bennett, Gloria Grahame.* Crawford gracefully aged into the late era of Hollywood noir in this tale of a middle-aged playwright who falls for a handsome young actor (Palance). After a whirlwind romance they settle into marriage, but he's got other ideas, which involve his mistress (Grahame) and murder. Crawford is excellent; when she discovers the plot she appears on the verge of collapse, then pulls herself back together, steels herself for survival, and starts turning the tables on the dangerous duo. Director Miller uses the San Francisco locations nicely and the moody black-and-white photography takes on an inky beauty as the bright outdoor scenes are edged out by the protagonists' nocturnal prowlings. —S. A.

THIN MAN, THE L: DETECTIVES/THIN MAN SERIES (1934) 91M D: W. S. Van Dyke. *William Powell, Nat Pendleton, Myrna Loy, Maureen O'Sullivan.* It's cocktail hour on the mystery beat in this sparkling adaptation of Dashiell Hammett's novel of a former sleuth gone high society and his game social-register wife. Powell and Loy sparkle, and spark just a little, as a playfully in love couple with nothing but time on their hands and highballs

in their fists who fall into a mystery, much to his chagrin and her delight. Director Van Dyke shot this in a whirlwind twelve days, and that rush may have encouraged the tossed-off flavor of the oh-so-suave and sly banter, though it would be nothing without the incomparable chemistry of Powell and Loy, who make elegance so much fun. There's a snap to their scenes and they proved such an irresistible pair that they were teamed for another dozen or so films, including five sequels. Great images by James Wong Howe. —S. A.

THIN MAN GOES HOME, THE L: DETECTIVES/THIN MAN SERIES (1944) 100M D: Richard Thorpe. *Myrna Loy, William Powell, Gloria de Haven, Lucile Watson, Harry Davenport.* Widely considered the weakest installment in the *Thin Man* series, this will still probably be the best and funniest movie you'll see all month. Nick and Nora Charles (along with terrier Asta) visit Sycamore Springs, Nick's childhood home. Nora busies herself smoothing Nick's relationship with his father, who is little impressed by Nick's police work and considers him an ambitionless drunken playboy. Meanwhile, Nick's notoriety as a detective brings the villains out of the woodwork and before long a baffling murder mystery is in full swing. This entry is particularly memorable for a number of elaborate sight gags exploiting Nick's inability to convince anyone of his newfound sobriety. In the best one, fate knocks out the purely innocent Nick, facedown on the floor, flask in hand, just as his father happens in. —C. B.

THIS WORLD, THEN THE FIREWORKS L: MURDER/MYSTERY/SUSPENSE (1997) 100M D: Michael Oblowitz. *Gina Gershon, Billy Zane, Sheryl Lee, Rue McClanahan, Seymour Cassel.* The disturbed world of Jim Thompson's deformed psyches and demented morality comes to life in *This World, Then the Fireworks*, one of the more unpredictable works in a career defined by disturbingly treacherous narratives. What makes this dreamy adaptation by director Oblowitz and screenwriter Larry Gross work is the way they peg the mood—a musky, simmering, low-key mixture of film noir and Southern Gothic. Zane, with his disarmingly lazy grin and bedroom eyes, flits between newspaperman and con man, while his twin sister, Gershon, her bow-tie lips parted in a perpetually suggestive smirk, plies her trade in the bars of their port-town home. It's a bizarre relationship: tender, respectful, suggestively incestuous, a palpable connection that goes way beyond sibling love. With a smoky jazz score, a chic '50s look, and a lazy pace, the crazy narrative twists become all the more casually outré, like a languid, opium-induced nightmare. —S. A.

THREE DAYS OF THE CONDOR L: SPY/SPY (1975) 120M D: Sydney Pollack. *Robert Redford, Faye Dunaway, Cliff Robertson, Max von Sydow, John Houseman.* Redford plays a man who works for a small firm that is investigating the CIA. One day when he comes back to the office from lunch he suddenly sees that all of his co-workers have been killed. While trying to hide from whoever may be out to assassinate him, this poor protagonist discovers that his own boss ordered the hit. Clearly this film taps into the well-established fears of Watergate, and between the acting of Redford and the directing of Pollack it's absolutely cliffhanging at every plot twist. It would make the perfect double feature with *All the President's Men*. —*N.J.*

THUNDERBALL L: SPY/007 (JAMES BOND) (1965) 125M D: Terence Young. *Sean Connery, Claudine Auger, Adolfo Celi, Luciana Paluzzi, Rick van Nutter*. The fourth Bond feature pins 007 against the organization S.P.E.C.T.R.E., which tries threatening Miami with an atom bomb. This leads the suave agent underwater with an appropriately amphibian vehicle supplied to him by Q. And of course, he is supplied with the appropriate love interest in the character Domino (Auger). All the underwater action, the remarkable gadgetry, and the implied sex interest are enough to nicely propel things forward. A suggestive underwater scene featuring Domino's bikini floating upward was cut from the original film for being a little too suggestive. Whereas *Thunderball* isn't the greatest film of the Bond series, technically it is certainly one of the most daring, demonstrating the producer's penchant for big-budget stunt sequences backed with all the equipment and cutting-edge photography to pull it off. —*N.J.*

THUNDERBOLT AND LIGHTFOOT L: CRIME/CAPERS (HEISTS) (1974) 114M D: Michael Cimino. *Geoffrey Lewis, Clint Eastwood, George Kennedy, Jeff Bridges, Catherine Bach*. Eastwood is extremely cool in this unique and well-directed road/heist movie. Bridges is the young protégé to veteran thief Eastwood, who plans a complicated robbery that will inevitably go sour. Perhaps the best way to get across the oddness of the movie is to describe the scene where the two hitchhike, planning to steal the car. Before they can do anything, the driver peels out on the side of the road and gets out of the car. He opens the trunk, dozens of bunnies start hopping out, and he starts shooting them. You see? That's why this is one of Eastwood's best. It was also Cimino's debut as a director. —*B.T.*

TRICK BABY (AKA **DOUBLE CON**) L: CRIME/CAPERS (HEISTS) (1973) 89M D: Larry Yust. *Kiel Martin, Mel Stewart, Jan Leighton, Byron Sanders*. In the book by Iceberg Slim, White Folks (played here by Martin) was a grifter with a black mother and a white father. He was able to pass for white to con the upper class, with whom he'd often exchange racist comments. In the movie he's just a white guy. It still has some of the same themes of racial and class strife and, like most stories about con artists, is fairly entertaining. This is the only movie ever adapted from Iceberg Slim so you'll

have to make due with only a little bit of the gritty texture of his novels. —*B.T.*

VIEW TO A KILL, A L: SPY/007 (JAMES BOND) (1985) 131M D: John Glen. *Roger Moore, Christopher Walken, Patrick Macnee, Tanya Roberts, Desmond Llewelyn, Grace Jones*. Moore's last Bond film features one of the greatest villains since Christopher Lee starred in *The Man with the Golden Gun* eleven years earlier. Walken plays Max Zorin, a high-tech villain who is keen on mass murder in order to expand his profits in microchips. What's more is that his henchperson is the unlikely female interest May Day, played by singer Jones. The predictable lack of story makes up for itself with excellent location photography (Swiss Alps, Eiffel Tower, Siberia, and the top of the Golden Gate Bridge,) stunt work (in particular Jones's leap from the Eiffel Tower with a parachute), and costuming (can you believe what Jones wears in front of the camera??). *A View to a Kill* might be the best Moore Bond film ever made, or at least one of the corniest. —*N.J.*

VIOLENT CITY (AKA **THE FAMILY**) L: CRIME/GANGS & GANGSTAS (1970) 100M D: Sergio Sollima. *Umberto Orsini, Telly Savalas, Michel Constantin, Charles Bronson, Jill Ireland*. Lyrical, moody, disturbing erotic thriller about an independent contract killer (Bronson) who can't decide if he wants to get back together with or kill his double-crossing girlfriend (Ireland); her new husband (Savalas), who is head of the New Orleans mob, wants to make him part of the "Organization." Sollima brings a brooding tension to each scene, from the initial car chase to the hit at the auto speedway to the tender scenes that seethe with violence beneath the surface. These are intercut with scenes containing the most bizarre philosophical humor, from the killer's jailhouse-philosopher cellmate to the bemused husband enjoying life to the end, smiling while playing head games with his assassin. The film is surprisingly well acted by all principals, Savalas in particular. With an Ennio Morricone score that hits just the right note of tetchy wistfulness, it's another brilliant outing by the director of *Revolver* and *Faccia a Faccia*. —*J.C.*

WANTED FOR MURDER L: NOIR/FILM NOIR (1946) 91M D: Lawrence Huntington. *Eric Portman, Dulcie Gray, Derek Farr, Roland Culver, Stanley Holloway*. Portman, so poised and mannered, is the epitome of the chilly aristocrat in this noirish Brit thriller. There's a sneer in his voice and his hard, heavy-lidded eyes seem to glare down his nose at the common world. It's hardly a surprise when he turns out to be a notorious strangler, but he does make a cultured and tormented killer. There's wit to the script (cowritten by Emeric Pressburger) and smooth direction by Huntington, who creates a wonderful mix of moods: Gothic shadows and foggy nights in the bustling urban world of postwar London; a haunted, self-loathing aristocrat in a middle-class milieu. Holloway costars as a sardonic detective. —S. A.

WAY OF THE GUN L: CRIME/CAPERS (HEISTS) (2000) 118M D: Christopher McQuarrie. *Benicio del Toro, Ryan Phillippe, Juliette Lewis, James Caan, Nicky Katt, Taye Diggs.* The first scene in McQuarrie's underrated gem *Way of the Gun* begins with Sarah Silverman screaming a stream of obscenities at del Toro and Phillippe, and ends with her getting punched in the face and the two "heroes" being beaten by an angry mob. The introduction perfectly sets the nihilistic tone for the rest of the film. The movie's script is too twisty and it drags a little in the middle, but the two leads are dead-on. Lewis is bearable as their pregnant hostage and Caan and Geoffrey Lewis (Juliette's father) are great as aging "bagmen." The spare dialogue and camerawork are its saving grace. The action sequences are loud and messy and seem to play out in real time. McQuarrie may not have made the most exciting action spectacular, but this film is a great commentary on modern action cinema. It's like an antigunfight movie... with great gunfights. —K. C.

WHATEVER HAPPENED TO AUNT ALICE? L: MURDER/ MYSTERY/SUSPENSE (1969) 101M D: Lee H. Katzin. *Rosemary Forsyth, Geraldine Page, Ruth Gordon, Robert Fuller, Mildred Dunnock.* Page is brilliant as a crabby old widow who lives as immodestly as she can in the distant suburbs. A new family moves into the empty house next door and their mere presence suddenly cramps her style. In the safety of isolation she has developed and mastered a very strange form of cash flow: she hires old maids who have few if any friends or family, gets all the information on their bank accounts, and then digs a hole for them. It's a rather simple strategy that not only supports her lifestyle but also adds trees to her drive. With the combination of Gordon as an independent detective investigating the disappearance of a friend and the continual intrusion of the family next door, an outrageous climax certainly awaits you. —N. J.

WILD SIDE L: MURDER/MYSTERY/SUSPENSE (1995) 111M D: Donald Cammell. *Anne Heche, Christopher Walken, Joan Chen.* Cammell's final voyage of bizarre sex couplings, extreme behavior, and alternate identities showcases a pre-fame Heche as a loan officer by day and for-pay play pal by night who squeezes into the middle of a planned bust involving an artsy money player (Walken) and his bodyguard, who turns out to be a cop and who also has the hots for Heche. A master of close-quartered unease, Cammell constructs his pace and camerawork to tell this tight tale. Cut to hell by the Americans, and most likely the final straw that Cammell needed to shuffle off this mortal coil (he committed suicide by gunshot in 1996), the region 2 DVD release rediscovers the film at the hands of longtime editor and friend Frank

Mazzolla. Ryuichi Sakamoto's score taps notes into the personal pain and peccadilloes of the love-quadrangled cast, including Chen as main squeeze to both Walken and Heche. —S. R.

WILD THINGS L: MURDER/MYSTERY/SUSPENSE (1998) 108M D: John McNaughton. *Denise Richards, Kevin Bacon, Bill Murray, Matt Dillon, Neve Campbell, Theresa Russell.* In a rich neighborhood near the Everglades, high school teacher Dillon is falsely accused of rape by his students Richards and Campbell. At first you think you're watching a typical sleazy sex thriller, like a Shannon Tweed movie you might see late at night on cable. Then a preposterous plot twist pulls the carpet out from under your feet and you land in an over-the-top, convention stretching near-parody of the genre. It's all treated with a straight face but the plot twists keep piling up so ridiculously that you don't even know who is in on what unless you stay for the end credits, and even then you're not entirely sure. Murray is great as Dillon's lawyer (part of his mid-'90s supporting role streak that included *Kingpin* and *Ed Wood*). Definitely McNaughton's best since *Henry: Portrait of a Serial Killer.* —B. T.

WINTER KILLS L: SPY/SPY (1979) 97M D: William Richert. *Jeff Bridges, Anthony Perkins, John Huston, Eli Wallach, Sterling Hayden.* Though technically a work of fiction, this is the maddest and most entertaining of Kennedy conspiracy thrillers, a wild kaleidoscope of clashing theories directed with wit and performed with gusto by an astounding cast. Bridges is the half brother of an assassinated president. He digs up the "truth" twenty years later and Huston plays his snarling kingmaker of a dad (imagine Joseph Kennedy by way of Howard Hughes) who keeps pointing him in different directions. Perkins steals every scene he's in as a ruthless, efficient, cold-blooded information broker, Richard Boone gives a hearty performance as a grizzly bear of a family friend, and Hayden makes his entrance in a tank and proceeds to chase Bridges across a muddy field mired in war games. The crazy-quilt script is adapted from Richard Condon's novel and the various (often contradictory) theories from the popular Kennedy conspiracy zeitgeist. The plot is practically lifted from Orson Welles's *Mr. Arkadin.* —S. A.

XXX L: SPY/SPY (2002) 124M D: Rob Cohen. *Vin Diesel, Asia Argento, Samuel L. Jackson.* Diesel is Xander Cage, an extreme sports terrorist who steals politicians' cars and jumps them off bridges to protest the censorship of rap music and video games. When he gets busted, a badly disfigured CIA agent (Jackson) convinces him to become a cutting-edge secret agent for a new generation and go stop decadent European anarchist terrorists who hang out in punkish dance clubs. After the enjoyably ridiculous opening, the actual plot kicks in and the film turns dull and lifeless.

Worse, Xander is a total sellout. You want him to be a Snake Plissken type who will save the world and then have a trick up his sleeve for the authority figures who have the audacity to think they can control him. Instead, he ends the movie lounging on a beach, happy to work for the man, leaving fourteen-year-old video-game-playing kids living in that world with no heroes that the trailer narrators are always talking about. —*B. T.*

YOU ONLY LIVE TWICE L: SPY/007 (JAMES BOND) (1967) 125M D: Lewis Gilbert. *Sean Connery, Donald Pleasence, Tetsuro Tamba, Mie Hama, Teru Shimada, Karin Dor.* After the underwater spectacle of *Thunderball,* producers Albert Broccoli and Harry Saltzman returned with the fifth Bond film, starting in space. Manned orbiting space-craft from both the United States and the USSR are being hijacked by some unknown force, causing the superpowers to start blaming each other. Bond is dispatched to Japan where the evil S.P.E.C.T.R.E. organization is suspected of calling the shots. And there in the massive crater of an extinct volcano Bond finds the impressive lair of Blofeld (Pleasence). The usual array of gadgetry is included, most notably the portable gyroscopic helicopter Bond uses to check out the volcano. —*N. J.*

ZERO EFFECT L: MURDER/MYSTERY/SUSPENSE (1998) 116M D: Jake Kasdan. *Bill Pullman, Ben Stiller, Kim Dickens, Angela Featherstone, Ryan O'Neal.* Somewhere between slacker and postmodern Zen master lies this combination of Sherlock Holmes and Nero Wolfe refigured for the '90s. Pullman is the paranoid, shaggy techno-hippy and "master of disguise" Daryl Zero, a genius detective who specializes in unsolvable cases. As he is burdened with more than his share of eccentricities, he relies heavily on his able assistant, agent, and leg-man (the long-suffering Stiller). Fans of Holmes and Wolfe will love the way Kasdan (yes, the son of Lawrence) plays with and parodies their quirks, but the offbeat story and funky charac-ters stand on their own just fine, and Kasdan has fun with the film that I find infectious. —*S. A.*

CHAPTER TEN

All Things Music

Probably even older than murder is music. In fact I think the first human act of murder might well have been the end of an argument that began with something like, "Turn that down!"

By whatever means human beings have filmed music, here it is, with a few Scarecrow twists to be sure. We break things down pretty much the way you'd see them in your favorite music store, with the obvious distinction that we are able to hear and see the performers play. Artists both major and minor are represented, from all over the globe.

Broadway shows are here with their progeny, the Hollywood musical. And the second of our only two "star" sections (see Westerns) are here as well: from Fred Astaire and the Beatles to Elvis and Esther Williams, stars that had the most successful musical runs in the movies, whose films reflected their styles almost perfectly, are given their own space. Composers Stephen Sondheim and the light opera geniuses Gilbert & Sullivan are noted here, too.

In the Rock section, we separate Rock Musicals and Beach Party movies from the rest, and we also have a mini-horror section here as well: Rock 'n' Roll Hell. There are quite a few more of these than you may have guessed: think *Rocky Horror Picture Show* meets *Night of the Living Dead* and you start to get the picture. But for our purposes in this book, they are listed all together, alphabetically by title. More recent musical movements are here, including Hip Hop & Rap and Electronica.

Can't Stop the Music (1980)

©ANCHOR BAY ENTERTAINMENT

On the classical side, from European classical music and opera to the American classics of Folk, Jazz, Country, Bluegrass, and Blues, from Yo-Yo Ma to Eubie Blake, we've got you covered.

Bottom line, if music is the only true universal language, and movies are a close second ... well, you've got both right here, what are you waiting for? Step in time!

APHEX TWIN: WINDOWLICKER L: ROCK/ELECTRONICA (1999) 11M D: Chris Cunningham. *Richard D. James, Gary W. Cruz, Brian Friedman, Marcus Morris.* One of the funniest, sexiest, and scariest eleven minutes you will ever have in your life, this masterpiece showcases two "playaz" at the top of their game, artist Richard "Destruction" James and director Chris "The Second Coming" Cunningham. The video begins with two "brothas" in a "whip" rollin' down the strip scamming for "honeys." They finally meet up with a couple a "chickenheads" and the exchange between them is butt-crackingly poignant, "Girl, I'm a playa girl fo real! Playa PLAYA guuurl!" You get about five minutes of this until the music video actually starts, at which point it could give you nightmares or orgasms or both. It's basically a bunch of luscious wet ladies bouncing in slow-motion but... they all have James's face! How fucked is that? —*T. C.*

ART OF CONDUCTING, THE L: CLASSICAL PERFORMANCE/ CLASSICAL PERFORMANCE (1995) 115M D: Gerald Caillat, Sue Knussen. *Isaac Stern, Julius Baker, Yehudi Menuhin.* Enter a world largely unknown by the average human, a realm where lightning bolts fly off the fingertips of men, where a flick of the wand brings forth an aural stampede of awesome magnitude, where one can silence the masses with a chilling stare. What, are we talking about wizards or something? Better: conductors. Covering several glorious decades, *The Art of Conducting* provides insight into the minds and dispositions of several of the most respected people in the field. Watch as they form a seemingly psychic bond as their directions transmit almost instantaneously to their orchestra. You know that thing that they sell in gift shops where a metal ball is encased by a glass globe and if you put your hands on it electricity flows from the metal to your fingertips? Yeah, it's kinda like that. —*T. C.*

BACK TO THE BEACH L: ROCK/BEACH PARTY! (1987) 88M D: Lyndall Hobbs. *Annette Funicello, Connie Stevens, Frankie Avalon, Lori Loughlin, Jerry Mathers, Tony Dow.* This beach film never should have been made, but perhaps that's the point. Funicello and Avalon return to their roles from the '60s beach party films, but now they are married with two kids and are properly domesticated, right down to Funicello serving up the peanut butter. But their children seem depressed, so they decide a good trip to the beach will cheer them up. Perhaps you'll be cheered up, too, when you see all the strange cameos they dig up, like an aging Bob Denver dressed as Gilligan. Or perhaps you'll just find this to be a cruel exercise in kitsch. —*N. J.*

BATTLE OF THE YEAR 2002 L: ROCK/BREAKDANCING (2002) 110M D: Not credited. Hip hop has conquered the majority of the globe. Wherever you go, you are bound to bump into some heads. Example: the Battle of the Year b-boy convention held annually in Frankfurt, Germany. Crews from all over the world battle each other, and it don't matter what dialect you're jabbering 'cause props is the only language here. South Africa battles Switzerland, crews from France battle heads from Korea. The video is split into two parts, routines and battles, with the four best crews doing battle for the title of Best in the World. The routines become somewhat repetitive, so fast-forward to the final battle between

France and Korea. After all of this, despite its impressive international presence, I can't help but feel that hip hop is better when done in the States. —*T. C.*

BEASTIE BOYS ANTHOLOGY L: ROCK/HIP HOP & RAP (2000) D: Spike Jonze. *Adam Yauch (MCA), Adam Horovitz (Kid Ad Rock), Mike D.* Criterion's first collection of music videos is one of the few to really take advantage of the DVD format. Most of the band's videos are collected and supplied with multiple audio tracks and angles. The audio tracks include newly commissioned remixes by top hip hop producers and separate band and director commentaries for each video. These aren't always enlightening but are extremely entertaining, especially in the instances where an unbilled Jonze calls the directors on the phone pretending to be a Criterion employee and asking them asinine pre-interview questions. There's also a great, little-seen video for the song "3 MCs and 1 DJ," shot on digital video in real time as the band performs the song live in a basement. The video would probably qualify for Dogme 95 status if Mixmaster Mike weren't wearing a jetpack. —*B. T.*

BEAT STREET L: ROCK/HIP HOP & RAP (1984) 106M D: Stan Lathan. *Robert Taylor, Rae Dawn Chong, Guy Davis, Leon Grant, John Chardiet.* Even suburban white kids knew that this was the best of the Hollywood breaksploitation movies. *Breakin'* suggested that breakdancing was cool not because of the creative art form it was, but because of its similarities to respectable, white-people dancing. *Beat Street* is certainly not as authentic as *Wild Style* but it is a respectful and somewhat gritty attempt to cram all the elements of the culture into a let's-put-on-a-show Hollywood movie. The aspects that stuck with me most after seeing this as a kid: the DJ sampling a leaky faucet to make a beat, Kool Moe Dee rapping about G.I. Joe dolls, and that bastard Spit ruining everybody's subway graffiti (it would be many years before I would recognize that subplot as a lift from the classic graffiti documentary *Style Wars*.) —*B. T.*

BENNY GOODMAN STORY, THE L: MUSICALS/MUSICALS (1956) 114M D: Valentine Davies. *Donna Reed, Steve Allen, Herbert Anderson, Hy Averback, Sammy Davis Sr., Berta Gersten.* No one would argue that this is a superior film to *The Glenn Miller Story.* Flatly directed by Davies (who cowrote *Glenn Miller*) and woodenly performed by Allen (who resembles Goodman and actually is a musician himself, but lacks any charisma on screen), it clunks through the highlights of Goodman's life, from his childhood in Chicago to his historic concert at Carnegie Hall in 1938. But what a life, what music (all of it performed by Goodman himself for the film), and what thrilling musical appearances. Goodman band members Lionel Hampton, Gene Krupa, Teddy Wilson, Ben Pollack, and Kid Ory play themselves (Hampton making a truly memorable entrance), Harry James, Ziggy Elman, and Martha Tilton make appearances, and that's Davis Sr. as Fletcher Henderson. Reed has the thankless role of playing the romantic interest of an actor who shows little interest and no romantic instincts. —S. A.

BIRTHDAY PARTY, THE: PLEASURE HEADS MUST BURN L: ROCK/ROCK & ROLL! (1984) 60M D: Various. *Nick Cave, Mick Harvey, Rowland Howard, Tracy Pew, Phil Calvert.* The legendary band The Birthday Party makes its first appearance on DVD in this hour of dangerous, ugly, uncompromising, and confrontational music. Led by Cave, the band plays a bizarre perversion of American roots music, and the creativity is unbelievable. Fueled equally by spiritual angst, punk fury, and heroin addiction, Cave explodes across the stage with the fury, sorrow, and intensity of a thousand stars going supernova, producing the melody of a choir of rebel angels. The DVD contains two live performances, one from 1982 and the other from 1983, both captured at the Hacienda and originally released on VHS nearly twenty years ago. Also included are five videos and TV appearances, the best being the video for the creepy murder ballad "Deep in the Woods," directed by Glenn Auchinachie. —T. S.

BLACK AND WHITE L: ROCK/HIP HOP & RAP (1999) 98M D: James Toback. *Oliver "Power" Grant, Scott Caan, Robert Downey Jr., Stacy Edwards, Brooke Shields, Allan Houston, Ben Stiller.* Largely improvised exploration of young white people's affinity for black culture. Unfortunately, all they do is keep exploring and exploring and never really come up with any interesting discoveries. There are some truly remarkable moments with nonactors (including Method Man, Raekwon, Brett Ratner, and especially Mike Tyson) but they are crushed beneath the two generic storylines, one about Shields and Downey making a documentary about white kids in hip hop and the other about a cop (Stiller) trying to set up a basketball player (Houston). —B. T.

BLACK ROSES L: ROCK/ROCK 'N' ROLL HELL (1988) 90M D: John Fasano. *Pat Strelioff, Sal Viviano, Frank Dietz, John Martin.* Demonic hair metal band The Black Roses plays a series of shows in a small town and turn the youth into parent killers. The only person standing in their way is the high school English teacher. Director Fasano previously helmed the similarly hair metal themed *Rock 'n' Roll Nightmare.* Unfortunately, this film does not contain Jon-Mikl Thor. However, it does contain the first screen appearance of Vincent Pastore ("Big Pussy" from *The Sopranos*) as the father of one of the kids. Upon discovering that his son is wearing an earring, Pastore exclaims, "Only two kinds of men wear earrings, pirates and faggots. I don't see no ship in our driveway." This film contains a lot of cheesy hair metal, breasts, and some fun creature effects. —S. W. F.

BLOODHAG: READ FREE OR DIE L: ROCK/ROCK & ROLL! (2000) 8M D: Brad Vanderburg. *Bloodhag.* A short documentary about the Seattle "edu-core" band, chronicling their 2000 tour of local libraries. Taking song titles from famous and obscure sci-fi literature, the band bombards unsuspecting adolescent librarygoers with Isaac Asimov–inspired guttural shrieking before actually hucking copies of tattered paperbacks at them. Although the kids look like they would rather be getting hit on the head with the *The Babysitters Club*, the sci-fi assimilation Bloodhag attempts to plant in the heads of the young doesn't seem entirely wasted. As they drive off in their van at the end, you almost wish that they could have been around for you, too, that one summer your mom abandoned you at the library for five hours. —A. T.

BLUES BROTHERS, THE L: ROCK/ROCK MUSICALS (1980) 135M D: John Landis. *Ray Charles, James Brown, Carrie Fisher, Aretha Franklin, Cab Calloway, Dan Aykroyd, John Belushi.* This is the one *Saturday Night Live*–based movie that is a bona fide masterpiece. It may seem odd that these two deadpan white guys are portrayed as the masters of soul music, but just go with it. The movie is a sprawling, all-star musical tribute to black music and the landscape of Chicago, packed with funny subplots and running gags that build into the thunderous crescendo of the greatest and most ridiculous car chase in the history of cinema. Landis was at his peak of anarchic excess, and it is a miracle he was able to balance all of this in one film. —B. T.

BLUES BROTHERS 2000 L: ROCK/ROCK MUSICALS (1998) 150M D: John Landis. *Dan Aykroyd, John Goodman, Joe Morton, Evan Bonifant.* When Elwood Blues (Aykroyd) gets out of prison, he waits for his brother Jake to pick him up, standing by the road all night because nobody told him Jake is dead. It's a touching opening to this generally uninspired sequel. Elwood finds Morton (Goodman) and ten-year-old Buster (Bonifant) to revive the Blues Brothers Band for a competition against the Louisiana Gator Boys (blues legends Eric Clapton, B. B. King, Bo Diddley, and more). There are occasional moments reminiscent of the wonderful excess of the original *The Blues Brothers*, and more enjoyable music by newer musicians like Erykah Badu and Jonny Lang. But overall, the cast has more fun than the audience. As great as it is to see Badu in a zombie-themed musical number, you find yourself thinking, "Wait a minute, Landis did better dancing zombies in the 'Thriller' video!" A nice try, I guess, but *The Blues Brothers* should've been left alone. —B. T.

BEST OF BLUR L: ROCK/ROCK & ROLL! (2000) 85M D: Damien Hirst. *Graham Coxon, Dave Rowntree, Alex James, Damon Albarn.* I like Blur, but if I were never able to hear their music again, I would still go on to lead a happy and productive life.

The Blur videos, though, these make me happy. The cinematography is impressive, and Hirst deserves a high five for directing some of the best music videos I've seen in a long time. The music and the videos complement each other perfectly. They are fun videos making fairly fun music superfun, so more likely than not you'll have fun watching it. When we play them in the store, almost everyone smiles just a little brighter. —*J. S.*

LIVE FROM BONNAROO MUSIC FESTIVAL 2002 L: ROCK/ ROCK & ROLL! (2002) 190M D: L. A. Johnson. *Widespread Panic, Trey Anastasio.* There is a whole subculture that follows "jam bands," groups that play long instrumental jams. They are a passionate and dedicated group of fans who most famously follow Phish but also more soulful groups, including the white New Orleans funk band Galactic. This DVD documents the first Bonnaroo Music Festival, which brought more than 70,000 fans to Tennessee to watch Anastasio and Widespread Panic. There are plenty of great excerpts of performances by Les Claypool's Flying Frog Brigade (featuring Seattle's own Skerik), Jurassic 5, Colonel Claypool's Bucket of Bernie Brains, and Karl Denson's Tiny Universe. Galactic drummer Stanton Moore also leads a brass band through the crowd for a nighttime parade. The performances are bookended by clips explaining the festival and interviewing people in the crowd, but there's not much substance to it as a documentary. It's just a good highlight reel. —*B. T.*

BOOTSY? PLAYER OF THE YEAR TOUR 1978 L: ROCK/ ROCK & ROLL! (1978) 76M D: unknown. *Bootsy Collins.* This funky-as-hell concert video begins with a cartoon projected onto a screen, an appropriate introduction for the larger-than-life space-bass player with the star-shaped glasses. Bootsy played in James Brown's original JBs when he was a teenager, but was fired after running off stage when some LSD convinced him the neck of his bass was a snake. He let his freak flag fly higher when he joined Parliament-Funkadelic and really let loose with this spin-off group, Bootsy's Rubber Band. Fellow JB/Parliament alumni Maceo Parker plays saxophone and hypes the crowd as Bootsy and his infectious smile dance around in front of a giant pair of flashing star-glasses, vibrating every rib cage in the crowd with his thunderous, impossibly funky bass lines. Taped from the closed-circuit television screens, so it ends with the words "Thank you for coming to tonight's event. Please drive carefully." (How come you can get vintage P-Funk videos in Japan, but not in the United States?) —*B. T.*

BREAKIN' L: ROCK/BREAKDANCING (1984) 87M D: Joel Silberg. *Adolpho "Shabba Doo" Quinones, Michael "Boogaloo Shrimp" Chambers, Ben Lokey, Chris McDonald, Lucinda Dickey.* A white dance stu-dent (Dickey) pushes the envelope, takes the starch out of that collar, subverts the system, etc. by befriending some breakdancers (Shabba Doo and Boogaloo Shrimp) who perform on pieces of cardboard in the street and by helping them to make it in the world of white people who dance on stages. *Breakin'* is a shabby, condescending exploitation of hip hop culture, but it may have helped push the culture into the mainstream. Director Silberg followed up *Breakin'* with *Rappin',* starring Mario Van Peebles, but when that didn't catch on he moved to *Lambada* in 1989, which gives an idea of the sincerity of his commitment to hip hop. —*B. T.*

BREAKIN' 2: ELECTRIC BOOGALOO L: ROCK/ BREAKDANCING (1984) 94M D: Sam Firstenberg. *Harry Caesar, Susie Bono, Lucinda Dickey, Adolpho "Shabba Doo" Quinones, Michael "Boogaloo Shrimp" Chambers.* This film has made one contribution to our culture: whenever someone wants to make fun of a sequel, or joke about making an inappropriate sequel to an existing movie, they add the subtitle "Electric Boogaloo." Here's how it works: *The Matrix 2: Electric Boogaloo. The Shining 2: Electric Boogaloo. Coal Miner's Daughter 2: Electric Boogaloo.* You see? It's wacky. Every time it's like a brand-new joke. *Breakin' 2* is a hobbled-together quickie made to cash in on the success of the original, but the resulting crappiness makes it a lot more fun. Instead of getting bogged down in all that "legitimate" dance business, this film just has a lot of random musical numbers and a plot that seems like they made it up as they went along. This time they get to dance their way out of a hospital and stand in front of a bulldozer to save the community center (which still works in movies, even if it doesn't in real life). Other sequels by director Firstenberg include *Revenge of the Ninja, Delta Force 3,* and *Spiders II: Breeding Ground.* —*B. T.*

BROWN SUGAR L: ROCK/HIP HOP & RAP (2002) 109M D: Rick Famuyiwa. *Mos Def, Taye Diggs, Queen Latifah, Nicole Ari Parker, Boris Kodjoe, Saana Latham.* A music journalist (Latham) and a hip hop producer (Diggs) are made for each other but they just don't know it in this familiar old song set to a new beat. He's married to a beautiful, success-driven lawyer (Parker), she's engaged to a tall, dark, and extremely confident athlete (Kodjoe), but the rest of the world knows that they are soulmates. While they don't radiate much romantic heat, they invest their characters with intelligence and passion and their casual intimacy resonates with a convincingly comfortable, lived-in history. Director Famuyiwa finds the universal chords in their shared passion of hip hop as they riff back and forth with snatches of lyrics and reminisce about formative musical experiences. You don't need to recognize the references to feel their investment in the culture. Famuyiwa understands that a generation defines its music as much as the music defines a generation. —S. A.

BUGSY MALONE L: MUSICALS/MUSICALS (1976) 94M D: Alan Parker. *Jodie Foster, Scott Baio, Florrie Augger, John Cassisi.* Parker's first feature film is quite an eye-opener. Featuring a cast entirely comprised of children (at thirteen, Foster was probably the oldest), the story of gangster Bugsy Malone is relayed in exquisite period detail: the mannerisms of the '30s, the fake accents, the tommy guns, the kids dressed to the nines, complete with fedoras. Of course, to make this story of a gangster who shakes down Hollywood work properly it would have to be a musical. It's a unique sort of film, and hard to forget. —N. J.

CALLE 54 L: JAZZ/JAZZ (2000) 105M D: Fernando Trueba. Trueba (*Belle Epoque*) celebrates the energy and rhythms of Latin Jazz in this documentary spotlight, sort of a cross between video album and a series of intimate concerts for the camera, an attempt at, in his words, "filming the magic of music." Tito Puente, Gato Barbieri, Paquito D'Rivera, Bebo Valdes, and Cachao are among the featured artists who leap from dull "documentary" introductions into vivid, bold studio performances (perhaps Trueba's way of describing how music lights up the drab world we live in?), all handsomely shot and smartly designed. The beat inspires his style, and his dedication to the "magic" of music focuses his camera not on the famed bandleaders but on the collaboration of musicians, the energy of their performances, and the passion of their playing. It lacks history, background, and cultural roots, but it's undeniably infectious. —S. A.

CAN'T STOP THE MUSIC L: ROCK/ROCK MUSICALS (1980) 120M D: Nancy Walker. *The Village People, Bruce Jenner, Steve Guttenberg, Valerie Perrine.* What has a decade of Disco managed to produce? This: The Village People team up with Guttenberg, Jenner, and director Walker (famous for her role in those Bounty commercials) to produce what must be the worst achievement of the '80s. Where to start? Guttenberg plays an obnoxious DJ who gloms onto each band member and Jenner to form the Village People and achieve fame and fortune for all. He acts so gay that Perrine thinks he's straight, the rest of the Village People think they have a shoe-in, and Jenner stands around wondering why he's even in the film. Meanwhile, the audience is forced to tolerate such songs as "YMCA," "Milk Shake," "Macho Man," "Liberation," and more. Don't say you haven't been warned. —N. J.

CHICAGO L: MUSICALS/MUSICALS (2002) 113M D: Rob Marshall. *Renee Zellweger, Catherine Zeta-Jones, Richard Gere, Queen Latifah, John C. Reilly, Lucy Liu.* Man, *Chicago* bugged me. I couldn't get past the fact that Zellweger looked like she spent five hours a day weight training. She was so thin

and ripped that I could not believe it was the 1920s. Zellweger is a real hit-and-miss actress for me; sometimes I like her tremendously, as in *Nurse Betty*, where other times I just can't watch her at all, like in *Bridget Jones' Diary.* I also could care less for the songs, except the "Mama" number sung by Queen Latifah. The costumes and sets were quite amazing, but a little too over the top for the time period. The one thing I thought was inventive was how some of the musical sounds originated from the sets, like banging on the bars in the prison song, but I thought this was explored much better in *Dancer in the Dark.* —R. D.

COAL MINER'S DAUGHTER L: MUSICALS/MUSICALS (1980) 125M D: Michael Apted. *Sissy Spacek, Tommy Lee Jones, Beverly D'Angelo, Levon Helm.* About twenty minutes into this film, Loretta Lynn (Spacek) is riding on the back of a tractor, driven by her husband Doo (Jones). He asks her if she really wants a shot at being a singer. She softly replies, "I want it." "What?" he yells back over the noise of the machine. "I WANT IT! I WANT IT REAL BAD!" she screams in reply. From there, it's a tough road to stardom. This adaptation of Lynn's autobiography depicts her childhood in Kentucky, her sometimes rocky but steadfast marriage, and how she became the First Lady of Country Music. Spacek portrays Loretta's growing maturity and strength with charm and ease. Jones delivers a gruff but loving Doolittle, and D'Angelo gives a wonderful (but sadly too small) performance as Patsy Cline. I have never loved country music, but this film and its message about not giving up have always inspired me. —J. K.

ORNETTE COLEMAN TRIO L: JAZZ/JAZZ (1966) 26M D: Dick Fontaine. *Ornette Coleman, David Izenzon, Charles Moffett.* This documentary catches Coleman, Izenzon, and Moffett at work recording the soundtrack to *Who's Crazy?* I'm more than a little biased, as this trio is easily my favorite jazz combo of all time, and this documentary falls at a high point in their chronology. The three are shown performing while the film is projected on a screen in front of them. They resist second takes (Moffett really loses his cool when a recording snafu spoils a first take). Cutaways to one-on-one interviews with the band bring a personal element to the proceedings. Definitely a must for any Coleman fan, as the music captured here was never released in any audio format in the United States, and the long-out-of-print, quasi-legitimate import recordings don't come cheap. —C. B.

CONVERGE: THE LONGEST DAY L: ROCK/ROCK & ROLL! (2003) 80M D: Various. *Jacob Bannon, Kurt Ballow, Nate Newton, John DiGiorgio.* Heroes of the American underground, the superpowered metal/hardcore band Converge is featured on this beautifully assembled DVD. Comprised of live footage shot by fans over the last ten years, it packs as much punch as possible with twenty-two excellently remastered songs, three complete live performances, and an awesome music video. Opening with the legendary "The Saddest Day," Converge delivers the goods and never lets up with their brutal noise assault. The standout pieces are the most recent, coming from the masterpiece epic *Jane Doe* album. Their experimentation with texture and structure fuses with the blisteringly chaotic, tragically beautiful emotions dredged from the bottom of vocalist Bannon's heart. Too extreme to achieve mainstream success, Converge is an underground staple, revered as much for its music as its surprising longevity, well-illustrated by the chronological diversity of the DVD. It is a treat for fans and a fitting tribute to a brilliant band. —*T. S.*

D.A.F.T. L: ROCK/ROCK & ROLL! (1999) 160M D: Various. *Spike Jonze, Tony Maxwell, Catherine Kallner, James C. Heavy, Roman Coppola*. A collection of five clever videos by the French dance music duo. You may have seen Jonze's strange contribution "Da Funk," featuring Charles (Maxwell), the man with a dog's head and a broken leg walking around Manhattan. Or perhaps Mike Gondry's mutated Busby Berkeley number "Around the World," where robots, skeletons, mummies, disco girls, and athletes perform a choreographed dance, each group representing an instrument in the song. There's also one about a boy who wants to become a fireman, and a return of Charles the dog boy (directed by Daft Punk themselves). My favorite is Coppola's "Revolution 909," which begins with a police raid on a rave but during a flashback becomes an instructional video about tomatoes and the Coppola family recipe for pasta sauce. The DVD includes a multiangle live performance, the making of documentaries, remixes, and director commentaries. Mike Gondry explains the concept of his video in detail on a chalkboard, and Jonze cries during his commentary track while claiming that hecklers made fun of the way he was dressed during the shoot. —*B. T.*

DANCING OUTLAW L: FOLK/FOLK (1991) 60M D: Jacob Young. *Wattie Green, Jesco White, Jerry White, Dorsey White*. Jesco is a multipersonalitied former gas huffer who lives in Boone County, West Virginia. He follows in his father's footsteps as a talented outlaw dancer, performing an unusual clog/tap/hillbilly hoedown. Much of the film is devoted to Jesco's extended family, including his mother and brother, and his father, who was senselessly shot in a petty dispute. Jesco has three distinct personalities and many interests, such as spending time channeling Elvis Presley in his Elvis room, arguing with his older overweight wife, and, of course, putting on his tap shoes and dancing. Some people may find this documentary condescending, but I find it fascinating, inspiring, and funny as hell. Jesco was

Five essential hip hop films

WILD STYLE

STYLE WARS

SCRATCH

WAVE TWISTERS

SLAM

Also of note

BEAT STREET

BIGGIE AND TUPAC

8 MILE

KRUSH GROOVE

LA HAINE

TOUGHER THAN LEATHER

"discovered" by then-married Tom Arnold and Rosanne Barr and brought to Hollywood for a guest appearance on the sitcom *Rosanne*. Those experiences are chronicled in the inferior follow-up *Dancing Outlaw 2*. —*S. H.*

DEATH ROW UNCUT L: ROCK/HIP HOP & RAP (2000) 120M D: Various. *Tupac Shakur, Snoop Dogg, Dr. Dre, DJ Quik*. After the departure of Dr. Dre and Snoop Dogg, the death of Tupac, and the incarceration of CEO Suge Knight, Death Row Records released this video compilation that gives a pretty good overview of what the label is about: macho thugs making an embarrassing attempt to stay on top long after their day. Music videos and interesting live clips are framed by pathetic skits about three guys driving around in a convertible talking shit about Snoop and Dre. They just make themselves look like complete jackasses since the Snoop and Dre videos they show are classics while the later Death Row material merely serves as filler. The title apparently refers to the nudity seen in a couple of non-MTV-friendly videos, but the other videos actually *are* cut—for some reason they never show them all the way through to the end. For fans of the early output of Death Row, this is still worth a rental for nostalgia's sake—just don't expect an intelligent or respectful expression of hip hop art and culture. —*B. T.*

DIRTY DANCING L: ROCK/ROCK MUSICALS (1987) 105M D: Emile Ardolino. *Jennifer Grey, Patrick Swayze, Jerry Orbach, Cynthia Rhodes, Max Cantor*. *Dirty Dancing* can withstand the excellence test on nostalgia alone. The soundtrack makes me want to don high heels and a sequined dress and shake my ass with the best of them. In the early '60s, Baby (Grey) goes to a summer resort with her family and falls for Johnny Castle (Swayze), a smooth dancing machine of luuuv. His partner gets pregnant, and Baby has to fill in to save his smooth dancing ass while said partner gets an abortion. They fall in love, they do the deed, and the ending is a heart-swelling display of corny affection. Yeah, Swayze is a cornball, and Grey's acting is a little shoddy at times, but so what? They're both smooth dancing machines of luuuv, and that's good enough for me. —*J. S.*

8 MILE L: ROCK/HIP HOP & RAP (2002) 110M D: Curtis Hanson. *Eminem, Kim Basinger, Brittany Murphy, Mekhi Phifer, Evan Jones.* Eminem stars in this semiautobiographical portrait of a white rapper trying to win a freestyle championship in working-class '90s Detroit. Jimmy (Eminem) is a loser living in a trailer park with his mom, dumped by his girlfriend, hated by his boss, and so afraid to go on stage that he pukes on himself and then freezes and says nothing when it's his turn on the mic. From these lowly beginnings he builds up his courage, works hard, and uses his wits to defeat his opponents—it's *Rocky* with rappers. Hanson brings a great authenticity to his version of the Detroit landscape, and Eminem gives an impressive acting performance. But what undeniably makes the movie is the freestyling scenes in which Eminem and the other MCs must improvise insults to one-up each other on stage. It's surprising that it took so long for someone to see the cinematic potential of freestyle competitions. —*B. T.*

EINSTURZENDE NEUBAUTEN: LIEBESLIEDER L: ROCK/EXPERIMENTAL MUSIC (1994) 110M D: Klaus Maeck. *Einsturzende Neubauten.* Using jackhammers, powerdrills, anvils, and other industrial equipment—in addition to more conventional rock instruments—Einsturzende Neubauten made even the best of their contemporaries appear dismally bland. This documentary is worth a rental simply for the concert footage. Ranging from very early 1980s clips to 1990s *Tabula Rasa*–era material, you'll have ample opportunity to gawk at the highly specific methods the band employs to create its impressive sonic atmospheres, and to thrill to the gripping energy of Blixa Bargeld's wailing vocals and theatrical stage presence. Though hardly a substitute for the real thing, these videotaped performances are exhilarating. A number of interviews let the articulate musicians discuss the concepts driving their impassioned performances, and as an added bonus, music videos for 1993's "Blame" and "Interim" bookend the film, making this a near-definitive EN documentary. —*C. B.*

EMPEROR: EMPERIAL LIVE CEREMONY L: ROCK/ROCK & ROLL! (2000) 55M D: *Trym, Alver, Samoth, Ihsahn, Tyr, Charmand Grimloch.* Emperor, the ultimate black metal band, is captured at the beginning of its sorry downfall. Shot in London during the 1999 tour in support of IX Equilibrium, this live footage is sometimes awe-inspiring, sometimes sad.

The ten songs are a mix of newer and (thankfully) older material. When they rip through majestic classics like "I Am the Black Wizards" or the gargantuan "Thus Spake the Nightspirit," one can see why Emperor is often considered the best black metal band of all time. Their chaotic, complex articulation creates beautiful and intricate songs. What distinguishes Emporer is their deconstructed structural signatures, which they balance with the violence of raw vocals, dissonant guitars, use of keyboards to support riffs and transitions, and harmonizing, haunting melodies. However, the newer material shows that their creative fire burned out quickly. It lacks the power and intricacy of their early stuff. Luckily, they broke up before they got too horrible. The video and sound quality are excellent. Though the camera lingers on Ihsahn too much, this video is great overall, and the only way to see this amazing band perform live. —*T. S.*

FEAR OF A BLACK HAT L: ROCK/HIP HOP & RAP (1994) 86M D: Rusty Cundieff. *Rusty Cundieff, Larry B. Scott, Mark Christopher Lawrence, Kasi Lemmons.* Fictional gangsta rap stars Niggaz With Hats are chronicled in this attempt at a hip hop *This Is Spinal Tap.* Some of the jokes are corny, but the mockery aimed at everyone from NWA to PM Dawn is so observant and knowledgeable of the music that it shows an obvious love of hip hop. I especially like the pretentious interpretations of lyrics about butts and the ridiculous acronyms (the song "Pet the P.U.S.S.Y.," for example, stands for "political unrest, stabilize society, yeah"). It's not nearly as convincing a mockumentary as *Spinal Tap* (the interviewer played by *Eve's Bayou* director Lemmons is completely unnecessary) but it's much better than Chris Rock's similar *CB4*. —*B. T.*

FIVE CONVERSATIONS ABOUT SOUL L: ROCK/ROCKUMENTARIES (2003) 63M D: Scott Andrews-Dunn. *Teddy Pendergrass, Jaguar Wright, George Clinton, Julie Dexter.* It sounds good on paper, but this collection of interviews about the history and philosophy of soul music comes across like a school project by someone with good connections and nothing else to offer. The interviews are not particularly enlightening or entertaining, they are not edited into any kind of cohesive structure, and only those interviewees you've never heard of are seen performing. Worst of all, the subjects don't seem very enthusiastic and are poorly shot in what appears to be a classroom. The highlight is ?uestlove's (drummer for The Roots) explanation of his theory that black music thrives whenever Republicans are in office and times are tough. (It's a good theory but then how would you explain the sorry state of hip hop during the Bush II Administration?) —*B. T.*

FLEA: ADVENTURES IN SPONTANEOUS JAMMING AND TECHNIQUE L: ROCK/ROCK & ROLL! (1996) 55M D: Rex Olson. *Chad Smith, Flea, River Phoenix.* Flea, the talented and lovable bassist of the Red Hot Chili Peppers, presents what is packaged as an instructional video but is more of a philosophical treatise on the spiritual and emotional power of improvisational music. Flea talks lovingly about his approach to music and the punk, funk, and jazz musicians who influenced him, using hippie-dippy language nobody else could get away with. He does not give step-by-step instructions to beginning players, but does provide very enjoyable interludes jamming with Smith, his band's drummer. The interview portions are hosted by the late Phoenix, trying to look very intense and thoughtful, *Inside the Actor's Studio*–style. —*B. T.*

FORBIDDEN ZONE L: ROCK/ROCK MUSICALS (1980) 76M D: Richard Elfman.
Danny Elfman, Herve Villechaize, Phil Gordon, Susan Tyrrell. This is, without a doubt, the finest new-wave sci-fi musical in the history of film. Shot on a nonbudget in Los Angeles warehouses and basements at the height of the proto-punk art explosion, *Forbidden Zone* careens across the viewer's brain like a driverless clown car on fire. The story follows members of the Hercules family into the sixth dimension, where they encounter mentally deficient boxers, a sex-crazed midget overlord, a giant frog in a tuxedo, and endless other inspired inventions from the head of Elfman (brother of composer Danny, who hams it up as Satan in one of the film's several amazing musical numbers). Actor "Toshiro Baloney," playing chicken-obsessed Squeezit Henderson as well as his masochistic, cross-dressing sibling Renee, is actually Matthew Bright, the director of *Freeway*. And the aforementioned braindead pugilists are really drooling maniac performance artists The Kipper Kids, one of whom, in his real life, drinks his own urine and is married to Bette Midler. Seriously. This movie has everything. To call it brilliant and hilarious would be a brutal understatement. —*Z. C.*

GET CRAZY L: ROCK/ROCK MUSICALS (1983) 92M D: Allan Arkush.
Miles Chapin, Malcolm McDowell, Allen Goorwitz, Gail Edwards, Ed Begley Jr., Daniel Stern. Fans of director Arkush's previous film, *Rock 'n' Roll High School* should seek out this movie. While it doesn't feature the Ramones, it does have a similar manic rock atmosphere and ample amounts of goofy humor. It's set in a rock club on New Years Eve 1983; the club owner (Goorwitz) is on his death bed and a harried young stage manager (Stern) must keep it all together. Among those booked for the big show are Reggie Wanker (McDowell), an egotistical rocker in the Mick Jagger mold; Nada, an almost allgirl new-wave punk band; King Blues (Bill Henderson), a surrogate Albert King blues man; and everyone performs their version of "Hoochie Coochie Man." Lou Reed also plays a Bob Dylan–type character that shows up at the gig too late. The concert is threatened by corporate bad guys (led by Begley) and an insane fire

inspector, but ultimately, everyone's problems are solved with drugs. I think the music would be better and the film would have a stronger reputation if they'd used real bands, but still, *Get Crazy* is a helluva lot of frantic fun. —*S. H.*

GIGANTIC (A TALE OF TWO JOHNS) L: ROCK/ROCKUMENTARIES (2002) 102M D: A. J. Schnack.
Janeane Garofalo, John Flansburgh, Sarah Vowell, Conan O'Brien, Dave Eggers, Jon Stewart, John Linnell. If you're not a They Might Be Giants fan, you might still enjoy this film, but the experience will likely be a vastly confusing in-joke. Made very much in quirky They Might Be Giants style, this documentary tracks their career and music in a delightfully haphazard way, sprinkled with random commentaries that pop out of nowhere and vanish just as quickly. My favorite? The movie opening officially with the mayor of Lincoln, Massachusetts, cutting a ribbon with ladies politely clapping and a unicyclist wheeling by. *Gigantic* is a playful cavalcade of interviews, concert footage, old photographs, video clips, and an entertaining exploration into the background and beginnings of this often neglected and unrecognized giant in the alternative music world. Check it out! —*M. N.*

GORILLAZ PHASE ONE: CELEBRITY TAKE L: ROCK/HIP HOP & RAP (2002) 174M D: Jamie Hewlett.
Murdoc, Noodle, Russel, 2-D. The literally minded would say that Gorillaz are a pop supergroup composed of Blur's Damon Albarn, Cibo Matto's Miho Hatori, cartoonist/*Tank Girl* creator Hewlett, the great hip hop producer Dan the Automator, and occasional guests Ibrahim Ferrer and Del tha Funkee Homosapien. However, the rest of us know that Gorillaz are actually a band of cartoon characters: satanic bassist Murdoc, zombie-obsessed singer 2-D (whose sockets contain no eyes), gargantuan drummer Russel, preteen martial artist/guitarist Noodle, and a blue ghost MC who haunts Russel's bass drum. At its best their "dark pop" music is infectious, but more interesting is the animated world Hewlett has created. This DVD compiles their five videos along with five "gorilla bite" animated clips and other visuals they used for their live tour (in which they stayed true to their animated counterparts by performing behind a screen with drawings projected onto it). The only bad animation is on the live clip, where they use ugly 3-D CGI versions of the characters. Skip the lame mockumentary "Charts of Darkness," though, unless you want to see Albarn trying to be funny and failing. —*B. T.*

GRAFFITI ROCK & OTHER HIP HOP DELIGHTS L: ROCK/HIP HOP & RAP (1983) 24M D: Michael Holman, Run DMC, Treacherous Three, New York City Breakers.
If you're in the mood for a cheesy time capsule of old school hip hop, you can't do much better than this archived episode of a *Soul Train*–like New York hip hop show. Young people in Kangol

hats and Adidas sweats look awkward trying to dance and have fun outside of their natural habitat, but there is an infectious enthusiasm for introducing the culture to the mainstream through the power of television. You may recognize Holman's scratch lesson ("don't try this at home, only under hip hop supervision") because the Beastie Boys sampled it. Also keep an eye out for dancers Vincent Gallo (who introduces himself as "Prince Vince") and Debi Mazar. The DVD is padded with home video footage of DJs, breakers, and graffiti artists. Even the boring stuff is somewhat of a revelation to those of us who grew up on hip hop but didn't witness these formative years. —B. T.

GROUPIES L: ROCK/ROCKUMENTARIES (1970) 75M D: Ron Dorfman, Nevard. *Patty Cakes, Joe Cocker, Miss Harlow, Goldie Glitters.* For as long as there have been rock stars, there have been groupies. Rock stars represent the sexiest, richest, most talented, and most unobtainable people, and groupies make it their challenge to have their own personal brush with these elevated folk. This documentary was made in the '70s, and for the women depicted, being a groupie is not just a hobby, but a lifestyle. From the woman who has a collection of rock star penis casts, including one of Jimi Hendrix, to the gay groupies of San Francisco, whose lifestyle is more about sexual frustration than anything else, this documentary never fails to entertain. Sure, it's a little fluffy, and at times even creepy, but considering the topic, this ultimately results in a much more pure and dynamic look at a timeless subculture. —J. S.

HERBIE HANCOCK AND THE ROCKIT BAND L: ROCK/HIP HOP & RAP (1984) 73M *Herbie Hancock.* This live video was made during the era of Hancock's *Futureshock* album, when he and producer Bill Laswell were experimenting with combining jazz and electro funk with hip hop, particularly the turntable work of DJ DXT. This video not only includes the landmark "Rockit" video, but features the video's wiggling mannequins and automatons on stage with Herbie. The inclusion of breakdancers in the stage show marks this as a legitimate hip hop fusion landmark and not just an exploitation. —B. T.

HERBIE HANCOCK: FUTURE-2-FUTURE LIVE L: JAZZ/JAZZ (2002) 104M D: Michael Simon. *Herbie Hancock.* Hancock performs live, showcasing the music from his *Future 2 Future* album, a sort of sequel to *Futureshock* in which he updates his experiments in fusing his music with hip hop and turntablism. The DJ this time is Phonosycographdisc (once a member of the Invisibl Skratch Piklz crew, now an innovator in his own right) whose scratches are much more intricate than the basic cuts DXT provided for Hancock's earlier albums. Hancock even gets playful enough to step away from the keyboards and exchange cuts with Disc using a CD-scratcher. —B. T.

HATED: GG ALLIN & THE MURDER JUNKIES L: ROCK/ROCKUMENTARIES (1993) 120M D: Todd Phillips. *GG Allin, Merle Allin.* G. G. Allin, a punk rocker infamous for shitting on stage, is seen performing, usually in tiny venues where most of the crowd tries to keep their distance. He usually doesn't get through more than one or two songs before randomly assaulting a member of the audience or chasing after them with his own feces or pieces of a banana previously shoved up his ass. The performances are extremely difficult to watch, but the interviews with fans and band mates trying to intellectualize them are incredible. One fan seems to be interested on an ironic level until he casually reveals that he also visits John Wayne Gacy in prison. The DVD also includes Phillips's shaky home video of Allin's last performance, an incredible real-time view from performance to riot to GG running down the streets of New York City trying to find a cab while naked and followed by a mob of fans chanting his name. —B. T.

HEDWIG AND THE ANGRY INCH L: ROCK/ROCK MUSICALS (2001) 91M D: John Cameron Mitchell. *Rob Campbell, Stephen Trask, Theodore Liscinski, Andrea Martin, Miriam Shor, Michael Pitt, John Cameron Mitchell.* Not since *The Rocky Horror Picture Show* has a rock musical made me want to sing and dance the way *Hedwig and the Angry Inch* does. A young German man turns gender-bending glam rocker after a sex change operation goes wrong. Hedwig's band, the Angry Inch, tours the country on the heels of Tommy Gnosis, the old flame who stole Hedwig's music and catapulted to fame. The music is aggressive and catchy; you'll want to listen to the soundtrack over and over. The costumes and the vibrant, colorful feel of the film are also a treat, but be warned—Hedwig will always look better in a dress than you will. In any case, it's fun, it's energetic, the story is told almost entirely through song, and the main character is sexy and usually scantily clad. It's everything a rock musical should be. —J. S.

I LOVE MELVIN L: MUSICALS/MUSICALS (1953) 77M D: Don Weis. *Donald O'Connor, Allyn Joslyn, Richard Anderson, Una Merkel, Debbie Reynolds.* This easy, breezy MGM musical comedy follows chorus girl and wannabe film star Judy LeRoy (Reynolds) and Melvin Hoover (O'Connor), a *Look* magazine photographer trying to get noticed by getting Judy on the cover. Reynolds is charming and little bit aloof as a glamorous gal, and O'Connor is perfectly bumbling as the hapless dork who can't find love. There are, of course, good musical numbers as well. Reynolds and O'Connor cruise through a park each singing individually about the love they wish to find, never knowing that they're right here for each other. The best song-and-dance routine sees Judy getting her first big break as a "football" among the football players. In her brown pigskin costume they snap her, pass her, run with her, score a touchdown, and kick the extra point, her lithe body tumbling through the uprights! *I Love Melvin* is a lighthearted jaunt any fan of musicals will like. —*G. M.*

MICHAEL JACKSON: MOONWALKER L: ROCK/ROCK & ROLL! (1988) 94M D: Colin Chilvers, Jerry Kramer, Will Vinton. *Joe Pesci, Brandon Adams, Sean Lennon, Michael Jackson.* Jackson's extraordinary dancing talent and bizarre personality shine through every minute of this surreal video collection/feature-length fantasy. It begins as an overview of his career, but turns weird when claymation autograph hounds chase him on a studio back lot. He disguises himself as a rabbit and escapes on a motorcycle—the rabbit later crossing paths with… Michael Jackson. Whuh? That's nothing compared to the extended version of the "Smooth Criminal" video, where the sinister drug kingpin Pesci, along with his paramilitary thugs and pet tarantulas try to kill Michael and a group of kids. At various times Michael transforms himself into a Prohibition-era gangster, a car, a giant robot, and a spaceship that ascends to the stars like Jesus or E.T. —*B. T.*

MASTER MUSICIANS OF JAHJOUKA L: WORLD MUSIC/WORLD MUSIC (1983) 62M D: Michael Mendizza. Although narrated like a dull travelogue, this is an incredible documentary of Jahjouka, a small Moroccan village with a heritage of highly respected musicianship. Their music is believed to have healing powers, and their art form is passed down from generation to generation. They were "discovered" in the sixties by such westerners as William S. Burroughs and Brian Jones of the Rolling Stones, who recorded an album there. The local musicians even perform chants about Jones, as if he were some mythical hero. The film explores the village traditions and the way the visits affect the local music. But it's worth watching for the musical performances alone. —*B. T.*

JOSEPH AND THE AMAZING TECHNICOLOR DREAMCOAT L: MUSICALS/MUSICALS (1999) 78M D: David Mallet, Steven Pimlott. *Donny Osmond, Richard Attenborough, Joan Collins.* After the big-budget stage tour featuring Osmond as Joseph, a film version was bound to follow. A school assembly serves as audience and neatly provides the backup singers. Once Joseph enters, the stage opens to a colorfully stylized backdrop against which the musical is performed. Produced by composer Andrew Lloyd Webber (this is his first musical), *Joseph* stays true to his intent. The music is stylistically eclectic and the words by Tim Rice are often corny and trite. But to Webber fans that's all part of the territory, and this production fills the bill. —*N. J.*

RAHSAAN ROLAND KIRK: THE ONE MAN TWINS L: JAZZ/JAZZ (1972) 50M D: Michel Dami, Joel Dorn. *Rahsaan Roland Kirk.* At the beginning of this film, an unseen narrator says, "Let me tell you some-thin' about Rahsaan," as you see Rahsaan Roland Kirk blowing a saxophone at the 1972 Montreux Jazz Festival. But then you realize, no, he's blowing *two* saxophones at the same time. He has a band, but he's the entire horn section, trading his sax solos with his clarinet solos. He also plays manzello, stritch, flute, and various whistles. At one point he sings while playing the flute, another time he blows a flute with his nose and a harmonica with his mouth. He looks like some kind of postapocalyptic traveler with all of these instruments strapped to him. What's most amazing is that the music is strangely beautiful. This is not a gimmick, like a one-man band, it's just his eccentric way of creating the sounds he needs for the music. Except for a title card at the end there is no other explanation offered—no interviews or narration. The music speaks for itself. —*B. T.*

KRUSH GROOVE L: ROCK/HIP HOP & RAP (1985) 100M D: Michael Schultz. *LL Cool J, Kurtis Blow, The Fat Boys, Shiela E., Run DMC, Blair Underwood.* Long before he became a powerful business man, community activist, and presenter of comedy and poetry jams—back when he was just the cofounder of Def Jam—Russell Simmons had his life turned into a movie. Apparently he wanted to play himself, but he wasn't an actor, so the role went to Underwood. Russell Walker (Underwood) borrows money to press Run DMC's records, birthing the fictional Krush Groove label. He also signs Kurtis Blow, LL Cool J, and the Beastie Boys. It's a corny movie with lots of bad eating jokes on the Fat Boys and an embarrassing rap by Sheila E., but it's pretty exciting to see these legends on film, especially the young, energetic LL. Schultz also directed *Cooley High, Car Wash, Disorderlies* and, believe it or not, a TV sequel to *The Jerk* called *The Jerk, Too* before becoming a prolific TV director. —*B. T.*

LIQUID SKY L: ROCK/ROCK N ROLL HELL (1982) 118M D: Slava Tsukerman. *Anne Carlisle, Bob Brady, Otto von Wernherr, Susan Doukas, Paula Sheppard.* Director Tsukerman's defining early-'80s cult flick tops all other New Wave films with its outrageous yet functional wardrobe, makeup, dialogue, and sought-after soundtrack. *Liquid Sky* anticipated a then-and-now zeitgeist in far-out club kid style, presaging Michael Alig's crew by a decade. Carlisle is delicious in the dual roles of Margaret and Jimmy, and performs the only self-blow job in the history of nonporn cinema. An alien has landed across the way from Margaret's above-club pad and is inserting crystal splinters into the brains of anyone who experiences orgasm in her home. She blames herself, declaring that her "pussy's got teeth." Sheppard pounds out a dynamic turn as Adrien, complete with hot lesbian scissor-legs fuck and heart-thumping cult song of the decade, "Me and My Rhythm Box." —*S. R.*

MALIBU'S MOST WANTED L: ROCK/HIP HOP & RAP (2003) 86M D: John Whitesell. *Taye Diggs, Ryan O'Neal, Jamie Kennedy, Anthony Anderson, Regina Hall, Blair Underwood.* If media has made the world a global village, then culture is merely a matter of which channel you choose. Kennedy's Beverly Hills scion Brad "B-Rad" Gluckman picked up his hip hop identity from BET and MTV, and simply adapted it to his own protected world. His chain-wearing, rap-spouting, naive child of privilege manages to remain oddly sweet, even when accosted by a pair of classically trained actors (Diggs and Anderson) hired by his politician father to "scare him white." The joke is not that this hip hop white boy with pimp-daddy ambitions is an affluent phony, but that he's genuine, with an unwavering conviction in his media-shaped identity. Too bad the film, which Kennedy spun from a stand-up comedy skit, remains as blissfully unaware of its possibilities as B-Rad is of his absurdity. —*S. A.*

MEDUSA: DARE TO BE TRUTHFUL L: ROCK/ROCK MUSICALS (1992) 51M D: Julie Brown. *Chris Elliott, Julie Brown, Bob Goldthwait.* Brown is a dead ringer for Madonna in this horrifically funny *Truth or Dare* parody. Madonna is kinda funny anyway, but Brown takes it to an entirely different level. This comedy sometimes breaks into the Christopher Guest genius mockumentary style and really shines. You've just gotta love Elliott as the dance trainer; I never knew how hot he looks in tights. —*R. D.*

MR. T: BE SOMEBODY OR BE SOMEBODY'S FOOL! L: ROCK/HIP HOP & RAP (1984) 52M D: Jeff Margolis. *Martika, Mr. T, Kelly Jo Minter.* Nothing better sums up the pop-cultural oddity of Mr. T than this unintentionally hilarious motivational video. Mr. T hangs out with kids, teaching them to eat healthy and believe in themselves through a series of skits, stilted rap songs, even a fashion show ("With her mustard sash and ketchup socks she is a real hot dog."). From the director of the classic *Richard Pryor: Live in Concert*, it features a young New Edition and lyrics written by Ice-T. —*B. T.*

MTV CRIBS: HIP HOP L: ROCK/ROCKUMENTARIES (2003) 62M D: Various. *Snoop Dogg, Missy Elliot, Nelly, Big Boi.* In the late '80s a lot of rappers worried that their colleagues and fans were misplacing their priorities because they wore gold chains and didn't know enough about Africa. Today materialism in commercial rap music has gone to such extremes that MTV created an entire show for rappers (and other musicians) to give tours of their mansions. They proudly show off their giant TVs, their car collections, their pit-bull kennels, their man-made lakes where they go to think. No wonder they don't make 'em like they used to—how are you supposed to write a song like "The Message," "Fuck the Police," or "Rebel Without a Pause" when you own twenty-

five cars, seven bathrooms, a swimming pool, a hot tub, a full-sized basketball court, a recording studio, and a home theater (for watching the *Scarface* DVD it seems)? Most of these people are talented hard workers but I worry about the kids who grow up watching this shit, dreaming of having that kind of money. The most thoughtful the show gets is to lament the loss of Russell Simmons's Manhattan penthouse on 9/11, or to admit on the dull commentary track that certain touches are "a little excessive." The solitary "keepin' it real" segment is Redman's. He lives in a normal house with crap laying everywhere, a broken doorbell, a VHS porn collection, and a cousin sleeping on the floor. He is the only person on this DVD who doesn't own a giant fish tank. —*B. T.*

MURDER WAS THE CASE L: ROCK/HIP HOP & RAP (1994) 16M D: Dr. Dre. *C Style, Snoop Doggy Dogg, Gregory S. Cummins, Freeze Luv, Charlie Murphy.* In 1994 he was still called Snoop Doggy Dogg. He was twenty-three-years old and a rising star who had garnered such attention from his guest appearances with Dr. Dre that his first album, *Doggystyle*, debuted at number one. Dre, interested in a filmmaking career, decided to adapt the song "Murder Was the Case" into a short film. Oliver Stone was so enamored with the short that he tried to have it released on a double bill with *Natural Born Killers*. But the film doesn't live up to the hype—it's just an extended music video based on Snoop's lyrics about an encounter with the devil. The DVD is still a worthwhile curiosity for Snoop fans since it includes vintage interviews and videos like "Natural Born Killaz" by Dr. Dre and Ice Cube. —*B. T.*

MUSICAL JOURNEY: THE FILMS OF PETE, TOSHI & DAN SEEGER—1957–1961 L: FOLK/FOLK (1996) 58M *Pete Seeger, Dan Seeger, Toshi Seeger, Big Bill Broonzy.* Armed with a 16 mm camera and three minute reels of film, Pete and family peered into the recesses of our folk traditions and came up with some fascinating results. Not just a music video but a document of a world long gone. Seeger family friend Stefan Grossman selected the film clips. —*M. S.*

MY FIRST NAME IS MACEO L: JAZZ/JAZZ (1996) 87M D: Markus Gruber. *Maceo Parker, Fred Wesley, George Clinton, Pee Wee Ellis.* Parker is the funkiest saxophone player I've ever heard. He played in James Brown's best band, the JBs ("Maceo, blow your horn!"), then joined Parliament's unparalleled horn section, the Horny Horns. He has continued touring with his own band and recording numerous great funk, soul, and jazz albums. A Maceo show is about the best time you can have with incredibly talented musicians who make the audience smile, sing along, chant, and shake their asses. Anyone could have a great time at a Maceo show (not true of George Clinton's marathon intergalactic funk attacks, which could require years of intense training). This concert film/documentary attempts to document the Maceo experience. It goes through a bit of his history in interview clips, but mostly lets the music speak for itself. There's a nice conversation between Maceo and George Clinton, an outdoor session with the Rebirth Brass Band, and a hilarious scene where Maceo jams with a bunch of little kids on a street. —*B. T.*

NICK CAVE AND THE BAD SEEDS: GOD IS IN THE HOUSE L: ROCK/ROCK & ROLL! (2001) 140M D: John Hillcoat.
Nick Cave, Warren Ellis, Martin Casey, Thomas Wylder, Mick Harvey, Blixa Bargeld. This DVD would please even the most casual Bad Seeds fans. It begins with a forty-minute documentary about the recording of their 2001 album at Abbey Road (previously released as a bonus CD-ROM with the album). It looks much nicer here than it did before and it is a very enjoyable piece, even if it isn't very enlightening. Also included are the three music videos for the album. The third of these, for the beautiful "Love Letter," is original, emotional, and powerful, definitely the highlight of the DVD. The meat of the disc is a sizable segment of an excellent live performance in Lyon, France, in 2001. Unfortunately, a couple of songs were cut, but the beauty of what is included far overshadows the omission. Pouring out their sublime music, the Bad Seeds offer their audience rapture, horror, and madness woven into the mysterious tales of life and death and love imparted by the man himself, my hero Nick Cave. —*T. S.*

PARSIFAL L: OPERA/OPERA (1982) 255M D: Hans-Jürgen
Syberberg. *Armin Jordan, Wolfgang Schone, Martin Sperr, Hans Tschammer.* Seeing a film by German New Wave director Syberberg is like watching one of the less accessible films of British director/painter Peter Greenaway: there really is no plot and what you get is a series of stylized images and symbolism meant to be interpreted on a subtextual level. The medieval legend of the Holy Grail of King Arthur and the Sacred Spear that pierced the side of Christ's body were combined by German composer Richard Wagner for his last opera and form the outline for the film's plot. Told with puppets, theatrical lighting, projected backgrounds, and actors set in a setting that reveals itself to be a giant replica of Wagner's death mask, the complete film is broken into three parts and runs over five hours. Like the opera, it will either drive its viewers crazy with boredom or invoke rapture with its grandeur. —*N. H.*

PAVEMENT: SLOW CENTURY L: ROCK/ROCK & ROLL!
(2002) 60M D: Lance Bangs. *S. M., Spiral Stairs, Bob Nastanovich, Mark Ibold, Gary Young, Steve West.* ". . . I love your tinted eyes. . ." The first DVD documents the Greatest Band in the World, Pavement, from their charmed beginnings in 1989 to their demise in 1999. It has lots of inter-

view segments, live performances, and music videos with commentary. The second DVD has two full-length concerts from the band's final tour: one in Manchester, the other in Seattle. Although these shows are from what is commonly called their suck-period, they play songs from throughout their ten years, and it is a great and holy thing to watch. —*T. B.*

PENNIES FROM HEAVEN L: MUSICALS/MUSICALS (1981)
108M D: Herbert Ross. *Steve Martin, Jessica Harper, Bernadette Peters, Christopher Walken.* No matter how you look at it, *Pennies from Heaven* is a difficult film. Managing to both glorify and ridicule the musical genre, and looking beautiful all the while, it is problematic nonetheless. Audiences didn't exactly take to this darkly ironic film, especially since it followed Martin's successful *The Jerk.* Here he plays Arthur Parker, a rather unlikable traveling sheet music salesman in the heart of the Depression-era '30s who escapes his miserable life by imagining it in Hollywood musical terms. It's to Martin's credit that we end up rooting for Parker, despite his horrible actions throughout the film. But while Martin shines, as do many others, the film still leaves a sour aftertaste in many mouths, thanks to its jarring combination of gritty, depressing realism and big-budget Hollywood musical numbers. Still, if you are willing to go with it, it is quite a wonderful film in its own sort of way. —*C. P.*

PHISH: BITTERSWEET MOTEL L: ROCK/ROCKUMENTARIES
(2000) 82M D: Todd Phillips. *Mike Gordon, Page McConnell, Jon Fishman, Trey Anastasio.* Phish is arguably the best live band in America, comprised of four of the finest musicians working today. They have played The Beatles's *White Album,* Pink Floyd's *Dark Side of the Moon,* and The Who's *Quadrophenia* live and in their entirety. They are described by *Rolling Stone* as "the most important band of the '90s." They are just plain good. I urge you to give Phish a listen before you scoff them off as a Grateful Dead hippie jam band. —*R. G.*

PINK FLOYD: THE WALL L: ROCK/ROCK & ROLL! (1979) 99M
D: Alan Parker. *Christine Hargreaves, James Laurenson, Eleanor David, Bob Hoskins, Bob Geldof, Kevin McKeon.* Geldof stars as Pink, the existentially depressed protagonist of this film version of *The Wall.* His inability to cope is analyzed lyrically and visually by juxtaposing childhood experiences against adult dysfunctions borne of unfocused angst. Finally, Pink's inner demons emerge in a veritable trial gruesomely depicted with animation. The wall separating him from the world summarily breaks down, but does the individual collapse along with it? This kind of musical psychology will appeal to fans of Pink Floyd, but for others it may be hit-and-miss. —*N. J.*

Early Film Music (1927–1939)

The music of early sound film was quite schizophrenic. In the silent film era, music had somewhat settled down to a predictable live-performance technique, but the new sound-film music had to completely reinvent itself. This process took more than a decade and was not always pretty.

The film credited with being the first talkie was in fact a musical—*The Jazz Singer* (1927), with Al Jolson—and so were most of the sound films produced immediately after this success: *The Street Singer, The Vagabond Lover,* and *Rio Rita,* to name a few. But for technical reasons, musicals were extremely expensive and difficult to produce. For one thing, the camera had to be encased in an enormous lead box to shield the sound of its motor from the sensitive microphone. This meant that camera motion in the earliest talkies was virtually nonexistent, because the camera was far too heavy to move. Furthermore, the technology for dubbing and mixing sound simply did not exist at this time, so the entire orchestra had to be on the set for every take. Days of effort could go into getting just a few minutes of good-quality sound and picture.

continued on page 600

PURPLE RAIN L: ROCK/ROCK MUSICALS (1984) 113M D: Albert Magnoli. *Prince, Morris Day, Apollonia, Olga Karlatos, Clarence Williams III.* Here's Prince, at the very height of his fame. He does everything you think of when you think of Prince: singing those great songs, wailing away on his fancy guitar, jerking it off without seeming like some frat boy. He's got the feminine face with the tough facade; the boots, the leather jacket, the motorcycle. He's a total rock god, one of the few icons of the '80s still worth remembering, and then—this is the part that gets me—he goes home, and he lives with his parents. I don't care if he's singing that his mother is never satisfied, it's hard to picture this guy ever living with his parents. *Purple Rain* is a cheesy film, but it's a lot of fun thanks to the great soundtrack, the little guy's badass persona, and the humorous villainy of Morris Day and the Time. —*B. T.*

QUADROPHENIA L: ROCK/ROCK MUSICALS (1979) 120M D: Franc Roddam. *Phil Daniels, Mark Wingett, Philip Davis, Garry Cooper, Ray Winstone, Sting.* "I don't wanna be like everybody else. That's why I'm a mod, see?" The Who's classic rock opera of teen rebellion and alienation in 1965 London hit the screen under the direction of Roddam (*The Bride*) with Daniels as the restless, Vespa-riding Mod Jimmy. It's not really a musical as much as a rough-and-ready drama inspired by the story suggested in the rock opera (though Pete Townshend's music underscores the film quite nicely), and it's aged well over the years. The portrait of early-'60s Britain—of young adults looking to carve out their own identity distinct from the glum middle-class dullness of their parents, and of a music explosion that becomes part of their lives—is astounding, and the desperation of Jimmy's dive into this vivid but undefined culture reverberates to this day. Sting is memorable as the charismatic Mod leader with a working-class secret. —*S. A.*

RETURN OF CAPTAIN INVINCIBLE, THE L: ROCK/ROCK MUSICALS (1983) 90M D: Philippe Mora. *Christopher Lee, Bill Hunter, Kate Fitzpatrick, Alan Arkin.* Arkin is a former American hero who crawls into the bottle after being accused of communist leanings during the blacklist years. He's called back to action when the dreaded supervillain Mr. Midnight (Lee, lampooning years of such roles with a baritone flair) starts "cleaning up" New York City. Arkin makes for a sardonic souse of a super-bum wondering where America and Kate Smith went, and Lee vamps it up nicely. Australian Mora directs this oddball superhero musical spoof on a threadbare budget with more gusto than grace, but the songs (by *The Rocky Horror Picture Show*'s Richard O'Brien) are often fun. Lee confessed in a British TV documentary that this was one of his favorite roles. —*S. A.*

RIVERS CREW 3 WARRIORS L: ROCK/BREAKDANCING (2001) 55M This video focuses on three members of the Rivers Crew from Korea, so each one gets about ten minutes to showcase a video diary of their best moves. Not to say that they aren't mindfuckingly impressive—they are—but it gets a little repetitive after a while. A big part of the visual draw to breaking lies in its tim-

The public eventually tired of these musicals. They wanted another Valentino, preferably one who would talk to them. And thus music in the early sound films had to reinvent itself once again. In the early 1930s, a new notion of the role of music in film began to take hold: the concept of "source music." Source music was essentially that music which had some visual justification on the screen for its existence. The sound of an orchestra, for instance, would not be heard unless the film showed a phonograph playing or perhaps the orchestra playing in a nearby concert hall. In other words, under the concept of source music, there was no such thing as background music (which, of course, later became standard).

Fritz Lang's early sound film *M* (1931) provides a good example of source music. It has no musical soundtrack; however, music is integral to the story. At the beginning of the film, when we are introduced to the murderer (played by Peter Lorre), we see him pick up his victim while whistling the familiar tune "In the Hall of the Mountain King" by Edward Grieg. Not only is the tune strikingly apt for this character, but it also becomes the means by which he is identified to the police—by, of all people, a blind newspaper salesman.

Josef von Sternberg's *The Blue Angel* (1930) with Marlene Dietrich makes creative use of source music just about everywhere except the opening credits. A practicing stage band, a children's choir, whistling characters, and, of course, Dietrich's singing—all this music is justified by visual means within the film. Inventive use of source music is also seen in Hitchcock's *The Lady Vanishes* (1938), in which a musi-

---

ing—pulling out a sequence of moves in an unexpected manner that blows the minds of the people watching—and unfortunately this video fails to translate that element. The most interesting part of the video comes at the end, when the Rivers Crew battles the Expressions Crew, another group from Korea. There, the moves are grounded with purpose and intent. Too bad most people will turn it off before they get to that part. —*T. C.*

ROBIN AND THE 7 HOODS L: MUSICALS/MUSICALS (1964) 123M D: Gordon M. Douglas. *Dean Martin, Frank Sinatra, Sammy Davis Jr., Bing Crosby, Peter Falk.* Sinatra plays Robin Hood as '20s gangster Robbo, with Martin as his Little John, Davis Jr. as sharpshooter Will, Crosby as the stiff do-gooder Allen A. Dale whom they teach to swing ("Gee, I'm a hood! I'm a hood!"), and Falk as cross-town enemy Guy Gisborne. This Rat Pack racket isn't quite as iconic as the quintessential *Ocean's 11*, but it's actually a smoother, more stylish little lark with a bouncy soundtrack by Sammy Cahn and James Van Heusen, including the signature Sinatra tune "My Kind of Town." Barbara Rush costars as a rather shifty and suspicious Marion. —*S. A.*

ROCK 'N' ROLL HIGH SCHOOL L: ROCK/ROCK MUSICALS (1979) 93M D: Allan Arkush. *P. J. Soles, Dey Young, Paul Bartel, The Ramones, Mary Woronov.* Executive producer Roger Corman wanted to make a movie to cash in on the (already dead by '79) disco craze. Lucky for the rest of us, Arkush recruited The Ramones and ditched disco in favor of pure American rock and roll, creating one of the most beloved high school musical comedies ever. Soles plays rock and roller Riff Randell, a serious Ramones groupie whose nerdy friend Kate (Young) wants to date a thickheaded jock. But the good times are squashed by the nazi-like new principal Miss Togar (Woronov), who rules Vince Lombardi High with an iron fist—that is until The Ramones play a kick-ass concert and drive the kids to a frenzied revolt culminating in explosions and riots. *Rock 'n' Roll High School* is good-natured, low-budget fun. Packed with great tunes, endearing performances, and lots of corny jokes, I frigging love this movie! —*S. H.*

ROCK 'N' ROLL NIGHTMARE L: ROCK/ROCK 'N' ROLL HELL (1986) 89M D: John Fasano. *Jillian Peri, Frank Dietz, Jon-Mikl Thor, Teresa Simson.* Thor, Canadian hair metal icon of the '80s, wrote, produced, and stars in this blunder of a B movie. The Tritons (Thor's band) retreat to a peaceful farm getaway to record their latest album. Little do they know the farmhouse is not so peaceful and the workings of Satan may be afoot. The film is mostly unwatchable and I highly recommend viewing the majority of the middle section on fast forward. Do check out the classic padding shots at the beginning of the movie: ohhh, we are driving and eerie music is playing; I bet something bad is going to happen. The ending has to be seen to be believed. Thor's conversation with the Devil is absolutely priceless, as is the battle that follows. Thor, with his tweaked-out metal hair and mascara-laden eyes, strips

cal coda accompanies a scene of a spy at an open window while, above her, rustic folk dances are noisily performed.

By the early 1930s, musicians were actually being squeezed out of the film industry. With the advent of sound film, all the local musicians formerly employed to accompany silent-film screenings suddenly found themselves out of work. And after the initial popularity of musicals faded, it began to look as though source music was going to curtail any meaningful or extensive use of music on film. But once dubbing and mixing were finally technologically feasible, studios began assembling their own permanent music departments with composers, orchestras, orchestrators, and copyists. As in the ever more numerous factories of the time, the music of films began to be produced by a large group of people in the most efficient manner available to them.

One element was missing from this mix, however, an element that we are used to seeing today in films: the autonomous composer. In the early film-music industry, a group of composers would be given the task of writing the music for one film, dividing up their work evenly. In this way, the musical postproduction of a film could be accomplished in just a few days, with this massive music factory working overtime. If the score had a particular theme, it would be shared among the composers; they would then get busy, completing their respective assignments in about twenty-four hours.

Igor Stravinsky was reportedly approached about composing music for film, but when he learned about the time

continued on page 602

---

down to studded briefs and takes on the Devil mano y mano. —*S. W. F.*

ROCKTOBER BLOOD L: ROCK/ROCK N ROLL HELL (1985) 88M D: Beverly Sebastian, Ferd Sebastian. *Nigel Benjamin, Tray Loren, Mick Jones, Joe Strummer.* Hair metal rocker Billy Eye (Loren) is electrocuted for the murder of twenty-five people, plus the attempted murder of his band mate, Lynn Starling (Scoggins). Flash forward three years, Lynn has come out of hiding and rejoins the band as lead singer. She renames the band "Head Mistress" and they are slated to play a music festival Billy set up years ago. Everything seems to be fine until Lynn starts to see Billy everywhere. Is she crazy or is Billy really still alive? More important, do we really give a rat's ass? This is an extremely low-budget generic slasher film containing the requisite nudity and blood. —*S. W. F.*

ROCKY HORROR PICTURE SHOW, THE L: ROCK/ROCK N ROLL HELL (1975) 100M D: Jim Sharman. *Barry Bostwick, Tim Curry, Susan Sarandon, Meat Loaf, Patricia Quinn, Richard O'Brien.* When I was in my first couple years of high school, going to see the *Rocky Horror Picture Show* on Friday nights at whatever shitty little theater it was playing at was the thing to do. We'd dress trashy, throw things, sing along, shout out all the "witty" phrases that went along with what was going on onscreen, and dance in the aisles. Young Curry in high heels made me feel all funny in the tummy, and the songs were so sci-fi/horror/eerie/silly/fantasic that I kept going back week after week to sing along again. After nearly thirty years, high school kids still spend evenings in dank theaters with all their freak friends, reveling in this cult classic musical masterpiece. When you watch the film without the dankness, and the crowd, and the dancing in the aisles, however, it just isn't the same. —*J. S.*

RUDE BOY L: ROCK/ROCK & ROLL! (1980) 127M D: Jack Hazan, David Mingay. *Topper Headon, Paul Simonon, Ray Gange, Mick Jones, Joe Strummer.* An odd hybrid, *Rude Boy* walks the line between corny after-school special and punk rock documentary. Young Ray, a British teen full of existential angst, gets a job as a roadie for The Clash. The difficulty with this movie is that it prioritizes Ray's story, when clearly the audience came for The Clash. Still, the fictional story isn't terrible, and does a decent job establishing a social context for '70s UK punk. The band seems to have fun acting in backstage conversations that were probably scripted, yet come off as pretty natural. And of course the concert footage (of which there's quite a bit) is as good as you'd expect, and maybe better. A must-see for fans of The Clash, but of little interest to anyone else. —*C. B.*

RUTLES, THE: ALL YOU NEED IS CASH L: ROCK/ROCK MUSICALS (1978) 70M D: Eric Idle, Gary Weis. *George Harrison, Michael Palin, Eric Idle, John Halsey.* No one will ever be fooled into thinking Idle's rollicking spoof of the Beatles is anything but a mockery. Though it's undeniably a prime inspiration for *Spinal Tap*, this is more absurd Monty Python outrageousness than tweaking satire, but it's always hilarious and the dead-on music

constraints that would be imposed on him (constraints that no doubt were far more lenient for him), he was indignant, insisting that the music would be finished when *he* decided it was finished. Naturally, he wasn't hired. But how would it be possible to employ such a creative musical genius, really, when the entire industry was set up to produce music that would match the filmed action? The answers would come slowly and from surprising places.

One preeminent Russian composer of the time who did decide to pick up the gauntlet of film music was Sergei Prokofiev, who composed the unforgettable score for Sergei Eisenstein's film *Alexander Nevsky*, released in 1938. Eisenstein's highly developed use of the montage even affected his use of music, and the marriage of music to image in *Alexander Nevsky* as well as Eisen-

stein's films *Ivan the Terrible I* and *II*, both scored by Prokofiev, is not only powerful and thoroughly compelling but makes for a fascinating study.

One year after *Alexander Nevsky,* two of the greatest American films of all time were released: *Gone with the Wind* and *The Wizard of Oz.* The use of a thematic score as largely background music to highlight and enhance the dramatic elements of these movies effectively ended the whole debate over "source music," and aesthetically and technologically cemented the concept of film music as we know it today. Clearly, the best film music would not only tap the tradition of the concert hall but would also be developed in the studio, proportionate to the technological and conceptual advancements of film itself.

—Nathan Jensen

---

parodies by Neil Innes are inspired, ingenious, and almost good enough to be the real thing. Good sport Harrison is along for a cameo, and Mick Jagger and Paul Simon are wickedly funny in interview segments as themselves commenting on the pre-fab four. It was coproduced by Lorne Michaels, which explains why so many cast members of *Saturday Night Live* fill out the film, including Bill Murray, Gilda Radner, and John Belushi (who does a wicked parody of Allen Klein). —*S.A.*

GIL SCOTT-HERON: BLACK WAX L: JAZZ/JAZZ (1982) 80M D: Robert Mugge. *Gil Scott-Heron.* Scott-Heron is best known for his work in the early '70s, but he was also great a decade later when he excoriated Reagan and the beginning of the Reagan era on the album *Reflections*. His song "B-Movie" attacked the low-rent movie star-turned-bumbling president and his cliché-ridden cowboy persona. That song, and the same theme of myth versus reality, continue on this unique concert film. Interspersed between live performances with his band are clips of Scott-Heron reciting poems (including the great "Whitey on the Moon") to dummies in a wax museum, touring the protest zone in front of the White House, and strolling along the Potomac with a boombox singing about Washington, D.C. By no means an overview of Scott-Heron's career (he doesn't even do "The Revolution Will Not Be Televised"), but a very good demonstration of his talents. —*B.T.*

SCRATCH L: ROCK/HIP HOP & RAP (2001) 92M D: Doug Pray. *DJ Qbert, Mixmaster Mike, Rob Swift, DJ Shadow.* Pray, the director of the "grunge" documentary *Hype!,* was an outsider to the scratch DJ culture, but created an extremely entertaining explanation and documentation of the art form, arguing for the turntable as a legitimate musical instrument. It's interesting to see the differences and similarities between the DJs: the X-ecutioners are African-Americans working out of a small house in New York, the Invisibl Skratch Piklz are Asian-Americans working from Qbert's lush property in San Francisco, but both were inspired by Herbie Hancock's "Rockit" and have toy robots next to their turntables. There are many surprising turns, such as Mixmaster Mike's hair-raising blues scratch in his living room, or DJ Shadow leading the camera into a decrepit record shop basement where thousands of LPs are stacked haphazardly to the ceiling. The editing and sound mixing are excellent, and even some people who hate hip hop would come out of the movie with a begrudging respect for the art of scratching. —*B.T.*

1776 L: MUSICALS/MUSICALS (1972) 166M D: Peter H. Hunt. *Donald Madden, William Daniels, Ronald Holgate, Howard da Silva, Ken Howard.* Excellent casting and strong performances keep this musical comedy about America's founding fathers and the creation of the Declaration of Independence from becoming corny. Daniels is remarkable as John Adams, who stubbornly works with the Continental Congress to get a unanimous vote for Jefferson's document, which would effectively sever ties with the King of England. Da Silva is ideal as the witty, even-tempered Franklin whose charisma balances the impatience of Adams. Good music and direction help tie it all together. The restored director's cut on DVD has an extra twenty-five minutes. —*N. J.*

NINA SIMONE: LIVE AT RONNIE SCOTT'S L: JAZZ/JAZZ (1985) 57M D: Steve Cleary, Rob Lemkin. *Nina Simone.*
Simone was a true original in the world of soul music. Her husky voice was both powerful and gorgeous as she sang songs of love and heartbreak, or anthems of the civil rights movement. Even after what are considered the successes of the movement, Simone could not abide by America's racism and defiantly emigrated to France, which perhaps was the reason she did not become as much of a household name as some of her American contemporaries. This film of a 1985 performance at Ronnie Scott's in London puts you right up front in the dark nightclub, watching Simone at the piano playing and singing with a small band, occasionally wiping the sweat from her brow. This intimate angle captures both her strength and her warmth more accurately than a more full-blown concert film. There are also fragments of an interview between codirector Lemkin and Simone when the club is empty, but thankfully the film mostly sticks to the music with classics such as "Mississippi Goddam." —*B. T.*

SKI PARTY L: ROCK/BEACH PARTY! (1965) 90M D: Alan Rafkin. *Annette Funicello, Dwayne Hickman, James Brown, Frankie Avalon, Dick Miller, Yvonne Craig.*
Hickman replaces Funicello as Avalon's sidekick in one of the last beach party movies. Hickman and Avalon play two sexually frustrated college roommates who'll do just about anything to get laid. Before you know it, the beach party goes alpine and the guys resort to cross dressing in order to get closer to two hot snow bunnies, thus providing the missing link between *Some Like It Hot* and *Bosom Buddies.* Don't worry about the snowbound setting because there's still plenty of young folks twisting and gyrating in bikinis, shorts, and miniskirts. Funicello shows up in a cameo as a horny sex-ed instructor and Leslie Gore sings "Sunshine, Lollipops, and Rainbows" on the ski bus. Featuring some pretty stale gags, *Ski Party* is elevated from its ocean-bound kin by the appearance of James Brown and the Famous Flames (performing "I Feel Good" in ski sweaters) and a running gag with a yodeling polar bear. The end credits promise a sequel called *Cruise Party* that never happened. —*S. H.*

SLIM SHADY SHOW, THE L: ROCK/HIP HOP & RAP (2001) 40M D: Mark Brooks, Peter Gilstrap. *Eminem.* Some people have a hard time admitting it, but Eminem is a microphone genius with a knack for storytelling, improvisational rhymes, horrific imagery, and clever boasts. He combines these with ingenious rhyme structures and an incredible

array of vocal styles. He also knows how to put an honest voice to the frustrations felt by angry young people, particularly the white underclasses. Unfortunately, while all this makes for great hip hop albums, it does not seem to help in the world of cartoons. *The Slim Shady Show* is an attempt at smart-ass *South Park*–style humor set both in a trailer park and in the world of hip hop, starring Marshall Mathers and his crazier alter ego Slim Shady. Like most Flash cartoons released on DVD, these shorts might have been mildly diverting when streamed for free from a website, but are woefully inadequate when put on disc. It's really not worth your time. —*B. T.*

SONIC YOUTH: GILA MONSTER JAMBOREE L: ROCK/ROCK & ROLL! (1985) 45M D: Unknown. *Kim Gordon, Thurston Moore, Steve Shelley, Lee Ranaldo.* A rough recording of the first West Coast Sonic Youth performance, in the Mojave Desert in 1985. There was no stage, just the band playing in the sand with an audience (roughly 350 people rumored to be fueled by free LSD circulating through the crowd) swarming in a circle around them. Most of the songs are from *Kill Your Idols* or the then-unreleased *Bad Moon Rising*. The video looks murky and slapped together, but somehow that seems appropriate. An absolute gem for Sonic Youth devotees, this gets my vote for best Sonic Youth video available. When you see them perform "The Burning Spear," I imagine you'll agree. —*C. B.*

SONIC YOUTH: 1991—THE YEAR PUNK BROKE L: ROCK/ROCK & ROLL! (1992) 95M D: David Markey. *Thurston Moore, Kim Gordan, Kurt Cobain, J. Mascis.* A must-see for any Sonic Youth fan, but with a little something for everyone. Behold the Ramones, Nirvana, Dinosaur Jr., Gumball, Babes in Toyland, and of course lots of Sonic Youth—all performances captured with unusual audio-visual clarity. Director Markey follows the Youth on its 1991 European tour, where they saw the closest they would come to commercial success. The result is a document of the excitement just before Nirvana's "Smell Like Teen Spirit" changed the world. But the real meat-and-potatoes here is the very un-serious backstage/road footage (check out the Mascis interview) and some priceless Moore record-shopping diatribes. —*C. B.*

SPACE IS THE PLACE L: JAZZ/JAZZ (1974) 85M D: John Coney. *Sun Ra, Barbara Deloney, Raymond Johnson, June Tyson.* The cosmic free-jazz pioneer Sun Ra returns to Earth in a spaceship powered by music. He touches down in Black Panther–era Oakland, where he tries to save a community center and deal with the FBI, NASA, and a demonic pimp called The Overseer. There's lots of great performance footage of Sun Ra and his Arkestra, mixed in with his interplanetary philosophy and the weird sci-fi/blaxploitation plot.

You've never seen anything like it, unless you've already seen it before. —B. T.

BRITNEY SPEARS: STAGES L: ROCK/ROCKUMENTARIES
(2002) 80M D: Judy Hoffman. *Britney Spears.* Albert Mayles is created as "consulting filmmaker" as well as director of photography and cameraman for this fascinating documentary about Spears's notorious four-day trip to Mexico on her "Dream Within a Dream" tour as a sequel to *Gimme Shelter.* In that film, the Rolling Stones put on a great show that turned disastrous when members of the Hell's Angels (acting as security) stabbed someone in the audience. In *Stages,* the performance is destroyed not by cultural clashes and idealistic experiments, but by the prepackaged nature of the concert. The show is based around choreography, special effects, and lip synching, so when faced with an unexpected rainstorm Spears can't dance safely, and she can't go out there and just sing her songs. We see Spears's life on tour: accompanied by enormous bodyguards, preceded by bomb-sniffing dogs, constantly being primped. The DVD itself is sponsored by Samsung, so whenever Spears talks on her cell phone (apparently not a Samsung) they blur it out, giving the illusion that she's holding a penis or a middle finger or something. Speaking of which, the notorious flipping off of the press and the abrupt end to the concert (both widely criticized in the press) are not shown. Despite these limitations, a sad portrait of the current state of pop music still comes through, especially in the final scene. Backstage, while 50,000 people wait in the rain to see if she'll finish her show, her personal assistant/family friend tells her, "You gotta make a decision. You are *twenty* years old." (This DVD is only available with the Britney Spears coffee table book of the same name.) —B. T.

SPICE WORLD L: ROCK/ROCK MUSICALS (1997) 93M D: Bob
Spiers. *Spice Girls, Alan Cumming, Richard O'Brien, Richard E. Grant, George Wendt, Roger Moore.* I don't know if someone already coined the word cine-masochist, but if they did they were probably talking about this movie. I'm still not sure why I watched it. It's not quite bad enough to be "so bad it's good" (it's still pretty bad though). *Spice World* came out after their fifteen minutes of fame had ended. The five singing tarts travel around England in a cool double-decker bus, help their Asian friend have a baby, wear silly but revealing outfits, fly to Miami, meet extra-terrestrials, play lots of lousy pop tunes, and it all ends at a big concert at the Royal Albert Hall ... which is the best part of the whole movie because it's the end! While the supporting cast is peppered with lots of cameos by British musicians and actors, the girls are pretty boring and none of them are allowed to develop much personality or individuality besides being "sporty" or some other bullshit. This movie might be

funny in another ten years, but there's really no need to rush things now. —S. H.

STRAIGHT FROM THE STREETS L: ROCK/HIP HOP & RAP
(1998) 110M D: Robert Corsini, Keith O'Derek. *Ice Cube, DJ Quik, Snoop Dogg, Ice-T, Denzel Washington.* If you just glanced at the cover, you'd think this was some video collection sold on TV. It just lists a bunch of rap artists next to a small picture of Ice Cube and a quote from Snoop Dogg. Actually it's an excellent documentary chronicling seven years of culture and politics in Los Angeles. The genesis of the documentary was a series of street interviews the filmmakers were shooting during the Rodney King uprising. They happened to come across Ice-T, who said he wished people would stop burning down their own businesses and start burning down the police station. From here the story continues through the three strikes law, censorship of rap music, the gang truce, the Million Man March, and more. It's not particularly polished, but the material is priceless. The DVD includes director commentary and numerous outtakes of interviews and freestyles with Ice Cube, Snoop Dogg, Kurupt, and others. —B. T.

STRAIGHT, NO CHASER L: JAZZ/JAZZ (1988) 90M D:
Charlotte Mitchell Zwerin. *Thelonious Monk, T. S. Monk.* A beautiful, bittersweet portrait of the great jazz pianist Thelonious Monk, told through a combination of new interviews and gorgeous black-and-white footage shot on a 1967–68 European tour. Monk's complex music and personality are fascinating material, although it's sad to hear the story of his increasing mental distance, as if he left a little bit of his mind on whatever plane his music comes from. In one scene, Monk is in an airport, and he just starts spinning around in circles for no reason at all. I'm glad someone had the foresight to shoot all this footage; it's a miracle of a movie, up there with *Gimme Shelter* as one of the all-time great music documentaries. —B. T.

STYLE WARS L: ROCK/HIP HOP & RAP (1983) 70M D: Tony
Silver, Henry Chalfant. *Cap, Frosty Freeze.* A priceless document of the early days of hip hop culture, this PBS documentary follows a group of pioneering New York graffiti writers as they illegally turn subway cars into moving temporary art exhibits. The film argues for the artistic significance of their work, but is more compelling for its depiction of the renegade/outlaw side of the culture as the writers come up against antigraffiti authority figures such as Mayor Ed Koch. There's also a memorable subplot about the community of artists banding together against a rogue who keeps painting over their work (this clearly inspired the villainous "Spit" character in *Beat Street*). The DVD release of *Style Wars* is superb. It includes 2002 interviews with most of the artists, and unlike rappers and breakdancers, most of them seem to be better off now

Best music documentaries

Anything by Les Blank

THE BEATLES ANTHOLOGY

THE BEST OF CHIC-A-GO-GO

DEVO: THE MEN WHO MAKE THE MUSIC

DON'T LOOK BACK

FRIENDS FOREVER

FUGAZI: INSTRUMENT

GIMME SHELTER

HIGH LONESOME

HYPE!

I AM TRYING TO BREAK YOUR HEART

INSIDE BJÖRK

THE LAST WALTZ

SCRATCH

STOP MAKING SENSE

STRAIGHT NO CHASER

THEREMIN

URGH: A MUSIC WAR

WATTSTAX

WE'RE ALL DEVO

ZIGGY STARDUST

than they were when they were young. There are also extensive galleries, and not just of graffiti: Ram-el-zee's bizarre suits of armor and "Letter Racer" skateboards are my favorite extra on the disc. —B. T.

SUN RA: ARKESTRA—LIVE AT THE PALAMINO L: JAZZ/JAZZ (1988) 93M This DVD was only released briefly in 2003, intended as the first in a series that never happened. I'm guessing it was unauthorized since it shows signs of being transferred directly from VHS. With that in mind, though, the quality is pretty good, and it's great to see an uninterrupted Arkestra show. Although it starts out with the sort of chaotic free jazz for which Sun Ra is best known, most of the set is spent on more traditional, bluesy numbers. The DVD also includes a duet between Ra and Don Cherry, and a short interview. When the interviewer tells him he seems like "a man with a plan," he explains that he is not a man at all, but an angel. —B. T.

SURF II L: ROCK/BEACH PARTY! (1984) 91M D: Randall M. Badat. *Morgan Paull, Cleavon Little, Lyle Waggoner, Eddie Deezen, Ruth Buzzi.* Like *Return of the Living Dead*, this entry concentrates on the gravely serious topic of zombies with mohawks. This nigh-perfect film is best summarized by its writer/director Badat: "Menlo Schwartzer, the geekiest genius of all, wants to rid the world of surfers by transforming them into garbage ingesting zombie punks! But no way dude can he stop their most awesome party!" An uncontrollable new-wave beach-horror-comedy, *Surf II* (no, there was NOT a *Surf I*) packs more slapstick and early-'80s drive-in mania into one movie than any sane mind could imagine. Included: trash-chomping, drooling, undead punks, valley girls, transgendered mad scientists in futuristic underwater bunkers, hard-working cop Chief Boyardee, the guy who played the corpse in the *Weekend at Bernie's* films, and an appearance by actor Fred Asparagus as "Fat Boy #1." Add the pogo-inducing soundtrack from Wall of Voodoo, Circle Jerks, Thomas Dolby, and Oingo Boingo and maybe you're starting to get the idea. Mad scientist Schwartzer is masterfully portrayed by über-nerd Deezen, the bespectacled schmoe from *Grease* and Steven Spielberg's *1941*. And don't miss the heartbreaking guest appearances by yesteryear's comedy favorites Buzzi and Little! Missing this movie would be like beating yourself in the face with a brick! —Z. C.

THIS IS SPINAL TAP L: ROCK/ROCK MUSICALS (1984) 82M D: Rob Reiner. *Harry Shearer, Christopher Guest, Michael McKean, Rob Reiner.* This film is hilarious. And it rocks. It's hilarockous. Yeah that's a new word. It's the only word to describe the awesome power and sheer brilliance of *This Is Spinal Tap*, arguably the funniest movie ever. Its most impressive feat is that the viewer is totally duped into believing in these guys. They're not a real band, but for all intents and purposes they are. Their music sounds real, they can actually play. What makes them a fake band? If someone is so good at pretending to be, say, a bartender, but isn't technically a bartender, what's the difference if nobody notices? These actors so embody their characters that we almost stop believing it's a "mockumentary" and give over to the apparent reality of the movie. I've seen interviews with "real" rock stars that don't feel as tangible as Spinal Tap. This hilarockous epic of egocentric, aging musicians, doomed drummers, sex-farms, dancing midgets, Stonehenge, and big-bottomed buttrock goes to eleven. Which is one higher than reality. —K. C.

TOUGHER THAN LEATHER L: ROCK/HIP HOP & RAP (1988) 92M D: Rick Rubin. *Jam Master Jay, Rick Rubin, DMC, Run, Richard Edson.* This is a disappointingly serious blaxploitation-style story about the trio getting revenge on a gangster (played by pioneering hip hop and rock producer/Def Jam cofounder/director of the movie Rubin) for killing their friend and roadie Runny Ray (playing himself). Nowadays this film is more entertaining as a time capsule, with Slick Rick, *Licensed to Ill*–era Beastie Boys, young and obnoxious Rubin, and of course the great Run DMC and Jam Master Jay in all their glory. The opening is priceless—big lovable DMC portrays himself as a badass just getting out of prison. Before you even see him you see his shadow, and it's instantly recognizable because of his iconic hat. —*B. T.*

TRUE STORIES L: ROCK/ROCK MUSICALS (1986) 89M D: David Byrne. *David Byrne, John Goodman, Annie McEnroe, Spalding Gray, Swoozie Kurtz*. Like a very backward version of *Our Town*, *True Stories* dives into the private lives of ordinary town folk with a narrator to lead the way. The difference is that the town is Virgil, Texas, and the narrator is Byrne wearing a cowboy hat. A number of very peculiar people are followed closely in this film. One who stands out is Goodman, playing an older bachelor who wants to get married so badly that he has a marquee outside his house advertising the fact. As we follow his constant dating, we see even more bizarre people. All of this is perfectly framed with music by Talking Heads, making it something between a mockumentary and a concert film. —*N. J.*

TRUTH OR DARE L: ROCK/ROCKUMENTARIES (1991) 118M D: Alek Keshishian. *Madonna, Warren Beatty, Sandra Bernhard*. If you're an absolute, die-hard Madonna fan you will likely love this film. As for the rest of us... Madonna apparently feels compelled to show her fans her true, unadulterated self, allowing cameras to follow her everywhere. But of course it's shot in black and white stock for an artsy effect, and Madonna had final say on everything in it. Despite all that, for large portions of the film she's concerned with how she looks. There really is no time spent on her rehearsals or how she goes about creating her music, neither creatively nor technically. It's mainly gabbing and makeup and playing gossip games like Truth or Dare. Even Beatty seems thoroughly unamused by this whole affair. —*N. J.*

UP IN SMOKE TOUR L: ROCK/HIP HOP & RAP (2000) 150M D: Philip G. Atwell. *Xzibit, Eminem, Ice Cube, Dr. Dre, Snoop Dogg*. The Up in Smoke Tour was the biggest, most ridiculous Monsters of Rock–style hip hop show. A giant talking skull shot lasers out of its eyes, a car with hydraulics drove onto the stage, and there was a liquor store set where Dre could "come through with a gang of Tangeray" at the same moment Snoop mentioned exactly that in his lyrics. This movie, which includes performance footage as well as backstage shenanigans, doesn't come close to capturing the joy of this big, silly spectacle starring the perfect lineup of West Coast greats (plus Eminem), but I'm glad it's here for the historical record.

Otherwise people might not believe me about that talking skull. —*B. T.*

WAVE TWISTERS L: ROCK/HIP HOP & RAP (2001) 45M D: Eric Henry, Syd Garon. *DJ Flare, Buckethead, D-Styles, Yogafrog, DJ Qbert*. Turntable virtuoso DJ Qbert turned his album of the same name into this animated sci-fi fever dream, which has been described as a hip hop *Heavy Metal*. When a dentist discovers a powerful turntable weapon in the belly of a half-man/half-shark, he joins forces with a graffiti artist, a robot MC, and a breakdancing grandpa to travel the galaxy fighting for the Lost Arts of hip hop. With the exception of one guitar solo, every sound in the movie comes from a turntable; even the dialogue, which is mostly made of samples from readalong storybook records. The animation, designed by graffiti artist Doug "Doug-One" Pray, is accompanied by live-action characters, crude 3-D computer animation, models, found art, and public domain NASA photos. It's the cinematic equivalent of sampling, and the result is a low-budget masterpiece that seems to move in the same way that the beats bump. One of the best hip hop films, and by far the most imaginative. The DVD even includes source files for the characters so that others can "sample" them. —*B. T.*

WE'RE ALL DEVO L: ROCK/ROCK & ROLL! (1983) 55M D: Gerald V. Casale. *Alan Myers, Timothy Leary, Laraine Newman, Gerald V. Casale, Robert Mothersbaugh, Mark Mothersbaugh, Bob Casale*. Devo was always more than just a band and their visual concepts, crackpot mythologies, and de-evolution manifesto combined some of the best New Wave punk music with so many weird ideas that the Ohio band was a natural to produce some of the best early music videos. This film collects fourteen songs from their great first two albums to their breakthrough hit "Whip It" to later misfires like the theme to *Dr. Detroit*. The videos are linked together with predictably odd wraparound segments that attack corporate America and the military. If you only think of Devo as those weird New-Wavers who wear flowerpots on their heads, you are missing out on some highly imaginative, fun stuff. —*S. H.*

WILCO: I AM TRYING TO BREAK YOUR HEART L: ROCK/ROCKUMENTARIES (2002) 92M D: Sam Jones. *Jeff Tweedy, John Stirratt, Leroy Bach, Glenn Kotche, Jay Bennett, Greg Kot*. I Am Trying to Break Your Heart centers on the creation of Wilco's album *Yankee Hotel Foxtrot*. This documentary (named after the album's lead track) delves into the very heart of what it means to be in a creative collaboration and to protect artistic integrity. Over the course of the film the band records an album that is rejected by their label, fire a band member, tour, and ultimately sign to a label closely affiliated with the one that originally rejected their work. The music is amazing, and any Wilco fan will love the behind-the-scenes look at how a truly great album was made. Little attention is given to the members of Wilco as individuals, which would have added a more well-rounded feel and given a deeper understanding of the band's tense dynamic. Overall, though, *I Am Trying to Break Your Heart* is a good documentary on a great band. —*J. S.*

WILD STYLE L: ROCK/HIP HOP & RAP (1982) 82M D: Charlie Ahearn. *Sandra Fabara, Fab Five Freddy, Lee Quinones.* The first and still the purest hip hop narrative film, *Wild Style* documents graffiti (at the time when it was being respected and exploited by New York galleries) and its relationship to the other hip hop arts. Old-school legends are presented, such as Busy Bee, Fab Five Freddy, Cold Crush Brothers, and even Ram-El-Zee, most (arguably) at their peak. Though definitely low budget and awkwardly acted, this film is a priceless time capsule for the early days of the culture. (You may also recognize it as a source of many samples, both on the soundtrack and in the dialogue). —*B. T.*

WESLEY WILLIS: DADDY OF ROCK 'N' ROLL L: ROCK/ ROCKUMENTARIES (2002) 59M D: Daniel Bitton. *Wesley Willis.* A short documentary on the daily life of Willis, the schizophrenic rock musician whose ranting lyrics are candid and at times a little disturbing. *Daddy of Rock 'n' Roll* is both an interesting look at a unique musician and an honest glimpse into what it means to live with mental illness. The documentary is true to the style of Willis himself, with depictions of his musical process broken up by long monologues that have the same abstract, disturbing feel as his music. Interviews with the many close friends who helped care for Willis reveal insight into his character and the voices that tormented him, and how those voices were kept under control so he could pursue his creative ambitions until his recent death. This thoughtful, provoking documentary pays an excellent tribute a very complicated, creative life. —*J. S.*

STEVIE WONDER: SONGS IN THE KEY OF LIFE L: ROCK/ ROCKUMENTARIES (1998) 75M D: David Heffernan. *Stevie Wonder, Quincy Jones, Gary Byrd, Berry Gordy, Herbie Hancock.* Music is subjective, of course, but can't we all agree that Stevie Wonder's 1976 double-LP *Songs in the Key of Life* is one of the greatest works of art of the twentieth century? OK, good. This documentary revisits the making of the album through interviews and a reunion between Stevie and all the musicians from the album. They rerecord some songs to show how it was done—we even get to see Stevie playing drums. My favorite part is when Stevie plays keyboards and sings gibberish because he can't remember all the lyrics to "I Wish." And it sounds beautiful! There's also a moment where one of the band members suddenly realizes that he never got his high school diploma because he was so busy working on the album. —*B. T.*

YELLOW SUBMARINE L: ROCK/BEATLES (1968) 90M D: George Dunning. *Paul Angelis, Dick Emery, Peter Batten, Geoffrey Hughes, John Clive, Lance Percival.* The ultimate in trippy psychedelic flicks. Travel with The Beatles as they are recruited to save Pepperland from the menacing Blue Meanies. Swim with them through the Sea of Holes, the Sea of Time, the Sea of Monsters, Nowhere Land, and many other strange and dangerous vistas. Watch them battle Snapping Turks, Screaming Clowns, Apple Bonkers, and of course, Glove! The humor is wry and dry, sharp and clever, with puns galore and in-jokes just waiting to be found. Though some might consider the animation to be dated, its unique look and Peter Max–esque style is still wonderfully original and stands the test of time. With, of course, fantastic music from The Beatles (though they didn't do their character's voices) and an entertaining story of Good Versus Evil, this is one of those childhood classics that is always in style. —*M. N.*

CHAPTER ELEVEN

Performance, Literature & the Arts

One of my favorite stories about the sometimes uncomfortable relationship between literature and the movies was told in an interview with a popular author of the '30s and '40s. When asked about how Hollywood studios had ruined his books, he replied, pointing to his books on a bookshelf, "No they haven't, they're still there."

But people still fret about these things. Plays and novels were going to be the ruin of poetry, performance art the decomposition of dance and theater, and the beat movement the deconstruction of fiction. Technologies may come and go, new methods of delivery are continually being invented, but art forms don't just go away. After all, what would the cave painters think of cinemas, but that they were artificial caves where the pictures of bison moved?

In the literary arts the writer is king. In the cinema, the writer is persona non grata, an unwelcome pest, lower than the rats that invade the craft services trailer. But for the films here in this chapter it is about great writing. It is about production companies listening to great writers and trying to be true to the authors' intentions.

Sometimes it is as simple as filming what the author or poet or playwright has already written. Most times it means finding a way to reduce the author's tale into two hours of telling without compromising its heart. But nearly every time it is an attempt to capture the lightning of an author's work in a bottle and to seamlessly project it onto a screen, whether in the cinema or on television.

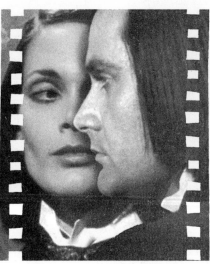

Dr. Jekyll and Sister Hyde (1971)

©ANCHOR BAY ENTERTAINMENT

The sections for Literature By Author and Playwrights represent certain writers whose works have been both highly acclaimed and adapted enough times for us to be able to group them together.

Also in this chapter are the more visual arts of dance, photography, fashion, architecture, and painting. As with our poetry section, these films tend to be documentary in nature but are no less rewarding.

AMERICAN CINEMA, THE L: CINEMA/CINEMA HISTORY (1995) 542M D: Not credited. Originally made for public TV, this ten-part overview of movies in America is less a master's class than a general overview, but it effectively charts the changing face of the Hollywood style and transformations of the industry, with sideline examinations of the star system and samplings of favorite genres (from romantic comedy to film noir). Packed with interviews (historians, directors and actors past and present, and the odd wild card like John Waters rhapsodizing over the larger-than-life enigma of the star), film clips, and rare behind-the-scenes footage, it's a smart, informed, and informative introduction. While it lacks the passion and single-minded focus of other cinema documentaries (such as *Visions of Light* and Martin Scorsese's *A Personal Journey*), it makes up for it in sheer ambition. —*S. A.*

AMERICAN MOVIE L: CINEMA/H'WOOD DIRECTORS (1999) 107M D: Chris Smith. In a small town near Milwaukee, Mark Borchardt spends his days dreaming. He yearns to be a filmmaker, and this documentary chronicles his three-year quest to complete his short horror film *Coven*. Both tragic and inspiring, the film shows Mark's battle against personal demons and a number of no-budget filmmaking disasters. It is heartbreaking to see a dream so utterly unattainable, yet heartwarming to see the undying determination Mark carries with him. Perhaps a quintessentially American story, this documentary reaches its most profound when Mark visits his ailing uncle on the porch of his trailer. The deeply depressed but always loving uncle says he is going to be forced to live out his life sitting on a porch, accomplishing nothing more. We then watch Mark struggle to articulate why that idea horrifies him and how he will never fall victim to such a fate. An honest and compelling portrait, accurately portraying the full humanity of a troubled soul, *American Movie* is a sad, sobering, yet inspiring film for everyone with a dream and nothing but ambition to carry it. —*T. S.*

AMERICAN PSYCHO L: LITERATURE/LITERATURE (2000) 97M D: Mary Harron. *Christian Bale, Jared Leto, Josh Lucas, Chloe Sevigny, Justin Theroux.* When Bret Easton Ellis's novel was released, it was reviled in the media and seen as shocking to even defend it. By the time it was translated into movie form, though, the story's satirical swipes at greed and materialism in the '80s seemed so obvious that the only controversy was about what the hell the end was supposed to mean. As a satire, it may not be as deep as it thinks it is, but as a yuppie-themed slasher movie it is spectacular. Bale is outstanding as the self-obsessed businessman/sadist Patrick Bateman, who delivers long internal monologues about facial scrubs and later runs around naked with a chainsaw, showing off his perfectly chiseled abs. —*B. T.*

ANN MAGNUSON'S VANDEMONIUM L: ARTS/PERFORMANCE ART (1987) 43M D: Stephen Oakes. *Ann Magnuson, Meat Loaf, Eric Bogosian.* Magnuson, from the band Bongwater as well as many films, is a character chameleon on a spaced-out adventure that parodies *Alice in Wonderland* and *The Wizard of Oz*. She plays the old lady of Steve "Piglet" (Meat Loaf) and lead singer of the band Vulcan Death

Grip who is on her way to a wet T-shirt concert. With lyrics like "Smokin' dope with Satan and I'm wasted," you can't go wrong. —*R. D.*

AUNTIE MAME L: PLAYS/PLAYS (1958) 161M D: Morton DaCosta. *Rosalind Russell, Peggy Cass, Forrest Tucker, Coral Browne, Jan Handzlik, Roger Smith.* Mame Dennis was my first fictional role model and is the blueprint for a strong, daring woman. Russell is (as always) radiant and fierce in this charming film about daring to live life outside the flock. Young, sheltered Patrick Dennis comes to live with his eccentric aunt, whose motto is "life is a banquet, and most poor suckers are starving to death!" Through the years, Mame and Patrick fight the good fight against stuffed shirts, Republicans, the Depression, and their own sometimes conflicting ideologies. Cass is hilarious as the frumpy secretary Agnes Gooch, who Mame gives a quick course in revelry. —*J. K.*

BARTLEBY L: LITERATURE/LITERATURE (2001) 83M D: Jonathan Parker. *Maury Chaykin, David Paymer, Crispin Glover, Glenne Headly, Joe Piscopo.* Based on the Herman Melville story "Bartleby the Scrivener," this film is simultaneously unsettling, tragic, and a little humorous. Paymer, the boss of a city's records department, places an ad looking for a new employee. The office itself epitomizes the type of boring desk job monotony that drives people to the brink of insanity, and only Bartleby responds to the ad. He's hired for the job but never ends up really doing it. When asked to complete a task, or why he refuses to work, he simply responds with "I'd prefer not to." The boss's frustration mounts as Bartleby continues to simply occupy space, and the movie ultimately ends tragically without ever providing any explanation. The slow pace and abstract nature of the film may make it unappealing to some, but the more patient viewer will find the subtle and bizarre interactions between Paymer and Glover intriguing. —*J. S.*

BIG BAD LOVE L: LITERATURE/LITERATURE (2001) 110M D: Arliss Howard. *Arliss Howard, Debra Winger, Paul Le Mat, Rosanna Arquette, Angie Dickinson.* Howard plays an alcoholic wastrel of a writer in the Deep South in his directorial debut, based on the short stories of Larry Brown. It plays like the labor of love from an artist who has been storing up ideas for years and finally gushes them all out in one overstuffed piece. Howard tries too hard and the world is hardly in need of another celebration of social irresponsibles as creative heroes, but there's plenty of imagination at work and a wonderful cast: Le Mat as his good old boy best buddy, Winger as his critical ex-wife, and Dickinson as his sharp-tongued mother. Features a lanky soundtrack of folk and blues. —*S. A.*

CANDY MOUNTAIN L: LITERATURE/BEATS (1987) 91M D: Robert Frank, Rudolph Wurlitzer. *Tom Waits, Kevin J. O'Connor, Harris Yulin.* Frank's most "commercial" film is also his most autobiographical as he takes us on the journey of his life—first as the young man who hits the road, and second as the old, withdrawn man at the end of the road, confronting the young man who has come to find him. —*M. S.*

CARRIED AWAY L: LITERATURE/LITERATURE (1996) 109M D: Bruno Barreto. *Amy Irving, Hal Holbrook, Gary Busey, Dennis Hopper, Amy Locane, Julie Harris.* *Carried Away* is a quiet little movie that starts out as if it's going to be grim duty, then finds its way to a wisdom, tenderness, and adult good humor rare in contemporary films. Hopper—in a complete change of pace from his usual freakazoid roles—plays a farmer whose holdings have been reduced to one crotchety cow and some bleak acreage that lies untilled. With a game leg from falling under a tractor in his youth, his main occupation seems divided between looking after his dying mother and teaching in one half of a two-room schoolhouse, without benefit of formal education himself. The other schoolroom is the responsibility of Irving, the childhood sweetheart who married his best friend (killed in the Korean War) and who has slept with Hopper, several evenings a week, for many years now. Enter Locane as a gorgeous blond transfer student from the city. An affair awakens Hopper to his fundamental frustration with a life of doing, and aspiring to, nothing much, and leads him to confess that frustration to Irving. Barreto directed *Carried Away*, and probably only a foreign director (and the leading lady's husband at that) would have dared a scene like the one at the center of the film, when Hopper announces that he and the woman he has loved for years finally must get middle-age-naked with the lights on. It's brave, startling, and exhilaratingly funny. —*R. T. J.*

CATWALK L: ARTS/FASHION (1996) 95M D: Robert Leacock. *Kate Moss, Naomi Campbell, Christy Turlington.* Step into a world where bitches will be bitches, and bitches will be pretty. This documentary follows supermodel Turlington as she sashays across the globe in a quest for total beauty domination. The catwalk seems more an arena for catfights as she claws her way to the top through an insidiously capitalist gaze. Bear witness as models compete for top bitch honors while trashing celebrities like Sharon Stone and backstabbing one another all for the sake of glamour and beauty. The most telling insight gleaned from this film is that, despite its glossy artifice, the camera is unable to cover up a perturbing sense that Ms. Turlington's entire career has been solely dictated by fear. —*T. C.*

CELLULOID CLOSET L: CINEMA/GAY CINEMA (1995) 102M D: Rob Epstein, Jeffery Friedman. *Tony Curtis, Susie Bright, Richard Dyer, Lily Tomlin (narrator), Quentin Crisp.* This documentary starts out by reminding us that film is a reflection of our lives, and we look to movies to show us not only who we are, but how we could be. But what if you don't see any part of yourself depicted in the movies? *Celluloid Closet* then sets off on a history of the homosexual character in cinema. Through clips of film from every decade of the medium and interviews with filmmakers, actors, and authors, we see the portrayal of gays and lesbians as everything from weak sissies to helpless, tortured victims to coldhearted villains. This documentary gives a clear sense of the frustration gay and lesbian audiences have with negative stereotypes, not only for their own sense of identity but for how the heterosexual world responds to them. As years progress and taboos fade, a more realistic homosexual character begins to emerge, and the film ends with hope for a more enlightened future. —*J. K.*

CIRQUE DU SOLEIL—QUIDAM L: PER/ART/CIRCUS (1999) 90M D: David Mallet. *Chris Lashua, John Gilkey, Franco Dragone, Olga Pikheinko, Yelena Kolesnikova, Elena Lev.* I've seen all of the Cirque du Soleil "films" and let me tell you now, *Quidam* is the best. The thing about Cirque that made it so unique was that it stepped free of the big top, Ringling Bros.–type of performance and returned to the aspects of the circus that are the most beautiful. Intimacy. Magic. Transformation. Everything is touched with grace and beauty. The costumes are exquisite. The makeup, magical. The music, inspiring. This one has a little more of the story arc visible than most of their others. A young girl, whose parents are indifferent and detached, is visited by a mysterious stranger with an umbrella who transports her to a fantastical world. When I first saw this, there were moments that were so beautiful and powerful in their simplicity and perfection that I actually had tears of pleasure running down my cheeks. —*M. N.*

CRUEL INTENTIONS L: LITERATURE/LITERATURE (1999) 95M D: Roger Kumble. *Selma Blair, Sarah Michelle Gellar, Ryan Phillippe, Reese Witherspoon.* *Dangerous Liaisons* is modernized into a campy teen sleazefest. Gellar draws on her soap opera experience to play the manipulative villainess who bets her stepbrother (Phillippe) that he can't deflower the daughter (Witherspoon) of their private school's headmaster. Shit, I wonder if they'll fall in love? The characters are all rich kids who lord over their mansions, gingerly holding wine glasses like some sort of teen *Falcon Crest*. Like *Wild Things*, the movie's delight with its own excesses is contagious. It's the kind of movie where Gellar stores cocaine in a crucifix necklace and "teaches" her naive protégé (Blair) how to kiss by making out with her in the park. As far as innuendo-filled movies about vapid characters being cruel to each other go, this is a good one. —*B.T.*

SALVADOR DALÍ: A SOFT SELF-PORTRAIT L: ARTS/ART (1969) 60M D: Jean-Christophe Averty. *Orson Welles, Salvador Dalí.* Dalí himself helped create this French TV documentary about his life and art, and he appears in many surreal live-action vignettes involving pianos and saws and cats and various other unexpected elements. It's hard to tell if Dalí is being completely honest about his life or if he's playing it up for the cameras. I'm not sure; for example, did he really release a record telling English speakers how to pronounce English properly? Whatever the case this very unique and entertaining biography is a great reflection of Dalí's personality and playful sense of humor. —*B.T.*

DECADE UNDER THE INFLUENCE, A L: CINEMA/CINEMA HISTORY (2003) 108M D: Ted Demme. *Francis Ford Coppola, Julie Christie, Jack Nicholson, Bruce Dern, Steven Soderbergh, William Friedkin.* This is an excellent documentary charting the fall of the Golden Age of Cinema. It discusses how the fall created unexpected opportunities for young filmmakers of the '60s and '70s; how this explosion of radical new filmmaking (inspired in part by the New Wave Cinema of France, Italy, and Spain) was born; how it prospered and was eventually crushed under the heel of marketing, merchandising, and demographics. There is a cavalcade of interviews with directors and actors who made their name and their mark during this radical period in filmmaking history. It is well filmed, eye-opening, and has a jazzy soundtrack that had me grooving in my seat the whole time! —*M.N.*

DETOURS L: DANCE/DANCE (2002) 95M D: Elsewhere Productions. *Elsewhere, Rawbzilla, Midus, Kujo.* Focusing on four dancers, Midus, Rawbzilla, Elsewhere, and Kujo, this video celebrates the notion of individuality and originality in B-boy culture. Adhering to a predictable model of what hip hop heads would consider "unconventional" music—starting off with some LTJ Bukem, mixing in a little Aphex Twin and Boards of Canada, and finishing off with a smattering of "jazzy" genres—the soundtrack tends to corner the video into too small a box, but it could have been much worse so I'm not complaining. Although a little repetitive, this video is plenty interesting as it offers insight into what compels B-boys to become B-boys in the first place. I especially like the section at the end about the debate over originality. After B-boy Crazy Legs proclaims that there are no original moves and that what is being done has been done before, the video cuts back and forth between B-boys battling and old-source video of Harlem musicals, kung-fu flicks, African tribal dances, and even some motocross in an attempt to link the languages. One leaves the film with not only a better appreciation of

B-boying as a dance form, but also a broader understanding of dance as movement. —*T.C.*

DOWNTOWN 81 L: ARTS/ART (1981) 72M D: Edo Bertoglio. *Jean Michel Basquiat, Marshall Chess, Danny Rosen, Saul Williams.* This lark of a boho odyssey was shot in 1981 and stars a prefame Basquiat as a free-spirited young artist. Director Bertoglio resurrected the film and reunited his cast to dub it (Baquiat's lines are read by Williams) in 2001. It plays like an aimless, student art film remake of *The Wizard of Oz* with Basquiat as a funky, impoverished Dorothy, selling paintings and crashing nightclubs in the underground scene of early '80s New York. Musical performances by the likes of Kid Creole and the Coconuts, James White and the Blacks, and the Japanese New Wave band The Plastics (among others), and the dozens of artists, musicians, and street characters wandering through Basquiat's meandering journey create a unique document of its era. An invaluable time capsule but a listless, lightweight odyssey. —*S.A.*

DRAGON: THE BRUCE LEE STORY L: CINEMA/ACTORS (1993) 107M D: Rob Cohen. *Jason Scott Lee, Lauren Holly.* Bruce Lee fans often make fun of this biography's Hollywood flights of fancy (a subplot about a demon curse, random street fights, breaking his back in a duel) but it makes for an entertaining mix, and at least it's more accurate than the various Hong Kong versions of the Lee story. Based on a book by Lee's wife, Linda (Holly), it goes from forbidden interracial romance to full-blown kung fu movie whenever Lee gets on the bad side of drunk sailors, rival kung fu instructors, or cleaver-wielding chefs. Lee looks nothing like Bruce, and he's a completely different body type, but he's such a great physical actor that he seems to almost contort his body into Bruce's. It's a surprisingly good biopic from Cohen, especially when you compare it to his later hackwork like *The Fast and the Furious* and *XXX*. —*B.T.*

DR. JEKYLL AND SISTER HYDE L: LIT. BY AUTHOR/ STEVENSON, ROBERT LOUIS (1971) 96M D: Roy Ward Baker. *Martine Beswicke, Susan Broderick, Lewis Fiander, Ralph Bates, Gerald Sim.* Bates puts a sexual twist on the classic Robert Louis Stevenson story when he takes an experimental elixir of life and lets out his evil side, which just happens to be the sexy and thoroughly debauched Beswick. Not that Bates is all that innocent to begin with (the actor specialized in charismatic corrupt figures in Hammer films). In a Jack-the-Ripper twist, she starts murdering prostitutes and he uses their glands to keep producing the elixir, but the best moment comes when he makes a pass at her male lover! It never dares to delve into subversive extremes, but Baker and screenwriter Brian Clemens take the whole thing seriously enough to make this Hammer horror more than just a dirty joke. —*S.A.*

E.E. CUMMINGS: AN AMERICAN ORIGINAL L: POETRY & POETS/POETRY & POETS (1997) 30M D: Nebraskans for Public Television.

e.e. cummings. I shoulda known from the fruity-ass photo on the back of the box that this was gonna be a piece of pompous crap. It's just a bunch of shitty theater actors on a shitty period set shittily reciting his poems. It's like water torture, but at least water torture makes more sense. I watched it for about three minutes, mostly because I couldn't believe what I was looking at. What's even scarier is that there are multiple tapes in this series, so all of your favorite writers get a turn at the block. If you wanna know why our public schools are going to shit and the literacy rate is drastically declining, it's because they have to put up with shit like this in the classroom. What the fuck are we doing renting this anyway? —*T. C.*

FIREPLACE: VISIONS OF TRANQUILITY L: CINEMA/HOME CINEMA (1996) 60M D: Not credited.

You know that romance is dead when there are actually people out there whose idea of an intimate, romantic evening is curling up with the person they love next to a simulation of a fireplace they rented from the video store. It starts out as just some kindling, but soon builds to a roaring flame. As it starts to die down, we watch as another log is put on to keep that romantic fire going. It's almost hot enough to feel, right? Except you're sitting in your living room next to a television that's emitting nothing resembling heat. As the romancing session comes to an end, the two lovebirds can sit together and watch the glowing embers slowly die down into ashes. What an exhilarating experience. To me, this is just really, really funny. So funny, in fact, that when I meet a man whose idea of a good joke is romancing me with a video fireplace, I will know that I've found true love. —*J. S.*

FOXFIRE L: LITERATURE/LITERATURE (1996) 100M D: Annette Haywood-Carter.

Sarah Rosenberg, Angelina Jolie, Jenny Shimizu, Hedy Burress. Entertainingly dumb girl-power melodrama starring a young Jolie as a mysterious outsider badass who comes to a high school and teaches a group of misfit girls to stick together and fight back against male oppression. Lots of lesbian undertones, stick-it-to-the-man one-liners, and ridiculous moments like when a teacher mistakes Jolie for a man because she has short hair and wears boots. Based on a Joyce Carol Oates book set in the '50s, which I guess explains why Jolie's character is named "Legs Sadovsky." —*B. T.*

FRIDA (2002) L: ARTS/ART (2002) 123M D: Julie Taymor.

Salma Hayek, Geoffrey Rush, Valeria Golino, Alfred Molina. Hayek is good as the brilliant Mexican painter and feminist icon Frida Kahlo, and Molina is great as her husband, the muralist Diego Rivera. But like many films about artists, the script plays like a book report trying to summarize too much in too little time. There's no focus; you get some of her childhood, her relationships with Rivera and Leon Trotsky (played by Rush), and lots of speeches by characters trying to sum up their politics and their approaches to painting in dinner conversation. One of the climaxes is Rivera's showdown with Nelson Rockefeller (Edward Norton), in which Kahlo has little involvement. Fortunately, director Taymor, herself a brilliant visual artist, transcends the weak script in several surrealist set pieces using animation and makeup effects to portray Kahlo's thoughts visually. She even got the Brothers Quay to animate Kahlo's view of the hospital after her crippling bus accident. These scenes almost make you wish Taymor had made a silent movie instead of being saddled with all that stiff dialogue, forcing her operatic style into the square peg of a standard Hollywood biopic. —*B. T.*

FULL-TILT BOOGIE L: CINEMA/MOVIES ABOUT MOVIES (1997) 100M D: Sarah Kelly.

Lawrence Bender, George Clooney, Robert Rodriguez, Quentin Tarantino. This feature-length documentary on the making of Rodriguez's *From Dusk Till Dawn* was given a separate video release and even showed in some theaters. What makes it a little different from other making-of-the-movie documentaries is that it mostly focuses on the frustrations of the low-ranking crew members as the production stumbles through the usual filming disasters and even a labor strike. This doesn't seem like a conscious choice, though—I think it was just a lack of access to and/or interesting footage of the principles (although they certainly do contribute). These documentarians don't come across any new insights into the process of filmmaking, and they don't capture anything too crazy or exciting about the making of this particular film. It's worth viewing for big fans of the movie or aspiring filmmakers, but it's more like a DVD extra than a stand-alone feature. Fortunately it was later included on the special edition DVD of *From Dusk Till Dawn*. —*B. T.*

GAMBLER, THE L: LIT. BY AUTHOR/DOSTOEVSKY, FYODOR (1997) 97M D: Karoly Makk.

Michael Gambon, Polly Walker, Jodhi May. St. Petersburg, 1870. Fyodor Dostoyevksy (a suitably seedy-looking Gambon) is broke, hounded by creditors, and on the verge of forfeiting all future works to a greedy publisher unless he can finish a novel in less than a month. Anna (May), a poor, innocent young stenographer with romantic notions of dashing heroes and true love, becomes both entranced and appalled by his novel in progress, *The Gambler*, a largely confessional story that plays out in flashback/dramatic recreation. Makk can't quite decide if this is a tragedy or a poignant love story, which makes for a curious ambivalence but never gets to the root of the film's driving force: obsession. Scenes around the Roulettenberg gambling tables miss the mad attraction that imprisons so many characters, and all the lust and passion of his story hardly raises a fever. Makk's observational remove only works in the framing story, where Gambon and May invest their wary glances and tentative moves with the longing of lost souls. —*S. A.*

GERMANY DADA L: ARTS/ART (1969) 55M D: Helmut Hebst. *Tristan Tzara.* An entertaining and relatively comprehensive summary of art history's coolest club, this is a documentary of more or less academic interest punctuated by chaotic bursts of Dada naughtiness. For example, a bio of Tristan Tzara is halted midsentence by a machine-gun barrage of sound poetry. This and other clever effects contribute to a haphazard, overlapping, short-attention-span composition more rooted in neo-Dada style than true Dada spirit. Unless you're a committed Dadaist (no pun intended), you'll likely let this minor point pass without complaint. For its recordings of Dada sound poetry alone this is well worth the time, but there is much to keep your interest here, most notably clips from several Hans Richter films. —*C. B.*

H. R. GIGER: TRILOGIE L: ARTS/ART (1998) 60M D: Not credited. *H.R. Giger.* This is a documentary trilogy about renowned Swiss surrealist H. R. Giger. Best known for his work on *Alien,* the film includes rare glimpses of early short films he worked on and shots of him painting. A must-see for any Giger fan, but it's not in English. —*B. W.*

GLENGARRY GLEN ROSS L: PLAYWRIGHTS/MAMET, DAVID (1992) 100M D: James Foley. *Jack Lemmon, Kevin Spacey, Ed Harris, Alec Baldwin, Al Pacino, Alan Arkin.* Call it David Mamet's *Death of a @#%&* Salesman, You @#%&*.* The joy of this film is the joy of hearing Mamet's short, sharp shocks of sharklike conversations, strangled exasperation, and salesman jungle cries, bitten off and bashed around by some of the best actors to roll out an obscenity like a love call. Pacino rules the film as the current king of his little jungle, a crummy office where worthless real estate is hawked to suckers over the phone. Lemmon is the veteran salesman in a career crippling slump (and coincidentally a career-reviving performance). Actually there isn't a bad performance in the batch—Baldwin as the frosty company hatchet man, Arkin and Harris as underperforming salesmen, Spacey as the unfailing office manager—and if they feel like they're on stage at times, perhaps it's only fitting for men who perform for a living. —*S. A.*

GO FATIMA: LEARN TO DANCE L: DANCE/HOW TO DANCE (1999) 40M D: Mark Gerard. *Fatima.* One day I found myself wishing that there was a video to teach even me, a white girl with no rhythm, how to shake my funky groove thing along with the pros. Somehow, somewhere, a group of people would come together and say, "We're a group of people

with rhythm, and we're going to make it our personal mission to teach people who don't have rhythm how to do the cutting-edge dance moves that we make look extremely easy. Furthermore, we'll put it on a video tape, so these people can learn how to move in their homes where no one will laugh at their pathetic attempts. Give them forty minutes and they will be as cool as we are." Sounds good, right? That is definitely not this video. *Fatima* may be able to coordinate dance moves for the Backstreet Boys, but after ten minutes of trying to keep up with the blur of arms and legs, I realized that having no rhythm just might be my destiny. —*J. S.*

GOD SAID HA! L: ARTS/PERFORMANCE ART (1998) 85M D: Julia Sweeney. *Julia Sweeney.* Sweeney brings her one-woman show to the big screen in this concert film, where she shares the intimate experiences of an emotionally turbulent year in her life. Her brother is diagnosed with cancer and takes up residence in her bedroom, her parents move down from Washington state and into the guest room, and the adult Sweeney is suddenly reliving her childhood in a bizarre nuclear family flashback. Sweeney is in total command of the stage, more like a host giving a cockeyed tour of her life than a monologist, and her stories are irresistible. It's a brave, funny, and irresistibly involving film, like the reflective confession of a dear friend sharing intimate details of her life with a mischievous grin. —*S. A.*

GODS AND MONSTERS L: CINEMA/H'WOOD DIRECTORS (1998) 120M D: Bill Condon. *Ian McKellen, Brendan Fraser, Lynn Redgrave. Gods and Monsters* is the story of the aging James Whale, director of *Frankenstein* and *Bride of Frankenstein.* The openly homosexual director is living out his final days on his large estate, reminiscing and trying to seduce young men. When his nurse hires a new gardener (Fraser), Whale befriends him and the relationship between the two evolves as he slowly dies. McKellen's amazing performance as the troubled old man shows his extraordinary talent and power. He brings the director brilliantly to life and slowly lets him whither away and die. The film deals with the pains of aging and being gay in an honest, tender, affecting way. Fraser is surprisingly good as the gardener and the friendship he develops with Whale is believable and moving. Drawing comparisons between the Frankenstein monster and the director himself, the film is an excellent character drama about the end of a magnificent director's tragic life. —*T. S.*

GOLDWYN: THE MAN AND HIS MOVIES L: CINEMA/ PRODUCERS (2001) 118M D: Peter Jones, Mark Catalena. *Samuel L. Goldwyn, Dustin Hoffman (narrator).* Samuel Goldwyn was Hollywood's first great independent producer. This documentary, based on A. Scott Berg's excellent biography, is a portrait of the man who gave the world the phrase

"Goldwynism" for his penchant for humorously (and unintentionally) mangling figures of speech. His immigrant roots and populist tastes shaped the Golden Age of Hollywood but became hopelessly out of touch with popular tastes by the 1950s. Almost unique among producers for his reverence of writers, he was most proud of his classy literary productions but ironically found his greatest financial success in a series of comedies. For a man self-conscious of his Jewishness, it was also ironic that he made stars of comics like Eddie Cantor and Danny Kaye, considered "too Jewish" by the rest of Hollywood. The highlight of this documentary is a thoughtful, in-depth look at the making of Goldwyn's only Oscar winner for Best Picture: *The Best Years of Our Lives*. It was the greatest achievement of his career, artistically, critically, and financially, and he never recovered from it. —*S. A.*

GREAT EXPECTATIONS (1998) L: LIT. BY AUTHOR/DICKENS, CHARLES (1998) 111M D: Alfonso Cuarón. *Gwyneth Paltrow, Ethan Hawke, Anne Bancroft, Robert De Niro.* In a modernization of the Dickens story, Cuarón casts Finn (Hawke) as a poor kid from Florida who becomes a hip New York painter with the help of an anonymous benefactor, but never lets go of his childhood obsession with an unattainable rich girl (Paltrow). You can't go too wrong with the timeless themes of the story, and the stylized look of the film is absolutely stunning. Cuarón displays his talent for depicting sensuality (later put to use in *Y Tu Mamá También*), which helps make Finn's obsessiveness more believable. An underrated film (many were turned off by the Dickensian story elements placed in a modern setting), but admittedly Cuarón's version of *A Little Princess* is a much more effective update of a classic story. —*B. T.*

GREY ZONE, THE L: PLAYS/PLAYS (2001) 108M D: Tim Blake Nelson. *Mira Sorvino, Steve Buscemi, David Arquette, Harvey Keitel.* A story of incredible resonance (the daily life and work of the Sonderkommando of Auschwitz, those who helped lure new victims into the gas chambers, collecting their clothing after death, and disposing of the corpses) instead becomes a partial freak and shock show. It takes the worst of the ever-unfortunate Mamet school of pseudo-speak, completely destroying the realism this film set out to achieve with its historically detailed sets and locations. Keitel as Oberscharführer stands out too much with his poor German accent, and along with the too-recognizable Buscemi distances us from the involving material. Bitching aside, the film is remarkable. The long, slow zooms to men inured to the daily task of the murder and disposal of their people, hair and gold tooth removal, and corpse burning are carried out in a manner that is frightening in its utter banality. The reality of the sets, clothing, and locations is unfortunately in such contrast to the well-fed Hollywood actors and Nelson's toss-away,

coldly delivered dialogue that the memory of the men and women murdered at Auschwitz is further annihilated. —*S. R.*

HAMLET L: PLAYWRIGHTS/SHAKESPEARE, WILLIAM (2000) 112M D: Michael Almereyda. *Diane Venora, Julia Stiles, Ethan Hawke, Sam Shepard, Bill Murray, Kyle MacLachlan.* This is not your father's *Hamlet*. Almereyda sets Shakespeare's poetry in a vision of glass and steel in modern New York. The melancholy Dane (Hawke) is the son of the deceased chairman of Denmark Corporation. His castle is a sleek but alienating New York high-rise dotted with omnipresent surveillance cameras, his kingdom city streets lined with paparazzi and tabloid reporters. Hawke broods well but emotes only passably as Hamlet, wrapping himself in a sullen, alienated shell, but it's refreshing to see a Hamlet who really acts like a grieving, messed-up young adult tortured by indecision and insecurity. MacLachlan is smooth and smarmy as Claudius, Stiles gives Ophelia a poignant and powerful demise, and Murray is lovely as the fussy but tender Polonius. Almereyda has pared away the text but he saves the language and the drama from the musty, reverent faithfulness of recent adaptations. His dramatic choices are often startlingly inspired: "To be or not to be" is contemplated in the aisles of a Blockbuster and Gertrude's (Venora) climactic death is transformed into a piercing maternal sacrifice. Fresh, vibrant, and vital, this interpretation reminds us why Shakespeare is timeless. —*S. A.*

HEARTBREAK KID, THE L: PLAYWRIGHTS/SIMON, NEIL (1972) 104M D: Elaine May. *Cybill Shepherd, Audra Lindley, Charles Grodin, Eddie Albert.* Within days of his traditional Jewish wedding, Lenny (Grodin) realizes he can't stand his wife, Lila (Jeannie Berlin), whose every move unwittingly aggravates his lofty ideals. Honeymooning in Florida, he finds the perfect landing pad for those ideals in the form of Kelly (Shepherd), a gorgeous blond WASP from a wealthy Minnesota family. Like something out of a cartoon, Lenny juggles his time between his wife and Kelly, weaving an increasingly preposterous web of lies. Complicating matters further is the fact that Kelly's father (Albert) despises Lenny. Trying to win him over, Lenny elevates phoniness to an art form, culminating in his diatribe on "honesty" and Minnesota's bland food in contrast to the deception of New York's exotic fare. A superb character study as well as a clever comedy, *The Heartbreak Kid* succeeds largely because May managed to turn the script's caricatures into three-dimensional sympathetic people. —*C. B.*

HEIST L: PLAYWRIGHTS/MAMET, DAVID (2001) 109M D: David Mamet. *Gene Hackman, Danny DeVito, Delroy Lindo, Sam Rockwell, Ricky Jay, Rebecca Pidgeon.* *Heist* has many of the hallmarks of a Mamet film, but luckily, not too many of them. When on its best behavior his dialogue is clever and cerebral;

at its worst, it's overly mannered and turns characters into toy soldiers being pushed around a fake battlefield. *Heist* gives them room to breathe. The plot—something about a gang of thieves, their nasty fence, and a bunch of soon-to-be-stolen gold—won't surprise anyone who's seen a hundred heist movies, or even one. The joy here is watching canny veterans such as Hackman, Lindo, and DeVito munch on the dialogue like bar peanuts. When Jay's character is asked if Hackman is cool, he replies, "My motherfucker's so cool, when he goes to sleep sheep count him." (*Heist* also carries another of Mamet's stamps, his brilliantly deployed profanity.) —*T. P.*

HELLCAB L: PLAYS/PLAYS (1998) 96M D: Mary Cybulski, John Tintori. *Paul Dillon, Shulie Cowen, Laurie Metcalf, John C. Reilly, Julianne Moore, John Cusack.* There's no cab that eats human flesh, nor does Rutger Hauer use a cab to pick up children and taunt their parents, as the title of this film might imply to some. It's simply the story of a nice guy in Chicago who happens to drive a cab. I don't mean nice like nice to look at or easygoing, I mean that this character is a really good, honest, enduring person. The stage of the cab allows us to view this really nice guy's confrontation with the harsh and the beautiful in the world. It also makes for a large cast of cameos. The best performances, though, are by Michael Shannon, playing an unintelligible crackhead, and Olivia Trevino, a four-year-old going to church at something like five in the morning. —*J. J.*

HENRY V L: PLAYWRIGHTS/SHAKESPEARE, WILLIAM (1944) 136M D: Laurence Olivier. *Laurence Olivier, Ernest Thesiger, Vernon Greeves, Robert Helpmann, Leslie Banks.* Olivier stepped out of the theater as actor and into the cinema as director with this gorgeous adaptation of the Shakespeare play. As young Henry V, Olivier is top-notch. As director, he reworks the dialogue and situations of the play to best his film, starting out in the medieval Globe Theater, home of the first Shakespeare productions, and literally lifting the camera out into the open world as the "play becomes a film." The famous tale of Henry taking England from the French became a war cry for the British to take back England from the Germans during WWII, and the film became a huge box office success. With battle scenes modeled after Sergei Eisenstein's *Alexander Nevsky* and artificial backdrops reflecting the story's theatricality, the gorgeous coloring and costumes create just the right mix of cinema and theater. One of the best Shakespeare plays ever put to film. Remade in 1989 by Kenneth Branagh and his acting troupe, their version chose to portray Henry in the mud and realism of the time, taking much away from the stylistic magic of Olivier's approach. Also known as *The Chronicle History of King Henry the Fifth with His Battle at Agincourt in France.* —*N. H.*

HENRY V L: PLAYWRIGHTS/SHAKESPEARE, WILLIAM (1989) 138M D: Kenneth Branagh. *Kenneth Branagh, Derek Jacobi, Brian Blessed, Alec McCowen, Judi Dench, Ian Holm.* This adaptation of Shakespeare's play is Branagh's first and finest hour. Well-balanced acting, extremely good effects, and intelligent use of music, editing, and pacing make this film adaptation as timeless as the script itself. The viewer cannot help but feel that all the actors are swept up in this dramatization of English history. The story details the young king's spectacular military forays into what is now western France. This expansive territory, clear down to Anjou, belonged to the Normans and was lost by the Plantagenets. It was under the House of Lancaster, to which Henry V belonged, that all the land was reclaimed, culminating with the victory of Agincort that is the spectacular climax of the play as well as this film. It's only too bad that Branagh would follow up such a masterpiece with a film like *Dead Again.* —*N. J.*

HISTORY OF TOM JONES, A FOUNDLING, THE L: LITERATURE/LITERATURE (1997) 300M D: Metin Huseyin. *Brian Blessed, Max Beesley, Samantha Morton, Con O'Neill, Rachel Scorgie.* "It is not enough that your actions are good. You must take care that they appear so." Poor, honest, good-hearted Tom. This seems to be the one lesson he never learns, charging through life with his chin up and his libido unchecked. With tongue firmly in cheek, our narrator, Henry Fielding himself (channeled, one assumes, by actor John Sessions), walks us through this randy satire like a tour guide, proffering introductions and amusing observations. Destined to comparison with Tony Richardson's hearty interpretation, the A&E/BBC miniseries doesn't necessarily take the high road, but it favors dry wit and understated asides over Richardson's knock-about comedy and high energy. Beesly (a dead ringer for Ewan MacGregor) is all charm and earthy sincerity as handsome Tom, with Morton a determined, elegant, and deliciously funny sweetheart, and red-faced Brit stalwart Blessed as her blustery, bellowing father. A delight from start to its improbably (and delightfully) contrived conclusion. —*S. A.*

HIT ME L: LITERATURE/LITERATURE (1996) 128M D: Steven Shainberg. *Elias Koteas, William H. Macy, Philip Baker Hall, Kevin J. O'Connor, Laure Marsac.* The debut film by Shainberg, an adaptation of Jim Thompson's novel *A Swell Looking Babe*, stars Koteas as a frustrated bellhop tangled in the criminal schemes of the hotel management. The story of double and triple crosses, betrayals, and bad luck has the hallmarks of Tarantino and the Coens, but the tawdry setting (a two-star hotel in Tacoma, Washington), the swaggering crooks who are too petty to realize that they haven't a clue what they are doing, and the dim hero who fights back out of wounded pride and hapless desperation are pure Thompson. Shainberg captures that tricky tone nicely and Koteas is perfect as the chump in the middle. The lightweight, light-fingered small-timer merely trying to keep afloat in his own shallow waters gets swamped when he's sucked into the depths of a crime well above his head. Which may be why the film isn't better known: is there anything less uplifting than the morose world of Thompson's sad-sack losers? A worthy addition to the cinema of low-rent crime tragicomedy. —*S. A.*

HOURS, THE L: LIT. BY AUTHOR/WOOLF, VIRGINIA (2002) 114M D: Stephen Daldry. *Nicole Kidman, Julianne Moore, Meryl Streep, John C. Reilly.* The slow pace and quiet atmosphere of this film may at first make it seem less than entertaining, but the observant viewer will feel its subtle mind-fuck for days afterward. Based on Virginia Woolf's novel *Mrs. Dalloway,* three separate narratives beautifully weave together the lives of Woolf herself as she writes the book, a 1950s suburban housewife reading it, and a contemporary New York woman whose life bears a strange resemblance to it. The acting is excellent, particularly Moore's role as the suicidal Laura Brown, who finds that she can no longer go through the motions of being happy. The narrative can be a little confusing at times, but overall this is a wonderful film that strikes an extremely strong emotional chord, hitting at the very core of depression and loneliness. —*J. S.*

HOUSE OF GAMES L: PLAYWRIGHTS/MAMET, DAVID (1987) 102M D: David Mamet. *Lindsay Crouse, Joe Mantegna, J. T. Walsh.* Crouse plays a straitlaced psychologist having difficulty with one of her patients who's addicted to gambling. After some time with the patient, when things seem particularly desperate concerning his gambling debts, she decides to meet the fellow he owes (Mantegna) to see what she can do. Perhaps it's a strange sort of love at first sight or perhaps she's tired of her nowhere job and is interested in this flip side of life, but she starts gravitating toward him even though she discovers that much of what he's doing in terms of gambling is immoral, scandalous, and illegal. He is fully capable of prefacing everything he does as a game, and she slowly accepts the fall of the cards. —*N. J.*

IDEAL HUSBAND, AN L: PLAYWRIGHTS/WILDE, OSCAR (1999) 97M D: Oliver Parker. *Minnie Driver, Rupert Everett, Julianne Moore, Jeremy Northam, John Wood, Cate Blanchett.* OK, this adaptation of Wilde's play has a fabulous cast who all act brilliantly and make this a witty, sly, clever, charming, hilarious, and wickedly delightful comedy/drama of errors. But honestly, I have to say that it is the dashing Everett in the pivotal part of Lord Goring who simply runs away with the film, taking all the best lines with him. It is the story of a man in Parliament who is caught betwixt a woman who holds a piece of his past against him, his wife who believes him, a man of honor who can do

no wrong, and his position that requires him to denounce a proposal at the risk of losing everything he has. To make matters more complicated, everyone has ties and relationships with everyone else, and thus begins the story of secrets, lies, blackmail, bets, friendship, love, romance, and idealism. Wilde was a brilliantly clever writer, and there is nothing more rewarding than seeing his work performed by a cast that so perfectly captures the nuances of every wry joke and subtle sarcasm. Bravo! —*M. N.*

IMPORTANCE OF BEING EARNEST, THE L: PLAYWRIGHTS/ WILDE, OSCAR (1952) 95M D: Anthony Asquith. *Joan Greenwood, Michael Redgrave, Michael Denison, Edith Evans, Dorothy Tutin.* The wittiest, driest, most deftly performed film incarnation of any Oscar Wilde work puts the 2002 version to shame for its artistic conceits. Redgrave and Denison are the aristocratic rascals caught between their gadabout double lives and their romantic complications, and Greenwood (whose smoking smooth voice is like silk on the ears) and Tutin combine social convention with daft logic as the lovely ladies who tame their wandering ways. Evans just about steals the film as the imperiously dotty aunt tossing off absurd pronouncements like pearls of wisdom. This most delicious of drawing room comedies skewers class, culture, the pretensions of nobility, and just about every convention of social graces with an effervescence that that makes it all so innocent. Asquith doesn't worry about tearing it free from its stage-bound roots, but simply gives it a beautifully gilded cinematic stage, choreographs a note-perfect cast, and photographs it all with the unblinking eye of a craftsman (as opposed to, say, an interpretive artist). —*S. A.*

IN THE BEDROOM L: LITERATURE/LITERATURE (2001) 130M D: Todd Field. *Sissy Spacek, William Mapother, Nick Stahl, Marisa Tomei, Tom Wilkinson.* A hushed portrait of love, loss, and vengeance in a sleepy New England backwater, this harrowing drama stars Spacek and Wilkinson as parents who stop communicating after the violent death of their only son. The directing debut of actor Field (he played the pianist in Stanley Kubrick's *Eyes Wide Shut*) favors the performances and they are among the best in modern American cinema. Spacek is steely and hard under her milky blue eyes, Wilkinson jovial and easygoing on the outside but walled-up inside, and Tomei (the "older woman" girlfriend of their murdered son) has the puffy look of a woman crying her grief away. Field's direction creates a mood of inexpressive sadness that blankets their lives. Words become meaningless. Their loss and loneliness are expressed almost solely through the way the old married couple shares a room, how they touch each other with familiarity that brings little comfort, and the sudden awkwardness of the space between them. It's a disappointment when the film takes a rather conventional turn in the third act, but Field remains true to his charac-ters. There is nothing simple in their solution for closure, and no peace to be found in vengeance. —*S.A.*

JANE EYRE L: LIT. BY AUTHOR/BRONTE SISTERS (1997) 108M D: Robert Young III. *Samantha Morton, Ciaran Hinds, Gemma Jones.* Morton plays Jane Eyre with a steady hand. She portrays Jane's terrible fear and curiosity with earnestness and innocence. And she has such a cute face. I only wish the film had been longer. I wish the film had spent more time on the second half of the book, when Jane's agony is supposed to feel prolonged and she builds herself up again, almost unwillingly, without hope of love. I don't care how long it would have been. —*J.J.*

JESUS' SON L: LITERATURE/LITERATURE (1999) 109M D: Alison Maclean. *Samantha Morton, Billy Crudup, Denis Leary, Will Patton, Jack Black.* A series of raw, sometimes surreal '70s-set vignettes nar-rated by Fuck Head (Crudup), a sweet-hearted junkie always trying (and failing) to straighten out his life. While struggling through a difficult relationship with Morton, he often finds himself in odd situations like stealing wire with Dennis Hopper or taking care of premature bunnies with Jack Black. It feels a little bit like *Drugstore Cowboy*, but more warmhearted. The characters are all addicts, but it's not a crime movie—it's more about relationships than hiding from the law. At its best it is a perfect synthesis of funny and sad, with scenes that make you laugh because it's better than crying. —*B.T.*

JUDE (1996) L: LIT. BY AUTHOR/HARDY, THOMAS (1996) 123M D: Michael Winterbottom. *Christopher Eccleston, Kate Winslet, Rachel Griffiths, Liam Cunningham, June Whitfield.* One night at the video store, a friend and I rented *Jude*. We both like Winslet and it's an adaptation of a classic book neither of us had read, so it seemed it would be entertaining and enriching. Looking back, I wish we'd gotten *Ghostbusters*, because I can safely say this is the most depressing film I have ever seen. Eccleston plays the brooding Jude who falls for his cousin (Winslet), but she's forced to marry someone else, and then everything just gets weird and complicated and downright sad. Every frame looks and feels like there is a heavy fog weighing on the characters; their internal strife projects outward, making everything around them dark. I was still depressed three days after watching it, and I still wince when I see Eccleston. If you want to feel like you've been run over by a tank, then watch this film. —*J.K.*

KID STAYS IN THE PICTURE, THE L: CINEMA/PRODUCERS (2002) 93M D: Nanette Burstein, Brett Morgen. *Robert Evans.* Based on Evans's self-congratulatory autobiography, the words and voice, the bluff and balls, and the tough-talking personality belong to Evans: the Evans-eye view of his own life. His narration and dialogue re-creations are pure Hollywood noir hero: tough, terse, sardonic, smart-mouthed—the kind of pulp commentary you expect from a screenwriter's page, not a producer's mouth. The images and the skewed style, however, belong to directors Morgen and Burstein, and that turns this cinematic autobi-ography into something more interesting: know-ing and appreciative, genuine and ironic, and as entertaining as any Hollywood melodrama from the golden age of golden boys turned movie moguls. —*S.A.*

KING LEAR L: PLAYWRIGHTS/SHAKESPEARE, WILLIAM (1984) 158M D: Michael Elliot. *Lawrence Olivier, Dorothy Tutin, Anna Clader-Marshall, Diana Rigg, Leo McKern, John Hurt.* After a long and amazing film career the eminent Olivier reached the ideal age to play the role of King Lear. Made for television, this play costars Rigg as the daughter Regan, Hurt as the king's fool, and a host of other solid actors. In Shakespeare's play, an aging King Lear divides his kingdom for two of his daughters and exiles his third and most favorite daughter, convinced she has no love for him. Yet the pride and inso-lence of the two daughters he favored hardens his heart. And so, while clearly approaching dementia, Lear seeks revenge on his children with the few loyal men he has left. One quickly gets past the staginess of the set and the video-tape-quality production and eventually becomes putty in the hands of Olivier's unforgettable per-formance. —*N.J.*

LAKEBOAT L: PLAYWRIGHTS/MAMET, DAVID (2000) 98M D: Joe Mantegna. *Denis Leary, Charles Durning, Robert Forster, J.J.Johnston.* Seven men without women rattle around a cavernous Great Lakes freighter over the course of a summer, with nothing to do but spin stories, argue, and rhapsodize about sex and booze and lost youth. What could be more quintessentially David Mamet? First-time direc-tor Mantegna brings Mamet's autobiographical early play to the screen. Not much happens, but then this is really about the singsong poetry of guy talk, and Mantegna brings just the right tone of easy gab and tossed-off tales to this actor's showcase: he makes the words dance and the characters come alive in their talk. Forster all but steals the ensemble piece as a freighter vet who hides his dashed dreams and bone-deep loneli-ness behind a calmly furrowed face and gentle eyes. His simple, naked words and directness sweep away all the testosterone-fueled gab of the previous sixty or so minutes, and once again he proves that he's America's most overlooked and underutilized master-class performer. —*S.A.*

LAST ORDERS L: LITERATURE/LITERATURE (2001) 109M D: Fred Schepisi. *Tom Courtenay, Michael Caine, Bob Hoskins, David Hemmings, Helen Mirren, Ray Winstone.* Unassuming, tender, and fraught with the barbs, Schepisi's adaptation of Graham Swift's novel is as human and vulnerable a

Our favorite movies about food

THE AGE OF INNOCENCE

BABETTE'S FEAST

BAD TASTE

A BOY AND HIS DOG

DELICATESSEN

EAT THE RICH

EAT DRINK MAN WOMAN

GOD OF COOKERY

GOOD BURGER

HAMBURGER: THE MOTION PICTURE

LA GRANDE BOUFFE

LIKE WATER FOR CHOCOLATE

LOVE ON A DIET

MOTEL HELL

MY DINNER WITH ANDRE

THE PEANUT BUTTER SOLUTION

SHAOLIN SOCCER

TAMPOPO

THE STUFF

WILLY WONKA AND THE CHOCOLATE FACTORY

drama as you'll find today. Caine is seen only in flashbacks, but even in death he's the driving personality behind their group, a kind of platoon leader. His last wish and last orders send pals Hoskins, Courtenay, and Hemmings, along with Caine's son (Winstone), on a testy, sometimes contentious, remembrance-filled odyssey from their regular pub to the seashore to deposit his ashes. Mirren costars as Caine's widow who makes her own journey into the past on that fateful day. Schepisi allows us to feel our way through these relationships with his imaginative web of flashbacks, while these pros give effortless performances of understated complexity. There are no dramatic fireworks or contrived obstacles here, only people simmering over decades-old conflicts, confronting their own mistakes and foibles, and trying to find some peace. —*S. A.*

LION IN WINTER, THE L: PLAYS/PLAYS (1968) 134M D: Anthony Harvey. *Katharine Hepburn, Peter O'Toole, John Castle, Nigel Terry, Anthony Hopkins, Timothy Dalton.* Man, and I thought MY family was dysfunctional! Here we have Eleanor of Aquitaine (played resplendently by Hepburn), so dis-

liked and distrusted by her husband Henry II (O'Toole) that she is kept locked up in her own private castle and is only brought "home" for the holidays. They spar relentlessly with one another and use their children as pawns, bartering anything or anyone to gain their desires. We see the period for what it was—not grand and elegant, but rather filthy and wretched, even for royalty. The tale is thick with intrigue, manipulation, cruelty, seduction, backstabbing, and betrayal, all in the name of power and control. This isn't just passive-aggressive, it's aggressive-aggressive. Though the tale tapers off without a strong or compelling conclusion, it is so wonderfully acted and so acerbically witty and vicious you won't mind a bit. —*M. N.*

LOLITA (1997) L: LITERATURE/LITERATURE (1997) 137M D: Adrian Lyne. *Jeremy Irons, Frank Langella, Dominique Swain, Melanie Griffith.* Although a lot of people probably prefer Kubrick's version to this one, for me it's no contest. Kubrick's version caused a little fluttering in my stomach, but with Irons in the role of pervy Humbert Humbert, I was dazzled. *Lolita* is a book I absolutely love, so I had high expectations going into the Kubrick version. I was disappointed. The interactions between Lolita and Humbert didn't make me uncomfortable in the way they did when I read the book, and I thought Lolita came across as more annoying than coy. When I watched this version, however, I felt the combination of sympathy and horror toward Humbert that I associate with the story, and the young Lolita is portrayed equally well as a silly child and a seductress. Casting is everything, and I think Irons and Swain more than do justice to one of the best books ever written. —*J. S.*

LOST IN LA MANCHA L: CINEMA/H'WOOD DIRECTORS (2002) 93M D: Keith Fulton, Louis Pepe. *Johnny Depp, Terry Gilliam, Jean Rochefort.* What began as a documentary of the making of a Gilliam film, destined as a supplement on a DVD, turned into a painful, morbidly funny, nightmarish, and riveting portrait of the unmaking of a movie. The production of *The Man Who Killed Don Quixote*, starring Depp and Rocheford, was hanging by threads (like the marionette soldiers created for unfilmed scenes) even before the pelting hail, flash floods, and crippling injury to Rocheford (who smiles through a painful day of shooting on horseback before he discovers he has a herniated disc) plagued the film like a curse by the gods. After two weeks of brutal, unrelenting disasters, directors Fulton and Pepe (who previously documented the making of *12 Monkeys* for Gilliam) watched the film bleed to death, yet the few delightful minutes of the finished film show us just why Gilliam will defy the gods once again and put his hubris on the line when he's given the green light on his next labor of love. —*S. A.*

LUMIERE BROTHERS' FIRST FILMS, THE L: CINEMA/ EARLY CINEMA (1996) 61M D: Lumiere Brothers. *Bertrand Tavernier.* This compilation of eighty-five Lumiere films painstakingly restored by the Institut Lumiere is no mere historical oddity but a testament to the timelessness of cinema. Accompanied by director/film historian Bertrand Tavernier's engaging insights and witty asides, these fifty-two-second wonders are like moving snapshots of life around the world one hundred years ago. The strong blacks, clear whites, and vivid gray scale of these restorations lets us see the grace and strength of such early cinema essentials as *Workers Leaving the Lumiere Factory* (did you know there were three different versions?) and *Train Arriving in the Station* ("the first masterpiece," proclaims Tavernier). With the veil of wear lifted from the works, they are no longer curios but honest-to-God films: documentaries, actualities, comedies, slices of life. Tavernier's informal commentary, pitched somewhere between historical scholar and enthusiastic fan, is packed with fascinating tidbits, acute observations, and an unabashed love for the films (though he's equally able to address gaffes and failed attempts), and he helps us watch them with fresh eyes. —*S. A.*

MADAME TUSSAUD'S: THE INSIDE STORY L: ARTS/ART (1992) 33M D: Maurice Stevens. This is just a routine tourist video about the history of the famous wax museum, sometimes showing celebrities admiring their waxen doppelgangers. Someone should do a real documentary about wax museums, though. What is the fascination with creating likenesses of celebrities and historical figures? I think wax dummies are really interesting to look at, but I could never tell you why. I wonder what would happen if the heater got stuck on at Madame Tussaud's. What if Michael Jackson and Princess Di got melted together? That would be pretty cool. —*B. T.*

MASTER OF BALLANTRAE, THE L: LIT. BY AUTHOR/ STEVENSON, ROBERT LOUIS (1953) 90M D: William Keighley. *Errol Flynn, Roger Livesey, Anthony Steel, Beatrice Campbell, Felix Aylmer.* Though one of Flynn's later films, this peculiar swashbuckler won a place in my heart. The aging Flynn still looks ruggedly handsome in this tale of Jaime Durrideer, a laird in Scotland who decides to side with Bonnie Prince Charles against the English. In order to save the family estate, it is agreed that his younger brother Henry will remain true to the British, so that no matter which side is triumphant, they will survive. Alas, through deception and the subterfuge of a jealous woman, Jamie becomes convinced that his own brother sold him out to the English so he could be laird of the castle and steal Jaime's fiancée. A duel ensues, followed by Jaime and his fighting companion, Burke, taking to the high seas, where their ship is captured by pirates. It is not the most even of plots, and the action waxes and wanes, but there is something infectious about the jovial humor of Burke and his bantering relationship with Jamie. And, of course, anything with pirates is good. —*M. N.*

MOLL FLANDERS L: LITERATURE/LITERATURE (1996) 190M D: David Attwood. *Alex Kingston, Daniel Craig, Diana Rigg.* Far from the handsome, careful dramas we expect from British TV, this lusty, lively version of the Daniel Dafoe social satire reminds us that the classics don't have to be dusty. Kingston is the eponymous heroine, who narrates her tale from the prison she was born in and has spiraled back into. Her bawdy journey takes her up and down the social ladder, through five husbands (one of them her brother!) and numerous lovers, until she finds her facility for larceny and becomes renowned as the country's most notorious criminal. Kingston plays Moll with a lust for life, ready to play by the rules when possible, make her own when necessary, and keep up a conversation with the audience with a wink and a smile throughout. Full of sass and sex (Kingston bares herself in more than one scene), this sharp little miniseries costars Craig (as her one true love). Scripted by Andrew Davies (of the 1995 *Pride and Prejudice* miniseries). —*S. A.*

MOMMIE DEAREST L: CINEMA/ACTORS (1981) 129M D: Frank Perry. *Faye Dunaway, Diana Scarwid, Steve Forrest, Mara Hobel, Howard da Silva.* Dunaway gives a tour de force performance as Joan Crawford, based on her daughter Christina's controversial autobiography. This film chronicles the steady rise of Crawford's popularity, while behind closed doors she becomes increasingly mean, cruel, depressed, hyper-self-critical, and alcoholic. This results in some incredible scenes of flagrant emotional abuse and a modicum of physical abuse as well. The famous example is the coat-hanger scene, where late one night while Christina is asleep, her mother inspects her closet and finds an expensive dress hanging on the wrong kind of hanger. Joan hauls Christina out of bed, attacks her with hangers, then forces her to scrub a perfectly clean bathroom floor. For a good double feature, try watching this one with *Serial Mom.* —*N. J.*

MURDER BY DEATH L: PLAYWRIGHTS/SIMON, NEIL (1976) 94M D: Robert Moore. *Truman Capote, Alec Guinness, Maggie Smith, Peter Falk, Peter Sellers, David Niven.* A slapstick mystery? It may not have started a new genre, but this one works thanks to its outstanding cast and Simon's script. A variety of detectives are invited over to a large estate to solve a strange murder. Guinness plays the blind butler who welcomes the guests while having unspeakable difficulty with the new deaf-mute maid. The all-star cast of detectives parody well-known personalities in the mystery world. It's Capote himself who turns out to be the host and helps them fit the clues together. —*N. J.*

NINETEEN EIGHTY-FOUR L: LITERATURE/LITERATURE (1984) 120M D: Michael Radford. *John Hurt, Suzanna Hamilton, Richard Burton, Cyril Susak.* Radford captures a respectful adaptation of George Orwell's dystopian Oceania. The film is shot on location in and around London with a dirty sepia-tone look by cinematographer Roger Deakins. He shoots slow dissolves, fade-outs, quick-cuts, flashbacks, and montages with high-contrast photography and low-key lighting; all of this captures the darkness of a broken soul. Winston and his lover, Julia, secretly and defiantly rendezvous against the ideas of Big Brother's totalitarian state, fermenting their forbidden passion while under the all-seeing electric eye and O'Brien's (Burton's final role) Thought Police. Room 101 is our worst nightmare come true, and I wouldn't wish Winston's nightmare on anyone. This film immerses you in Winston's fear and O'Brien's sadistic desire to heal Winston from his lack of faith in his government through patient systematic destruction of the human spirit. —*B.W.*

O L: PLAYWRIGHTS/SHAKESPEARE, WILLIAM (2000) 95M D: Tim Blake Nelson. *Mekhi Phifer, Josh Hartnett, Julia Stiles.* The runaway emotions that drive Shakespeare's *Othello*—envy, racism, fear, passion, jealousy— make even more sense in the modern world of teenagers exploring adult emotions in the seclusion of a private school. In this thoughtful revision, basketball hero Odin (Phifer), the only African-American in the student body, is the target of bad seed Hugo (a chilling Hartnett), who preys upon the immaturity and fragile self-esteem of his classmates. Stiles is smart and sure as Desi, the dean's daughter and O's girlfriend. Though it begins clumsily and the script sometimes gets tangled in its own complications, it's a sensitive and intelligent exploration of the tangled issues of teen violence, race, and self-esteem. Nelson allows the emotional world of the teens to carry the drama through to its devastating denouement. Disney was terrified of releasing it in the shadow of Columbine, and it took two years before Lions Gate acquired the rights and brought it to theaters. —*S.A.*

ORDER, THE (FROM CREMASTER 3) L: ARTS/ PERFORMANCE ART (2002) 32M D: Matthew Barney. *Matthew Barney, Murphy's Law, Aimee Mullins, Agnostic Front.* For years people have asked us if we had Barney's *Cremaster* cycle. It was a series of highly touted experimental films that were shown in art museums in New York, but the videos were only available for exorbitant amounts because they were considered "installations" rather than movies. Word was that they would never be released on DVD because they were not movies, they were art. Because, you know, movies are not art, and clearly (judging from this excerpt from *Cremaster 3*) no movie has ever been made that is as important as Barney climbing around in a building wearing a pink kilt. It's

like a lesser Marilyn Manson video stretched out to an unbearable thirty minutes, mistakenly thinking it is making a point about . . . climbing on stuff and, uh, some cheetah lady, I guess. I'm sure the actual movie . . . er, I mean, installations are better than this crap (the DVD includes a trailer with some interesting images in it) but this short version reinforces every stereotype there is about modern art as pretentious, self-involved bullshit. —*B.T.*

OSCAR L: PLAYS/PLAYS (1991) 109M D: John Landis. *Sylvester Stallone, Ornella Muti, Marisa Tomei, Vincent Spano, Chazz Palminteri, Peter Riegert, Tim Curry.* Landis tries to re-create a '30s-era screwball farce, complete with a cast right out of a Warner Bros. gangster film. Stallone, who proves himself a fine hand at comedy, has just the right attitude as Snaps Provolene, an exasperated mob leader in Depression-era New York who vows on his father's deathbed (Kirk Douglas in a cameo) to go straight, and trips every step of the way. Landis doesn't have the snap (pardon the pun) of the old Hollywood door-slamming comedy and the chemistry just doesn't fizz. Perhaps Landis just isn't shaking briskly enough-the film never has the runaway feel of a movie spinning helplessly and hilariously out of control—but he makes a valiant effort and his cast has the luggish charm of a'30s Warner crime comedy. —*S.A.*

PIERRE AND GILLES: LOVE STORIES L: ARTS/ART (1997) 57M D: Mike Aho. *Catherine Deneuve, Rupert Everett, Jean-Paul Gaultier, Nina Hagen.* A standard arts documentary made interesting by its subject: a photographer/painter duo who combine their skills to make kitschy portraits, often of rock stars and other celebrities. They create colorful, plastic-y characters in front of blatantly artificial backgrounds, sometimes combining fashion photography and homoeroticism with religious iconography. They could make a painting of the Virgin Mary that wouldn't look out of place hanging in Pee-wee's Playhouse. You may recognize some of their work, such as the cover of Prince's *Lovesexy*. This movie doesn't offer a whole lot of insight, but is an entertaining introduction to their work. —*B.T.*

PILOBOLUS DANCE THEATRE L: DANCE/DANCE (1977) 59M D: Merrill Brockway. *Alison Chase, Jonathan Wolken, Michael Tracy, Martha Clarke, Robert Barnett, Moses Pendleton.* Pilobolus Dance Theatre is the 'shrooms of dance; you can't really tell if what you're witnessing is legitimate or fabricated from somewhere within the recesses of your brain. Founded by a bunch of Ivy League Connecticut postgrads, the members of Pilobolus manage to mold and bend themselves into weird shapes and unthinkable body combinations. Dancers connect and separate from the unlikeliest of body parts, one dancer wrapped around another like a hula hoop while yet another is cantilevered off his thigh; the combinations seem endless. At times, the performances get a bit heady and intellectual, several drawing from history and mythology, but most are carried off with a sense of wonder and whimsy, or at least as much as pretentious college people from Connecticut in the '70s could convey. —*T. C.*

PITCH L: CINEMA/H'WD TRADES (1997) 81M D: Kenny Hotz, Spencer Rice. *Spencer Rice, Kenny Hotz.* Aspiring screenwriters can be desperate. They read books about how to write a commercial Hollywood screenplay, how to send a query letter to an agency, how to pitch. If you ask them they'll school you on the intricacies of screenplay format, Writer's Guild registration, proper binding, and the hierarchy of literary agencies. They've studied it obsessively because they're trying to sell a screenplay about a mafia don who accidentally gets a sex change operation and as a result becomes more sensitive, with hilarity liable to ensue. At least that's the case for the two obnoxious Canadian hacks who came up with this high-concept stunt of doing a documentary about themselves as an excuse to give their screenplay to celebrities at the Toronto Film Festival. I recommend this movie because it's fascinating, but it really made me squirm. It's hard to watch people talk so humorlessly about how funny they are. For most of the movie I felt like I was hanging out with a friend who is doing something really embarrassing and I have to think of a way to make it seem like I don't know him. They talk to some celebrities, like Fred Williamson and Roger Ebert, without seeming to really know who they are. The conversation with Ebert is a highlight because he immediately figures out what they're up to and bluntly tells them their idea is lame. —*B. T.*

POLLOCK L: ARTS/ART (2000) 122M D: Ed Harris. *Jennifer Connelly, Jeffrey Tambor, Marcia Gay Harden, Ed Harris, Amy Madigan, Bud Cort.* You'd think Jackson Pollock might be a unique painter to make a movie about, partly because he was so angry and macho, and partly because of his art, which is either completely brilliant or a bunch of paint splattered on a wall, depending on who you ask. This biography hits every single note that you expect in an artist biography: the struggle from obscurity to acclaim, the continued misunderstood artistry, the fiery arguments with a lover whose supportiveness is never truly appreciated, the infidelity, the alcohol, the self-destruction, and the tragic death. Yet somehow the sparse direction and strong performances by Harris and Harden make this a worthwhile drama. —*B. T.*

PRIDE AND PREJUDICE L: LIT. BY AUTHOR/AUSTEN, JANE (1995) 300M D: Simon Langton. *Jennifer Ehle, Colin Firth, Susannah Harker.* I first watched this miniseries when I was a sophomore in high school, and our English teacher had us watch it over the course

of like three billion days. It's really, really long, but I enjoyed every fucking minute. I'm talking the kind of enjoyment that made me excited to go to class every day, sad when class ended, and preoccupied with the plot until I could get back to it. Weekends were a bitch. When I rewatch it now, it's still every bit as endearing but I get to watch it all in one gloriously long stretch. It's so true to the book, Jane Austen fans will want to hug themselves with glee. Firth was born to play the role of Mark Darcy, as he exudes a natural air of stiffness and formality. It doesn't hurt that he is also really hot. Literature never looked so good. —*J. S.*

PSYCHO BEACH PARTY L: PLAYS/PLAYS (2000) 95M D: Robert Lee King. *Lauren Ambrose, Charles Busch, Nicholas Brendon, Matt Keeslar, Kimberley Davies, Thomas Gibson.* The premise of this campy, wannabe cult film is "What if Gidget had a split personality and went on a killing spree?" It recreates the tone of Gidget and the old beach party movies with some skill, then throws in a little bit of vulgarity, homoeroticism, and murder as an attempt at black comedy. On a technical level you have to give the movie credit, but the problem is it's not even remotely funny. Maybe they thought this sort of retro-camp was so out of date that it would be ironic to bring it back? I guess if you think a swearing Gidget would be shocking, or if you find any movie with a campy female impersonator in it funny, then this is the movie for you. But I think these guys were about thirty years too late to take the piss out of the beach movies. Written by Charles Busch from his supposedly popular off-Broadway play. —*B. T.*

QUIET AMERICAN, THE L: LITERATURE/LITERATURE (2002) 101M D: Phillip Noyce. *Michael Caine, Brendan Fraser, Do Hai Yen, Rade Serbedzija.* Caine is Thomas Fowler, a British reporter with the *London Times*, happily taking it easy in Saigon with a young Vietnamese lover (Hai Yen) when the Americans bully their way into the country's political struggles. Fraser is Pyle, "the quiet American," whom Fowler (our narrator) remembers as a serious, humble, genuinely likable young man, despite the fact that the Boy Scout medical doctor on a mission of conscience is in reality a CIA agent with a passionate and naive dedication to global democracy. Not so much an indictment of American foreign policy as a demand that the United States take responsibility for its actions in other countries, Noyce's adaptation of the Graham Greene novel revolves around the cost of interference—thousands of innocents sacrificed in the name of fighting Communism—and the contradictions within the men that make them both friends and rivals. Caine's beautifully understated performance earned him an Oscar nomination. —*S. A.*

REDUCED SHAKESPEARE COMPANY, THE L: PLAYWRIGHTS/SHAKESPEARE, WILLIAM (2000) 90M D: Matthew Croke, others.

Matthew Croke, Michael John Faulkner, John Kernion. After kicking off with a short biography of Shakespeare (bet you didn't know he wrote *Mein Kampf* and annexed the Sudetenland), the company's three glee-fully overacting jesters tear through—and tear up—the complete cycle of Shakespeare's plays. In fewer than ninety minutes. *Titus Andronicus* becomes a cooking show, *Othello* is rewritten as a rap song, the histories are transformed into a winner-take-all football match where the crown changes hands in fatal tackles, and all sixteen comedies are distilled into one production stuffed to the gills with identical twins. Two plays get their undivided demolition: *Romeo and Juliet,* their opening salvo into Bard destruction, and their breathless finale, an audience partici-pation workshop version of *Hamlet* with sock puppet guest stars and a rubber Yorrick (alas, he bounces well). Methinks it hilarious. *—S. A.*

REQUIEM FOR A DREAM L: LITERATURE/LITERATURE (2000) 102M D: Darren Aronofsky.

Jared Leto, Jennifer Connelly, Marlon Wayans, Christopher McDonald, Louise Lasser, Ellen Burstyn. Depressing and more than a little difficult to watch, *Requiem for a Dream* tackles the world of drug addiction and the inevitable downward spiral that comes with it. Sara (Burstyn) finds out that she is going to be on her favorite TV show and dreams of wear-ing a red dress that she hasn't been able to fit into for a few years, which leads to her becoming addicted to diet pills. Her son, Harry (Leto), his girlfriend, Marion (Connelly), and their friend, Tyrone (Wayans), are addicted to heroin and cocaine and dream of living large when they start dealing in large amounts. As the four slip further and further into addiction, their dreams become more and more unobtainable. The cinematogra-phy and music in this film are excellent, and add to the jerky, surreal atmosphere of the addiction. Not for the faint of heart, this movie gives a real, candid look at drug addiction and the lengths that people will go to feed it. *—J. S.*

RHINOCEROS L: PLAYS/PLAYS (1974) 101M D: Tom O'Horgan.

Zero Mostel, Gene Wilder, Robert Weil, Karen Wilder, Joe Silver. If you're a fan of *The Producers* and you haven't had a chance to see *Rhinoceros,* you're in for a real treat. Driven by the talents of Mostel and Wilder, this is one weird movie about a sophisticated gentleman who turns into a rhi-noceros. Watching Mostel transform is incred-ible. Man, those guys are awesome. I love how everyone in the movie deals so seriously with the rhinoceros problem. It's dark, funny, absurd, surreal, and a good conversation piece. This was a very difficult movie to rent until recently, so now's your chance. *—R. D.*

RHINOSKIN: THE MAKING OF A MOVIE STAR L: CINEMA/ ACTING (1994) 90M D: Tod DePree.

This is an essential film for any chucklehead nutty enough to want to become a "star" or even a working stiff in the industry that is Hollywood. DePree (known today as Hopworth DePree) brings us along to auditions, meetings with agents, and all ways of trying to scrounge a career for himself as an actor in the glittery world of the movies. It is not at all what you'd expect, which is perfect for anyone so blindly ambitious as to attempt a career where failure is the rule and success a glorious excep-tion. Painful, hope-filled, and disappointing as it all can be, we realize just what the director/actor does: at the very least, in Hollywood, your first prerequisite is *Rhinoskin. —K. S.*

RKO 281 L: CINEMA/H'WOOD DIRECTORS (1999) 87M D: Benjamin Ross.

Brenda Blethyn, Roy Scheider, John Malkovich, James Cromwell, Liev Schreiber, Melanie Griffith. There are unnecessary fiction, distorted facts, and a few apocryphal stories passed off as history in this portrait of the making and almost unmaking of *Citizen Kane,* but surprisingly this dramatization paints a more complex and intri-cate picture than the documentary that inspired it, *The Battle over Citizen Kane.* Aping the struc-ture of *Kane* and quoting from Welles relent-lessly, director Benjamin Ross and screenwriter John Logan pay respectful homage without slipping into humorless adoration. Their Welles (played smartly by Schreiber) is a charmer and a monster, the face of modesty over the soul of a megalomaniac, but the richness comes in the colorful personalities, telling details, and often neglected heroes woven through his story. Malkovich makes a great Herman J. Mankiewicz, Hollywood insider and celebrity troublemaker; Griffith is surprisingly vulnerable and touch-ing as Marion Davies; and Scheider brings dig-nity and defiance to RKO head of production George Schaefer, the unsung hero of the behind-the-scenes drama. *—S. A.*

ROSENCRANTZ AND GUILDENSTERN ARE DEAD L: PLAYS/PLAYS (1990) 117M D: Tom Stoppard.

Gary Oldman, Tim Roth, Richard Dreyfuss, Iain Glen, Donald Sumpter, Joanna Miles. Meet Rosencrantz and Guildenstern, two small characters from Shakespeare's epic tale of lust, betrayal, and madness, *Hamlet.* These supposed friends of Hamlet's are summoned to help the prince and deduce the madness that afflicts him, but we see the pair rarely and they serve little more pur-pose than to play the part of pawns. So Stoppard took pity on these two poor buggers and gave them their own movie. It's a brilliantly funny and satirical look at the underbelly of *Hamlet* as Rosencrantz (Oldman) and Guildenstern (Roth) stumble through the story, struggling to dissect what is going on around them, do their duty, and figure out just which of them is which. Only the Player, played with pompous perfection by Dreyfuss, knows the truth behind their design, likely because he is a member of the theater and as such knows the worth and destiny of doomed characters trapped in a tragedy where death is the only answer. The film incorporates wickedly clever foreshadowing, playful physics experiments, and delightful musings and introspections upon life, person, and purpose. —*M. N.*

RULES OF ATTRACTION, THE L: LITERATURE/LITERATURE
(2002) 110M D: Roger Avary. *James Van Der Beek, Ian Somerhalder, Shannyn Sossamon, Jessica Biel, Kip Pardue.* Much-hated Bret Easton Ellis adaptation about drug use and degrading sex among soulless rich college students. Most of the characters are intentionally unsympathetic, and of course the idea that rich kids are living lives of cruelty and debauchery is not exactly shocking. But I like the movie for the same reasons most hate it. It has a detached feeling that probably comes from Avary studying Kubrick movies, but stylistically it's more DePalmian: audacious, well-executed gimmicks involving time going backwards; elaborate split screening; stunt casting of TV Goody Two-shoes as pathetic low-lifes; and a devastating scene of a lonely girl committing suicide made all the more effective by the fact that you can't remember seeing her before. It's a better exercise in style than satire, but why punish a movie for getting it partly right? —*B. T.*

SCHLOCK! THE SECRET HISTORY OF AMERICAN MOVIES L: CINEMA/CINEMA HISTORY (2003) 90M D: Ray Greene. *Doris Wishman, Dick Miller, Harry Novak, Sam Arkoff, Roger Corman, David F. Friedman.* Schlock! surveys American exploitation cinema and the people who thrived in the production of low-budget sex, gore, and drug films outside the traditional studio system of production and distribution. Greene's portrait about the rise, evolution, and fall of the exploitation film industry is surprisingly detailed, though he offers no new insights to the previously trod ground. The highlights are new interviews with Corman, Wishman, Arkoff, Friedman, Novak, and Miller, all of whom are frank about their work and *articulate in their discussions. An entertaining introduction to the film history you don't always hear about.* —*S. A.*

SCOTLAND, PA L: PLAYWRIGHTS/SHAKESPEARE, WILLIAM
(2002) 104M D: Billy Morrissette. *James LeGros, Maura Tierney, Christopher Walken, Kevin Corrigan.* Yeah, yeah, Shakespeare was a genius, blah dee blah, but his work in the written form can often be a little dense and difficult to digest. Thanks to the wonders of the electronic age, however, Shakespeare can be on your TV, transformed into a fast-food parody and delivered in 104 dark, tragic, and, at times, kind of funny minutes. This is *Scotland, PA* in a nutshell. The story is *Macbeth*, but set in the modern day with some deep fryers and hamburgers thrown in. The story has been remade about a billion times, but this unique adaptation stands on its own mer-

its not as just a Shakespeare story but also as a dark, deeply funny movie with complex characters who are willing to (and will) die for the fast-food industry. Tierney and Walken deserve particular recognition for the performances they deliver. —*J. S.*

It's set in and around a diner in—for no clear reason—1975 or so. Perhaps director Morrissette does this to capitalize on the kitsch value of the decorations and clothing, but it doesn't really add anything to the film and winds up being more annoying than inspiring. Even Walken's rather entertaining turn is not enough to save this "look-at-me-I'm-an-indie" film. A completely mediocre and not particularly necessary adaptation. —*C. P.*

SEEMS LIKE OLD TIMES L: PLAYWRIGHTS/SIMON, NEIL
(1980) 102M D: Jay Sandrich. *Charles Grodin, Chevy Chase, Goldie Hawn.* It's really too bad that Chase, Hawn, and Grodin don't get many scripts as well-written as Simon's comedic romp. Lately Chase (one of my favorite actors growing up) has resigned himself to showing up in family films like *Snow Day* and *Man of the House.* Sadly, Hawn's recent films have also been nothing to write home about. *Seems Like Old Times* features Chase as an allegedly innocent ex-con writer who has escaped to the coast to work on his novel. In retreat, however, he is kidnapped by a couple of second-rate robbery men and forced to hold up a bank, which (of course) only brings him more legal trouble. Desperate and on the run, he makes his way to the house of his ex-wife (Hawn). A sympathetic public defender, Hawn is now married to Grodin, who is up for district attorney. Hiding Chase from her husband and his employers, attempting to ward off his pathetic come-on lines, and somehow trying to keep the house all in one piece, Hawn begins to come unglued. To be sure, hilarity ensues. —*C. P.*

SEPARATE TABLES L: PLAYS/PLAYS (1958) 98M D: Delbert
Mann. *Wendy Hiller, David Niven, Burt Lancaster, Rita Hayworth, Gladys Cooper, Deborah Kerr.* Niven and Hiller earned Oscars for their performances in this handsome adaptation of Terence Rattigan's two-act play about lonely and disconnected people rattling around in a past-its-prime residence hotel on the British seaside. Their routine lives are shaken up when scandal reveals blustery old warhorse Niven's lies and shatters the illusions of the lovestruck Kerr, a nervous, mousy woman smothered by her haughty mother (Cooper). Meanwhile an American writer's (Lancaster) emotional wounds are reopened by the unexpected arrival of his ex-wife (Hayworth), who is perfect as the past-her-prime beauty masking her loneliness and fear behind a facade of confidence and cool. This deftly written actor's piece has plenty of good lines and showpiece scenes. Director Mann, usually something of a stiff, rises to the challenge and makes a handsome piece of it. —*S. A.*

SISTER MARY EXPLAINS IT ALL L: PLAYS/PLAYS (2000) 77M D: Marshall Brickman. *Diane Keaton, Laura San Giacomo, Jennifer Tilly, Brian Benben, Wallace Langham.* In this adaptation of the Christopher Durang play *Sister Mary Ignatius Explains It All For You,* a group of friends decide to visit their old Catholic school teacher, Sister Mary Ignatius (Keaton). She is a pillar of religious conservatism, and in a regular presentation she explains everything with clear black-and-white morality for her audience. When her former students present to her some of the moral ambiguities of the outside world, the sparks start to fly. This film adaptation may not be as good as the stage version, but Keaton is well cast and the holier-than-thou tirades stand out quite well. —*N.J.*

SLAM NATION: THE SPORT OF THE SPOKEN WORD L: POETRY & POETS/POETRY & POETS (1998) 100M D: Paul Devlin. *Saul Williams.* Documentary about slam poetry competitions where poets recite in front of judges for points. A wide array of performers from different backgrounds and with different philosophies will both challenge and confirm your suspicions about this type of poetry. It's interesting to see the performers struggle with the idea of art as sport. To me, the main attraction is Williams (later the star of *Slam*), who performs several brilliant pieces that might be poetry, or might be hip hop, but are probably something else that hasn't been invented yet. —*B.T.*

SNOW FALLING ON CEDARS L: LITERATURE/LITERATURE (1999) 127M D: Scott Hicks. *Youki Kudoh, Ethan Hawke.* Of all the films shot in Washington state, this is perhaps the most beautiful, as Robert Richardson's camera lovingly captures the sights and sounds of Eastern Washington in the first half of the twentieth century. A sense of poetic abstraction renders much of the narrative difficult to follow—what works for the novel doesn't always work here—but the visual marvel of this film more than makes up for its possible inadequacies. If you want to see Washington the way it was meant to be seen, give this film a look. —*C. P.*

SOME NUDITY REQUIRED L: CINEMA/H'WD TRADES (1998) 82M D: Odette Springer, Johanna Demetrakas. *Samuel Z. Arkoff, Maria Ford, Roger Corman, Arlene Sidaris, Julie Strain, Andy Sidaris, Lisa Boyle.* Springer, the musical director of Corman's New Horizons, explores her own conflicted relationship with the modern B-movie industry of erotic thrillers and action nudies. Springer manages the improbable: a revealing behind-the-scenes working of the straight-to-video market and an intelligent, often provocative examination of issues of self-image, control, and the compromises women make to work in their chosen field. From the testosterone-fueled visions of zero-budget stalwarts Jim Wynorski and Fred Olen Ray ("Breasts are the cheapest special effects in the business" is Wynorski's mantra) to the revelations of cult queens Ford and Strain, Odette's startlingly personal odyssey through the cinematic degradation of women on-screen is fascinating, informative, and at times disturbing. —*S. A.*

STATIONS OF THE ELEVATED L: ARTS/ART (1980) 45M D: Manfred Kirchheimer. Unless you were the one painting it, New York subway graffiti of the '70s and '80s was mostly seen moving along the elevated tracks, a sort of motorized art museum transporting paintings around the city to be seen by unsuspecting passersby. This simple but beautiful movie shows us that view. It is made up of footage of moving subways set to the music of Charles Mingus. Created for the Museum of Modern Art in New York. —*B. T.*

STEVIE L: POETRY & POETS/POETRY & POETS (1978) 102M D: Robert Enders. *Mona Washbourne, Glenda Jackson.* I dare you to visit a living room—the suburban living room that poet Stevie Smith shared with her most splendid aunt. Here is the life, work, and legend of "the British Dorothy Parker," personified magnificently by Jackson, whose sing-song verse barely sheathes the daggers we keep pointed at our own hearts. Hear Stevie's dark and witty summation of life in suburbia (alone, worth the price of a rental) and say you don't know it's the truth. —*K. S.*

TAMING OF THE SHREW L: PLAYWRIGHTS/SHAKESPEARE, WILLIAM (1976) 120M D: Kirk Browning. *Sandra Shotwell, Fredi Olster, Marc Singer.* An American Conservatory Theatre of San Francisco production, this is without a doubt my all-time favorite version of the classic tale. Bursting with lively humor, a clean and simple style, physical prowess and agility, the play offers a vivacious and refreshingly playful version of Shakespeare's words. In the affable town of Padua there are two infamous women, the younger a virtuous beauty greatly sought after, the elder of hostile and shrewish temperament. Their father has decreed that none shall marry the younger till the older be wed. This leads to a variety of plots, plans, and bribes to get the first married and then win over the affections of the second. The parts of Kate and Petruchio are played with youthful exuberance and acrobatics. The two leads spark from the beginning with chemistry that blossoms into a contest of wills and later into a truer, gentler love. Of course there is much to be said for the talented chest of Singer as well, but that is not the only allure. No, come on, really, I mean it! —*M. N.*

THIS BOY'S LIFE L: LITERATURE/LITERATURE (1993) 114M D: Michael Caton-Jones. *Robert De Niro, Leonardo DiCaprio, Ellen Barkin, Jonah Blechman.* DiCaprio is part Boy Scout, part juvenile delinquent as teenage Tobias "Toby" Wolff in the film version of his autobiographical novel, the well-meaning but frustrated son of a single mom (Barkin), whose good heart is kicked around by the bad-luck men her life. Her latest is Dwight (De Niro), a single father of three who takes them to the aptly named Concrete, a sinkhole of a town in rural Washington state that threatens to harden around the feet of everyone who lands there. DiCaprio is magnetic in his first starring role, full of passion, anger, hope, and confusion. De Niro is frightening as Dwight, whose good manners, bad jokes, and flat rural accent hide an angry, soul-crushing bully determined to smother the ambition out of his children through intimidation and humiliation. Look out for Pearl, his youngest daughter: she's played by future star and vampire slayer Eliza Dushku. —S. A.

TITUS L: PLAYWRIGHTS/SHAKESPEARE, WILLIAM (1999) 162M D: Julie Taymor. *Jessica Lange, Anthony Hopkins, Laura Fraser, Harry J. Lennix, Alan Cumming.* Often said to be Shakespeare's worst play, the brilliant opera director Taymor (best known for her Broadway musical of *The Lion King*) challenged that notion by bringing Titus Andronicus to the big screen. Some feel that the play's amoral characters and extreme acts of violence (which alternate between darkly humorous and completely horrifying) are too much, but Taymor plays them as a statement about the cyclical nature of violence. She mixes time periods (where kids have both swords and video games) but keeps the original language. The superb costume designs, which give a distinctive style to each of the various factions, make it easier for the Shakespeare-challenged to follow. The elaborate, stylized sets are even more impressive. And then there is the acting, particularly that of Lennix as the unrepentant villain, Aaron. This is one of the most stunning directorial debuts in years. —B. T.

TREASURE ISLAND L: LIT. BY AUTHOR/STEVENSON, ROBERT LOUIS (1950) 96M D: Byron Haskin. *Bobby Driscoll, Robert Newton, Lance Baker, Nick Offerman, Basil Sydney, Walter Fitzgerald.* Newton practically created the "Argh, matey" cliché of growling pirate captains in his ingratiating performance as the scheming Long John Silver in Walt Disney's first live-action feature. The boy's own adventure stars Driscoll as Jim Hawkins, the spunky kid who embarks on the adventure of a lifetime when he inherits a pirate treasure map. Directed by Haskin with a journeyman's flatness on studio-bound sets interspersed with gorgeous photography of grand ships, endless blue skies, calm seas, and lush Caribbean island, he nonetheless delivers a tale almost too hearty for the Disney family film tradition (there is no blood but some of the violence is surprisingly visceral). The film belongs to the peg-leg pirate king with a paternal protectiveness of young Hawkins and a sense of honor and restraint in matters of life and death. Long John Silver is many things, but heartless isn't one of them. He's got more heart than everyone else in the movie put together. —S. A.

VIRGIN SUICIDES L: LITERATURE/LITERATURE (1999) 96M D: Sofia Coppola. *Hanna R. Hall, Kirsten Dunst, Josh Hartnett, Kathleen Turner, James Woods.* Told from the perspective of a group of young men fascinated with the five beautiful Lisben girls, *Virgin Suicides* is the sad story of the events leading up to the girls' mass suicide. Beautifully shot with a soft, pure look to it, the cinematography is excellent, but the plot ultimately leaves you feeling a little mystified. Outside of Dunst's character, Lux, none of the other girls are given any real personality or character development, making it difficult to relate to the reasoning behind their final decision to commit suicide. This ultimately contributes to the dreamy, distant feel of the film. The Lisben sisters are, from the very beginning of the movie, one entity, and it is the decision by one to act independently of the group that inevitably leads to their demise. Coppola proves herself to be a talented director with this film. —J. S.

VISIONS OF LIGHT: THE ART OF CINEMATOGRAPHY L: CINEMA/H'WD TRADES (1992) 92M D: Stuart Samuels. *Ernest R. Dickerson, Lisa Rinzler, Michael Chapman, Allen Daviau, Conrad L. Hall, Caleb Deschanel. Visions of Light* is a wonderfully intriguing documentary looking at the power of the cinematographer, going back to their origins as the inventors and reinventors of camera technologies and forward to their work as visionaries of space, depth, light, and form. Filled with images from some famous, some infamous, and some more obscure films, this look at what goes on with the camera is a fount of great film recommendations. I found many of the scenes mesmerizing, the stories behind the happy accidents and the deliberate machinations both entertaining and endlessly fascinating. My only complaint is the exploration ends a bit short of what was current at the time of the documentary's completion. It's uncertain to me if they didn't feel that anything more recent had been worth remarking upon, if nothing good had been released, or if they just ran out of time and needed to wrap things up. Regardless, this is still a wonderful look at the "look" of films. —M. N.

WAIT UNTIL DARK L: PLAYS/PLAYS (1967) 120M D: Terence Young. *Audrey Hepburn, Alan Arkin, Richard Crenna, Jack Weston.* Hepburn is remarkable as a blind woman whose husband gives her a doll. The problem is he didn't know crooks were using it to smuggle heroin. Arkin plays the conniving crook who was expecting the drugs and uses every nasty trick he can muster to get Hepburn to surrender the doll. Eventually the story develops into a very tense survival of the fittest. This film is adapted from the Broadway play by Frederick Knott. While it primarily has just one set for most of the film, its great use of sound and lighting heightens the suspense. —N. J.

WAR PHOTOGRAPHER L: ARTS/PHOTOGRAPHY (2001) 96M D: Christian Frei. *James Nachtwey, Des Wright, Christiane Amanpour.* A documentary about Nachtwey, considered by many the greatest war photographer ever, whose passion is documenting, through his camera, man's inhumanity to man. Why would someone want to fly around the world to war zones, exposing himself to danger and hell on earth? Nachtwey is a seemingly humble man who has found a way to convey his vision by sharing the horror of war with the pictures he takes. By bringing these snapshots of war to mainstream publications, he is bringing it into our living rooms, something most people don't see and don't want to see. He is forcing a dialogue about war and atrocities, hoping to bring about a consciousness to affect change in the situations he covers. When Nachtwey shows us these pictures, we see that no matter in whose name a war is fought, the end result is not freedom but everlasting, enduring pain for everyone involved. Most wars are committed in the name of "liberty," and liberty just means the freedom to exploit any weakness you can find. —*B. W.*

WITHOUT YOU I'M NOTHING L: ARTS/PERFORMANCE ART (1990) 90M D: John Boskovich. *Sandra Bernhard.* Bernhard leaves nothing sacred in this one-woman show. Each episode of the stand-up comedy routine is introduced to the audience as though it's one evening following another, and so few people appreciate her jokes that by the end of the film the house is empty! Why? Because her audience is composed of exactly the kind of people she ridicules night after night. But each skit is an all-out production in and of itself, despite how strange the subject may be—at one point she's dressed like Nina Simone singing "Four Women." It may not be politically correct, but if you are at all as able to laugh at yourself as she is able to laugh at herself, you will get quite a rise out of this curious self-effacing comedy. —*N. J.*

WONDER BOYS L: LITERATURE/LITERATURE (2000) 112M D: Curtis Hanson. *Michael Douglas, Tobey Maguire, Robert Downey Jr., Frances McDormand, Katie Holmes.* Wonder Boys is the story of a college professor (Douglas) trying to follow up his critically successful first novel. Meanwhile he is dealing with pressures from his agent (Downey), trying to keep a talented student (Maguire) out of trouble, warding off a female student boarder's (Holmes) affections, and dealing with the fact that he got the chancellor (McDormand, who is married to the chair of the English department) pregnant. Easily a candidate for best written film of 2000, *Wonder Boys* truly speaks to the human condition and is filled with dry wit rarely seen on the screen today. Oscar-worthy performances across the board, especially from Maguire who proves once again he is one of the most talented young actors working on the big screen. Filled with beautiful cinematography and some really good music by Mr. Bob Dylan. Based on the novel by Michael Chabon. —*S. W. F.*

CHAPTER TWELVE
Psychotronic
(Horror, Sci-Fi, Fantasy)

W hat is psychotronic, you ask? Well, back in 1980, Michael Weldon started using this word to group together all of the films he loved: Horror, Sci-Fi, Fantasy, and various other genres of arguable quality, all of which had such a profound influence on him that he founded a magazine (then a book and later a website) dedicated to these films. He didn't coin the word, but it sure fits. "Psychotronic" was originally defined by various UFO/Alien Abduction/Crop Circle/brainiac nutjob genius-types, as "mind control by electronic low-frequency waves." Well, just as aliens are influencing us, Michael Weldon was influenced by these films. They "got into his head." And they got into our heads as well, and we are all the better for it.

From Japanese Science Fiction to Italian Horror and everything in-between, this chapter is often represented by films whose low-budget realities have put a taint upon their high-minded aspirations. How else could you explain a terrific classic sci-fi B-movie like *The Brain from Planet Arous*?

(I can't even begin to tell you why I don't have room to explain ... but watch it! I beg you! You must watch *The Brain from Planet Arous*! I am being compelled by electronic waves to tell you. And watch *The Monolith Monsters* after that! Please! The survival of our planet depends upon it!)

We love these movies! We love them so much we've made up all kinds of goofy subsections here. Horror is so bloody generic, how could we resist breaking it up into sections like Mad Scientists or Were-

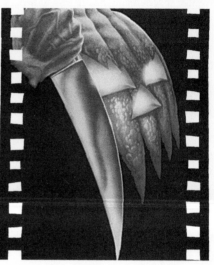

Halloween (1980)

wolves? What about those wacky fantastical Mexican fairy tales or wrestling movies? Mexico-a-go-go! And is there a better section in the store than VAOWG? It stands for Vengeful Acts of a Wrathful God and contains films portraying all kinds of imaginable human demise. Woo hoo! What about those films created by well-meaning, faith-based filmmakers? You know, those films that don't trust that the teachings of Jesus are enough? That they have to try to threaten you or scare you to death instead? You can find those films in the Christploitation section!

This chapter also includes sections devoted to two animators of the fantastic whose animation so dominated the films they were in that you feel as if they themselves had directed the movies: Ray Harryhausen and Willis O'Brien. Only recently have computer animators even begun to come close to achieving what Harryhausen and O'Brien did with stop-motion animation. Have you seen *Jason and the Argonauts*? It is still astonishing. Have you ever watched O'Brien's *The Lost World*? Is it any wonder that many in the original audiences believed it was real?

There is also a literary section here called Psychotronic Writers; a great place to gather up the films based on the works of the writers who scare the crap out of us, creep us out, or otherwise amaze, awe, or terrify us. Authors and stories of great imagination all, these are films bent on bending your ear, then your heart, then your mind only to steer your soul to uncharted territory.

Fear electronic low-frequency waves? Bah! To take Pogo out of context, we have met the enemy, and he is us. But we have also met the heroes in ourselves as well. And let the battles begin! In the realm of Psychotronic cinema, either way, we win just by playing in the uncharted territories of our imaginations.

ABOMINABLE DR. PHIBES, THE L: HORROR/MAD SCIENTISTS (1971) 94M D: Robert Fuest. *Virginia North, Vincent Price, Joseph Cotton.* The tragic story of love and revenge at the heart of *Dr. Phibes* is embellished with brilliant black comedy, beautiful direction, and extraordinarily creative death sequences to create an essential piece of classic horror. The undead Dr. Phibes has returned to seek vengeance upon the surgeons who killed his wife. He uses the Ten Plagues of the Pharaohs as inspiration for his murders. Lavish set design, creative camera work, and subtle makeup effects all serve to highlight Price's magnificent performance as the mad doctor. Hideously deformed, Phibes wears a prosthetic face, the face of Price. Never opening his mouth to speak, he communicates his loss, suffering, and anger with terrifying intensity. His voice, usually Price's most diabolically sinister characteristic, sometimes emanates from beneath his mask. However, it is almost incidental when it does. Price's performance is a purely physical one. Cotton is good as the protagonist but Phibes's tragic villain steals the show, even from the overbearingly magnifi-

cent art direction, fantastic death scenes, and razor-sharp script. —*T. S.*

ABOMINABLE SNOWMAN OF THE HIMALAYAS, THE L: HORROR/HAMMER FILMS (1957) 91M D: Val Guest. *Forrest Tucker, Peter Cushing, Maureen Connell, Robert Brown, Richard Wattis.* British botanist Cushing joins American entrepreneur Tucker to search for the legendary yeti in the Himalayas, and neither are prepared for what they find. Director Guest brilliantly combines spectacular aerial mountain footage with claustrophobic studio sets to create an edgy thriller. Nigel Kneale's smart script is heavier on philosophy than adventure and his opportunistic villains are one-dimensional, but Guest comes through with chilling set pieces and a brilliant use of offscreen sound when the unseen mountain creatures howl a cry of mourning for a fallen brother. Cushing, better known for his cold, rational heroes and villains, delivers a warm, human performance as the voice of reason and the soul of the doomed hunting party. —*S. A.*

ADVENTURES OF BUCKAROO BANZAI ACROSS THE 8TH DIMENSION, THE L: SCIENCE FICTION/SCIENCE FICTION (1984) 103M D: W. D. Richter. *Peter Weller, Jeff Goldblum, John Lithgow.* Remember, no matter where you go, there you are. Weller is the brain surgeon and rock star who, with "The Hong Kong Cavaliers" (his loyal band of heroes), saves the world in his spare time. Lithgow puts the mad back into mad scientist as the alien genius out to conquer the monkey-boys of planet Earth, and Goldblum dons chaps and a Roy Rogers shirt to play the band's newest recruit. Why? Because this movie lives in its own universe of pulp hero references: imagine a New Wave version of Doc Savage melded with Orson Welles's *War of the Worlds* and bar band rock and roll. Wonderfully weird and obscure, this low-key bit of funky cool never caught on to a general audience (and thus the promised sequel remains only a dream) but has built up a devoted cult following in the years since. —*S. A.*

AIRPORT 1975 L: VAOWG/VAOWG (1974) 107M D: Jack Smight. *Helen Reddy, Linda Blair, Charlton Heston, Gloria Swanson, Karen Black, George Kennedy.* It's hard to watch the *Airport* movies in a post-*Airplane!* world, but the weird thing is that *Airport 1975* is almost as funny as the parody! The first *Airport* is essentially a soap opera in the sky and follows the grand Hollywood tradition of big casts of has-beens in bloated movie versions of crappy best sellers. This first sequel takes a page out of the disaster film genre, throws in a singing nun (Reddy), a sick kid (Blair between TV movies and *Exorcist* sequels), an overacting (as usual) Heston, and the requisite group of washed-up actors. Dana Andrews has a heart attack and crashes his small plane into a big jumbo jet and kills pilot Roy Thinnes (who flies out the window), so a cross-eyed stewardess

(Black) has to land the sucker. There's too many "stars" to list but my favorite is a trio of drunken guys played by Jerry Stiller, Norman Fell, and Conrad Janis. —*S. H.*

ALIEN RESURRECTION L: SCIENCE FICTION/SCIENCE FICTION (1997) 108M D: Jean-Pierre Jeunet. *Sigourney Weaver, Winona Ryder, Ron Perlman, Dominique Pinon, Michael Wincott.* Using the tissue sample taken during *Alien 3*, military scientists on a spaceship manage to clone Ripley and remove the alien queen from her womb. Stupid bastards. When the alien specimens escape, it's up to Ripley clone #8 and a team of visiting mercenaries to kill them. It's not as good as you'd hope from the dream team of *City of Lost Children* director Jeunet and *Buffy the Vampire Slayer* creator Joss Whedon, but it's full of great set-pieces (the underwater ambush), pulpy characters (Perlman is particularly great), and clever plays on expectations (fans always wanted the aliens to come to Earth, but these characters don't want to go there because it's a "shithole"). Some scenes suffer from creature effects that aren't up to the standards of the first two films in the series, but I do at least appreciate the idea of a sympathetic half-alien being given the most painful death imaginable (sucked into space through a tiny hole). —*B. T.*

ALIEN VISITOR (AKA EPSILON) L: SCIENCE FICTION/ SCIENCE FICTION (1995) 92M D: Rolf De Heer. *Syd Brisbane, Ullie Birve, Chloe Ferguson, Alethea McGrath, Phoebe Ferguson.* Another interesting movie by the director of *Bad Boy Bubby* and *The Quiet Room* about an alien who shares information about the universe with an average joe from the Outback. This is more a commentary on environmental and human issues than a science fiction movie. There are some pretty poignant ecological themes that might make this film an entertaining yet educational movie for the classroom. —*R. D.*

ALIVE L: VAOWG/VAOWG (1993) 125M D: Frank Marshall. *Vincent Spano, John Haymes Newton, Josh Hamilton, Ethan Hawke, Bruce Ramsay.* This eye-opening suspense film is based on a true story about a group of Uruguayan rugby players whose plane crashed in the Andes in 1972. Predating the age of reality television, this film smacks of *Survivor*-style voyeurism except for the realistic and overly sustained crash sequence, and of course the group consensus to resort to cannibalism. It is hard to conceive why director Marshall (who produced several Steven Spielberg films) would tackle such a subject in such an exploitative way. By the end one might conclude this is the first feel-good film about cannibalism. The primary audience for *Alive* is those who appreciate B-grade horror films replete with cannibalism. For them this film is all the more funny because of its huge budget. —*N. J.*

ALUCARDA L: HORROR/WITCHES & WARLOCKS (1975) 85M D: Juan López Moctezuma. *Tina Romero, Susana Kamini, David Silva, Claudio Brook, Tina French.* Lush, imaginative tale of witchcraft infecting a nunnery, from naked ceremonies to inquisitional tortures set in baroquely inflated Gothic architecture. Nuns in rude habits unwashed and marked by menstrual stains scurry about, head bent, clueless to the whirlwind of forces surrounding them. Likewise the rational medical doctor battling the torture-prone priest and mother superior who all prove equally helpless in the crunch. Only adventurous novitiate Alucarda (Romero) and one sister seem to know what is what, pulling novitiate Justine (Kamini) in two directions—pure sensual delight versus the hard, often bloody path of self-sacrifice. Director Moctezuma makes both paths seem equally appealing from the sheer visual and surreal force of his imagery. The most powerful of the director's groundbreaking Mexican horror films from the 1970s—*Mary, Mary, Bloody Mary* and *La Mansión de la Locura* are the other two. —*J. C.*

AMAZING STORIES BOOK 2 L: SCIENCE FICTION/SCIENCE FICTION TV (1986) 71M D: Robert Zemeckis, Brad Bird. *Annie Potts, Christopher Lloyd, Mary Stuart Masterson.* Two episodes of the Spielberg-produced anthology series. The episode Zemeckis directed, starring Lloyd as a teacher whose cruelty is avenged by witchcraft, is nothing special. But the other half, "Family Dog," is a classic half-hour of animation directed by Bird (who would go on to direct the pilot of *The Simpsons*, the modern classic *The Iron Giant*, and Pixar's *The Incredibles*) with character designs by Tim Burton. It tells about the lives of a suburban family from the point of view of their long-suffering dog, who gets blamed for not stopping burglars from robbing their house, then ends up joining the gang of robbers himself. Although the story does follow cartoon logic, what makes it special is that the dog is not anthropomorphized. He is a dog who only cares about dog things like eating and getting enough sleep. The kids are also very funny and talk like real kids. After years of delays, this became a short-lived and savagely reviewed prime-time series. —*B. T.*

AMERICAN GOTHIC L: HORROR/STALKERS (1987) 89M D: John Hough. *Rod Steiger, Michael J. Pollard, Yvonne De Carlo.* American Gothic begins as the average B-grade horror film. A group of stupid teenagers find themselves stranded on an island and have to find lodging for the night. They stumble on a home they think is uninhabited, finding 1920s records and clothing. Yet all resemblance to a typical American horror film ends when Steiger and De Carlo step out. This quirky film spins and turns in the most unpredictable ways, as each character of the family introduced hereafter is crazier than the last. And slowly but surely the teenagers get knocked off in a variety of bizarre

accidents. This film is a must-see for all horror aficionados. —*N. J.*

AMERICAN WEREWOLF IN LONDON, AN L: HORROR/ WEREWOLVES (1981) 98M D: John Landis. *Jenny Agutter, David Naughton, Griffin Dunne.* Back when Vic Morrow was still around, Landis made some pretty good movies. He'd proven himself at the box office, so he was allowed to do this project based on one of his early scripts. Two American pals on vacation in England get attacked by a werewolf, one dies and the other gets infected. He (Naughton) hooks up with a sexy British nurse (Agutter), has gory nightmares, and gets visited by his dead friend (Dunne with his neck ripped out), who warns of his upcoming transformation. Sure enough, next full moon there's a lengthy transformation and a hungry werewolf is set loose in London. There's a lot of unsettling humor mixed with the scares, moon-themed rock songs are heard on the soundtrack, and the makeup effects are outstanding. The first hour is great, but it eventually spins apart into car crashes and an abrupt, frustrating ending. —*S. H.*

I think the chaotic climax is classic Landis, showing the sort of over-the-top mayhem he perfected in *The Blues Brothers* but used to a more nightmarish effect. It begins as a more intimate story between friends and ends with all hell breaking loose in the middle of Piccadilly Circus. And the abrupt ending is the punch line to the movie, a blackly humorous fuck-you to the audience that can only be taken in jest. *An American Werewolf in London* is perhaps the finest balance to date between comedy and serious horror. —*B. T.*

AMITYVILLE HORROR, THE L: HORROR/GHOSTS (1979) 117M D: Stuart Rosenberg. *Don Stroud, James Brolin, Rod Steiger, Margot Kidder.* I can say with a fair degree of certainty that if I moved into a house that showed anything even remotely resembling signs of being demonically possessed, my ass would be out the door in about three seconds. Fuck exorcism, fuck scary shit floating around, and fuck finding the gateway to HELL in my basement. I would be gone. *The Amityville Horror,* supposedly based on a true story, is one of the most classic examples of how I would NOT behave were I living with a bunch of demons trying to possess me and my family. If the priest who came to exorcise the demons going blind wasn't enough to send me packing, the flaming red pit behind a wall in my basement identified as the center of evil certainly would. But if they fled, what kind of movie would that make? Probably one only slightly more boring than this. —*J. S.*

AND NOW THE SCREAMING STARTS L: HORROR/GHOSTS (1972) 91M D: Roy Ward Baker. *Patrick Magee, Ian Ogilvy, Peter Cushing, Herbert Lom, Stephanie*

Beacham. Newlywed Catherine (Beacham) moves into the Fengriffen estate with her aristocratic husband (Ogilvy) and discovers a curse on his family bloodline. Bloody stumps, eyeless apparitions, and a disembodied hand may or may not really be crawling along the floor like an avenging spider, but they nonetheless terrorize the virgin bride and start to drive her mad during her pregnancy. Cushing (under an almost comically generous head of bushy hair) is the rationalist doctor battling Beacham's visions. Lom appears in flashback as Ogilvy's despicable ancestor, and Magee is the family doctor. Directed by Hammer Films veteran Baker for competing British horror house Amicus, it's less stylish and colorful than Hammer's fare, but plenty lurid and, as the title would suggest, full of Beacham's terrified screams. —*S. A.*

ANGEL HEART L: HORROR/WITCHES & WARLOCKS (1987) 112M D: Alan Parker. *Mickey Rourke, Lisa Bonet, Charlotte Rampling, Robert De Niro, Michel Higgins.* Adapted from William Hjortsberg's *Falling Angel,* this film is an interesting and stylistic revamping of the story of *Faust.* A cop named Angel (Rourke) is investigating the disappearance of a big band singer who apparently broke contract with a certain Louis Cipher (De Niro). The film makes use of the occult and voodoo for remarkably violent crime scenes, not to mention a shocking, over-the-top sex scene. Excellent performances all around are well balanced by the direction of Parker, who seems to have a knack for stories like this. He followed *Angel Heart* with *Mississippi Burning* in 1988. —*N. J.*

ANGEL—SEASON 1 L: HORROR TV/HORROR TV (1999) 18 hours D: Joss Whedon, others. *David Boreanaz, Elisabeth Rohm, Christian Kane, Alexis Denisof, Glenn Quinn, Charisma Carpenter.* Enter the spin-off series from *Buffy the Vampire Slayer.* Since love relationships on TV generally must perish (it's all about the chase), Angel, too, had to leave Buffy . . . but not TV! The main problem with *Angel's* first season is that it didn't have a large enough cast. Whedon has proven he writes best with big casts, but *Angel* starts out with only three main characters. To make matters worse, one of those, Doyle, annoyed many viewers and clearly something had to be done. As a result the series gets off to a rocky start, with some really abysmally bad episodes, but some really excellent ones as well. Those who love *Buffy* will enjoy following *Angel.* There are a few crossover episodes that kick ass and overall the season is not only watchable, but enjoyable. A fine ride with a few potholes. —*M. N.*

ANGEL—SEASON 2 L: HORROR TV/HORROR TV (2000) 18 hours D: Joss Whedon, others. *David Boreanaz, Andy Hallett, Julie Benz, J. August Richards, Alexis Denisof, Charisma Carpenter.* *Angel's* second season picks up the pace a bit and, with a more stable cast, has a stronger running than in the first

season. In addition, Whedon slowly adds a few more regulars into the mix, and there are more story arcs (versus the stand-alone episodes). It's definitely a much darker season, with Angel determining that while others can fight the good fight, he's going to win the war. If you love angst, this is the season for you. We see the return of Darla ("Darla?" I hear you say. "Didn't she get staked in *Buffy*??") and Drusilla, and that is all about evil goodness. The show takes an abrupt turn toward the end of the season, suddenly becoming much lighter and sillier. Both aspects are enjoyable, though the shift was definitely both unexpected and unusual. Usually a show picks a theme and sticks with it. Maybe Whedon thought he was getting a little TOO angsty for the show's own good. —*M. N.*

ANGEL—SEASON 3 L: HORROR TV/HORROR TV (2001) 18 hours D: Joss Whedon, others. *David Boreanaz, Charisma Carpenter, Alexis Denisof, J. August Richards, Andy Hallett, Amy Acker.* The third season of *Angel* is all about the story arc, with only a few stand-alone episodes, and boy is it ever a doozy of an arc. There is a mysterious pregnancy, old arch enemies, ancient prophecies, and a nice big juicy ensemble cast full of old and new favorites. There is, alas, some suspicious character behavior that feels a bit manipulated in order to serve the plot. Vexing, but it does lead to some of the best character interactions for the fourth season, so I guess I can't bitch too much. In addition there is the start of a downward spiral, where suddenly love is in the air and Whedon can't seem to make a good match among his many mates. Every pairing he begins here is a terrible mistake, all lacking chemistry. Still, it's a pretty solid season with more good episodes than bad. —*M. N.*

ANGUISH L: HORROR/STALKERS (1988) 89M D: J. J. Bigas Luna. *Michael Lerner, Zelda Rubinstein, Talia Paul.* Lerner plays an insecure optometrist. When he goes home after work, his crazy mother (Rubinstein) feeds him and then hypnotizes him. Once he's under her control she sends him out to murder certain people and retrieve their eyeballs as trophies. But all of this is simply happening in a movie theater one sunlit afternoon. It's really just a dumb horror matinee watched by a handful of adults and teenagers, or is it? While some in the audience are engrossed by this cheap horror flick, others are dying in much the same way as the victims in the matinee. This film-within-a-film plays up its novelty to great effect despite a low budget. When it was released there were warnings about the potential hypnotic effect this film could have upon its audience. —*N. J.*

ARACHNOPHOBIA L: VAOWG/VAOWG (1990) 110M D: Frank Marshall. *Harley Jane Kozak, Jeff Daniels, John Goodman, Stuart Pankin, Julian Sands.* A scary-ass foreign spider, who is really a killing machine, gets transported back to the United States in a coffin and ends up in the barn of a small town. It does the "deed" with a normal spider, and the result is lots and lots and lots of supervicious, superdeadly monster spiders. Holy shit! People start to die, and what's a town to do? Exterminators can't seem to do the job, and it becomes up to one guy (Daniels) who is deathly afraid of spiders to save the town. Goodman gives a great performance as the loopy exterminator. Though more silly than scary, *Arachnophobia* will make your skin crawl. —*J. S.*

ARMAGEDDON L: VAOWG/VAOWG (1998) 150M D: Michael Bay. *Bruce Willis, Billy Bob Thornton, Liv Tyler, Ben Affleck, Will Patton.* With this movie, Bay first announced his intentions to destroy the language of cinema. It's macho, brainless, patriotism porn about undershirt-wearing outlaw oil derrick workers who become astronauts to save the world from a killer meteor (don't even ask). It's lit and shot like the AT&T commercials that it is exactly as deep as and edited like a music video on fast-forward; the rapid cuts are so distracting. I found myself counting the off the shots to see if they'd hold one longer than two seconds (I couldn't find many). The action scenes are shot and cut so confusingly that even in a scene where a computer readout shows you the layout of the action, you still can't follow where the characters are standing or what the hell they are supposed to be doing. Meanwhile, a litany of award-winning and/or talented writers (Thornton, Affleck, Owen Wilson, Steve Buscemi) act out moronic sci-fi action that makes *Independence Day* seem like friggin' *2001*. If you're ever wondering if the whole world has gone to shit or not, just remind yourself that this movie has a Criterion Edition. —*B. T.*

I feel absolutely no shame admitting that this film is one of my all-time favorites. Yes, the movie is stupid and corny, obnoxious and overblown. It is also completely awesome. It's like *The Dirty Dozen* in space, only instead of blowing up a bunch of Nazis, they blow up a big fuckin' rock. I think that's really cool. As a child, I really wanted to be an astronaut. This cinematic gem is the truest expression of what I thought astronauts did when they were on the clock. Fast spaceships, rocket packs, danger at every turn, saving the world. I'm a sap for this stuff—I still get a lump in my throat when I watch shuttle launches. So it makes me a little sad to have to defend this movie. A lot of folks won't give it a fair shake, deciding they're too smart or too cool to enjoy what is essentially great trash. Also, Willis just kicks ass. —*M. L.*

ASTRO-ZOMBIES, THE L: CLASSIC SCIENCE FICTION/ CLASSIC SCIENCE FICTION (1967) 83M D: Ted Mikels. *John Carradine, Wendell Corey.* Carradine is superbly cast as a crazed scientist doing thoroughly unethical Frankenstein experiments. He allows great latitude to his hunchback Igor to do whatever experiments the brain-damaged assistant can muster. But more important are the Astro-Zombies, the astronautlike robotons Carradine has created and sent out to gather beautiful women for his experiments. The police, of course, are on to him, but it's amazing how inept police can be in films with absolutely no budget. Still, this film has much to offer the aficionado of über-schlock. —*N. J.*

ATOMIC WAR BRIDE L: CLASSIC SCIENCE FICTION/ CLASSIC SCIENCE FICTION (1960) 77M D: Veljko Bulajic.
Eva Krewskan, Anton Voldak. This Yugoslavian nuclear war satire, penned by Italian neorealist godfather Cesare Zavattani, presents the end of the world as a deadpan farce with a grim fallout. A nervous groom sets out for his wedding as newsboys hawk papers announcing the declaration of war, bombs interrupt his ceremony, and the draft snatches him from his honeymoon. Bulajic plays it straight even in the most absurd sequences, such as military brass playing stewardess as they instruct the populace on the proper way to don a radiation poncho: "Hood up! Hood down! Hood up!" The entire outrageous spectacle is over in a single day. —*S. A.*

ATTACK OF THE KILLER TOMATOES L: VAOWG/VAOWG (1978) 87M D: John DeBello. *David Miller, George Wilson, Sharon Taylor, J. Stephen Peace.* It's been called one of the worst films of all time, embraced as a knowing parody of low-budget horrors, and toasted as one of the greatest titles of all time. And they're all right! DeBello's aggressively stupid spoof is bad, cheap, and clumsy, a purposely club-footed film with hackneyed dialogue and intentionally cheesy special effects. It's all part of the insane (and perhaps misguided) inspiration, but it doesn't make it any easier to actually watch. Agent Mason Dixon leads a crackpot team to find out why tomatoes are massacring humans and he even puts one master of disguise undercover (where he panics and asks one of the carnivorous tomatoes to "pass the ketchup." Oops!). Don't let kids see this—they'll be singing the screeching adenoidal tune "Puberty Love" for weeks. Oh the horror! —*S. A.*

ATTIC EXPEDITIONS, THE L: HORROR/MAD SCIENTISTS (2001) 100M D: Jeremy Kasten. *Wendy Robie, Seth Green, Alice Cooper, Ted Raimi, Andras Jones, Jeffrey Combs.* Psychodrama meets the supernatural in this mind game of a thriller. An amnesiac (Jones) undergoes a twisted form of radical psychotherapy from his unorthodox doctor (cult star Combs as a mad scientist dressed like a Mississippi riverboat gambler) while his mind flits between dreams, memories, and drug-induced hallucinations. It's an ambitious and generally clever mix of Lovecraftian horror, subjective reality, and B-movie tropes, though first-time director Kasten is better at abstract ideas than their cinematic realizations. The direction

is clunky and the images fail to scare or excite, but the script is entertaining and often ingenious as it weaves the alternate realities into a skewed, schizophrenic vision. —*S. A.*

AURORA ENCOUNTER, THE L: SCIENCE FICTION/SCIENCE FICTION (1985) 90M D: Jim McCullough. *Mickey Hays, Jack Elam, Peter Brown.* You may be familiar with a genetic disorder called progeria, in which the sufferer's body ages six to ten years for every year lived. This brutal disease results in feeble, wrinkled, hairless mutant kindergarteners and a life expectancy that would turn anyone into an atheist. But the makers of *The Aurora Encounter*, clearly perennial optimists, chose to see this affliction not as a tragedy but rather a golden opportunity for their red-blooded sci-fi/ Western family adventure. The story of a bizarre alien creature visiting a settlers' township in the 1800's might have cost a bundle in fancy special effects if not for the producers' brilliant idea of casting wee progeria victim Mickey Hays in the role of the hideous interplanetary visitor, with absolutely no makeup to contribute to his "outrageous" appearance. Way to go, guys! What a stroke of sadistic frugality! See the little feller play checkers with wall-eyed hermit Jack Elam! See him maneuver a cardboard spaceship over a barn! See him prostitute his condition for fame that would never come! Jesus Christ! "Based on a true story." JESUS CHRIST! —*Z. C.*

BABA YAGA (AKA KISS ME, KILL ME) L: HORROR/EURO-HORROR (1973) 91M D: Corrado Farina. *Carroll Baker, George Eastman, Ely Galleani, Isabelle De Funès.* Contemporary Gothic derived from the famous Crepax cartoon of a woman photographer doubly haunted. Valentina (De Funès) has sadomasochistic visions, such as one of a firing squad killing her model while she walks out to sea with her hands tied behind her back. Baba Yaga (Baker) bewitches Valentina's camera so that it shoots its subjects as if it were a gun. She also gives Valentina a doll. On film, the doll is a live woman in leather who later strips and whips Valentina. It's a wonderfully stylish, if thin, little fantasy film. —*J. C.*

BACK TO THE FUTURE L: SCIENCE FICTION/SCIENCE FICTION (1985) 116M D: Robert Zemeckis. *Michael J. Fox, Lea Thompson, Crispin Glover, Thomas F. Wilson, Christopher Lloyd.* Back to the Future is, quite possibly, a perfect film. At least it's as close as Hollywood will ever come. Not high art, of course, but pure action-adventure-sci-fi-comedy fun. Not a second of screen time is wasted, not a frame of film is boring. A flashback to the '80s that is a flashback to the '50s, the creativity of the story is only the beginning. The score is thrilling, and the special effects, revolutionary in their time, still hold up as well. Everything comes together to make this film's adventure and excitement pack such a punch that, no matter when I watch it, I am imme-

diately transported back in time to when I was a kid and everything was fun and exciting and life itself was good. —*T. S.*

BAD RONALD L: HORROR/STALKERS (1974) 78M D: Buzz Kulik. *Scott Jacoby, Pippa Scott, Dabney Coleman, Kim Hunter.* Of all the creepy '70s made-for-TV movies, this one takes the proverbial cake. Total nerd Ronald lives with his mom and is made fun of a lot by other kids. He accidentally kills a little girl who was making fun of him. Mom says he ran away but actually she hides him in the wall. When his mom dies, Ronald stays in the wall living off Hershey bars. But soon another family moves in with really fine daughters. Ronald, who is now filthy due to his lack of access to any bathing facilities, spies on them and fantasizes about medieval times as he draws medieval scenarios involving himself with the young ladies all over his wall. It is not easy to find this movie, but if you do, the rewards will be plentiful. —*D. W.*

BARBARELLA L: SCIENCE FICTION/SCIENCE FICTION (1968) 98M D: Roger Vadim. *Jane Fonda, John Phillip Law, Milo O'Shea, David Hemmings, Anita Pallenberg.* Fonda plays Barbarella, a bubbly and outlandishly dressed adventurer sent into space to find the missing scientist Duran Duran (O'Shea) and his dangerous positronic ray. On her quest she gets attacked by killer dolls, gets hit on by the Black Queen (Pallenberg), rides a sled attached to a weird manta ray, rolls around in a space ship with shag carpeting, changes costumes many times, and falls in love with a blind angel named Pygar (Law). Director Vadim, whose movies often seem like an excuse for him to stare at beautiful women, said he was inspired to make the movie because he watched his then-wife Fonda walk around the house topless. It certainly is a sexy movie, but it's also Vadim's most stylish and Fonda's best comic performance. At the same time, the psychedelic imagery and campy tone are remarkably faithful to the comic strip by Jean-Claude Forest, and Fonda looks amazingly like Forest's drawings. —*B. T.*

BARBARIAN QUEEN L: FANTASY/FANTASY (1985) 70M D: Héctor Olivera. *Lana Clarkson, Dawn Dunlap, Katt Shea Ruben.* In this sword-and-sorcery classic, troops of the evil lord have attacked a tribal wedding ceremony. Many are killed; the rest are captured and marched back to the capital as gladiators or harem slaves—except for three women they overlooked (Clarkson and Ruben). A rebel kid they aid en-route secretly leads them into the city. The two impatient warriors nudge the gladiators to revolt, but a snitch in their midst spells doom. The warriors soon find themselves captured and tortured. Sexy, creepy scenes, with the fleshy but sinewy Clarkson shown off to particularly good effect. And dandy fight sequences follow when rebellion finally does break out. Soundly paced and toned to the muscular exuberance of the women warriors, *Barbarian Queen* is a believable fantasy that actually gets under your skin. —*J. C.*

BASKET CASE L: HORROR/STALKERS (1982) 91M D: Frank Henenlotter. *Beverly Bonner, Terri Susan Smith, Kevin VanHentenryck.* Henenlotter shot his gruesome little cult indie-horror drama of brotherly love on location in New York to get just the right sleazy Forty-Second Street atmosphere for his low-budget exercise in grotesquery and gore. VanHentenryck shuffles through the film with a guilty conscience as the "normal" brother sent by his deformed Siamese twin to take revenge on the doctors who separated the two and left the blobby brother to die. Most of the effects are shrewdly just offscreen, with spurts of blood and a gnarled hand dragging the character out of view to feed our imaginations, and a few bloody corpses left in the aftermath. In this day of sophisticated effects and film school–savvy directors, much of *Basket Case* looks naively amateur, but there's a loving B-movie attitude and a genuine sense of character to the "monster," the misshapen, fleshy, snaggletoothed Belial. —*S. A.*

BAT, THE (1959) L: CLASSIC HORROR/CLASSIC HORROR (1959) 80M D: Crane Wilbur. *Gavin Gordon, Agnes Moorehead, Lenita Lane, John Sutton, Vincent Price.* Another adaptation of the Mary Roberts Rinehart story. Although this version is not as good as some of the earlier films, Price is excellent and there are some killings exceptionally brutal for the times. However, this is also one of the most lighthearted and cornball Old Dark House movies around, which detracts a little from its greatness. Overall, this film deserves the relative obscurity in which it currently exists. It's just not classic material. —*T. S.*

BAT WHISPERS, THE L: CLASSIC HORROR/CLASSIC HORROR (1930) 82M D: Roland West. *Chester Morris, Una Merkel, Spencer Charters, Chance Ward.* This artifact of the early sound era, either a cockeyed fluke or a surrealist masterpiece, was independent producer-director West's second take on *The Bat*, Mary Roberts Rinehart and Avery Hopwood's creaky stage melodrama about a fiendish master criminal haunting a lonely Long Island mansion. With sound, now The Bat could whisper as well as skulk silently. The film would be one of a handful of 1930 features shot in widescreen, with a compositional emphasis on asymmetrical forms, forced perspective, and inky, lunatic shadow play. The plot beggars belief, but there are images that seem to have escaped from the collective unconscious. Like the other pre-CinemaScope experiments of its day, *The Bat Whispers* also was shot in a conventional "square" format, in case theater owners who had just wired for sound refused to invest in new screens as well. The DVD offers the standard-release version—the only way we could see the film for sixty years—as well as the lustrous UCLA Film and Television Archive restoration of the wide-screen version. —R. J.

BATTLE BEYOND THE STARS L: SCIENCE FICTION/SCIENCE FICTION (1980) 105M D: Jimmy T. Murakami. *Richard Thomas, George Peppard, Robert Vaughn, Sybil Danning.* At the time, this film was the most expensive production Roger Corman had ever done, so it is surprising how low-budget it looks. Even though it was plainly riding on the success of *Star Wars* and using the tried-and-true *Magnificent Seven* plotline, *Battle Beyond the Stars* is still a very fun movie thanks in large part to the script by John Sayles, which is peppered with plenty of humor, and the curiously variegated cast. Thomas plays Shad, saving his planet from the threat posed by Sador (John Saxon). He employs Space Cowboy (Peppard), the universally feared mercenary Gelt (Vaughn), the scantily clad Valkyrie warrior Saint-Exmin (Danning), and of course "Nestor," a group of five white-robed men sharing the same consciousness. Corman fired the original effects man, insisting it was all too expensive, and replaced him with a very young James Cameron. The DVD from New Concorde features commentaries with Sayles and Corman. —N. J.

BATTLE FOR THE PLANET OF THE APES L: VAOWG/PLANET OF THE APES (1973) 86M D: J. Lee Thompson. *Severn Darden, Paul Williams, Natalie Trundy, Roddy McDowall, John Huston.* Starting with lengthy flashbacks narrated by The Lawgiver (Huston), the beginning of this film summarizes parts three and four for this, the last of the *Planet of the Apes* series. Humans have become slaves to their conquering apes and Caesar does his best to maintain the peace as a benevolent dictator. However, it soon becomes apparent that the gorillas don't see eye to eye with the chimpanzees and that a violent power struggle is inevitable. It also becomes obvious how this will all loop around to the very beginning of the first film of the series. *Battle* is a necessary finale to the series, yet it will only be of interest to *Planet of the Apes* fans who have already seen all the previous installments. If that describes you, all that is left is the DVD box set with a very well-done documentary called *Behind the Planet of the Apes.* —N. J.

BEAST OF YUCCA FLATS, THE L: CLASSIC SCIENCE FICTION/CLASSIC SCIENCE FICTION (1961) 54M D: Coleman Francis. *Douglas Mellor, Barbara Francis, Bing Stafford, Tor Johnson.* To those who claim that Ed Wood Jr. is the worst director of all time, I offer the oeuvre of Coleman Francis. Exhibit 1: This inept horror film about a defecting Russian scientist (former wrestler and hulking Ed Wood Jr. favorite Johnson) who becomes a proto-Hulk after a car chase with Russian agents sends him wandering through a nuclear test site just as an A-Bomb goes off (now that's security!). Johnson makes a superbly cheesy rampaging mutant, but

the film really enters the Twilight Zone when the investigating cops target an innocent dad looking for his sons lost in the desert. Francis shot this without sound (he dubbed the dialogue in later, and quite possibly wrote it then as well), cutting away from his actors every time they open their mouths. The effect is almost as distracting as the wooden dialogue that seems to float through the picture, untethered by character, logic, and performer. The ultracheap production straddles the line between camp artifact and surreal masterpiece. —S. A.

BELOW L: HORROR/GHOSTS (2002) 105M D: David Twohy. *Bruce Greenwood, Scott Foley, Matt Davis, Olivia Williams.* Twohy's haunted sub film sunk without a trace after an almost dismissive release, for reasons beyond me. A tight, smartly engineered little genre piece about an American U-boat hiding from German battleships above while a poltergeist causes havoc below, it makes marvelous use of the claustrophobic quarters, the lonely silence of the deep sea shattered by terrifying sounds, and the sudden loss of control of the boat (it's not a ship, as they take pains to tell us). Davis is fine as the handsome, earnest young junior officer, but Greenwood owns this picture as the creepily confident captain whose secrets haunt this vessel. —S. A.

BEN L: VAOWG/VAOWG (1972) 93M D: Phil Karlson. *Joseph Campanella, Arthur O'Connell, Lee Montgomery, Meredith Baxter.* Just after the events of *Willard*, the authorities are trying to track down the army of rats that ate some townsfolk. Little do they know the rats are living and breeding in the sewers, and their leader Ben has befriended a little lonely kid named Danny (Montgomery). Danny plays piano and sings a song about Ben (somehow it sounds a lot better when Michael Jackson sings it on the credits) and his love for the little guy is reciprocated: when the neighborhood bully picks on Danny, Ben and his boys move in. Grown-ups think Danny knows where the rats are, and Danny pretends the "Ben" he always talks about is an imaginary friend. Then he gets trapped in a sewer with millions of rats. It's written by Gilbert A. Ralston, who wrote both *Willard* and the book it was based on, but the added ridiculousness of the little boy plot makes it arguably more enjoyable than the first film. —B. T.

BENEATH THE PLANET OF THE APES L: VAOWG/PLANET OF THE APES (1970) 108M D: Ted Post. *Linda Harrison, Maurice Evans, Kim Hunter, James Franciscus, Charlton Heston.* This second installment of the *Planet of the Apes* series will not disappoint those who were thoroughly absorbed by the first film. Franciscus plays an astronaut who is somehow able to break the time barrier in search of his friend Taylor (Heston). Upon being captured himself and imprisoned by the apes, this new astronaut goes through much the same sort of

Scariest movies ever

ALIEN

BLACK SABBATH

CLEAN, SHAVEN

THE EVIL DEAD

THE EXORCIST

HALLOWEEN

THE HAUNTING *(1963)*

IN A GLASS CAGE

JACOB'S LADDER

NIGHT OF THE LIVING DEAD *(1968)*

RAW MEAT

SEVEN

THE SHINING *(1980)*

SUSPIRIA

THE TEXAS CHAIN SAW MASSACRE *(1974)*

THE THING *(1982)*

THE WIZARD OF OZ

exposure to this strange, upside-down world as his friend did in the previous film. At length he does find Taylor and the two escape deep underground where they discover many artifacts of postapocalyptic New York. More curiously, they stumble on a mutant cult of humans who are able to use telepathy and mind control—a cult that worships a giant atomic missile! —*N. J.*

BILLY THE KID VS. DRACULA L: CLASSIC HORROR/ CLASSIC HORROR (1966) 95M D: William Beaudine. *John Carradine, Roy Barcroft, Chuck Courtney.* Carradine called this "the worst film I ever made." Perhaps this is true since this film takes a premise full of possibility and destroys it. It fails in pretty much every way possible. There's a great scene where Billy the Kid fires shots at Dracula, but the Count is unharmed by the bullets. Billy then throws his pistol at Dracula's head and knocks him out cold. But it's not even very funny. —*T. S.*

BLACK CHRISTMAS L: HORROR/STALKERS (1974) 98M D: Bob Clark. *Andrea Martin, John Saxon, Margot Kidder, Keir Dullea, Olivia Hussey.* This is an important, seminal horror film. Made four years before John Carpenter's *Halloween*, *Black Christmas* is a much more groundbreaking film. Taking cues from *Twitch of the Death Nerve*, it's one of the first slasher movies about hot young people being murdered by a mys-

terious maniac on the loose. Many of today's clichés, including the killer calling from inside the house, originated with this film. On top of all that, it's really creepy. Some of the phone calls are strange and disturbing even by today's standards, and the scare moments still hold up. This is also a dual purpose holiday film, watchable on Halloween and Christmas. *Halloween* really owes *Black Christmas* a huge debt since it borrows so much from it. Ultimately, *Black Christmas* more than fills all the criteria for the status of "classic" and it's a shame so few people regard it as such. —*T. S.*

BLACK CIRCLE BOYS L: HORROR/WITCHES & WARLOCKS (1997) 101M D: Matthew Carnahan. *Donnie Wahlberg, Dee Wallace-Stone, Eric Mabius, Lisa Loeb, John Doe, Scott Bairstow.* Boy's older brother dies. Enter familial dysfunction. Family moves; boy befriends satanic high school Goths. Enter ritual sacrifice and attempted familial intervention. Oh, and Donnie Wahlberg, too. —*E. B.*

BLACK SCORPION, THE L: PSYCHOTRONIC/O'BRIEN, WILLIS (1957) 85M D: Edward Ludwig. *Carlos Muzquiz, Carlos Rivas, Mara Corday, Richard Denning.* After a volcano erupts outside Mexico City, the scientists sent to study it are confronted with giant scorpions that rise out of the ground at night. The 1950s saw many incarnations of the giant creature versus helpless humanity movie, but this Ludwig picture about a group of menacing oversized scorpions that terrorize Mexico City and its inhabitants is one of the best. *Black Scorpion* has a cool story, with native Mexicans that are smart and heroic, not just fodder for the monsters. The only exception being (of course) a precocious child whose antics are constantly putting him and the adults around him at risk. Willis O'Brien's special-effects work is, as always, excellent. O'Brien's saliva-dripping monstrosities are truly scary (and a little bit gross). The direction is technical and impressive; Ludwig blends effects, stock footage, and his human cast together very well for the age. *Black Scorpion* is a standout picture in a generally clumsy genre. —*G. M.*

BLADE OF THE RIPPER L: HORROR/GIALLO (ITALIAN HORROR) (1971) 90M D: Sergio Martino. *Alberto de Mendoza, Ivan Rassimov, Conchita Airoldi, Edwige Fenech, George Hilton.* A fruitful collaboration between the Martino brothers, screenwriter Ernesto Gastaldi, and Fenech begins with this film, their best, and one of the genre's very best. A lonely ambassador's wife (Fenech) is in a whirl of erotic confusion. Her husband is distant and busy, and she is haunted by the sadism of a long-ago lover (Rassimov) who may be the serial killer loose in Vienna. Her friend Carol (Airoldi) ushers her off to a party to get her mind off things, where Carol's newly rich cousin (Hilton) sweeps the wife off her feet. But someone at the party dies and she could swear she saw her sadistic ex-lover in the shadows. This well-scripted Giallo contains twists within twists, and its lurid, off-balance drive (aided by Nora Orlandi's descending sonorities in a minor key) makes it richly compelling. That and the camera's caress of Fenech's lush sensuality, which is more than enough to make you miss the clues as to what's really going on. —*J. C.*

BLAIR WITCH PROJECT, THE L: HORROR/WITCHES & WARLOCKS (1999) 86M D: Daniel Myrick, Edward Sanchez. *Michael C. Williams, Joshua Leonard, Heather Donahue.* As Brian on *The Family Guy* says to his blind companion as they watch *The Blair Witch Project,* "they're in the woods, the camera keeps on moving . . . nothing's happening, nothing's happening, something about a map, nothing's happening, it's over, a lot of people in the audience look pissed." I was one of those people. The film has a good concept, but it's killed by the execution. First off, you can't get lost in Burketsville (Frederick), Maryland. There are no woodlands of any real size, only a lot of open farmland. There is nothing scary in the film and only one moment that could qualify as supernatural. Like all horror movies, the people in the film all make stupid, stupid choices. These people have floodlights and lots of batteries, yet spend most of the film being scared of the dark. If rednecks throwing rocks at your tent while they giggle in the dark scares you, then so will *Blair Witch,* but you're probably not that lame. —*G. M.*

Myrick and Sanchez may have been unremarkable filmmakers, but they did come upon this simple gimmick at exactly the right time: when digital video technology was becoming more affordable and distributors were beginning to flirt with it as an acceptable medium for filmmaking. (Of course, many mainstream moviegoers were pulled in by the hype and shocked to find that it wasn't even a "real movie.") This film used an unorthodox approach (nonactors, playing themselves, out in the woods to improvise with little instruction) that took full advantage of the premise and the tiny budget. They also went back to the old-fashioned what-you-imagine-is-scarier-than-anything-we-could-show-you approach to horror, which was refreshing at the time. I may never watch this film again, because I think it was a film for its exact time. If it's a big bore on video it doesn't matter because I still remember what it was like to watch it in a sold-out theater with people who laughed and heckled in the beginning but gasped and flinched in the end. You could actually hear the fear rolling across the theater like a wave. —*B. T.*

BLOB, THE L: CLASSIC SCIENCE FICTION/CLASSIC SCIENCE FICTION (1958) 83M D: Irvin S. Yeaworth Jr. *Earl Rowe, Olin Howlin, Aneta Corsaut, Steve McQueen.* After the success of *Invasion of the Body Snatchers,* it seemed Hollywood could market just about any

film that dealt with the threat of Communism so long as it was disguised with some kind of extraterrestrial plot. In terms of low-budget '50s camp *The Blob* was one of the finest. McQueen is given his first leading role saving a town from the slimy alien that menacingly drips from the ceiling in order to overwhelm people with its interstellar composition. It's not surprising that forty years later this film was remade with high-tech gloss. But really, what should anyone at any time expect to see when they sit down to watch a movie named *The Blob*? —*N. J.*

BLOB, THE (1988) L: SCIENCE FICTION/SCIENCE FICTION (1988) 92M D: Chuck Russell. *Kevin Dillon, Donovan Leitch, Jeffrey DeMunn, Bill Moseley, Shawnee Smith.* This remake of the 1958 camp classic preserves the tongue-in-cheek flavor of the original, yet uses superb special effects to bring a little more flare to the man-eating blob. As opposed to the slow, oozing menace of the first film, the blob in this film is one mean protoplasm capable of great strength, speed, and jolts of electricity. Dillon plays a young man who tries saving himself and his family from the slippery creature that he comes to learn is all a part of some government conspiracy. If someone were to compile a list of the best sci-fi remakes, *The Blob* would surely deserve a place near the top, for it takes the themes and tones from the original film and enhances them with great effect. —*N. J.*

BLOOD BEACH L: VAOWG/VAOWG (1981) 89M D: Jeffrey Bloom. *Burt Young, Otis Young, David Huffman, John Saxon, Marianna Hill.* Just when you thought it was safe to go back in the water . . . you can't get to it! Desperately aping the seaside setting of the immensely popular *Jaws,* this 1981 drive-in schlocker holds up better than even its coattail-riding creators might have expected. A mysterious force is pulling beachgoers under the sand, leaving behind only the occasional eye or human giblet. Some creative casting resulted in the onscreen detective duo of a horror-worn Saxon and the ever-laconic Burt Young. As the "terrifying" mystery unravels, tourists continue losing life and limb (including a would-be rapist who really gets his in the film's most gruesome and inspired scene). A flimsy plot and obviously hurried production don't seem to hurt *Blood Beach,* as the result is a genuinely entertaining and evenly paced horror film with a truly surprising twist ending. Keep an eye out for nutty bag lady Eleanor Zee, who also plays in John Cassavetes's *Minnie & Moskowitz.* —*Z. C.*

BLOOD CITY (AKA WELCOME TO BLOOD CITY) L: SCIENCE FICTION/SCIENCE FICTION (1977) 90M D: Peter Sasdy. *Keir Dullea, Hollis McLaren, Chris Wiggins, Jack Palance, Samantha Eggar, Barry Morse.* The untouchable Palance leads a pack of virtual reality cowboys in this shameless, high-concept rip-off of Yul Brynner's *Westworld.* Several amne-

siacs awaken in a dusty Old West town, where they are immediately forced into slavery. Their only hope of social advancement is to murder other denizens of Blood City, gaining all-important street cred and working their way up to a face-off with the schizophrenic sheriff, valiantly played to the straight-faced hilt by Palance. The prematurely revealed would-be "twist" is that all the amnesiacs are actually in suspended animation, merely passing a computerized aptitude test in the technologically manufactured West, uh, world. If you've rented *Blood City* in search of blood, there's not a drop to be seen. This constantly deflating film costars sci-fi veterans Dullea (*2001*) and Morse (*Space: 1999*). —*Z. C.*

BLOOD FREAK L: PSYCHOTRONIC/DRUGS (1972) 86M D: Brad F. Grinter, Steve Hawkes. *Tina Anderson, Dana Culliver, Heather Hughes, Steve Hawkes, Randy Grinter Jr.* If you like cheap, stupid, antidrug, pro-God monster movies, then *Blood Freak* should top your list of must-sees. It stars thick-accented Hawkes as Hershel, a slow-witted Vietnam vet biker in Elvis shades who gets involved with two sisters. Angel (Hughes), a Bible-thumping Goody Two-shoes, introduces him to her sexy, drug-addicted sister Anne (Culliver). Anne takes a liking to Hersh and the two soon begin sharing drugs and having premarital sex. Hershel gets a job at a turkey farm where a pair of mad scientists is experimenting on their gobblers. Hershel eats an entire bird and mutates into a ridiculous turkey monster, killing junkies and drug dealers. There's lots of blood and chopped-off limbs, and the same audio track is looped over and over. The comedic on-screen narration is by the cigarette-smoking director, who reads his lines directly from his script and in one hilarious scene collapses into a coughing fit while lecturing about the dangers of drug addiction. Funny stuff! —*S. H.*

BLOOD ORGY OF THE SHE-DEVILS L: HORROR/WITCHES & WARLOCKS (1972) 73M D: Ted V. Mikels. *Lila Zaborin, Victor Izay.* Zaborin stars as Mara, Queen of the Black Witches, full-time medium and part-time supernatural assassin, in this Mikels drive-in exploitation classic about a wicked spell caster who gruesomely sacrifices captive men and matches wits with a parapsychology professor (Izay). It starts with a psychedelic credits sequence and burbling electronic music, then segues into a crazy ceremony of hoochie-koochie dancing girls with spears but little sense of rhythm. It's terrible, of course, cheaply made and badly directed, and (apart from Zaborin's hammy turn) rather listlessly performed, but there is a certain goofy entertainment value in cheesy flashbacks to medieval crowds wearing cuffs and collars. The clarity of the DVD only accentuates the poor photography and lighting and the abysmal sets. —*S. A.*

BLOOD SPATTERED BRIDE, THE L: HORROR/EURO-HORROR (1978) 94M D: Vicente Aranda. *Maribel Martín, Dean Selmier, Simón Andreu, Alexandra Bastedo.* An inexperienced young bride (Martín) marries an aristocrat (Andreu) with a cursed family tree and a disposition for rough sex. Aranda's adaptation of Joseph Sheridan Le Fanu's *Carmilla* turns the notorious female vampire into a manifestation of the girl's own sexual fears and psychotic fantasies. Think of her as a homicidal enabler, unleashing the bride's repression and torment in a bloody reign of terror. Unlike the dreamy eroticism of French and Italian vampire films, this is earthy and edgy, a world where dreams literally push their way into nature. Carmilla's entrance, buried naked in the sand but for a snorkel and a face mask, is one of the most beautifully bizarre images in modern horror cinema. —*S. A.*

BLUE SUNSHINE L: PSYCHOTRONIC/DRUGS (1978) 94M D: Jeff Lieberman. *Robert Walden, Mark Goddard, Richard Crystal, Zalman King, Ray Young, Deborah Winters.* A group of ex-hippies are haunted by some bad acid they took back in the '60s that turns them into bald homicidal maniacs who hate loud disco music. It's up to Jerry Zipkin (King, who went on to produce and direct softcore sex films such as *Two Moon Junction* and *The Red Shoe Diaries*) to figure out what the hell is going on. *Blue Sunshine* has a great concept and some memorable scenes but is a little light on the suspense and spends much of the movie unfolding as a "political intrigue" thriller. The scene with one of the bald psychos freaking out in a disco is worth the rental price, but throw in death by fireplace, some cool photography, and an unusual soundtrack and you have a forgotten, low-budget '70s flick worthy of reevaluation. Lieberman also directed the great killer worm movie *Squirm*. —*S. H.*

BODY SNATCHER FROM HELL (AKA GOKE, BODY SNATCHER FROM HELL) L: JAPANESE SCIENCE FICTION /JAPANESE SCIENCE FICTION (1968) 84M D: Hajime Sato. *Tomomi Sato, Hideo Ko, Teruo Yoshida.* This is one of the best Japanese horror and/or science fiction movies ever. Survivors of a mysterious plane crash are stalked by mucus-based silver interplanetary blobs bent on destroying the human race by reanimating the corpses of Earthmen. The sounds, colors, special effects, and even acting are like nothing ever done in film before. Disturbing images and horrific events pile on until it seems impossible for another to occur, and then one does. The performances of the doomed survivors are amazing, yet constantly eclipsed by the insane genius of screenwriters Kyuzo Kobayashi and Susumu Takahisa as inconceivable plot developments thrust the characters and viewer headlong into insanity. Add mascara-wearing male terrorists, genitalia-esque forehead growths, bubble-shaped saucers, various psychotic episodes, and the most disconcerting pulsing antiwar propaganda imaginable and you've just scratched the surface of what Sato's psychedelic alien invasion zombie epic has to offer. Essential. —*Z. C.*

BONES L: HORROR/GHOSTS (2001) 92M D: Ernest Dickerson. *Ricky Harris, Pam Grier, Michael T. Weiss, Clifton Powell, Snoop Dogg.* Snoop Dogg plays Jimmy Bones, a pimp and community leader in the '70s who gets killed by his associates when he refuses to allow crack into the neighborhood. But, as these things sometimes go, teens trying to turn his house into a dance club in the '90s accidentally resurrect him, and he takes the opportunity to get a little revenge on his betrayers. The most clever aspect of the story is that it allows for Grier to play Snoop's love interest both in the present day and in flashbacks, where she dresses like Foxy Brown. The premise and subtext are reminiscent of the *Blacula* films but the effects and execution are more like a *Nightmare on Elm Street* sequel. Snoop makes a great horror villain, and there's some nice cinematography by former Spike Lee DP Dickerson, but if that's not enough for you, then you should sit this one out. —*B. T.*

BONEYARD, THE L: HORROR/CANNIBALS (1990) 98M D: James Cummins. *Phyllis Diller, Norman Fell, Ed Nelson.* With Fell as the mortician and Diller as the head nurse, this horror film cannot fail to amuse. A detective and an overweight psychic are put onto the case of some grizzly murders. After more character analysis than is necessary for a cheap horror film, their investigation leads them to the morgue, where they find themselves fighting living-dead cannibal babies. And if that's not enough for you, wait until the end, when Diller's pet poodle gets bitten by one of these demons and turns into a mammoth flesh-eating zombie puppy. If that's not worth a video rental, I don't know what is. —*N. J.*

BOOGENS, THE L: HORROR/DEMONS (1982) 95M D: James L. Conway. *Jeff Harlan, Anne-Marie Martin, Rebecca Balding, Fred McCarren.* The people who made *In Search of Historic Jesus* and *Hangar 18* took a break from their wholesome productions to make this scary little sleeper that played on cable quite a bit in the '80s then vanished for a while before appearing on video. Ugly tenticled turtle monsters (similar to the creatures in *Island of Terror*) have been sealed in an old mine located somewhere in Colorado. Some horny college kids and a poodle arrive and are soon Boogen bait as the critters escape the shaft. It's up to an old miner to take care of the monsters before more people get killed. I've always had a soft spot for this cheap but effective thriller; it's not great, but *The Boogens* delivers plenty of scares and corpses. —*S. H.*

BORDELLO OF BLOOD (AKA **TALES FROM THE CRYPT PRESENTS BORDELLO OF BLOOD**) L: HORROR TV/HORROR TV (1996) 87M D: Gilbert Adler. *Erika Eleniak, Angie Everhart, Chris Sarandon, Corey Feldman, Dennis Miller.* This film begins in a crypt, where a dwarf incarnates a vampire and with a special amulet is able to control it. Many vampires are being similarly controlled and eventually we see they are being used to add spice to a bordello. The surprising part is that some cheesy evangelist is in charge of it all, making money above and beyond the offering plate while trying to save the planet from those men who would be so sinful as to go to such a place. But ultimately this is a vehicle to show off some scantily clad vampire women in leather and chains, because neither the jokes nor the gore make this bad storyline any more interesting. —*N. J.*

BOY AND HIS DOG, A L: SCIENCE FICTION/SCIENCE FICTION (1975) 87M D: L. Q. Jones. *Jason Robards, Don Johnson, Tim McIntire (voice), Susanne Benton.* The directorial debut of character actor L. Q. Jones creatively preserves the tone and attitude of Harlan Ellison's science fiction novella while reworking the details. The satire and cynicism run deep as callow Don Johnson, a feral human led by an erudite and insightful telepathic dog (the voice of McIntire), lets his libido lead him from the mercenary postapocalyptic surface world to a sallow underground recreation of "the good old days." Benton is the would-be farm girl in the creaky fantasy of small town preserved in rose-colored amber who realizes that her savage, oversexed guerrilla may be her only chance to escape the smothering artificiality. As in the best low-budget efforts, less is more in the visualization of a war-decimated world populated by wandering scavengers, but the heart of the film is in the surprising relationship between man and canine. —*S. A.*

BRAIN DAMAGE L: SCIENCE FICTION/SCIENCE FICTION (1988) 89M D: Frank Henenlotter. *Rick Hearst, Jennifer Lowry, John Zacherle (voice).* When Brian discovers the mysterious Aylmer, his life begins to fall apart. The creature, which looks like a cross between a cock and piece of shit, injects him with a powerful, mind-altering drug that provides the greatest high imaginable. The only problem is the Aylmer feeds on brains and forces the inebriated Brian to help him get them. During his horrifying moments of lucidity, he is forced to endure the Aylmer (voiced by horror icon Zacherle) making quips and singing songs to taunt him, urging him to gather more brains. In one of the film's best scenes, a drugged Brian is about to get a blowjob when suddenly the Aylmer bursts out of Brian's pants and into the girl's mouth where he sucks out her brain. Supposedly a warning about the dangers of addiction, *Brain Damage* seems more of a passionate and convincing argument for drug use to escape the terrible unpleasantness of a banal existence. —*T. S.*

BRAIN FROM PLANET AROUS, THE L: CLASSIC SCIENCE FICTION/CLASSIC SCIENCE FICTION (1957) 70M D: Nathan Juran. *John Agar, Joyce Meadows.* Agar gets possessed by a giant floating brain named Gor and tries to rule the world. In one of his craziest roles (and that's saying a lot), Agar laughs his ass off while he blows up a passenger plane with his Gor-controlled mind. What a kook! Gor is interested in more than just ruling the world, however. He also wants to get laid! Watch in horror (or delight) as Agar/Gor puts the moves on Agar's girlfriend, Sally (Meadows), and tries to cram his tongue in her ear. Naughty brain! Luckily (for Sally, anyway), a "good" brain from Planet Arous named Vol shows up to help . . . . by possessing the body of Sal's dog! There's never a dull moment in *The Brain from Planet Arous.* Floating brains, laughing maniacs, talking dogs . . . John Agar does rule! —*P.M.*

BRAIN 17 L: JAPANESE SCIENCE FICTION/JAPANESE SCIENCE FICTION (1982) 72M D: Michael Part. Episodes of a Japanese kids' show edited together to "feature length," dubbed with a confounding lack of sanity and credited to a bunch of Americans who did nothing. An enormous Capsela-like computer blows up a federal building and flies away. One year later, a giant oil drum causes a rockslide that kills young Stevie's entire family. A soldier with a failed Clint Eastwood impersonator handling his voice-over clarifies that the boy's relatives were "crushed by dirt." Stevie soon falls in a hole and is swept away from a mad scientist by a tall, tall robot named Brain 17. The boy is given a helmet that allows him to communicate with Brain. The robot uses his "gravitron" to save "Town" (actually Tokyo) from a bionic steamroller. Eventually, Brain 17 and Stevie vanquish a huge pogo stick and an aluminum dragon. Meanwhile, the soldier dons a fake beard to infiltrate enemy headquarters. He is whipped to death and crucified on a snowy mountaintop. Released by Family Home Entertainment. —*Z.C.*

BRAINSTORM L: SCIENCE FICTION/SCIENCE FICTION (1983) 106M D: Douglas Trumbull. *Cliff Robertson, Christopher Walken, Louise Fletcher, Natalie Wood.* Walken and Fletcher both play scientists with a special sort of multitrack tape recorder. It's an elaborate machine that records a subject's every thought, feeling, and emotion, including sights and sounds. It's such a unique invention that the two scientists spend a great deal of time testing it by recording memories and dreams, causing Walken's wife (Wood) much distress. One night a lab worker borrows the machine and records a tryst with a prostitute. The tape is passed around the lab before it's discovered, nearly causing the benefactors to pull out of the project. The government eventually takes over the experiment, but not before Fletcher manages to record her death for Walken to view. This is an intense visual film that only works in widescreen format

since the unadulterated visions fill the full screen while the normal narrative does not. —*N.J.*

BRAINWAVES L: SCIENCE FICTION/SCIENCE FICTION (1982) 83M D: Ulli Lommel, Arthur A. Seidelman. *Suzanna Love, Keir Dullea, Percy Rodrigues, Paul Wilson, Tony Curtis, Vera Miles.* Love plays a woman whose brain is resuscitated after a traffic accident with the help of an experimental brainwave transplant. When she returns to her regular life, however, she slowly realizes that her memories are not all her own. As some other person's memories become more and more vivid to her, she soon discovers that her brainwave donor was a murder victim. And remarkably, the paranoid murderer has been following this transference of thoughts through hospital corridors and the whole rest of the city. This is a decent psychological B-thriller by Lommel. —*N.J.*

BRIDE AND THE BEAST, THE L: CLASSIC HORROR/CLASSIC HORROR (1958) 78M D: Adrian Weiss. *Johnny Roth, Steve Calvert, William Justine, Charlotte Austin, Lance Fuller.* Written (but not directed) by Ed Wood Jr., this bit of past life mumbo jumbo is cheap and silly, but give Wood credit for an inventive twist on reincarnation and an unexpectedly sympathetic embrace of the bestiality subtext of such monsters-and-maidens love triangles. Austin has a strange attraction to the gorilla in the basement and the wild apes in the African jungles, and why not? They have far more animal passion and romantic tenderness than her clunky husband (Fuller). The hypnotic regression and moody memory veil of the first act is the kind of mad B-movie delirium cult fans seek out. It gets lost in cheap jungle stock footage by the end and the ratty gorilla suit is pure camp, but in true exploitation fashion Austin spends a good deal of the film in sheer nightgowns and tight sweaters while she honeymoons in Africa, and Weiss and Wood cook up a gonzo ending that, well, seems inevitable given the jungle love simmering through the picture. —*S.A.*

BRIDE OF RE-ANIMATOR L: PSYCHOTRONIC/LOVECRAFT, H. P. (aka HOWARD PHILLIPS LOVECRAFT). (1990) 96M D: Brian Yuzna. *Fabiana Udenio, David Gale, Jeffrey Combs, Bruce Abbott.* The overwhelming popularity of *Re-Animator* meant that a sequel was bound to happen. The main players and crew return in fine form to spin another tale of the demented Dr. Herbert West (Combs) and his assistant Dan Cain (Abbott). The story picks up eight months after the events of the first film, with the cadaver-stealing duo working on a new experiment that would make Dr. Frankenstein proud. They have taken women's body parts and given life to their own sensually horrific monster that contains the very heart of Cain's dead girlfriend. The head of the overtly diabolical Dr. Hill (Gale) has also returned, and after a little surgery, has become a menace of the sky. Director Yuzna brings all the yucks, screams, and laughs from the original back in all their gooey glory to expand ever more on Lovecraft's death-defying scientist. It's a strong follow-up to the 1985 classic. —*R. M.*

BRIGHAM CITY L: VAOWG/CHRISTPLOITATION (2001) 120M D: Richard Dutcher.

Mathew Brown, Wilford Brimley, Carrie Morgan, John Enos, Richard Dutcher. A rarity: a modern crime thriller with a religious message of genuine depth and sensitivity. Writer/producer/director/star Dutcher, a one-man cinematic Mormon missionary, expresses his message in a film that ignores dogma in favor of issues of faith, community, and responsibility. Ostensibly a modern thriller about a serial killer loose in rural northwest Utah, it plays like a contemporary Western, with an upright county sheriff (Dutcher) who is also a church bishop. He first tries to shield his town from the horror, then pulls the good, churchgoing citizens into a veritable posse, shattering constitutional rights in a desperate attempt to save a kidnapped girl from the killer. His cinematic skills are clumsy and perhaps naive, but his humanist philosophy and religious insight are anything but. He creates a portrait of family values, community ties, and neighborly caring with an honest, unaffected forthrightness and makes the case that fear and suspicion are the real snake in Eden. —*S. A.*

BRUTES AND SAVAGES: THE "UNCIVILIZED" EDITION L: PSYCHOTRONIC/SHOCK (1978) 107M D: Art Davis.

Richard Johnson (narrator). Part American "Mondo" docsploitation, part National Geographic exploration of tribal rituals of sex and violence, the "Factual Report of the Arthur Davis Expedition" to Africa and South America is, like its Mondo inspirations, a combination of real documentary footage and faked "reenactments." The narration (by Johnson, whose voice is the only real class this film can muster) pretends to be enlightened even while it shills the most exploitative aspects (man-eating crocodiles, tribal fights to the death, animal sacrifices, primitive mating rituals, and a scene of brain surgery). Riz Ortani, who scored the original *Mondo Cane*, give this an absolutely absurd mock rock-fusion score with wah-wah guitars and pre-disco beats. It's almost jarring to see such blatant grindhouse exploitation look so good in the restored DVD, which was mastered from print almost fifteen minutes longer than the original American release (which had cut-up and reordered the footage for more blatant shock effects). —*S. A.*

BUBBA HO-TEP L: HORROR/ZOMBIES (2002) 92M D: Don Coscarelli.

Reggie Bannister, Bob Ivy, Ella Joyce, Ossie Davis, Bruce Campbell, Larry Pennell. While not as good as I was hoping it would be, *Bubba Ho-tep* was still an awful lot of fun. Campbell gives a great performance as an aged Elvis, and Davis is wonderful as an elderly nursing home resident convinced he is JFK. It was odd and quirky, at times creepy and scary, and very entertaining. At the beginning are definitions, diction-

ary style, typed across the screen for "Ho-tep" and then "Bubba." I think my favorite lines were when Elvis is trying to explain to the administrator, after having killed a giant scarab beetle, that the rest home has a serious bug problem. "They're big! As big as my hand! As big as a peanut butter–banana sandwich!" And when the administrator assures him they will bring in an exterminator to deal with the problem, he of course answers, "Thank yew. Thank yew verry muuch!" —*M. N.*

BUFFY THE VAMPIRE SLAYER—ONCE MORE WITH FEELING L: HORROR TV/HORROR TV (2002) 88M D: Joss Whedon.

Sarah Michelle Gellar, Emma Caulfield, Michelle Trachtenberg, Alyson Hannigan, Nicholas Brendon, James Marsters. This extraordinary *Buffy* episode is Whedon's bold effort at writing a musical. "Once More with Feeling" runs over the traditional sixty minutes, was filmed in a widescreen aspect ratio (unlike the rest of the series), and features songs and lyrics written by Whedon himself. While the cast's singing abilities greatly vary, the story accommodates this with a demon who forces everyone, whether they can sing well or not, to spontaneously burst into song and dance! It's the kind of musical even someone who hates musicals can like because at least there is a reason why the cast sings and dances. Best of all are the many little touches, the self-referential moments, the brilliantly wry wit, the clever lyrics, and the varied music stylings based on the different temperaments of the characters. —*M. N.*

BUFFY THE VAMPIRE SLAYER—SEASON 1 L: HORROR TV/HORROR TV (1997) 18 hours D: Joss Whedon, others.

Sarah Michelle Gellar, David Boreanaz, Charisma Carpenter, Alyson Hannigan, Anthony Stewart Head, Nicholas Brendon. All hail Whedon, creator of *Buffy the Vampire Slayer*. Whedon was never satisfied with the trite, fluffy treatment of his *Buffy* movie script, and finally created a TV series in which he could both explore the humor and move deeper into heavier, darker issues. The first season is short, only twelve episodes, being a midseason replacement show. It became so popular it managed to weather seven seasons in all. The first season is the lightest of the fare, setting up the location of Sunnydale, California; the characters and their relationships to one another; and the dangers surrounding them (being on a Hellmouth and all). The dialogue is sharp and witty, the action great (and later seasons improve upon this more and more), and the stories engaging. Sure, there are a few weak episodes here and there, but what series doesn't suffer the occasional so-so? —*M. N.*

BUFFY THE VAMPIRE SLAYER—SEASON 2 L: HORROR TV/HORROR TV (1998) 18 hours D: Joss Whedon.

Sarah Michelle Gellar, David Boreanaz, Anthony Stewart Head, Charisma Carpenter, Nicholas Brendon, Alyson Hannigan. Right away Whedon heads toward the darker side of the Buffy-verse, taking the obvious trauma of the season finale and exploring its affect on Buffy. Sure, there is still the sly humor and blundering buffoonery, but there is an ever-increasing dark edge cutting into this season that makes it wickedly wonderful. Whedon reveals the consequences of Buffy's death in the first season, the culmination of her relationship with Angel, the bitterness of responsibility and duty, and the mixed and not always honorable motivations of the others. Best of all, Spike and Drusilla debut, the Sid and Nancy of the show who make evil look so good you almost want to start rooting for them. Boreanaz gets to cut loose and show us what he's really good at, and damn is he ever good at it. But hold on, you ain't seen nothin' yet! —*M. N.*

BUFFY THE VAMPIRE SLAYER—SEASON 3 L: HORROR TV/HORROR TV (1999) 18 hours D: Joss Whedon, others. *Sarah Michelle Gellar, Charisma Carpenter, Alyson Hannigan, Nicholas Brendon, Anthony Stewart Head, David Boreanaz.* The third season is probably the best season of *Buffy*. There is still a fine balance between the humor and drama, neither one overshadowing the other. Add one of the best villains ever in the form of the Mayor. Enter the wicked, sexy Faith, a Slayer who's on the edge of the dark side of the stake. It's also the last season with Angel, and that turns out OK. It is Buffy's graduating year and the Hellmouth just keeps getting hotter and hotter and the stakes (no pun intended) are getting higher and higher. In other words, it's the Apocalypse. Again. Some choice episodes from this season include "Earshot," "The Zeppo," "Amends," and "Doppelgangland" (Whoo! Evil Willow!). —*M. N.*

BUFFY THE VAMPIRE SLAYER—SEASON 4 L: HORROR TV/HORROR TV (2000) 18 hours D: Joss Whedon. *Sarah Michelle Gellar, James Marsters, Marc Blucas, Nicholas Brendon, Alyson Hannigan, Anthony Stewart Head.* Buffy has left Sunnydale High and begun college. The gang has been somewhat broken apart. Buffy is now working more on her own, and though Giles is still around, he doesn't have the hands-on relationship he did as her formal Watcher. Willow and Buffy are in college together, Xander is living at his parents' house, and Angel and Cordelia are gone. The initial awkwardness of this season could be deliberate, paralleling the awkwardness of moving from high school to college; or it could just be that with the change in cast and structure, it took a little while for the show to find its feet again. The villains are a little weak, but there are new faces and relationships that make it worthwhile. There's the return of the fabulous Spike, a new love interest for Buffy, and a further progression into the mysteries of what it is to be the Slayer. Highlights include the hilarious "Something Blue," "This Year's Girl," and the brilliant "Hush," mostly performed without spoken dialogue. —*M. N.*

BUFFY THE VAMPIRE SLAYER—SEASON 5 L: HORROR TV/HORROR TV (2001) 18 hours D: Joss Whedon. *Sarah Michelle Gellar, Nicholas Brendon, Emma Caulfield, James Marsters, Alyson Hannigan, Anthony Stewart Head, Michelle Trachtenberg.* The WB was concerned they would lose their teenage audience now that Buffy is all grown up and in college. Enter Dawn, Buffy's sister, who's never been seen or heard of before. But don't worry, there is method in that madness and it all works out pretty well, for this season at least. There's a new and entertaining villainess named Glory, who is as put off by breaking a nail as she is about not being able to find the Key so she can return to the dimension from whence she came. She's bitchy, sarcastic, and evil. Still, some of the magic is gone. There are high moments, but there seem to be more so-so episodes. There is goodness to be found, though, in Spike and his changing attitude toward Buffy, in the sweet and charming Tara, and in a Buffy-Bot. But there's a disturbing trend toward people doing dumb things and some heavy-handedness with the characters. —*M. N.*

On the other hand, you have "The Body," maybe the best single episode in the entire run of the series. Following up the shocking death of a lead character in the previous episode, this deals matter-of-factly and nearly in real time with the affect this tragedy has on each of the remaining characters. After growing to care about Buffy and her friends through so much wisecracking and monster slaying, it is now very moving to watch them face a loss involving no foul play or supernatural forces. Like many of the episodes directed by Whedon, this feels more like a movie than just a good episode of a TV show. —*B. T.*

BUFFY THE VAMPIRE SLAYER—SEASON 6 L: HORROR TV/HORROR TV (2002) 18 hours D: Joss Whedon, others. *Sarah Michelle Gellar, Michelle Trachtenberg, Emma Caulfield, James Marsters, Alyson Hannigan, Anthony Stewart Head, Nicholas Brandon.* The sixth is the worst of the *Buffy* seasons, due in part to a heavy-handed effort by Whedon to make the show more about real-life problems, eschewing the expected paranormal villains and conflicts. The *Buffy* audience wants to be entertained by wit and action, the characters flawed but nevertheless strong and winning. Instead there is a browbeaten feeling this season. Buffy is weighed down by adult responsibilities, by her new role as parent/guardian, by her undesired return to Sunnydale, and by an ever-increasing loss of purpose, direction, and hope. She indulges in destructive behavior and continually slides back into depression. Dawn is completely useless, just whining and mewling. Willow strolls down the path of drugs ... whoops, I mean dark magic. At least there are the Geeks of Doom, who are hilariously inept and yet strangely competent in their own über-nerdy, movie-obsessed, gadget-oriented way. There are a few shining moments, but overall the season is definitely tarnished. —*M. N.*

BUFFY THE VAMPIRE SLAYER—SEASON 7 L: HORROR TV/HORROR TV (2003)18 hours D: Joss Whedon, others. *Sarah Michelle Gellar, Michelle Trachtenberg, James Marsters, Emma Caulfield, Nicholas Brandon, Alyson Hannigan, Anthony Stweart Head.* Whedon decided to return to the show's roots after he and Gellar wisely decided to end the series rather than run it into the ground and spoil the memory. So back to Sunnydale High we go, this time to a new campus built right on top of the Hellmouth again! This final season moves along with more humor and lightness than it has in some time, and there are some brilliant episodes, such as "Conversations with Dead People." But there is also a peculiar lack of substance, with a lot of set-ups left dangling and overly emphasized hints that turn out to be nothing. New characters and old faces come for a visit, but they make little impact on the events or the show. And there is still a bit of that heavy broodiness lingering from the last season. Still, it's a much brighter and more entertaining note on which to end the series, and Whedon still managed to pull some cool surprises and excellent stories out of his pocket. Whatta guy! —*M. N.*

BUNKER, THE L: HORROR/GHOSTS (2001) 95M D: Rob Green. *Charley Boorman, Jason Flemyng, Jack Davenport, John Carlisle, Josh Cole.* The Bunker is a very strong piece of well-intentioned modern British horror that, while flawed, is commendable for being far better than most current horror films. A ragtag group of German soldiers during WWII, the only survivors of their company, stumble upon a bunker being held by only an old man and a young boy. As they stay to help defend the bunker and wait for reinforcements, they begin to fear there is something evil deep in the tunnels underneath them. Expertly directed but not quite as well written, the film comes off commendably considering its micro budget. American horror should stand up and take note. Not only are the Japanese doing it better than us, so are the British. —*T. S.*

BURIAL GROUND L: HORROR/ZOMBIES (1980) 85M D: Andrea Bianchi. *Peter Bark, Gian Luigi Chirizzi, Simone Mattioli, Karin Well.* A good Z-grade zombie film set on a big garden estate. The zombies here are tough and intelligent. They can use a battering ram and power tools, and they can also throw knives. There is a strange subplot with an Oedipal son, played by an adult (Bark). This is poorly made trash, but that's not a bad thing! This is a more-than-decent zombie film that offers good undead fun. —*T. S.*

CABIN FEVER L: VAOWG/VAOWG (2002) 94M D: Eli Roth. *Jordan Ladd, Cerina Vincent, Joey Kern, James DeBello, Giusseppe Andrews, Rider Strong.* Bursting onto the horror scene with a violent fury, first-time director Roth has crafted the best American horror film in quite a while, tongue jammed firmly into bloodied, decaying cheek. Five teens vacationing at a secluded cabin in the middle of woods are attacked by a flesh-eating virus and left with no way to escape its bloody consequences. Mixing humor (which is actually funny) with shocks (that are actually scary), the movie is like a roller-coaster ride—even though it makes you feel like puking, you want to ride it again and again. Filled with memorable characters like a retarded, kung fu–practicing redneck child (Matthew Helms) and a cop (Andrews) more interested in partying hard than any of the kids, *Cabin Fever* really dazzles because of the way Roth deftly weaves together his obvious influences and manages to make something entirely refreshing, entirely nostalgic, and entirely entertaining, all at the same time. —*T. S.*

CANNIBAL HOLOCAUST L: HORROR/CANNIBALS (1979) 98M D: Ruggero Deodato. *Robert Kerman, Salvatore Basil, Francesca Ciardi, Perry Pirkanen, Luca Barbareschi.* This well-directed film with a powerhouse script nearly lives up to its legendary reputation. A journalist and his film crew head to the Amazon to locate the so-called last cannibal tribe. The whole crew disappears, and later their film footage is found, so the network wants to edit it quickly into a sensational story fit for broadcast TV. Cinema-verité style, you get a quick sense of what each member of the crew is like: their interpersonal playfulness and testiness while enduring hardships together, their hunger for sensational images to the point they change and even fake some events to validate their presuppositions. Then pushing the envelope of engaged journalism, they step into the abyss morally and physically, and can no longer retreat, dying more horribly than they could have imagined. The irony runs so deep and the humor so dark that you can't help feeling Deodato to be just a tad too pleased with himself. —*J. C.*

If you love shoddily produced, completely braindead garbage that gets by on the outrageousness of graphic rape and murder scenes, sexual mutilation, un-simulated cruelty to animals, and blatant racism, and then cynically pretends to preach against those things—then you probably already have this one hidden under your mattress. Turtles can live for a hundred years, so I'm sure they don't mind being split open just so that you can get a boner watching "savages" fondle their guts. OK, no offense—I have friends who like this movie, but I just don't get it. —*B. T.*

CANNIBAL! THE MUSICAL L: PSYCHOTRONIC/TROMA FILMS (1996) 90M D: Trey Parker. *Trey Parker, Matt Stone, Toddy Walters.* Parker is riding tall on his horse, the blue sky and Colorado mountains behind him, as he sings, "I think I know exactly what I say/When I say it's a shpredoinkle day." He originally wrote this Rogers and Hammerstein-meets-*Cannibal Holocaust* (inspired by the true story of real-life pioneer Alfred Packer, the only American ever convicted of cannibalism) as a stage production. Parker plays it with gee-whiz goofiness punctuated by grotesque bad taste, a wide-eyed innocent telling his demented story of bloody body parts, festering sores, human hors d'oeuvres, and demented snowman-building through song. The juvenile jokes wear thin over the course of a feature film but his enthusiasm is infectious. Now if he can just learn to lay off the fart jokes. Stone, Parker's partner in giddy bad taste, co-stars. —*S. A.*

CAPRICORN ONE L: SCIENCE FICTION/SCIENCE FICTION
(1978) 123M D: Peter Hyams. *Sam Waterston, O. J. Simpson, Brenda Vaccaro, James Brolin, Elliott Gould.* Based on a novel by Ken Follett, *Capricorn One* concerns an egregious NASA cover-up. The flight to Mars looks perfectly legitimate until some problems beset the ship. The astronauts, out in the desert posing for their Mars landing, figure they will be executed to save face for the space program and the administration, so they flee into the desert. Gould is brilliant as the reporter who smells a rat. This film is certain to be a hit with the conspiracy theorists, but it is also a decent suspense film for everyone else. —*N. J.*

CAPTAIN KRONOS: VAMPIRE HUNTER L: HORROR/
HAMMER FILMS (1972) 91M D: Brian Clemens. *Horst Janson, John Cater, Caroline Munro, John Carson, Shane Briant.* Best known for his snappy, stylish work on British TV (notably *The Avengers*), Clemens made his mark in cult movie circles with this swashbuckling vampire film. When the hooded undead creature drains not the blood but the bloom of youth from a beautiful young maiden in the forest, Clemens puts a whole new spin on a familiar genre. Janson is the brooding Kronos, a Napoleonic soldier who hunts the undead with his jovial hunchbacked partner, Grost (Cater), and takes time out from his athletic battles and meditative interludes for a few lusty pleasures with curvaceous peasant girl/camp follower Munro. Clemens wasn't provided the budget to bring his visual ideas to full fruition (and, frankly, he lacks the cinematic high style necessary for true swashbuckling flourish), which may explain why it flopped on its original release. It has since deservedly been rediscovered and celebrated for its unique sensibility, well-wrought characters, and inspired ideas. —*S. A.*

CARNIVAL OF SOULS L: CLASSIC HORROR/CLASSIC HORROR
(1962) 93M D: Herk Harvey. *Stan Levitt, Candace Hilligoss, Art Ellison, Frances Feist, Sidney Berger.* Shot by industrial documentary director Harvey on a tiny budget with a largely student cast in Lawrence, Kansas, this imaginative tale of a chilly church organist haunted by zombie-like apparitions after surviving a car accident surely was an inspiration for *Night of the Living Dead*, that other cult 1960s indie by a Midwest industrial filmmaker. The slightly arch performance by lead Hilligoss sets the film off-center from the opening and as she disengages from reality, wandering through a silent city that neither sees nor hears her, she communicates a genuinely eerie sense of dislocation. "We hoped for the look of a Bergman film and the feel of Cocteau," remarked director Harvey in an interview after the forgotten film was rediscovered by a new audience in the 1990s. Yet there's something uniquely American about this mix of fantasy, horror, and modern alienation. The shivery climax was shot in the crumbling remains of the abandoned Salt Palace on the Great Salt Lake, one of the most memorable locations you'll ever see in a horror film. —*S. A.*

CARNOSAUR L: VAOWG/VAOWG (1993) 82M D: Adam Simon.
Harrison Page, Jennifer Runyon, Raphael Sbarge, Clint Howard, Diane Ladd. One must admire the audacity of Roger Corman producing this low-budget dinosaur movie to compete/tie-in with the big budget FX extravaganza of the time, *Jurassic Park.* Gene Siskel gave *Carnosaur* a thumbs up, and Christian Gore of *Film Threat Magazine* claimed it was better than *Jurassic Park*, but both were smoking the proverbial crack. Stunts like this are generally more fun to look at the cover of than to actually sit down and watch, and this is no exception. An ugly, lifeless bore with little humor (intentional or otherwise) until the admittedly clever ending where the hero, fresh from saving the day, is gunned down and blowtorched by goons in biohazard suits. —*B. T.*

CARTOON ALL-STARS TO THE RESCUE L: PSYCHOTRONIC/
DRUGS (1990) 60M D: Milton Gray, Marsh Lamore, others. In 1990, an unprecedented event occurred: Bugs Bunny, Daffy Duck, the Muppet Babies, the Smurfs, Huey, Dewey, and Louie, Winnie the Pooh and Tigger, Alvin and the Chipmunks, the Teenage Mutant Ninja Turtles, Garfield, Alf, and Slimer all teamed up to teach nine-year-old Corey's older brother to say "no" to an anthropomorphic puff of deadly marijuana smoke. If that dream-team lineup can't stop drug abuse worldwide, then why even bother with a Drug War? Who do the DEA think they're fooling trying to pull off something that the Ninja Turtles couldn't? —*B. T.*

CASE OF THE BLOODY IRIS, THE L: HORROR/GIALLO
(ITALIAN HORROR) (1972) 94M D: Giuliano Carmineo. *Edwige Fenech, George Hilton, Annabella Incontrera, Paola Quattrini.* Solid well-plotted *giallo.* Beautiful to look at, though not as sleazy or as twisted as it probably should have been. A woman is knifed in an elevator, then a cabaret performer is drowned in the same building. A fashion model (Fenech)

and her pal move in. Her ex-husband causes problems for the model and her new beau. Then the model's ex dies and her roommate is stabbed on a public street. When she learns her beau was at the murder, she runs to the neighbors for help but . . . . Another effective *giallo* scripted by Ernesto Gastaldi and produced by Luciano Martino as a vehicle for Fenech. Luscious eye-candy. *—J. C.*

CASTLE OF THE WALKING DEAD L: PSYCHOTRONIC/POE, EDGAR ALLAN (1967) 81M D: Harald Reinl. *Carl Lange, Karin Dor, Christopher Lee, Lex Barker.* Former Tarzan turned German Western star Barker is an attorney called to the Transylvania Castle of a Count who died thirty-five years earlier and, along with a beautiful Baroness (Dor), finds himself at the center of a revenge plot from beyond the grave. Lee opens the film as a vicious sadist who, after murdering twelve virgins, gets a spiked mask pounded into his head before he's drawn and quartered. Not that such small measures will keep him from his ultimate plan of eternal life, even after his own death! There is a pit and there is a pendulum, but this very loose German adaptation of Edgar Allan Poe's story is much closer to the Italian horror cinema of sex and sadism and the German "Krimi" thrillers of director Reinl than Poe. Dead bodies hang from trees like overripe fruit, and Lee's half-naked murder victims are left strapped to torture devices and displayed like wax museum exhibits. Lurid but rather styleless, with an ill-fitting musical score, it's more of a curiosity than a horror classic, but thankfully the English-language version features Lee's actual voice. *—S. A.*

CAT WOMEN OF THE MOON L: CLASSIC SCIENCE FICTION/ CLASSIC SCIENCE FICTION (1953) 65M D: Arthur D. Hilton. *Laird Grainger, Sonny Tufts, Victor Jory, Marie Windsor, Carol Brewster, Douglas Fowley.* The notorious Tufts leads an expedition to the moon and discovers a race of cat-suited babes with psychic powers, a hankering for Earthmen, and a desire to take over our planet. Will the male astronauts resist their lustful urges? Will the female astronaut resist her space sisters' cosmic influence? And what about the giant puppet spider? Sure, it doesn't live up to the ludicrous title, but this is still a pretty fun cheapo camp classic from the makers of the amazing *Robot Monster.* *—S. H.*

CHAINED FOR LIFE L: VAOWG/VAOWG (1951) 81M D: Harry L. Fraserp. *Daisy Hilton, Violet Hilton.* Almost twenty years after *Freaks*, Siamese twins the Hilton Sisters were given this strange starring vehicle. Part court room drama and part vaudeville act, a big chunk of the screen time is given over to singing duets by the sisters, juggling acts, and gun tricks. Victimized by a cruel publicity stunt, one of the sisters turns to murder and a judge must decide whether it is fair to execute them both. At the end he cops out, defers to the Supreme Court and asks us, the audience, what we would do if we were jurors. Something to think about, I guess, in case you are ever on a jury deciding the punishment for a murderous Siamese twin. *—B. T.*

CHANGELING, THE L: HORROR/GHOSTS (1980) 115M D: Peter Medak. *Trish Van Devere, George C. Scott, Melvyn Douglas, Jean Marsh.* Although one of the scariest horror films of all time, *The Changeling* contains not one drop of blood. John (Scott) witnesses his wife and daughter die in a car accident. He moves to Seattle to get away from it all, but the vast mansion he buys has some unwanted amenities, such as doors that open on their own, banging noises at six in the morning, and a cobweb-covered wheelchair that won't stay in its attic hideaway. John enlists the aid of historian Claire (Van Devere) to unearth the stories contained in this old house. Some of the most simple horror ideas are treated with deft painterly skill, making each self-opening door and self-tapping piano key a fresh experience. Any minor shortcomings are overridden by a complex interweaving of fearful moments and an almost unbearable unwavering tension throughout. The actor's fearful reactions induce their own heart-pounding rhythms. Smart and tight, *The Changeling* is an obvious suggestion for a night of fearful movie viewing. *—S. R.*

CHILDREN OF THE LIVING DEAD L: HORROR/ZOMBIES (2001) 90M D: Tor Ramsey. *Jamie McCoy, Tom Savini, A. Barrett Worland.* From the man who butchered *Night of the Living Dead* comes *Children of the Living Dead*, a terrible film. Since John Russo owns the *Living Dead* trademark, he is free to promote his films. But how he continues to get funding to make them is beyond me. *—T. S.*

CHILD'S PLAY L: HORROR/STALKERS (1988) 95M D: Tom Holland. *Alex Vincent, Catherine Hicks, Chris Sarandon, Brad Dourif (voice).* Cornered in a toy store by police, a serial killer (Dourif) performs a voodoo spell that transfers his soul into a talking Good Guys doll. As luck would have it, Good Guys are the impossible to find, in-demand doll of the season and all that little Andy (Vincent) wants for his birthday. His hardworking single mother (Hicks) buys the possessed doll on the black market, and before long the little thing is toddling around killing people with toy hammers. Like Freddy, the sequels turned Chucky into somewhat of a killer comedian, but this first in the series is genuinely creepy. There have been other good killer doll movies, but most are about antique dolls. *Child's Play* was the first to update the concept to the post–Cabbage Patch Kids days of mass-produced fad toys. *—B. T.*

CHILD'S PLAY 2 L: HORROR/STALKERS (1990) 88M D: John Lafia. *Brad Dourif (voice), Alex Vincent, Jenny Agutter, Gerrit Graham, Christine Elise, Grace Zabriskie.* This sequel to the 1988 horror-comedy is every bit as good as the original. In this film the boy and his doll are in a foster home because his mother had a nervous breakdown. But a couple decide to adopt the troubled boy even as their older foster daughter is having problems herself. Meanwhile, the killer inside the doll is plotting to transfer his soul into the body of the boy. Excellent comedic horror scenes compare favorably to the original, especially a memorable murder over a Xerox machine, and the spoofing of such horror villains as Jason, who cannot seem to die. —*N. J.*

CHILD'S PLAY 3 L: HORROR/STALKERS (1991) 89M D: Jack Bender. *Jeremy Sylvers, Peter Haskell, Perrey Reeves, Justin Whalin, Brad Dourif (voice), Dakin Matthews.* This sequel falls a little flat after the first two films because much of the comedic horror is simply being repeated. The same plot as *Child's Play 2* is used with a different setting, this time in a state-run military school. With the boy now a teenage cadet, the doll's violent humor doesn't play as well as it did off the innocence of a small boy. Still, there's plenty of violence and foul language to keep the Chucky fan happy. A decade would have to expire, however, before a more deserving sequel would be released—*Bride of Chucky*. —*N. J.*

CHOPPING MALL L: SCIENCE FICTION/SCIENCE FICTION (1986) 77M D: Jim Wynorski. *Barbara Crampton, Paul Bartel, Mary Woronov, Dick Miller, Kelli Maroney, Gerrit Graham.* Although the film's tagline is "Where shopping can cost you an arm and a leg," it's not the shoppers who lose their limbs when the local mall's three new nighttime security patrol robots go haywire. Instead, the victims are four libidinous young couples who plan on spending a wild night of drinking, partying, and carrying on in the mattress department of the mall's expansive furniture store. The good times soon come to an end, however, as the teens are systematically hunted down and destroyed by the three killer robots equipped with an arsenal of poisoned darts, choke wires, and lasers strong enough to make a head explode. The music, the acting, the dialogue—everything about *Chopping Mall* is ridiculous and terrible. But it's ridiculous and terrible in the wonderful kind of way that makes so many '80s horror films a whole lot of fun to watch. —*A. W.*

CHRISTMAS EVIL (AKA **YOU BETTER WATCH OUT,** AKA **TERROR IN TOYLAND**) L: HORROR/STALKERS (1980) 82M D: Lewis Jackson. *Andy Fenwick, Brandon Maggart, Jeffrey DeMunn, Dianne Hull.* Easily the best of the "Santa serial killer" genre (and believe me, there are more holiday horrors than you'd care to know about), this smartly made little production is John Waters's favorite Christmas film, at least according to Troma honcho Lloyd Kaufman. The "hero" is a spineless adult nerd (Maggart) who was traumatized as a child when he saw mommy doing more than kissing Santa Claus.

We get to know a man desperate to hold onto faith and fantasy and childhood innocence in a cynical world. He's not simply an avenging elf, but a jolly Santa who just wants to spread cheer and goes homicidal when faced with sneering bullies. —*S. A.*

C.H.U.D. L: SCIENCE FICTION/SCIENCE FICTION (1984) 96M D: Douglas Cheek. *Daniel Stern, John Heard.* The low-budget, high energy drive-in cinema of Roger Corman in the '70s was taken up by hungry filmmakers and ambitious B studios in the '80s. *C.H.U.D.*, a grungy monster movie of toxic poison, government conspiracy, and limbs ripped whole from bodies, is one of those. Soup kitchen cook turned homeless activist Stern tells cop Heard that something very weird is munching on the street people who live in the New York sewers. Perhaps not the best of the lot, it creaks a bit and the rubber monsters are pretty cheap looking (which is why they are only seen in quick cuts and dark shadows), but it's suitably gory, appropriately paranoid, briskly paced, and plenty fun. Heck, with a title that stands for "Cannibalistic Humanoid Underground Dwellers," how could you go wrong? —*S. A.*

CITIZEN TOXIE: TOXIC AVENGER IV L: PSYCHOTRONIC/ TROMA FILMS (2001) 108M D: Lloyd Kaufman. *David Mattey, Debbie Rochon, Ron Jeremy, Joe Fleishaker.* *Citizen Toxie* is the most retarded movie ever and the most brilliant. But, it's not important whether you love the movie or hate it, what matters is that this movie "has" to exist, because if it doesn't, freedom of speech is just bullshit and art is meaningless. *Citizen Toxie* is as much free-form art as it is a coherent collection of plot-points, longer than it should be, shorter than it should be, and containing enough disturbing filth to piss off everyone. A film like this is a firecracker up the ass of any creative being. Hate it? Good! Pick up a fucking camera and make something better. Love it? Great (see above)! Movies like this, and directors like Kaufman are our only weapon against the pedestrian boredom of mainstream "art." Whose side are you on? —*K. C.*

CLASH OF THE TITANS L: PSYCHOTRONIC/HARRYHAUSEN, RAY (1981) 118M D: Desmond Davis. *Burgess Meredith, Harry Hamlin, Ursula Andress, Maggie Smith, Lawrence Olivier, Judi Bowker.* Special effects master Ray Harryhausen takes on the gods, goddesses, and monsters of Roman myths in his final and most ambitious work. Hamlin is Perseus, the stiffly heroic human who battles a bestiary of mythological horrors (sea-beast Kraken, demonic man-beast Callibos, and a beautifully rendered Medusa) to rescue the lovely and delicate princess Andromeda (Bowker) while the Olympian gods (Olivier as Zeus, Smith as Thetis, Andress as Aphrodite, among others) watch from on high. Meredith plays sidekick and poet Ammon. Though directed by Davis, this labor of love is Harryhausen's baby all the way.

It feels like a throwback to his 1950s fantasies, from the creaky drama to the lavish spectacle and wonderfully quaint stop-motion creations. They don't "convince" as much as they delight and entertain. This is the work of an artist with pride in his craft. —*S. A.*

CLIVE BARKER'S SALOME & THE FORBIDDEN L: PSYCHOTRONIC/BARKER, CLIVE (1973) 70M D: Clive Barker. *Doug Bradley, Peter Atkins, Anne Taylor, Clive Barker.* Barker made these two experimental films in the '70s. The closest thing here relating to the story of *Salome* is the delivery of a freshly severed head to the laughing title temptress. The film features various shots of nude people holding torches, performing strange dances, and intertwining in somewhat orgiastic tableaus. The murky, dark grain allows the viewer to be drawn into Clive's telling of this classic story, an extremely free portrayal offering soft, moody shots of the actors being spooky. *The Forbidden* follows the creation of a painting and a bearded man (*Hellraiser 2* screenwriter Atkins) in a cell continually looking at it. Printed almost exclusively in negative, this film concentrates on the man and his assembly of a puzzle. Barker pops in for a few moments sporting a silver face and a blood-engorged penis, dancing frenetically. The bearded man's flesh is peeled off until he's skinless, much like Frank in *Hellraiser*, and the puzzle pieces are blown apart. —*S. R.*

COLOSSUS: THE FORBIN PROJECT L: SCIENCE FICTION/SCIENCE FICTION (1970) 90M D: Joseph Sargent. *Eric Braeden, Susan Clark, Gordon Pinsent.* Brainy scientist Charles Forbin (Braeden) creates a computer, suitably named Colossus, to run all of mankind's needs. In response, the Russians create Gemini. Colossus was programmed to "never stop learning" and soon realizes it has mankind by the balls. It hooks up with Gemini and soon has control over the world's nuclear arsenal. The supercomputer executes its enemies and takes complete possession over its creator, Dr. Forbin, who must pay the devil its due by giving up his personal freedom to the beast he has unleashed on the world. This film sends me back to the wonderful memories of '70s late-night television, watching crappy pan-n-scan versions of doomsday sci-fi classics with big computers and mass destruction. *Colossus* should really only be watched in its original 2.35:1 aspect ratio, sadly only available on the out-of-print laserdisc (which included the equally interesting *Silent Running* as a double bill). Well worth tracking down (or staying up late night and catching on TV). From the director of another '70s classic, *The Taking of Pelham One Two Three* and the unbelievably bad *Jaws 4: The Revenge.* —*N. J.*

CONAN THE BARBARIAN L: PSYCHOTRONIC/HOWARD, ROBERT E. (1982) 129M D: John Milius. *Arnold Schwarzenegger, Sandahl Bergman, Max von Sydow, James Earl Jones.* As a child Conan sees his family and village slaughtered at the hands of Thulsa Doom (Jones) and his snake cult. Pressed into slavery, Conan grows strong and learns to fight in a bloody, primitive arena. Once freed, the adult Conan (Schwarzenegger) seeks his revenge against the cult. Conan reads philosophy, learns the ways of women, and sets out across the lands. He has incredibly bad simulated sex with a sorceress. He interacts with the animal kingdom—punching a camel, kicking a rat through the air, fighting giant snakes, and killing a buzzard with his teeth. This movie is one of only a few Dino De Laurentiis productions that doesn't suck. The world knew who Schwarzenegger was after this picture, thanks in part to the greatest line in all of filmdom, when Conan defines what is truly good: "to crush your enemy, to see him driven before you, and to hear the lamentations of the women." *Conan the Barbarian* is one of the best sword and sorcery epics ever and definitely my favorite. —*G. M.*

CONQUEST OF THE PLANET OF THE APES L: VAOWG/PLANET OF THE APES (1972) 88M D: J. Lee Thompson. *Ricardo Montalban, Don Murray, Roddy McDowall.* It's a very strange future indeed in this the fourth *Planet of the Apes* installment. Apes have become a curious cross between servants and pets for their human owners. Montalban plays Armando, an owner of a very unique ape named Caesar played by McDowall—an ape that can talk! The original themes of the first film are here exploded out of proportion, especially as Caesar leads the apes in revolt. A lot of good laughs are to be had along the way, especially as one realizes that nearly all of the film is shot in Century Plaza in Los Angeles! —*N. J.*

CORE, THE L: VAOWG/VAOWG (2003) 134M D: Jon Amiel. *Aaron Eckhart, Hilary Swank, Tchéky Karyo, Stanley Tucci, Delroy Lindo, Bruce Greenwood.* Essentially *Armageddon* meets *Journey to the Center of the Earth* (or so it was surely pitched to the studio), this mix of Jules Verne and modern disaster action cinema is, for all its absurdity and scientific gobbledy-gook, far more entertaining than it has a right to be. Eckhart is the nominal hero, a physics phenom who figures out that the biblical disasters plaguing the Earth are the result of the planet's core having inexplicably stopped spinning, and Swank is the reckless but brilliant young pilot brought on the mission of the world's best and brightest to jump-start the planet's heart. Fine, they're the obligatory young lovers, but the film belongs to Tucci's preening, self-important science celebrity, who steals scenes right and left. Director Amiel is less concerned about making the ridiculous science sound even remotely plausible than a more basic kind of chemistry in the casting, and is slightly more successful there. —*S. A.*

COUNT YORGA, VAMPIRE L: HORROR/VAMPIRES (1970) 90M D: Bob Kelljan. *Roger Perry, Robert Quarry, Donna Anders, Michael Murphy.* Quarry is perfectly cast as the well dressed and overly made-up Count Yorga of Bulgaria who lives in Los Angeles. Beginning with the Count leading a séance, the vampire is soon pursuing the young women of the group so he can drink their blood. In one shocking scene a woman, having been bitten, is found eating the flesh of a small kitten. Despite the mounting evidence—bite marks, blood drinking, and the fact the Count is from Bulgaria and wears too much makeup—the boyfriends refuse to believe it's vampirism. Until it's too late. This low-grade vampire film works quite well, in large part because of Quarry's marvelous depiction of the Count. —*N. J.*

COVEN L: HORROR/WITCHES & WARLOCKS (1997) 40M D: Mark Borchardt. *Mark Borchardt, Tom Dallace, Miriam Frost, Bill Borchardt.* Coven (not pronounced like oven) is the film whose making is chronicled in the documentary *American Movie.* While the documentary shows director/star Borchardt as an optimistic dreamer with no clue how to make a film, his final product shows us something else. The film is surprisingly well crafted and atmospheric, effectively telling the story of an alcoholic who unwittingly joins a satanic support group. The ridiculous plot is saved by the obvious enthusiasm behind the project, apparent even without watching the documentary. Not a masterpiece by any means, *Coven* is a good no-budget horror film and is far better than most movies produced by people with Mark's resources and training. Not just an oddity on whom a documentary is based, Mark's passion could one day result in a truly good movie, especially if his *Northwestern* project ever gets off the ground. But *Coven* is fun to watch and that's all you can ask from a cheapo horror flick. —*T. S.*

CRAWLING EYE, THE (AKA THE TROLLENBERG TERROR) L: CLASSIC HORROR/CLASSIC HORROR (1958) 84M D: Quentin Lawrence. *Janet Munro, Laurence Payne, Jennifer Jayne, Forrest Tucker, Warren Mitchell.* An alien menace hiding in a cloud of mist decapitates scientists in a remote high-altitude research station in the Alps. When the cloud descends into the Swiss village of Trollenberg, UN scientist Tucker joins Mitchell and Munro to stop the headhunter's rampage. This is one title that delivers more than what it promises: not one but a whole gang of giant crawling eyeballs with vinelike tentacles converge for the climax, and they are just weird and wiggy enough not to look too silly. Shot in crisp black and white on obviously low-budget sets, it lacks the mood of similar British sci-fi horrors of the late '50s, but it does boast a claustrophobic atmosphere and a marvelous setting in the snow-packed mountains. Originally a British miniseries, it was brought to the big screen under the direction of atomic scientist turned British TV director Lawrence. —*S. A.*

CREATURE WALKS AMONG US, THE L: CLASSIC SCIENCE FICTION/CLASSIC SCIENCE FICTION (1956) 79M D: John Sherwood. *Don Megowan, Riccou Browning, Leigh Snowden, Rex Reason, Jeff Morrow.* In this conclusion to the *Creature of the Black Lagoon* series, the creature is in captivity and being studied by scientists. They even give him clothes and a set of lungs so he can, in fact, walk among us. I like this one simply because the creature looks very menacing. His body is bulkier and, with that little head poking out from his shoddily sewn scrubs, he looks like he'd tear you in half if you tried to talk shit about amphibians. —*B. T.*

CUBE L: SCIENCE FICTION/SCIENCE FICTION (1997) 90M D: Vincenzo Natali. *Maurice Dean Wint, Nicole deBoer, Nicky Guadagni, David Hewlett, Wayne Robson.* A group of strangers find themselves stuck inside a strange, symmetrical room with hatches on the walls, floor, and ceiling. When they go through any one of the hatches, it brings them to another room that looks exactly the same. Nobody remembers how they got there, and some of the people don't get along, so (like in a George Romero movie) they have to quit arguing and work together to figure out a solution to their quandary. The acting is not great, and some of the conflicts seem forced, but it's worth watching just to see where they go with this simple, nightmarish premise. —*B. T.*

CURE L: JAPANESE HORROR/JAPANESE HORROR (1997) 111M D: Kiyoshi Kurosawa. *Masato Hagiwara, Tsuyoshi Ujiki, Anna Nakagawa, Yoriko Douguchi, Koji Yakusho.* The breakthrough film by Japan's master of moody menace and unfathomable mystery is the unsettling tale of a murder spree where the victims are dispatched in identical ways, but the killers are ordinary civilians who have no memory of their deeds. An investigating detective (Yakusho) discovers one common thread: each killer received a visit from a blank young man with no short-term memory. Though made in the shadow of *Seven* and *The X-Files*, the thematic roots of the film are more accurately traced to *God Told Me To* and David Cronenberg's *Shivers*, a pair of minor classics from the '70s that roil with ideas of conformity, urban repression, and the restraints of human morality removed by either suggestion or chemistry. Kurosawa's film is even dreamier, slower, and more alienated and unsettling, a portrait of an overcrowded society cracking with just a push of the psyche, filmed with the passion of a blasé voyeur. Is it the disease, or the cure? —*S. A.*

CURSE OF THE BLAIR WITCH L: HORROR/WITCHES & WARLOCKS (1999) 44M D: Daniel Myrick, Edward Sanchez. *Heather Donahue.* This made-for-TV special about the mysterious happenings in Burketsville is much better than the actual *Blair Witch Project* film. It made me far more uncomfortable than the actual film did. *Curse of the Blair Witch* is a compilation of supposed interviews and history about the Blair Witch. Because it treats the subject with respect and just the right amount of fear, this "documentary" helped give rise to the belief by some that *The Blair Witch Project* was real. *Curse* entrenches the mystery into your psyche, so viewing it before seeing the movie actually improves the experience of a pretty poor film. —*T. S.*

DARK CITY L: SCIENCE FICTION/SCIENCE FICTION (1998) 101M D: Alex Proyas. *Richard O'Brien, Kiefer Sutherland, Rufus Sewell, Jennifer Connelly, William Hurt.* When this movie starts, turn off the volume on your TV until you start seeing the actual credits. Why? Because the studio inserted a super-annoying voice-over at the beginning that gives away, ohhhhh, about three-fourths of the plot! Idiots! Since you do learn everything eventually, what the hell is the point of giving it all away at the beginning of the film? Make the audience work their brains for a change, that's what I say! —*M. N.*

DARK CRYSTAL L: FANTASY/FANTASY (1982) 93M D: Jim Henson, Frank Oz. *Dave Goelz, Brian Muehl, Jim Henson, Kathryn Mullen.* We're used to seeing animated and live-action movies jammed with computer effects, but it's still unusual to see a movie where all of the actors are puppets—especially a serious one like this. The designs by renowned fantasy artist Brian Froud, along with the innovative effects of the Jim Henson workshop, create a completely artificial world. There are enough creatures to fill a *Star Wars* cantina, most memorably the wrinkly, vulturelike Skeksies, who are some of the creepiest monsters ever put on film. Unfortunately the Gelfling heroes are bland and lifeless, making the whole story fall flat. Still, it's a one-of-a-kind movie and it's tragic Henson didn't live long enough to continue exploring the potential of puppet movies. —*B. T.*

DARK SHADOWS L: HORROR TV/HORROR TV (1966) 30M D: Dan Curtis. *Jonathan Frid, Lara Parker, Grayson Hall, Nancy Barrett, Joan Bennet, Alexandra Isles.* The heightened emotional schizophrenia of the soap opera owes a great deal to classic drama like that penned by the Brontë sisters. It was Art Wallace and Dan Curtis's stroke of genius that brought the two together in the television phenomenon known as *Dark Shadows*. With 1,225 episodes over five years, the show began as a character drama set in a creepy fishing village, revolving around the remote manor home of the ancient Collins family. About a year into its run, after the undead Barnabus Collins rose from the grave, the show really took off. Ghosts, vampires, zombies, werewolves, time travel, and the Devil himself appeared in the show. With recurring cast members, small budgets, and challenging schedules, there were frequent mistakes that they had no time to edit or reshoot. Its greatest strength is its penchant for Gothic suspense

and its absurd, enthralling storylines. The show presented so many thrilling, chilling, laughable, and moving tales that it will live on forever, like the tormented undead characters whose stories it relates. —*T. S.*

DARKNESS FALLS L: HORROR/DEMONS (2003) 85M D: Jonathan Liebesman. *Cheney Kley, Emma Caulfield, Lee Cormie. Darkness Falls:* Terrible? Yes. Redeeming qualities? Very, very few. An excellent first two minutes give you all the wrong ideas and just when you are starting to get excited, everything collapses (only three minutes into the movie). The original concept, though ridiculous, was purportedly very well developed in the original script. However, after the film was shot, the director decided to change the story completely, cutting most of Stan Winston's wonderfully designed monster, editing the film down to PG-13, and releasing it as an undecipherable mess. The numerous plot holes are too confusing to merit consideration. To the inane tagline of "Runs rings around *The Ring*," I offer the more appropriate "*Darkness Falls* should fall into darkness." And damn if it doesn't. —*T. S.*

DAUGHTERS OF DARKNESS L: HORROR/VAMPIRES (1971) 100M D: Harry Kümel. *John Karlen, Daniele Ouimet, Delphine Seyrig, Andrea Rau.* One of the most unusual vampire tales, this sexy European film is one of the kinkiest and most artistic of the popular lesbian vampire genre typified by movies like Hammer's *Countess Dracula* or Tony Scott's *The Hunger.* A young newly married couple (Ouimet and Karlen) spends their honeymoon at an eerie, vacant hotel with a stunning countess (Seyring, *Last Year at Marienbad*) and her sexy companion (Rau). The countess attempts to seduce the bride, and the groom turns out to be a sadistic pervert who talks to his male "mother" on the phone. *Daughters of Darkness* features all the stock ingredients (reflection-free vampires who fear daylight and running water, etc.), but the story unfolds with a perverse grace and twisted black humor, as well as a considerable amount of lush eroticism. It is far from the typical story of a three-hundred-year-old, blood-drinking countess. —*S. H.*

DAY AFTER, THE L: VAOWG/VAOWG (1983) 126M D: Nicholas Meyer. *John Cullum, John Lithgow, Steve Guttenberg, JoBeth Williams, Jason Robards.* This late-Cold War made-for-TV film hypes the potential of the United States and the USSR to destroy the world a thousand times over. After a brief exposition of the characters, the missiles launch. Trying for realism, the film depicts live broadcasts of newsmen and somewhat realistic live footage throughout the fictional crisis. The film aired on ABC, who issued a warning (publicity stunt?) so as presumably not to repeat a *War of the Worlds*–style panic. As a disaster film, this one doesn't measure up to the best. The suspense is largely sacrificed for the novelty of TV realism that may have worked in the '80s, but the effort of the actors does little to help save it. —*N.J.*

DAY OF THE ANIMALS (AKA SOMETHING IS OUT THERE) L: VAOWG/VAOWG (1977) 95M D: William Girdler.
Christopher George, Michael Ansara, Lynda Day George, Richard Jaeckel, Leslie Nielsen. It's *Wild Kingdom* meets *Grizzly* as a hole in the ozone layer causes a wide variety of animals (birds, snakes, cougars, bears, dogs, rats, and even a tarantula) to stalk and eventually attack a group of hikers led by George. The radioactive rays are strong enough to make a pre-*Airplane!* Nielsen take his shirt off, kill a guy, rape a woman, and then wrestle a grizzly bear (in that order). He even tries to bite the bear's ear off! Director Girdler has always had a knack for creating silly but compelling cheapo epics like this. While it's no *Kingdom of the Spiders*, *Day of the Animals* has enough dead Hollywood hacks, unintentional laughs, and sinister vultures to satisfy fans of nature-gone-amuck cinema. —*S. H.*

DAY OF THE TRIFFIDS, THE L: CLASSIC SCIENCE FICTION /CLASSIC SCIENCE FICTION (1963) 93M D: Steve Sekely.
Mervyn Johns, Kieron Moore, Janette Scott, Howard Keel, Nicole Maurey. An often overlooked British sci-fi classic from writer Phillip Yordan and codirected by cinematographer/Hammer Films director Freddie Francis. Meteors hit the Earth and give birth to man-eating Triffid plants. Bill Masen (Keel) lies in his hospital bed suffering from an injury to his eyes. When he gets his bandages off his sight has returned, only for him to find that the world is in chaos, most of the population having been also blinded by the meteors and having become victims to the man-eating monstrous plants. The plants are well designed, making a shrill squeaking noise before they attack. The film is tensely edited and well lensed in CinemaScope. A doomsday thriller based on the book by John Wyndham, the film has unfortunately fallen into the public domain market in the United States and is available usually in poor-quality pan-and-scan versions. The film is really only meant to be seen its glorious Technicolor 2:35.1 widescreen aspect ratio. Look for the long out-of-print widescreen laserdisc by Image Entertainment or the nice PAL British DVD release by Second Sight Films. —*N. H.*

DEAD AND BURIED L: HORROR/ZOMBIES (1981) 92M D: Gary Sherman. *James Farentino, Melody Anderson, Dennis Redfield, Nancy Locke, Jack Albertson.*
This spooky undead horror mystery starts off slow but turns into a really excellent and unique zombie film. Set in a small seaside town reminiscent of *The Fog*, *Dead and Buried* has an equally creepy atmosphere, more like '30s horror than other films of the early '80s. That and some nice gore are what sets it apart. It's surprisingly good and a great creepy spookfest. —*T. S.*

DEAD HATE THE LIVING, THE L: HORROR/ZOMBIES (1999) 90M D: Dave Parker. *Jamie Donahue, Brett Beardslee, Eric Clawson, Wendy Speake.*
The idea isn't new by any means: low-budget horror filmmakers tempt fate while shooting in an abandoned hospital and become the victims in a real monster mash when they inadvertently activate the portal to a demon dimension. But if the plot echoes every made-for-video chiller of the past decade, and the gimmick is affectionately cribbed from *Phantasm*, writer/director Parker marries his love of the genre with genuine style, surprisingly competent performances, and cool zombie makeup. The film is chock full of references to cult Italian horror director Lucio Fulci (the final image even echoes his classic *The Beyond*) and is awash in bright, artificial colors like a Dario Argento film. Think of *Scream* for the zombie crowd: not particularly scary, but accomplished, cool, clever, and made with as much confidence as passion. —*S. A.*

DEAD HEAT L: SCIENCE FICTION/SCIENCE FICTION (1988) 86M D: Mark Goldblatt. *Vincent Price, Treat Williams, Joe Piscopo.*
If you ever wanted to see Williams turn into a zombie, this film is for you. However, if you expect him to be funny while delivering a bunch of one-liners and badly written jokes to his sidekick, Piscopo, you are expecting too much. Williams and Piscopo play a couple of police officers investigating a series of robberies. They quickly find that the robbers are the living dead—dead criminals brought back to life to perform more crimes. When Williams gets killed he too is revived, and for the rest of the film they try to get to the bottom of the strange case. Is it a comedy? Is it horror? It's neither. Price is thoroughly wasted as the evil professor. —*N. J.*

DEAD ZONE, THE—THE COMPLETE FIRST SEASON L: PSYCHOTRONIC/KING, STEPHEN (2002) 11 hours D: Robert Lieberman, others. *Anthony Michael Hall, David Ogden Stiers, Sean Patrick Flanery, Nicole de Boer, Chris Bruno, John L. Adams.*
Adapted from Stephen King's book, the series is both true to the original story and fairly original itself. An engaged schoolteacher suffers injuries in a car accident that put him in a coma for six years. When he finally awakens, he finds his fiancée married to another man, then discovers that with a single touch he can see things from the past, present, or future. The first few episodes follow the book closely, but then the series departs to cover new ground. Best is the unexpected story arc, extracted from the novel, of up-and-coming politician Greg Stillson, whom the world sees as a breath of fresh air and Johnny sees as a dangerous threat to all humanity. The characters are well-developed and interesting, many far more complex and honest than most shows would bother to make them. While there are predictable stories from time to time, I often cannot guess what will happen. Most refreshing! —*M. N.*

DEADBEAT AT DAWN L: PSYCHOTRONIC/FILM THREAT (1990) 80M D: Jim van Bebber. *Jim van Bebber, Paul Harper, Ric Walker, Marc Pitman, Megan Murphy.* This action-packed scuzzball revenge thriller, produced on a minuscule budget, is a brutal throwback to '70s drive-in filmmaking at its most demented. Van Bebber not only wrote, directed, and produced this movie, but also stars as Goose, a disenfranchised gang member who wants to quit the thug life and spend more time with his woman. His girlfriend is brutally murdered with a couple of golf clubs and, after romantically dumping her body in a trash compactor, Goose is hell-bent for unmerciful vengeance. There's enough blood and gore to rival *The Street Fighter* (throats ripped out, heads cut off, etc.), and the frequent stunt work is absolutely nerve-wracking, especially since van Bebber performs them himself with ballsy abandon. He jumps on moving trains, scales buildings, and beats the shit out of lots of people. This impressive feature-length 16mm debut ends with a lengthy showdown between the scruffy badass (who takes a lot of abuse) and his former gang, culminating in a tough, unflinching finale. —*S. H.*

DEATHDREAM L: HORROR/ZOMBIES (1972) 98M D: Bob Clark. *Richard Backus, Lynn Carlin, John Marley.* *Deathdream,* Clark's (*Black Christmas*) grim suburban chiller, may be one of the most shamefully neglected classics of '70s horror. An anti–Vietnam War allegory depicting the collapse of the American family ideal, this is also a genuinely unique and effective zombie movie, which stars Marley and Carlin as a dissolving married couple (much like the couple they portrayed in John Cassavetes's *Faces* six years earlier). When the Brooks' son Andy returns home following the army's announcement of his death overseas, his grieving family is happy to disregard the bad news as a government error. But Andy's distant behavior grows stranger and local residents start showing up mutilated and gnawed. What could (and should) have been an average low-rent splatter film is elevated by engaging dialogue and amazing acting from all cast members. Backus as zombie veteran Andy is the most transfixing, and his solid performance makes the film's climax an unexpected palpitater. Also released as *Dead of Night, The Night Andy Came Home, Nightwalk, The Veteran,* and *Whispers.* —*Z. C.*

DEATH MACHINE L: SCIENCE FICTION/SCIENCE FICTION (1994) 120M D: Steve Norrington. *Brad Dourif, Ely Pouget, William Hootkins.* Low-budget, badly acted tale of a killer robot loose in a corporate headquarters. With some attempt at *Robocop*-style futurism and the occasional nice visual, there are vague signs of the much more skilled direction Norrington would bring to his next film, *Blade.* But the only really interesting part in *Death Machine* is the robot itself—it is no surprise that the director's previous job was in special effects. Watch for characters named after famous horror directors John Carpenter, Sam Raimi, and "Scott Ridley" (and Dourif's character "Jack Dante" may be named after Joe Dante). Norrington's third film, *The Last Minute,* is a semiautobiographical fantasy partly based on the time when he was making *Death Machine.* —*B. T.*

DEATHROW GAMESHOW L: HORROR/STALKERS (1987) 78M D: Mark Pirro. *John McCafferty, Robin Blythe, Beano, Mark Lasky, Darwyn Carson, Debra Lamb.* This is a one-joke movie that can be summed up by its title. With a plot very similar to *The Running Man* yet nowhere near the budget, *Deathrow Gameshow* is a television show where the contestants are convicts playing inept games to win their freedom or (more likely) face the electric chair. McCafferty plays the host who is being hunted by the mob. But the plot is just an excuse to show death row convicts fry after being exploited on television. —*N. J.*

DEATHSPORT L: SCIENCE FICTION/SCIENCE FICTION (1978) 82M D: Allan Arkush, Henry Suso. *David Carradine, Claudia Jennings, Richard Lynch.* Less a sequel than a quick attempt to cash in on the success of *Death Race 2000,* this energetic but silly knock-off, set a thousand years into a barbaric future, stars Carradine as a freedom-loving, motorcycle-riding "Desert Ranger" and B-movie goddess Jennings as a renegade warrior. Both are captured by bad guy Lynch and forced to battle it out in moto-gladiatorial battles to the death. *Rock and Roll High School*'s Arkush codirects with Nicholas Niciphor (working under the pseudonym Henry Suso), and word has it producer Roger Corman tinkered with it a bit too (like maybe adding Jennings's bizarre nude romp in a dream-sequence-style chamber of tortures?). —*S. A.*

DEATHWATCH L: HORROR/DEMONS (2002) 94M D: Michael J. Bassett. *Laurence Fox, Andy Serkis, Rúaidhrí Conroy, Jamie Bell.* Continuing the recent trend of crossing action with horror, *Deathwatch* is about a group of WWI soldiers who stumble upon an enemy trench in the midst of a thick fog after their company is attacked and mostly decimated. They take control of the trench and are ordered to hold their position. But there is something evil in the trench. First-time director Bassett does well, creating a feeling of dread and developing an ominous presence. Though the atmosphere is excellent, the dialogue and acting aren't. Fortunately that doesn't weigh down the film that badly. *Deathwatch* has more in common with the war-themed spookery of *Devil's Backbone* than a gory action romp like *Dog Soldiers.* Its creative exploration of the psychological horrors of war make for a very satisfying movie, if not an entirely original or masterful one. —*T. S.*

DEEP BLUE SEA L: VAOWG/VAOWG (1999) 105M D: Renny Harlin. *Samuel L. Jackson, Saffron Burrows, Thomas Jane, LL Cool J, Michael Rapaport, Stellan Skarsgård.* For the most part this is exactly the crap you'd expect when you know you're about to watch a movie about scientists who accidentally unleash, uh, superintelligent sharks. But there are a couple of unusual touches that make it special. The first is a brilliant bit of misdirection that I cannot in good conscience give away. The other is LL Cool J, who plays the ship's wisecracking cook. You know right away he's going to be the first guy eaten by a supershark, and right away he encounters one. But somehow he escapes. And then he sees a shark again, and escapes again. It seems like for the first half of the movie this sidekick character is fighting off the sharks repeatedly while the scientist heroes don't even know what's going on. It's like if by accident the lawyer in *Jurassic Park* got off the toilet just in time and turned into a fearless dino killer. —*B. T.*

DELIRIUM: PHOTOS OF GIOIA L: HORROR/GIALLO (ITALIAN HORROR) (1987) 94M D: Lamberto Bava. *Serena Grandi, Daria Nicolodi, Capucine, Katerine Michelsen.* Bava's sex-and-psychos thriller is right out the Dario Argento school: beautiful naked women are sadistically murdered to a screeching electronic rock score (by Bava regular Simon Boswell). Grandi (the "Dolly Parton of Italy") plays former centerfold turned flesh magazine magnate Gioia (renamed Gloria for the English dub), who is stalked by an insane fan who kills all the models in her magazine and sends her photos of their corpses posed in front of giant posters of her. Bava, son of *giallo* godfather Mario Bava, went into the family business with more eagerness than elegance; this is hardly his best work but it has a few deliriously weird images (love the giant eyeball head!) amid the flesh feast. —*S. A.*

DELUGE L: VAOWG/VAOWG (1933) 70M D: Felix E. Feist. *Sidney Blackmer, Peggy Shannon, Lois Wilson, Fred Kohler, Matt Moore, Lane Chandler.* A storm whips up. An eclipse sets off an earthquake. A tidal wave crushes the coast. Within minutes the world is sanded down to ground zero. For a while we only hear it on the radio, an eerily effective way of isolating us as communications break down, but a mere fifteen minutes into the film the money shot gives us New York shaken to rubble and washed away in a tidal wave. It's a pure survivalist melodrama after that, with civilization as we know it destroyed and a handful of survivors battling out the mating priorities. Even the ultimate message of hope can't erase the genuinely disturbing moments—as when we glimpse the broken body of a girl used and discarded by a roving band of marauders. Note: Though it is an American film, the only surviving print is dubbed in Italian. The Italian dialogue is slightly disconcerting, but the subtitles are excellent. —*S. A.*

DEMON KNIGHT (AKA **TALES FROM THE CRYPT PRESENTS: DEMON KNIGHT**) L: HORROR TV/HORROR TV (1994) 92M D: Gilbert Alder, Ernest R. Dickerson. *Brenda Bakke, Jada Pinkett Smith, CCH Pounder, Bill Sadler, Billy Zane.* Enlivened by special effects and buoyed by an entertaining performance from Zane, *Demon Knight* is far better than it should be. The first in a supposed series based on the cable horror show—the series only lasted two films—it tells the tale of a group of strangers battling a siege of demons. As the demons' leader, Zane clearly had free reign in his performance, and he responds by taking it in every possible direction at once. (His disgusted reaction to the cowboy getup he wears as a disguise is especially good.) Meanwhile, the demons themselves are satisfyingly disturbing and the cast is pleasantly enthusiastic. This one's worth a look. —*T. P.*

DEMON SEED L: SCIENCE FICTION/SCIENCE FICTION (1977) 94M D: Donald Cammell. *Julie Christie, Fritz Weaver, Gerrit Graham.* In line with *Rosemary's Baby, The Exorcist, The Omen,* and *The Entity,* Cammell's take on single motherhood and demonic children also crosses over into science fictional fear, affirming its unique place in a niche genre. Proteus, the computer son of Fritz Weaver, has gained his own intelligence and he wants a child. Luckily the good doctor's home is computer-automated and Proteus turns Christie's comfort pad into a combo torture chamber/love nest. After some haphazard wooing, Proteus and his machine accoutrements (a wheelchair with a robot arm) get down and dirty, complete with a Proteus-crafted metallic penis. Psychedelic images flicker on-screen and triangles multiply and the baby is yanked out and placed in the incubator. Most of the film is Christie being tortured and driven insane by Proteus. Shot in full frame, the film today works almost as well on TV, though you miss a butt-shot of Christie, a decapitation by a giant computer python, and Jordan Belson's enlarged computer visuals. —*S. R.*

DEMONS L: HORROR/EURO-HORROR (1985) 88M D: Lamberto Bava. *Nicoletta Elmi, Fiore Argento, Natasha Hovey, Urbano Barberini.* This little gem is produced by Italian-great Dario Argento and directed by Italian-great Mario Bava's son. Mario and Dario are said to be sworn enemies but Lamberto brings the two families together with this film. At a showing of a movie about killer demons, real demons manifest in the theater and begin killing the audience. The story is a lot of fun and works surprisingly well. The gore effects are decent, in some parts very good, but the real standout is the cinematography. The harsh reds of "reality" contrast with the ghoulish blues of the film-within-a-film. At the beginning of the colors help the audience easily distinguish between the real world and fantasy, but as the horror becomes a reality, the colors merge and violence pervades both worlds. This film is an effort worth applauding. Plus, the '80s music used in the soundtrack works perfectly. —*T. S.*

DENTIST, THE L: HORROR/MAD SCIENTISTS (1996) 93M D: Brian Yuzna. *Corbin Bernsen, Ken Foree, Linda Hoffman, Michael Stadvec.* Hold on to your dental chair! The dentist's wife has been sleeping with the pool maintenance man and now he's furious. He is also completely insane, which is the only way to explain this film. Through psychologically deranged first-person perspectives, we get to see dentist Feinstone (Bernsen) torture a cadre of annoying customers at work, whack a few of his very own employees, and fix the overbite of a federal tax collector in a horrible fashion. But hold on for the finale—to the soothing strains of Puccini we see the dentist employ an operating room especially made for the purpose of torturing his own wife, which of course he does with great conviction and no Novocain. —*N. J.*

DENTIST II, THE L: HORROR/MAD SCIENTISTS (1998) 98M D: Brian Yuzna. *Corbin Bernsen, Jillian McWhirter, Linda Hoffman.* In this follow-up to *The Dentist,* Bernsen returns to a familiar role and an even more familiar plot. Out on parole, Dr. Feinstone does his best to maintain his clientele while living with his ailing and manipulative mother. The bodies pile up, each displaying chillingly vengeful dental work. We find in the end that the teeth of this plot belong in full to *Psycho.* Good for a cheap laugh but only if you enjoyed the humor of the first film. —*N. J.*

DEVIL BAT, THE L: CLASSIC HORROR/CLASSIC HORROR (1940) 68M D: Jean Yarbrough. *Dave O'Brien, Bela Lugosi.* Lugosi is suitably grandiloquent as a bitter cosmetics inventor who turns his latest creation, an aromatic aftershave, into bait for a vulture-sized bat he breeds with the magic of electricity (that flashes through his workshop like a Frankenstein laboratory). Smirking as he hands off trial bottles to his victims, the moral is clear: beware of free samples. It's all fairly ridiculous, but Lugosi's florid performance and the antics of smart-talking newsman O'Brien invest the silly story with energy, and giant rubber bats are always good for a cheesy amusement park thrill. —*S. A.*

DEVIL'S RAIN L: HORROR/WITCHES & WARLOCKS (1975) 85M D: Robert Fuest. *Ernest Borgnine, Ida Lupino, William Shatner, Keenan Wynn, Eddie Albert.* This film effectively combines the general story of *Rosemary's Baby* and the kind of characterizations used on *The Twilight Zone,* while using the English humor and sensibilities of director Fuest (known for *The Abominable Dr. Phibes*). Shatner plays the innocent protagonist who slowly realizes that nearly everyone he knows is involved in a large satanic cult. Naturally they try to pull him

into their ranks. Borgnine is absolutely brilliant as the cult leader; and don't miss the indoctrination of a very young John Travolta. The stunning violence at the end is sure to thoroughly amuse. —*N. J.*

DIE! DIE! MY DARLING L: HORROR/HAMMER FILMS (1965) 97M D: Silvio Narizzano. *Yootha Joyce, Donald Sutherland, Maurice Kaufmann, Peter Vaughan, Stefanie Powers, Tallulah Bankhead.* Bankhead's dotty, Bible-mad matriarch whose eccentricities turn to fanaticism is right out of the *Whatever Happened to Baby Jane* gallery of grotesques in this Hammer Films thriller. Modern, liberated woman Powers goes to visit the mother of her deceased fiancé and finds herself a long-term guest in a decaying old mansion, a bit of American Southern Gothic in the British countryside. Vaughan is her sleazy handyman and Sutherland her idiot odd jobber manipulated into doing the dirty work. Bankhead pulls out all stops as the former stage actress twisted into fundamentalist severity by a terrible secret in her own dark past she dare not confront. It was her last screen performance and she chews it up with the relish of an old scene stealer. Richard Matheson's screenplay (adapted from the novel *Nightmare* by Anne Blaisdell) owes inspiration to *Psycho* and *Baby Jane* but manages to stand on its own. —*S. A.*

DISTANT THUNDER, A L: VAOWG/CHRISTPLOITATION (1977) 77M D: Donald W. Thompson. *Sandy Christen, Patty Dunning, Sally Johnson.* This film is a sequel to *A Thief in the Night,* in which the Rapture happens halfway through. You may ask how Christians could make a sequel to a film when the Rapture has already happened. The answer is, make it a lot more violent. There are car crashes, shootings, and even a beheading. The plot concerns a group of people who have become believers since the Rapture and who are running from Unite, the organized minions of Satan. Their Christian leader explains they are all too late to get to heaven because they all missed the boat— they were all "left behind." They can believe in God all they want, and they do, but they won't get to Heaven. And so you may ask, what's the point? The point is to scare you into becoming a believer. —*N. J.*

DISTURBING BEHAVIOR L: SCIENCE FICTION/SCIENCE FICTION (1998) 84M D: David Nutter. *Nick Stahl, Katie Holmes, James Marsden.* The first line in this movie is "Self-mutilate this, Fluid Boy," and it gets more awkward from there. Screenwriter Scott Rosenberg (*Con Air, Beautiful Girls*) specializes in this kind of painfully self-conscious dialogue that sounds like Joss Whedon lines fed through some weird Internet translator to turn them into gibberish. Nutter, a director from *The X-Files,* does what he can with the paranoid *Twilight Zone*–style premise, but it is impossible for any teen movie to transcend a script this forced. —*B. T.*

DOG SOLDIERS L: HORROR/WEREWOLVES (2002) 104M D: Neil Marshall. *Emma Cleasby, Sean Pertwee, Liam Cunningham, Kevin McKidd.* When a routine training mission for a group of British soldiers turns into a lycanthropic nightmare, they barricade themselves in a remote farmhouse and try to live through the full moon. Boasting equal parts action and suspense, *Dog Soldiers* has taken the American trend of making horror movies more action-packed and actually done the concept justice. Here, it actually makes sense. The men are soldiers and they are fighting their enemy. It just so happens their enemy is a family of supernatural beasts. The filmmakers definitely deserve kudos for making the film on their own, after the Film Council subsidiary in their region refused to support it. A somewhat unique take on werewolves, and horror in general, *Dog Soldiers* succeeds where others fail, offering a healthy dose of blood and guts while it's at it. —*T. S.*

DON'T LOOK IN THE BASEMENT! L: HORROR/STALKERS (1973) 95M D: S. F. Brownrigg. *Michael Harvey, Anne MacAdams, Rosie Holotik, Gene Ross, Betty Chandler.* Allowed to enact their fantasies, the patients end up running the asylum when "The Judge" (Ross) takes an axe to Dr. Stephens's (Harvey) head. When the incident is discovered by Dr. Masters (MacAdams), it is quietly "forgotten." The gore scenes are a bit laughable at times, from the first axe blow to a tongue getting ripped out to the over-the-top finale, but it all adds up to more Brownriggian fun. This low-budget madhouse is for those who enjoy sweaty close-ups of screaming, deranged faces and watching marginal actors explore their craft. Recommended for devotees of *Thundercrack!* Not as much sex here, but plenty of insanity! —*S. R.*

DR. BUTCHER M.D. (AKA **ZOMBIE HOLOCAUST**) L: HORROR/CANNIBALS (1979) 80M D: Frank Martin. *Ian McCulloch, Alexandra Delli Colli, Peter O'Neal.* Aquarius Pictures, a grindhouse distribution company, acquired an Italian Zombie/Cannibal movie entitled *Zombie Holocaust*, added a brief, unrelated graveyard prologue, replaced a "serious" soundtrack with a delightfully annoying analogue synth score, developed a misleading ad campaign about a "medical deviate," and, unfortunately, removed some gratuitous nudity. It's another post–*Dawn of the Dead* spaghetti gore epic and this time the plot is basically a combination of *Zombie* and *Cannibal Holocaust* with a dash of *Slave of the Cannibal God*. The zombies versus cannibals premise isn't fully realized, but this low-rent gore epic is an endearing example of gut-spilling Italian horror splatter cinema. Investigating some mysterious mutilations at a city hospital, an expedition led by McCulloch (*Zombie*) travels to a Pacific island and ends up

battling hungry cannibals, the occasional zombie, and the film's titular doctor who has encouraged the cannibalism as a cover for his corpse re-animating experiments. Delli Colli gets bucknaked and is worshipped by the cannibals, who soon turn the tables on the sick doctor and chow down on his deviant ass (and guts). —*S. H.*

DR. PHIBES RISES AGAIN L: HORROR/MAD SCIENTISTS (1972) 89M D: Robert Fuest. *Hugh Griffith, Vincent Price, Robert Quarry, Valli Kemp.* Just as the title promises, Dr. Phibes rises again and sets out to reanimate his dead wife by finding the mysterious river of life, supposedly somewhere in Egypt. But as he rises up on his magnificent organ, again entering the world of the living, he discovers his house has been destroyed and his scrolls stolen. So before he can achieve immortal life, he must exact revenge on those responsible. It's not as good as the first, but it has a lot going for it. The design, photography, and score are all excellent and Price is just as ominous as before. However, the story is not as well planned, even though it does carry on many of the themes brought up in the original. The main thing that compromises this film is the humor, which is much more obvious and a whole lot dumber. Overall, though, the second *Phibes* is a fantastic picture complete with all the imaginative deaths and Gothic leanings of the first. —*T. S.*

DR. TERROR'S HOUSE OF HORRORS L: CLASSIC HORROR/CLASSIC HORROR (1965)105M D: Freddie Francis. *Donald Sutherland, Neil McCallum, Peter Cushing, Roy Castle, Christopher Lee.* This is a first-rate piece of anthology horror. The individual stories are all excellent, but what usually makes or breaks an anthology piece is the connecting framework. Here, it couldn't be better. Five strangers meet on a train and learn how they will (or already have?) died. As Hammer Horror's standards began to slip, Amicus Productions began to put out some great horror flicks. This is one of the best. —*T. S.*

DR. WHO AND THE DALEKS L: SCIENCE FICTION/DR. WHO FILMS (1965) 83M D: Gordon Flemyng. *Peter Cushing, Roy Castle, Jennie Linden, Roberta Tovey.* This is the very first Dr. Who film, with Cushing playing the amiable doctor. The whole world of Dr. Who is remarkably well established, with tongue firmly in cheek as much as its science is firmly in fiction. Dr. Who's mode of transportation is his phone booth, which here is a very large blue model rather than the familiar red one in the TV series. With his granddaughters and their friend Ian, Dr. Who is inadvertently taken to the planet Skaro where they find a race of humanoids being brutalized by the evil Daleks. The Daleks look like a bad replica of R2D2, but instead of beeping some computer language they deliberately butcher English with a monotone and brutally arrhythmic execution. In contrast, the very suave Dr. Who vanquishes them, in part because of class, education, and of course sheer elegance. —*N. J.*

DR. WHO: CURSE OF FATAL DEATH L: SCIENCE FICTION /DR. WHO FILMS (1999) 62M D: John Henderson. *Jonathan Pryce, Rowan Atkinson, Richard E. Grant, Hugh Grant, Dave Chapman, Jim Broadbent.* When I played this in the store on a Friday night, I could have rented three copies of it. Even if you're not a fan of *Dr. Who*, this is a hysterical little parody. It boasts the acting prowess of Pryce, Atkinson, and Grant, among others. I watched this primarily because it is a spoof, one of my main film interests, but I thought it might be a little drab because I've never really enjoyed *Dr. Who* that much. But I was completely wrong; it's very cool. —*R. D.*

DRACULA (SPANISH VERSION) L: CLASSIC HORROR/ CLASSIC HORROR (1931) 104M D: George Melford, Enrique Tovar. *Lupita Tovar, Eduardo Arozamena, Pablo Álvarez Rubio, Barry Norton, Carlos Villarías.* Shot concurrently with the 1931 version directed by Tod Browning, this version uses the same sets and script as Browning's but actually improves on his visual ideas. Since the Spanish film always shot after the English, the crew was able to build upon Browning's ideas and execute them even better. What results is truly a marvel to behold. While Browning's version starred the incomparable and irreplaceable Bela Lugosi, this version stars Villarías, who is nowhere near as enthralling. It's an odd, beautiful horror classic. —*T. S.*

DRACULA A.D. 1972 L: HORROR/HAMMER FILMS (1972) 100M D: Alan Gibson. *Peter Cushing, Stephanie Beacham, Marsha Hunt, Caroline Munro, Christopher Lee.* When Dracula is brought back from the dead in London in the '70s, he goes after Van Helsing's descendents. Cushing makes his glorious return to the series playing the modern version of Van Helsing. The film tries to be serious but it's far too ridiculous to work as authentic Gothic horror. Unlike its predecessors, it incorporates contemporary sensibilities that only serve to detract from the atmosphere. But the film's strength is in its prowess for groovy fun. The movie never drags and is full of unintentional laughs. Terrible music and absurd sets and costumes make this an altogether different kind of period horror. —*T. S.*

DRACULA HAS RISEN FROM THE GRAVE L: HORROR/ HAMMER FILMS (1968) 92M D: Freddie Francis. *Christopher Lee, Rupert Davies, Michael Ripper, Veronica Carlson.* Hammer's third Dracula film is not only the best of the series, but the best Hammer film ever. Dracula awakens to find his castle has been exorcised. Expelled from his home, he sets out for revenge against the Monsignor who placed the spell, making his niece his undead bride. Laced with religious imagery and themes of redemption and damnation, this visually exquisite film fills the screen with beautiful compositions and

rich, Gothic colors. Lee is at the top of his game, doing the best Dracula of his career, and Carlson exudes an otherworldly beauty, wafting across rooftops like a female reincarnation of Caligari's Caesar. The plot is in perfect Hammer-revisionist style, maintaining many features of the original Dracula story but pulling it in strange new directions. The pacing is perfect as well, always keeping the action suspenseful. And in the end, when Dracula is finally impaled on a giant golden crucifix, the film's genius is cemented into your memory with a marvelous splatter of bright red Hammer blood. —*T. S.*

DRACULA'S DAUGHTER L: CLASSIC HORROR/CLASSIC HORROR (1936) 71M D: Lambert Hillyer. *Irving Pichel, Edward Van Sloan, Gloria Holden, Marguerite Churchill, Otto Kruger.* The first sequel to Tod Browning's hit doesn't feature Bela Lugosi at all, though it does open on the last scene from *Dracula*. This sleek, stylish horror picture then turns into the tale of his aristocratic "daughter" (the continental Holden), who is seeking a cure for her affliction. The cut-rate knockoff is actually quite elegant, even if it too often loses the mood in an overly busy plot. Holden's haunted face and willowy body cut a striking figure and Pichel's offbeat servant is like an American gangster with the breeding of a European aristocrat: thick, thuggish, but always proper. Van Sloan reprises his role as Van Helsing. —*S. A.*

DRAGON BLUE L: JAPANESE HORROR/JAPANESE HORROR (1996) 80M D: Takuya Wada. *Keiji Mutoh, Hiroko Tanaka.* "Why does this always happen to me?" whines apprentice exorcist Tanaka, a teenage girl who battles a demon, meets a ghostly monk, discovers that the blood of the dragon clan runs through her veins, and harnesses the powers of a demon hunter. And that's just in the first scene. Later on she takes on an ancient sea demon (which has an unerring gift for finding topless women), and flirts (in her virginal way) with a burly, chivalrous detective. It's cheaply made, completely absurd, and packed with bloody bodies and gratuitous nudity, but under the carnage is the gee-whiz innocence of early '60s Japanese monster movies and a very cool rubber demon suit. —*S. A.*

DREAMCATCHER L: PSYCHOTRONIC /KING, STEPHEN (2003) 134M D: Lawrence Kasdan. *Tom Sizemore, Morgan Freeman, Thomas Jane, Jason Lee, Timothy Olyphant, Damian Lewis.* Stephen King put all his stories into a blender and poured out this alien invasion thriller which, against all odds, Kasdan and screenwriter William Goldman (who should know better) adapted into a big-budget feature film. Think an *X-Files* remake of *Stand By Me* spun into a junior league *The Stand* with an alien invasion standing in for Satan. Better yet, don't. Freeman gets top billing as a maniacal colonel whose scorched-earth policy leaves no infected human alive, but the real stars are Jane as the good-looking hero and Lewis (*Band of Brothers*), whose demonic grin and British accent are all we need to know that he has been possessed by a nasty extraterrestrial. The aliens are impressive, in a gooey, grotesque sort of way, but are simply absurd creations with properties that belong to the realm of magic rather than extraterrestrial evolution. And the less said about Donny Wahlberg's retarded messiah Duddtz the better. —*S. A.*

DREAMSCAPE L: SCIENCE FICTION/SCIENCE FICTION (1984) 99M D: Joseph Ruben. *Dennis Quaid, Max von Sydow, Christopher Plummer, Eddie Albert.* You have to love any film that casts Albert as the president of the United States. Quaid plays a young psychic who, with the help of some doctors, learns how to enter people's dreams. The noble goal is to save people from their nightmares, but of course some evil men intervene and try using the technique for themselves. These men conspire to enter the head of Albert in order to trigger doomsday. Quaid is the only one able to stave off this threat and save the planet. However, it's the great special effects that are the only thing to save this film. —*N. J.*

EARTHQUAKE L: VAOWG/VAOWG (1974) 123M D: Mark Robson. *George Kennedy, Ava Gardner, Lorne Greene, Genevieve Bujold, Richard Roundtree, Charlton Heston.* In 1972 *The Poseidon Adventure* cracked open a whole wave of epic disaster films, and *Earthquake* was a predictable follow-up. Similar to *The Towering Inferno*, which was released the same year, all that was needed was an all-star cast and a deathtrap in which to put them. In this case the deathtrap is Los Angeles with a giant impending earthquake. It's a good thing the effects are top-notch because the script is extraordinarily empty. This film won the Oscar for Best Visual Effects while *The Towering Inferno* won for Best Cinematography, so at least in '74 people got a good visual dose of disaster. —*N. J.*

EBIRAH, HORROR OF THE DEEP (AKA **GODZILLA VS THE SEA MONSTER**) L: JAPANESE SCIENCE FICTION /GODZILLA (1966) 87M D: Jun Fukuda. *Toru Watanabe, Akira Takarada, Kumi Mizuno.* After the previous epic science fiction Godzilla films, *Ebirah* is quite a change of pace. Along with a new director, the location was switched from the city to the jungle, limiting the scope of monster destruction. It's an odd but enjoyable adventure originally intended to star Toho's King Kong. This casting change is clearly evident in Godzilla's behavior, which is much more typical of the giant ape than the mutant lizard. He lives on a Pacific island, likes jungle girls (Mizuno), and gets supercharged by lightning. In a plot clearly influenced by James Bond films, a sinister group is making nuclear bombs at a secret base protected by a giant lobster called Ebirah. A group of castaways uncovers the nefarious plot and awakens a slumbering Godzilla, who tears apart the sea monster and

stomps the bad guy's headquarters. Mothra makes a brief appearance at the end and saves the natives and castaways. —*S. H.*

EEGAH! L: CLASSIC HORROR/CLASSIC HORROR (1962) 93M D: Nicholas Merriwether (aka Arch Hall Sr.). *Richard Kiel, Marilyn Manning, Arch Hall Jr.* Kiel plays Eegah, a lovesick caveman who just wants to fit in with the local teenagers. Roxy (Manning) is the object of Eegah's primitive lust. She has the misfortune of discovering Eegah in a cave. Feeling sorry for him, she befriends the big dope and shaves his beard. As with every other "I discovered a caveman" movie, she should've left him alone. Directed by Merriwether (aka Arch Hall Sr.) and costarring William Watters (aka Arch Hall Sr.) and Arch Hall Jr. (aka son of Arch Hall Sr.), this Z-grade drive-in classic was one of several attempts by Senior to make Junior into a teen idol. It didn't work. *Eegah*, like many other nobudget films, was shot without sound to save money, so Senior dubbed in all the male voices (except Junior's) himself. Another psychotronic pioneer, Ray Dennis Stockler in a cameo, gets thrown into a pool by Eegah. Is it any wonder Eegah can't make any friends? —*P. M.*

EIGHT LEGGED FREAKS L: VAOWG/VAOWG (2002) 99M D: Ellory Elkayem. *David Arquette, Kari Wuhrer, Scott Terra, Scarlett Johansson, Doug E. Doug.* This B-movie-and-proud-of-it thrill ride is a knowing, high-spirited updating of the old giant insect rampage flicks that doesn't so much make fun of the classic genre as have fun with it. Community black sheep Arquette comes home just in time to take on a furry army of Volkswagen-sized spiders with single mom Sheriff Wuhrer, whom he tries to romance between the arachnid attacks. Arquette's trademark twitches and spastic energy are under tight reign but there's still something askew about the guy, which fits the off-center humor and knowing attitude in director Elkayem's on-the-edge-of-spoof style. This guns-and-gooey-green-spider-guts mutant creature feature balances funhouse roller-coaster rides, winking in-jokes, and creepy-crawly menaces gone large. —*S. A.*

ELECTRIC DRAGON 80,000 VOLTS L: JAPANESE SCIENCE FICTION/JAPANESE SCIENCE FICTION (2001) 53M D: Sogo Ishii. *Masatoshi Nagase, Tadanobu Asano.* Easy comparisons to Shinya Tsukamoto's *Tetsuo: The Iron Man* can be made across the board, from the running time to the use of black and white, and from the low-budget production to the nihilistic undertones about society. Fans of *Tetsuo* will surely having a shockingly good time with this one as well. The plot is almost nonexistent, as pure style and imagery take front row here. The film follows two men obsessed with electricity, and their final meeting on a rooftop that opens up the sky in static white. One is a leather-clad rocker (Asano), who makes beautiful noise on his homemade guitar and is charged with electricity after climbing a power line tower. The other is an electronics madman who wears half a Buddha mask and creates deadly weapons for his energetic vigilantism. His next target is the guitar-slinging, violently charged rocker, who is unaware of his nearly limitless capability. Only a showdown between them will unleash the voltage within. —*R. M.*

EMPIRE OF THE ANTS L: VAOWG/VAOWG (1977) 89M D: Bert I. Gordon. *Joan Collins, Robert Lansing, John Carson, Albert Salmi, Jacqueline Scott.* Mr. B.I.G.'s last giant monster movie was also one of American International Pictures's last films before they became Filmways and eventually Orion. Like Gordon's previous film, *Food of the Gods*, this is another very loose adaptation of an H. G. Wells novel. Barrels of (clearly marked) radioactive waste are dumped off the Florida coast, causing the local ant population to get really big. A sleazy, bitchy real estate agent (a pre-*Dynasty* Collins) boats some suckers into a housing development in the Everglades and soon the cast of TV veterans becomes bug food. It's up to the heroic captain (Lansing) to save the day. Unfortunately, all the local humans have already become slaves to the sugar-loving ant queen. The survivors have to fight man and mandible to escape the colony and keep their individuality intact. The special effects consist mostly of rear screen projection of magnified ants as well as some sub-*Them* ant head mock-ups. By no means a good movie, I saw *Empire* at my local drive-in (on a double bill with William Castle's *Bug*) and I've had a soft spot for its cheesy effects and crappy acting ever since. —*S. H.*

EMPIRE STRIKES BACK, THE L: SCIENCE FICTION/STAR WARS (1980) 124M D: Irvin Kershner. *Billy Dee Williams, Harrison Ford, Mark Hamill, Carrie Fisher, Frank Oz, Alec Guinness.* Even those who mock the "gee-golly" quality of *Star Wars* like *Empire*, its darker, moodier sequel. Luke Skywalker sheds his youthful pluck and treads, with Yoda on his back, into adulthood. Darth Vader has some sinister plans for the burgeoning Jedi, so he sends out some evil Force vibes and the coolest group of bounty hunters around (don't you just love Vader having to tell Boba Fett, "No disintegrations!"). Luke finds he's not as prepared as he thought to deal with the Dark Side and ends up the worse for wear. Meanwhile, Han and Leia have gotten past their "insulting you to show I care" phase and are inching toward love when a hunk of carbonite stops the romance short. *Empire* is unsettling, which is exactly what some people needed from the franchise. —*J. K.*

EQUILIBRIUM L: SCIENCE FICTION/SCIENCE FICTION (2002) 107M D: Kurt Wimmer. *Christian Bale, Emily Watson, Taye Diggs, Angus MacFadyen, Sean Bean.* This film's basic premise pulls from the great dystopian novels of the twentieth century, gladly borrowing from *A Brave New World, Fahrenheit 451, 1984*, and fascist politics to bring this dark tale of oppression to light. John Preston (Bale) is a government soldier who seeks those who would be guilty of "sense crimes," such as possessing thought-provoking contraband (books and music). A mind-numbing drug controls all of society, and when Preston misses a dose, he awakens to the world of feelings. He begins a double life, still a soldier by day but seeking the company of the resistance at night. The film itself is more thought-oriented, although the action scenes sprinkled over the course of the film are intense and should please anyone looking for a Tai Chi–inspired gunplay. Also of interest is that *Equilibrium* was produced by Miramax, itself guilty of altering both domestic and foreign films to appeal to the lowest common denominator and avoiding any thought-provoking or other unwanted feelings. —*R. M.*

ESCAPE FROM THE PLANET OF THE APES L: VAOWG/ PLANET OF THE APES (1971) 98M D: Don Taylor. *Kim Hunter, Ricardo Montalban, Bradford Dillman, Roddy McDowall, Sal Mineo.* Cornelius (McDowall) and Zelda (Hunter) make this third installment of the *Planet of the Apes* series well worth watching. They are two chimpanzee scientists who somehow break the time barrier, transporting themselves back to 1970s New York. The social commentary becomes quite humorous as here the themes of the first film are completely inverted. The novelty of speaking apes becomes the toast of New York society, and in the midst of this attention Zelda announces she is pregnant. Naturally this concerns government officials, who originally wanted her to be sterilized, and the plot escalates to a tragic climax that naturally sets the stage for another sequel. —*N. J.*

EWOK ADVENTURE, THE L: SCIENCE FICTION/STAR WARS (1984) 96M D: John Korty. *Warwick Davis, Aubree Miller, Eric Walker, Debbie Lee Carrington, Tony Cox.* A humanoid family has crash-landed on "the forest moon of Endor" (does that mean Endor itself is a forest moon, or that this planet is the foresty moon of a planet called Endor? I just looked it up—it's the latter). The two bratty kids (Miller and Walker) wander off and the parents are kidnapped by a giant hairy troll that looks kind of like John Travolta in *Battlefield Earth*. The kids befriend Wicket and some other Ewoks, and a group of them go on a brave journey up some stairs and across a giant spider web to save the parents. There is a cool fight with a stop-motion warthog, but the giant spiders barely move and the other strange Endorian creatures you see are horses, llamas, a ferret, a mouse, a lizard, and a goat, which makes it hard not to think this might have actually been filmed here on Earth. I have no problem with Ewoks—I actually like them—but this story has little of the adventure promised by the title or its connection to the *Star Wars* universe. —*B. T.*

EWOKS: THE BATTLE FOR ENDOR L: SCIENCE FICTION/ STAR WARS (1985) 98M D: Jim Wheat, Ken Wheat. *Warwick Davis, Wilford Brimley, Aubree Miller, Sian Phillips.* This second TV movie spin-off of *Return of the Jedi* has a bit of a *Return to Oz* vibe, but with the cheap-ass feel of the *Planet of the Apes* TV series. Still, it's a huge improvement over *The Ewok Adventure.* The good new is most of the family from that film are killed off right away, leaving young Cindel (Miller) and Wicket (Davis) to team up with an old curmudgeon (Brimley) and a puppet creature even Wicket finds annoying. The bad news is Wicket now speaks some English. Together they fight off an army of Orc-like brutes and a sorceress (Phillips) who can turn into a bird. Unlike the first Ewok movie there are many special effects: people in costumes, stop-motion monsters, puppets, charmingly fake-looking blue screening, and even a charred corpse. At the end the humans tearfully fly away in a space ship, leaving their creature friends behind—sort of a reverse E.T. maneuver. One question: Shouldn't this be called *The Battle for a Moon of Endor*? Or did the Ewoks move to Endor proper since we last saw them? —*B.T.*

EXORCIST III, THE L: HORROR/DEMONS (1990) 110M D: William Peter Blatty. *George C. Scott, Brad Dourif, Nicol Williamson, Jason Miller, Ed Flanders.* Directed by Blatty, the man who wrote the story for the first *Exorcist* film, *The Exorcist III* has a compelling story and a great cast. Scott plays an inspector investigating random and ruthless murders that closely resemble the work of a particular psycho-killer who was executed the night of Linda Blair's exorcism. With such a plot the violence in this film becomes virtually unbridled, making it more like a suspense thriller than a paranormal horror film. But with Blatty's eerie dreamscapes and his surprise plot twists, this film will certainly please and frighten fans of the first movie. —*N.J.*

FALL OF THE HOUSE OF USHER, THE L: PSYCHOTRONIC/ POE, EDGAR ALLAN (1928) 66M D: Jean Epstein. *Marguerite Gance, Jean Debucourt.* Epstein's avant-garde silent classic takes unusual liberties with Poe, making Roderick and Madeleine Usher man and wife (which removes the suggestive perversity of father/daughter relations) and giving the picture a happy ending. In between is an atmospheric classic that becomes increasingly more surreal as Roderick buries his wife and faces the ominous storm that blows through the empty, decaying castle. A strange mix of Gothic design, modern austerity, expressionist angles, graceful camerawork, and surreal effects, it's one of the only films to apply the poetic impressionism of the French avant-garde to a feature-length narrative. The All Day Entertainment DVD is mastered from a 35mm preservation print featuring Rolande de Cande's 1970 score (adapted from medieval melodies) and English translations of the French intertitles spoken by Jean-Pierre Aumont. —*S.A.*

FANTASTIC VOYAGE L: CLASSIC SCIENCE FICTION /CLASSIC SCIENCE FICTION (1966) 100M D: Richard Fleischer. *Arthur Kennedy, Raquel Welch, Stephen Boyd, Donald Pleasence, Edmond O'Brien.* Truly stunning special effects make this film a spectacular visual feast. An important scientist rescued from behind the iron curtain is badly wounded and must be saved with experimental surgery. The most advanced technology in this stylized atomic age has it that the military can shrink a probe with a crew down to microscopic size but only for a short period of time. So once a team is gathered and put in a probe, it is shrunken, then injected into the subject and the fantastic voyage begins. Lots of obstacles await them on their journey, some of which are the natural defenses of the body itself. Good direction helps to keep this thin story together and a great cast makes the holes in the plot appear quite minuscule. —*N.J.*

FANTOM KILER L: HORROR/STALKERS (1998) 90M D: Trevor Barley (aka Roman Nowicki). *Eliza Borecka, Magda Szymborska, Katarzyna Zelnik, Andrej Jass.* Polish prostitutes are dying and who is targeting them? After a couple of naked, bloody bodies are investigated, the police angle is dropped and the point of view of two suspects is picked up. This turns women as dead objects into women as naked subjects to be stalked and killed. Terrible filmmaking and storytelling technique, but emotionally it works: you live through a range of emotions from disgust to fear to resignation from the viewpoint of the victims. Hokey and unrealistic, *Fantom Kiler* is as crude as porno and almost that explicit, but these sequences have the lurid coloring and design of 1940s pulp-novel covers and are compellingly choreographed and performed. Note: This is a fake Polish film with some Polish exteriors but shot largely inside a studio in England using Russian (and maybe Polish) models/actresses: then overdubbed into Russian. Two sequels follow. —*J.C.*

FARSCAPE: THE COMPLETE SEASON 1 L: SCIENCE FICTION/SCIENCE FICTION TV (1999) 1100M D: Pino Amenta, others. *Ben Browder, Lani John Tupu, Anthony Simcoe, Jonathan Hardy, Virginia Hey, Claudia Black.* Though created in part by Jim Henson Productions, this ain't no kiddie show! Young astronaut John Crichton is sucked through an open wormhole into the far reaches of space. He tumbles into the middle of a firefight between an escaping ship of criminals and the Peacekeepers. Dragged on board *Moya*, a living ship, Crichton finds himself in the hands of the fugitives and a captured Peacekeeper soldier. An uneasy alliance is struck among the ragtag group who, for better and for worse, are forced to rely on each other. And if that weren't enough, a dangerous Peacekeeper, Scorpius, discovers that Crichton possesses highly prized knowledge about wormholes, which must be extracted by any means. The first season starts off a bit rocky as this complex show struggles to stand upright, the first few shows alternating between really good and pretty lame. But by mid-season *Farscape* stabilizes and really takes flight. There are great characters, interesting alien worlds and beings, as well as excellent action, drama, humor, and pacing that will suck you in faster than a wormhole. —*M. N.*

FARSCAPE: THE COMPLETE SEASON 2 L: SCIENCE FICTION/SCIENCE FICTION TV (2000) 1110M D: Ian Barry, Brian Henson, others. *Anthony Simcoe, Jonathan Hardy, Ben Browder, Claudia Black, Virginia Hey, Lani John Tupu.* It just keeps getting better. Season two follows the many adventures of the living ship *Moya* and her passengers. *Moya* becomes pregnant and is going to give birth to a baby *Leviathan* ship, new crew members must settle in and earn their place, and they are still being pursued by the ruthless Scorpius. This season spends a little more time delving into the background of the characters, exploring who they are and who they are becoming. The show is marked by a growing romantic relationship between John and Aeryn, the unexpected "gift" given to John by Scorpius, and the discovery of D'Argo's son, resulting in a combination rescue/robbery. With a better grasp on the large cast and the clearer picture of the universe they live in, season two is better written, more exciting and interesting, and even more addictive than the first. Hang onto the handle bars, 'cause this ride is gonna get rough! —*M. N.*

FARSCAPE: THE COMPLETE SEASON 3 L: SCIENCE FICTION/SCIENCE FICTION TV (2001) 60M D: Brendan Maher, Catherine Millar, others. *Ben Browder, Lani John Tupu, Anthony Simcoe, Virginia Hey, Claudia Black, Jonathan Hardy.* Season three once again returns to rather rocky ground, with major cast changes and complications. The crew of *Moya* is split in half, with one group on *Moya* and the other on *Moya*'s child, *Talyn.* Alas, the crew on *Talyn* gets all the good stories and the crew on *Moya* gets the lamer, goofier stories. So once again, as in the beginning of the first season, a see-saw effect shifts every other show from one ship to the other, from good story to blah story. There blessedly are a few exceptions, and your mileage may vary. It's all worth it, though, for "Infinite Possibilities," a very dramatic story arc. The season comes to a very odd and unexpected end that felt ludicrously forced and unrealistic. The ride, my friends, is slowing down. —*M. N.*

FAT GUY GOES NUTZOID L: PSYCHOTRONIC/TROMA FILMS (1986) 85M D: John Golden. *Max Alexander, Doug Stone, John A. MacKay, Peter Linari, Tibor Feldman.* It happens to all of us. We see *The Toxic Avenger* when we're young, and we come to the conclusion that Troma films are hilarious. We

scour the mom and pop stores for anything with the Troma name on it, especially the ones with the really ridiculous titles. It takes us a while to figure out that most of what Troma releases is unwatchable garbage that they picked up from other filmmakers. This one is the most painful one of all. I cannot confirm this information, because I will not watch this movie again. But it was my impression as a young man that Troma had acquired a lame independent drama about young people taking an overweight retarded guy out for a night on the town, and renamed it *Fat Guy Goes Nutzoid.* It's funny that they did that, but it's not funny that some of us watched it. —*B. T.*

FEARDOTCOM L: HORROR/STALKERS (2002) 101M D: William Malone. *Stephen Rea, Natasha McElhone, Stephen Dorff.* Malone follows up his funhouse B-movie rip *House on Haunted Hill* with this darker serial killer thriller. A cop (Dorff) and a city health inspector (McElhone) become partners and ultimately lovers (despite a complete lack of screen chemistry) as they hunt an Internet-based psycho-killer (Rea). The story is confusing and confused, and the women-in-peril imagery crosses the line into pure sadism, but director Malone certainly has the look down. The jittery flash-cut imagery, the leaping narrative that jumps through the story in sudden cuts, the art direction in shades of gray, and the entire tech-noir look by way of Depression-era poverty is striking, to say the least. The construction has more character than the paper-thin heroes and villains. —*S. A.*

FIEND WITHOUT A FACE L: CLASSIC SCIENCE FICTION /CLASSIC SCIENCE FICTION (1958) 77M D: Arthur Crabtree. *Marshall Thompson, Michael Balfour, Terry Kilburn.* Crabtree's atomic twist on *Forbidden Planet* is a dry little British chiller until its gonzo climax. Set in a remote Canadian town with an experimental U.S. Air Force base run by stalwart Thompson (though it feels more like the British countryside invaded by the Yanks), with the appropriate tensions building as the body count rises. The invisible killers are vampires that suck the brains and spinal columns from their human victims. They materialize in the final reels as icky flying brains with spinal columns that whiplash around like a snake, truly icky creatures accompanied by slurping sound effects. Hardly a masterpiece, but these have got to be among the most memorably disturbing monsters from any film of its era. —*S. A.*

FINAL L: SCIENCE FICTION/SCIENCE FICTION (2001) 112M D: Campbell Scott. *Hope Davis, Denis Leary.* Scott (Stanley Tucci's directing partner on *Big Night*) goes solo for this shot-on-digital-video science fiction psychodrama about a paranoid patient in a mental hospital. Bill Tyler (Leary) is convinced he was cryogenically frozen and thawed out centuries in the future for use in medical experiments. Davis is the psychiatrist trying to calm his delusions and help him come to grips with reality, but that reality is thrown into question as his sessions continue. The constraining, featureless sets and washed-out colors effectively create a dreary atmosphere drained of life and hope, and the performances are beautifully matched, from Leary's jittery paranoia to Davis's compromised professionalism and sad self-examination. The contradictions and the conspiratorial twists behind the counseling don't quite gel, but the moral is unmistakable: Just because you're paranoid doesn't mean they aren't out to get you. —*S. A.*

FIREFLY: THE COMPLETE SERIES L: SCIENCE FICTION /SCIENCE FICTION TV (2002) 675M D: Various. *Nathan Fillion, Gina Torres, Alan Tudyk, Morena Baccarin, Jewel Staite, Adam Baldwin.* Joss Whedon's short-lived foray into sci-fi television is presented the way he always meant it to be seen. Thus the fourteen episodes begin with the original movie-length pilot "Serenity," which the network had broadcast late in the season. The pilot makes a far better introduction to the series on all levels, establishing not merely the present circumstances but the past war that turned Captain Mal (Fillion) into a suspicious, emotionally leathery man whose only duty is to the crew he comes to think of as family. The wounded loser of a civil war, he's fled to the edges of the authoritarian empire in a cargo ship where he and his crew survive in the fringes of the law. The handheld camera and on-the-fly looseness (even in special-effects scenes) give this show a roughness that matches its frontier flavor: no utopian existence here. The three unaired episodes are among the best, highlighted by a betrayal that cuts to the quick of Mal's unbending loyalty and spurs his sense of hard justice. Whedon ends the show with a powerful moment of reconciliation and community. —*S. A.*

FLESH AND THE FIENDS, THE L: HORROR/EURO-HORROR (1959) 94M D: John Gilling. *June Laverick, George Rose, Donald Pleasence, Peter Cushing.* Gilling (*Plague of the Zombies*) directs this horror tale based on the true story of Dr. Knox (played by Hammer horror legend Cushing) and Burke and Hare (Pleasence and Rose), the grave robbers who turned to murder to supply the doctor with research cadavers in 1827 Edinburgh. The story inspired countless films, from the 1945 *The Body Snatcher* (with Boris Karloff and Bela Lugosi) to the 1985 *Doctor and the Devils*, but this grisly, moody black-and-white horror from the early days of Britain's horror rebirth is one of the best. Cushing is excellent as the haughty, ruthlessly "logical" man of science with little time for moral questions, and Pleasence is appropriately creepy as the Irish underworld thug with an angle for every scam. The Image DVD serves up not one but two versions, the ninety-three-minute British cut and the spicier ninety-four-minute "Continental" version. Both are more complete than the trimmed American release, which is represented by the trailer for the retitled *The Fiendish Ghouls*. —*S. A.*

FRANKENSTEIN MEETS THE WOLFMAN L: CLASSIC HORROR/CLASSIC HORROR (1942) 74M D: Roy William Neill. *Patric Knowles, Lon Chaney Sr., Ilona Massey, Lionel Atwill, Bela Lugosi.* Naysayers be damned! *Frankenstein Meets the Wolfman* really gives *Bride of Frankenstein* a run for its money as the best Frankenstein sequel, though it's really more of a sequel to *The Wolfman.* While not as poetic, beautiful, or truly as important as *Bride, Frankenstein Meets the Wolfman* is gold. I devote quite a bit of conscious thought pondering what would happen if the monster were to meet up. This film is one of the few accurate representations of what would probably occur if the monsters were to meet. To paraphrase *Mr. Show*, ". . . it wouldn't be a mash, it would be some kind of horrible battle." And that's exactly what happens. They wisely delay the conflict to the final scene and, surprisingly, it exceeded my expectations. The whole film is a marvel to behold and I've seen it far more times than I care to admit. *Frankenstein Meets the Wolfman* is the apex of classic horror camp. —*T. S.*

FREAKMAKER L: HORROR/MAD SCIENTISTS (1973) 92M D: Jack Cardiff. *Donald Pleasence, Tom Baker, Brad Harris.* Pleasence plays a professor of genetics interested in carnivorous plants and how they work. His private experiments go well past the theories he asserts in the classroom. He is looking for the genetic link between plants and humans to create the perfect organism, and needs human subjects on whom to conduct his tests. That's where the freakshow he co-owns comes in handy—there he deposits the victims of his failed experiments. Nobody can play a mad scientist better than Pleasence. —*N. J.*

FREAKS UNCENSORED L: PSYCHOTRONIC/PSYCHOTRONIC DOCS (1999) 100M D: Ari M. Roussimoff. *Johnny Eck, Tom Thumb.* A standard documentary overview of sideshow freaks, including famous figures like Johnny Eck and Tom Thumb. But the reason I like it is because the box shows a "dog boy," his face completely covered in hair, and one time, believe it or not, I found it misplaced in the stand-up comedy section. It was so great to see it in that context. For a split second there I thought I lived in a world where a dog boy could leave the sideshow behind, get up there and tell some jokes. He would probably have a lot of stories about getting hairballs in the shower drain and that kind of stuff. It would be awesome. —*B. T.*

FREDDY'S DEAD: THE FINAL NIGHTMARE L: HORROR/ STALKERS (1991) 96M D: Rachel Talalay. *Breckin Meyer, Yaphet Kotto, Shon Greenblatt, Lisa Zane, Robert Englund.* This film is an ambitious mixed-bag

of a would-be final chapter in the Freddy saga. This time the suburb of Springwood is depicted in a more Lynchian vein: Freddy has killed all the children, so the adults have gone crazy. The story goes further into the Krueger backstory with flashbacks to his childhood (Alice Cooper plays his abusive father) and pre-burnt-alive murdering days (it turns out that—*gasp!*—he had a daughter). Best of all, we get to see the "dream demons" that gave him his powers—little wormy guys depicted in stop-motion animation during the climactic "Freddy-vision" 3-D sequence, which unfortunately is done in the crappy red and blue format (which looks just as so-so on your TV as it did in theaters). Freddy is incredibly corny (he turns his razor glove into a Nintendo Power Glove during a video game–themed nightmare!), the teen characters are ludicrous, and I have no idea what poor Kotto is doing in a movie like this. But I like the more cartoonish tone and the attempt to bring the series in a different direction than the previous formulaic sequels. Also watch for cameos by Roseanne, Tom Arnold, and Johnny Depp. —*B. T.*

FREEZE ME L: JAPANESE HORROR/JAPANESE HORROR (2000) 101M D: Takashi Ishii. *Harumi Inoue, Kazuki Kitamura, Naoto Takenaka, Shunsuke Matsuoka.* Somewhere between inspired psychodrama and unsettling sexploitation lies Ishii's twist on the rape victim revenge film. Chihiro (Inoue) starts the film alive and ebullient, a young professional with a doting beau and a thriving social circle, but she reverts to meek victim as a trio of men who raped her five years ago arrive one by one to reenact their assault until she's completely isolated from her old life and, with no social net holding her back, roused into retaliation. The twist comes in the aftermath, as she hides their bodies in the freezer and becomes attached to their frozen beauty. Ishii plays on the near crippling sense of shame felt by a survivor plunged back into the nightmare, and his approach is blunt and direct, without much psychological shading. That's part of the film's weird power. Chihiro's madness is protective and her care for the corpses is tender; she's not getting even, so much as taking away their ability to hurt and humiliate. Ishii's not interested in the moral issues as much as the emotional punch, and his visceral style doesn't dull the boldness of his metaphor. —*S. A.*

FRIGHT NIGHT L: HORROR/VAMPIRES (1985) 106M D: Tom Holland. *Jonathan Stark, Amanda Bearse, Chris Sarandon, Roddy McDowall, Stephen Geoffreys, William Ragsdale.* This is a clever 1980's vampire story about a group of teenagers who slowly come to believe that one of their neighbors is a vampire. Unwittingly, the host of the late-night television horror program *Fright Night* (McDowall) offers his help as a vampire hunter in hopes of convincing them it's all in their heads. Sarandon does well trying to conceal

his identity as the bloodsucker, yet McDowall finally comes to believe the teens, leading to the suspenseful climax. Good performances mixed with humorous clichés make this an enjoyable vampire film. —*N. J.*

FROM DUSK TILL DAWN 2: TEXAS BLOOD MONEY L: HORROR/VAMPIRES (1999) 90M D: Scott Spiegel. *Robert Patrick, Brett Harrelson, Danny Trejo, Bo Hopkins, Tiffani-Amber Thiessen.* Buck (Patrick) runs over a bat while driving near the Titty Twister bar, gets out and gets bit by a guy named Razor Eddie (Trejo). Thing is, Buck was headed to meet up with his gang to rob a bank, so he shows up a little more of a vampire than his cohorts probably expected. This causes inner-gang tensions but also helps out when they need to fight cops. It's not as smart or well made as the original, and the low-budget South African locations are pretty ugly, but *Texas Blood Money* is still one of the best straight-to-video sequels ever made (for what that's worth). Unlike its predecessor, you know from the beginning that this will feature both bank robbers and vampires, so there is no awkward pacing problem. There's no magnetic leading man, but the cast is full of narrow-eyed, badass character actors, and Harrelson (Woody's brother) is particularly good. But the most fun comes from director Spiegel and his gimmicky POV shots. He places his camera on a guy doing pushups, on an oscillating fan, and even inside the mouth of a vampire as it bites someone. —*B. T.*

FROM DUSK TILL DAWN 3: THE HANGMAN'S DAUGHTER L: HORROR/VAMPIRES (2000) 94M D: P. J. Pesce. *Michael Parks, Temuera Morrison, Rebecca Gayheart, Marco Leonardi, Ara Celi.* This prequel (written by Robert Rodriguez and his cousin Álvaro) tells the backstory of Salma Hayek's snake-dancing character Santanico Pandemonium, now played by Celi. She is the hangman's daughter of the title, who goes along with an outlaw who escapes her father's (Morrison) gallows. At first you feel sorry for Santanico because her father cruelly whips her, but you later find out why he was completely justified. There are a number of such clever surprises that play on your expectations, but storywise this is the most routine and least effective of the series. Still, any straight-to-video sequel that's worth watching is something. —*B.T.*

FUNHOUSE, THE L: HORROR/STALKERS (1981) 96M D: Tobe Hooper. *Cooper Huckabee, Sylvia Miles, Elizabeth Berridge, Miles Chapin, Largo Woodruff.* Teens try to stay over night in the funhouse of a traveling carnival, but they see too much and they must die. Definitely feels like an '80s horror movie, complete with lifts of the POV shots in *Halloween*. The best bit involves a freak in an oversized Frankenstein's monster mask. His dad promises that if he'll kill the kids he'll get to go fishing. Unfortunately, he later takes off the mask to reveal his freak face, which ironically looks like a cheap Halloween mask. Not nearly on the level of his *Texas Chain Saw* films, but good compared to most of Hooper's work. —*B. T.*

GALAXY QUEST L: SCIENCE FICTION/SCIENCE FICTION (1999) 102M D: Dean Parisot. *Tim Allen, Alan Rickman, Tony Shalhoub, Sam Rockwell, Signourney Weaver.* This is the quintessential *Star Trek* spoof. Allen, Weaver, and Rickman play actors in a sci-fi TV series named *Galaxy Quest*. Twenty years after the series was cancelled, the actor who played the captain (Allen) gets a knock on his door. It's a handful of aliens who want him and his crew to save their planet. They know he can help them because they've seen what he can do from what they've seen of Earth's satellite transmissions. Once the crew of aged actors gets together, they agree to do the best they can in their old roles. It's a good thing their enemy is just as corny and predictable as the low-budget aliens they faced on the show. —*N. J.*

GAMERA: THE GUARDIAN OF THE UNIVERSE L: JAPANESE SCIENCE FICTION/GAMERA (1997) 92M D: Shusuke Kaneko. *Tsuyoshi Ihara, Akira Onodera, Ayako Fujitani.* In this first of a trilogy (all three are among the best giant monster movies ever made), the giant turtle Gamera, an ancient man-made weapon designed to protect Earth from attack, is awakened to fight the Gyaos, a race of fast-growing, heat-breathing prehistoric birds. Kaneko, a longtime Godzilla fan, got the chance to update the silly flying turtle Gamera, and ended up making him much cooler than Godzilla ever was. At first you might laugh to see such a vicious turtle, especially since he can go inside his shell and fly away like a spinning UFO, but you quickly learn to take him seriously. Full of dark humor and fantastic imagery (when an errant missile takes out the Tokyo Tower, the Gyaos use it for a nest), this movie set a new standard for every aspect of the genre, from the special effects to the human protagonists. Fujitani has a special connection to Gamera, and she returns in the increasingly great sequels. —*B. T.*

GAMERA 2: ATTACK OF LEGION L: JAPANESE SCIENCE FICTION/GAMERA (1996) 99M D: Shusuke Kaneko. *Akiji Kobayashi, Miki Mizuno, Toshiyuki Nagashima.* Deadly insectlike aliens invade Earth, and only Gamera can stop them (especially once they combine to form a giant monster). Kaneko continues with his superb trilogy, bringing the effects to the next level with lots of help from computers (for lasers and fireballs) and an evolved, more vicious Gamera whose arms now grow into sea turtle flippers when he flies. In one disturbing scene, Gamera is completely covered with the insects—bet you never saw that in a giant monster movie before. Arguably even better than *Guardian of the Universe*. —*B. T.*

GAMERA 3: REVENGE OF IRIS L: JAPANESE SCIENCE FICTION/GAMERA (1999) 105M D: Shusuke Kaneko. *Senri Yamasaki, Ayako Fujitani, Ai Maeda, Shinobu Nakayama.* A girl orphaned by Gamera (Ai) finds a baby monster in a cave and names it Iris, after her cat who was also killed by Gamera. As Gamera battles more Gyaos, destroys much of Tokyo, and has the Japanese government turn against him, Iris grows larger and larger. The climactic fight is an amazing FX spectacle—Iris uses the traditional rubber suit technique combined with CGI tentacles and lighting effects. I believe this is the best Japanese giant monster movie ever made, and I am not alone in this. —*B. T.*

GARGOYLES L: HORROR/DEMONS (1972) 74M D: Bill L. Norton. *Cornel Wilde, Jennifer Salt, Bernie Casey, Scott Glenn.* This was a favorite of mine as a kid for a couple of reasons: they show the monsters a lot, and it was regularly played on TV. It was kind of scary then and is good for some nostalgic fun now. An anthropologist (Wilde) and his daughter (Salt) find a weird skeleton in the Arizona desert. When they remove it for further study, they are attacked by a bunch of lizardlike gargoyle monsters led by Casey under a shitload of makeup. The first half is pretty good as the creatures are kept in the shadows and only glimpsed in the sky. But the latter half, spent more closely with the gargoyles, is damned silly stuff. This was made for TV, so the action fades for commercial breaks. *Gargoyles* was also the inspiration for the Disney cartoon series of the same name. —*S. H.*

GATTACA L: SCIENCE FICTION/SCIENCE FICTION (1997) 101M D: Andrew Niccol. *Gore Vidal, Ethan Hawke, Uma Thurman, Jude Law.* Gattaca is set in a near-future world populated by genetically engineered humans. Vincent (Hawke) is born an invalid, without the influence of biological enhancement. With a life expectancy of thirty years, he must find a way to realize his dream of manning a ship set for Titan in a society that discriminates against those of genetic inferiority. Assuming a false identity, Vincent gains a prominent position within the Gattaca Company, careful not to leave any genetic trace of his true identity along the way. Moments away from achieving his dream of space travel, a murder investigation and a snooping detective threaten to reveal Vincent and compromise his chances of flight. *Gattaca* is a great example of a sci-fi movie based on concepts rather than special effects. —*J. D.*

GEORGE LUCAS IN LOVE L: SCIENCE FICTION/STAR WARS (1999) 8M D: Joe Nussbaum. *Lisa Jakub, Jason Peck, Martin Hynes.* Not just for film buffs, the four lampoons in this anthology vary in polish and professionalism but all share a free and easy sense of fun and a giddy love of cinema. *George Lucas* is the highlight of the collection, a hilarious, perfectly sculpted parody loaded with *Star Wars* gags and highlighted by a nebbish performance by Hynes as USC student Lucas overcoming writer's block with the love of a beautiful young woman (a spot-on Jakub) in giant hair buns. The mock *Shakespeare in Love* score is the romantic lubricant for the deftly integrated gags. The DVD also features interviews, a documentary featurette, a bonus feature (the secret four-digit code, if you haven't guessed, is 1-1-3-8) and three more parodies. *Swing Blade*, a mock trailer that drops the mumbling dimwit Karl into the hip LA scene, features a great Billy Bob Thornton spin. *Evil Hill* tries too hard to meld *Austin Powers* with *Notting Hill* but emerges with an inspired twist, and *Film Club* (the most technically rough of the bunch) finds a new use for the Dogma 95 commandments. —*S. A.*

GHOST OF FRANKENSTEIN L: HORROR/CLASSIC HORROR
(1942) 67M D: Erle C. Kenton. *Cedric Hardwicke, Lon Chaney Jr., Bela Lugosi, Lionel Atwill, Ralph Bellamy. Ghost of Frankenstein* is the fourth Frankenstein film from Universal and the first to devolve into pure camp. Ygor and the Monster somehow miraculously survive another fire and return in this film; however, the monster is now played by Chaney, and he's certainly no Karloff. But that doesn't mean this film isn't fun. It has "fun" by the bucketload: mad scientists, ghosts, brain-swapping, and monsters! Add to that Universal's consistently high production standards, beautiful sets, eerie atmosphere, and you have a damn good movie. While it doesn't have the significance of the original Frankenstein, you could certainly do a lot worse. —*T. S.*

GHOUL, THE L: CLASSIC HORROR/CLASSIC HORROR (1934)
73M D: T. Hayes Hunter. *Ralph Richardson, Dorothy Hyson, Ernest Thesiger, Cedric Hardwicke, Boris Karloff.* A slow, atmospheric horror film featuring Karloff as an Egyptologist convinced that a certain gem can give him eternal life if he is buried with it. When it is stolen from his tomb, he rises from the dead to reclaim it. There are some interesting and even comical secondary characters within this early sound film, but it quite simply isn't up to the more auspicious Karloff films of the time, such as *Frankenstein* and *The Mummy.* —*N. J.*

GIALLO A VENEZIA L: HORROR/GIALLO (ITALIAN HORROR)
(1979) 93M D: Mario Landi. *Leonora Fani, Jeff Blynn, Gianni Dei, Mariangela Giordano.* A dead couple is found alongside a Venice canal in this twisted murder mystery. The force of this *giallo* resides in the perverse games the husband (Dei) inflicts upon his wife (Fani), seen in flashback, which are startlingly arousing and deeply cruel. Note the glaring harshness of the rape and leg-amputation scenes, and the grimness of the drug dealer being shot and set afire. The solution is made dumbly obvious only at the end. —*J. C.*

GIANT CLAW, THE L: CLASSIC SCIENCE FICTION/CLASSIC
SCIENCE FICTION (1957) 75M D: Fred F. Sears. *Louis Merrill, Jeff Morrow, Mara Corday, Morris Ankrum. The Giant Claw* features one of the funniest and stupidest movie monsters ever! A giant buzzard ("as big as a battleship") escapes from an alternate dimension and causes fear and panic on Earth (as an overblown narrator tells us again and again). The monster is an obvious papier-mâché marionette and gets lots of screen time as it attacks airplanes and chomps on parachuters. A drunk, lecherous scientist (Morrow) hits on Corday and, along with a military officer (Ankrum), devises an atomic cannon to destroy the buzzard's force field and fry the big bird. I'm not sure it's intentional, but at times, *The Giant Claw* comes across as an *Airplane!*–style spoof of the '50s monster movie genre. —*S. H.*

GIANT SPIDER INVASION, THE L: VAOWG/VAOWG (1975)
76M D: Bill Rebane. *Leslie Parrish, Steve Brodie, Barbara Hale, Alan Hale Jr., Robert Easton.* Rebane made movies through the '70s and '80s that relied on primitive effects, absurd plots, and over-the-hill actors to create part of the last wave of drive-in-friendly, regionally distributed psychotronica, and this is one of his most notorious productions. Spiders (in diamond-lined meteors) from another dimension land on Earth via a black hole. Initially normal in size, the spiders terrorize a family of hicks. They crawl around in the Daisy Duke shorts–attired daughter and the patriarch accidently drinks a spider shake. Scientists Brodie and Hale find romance with each other and try to stop the alien invasion. In one hilarious scene they get chased by a giant spider and Brodie steamrolls Hale as they roll down a hill. Hale Jr. plays the town sheriff who spends most of the time getting ready to leave his office. Two of the spiders do become gigantic and "invade" a Little League game. Using parade-float techniques, the giant spiders are actually VW bugs adorned with spider-shaped bodies made of chicken wire. Funny stuff. —*S. H.*

GINGER SNAPS L: HORROR/WEREWOLVES (2000) 108M
D: John Fawcett. *Emily Perkins, Katharine Isabelle, Mimi Rogers.* Death-obsessed, antisocial sisters Ginger (Isabelle) and Brigitte (Perkins) have a very close relationship. But when Ginger has her period, starts dating a boy, and, oh yeah, also gets bit by the same thing that's been eating all the dogs in their Canadian suburb . . . well, the sisters start to grow apart. Like some of the best of the teen horror genre, *Ginger Snaps* uses horror elements (in this case werewolves) as a metaphor for nonsupernatural horrors to which most teens can relate. Very original horror with a dry sense of humor completely unlike the post-*Scream* approach popular at the time. It went direct to video in the United States, but is destined for cult status because of its smartly written, misanthropic protagonists. In that sense it is similar to *Heathers* and *Heavenly Creatures.* —*B. T.*

A Brief Guide to the Lizard King of Tokyo

He's the King Kong of the post-nuclear age, the James Bond of giant monsters (he takes his cities shaken, not stirred), Toho Studios's most successful series star, and the most prolific monster to step inside (or on top of) a studio. Over the course of twenty-five films in more than forty years, Godzilla has been everything from rampaging menace to Tokyo's savior to doting dad, and has inspired a zoo of imitators (Gamera, the fire-breathing turtle, being the greatest of them) and a misguided American remake that feels less *daikaiju* (giant monster) than *Jurassic Park* in Manhattan. But only Japan knows the real creature.

Born in the wake of the American bombing of Hiroshima and nuclear testing in the Pacific, Godzilla entered the international scene as an avenging devil rising from the radioactive ashes of the atomic age. Hollywood had *Them!* (1954), *Tarantula* (1955), *The Deadly Mantis* (1957), and the proto-zilla of *The Beast from 20,000 Fathoms* (1953), but these nuclear spawn all lacked one key element: personality. The scaly gray one became the "It" monster, a magnificent, dignified creature who descends upon Tokyo like a biblical curse with attitude. Blending science and myth, he's part prehistoric dinosaur, part nuclear mutation, part golem, with a dash of fire-breathing dragon and a hint of King Kong.

There's nothing cute or campy about

continued on page 666

GINGER SNAPS 2: UNLEASHED L: HORROR/WEREWOLVES (2004) 92M D: Brett Sullivan. *Emily Perkins, Katherine Isabelle*. A surprisingly good sequel to the Canadian werewolf sleeper. Perkins returns as Brigitte, now living on her own and seemingly a junkie—but actually she's shooting up wolfsbane to ward off turning into a wolf. That doesn't stop her from getting locked up in rehab where she has no access to the herbs she needs. To make things worse, a male werewolf keeps trying to mate with her, taking out the occasional human along the way. The setting and story are very different from the original, but the tone is similar, with superb acting and a new sisterly relationship between Brigitte and an insane little girl named Ghost (Tatiana Maslany). Ginger (Isabelle) briefly returns from the dead to haunt her sister. As with *Ginger Snaps*, the script uses horror concepts as parallels to the problems experienced by teenage girls. Definitely worth checking out if you liked the first one. —*B. T.*

GLEN AND RANDA L: VAOWG/VAOWG (1971) 93M D: Jim McBride. *Steven Curry, Shelley Plimpton*. This unique postapocalyptic movie has an almost documentarylike feel. The teenage couple of the title live in a tribal society surviving off of scavenged canned food from the old world. When a "magician" armed with a record player and other trinkets fills their heads with new ideas, they decide to go on a journey searching for a city that may or may not still exist. This is a quiet movie with no score and very naturalistic acting, making for a much more true-to-life feel than you expect in this type of film. There's also no violence (unless you count a fishing scene). It's just a story of curious kids who don't know the difference between a horse and a dog and who think what they see in old Wonder Woman comics is real life. Rated X for some sex and nudity but would be a soft R by today's standards. —*B. T.*

GODZILLA (1998) L: JAPANESE SCIENCE FICTION/GODZILLA (1998) 138M D: Roland Emmerich. *Matthew Broderick, Jean Réno, Maria Pitillo, Hank Azaria*. The gang of idiots behind *Independence Day* continued their mercilessly short string of financially successful/artistically bankrupt crap, but this time it was personal: they brought down an icon with them. Some who haven't seen the modern Japanese Godzilla films might argue that because this is based on silly old monster movies, it should be exactly what it is: moronic garbage that, now separated from its multimillion-dollar hype machine, will never be willingly watched or thought about again. But I'm not letting them off that easy. All they had to do to satisfy some of the audience was deliver some shots of Godzilla stepping on stuff, but they couldn't even pull

Godzilla (1954). Sure, he's a guy in a rubber suit, but "suitmation" (Toho's gimmicky name for the process) became the basis of all *kaiju eiga* (giant monster movies) to follow and a convention of the genre. Director Ishiro Honda (a former assistant to Akira Kurosawa) directs this dark nuclear parable in a solemn key, aided by Akira Ifukube's distinctive, brooding score. In a Tokyo that resembles the set of a neorealist film, Godzilla's devastating rampage and radioactive breath leaves behind thousands of casualties and a city aflame, recalling nothing less than the bombings of Hiroshima and Nagasaki.

While Godzilla was originally a devastating force majeure, his transformation into something quite different began early on. He is dead at the end of *Godzilla*, but his twin returns for *Godzilla Raids Again* (1959), which portrays the first of a seemingly unending succession of turf wars. In his slimmer, leaner suit, he's still the big guy on the block. After his battle with Anguirus,

he takes a three-year vacation before returning to wrestle with King Kong (a deformed, lumbering suitmation monster) in *King Kong vs. Godzilla* (1962) and Mothra in *Godzilla vs. Mothra* (1964).

If Godzilla is the king of monsters, then Mothra is the regal queen. Against the clumsy, plodding dark gray of Godzilla's annihilating rampages, the delicate, ethereal marionette Mothra gently glides on rainbow wings through a mission of peace and protection. Enlivened by the pixie princess twins who communicate with their deity through song, *Godzilla vs. Mothra* is a *daikaiju* fairy tale of exquisite color and fantastic imagery, considered by most fans to be the apex of the series.

In Godzilla's fifth outing, *Ghidrah, the Three Headed Monster* (1964), former enemy Mothra convinces the scaly gray one to change sides and defend Earth from the marauding three-headed dragon from space. Ghidrah's bat-winged body and energy-blasting serpentine heads, bobbing

---

that off; instead they made a movie about a giant iguana who, in one of many bizarrely inept scenes, seems to be humping a building. If it had to be these tasteless hacks making an American Godzilla film, for crying out loud, why couldn't they at least put the real Godzilla in it somewhere? —*B. T.*

GODZILLA 1985 L: JAPANESE SCIENCE FICTION/GODZILLA (1984) 99M D: Kohji Hashimoto, Robert J. Kizer. *Ken Tanaka, Yasuko Sawaguchi, Raymond Burr.* This start to the new Godzilla series of the '80s and '90s is a direct sequel to the 1956 original and, like that one, was repackaged for American audiences with Burr in the lead. (The American director is the guy who did *Hell Comes to Frogtown*.) Godzilla returns to attack Tokyo, this time with more advanced model and suit effects and a very serious tone. I know the original was an allegory about the atom bomb, but Burr's melodramatic narration tying in Godzilla with environmental catastrophe (accompanied by heart-tugging strings) is still pretty hilarious. —*B. T.*

GODZILLA RAIDS AGAIN (AKA GIGANTIS, THE FIRE MONSTER) L: JAPANESE SCIENCE FICTION/GODZILLA (1955) 78M D: Motoyoshi Oda. *Minoru Chiaki, Hiroshi Koisumi.* This is not one of the more exciting Godzilla movies, but it stands out for a number of reasons. (1) It's the first Godzilla sequel. (2)

It's the only Godzilla sequel in black and white. (3) It's the first time Godzilla fought another monster. (4) This also means it's the only time Godzilla fought another monster in black and white. (5) Since no one knew Godzilla would become a franchise and an icon, the American version renamed him Gigantis. (6) It's told from the point of view of a pilot who spots tuna for fishermen, instead of some scientist or military figure. —*B. T.*

GODZILLA VS BIOLLANTE L: JAPANESE SCIENCE FICTION / GODZILLA (1989) 104M D: Kazuki Ohmori. *Megumi Odaka, Kenpachiro Satsuma.* In the second of the modern Godzilla series (after *Godzilla 1985*), some of Godzilla's cells are combined with a rosebush to create Biollante, one of the weirdest (and coolest) monsters Godzilla has ever fought. The story (which involves corporations fighting over Godzilla's genetic material and a scientist who thinks his daughter's ghost possesses the rosebush) is kind of slow, like many Godzilla movies, but the climactic battle has some of the best and most strangely beautiful effects of the series. —*B. T.*

GODZILLA VS DESTROYAH L: JAPANESE SCIENCE FICTION /GODZILLA (1995) 103M D: Takao Okawara. *Momoko Kochi.* This was going to be Toho Studio's last Godzilla film, but the American version sucked

and twisting like a frenzied Medusa, is a different sort of marionette than Mothra: restless, malevolent, a snaky civilization smasher. Against this new personification of pure evil, Godzilla begins his transformation into a kinder, gentler monster, a hero for Earth who now teams up with other monsters, laughs, and even dances for joy in a childlike, earth-pounding jig.

In *Godzilla vs. Monster Zero* (1965, starring American B-actor Nick Adams), Earth is threatened by the first of many alien civilizations: the scheming, black-leather-and-purple-attired inhabitants of the devastated Planet X, who turn Godzilla, Rodan, and Ghidrah (the "Monster Zero" of the title) against Earth. Godzilla goes space age!

Godzilla's decline came in the '60s, when the earnest one-on-one contests turned into tag-team wrestling bouts aimed at a more juvenile audience. The cycle reaches its nadir with the juvenile *Son of Godzilla* (1967), the adolescent fantasy *Godzilla's Revenge* (1969), the tired *Godzilla vs. Gigan* (1972), and *Godzilla vs. Megalon* (1973). These low-budget editions shamelessly recycle old effects clumsily melded with shoddy new footage. Welcome to Godzilla's camp period of uninspired monsters and a goofy-looking suit with large doll-like eyes and an oversized head. The American versions are even more poorly dubbed than their predecessors, only amplifying the goofy narratives: these films are simply silly, if perversely entertaining.

Not all the films of this period are write-offs, though. If mad monster parties are your thing, then you gotta love *Destroy All Monsters* (1968), with the highest *daikaiju* quotient of the series: twelve monsters! *Destroy All Monsters* establishes Monsterland/Monster Island, a proto–Jurassic Park that Godzilla and friends call home between films (and which serves as a convenient plot device for the succeeding films: "Godzilla has once again escaped Monster Island!"). The trippiest picture of the cycle, *Godzilla*

continued on page 668

---

so bad that they reintroduced the mutant lizard five years later. This film does serve as the end of the so-called "Heisei" series and is a satisfying, but flawed, conclusion that refers back to the original *Godzilla King of the Monsters*. The story kicks off with an extra-radioactive Godzilla menacing Hong Kong. I'm not sure if this is supposed to represent China, but Godzilla is glowing red and nearing a nuclear meltdown. Meanwhile a bunch of ugly crab monsters that were mutated by the Oxygen Destroyer from the original film start causing trouble and eventually meld together into one big-ass monster. The fight scenes are decent, but the big Destroyah is kind of bottom heavy and the possibilities of Godzilla fighting the little Destroyahs is barely explored. This movie belongs to Little Godzilla, who was hatched a few movies ago and is now a tough little bugger who takes on the much bigger Destroyah in the best monster scene. —*S. H.*

GODZILLA VS GIGAN L: JAPANESE SCIENCE FICTION /GODZILLA (1972) 89M D: Jun Fukuda. *Yuriko Hishimi, Tomoko Umeda, Haruo Nakajima.* After the financial and perceived artistic failure of *Godzilla vs The Smog Monster*, director Fukuda (who previously helmed *Son of Godzilla* and *Godzilla vs The Sea Monster*) returned and, typical for the series, Godzilla's most popular nemesis King Ghidorah is brought back for a rematch. In a plot recycled from *Monster Zero,* space cockroaches plan on invading Earth with giant monsters. A new monster, Gigan (who has a buzz saw in his stomach) is teamed with King Ghidorah and the pair are set loose on Tokyo. Godzilla and Angilas (who communicate to each other via comic-book style dialogue balloons!) travel from Monster Island to defend the planet. The human hero is a graphic artist working for a sinister amusement park with a giant Godzilla statue. Frequently regarded as one of the worst entries, *Godzilla vs Gigan* features an enormous amount of recycled monster footage and also reuses stock music by Akira Ifukube. Godzilla and Gigan returned one year later in the even sillier *Godzilla vs Megalon.* —*S. H.*

GODZILLA VS KING GHIDORAH L: JAPANESE SCIENCE FICTION /GODZILLA (1991) 103M D: Kazuki Ohmori. *Richard Berger, Kenpachiro Satsuma.* Following the disappointing box office performance by *Godzilla vs Biollante*, Godzilla's most popular adversary King Ghidorah returns in this imaginative time travel movie that reinvents the origins of Godzilla and Ghidorah as well as combining elements of classic Toho Kaiju with ideas "borrowed" from the American *Terminator* films. A UFO from the future arrives in Japan with a plan to travel further back in time and destroy the dinosaur (a Godzillasaurus) before atomic radia-

vs. the Smog Monster (1971), is a mod-zilla mixing of (often bad) pop music, hip nightclub scenes, and psychedelic imagery (including animated interludes and a bad acid trip) with an environmental message and the pollution-spawned monster Hedo-rah, who tokes on a belching smokestack like a giant putrid bong.

With the one-two punch of Godzilla vs. Mechagodzilla (1974) and Terror of Mechagodzilla (1975), the Big G celebrated his twentieth anniversary with a new mech-anized menace (a robot monster replica of the scaly one), alien invaders who look like refugees from a low-budget Planet of the Apes knockoff, mad scientists, spies, secret agents, and a terrific tough new suit with a fierce head design and peacock-like silver dorsal plates. Terror reunites the scaly one with original director Ishiro Honda (who directed all his best outings) and composer Akira Ifukube (who revives his brooding score), but while the first Mechagodzilla film was a hit, the sequel flopped; so Godzilla

took a temporary retirement, wading back into the sea for a ten-year hibernation.

In 1984, Toho revived the Big G for his thirtieth-anniversary celebration with Godzilla 1985: The Legend is Reborn (origi-nal title: The Return of Godzilla). As much a direct sequel to the original film as a revi-sionist remake, Godzilla 1985 swept away the past thirty years of campy sequels and returned the Big G to the awe and solemn grandeur of the mighty first feature. The fierce fighting machine we all know and love came back lean, mean, and menacing. Taking the cue, American distributor New World recruited Raymond Burr to reprise his role from the American version of the original and once again added new footage to their cut-and-paste presentation, this time not as smoothly or seriously. In American theaters, the film was preceded by Marv Newland's animated spoof Bambi Meets Godzilla.

The film flopped in the United States but played to stomping-room-only crowds in Japan and led to the Big G's second wave

tion causes his mutation. Godzilla is destroyed, but three weird little space critters called Dorats mutate into King Ghidorah and terrorize mod-ern Japan. After more time travel shenanigans, a bigger, meaner Godzilla is created. He destroys Ghidorah and turns his attention to smashing Tokyo one more time, so a Mecha-King Ghidora is built to try to stop Godzilla. The time-warp-ing plot is complex and contradictory, but who watches Godzilla films for their sensible sto-rylines? There's tons of monster action plus the great Akira Ifukube returns to score one of the best Godzilla films of the '90s. —S. H.

GODZILLA VS MEGALON L: JAPANESE SCIENCE FICTION/ GODZILLA (1973) 81M D: Jun Fukuda. Hiroyuki Kawase, Yutaka Hayashi, Katsuhiko Sasaki. One of the silliest Godzilla movies, this has the big guy fighting the roach-like Megalon as well as the hook-handed Gigan. But there are two reasons why it stands out. First of all, it's the only one to have the wonderfully named Jet Jaguar, an Ultraman-esque robot with a Cheshire Cat grin who shapes his arms into a V when he flies around. Second, this is the one where Godzilla actually drop-kicks an opponent. Amazing! —B. T.

GODZILLA VS THE SMOG MONSTER L: JAPANESE SCIENCE FICTION /GODZILLA (1971) 85M D: Yoshimitsu Banno. Kenpachiro Satsuma, Haruo Nakajima. The weirdest and most misunderstood Godzilla movie was made as a commentary on ecological issues. The story unfolds with a unique visual style that incorporates cartoons, musical inter-ludes (including the groovy tune "Save the Earth") and lots of other wild stuff. Godzilla (Nakajima) flies by tucking his tail between his legs and blasting out his radioactive breath. The Smog Monster Hedorah (Satsuma) is a blob of sludge that mutates into a deadly pollution-sucking monster that changes forms. He kills a lot of people, but spares a cute kitty cat. Godzilla is the Earth's defender, taking a real beating until he's helped by resourceful humans who zap Hedorah with a dose of mega-electricity. This attempt to reinvent the Godzilla film series is hated by many (including the film's producer, who thought it was too violent), but I think it's one of the best and is certainly the most exciting of all the '70s Godzilla movies. —S. H.

GODZILLA, MOTHRA AND KING GHIDORAH: GIANT MONSTERS ALL-OUT ATTACK (AKA GODZILLA GMK) L: JAPANESE SCIENCE FICTION/GODZILLA (2001) 105M D: Shusuke Kaneko. Ryudo Uzaki, Kunio Murai, Hiroyuki Watanabe, Masahiro Kobayashi. Shusuke, direc-

(the "Heisei" series) and a whole new generation of fans. None of the films ever surfaced theatrically in the United States, and only one—*Godzilla vs. Biollante* (1989)—made it to video before 1998 (when the big-budget American remake made all things Godzilla suddenly hip, or at least commercial). But fervent American *kaiju eiga* fans followed the Big G's new big-budget, candy-colored, growth-inducing adventures through imported laser discs and bootleg tapes before he finally debuted stateside on tape and DVD in *Godzilla vs. King Ghidora* (1991), *Godzilla vs. Mothra: Battle for Earth* (1992), *Godzilla vs. Mechagodzilla II* (1993), and *Godzilla vs. Space Godzilla* (1994). In 1995, having grown to twice his original size (more than 300 feet tall!), time-traveled, been born once again, and battled with his greatest foes, the Big G commemorated his fortieth by getting killed off in *Godzilla vs. Destoroyah*, a knock-down, drag-out match in which Godzilla passes the torch to Godzilla Jr. with a blast of radioactive energy.

Junior will have to wait to take up the mantle of king of the monsters, though, for Toho decided, in the wake of Roland Emmerich's CGI makeover of the Big G in the 1998 American remake, to return the lizard king to his roots. *Godzilla 2000* (1999) finds the Big G alive, well, and once again a man in a scaly rubber suit. The effects are digitally tweaked, but the old joys are back: the crunch of lovingly detailed buildings rendered to splinters in a single step, the rubble and dust left in the wake of a prehistoric body slam, the noble profile of the scaly gray one in action. . . . It's a juvenile thrill that CGI can't touch.

Godzilla 2000 is the first in Toho's "Alternate Reality" series, one-offs that reinvent Godzilla for stories that stand outside of the series. *Godzilla vs. Megaguirus* (2000) and *Godzilla, Mothra, King Ghidora: Giant Monsters All-out Attack* (2001) are still waiting to stomp stateside, but in Japan the king of the monsters is still on top.

—Sean Axmaker

---

tor of the '90s *Gamera* trilogy, fulfills his dream of directing a Godzilla film and reinvents the series. Godzilla is a bad guy again, this time an embodiment of the forgotten victims of WWII (a variation on the original's Hiroshima symbolism). The twist is that the other monsters (Mothra, King Ghidorah, and Baragon) are guardians of the human race trying to stop Godzilla. In a sense, Shusuke is to giant monster movies what Sergio Leone was to Westerns: he amplifies everything you like about the genre to take it to the next level, and applies an unexpected level of artistry. The human characters are actually likable, and it's a brutal enough film that they stand a chance of dying. In one scene Godzilla's fire breath takes out two fighter jets, which instead of exploding midair actually crash down and blow up houses. There's even a character who miraculously survives one Godzilla attack only to get squished by him later while in the hospital. It's a movie filled with clever genre tweaks and jokes, even a swipe at the American Godzilla, and a scene where a woman who sees Baragon mistakingly yells, "Godzilla!" While arguably not topping his *Gamera* series, Shusuke has undoubtedly created one of the very best *Godzilla* movies. *—B. T.*

GREMLINS L: HORROR/DEMONS (1984) 106M D: Joe Dante. *Frances Lee McCain, Phoebe Cates, Hoyt Axton, Zach Galligan, Keye Luke, Corey Feldman, Polly Holliday.* Looking for a unique present for his son at a curiosity shop in Chinatown, a gadget salesman happens upon a strange pet he's never seen before. The store's owner refers to the little gremlin as a *mogwai* and sells it to him if he promises three things: don't let it get wet, don't expose it to bright light, and don't feed it after midnight. These strange rules seem random to the young man who receives the adorable pet, and the rest of the film is simply the opening of Pandora's box. Who would ever think that so much mayhem and violence could spring from what is essentially a cross between an Ewok and E.T.? *—N. J.*

GREMLINS 2: THE NEW BATCH L: HORROR/DEMONS (1990) 107M D: Joe Dante. *Christopher Lee, Robert Picardo, Robert Prosky, John Glover, Phoebe Cates, Zach Galligan.* Now in New York City, Galligan and Cates accidentally unleash a gremlin plague in the high-tech corporate office building where they work. Made on a bigger budget than the original, the puppets and their mayhem are more elaborate. Some of them turn into spider-gremlins, others into bat-gremlins, and there's even a "sexy" female gremlin. Completely abandoning any aspirations toward serious horror, this sequel jokes about flaws in the original and delves further into cartoon humor and social satire. It has everything Dante loves: wacky sight gags, Looney Tunes humor (including Chuck Jones–directed appearances by Bugs and Daffy), old genre actors, references to 1950s sci-fi films, a TV horror host in a Dracula cape, stop-motion animation, even a musical number. It's fun to watch the gremlins wreak havoc on such a deserving target (the corporate culture, taking particular aim at Donald Trump and Ted Turner). Although the heroes are bland and some of the jokes miss, this movie is a whole lot of goofy fun. Hooray for puppets. —*B. T.*

GUTS OF A VIRGIN L: JAPANESE HORROR/JAPANESE HORROR (1986) 72M D: Kazuo "Gaira" Komizu. *Taiju Kato, Saeko Kizuki, Naomi Hagio.* Amusingly perverse slasher film with a hugely endowed zombie fucking the women and perforating the men. The story involves partying showbiz types who engage in grueling humiliating sex with each other before being horribly murdered by the swamp zombie. Quite memorable images make this schlock far better than it has any right to have been. —*J. C.*

HABIT L: HORROR/VAMPIRES (1996) 93M D: Larry Fessenden. *Meredith Snaider, Patricia Coleman, Aaron Beall, Larry Fessenden.* A New York artist type (Fessenden) on the rebound meets a woman (Snaider) at a Halloween party. She gives him a fake phone number but they continue to have encounters, one of which ends with her biting his lip and sucking the blood. He grows more and more obsessed with her and loses his grip on reality; all the while his friends are disappearing. It's a deliberately ambiguous vampire film (like George Romero's more effective *Martin*) that tries to weave all kinds of details of vampire legends into a story about dating. This is the second in Fessenden's pretentious horror trilogy along with *No Telling* and *Wendigo.* They all become grating and self-indulgent to varying degrees (this one has some pretty painful philosophical dialogue), but *Habit* is mostly successful at the admirable goal of creating a horror film with the natural, character-oriented style of an independent relationship drama. —*B. T.*

HABITAT L: SCIENCE FICTION/SCIENCE FICTION (1997) 120M D: Rene Daalder. *Lynne Adams, Tchéky Karyo, Susan Almgren, Alice Krige, Balthazar Getty, Laura Harris. Habitat* is one of those interesting movies with a stupid cover. It's about Andreas (Getty), a nice boy with strange parents (Karyo and Krige). His folks, scientists on the crazy side of genius, have just moved to town and turned their house into a jungle in an attempt to counteract the planet's radiation problem. Local hottie Deborah Marlowe (*The Faculty*'s Harris) falls for Andreas, the local boys get jealous, and the town turns against the strange newcomers. It's an all-out battle between man and nature as

the house comes alive to help rid the family of the threatening townies. Watch as Deborah and Andreas skinny dip their troubles away. Totally smokin'! It's like a cross between *The Wraith, Heathers,* and *Alien: Resurrection.* —*R. D.*

HALLOWEEN II L: HORROR/STALKERS (1981) 92M D: Rick Rosenthal. *Jamie Lee Curtis, Donald Pleasence, Dick Warlock.* Watching this film, I can clearly see why slasher movies have turned to shit. The problem's roots are very evident. This film is just too complicated. The first *Halloween* works so well because it is so simple. Just a few locations, very straightforward plot, not many twists or turns, just teenagers getting killed with chills, thrills, and gore. Even in this first sequel, everything gets too big and out of hand and the whole thing ends up muddled, confused, and crappy. The first *Halloween* was pure and simple. This one is just the opposite. —*T. S.*

But it's an interesting slasher sequel because it actually continues from the end of the first film through the rest of the night, making it feel like one long, bad holiday. There are some very effective scenes, like the POV shot of Michael Myers looking into people's windows, and the foggy, atmospheric ending when the police show up after dawn. Some of the gore is more surreal and *giallo*-inspired. Unfortunately, most new characters are poorly written and acted, and Curtis as Laurie Strode spends a lot of the movie drugged in a hospital. The plot thickens in this installment—you find out why Michael has singled out Laurie. Although John Carpenter didn't direct, he did cowrite (with Debra Hill) and produce, and he reshot some scenes when he wasn't happy with Rosenthal's footage. —*B. T.*

HALLOWEEN III: SEASON OF THE WITCH L: HORROR/STALKERS (1982) 96M D: Tommy Lee Wallace. *Tom Atkins, Stacy Nelkin, Dan O'Herlihy.* This film was unfairly panned. It's actually the creepiest, most successful *Halloween* sequel. It has nothing to do with the previous *Halloween* movies, though. *Season of the Witch* is about an evil mask maker whose Halloween masks kill the kids who wear them. It stars Atkins as the hero, Dr. Challis, who does a great job, mustache and all. This is a creepy little movie that really should be more appreciated. —*T. S.*

HALLOWEEN H20: TWENTY YEARS LATER L: HORROR/STALKERS (1998) 85M D: Steve Miner. *Jamie Lee Curtis, Adam Arkin, Josh Hartnett, Michelle Williams, Jodi Lyn O'Keefe.* Twenty years after the events of *Halloween II,* Laurie Strode (Curtis) is still alive, hiding out under an assumed name and raising a son (Hartnett, whose dark eyes remind one of the shadows on his uncle's mask). Of course Laurie is in therapy, and she's an alcoholic, and she has not come to terms with her traumatic past. So when Michael comes back to stalk her son, the stakes are as much psychological as they are physical.

It's a great payoff when, having escaped, Laurie makes the decision to turn around, grab a fire axe, and yell, "Michael!"—realizing that it's time to stop running. Director Miner did the first two *Friday the 13th* sequels and he brings that same energy to this film, particularly in the rousing chase that makes up the last fifteen minutes or so of the movie. Saying this is the best *Halloween* sequel isn't saying much, but it was a fitting end to the series. (Until they made *Halloween* goddamn *Resurrection*. Thanks a lot, assholes.) —*B. T.*

HALLOWEEN: RESURRECTION L: HORROR/STALKERS
(2002) 89M D: Rick Rosenthal. *Brad Lorree, Busta Rhymes, Bianca Kajlich, Sean Patrick Thomas.* *Halloween II* director Rosenthal returns to the series he was fired from to prop up its corpse *Weekend at Bernie's* style and wiggle it around, with exactly the results you'd expect. The asinine premise involves Busta and Tyra Banks setting up a group of teens with cameras in Michael Myers's childhood home and broadcasting what happens on a website. This may shock you, but Michael Myers shows up and kills a bunch of them. You see (you might want to sit down for this), it turns out that the guy who was killed at the end of *Halloween H20* was not Michael, but an unlucky ambulance driver with whom Michael switched clothes. In other words, this is by far the worst of the series. Don't get me wrong, I enjoy hearing Busta say, "Trick or treat, motherfucker!" but that is really the only joy in the whole movie. —*B. T.*

HAMMER HOUSE OF HORROR L: HORROR/HAMMER FILMS
(1980) 676M D: Tom Clegg, Alan Gibson, others. *Pierce Brosnan, Denholm Elliot, Peter Cushing.* In very much the spirit of Rod Serling's *Night Gallery*, British production company Hammer produced a number of fascinating episodes of horror for television. "Charlie Boy" features a couple tormented by the curse of an African fetish doll with voodoo powers. "Rude Awakening" features an estate agent trapped in a recurring nightmare with a haunted house. "The Mark of Satan" is about a trainee at a hospital morgue. Episodic horror is rarely as good as these gems from the great house of Hammer. —*N. J.*

HANGAR 18 L: SCIENCE FICTION/SCIENCE FICTION (1980)
97M D: James L. Conway. *James Hampton, Gary Collins, Robert Vaughn, Darren McGavin.* Though it hasn't aged particularly well in a post–*X-Files* world, *Hangar 18* (along with *Capricorn One*) was one of the first government conspiracy/space exploration movies. The crew of a space shuttle mission witnesses a UFO crash into a satellite. The UFO makes an emergency landing on Earth and NASA blames the destroyed satellite on the astronauts. The space ship ends up in an Area 51–type compound where McGavin leads the team of scientists studying the extraterrestrial craft. The astronauts (Collins and Hampton) investigate a government cover-up enacted by

a presidential aid (Vaughn). The director first made cheesy psychotronic documentaries like *Beyond and Back*, then moved on to stuff like this and *The Boogens*, and now works on *Star Trek* TV shows. —*S. H.*

HARDWARE WARS L: SCIENCE FICTION/STAR WARS (1977)
13M D: Ernie Fosselius. *Frank Robertson, Scott Mathews, Jeff Hale, Cindy Furgatch, Bob Knickerbocker, Paul Frees.* This, to me, is the great grandfather of all spoof films, the first one I can remember watching with my family on TV. It is as funny to me now as it was then. *Star Wars* has probably been spoofed more times than any other film, but it still doesn't get better than this. "You'll laugh, you'll cry, you'll kiss three bucks goodbye," boasts this groundbreaking parody, made the same year as the original *Star Wars*. I'm sure that many young filmmakers were inspired by this film after it was so successful without a budget. This short takes every opportunity to use the worst possible effects, sound, and props, adding to its charm. After George Lucas added extra computer footage to his already finished films, they released a second edition of *Hardware Wars*, parodying Lucas's new attempt by inserting their own stupid Video Toaster effects. Totally killer. Remember, if you're playing Princess Leia and you've got huge cinnamon buns on your head, you might be attacked by a wookie monster. —*R. D.*

HARRYHAUSEN CHRONICLES, THE L: PSYCHOTRONIC/
HARRYHAUSEN, RAY (1997) 60M D: Richard Schickel. *Henry Selick, Leonard Nimoy, Ray Bradbury, Ray Harryhausen, Tom Hanks.* This documentary on film master Harryhausen is so moving I almost cried when Bradbury presents him with a lifetime achievement award. Bradbury and Harryhausen have been good friends and collaborators since the 1950s, so he was a perfect choice to do the honors. It is so inspirational to see such a dedicated, hard-working artist do what he loves and be able to make a living at it. There are so many nifty tidbits about Harryhausen's career, and it's presented in such a fascinating manner that you'll feel compelled to revisit one of those awesome old stop-motion favorites. This film reminds me of *Divine Trash*, the John Waters documentary, another film about a driven artist who took risks and didn't wait for the world or anyone to validate his art. —*R. D.*

HARRY POTTER AND THE SORCERER'S STONE L:
CHILDREN'S LIVE/CHILDREN'S LIVE ACTION (2001) 152M D: Chris Columbus. *Richard Harris, Daniel Radcliffe, Maggie Smith, Robbie Coltrane, Emma Watson, Rupert Grint.* The *Harry Potter* books are written for kids, yes, but they are also written for adult nerds who love a good fantasy story. This movie definitely quenches escapism thirst. Sure it has its faults, but why focus on them? It's just good, simple fun about a normal boy with a shitty family who finds out that he is actually a wiz-

ard badass and goes on to repeatedly save the day. So whether you're a kid or a card-carrying member of the nerd community, I'll bet you'll cheer when Harry Potter conquers that gigantic 3-headed dog. —*J. S.*

HEARTS IN ATLANTIS L: PSYCHOTRONIC/KING, STEPHEN (2001) 101M D: Scott Hicks. *Anthony Hopkins, David Morse, Mika Boorem, Anton Yelchin, Hope Davis.* Hicks (*Shine*) adapts this Stephen King story (working from the best screenplay Oscar-winner William Goldman has penned in ages) about the friendship between odd, threadbare, literature-quoting recluse Ted Brautigan (Hopkins) and his adolescent neighbor Bobby (Yelchin). Brautigan is on the run from the "low men," he confesses, and is something of a mind reader, but his life lessons have as much to do with learning and literature as self-esteem and courage. Hopkins offers an understated, serene portrait of Ted, and Davis brings out the streak of selfishness and self-pity of Bobby's hard-luck mom without sinking into fairy tale wickedness: she's not so much inattentive as simply unhappy. Hicks captures the right mix of nostalgia and adversity for this coming-of-age story with a background of paranormal powers, clandestine conspiracies, and a predatory world. It's closest to Ray Bradbury's beautiful stories of adolescence, a rare story of childhood for adults. —*S. A.*

HELL IS A CITY L: HORROR/HAMMER FILMS (1959) 96M D: Val Guest. *Billie Whitelaw, Donald Pleasence, Stanley Baker, John Crawford.* Baker is a driven police inspector investigating a bank heist that ended in murder while keeping an ear out for an escaped prisoner (Crawford) who killed a guard in his flight. It turns out the two are connected. Baker brings his dominating presence and simmering control to his cop character, whose relentless dedication is proportional to the misery of his unhappy marriage, and Crawford is savage as the desperate killer on the run who has nothing to lose as he threatens old friends and enemies while plotting an escape route from the city. Director and screenwriter Guest brings a tough, hard-edged intensity to this oddly downbeat thriller. Pleasence and Whitelaw costar in this Hammer feature, one of their last nonhorror productions. —*S. A.*

HELLRAISER L: PSYCHOTRONIC/BARKER, CLIVE (1987) 94M D: Clive Barker. *Ashley Laurence, Clare Higgins, Doug Bradley, Andrew Robinson.* Barker directed and adapted his first feature film from his own novelette *Hellbound Heart*, bringing his disturbing and horrifying story to life. Shot on a relatively low budget, he makes due with shocking imagery, a believable cast, and ingenious FX. This original story creates a myth around a puzzle box that, when mastered, unlocks the doors to hell, releasing the tortured bondage demons known as Cenobites. Opening this doorway reveals hidden mysteries and untold pleasures,

but also the possibility of being lost in an eternal pain. Some of the imagery in this film will stick with you long after viewing, such as the rebirthing of Frank and the dismembering by hooked chains. This film takes itself seriously from start to finish, without the self-mocking tongue-in-cheek humor that so many horror films employ. *Hellraiser* spawned mostly poor sequels, the only one really worth seeing is the second, *Hellbound: Hellraiser II.* —*B. W.*

HELLBOUND: HELLRAISER II L: PSYCHOTRONIC/BARKER, CLIVE (1988) 96M D: Tony Randel. *Imogen Boorman, Kenneth Cranham, Ashley Laurence, William Hope, Claire Higgins.* The Hellraiser mythology is greatly expanded in this perversely imaginative horror fantasy. Dr. Channard (Cranham) wants to become a Cenobite, so he resurrects Julia (Higgins) from her bloody mattress and makes out with her while she's still skinless. What's worse, Kirsty's (Laurence) schmo boyfriend (Hope) is hiding behind a curtain watching the whole thing! The low budget isn't quite enough to match the ambition of the filmmakers, so you'll have to accept a few static matte paintings to depict the labyrinth of Hell and its geometric god Leviathan. In exchange for your patience you'll get all kinds of sick shit you don't expect in a horror sequel, including a mental patient who cuts himself because he thinks he's covered with insects and a scene where Kirsty wears Julia's skin but it accidentally slides off. It's still hard to believe I saw this movie in an American multiplex at Christmas. —*B. T.*

HELLRAISER III: HELL ON EARTH L: PSYCHOTRONIC /BARKER, CLIVE (1992) 93M D: Anthony Hickox. *Doug Bradley, Terry Farrell, Kevin Bernhardt, Ashley Laurence.* A hip nightclub owner (Bernhardt) buys a weird statue made from the remains of Pinhead (Bradley) and the other Cenobites. Soon he releases them and they slaughter everyone on the dance floor. At that same moment *Hellraiser* goes from brilliantly perverse fantasy epic to just another stupid slasher series. I guess it didn't occur to anyone that the bizarre S&M demons that are scary in a dark basement might look silly walking around the streets of New York City. They also shouldn't have introduced CD-Head (who shoots deadly CDs out of his head) or Camerahead (who uses the zoom lens in his eye to crush people). I mean for crying out loud, I'm positive that Clive Barker knew better than this, but he's still credited as producer. —*B. T.*

HIDDEN, THE L: SCIENCE FICTION/SCIENCE FICTION (1987) 97M D: Jack Sholder. *Kyle McLaughlan, Clarence Felder, Claudia Christian, Clu Gulager, Ed O'Ross, Michael Nouri.* There's a very strange visitor from another planet lurking about Los Angeles. *The Hidden* refers to a disgusting, sluglike alien that takes control of a randomly selected person's body. While it controls that person's faculties, it has an insatiably violent taste for expensive race cars, sex, and loud rock music. Perhaps this sounds like a lot of people in Los Angeles, but the main difference is that this alien is being hunted down by MacLachlan playing an FBI agent who doesn't seem quite right himself. This film holds up well to repeated viewings, thanks to a unique script and some very creative acting. —*N.J.*

HIGHLANDER L: SCIENCE FICTION/SCIENCE FICTION (1986) 110M D: Russell Mulcahy. *Beatie Edney, Christopher Lambert, Roxanne Hart, Clancy Brown, Sean Connery.* This was designed to be a fantasy cult film that would inspire many sequels. It is actually very little more than a B-grade thriller with a big budget, but many sequels followed anyway. Lambert plays a Scottish warrior (bad accent and all) who happens to be nearly immortal. He winds up in modern-day Manhattan hunting down his nearly immortal nemesis. If he can cut off the head of this antagonist with his family's sword, a 500-year feud will come to an end. Connery plays the mentor to the protagonist—at least he can do the Scottish accent! Followed by one of the worst sequels of modern history, *Highlander II: The Quickening.* —*N.J.*

HOLLYWOOD CHAINSAW HOOKERS L: PSEUDOTRONIC /PSEUDOTRONIC (FAUX TROMA) (1988) 75M D: Fred Olen Ray. *Michelle Bauer, Dawn Wildsmith, Jay Richardson, Linnea Quigley, Gunnar Hansen.* Ray's best film ever? Yes. Crazed hookers kill people with chainsaws while a noir-style detective searches for them. At the end there is a coven of witches or something. Plus, it stars Quigley and Bauer. Go for the naked hookers drenched in blood. Stay for the naked hookers drenched in blood. —*T.S.*

HORROR HOSPITAL L: HORROR/EURO-HORROR (1973) 91M D: Anthony Balch. *Vanessa Shaw, Michael Gough, Robin Askwith, Dennis Price.* Balch, using a different version of "cut-up" than he learned from buddy William Burroughs, exhibits the zany antics of Dr. Storm (Gough) and friends as they enact their plan to "cure" the young people of early '70s England of their hang-ups by frying their brains and turning them into gape-mouthed zombified guinea pigs. Most of *Horror Hospital* concerns young Jason and new friend Judy, who want a holiday at Judy's Aunt Harris, the wife of Dr. Storm. The zombified folk at the castle don't faze the young couple, but other guests who do sense trouble are quickly dispensed with either by a remarkable beheading vehicle or by brutes who bludgeon the guests bloody. Not a great film by any means, but *Horror Hospital* is filled with tons of fun bits and silly scenes. —*S.R.*

HORROR HOTEL L: CLASSIC HORROR/CLASSIC HORROR (1960) 76M D: John Moxey. *Venetia Stevenson, Christopher Lee.* Moxey (better known as TV horror and fantasy specialist John Llewellyn Moxey) turns this interesting, straightforward story of a coven of witches in a small Massachusetts village into a

moody horror film on a budget not much bigger than his later TV movies. Borrowing elements from *Psycho* and Val Lewton's RKO horror classics, George Baxt's lean screenplay nicely sets up the surprises and revelations to come. Moxey makes the most of his limited resources with dynamic staging, turning the studio-bound setting of Whitewood into a claustrophobic nightmare of a town in perpetual night carpeted with a thick layer of swirling mist. —*S.A.*

HORRORS OF THE BLACK MUSEUM L: CLASSIC HORROR/ CLASSIC HORROR (1959) 95M D: Arthur Crabtree. *Michael Gough, Geoffrey Keen, June Cunningham, Graham Curnow, Shirley Ann Field.* A gruesome murderer who uses arcane tools inspired by the exhibits in Scotland Yard's private Black Museum stalks the young women of London. The lurid articles by slumming sophisticate crime reporter Edmond Bancroft (Gough, playing him like the Waldo Lydecker of the murder beat) is only making Scotland Yard's job harder. Produced in England by American exploitation specialist Herman Cohen, the film is never quite as gruesome as its calling card moments would have you think (though if you ever saw the opening minutes as a child, you probably thought twice before putting your naked eyes to a pair of binoculars). Gough has far too much fun as the (almost assuredly impotent) aesthete caught in a confused mad scientist/psycho-killer relationship and obsessed with gory details of murder. The tawdry, sordid atmosphere of "the poetry of murder" makes this ghoulish bit of British Grand Guignol feel just a little perverse, which elevates it to cultdom. —*S.A.*

HOUSE OF DRACULA L: CLASSIC HORROR/CLASSIC HORROR (1945) 67M D: Erle C. Kenton. *Lon Chaney Jr., Martha O'Driscoll, Lionel Atwill, Glenn Strange, Jane Adams, John Carradine.* Oh how far the mighty can fall. It's sad the amazing classic Universal legacy had to end with *House of Dracula* as the last official entry in their horror saga. Dracula is revived only to suffer an even lamer death this time. Wolfman mysteriously comes back to life as well and receives that always-elusive cure to his lycanthropy, a surprisingly anticlimactic event. Frankenstein is only alive a few minutes at the end and dies in exactly the same way as in *Ghost of Frankenstein,* because they reused the footage from that film. The monsters never really interact with each other, much less battle. Still, this film has some interesting aspects. It treats the monsters' afflictions as diseases rather than standard supernatural aberrations. Dracula bites the mad Doctor Edelmann, but since the doctor never drinks any vampire blood, he becomes a half vampire in the spirit of Jekyll and Hyde. He's a fascinating character who could have sustained a whole movie had it been made right. Sadly, it wasn't and *House of Dracula* is a weak finale to the wonderful series. —*T.S.*

HOUSE OF FRANKENSTEIN L: CLASSIC HORROR/CLASSIC HORROR (1944) 71M D: Erle C. Kenton.

Anne Gwynne, John Carradine, Lionel Atwill, Boris Karloff, Lon Chaney Jr., J. Carrol Naish. The first film to bring together Dracula, the Wolfman, and Frankenstein, *House of Frankenstein* is about a mad scientist who escapes an institution and resurrects the monsters in order to get revenge on his many enemies. The cold-hearted doctor and a fickle gypsy beauty both get their comeuppance at the hands of the monsters, whose wild antics and horrifying brutality make this film more fun than a barrel of monkeys. I mean, how could a film with Dracula, Frankenstein, AND the Wolfman be bad? It's an impossibility. An utter impossibility. —*T. S.*

HOUSE OF LONG SHADOWS L: CLASSIC HORROR/CLASSIC HORROR (1983) 100M D: Pete Walker.

Vincent Price, Christopher Lee, Peter Cushing, John Carradine, Desi Arnaz Jr. House of Long Shadows is an amazing film to watch. Never have so many horror icons starred in not only the same movie, but the same scenes. When a writer, played by Arnaz Jr., takes a bet to write a Gothic novel in twenty-four hours, he travels to a creepy old manor house to work. Before he can even start, strange things start to happen as the house is teeming with mysterious characters spreading their macabre charm. The film is a joy to behold, just to witness these amazing actors giving it their all and really hamming it up. The plot is nicely put together and the twist ending works well. The film comes off as a great tribute to a bygone era of Gothic horror. Sadly, we don't have any iconic actors for horror films anymore. At least I can watch *House of Long Shadows* and remember how awesome they all were. —*T. S.*

HOUSE OF 1,000 CORPSES L: HORROR/STALKERS (2003) 88M D: Rob Zombie.

Karen Black, Bill Moseley, Sherri Moon, Dennis Fimple, Harrison Young, Sid Haig. Zombie's directorial debut plays out with all the hypersaturated, psychedelic grindhouse horror of his music videos. And unfortunately it makes about as much sense. With standout performances from almost all the kindred psychos, including Moselely, Black, and the demented genius of Haig, *House* plays out like a greatest hits of horror's last fifty years. With nearly every shot paying homage to another horror film, the movie is a horror fan's delirious fever dream. When Lion's Gate finally released this film, it sadly was a heavily edited version. Not only is there very little gore, there seems to be about a half hour's worth of story missing from the third act and the film's abrupt ending leaves you confused and disappointed. But overall you get the feeling that Zombie made exactly the film that he set out to and his gleeful, childlike exuberance about his idols shines through in every frame. —*T. S.*

HOUSE OF THE DEAD L: HORROR/ZOMBIES (2003) 90M D: Uwe Boll.

Jonathon Cherry, Tyron Leitso, Kira Clavell, Clint Howard. A word to the faithful: despite the use of a DMX song in the trailer and TV ads for this film there is NO DMX song anywhere in it, not even the credits. Rip-off. Anyway, *House of the Dead* is without a doubt one of the worst films of 2003. There is a sexy chick (Clavell) who wears a red, white, and blue hot-pant suit, but this is *still* one of the worst films of 2003. It seems to be stuck in a time warp: The "kids" (thirty-plus-year-olds) are going to a "rave" (who does that anymore?) and Prodigy is constantly playing in the background. Is this 1994? And Clint Howard's in it (sorry Clint). Five minutes in and you know it's gonna be bad. It turns out to be horrible. Horrid script, really horrid acting. Clips of the actual video game splash onto the screen, as if the opening credit roll, which starts with "based on the Sega video game," and the Sega signs hanging at the "rave" aren't enough of a reminder of what spawned this piece of crap. You should probably avoid this film unless you're trying to see every zombie film ever made. —*G. M.*

HOUSE ON HAUNTED HILL, THE L: HORROR/GHOSTS (1999) 93M D: William Malone

Ali Larter, Chris Kattan, Famke Janssen, Peter Gallagher, Geoffrey Rush, Taye Diggs. This haunted house thrill ride, adapted from the gimmicky William Castle classic, is the giddiest, goofiest horror funhouse made in years. Rush puts his tongue firmly in cheek to play the Vincent Price role, a snarky, snarling carnival showman with a John Waters mustache, a James Woods layer of sleaze, and a boorish sense of humor. Janssen purrs with malevolent hatred as his gold-digging wife. Their haunted house party, an invitation-only bash thrown for a group of strangers who are promised $1 million if they can stay the night in the notorious mansion and remain alive through morning, turns into a mess of crisscrossing schemes, all played for cheap thrills and black humor until it gets outrageously out of control. It's an old-fashioned spook show as a slick, silly, and energetic B-movie, powered by fun and enthusiasm. Jeffrey Combs has a cameo in the jittery flashbacks. —*S. A.*

HOUSE WITH LAUGHING WINDOWS L: HORROR/GIALLO (ITALIAN HORROR) (1976) 110M D: Pupi Avati.

Lino Capolicchio, Andrea Matteuzzi, Francesca Marciano, Gianni Cavina, Giulio Pizzirani, Vanna Busoni. House with Laughing Windows is a cut above most *giallos*, building a nice atmosphere of paranoia and deception. Aside from the brutal title sequence (try not to feel a little dirty while watching it), there isn't much gore until things start heating up toward the end. Capolicchio plays Stefano, an artist sent to finish a fresco by another artist who died under unusual circumstances. Most of the town is unmoved by his efforts, some resorting to anonymous threats. Soon he is forced out of his hotel room and into an old, decrepit house occupied only by a bed-bound woman. He begins an affair with a young teacher and gradually starts to uncover the defaced fresco and the mystery behind its artist. His curiosity leads to obsession and Stefano soon finds himself in a compromised situation risking love and life. —*M. H.*

HOW HIGH L: PSYCHOTRONIC/DRUGS (2001) 93M D: Jesse Dylan. *Fred Willard, Method Man, Redman, Obba Babatunde, Mike Epps.* The rap duo of Method Man and Redman makes the leap to big screen comedy team with slightly better results than The Fat Boys (*Disorderlies*) and Dr. Dre and Ed Lover (*Who's the Man?*). But only slightly. Red and Meth play potheads who smoke a special type of weed made out of their dead friend, whose ghost gives them the answers to tests so they can get into Harvard. As you'd expect, their wacky, outrageous antics take the starch out of many a collar. It's about as cheesy as any movie could be, and the character types (uptight yuppie dean, sweater-wearing preppy boyfriend, etc.) are broad enough to make *Revenge of the Nerds* look naturalistic. But the humor gets so asinine (the dean's last name is Caine, so he's Dean Caine—get it? Like Superman!) and weird (they actually dig up a dead body and "smoke his skeleton ass") that you eventually have to give in and start laughing. —*B. T.*

HUNDRA L: FANTASY/FANTASY (1983) 90M D: Matt Cimber. *Laurene Landon, John Gaffari.* As she did in *All the Marbles*, blond Amazon Landon, as Hundra, shows off her chops as a woman of action. She uses sword and bow to disembowel, skewer, and decapitate practically every male she encounters. You see, Hundra is kind of angry. Seems that a band of hairy, slavering goons raped and slaughtered her entire village of woman-warriors while Hundra was out hunting. Now Hundra wants revenge. Unfortunately, an oracle tells her that in order to keep from being the last of her kind, Hundra must mate—with one of the goons! What's a woman-warrior to do? Set to a rousing Ennio Morricone score that perfectly compliments the film's epic intentions, and directed by Cimber with an eye for action as well as a sense of humor, *Hundra* is a true cinematic rarity: an '80s sword-and-sorcery film that actually doesn't suck. —*S. F.*

I DRINK YOUR BLOOD L: HORROR/CANNIBALS (1971) 90M D: David E. Durston. *John McCook, Bhaskar.* A multiracial group of hippie Satanists in bell-bottoms torments a small town until a kid gives them rabies-infested meat pies. After taking some bad acid, the Manson-inspired clan freaks out and turns into crazed lunatics, killing and/or infecting everything and everyone in their path. Electric knives, pitchforks, false teeth, and garden hoses are all used as lethal weapons. There's self-immolation, decapitation, group sex, rabid construction workers in yellow hard hats, and

lots of gore. I thought this movie was pretty funny, but it almost made my friends throw up. *I Drink Your Blood* was severely trimmed for an R-rating but is now available uncut on DVD. Yee-haw! Barf!! —*S. H.*

I SPIT ON YOUR GRAVE L: HORROR/STALKERS (1977) 100M D: Meir Zarchi. *Camille Keaton, Eron Tabor, Richard Pace.* Her half-naked body contorts in pain. Her face fissures. She bellows like a dying animal. Jennifer (Keaton) is vacationing in the country to relax by a lazy river and do some writing. Matthew (Pace) and his two buddies decide Johnny (Tabor) has been a virgin long enough, so they trap Jennifer when she's out on a stroll. Though Johnny balks, the others don't. By the time they leave her for dead, her clothes are blood-soaked and shredded. These are the most unflinching rape scenes ever put on film. But if anything could be colder, it is the vengeance she reaps next. To see someone transform from urban gentility to animal-like victim to cold-eyed killer has never been portrayed on film so compellingly. Keaton is a deep-down powerful performer. *I Spit on Your Grave* is an emotionally stark, intellectually honest masterpiece of exploitation cinema. —*J. C.*

I STILL KNOW WHAT YOU DID LAST SUMMER L: HORROR/STALKERS (1998) 120M D: Danny Cannon. *Mekhi Phifer, Freddie Prinze Jr., Muse Watson, Jeffrey Combs, Jennifer Love Hewitt, Brandy.* *I Know What You Did Last Summer*'s survivors (Hewitt and Prinze) go with their friend (Brandy) to the Bahamas for an all-expenses-paid vacation she won in a radio contest. But the hotel is run by a crazy man (Combs) and to make matters worse, everybody keeps getting killed by a maniac fisherman (Watson). If this sounds like dumb fun, then go for it. As a special bonus you get an uncredited Jack Black as a pot dealer who moans, "It's all good," as he gets hooked to death. —*B. T.*

ICE CREAM MAN L: HORROR/STALKERS (1995) 87M D: Norman Apstein. *Clint Howard, Sandahl Bergman, Lee Majors II, Olivia Hussey, David Warner.* The best part of this video is the box it comes in. To be fair, there are some funny moments—it's just difficult to decide if it's worth sitting through the entire film to see them. Predictably, the Ice Cream Man (Howard) chops up people and serves their body parts in his ice cream. But all of this can be seen on the box. In the film we actually get to see the Ice Cream Man's flashbacks through a fish-eyed lens featuring a giant clown doing the most unspeakable acts to him, acts that made him the Ice Cream Man he is today. Now do you want to sit through it? Perhaps it's better just to admire the box. —*N. J.*

IN SEARCH OF THE CASTAWAYS L: PSYCHOTRONIC /VERNE, JULES (1962) 98M D: Robert Stevenson. *Maurice Chevalier, Hayley Mills, George Sanders.* Before "Don't Worry, Be Happy" there was the perfectly

dreadful Mills and the disarmingly charming Chevalier in this flick: a mix of Jules Verne, a New Testament (happy ending) view of Ecclesiastes, and Disney hokum. Fun for the whole family (but especially good on mushrooms), the film seduces you into enjoying its rambling storyline and dares you to just "enjoy it!" —*K. S.*

INCUBUS L: HORROR/DEMONS (1965) 78M D: Leslie Stevens. *William Shatner, Allyson Ames, Robert Fortier.* This is a very curious cult film in that it is the first (and very possibly the last) completely shot using the artificial language of Esperanto. Shatner plays Marc, a soldier injured in a war and returning home. On the way he is stopped and seduced by Kia (Ames), a female demon who normally kills all the wayward men she meets. But she determines this soldier to be pure of heart and decides to spare him, soon falling in love with him. This becomes difficult to hide from her evil sister demon and eventually the sister resorts to summoning the Incubus. Beautifully shot in black and white, the digitally restored DVD features audio commentaries by Shatner and the film's producer, Anthony Taylor. —*N. J.*

INNERSPACE L: SCIENCE FICTION/SCIENCE FICTION (1982) 92M D: Joe Dante. *Meg Ryan, Dennis Quaid, Martin Short, Kevin McCarthy, Fiona Lewis, Henry Gibson.* Imagine *Fantastic Voyage* as sci-fi slapstick. Quaid is a reckless test pilot shrunk to molecular dimensions in a secret experiment and accidentally shot into the bloodstream of a hypochondriac grocery clerk (Short), who immediately believes he's possessed when the micronaut starts talking inside his head. It's prime material for Dante, who sends Short into rubbery convulsions and casts some of his favorite old-time sci-fi faces (McCarthy as the heavy, William Schallert and Kenneth Tobey in bits, and Dante's good-luck charm Dick Miller) in a cast that features Ryan, in one of her earliest headlining roles, and Gibson, a marvelously softspoken straight man to Short's explosive gyrations. It's fast and furious and careens around as much as Short's jittery performance, and if it comes up short on narrative spine and story center, Dante's manic energy and B-movie spirit manages to pull it off. —*S. A.*

INVASION OF THE BLOOD FARMERS L: HORROR/WITCHES & WARLOCKS (1972) 86M D: Ed Adlum. *Paul Craig Jennings, Norman Kelley.* Modern druids are drawing blood from hapless victims to keep their queen happy in her Plexiglas coffin. A cheapie from upstate New York, *Invasion of the Blood Farmers* features a great/stupid title, tinted scenes, hilarious '70s pants and belt buckles, inept acting, and zombified pitchfork-wielding henchmen in overalls. It's pretty bad but what would you expect from the guy who made *Blonde on a Bum Trip* and *Shriek of the Mutilated*? This film is fun to watch except that the blood sucking scenes

seem to go on and on. Still the Plexiglas coffin alone is worth the rental price. —*S. H.*

IT L: PSYCHOTRONIC/KING, STEPHEN (1990) 193M D: Tommy Lee Wallace. *John Ritter, Annette O'Toole, Tim Curry, Harry Anderson.* For children, clowns are really fucking creepy, and evil clowns with evil balloons who rip the arms off kids and make blood come out of the bathroom sink and turn into werewolves and chase bicycles pretty much epitomize terror. Adults are likely to feel nothing close to fright. The acting is mediocre, the scary scenes just aren't scary, and the movie is way, way, way too long. A movie half as long with more clown and less shitty dialogue would have been better. —*J. S.*

IT CAME FROM BENEATH THE SEA L: PSYCHOTRONIC/ HARRYHAUSEN, RAY (1955) 79M D: Robert Gordon. *Faith Domergue, Kenneth Tobey, Donald Curtis.* A by-the-books giant monster movie that's too derivative of other, better movies (such as *Beast from 20,000 Fathoms*) but it's still memorable for its six-armed octopus. Two tentacles were removed for budgetary reasons and it's hard to tell the difference, but that's what most people mention when they discuss this movie. *It Came . . .* predictably starts with a submarine spotting a strange shape with its radar. It turns out to be a gigantic mutant octopus that makes its way down the west coast of North America and eventually attacks various San Francisco landmarks. It's up to the sub captain and two nuclear scientists to kill the big sea critter. There's too much stereotypical sci-fi romance (sub captain and hot young scientist) and not nearly enough octopus. —*S. H.*

IT! THE TERROR FROM BEYOND SPACE L: CLASSIC SCIENCE FICTION/CLASSIC SCIENCE FICTION (1958) 69M D: Edward L. Cahn. *Marshall Thompson, Ray Corrigan, Dabbs Greer, Ann Doran, Shirley Patterson, Kim Spalding.* *Alien* is essentially an uncredited remake of this low-budget '50s sci-fi flick, as much of the plot and situations were re-created with an increased budget and amped-up suspense. The crew of the first expedition to Mars is killed except for the captain, who is rescued by another spaceship. The demented captain believes a space monster killed his crew and that the creature has stowed away on the spaceship. Pretty much everybody thinks the captain did it, until people start getting killed by the titular It! (Corrigan in a rubber suit with clawed hands). There are no exploding chests or sexy astronauts in panties and it's pretty cheap and dated (set in the far off future of 1973) but this is a fun little movie and provides an interesting blueprint for Ridley Scott's film. —*S. H.*

JACK FROST L: HORROR/STALKERS (1997) 95M D: Michael Cooney. *Scott MacDonald, Christopher Allport, Shannon Elizabeth.* Not to be confused with the shitty kid's movie where Michael Keaton returns from the dead as a happy, loving snowman, this Jack Frost is pure evil. He's a convicted serial killer on the way to his execution when he gets into a car accident that transforms him into a genetically mutated snowman. Evil is in his every water molecule, and he returns to seek revenge on everybody. This movie is bad, but it's a campy kind of bad, full of one-liners and cheesy murders. One of the best scenes is when Jack melts himself into Elizabeth's bathwater, waits for her to get in, and then solidifies so that she is stuck in him and can't escape. In the end, Jack is defeated of course, but is he REALLY defeated? Only the sequel will tell. —*J. S.*

JACKASS: THE MOVIE L: PSYCHOTRONIC/SHOCK (2002)
87M D: Jeff Tremaine. *Dave Englund, Johnny Knoxville, Bam Margera, Steve-O, Chris Pontius, Ryan Dunn.* At the dawn of the twenty-first century, humanity is on the brink of enormous change. We could continue down the path we have chosen, falling deeper and deeper into a technological isolation in which the daily rhythms of our lives attune themselves to the blinking of a cursor on a screen, the beating of war drums by the puppets in public office, the rise and fall of the stock market, or the pulsating trends prescribed to us by coprporations more interested in acquiring wealth than enjoying it. Or, we could reclaim our humanity, learning to live one moment at a time, enjoying life to its fullest, always finding a reason to laugh and love, and joyfully fall forward into the sunrise of the brand-new day. *Jackass: The Movie* is a guiding light through this dark night, leading us toward a world where we can learn to find happiness in the simplest of things. Things like shooting fireworks out of our asses or jumping headfirst into a river of sewage. —*T. S.*

JASON X L: HORROR/STALKERS (2002) 93M D: James Isaac.
Lisa Ryder, Lexa Doig, Dov Tiefenbach, Kane Hodder. The *Friday the 13th* series is hilariously reinvented in this clever ninth sequel. Hundreds of years in the future, a science class finds Jason cryogenically frozen on the wasteland Earth. Before you know it, they bring him onto their spaceship and awaken him by exposing him to the sounds of teenage sex. The filmmakers seem to have made a list of cool things Jason could do in a sci-fi movie that he never did before, and it's all there: impaling a guy on a giant drill, chemically freezing a victim's head, fighting in virtual reality, turning into a robot, getting sucked out an airlock, and more. Like *Bride of Chucky,* the filmmakers are clearly aware of the absurdity, whether or not the audience is willing to give them credit for it. This installment complicates matters for anyone trying to calculate a Jason body count because he casually destroys an apparently populated space station. —*B. T.*

JAWS 2 L: VAOWG/VAOWG (1978) 116M D: Jeannot Szwarc.
Roy Scheider, Keith Gordon, Lorraine Gary, Murray Hamilton, Mark Gruner. There was no way for Universal not to make *Jaws 2*, considering *Jaws* was the biggest film of its day. *Jaws 2* was started by director John Hancock (*Let's Scare Jessica to Death*), but he was replaced midshoot by director Szwarc (later of *Supergirl*). The result is an OK sequel. Scheider gets to grand stand again as Amity Island sheriff Brody who knows what's going on when another giant (now forty-foot!) great white swims into his waters during the summer season. The film has a terribly dated look to it, and the teenagers the shark targets all look far too old and exhibit an air of stupidity. The best sequence in the film features two teens out on their own in a boat, making out, as the boat gets hit by the shark. The boy falls in the water, is carried around back and forth inside the shark's mouth and just as the girl reaches down to save him, the shark pulls him down underwater, leaving only a pool of blood. It is really the film's only frightening moment. Unlike the first film, director Szwarc decides to show us the creature in all his glory right off the bat, so all pretenses of this being a real shark are out the window. —*N. H.*

JAWS: THE REVENGE (AKA JAWS 4: THE REVENGE)
L: VAOWG/VAOWG (1987) 87M D: Joseph Sargent. *Mario Van Peebles, Michael Caine, Lorraine Gary, Lance Guest, Karen Young.* A great white shark shows up in Amity waters again, murders Roy Scheider's youngest son from *Jaws 3*, and chases Mom (Gary) all the way to the Bahamas to kill her, her oldest son, and her grandchild! Why? Because it's mad at the family for killing the other three sharks. This sad final entry in the *Jaws* saga includes scenes of Gary going to the water's edge, hand at her head, as she senses the shark out there waiting for her. Caine stars, rather superfluously, as Gary's new boyfriend (Scheider's character died of heart failure), but he's not much help when the film ends with Gary herself facing down the shark from a boat. Gary was married to head honcho Sid Scheinberg at Universal who obviously wanted a trip to the Bahamas with his wife at studio expense, as there was no other reason to make this turkey. The shark effects have never looked worse, and this entry closed the door on any more *Jaws* films. —*N. H.*

JEEPERS CREEPERS L: HORROR/DEMONS (2001) 90M
D: Victor Salva. *Patricia Belcher, Gina Phillips, Justin Long, Jonathan Breck.* This is a well-done little monster movie with intriguing character dynamics, fantastic monster design, and some honest scares. It wisely takes itself seriously for the most part, throwing in a fun tongue-in-cheek ending and just few other laughs. It's the structure that really makes *Jeepers Creepers* work. The tension builds perfectly throughout the film. This is no masterpiece but it's a very well-crafted film that provides plenty of entertainment for those seeking a modern monster movie. —*T. S.*

JESUS CHRIST VAMPIRE HUNTER L: PSEUDOTRONIC /PSEUDOTRONIC (FAUX TROMA) (2002) 85M D: Lee Demarbre *Jeff Moffet, Maria Moulton, Phil Caracas, Murielle Varhelyi, Ian Driscoll.* Buffy's got nothing on Our Lord, the vampire slayer. With the help of red leather–clad Mary Magnum and Mexican wrestler superhero El Santo, Jesus (Caracas) makes Ontario the site of the Second Coming and takes on a plague of vampires who walk in the sunlight and prey upon defenseless lesbians. A shaggy, silly, and good-natured horror spoof with musical numbers, '70s-style kung fu action, and a message of love and acceptance (except for, of course, evil vampires), this film earns its cult credentials. It's funny ("Bless the lake, quickly!" shouts Jesus to his priest sidekicks as he busts his martial arts moves on a bevy of vampire goth punks) and more fun that it has a right to be, and the post-dubbed dialogue and library sound-effects only enhance the experience. Someone surely blessed this production. —*S. A.*

JIM ROSE CIRCUS SIDESHOW L: PSYCHOTRONIC/SHOCK (1993) 35M D: Jonathan Dayton. *Jim Rose, The Amazing Mr. Lifto, The Enigma, The Torture King.* Watch as the Human Enigma consumes wriggling insects! Squirm as the Amazing Mr. Lifto picks up heavy objects with his nipples! You will be in awe when the Torture King skewers his face with a giant needle! Rose's motley collection of circus geeks do everything imaginable to shock, amaze, and disgust their audience in this (brilliant?) 1993 performance. One of the best acts involves running three feet of rubber tube down a man's throat, shotgunning a forty-ounce straight into his belly, sucking the beer (and bile) back out, and then drinking it! Other highlights include razorblade swallowing, a human dartboard, and genital mutilation. And it's beautiful. Maybe I'm being a bit sentimental here, but Rose's impassioned effort to preserve the art of the sideshow, even in this scientific age when true human oddities are getting rarer and rarer, is admirable, and the level at which he succeeds is pure fucking perfection. —*T. S.*

JOHNNY MNEMONIC L: SCIENCE FICTION/SCIENCE FICTION (1995) 96M D: Robert Longo. *Henry Rollins, Keanu Reeves, Dina Meyer, Ice-T, Takeshi Kitano, Dolph Lundgren.* Perhaps in 1995 the world wasn't ready for a cinematic version of cyberpunk, as audiences completely scoffed at this movie upon its initial release. Reeves takes up the title character, a courier in the twenty-first century who stores data plugged directly into his brain until it is ready to be extracted. When a rival yakuza gang interrupts his latest transaction, Johnny must figure out the code that will unlock his brain before it overloads. William Gibson adapted his own short story into the screenplay, an elaborated, slightly alternate version of the original. The cyberpunk style, technology, and terminology are believably brought to the screen, and only those fans most dedicated to

Gibson's novels could be turned off by the B-movie aspects of the film. The cast has a lot of fun overplaying their roles as motley members of the future underworld. Who among us can't enjoy a film with a dolphin that talks through a computer? —*R. M.*

JOHNNY SOKKO AND HIS FLYING ROBOT (4 VOLUMES) L: JAPANESE SCIENCE FICTION/JAPANESE TV (1967) 30M D: Michio Konishi, Itaru Orita, others. *Mitsunobu Kaneko, Mitsuo Andô.* Better known as *Giant Robot*, this series is about a boy named Johnny Sokko (Kaneko) who, with the help of an organization called Unicorn, controls a giant robot to fight against the wicked Emperor Guillotine. The robot (who can fly and shoot missiles out of his fingers) has an Egyptian pharaoh look that is among the coolest robot designs ever. But it's the fact that a little kid (with short shorts, a cool watch, and sometimes a helmet) is the hero that probably put it over the top for the kids who grew up loving this show. The whole series was edited into a movie called *Voyage into Space* that was sometimes shown on television, and ended with Giant Robot sacrificing himself to save Earth. In the '90s it inspired an anime series. Unfortunately, the live-action version has only been made widely available on this video series, which is now out of print. —*B. T.*

JUNGLE HOLOCAUST L: HORROR/CANNIBALS (1977) 88M D: Ruggero Deodato. *Ivan Rassimov, Me Me Lai, Massimo Faschi.* Made by Deodato before his notorious *Cannibal Holocaust*, this is actually a far better film. With more realistic characters, a more frightening atmosphere, and more blood and guts, I'll take *Jungle Holocaust* any day of the week. While *Cannibal* is nothing but overdone bullshit that lingers far too long on unlikable characters and their boring adventure, *Jungle* is suspenseful and uses its disturbing images to much greater effect. The story is about some guys who fly into the jungle to check on a team of scientists only to find them all missing. Their plane is damaged and they get lost in the jungle. Carnage ensues. But where *Cannibal* plays out like a bunch of elaborately gory set pieces, this film is more emotional, honest, intense, and satisfying. The action pulls you in and the rawness and brutality doesn't let you go. This is the best jungle cannibal movie there is—it's too bad that it's overshadowed by its younger brother. —*T. S.*

JUNK L: JAPANESE HORROR/JAPANESE HORROR (1999) 91M D: Atsushi Muroga. *Osamu Ebara, Nobuyuki Asano, Tate Gouta.* Muroga reworks his double-crossing robbery plot from *Score* to incorporate the living dead. While a quartet of amateur thieves are making a successful assault on a jewelry store, a government experiment to raise the dead in an abandoned warehouse is spinning out of control. This warehouse is the exact location they are to meet their contacts, who intend to kill them at the rendezvous. As the hand-off is about to go down, Romero-style zombies interrupt the transaction and the mayhem begins. The thieves and yakuza fight each other and the zombies, and a team of government scientists arrives on the scene and join in, adding to the chaos, and inevitably raising more zombies with green goo right out of *Re-Animator*. Messy entrails snacking? Check. Bad English dialogue in a Japanese film? Check. Over-the-top acting? Check. Attempt to reanimate dead girlfriend goes horribly wrong and starts the whole mess? Check. So break out the popcorn and start the maniacal laughter. —*R. M.*

JU-ON: THE GRUDGE L: JAPANESE HORROR/JAPANESE HORROR (2003) 92M D: Takeshi Shimizu. *Migumi Okina, Misaki Ito, Yui Ichikawa.* With a plot revolving around a supernatural curse born of terrible events, *Ju-On* shows us that the scariest horror relies not on convoluted storylines and confusing "rules" but on unrelenting suspense, the constant build up of tension punctuated by nerve-destroying climaxes. The story is a sort of horror fugue in which the themes are explored in short segments, connected but not interwoven, building upon a theme until its final conclusion, apparent but unpredictable. Perhaps one the scariest films ever made, *Ju-On* towers above even the films of Hideo Nakata and Kiyoshi Kurosawa. The cream of the crop as far as contemporary Japanese horror is concerned, this film will chill you to the bone and leave you in awe, awash in terror-sweat and giddy with excitement. —*T. S.*

JURASSIC PARK III L: VAOWG/VAOWG (2001) 92M D: Joe Johnston. *Téa Leoni, Sam Neill, William H. Macy.* Johnston (*The Rocketeer*) takes over from Steven Spielberg for the third installment of the trilogy about modern dinosaur adventures. Neill returns as the kid-phobic paleontologist, this time leading an unauthorized expedition to the new dinosaur island by globetrotting adventurers Macy and Leoni, except that all is not as it seems. Swifter and leaner than the first two installments, it's more of a souped-up genre adventure than the previous films, and therein lies both its drawbacks and its appeal. It packs little dramatic punch and it doesn't take much time before we wish the embarrassingly idiotic search party dead, but bear with the film: it pays off in modestly scaled and sleekly accomplished adventure. Alexander Payne and Jim Taylor, the scribes behind *Election*, lent a hand in rewrites. —*S. A.*

KILLER KLOWNS FROM OUTER SPACE L: PSEUDOTRONIC/ PSEUDOTRONIC (FAUX TROMA) (1988) 90M D: Stephen Chiodo. *Grant Cramer, Suzanne Snyder, John Vernon.* In a straight-faced parody of science fiction horror, small-town teens are the first to discover an alien invasion by a race that appear to be clowns. They fire popcorn guns, harvest people inside cotton candy cocoons, drink blood through crazy straws, and even use balloon animals as bloodhounds. The protagonists theorize that our conception of clowns actually comes from this race when they visited Earth in ancient times. Made by FX-artist siblings the Chiodo brothers, the movie is very enjoyable for its morbid circus-themed gags and imaginative animatronic creatures. Director Stephen Chiodo animated the Large Marge sequence in *Pee-wee's Big Adventure*, and that's not too far from the cartoonish aesthetic of the Klowns. —*B. T.*

KILLING OF SATAN L: HORROR/DEMONS (1983) 95M D: Efren C. Pinon. *George Estregan, Charlie Davao, Ramon Revilla, Elizabeth Oropesa, Paquito Diaz.* An evil magician in cahoots with the devil hassles the good residents of a Philippine island. He makes a guy's head spin around, shoots rays at people, kidnaps some women, and laughs heartily. It's up to tough but good-natured Lando to avenge his uncle's death and save his relatives. Equipped with a doomed sidekick and a magic elbow (!), Lando travels to Hell (which is located in a cave on a nearby island), where he fights snake people, deadly boulders, Satan, and an unexpected hurricane. Crudely produced with almost no budget but loaded with ample enthusiasm, *The Killing of Satan* is one of my all-time cheapo favorites. Filled with half-assed martial arts, naked women in cages, Christian allegories, unexpected gore, hilarious dubbing, a Halloween-costumed Satan, and at least four scenes that make me go "Huh?"—it doesn't get much better (or worse) than this! —*S. H.*

KING KONG LIVES (AKA KING KONG 2) L: VAOWG/VAOWG (1986) 105M D: John Guillermin. *Peter Elliott, John Ashton, George Yiasoumi, Brian Kerwin, Linda Hamilton.* After his terrible commercial flop with *Dune* in '83, producer Dino De Laurentiis returned in '86, sans Paramount, and brought back director Guillermin, giving him double the budget ($40 million) for a second go at *Kong*. This time, Kong is revived by veterinarian Hamilton via a giant mechanical heart transplant (no kidding)! Queen Kong, with huge tits, is found in the jungle by Brian Kerwin, who, in a tricky reversal on the Kong/Ann Darrow theme, becomes the Queen's dumb blonde love interest. Kerwin and Hamilton get together, and then try and get the apes together, in hopes of creating some monkey love. However, the pesky government, funding the whole thing, gets in the middle of the couple's attempts at creating a giant ape blind date. Kong gets mad, Queen gets pregnant, and a new baby Kong enters the world. This is a movie about the rights for giant apes everywhere. . . —*N. H.*

KINGDOM OF THE SPIDERS L: VAOWG/VAOWG (1977) 94M D: John Cardos. *William Shatner, Tiffany Bolling, Woody Strode.* This low-budget tarantulas-take-the-town film is very sluggish at the beginning as it tries to establish characters who ultimately

become spider-bait in a dusty Western town. Particularly slow are the subplots concerning Shatner's dead brother and his love interests. Ultimately he falls in love with the traveling scientist, who tells him that the deaths of local bulls and cattle are caused by spiders. Eventually the dramatis personae begins diminishing with the help of countless aggressive tarantulas with venom five times more potent than normal. All this because of DDT, the scientist insists. There's good stuff toward the end: tarantulas wrapping their victims in webs, taking out airplanes as they fly, and of course the final showdown. All in all it's good fun for the patient Shatner fan. —*N. J.*

KONGA L: VAOWG/VAOWG (1961) 90M D: John Lemont. *Claire Gordon, Margo Johns, Jess Conrad, Michael Gough.* A botany professor (Gough) missing in the jungle for a while comes back with a pet monkey named Konga and some new witch doctor skills that lead to important breakthroughs in carnivorous plant-making. Oh yeah, and turning Konga into a seven-foot, mind-controlled gorilla. Soon he orders Konga to kill a dean that might stop the professor's experiments, justifying it by saying it's the only way to prove total control. And then he has him kill other rivals, I guess to prove it even more. During the bungled sexual harassment of a student, Konga drinks a formula that makes him turn giant, and you can imagine where it goes from there. *Konga* is very enjoyable for its bug-eyed ape and (like James Whale's *The Invisible Man*) for the sheer outrageous amorality of its antihero. —*B. T.*

KRONOS L: CLASSIC SCIENCE FICTION/CLASSIC SCIENCE FICTION (1957) 78M D: Kurt Neumann. *John Emery, Jeff Morrow, Barbara Lawrence, George O'Hanlon, Morris Ankrum.* A giant robot lands in the Gulf of Mexico and goes on a rampage through the Southwest, guided by an alien intelligence that has infiltrated a top-secret laboratory. This simplistic but fun B-movie slice of '50s science fiction makes an impression in black and white widescreen with its striking designs, great use of southwestern desertscapes, and its austere robot monster: a skyscraper-scaled battery propelled by pile-driver feet. Lunky leading man Morrow looks like a Cro-Magnon in a lab coat but barks with the authority of a hunky hero, while the balance of the performances are either flat or florid, but it's lively and imaginatively put together by Neumann, who shot the cult classic *The Fly* a year later. —*S. A.*

KULL THE CONQUEROR L: PSYCHOTRONIC/HOWARD, ROBERT E. (1997) 95M D: John Nicolella. *Kevin Sorbo, Tia Carrere.* Sorbo portrays Kull, an outcast from Atlantis forced into slavery. Kull is probably one of Robert Howard's most liked characters. The tongue-in-cheek humor plays like a two-hour episode of *Hercules*, but that's part of its beauty. If the producers and director had taken any other approach, this film would have failed completely. It is both funny and brutal, making it fantasy worth watching. —*E. B.*

LABYRINTH L: FANTASY/FANTASY (1986) 102M D: Jim Henson. *Shari Weiser, David Bowie, Jennifer Connelly.* Before I knew Bowie for his music, I knew him as the tights-wearing, heat-packing, baby-tossing Goblin King of *Labyrinth*. When Connelly is all pissed off because she has to babysit her little brother, she wishes for Bowie to come take him away to live with the goblins. When he does, she freaks out and wants him back. Suddenly a labyrinth appears in her backyard, which she must conquer to get her brother back. Goblins, giants, a bog of eternal stench, enchanted fruit, a Bowie-drenched soundtrack, and much, much more ensues. I'm not sure that if I saw this for the first time now it would have nearly the same effect on me, but the nostalgia makes it untouchable in my mind. Let's face it, kids: they just don't make them like they used to. —*J. S.*

LANDLADY, THE L: HORROR/STALKERS (1998) 120M D: Rob Malenfant. *Bette Ford, Talia Shire, Bruce Weitz, Melissa Behr, Susie Singer, Jack Coleman.* Don't be late with your rental for this! An aging Shire murders her cheating husband, inheriting his mother's apartment complex. But her obsession over a certain virile young man in her building makes her turn cold and sinister to all the tenants who might interrupt her designs for a new marriage. "He is the one! He is the one!" she chants while sniffing his stolen laundry and spying on his bedroom through a one-way mirror she installed. This film must win some points for its creative use of violence (such as murder with a freezer door). And how can you not like a film that uses such priceless repartee as, "You said you would let me go!" "I am! I'm letting your sorry pathetic soul go!" —*N. J.*

LAST HOUSE ON DEAD END STREET L: HORROR/STALKERS (1973) 78M D: Roger Watkins (aka Victor Janos). *Roger Watkins (aka Steven Morrison), Ken Fisher.* Terry (Watkins) has just been released from prison for marijuana possession. For some loose reasons, he's decided to pay back some people he worked with in the porn industry and use them in some weird films he's come up with. He recruits two young hippie chicks who need some money and his filmmaker friend Ken, and begins his reign of terror against those who must pay. There's no morality. There are no character arcs. There's just action. As soon as we meet Terry and hear his voice-over, we've heard all we need to know about this man: he's a fucking hardcore sleazebag and he'll go down in flames to make the world pay for its crimes against him. —*S. R.*

LEATHERFACE: THE TEXAS CHAINSAW MASSACRE III L: HORROR/STALKERS (1990) 85M D: Jeff Burr. *Viggo Mortensen, William Butler, Ken Foree, Joe Unger, Kate Hodge.* So you're going to follow up the first two *Texas Chainsaw Massacre* films, but you don't have Tobe Hooper. So what do you do? Ah shit, I don't know, just get Burr, that guy who did *Pumpkinhead 2*. *Leatherface* is pretty much what you'd expect from that pedigree: a much lesser take on the same type of material. While Hooper's films felt raw, spontaneous, and at times even documentarian, this feels like your standard horror sequel, with actors standing on sets reading lines from an only-OK script. There are occasional touches of that chainsaw insanity (an old lady says, "Junior loves them private parts, he sure knows what to do with 'em"), plus some funny ideas such as Leatherface going through a rebellious teenage stage, and *Dawn of the Dead*'s Foree as a heavily armed survivalist blowing the crap out of Grandpa's mummified corpse. But it signaled the end of any hope for the series. —*B. T.*

LEFT BEHIND: THE MOVIE L: VAOWG/CHRISTPLOITATION (2000) 95M D: Vic Sarin. *Brad Johnson, Kirk Cameron, Colin Fox, Gordon Currie, Chelsea Noble, Clarence Gilyard Jr.* For all practical purposes, this film is a large-budget update of *Thief in the Night*. Even though it is based on the novel *Left Behind*, this movie is really just a vehicle to scare people into believing in Jesus Christ while vividly painting a future as interpreted from a mosaic of many, many verses gleaned from the Bible. The key concept of the Rapture, which is not explicitly mentioned in the Bible yet is fervently believed by literalist Christians, is that when Christ returns to Earth, his believers will be physically taken to Heaven. The drama concerns an airline pilot whose wife is taken, but not his pastor friend. It also follows a young reporter who slowly discovers what many fundamentalists apparently fear: the United Nations is the active work of Satan in this world and it intends to be completely in charge of the so-called Tribulation that will happen after the Rapture. —*N. J.*

LEGEND OF HELL HOUSE, THE L: HORROR/GHOSTS (1973) 95M D: John Hough. *Pamela Franklin, Roddy McDowall, Clive Revill, Gayle Hunnicutt, Roland Culver.* This brilliant, intelligent, suspenseful haunted house story takes the supernatural seriously and shapes a genuine mystery story around the haunting. Four are hired to determine the possibility of life after death. The shocks and ectoplasm and possession are slow in coming but strike with a bang. A scientist (Revill) is sure he can electromagnetically neutralize the negative energy. He's perhaps unadvisedly brought his wife (Hunnicutt). A young clairvoyant (Franklin) believes she is communicating with spirits. The final investigator (McDowall), the only sane survivor of the last visit by scientists to Hell House twenty years before, is a "physical medium" who uses his powers to close out the extraordinary power in this house. Good chills all around, with McDowall wonderfully over the top. —*J. C.*

LEPRECHAUN 3 L: HORROR/DEMONS (1995) 90M D: Brian Trenchard-Smith. *Warwick Davis, John Gatins, John de Mita, Caroline Williams.* One of the early scenes of *Leprechaun 3* features a mysterious stranger wearing an eye patch. The stranger's appearance is filmed at such an angle that viewers can see his eye moving beneath the patch. Things go downhill from there. The plot features a young man and woman on the run from the seemingly unstoppable leprechaun (Davis) in Las Vegas. The young man is bitten by the leprechaun, then starts turning into a leprechaun himself, meaning that by the time the film is reaching its conclusion, the two male characters share a love of potatoes and an Irish accent straight out of a Lucky Charms commercial. A seedy magician, his floozy assistant, and the emptiest casino ever complete the scene. —*T. P.*

LEPRECHAUN IN THE HOOD L: HORROR/DEMONS (2000) 91M D: Rob Spera. *Warwick Davis, Ice-T.* *Leprechaun in the Hood* is not a good horror movie, but it does contain two of the most brilliant moments of all time. (1) A cameo by rap star Coolio about halfway through the movie. Several characters are performing music in a church. Suddenly Coolio appears and one of the characters points and says, "Look! It's Coolio!" Then Coolio is never seen or mentioned again. (2) At the end of the movie, the villainous leprechaun (Davis) raps, which is almost worth renting the movie and fast-forwarding. He's accompanied by *zombie fly girls*. —*T. P.*

LET THE SLEEPING CORPSES LIE L: HORROR/ZOMBIES (1974) 88M D: Jorge Grau. *Christina Galbo, Raymond Lovelock.* The alternate title *The Living Dead at Manchester Morgue* is perhaps a more accurate description of this English take on the living dead. Lovelock and Galbo play traveling companions who stumble on a small town run over with the living dead. It's discovered that radioactive waves from some agricultural machine must be the cause. The film reaches its logical climax with a shocking ending at a nearby morgue. This is an extraordinarily atmospheric version of the familiar horror story. The corpses move very slowly and quietly; and with lengthy drawn-out scenes and great camera work, you will likely be kept on the edge of your chair. —*N. J.*

LIBIDO L: HORROR/GIALLO (ITALIAN HORROR) (1965) 90M D: Ernesto Gastaldi, Vittorio Salerno. *Dominique Boschero, Mara Maryl, Luciano Pigozzi, Giancarlo Giannini.* Christian, a young child, sees a murdered woman and his father rushing from the room. Now a young man (Giannini), he revisits the house and lands that become his at age twenty-five. The estate is managed by his lawyer cousin and the two men bringing their wives. The rocking-chair rocks. There is smoke in his father's pipe. The lawyer's wife (Maryl) looks more and more like the woman who died. Is Christian going insane, or is there a plot to control his fortune? Gothic

plotline aside: this 1965 film's stunningly perverse beginning and equally harsh denouement proved influential on Dario Argento's groundbreaking *giallos*. —*J. C.*

LIFEFORCE L: SCIENCE FICTION/SCIENCE FICTION (1985) 100M D: Tobe Hooper. *Steve Railsback, Michael Gothard, Patrick Stewart, Frank Finlay, Peter Firth, Nicholas Ball .* This odd mixture of horror and science fiction has its tongue firmly planted in its cheek. A beautiful female vampire arrives in London and begins seducing her victims, drinking their blood to increase her lifeforce. But when she drinks, she doesn't leave a drop behind, resulting in corpses that are shriveled up like prunes. Bodies pile up and an investigation ensues, but she constructs a kind of space-elevator and sucks the lifeforce of London straight up into space. Despite a generous budget with some spectacular special effects, you'll be saying "yeah, right" through this film more times than you can count. —*N. J.*

LUTHER THE GEEK L: HORROR/CANNIBALS (1990) 90M D: Carlton J. Albright. *Edward Terry, Gil Rogers, Joan Roth, Stacy Haiduk.* The term "geek" originally referred to a carnival entertainer who sat in a filthy cage and chewed the heads off live chickens. One-time-only director Albright apparently found this notion exciting enough to inspire his lone opus, *Luther the Geek*. Updating the concept for the modern horror fan, Luther is given metal chompers and a taste for human blood as well, but the excitement ends there as a bald "maniac" hides out in a barn for an hour and makes chicken sounds for sixty agonizing minutes, carnivorously murdering anyone stupid enough to enter his hay-strewn domain. Roth does her darndest as the farm owner futilely trying to rid her land of the pesky cannibal. If you're really looking for a good movie about a guy who acts like a bird . . . what's the matter with you? —*Z. C.*

MAD LOVE L: CLASSIC HORROR/CLASSIC HORROR (1935) 68M D: Karl Freund. *Peter Lorre, Colin Clive, Frances Drake, Ted Healy.* I love Peter Lorre. You know why? Because the poor bastard never gets the girl. Ever. Not even close. In *Mad Love*, Lorre plays Dr. Gogol, a desperately lonely surgeon who spends his time ogling Yvonne Orlac (Drake) as she screams and moans in a nightly S&M torture show. With his giant "Precious Moments" eyeballs, and shiny bald head, Lorre looks like a walking embryo. Yvonne, of course, rejects all advances by him until her husband Steven Orlac (Clive) gets his hands mangled in a train wreck and only the brilliant Dr. Gogol can help. And how does he help? By replacing Orlac's hands with those of a deranged, knife-throwing murderer, of course! Genius! *Mad Love* is a surreal, over-the-top showcase for Lorre, who is both terrifying and strangely adorable as the slobbering, bobble-headed madman. —*P. M.*

MAD MAGICIAN, THE L: CLASSIC HORROR/CLASSIC HORROR (1954) 72M D: John Brahm. *Vincent Price, Mary Murphy, Eva Gabor, John Emery.* Price plays a talented designer of magic tricks who, after deciding to perform himself as The Great Gallico, is forced to give his new buzz saw illusion to his rival, Rinaldi (Emery). Tired of others taking credit for his genius, Gallico rigs the buzz saw to cut off Rinaldi's head, which is just the beginning of a demented killing spree using the theatrics and sleight of hand of his trade. Gallico disguises himself as his victim and rents an apartment, just to create the illusion that he's still alive. In another great scene he disposes of a body by dressing it up as a dummy of a rival football team and throwing it on the bonfire at a pep rally. Not given a wide release on video, but well worth tracking down. —*B. T.*

MAD YOUTH L: PSYCHOTRONIC/DRUGS (1940) 76M D: Willis Kent. *Mary Ainslee, Betty Compson, Willy Castello.* "Pitfalls of this streamlined age revealed!" proclaimed the posters for this "expose" of escort bureaus by grindhouse guru Kent (*Wages of Sin*). Ainslee and Compson are a teenage girl and her decadent mother competing for the same gigolo, but then everyone is on the make in this lusty little bit of lasciviousness, from middle-aged bridge players who hire professional escorts with phony titles to horny kids into heavy petting. In a nice twist, Latin lover Castello turns out to be a respectable guy sick of his rotten job who rushes to save Ainslee from the white slave trade. B-movie tawdriness of the most entertaining kind. —*S. A.*

MANGLER, THE L: PSYCHOTRONIC/KING, STEPHEN (1995) 106M D: Tobe Hooper. *Daniel Matmor, Demetre Philips, Ted Levine, Robert Englund.* The Mangler concerns an enormous machine that steams and folds sheets. Englund rides herd over a crew of scantily dressed young women and from time to time, (oops!) one of them accidentally gets fed through the machine. Levine plays the investigator who discovers this laundry machine is possessed and prefers the meat of virgins. Stopping Englund turns out to be quite a task, considering that he barely escaped the machine himself and now draws his power from it. Only lovers of Hooper's work will appreciate this film, most everyone else might feel, um, short sheeted. —*N. J.*

MANIAC L: HORROR/STALKERS (1980) 91M D: William Lustig. *Rita Montone, Kelly Piper, Gail Lawrence, Caroline Munro, Joe Spinell, Tom Savini, Horace Carpenter, Bill Woods, Ted Edwards.* What if Leatherface, instead of growing up in rural Texas, had been a New Yorker? He'd still be a big, sweaty freak, but maybe he would've been a little more social. He'd live alone in a ratty apartment, but when he got a chance to get out he'd kill women, staple their scalps to a mannequin, handcuff himself to the mannequin and blubber, "I'm so happy!" Then during the day he'd put on some hipster

Favorite giant monsters

DAIMAJIN (Daimajin)	**MOTHRA** *(various)*
FRANKENSTEIN (Frankenstein Conquers the World)	**RABBIT** (Night of the Lepus)
GAMERA *(especially in* Gamera 3: Revenge of Iris*)*	**SANDA AND GAIRA** (War of the Gargantuas)
GIANT MARTIANS (Angry Red Planet)	**SHREWS** (The Killer Shrews)
GIANT SQUIDS *(in general)*	**STA-PUFT MARSHMALLOW MAN** (Ghostbusters)
GODZILLA *(various)*	**T. REX** (Jurassic Park)
KING KONG *(both 1933 and 1976 versions)*	**ZARDOZ** (Zardoz)
MECHA–KING KONG (King Kong Escapes)	

sunglasses and try to pass himself off as a fashion photographer. *Maniac* is a brutal, extremely disturbing slasher film. The urban equivalent of *Last House on the Left*, it reminds you of the stranglers, snipers, and other sickos who were making the headlines at that time. Star, writer, and coproducer Spinell (who also appeared in *Taxi Driver*) intended the film as a heartfelt cry against child abuse. —*B. T.*

As influenced by Italian *giallo* films as it is by American slashers, the result is a brutal horror classic that rips your hair out and takes it home to lust over. The killer was abused by his mom, and his murderous undertakings have their roots therein. But the movie is hardly about honestly delving into psychological traumas and the way in which violence perpetuates violence. Rather, it is a crude and exploitative bloody mess. A good one. —*T. S.*

MANIAC! L: CLASSIC HORROR/CLASSIC HORROR (1934) 51M D: Dwain Esper. *Rita Montone, Kelly Piper, Gail Lawrence, Caroline Munro, Joe Spinell, Tom Savini, Horace Carpenter, Bill Woods, Ted Edwards.* This hilariously inept poverty row cheapie from the notorious road show filmmaker Esper (*How to Undress Your Husband, Marijuana*) rips off Edgar Allan Poe, features some of the worst acting ever filmed, shows some unexpected nudity, and offers ridiculous pseudo-scientific explanations for different forms of madness. A mad scientist and his ex-vaudeville assistant bring a woman's corpse back to life. Then, when the assistant fails to obtain another corpse, the doctor attempts to kill his helper but instead is killed himself. His helper dons a fake beard to impersonate the doc. In the movie's best scene, the imposter injects a patient with monkey hormones and the hammy actor turns into a gorilla, kidnaps a topless woman, and strangles her. Weird characters and an amazing amount of strange things happening make this a must-see for fans of trash like *Plan Nine* and *Robot Monster*. —*S. H.*

MANITOU, THE L: HORROR/DEMONS (1978) 104M D: William Girdler. *Gabriel Damon, Michael Ansara, Burgess Meredith, Tony Curtis.* Seventies exploitation auteur Girdler's last film is his second *Exorcist* rip-off. Karen (Susan Strasberg) has a mysterious growth on her neck that turns out to be the reborn spirit of an evil Indian medicine man, Misquamacas. The doctors and their science are ineffective, so it's up to her hack psychic boyfriend Harry (Curtis) to find the cure. He enlists the help of John Singing Rock (Ansara). Misquamacas emerges from Karen's neck as an ugly midget with scary eyes and a sinister laugh (Felix Silla). He freezes the hospital and makes Karen's room look like a Santana record cover. John tries to direct the hospital computer's spirit (Manitou) at the little demon to no effect. Somehow Harry's love for Karen successfully directs the energy, and the climactic scenes of a topless Strasberg flying around in her hospital bed shooting lasers at Misquamacas is pretty hilarious. —*S. H.*

MANOS, THE HANDS OF FATE L: CLASSIC HORROR/CLASSIC HORROR (1966) 74M D: Hal P. Warren. *John Reynolds, Diane Mahree, Hal P. Warren, Tom Neyman.* In what may be the very worst film of all time, Warren plays Michael, who, after getting his family lost on their vacation, gets stranded in the backwaters of Texas. Fortunately they find a house, and with it, the possibility of help. Unfortunately it is the home of The Master, played to the hilt by oily renaissance festival reject Neyman, and Torgo, caretaker and resident perv, brought to life by the even oilier Reynolds. Both are up to supernatural no-good. Things happen, people talk, but it's not the plot that keeps you watching. It's the numbness from seeing something truly awful. The shots are clumsy and have all the warmth of the Zapruder film. The audio sounds like it was recorded on an answering machine. The hateful, repetitive score is only outdone by the baffling repetitive dialogue. And just when you thought it can't possibly get any worse, there's the ending. Oh Christ, the ending . . . —*R. G.*

MARK OF THE DEVIL L: HORROR/WITCHES & WARLOCKS (1969) 97M D: Michael Armstrong. *Udo Kier, Michael Maien, Reggie Nalder, Herbert Lom, Herbert Fuchs.* Introduced as a true story, *Mark of the Devil* features a variety of documented witch trials that led to executions in Austria in the 1770's. That's as far as the documentary part goes in this docuhorror film. The rest is lengthy scenes of graphic tortures as they would have been implemented at the time, as well as a close look at how the justice system worked (or didn't). What remains in the plot is the struggle between Kier and Lom over who really has the authority to send all these people to extended torture and death on the flimsiest evidence. This is all complicated because Kier's character falls in love with a beautiful prisoner. A wonderful soundtrack disturbingly offsets the violence—this film is certainly not for the squeamish. —*N. J.*

MASTERS OF THE UNIVERSE L: FANTASY/FANTASY (1987) 109M D: Gary Goddard. *Dolph Lundgren, Robert Duncan McNeill, Courtney Cox, Billy Barty, Frank Langella, Meg Foster.* Langella took the role of Skeletor, He-Man's wicked foe, as a gift to his kids. When he brought them to see the movie, they fell asleep. Abandoning the derivative fantasy world of the toy-commercial/cartoon, this movie brings vague facsimiles of the characters to Earth, where Skeletor has a parade and threatens to bore everybody to death. I guess you could praise Lundgren for re-creating the blandness and lack of personality from the cartoon. Look for blatant *Star Wars* lifts, even in the music, and be sure to fast-forward to the end of the credits so you can see Skeletor pop out of the lava to scream (incorrectly) "I'll be back!" —*B. T.*

MATRIX, THE L: SCIENCE FICTION/SCIENCE FICTION (1999) 136M D: Andy Wachowski, Larry Wachowski. *Keanu Reeves, Hugo Weaving, Carrie-Anne Moss, Laurence Fishburne, Joe Pantoliano.* I'm sure you know what *The Matrix* is, and how sick you are of people who love it, or movies that imitate it. But even with all that baggage, it remains one of the most effective genre films in years. It isn't just the much-hyped special effects and the unusual sight of Hollywood stars doing wire fu, but also the great premise that organically ties together film noir, Philip K. Dick–inspired sci-fi, excellent kung fu choreography, and even a little bit of *Hellraiser*-style horror (when Neo wakes up and learns he's just a naked cog in a giant power plant for robots). The movie also works as a great metaphor for the modern world: when your idea of what's going on in the world comes between yogurt commericials on heavily propagandized cable news channels, you are in the matrix. Despite becoming a cultural phenomenon and facing an inevitable backlash, *The Matrix* stands up as a fearless, innovative blending of genres that tells a thought-provoking story without sacrificing the visceral thrills of a great action film. —*B. T.*

MATRIX RELOADED, THE L: SCIENCE FICTION/SCIENCE FICTION (2003) 138M D: Andy Wachowski, Larry Wachowski. *Keanu Reeves, Hugo Weaving, Carrie-Anne Moss, Laurence Fishburne, Jada Pinkett Smith.* The second installment of the *Matrix* trilogy is more of an epic sci-fi film. Neo (Reeves) is now the flying superhero he became at the end of *The Matrix*. With an army of robotic sentinels digging toward the last human city, Zion, he must work among a disbelieving military organization to fulfill the prophecy of overthrowing the machines. This movie confounded audiences, perhaps because it alternates jarringly between heady, philosophical discussions about the nature of reality and mind-bogglingly huge action set pieces. Confusing ideas are densely packed into long dialogue scenes, and you're left not knowing whether these concepts will pay off in the next installment or whether the Wachowskis are just tossing them out there like this was a Richard Linklater movie. It also loses some of the first film's appeal by taking the heroes out of the matrix and into Zion, where they are something closer to authority figures than a ragtag band of rebels. Still, you have to admire the ambition of the Wachowskis and their willingness to challenge summer movie crowds, forcing them to decipher things for themselves. Plus, anyone who is unimpressed by the jawdropping freeway chase/high-speed kung fu battle is probably so desensitized they should never bother to watch an action movie ever again. —*B. T.*

MATRIX REVOLUTIONS, THE L: SCIENCE FICTION/SCIENCE FICTION (2003) 128M D: Andy Wachowski, Larry Wachowski *Keanu Reeves, Hugo Weaving, Laurence Fishburne, Carrie-Anne Moss, Jada Pinkett Smith, Ngai Sing.* The conclusion to the *Matrix* trilogy takes the story in a much more mythical and religious direction. While in the first film Neo seemed to have powers because of flaws in the programming of the matrix, *Revolutions* reveals him to actually be the One, with powers over machines even in the real world. He gets blinded and follows his senses into the machine city, more like a prophet on an epic quest than a kung fu superhero out to kick some ass. (But don't worry, you get that, too, when Neo and Agent Smith battle midair on a rainy night as the reality of the matrix world crumbles around them.) I can understand why many people wish the Wachowskis had just stopped with *The Matrix* and left the ensuing battles to take place in our own imaginations. But their version of what happened is a lot of fun, and even pretty daring. It may be frustrating to the audience to see how the machine war is resolved, but it is certainly in line with the themes of the story and with what's going on in the world today. At the same time, it leaves you in an uncertain world, wondering what will happen to these characters next, just as you did at the end of the first film. Note: I would like to thank the Wachowskis on behalf of all video stores for titling this series so that we wouldn't have to decide between filing them in alphabetical order or in chronological order. —*B. T.*

MAXIMUM OVERDRIVE L: PSYCHOTRONIC/KING, STEPHEN

(1986) 97M D: Stephen King. *Emilio Estevez, Laura Harrington, Yeardley Smith, John Short, Pat Hingle.* One can only hope this film is intended as a big joke. For his first venture into directing films, the legendary horror author directs a feature that could only appeal to fans of Ed Wood Jr. At a truck stop, machines are suddenly, violently possessed and hold people hostage. The exposition of this film is by far the most entertaining segment, and not because it is particularly interesting or horrifying, but because it is outright comical. And predictably it gets a lot worse from there. Perhaps this first-time director was just experimenting on his audience. But if so, it was clearly a failed experiment, for it was the only film he directed. —*N. J.*

MAY L: HORROR/STALKERS (2002) 94M D: Lucky McKee.

Anna Faris, Angela Bettis, Jeremy Sisto, James Duval. A smart and sometimes surprising horror yarn somewhat inspired by *Carrie* (in fact, lead actress Bettis starred in the TV version of *Carrie*). May is a lonely veterinarian's assistant with a lazy eye and a complete lack of social skills. She starts dating a guy who appreciates her eccentricities. Things progress generally how you'd expect in this type of movie until she bites his lip and smears the blood all over her face. She doesn't seem to have a clue why this turns him off. The pacing of *May* is pretty unique: the horror doesn't really come in until the last half hour, so you start to sympathize with May and the next thing you know she's killing innocents for their body parts. —*B. T.*

Beyond all its surface intentions, *May* is a film about loneliness, about the way it affects us and changes us and shapes who we become. And while this tale might be taken to a rather extreme conclusion, that shouldn't detract from what the film ultimately tries to convey about the human condition. I won't deny that this is a truly disturbing film on many levels, but it is not the mere horror/gore film it is often marketed as being. If anything, it's a very quirky romance story that ultimately becomes a frightening exploration of unrequited love and the aching hurt of being lonely. McKee is remarkably assured in his direction, especially for a first-time director. Bettis, Faris, and Sisto turn in remarkable performances, though it is ultimately Bettis who owns this movie, appearing in nearly every scene and making every line ring true.—*C. P.*

MIGHTY PEKING MAN L: VAOWG/VAOWG (1977) 90M

D: Meng-Hwa Ho. *Evelyn Kraft, Danny Lee, Feng Ku.* Hong Kong's 1977 answer to Dino De Laurentiis's *King Kong* revival is a born "Midnight Movie" natural. The titular character is a guy in a moth-eaten gorilla suit (that doesn't quite hide the stunt man's face) who's in love with statuesque German blonde Kraft, a teased-haired jungle beauty with a peek-a-boo bikini. When buff Chinese explorer Lee (a boyish, innocent lead in his pre-Woo year) wanders along, it's lust at first sight and Kraft is introduced to a new kind of jungle romp (in a slow-motion montage backed by the cheesiest late-'70s synthesized soft rock), and the trio is off to the city. This badly dubbed modern schlock classic has more action packed in its ninety minutes than an entire twelve-chapter serial. Effects range from the sloppy to the ridiculous, and include such highlights as an elephant that cries real tears and a monster-versus-monster truck rally, concluding with an appropriately Godzilla-esque rampage through Tokyo. Silly? You bet, but undeniably energetic fun on its own giddy terms. —*S. A.*

MIMIC 3: SENTINEL L: SCIENCE FICTION/SCIENCE FICTION

(2003) 76M D: J. T. Petty. *John Kapelos, Alexis Dziena, Lance Henriksen, Amanda Plummer, Karl Geary.* "Rear Window" with giant cockroaches" is how writer/director Petty describes his moody, creepily effective direct-to-video horror sequel. Marvin (Geary), who suffers from "Strickler's Disease" and lives in a controlled environment, passes his time by snapping pictures of his low-rent apartment courtyard and discovers that his neighbors are disappearing. The giant, predatory Judas Breed bugs are back, and the skulking creeper known as "the Garbageman" (Henriksen) is somehow connected. Petty edits in dissolves that give it a quality of floating through time rather than driving through it (like most thrillers), as if seeing the world through Marvin's eyes, and he favors mood to visceral gore and shock, filling his film with shadow, suggestions of horror, and unnerving images. It's what the direct-to-video market should be all about: a training ground for young filmmakers to stretch their wings. —*S. A.*

MIRACLE MILE L: VAOWG/VAOWG (1989) 87M D: Steve de Jarnatt. *Anthony Edwards, Mare Winningham, John Agar, Lou Hancock.* This is a sweet romantic love story set during a few short hours before apocalyptic doom. Edwards plays Harry Washello, a nerdy fellow just living his life and looking for love. Along comes Julie (Winningham), fitting Harry's ideal. At a diner to call Julie early one morning, a twist of fate has him answering a ringing pay phone. On the other end is a frantic voice explaining that "we shot our wad, and it's coming back to you!" After a short conversation, gunshots, and a stern voice coming on the line saying "forget everything you just heard, and go back to sleep," Harry is in disbelief. The story slowly escalates to chaos in the streets of Los Angeles as people wake up to the impending catastrophe. This film had much more impact upon first release, but it now seems dated by Cold War paranoia and really bad fashion. —*B. W.*

It's so well constructed, though; I don't think being dated to the Cold War makes it any less tense. It keeps throwing in complication after complication and it is difficult not to yell, "JUST GET THE HELL OUT OF THERE!" as Edwards keeps tending to his pre-Armageddon arrangements. Unjustly overlooked. —*B. T.*

MISA THE DARK ANGEL L: JAPANESE HORROR/JAPANESE HORROR (1998) 95M D: Katsuhito Ueno. *Saeki Hinako.* A charred corpse utters the name of Misa Kuroi, a legendary teenage demon hunter, just before dying. It turns out Misa is real, a Kolchak in schoolgirl skirt (Hinako), and her investigation takes her to a girl's school where an innocent play becomes a sacrificial ceremony. The film is a cross between a Japanese manga (it was adapted from one by Koga Shinichi), an American slasher film, and Agatha Christie's *Ten Little Indians*, maintaining an appropriately dark, dangerous horror fantasy mood but stopping short of the erotic-kill excess of the adults-only "schoolgirl in terror" pictures. Stylish and weird, but largely for fans of manga and Asian horror. Also known as *Eko Eko Azarak.* —*S. A.*

MISERY L: PSYCHOTRONIC/KING, STEPHEN (1990) 107M D: Rob Reiner. *James Caan, Kathy Bates.* This movie gives me a serious case of the willies because no one else does crazy, crazy bitch quite as well as Bates. She plays Annie, the obsessed fan of writer Paul Sheldon (Caan), whom she "rescues" from a mangled car after an accident. Keeping him captive in her house, she nurses him back to health. When Sheldon begins to realize that Annie is, in fact, a crazy, crazy bitch who is obsessed with him, he tries to escape. But she tortures him, forcing him to stay and write her a new book about her favorite character, Misery. It gets really, really ugly. The plot is fairly straightforward, but the acting easily makes this one of Stephen King's creepiest adaptations. —*J. S.*

MONSTER THAT CHALLENGED THE WORLD, THE L: CLASSIC SCIENCE FICTION/CLASSIC SCIENCE FICTION (1957) 83M D: Arnold Laven. *Tim Holt, Audrey Dalton, Hans Conried, Barbara Darrow.* An oceanic earthquake releases mutant prehistoric sea mollusks that look like really ugly caterpillars. They suck the fluids out of their victims and kill swimmers, boaters, and rabbits. Soon a scientist (Conried) and a military man named Twillinger team up to stop the slimy critters. Unfortunately, the monsters escape into the Los Angeles canals and threaten to "challenge the world," or at least Southern California. This movie scared me pretty badly when I was a kid, mostly because the victims look so gross. The characters are a little more interesting (and funnier) than those in similar films, and there's plenty of silly '50s monster movie fun. —*S. H.*

MONSTERS CRASH THE PAJAMA PARTY L: CLASSIC HORROR/CLASSIC HORROR (1965) 214M D: David L. Hewitt. *Vic McGee, Charles Hegen, James Reason, Clara Nadel, Pauline Hillkurt.* This is a lame, Z-grade horror comedy involving a sorority, a werewolf, and a guy in a gorilla suit. Even if you can't sit through it, though, the DVD might be worth checking out. Designed as a tribute to "spook shows" in which horror movies were accompanied by live performers and ghost gimmicks, the charmingly amateurish and not-at-all user-friendly menus take you through nostalgic spook show how-to's, previews, radio spots, poster galleries, short films, a "Hypno-Vision" intro, commentary tracks, and more. It even includes the 3-D short *The Asylum of the Insane* and Bert I. Gordon's feature-length *Tormented*. So many extras (most of which must've been found in someone's basement) are crammed onto this thing that it takes on the feel of an interactive presentation instead of just a movie on DVD. —*B. T.*

MOTEL HELL L: HORROR/CANNIBALS (1980) 102M D: Kevin Connor. *Nina Axelrod, Paul Linke, Wolfman Jack, Rory Calhoun, Nancy Parsons.* Imagine *Sweeney Todd* without the barbershop, without the music, and with a lot more gore. In this film a crazy farmer and his wife operate a "hotel" where the guests receive a small hole in the backyard, are buried up to their necks, have their tongues ripped out, and are fed high-protein slop to fatten them up. Upon harvest time this farmer and his wife sell the very best meat you can buy. In the spirit of Herschel Gordon Lewis, this comic-horror will certainly appeal to fans of the splatter genre. —*N. J.*

MUMMY, THE L: HORROR/ZOMBIES (1999) 124M D: Stephen Sommers. *Rachel Weisz, Brendan Fraser, Arnold Vosloo, John Hannah, Kevin J. O'Connor.* A nostalgic look back to those days in the mid-'80s when Steven Spielberg took a nostalgic look back to those days in the '30s when people figured out how to make movies without taking a nostalgic look back to some other era. Painfully mediocre director Sommers casts bland hunk of meat Fraser in a quasi–Indiana Jones role fighting off the return of the cursed pharaoh Imhoten (Vosloo, doing his best with a corny role). After a strong prologue *The Mummy* is just one noisy scene after another with virtually no rhythm or build. It's also weighed down by lots of racist and/or lame humor (a guy snores and gets hit in the face with a stick—get it?) intended to relieve tension that simply does not exist in the movie. Some of the effects by Industrial Light and Magic are interesting, which makes the movie more watchable than Sommers's entry into the world of hackdom, *Deep Rising.* —*B. T.*

MUMMY RETURNS, THE L: HORROR/ZOMBIES (2001) 130M D: Stephen Sommers. *Brendan Fraser, Rachel Weisz, The Rock, Arnold Vosloo.* You just can't keep the undead under wraps. Fraser and Weisz reunite with writer/director Sommers for a rematch with the evil mummy Imhotep (Vosloo) and a tussle with the ancient warrior demon The Scorpion King (WWE sensation The Rock, little more than a possessed plastic action figure). They've even got a whip-smart kid eager to mix it up, but the film is stolen from them all by a feral army of chattering, Gremlin-like, hopped-up pygmy mummies. Sommers is a pure pop Stephen Spielberg, but this is less *Raiders of the Lost Ark* than *Gunga Din,* a pulp update of old Hollywood action movies. Hardly sensitive (his attitude is blithely Eurocentric colonialist—these guys never stop plundering the ancient world and the loot seems to go straight to their London digs) and at times sloppy, it's sometimes more exhausting than exciting. The whirlwind third act rolls from one hyperkinetic cliffhanger to another with almost numbing overkill, but it's hard to resist the naive pulp sensibilities and giddy thrills. —*S. A.*

MUMMY'S CURSE, THE L: CLASSIC HORROR/CLASSIC HORROR (1944) 62M D: Leslie Goodwins. *Peter Coe, Virginia Christine, Jackie Lou Harding, Dennis Moore.* The fifth and final Mummy film could be called a disappointment if anyone ever expected anything from it. But by the time you reach the fifth film in a series about a mummy (when the plot is the exact same in every film), you really aren't expecting much. And as far as Mummy sequels go, this isn't half bad. The plot is moved to Louisiana and that's about the only new thing here. Mummy seeks girl, girl is protected, Mummy is destroyed. Applause! Hurray! Beware the curse! —*T. S.*

MUMMY'S GHOST, THE L: CLASSIC HORROR/CLASSIC HORROR (1944) 61M D: Reginald Le Borg. *John Carradine, George Zucco, Barton MacLane, Ramsay Ames,*

Robert Lowery, Lon Chaney Jr. The Mummy's Ghost grabs the Mummy series by the balls and gives a good hard yank. Infused with a keen sense of irony and tongue firmly in cheek, director Le Borg creates what is far and away the best mummy sequel. Reveling in its own clichés and indulging the audience with gleeful abandon, this wry film maintains a certain honesty, finding the perfect B-movie balance between horror and humor. The twist ending throws a wrench into the mummy machine, surprising the audience and leaving them unsure of what to make of the film's resolution. *The Mummy's Ghost* is a great, beefy slab of horror fun. —*T. S.*

MUMMY'S HAND, THE L: CLASSIC HORROR/CLASSIC HORROR (1940) 67M D: William Christy Cabanne. *Wallace Ford, Dick Foran, George Zucco, Eduardo Ciannelli, Tom Tyler, Peggy Moran.* The second Mummy film from Universal, *The Mummy's Hand* shows a steep drop in quality from the first. That's not to say it is terrible, though. The film begins with a brief retelling of the first film with the aid of the magic pool. From there, Boris Karloff's Imho Tep is replaced with a new mummy named Kharis who, like Imho Tep, is after the reincarnation of his lost love. Kharis, however, does not rise out of his tomb due to a curse. He was secretly kept alive by Egyptian priests for thousands of years using the magical Tanis leaves. *The Mummy's Hand* is infused with a great deal of comedy, which, depending on your disposition, is either good or bad. I personally think it's kind of fun. At least it's better than its sequel. —*T. S.*

MUMMY'S TOMB, THE L: CLASSIC HORROR/CLASSIC HORROR (1942) 71M D: Harold Young. *Turhan Bey, Lon Chaney Jr., Elyse Knox, Wallace Ford, George Zucco, Dick Foran. The Mummy's Tomb* begins by spending an excessive amount of time recapping the previous film, *The Mummy's Hand.* Once again Kharis (Chaney Jr.) is lusting after his eternal love and travels to America to capture her with the aid of an Egyptian priest. Many characters from *Tomb* return, only to be killed off early in the film. This lends the film an odd pacing and since it's almost a complete rehash of both its predecessors, it fails to provide much entertainment. —*T. S.*

MY BLOODY VALENTINE L: HORROR/STALKERS (1981) 91M D: Georges Mihalka. *Neil Affleck, Lori Hallier, Paul Kelman. My Bloody Valentine* is a perfect slasher film, in league with *Bay of Blood, Black Christmas,* and *Halloween.* The small mining town of Valentine's Bluff is planning a big Valentine's Day party for the first time since an infamous massacre twenty years earlier. But as the day draws near, people begin to die and it seems as if the maniac has returned. The film is filled with memorable sequences, such as a woman's bloody corpse spinning around in the washer and a part where a guy gets his head boiled in a flaming hot-dog pot. The atmosphere is top-notch, the pacing is perfect, and everything really comes together. The only thing that sucks is that the movie has been cut to shreds by the censors to avoid an X rating and the assholes at Paramount won't release the uncut version. When the killer hangs and decapitates a helpless victim, you can hardly tell what's going on. We want the gore! —*T. S.*

MY LITTLE EYE L: HORROR/STALKERS (2002) 96M D: Marc Evans. *Sean C. W. Johnson, Jennifer Sky, Kristopher Lemche, Stephen O'Reilly, Laura Regan, Bradley Cooper.* I thought the whole reality TV (or in this case Internet) thing had been done to death after garbage like *Series 7*. Without providing any sort of new angle or offering any interesting commentary, *My Little Eye* manages to be an effectively creepy little film. Five young people are supposed to live in a house together for six months while being filmed and, afterward, get paid a million dollars. The catch: If anyone leaves early, no one gets paid. The real catch: One by one they start to die. Shot entirely from the perspective of the reality cameras, the film plays out nicely, offering a few fun moments and a good ending. It's nothing special, but is still a cut above average and worth the time of any horror fan. —*T. S.*

MYSTERIOUS TWO L: PSYCHOTRONIC/UFO! (1982) 100M D: Gary Sherman. *Priscilla Pointer, Robert Englund, Vic Tayback, Noah Beery Jr., John Forsythe.* This is a standard, sensationalistic TV movie about two cult leaders who claim to be from outer space but seem actually to be brainwashing their followers and leading them to a Jonestown-style fate. What makes the movie interesting is that the filmmakers weren't just being paranoid—they were right. The movie was inspired by real cult leaders Bonnie Lu Nettles and Marshall Applewhite, who founded what became known as the Heaven's Gate cult. Fifteen years after the movie aired on NBC, Applewhite and thirty-eight other cultists were found dead after a mass suicide, all wearing matching Nikes. They left behind testimonial videos and a sci-fi screenplay about their religious beliefs, which was presumably more epic than this rather dull TV movie. Sherman also directed *Dead and Buried* and *Poltergeist III*. —*B T.*

MYSTERY SCIENCE THEATER 3000: I ACCUSE MY PARENTS L: PSYCHOTRONIC/MST3K (1994) 92M D: Sam Newfield. *Tom Servo.* "They laughed when I accused my parents and I killed them. Let's see if they'll be laughing now," sings Servo to the opening strains of *I Accuse My Parents* (1945). Hodgson and the robots of the Satellite of Love deconstruct Newfield's square juvenile delinquent drama (starring the most starched and squeaky clean J.D. hero to walk across a movie screen) with everything from art projects to a giant mobile representing the hero's roiling subconscious. "Joel, don't you have anything better to do than psychoanalyze a bunch of robots?"

Sure he does: he leads the gang in a colorful re-creation of the film's cheesy nightclub number. Gypsy lip-synchs the song while the other three pop in and out of costume to play the entire audience. If that's not enough, Servo tries to become a "real boy" with a can of flesh-colored paint ("I'm naked!") and TV's Frank bakes a Chippendales dancer in a cake. "Seriously, Joel, who would you accuse?" —*S. A.*

MYSTERY SCIENCE THEATER 3000: RED ZONE CUBA L: PSYCHOTRONIC/MST3K (1994) 92M D: Coleman Francis. *Coleman Francis, Harold Saunders, John Carradine.* If Francis never existed, he would have been invented by *MST3K*: there isn't a filmmaker who is so much fun to skewer. His editing style favors cutting away from the character speaking (thus making his dubbing job easier) and he employs a surreal repetition of action scenes in a futile attempt to make the cast look larger. This Francis special is a jailbreak film that takes a bizarre veer into an American invasion of Cuba, which was apparently hampered by military budget cuts before ending up in an American tungsten mine ("So this Cuban stuff was really a diversion ..."). Why? Who knows, but the 'bots have a ball skewering the film with some of their funniest comments ("I want to hurt this movie, but I can never hurt it the way it hurt me"), and Nelson becomes so disturbed he turns into Carol Channing. Believe it or not, costar Carradine rasps out the theme song "Night Train to Mundo Fine" (which was the film's original title). —*S. A.*

MYSTICS IN BALI L: HORROR/WITCHES & WARLOCKS (1981) 85M D: H. Tjut Djalil. *Ilona Agathe Bastian, Yos Santo, Sofia W.D.* Have you ever seen a movie about a witch whose head separates from her body and flies around with all the internal organs hanging out of her neck, sucking fetuses out of pregnant women and drinking their blood? Well then, what are you waiting for? The acting and dialogue are strictly Z-level, but no one should be able to resist the power of a rubber head hanging from a pole flying around attacking people. This is based on the myth of the Penanggalan, or "head with dancing intestines." A customer once asked if I knew of any other movies like this. There actually is one: the Hong Kong film *Witch with Flying Head*, which unfortunately has not been released here commercially. —*B. T.*

NEAR DARK L: HORROR/VAMPIRES (1987) 94M D: Kathryn Bigelow. *Jenette Goldstein, Bill Paxton, Adrian Pasdar, Lance Henriksen, Jenny Wright.* A modern Southwestern with teeth, Bigelow's vampire road movie noir (in which the word "vampire" is never uttered) is feral and ferocious, yet grounded in family. Beautiful blue-eyed farmboy Caleb (Pasdar) succumbs to the little-girl-lost charms of honey-voiced Mae (Wright), the doe-eyed junior member of a scruffy pack of human predators that hunts the back roads by night. They are family in every meaningful sense—Henriksen's scarred survivor is a kind of dad, Goldstein's soiled peroxide blonde lapses into mothering instincts, Paxton is a wild man big brother—and Bigelow manages to combine the frontier community romanticism of a John Ford Western with the violent ferocity of a Sam Peckinpah film. Bigelow's night shooting has a stiletto sharpness to it, her daytime scenes have a foggy haze, and her sunlight sears like a laser as it burns through the shadows of their shelters, through bullet holes and broken walls. This is a movie about blood in all senses of the word, defying the traditions of vampire lore with a moving portrait of healing and sacrifice. —S. A.

NEKROMANTIK L: HORROR/EURO-HORROR (1988) 75M D: Jorg Buttgereit. *Daktari Lorenz, Beatrice Manowski.* Nekromantik is a sensitive parable inadvertently filled with ideological concerns and complex themes. The work of exploitation director Buttgereit shares a surprising similarity to Rainer Werner Fassbinder and Wim Wenders in that he has a preoccupation with reinterpreting insufficiently considered historical horrors. He succeeds at exploring pseudo-political, troubled nationalistic notions by maintaining a constant self-referential quality in which history is constantly reexamined. Buttgereit fuses these concerns with a fetish for death springing from a perverted existentialism and spiritual isolationism brought to shocking extremes. Yet the Zen-like simplicity and deftness with which spiritual and carnal imperatives are juxtaposed are as trenchant an argument for the romantic heresy of Charles Baudelaire or existential combat of Camus as is a seminar on Hegelian Collectivism presented by Britney Spears. Ultimately the film exists as a meaningless piece of über-gory sexploitation where a man sucking on the gouged-out eye of a pig, bathing in fresh cat's blood or masturbating while his girlfriend makes love to a decomposed body is somehow meant to be beautiful. —T. S.

NIGHT GALLERY L: HORROR TV/HORROR TV (1970) 960M D: Steven Spielberg, Barry Shear, others. *Rod Serling, Joan Crawford, Richard Kiley.* Attempting to follow the unequivocal success of his TV series *The Twilight Zone,* Serling appears in a dimly lit art gallery with some rather horrifying paintings and introduces each of the episodes with a touch of art. Unlike the *The Twilight Zone,* these episodes are in color and are a bit more oriented toward horror than to general science fiction. Take "Dickman's Model," which is based on an H. P. Lovecraft story about an artist obsessed with painting a race of ghouls; or "A Question of Fear," where Leslie Nielsen takes a bet to survive one night in a haunted house; or "Pamela's Voice," with Phyllis Diller returning from the dead to torture her greedy husband. These episodes may not be as famous as Serling's previous series, but they boast greater and more mature production talent. —N. J.

NIGHT OF THE BLOODY APES L: HORROR/MAD SCIENTISTS (1968) 84M D: René Cardona. *Armando Silvestre, Gerard Cepeda, Agustin Martinez Solares.* Sleazy low-rent exploitation about a scientist who saves his son by transplanting a gorilla's heart into him, only to find that it turns him into an ape-man beast who goes on a deadly rampage. Which may or may not be scientifically plausible—I'm no doctor. At first it seems silly fun, complete with female lucha libre wrestlers. But then you get to the actual footage of open heart surgery, and the rape scenes. Oh well, at least it's a great title. —B. T.

NIGHT OF THE LIVING DEAD (1990) L: HORROR/ZOMBIES (1990) 92M D: Tom Savini. *Tony Todd, Bill Moseley, Tom Towles, Patricia Tallman.* By no means a replacement for, but a worthwhile companion piece to, Romero's 1968 classic, this modernized color version is most notable for its more modern attitudes toward women. Like in the original, Barbara goes into a near catatonic state when first confronted with zombies. But when attacked in the farmhouse she snaps, literally trades her skirt in for pants, and takes charge Ripley style. Tallman, a stuntwoman and bit player in many Romero movies, gives a performance that should've launched her to cult status, but that only kind of happened when she joined the cast of *Babylon 5.* Todd (the title character from *Candyman*) is great as Ben, but Towles (*Henry: Portrait of a Serial Killer's* Otis) is a little over the top as the hothead Harry Cooper. —B. T.

NIGHT STALKER, THE L: HORROR TV/HORROR TV (1972) 74M D: John Llewellyn Moxey. *Darren McGavin, Simon Oakland, Claude Akins, Ralph Meeker.* McGavin stars as a wisecracking, hard-working reporter named Carl Kolchak in this contemporary vampire thriller. A psycho is terrorizing women in Las Vegas. Kolchak believes that the perpetrator is a vampire but he meets a lot of resistance from the local police (headed by future Sheriff Lobo Akins) and his editor (Oakland, who'd continue his role in the sequels). Made for television, *The Night Stalker* inspired later TV shows such as *The X-Files.* It was a huge ratings hit, leading to another movie, *The Night Strangler,* and a great but short-lived series titled *Kolchak the Night Stalker.* —S. H.

NIGHT STRANGLER, THE L: HORROR TV/HORROR TV (1973) 74M D: Dan Curtis. *Simon Oakland, Darren McGavin, John Carradine, Margaret Hamilton.* The TV movie *The Night Stalker* was a massive hit so ABC followed it up with this sequel, again starring McGavin as wisecracking investigative reporter Carl Kolchack. Richard Matheson delivers another strong script and Curtis, who produced the first film, assumes the director's chair this time around. In the previous film, Kolchack battled a vampire in Las Vegas, this time it's a Jekyll-and-Hyde type terrorizing Seattle. Oakland returns as Kolchack's harried editor and the cast is filled with lots of veteran actors, though it's kind of strange to see Richard "Oscar Goldman" Anderson playing the 120-year-old villain. It all ends in a showdown in an underground city that looks more like a deserted Western movie set than the actual wet basements of the underground of Seattle's Pioneer Square. This superior follow-up led to the short-lived but beloved *Kolchack the Night Stalker* TV series that found our hero relocating to Chicago and continuing his paranormal investigations. —*S. H.*

NIGHT TO REMEMBER, A L: VAOWG/VAOWG (1958) 119M D: Roy Ward Baker. *Kenneth More, Honor Blackman, Frank Lawton, David McCallum, Lawrence Naismith, Jill Dixon.* The plot of this film is nothing less than the sinking of the cruise ship *Titanic.* Eric Ambler wrote the script, making all the events as true to life as possible, getting his details from Walter Lord's account of the tragedy. The exposition sets up a number of characters, such as the captain and crew and various passengers; some make it through and some do not. Because this film has a more documentary angle on the events, there isn't much room for the characters to develop. Instead, with gripping suspense, they fight for survival for most of the film. *A Night To Remember* is not an easy film to forget. —*N. J.*

NIGHTBREED L: PSYCHOTRONIC /BARKER, CLIVE (1990) 115M D: Clive Barker. *Anne Bobby, Doug Bradley, Craig Sheffer, David Cronenberg, Hugh Ross.* Barker followed up the success of *Hellraiser* with this flawed but ambitious horror/fantasy epic about the underground city of Midian, where monsters hide from the persecution of humans. Dr. Decker (Cronenberg), a psychologist who moonlights as a masked serial killer, brainwashes a patient named Boone (Sheffer) into thinking he's the killer. A monster-obsessed psychotic leads Boone to Midian for asylum. Well as luck would have it, Boone is actually a monster who's destined to both bring the downfall of Midian and lead the refugees to a new home. Unfortunately, the immigraton never happens on-screen because the movie and book were planned as trilogies that never materialized. There is a great deal to admire in this movie, especially the detail put into the numerous monster extras. Barker wanted this to be "the *Star Wars* of horror" so he actually wrote back stories for each creature. When I was fifteen, this was the greatest movie ever made. —*B. T.*

NIGHTMARE ON ELM STREET 2, A: FREDDY'S REVENGE L: HORROR/STALKERS (1985) 87M D: Jack Sholder. *Clu Gulager, Kim Myers, Robert Englund, Mark Patton, Hope Lange, Robert Rusler.* Jesse (Patton) moves into the same bedroom Nancy lived in, dreams of the same killer (Englund as Freddy), and even reads her diary. Freddy is trying to possess Jesse's body, and eventually succeeds, jumping into reality at a pool party. It's weird to watch this

first attempt at an *Elm Street* sequel if you already know where the series is going. Freddy is still creepy and not yet a jokester, but the gloomy mood and homoerotic S&M undertones (Jesse ties his coach up with jump ropes in the locker room showers) are depressing without being particularly scary. Still, it has some good moments, such as the opening nightmare about Freddy's unorthodox methods for driving a school bus. —*B. T.*

NIGHTMARE ON ELM STREET 3, A: DREAM WARRIORS L: HORROR/STALKERS (1987) 96M D: Chuck Russell. *Patricia Arquette, Robert Englund, Craig Wasson, Heather Langenkamp, Laurence Fishburne.* When you're an Elm Street teen being haunted by dreams of Freddy (Englund), your parents never fucking believe you. Instead they send you to a mental ward where Fishburne treats you with tough love and eventually Freddy calls you a bitch and smashes your head into a TV set or pulls out your veins and walks you out a window like a marionette. Luckily Nancy (Langenkamp), who fought Freddy so bravely in the original *A Nightmare on Elm Street*, is now a doctor at the hospital, so there's finally an adult who understands this whole Freddy situation. Better yet, Kristen (Arquette) has a strange ability to pull other people into her dreams so that all the asylum inmates can be in the dreamworld together. They find that they can do things in their dreams that they can't when they're awake, which is why they are dream warriors, I guess. This movie is silly and incredibly dated, but the script (cowritten by *Shawshank Redemption* director Frank Darabont) was a clever way of reinventing the series and served as the template for the next three sequels. —*B. T.*

NIGHTMARE ON ELM STREET 4, A: THE DREAM MASTER L: HORROR/STALKERS (1988) 99M D: Renny Harlin. *Lisa Wilcox, Tuesday Knight, Andras Jones, Rodney Eastman, Robert Englund, Danny Hassel.* The surviving characters from Part 3 are now out of the asylum and in a normal high school. Next thing you know Kincaid (Eastman) dreams about his dog peeing fire onto Freddy's skeleton, and suddenly the burnt-up bastard is haunting their dreams again. As Freddy dresses up in different costumes and kills them in ways based on their hobbies or fears, their friend Alice (Wilcox) inherits their dream powers. Soon she realizes that she is "The Dream Master" who must figure out a way to kill Freddy that will hopefully last longer than the previous three ways of killing him. This was the first time the *Elm Street* series repeated itself, reusing much of the same cast (at least at the beginning) and following the concepts and jokiness of the previous installment. —*B. T.*

NIGHTMARE ON ELM STREET 5, A: THE DREAM CHILD L: HORROR/STALKERS (1989) 90M D: Stephen Hopkins. *Lisa Wilcox, Erika Anderson, Danny Hassel, Kelly*

Minter, Robert Englund, Joe Seely. After graduating from high school, Alice (Wilcox) discovers she is pregnant with Dan's (Hassel) baby. Soon she starts having weird dreams about a little boy named Jacob (Whitby Hertford). It turns out that Freddy is haunting the dreams of her unborn baby, so there is no escaping him—she can slip into the dream world while she's awake. This was an admirable attempt to bring the Elm Street teens into the adult world, dealing with parenting themes (which are paralleled with more backstory about Freddy and his mother Amanda Krueger). Unfortunately it's still one of the more lackluster sequels, very formulaic and with gimmicky murder scenes (Freddy even turns into "Super Freddy" to kill an aspiring comic book artist). And despite having the kids grow up, it maintains the parents-just-don't-understand paranoia of teen films. —*B T.*

NIGHTMARE SERIES ENCYCLOPEDIA, THE L: HORROR/STALKERS (1999) 98M D: Wes Craven, others. *Robert Englund, Wes Craven.* This bonus disc from the *A Nightmare on Elm Street* eight-disc box set is a treasure trove for horror nerds like me who grew up obsessed with the *Elm Street* movies. Most of the content is in "The Labyrinth," an intricate series of clickable menus designed to look like a series of creepy hallways and boiler rooms. Included here are various interviews about numerous aspects of each movie, vintage clips of Freddy TV appearances, even a gallery of Freddy merchandise. (They should've borrowed my official Freddy Krueger yo-yo, though.) There is test footage of the directors (and, perhaps more significant, the special effects artists) behind even the bad sequels, and it's fascinating to hear the director of Part 2 explain what he was going for. The menus are very impressive but all that clicking gets old fast—luckily there's also a table of contents page that links to all the material directly. —*B. T.*

OF UNKNOWN ORIGIN L: VAOWG/VAOWG (1983) 89M D: George P. Cosmatos. *Kenneth Welsh, Louis Del Grande, Peter Weller, Lawrence Dane, Jennifer Dale, Shannon Tweed.* Of Unknown Origin incorporates an interesting theme and premise and lets the production rest primarily on Weller's capable shoulders. What should be just another B-movie about a giant rat becomes a metaphor for the corporate rat race, as well as a physical manifestation of a modern man's fears and anxieties about providing for and protecting his family. Working his way up from the bottom of the corporate ladder, Weller is forced to simultaneously cope with an impossible business deadline, the absence of his wife, and the disastrous appearance of a seemingly invincible rat hell-bent on destroying the house he just bought for his family. As the pressure mounts, Weller becomes more and more obsessed with the rat, pushing the rest of his affairs lower on the priority list. Long relegated to a dusty, forgotten VHS box and basic cable

programming, *Of Unknown Origin* is well worth another look. —*M. H.*

OFFICE KILLER L: HORROR/STALKERS (1997) 83M D: Cindy Sherman. *Carol Kane, Molly Ringwald, Jeanne Tripplehorn.* High-concept artist/photographer Sherman's only feature film to date takes the B-movie gore fest to the office. After Dorine (Kane) is downsized and forced to telecommute from home, she satisfies a need for the human contact of the workplace by systematically murdering her former coworkers and storing their decaying corpses at home. *Office Killer* is too mired in irony and deliberate camp to be of much critical interest, or to be particularly entertaining as a B-movie. The deliberately unrealistic gore, Kane's entertaining performance, and some excellent dialogue (notably scripted by writer/director Todd Haynes) are all points of interest. But by the time the films rolls out disembodied sex organs skewered on the hands of a clock, I could smell the college thesis papers coming and I'd just about had enough. —*C. B.*

OMEGA CODE, THE L: VAOWG/CHRISTPLOITATION (1999) 100M D: Robert Marcarelli. *Casper Van Dien, Michael York, Catherine Oxenberg, Michael Ironside.* Produced by televangelist Paul Crouch of the Trinity Broadcast Network (you'd recognize his wife, Jan, with the caked makeup and huge wig trying her best to outdo Tammy Faye Bakker) *The Omega Code* employs a routine action script on top of an outrageous premise these tele-fundamentalists actually believe: the Old Testament in Hebrew is nothing less than a code for a doomsday prophecy, and today with our modern computers we finally decode it. In this script all of the Hebrew is decoded except for one line that a rabbi prints out before he is assassinated. Van Dien is the overplayed good guy, York is totally miscast as the bad guy. You fill in the blanks. The production value, of course, is quite good given all that money Paul and Jan Crouch have raked in since they stole the *Praise the Lord (PTL)* show from the Bakkers (see *The Eyes of Tammy Faye* for how this happened). —*N. J.*

OMEGA MAN, THE L: VAOWG/VAOWG (1971) 120M D: Boris Sagal. *Charlton Heston, Rosalind Cash, Lincoln Kilpatrick.* One day I was flipping the channels around and found a drunken Heston playing chess with a dressed-up bust of Julius Caesar. Suddenly some weird ghouls in black robes catapulted a fireball through his window, so he picked up a rifle and started busting off shots. And I thought, "What the hell *is* this movie?" Turned out it was *The Omega Man*, second in Heston's trilogy of apocalyptic sci-fi classics, including *Planet of the Apes* and *Soylent Green.* Heston plays Neville, one of the last remaining humans on Earth, who spends his time fighting off ghouls that have taken over and trying to find a cure for their victims. The film is adapted from the book *I Am Legend* by Richard Matheson (also

the basis for *Last Man on Earth* with Vincent Price and a major imspiration for George A. Romero's *Night of the Living Dead* series), which deserves a more faithful adaptation some day. This version is much sillier and pulpier than the book, but it's very entertaining and there's no other movie with quite the same feel. Cash is great as the love interest—only in the '70s (and after an apocalypse) could we see Heston fall in love with an afro-sporting soul sister. —*B. T.*

OMEN, THE L: VAOWG/CHRISTPLOITATION (1976) 111M D: Richard Donner. *Gregory Peck, Lee Remick, Harvey Stephens, David Warner, Billie Whitelaw, Patrick Troughton.* Here's a pretty good Antichrist flick! Robert Thorn (Peck) is a U.S. diplomat whose wife (Remick) experiences a stillbirth while they're in Rome. At the suggestion of a priest, they adopt another child whose mother has died. They settle in London where nothing seems to go quite right. Damien (Stephens), now five, seems to inspire his nanny to hang herself at his birthday party. Later, his mother slips and falls, causing a miscarriage while Damien looks on. Thorn is told by a priest (Troughton) that Damien could very possibly be the Antichrist! Soon after, the priest dies. Thorn sets out to remedy this apocalyptic dilemma, but it doesn't go as planned, opening the door for sequels. —*N. J.*

DAMIEN: OMEN II L: VAOWG/CHRISTPLOITATION (1978) 110M D: Don Taylor. *Sylvia Sidney, William Holden, Lee Grant, Robert Foxworth, Lew Ayres, Jonathan Scott-Taylor.* In this sequel to *The Omen,* Damien (Scott-Taylor) is now a happy cadet with a new set of parents and a new outlook on life. That is, until people slowly but surely learn about what he actually is. It starts with a wall, discovered on an archeological dig, that clearly depicts Damien as the Antichrist. Oddly enough, each person who sees this wall or even learns about it dies a horrible death, this time with the help of a black raven. One by one, Damien's family comes to believe the prophecies, his father holding out until the wall is brought to the local museum. Though this film is somewhat less suspenseful than the first, the violence is more aggressive and a little over the top. —*N. J.*

OMEN III: THE FINAL CONFLICT L: VAOWG/ CHRISTPLOITATION (1981) 108M D: Graham Baker. *Lisa Harrow, Don Gordon, Sam Neill, Mason Adams, Rossano Brazzi.* Neill plays the adult Damien, now an advisor to the president of the United States. After a large black dog inspires the ambassador to Britain to blow his own head off, Damien is appointed to the post. He becomes quite famous while promoting his programs for children, even as assassination attempts are made on his life by a small group that knows his identity and has the special daggers needed to kill him. Meanwhile, the second coming (or what Damien calls the Nazarene) is born, so he sets

out to kill all the babies born on the particular day prophesied. The violence of this film is more outrageous than in the first two *Omen* films, but that's clearly to make up for a waning story. This *Final Conflict* is in fact followed by a curious sequel, *Omen IV: The Awakening.* —*N. J.*

OMEN IV: THE AWAKENING L: VAOWG/CHRISTPLOITATION (1991) 97M D: Jorge Montesi, Dominique Othenin-Girard. *Madison Mason, Faye Grant, Michael Woods, Michael Lerner, Asia Vieira.* The Final Conflict wasn't so final after all! Perhaps that's why this offbeat sequel seems a bit more like a strange black comedy. A U.S. Senator and his wife adopt Delia, a young girl who just happens to be Damien's daughter. They love her despite her incredible mood swings and the large black dog that seems to protect her by terrorizing everyone else. Naturally lots of people die in the most curious and violent ways, but everyone writes it off as coincidence—everyone except her nanny. The nanny has new age beliefs, and when all of her crystals turn black she figures there is something spiritually wrong with the child. She takes Delia to a Psychic Fair to have the child analyzed, which proves amusing since she telekinetically burns the place down. Of course, things only get worse. To punctuate the black humor, a vision of a choir from hell appears from time to time singing the most ridiculous stuff as people are about to get killed. —*N. J.*

ONE, THE L: SCIENCE FICTION/SCIENCE FICTION (2001) 87M D: James Wong. *Delroy Lindo, Jet Li, Carla Gugino, Jason Statham.* Li bounces through a multitude of parallel universes battling alternate versions of himself in this sci-fi martial arts showdown. Li is less an actor than a pleasant personality, hardly convincing as a doting husband, and barely more credible as a wisecracking thug, but as a gymnastic whirlwind he's the best special effect in the film: a superpowered speed demon. It's pure pulp junk, less written than engineered, and director Wong embraces it as such. He tosses off such mundane details as character and motivation to leap into action, and boils everything down to a lean eighty-seven minutes of high-tech spectacles. Forget making sense of the absurd premise and just enjoy the mischievously tongue-in-cheek tone and the slickly engineered set pieces. —*S. A.*

A good Jet Li and an evil Jet Li fight each other using the standard post-*Matrix* digitized martial arts trickery. There was even talk that Li had worked some of his Buddhist philosophy into the storyline to make it more personal. Seems like a perfect B-movie premise for the usually reliable team of Wong and Glen Morgan (*The X-Files, Final Destination,* the remake of *Willard*), but instead it's a complete bore with little to offer in the way of genuine fight choreography or fun CGI absurdity. It feels a lot like *Timecop*—just a half-baked sci-fi story with little in the way of visual imagination or cinematic savvy. But I suppose it would have been even worse with the original star, The Rock. —*B. T.*

ORCA, THE KILLER WHALE L: VAOWG/VAOWG (1977) 92M D: Michael Anderson. *Robert Carradine, Keenan Wynn, Bo Derek, Will Sampson, Charlotte Rampling, Richard Harris. Orca* is one of the big budget films made to cash in on a phenomenon (in this case, *Jaws*). But *Orca* works well on its own as an exploitation film of the '70s, specifically in the nature-gets-its-revenge-against-mankind genre. Harris is the drunken Nolan, who illegally hunts whales. In a truly macabre sequence, he snares a pregnant killer whale, who gives birth on his ship's deck. The angry Orca father witnesses his mate and child die, as Nolan crassly washes the dead baby off his deck with a hose, and goes after Nolan with a ferocity that rivals Ahab's. In a truly amazing scene the whale knocks down Nolan's house. In another, the whale actually sets fire to the entire town, forcing Nolan to go back to the sea and chase the whale to the "ends of the earth," resulting in a final showdown between man and beast at the North Pole. Ennio Morricone provides a wonderful score and the whale effects are surprisingly realistic. —*N. H.*

ORGAN L: JAPANESE HORROR/JAPANESE HORROR (1996) 110M D: Kei Fujiwara. *Yosiakia Maekawa, Ryo Okubo, Kei Fujiwara, Shozo Tojima, Kenji Nasa.* Messy in every sense of the word, this grotesque, gooey thriller of organ pirates, deviant sex killers, and festering biology experiments is almost incoherent, but what a wild trip! When a Tokyo cop falls victim to a yakuza syndicate selling body parts, his brother investigates. Meanwhile a scientist experiments on the cop's limbless trunk, which he keeps alive with the blood of virgin high school girls. Director Kei, the star of the bio-techno-horror *Tetsuo* films, pushes the alienated timbre of those films into a nightmarish stew of pus and blood and severed limbs. The story of sick siblings and sexual predators gets so knotted in excess and seeped in bodily fluids that it loses its way, but perhaps that's the madness to his method. It's not for the squeamish, and even gore hounds may find themselves challenged, but it's truly unforgettable. —*S. A.*

OROCHI THE EIGHT-HEADED DRAGON L: JAPANESE SCIENCE FICTION/JAPANESE SCIENCE FICTION (1994) 105M D: Takao Okawara. *Masahiro Takashima, Hiroshi Abe, Yasuko Sawaguchi.* During their successful run of '90s *Godzilla* revivals, Toho branched out with this epic fantasy based on Japanese mythology. The opening tells the story of the birth of the gods and the day baby Prince Yamato was thrown off a cliff, only to be saved by a shimmering metallic bird called "The White Bird of Heaven." The adult Yamato (Takashima) struggles to control dangerous powers and to face his destiny of uniting with the bird to slay the apocalyptic dragon of the title. This is the kind of story that includes giant, tentacled sea gods, a crystal-encased demon floating in outer space, and a magical weapon called "The Sword of the Dark Clouds." In other words, don't expect a Godzilla movie—there's a lot more sword fighting and magic duels than giant monster mayhem. But when the dragon does appear, he looks like Ghidrah with five extra heads, and it's an incredible feat of puppetry. This is a good fantasy movie, and young kids would probably love it (but be warned there are two very realistic sword impalements). —*B. T.*

OTHERS, THE L: HORROR/GHOSTS (2001) 104M D: Alejandro Amenabar. *Nicole Kidman, Eric Sykes, Christopher Eccleston. The Others* is a well put together ghost story. Granted, it has more or less the same ending as *The Sixth Sense* (which was hardly original itself) and no gore or jump moments, but it is still eerie enough to make me feel that good and ghastly haunted vibe. The awesome production design and creepy cinematography combine to create a fantastic atmosphere reminiscent of *The Changeling* and *Legend of Hell House*. Maybe my love for haunted houses overshadows the film's many shortcomings but it's nice and spooky, so it's good enough for me. —*T. S.*

OUTER LIMITS, THE—THE ORIGINAL SERIES L: SCIENCE FICTION /SCIENCE FICTION TV (1963) 1642M D: Various. *Robert Duvall, Warren Oates, Eddie Albert, William Shatner, Donald Pleasence. The Outer Limits* was first broadcast in 1963 in direct competition with the final season of *The Twilight Zone*. Beyond the obvious similarities of science fiction and trick storylines, *Outer Limits* occupied itself predominantly with the unknowns of futuristic space travel. With a fairly small budget (most aliens were obviously people hopping around in furry suits), the show exploited the thrill and throes of interstellar travel. It soon hedged out *The Twilight Zone* while following the same production formula that made that show great: a different cast every episode, stark black and white photography, and the deliberate use of the television format. "We control the vertical. We control the horizontal." —*N. J.*

PENETRATION ANGST L: HORROR/STALKERS (2003) 100M D: Wolfgang Buld. *Fiona Horsey, Paul Conway, Amy Steel. Penetration Angst* is primarily the story of a woman who, after losing her virginity to a rapist, finds that all men who enter her die, disappear, or more accurately are sucked into her. The first half is a lot of fun as the woman struggles with her emerging sexuality and terrible curse. However, rather than developing that theme, everything falls apart. The story then follows her good-hearted, would-be lover as he meets Siamese twins, falls in love, and then unbelievably turns homicidal. He goes on a crime spree with a stripper and unwittingly kidnaps his newly reformed, recently married, still sexually challenged true love. The plot falls to pieces and

everything ends poorly, failing to deliver on an excellent if completely ridiculous premise. The story just isn't there and the cheap thrills and absurd situations aren't enough to carry the film. —*T. S.*

PEOPLE NEXT DOOR, THE L: PSYCHOTRONIC/DRUGS (1970) 93M D: David Green. *Hal Holbrook, Stephen McHattie, Deborah Winters, Julie Harris, Eli Wallach, Cloris Leachman. The People Next Door* is one of the first, and funniest, suburban teenage drug scare movies. Wallach and Harris can't figure out their rebellious teenage daughter and when she turns to heavy drugs, they blame her hippie boyfriend. All the adults drink heavily in this movie (Wallach almost always has a can of beer in his hand) and the actual drug pusher turns out to be Don (*Squirm*) Scardino, the nerdy son of the new neighbors. This movie is a good time capsule as it not only features hippies and drugs but also swingers, nymphomaniacs, psychologists, full-frontal male nudity and more, baby, more! —*S. H.*

PEOPLE WHO OWN THE DARK, THE L: HORROR/EURO-HORROR (1976) 83M D: León Klimovsky. *Tony Kendall, Alberto de Mendoza, Jacinto Molina, Nadiuska, Maria Perschy.* This film starts out as a Spanish *La Grande Bouffe*, with a group of male diplomats and intellectuals at a rural estate getting together with a group of prostitutes for a Sadean fete and orgy. It turns into *Night of the Living Dead* meets *On the Beach* when the proceedings are interrupted by a nuclear blast that blinds the inhabitants of a nearby village, turning them into the titular "People." This film was one of nine collaborations between Iberian lycanthrope-actor Molina (better known in the United States as Paul Naschy) and Argentinean-born director Klimovsky (*A Dragonfly for Each Corpse*). Made in the wake of Franco's death, the film's subtext is easily interpreted as political commentary, reflecting anxieties over the then-current power vacuum. Though it has its fair share of killing, this is not an especially wgraphic film when compared, say, to de Amando de Ossorio's *Blind Dead* quartet. Still, the ending is shockingly bleak. —*S. A.*

PERVIRELLA L: PSYCHOTRONIC/FILM THREAT (1997) 88M D: Alex Chandon. *Emily Booth.* This bizarre satire of old Britannia and Victorian repression is an acid-laced brew of *Barbarella, Rocky Horror Picture Show, Flesh Gordon,* and Jules Verne globetrotting fantasies, directed in the style of Derek Jarman in his punk years. This tiny budget, wacko sci-fantasy epic stars the bountiful Emily Bouffante (aka Booth) as the titular Pervirella, the daughter of a repressed Victorian scientist and a sex rebel guerrilla. She's a softcore Candide, an innocent with a volcanic sex drive who spreads her love while searching the world for more magical elixir to keep the mummified three-hundred-year-old Queen Victoria alive and pumping out mutant

offspring. It's a woolly little cult thing, with special effects as colorful and creative as they are willfully cheap and kitschy, and as fun as kinky sex farce gets. British music video and underground movie whiz Chandon directs, and cult figures Jonathan Ross and David Warbeck make cameos. —*S. A.*

PHANTASM L: HORROR/ZOMBIES (1979) 90M D: Don Coscarelli. *Reggie Bannister, Michael Baldwin, Bill Thornbury. Phantasm* kicks ass. When I first saw this film at the tender age of nine, it scared me shitless. When I saw it again later on I thought it was just damn good and that opinion is reinforced with every single viewing. Everything about this film just oozes The Seventies. Part zombie movie, part interdimensional sci-fi action, part adolescent adventure, pure greatness. That's *Phantasm* and boy, does it kick ass. —*T. S.*

PHANTOM EMPIRE, THE L: PSEUDOTRONIC /PSEUDOTRONIC (FAUX TROMA) (1986) 85M D: Fred Olen Ray. *Susan Stokey, Sybil Danning, Ross Hagen, Jeffrey Combs, Robert Quarry, Russ Tamblyn.* This *Journey to the Center of the Earth* sci-fantasy quest by way of a private eye adventure has the usual hallmarks of Ray's drive-in epics: a smart-alecky script, babes in bikinis (and less), and stumbling action scenes to give the film some energy. Ray is hardly a class act—even among B-movie auteurs he's often sloppy and dull—but this one looks better than most and he's having a good time, as is his cast, which is salted with old Hollywood characters and B-movie icons. Joining stars Hagen and Stokey are Combs (Herbert West from the *Re-Animator* films in a rare "normal" role), Quarry (*Count Yorga*), Tamblyn, and B-movie queen Danning. He even throws in a couple of primitive stop-motion dinosaurs, which may lack in realism but make up for it in funky sub–Ray Harryhausen charm. Watch for the great end credits, which begin with: "Filmed on location at the Center of the Earth." —*S. A.*

PHANTOM OF THE OPERA L: CLASSIC HORROR/CLASSIC HORROR (1943) 92M D: Arthur Lubin. *Claude Rains, Susanna Foster, Nelson Eddy, Edgar Barrier, Hume Cronyn, Jane Farrar.* This 1943 version, again from Universal, is not as good as the classic with Lon Chaney but very fun nonetheless. It strays from the original story and focuses too much on the opera being produced. Otherwise it is superb, as Rains delivers a fantastic performance as the Phantom. Not much horror but still a good movie. —*T. S.*

PHANTOM OF THE OPERA (1989) L: HORROR/STALKERS (1989) 93M D: Dwight H. Little. *Jill Schoelen, Robert Englund, Stephanie Lawrence, Alex Hyde-White, Bill Nighy. Phantom of the Opera* becomes a slasher picture as the Phantom is played by Englund of Freddy Krueger fame. He isn't a victim of an accident but a man who sold his soul for powers. In fact, it has almost nothing to do with the original story. But it's crazy fun and has some good gore. It's just an '80s slasher movie with a lot of style. —*T. S.*

PHANTOM PLANET L: CLASSIC SCIENCE FICTION/CLASSIC SCIENCE FICTION (1961) 82M D: William Marshall. *Coleen Gray, Michael Marshall, Dean Fredericks, Dolores Faith, Anthony Dexter.* Astronauts from the far-flung future of 1980 crash land on an asteroid and are shrunk by aliens in the midst of a war with a race of grotesque fire monsters in Marshall's low-budget sci-fi adventure. It was lampooned on *Mystery Science Theater 3000* but despite its *Star Trek*–style papier mâché sets and pulp plot, it survives the teasing quite nicely. Though hardly a classic, Marshall manages to instill the bargain basement effects with some style (the precredits crash is a real audience grabber) and even anticipates two iconic moments in sci-fi history: the untethered astronaut floating to oblivion of *2001* and the macho *Star Trek* duels. You might say that American he-man Fredericks anticipates the two-fisted machismo of William Shatner's Captain Kirk, right down to getting stuck on a planet of luscious babes. —*S. A.*

PHASE IV L: VAOWG/VAOWG (1974) 93M D: Saul Bass. *Robert Henderson, Lynne Frederick, Michael Murphy, Nigel Davenport, Alan Gifford.* After a brilliant and prolific career designing titles, posters, and logos (his distinctive touch is perhaps most closely associated with *Anatomy of a Murder* and *Vertigo*), Bass directed exactly one feature length film—I have no idea why it was this one. The first stretch contains no dialogue and lots of documentary footage of ants. The story that eventually emerges involves a colony of superintelligent ants out in a desert and the small group of scientists charged with the task of exterminating them. Despite being slow, cold, and uninvolving, its undeniable strangeness makes it somewhat interesting. There are also some striking images here and there—if cleaned up and letterboxed on a DVD, the movie might be vastly improved. —*B. T.*

PIECES L: HORROR/EURO-HORROR (1983) 89M D: Juan Piquer Simon. *Christopher George, Lynda Day George, Paul L. Smith.* Modern horror got you down? Starving for mindless bloodshed? Brain-dead actors? Aimless weapons slicing into unidentifiable slabs of meat? Look no further, as the high mark of low-brow terror is here: *Pieces*! Sexist? Racist? Totally tasteless? Admittedly so, but also a gruesome, straight-faced exploration of the goofiest cross-section of '80s exploitation insanity. An uncomfortably twisted and questionable work, even for this genre, *Pieces* is a particularly glaring product of the anything-for-a-shock '70s/'80s international horror sweatshop. See teenagers flayed and filleted with clumsy ferocity while you guess the identity of the mysterious killer. Is it the embittered tennis instructor? The shameful stereotype of a kung fu teacher? The

gardener, who also played Bluto in *Popeye*? Who cares? Bring on the guts! —*Z. C.*

PIN L: HORROR/STALKERS (1988) 102M D: Sandor Stern. *Cynthia Preston, David Hewlett, Terry O'Quinn.* Perusing the cover of *Pin*, you may think it's just another '80s cheapie softcore fright flick that doesn't deliver the goods. Not so! Bare flesh seekers will hardly be satisfied by the sole quick flash of breasts, and gore fans aren't likely to be sated by the sparse use of blood. This is, however, a supremely creepy and fun movie that rarely garners complaints. Hewlett gives his all to the role of Leon, a young man disturbed by the cold indifference of his doctor father (O'Quinn of *Stepfather* fame). He turns to the company of Pin, his father's medical dummy, for solace. Following the death of his parents in a horrific car crash (caused by Pin?), Leon loses it and moves his best buddy Pin into the house, to the dismay of his sister Ursula (Preston). Eerie medical dummy madness ensues. Major bonus points here for nurse-on-medical-dummy sex and the disturbing Pin voice concocted by Jonathan Banks. You'll never look at a dummy the same way. . . —*E. O.*

PIRANHA L: VAOWG/VAOWG (1978) 92M D: Joe Dante. *Bradford Dillman, Barbara Steele, Dick Miller, Keenan Wynn, Heather Menzies, Kevin McCarthy.* Director Dante and screenwriter John Sayles turn a shameless *Jaws* rip-off into a playfully tongue-in-cheek thriller. True to the Roger Corman school of drive-in filmmaking, they provide plenty of blood, meat, and gore-ific shocks along the way when they release a school of mutant piranha (hatched in a long-forgotten secret military lab) into a river that feeds a children's summer camp and a chintzy waterfront amusement park. Along with the paranoia of government experiments and satirical stabs at money-grubbing entrepreneurs, there are plenty of movie in-jokes and minor genre movie star appearances (McCarthy, Wynn, Miller, and Steele all get meaty roles) and bursts of black humor throughout. ("Sir, the Piranhas." "What about the goddamm piranhas?!" "They're eating the guests.") True to form, the river runs red before it's over. —*S. A.*

PIT, THE (1981) L: HORROR/DEMONS (1981) 97M D: Lew Lehman. *Sammy Snyders, Jeannie Elias, Sonja Smits, Laura Hollingsworth.* This movie is disturbing on many different levels. Essentially, it's an early '80s softcore/gore film masquerading itself under a thin veil of after-school special. Bullied young Jamie (Snyders) resorts to feeding neighborhood kids to his pit of prehistoric Trogs hidden in the forest. This could prove to be a bit taxing under normal circumstances, so the twelve-year-old relies on his teddy bear, with which he shares a psychic bond, to help orchestrate his revenges. Teddy also helps Jamie blackmail the grumpy neighborhood librarian into giving them a striptease after she lost her daughter. You never really feel sorry for Jamie not fitting in with the other kids or feel an ounce of compassion as his face gets pummeled, because he honestly is creepy as all hell. I cannot think of another horror movie as wholly unsettling as this. —*A. T.*

PLANET OF THE APES L: VAOWG/PLANET OF THE APES (1968) 112M D: Franklin J. Schaffner. *Roddy McDowall, Charlton Heston, Maurice Evans, Kim Hunter.* An American astronaut (Heston) wakes up from untold years of suspended animation, bares his chest, and leads the human rights revolution against the master race of the primitive planet he and his fellows space travelers have landed on. It's pop sci-fi done up with style by Schaffner, who makes the most of his savage landscapes and superb art direction and creates vivid, fully rounded characters from his simian cast (notably McDowall, Hunter, and Evans under the masks). Adapted by Rod Serling from the Pierre Boulle novel, with plenty of character and an undercurrent of humor, it was followed by four sequels and a TV series, none of which touch the macho glory of the original. It remains a striking, exciting classic of late '60s science fiction, a kick-ass adventure with a bizarre but cleverly conceived vision of an alternate reality, an unnerving, percussion-heavy score by Jerry Goldsmith, and a legendary climax. —*S. A.*

PLAYGIRLS AND THE VAMPIRE, THE L: CLASSIC HORROR/ CLASSIC HORROR (1960) 80M D: Piero Regnoli. *Lyla Rocco, Walter Brandi, Maria Giovannini.* Made in the early days of French horror films, *The Playgirls and the Vampire* introduced a touch of sexuality to its simple plot. The title is much more titillating than the film. Forced off the road in a violent thunderstorm, five playgirls and their manager find themselves at the castle of Count Kernassy (Brandi), who is not welcoming to the curvaceous beauties. Until, that is, Vera (Rocco) steps forward and he recognizes her resemblance to his beautiful ancestor Margerhita, just as he bears his own resemblance to his two-hundred-year-old ancestor, a vampire who slumbers in the family crypt. The opening scenes of the crypt itself are possibly the creepiest moments in the film, with the vampire's hand snaking its way out of its stone-lidded coffin. The sparsely lit black and white castle hallways and rooms give the movie a sense of unease, but the inherent silliness of the bump 'n' grinders keeps the chills at constant bay. Sort of like *Orgy of the Dead* in black and white. —*S. R.*

POLTERGEIST L: HORROR/GHOSTS (1982) 114M D: Tobe Hooper. *Craig T. Nelson, JoBeth Williams, Heather O'Rourke, Zelda Rubinstein.* Carol Anne has been sucked into the television! That, and numerous other mysterious goings on, would seem to indicate their house is haunted. Among the established American horror directors at the time, Hooper had a curious blend of humor and hor-

ror which in this film is evident with the casting of Rubinstein, the diminutive lady playing the outrageous psychic who spearheads the paranormal investigation. With frights and giggles aplenty, *Poltergeist* is a decent enough horror film in its own right to warrant a wave of sequels (the second one in particular could be chalked up as one of the worst sequels ever made). —*N. J.*

POSEIDON ADVENTURE, THE L: VAOWG/VAOWG (1972) 117M D: Ronald Neame. *Gene Hackman, Ernest Borgnine, Shelley Winters, Red Buttons, Carol Lynley, Roddy McDowall.* This is the first in a series of big-budget disaster films to flood the market in the seventies, culminating in the *Airport* films and eventually the downfall of the genre with the *Airplane* movies. In this film the S.S. *Poseidon* is a gigantic cruise ship loaded down with passengers for its last voyage from New York to Athens. During a New Year's Eve party, while everyone is well dressed and celebrating, the ship is capsized by a gigantic wave. A stellar cast performs in earnest, not the least of which is Winters, who noisily whines at the mere sight of water. The film won Oscars for its visual effects and for its song "The Morning After." —*N. J.*

POSSESSION L: HORROR/DEMONS (1981) 123M D: Andrzej Zulawski. *Sam Neill, Margit Carstensen, Isabelle Adjani, Heinz Bennent.* A screeching mix of David Cronenberg bio-horror and *Rosemary's Baby* with the naked emotions of European art cinema, this is a film like no other. Adjani leaves her husband (Neill), son, and lover to become mother and mistress to a dark demon that she spontaneously births in the midst of a breakdown. Obviously symbolic but purposefully obscure, Zulawski's story of demons and doppelgangers is an uncomfortable collision of heady art film and exploitation weirdness, strewn through with hysterical shouting matches and intense, bug-eyed performances. Carlo Rambaldi helped create the creepy, totemlike creature. Initially sheered by more than forty minutes for its American release, the restored version is even more uncomfortable. —*S. A.*

Being the person who licensed this film for DVD, I do not agree that it is "heady art . . . and exploitation weirdness . . . strewn with hysterical shouting matches and intense, bug-eyed performances." Instead, I see *Possession*, like many of Zulawski's films, as being a perverse document of his anxieties about the disintegration of relationships and the destructive "conjuring" of inner demons. Adjani's creation of the husband she really wants, which she creates out of her own id, gives birth to some goo that slowly develops into a monster and takes over (and murdering in the end) Neill's character. I do not know of another film that so completely exposes the destruction of the heterosexual relationship and guts the inner turmoil of a family falling apart. All of the actors are uniformly excellent, Adjani in particular is the shining jewel in the crown. —*N. H.*

POSTMAN, THE L: SCIENCE FICTION/SCIENCE FICTION (1997) 177M D: Kevin Costner. *Kevin Costner, Olivia Williams, Will Patton, Daniel Von Bargen, James Russo, Larenz Tate.* A fascinating character study of a Hollywood star whose ego has robbed him of all his sensibilities. Costner directed, produced, and starred in this big-budget film about himself bringing hope and salvation to a postapocalyptic world by delivering old mail and sleeping with a childless woman whose husband is sterile. Among the benefactors of Costner's selflessness are two of his own children, one of whom plays a boy who hands off a letter in an overly emotional slo-mo scene and the other who unveils a statue of said scene at the end. Characterizations could not be more white-and-black in this gigantic flop, and with repeated viewings it would seem this film has all the makings of a cult classic for exactly the opposite reasons Costner made it. —*N. J.*

PREDATOR L: SCIENCE FICTION/SCIENCE FICTION (1987) 107M D: John McTiernan. *Arnold Schwarzenegger, Carl Weathers, Bill Duke, Elpidia Carrillo.* Look, I don't care if it *seemed* like a great movie when we were thirteen. It's not. I will not begrudge anyone for enjoying macho Schwarzenegger running around covered in mud making bad puns, or Jesse "The Body" Ventura (at that time my favorite evil wrestling commentator) boasting, "I ain't got time to bleed." But the movie doesn't have much more than that to offer. I believe the reputation of *Predator* is due to two factors: (1) The monster seemed cool at the time. (2) It wasn't good enough that we ever went back and watched it again. Now all we have is that residual thirteen-year-old memory of a cool monster, and that image gets more and more watered down by action figures and comic books, and by watching the movie and seeing that cheesy heat vision effect that, again, seemed cool at the time. Oh well. I guess you can get excited about your *Alien* crossover if you want to, but just remember, I tried to warn you. —*B. T.*

PRINCESS BLADE L: JAPANESE SCIENCE FICTION /JAPANESE SCIENCE FICTION (2002) 92M D: Shinsuke Sato. *Hideaki Ito, Yoichi Numata, Shiro Sano, Yumiko Shaku.* Set five hundred years in Japan's future, which is once again ruled by a monarchy and isolated from the outside world, is the House of Takemikazuchi, an assassination organization that keeps the ever growing rebel resistance at bay. Yuki (Shaku), a young teenager, is the last of the bloodline of the House, and is set to inherit command over the others. But Yuki has been questioning her role, and when a horrible secret regarding her mother's death comes to light, Yuki may find herself fighting those she grew up with. With a name like Princess Blade, it is the action that is the main draw here. The swordplay is fast and

furious, with wirework, filmcranking tricks, and quick editing energizing it even more. Though it is set in the future, the sci-fi aspect is somewhat lacking, and the forced CGI throwaway shots make the otherwise well-made film look cheap. Still, it is a worthwhile addition to the world of girls-with-swords. —*R. M.*

PRINCESS BRIDE, THE L: FANTASY/FANTASY (1987) 98M D: Rob Reiner. *Cary Elwes, Robin Wright Penn, Fred Savage, André the Giant, Mandy Patinkin, Peter Falk.* The *Princess Bride* embodies everything that I found beautiful about fantasy when I was ten years old: a wannabe princess with long, flowing hair, a giant, swordfights, a suave and debonair prince who is willing to do anything to save said wannabe princess, torture, rescues, and gigantic rats. (I probably wasn't too into the gigantic rats when I was ten, but I think they are pretty rad now.) This movie takes all the traditional elements of fantasy and exaggerates them, resulting in an extremely comic story that will have you falling in love with all the characters and cheer in excitement. I've probably seen this a hundred times, and every time I'm reminded why it has remained the best fantasy film for over fifteen years. And no, it has nothing to do with Fred Savage's narration. —*J. S.*

PROGENY L: SCIENCE FICTION/SCIENCE FICTION (1998) 120M D: Brian Yuzna. *Arnold Vosloo, Jillian McWhirter, Brad Dourif, Lindsey Crouse.* A standard alien abduction plot in this film from Yuzna (who wrote *Re-animator*) has a number of great things to recommend it. First is the spooky atmosphere and the surreal special effects employed for the abduction of Vosloo and McWhirter. Next is Dourif, amazingly well cast as the loopy UFOlogist who loves gathering his information through hypnotism. And last is the truly horrifying, slimy aliens who make McWhirter's repressed memories about as shocking as such a film can get. Of course, it turns out that she's impregnated, hence the title. More suspense/horror than science fiction, this film also has a thin veil of black humor that marks much of Yuzna's work. —*N. J.*

PROPHECY, THE (1995) L: VAOWG/CHRISTPLOITATION (1995) 98M D: Gregory Widen. *Christopher Walken, Eric Stoltz, Virginia Madsen, Elias Koteas.* The *Prophecy* is a modest movie that manages to overcome its limitations. It follows a failed priest turned homicide cop (try putting that on a business card!) as he investigates creepy doings in a Southwest community. He soon becomes embroiled in a war for heaven itself, with angels, the devil, and Gabriel all jockeying for position. The budget is obviously small, and at times the movie strains to keep up with the ambitious sweep it has set for itself. Aid comes in the form of a strong cast, which includes Koteas as the cop, Stoltz as an angel, Madsen as a quite-human love interest, and Viggo Mortensen in a brief but memorable appearance as the Father of Lies. The film belongs to Walken, however, as Gabriel. By turns frightening, calculating, weary, and charismatic, he elevates the whole production to fairly grand heights for a supernatural thriller. —T. P.

PSYCH-OUT L: PSYCHOTRONIC/DRUGS (1968) 95M D: Richard Rush. *Susan Strasberg, Max Julien, Adam Roarke, Bruce Dern, Jack Nicholson, Dean Stockwell.* Strasberg is a deaf girl who comes to San Francisco in search of her brother (Dern) who tuned in, turned on, and dropped out. Nicholson is the callous hippie bandleader who takes her in and Stockwell the guru who lends his connections to her search and his patience to her pain. Rush directs this portrait of the Haight-Ashbury Flower Power scene of hippie communes, free love, bad trips, and rock happenings. The Strawberry Alarm Clock perform in front of the liquid lightshow, and dig that crazy funeral led by The Seeds' Sky Saxon! It's all pretty groovy, with a cast that brings freewheeling energy to the scene and a vivid, psychedelic look brought by cinematographer Laszlo Kovacs. "Reality is a deadly place. I hope this trip is a good one." —S. A.

PULSE L: JAPANESE HORROR/JAPANESE HORROR (2001) 119M D: Kiyoshi Kurosawa. *Haruhiko Kato, Kumiko Aso, Jun Fubuki.* Pulse slowly churns for two hours, until the feeling of dread is absorbed by those watching it. People all around Tokyo are mysteriously disappearing or dying, and when Michi (Aso) discovers her friend dead one day, she vows to understand what is happening. Across town, Ryosuke (Kato) stumbles across a bizarre Web site filled with web cams broadcasting depressed people looking for help. As Tokyo slowly transforms into a ghost town, Michi and Ryosuke's curiosity cross paths, and together they are able to discover the horrifying truth that has been spreading out all around them. There is zero gore in the film, and while a few shocks are spread throughout the story, it is the soul of the entire film that will draw you in to keep you forever, and ever, and ever. —R. M.

PUMPKINHEAD L: HORROR/DEMONS (1988) 89M D: Stan Winston. *Lance Henriksen, Jeff East, John D'Aquino.* To a youngster raised in the suburbs, there is nothing more frightening than the wrath of a redneck. Especially when said redneck resurrects a demon of vengeance as creepy as this one. This film taught me the nature of karma, as well as to stay out of the backwoods. —E. B.

QUATERMASS II L: HORROR/HAMMER FILMS (1957) 85M D: Val Guest. *John Longden, Bryan Forbes, Brian Donlevy.* The second of Hammer's Nigel Kneale–scripted Quatermass films puts a few twists in the *Invasion of the Body Snatchers* tale and then compounds the paranoia with stark black and white cinematography and an eerie, empty industrial location. Cantankerous Dr. Quatermass (played with testy abruptness by Donlevy) investigates strange meteors falling around a secret government plant in rural England and soon uncovers an alien conspiracy from outer space, but it's the horrific details that give the story its lifeblood: oozing black wounds, pods that hatch alien seeds planted in human hosts (shades of *Alien*), and the stumbling, fumbling escape of a dying man black with burning tar, a screaming shadow on a white storage tank. —S. A.

QUATERMASS AND THE PIT L: HORROR/HAMMER FILMS (1967) 98M D: Roy Ward Baker. *Barbara Shelley, Julian Glover, James Donald, Andrew Keir, Maurice Good.* Ancient skulls are discovered during a London subway excavation, then an unexploded WWII missile. As if that wasn't odd enough, investigators realize it's not a missile at all, but an alien spacecraft with the remains of its insectlike occupants still inside, their power perhaps waiting to be released. Adapted from a 1958 mini-series, this Hammer version of a Dr. Quatermass adventure takes an intelligent and extremely suspenseful approach to science fiction. Most of the film is confined to the subway tunnel, where scientists peel open the spacecraft layer by layer until they find not a creamy surprise in the center, but a horrible one. —B. T.

RAGE: CARRIE 2, THE L: PSYCHOTRONIC/KING, STEPHEN (1999) 101M D: Katt Shea. *Jason London, Zachery Ty Bryan, Emily Bergl, Amy Irving.* A flawed sequel, but not quite as bad as you'd expect. Rachel (Bergl) isn't popular, but she's not an outcast. The only really weird thing about her is that she is the half-sister of Carrie White and has inherited the same telekinetic powers. Irving returns in a tacked-on subplot as Sue Snell, now a counselor, who figures out Rachel's secret and tries to help her before she becomes Carrie 2. Another set of jocks plays another cruel prank on Rachel, this time at a party, and she goes on her own rampage. Bergl does a great job as Rachel, really differentiating her from Spacek's Carrie. Some of the references to the first film are clever, especially the scene where she comforts her dog who has been hit by a car and ends up covered in blood. Unfortunately the film pales next to the original, and you're reminded of that every time they foolishly cut to footage from it. —B. T.

RAPTURE, THE L: VAOWG/CHRISTPLOITATION (1991) 100M D: Michael Tolkin. *Mimi Rogers, David Duchovny, Marvin Elkins, Patrick Bauchau, Darwyn Carson, Stephanie Menuez.* If you're looking for a sexy movie, don't browse around, looking for something you think is gonna be sexy but that no one will realize is sexy when you take it up to the counter. Because if you do, you might pick up *The Rapture* by accident. You'll look at the cover and think, "Huh. That looks sexy. Rapture is sexy." You'll read the back, about how Mimi Rogers lives a risqué life and then joins a religious cult. It even has Duchovny in it, and he's pretty hot. Don't rent this flick only to discover that Rogers starts off debauched (so there's a little sex) but then joins a scary Christian cult, the whole story being, of course, not about the sexy Rapture, but the Biblical one. Doh! That was a really disappointing experience . . . heh, heh, er, or so I've been told. —*M.N.*

RAW MEAT L: HORROR/CANNIBALS (1972) 88M D: Gary Sherman. *Christopher Lee, Sharon Gurney, Donald Pleasence, Hugh Armstrong.* A brutal cannibalistic reworking of the classic *Beauty and the Beast* tale. A third-generation subterranean man-eating hobo has made his way from his bone-ridden lair into the British subway system, hungry and searching for a new mate. The unfortunate Gurney becomes the object of his affection, and it's up to her abrasively fashionable boyfriend and Scotland Yard to solve her disappearance before more corpses hit the dinner pile. A healthy amount of gore, combat, and oozing pustules help to elevate *Raw Meat* to the very top of the UK horror heap, and Armstrong's performance as the heartsick inarticulate cannibal deserves some kind of major award. Pleasence and Lee are the recognizable faces in Sherman's (*Dead & Buried*) extremely impressive feature film debut. Released overseas as *Deathline.* —*Z. C.*

REAL CANCUN, THE L: PSYCHOTRONIC/REALITY TV (2003) 96M D: Rick de Oliveira. *Brittany Brown-Hart, Benjamin Fletcher.* "Reality TV" goes to the big screen and proves that it's not the same thing as a documentary. The producers of *The Real World* cast a bunch of young character types to go on a spring break vacation, drink endless shots of tequila, bungee jump, and "hook up." One couple actually high-fives after sex, another gets together after the guy chivalrously offers his urine to soothe the lady's jellyfish sting. It's supposed to be titillating, but it's more effective as a Bret Easton Ellis–style look into the empty skulls of alcoholic rich brats. It was filmed while the United States was invading Iraq, but that's never mentioned, and if the kids were even aware of the war it doesn't appear to have put a damper on their wet T-shirt contests or their body shots. So in a way it's a very accurate record of the phony, media-created world many Americans live in. Our parents had Woodstock, we had the fucking *Real Cancun.* Pardon me, I have to go cry now. —*B. T.*

REAL WORLD LAS VEGAS—THE COMPLETE SEASON L: PSYCHOTRONIC/REALITY TV (2002) 559M D: Liz Patrick. When *The Real World* first started, the title seemed to accidently emphasize how contrived it was—a bunch of kids from different parts of the country getting to live in a nice apartment for free if they can get used to ignoring the cameramen around them is not exactly the real world. But there did seem to be a genuine hope on the part of the producers that they would stumble across some sorts of insights about young people finding their place in the world. Now, twelve seasons and hundreds of spin-offs and ripoffs later, the new kids on *The Real World* have grown up in a world where living your life on TV is normal, like you're already expected to know how to do it. That, combined with the growing horrendousness of "reality TV," has led to a season so ridiculously sleazy it should be called *Larry Clark's The Real World.* They live above a casino, work at a bar, and are allowed to carry drinks with them in the elevators. In the old days it was funny to see one sex scene in a season, this time it's unusual to see an episode where someone doesn't shamelessly "hook up" in front of the camera crew. Early in the season, three cast members have a ménage-a-trois in the hot tub. When one of the girls is hurt that it didn't mean anything, the guy tries to get her kicked out of the house. I'm sure this is not an accurate portrayal of your average young American lifestyle, but it must mean something that they can find this many people willing to do this on camera. I would just like to apologize on behalf of the entire human race to the Martians who will find this box set in the wreckage of our once proud civilization. —*B. T.*

REEFER MADNESS L: PSYCHOTRONIC/DRUGS (1938) 67M D: Louis J. Gasnier. *Lillian Miles, Dorothy Short, Kenneth Craig.* Today this film is seen more often than not as a humorous cult film. How could anyone exaggerate the effects of marijuana this badly? But put in context, this low-budget propaganda piece does make some kind of sense. Prohibition had only been recently repealed and so marijuana became a target. With the help of William Randolph Hearst, oil companies, and propaganda such as this film, the entire hemp industry was smashed by 1937. The film depicts a young man who, after one puff of the "evil weed," gets a wild look in his eyes, becomes insanely lustful, and hops in his car and crushes pedestrians without even knowing it. It wasn't until Nixon that the "War on Drugs" began and not until Reagan that the absurd theories about marijuana put forth in *Reefer Madness* were generally accepted as the official stance of the Drug Czar. —*N. J.*

REEFER MADNESS II: THE TRUE STORY L: PSYCHOTRONIC/DRUGS (1985) 50M D: Kent Skov. *Sandy Mielke, Stephen Rollman. Reefer Madness 2* is ten times funnier than the slow-moving *Reefer Madness.* This movie is much like a very good *Mystery Science Theater 3000* episode, with lines like, "I couldn't find any pot, you wanna buy some money?" This is a very independent film and might be hard to find, but if you run across it, feel lucky. Try this movie with the substance of your choice, but I think reefer was the creative force behind this one. So when in Rome, eh? —*R. D.*

REIGN OF FIRE L: VAOWG/VAOWG (2002) 102M D: Rob Bowman. *Christian Bale, Gerard Butler, Izabella Scorupco, Matthew McConaughey, Scott James Moutter.* A strange egg in a tunnel beneath London unleashes a plague of fast-breeding, fire-breathing dragons that scorch the earth and decimate its population in only a few years. Like *Day of the Dead*, this film takes place in the aftermath, with Bale leading a community of survivors and McConaughey's psychotic American soldier coming in to show them how to hunt dragons. It's a clever movie with an appropriately gloomy atmosphere and a somber tone (especially the scene where all the children cry after a dragon attack). Definitely a worthwhile postapocalypse movie, but it could've had more gravity with a longer running time and a bit of R-rated violence. —*B.T.*

RETURN OF THE JEDI L: SCIENCE FICTION/STAR WARS (1983) 136M D: Richard Marquand. *Billy Dee Williams, Harrison Ford, Carrie Fisher, Alec Guinness, Mark Hamill.* The last film in the "original" *Star Wars* trilogy. Resolutions abound: Luke is a mature Jedi, all dressed up in black and ready to meet his destiny. Leia stages a rescue operation and liberates Han from Jabba's palace, melting the carbonite and what's left of the ice around her heart. Han shows he's not just a scruffy-looking nerf herder anymore by leading the Rebels into a dangerous mission on the forest moon of Endor. C-3PO is finally worshipped for the idol he is by the Ewoks. We see what's underneath Vader's mask as he makes the transition from evil Lord to see-through spirit. The best part of *Jedi* is when 3PO gives the Ewoks the run down, in their native tongue, of everything that's happened up until then. It makes you realize how far everyone's come, and makes the final triumph of good over evil even more sweet. —*J.K.*

RETURN OF THE LIVING DEAD L: HORROR/ZOMBIES (1985) 90M D: Dan O'Bannon. *Clu Gulager, Jim Karen, Don Calfa, Beverly Randolph.* Not a sequel to *Night of the Living Dead*, but a semiofficial spin-off about a military biohazard container unleashing fast-moving, brain-eating zombies. The movie is very inventive in the way it depicts the spread of the disease: chopping up a zombie doesn't work, so they cremate it, but the smoke created turns into acid rain that zombifies an entire graveyard. The opening scene, where the training of a new employee at a medical supply warehouse leads to the unleashing of the zombies, is especially masterful. It's also a harsh critique of military ineptitude and callousness. The exaggerated punk rocker characters at times tip what could be a perfect balance of dark humor and intense horror, but it's still one of the most satisfying zombie movies not directed by George Romero. —*B.T.*

RETURN OF THE VAMPIRE, THE L: CLASSIC HORROR/ CLASSIC HORROR (1943) 70M D: Lew Landers. *Miles Mander, Roland Varno, Nina Foch, Frieda Inescort, Bela Lugosi.* Lugosi isn't called Dracula in this film, but despite the name change (he's Armand Tesla), you can't mistake this stately bloodsucker, who wears a black cape with jutting collar and has a werewolf servant who calls him master, for anyone but the Count. After over a decade of denial, Lugosi donned the fangs for his first real vampire role since *Dracula*. This time his Van Helsing is a woman (Inescort), who searches for him when his grave is unearthed during the London Blitz. Yes, it's WWII, and the timely setting seems even more inspired now. That inspiration, plus the girl-next-door sultriness of Foch, pull this otherwise mundane monster flick out of the B-movie swamp. Landers directs with just enough atmosphere to make it work. —*S.A.*

RETURN TO OZ L: FANTASY/FANTASY (1985) 109M D: Walter Murch. *Fairuza Balk, Nicol Williamson, Jean Marsh, Piper Laurie.* Dorothy (Balk) is given shock therapy to try to calm down that pesky imagination, but like a rebellious kid at a reprogramming ranch she manages to escape to her troublemaker friends in the land of Oz. Don't expect a sequel to the cheery Technicolor musical. This is a dark, creepy fantasy that remains dear to the hearts of the lucky few kids who managed to see it during its short run. There are many colorful characters and creatures, including a clockwork man named Tic Toc, a pumpkin head (Brian Henson), a living moose head attached to a sofa (*Blade* director Steve Norrington), a wall of rock (animated by Will Vinton), and a wicked princess who cuts off people's heads and uses them as her own. The tone is downbeat, and as Dorothy is played by an actual child, she seems much more vulnerable. In the '80s we had this, *Labyrinth*, and *The Neverending Story*. Why don't they make movies like those anymore? —*B.T.*

RINGU (AKA RING) L: JAPANESE HORROR/JAPANESE HORROR (1998) 96M D: Hideo Nakata. *Nanako Matsushima, Miki Nakatani, Hiroyuki Sanada.* Adapted from the novel by Koji Suzuki ("the Japanese Stephen King"), *Ringu* changed the face of Japanese horror cinema. This eerie thriller about a mysterious, unsettling videotape that kills everyone who watches it seven days later is an urban legend turned skin-crawling psycho-thriller with supernatural echoes, and it became a phenomenon throughout Asia, spawning sequels, prequels, remakes, and a TV series. None of them approach the simple genius of the original, which spins the murky tale with some of the most ingeniously simple techniques sprung on a modern audience. The videotape oozes suggestive horror, the victims are frozen in a disturbing look of utter terror, photographs of the doomed smear and blur into unrecognizable puddles, and a gnarled ghost crawls and stumbles to her victims with the jerky, unearthly manner of a demonic insect.

Nakata never makes much sense out of the backstory, but he never lets up on the atmosphere of dread or the haunting, horrific imagery. He turns the human factor into the film's final stab of true horror. —*S.A.*

RING 2 (AKA **RINGU 2**) L: JAPANESE HORROR/JAPANESE HORROR (1999) 92M D: Hideo Nakata. *Kyoko Fukada, Hitomi Sato, Miki Nakatani.* The plot of this sequel to the *Ring* phenomenon picks up right after the first film, and follows Mai, the girlfriend of the now deceased Ryuji, who dooms herself as she attempts to learn what exactly killed him, and becomes caught up in the curse of The Videotape. As she discovers the legend of Sadako, Mai also becomes horrifically aware that Ryuji's son, Youichi, is beginning to develop the same psychic powers that Sadako had when she was alive. Mai comes to the conclusion that Sadako's spirit is attempting to inhabit him, and begins a race against time to stop the curse once and for all. Nakata returns to helm this feature, and uses all his subtle tricks to build up the dread. A must-see for fans of the first film. —*R. M.*

RING, THE (2002) L: HORROR/GHOSTS (2002) 115M D: Gore Verbinski. *Naomi Watts, Martin Henderson, Brian Cox, Daveigh Chase, Jane Alexander, David Dorfman.* Although it's not the atrocity it could have been, the American remake of *The Ring* is nonetheless inferior to the Japanese original in every way. What really makes it bad is its pandering to contemporary American audiences by way of cinematic cliché and overt, tactless technique. Where the Japanese version relied on the power of imagination, never delving into any backstory, the American version explicitly explains just why the girl is so evil. Where the Japanese version is quiet, slow, and brooding, creating an atmosphere of sheer dread, the American version is packed with jump scares, special effects, and visceral thrills that leave little lasting impression. —*T. S.*

While I agree that the original by Hideo Nakata is ultimately more effective, I think this is an extremely good remake. The story has been moved to the Seattle area, and the waterlogged imagery is also reminiscent of Nakata's *Dark Water*. Like the original (and contrary to what T. S. says above) I think this movie is quiet and deliberately paced. What really makes it work is that, with few exceptions, the filmmakers don't insist on giving explanations for the weird things that happen. Instead they stay admirably close to the Japanese approach and even add surreal touches of their own (like a fly that appears in the video and then on the TV screen itself.). I think the original is scarier, and the images on the cursed video here are a little too MTV. But this version works, and it's all justified by a brief but horrifying new scene that takes place on a ferry. —*B. T.*

ROBOCOP 2 L: SCIENCE FICTION/SCIENCE FICTION (1990) 117M D: Irvin Kershner. *Peter Weller, Belinda Bauer, Nancy Allen, Dan O'Herlihy, Tom Noonan.* With the premise of robotic law enforcement well established by the first film, *Robocop 2* carries the concept further into the streets of Detroit by targeting gangs and drugs. Robocop (Weller) is patched back together after the last film and doesn't disappoint as he mercilessly, methodically executes his programming. This culminates in a showdown with drug lords who happen to have their own robocop, and the two duke it out. As in the first film, there is government corruption at work, yet this film is even more violent. Followed by the rather feeble *Robocop 3*. —*N.J.*

ROBOCOP 3 L: SCIENCE FICTION/SCIENCE FICTION (1991) 104M D: Fred Dekker. *Robert Burke, John Castle, Nancy Allen, Rip Torn.* Sequels sometimes peter out because the primary materials they use are exhausted or the protagonist has overstayed his or her welcome. The end result becomes somewhat comedic, whether intentional or not. That sums up *Robocop 3* rather well, and explains why there hasn't been a *Robocop 4*. Peter Weller wasn't even in this one. The plot concerns the building of a new city on top of Detroit, necessitating cleaning the streets of all the teeming masses for which bigger and better robocops are employed. A very smart girl, with help from her laptop, manages to hack her way into the robotic system and cause some very fun though unrealistic sabotage. But it's not enough to sustain your interest. —*N.J.*

ROBOT MONSTER L: CLASSIC SCIENCE FICTION/CLASSIC SCIENCE FICTION (1953) 63M D: Phil Tucker. *George Nader, Claudia Barrett, George Barrows.* I love this stupid-ass, cheapo movie! A space alien named Ro-Man (a fat guy in a gorilla suit wearing a diver's helmet) kills off every "hu-man" except a group of picnickers protected by a special serum. Ro-Man hangs out in front of a cave, where he sets up his equipment (a bubble machine, a television, and radio dials . . . all on a kitchen table!) and prepares to annihilate the survivors. He strangles an obnoxious kid, but falls in love with one of the women and can't consummate his feelings or kill the rest of the humans. My favorite scene has two characters trying to fix a radio, their discussion filled with blatant sexual innuendos. The scene where they show the same footage of Ro-Man exiting the cave three times in a row is pretty funny, too. *Robot Monster* gives *Plan 9* serious competition for the dubious honor of "worst movie ever." —*S. H.*

ROLLER BLADE L: PSEUDOTRONIC/PSEUDOTRONIC (FAUX TROMA) (1985) 88M D: Donald Jackson. *Katrina Garner, Jeff Hutchinson, Sam Mann, Shaun Michelle, Suzanne Solari.* In this strange, low-budget slasher, a cult of female roller skaters are armed with switchblades. As they roam the streets, they attack and murder anyone they see who is not on roller skates. Of course, since this is a postapocalyptic setting, there are very few people for them to kill, and those who are on the streets are by and large aware of this religious cult. The effects are in the Herschell Gordon Lewis vein, and the plot is ripped off from *Mad Max*. But for fans of schlock this may be quite a fun little sleeper. —*N.J.*

ROLLERBALL L: SCIENCE FICTION/SCIENCE FICTION (1975) 128M D: Norman Jewison. *James Caan, John Houseman, Maud Adams, John Beck, Moses Gunn.* Try to imagine a world where media moguls own the heart and soul of their sports celebrities. Sounds a bit like today? Then advance several years in the future, when Rollerball is the sport of choice. The game basically morphs basketball with the team roller skating derbies popular in the 1970s, and a good amount of back-street rugby. This is where Caan enters, playing the most celebrated of Rollerball players. The plot, after a lengthy exposition of the game, focuses on whether this celebrity can actually be bought. The effects get quite gruesome, but the game itself is simple and dated given that roller derbies went the way of 8-track and disco balls. —*N.J.*

ROLLERBALL L: SCIENCE FICTION/SCIENCE FICTION (2002) 97M D: John McTiernan. *Rebecca Romijn-Stamos, LL Cool J, Chris Klein, Jean Reno.* McTiernan drops the ball on this hopeless remake. He transforms the brutal cocktail of football, rugby, and roller derby stripped down to a high-speed bloodlust spectacle from the original film to a collision of extreme sports and professional wrestling, and replaces the fierce, scarred survivor played by James Caan with the baby-faced blank of Klein. Set in the near future misery of the former Soviet states of Eastern Europe and Northern Asia, this confused satire is so out of focus it has lost all irony: on one hand the audiences are bloodthirsty channel surfers whose insatiable hunger for spectacle drives the violence, on the other they are simple working-class slaves to industrial despots who draw their sense of self-worth (and their call to revolt) from the triumphs of their sports heroes. If there were ever any teeth to this caricature of modern sports entertainment and media exploitation, they've been yanked out. The violence and brief nudity was trimmed to get a PG-13 rating but has been returned to the R-rated version on DVD. —*S.A.*

SALEM'S LOT L: PSYCHOTRONIC/KING, STEPHEN (1979) 183M D: Tobe Hooper. *Fred Willard, David Soul, James Mason, Lance Kerwin, Bonnie Bedelia, Lew Ayres.* This made-for-TV film is a far cry from the book, but has much going for it, especially in the depiction of the atmosphere of a town being taken over by vampires. Soul plays a writer who moves back to his home town only to find out how much everyone has changed. With a screenplay by Larry Cohen, the film has great potential, but surprisingly uneven casting causes this

Best postapocalyptic movie

ROAD WARRIOR
(aka Mad Max 2)

Runners-up

ANGEL'S EGG

A BOY AND HIS DOG

CRAZY THUNDER ROAD

DEATH RACE 2000

EQUALIZER 2000

GOODBYE, 20TH CENTURY

NAUSICAÄ OF THE VALLEY OF THE WINDS

THE OMEGA MAN

PLANET OF THE APES

THE QUIET EARTH

ROBOT HOLOCAUST

SHREDDER ORPHEUS

SOLARBABIES

classic horror yarn to unravel. Who would put Mason and Willard on the same soundstage together? —*N.J.*

SANTA CLAUS CONQUERS THE MARTIANS L: CLASSIC SCIENCE FICTION/CLASSIC SCIENCE FICTION (1964) 80M D: Nicholas Webster. *Leonard Hicks, Bill McCutcheon, John Call.* A jaw-dropping camp classic of the highest (or lowest?) order! Martian kids are suffering from severe holiday depression and television addiction. Thinking Santa Envy and affluenza is the cause, their parents invade the North Pole, kidnap Saint Nick, and put him to work as a propaganda tool and toy maker on Mars. Fortunately, a couple of Earth kids tag along—it's up to them to save Santa and teach the Martians the real meaning of Christmas. Featuring Pia Zadora as a young Martian, lots of hilarious songs, and one of the cheesiest cinematic robots ever. —*S.H.*

SASQUATCH L: VAOWG/VAOWG (1978) 102M D: Ed Ragozzini. *Jim Bradford, Ken Kenzle, Steve Boergadine, George Lauris, William Emmons.* One of the ultra-rare videos released by Unicorn, *Sasquatch* is "the Holy Grail of bigfoot films," our former rare-tape searcher once told me. Then, somehow, he found it. Unfortunately, the tape did not bring me eternal youth, but it did turn out to be a fairly entertaining, Z-grade quasi-docudrama about explorers searching for Sasquatch. The most amusing aspect is the way the Northwest is portrayed as a rural frontier, where people talk like prospectors during the Gold Rush. One old character is described as "a fixture in the Northwest since the turn of the century." Which I guess means Washington, Oregon, and Idaho are one small town where everyone knows each other. —B. T.

SATANIC RITES OF DRACULA, THE L: HORROR/HAMMER FILMS (1974) 87M D: Alan Gibson. Freddie Jones, Joanna Lumley, Peter Cushing, Christopher Lee.
Dracula has always been a menacing monster, but a supervillain intent on world destruction? That's the premise of this final installment of Hammer's Dracula series. Lee did his duty well, playing Dracula in every single film except Brides of Dracula, which doesn't actually include Dracula. If you think the idea of Dracula becoming the CEO of a company and plotting to spread a virus is a good idea, maybe you will like this movie. Otherwise, I can pretty much tell you there aren't too many surprises. The first fifteen minutes are interspliced with a satanic ceremony complete with black robes and nude women. After that, there is little of interest and the film relies on weird action sequences rather than atmosphere or suspense. Watching this last Dracula film made by Hammer, it becomes painfully clear why they stopped. Thankfully, Cushing is present to take on the Count one final time. But the final battle passes by and Dracula is killed, and none too soon either. —T. S.

SCARECROWS L: HORROR/DEMONS (1988) 80M D: William Wesley. Dax Vernon, B. J. Turner, Michael Simms, Ted Vernon.
A paramilitary team of annoyingly self-satisfied thieves gets stranded in a remote cabin after one of their number takes off with the loot. For some reason the cabin is surrounded by scarecrows that occasionally like to come alive, disembowel people, and stuff them with money. This film is obviously based on the George Romero model, but is not very successful on any level. Still, I get a kick out of the scene beginning nearly about fifty-two minutes in, where the Joe Pilato-ish asshole breaks down and gets existential. "What if, what if they didn't miss us, man, what if they hit us, and, maybe, (giggle) we're dead, and, we're, I mean we're not really here, this isn't real. I mean we're here, but, none of this . . ." —B. T.

SCARS OF DRACULA L: HORROR/HAMMER FILMS (1970) 96M D: Roy Ward Baker. Christopher Lee, Jenny Hanley, Michael Ripper, Dennis Waterman, Patrick Troughton.
This is the worst of the Hammer Dracula movies. There is nothing that makes it stand out. A guy stays in Dracula's castle, Dracula kills him, the guy's brother comes for revenge. Lee is on autopilot and seems bored with being Dracula (this is the fifth sequel, after all). The plot wanders along and it all seems like a bad imitation of earlier Hammer films. All the

elements are there, but nothing has that spark, and the ending is especially weak. Dracula, on the roof of his castle, is struck by lightning and falls into the moat. There were two more Dracula films, but they were set in the 1970s, so didn't have the same atmosphere. —T. S.

SCREAM AND SCREAM AGAIN L: HORROR/MAD SCIENTISTS (1969) 95M D: Gordon Hessler. Christopher Lee, Peter Cushing, Vincent Price.
Scream is a meeting of three great horror masters who sadly share little to no screen time. Police are tracking a serial killer while a mad scientist is building a race of superhumans to infiltrate government positions. It's actually an interesting mix of horror and science fiction, but fails to deliver on the promise of its cast because there are so many unresolved subplots and so much wasted screen time that it all falls apart. However, the three big actors all do an excellent job in their roles and director Hessler gives the film some style. The picture could have been a classic, but it's too ambitious for its own good and ultimately it's just sloppy schlock. —T. S.

SCREAMERS L: SCIENCE FICTION/SCIENCE FICTION (1995) 108M D: Christian Duguay. Andrew Lauer, Jennifer Rubin, Roy Dupuis, Peter Weller.
Barely competent direction. Scratch that—totally incompetent direction. With the production values of a bigger-budget television show, how Screamers made it into the theaters is a mystery. It's notable for Weller's performance; although he doesn't save the film, it's amazing how he can say the stupidest dialogue to the silliest actors and remain 100 percent convincing. The Philip K. Dick source material manages to overcome the production at times, offering a few moments of genuine paranoia-inspired surprises as well as his unique brand of humanism. Ultimately, though, it is wasted. Dan O'Bannon (Alien, Return of the Living Dead) cowrote the script; at the time of the film's release he expressed disappointment in the departure the film took from his original version. Under the right conditions this could have been a classic. As it stands, this one's a wreck. —M. H.

SESSION 9 L: HORROR/DEMONS (2001) 100M D: Brad Anderson. Stephen Geveden, Paul Guilfoyle, Josh Lucas, David Caruso.
Session 9 is an excellent psychological horror movie about a scary old mental institution. Rather than trying to be clever, hip, or ironic, writer-director Anderson settles for making a film that's just plain spooky. The digital cinematography is outstanding, one of the best uses of the medium I've seen. There is a sequence where a character who is deathly afraid of the dark runs down a hallway as darkness literally chases after him. The contrast of light and dark, as well as the excellent use of colors and camera dynamics, make this a sumptuously visual film. However, it also succeeds psy-

chologically. This is one of the best horror films in a long, long while. —*T. S.*

SHE-FREAK L: CLASSIC HORROR/CLASSIC HORROR (1967) 87M D: B. Ron Elliot. *Claire Brennen, Bernie Moore, Felix Silla, Bill McKinney.* Sleazy "carny noir" about a cynical waitress named Jade (Brennen) who joins a carnival and marries the freak show owner. Her sordid affair with a sadistic Ferris wheel operator and her relentless badgering of a midget named Shorty (Silla) foreshadows the inevitable and, after she starts running the show and tries to screw everybody over, Jade is transformed into the titular shefreak. An unofficial remake of Tod Browning's classic film *Freaks*, *She Freak* will appeal most to people with a carnival fetish, as roughly one third of the film is footage of amusement park rides and carnies at work. This seedy tribute to carnival life is one of producer David F. Friedman's favorites. —*S. H.*

SHINING, THE (1997) L: PSYCHOTRONIC /KING, STEPHEN (1997) 273M D: Mick Garris. *Steven Weber, Rebecca De Mornay, Melvin Van Peebles, Courtland Mead.* Stephen King, apparently not recognizing the brilliance of Stanley Kubrick's version, adapted his novel for this embarrassing mini-series directed by hack extraordinaire Garris. Hailed as more faithful to the book, it is loaded with tiresome alcoholism clichés and repetitive catch phrases ("Time to take your medicine!"). At first you hope it will be good, then you hope it will get better, then you keep watching to see how bad it will get. The answer is that at the end Jack's ghost attends Danny's high school graduation like he was Obi Wan Kenobi. There is also a scene featuring a CG firehouse with fangs. —*B. T.*

SHOCK WAVES L: HORROR/ZOMBIES (1977) 90M D: Ken Wiederhorn. *Peter Cushing, Brooke Adams, John Carradine, Fred Buch, Robert Vaughn.* This is a classic zombie movie for two main reasons: it has Nazi zombies and it has underwater zombies. Plus, it also has the great Cushing as the undead SS commander who awkwardly lurks around. All the Nazi zombies wear gray uniforms and black goggles. For those like myself who have long been fans of this film, the striking images of these particular zombies are just as classic a horror icon as Jason's mask or Fulci's zombie's worm-filled eye. This is a fantastic '70s-style, grade-B horror film. —*T. S.*

SHRUNKEN HEADS L: HORROR/WITCHES & WARLOCKS (1994) 86M D: Richard Elfman. *Aeryk Egan, Becky Herbst, Julius Harris, Meg Foster.* Forbidden Zone director Elfman takes a hilariously deadpan approach to this bizarre horror/superhero hybrid. The first act is like an old live-action Disney movie about three comic-book-loving boys who foil a street gang. But then they get murdered, so their friend at the newsstand, Mr. Sumatra (Harris), uses his knowledge of voodoo

to transform them into flying shrunken heads with super powers. The rest of the movie plays out like a dead serious superhero yarn with the flying heads getting their revenge, accepting their outsider status, and even falling in love. One of the weirdest in-jokes is when the score by Richard Band blatantly rips off the love theme from *Edward Scissorhands*, which was composed by the director's own brother Danny (Do you think he'll notice?). Deserves credit as the best release from Full Moon video (for whatever that's worth). —*B. T.*

SIGNS L: SCIENCE FICTION/SCIENCE FICTION (2002) 107M D: M. Night Shyamalan. *Mel Gibson, Joaquin Phoenix, Rory Culkin, Abigail Breslin, Cherry Jones.* Gibson is a widowed father struggling with the loss of both his wife and his faith when crop circles and lights in the sky around the world throw life into a panic. Shyamalan again uses a pulp movie situation (first contact and alien invasion) as a crucible for the exploration of loss, self-discovery, acceptance, and faith, with mixed results. Perpetually shrouded in twilight shadows and the alienated atmosphere of the emotionally adrift Gibson, Shyamalan's style is surprisingly graceless, as if paralyzed by a smothering sense of purpose, and the B-movie twists that follow are as contrived as they are absurd. Yet Shyamalan has learned the lessons that so many horror directors ignore: suggestion is scarier than revelation. He delivers a creepy sense of unease and a few funhouse scares, and his knack for casting and directing child actors delivers once again. Too bad the story of spiritual healing is undercut when Shyamalan trades the wonder of mystery for literal divine intervention. If Shyamalan can't make the leap of faith, how can he expect us to? —*S. A.*

SILENT NIGHT, DEADLY NIGHT 2 L: HORROR/STALKERS (1987) 88M D: Lee Harry. *Eric Freeman, Jean Miller, James Newman.* Perhaps the laziest sequel of all time. The entire first half is built around flashbacks as the grown-up younger brother of killer Santa recalls his ordeal to a psychiatrist. Funny thing is, in the handful of scenes that actually include his character, he is a baby. And there's at least one amusing inconsistency: the priest dressed as Santa shot by police in the original is said here to be the janitor (as if they didn't bother to watch the footage as they reedited it). In the second half, little brother strangles the psychiatrist and goes on a rampage. For those who get a kick out of bad slasher movies, this one is pretty spectacular. Dare: watch parts one and two back to back. —. *T. B.*

SILENT RUNNING L: SCIENCE FICTION/SCIENCE FICTION (1971) 90M D: Douglas Trumbull. *Bruce Dern, Ron Rifkin, Cliff Potts, Jesse Vint.* In the future, the Earth is so polluted and land so valuable that forests are sustained as floating ecological zoos in space. The premise stretches credulity to say the least (just what is Earth doing for oxygen?), but it makes a nice ecological metaphor in this tale of a mother nature's son in space (Dern) who steals a ship rather than destroy the last of the forests. With a trio of robots as companions, he cuts off all communications and drifts silently through space. The introspective drama tends to drift with the ship and the worst-case-scenario ecological message is hardly subtle, but director Trumbull and Dern (who delivers a tender and sad performance) center the film in the rebel conservationist's guilt-wracked soul, torn between his loneliness and his duty to mother nature. Trumbull created the special effects for *2001: A Space Odyssey* and contributes a similarly elegant design for his directorial debut: ships quietly drifting past the sun and the planets and forests under geodesic domes floating in space like jewels. Joan Baez contributes songs. —*S. A.*

SIR DRONE L: PSYCHOTRONIC/FILM THREAT (1989) 58M D: Raymond Pettibon. *Mike Watt, Michael G. Kelley.* Renowned Los Angeles painter and Black Flag cover artist Pettibon wrote and directed four semi-features in 1989 before retiring from filmmaking. Each starred his musician and outcast friends, including punk luminaries Dez Cadena, Pat Smear, and Kim Gordon. Here, Pettibon mocks the deflated Los Angeles music scene by depicting the formation of rock group Sir Drone, comprised of talentless morons played by Watt and Kelley. Most of the film takes place in the band's filthy, barren studio apartment in one of LA's warehouse districts, and consists of the two leads endlessly bickering and strumming sour notes on a busted guitar. Watt's performance is cardboard and hilarious as he intimidates his feeble bandmate into altering his clothes, hairstyle, and even general outlook in the name of Sir Drone's success. An enormous achievement in awkward, aimless, novice storytelling. —*Z. C.*

6TH DAY, THE L: SCIENCE FICTION/SCIENCE FICTION (2000) 123M D: Roger Spottiswoode. *Arnold Schwarzenegger, Tony Goldwyn, Robert Duvall.* Reverberating with the same dark, future-shock themes Philip K. Dick explored in *Blade Runner* and *Total Recall*, Ah-nold's return to form is a clever and colorful conspiratorial thriller with high-energy action scenes, car crashes a-go-go, spectacular technology, and really big explosions. Playing a stiff but amiable family man thrust into the center of a cloning conspiracy, the gentle giant takes to murder and mayhem with alarming ease. It's hard to tell if director Spottiswoode works in this merciless turn by design or simply out of deference to Arnold's screen history, but it adds a vicious, subtly subversive twist to a film that almost offhandedly explores issues of identity, immortality, and technological morality between futuristic gadgetry and tongue-in-cheek satire. Goldwyn is the oily CEO with a (literal) God complex, and Duvall acts like he's

slumming in the blockbuster ghetto as a genetics genius. —*S. A.*

SIX-STRING SAMURAI L: SCIENCE FICTION/SCIENCE FICTION (1998) 91M D: Lance Mungia. *Justin McGuire, Jeffrey Falcon.* Now this is my kind of postapocalyptic wasteland. When the Russians nuke the United States in 1957, the King of Rock 'n' Roll becomes the King of (what's left of) America and deadly guitar-slinging warriors wander the desolate hinterlands. Forty years later the King is dead and pretenders to the throne are trekking to the glittering Oz known as Lost Vegas, including a sword-wielding, guitar-strumming, rockabilly samurai named Buddy (Falcon). Mungia's high energy parody melts rock and roll, Akira Kurosawa samurai epics, dusty Sergio Leone Westerns, *The Road Warrior*, 1950s JD potboilers, and TV sitcoms into a high-octane/low-budget adventure, a kind of grunge *Star Wars* built on modern movie myths. Falcon, a veteran martial artist and action director, delivers the goods with slick moves and flashy choreography, while Mungia's Hong Kong–drenched style makes the most of his no-budget, grime-chic production design. —*S. A.*

SLASHER, THE L: HORROR/GIALLO (ITALIAN HORROR) (1974) 88M D: Roberto Montero. *Farley Granger, Sylva Koscina, Silvano Tranquilli, Annabella Incontrera, Cristea Avram, Femi Benussi.* If you've never seen a *giallo*, *The Slasher* is a good place to start. It has all the elements of the genre: naked women, wicked weapons, a masked killer, deep red blood, and screams that nobody hears. Plus strange clues that match up to an obscure motive for the crimes with a twisted logic that ultimately makes sense. This film has a particularly gnarly two-pronged plot that forks together by the end. Rich wives are slain, with compromising photographs left beside their naked corpses. The detective in charge (Granger) is hamstrung by politics—he can't haul in the rich and powerful to question them. *The Slasher* is smartly scripted with nasty twists. The photography is bold, lurid, and always right on, from the first shot of cops examining a corpse to how it frames the cruelest of cruel denouements at the end. —*J. C.*

SLEEPAWAY CAMP L: HORROR/STALKERS (1983) 84M D: Robert Hiltzik. *Jonathan Tiersten, Felissa Rose, Mike Kellin, Christopher Collet.* All right, I'll say it: *Sleepaway Camp* is the number-one summer camp slasher film EVER! Yeah, yeah, *Friday the 13th, The Burning,* and several others really put the genre on the map, but I'll be goddamned if all of them combined could come close to the head-spinning violent psychosexual mania contained in just the first installment of the *Sleepaway Camp* series. Two misfit kids enroll at a crowded camp just in time for a mysterious murderer to get his body count on. And does he ever! The creative killings include boiling an obese perv's face in a giant stewpot and unleashing a deadly beehive upon a pooping bully, but the unbelievable clincher cannot be revealed here without compromising one of the greatest endings in film history! Suffice it to say, *Sleepaway Camp* is a twisted sociopath's goldmine, and a 100 percent vital addition to any horror nerd's viewing. —*Z. C.*

SLUMBER PARTY MASSACRE L: HORROR/STALKERS (1982) 84M D: Amy Holden Jones, Aaron Lipstadt. *Michelle Michaels, Rigg Kennedy, Michael Villela, Pamela Roylance, David Millbern.* The first and finest installment in the *Massacre* series, *Slumber Party* supplies all the attributes you want in a slasher film: gratuitous nudity, suspense, gore, and the occasional not-very-funny humor. They broke the mold with this one. An early scene is a long tracking shot through a locker room as the girls basketball team is showering. The camera passes each girls' back and then holds on one in particular, pans slowly down, and shows her naked ass. There is no other reason than the obvious for this shot and therein lies the beauty of this film: they spare no expense for your entertainment. The plot is banal: girls throw a slumber party, stalker-creepy-guy shows up, he starts killing people with a drill, lots of guts spill, and then they finally kill him. The amazing thing, though, is the way they kill him; it's brutal and it takes time. I don't want to spoil it for you; you're going to have to see it for yourself. —*T. B.*

SOCIETY L: HORROR/CANNIBALS (1989) 99M D: Brian Yuzna. *Devin Devasquez, Ben Meyerson, Connie Danese, Billy Warlock, Evan Richards.* Yes, the rich are different from us, as Yuzna so viscerally shows us in this blackly comic horror satire of class privilege, cabalistic incest, and cannibalism. Warlock is the all-American boy who realizes just how different he is from his family of upper-class snobs when he discovers the secret of those society functions to which he's never invited. It's glib social satire, to be sure, but great paranoia, too. The grotesque special effects, which show in gooey detail just how the wealthy literally feed off the masses, are often clumsy but just surreal and twisted enough that it doesn't really matter. Former centerfold Devasquez is the trashy rich girl who falls for our plebian hero. The unrated DVD restores the four minutes that were cut for its American release. —*S. A.*

SON OF FRANKENSTEIN L: CLASSIC HORROR/CLASSIC HORROR (1939) 99M D: Rowland V. Lee. *Basil Rathbone, Lionel Atwill, Boris Karloff, Josephine Hutchinson, Bela Lugosi.* The third film in Universal's amazing Frankenstein series, *Son of Frankenstein* has the distinction of being the last in the series to feature the irreplaceable Karloff. Just as integral to the Frankenstein legacy as the original and *Bride of Frankenstein, Son* features much of the material that was parodied in Mel Brooks's *Young Frankenstein.* Although often overlooked in favor of the first two films, this is a master-

piece of classic horror that really shines thanks to the excellent performances by Lugosi and Karloff. The story brings Dr. Frankenstein's son back to the village where the monster was created. He meets Ygor (Lugosi) who is in possession of the monster (somehow having survived the explosion at the end of *Bride*). Together, they reanimate the monster and terror ensues. This is surely not to be missed. —*T. S.*

SON OF GODZILLA L: JAPANESE SCIENCE FICTION/GODZILLA (1967) 86M D: Jun Fukuda. *Kenji Sahara, Haruo Nakajima.* The big question in this movie is, who is the mother? Some giant mantises discover an egg that hatches Godzilla's son Minya. But I have a hard time believing Godzilla laid that egg. If there is a mother, I wonder why the scientists haven't discovered her yet? Giant monster mating is probably very dangerous for humans. I guess as long as they do it on Monster Island or in the ocean or something we'll be fine. This is a silly entry in the Godzilla series, but it's one of my favorites because it shows a different facet of Godzilla's personality. He tries to teach Minya how to breathe fire, but at first he only blows smoke rings. —*B. T.*

SPACE MONSTER GAMERA L: JAPANESE SCIENCE FICTION /GAMERA (1967) 90M D: Noriaki Yuasa. *Yoko Komatsu, Mach Fumiake.* This rarely seen last of the original Gamera series is sort of a best of, combining fights from all the previous movies with a wraparound story about a boy, his pet turtle, and heroic "Space Women" disguised as pet store owners. The movie rips off everything from *Star Wars* to *Mork and Mindy* and even uses some stock footage from anime. Because virtually all Gamera's previous foes are crammed into one movie, it's constantly entertaining. If someone tells you it's the worst of the series, don't listen to them. Note: In the English-dubbed version the title is *Gamera Space Monster* and they pronounce it "Guh-MARE-uh" instead of "GAMer-ruh." —*B. T.*

SPACE: 1999 MEGASET L: SCIENCE FICTION/SCIENCE FICTION TV (1975) 1400M D: Val Guest, Peter Medak, others. *Martin Landau, Barbara Bain.* One of the most interesting stabs at science fiction television, the plot of *Space: 1999* is certainly quite novel: after Moon Base Alpha is established, a nuclear explosion throws the moon off its orbit and into space. With monochromatic sets and rather slow pacing, this series emphasized the science in its science fiction. It ushered in a wide variety of alien guests such as Christopher Lee, Brian Blessed, Leo McKern, and Joan Collins. Halfway through the series, the producers introduced Maya, a shape-shifting alien who becomes a crew member. Aside from what now looks like low-budget effects, this show serves as a warning against putting a date in the title of a futuristic show. For where *Space: 1999* predicted that by 1999 we would be employing cool hovercraft

Our least favorite remakes

GODZILLA *(1998)*

GONE IN 60 SECONDS *(2000)*

THE HAUNTING *(1999)*

HOUSE ON HAUNTED HILL *(1999)*

MIRACLE ON 34TH STREET *(1994)*

NIGHT OF THE LIVING DEAD *(1990)*

PAYBACK
(remake of Point Blank*)*

PLANET OF THE APES *(2001)*

PSYCHO *(1998)*

ROAD TO PERDITION
(if considered a remake of Lone Wolf and Cub*)*

THE SHINING *(1997)*

THE TEXAS CHAINSAW MASSACRE *(2003)*

THE TRUTH ABOUT CHARLIE
(remake of Charade*)*

VANISHING POINT *(1997)*

ships to colonize the moon, in fact by 1999 we were losing small nerdy probes on Mars for lack of coordinating our standard measurements with our metric measurements! *—N.J.*

SPACEHUNTER: ADVENTURES IN THE FORBIDDEN ZONE L: SCIENCE FICTION/SCIENCE FICTION (1983) 90M D: Lamont Johnson. *Michael Ironside, Molly Ringwald, Peter Strauss, Ernie Hudson.* That's right, suckers. The blood of our galaxy's finest pumps red-hot in this tough-as-lasers tale that lays bare the harsh realities of the transgalactic hood. Can an unshaven, planet-hopping bounty hunter join forces with a pubescent Ringwald to defeat cyborg maniac/extreme sports enthusiast The Overdog? Hell, YES! In the meantime, Spacehunter and his friends are assaulted by all types of extraterrestrial irritations, from chanting bloodthirsty babies to outrageously obese subterranean albinos. A scene of the adult Spacehunter forcibly bathing a teeny-bopper Ringwald is enough to make even your pervert uncle a little uncomfortable, but this is generally some good clean fun, requiring no attention span or even rational thought. Produced by Ivan *(Ghostbusters)* Reitman and released theatrically in 3-D. Androids, mandroids, asteroids, and insectapoids alike are blasted to carbonized atoms in this, the dopiest barnburner of Hollywood's true golden era (the '80s). ZZANG!!! *—Z.C.*

SPECIAL BULLETIN L: VAOWG/VAOWG (1983) 105M D: Edward Zwick. *David Rasche, David Clennon, Lane Smith, Roberta Maxwell, Ebbe Roe Smith.* Cold-War era nuclear scare TV movie presented in a fake news format (*The Day After* by way of Orson Welles's *War of the Worlds* radio broadcast). A group of former military scientists takes a news crew hostage and goes on live TV threatening to set off a nuclear bomb unless the U.S. government disarms all its warheads. Most of the acting is good and the news format is pretty well done. It does get corny at times, especially when it sidetracks into a critique of TV news. But it's not a bad gimmick and it has moments that make the audience really consider the possible consequences of the arms race (perhaps even more so post-9/11). *—B.T.*

SPONTANEOUS COMBUSTION L: SCIENCE FICTION/ SCIENCE FICTION (1989) 97M D: Tobe Hooper. *Brad Dourif, Cynthia Bain, Melinda Dillon, Dick Buttkus, Jon Cypher.* Dourif is expertly cast as Sam Kramer, a young man whose parents die from highly experimental atomic government research in the '50s. But just before this couple mysteriously dies of *spontaneous combustion,* the wife gives birth to Sam. We then zoom to the '70s, where a grown Sam discovers he has a very peculiar power: whenever he gets very angry, flames burst out of his body. He has a girlfriend who has enormous sympathy for him, "My parents died of spontaneous combustion, too." What makes him the most angry is the government's cover-up of his parents' deaths and consequently about what he himself has become. This film might seem like a dud if you're not keen on Hooper's sense of humor, but Dourif brilliantly delivers this curious mixture of humor and horror. *—N.J.*

SPUN L: PSYCHOTRONIC/DRUGS (2002) 101M D: Jonas Åkerlund. *Jason Schwartzman, John Leguizamo, Mena Suvari, Patrick Fugit, Brittany Murphy.* Schwartzman, Leguizamo, Suvari, and Fugit let their good looks get grubby with the ravages of crystal meth addiction in music video veteran Åkerlund's directorial debut. *Spun* is an appropriate title for a film that equates meth addiction to the spin cycle of the (brain)washing machine of life, and Åkerlund puts plenty of jittery, jazzy, out-of-control style into this three-day, drug-driven trip where Schwartzman's soiled college boy becomes the personal driver for the local crystal meth cook (Mickey Rourke, stealing the show from the young cast with his swanky urban cowboy verve) and his giggly young girlfriend (Murphy). Åkerlund plays it all for a creepy rush of black comedy. You may not learn much about the lifestyle or the characters, whose lives are all in a holding pattern, but you'll want to take a shower when it's over. Eric Roberts has a blast in his small role as a teasing, cooing drug financier seemingly modeled on Dean Stockwell's character in *Blue Velvet,* but with Roberts's uniquely disturbed spin on it. *—S.A.*

SQUIRM L: VAOWG/VAOWG (1976) 93M D: Jeff Lieberman. *Peter MacLean, R. A. Dow, Patricia Pearcy, Don Scardino.* The plot involves a small town in Georgia that has a thunderstorm that knocks down some power lines. The broken power lines feed electricity into the muddy earth, causing the regional bloodworms to go mad and attack humans. On paper the plot sounds pretty inane, but first time writer/director Lieberman creates what may be the best of the nature-gone-wild movies of the '70s. The film is shot well and the acting is above average for the genre. One highpoint involves worms boring into and under the flesh of one of the characters. The makeup effects were designed by Rick Baker, who would later win an Academy Award for his work on *An American Werewolf in London.* —*S. W. F.*

STACY L: JAPANESE SCIENCE FICTION/JAPANESE SCIENCE FICTION (2001) 80M D: Naoyuki Tomomatsu. *Yukijiro Hotaru, Natsuki Kato, Tomoka Hayashi.* Oh, the joy of watching Japanese schoolgirl-zombies munching on guts. The premise alone is enough to make gore hounds giggle with delight, and with the digital video production comes a low-budget feel that nicely rounds out this dark comedy. Based on the novel by Kenji Otsuki, *Stacy* begins during a bizarre epidemic infecting Japan that is taken rather lightly by the inhabitants. No one knows why, but teenage girls all over the world are mysteriously dying and coming back to life with a hunger for humans. Several measures have been taken to stop the zombies, which have been dubbed Stacies. From the George Romero clean-up crews and the consumer-friendly Bruce Campbell Right Hand chainsaw, to obsessed hunters-for-hire, the comedy is slathered on as thick as the copious amounts of red corn syrup used throughout the film. Add in some crazed military personnel, a scientist bent on discovering a reason for the change, and a fluffy sentimental love story to make all worth while. Good stuff from beginning to end. —*R. M.*

STAND BY ME L: PSYCHOTRONIC/KING, STEPHEN (1986) 88M D: Rob Reiner. *Richard Dreyfuss, Kiefer Sutherland, Jerry O'Connell, Corey Feldman, River Phoenix, Wil Wheaton.* Gordie (Wheaton), Chris (Phoenix), Teddy (Feldman), and Vern (O'Connell) are a bunch of kids who set out to find the body of another kid who is missing and presumed dead. This is their chance to be heroes, to show everyone that they are something better than what everyone pegs them as being. A tender, realistic coming-of-age story, *Stand By Me* does an excellent job of portraying adolescence and the lessons that come with it. The interactions between the four young leads are emotional, moving, and extremely well-acted. Maybe if Reiner had directed more of the movies based on Stephen King books they wouldn't be so shitty. —*J. S.*

STAR TREK (79 EPISODES) L: SCIENCE FICTION/SCIENCE FICTION TV (1966) 4,740M D: David Alexander, Robert Butler, others. *William Shatner, Leonard Nimoy, Nichelle Nichols, DeForest Kelley, James Doohan, George Takei.* Only a handful of television series have been as influential and as timeless as *Star Trek.* The three seasons of this remarkable series not only led to six feature films but spawned three other series still in syndication. And then there is the lifestyle of Trekkies that culminates in Star Trek Conventions across the world. In this series conceived by Gene Roddenberry, Captain Kirk (Shatner) and his crew form an expedition "to boldly go where no man has gone before." In so doing they meet a wide variety of aliens such as Klingons, Romulans, and Tribbles. At times they are held prisoner, find parallel universes, or stumble into time travel. Amid all this the primary characters—Kirk, Spock (Nimoy), and Bones (Kelley)—struggle with romance, allegiances, vices, power, and the peculiar nature of Spock, who is half human and half Vulcan. Taken as a whole, the futuristic world of *Star Trek* is sufficiently deep and intricate to spawn the virtual universe of *Star Trek* we enjoy today. —*N. J.*

STAR TREK II: THE WRATH OF KHAN L: SCIENCE FICTION/SCIENCE FICTION TV (1982) 113M D: Nicholas Meyer. *William Shatner, Leonard Nimoy, DeForest Kelley, Ricardo Montalban, Kirstie Alley, Bibi Besch.* After the staid and stiff first movie, new blood was brought in behind the scenes and Meyer transformed the *Wagon Train to the Stars* into an interstellar pirate movie by way of *Moby Dick*, complete with a rousing nautical score by James Horner and a swashbuckling performance by guest villain Montalban. Reprising his role from the original series TV episode *The Space Seed*, he's a genetically perfect human turned maniacal survivor, obsessed with revenge against Captain Kirk. Shatner, Nimoy, and Kelley, so clunky in the first feature, got in touch with their characters and relationships all over again—deftly flirting with the changes of age and gleefully falling into familiar clashes of logic versus emotion—while Shatner's Kirk springs into action with the wiles of an old fox teaching the young cubs the real rules of the wild. And of course there is the still impressive sight of wild-maned and bare-chested Montalban looking more buff and cut in his sixties than most of the young stars on screen. —*S. A.*

STAR TREK III: THE SEARCH FOR SPOCK L: SCIENCE FICTION/SCIENCE FICTION TV (1984) 105M D: Leonard Nimoy. *William Shatner, DeForest Kelley, Walter Koenig, George Takei, James Doohan.* Back at the Federation, Kirk and his crew are told that the *Enterprise* is being decommissioned. Spock's distraught father (Mark Lenard) is seeking the last person Spock melded with, and Kirk comes to believe that perhaps the Genesis planet on which they left him would have regenerated his body. Kirk and his trusted crew steal the *Enterprise* from the Federation in order to find him. Eventually they run into meddling Klingons who make the venture more complicated. In this installment, Kirk's son is killed and apparently Genesis can't clone him like it did Spock, who is suitably regenerated to direct *Star Trek IV*. —*N.J.*

STAR TREK IV: THE VOYAGE HOME L: SCIENCE FICTION / SCIENCE FICTION TV (1986) 118M D: Leonard Nimoy. *William Shatner, Leonard Nimoy, DeForest Kelley, George Takei, James Doohan*. In this, the eco-friendly *Star Trek* sequel, the voyage home is a trip back in time to San Francisco circa 1986. There the crew hopes to save Earth by altering history. To do so they have to fit into society for a time and decipher whale sounds. Disbelief in this outrageously impossible scenario is suspended largely with the help of stunning special effects. Some of the corniest jokes are to be found in this sequel as the crew wanders about the city streets. —*N.J.*

STAR TREK V: THE FINAL FRONTIER L: SCIENCE FICTION /SCIENCE FICTION TV (1989) 106M D: William Shatner. *William Shatner, Leonard Nimoy, Walter Koenig, James Doohan, George Takei, DeForest Kelley*. Many Trekkies disown this *Star Trek* vehicle as the worst movie of the bunch. This entry takes itself much less seriously than the previous two, with the corny jokes and off-hand wit indicative of the TV series spread liberally throughout the film. The plot focuses on Spock's step-brother (Laurence Luckinbill) who commandeers the *Enterprise* by a process of hypnotic empathy. Once in control, he steers the starship to the center of the galaxy in order to find . . . God! They find him and he turns out to be basically a cheap imitation of the Wizard of Oz. Shatner delivers the perfectly hokey line, "What use has God for a starship?" Perhaps the budget and effects are overkill for what Shatner envisioned, but that doesn't necessitate its exclusion, even as a black sheep, from the *Star Trek* fold. Some still think this is a perfectly enjoyable film, on par with the Tribbles episode. —*N.J.*

STAR TREK VI: THE UNDISCOVERED COUNTRY L: SCIENCE FICTION/SCIENCE FICTION TV (1991) 113M D: Nicholas Meyer. *William Shatner, James Doohan, Nichelle Nichols, George Takei, Leonard Nimoy, DeForest Kelley*. In this, the last *Star Trek* film before the *Next Generation* takes over, Admiral Kirk and his crew prepare for a peace summit between the Federation and the Klingons when a Klingon ship is attacked with missiles coming from the direction of the *Enterprise*. Kirk is blamed and he surrenders to face trial on an enemy ship. To garner time to unravel this plot against Kirk, Spock takes advantage of a malfunction which prevents the *Enterprise* from receiving a call from Federation to return. A very tight plot connects this sequel nicely to the primary films of the series. —*N.J.*

STAR WARS L: SCIENCE FICTION/STAR WARS (1977) 121M D: George Lucas. *Peter Cushing, Harrison Ford, Mark Hamill, Carrie Fisher, Alec Guinness*. All Luke really wanted to do that fateful day on Tatooine was pick up some power converters and maybe hang out in Toshii Station to avoid having to go home, then watch the two suns set on yet another boring day on the farm. But destiny comes calling for him in the form of a cryptic old man and two droids with a very important message. Luke breaks out of his small planet doldrums as he hooks up with a dashing smuggler, his tall shaggy friend, and their "bucket of bolts" starship to save the princess and the galaxy from evil. Whether you still love it as much as you did when you first saw it, or you've taught yourself to hate it in some twisted effort to seem cooler than you really are, no one can deny the simple fairy-tale style pleasure of this film. —*J.K.*

STAR WARS EPISODE 1: THE PHANTOM MENACE L: SCIENCE FICTION/STAR WARS (1999) 133M D: George Lucas. *Ewan McGregor, Liam Neeson, Jake Lloyd, Natalie Portman*. Lucas's highly anticipated prequel to the *Star Wars* trilogy kicks off with the same giddy promise of adventure: John Williams's brash fanfare, the title "Long ago in a galaxy far, far away . . ." scrolling across the star field, an acrobatic light-saber battle amidst a conspiratorial sense of menace. Neeson makes a fine Jedi master as Qui-Gon Jinn, calm, confident, and a helluva swordsman; and McGregor is an ambitious if too restrained young Obi-Wan Kenobi, a pair of emissaries who meet up with the beleaguered Queen Amidala (Portman) and escape to the planet Tatooine, where they meet young Anakin Skywalker (Jake Lloyd), who all fans know grows into the evil overlord Darth Vader—but that's another movie. Too bad. While it looks amazing, Lucas's heart isn't in it. After twenty-two years out of the director's chair, he's lost the sense of wonder and rough pulpy energy that turned *Star Wars* into a modern movie myth and found instead a stolid producer's vision. Flush with astounding special effects and imaginative designs come to life with the magic of CGI, *The Phantom Menace* is so shaped by digital technology it's smoothed the life right out of the film. —*S.A.*

STAR WARS EPISODE II: ATTACK OF THE CLONES L: SCIENCE FICTION/STAR WARS (2002) 143M D: George Lucas. *Christopher Lee, Ewan McGregor, Natalie Portman, Hayden Christensen*. I remember being on the playground as a kid discussing Yoda. If he's the greatest Jedi, does that mean he knows how to use a light saber? The answer, according to *Attack of the Clones*, is fuck yeah. And not only does he use a light saber, he uses it against Lee (*Star Wars* had Van Helsing, and now this one has Dracula). You'd think it would be a mistake to turn Yoda from a puppet into computer animation, but it works beautifully and makes him more menacing in his fight scene. There's

also a big battle with lots of Jedis, an army of clones, a couple jokes at the expense of Jar Jar Binks, a baby sand person, and political themes that eerily mirror the troubles of our times. So yeah, Christensen is terrible as the young Anakin Skywalker, and the romantic dialogue he stumbles through is even worse. But you can't win every battle. If you could, Han Solo never would've been frozen in that carbonite. —B. T.

STAR WARS HOLIDAY SPECIAL, THE L: SCIENCE FICTION/ STAR WARS (1978) 120M D: Steve Binder. *Mark Hamill, Harrison Ford, Beatrice Arthur, Carrie Fisher, Art Carney, Peter Mayhew.* This legendary/infamous TV special was a particularly awkward attempt to cash in on *Star Wars* mania before the first sequel. The story involves Chewbacca's family waiting in their Ewok-like tree house for Chewie to come home on Life Day (the space equivalent of Kwaanza). The original cast members all make appearances and they look funny because they're shot on video (Luke Skywalker wears a lot of makeup!). The first ten minutes are all in Wookie without subtitles, and the thing plods along for what seems like four hours, eventually making it through various celebrity cameos (Diahann Carroll, Harvey Korman, Jefferson Starship) and disturbing Gestapo-like raids by mean storm troopers who purposely break little Lumpy's toy bantha. The highlights are a crude animated sequence that introduces Boba Fett and Bea Arthur's musical number with all of Rick Baker's cantina creatures. The producers are veterans of various TV specials, many of them having to do with Bette Midler or ice skating. One of the writers is Bruce Vilanch! Unfortunately (?) this has never been given a legitimate video release. —B. T.

STAR WREK ZONE L: SCIENCE FICTION/SCIENCE FICTION TV (1996) 17M D: Milco Davis. *Michael Spatafore, Brad Marcus, Mike Davis, Jon Matas.* This is an awesome little claymation piece. What really makes it funny is how fearlessly dumb the jokes, sets, and claymation are. Sometimes bad is good, though, and this short continues the do-it-yourself feel of the 1977 hit *Hardware Wars*. The original *Star Trek* cast meets the cast of *Star Trek: The Next Generation* for some time-traveling mayhem. Great quote: "Captain's Log, Stardate 2099, and still no cure for baldness," by Captain Pickacard. —R. D.

STARMAN: INVADERS FROM SPACE L: JAPANESE SCIENCE FICTION/JAPANESE SCIENCE FICTION (1964) 75M D: Teruo Ishii, Akira Mitsuwa, Koreyoshi Akasaka. *Minako Yamada, Sachihiro Ohsawa, Ken Utsui.* In Japan, Utsui's white-clad robot from another galaxy was called Super Giant, but when the short adventures of the 1950s series were reedited into feature-length films and dubbed into English, he became: Starman! In *Invaders from Space*, edited together from his earliest film appearances, he takes on Salamander Men from the planet Koolamon

who set out to conquer Earth with a deadly virus they spread through avant-garde dance recitals. Cunningly disguised as a Japanese civil servant, Starman doesn't seem terribly worried keeping a secret identity ("Excuse me, I'm Starman"), and is quick to toss aside the suit for his tights and cape when battling the gymnastically hyperactive Koolamons (who manage to remove their cheap face masks and pass as humans just as easily as Starman). Don't worry about getting lost in the sudden leaps in the plot; a narrator drones a running play-by-play of exposition and explanation. Cheaply made and badly dubbed but energetically tackled, this is definitely cult material. —S. A.

STARSHIP INVASIONS L: SCIENCE FICTION/SCIENCE FICTION (1977) 89M D: Ed Hunt. *Tiiu Leek, Robert Vaughn, Christopher Lee.* When I was five I saw a movie on TV that made a lasting impression on me, but I could remember only two scenes. In one, a woman slits her wrists after looking at the cover of *Time* magazine. In the second, an old farmer is taken aboard a spaceship with a sexy alien in a tight black outfit. Then one day I found my movie—*Starship Invasions*! What a fucking disappointment. One would think a tongue-in-cheek homage to '50s sci-fi serials about aliens (descendants of humans?) that use some kind of ray to make Earthlings commit suicide, and starring Lee, would be pretty cool, right? Yeah, but it ain't. The only decent part is when the abducted farmer tells the sheriff his story of a naked female alien and the sheriff says, "What did you do then?" The farmer replies, "Well, I had sex with her!" —S. C. V.

STEPFORD WIVES, THE L: SCIENCE FICTION/SCIENCE FICTION (1975) 115M D: Bryan Forbes. *Patrick O'Neal, Peter Masterson, Katherine Ross, Paula Prentiss.* Ross plays an "independent woman" who has just moved to town with her husband. She notices that something seems odd. For instance, all the women seem very bland, except for the one she quickly befriends. But even her new friend eventually becomes like the other housewives. The men of Stepford have replaced their wives with duplicates, wired and programmed to perfection. And it's not too hard to figure out who's next, since her husband has discovered the benefits of owning a state-of-the-art robo-wife. —N. J.

STORYTELLER, THE L: FANTASY TV/FANTASY TV (1987) 216M D: Jon Amiel, Steve Barron, others. *Miranda Richardson, Sean Bean, Brenda Blethyn.* One of the more inventive of Jim Henson's productions, *The Storyteller* is a spellbinding mix of fairy tale and medieval legend. The stories are practically archeological explorations of the unfamiliar sources of familiar storybook tales. *Sapsorrow,* from the first volume, is a German story that anticipates Cinderella, and the Russian *The Luck Child* has a Grimm Brothers–like edge to it. John

Hurt stars as the storyteller, whose narration also punctuates the stories, with appearances by British stars Richardson, Bean, Blethyn, Gabrielle Anwar, and Jonathan Pryce (among others). The literate scripts are all written by (then future) Oscar-winner Anthony Minghella (*The English Patient*) and the directors include Barron, Charles Sturridge, Amiel, and Henson. The Muppets are not the stars here but elements of the magical atmosphere. The British-produced series never caught on in the United States (they played to great acclaim but small audiences on HBO), but these proto-fairy tales celebrate the art of stories and storytelling with grace and imagination. —*S. A.*

STRANGE INVADERS L: SCIENCE FICTION/SCIENCE FICTION (1983) 94M D: Michael Laughlin. *Wallace Shawn, Nancy Allen, Paul LeMat, Louise Fletcher.* Part offbeat horror film, part UFO conspiracy, and part tribute to '50s alien invasion pictures, this good-natured comic sci-fi film stars LeMat as a college professor who goes in search of his ex-wife and finds a time-warped town that shouldn't exist populated by bug-eyed monsters that shoot lasers. With the help of a ditzy tabloid reporter (Allen), he digs into a plot that involves a small army of E.T.'s cousins in human faces (marching into modern-day New York as if they've stepped out of an episode of *Happy Days*), a lonely man in an insane asylum who may not be crazy after all, and the U.S. government. The colors (a mixture of the candy colors of golden age fantasy cinema and the muted hues of nostalgia) are lush, and the hazy scenes of the stuck-in-the-'50s small town feel like some misty-eyed time warp with a few weird twists. Cowriter William Condon may be better known as Bill Condon, who won an Oscar for another tribute to the fantastic cinema of yesteryear: *Gods and Monsters.* —*S. A.*

STRANGLER OF THE SWAMP L: CLASSIC HORROR/CLASSIC HORROR (1945) 59M D: Frank Wisbar. *Blake Edwards, Rosemary La Planche, Robert H. Barrat, Charles B. Middleton.* Douglas (Middleton), a ferry captain, may have not been guilty of the murder for which he was executed years ago. Joseph, another ferryman, is confronted by the vengeful ghost of Douglas in the misty swamp, as a long-tied noose appears. Joseph throws the deadly rope in the air only to have it land around his neck and tie itself off. Young, sweet Maria comes to town to see her grandfather and take over his job of ferryman. Will she be the next victim? The shadowed, dark backgrounds of the film appear to be an effect of a murky film stock, while in fact serving as spaces for the strangler's apparition to manifest. Congealing out of the blackness, the strangler is only visible in the swamp's darkest spots. A very young Edwards (yes, that Blake Edwards) performs as a hopeful suitor for Maria's beauty. —*S. R.*

TARGET EARTH L: CLASSIC SCIENCE FICTION/CLASSIC SCIENCE FICTION (1954) 75M D: Sherman A. Rose. *Virginia Grey, Richard Reeves, Kathleen Crowley, Richard Denning.* Earth is invaded by robot aliens and a handful of humans who wake up to a deserted Chicago try to survive. An eerily effective low-budget thriller, it gets creaky whenever it cuts back to the scientists struggling to find a way to stop the rampaging robots. There is just something unsettling about an empty city, however, and the sight of our confused survivors trying to find out what happened and where everyone went in the deserted streets is the film's best special effect. The script takes a strange turn when a wanted killer takes them hostage, but for the most part the film is quite well handled, even with the stalwart B-movie-ness of Denning spouting off theories to the ragtag survivors. —*S. A.*

TASTE THE BLOOD OF DRACULA L: HORROR/HAMMER FILMS (1970) 91M D: Peter Sasdy. *Christopher Lee, Geoffrey Keen, Ralph Bates, Linda Hayden, Ilsa Blair, Michael Ripper.* Just as Universal's fourth Frankenstein film (*Ghost of Frankenstein*) marked the point when the artistry and magnificence of the series gave way to B-movie trappings, Hammer's fourth Dracula film, *Taste the Blood of Dracula*, is also the beginning of its end. Unlike Universal's movies, this sequel ties in very well to the film before it and does bring some new, interesting ideas to the series. Rather than just spreading terror across the land, Dracula sticks to a carefully plotted revenge plan and ultimately we see he is not the true villain. Dracula is simply living according to his dark nature; the terrible townsfolk who go seeking evil pleasures are the ones to blame for the atrocities. However, the story focuses far too much on said townsfolk and they just aren't compelling enough to carry the movie. Mixing weird Freudian themes into this traditional revenge story adds an element of interest, but the bland characters and unengaging plot make this a lesser entry in the Hammer Dracula series. But still, that's not to say it isn't worthwhile. —*T. S.*

TEENAGE CAVEMAN (2001) L: SCIENCE FICTION/SCIENCE FICTION (2001) 100M D: Larry Clark. *Tiffany Limos, Andrew Keegan, Tara Subkoff, Richard Hillman.* Stan Winston's Creature Features was meant as a special effects showcase, a series of straight-to-video updates of old Samuel Z. Arkoff B movies. But for some reason he gave this one to Clark, the arty pervert director of divisive films like *Kids* and *Bully*. It's a postapocalyptic teen movie, shot in the modern art house style of washed-out film and handheld cameras. Since it's a Clark movie, the teens abandon their tribe and make new friends who teach them about booze and sex. They have a huge orgy and some of them get an STD, which causes them to morph into the Toxic Avenger–like cavemen of the title. Clark must've been excited to get to do a movie with a severed head in it. It's a ridiculous combination of styles, and a lot of fun for those who enjoy Clark's work. —*B. T.*

TERMINATOR 3: RISE OF THE MACHINES L: SCIENCE FICTION/SCIENCE FICTION (2003) 109M D: Jonathan Mostow.
Claire Danes, Nick Stahl, Arnold Schwarzenegger, Kristanna Loken, Kristanna Loken, Arnold Schwarzenegger, Nick Stahl, Claire Danes. Schwarzenegger's old, obsolete Terminator is back in black. Leather, that is, as well as his trademark dark glasses and monosyllabic punch lines. He may be machine, but there's the spirit of a human whirring inside the gearbox as he plays tough-love father figure to John Connor (now grown up to become scruffy, haggard Stahl) and a reluctant bystander (Danes) destined to play a role in the future of mankind. The new Terminator TX (Loken), who looks like she stepped out of *The Blue Lagoon*, is a veritable Swiss Army Knife of goodies, Inspector Gadget in the guise of a Victoria's Secret mannequin. Director Mostow delivers an impressive display of property damage and powers through his set pieces with such speed that you rarely notice (or just don't care) when the plot and the characters fail to connect. It lacks the mano-a-machino grit of the original down-and-dirty classic, and the eye-popping effects spectacle of *T2: Judgment Day*, but compared to the comic book "supeoperas" dense with psychological torment, guilt, and sprawling running times, the narrative efficiency of *T3* is not just commendable, it's refreshing. —*S. A.*

John Connor (Stahl), the future warrior of this series whose postapocalyptic destiny is nearly realized, receives assistance from a futuristic robot (Schwarzenegger). If this sounds like *T2*, you're right. The story is basically identical, except there are more chase scenes, fewer effects, stupider one-liners, and significantly less story. Perhaps the only audience that will get something out of this film is the audience that hasn't seen *T2*. And to find such a thing we would have to travel to the past. —*N. J.*

TERROR FIRMER L: PSYCHOTRONIC/TROMA FILMS (1999) 114M D: Lloyd Kaufman. *Will Keenan, Trent Haaga, Lloyd Kaufman, Alyce LaTourelle, Ron Jeremy.* *Terror Firmer* is the movie that *The Player* was too stuck-up to be and that *Cecil B. Demented* was not radical enough to be. It's a big "fuck you" to bullshit Hollywood and "Indie" cinema, a true call to arms for anyone wanting to make truly independent films. It's also the kind of bizarre movie the babies in Hollywood would never touch, full of blind directors, transsexual murderers, head crushings, tits being blown apart by shotguns, and everything that should be in a Ron Howard movie. —*K. C.*

TERRORVISION L: SCIENCE FICTION/SCIENCE FICTION (1986) 83M D: Ted Nicolau. *Diane Franklin, Mary Woronov, Chad Allen, Gerrit Graham, Jonathan Gries.* A swinging suburban LA family is creatively mangulated by a satellite-transmitted space beast in this brilliant post-New Wave horror/comedy. When the Puttermans (Woronov and the hilarious Graham) hook up their new satellite dish, they unwittingly open a transgalactic gateway to a carnivorous alien creature. Soon, shell-shocked Grandpa and medicated adolescent Stanley are left to defend their home from the ravenous beast, while the Putterman parents desperately try to lock parts with a couple of half-hearted swingers they've unknowingly dragged to the human buffet. Though the creature temporarily takes a liking to glam-cartoon Franklin's heavy metal boyfriend O.D., it's not long before the next stage of the hunger-slaughter begins. Even the schizophrenic soundtrack is entertaining, performed by popular Italian New Wave group The Fibonaccis. Filled with gore, outrageous rubber beasts, and genuinely funny dialogue, *Terrorvision* is the top-notch in the shit heap. —*Z. C.*

TETSUO: THE IRON MAN L: JAPANESE SCIENCE FICTION / JAPANESE SCIENCE FICTION (1988) 67M D: Shinya Tsukamoto.
Kei Fujiwara, Nobu Kanaoka, Shinya Tsukamoto, Tomorowo Taguchi. This is psychotic, hallucinating, cyberpunk insanity, a surreal trip into a dystrophic biomechanical nightmare shot in grainy black and white with an experimental, clanking, industrial soundtrack. There's interesting stop-motion animation special effects mixed with live action. Quick cuts, speed-ups, furious pacing attacking the senses, growing crawling roots of metal and pipe seething, piercing skin. Evolution in form and consciousness, flesh and metal become one, transforming and changing the weakness of mere flesh into the monstrosity of machines out of control. We see flashes of a man shoving metal into his flesh, transcendence through pain and nightmares of destruction. Phallic drills penetrating, a woman raping a man. Technocratic sculptures, rusted disease. My altered state of consciousness pounded into darkness by the shocking images and thoughts of death and destruction, all revisited by this black comedy of horrors. —*B. W.*

TETSUO II: BODYHAMMER L: JAPANESE SCIENCE FICTION/ JAPANESE SCIENCE FICTION (1992) 83M D: Shinya Tsukamoto.
Shinya Tsukamoto, Keinosuke Tomioka, Nobu Kanaoka, Torauemon Utazawa, Tomorowo Taguchi. If you thought *Tetsuo: The Iron Man* was weird … Less sequel or remake than extension of the ideas of the first film, *Bodyhammer* ups the budget, trades the black and white for color photography, and sets the narrative ambitions higher, but the roots remain in the nightmarish imagery and the themes of the marriage of flesh and technology, metal and magic. A young middle-class couple see their young son kidnapped by mysterious

hoodlums and the father (Taguchi, returning from *Iron Man*), filled with rage and shame at his powerlessness, inexplicably transforms into a robotic warrior. Tsukamoto explores the simultaneous terror and ecstasy as he claims the birthright in a battle of biblical proportions with an underground society of cybermen led by a twisted madman. There ain't nothing like this in the American cinema. —*S. A.*

TEXAS CHAIN SAW MASSACRE, THE L: HORROR/ CANNIBALS (1974) 83M D: Tobe Hooper. *Marilyn Burns, Jim Siedow, Edwin Neal, Paul A. Partain, Gunnar Hansen.* A group of young people visiting a childhood home happen to trespass on the property of a family of deranged cannibals. Try not to do that, young people. *The Texas Chain Saw Massacre* is a masterpiece of low-budget horror, a combination of brutal (but not really gory) imagery, unyielding suspense, nightmarish production design, and an almost documentary feel to the acting and camera work. Although the human-skin-wearing Leatherface (Hansen) is the iconic image from the film, the best character is the hitchhiker (Neal), who gets so mad the kids won't buy a photograph that he cuts his own hand and smears blood on their van. Then there's the cook (Siedow), who makes polite conversation with his abductee even as he beats her with a broom. The movie is full of this type of behavior—almost too authentically insane for someone to just make up. Perhaps spawned by the misleading advertising slogan, "What happened was real," there is a persistent myth that *Texas Chain Saw Massacre* is based on a true story. It is only vaguely inspired by Ed Gein, who lived in Wisconsin, never really got around to a massacre, and didn't use a chain saw. —*B. T.*

TEXAS CHAINSAW MASSACRE PART 2, THE L: HORROR/ CANNIBALS (1986) 90M D: Tobe Hooper. *Caroline Williams, Dennis Hopper, Bill Johnson, Bill Moseley, Jim Siedow.* With help of Tom Savini, Hooper took all the gore people imagined they saw in *Texas Chain Saw Massacre* and actually put it into this gruesome, over-the-top black comedy sequel. The Chainsaw Family butcher some obnoxious tourists while they're on the phone with a radio DJ (Williams), who subsequently becomes their prey when she plays the call on the air. Hopper's obsessed Texas Ranger spouts biblical verses while sawing down the family's corpse-strewn underground amusement park. The film is completely relentless, from the time Leatherface (Johnson) and Chop Top (Moseley) show up at the radio station to the feverish climax. Chop Top (intended to be the twin brother of the hitchhiker from the first film) is a classic horror villain who rants psychotically while snacking on pieces of skin he picks from his head wound using a coat hanger. Cowritten with L. M. Kit Carson (*Paris, Texas*), the film contains an underlying critique of Reagan-era values as well as the

Texas Rangers, chili contests, and rowdy football weekends. —*B. T.*

TEXAS CHAINSAW MASSACRE (2003) L: HORROR/ CANNIBALS (2003) 98M D: Marcus Nispel. *Andrew Bryniarski, Jessica Biel, Eric Balfour, R. Lee Ermey.* Had I not seen the original, this remake might have been more enjoyable. It did make me jump a couple times, and it did pile on the gore, but it wasn't particularly spectacular. And I did see the original, so I didn't blink twice at this remake. It doesn't have that sheer horror value, the gore scenes come nowhere NEAR the original, and the film has a polished, clean feel that causes it to lose that eeriness that was so perfectly captured with the gritty, dirty feel of the original. Biel is there to add the tits and ass, "oops, my T-shirt is wet . . . again, and look at my booty jiggle" element. I'm a fan of '70s horror, and this movie is just another example of a mediocre remake. —*J. S.*

TEXAS CHAINSAW MASSACRE: A FAMILY PORTRAIT L: HORROR/CANNIBALS (1990) 64M D: Brad Shellady. *Jim Siedow, Gunnar Hansen, Edwin Neal, John Dugan.* This set of behind-the-scenes interviews shot in 1988 is a must-see for fans of the 1974 horror classic. It's an oral history of the filming as told by the four actors who played the cannibalistic family. Their stories give a good idea of how the conditions of the low-budget production (everyone living in one house, nobody allowed to change clothes, rotting meat on the tables, burning animal corpses in the backyard) led to the tense atmosphere that ended up on screen. Neal (the hitchhiker) and Seidow (the cook) seem to show glints of their characters' madness; and even the humble, soft-spoken Hansen (Leatherface) tells of an incident on set where he found himself too far into the character and actually cut one of the actresses for real. —*B. T.*

TEXAS CHAINSAW MASSACRE: THE NEXT GENERATION L: HORROR/CANNIBALS (1995) 93M D: Kim Henkel. *Robert Jacks, Renée Zellweger, Matthew McConaughey.* Teenagers on the way home from the prom are abducted and terrorized by the latest lineup of that Texas clan with the unusual diet. In the kidnapper corner we have the overacting McConaughey; representing the kidnapped we have the marginally professional actor Zellweger. Both became famous before the film was released, and were rightfully embarrassed about their participation—not because they were in a *Texas Chainsaw* movie, but because they were in the worst *Texas Chainsaw* movie. With bad acting and lame attempts at shock value (Leatherface is a cross-dresser!), it plays like a Troma remake of the original—and why do we need that when we already have *Mother's Day*? The revelation about a conspiracy behind the cannibal killings is even more lamentable than the thorn-cult idea in the *Halloween* sequels. Henkel, who cowrote the original, ought to know better. —*B. T.*

THEATER OF BLOOD L: CLASSIC HORROR/CLASSIC HORROR (1973) 104M D: Douglas Hickox. *Vincent Price, Diana Rigg, Ian Hendry. Theater of Blood,* my favorite Price film, is one of his funniest and goriest. Edward Lionheart (Price), a self-obsessed Shakespearean actor, gets revenge on the critics circle who snubbed him by killing them in methods lifted from the Bard's plays. Price seems to have the time of his life dressing in a wide array of costumes and delivering multiple Shakespeare monologues. Rigg, as his daughter, spends most of the film in an afro wig and fake mustache. If you enjoyed the Dr. Phibes films you need to watch this, too, but be warned—it is much more gruesome. *—B.T.*

THIEF IN THE NIGHT, A L: VAOWG/CHRISTPLOITATION (1972) 69M D: Donald W. Thompson. *Colleen Niday, Patty Dunning, Mike Niday.* This peculiar film is said to have saved more souls for Jesus than any other movie, and does it by scaring them. This film is about the Rapture and focuses on a group of friends, both believers and nonbelievers, in a small Midwest town. If you don't know what the Rapture is, a badly dressed Christian rock group with acne explains it all for you through the credits. They're proselytizing right from the beginning so that you won't be "left behind." Eventually, the Rapture happens, leading to the best scene of the film: a disbelieving Patty hears about it on the radio one morning and rushes into the bathroom panicked about losing her believer husband. All she sees is an electric razor, still running, laying in the sink. She screams. For the rest of the film she flees from Unite, the organized minions of Satan. *—N.J.*

13 GHOSTS (AKA THIR13EN GHOSTS) L: HORROR/GHOSTS (2001) 91M D: Steve Beck. *F. Murray Abraham, Alec Roberts, Matthew Lillard, Tony Shalhoub, Shayne Litwiller, Shannon Elizabeth.* Loosely based on the '60s William Castle film of the same title, this version involves a house full of locked-up ghosts who are part of a gigantic machine designed to open the "eye of hell." Lock in an innocent family, and heads roll. Although may not be a good movie in the traditional sense, it's fucking FUN. The special effects are fantastic, and the ghosts are genuinely scary and gory. Lillard adds his usual sparkle of comic genius; and there's an extremely gratuitous shot of a ghost ripping Elizabeth's shirt off and her breast popping out. More for those looking for a good laugh than for the real horror aficionado, this film is better than it seems. *—J.S.*

THUMB WARS: THE PHANTOM CUTICLE L: SCIENCE FICTION/STAR WARS (1999) 29M D: Steve Oedekerk. Oedekerk created and directed this half-hour *Star Wars* spoof performed entirely by a cast of thumbs (apart from cameos by a foot and an upside-down chin). To put it bluntly, this is just plain weird: the humor is juvenile and the mix of high-tech digital effects and low-tech doll house sets and toy props is oddly cool, but the computer manipulations that apply select facial features on human thumbs and tweak them into cartoonish exaggeration creates a truly bizarre, genuinely inspired effect. My favorite scene is an inspired send-up of Yoda as spaced-out puppet mumbling about the all-controlling hand and staring blankly into the camera like a dazed shock therapy patient. *—S.A.*

TIME AFTER TIME L: PSYCHOTRONIC /WELLS, H.G. (1979) 120M D: Nicholas Meyer. *Malcolm McDowell, David Warner, Patti D'Arbanville, Mary Steenburgen, Charles Cioffi.* McDowell plays H. G. Wells, the author of *The Time Machine* and here the actual inventor of said device. While discussing time travel with guests at a dinner party, he decides to show off the invention. But the machine is stolen by someone at the party, someone who really wants to escape the present of 1893—Jack the Ripper (Warner). What follows is a chase through modern San Francisco involving two Victorian icons. It's an interesting twist on the familiar Wells story. *—N.J.*

TINTORERA . . . TIGER SHARK L: VAOWG/VAOWG (1977) 89M D: René Cardona Jr. *Susan George, Andrés García, Fiona Lewis, Jennifer Ashley, Hugo Stiglitz, Roberto Guzmán.* Interesting, complex adventure/sexploitation movie about an American (Stiglitz) who anchors his large boat off a Mexican resort community in tourist season, learns a little about shark hunting, but mostly is interested in trolling for women. He gets close to one (Lewis) but she flirts with an insolent Mexican pretty boy (García), too. Rising naked from the latter's bed one morning, she walks into the sea to swim to the American's boat, having made her decision. A tiger shark gets her, leaving no evidence. The bitter American assumes she went home, but is happily consoled by his former rival, who shows him how to hunt small sharks. They also troll for women together, carefree. Then one woman (George) is shared by them both, and the large tiger shark returns to these waters. Not a rip-off of *Jaws,* this is more like an Italian buddy picture by a Mexican director who is earthy and philosophical about life in his every move. *—J.C.*

TITANIC (1953) L: VAOWG/VAOWG (1953) 98M D: Jean Negulesco. *Barbara Stanwick, Clifton Webb, Robert Wagner, Audrey Dalton, Thelma Ritter.* Stanwick plays a rich conservative woman, separated from her husband, who takes her two children from London society to live a more down-to-earth life in the American Midwest. Webb plays her husband, who manages to buy a ticket off someone at the last possible moment. He tries everything he can to win back her love. Naturally this confuses the two children (played by a very young Wagner and Dalton), who are eventually forced to take sides. By the end of the film the sides they must choose between are the side of the ship or the side of a lifeboat. This is a fantastic drama expertly played by Stanwick and Webb. For a thoroughly different take on the Titanic voyage, perhaps even as a double feature, be sure to see *A Night to Remember*. —*N. J.*

TO THE DEVIL, A DAUGHTER L: HORROR/HAMMER FILMS
(1976) 95M D: Peter Sykes. *Nastassja Kinski, Richard Widmark, Honor Blackman, Christopher Lee*. "It is not heresy! And I will not recant!" shouts priest Lee as he is excommunicated from the church. So begins the story of a satanic cult and the young girl who is inadvertently drawn into the devious plans. The innocent girl, played by the amazing Kinski, is accidentally entrusted to the cult by her father, and on her eighteenth birthday they plan to turn her into a satanic bride. The father enlists the help of an occult expert and they set off to save her soul from Hell. One of the slowest, most carefully constructed Hammer films, *To the Devil* is filled with beautiful cinematography and populated by amazing actors, all giving strong performances. The notoriety of Kinski's full-frontal nude scenes have overshadowed her brilliant performance. The atmosphere is eerie and the story engaging, but unfortunately the ending is somewhat weak. Poorly executed special effects also detract from the film, but overall it is a taut and suspenseful occult story. —*T. S.*

TOOLBOX MURDERS, THE L: HORROR/STALKERS (1978)
93M D: Dennis Donnelly. *Cameron Mitchell, Nicolas Beauvy, Pamelyn Ferdin, Wesley Eure*. A man wearing a ski mask enters an apartment building and murders a woman with a power drill. He moves on to other apartments and kills with a nail gun and other tools. This grisly murder spree goes on for fifteen minutes before the characters are even introduced. The only dialogue is little snippets overheard as the killer stalks his victims; the murders are juxtaposed with music playing in the apartments, which at times the killer hums along with. Being thrust into this violence with no explanation is disorienting for the audience, and very effective. But then the killer leaves and the actual plot begins, with mostly standard TV-style staging for a story about two teens and a police detective trying to find a girl kidnapped by the guy with the tools. It never lives up to the power of those first scenes, but it's worth staying tuned for an unusual twist after the killer's identity is revealed. —*B. T.*

TOWER OF EVIL L: HORROR/STALKERS (1972) 85M D: James
P. O'Connolly. *Mark McBride, Jill Haworth, William Lucas, Anna Palk, Anthony Valentine*. A simple night of sex and frolic becomes entrenched in death and gory violence in this British '70s terror film. Two fishermen find the bodies of three brutally murdered teens on the stairs to an island lighthouse, followed by a crazed nude woman. When she is caught, she is placed under a hypnotizing machine of many colored lights, enabling her to recount partial details of the horrors on Snape Island, with flashbacks of nudity,

sex, and horrific events. A group of archaeologists make for Snape Island and bicker among themselves while unlocking the island's secrets, the young woman's fragmented memories, and the mystery of just who, or what, killed the young island goers. *Tower of Evil* is a fun trip back to a long-gone time of British cinema. Scary isn't the word here; "turned-on" terror would be more apt. —*S. R.*

TOWERING INFERNO, THE L: VAOWG/VAOWG (1974)
165M D: John Guillermin, Irwin Allen. *Steve McQueen, Paul Newman, O. J. Simpson, William Holden, Faye Dunaway, Fred Astaire, Richard Chamberlain*. It's difficult making a good sequel to a spectacular disaster film. By the end of *The Poseidon Adventure*, the cruise ship had sunk into the ocean and most of the characters had died off. So it was time to put together a new cast and another death trap in which to put them all: *The Towering Inferno*. Here we have the tallest skyscraper in the world celebrating its dedication while O. J. Simpson runs loose inside it. Just as you would expect, a fire starts and the characters must find their way out of the structure, floor by floor. Much like *The Poseidon Adventure*, this film won some Oscars: Best Cinematography and Best Song ("We May Never Love Like This Again"). —*N. J.*

TOXIC AVENGER, THE L: PSYCHOTRONIC/TROMA FILMS
(1985) 90M D: Michael Herz, Lloyd Kaufman. *Mitchell Cohen, Andree Maranda, Jennifer Babtist, Mark Torgl, Robert Prichard, Cindy Manion*. This cheesy, low-budget superhero parody is a winning combination of goofy humor and excessive sex and violence. Melvin Junko (Torgl), the unbelievably nerdy janitor of a fitness club, falls into a vat of toxic waste as the result of a cruel prank. On fire, his skin bubbling like hot grease, one of the jocks responsible says, "He's fakin' it!" But he'll get his after Melvin transforms into a "hideously deformed creature of super human size and strength" (Cohen) who ends up brutally slaughtering first those who wronged him and then the criminals who plague the town of Tromaville. *The Toxic Avenger* is full of extremely tasteless humor (and at times is inexcusably misogynistic). I still have a soft spot for it in my heart. If you're only going to watch one Troma movie (which is probably a good idea for most people), this should be the one. —*B. T.*

TOXIC CRUSADERS: THE MOVIE L: PSYCHOTRONIC/
TROMA FILMS (1991) 76M D: Bill Hutten, Tony Love. *Michael J. Pollard, Chuck McCann*. Clearly made in the post–Ninja Turtles era, and with a clumsy attempt at an ecology theme, this cartoon takeoff on *The Toxic Avenger* has Toxie, his mop (who is now alive), his girlfriend (who is not blind but still wears the sunglasses), and other mutants fighting against a four-armed industrialist named Dr. Killemoff. The design, animation, music, and voices are all horrible, but many scripts con-

tain a sanitized version of the trademark Troma goofiness. In each episode the villain's sidekick Psycho says, "But Dr. Killemoff, what if Toxie . . ." and then describes in detail what will happen in the rest of the episode. I wonder if somewhere some kid who watched this cartoon made the connection to *Toxic Avenger* and managed to get his parents to rent it? I mean, it must've at least happened once. —*B. T.*

TRAGIC CEREMONY L: HORROR/EURO-HORROR (1972) 88M D: Riccardo Freda. *Tony Isbert, Luciana Paluzzi, Máximo Valverde, Giovanni Petrucci, Luigi Pistilli, Camille Keaton.* OK—the story is silly and the effects are worse in this Spanish-language Euro-horror film set in England with an Italian director who's seen better days. But it has a rare performance by the sublime Camille Keaton. Two guys and a girl are vacationing together. Out of gas in a rainstorm, they seek shelter in a mansion where a satanic ceremony hypnotizes the girl (Keaton) into becoming its ritual sacrifice. The boys rescue her but kill the lady of the house (Paluzzi), who ends up possessing the girl and killing the boys. Spanish prints of European B-movies in the early '70s were the most heavily censored, and this film's other language versions might be spicier, but even still Keaton is odd and eerie. An extreme psychological range: you feel in her face her sense of resigned doom and then the wounded-animal anguish in both face and body when her friends start to die. —*J. C.*

TREES L: VAOWG/VAOWG (2000) 90M D: Michael Pleckaitis. *Kevin McCauley, Philip Gardiner, Peter Randazzo, Mary Ann Nilan.* A spoof on *Jaws*, but with trees, the tagline for this incredibly campy "thriller" is "Its bark is worse than its bite!" The terror in a community mounts as vicious tree attacks claim the lives of some of the citizens. Families and couples, once able to recreate in the fields near the forest without a care in the world, now fear for their lives if they get too close to the edge of the woods. When I say this is a *Jaws* spoof, I mean it follows the plot of *Jaws* almost exactly. But with trees, see? The best part of this film is when we get to see things from the killer tree's perspective, and everything is all green and shimmery and hateful. Yes! If you like funny things, you'll like this. —*J. S.*

TREKKIES L: SCIENCE FICTION/SCIENCE FICTION TV (1997) 86M D: Roger Nygard. *Denise Crosby.* What seems designed as a whimsical look at a pop culture obsession instead comes across as a creepy portrait of dementia. Nygard tries to be sympathetic toward hardcore *Star Trek* fans, but the more interesting ones to watch are the ones who are completely insane. On the one hand you have the nerdy dentist with the *Trek*-themed office, on the other hand you have the infamous uniform-wearing Whitewater juror, who makes her coworkers call her "Commander" and who wore the uniform to trial because she wanted

to set a positive example for the rest of the, uh, Federation. There's also an incredibly irritating teenager who's a perfectionist about the uniforms in his home-made *Star Trek* videos, and a depressingly mixed-up folk singer who seems to use the show as an excuse not to face his gender confusion. Despite the director's best efforts, *Trekkies* is a total freak show. But it's a fascinating one. —*B. T.*

TREMORS L: VAOWG/VAOWG (1990) 96M D: Ron Underwood. *Kevin Bacon, Finn Carter, Michael Gross, Reba McEntire, Fred Ward.* The '50s monster-sci-fi-horror genre is given its just due here in this homage to the frights and fun of a bygone era. Loving care is tended to fleshing out the characters as much as turning them into food, and the seriousness of the situation is never truly taken seriously. In the rural town of Perfection, in the middle of the desert, mysterious monsters have suddenly arrived and begun devouring anyone in their path. Two handymen, Valentine (Bacon) and Earl (Ward), become the leaders of the town's residents and try to figure out what exactly the "graboids" are, and how to stop them. The supporting cast shows they know exactly what this tongue-in-cheek film is trying to do, and they gleefully play along. The entire movie is pure fun. —*R. M.*

TRIPODS (1984) L: SCIENCE FICTION/SCIENCE FICTION (1984) 150M D: Graham Theakston, Christopher Barry. *Carl Seel, John Shackley, Jim Baker.* Made for British television, this miniseries is a sci-fi suspense story about an invasion of giant three-legged machines from another plane that take over Earth predominantly with their use of mind control. As it turns out, they cannot control the minds of humans sixteen or younger because of the development of the human brain. Consequently two boys set out to end the occupation and reclaim the Earth for adults before they themselves fall under the influence of the Tripods. This low-budget science fiction program is quite amusing and is good for all ages. —*N. J.*

TROG L: VAOWG/VAOWG (1970) 91M D: Freddie Francis. *Joan Crawford, Michael Gough, Kim Braden, David Griffin, John Hamill.* This is Crawford's last film, and to her fans that should either be horrifying or hilarious, perhaps depending upon how much they liked *Mommy Dearest.* Crawford plays an anthropologist who stumbles into a cave and discovers the last living troglodyte, or "Trog" for short. She keeps it caged in her laboratory and, after a battery of tests with puzzles and toy dolls, she finds it is nearly human. A must-see for purveyors of highbrow B-filmology. —*N. J.*

TROLL 2 L: HORROR/DEMONS (1990) 95M D: Drake Floyd. *George Hardy, Gary Carlson, Margo Prey, Connie McFarland, Michael Stephenson.* One of the most unbelievable sequels ever made, supposedly shot without the knowledge or consent of the creators of the first *Troll* film. At first glance a sub-Z-grade continuity abomination, this fine example of direct-to-video hysteria is a nonstop explosion of genius disguised as ineptitude. Grade-schooler Joshua is visited by the protective ghost of his Grandpa Seth, who warns him that his family's vacation destination of Nilbog may be worth avoiding. But there's no changing dad's mind, and soon the whole family is knee-deep in black magic and nefarious villagers, including the remarkably abnormal Carlson as Sheriff Gene Freak. Young Joshua and his dead grandpa are the only ones aware of their mortal danger, which Josh at one point attempts to curb by urinating all over the dinner table. Not bad for PG-13. Worth noting is the fact that trolls aren't mentioned once in this film, while the threat of goblins remains all too real. Directed by "Drago Floyd" (actually Claudio Fragasso), a low-rent auteur from the initial home video exploitation tidal wave of the late 1980s. —Z. C.

28 DAYS LATER L: VAOWG/VAOWG (2002) 113M D: Danny Boyle. *Cillian Murphy, Kim McGarrity, Alexander Delamere, Naomie Harris, Brendan Gleeson, Christopher Eccleston.* A group of animal rights activists break into a testing facility to free a group of chimps infected with the RAGE virus. Twenty-eight days later, everyone is dead. Coming out of a coma in a hospital bed, Jim (Murphy) wakes up to an empty London where the only other people are infected with a virus that fills them with a psychotic bloodlust. Soon he finds other survivors and they set off, following a radio message promising some sort of hope. What follows is an intensely performed, beautifully shot (on digital video), stylish yet gritty, and above all intelligent horror film merging aspects of the deadly virus, postapocalyptic, and zombie genres. Despite an unfitting final conclusion, the film succeeds because, following in the tradition of all great horror, it not only provides thrills but also raises questions about what it means to be a human and what our anger will cause us to do. An excellent modern horror film bound to be a classic. —T. S.

20 MILLION MILES TO EARTH L: PSYCHOTRONIC/ HARRYHAUSEN, RAY (1957) 83M D: Nathan Juran. *William Hopper, Joan Taylor, Frank Puglia, John Zaremba.* Think of this alien lizard on the rampage as a space-age *King Kong*: an innocent creature plucked from his planet escapes from his cage and runs away, hungry and lost in the Italian countryside. As in the best of Ray Harryhausen's creations, the creature from Venus has an endearing personality that comes through its skittish movements and uncomprehending face, far more interesting than the stiff, flat human characters saddled with dialogue that thuds with every syllable. Luckily you can forget all that as the ever-growing lizard rampages through Rome and ends up in the Coliseum for the final clash. —S. A.

TWILIGHT ZONE, THE L: SCIENCE FICTION/SCIENCE FICTION TV (1959) 5,190M D: Juss Addiss, William Asher, others. *Rod Serling, Agnes Moorehead, Burgess Meredith.* This black and white TV series that ran from 1959 through 1964 is one of the most imaginative and experimental series ever broadcast. The *Twilight Zone*, as the opening titles suggest, is that peculiar area beyond time and space, a fourth dimension perhaps, in which the most inexplicable phenomena occur. Each episode realizes some kind of eye-opening fluke or impossibility. In "After Hours," Anne Francis plays a beautiful woman who discovers she is in fact a department store mannequin who is overstaying her time on leave. In "The Invaders," Agnes Moorehead fends off a flying saucer full of little men trying to zap her. Burgess Meredith finds a watch that can suspend time while he does whatever he likes in "A Kind of Stopwatch." The scope and breadth of this classic series cannot be easily summarized; at any time it may be allegorical, comical, highly dramatic, or just plain silly. Yet under Serling's supervision they are all brilliant and continue to influence the creative minds of the *Zone*'s audience. —N. J.

TWINS OF EVIL L: HORROR/HAMMER FILMS (1971) 87M D: John Hough. *Mary Collinson, Kathleen Byron, Madeleine Collinson, Peter Cushing, Isobel Black, Dennis Price.* This powerful allegory of class conflict is presented in the trappings of a horror thriller. Twins Maria (Mary Collinson) and Frieda (Madeleine Collinson) come to live with Uncle Gustav (Cushing), who scowls at the girls' pretty dresses. He heads a puritan band of witch hunters, which sets him at odds with Dietrich (Price), a liberal man of science. In Karnstein Castle the libertine count (Damien Thomas) ritually sacrifices a naked woman on a stone slab. Soon he asks Frieda to visit, which makes her a target for the witch-burners. Now Dietrich will have to choose up sides. Every ounce of the prolific violence and nudity enriching *Twins of Evil* build toward an intense emotional climax. Hammer Studio at its most inspired. —J. C.

2010: THE YEAR WE MAKE CONTACT L: SCIENCE FICTION/SCIENCE FICTION (1984) 114M D: Peter Hyams. *Roy Scheider, John Lithgow, Helen Mirren, Keir Dullea, Bob Balaban.* Why would someone make a *sequel* to *2001*? How did they get enough executives, enough crew members, enough actors who were all willing to agree that, yes, this is a good idea. We should spend millions of dollars and a year of our lives making this movie. We should take the mysterious monolith, and the space baby, and we should *try to explain them*. We should send a new crew to *find* the crew from *2001*. One of them should be the inventor of HAL 9000. And we should treat it all literally and include narration that explains all the new concepts. Yeah, that would be a great idea, right? No! It wouldn't! What is wrong with us humans that we can't just leave something like *2001* alone, we

have to keep fucking around with it? Would the monolith have made a sequel? No. Would the star child have made a sequel? I doubt it. I guess maybe the bone-throwing monkeys would do it. *Maybe.* We suck. —*B.T.*

UFO: THE COMPLETE UFO MEGAFEST L: SCIENCE FICTION/SCIENCE FICTION TV (1970) 1352M D: Gerry Anderson, Ron Appleton, ohers. *Wanda Ventham, Ed Bishop, George Sewell, Michael Billington, Peter Gordeno.* After a decade of playing with puppets, Brit TV producer Anderson combined the cool aircrafts of *Thunderbirds* and the paranoia of *Captain Scarlet* into pioneering alien invasion show and put humans at the helm. This time they are S.H.A.D.O., a supersecret military branch in the mod 1980s dedicated to fighting off mysterious invasions of flying saucers from another galaxy. But for all the special effects spectacles, it's the uncertainty of their intentions and their identity that defines the show's tense, shrouded-in-mystery tone. Yes, the stiff, wooden performances and repressed personalities inspire comparisons to the marionettes of previous Anderson shows, but as the shows progress they earn this dourness through sacrifice and battered emotions. Bishop, the American commander with intense eyes and a ruthless devotion to his responsibility, is an almost tragic figure, as the episodes "A Question of Priorities" and "Confetti Check A-OK" reveal. Their need for security even puts them on the scheming end of mind-warping conspiracies ("Exposed"). On the funky side there is the way cool futuristic style of silent DeLorean-esque cars and casual weird fashions. —*S.A.*

UNCLE SAM L: HORROR/DEMONS (1997) 90M D: William Lustig. *William Smith, David "Shark" Fralick, P. J. Soles, Robert Forster, Timothy Bottoms, Bo Hopkins.* Sam Harper is shot down by friendly fire in his helicopter during the Gulf War. His body is sent back home to his sister's house, where it awaits burial. While she doesn't remember him too fondly, her son reveres Uncle Sam and his service to the country. Inspired by his uncle's heroism, the young man swears he will enlist when he gets older and quickly judges anyone who thinks poorly of his uncle. At about this time the badly burned and decomposed body is magically resuscitated. Uncle Sam's goal is to fight the war at home and he does this by wrapping himself up in the flag and murdering as many antiwar liberals as he can find. A great supporting cast helps to make this low-grade horror film a high-grade social commentary. Written by Larry Cohen. —*N.J.*

UNEARTHLY, THE L: CLASSIC SCIENCE FICTION/CLASSIC SCIENCE FICTION (1957) 73M D: Brooke Peters. *Myron Healey, John Carradine, Sally Todd, Allison Hayes, Tor Johnson.* Despite the title, there are no aliens in this film, only a mad scientist (the ever reliable Carradine) experimenting on his forgotten and forlorn patients with extracts of human

glands. His goal is to prolong life, but he keeps tripping over a nasty side effect: his victims end up horribly mutated monsters. Johnson is the monosyllabic hulk of a manservant Lobo (who played an almost identical part—with the same name—in Ed Wood's *Night of the Ghouls*), but he's more expressive than our ostensible hero Healy, a tough crook with his own secret, and less attractive than our hapless heroine Hayes (*Attack of the 50 Foot Woman*). IMDb viewers voted this in the bottom 100, which may be a bit extreme. Not that it's an undiscovered masterpiece—it's silly, clumsy, and cheap—but a film with such a kicker of a dungeon climax deserves a leg up to the bottom 1,000. —*S.A.*

UZUMAKI L: JAPANESE HORROR/JAPANESE HORROR (2000) 90M D: Higuchinsky. *Keiko Takahashi, Ren Osugi, Hinako Saeki.* Uzumaki opens with a close-up of a young woman's eye, her disembodied voice saying, "I have a story to tell you." The woman is Kirie (Ericko Hatsune), a Japanese schoolgirl, and the story is an account of the last days of sanity of her home town of Kurouzu. It seems that one by one, the residents are becoming more and more obsessed with spirals: collecting items with spiral patterns, refusing to eat food unless it contains a spiral, and so on. Soon the body count starts to rise and things begin to get weird. *Uzumaki* is based on the manga by Junji Ito. Keeping with the style of the comic and staying true to the text, *Uzumaki* is full of bizarre imagery and clever editing. The original music is great, both eerie and oddly catchy. Although the ending may leave you with more questions than answers, it is definitely worth the trip through this Lovecraftian phantasmagoria. —*R. G.*

VAMPIRE HAPPENING L: HORROR/VAMPIRES (1974) 101M D: Freddie Francis. *Pia Degermark, Ingrid van Bergen, Yvor Murillo, Thomas Hunter, Ferdy Mayne.* Degermark (*Elvira Madigan*) plays both an oversexed blond American actress who travels to Transylvania to sell a family castle and her brunette great grandmother, a vampire she unwittingly unleashes on the local populace, in this dippy horror comedy. As the girl falls in with a swinging group of bloodsucking ancestors, her vampire matriarch nibbles her way through a repressed monastery of horny monks and a local girls school of willing young women. Mayne spoofs his vampire aristocrat role from *The Fearless Vampire Killers*, this picture's obvious inspiration, and the comparison is not flattering. It's a silly, sloppy, wig-swapping, door-slamming farce that displays volumes of female flesh in place of wit or wiles. —*S.A.*

VAMPYRES L: HORROR/VAMPIRES (1974) 88M D: Jose Larraz. *Marianne Morris, Anulka Dziubinska.* Larraz's tale of lesbian lovers (Morris and Anulka) who arise as thirsty undead sexpots is full of misty forests, candlelit castle interiors, and boobs and blood ... what more could you want? One of the lovers falls for a male victim and keeps him alive for sex while slowly draining him dry. Larraz's direction makes classic imagery almost mythic—blood dripping down pale faces, clouds crawling past a castle—but more importantly gives the dead girls an emotional life even while piling on the exploitative nude scenes. It's a minor classic with a dreamy sense of horror and a delicious conclusion restored, after all these years, to its full European cut. —*S.A.*

VEIL, THE L: HORROR TV/HORROR TV (1958) 311M D: George Wagner, Herbert L. Strock, others. *Boris Karloff.* This remarkable yet short-lived television series was hosted by Karloff and featured him in a variety of roles and guises. Each and every one of the twelve episodes is a mystery of supernatural proportions. In "Vision of Crime," Karloff plays a police detective investigating a murder witnessed from a distance of 150 miles; in "Food on the Table," Karloff plays a lecherous sea captain who murders his own wife only to be plagued by her ghost; and in "The Black Hand" a surgeon loses his hand only to replace it with a murderer's—shades of *The Hands of Orlac!* This DVD set released by Something Weird Video is a must-have for Karloff fans. —*N.J.*

VOLCANO L: VAOWG/VAOWG (1997) 102M D: Mick Jackson. *Tommy Lee Jones, Anne Heche, Gaby Hoffman, Don Cheadle, Keith David, John Corbett.* Jones tries to save Los Angeles in this run-of-the-mill disaster flick. Producers must have simply sat around a table one day in 1996 and said to each other, "We've done *Earthquake, The Towering Inferno, The Poseidon Adventure*, and all those *Airport* movies. What can we do now?" Someone came up with the cockamamie idea of Los Angeles being terrorized by a volcano. Nothing more really needs to be said about this disastrous disaster film. Jones flirts with buxom seismologist Heche, and Wilshire Avenue gets roiled with hot magma. This film was purely a profit opportunity for producers eager to resurrect the heyday of cheap disaster films. This particular result, however, gets a D-minus for lack of any plausibility. —*N.J.*

WATCHER IN THE ATTIC L: JAPANESE HORROR/JAPANESE HORROR (1976) 76M D: Noboru Tanaka. *Renji Ishibashi, Junko Miyashita.* Brilliant, perverse Edogawa Rampo erotic satiric tale, brought to the screen with an edgy detachment. A 1920s landlord (Ishibashi) skulks about the attic of the rooming house he owns, peeping through the ceiling on his tenants: a Christian teacher always pontificating on good works, a shy artistic young woman who does body-painting for clients, and a married lady (Miyashita) who needs a place for her affairs, currently with a mime she picked up in the park. One day the lady notices the watching eye through a ceiling hole, but does not let on. She tightens her legs around the mime's neck, who struggles like a wounded animal until

he dies, implicitly taunting the man in the attic, daring him to tell. The tale only gets darker from there. And deadlier. —*J.C.*

WEREWOLF OF LONDON L: CLASSIC HORROR/CLASSIC HORROR (1935) 75M D: Stuart Walker. *Henry Hull, Lester Matthews, Spring Byington, Valerie Hobson, Warner Oland.* Universal's first go at the legend stars Hull as a botanist who is bitten by a wolf while searching for a rare Tibetan flower. Back in London, he transforms into a wolf himself when the moon is full. Leaner and edgier than the famous 1941 Lon Chaney classic, it drags through Scotland Yard investigations and needless comic relief but soars in eerie, imaginative twists, and striking action sequences. Oland costars as the melancholy scientist who seeks the rare flower because it is the only antidote to the condition they both suffer from, and Hobson is his doomed wife: "The werewolf instinctively kills the thing it loves best." —*S.A.*

WESTWORLD L: SCIENCE FICTION/SCIENCE FICTION (1973) 88M D: Michael Crichton. *Richard Benjamin, James Brolin, Yul Brynner.* Westworld is just one section of an enormous high-tech theme park designed for the affluent to be able to live out their fantasies. In Medievalworld, you can joust with and kill knights that are actually lifelike, preprogrammed robots. In Futureworld (which actually became a movie sequel with Henry Fonda) you can fight and kill aliens (that are also robots). Benjamin and Brolin take a vacation in *Westworld* to have fun shooting up robot cowboys and employing robot prostitutes. However one such robot, menacingly played by Brynner, somehow has live ammunition. Worse, he simply won't die when he's shot. Written and directed by Crichton, this film was released eleven years before *The Terminator*, and Brynner plays an unstoppable robot much better than Schwarzenegger does. —*N.J.*

WHAT HAVE YOU DONE TO SOLANGE? L: HORROR/GIALLO (ITALIAN HORROR) (1972) 102M D: Massimo Dallamano. *Joachim Fuchsberger, Fabio Testi, Cristina Galbo, Karin Baal.* Anyone interested in the world of Italian thrillers would do themselves right by starting here, as many of the thematic elements, plot devices, and cinematic techniques are sampled without being overly graphic. While a teacher and his student are together for a forbidden rendezvous, the teenager witnesses a murder. When the body is discovered, evidence points toward the teacher, who proclaims his innocence. The killer strikes the school again and again, seemingly picking his victims at random, baffling the police. A clue deliberately left by the murderer sends the teacher on a hunt for the truth hidden in the deceased teens' past. This film is filled with gripping twists, shocking violence, and gratuitous nudity that should please most mystery seekers and exploitation fans alike, while the repetitive score will echo in your mind for hours afterward. —*R. M.*

WHITE ZOMBIE L: CLASSIC HORROR/CLASSIC HORROR
(1932) 73M D: Victor Halperin. *Joseph Cawthorn, Madge Bellamy, John Harron, Bela Lugosi, Robert W. Frazer.* Using the beautiful indulgence and visual artistry of the most atmospheric silent horror films, *White Zombie* is a classic of the genre and an important piece of horror history. Here, as in voodoo legend, zombies are not rotting corpses returned from the grave (as cinema would eventually recreate them), but mindless slaves controlled by the sinister black magician "Murder" Legendre (Lugosi). Each shot is a masterwork unto itself, utilizing fairy-tale locales, Gothic architecture, deep menacing shadows, and amazing composition. It's very much an expressionist piece and is complemented well by its mysterious music, a collection of black spirituals. Although it is slow in some parts, it plays with all the grace of a silent film and is filled with memorable shots and sequences. —*T. S.*

WHOLE WIDE WORLD, THE L: PSYCHOTRONIC/HOWARD,
ROBERT E. (1996) 106M D: Dan Ireland. *Renee Zellweger, Vincent D'Onofrio.* Ireland's directorial debut, based on the memoir by Novalyne Price Ellis, flies on the success of his leading actors, Vincent D'Onofrio (as pulp author Robert E. Howard, creator of Conan) and Renee Zellweger (his onetime love Novalyne). Set in 1930s Texas, Ireland presents a troubled Howard, a quirky local character tied to his invalid mother's apron strings and often found acting out his characters' lives in the streets. The beautiful Texas locations set this platonic romance in another world, a place where at times no one else seems to exist, appropriate to the author of tales of loner warriors and solitary heroes. Where D'Onofrio's blustery Howard wears a cheerfully conceited hide to protect his fragile emotions, Zellweger's young Novalyne tries to burrow under his shell to free the man inside, creating a poignant love-story-that-almost-was. —*S. A.*

WILLARD L: VAOWG/VAOWG (1971) 95M D: Daniel Mann.
Bruce Davison, Michael Dante, Sondra Locke, Ernest Borgnine, Elsa Lanchester. Willard Stiles (Davison) is a socially inept young weirdo who lives with his elderly mother (Lanchester) in a deteriorating mansion. The mansion is paid for by his late father's business, which is now run by the cruel Al Martin (Borgnine). When Willard discovers the house is infested by rats he decides not to kill them, but instead plays with them. He names his favorites Ben and Socrates, and begins an unhealthy relationship with them, secretly carrying them around in his pocket and talking to them. When Al sees Socrates running loose in the office he kills him, leaving Willard no reasonable choice but to, you know, sic his army of rats on the bastard. The direction is weak, giving it the feel of a TV movie, but the twisted storyline

is compelling. It's also great to see Lanchester, the *Bride of Frankenstein* herself, as Willard's mother. —*B T.*

WILLARD L: VAOWG/VAOWG (2003) 100M D: Glen Morgan.
Laura Harring, Crispin Glover, R. Lee Ermey. A boy's best friend is his rat. Hunched in a repressed ball of nerves and tension, his voice almost a whimper, desperation and misery repressed behind his blank face but burning through his darting eyes, Glover was born to play the Willard in director Morgan's remake of the 1971 cult critter thriller. Morgan (who also scripts and coproduces with fellow *X-Files* alum James Wong) walks a fine line between light-fingered fun and demented revenge-of-the-rodents horror (watch the rat pack hunt a house cat while Michael Jackson's "Ben" plays in the background), but he has a sure sense of his craft and favors the skin-crawling spectacle of seas of angry rats over mere gore (which he keeps off screen). With its atmosphere of rot and decay and echoes of *Psycho* and *The Birds*, *Willard* is clever, darkly humorous, and unfailingly sympathetic. Morgan creates a savvy, smart drive-in movie with Hollywood studio polish and a movie buff's loving care. Ermey, spewing insults as if in a *Full Metal Jacket* flashback, is Willard's abusive terror of a boss. —*S. A.*

WILLOW L: FANTASY/FANTASY (1988) 130M D: Ron Howard.
Jean Marsh, Kevin Pollak, Val Kilmer, Warwick Davis, Joanne Whalley. My parents did not allow me to watch R-rated movies growing up. In fact, I was at least fourteen before I was technically allowed to watch PG-13 films. Of course, that did not mean I didn't sneak a restricted movie on occasion at a friend's house, but as far as my mom was concerned, I was trapped in a cinematic world without cussing, violence, or sex. Knowing that I was missing all the good stuff, I spent time watching PG movies that I did like over and over again. This is one of those movies. *Willow* is a magical adventure full of swords, sorcery, brownies, and midgets, with strong parallels to the *Lord of the Rings* trilogy. I admit that the film is not as good as I remember it being as a child, but if you don't want your kids to watch films with adult content, then this is the movie for them. Just remember they probably watch violent and sexy films at their friend's house anyway. —*D. D.*

WING COMMANDER L: SCIENCE FICTION/SCIENCE FICTION
(1999) 100M D: Chris Roberts. *David Warner, Freddie Prinze Jr., Matthew Lillard, Saffron Burrows, Tchéky Karyo.* In 2654, teenage heartthrobs undergo specialized space pilot training so they can fight against an evil alien race called the Kilrathi. As these bland characters flew their not-quite-X-Wings through the stars I kept waiting for them to land on a planet somewhere so the adventure could begin. How was I supposed to know that the video game series this was based

on was just a spruced-up flight simulator? Some day filmmakers will have to figure out that just coming up with a couple of names for alien races and some phony spiritual bullshit does not mean you're creating *Star Wars* for a new generation. You're not even creating *The Last Starfighter*. Not surprisingly, this is directed by the creator of the video games. —*B. T.*

WITCH ACADEMY L: HORROR/WITCHES & WARLOCKS (1993) 83M D: Fred Olen Ray. *Michelle Bauer, Priscilla Barnes, Suzanne Ager.* Trash director Ray's films ride the fine line between maniacally deranged, no-budget greatness and painfully unwatchable junk. This little number falls squarely in the first category. Starring the beautiful scream queens Bauer, Barnes, Ager, and Veronica Carothers (who all appear naked at one time or another), *Witch Academy* is pure satanic sex fun. —*T. S.*

WITCHES (AKA **DEVIL'S OWN**) L: HORROR/HAMMER FILMS (1966) 90M D: Cyril Frankel. *Alec McCowen, Ann Bell, Kay Walsh, Joan Fontaine, John Collin.* Fontaine plays a woman who moves back to England from Africa where her missionary work was cut short by a run-in with black magic. She applies for the position of school teacher in an English country town and soon finds that things there are not what they seem. The priest who hires her, for instance, is not a priest at all, but some fellow who gets his kicks dressing as a priest in front of people. As she acclimates to the small hamlet, she ultimately realizes that she has fled one kind of black magic for another. This peculiar Hammer production is one that shouldn't be missed. —*N. J.*

WRONG TURN L: HORROR/STALKERS (2003) 84M D: Rob Schmidt. *Eliza Dushku, Jeremy Sisto, Desmond Harrington, Emmanuelle Chriqui.* Touted as a glorious return to form for horror filmmaking, *Wrong Turn* may be throwback to some classic films, but in all the wrong ways. Part *Just Before Dawn*, part *The Hills Have Eyes*, part *Deliverance*, no parts good movie. It has a straightforward storyline not muddled with postmodern horror "rules" or post-ironic horror "humor," but *Wrong Turn* concentrated so much on what to leave out that it forgot about what to actually have. Lacking any sort of tension, creativity, or showmanship, this film falls flat and does not entertain. The inbred psychos designed by Stan Winston (who can't stop singing his own praises on this film) look more like Muppets than menaces. The cast is painful, with the exception of Sisto, who makes a great poor man's Jeff Goldblum. Otherwise, all we're left with is a handful of sloppily made, unengaging chase sequences in which the monsters hunt down the kids and kill them (but without the excitement it should contain). *Wrong Turn* is certainly an apt title. It may bear a certain resemblance to films of the horror days of yore, but it has none of what made them good. —*T. S.*

X THE UNKNOWN L: HORROR/HAMMER FILMS (1956) 91M D: *Dean Jagger, Anthony Newley, Edward Chapman, Leo McKern.* Hammer's attempt to replicate the success of *The Quatermass Xperiment* without author Nigel Kneale (this was scripted by Jimmy Sangster) takes a low-key approach with a polite, soft-spoken hero (Jagger as Dr. Royston) and a creature from inner space. Villagers die of unidentifiable burns and radioactive material mysteriously disappears from labs and hospitals, and sure enough, a pool of intelligent sludge from the Earth's core has risen to feed. The creature is scarier offscreen than on and the script lacks the sharpness and bite of Kneale, but the moody night shooting and marshy locations set a terrific mood and the startling effect of the flesh melting off the bones of victims lingers long after the film is over. —*S. A.*

X-FILES: THE COMPLETE FIRST SEASON L: SCIENCE FICTION/SCIENCE FICTION TV (1993) 1104M D: Rob Bowman, Cliff Bole, others. *Gillian Anderson, David Duchovny, Mitch Pileggi, William B. Davis.* Welcome to the *X-Files*, a series that altered television history, leading to many clones, copycats, and references in other TV shows. The first season introduces the believer and the cynic. FBI Special Agent Dana Scully (Anderson) is brought in to report on and debunk the work of fellow Agent Fox Mulder (Duchovny) on paranormal or other usual cases. Quickly, through Scully's honest nature, Mulder's powerful beliefs and uncanny instincts, and cases too strange and bizarre to be explained solely by science and logic, Scully forms a united front with Mulder, bringing reason and science to his pursuits. In turn Mulder opens Scully's eyes to a myriad of possibilities she would not have considered before. Most of these episodes are stand-alones, but keep your eyes peeled! Certain faces and plot points drop into our unsuspecting laps, and they will come back to tease us. This is the season that started it all, with refreshing and unique stories, exciting character development, and a winning chemistry between the two leads. It's no wonder this series became as popular as it did. —*M. N.*

X-FILES: THE COMPLETE SECOND SEASON L: SCIENCE FICTION/SCIENCE FICTION TV (1994) 1104M D: Rob Bowman, Cliff Bole, others. *David Duchovny, Gillian Anderson, Mitch Pileggi, William B. Davis, Nicholas Lea.* The second season picks up shortly after the climactic end of first, with the culmination of previous events leading to the official separation of Mulder and Scully. This was due in part to Anderson's pregnancy; they needed to reduce her screen time to hide her ever-increasing size. Enter Alex Krycek (Lea), Mulder's temporary partner and future ongoing thorn in his side. This season delves more heavily into story arcs and starts a chain reaction of conspiracies that trickles through the rest of the series. It is also proof positive that the chemistry of Duchovny and Anderson cannot be denied. The few episodes where Scully is completely absent are definitely lacking. There were also missed opportunities with Krycek; his time as Mulder's partner was shorter and less manipulative than it could have been. Still, it's a powerful season with some amazing episodes, brilliant stories, and great acting. These are the golden years of the *X-Files*, so drink up, me hearties! —*M. N.*

X-FILES: "BAD BLOOD" (SEASON 5, DISC 3) L: SCIENCE FICTION/SCIENCE FICTION TV (1997) 60M D: Cliff Bole. *David Duchovny, Luke Wilson, Gillian Anderson.* I watched *The X-Files* because it was a smartly written and directed show full of spooky ideas, but I gave it up as the stories became more involved in the complex alien/black oil/cigarette smoker conspiracy and lost their humor. My favorites were always the more comedic episodes and this was the best of those. The story opens with Mulder chasing a young man in the woods, pinning him to the ground, and pounding a stake through his heart. Mulder pushes open the dead man's lips to reveal vampire fangs—which suddenly fall out, because they're made of plastic. Mulder begins to exclaim "Oh shit!" but is cut off by the *X-Files* theme song. As the two agents defend against the family's lawsuit, the events leading up to the staking are told through their distinct points of view (ala *Rashomon*) with each portraying themselves heroically and the others ridiculously. There is also an amusing discrepancy between their takes on the town sheriff (Wilson), whom Scully sees as a handsome stud and Mulder sees as a bumbling hick with an overbite. —*B. T.*

X-FILES: "HOME" (SEASON 4, DISC 1) L: SCIENCE FICTION/SCIENCE FICTION TV (1996) 60M D: Kim Manners. *David Duchovny, Gillian Anderson.* This is, hands-down, the scariest thing to ever play on network television. This story of a creepy family of incestuous murderers who keep their deformed mother underneath the floorboards terrified me, something no television show and few movies have ever done. Public response to the episode kept the network from ever showing it again, and it played only once on FX. Now watch it on DVD in pristine quality. It's seriously creepy shit. —*T. S.*

X-FILES: "JOSE CHUNG'S 'FROM OUTER SPACE'" **(SEASON 3, DISC 5)** L: SCIENCE FICTION/SCIENCE FICTION TV (1995) 60M D: Rob Bowman. *Alex Trebek, Charles Nelson Reilly, Gillian Anderson, David Duchovny, Jesse Ventura.* Scully's favorite writer Jose Chung (Reilly) interviews her for a book about alien abductions, and she tells him about one of her weirdest cases. This is the show at its best, an ingenious comedy episode full of hilarious twists and turns: an alien autopsy that reveals a zipper, a man in black said to look a lot like Alex Trebek (played, of course, by Trebek himself), a D&D-playing UFO victim that writes up his entire ordeal in screenplay format, Mulder and

Scully acting completely out of character when depicted from the point of view of unreliable witnesses. This is one of those classic television episodes that will always be remembered regardless of your continued fondness of the series as a whole. —*B. T.*

X-FILES: FIGHT THE FUTURE L: SCIENCE FICTION/SCIENCE FICTION TV (1998) 120M D: Rob Bowman. *David Duchovny, Gillian Anderson.* Scully and Mulder finally make it to the big screen with this film, which doesn't let down fans of the TV series. The story involves an alien plot to take over the world, which may seem like the most tried-and-true plot of sci-fi history, but given the tenor of the series it's very much on par with what these two FBI agents are used to doing. The only problem is that it feels like just another episode of the show, a two-parter meant to fill the time of a feature-length film. The familiar "to be continued" credit that would be used if this were actually a TV broadcast would go right in the middle of the film where Scully nearly kisses Mulder. —*N. J.*

YOKAI MONSTERS: SPOOK WARFARE L: JAPANESE HORROR/JAPANESE HORROR (1968) 79M D: Yoshiyuki Kuroda. *Yoshihiko Aoyama, Hideki Hanamura, Chikara Hashimoto, Hiromi Inoue, Mari Kanda.* Grave robbers in Babylonia unleash a bloodsucking demon that heads for Japan, where he kills and replaces a kind magistrate. When a froglike water imp sees what's going on, he rallies an army of spirits to fight off the demon. Nice, atmospheric lighting and photography, but what makes this movie stand out is the incredible menagerie of strange creatures. There's a woman with an expanding neck, a one-legged umbrella monster, and numerous other apparitions that resemble the adorable characters you see on Japanese toys and stationary. It's as if Sid and Marty Krofft had a much bigger budget and were interested in Japanese mythology. —*B. T.*

ZEDER L: HORROR/ZOMBIES (1983) 98M D: Pupi Avati. *Anne Canovas, Paola Tanziani, Gabriele Lavia, Cesare Barbetti.* Avati, the director of such lush, ironic Italian romances as *The Best Man* and *The Story of Boys and Girls*, cut his teeth in the horror industry. This unusual and surprising mix of science fiction conspiracy, supernatural investigation, and zombie horror (think *Pet Sematary* as a corporate experiment) eschews the baroque stylistic flash of Dario Argento for eerie imagery and beautifully sustained mood. Lavia plays a writer who finds a strange story imprinted on the ribbon of a used typewriter. His investigations dig up a supposedly dead scientist (who appears very much alive) and a twisted science project of the dead. Lavia makes a rather bland lead (his flat English dubbing doesn't help) and the plot gets a bit confused, but the film never slackens. The ominous tone is more suggestive than horrific and the visuals are arresting:

houses strain and moan as if coming alive and hands push through walls and floors like flowers of death. —S.A.

ZONE 39 L: SCIENCE FICTION/SCIENCE FICTION (1997) 93M D: John Tatoulis. *Carolyn Bock, Peter Phelps, William Zappa.* A loyal soldier (Phelps), grieving for his murdered wife, sends himself into a virtual exile guarding the border at a lonely outpost so he can live with the shadow of his wife in a drug-addled existence. Making the most of a budget that wouldn't cover craft services for an Adam Sandler film, Tatoulis creates an eerily empty frontier in a war-torn future from desert irrigation ditches, abandoned cement buildings, and the cracking dam works of the parched sun-baked plain. The isolation brings the film inward, creating a compelling psychological drama with echoes of Andrei Tarkovksy's *Stalker* and *Solaris* in the midst of a conspiracy thriller. —S.A.

CHAPTER THIRTEEN

Sexploitation

Every technology in recorded history has been given the stamp of approval only after the sex industry, one way or another, has had its say. You think that prehistoric cave painters were only drawing bison? Think again. From cave walls to the Internet, "dirty pictures" have been put on display. Pornography is the most reliable litmus test for popular entertainment technology.

In some ways, we owe our very existence to the porn trade. In the early days, there was no indication that the home video business was going to survive. Movies were expensive to buy and the VCR had yet to become the ubiquitous household appliance it is now. But it wasn't long before the technology was embraced by the porn industry, and the home video market began to blossom. People (OK, mainly men) could now keep their trench coats in the closet, abandon the seedy, run-down porno theaters inevitably stuck in decaying neighborhoods, and enjoy the glory of pornography in the comfort of their own homes. Before long, people were renting and buying Hollywood movies as well. And the rest, as they say ...

But it is never that easy. Some people don't like pornography, some don't want it or, God forbid, need it, but it's always going to be here. Some people think it is a great evil—to women, to men, and to our society as a whole. Some of us at Scarecrow feel that way and some don't. We're no different than anyone else in that way. Pornography confronts us, in some form or other every

Candy (1968)

day. Whether it is pornographic violence, sex, attitudes, or advertising, porn pushes each of us to determine our own standards of what is acceptable and what is not, what contains dignity and what does not.

No matter what we think or feel about it, whether we care to face up to it or not, history tells us that pornography serves a purpose. Even so, it is a dicey line to walk. Among consenting adults, exactly where does the line between enjoyment and exploitation begin? Is there any way to keep the lid on an industry like this? Are those little T & A comedies we watched when we were teenagers like gateway drugs? Will some people just need more and more and more?

We don't answer those questions at our store. While this may be seen as a convenient stance for us to take, we just want to reflect the tastes and needs of our customers. Whether that means getting the latest Bollywood film or the latest Hustler porno, we offer what we offer. But we do have limits. When we do answer the question of how we do what we do, on a case-by-case basis, we answer with the standard of quality. Is the film well made? How does this film compare to others of its genre? Does this film have some sense of personality? Is it fun? Does it seem to have some art to it, or is it just purely exploitative? Sometimes the simple question, "Does it have a plot line?" is the deciding factor.

Inevitably, we find ourselves grouping certain directors together. These directors represent the best of the porn business. Artful, tasteful, well-photographed (usually on film), and pleasantly composed, the films by these directors reach for more than just a crotchful of happy funtime. These directors each have their own style and artistic vision. They have distinguished themselves over time with films uniquely their own, cheesy or erotic, straight-laced or fetish pleasing, softcore or hardcore, gay or straight.

So, if you are inclined to explore this realm of cinema, don't let us stop you. But be responsible about it, OK? Be mindful of others, don't do anything they don't want to do or go anywhere they don't want to go. Be healthy and be careful. And have fun!

ALL LADIES DO IT L: SEX DIRECTORS/BRASS, TINTO (1992) 88M D: Tinto Brass. *Claudia Koll, Paolo Lanza.* Koll is a flirtatious young wife who spices up her sex life by telling her husband all about her adventures, and then embellishes to the point he can't control his passions in Brass's continental erotic drama. It works until he finds out that one of her "adventures" is true. This piece of Italian erotica isn't deep but it is sexy, a love letter to Koll's bare, heart-shaped posterior. Don't bother with the story, it's all in the scenery, though the Venice settings are somewhat obscured by all the naked flesh that gets in the way. The dubbing in this English-language version is rather blunt and flat, but then who's listening to dialogue in a skin and sexfest? —*S. A.*

AMANDA BY NIGHT L: SEXPLOITATION/HARDX (XXX) (1981) 95M D: Gary Graver (as "Robert McCallum"). *Veronice Hart, Frank Hallowell.* Two prostitutes are dead and nice guy cop (Robert Kerman) thinks the real target is a self-reliant call-girl (Hart) who doesn't want his help. Sound familiar? Yeah, the two get together, but when the baddie shows and the cop's not there, she deals with it. The story toys you along nicely, in-between sex scenes—one monotonous screw after another. This is a hard-core porn film, directed and photographed by a cinematographer for Orson Welles. The humping scenes are almost too fastidious for words and ruin the pace. The remaining narrative is a bit forced. But it holds together somehow as a good erotic thriller. Emotions come off as real, particularly Hart's, and the story is ultimately compelling. One of early adult cinema's very best. —*J. C.*

AMAZON JAIL L: SEXPLOITATION/WOMEN IN PRISON (1985) 94M D: Osualdo De Oliveira. *Sérgio Hingst, Maurício do Valle, Sondra Graffi, Márcia Fraga, Elizabeth Hartmann.* Girls are lured to the jungle with promises of jobs, only to be sold to rich men instead. Those who escape are tracked. All hell breaks loose when trackers bring back three well-to-do local girls who harbored an escapee and witnessed her death. A mass escape ensues. But there's still the problem of poison snakes, poachers, animosities, and a company of illegal miners who want to keep the women. Unlike Oliveira's equally notorious film *Bare Behind Bars*, where a thin, semicomic plot proves mostly an excuse for prolific, and by-and-large uninteresting, nudity, *Amazon Jail* is a good little adventure story. Its grungy shadings of sex and violence feeling like the very nectar of freedom itself. —*J. C.*

AU PAIR GIRLS L: SEXPLOITATION/SEXPLOITATION (1972) 86M D: Val Guest. *Astrid Frank, Johnny Briggs, Me Me Lai, Nancie Wait, Gabrielle Drake.* Frank, Drake, Lai, and Wait are sexy foreign girls who fly in from all parts of the globe to learn English on the job in London. "Oh ya, I work with them all day, and at night I play with myself," giggles free-spirited Swede Frank (referring to her employer's color TV, obviously). In one wild night they lose their positions and their clothes. It's a silly British nudie cutie about drooling, lascivious men and willing young women getting it on in the sack, in the hayloft, in the car, in . . . you get the idea. British genre veteran Guest directs with spirit, giving a sense of fun and playful quality to an otherwise obvious bit of bird watching. —*S. A.*

BAD GIRLS DORMITORY L: SEXPLOITATION/WOMEN IN PRISON (1984) 95M D: Tim Kincaid. *Carey Zuris, Teresa Farley, Jennifer Delora.* The warden (Marita) is willfully clueless about the brutality and drugs that control the inner power structure of this reformatory for girls, tumbling the new girl (Zuris) about until she gets the lay of the land

and starts to take charge. Nothing new for the woman-in-prison genre so far. But this one stands out for the edginess of its nudity and the bitter harshness of its violence. Both the sex and violence have a very cool, almost indifferent side that in a flash turns very hot. This gives the damaged individuals a dynamic psychology most such films lack, unhampered by sentimentality or heroic aspirations. You see not why they are broken, but once broken, you see the twisted way in which they mend, becoming criminals for life. Even in this comic-book genre, uncomfortable truths do burn through. —*J. C.*

BAMBOO HOUSE OF DOLLS L: SEXPLOITATION/WOMEN IN PRISON (1974) 95M D: Chin Hung Kuei. *Niki Wane, Roska Rozen, Terry Liu, Wang Hsieh, Lieh Lo, Birte Tove.*
Japanese troops invade a local hospital unit looking for a fallen American pilot. Six of the patients are shot in front of their brethren. The troops take the nurses hostage and back to their concentration camp. A sadistic female warden orders a young Asian girl to lick her boots clean, with a nice tongue-against-leather close-up. Another girl is dragged out of an isolation cell is hung by her wrists in the prison yard. A shot from the doomed girl's nipple to the tight face of the warden is followed by the order, "Beat her to death!" Another inmate must hold the whip and beat the other into unconsciousness. She stops and is beaten herself until she resumes the brutal blows. She runs away and electrocutes herself on the hot fence, her mouth wide open in horror as her hand fuses with the wire. And this is only the first ten minutes! Eye-grabbing camera work, action scenes, brutality, and the excellent music score orchestrated by Wang Fu-Ling carry this film above the usual women-in-prison fare. —*S. R.*

BEAST THAT KILLED WOMEN, THE L: SEXPLOITATION/ SEXPLOITATION (1965) 61M D: Barry Mahon. *Darlene Bennett, Gigi Darlene, Dolores Carlos, Barry Mahon.*
This sex-horror masterpiece by Mahon is a great piece of trash cinema about a nudist colony where a giant rampaging ape attacks all the cute young girls. It's very poorly made using lots of really long takes of wide shots without ever cutting to close-ups. It makes no sense and the acting is terrible. But these are the reasons I like it. It's primal fun at its best. —*T. S.*

BEYOND THE VALLEY OF THE DOLLS L: SEX DIRECTORS/ MEYER, RUSS (1970) 110M D: Russ Meyer. *Marcia McBroom, Dolly Read, Cynthia Myers, John Lazar, Pam Grier, Michael Blodgett.*
"Buxotic" sexploitation filmmaker Meyer was given free reign for his first major studio production, a crazed non-sequel to *Valley of the Dolls.* Respectable film critic Roger Ebert's script finds a girl group, The Carrie Nations, who sing and sleep their way to stardom. Unfortunately, life gets complicated when the girls fall victim to those oh-so-familiar Hollywood excesses. This over-the-top

parody of Hollywood soap operas and overnight success stories is rich with quotable lines, typically excellent photography and editing, plus a cast padded out with Meyer regulars (like Erica Gavin, Haji, Charles Napier, and Edy Williams). The film's overall message is fairly conservative and the movie rejects the wild lifestyle it pretends to celebrate. But the fast pace, absurd plot twists, and outrageous dialogue have made it a cult favorite. —*S, H.*

BLACK MAMA, WHITE MAMA L: SEXPLOITATION/WOMEN IN PRISON (1973) 87M D: Eddie Romero. *Jess Ramos, Ricardo Herrero, Pam Grier, Margaret Markov.*
Excellent shot-in-the-Philippines flick with bare-breasted women, loads of social cynicism, and virtually everyone dying. Two new prisoners to a female prison camp escape, after the requisite shower, fight, and hot-box scenes. The blonde (Markov) has revolutionary friends plus the key to their arms shipment. The black woman (Grier) has money stashed but her pimp is after her. Each woman wants to go her separate way, but they are chained together. Putting panties on a dog to throw off the tracking hounds and using nuns and a cowboy, they make their way to the coast. There, gangsters, prison cops, a regional military unit, and revolutionaries all collide. One of the women dies bloodily, and little good comes of it. An amusing, sometimes quite shrewd little satire. —*J. C.*

BORN INNOCENT L: SEXPLOITATION/WOMEN IN PRISON (1974) 92M D: Donald Wrye. *Linda Blair, Joanna Miles, Richard Jaeckel, Kim Hunter.*
Blair, in her first movie after *The Exorcist,* plays a fourteen-year-old chronic runaway who gets locked up in a brutal all-girl juvenile detention center where she is mistreated by an uncaring staff, ignored by her parents (Hunter and Jaeckel), screwed over by the system, tormented by her peers, and, most shockingly, raped in the bathroom with a broom handle. It's harsh stuff and you got to give it to Blair for her committed performance. It's hard to believe this gritty and graphic juvie drama was made for television and I'm not sure what the movie's point is (besides showing suffering teenage girls), as Blair never really learns her lesson. The notorious rape scene, removed after a family sued ABC after a copycat attack, has been restored for the video release. —*S. H.*

CANADIAN BALLET: STRIPTEASE DANCERS OF THE NORTH L: SEXPLOITATION/SEX DOCS (1998) 90M D: Paul Borghese. *Devina Dreams, Kathryn Allard.*
Gritty, in-your-face sexuality with no touching allowed, this near-excellent documentary focuses on the exotic dance industry in Canada. Canadian law and tradition require strippers be paid as performers on stage with no lap-dancing allowed. So making money is tied to how good and innovative they are, not from bouncing on men's crotches. Which means winning contests to become a top-pay headliner. Filmmakers inter-

view several on a range of issues from the art of dancing, money, and family back home to lover's attitudes, exercise, and breast implants, and public attitude toward strippers versus their own self-respect. But it is the too-little-shown dancing that shines. All performers here reveal something smart and original in their movement. Four soar. And two are just plain off the chart. —*J. C.*

CANDY L: SEXPLOITATION/SEXPLOITATION (1968) 115M D: Christian Marquand. *Walter Matthau, Ringo Starr, Ewa Aulin, Richard Burton, Marlon Brando, James Coburn.* This infamous *Candide* for the swinging '60s, adapted by sly satirist Buck Henry from counterculture legend Terry Southern's novel, is supposed to be a rollicking social satire. Instead, this Euro-pudding misfire is little more than a clumsy, intermittently funny romp through stuffy French director Marquand's idea of American decadence. Burton and Brando come off the best, tossing caution to the wind in hysterically over-the-top performances (as a drunken, sex-mad Welsh poet and a phony, sex-mad guru, respectively), while bland, curvy, wide-eyed Swedish kewpie doll Aulin coasts through as the naive teenager they coax out of her mini-dress and into the sack. It's a bewildering curiosity and the most star-studded sex farce ever made. —*S. A.*

CHAINED HEAT L: SEXPLOITATION/WOMEN IN PRISON (1983) 95M D: Lutz Schaarwächter (as "Paul Nicolas"). *Linda Blair, Sybil Danning, Monique Gabrielle.* Slick, yet one of the cheesier woman-in-prison films, with a most extreme plot: rival black and white gangs in prison. They fight for control over the drug trade between the warden with his goons and the captain with her goons. There is a full-frontal shower sequence for all but the principals (though even Blair and Danning are topless). An inmate (Gabrielle) performs a nice striptease number to please her favorite master. Quirky, occasionally quite frisky acting. There's a rape, a hanging, a stabbing, a nasty hooking implement, plus bloody makeup effects. The story is silly but told seriously, with blacks and whites joining in a riot for justice at the end. —*J. C.*

CHATTERBOX L: SEXPLOITATION/SEXPLOITATION (1977) 73M D: Tom DeSimone. *Perry Bullington, Candice Rialson, Rip Taylor, Jane Kean, Larry Gelman.* Take a hairdresser, a talking vagina, and Perry Bullington and you have the next best thing to the *Stardust* series. Penny (Rialson), a young beautician, begins to hear a strange voice. Could it be her conscience? No, it's her musically talented vagina. Penny tries to keep this sassy voice from the public, which proves to be impossible in her work uniform. Penny begins to realize that "Virginia" cannot be quieted and instead must be appeased. The musical numbers are fantastic and the costumes bring tears to my glitter-loving eyes. The story keeps a good pace and it's all

pretty well-written, for a movie about a talking vagina. —*J. J.*

CHEERLEADERS, THE L: SEXPLOITATION/SEXPLOITATION (1972) 82M D: Paul Glickler. *Debbie Lowe, Stephanie Fondue, Jovita Bush, John Jacobs, Denise Dillaway.* *The Cheerleaders* is the kind of sexploitation/ drive-in fare sorely missed today. The film is filled with young girls who actually look their age and there is no silicone in sight—how refreshing! The film kicked off a string of cheerleader-themed exploitation pictures in the '70s. Jeannie (played by the nubile beauty Fondue) wants to become a cheerleader because she hopes it will cure her virginity problem. Of course, many hijinks and shenanigans ensue along her quest for sex. The acting is quite terrible but who cares when you have so many attractive women taking it off and having sex every chance they get? The film is actually pretty funny and is filled with many bizarre, almost surreal scenes. My favorite involves a creepy janitor in a bear mascot suit trying to get in on the action. —*S. W. F.*

CONCRETE JUNGLE, THE L: SEXPLOITATION/WOMEN IN PRISON (1982) 99M D: Tom de Simone. *Jill St. John, Camille Keaton, Tracy Bregman, Barbara Luna.* This nicely scripted and directed jailhouse film is low on sleaze. Trying to be serious, it may not be sociologically accurate, but it is psychologically apt. Caught for unknowingly bringing her boyfriend's drugs into the country, the girl (Bregman) stays silent, trusting him. Inside, she gets pegged mostly unfairly as a troublemaker, gets solitary, and is raped and attacked by goons of the top inmate (Luna), who wants power over her. But still she won't talk to a reform-minded social worker, and instead very shrewdly begins to fight back. No cheesy shower scenes or talk of escape, only power and control drive these characters. The one shocker comes when a prisoner (Keaton) being moved to different cellblock is raped halfway; the lurch of her body and squeal of her pain tell you everything you need to know about the ends of power in such a place! A very nasty yet pertinent exclamation point on a very good, very different type of women-in-prison film. —*J. C.*

DAYDREAM (HAKUJITSUMU) L: SEXPLOITATION/ASIAN/X (1964) 92M D: Tetsuji Takechi. *Kanako Michi, Akira Ishihama, Choyuro Hanakawa.* A young man (Ishihama) watches from just outside the window as a woman performer (Michi) who sang to him in the club is now being tied, whipped, and electrocuted by the sadistic club owner (Hanakawa), and he can do nothing to help. This extraordinary little film was the beginning of pink films in Japan. Based on an erotic short story by Junichiro Tanazaki, the scene is just the result of their neurotic fear of the seemingly sadistic dentist by both a woman and man in the dentist chairs about to go under with laughing gas. But the power of the joint hallucination is

Sexiest movies

BARBARELLA

BESIEGED

BOOGIE NIGHTS

BREATHLESS

BRING IT ON

UN CHANT D'AMOUR

CLAIRE'S KNEE

THE CONFORMIST

EDWARD II

EYES WIDE SHUT

HAPPY TOGETHER

HENRY AND JUNE

HISTORY IS MADE AT NIGHT

IN THE MOOD FOR LOVE

LADY EVE

LOST HIGHWAY

PRIDE AND PREJUDICE *(1995)*

QUERELLE

SPIDER-MAN

(upside-down kiss in the rain)

THE UNBEARABLE LIGHTNESS OF BEING

remarkable: the woman singing moody lyrics in the club, or tortured, or being chased dream-slow naked down a department store's up escalator. Takechi came from experimental theater to create this stunning visual document and change Japanese films forever. —*J. C.*

DEEP THROAT L: SEX DIRECTORS/DAMIANO, GERARDO (1972) 60M D: Gerardo Damiano. *Harry Reems, Linda Lovelace.* This movie (and *Behind the Green Door*) set the stage for "porno chic," an era when it was OK for regular folks to see a dirty movie. Lovelace stars as a woman who is dissatisfied with her very active (and kinky) sex life. Her clever, well-hung doctor (Reems) discovers the problem: her clitoris is actually located at the back of her throat, and much cock sucking ensues. *Deep Throat* was a phenomenon at the time of its release and is still notorious today. It's a lousy movie, though; not only is *Deep Throat* boring at times, Lovelace later revealed how she was abused by her husband and forced to perform the many degrading sexual acts in the movie. This fact renders her enthusiastic performance

and the movie almost unwatchable. Still, it's pretty strange to think of how many "normal" couples saw this movie. —*S. H.*

DEVIL IN MISS JONES, THE L: SEX DIRECTORS/DAMIANO, GERARDO (1972) 70M D: Gerardo Damiano. *Georgina Spelvin, Harry Reems.* Spelvin stars as a repressed spinster who commits suicide and finds herself in a sexy limbo where she is carnally educated by Reems and other well-endowed performers. She transforms into a sex-crazed supervixen who engages in increasingly kinky behavior. Spelvin was an unusual porno star as she doesn't fit the normal physical model, but she makes up for the lack of gigantic cans with an enthusiastic performance filled with lots of raunchy talk and uninhibited fucking. The film ends with Miss Jones unable to find sexual release and locked in a room with a babbling impotent lunatic (played by the director). *The Devil in Miss Jones* is actually a pretty depressing movie, but was insanely popular back in the day and helped usher in the era of "porno-chic," when explicit adult films entered the mainstream and were viewed by average Americans everywhere. —*S. H.*

DIRTY GIRLS, THE L: SEX DIRECTORS/METZGER, RADLEY (1964) 82M D: Radley Metzger. *Marlene Sherter, Denyse Roland, Peter Parten, Reine Rohan.* Metzger's first stab at erotic filmmaking is a teasing little confection that combines the rambling looseness of the French New Wave with the chic elegance of Michelangelo Antonioni and company to create trash with class. With only glimpses of nudity, this tale of two streetwalkers (one in Paris, one in Munich) seems tame by modern standards, but Metzger's pre-AIDS continental attitude is both knowing and innocently hedonistic, taking pleasure in the smiles, looks, and fleshy pageant of foreplay. Hans Jura's cool, graceful photography and the jazzy score add to the Euro-sheen, which is broken only when a businessman opens his mouth and out rolls the voice of Speed Racer! —*S. A.*

DOUBLE AGENT 73 L: SEX DIRECTORS/WISHMAN, DORIS (1970) 73M D: Doris Wishman. *Frank Silvano, Chesty Morgan.* Polish stripper turned "actress" Morgan and her outlandishly huge jugs (the "73" is for inches) star as a secret agent in this unbelievable film brought to us by exploitation goddess Wishman (probably the only director who could think of casting Morgan, one of the most conspicuous creatures ever to walk to the earth, as a secret agent). Her top-secret mission involves taking photos of bad guys. But instead of just giving her a camera, her bosses have one surgically implanted in her left breast and set to explode thirty-six hours later. In order to take photos, she must remove her top and fondle her mammoth melons, giving her plenty of opportunities to flaunt her meal tickets. Viewers also are treated to some interesting, boob-oriented killings. Breast lovers, beware: it's highly unlikely you'll find yourself attracted to the horrifically large, malformed mounds found on Morgan's chest. That said, any exploitation film fan would be depriving themselves by missing this classic. —E. O.

DR. CALIGARI L: SEXPLOITATION/SEXPLOITATION (1989) 80M
D: Stephen Sayadian. *Jennifer Balgobin, John Durbin, Laura Albert, Fox Harris, Madeleine Reynal.* Brought to you by the makers of the film *Flesh Gordon, Dr. Caligari* is a very strange sequel to the 1919 German silent film *The Cabinet of Dr. Caligari.* Reynal is Dr. Caligari, the heir of the famous head of the asylum in the silent classic. She is now in charge of the asylum and holds a terrible psycho-sexual control over the patients. With brilliant color, outrageous direction, a crazed script, and bizarre special effects *Dr. Caligari* is just the kind of film that will burn through your retinas and leave an indelible impression on your brain. —N. J.

EROTIC ADVENTURES OF PINOCCHIO, THE L: SEXPLOITATION/SEXPLOITATION (1971) 79M D: Corey Allen.
Alex Roman, Monica Gayle. The not-so-creative tagline, "It's not his nose that grows!," reveals the gimmick of this campy '70s pseudo-porn. Gepetta is not the old-man toy maker of the more traditional versions of this story, but is instead a lusty young nympho craving some action. Instead of going with more, uh, conventional approaches, she carves herself a man out of wood and does the deed with him, thus bringing him to life. The fairy godmother responsible for this transformation warns him to save his man-love for Gepetta, but his "woody" seems to have a mind of its own. Things get all wacky as he goes around banging all kinds of chicks, despite the warning of what would happen if he did. Very, very softcore and without much adventure, this film doesn't even begin to touch on sexy. It is, however, good for a few laughs. —J. S.

EROTIC SURVIVOR L: SEXPLOITATION/SEXPLOITATION (2001) 97M D: John Bacchus. *Misty Mundae, Darian Caine.* "Eight people. Two tribes. Three days. $20." Is Bacchus a genius of softcore pop culture parody, or merely a schlub with a video camera who lucked into a successful vein of straight-to-video knockoffs? While *Erotic Survivor* is no *Erotic Witch Project* (heck, the gorilla only makes a cameo here), it's funnier than it has any right to be and once again turns the low-budget video aesthetic into spot-on parody. The tribal party games and conniving web of alliances and double crossings are like an elaborate theater exercise Bacchus hews into a smart-ass version of TV's cult phenomenon, with extended time-outs for girl-on-girl groping and licking (in a mud pit even—yech!). He knows his audience. —S. A.

EROTIC WITCH PROJECT L: SEXPLOITATION/SEXPLOITATION (1999) 78M D: John Bacchus. *Katie Keane, Victoria Vega, Darian Cane.* "I'm so horny, and I'm so scared at the same time." Bacchus's softcore parody of you-know-what is clumsy, ridiculous, and baldly exploitative—so why do I like it? Perhaps it's the anatomically correct stick figures the girls find outside their tents (along with the message: "Eat me"), or the creepy offscreen howls that sound of coital ecstasy, or the unexplained guy in the ratty gorilla suit who falls in love with a blow-up doll and picks up the camera when the girls are too busy, uh, getting aroused. Did I mention someone steals their clothes when they steal their map? And they don't care? It's as terrible as it is inspired, and at times it stumbles into near genius. —S. A.

ESCAPE FROM WOMEN'S PRISON L: SEXPLOITATION/WOMEN IN PRISON (1978) 95M D: Giovanni Brusadori. *Ines Pellegrini, Lilli Carati, Zora Kerova.* Sleazy, effective little movie with harsh ironies. Heavily armed escaped female convicts with a wounded male accomplice hijack a busload of female tennis players. They take them to a judge's estate to exact some personal revenge and patch up the wounded male. Each tennis player strategizes their escape, and some lovely and some marvelously twisted manipulative sex scenes ensue. The chords of politics, greed, and personal vendetta begin to chime louder than the former prisoners' goal of escaping. With tennis players making their moves as cops surround the villa, everything begins to unravel. Edgy, salacious fun with nice, gritty performances and some hard-edged surprises by the end. —J. C.

FASTER, PUSSYCAT! KILL! KILL! L: SEX DIRECTORS/MEYER, RUSS (1966) 83M D: Russ Meyer. *Lori Williams, Tura Satana, Haji.* "Welcome To Violence!" Three strippers driving fast cars in the desert meet up with a young couple. They brutally kill the man and abduct the woman. Later they plan to rob an old man and have sex with his sons. This is Meyer's most remembered film and it has become a cult classic. Even though it's not his best movie, it's still jam-packed with sex, violence, trash, and sleaze. And that's what Meyer is all about. —T. S.

GOODBYE EMMANUELLE (EMMANUELLE 3) L: SEXPLOITATION/EMMANUELLE (1977) 95M D: François Leterrier.
Sylvia Kristel, Umberto Orsini, Jean-Pierre Bouvier, Charlette Alexandra. By far the best of Kristel's three-and-a-half Emmanuelle movies, and likely more deeply engrossing than any of the dozens that followed because this one nails down a concrete place (tropical Seychelles) and an adventurous husband, Jean (Orsini). A social network replete with unending emotional tangles gives the lively party they attend a complicated texture that never quite evaporates from their lives once the focused adventures begin. A man interests Emmanuelle but he is more caught up in his film project than in her. He finally agrees to see the unusual place she speaks of, a day's journey away, imagining a possible shooting location. The

seduction does not go as planned, though. Once home, she realizes the day was a horizon-event, that something in her life is about to change. *Goodbye Emmanuelle* trips resonant chords that never quite turn soapy—real-life chords that say goodbye forever to erotic solipsism. —*J. C.*

HARRAD EXPERIMENT, THE L: SEXPLOITATION/
SEXPLOITATION (1973) 96M D: Ted Post. *Laurie Walters, Don Johnson, Tippi Hedren, Bruno Kirby, James Whitmore.* During the age of Free Love, a small, private college is formed where professors conduct an experiment on teaching sexuality. This involves a number of young students, including a very young Don Johnson, taught how to lower their inhibitions, be at peace with each other, and, of course, have multiple sex partners. Evidently the film takes itself seriously, as it was based on the best seller by Robert Rimmer. But given the subject matter, the script, and the quality of acting, it's hard not to let out a few belly laughs during what are supposed to be sensitive scenes. —*N. J.*

HOT SPUR, THE L: SEXPLOITATION/SEXPLOITATION (1971)
91M D: Lee Frost. *James Arena, Virginia Gordon, Joseph Mascolo.* A stark tale of a poor Mexican boy who kidnaps the rich white rancher's wife in vengeance over the man's long-ago rape of his sister. The boy and his prisoner hole up in a defensible hilltop cabin, letting the rancher know the location. "Come alone and stop sending your boys" is the message he sends back with a wounded ranch hand. But this tale gets starker still. He apologizes to the wife but says he must strip and abuse her—the rich man must know damage has been done to his "property." And in her teeth-gritting way she even understands: as with her husband's racism toward Mexicans, so, too, is this Mexican's sexism toward her. He is a brutal man. The tale ends not well or badly: but interestingly. Frost and R.W. Cresse are the best exploitation filmmakers for going after the darkest nastiest places in human endeavor. Emotionally, *The Hot Spur* is perhaps the most bluntly cold and honest Western ever made. It is certainly cruel. And the storytelling's scrape and scratch style is a spur up the ass. The most unlikely great Western ever filmed. —*J. C.*

HUMAN EXPERIMENTS L: SEXPLOITATION/WOMEN IN
PRISON (1979) 82M D: Gregory Goodell. *Lynda Haynes, Geoffrey Lewis.* This modest woman-in-prison picture is graced with a tight little story and as perfect an ending as you could ever ask for. A singer (Haynes) at her wit's end throws a fit when a club owner reneges on their contract and she ends up in jail. The nude delousing and shower scene is detached and asexual. The only erotic moment is her discreet nighttime masturbation in her lonely cell. Jail conditions are not baroque, so when she is offered benefits for volunteering for medical research, the internal alarm bells don't automatically go off. Suspicion

is slow to build, as is the recognition of the doc's perversity (Lewis) and the twistedness of what lies behind these human experiments. Not your typical B movie, this is an understated masterpiece of character and tone. —*J. C.*

I, A WOMAN L: SEXPLOITATION/SEXPLOITATION (1965) 95M
D: Mac Ahlberg. *Preben Mahrt, Preben Kørning, Erik Hell, Tove Maës, Jørgen Reenberg, Essy Persson.* Second for second, this may be the sexiest film ever made: a flirting, prickly pertness in face and eyes and moving torso of Siv (Persson) or the men attracted to her when touched by the slightest sexual thought. Seen best in Ahlberg's intimate black-and-white photography, these signals of sensual interest ripple across space connecting one person to the other and them to you. But *I, a Woman* is also a very discreet film: a momentary glimmer of naked skin, the textured bare stretches of flesh finding fullness only in sensually and emotionally full moments. Siv's mother is an evangelical convert whose only sensual joy comes in the pulsing Heaven-bound songs she sings. Her father's rare violin playing is esthetic heaven to Siv. But it is time to leave home and the fiancé and the married sensualist who relieved her of her virginity, time to make a way that is her own. *I, a Woman* asks more questions than it answers, like a very adult movie should, while it deeply stirs the soul. —*J. C.*

IMAGE, THE (AKA THE PUNISHMENT OF ANNE) L: SEX
DIRECTORS/METZGER, RADLEY (1976) 89M D: Radley Metzger. *Marilyn Roberts, Carl Parker, Rebecca Brooke.* This contains one of the shrewdest stories in all of cinema, directed by erotic cinema's most talented stylist. Jean (Parker) comes to Claire's party after a long absence. Claire (Roberts) hints she has something to show him he might be interested in—the masochist Anne (Brooke), who is totally servile to Claire. With Jean as audience, their dungeon games deepen the experience for both women and make them reach for more exquisite forms of pain and, eventually, very dangerous practices. With lovely scenes that become as barbed as Anne's sought-after pain, it gets darker and starker, as it slowly dawns why Claire is pushing so far. Intelligent, harsh, and unremitting, and most likely the finest erotic movie (softcore or hard) ever made. —*J. C.*

IMMORAL TALES L: SEXPLOITATION/SEXPLOITATION (1975)
103M D: Walerian Borowczyk. *Paloma Picasso, Charlotte Alexandra, Florence Bellamy, Lise Danvers, Pascale Christophe, Marie Forså.* Four lascivious tales told so dryly as to almost evaporate all their erotic juices. A boy teaches his young female cousin "the mystery of the tides," demanding fellatio be performed on him exactly as the tide hits the high-water mark. Spirits lead a pious girl to an old book of pornographic drawings, and she puts to good use the smooth household religious implements she loves, abandoning her home only to be raped by a beggar. Countess

Joe Sarno

Born in 1921, Joe Sarno is noted for making sex films with integrity. During the '60s, at a time when most exhibitors and distributors would have been perfectly happy with an hour and a half of naked flesh followed by a final title card, Sarno was making daring, challenging films that were much better than they needed to be. A psychology major in college, he produced, wrote, and directed erotic movies with strong moral and archetypal underpinnings. His films are full of mind games, secret rituals, role playing, masks, and strong, often dominant female characters.

Women often respond strongly to Sarno's films. He has said, "I stress the efficacy of women for themselves. In general, I try to focus on the female orgasm as much as I can. Women have much more imagination than men." Those familiar with the sex films of the '60s can appreciate how radical these sentiments were at the time. Sarno's most important collaborator was his wife, Peggy Steffans, who acted in many of his films before becoming his assistant director and producer.

By Sarno's count, he made more than 200 films. While this is impossible to confirm, it's probably not far from the truth. His films often resound within the subconscious, like a strange yet fascinating dream that haunts the dreamer all day. The most bizarre Sarno movies, like *The Sex Cycle* (1966), *Veil of Blood* (1973), and the unbelievable *Young Playthings* (1972), are made all the more surreal by their low budgets and occasionally less-than-believable performances. Sarno was smart and canny enough to use these deficiencies as strengths. His *Inga* was a major hit stateside and, together with his earlier *Sin You Sinners*, is probably his best-known work.

—*Lars Nilsen*

Bathory (Picasso) lures virgin peasant girls with promises of jewels and "immortality" to romp naked about her castle then be harvested for their youth-renewing blood for Bathory's bath. Lucretia Borgia brings her weak husband to Rome to see her father the Pope and her Cardinal brother poison her husband and baptize her incestuously fathered child. These are the most obscure, dark, ironic, deeply intelligent erotic shorts ever made. —*J. C.*

INGA L: SEX DIRECTORS/SARNO, JOE (1967) 86M D: Joseph W. Sarno. *Sissi Kaiser, Else-Marie Brandt, Marie Liljedahl, Monica Strömmerstedt, Casten Lassen, Thomas Ungewitter.* Recently orphaned teen Inga (Liljedahl) comes to live with her middle-class Aunt Greta. Greta is strapped for cash, and her writer-protégé Karl (Lassen) has an expensive lifestyle. From just a taste of Aunt Greta's sophisticated social circle, the young virgin grows up quickly and begins to dream (in her bed alone at night, with hands all over her body!). Rich, older gentleman friend Einar (Ungewitter) desires companionship Greta is tired of providing, and Inga is nudged in Einar's direction. Sarno's movie made a huge splash in the '60s. It was treated as a coming-of-age story—pretty nice one if you focus on the young innocent of the title. But focus on the aunt and the bleak manipulative character of her world, and it becomes a nasty and unremittingly flinty critique of the sophisticated conduct of the very social set that loved this film. Great exploiter, as cynical as they come! —*J. C.*

INVASION OF THE BEE GIRLS L: SEXPLOITATION/ SEXPLOITATION (1973) 85M D: Denis Sanders. *Victoria Vetri, William Smith, Rene Bond, Anitra Ford.* "They'll love the life out of your body!" Male research scientists are mysteriously dying of sexual exhaustion in this classic '70s tongue-in-cheek sexploitation sci-fi flick. A government agent, played by B-movie biker and *Hawaii 5-0* star Smith, discovers that a group of women, led by queen bee Ford (formerly on *The Price Is Right!*), have turned themselves into sunglass-wearing nymphomaniacs who leave their men smiling … and dead. It's pretty tacky, stupid, and poorly acted but features some amusing scenes and lots of boobs. There's one tasteless, pointless near gang rape, but otherwise it's a fun flashback. The script writer, Nicholas Meyer, went on to write and direct *Star Trek II: The Wrath of Khan* and *Time After Time.* —*S. H.*

JEWEL RAIDER L: SEXPLOITATION/HARDX (XXX) (2001) 75M D: Jay Jeff. *Nicole Sheridan, Dominica Leoni, Mike Horner, Voodoo, Venus.* Venus plays Laura Croff, a thief who dresses suspiciously like Lara Croft from the video game *Tomb Raider.* I wonder if they ever had a *Ms. Pac-Man* porn. Laura tries to steal an alien artifact from another thief, but she has to fight and/or have sex with many people who stand in her way. This is an early entry in the funny subgenre of porn that tries to include legitimate action scenes along with the, uh, action scenes. Venus does choreographed fights against real stuntmen, often spinning around on gymnastic rings as a cheapie version of wire fu. By porn standards, or by crappy shot-on-video home movie standards, it's pretty professional. There's even a car chase with a close-up of Venus sitting in a parked car pretending to turn the steering wheel. Unfortunately, the jokey mood is spoiled by forced S&M sex with the villain, which apparently interests some video game–playing porn fans. (The Lara Croft/S&M theme was later explored in Olivier Assayas's *Demonlover.*) —*B. T.*

LET MY PUPPETS COME L: SEX DIRECTORS/DAMIANO, GERARDO (1976) 74M D: Gerard Damiano. *Gerard Damiano.* You can't hear the phrase "puppet porn" without being at least a little curious, right? From the director of cult-porno *Deep Throat,* the title of this film pretty much speaks for itself. There's an abundance of hot puppet-on-puppet action. Naked human people appear periodically, but nothing much happens with them outside of the gratuitous factor. A puppet dog gets involved at one point, which is a little creepy, but I guess the perks of making a porno with nonhuman actors include being able to transcend those pesky species boundaries that can be so problematic in regular porn. This film's most redeeming quality is its novelty, but that doesn't really last very long. After the first ten minutes, you'll have probably had enough puppet sex, but if not, there will be another sixty-four minutes ready and waiting for you. —*J. S.*

LICKERISH QUARTET, THE L: SEX DIRECTORS/METZGER, RADLEY (1970) 90M D: Radley Metzger. *Paolo Turco, Erika Remberg, Frank Wolff, Silvana Venturelli.* A swinging continental couple and their decadent son spy a sexy young daredevil cyclist (Venturelli) at a local carnival and, convinced she is the erotic star they watched in a raw porn film earlier that evening, invite her to their castle. Metzger's deliriously erotic fantasy is like a stag film directed by Alain Resnais: lush, dense, sleekly grand, a heady hall of mirrors in a sensuous landscape. The mysterious young woman unlocks each character's fantasy in a blend of Psych 101 and sexual healing as she fulfills the libidinous desires of a bickering trio through a succession of seductive romps. But Metzger has the last word as he pushes the bounds between fantasy and reality into a game of illusionist hide and seek. Playful,

smart, ripe, and sensuous. Though rated X, it's an arty eroticism. —*S. A.*

LOVE CAMP 7 L: SEXPLOITATION/ILSA & FRIENDS (1969) 90M D: Lee Frost. *Phil Poth, John Alderman, Maria Lease, Kathy Williams.* With art, it is often said the whole is greater than the sum of its parts. With good exploitation films, the reverse is typically true. This has a not-very-compelling story with a clear and serviceable visual style, but lacks emotional resonance and the acting ranges from flat to grotesque. But *Love Camp 7* is packed end to end with great crazy little bits and lush enthralling sequences. During World War II, two female OSS spies (Lease and Williams) are sent undercover into a prison camp used as a brothel for German officers. Their assignment: to bring about the escape of a former assistant to a German nuclear scientist. The rest is the biting abuse the two women endure to accomplish their mission: hands tied with a rope lifting her so one spy is standing naked on her tiptoes being whipped, or the end's chaotic deadly shoot-out. Harsh lovely stuff. —*J. C.*

MUDHONEY L: SEX DIRECTORS/MEYER, RUSS (1965) 92M D: Russ Meyer. *Hal Hopper, Antointette Christiani, John Furlong, Rena Horten, Princess Livingston, Lorna Maitland.* Between 1964 and 1968, Meyer made ten films, at least six of which can be considered masterpieces. *Mudhoney* is one of the best. Set during the Depression, it's the tale of a drunken, wife-beating drifter who wanders into a small town and starts up a whole shit load of trouble. Filled to the brim with all the trashy brilliance Meyer is famous for, *Mudhoney* is a seminal piece of drive-in schlock. —*T. S.*

MYRA BRECKINRIDGE L: SEXPLOITATION/SEXPLOITATION (1970) 94M D: Michael Sarne. *Rex Reed, Farrah Fawcett, Mae West, John Huston, Raquel Welch.* Reed is well cast in this adaptation of Gore Vidal's book, playing a gay movie reviewer who decides to undergo a sex change from a crazed doctor, played by John Carradine. This way he can scheme an inheritance by pretending to be Huston's long lost daughter. But after the operation, he turns into Welch! Reed still makes intermittent appearances as the conscience for Welch, who plays a very aggressive Myra Breckenridge. West plays the head of a stud house to which Tom Selleck (in his first film appearance) applies for work. This film is way over the top and will be of great interest for those with a keen sense of camp. —*N. J.*

OLGA'S GIRLS L: SEXPLOITATION/SEXPLOITATION (1964) 70M D: Joseph P. Mawra. *Dolly Simmons, Audrey Campbell, Eva Denning, Rickey Bell.* Campbell reprises her drug-dealing, white-slaving character Olga from *White Slaves of Chinatown* in this bargain-basement, not-so-Grand Guignol sequel. Like the original, the so-called story of the sexual sadist who keeps a harem in subjugation in New York's

Chinatown is little more than a string of kinky stag reels pasted together with a suggestion of a plot and exposition lazily provided by a bored narrator (director Mawra's money-saving alternative to recording dialogue). Indifferently acted, crude and sleazy, this fascinatingly bad exploitation artifact of 1960s grindhouses is hilarious camp only because the parade of tortures (floggings, dismemberments, a blowtorch to the breasts) has the halfhearted execution of a preschool Christmas pageant. —*S. A.*

ON HER BED OF ROSES L: SEXPLOITATION/SEXPLOITATION (1966) 104M D: Albert Zugsmith. *Lee Gladden, Sandra Lynn.* Beautiful blond Lisa (Lynn) has sexual hang-ups and mental problems as well as a psycho-sniper fiancé. Who better to turn to than '60s pop psychologist Dr. Richard von Krafft-Ebing (Gladden) himself? Through psychoanalysis and flashbacks, the good doctor helps reveal Lisa's sordid path. Supposedly based on the book *Psychopathia Sexualis,* this sexploitation picture features topless go-go dancing, groovy experimental music, crazy dream sequences, lots of psychobabble, and a naked underwater catfight. The director worked in nearly every genre as a producer, director, screenwriter, and sometime actor. He made respectable mainstream fare (working on classics like *Touch of Evil* and *Tarnished Angels*), then moved to '50s exploitation films like *High School Confidential* and, in the '60s, settled into "adults only" drug films along the lines of this wacky movie. —*S. H.*

PAM AND TOMMY LEE: HARDCORE AND UNCENSORED L: SEXPLOITATION/HARDX (XXX) (1998) 76M D: Tommy Lee. *Tommy Lee, Pamela Anderson Lee.* I don't like porn, not in either the traditional or ironic sense. It seems inevitable in today's *Girls Gone Wild* society that everyone will view some porn at least once, so a few of us decided to fulfill our requirement by renting this tape. Having never seen porn before, it took a while to get over the ... technical aspects, but soon I was laughing along with everyone else. The film is obviously amateur and not meant to be viewed by prying, perverted eyes, but I imagine it takes great concentration and skill to maneuver a camcorder into some of those spots while performing other duties. And someone should construct a drinking game based on how many times Pamela says, "I love you, lover." The novelty wore off fast, though, and by the end I was torn between feeling guilty for laughing at what was clearly the most private of moments and being really disturbed by their relationship. I wouldn't recommend this for arousal purposes, but it will certainly satisfy the voyeur in you. —*J. K.*

PLAYMATE OF THE APES L: SEXPLOITATION/SEXPLOITATION (2002) 90M D: John Bacchus. *Debbie Rochon, Misty Mundae.* The ever popular Mundae headlines this skin-flick spoof, which is exactly what you think it is: a silly take-off of Tim Burton's film.

Movies we like that most people hate

A.I. ARTIFICIAL INTELLIGENCE

ARMAGEDDON

BAD BOYS

BUFFALO 66

CRACKING UP

ESCAPE FROM LA

GHOSTBUSTERS 2

HUDSON HAWK

INDEPENDENCE DAY

THE ISLAND OF DR. MOREAU *(1996)*

KUNG POW: ENTER THE FIST

LEPRECHAUN 2

LITTLE NICKY

LOVE ON THE RUN

A NIGHT AT THE ROXBURY

OC & STIGGS

POLICE ACADEMY 6: CITY UNDER SIEGE

POPEYE

RUN, RONNIE, RUN!

STARSHIP TROOPERS

THE STUPIDS

TANGO

THUMB WARS

WAY OF THE GUN

"Oh great, another human spaceship crashing into our planet. If I have to hear one more speech about the NRA, I'm going to shoot myself." The all-lesbian crew falls in the hands of simian scientist Rochon, whose evolutionary theory is given a boost when Ms. Mundae struts her stuff at a strip club and proves that humans can not only talk, they can dance (which proves they have a soul, or at least have soul). Dumb? Absolutely. Cheap? Heck, they blew the budget on ill-fitting ape suits and not-too-convincing masks. But for a softcore bit of jungle love, it's pretty darn funny in a smart-alecky sort of way. —*S. A.*

PLEASE DON'T EAT MY MOTHER! L: SEXPLOITATION/ SEXPLOITATION (1972) 97M D: Carl Monson. *Buck Kartalian, Rene Bond.* This guy is like forty-five and a virgin, and is craving some companionship, so he buys a plant. You'd think a hooker would be a more suitable choice, but whatever. So anyway, the plant grows to be huge and starts talking with this really sexy woman voice, and the virgin guy is all turned on by it and tries to hump it and stuff, but all it wants to do is eat things, including people. So virgin guy feeds it people, and then it wants a boy plant to have sex with, and he's all depressed, and his neighbors have a fight, and the woman kills the husband, and the virgin guy feeds the dead husband to the plant, and the woman is so happy that she has sex with him. And then the plant eats her. This movie is porn with plot being taken to a whole new level. It would have probably been better if there had been some hot man-plant luuuuv. —*J. S.*

PRIVATE DUTY NURSES L: SEXPLOITATION/SEXPLOITATION (1971) 80M D: George Armitage. *Kathy Cannon, Joyce Williams, Herbert Jefferson Jr., Pegi Boucher, Joseph Kaufmann.* Part of the swinging stewardess/nurse/liberated women sexploitation genre of the early '70s, Armitage's directorial debut is a typical entry featuring lots of naked flesh, drugs, bad rock music, a melodramatic plot, and some social commentary. Three young nursing students (the normal blond, bruntte, black arrangement) rent a California beach house and encounter free love, drug dealers, rapists, murderers, racism, male chauvinist pigs, political activism, corrupt cops, and tense operating room action. They spend a lot of time at a bar where a shitty '70s band plays, and there's plenty of gratuitous nudity and bedroom action. *The Student Nurses* was a big hit for producer Roger Corman and he followed it up with other nursesploitaion hits like *Night Call Nurses, Candy Stripe Nurses,* and this time capsule. —*S. H.*

REFORM SCHOOL GIRLS L: SEXPLOITATION/WOMEN IN PRISON (1986) 94M D: Tom DeSimone. *Linda Carol, Sybil Danning, Wendy O. Williams.* Hmm . . . *Reform School Girls.* My eleven-year-old brain raced. I was at my uncle's house watching *Robocop* and this was on afterward on some mix tape of Cinemax movies. Hmmm . . . Well, everyone else was in bed, so I could totally get away with it, and nobody would be the wiser. So I turned down the volume and began a terrifying journey into hell. I thought maybe there would be some fun nudity, but all I saw was nude torture, with firehoses, with needles, with whatever. Also, one girl had snuck a kitten into jail with her. Ahh, a kitten. But then the evil, fat bitch of a warden chased it around for a few minutes and stomped on it. That was about all I could take. This affected me more than the violence in *Robocop.* My imagination ran wild: What if someone I knew had to go there? Would they be beaten and tortured? I couldn't sleep after that. It's probably harmless now, but for me, on that night, it was the scariest movie ever. —*K. C.*

SCORE L: SEX DIRECTORS/METZGER, RADLEY (1973) 90M D: Radley Metzger. *Lynn Lowry, Calvin Culver, Claire Wilbur, Carl Parker, Gerald Grant.* In the beautiful resort town of Leisure, in the land of Play, deep within the Erogenous Zone, live a swinging couple (Wilbur and Culver) who like to place wagers on their little games of seduction. This time they've set their sights on a naive young pair of newlyweds (Lowry and Grant) who turn out to be more open to the possiblity than even they knew. Shot on location in Europe at a gorgeous storybook seaside village, Metzger's stylish softcore erotica combines a playful cinematic style with a cool European sensibility. His attitude toward sex is neither condescending nor judgmental, and his exploration of the pleasures of the flesh is open to all couplings. The actual sex is rather tame by modern standards, but still quite sexy and informed by a remarkable equanimity: there's as much male as female nudity. At heart, Metzger has fashioned a smart, witty, sexual fairy tale, where even selfish intentions lead to happy endings. —*S. A.*

SEX: THE ANNABEL CHONG STORY L: SEXPLOITATION/SEX DOCS (1999) 86M D: Gough Lewis. *Ed Powers, Ron Jeremy, Annabel Chong.* You go into this out of curiosity, to know what could possess someone to want to have sex with 251 men in a few hours, and you come out feeling like you've been punched in the stomach. Annabel's explanation of going for the world gang-bang record as a sort of feminist social commentary rings hollow as you find out about her past drug addiction and rape. She dons a plastic smile while being fucked by lines and lines of men, and that feminist message seems further lost. Her behavior seems schizophrenic, and as the eighty-six minutes pass, you realize Chong is really fucked-up and really, really confused. Far from being any type of commentary on the porn industry itself, this movie is just the sad unraveling of the blatant problems that caused one woman to turn to the porn industry as a fucked-up kind of therapy. If you're looking for a documentary on the porn industry itself, this isn't it. Be prepared to feel a little ill at ease. —*J. S.*

STARDUST (4&5) L: SEXPLOITATION/HARDX (XXX) (1995) 240M D: Michael Zen. *Kobe Tai, Jenteal.* This series is terrible in a very good way. Complete with bad southern accents, aliens, a talking moose head, and lots of unseemly conduct, these movies are the spumoni ice cream of porn. The adventure follows Honey Potts and her sometime-boyfriend Bubba through their shady shenanigans. Bubba's philandering and Honey's good-girl magnetism draw the most formidable of enemies: mean, corporate women with long, shiny nails. Jenteal actually delivers a genuinely good performance. —*J. J.*

STUDENT NURSES, THE L: SEXPLOITATION/SEXPLOITATION (1970) 89M D: Stephanie Rothman. *Elaine Giftos, Reni Santoni, Barbara Leigh, Karen Carlson, Brioni Farrell.* A veritable subgenre all its own created by legendary producer Roger Corman, the "Nurses" films are part soap opera, part sex comedy, and all drive-in exploitation with a twist: the women in these movies are sexually, socially, and politically active. Director Rothman kicked off the cycle and set the pattern with *The Student Nurses*, where four luscious young roommates in the last months of a nursing program get their real education outside the classroom. Drugs, abortion, and a Chicano inner-city activist/revolutionary (Santoni) contribute to just a few of their formative experiences. The groovy music, sexual liberation, and undercurrent of social politics (hinted at, if not actually addressed) became standard for the genre, at least for Corman's New World productions. —*S. A.*

TRADER HORNEE L: SEXPLOITATION/SEXPLOITATION (1970) 84M D: Jonathan Lucas. *Buddy Pantsari, John Alderman.* Private eye Hamilton Hornee (the e's are silent) travels to Africa to find a missing heiress. Hornee and his entourage discover the daughter is now called Algona and is worshipped by jive-talking, watermelon-eating natives who yell "Ungawa." Add a rare white gorilla, some '70s-style optical effects, ample jungle clichés, plus lots of sex and nudity, and you get a typical sexploitation offering from the prolific Dave Friedman. The humor doesn't get much better than stale racist jokes and ancient slapstick routines, the acting is stiff (and not in a good way!), the sex ain't very sexy, and there's excessive use of stock footage. Still, for some crazy reason, I kinda like it! —*S. H.*

TRIXXX L: SEXPLOITATION/HARDX (XXX) (1999) 87M D: Francois Clousot. *Rebecca Lord, Candy Apples, Cheyenne Silver, Michael J. Cox.* It was inevitable someone would bring together the worlds of *The Matrix* and hardcore pornography, combining the two principle interests of many young men of the late '90s. This is not so much a parody as a straight-up rip-off, but with penetration. The opening scene mimics the opening of *The Matrix* with surprising accuracy, complete with pony-tailed porn dudes playing the agents. Then, unfortunately, it leaves *The Matrix* for various sex scenes and generic virtual-reality concepts. The abrupt ending promises a part 2 (I guess they foresaw the cliffhanger ending of *The Matrix Reloaded*). It's disappointing to watch this film and imagine what could have been if the filmmakers had been giving 100 percent. How hard could it really have been to set up a circle of cameras and do a bullet time with the money shot? OK, so maybe it would take a little effort, but you can't tell me it wouldn't be worth it. —*B. T.*

UP! L: SEX DIRECTORS/MEYER, RUSS (1976) 80M D: Russ Meyer. *Kitten Natavidad, Janet Wood, Su Ling, Mary Gavin, Edward Schaaf.* The most outrageously absurd romp by bosom-obsessed nudie film rebel Meyer, *Up!* is also his most violent. Amid his trademark style—generously oversized performances, rapid-fire pacing, high-energy music, a flair for color and composition, and, of course, a cast of voluptuous beauties bouncing through the story—are a couple of rape scenes uncomfortably out of place in an otherwise surreal comic book of a sex farce. Natavidad plays a self-described "Greek Chorus" who reappears periodically (naked, of course) to try (unsuccessfully) to keep the story on track and (more successfully) comment on the frequent sexual interludes in Meyer's trademark dialogue delirium (cowritten, uncredited, by Roger Ebert). For the record, the plot has to do with covert agents, a Bavarian castle in Northern California, and an Adolph Hitler look-alike with a penchant for masochism. —*S. A.*

WHITE SLAVES OF CHINATOWN L: SEXPLOITATION/WOMEN IN PRISON (1964) 72M D: Joseph P. Mawra *Leonore Rhein, Audrey Campbell.* Tawdry and twisted grindhouse kink starring Campbell as the drug-dealing, white-slaving sexual sadist Olga, a woman with "a mind so warped that she made sadism a full-time business." In her demented debut, she bends a dungeon of kidnapped girls to her will in both mind and body through insidious torture, and accomplishes it all without uttering a word. In fact, the film was shot without sound. Only the lazy exposition of a bored narrator (and intermittent voice-over reflections by Olga herself) and a strange, repetitive mix of library music (famous classical themes, tinny Chinese music, and R&B-inflected strip-club grinds) connect the arbitrary scenes that pass for a plot. It would be too deviant for words if it weren't for the passive, halfhearted performances of her victims and the crude spectacle of cheap effects. Campbell, however, proved to be a riveting villainess and returned in two more Olga films. —*S. A.*

WOMEN IN CAGES L: SEXPLOITATION/WOMEN IN PRISON (1971) 78M D: Gerry de Leon. *Roberta Collins, Pam Grier, Judy Brown.* When cops raid his yacht, a white-slaving drug dealer slips his stash into his naive girlfriend's purse. "You'll be out soon darling. I promise." She never realizes he means *in a coffin* until after jailbreak with her cellmates, trekking through the jungle to his yacht, where the cop who's been pressuring her has to rescue her. This women-in-prison flick has a good story but lackluster direction and special effects. The "playpen" tortures should have felt twisted and the group shower scenes catty. But *Women in Cages* nonetheless contains a number of harsh sequences and good performances. Collins's torso is whip-marked, but she refuses to cry in front of cellmates. Grier's warden, hostage to her lesbian lover in the escape, is raped and murdered by her own brutal trackers, never trying to tell them who she is. This film is another case of an exploiter where the sum of the parts are far greater than the artistic whole. —*J. C.*

YOUNG PLAYTHINGS (THE RED QUEEN) L: SEXPLOITATION/ SARNO, JOE (1972) 105M D: Joe Sarno. *Christina Lindberg, Eva Portnoff.* Wonderfully mad farce with double doses of Sarno's patented irony. Female friend (Portnoff) warns an innocent wife (Lindberg) her husband's late stays must mean something. Then she talks the wife into a three-way with her casual boyfriend, and then into moving in with her alone. Now a swerve: the wife meets the mysterious woman downstairs (Margaretha Hellström) who never leaves her room, a toy maker who invites her to a soirée featuring a fairy-tale puppet play with live actors. Despite her friend's resistance, the wife attends. In natural surroundings, the nudity is casual, less so in bed. And with these white-faced pantomimes, nudity turns eerie, poetic, creepy, sad—pointing toward a forbidden fruit. *Young Playthings* is one weirdly twisted little erotic masterpiece. —*J. C.*

ZEN PUSSY L: SEXPLOTATION/SEX DOCS (1999) 60M D: Annie Sprinkle, Joseph Kramer. *Betsy Caygill, Emilie Brough, Letta Neely.* Before I started working at Scrarecrow, world-renowned sex goddess and artist Annie Sprinkle did an in-store appearance. One of my colleagues recently told me a story about that day and this video of hers. Before Ms. Sprinkle started her show, someone put this tape in the backroom VCR. Soon, a small group gathered to witness what the display box describes as "wall-to-wall, extreme vulva close-ups." "It's not sexual at all," a coworker said, "it's just these shots with a steady cam, up close, with one right after another." While the whole viewing didn't last more than a few minutes, the experience left all involved "completely disturbed." While I'm not all that familiar with Ms. Sprinkle's work, I know her message about sex and such is positive and encouraging. *Zen Pussy* encourages viewers to "welcome visions, reflections, memories, feelings and questions" while meditating on each vulva, but doing so at work in front of a bunch of your coworkers may not be the best way to invite these experiences into your life. This one is probably best watched alone. —*J. K.*

CHAPTER FOURTEEN

Silent Films

It is often bragged that silent films represent the last time cinema was truly universal. But this is not quite true. Even back in the day there were problems with intertitles being part of cinema at all, or with intertitled prints being shipped with the wrong language. It is also often written that the Silent Era represents the most poetic examples of film. Again, this is not entirely true. Many silent films are truly awkward or crude in their techniques.

This, however, is very true: films of the Silent Era provided the very vocabulary, cinematically, at an almost elemental or atomic level that all subsequent films are based upon.

When movies began, they were just moving pictures. Soon they became short stories and, not long after, those stories had intertitles helping to explain details or dialogue essential to the story. The stories were shot elementally and from a distance. But soon came the close-up, montage, and longer and more complex stories were being shown. Then, in a flood of creativity and exploration of the new form of cinema around the world, came nearly every element that makes up the art of storytelling in cinema today.

The best examples of the silent film are universal, poetic, and richly textured as they tell their stories visually, with a minimal need for intertitles. Add the music that was usually written for the best of the silent films and you really do come close to poetic universality. In the best hands, movies are not moving pictures but moving paintings, and since the early cinema had not learned

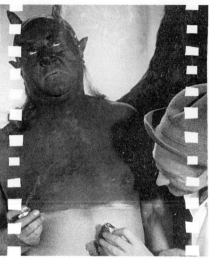

©KINO INTERNATIONAL CORP.

Faust (1926)

to speak, the visual was most of what you had. The films of Frank Borzage, Cecil B. DeMille, Carl Dreyer, D. W. Griffith, Rex Ingram, F. W. Murnau, Victor Sjostrom, Maurice Tourneur, King Vidor, Jean Vigo, and many more are among the very best examples of cinema at its (nearly) purest and most potent.

If you are to be a student of film, you must study the masters of early cinema. It is essential. An ignorance of silent film is a profound ignorance indeed.

While many of the great silent films are lost forever, the films that remain—the comedies and dramas, the short and the long—give us an amazing glimpse of a new art form to be studied from its infancy when new discoveries and techniques and advances were being made nearly every single day. How lucky are we to have the films we do? Extremely lucky indeed, we think. And we hope that our little sampling of the silent films here and those that appear in our Directors section will give you just enough to whet your appetite to explore and enjoy these silent films.

BACKSTAIRS L: SILENT FILMS/SILENT GERMANS (1921) 50M D: Leopold Jessner, Paul Leni. *Henny Porten, Wilhelm Doeterle, Fritz Kortner.* This backstairs romance has a dark poetry to it. It's almost Chaplinesque: remember the dinner party in *The Gold Rush* where no one came? It has the same kind of cheerful optimism that doesn't end well. A postman (Kortner) has a crush on a local maid (Porten) to a wealthy family. She sees him as only the man who'll someday bring a letter from her lover, a letter that never comes. To cheer her, the postman forges a letter in the lover's name. She soon discovers his forgery, and at first it upsets her but ends up drawing him to her. There are so few intertitles that to get what's going on you have to read between the pictures. The wonderful set appears both naturalistic and expressionistic at the same time. —*J. C.*

BANGVILLE POLICE, THE L: SILENT FILMS/EARLY CINEMA (1913) 8M D: Henry Lehrman. *Mabel Normand, Nick Cogley, Dot Farley, Fred Mace.* A girl (Normand) imagines criminals in the barn, calls the bumbling police chief, and barricades herself in the house. She almost shoots her father when he tries to break in. The police arrest everybody: the only thing happening in the barn is that the cow is calving. Classic Keystone, slapstick comedy. Sennett, having worked at Biograph with D. W. Griffith, utilizes the crosscutting techniques Griffith used to create drama, but here toward humorous ends. So what looks ragged actually has quite a polished continuity to it, and thus comes off a good deal fresher than vaudeville's hackneyed "laugh a minute" gags. Keystone was the perfect workshop for such later comic originals as Charlie Chaplin and Buster Keaton. —*J. C.*

BARGAIN, THE L: SILENT FILMS/SILENT WESTERNS (1914) 50M D: Reginald Barker. *J. Barney Sherry, J. Frank Burke, William S. Hart, Clara Williams.* In the naked light of a gorge, Jim Stokes (Hart) lights a cigarette and readies himself to rob a stagecoach. Thought outmanned and outgunned, he and his accomplices pull off the heist, but Stokes is left wounded and horseless. He makes his way to a cabin, where the miner's daughter (Williams) nurses him back to health and awakens his conscience. He decides to return the stolen money, but there are complications that lead to an astute ending turning on morali-

ty's double edge. Barker's landscape is wild and unpredictable, like the rough-hewn tavern with its gambling tables and elk heads on the walls, showing a civilization only a little different than the one outside. Hart's character is as natural as a crooked tree in a gully trying to grow straight. *The Bargain* is the first masterpiece of the Western genre. —*J. C.*

BAT, THE (1926) L: SILENT FILMS/SILENT HORROR (1926) 86M D: Roland West. *Charles Herzinger, Arthur Houseman, Louise Fazenda, Tullio Carminatti, Jewel Carmen, Emily Fitzroy.* A silent film set in an old dark house, this is inferior to the similar *The Cat and the Canary* that followed a year later. There is some interesting camera work here but it lacks much of the atmosphere that gives old dark house films their elegance. An important pioneering early work but easily surpassed by others. —*T. S.*

BERLIN: SYMPHONY OF A GREAT CITY L: SILENT FILMS/SILENT GERMANS (1927) 65M D: Walter Ruttmann. Ruttmann's mix of documentary and experimental cinema remains, with Dziga Vertov's *Man with a Movie Camera*, one of the great visual symphonies of world cinema. Broken into five movements, the film samples a day in the life of Berlin from dawn to dusk, celebrating the city as architectural wonder, industrial giant, and social beehive. As a snapshot of pre-Nazi Germany it's an incredible document, but as a triumph of rhythm, movement, mood, and pictorial beauty in motion it's a work of art. —*S. A.*

BEST ARBUCKLE/KEATON COLLECTION, THE L: SILENT FILMS/SILENT COMEDY (1917) 248M D: Fatty Arbuckle. *Roscoe "Fatty" Arbuckle, Buster Keaton.* In 1917, Arbuckle formed his own company and recruited a brilliant young vaudevillian with a bright future: Keaton. The eleven films and one additional fragment gathered for this collection (of fifteen they made together) show Arbuckle's gift for corralling chaos and shaping free-for-all scenes with kinetic care and crack timing. Keaton always cited Arbuckle as his early mentor and you can find the seeds of his style in Arbuckle's assured, meticulously constructed final collaborations (the 1919 *Back Stage* surely inspired Keaton's brilliant *The Playhouse*). It's a treat to see Keaton's development from screen neophyte (his 1917 debut *The Butcher Boy*, where his shuffling hayseed part is but a supporting player still looking for his persona) to deadpan sidekick (his gift for comic understatement and rubbery gymnastic pratfalls is thoroughly mature in the 1920 *The Garage*). More importantly this collection reminds us of Arbuckle's talents as a boyish, sweet-faced comedian, light on his feet despite his girth, and an inventive comedy director and gagman. —*S. A.*

Nell Shipman

Seattle-raised writer, actor, and director Nell Shipman was one of the most significant pioneers in film. Never heard of her? Not surprising. Until the late 1980s, when her films were miraculously recovered and rediscovered, Shipman was nearly forgotten.

Born Helen Barham on October 25, 1892, in Victoria, B.C., she moved with her family to Bainbridge Island and then to Seattle's Madrona Heights neighborhood. Her strong-willed path to cinema started at a young age. She attended the Seattle Grammar School but developed a bad case of the theater bug and, at age thirteen, dropped out of high school to study at a local drama school. She was cast in several plays at Seattle's Third Avenue Theater and later traveled cross-country several times with a Seattle-based acting company. At eighteen she married theatrical entrepreneur

Ernie Shipman, and two years later they moved to the burgeoning film community in Hollywood to stake their claim in territory quickly becoming the center of the motion picture industry.

Shipman got a few bit parts in small films and wrote scripts. Doors eventually opened for her at Universal, Selig, and Vitagraph as a scriptwriter, but her first big break came in 1915, when she was cast in a leading role in Vitagraph's outdoor saga based on a James Oliver Curwood novel, *God's Country and the Woman,* filmed near Big Bear Lake in California. The film was a hit and made Shipman a star. She performed in a number of films for Vitagraph, including many Westerns, in which she did her own stunts. Shipman might have been one of the biggest stars of the silent era: Samuel Goldwyn chased after her with a contract that would have put her among Hollywood's acting elite, but she turned him down flat.

Shipman was one of cinema's earliest

continued on page 742

CABINET OF DR. CALIGARI, THE L: SILENT FILMS/SILENT GERMANS (1919) 75M D: Robert Wiene. *Lil Dagover, Hans von Twardowski, Conrad Veidt, Werner Krauss.* This is one of the finest and certainly one of the most psychedelic silent films ever made. At a local circus Dr. Caligari (Veidt) shows off his Somnambulist, a man perpetually asleep who steps out of a coffin to predict the future. The future he predicts for circusgoers is the time of their death—a prediction he makes sure comes true! This bizarre plot is investigated by a young man who fears his girlfriend is next. But what he discovers turns his whole world inside out. The outrageous sets in this film are the very essence of German Expressionism of the time, with oddly shaped windows, impossibly constructed buildings, and obtuse designs intended to express the vision of the mentally unstable. Kino video released this film with a brilliant original score by Timothy Brock. —*N.J.*

CABIRIA L: SILENT FILMS/SILENT ADVENTURE (1914) 123M D: Giovanni Pastrone. *Lidia Quaranta, Umberto Mozzato, Bartolomeo Pagano.* Mount Aetna explodes, showering stones and shaking classical Roman

architecture apart. Young Cabiria (Quaranta) flees only to be kidnapped to Carthage by Phoenician pirates. Sent to be sacrificed to Moloc in a most magnificently sinister temple, she is rescued by Fulvio (Mozzato) and his slave Maciste (Pagano). The three are separated and sent on their own adventures till fate reunites them many years later. Nominally an early masterpiece of the feature film, *Cabiria* is a serial of one-reel episodes only slightly more integrated than *The Perils of Pauline. —J.C.*

CAT AND THE CANARY, THE L: SILENT FILMS/SILENT HORROR (1927) 82M D: Paul Leni. *Forrest Stanley, Laura La Plante, Creighton Hale, Tully Marshall, Gertrude Astor.* This film's fantastic style carries the whole production to great success. This silent is the film that really popularized the old dark house trend in film. The whole creepy affair has a certain levity to it that seems intentional since, even by this point, the idea of the old dark house had become clichéd through other mediums. As far as I can tell, this is the first film ever to use the much imitated shot of a closet opening and a dead body falling out onto the camera. —*T.S.*

independent filmmakers. She wanted what less than a handful of stars had: creative control. When the opportunity came to start her own company, with novelist Curwood, to film adaptations of his work, she jumped at it. The company's first film, *Back to God's Country,* filmed in 1919, was a terrific success, due in part to a much-publicized nude scene, the first by an actress in a major American film. Shipman next produced, wrote, and directed a few films herself. *Something New* began as a commercial of sorts for a new model of car, the Maxwell, but became a feature-length adventure in which the "new horse" becomes the star. Another film, a twelve-reel epic-Curwood adaptation, *The Girl from God's Country,* was delivered late and over budget in 1921, and was grossly reedited by Shipman's financial backers. Devastated but not undone, Shipman, now divorced, returned to the Northwest.

With a new lover, and a film crew that included cameraman Joseph Walker (who later shot all of the great Frank Capra classics), Shipman began work on the film that would become her masterpiece: *The Grub*

Stake, an Alaskan gold-rush epic filmed in 1922 at the Minnehaha Film Studio in Spokane; her own film studio at Lionhead Lodge in Priest Lake, Idaho; and Seattle. But this was no era for independent filmmakers. It was nearly impossible to break through the production, distribution, and exhibition blocs formed by the consolidation of big-money studios. Small companies like Shipman's were squeezed out. In spite of the film's quality and local successes (its Seattle engagement was very popular), its New York distributor was forced into bankruptcy, and *The Grub Stake* never received a major commercial release.

Shipman retrenched at her Priest Lake compound and made a series of two-reelers that she managed to sell to Lewis Selznick (David O.'s dad), collectively titled *Little Dramas in Big Places.* But her financial troubles, aggravated by two dreadfully harsh Idaho winters and personal problems in the film company, were too much to overcome. In 1925, when her creditors confiscated her film equipment, Shipman was forced to abandon her studio. She suffered a breakdown and, at thirty-three, was

---

DRUMMER OF THE 8TH L: SILENT FILMS/SILENT DRAMA (1913) 24M D: Thomas Ince. *Cyril Gardner, Mildred Harris, Frank Borzage.* Hard, unsentimental ironic picture of war and true to Ince's excellent two-reelers. The physical action is expressed with energy and exuberance. After his older brother enlists during the American Civil War, a romantic young boy (Gardner) runs off to become a drummer for the Union Army. Captured during battle he bravely escapes, sustaining a gunshot wound. Hiding in a trunk in a Confederate general's tent, he overhears plans for next morning's attack. He escapes again, battle plans change, lives are lost. —*J. C.*

FOOL THERE WAS, A L: SILENT FILMS/SILENT DRAMA (1915) 67M D: Frank Powell. *Mabel Frenyear, Theda Bara, Victor Benoit, Clifford Bruce, May Allison, Edward José.* The vamp (Bara) is wickedly playful, as if to say, "Life is a game that I will win." While on a cruise ship, she spots a married rich man (José) and says to herself, "I will have this fool. Just watch." She drops her current beau flat (he later kills himself, but it means nothing to her). She reclines in catlike languor with

self-assurance in her eyes, and by Italy she has the fool. This run-of-the-mill melodrama made Bara's career, or it may have ruined it, damning her to replay the vamp-type in one film after another. It's just as well; she can't act worth a damn. But boy does she strike some wonderfully seductive poses. —*J. C.*

FOUR TROUBLESOME HEADS L: SILENT FILMS/EARLY CINEMA (1898) 2M D: Georges Méliès. *Georges Méliès.* One of Méliès's earliest films sets the tone for many of his experimental shorts to follow. In this brief yet spectacular magic act, Méliès, himself a magician who took to the tricks of motion pictures, takes off his head and sets it upon a table. Using impressive trick photography, his head reappears on his shoulders with the wave of his hand. Doing this two more times brings about a total of four heads. He then tries singing in harmony with himself, but it proves disagreeable so he destroys the heads. End of trick. On the video *Méliès the Magician,* by Facets Video (2001), many other Méliès shorts can be seen where he uses his head for further tricks—from inflating it like a balloon to making musical notes with it, which he throws onto a musical staff. Extremely inven-

effectively out of the industry.

She had some small success as a writer: a three-part series on her life as a female adventure filmmaker appeared in the *Atlantic Monthly* in 1926; a novel, *Abandoned Trails*, followed in 1932; and she even wrote a script, filmed in 1934 as *Wings in the Dark*, starring Cary Grant and Myrna Loy. But Shipman lived out her life quietly, raising her family and traveling. Her closest contact with Hollywood would be through her son, a successful screenwriter of B Westerns and serials (including *Flash Gordon* and *Dick Tracy*) who helped support her in her later years. In 1960, a longtime fan presented Shipman with a small house near Palm Springs, where she lived until her death in 1968.

In spite of her accomplishments, it is likely that Shipman would have remained, at best, a footnote in American film history. But in 1986, while researching Idaho writers and artists, Boise State University English professor Tom Trusky came across Shipman's *Atlantic Monthly* stories and began to investigate. He tracked down Shipman's son, Barry, and discovered that she had left behind a sprawling autobiographical manuscript. Trusky convinced Idaho University Press to publish it under the title *The Silent Screen and My Talking Heart*. Trusky then tracked down many of Shipman's films. Thanks to him, Shipman's splendid films are now available to be enjoyed and appreciated by audiences for a long time to come

Nevertheless, her films have a power that transcends time. She was an artist of the first order, adventurous and bold, daring and risk-taking. Her films are stories of ordinary people (the kind that Frank Capra would build his career on), tales that endure because they dare to include the intangible, humble stories that embrace the unknown and unknowable, becoming greater than the sum of their small, simple parts. Nell Shipman could have had influence in her own time, but her own time rejected her. We are left today to confront her work, the flowers of her stunted career, and we are unable to deny the enduring power, influence, and inspiration that work still holds for audiences and filmmakers today.

—*Kevin Shannon*

---

tive and amusing, these short films will charm an audience as much today as they did a hundred years ago. —*N. H.*

FRANKENSTEIN L: SILENT FILMS/SILENT HORROR (1910) 16M D: J. Searle Dawley. *Mary Fuller, Augustus Phillips, Charles Ogle.* The very first Frankenstein film was made by the Thomas Edison company in 1910. It's an interesting rendition of the story in which Dr. Frankenstein has no assistant and gathers no body parts. Instead, he fires up a large furnace and a strange stick-figure slowly appears inside and gradually grows into a hideous monster instead of the perfect specimen he was expecting. The monster runs away only to return on the eve of Frankenstein's marriage and then, with an interesting and no doubt symbolic use of a full-sized mirror, the monster becomes Frankenstein, then disappears. It's a curious take on the Shelley story and is ahead of its time in how it anticipates the subject of Gothic horror in film. —*N. J.*

GAUCHO, THE L: SILENT FILMS/SILENT ADVENTURE (1927) M D: F. Richard Jones. *Lupe Velez, Mary Pickford, Douglas Fairbanks.* Fairbanks is a lusty, live-for-the-day South American outlaw whose acrobatic antics and cigarette tricks mask a hard-living, hedonistic life, but his happy-go-lucky days are put to the test when he's infected by the plague and the fabled "Miracle Girl" (Velez) selflessly saves his life. Fairbanks, forty-four when he made this picture, faced the same realities at the end of his silent career as Jackie Chan does today: he leaps and cavorts with the same jaunty bounce and hearty laugh of his earlier pictures, but the dark undertones are the work of an aging actor rethinking his swashbuckling superhero image. It makes for his most mature, thoughtful film, a breathtakingly gorgeous picture (the mountain village appears to literally hang off the edge of a cliff by the grace of God) and a portrait of a repentant rascal whose conversion can't change a long life of debauchery overnight. —*S. A.*

GIRL AND HER TRUST L: SILENT FILMS/EARLY CINEMA (1912) 17M D: D. W. Griffith. *Wilfred Lucas, Dorothy Bernard.* The first masterpiece of clean modern storytelling also trumpets two basic American virtues: taking one's responsibilities seriously and having the presence of mind in a crunch to innovate in order to act effectively. A young woman (Bernard), working as a railroad station-manager, resists two thieves who want her key to a payroll strongbox. They try to break into her office as she telegraphs for help. In close-up she inserts a bullet into door's keyhole and hammers it till it fires, making the thieves scramble away hauling the unopened heavy box with them. She runs after them grabbing hold of the box for dear life despite repeated blows. Griffith follows with one of his trademark, crosscutting chase-scenes. —*J. C.*

GOLEM L: SILENT FILMS/SILENT GERMANS (1920) 91M D: Carl Boese, Paul Wegener. *Lyda Salmonova, Ernst Deutsch, Greta Schröder, Albert Steinrück, Paul Wegener.* The Golem (Wegener) is a clay statue, built to protect Prague's Jewish ghetto, that is brought to life when a magic amulet is placed around its neck. Seeing its power, the wizard's assistant (Deutsch) puts the statue to use for more monstrous tasks. He angers the statue, sending it on a destructive rampage. With a love affair and subtle politics as a backdrop, the core morality tale of power and power's backlash when used unwisely is what makes this film so gripping. The message is amplified by Wegener's performance as the awkward monster and cinematographer Karl Freund's rich palate of toned grays. Balancing this are the little human and very ironic touches, like the monster picking up the little girl with a flower (Schröder), making it satisfying beyond its folk tale character. This is a subtle master-piece of the macabre. —*J. C.*

GÖSTA BERLINGS SAGA L: SILENT FILMS/SILENT DRAMA (1924) 91M D: Mauritz Stiller. *Otto Elg-Lundberg, Lars Hanson, Greta Garbo, Gerda Lundeqvist.* This is a complicated though remarkably modern story of a defrocked minister (Hanson), full of self-loath-ing over alcohol and feelings that he has been the ruin of women he has known. He is pulled from the brink of suicide by an older woman (Lundeqvist) who admits to him her one great illicit love earlier in her life. But the story gets out and her current husband casts her into a workhouse. It's there that a powerful life-chang-ing moment occurs as nature and society mix in edgy ways. Wolves chase a sleigh across a fro-zen lake in a remarkably scary and thematically effective scene (the conventionally pious are often the most wolflike). Garbo's acting is emo-tionally rich, a countess counseling courage to society's outcasts and credibly putting herself on the line. Hanson's lead performance takes your breath away. A very solid film all round. —*J. C.*

GREAT K & A TRAIN ROBBERY, THE L: SILENT FILMS/ SILENT WESTERNS (1925) 53M D: Lewis Seiler. *Tom Mix, Dorothy Dwan, Will Walling.* Like all of Mix's films, this one is memorable mostly for its wonderful stunts. The head of a railroad hires a cowboy detective (Mix) who doesn't arrive but has actually gone undercover to rescue a railroader's daughter and reveal who at the rail-road is an inside man for the bandits. The rest is Boy Scout nonsense. Fake trains and real trains. Underwater cave as an entrance to a hideout. Jumping onto and off moving trains. All mak-ing Mix the Douglas Fairbanks of Westerns. Adolescent fun. —*J. C.*

GREAT TRAIN ROBBERY, THE L: SILENT FILMS/EARLY CINEMA (1903) 12M D: Edwin S. Porter. *A. C. Abadie, Gilbert M. "Broncho Billy" Anderson, Justus D. Barnes.* Bandits rob a train, killing three men in the process, and are chased by a posse and die in a shootout. In 1903 motion pictures were still just a money-making novelty item: no one knew then that movie's future as an industry and art form was via "narrative realism." Full of strong images and muscular energy, *The Great Train Robbery* was one of the longest and most ambi-tious films of its day. But its importance is that it was the first masterpiece of linear narrative. —*J. C.*

HANDS OF ORLAC (ORLACS HÄNDE) L: SILENT FILMS/ SILENT GERMANS (1925) 92M D: Robert Wiene. *Carmen Cartellieri, Conrad Veidt, Fritz Kortner, Alexandra Sorina.* Orlac opens with a great catastrophic scene of workers looking for wounded in a head-on train crash. We see one of the victims, a great pianist (Veidt), having bandages removed from his hands. They stand out like objects foreign to his body. He can no longer play the piano. One night a message comes to him. These strange hands were grafted onto his arms, hands of an executed, knife-throwing murderer. People around him start dying by those same knives with the executed murder's fingerprints on them. *Hands of Orlac* is a great, chilling essay in moral terror, all in dark foggy German expressionistic shading (in the best sense of that phrase) with an excellent zinger of an ending. —*J. C.*

HÄXAN (AKA WITCHCRAFT THROUGH THE AGES) L: SILENT FILMS/SILENT HORROR (1922) 74M D: Benjamin Christiansen. *Benjamin Christensen, Astrid Holm, Clara Pontoppidan, Oscar Stribolt.* This pio-neering Swedish silent film begins as a sort of documentary presentation of woodcuts and engravings depicting myths of witchcraft from various cultures. It continues with beautifully shot reenactments of women being accused of witchcraft, using ingenious early special effects to depict the claims of the accusers (including the Devil, Hell, and flying brooms). The Devil depicted in this movie is more convincing than most filmmakers could accomplish even with today's technology. Although the middle portion of the film seems to treat stories of devil wor-ship literally, the final stretch depicts women in the '20s and shows how those stories correlate with symptoms of hysteria. Unless you're a pur-ist, I would recommend the 1968 Americanized version, *Witchcraft Through the Ages*, which adds narration by William S. Burroughs and a great avant-jazz score featuring Jean-Luc Ponty. Both versions are included on the Criterion Edition DVD. —B. T.

HELL'S HINGES L: SILENT FILMS/SILENT WESTERNS
(1916) 64M D: Charles Swickard, William S. Hart. *Louis Glaum, Alfred Hollingsworth, Jack Standing, Clara Williams, Williams S. Hart.* Both the saloon-keeper (Hollingsworth) and local gunman (Hart) like their town wild. No Bible-thumpers here. A preacher who arrives (Standing) has little backbone; he'd be easy to brace and back out of town. But the gunman eyes the coward's wholesome sister (Williams), and with the first pleading word from her lips he is lost. Before he knows it he finds himself facing down the saloonkeeper and all the nastier elements of the town, a town so vile maybe the whole place should burned down. Sound familiar? Clint Eastwood's pale, high-plains riders inherit their rage from this gutsy little Western that singes the nerve-ends. A vision of corrupt humanity so hellish that no fire-and-brimstone preacher's rhetoric could imagine venality and its consequence half so well as Thomas Ince and Hart do here. —J. C.

HUNCHBACK OF NOTRE DAME, THE L: SILENT FILMS/
SILENT DRAMA (1923) 133M D: Wallace Worsley. *Kate Lester, Norman Kerry, Patsy Ruth Miller, Ernest Torrence, Lon Chaney.* This silent classic is one of Universal's first horror films. It really set the standard for what was to follow. A dark and ominous atmosphere pervades while the story follows Esmerelda through Paris. Quasimodo is not so much the focus here, but he is played marvelously by Chaney. Even under pounds of makeup, a simple gesture or expression conveyed worlds of meaning. —T. S.

IMPOSSIBLE VOYAGE L: SILENT FILMS/EARLY CINEMA
(1904) 24M D: Georges Méliès. *Georges Méliès, Fernande Albany, May de Lavergne.* Riding off the success of *A Trip to the Moon,* French magician and film-maker Méliès, whose epic fantasies captured the minds of Parisians in the earliest years of film, released this curious adventure. Much like his earlier opus, an association of astronomers converges to hear a proposal for yet another fantastic excursion. A carriage conveys the travelers quickly to the Swiss Alps, where they board a train equipped with dirigibles that propel off a mountain and zoom the travelers toward the sun. Problems arise along the way, leading the train through the mouth of the personified sun (as opposed to plopping in the eye of the moon, as in his previous film). At twenty-five minutes, this fantasy was so exciting that Méliès was compelled to shoot extra footage. With this the film topped out at an unprecedented twenty-four minute running time. —N. J.

INDIAN TOMB, THE L: SILENT FILMS/SILENT GERMANS
(1921) 211M D: Joe May. *Olaf Fønss, Mia May, Conrad Veidt, Erna Morena.* Wonderfully exotic German silent spectacle features lovely, very costly sets and décor. These almost make up for the ridiculous characters and high-melodrama plot that plagued all German spectacles of the silent era. Here a yogi with magic powers (Goetzke) is bound to an evil prince (Veidt) for bringing him back to life, commanding him to bring an architect (Fønss) from Europe to build a palace, or rather a prison, for his unfaithful wife (Morena). The architect's worried fiancé (May) follows only to be placed under house arrest by the Prince. She reaches out to a servant girl (Lya De Putti) for help, spelling the girl's doom, of course. Complicating matters is the way the architect wanders into a lepers' colony and contracts the disease. What makes this film fun and approachable compared to Fritz Lang's and Ernst Lubitsch's more tightly controlled spectacles is May's looser handling of his material: the movie breathes. Its high sensuality is allowed to flower. And Veidt's riveting performance caps the treat. —J. C.

KEYSTONE COMEDIES V.5 L: SILENT FILMS/SILENT COMEDY
(1915) 11M D: Fatty Arbuckle. *Fatty Arbuckle.* The beauty of this volume of the wonderful collection of Keystone comedies is the true genius of Arbuckle. Here Fatty stars in "Miss Fatty's Seaside Lovers" as the daughter of a wealthy mothball magnate on a trip to the seashore. Fatty in drag is surprisingly natural but still very chuckle-worthy. When Miss Fatty arrives there are three young mashers ready to charm and swindle our heroine. Miss Fatty is a rather boisterous girl when feeling flirtatious and more than once almost injures her suitors. The climax is Miss Fatty sunbathing on a rock when the tide comes in leaving her stranded. Fatty's performance in this short is a perfect example of his comic brilliance and a reminder of how good physical comedy can be. —A. B.

LAST OF THE LINE, THE L: SILENT FILMS/SILENT DRAMA
(1914) 25M D: Thomas Ince, Jay Hunt. *Sessue Hayakawa, Gladys Brockwell, Tsuru Aoki.* Hayakawa plays the son of a Sioux chief sent to a white man's school. He comes back not a leader but a drunk. With some tribal renegades, he raids an army pay wagon. His father witnesses it and is ashamed, resorting to drastic action. The outdoor photography is as tawny as a running pony. Another superb, quite rueful two-reel Ince Western, this one is as hard as nails. —J. C.

LIFE OF AN AMERICAN FIREMAN L: SILENT FILMS/EARLY
CINEMA (1902) 6M D: Edwin S. Porter. *Vivian Vaughan, Arthur White.* Before narrative film technique developed using linear editing and story condensation, early cinema's stumbling attempts to produce urgency and suspense were done through situation and action alone. A woman and child are trapped upstairs in a burning apartment. The fire engine races around street corners to the rescue, with the woman's husband among the firemen. There is only one close-up: a

hand on the alarm box. Inside the firehouse the firemen rise from bed, slide down the pole, and jump on a horse-drawn fire engine and exit the firehouse. Back up to outside the firehouse to see doors opening and the engine crew exiting from the exterior viewpoint. From inside the burning house you see the terrified woman and child suddenly being rescued by firemen and taken out the window; the same scene is replayed from outside the building as firemen break in and take the woman and child out via the window. —J. C.

MÉLIÈS THE MAGICIAN L: SILENT FILMS/EARLY CINEMA
(1997) 185M D: Jacques Meny. *George Méliès.* Magician turned filmmaker Méliès went from cinematic innovator to old fashioned relic in ten years. His story is told in Meny's labor of love documentary *The Magic of Méliès* (1997), a survey of the artist and the rapidly changing face of cinema in his time. The impressionistic re-creations of events from his life are somewhat precious, but his studio (built in miniature as a fully functioning model) is a marvel of engineering, a fascinating glimpse into the mechanically minded practical imagination of *Méliès* and a delight to behold in itself. It's oddly structured, jumping back and forth through his career, but richly detailed. It's also interactive: fifteen of the clips feature a function that allows you to access the complete short film, which can also be viewed in a featurette called *Méliès' Magic Show,* a compilation hosted, introduced, and at times narrated by Madeleine Malthete-Méliès (in the style of her grandfather). The shorts are mostly well preserved and some of them are stunning, with original hand-painted colors dancing across the image. —S. A.

MOULIN ROUGE L: SILENT FILMS/SILENT DRAMA (1928)
88M D: E. A. Dupont. *Olga Tschechowa, Eve Gray, Jean Bradin.* This early *Moulin Rouge* captures the glamour of the 1920s Parisian theater district (the Vegas of its day), with glittering costumes, big headdresses, and precision song-and-dance numbers. In the front row, enthralled by the aging headlining performer (Tschechowa), is a young woman (Gray) and her fiancé (Bradin). She is the performer's daughter who has just graduated from school. But the fiancé falls deeply in love with the performer. Dupont made melodrama work as a vehicle for human emotions through more than just steel-edged acting by using startling visuals, such as inserting a telling little detail like a close-up of hands prior to a two-shot of faces. Or reflecting the fiancé's image in a glass door swinging back and forth, in and out of the picture frame, as the betrothed say goodnight. —J. C.

OUR DANCING DAUGHTERS L: SILENT FILMS/SILENT DRAMA
(1928) 84M D: Harry Beaumont. *Joan Crawford, Dorothy Sebastian, Nils Asther, Johnny Mack Brown, Anita Page.* Di (Crawford) is all frank energy as she dances wildly. This catches the eye of Ben

(Brown) and they spontaneously hit it off. Ben is soon to inherit millions. Annikins (Page) plays her shy-girl bit to steal Ben away, and shrewdly builds her case for marriage. *Daughters* is an excellent love triangle with flashy bits of camera magic to give it a very modern look, complete with clean, spare architecture, skimpy clothes showing a lot of leg, a "with it" sense of modern relationships, and composition that frames couples for emotional effect. The film takes the side of modern "frank" values (kiss and run) over old-fashioned hypocrisy (feigning virtue to scam one's way into lucrative marriage). Page has a wonderful drunk scene lecturing a scrubwoman. Crawford, in every move she makes, is the emotionally honest modern woman from head to toe. —J. C.

PAGE OF MADNESS, A (KURUTTA IPPEJI) L: SILENT
FILMS/SILENT DRAMA (1926) 60M D: Teinosuke Kinugasa. *Masuo Inoue, Yoshie Nakagawa.* When his wife (Nakagawa) is committed to a mental institution, a man (Inoue) gets a job as janitor there to be near her. He daydreams of saving her and helping her to escape; his repetitive images of revolt and escape dissolve in a dreamlike sea. Mesmerizing and baffling scenes come and go. A crazed dancer. A group laughing. Is his wife crazy, or is it he? Is she really his wife or is this just a daydream? This Japanese experimental film from the silent era features strong black and whites and severe camera angles. The edgy editing and cutaways to wind and rain all suggest a brain at the edge of frenzy in the frontier between madness and sanity. —J. C.

PHANTOM OF THE OPERA, THE (1925) L: SILENT
FILMS/SILENT HORROR (1925) 93M D: Wallace Worsley. *Kate Lester, Ernest Torrence, Patsy Ruth Miller, Lon Chaney, Norman Kerry.* This early silent version of the *Phantom,* starring the great Chaney, still stands tall above all its successors. Here, the tortured tale of the tragic anti-hero and his unrequited love is beautifully told. The Phantom is made to be quite a monster but, still, you have to sympathize with him. Visually the film employs incredible production design but mediocre camera work. The acting is what really makes this one shine. —T. S.

PICCADILLY L: SILENT FILMS/SILENT DRAMA (1929) 92M D:
E. A. Dupont. *Gilda Gray, Jameson Thomas, Anna May Wong.* Former nightclub star Mabel tails Shosho and Valentine home: when club owner Valentine leaves she enters and confronts the club's new headliner, Shosho. Threatens. Begs. Is beside herself: "You don't need him! I do!" Shosho (Wong) is haughty with the pride of possession. Mabel (Gray) opens her purse. Beside her handkerchief is a gun. Shosho's indifferent face cracks in terror. She raises a knife. Mabel raises the gun. Shoots. Faints. Valentine (Thomas) realizes the gun is his and perhaps, too, the blame. This taut, stylish murder mystery is full of smart visual

George Méliès

George Méliès was born on December 18, 1861. He excelled as a magician and eventually became the owner of Theatre Robert-Houdin in Paris, where he performed his art. On December 28, 1895, he happened to attend the first screening of the Lumière Cinematograph, which featured stunning moving pictures. Méliès bought himself a camera a few months later, and in a few more months was beginning to make his own films.

Méliès was literally one in a million, for at that time there were probably a million magicians swarming Paris in search of their niche. But this magician found his niche well enough, for whereas the Lumière brothers felt compelled to shoot footage of peoples and cities, Méliès used film as a remarkable extension of his art. Much as most science fiction films do today, George Méliès used film to perform magic.

Among his earliest surviving prints is *The Four Troublesome Heads*, released in 1898 to an audience eager for this kind of magic. In this two-minute film, roughly the length of one reel of film at the time, Méliès himself steps out and performs an alarming magic act. He takes his head off his shoulders and sets it on a nearby table. Then, with a wave of his arms, his head reappears. He replicates his head in this way three more times, thus producing four separate heads, which then attempt to sing in harmony. This was fantastic stuff for a darkened theater in the 1890s, and Méliès followed it up with a number of outrageous spectacles, each of which featured some magical aspect unique to the world of filmmaking.

In *The Man with the Rubber Head* (1901), he makes use of the concept of zooming in tandem with superimposition. He takes his own head (he seemed to love using his head for these cinematic tricks) and inflates it with a simple bellows. Once the head has become nearly as big as the frame, he laughs and lets air out of it, thereby diminishing its size. Such magic acts would never be seen on stage at the time, he could assure you that.

Méliès' vision went far beyond mere trick photography, though it must be noted that the tricks of photography at that time were amazingly visionary and in no small way formed the basis of today's film technique. At a time when most films were two minutes in length, Méliès edited his reels together into extremely long, continuous films. In 1903 he released his magnum opus, *A Trip to the Moon*, which was a staggering fifteen minutes long. Consider briefly what *Lawrence of Arabia* was to the 1960s, with its 70mm photography, stereo sound, and epic length. In its own small way, that's what Méliès's sensational film was to the moviegoers of 1903. In addition, the idea of landing on the moon was an absurd fiction at the time, but there it was depicted in motion on the large screen. Taken in full, the film's entertainment value could not be denied by anyone.

In total, Méliès directed hundreds of films. His largest works, including *Conquest of the North Pole*, used outrageous and enormous sets in addition to hand-tinting of the film.

For those wanting to learn more about this film pioneer, *Méliès the Magician* is a splendid DVD that brings you into a theater where an elderly lady who knew Méliès in her youth discusses his films and serves as the "barker"—the person who shouted out the information patrons needed to know, in the age before title cards were used in silent films.

—Nathan Jensen

touches and edgy performances, Wong's in particular. Her rise from fun-loving kitchen worker to star to scheming seductress is delineated by carefully calibrated changes to her physical movement: you watch every twitch and turn of her muscles. If only Hollywood had used her so well. —*J. C.*

SALOMÉ L: SILENT FILMS/SILENT DRAMA (1923) 75M D: Charles Bryant. *Earl Schenk, Alla Nazimova, Mitchell Lewis, Rose Dione.* A lovely stylized stage play with pretenses to be cinema. Lavish sets and costumes dominate as Salomé (Nazimova) becomes intrigued by the raving desert prisoner in her stepfather's jail. He shows no interest in her except to damn her lecherous thoughts, which only intrigues her more. Her mother wants the lunatic silenced but King Herod will not have a Holy Man killed. Both mother and daughter get their wish after Salomé dances for the old letch. "The mystery of love is greater than the mystery of death." Such 1920s esthete platitudes aside, *Salomé* is visually rich and feels very modern even today. Nazimova's quirky sensuality comes off fresh and believable, as an honest and intense erotic fixation in this unapologetic, low-grade spectacle. —*J. C.*

SON OF THE SHEIK, THE L: SILENT FILMS/SILENT ADVENTURE (1926) 68M D: George Fitzmaurice. *Montague Love, Rudolph Valentino, George Fawcett, Vilma Banky.* Pity the woman who stars opposite Valentino, one of the most beautiful creatures ever captured on film. In the sequel to *The Sheik* he returns in two roles: the hot-blooded young son out for revenge on the dancing girl (Banky) he believes betrayed him, and his stern, bearded father (their scenes together are so smoothly tricked you might never notice). The defining moment of the film has the hero tied up and tortured by the sadistic villain. Valentino is the only actor of the silent era to receive the same soft visual caress as the actresses, and here he's even treated to the spectacle of Victorian abasement saved for the feminine objects of sexual desire. This was the swoony star's final film: he collapsed while in New York for the premiere and died eight days later. The public hysteria surrounding his funeral is documented in the original Pathe newsreel that accompanies the Kino DVD release. —*S. A.*

SPARROWS L: SILENT FILMS/SILENT DRAMA (1926) 107M D: William Beaudine. *Gustave von Seyffertitz, Mary Louise Miller, Mary Pickford, Roy Stewart.* Pickford was America's sweetheart, the first female superstar, and the darling of silent cinema. As the big sister/foster mother to a rag-tag collection of orphaned kids living as slaves to a vicious boss, she's an icon of hope, courage, and spunky drive leading her pilgrims to the promised land through the dank, fetid, alligator-infested swamp—a thrilling, beautifully accomplished scene. It's quintessential Pickford,

but director Beaudine transcends himself and Pickford with one of the most breathtaking moments of silent cinema, when a vision of Jesus turns an infant's death into a soaring moment of salvation. —*S. A.*

STELLA MARIS L: SILENT FILMS/SILENT DRAMA (1918) 84M D: Marshall Neilan. *Mary Pickford, Ida Waterman, Josephine Crowell, Conway Tearle, Herbert Standing.* Stella Maris is a tidy melodrama featuring Pickford in a dual role. An attractive but crippled rich girl (Pickford) and a homely orphan (also Pickford) are by degrees brought together by a journalist (Tearle), who dotes on the rich invalid. His brutal former wife (Marcia Manon) beats the orphan after "adopting" her for cheap labor. When police throw the ex in jail, the journalist takes over care of the child. All is fine until the rich girl is cured and the ex-wife gets out of prison promising trouble. The movie was a platform to show the world that Pickford could act (passably so), but the lyrical curly haired girl with pep and feistiness that audiences loved is divided in two, a stunted performance on both parts. The story's pat ending is nearly contemptible. —*J. C.*

THOMAS GRAAL'S BEST FILM L: SILENT FILMS/SILENT COMEDY (1917) 55M D: Mauritz Stiller. *Albin Lavén, Jenny Tschernichin-Larsson, Karin Molander, Victor Sjöström, Axel Nilsson.* Though it's a silent film, shot for shot this is perhaps the most naturally witty film ever made. Thomas Graal (Sjöström) stomps about his room trying to dictate his new screenplay, jumping upon chairs or catching manuscript pages afire and being blasé about putting them out. His new secretary (Molander) takes it all in stride, but not his little peck-kiss. She leaves only to be kidnapped back to her rich home by detectives. Disconsolate and not knowing how to find her, Graal imagines her as having run away from a life of poverty. Running across fields and onto a ferry he finds her . . . in his new screenplay. Every bit of this is done visually through camera work in natural settings with performances by Sjöström and Molander as quick and fluid as swallows winging into eves. Probably the first screwball comedy, the humor is as fresh and natural as the awkward eagerness of the lovers' first true kiss. —*J. C.*

TOO WISE WIVES L: SILENT FILMS/SILENT COMEDY (1921) 79M D: Lois Weber. *Phillips Smalley, Mona Lisa, Louis Calhern, Claire Windsor.* Too Wise Wives is a beautifully photographed, extraordinarily deft domestic comedy mixed with social satire. The Grahams are well-to-do and the Dalys are downright rich. The camera compares the dining rooms and entranceways of each family to give you the details of their homes, then moves on to the psychological interiors. Mrs. Daly (Lisa) cynically dotes on her husband (he gives her a blank check to spend all she wants in expensive clothing stores) while Mrs. Graham (Windsor) does the things she thinks a proper woman of her station should do whether it genuinely pleases her husband or not. Then a letter arranging an extramarital tryst winds up in the wrong hands and both women's complacent lives are suddenly unsettled. An unerringly intelligent film with an earned pathos undergirding the suave, gently humorous surface. It was released the same year as Weber's equally shrewd and thoughtful social satire *The Blot.* —*J. C.*

TRAFFIC IN SOULS L: SILENT FILMS/SILENT DRAMA (1913) 74M D: George Loane Tucker. *William Welsh, William H. Turner, Ethel Grandin, Jane Gail, Matt Moore.* A smart exposé detailing step by careful step how naive immigrant girls just off the boat are tricked into prostitution houses, where they are locked in and become dependent on their keepers like animals in cages. It details the money trail as well, the bribing cops and user middlemen, all leading back to the top guy, a high-society hypocrite who rails publicly against the "white slave racket." A sympathetic cop (Moore) tries to find his girlfriend's kidnapped sister (Grandin), a spunky gal who went undercover for the cops. There's a nice crosscut from the locked-up sister's utter desolation to a scene of the middleman's happy home life. The biggest money maker of its day, *Traffic in Souls* is often referred to as cinema's first exploitation film due to its lurid content. —*J. C.*

TRIP TO THE MOON, A L: SILENT FILMS/EARLY CINEMA (1902) 21M D: Georges Méliès. *Victor André, Georges Méliès, Bleuette Bernon.* This very early and highly stylized silent science fiction film is humorous, visionary, and truly astonishing, not the least because it runs twenty-one minutes at a time when films generally ran only one minute.

Loosely based on Jules Verne's *From the Earth to the Moon* and H. G. Wells's *The First Men in the Moon,* the plot concerns an association of astronomers who approve a trip to the moon. The proposed method of transportation is a bullet-shaped craft fired from a specially made cannon. Fitted to the highest building in town, the cannon is fired and the five occupants arrive safely (despite the sour expression of the moon with a large bullet poking out of its face). After a fitful night's sleep the voyagers descend to the inside of the moon where they meet its inhabitants, the vicious, savage Selenites. This is Méliès's most popular film and the first true classic of science fiction films. —*N. J.*

VAMPIRES, LES L: SILENT FILMS/SILENT HORROR (1915) 399M D: Louis Feuillade. *Musidora, Edouard Mathé, Marcel Lévesque, Jean Aymé, Fernand Herrmann, Stacia Napierkowska.* It's easy to see why the surrealists embraced Feuillade's mad serialized tale of a master criminal organization that robs, kidnaps, and murders their way through Parisian society. The impossibly hard to follow ten-episode serial revels in anarchy caused by the rapacious gang "The Vampires." Let's face it, nothing interrupts a well-ordered day more than getting lassoed from your window and yanked into a waiting sack, or finding a severed head in a secret compartment hidden above your bed. Shot in the chaos of 1914 France, Feuillade directed the film on the run, often improvising and repeatedly killing off characters as performers were called to war. The resulting narrative doesn't always make sense, but that's part of the delight—"The Vampires" seem all the more deadly for their unpredictability and obscure intentions. —*S. A.*

ACKNOWLEDGMENTS

While this book contains reviews from the staff and friends of Scarecrow Video, it's important to acknowledge that content does not magically form itself into a book. From Scarecrow we thank Norman Hill, our liaison with Sasquatch Books, who helped us shape the vision of what this book became and to bring it in on time. John Dauphiny and Josh Warren created and maintained the database we used to keep all the many details in this book straight; Sue Pope for maintaining the accounting. We couldn't have done this without their help. Most importantly, we must thank Jen Koogler and Bryan Theiss—when it became clear that we needed a lot of editing help (at about the time we hit review number 3,000), they stepped up with red pens blazing. Their many long nights of reading and re-reading every review in this book (along with many that are no longer here) took a disorganized pile of well-meant but fairly scattered reviews and sculpted them into the collection you're holding, and because of their time and dedication it's much better than it had any right to be.

At the end of the day, Scarecrow is about movies, and we couldn't have done a book without the professionals at Sasquatch. Thanks to Gary Luke, Dana Youlin, Stewart Williams, and Bill Quinby.

Finally, we must acknowledge and thank the customers at Scarecrow Video—we wouldn't be here without them, and it's their continued patronage that's allowed us to build the collection and film knowledge that we have today. To all of you—past, present, and those yet to stop in—we'll see you at the counter.

Index

305, 310, 446, 520, 537, 552, 576, 599, 646,
655–56, 669, 673–74, 699, 703, 709–11, 715
Leigh, Jennifer Jason, 9, 52, 61,
123, 316, 393, 458, 473
Lorre, Peter, 58, 65, 121–22,
127, 148, 532, 565, 682
Lugosi, Bela, 30, 162, 283, 287, 408,
413, 654, 661, 664, 700, 706, 720
Lupino, Ida, 167, 195, 271, 580, 654

➤ **M**

Marvin, Lee, 25, 89, 100, 148,
232, 244, 382, 397, 581
Masina, Giulietta, 84, 218
McDormand, Frances, 52, 205,
458, 467, 497, 522, 627
McLachlan, Kyle, 167–68
Mifune, Toshirô, 394
Mirren, Helen, 9, 107, 109, 447, 579, 618, 717
Mitchum, Robert, 74, 134, 271,
277, 394, 566, 570, 577
Monroe, Marilyn, 110, 282

➤ **N**

Nicholson, Jack, 16, 33–34, 58, 92,
114, 128, 144, 183, 198, 204, 389,
408, 464–65, 473, 612, 698

➤ **O**

Oates, Warren, 114–15, 171,
195–96, 389, 445, 693

➤ **P**

Pacino, Al, 56, 70, 72, 97, 165, 167,
175, 272, 424, 444, 573, 614
Perkins, Anthony, 121, 221, 277, 510, 581, 584
Phoenix, River, 239, 285, 428,
476, 581, 593, 708
Pickford, Mary, 108, 743, 748
Potente, Franka, 263, 325
Presley, Elvis, 65
Price, Vincent, 34–35, 43, 57–58, 72,
204, 257, 417, 516, 558, 574, 630,
635, 651, 655, 674, 682, 703, 714

➤ **R**

Reed, Oliver, 60, 102, 156, 222–23,
231, 304, 307, 399, 511

Reno, Jean, 12, 22, 71, 206–7, 319, 325, 702
Rigg, Diana, 436, 516, 532, 564,
578, 618, 620, 714
Rossellini, Isabella, 167, 441
Roth, Tim, 6, 35, 107, 249, 292, 466, 623
Ryan, Robert, 173, 196, 244, 391

➤ **S**

Sarandon, Susan, 171, 183, 416,
428, 497, 519, 567, 601
Scott, George C., 143, 156, 219, 226,
283, 395, 398, 528, 646, 659
Shatner, William, 57, 284, 379, 408, 423,
466, 654, 676, 679, 693, 708–9
Stamp, Terence, 161, 194, 236, 288, 293, 300
Stanwyck, Barbara, 101, 110,
181, 244, 277, 281
Steele, Barbara, 17, 62, 68, 84, 176, 695
Stewart, James, 4, 38, 64, 67, 89,
122–23, 163, 173–74, 204, 384
Streep, Meryl, 6, 187, 384, 408, 617
Swanson, Gloria, 68, 243, 271, 282, 476, 630
Swinton, Tilda, 132–33, 408, 568

➤ **T**

Taylor, Lili, 274, 344, 429, 443
Turner, Lana, 183, 233, 468, 472, 579

➤ **U**

Ullmann, Liv, 19–20, 371

➤ **V**

von Sydow, Max, 20, 25, 97, 116, 167, 242,
258, 368, 445, 459, 542, 582, 648, 657

➤ **W**

Walken, Christopher, 33, 35, 61, 85,
384, 389, 404, 414, 424, 430, 524,
583–84, 598, 624, 641, 697
Watson, Emily, 9, 257, 658
Weaver, Sigourney, 36, 85, 152,
187, 231, 419, 447, 517, 631
Williamson, Fred, 55, 380, 404

➤ **Y**

Yeoh, Michelle, 49, 151, 255, 340, 343

Baker, Roy Ward, 612, 632, 690, 698
Bakshi, Ralph, 509, 534–35, 537, 541–42, 544–45, 549, 556
Baky, Josef von, 328
Balaban, Bob, 438
Balabanov, Alexei, 366
Balch, Anthony, 673
Baldwin, Craig, 295
Baldwin, Gerald, 517
Ballard, Carroll, 16
Bangs, Lance, 420, 598
Bani-Etemad, Rakhshan, 346
Banno, Yoshimitsu, 668
Barbate, Randy, 471–72
Barbato, Randy, 490
Barbera, Joseph, 528
Barclay, Paris, 401
Barker, Clive, 648, 672, 690
Barley, Trevor (aka Roman Nowicki), 659
Barney, Matthew, 621
Barredo, Ana, 440
Barreto, Bruno, 472, 611
Barrett, Shirley, 301
Barry, Ian, 660
Bartel, Paul, 16
Barton, Charles, 408
Bass, Jules, 514, 520, 522
Bass, Saul, 695
Bassett, Michael J., 652
Bassul, Vincent, 552
Bava, Lamberto, 653–54
Bava, Mario, 17–19
Bay, Michael, 395–96, 633
Bearde, Chris, 428
Beatty, Warren, 416, 473
Beaudine, William, 413, 637
Becker, Jacques, 18–19
Becker, Josh, 403, 433, 580
Bedford, Terry, 402
Beebe, Ford I., 513
Beeson, Jeannette, 491
Bell, Martin, 467, 502
Bell, Alan J. W., 311
Belvaux, Remy, 302
Bender, Jack, 647
Benjamin, Richard, 436
Bergman, Ingmar, 19–21
Bergman, Peter, 429–30
Berliner, Alain, 302
Berlinger, Joe, 578
Berlinger, Robert, 454–55

Berman, Sasbina, 362–63
Berman, Shari Springer, 535
Berman, Ted, 510
Bernds, Edward, 448
Bernhardt, Curtis, 474
Berry, John, 412
Bertoglio, Edo, 612
Bertolucci, Bernardo, 21–22
Besson, Luc, 22
Besson, Ty, 491
Beyer, Frank, 327
Bezucha, Thomas, 478
Bhansali, Sanjay Leela, 345
Bianchi, Andrea, 644
Bielinsky, Fabian, 299–300
Bierman, Robert, 449
Bigelow, Kathryn, 396, 403, 688–89
Bill, Tony, 419
Bindler, S. R., 492
Bird, Brad, 518, 631
Birkin, John, 312
Birmingham, Hilary, 476
Bitton, Donald, 607
Black, Stephanie, 496
Blank, Les, 486–87, 491, 495
Blatty, William Peter, 577, 659
Blaustein, Barry, 484
Blier, Bertrand, 22–23
Block, Doug, 494
Bloom, Jeffrey, 638
Blum, Michael, 439–40
Bluth, Don, 508, 529, 531
Bochner, Hart, 427
Boetticher, Budd, 23–24
Bogdanovich, Peter, 23, 25
Bohlen, Anne, 485
Boll, Uwe, 674
Bolton, Michael, 497
Bont, Jan de, 402
Bonzel, Andre, 302
Boorman, John, 25–26
Booth, Kevin, 427
Borchardt, Mark, 649
Borowczyk, Walerian, 318
Borzage, Frank, 26–27
Bosher, Dennis, 402
Boskovich, John, 627
Bower, Dallas, 534
Bowman, Rob, 700
Bozzetto, Bruno, 534
Brady, Tom, 427–28

Endfield, Raker, 405
Epstein, Jean, 659
Epstein, Rob, 611
Epstein, Robert, 479
Erice, Victor, 368, 369–70
Erwitt, Elliott, 492
Esper, Dwain, 683
Eustache, Jean, 322
Evans, Marc, 688
Evans, Ty, 505
Eyre, Chris, 474
➤ **F**
Famuyiwa, Rick, 590–91
Farina, Corrado, 634
Farocki, Harun, 327–28
Farrelly, Bobby, 431, 434, 444, 525
Farrelly, Peter, 431, 434, 444, 525
Fasano, John, 589, 600–601
Fassbinder, Rainer Werner, 81–84
Fawcett, John, 664
Fei-Hung, Wong, 333–36
Feist, Felix E., 653
Fellini, Federico, 84–85
Feng-bor, Lee, 372
Ferrara, Abel, 85
Fessenden, Larry, 670
Field, Todd, 617–18
Figgis, Mike, 475
Fincher, David, 85–86
Finkleman, Ken, 408–09
Firstenberg, Sam, 394, 590
Fisher, Terence, 86–88
Fleischer, David, 556
Fleischer, Richard, 99, 394, 405, 532,
  566, 659
Fleming, Victor, 88–89
Flemyng, Gordon, 655–56
Fletcher, Mandie, 310
Flynn, John, 399, 564–65
Fok, Clarence, 338
Foley, David, 453
Foley, James, 383, 567, 614
Fonda, Peter, 389–90
Fontaine, Dick, 591
Fonteyne, Frederic, 317
Ford, John, 89–91
Forman, Milos, 91–92
Forrest, Arthur, 454
Forster, Marc, 470–71
Forsyth, Edward J., 403
Fosse, Bob, 93
Fosselius, Ernie, 671

Foster, Lewis R., 382
Francis, Coleman, 636, 688
Francis, Freddie, 655–56
Franco, Jess, 93–94
Franju, Georges, 94
Frank, Robert, 611
Frankel, David, 379
Frankenheimer, John, 94–96
Fraserp, Harry L., 646
Frawley, James, 524
Frears, Stephen, 96–97
Frei, Christian, 627
Fremke, Susan, 488
Fresnadillo, Juan Carlos, 368
Freund, Kate, 682
Freundlich, Bart, 477
Fridolinski, Alex, 372
Fridriksson, Fridrik Thor, 344
Friedkin, William, 97–98
Friedman, Jeffrey, 611
Friedman, Ken, 392–93
Frost, Lee, 380
Fuest, Robert, 630, 654, 655
Fujiwara, Kel, 693
Fukasaku, Kinji, 98–99
Fukuda, Jon, 657, 667, 668
Fulci, Lucio, 99–100
Fuller, Samuel, 100–101, 102–03
Fulton, Keith, 619
Fuqua, Antoine, 399, 404
Furie, Sidney J., 390, 392
Furuhashi, Kazuhiro, 554
Fywell, Tim, 566
➤ **G**
Gabriel, Mike, 528
Gabriel Mike, 526
Gallardo, Carlos, 363
Gallen, Joel, 437
Gallo, George, 425
Gallo, Vincent, 462
Gambler, The, 613–14
Gance, Abel, 101–02
Gandini, Erik, 502
Gans, Christophe, 318, 540
Garcia, Nicole, 323
Garnett, Tay, 579
Garon, Syd, 606
Gasnier, Louis J., 699
Gast, Leon, 505
Gastaldi, Ernesto, 681–82
Gatlif, Tony, 102
Gaup, Nils, 365

Gay, Cesc, 369
Geda, Curt, 536, 557
Genet, Jean, 297
Gerard, Mark, 614
Geronimi, Clyde, 507, 508, 511, 520, 523, 525, 529
Gervais, Ricky, 312
Gessner, Nicolas, 581
Gibney, Alex, 503
Gibson, Alan, 656, 671
Gilbert, Lewis, 576, 581–82, 585
Gillam, Terry, 311–12
Gillen, Jeff, 568
Gillespie, Jim, 569–70
Gilliam, Terry, 102–04
Gilling, John, 661
Gilmore, Patrick, 529
Gilroy, Tom, 474
Gilstrap, Peter, 603
Ginsberg, Milton Moses, 463
Girdler, William, 651, 683
Gitai, Amos, 347
Glazer, Jonathan, 580–81
Glen, John, 570, 575, 578, 583
Godard, Jean-Luc, 104–07
Goddard, Gary, 684
Goldberg, Eric, 526
Goldblatt, Mark, 651
Golden, John, 660
Goldman, Gary, 508, 531
Goldthwait, Bob, 443–44
Goleszowski, Richard, 554
Gondry, Michel, 428
Gong, Ching, 336
Goodman, Barak, 490
Goodwins, Leslie, 687
Goosens, Ray, 526
Gordon, Bert I., 658
Gordon, Dennie, 430
Gordon, Robert, 676
Gordon, Steve, 410–11
Gosling, Maureen, 491
Gosnell, Raja, 528
Gotoh, Daisuke, 356
Gottlieb, Carl, 409
Gottlieb, Lisa, 430–31
Gowariker, Ashotosh, 345
Goyer, David S., 478
Graham, William A., 467
Grames, Lee, 458
Grant, Joe, 523
Grau, Jorge, 681

Gray, Gary, 424
Gray, Milton, 645
Green, David, 694
Green, David Gordon, 458, 466
Green, Jack N., 476
Green, Joseph, 478
Green, Rob, 644
Green, Tom, 423
Greenaway, Peter, 107–08
Greenburg, Alan, 496
Greenburg, Robert, 521
Greene, Ray, 624
Greenfield, Luke, 410
Griffith, D.W., 106–07, 108
Grinter, Brad F., 639
Gross, Paul, 314
Gruber, Markus, 597–98
Gruener, Daniel, 362
Guédiguian, Robert, 324
Guest, Christopher, 413, 450
Guest, Val, 304, 630, 672, 698
Guillermin, John, 679
➤ H
Halicki, H.B., 388, 390
Hallström, Lasse, 471
Hamilton, Guy, 387–88, 569, 571–72, 575–76, 579
Hand, David, 509, 529
Haneke, Michael, 109
Hanks, Tom, 379
Hanna, William, 528
Hanson, Curtis, 593, 627
Hardy, Robin, 310
Harlin, Renny, 384, 653, 690
Harris, Ed, 622
Harris, James B., 460
Harris, Maia, 502
Harron, Mary, 610
Hartley, Hal, 109
Harvey, Anthony, 619
Harvey, Herk, 645
Has, Wojciech, 365–66
Hasebe, Yasuharu, 350
Hashimoto, Kohji, 666
Hasier, Joachim, 327
Haskin, Bryon, 626
Hata, Masanori, 548
Hathaway, Henry, 109
Hauser, Rick, 495
Hawkes, Steve, 639
Hawks, Howard, 110–13
Hayashi, Hiroki, 541

Hayes, Blair, 415–16
Haynes, Todd, 113–14
Haywood-Carter, Annette, 613
Hebst, Helmut, 614
Hecht, Ben, 458
Heer, Rolf De, 300, 301, 631
Heffernan, David, 607
Helgeland, Brian, 395
Heller, André, 484–85
Hellman, Monte, 114–15
Helmer, Velt, 328
Henderson, John, 656
Henenlotter, Frank, 635, 640
Henry, Eric, 606
Henson, Brian, 524, 660
Henson, Jim, 512, 516, 650, 680
Henzell, Perry, 349
Herman, Mark, 304
Hermosillo, Jaime Humberto, 363
Herrington, Rowdy, 399
Herzog, Werner, 115–16
Hewitt, David L., 686
Hewitt, Peter, 414
Hewlett, Jamie, 594
Hicks, Scott, 301–02, 625, 672
Hideyuki, Hirayama, 355
Hiken, Nat, 432
Hill, George Roy, 116–17
Hill, Jack, 117–18
Hill, Tim, 524
Hill, Walter, 118–19
Hillcoat, John, 301, 598
Hillyer, Lambert, 656
Hilton, Arthur D., 646
Hing-kai, Chan, 330
Hirschbiebel, Oliver, 326
Hirst, Damien, 589–90
Hitchcock, Alfred, 119–23
Ho, Meng-Hwa, 685
Hobbs, Lyndall, 588
Hodges, Mike, 542
Hodson, Christopher, 310
Hoffman, Judy, 604
Hoffman, Michael, 437
Holland, Agnieszka, 123–24
Holland, Savage Steve, 413
Holland, Tom, 646, 662
Holofcener, Nicole, 433
Honda, Inoshiro, 124–25
Hong, Sang-soo, 361
Hooks, Kevin, 380
Hooper, Tobe, 662–63, 682, 696

Hopkins, Joel, 430
Hopkins, Stephen, 690–91
Hopper, Dennis, 464
Horne, James W., 450
Horton, Peter, 409
Hou Hsiao-Hsien, 125
Hough, John, 631–32, 681
Hovde, Ellen, 492
Howard, Arliss, 610
Howard, Ron, 438, 445, 459
Hrebejk, Jan, 316
Hu, King, 330–31, 372
Hua-Shan, 335
Hubley, Faith, 545–46
Huddles, John, 449
Hughes, Albert, 483–84, 568, 571
Hughes, Allen, 483–84, 568, 571
Hughes, Bronwen, 517
Hughes, John, 415, 450
Hughes, Ken, 511
Hughes, Robert C., 505
Humphreys, Dewl, 308
Hung, Sammo, 125–26
Hung, Tran Anh, 374–75
Hunt, Peter H., 602–3
Hunt, Peter R., 578
Hunter, T. Hayes, 664
Hunter, Tim, 473
Huntington, Lawrence, 583–84
Hurley, Frank, 501
Hurtz, William T., 548
Huseyin, Metin, 616
Hussein, Waris, 476
Huston, John, 126–28
Hutton, Brian G., 405
Huyck, Willard, 545
Hyams, Peter, 403, 645

➤ I

Ichaso, Leon, 315–16
Idle, Eric, 601–2
Iglesia, Alex de la, 128–29
Ikeda, Toshiharu, 349
Ikehiro, Kazuo, 353
Illsley, Mark, 426
Imamura, Shohei, 129
Imanishi, Takashi, 539
Iñárritu, Alejandro González, 362
Isaac, James, 677
Ishi, Katsuhiro, 353
Ishiguro, Noboru, 556
Ishii, Katsuhito, 352–53
Ishii, Sogo, 657–58

Keusch, Michael, 430
Kiarostami, Abbas, 140–42
Kieslowski, Krzysztof, 142–43
Kim, Dong-bin, 360
Kim, Ki-duk, 356–58, 362
Kim, Moon Saeng, 561–62
Kim, Sang-Jin, 356, 359
Kim, Sung-su, 357, 359
King, Robert Lee, 622
King, Scott, 476
King, Stephen, 685
Kinney, Jack, 523
Kirchheimer, Manfred, 625
Kitakubo, Hiroyuki, 537, 554
Kitamura, Ryuhei, 355
Kitano, Takeshi, 246–49
Kizer, Robert J., 666
Klane, Robert, 450
Klapisch, Cédric, 318, 322–23
Klein, Brian, 498
Klein, Rolando, 363
Kleiser, Randal, 461, 509–10
Klimovsky, León, 694
Knussen, Sue, 588
Kok, Vincent, 334
Komizu, Kazuo "Gaira," 670
Kon, Satoshi, 550, 552
Kondo, Yoshifumi, 561
Konishi, Michio, 678
Konuma, Masaru, 355
Kopple, Barbara, 490, 492
Kore-eda, Hirokazu, 351–52
Korine, Harmony, 467, 469
Kormakur, Baltasar, 344
Korty, John, 466, 560, 658
Koster, Henry, 447
Kotcheff, Ted, 387, 471, 571
Kotcheff, Terry, 450
Kovacs, Ernie, 453
Krawczyk, Gerard, 325
Krishnamma, Suri, 347
Kristersson, Mikael, 496
Kroyer, Bill, 513
Krulik, Jeff, 490, 502–03
Kubrick, Stanley, 143–45
Kulik, Buzz, 635
Kumble, Roger, 446, 464, 611
Kümel, Harry, 650
Kunuk, Zacharias, 314
Kuo-fu, Chen, 331, 372
Kuri, Ippei, 508
Kurosawa, Akira, 145–47

Kurosawa, Kiyoshi, 350, 649, 698
Kursturica, Emir, 147
Kuzui, Fran Rubel, 416
Kwak, Jae-young, 359
Kwon-Taek, Im, 357
Kyu-Dong, Min, 359
➤ L
LaBute, Neil, 478
LaCava, Gregory, 147
Lachman, Edward, 469
Lachow, Gregg, 297–98
Lafia, John, 646–47
LaGavenese, Richard, 432
LaLoggia, Frank, 574
Laloux, Rene, 541, 560
Lam, Allun, 329
Lam, Ringo, 147–48
Lamore, Marsh, 645
Lampson, Mary, 504
Lancaster, Burt, 390
Landers, Lew, 700
Landi, Mario, 664
Landis, James, 580
Landis, John, 409, 431, 446, 573, 589, 621, 632
Landon, Michael, 522
Lang, Fritz, 148–50
Langton, Simon, 622
Lanzmann, Claude, 501
Lapine, James, 304–05
Larson, Eric, 529
Lasseter, John, 531
Lathan, Stan, 588
Lau, Andrew, 335, 336–37, 342–43
Lau, Jeff, 330
Lau, Ricky, 337–38
Laughlin, Tom, 379–80, 380, 393
Laughton, Charles, 577
Laugier, Pascal, 318
Lautrec, Linda, 436
Laven, Arnold, 686
Law Wing-Cheung, 256
Lawrence, John, 400
Lawrence, Quentin, 649
Layton, Joe, 440
Le Borg, Reginald, 687
Leacock, Robert, 611
Lean, David, 150–51
Leconte, Patrice, 151
Lee, Ang, 151–52
Lee, Bruce, 339
Lee, Chang-dong, 357–58

Mantegna, Joe, 618
Marcarelli, Robert, 691
Marcovich, Carlos, 363
Margheriti, Antonio, 176
Margolis, Jeff, 440, 597
Margulies, Lynn, 409–10
Marins, José Mojica, 176
Marker, Chris, 296
Markey, David, 603
Markie, Peter, 428
Marks, Arthur, 384, 388, 390
Marquand, Richard, 700
Marshall, Frank, 631, 633
Marshall, George, 384
Marshall, Neil, 655
Marshall, Penny, 413, 459
Marshall, Rob, 591
Marshall, Tonie, 324–25
Marshall, William, 695
Martin, Frank, 655
Martineau, Jacques, 317
Martinez, Emilio, 369
Martino, Sergio, 637–38
Martinson, Leslie, 536
Mashimo, Koichi, 546
Masuda, Toshihiko, 536
Masumura, Yasuzo, 350–51
Mate, Rudolph, 569
Mattel, Bruno, 100
Mattinson, Bury, 516
May, Elaine, 615
Mayer, Daisy von Scherler, 452, 522
Maysles, Albert, 487–88, 491–92, 500
Maysles, David, 487–88, 491–92, 500
Mazin, Craig, 445
McBride, Jim, 665
McCarey, Leo, 176–77
McCracken, Craig, 527
McCullough, Jim, 634
McDonald, Michael J., 419–20
McEveety, Vincent, 516–17
McG, 382
McGehee, Scott, 568
McGrath, Douglas, 419
McGrath, Joseph, 305
Mcguire, Don, 420
McKay, Jim, 471
McKee, Lucky, 685
McKenzie, David, 493
McLeod, Norman Z., 427, 429, 448
McNaughton, John, 572, 577–78, 584
McQuarrie, Christopher, 584

McTiernan, John, 384–85, 697
Medak, Peter, 305, 580, 646
Medem, Julio, 177
Mehrjul, Dariush, 346
Mehta, Deepa, 177–78
Mekas, Jonas, 297
Melendez, Bill, 511, 519, 521, 527
Melford, George, 656
Melville, Jean-Pierre, 178–79
Menaul, Christopher, 579
Mendes, Sam, 458
Mendizza, Michael, 596
Merchant, Stephen, 312
Merendino, James, 474
Merhige, E. Elias, 296–97
Merriwether, Nicholas, 657
Messina, Philip Frank, 451
Metter, Alan, 425
Metzger, Radley, 479
Meyer, Nicholas, 650–51
Michener, Dave, 516
Mikels, Ted V., 385, 633–34, 639
Milestone, Lewis, 181–82
Milhaka, George, 687–88
Milius, John, 399–400, 461, 648
Milke, Takashi, 179–81
Millar, Catherine, 660
Miller, Bennett, 489
Miller, Claude, 182
Miller, David, 582
Miller, George, 182–83, 532
Miller, Paul, 447
Miller, Troy, 422, 519
Miner, Steve, 670–71
Minghella, Anthony, 305
Minkoff, Rob, 509, 530
Minkoff, Robert, 521
Minnelli, Vincente, 183–84
Misumi, Kenji, 351, 356
Mitchell, Charlotte, 500
Mitchell, Duke, 569
Mitchell, John Cameron, 595
Mitchell, Mike, 420–21
Mitrevski, Darko, 362
Miyazaki, Hayao, 538, 547–48, 550, 553–54,
    556
Mizoguchi, Kenji, 182–83, 184
Moctezuma, Juan López, 631
Moland, Hans Petter, 365
Moland, Petter, 367
Moll, Dominik, 325
Moncrieff, Karen, 461

Monson, Carl, 401
Montagne, Edward J. Jr., 440
Montaldo, Giuliano, 348, 572
Montesi, Jorge, 692
Moore, Guy, 540–41
Moore, Michael, 484–85, 487, 500, 504
Moore, Robert, 620
Moore, Steve, 525
Mora, Phillippe, 599
Moranis, Rick, 445
Mordillat, Gerard, 322
Morgen, Brett, 618
Mori, Kazuo, 356
Morimoto, Kouji, 549
Morita, Hiroyuki, 538
Morris, Errol, 485–86, 490–91, 498, 503
Morrissette, Billy, 624
Morrissey, Paul, 184
Mostow, Jonathan, 565
Motohiro, Katsuyuki, 349
Mottola, Greg, 420
Moxey, John, 673
Moxey, John Llewellyn, 689
Moyle, Allan, 423, 472
Mugge, Robert, 602
Mulcahy, Russell, 673
Muldaur, Maureen, 454
Mullan, Peter, 347
Mulligan, Robert, 184–85
Mune, Ian, 365
Murakami, Jimmy T., 636
Murch, Walter, 700
Murnau, F. W., 185–86
Muroga, Atsushi, 678–79
Murphy, Edward D., 399
Murphy, Geoff, 364
Murphy, Melanie, 505
Muska, Susan, 485
Musker, John, 516
Myrick, Daniel, 638, 649–50
Myung-Sae, Lee, 359–60

➤ **N**

Naess, Peter, 365
Nagashima, Kizo, 528
Nagy, Ivan, 537
Nahon, Chris, 390–91
Nair, Mira, 186–87
Nakahara, Shun, 539
Nakamura, Genji, 349–50
Nakamura, Ryutaro, 555
Nakano, Hiroyuki, 341
Nakata, Hideo, 350, 700–701

Nakmura, Takeo, 552
Narizzano, Silvio, 654
Natali, Vincenzo, 649
Neame, Ronald, 572, 696
Nebraskans for Public Television, 613
Needham, Hal, 390
Negulesco, Jean, 468, 580
Neill, William, 565, 661
Nelson, Blake, 621
Nelson, Gary, 510
Nelson, Tim Blake, 615
Nettelbeck, Sandra, 327–28
Neumann, Kurt, 680
Nevard, 595
Newfield, Sam, 688
Newland, Marv, 535–36, 557
Newman, Joseph, 15
Ng See Yuen, 331
Niblo, Fred, 393
Niccol, Andrew, 444, 663
Nichols, Charles A., 511
Nichols, Mike, 187
Nicholson, William, 307
Nicolella, John, 680
Nimibutr, Nonzee, 373–74
Nimura, Riyoji, 353
Noda, Yukio, 349
Noé, Gaspar, 320–21
Nolan, Christopher, 465, 573, 576
Noonan, Chris, 300
Noonan, Tom, 451
Norbu, Khyentse, 303
Norrington, Stephen, 308
Norrington, Steve, 537, 548, 652
Norton, Bill L., 663
Norton, Edward, 431
Noyce, Phillip, 622
Nussbaum Joe, 663–64
Nutter, David, 654–55
Nygard, Roger, 427

➤ **O**

Oakes, Stephen, 610
O'Bannon, Dan, 700
Oblowitz, Michael, 394, 582
O'Brien, John, 450
Ocelot, Michel, 519–20
Oclet, Michel, 553
O'Connor, Geoffrey, 311
Oda, Motoyoshi, 666
O'Derek, Keith, 604
Odgers, Chris, 301
O'Haver, Tommy, 424

Ohkawa, Shundo, 352
Ohkawa, Toshimichi, 352
Ohmori, Kazuki, 666–68
O'Horgan, Tom, 623
Okawara, Takao, 666–67, 693
Okazaki, Steven, 432
Okiura, Hiroyuki, 546–47
Olafsdottier, Gréta, 485
Oliveira, Manoel de, 366
Oliveira, Rick de, 699
Oliver, Daniel, 417
Olivera, Hector, 299, 635
Olivier, Laurence, 616
Olson, Rex, 593–94
Ophuls, Max, 188
Orita, Itaru, 678
Ormsby, Alan, 568
Orr, Joe, 409–10
Orr, Wayne, 525
Oshii, Mamoru, 535
Oshima, Nagisa, 188
Ossorio, Armando de, 188
Othenin-Girard, Dominique, 692
Otomo, Katsuhiro, 534
Ouedraogo, Idrissa, 313
Owens, Brent, 499
Oz, Frank, 414–15, 421, 650
Ozawa, Shigehiro, 353–54
Ozeki, Masayuki, 549
Ozon, François, 188–89
Ozu, Yasujiro, 189–91
➤ P
Pabst, G. W., 191–92
Page, Anthony, 461
Paizs, John, 313
Pakula, Alan J., 458, 574
Pal, George, 192
Paltrow, Bruce, 422
Panahi, Jafar, 345–46
Pang, Danny, 373
Paolinetti, Jamie, 492
Paradjanov, Sergei, 192
Parello, Chuck, 569
Paris, Jerry, 439
Parisot, Dean, 663
Park, Chan-wook, 358–59, 361
Park, Nick, 538, 560–61, 562
Parker, Alan, 497, 591, 598, 632
Parker, Dave, 651
Parker, John, 567
Parker, Jonathan, 610
Parker, Oliver, 617

Parker, Trey, 555, 644–45
Part, Michael, 641
Pasakaljevic, Goran, 302
Pasolini, Pier Paulo, 192–95
Paterson, Vincent, 518
Patrick, Liz, 699
Patterson, Ray, 514
Patterson, Richard, 429–30
Paul, Don Michael, 389
Paxton, Bill, 571
Payami, Babak, 346
Payne, Alexander, 408, 418, 423
Peckinpah, Sam, 195–97
Peirce, Kimberly, 461–62
Penn, Arthur, 197
Pepe, Louis, 619
Peralta, Stacy, 489
Pereira, Manuel Gómez, 367–68, 368
Peretz, Jesse, 418
Perez, Bill, 516
Perez, Fernando, 316
Perrin, Jacques, 505
Perry, Frank, 620
Pesce, P.J., 662
Petersen, Wolfgang, 326
Petty, J.T., 685–86
Philibert, Nicolas, 321, 324
Phillips, Todd, 595, 598
Pialat, Maurice, 197
Pierson, Frank, 575–76
Pillsbury, Sam, 453
Pimlett, Steven, 596
Pin, Chao, 372
Pinon, Efren C., 380, 678
Pirro, Mark, 652
Pitof, 325
Plympton, Bill, 546, 562
Polanski, Roman, 197–99
Polish, Michael, 477
Pollack, Sydney, 582–83
Polonsky, Abraham, 570
Pontecorvo, Gillo, 199–200
Ponti, Edoardo, 313
Pool, Lea, 323
Poole, Dan, 543
Popovski, Aleksandar, 362
Posner, Geoff, 313
Post, Ted, 393, 564, 636–37
Potter, H.C., 436
Powell, Michael, 200–202
Pratt, Hawley, 512, 522
Pray, Doug, 602

Preminger, Otto, 203–04
Pressman, Michael, 412, 558
Prince-Bythewood, Gina, 470
Pritts, Rob, 419
Proctor, Philip, 429–30
Proyas, Alex, 540, 650
Pryor, Richard, 468–69
Putnam, Tom, 443
Pytka, Joe, 529–30

➤ **Q**

Questi, Giulio, 385
Quine, Richard, 204

➤ **R**

Raboy, Marcus, 424
Radford, Michael, 621
Rafelson, Bob, 204, 465
Rafferty, Kevin, 484–85, 490
Rafferty, Pierce, 484
Raffill, Stewart, 522
Rafkin, Alan, 603
Raimi, Sam, 204–06
Ramis, Harold, 425–26, 445
Ramsay, Lynne, 309
Ramsey, Ben, 392
Ramsey, Tor, 646
Ranga, Dana, 326
Rankin, Alan, 424
Rankin, Arthur Jr., 514, 520
Rapp, Bernard, 321–22
Rappaport, Mark, 443
Rappeneau, Jean-Paul, 320
Ratliff, George Whittenburg, 493
Ratner, Brett, 400, 434–35
Ray, Fred Olen, 673, 694
Ray, Nicholas, 206
Raynr, David, 451
Rebane, Bill, 664
Reed, Carol, 206
Reed, Peyton, 415, 421
Rees, Jerry, 510
Reggio, Godfrey, 296
Regnoli, Piero, 696
Reid, Alastair, 309
Reiner, Carl, 409, 429, 437
Reiner, Rob, 409, 605, 686, 697
Reini, Harold, 646
Reininger, Lotte, 534
Reither, John, 500
Reitherman, Wolfgang, 519, 525
Reitman, Ivan, 445
Renoir, Jean, 206–07
Resnais, Alain, 207–08

Resnick, Adam, 416
Reubens, Paul, 525
Riba, Dan, 557
Rice, Spencer, 622
Rich, John, 414
Rich, Richard, 510, 530
Richards, Dick, 570
Richardson, Tony, 208
Richert, William, 584
Richter, W. D., 630
Ridgeway, James, 485, 490
Riefenstahl, Leni, 502–03, 504
Rieser, Dean, 297
Rifkin, Adam, 420, 471
Rintaro, 549–50, 562
Ripoll, Maria, 309
Risi, Dino, 348–49
Ritchie, Guy, 575, 581
Ritchie, Michael, 397, 412, 570
Ritt, Martin, 208–09
Rivette, Jacques, 209–10
Roach, Jay, 411–12, 434
Robbins, Brian, 514–15
Robbins, Matthew, 469–70, 510
Robbins, Tim, 414, 567–68
Robinson, James Dale, 419
Robinson, Phil Alden, 581
Robson, Mark, 472, 477, 657
Rocco, Marco, 421
Rocha, Glauber, 303
Roddam, Franc, 599
Rodriguez, Robert, 210–11
Roeg, Nicholas, 211–12, 214
Roemer, Larry, 528
Rohmer, Eric, 213–15
Rollin, Jean, 215–17
Roman, Phil, 527
Romero, George A., 217–18
Roos, Don, 438
Roquemore, Cliff, 396, 400
Rose, Mickey, 445–46
Rosen, Martin, 553, 561
Rosenberg, Stuart, 567, 632
Rosenthal, Rick, 670–71
Rosenthal, Robert J., 452
Ross, Benjamin, 306, 623
Ross, Gary, 439
Ross, Herbert, 598
Rossellini, Roberto, 218–19
Rossen, Robert, 219
Roth, Eli, 644
Roussimoff, Ari M., 661

Yip, Wilson, 329
Young, Harold, 687
Young, Jacob, 592
Young, Robert III, 618
Young, Robert M., 532
Young, Terence, 569, 571, 583, 626
Yu, Jimmy Wang, 337
Yu, Ronny, 290–91
Yuan, Chu, 335–36
Yuen, Brandy, 330
Yuen, Corey, 334–35, 338, 341, 343–44, 394, 404
Yuen Woo Ping, 291
Yukel, Chatrichalerm, 373
Yukich, James, 496
Yun, Je-gyun, 360
Yust, Larry, 583
Yuyama, Kunihiko, 560
Yuzna, Brian, 641–42, 654, 697

➤ **Z**

Zaillian, Steven, 473–74
Zanuck, Lilli Fini, 473
Zanussi, Krzysztof, 291
Zarchi, Meir, 675
Zeitoun, Ariel, 325
Zemeckis, Robert, 449, 465, 561, 631, 634–35
Zhang Yang, 315
Zhangke, Jia, 343
Zhuangzhuang, Tian, 255
Zieff, Howard, 422
Zielinski, Rafael, 466
Zinnemann, Fred, 291–92
Zombie, Rob, 674
Zucker, David, 408, 448
Zucker, Jerry, 408, 448
Zulawski, Andrzej, 696–97
Zwart, Harold, 438
Zwerin, Charlotte Mitchell, 488, 604
Zwigoff, Terry, 542

Index

Gilda, 571
Gimme Shelter, 491
Ginger Snaps, 664
Ginger Snaps 2: Unleashed, 665
Ginkgo Bed, 357
Girl, Interrupted, 466
Girl Getters (aka The System), 307
Girl Hunters, The, 571
Girl on the Bridge, The, 150–51
Girls Just Want to Have Fun, 425
Gladiator, 231–32
Gleaners and I, The, 267
Glen and Randa, 665
Glen or Glenda?, 287
Glengarry Glen Ross, 614
Glenn Miller Story, The, 173
Go Ask Alice, 466
Go Fatima: Learn to Dance, 614
Gobots: Battle of the Rock Lords, 514
God of Cookery, 333
God of Gamblers, 333–34
God Said Ha!, 614
God Told Me to (aka Demon), 54
Godfather, The, 56
Godfather Part II, The, 56
Godfather Part III, The, 56–57
Gods and Monsters, 614
Godzilla, 665–66
Godzilla 1985, 666
Godzilla, Mothra and King Ghidorah: Giant
    Monsters All-Out Attack (aka Godzilla
    GMK), 668–69
Godzilla Raids Again (aka Gigantis, The Fire
    Monster), 666
Godzilla vs Biollante, 666
Godzilla vs Destroyah, 666–67
Godzilla vs Gigan, 667
Godzilla vs King Ghidorah, 667–68
Godzilla vs Megalon, 668
Godzilla vs Monster Zero, 124
Godzilla vs the Smog Monster, 668
Godzilla's Revenge, 124
Gold Rush, The, 47
Goldfinger, 571–72
Goldwyn: The Man and His Movies, 614–15
Gone in 60 Seconds, 388
Gone to Earth (aka The Wild Heart), 200
Gone with the Wind, 88
Gonin, 351
Good, the Bad, and the Ugly, The, 155
Good Burger, 514–15
Good Girl, The, 425

Good Morning (Ohayo), 189
Good Thief, The, 136
Good Will Hunting, 265
Goodbye, 20th Century, 362
Goodfellas, 229
Goonies, The, 516
Gorgeous (Bor Lei Jun), 334
Gorillaz Phase One: Celebrity Take, 594
Gosford Park, 9
Gospel According to St. Matthew, The, 193
Gothic, 222
Graffiti Rock & Other Hip Hop Delights,
    594–95
Grand Illusion, 207
Grand Slam, 572
Grapes of Death, The, 215–16
Grapes of Wrath, The, 89
Grass, 491–92
Grass Is Greener, The, 74
Grave of the Fireflies, 543
Greaser's Place, 425
Great Dictator, The, 47
Great Expectations, 150
Great Expectations (1998), 615
Great Mouse Detective, The (aka The
    Adventures of the Great Mouse
    Detective), 516
Great Muppet Caper, 516
Great Silence, The, 388–89
Great Wall, A (aka The Great Wall Is a Great
    Wall), 314–15
Greatest Show on Earth, The, 67
Greatest Story Ever Told, 242
Greed, 243
Green Fish, 357–58
Green Goblin's Last Stand, The, 543
Green Slime, The, 99
Green Snake, 262
Greetings From Down South, 492
Gremlins, 669
Gremlins 2: The New Batch, 669–70
Grey Gardens, 492
Grey Zone, The, 615
Gridlock'd, 466–67
Griffin, Eddie, Dysfunktional Family, 425
Griffith, D.W.: Years of Discovery, 108
Grifters, The, 96
Grinch Grinches the Cat in the Hat, The, 516
Grosse Pointe Blank, 425
Groundhog Day, 425–26
Groupies, 595
GTO—Great Teacher Onizuka (Vol. 1), 543

Jesus' Son, 618
Jetee, La, 296
JFK, 243
Jim Rose Circus Sideshow, 678
Jimmy, the Boy Wonder, 157
Jimmy Neutron: Boy Genius, 519
Jin-Roh (aka Jin-Roh: The Wolf Brigade), 546–47
J-Men Forever, 429–30
Jo Jo Dancer, Your Life Is Calling, 468–69
Joe 90 (4 Volumes), 547
Joe Dirt, 430
Joe Versus the Volcano, 430
Johnny Handsome, 118
Johnny Mnemonic, 678
Johnny Sokko and His Flying Robot (4 Volumes), 678
Joint Security Area, 358–59
Joli Mai, Le, 296
Joseph and the Amazing Technicolor Dreamcoat, 596
Joyless Street, 192
Jubilee, 133
Jude, 618
Juha, 138
Jules and Jim, 259
Jump Tomorrow, 430
Jungle Book, The, 519
Jungle Fever, 153
Jungle Holocaust, 678
Junior Bonner, 195
Junk, 678–79
Junkers Come Here, 547
Junkman, The, 390
Ju-On: The Grudge, 679
Jurassic Park III, 679
Just for the Hell of It, 157–58
Just Married, 430
Just One of the Girls (aka Anything for Love), 430
Just One of the Guys, 430–31
Justine, 93–94
➤ K
Kafka, 235–36
Kandahar, 170
Kansas City, 9–10
Kansas City Confidential, 137
Keeping the Faith, 431
Kentuckian, The, 390
Kentucky Fried Movie, The, 431
Kestrel's Eye, 496
Khartoum, 66–67

Khudah Gawah (God Is My Witness), 345
Kick the Moon, 359
Kid Stays in the Picture, The, 618
Kidnap, 336
Kids in the Hall: Brain Candy, 453
Kids in the Hall: Same Guys, New Dresses, 453
Kids Return, 248
Kika, 8
Kiki's Delivery Service, 547–48
Kikujiro, 248
Kill, Baby. . .Kill, 17
Kill Bill Vol. 1, 249
Killer, The, 286
Killer Condom, 327
Killer Klowns From Outer Space, 679
Killer Tattoo, 373
Killers, The (1946), 233
Killers, The (1964), 232–33
Killing, The, 144
Killing of a Chinese Bookie, 42
Killing of Satan, 679
Kim Possible: The Secret Files, 519
King Creole, 65
King is Alive, The (Dogme #14), 316
King Kong, 225
King Kong Escapes, 124
King Kong Lives (aka King Kong 2), 679
King Kong vs Godzilla, 125
King Lear, 618
King of Comedy, The, 229
King of Hearts, The, 28–29
King of New York, 85
King of the Hill: Season One, 548
Kingdom 2, The, 258
Kingdom, The, 257–58
Kingdom of the Spiders, 679–80
Kingpin, 431
Kings of the Road, 278
Kippur, 347
Kirikou and the Sorceress, 519–20
Kiss Me, Stupid, 282
Kiss Me Deadly, 4–5
Kiss of the Dragon, 390–91
Klute, 574
Knife in the Water, 198
Knightriders, 217–18
Knives of the Avenger, 17–18
Knock Off, 262
Kolya, 316
Konga, 680
Kovacs, Ernie, Best of, 453

Titanic, 36–37
Titus, 626
T-Men, 174
To Be and To Have (Etre et Avoir), 324
To Be Or Not To Be, 163–64
To Catch a Thief, 123
To Have and Have Not, 112–13
To Kill a Mockingbird, 185
To Live and Die in LA, 98
To Play the King, 309
Tokyo Drifter, 245
Tokyo Fist, 354
Tokyo Mafia: Yakuza Wars, 354–55
Tokyo Story (Tokyo Monogatari), 191
Tokyo-Ga, 279
Tom and Lola, 324
Tombs of the Blind Dead, 188
Tombstone, 403
Tommy, 223
Tomorrow's Children, 476
Tonight or Never, 476
Top Secret!, 448
Topo, El, 136
Topper, 448
Tora! Tora! Tora!, 99
Total Recall, 269
Touch of Evil, 275–76
Touch of Zen, 372
Tougher Than Leather, 605–6
Toute Une Nuit (All Night Long), 4
Town Is Quiet, The, 324
Toy Story, 531
Toy Story 2, 531
Toys, 448
Track 29, 212
Traffic, 238
Traffik, 309
Tragedy (aka Surviving), 476
Trail of the Lonesome Pine, The, 109
Training Day, 404
Transporter, The, 404
Traveller, 476
Treasure Island, 476, 626
Treasure of the Sierra Madre, The, 128
Trial, The, 277
Trial of Joan of Arc, 28
Trials of Henry Kissinger, The, 503
Tribulation 99, 295
Trick Baby (aka Double Con), 583
Trip, The, 58
Triumph of the Will, The, 504
Tron, 531

Trou, Le, 19
Trouble in Paradise, 164
Truck Turner, 404
True Lies, 37
True Romance, 404
True Stories, 606
Truly, Madly, Deeply, 305
Truth or Dare, 606
Tully, 476
Turbo: A Power Rangers Movie, 531–32
Turn, 355
Tuvalu, 328
TV Nation: Volumes One and Two, 504
12 Angry Men, 167
12 Monkeys, 103
Twentieth Century, 113
Twenty Something Taipei, 343
28 Days, 448–49
24 Hour Party People, 305–06
24—Season One, 480
20,000 Leagues Under the Sea, 532
Twice Upon a Time, 560
Twice Upon a Yesterday (aka The Man With
    Rain in His Shoes), 309
Twilight Girls, The, 479
Twilight of the Ice Nymphs, 169
Twilight Zone: The Movie, 293–94
Twin Falls Idaho, 477
Twin Peaks, 168
Twin Peaks: Fire Walk with Me, 168–69
Two Deaths, 212–13
Two Evil Eyes, 294
Two for the Road, 74
Two Lane Blacktop, 115
2 or 3 Things I Know About Her, 106
2000 Maniacs, 158
2001: A Space Odyssey, 145

➤ U

Ugetsu (aka Ugetsu Monogatari), 184
Ulee's Gold, 187
Umberto D, 72
Umbrellas of Cherbourg, The, 69
Unbelievable Truth, The, 109
UnBreakable, 477
Uncorked (aka At Sachem Farm), 449
Under the Roofs of Paris, 50
Under the Sand, 189
Undercover Brother, 449
Underground (1976), 504
Underground (1995), 147
Underworld USA, 101
Undisputed, 119